NnOoPp
QqRr
SsTtUu
VvWw
XxYyZz

 Published in the United States by Random House, Inc., New York, and simultaneously in Canada by Random House of Canada Limited, Toronto, in conjunction with the Children's Television Workshop. Distributed by Funk & Wagnalls, Inc., New York, N.Y.
Manufactured in the United States of America. 8 9 0 0-394-84942-6

volume 2

BIG BIRD'S SESAME STREET® DICTIONARY

FEATURING JIM HENSON'S SESAME STREET MUPPETS

LETTERS C–D

by Linda Hayward
illustrated by Joe Mathieu
Editor in Chief: Sharon Lerner

Art Directors: Grace Clarke and Cathy Goldsmith
with special thanks to Judith M. Leary

Funk & Wagnalls, Inc./Children's Television Workshop

A B C D E F G H I J K L M N O P Q R S T U V W X Y Z

cake A cake is something sweet to eat. It is usually made with flour, eggs, butter, sugar, and other things.

calendar A calendar tells you what day it is. It shows the months, weeks, and days of the year. There are seven days in a week and twelve months in a year.

The days of the week are Sunday, Monday, Tuesday, Wednesday, Thursday, Friday, and Saturday.

The months of the year are January, February, March, April, May, June, July, August, September, October, November, and December.

call When you call someone, you use a loud voice.

call When you call on a telephone, you use a telephone to speak to someone.

can A can is a kind of container, usually made of metal. It is used to hold things.

Bert is opening a **can** of soup.

can When you can do something, it is possible for you to do it. You are able to do it.

Big Bird **can** reach the shelf.

Little Bird **can**not.

cap A cap is a kind of lid. It covers the top of something else.

Ernie just took the **cap** off a bottle of Figgy Fizz.

cap A cap is also something to wear on your head.

Bert is wearing a shower **cap.**

cape A cape is a coat without sleeves.

Super Grover wears a pink **cape.**

car A car is something that you ride in.

card A card is a flat, stiff piece of paper. Often it has words and pictures on it.

Big Bird is making a birthday **card** for his friend Snuffle-upagus.

Rodeo Rosie and Bad Bart are playing a game with **cards.**

careful When you are careful, you pay attention to what you are doing.

carpenter A carpenter is someone who builds things with wood.

Bert the **carpenter** uses a saw to cut the wood. He uses a hammer to pound in the nails.

carpet A carpet is a cover for the floor.

Barkley likes to roll around on the **carpet.**

carrot A carrot is a vegetable. Carrots are orange and grow in the ground.

Farmer Grover is pulling up some **carrots** for dinner.

carry When you carry something, you pick it up and take it somewhere.

Herry Monster is very strong. He can **carry** a lot.

carton A carton is a kind of container. It can hold things.

Bert is carrying the groceries in a **carton.**

castle A castle is a very big building with tall towers and thick walls.

cat A cat is a furry animal with claws.

Some **cats** are small and tame

Some **cats** are big and wild.

catch When you catch something, you grab it as it comes to you.

Ernie can **catch** a football.

cave A cave is a big hole under the ground or in the side of a hill.

Snuffle-upagus lives in a **cave.**

cent One cent is the smallest amount of money you can spend. If you have a penny, you have one cent.

A one-**cent** cookie costs a penny.

ceiling The ceiling is the part of the room you see when you look up.

Prairie Dawn is painting the **ceiling.**

center The center is the place in the middle.

A doughnut has a hole in the **center.**

cereal Cereal is a food made from grain.

Ernie and Bert are eating **cereal** for breakfast. Bert is having oatmeal. Ernie is having crispies with milk.

certain When you are certain about something, you are very sure of it.

chair A chair is a piece of furniture that you sit on. A chair has a back to lean against.

change When you change something, you make it different.

chase When you chase something, you go after it.

Marshal Grover has to **chase** his horse, Fred.

cheek Your cheeks are the sides of your face. Look up the word face.

Roosevelt Franklin is kissing his mother on her **cheek.**

cheese Cheese is a food made from milk.

Prairie Dawn is having a picnic. She is eating **cheese** and crackers.

chest Your chest is the front part of your body between your neck and your stomach. Look up the word body.

The letter G is on Super Grover's **chest.**

chest A chest is also a kind of container. It is used to hold things.

Bert keeps his socks in a **chest** of drawers.

Herry Monster found a **chest** full of treasure.

chew When you chew, you mash up food with your teeth.

Fred likes to **chew** on a carrot.

chicken A chicken is a kind of bird. Some chickens live on farms. Their eggs are good to eat.

child A child is a young boy or girl.

Charlie is the last **child** in line. There are three **children** in front of him.

chilly When you are chilly, you are too cool to be comfortable.

chin Your chin is the part of your face below your mouth. Look up the word face.

The Count has a beard on his **chin.**

choose When you choose, you pick one or the other.

circle A circle is a kind of shape. A circle is round.

Ernie is drawing a **circle** on the blackboard.

circus A circus is a special kind of show.

At the **circus** you can see clowns and acrobats and jugglers.

Circus animals do tricks.

The Sesame Street Circus

city A city is a place where many people live and work.

Grover is flying his airplane over the **city.**

clean When something is clean, it is not dirty.

climb When you climb, you move up toward the top.

The Count has to **climb** up the tree to get his cat.

clock A clock is a kind of machine that shows you what time it is.

close When you close something, you shut it.

Bert had to **close** the window.

close When two things are close, they are near each other.

Oscar's trash can is **close** to Ernie and Bert's apartment.

closet A closet is a tiny room where you can keep things—especially clothes.

clothes Clothes are what people wear. Most clothes are made from cloth.

cloud A cloud is made of tiny drops of water. Clouds float in the sky.

Grover can fly his airplane through a **cloud.**

coat A coat is a piece of clothing. You wear a coat over your other clothes.

The salesman has a letter C inside his **coat.**

coin A coin is a piece of money made from metal.

cold When the air is cold, you feel chilly.

collection A collection is a group of things that are alike in some way.

color Color is all around us. The grass is green. The sky is blue. Red, yellow, orange, and purple are some of the other colors you see every day.

I, the Amazing Mumford, will now pull from this perfectly empty hat... one purple thing, one red thing, one blue thing, one yellow thing, one green thing, and one orange thing.

A LA PEANUT BUTTER SANDWICHES!

THING
THING
THING
THING
THING
THING

Wow! Each thing is a different **color**!

come To come is to move from there to here.

Can you
mix colors?
yellow + red = orange
red + blue = purple
blue + yellow = green
Yellow
Green
Orange
Blue
Purple
Red

comfortable When you are comfortable, you feel good.

Big Bird is resting in his nest. He feels **comfortable.**

complain When you complain, you make a fuss about how things are.

container A container is something that can hold something else. There are many kinds of containers.

cook When you cook, you use heat to prepare food to eat.

cook A cook is someone who cooks.

cookie A cookie is something to eat. It is usually small, flat, and sweet.

Cookies are **Cookie** Monster's favorite food.

cool When something feels cool, it is more cold than hot.

cooperate When you cooperate, you work together with someone to do something.

Fire fighters have to **cooperate** to put out a fire.

corner A corner is the point where two sides come together.

The **corner** of a room is the place where one wall meets another.

The **corner** of a triangle is the place where one line meets another.

A **corner** is also the place where two streets meet.

costume A costume is something to wear. It can help you pretend to be someone else.

Grover's mommy made him a Halloween **costume.**

count When you count, you say numbers in order. Counting can help you find out how many things there are all together.

country A country is a place where many people live. Some countries are large. Some are small.

country Country is also a name for a place that is not like the city. In the country there is usually a lot of grass and trees, but not many buildings.

cousin The child of your aunt and uncle is your cousin.

cover When you cover people or things, you put something over them.

Ernie likes to **cover** Bert with sand at the beach.

cow A cow is an animal that usually lives on a farm and gives milk.

crab A crab is an animal that lives in or near the water. A crab has a hard shell, eight legs, and two claws.

crack When something cracks, it starts to break.

crash When one thing hits another with a loud noise, it crashes.

crawl When you crawl, you move on your hands and your knees.

Grover has to **crawl** out of his airplane.

crayon A crayon is a stick of colored wax used to draw on paper.

crowd A crowd is a lot of people together.

A **crowd** is waiting for a bus.

cream Cream is the thick part of milk that is made into butter.

There is already a **crowd** on the bus.

cross When you cross something, you go from one side of it to the other.

cry When you cry, tears come from your eyes.

Grover spilled his milk and began to **cry.**

cup A cup is a container to drink from. Usually it has a handle.

Snuffle-upagus has a very large **cup.**

curious When you are curious, you wonder about something.

Prairie Dawn is **curious.**

cut When you cut something, you divide it into pieces. Most often you use scissors or a knife.

Big Bird can **cut** out paper dolls with scissors.

Cookie the baker **cuts** his cookie dough with a knife.

How Many Things That Begin with **C** Can You Find?

dance When you dance, you move with rhythm. Usually you dance to music.

dancer A dancer is someone who dances.

The piper is piping. The **dancer** is **dancing.**

danger If there is danger, there is a chance that someone may get hurt.

dark When it is dark, there is no light.

date The date is the day, month, and year when something happens.

daughter A girl or a woman is the daughter of her mother and father.

dawn Dawn is the time when the sun begins to light up the sky.

Farmer Grover's rooster crows at **dawn.** It is time for Farmer Grover to wake up.

day A day is twenty-four hours long. Morning, afternoon, and night are all parts of a day.

deaf A person who is deaf cannot hear.

If you know sign language, you can talk to a **deaf** person with your hands.

decide When you decide, you make up your mind.

Cookie Monster cannot **decide** what to eat.

Cookie Monster **decided** to eat both.

decorate When you decorate something, you make it pretty.

Cookie the baker is going to **decorate** a cake.

deep When something is deep, the bottom is far below the top.

deer A deer is an animal with four legs. Most deer live in the forest. The father deer has antlers on his head.

delicious When food is delicious, it tastes good.

deliver When you deliver something, you take it to a place or person.

dentist A dentist is someone who helps you take care of your teeth.

The **dentist** is counting and cleaning Farley's teeth.

describe When you describe people or things, you tell about them.

Fast, smart, brave, and cute are words that **describe** Super Grover.

desert A desert is a place with very little water. Most deserts are covered with sand.

Cactus plants can grow in the **desert** because they do not need much water.

desk A desk is a special table where you can write or draw.

Farley is sitting at his **desk** and writing a letter.

dessert A dessert is a special food that you eat at the end of a meal.

Cookie Monster is having cookies for **dessert**.

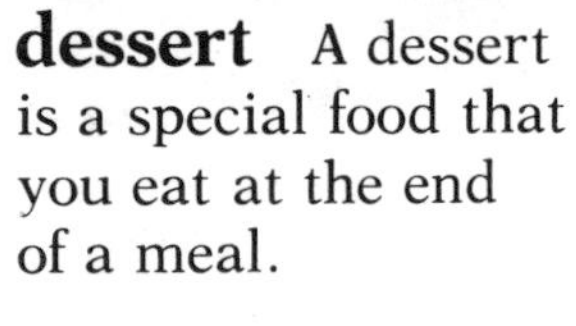

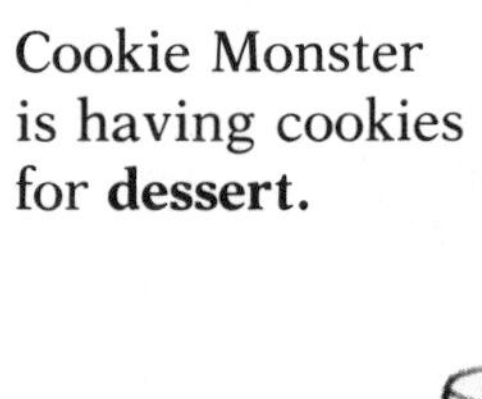

detective A detective is someone who tries to find the answer to a mystery.

Sherlock Hemlock is a **detective.** He is looking for clues.

dictionary A dictionary is a book that tells the meanings of words.

This book is a **dictionary.**

die When things die, they stop living.

different When things are different, they are not the same.

Big Bird is big.
Little Bird is small.
Big Bird and Little Bird are **different** sizes.

difficult When something is difficult, it is hard to do.

It is **difficult** for Big Bird to fit into a phone booth.

dig When you dig in the ground, you scoop up dirt.

Barkley likes to **dig** holes. He has already **dug** three.

dime A dime is a coin. A dime is equal to ten cents. Look up the word coin.

Each of the Busby twins has ten cents.

dinner Dinner is usually the biggest meal of the day.

Cookie Monster has a well-balanced **dinner.**

dinosaur A dinosaur is a kind of animal that lived millions of years ago.

Different Dinosaurs

direct When you direct people, you show them the way.

direction A direction is a way to go.

director A director is someone who directs.

The policewoman is a traffic **director**. She has to **direct** the traffic in four different **directions.**

dirt Dirt is the earth you scoop up when you dig in the ground.

dirty When something is dirty, it has dirt on it or it is not clean.

Farmer Grover has been working in the field. His overalls are **dirty.**

disagree When people disagree, they want different things or their ideas are not the same.

The Busby twins **disagree.**

disappear When something disappears, you cannot see it anymore.

disappointed You feel disappointed when something you want to happen does not happen.

Big Bird did not find any mail in his mailbox. He was **disappointed.**

discover When you discover something, you find it.

Zounds! Two suspicious-looking feet. I must **discover** whose they are.

disguise You wear a disguise to look like something or someone else.

The Big Bad Wolf is wearing a **disguise** to look like Grandma.

dish A dish is a kind of container to hold food.

Frazzle is taking a **dish** out of the cupboard.

distance Distance is the amount of space between two places or things.

The **distance** from Oscar's mud box to the fire hydrant is six feet.

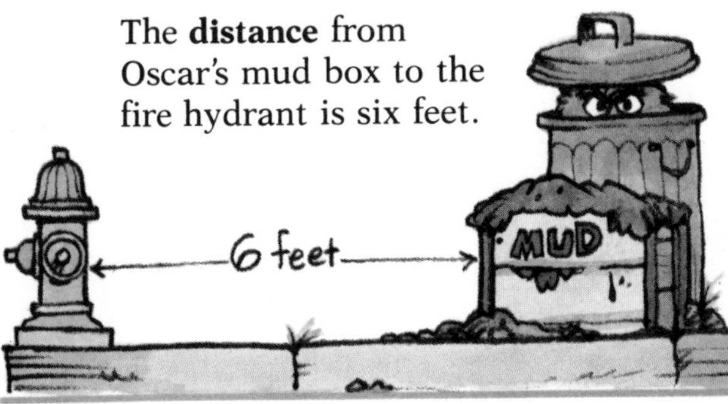

divide When you divide something, you separate it into parts.

do When you do something, you act in a certain way or you make something happen.

doctor A doctor is someone who helps people stay healthy. Doctors also help sick people get well.

The **doctor** is listening to Farley's heart with a stethoscope.

dog A dog is a kind of furry animal with a tail. Most dogs bark.

One of these things does not belong here.

A collie, a dachshund, and a poodle are all **dogs.** A turkey is a bird. The turkey does not belong.

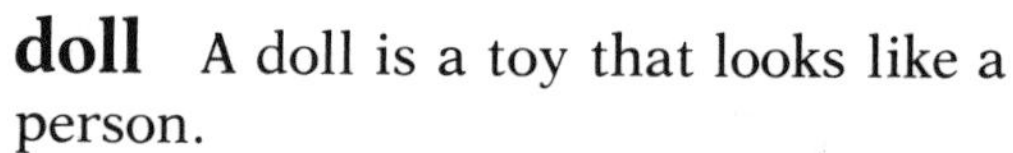

doll A doll is a toy that looks like a person.

Herry Monster's **doll** has red hair.

dollar A dollar is an amount of money. A dollar bill is a piece of paper money equal to one hundred cents.

done When something is done, it is finished.

door A door is used to close off the way into something.

doorknob A doorknob is a handle on a door.

dot A dot is a very tiny round mark.

Sherlock Hemlock is looking at a **dot** on a piece of paper through his magnifying glass.

double When something is double, there are two instead of one.

down When you go down, you move to a lower place.

Bert is going **down** the steps.

dozen When you have twelve things, you have a dozen of them.

dragon A dragon is an imaginary animal that has wings and breathes fire.

Roosevelt Franklin is reading a book about a **dragon.**

draw When you draw, you make a picture. You can draw with a pencil or a pen or a crayon.

Roosevelt Franklin can **draw** a picture of a dragon.

drawer A drawer is a kind of container that slides in and out of a piece of furniture. You can keep things in a drawer.

Bert is folding his socks and putting them into his **drawer.**

dream When you dream, you see, think, and feel things while you sleep.

Cookie Monster likes to **dream** about his favorite thing.

dress A dress is something to wear.

Betty Lou is putting on a **dress.**

dress When you dress, you put on clothes.

drink When you drink, you swallow a liquid.

drive When you drive something, you make it go and steer it.

driver The driver is the one who is driving.

Grover Knover can **drive** his motorcycle over ten barrels. Grover Knover is a good **driver.**

drop A drop is a small amount of liquid.

Sherlock Hemlock is looking at a **drop** of rain.

drop When you drop something, you let it fall.

drum A drum is a musical instrument. When you play a drum, you hit it with your hands or with drumsticks.

Ernie is playing the **drum.**

dry When something is dry, it is not wet.

It is raining, but my little umbrella keeps me **dry.**

Now I am all wet. Next time I will wear my raincoat.

dry When you dry something, you take away the water.

Biff likes to wash the dishes. Sully likes to **dry** them.

duck A duck is a kind of bird. Ducks have webbed feet. Ducks can fly or walk or swim.

I am the **duck**ling's father. I am a drake.

I am a baby **duck.** I am a **duck**ling.

Farmer Grover's **ducks** are swimming in the pond.

I am the **duck**ling's mother. I am a **duck.**

duckie A duckie is a toy duck.

Rubber **Duckie** is a toy that floats in Ernie's bathtub.

dump The dump is a place for garbage.

dump When you dump something, you get rid of it.

I love to visit the **dump**! It is one of my favorite places.

The garbage truck takes the garbage to the **dump** to **dump** it.

during During is a word that means between the beginning and the end.

dust Dust is very small bits of dirt.

Oscar loves to have **dust** in his can.

How Many Things That Begin with **D** Can You Find?

A Delightful D Story

One **dull dark day,**
Grover had nothing to **do.**
So he **decided** to **draw**
at his **desk.** First he
drew a **duck.** Then he
drew a **dog digging.**

"Now I want to **draw** something really **different,"** he said. So he **drew** a **dragon.** It was **difficult** to **draw** and it made Grover **drowsy.** Suddenly the **desk disappeared,** but the **dragon did** not! The **dragon** looked very **dangerous.**

travelling was a sad sight to see. Black flags hung from the windows, and the sound of lamentation was to be heard on all sides. An evil nine-headed dragon had moved into the once-happy land, and had threatened to destroy the entire kingdom if the king did not bring his three daughters to the dragon's lair the morning before the full moon. Only the boldest of the knights had dared to challenge the fearful monster, and not one had returned alive. All this the prince learned from the citizens as he made his way to the royal palace. In the palace gardens he came across the three hapless princesses. The most beautiful of them was the youngest, Princess Rosalinda. He plucked her a white rose, and smiled at her. "Your smile warms the heart," she whispered. "What is your name?"
"Bah-yah-yah," replied the prince. "Oh, you poor mute. Stay here with us in the palace until we go to meet our fate. You will cheer us with your smile." The prince willingly agreed. The girls often asked him who he was and where he came from, but he would only say, "bah-yah-yah". So he came to be called Bajaja. His smile allayed their grief, so that they almost forgot the cruel destiny that awaited them. But on the last evening before the full moon, amid weeping and wailing, the prince slipped out of the palace and set off to consult his wise friend, the horse.
"In the chest by the wall you will find a suit of magic armour," the white stallion told him when, in the golden cavern, the prince had related the whole sad tale. "Before sunrise we shall ride into battle. But now it is time to sleep."

7 JANUARY

How Prince Bajaja Fought the Nine-Headed Dragon

The next day before cockcrow the old king and his unhappy daughters made their way to the dragon's lair. They were greeted by nine fierce roars, and from out of the rocks nine hideous heads appeared. The princesses almost fainted with terror, but—out of nowhere, it seemed—a strange knight appeared on a fine white horse. Vizor lowered and sword drawn, he rode full tilt at the monster. Who would have thought that this bold deliverer might be the dumb page Bajaja? The monster roared furiously, its nine throats hurling fire at the prince; but Bajaja never flinched. He felled the dragon heads bravely, until the blood spurted out. But scarcely had one head rolled to the ground, when another grew in its place. Bajaja was growing weary, but just as it seemed it was all over with him, the youngest princess tossed him her white rose, whereupon he suddenly found new strength, and took up the fight again. Dragon heads tumbled like corn beneath the scythe, and before long the last of them was lying bloody on the ground. The prince cut out the tongue, pushed it into his saddle-bag and, without so much as a word of farewell, was gone as swiftly as he had come. When the joyful princesses arrived back at the

palace with their father, the dumb page Bajaja was at the gate to greet them with a happy smile.

"Oh, you ungrateful wretch," Rosalinda scolded him, playfully, "to leave us at our time of greatest need. But for your smile I forgive you." "Bah-yah-yah," replied the prince, smiling broadly. That evening the princess found a white rose on her pillow. Now, who do you think had left it there?

8 JANUARY

Prince Bajaja and the Golden Apple

The youngest princess could not forget her saviour. Day after day she languished, until at last the king called his daughters to the throne and told them, "Our land has seen grief enough. The time has come to find you husbands." He ordered the most handsome princes from all around to be invited to his palace, and thrust a golden apple into each one's hand. The dumb Bajaja crept among them and he, too, put out his hand for an apple. The king declared: "Whoever rolls his apple to one of my daughters shall have her for his wife." For a long time the noble princes tried in vain. Then at last the apples of the two most handsome princes found their way to the feet of the elder sisters. Then Prince Bajaja threw his apple, which rolled to the feet of the youngest and most beautiful of all. The poor girl burst into tears. How she had dreamed of her bold deliverer, and now she was fated to marry the dumb Bajaja! But the page disappeared as if the ground had swallowed him up. They asked after him in vain. Then, one day, a fine prince on a spirited white stallion came riding with a flourish into the palace courtyard. "I am Bajaja, your

bridegroom and saviour," he proclaimed, drawing the dragon's tongue from his saddle-bag to prove it. "If you do not want me for your husband, then I release you from the promise given by the king himself!" But Rosalinda threw herself at once into the arms of her deliverer. Thus it was that Prince Bajaja found his fortune in the world. And his faithful white stallion? He disappeared like a puff of smoke. Perhaps he is in his golden cavern to this day, waiting for someone to ask his help.

9 JANUARY

The Little Shepherd Boy

Have you ever heard of the clever little shepherd boy? His sheep were so inquisitive that he could scarcely keep up with their questions. Soon he knew the answer to every question in the world. The king himself heard of his wisdom. He summoned him to the palace and told him, "If you can answer three questions, I shall adopt you as my own son." And right away he began with the first question: "How many drops of water are there in the sea?" — "A difficult question indeed, Sire," replied the boy. "But if you were to have all the rivers of the world blocked up, that the sea might grow no larger, then I should count them for you." The king said nothing, but asked again: "How many stars are there in the sky?" The shepherd boy took from his tunic three bags of poppy-seed and spread it over the ground. "There are as many stars in the sky as there are poppy seeds here, and you may count them yourself!" he said. The king smiled. "Very well, but now you must tell me how many seconds there are in eternity." The shepherd boy replied, "Sire, at the end of the Earth stands a diamond mountain, an hour's journey high, an hour's journey deep, and an hour's journey broad. Once in a hundred years a bird flies to the mountain and sharpens its beak on it. When the whole mountain has been worn away, the first second of eternity will have passed. Why do we not, Sire, wait together for all eternity, so that we may count the seconds?" The king broke into laughter. "You wise young fellow," he said. "I will adopt you as my own."—"But you must take my sheep, too," replied the shepherd boy. And so it was. The shepherd boy ruled the land, and the king watched over his sheep.

10 JANUARY

The Two Hens

What do you think? Two hens quarrelled over a grain of corn, and hurried off to complain to the cock. "Bring me the grain!" ordered the cock. The hens obeyed, the cock gave a quick peck, and the grain of corn was gone. "How unfair!" shrieked the hens, and they scurried off into the forest to tell the fox. "Bring me the cock," said the fox, smacking his lips. "He is surely plumper than you are. The grain will lie heavy in his stomach for nothing." The hens returned home and lured the cock into the forest. The fox's jaws snapped shut once or twice, and that was the end of the cock. "How unfair!" grumbled the hens, and off they went to complain to the wolf. "Bring me the fox," snarled the wolf. The hens enticed the fox into the wolf's lair, the wolf bit and chewed a few times, and that was the end of the fox. "How unfair!" clucked the hens, and scampered away to see the bear. "We quarrelled over a grain of corn, and the cock pecked it up. The fox swallowed the cock. The wolf ate the fox. How unfair it is!" they complained. "Bring me the wolf!" growled the bear. A couple of mouthfuls, and the wolf was in his stomach. "And now be off with you, before I eat you up too!" he threatened. Away they ran, as fast as their legs could carry them. "Well, there's a fine thing," grumbled the hens. "One little grain of corn, and see how many animals have eaten their fill! Only we, who quarrelled over it, have gone hungry. How unfair it is!"

11 JANUARY

The Fox and the Cat

The fox was known for her airs and graces. There was not a ball in the forest that she did not attend; she went about dressed up like a courtier, and held her nose higher in the air than any princess. "I am the most beautiful of all the animals," she would boast to all she met. One day a poor cat saw her and said, admiringly, "My, my, dear fox, how fine you look today, as always! How do you come to do so well for yourself? How I wish I could be as well-to-do as you." The fox nearly burst with pride. "He who has a bad time of it is a fool," she said, haughtily. "Can you do anything clever at all, you good-for-nothing cat?"—"No, indeed," replied the cat. "It is enough for me that I can jump into a tree whenever I catch sight of a dog."—"Well, there you are, then," sneered the fox. "For I have a whole sackful of tricks, ruses and clever ideas up my sleeve for any dog that comes along. Come with me, and see how I put dogs in their place!" Just then a group of hunters and their dogs came into the forest. As soon as the hounds picked up the fox's trail, things looked black. Without more ado the cat jumped into a tree. "Quickly, cousin fox," she called. "Open up your bag of tricks!" But the dogs soon caught the proud fox, and throttled her to death. "There you are, you see, madam fox," purred the cat. "My one little trick was worth a whole sackful of your cleverness." And she curled up in the tree and slept, and slept.

12 JANUARY

The Goose Princesses

There was once a king who had two naughty little daughters. He didn't know what to do with them—even a sound beating did no good at all—so he simply sat on his throne and shook his head, saying, "Children, children, whatever will you grow up into!" One day, down by the palace lake, a wild goose appeared with her goslings. The moment the princesses saw them they started throwing stones at them. "You'll be sorry, just you wait!" cackled the goose. But the princesses only laughed at her. The next morning, when they woke up, they found to their horror that they were covered all over with feathers, and had bright orange beaks where their mouths should be. "Heavens, we are turned into geese!" they gaggled. What a weeping and wailing there was throughout the kingdom! Wherever he went, the king asked, "How are their Highnesses the princesses?" His unfortunate servants would reply, "Begging your pardon, Your Majesty, they are, one might say, in high feather, if Your Majesty will pardon the expression." One day a certain scatterbrained housemaid wished to stuff

a pillow. She caught hold of the first two geese she came across, and began to pluck them alive. The geese cackled with pain till they were blue in the face, but all to no avail—the girl soon plucked them quite bare. No sooner had she torn off the last little feather than—what should she see but, there, standing before her as bald as two coots, the naughty little princesses. "Begging your pardon, Your Highnesses the geese . . . er, Your Highnesses the princesses," she stammered, "but I wasn't to know you were geese . . . er, I mean princesses." But the princesses just burst into tears and hid under the bed. They may very well be there to this day—or do you suppose their hair has grown by now?

13 JANUARY

The Devil's Bride

There was once a clever piper who had a beautiful daughter. The fame of her beauty spread to hell itself. Now, there happened to be in hell at the time a stupid devil who had thoughts of marrying, and it occurred to him that such a wife would be the envy of all who set eyes on her. So without delay he set out to visit the piper. He flew down the chimney straight into the parlour, and, paying no regard to formalities, shouted at the musician: "Give me your daughter for my wife, or I shall carry you off to hell!" As it happened, the beautiful maiden was not at home, having gone down to the well on the village green to draw water, so the wily piper just went calmly on filling his pipe, and said: "And why not, my friend? But she is not here just at the moment. She was disobedient, so I locked her up in the shed out in the yard." As soon as the devil heard this, he rushed into the back yard to do his courting. A bearded billy-goat's head appeared from the shed. He was getting on in years, and was grumpy and didn't have much time for jokes. "By Hades, a truly devilish beauty!" exclaimed the demon with satisfaction. "Horns like Lucifer himself, a chin as hairy as a tinker's—how the other devils will envy me such a bride." And at once he begged a kiss! The billy-goat bleated angrily and butted the devil so hard that he flew all the way back to hell. Just then the sky clouded over like doomsday, and a passing shepherd called in to the piper, "This must be the devil's wedding day!" —which is what the local people say when the sky is very black. "Indeed it is, neighbour, for he is marrying our old billy-goat!" replied the clever piper. And with a smile of satisfaction he stretched himself out in front of the fire.

14 JANUARY

The Magic Flute

Over nine rivers there lived, until not very long ago, a proud princess. Nothing was to her taste; she turned her nose up at everything. One day a little vagabond passed by, and he had a magic flute. He played to a white rose, and out of it stepped a white doll, which bowed three times and pirouetted three times. He played to the blue forget-me-not, and out jumped a little knight in blue armour, who waved his sword three times and raised his lance three times. "Oh, what a beautiful toy!" cried the princess from the palace window. "I must have it, whatever it costs!"—"You may have it for nothing," smiled the vagabond, "if you promise to play for the joy of people and flowers." The princess promised, but she did not keep her word. She wanted to play the flute only for her own amusement. She played once, and out crawled a black spider, which bowed three times and three times spun her a black web. She played a second time, and out flew a yellow wasp, which circled three times and then stung the princess three times. She started to cry and, throwing down the flute, ran indoors to complain. "The flute's magic is only for those who have a good heart," the little vagabond called after her, picking up the flute and setting it to his lips again. Wherever he went, the flowers danced; wherever he turned, all the birds of the air flew after him. Perhaps one day he will come your way.

15 JANUARY

The Musicians of Bremen

There was once a donkey who had toiled away all his life in a mill. Now that he was old and weak the miller wanted to have him put down. "What an ass I should be to wait for such a reward," the poor creature thought to himself. "I shall instead run away to Bremen to join the musicians." And so he did. On the way he was joined by an old dog, a homeless cat and a lame goat, all of which had been condemned to die. They walked and walked, and as they walked they made music. The donkey brayed, the dog howled, the cat mewed and the goat bleated until your ears would have split. On the fence of a farmstead a cock was crowing for all he was worth, singing his last song before the farmer's wife slit his throat. "Come along to Bremen with us, for it is a fine place, and we shall be musicians there," the donkey told him, and the cock did not wait to be asked twice. Night had fallen by the time they reached the cottage of a band of

robbers. The donkey peeped in at the window and saw the robbers feasting at a richly-spread table. "Let us play these good people a tune: surely they will not turn us away hungry from their doorstep," he said, and he began to beat time with his hoof. What a racket! The animals' music was enough to set the robbers' hair standing on end, and without more ado they fled the cottage like bats out of hell. So our fine musicians scampered over each other towards the table, where they ate, drank and made merry, and then dropped contentedly off to sleep.

16 JANUARY

The Musicians of Bremen

The robbers had run away from the cottage as if the devil himself were at their heels. Their ears were so sore from the music that they thought their heads would burst. But in the end they came together again in the forest to discuss what they must do. In time the pain in their ears subsided. "Who were you running away from, you oafs?" demanded their leader, angrily. "We?" the others retorted. "We were running after you!" And they began to argue so fiercely that they nearly flew at each other's throats. In the end their leader crept back alone to see what was going on. The cottage was now as dark and as quiet as the grave. On tiptoe, the robber stole inside and made straight for the hearth, where two bright embers were still glowing, to blow the fire into life. Alas! They were not glowing embers, but the cat's eyes, and, hissing and spitting in the dark, she tore angrily at his beard with her claws. Startled out of his wits, the robber chief once more took to his heels. But as he crossed the doorstep he trod on the sleeping dog's tail. The creature was far from pleased and, howling and whining like the devil himself, he sank his teeth into the robber's leg. The noise woke the donkey as he lay outside on the manure heap, and he began to beat a tattoo on the robber's back with his hooves, which in turn brought the lame goat hobbling along to

butt the intruder. Then the cock flew up and attacked the robber with his beak. "Cock-a-doodle-do!" he crowed. "Thieves, robbers! Beat them! Beat them!" Battered and bruised, the unhappy bandit ran into the forest, calling to his men: "Run for your lives! The cottage is full of demons. They chop and tear, spear with pitchforks and beat with clubs." As soon as the robbers heard this they turned tail and ran, and this time they did not return. And the musicians of Bremen? They never reached that town. Maybe they are still keeping house in the robbers' cottage.

17 JANUARY

Snow-White and Rose-Red

Once upon a time there was a little cottage; beside the cottage was a little garden, and in the garden were two rose bushes. One of them bore white roses, the other red. In the cottage lived a poor widow who had two beautiful daughters. The first of them was called Snow-White, because her skin was as white as the whitest rosebud, and the second was known as Rose-Red, since she ran about so tirelessly that she was always flushed like a scarlet rose. The two girls and their mother worked hard, and when their work was over the sisters would go into the forest to play

with the birds and animals, often sleeping among them in the soft green moss the whole night through. There was not an animal in the forest that would hurt a hair of their heads. When the first roses of summer blossomed in the garden, Rose-Red would carry whole armfuls of them into the parlour, till the entire cottage smelt like a bed of roses. And each bunch of roses would have a white rosebud for Snow-White, a red one for Rose-Red, and one, the loveliest of all, for their mother. They lived together happily in the little cottage.

One year there was a particularly hard winter, and on an evening when the frost chilled to the marrow and the wind thrust snowy fingers through every crack, there was a sudden thumping at the door, and a huge bear pushed his head into the parlour. "Let me warm myself by your fire, good folk!" he begged, in a human voice. The little white dove cooed with fear and huddled into a corner, followed by the sheep, followed by Snow-White and Rose-Red. They shivered with fright. "Don't be afraid, my dears," their mother reassured them, "the bear will not harm you." The girls took heart, brushed the snow from the poor animal's fur, and made him a bed by the hearth.

They were soon great friends, and the bear stayed with them in the cottage the whole winter.

18 JANUARY

Snow-White and Rose-Red

What a merry time they had in the little cottage! How Snow-White and Rose-Red played with the bear and teased him — they almost smothered him with love, so that from time to time he had to scold them mildly:

"Snow-White, take care —
Rose-Red, by gentle in your play,
'Twere sad to slay the husband
before the wedding day!"

The girls laughed gaily at this. But when spring came the bear could not be persuaded to stay. "I must guard my treasure from the wicked dwarfs. While the ground was frozen, they could not dig, but now they will again steal whatever they can lay their hands on," he explained, and took his leave of them graciously. As he passed through the door, he tore his skin on an old nail, and for a moment they saw a gleam like pure gold under his fur. But before the girls could ask about it, he was gone.

One day Snow-White and Rose-Red went into the forest to gather kindling-wood. In a clearing they came across an ugly dwarf, jumping about and screeching angrily. He had got his beard caught in a crack in a tree stump, and he could not get it out again. The girls ran willingly to his aid, but though they tugged and tugged they could not pull him loose. In the end Snow-White had to cut off the tip of his beard. "Oh, you horrible children, to disgrace me so!" he hissed, and without even bothering to thank them he snatched up a pot of gold from the grass and disappeared beneath the ground. Another time they found the ungrateful manikin down by the river. This time his beard was caught up in his fishing line, and a great fish was dragging him into the deep water. "Help!" he called, desperately. Again the girls took pity on him, and, since they couldn't untangle his beard, they had to cut it off right at the top. The dwarf insulted them at the top of his voice, grabbed a sack of pearls from the reeds, made a rude face at them, and once more the earth swallowed him up. "That's the last time we help him, ungrateful fellow," resolved the girls, and they went home to bed.

19 JANUARY

Snow-White and Rose-Red

One day Snow-White and Rose-Red were on their way to town to do some shopping. All at once they saw the thankless dwarf struggling vainly with a huge eagle. Forgetting their resolve, the girls prized him out of the bird's claws. "Fie! You horrid little wretches, you've ruined my tunic!" he hissed at them, throwing a sack of jewels across his shoulder and disappearing as before. Towards evening, as they returned home, they spied him playing with diamonds on a patch of ground he had cleared. "What are you staring at?" he squealed, angrily. Just then a huge bear emerged from the forest, making straight for the dwarf. "Eat those horrid girls, not me!" pleaded the little man, but the bear struck him a great blow with his huge paw, laying him dead in the grass. Snow-White and Rose-Red took to their heels, but they heard a voice call: "Do not be afraid, it is I, your friend the bear!" They turned around and, lo and behold! The black bear skin had fallen away, and there stood a prince dressed all in gold. "The wicked dwarf once stole all my treasures and turned

me into a bear," he said. "Now that he is dead, the spell is broken." As he spoke these words a golden coach appeared by magic; the three of them sat in it and set off for the cottage to pick up mother, the sheep and the white dove. Then they all drove together to the prince's palace. The prince took Snow-White for his wife, and Rose-Red was married to his brother. They brought the two rose bushes from the little cottage garden and planted them in front of the palace. And whenever a rose-bud blossoms on them, a little child is born at the palace. Sometimes it is as white as snow, sometimes as red as a rose.

20 JANUARY

Thumbling

In a cottage on the hillside lived a peasant and his wife. It was a sad household, for they had no children. "If only we could have a child, even if he were as tiny as a pea," the woman would sometimes sigh to herself. Now, what we say and think is sometimes not as unlikely as we suppose. And so one winter's day it happened that a little boy was born in the cottage. He was no larger than your thumb, and though he ate enough for two, he never grew so much as a hair's breadth taller. He wore a tunic sewn from a single mouse-skin. But he was soon all over the parlour, and was full of fun and no trouble to anyone—in short, as lively a lad as ever you saw! They started to call him Thumbling. One day, when his father had gone to collect firewood, towards midday Thumbling said to his mother: "Harness up the horse, I shall take the cart to meet father." His mother clasped her hands in dismay. "My poor child, you will never hold the rein!" But Thumbling begged her to set him in the horse's ear, and as soon as she had done this, hey-up! Off went the horse at a trot. Oh, what a ride! They went like the wind. On the way they passed a couple of rogues, who stared in wonder and said: "A cart without a carter, but still someone is shouting the horse on. What wonder is this?" And they ran after the cart curiously, until it reached the clearing. What should they see there? Out of the horse's ear popped a tiny boy, and leapt into his father's palm. You can imagine how proud the peasant was of his little son.

21 JANUARY

Thumbling

The moment the two rogues set eyes on Thumbling, it occurred to them that they might make a good living for themselves by showing him at fairs, and they at once begged the good-natured peasant to sell them his son. "Not for the world," the peasant told them, but Thumbling crawled up his sleeve to his shoulder and whispered in his ear, "Sell me, father: you shall not regret it!" The peasant hesitated, but in the end he agreed to sell, and made a tidy little sum out of the deal. One of the travellers then stowed Thumbling away in his knapsack. It was packed full of gold pieces! The clever Thumbling threw one ducat after another out onto the path where he knew his father would go on his way home. When the knapsack was empty, he demanded to be let out of it, saying he had had enough of sitting in the dark, and asked to ride on the brim of the man's hat. There he strutted up and down like a squire, and gazed merrily around him at the passing countryside. But as soon as they had gone some distance thus, the lad began to cry out, "Help, let me down, my stomach hurts me so!" The moment the travellers put him on the ground, he slipped into the nearest mousehole and made his way to safety through the underground passages. When he finally came out into the sunlight again, he curled up in an empty snail's shell and slept like a tiny log.

22 JANUARY

Thumbling

The sparrows on the fences were already chattering nineteen to the dozen when Thumbling woke up. He could hear voices not far away. Two robbers were arguing over how best to rob a nearby parsonage. "Take me with you, I shall help you!" called Thumbling, in a thin little voice. When the startled robbers saw him crawling out of a snail shell, they burst out laughing. "What use to us are you, little man?" they jeered. But Thumbling offered to squeeze through the grille on the parsonage window and throw the booty out to them. The robbers liked the idea. When night fell, one of them took him in his coat pocket, and when they got to the parsonage they pushed him through the window-bars into the drawing-room. The boy began to shout, "Do you want everything that is here?" "Quiet, you fool!" called the robbers, softly. But Thumbling pretended not to hear, and went on yelling. This woke up the cook, who went to see what was going on. The robbers fled. And Thumbling? He slipped through the cook's legs into the yard and buried himself contentedly in a haystack, where he went to sleep again!

23 JANUARY

Thumbling

Early next morning the servant-girl went to feed the animals. She gathered up an armful of hay with Thumbling inside and dropped it in the cow's manger. The cow munched hungrily, and before you could say Jack Robinson Thumbling found himself in the cow's stomach. How dark it was there! "They must have forgotten to put windows in this room," he thought to himself, but as one mouthful of hay after another came tumbling down on his head, it was a wonder he did not suffocate. The clever lad began to shout at the top of his voice, "Enough, enough! Feed me no more!" The girl was frightened to death. "Save us, our cow can speak!" she called out, and ran to tell the parson. The parson crossed himself, and called the butcher to slaughter the possessed animal. When he had done so, the butcher threw the stomach with Thumbling inside it on the manure heap. A passing wolf, being very fond of tripe, was not slow to devour this titbit, little boy and all. But Thumbling soon had a bright idea. "Brother wolf," he called, "why do you not go to our cottage, mother's larder is full of good things to eat!" The wolf needed no further persuasion; he slipped in through the larder window, and ate and ate until he was so bloated he was unable to get out again. Then Thumbling began to shout, "Father, help! The wolf has me in his stomach!" When his father heard this, he slew the wolf with an axe, slit open its stomach and set his son free. What a joyful reunion it was! The boy related his adventures over and over again. But from then on he was content to stay at home.

24 JANUARY

The Sea-Princess's Gift

Far out on the open sea, a young fisherman cast his nets. Drawing them in, he caught sight of a strange fish, with lovely human eyes, and a golden key hanging round its neck. All at once, it spoke: "I am the sea-king's daughter: if you set me free, I shall take you with me to his palace beneath the waves, where you shall be richly rewarded." The fisherman agreed; he took hold of a fin, and the fish plunged beneath the surface, dragging him along. He was quite unharmed by the water, and they swam past placid underwater scenes, through shoals of merry fish, gliding by dancing octopuses and grim-faced sharks, till they came to a palace built of pearls and red coral. No sooner had they passed through its gates, than the fish changed into a beautiful princess. She led him through mother-of-pearl chambers, where people like fish were dancing, and into a golden hall, filled with riches of all the seas. "Choose what you wish," said the princess, handing him the golden key to the treasure chests. The fisherman did not know which way to look first, but just then

a lovely young girl, set all over with silver fish-scales, danced up to him, and whispered in his ear: "Take only one old mussel!" The fisherman did as he was told, and when the sea-princess learnt of his wish, she only smiled at him kindly, and took him to the palace gate. From there the girl with the silver scales accompanied him to the shore: but scarcely had they passed through the gates, when she changed into a silvery fish.

25 JANUARY

The Sea-Princess's Gift

The fish-girl was so kind and beautiful that the young man fell in love with her before they reached the shore. "What a pity you may not live on land," he mourned. "I should like you to be my wife." But the fish only smiled, and

answered: "Trust in your mussel, it will fulfil your every wish!" So the fisherman told the mussel his wish and, lo and behold—when they reached the shallows the silvery fish again changed into a beautiful girl, and she stepped out onto the shore with him. But the fisherman looked around in vain for his cottage home. While he had been in the palace beneath the waves, a hundred long years had passed in the world above. The young man was startled. "If only my old mother and father were here," he exclaimed, bitterly. The moment he had said this—wonder of wonders—the family cottage appeared before his very eyes, and on the doorstep an old couple began to wake from a deep sleep. "How soundly we have slept," they yawned in wonder, and at once they warmly greeted their son and his bride. From then on they all lived in happiness and

contentment. The magic mussel fulfilled their each and every wish; and when, one day, the envious king of that land heard of their riches, and tried to steal away the magic mussel by force, a great wave from the sea swept the king and all his soldiers into the depths of the ocean. Then the poor fisherman became ruler of the whole country, and the beautiful fish-girl his queen.

26 JANUARY

The Old Woman and the Mouse

In a little paper house on a little paper hill lived a kind old woman. One day a cheeky

little mouse moved in with her. “I’m going to stay here and live with you, granny,” he told her coarsely, “and if you don’t like it I shall chew your little house to pieces!”—“I don’t mind,” smiled the clever old woman. “At least I shan’t be lonely here on my own. If you like, we can ask each other riddles.” The mouse agreed, and perched haughtily on the woman’s outstretched palm. “I shall begin,” he squeaked. “Tell me, old woman, tell me, how many steps does a sparrow take, to cross an acre field?” “An easy one,” replied the old woman. “None at all. A sparrow doesn’t step, it only hops. But now listen carefully to my riddle! Ears like a mouse, claws like a mouse, whiskers like a mouse, but it isn’t a mouse. What is it?”—“I give up,” said the mouse. “No, no,” said the old woman, shaking her head. “You must keep guessing. Let’s try it another way. What is it? Eyes like a cat, legs like a cat, tail like a cat, voice like a cat, and right now it’s getting ready to jump on your back!” “C-c-c-c-cat!” shrieked the mouse, and was off and out of the little house in a flash. “Dear me, wherever would a cat appear from in my house—it was only a riddle,” smiled the old woman, thinking to herself how glad she was to see the last of the silly little mouse.

27 JANUARY

The Master of the Robber’s Trade

Once upon a time, a cottager was out in his garden planting trees, when a stranger rode by. He had the look of a gentleman, but there was something roguish about his eyes. “What, have you no son to help you in your work?” he called out to the cottager. “Indeed, I have a son,” said the cottager. “But he was good-for-nothing, and ran away from home.” The stranger smiled, and asked if the cottager’s wife might cook him some simple peasant food. “I have had enough of fine delicacies,” he said, with a sigh. While the woman was cooking him a dish of dumplings, he stood in the porch, watching the cottager tying back young trees. “Why do you not tie up that old, crooked tree?” he asked in surprise. “It is clear that you are no nurseryman,” replied the cottager. “Old wood cannot be straightened. If you wish to have straight trees, you must tie them back from the start.” At this the unknown traveller pushed his hat to the back of his head and said: “So is it also with people, father! I am your long-lost son. Had you bound me to honesty from the very start by using a firm hand, I might have been an upright man. As it is, I have learnt the robber’s trade: mind you, I am master of it now, and make a good living by it.”
The cottager and his wife were filled with horror. “What would your godfather, the noble duke, say to all this?” they cried in despair. “He would surely have you swing

from a gibbet!" But the wayward son only smiled, and said, "What of it? He, too, is grown rich otherwise than by honest work. Tomorrow I shall go to visit him." And he did.

28 JANUARY

The Master of the Robber's Trade

The next day, when the cottager's son had himself announced at the mansion of his godfather, the duke, and told him what trade he had learnt, the stern nobleman frowned darkly. "I should hand you over to the executioner without delay," he said, "but since you are my godson, I shall be merciful to you if you fulfil three commands. First you must

steal from my stables my favourite horse. If you succeed, then you shall enter my bedchamber and steal the ring from my wife's finger and the sheet on which she lies. If you manage this second task, then you must steal from the parsonage the parson and his sexton. If you are able to perform all these feats, then you are truly a master of the robber's trade. If you do not, then you will be shorter by a head!" The clever thief was not dismayed. That evening he dressed up as an old woman, took a skin of wine, added to it a strong sleeping draught, and hobbled off towards the duke's stable. The duke's soldiers were on guard there. One sat on the horse, a second

held its rein, and just to make sure, a third was holding it by the tail. "Hey, old woman, where are you going with that bottle?" they called. "To you, my dears," the old woman croaked. "The duke sends you some of his own wine to warm you." The soldiers needed no encouragement; they drank, and drank, and soon were sleeping soundly. The one who sat on the horse, the robber tied to a beam; the second he gave a piece of string to hold instead of the rein, and the one who had held the tail snored on contentedly, grasping a bunch of straw. When the duke came into the stable the next morning, he could not help laughing at the way the robber had fooled them. "But just you wait, you rogue! Tonight I shall keep watch a good deal better!"

29 JANUARY

The Master of the Robber's Trade

That evening the duke sat by his wife's bed with a blunderbuss in his hand and his eyes peeled for the robber. But the young man had hurried off to the execution yard, where he cut one of the victims down from the gallows and carried him off to a spot below the mansion windows. When midnight came, he placed a ladder against the wall and dragged the hanged man's body up it, pushing its head in front of the bedroom window. Scarcely had he done so, when the duke let fly from his gun, and then rushed off to see the results of his marksmanship. He found the body beneath the window. "Poor fellow," he thought to himself, "he brought about his own undoing in the end." And he began to dig him a grave. In the meantime the robber had entered the bedroom, where he whispered to the duchess: "Do not be afraid, it is I, your husband. You need fear no more, I have shot the robber dead. But he was, after all, my godson, and he deserves a Christian burial. Give me your bedsheet to wrap him in, and your ring, that he may at least take with him to the grave that for which he died." The duchess obliged, and the clever thief was gone like the wind. When the duke returned to his bedchamber, he could not believe his eyes. "Is that rogue a wizard, too?" he wondered. "Did I not bury him with my own hands?" The next day the robber brought him the ring and the sheet, smiling beneath his beard. "Just you wait, my clever lad, the third time you shall not be so lucky," warned the duke. But what can one do with robbers?

30 JANUARY

The Master of the Robber's Trade

Late that night the robber made his way to the parsonage with a bag of crayfish he had caught. Onto the backs of the crayfish he stuck lighted candles, and set them among the graves in the churchyard. Then he dressed in a black smock, and, holding a large sack at the ready, climbed up into the pulpit. He began to shout, "Hurry, hurry; the end of the world is at hand! See how the dead leave their graves on their way to the heavenly kingdom! I am Peter, who guards the golden gate. Whosoever wishes to enter the kingdom before the end of the world, let him climb into my sack!" The parson and the sexton heard this and, looking towards the churchyard, saw the strange lights moving to and fro among the gravestones. Without more ado they jumped into the robber's sack, anxious to be the first. The robber dragged them down the steps until their heads banged this way and that, calling out to them: "Now we are floating above the mountains!" Then he dragged them through a puddle, and cried: "Now we are passing through rainclouds!" When he had given them another good shaking on the steps of the ducal mansion, he shoved the sack into the dovecote. "Can you hear the beating of angels' wings?" he whispered. "Why, of course," replied the parson. "I beg your pardon, St. Peter," said the unhappy sexton, "but it stinks here in heaven like some pigeon-house!" The robber laughed till he almost dropped. When, the next morning, he showed the duke his night's booty, his lordship was forced to laugh, too. When he untied the sack, the two foolish prisoners thrust out their heads and said in surprise, "By all the saints, Your Lordship, are you in heaven already?" What was the duke to do? He gave the clever robber a chest full of gold coins, and told him, "You are indeed a master of the robber's trade; but be gone with you from my dukedom, never to return, or it will go ill with you!" The rogue thanked him, left his parents money enough to live in comfort, and disappeared into the world. Who knows what has become of him since. Perhaps he has retired from robbery, and turned his hand to playing the lute and singing robbers' songs!

31 JANUARY

The Bowl of Milk

A cat and a pig set off together into the world one day. Soon both of them began to feel quite hungry. They met an old goat. "Give us a little milk, mother goat!" they begged her. "If you first dig my garden," bleated the goat. The pig set to at once, but the cat mewed that she must first take a rest. She lay down in the sun, stretched herself out, and spent a long while cleaning her fur with her pink tongue. When noon came, the goat brought along a bowl of cream. "This is for the one who has done the most work in my garden," she said. The pig, who was covered in earth, rushed towards the bowl. "I have dug the whole garden on my own," he grunted. The goat shook her head. "You have the manners of a pig," she said. "Is that any way to come to lunch?" Then she looked at the cat. "And what did you do all morning?" she asked. "I?" said the cat. "Why, I washed myself instead of the pig." The goat thought for a while. "The cat shall have the cream," she said at last. "For she has worked for both." And that has been the way of the world ever since. While one does all the work, another laps up the cream. And all because of the stupid goat.

FEBRUARY

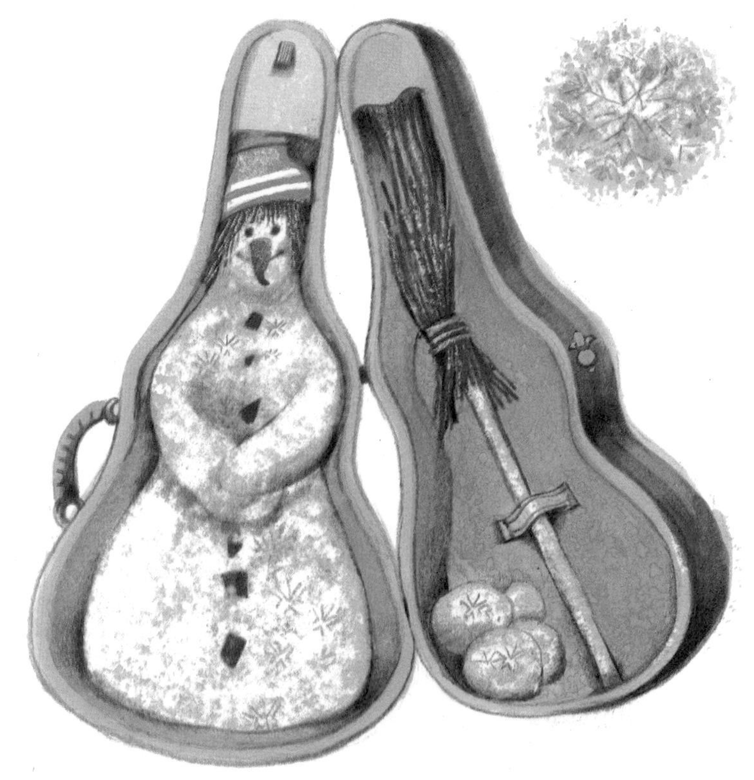

1 FEBRUARY

Ali Baba and the Forty Thieves

In a land far away to the east, where the sun blazes down like a huge red jewel over the glaring white cities, there lived, long ago, two brothers, called Kassim and Ali Baba. Kassim was a rich merchant, but Ali Baba was as poor as a church mouse. He was just able to support his family by gathering dry sticks to sell as firewood. One day his work took him far beyond the city, where the sand and scorched rocks of the desert begin. He was just tying the last armful of sticks up in his bundle, when he heard in the distance the thunder of a great troop of horses. Ali Baba hid himself in the bushes, and waited to see what would happen. A band of robbers came riding up in a cloud of dust. Not counting their leader, there were exactly forty of them. They leapt down from their horses and gathered around one of the rocks, and in a fearful voice their leader called out, "Open, sesame!" In the twinkling of an eye the rock face opened up before them, and the robbers poured into a secret cave. Ali Baba waited, and watched. After a while the rocks again opened up; the robbers came out, mounted their horses and galloped off. Ali Baba could not contain his curiosity; he went up to the cliff and called out, "Open, sesame!" To his surprise the hard stone wall parted to let him into an exquisite cave, filled with gold and precious stones. The cliff face crashed shut behind him.

2 FEBRUARY

Ali Baba and the Forty Thieves

Ali Baba was dazzled by the beauty and richness of what he saw, but he wasted no time, caught up as much gold and jewels as he could carry, and ordered the rocks to release him again. He shoved the treasure into his bundles of firewood, loaded them onto his donkey, and hurried home. His wife could not believe her eyes when she saw the riches he had brought. She ran off at once to her sister-in-law, Kassim's wife, to borrow a grain measure, in order to measure their new-found wealth. But Kassim's wife was curious to know why the poor folk needed a grain measure, when they scarcely had enough to keep body and soul together, so she spread a little honey on the bottom of the measure. When she got the measure back again, she found a tiny gold coin stuck to the honey. As soon as Kassim heard from his wife that Ali Baba the pauper had been using a grain measure to take stock of his gold coins, he went off and demanded that his brother should tell him where he had come by such wealth. The good-hearted Ali Baba told him everything, and the greedy Kassim rode off at once towards the secret cave. "Open, sesame!" he called out to the rock face, and it opened to let him in. The miserly merchant could not bring himself to go away and leave such treasures. He played with the tinkling gold pieces for so long that the robbers, returning to their cave, found him there and cut his throat.

3 FEBRUARY

Ali Baba and the Forty Thieves

When Kassim did not return for a long time, Ali Baba went out to the rocks to look for him. But in the cave he found only his brother's lifeless body. Sadly, he slung the dead man over his donkey and carried him back to the city, where the family buried him. He and his wife and children then moved into his brother's house. Meanwhile, the robbers had returned to their cave from another expedition, and when they saw that Kassim's body had disappeared, they realized that someone else must also know their secret. Their chieftain ordered one of his cut-throats to go into the city and find out who had dared to enter their cave. The robber stood in the market-place asking questions, until at last he heard how a poor man called Ali Baba had recently buried his brother, and had come by mysterious wealth. The robber made a chalk cross on the door of Ali Baba's house in order to remember where he lived, and went to report to his leader. But Ali Baba had a clever servant-girl called Morgiana. She noticed the chalkmark at once and, suspecting foul play, made crosses on all the doors in the street. When, that night, the robbers stole into the city, they could not find Ali Baba's house. The robber chieftain was so angry with his spy that he had the poor man's head cut off on the spot.

4 FEBRUARY

Ali Baba and the Forty Thieves

The robbers' leader stayed behind in the city himself, until he had again found the house he wanted. He went back to his men and ordered them to load forty skins and jars onto a train of mules. He filled one of them with olive oil, but in each of the others he hid one of his men. They agreed on a signal, at which they would leap out to attack Ali Baba's house. Then the

robber chief disguised himself as a merchant, made his way with his caravan to Ali Baba's house, and asked for a bed for the night. Ali Baba willingly took the stranger into his house. While they were talking together, the lamp in the kitchen went out, and the servant-girl Morgiana went to fill it with oil. She remembered that the merchant had left his jars of oil in the courtyard, and she went up to them. When the hidden robbers heard footsteps in the yard, they asked in a whisper: "Is it time, master?" The clever girl suspected a trap, and whispered in a deep voice: "No, not yet!" She felt the skins until she found the one which was full of oil, which she then boiled in a cauldron and poured into all the other vessels, scalding the robbers to death. Then she called the soldiers, who recognizea the robber chief and executed him on the spot. Thus it was that once again the clever Morgiana saved Ali Baba and his family, and he rewarded her richly for her courage and faithfulness.

5 FEBRUARY

The Magic Pot

Once upon a time a poor girl went into the forest to gather wild strawberries, and there she met an old woman. "Give me at least a poor crust of bread, my girl, for I am so hungry I can scarcely stand," the woman begged. The kindhearted girl shared with her the little food she had, and for her generosity the old woman made her a present of a cooking pot. "It is magic," she explained. "If you say to it 'pot, cook gruel', it will cook as much gruel as you could wish for." The girl thanked her kindly and went home, and she and her mother cooked sweet, wholesome gruel until they could eat no more. From then on they were never short of food. One day, the girl had gone on some errand or other, when her mother began to feel hungry. She put the pot on the hearth, so that the gruel would be nice and warm, and told it, "Pot, cook gruel!" The pot cooked and cooked, until the gruel ran out of it and onto the floor, then out of the door into the garden. The girl's mother was so upset that she forgot how to stop the pot from cooking. She took a broom and brushed the gruel out of the hallway, but to no avail: soon the parlour was full of gruel, then it flowed out of the window, down onto the village green. At that moment the girl came running in, and told the pot, "Pot, enough!" But by that time there was so much gruel on the village green that the farmers and their horses could not get by, and had to eat their way through the sweet morass.

6 FEBRUARY

Primrose

There once lived a poor, but hard-working young girl whom everyone called Primrose, for though she was very beautiful, she was as humble as that lovely flower. Whenever she went into town she would hide her face behind a veil, being too modest to show her beauty. One day the king's son himself saw

her, and he asked the people why she did not show her face. "She is beautiful, but modest," they replied. The prince was burning with curiosity and, determined to see the girl's beauty for himself, he sent a servant to her cottage with a golden ring and a message that she should meet him at sunset beneath the great oak tree. Thinking that those in the palace were going to give her some work to do, she waited beneath the tree at the appointed hour. When the prince saw her without her veil, he was so enchanted with her beauty that he wanted to take her off to the royal castle without delay. But Primrose refused to go with him, saying, "I am a poor girl, and your father would surely be angry to know whom you had chosen for your bride. Let me have at least a few days to consider." Unwillingly, the prince agreed. Soon afterwards, he sent a servant to her cottage with a pair of silver shoes, and again asked her to meet him beneath the old oak. She went to meet him, but again he was unable to persuade her to go with him, try as he might. And when the prince sent her a present of a golden gown, she did not even go to the tree to meet him, because she was so afraid of the king.

7 FEBRUARY

Primrose

One day the king did indeed hear of his son's meetings with a poor peasant-girl. His anger was truly great, for he had chosen the daughter of a powerful neighbouring king to marry his heir. So he ordered his soldiers to burn down the roof over her head. "Let her burn along with her cottage!" he thundered. The soldiers went and carried out his command. Primrose was busy sewing, her beloved songbird beside her in its cage. Suddenly, flames licked at her from all sides. She ran to the door, and saw that the cottage was surrounded by the king's soldiers. So, without more ado, she caught up the birdcage and leapt straight from the window into the old well. There she lay hidden for many days, crying her eyes out with grief. She was sad to lose her little cottage, but she was even sadder to think that she might never see the prince again. In the end she took heart again, dressed herself in boy's clothes, and set off for the royal castle to ask to be taken into service. The comely page at once caught the king's eye. "What is your name?" he asked. "I am

called Misfortune," the girl replied. "That is not a pretty name," said the king, shaking his head, "but I shall take you into my service if you sing me a pretty song." Primrose and her songbird sang a song so beautiful and so sad that the king's heart was moved. From then on the new page was treated like the king's own son.

8 FEBRUARY

Primrose

When the unhappy prince heard that Primrose had gone up in flames with her cottage, it was a wonder his heart did not break, such was his grief. When at last his suffering eased a little, the king decided that his wedding with the princess should be delayed no longer. So he set off with his entire court in a magnificent procession to the neighbouring kingdom. At the rear of the royal train came Primrose in her page's dress, riding on a horse. She felt very melancholy, so to cheer her heart she began to sing: "For Misfortune, Prince, to wear, tie a primrose in my hair."—"Who is it that sings so sad a song?" asked the prince, in surprise. "It is Misfortune, my servant," his father told him. Unable to resist the plaintive refrain, the prince plucked from the wayside a primrose and rode up to the page. He recognized his gold ring, gleaming on the girl's finger, and knew she was his chosen love. He smiled at her, but said nothing. When all had taken their seats for a great feast at the palace of the neighbouring king, their host said to them: "Come, let us tell riddles!" The prince was not slow to pose one: "Sire, in my castle I have a golden casket, from which I lost the key. They promised to make me a new one, but now I have found the old. Tell me, my lord, which key should I keep—the old or the new?"—"Why, the old, of course," replied the king. Then the prince took Primrose by the hand, and proclaimed, "You yourself have decided the matter, my lord! I cannot marry your daughter. For here is the key which I lost, and have found again." When all had seen the lovely Primrose and heard her tale, anger was forgotten, and a magnificent wedding prepared. When the celebrations were over, the prince returned to his palace with his happy bride.

9 FEBRUARY

The Three Wood-Elves

Once upon a time there was a widower who had a beautiful daughter. Not far from them lived a widow who also had a daughter, but she was ugly and selfish. The two girls had known each other since they were little, and from time to time they would visit each other. One day the widow told her neighbour's daughter, "If your father were to take me as his wife, you would not be sorry. You could bathe every day in milk, and drink good wine; I should treat you better than my own

daughter. Perhaps you might speak a word in his ear." The girl did as the old woman told her. But the old man did not too much like the idea of marrying again, and he said: "We shall let Fate decide." Thinking to make an end of the matter, he took an old shoe, hung it from a beam in the attic, and filled it with water. "If the water remains in the shoe until morning, it shall be a sign that I am to marry again," he said. The old shoe was full of holes, so he thought he had nothing to fear. But the water made the shoe swell, the holes closed up, and in the morning the water was still there. What could the old man do? He had to marry the widow, as he had promised. The first day after the wedding his new wife treated her stepdaughter like a rare gift from heaven, but it was not long at all before she had changed her tune. Her own daughter she spoilt endlessly, but the old man's child began to wish she had never been born.

10 FEBRUARY

The Three Wood-Elves

Winter came, and the frost bit deep. The cruel stepmother sewed a dress from paper, put it on her stepdaughter, and ordered her, "Go out into the forest, and bring home a basket of strawberries; otherwise you need not return at all!" What was the poor child to do? She wandered through the snowy wastes, icy tears running down her cheeks. Somewhere in the

depths of the forest, where she no longer knew her way at all, she came across a little cottage. It was the home of three little wood-elves. The hapless child begged them to let her warm herself by their fire. They frowned at her, but let her in. She crouched gratefully in front of the flaming logs, and took out a crust of dry bread. "Give us some too," said the elves, quite sternly, and the girl was only too willing to share what little she had. Then she told them how she came to be in the forest in such cruel weather. "Take the broom and sweep away the snow behind our cottage!" the elves ordered her. She did as she was told, and when she went out, the elves discussed how they might reward her for her obedience. The first of them said: "My gift shall be for her to grow lovelier day by day." The second said: "My gift shall be for gold pieces to fall from her mouth each time she speaks." And the third declared: "My gift shall be for a king to come and take her for his wife." Meanwhile, the girl had swept away the snow as she had been bidden, and what do you suppose she found buried under the snow? Ripe red strawberries! She thanked the elves for their kindness, and hurried home.

11 FEBRUARY

The Three Wood-Elves

The girl had hardly reached home with the strawberries and spoken a word of greeting,

when a shining gold piece fell out of her mouth. And when she told them of all that happened in the forest, the kitchen floor became littered with gold coins. The stepmother and her daughter were quite green with envy. And to make things worse for them, the good child grew more beautiful every day. One day the ugly sister resolved that she, too, would go off into the forest in search of strawberries. She put on a warm fur coat, took a basket of cakes for the journey, and made straight for the wood-elves' cottage. Without a word she sat herself down in front of the fire and began to eat. "Give us some too!" called the elves, but she did not even look their way. When she had finally eaten her fill, the elves told her to sweep away the snow from the garden path. But work was not to her liking at all, so she decided it was time to go home. The elves were furious. "My gift shall be for her to grow uglier every day!" scowled the first. "My gift shall be for a toad to fall out of her mouth every time she speaks," said the second, and the third added: "My gift shall be for her to meet a cruel fate." And so it happened that when the ugly girl came home, with the first word she spoke a toad leapt out of her mouth. In a short while the parlour was thicker with toads than a woodland pond.

12 FEBRUARY

The Three Wood-Elves

It was then that life really became difficult for the girl with the golden tongue. But one day, when the stepmother had sent her down to the frozen stream to wring out the washing, the king himself passed by. The girl greeted him politely, and gold pieces fell from her mouth as she spoke. "Such a beautiful and rich bride deserves to marry no less than the king himself," he said, and took her off to his castle to be his wife. Before the year was out a child was born to the young queen. The moment the stepmother heard this, she hurried off to the palace with her own daughter to visit the royal mother. But when the king left them alone in the bedchamber, the wicked women dragged her from her bed and threw her from a window into the river below. The ugly girl climbed into bed in her place, pulling the sheets up over her face. When the king

returned to the chamber, the stepmother told him his wife had suddenly become ill. The king was deceived, but when she did not rise from her bed the next day, he went to inquire after her health. The moment she spoke, toads began to drop from her mouth instead of gold. "It is on account of the fever," the stepmother declared. But that evening a small duck waddled into the royal kitchens. "How is my child?" she asked. The cook recognized the young queen's voice, and he replied, "He is asleep in his cradle." He hurried off to tell the king, and led him into the kitchen to see the wonder for himself. The duck begged the king to pass his sword three times over her head, and no sooner had he done so, than there in front of him stood his golden-tongued wife. And what of the stepmother and her ugly daughter? So afraid were they of the wrath of the king that they leapt out of the window of their own accord, and drowned in the river below.

13 FEBRUARY

The Ugly Duckling

Underneath a burdock leaf a duck was sitting on her eggs. She could hardly wait for the ducklings to burst out of their shells. Then at last they began to hatch. "Peep, peep, peep," they said, as they pushed their little heads out into the big world. But there was only one strange, large egg that somehow refused to hatch. "Sure to be a turkey's egg, my dear," whispered a neighbour to the mother duck.

"They once gave me one of those. Better leave it be and teach your dear little ducklings to swim." The mother duck decided not to abandon the last egg, and at last the strange egg hatched. But what was this? Out of the shell came such an ugly, gawky duckling that the mother duck was quite dismayed. "Perhaps it is a turkey chick, after all," she said to herself. "But we'll soon see." And she took the whole family off to the pond and went splash! into the water. One by one, the ducklings plopped in after her, the big, ugly one as well. "That's no turkey, dear, it's one of your very own," said the old goose. "See how beautifully he swims," the mother duck said proudly, and she led her family off to meet the other ducks, especially their queen. She was a noble duck with a ribbon on one of her legs, and had Spanish blood in her veins. She looked the ducklings over for a long time.

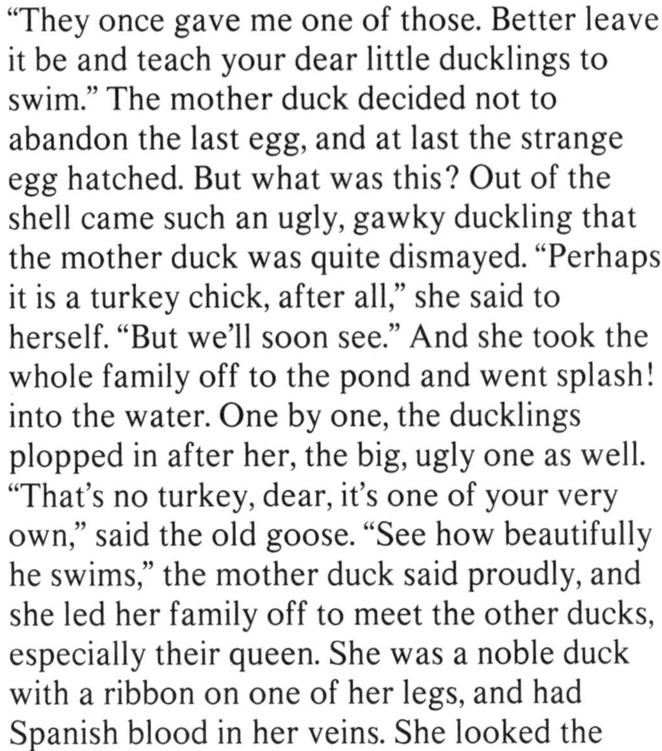

14 FEBRUARY

The Ugly Duckling

When the queen had had a good look at the duck family, she said, "You have indeed pretty children, my dear, except for the last one, that big one; he is terribly ugly. Never in my life have I seen such an ugly little thing!"
When the other ducks heard this, they began to peck the poor duckling, and pinch him, and the geese and the hens joined in; and the old turkey, who thought he was emperor, charged at him, crimson with rage and gobbling fiercely. Even the poor creature's brothers and sisters laughed at him, and his mother cried. She secretly wished he would wander off somewhere and never return. One day, when the ugly duckling could stand it no longer, he

ran away in a flood of tears. He flew over the fence, and on, and on, to the great marshes where the wild ducks lived. "Oh, how ugly you are!" they said to him. "But we don't mind, as long as you don't marry into the family." Just then a pair of wild ganders flew by. "You are so ugly that we quite like you," they cackled. "Wouldn't you like to come along with us and be a bird of passage?" But the ugly duckling just hung his head sadly.

15 FEBRUARY

The Ugly Duckling

The two wild ganders did not get far. A shooting party was lying in wait in the marshes and, bang! bang!—the ganders plummetted into the water. Then retriever dogs came charging through the rushes, medals around their necks. The duckling hid in the bushes, but it was no use. Suddenly a huge dog was standing over him, tongue hanging out and eyes glinting threateningly. He touched the duckling with his nose, licked him with his tongue, and then was gone again in a flash. "Oh dear," said the duckling to himself, mournfully, "I am so ugly that even a dog shrinks away from me!" And he flew away. Towards evening he reached a little cottage. In it lived an old woman who had a cat and a hen. The cat could arch her back and purr, and if you stroked her the wrong way she could even give off sparks. The hen laid beautiful eggs. Both were very proud of themselves, and thought themselves the most intelligent creatures in the world. The old woman took the duckling in, thinking he would learn to lay eggs. But he soon seemed not only ugly, but also quite useless, and the cat and the hen made so much of his stupidity and of their own wisdom and skill that one day he was forced to run away again. "It serves you right for being so ugly!" they called after him.

16 FEBRUARY

The Ugly Duckling

The unhappy duckling again wandered

aimlessly through the world. No one wanted him, and all the animals despised him for his ugliness. Summer passed, and autumn, and then cruel winter came along. The duckling shivered with cold. Words cannot describe his suffering during that harsh winter. It was a wonder he did not freeze to death on the frozen lake.

But then spring arrived, and with a strength which surprised him the duckling took to the air. One day he alighted on an ornamental lake in a beautiful garden. On it there swam magnificent white birds with long necks. They were swans, although the duckling did not know it. He felt only a great joy, and a wish to join the lovely creatures. He swam shyly towards them. He was afraid they would drive him away for his ugliness, but they leaned towards him and welcomed him. Suddenly, the duckling saw his own reflection in the water. It was not that of an ugly duckling, but of a splendid white swan. Just then some children ran up to the lakeside, calling out: "There is a new swan—look, it is the most beautiful of all!" The young swan was so happy he burst into song. "Never did I dream of such happiness, when I was an ugly duckling!" he thought to himself joyfully, and proudly swam about the lake with his companions.

17 FEBRUARY

The Candle-Flame Fairy Tale

In a certain little cottage lived an old woman who had a magic candlestick. A candle burned there day and night, and never burned down. Whoever gazed into the flame of that candle would dream a fairy tale at night. And which fairy tale? Why, this one: Once upon a time there was a little prince called Rini. He lived inside a hazel nut, in a diamond chamber inside a golden palace. The silver flowers beneath his window were watered and cared for by a little gardener-girl called Lini. The two of them were always quarrelling. One time it would be over which of them was taller, another time who was smaller, another who had more freckles, how to make doughnuts, or whatever. They quarrelled so much that in the end they fell in love with each other—but please don't tell anyone, or they would be terribly ashamed. One day the little prince went out hunting. What was it he

went to hunt? I can't remember exactly—it was probably mosquitoes. But just as the chase was at its most exciting, from out of nowhere two giantesses appeared. One of them caught the prince in her hand like a butterfly; the other lifted the first onto her shoulders, and off they went! The king proclaimed to the whole world that he would give half his kingdom and a quarter of a curd tart to whoever brought the prince back home; but to no avail, for no one could find him. "I shall bring him home," declared Lini, the little gardener, one day. "Simply because I have no one to quarrel with any more." And she put on her gossamer shoes and set off.

18 FEBRUARY

The Candle-Flame Fairy Tale

Do you know where Lini went? Why, she followed her nose, of course, so as not to go and get lost. After some time she came to an ice-cave. Inside were golden icicles, and in the middle a cot. There were paintings of flowers on the front of it, and on the back two white swans, and beneath the swans a magic inscription, written upside-down so that no one could understand it. In the cot lay little Prince Rini. He was sleeping like a log. Little Lini pulled his nose, then his big toe, but Rini did not move, or so much as bat an eyelid. Just then there were thundrous footsteps outside the cave, and in came the two ugly giantesses.

Lini just managed to hide behind an icicle in time. The giantesses leaned over the cot and called out, "Swans, within whose cot he lies, Sing, that sleep may leave his eyes!" The swans sang, the prince woke up, and the giantesses growled at him, "Will you take one of us for your wife?" The little prince put out his tongue and said, "Pigs might fly!" At this the giantesses flew into a rage and shouted: "Swans, within whose cot he lies, Sing, that sleep may close his eyes!" The prince fell fast asleep again, and the giantesses left the cave.

19 FEBRUARY

The Candle-Flame Fairy Tale

As soon as the giantesses had disappeared from sight, Lini ran up to the cot and ordered the swans to wake the prince. When he had opened his eyes, he and Lini embraced, then quarrelled a little, and then made up again. Then Lini told him that next time he should pretend to promise that he would marry one of the giantesses, but only if they told him what they did when they were not in the cave, and what the secret writing on the cot meant. At that moment they heard the giantesses coming back, and Lini slipped behind an icicle again. As before, the giantesses asked him roughly if he had not changed his mind. "I shall take one of you for my wife," answered the little prince, "but you must tell me where you go when you are not at home, and what is written on the cot." The giantesses were pleased, and they revealed that they went to a nearby wood to play with a golden egg. "If anyone were to smash the egg, we should turn into a couple of black crows," they told him. Then they read him the inscription on the cot. It said: "Magic cot, without delay, Carry me off wherever I say!" Then they put the prince back to sleep, and hurried off to the wood to play with their golden egg.

20 FEBRUARY

The Candle-Flame Fairy Tale

Lini stayed hidden until the giantesses' footsteps had died away. Then she ordered the swans to wake the prince, jumped into the cot beside him, and called out, "Magic cot, without delay, Carry us off to where I say!" And she ordered it to take them to the giantesses' wood. The cot soared into the air, and flew and flew until they reached a black wood. There Rini and Lini hid in the crown of a tall tree. Rini broke off a thick branch and made himself a sturdy spear. Before long the ogresses arrived. They sat down beneath the very tree in which the prince and the little gardener were crouching, and began to throw the golden egg to each other. Prince Rini aimed his spear carefully and, smack! The golden egg was shattered to a thousand pieces, and the giantesses were turned into black crows. Without delay, Rini and Lini ordered the cot to take them back to the cave; there they filled their pockets with gold and precious stones, and then ordered the cot to take them home. What a celebration there was, when they both returned safe and well! The king prepared a grand wedding for them, and gave them his whole kingdom, leaving himself only the curd tart. And Rini and Lini? They have stopped quarrelling. Lini sits on the throne ruling the kingdom, and Prince Rini does all the sleeping for her in the little cot.

21 FEBRUARY

The Dumb Child

A son was born to a farmer and his wife. He grew into a fine young lad, but, sad to relate, he did not speak a word. Hither and thither they took him, to see doctors and herbalists, sought the advice of the parson, the schoolteacher and the old woman who cast out devils, but the boy spoke never a word, and went on being as dumb as a fish. When he grew up, his parents looked around for a wife for him. Since they had a good-sized farm, they did not have to look far. In the end they chose a scatterbrained girl who spoke very little herself. "At least they will not quarrel together," they thought to themselves. Then there was a wedding the villagers recall to this day. The young bride baked basketfuls of little

cakes and carried them to the table. And, as was the custom in that part of the world, she also cooked a pot of millet gruel, so that folk would not forget everyday things even at the wedding. She put a bowl of this gruel in front of the dumb bridegroom. But the moment he tasted it he cried out in disgust, "The gruel is not sweet enough!" All the guests gathered around him. "How do you come to speak now, when you have never before so much as murmured?" they asked, excitedly. The dumb husband wiped his mouth on the back of his hand and said, "What reason had I to say anything, when the gruel was always sweet enough?"

22 FEBRUARY

The Seven Swabians

There were once seven cowards from the German land of Schwaben, who never tired of boasting of their bravery. One day, the most talkative of them all, Schulz, said to the others, "Bold Swabians, why do we not set off on our travels, that we may show the world what fine fellows and heroes the men of Schwaben are?" All agreed enthusiastically. So that they would not be afraid, they made themselves a lance, so long that all seven of them had to carry it at once. Out at the front was Schulz, followed by the biggest of the Swabians, then the next, then the next, down to the smallest at the back. This last was almost lost among the clover, but judging by his words, he had courage enough for three. They came to a great meadow, and there they disturbed a hornet, which buzzed angrily around their ears. "Halt!" cried Schulz, startled. "Can you hear? The enemy's drums are beating the advance!" Just then the wind blew the smoke from a chimney in a nearby village towards them. "You are right, Schulz, for I can smell gunpowder!" cried the second hero. "Forward to battle!" yelled the seventh, the smallest, hidden behind the others' backs. His knees

were knocking with fright. Schulz got such a shock that he jumped so high that we shall have to wait till he comes down before going on with the story.

23 FEBRUARY

The Seven Swabians

By a piece of bad luck, Schulz came down right on a rake which happened to be lying there. The handle flew up and hit him right between the eyes. "Help! I surrender!" he cried with a will. When the others heard this, they leapt head-first into a hayrick and called out, "We surrender too, mercy, mercy!" When nothing happened for some time, they cautiously stuck their heads out of the hay. The enemy was neither to be seen nor heard. "What a glorious victory we have won," the Swabians congratulated themselves, and went on their way. They stamped and swanked along like a whole army. Under a wild rose in the hedgerow a fine, fat hare was sleeping. "Halt!" called Schulz. "What creature is crouching there in the bushes?" The hare had his ears pricked and his eyes wide open. To the Swabians he seemed like a monster. "It is a dragon," stammered one of the heroes. "Dragons are not hairy," squeaked another. "Lord save us, it is the devil himself, or at least his grandmother!"—"Forward, upon him!" yelled the smallest, from the rear. "Hack him to pieces!"—"Then you go first," they told him. "No fear," the little fellow replied, "let Schulz go first!" What could he do? Step by step Schulz, the leader of the heroes, went up to the hare, his valiant rabble following behind. As he drew near, his legs almost gave way beneath him with fear, and he cried out "Oh, oh, oh!" This woke up the hare, who ran off as fast as his legs could carry him. Again the bold Swabians celebrated a great victory!

24 FEBRUARY

The Seven Swabians

After their triumph over the hare, the Swabians went in search of further adventure. Soon they came to a field of hemp, which was in flower. "What is it?" cried Schulz in amazement. "It is blue, it is large, and I cannot see to the end of it!"—"It is the sea!" shouted the others behind, pleased at having answered their leader's riddle. Schulz took a couple of gingerly steps into the sea of hemp, but soon found it was only up to his knees. "How foolish people are!" he laughed. "They build great ships just to cross the sea, and we wade across it as if it were nothing. What heroes the Swabians are!" When they had made their way safely across the field of hemp, they came to a deep river. "How can we get across?" they called out to a ferry-man over on the other side. "Wait for me!" he called back, but the wind made it difficult to hear, and they thought he said "wade to me". So the brave Swabians set off into the deep water. "We waded across the sea," they said to each other, "so why should we not wade across an ordinary river?" And one after the other they drowned. But for this unfortunate accident they would surely have conquered the whole world.

25 FEBRUARY

The Mighty Tailor

Once upon a time there was a tailor who grew tired of pricking his fingers with the needle, so he took his grandfather's old sabre out of the chest, dressed up like a general, and set off into the world. "Something will turn up," he said to himself. He walked for a long time and, since he was not used to such treks, his feet began to hurt him. He took off his shoes, sat down on a bank, and began to cool his blistered soles in the wet grass. Soon a swarm of gnats flew out of the grass, and began to bite him on his bare feet. The tailor took a swing at them and squashed a round two dozen. "Gracious, how many other men could kill so many with a single blow?" he said proudly, and he took his tailor's chalk and

wrote on his tall hat: "Killed twenty-four with one blow!" Then he set off again. Before long he came to a strange town. The people looked at him queerly; they didn't want anything to do with such a strong fellow, and when he asked the way to nowhere in particular, they sent him on purpose to the dark forest where a wild boar was known to roam. They thought the beast would tear the mighty stranger to pieces. No sooner had the tailor gone into the trees, than the old boar came charging at him. The strong-man took to his heels and ran, and ran, and ran.

26 FEBRUARY

The Mighty Tailor

The wild boar had almost caught up with the tailor, when they came to a little wayside chapel. The tailor just managed to hide behind the door before the bloodthirsty creature came hurtling in after him. Before the animal was able to stop and turn around, the tailor dashed out again and slammed the chapel door. Then he went back to the town and told everyone he met how he had taken the boar by the ears and flung him into the chapel so that he would not escape. The people were amazed to hear what a courageous fellow he was! Before long the king himself had heard of the tailor's brave deed. He sent for him and said, "My strong fellow, a terrible unicorn has come to my kingdom, and is causing great damage. If you kill him, you shall have my daughter for your wife." "Why not?" replied the tailor. He asked for a gold piece or two for the journey, and looked for the quickest way out of the palace. He had not the slightest wish to pick a quarrel with a unicorn. Swatting flies was much more in his line. But he had scarcely left the palace gate when there was the monster itself, making straight for him! He just managed at the last moment to jump behind a huge oak tree. The angry unicorn stuck its horn so deep into the tree trunk that it could not move from the spot. The tailor

was not slow to tie its legs with his belt, and he hurried off to boast of his success to the king.

27 FEBRUARY

The Mighty Tailor

The tailor told the king a fine tale of his courage; how he had caught the unicorn by the tail and flung it against the tree with such might that it was a wonder the creature had not been killed at once. And right away the hero was anxious to marry the princess. But the king had other ideas. "If I were to have such a strong fellow about the place, I should not be king for very long," he thought to himself. And he told the tailor he must first deal with three wicked giants who were wreaking havoc in his kingdom. He supposed he was sending the tailor to a certain death. The tailor did not hesitate. He tied a couple of cheeses up in his bundle, threw in a few gold pieces, and as soon as he got out of the palace set off quickly, so as to be clear of danger as soon as possible. He did not give a thought to any giants. As he walked, he heard a rustling in the bushes. A little bird had got caught among some twigs and couldn't get out. The tailor put the bird in his bundle. "Perhaps I can sell it to some bird-catcher," he thought to himself. Before he had gone a hundred paces, he heard a roar of thunder. But this was no thunder! A giant was stamping down the road, until the trees cracked beneath his feet. "Little man," roared the giant, "let us try our strength! If you lose, I shall swallow you like a raspberry." What was the tailor to do? He thought it was the end of him.

28 FEBRUARY

The Mighty Tailor

The giant said to the tailor, "Let us see who can throw the highest!" And he picked up

a great boulder as if it were a pebble, and hurled it into the sky. It was a quarter of an hour before it came down again. But the tailor took the little bird from his bundle and threw it in the air. "The devil take me, if that stone ever comes down again," he said, jauntily. Nor did it. "Very well, you win," said the giant, gruffly, and, picking up a stone, squeezed it until drops of water fell from it. The tailor only laughed. "That is nothing, my friend," he said, and he squeezed one of the cheeses from his bundle until the whey poured out of it. The giant could not believe his eyes. "Then let us see who can jump higher," he said. And with one great leap he reached the top of the cliff on which the giants' castle stood. But the clever tailor caught hold of the tip of a tall fir tree which the giant had kicked over as he jumped, and it sprang him to the very battlements of the castle. "I see that you are indeed a strong fellow," said the giant. "Come into our castle and meet my brothers." The giants sat and feasted with the tailor until late into the night, then made up a bed for him in the hall. But the tailor did not lie in it; instead he hid behind the stove. Soon the giants crept up to his bed. "Are you sleeping?" they asked, and when the tailor did not answer, they dropped a millstone on his bed in the dark. "What a trick to play, laying such a hard eiderdown on me!" cried the tailor. The giants were so startled that they leapt out of the window, straight into the abyss, and broke their necks. The tailor returned proudly to the royal palace, and the king was so afraid of him that he handed over his throne to him. The little tailor rules there to this day.

end he let Jack have his way. Jack took the cow on a piece of rope, and set off behind the cottage. But all they found there was thistles and nettles. "Only be patient, cow, I shall find you better fare," thought the lad, and he took the cow down to the river. No sooner had they reached the bank, than the cow jumped into the water and set out to swim to the other side. It was all Jack could do to catch her by the tail. "Stop, you stupid creature," cried Jack, angrily, but the cow took no notice, and dragged him along through field and hedgerow until they reached a fine castle. All things in it were of silver and gold, and the stables had the scent of fresh hay. The cow went up to a manger and began to munch contentedly. As soon as she had eaten her fill, she let Jack lead her home again. His father was amazed at how well-fed the cow looked, and he praised his stupid son highly.

21 MARCH

How the Fool Freed a Princess

From then on only Jack took the cow to pasture. His elder brothers were angry and envious, but to no avail. Their father was full of praise for how fat the cow was looking, as round as a beer-cask, and he would not hear a word spoken against his youngest son. One day, as Jack arrived at the golden castle with the cow, a little black dog ran up to them. Jack was about to drive the dog away, but she spoke to Jack in a human voice. "Tomorrow, when you come with the cow to my castle, bring with you an axe!" Jack asked no questions, and did as he was told. The next day, as soon as he reached the castle, the dog ran up to him and said, "Cut off my head!" Jack hesitated, for he had a gentle nature, but when the dog insisted, he did as he was asked. Scarcely had the blow fallen, when the earth trembled, and there in front of Jack stood a beautiful princess. She fell into his arms, and with tears in her eyes thanked him for releasing her from the spell. Then she took him by the hand and sat him down beside her

on a golden throne. And so Jack Simple became king. Believe it or not, he even learnt to count to five in time! And he ruled wisely and well.

22 MARCH

One-Eye, Two-Eyes and Three-Eyes

Once upon a time, in a certain cottage, there lived a woman who had three daughters. The eldest was called One-Eye, because she had a single eye in the middle of her forehead. The middle one was called Two-Eyes, because she had two eyes, just like other people. The youngest had an extra eye, and so she was called Three-Eyes. Two-Eyes had a hard time of it. Her mother hated her, and her sisters were unkind to her. They envied her because she was the most beautiful. They gave her the worst clothes, and all she got to eat was what was left over when the others had finished. Every morning the poor girl had to take the goat off to graze, and she was allowed to return only after sunset, when there was almost nothing left on the plate. No wonder she was always weeping! One day a strange woman met her in the meadows, and asked her, "Why do you cry so, Two-Eyes?" Two-Eyes told her of her troubles. Then the woman stroked her hair, and said, "Do not be sad, Two-Eyes! Whenever you are hungry,

just say to your goat: 'Dearest goat, as you are able, Fill with food your little table!' And you shall have whatever food you wish." Two-Eyes did as the lady told her, and in a trice a small table appeared, heaped with the most delicious foods. The girl ate her fill, and the unknown woman said: "Dearest goat, as you are able, Clear away your little table!" At that the table disappeared, and the strange woman with it.

23 MARCH

One-Eye, Two-Eyes and Three-Eyes

From then on Two-Eyes was much happier. But it seemed curious to her sisters and her mother that she no longer ate hungrily what little they left her on her return from the pastures. So their mother sent One-Eye with her to the meadows. Two-Eyes soon felt hungry, and she wished to ask the goat for something to eat. But first she sat down next to her sister and said: "Sister, I shall sing you a pretty little song." And she sang, over and over again: "One-Eye, now your vigil keeping, One-Eye, now so softly sleeping." It was not long before One-Eye fell asleep. Two-Eyes quickly asked the goat to lay the little table, and when she had eaten her fill she sent it away again. Towards evening she woke her sister up and they hurried home. One-Eye was forced to admit to their mother that she had slept, and had seen nothing at all. Her mother was very angry with her, and the next day sent Three-Eyes instead. Two-Eyes sat beside her in the grass, and in a while began to sing: "Three-Eyes, now your vigil keeping," but by mistake she sang, "Two-Eyes, now so softly sleeping." And so it happened that Three-Eyes seemed to fall asleep, but her third eye, which had not been mentioned in the song, she only pretended to close, and with it she saw all that took place. As soon as they got home, she told their mother how their goat had given Two-Eyes all manner of good things to eat.

24 MARCH

One-Eye, Two-Eyes and Three-Eyes

When the girls' mother heard how the goat

had been treating Two-Eyes to such delicacies down in the meadows, she was so angry she had the poor creature's throat cut at once. Poor Two-Eyes was broken-hearted. But the kind woman appeared before her again, and said: "Do not cry, Two-Eyes. Take a horn from your poor goat and plant it beside the front door." At that she was gone again. Two-Eyes did as she had been told and, wondrous to behold, a beautiful tree bearing golden apples grew up there overnight. Her mother and her two sisters rushed to pick the fruit, but the branches slipped out of their hands as if they did not wish to be touched by them. But when Two-Eyes came up to the tree, the apples seemed to fall right into her lap. However, her mother and her sisters took them all away for themselves. One day, a handsome young knight rode by. Her mother and sisters shoved Two-Eyes under an old tub, saying that they were ashamed of her, and themselves bowed to the rider from afar. "Whose is that beautiful tree?" the knight asked in wonder. "I will give any reward you ask, if you give me a branch from it." The two sisters cried each other down, saying the tree was theirs, but the branches always slipped out of their hands. Then a golden apple fell from the tree and rolled straight to the upturned tub where Two-Eyes was hidden. The knight lifted the tub, and when he saw Two-Eyes beneath it, he asked her for a branch from the tree. This she was happy to give him. "Now I know to whom the tree belongs," he said, and to the disgust of the wicked mother and sisters, he took the beautiful Two-Eyes off with him to his castle. And the magic tree? That uprooted itself and followed her to her new home, where it bears golden apples to this day.

25 MARCH

The Two Musicians

Two poor musicians were wandering through the world. One played the trumpet and the other beat the drum, until the glass rattled in the windows. One day their wanderings brought them to a woodland spring. Fairies were dancing around it. "Play for us, musicians," begged the fairy queen. The trumpeter began to play a merry dance. But the drummer refused to play, saying he would not beat his drum for nothing, and that anyway he was so hungry he could scarcely raise his arms. He lay down in the grass and went to sleep. The fairies danced to the trumpeter's tune, and when they had danced enough, their queen said: "Now you shall both have your rewards." She touched the trumpet with a golden primrose, and beat the drum with a dry thistle. "You may keep such a reward as this," said the drummer, turning up his nose. But the trumpeter smiled warmly at the fairies and said, "You have rewarded me well. I am well satisfied if your feet keep time to my music." And the musicians went their way. They came to a village where a festival was in progress. The trumpeter blew into his

trumpet and the drummer twirled his drumsticks, and—what do you suppose? From out of the trumpet gold pieces began to fall, and they went on tinkling to the ground as long as the trumpeter played. But a swarm of wasps flew out of the drum, and drove the drummer up hill and down dale, away out of the village.

26 MARCH

The Two Musicians

The worthy trumpeter stayed on in the village and married the mayor's daughter. Never did he turn a poor man from his door, and he trumpeted on his way any beggar who came along and gave him a couple of gold pieces for his journey. But for the drummer things went from bad to worse. He threw the accursed drum away, and was left with no way of making a living. One day he happened to wander by the woodland spring again. Suddenly, the fairies appeared. "Play for us as we dance," they begged him. "If you were to give me a magic trumpet such as you gave my companion, I should play for you from morning till night," he said. The fairy queen only smiled, plucked a reed from the waterside, and struck it with a dry thistle. The reed turned into a golden trumpet that was a delight to behold. The musician snatched it up and, before the fairies could change their minds, made off. After a while he could wait no longer, so he stopped by the wayside and blew a few notes. But what an unpleasant surprise! Strange things began to happen to him. His whole body was suddenly covered in hair; claws grew out from his fingers and toes, and his nose got longer and longer, until it was like a bird's beak. The musician looked at himself in a lake, and almost fainted with horror. He had turned into a horrible spectre. Ever since then, on a moonlit night, a strange hooting can be heard from the woods. People say it is the tawny owl, but do not believe them! It is the selfish musician, playing his trumpet as the fairies dance, and waiting for them to take pity on him.

27 MARCH

The Iron Box

One day a poor peasant went into the forest to gather firewood. Among the roots of an old tree he found a locked iron box. "Whatever could be inside?" he thought to himself. At that moment an old woman appeared from nowhere beside him. "The box is full of thalers," she told him. "They belong to me, but you may take them if you wish. Only you must speak to no one about it, otherwise it will go ill with you!" And with these words she was gone. The peasant hurried home with the box and smashed it open with an axe. The old woman had, to be sure, told the truth. The peasant rushed off to tell his wife. "But you must tell no one!" he warned her. The woman promised, and went off to buy meat and flour; then she baked, and roasted, and fried. Soon there was such a wonderful smell of cooking from the cottage that the neighbours' mouths watered. "What good things are you cooking?" asked one. The peasant's wife had never kept a secret in her life, and soon she told the whole story. "My husband found a box full of money: I am cooking him a meal to celebrate. Mind you, you must tell no one!" The neighbour promised, but because he was related to her, she didn't really count the gravedigger, so she told him. He told the sexton, and the sexton told the parson. The parson at once ran off to tell the judge while the news was fresh.

28 MARCH

The Iron Box

The moment the judge heard from the parson of the peasant's new-found riches, he sent for the man and began to question him harshly. "Listen, you cunning fox. I hear you have stolen a pile of money somewhere or other. Your own wife said so. Now, tell me where you stole it!" But the peasant would admit

nothing. "Your honour should not set such store by a woman's words," he said. "My wife is a little mad."—"Mad, is she?" the judge retorted. "Then I shall have her brought to court in fourteen days' time, and we'll see how mad she is!" The unfortunate peasant racked his brains for a way out of the mess he was in. Then he had a bright idea. He bought pretzels and cakes from all the bakers in town, took them home and scattered them about the garden, throwing a few onto the roof; then he called to his wife in the kitchen. "A poor housekeeper you are, wife! It has been raining cakes and pretzels, and you do not even come to gather them up!" The woman was filled with amazement, but she wasted no time, and soon she had a sackful of pastries. The next day her husband said, "Hurry, mother, hide under the washtub! The king's soldiers are coming to the village. They have long iron beaks instead of mouths, and they peck almost to death any woman they see!" Without delay his wife crawled under the washtub, and waited to see what would happen.

29 MARCH

The Iron Box

While the peasant's wife was crouched beneath the washtub, shivering with fear, her husband poured a sackful of corn over her and let the chickens into the yard. They ran up and pecked at the corn, tap, tap, tap!—until it was all gone. Only then did the peasant lift up the tub and call out, "Come on out, mother, the soldiers have gone!"—"Thank the lord," the woman sighed with relief. "How scared I was when they were pecking at me with their iron beaks!" The peasant just smiled quietly to himself. In two weeks' time the judge summoned her to court. "Tell me about the money," he ordered. The woman answered fearfully that her husband had brought a box full of thalers from somewhere. "Do not believe her, my lord!" cried the peasant. "Can't you see that she is mad?" And he asked his wife, "When do you say I brought the money?" His wife answered, "Do you not remember? The next day it rained pretzels, and the day after that the king's soldiers came with their iron beaks, and I had to hide from them under the washtub. Even now I shake with fear when I recall how their beaks pecked at me, tap, tap, tap!" The judges decided that she really was crazy, and they let the peasant go free.

30 MARCH

The Foolish Bride

There was once a miller's daughter who was so foolish that the young men from miles around kept well out of her way. One day a farmhand was passing by the mill. "Better a poor husband than none at all," thought the girl's mother, and she invited the young man to eat with them. They got talking, and by and by the lad promised to marry the miller's daughter. Her mother sent her to the cellar to draw a jug of ale with which to seal the bargain. The foolish girl set the jug on the floor, turned the tap, and began to look around her aimlessly. She noticed an axe wedged in a beam. "Mercy!" she cried in horror. "What if we should have a baby, and the axe should fall on his head! What a misfortune!" And she burst into tears. The beer was lapping about her ankles. Just then her mother arrived. "What is the matter?" she asked in surprise. Right away the girl told her of the terrible misfortune which threatened the miller's future grandchild, and the mother, too, began to cry. The beer foamed around their knees. Before long the miller himself came on the scene. As soon as he heard the fearful tale, the miller sat down beside them and began to mourn the poor child. Just then the farmhand came to see what was keeping them. They all spoke at once, telling him of the danger that threatened his unborn child. The lad began to laugh: "Better wed to poverty, than such a stupid wife," he said, and moved on.

31 MARCH

Father Gold, Mother Silver and Son Copper

Far across the sea there lived two brothers—one poor and the other rich. One day the poor man found a silver piece by the wayside. He took it to his rich brother. "Brother, I bring you a bride for your gold pieces," he said. "If you put one of them in my care, I shall marry him to my silver piece. When they have a child, I shall bring you the whole family." The rich man hesitated, but because he was greedy, he finally agreed. By and by his brother brought him one gold piece, one silver piece and one copper piece. "See," he said, "our coins are blessed with a copper son. A pity that both were not gold, for you might have had more gold pieces." The rich man could not believe his eyes. "Brother," he said, "I shall give you all my gold pieces; marry them off, and let them have an abundance of children!"—"Why not?" the poor man agreed, taking the gold pieces and going his way. When he did not return for a long time, his brother went to see him. "Where is my money?" he asked. "My condolences," said the poor brother sadly, "all your gold pieces have passed away." "Fool," fumed the rich man. "How can money die?"—"If it can have children, then why should it not die?" smiled the clever brother, and the local judge laughed, and had to agree. So it was that a rich man became poor, and a poor man rich.

APRIL

1 APRIL

The Cat and the Mouse Join Forces

Once upon a time there was a cat who managed to persuade a mouse to come and live with her. "It will be just like a wedding breakfast," she told the mouse. "We shall play and dance together, eat, drink and make merry." The mouse decided it might really be a good idea, and so she moved in with the cat. So as not to go hungry in the wintertime, they put a pot of dripping aside for a rainy day. "But where shall we hide it?" asked the cat. The mouse thought of putting it under the altar in the church, saying that it was sure to be safe from thieves. The cat agreed. But after some time she took a fancy to a little dripping. "Dear mouse, my cousin has a baby son," she lied. "I must go to the church for the christening." "Have a good time," the mouse told her, kindheartedly. The cat ran along to the church and licked the top of the bowl of dripping clean away. "What is your godson's name?" asked the mouse when the cat came home. "Er—Topgone," said the cat, hurriedly. "What a strange name," said the mouse, raising her eyebrows. "Oh, what's in a name," purred the cat. "Anyway, it is no stranger than Crumbscavenger, as your godchildren are called." And she curled up, and slept, and slept.

2 APRIL

The Cat and the Mouse Join Forces

Before very long the greedy cat thought up another christening, and this time she ate a full half of the dripping. "What is the baby called this time?" asked the mouse. "Halfgone," the cat told her. The mouse shook her head. By and by the cat again had to go to the church to be godmother. This time she licked the bowl clean. "What is the baby's name?" inquired the mouse, as usual. "Allgone," mewed the cat. "Allgone? Never in my life have I heard such a name!" the mouse said in wonder, but the cat just smiled secretly to herself. When winter came along they had nothing to eat, and the mouse, remembering the bowl of dripping, set off for the church with the cat. But the bowl was quite, quite empty. Suddenly the mouse realized what had been happening. "So that's it! You have eaten it all yourself," she chided the cat angrily. "First the top gone, then half gone . . .!"—"Keep quiet," hissed the cat, "or I'll eat you up too!" But it was too late for the mouse to stop herself from finishing what she wanted to say: ". . . and then all gone!" she squeaked. No sooner had she said the last word, than the cat pounced on her and swallowed the poor mouse at one gulp. There you are, you see: if the cat the mouse befriend, the mouse shall rue it in the end!—anyway, that's what the dog says.

3 APRIL

The Ram's Head

A father sent his greedy son to market to buy a roast ram's head. The boy hurried along, anxious to please his father. But on the way back he did not walk so fast. The roast meat smelt so delicious, it made his mouth water. He dillied and dallied, and, being greedy, pulled off pieces of meat all the way, until

only the bones were left. In the end he brought home a bare ram's skull. "What is this you have brought me?" his father asked in surprise. "Why, a ram's head, of course," his greedy son replied. "And where are its eyes?" asked his father. "Oh, father, the ram was blind," the boy told him. His father frowned like thunder. "Then where are its ears, my clever lad?" he said, gruffly. "Oh, father, the ram was deaf," the boy persisted. "And its tongue?"—"Father, the ram was dumb, too!"—"Why has it no skin on its head?" his father asked, angrily. "Father, dear father, the ram was quite bald!" the greedy boy replied, and dashed off to his mother to beg a cake.

4 APRIL

The Waterman Who Couldn't Sleep

In a lake below the forest lived an old, bad-tempered waterman. A mischievous fish had once stolen his sleep, and since then he had been unable to sleep a wink. One night a merry journeyman passed by the lakeside. The waterman thrust his green fingers out of the water and grabbed the traveller by the leg. "I've got you!" he croaked. "Unless you tell me where I can find sleep, I shall take you to the bottom of the lake!" The journeyman was frightened, but he quickly recovered himself. "You cannot sleep at night?" he asked, pretending to be surprised. "Then, what kind of water do you place beneath your head?"—"Why, water from the spring," the waterman said. "Ah, then that's it! You must make your bed with marsh water, for spring water is much too hard," the clever journeyman told him. The waterman thanked him for his advice and let him go. That night he made his bed with marsh water, but again he did not sleep a wink. One day he caught the journeyman again as he was passing by the lake. "You gave me bad advice," he said, "I shall drag you to the bottom!" But the journeyman was undismayed. "Then I'll tell you what to do," he said. "Call together all the frogs and watermen to sing you a lullaby!" The waterman allowed himself to be persuaded, and the next evening all the frogs and watermen made music enough to crack the eardrums. It was a terrible croaking and wailing, but the waterman in his willow tree felt his eyelids grow heavy, and soon he dropped off into a deep sleep. Ever since then, on a moonlit night you can hear the waterman's choir croaking its harsh song down by the waterside.

5 APRIL

How Foolish Jacob Learnt to be a Robber

In the dark forest over the hills lived an old robber and his foolish son, Jacob. One day the old man said to his son, "Son, my eyes are beginning to fail me, and I can no longer shoot straight, it is time you learned my trade. You must earn your own living soon!" So what was Jacob to do? He yawned widely, pulled his feathered hat down over his eyes, and, so as not to have to walk, rolled down the hillside into the valley. A penniless vagabond was just passing that way, pockets so full of holes the wind whistled through them, and they wouldn't have known what a farthing was if they had seen one. "Your money or your life!" shouted Jacob, just as his father had taught him. The vagabond was startled, but he soon recovered himself. "Most esteemed robber," he said, bowing. "I have but one life and, little as it is worth, I should rather hang on to it, but you may have all the money I have in my pockets. Only have a care, for it is wind money, which I was given by the wind king. If you were to take it from my pockets to put into yours, it might blow away—feel how it flies about in there! It were better to change your clothes with mine." The foolish Jacob liked the idea, so he put on the vagabond's rags, leaving the clever fellow his fine robber's clothes. You can imagine the welcome he got when he came home!

6 APRIL

Little Pip

In a far-off land there lived a small fellow who went by the name of little Pip. His parents died, so Pip set off into the world on his pony to seek his fortune. On the way he wandered into a beautiful city. In it there lived an old woman who had a house full of cats and dogs. She took little Pip into her service, and told him to look after her animals well. He was happy there, and before long all the animals liked him. His greatest friend was a lame little dog. One day the dog led little Pip into a secret chamber. The only things in it were a large pair of slippers and a strange stick. "The stick is magic," the dog told him, in a human voice. "Wherever there is gold to be dug, the stick will tap the ground three times. If it taps twice, you will find silver beneath." Little Pip thanked the dog and started to leave, but the dog said to him, "Do not forget the magic slippers. If you turn on your heels in them three times, they will carry you wherever you wish." The dog had spoken truly. Before long Pip had more gold and silver than he could carry. One day, he turned his pony loose, put on the magic slippers, turned three times on his heels, and ordered the slippers to take him to the royal palace. There he offered his services to the king as the swiftest runner in the land.

7 APRIL

Little Pip

When the king saw little Pip, he burst out laughing. But Pip pleaded so touchingly to be allowed to take part in the next races that in the end the king took pity on him. The next day there was a great celebration at the palace. When the feasting was over, all the best runners in the world gathered in the royal gardens for a race to see who was the fastest. With a smile, little Pip put on his magic slippers, turned on his heels three times, and before the other runners knew what was happening was at the finish. The king could not believe his eyes, but when he had got over his surprise he appointed little Pip his chief runner and messenger. But the boy's happiness was short-lived. It was not long before envious folk noticed that the strange little fellow had all the gold and silver he might wish for, and they began to spread tales about him throughout the city. At first Pip thought he could silence them by his generosity, but the more he gave away, the more his rivals hated him. Finally, word came to the king that Pip's riches were stolen from the royal coffers. The king was enraged, and had Pip thrown in gaol.

8 APRIL

Little Pip

Poor little Pip. He believed the king to be a just man, and thought that if he revealed the secret of the magic stick and slippers he would be set free. But, alas! The ungrateful king kept the magic gifts for himself and drove Pip from his palace without a penny to his name. He wandered miserably about the world for a long time, until he came to a secret forest where beautiful fig-trees grew. But no sooner had the hungry Pip eaten a few mouthfuls of the fruit, than he found that he had grown enormous ears and a long nose. He began to cry. Bemoaning his cruel fate, he carelessly chewed the fruit of another fig-tree, and to his amazement his nose and ears returned to their usual size. This gave Pip an idea as to how he might revenge himself. He returned to the royal city and offered the palace cook the fruit of the first fig-tree. The moment the king tasted the figs after his supper, he thought he would die of shame! Not even the royal elephant had such a nose and ears. What lamentation there was in the royal household! Then along came Pip, dressed as a doctor. "Sire, I will rid you of your unsightly ornaments, if I may choose from your treasures whatever I will," he told the king. The king agreed, and led him to his treasure-house. There Pip spied his magic slippers and stick. Quickly, he picked up the stick and put on the slippers and called out, "For your treachery you shall keep your ass's nose and elephant's ears, ungrateful king!" And with these words he turned three times on his heels and disappeared, no one knows where. Perhaps somewhere his faithful pony was waiting for him.

9 APRIL

Cinderella

There was once a rich merchant who had all he could wish for; money to burn, a good and beautiful wife, and an even more beautiful daughter. But misfortune often strikes where least expected, and one day his beloved wife died. His daughter visited her mother's grave every day, day after day, and wept long and bitterly at their sad loss. The merchant thought it wrong that one so young should grieve so long, and, so that she might not grow up without a mother's care, he took a second wife. The stepmother had two pretty daughters of her own. They looked like a pair of rosebuds, but their hearts were filled with envy and hatred. The moment their stepfather left the house, they would turn on their new sister. "Just look at the proud little princess! How finely she dresses! But from now on you shall earn your bread in this house." They took away all her beautiful clothes, gave her a pair of old wooden shoes, and made her wear a tattered smock. Then they shut her up in the kitchen and gave her all the most unpleasant tasks to do. And as if that were not enough, they would drop peas and lentils in the ashes, and make the poor little girl pick every last one out again. Even when her dreary day's work was ended they gave her no peace, and instead of her feather bed, she was made to sleep among the ashes in the fireplace. Because the poor girl was always smutty, they started to call her Cinderella.

10 APRIL

Cinderella

Poor Cinderella! She was afraid to tell her father, in case her stepmother and the two wicked sisters mistreated her even more. One day, as the merchant was setting off into the city, he asked his stepdaughters what presents he should bring them. They asked for fine robes and jewels, necklaces, bracelets, and all manner of vanity. But Cinderella told him to bring her the first twig to catch against his hat as he was returning home. This happened to be a hazel twig, and he brought it to Cinderella as she had asked. She planted it on her mother's grave and watered it with her tears. In the twinkling of an eye a splendid hazel bush grew up, and on it alighted a little white bird, which said, "Cinderella, I shall grant your every wish!" But the modest child wanted no more than to remember her poor mother. One day, she came home from the churchyard to find her stepmother and two wicked sisters getting ready for a grand ball at the royal palace. It was to last three whole

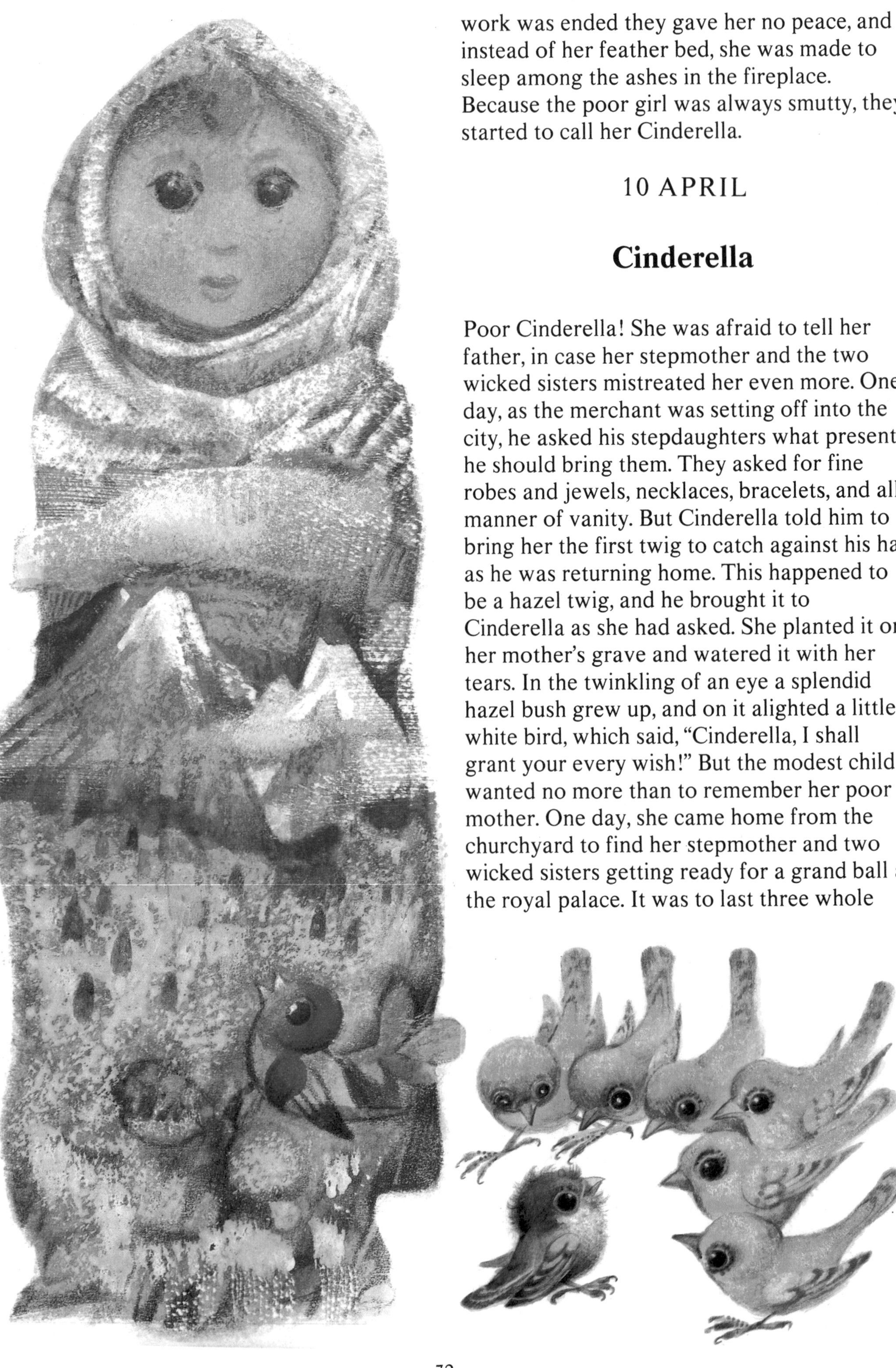

days, and the young prince was to choose himself a bride there. Cinderella begged them to take her with them, but her stepmother only laughed and, tipping a bowl of lentils into the ashes, said, "If you can pick them out again in one hour, we shall see!" Cinderella ran into the garden and begged the birds to help her. The birds set to with a will, and soon all the lentils were back in the bowl. But the stepmother was only angry with her, and shouted, "You shall go nowhere, you would only bring shame on us, you ragamuffin!" So the poor girl had to stay at home.

11 APRIL

Cinderella

As soon as her stepmother and the wicked sisters had set off for the ball, Cinderella ran all the way to her mother's grave, and begged the hazel bush: "Give me a gown to please a prince's eye, dear hazel." The bush shook itself, and the little white bird threw into Cinderella's lap a gold and silver gown and a pair of velvet slippers. Quickly, she changed her clothes and set off for the royal castle. All the guests at the ball were astounded at her beauty, and even the stepmother and the wicked sisters could scarcely take their envious eyes off her. Whoever would have thought that this beautiful princess could be their poor Cinderella? As for the prince, he would dance with no other the whole evening. But as midnight approached, Cinderella slipped from his arms and hurried off home again. The prince galloped after her on his horse, but Cinderella was as swift as a bird, and when she reached the courtyard of her father's house she hid in the dovecote. Just then her father arrived home from his travels, and the prince told him of the beautiful girl who was hiding in his dovecote. "Could it be Cinderella?" her father thought to himself, and he threw the dovecote to the ground and chopped it to pieces with an axe. But Cinderella? She was already asleep among the ashes, smiling in her dreams. The prince returned to his castle empty-handed.

12 APRIL

Cinderella

The next day the hazel bush gave Cinderella an even lovelier gown and a pair of silver slippers, and again the prince danced away the whole evening with her. Towards midnight she slipped away again, and this time she hid in the crown of an old pear tree. But before the prince could climb up after her she jumped down and curled up among the cinders.
On the third evening the prince had the palace

steps spread with gum, and when Cinderella, this time in golden slippers, again ran away from him, one of the slippers remained stuck to the steps. The prince picked it up, and at once made straight for Cinderella's house. He bowed to the wicked stepsisters, and said, "Whichever of you the slipper fits, shall become my wife." Cinderella was nowhere to be seen. The two sisters tried every way they could think of to get the slipper on, but to no avail. Then the younger one, taking her mother's advice, chopped off one of her toes, and managed to get her foot inside. The prince would have taken her back to his castle with him, but at that moment a white dove appeared and began to coo:

"Has not the bride a toe too
few-oo-oo,
Who cut the foot to fit the
shoe-oo-oo?"

The prince had a look, and sent the cheating sister away in disgrace. Nor did the other stepsister come off any better when she sliced off a piece of her heel. She, too, was given away by the dove. Then Cinderella appeared, and asked to be allowed to try on the shoe, and to the wonder of all those present it fitted like a glove. The prince took a good look at the ragged girl, and recognized his lovely dancing partner. "She is the one I shall marry, and no other!" he cried, and he took the smiling Cinderella off to his royal palace.

13 APRIL

The Magic Merry-Go-Round

Once upon a time there was a little boy who had a kitten he loved more than anything in the world. But one day the kitten wandered off somewhere and did not come back again. The little boy was heartbroken. He cried, and cried, and could not be comforted. Some time later an old man with a merry-go-round came to the village, ringing a silver bell and calling out: "Come and take your seats! My magic merry-go-round will take you wherever you please!" The children had lots of wishes, one of them wanting to go to America, another to a gingerbread cottage; but our little boy wanted only to go to his little lost kitten. No sooner had he wished, than the wooden horse he was sitting on galloped away with him. Before very long, they arrived in a strange land. There were many people and animals there, but they all looked like shadows. Suddenly, along came the little kitten. "Where am I?" asked the boy in wonder. "In the land of memories," replied the kitten in a human voice. "All those who are sadly missed in the world come here. But they may live only so long as someone remembers them." The boy would have taken his kitten home with him, but the kitten told him, "I cannot go with you. But if you call my name before you go to sleep, I shall come to you in your dreams." The boy played with her for a while, then he jumped back on the merry-go-round horse, and before he knew it he was standing on the village green. Strange to say, the magic

merry-go-round had disappeared from sight. When the boy told his mother of his journey, she did not believe him. But when he called the kitten's name before he went to sleep, she came to him in his dreams. And he never forgot her.

14 APRIL

The Tale of the Wicked Goat

In a little painted cottage lived a kind old woman. One day a wicked goat came along and begged to be allowed to warm herself in front of the fire. But as soon as the old woman let her in the goat attacked her with her horns and drove her out of the little house. In tears, the old woman turned to the brave donkey for help. He rapped on the door with his hooves, and called out, "Open up, you stupid goat, or I shall trample you underfoot!" The goat stuck her head out of the door and butted the donkey so hard his bones rattled. The unhappy woman appealed to the bear, but he came off no better. To this day the forest spiders are busy mending his fur. Now the old woman did not know what to do. She wept and wandered about, and came across a little hedgehog. "Dry your tears, old woman," said

the hedgehog, "I shall see to the goat!" He knocked gently at the cottage door, and rolled up into a ball. When the goat charged at him she pricked herself so cruelly on his sharp spines that tears came to her eyes. Bleating with pain, she took to her heels. Overjoyed, the old woman moved back into her cottage, and she gave the bold hedgehog a bowlful of apples as a reward.

15 APRIL

The Old Flower-Seller

In a far-off kingdom, long ago, ruled a foolish and capricious king. One day he made a law that all his people must be happy. It was forbidden for anyone to cry. From then on everyone had to smile, even if there was nothing to smile about at all, and if anyone was sad, he had to hide away in a corner somewhere until his tears were dry. But the more people smiled, the sadder their hearts became, and the saddest of all was the king. One day an old flower-seller set up her stall beneath the palace windows. On it were the most beautiful of flowers, but all of them sad and drooping. "Why are those flowers not smiling?" roared the king from one of the windows. "Do you not know that all creatures in my kingdom must be happy?" The old woman shook her white head. "Happiness is not made by royal decree, my lord! Whoever wishes to know true joy must be able to cure a sad heart with tears. My flowers languish because they lack the very thing you have forbidden, human tears." Just then one of the flower-buds began to sing. It sang so sweetly and plaintively that tears came to the foolish sovereign's eyes, and when his subjects saw this, they, too, began to cry. All at once they could feel their tears washing a heavy burden from their hearts, and soon their faces broke into the first real smiles they had smiled for years. All the flowers opened out in wondrous beauty, but the wise old woman had vanished like a summer breeze.

16 APRIL

King Wren

Long, long ago, everything on earth could speak, and every sound had a meaning. So when the blacksmith brought his great hammer down on the anvil, the hammer would call out over and over again, "Stand! Stand! Stand!" and the anvil would reply, "Swing! Swing! Swing!" The carpenter's saw would exhort its master, "Rip—through, rip—through!" And as the mill-wheel began to turn it would boast, "Forty sacks a day, forty sacks a day!" In those days the birds, too, had their own language, and everyone understood them well. At that time the birds decided to choose a king from their number. From field and forest alike, all feathered creatures came flying to the meeting: the eagle and the finch, the owl and the crow, the sparrow and the lark, the cuckoo and the hoopoe, and one tiny bird who did not even have a name. Only the lapwing was not too happy with the idea of having a king, and flew off in the opposite direction in search of peace and quiet. "We'll see, we'll see," she called, disdainfully, finding herself a lonely spot in the marshes, away from them all. Meanwhile, the birds warbled and chirped and debated, until they decided that whichever of them could fly the highest should become their king. The hen was somewhat hard of hearing, and kept asking the cock: "What? What? What, Co-Co-Cock?"—"What to do, to do," the cock explained, and told her how the matter was to be decided. "Hurrah! Hurrah! Hurrah!" exclaimed the crow, who couldn't wait for the fun to begin.

17 APRIL

King Wren

Early the next morning, a flock of birds like a great black cloud rose slowly up to the sky. Each tried his utmost to win the crown, but soon one after the other fell back, exhausted, until at last the eagle soared high above them all. "You shall be our king," the others called to him, "for none has flown higher than you."—"Only I," piped a thin little voice, and there above the eagle circled the little bird without a name. The cunning creature had

you suppose he bothered to rule anybody? Not a bit of it; he spent his days greedily licking honey from a golden spoon!

15 MAY

Which is the Strongest of All the Birds?

There was once a mother bird who had six sons, all little brother birds. All of them would shout at once, boasting that they were the strongest birds in the world. One day their mother saw a worm poking its head out of the grass. She caught it in her beak and pulled, and pulled, but she could not pull it out. "Wait, mother, I'll help you," twittered her eldest son, "for am I not the strongest bird in the world?" They pulled, and pulled, but they could not pull the worm out. Her second son came flying up. "Wait, mother, I'll help you. I am stronger than the strongest of my brothers," he boasted. They pulled, and pulled, but they could not pull the worm out. The third, fourth and fifth brothers all flew up, and they pulled, and pulled, but they could not pull the worm out. "What heroes you are," mocked the youngest of the brothers. "You will see that I am the strongest in the world." He stood at the end of the line, and they all pulled, and pulled, but they could not pull the worm out. Then a little fly caught hold of the last bird's tail. He was so small that they could not even see him. He took hold of a feather, and they all pulled and pulled, and pulled the worm out, and fell back onto the ground. "I am the strongest in the world!" shouted all the birds at once. Do you think they were right?

16 MAY

The Imp in the Box

In an old ring-box lived a wicked little magic imp. He had an enchanted mirror which swallowed up anyone he pointed it at, and would not let them go. They became a little glass picture. You would not believe how many people and things the magic mirror had imprisoned. There was a king with the whole of his palace, a princess with a golden star on her forehead, a phoenix, a blue parasol, and all manner of other things. One day the ring-box was found by a little glass doll from the kingdom of glass. The moment she opened the box, the wicked imp peeped out and pointed the magic mirror at her. But since she was made of glass, and was clear and quite invisible, the mirror could not see her, and could not swallow her up. "Oh, what beautiful little glass pictures there are there!" she cried, excitedly, as she looked into the mirror. And she put her hand in and, one by one, drew them all out to safety. The imp lost his temper, and wanted to destroy the mirror. But when he turned it round, the mirror swallowed him up. He became a little glass picture. Now that picture hangs in a glass palace in a certain fairytale kingdom. The ruler of the kingdom is the little glass doll. Why don't you go and see her sometime?

17 MAY

The Bearskin

Back in the days when the rivers ran uphill and the rain fell from the earth to the sky, an old soldier was wandering about the world. At noon one day he was resting under an old oak tree and trying to recall what army rations tasted like. Suddenly there was a rustling in the branches, and an acorn came tumbling to the ground. No sooner had it landed, than a strange, strange little man leapt out of it. He had a short green coat and a hoof on one leg, and looked a little like a water sprite. "Afternoon; and who the devil might you be?" the soldier asked. "Might be, might not be, but the devil I am, in disguise," said the little fellow, gruffly. "My compliments," said the soldier, "and how might I be of service?" The devil grimaced as if he had bitten on an aching tooth. "Well," he said, "I really can't imagine what the likes of you might do for me. But I may be of use to you. First, though, you must show that you are not afraid. Take a look over your shoulder!" The soldier looked round, and what should he see! A huge bear was

lumbering toward him. Without hesitation he levelled his rifle and laid the creature to the ground with a single shot. "I see that you are no coward," said the demon. "Come to the oak again tomorrow, and we shall sign a devil's contract. Now I must go to hell."

18 MAY

The Bearskin

The next day the soldier sat beneath the old oak tree and waited. Before long an acorn fell to the ground, and out crept the little green man. "Hear me well, old soldier," he said. "I shall give you my green jacket. Whenever you reach in the pocket, you will find a handful of gold pieces. In return you must wear the same clothes for a full seven years. You must not wash, shave, or cut your hair. And for a cloak you must wear the skin of the bear you shot yesterday. If you can do this for seven years, you'll be free. Otherwise I'll carry you off to hell." The soldier needed no second asking. He put on the green jacket, skinned the bear, and flung the skin across his shoulders. As soon as he put his hand in the pocket of the green jacket, he felt a pile of gold pieces there. "Now I shall have a fine time!" he hooted. And indeed he did. But not for ever. Before a year was out, he had changed beyond all recognition. Unwashed and unkempt, claws on his hands and feet like a wild animal—what a sight he was! Wherever he went, people ran away from him; children threw stones at him, and he had nowhere to lay his head. True, he had money to burn, but what use was it to him, when everyone shouted at him: "Be off with you, you old bearskin, don't you dare show your face here again!"

19 MAY

The Bearskin

For more than two years the old soldier had roamed the world in his bearskin. Winter came and the frost bit, and the poor fellow knocked desperately at a cottage door. A peasant with tears in his eyes opened it; he was at the end of his tether. The soldier asked him for shelter. "Poor wretch," the peasant moaned. "What a refuge you have found! Here you will not get a bite to eat, for we are starving to death ourselves. The waters carried away our crops, and if I do not pay my master what I owe on the morrow, I shall be thrown in gaol. But if you will make your bed on the bare boards, you are welcome beneath our roof. Indeed, you seem still less fortunate than I." The soldier thanked him, and huddled in a corner of the parlour. When they arose in the morning, the soldier dipped his hand in the pocket of the devil's coat and strewed a pile of gold pieces in front of the peasant. "Go and pay your debts," he told him, "and you shall have enough for a good living besides!" The peasant could not believe his eyes. When he

had come to his senses, he said: "I thank you, kind sir! But I shall repay this debt. Take whichever of my three daughters you please to be your wife." And he led the soldier in his bearskin off to meet his daughters.

20 MAY

The Bearskin

When the peasant's daughters set eyes on the beast in the bearskin, they almost fainted with horror. They did not want to hear of marrying him. But in the end the youngest of them took pity on him, and promised to be his bride. Then the soldier broke a golden ring in two and said: "There is time enough for marrying; I must first go out into the world again. Whoever brings you half of my ring four years from now, you shall take him as your husband." With these words he left them. He had a harder time of it than ever in the wide world, but finally the seven long years were up, and the soldier returned to the old oak tree. An acorn fell from the tree, and out jumped the little green man. "You have kept our bargain, soldier," he said. "Now I must fulfil one more wish for you." With a laugh the soldier told the devil to wash him, shave him, and to cut and comb his hair. What else could the little devil do? He set to work at once. And as soon as the soldier had again turned into a handsome young fellow, he set off for the home of his bride-to-be. On the way he got himself a fine suit of clothes, and he knocked at the peasant's door looking a fine gentleman. The moment he showed his loved one the ring, she threw herself in his arms—and they were married and lived happily ever after.

21 MAY

The Forgetful Elephant

Deep inside the jungle lived a foolish elephant. He was so forgetful that he would forget to get up in the morning, and forget to go to bed at night; he didn't remember to wash himself, or when to eat his meals. The monkeys would laugh at him and shout: "Brother elephant, where have you left your head again?" The angry elephant would suck up a trunkful of water and spray the mischievous monkeys from head to foot. The monkeys tried to think of a way to get their own back on him. One old monkey had a bright idea. "Brother elephant," he called out from the branches, "why not tie a knot in your trunk, so as to remember what not to forget?"—"A good idea," the elephant thought to himself, and he asked the monkey to do it for him. But no sooner was the knot tied, than the monkeys began to laugh at him again, and dropped coconuts on his head. "Why have you a knot in your trunk, brother elephant?" they shrieked. "I don't know," said the poor elephant, "I can't remember." And he began to cry noisily. In the end the monkeys took pity on him and untied his trunk. "But you must promise not to splash us with water," they told him. "Of course, of course, I promise," said the elephant, and he sucked up a trunkful of water and sprayed the monkeys until they nearly choked. You see, he really was a forgetful elephant: he had already forgotten his promise.

22 MAY

The Two Fishermen

Long ago, in a poor hut by the sea shore, lived a fisherman. Though he cast his nets from morning till night, he was unable to catch anything. He almost died of hunger. One evening he was sitting on the shore, sadly pondering his fate, when he saw a flame shoot out of the water. "Might there not be some sunken treasure there?" he thought to himself. "But I want nothing to do with it; upon my faith, the devil's hand is in such a thing!" And he turned on his heels and walked quickly towards his hut. But a voice behind him said: "Do not go away, fisherman!" The young man turned round. A strange figure with long blue hair and wearing a tail-coat was stepping out from the sea. His arms were stretched out in front of him, as if he could not see where he was going. "Andrew," the stranger addressed the fisherman, "I know you are troubled by poverty and hunger. If you wish, I shall help you. Take my brass ring and come here again tomorrow at midnight. You will see a flame on the sea. Go straight to it. Beneath it you will find three upturned pots. Lift the middle one, and you will release the soul of a drowned man; but you must speak to no one on the way. You will see how your fortunes will change." But the fisherman thought that Lucifer himself was tempting him, and he rushed home to his hut.

23 MAY

The Two Fishermen

No sooner had the fisherman reached his bed, than he became ill, and he was ill the whole

year. He had to sell his boat and nets, and even his poor wooden hut. He was left with only a beggar's staff. Exactly a year later, on St. Andrew's eve, he was again sitting sadly by the shore, when a flame suddenly shot out from the waves. From out of the flame the strange man appeared again. "It is a year since we spoke together, Andrew," he smiled. "Will you not change your mind?" The fisherman, thinking that even hell could be no worse than his present plight, promised to return at midnight the next night to release the soul of one of the drowned. The stranger slipped a brass ring on his finger and disappeared into the sea. The next day at midnight the fisherman set off into the waves. Far off over the sea he saw a mysterious light, and he headed towards it. He thought he would have to swim, but the water came up no higher as he walked, and in a while, to his amazement, he came upon a beautiful meadow. There were mowers there, merrily scything the grass and singing with joy. The fisherman recognized people from the villages around his home who had been drowned at sea, but he did not stop to speak to them. Nor did he stop at a beautiful house from which a young girl was calling to him. Instead he hurried on to the upturned pots, and set free from the middle one the soul of a drowned man. At that moment all the mowers ran towards him, shouting and wailing. The fisherman thought his hour had come, and he fainted with terror. When he awoke, he was lying on the beach, his whole body aching and sore. To his astonishment he saw that he was covered in scales, and that the scales were of pure gold. From that moment he never knew want again.

24 MAY

The Two Fishermen

The news of the sudden good fortune of fisherman Andrew soon spread up and down the whole coast. One of those who heard the tale was Peter the fisherman. He was a lazy, envious fellow, and to make matters worse he had a wicked, nagging wife. So he drank away what he earned down at the local tavern. One day his neighbour came rushing into the tavern to tell him his wife had drowned in an accident. "What God gave, he has taken unto his own," thought Peter. "But if golden scales were to grow on me, like on fisherman Andrew, I should have a merry time of it now, without my nagging wife." And towards evening he set off down to the sea to look for the mysterious flame. It was not long before a flame leapt up, and out of it stepped the curious stranger. "I, too, should like to free the soul of a drowned man," fisherman Peter grunted at him. The stranger threw a brass ring at his feet without a word, and disappeared into the waves. The next day at midnight, Peter set off into the waves. The sea parted in front of him, and before long he had reached the beautiful meadow, where the mowers reaped and sang merrily in the green grass. At the edge of the meadow stood a fine house. "That would be the place to live," thought Peter to himself, and he knocked at the door. Rat-a-tat-tat! Who do you suppose will come and open it?

25 MAY

The Two Fishermen

As soon as the fisherman knocked, the door flew open, and there stood a giantess, grinning from ear to ear. "Good lady," stammered the fisherman, "do you not know where I might find three upturned pots?"—"Just you wait, I'll show you," shrieked the giantess. "Marry me

you will not, but bang and make a racket, that's what you like to do!" And she chased after the fisherman, followed by the mowers, who came running as if summoned. The fisherman took to his heels. He ran like the wind; then, suddenly, he saw in front of him three upturned pots. Straight away he turned over the nearest of them, and at that moment it seemed as if the sky fell in on him. "This is the end of me," thought Peter to himself, and he fell into a dead faint. When he awoke, he was lying on the beach, aching all over. He felt his skin quickly, and what do you suppose? There were scales on his body, all right, but not of gold! They were quite ordinary fish scales. "Perhaps I shall have some gold pieces at home, at least," he thought, and set off for his cottage with tears in his eyes. He saw something shining from the window, and he thought it must surely be the gleam of gold. But when he reached his doorstep, what should he see but his nagging wife, waiting for him with her arms folded. You can imagine the welcome he got! He remembers it to this day.

26 MAY

The Singing River

On the banks of a crystal river a young Indian maiden lived. She was called Morning Dew. When the sun rose in the morning, Morning Dew began to sing, and she sang so sweetly that every day the chief of all the gods would stop all life on earth for an instant to listen to her song. Since then there has always been a moment of sacred silence just before daybreak. Morning Dew loved the most courageous of all the Indian braves, and she had promised to become his squaw. But one day the young man took his canoe down the river and forgot to greet the powerful god of the waters. The river grew angry, overturned the canoe, and dragged the young brave to the bottom. There he turned into a rainbow trout. Morning Dew, in tears, begged the river to give her back her loved one, but the river just

flowed quietly on down to the distant Lake of Shadows, and the waves did not reply. So the maiden flung herself into the water, and tearfully begged the crystal waters to take her life. The spirits of the waters took pity on her for her grief, and changed her into a white waterfall. Every year a rainbow trout swims up to the waterfall, basks in its waters, and whispers with its eddies. Since then the crystal river has sung a song at daybreak. Its voice is like that of Morning Dew.

27 MAY

The Clever Schoolmaster and the Stupid Shark

In a certain fishing village there lived a wise schoolteacher. He read old books, and could do many strange things. He knew how to

count to five, sleep on his left ear, speak underwater, and sneeze into a handkerchief. The strangest thing of all was that he wore a hat on his head even when it was not raining. The people of the village used to say that perhaps he even knew magic. One day, he was passing the time by sunning himself in a little boat near to the shore. Along came a shark, turned the boat over, and dragged the teacher by the leg to the bottom of the sea. His hat was left floating on the surface. "What a foolish shark you are," said the schoolmaster, beneath the waves. "Can you not see that my head has floated away? Why, that is the best part of me—it is a full of good things: my eyes, my ears, my nose and my brain." The shark looked up, and, sure enough, something was floating on the surface of the waves. He left the schoolmaster behind and shot off to catch his head. Meanwhile, the clever teacher swam to the surface and made quickly for the shore. Now he tells everyone the story of the stupid shark. People laugh and say it is a very tall story indeed. But what if it is true? If you ever see a shark wearing a hat, it might be that one, looking for the schoolmaster whose head floated away.

28 MAY

The Princess and the Pea

There once lived a prince who wanted only a real princess for his wife. So he went out into the world to seek his bride. There were princesses everywhere he looked, like flowers in the meadows, but none of them seemed to the young prince to be quite the real thing; each and every one of them had at least some little fault. He returned home sadly. Then, one evening, in the midst of a terrible storm, somebody came knocking at the palace door. The queen opened it. On the doorstep stood a beautiful young girl, soaked from head to foot like a flower the gardener has just watered. If she had wrung out her clothes, it would have left her standing in a proper little lake. She asked the queen for a bed for the

night. "Who are you?" asked the queen. "A princess," the girl replied, "a real princess." All in the palace were overjoyed to hear that a real princess had arrived, but the queen was not just going to take her word for it. She took a little pea and placed it on the princess's bed. On it she laid twenty mattresses and twice twenty cushions, and then she bade the princess good-night. The next morning, she asked her how she had slept. "Oh," sighed the princess. "Oh, my poor back. I did not sleep a wink all night; there was something so terribly hard in my bed!" Then they all knew that she was a real princess, and it was not long before a grand wedding was celebrated at the palace.

29 MAY

The Danced-Away Shoes

There was once a king who had twelve daughters, each of them lovelier than the next. They all slept in the same bedchamber, and every night the king locked the door with seven locks, to make sure that his daughters did not stray from their beds. But it was all to no avail; every morning the princesses' shoes were worn down, as if they had danced the night away somewhere. One day the enraged king proclaimed throughout the land that he would give one of his daughters and his whole kingdom to anyone who could discover where the princesses went to dance every night. Princes and knights began to assemble from all around to watch over the king's restless daughters. Each of them took his place by the door of the princesses' bedchamber, but the moment the clock struck midnight, it was always the same story. Each of the royal suitors would mysteriously close his eyes, and sleep, and sleep, and sleep. In the morning, the princesses' shoes would be danced away as before. One after the other, the king had the careless sentries banished from the land, and he sat on his throne and lamented until all the servants and courtiers stopped up their ears. Once a poor soldier was passing that way. As he walked beneath the palace windows he heard the royal groans, and said to himself: "Why should I not try my luck? I shall go and guard the restless princesses; anyway, I have nothing better to do." And he set off for the palace gates.

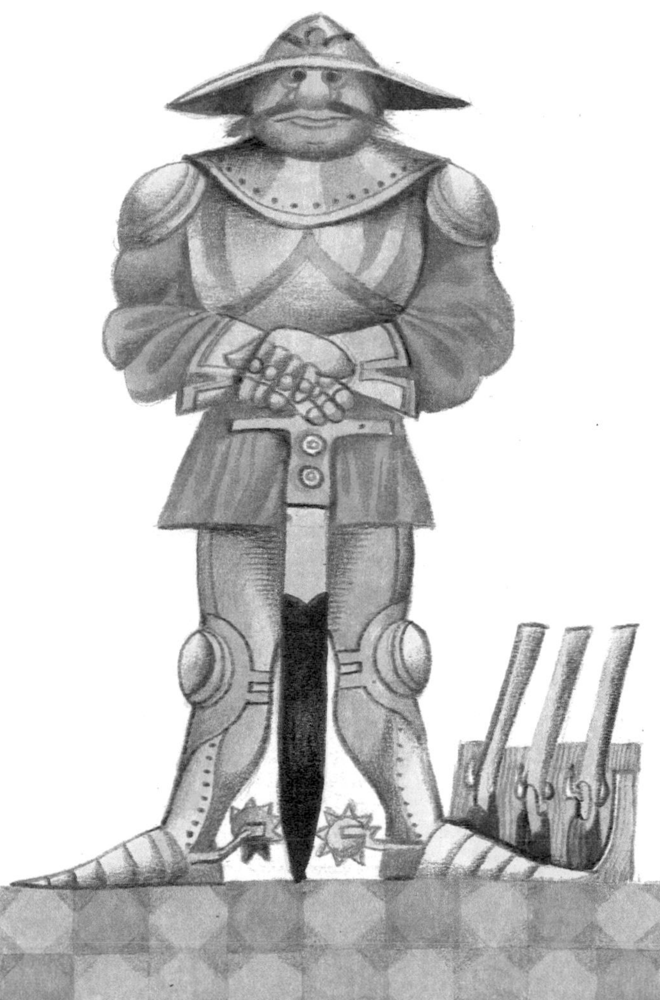

30 MAY

The Danced-Away Shoes

On his way to the king, the soldier met an old woman. He gave her a friendly greeting, and the woman smiled and said to him: "A kind word is like a mother's caress. I shall reward you for your greeting. I know where you are going, soldier! When you go to guard the princesses' chamber, you must not take the wine they will offer you! If you heed my words, you will not blink an eye till morning. But you must pretend to be asleep. Take this magic cloak. If you throw it across your shoulders, you will become invisible, and you may watch secretly to see where the princesses wander at night." The soldier thanked her kindly, and went to seek an audience with the king. The servants dressed him in splendid clothes, and when evening came they sat him down by the door of the princesses' bedchamber. "If you fail in your task, you will lose your head," the king warned him. But the soldier only smiled. When, just before midnight, the youngest of the princesses offered him a goblet of wine, he pretended to drink it; but he poured the wine into an old sponge which he wore around his neck. Then he lay stretched out on the floor and snored until the windows rattled. When midnight struck, the eldest of the princesses lit a candle and knocked three times her bed; the bed fell through the floor and, one after the other, the princesses climbed down through the hole into the ground. The soldier threw the magic cloak over his shoulders and went after them.

31 MAY

The Danced-Away Shoes

As the princesses ran down a flight of underground steps, the invisible soldier accidentally trod on the last one's train. "Sisters, someone is following us!" she cried in dismay; but the others reassured her, saying: "It was only a nail in the floor!" In a while they came to an enchanted garden. Exquisite trees grew there, with gold and silver branches, and a little bird all covered in diamonds was singing on a glistening tree-stump. The soldier snapped off a twig from each tree he passed, so that he might prove his story to the king. "What is that crackling behind us?" asked the princesses, nervously. "It is probably the enchanted princes firing a salute in our honour," their eldest sister said, soothingly. They hurried on to the banks of a broad lake. There twelve princes stood waiting with twelve little boats; they took the princesses aboard, and sailed towards a rainbow palace in the middle of the underground lake. "Princess, why are you so heavy today? You quite weigh my boat down," declared the prince who had the extra passenger, hidden by his magic cloak. At last they reached the palace, and began to dance. The invisible soldier danced along with them, and if one of the princesses happened to be holding a goblet of wine, he would drain it at a gulp. "What strange magic is this?" wondered the princesses. This went on all night; then, just before dawn, the princes took their partners back across the lake, and the girls hurried back to their chamber. But the soldier got to the palace first, and went to tell the king. He told the girls' father everything, and showed him the splendid twigs and a wine-goblet he had kept as a souvenir. The grateful king had the enchanted passage walled up, married the soldier to the most beautiful of his daughters, and found the rest of them soldiers for husbands, too. And the enchanted princes? They dance with the midnight fairies in their rainbow palace, and I daresay they don't even want to be set free any more.

JUNE

1 JUNE

The Magic Flower

Once upon a time there was a king who resolved to find out how his soldiers lived and what they thought of him. So he dressed as a beggar and knocked at the door of his trustiest corporal, asking for a bed for the night. "To be sure, you may make your bed here in the straw," the young man agreed. But the king had scarcely closed his eyes, when the soldier shook him awake again. "I can see, old man, that the world has not treated you too well," he said. "Come along with me to the town square. I have a magic flower, which opens all locks." The king was curious, and he agreed at once. They came to a shop; the soldier opened the lock with his magic flower, and took all the money out of the shopkeeper's strong-box. He counted it carefully, and divided it into three piles. "This pile is the money the shopkeeper paid for his goods," the soldier explained. "The second pile is money honestly earned. But the third pile we shall keep, for it is money the shopkeeper obtained by cheating his customers." They continued thus until they had been to all the shops in the square, and then the soldier led the king to the royal treasury itself. The king pretended to fill his pockets greedily, but the soldier gave him such a slap in the face that his ears rang. "This money goes to the keep of all the king's soldiers; you must not touch it!" he scolded. "Take your share of what he spends on his extravagant courtiers." And the soldier was as good as his word. Afterwards they parted. The next day the king summoned his corporal and revealed all. The soldier thought it was the end of him, but the king said to him: "Soldier, I pardon you, for you are a just man. In return for an honest slap in the face, I shall make you general of all my forces."

2 JUNE

The Parrot's Story

Once a young man bought himself a parrot in the marketplace. He knew how to tell stories, and this is one of them: When I was small, a young parrot scarcely fledged, I lived in a golden cage, in the chamber of a certain proud princess. She was so beautiful that all the flowers bowed to her as she passed, and even the most splendid peacocks in the royal gardens would hide themselves in shame behind their splendid fans. But she was as

cruel and capricious as she was beautiful. There was not a jewel that was precious to her, nor did the finest gifts earn her gratitude. She wore a robe embroidered with stars, a veil of butterfly wings, and sparkling slippers hollowed out from huge diamonds. She bathed in the tears of her chambermaids, and slept beneath a gossamer bedspread spun from maidens' hair. Her father, a powerful king, granted her every wish. One day, just before dawn, the proud princess went out into the garden, so as to enjoy the sunrise for the first time in her life. The grass and flowers were covered in dew. Then the sun sprang up over the horizon, and at once the dewdrops glittered like rainbow diamonds. It was so bright and beautiful that the princess had to close her eyes so as not to be blinded by the dancing, dazzling colours. When she came to herself again, she ran off, calling, "Father, I must have a diadem of morning dew, or I shall die!"

3 JUNE

The Parrot's Story

No sooner had the king heard his daughter's wish, than he summoned all the goldsmiths in the city and ordered them to make the princess a diadem of dewdrops by the very next day, or he would have their heads cut off. The jewellers made their way sadly back to their homes. They knew that none of them could fulfil the princess's wish. The next day, before dawn, as they stood before their ruler with tears in their eyes, they had already in their hearts taken leave of this life. "Have you brought the diadem of dew?" the king asked them sternly. They shook their heads mournfully. Just then the voice of an old stranger was heard from a corner of the chamber. "I shall make the princess the diadem she desires; but first she herself must gather the most beautiful of the diamond dewdrops." When she heard this, the princess ran out into the garden, ready to catch the gleaming drops in her palm. But the moment

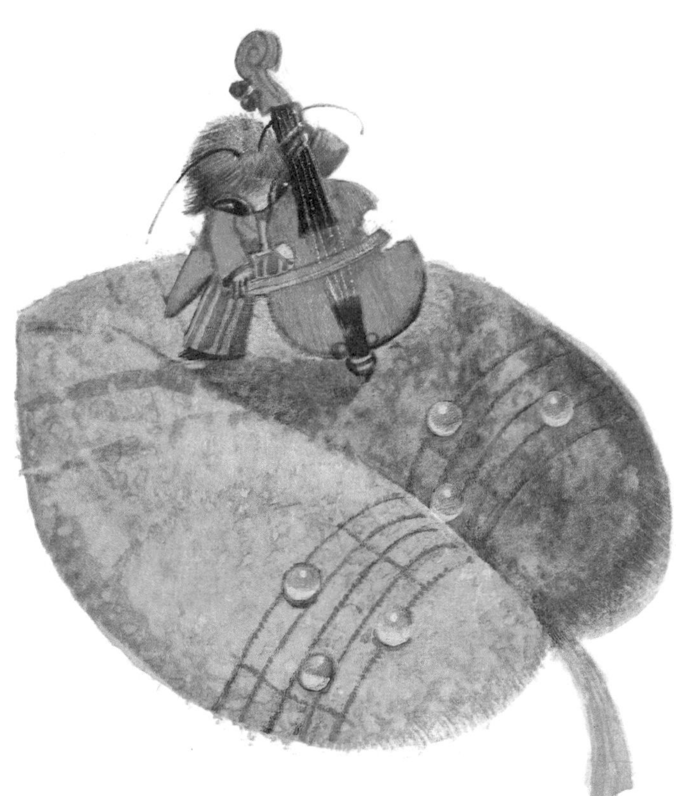

she touched them, they disappeared beneath her fingers. "Do not require of others what you cannot do yourself," the old man said, and was gone in an instant, like the morning dew itself. The princess was ashamed, and ran tearfully into the palace, where she rewarded the frightened jewellers with gold and precious stones. From then on, she was proud no more.

4 JUNE

The Lucky Shepherd

Once a shepherd was grazing his sheep when a naughty little lamb wandered off from the flock. The shepherd followed him into the forest. Suddenly he saw a cooking-pot in a tree. A wonderful smell came from inside it. The shepherd did not hesitate, but took a mouthful from the pot with his wooden spoon and tasted it. It was meat, but it wasn't meat; it was pudding, but it wasn't pudding: all he knew was that he had never tasted anything so good in all his life. Suddenly, there was a rustling in the bushes; the shepherd took fright, and hid in the branches of the tree. He was sure that robbers were coming. But it was only an ordinary cat! The cat looked into

the pot, then up into the branches, and said, "So, my fine shepherd, you have been stealing from my cooking-pot!" The shepherd was so astonished he could not even reply, so the cat smiled and said, "Come down here, I have work for you. If you can chop down the whole forest by nightfall, I shall give you twelve hundred gold pieces!" Well, that is not the sort of money you find lying in the street, so the shepherd set to. He felled trees for half the day, but it always seemed that there were still as many as before. "Wait a moment, shepherd; I'll help you," said the cat. She took the axe, and in a twinkling trees began to fall like corn beneath a scythe. Before long the whole forest lay on the ground. "Now we shall sleep," said the cat, "but tomorrow you'll pile the trees up. Then you will receive another twelve hundred pieces of gold."

5 JUNE

The Lucky Shepherd

Early the next morning the shepherd went to work again, but if the cat had not helped him, he would have been piling up trees to this day. When all the trunks were stacked in a heap, the cat told him to set light to it, and to throw her on the fire. When she insisted, the shepherd did as he was asked. All of a sudden, there in front of him stood the loveliest princess you have ever seen. "Thank you for setting me free," she said with a smile. "Now, come with me to my castle and become my husband."—"Why not?" said the shepherd, gladly. And off they went. On the way they met a rider on a horse. The stranger jumped down and said to the shepherd: "Hold my horse till I return, my lad." The shepherd did as he was asked, but as soon as the man had disappeared into the forest, he leapt on the horse with the princess and galloped away to her castle. They came to a river, where the shepherd cut off the horse's tail and threw it in the water. Then they rode to the other side. Meanwhile, the stranger was looking for his horse. He ran to the river, saw the horse's tail,

and thought that the shepherd and the horse had both drowned, so he went to look for a bridge across the river. The shepherd rode a little way, but then he remembered that he had left his cap on the opposite bank. He asked the princess to hold the horse for a moment, and went to look for the cap. While he was looking for it, the stranger spied his horse, leapt upon it, and rode off with the princess to her castle. But at least the shepherd found his cap!

6 JUNE

The Wise Peasant

A certain peasant was once riding to the mill on his pony. In order to take weight off the pony, he slung his bag of grain over his shoulder. On the way he met a clever tinker. “Hey, farmer,” said the tinker, “that sack is heavy enough. Do you want to break your pony’s back? Why do you not walk, and leave the pony to carry the sack?” “Fool,” said the peasant, “can you not see that I am carrying the sack, and not my pony?” The tinker saw at once that the peasant was a little short of sense, and decided to play a trick on him. As they went, he asked where the peasant lived, and made straight for the cottage. He said to the peasant’s wife, “Mother, your husband sends greetings and a farewell kiss. He has had enough of his ungrateful family, and wishes to see the world a little. So that you may not be lonely, I am to keep house with you until he returns.” The farmer’s wife liked the tinker, and she gladly agreed. The tinker at once began to make himself at home. First of all he had the peasant’s family cut down the two linden trees which stood in front of the cottage, saying they cast too much shade. Hardly had they done so, when the peasant returned with his flour. The pony recognized his home, but the peasant shouted at him, “Whoa, where are you going, you oaf? Do you not know where we live? There are two linden trees in front of the gates. This is not our farm. We must have wandered into another village.” And with these words the peasant set off into the world to seek his home.

7 JUNE

The Wise Peasant

As he rode, the peasant wondered how it could be that he could not find his home. When he grew tired of plodding along, he stopped at a wayside tavern. As he sat there,

a cottager came running up to him. "Help me, good fellow," he said to the peasant. "My fine mare is lying in her stable, and will not get up." The peasant allowed himself to be persuaded, and he hurried off to look at the mare. He knelt down beside her and whispered, "If you are tired of life, then there are plenty of dogs which will be glad of your meat. But if you want to live, there is grass enough for you to eat." The mare was not sick, but only lazy. As soon as the peasant began to speak of feeding the dogs, she jumped up and began to canter. The cottager's mouth fell open in wonder. "Who are you, that you can cure a horse just by speaking to it?" he asked in astonishment. Before long the tale of the wise doctor had spread to the king himself. He invited the sage to his palace. When the peasant arrived, the king happened to be sitting in his summer-house. The weather was close, for a storm was brewing, and the peasant waved away mosquitoes as he walked. The king thought the man was waving his hands at him, and went to meet him. At that moment a bolt of lightning flew down and struck the summer-house. "So that was why you were waving to me, oh greatest of sages!" said the king, delighted that his life had been saved. "You shall be richly rewarded for delivering me from the lightning." And he appointed the peasant his chief counsellor.

8 JUNE

The Bagpiper

A young bagpiper was on his way to a village festival when a black egg rolled onto his path. "Let me out!" called a thin little voice. The piper cracked the egg open, and out jumped a little imp. "I shall reward you well, bagpiper," he promised, and he cracked a hair from his mouse's tail like a little whip, over the musician's pipes. As soon as he had done this he disappeared like the steam from a kettle. "Well, a fine reward!" thought the piper, and went to play in the village. The moment he squeezed the bladder, out of the pipes leapt the little imp, and began to sing, "Ill-gotten riches, wherever you be, Fly from your masters and hurry to me!" No sooner had he said this, than the gold and silver of the grasping landlords, dishonest merchants and crooked dealers of the village jumped from their pockets and purses, came rolling and tumbling along to the feet of the startled piper, and leapt into his enchanted pipes. "Stop, thief!" cried the scoundrels who had paid for this wonderful entertainment, and they tried to run after their money; but they

stood on the spot as if enchanted, unable to lift a finger or a foot. "The thief cries: stop, thief," grinned the imp. "It has ever been so in this world." The piper frowned. "I see you do not have too good an opinion of people," he said, and he tipped the money onto the ground and gave it away to the poor. "Let the money be returned to those it rightfully belongs to," he added. "You have done the right thing, piper," the imp told him, approvingly. "If you had kept dishonest money, you would have sold your soul to the devil." The piper smiled, squeezed the bag of his pipes, and played until every foot began to dance. Perhaps he is playing to this day.

9 JUNE

The Green Goose

Long, long ago, in times beyond memory, there was a cottager who had twelve daughters, whom he and his wife were scarcely able to keep. One day the cottager was out in the forest with his eldest daughter, gathering firewood into bundles so that they might at least warm themselves, even if their stomachs were empty. Suddenly a golden carriage appeared before them, and out from it leaned a beautiful maiden, green all over like a frog. "I know of your troubles, good fellow," she said. "But if you will put your eldest daughter in my service for seven years, you shall have a larder full of food and drink, which will never grow empty." The cottager did not know what he was to do, but when his daughter beseeched him to do as the green maiden had asked, he unwillingly agreed. The maiden took his daughter into her coach and, before the cottager knew it, they were gone. When he returned home, he told his wife, "Bring from the larder our best food and drink!" The poor woman burst into tears, thinking her husband had gone off his head from want and hunger; but in the end she went to look in the larder. She almost fell down the steps with wonder and joy! The larder was stacked from floor to ceiling with food and drink fit for a king. From then on they lived in the little cottage like lords.

10 JUNE

The Green Goose

Meanwhile, the green maiden took the cottager's eldest daughter to a golden palace on a silver pillar. There were more rooms in the palace than cherries on a tree. The maiden stroked the poor girl's hair and said: "Here are the keys to all chambers; for a whole seven years you shall dust the rooms and clean them and make the diamond-studded beds. But do not enter the last of the chambers, or it will go ill with you." The girl promised, and set to work, as she had done since she was a small child. Six years passed like six months, and in all that time the cottager's daughter never met a soul in the palace: but each morning the beds were crumpled, as if they had been slept in. As the seventh year drew near, the girl was overcome with curiosity, and she opened the door of the forbidden chamber just a crack, and peeped inside. She saw there a huge golden hall with an enormous pond in the middle; on the pond a green goose was swimming. The moment she saw the girl, the goose called out sadly, "Alas! You hapless child; if you had obeyed, I should have been released from the spell. Now I must wait another hundred years." Before the astonished girl had come to her senses, she was again standing in her poor cottage home. All the good things had disappeared from the larder, and again the cottager and his family were as poor as church mice.

11 JUNE

Tall, Broad and Sharpsighted

Once upon a time there was an old king who only had one son. One day he called the young man to him and said, "My son, it is time for you to choose a bride. Take this key and go to the thirteenth chamber, where you will find the portraits of all the most beautiful princesses. Whichever of them you choose shall become your wife." The prince obeyed, and when he entered the secret chamber he found twelve magnificent gold frames. Eleven of them contained the portraits of princesses, each more lovely than the next, but the twelfth was covered over with a black drape. The prince was curious, and drew back the cloth. The beauty of the face beneath took his breath away. But the girl's face was as pale as wax, and her eyes shed real tears. "This one, and no other!" breathed the prince, enchanted by her beauty. At these words the sad princess smiled, and the portrait disappeared. When the prince told his father of his decision, the old man was saddened. "You have not chosen wisely, my son," he said. "Your bride is a prisoner in the castle of the Black Wizard. Many a brave knight has tried to set her free, but none has returned." But the young prince was not to be deterred. He quickly took leave of his unhappy father and set out into the world to seek the sad princess.

12 JUNE

Tall, Broad and Sharpsighted

For a long time the prince roamed the world, not knowing where to turn. Then, in a deep forest, he came across three strange fellows. One was as tall as a fir tree, the second as round as a pumpkin, and the third wore a black scarf across his eyes. "Hold fast, noble prince! Take us into your service," called the tall one. "Who are you, and what can you do?" asked the prince. "We are called Tall, Broad and Sharpsighted," replied the lanky fellow. "I am able to stretch myself up to the clouds. Broad can drink up the whole sea, and when he has taken his fill, his stomach flattens all living things around him. Sharpsighted can see to the end of the world, and if he takes the

scarf from his eyes, his very glance can crack open the hardest rock." And the three strange fellows at once showed him their skills. "Very well," said the prince, impressed by their tricks, "I shall take you into my service, if you tell me where I may find the Black Wizard's castle." At this Sharpsighted peered all around; the rocks cracked open, and soon he called out: "Now I see it; but we should not reach it if we walked to the end of our lives, were we to go on foot. Tall shall take us all on his shoulders!" And so it happened. Tall stretched himself out until his head disappeared into the clouds, and off they went, the others sitting on his shoulders. A score of miles he strode with every step, and before evening they were standing before the castle of the Black Wizard.

13 JUNE

Tall, Broad and Sharpsighted

Inside the gates there was a deathly stillness. The only things to be seen in the courtyard were the strange statues of knights in full armour, looking as though they had suddenly been turned to stone. One held a half-drawn sword, another's mouth was open wide, while a third looked as if he had just stumbled, but had not yet fallen to the ground. But the prince and his companions went on boldly into the banqueting hall, and sat down at the great oak table. Strange to relate, at that moment the empty plates were filled with delicacies, and the pewter goblets contained good wine. Putting all else out of their minds, the weary travellers set to with a will. No sooner had they finished their meal, than with a bang and a flash the wall parted and into the hall stepped the Black Wizard himself. He had a long black beard, and around his waist he wore an iron band. He was leading the sad princess by the hand. "I know why you have come," he snarled. "If you are able, oh prince, to guard the princess in this hall until daybreak, she is yours. Otherwise you shall all be turned to stone!" He led the girl to the

centre of the room, laughed fiendishly, and was gone in a puff of smoke. The prince tried in vain to speak to the maiden; she lay as if asleep, but with tears glistening in her eyes. Then Tall stretched himself round the room like a belt, Broad blew himself out in the doorway like a great barrel, and the prince took the beautiful princess by the hand. They promised each other that none would sleep a wink, but before many moments had passed they all fell into a deep slumber.

14 JUNE

Tall, Broad and Sharpsighted

When, just before dawn, the prince awoke from his sleep, the princess was nowhere to be seen. "Have no fear," Sharpsighted assured him, "I shall soon find her." He looked out through the window into the world, gazing until the rocks cracked open; suddenly he

cried, "Now I see her! Far away from here, on the bottom of a black sea, lies a golden ring, and that ring is the enchanted princess." At this Tall took Broad and Sharpsighted upon his shoulders, stretched himself out, and off he went. Thirty miles with every step, and soon they reached their goal. But alas, however Tall stretched himself on the shore of the black sea, he was unable to reach the ring. Then Broad puffed himself up like a huge cask, and with a single draught he drained the sea. Now they had no difficulty in getting the ring, and soon Tall had again taken them on his back and set off for the castle. But Broad was now so heavy that he had to put him down again, and the sea ran back out and down to where it had come from. At that moment the first rays of dawn began to appear in the sky. Without delay Tall reached out and dropped the golden ring through the window of the Black Wizard's banqueting hall. The moment it touched the ground it changed into the beautiful princess. When the wicked magician saw this, he roared with anger, the iron band around his waist snapped in half, and he changed into a raven. Immediately, all the stony knights came alive, and led the prince and princess in triumph to the prince's castle. Only Tall, Broad and Sharpsighted went their own way, off into the world again to help good people everywhere.

15 JUNE

The Swede

There once lived two brothers, one of them rich and the other one poor, as is the way of the world. Both of them served in the army. But the poor brother soon tired of a soldier's life, and he turned to farming instead. He dug a tiny field and sowed it with swedes. Before he knew it, a swede had grown up so large that he could only pull it up with the help of a pair of oxen. "What am I to do with such a monster?" said the poor man in dismay. "I shall not eat it as long as I live, and no one will buy it from me." Then an idea came to him. "I shall give it as a present to the king!"

he said to himself. And so he did. When he saw the giant swede, the king was astonished. "You must have been born under a lucky star, that your fields give you such a harvest," he told the man. "Indeed not sire, for I have known only hunger and want since my childhood," was the reply. "But my brother, the captain—there is a lordly fellow. Gold pieces fall into his lap!" The king took pity on the poor man. "If you are indeed so poor, then take what gold you can carry from my coffers!" he told him, and gave him a fine piece of farmland as well. When his brother heard of this good fortune, he said to himself, "If the king gave my brother such riches in return for an ordinary swede, then I shall bring him far richer gifts, and shall surely have a much greater reward!" He bought jewels and rings, loaded them on fine black horses, and took them off to the palace. The king shook his head over the gifts. "Whoever can offer such gifts must be richer than the king himself, and wants for nothing," he said. "But I shall reward you." And do you know what he ordered his servants to bring? Why, the huge swede, of course. It took the rich captain weeks to roll his present home!

16 JUNE

Lazy Hans

There was never a fellow as lazy as Hans. So that he should not have to take the goat to pasture, he preferred to marry fat Trina. He thought she would look after the goat for him, and at first that is how it was. Trina would take the goat to graze, and Hans would lie in his bed till mid-day, in order not to waste good food on breakfast. But Trina was not too fond of work either. One day she said to Hans, "Let us exchange the goat for our neighbour's beehive. Bees do not have to be taken to the pastures—they fly there on their own. And we shall have a pot full of honey." Hans liked the idea. "Anyway, honey tastes better than goat's milk," he piped in, and went to change the goat for the bees. By autumn they had a pot full of honey. Trina put it down by the foot of the bed with the hive beside it, so that no one might steal their honey, and the two of them lazed among the bedclothes all day long. "Dear me," said Hans one day. "Trina has a sweet tooth; she is sure to eat all the honey herself, and there will be none left for me. Let us rather exchange it for a goose and goslings."—"Very well," Trina replied, "but not before we have children, for who is to take the geese to grass?" Hans frowned. "Children are no good at working," he said. "They will only go chasing butterflies." "Let them try," said Trina. "I should soon smack their bottoms for them! Like this!" And she caught up a stick, swung it down, and, crash! The pot of honey smashed to pieces. "Well, that is the end of our goose and goslings," said Hans. "Now no one will have to look after them. How well we have settled the matter!" And they licked the honey from the pieces of the pot, and went to bed. There was nothing for them to do anyway.

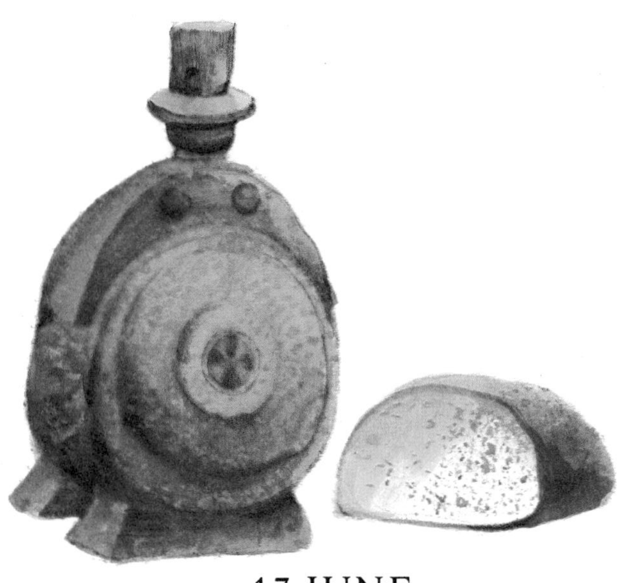

17 JUNE

The Loaf and the Flask

A miser and a generous man were travelling through the world together. Neither of them had two coins to rub together, but the generous man always divided the little he had with anyone who cared to share it, while the miserly fellow would not have given a flea from his head. One day they found they had just three crusts of bread left in their bundle. Suddenly, a white-haired old man appeared beside them. "Give me a little of your bread," he pleaded. "Not a morsel has passed my lips for three whole days."—"Why should we?" the miser said to him roughly, and he quickly ate two of the crusts, to make sure he did not go short. But the generous one shared the last crust with the old man. "I shall reward you both well," the stranger told them, as they prepared to go their way. "Here is a loaf of bread and a pocket-flask. Whoever swallows a piece of the loaf, the mouthful will turn into pure gold. In the flask is the water of life. It is able to cure any ailment. You may share the gifts as you wish."—"What are the sick to me?" thought the miser to himself. "I shall take the magic loaf." The old man only smiled, and disappeared. The miser at once began to eat. He swallowed greedily; the bread turned to gold in his throat, until he could not even stand up, and had to roll along instead. He rolled onto a bridge, but it gave way beneath his great weight, and the gold dragged the miser to the bottom of the river. The fellow with the generous heart wandered the world, curing the sick everywhere he went with his wonderful water. In the end he cured a beautiful princess, and so became king.

18 JUNE

Beautiful Vasilisa

There once lived a beautiful girl called Vasilisa. There was not another maiden for miles around whose beauty could compare with hers. She wanted for nothing. But one sad day her dear mother lay on her deathbed. Before she died, she gave Vasilisa a little doll. "Care for her as if she were your very own child," her mother told her. "Whenever times are hard for you, give her food and drink, and she will comfort you." With these words she gave up the ghost. Vasilisa cried until she had no tears left to cry; but misfortunes never come singly, and before long her father brought home a stepmother and two ugly stepdaughters. They hated Vasilisa so much that they would have starved her to death. They gave her all the most unpleasant work to do, and beat her frequently. Whenever her heart was heavy with sadness, she would feed her doll with milk, and the doll would sing her her mother's song to comfort her. But one day her father left home to go on a journey. The stepmother and her daughters lay in bed all

day, and Vasilisa had to wait on them hand and foot. She had so much to do that she let the fire go out. "Off with you to Yagga the Hag herself to get fire!" the women shouted at her. "But don't you dare come back from the old ogress without it!" What else could the poor girl do? She set off into the dark night to visit Yagga the Hag.

19 JUNE

Beautiful Vasilisa

Poor Vasilisa walked, and walked, until she came to a black forest. A black rider on a black horse rode past her, and human skulls shone white from all the trees. Terrified, Vasilisa began to run, until she arrived, breathless, at a gate made of human bones. Beyond the gate stood a birch tree, and on the other side of the tree a strange cottage was turning around on a chicken's leg. Out of it jumped a black dog and a black cat, their jaws covered in blood and their claws glowing like hot coals. They rushed towards Vasilisa, ready to tear her throat out. But just then a black-eyed dwarf-girl looked out of the window and called the beasts off. "What are you doing here, poor child?" she asked Vasilisa. The hapless girl told her tearfully why she had come. "Dear me, child, I really don't know if you will leave here alive," sighed the black-eyed girl. "Yagga the Hag, my mistress, lives on human meat and dresses in human skins." But at that moment there was a roar in the air like the draught up some dark chimney, and Yagga the Hag herself came flying up astride a broomstick, sweeping black clouds behind her. "What are you doing here, you skinny little worm?" she asked, with a snivel. Vasilisa begged the hag on her bended knees to give her a little fire, saying that she must not go home without it. "Very well," said the ogress. "If you serve me well, you shall have what you ask. Otherwise I shall roast you for dinner." And she made Vasilisa a bed for the night in a black mousehole.

20 JUNE

Beautiful Vasilisa

When Vasilisa got up in the morning, Yagga the Hag tipped a sackful of peas and poppy seed on the floor in front of her and told the girl: "If you have not picked out the peas

before a red rider on a red horse passes by my gate, you shall not leave here alive!" With these words she flew off on her broomstick, making a terrible roar. Poor Vasilisa started to cry. "I shall not finish this work till the end of my life," she wailed. And she took her little doll on her knee, gave her a little milk, and poured out her heart to her. "Do not be afraid," the doll said. "Everything will be all right." Then the doll called all the birds of the forest, and in no time at all they had picked out the peas from the poppy seed. When Yagga the Hag returned, she could hardly believe her eyes. "Very well," she muttered. "I have a still harder task for you. Before a black rider on a black horse passes by my gate, you must shell all my nuts." And she tipped thirty sacks of golden nuts on the floor in front of Vasilisa; then she flew off again. Again the girl wanted to cry, but the doll helped her again. She clapped, and sang, and all of a sudden the cottage was full of mice, and before evening all the nuts were shelled. By that time the black rider was on his way, and Yagga the Hag was flying home. When she saw that Vasilisa had again finished her work, she scowled with disappointment and sent the child off to her mousehole.

21 JUNE

Beautiful Vasilisa

In the night the hag woke up her black-eyed servant and told her to light a fire under the oven so that she might roast Vasilisa for breakfast. Then she stretched out on her bed, laid her broomstick over herself, and was soon fast asleep. But Vasilisa had heard the ogress, and she pleaded with the black-eyed dwarf, and said, "I'll give you my silk scarf if you set me free." The dwarf-girl had a kind heart, and she agreed. The dog and the cat ran after Vasilisa, and would have torn her to pieces, but Vasilisa threw them a piroschek and hurried towards the gate. There the birch tree wound its branches into her hair, and the gate slammed in her face. She tied the branches back with a silk ribbon and greased the hinges of the gate with butter. The tree and the gate thanked her and let her go free. She ran as fast as if she had wings. So that she could find her way, she stuck a skull with shining eyes onto a long stick, and was able to see the path in front of her as she ran through the dark forest. In the morning, when Yagga the Hag awoke and found Vasilisa gone, she turned angrily on the black-eyed dwarf, the poor animals, the tree and the gate; but they replied that in all the years they had served her faithfully she had never given them anything, while Vasilisa had rewarded all of them. The hag was so angry that she fell into the ground and was swallowed up. When Vasilisa got home, her stepmother and the two sisters gave her a warm welcome. "Where have you been so long?" they shrieked at her, and would have punished the poor girl. But the skull turned its glowing eyes on them, and the wicked women were burned to ashes. After that Vasilisa lived in the little house in happiness and contentment. One day a young prince passed by, and was so enchanted by her beauty that he carried her off to his castle.

22 JUNE

The Lad Who Wanted to Learn to Fear

There were once two brothers, one of them clever and the other foolish. But the clever brother was a terrible coward. "If he has to cross the yard at night, he shakes with fear!" people would say. "What a wise fellow my brother is, that he is able to shake with fear," the foolish fellow complained sadly to his dog. "How I should like to know how to do it!" The sexton heard him say this, and he told the simpleton to come to the church belfry at midnight to ring the bells. That night the sexton dressed in a white sheet, thinking he would scare the fellow to death. But it was no use; the lad just shouted at him, "Go away, you silly old ghost. I haven't time for you—I must ring the bells so that I may learn to shake with fear!" But when the sexton went on howling and wailing, the foolish lad gave him such a clout across the ear that he rolled down the stairs and broke all his ribs. In the end the lad gave up in disappointment and went home. His father gave him a good scolding when he heard what he had done to the sexton. He put a purse with fifty thalers in it in the boy's hand, and sent him out into the world so that he might not bring disgrace on the family. As he went on his way the foolish fellow said to himself aloud, "I should have to be the devil himself not to be able to fear in the wide world!" A passing wayfarer heard these words and, smiling to himself, led the young man to a gallows. "Stay here till morning," he told him, "and you will soon know what fear is." And he went his way.

23 JUNE

The Lad Who Wanted to Learn to Fear

The simpleton sat down beneath the gallows and lit a fire. The night was cold; seven corpses swung from the beams until their bones creaked, and shadowy bats flitted past.

"Dear me, those fellows will catch their deaths of cold," thought the lad, and since he had a good heart he untied the corpses and sat them down beside him round the fire. In a little while their rotten clothes began to smoulder, but the hanged men did not move a muscle. "Stupid fellows, must I do everything for you?" the boy scolded them, beating sparks from the glowing cloth; and he hung his silent companions back on the gallows. The wayfarer again came by in the morning. "Well, my good fellow, have you learnt to be afraid?" he asked, with a smile. "It was no good," said the simpleton. "And even those fellows up there did nothing to help, though I sat them down beside me." The wayfarer was astonished. "Never have I seen such a fearless lad," he said. And he took the boy off to see the king. The king listened to the tale of the young fellow's heroism, then said, "So you wish at all costs to learn to shake with fear? Very well! Not far from here is a haunted castle. Demons guard a great treasure there. If you can stay there for three nights, you shall have my daughter for your wife. But you may take only three things with you."

24 JUNE

The Lad Who Wanted to Learn to Fear

The next day the simpleton ordered the servants to bring along a vice, a spokeshave and a lathe, and they set off for the haunted castle. Night fell, and the lad lit a fire in the hearth and waited to see what would happen. Midnight struck, and into the chamber rushed a dog with bloody fangs and a cat with fiery eyes. They spoke fiercely, saying, "Come and play cards with us. If you lose, we shall tear you to pieces!"—"Why not?" said the lad. "But your long claws might tear the cards. First I must trim them a little with the spokeshave!" The dog and the cat obediently put their paws in the vice; the simpleton screwed it down on their claws, and cut both their throats with the spokeshave. Then he went contentedly to bed.

But the bed began to toss and turn like a stick in a stream, spinning round first one way, then the other, and finally overturned in a tub of grease. "Phew, what a ride that was!" the lad said with satisfaction, and slept like a log. When the king came the next morning he thought the young fellow was dead. But then he opened his eyes and said, "I wonder if I shall learn to shake with fear tomorrow at least!" And that evening he set off for the haunted castle again.

25 JUNE

The Lad Who Wanted to Learn to Fear

At midnight there was a rattling in the chimney, and out of it fell, first a pair of man's legs, then a head, then the trunk to go in between them. Soon the apparition had put himself together, and without invitation he sat down at the table. In a while came a second, then a third and a fourth. Ghost after ghost! They began to throw human skulls from one to the other. "Come and play skittles with us!" they whined at the young man. "Why not?" he answered. "But the balls are not quite round; I must grind them a little." And he put the skulls in his lathe and made them nice and round. They began to play, and when the cock crew the ghosts disappeared. "Oh dear, shall I never learn to shake with fear?" grieved the simple lad. The next night there was again a terrible noise in the chimney, and down came a coffin containing the body of a bearded old gaoler. "My, how cold you are, old man," said the boy, feeling sorry for him; and he laid the corpse beside him in his bed. As soon as the body warmed up a little, it came to life, and the old man grabbed hold of the boy. "Come and try your strength with me," he grunted. "If you do not shake with fear, you shall die!"—"Indeed, that is why I am here," replied the lad. The corpse led him off through secret passages to the dungeons. There it thrust an iron pillory into the ground with a single blow. "I can do better than that," smiled the lad, and he swung an axe and caught the old man's long beard in the pillory. At once there was a noise like thunder, and in the place where the old man had stood was a huge, sparkling heap of gold and diamonds. When the king came the next morning he could not believe his eyes, and he gladly gave the young man his daughter's hand. Believe it or not, she taught him to shake until his teeth rattled. How? Every morning she poured a bucket of icy water into his bed. Thus it was that the lad finally learned to do what he had wanted to for so long.

26 JUNE

King Ragbeard

A certain king once held a great tournament in order to choose a bridegroom for his proud daughter. Princes, knights and even kings gathered from all corners of the earth to joust and win the favour of the beautiful princess. But the proud young lady only laughed at them all. One was too short, another too tall; this one too thin, that one too fat—and so it went on. But most of all she mocked the young king who was the boldest and most handsome of all, for, while hunting, he had been wounded on the cheek by a savage bear. He defeated all his rivals in the tournament; but that was not enough for the princess. "Dear Heavens, not to save my life, would I become that ragbeard's wife!" she giggled, and from then on the name stuck, and the unfortunate king was known as Ragbeard. In the end all the suitors were so insulted that

they left in disgust. The king was angry with his proud daughter, and said to her, "I shall punish you for your pride. You shall become the wife of the first wandering vagabond who comes to the palace gates." At that very moment a poor minstrel struck up a tune beneath the windows of the royal chamber. He sang so beautifully that the soft notes smoothed away the anger from the monarch's brow. "That is the husband for you, proud child," he exclaimed, and he had the wedding made ready without delay.

27 JUNE

King Ragbeard

The princess wept bitterly, and begged her father to take pity on her, but to no avail. The moment she was married, he sent her away from the royal castle. "Go with your poor husband wherever you will," he told her. "But do not show you face here again." The princess walked along miserably behind her husband, up hill and down dale, until they came to a beautiful country with rich forests, fields and meadows. Not far away they could see a royal city, sparkling proudly in the sunshine. "What is this lovely country?" the princess asked, sighing. "It is the kingdom of King Ragbeard," her husband replied. "Alas! If only I had known; I might have sat upon its throne," the princess sobbed. "You are my wife, proud princess; I will not have you lamenting for another!" the minstrel rebuked her sternly, and he led her to a poor little cottage, so low that she had to crawl into it on her hands and knees. "This is our home," the minstrel told her. "From now on you must work your fingers to the bone so that we may have enough to eat." And he began at once to teach her to weave baskets, knead bread and clean and tidy the cottage. But soon her soft hands were torn and bleeding. "You are no use at all," her husband said with a scowl. "Go at least to market to sell a couple of earthenware jugs!" She did as she was told, and laid out her

wares at the corner of the market square. But suddenly a drunken hussar appeared on his horse, and trampled the jugs to smithereens. "You good-for-nothing!" her husband shouted at her when she came home. "You would do better to wash the dishes in the royal kitchens." And so it was to be.

28 JUNE

King Ragbeard

Now the princess really had a hard time of it. She was rushed off her feet from morning till night, and had never a kind word from the royal cook. But she managed now and then to save a few poor scraps in a pot she carried tied beneath her apron, so they did not go hungry, anyway. One day, the chief steward ordered the cook to prepare a great feast. The young king, whom the princess had never set eyes on since she came to the palace, was to bring home his bride. That day in the kitchen she didn't have time to turn round, but when evening came, and she was setting off home, exhausted, with her secret jar of food full to the brim, she could not resist just a peep into the banqueting hall through a crack in the door. Just then a pair of arms caught her around the waist from behind; she turned, and could not believe her eyes, for it was none other than King Ragbeard himself, and he took her in his arms to dance. He tripped and whirled with her so gaily that the jar of food came unfastened, and all the scraps she had hidden went flying across the floor. The princess nearly died of shame, and wanted to run away, but the king held her fast and said, kindly: "Do you not recognize your own husband from the poor cottage? Your father and I wanted to punish you for your pride. The hussar whose horse stamped upon your jugs—that was also I! But because a kind heart beat within your proud bosom, you have passed the test. Now we shall never again be parted." And the princess fell into his arms.

29 JUNE

A Little Mouse Story

Once upon a time there was a mouse kingdom, in which there lived a mouse who was never satisfied. Nothing was to her liking: she turned up her nose at everything. One day she decided to go out into the world. She crept quietly past the guards and peeped out of the mousehole at the world outside. Not far away in the grass she could see a bird's nest. "Ah, what a splendid palace! I should like to live there," she whispered. Just then a little bird flew out of the nest and up into the sky. "That is surely the king of the birds himself—what fine robes he wears!" sighed the mouse. "How much more splendid they are than the dirty grey coat worn by the mouse-king." And

before you could blink an eyelid, she had jumped into the nest and was making herself at home. "Now I am queen. Don't you dare disturb me!" she said to the astonished birds. They flew off to tell the falcon. "A fine state of affairs," said the falcon, angrily. "A mouse, queen of the birds? I'll show her!" But as soon as he came into sight above the nest, the mouse called out, "There he is, hunter: aim your gun and fire!" The falcon took fright and flew away. Just then a little boy went by; he saw the mouse and mewed softly like a cat. The mouse was off down the nearest mousehole as if the devil himself were after her. The birds were so pleased to see the last of her that each of them dropped the little boy a feather into the grass.

30 JUNE

The Thief Robbed

There once lived a foolish country lad, who was so lazy that he would have ridden to church in his bed if he had been able. "Begone from my sight, lazybones!" his father roared at him one day. "If you cannot do an honest day's work, then go and learn the highwayman's trade at least!" The lad was not against the idea. He took his grandfather's old pistol from the chest in the attic, thrust a rusty knife into his belt, and crouched beside the old well at the end of the parish field. He was in luck right away. The merchants and farmers were just making their way home from market, and when the lad called out in his best robber's voice "Your money or your lives!", they pacified him with gold pieces. Before long he had money by the sackful. Then along came the king himself in his coach. "Your money or your life!" cried the stupid lad. But the king was no fool. "Dear me; all I possess is yours, Most Esteemed Highwayman," he said. "But all my riches are hidden in this old well, and neither I nor my coachman can swim. Why do you not go into the well yourself to bring out the treasure?" The lad did not hesitate, but took off his clothes, filled with stolen gold, and leapt into the well. The king laughed until his sides ached. "You fool; did you not know that the king is always the greatest robber in the land?" he chuckled, and he picked up the highwayman's booty and was gone.

AUGUST

1 AUGUST

The Clever Peasant-Girl

There was once a poor cottager who had nothing in the world but his beautiful and clever daughter. "If only the king would be pleased to give us a little piece of land, so that we might not die of hunger!" he sighed one day. Who knows how the king came to hear of it, but he did, and he granted the poor man's wish. The peasant set to work joyfully. Suddenly something rang out beneath his mattock. The man bent down and, what should he see but a golden mortar! "I shall take it as a present to the king in return for the field he gave us," said the poor cottager. But his clever daughter warned him: "Father, if you take the king the mortar, he will want a pestle, too; you would do better to keep it!" But the man took no heed of his daughter's words, and carried his rare find to the royal castle. "Where is the pestle to go with this mortar?" asked the king, sternly. And, though the cottager solemnly swore that he had found no pestle, the king would not believe him, and had him thrown in gaol. How the poor fellow wept and wailed! "Why did I not heed my daughter's words?" he lamented. One day the king himself heard his groans, and had him summoned again. "Why do you call on your daughter so?" he asked. The cottager told him everything, and the king pondered awhile and then said, "If your daughter is indeed so wise, then send her to me here. If she can guess my riddle, then I shall take her for my wife."

2 AUGUST

The Clever Peasant-Girl

The next day, when the cottager's daughter came to the castle, the king said to her: "I shall fulfil my promise and take you for my wife if you come to me tomorrow, not dressed, not naked, not on horseback, not on foot, not in a cart, not by road, and not by field." The girl only smiled. The next morning she took off her clothes, so as not to be dressed. Then she put on a fishing-net, so as not to be naked, and tied the net to the donkey's tail. Then the donkey dragged her along the ditch to the king's palace. Thus she went neither on horseback, nor on foot, nor in a cart. She travelled neither by road, nor by field, but in between the two. When the king saw her from the window, he smiled and said: "Indeed you are a wise girl; you deserve to be queen. But, mark my words, you are not to meddle in affairs of state!" And so before very long the cottager's daughter was sitting on the throne beside the king.

hands, and pretended to catch fish. "Fool!" called the king from the window. "How can you catch fish here?" But the peasant replied: "If a pair of oxen may have a foal, why should I not catch fish in the street?" The king smiled, but then he said sternly, "This was not your own idea; who told you to do it?" At first the peasant would not tell, but after being given a sound beating he gave the queen away. The king flew into a rage, and told the queen: "You have not kept your promise. Tomorrow you shall return to your home. You may take with you from the palace whatever is dearest to you." The clever queen got the king to drink with her that evening for the last time, and made him drunk. In the morning she put him on a handcart and took him off to her cottage. When he woke up, she smiled and said to him: "You are dearest of all to me, so I have brought you with me." The king laughed heartily at her cleverness and took her back to the palace with him. From then on the king always took his queen's advice, and they lived happily ever after.

3 AUGUST

The Clever Peasant-Girl

One day there was a great market in the royal city. During the night a fine foal was born to a certain farmer's mare, but it wandered off and lay down between a couple of oxen. In the morning, when the owner of the oxen found the foal, he wished to keep it for himself. He and the rightful owner argued for so long that the king himself heard of their quarrel. "The foal belongs to him with whose beasts it lay!" was the judgement of the king. When the queen heard this unjust verdict, she secretly called the wronged peasant to her, and said to him: "If you tell no one, I shall advise you how to get your foal back again." Then she whispered something in his ear. The next day the foal's owner sat down in the middle of the road in front of the palace with a rod in his

4 AUGUST

The Three Magic Gifts

A soldier was returning from the wars. All he had been given by the emperor in return for his brave and faithful service was five groschen. As he was walking along he came across a large fishpond. On its surface stood a table, and round it sat four watermen, green and ghostly. "Be a good fellow, and take pity on us," they croaked. "We are out of tobacco, our wine-jug is empty, and for our fish-scales

we cannot even buy a piece of dry cheese! Give us just a groschen!" The soldier scratched his ear. "This is a fine thing," he said. "But what am I to do with you, my good fellows! Here is a groschen for each of you, that you may drink to my health." The watermen thanked him kindly, and the eldest of them said to him, "Since you have such a kind heart, my son, we shall grant you three wishes." The soldier scratched his ear again for a moment, then said, "Well, if that is to be, then give me a pipe which is always full, a pack of cards with which I may always win and . . . and a sack to which I may say only 'In you go!' and into it will fly anything or anyone I wish to get rid of!" The watermen smiled and gave him what he asked for, and the soldier went his way.

5 AUGUST

The Three Magic Gifts

The sun was soon sinking in the west, and the soldier looked around him for a place to lay his head for the night. At length he came to an inn. He said to the innkeeper, "Here you have my last groschen—let me sleep here tonight." But the innkeeper frowned and said, "Whatever are you thinking of? Every night, just before midnight, the devils come to my inn. I myself always run away at night. But if you will, you may stay here for nothing." The soldier thanked him, and when the innkeeper had left, he lay down on a bench in the taproom and fell fast asleep. Scarcely had the clock struck eleven, when down the chimney and into the room swept a whole swarm of devils. "Come and play cards with us, or we shall tear you to pieces!" they screamed at the soldier. "Why not?" grinned the soldier, taking out his magic cards; and the game began. Soon the soldier had all the devils' gold piled in front of him on the table. The devils lost their tempers. "We'll carry you off to hell for this!" they threatened him. "Just you try, you ill-mannered louts!" said the soldier with a smile, and he pulled out his magic sack and called out, "In you go!" In a brace of shakes

the devils were wrapped and tied in the old sack. When the innkeeper came home in the morning, he was astonished to find the soldier still in one piece. But the soldier just smiled, and told the innkeeper to give the old sack a good beating with a stout stick. You should have heard how the devils squealed and yelled! And when the soldier finally took pity on them and let them out of the sack, they did not so much as stop for breath until they reached the gates of hell.

6 AUGUST

The Three Magic Gifts

The soldier went on wandering the world for a while, but then he bought himself a nice little farm with the devils' gold, and lived there in peace and happiness. But time does not stand still, and by and by the soldier grew old. Then, one day, whom should he see sitting in the pear tree in the garden, but Lady Death herself, looking like a great black bat. "I have come for you," she croaked. But the soldier was none too keen to leave this world for the next just yet, so he grabbed his magic sack and cried: "In you go!" And Death was in the trap. The soldier took the sack and threw it down the well, then filled the well with stones just to make sure. That very day one of the village lasses went to cut the goose's throat in the back yard; but no sooner had she drawn the knife across the bird's neck, than the goose's head jumped back into place, and off it flew. Just then the butcher came running by, waving his arms and shouting: "Save us! A slaughtered pig is chasing me!" To cut a long story short, nothing died any more, and before very long people were swarming about the world like flies, and it was a wonder they did not start to eat each other up. "It's no good, this can't go on," said the soldier to himself, and he went and set Death free again; no sooner was she out of the bag than she grabbed the soldier, and that was the end of him. The moment he was dead he made straight for heaven, but St. Peter did not want to let him in, saying that he had been a drinker and a gambler and heaven knows what else.

What now? The soldier had no wish to try his luck in hell, for the devils had surely not forgotten their beating at the inn; so he was relieved to bump into the village parson. "Reverend," he begged him, "would you mind taking this old sack to heaven for me?" The parson had no objection, but he had scarcely taken three paces when the soldier pointed a finger at himself and said: "In you go!" And in he went. The parson was quite out of breath by the time they reached the pearly gates, but the soldier got to heaven all right in the end.

7 AUGUST

Smuttikin

Smuttikin the urchin lived in the forest with a stag who had golden antlers. Who knows how Smuttikin got there; maybe one day the

golden-haired wood-nymphs set him down on the doorstep, but no one can remember any more. The important thing was that he was happy there. When he was at home on his own, he would play the violin, and all the birds of the forest would sing along to the tune. Or else he would ride around the parlour on his tame squirrel's tail. During the day the stag would go to pasture, and he always reminded Smuttikin sternly not to open the door to strangers. But one day there was a knocking at the door and silky little voices from outside called to him, "Smuttikin the urchin, open up the door; we would only warm our fingers before your parlour fire." Smuttikin felt sorry for the soft-spoken strangers out in the cold, but he remembered the stag's warning and did not open the door. "It was well done," the stag praised him when he heard the boy's tale that evening. "Those were evil fairies, the Cavies. If you had opened the door to them, they would have carried you off to their den and roasted you for supper." Smuttikin cuddled up happily against the stag, and the stag told him a fairy tale.

8 AUGUST
Smuttikin

The next morning the stag with the golden antlers again set off somewhere to pasture, and to pass the time Smuttikin began to play

the violin. Then he heard from the other side of the door voices even softer than those of the day before. "Smuttikin the urchin," they called. "Open up the door; we would only warm our fingers before your parlour fire." Smuttikin would so have liked just to see the Cavies, but he did not open the door. Then the fairies outside the door began to cry; they shivered with cold and moaned softly until Smuttikin felt so sorry for them that he forgot the wise stag's warning, and opened the door just a crack. The Cavies pushed their fingers through the door, then their hands, and before he knew it they were in the parlour. They grabbed hold of Smuttikin and ran off with him into the forest. But the boy began to play a sad lament on his violin: "From o'er the hills and far away, among your pastures green, come hither, golden stag, to me, and save your Smuttikin!" The stag with the golden antlers heard this plea and came thundering through the forest like a gust of wind; he took Smuttikin up on his antlers and carried him to safety. When they reached home, the lad got a good scolding. "Never open the door to strangers again!" the stag told him, angrily. Do you think Smuttikin will obey him?

9 AUGUST
Smuttikin

Not many days had passed before there was again a whimpering at the door: "Smuttikin the urchin, open up the door; we would only warm our fingers before your parlour fire!" The boy tried to pretend not to hear, but when the wicked fairies began to weep and wail, and promised to play with him and give him nice things to eat and drink, he relented and opened the door again. Quick as a flash, the Cavies grabbed hold of him and ran off into the forest. Smuttikin wept bitterly and called to the stag, but he was grazing far off in the valley and did not hear the boy's cries. So the fairies took him off to their woodland lair. At first he had nothing to complain of: they gave

him all manner of good things to eat to fatten him up before roasting him. When he seemed nice and plump, they laid him in a dish and carried him to the oven. But Smuttikin begged them in tears to let him play his violin once more before they ate him; when they heard his plea, he again struck up his sad song: "From o'er the hills and far away, among your pastures green, come hither, golden stag, to me, and save your Smuttikin!" Before he had finished there was a pounding of hooves; out of the trees charged the stag with the golden antlers, drove the wicked fairies this way and that, and carried the boy off home. But what a scolding he had this time! He remembered it for the rest of his life, and he never, never opened the door to a stranger again.

10 AUGUST

Goldenhair

There was a king who caught a strange and exotic bird in his garden one day. Under its wing the bird held a golden key. The king tried in vain to think what the key might fit. Then one day the bird laid a golden egg, and in that egg was a keyhole. The king tried the golden key in it, and as if by magic the egg flew open and out stepped a bearded little manikin. In his hand he held a fish on a tray. "Sire, I am the servant of the queen of the fishes," he said. "If you eat this fish, you will understand the language of all the animals." And with that he disappeared without trace. The monarch told Jack, the young cook, to fry the fish for his lunch. "But mind you, you are not to taste the fish!" he told him. What sort of a cook could prepare a dish without even tasting it? When no one was looking, the lad slipped a small piece of the tail into his mouth. Just then a couple of flies flew by. "Leave some for us, leave some for us!" they pleaded. Jack was amazed that he could understand what they were saying. "So that is the dish which the king is to eat," he said to himself. He took another mouthful and hurried off to the king with the fish. After lunch, the king ordered the young cook to accompany him in his hunting. As they were riding through a grove of oaks, Jack's horse neighed merrily: "How light are my hooves today! I could leap over hill and dale." But the king's horse replied, gruffly: "It is all very well for you; but if you had on your back such a fat fellow as I, you would speak differently. If only the old fool would fall and break his neck!" The king frowned darkly, but young Jack laughed gaily at the horses' talk. The king looked at him suspiciously, and at once gave orders that they should return to the castle.

11 AUGUST

Goldenhair

The king resolved to find out why Jack had laughed. "I shall make a test to see whether he tasted the fish," he said to himself, and he ordered Jack to fill his goblet with wine. "But if you spill the wine, or do not fill the cup to the brim, it shall cost you your head," he told him. Then he opened the window and let two small birds into the chamber. One was holding in its beak three golden hairs. "These are the hairs of Princess Goldenhair," it twittered. "Show me, show me," chirped the other, curiously, and chased the first all around the chamber. Jack listened with a smile as they squabbled, watching them flying about, and — the wine ran over the brim of the goblet. "So! Your head is forfeit!" cried the king. "But I shall show you mercy. If you bring to my palace the golden-haired maiden, you will be pardoned." And there was nothing for it but for Jack to set off into the world. Before very long he rode into a dark forest. There, beneath a tree, he found a couple of young ravens that had fallen from their nest. "Help us, good fellow," they beseeched him. Jack willingly picked them up and put them back in their nest, and the birds croaked, "When you have need of us, think of us." Jack waved to them and went his way. He came to the shore of a black sea. Two fishermen were arguing over a little fish. "Sell it to me," he told the men. He gave each of them a golden ducat and threw the fish back in the sea. "When you have need of me, think of me," called the fish, and disappeared into the waves. And Jack rode on boldly.

12 AUGUST

Goldenhair

Jack wandered far and wide, until at last he came to a lakeside palace. It was the palace of King Little, who was no bigger than a thimble. He had twelve daughters, each of them prettier than the next; but the most beautiful of all was Goldenhair. When King Little heard why Jack had come, he said to him, "Very well, I shall give my golden-haired daughter in marriage to your master, but first you must carry out three commands. This morning, as Goldenhair was bathing in the sea, she lost her gold ring. Go, and bring it to me!" Jack wandered sadly down to the seashore, an looked out over the dark waters. "If only the little fish were here," he thought to himself, and before he knew it the little fish had poked its head out of the water, and was holding the gold ring in its jaws. King Little was pleased, but he said, "Before you may win the golden-haired maiden, you must bring from the spring at the end of the world the waters of life and death." "How am I to get to the end of the world?" sighed the unhappy Jack. "Unless, perhaps, my little ravens were to fly there." Scarcely had he thought this, when a whole flock of ravens came flying up, bringing him the waters of life and death in two little phials. Jack turned back merrily towards the lakeside palace. On the way he saw a spider, about to make a feast of a golden fly that was caught in its web. The young man sprinkled the fly with the water of life, and when it had come back to life again he set it free. "When you have need of me, think of me," it called to him. Jack waved to the fly and hurried back to King Little.

13 AUGUST

Goldenhair

"You are a bold young fellow," King Little told the lad. "But if you would take away my Goldenhair, you must first pick her out from among my other daughters." And he led Jack to a chamber where twelve maidens stood, covered from head to foot in white sheets.

"Which is she?" asked the king. Just at that moment the golden fly whose life he had saved came buzzing around Jack's head. "Not that one; not that one; not that one either," it whispered to him. "This is she!" cried Jack triumphantly, as the golden fly alighted on one of the girls' veils. And it was indeed Princess Goldenhair. Now there was nothing for it but for King Little to bid farewell to the dearest of his daughters. When Jack brought Goldenhair back to the king, his master was so taken with her beauty that he almost forgot to breathe. Then he said to Jack with a cruel smile: "Since you have served me well, they shall cut off your body instead of your head!" And the executioner carried out the king's order without delay. But at midnight Princess Goldenhair came to where they had laid his body and sprinkled it with the water of death; as soon as she had done so the head grew back onto the body. Then she sprinkled him with the water of life, and Jack opened his eyes and sat up as healthy as ever, only twice as handsome as before. "Oh, how deeply I have slept!" he said in wonder. When the old king saw how Jack had come to life, looking younger and more dashing than ever, he had them cut his own head off, but then they found that the phials of wonderful water were empty. And so it was that the bold Jack himself became king—for did he not have the most beautiful of princesses at his side?

14 AUGUST

The Giant Pig

Once upon a time a farmer found a china pig on the rubbish heap. As a jest he laid it down on some straw in the pigsty and told his swineherd to put some acorns in its trough. As soon as people got to hear of this, they laughed at the farmer: "The old miser! He wants to fatten himself up a china pig!" But, believe it or not, the pig grew, and grew, and was soon so big that it knocked down the whole sty. The farmer drove it into the parlour and filled the washtub with acorns for it. But the pig ate and ate, until soon it brought the whole farmhouse tumbling down, chimney and all. "See what a fine fellow he is growing into!" said the farmer gleefully, and he drove it into the barn. Then he brought it a cartload of potatoes. The pig munched, and crunched, and it was not long before it brought the whole barn crashing down around it. Now the farmer had nothing but the pig, so he called the butcher to come and make china sausages of it, but the pig gobbled up the butcher like a raspberry. Then it swallowed the swineherd, the milkmaid, a hunter, and a whole regiment of dragoons. In the end the royal artillery had to come, and the gunners fired their cannon all day and all night, until at last they blew the pig to pieces and let all the poor folk out. All the farmer had left was a huge pile of broken china. Believe it or not, in the middle of it he found a little china pig. But this time he isn't feeding it; he is saving up his money in it to buy a new farm.

15 AUGUST

The Biggest Fool in the World

There was once a merry kingdom where the king laughed at everything, and was forever thinking up new jokes, games and pastimes.

He would sit on a throne made of lemon cheese, sleep in a whipped cream bed, and go around wearing a suit of curds. One day, the king decided to give his only daughter in marriage to whomever brought him the biggest fool in the world. A certain trickster heard of this, and said to himself: "Why should I not try my luck? I shall go into the world and look for the biggest fool: he is sure to cross my path some day." And go he did. At one crossroads he came to he saw a fellow who was harnessing a horse to a cart back-to-front. "Whatever are you up to, you dunce?" laughed the trickster. "Simple," the other returned. "I must go back home, for I forgot to wish my wife good day." "Then why do you not turn the whole cart around?" asked the young man in surprise. "Indeed, I had not thought of that," the stupid fellow replied. "Thank you for your good advice. So that you may know I am not ungrateful, I shall give you my horse and cart in return and I shall go on foot." The trickster laughed. "Surely he is the biggest fool in the world," he thought to himself, and told the fellow: "If you insist, then I shall take your horse and cart: but sit in the back—for your kindness I shall drive you home." With tears of gratitude in his eyes the fool thanked him and sat down.

16 AUGUST

The Biggest Fool in the World

The trickster had not driven far when he came upon a strange sight. Beneath a big oak tree a man was trying to teach his pig to climb up. "Fool!" called the trickster. "Why do you vex the poor creature so?"—"Am I to let it die of hunger?" replied the man, gruffly. "He must climb the tree and feed on the acorns there!"—"Why do you not shake them down to the ground?" asked the young man. "Indeed, I had not thought of it," the fellow said with a grin. "Thank you for your good advice, stranger!" The trickster laughed until his sides ached. "He must surely be a greater fool than the first," he thought, and he invited

the fellow to sit down in the cart, saying he would take him to see the king. Before they had gone very far, they saw a fisherman in a boat on the river. Each time he caught a fish on his hook, he took off his clothes, held his nose, and jumped in to get the fish. "Why do you not haul it in on the line?" asked the trickster. "Indeed, I had not thought of that," the fisherman replied. "Thank you for your good advice."—"I shall not find another such fool in a hurry," thought the young man, and he invited the fisherman to come along with them to see the king.

17 AUGUST

The Biggest Fool in the World

On the way to the king's palace, the trickster and his companions strayed into a queer city. The trees there were planted roots upwards, and the houses built with their roofs pointing down. Just at that moment there was a great to-do in the town square, with people putting their bottles, buckets and pots out in the sun and then carrying them off into the town-hall. One old citizen explained to the youth what

was happening: "We have built a new town-hall, but we must carry the sunshine inside; for some reason or other it is quite dark in there!"—"Fools!" cried the trickster. "You have forgotten to make windows in it. Knock them through, and you shall have all the light you could wish for!"—"Indeed, we never thought of that," said the old man in surprise. "Since you are so wise, young stranger, tell us how to move the town-hall a little to one side, for we have built it right in the road."—"That is a simple matter," said the trickster. "You must all push on one side of the town-hall; I shall place my coat on the other side, so that we may see how much it has moved." So all the citizens went to the other side and pushed. In a little while the trickster secretly folded his coat in half. "See," he called out, "it is moving already, for half of my coat is under it." The people spat on their hands and set to again with a will. Meanwhile, the young man slipped his coat into the cart. "Enough!" he cried. "My coat has quite disappeared beneath the building." All the citizens embraced him, and the trickster said to himself: "The world is full of fools: why should I seek the biggest of them? It would be better to stay here and become mayor of the city. Fools are easily governed." And so he never returned to the merry kingdom. To this day he is mayor of that city. Do you want to go and see him? You must go to the end of the world on the train that brings the fairy tales.

18 AUGUST

The Fearless Princess

Once upon a time there was a village lad called Jake, for whom life was no bed of roses. His parents had long since died, leaving behind them only the poverty they had always known. None of the village girls would so much as look him over, for who in her right mind would take on such a penniless fellow for a husband? So poor Jake lived by himself in his little turf cottage by the wild rose bush. So that he would not be lonely, he tamed a little mouse, and carried him around in his pocket wherever he went. One day his godfather called the lad to him and said:

"Young fellow, I can no longer bear to see how poorly you live. Take my old cornet and go out into the world to seek your fortune. It is no ordinary cornet. When you blow it, all who hear it must follow you wherever you lead them." Jake thanked him, took the cornet, and set off into the wide world. When he played it, people came running up to him and walked behind him like a procession. "A fine thing my godfather has given me," thought Jake to himself. "Am I to wander about the world with folk treading on my heels, as though I were some general or other? I had better stop playing the devilish instrument." So stop he did; at once the people ran off in all directions to their homes, and Jake stretched himself out in a clearing in the forest, and fell fast asleep.

19 AUGUST

The Fearless Princess

When Jake woke up, it was just on midnight. At that moment little fires appeared all over the woods, and weird spectres began to enter the clearing from all sides. Goblins and werewolves, hullabaloos and will-o-the-wisps, fiery-eyed bats, pixies with mouse's tails, strange animals with human heads, watermen, trolls and flibbertigibbets and all manner of other horrible creatures. Jake began to shake with fear, until the little mouse's teeth rattled in his pocket. The demons began their council. "I wonder if you know," croaked a waterman, "that there is a princess in the castle beyond the haunted wood who is not afraid of the devil himself? They have tried a seven-headed dragon on her, a headless horseman and a horseless headman, but she only laughs and says that ghosts don't exist. She says that anyone who can frighten her may have her for his wife." Jake listened without moving a muscle. "I should dearly like to become king," he thought to himself. And at once he had an idea. He put the cornet carefully to his lips and began to blow with all his might. As soon as the spectres heard this, they gathered around him on all sides; but young Jake looked straight ahead of him and set off briskly towards the castle with his ghostly train.

20 AUGUST

The Fearless Princess

The fearless princess was just listening to her suitors reading a frightening tale about a terrible ogre. "That's nothing to be scared of!" she laughed. "If he were to come to me, I should give him a nice kiss. But I should have to stand on tiptoe!" The young men racked their brains for something to frighten her with. It was then that young Jake appeared in the chamber with his procession of assorted apparitions. "I'll scare you all right, princess!" he called out, and he blew his cornet until the forest had emptied all its most horrible creatures into the princess's chamber. They gave out a wailing and hooting and hullabalooing and shrieking, rolled their heads around the marble floor, spat fire, and all in all played every demonic trick they knew, until all the princes and bold knights ran and hid themselves inside, under and behind anything they could find. But the princess only laughed and clapped her hands. "Oh, what dear little creatures!" she cried. "I never saw such a fine thing in my life." Now even young Jake did not know what to do. But suddenly the princess's necklace burst with her laughing, and one of the little jewels rolled under her gown. Jake's little mouse spotted it at once as he peeped out of the lad's pocket, and quick as a flash he was after it. "He-e-e-lp! A mouse!" screamed the princess in horror, and fainted quite away. When she came round, she could hardly catch her breath. "Oh, Jake, how you frightened me!" she gasped. "You shall be my husband." And she flung her arms round his neck. So it was that poor Jake became king. But first of all he had to have his pocket sewn up, so that his little mouse could not get out.

21 AUGUST

Hansel and Gretel

In a cottage by the forest there once lived a poor woodcutter. His wife had died, leaving him alone in the world with their two children, Hansel and Gretel. So that they might have someone to look after them, one day he brought home to their little cottage a stepmother. That year a great famine came upon the land, and it was not long before the woodcutter and his family were down to their last loaf of bread. As they were going to bed that night, the stepmother said to her husband: "Unless we do something, we shall all die of hunger. Let us take the children into the forest tomorrow morning and leave them there: Providence will take care of them." The woodcutter did not want to hear of it, but when his wife continued to pester him, with tears in his eyes he finally agreed. The children were so hungry they could not sleep, and they heard all that their parents were saying. Gretel began to cry bitterly, but Hansel whispered words of comfort, "Do not weep, dear sister, I shall think of something." And when the adults were asleep, he crept quietly out of the cottage and filled his pockets with shiny pebbles. Then he slipped back inside. No sooner had dawn broken, than the stepmother roughly shook the children awake, gave each of them a slice of dry bread, and told them to make ready to go into the forest. "We shall go to gather firewood," she lied to them. "But do not eat your bread all at once, for you will get no more today." And off into the forest they went, the woodcutter, the stepmother, and the two children.

22 AUGUST

Hansel and Gretel

As they walked into the forest, Hansel kept stopping and turning round. "Hansel, why do you tarry so?" his father scolded him. "I am looking at my little white cat, sitting on the roof of our cottage and watching me," the boy told him, but he was really dropping the pebbles from his pockets on the path. "It is not

your cat, but only the morning sun shining on the chimney," said his stepmother, sharply. On and on they walked, until at last, deep in the forest, the woodcutter made a fire and told the children to wait there until he and their stepmother came back again. To pass the time Hansel and Gretel began to pick strawberries, but when their parents did not return, they sat down by the fire and waited. They thought they could hear the blows of an axe in the forest nearby, but it was only a dry branch which their father had hung from a tree, banging in the wind. Before long the children's eyes grew heavy, and they dropped off to sleep. When they awoke, it was night-time, and the forest was pitch-dark. Gretel burst out crying with fear, but just then the moon came out, and they saw the pebbles shining along the path; they glistened in the moonlight like pure silver. Hansel and Gretel took each other by the hand, and the silver trail led them safely back to their cottage. How angry their stepmother was to see them safe and sound!

23 AUGUST

Hansel and Gretel

It was not long before the children, as they lay in bed, heard their stepmother telling their father to lead them even deeper into the woods the next day. "We have only half a loaf of bread in the cottage," she wailed. "If we do not rid ourselves of the children, we shall all die of hunger." In the end the unhappy woodcutter again agreed. The moment their father and stepmother had fallen asleep, Hansel stole out of bed and went to fetch some more pebbles. But, alas! The door was locked. Gretel again began to cry, but Hansel comforted her once more, "Don't be afraid: by morning I shall have thought of something." Early the next morning their stepmother again got them ready to go into the forest. This time she gave each of them an even smaller piece of bread. Hansel crumbled the bread in his pocket, and kept turning round and dropping the crumbs onto the path. "Why are you

stopping and looking round?" his father asked, crossly. "I am looking at my little white dove, sitting on the roof of our cottage and watching me," said the boy. "That is no dove, you foolish child, but only the morning sun shining on the chimney!" snapped his stepmother. And when they came to the darkest part of the whole forest, she told the children to wait by the fire until she and their father returned. Hansel and Gretel lay down in the grass, and they were so tired from their long walk that they soon fell fast asleep. When they woke up, black night had again descended on the forest. "Do not be afraid, Gretel," Hansel again soothed his sister. "When the moon comes out we shall find the breadcrumbs, and they will lead us back home."

24 AUGUST

Hansel and Gretel

The moon rose over the dark forest, but the breadcrumbs were nowhere to be seen. The woodland birds had pecked them all up! "Don't be afraid," Hansel told his sister. "We shall find our way without them." But this time it was no easy matter; they walked all night, and all the next day, too. Evening was falling once again, and the end of the forest was nowhere in sight. Finally the children huddled together among the ferns and cried themselves to sleep. No sooner had they woken up the next morning, than a beautiful white bird appeared. It flew in front of them as if to show them the way, and sang so sweetly that the children ran after it. Soon they came to a clearing, and in the clearing stood a cottage. Now, the cottage was quite different from its owner: how beautiful it looked, and how wonderful it smelled! "See, Gretel, the walls are made of bread and cakes!" gasped Hansel. "And the roof of marzipan! And the windows of clear sugar crystals!" cried Gretel. Hansel had an idea at once. "I'll eat a piece of the roof, and you break off a piece of the shutters!" he told his sister. And straight away he began munching marzipan, while Gretel stood beneath a window and crunched away at the sparkling sugar, licking her fingers and smacking her lips. What a feast they had! Suddenly they heard a voice from inside the cottage say: "Are those little teeth I hear, nibbling at my cottage dear?" And the children replied: "It is only the wind as it blusters and squalls, tearing the gingerbread down from the walls." And they went on eating as if nothing had happened.

25 AUGUST

Hansel and Gretel

The children were having the time of their lives nibbling away at the sweet-tasting

cottage, when the door flew open, and there in the porch stood a wrinkled old hag. She was leaning on a stick. "Well, well, and how did you get here?" she asked in surprise. "Come along inside, you will like it here." She took the children by the hand and led them to the table, where she fed them on all sorts of goodies; then she put them to bed under a soft eiderdown. But before they could rub the sleep from their eyes the next morning she grabbed hold of Hansel and shoved him into a little wooden pen to fatten him up for the oven. From then on Gretel had to take him the finest of foods, but she got only a few poor scraps that were left. Every day the wicked witch went to the pen and called to him, "Hansel, put out your finger, that I may feel how fat you have got!" But each time the clever lad pushed only a dry old bone through the bars of the pen. In the end the witch could wait no longer. "Fat or thin, I shall roast you anyway," she said, and ordered Gretel to light the fire under the oven. "Get inside the oven to see if it is hot enough, my dear," the old hag told her; but Gretel made excuses, saying she did not know how to get in, that the door was too small, and such, until at last the witch lost her temper. "I shall show you, foolish child," she said, and pushed her head inside the oven. Then Gretel gave the old hag a good push, and into the oven she went. Right away the girl opened the pen to let her brother out; then they broke off a few mouthfuls of gingerbread, filled their pockets with jewels from the witch's chest, and hurried off home. They would never have got there, if a kindly white duck had not carried them across an enchanted lake; but at last they arrived at their own little cottage, where their father greeted them joyfully. Their wicked stepmother had died while they were away, and so they lived happily with their father again. They sold the witch's jewels, and built themselves a gingerbread cottage out of the proceeds.

26 AUGUST

Waterman William

There once lived a lazy waterman called William. During the day he would sleep soundly on the bottom of the woodland lake with frothy water for an eiderdown, dreaming his watery dreams. And what sort of dreams were they? Well, they were as dumb as fish; they even had fishes' scales, and up above them little rings of ripples spread across the water. For a waterman dreams as many water dreams as there are rippling rainbow rings on the surface of the lake. When evening fell and the moon slid out into the sky, daddy waterman would send sleepy waterman William off to school. And where was the school? Why, up in the old willow tree on the bank of the little lake. The waterman would sit there, open his waterman's reading book and study his waterman's ABC. There he would find everything, right from A to Z. How to stop the miller's water-wheel, how to light will-o-the-wisps, how to make mist over the water, why dogs bark and cats climb, how to tie ribbons on a willow wand, how to guard people's souls under upturned pots after drowning them, how many fingers there are on a hand and jars in the larder, and all manner of other things. But William was not very good at his lessons. One night, as he was sitting sadly in the willow, he heard a thin little voice in the grass down below saying, "Teach me to read! Teach me to read!" William looked down and, what should he see! A little maiden in a frog's skin, with frog's eyes and a frog's smile. And what sort of smile is that? Why, from ear to ear! The waterman liked the little maiden, and promised to teach her to read the very next day.

27 AUGUST

Waterman William

Believe it or not, the frog maiden learnt her lessons as if there were nothing easier in the whole world. Daddy waterman himself thrust his head out of the water and said to himself, "Now, that would be a fine wife for my son! All green, soft as the grass—in a word, a real beauty!" When he suggested it to his son, the

lad was willing. Why should he not marry? Why, he was three years, three months, three weeks and three days old, and that was the best age of all to be marrying. So the next time the frog maiden came for her lessons he told her he would like to have her for his wife. The maiden smiled a smile like when the dew tinkles on a snowdrop, and said, "I should be glad to be your wife, if you fulfilled one wish for me." And she reached in the pocket of her apron and pulled out three hazel nuts. "Take the darkness out of these nuts and sew it into a coat that will keep out the cold when I am under the water," she said. Waterman William grew sad. "How on earth do you get the darkness out of a nut?" he thought, puzzled; then he took a stone and cracked open one of the nuts. But the darkness was gone without trace. "Maybe there is something about it in the waterman's reading book," he thought to himself, suddenly. And he began to study until his head ached, and soon knew the waterman's ABC back to front and better than all the other watermen put together. But he could find no mention at all of how to get the dark out of nuts. He was so sad he could have cried.

28 AUGUST

Waterman William

The frog maiden frowned when the young waterman told her he couldn't fulfil her wish. "You must have slacked at school," she told him. "Go out into the world and open up your eyes, lazybones! Otherwise I shall not marry you." So the waterman went. He met a little mouse and told her of his troubles. "If you help me carry grain into my hole, I shall tell you how to get the dark out of nuts," promised the mouse. But as soon as the work was finished the mouse laughed at the waterman. "Fool! No one in the world can learn the impossible. It is clear that you are still very stupid," she told him. The disappointed waterman met a hedgehog. "If you help me clean out my hole, I shall tell you," he offered. But when the waterman had worked his fingers to the bone and the job was done, the hedgehog laughed at him, too. The same thing happened when he visited the fox, the squirrel,

the goat and the horned stag. He helped them all, but they only laughed at him. In the end he went back to the frog maiden and told her: "I can do everything in the world: carry grain, clean and tidy, get the seeds out of pine-cones, dry hay, feed stags—but I cannot get the darkness out of nuts. It is quite impossible." The little maiden smiled at him and said: "I shall take you as my husband, since you have learnt the greatest wisdom of all: Let alone the impossible and learn at least the useful." And so waterman William at last married the little frog maiden. By and by two little water-children were born to them, and grandfather waterman taught them the waterman's ABC.

29 AUGUST

The Three Spinstresses

There was once an old spinstress who had a very lazy daughter. She would not take to spinning, no matter how her mother tried to persuade her. One day the old woman lost her patience and began to beat the lazy child. The girl began to shout and scream terribly. Just at that moment the queen herself happened to be passing by the cottage. "Why do you beat the poor child so?" the queen chided the spinstress, sternly. The woman was ashamed to admit how lazy her daughter was, and she lied instead. "Why should I not beat her, when she will not stop working? She spins and spins all day; where is a poor woman to get so much flax?" The queen comforted the poor girl, and told her; "I like to see the spinners at work; the whirr of their wheels is like music to my ears." And she asked the girl's mother to let her take her daughter back to the castle with her. The woman was only too glad to see the back of the lazy child. When they got to the palace, the queen led the girl to three chambers, filled from floor to ceiling with the finest flax. "If you spin this flax for me as quickly as you can, you shall have my eldest son for your husband, for a woman's industry is more than any dowry." The girl was dismayed. She would never spin so much flax if she worked till the day she died. She went over to the window and began to cry.

30 AUGUST

The Three Spinstresses

As the girl stood by the window and wept, down by the palace gate she spied three strange old women. One of them had a foot the size of a mill wheel; another had a lower lip so long that it hung below her chin; the third had a thumb as thick as tree-trunk. "Why are you weeping so?" they called through the window to the unhappy spinstress. She told them of her troubles; the old women smiled and said to her: "If you promise to invite us to your wedding and not to be ashamed of us, but own us as your aunts and sit us down beside you at table, we shall spin the flax for you right away." The girl was happy to promise, and she let the three strange women into the palace. No sooner had they sat down in the first chamber than the spinning-wheel began to sing its merry song: "Tittity, tittity, tittity-tee; the spokes they shall turn and the bobbin shall spin, and the beautiful spinster be wife to a king!" The old woman with the huge foot smiled and stepped on the treadle; the one with the great lip smiled and wet the yarn, and the one with the thick thumb wound it up and tapped it against the table. Whenever she did so a skein fell to the floor, and the yarn on it was as fine as gossamer. They spun and spun the whole night through.

The Three Spinstresses

Before the sun rose the next morning, the flax in all three chambers was spun. The three old women said farewell to the girl. "Do not forget your promise," they reminded her. "It shall be to your profit." Then they disappeared. The moment the queen saw the pile of yarn she had the wedding prepared without delay. The prince, too, was delighted that he should have such a beautiful and hard-working wife. He praised her to the skies. Then the girl said, "I have three aunts who have been of great service to me, my lady, and I should like to reward them. Might I invite them to sit beside me at table when the wedding feast is held?" The queen and the prince agreed. When the ceremony was over and the banquet had begun, into the hall came the three spinstresses, dressed in clothes that must have been older than the Ark. "Welcome, dear aunts," called the bride, but the prince frowned. "What ugly creatures are these?" he wondered, and at once he asked the first of the women, "Why is your foot so broad?"—"From working the treadle of the spinning-wheel," she told him. "And why is your lip so large?" he asked the second. "From wetting the thread," she told him. "And my thumb is so thick from spinning," the third woman told him. The prince was astonished, and said right away, "From this day on my beautiful wife shall never touch a spinning wheel again!" Do you suppose his bride was disappointed?

SEPTEMBER

1 SEPTEMBER

The Boy Who Was Looking for His Eyes

Once upon a time there was a little boy who was always crying, even though there was nothing to cry about at all. In short, he liked it when everyone was sorry for him and tried to comfort him. The more they spoiled him, the more plaintively he wailed and tried his poor mother. One day she lost her patience with him, and said, "Just you be careful, little cry-baby! He who cries for nothing will cry away all his tears. Then the little goblins will come creeping up in the night, steal the eyes from his head, and take them far, far away to the secret forest spring which is guarded by the snake with an enchanted elder sprig. The snake touches the eyes with the sprig, and they turn into precious stones and fall to the bottom of the deep water. There they stay until someone comes along to fill them again with tears. But first he must outwit the wicked snake and take away his enchanted sprig." When his mother had finished telling him this, the boy began to cry louder than ever. He cried and cried, until the Dream Maker awoke and locked up his tearful eyes with a golden key. Then he laid the key on the pillow, where it was found by the goblins from the far-off land of springs and sparkling pools. They opened up the boy's eyes with the key and carried them off to the snake sentry of the pool.

2 SEPTEMBER

The Boy Who Was Looking for His Eyes

The next morning, when the boy awoke, he felt the warm sunbeams on his cheeks, but all around him was as dark as the bottom of a well. "Mother, I have no eyes!" he called out, and tried to burst into tears, but there were no tears to cry any more. His unhappy mother tried her best to comfort him, but she did not know what to do. From then on the boy was blind, and grew sadder day by day. Then, one day, he took courage, wrapped a scarf around his empty eye-sockets, and when no one was looking he slipped out into the world to go searching for the enchanted well. He felt with his hands in front of him, and stumbled along through the black, black darkness, and he would surely have not got very far at all, had he not suddenly heard a quiet little voice say: "Ow! You are standing on my foot!" The boy bent down, and there, at his feet, he felt a little frog. "Do not hurt me," he begged. But the blind boy took the frog gently in his hand and blew his poor little leg better. "You have a kind heart, my boy," said the frog. "For that I shall reward you." When the boy told the frog of his troubles, the frog leapt from his hand and under a burdock leaf, and pulled out a ball of blue string. "Take the end of the string in your hand and hold it tight," the frog told him. Then he flung the ball down the bank and croaked: "Froggy skip and froggy hop, down the stream and never stop." At these words the string turned into a babbling brook, which seethed over stones and through hollows and led the blind boy and his friend the frog right to the snake's pool.

3 SEPTEMBER

The Boy Who Was Looking for His Eyes

On the way the frog said to the boy, "When we get to the spring, tell the snake you have brought him food, and throw me in front of him. When he opens his mouth to swallow me, the elder sprig will fall from it. You must throw it into the water without delay."—"I cannot do such a thing, for you have been so good to me," the boy told him, but the frog insisted. When at last they reached the spring, the snake reared up in front of them and hissed: "Hsss, hsss; my sharp fangs' poison, in a trice, will turn you to a block of ice!" But the boy was not afraid, and said: "I have here food for you, sentry-snake!" and he threw the frog to the ground. The snake dropped the elder sprig and pounced on the frog; but in an instant the frog changed into a white-hot pebble, and as soon as the beast swallowed this he burned to a cinder. The blind boy felt for the elder sprig and threw it into the spring. There was a brilliant flash of light, and the water began to bubble and seethe with human eyes turned into precious stones. One by one

the boy took them out and tried them until he found his own. Then he burst into tears of joy, but because he was not crying for nothing this time, his eyes grew brighter and more beautiful than ever, and the tears on his cheeks turned to pearls. The little frog was nowhere to be seen. The boy filled his scarf with jewelled eyes, and gave them to all the blind children he met on his way home.

4 SEPTEMBER

The Little Glass Fairy

When I was quite, quite small, I had my own little brittle glass fairy which none of the grown-ups could see. She was clear and colourless and quite invisible. A little glass butterfly sat in her hair, and a red glass heart beat quietly in her breast. Pink, pink, pink tinkled that little red heart. The fairy lived in our garden inside a little glass tulip. We liked each other very much. One day we were playing together underneath the dog-rose bush which knew how to speak. I don't know where he had learnt it; maybe from the little children who used to pass by our garden fence, because he had a terrible lisp. The glass fairy would tease him about it; she told him he had a knot in his tongue, and laughed at him. "Briar, dear briar, say 'the seething sea ceaseth'," she would nettle him. "I am not a briar, I am a rothe," the proud and prickly

bush would snap back. "And I than't thay anything for you, tho there!" The glass fairy put her hand on her little glass heart and promised not to laugh, but the dog-rose was adamant, and would not be friends with us at all. Just to spite him, the fairy picked his most lovely flower, the one of which he was so proud. She ran across the grass with it, and planted it at once beside her own little glass tulip.

5 SEPTEMBER

The Little Glass Fairy

When the little glass fairy picked the most beautiful flower on the briar rose-bush, the rose-bush lost his temper: "I'll tell on you, you little thcamp!" And since mother came into the garden at that very moment, he wasted no time in telling her all about it. Only mother couldn't hear him. I don't know why it is that grown-ups can never hear the voices of the flowers, or of the birds and the animals, or of toys. How sad the world must be for them. But this time I was glad my mother couldn't hear, because she would have been cross with me and that would have upset me. So I pulled a face at the rose-bush, and the glass fairy and I joined hands and danced around the rose. "Little Tommy Tell-Tale," we chanted. The bush began to cry, until his leaves shook with sobbing. Then he dried his tears in the sun and began to whisper with someone. "Shhh, shhh, shhh," whispered the bush. Full of curiosity, the glass fairy stretched out her ear, but she could understand not a word. So she crept nearer and nearer, holding a hand against her glass skirt so that it would not jingle, though now and again her glass hair did tinkle softly. The bush pretended not to hear, and just went on whispering "shhh, shhh, shhh" importantly to someone or other, maybe the bees.

6 SEPTEMBER

The Little Glass Fairy

As the dog-rose went on with his secret whispering, out of the bush flew a magpie, the bird which steals everything it sees which is small and shiny. "Run!" I shouted to the glass fairy, but she was frozen with fear. It was a wonder her little glass heart did not stop beating; little glass tears began to run down her cheeks, shattering on the stones as they fell to the ground. Ting, ting, ting they tinkled as they smashed. The thieving magpie almost had the little fairy in her beak, when the glass butterfly in her hair woke up. "Get off, you thieving devil!" it screeched at the magpie, and brrrh!—off it fluttered into the sky. How its little glass wings glittered in the sun! When the magpie saw this shimmering splendour, she left the fairy alone and flew off after the butterfly. Both of them soon disappeared in the distance. I wasted no time at all and, snatching up the little glass fairy, I hurried off with her to the glass tulip. There I sat her down in her parlour in the cup of the flower and begged the glass petals to shut over her as if dark were falling. Then I sat down by the tulip to keep watch.

7 SEPTEMBER

The Little Glass Fairy

As I sat watching over the glass tulip, a soft sobbing came to my ears. "Why are you crying, little glass fairy?" I asked. "O-o-o-oh," she moaned from her little glass parlour, "I am not beautiful any more!"—"Why ever not?" I asked. "Because the glass butterfly from my hair has flown away," she whimpered. "Then I shall catch you another—a real live one," I promised, but she would not hear of it. She wanted nothing but to die of a broken heart, she told me, and other such things. This upset me. If my little glass fairy were to die, I should never be able to imagine another one, since she was the only one I loved. I looked round the garden unhappily. Suddenly something glinted like a rainbow across the other side. What else but the glass butterfly! There it was, playing with its live companions, as if nothing were the matter at all; now bobbing up and down on a rose, now licking away from the cup of an acacia flower, flitting here, there and everywhere—just like any butterfly! "Come back at once, you rascal!" I called to it. "Don't you know the little glass fairy is crying for you?"—"Indeed!" the butterfly replied. "But I am not tame any more, and I want to play here with the others!" The little glass fairy peeped out of the tulip. "Does it mean nothing to you that I am not beautiful any more?" she asked. "Nothing at all," replied the butterfly, and dived straight into a peony. The glass fairy burst into tears again. Can you hear her tears falling? Ting! Ting! Ting!

8 SEPTEMBER

The Little Glass Fairy

Everyone tried to comfort the little glass fairy. The golden pheasant from the gamekeeper's lodge brought her a pretty feather for her hair, and gave the thieving magpie a good

scolding. The little hedgehog brought her the most beautiful water-lily he could find, and the green frogs came hopping along with a fiery poppy, which they first had to quench in the water so that it would not burn her. But the glass fairy could not be comforted. When she had cried away all her little glass tears, though, she flew into a rage, caught up her little glass skirt and leapt straight out of her little glass parlour into the grass. Off we went to chase the butterfly. But the butterfly only laughed, flitted on his glass wings from flower to flower, and made funny faces at us. The glass fairy was soon in tears again. Then a golden spider called out from the dog-rose, "Don't cry, glass fairy, I'll catch your butterfly for you!" And he set to work busily. He spun, and spun, until he had spun a huge web over the rose-bush. It was as clear and invisible as the glass fairy herself. Then the rose-bush said, "Forgive me, little fairy, for thending the wicked magpie to get you; I'll never do it again." The fairy forgave him gladly, and the bush called out to the butterfly: "Come here, you rathcal; I shall give you the sweetest of honey to drink." The butterfly did not wait to be asked twice, and flew straight into the bush's branches. Before he knew it, he was fluttering hopelessly in the spider's web.

9 SEPTEMBER

The Little Glass Fairy

The glass fairy thanked the rose-bush and the spider kindly, tied the little glass butterfly back in her glass hair, and said: "You just wait, you little scamp: I'll soon have you tamed again!" But the butterfly replied: "I was getting homesick anyway, and I am glad that you are beautiful again." I ran to fetch my mother, so that she might look at my little glass fairy, but she just let down her own honey-coloured hair in the sunshine, smiled, and said, a little sadly: "I can't see your little glass fairy, I'm too big." And she gave me two sweet-smelling rhubarb tarts. "One for you and one for your fairy," she said, stroking me on the head. I took the fairy her tart. "Mmmm, that's good," she said, licking her lips with her little glass tongue until they tinkled. "It is strange, but big people often can't see the purest things in the world. Just remember that. Then they are always sad. But then you too will stop seeing me one day, though I shall always be here with you." I did not believe her, then. We spent many happy days together. But one day I came into the garden, and the little fairy and the glass tulip had disappeared as though the ground had swallowed them up, though to this day, when white birds wing their way across the sky, I sometimes hear the beating of her little glass heart, somewhere near to me. Pink, pink, pink.

10 SEPTEMBER

The Tale of a Circus

One day the circus came to town. Elephants and monkeys strolled through the streets, and acrobats in golden suits turned somersaults on horseback. What a fine sight it was! "Come to the circus, see the magic and the wonders!" called the clowns, tears of laughter streaming down their cheeks and glowing red smiles on their lips like many-coloured butterflies. In the town there lived a little boy who longed to go and see the wonderful circus. He begged his mother for the money to buy a ticket, but before he reached the big top the coins had fallen out of a hole in his pocket and rolled away somewhere. He stood miserably outside, peeping enviously now and then through a hole in the canvas. It was marvellous! High above the ground slender fairies danced on a silver thread, shining like snowflakes and flying through the air like glistening strands of gossamer. Beautiful princesses in colourful costumes rode along on white horses with flying plumes, and frowning wizards swallowed fire, leapt through flaming hoops, or had steel swords plunged into their breasts. "If only, just for a moment, I could enter the forbidden world of magic," thought the boy. Then a wonder came to pass!

11 SEPTEMBER

The Tale of a Circus

As the boy was gazing wistfully at the prancing horses, a strange old man appeared before his eyes. He had big paper boots and a red paper nose on his face. On his white-painted face there was the orange glow of laughter, like the flame of a candle. He stroked the boy with a transparent hand and said, "I am Pepe the conjurer. I see that you would like to visit the world of magic and wonders. If you like, I shall change you into an elephant, and you may walk through the sawdust ring like the king of the jungle."— "I would rather you conjured up the money for me to buy a ticket," said the boy, who was not too sure he wanted to be turned into an animal. But the old man replied, "It is easy to turn small things into larger ones, but it is much more difficult to make small ones from big ones. There are many folk who make small deeds into something wonderful, but few know how to make trifles of great deeds. It is the same with magicians. Choose what you would like to be, but do not ask me to make you smaller than you are." The boy did not understand the old man's words too well, but just then the roar of a big cat could be heard coming from the tent. "I should like to be a tiger-tamer," he said, softly. And before he knew what was happening he was standing in the middle of the ring in a splendid braided uniform with a goad in one hand and a whip in the other. All around him huge striped cats were creeping menacingly.

12 SEPTEMBER

The Tale of a Circus

As the boy stood in the middle of the floodlit ring of sawdust, surrounded by bloodthirsty tigers, his heart sank with terror. The big cats bared their fangs at him, and great bloodied tongues hung from their jaws. "Pepe, Pepe the Magician!" he called out desperately. "Turn me into something huge, so that I need not be afraid!" But the old man in the paper shoes and the red paper nose replied, "There is nothing as enormous as fear. Only you can make yourself bigger!" The tigers roared fiercely and clawed the air. The boy glanced miserably up towards the roof of the big top, and there he saw a tiny, beautiful princess, dancing high above the ground on a flying trapeze. In her hand she held a white parasol. Suddenly her delicate little foot slipped, and the slender princess came floating down on her parasol like a snowflake, right into the middle of the snarling beasts. The strange white shape annoyed the tigers. They roared fearfully and leapt towards her. At that the boy overcame his fear; he cracked his whip and goaded the animals into their cage. He could hear a great clapping and cheering, but he hardly noticed anything but the delicate arms that were flung around his neck. "It was nothing," he said. Just at that moment Pepe the Magician, the man with the paper shoes and paper nose, clapped his hands, and the boy found himself at home in bed. Beside him lay a little doll with a white parasol.

13 SEPTEMBER

The Sleepy Bear

In a certain forest there lived with his mother a certain little bear. He liked nothing better in the world than eating honey and sleeping in the sun. One day his mother told him a story about the kingdom of honey. It is ruled over by the queen bee, and anyone who is disobedient must for his punishment eat a whole pot of honey, sleep in the sun, and listen to fairy tales. "Oo, how I should like that!" thought the little bear, and when his mother wasn't looking, he set off to look for the kingdom of honey. He walked, and walked, until he came to the shore of a great sea. Close at hand a fisherman was mending his boat. "Good day," the bear greeted him. "Do you by any chance happen to know how one is supposed to get to the kingdom of honey?" Now the fisherman was a sly old fellow, and it occurred to him at once that he might put the young bear to work for him. "Why, of course I know," he said. "If you untangle this big ball of twine and find the end

for me, I shall show you how to get there." And he showed the bear what to do. The ball of twine was huge, and the little bear did not feel a bit like working so hard. "Why should I ravel and twist for nothing, when every piece of string has an end at both ends," he thought to himself, and he caught the end that was at the beginning between his teeth. Then, since the sun was shining so brightly, he curled up and fell fast asleep. When the fisherman came back, he said crossly: "A fine worker you are! Where is the end of the string?"—"Why, here, of course," replied the clever bear. "I found it right at the beginning." The fisherman smiled. "Very well," he said. "Come with me; I shall take you to the kingdom of honey." He led the bear to a beehive, gave it a good bang with his fist, and ran off. You should have seen how the bees chased that poor little bear! He ran back to his mother in tears, and did not even want to hear fairy tales about the kingdom of honey any more.

14 SEPTEMBER

The Little Big Prince

Once upon a time there was a tiny little prince. He was so small that even on tiptoe he could see no further than the end of his nose. Everyone laughed at him. While the rest of the princes fought with seven-headed dragons, delivered enchanted princesses and pulled the tails of the palace cats, Prince Little, as they used to call him, could not even face up to a mouse. Instead of a horse he would ride on a grasshopper, and instead of a sword his mother gave him a rusty old needle. One day he was sitting sadly in the palace gardens on an upturned thimble and watching the birds pecking away at the ripe poppy heads. One of the little poppy seeds fell and rolled to the prince's feet. He picked it up and ate it, and, what do you think? Suddenly he felt his body stretching out, and before he knew it his head was high above the clouds. When he looked down and saw how tiny everything on the ground seemed from up there, he had to burst

out laughing. But it was not long before he felt anxious. "How am I to live like this?" he thought. "Feet on the ground, head in the clouds! I should rather be tiny, as I was before!" Scarcely had he thought this to himself, when he shrank back to his former size. "It must have been the poppy seed that did it," he thought, and he quickly picked up some more and put them in his pocket.

15 SEPTEMBER

The Little Big Prince

Now that the little prince had found out how to be big when he wanted to, he decided to go out into the world like the other princes. He saddled his grasshopper, sharpened his rusty needle, and with a "gee-up, there!" went riding out of the palace gates. On the way he met some boys who were racing on their hobby-horses. "Who will be there first?" he called to them, and spurred on his mount. The boys shot after him as fast as they could, but Prince Little beat them all and was there first. Where? They hadn't the slightest idea. There were iron trees and stone flowers growing there, and a troop of wooden soldiers marching along the road. "Halt!" called their leader. "What will you here?" Prince Little replied boldly that they were seeking their fortune in the world. The soldier was pleased, and took the prince and his friends to see the king right away. The king was also made of wood, and every time he took a step he creaked like anything. "I am glad," said he, in his wooden voice, when the soldier had made his report. "I have a daughter named Fortune. An evil wizard has taken her off to a paper island on a paper sea. He put her on a paper rose, which has grown to the sky. There she sits and weeps and waits for her deliverer. She is afraid to jump down lest the paper island should give way beneath her."—"Have no fear," said Prince Little, "I shall have her free in no time at all." And he and the boys went off to the paper sea.

16 SEPTEMBER

The Little Big Prince

Beside the shore of the paper sea two small boats were rocking at anchor. They were sisters, and they held hands all the time. "How are we all to get in?" said the boys on the hobby-horses. "Just wait and see!" laughed Prince Little. He lay across both the boats and swallowed a grain of poppy-seed; at that he began to stretch out, and the boats with him, until they made a wooden bridge to the paper island. The boys rode across, and then Prince Little and his army banged on the door of the wizard's paper castle. "We are come to free Princess Fortune!" the prince called out sternly. "Help yourselves!" chuckled the magician. "She is sitting up there in the paper rose." Prince Little stretched out his arm, but he could not reach the top of the rose. So he quickly swallowed another grain of poppy-seed, and at once was twice as tall as before. Then he took Princess Fortune in his hand and lowered her gently to the paper island. They and the boys set off at once for the opposite shore, with the wizard following. But the moment they had reached dry land the prince thought to himself, "Let me be as small as before!" At that the bridge again shrank into a pair of little boats again. These could not bear the wizard's weight, and sank in the paper sea, taking the evil magician with them. Strange to say, Princess Fortune was also no bigger than your little finger, so she and the prince were wed; but when he wanted to tease her, he would eat a grain of poppy-seed and grow to the sky.

17 SEPTEMBER

The Table, the Ass and the Cudgel

Long, long ago there lived a tailor who had three sons. Every day one of them would take the goat to pasture. One day the eldest brother took her to the cemetery, where the grass was as soft as silk, and left her to eat her fill. When evening drew near, he asked her: "Well, goat, have you had enough?" And the goat replied, "Master, even if we stayed, I could not eat another blade." The lad was pleased, and led the animal home. But after supper his father went and asked the goat, "Well, goat, how did you eat today?" And the goat replied, "Master, how was I to eat, when instead of pastures sweet, I was grazing all the day, in among the tombstones grey?" The tailor flew into a rage and turned his eldest son out of the house. The next day the middle son took the goat to pasture. He led her to a meadow full of sweet clover. Before long she had munched it bare. "Well, goat, have you had enough?" the second son asked her towards evening. "Master, even if we stayed, I could not eat another blade," the goat

replied. So the young man took the creature home again; but his father did not trust him, and went to ask the goat, "Well, how did you eat today?" "Master, how was I to eat, when instead of pastures sweet, I was grazing all the day, in a field of stones and clay?" The tailor was again enraged, and drove his middle son away, too.

18 SEPTEMBER

The Table, the Ass and the Cudgel

On the third day the youngest son was sent to pasture the goat. He found her a spinney where the leaves were green and juicy, and as evening fell the goat told him how well she had eaten. But the moment they got back home, the goat complained bitterly to the tailor: "Master, how was I to eat, when instead of pastures sweet, I was grazing all the day, where the fallen leaves decay?" As soon as the tailor heard this, he sent the youngest son out into the world to fend for himself. The next day he set off to take the goat to pasture himself; he took her where all the most luscious goat delicacies grow, and she munched away greedily. When evening came she said contentedly, "Master, even if we stayed, I could not eat another blade!" The tailor led her home jauntily and tied her up in the shed. "Well, goat, at last you have eaten your fill!" he said to her. But the mischievous goat replied, "Master, how was I to eat, when instead of pàstures sweet, I was grazing all the day, where the grass was dry as hay?" Then at last the tailor realized how he had been taken in by the deceitful creature. He gave her a good beating with a stick, and shaved her head till she was quite bald; but what good did it do? It would not bring his sons back again.

19 SEPTEMBER

The Table, the Ass and the Cudgel

Meanwhile the three sons were not doing too badly for themselves in the world. The eldest became apprenticed to a carpenter, and so skilfully did he work, that his master soon took a liking to him. When his apprenticeship was over, the carpenter gave him as a parting gift a little wooden table. "It is no ordinary table," he told him. "If you tell it 'Table, be laid!', it will fill itself with whatever foods you fancy." The young man thanked him and set off home. When he grew hungry, all he had to do was to give the order to the table, and it was at once full of the most delicious titbits. On the way home the lad stopped by at an inn. The inn was full of guests, but the landlord had run out of food and drink. So the young man set the table down in the middle of the dining-room and ordered it: "Table, be laid!" Soon all the guests were eating and drinking as though it were Shrove Tuesday. Among them sat a band of wandering gipsies. They ate so well that when they had finished they spread themselves out around an empty cask in front of the inn, and fell fast asleep.
"I should dearly like to have such a wooden cook," thought the innkeeper to himself, and when the lad, too, had dropped off, he changed the table for another just like it. In the morning the young man set off for home with the innkeeper's table under his arm. His father greeted him with open arms. "I have learned the carpenter's trade," his son told him proudly. "Invite all our relations, and you shall see how I shall wine and dine them," he bragged. When all the relatives arrived, the eldest son placed the table in the midst of them and ordered it: "Table, be laid!" But, of course, nothing happened at all! How ashamed the young man was!

20 SEPTEMBER

The Table, the Ass and the Cudgel

The second son became apprentice to a miller. When his time was served, the miller rewarded him for his service with an ass. "But it is no ordinary ass," he told him. "If you say to it 'Ass, give me gold!', it will drop gold coins from its mouth faster than you can gather them up." The boy thanked the miller and set off home, leading the ass behind him. Soon he chanced to arrive at the same wayside inn where his brother had been robbed of his magic table. He tied the ass up in the stable and went to ask for a bed for the night. "First you must pay!" the landlord told him. "I am not having you making off in the morning without paying." So the young man borrowed a tablecloth from the innkeeper, saying he would fetch some money. The innkeeper was puzzled, and secretly followed the boy to see what he was up to. He saw the ass fill the tablecloth with gold pieces. "I should dearly like to have such a money-mint for myself," he thought, and that night, when the lad was asleep, he swapped the ass for another. It was this other animal that the young man led home to his father, who welcomed him with tears in his eyes. "What have you brought me, son?" he asked. "Wait and see, father," the middle son told him. "You must invite all our relations, and I shall give them more gold than they have seen in their lives!" When the family was assembled, he said, "Ass, give me gold!" But the only thing the ass could offer was something that was nothing at all like gold. What a scandal there was again!

21 SEPTEMBER

The Table, the Ass and the Cudgel

The youngest son learned the turner's trade. His master gave him a wooden cudgel in a sack as he was leaving. "If you tell it 'Cudgel, out you come!', it will jump out and beat your enemies soundly," he said to the lad. The young man thanked him, and because his brothers had written to tell him how the innkeeper had swindled them, he made straight for the fellow's inn. There he got talking to the landlord. "Here in this sack I have a prize far more precious than any bountiful table or golden-mouthed ass," he told the greedy fellow, casually. When the lad had eaten his fill, he lay down on a bench and put the sack under his head. Soon he pretended to be fast asleep. The innkeeper crept up on tiptoe and tried to get the sack from him. But the youngest brother shouted out "Cudgel, out you come!" and the wooden cudgel set about the dishonest landlord until he was black and blue. The lad would not call the cudgel off until he had returned the magic ass and table. What a homecoming it was when the youngest son arrived at his father's house! They invited all the relations once more, laid out a great feast, and gave them all as much gold as they could carry to take home with them. From then on life was like a fairy tale.

Do you know where I heard this tale? It was told by a father starling to his little ones, and before he had quite finished they were all of them fast asleep.

22 SEPTEMBER

The Table, the Ass and the Cudgel

Now it only remains to be told what happened to the mischievous goat. When the tailor beat her with his stick and shaved her head with his razor, she was so ashamed that she ran off into the woods and hid herself in a fox's lair. When the fox came home, a pair of huge eyes shone from her lair, a pair of horns creaked at her, and a set of hooves beat the ground menacingly. The fox ran away in tears. "Why are you crying, sister fox?" the bear asked her. "Why would I not cry, when the devil himself has moved into my lair, with his fiery eyes, his goat's horns and his satanic hooves!" the fox told him. "Dry your eyes, sister fox," said the bear. "You shall see how I get the rascal out of there." And he went straight to the fox's lair. But when he saw the fiery eyes himself, he, too, took to his heels. He met a little bee. "Why so sad, Bruno?" asked the bee. The bear told her all, and the bee smiled. "A fine couple of heroes you are!" she said. "I'll show the fellow!" She flew into the lair and stung the goat on her bald head so terribly that she bleated with pain and ran off into the trees. That was the last that was ever seen of her.

23 SEPTEMBER

The Tale of the Mouse

Once I met a little boy who was holding in his hand a little brown mouse. When he saw me, he put the mouse down in the grass and said, "Help me build a mountain of pebbles. When it is finished we shall climb to the top with my little mouse and see what it is like up there, high above the clouds. Perhaps my little sister will come up afterwards, but she can't just yet, because she is poorly. What do you suppose the sky is made of? Won't we fall through it?"—"I don't know," I told him, "I have never been there. Perhaps it is a great big meadow with stars growing on it."—"Meadows are green," he said, wisely. "You never know," I said. "Maybe some meadows have grass that is quite, quite blue. There are little white sheep grazing there, and round their necks they have little glass bells. When the bells ring the sun comes up, and it is morning."—"Why is it morning?" he asked, curiously. "Because the flowers have dropped their petals."—"Why do they drop their petals?"—"Because they only

flower at night." "Why do they only flower at night?" he asked. "Why? Because!" I said, crossly. "You keep on asking questions as though you had nothing better to do. You had better grow up soon. Grown-ups are not surprised at anything."—"Why aren't they?" he wondered. I told him I should rather help him build his pebble mountain than answer his questions. While he worked, he told me the tale of his little mouse.

24 SEPTEMBER

The Tale of the Mouse

Once upon a time there was a little mouse. One night he slipped out of his hole and began to gnaw at some sweet ears of corn. Suddenly he heard a whispering, and all at once a tiny voice called out, "Let us be, you are ruining our house!" "Who can it be?" thought the mouse in surprise. "We are the little grain fairies. One of us lives in each grain, and we look after the ears. If you do not harm us, we'll show you a magic footpath." The mouse promised to leave them alone, and out of the grains of corn jumped little fairies in white caps and white lace aprons. In their hands they held dandelion-down parasols, and floated down to the ground on them like little snowflakes. They sat on the mouse's tail and showed him how to get to the magic footpath. "There it is!" they shouted, when they came to a grassy ridge. And indeed it was. A tiny little path stretched out like a stream of tears between the stalks and bushes, over field and through forest, and at the end of it the great full moon was shining. "Where does it lead to?" asked the mouse. "We don't know," said the grain fairies, but it wasn't true. They had heard that whoever sets out on that path wanders far into the wide world. And since they did not want the mouse to come back and chew their ears of corn again, they had decided to show him the enchanted footpath. Now, where do you suppose it will lead to?

25 SEPTEMBER

The Tale of the Mouse

The mouse walked and walked, and was just beginning to feel sad and lonely when he met a little frog. "Where does this path lead to?" he called out. The frog started, but when he saw that it was only a little mouse speaking, he took heart, and replied, "I don't know; I have been hopping along it for a long time, but it seems to have no end. Perhaps it leads to the sky itself. If you like, we may go together, so that we won't be afraid." The mouse agreed. Soon they reached the kingdom of marsh-marigolds. The king sat in a golden flower with a tame bee on his lap. He was giving her honey from a crystal goblet, and the bee was fanning him with her wings.

With one hand the king was turning the pages of a great book, made of marsh-marigold leaves bound together. "Halt!" the king ordered the mouse and the frog. "Whoever enters the kingdom of marsh-marigolds by the enchanted path shall at once, immediately and without delay be turned into a marsh-marigold! Thus it is written in the book of marsh-marigold laws. Here, you may see for yourselves!" The mouse and the frog took a courteous peep. "We cannot read, Your Majesty," they said. "Oh, what a pity!" sighed the king of the marsh-marigolds. "I was hoping you would read the rest of this book to me, for I am tired of reading it. But if you cannot read, then get out of my sight. Where are you going to, anyway?"—"To the sky," replied the mouse. "This way, please," said the king, and pointed towards the moon. So that was the way they went.

26 SEPTEMBER

The Tale of the Mouse

The mouse and the frog could scarcely put one foot in front of the other, but they seemed to be no nearer the sky. "I wonder what the sky is like," said the mouse. And the frog said, "I suppose it is like a great puddle, with a beautiful water-lily floating on it. On the water-lily sits the queen of the frogs, looking after the little star-frogs. She has one silver eye and one golden one. She looks through one of them at night and the other in the daytime. When she closes her eyes, it is dark here on earth."—"Oh, no," said the mouse, shaking his head. "The sky is sure to be as dry as a mouse's hole."—"Then why does it rain from there?" asked the frog, a little crossly. "It is a great puddle, I tell you!" They would probably have fallen out altogether, if something had not hissed beside them in the grass, and a pair of devilish eyes had not shone at them out of the dark. One of them was silver, the other golden. "Hurrah, we're here," shouted the frog. "I told you so!" He wanted to jump forward, but he couldn't even move. The mouse, too, was fixed to the spot. It was as though they were both turned to stone. For out of the grass poked a hideous snake's head, its forked tongue swishing through the air. The snake opened his mouth wide and hissed, "Just you come along into my splendid jaws, and make yourselves at home. Whoever would get to the end of the path of wandering must pass through my stomach." Just then the shadow of an owl fell across the path, and the snake's bright eyes dulled with fear. The mouse and the frog waited for nothing and dashed to safety.

27 SEPTEMBER

The Tale of the Mouse

The two animals plodded along that enchanted path, and began to feel very sorry for themselves. "Are we nearly there?" asked the frog. "Is it far now?" he panted. But there were no words of comfort for the little mouse to offer. Then they came to a great lake. The whole of the night sky was reflected in its water, the stars glittering on its surface like tiny bits of mother-of-pearl. "Hurrah, we're here at last!" cried the frog, joyfully. "I told you the sky was a great puddle." And before the mouse could say a word, the frog had leapt into the lake and disappeared into the depths. The mouse waited, and waited for the frog to come up again, but there was no sign

of him. "Perhaps there is one sky for frogs, and another for mice," he thought to himself. Suddenly he felt very homesick. As he turned around, he suddenly saw nearby a little passage like a mousehole. "Maybe I shall find a friendly mouse there who will take me in," he thought to himself, and stuck his head in the hole. But out of the passage came a buzzing sound, which grew louder and louder, then out of the hole flew a swarm of angry bumble-bees. They settled all around the poor wanderer, and the queen said angrily, "How dare you disturb our kingdom? As a punishment we shall shut you up in the underground cells!" And they drove the poor creature down the passage and walled it up with earth and wax.

The Tale of the Mouse

Luckily, mice are not the least bit helpless under the ground. As soon as the little traveller had got over the shock of being thrown in a bee-dungeon, he began to dig and scrape, until at last he dug his way right out of the bees' nest. But there again was the endless lake, and the mouse began to cry hopelessly. "I shall never find out what the sky is like," he wailed. Just then a little boat made of a walnut shell came floating up in the breeze. The mouse begged it, "Take me with you, far, far away to where the sky is."—"I was just about to go there anyway," said the little boat, which knew how to talk and sing. "The two little children have sent me to see how far it is to the sky. But I have been sailing ten days and nights, and the clouds just run away from me. Come with me if you wish: at least we shall not be lonely." The mouse was pleased, and curled up contentedly in the bottom of the shell. It was a lovely day, and the sun shone so pleasantly that the mouse was soon sound asleep. Suddenly he was woken up by piercing cries. A flock of seagulls was circling over the little boat, and their king called out angrily: "Whoever values his life stays away from the kingdom of the water birds!" And he snatched at the little mouse with his beak. But the boat puffed out its sail and shot across the water like an arrow, until the birds were lost from sight.

29 SEPTEMBER

The Tale of the Mouse

Who knows how long the mouse and the little boat bobbed up and down over the waves; but the sky was always as far away as ever, and they never, never reached the place where it meets the water. In the end a fierce storm drove them back to the shore. There were two small children standing there, a boy and a girl. "Look!" called the boy. "Our little nutshell boat has come back again." The children were surprised to find the half-dead mouse inside, and they took him in their hands and warmed him gently. Then the little mouse told them how he had set out on the enchanted path to the sky, so as to find out what it was like up among the stars. Then the boy said: "I, too, should like to know what it is like up in the stars. I shall build a high mountain of pebbles, so high that it will reach into the sky. Then I shall go and become king of the stars. I shall rule wisely and fairly, and teach grown-ups to believe in miracles."—"Then take us with you," begged the little girl and the mouse. "We, too, should like to go higher and higher, to climb up with you along the magic pathway to the blue realm of the stars."—"I'll take you," said the boy. It was the same little boy I helped to build his pebble mountain. When it is finished, I'll tell you what it is like up there in the sky. But if we should grow old, and never manage to finish it, then you must go on building it, dear children. Perhaps there are even people like us living up there, and waiting to throw their arms around us.

30 SEPTEMBER

The Inquisitive Fish

There was once a little fish who just had to be everywhere, and hear everything. Her mother would say to her, "You know, curiosity killed the cat!" But the little fish would not listen, and swam hither and thither about the sea, so as to miss nothing. One day she came across a clump of sea-plants on her travels. "Clack, clack, clack," she heard from inside. An old crab was sharpening his claws. "Whatever can it be?" thought the curious little fish, and for a while she swam round and round, since she was a little afraid. But her curiosity got the better of her fear. When the tapping did not stop, she turned and swam up to the mysterious clump, just to take a peep. Now that was a mistake! The old crab did not take kindly to inquisitive visitors. He stuck out his pincers and, snap! He nipped the curious little fish on the nose until her eyes watered. You should have seen how she hurried home to her mother, weeping and wailing. True, her mother put a sticking plaster on her sore nose, but then she gave the little fish a good smacking with her fin, to teach her that it doesn't pay to be inquisitive. What about you, children? Are you inquisitive? You had better watch out; not only for crabs, but also in case a blackbird should come along and peck off your nose!

OCTOBER

1 OCTOBER

The Selfish Fox

Once upon a time a fox went to visit her godmother. She carried a sack of poppy-seed on her back, so that they might bake poppy-seed cakes. She met a little hedgehog. "Give me a handful of poppy-seed," begged the hedgehog, "so that I may bake a cake for my children. If you give it to me, your sack will grow heavier and heavier. If not, it will get lighter with every step." The selfish fox frowned. "Why should I want the sack to be heavier, when I have such a long journey before me? And what are your children to me, foolish hedgehog!" And she went on. The hedgehog hurried quietly after her, and slipped in front of her on the other side of the woods. He rolled himself up in a ball, until he looked like a little tree-stump. When the fox saw him, she said to herself: "I have walked long enough; now I shall have a rest." So she sat down in the grass, and rested her sack on the tree-stump. But the hedgehog stuck out his spines and pricked the sack all over. When the fox had rested, she set off again. She did not even notice the poppy-seed falling out of the sack, grain by grain. "The foolish hedgehog was right," she thought, in a little while. "The sack is growing lighter step by step. A good thing I didn't give him so much as a grain of the seed." But before she got to her godmother's, the sack was quite empty. There were no poppy-seed cakes that day. But the woodland birds had a fine feast, and thanked the hedgehog from their hearts.

2 OCTOBER

The Magic Arrow

A young Indian brave went out hunting one day. Suddenly he saw a splendid bird in a tree nearby. Instead of feathers, it was covered in wild roses. Right away the young hunter drew back an arrow in his bow. "Do not shoot!" called the bird. "I shall reward you." The Indian put back his arrow, and the bird said,

"It is well that you did not shoot, for had you killed me, you would have met with ill-fortune. Go to your tepee and you will find there a magic arrow. Whenever you seek something, loose the arrow into the sky, and it will show you the way." The bird had spoken truly. When the brave returned to his home, he found in his tepee a beautiful arrow, covered in wild roses. The days went by, and then the young brave fell in love with the witch-doctor's beautiful daughter. One evening he summoned up his courage, and went to ask her father for her hand. "I shall give you my daughter in marriage, if you can three times find her where I hide her," said the witch-doctor. The young man agreed. The next day he set out into the prairie to look for his loved one, but though he wandered back and forth he could find the young maiden nowhere. Then he remembered his magic arrow. He shot it up in the air; the arrow turned around and flew like a bolt of lightning into the throat of a little red bird. As soon as the bird hit the ground, it turned into the medicine-man's daughter.

3 OCTOBER

The Magic Arrow

When the young brave led the witch-doctor's daughter back to her father, the powerful magician was astonished, and said, sternly, "The second time you will not find her." But in the morning the young man did not hesitate, and shot his magic arrow straight for the sun. It flew for a long time, and as it flew it sang an Indian love-song, so that the young man might not lose sight of it. It fell into a deep lake, and soon a beautiful silver fish popped up out of the water. The arrow was stuck in its eye. The young brave pulled it out, and at once there stood before him the smiling beauty he loved. The witch-doctor frowned with anger. "You have not won her yet," he said. "If you do not find her a third time, I shall turn you into a wild wolf." The young man only smiled, undaunted. But when he shot his magic arrow the next day, it soon fell back at his feet. He drew his bow again, but again the arrow fell to the ground. "I cannot find your bride," it said in a human voice. "You must give me your blood to drink." The young man did not hesitate, but shot the arrow through his own leg. Then he again loosed it to the clouds. As it flew, it sang a sad song. Then it fell and pierced a dry white flower. The young man picked the flower, but nothing happened. "Pour your blood over it," said the arrow, and when the brave had done so, it turned into the beautiful Indian maiden. They embraced, and were never parted again.

4 OCTOBER

Sleeping Beauty

Once upon a time there lived a king and queen, who would say to themselves, day in,

day out: "If only we had a child." But their wish remained unfulfilled. Then one day, as the queen was bathing in the lake, a frog came hopping out of the water and said: "Your wish shall be fulfilled, o queen! Before the year is out, a daughter will be born to you." And as the frog had prophesied, so it came about. The royal couple had a little baby princess, as beautiful as a rosebud. The king ordered a grand christening to be prepared, and invited guests from far and wide. Among these guests were twelve powerful fairies; in actual fact there were thirteen of them in the kingdom, but the king had only a dozen golden plates, so he did not invite the thirteenth. When the banquet was over, one by one the fairies went up to the cradle and proclaimed the gifts they would give the child. The first gave her virtue, the second health, the third beauty unsurpassed, the fourth riches, and so it went on, until eleven of them had passed the cradle. Then, suddenly, there appeared in the hall the fairy who had not been invited, and she called out in a vengeful voice, "Since you have spurned me, proud king and queen, your rose shall be given but summers fifteen, wherein she may grow, and in loveliness bloom; till the prick of a spindle shall spell out her doom!" All those present were struck dumb with horror; before they could recover themselves, the fairy was gone.

5 OCTOBER

Sleeping Beauty

After the angry fairy's prophecy had been made, there was great sadness and mourning throughout the banqueting hall and the whole palace. But then the twelfth fairy stepped up to the cradle, for she had not yet pronounced her spell. In a clear voice she called out, "Though I may not decree that the spell be reversed, yet still can I lessen your tears; so with sleep and not death let the princess be cursed, sleep lasting for one hundred years." And the good fairies were gone like the morning mist. But the foreboding of the twelfth fairy did little to ease the king's mind, and he ordered that every spinning wheel in the kingdom be burnt or smashed to pieces. In the meantime his daughter grew up fast, and all the good wishes contained in the fairies' gifts came true. She was beautiful, wise and happy.

She grew into a lovely young maiden. It happened by chance that on the very day of her fifteenth birthday the king and queen had to leave the palace, and the princess stayed behind on her own. She began to wander about the castle, until she reached an old tower. There she found a strange little door, and, turning the rusty key in the lock, she found herself in a tiny chamber. There she saw an old woman sitting by a spinning-wheel with the spindle in her hand, and spinning merrily away. The princess could not take her eyes off her.

6 OCTOBER

Sleeping Beauty

"Good day, old woman," said the girl at last. "What a fine game you are playing; I should dearly like to try it." And at once she put out her hand towards the spindle. But the moment she touched it she pricked her finger, and fell onto a golden couch which stood beside the wheel, slipping into a deep, deep sleep. With her all else in the palace slept too: the king and queen, who had just returned; the courtiers; the horses in the stables; the dogs in the yard, the doves on the roof, the flies on the wall, even the fire in the hearth. Even the cook, who was about to clout the kitchen-boy, dropped off, as did the girl who was plucking a chicken for the royal supper. The very wind which was gently blowing past the palace at the time settled down in the bushes and went to sleep. Only the thick briars which grew around the castle walls were not still; these grew and grew until the whole palace was covered with an impenetrable layer of thorny branches, and then a great silence descended on the place. Many a bold knight or prince tried to cut his way through the prickly mass, but all were caught up in the terrible briars and none returned alive. The years came and went like passing dreams, and the people from the countryside around the palace began to tell the story of the sleeping princess to their children, though none knew what was really happening inside the palace. Then, one day, just one hundred years later, a handsome young prince happened to be passing through that land; he heard an old man telling his grandchildren the tale of the enchanted palace, and decided to see for himself.

7 OCTOBER

Sleeping Beauty

The young prince threw himself at the thorny thicket with drawn sword; but the briars parted to let him by, and wherever he passed beautiful roses burst into flower among the thorns. When he reached the palace, however, the prince could not find a single moving creature, for all was steeped in the deepest of deep sleeps. The astonished prince wandered from one chamber to the next, until at last he reached the old tower. There, lying upon the golden couch, he saw a princess so beautiful that it quite took his breath away. He leaned over and kissed her gently. "Awake from your dreams, o sleeping beauty sweet, and open your eyes, that they and mine may meet!" he breathed. Then the princess gave a long, deep sigh, opened her eyes, and smiled at the prince. "I have been dreaming of you," she said. "Ah, what a long and beautiful dream it was!" And at that moment everything in the palace awoke. The wind rose and shook the flags, the fire shot out red tongues of flame, the girl finished plucking the chicken, the kitchen boy got his clout over the head from the cook, the horses in the stables gave a merry neigh, the doves flew down from the roof, and the flies began to buzz around busily. The king and queen and all the courtiers rubbed the sleep from their eyes and called on everyone in the kingdom to acclaim the bold young prince. Nor was it long before they were celebrating a glorious wedding, and all twelve of the good fairies were there. The thirteenth had moved off to another kingdom, and only the birds would sometimes bring news of her.

8 OCTOBER

The Pot of Gruel

In the treasury of a certain kingdom the most precious treasure of all is a rusty old pot. The

old queen walks about the palace and tells all who stop to listen the tale of the pot of gruel. Long, long ago, there lived a miller who had fallen upon hard times. As if that were not enough he had a nagging wife, so that his only joy in the world was his beautiful daughter. When, one year, a famine came upon the land, even the mice in the miller's corn-loft started to go hungry. One day, the miller's wife cooked a pot of gruel from the last few handfuls of flour, set it down on the table, and said, "When we have eaten it, we may take our leave of this life, for this gruel is all we have in the world." When the miller heard this, he grabbed a wooden spoon, anxious to taste a last morsel before he set about the business of starving to death. But his quarrelsome wife would not let him near the pot, afraid lest he should leave none for her daughter and herself. When they had fought over the gruel for a long time, she suddenly grabbed the pot, put it on her head, and ran out of the mill. Waving the wooden spoon, the miller chased after her. When their daughter saw them, she did not even stop to put on her shoes, but took them in her hand and went after her parents. But they had disappeared from sight. Then, to cap it all, the poor girl dropped one of her shoes on the way, and couldn't find it again. She sat down on a bank and began to cry.

9 OCTOBER

The Pot of Gruel

Scarcely had the girl wept her last tear, when there beside her an old woman suddenly appeared. "Why were you weeping so?" she asked, kindly. The girl told her everything that had happened, and the old woman smiled at her. "Here you have another shoe," she said and, reaching into her bag, pulled out a slipper all of gold. "Go through the forest until you come to the king's castle," she told the miller's daughter. "Knock on the gate and ask for some clothes. But take only silk ones. If they ask you why, tell them you have worn silk all your life." When she had said this, the old woman disappeared. The girl did as she had been told, and when the servants had brought her silken robes, she looked like the most beautiful of princesses. The moment the prince saw her, he fell in love with her. The old king liked the girl too, and so a great wedding was prepared. While the cakes were being baked, the girl looked out of the window at the birds as they twittered to the parrot in his cage. Suddenly, she saw her mother running across the fields with the pot of gruel on her head and her father chasing after her with the wooden spoon. She could not help bursting out laughing. "What are you laughing at?" asked the prince in surprise. She told him a tale, since the truth was much too shameful. "Oh," she said, with a laugh, "I was just thinking how small this palace is for such a wedding. Wherever are we to put all our guests?" The prince fell into thought. What do you suppose he will think of?

10 OCTOBER

The Pot of Gruel

When the prince had thought for a long time and thought of nothing, he asked his bride, "Have you then a bigger palace than ours, that this one makes you laugh so?"—"Why, of course!" the miller's daughter told him proudly. The prince was glad to hear this. "Then we shall put the wedding off for a week, and invite the guests to your palace." And he rushed off to tell the king. His bride suddenly grew sad, and was sorry she had boasted to the prince so foolishly. Then, before her very eyes, the bird in the golden cage changed into the little old woman. "I heard all," she said. "But do not fear; next week you shall set off on your journey. A little dog will be waiting outside the city gates. No one will see him but yourself. He will lead you and the royal train to a great palace." Then the old woman disappeared again. And all was indeed as she had said. No sooner had the royal procession left the palace gates, than a little dog ran out of the bushes, and led the

miller's daughter to a magnificent castle. "This is my palace," said the bride to her guests, and they all went inside, sat down at a huge table, and ate, drank and made merry. Then the doors flew open, and into the banqueting hall ran a woman with a pot of gruel on her head. "Help! He will beat me!" she called out. The king, the queen and all the guests burst into roars of laughter, and in the end the young bride smiled and admitted that these were her dear parents. They all rejoiced, ate the gruel with the wooden spoon, and then placed the pot in the royal treasury.

11 OCTOBER

The Tale from the Zoo

There was once a beautiful zoo. There must have been animals there from all the world. They all liked it there, because no one did them any harm, they had plenty to eat, and the children and the adults would gaze at them admiringly all day long. One day a bold African lion was brought to the zoo. They shut him in a cage and gave him his breakfast. But the lion would not touch his food, frowned, and roared at the top of his voice, "I don't want to go to prison; I haven't done anything wrong."—"Don't be silly," the keeper told him. "This is not a prison, it's a zoo. Now you will be the most important of all the lions. You will get a fine-sounding name, like Julius Caesar or Jack the Ripper, the Count of Monte Christo or Harry Hawkins, and you will show all the children what a real, unstuffed lion looks like." The lion was flattered. "That's more like it," he said. "I know all about looking like a real lion; just as long as you don't want me to look like a real anything else, that will be all right. And you can call me Harry. I like that name." So they called him Harry. The children crowded round his cage, and the lion was proud enough to burst. But before very long there was a terrible mess all round his cage. The naughty children threw their rubbish on the ground, and the keeper could not clear it up fast enough. "Now that was all I needed," thought the keeper to himself, and he sat down to think.

12 OCTOBER

The Tale from the Zoo

When he had done all the thinking he intended to, the keeper said to the lion: "Dear, golden lion Harry; it seems to me we shall have to send you back to Africa again. The minute the children see you, they throw down their ice-cream cornets, sweet packets and lemonade cups, and come over to talk to you. Who is supposed to sweep all that lot up after them? It's not as if you knew what to do with a broom yourself." Harry the Lion grew very sad. He liked the zoo; he was pleased with all the attention he got from the children, and didn't much fancy going back to Africa. So he, too, began to think, and suddenly he said to the keeper: "What are those strange animals over there?"—"Why, kangaroos, of course," the keeper replied. "They have a pouch on their stomachs to carry their children."—"I know!" said the lion, brightly, and he whispered something in the keeper's ear. The keeper's face lit up, and he went off to get a brush and some paint. On either side of the lion's cage he placed a kangaroo, painted on his stomach the word "rubbish", and smiled with satisfaction as the children threw their junk into the kangaroos' pouches. When they were full, the kangaroos went off and emptied them, and then stood by the cage again. From then on the zoo was as spick and span as mother's back garden. And Harry the Lion was as pleased as Punch that he did not have to go back to Africa.

13 OCTOBER

Annie the Monkey, Chico the Parrot and Wally the Bear

Once upon a time there was a sailor who had sailed in a ship through all the seven seas. He had seen many strange countries and all the wonders of the world. But still he was sad and lonely, for he was all alone; he had no wife or children, and there was not a port that he could call home. One day, as he was sailing across the open sea, the ship ran into a huge storm. The waves towered over the ship like terrible mountains, and it bobbed up and down like a nutshell. Suddenly a giant wave washed over the deck, sweeping away the whole crew, along with the captain himself, all except for the sailor. Luckily the captain was smoking his pipe at the time, and the sailors swam after the puffs of smoke, until they all reached America safely. There they wrung out their clothes, dried their boots, and went to the cinema. Maybe they are there to this day. The sad sailor was quite alone on the ship. He was tossed here and there by the storm, until at last he arrived at an unknown island. "What am I to do without the captain and the crew?" he lamented, but just then a parrot alighted on a branch nearby and called out: "I am the admirrral! I am the admirrral!"—"Well, if I haven't got a captain, I shall have to make do with an admiral," thought the sailor to himself, and he took the parrot on board.

14 OCTOBER

Annie the Monkey, Chico the Parrot and Wally the Bear

The parrot was called Chico, and he knew as much about sailing as a cock does about laying eggs, but he was as stern and as self-important as the most captain-like of captains. All day long he would sit on the flagstaff and call out: "I am the admirrral, I am; full steam ahead as fast as you can!" The poor sailor had his work cut out to stoke up, draw water, swab the decks, cook and darn. "We can't go on like this," he said to himself one day. "We shall have to find a deck-hand somewhere." They were just coming to an unknown shore, and in a while they spotted a little bear collecting honey. "We have plenty of honey aboard!" the sailor shouted to him. "If you like you can have a white sailor's cap and you may work as a deck-hand." The bear liked the idea. "My name is Wally," he said, as he came aboard. It was merrier right away with three of them, but Wally the Bear was not one for hard work. He liked nothing better than snoozing or licking the dishes and snooping around looking for pots of honey. The sailor had to do everything else. "This is no good," he said to himself. "We must at least find ourselves a cook." And he steered for a nearby island.

15 OCTOBER

Annie the Monkey, Chico the Parrot and Wally the Bear

On the island they found a little monkey swinging from the trees. "What's your name?" the sailor called out, but the monkey did not reply. The sailor pulled a face at the impolite creature; the monkey did the same. The sailor put out his tongue; so did the monkey. Well, being a monkey, it could only monkey about. But the sailor took it aboard just the same. They started to call her Annie. They gave her a little white apron, and she became their cook. She was not the least bit lazy, but whatever the sailor wanted her to do, he first had to do it himself. Then the monkey would do it. That way they always cooked the same food twice; first the sailor, then the monkey. They ate so well that they always fell asleep on the spot; the parrot on the flagstaff, Wally the Bear in a tub of marmalade, Annie the Monkey hanging by her tail from the pendulum of the clock, and the sad sailor in a barrel of salted herrings. Once, as they were sleeping like that, their ship was spotted by pirates. They sailed closer, but could not see a soul on board. "Let us board her and plunder her, then we shall send her to the bottom," said the pirate chief. "Have at them!" he called, and the pirates began to hurl kegs of gunpowder aboard the other ship. Boom! Boom! Boom! they went.

16 OCTOBER

Annie the Monkey, Chico the Parrot and Wally the Bear

The first to wake up was Chico the Parrot. He blinked one eye and called out: "I am the admirrral, I am; full steam ahead, as fast as you can!" The pirates were startled. "Could it be the admiral's flagship?" they wondered. Then Wally the Bear crawled out of the marmalade tub. "He-e-elp!" cried the pirates. "A sea-devil!" At that Annie the monkey woke up, swung along on her tail and, seeing the pirates hurling kegs of powder at their ship, began to copy them and threw at them everything she could lay her paws on. Finally the sad sailor hauled himself out of the barrel of herrings. He was covered all over in fish-scales, and had a herring between his teeth. The pirates thought it was Neptune himself, and they were so scared they leapt into the water, and before they could swim ashore they were eaten by sharks. Then the sad sailor and his crew sailed to the pirates' island and raised their flag triumphantly. They

found chests full of gold there, and sweet nuts and pots of fine honey. They built themselves a cottage and the sad sailor scrubbed it from top to bottom. When the monkey saw this, she grabbed a hedgehog and tried to scrub the floor with that, but she pricked herself so badly on its spines that she never touched a scrubbing-brush again. They are living there together happily to this very day. Now the sad sailor has found himself a home port, and we have a secret island to send messages to by carrier pigeon.

17 OCTOBER

Why

In a far-off land to the east lived a ruler who loved to set his subjects riddles. One day he summoned the greatest sages in all the land and said to them: "Tell me, tell me, why has the camel got a hump? If you cannot answer in three days, you shall lose your heads." The learned men went off sadly. It had never occurred to them to wonder about such an obvious thing as that, and now they could not answer their monarch's riddle to save their lives. They hurried to their libraries to consult their learned books, but they could not find the answer. So they turned to the stars, but they were no help either. In the end the eldest of the sages called up powerful magicians, using ancient spells and incantations; they put their heads together, and gazed into their crystal balls, magic mirrors and fiendish flames, but all to no avail. After three days the ruler summoned the sages again and said: "Well, tell me why the camel has a hump!" The wise men stood in silence and secretly took their leave of this life. Just then a little boy ran into the chamber and called out, "Because its back is not straight!" "Indeed, I should not have thought of that myself!" laughed the ruler; he set the wise men free and gave the boy a splendid glass marble. So you see that there is nothing magic about cleverness!

18 OCTOBER

Woodkin

Long ago in a little cottage on the edge of the forest there lived a carpenter and his wife. They prayed in vain to the Lord to give them a little child. Then one day the woman forgot herself and cried out in her bitterness, "If the Lord will not give us a child, then may the Devil at least!" That evening her husband brought home from the forest a little tree-stump. It looked for all the world like a little baby; all he had to do was trim it a little and carve two holes for the eyes. The woman wrapped it in an eiderdown and began to rock it in her arms. "Rock-a-bye, baby Woodkin!" she sang. Then the wooden child opened his eyes and shouted, "Mummy, I'm hungry!" The joyous woman hurriedly cooked a pan of gruel, but before she could turn around the child had eaten it, pan and all. "Mummy, I'm hungry!" he called, as if he were starved to death. The woman sent her husband for a loaf of bread, but Woodkin swallowed it like a raspberry. "Mummy, I'm hungry!" he shrilled, growing before their very eyes at a tremendous rate. Before long he was as big as a well-fed pig. The carpenter rushed off to the shed to milk the goat, but when he got back there was no sign of his wife. "Where is Mummy?" he asked. "I've eaten a pan of gruel, a loaf of bread and Mummy, and I'll eat you up too!" called Woodkin, and he had scarcely finished speaking when he opened his mouth like a barn door and swallowed the carpenter, milk-jug and all.

19 OCTOBER

Woodkin

Now Woodkin was bigger than the old stove. Since there was nothing left to eat in the cottage, he set off for the village. On the green he came across a girl with a handcart. "My, how swollen your stomach is!" she cried. "Whatever have you eaten?" — "I have eaten a pan of gruel, a loaf of bread, a jug of milk, my mummy and daddy, and I shall eat you up too!" he cried. And before the girl knew it she, too, was in his stomach. Just then a farmer went by with a load of hay. "My, my, lad, what a stomach you have! What have you been eating?" said the farmer. "I have eaten a pan of gruel, a loaf of bread, a jug of milk, my mummy and daddy, a girl with a handcart, and I shall eat you up too!" said Woodkin, and with a glug! the farmer was in his stomach. As he went along he also ate a whole flock of

sheep, along with the shepherd and his dog. Then he rolled along to a field where an old woman was digging beet. "Well, well, my lad; you have a fine stomach indeed! What have you been eating?" she asked in wonder. "I have eaten a pan of gruel, a loaf of bread, a jug of milk, my mummy and daddy, a girl with a handcart, a farmer and his hay, a shepherd and his sheep, and I shall eat you up too!" said Woodkin. But the old woman did not wait to be swallowed, and she ripped his stomach open with her mattock. You should have seen the procession that came out! But it was the last time the carpenter's wife called on the devil. The owl told me this tale, to-whit, to-whoo; if you go and ask him, he'll tell you one too.

20 OCTOBER

Why the Ostrich Cannot Fly

Once upon a time, long long ago, the ostrich could fly just like all the other birds. It was in the days when the sun laid golden eggs and hatched out golden chickens from them. The chickens ran off across the sky in all directions; then people began to call them stars. The sun sent a little bird with a letter to the moon asking it to come and be godfather to the chickens. The little bird dashed over hill and dale to get to the moon before it hid behind the clouds, but soon his wings began to ache. Then he saw an ostrich down below on the ground. "Ostrich, dear ostrich," the little bird called. "Please would you carry me and my letter to the moon! My wings are aching so, I am sure they will drop off soon." The ostrich scowled, "Well, then, if your little wings are aching, what about me? I am much bigger and heavier, and it is terribly far to the moon. But if you like, you may sit on my back, and we shall go there slowly on foot. We are sure to get there in the end, anyway." And so it was. The ostrich had long legs, but they seemed to get no nearer their goal. Long before the moon got the letter, the christening was over. "You lazy ostrich!" cried the sun, angrily. "If you are too lazy to fly, then from this day forth your wings shall be but an ornament!" And since then the ostrich has had to walk.

21 OCTOBER

The Pen That Told Tales

There was once a naughty little girl. She obeyed nobody, never said good-day to anyone, and at school she read fairy tales underneath her desk. When the teacher asked her, she couldn't even say A, B, C, let alone all of the rest. But she knew how to tell lies all right. One day she lost her pen. At school she told the teacher someone had stolen it. "Are you sure?" her teacher asked, but she insisted that one of her schoolmates had taken it. The teacher smiled, and gave her a beautiful new pen, such as none of the children had ever seen before. When the little girl got home, she hurriedly scribbled her homework and ran out into the garden. She didn't even read her homework over. She was naughty all afternoon, and that evening she quarrelled with her little brother. The next day at school the teacher called her name. "Read me your homework!" he told her. The girl began to read, but soon she started to blush like a ripe cherry. The magic pen had written, instead of her homework, all the mischief she had got up to. From then on the little girl was much better behaved. She was afraid the magic pen would tell on her again.

22 OCTOBER

A Bull in a China Shop

Once upon a time a great kingdom stood on the point of a needle. The king had one daughter, as pretty as a picture. He wanted to marry her to the most powerful man on earth. Suitors came and went, but none was to the old king's liking. Then one day a mighty magician came along. He knew all there was to know about magic, and right away he threatened to turn the kingdom into a pool full of frogs if the king did not give him his daughter. The old king was no fool. "Very well," he said. "I shall give you my daughter and all my kingdom, if you can conjure up a china shop in which there shall be a fine black bull, and that bull shall dance the two-step in the china shop." The magician laughed, waved his magic wand, and said "abracadabra", and at once a shop full of fine china appeared. He waved his wand a second time, and in the middle of the shop a great black bull appeared. But before the magician had time to order the bull to dance the two-step, the restless animal had turned and shifted once or twice, and the beautiful china was smashed to smithereens. "You clumsy fool!" laughed the king at the magician, and the great conjurer was so ashamed that he hid himself away in his own pocket and disappeared to where he had come from. Since then, when people behave clumsily, we say that they are acting like a bull in a china shop.

23 OCTOBER

The Three Satchels and the Purse

Once upon a time there were four brothers. Three of them were strapping young lads, but the youngest of them scarcely reached halfway up to the front-door handle. Everyone

used to laugh at him, and he often felt sorry for himself. But what he minded most of all was that his brothers called him Halfling. One day their father called them to him and said, "Go out into the world and seek your brides. Whoever brings home the most beautiful girl shall have the cottage and a field to go with it." So off they went. Halfling called vainly after the others to wait for him; they only laughed and lengthened their stride. In a while they came to a field of peas. From one of the pods they heard a great clamour and rejoicing. "Whatever can it be?" wondered the brothers. They cracked open the pod and peeped inside; they were astonished at what they saw. Inside the peapod was a whole kingdom. There on a golden throne sat a tiny king; beside him was an even tinier queen, and beneath the throne three tiny princesses were dancing

with their bridegrooms. The tiny courtiers were clapping in time to the dance and calling, "Hurrah, hurrah!"—"Here we have our brides!" grinned the brothers, and they would have taken the peapod away. But at that moment Halfling caught up with them. "I want a bride too!" he called. What were they to do now? Bridegrooms all over the place, but only three brides to go round.

24 OCTOBER

The Three Satchels and the Purse

While the brothers were arguing over which of the pea-princesses they should each have as their brides, the tiny king said: "Gentlemen, what use would such tiny wives be to you? If you leave us in peace, I shall give you three magic satchels. The first contains plenty, the second more than enough, and the third a profusion." The greedy brothers agreed. But then Halfling spoke up: "There is no satchel for me, so I should like a bride at least. I am small, she is small; we shall want for nothing, and at least she will not bully me!" The king smiled, and said: "If you do not mind a tiny bride, then, very well. Here is a magic purse. It contains four painted eggs. Give them your broody hen to sit on when you get home; she will hatch you a bride, you shall see." Halfling agreed, took the purse, and hurried after his brothers. You should have seen how they laughed at him all the way! When they got home, the three elder brothers opened up their satchels with great excitement; but out leapt little green imps with cudgels, and began to beat the brothers mercilessly. One of them got plenty, another more than enough, and the third a profusion. But Halfling gave the painted eggs to the hen to hatch. From the first there hatched a golden castle; from the second a golden throne; from the third he got a golden crown, and from the fourth a lovely little half-girl hatched. The two of them were married, and to this day they live happily together in their little golden castle.

25 OCTOBER

The Goblin Iwouldeat

There was once an old woman who used to go into the forest to gather firewood. One day, when she had filled her shawl with brushwood and dry pine-cones, she sat down in a clearing to rest. She took out a piece of dry bread and began to eat. Suddenly, an acorn came tumbling to the ground in front of her, and out jumped a tattered little dwarf. "I am the goblin Iwouldeat!" he shrieked at the old woman. "Give me some food, or I shall eat you instead!" The old woman had only a crumb left over, so she threw it to him; but the goblin flew into a rage and said, "Do you not know that I cannot bear to eat bread? I shall eat you!" And he opened his mouth wide and moved towards the old woman; but she took to her heels. For a long time she did not dare to set foot again in the forest, but in the end her cottage grew so cold that she had to set off to gather wood again. When her shawl was full, she sat down to rest. Then the little goblin again leapt out of his acorn and screeched, "I am the goblin Iwouldeat! Give me food, or I shall eat you up!" The old woman quickly took out a jar of honey from her apron, and the goblin plunged his head into it greedily. The old woman turned the jar over on top of him and hurried off home. Since then the honey-pot has leapt about the forest, with a voice inside it saying, "I would eat, I would eat." If you value your life, be sure you don't turn it over!

26 OCTOBER

The Rajah's Bride

Far away in the middle of the jungle lived a foolish and lazy rajah, ruler of the Forgotten Empire. He would lounge all day on a cushion of bird-of-paradise feathers and let himself be fanned. One day he decided he would get married. He sent his counsellors and missives to all the corners of the earth to find him a bride; all of them were every bit as stupid as he was. "I want only a bride who can walk on the ground and fly through the air; one who looks like a human being, but does not look like a human being; one who has four hands and four feet," he ordered them. The envoys went sadly along until they met a wild boar. "Your Porcine Excellency," they addressed him, respectfully, "we are seeking a wife for His Magnificence the Rajah." And they told the boar what was required. "An easy matter," the boar told them. "You must take him a monkey. She will be just the bride he has asked for." The rajah's men did as he suggested: they caught a monkey in the jungle and took it back to the rajah. "Fools!" roared

the rajah. "It is an ordinary monkey!"—"But Your Royal Highness," replied the counsellors, "it is the only creature in the world which looks like a human being and does not look like one, which can fly through the air from tree to tree and walk on the ground, and which has four hands and at the same time four feet. Indeed, it is the very bride you asked for!" There was nothing for it for the rajah but to keep his word and to marry the strange creature. People would laugh at him behind his back and say: "See what a monkey of a wife he has!"

27 OCTOBER

The Gossamer Veil

Long, long ago, there lived a queen who had magic powers. Out of a thimble she conjured up a live doll, Gretel, so that she might have someone to play with. But because the queen was cruel and wanton, she teased the little doll, and set her impossible tasks. One winter's day she told Gretel she must weave her a veil of gossamer which would make her invisible. The poor girl wandered sadly through the frosty night, not knowing where to turn. All at once, a sturdy stag was standing in her path. "Tell me what troubles you, little girl," he said. When Gretel had told her sad tale, the stag just tossed his head, saying: "Don't worry, everything will be all right." Then he shook his antlers and, lo and behold, the snow suddenly thawed, and the trees were covered in blossom. Again he shook his antlers, and the trees were hung with fruit. He shook them a third time: the fruit ripened, the leaves began to turn yellow, and gossamer drifted through the air. Overjoyed, the girl gathered it up, and wove the magic veil. But instead of taking it to the queen, she threw it over herself, and at once became invisible. Then she returned to the palace. "Cruel queen, your days are numbered!" she cried out, in an eery voice. "Who speaks to me?" asked the witch. "Your sister, Death," replied Gretel. The queen was so startled that her wicked heart broke. So it was that little Gretel became queen, and from time to time the kind stag pays her a visit.

28 OCTOBER

The Bad-Tempered Admiral

Once upon a time there was a bad-tempered admiral. He and his ship sailed the seven seas and all the rivers, lakes, ponds and puddles of the world, and wherever he went he ranted and roared until earthquakes shook the land and volcanoes spewed out streams of lava and more ash than Granddad's pipe. The admiral's poor sailors could stand his endless bawling no longer, for their heads ached fit to split, and the only way to sleep was lying on both ears, and, as every sailor knows, that is no easy matter unless you happen to have both ears on the same side of your head. So one day they put their heads together, and when the admiral was sitting on shore and drinking his tenth keg of admiral's rum, they weighed anchor and made full steam ahead for the horizon. At that very moment the admiral happened to glance from the tavern window seaward, and he could not believe his eyes—there was his very own ship sailing off somewhere, straight along the equator. "Octopuses, sharks and anchovies!" he roared, turning purple with rage. "Why, stone the crows, they've made off with me ship, and me admiral's cap to boot!" And off he ran after it, sea or no sea, dashing over the waves to catch his ship. Since it was right on the equator, where the earth is fattest of all, he had a good long way to run, but he had nearly caught up with his ship when, from out of the crow's nest, the voice of Jack, the ship's boy, called, "Look out, Mr. Admiral sir, you're running across the sea!" The admiral looked down at his feet and, shiver his timbers, so he was! He got such a shock that he fell in the water and, since he couldn't swim, he altogether drowned. Well, he wasn't much of a sailor, anyway!

29 OCTOBER

The Starlings

In a certain city, where the houses grow up to the sky, an ordinary starling nesting-box hung from a tree. One autumn, when the starlings were flying off to the south as usual, the city fathers met down at the town hall, and pondered over why the starlings did not want to stay in the winter. "Who would want to stay in such an old-fashioned nesting-box," said the Civic Engineer. "We shall build them a modern starling housing-estate, and I shall be most surprised if they still fly away in winter." And so they did. In spring, when mother and father starling came back from their holiday in Africa, they were quite taken

aback. "Good heavens, which floor do we live on?" said daddy starling. "Right at the top, I think," replied the mother starling. "There is a good view from here, and we are nearer the sun."—"That is all very well," said the father. "But what if the lift breaks down?" And so they argued and quarrelled, and since they could not agree, they decided to move into the middle. They liked it there very much. But summer passed and autumn came along, and once more the starlings got ready to leave for the south. "Hold on!" the people called to them from the town-hall. "Why are you flying away?" Father starling waved a disdainful wing: "Central heating," he said, scornfully. "Playing up again." And with a mocking laugh they both flew away. Don't worry; when the warm sun returns, then so will they. But who knows, they may find themselves an ordinary nesting box again.

30 OCTOBER

Baron Redbeard and the Dog

Once upon a time there was a baron named Redbeard, who was stronger than the strongest of his subjects. All were afraid of him, for he was cruel, and mistreated both men and animals; most of all he liked to tease cats and dogs. One day he was walking through his domain when he came to a peasant's farm. A skinny little dog was tied up beside its kennel. "Listen, Baron Redbeard," the dog barked out suddenly. "If you can carry me on your back to your castle, I shall serve you faithfully for seven years without food. If you cannot, then you shall watch over my kennel for seven years." The baron laughed. "Very well," he said, and tried to lift the dog up on his shoulders. But the dog turned round on

his tail three times, and before the baron could catch his breath, there in front of him stood a dog the size of barn. He tried in vain to lift the creature. Then he ran off to his castle as fast as he could. He had the blacksmith make him a pair of iron boots, the tinker a suit of iron clothes, and ordered the servants to chain him to an iron bed. He was afraid the dog would carry him off to his kennel. In a little while he fell fast asleep. But the moment he shut his eyes, there in the chamber stood the gigantic dog. It bit through the iron chains as if they were paper, and made off with the baron, iron suit, iron boots and all. When the dog got to its kennel it tied the baron up, with a collar round his neck, and the wicked fellow had for seven years to serve the farmer who lived there. And since he was covered in iron from head to foot, by the end of the seven years he had quite rusted away.

31 OCTOBER

The Boats with Dewdrops Aboard

There was once a little boy who was building a mountain of pebbles so as to reach the sky. He went on building, and building, and when he was tired, he and his little sister went to play on the bank of a nearby lake so as to have a rest. Most of all he liked to sail little boats made of nutshells or pieces of pine bark. This time, too, he carved two pretty little boats and gave each of them a little paper sail; then he and his sister shook a tiny dewdrop into each of the little vessels. It was all the riches they possessed. "Sail away, little boats; as you voyage, find out what our pearls are worth in the world," said the boy. The boats sailed away obediently on a long voyage. It was a long time before they returned. They anchored quietly in the creek and called out, "Your pearls are like human tears, and so they are worth nothing. There are too many of them in the world, for there is a shortage of compassion." The boy thought for a moment, then said, "Very well! I do not know what compassion is, but when I grow up I shall find out. Then I shall spread it among people, so that they may know the value of tears." Then he saw that his little sister was crying. "Don't cry," he told her. "I love you." And the boats said, "You already know what compassion is. It is the wealth of the kind-hearted." And they quietly filled their sails and sailed away.

NOVEMBER

1 NOVEMBER

The Lad Who Learnt to Understand the Birds

There once lived a peasant who had a bright young son. One day he said to himself, "It would be a pity for such a clever lad to spend the rest of his life on the farm; I shall send him to get an education, so that he may wear shoes on his feet like a lord." His wife was willing, but she said, "What trade do you suppose he may learn?" The peasant scratched his head, but he could think of nothing. Then a little sparrow perched on the chimney and began to twitter some piece of news to the other birds. "Now I have it!" cried the peasant. "We shall send him to town to learn the language of the birds!" They gave him a sixpence to pay his fees, and bade their son farewell. By and by the lad returned to a joyful welcome. "Father, I have finished my studies," he said. "Now I can understand what the sparrows on the roof are chirping about!" he added, grinning from ear to ear. His father and mother put on their best wooden clogs as if they were going to church, and sat the boy down at the table they had spread to welcome him home. His father was impatient with curiosity. "Well, then, tell us what the sparrows are saying!" he said, excitedly. The lad stretched out his ears until they were longer than those of their old donkey, listened for a while, and said with a smile: "Believe it or not, father, the sparrows are telling each other how one day you will fetch me water in a copper basin, and how mother will dry my hands on the best tablecloth." The peasant almost burst his buttons with rage, and shouted at his son: "You mealy-mouthed good-for-nothing! Fine airs and graces you have taught yourself in the world! Get out of my house, and never come back again!"

2 NOVEMBER

The Lad Who Learnt to Understand the Birds

What was the poor lad to do? He wandered the world, offering his services everywhere. "What can you do?" they would ask him. But when he told them the truth, that he could understand the birds, he got short shrift. "Whoever needs to know the latest bird gossip!" they would say to him. In the end he became apprenticed to a poor cobbler. "At least I shall learn a proper trade," he thought. One day he was sitting on his shoemaker's stool patching up a pair of old boots, when a flea jumped into his shirt. "I'll show you, you cheeky little beast!" cried the lad, and laid his cobbler's strap square across the flea's head. The creature lost its appetite at once. It fell to the floor and lay there with its legs in the air. "My, what a beauty!" cried the lad gleefully; he measured the flea from head to toe and from toe to head, and then skinned it and sewed a fine pair of shoes from the hide. They

were so big that a band of dwarfs might have played skittles in them. "Only the king himself can have such feet," said the shoemaker's apprentice to himself. "Not for nothing is it said that where he has trod no grass grows for seven years!" And he loaded the shoes on a handcart and set off to take them to the king.

3 NOVEMBER

The Lad Who Learnt to Understand the Birds

The shoes fitted the king like a glove. "You are a clever lad," he said to the boy. "Can you do anything else?" The boy told him proudly how he could understand the song of the birds. The king's face lit up like the summer sun. "What a piece of luck," he said. "For three days three ravens have been flying beneath my windows, and I do not know what they want of me." The lad stuck his head out of the window, stretched out his ears until they were as long as a sexton's cold, and at once began to translate the ravens' cries: "The birds are a father, a mother and a son. Last year, when food was scarce, the mother left the youngster to die of hunger. But the father took care of him and brought him up. They are asking you, my lord, to whom the son belongs."—"Why, that is simple," replied the king. "To the father, who brought him up." When the ravens heard this judgement they stopped crowing and flew away. "You are the wisest of the wise, my son," said the king. "I shall give you my daughter's hand in marriage. She is quite stupid, and you have brains enough for two."—"Why not?" the lad agreed, and right after the wedding he set off in the royal carriage to his parents' cottage. When his mother and father saw their noble visitor they fell over each other to do him honour. They invited him inside; his father brought him water in a copper basin and his mother dried his hands with the best tablecloth. "There you are, you see, the birds were quite right," said the boy with a smile. Only then did they recognize their son, and how ashamed they were for having turned him away from their door. But the lad was not angry with them, and took them off to the palace in the royal carriage.

4 NOVEMBER

The Clockmaker Imp

There was once a very, very old town, in which there were thousands of towers. In the tallest of the towers, inside the big old clock, lived the clockmaker imp. He always made sure the clock was neither fast nor slow, wound it up, oiled it, and looked after its bells. Ding, dong, ding, dong the clock would strike contentedly, and the clockmaker imp would give a smile of satisfaction. But one day some

little boys passed by the clock tower on their way to school. They looked up at the clock and started. "The school bell will ring any minute!" cried one of them. "We shall be late, and the teacher will put us in disgrace."—"All because we played hide-and-seek!" another boy said. But a third boy had a clever idea. "Let us ask the clockmaker imp to put back the hands," he said. So they knelt down in front of the clock-tower and called, "Clockmaker imp, clockmaker imp, help us please! If you put back the hands for us, we will bring you a bag of humbugs." The imp had a sweet tooth, and he gladly helped the boys. In a flash all the clocks in the world were a minute slow, and the boys got to school on time.

5 NOVEMBER

The Clockmaker Imp

But the clockmaker imp in his tower waited in vain for his bag of humbugs. As soon as their fear was gone, the boys forgot all about their promise. This made the imp terribly angry. "So that is the ungrateful human race!" he scowled, and out of spite he began to turn the hands of the clock backwards. A fine mess that was! Everything in the world went back-to-front. People began to walk backwards instead of forwards; instead of tomorrow there was yesterday; the dead rose up from their graves, the sun crossed the sky from west to east, spring followed summer, winter spring and autumn winter; night followed morning, evening followed night, and so on. The old folk were naturally pleased that they were growing younger day by day, but the forgetful boys were quite upset. Instead of the third class at school they found themselves in the second, then in the first, and they were surely soon going to be little babies wrapped in shawls again, or even disappear to wherever they had been before they were born. Luckily one of them remembered that they had promised the clockmaker imp a bag of humbugs. He took a quarter of a pound of the best and went hurrying to the clock-tower. He laid the bag of humbugs down under the great clock. The clockmaker imp got his temper back at once, put the clock right, and made everything in the world the way it was before. Don't you ever go upsetting the clockmaker imp, will you!

6 NOVEMBER

The Stolen Tale of the Giant with the Golden Hair

There was once a little girl whose fairy godmother gave her a magic skipping-rope for her birthday. The moment she skipped over it there appeared in front of her a pair of terrifying robbers. They bowed right to the ground and said, "What is your command, most noble princess? May we have the honour of stealing something for you?" But the little girl waved her finger at them and said, "Stealing is wrong, you scoundrels! Think yourselves lucky I don't call a policeman. But since it is you, I shall let you steal a story for me from the realm of fairy tales. But be sure to take it back afterwards!" The robbers bowed and disappeared, but in a twinkling they were back again with a fairy tale under their arms. Which one? This one!

Long, long ago, a son was born in the cottage of a poor woodcutter. He was no ordinary boy. He had a golden star on his forehead, and what was more, he could lie on his tummy and on his back, wink his eyes, and yawn away like anything. Do you see? There he goes, yawning again. You'd better hide under the bedclothes before he swallows you up!

7 NOVEMBER

The Stolen Tale of the Giant with the Golden Hair

Well, let us continue. Where were we? When that wonderful little boy was born, the wise old fairy from the foxglove wood came along to be his godmother. She looked at the mark on his forehead, then up at the sky, and nodded her white head. "It is written in the stars that your son will take the king's daughter for his wife," she said. Word of this spread far and wide, until it came to the ears of the king himself. He heard it on the very day that a girl as pretty as a picture was born to the queen. The king frowned. "My noble daughter the wife of a poor woodcutter's son?" he said to himself. "That shall never be!" Then he dressed as a rich merchant and set off for the woodcutter's cottage. "You have a fine son," he flattered the parents. "Give him to me to bring up; I shall make a noble gentleman of him!" The woodcutter and his wife were unwilling, but in the end they agreed. The king took the cradle containing the little boy, and dropped it into a raging river from a bridge along the way. He was sure the child would be drowned in the torrent.

8 NOVEMBER

The Stolen Tale of the Giant with the Golden Hair

Strange to relate, the seething waters suddenly became slow and gentle, and rocked the child in his cradle as softly and safely as if he were in his mother's arms. By and by they carried the cradle down to an old mill. A poor miller and his wife lived there. They had no children of their own, and when they found the little boy they were happy to take him in and treat him as their own. Because he had come bobbing down the river to their mill, they called him Bobbikin. He grew like a healthy spruce, and before they knew it he

had turned into a fine young man, a pleasure to behold. When he was just sixteen, there was a great storm in the countryside thereabout. That day the king had been hunting in the forest close at hand, and he took shelter in the old mill. The moment he saw the young man with the golden star on his forehead, he asked whose son he was. The old miller, suspecting no evil, told the king how he had been brought to them by the river. At once the king guessed what had happened. Without delay he wrote a letter to the queen. In it he told her to have the head of the one who brought the letter cut off right away. Then he ordered Bobbikin to take the letter to the palace that very evening. The young man set off at once, but because the night was dark he got lost in the deep forest. Luckily he soon came to a strange cottage. A young girl, grubby and untidy, was looking out of the window; she was the daughter of a robber chief. "Go away from here, if you value your life!" she called to Bobbikin. "If the robbers catch you here, it will go ill with you!" But the lad was so tired he could go no further, and in the end the girl hid him behind the stove. Before long the robbers arrived.

9 NOVEMBER

The Stolen Tale of the Giant with the Golden Hair

As soon as the robbers arrived, one of them, who had a long nose, called out: "I smell a strange smell, like in the grinding-room of a mill!" And before he knew it, the long-nosed robber was dragging Bobbikin out from behind the stove. They would have killed him at once, but the girl beseeched them not to, so in the end they spared him. They went through his pockets, and found the letter from the king. When they had read it, they were angry at the cruel king's treachery. So they wrote another letter, saying that the queen was to marry her daughter right away to the man who brought the letter. Then they carefully put the king's seal on the new letter, and when dawn broke they sent Bobbikin off to the palace. When the queen read the letter, she was surprised, but, not daring to defy her husband, she did as she was asked. The marriage took place at once.

When the king returned, he was horrified, and wanted to punish his wife severely. But she showed him the letter bearing his seal, and the king was at a loss to understand who might wish him such mischief. So as to get rid of his unwanted son-in-law, he summoned him to the throne and said, "I order you to bring me three hairs from the head of the giant Tellitall. If you fail, you shall lose your head!" So poor Bobbikin set off.

10 NOVEMBER

The Stolen Tale of the Giant with the Golden Hair

For a long time Bobbikin wandered the world, until at last he reached a certain city. "Halt!" called the sentry at the city gates. "Where are you going?" Bobbikin said he was looking for the giant Tellitall, and the sentry told him joyfully: "If you promise to ask him why the spring of living water in our city has dried up, then you may pass." Bobbikin promised, and went his way. By and by he came to another city. There, too, the sentry stopped him, but when the lad had told him of his errand, he called out, "I shall let you pass if you promise to ask the giant why our city's wonderful golden apple tree has ceased to bear fruit." Bobbikin gave his word, and the sentry let him pass. As he made his way onward, he came to a broad river. Sitting in a boat by the bank was a downcast ferryman. "Tell me, friend, where can I find the golden-haired giant Tellitall?" Bobbikin called to him, and the ferryman replied, "On the far bank of the river is the golden cave where the giant lives with his mother. If you promise to ask him how much longer I shall have to ferry folk across the river, I shall take you there." Bobbikin promised, and the ferryman took him to the other bank.

11 NOVEMBER

The Stolen Tale of the Giant with the Golden Hair

The golden cave shone like the midday sun. Sitting in front of it, spinning golden thread, was a white-haired old woman. "What are you doing here, child?" she asked in surprise. "If you value your life, you will escape before my golden-haired son returns, or he is sure to make an end of you." But Bobbikin told her sadly that he had no choice. If he returned without three golden hairs he would be shorter by a head anyway. The old woman

took pity on him, and promised to help him. Bobbikin begged her to find out from the giant how much longer the ferryman had to carry people across the river, why the golden apple tree had ceased to bear fruit, and why the spring of living water had dried up. No sooner had he finished speaking, than the golden-haired giant came striding through the sky with huge steps. The old woman just managed to hide Bobbikin in the kneading-trough in time. "I smell human!" roared the golden-haired giant, but the old woman calmed him: "It is because you spend the whole day flying over men's dwellings." Then she laid his head in her lap and began to stroke his hair. Soon the giant dozed off. The old woman pulled out a golden hair. "Why do you wake me, mother?" asked the giant, irritably. "Oh, son, I fell asleep, and I dreamed of the ferryman; for age upon age he has had to ferry folk over the river." "He is a fool," laughed the giant, "for if he were to give someone the oars to hold and jump out onto the bank, then the other would have to take his place." And the giant was soon asleep again.

12 NOVEMBER

The Stolen Tale of the Giant with the Golden Hair

The kind-hearted old woman soon plucked another hair from the giant's head, then another. Each time she told him she had had a strange dream; in this way she found out that the golden apple tree has ceased to give fruit because a poisonous snake was nesting in its roots, and that the spring of living water was being swallowed by a fat frog. Then she left him in peace. When he had had a good sleep, he set off once more across the sky with his giant steps. Bobbikin took the three golden hairs from the old woman, thanked her kindly, and set off for home. The impatient ferryman was waiting for him. "When you have taken me across, I shall tell you what you want to know," Bobbikin told him, and when he was safely on the other bank he called out, "You must give one of your passengers the oars to hold and then jump out onto the bank; he will have to ferry in your stead!" When he got to the first city, he told the sentry why the apple tree gave no fruit. Without delay the citizens slew the snake, and at once the tree burst into golden blossom. They rewarded Bobbikin with three carts full of gold. He fared just as well in the second city. As soon as the citizens had, on his advice, slain the frog, the spring of living water shot up to the sky. The grateful citizens gave Bobbikin ten carts loaded with diamonds and pearls. So it was that he arrived home richer than the king himself. When the envious king saw his great wealth, he himself set off to visit the golden-haired giant, but when he reached the dark river, the ferryman gave him the oars to hold and leapt onto the bank. To this day the wicked king has to carry people across the river. Bobbikin and his beautiful wife have lived happily ever since.

When the robbers had finished their tale the little girl thanked them and sent them back to the realm of fairy tales to return the story to where it belonged. They have never been back since.

13 NOVEMBER

Baron Simple of Doltham

Once upon a time, beyond the dark forests, lived Baron Simple, Lord of Doltham. The baron was true to his name; he was so stupid that the sparrows on the roofs would twitter about his foolishness. Anyone who had any sense at all could catch him out with the simplest of ruses. No wonder he soon lost all that he owned to rogues and tricksters. What was left of his cloak just managed to keep the patches together. But the baron was as proud as any peacock, and thought himself the cleverest fellow in the world. One day a pair of poor old beggars came wandering up to his castle. The only thing they had in the world was a dog who had taken up with them along the road, knowing the beggars would treat him better than a rich master. The two old men banged on the blistered castle gate and asked the baron for alms. "Go away, you'll get nothing from me!" growled Baron Simple, waving a rusty sabre and slamming the gate in their faces. The beggars pleaded with him to give them at least a roof over their heads for the night, but the foolish baron would not soften. "You wait, you old miser, we'll show you!" warned the old men. They begged some old bones from the cottages nearby and threw them to the dog. What he did not eat, he buried in the ground. With each of the bones the clever beggars placed a copper coin they had begged. Then they knocked on the baron's gate again.

14 NOVEMBER

Baron Simple of Doltham

"You'll get nothing from me, I tell you!" shouted the baron again, when he saw the two beggars. "We have not come for alms," the old men said with a bow. "We have for sale a magic dog, which can find buried treasure. The first day he digs up copper pieces; the second day silver pieces, and the third day gold. We are too old now to run after him, but if you give us your poor domain, you may have our magic dog." The baron wanted to see for himself. The old men unleashed the hungry dog, and it began to scrabble away at the earth to uncover its buried bones. Every time it did so it dug up a copper coin. Baron Simple could not believe his eyes. "If tomorrow he

digs up silver, and the day after gold, I shall soon be able to buy a crystal castle, and shall be the richest noble in all the land," he thought to himself. Without delay he signed a contract with the two beggars, giving them his entire domain in return for their dog. Thus the two old men became the lords of Doltham. But it was in vain that the baron tried the next day to get the dog to dig up silver. In the end he had to beg the two old men to give him a roof over his head. They made him plead and beseech them, but in the end they took pity on him and relented. "You can keep your crumbling castle," they told him. "We shall make do with the blue sky above our heads." They took their beloved dog and went their way, and told everyone they met the story of the stupid baron.

15 NOVEMBER

Red Riding Hood

There once lived a little girl whom everyone liked, but most of all her grandmother. She sewed her little granddaughter a pretty little riding hood of red velvet, and it suited her so well that after that she never wanted to wear anything else on her head. So they started to call her Red Riding Hood. One day her mother asked her to take a basket to her grandmother. "Take these cakes and this bottle of wine to Granny," she told her. "She has been ill, and they will give her back her strength. But, mark my words, do not tarry on the way or wander from the path! And do not forget to greet politely anyone you meet." Red Riding Hood promised, and off she went. Her granny lived in the forest up above the village, and it was a good way to her little cottage. Scarcely had she reached the edge of the forest, when she met a wolf; but she was not afraid, since she did not know what a wicked creature it was. He asked her where she was going, and Red Riding Hood told him everything. The wolf licked his lips greedily, and at once began to ponder how he might eat up the grandmother and the little girl in one go. He trotted along beside her for a while, and then said: "See what pretty flowers are growing all around. And how sweetly the birds are singing! Why are you in such a hurry?" Red Riding Hood looked around her, and saw that the wolf was right. "What a nice posy I can pick for Granny!" she thought, and she started to run here and there gathering the wild forest flowers. Meanwhile, the wolf hurried on to the grandmother's cottage.

16 NOVEMBER

Red Riding Hood

When the wolf reached the cottage, he knocked at the door and called out: "It is I, Red Riding Hood!" "Lift the latch and come in, dear. I cannot get out of bed, for I am still weak from my illness," grandmother

answered. The wolf rushed inside and swallowed the old woman up. Then he put on her nightdress, pulled her night-cap down over his long ears, and lay down in her bed. Before long Red Riding Hood arrived. But what was this? The door was wide open, and her granny, lying there in bed, looked terribly strange. Red Riding Hood began to feel a little scared. "Good morning, Granny, what big ears you have today!" she said in surprise. "All the better to hear you with!" replied the wolf. "Dear me, Granny, what big eyes you have!"—"All the better to see you with!"— "And oh, what a big mouth you have!" said Red Riding Hood. "All the better to eat you with!" roared the wolf, and he leapt out of bed and swallowed her up. Then he stretched out on the bed and began to snore loudly.

A hunter happened to pass by the cottage, and he was surprised to hear the old lady snore so loudly. He peeped into the cottage, and recognized the wolf right away. "Just you wait, you old scoundrel!" he said to himself, and he quietly took a pair of scissors and cut open the wolf's stomach. Out jumped Red Riding Hood, and then Granny. "Dear me, how dark it was in there, and how afraid I was!" cried Red Riding Hood, and all three of them were so glad it was all over that they set to and ate all the cakes from the basket. Then they filled the wolf's stomach with stones, and sewed it up again. When the wolf woke up, he tried to run away, but the stones were so heavy that he crashed to the ground and killed himself. And Red Riding Hood? Do you know, after that she always did as she was told, and never tarried or wandered from the path again.

17 NOVEMBER

The Hare and the Fox

A certain deep forest was ruled over by a cruel fox. All the animals were afraid of him, and kept as far away from him as possible. On the edge of the forest, in a cosy little lair, there lived a clever hare. One day he got up early so as to go down to the fields for a taste of fresh cabbage. All of a sudden he found the fox standing in front of him, licking his lips greedily. "How dare you steal cabbages from another's field?" the fox snarled. "Take leave of this life, friend hare! For your impertinence I shall eat you!" The hare was frightened, but he soon recovered his wits, and said boldly, "Fool! Do you not know that these fields belong to my bride-to-be, the fairy of the lake? Just yesterday she sent for me; but I have no horse, as befits a rich bridegroom. If you carry me to her on your back, the fairy will reward you well." The foolish fox agreed. The hare smoothed down his coat like a noble gentleman, plucked a posy of flowers, and swung himself up on the fox's back. "Make way! I am on my way to visit my bride!" he called out, and he whipped the fox on until the hairs flew off his back. It was such a funny sight that all the animals rolled about with laughter.

18 NOVEMBER

The Hare and the Fox

When they reached the lake, the fox, his tongue hanging out, growled, "Where is your lake-fairy, hare? I want my reward!" The hare replied: "Dip your tail in the lake and wait; you will see that the fairy will hang something on it." No sooner had he said this, than he was gone. The foolish fox did as the hare told him, and waited, and waited. Days passed, then weeks, then months; winter came, and the lake froze over. "At last I have my reward," thought the fox, and he tried to pull his tail out of the lake, but it was stuck fast. "You have been too generous, lake-fairy," he whimpered. "I cannot lift your gifts; take some of them off!" But there was no fairy in the lake; it was only the clever hare's trick. In the end the dogs heard the cruel fox's cries, came running up, and tore him to pieces. From then on the animals of the forest had to put up with his tyranny no more.

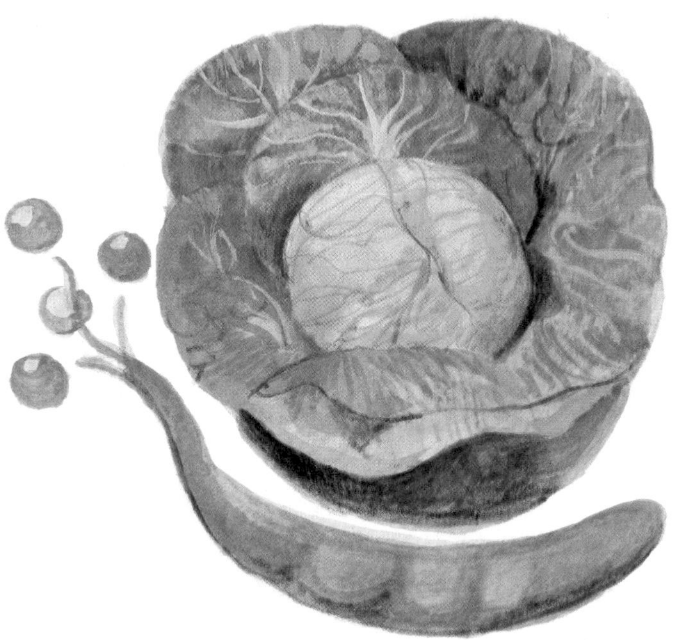

19 NOVEMBER

The Ungrateful Son

This is a tale the mother cat told her kittens. Listen: Once upon a time there was a poor widow who lived with her son on the shores of a great lake. The boy was called Si Angui. One day he asked his mother, "Mother, what is on the far side of the lake?" His mother sang to him: "On the far bank happiness abides, once he may cross over to our side."—"But, mother," said Si Angui in surprise, "does not happiness dwell with us? I have my own little cat and my own dear dog, my own mat to sleep on, and the tsai-tsai lizard; I have you to stroke my head when I am asleep."—"It was only a kind of fairy tale," his mother told him, hiding the tears of love behind her hand. So they lived happily. But as time went by, Si

Angui found himself more and more often sending his eyes like two little nutshell boats across to the far bank of the lake. "I wonder what the realm of happiness is like?" he reflected, and he grew more silent day by day. One evening, as his glance again wandered about the lake, he spotted against the starry sky a white sail. Nearer and nearer it sailed, shining like the smile of the sun, singing in the breeze like a reed flute. "Mother!" cried Si Angui, "happiness is coming to us!"

20 NOVEMBER

The Ungrateful Son

They stood by the shore, waiting for happiness to reach their hovel. Si Angui could not imagine what happiness might look like; perhaps like a young girl with a skirt of leaves and a white spider in her raven hair. Or perhaps like an orchid on the River of Shadows. But when the boat reached the bank, out stepped an ugly, bald-headed old man in a parrot-feather headband. Si Angui could feel tears of disappointment welling up in his eyes. But the old man smiled warmly, and his face grew in beauty like a kindled flame. "I am the richest merchant in the island empire," he said to the boy's mother. "I have heard on my travels that you live alone with your son in humble circumstances—nay, in poverty. I have no heir to my fortune, so I would ask you, mother, to put Si Angui in my care. I shall teach him to sell salt and buy pearls; I shall reveal to him how to grow riches from cocoa beans. Mother, let your son sail with me to the other side of the lake!" The boy's mother hesitated. "You who wear bird feathers on your head," she said, "Si Angui is happy here." But then Si Angui cried out eagerly: "Why do you hold me back, mother? Let me sail across the lake and buy happiness! When I have become the richest man in the island empire I shall build a palace of pink coral, and then return for you and my dear animals." His mother began to weep, but then she knelt down and kissed Si Angui's feet.

"May the good spirits keep you on your journey, my son!" she said. And so Si Angui set out for the far side of the lake to buy happiness.

21 NOVEMBER

The Ungrateful Son

For a long, long time Si Angui travelled from island to island with the old man. He came to know the glint of gold and the misty beauty of pearls, and piled up more and more wealth as the days went by. But he did not find happiness. The richer he grew, the more his heart turned to stone. The old man, his faithful teacher and guide, looked at him one day with sad eyes. "My days are numbered, Si Angui," he whispered. "But before I die, I want to tell

you that you are not the boy I thought you were. Riches and splendour have turned your heart to stone. I wished to teach you the knowledge that happiness cannot be bought; but you spurn wisdom as the night spurns the sun. You are the poorest fellow in the island empire, Si Angui the rich! If you would bring your heart back to life, fulfil the promise you made to your mother. Return to her. Your happiness is again on the other bank." The old man finished speaking, smiled grimly, and before Si Angui's astonished eyes turned into a heap of sparkling diamonds. Si Angui had forgotten how to cry. He disregarded the old man's words, and with a cry of joy grasped the fairy-tale wealth in his hands. When he had got over the thrill, he cried out, "I shall fulfil my promise; but first I shall build a palace of pink coral. Then I shall take my mother there and find happiness at last."

22 NOVEMBER

The Ungrateful Son

Si Angui achieved his ambition. He built a splendid palace, and the rajah himself, the king of kings, gave him his beautiful daughter for his wife. So Si Angui became king. But his heart froze like an icy stone. One day he said to his wife, "Far across the sea and the jungle my mother lives alone, waiting for me. I have promised that one day I shall take her to my palace of pink pearl; it is time now to set off." His queen was happy to agree, and they set off at the head of a great procession towards the far-off lake. When they reached its bank, Si Angui whispered: "On the far shore happiness abides; once he may cross over to our side."—"What did you say?" whispered his wife. "It is only a kind of fairy tale," Si Angui replied. As their boats approached the far bank, a weak old woman in frayed old rags came out to greet them with open arms. Alongside her limped a scrawny cat and dog. "Si Angui, my son," she cried, and kissed the ground where he had trod. "Have you at last found happiness?" At that moment Si Angui broke into tears. He bitterly regretted leaving his mother in such straits. He knelt and embraced her knees. "Forgive me, mother; forgive me, faithful animals," he said. "My happiness is here with you; here I have found that which I had lost, and have searched for in vain throughout the world." No sooner had he said this than the stony weight around his heart fell away. At last Si Angui was happy.

23 NOVEMBER

The Magic Pot and the Magic Balls

There was once a sexton who was as poor as . . . well, as poor as a church mouse. One winter's day, when there was scarcely a scrap of food left in their cottage, he sent his wife to town to sell the last of the chickens, so that they might pay off their debts. The woman was soon exhausted from plodding through the snow, and she sat down on the edge of the forest to take a rest. Suddenly a bearded little man appeared before her. "If you wish," he told her, "I shall give you this magic pot for your hen. All you have to do is to cover it and say 'pot-belly, fill yourself'. The pot will at once cook whatever you happen to fancy to eat. But mark my words, you must never wash the pot, or it will go ill with you!" The woman believed him, and gave the little fellow the hen in return for his pot. The strange man sat on the bird, spurred it on, and rode off into the forest. When she got home the sexton was angry with her, but she set the pot down on the table and ordered it: "Pot-belly, fill yourself!" In an instant the pot was filled with the most delicious foods. From then on the pot would cook them anything they cared to think of. But the sexton's wife was unhappy that the pot was getting dirtier day by day, and one day she could resist no longer: she put it in the wash-tub and began to scour it with sand, until it shone like gold. All of a sudden something or other struck her such a blow on the head that stars swam before her eyes, and the pot went bouncing off into the woods.

24 NOVEMBER

The Magic Pot and the Magic Balls

From the moment the magic pot disappeared into the forest, want and hunger came to the sexton's cottage again. One day the sexton led their lamb out of the shed and said to his wife: "I shall go and try my luck; perhaps I, too, may meet the little man." And off he went. On the edge of the forest he sat down on a fallen treetrunk and waited to see what would happen. Suddenly a voice said, "Welcome, sexton! If you wish, I shall give you this wooden ball in exchange for your lamb." The sexton turned, and saw standing behind him the magic little man. "A lamb for a wooden ball?" he wondered, but the little man smiled. "You will not be sorry, you'll see. When you get home, shut all the doors and windows carefully, place the ball on the floor, and tell it: 'bow politely, now'. You'll see what happens!" The sexton did not hesitate for long, and he gave the little man his lamb; the manikin sat on its back, spurred it on, and rode off into the forest. As soon as the sexton got home, he impatiently placed the wooden ball on the floor and ordered it to bow as the manikin had told him. The ball began to turn round and round, at first slowly, then gradually faster and faster; then, suddenly, it split in half like an apple, and out leapt tiny little dwarfs. Some were carrying a tablecloth, others gold plates, dishes and cutlery, and others tureens full of food. The sexton and his wife and children feasted as if they were at a royal banquet. When they had eaten and drunk their fill, the little men cleared the table and disappeared again into the wooden ball.

25 NOVEMBER

The Magic Pot and the Magic Balls

The sexton's good fortune was short-lived. The parson got to hear about his magic wooden ball. "It is surely the devil's work!" he cried, and took the magic ball away from him.

He promised to put up the sexton's wages, but he forgot to say when. As things grew worse and worse for the poor man and his family, he set off for the forest with their calf on a lead. Again the manikin appeared, and he gave the sexton for his calf another wooden ball, only

this time much larger than the first. When the sexton put it down on the floor, out of it jumped a pair of giants with clubs; they beat the unhappy sexton half to death, then disappeared back into the ball. The sexton had an idea. He took the wooden ball off to the parson. The parson had guests, and the little dwarfs could hardly keep up with their eating and drinking. "I have brought you something better!" the sexton told the parson. Filled with curiosity, the parson put the large ball on the floor, and ordered it, "Bow politely, now!" At his words out leapt the two giants and set about the parson and his guests without mercy. When they had finished, the sexton caught up both the balls and rushed off home. After that he and his family again wanted for nothing—but not for long. One day someone forgot to close the door; the magic balls rolled off into the forest, and were never seen again.

26 NOVEMBER

The Boy, His Sister and the Little Mouse

A long time ago, it must be two or three days now, a little mouse came floating along to a little boy in a little boat. The mouse had been all the way to the sky. Quite by chance, the little boy was just building a mountain of pebbles so that he could get to the sky. He took the mouse in and promised that one day, when he was bigger, he and the mouse and his sister would climb up together among the stars. They had not managed it yet, but the boy said that did not matter. It might be more fun to long for something than to have it. He took the old flute out of Grandfather's chest and began to play this and that. It sounded wonderful. The little mouse listened and listened, and then said, "I shall never forget that you wanted to take me to the skies. Even if we never got there, what a beautiful journey it has been! More beautiful than a dark mousehole, brighter than a golden grain of rye. Thank you for playing the flute." And he disappeared down a mousehole.

27 NOVEMBER

The Lost Letter

In a certain city the postboy was delivering the mail. There were sad letters and merry ones, ordinary ones and special ones, important ones and silly ones—in short, all sorts. Suddenly the wind blew the letters out of the postboy's bag. It wouldn't have mattered much, except for one little letter which was very important. It was written by a young prince who had gone out into the world, and it was to tell his princess that soon, very soon, he would return to make her his wife. The princess had waited in vain for news

of him, and she grew sadder day by day. No one was able to cheer her up. The young postboy was upset, too, that he hadn't delivered all the mail, the way a postboy is supposed to do, come rain or shine or earthquake. He was ashamed to go back to the postmaster, and he went off instead to look for the lost letters. He searched and searched, until finally he had found all those letters which were only ordinary, but not that one letter which was so important. It is a wonder the princess didn't cry her eyes out. But suddenly there appeared a carrier pigeon, carrying the letter in his beak. The postboy cried out with joy and took the letter to the sad princess; her tearstained cheeks burst into a smile like the cherry trees burst into bloom in spring. It was a stroke of luck, for otherwise the postboy would have had to roam the world back and forth to this very day. And what about the prince and the princess? Well, they got married, and sent letters to all good people to tell them.

28 NOVEMBER

The Little Spark-Girl

A couple of little urchins were sitting by the wayside thinking to themselves, "If only we had a little fire, we might cook ourselves some sausages!" Suddenly, out of nowhere, a little spark appeared on the ground in front of them. "I am the Spark-Girl," she said politely, and bowed to the boys. "Will you play with me if I light a fire for you?" The lads were only too happy to promise. They brought some dry twigs and branches, then the Spark-Girl danced a merry dance, and the fire was soon blazing brightly. When the boys had roasted their sausages and eaten their fill, the Spark-Girl begged them, "Come and play with me now for a while!"—"Huh! We don't play with girls," said the lads, putting out their tongues at her. And they began to jump and play about the fire. Now if sparks could cry, the little Spark-Girl would surely have burst into tears with disappointment; as it is, they must not, or they would put themselves out. She just frowned crossly, spun her fiery skirt around, and called out: "Abracadabra!" Then, as the boys were dancing around the fire, a shower of glowing embers leapt out of it and shot into their trousers. You should have seen them run for the stream! They sat down in the water with a hiss; but that did not mend the holes they had burnt in their trousers. They got a good hiding at home on top of their scorching, and they would gladly have begged the Spark-Girl's forgiveness, but she never appeared to them again.

29 NOVEMBER

The Queen of the Snakes

Once upon a time a young shepherd-girl found a snake under a briar. It was half-starved, and its skin had been torn by the talons of some voracious bird. The girl took pity on the snake, tended its wounds, and even gave it some milk to drink from her cup. The snake soon recovered a little and crawled away. The girl went on with her work. Some time later a poor young farm-lad came to ask her father for her hand. But her father was a rich peasant, and did not want such a poor fellow for his son-in-law, so he showed the lad the door. The shepherdess cried and begged her father in vain; she could not get him to change his mind. So she ran out of the house and into the fields, and sat down beneath the briar. Then a snake came crawling up to her and hissed: "What ails you, child? I shall help you if I can."—"How can you help," sighed the shepherd-girl; but she told the snake all about her troubles, just the same. "Make me a garland of wild flowers," the snake said, when it had heard her sad tale. The girl did as she was told, and the snake at once had another request: "Kiss my forehead, good child; I am alone in the world, and no one loves me." The shepherd-girl shuddered with disgust, but when she saw the sad snake's eyes, she overcame her horror and kissed it. In an instant flames flew out of the earth and burned her father's farm to the ground.

30 NOVEMBER

The Queen of the Snakes

When the young girl saw the terrible misfortune which had befallen her home, she wept more than ever. "You have rewarded me ill, ungrateful snake!" she complained, certain that it was the snake's doing. She ran home to offer at least words of comfort to her father; but words cannot make up for lost riches. The once-wealthy farmer had to set off into the world with his daughter at his side and a beggar's stick in his hand. From that time on he met with misfortune wherever he went, and at every turn a snake with a garland of wild flowers would appear before him. Meanwhile, the poor farmhand was getting on better every day, and before long he had become the richest farmer in the village. Folk told strange tales of him; they said that his fields were guarded by a fiery snake, and that it laid gold pieces on his doorstep at night. Before long the faithful young man came again to ask the now poor peasant for the hand of the beautiful shepherd-girl. This time the old man gave his blessing gratefully, and begged the young farmer for forgiveness. Before long there was a fine wedding in the village. When the celebrations were at their height, a snake came crawling up to their door, with a tiny fairy wearing a garland of wild flowers sitting on its back. "I am the queen of the snakes," she said to the bride. "I have rewarded you for your kind heart. Remember that it is an ill wind which blows no one any good. Only the want in which your father found himself softened his hard heart." Then the fairy smiled, and disappeared for ever.

DECEMBER

1 DECEMBER

The Tale from the Cottage in the Snows

Far away from here, in the midst of the deep snows, is a cottage where three little snowmen live. During the day they play just like other children, sledging, skating, and even bicycling into town for strawberry ice-cream; but the moment night falls and the moon lights up the icicles outside, they sit down at their snow-table and tell each other fairy tales from the land of snow and ice. I once went to visit them, so I can tell you one of those stories. Maybe this one:

Once upon a time there was a little girl called Nawarana. She lived in a little snow-house in a land far off to the north, where in summer the sun never sets and in winter it never even shows itself in the sky. Instead of the sun the sky is filled with twinkling stars, the moon shines, and the glimmering aurora thrusts out its luminous fingers. The long, crystal night holds sway. Throughout those endless winter nights Nawarana would sit in her snowy parlour, listening to tales of great polar bears that roam the skies, or of the white whale with the golden hair. Even though the frost outside was as keen as a knife, it was as warm and cosy in the little snow-house as in a feather-bed, and as Nawarana went to sleep, she would dream that the wise reindeer fairy had turned her into a beautiful snowflake, bringing people luck.

2 DECEMBER

The Tale from the Cottage in the Snows

Do you know who the reindeer fairy is? She is a kind, white reindeer hind who grants everyone's secret wishes. Nawarana knew this very well, which is why she dropped a glistening little tear into the flames of the fire every day. That was so that the reindeer magician in her silent realm of snow would hear the voices of people's dreams, as one wise old woman used to say. Nawarana was happy in her home made of frozen snow, and the only thing that troubled her was her mischievous elder brother. He was never up to any good. He would stick cold icicles in her hair and drop icy snow down the back of her reindeer-skin coat. Ow! How cold it was! Nawarana would have tears in her eyes, but she was afraid to tell anyone, in case her brother got his own back some way. One day, when their mother and father were out hunting on the frozen sea, her brother teased her so much that she could stand it no longer. She ran out in tears into the dark polar night, sobbing, "Reindeer fairy, reindeer fairy, take me off somewhere where my brother may no longer trouble me!" At that moment she thought she saw, far off across the tundra, the flash of a white reindeer hind. Around its head shone a veil of glimmering polar light.

3 DECEMBER

The Tale from the Cottage in the Snows

Little Nawarana flew along towards the shadow of the reindeer fairy like a little bird. She ran through the crystal polar night, calling, "Reindeer fairy, reindeer fairy, wait for little Nawarana!" But the white wraith suddenly dissolved like a cloud, and the aurora that surrounded it was extinguished. Nawarana wandered, lost, about the endless snowy plains. How long she trekked across those icy wastes she did not know herself. But she suddenly found herself at the foot of a range of tall mountains. Up and up she climbed, until at long last she arrived on a broad plain. But, strange to relate, the ground began to shudder beneath her feet, like when the crust of ice on the sea begins to crack. Boom, boom, boom! she heard from beneath. Startled, Nawarana began to run across the plain, but another tall mountain rose up in her path. It was covered all over in thick forests; in the midst of the forest yawned a fearsome gorge, out of which a fierce wind howled, like when a storm is blowing up at sea. Terrified, Nawarana climbed to the very peak of the mountain, whose sharp point thrust up out of the forest. Then a terrible voice roared out: "What will you here, hapless child? Am I to swallow you up?" Nawarana looked round fearfully, but she could see no one. Who was calling?

4 DECEMBER

The Tale from the Cottage in the Snows

When Nawarana heard that terrible voice, her knees shook with fear. "Who is calling me?" she piped up in a thin little voice. "Are you a good spirit, or an evil one?"—"Aah, foolish woman!" said the voice. "I am Kinak, the snow giant, and you are sitting on the end of my nose. It tickles so terribly that soon I shall sneeze!" And the giant gave such a sneeze that Nawarana just managed to hold on to a mole on the giant's nose, so as not to fall off. "You have been climbing over me for several days now," grunted Kinak. "You tickled me under the heart, and you crawled in my beard—just like a flea. Who might you be, anyway?" Nawarana told the giant who she was, and why she was wandering alone through the polar night. "I thought the reindeer fairy must have sent you to me," said Kinak. "She is my sister, and she knows well enough how lonely I am. I am so big that I cannot even stand up, so as not to trample on anyone, so I just lie here on my back the whole time, pining for someone I can be fond of. If you like, you may stay here; you can put up a tent right beside my nose. Only take care not to roll into my mouth!" It was only then that Nawarana realized that the terrible gorge from which the fierce wind was blowing was in fact the giant's huge mouth. But Kinak had such a kindly voice that she decided to stay.

5 DECEMBER

The Tale from the Cottage in the Snows

Nawarana put up a tent of reindeer skins beside the giant's nose, and lived there for a long time with her herd of reindeer, which the giant caught for her in the palm of his hand. She had a fine time. She told the snow-giant fairy tales she had heard at home, and as a reward he let her catch fish in his eyes, which were as deep as a couple of lakes. But one day Kinak heard a quiet sobbing. "What is the matter, Nawarana, are you homesick?" he asked. "Very homesick," she admitted. "Perhaps father and mother are already crying for me."—"Well," grunted the giant, "it would be better if you were to go back home. Anyway, I cannot move on your account, in case I might crush you, and I cannot sneeze, for fear of blowing you away. You will be better off at home. And if your brother should bother you again, just you call me!" Then he took Nawarana carefully in the palm of his hand, blew with all his might, and sent her floating through the air like a snowflake, right down to the door of her snow-house. "Where have you been so long?" her brother snapped at her angrily, and he was just about to teach her a lesson when she called out: "Kinak, Kinak, help me, my brother wants to hurt me!" At that moment the distant giant sneezed so mightily that the wicked brother rolled for three days and three nights across the snowfields. When he finally got back home, he never troubled Nawarana again. He believed that she was hand-in-glove with the spirits of the snows.

6 DECEMBER

The Waterman and the Dog

There was once a waterman called Walter. He loved to climb out of his stream at night

and go for a walk. His mother would warn him, "Don't you go wandering about on dry land, young man, you know very well that where there is no water it is no place for a waterman!" But Walter would not listen. One night he met a lonely little dog. "Let us be friends," said the dog. "I am quite alone in the world." The waterman took pity on the lonesome creature, and would play with him every night until his mother called him home. But one day some naughty boys saw him. "Look! A waterman!" they called. "Let us drive him away from the water; then we can tie him up with strips of bark and sell him to a circus!" And they ran after him. They drove him farther and farther from the water; the further away he got, the weaker he grew. He looked around desperately for some puddle or other, but there was not a drop of water in sight. He had given up all hope of ever being free again, when the faithful dog appeared, lifted his leg, and made a puddle. "Hurrah!" cried the waterman, wet himself all over, and dashed straight to the stream, where he splashed his way back home. But his mother had to give him a good wash. And you should have seen the scolding he got!

7 DECEMBER

The Tale of the Lost Alphabet

A long, long time ago there was only one single fairy tale in the whole wide world; but it

was so long that no one ever got to the end of it. All the fairy-tale stories that ever were fitted inside it. But one day a naughty wind came along and mischievously blew the fairy-tale alphabet off in all directions. Since then no one has been able to put the story together again. But whenever anyone comes across at least a letter of it, the letter tells him a little bit of that endless tale. Look, the dove, clever fellow, has just found the letter R.
I wonder what the R will tell us?
Once upon a time there were a young mother and father who had seven sons, but no daughter. They so wanted to have a daughter, and when at last a little girl was born, they looked after her like a crock of gold. One day the father sent his sons to bring water from the well, wishing to bathe his daughter in her little gold bath. But the boys began to play down at the well, and did not return for a long time. Their father said angrily, "I wish you lads would be turned into black rooks for this!" Scarcely had he said these words, when seven black rooks rose up from the well and began to fly in circles around the countryside, wailing loudly. And how does the story go on? This letter won't tell us any more; we'll have to wait for another one.

8 DECEMBER

The Tale of the Lost Alphabet

Look, a scruffy little bird is scrawling the letter S on the blackboard for us. Let us ask how the story goes on. Like this? When the hapless father found that his careless curse had really turned his sons into rooks, he nearly died of grief. Luckily his lovely little daughter remained to assuage his sadness. She grew and grew, and when she grew up into a young woman, she was beautiful beyond compare. One day she found seven boy's shirts in an old trunk, and her parents had to tell her all about her brothers. When the girl heard the story, she decided to go out into the world to seek her brothers. First she went to the sun. "Sun, dear sun, tell me where I may find my

enchanted brothers!" she called, but the sun did not answer and glared until her poor rags were burnt. She ran off in tears to see the moon, so that she might cool down. "Moon, kind moon, show me the way to my lost brothers," she begged. But such an icy blast of air came from the moon that the poor girl was changed into a silver snowgirl. At the end of her strength she just managed to reach the stars. But another letter will have to go on with the story now.

9 DECEMBER

The Tale of the Lost Alphabet

Oh, look! The busy birds have turned up a magic letter C somewhere or other. We can go on listening now. When the girl got to the stars, the Morning Star smiled at her sweetly and said, "Dear child, your brothers are prisoners in the glass mountain. I shall give

you a little bone to take with you. When you get to the glass mountain, you must use the bone to open it." Then she showed the girl the way, and took leave of her. A rainbow stretched itself across the sky; the little sister stepped onto it and walked across it like a bridge until she reached the glass mountain. But when she looked in her bundle for the bone the Morning Star had given her, she could not find it. She knew at once what she must do; she cut off her little finger and used it to open the gate in the glass mountain. In the courtyard on the other side stood an ugly dwarf. "I know why you are here," he told her. "But if you wish to release your brothers you must with your bare hands pick glass nettles, spin from them a glass thread, weave the thread into cloth, and from that cloth sew seven glass shirts. If you cannot do this by morning, you too will become a black rook, and will remain enchanted with your brothers for ever more."

10 DECEMBER

The Tale of the Lost Alphabet

See, that sooty little sparrow has found a magic letter K in the chimney. What story will it tell us? Maybe this one: The girl was not dismayed by the dwarf's words. With her bare hands she plucked glass nettles, paying no regard to the stinging pain; she spun glass thread, wove glass cloth, and sewed seven glass shirts. She sewed and sewed all night long, and nearly went quite blind from peering at her work. The sun was slowly thrusting golden fingers over the horizon; but the girl had one more sleeve to sew on the last of the seven shirts. Then she heard the beating of wings above her head, and seven rooks appeared. "Hurry, dear sister," they called. "The sun is rising!" Without delay the girl threw each of them a glass shirt. At that moment there was a thundrous roar; the glass mountain changed into a golden palace, and there, in front of the girl, stood seven sturdy young men, her brothers. Only the seventh, whose sleeve she had not finished, had a black wing instead of one of his arms; but this did nothing to spoil their joy. They all joined hands and hurried home to their mother and father. Then they all went together to the golden palace. They live there happily to this day. The ugly dwarf had disappeared, no one knows where to, and the magic letter did not tell us. Why don't you have a look for some more of the magic alphabet?

11 DECEMBER

The Otter Queen

In a certain woodland pool there once blossomed a lovely flower. It played and sang such beautiful songs that all who passed that way had to dance whether they liked it or not, until the flower strummed a quiet lullaby. A young king heard tell of this flower, and wanted to bring it to his palace. He journeyed to the pool, jumped in the water, and swam to the deepest part of the pool. But the moment he touched the flower an old otter thrust her head out of the water. "How dare you steal flowers from my royal treasury?" she asked, angrily; she touched the king with a reed wand, and he turned into a beautiful pearl. This sank slowly to the bottom of the pool. "You shall lie here until someone has shed for you as many tears as there are drops of water in this pool," the otter told him, and disappeared in the murky water.

12 DECEMBER

The Otter Queen

When the king did not return for a long time, his mother set out for the pool to seek him. The magic flower was singing a song about an enchanted pearl; when the king's mother heard the song, she sat down on the bank and began to weep. She wept until she had no more tears, but it was still not enough. Then drops of blood began to flow from her eyes. When she had cried away all the blood in her body, the old otter emerged from the water and dropped the pearl at her feet. It turned miraculously back into the young king. From the enchanted flower a beautiful young girl stepped out, swam to the bank, and kissed the dead queen. At that the queen opened her eyes and began to smile. "Thank you, mother, for setting us free," said the king and the young girl. All three of them joined hands and hurried to the royal castle. "May you live in happiness!" the otter queen called after them. And they did.

13 DECEMBER

The Clockwork Steamer

A little boy was once given a clockwork steamer by his grandfather. He filled the bath with water, wound it up, and off it steamed across the water. But what do you think? All of a sudden huge waves got up, and the little lake became the open sea. The toy steamer turned into a real steamer, smoke billowing from its funnel like from granddad's big cigar, and siren hooting fit to deafen you. The little boy clapped his hands gleefully at this wonder, and before you could count to five he had stepped aboard, strode up to the helm, and gave the order: "Full steam ahead!" The steamer leapt across the waves like a horse spurred on by its rider, and made for the horizon. Merry fishes scudded past in the water, seabirds wheeled above the waves, and the great ocean-going steamships greeted the steamer politely with their flags. "Where are you bound for?" the sailors called from the passing ships. The boy stood by the helm, saluted and proudly replied: "We are sailing to discover America!"—"Bon voyage!" called back the sailors, and waved them on their way. Then the steamer wound down, grew smaller and smaller, and once more became just an ordinary little toy steamer, and the great ocean changed back into an ordinary bath of water. What a pity! The boy would surely have discovered his America. No matter that Columbus has already discovered it long ago! Little boys will always discover it over and over again.

14 DECEMBER

The Queen and the Knight

Once a little girl found an old chess set in the attic. All the figures had long since been lost, except for a knight on a lame horse and a sad queen. The little girl played with them, but the queen grew sadder every day, and the knight looked so unhappy that the girl herself burst into tears. "It is raining!" said the sad queen, and she opened a little umbrella over her head. "Oh dear, raining," said the downfallen knight, and hurried to hide under an umbrella, too. The queen strutted up and down in the salty rain of tears, accompanied by her faithful knight, who reminded her of the good old days, when he and her lost husband would ride out into battle together. The more they remembered, the more abandoned they felt. The little girl did not know how to cheer them up. But one day she found the lost figures in an old cupboard, and laid them out on the squares of the chessboard. Soon there was the sound of joyful trumpet calls from the castle battlements; the queen smiled and she and the king embraced, sat down on their thrones, and ordered a magnificent tournament to begin. When the jousting was over, the old knight and the queen bowed graciously to the little girl, and gave her two little umbrellas as a keepsake. They never needed them again.

15 DECEMBER

How the Animals Wanted to Build a House

In a certain zoo there lived a giraffe, a monkey, a parrot and a sparrow. "Let us build ourselves a house!" they said one day, and at once began to discuss what sort of a house they were to build. The giraffe said, "It must have a roof up to the skies, so that I may get my head inside it."—"But inside it there must be trees with nuts and thick branches, so that I may swing from them by my tail," said the monkey. Then the parrot said that it should swing in the air like a cage, and have a perch and a grain trough and all sorts of other things. "Oh, no," said the sparrow. "Our house shall be of grass and twigs, and small and cosy like a sparrow's nest, so that the wind cannot get in." In the end they decided to build a house which would suit everyone. They built and built, but they never managed to build that house. It was either too big, or it was too small, or it was too this, or it was not enough that. "There is nothing for it," sighed

the monkey at last. "Only children can paint a house like that for everyone. When the children come, we shall ask them to think up a house for us." And to this day they are waiting for someone to come along and paint them a lovely house that will suit them all. When you wake up in the morning, why don't you try and paint it for them?

16 DECEMBER

Snow White and the Seven Dwarfs

Sitting beside the window, the happy queen sewed and sewed. Little coats and caps she sewed, and as she sewed she smiled sweetly to herself. She was looking forward to the baby that was soon to be born to her. It was winter, and outside the snow was falling and the little white flakes were settling on the black, black ebony window frames. Before she knew it, the daydreaming queen had pricked herself with the needle. She opened the window to cool the sore finger, and three little drops of crimson blood ran down into the snow. The queen smiled. "Oh, how I should like my child to be as white as the freshly fallen snow, with cheeks as red as blood and hair as black as ebony," she thought to herself. It was not long before her wish was granted. A little girl was born to her who looked just as she had hoped. They called her Snow White. But joy and grief go hand in hand in this world, and soon after the child was born her mother died. Before the year was out the king had brought a new wife to the palace. She was exceedingly lovely, but as she was beautiful, so was she cruel, proud and wanton. She knew spells and magic, and every morning she would look at herself in her magic mirror and ask it: "Mirror, mirror, on the wall, who is the fairest of us all?" And the mirror would reply: "Mistress, by my troth I vow, yours is far the fairest brow." And the proud queen would kiss the mirror.

17 DECEMBER

Snow White and the Seven Dwarfs

The years went by, and Snow White grew up into a lovely young girl. When she reached the age of seventeen she was as beautiful as a forest nymph, and far, far more beautiful than the queen herself. Then, one day, the queen again stood before her magic mirror and asked it with a smile: "Mirror, mirror, on the wall, who is the fairest of us all?" But the mirror darkened and said: "Mistress, by my troth I vow, Snow White is the fairest now!" The queen flew into such a rage that she could not sleep that night for envy and anger. The next day she called one of the royal hunters to her and ordered him to lead Snow White deep into the forest and to kill her there. "To prove that you have done it, you shall bring me her heart," she told him. What was the poor hunter to do? If he did not obey her, the queen would have his head cut off. So, like it or not, he had to lead Snow White off into the deepest and thickest part of the forest. The beautiful child suspected nothing, and she drew such pleasure from the song of the birds, the scent of the flowers and the antics of the woodland creatures that the hunter took pity on her. He told Snow White what fate her stepmother had ordained for her, and warned her not to return home. Then he shot a fawn and took its heart back to the wicked queen. She threw it into the fire with an evil smile.

18 DECEMBER

Snow White and the Seven Dwarfs

Poor Snow White wandered through the deep forest, not even able to see her way for tears. Finally she dragged her weary feet into a woodland clearing. In it stood a little cottage such as no human eye had ever seen before. It was all of moss and pine cones, and from the windows fireflies glowed. Snow White knocked gently, and when no one answered she tiptoed inside. How lovely it was in there! There was a tiny parlour, as spick and span as a gleaming new pin. In the middle of it stood a table, on which there lay a white tablecloth and seven little plates. Beside each plate was a golden knife, fork and spoon, and behind it a golden goblet. Over by the wall there were seven little beds with snowy sheets. The poor girl was so hungry and tired that she took a mouthful of food from each of the little plates, drank a sip from each of the goblets, so as not to leave anyone short, and then lay down in each of the little beds. In the seventh she curled up and fell fast asleep. When darkness fell, seven little dwarfs came marching and singing into the cottage, and

made straight for the table. Suddenly, they stood as if struck by lightning. Do you know why?

19 DECEMBER

Snow White and the Seven Dwarfs

The dwarfs stood gazing at the table with their mouths wide open. "Who's been sitting on my chair?" wondered the first. "Who's been eating from my plate?" grumbled the second. "Who has broken a piece off my bread?" asked the third. "Who has been eating my vegetables?" said the fourth. "Who has been using my fork?" complained the fifth. "Who has been cutting with my knife?" cried the sixth, and the seventh exclaimed, "Who has been drinking from my cup?" Then the first dwarf looked round and saw his ruffled bedsheets. "Someone has been lying in my bed!" he announced. "In mine too, in mine too!" called the next five, one after the other, but the seventh saw Snow White still lying in his bed. The others gathered round him and shone their firefly lamps on her. "How beautiful she is!" they breathed, and so as not to wake her they crept quietly into bed. The seventh dwarf slept for a while in each of his companions' beds, and so they all slept well. When Snow White woke up in the morning she was startled to see the seven little men, but they looked at her so affably that she tearfully told them her sad story. The dwarfs put their heads together, and then the first one said: "If you will keep house for us, wash, sew, cook and clean, then you may stay here. But do not open the door to anyone while we are out; your evil stepmother will soon find out that you have not perished in the forest." And so Snow White stayed on in the cottage of the seven dwarfs.

20 DECEMBER

Snow White and the Seven Dwarfs

One day the proud queen again stepped in front of the magic mirror and said: "Mirror, mirror, on the wall, who is the fairest of us all?" But the mirror darkened, and replied: "Mistress, by my troth I vow, Snow White is fairer still than thou!" The queen knew now that the hunter had tricked her, and she fell into such a rage that sparks flew from her wicked eyes. Without delay she dressed up as an old pedlar-woman and set out for the cottage of the seven dwarfs. The enchanted mirror had told her the way. When she got there, she knocked on the shutters and called out to Snow White in a sweet, enticing voice: "Buy a pretty lace for your bodice, my dear." Snow White did not recognize her wicked stepmother, and in the end she let herself be persuaded. She bought a golden lace for her bodice, and the old woman willingly offered to tie it for her. When the trustful girl agreed, her stepmother pulled the lace so tight that the poor child could not breathe, and fell lifeless to the ground. There the dwarfs found her that evening when they returned home from their underground caverns.

21 DECEMBER

Snow White and the Seven Dwarfs

When the dwarfs saw Snow White lying there in a deep faint, they quickly cut the lace of her bodice, and in a while she came to her senses. "Never open the door again!" her little friends warned her. Snow White was sure she would remember their advice. Meanwhile, back in the palace, the stepmother again asked the magic mirror who was the fairest. But again it told her: "Mistress, by my troth I vow, Snow White is fairer still than thou!" She was so enraged that her heart almost broke. She hurried to her magic chamber and prepared a silver comb covered in poison. Then she dressed up as a different pedlar-woman and set out for the cottage of the dwarfs. "Buy a pretty comb for your hair, my dear," she enticed her beautiful step-daughter. Snow White refused to open the door, but when the old woman coaxed her and cajoled her, she finally took the comb through the window and pushed it into her beautiful black hair. At once she fell to the ground and lay there motionless. When the dwarfs got home in the evening, they wrung their hands in despair over the poor girl. But the youngest and smallest of them found the poisoned comb in her hair and drew it out, and Snow White came to life again. You should have heard the scolding she got! In the meantime the queen had got back to the palace, and she rushed off to ask the mirror her question. But the mirror again replied: "Mistress, by my troth I vow, Snow White is fairer still than thou!" The queen turned white with anger.

22 DECEMBER

Snow White and the Seven Dwarfs

This time the wicked stepmother dressed up as a poor peasant woman. She took with her a basket of sweet-scented apples. Half of one of them contained a strong poison. When she got to the cottage she tried to persuade Snow White to buy the poisoned apple, but the girl was suspicious. "You need have no fear, my dear!" the envious queen told her, and took a bite herself from the good side of the apple. When Snow White saw this she was no longer afraid, and bit into the poisoned half of the apple. In an instant she fell dead. This time the dwarfs, do what they would, could not revive her; Snow White did not wake up. Weeping and wailing, the kindhearted dwarfs laid her in a silver coffin and placed a glass lid over it. Then they carried her to the top of a woodland mound, where the birds and animals of the forest guarded her night and day. One day a handsome young prince rode past, and when he saw the beautiful Snow White in her coffin, he begged them to allow him to carry the lovely creature off with him to his royal palace. The dwarfs would not hear of it at first, but finally they agreed. The prince's servants carried Snow White in her coffin along the forest paths. Suddenly, one of them stumbled over the root of a tree; the coffin fell to the ground, and the piece of

poisoned apple was jerked from Snow White's throat. She sat up and looked around her in astonishment. The prince and the dwarfs were struck dumb with joy. The prince led Snow White off to his castle, and before long a magnificent wedding had been prepared. Among those they invited was the wicked stepmother. She stood proudly in front of the magic mirror and asked who was the fairest. "Fairest is she who, though she died, now lives to be the prince's bride!" said the mirror. The queen was so furious that she hurled the mirror to the ground; at that moment her cruel heart shattered to a thousand pieces.

23 DECEMBER

The Tree of the Abandoned Children

When the first flakes of snow begin to fall and the frost glazes over the rivers and lakes, in a certain silent forest a magic tree lights up. Its candles kindle, its ornaments glitter, and on each little twig a beautiful present grows for some abandoned child. Day and night the birds fly to and fro, carrying the gifts all over the world. As soon as they pluck from it one of the toys, another grows in its place. Once upon a time there lived, not far from that forest, a rich little boy. I don't know how it came about, but one day he wandered into the woods and happened to come across the magic tree. "Oh, how beautiful it is! It must be just for me!" he cried, and he ran home to fetch a saw; then he cut the tree down and planted it in the garden in front of his window. In vain did the tree beg him and beseech him. That year not one sad, abandoned little child got a present for Christmas. The wicked boy could not wait for morning, so that he might pick what he fancied from the tree. But what a surprise the next day, when he found the tree withered and without a single present on it! And, strange to relate, the little boy himself was as dumb as a fish. "You shall not get back your speech until you take me back into the forest, and water me with your tears, so that I may grow green again," said the tree, sadly. The frightened boy carried the tree back into the forest and watered it with tears until its withered branches came back to life. At that instant he got back his speech. He hurried home to his mother and cried, "Mother, I do not want to be wicked any more!" And so once more the magic tree lights up in that forest every year. And every year the little boy comes along and hangs from its branches his own little present for the abandoned children.

24 DECEMBER

The Three Carollers

Once upon a time there was a little boy who simply could not wait for that silent, holy night to fall on the snow-covered countryside, and for that warm wish, "Peace to men of good will" to go echoing from each and every dwelling up to the starry skies. He stood alone in his room and gazed out of the frosted window at the gently falling snow. Whenever he breathed on the window-pane, new frost-flowers would grow there, and glisten in the light of the snow-decked street-lamps. They seemed to the boy to be playing a delicate, tinkling melody, which rose high, high up to the heavens, like a breeze. He smiled a happy smile. "I shall go to Bethlehem and play the baby Jesus a lullaby on my violin," he thought, suddenly. So he waited until all in the house were asleep, then he opened the window and, with his violin tucked under his arm, slid out into the street. He did not know which way to go, but he followed the wind which drove the little snowflakes, and soon it led him into a large and silent park. There, on a stone plinth, stood the statue of a beautiful young girl, softly plucking with her frozen fingers the strings of a lute. "Where are you going?" she asked the boy. "To Bethlehem, to play a lullaby on my violin for the baby Jesus," he replied. "I shall go with you," said the statue, tucking up her skirts and stepping down from her plinth. So off they went together to Bethlehem.

25 DECEMBER

The Three Carollers

For a long time they walked through the endless, frosty night. The boy began to grow afraid; his fingers and toes were cold, and tears came to his eyes like two clear little icicles. The stone girl comforted him, saying, "Don't cry, we shall soon be there!" but she did not know herself how far it was to Bethlehem, or whether they were going the right way, so she lightly plucked the strings of her lute to drive away their fear. They passed by a big snowman with a shining new coat of fresh-fallen flakes; they tried to speak to him, but he did not answer, for he was dreaming of the land of the great white clouds where his forefathers had come from. He only sighed happily and smiled in his sleep. Then the two of them spotted a little frozen bird on a branch nearby. "Come along with us!" they called. "We are off to Bethlehem to play for the baby Jesus."—"With pleasure," replied the bird, "for I am alone and sad." And so they wandered the darkened streets, full of hurrying people; but no one took any notice of them, and no one was surprised to meet a girl made of stone playing the lute, for on the nights before Christmas Eve miracles may happen in the world, and people may believe in them. Then the three lone wanderers left the town behind them and turned their steps towards the place where, on the distant horizon, an exquisite star was blazing.

26 DECEMBER

The Three Carollers

The pilgrims were at once sad and deeply happy. They had no idea how long they had walked when they saw before them a little cottage covered in snow. There was the scent of hay all around, and out of a shed came the

bleating of lambs and the braying of an ass. Just then the flame of a candle blazed up in the window, and it seemed to the lonely travellers that out of the flame there stepped a tiny Virgin Mary with Baby Jesus in her arms. She walked towards them and smiled sweetly. The little boy and the stone girl fell down on their knees, and whispered to the little bird to bow his head. He did it so beautifully that he was proud of himself. Then the girl struck the strings of her lute, the boy drew the bow across his violin, and the little bird sang a lullaby in a voice so sweet and pure that the very stars were moved to tears. When it had finished, all the bells in the land rang out and Christmas trees lit up everywhere. Then the whole world began to sing:

"Silent night, holy night . . ."

When the carol had died down, the pilgrims again bowed to the candle flame, and made their way home. The stone girl climbed back up on her plinth, the little bird went contentedly to sleep among the branches, and the little boy curled up in his mother's arms. When he woke up in the morning, he found beneath the Christmas tree the last five fairy tales. They were all stories he had never heard before, and the boy was happy.

27 DECEMBER

The Little Pine-Cone Sister

Once upon a time there were three little brothers. They were very fond of each other, but they were often sad just the same. "If only we had a little sister," they would say. One day they were walking in the woods, when a pine-cone tumbled down from one of the branches. "Here I am!" it called. The boys bent

over and, sure enough, it was no ordinary pine-cone, but a tiny girl in a skirt of cone-scales. The brothers were filled with joy. "Would you like to be our sister?" they asked. "I should love to," said the cone-girl, so with cries of glee the boys carried her off home. They looked after her, played with her, carved her a little bed from the bark of a pine tree; but all to no avail. After a while their little pine-cone sister began to hang her head, to cry and to waste away. "I am sad for my tree," she wailed one day. The boys put their heads together, then they set off for the woods again. "Forest, dear forest, give us a tree for our little sister!" they called. There was a rustle and a swish, and a beautiful little tree thudded to the ground. The brothers carried it home, planted it in the garden in front of their window, and hung the little cone-girl from one of the branches. Right away the colour came back to her cheeks; the little girl clapped her hands, laughed, and began to sing songs. Then all the birds came flying up and sang along with her. Since then the three little brothers have had in their garden a tree which is always singing.

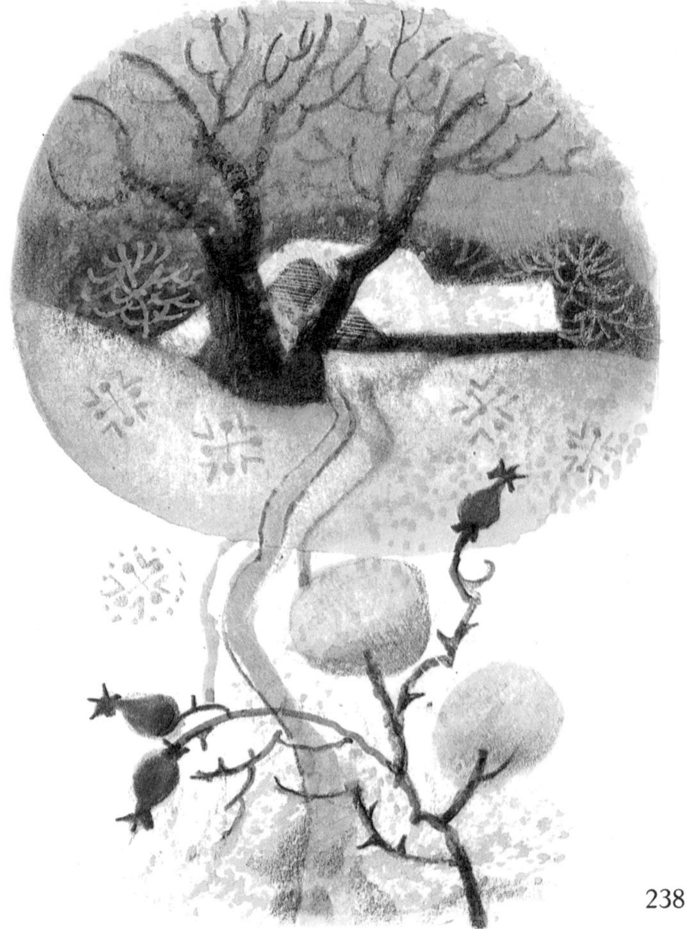

28 DECEMBER

The Ice Bird

There was once a little cottage where a wise old woman lived. She had two granddaughters, Sally and Polly. Sally was a good and obedient child, while Polly liked best of all to dress up, and did not help the old woman with anything. She declared that she was the most beautiful girl in the world, and that one day a fairytale prince would come to fetch her. One year the winter was particularly hard, and the snow covered the little cottage right to the eaves. Then a little bird came and perched in front of the cottage. He was made all of ice, and he sang so sadly and beautifully that your heart would break. "Poor thing," said Sally. "He must have been put under the ice-queen's spell. We shall set him free!" She and her sister ran out and Polly took the bird in her hands. "Brrrh, how cold he is!" she cried, and threw the bird down in the snow. He sang so sadly that tears came to Sally's eyes. She took the bird into the cottage, lay down in her bed, and clutched the poor creature to her heart. He chilled like ice, and Sally seemed to be turning into an icicle herself. She almost wept with cold and pain, but in the end she fell asleep. When she woke up in the morning, a golden-haired prince was lying beside her in her bed. "Thank you for setting me free," he

said. "You warmed me at your breast, and for that service I shall never leave you." And so it was not the wicked Polly but the good Sally who married a prince in the end.

29 DECEMBER

The Snow Princess

Long, long ago a poor potter lived all on his own. He had no one in the whole world, so on the long winter's evenings he often felt so sad he could have cried. One evening he went out onto the doorstep and watched the snow as it came tumbling down. He held out his hand, and one snowflake after another settled on his palm. The flakes quickly melted, but one of them suddenly changed into a beautiful little girl; she took hold of her white skirts and bowed politely. "I am the snow princess," she said, in a voice like tiny tinkling bells. "The winter queen has sent me to you, so that you may not be so lonely in the world." The potter rejoiced, and at once invited her into his warm parlour. "Oh dear, no!" she laughed. "If I were get just a little too warm I should melt away. Build me a little palace of snow; I shall live there, and you shall visit me every day. But don't forget your fur cap, so that your ears do not chap." The potter did as the snow princess asked, and he was no longer sad in the world. When spring came the snow palace melted in the sunshine, and the snow princess disappeared with it. But every year she returned, and she grew bigger and more beautiful every time. This went on for sixteen long years.

30 DECEMBER

The Snow Princess

Word soon got about that the poor potter had the most beautiful daughter of any in the land. Even the king himself heard the tale. He had a team of horses harnessed to a sleigh, and set off to see for himself. Oh, what a ride it was. The sleigh-bells jingled, and wherever the royal sleigh went flying past, the people fell to their knees and called: "Out of the way, the king is passing!" The monarch pulled up beside the snow princess's ice-palace, and out

stepped a girl as white and gleaming as fresh-fallen snow. The king could not take his eyes off her. "I want her for my wife, and no other," he cried. The potter was taken aback. The king was old and ugly, and people said he was cruel and ill-tempered to boot. No wonder the potter tried every way he could to get her out of it. But the king would not be dissuaded. "I shall give you whatever you ask for your daughter," he said. "If you refuse, you shall lose your head." Then the snow princess whispered in the potter's ear, "Do not worry, father. Take the king's signet ring and tell him I should like to receive him in my snow palace." The potter did as the snow princess had told him. He took the king's ring, and the king stepped proudly into the princess's chamber. At once the palace shone with icy hoarfrost, snow began to fall from the ceiling, and soon the cruel king turned into an icicle. His courtiers searched for him in vain. When spring came the sun's rays melted the snow palace and the princess and the wicked king with it. Because the potter had the king's seal, he became king. And the snow princess? The next year she came back again, and she was more beautiful than ever. But what had happened to the wicked king she did not say. Perhaps he has to serve the winter queen for ever more.

31 DECEMBER

The Dream Maker

Far, far away, in the starry realm of shadows, the Night Queen sits on her moon throne. In her clasped hands she holds, like a cup of holy water, a magic water-lily lake. The moment the sun has set on the Earth, the loveliest of the water-lilies spreads its petals, and on it there awake from their slumbers the Dream Maker and the kindly Night Fairy. Both of them are as transparent as a dewdrop, and

quite, quite invisible. The fairy's hair hangs in clear glass plaits, and her skirt is a crystal bell. The little Dream Maker will sprinkle stardust in her hair, or strike a tinkling note from her skirt with a slender moonbeam. Then the brittle melody rings out softly through the night, until sleep draws shut the eyelids of children the world over, as the Dream Maker croons his lullaby and stars drop from the heavens. Night is falling. The water-lily is spreading its petals. Can you hear? Out there in the distance someone is singing. The Dream Maker is calling you to his kingdom. Listen!

Ting-a-ling starbells, faintly ringing;
Moonshine, silver bright.
Fairy voices, softly singing,
Far off in the night.
Hush now, children, close your eyes:
Before your dreaming's done,
Dewdrops, tinkling from the skies,
Will greet the morning sun.

Contents

Chapters without author names were written by the editors.

See Targeted Therapy available online at **studentconsult.com**

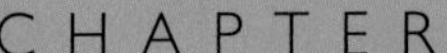

CHAPTER 1

Cell Injury, Cell Death, and Adaptations

CHAPTER CONTENTS

INTRODUCTION TO PATHOLOGY

Literally translated, *pathology* is the study (*logos*) of disease (*pathos*, suffering). It involves the investigation of the causes of disease and the associated changes at the levels of cells, tissues, and organs, which in turn give rise to the presenting signs and symptoms of the patient. There are two important terms that students will encounter throughout their study of pathology and medicine:

- *Etiology* is the origin of a disease, including the underlying causes and modifying factors. It is now clear that most common diseases, such as hypertension, diabetes, and cancer, are caused by a combination of inherited genetic susceptibility and various environmental triggers. Understanding the genetic and environmental factors underlying diseases is a major theme of modern medicine.
- *Pathogenesis* refers to the steps in the development of disease. It describes how etiologic factors trigger cellular and molecular changes that give rise to the specific functional and structural abnormalities that characterize the disease. Whereas etiology refers to *why* a disease arises, pathogenesis describes *how* a disease develops.

Defining the etiology and pathogenesis of disease not only is essential for understanding a disease but is also the basis for developing rational treatments. Thus, by explaining the causes and development of disease *pathology provides the scientific foundation for the practice of medicine.*

To render diagnoses and guide therapy in clinical practice, pathologists identify changes in the gross or microscopic appearance (*morphology*) of cells and tissues, and biochemical alterations in body fluids (such as blood and urine). Pathologists also use a variety of morphologic, molecular, microbiologic, and immunologic techniques to define the biochemical, structural, and functional changes that occur in cells, tissues, and organs in response to injury. Traditionally, the discipline is divided into general pathology and systemic pathology; the former focuses on the cellular and tissue alterations caused by pathologic stimuli in most tissues, while the latter examines the reactions and abnormalities of different specialized organs. In this book we first cover the broad principles of general pathology and then progress to specific disease processes in individual organs.

OVERVIEW OF CELLULAR RESPONSES TO STRESS AND NOXIOUS STIMULI

Cells are active participants in their environment, constantly adjusting their structure and function to accommodate changing demands and extracellular stresses. Cells normally maintain a steady state called *homeostasis* in which the intracellular milieu is kept within a fairly narrow range of physiologic parameters. As cells encounter physiologic stresses or pathologic stimuli, they can undergo adaptation, achieving a new steady state and preserving viability and function. The principal adaptive responses are *hypertrophy, hyperplasia, atrophy,* and *metaplasia.* If the adaptive capability is exceeded or if the external stress is inherently harmful, *cell injury* develops (Fig. 1–1). Within certain limits, injury is *reversible,* and cells return to a stable baseline; however, if the stress is severe, persistent and rapid in onset, it results in *irreversible injury* and death of the affected cells. *Cell death* is one of the most crucial events in the evolution of disease in any tissue or organ. It results from diverse causes, including ischemia (lack of blood flow), infections, toxins, and immune reactions. Cell death also is a normal and essential process in embryogenesis, the development of organs, and the maintenance of homeostasis.

The relationships among normal, adapted, and reversibly and irreversibly injured cells are well illustrated by the responses of the heart to different types of stress (Fig. 1–2). Myocardium subjected to persistent increased load, as in hypertension or with a narrowed (stenotic) valve, adapts by undergoing *hypertrophy*—an increase in the size of the individual cells and ultimately the entire heart—to generate the required higher contractile force. If the increased demand is not relieved, or if the myocardium is subjected to reduced blood flow (*ischemia*) from an occluded coronary artery, the muscle cells may undergo injury. Myocardium may be reversibly injured if the stress is mild or the arterial occlusion is incomplete or sufficiently brief, or it may undergo irreversible injury and cell death (*infarction*) after complete or prolonged occlusion. Also of note, stresses

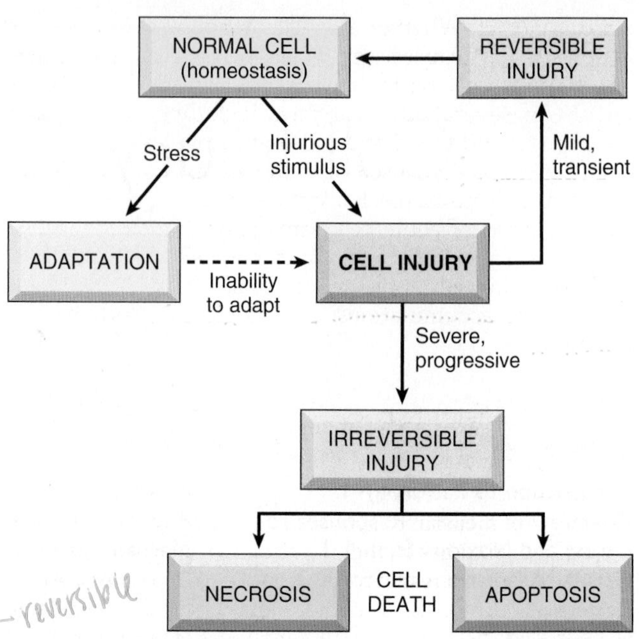

Figure 1–1 Stages in the cellular response to stress and injurious stimuli.

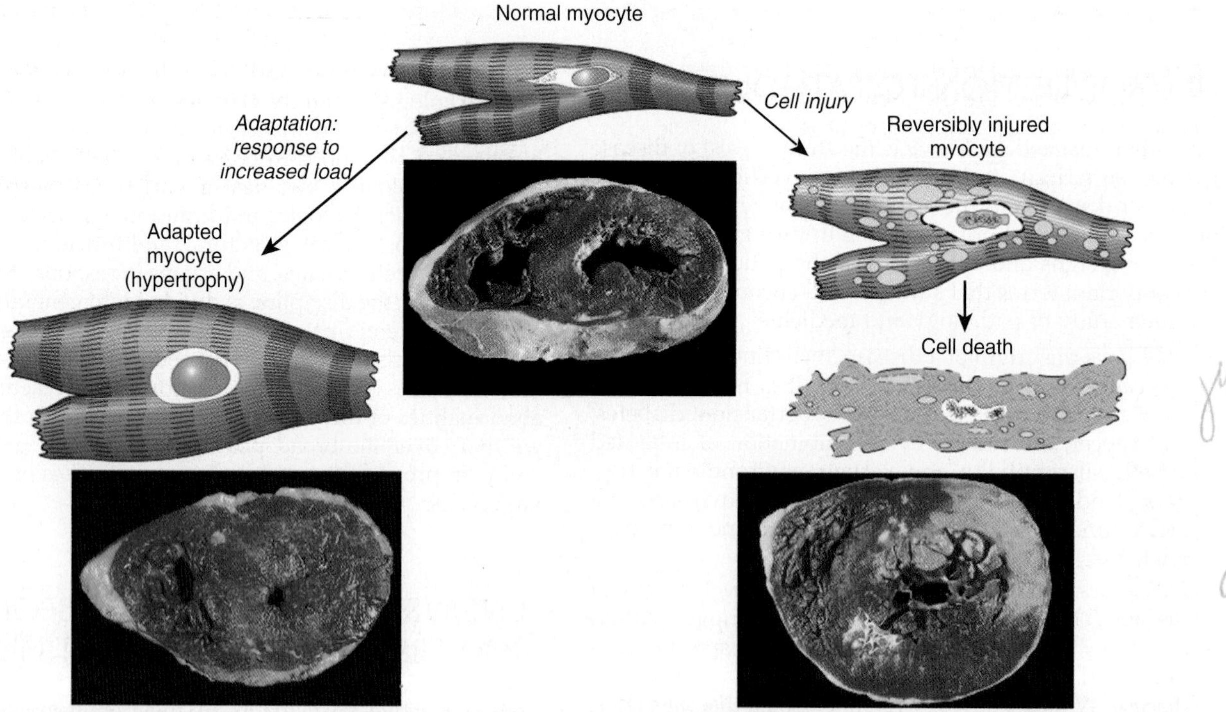

and injury affect not only the morphology but also the functional status of cells and tissues. Thus, reversibly injured myocytes are not dead and may resemble normal myocytes morphologically; however, they are transiently noncontractile, so even mild injury can have a significant

Figure 1–2 The relationship among normal, adapted, reversibly injured, and dead myocardial cells. The cellular adaptation depicted here is hypertrophy, the type of reversible injury is ischemia, and the irreversible injury is ischemic coagulative necrosis. In the example of myocardial hypertrophy (*lower left*), the left ventricular wall is thicker than 2 cm (normal, 1–1.5 cm). Reversibly injured myocardium shows functional effects without any gross or light microscopic changes, or reversible changes like cellular swelling and fatty change (*shown here*). In the specimen showing necrosis (*lower right*) the transmural light area in the posterolateral left ventricle represents an acute myocardial infarction. All three transverse sections of myocardium have been stained with triphenyltetrazolium chloride, an enzyme substrate that colors viable myocardium magenta. Failure to stain is due to enzyme loss after cell death.

clinical impact. Whether a specific form of stress induces adaptation or causes reversible or irreversible injury depends not only on the nature and severity of the stress but also on several other variables, including basal cellular metabolism and blood and nutrient supply.

In this chapter we discuss first how cells adapt to stresses and then the causes, mechanisms, and consequences of the various forms of acute cell damage, including reversible cell injury, subcellular alterations, and cell death. We conclude with three other processes that affect cells and tissues: intracellular accumulations, pathologic calcification, and cell aging.

CELLULAR ADAPTATIONS TO STRESS

Adaptations are reversible changes in the number, size, phenotype, metabolic activity, or functions of cells in response to changes in their environment. *Physiologic adaptations* usually represent responses of cells to normal stimulation by hormones or endogenous chemical mediators (e.g., the hormone-induced enlargement of the breast and uterus during pregnancy). *Pathologic adaptations* are responses to stress that allow cells to modulate their structure and function and thus escape injury. Such adaptations can take several distinct forms.

Hypertrophy

Hypertrophy is an increase in the size of cells resulting in increase in the size of the organ. In contrast, hyperplasia (discussed next) is characterized by an increase in cell number because of proliferation of differentiated cells and replacement by tissue stem cells. Stated another way, in pure hypertrophy there are no new cells, just bigger cells containing increased amounts of structural proteins and organelles. Hyperplasia is an adaptive response in cells capable of replication, whereas hypertrophy occurs when cells have a limited capacity to divide. Hypertrophy and hyperplasia also can occur together, and obviously both result in an enlarged (*hypertrophic*) organ.

Hypertrophy can be physiologic or pathologic and is caused either by increased functional demand or by growth factor or hormonal stimulation.

- The massive physiologic enlargement of the uterus during pregnancy occurs as a consequence of estrogen-stimulated smooth muscle hypertrophy and smooth muscle hyperplasia (Fig. 1–3). In contrast, in response to increased demand the striated muscle cells in both the skeletal muscle and the heart can undergo only hypertrophy because adult muscle cells have a limited capacity to divide. Therefore, the chiseled physique of the avid weightlifter stems solely from the hypertrophy of individual skeletal muscles.
- An example of pathologic cellular hypertrophy is the cardiac enlargement that occurs with hypertension or aortic valve disease (Fig. 1–2).

The mechanisms driving cardiac hypertrophy involve at least two types of signals: *mechanical triggers,* such as stretch, and *trophic triggers,* which typically are soluble mediators that stimulate cell growth, such as growth factors and adrenergic hormones. These stimuli turn on signal transduction pathways that lead to the induction of a number of genes, which in turn stimulate synthesis of many cellular proteins, including growth factors and structural proteins. The result is the synthesis of more proteins and myofilaments per cell, which increases the force generated with each contraction, enabling the cell to meet increased work demands. There may also be a switch of contractile proteins from adult to fetal or neonatal forms. For example, during muscle hypertrophy, the α-myosin heavy chain is replaced by the β form of the myosin heavy chain, which produces slower, more energetically economical contraction.

Whatever the exact mechanisms of hypertrophy, a limit is reached beyond which the enlargement of muscle mass

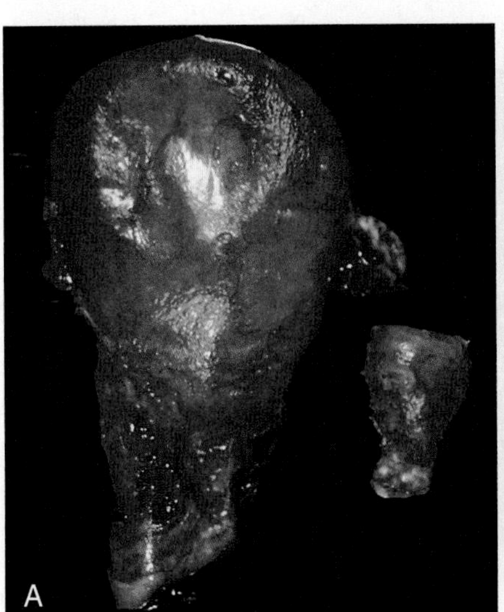

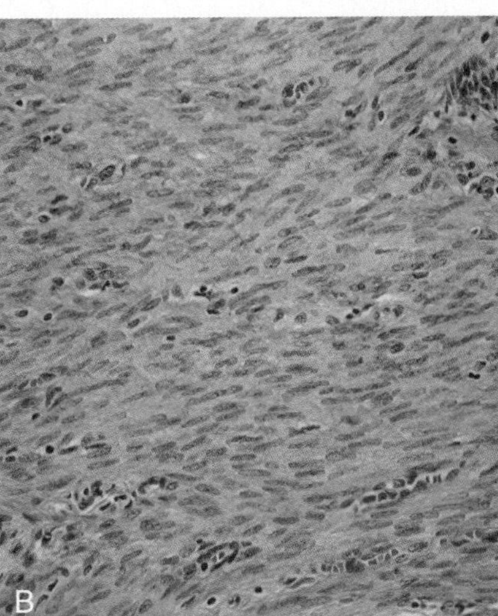

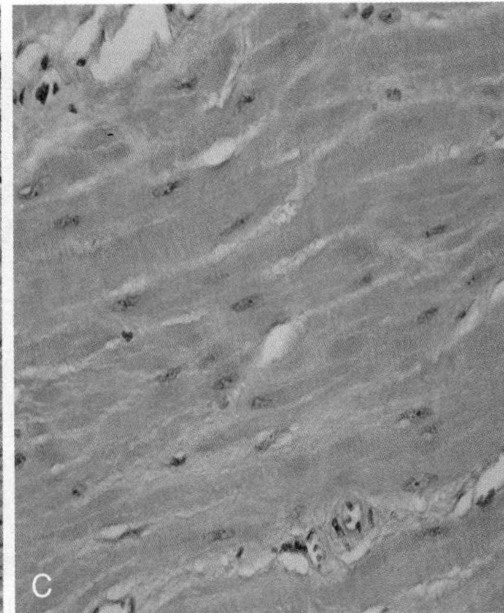

Figure 1–3 Physiologic hypertrophy of the uterus during pregnancy. **A,** Gross appearance of a normal uterus (*right*) and a gravid uterus (*left*) that was removed for postpartum bleeding. **B,** Small spindle-shaped uterine smooth muscle cells from a normal uterus. **C,** Large, plump hypertrophied smooth muscle cells from a gravid uterus; compare with **B.** (**B** and **C,** Same magnification.)

can no longer compensate for the increased burden. When this happens in the heart, several "degenerative" changes occur in the myocardial fibers, of which the most important are fragmentation and loss of myofibrillar contractile elements. The variables that limit continued hypertrophy and cause the regressive changes are incompletely understood. There may be finite limits of the vasculature to adequately supply the enlarged fibers, of the mitochondria to supply adenosine triphosphate (ATP), or of the biosynthetic machinery to provide the contractile proteins or other cytoskeletal elements. The net result of these changes is ventricular dilation and ultimately cardiac failure, a sequence of events that illustrates how *an adaptation to stress can progress to functionally significant cell injury if the stress is not relieved.*

Hyperplasia

As discussed earlier, hyperplasia takes place if the tissue contains cell populations capable of replication; it may occur concurrently with hypertrophy and often in response to the same stimuli.

Hyperplasia can be physiologic or pathologic. In both situations, cellular proliferation is stimulated by growth factors that are produced by a variety of cell types.

- The two types of *physiologic hyperplasia* are (1) *hormonal hyperplasia,* exemplified by the proliferation of the glandular epithelium of the female breast at puberty and during pregnancy, and (2) *compensatory hyperplasia,* in which residual tissue grows after removal or loss of part of an organ. For example, when part of a liver is resected, mitotic activity in the remaining cells begins as early as 12 hours later, eventually restoring the liver to its normal weight. The stimuli for hyperplasia in this setting are polypeptide growth factors produced by uninjured hepatocytes as well as nonparenchymal cells in the liver (Chapter 2). After restoration of the liver mass, cell proliferation is "turned off" by various growth inhibitors.
- Most forms of *pathologic hyperplasia* are caused by excessive hormonal or growth factor stimulation. For example, after a normal menstrual period there is a burst of uterine epithelial proliferation that is normally tightly regulated by stimulation through pituitary hormones and ovarian estrogen and by inhibition through progesterone. However, a disturbed balance between estrogen and progesterone causes endometrial hyperplasia, which is a common cause of abnormal menstrual bleeding. Hyperplasia also is an important response of connective tissue cells in wound healing, in which proliferating fibroblasts and blood vessels aid in repair (Chapter 2). In this process, growth factors are produced by white blood cells (leukocytes) responding to the injury and by cells in the extracellular matrix. Stimulation by growth factors also is involved in the hyperplasia that is associated with certain viral infections; for example, papillomaviruses cause skin warts and mucosal lesions composed of masses of hyperplastic epithelium. Here the growth factors may be encoded by viral genes or by the genes of the infected host cells.

An important point is that in all of these situations, *the hyperplastic process remains controlled; if the signals that initiate it abate, the hyperplasia disappears.* It is this responsiveness to normal regulatory control mechanisms that distinguishes pathologic hyperplasias from cancer, in which the growth control mechanisms become dysregulated or ineffective (Chapter 5). Nevertheless, in many cases, pathologic hyperplasia constitutes a fertile soil in which cancers may eventually arise. For example, patients with hyperplasia of the endometrium are at increased risk of developing endometrial cancer (Chapter 18).

Atrophy

Shrinkage in the size of the cell by the loss of cell substance is known as atrophy. When a sufficient number of cells are involved, the entire tissue or organ diminishes in size, becoming atrophic (Fig. 1–4). Although atrophic cells may have diminished function, they are not dead.

Causes of atrophy include a decreased workload (e.g., immobilization of a limb to permit healing of a fracture),

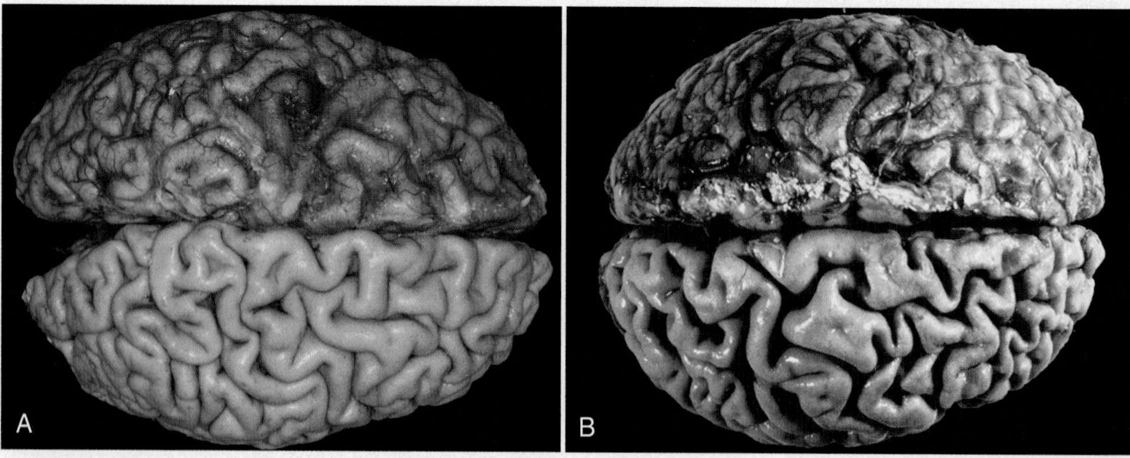

Figure 1–4 Atrophy as seen in the brain. **A,** Normal brain of a young adult. **B,** Atrophy of the brain in an 82-year-old man with atherosclerotic disease. Atrophy of the brain is due to aging and reduced blood supply. Note that loss of brain substance narrows the gyri and widens the sulci. The meninges have been stripped from the bottom half of each specimen to reveal the surface of the brain.

loss of innervation, diminished blood supply, inadequate nutrition, loss of endocrine stimulation, and aging (senile atrophy). Although some of these stimuli are physiologic (e.g., the loss of hormone stimulation in menopause) and others pathologic (e.g., denervation), the fundamental cellular changes are identical. They represent a retreat by the cell to a smaller size at which survival is still possible; a new equilibrium is achieved between cell size and diminished blood supply, nutrition, or trophic stimulation.

The mechanisms of atrophy consist of a combination of decreased protein synthesis and increased protein degradation in cells.

- Protein synthesis decreases because of reduced metabolic activity.
- The degradation of cellular proteins occurs mainly by the *ubiquitin-proteasome pathway*. Nutrient deficiency and disuse may activate ubiquitin ligases, which attach multiple copies of the small peptide ubiquitin to cellular proteins and target them for degradation in proteasomes. This pathway is also thought to be responsible for the accelerated proteolysis seen in a variety of catabolic conditions, including the cachexia associated with cancer.
- In many situations, atrophy is also accompanied by increased *autophagy*, with resulting increases in the number of *autophagic vacuoles*. Autophagy ("self-eating") is the process in which the starved cell eats its own components in an attempt to survive. We describe this process later in the chapter.

Metaplasia

Metaplasia is a reversible change in which one adult cell type (epithelial or mesenchymal) is replaced by another adult cell type. In this type of cellular adaptation, a cell type sensitive to a particular stress is replaced by another cell type better able to withstand the adverse environment. Metaplasia is thought to arise by reprogramming of stem cells to differentiate along a new pathway rather than a phenotypic change (transdifferentiation) of already differentiated cells.

Epithelial metaplasia is exemplified by the squamous change that occurs in the respiratory epithelium of habitual cigarette smokers (Fig. 1–5). The normal ciliated columnar epithelial cells of the trachea and bronchi are focally or widely replaced by stratified squamous epithelial cells. The rugged stratified squamous epithelium may be able to survive the noxious chemicals in cigarette smoke that the more fragile specialized epithelium would not tolerate. *Although the metaplastic squamous epithelium has survival advantages, important protective mechanisms are lost,* such as mucus secretion and ciliary clearance of particulate matter. Epithelial metaplasia is therefore a double-edged sword. Moreover, *the influences that induce metaplastic change, if persistent, may predispose to malignant transformation of the epithelium.* In fact, squamous metaplasia of the respiratory epithelium often coexists with lung cancers composed of malignant squamous cells. It is thought that cigarette smoking initially causes squamous metaplasia, and cancers arise later in some of these altered foci. Since vitamin A is essential for normal epithelial differentiation, its deficiency may also induce squamous metaplasia in the respiratory

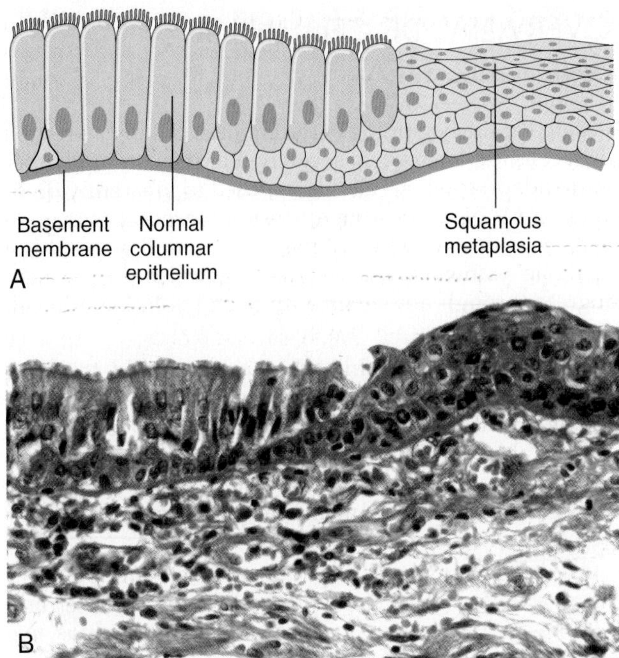

Figure 1–5 Metaplasia of normal columnar (*left*) to squamous epithelium (*right*) in a bronchus, shown schematically (**A**) and histologically (**B**).

epithelium. Metaplasia need not always occur in the direction of columnar to squamous epithelium; in chronic gastric reflux, the normal stratified squamous epithelium of the lower esophagus may undergo metaplastic transformation to gastric or intestinal-type columnar epithelium. Metaplasia may also occur in mesenchymal cells but in these situations it is generally a reaction to some pathologic alteration and not an adaptive response to stress. For example, bone is occasionally formed in soft tissues, particularly in foci of injury.

SUMMARY

Cellular Adaptations to Stress

- *Hypertrophy:* increased cell and organ size, often in response to increased workload; induced by growth factors produced in response to mechanical stress or other stimuli; occurs in tissues incapable of cell division
- *Hyperplasia:* increased cell numbers in response to hormones and other growth factors; occurs in tissues whose cells are able to divide or contain abundant tissue stem cells
- *Atrophy:* decreased cell and organ size, as a result of decreased nutrient supply or disuse; associated with decreased synthesis of cellular building blocks and increased breakdown of cellular organelles
- *Metaplasia:* change in phenotype of differentiated cells, often in response to chronic irritation, that makes cells better able to withstand the stress; usually induced by altered differentiation pathway of tissue stem cells; may result in reduced functions or increased propensity for malignant transformation

OVERVIEW OF CELL INJURY AND CELL DEATH

As stated at the beginning of the chapter, cell injury results when cells are stressed so severely that they are no longer able to adapt or when cells are exposed to inherently damaging agents or suffer from intrinsic abnormalities (e.g., in DNA or proteins). Different injurious stimuli affect many metabolic pathways and cellular organelles. Injury may progress through a reversible stage and culminate in cell death (Fig. 1–1).

- *Reversible cell injury.* In early stages or mild forms of injury the functional and morphologic changes are reversible if the damaging stimulus is removed. At this stage, although there may be significant structural and functional abnormalities, the injury has typically not progressed to severe membrane damage and nuclear dissolution.
- *Cell death.* With continuing damage, the injury becomes irreversible, at which time the cell cannot recover and it dies. *There are two types of cell death – necrosis and apoptosis – which differ in their mechanisms, morphology, and roles in disease and physiology* (Fig. 1–6 and Table 1–1). When damage to membranes is severe, enzymes leak out of lysosomes, enter the cytoplasm, and digest the cell, resulting in *necrosis.* Cellular contents also leak through the damaged plasma membrane into the extracellular space, where they elicit a host reaction (inflammation). Necrosis is the major pathway of cell death in many commonly encountered injuries, such as those resulting from ischemia, exposure to toxins, various infections, and trauma. When a cell is deprived of growth factors, or the cell's DNA or proteins are damaged beyond repair, typically the cell kills itself by another type of death, called *apoptosis,* which is characterized by nuclear dissolution without complete loss of membrane integrity. *Whereas necrosis is always a pathologic process, apoptosis serves many normal functions and is not necessarily associated with pathologic cell injury. Furthermore, in keeping with its role in certain physiologic processes, apoptosis does not elicit an inflammatory response.* The morphologic features, mechanisms, and significance of these two death pathways are discussed in more detail later in the chapter.

CAUSES OF CELL INJURY

The causes of cell injury range from the gross physical trauma of a motor vehicle accident to the single gene defect that results in a nonfunctional enzyme underlying a

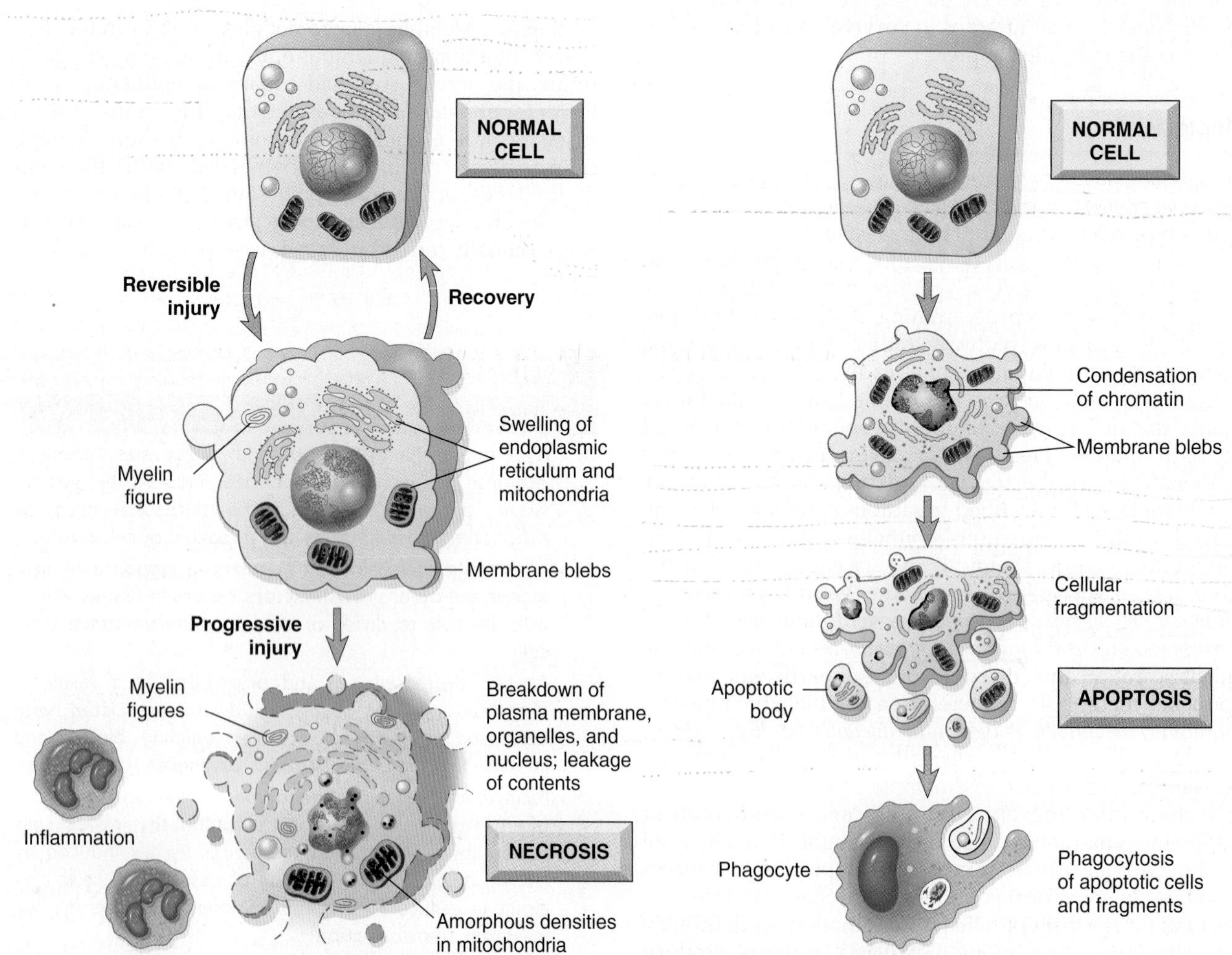

Figure 1–6 Cellular features of necrosis (*left*) and apoptosis (*right*).

Table 1–1 Features of Necrosis and Apoptosis

Feature	Necrosis	Apoptosis
Cell size	Enlarged (swelling)	Reduced (shrinkage)
Nucleus	Pyknosis → karyorrhexis → karyolysis	Fragmentation into nucleosome size fragments
Plasma membrane	Disrupted	Intact; altered structure, especially orientation of lipids
Cellular contents	Enzymatic digestion; may leak out of cell	Intact; may be released in apoptotic bodies
Adjacent inflammation	Frequent	No
Physiologic or pathologic role	Invariably pathologic (culmination of irreversible cell injury)	Often physiologic; means of eliminating unwanted cells; may be pathologic after some forms of cell injury, especially DNA and protein damage

DNA, deoxyribonucleic acid.

specific metabolic disease. Most injurious stimuli can be grouped into the following categories.

Oxygen Deprivation

Hypoxia, or oxygen deficiency, interferes with aerobic oxidative respiration and is an extremely important and common cause of cell injury and death. Hypoxia should be distinguished from *ischemia,* which is a loss of blood supply in a tissue due to impeded arterial flow or reduced venous drainage. While ischemia is the most common cause of hypoxia, oxygen deficiency can also result from inadequate oxygenation of the blood, as in pneumonia, or from reduction in the oxygen-carrying capacity of the blood, as in blood loss anemia or carbon monoxide (CO) poisoning. (CO forms a stable complex with hemoglobin that prevents oxygen binding.)

Chemical Agents

An increasing number of chemical substances that can injure cells are being recognized; even innocuous substances such as glucose, salt, or even water, if absorbed or administered in excess, can so derange the osmotic environment that cell injury or death results. Agents commonly known as poisons cause severe damage at the cellular level by altering membrane permeability, osmotic homeostasis, or the integrity of an enzyme or cofactor, and exposure to such poisons can culminate in the death of the whole organism. Other potentially toxic agents are encountered daily in the environment; these include air pollutants, insecticides, CO, asbestos, and "social stimuli" such as ethanol. Many therapeutic drugs can cause cell or tissue injury in a susceptible patient or if used excessively or inappropriately (Chapter 7). Even oxygen at sufficiently high partial pressures is toxic.

Infectious Agents

Agents of infection range from submicroscopic viruses to meter-long tapeworms; in between are the rickettsiae, bacteria, fungi, and protozoans. The diverse ways in which infectious pathogens cause injury are discussed in Chapter 8.

Immunologic Reactions

Although the immune system defends the body against pathogenic microbes, immune reactions can also result in cell and tissue injury. Examples are autoimmune reactions against one's own tissues and allergic reactions against environmental substances in genetically susceptible individuals (Chapter 4).

Genetic Factors

Genetic aberrations can result in pathologic changes as conspicuous as the congenital malformations associated with Down syndrome or as subtle as the single amino acid substitution in hemoglobin S giving rise to sickle cell anemia (Chapter 6). Genetic defects may cause cell injury as a consequence of deficiency of functional proteins, such as enzymes in inborn errors of metabolism, or accumulation of damaged DNA or misfolded proteins, both of which trigger cell death when they are beyond repair. Genetic variations (polymorphisms) contribute to the development of many complex diseases and can influence the susceptibility of cells to injury by chemicals and other environmental insults.

Nutritional Imbalances

Even in the current era of burgeoning global affluence, nutritional deficiencies remain a major cause of cell injury. Protein–calorie insufficiency among underprivileged populations is only the most obvious example; specific vitamin deficiencies are not uncommon even in developed countries with high standards of living (Chapter 7). Ironically, disorders of nutrition rather than lack of nutrients are also important causes of morbidity and mortality; for example, obesity markedly increases the risk for type 2 diabetes mellitus. Moreover, diets rich in animal fat are strongly implicated in the development of atherosclerosis as well as in increased vulnerability to many disorders, including cancer.

Physical Agents

Trauma, extremes of temperature, radiation, electric shock, and sudden changes in atmospheric pressure all have wide-ranging effects on cells (Chapter 7).

Aging

Cellular senescence leads to alterations in replicative and repair abilities of individual cells and tissues. All of these changes result in a diminished ability to respond to damage and, eventually, the death of cells and of the organism. The mechanisms underlying cellular aging are discussed separately at the end of the chapter.

THE MORPHOLOGY OF CELL AND TISSUE INJURY

It is useful to describe the structural alterations that occur in damaged cells before we discuss the biochemical mechanisms that bring about these changes. All stresses and noxious influences exert their effects first at the molecular or biochemical level. *Cellular function may be lost long before cell death occurs, and the morphologic changes of cell injury (or death) lag far behind both* (Fig. 1–7). For example, myocardial cells become noncontractile after 1 to 2 minutes of ischemia, although they do not die until 20 to 30 minutes of ischemia have elapsed. These myocytes may not appear dead by electron microscopy for 2 to 3 hours, or by light microscopy for 6 to 12 hours.

The cellular derangements of reversible injury can be corrected, and if the injurious stimulus abates, the cell can return to normalcy. Persistent or excessive injury, however, causes cells to pass the nebulous "point of no return" into *irreversible injury* and *cell death.* The events that determine when reversible injury becomes irreversible and progresses to cell death remain poorly understood. The clinical relevance of this question is obvious; if the biochemical and molecular changes that predict cell death can be identified with precision, it may be possible to devise strategies for preventing the transition from reversible to irreversible cell injury. Although there are no definitive morphologic or biochemical correlates of irreversibility, *two phenomena consistently characterize irreversibility: the inability to correct mitochondrial dysfunction* (lack of oxidative phosphorylation and ATP generation) even after resolution of the original injury, and *profound disturbances in membrane function.* As mentioned earlier, injury to lysosomal membranes results in the enzymatic dissolution of the injured cell, which is the culmination of injury progressing to necrosis.

As mentioned earlier, different injurious stimuli may induce death by necrosis or apoptosis (Fig. 1–6 and Table

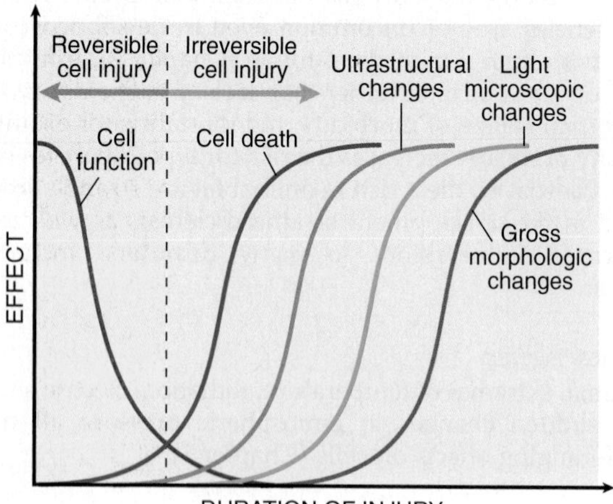

Figure 1–7 The relationship among cellular function, cell death, and the morphologic changes of cell injury. Note that cells may rapidly become nonfunctional after the onset of injury, although they are still viable, with potentially reversible damage; with a longer duration of injury, irreversible injury and cell death may result. Note also that cell death typically precedes ultrastructural, light microscopic, and grossly visible morphologic changes.

1–1). Below we describe the morphology of reversible cell injury and necrosis; the sequence of morphologic alterations in these processes is illustrated in Figure 1–6, *left.* Apoptosis has many unique features, and we describe it separately later in the chapter.

Reversible Injury

The two main morphologic correlates of reversible cell injury are *cellular swelling* and *fatty change.* Cellular swelling is the result of failure of energy-dependent ion pumps in the plasma membrane, leading to an inability to maintain ionic and fluid homeostasis. Fatty change occurs in hypoxic injury and in various forms of toxic or metabolic injury and is manifested by the appearance of small or large lipid vacuoles in the cytoplasm. The mechanisms of fatty change are discussed in Chapter 15.

In some situations, potentially injurious insults induce specific alterations in cellular organelles, like the ER. The smooth ER is involved in the metabolism of various chemicals, and cells exposed to these chemicals show hypertrophy of the ER as an adaptive response that may have important functional consequences. For instance, barbiturates are metabolized in the liver by the cytochrome P-450 mixed-function oxidase system found in the smooth ER. Protracted use of barbiturates leads to a state of tolerance, with a decrease in the effects of the drug and the need to use increasing doses. This adaptation is due to increased volume (hypertrophy) of the smooth ER of hepatocytes and consequent increased P-450 enzymatic activity. Although P-450–mediated modification is often thought of as "detoxification," many compounds are rendered *more* injurious by this process; one example is carbon tetrachloride (CCl_4), discussed later. In addition, the products formed by this oxidative metabolism include reactive oxygen species (ROS), which can injure the cell. Cells adapted to one drug have increased capacity to metabolize other compounds handled by the same system. Thus, if patients taking phenobarbital for epilepsy increase their alcohol intake, they may experience a drop in blood concentration of the antiseizure medication to subtherapeutic levels because of induction of smooth ER in response to the alcohol.

MORPHOLOGY

Cellular swelling (Fig. 1–8, *B*), the first manifestation of almost all forms of injury to cells, is a reversible alteration that may be difficult to appreciate with the light microscope, but it may be more apparent at the level of the whole organ. When it affects many cells in an organ, it causes some pallor (as a result of compression of capillaries), increased turgor, and increase in weight of the organ. Microscopic examination may reveal small, clear vacuoles within the cytoplasm; these represent distended and pinched-off segments of the endoplasmic reticulum (ER). This pattern of nonlethal injury is sometimes called **hydropic change** or **vacuolar degeneration. Fatty change** is manifested by the appearance of lipid vacuoles in the cytoplasm. It is principally encountered in cells participating in fat metabolism (e.g., hepatocytes, myocardial cells) and is also reversible. Injured cells may also show increased eosinophilic staining, which becomes much

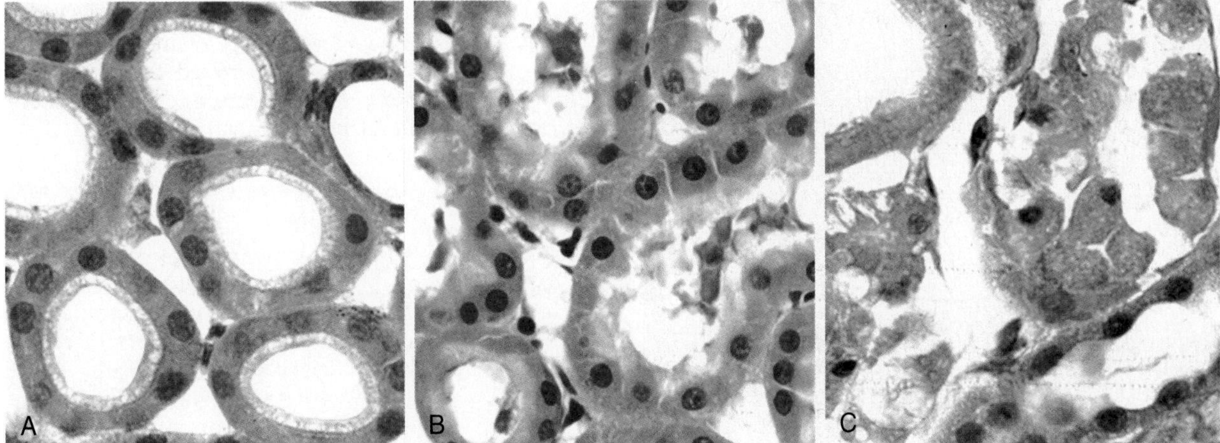

Figure 1–8 Morphologic changes in reversible and irreversible cell injury (necrosis). **A,** Normal kidney tubules with viable epithelial cells. **B,** Early (reversible) ischemic injury showing surface blebs, increased eosinophilia of cytoplasm, and swelling of occasional cells. **C,** Necrotic (irreversible) injury of epithelial cells, with loss of nuclei and fragmentation of cells and leakage of contents.
(Courtesy of Drs. Neal Pinckard and M.A. Venkatachalam, University of Texas Health Sciences Center, San Antonio, Tex.)

more pronounced with progression to necrosis (described further on).

The intracellular changes associated with reversible injury (Fig. 1–6) include (1) plasma membrane alterations such as blebbing, blunting, or distortion of microvilli, and loosening of intercellular attachments; (2) mitochondrial changes such as swelling and the appearance of phospholipid-rich amorphous densities; (3) dilation of the ER with detachment of ribosomes and dissociation of polysomes; and (4) nuclear alterations, with clumping of chromatin. The cytoplasm may contain phospholipid masses, called myelin figures, which are derived from damaged cellular membranes.

Necrosis

Necrosis is the type of cell death that is associated with loss of membrane integrity and leakage of cellular contents culminating in dissolution of cells, largely resulting from the degradative action of enzymes on lethally injured cells. The leaked cellular contents often elicit a local host reaction, called *inflammation,* that attempts to eliminate the dead cells and start the subsequent repair process (Chapter 2). The enzymes responsible for digestion of the cell may be derived from the lysosomes of the dying cells themselves and from the lysosomes of leukocytes that are recruited as part of the inflammatory reaction to the dead cells.

MORPHOLOGY

Necrosis is characterized by changes in the cytoplasm and nuclei of the injured cells (Figs. 1–6, *left,* and 1–8, *C*).

- **Cytoplasmic changes.** Necrotic cells show **increased eosinophilia** (i.e., pink staining from the eosin dye—the E in the hematoxylin and eosin [H&E] stain), attributable in part to increased binding of eosin to denatured cytoplasmic proteins and in part to loss of the basophilia that is normally imparted by the ribonucleic acid (RNA) in the cytoplasm (basophilia is the blue staining from the hematoxylin dye—the H in "H&E"). Compared with viable cells, the cell may have a more glassy, homogeneous appearance, mostly because of the loss of glycogen particles. Myelin figures are more prominent in necrotic cells than during reversible injury. When enzymes have digested cytoplasmic organelles, the cytoplasm becomes vacuolated and appears "moth-eaten." By electron microscopy, necrotic cells are characterized by discontinuities in plasma and organelle membranes, marked dilation of mitochondria with the appearance of large amorphous densities, disruption of lysosomes, and intracytoplasmic myelin figures.
- **Nuclear changes.** Nuclear changes assume one of three patterns, all due to breakdown of DNA and chromatin. The basophilia of the chromatin may fade **(karyolysis),** presumably secondary to deoxyribonuclease (DNase) activity. A second pattern is **pyknosis,** characterized by nuclear shrinkage and increased basophilia; the DNA condenses into a solid shrunken mass. In the third pattern, **karyorrhexis,** the pyknotic nucleus undergoes fragmentation. In 1 to 2 days, the nucleus in a dead cell may completely disappear. Electron microscopy reveals profound nuclear changes culminating in nuclear dissolution.
- **Fates of necrotic cells.** Necrotic cells may persist for some time or may be digested by enzymes and disappear. Dead cells may be replaced by myelin figures, which are either phagocytosed by other cells or further degraded into fatty acids. These fatty acids bind calcium salts, which may result in the dead cells ultimately becoming **calcified.**

Patterns of Tissue Necrosis

There are several morphologically distinct patterns of tissue necrosis, which may provide clues about the underlying cause. Although the terms that describe these patterns do not reflect underlying mechanisms, such terms are in common use, and their implications are understood by both pathologists and clinicians. Most of these types of necrosis have distinct gross appearance; fibrinoid necrosis is detected only by histologic examination.

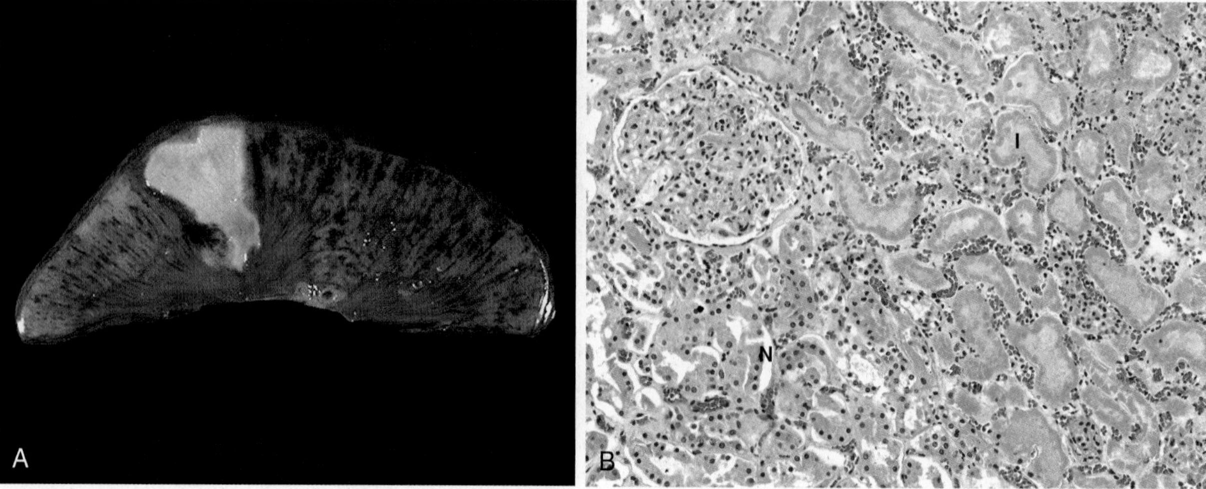

Figure 1–9 Coagulative necrosis. **A,** A wedge-shaped kidney infarct *(yellow)* with preservation of the outlines. **B,** Microscopic view of the edge of the infarct, with normal kidney *(N)* and necrotic cells in the infarct *(I)*. The necrotic cells show preserved outlines with loss of nuclei, and an inflammatory infiltrate is present (difficult to discern at this magnification).

MORPHOLOGY

- **Coagulative necrosis** is a form of necrosis in which the underlying tissue architecture is preserved for at least several days (Fig. 1–9). The affected tissues take on a firm texture. Presumably the injury denatures not only structural proteins but also enzymes, thereby blocking the proteolysis of the dead cells; as a result, eosinophilic, anucleate cells may persist for days or weeks. Leukocytes are recruited to the site of necrosis, and the dead cells are digested by the action of lysosomal enzymes of the leukocytes. The cellular debris is then removed by phagocytosis. Coagulative necrosis is characteristic of **infarcts** (areas of ischemic necrosis) in all of the solid organs except the brain.
- **Liquefactive necrosis** is seen in focal bacterial or, occasionally, fungal infections, because microbes stimulate the accumulation of inflammatory cells and the enzymes of leukocytes digest ("liquefy") the tissue. For obscure reasons, hypoxic death of cells within the central nervous system often evokes liquefactive necrosis (Fig. 1–10). Whatever the pathogenesis, the dead cells are completely digested, transforming the tissue into a liquid viscous mass. Eventually, the digested tissue is removed by phagocytes. If the process was initiated by acute inflammation, as in a bacterial infection, the material is frequently creamy yellow and is called pus (Chapter 2).
- Although **gangrenous necrosis** is not a distinctive pattern of cell death, the term is still commonly used in clinical practice. It usually refers to the condition of a limb, generally the lower leg, that has lost its blood supply and has undergone coagulative necrosis involving multiple tissue layers. When bacterial infection is superimposed, coagulative necrosis is modified by the liquefactive action of the bacteria and the attracted leukocytes (resulting in so-called **wet gangrene**).
- **Caseous necrosis** is encountered most often in foci of tuberculous infection. **Caseous** means "cheese-like," referring to the friable yellow-white appearance of the area of necrosis (Fig. 1–11). On microscopic examination, the necrotic focus appears as a collection of fragmented or lysed cells with an amorphous granular pink appearance in the usual H&E-stained tissue. Unlike with coagulative necrosis, the tissue architecture is completely obliterated and cellular outlines cannot be discerned. The area of caseous necrosis is often enclosed within a distinctive inflammatory border; this appearance is characteristic of a focus of inflammation known as a **granuloma** (Chapter 2).
- **Fat necrosis** refers to focal areas of fat destruction, typically resulting from release of activated pancreatic lipases into the substance of the pancreas and the peritoneal cavity. This occurs in the calamitous abdominal emergency known as acute pancreatitis (Chapter 16). In this disorder, pancreatic enzymes that have leaked out of acinar cells

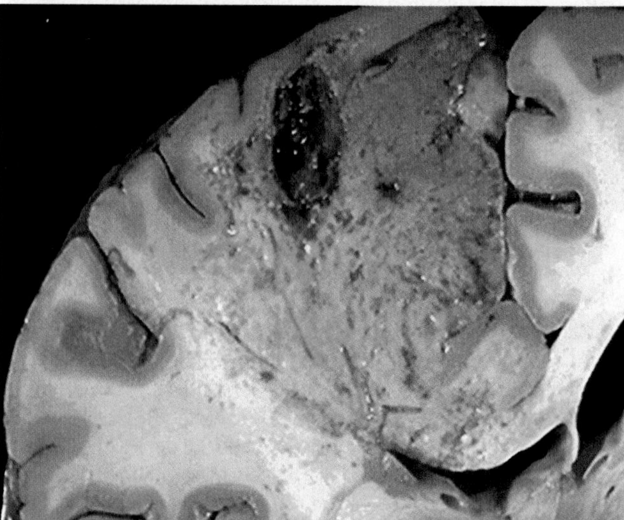

Figure 1–10 Liquefactive necrosis. An infarct in the brain showing dissolution of the tissue.

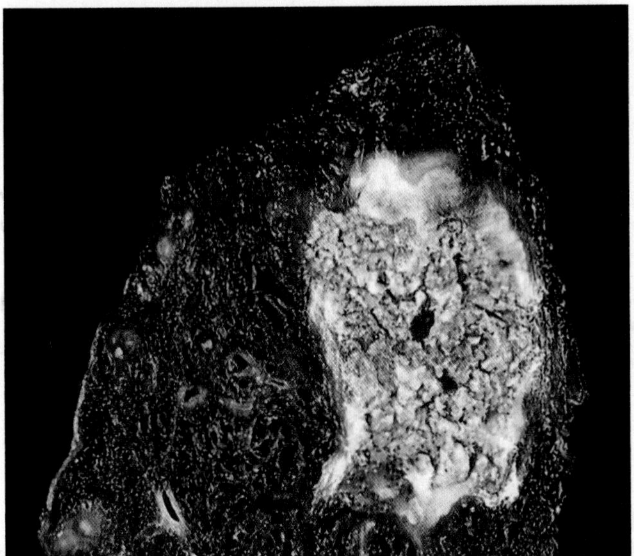

Figure 1–11 Caseous necrosis. Tuberculosis of the lung, with a large area of caseous necrosis containing yellow-white (cheesy) debris.

and ducts liquefy the membranes of fat cells in the peritoneum, and lipases split the triglyceride esters contained within fat cells. The released fatty acids combine with calcium to produce grossly visible chalky white areas (fat saponification), which enable the surgeon and the pathologist to identify the lesions (Fig. 1–12). On histologic examination, the foci of necrosis contain shadowy outlines of necrotic fat cells with basophilic calcium deposits, surrounded by an inflammatory reaction.

- **Fibrinoid necrosis** is a special form of necrosis, visible by light microscopy, usually in immune reactions in which complexes of antigens and antibodies are deposited in the walls of arteries. The deposited immune complexes, together with fibrin that has leaked out of vessels, produce a bright pink and amorphous appearance on H&E preparations called **fibrinoid** (fibrin-like) by pathologists (Fig. 1–13). The immunologically mediated diseases (e.g., polyarteritis nodosa) in which this type of necrosis is seen are described in Chapter 4.

Figure 1–12 Fat necrosis in acute pancreatitis. The areas of white chalky deposits represent foci of fat necrosis with calcium soap formation (saponification) at sites of lipid breakdown in the mesentery.

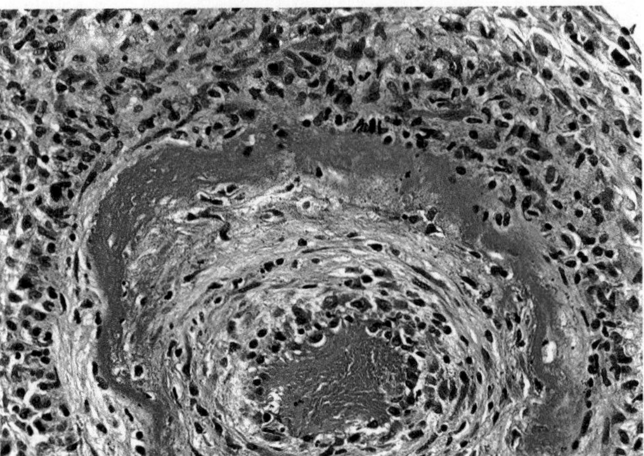

Figure 1–13 Fibrinoid necrosis in an artery in a patient with polyarteritis nodosa. The wall of the artery shows a circumferential bright pink area of necrosis with protein deposition and inflammation.

Leakage of intracellular proteins through the damaged cell membrane and ultimately into the circulation provides a means of detecting tissue-specific necrosis using blood or serum samples. Cardiac muscle, for example, contains a unique isoform of the enzyme creatine kinase and of the contractile protein troponin, whereas hepatic bile duct epithelium contains a temperature-resistant isoform of the enzyme alkaline phosphatase, and hepatocytes contain transaminases. Irreversible injury and cell death in these tissues result in increased serum levels of such proteins, and measurement of serum levels is used clinically to assess damage to these tissues.

SUMMARY

Morphologic Alterations in Injured Cells and Tissues

- *Reversible cell injury:* cell swelling, fatty change, plasma membrane blebbing and loss of microvilli, mitochondrial swelling, dilation of the ER, eosinophilia (due to decreased cytoplasmic RNA)
- *Necrosis:* increased eosinophilia; nuclear shrinkage, fragmentation, and dissolution; breakdown of plasma membrane and organellar membranes; abundant myelin figures; leakage and enzymatic digestion of cellular contents
- *Patterns of tissue necrosis:* Under different conditions, necrosis in tissues may assume specific patterns: coagulative, liquefactive, gangrenous, caseous, fat, and fibrinoid.

MECHANISMS OF CELL INJURY

Now that we have discussed the causes of cell injury and the morphologic changes in necrosis, we next consider in more detail the molecular basis of cell injury, and then illustrate the important principles with a few selected examples of common types of injury.

The biochemical mechanisms linking any given injury with the resulting cellular and tissue manifestations are complex, interconnected, and tightly interwoven with many intracellular metabolic pathways. Nevertheless, several general principles are relevant to most forms of cell injury:

- *The cellular response to injurious stimuli depends on the type of injury, its duration, and its severity.* Thus, low doses of toxins or a brief duration of ischemia may lead to reversible cell injury, whereas larger toxin doses or longer ischemic intervals may result in irreversible injury and cell death.
- *The consequences of an injurious stimulus depend on the type, status, adaptability, and genetic makeup of the injured cell.* The same injury has vastly different outcomes depending on the cell type; thus, striated skeletal muscle in the leg accommodates complete ischemia for 2 to 3 hours without irreversible injury, whereas cardiac muscle dies after only 20 to 30 minutes. The nutritional (or hormonal) status can also be important; clearly, a glycogen-replete hepatocyte will tolerate ischemia much better than one that has just burned its last glucose molecule. Genetically determined diversity in metabolic pathways can contribute to differences in responses to injurious stimuli. For instance, when exposed to the same dose of a toxin, individuals who inherit variants in genes encoding cytochrome P-450 may catabolize the toxin at different rates, leading to different outcomes. Much effort is now directed toward understanding the role of genetic polymorphisms in responses to drugs and toxins. The study of such interactions is called pharmacogenomics. In fact, genetic variations influence susceptibility to many complex diseases as well as responsiveness to various therapeutic agents. Using the genetic makeup of the individual patient to guide therapy is one example of "personalized medicine."
- *Cell injury results from functional and biochemical abnormalities in one or more of several essential cellular components* (Fig. 1–14). The principal targets and biochemical mechanisms of cell injury are: (1) mitochondria and their ability to generate ATP and ROS under pathologic conditions; (2) disturbance in calcium homeostasis; (3) damage to cellular (plasma and lysosomal) membranes; and (4) damage to DNA and misfolding of proteins.
- *Multiple biochemical alterations may be triggered by any one injurious insult.* It is therefore difficult to assign any one mechanism to a particular insult or clinical situation in which cell injury is prominent. For this reason, therapies that target individual mechanisms of cell injury may not be effective.

With this background, we can briefly discuss the major biochemical mechanisms of cell injury.

Depletion of ATP

ATP, the energy store of cells, is produced mainly by oxidative phosphorylation of adenosine diphosphate (ADP) during reduction of oxygen in the electron transport system of mitochondria. In addition, the glycolytic pathway can generate ATP in the absence of oxygen using glucose derived either from the circulation or from the hydrolysis of intracellular glycogen. The major causes of ATP depletion are reduced supply of oxygen and nutrients, mitochondrial damage, and the actions of some toxins (e.g., cyanide). Tissues with a greater glycolytic capacity (e.g., the liver) are able to survive loss of oxygen and decreased oxidative phosphorylation better than are tissues with limited capacity for glycolysis (e.g., the brain). High-energy phosphate in the form of ATP is required for virtually all synthetic and degradative processes within the cell, including membrane transport, protein synthesis, lipogenesis, and the deacylation-reacylation reactions necessary for phospholipid turnover. It is estimated that in total, the cells of a healthy human burn 50 to 75 kg of ATP every day!

Significant depletion of ATP has widespread effects on many critical cellular systems (Fig. 1–15):

- The activity of *plasma membrane ATP-dependent sodium pumps* is reduced, resulting in intracellular accumulation of sodium and efflux of potassium. The net gain of solute is accompanied by iso-osmotic gain of water, causing *cell swelling* and dilation of the ER.
- There is a compensatory *increase in anaerobic glycolysis* in an attempt to maintain the cell's energy sources. As a consequence, intracellular glycogen stores are rapidly depleted, and lactic acid accumulates, leading to decreased intracellular pH and decreased activity of many cellular enzymes.
- *Failure of ATP-dependent Ca^{2+} pumps* leads to influx of Ca^{2+}, with damaging effects on numerous cellular components, described later.

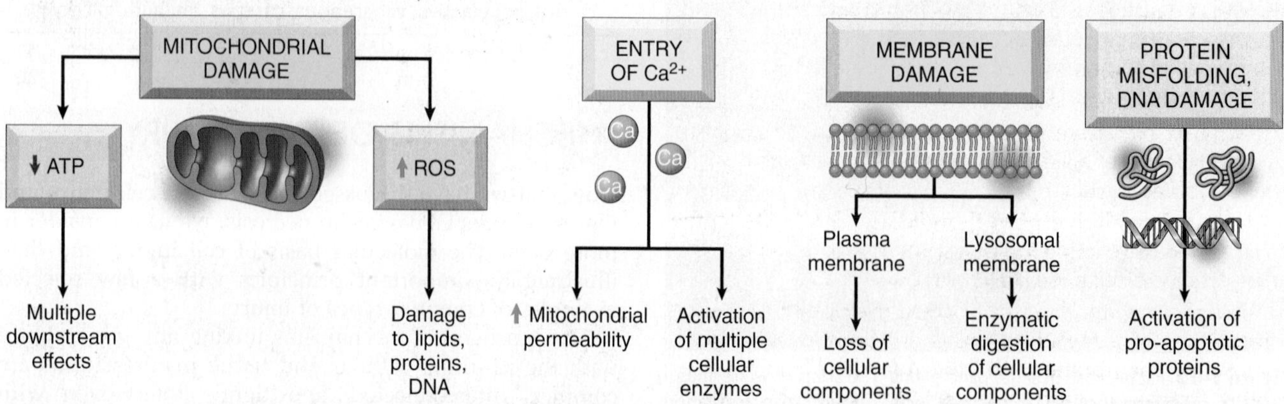

Figure 1–14 The principal biochemical mechanisms and sites of damage in cell injury. ATP, adenosine triphospate; ROS, reactive oxygen species.

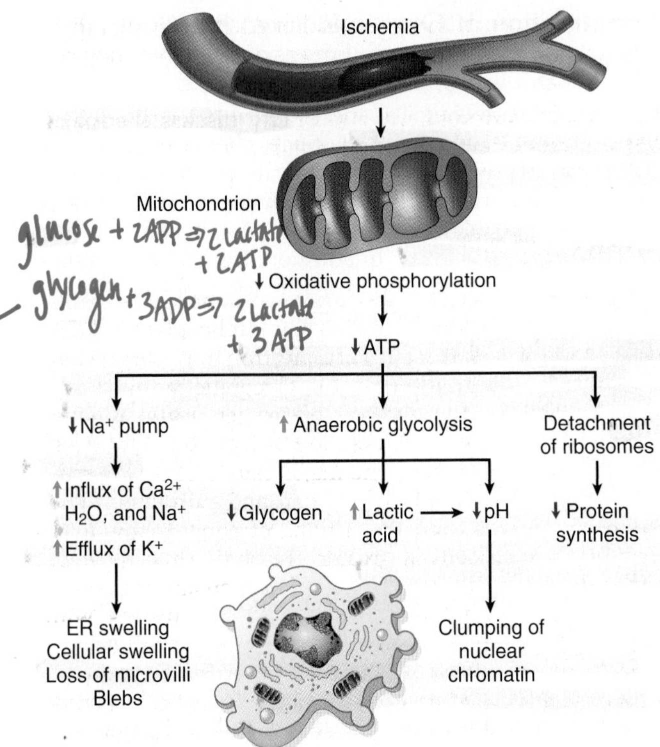

Figure 1–15 The functional and morphologic consequences of depletion of intracellular adenosine triphosphate (ATP). ER, endoplasmic reticulum.

- Prolonged or worsening depletion of ATP causes *structural disruption of the protein synthetic apparatus,* manifested as detachment of ribosomes from the rough ER (RER) and dissociation of polysomes into monosomes, with a consequent reduction in protein synthesis. Ultimately, there is irreversible damage to mitochondrial and lysosomal membranes, and the cell undergoes necrosis.

Mitochondrial Damage and Dysfunction

Mitochondria may be viewed as "mini-factories" that produce life-sustaining energy in the form of ATP. Not surprisingly, therefore, they are also critical players in cell injury and death (Fig. 1–16). Mitochondria are sensitive to many types of injurious stimuli, including hypoxia, chemical toxins, and radiation. Mitochondrial damage may result in several biochemical abnormalities:

- Failure of oxidative phosphorylation leads to progressive depletion of ATP, culminating in necrosis of the cell, as described earlier.
- Abnormal oxidative phosphorylation also leads to the formation of reactive oxygen species, which have many deleterious effects, described below.
- Damage to mitochondria is often associated with the formation of a high-conductance channel in the mitochondrial membrane, called the mitochondrial permeability transition pore. The opening of this channel leads to the loss of mitochondrial membrane potential and pH changes, further compromising oxidative phosphorylation.
- The mitochondria also contain several proteins that, when released into the cytoplasm, tell the cell there is internal injury and activate a pathway of apoptosis, discussed later.

Influx of Calcium

The importance of Ca^{2+} in cell injury was established by the experimental finding that depleting extracellular Ca^{2+} delays cell death after hypoxia and exposure to some toxins. Cytosolic free calcium is normally maintained by ATP-dependent calcium transporters at concentrations as much as 10,000 times lower than the concentration of extracellular calcium or of sequestered intracellular mitochondrial and ER calcium. Ischemia and certain toxins cause an increase in cytosolic calcium concentration, initially because of release of Ca^{2+} from the intracellular stores, and later resulting from increased influx across the plasma membrane. *Increased cytosolic Ca^{2+} activates a number of enzymes,* with potentially deleterious cellular effects (Fig. 1–17). These enzymes include phospholipases (which cause membrane damage), proteases (which break down both membrane and cytoskeletal proteins), endonucleases (which are responsible for DNA and chromatin fragmentation), and adenosine triphosphatases (ATPases) (thereby hastening ATP depletion). Increased intracellular Ca^{2+} levels may also induce apoptosis, by direct activation of caspases and by increasing mitochondrial permeability.

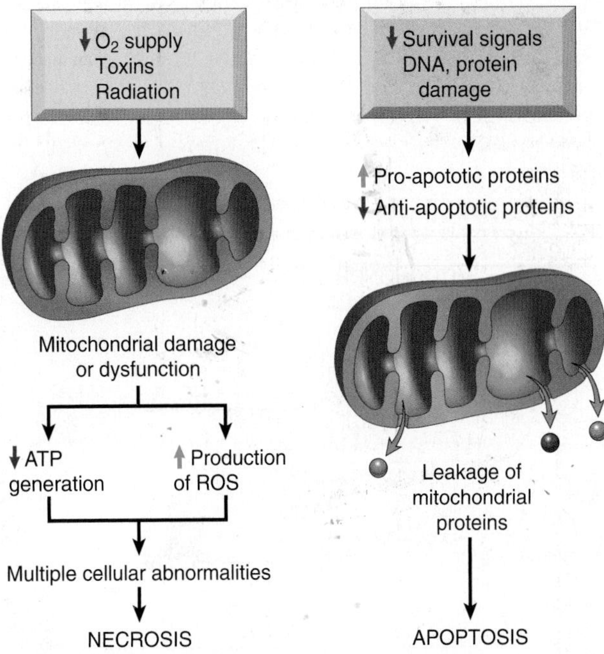

Figure 1–16 Role of mitochondria in cell injury and death. Mitochondria are affected by a variety of injurious stimuli and their abnormalities lead to necrosis or apoptosis. This pathway of apoptosis is described in more detail later. ATP, adenosine triphosphate; ROS, reactive oxygen species.

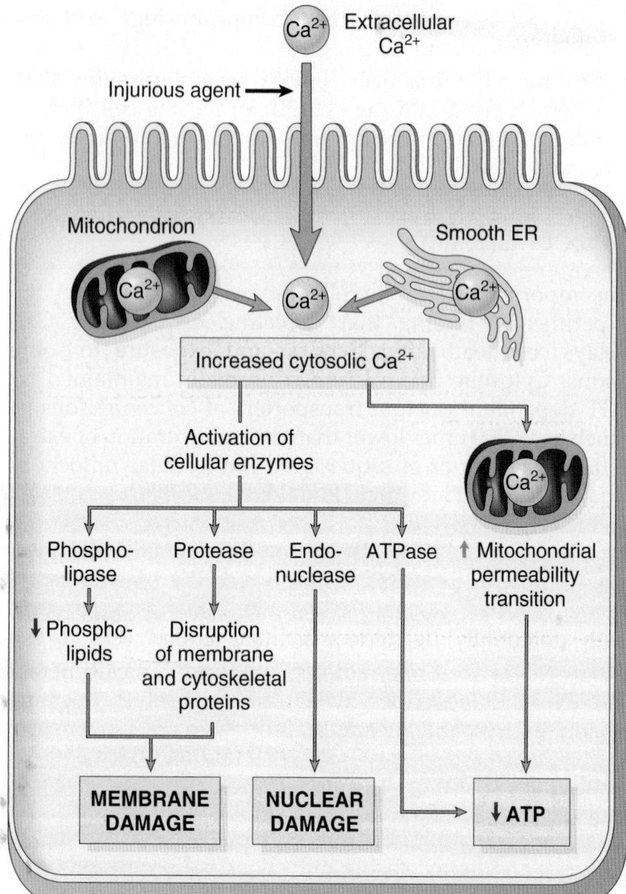

Figure 1–17 Sources and consequences of increased cytosolic calcium in cell injury. ATP, adenosine triphosphate; ATPase, adenosine triphosphatase.

Accumulation of Oxygen-Derived Free Radicals (Oxidative Stress)

Free radicals are chemical species with a single unpaired electron in an outer orbital. Such chemical states are extremely unstable, and free radicals readily react with inorganic and organic chemicals; when generated in cells, they avidly attack nucleic acids as well as a variety of cellular proteins and lipids. In addition, free radicals initiate reactions in which molecules that react with free radicals are themselves converted into other types of free radicals, thereby propagating the chain of damage.

Reactive oxygen species (ROS) are a type of oxygen-derived free radical whose role in cell injury is well established. Cell injury in many circumstances involves damage by free radicals; these situations include ischemia-reperfusion (discussed later on), chemical and radiation injury, toxicity from oxygen and other gases, cellular aging, microbial killing by phagocytic cells, and tissue injury caused by inflammatory cells.

There are different types of ROS, and they are produced by two major pathways (Fig. 1–18).

- *ROS are produced normally in small amounts in all cells during the reduction-oxidation (redox) reactions* that occur during mitochondrial respiration and energy generation. In this process, molecular oxygen is sequentially reduced in mitochondria by the addition of four electrons to generate water. This reaction is imperfect, however, and small amounts of highly reactive but short-lived toxic intermediates are generated when oxygen is only partially reduced. These intermediates include superoxide ($O_2^{\bullet}$), which is converted to hydrogen peroxide (H_2O_2) spontaneously and by the action of the enzyme superoxide dismutase. H_2O_2 is more stable than $O_2^{\bullet}$ and can cross biologic membranes. In the presence of metals, such as Fe^{2+}, H_2O_2 is converted to the highly reactive hydroxyl radical $^{\bullet}OH$ by the Fenton reaction.

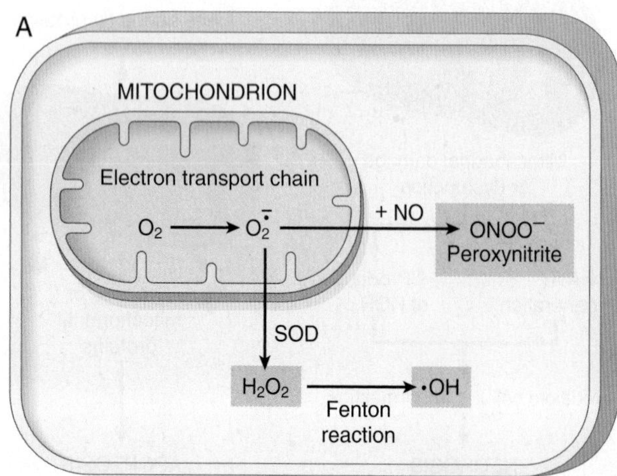

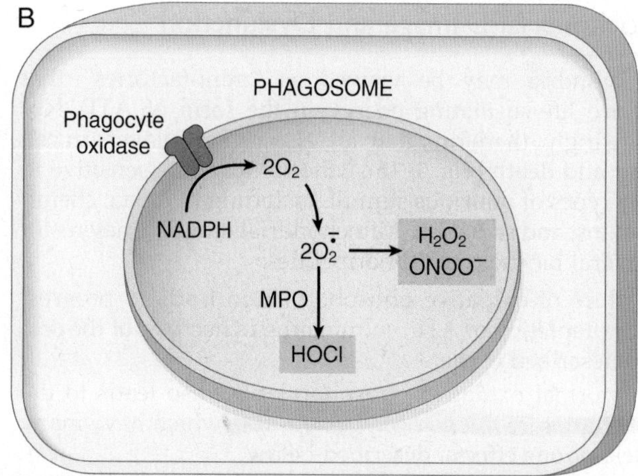

Figure 1–18 Pathways of production of reactive oxygen species. **A,** In all cells, superoxide ($O_2^{\bullet}$) is generated during mitochondrial respiration by the electron transport chain and may be converted to H_2O_2 and the hydroxyl ($^{\bullet}OH$) free radical or to peroxynitrite ($ONOO^-$). **B,** In leukocytes (mainly neutrophils and macrophages), the phagocyte oxidase enzyme in the phagosome membrane generates superoxide, which can be converted to other free radicals. Myeloperoxidase (MPO) in phagosomes also generates hypochlorite from reactive oxygen species (ROS). NO, nitric oxide; SOD, superoxide dismutase.

- *ROS are produced in phagocytic leukocytes, mainly neutrophils and macrophages,* as a weapon for destroying ingested microbes and other substances during inflammation and host defense (Chapter 2). The ROS are generated in the phagosomes and phagolysosomes of leukocytes by a process that is similar to mitochondrial respiration and is called the *respiratory burst* (or oxidative burst). In this process, a phagosome membrane enzyme catalyzes the generation of superoxide, which is converted to H_2O_2. H_2O_2 is in turn converted to a highly reactive compound hypochlorite (the major component of household bleach) by the enzyme myeloperoxidase, which is present in leukocytes. The role of ROS in inflammation is described in Chapter 2.
- *Nitric oxide (NO)* is another reactive free radical produced in leukocytes and other cells. It can react with $O_2^{\bullet-}$ to form a highly reactive compound, peroxynitrite, which also participates in cell injury.

The damage caused by free radicals is determined by their rates of production and removal (Fig. 1–19). When the production of ROS increases or the scavenging systems are ineffective, the result is an excess of these free radicals, leading to a condition called *oxidative stress.*

The generation of free radicals is increased under several circumstances:

- The absorption of radiant energy (e.g., ultraviolet light, x-rays). Ionizing radiation can hydrolyze water into hydroxyl ($^{\bullet}OH$) and hydrogen ($H^{\bullet}$) free radicals.
- The enzymatic metabolism of exogenous chemicals (e.g., carbon tetrachloride—see later)
- Inflammation, in which free radicals are produced by leukocytes (Chapter 2)

Cells have developed many *mechanisms to remove free radicals* and thereby minimize injury. Free radicals are inherently unstable and decay spontaneously. There are also nonenzymatic and enzymatic systems that contribute to inactivation of free radicals (Fig. 1–19).

- The rate of decay of superoxide is significantly increased by the action of superoxide dismutases (SODs) found in many cell types.
- Glutathione (GSH) peroxidases are a family of enzymes whose major function is to protect cells from oxidative damage. The most abundant member of this family, glutathione peroxidase 1, is found in the cytoplasm of all cells. It catalyzes the breakdown of H_2O_2 by the reaction 2 GSH (glutathione) + $H_2O_2 \rightarrow$ GS-SG + 2 H_2O. The intracellular ratio of oxidized glutathione (GSSG) to reduced glutathione (GSH) is a reflection of this enzyme's activity and thus of the cell's ability to catabolize free radicals.
- Catalase, present in peroxisomes, catalyzes the decomposition of hydrogen peroxide ($2H_2O_2 \rightarrow O_2 + 2H_2O$). It is one of the most active enzymes known, capable of degrading millions of molecules of H_2O_2 per second.
- Endogenous or exogenous antioxidants (e.g., vitamins E, A, and C and β-carotene) may either block the formation of free radicals or scavenge them once they have formed.

Reactive oxygen species cause cell injury by three main reactions (Fig. 1–19):

- *Lipid peroxidation of membranes.* Double bonds in membrane polyunsaturated lipids are vulnerable to attack by oxygen-derived free radicals. The lipid–radical interactions yield peroxides, which are themselves unstable and reactive, and an autocatalytic chain reaction ensues.
- *Cross-linking and other changes in proteins.* Free radicals promote sulfhydryl-mediated protein cross-linking, resulting in enhanced degradation or loss of enzymatic activity. Free radical reactions may also directly cause polypeptide fragmentation.
- *DNA damage.* Free radical reactions with thymine in nuclear and mitochondrial DNA produce single-strand breaks. Such DNA damage has been implicated in cell death, aging, and malignant transformation of cells.

In addition to the role of ROS in cell injury and killing of microbes, low concentrations of ROS are involved in numerous signaling pathways in cells and thus in many physiologic reactions. Therefore, these molecules are produced normally but, to avoid their harmful effects, their intracellular concentrations are tightly regulated in healthy cells.

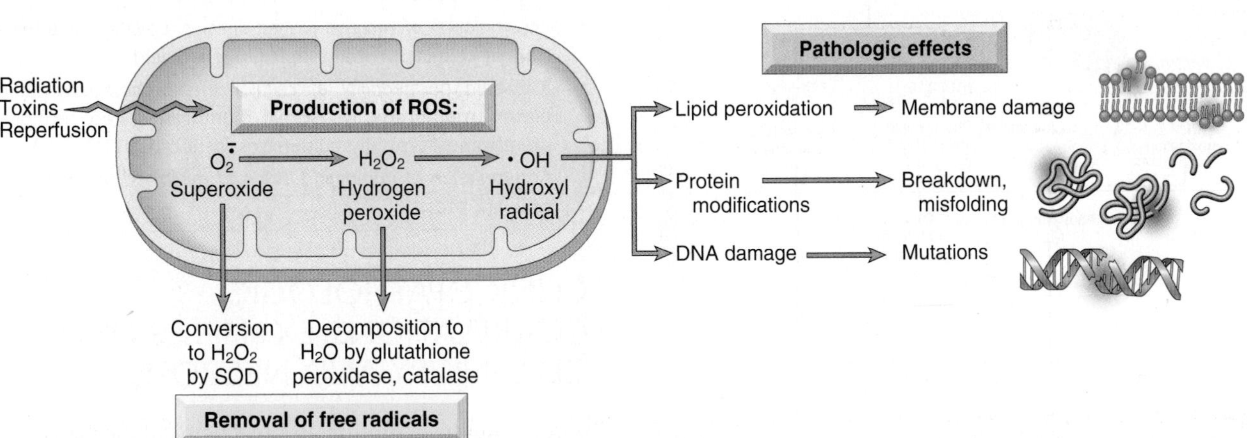

Figure 1–19 The generation, removal, and role of reactive oxygen species (ROS) in cell injury. The production of ROS is increased by many injurious stimuli. These free radicals are removed by spontaneous decay and by specialized enzymatic systems. Excessive production or inadequate removal leads to accumulation of free radicals in cells, which may damage lipids (by peroxidation), proteins, and deoxyribonucleic acid (DNA), resulting in cell injury.

Defects in Membrane Permeability

Increased membrane permeability leading ultimately to overt membrane damage is a consistent feature of most forms of cell injury that culminate in necrosis. The plasma membrane can be damaged by ischemia, various microbial toxins, lytic complement components, and a variety of physical and chemical agents. Several biochemical mechanisms may contribute to membrane damage (Fig. 1–20):

- *Decreased phospholipid synthesis.* The production of phospholipids in cells may be reduced whenever there is a fall in ATP levels, leading to decreased energy-dependent enzymatic activities. The reduced phospholipid synthesis may affect all cellular membranes, including the membranes of mitochondria, thus exacerbating the loss of ATP.
- *Increased phospholipid breakdown.* Severe cell injury is associated with increased degradation of membrane phospholipids, probably owing to activation of endogenous phospholipases by increased levels of cytosolic Ca^{2+}.
- *ROS.* Oxygen free radicals cause injury to cell membranes by lipid peroxidation, discussed earlier.
- *Cytoskeletal abnormalities.* Cytoskeletal filaments act as anchors connecting the plasma membrane to the cell interior, and serve many functions in maintaining normal cellular architecture, motility, and signaling. Activation of proteases by increased cytosolic Ca^{2+} may cause damage to elements of the cytoskeleton, leading to membrane damage.
- *Lipid breakdown products.* These include unesterified free fatty acids, acyl carnitine, and lysophospholipids, all of which accumulate in injured cells as a result of phospholipid degradation. These catabolic products have a detergent effect on membranes. They may also either insert into the lipid bilayer of the membrane or exchange with membrane phospholipids, causing changes in permeability and electrophysiologic alterations.

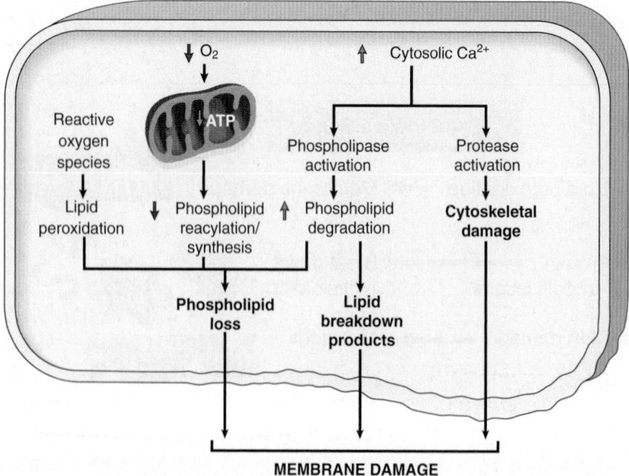

Figure 1–20 Mechanisms of membrane damage in cell injury. Decreased O_2 and increased cytosolic Ca^{2+} typically are seen in ischemia but may accompany other forms of cell injury. Reactive oxygen species, which often are produced on reperfusion of ischemic tissues, also cause membrane damage (*not shown*).

The most important sites of membrane damage during cell injury are the mitochondrial membrane, the plasma membrane, and membranes of lysosomes.

- *Mitochondrial membrane damage.* As discussed earlier, damage to mitochondrial membranes results in decreased production of ATP, with many deleterious effects culminating in necrosis.
- *Plasma membrane damage.* Plasma membrane damage leads to loss of osmotic balance and influx of fluids and ions, as well as loss of cellular contents. The cells may also leak metabolites that are vital for the reconstitution of ATP, thus further depleting energy stores.
- *Injury to lysosomal membranes* results in leakage of their enzymes into the cytoplasm and activation of the acid hydrolases in the acidic intracellular pH of the injured (e.g., ischemic) cell. Lysosomes contain ribonucleases (RNases), DNases, proteases, glucosidases, and other enzymes. Activation of these enzymes leads to enzymatic digestion of cell components, and the cells die by necrosis.

Damage to DNA and Proteins

Cells have mechanisms that repair damage to DNA, but if this damage is too severe to be corrected (e.g., after radiation injury or oxidative stress), the cell initiates its suicide program and dies by apoptosis. A similar reaction is triggered by the accumulation of improperly folded proteins, which may result from inherited mutations or external triggers such as free radicals. Since these mechanisms of cell injury typically cause apoptosis, they are discussed later in the chapter.

SUMMARY

Mechanisms of Cell Injury

- *ATP depletion:* failure of energy-dependent functions → reversible injury → necrosis
- *Mitochondrial damage:* ATP depletion → failure of energy-dependent cellular functions → ultimately, necrosis; under some conditions, leakage of mitochondrial proteins that cause apoptosis
- *Influx of calcium:* activation of enzymes that damage cellular components and may also trigger apoptosis
- *Accumulation of reactive oxygen species:* covalent modification of cellular proteins, lipids, nucleic acids
- *Increased permeability of cellular membranes:* may affect plasma membrane, lysosomal membranes, mitochondrial membranes; typically culminates in necrosis
- *Accumulation of damaged DNA and misfolded proteins:* triggers apoptosis

CLINICOPATHOLOGIC CORRELATIONS: EXAMPLES OF CELL INJURY AND NECROSIS

To illustrate the evolution and biochemical mechanisms of cell injury, we conclude this section by discussing some commonly encountered examples of reversible cell injury and necrosis.

Ischemic and Hypoxic Injury

Ischemia, or diminished blood flow to a tissue, is a common cause of acute cell injury underlying human disease. In contrast with hypoxia, in which energy generation by anaerobic glycolysis can continue (albeit less efficiently than by oxidative pathways), ischemia, because of reduced blood supply, also compromises the delivery of substrates for glycolysis. Consequently, anaerobic energy generation also ceases in ischemic tissues after potential substrates are exhausted or when glycolysis is inhibited by the accumulation of metabolites that would normally be removed by blood flow. Therefore, *ischemia injures tissues faster and usually more severely than does hypoxia.* The major cellular abnormalities in oxygen-deprived cells are decreased ATP generation, mitochondrial damage, and accumulation of ROS, with its downstream consequences.

The most important biochemical abnormality in hypoxic cells that leads to cell injury is reduced intracellular generation of ATP, as a consequence of reduced supply of oxygen. As described above, loss of ATP leads to the failure of many energy-dependent cellular systems, including (1) ion pumps (leading to cell swelling, and influx of Ca^{2+}, with its deleterious consequences); (2) depletion of glycogen stores and accumulation of lactic acid, thus lowering the intracellular pH; and (3) reduction in protein synthesis.

The functional consequences may be severe at this stage. For instance, heart muscle ceases to contract within 60 seconds of coronary occlusion. If hypoxia continues, worsening ATP depletion causes further deterioration, with loss of microvilli and the formation of "blebs" (Fig. 1–6). At this time, the entire cell and its organelles (mitochondria, ER) are markedly swollen, with increased concentrations of water, sodium, and chloride and a decreased concentration of potassium. *If oxygen is restored, all of these disturbances are reversible,* and in the case of myocardium, contractility returns.

If ischemia persists, irreversible injury and necrosis ensue. Irreversible injury is associated with severe swelling of mitochondria, extensive damage to plasma membranes, and swelling of lysosomes. ROS accumulate in cells, and massive influx of calcium may occur. Death is mainly by necrosis, but apoptosis also contributes; the apoptotic pathway is activated by release of pro-apoptotic molecules from mitochondria. The cell's components are progressively degraded, and there is widespread leakage of cellular enzymes into the extracellular space. Finally, the dead cells may become replaced by large masses composed of phospholipids in the form of myelin figures. These are then either phagocytosed by leukocytes or degraded further into fatty acids that may become calcified.

Ischemia-Reperfusion Injury

If cells are reversibly injured, the restoration of blood flow can result in cell recovery. However, under certain circumstances, *the restoration of blood flow to ischemic but viable tissues results, paradoxically, in the death of cells that are not otherwise irreversibly injured.* This so-called *ischemia-reperfusion injury* is a clinically important process that may contribute significantly to tissue damage in myocardial and cerebral ischemia.

Several mechanisms may account for the exacerbation of cell injury resulting from reperfusion into ischemic tissues:

- New damage may be initiated during reoxygenation by increased generation of *ROS* from parenchymal and endothelial cells and from infiltrating leukocytes. When the supply of oxygen is increased, there may be a corresponding increase in the production of ROS, especially because mitochondrial damage leads to incomplete reduction of oxygen, and because of the action of oxidases in leukocytes, endothelial cells, or parenchymal cells. Cellular antioxidant defense mechanisms may also be compromised by ischemia, favoring the accumulation of free radicals.
- The *inflammation* that is induced by ischemic injury may increase with reperfusion because of increased influx of leukocytes and plasma proteins. The products of activated leukocytes may cause additional tissue injury (Chapter 2). Activation of the *complement system* may also contribute to ischemia-reperfusion injury. Complement proteins may bind in the injured tissues, or to antibodies that are deposited in the tissues, and subsequent complement activation generates by-products that exacerbate the cell injury and inflammation.

Chemical (Toxic) Injury

Chemicals induce cell injury by one of two general mechanisms:

- *Some chemicals act directly by combining with a critical molecular component or cellular organelle.* For example, in mercuric chloride poisoning (as may occur from ingestion of contaminated seafood) (Chapter 7), mercury binds to the sulfhydryl groups of various cell membrane proteins, causing inhibition of ATP-dependent transport and increased membrane permeability. Many antineoplastic chemotherapeutic agents also induce cell damage by direct cytotoxic effects. In such instances, the *greatest damage is sustained by the cells that use, absorb, excrete, or concentrate the compounds.*
- *Many other chemicals are not intrinsically biologically active but must be first converted to reactive toxic metabolites, which then act on target cells.* This modification is usually accomplished by the cytochrome P-450 in the smooth ER of the liver and other organs. Although the metabolites might cause membrane damage and cell injury by direct covalent binding to protein and lipids, the most important mechanism of cell injury involves the formation of free radicals. *Carbon tetrachloride* (CCl_4)—once widely used in the dry cleaning industry but now banned—and the analgesic *acetaminophen* belong in this category. The effect of CCl_4 is still instructive as an example of chemical injury. CCl_4 is converted to the toxic free radical $CCl_3^{\bullet}$, principally in the liver, and this free radical is the cause of cell injury, mainly by membrane phospholipid peroxidation. In less than 30 minutes after exposure to CCl_4, there is breakdown of ER membranes with a decline in hepatic protein synthesis of enzymes and plasma proteins; within 2 hours, swelling of the smooth ER and dissociation of ribosomes from the smooth ER have occurred. There is reduced lipid export from the hepatocytes, as a result of their inability to synthesize

apoprotein to form complexes with triglycerides and thereby facilitate lipoprotein secretion; the result is the "fatty liver" of CCl_4 poisoning. Mitochondrial injury follows, and subsequently diminished ATP stores result in defective ion transport and progressive cell swelling; the plasma membranes are further damaged by fatty aldehydes produced by lipid peroxidation in the ER. The end result can be calcium influx and eventually cell death.

APOPTOSIS

Apoptosis is a pathway of cell death in which cells activate enzymes that degrade the cells' own nuclear DNA and nuclear and cytoplasmic proteins. Fragments of the apoptotic cells then break off, giving the appearance that is responsible for the name (*apoptosis,* "falling off"). The plasma membrane of the apoptotic cell remains intact, but the membrane is altered in such a way that the cell and its fragments become avid targets for phagocytes. The dead cell and its fragments are rapidly cleared before cellular contents have leaked out, so *apoptotic cell death does not elicit an inflammatory reaction in the host.* Apoptosis differs in this respect from necrosis, which is characterized by loss of membrane integrity, enzymatic digestion of cells, leakage of cellular contents, and frequently a host reaction (Fig. 1–6 and Table 1–1). However, apoptosis and necrosis sometimes coexist, and apoptosis induced by some pathologic stimuli may progress to necrosis.

Causes of Apoptosis

Apoptosis occurs in many normal situations and serves to eliminate potentially harmful cells and cells that have outlived their usefulness. It also occurs as a pathologic event when cells are damaged beyond repair, especially when the damage affects the cell's DNA or proteins; in these situations, the irreparably damaged cell is eliminated.

Apoptosis in Physiologic Situations

Death by apoptosis is a normal phenomenon that serves to eliminate cells that are no longer needed and to maintain a constant number of cells of various types in tissues. It is important in the following physiologic situations:

- *The programmed destruction of cells during embryogenesis.* Normal development is associated with the death of some cells and the appearance of new cells and tissues. The term *programmed cell death* was originally coined to denote this death of specific cell types at defined times during the development of an organism. Apoptosis is a generic term for this pattern of cell death, regardless of the context, but it is often used interchangeably with programmed cell death.
- *Involution of hormone-dependent tissues upon hormone deprivation,* such as endometrial cell breakdown during the menstrual cycle, and regression of the lactating breast after weaning
- *Cell loss in proliferating cell populations,* such as intestinal crypt epithelia, in order to maintain a constant number
- *Elimination of cells that have served their useful purpose,* such as neutrophils in an acute inflammatory response and lymphocytes at the end of an immune response. In these situations, cells undergo apoptosis because they are deprived of necessary survival signals, such as growth factors.
- *Elimination of potentially harmful self-reactive lymphocytes,* either before or after they have completed their maturation, in order to prevent reactions against the body's own tissues (Chapter 4)
- *Cell death induced by cytotoxic T lymphocytes,* a defense mechanism against viruses and tumors that serves to kill virus-infected and neoplastic cells (Chapter 4)

Apoptosis in Pathologic Conditions

Apoptosis eliminates cells that are genetically altered or injured beyond repair and does so without eliciting a severe host reaction, thereby keeping the extent of tissue damage to a minimum. Death by apoptosis is responsible for loss of cells in a variety of pathologic states:

- *DNA damage.* Radiation, cytotoxic anticancer drugs, extremes of temperature, and even hypoxia can damage DNA, either directly or through production of free radicals. If repair mechanisms cannot cope with the injury, the cell triggers intrinsic mechanisms that induce apoptosis. In these situations, elimination of the cell may be a better alternative than risking mutations in the damaged DNA, which may progress to malignant transformation. These injurious stimuli cause apoptosis if the insult is mild, but larger doses of the same stimuli result in necrotic cell death. Inducing apoptosis of cancer cells is a desired effect of chemotherapeutic agents, many of which work by damaging DNA.
- *Accumulation of misfolded proteins.* Improperly folded proteins may arise because of mutations in the genes encoding these proteins or because of extrinsic factors, such as damage caused by free radicals. Excessive accumulation of these proteins in the ER leads to a condition called *ER stress,* which culminates in apoptotic death of cells.
- *Cell injury in certain infections,* particularly viral infections, in which loss of infected cells is largely due to apoptotic death that may be induced by the virus (as in adenovirus and human immunodeficiency virus infections) or by the host immune response (as in viral hepatitis).
- *Pathologic atrophy in parenchymal organs after duct obstruction,* such as occurs in the pancreas, parotid gland, and kidney

MORPHOLOGY

In H&E-stained tissue sections, the nuclei of apoptotic cells show various stages of chromatin condensation and aggregation and, ultimately, karyorrhexis (Fig. 1–21); at the molecular level this is reflected in fragmentation of DNA into nucleosome-sized pieces. The cells rapidly shrink, form cytoplasmic buds, and fragment into **apoptotic bodies** composed of membrane-bound vesicles of cytosol and organelles (Fig. 1–6). Because these fragments are quickly extruded and phagocytosed without eliciting an inflammatory response, even substantial apoptosis may be histologically undetectable.

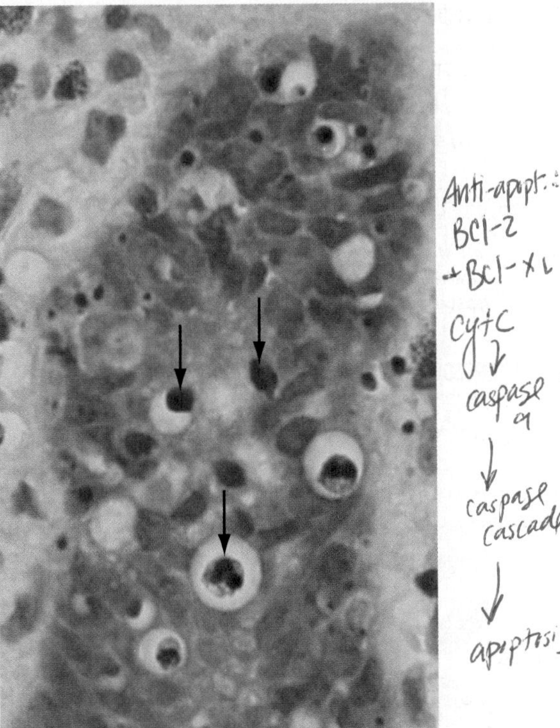

Figure 1–21 Morphologic appearance of apoptotic cells. Apoptotic cells (some indicated by *arrows*) in a normal crypt in the colonic epithelium are shown. (The preparative regimen for colonoscopy frequently induces apoptosis in epithelial cells, which explains the abundance of dead cells in this normal tissue.) Note the fragmented nuclei with condensed chromatin and the shrunken cell bodies, some with pieces falling off.

(Courtesy of Dr. Sanjay Kakar, Department of Pathology, University of California San Francisco, San Francisco, Calif.)

Mechanisms of Apoptosis

Apoptosis results from the activation of enzymes called caspases (so named because they are *c*ysteine proteases that cleave proteins after *asp*artic residues). The activation of caspases depends on a finely tuned balance between production of pro- and anti-apoptotic proteins. Two distinct pathways converge on caspase activation: the *mitochondrial pathway* and the *death receptor pathway* (Fig. 1–22). Although these pathways can intersect, they are generally induced under different conditions, involve different molecules, and serve distinct roles in physiology and disease.

The Mitochondrial (Intrinsic) Pathway of Apoptosis

Mitochondria contain several proteins that are capable of inducing apoptosis; these proteins include cytochrome c and other proteins that neutralize endogenous inhibitors of apoptosis. The choice between cell survival and death is determined by the permeability of mitochondria, which is controlled by a family of more than 20 proteins, the prototype of which is Bcl-2 (Fig. 1–23). When cells are deprived of growth factors and other survival signals, or are exposed to agents that damage DNA, or accumulate unacceptable amounts of misfolded proteins, a number of sensors are activated. These sensors are members of the Bcl-2 family called "BH3 proteins" (because they contain only the third of multiple conserved domains of the Bcl-2 family). They in turn activate two pro-apoptotic members of the family called Bax and Bak, which dimerize, insert into the mitochondrial membrane, and form channels through which cytochrome c and other mitochondrial proteins escape into the cytosol. These sensors also inhibit the anti-apoptotic molecules Bcl-2 and Bcl-x_L (see further on), enhancing the leakage of mitochondrial proteins. Cytochrome c, together with some cofactors, activates caspase-9. Other proteins that leak out of mitochondria block the activities of caspase antagonists that function as physiologic inhibitors of apoptosis. The net result is the activation of the caspase cascade, ultimately leading to nuclear fragmentation. Conversely, if cells are exposed to growth factors and other survival signals, they synthesize anti-apoptotic members of the Bcl-2 family, the two main ones of which are Bcl-2 itself and Bcl-x_L. These proteins antagonize Bax and Bak, and thus limit the escape of the mitochondrial pro-apoptotic proteins. Cells deprived of growth factors not only activate the pro-apoptotic Bax and Bak but also show reduced levels of Bcl-2 and Bcl-x_L, thus further tilting the balance toward death. The mitochondrial pathway seems to be the pathway that is responsible for apoptosis in most situations, as we discuss later.

The Death Receptor (Extrinsic) Pathway of Apoptosis

Many cells express surface molecules, called death receptors, that trigger apoptosis. Most of these are members of the tumor necrosis factor (TNF) receptor family, which contain in their cytoplasmic regions a conserved "death domain," so named because it mediates interaction with other proteins involved in cell death. The prototypic death receptors are the type I TNF receptor and Fas (CD95). Fas ligand (FasL) is a membrane protein expressed mainly on activated T lymphocytes. When these T cells recognize Fas-expressing targets, Fas molecules are cross-linked by FasL and bind adaptor proteins via the death domain. These in turn recruit and activate caspase-8. In many cell types caspase-8 may cleave and activate a pro-apoptotic member of the Bcl-2 family called Bid, thus feeding into the mitochondrial pathway. The combined activation of both pathways delivers a lethal blow to the cell. Cellular proteins, notably a caspase antagonist called FLIP, block activation of caspases downstream of death receptors. Interestingly, some viruses produce homologues of FLIP, and it is suggested that this is a mechanism that viruses use to keep infected cells alive. The death receptor pathway is involved in elimination of self-reactive lymphocytes and in killing of target cells by some cytotoxic T lymphocytes.

Activation and Function of Caspases

The mitochondrial and death receptor pathways lead to the activation of the *initiator caspases*, caspase-9 and -8, respectively. Active forms of these enzymes are produced, and these cleave and thereby activate another series of caspases that are called the *executioner caspases*. These activated caspases cleave numerous targets, culminating in activation of nucleases that degrade DNA and nucleoproteins. Caspases also degrade components of the nuclear matrix and cytoskeleton, leading to fragmentation of cells.

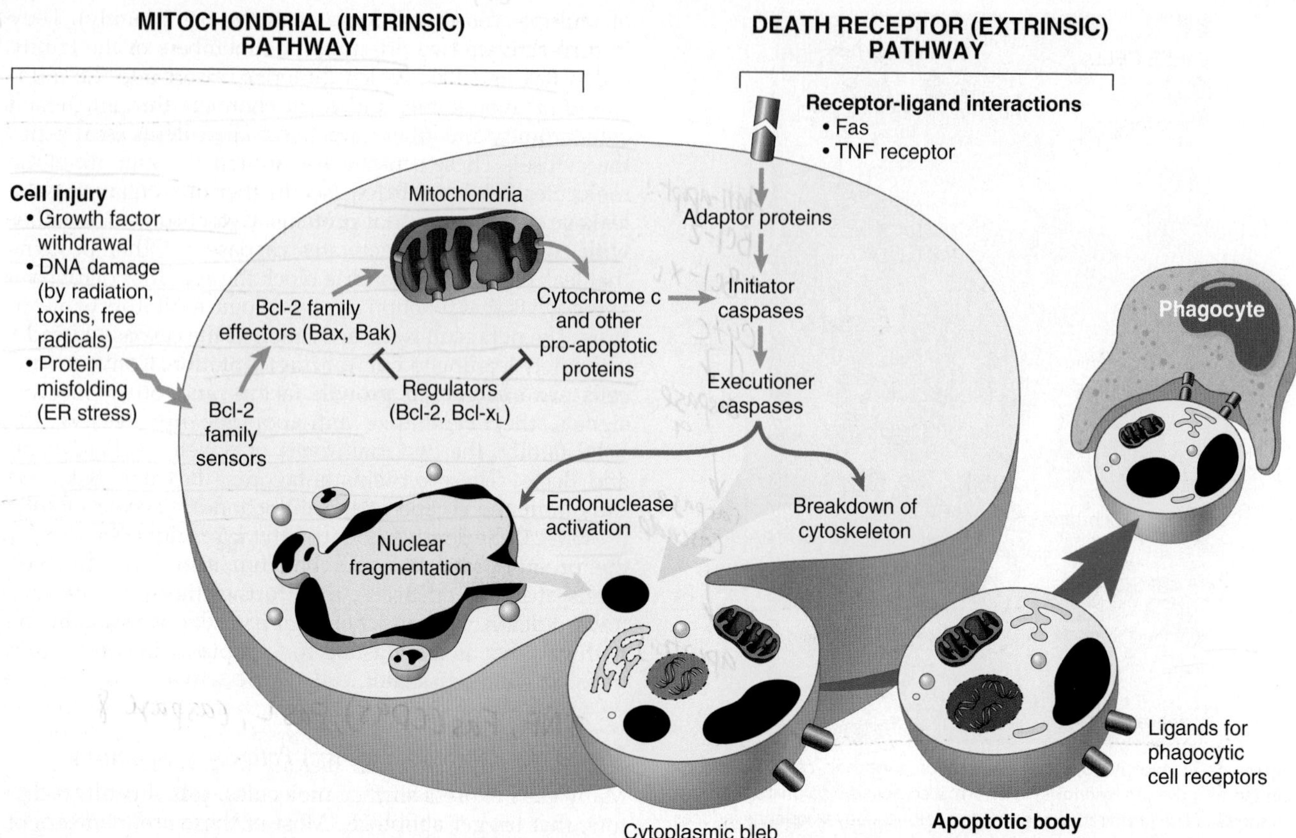

Figure 1–22 Mechanisms of apoptosis. The two pathways of apoptosis differ in their induction and regulation, and both culminate in the activation of caspases. In the mitochondrial pathway, proteins of the Bcl-2 family, which regulate mitochondrial permeability, become imbalanced and leakage of various substances from mitochondria leads to caspase activation. In the death receptor pathway, signals from plasma membrane receptors lead to the assembly of adaptor proteins into a "death-inducing signaling complex," which activates caspases, and the end result is the same.

Clearance of Apoptotic Cells

Apoptotic cells entice phagocytes by producing "eat-me" signals. In normal cells phosphatidylserine is present on the inner leaflet of the plasma membrane, but in apoptotic cells this phospholipid "flips" to the outer leaflet, where it is recognized by tissue macrophages and leads to phagocytosis of the apoptotic cells. Cells that are dying by apoptosis also secrete soluble factors that recruit phagocytes. This facilitates prompt clearance of the dead cells before they undergo secondary membrane damage and release their cellular contents (which can induce inflammation). Some apoptotic bodies express adhesive glycoproteins that are recognized by phagocytes, and macrophages themselves may produce proteins that bind to apoptotic cells (but not to live cells) and target the dead cells for engulfment. Numerous macrophage receptors have been shown to be involved in the binding and engulfment of apoptotic cells. This process of phagocytosis of apoptotic cells is so efficient that dead cells disappear without leaving a trace, and inflammation is virtually absent.

Although we have emphasized the distinctions between necrosis and apoptosis, these two forms of cell death may coexist and be related mechanistically. For instance, DNA damage (seen in apoptosis) activates an enzyme called poly-ADP(ribose) polymerase, which depletes cellular supplies of nicotinamide adenine dinucleotide, leading to a fall in ATP levels and ultimately necrosis. In fact, even in common situations such as ischemia, it has been suggested that early cell death can be partly attributed to apoptosis, with necrosis supervening later as ischemia worsens.

Examples of Apoptosis

Cell death in many situations is caused by apoptosis. The examples listed next illustrate the role of the two pathways of apoptosis in normal physiology and in disease.

Growth Factor Deprivation

Hormone-sensitive cells deprived of the relevant hormone, lymphocytes that are not stimulated by antigens and cytokines, and neurons deprived of nerve growth factor die by apoptosis. In all these situations, apoptosis is triggered by the mitochondrial pathway and is attributable to activation of pro-apoptotic members of the Bcl-2 family and decreased synthesis of Bcl-2 and Bcl-x_L.

DNA Damage

Exposure of cells to radiation or chemotherapeutic agents induces DNA damage, which if severe may trigger apoptotic death. When DNA is damaged, the p53 protein accumulates in cells. It first arrests the cell cycle (at the G_1 phase) to allow the DNA to be repaired before it is replicated (Chapter 5). However, if the damage is too great to be

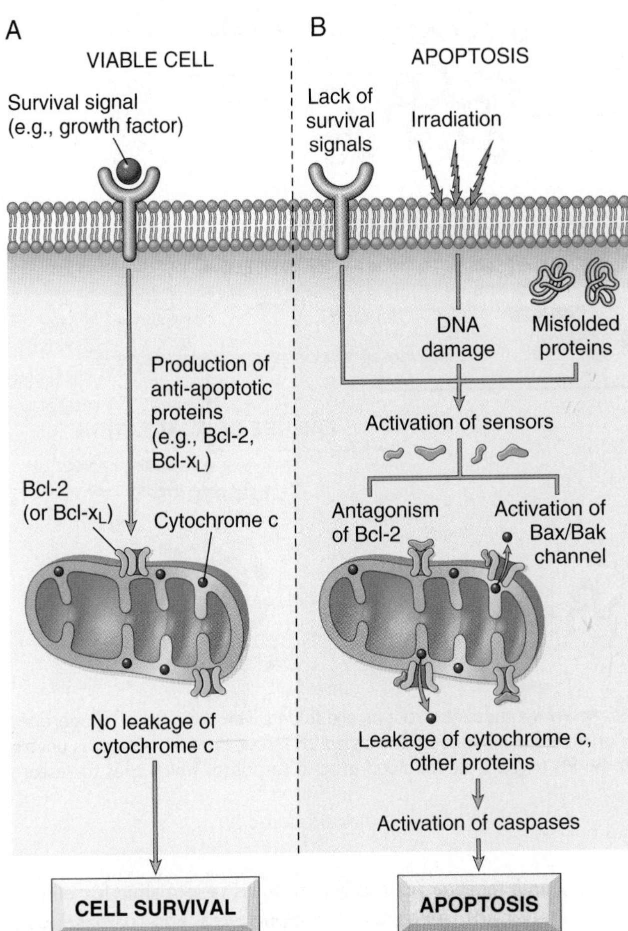

Figure 1–23 The mitochondrial pathway of apoptosis. The induction of apoptosis by the mitochondrial pathway is dependent on a balance between pro- and anti-apoptotic proteins of the Bcl family. The pro-apoptotic proteins include some (sensors) that sense DNA and protein damage and trigger apoptosis and others (effectors) that insert in the mitochondrial membrane and promote leakage of mitochondrial proteins. **A,** In a viable cell, anti-apoptotic members of the Bcl-2 family prevent leakage of mitochondrial proteins. **B,** Various injurious stimuli activate cytoplasmic sensors and lead to reduced production of these anti-apoptotic proteins and increased amounts of pro-apoptotic proteins, resulting in leakage of proteins that are normally sequestered within mitochondria. The mitochondrial proteins that leak out activate a series of caspases, first the initiators and then the executioners, and these enzymes cause fragmentation of the nucleus and ultimately the cell.

repaired successfully, p53 triggers apoptosis, mainly by stimulating sensors that ultimately activate Bax and Bak, and by increasing the synthesis of pro-apoptotic members of the Bcl-2 family. When p53 is mutated or absent (as it is in certain cancers), cells with damaged DNA that would otherwise undergo apoptosis survive. In such cells, the DNA damage may result in mutations or DNA rearrangements (e.g., translocations) that lead to neoplastic transformation (Chapter 5).

Accumulation of Misfolded Proteins: ER Stress

During normal protein synthesis, chaperones in the ER control the proper folding of newly synthesized proteins, and misfolded polypeptides are ubiquitinated and targeted for proteolysis. If, however, unfolded or misfolded proteins accumulate in the ER because of inherited mutations or environmental perturbations, they induce a protective cellular response that is called the *unfolded protein response* (Fig. 1–24). This response activates signaling pathways that increase the production of chaperones and retard protein translation, thus reducing the levels of misfolded proteins in the cell. In circumstances in which the accumulation of misfolded proteins overwhelms these adaptations, the result is *ER stress*, which leads to the activation of caspases and ultimately apoptosis. Intracellular accumulation of abnormally folded proteins, caused by mutations, aging, or unknown environmental factors, may cause diseases by reducing the availability of the normal protein or by inducing cell injury (Table 1–2). Cell death as a result of protein misfolding is now recognized as a feature of a number of neurodegenerative diseases, including Alzheimer, Huntington, and Parkinson diseases, and possibly type 2 diabetes. Deprivation of glucose and oxygen and stresses such as infections also result in protein misfolding, culminating in cell injury and death.

Apoptosis of Self-Reactive Lymphocytes

Lymphocytes capable of recognizing self antigens are normally produced in all individuals. If these lymphocytes encounter self antigens, the cells die by apoptosis. Both the mitochondrial pathway and the Fas death receptor pathway have been implicated in this process (Chapter 4). Failure of apoptosis of self-reactive lymphocytes is one of the causes of autoimmune diseases.

Table 1–2 Diseases Caused by Misfolding of Proteins

Disease	Affected Protein	Pathogenesis
Cystic fibrosis	Cystic fibrosis transmembrane conductance regulator (CFTR)	Loss of CFTR leads to defects in chloride transport
Familial hypercholesterolemia	LDL receptor	Loss of LDL receptor leading to hypercholesterolemia
Tay-Sachs disease	Hexosaminidase β subunit	Lack of the lysosomal enzyme leads to storage of GM_2 gangliosides in neurons
Alpha-1-antitrypsin deficiency	α-1 antitrypsin	Storage of nonfunctional protein in hepatocytes causes apoptosis; absence of enzymatic activity in lungs causes destruction of elastic tissue giving rise to emphysema
Creutzfeld-Jacob disease	Prions	Abnormal folding of PrP^{sc} causes neuronal cell death
Alzheimer disease	A_β peptide	Abnormal folding of A_β peptides causes aggregation within neurons and apoptosis

Shown are selected illustrative examples of diseases in which protein misfolding is thought to be the major mechanism of functional derangement or cell or tissue injury.

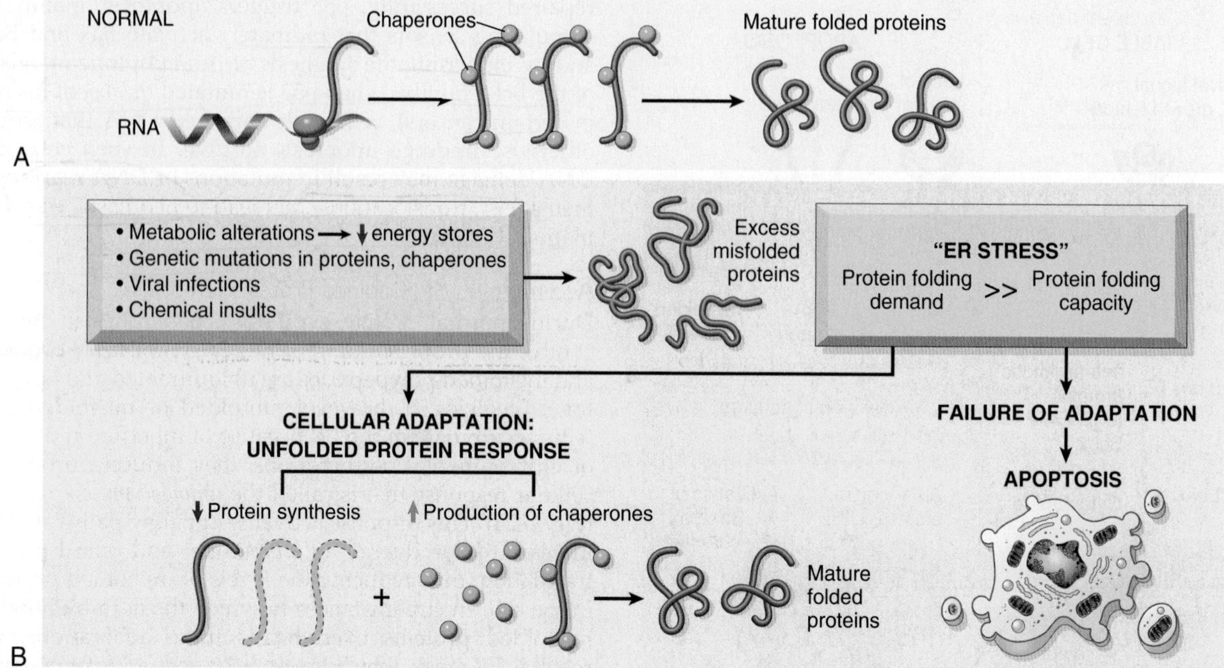

Figure 1–24 The unfolded protein response and ER stress. **A,** In healthy cells, newly synthesized proteins are folded with the help of chaperones and are then incorporated into the cell or secreted. **B,** Various external stresses or mutations induce a state called ER stress, in which the cell is unable to cope with the load of misfolded proteins. Accumulation of these proteins in the ER triggers the unfolded protein response, which tries to restore protein homeostasis; if this response is inadequate, the cell dies by apoptosis.

Cytotoxic T Lymphocyte–Mediated Apoptosis

Cytotoxic T lymphocytes (CTLs) recognize foreign antigens presented on the surface of infected host cells and tumor cells (Chapter 4). On activation, CTL granule proteases called *granzymes* enter the target cells. Granzymes cleave proteins at aspartate residues and are able to activate cellular caspases. In this way, the CTL kills target cells by directly inducing the effector phase of apoptosis, without engaging mitochondria or death receptors. CTLs also express FasL on their surface and may kill target cells by ligation of Fas receptors.

SUMMARY

Apoptosis

- Regulated mechanism of cell death that serves to eliminate unwanted and irreparably damaged cells, with the least possible host reaction
- Characterized by enzymatic degradation of proteins and DNA, initiated by caspases; and by recognition and removal of dead cells by phagocytes
- Initiated by two major pathways:
  - *Mitochondrial (intrinsic) pathway* is triggered by loss of survival signals, DNA damage and accumulation of misfolded proteins (ER stress); associated with leakage of pro-apoptotic proteins from mitochondrial membrane into the cytoplasm, where they trigger caspase activation; inhibited by anti-apoptotic members of the Bcl family, which are induced by survival signals including growth factors.
  - *Death receptor (extrinsic) pathway* is responsible for elimination of self-reactive lymphocytes and damage by cytotoxic T lymphocytes; is initiated by engagement of death receptors (members of the TNF receptor family) by ligands on adjacent cells.

AUTOPHAGY

Autophagy ("self-eating") refers to lysosomal digestion of the cell's own components. It is a survival mechanism in times of nutrient deprivation, such that the starved cell subsists by eating its own contents and recycling these contents to provide nutrients and energy. In this process, intracellular organelles and portions of cytosol are first sequestered within an *autophagic vacuole,* which is postulated to be formed from ribosome-free regions of the ER (Fig. 1–25). The vacuole fuses with lysosomes to form an *autophagolysosome,* in which lysosomal enzymes digest the cellular components. Autophagy is initiated by multiprotein complexes that sense nutrient deprivation and stimulate formation of the autophagic vacuole. With time, the starved cell eventually can no longer cope by devouring itself; at this stage, autophagy may also signal cell death by apoptosis.

Autophagy is also involved in the clearance of misfolded proteins, for instance, in neurons and hepatocytes. Therefore, defective autophagy may be a cause of neuronal death induced by accumulation of these proteins and, subsequently, neurodegenerative diseases. Conversely, pharmacologic activation of autophagy limits the build-up of misfolded proteins in liver cells in animal models,

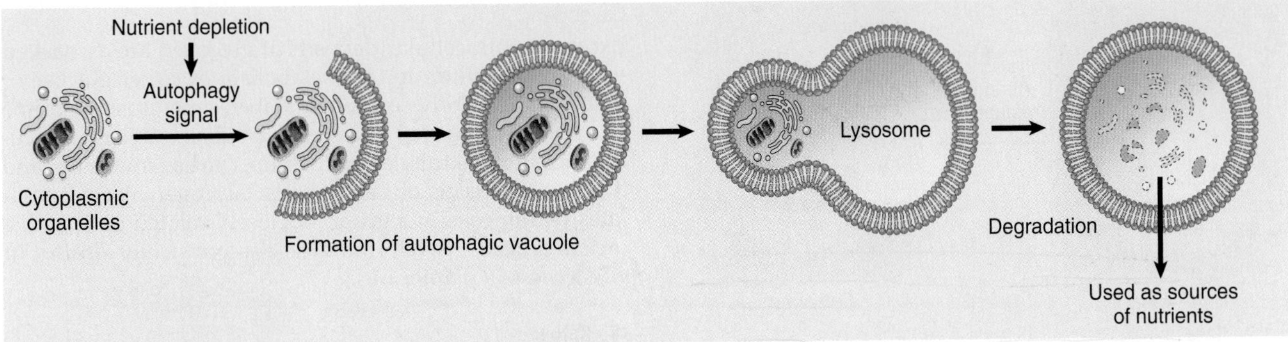

Figure 1–25 Autophagy. Cellular stresses, such as nutrient deprivation, activate autophagy genes (*Atg* genes), which initiate the formation of membrane-bound vesicles in which cellular organelles are sequestered. These vesicles fuse with lysosomes, in which the organelles are digested, and the products are used to provide nutrients for the cell. The same process can trigger apoptosis, by mechanisms that are not well defined.

thereby reducing liver fibrosis. Polymorphisms in a gene involved in autophagy have been associated with inflammatory bowel disease, but the mechanistic link between autophagy and intestinal inflammation is not known. The role of autophagy in cancer is discussed in Chapter 5. Thus, a once little-appreciated survival pathway in cells may prove to have wide-ranging roles in human disease.

We have now concluded the discussion of cell injury and cell death. As we have seen, these processes are the root cause of many common diseases. We end this chapter with brief considerations of three other processes: intracellular accumulations of various substances and extracellular deposition of calcium, both of which are often associated with cell injury, and aging.

INTRACELLULAR ACCUMULATIONS

Under some circumstances cells may accumulate abnormal amounts of various substances, which may be harmless or associated with varying degrees of injury. The substance may be located in the cytoplasm, within organelles (typically lysosomes), or in the nucleus, and it may be synthesized by the affected cells or may be produced elsewhere.

There are four main pathways of abnormal intracellular accumulations (Fig. 1–26):

- Inadequate removal of a normal substance secondary to defects in mechanisms of packaging and transport, as in fatty change in the liver
- Accumulation of an abnormal endogenous substance as a result of genetic or acquired defects in its folding, packaging, transport, or secretion, as with certain mutated forms of α_1-antitrypsin
- Failure to degrade a metabolite due to inherited enzyme deficiencies. The resulting disorders are called *storage diseases* (Chapter 6).
- Deposition and accumulation of an abnormal exogenous substance when the cell has neither the enzymatic machinery to degrade the substance nor the ability to transport it to other sites. Accumulation of carbon or silica particles is an example of this type of alteration.

Fatty Change (Steatosis)

Fatty change refers to any abnormal accumulation of triglycerides within parenchymal cells. It is most often seen in the liver, since this is the major organ involved in fat metabolism, but it may also occur in heart, skeletal muscle, kidney, and other organs. Steatosis may be caused by toxins, protein malnutrition, diabetes mellitus, obesity, or anoxia. *Alcohol abuse and diabetes associated with obesity are the most common causes of fatty change in the liver* (fatty liver) in industrialized nations. This process is discussed in more detail in Chapter 15.

Cholesterol and Cholesteryl Esters

Cellular cholesterol metabolism is tightly regulated to ensure normal cell membrane synthesis without significant intracellular accumulation. However, phagocytic cells may become overloaded with lipid (triglycerides, cholesterol, and cholesteryl esters) in several different pathologic processes. Of these, atherosclerosis is the most important. The role of lipid and cholesterol deposition in the pathogenesis of atherosclerosis is discussed in Chapter 9.

Proteins

Morphologically visible protein accumulations are much less common than lipid accumulations; they may occur when excesses are presented to the cells or if the cells synthesize excessive amounts. In the kidney, for example, trace amounts of albumin filtered through the glomerulus are normally reabsorbed by pinocytosis in the proximal convoluted tubules. However, in disorders with heavy protein leakage across the glomerular filter (e.g., nephrotic syndrome), there is a much larger reabsorption of the protein, and vesicles containing this protein accumulate, giving the histologic appearance of pink, hyaline cytoplasmic droplets. The process is reversible: If the proteinuria abates, the protein droplets are metabolized and disappear. Another example is the marked accumulation of newly synthesized immunoglobulins that may occur in the RER of some plasma cells, forming rounded, eosinophilic *Russell bodies.* Other examples of protein aggregation are discussed elsewhere in this book (e.g., "alcoholic hyaline" in the liver in Chapter 15; neurofibrillary tangles in neurons in Chapter 22).

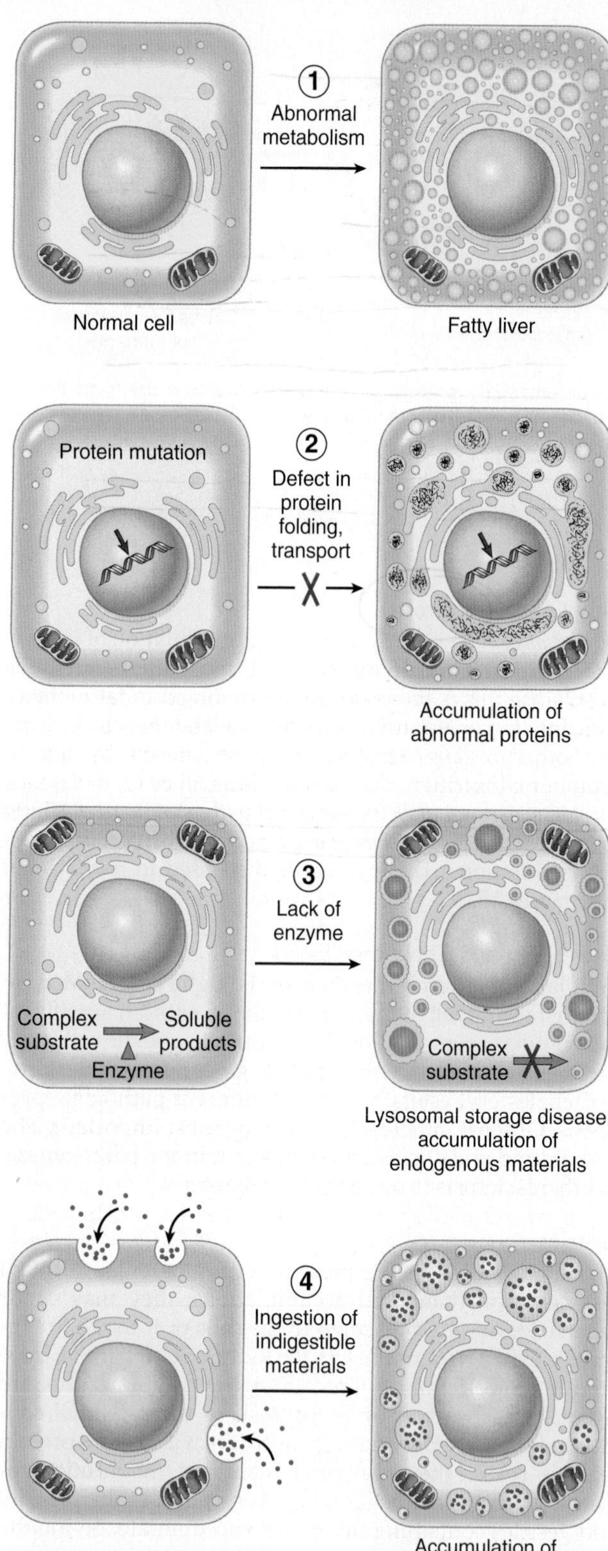

Figure 1–26 Mechanisms of intracellular accumulation: *(1)* Abnormal metabolism, as in fatty change in the liver. *(2)* Mutations causing alterations in protein folding and transport, so that defective molecules accumulate intracellularly. *(3)* A deficiency of critical enzymes responsible for breaking down certain compounds, causing substrates to accumulate in lysosomes, as in lysosomal storage diseases. *(4)* An inability to degrade phagocytosed particles, as in carbon pigment accumulation.

Glycogen

Excessive intracellular deposits of glycogen are associated with abnormalities in the metabolism of either glucose or glycogen. In poorly controlled diabetes mellitus, the prime example of abnormal glucose metabolism, glycogen accumulates in renal tubular epithelium, cardiac myocytes, and β cells of the islets of Langerhans. Glycogen also accumulates within cells in a group of closely related genetic disorders collectively referred to as *glycogen storage diseases,* or *glycogenoses* (Chapter 6).

Pigments

Pigments are colored substances that are either exogenous, coming from outside the body, such as carbon, or endogenous, synthesized within the body itself, such as lipofuscin, melanin, and certain derivatives of hemoglobin.

- The most common exogenous pigment is *carbon* (an example is coal dust), a ubiquitous air pollutant of urban life. When inhaled, it is phagocytosed by alveolar macrophages and transported through lymphatic channels to the regional tracheobronchial lymph nodes. Aggregates of the pigment blacken the draining lymph nodes and pulmonary parenchyma (*anthracosis*) (Chapter 12).
- *Lipofuscin,* or "wear-and-tear pigment," is an insoluble brownish-yellow granular intracellular material that accumulates in a variety of tissues (particularly the heart, liver, and brain) as a function of age or atrophy. Lipofuscin represents complexes of lipid and protein that derive from the free radical–catalyzed peroxidation of polyunsaturated lipids of subcellular membranes. It is not injurious to the cell but is a marker of past free radical injury. The brown pigment (Fig. 1–27), when present in large amounts, imparts an appearance to the tissue that is called *brown atrophy.* By electron microscopy, the pigment appears as perinuclear electron-dense granules (Fig. 1–27, *B*).
- *Melanin* is an endogenous, brown-black pigment that is synthesized by melanocytes located in the epidermis and acts as a screen against harmful ultraviolet radiation. Although melanocytes are the only source of melanin, adjacent basal keratinocytes in the skin can accumulate the pigment (e.g., in freckles), as can dermal macrophages.
- *Hemosiderin* is a hemoglobin-derived granular pigment that is golden yellow to brown and accumulates in tissues when there is a local or systemic excess of iron. Iron is normally stored within cells in association with the protein *apoferritin,* forming ferritin micelles. Hemosiderin pigment represents large aggregates of these ferritin micelles, readily visualized by light and electron microscopy; the iron can be unambiguously identified by the Prussian blue histochemical reaction (Fig. 1–28). Although hemosiderin accumulation is usually pathologic, small amounts of this pigment are normal in the mononuclear phagocytes of the bone marrow, spleen, and liver, where aging red cells are normally degraded. Excessive deposition of hemosiderin, called *hemosiderosis,* and more extensive accumulations of iron seen in *hereditary hemochromatosis,* are described in Chapter 15.

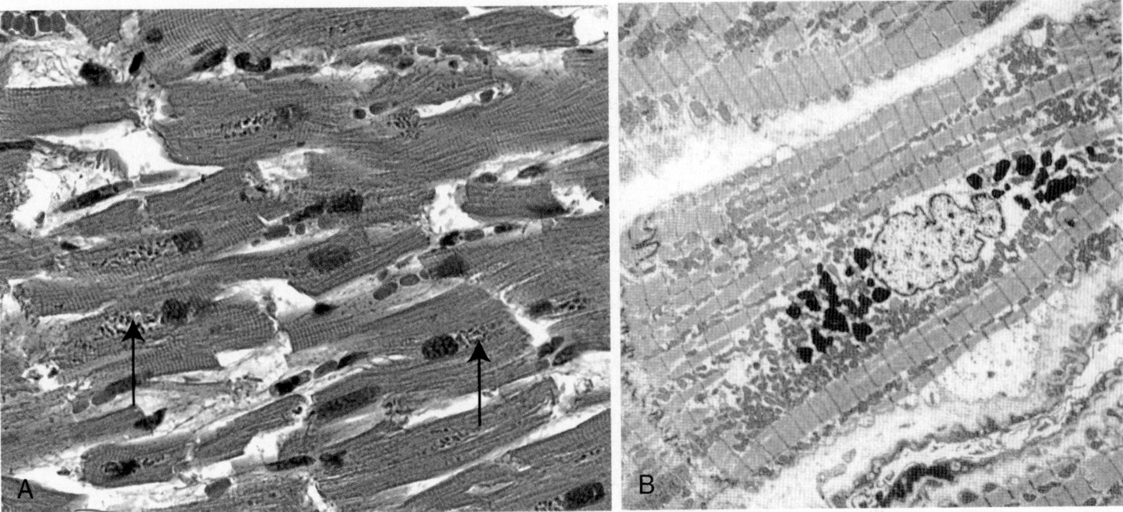

Figure 1–27 Lipofuscin granules in a cardiac myocyte. **A,** Light microscopy (deposits indicated by *arrows*). **B,** Electron microscopy. Note the perinuclear, intralysosomal location.

PATHOLOGIC CALCIFICATION

Pathologic calcification is a common process in a wide variety of disease states; it implies the abnormal deposition of calcium salts, together with smaller amounts of iron, magnesium, and other minerals. When the deposition occurs in dead or dying tissues, it is called *dystrophic calcification; it occurs in the absence of derangements in calcium metabolism* (i.e., with normal serum levels of calcium). In contrast, the deposition of calcium salts in normal tissues is known as *metastatic calcification and is almost always secondary to some derangement in calcium metabolism (hypercalcemia).* Of note, while hypercalcemia is not a prerequisite for dystrophic calcification, it can exacerbate it.

Dystrophic Calcification

Dystrophic calcification is encountered in areas of necrosis of any type. It is virtually inevitable in the *atheromas* of advanced atherosclerosis, associated with intimal injury in the aorta and large arteries and characterized by accumulation of lipids (Chapter 9). Although dystrophic calcification may be an incidental finding indicating insignificant past cell injury, it may also be a cause of organ dysfunction. For example, calcification can develop in aging or damaged heart valves, resulting in severely compromised valve motion. Dystrophic calcification of the aortic valves is an important cause of aortic stenosis in elderly persons (Fig. 10-17, Chapter 10).

The pathogenesis of dystrophic calcification involves *initiation* (or nucleation) and *propagation,* both of which may be either intracellular or extracellular; the ultimate end product is the formation of crystalline *calcium phosphate.* Initiation in extracellular sites occurs in membrane-bound vesicles about 200 nm in diameter; in normal cartilage and bone they are known as *matrix vesicles,* and in pathologic calcification they derive from degenerating cells. It is thought that calcium is initially concentrated in these vesicles by its affinity for membrane phospholipids, while phosphates accumulate as a result of the action of membrane-bound phosphatases. Initiation of intracellular calcification occurs in the mitochondria of dead or dying

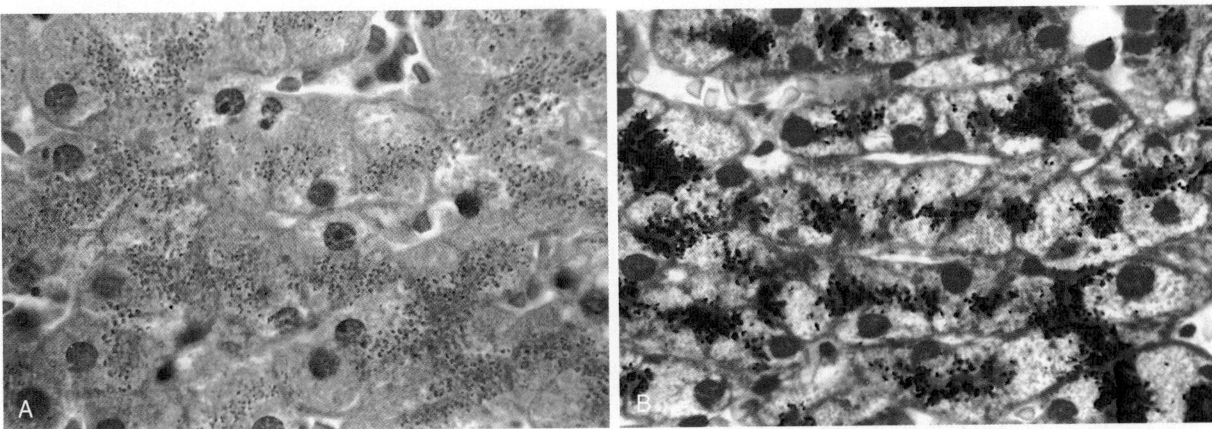

Figure 1–28 Hemosiderin granules in liver cells. **A,** Hematoxylin-eosin–stained section showing golden-brown, finely granular pigment. **B,** Iron deposits revealed by a special staining process called the Prussian blue reaction.

cells that have lost their ability to regulate intracellular calcium. After initiation in either location, propagation of crystal formation occurs. This is dependent on the concentration of Ca^{2+} and PO_4^-, the presence of mineral inhibitors, and the degree of collagenization, which enhances the rate of crystal growth.

Metastatic Calcification

Metastatic calcification can occur in normal tissues whenever there is hypercalcemia. The major causes of hypercalcemia are (1) *increased secretion of parathyroid hormone,* due to either primary parathyroid tumors or production of parathyroid hormone–related protein by other malignant tumors; (2) *destruction of bone* due to the effects of accelerated turnover (e.g., *Paget disease*), immobilization, or tumors (increased bone catabolism associated with multiple myeloma, leukemia, or diffuse skeletal metastases); (3) *vitamin D–related disorders* including vitamin D intoxication and *sarcoidosis* (in which macrophages activate a vitamin D precursor); and (4) *renal failure,* in which phosphate retention leads to *secondary hyperparathyroidism.*

MORPHOLOGY

Regardless of the site, calcium salts are seen on gross examination as fine white granules or clumps, often felt as gritty deposits. Dystrophic calcification is common in areas of caseous necrosis in tuberculosis. Sometimes a tuberculous lymph node is essentially converted to radiopaque stone. On histologic examination, calcification appears as intracellular and/or extracellular basophilic deposits. Over time, heterotopic bone may be formed in the focus of calcification.

Metastatic calcification can occur widely throughout the body but principally affects the interstitial tissues of the vasculature, kidneys, lungs, and gastric mucosa. The calcium deposits morphologically resemble those described in dystrophic calcification. Although they generally do not cause clinical dysfunction, extensive calcifications in the lungs may be evident on radiographs and may produce respiratory deficits, and massive deposits in the kidney **(nephrocalcinosis)** can lead to renal damage.

SUMMARY

Abnormal Intracellular Depositions and Calcifications

Abnormal deposits of materials in cells and tissues are the result of excessive intake or defective transport or catabolism.

- Depositions of *lipids*
  - *Fatty change:* accumulation of free triglycerides in cells, resulting from excessive intake or defective transport (often because of defects in synthesis of transport proteins); manifestation of reversible cell injury
  - *Cholesterol deposition:* result of defective catabolism and excessive intake; in macrophages and smooth muscle cells of vessel walls in atherosclerosis
- Deposition of *proteins:* reabsorbed proteins in kidney tubules; immunoglobulins in plasma cells
- Deposition of *glycogen:* in macrophages of patients with defects in lysosomal enzymes that break down glycogen (glycogen storage diseases)
- Deposition of *pigments:* typically indigestible pigments, such as carbon, lipofuscin (breakdown product of lipid peroxidation), or iron (usually due to overload, as in hemosiderosis)
- Pathologic calcifications
  - *Dystrophic calcification:* deposition of calcium at sites of cell injury and necrosis
  - *Metastatic calcification:* deposition of calcium in normal tissues, caused by hypercalcemia (usually a consequence of parathyroid hormone excess)

CELLULAR AGING

Individuals age because their cells age. Although public attention on the aging process has traditionally focused on its cosmetic manifestations, aging has important health consequences, because age is one of the strongest independent risk factors for many chronic diseases, such as cancer, Alzheimer disease, and ischemic heart disease. Perhaps one of the most striking discoveries about cellular aging is that it is not simply a consequence of cells' "running out of steam," but in fact is regulated by a limited number of genes and signaling pathways that are evolutionarily conserved from yeast to mammals.

Cellular aging is the result of a progressive decline in the life span and functional capacity of cells. Several mechanisms are thought to be responsible for cellular aging (Fig. 1–29):

- *DNA damage.* A variety of metabolic insults that accumulate over time may result in damage to nuclear and mitochondrial DNA. Although most DNA damage is repaired by DNA repair enzymes, some persists and accumulates as cells age. Some aging syndromes are associated with defects in DNA repair mechanisms, and the life span of experimental animals in some models can be increased if responses to DNA damage are enhanced or proteins that stabilize DNA are introduced. A role of free radicals in DNA damage leading to aging has been postulated but remains controversial.
- *Decreased cellular replication.* All normal cells have a limited capacity for replication, and after a fixed number of divisions cells become arrested in a terminally nondividing state, known as *replicative senescence.* Aging is associated with progressive replicative senescence of cells. Cells from children have the capacity to undergo more rounds of replication than do cells from older people. In contrast, cells from patients with *Werner syndrome,* a rare disease characterized by premature aging, have a markedly reduced in vitro life span. In human cells, the mechanism of replicative senescence involves progressive shortening of telomeres, which ultimately results in cell cycle arrest. *Telomeres* are short repeated sequences of DNA present at the ends of linear chromosomes that are important for ensuring the complete replication of chromosome ends and for protecting the ends from fusion and degradation. When somatic cells replicate, a small section of the telomere is not duplicated,

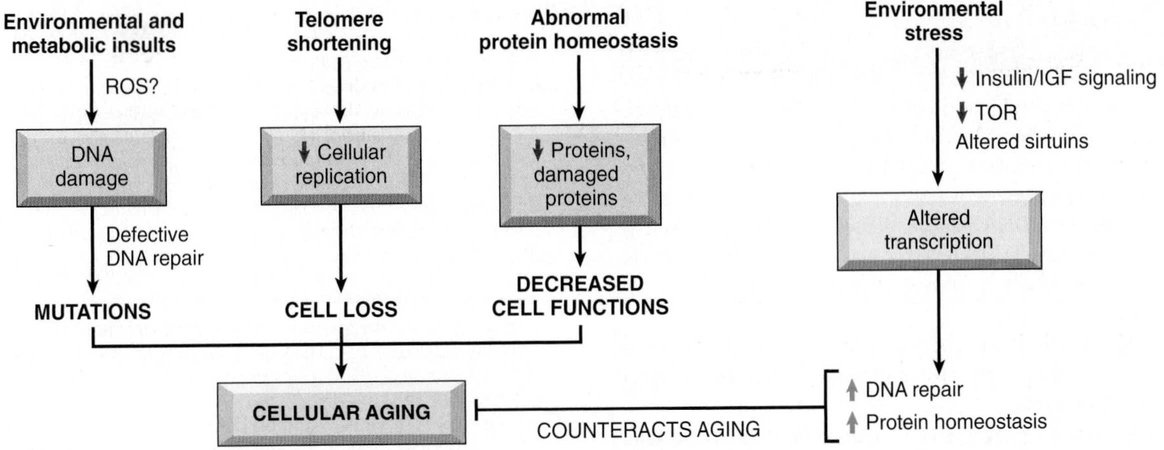

Figure 1–29 Mechanisms that cause and counteract cellular aging. DNA damage, replicative senescence, and decreased and misfolded proteins are among the best described mechanisms of cellular aging. Some environmental stresses, such as calorie restriction, counteract aging by activating various signaling pathways and transcription factors. IGF, insulin-like growth factor; TOR, target of rapamycin.

and telomeres become progressively shortened. As the telomeres become shorter, the ends of chromosomes cannot be protected and are seen as broken DNA, which signals cell cycle arrest. Telomere length is maintained by nucleotide addition mediated by an enzyme called *telomerase*. Telomerase is a specialized RNA-protein complex that uses its own RNA as a template for adding nucleotides to the ends of chromosomes. Telomerase activity is expressed in germ cells and is present at low levels in stem cells, but it is absent in most somatic tissues (Fig. 1-30). Therefore, as most somatic cells age their telomeres become shorter and they exit the cell cycle, resulting in an inability to generate new cells to replace damaged ones. Conversely, in immortalized cancer cells, telomerase is usually reactivated and

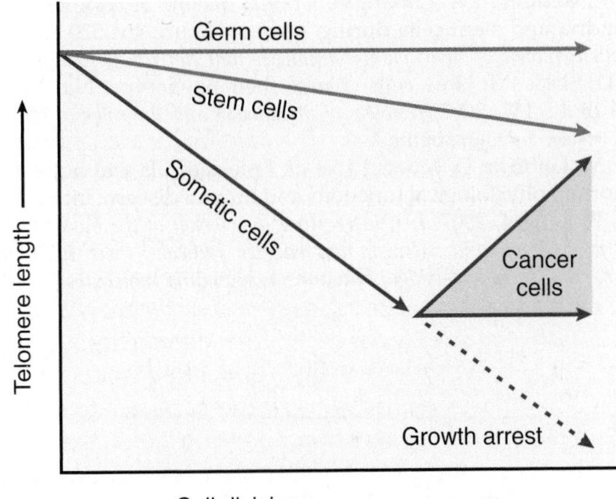

Figure 1–30 The role of telomeres and telomerase in replicative senescence of cells. Telomere length is plotted against the number of cell divisions. In most normal somatic cells there is no telomerase activity, and telomeres progressively shorten with increasing cell divisions until growth arrest, or senescence, occurs. Germ cells and stem cells both contain active telomerase, but only the germ cells have sufficient levels of the enzyme to stabilize telomere length completely. In cancer cells, telomerase is often reactivated.

(Data from Macmillan Publishers Ltd, from Holt SE, et al: Refining the telomer-telomerase hypothesis of aging and cancer. Nat Biotechnol 14:836, 1996.)

telomere length is stabilized, allowing the cells to proliferate indefinitely. This is discussed more fully in Chapter 5. Telomere shortening may also decrease the regenerative capacity of stem cells, further contributing to cellular aging. Despite such alluring observations, however, the relationship of telomerase activity and telomere length to aging has yet to be fully established.

- *Defective protein homeostasis.* Over time, cells are unable to maintain normal protein homeostasis, because of increased turnover and decreased synthesis caused by reduced translation of proteins and defective activity of chaperones (which promote normal protein folding), proteasomes (which destroy misfolded proteins) and repair enzymes. Abnormal protein homeostasis can have many effects on cell survival, replication, and functions. In addition, it may lead to accumulation of misfolded proteins, which can trigger pathways of apoptosis.

There has been great interest in defining signaling pathways that counteract the aging process, not only because of their obvious therapeutic potential (the search for the "elixir of youth") but also because elucidating these pathways might tell us about the mechanisms that cause aging. It is now thought that certain *environmental stresses, such as calorie restriction, alter signaling pathways that influence aging* (Fig. 1-29). Among the biochemical alterations that have been described as playing a role in counteracting the aging process are reduced signaling by insulin-like growth factor receptors, reduced activation of kinases (notably the "target of rapamycin," [TOR], and the AKT kinase), and altered transcriptional activity. Ultimately these changes lead to improved DNA repair and protein homeostasis and enhanced immunity, all of which inhibit aging. Environmental stresses may also activate proteins of the Sirtuin family, such as Sir2, which function as protein deacetylases. These proteins may deacetylate and thereby activate DNA repair enzymes, thus stabilizing the DNA; in the absence of these proteins, DNA is more prone to damage. Although the role of sirtuins has received a great deal of attention recently, their importance in the aging process is not yet established.

SUMMARY

Cellular Aging

- Results from combination of accumulating cellular damage (e.g., by free radicals), reduced capacity to divide (replicative senescence), and reduced ability to repair damaged DNA
- *Accumulation of DNA damage:* defective DNA repair mechanisms; conversely DNA repair may be activated by calorie restriction, which is known to prolong aging in model organisms
- *Replicative senescence:* reduced capacity of cells to divide secondary to progressive shortening of chromosomal ends (telomeres)
- *Other factors:* progressive accumulation of metabolic damage; possible roles of growth factors that promote aging in simple model organisms

It should be apparent that the various forms of cellular derangements and adaptations described in this chapter cover a wide spectrum, ranging from adaptations in cell size, growth, and function, to the reversible and irreversible forms of acute cell injury, to the regulated type of cell death represented by apoptosis. Reference is made to these many different alterations throughout this book, because all instances of organ injury and ultimately all cases of clinical disease arise from derangements in cell structure and function.

BIBLIOGRAPHY

Auten RL, Davis JM: Oxygen toxicity and reactive oxygen species: the devil is in the details. Pediatr Res 66:121, 2009. *[A review of the production and degradation of reactive oxygen species, and their roles in cell injury.]*

Balaban RS, Nemoto S, Finkel T: Mitochondria, oxidants, and aging. Cell 120:483, 2005. *[A good review of the role of free radicals in aging.]*

Calado RT, Young NS: Telomere diseases. N Engl J Med 361:2353, 2009. *[An excellent review of the basic biology of telomeres, and how their abnormalities may contribute to cancer, aging, and other diseases.]*

Chipuk JE, Moldoveanu T, Llambl F, et al: The BCL-2 family reunion. Mol Cell 37:299, 2010. *[A review of the biochemistry and biology of the BCL-2 family of apoptosis-regulating proteins.]*

de Groot H, Rauen U: Ischemia-reperfusion injury: processes in pathogenetic networks: a review. Transplant Proc 39:481, 2007. *[A review of the roles of intrinsic cell injury and the inflammatory response in ischemia-reperfusion injury.]*

Dong Z, Saikumar P, Weinberg JM, Venkatachalam MA: Calcium in cell injury and death. Annu Rev Pathol 1:405, 2006. *[A review of the links between calcium and cell injury.]*

Elliott MR, Ravichandran KS: Clearance of apoptotic cells: implications in health and disease. J Cell Biol 189:1059, 2010. *[An excellent review of the mechanisms by which apoptotic cells are cleared, and how abnormalities in these clearance pathways may result in disease.]*

Frey N, Olson EN: Cardiac hypertrophy: the good, the bad, and the ugly. Annu Rev Physiol 65:45, 2003. *[Excellent discussion of the mechanisms of muscle hypertrophy, using the heart as the paradigm.]*

Galluzzi L, Aaronson SA, Abrams J, et al: Guidelines for the use and interpretation of assays for monitoring cell death in higher eukaryotes. Cell Death Differ 16:1093, 2009. *[A practical summary of the morphologic and other techniques for detecting and quantifying dead cells.]*

Haigis MC, Yankner BA: The aging stress response. Mol Cell 40:333, 2010. *[A review of the role of cellular stresses in controlling the aging process.]*

Hotchkiss RS, Strasser A, McDunn JE, Swanson PE: Cell death. N Engl J Med 361:1570, 2009. *[Excellent review of the major pathways of cell death (necrosis, apoptosis, and autophagy-associated death), and their clinical implications and therapeutic targeting.]*

Kenyon CJ: The genetics of ageing. Nature 464:504, 2010. *[An excellent review of the genes that influence aging, based on human genetic syndromes and studies with mutant model organisms.]*

Kroemer G, Marino G, Levine B: Autophagy and the integrated stress response. Mol Cell 40:280, 2010. *[An excellent discussion of the biology, biochemical pathways, and physiologic roles of autophagy.]*

Kundu M, Thompson CB: Autophagy: basic principles and relevance to disease. Annu Rev Pathol 3:427, 2008. *[A discussion of the biology of autophagy and its potential contribution to a variety of disease states.]*

Lin JH, Walter P, Yen TSB: Endoplasmic reticulum stress in disease pathogenesis. Annu Rev Pathol 3:399, 2008. *[A review of the biology and disease relevance of the unfolded protein response and ER stress induced by unfolded proteins.]*

Lombard DB, Chua KF, Mostoslavsky R, et al: DNA repair, genome stability, and aging. Cell 120:497, 2005. *[The role of DNA damage in cellular aging.]*

McKinnell IW, Rudnicki MA: Molecular mechanisms of muscle atrophy. Cell 119:907, 2004. *[Discussion of the mechanisms of cellular atrophy.]*

Newmeyer DD, Ferguson-Miller S: Mitochondria: releasing power for life and unleashing the machineries of death. Cell 112:481, 2003. *[Excellent review of the many functions of mitochondria, with an emphasis on their role in cell death.]*

Sahin E, DePinho RA: Linking functional decline of telomeres, mitochondria and stem cells during ageing. Nature 464:520, 2010. *[An excellent review of stem cell abnormalities that contribute to aging.]*

Tosh D, Slack JM: How cells change their phenotype. Nat Rev Mol Cell Biol 3:187, 2002. *[Review of metaplasia and the roles of stem cells and genetic reprogramming.]*

Valko M, Leibfritz D, Moncol J, et al: Free radicals and antioxidants in normal physiological functions and human disease. Int J Biochem Cell Biol 39:44, 2007. *[An interesting discussion of the biochemistry of reactive oxygen and nitrogen-derived free radicals, their roles in cell injury, and their physiologic functions as signaling molecules.]*

See Targeted Therapy available online at
studentconsult.com

CHAPTER 2

Inflammation and Repair

CHAPTER CONTENTS

OVERVIEW OF INFLAMMATION AND TISSUE REPAIR

The survival of all organisms requires that they eliminate foreign invaders, such as infectious agents, and damaged tissues. These functions are mediated by a complex host response called *inflammation. Inflammation is a protective response involving host cells, blood vessels, and proteins and other mediators that is intended to eliminate the initial cause of cell injury, as well as the necrotic cells and tissues resulting from the original insult, and to initiate the process of repair.* Inflammation accomplishes its protective mission by first diluting, destroying, or otherwise neutralizing harmful agents (e.g., microbes, toxins). It then sets into motion the events that eventually heal and repair the sites of injury. Without inflammation, infections would go unchecked and wounds would never heal. In the context of infections, inflammation is one component of a protective response that immunologists refer to as innate immunity (Chapter 4).

Although inflammation helps clear infections and other noxious stimuli and initiates repair, the inflammatory reaction and the subsequent repair process can themselves cause considerable harm. The components of the inflammatory reaction that destroy and eliminate microbes and dead tissues are also capable of injuring normal tissues. Therefore, injury may accompany entirely normal, beneficial inflammatory reactions, and the damage may even become the dominant feature if the reaction is very strong (e.g., when the infection is severe), prolonged (e.g., when the eliciting agent resists eradication), or inappropriate (e.g., when it is directed against self-antigens in autoimmune diseases, or against usually harmless environmental antigens (e.g., in allergic disorders). Some of the most vexing diseases of humans are disorders that result from inappropriate, often chronic, inflammation. Thus, the process of inflammation is fundamental to virtually all of clinical medicine.

The cells and molecules of host defense, including leukocytes and plasma proteins, normally circulate in the blood, and the goal of the inflammatory reaction is to bring them to the site of infection or tissue damage. In addition, resident cells of vascular walls and the cells and proteins of the extracellular matrix (ECM) are also involved in inflammation and repair (Fig. 2–1). Before we describe the process of inflammation in detail, some of the basic features will be highlighted.

Inflammation can be acute or chronic (Table 2–1). Acute inflammation is rapid in onset and of short duration, lasting

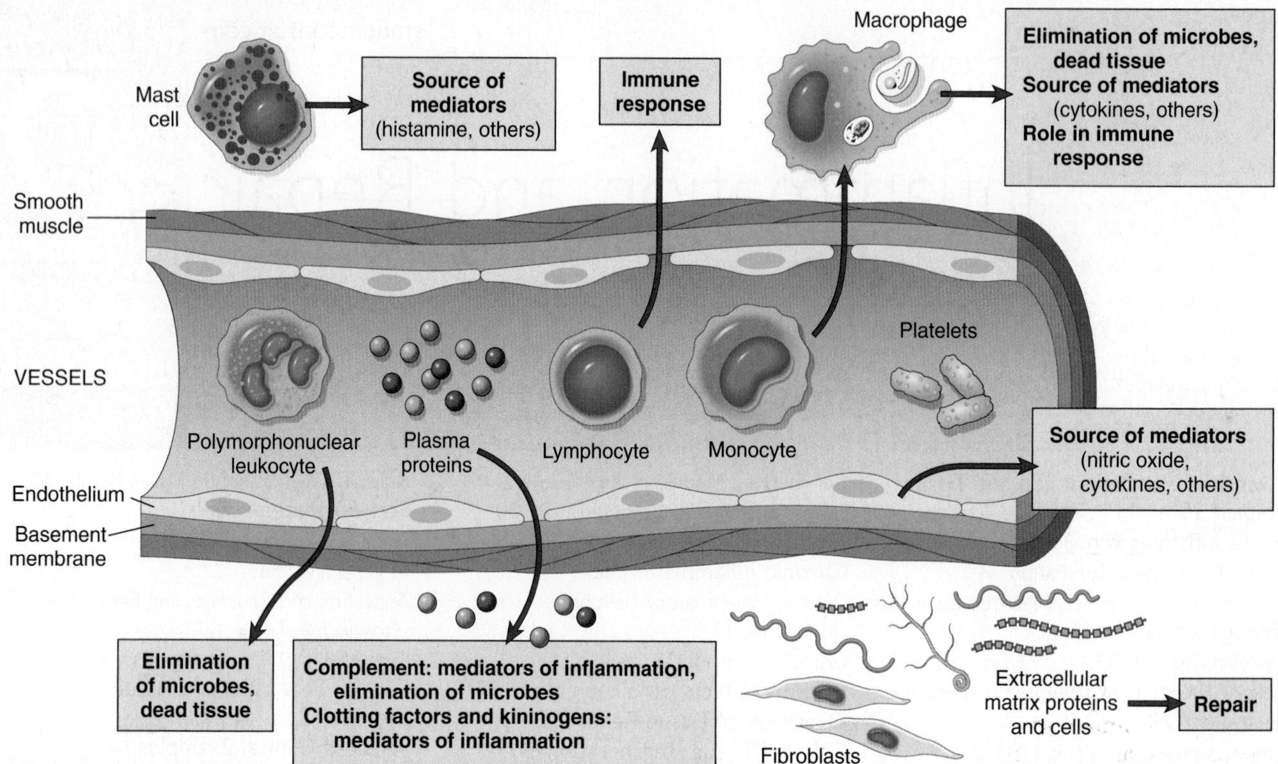

Figure 2–1 The components of acute and chronic inflammatory responses and their principal functions. The roles of these cells and molecules in inflammation are described in this chapter.

from a few minutes to as long as a few days, and is characterized by fluid and plasma protein exudation and a predominantly neutrophilic leukocyte accumulation. Chronic inflammation may be more insidious, is of longer duration (days to years), and is typified by influx of lymphocytes and macrophages with associated vascular proliferation and fibrosis (scarring). As we shall see later, however, these two basic forms of inflammation may coexist, and many variables modify their course and histologic appearance.

Inflammation is induced by chemical mediators that are produced by host cells in response to injurious stimuli. When a microbe enters a tissue or the tissue is injured, the presence of the infection or damage is sensed by resident cells, mainly macrophages, but also dendritic cells, mast cells, and other cell types. These cells secrete molecules (cytokines and other mediators) that induce and regulate the subsequent inflammatory response. Inflammatory mediators are also produced from plasma proteins that react with the microbes or to injured tissues. Some of these mediators promote the efflux of plasma and the recruitment of circulating leukocytes to the site where the offending agent is located. The recruited leukocytes are activated and they try to remove the offending agent by phagocytosis. An unfortunate side effect of the activation of leukocytes may be damage to normal host tissues.

The external manifestations of inflammation, often called its cardinal signs, are heat (calor), redness (rubor), swelling (tumor), pain (dolor), and loss of function (functio laesa). The first four of these were described more than 2000 years ago by a Roman encyclopedist named Celsus, who wrote the then-famous text *De Medicina,* and the fifth was added in the late 19th century by Rudolf Virchow, known as the "father of modern pathology." These manifestations occur as consequences of the vascular changes and leukocyte recruitment and activation, as will be evident from the discussion that follows.

Inflammation is normally controlled and self-limited. The mediators and cells are activated only in response to the injurious stimulus and are short-lived, and they are degraded or become inactive as the injurious agent is eliminated. In addition, various anti-inflammatory mechanisms become active. If the injurious agent cannot be quickly eliminated, the result may be chronic inflammation, which can have serious pathologic consequences.

Table 2–1 Features of Acute and Chronic Inflammation

Feature	Acute	Chronic
Onset	Fast: minutes or hours	Slow: days
Cellular infiltrate	Mainly neutrophils	Monocytes/macrophages and lymphocytes
Tissue injury, fibrosis	Usually mild and self-limited	Often severe and progressive
Local and systemic signs	Prominent	Less prominent; may be subtle

> **SUMMARY**
> **General Features of Inflammation**
>
> - Inflammation is a defensive host response to foreign invaders and necrotic tissue, but it is itself capable of causing tissue damage.
> - The main components of inflammation are a vascular reaction and a cellular response; both are activated by mediators derived from plasma proteins and various cells.
> - The steps of the inflammatory response can be remembered as the five *R*s: (1) *r*ecognition of the injurious agent, (2) *r*ecruitment of leukocytes, (3) *r*emoval of the agent, (4) *r*egulation (control) of the response, and (5) *r*esolution (repair).
> - The outcome of acute inflammation is either elimination of the noxious stimulus, followed by decline of the reaction and repair of the damaged tissue, or persistent injury resulting in chronic inflammation.

ACUTE INFLAMMATION

The acute inflammatory response rapidly delivers leukocytes and plasma proteins to sites of injury. Once there, leukocytes clear the invaders and begin the process of digesting and getting rid of necrotic tissues.

Acute inflammation has two major components (Fig. 2–2):

- *Vascular changes:* alterations in vessel caliber resulting in increased blood flow (vasodilation) and changes in the vessel wall that permit plasma proteins to leave the circulation (increased vascular permeability). In addition, endothelial cells are activated, resulting in increased adhesion of leukocytes and migration of the leukocytes through the vessel wall.
- *Cellular events:* emigration of the leukocytes from the circulation and accumulation in the focus of injury (cellular recruitment), followed by activation of the leukocytes, enabling them to eliminate the offending agent. The principal leukocytes in acute inflammation are neutrophils (polymorphonuclear leukocytes).

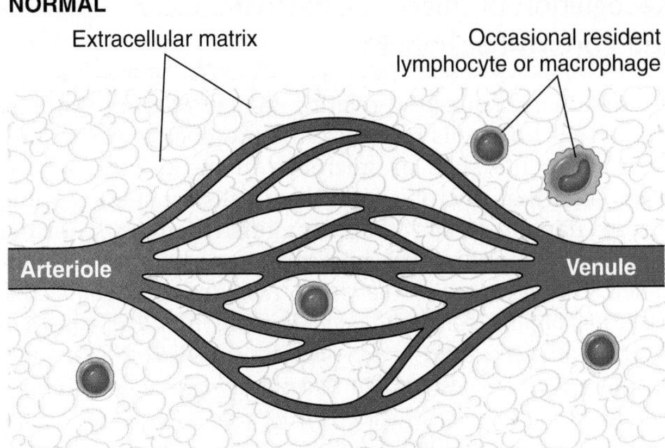

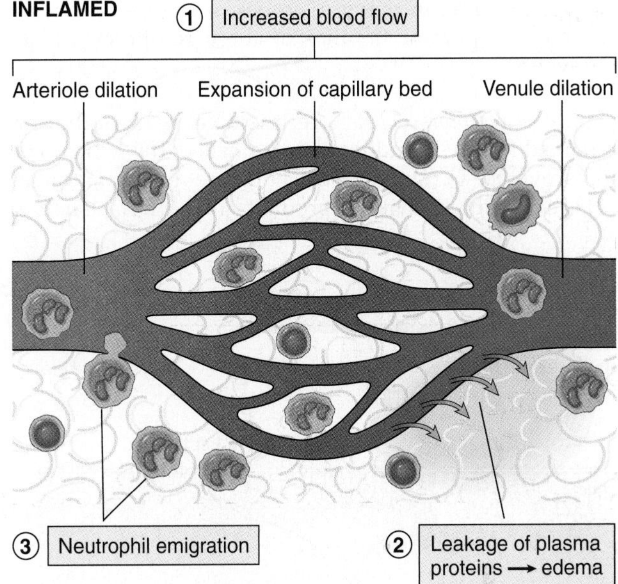

Figure 2–2 Vascular and cellular reactions of acute inflammation. The major local manifestations of acute inflammation, compared with normal, are *(1)* vascular dilation and increased blood flow (causing erythema and warmth), *(2)* extravasation of plasma fluid and proteins (edema), and *(3)* leukocyte (mainly neutrophil) emigration and accumulation.

Stimuli for Acute Inflammation

Acute inflammatory reactions may be triggered by a variety of stimuli:

- *Infections* (bacterial, viral, fungal, parasitic) are among the most common and medically important causes of inflammation.
- *Trauma* (blunt and penetrating) and various physical and chemical agents (e.g., thermal injury, such as burns or frostbite; irradiation; toxicity from certain environmental chemicals) injure host cells and elicit inflammatory reactions.
- *Tissue necrosis* (from any cause), including ischemia (as in a myocardial infarct) and physical and chemical injury
- *Foreign bodies* (splinters, dirt, sutures, crystal deposits)
- *Immune reactions* (also called *hypersensitivity reactions*) against environmental substances or against "self" tissues. Because the stimuli for these inflammatory responses often cannot be eliminated or avoided, such reactions tend to persist, with features of chronic inflammation. The term "immune-mediated inflammatory disease" is sometimes used to refer to this group of disorders.

Although each of these stimuli may induce reactions with some distinctive characteristics, in general, all inflammatory reactions have the same basic features.

In this section, we describe first how inflammatory stimuli are recognized by the host, then the typical reactions of acute inflammation and its morphologic features, and finally the chemical mediators responsible for these reactions.

Recognition of Microbes, Necrotic Cells, and Foreign Substances

A fundamental question relating to activation of the host response is how cells recognize the presence of potentially harmful agents such as microbes in the tissues. It was postulated that microbes and dead cells must elicit some sort of "danger signals" that distinguish them from normal tissues and mobilize the host response. It is now established that *phagocytes, dendritic cells (cells in connective tissue and organs that capture microbes and initiate responses to them), and many other cells, such as epithelial cells, express receptors that are designed to sense the presence of infectious pathogens and substances released from dead cells.* These receptors have been called "pattern recognition receptors" because they recognize structures (i.e., molecular patterns) that are common to many microbes or to dead cells. The two most important families of these receptors are the following:

- *Toll-like receptors (TLRs)* are microbial sensors that are named for the founding member called *Toll,* which was discovered in *Drosophila.* There are ten mammalian TLRs, which recognize products of bacteria (such as endotoxin and bacterial DNA), viruses (such as double-stranded RNA), and other pathogens (Fig. 2–3, *A*). TLRs are located in plasma membranes and endosomes, so they are able to detect extracellular and ingested microbes. They are complemented by cytoplasmic and membrane molecules, from several other families, that also recognize microbial products. TLRs and the other receptors recognize products of different types of microbes and thus provide defense against essentially all classes of infectious pathogens. Recognition of microbes by these receptors activates transcription factors that stimulate the production of a number of secreted and membrane proteins. These proteins include mediators of inflammation, antiviral cytokines (interferons), and proteins that promote lymphocyte activation and even more potent immune responses. We return to TLRs in Chapter 4, when we discuss innate immunity, the early defense against infections.
- The *inflammasome* is a multi-protein cytoplasmic complex that recognizes products of dead cells, such as uric acid and extracellular ATP, as well as crystals and some microbial products. Triggering of the inflammasome results in activation of an enzyme called caspase-1, which cleaves precursor forms of the inflammatory

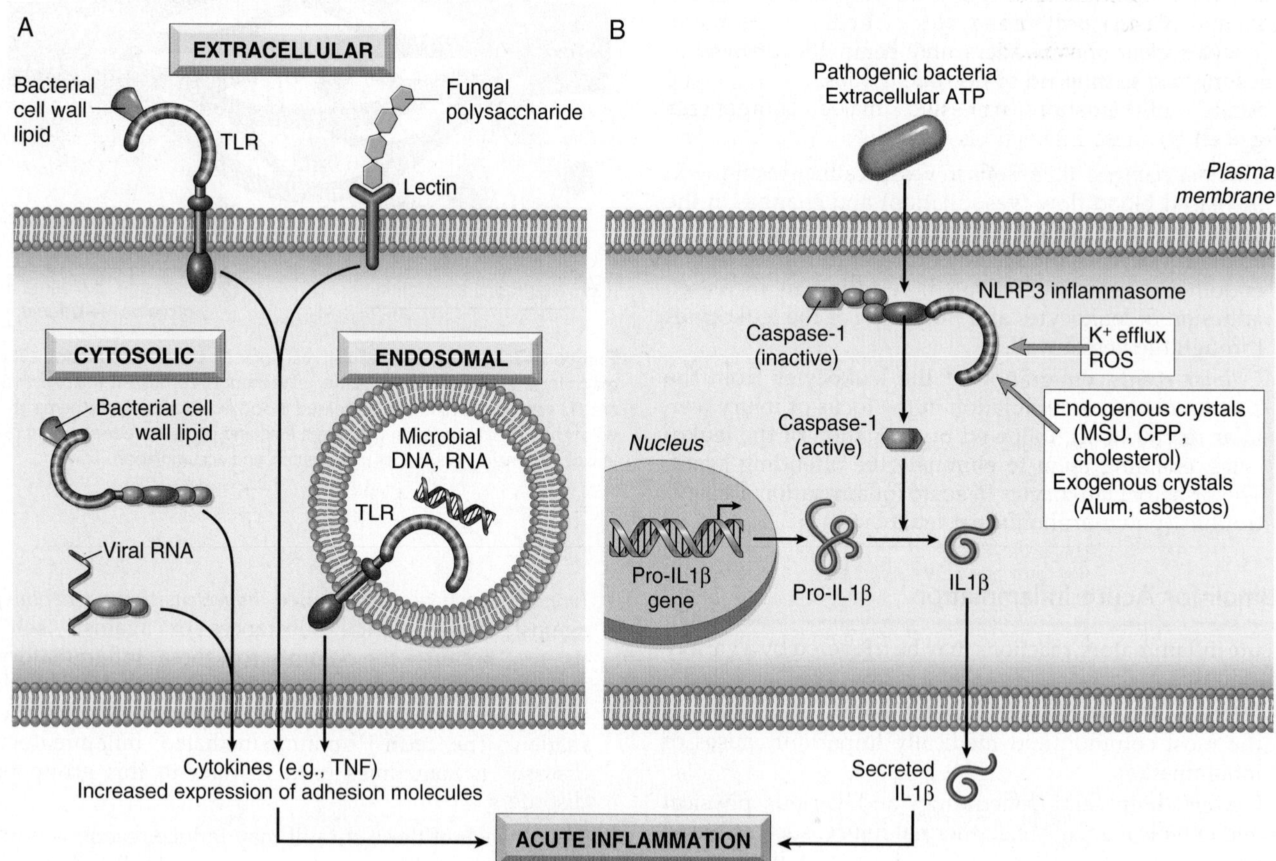

Figure 2–3 Sensors of microbes and dead cells: Phagocytes, dendritic cells, and many types of epithelial cells express different classes of receptors that sense the presence of microbes and dead cells. **A, Toll-like receptors** (TLRs) located in the plasma membrane and endosomes and other cytoplasmic and plasma membrane receptors (members of families other than TLRs) recognize products of different classes of microbes. The proteins produced by TLR activation have numerous functions; only their role in inflammation is shown. **B,** The **inflammasome** is a protein complex that recognizes products of dead cells and some microbes and induces the secretion of biologically active interleukin-1 (IL-1). The inflammasome consists of a sensor protein (a leucine-rich protein called NLRP3), an adaptor, and the enzyme caspase-1, which is converted from an inactive to an active form. (Note that the inflammasome is distinct from phagolysosomes, which also are present in the cytoplasm but are vesicles that serve different functions in inflammation, as discussed later in the chapter.) CPP, calcium pyrophosphate; MSU, monosodium urate.

cytokine interleukin-1β (IL-1β) into its biologically active form (Fig. 2–3, *B*). As discussed later, IL-1 is an important mediator of leukocyte recruitment in the acute inflammatory response, and the leukocytes phagocytose and destroy dead cells. The joint disease, gout, is caused by deposition of urate crystals, which are ingested by phagocytes and activate the inflammasome, resulting in IL-1 production and acute inflammation. IL-1 antagonists are effective treatments in cases of gout that are resistant to conventional anti-inflammatory therapy. Recent studies have shown that cholesterol crystals and free fatty acids also activate the inflammasome, suggesting that IL-1 plays a role in common diseases such as atherosclerosis (associated with deposition of cholesterol crystals in vessel walls) and obesity-associated type 2 diabetes. This finding raises the possibility of treating these diseases by blocking IL-1.

The functions of these sensors are referred to throughout the chapter. We now proceed with a discussion of the principal reactions of acute inflammation.

Vascular Changes

The main vascular reactions of acute inflammation are increased blood flow secondary to vasodilation and increased vascular permeability, both designed to bring blood cells and proteins to sites of infection or injury. While the initial encounter of an injurious stimulus, such as a microbe, is with macrophages and other cells in the connective tissue, the vascular reactions triggered by these interactions soon follow and dominate the early phase of the response.

Changes in Vascular Caliber and Flow

Changes in blood vessels are initiated rapidly after infection or injury but evolve at variable rates, depending on the nature and severity of the original inflammatory stimulus.

- After transient vasoconstriction (lasting only for seconds), arteriolar vasodilation occurs, resulting in locally increased blood flow and engorgement of the down-stream capillary beds (Fig. 2–2). This vascular expansion is the cause of the redness (*erythema*) and warmth characteristic of acute inflammation, and mentioned previously as two of the cardinal signs of inflammation.
- The microvasculature becomes more permeable, and protein-rich fluid moves into the extravascular tissues. This causes the red cells in the flowing blood to become more concentrated, thereby increasing blood viscosity and slowing the circulation. These changes are reflected microscopically by numerous dilated small vessels packed with red blood cells, called *stasis.*
- As stasis develops, leukocytes (principally neutrophils) begin to accumulate along the vascular endothelial surface—a process called *margination.* This is the first step in the journey of the leukocytes through the vascular wall into the interstitial tissue (described later).

Increased Vascular Permeability

Increasing vascular permeability leads to the movement of protein-rich fluid and even blood cells into the extravascular tissues (Fig. 2–4). This in turn increases the osmotic pressure of the interstitial fluid, leading to more outflow of

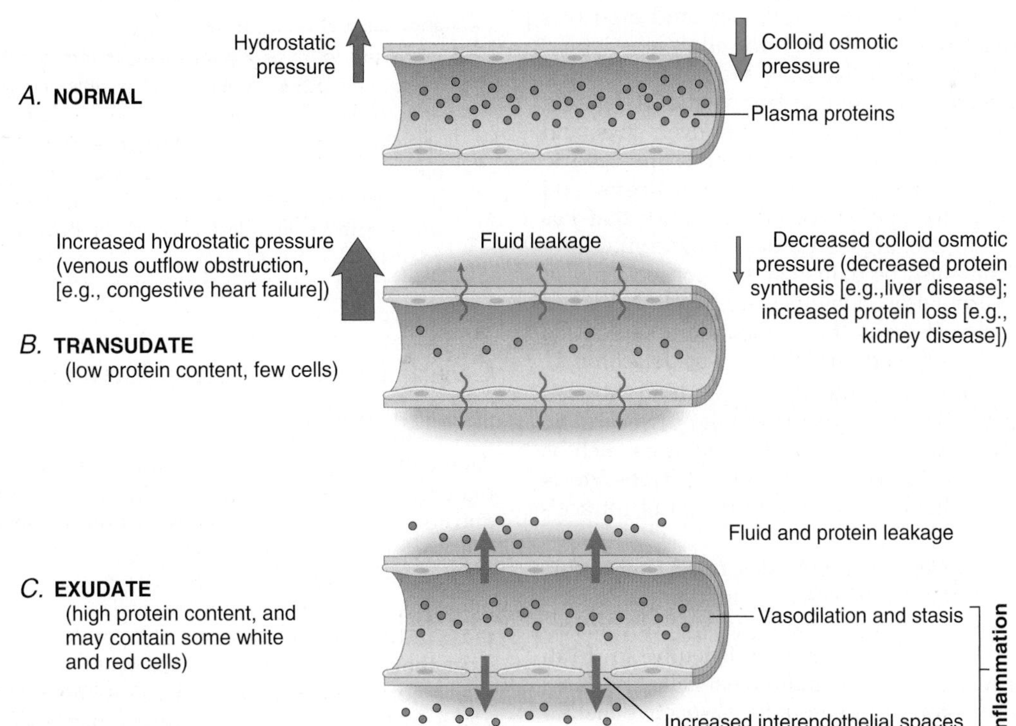

Figure 2–4 Formation of transudates and exudates. *A,* Normal hydrostatic pressure (*blue arrows*) is approximately 32 mm Hg at the arterial end of a capillary bed and 12 mm Hg at the venous end; the mean colloid osmotic pressure of tissues is approximately 25 mm Hg (*green arrows*), which is nearly equal to the mean capillary pressure. Therefore, the net flow of fluid across the vascular bed is almost nil. *B,* A transudate is formed when fluid leaks out because of increased hydrostatic pressure or decreased osmotic pressure. *C,* An exudate is formed in inflammation because vascular permeability increases as a result of the increase in interendothelial spaces.

water from the blood into the tissues. The resulting protein-rich fluid accumulation is called an *exudate*. Exudates must be distinguished from *transudates,* which are interstitial fluid accumulations caused by increased hydrostatic pressure, usually a consequence of reduced venous return. Transudates typically contain low concentrations of protein and few or no blood cells. Fluid accumulation in extravascular spaces, whether from an exudate or a transudate, produces tissue *edema.* Whereas exudates are typical of inflammation, transudates accumulate in various noninflammatory conditions, which are mentioned in Figure 2–4 and described in more detail in Chapter 3.

Several mechanisms may contribute to increased vascular permeability in acute inflammatory reactions:

- *Endothelial cell contraction leading to intercellular gaps in postcapillary venules* is the most common cause of increased vascular permeability. Endothelial cell contraction occurs rapidly after binding of histamine, bradykinin, leukotrienes, and many other mediators to specific receptors, and is usually short-lived (15 to 30 minutes). A slower and more prolonged retraction of endothelial cells, resulting from changes in the cytoskeleton, may be induced by cytokines such as tumor necrosis factor (TNF) and interleukin-1 (IL-1). This reaction may take 4 to 6 hours to develop after the initial trigger and persist for 24 hours or more.
- *Endothelial injury* results in vascular leakage by causing endothelial cell necrosis and detachment. Endothelial cells are damaged after severe injury such as with burns and some infections. In most cases, leakage begins immediately after the injury and persists for several hours (or days) until the damaged vessels are thrombosed or repaired. Venules, capillaries, and arterioles can all be affected, depending on the site of the injury. Direct injury to endothelial cells may also induce a delayed prolonged leakage that begins after a delay of 2 to 12 hours, lasts for several hours or even days, and involves venules and capillaries. Examples are mild to moderate thermal injury, certain bacterial toxins, and x- or ultraviolet irradiation (i.e., the sunburn that has spoiled many an evening after a day in the sun). Endothelial cells may also be damaged as a consequence of leukocyte accumulation along the vessel wall. Activated leukocytes release many toxic mediators, discussed later, that may cause endothelial injury or detachment.
- *Increased transcytosis* of proteins by way of an intracellular vesicular pathway augments venular permeability, especially after exposure to certain mediators such as vascular endothelial growth factor (VEGF). Transcytosis occurs through channels formed by fusion of intracellular vesicles.
- *Leakage from new blood vessels.* As described later, tissue repair involves new blood vessel formation (angiogenesis). These vessel sprouts remain leaky until proliferating endothelial cells mature sufficiently to form intercellular junctions. New endothelial cells also have increased expression of receptors for vasoactive mediators, and some of the factors that stimulate angiogenesis (e.g., VEGF) also directly induce increased vascular permeability.

Although these mechanisms of vascular permeability are separable, all of them may participate in the response to a particular stimulus. For example, in a thermal burn, leakage results from chemically mediated endothelial contraction, as well as from direct injury and leukocyte-mediated endothelial damage.

Responses of Lymphatic Vessels

In addition to blood vessels, lymphatic vessels also participate in the inflammatory response. In inflammation, lymph flow is increased and helps drain edema fluid, leukocytes, and cell debris from the extravascular space. In severe inflammatory reactions, especially to microbes, the lymphatics may transport the offending agent, contributing to its dissemination. The lymphatics may become secondarily inflamed (*lymphangitis*), as may the draining lymph nodes (*lymphadenitis*). Inflamed lymph nodes are often enlarged because of hyperplasia of the lymphoid follicles and increased numbers of lymphocytes and phagocytic cells lining the sinuses of the lymph nodes. This constellation of pathologic changes is termed reactive, or inflammatory, lymphadenitis (Chapter 11). For clinicians, the presence of red streaks near a skin wound is a telltale sign of an infection in the wound. This streaking follows the course of the lymphatic channels and is diagnostic of lymphangitis; it may be accompanied by painful enlargement of the draining lymph nodes, indicating lymphadenitis.

SUMMARY

Vascular Reactions in Acute Inflammation

- Vasodilation is induced by chemical mediators such as histamine (described later) and is the cause of erythema and stasis of blood flow.
- Increased vascular permeability is induced by histamine, kinins, and other mediators that produce gaps between endothelial cells; by direct or leukocyte-induced endothelial injury; and by increased passage of fluids through the endothelium. This increased permeability allows plasma proteins and leukocytes to enter sites of infection or tissue damage; fluid leak through blood vessels results in edema.

Cellular Events: Leukocyte Recruitment and Activation

As mentioned earlier, an important function of the inflammatory response is to deliver leukocytes to the site of injury and to activate them. Leukocytes ingest offending agents, kill bacteria and other microbes, and eliminate necrotic tissue and foreign substances. A price that is paid for the defensive potency of leukocytes is that once activated, they may induce tissue damage and prolong inflammation, since the leukocyte products that destroy microbes can also injure normal host tissues. Therefore, host defense mechanisms include checks and balances that ensure that leukocytes are recruited and activated only when and where they are needed (i.e., in response to foreign invaders and dead tissues). Systemic activation of leukocytes can, in fact, have detrimental consequences, as in septic shock (Chapter 3).

Leukocyte Recruitment

Leukocytes normally flow rapidly in the blood, and in inflammation, they have to be stopped and brought to the offending agent or the site of tissue damage, which are typically outside the vessels. The sequence of events in the recruitment of leukocytes from the vascular lumen to the extravascular space consists of (1) margination and rolling along the vessel wall; (2) firm adhesion to the endothelium; (3) transmigration between endothelial cells; and (4) migration in interstitial tissues toward a chemotactic stimulus (Fig. 2–5). Rolling, adhesion, and transmigration are mediated by the interactions of adhesion molecules on leukocytes and endothelial surfaces (see later on). Chemical mediators—chemoattractants and certain cytokines—affect these processes by modulating the surface expression and binding affinity of the adhesion molecules and by stimulating directional movement of the leukocytes.

Margination and Rolling. As blood flows from capillaries into postcapillary venules, circulating cells are swept by laminar flow against the vessel wall. Because the smaller red cells tend to move faster than the larger white cells, leukocytes are pushed out of the central axial column and thus have a better opportunity to interact with lining endothelial cells, especially as stasis sets in. This process of leukocyte accumulation at the periphery of vessels is called *margination.* If the endothelial cells are activated by cytokines and other mediators produced locally, they express adhesion molecules to which the leukocytes attach loosely. These cells bind and detach and thus begin to tumble on the endothelial surface, a process called *rolling.*

The weak and transient interactions involved in rolling are mediated by the *selectin* family of adhesion molecules (Table 2–2). Selectins are receptors expressed on leukocytes and endothelium that contain an extracellular domain that binds sugars (hence the lectin part of the name). The three members of this family are E-selectin (also called CD62E), expressed on endothelial cells; P-selectin (CD62P), present on platelets and endothelium; and L-selectin (CD62L), on the surface of most leukocytes. Selectins bind sialylated oligosaccharides (e.g., sialyl-Lewis X on leukocytes) that are attached to mucin-like glycoproteins on various cells. The endothelial selectins are typically expressed at low levels or are not present at all on unactivated endothelium, and are up-regulated after stimulation by cytokines and other mediators. Therefore, binding of leukocytes is largely restricted to endothelium at sites of infection or tissue injury (where the mediators are produced). For example, in unactivated endothelial cells, P-selectin is found primarily in intracellular Weibel-Palade bodies; however, within minutes of exposure to mediators such as histamine or thrombin, P-selectin is distributed to the cell surface, where it can facilitate leukocyte binding. Similarly, E-selectin and the ligand for L-selectin, which are not expressed on normal endothelium, are induced after stimulation by the cytokines IL-1 and TNF.

Adhesion. The rolling leukocytes are able to sense changes in the endothelium that initiate the next step in the reaction of leukocytes, which is firm *adhesion* to endothelial surfaces. This adhesion is mediated by *integrins* expressed on leukocyte cell surfaces interacting with their ligands on endothelial cells (Fig. 2–5 and Table 2–2). Integrins are

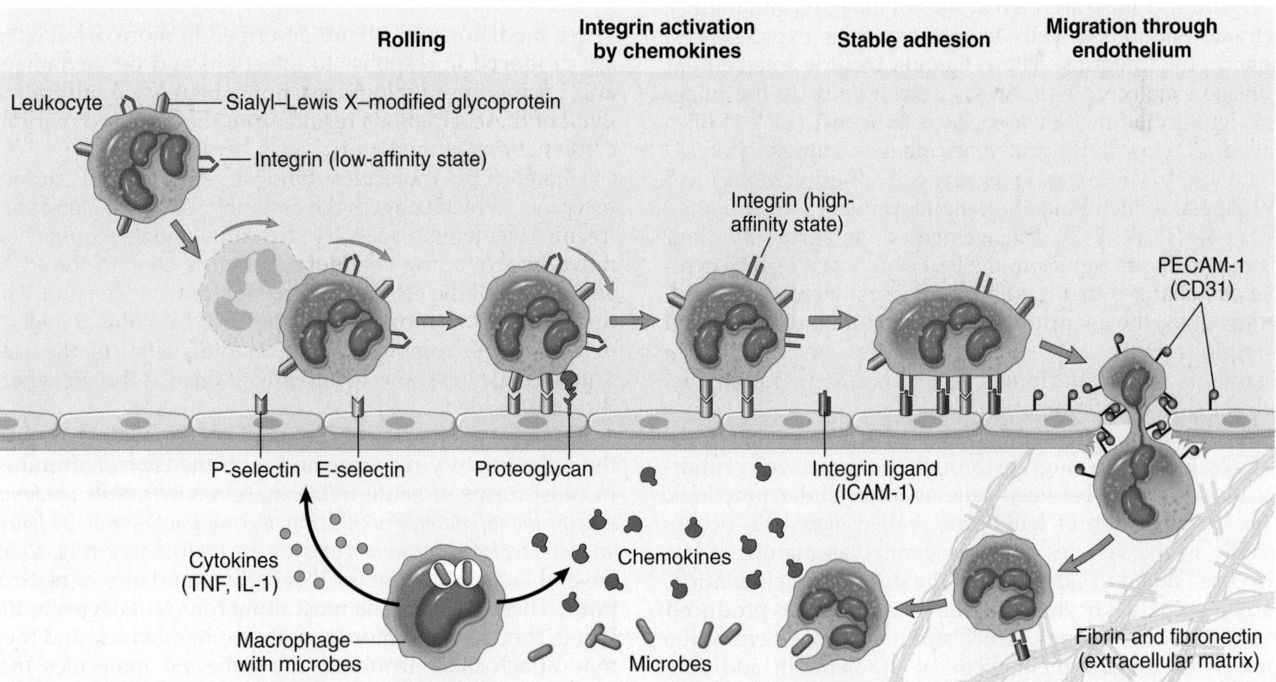

Figure 2–5 Mechanisms of leukocyte migration through blood vessels. The leukocytes (neutrophils shown here) first roll, then become activated and adhere to endothelium, then transmigrate across the endothelium, pierce the basement membrane, and migrate toward chemoattractants emanating from the source of injury. Different molecules play predominant roles in different steps of this process: selectins in rolling; chemokines (usually displayed bound to proteoglycans) in activating the neutrophils to increase avidity of integrins; integrins in firm adhesion; and CD31 (PECAM-1) in transmigration. ICAM-1, intercellular adhesion molecule-1; IL-1, interleukin-1; PECAM-1, platelet endothelial cell adhesion molecule-1; TNF, tumor necrosis factor.

Table 2–2 Endothelial and Leukocyte Adhesion Molecules

Endothelial Molecule	Leukocyte Molecule	Major Role(s)
Selectins and Selectin Ligands		
P-selectin	Sialyl–Lewis X–modified proteins	Rolling
E-selectin	Sialyl–Lewis X–modified proteins	Rolling and adhesion
GlyCam-1, CD34	L-selectin*	Rolling (neutrophils, monocytes)
Integrins and Integrin Ligands		
ICAM-1 (immunoglobulin family)	CD11/CD18 integrins (LFA-1, Mac-1)	Firm adhesion, arrest, transmigration
VCAM-1 (immunoglobulin family)	VLA-4 integrin	Adhesion
Others		
CD31	CD31 (homotypic interaction)	Transmigration of leukocytes through endothelium

*L-selectin is also involved in the binding of circulating lymphocytes to the high endothelial venules in lymph nodes and mucosal lymphoid tissues, and subsequent homing of lymphocytes to these tissues.
ICAM-1, intercellular adhesion molecule-1; LFA-1, leukocyte function–associated antigen-1; Mac-1, macrophage-1 antigen; VCAM-1, vascular cell adhesion molecule-1; VLA-4, very late antigen-4.

transmembrane heterodimeric glycoproteins that mediate the adhesion of leukocytes to endothelium and of various cells to the extracellular matrix. They are normally expressed on leukocyte plasma membranes in a low-affinity form and do not adhere to their specific ligands until the leukocytes are activated by chemokines.

Chemokines are chemoattractant cytokines that are secreted by many cells at sites of inflammation and are displayed on the endothelial surface. (Cytokines are described later in the chapter.) When the adherent leukocytes encounter the displayed chemokines, the cells are activated, and their integrins undergo conformational changes and cluster together, thus converting to a high-affinity form. At the same time, other cytokines, notably TNF and IL-1 (also secreted at sites of infection and injury), activate endothelial cells to increase their expression of ligands for integrins. These ligands include intercellular adhesion molecule-1 (ICAM-1), which binds to the integrins leukocyte function–associated antigen-1 (LFA-1) (also called CD11a/CD18) and macrophage-1 antigen (Mac-1) (i.e., CD11b/CD18), and vascular cell adhesion molecule-1 (VCAM-1), which binds to the integrin very late antigen-4 (VLA-4) (Table 2–2). Engagement of integrins by their ligands delivers signals to the leukocytes that lead to cytoskeletal changes that mediate firm attachment to the substrate. Thus, the net result of cytokine-stimulated increased integrin affinity and increased expression of integrin ligands is stable attachment of leukocytes to endothelial cells at sites of inflammation.

Transmigration. After being arrested on the endothelial surface, leukocytes migrate through the vessel wall primarily by squeezing between cells at intercellular junctions. This extravasation of leukocytes, called *diapedesis,* occurs mainly in the venules of the systemic vasculature; it has also been noted in capillaries in the pulmonary circulation. Migration of leukocytes is driven by chemokines produced in extravascular tissues, which stimulate movement of the leukocytes toward their chemical gradient. In addition, platelet endothelial cell adhesion molecule-1 (PECAM-1) (also called CD31), a cellular adhesion molecule expressed on leukocytes and endothelial cells, mediates the binding events needed for leukocytes to traverse the endothelium. After passing through the endothelium, leukocytes secrete collagenases that enable them to pass through the vascular basement membrane.

Chemotaxis. After extravasating from the blood, leukocytes move toward sites of infection or injury along a chemical gradient by a process called *chemotaxis*. Both exogenous and endogenous substances can be chemotactic for leukocytes, including the following:

- Bacterial products, particularly peptides with *N*-formylmethionine termini
- Cytokines, especially those of the *chemokine* family
- Components of the complement system, particularly C5
- Products of the lipoxygenase pathway of arachidonic acid (AA) metabolism, particularly leukotriene B4 (LTB4)

These mediators, which are described in more detail later, are produced in response to infections and tissue damage and during immunologic reactions. Leukocyte infiltration in all of these situations results from the actions of various combinations of mediators.

Chemotactic molecules bind to specific cell surface receptors, which triggers the assembly of cytoskeletal contractile elements necessary for movement. Leukocytes move by extending pseudopods that anchor to the ECM and then pull the cell in the direction of the extension. The direction of such movement is specified by a higher density of chemokine receptors at the leading edge of the cell. Thus, leukocytes move to and are retained at the site where they are needed.

The type of emigrating leukocyte varies with the age of the inflammatory response and with the type of stimulus. In most forms of acute inflammation, *neutrophils predominate in the inflammatory infiltrate during the first 6 to 24 hours and are replaced by monocytes in 24 to 48 hours* (Fig. 2–6). Several factors account for this early abundance of neutrophils: These cells are the most numerous leukocytes in the blood, they respond more rapidly to chemokines, and they may attach more firmly to the adhesion molecules that are rapidly induced on endothelial cells, such as P- and E-selectins. In addition, after entering tissues, neutrophils are short-lived—they die by apoptosis and disappear within 24 to 48 hours—while monocytes survive longer. There are exceptions to this pattern of cellular infiltration, however.

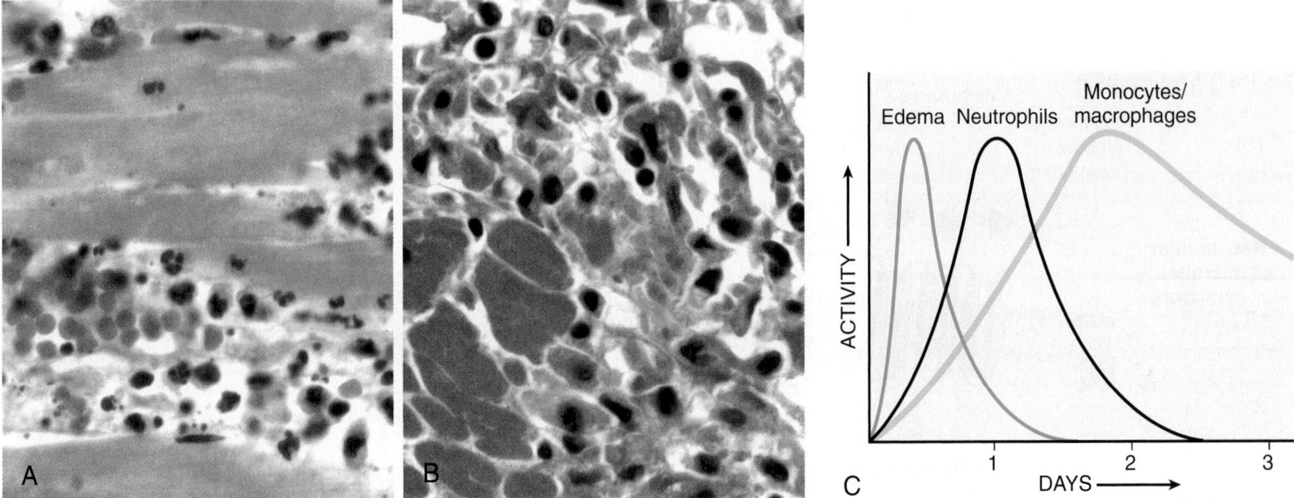

Figure 2–6 Nature of leukocyte infiltrates in inflammatory reactions. The photomicrographs show an inflammatory reaction in the myocardium after ischemic necrosis (infarction). **A,** Early (neutrophilic) infiltrates and congested blood vessels. **B,** Later (mononuclear) cellular infiltrates. **C,** The approximate kinetics of edema and cellular infiltration. For sake of simplicity, edema is shown as an acute transient response, although secondary waves of delayed edema and neutrophil infiltration also can occur.

In certain infections (e.g., those caused by *Pseudomonas* organisms), the cellular infiltrate is dominated by continuously recruited neutrophils for several days; in viral infections, lymphocytes may be the first cells to arrive; and in some hypersensitivity reactions, eosinophils may be the main cell type.

SUMMARY

Leukocyte Recruitment to Sites of Inflammation

- Leukocytes are recruited from the blood into the extravascular tissue, where infectious pathogens or damaged tissues may be located, and are activated to perform their functions.
- Leukocyte recruitment is a multi-step process consisting of loose attachment to and rolling on endothelium (mediated by selectins); firm attachment to endothelium (mediated by integrins); and migration through interendothelial spaces.
- Various cytokines promote expression of selectins and integrin ligands on endothelium (TNF, IL-1), increase the avidity of integrins for their ligands (chemokines), and promote directional migration of leukocytes (also chemokines); many of these cytokines are produced by tissue macrophages and other cells responding to pathogens or damaged tissues.
- Neutrophils predominate in the early inflammatory infiltrate and are later replaced by macrophages.

Leukocyte Activation

Once leukocytes have been recruited to the site of infection or tissue necrosis, they must be activated to perform their functions. Stimuli for activation include microbes, products of necrotic cells, and several mediators that are described later. As described earlier, leukocytes use various receptors to sense the presence of microbes, dead cells, and foreign substances. Engagement of these cellular receptors induces a number of responses in leukocytes that are part of their normal defensive functions and are grouped under the term *leukocyte activation* (Fig. 2–7). Leukocyte activation results in the enhancement of the following functions:

- *Phagocytosis* of particles
- *Intracellular destruction of phagocytosed microbes and dead cells* by substances produced in phagosomes, including reactive oxygen and nitrogen species and lysosomal enzymes
- *Liberation of substances that destroy extracellular microbes and dead tissues,* which are largely the same as the substances produced within phagocytic vesicles. A recently discovered mechanism by which neutrophils destroy extracellular microbes is the formation of extracellular "traps."
- *Production of mediators,* including arachidonic acid metabolites and cytokines, that amplify the inflammatory reaction, by recruiting and activating more leukocytes

Phagocytosis. *Phagocytosis consists of three steps* (Fig. 2–8): *(1) recognition and attachment of the particle to the ingesting leukocyte; (2) engulfment, with subsequent formation of a phagocytic vacuole; and (3) killing and degradation of the ingested material.*

Leukocytes bind and ingest most microorganisms and dead cells by means of specific surface receptors. Some of these receptors recognize components of the microbes and dead cells and other receptors recognize host proteins, called *opsonins,* that coat microbes and target them for phagocytosis (the process called *opsonization*). The most important opsonins are antibodies of the immunoglobulin G (IgG) class that bind to microbial surface antigens, breakdown products of the complement protein C3 (described later), and plasma carbohydrate-binding lectins called collectins, which bind to microbial cell wall sugar groups. These opsonins either are present in the blood ready to coat

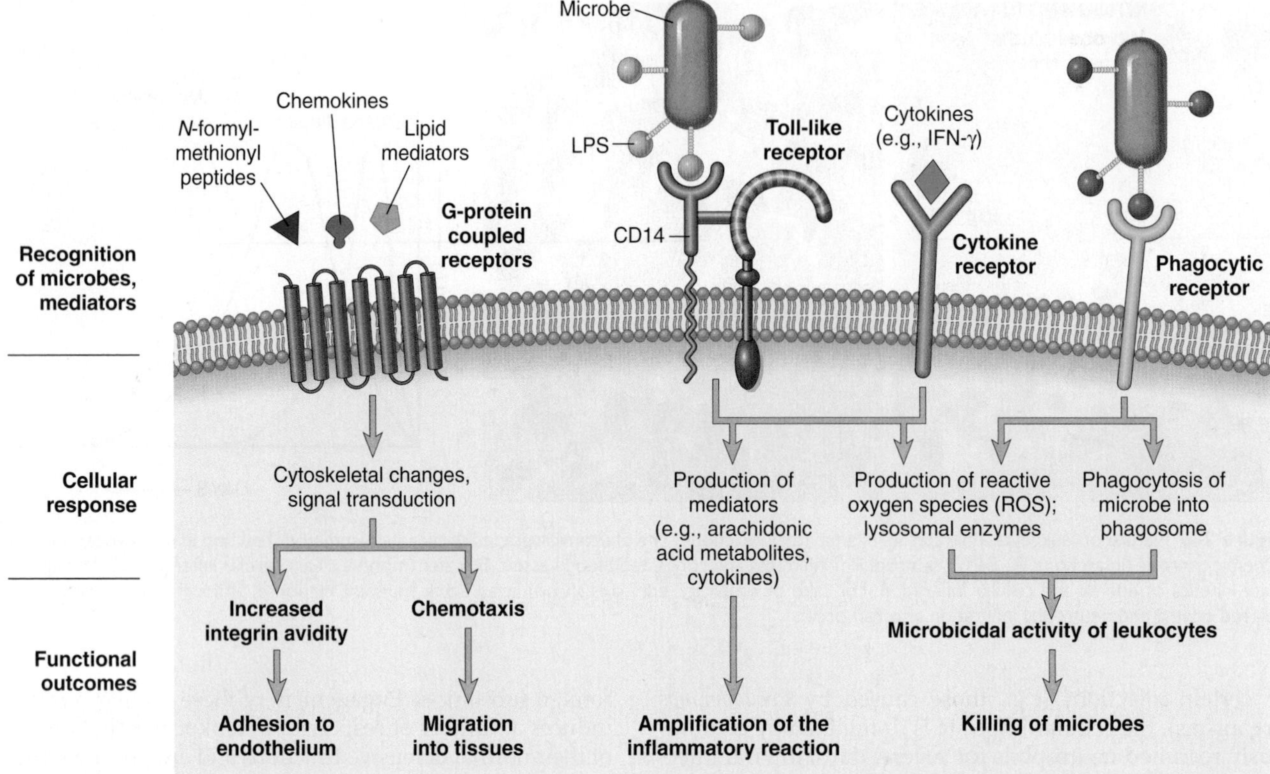

Figure 2–7 Leukocyte activation. Different classes of cell surface receptors of leukocytes recognize different stimuli. The receptors initiate responses that mediate the functions of the leukocytes. Only some receptors are depicted (see text for details). Lipopolysaccharide (LPS) first binds to a circulating LPS-binding protein (*not shown*). IFN-γ, interferon-γ.

microbes or are produced in response to the microbes. Leukocytes express receptors for opsonins that facilitate rapid phagocytosis of the coated microbes. These receptors include the Fc receptor for IgG (called FcγRI), complement receptors 1 and 3 (CR1 and CR3) for complement fragments, and C1q for the collectins.

Binding of opsonized particles to these receptors triggers engulfment and induces cellular activation that enhances degradation of ingested microbes. In engulfment, pseudopods are extended around the object, eventually forming a phagocytic vacuole. The membrane of the vacuole then fuses with the membrane of a lysosomal granule, resulting in discharge of the granule's contents into the *phagolysosome*.

Killing and Degradation of Phagocytosed Microbes. The culmination of the phagocytosis of microbes is killing and degradation of the ingested particles. The key steps in this reaction are the production of microbicidal substances within lysosomes and fusion of the lysosomes with phagosomes, thus exposing the ingested particles to the destructive mechanisms of the leukocytes (Fig. 2–8). The most important microbicidal substances are reactive oxygen species (ROS) and lysosomal enzymes. The production of ROS involves the following steps:

- Phagocytosis and the engagement of various cellular receptors stimulate an *oxidative burst,* also called the *respiratory burst,* which is characterized by a rapid increase in oxygen consumption, glycogen catabolism (glycogenolysis), increased glucose oxidation, and production of ROS. The generation of the oxygen metabolites is due to rapid activation of a leukocyte NADPH oxidase, called the *phagocyte oxidase,* which oxidizes NADPH (reduced nicotinamide adenine dinucleotide phosphate) and, in the process, converts oxygen to superoxide ion ($O_2^{\bullet}$) (see Fig. 1–18, *B*, Chapter 1).
- Superoxide is then converted by spontaneous dismutation into hydrogen peroxide ($O_2^{\bullet} + 2H^+ \rightarrow H_2O_2$). These ROS act as free radicals and destroy microbes by mechanisms that were described in Chapter 1.
- The quantities of H_2O_2 produced generally are insufficient to kill most bacteria (although superoxide and hydroxyl radical formation may be sufficient to do so). However, the lysosomes of neutrophils (called *azurophilic granules*) contain the enzyme myeloperoxidase (MPO), and in the presence of a halide such as Cl^-, MPO converts H_2O_2 to $HOCl^{\bullet}$ (hypochlorous radical). $HOCl^{\bullet}$ is a powerful oxidant and antimicrobial agent (NaOCl is the active ingredient in chlorine bleach) that kills bacteria by halogenation, or by protein and lipid peroxidation.

Fortunately, the phagocyte oxidase is active only after its cytosolic subunit translocates to the membrane of the phagolysosome; thus, the reactive end products are generated mainly within the vesicles, and the phagocyte itself is not damaged. H_2O_2 is eventually broken down to water and O_2 by the actions of catalase, and the other ROS also are degraded (Chapter 1). Reactive nitrogen species, particularly nitric oxide (NO), act in the same way as that described for ROS.

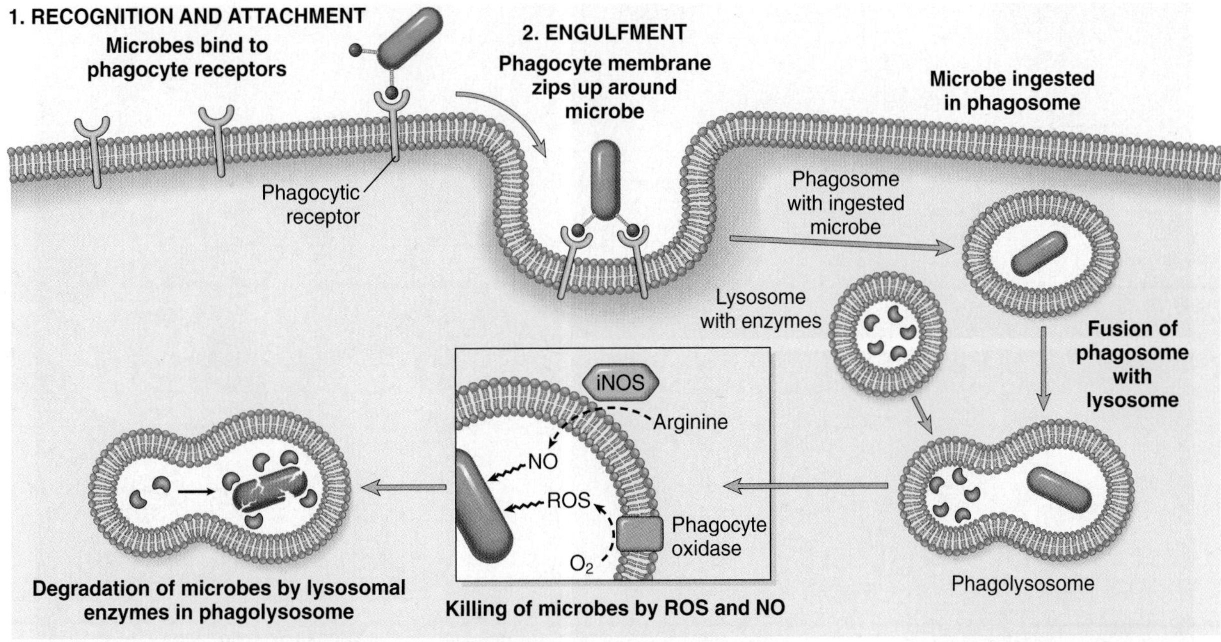

Figure 2–8 Phagocytosis. Phagocytosis of a particle (e.g., a bacterium) involves (*1*) attachment and binding of the particle to receptors on the leukocyte surface, (*2*) engulfment and fusion of the phagocytic vacuole with granules (lysosomes), and (*3*) destruction of the ingested particle. iNOS, inducible nitric oxide synthase; NO, nitric oxide; ROS, reactive oxygen species.

The dead microorganisms are then degraded by the action of lysosomal acid hydrolases. Perhaps the most important lysosomal enzyme involved in bacterial killing is elastase.

Of note, in addition to ROS and enzymes, several other constituents of leukocyte granules are capable of killing infectious pathogens. These include bactericidal permeability-increasing protein (causing phospholipase activation and membrane phospholipid degradation), lysozyme (causing degradation of bacterial coat oligosaccharides), major basic protein (an important eosinophil granule constituent that is cytotoxic for parasites), and defensins (peptides that kill microbes by creating holes in their membranes).

Secretion of Microbicidal Substances. The microbicidal mechanisms of phagocytes are largely sequestered within phagolysosomes in order to protect the leukocytes from damaging themselves. Leukocytes also actively secrete granule components including enzymes such as elastase, which destroy and digest extracellular microbes and dead tissues, as well as antimicrobial peptides. The contents of lysosomal granules are secreted by leukocytes into the extracellular milieu by several mechanisms:

- The phagocytic vacuole may remain transiently open to the outside before complete closure of the phagolysosome (regurgitation during feeding).
- If cells encounter materials that cannot be easily ingested, such as immune complexes deposited on immovable surfaces (e.g., glomerular basement membrane), the attempt to phagocytose these substances (frustrated phagocytosis) triggers strong leukocyte activation, and lysosomal enzymes are released into the surrounding tissue or lumen.
- The membrane of the phagolysosome may be damaged if potentially injurious substances, such as silica particles, are phagocytosed.

Neutrophil Extracellular Traps (NETs). These "traps" are extracellular fibrillar networks that are produced by neutrophils in response to infectious pathogens (mainly bacteria and fungi) and inflammatory mediators (such as chemokines, cytokines, complement proteins, and ROS). NETs contain a framework of nuclear chromatin with embedded granule proteins, such as antimicrobial peptides and enzymes (Fig. 2–9). The traps provide a high concentration of antimicrobial substances at sites of infection, and prevent the spread of the microbes by trapping them in the fibrils. In the process, the nuclei of the neutrophils are lost, leading to death of the cells. NETs also have been detected in blood neutrophils during sepsis. The nuclear chromatin in the NETs, which includes histones and associated DNA, has been postulated to be a source of nuclear antigens in systemic autoimmune diseases, particularly lupus, in which affected persons react against their own DNA and nucleoproteins (Chapter 4).

Leukocyte-Induced Tissue Injury

Because leukocytes are capable of secreting potentially harmful substances such as enzymes and ROS, they are important causes of injury to normal cells and tissues under several circumstances:

- As part of a normal defense reaction against infectious microbes, when "bystander" tissues are injured. In certain infections that are difficult to eradicate, such as tuberculosis and some viral diseases, the host response

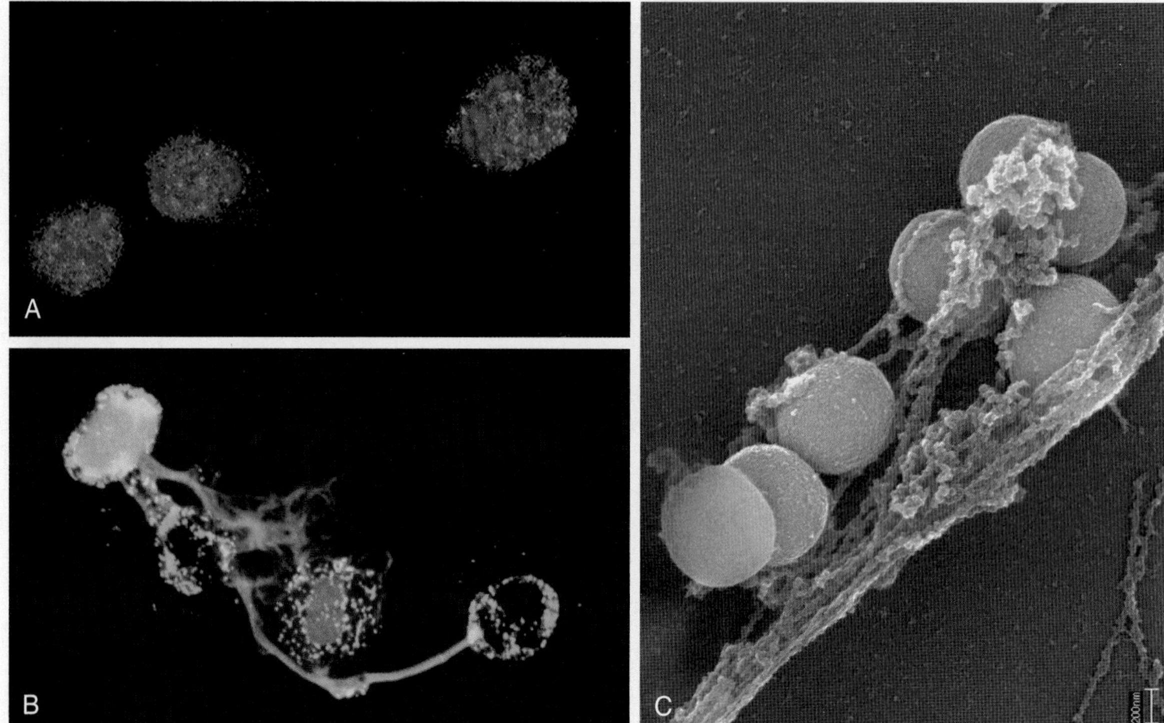

Figure 2–9 Neutrophil extracellular traps (NETs). **A,** Healthy neutrophils with nuclei stained red and cytoplasm green. **B,** Release of nuclear material from neutrophils (note that two have lost their nuclei), forming extracellular traps. **C,** An electron micrograph of bacteria (staphylococci) trapped in NETs.

(From Brinkmann V, Zychlinsky A: Beneficial suicide: why neutrophils die to make NETs. Nat Rev Microbiol 5:577, 2007, with the permission of the authors and publisher.)

contributes more to the pathologic process than does the microbe itself.

- As a normal attempt to clear damaged and dead tissues (e.g., after a myocardial infarction). In an infarct, inflammation may prolong and exacerbate the injurious consequences of the ischemia, especially upon reperfusion (Chapter 1).
- When the inflammatory response is inappropriately directed against host tissues, as in certain autoimmune diseases, or when the host reacts excessively against nontoxic environmental substances, such as allergic diseases including asthma (discussed in Chapter 4)

In all of these situations, the mechanisms by which leukocytes damage normal tissues are the same as the mechanisms involved in the clearance of microbes and dead tissues, because once the leukocytes are activated, their effector mechanisms do not distinguish between offender and host. In fact, if unchecked or inappropriately directed against host tissues, leukocytes themselves become the main offenders. Leukocyte-dependent tissue injury underlies many acute and chronic human diseases (Table 2-3), as is evident in discussions of specific disorders throughout this book.

Activated leukocytes, especially macrophages, also secrete many cytokines, which stimulate further inflammation and have important systemic effects, to be discussed later.

SUMMARY

Leukocyte Effector Mechanisms

- Leukocytes can eliminate microbes and dead cells by phagocytosis, followed by their destruction in phagolysosomes.
- Destruction is caused by free radicals (ROS, NO) generated in activated leukocytes and lysosomal enzymes.
- Enzymes and ROS may be released into the extracellular environment.
- The mechanisms that function to eliminate microbes and dead cells (the physiologic role of inflammation) are also capable of damaging normal tissues (the pathologic consequences of inflammation).

Defects in Leukocyte Function

Since leukocytes play a central role in host defense, it is not surprising that defects in leukocyte function, both acquired and inherited, lead to increased susceptibility to infections, which may be recurrent and life-threatening (Table 2–4). The most common causes of defective inflammation are bone marrow suppression caused by tumors or treatment with chemotherapy or radiation (resulting in decreased leukocyte numbers) and metabolic diseases such as

Table 2–3 Clinical Examples of Leukocyte-Induced Injury

Disorder*	Cells and Molecules Involved in Injury
Acute	
Acute respiratory distress syndrome	Neutrophils
Acute transplant rejection	Lymphocytes; antibodies and complement
Asthma	Eosinophils; IgE antibodies
Glomerulonephritis	Antibodies and complement; neutrophils, monocytes
Septic shock	Cytokines
Chronic	
Rheumatoid arthritis	Lymphocytes, macrophages; antibodies?
Asthma	Eosinophils; IgE antibodies
Atherosclerosis	Macrophages; lymphocytes?
Chronic transplant rejection	Lymphocytes, macrophages; cytokines
Pulmonary fibrosis	Macrophages; fibroblasts

*Listed are selected examples of diseases in which the host response plays a significant role in tissue injury. Some, such as asthma, can manifest with acute inflammation or a chronic illness with repeated bouts of acute exacerbation. These diseases and their pathogenesis are discussed in much more detail in relevant chapters.
IgE, immunoglobulin E.

Table 2–4 Defects in Leukocyte Functions

Disease	Defect
Acquired	
Bone marrow suppression: tumors (including leukemias), radiation, and chemotherapy	Production of leukocytes
Diabetes, malignancy, sepsis, chronic dialysis	Adhesion and chemotaxis
Anemia, sepsis, diabetes, malnutrition	Phagocytosis and microbicidal activity
Genetic	
Leukocyte adhesion deficiency 1	Defective leukocyte adhesion because of mutations in β chain of CD11/CD18 integrins
Leukocyte adhesion deficiency 2	Defective leukocyte adhesion because of mutations in fucosyl transferase required for synthesis of sialylated oligosaccharide (receptor for selectins)
Chronic granulomatous disease	Decreased oxidative burst
X-linked	Phagocyte oxidase (membrane component)
Autosomal recessive	Phagocyte oxidase (cytoplasmic components)
Myeloperoxidase deficiency	Decreased microbial killing because of defective MPO–H_2O_2 system
Chédiak-Higashi syndrome	Decreased leukocyte functions because of mutations affecting protein involved in lysosomal membrane traffic

H_2O_2, hydrogen peroxide; MPO, myeloperoxidase.
Modified from Gallin JI: Disorders of phagocytic cells. In Gallin JI, et al (eds): Inflammation: Basic Principles and Clinical Correlates, 2nd ed. New York, Raven Press, 1992, pp 860, 861.

diabetes (causing abnormal leukocyte functions). These are described elsewhere in the book.

The genetic disorders, although individually rare, illustrate the importance of particular molecular pathways in the complex inflammatory response. Some of the better understood inherited diseases are the following:

- *Defects in leukocyte adhesion.* In *leukocyte adhesion deficiency type 1 (LAD-1)*, defective synthesis of the CD18 β subunit of the leukocyte integrins LFA-1 and Mac-1 leads to impaired leukocyte adhesion to and migration through endothelium, and defective phagocytosis and generation of an oxidative burst. *Leukocyte adhesion deficiency type 2 (LAD-2)* is caused by a defect in fucose metabolism resulting in the absence of sialyl–Lewis X, the oligosaccharide on leukocytes that binds to selectins on activated endothelium. Its clinical manifestations are similar to but milder than those of LAD-1.
- *Defects in microbicidal activity.* An example is *chronic granulomatous disease,* a genetic deficiency in one of the several components of the phagocyte oxidase enzyme that is responsible for generating ROS. In these patients, engulfment of bacteria does not result in activation of oxygen-dependent killing mechanisms. In an attempt to control these infections, the microbes are surrounded by activated macrophages, forming the "granulomas" (see later) that give the disease its distinctive pathologic features and its somewhat misleading name.
- *Defects in phagolysosome formation.* One such disorder, *Chédiak-Higashi syndrome,* is an autosomal recessive disease that results from disordered intracellular trafficking of organelles, ultimately impairing the fusion of lysosomes with phagosomes. The secretion of lytic secretory granules by cytotoxic T lymphocytes is also affected, explaining the severe immunodeficiency typical of the disorder.
- Rare patients with defective host defenses have been shown to carry *mutations in TLR signaling pathways.* Inherited defects in components of adaptive immune responses also result in increased susceptibility to infections. These are described in Chapter 4.
- *Gain-of-function mutations in genes encoding some components of the inflammasome,* one of which is called *cryopyrin,* are responsible for rare but serious diseases called cryopyrin-associated periodic fever syndromes (CAPSs), which manifest with unrelenting fevers and other signs of inflammation and respond well to treatment with IL-1 antagonists.

Outcomes of Acute Inflammation

Although the consequences of acute inflammation are modified by the nature and intensity of the injury, the site and tissue affected, and the ability of the host to mount a response, *acute inflammation generally has one of three outcomes* (Fig. 2–10):

- *Resolution: Regeneration and repair.* When the injury is limited or short-lived, when there has been no or minimal tissue damage, and when the injured tissue is capable of regenerating, the usual outcome is restoration

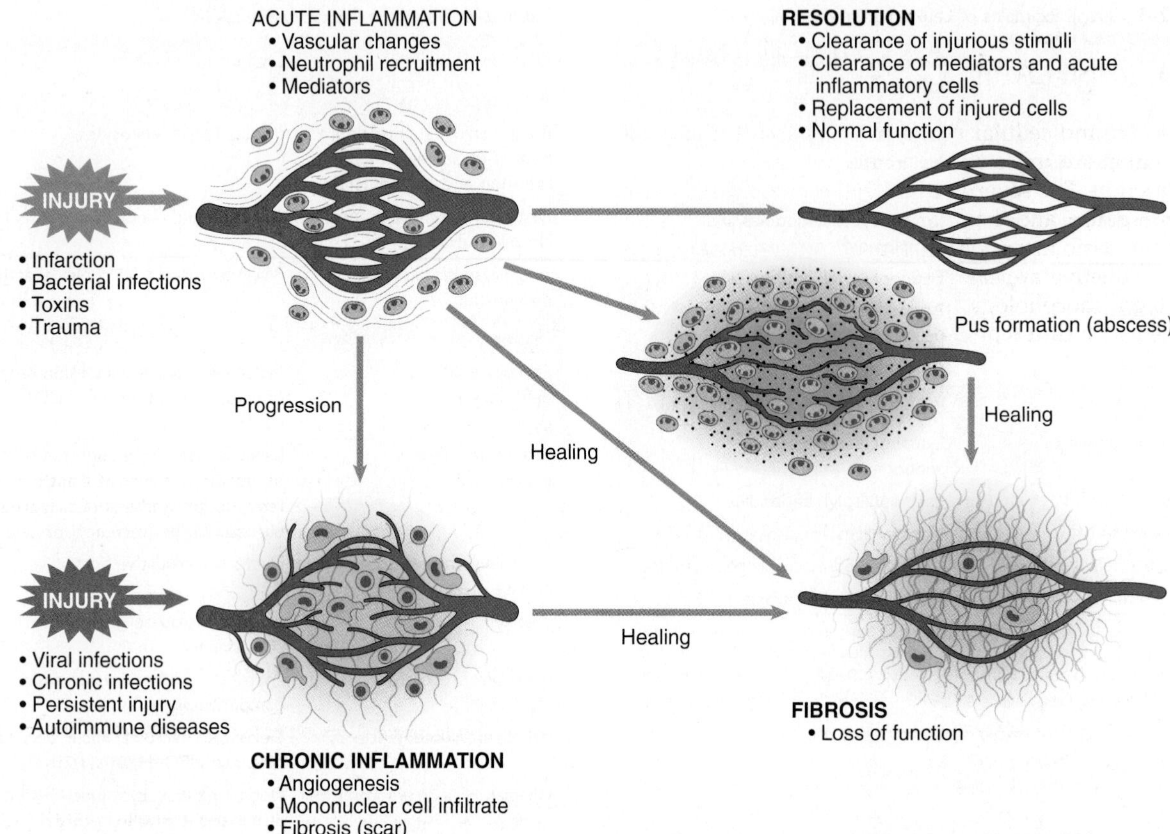

Figure 2–10 Outcomes of acute inflammation: resolution, healing by scarring (fibrosis), or chronic inflammation (see text).

to structural and functional normalcy. Before the process of resolution can start, the acute inflammatory response has to be terminated. This involves neutralization, decay, or enzymatic degradation of the various chemical mediators; normalization of vascular permeability; and cessation of leukocyte emigration, with subsequent death (by apoptosis) of extravasated neutrophils. Furthermore, leukocytes begin to produce mediators that inhibit inflammation, thereby limiting the reaction. The necrotic debris, edema fluid, and inflammatory cells are cleared by phagocytes and lymphatic drainage, eliminating the detritus from the battlefield. Leukocytes secrete cytokines that initiate the subsequent repair process, in which new blood vessels grow into the injured tissue to provide nutrients, growth factors stimulate the proliferation of fibroblasts and laying down of collagen to fill defects, and residual tissue cells proliferate to restore structural integrity. This process is described later in the chapter.

- *Chronic inflammation* may follow acute inflammation if the offending agent is not removed, or it may be present from the onset of injury (e.g., in viral infections or immune responses to self-antigens). Depending on the extent of the initial and continuing tissue injury, as well as the capacity of the affected tissues to regrow, chronic inflammation may be followed by restoration of normal structure and function or may lead to scarring.
- *Scarring* is a type of repair after substantial tissue destruction (as in abscess formation, discussed later) or when inflammation occurs in tissues that do not regenerate, in which the injured tissue is filled in by connective tissue. In organs in which extensive connective tissue deposition occurs in attempts to heal the damage or as a consequence of chronic inflammation, the outcome is *fibrosis,* a process that can significantly compromise function.

SUMMARY

Sequence of Events in Acute Inflammation

- The vascular changes in acute inflammation are characterized by increased blood flow secondary to arteriolar and capillary bed dilation (erythema and warmth).
- Increased vascular permeability, as a consequence of either widening of interendothelial cell junctions of the venules or direct endothelial cell injury, results in an exudate of protein-rich extravascular fluid (tissue edema).
- The leukocytes, initially predominantly neutrophils, adhere to the endothelium via adhesion molecules and then leave the microvasculature and migrate to the site of injury under the influence of chemotactic agents.
- Phagocytosis, killing, and degradation of the offending agent follow.
- Genetic or acquired defects in leukocyte functions give rise to recurrent infections.
- The outcome of acute inflammation may be removal of the exudate with restoration of normal tissue architecture (resolution); transition to chronic inflammation; or extensive destruction of the tissue resulting in scarring.

MORPHOLOGIC PATTERNS OF ACUTE INFLAMMATION

The vascular and cellular reactions that characterize acute inflammation are reflected in the morphologic appearance of the reaction. The severity of the inflammatory response, its specific cause, and the particular tissue involved all can modify the basic morphology of acute inflammation, producing distinctive appearances. The importance of recognizing these morphologic patterns is that they are often associated with different etiology and clinical situations.

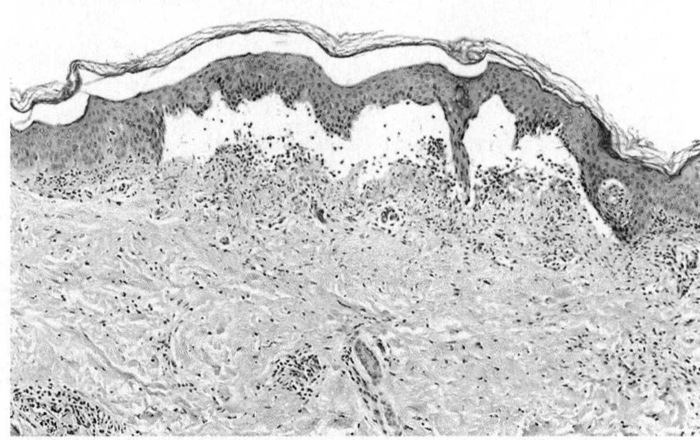

Figure 2–11 Serous inflammation. Low-power view of a cross-section of a skin blister showing the epidermis separated from the dermis by a focal collection of serous effusion.

MORPHOLOGY

- **Serous inflammation** is characterized by the outpouring of a watery, relatively protein-poor fluid that, depending on the site of injury, derives either from the plasma or from the secretions of mesothelial cells lining the peritoneal, pleural, and pericardial cavities. The skin blister resulting from a burn or viral infection is a good example of the accumulation of a serous effusion either within or immediately beneath the epidermis of the skin (Fig. 2–11). Fluid in a serous cavity is called an **effusion.**
- **Fibrinous inflammation** occurs as a consequence of more severe injuries, resulting in greater vascular permeability that allows large molecules (such as fibrinogen) to pass the endothelial barrier. Histologically, the accumulated extravascular fibrin appears as an eosinophilic meshwork of threads or sometimes as an amorphous coagulum (Fig. 2–12). A fibrinous exudate is characteristic of inflammation in the lining of body cavities, such as the meninges, pericardium, and pleura. Such exudates may be degraded by fibrinolysis, and the accumulated debris may be removed by macrophages, resulting in restoration of the normal tissue structure **(resolution).** However, extensive fibrin-rich exudates may not be completely removed, and are replaced by an ingrowth of fibroblasts and blood vessels **(organization),** leading ultimately to scarring that may have significant clinical consequences. For example, organization of a fibrinous pericardial exudate forms dense fibrous scar tissue that bridges or obliterates the pericardial space and restricts myocardial function.
- **Suppurative (purulent) inflammation and abscess formation.** These are manifested by the collection of large amounts of purulent exudate (pus) consisting of neutrophils, necrotic cells, and edema fluid. Certain organisms (e.g., staphylococci) are more likely to induce such localized suppuration and are therefore referred to as pyogenic (pus-forming). **Abscesses** are focal collections of pus that may be caused by seeding of pyogenic organisms into a tissue or by secondary infections of necrotic foci. Abscesses typically have a central, largely necrotic region rimmed by a layer of preserved neutrophils (Fig. 2–13), with a surrounding zone of dilated vessels and fibroblast proliferation indicative of attempted repair. As time passes, the abscess may become completely walled off and eventually be replaced by connective tissue. Because of the underlying tissue destruction, the usual outcome with abscess formation is scarring.

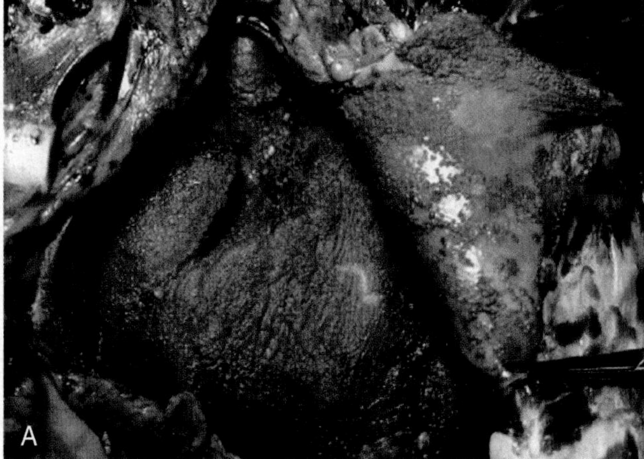

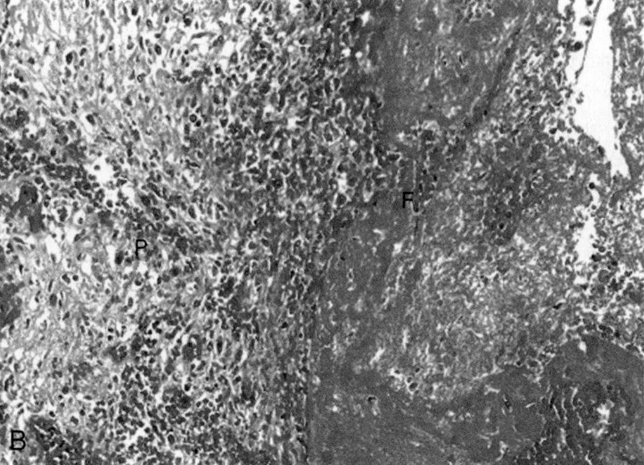

Figure 2–12 Fibrinous pericarditis. **A,** Deposits of fibrin on the pericardium. **B,** A pink meshwork of fibrin exudate *(F)* overlies the pericardial surface *(P)*.

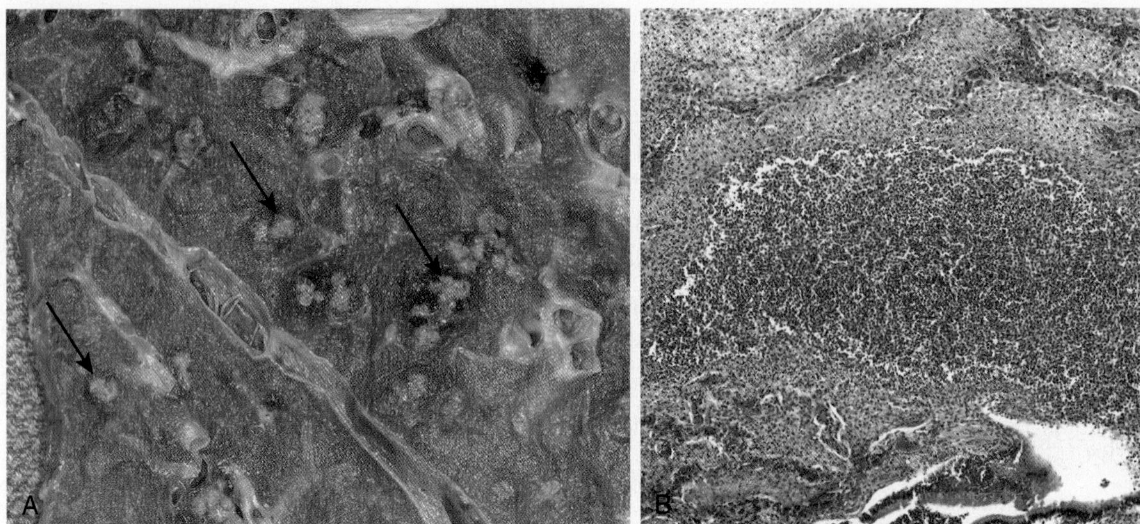

Figure 2–13 Purulent inflammation with abscess formation. **A,** Multiple bacterial abscesses in the lung (*arrows*) in a case of bronchopneumonia. **B,** The abscess contains neutrophils and cellular debris and is surrounded by congested blood vessels.

- An **ulcer** is a local defect, or excavation, of the surface of an organ or tissue that is produced by necrosis of cells and sloughing (shedding) of necrotic and inflammatory tissue (Fig. 2–14). Ulceration can occur only when tissue necrosis and resultant inflammation exist on or near a surface. Ulcers are most commonly encountered in (1) the mucosa of the mouth, stomach, intestines, or genitourinary tract and (2) in the subcutaneous tissues of the lower extremities in older persons who have circulatory disturbances predisposing affected tissue to extensive necrosis. Ulcerations are best exemplified by peptic ulcer of the stomach or duodenum, in which acute and chronic inflammation coexist. During the acute stage, there is intense polymorphonuclear infiltration and vascular dilation in the margins of the defect. With chronicity, the margins and base of the ulcer develop scarring with accumulation of lymphocytes, macrophages, and plasma cells.

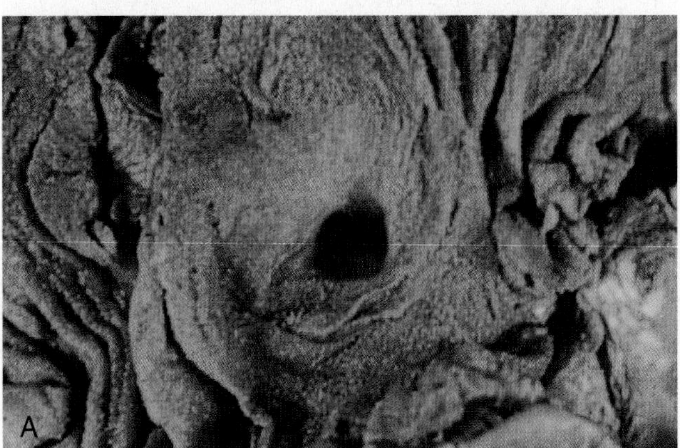

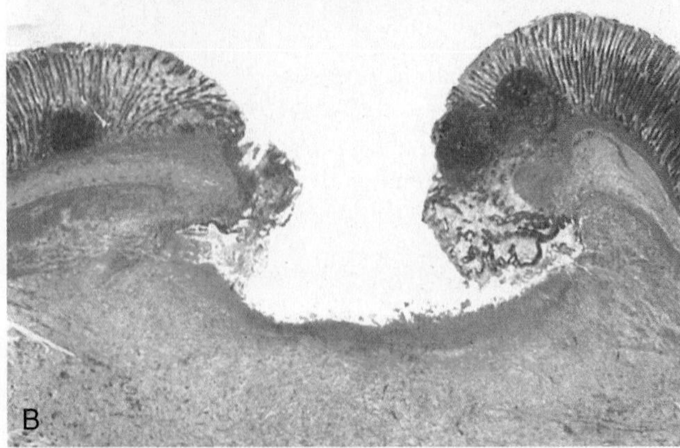

Figure 2–14 Ulcer. **A,** A chronic duodenal ulcer. **B,** Low-power cross-section of a duodenal ulcer crater with an acute inflammatory exudate in the base.

CHEMICAL MEDIATORS AND REGULATORS OF INFLAMMATION

Having described the vascular and cellular events in acute inflammation, and the accompanying morphologic alterations, we next discuss the chemical mediators that are responsible for these events. While the harried student may find this list daunting (as do the professors!), it is worthy of note that this knowledge has been used to design a large armamentarium of anti-inflammatory drugs, which are used every day by large numbers of people and include familiar drugs like aspirin and acetaminophen. In this section, we emphasize general properties of the mediators of inflammation and highlight only some of the more important molecules. We also touch upon some of the mechanisms that limit and terminate inflammatory reactions.

- *Mediators may be produced locally by cells at the site of inflammation, or may be derived from circulating inactive precursors (typically synthesized by the liver) that are activated at the site of inflammation* (Fig. 2–15 and Table 2–5). Cell-derived mediators are normally sequestered in intracellular granules and are rapidly secreted upon cellular activation (e.g., histamine in mast cells) or are

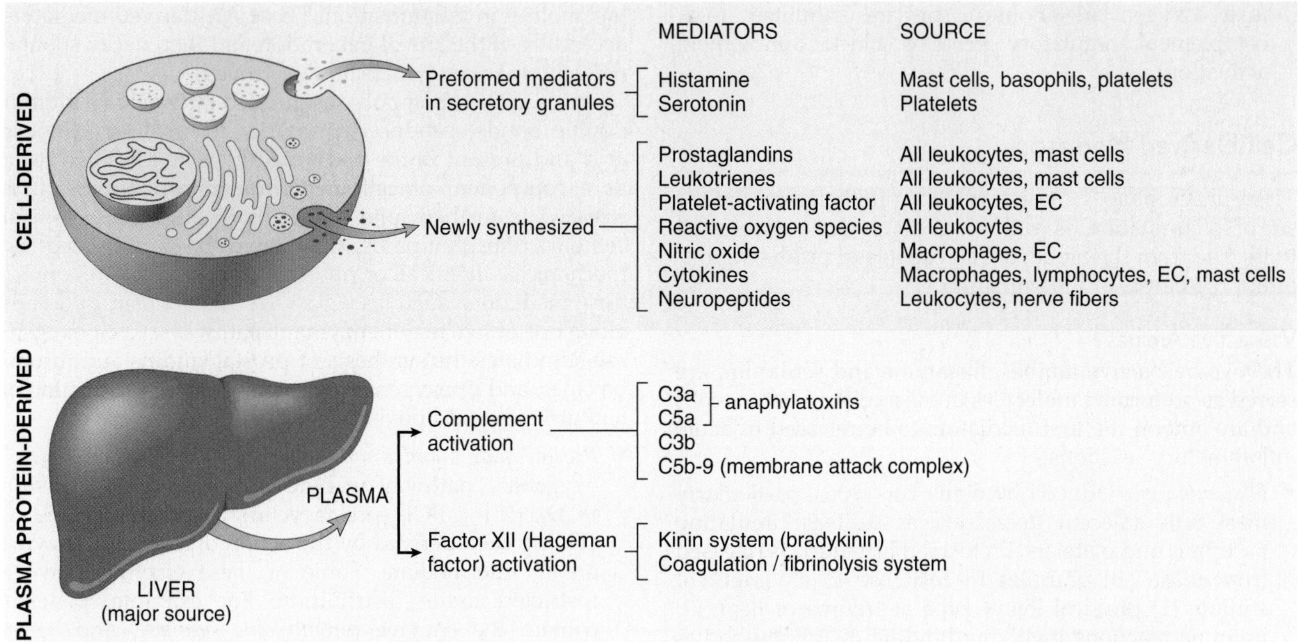

Figure 2–15 Mediators of inflammation. The principal cell-derived and plasma protein mediators are shown. EC, endothelial cells.

synthesized de novo in response to a stimulus (e.g., prostaglandins and cytokines produced by leukocytes and other cells). Plasma protein–derived mediators (complement proteins, kinins) circulate in an inactive form and typically undergo proteolytic cleavage to acquire their biologic activities.

- *Most mediators act by binding to specific receptors on different target cells.* Such mediators may act on only one or a very few cell types, or they may have diverse actions, with differing outcomes depending on which cell type they affect. Other mediators (e.g., lysosomal proteases, ROS) have direct enzymatic and/or toxic activities that do not require binding to specific receptors.
- *The actions of most mediators are tightly regulated and short-lived.* Once activated and released from the cell, mediators quickly decay (e.g., arachidonic acid metabolites), are inactivated by enzymes (e.g., kininase inactivates bradykinin), are eliminated (e.g., antioxidants scavenge

Table 2–5 Actions of the Principal Mediators of Inflammation

Mediator	Source(s)	Actions
Cell-Derived		
Histamine	Mast cells, basophils, platelets	Vasodilation, increased vascular permeability, endothelial activation
Serotonin	Platelets	Vasoconstriction
Prostaglandins	Mast cells, leukocytes	Vasodilation, pain, fever
Leukotrienes	Mast cells, leukocytes	Increased vascular permeability, chemotaxis, leukocyte adhesion and activation
Platelet-activating factor	Leukocytes, mast cells	Vasodilation, increased vascular permeability, leukocyte adhesion, chemotaxis, degranulation, oxidative burst
Reactive oxygen species	Leukocytes	Killing of microbes, tissue damage
Nitric oxide	Endothelium, macrophages	Vascular smooth muscle relaxation; killing of microbes
Cytokines (TNF, IL-1, IL-6)	Macrophages, endothelial cells, mast cells	*Local*: endothelial activation (expression of adhesion molecules). *Systemic*: fever, metabolic abnormalities, hypotension (shock)
Chemokines	Leukocytes, activated macrophages	Chemotaxis, leukocyte activation
Plasma Protein–Derived		
Complement	Plasma (produced in liver)	Leukocyte chemotaxis and activation, direct target killing (MAC), vasodilation (mast cell stimulation)
Kinins	Plasma (produced in liver)	Increased vascular permeability, smooth muscle contraction, vasodilation, pain
Proteases activated during coagulation	Plasma (produced in liver)	Endothelial activation, leukocyte recruitment

IL-1, IL-6, interleukin-1 and -6; MAC, membrane attack complex; TNF, tumor necrosis factor.

toxic oxygen metabolites), or are inhibited (e.g., complement regulatory proteins block complement activation).

Cell-Derived Mediators

Tissue macrophages, mast cells, and endothelial cells at the site of inflammation, as well as leukocytes that are recruited to the site from the blood, are all capable of producing different mediators of inflammation.

Vasoactive Amines

The two vasoactive amines, histamine and serotonin, are stored as preformed molecules in mast cells and other cells and are among the first mediators to be released in acute inflammatory reactions.

- *Histamine* is produced by many cell types, particularly mast cells adjacent to vessels, as well as circulating basophils and platelets. Preformed histamine is released from mast cell granules in response to a variety of stimuli: (1) physical injury such as trauma or heat; (2) immune reactions involving binding of IgE antibodies to Fc receptors on mast cells (Chapter 4); (3) C3a and C5a fragments of complement, the so-called anaphylatoxins (see later); (4) leukocyte-derived histamine-releasing proteins; (5) neuropeptides (e.g., substance P); and (6) certain cytokines (e.g., IL-1, IL-8). In humans, histamine causes arteriolar dilation and rapidly increases vascular permeability by inducing venular endothelial contraction and formation of interendothelial gaps. Soon after its release, histamine is inactivated by histaminase.
- *Serotonin* (5-hydroxytryptamine) is a preformed vasoactive mediator found within platelet granules that is released during platelet aggregation (Chapter 3). It induces vasoconstriction during clotting. It is produced mainly in some neurons and enterochromaffin cells, and is a neurotransmitter and regulates intestinal motility.

Arachidonic Acid Metabolites: Prostaglandins, Leukotrienes, and Lipoxins

Products derived from the metabolism of AA affect a variety of biologic processes, including inflammation and hemostasis. AA metabolites, also called *eicosanoids* (because they are derived from 20-carbon fatty acids—Greek *eicosa,* "twenty"), can mediate virtually every step of inflammation (Table 2–6); their synthesis is increased at sites of inflammatory response, and agents that inhibit their synthesis also diminish inflammation. Leukocytes, mast cells, endothelial cells, and platelets are the major sources of AA metabolites in inflammation. These AA-derived mediators act locally at the site of generation and then decay spontaneously or are enzymatically destroyed.

Table 2–6 Principal Inflammatory Actions of Arachidonic Acid Metabolites (Eicosanoids)

Action	Eicosanoid
Vasodilation	Prostaglandins PGI_2 (prostacyclin), PGE_1, PGE_2, PGD_2
Vasoconstriction	Thromboxane A_2, leukotrienes C_4, D_4, E_4
Increased vascular permeability	Leukotrienes C_4, D_4, E_4
Chemotaxis, leukocyte adhesion	Leukotriene B_4, HETE

HETE, hydroxyeicosatetraenoic acid.

AA is a 20-carbon polyunsaturated fatty acid (with four double bonds) produced primarily from dietary linoleic acid and present in the body mainly in its esterified form as a component of cell membrane phospholipids. It is released from these phospholipids through the action of cellular phospholipases that have been activated by mechanical, chemical, or physical stimuli, or by inflammatory mediators such as C5a. AA metabolism proceeds along one of two major enzymatic pathways: Cyclooxygenase stimulates the synthesis of prostaglandins and thromboxanes, and lipoxygenase is responsible for production of leukotrienes and lipoxins (Fig. 2–16).

- *Prostaglandins and thromboxanes.* Products of the cyclooxygenase pathway include prostaglandin E_2 (PGE_2), PGD_2, $PGF_{2\alpha}$, PGI_2 (prostacyclin), and thromboxane A_2 (TXA_2), each derived by the action of a specific enzyme on an intermediate. Some of these enzymes have a restricted tissue distribution. For example, platelets contain the enzyme *thromboxane synthase,* and hence TXA_2, a potent platelet-aggregating agent and vasoconstrictor, is the major prostaglandin produced in these cells. Endothelial cells, on the other hand, lack thromboxane synthase but contain prostacyclin synthase, which is responsible for the formation of PGI_2, a vasodilator and a potent inhibitor of platelet aggregation. The opposing roles of TXA_2 and PGI_2 in hemostasis are discussed further in Chapter 3. PGD_2 is the major metabolite of the cyclooxygenase pathway in mast cells; along with PGE_2 and $PGF_{2\alpha}$ (which are more widely distributed), it causes vasodilation and potentiates edema formation. The prostaglandins also contribute to the pain and fever that accompany inflammation; PGE_2 augments pain sensitivity to a variety of other stimuli and interacts with cytokines to cause fever.
- *Leukotrienes.* Leukotrienes are produced by the action of 5-lipoxygenase, the major AA-metabolizing enzyme in neutrophils. The synthesis of leukotrienes involves multiple steps (Fig. 2–16). The first step generates leukotriene A_4 (LTA_4), which in turn gives rise to LTB_4 or LTC_4. LTB_4 is produced by neutrophils and some macrophages and is a potent chemotactic agent for neutrophils. LTC_4 and its subsequent metabolites, LTD_4 and LTE_4, are produced mainly in mast cells and cause bronchoconstriction and increased vascular permeability.
- *Lipoxins.* Once leukocytes enter tissues, they gradually change their major lipoxygenase-derived AA products from leukotrienes to anti-inflammatory mediators called lipoxins, which inhibit neutrophil chemotaxis and adhesion to endothelium and thus serve as endogenous antagonists of leukotrienes. Platelets that are activated and adherent to leukocytes also are important sources of lipoxins. Platelets alone cannot synthesize lipoxins A_4 and B_4 (LXA_4 and LXB_4), but they can form these mediators from an intermediate derived from adjacent neutrophils, by a transcellular biosynthetic pathway. By this mechanism, AA products can pass from one cell type to another.

Anti-inflammatory Drugs That Block Prostaglandin Production. The central role of eicosanoids in inflammatory

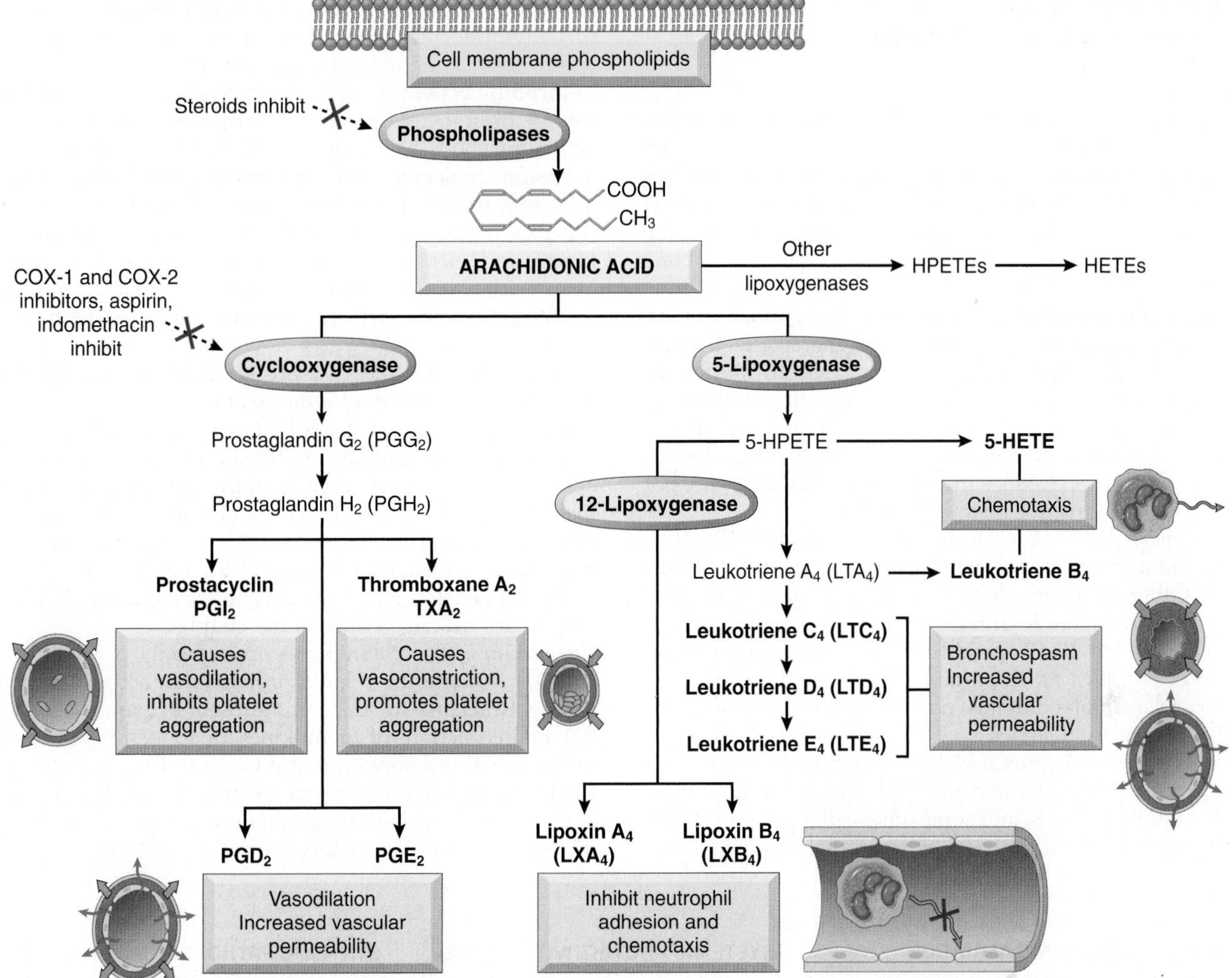

Figure 2–16 Production of arachidonic acid metabolites and their roles in inflammation. Note the enzymatic activities whose inhibition through pharmacologic intervention blocks major pathways (denoted with a *red X*). COX-1, COX-2, cyclooxygenases 1 and 2; HETE, hydroxyeicosatetraenoic acid; HPETE, hydroperoxyeicosatetraenoic acid.

processes is emphasized by the clinical utility of agents that block eicosanoid synthesis. Nonsteroidal anti-inflammatory drugs (NSAIDs), such as aspirin and ibuprofen, inhibit cyclooxygenase activity, thereby blocking all prostaglandin synthesis (hence their efficacy in treating pain and fever). There are two forms of the cyclooxygenase enzyme, COX-1 and COX-2. COX-1 is produced in response to inflammatory stimuli and also is constitutively expressed in most tissues, where it stimulates the production of prostaglandins that serve a homeostatic function (e.g., fluid and electrolyte balance in the kidneys, cytoprotection in the gastrointestinal tract). By contrast, COX-2 is induced by inflammatory stimuli but it is absent from most normal tissues. Therefore, COX-2 inhibitors have been developed with the expectation that they will inhibit harmful inflammation but will not block the protective effects of constitutively produced prostaglandins. These distinctions between the roles of the two cyclooxygenases are not absolute, however. Furthermore, COX-2 inhibitors may increase the risk for cardiovascular and cerebrovascular events, possibly because they impair endothelial cell production of prostacyclin (PGI_2), an inhibitor of platelet aggregation, but leave intact the COX-1–mediated production by platelets of TXA_2, a mediator of platelet aggregation. Glucocorticoids, which are powerful anti-inflammatory agents, act in part by inhibiting the activity of phospholipase A_2 and thus the release of AA from membrane lipids.

Platelet-Activating Factor

Originally named for its ability to aggregate platelets and cause their degranulation, platelet-activating factor (PAF) is another phospholipid-derived mediator with a broad spectrum of inflammatory effects. PAF is acetyl glycerol ether phosphocholine; it is generated from the membrane phospholipids of neutrophils, monocytes, basophils, endothelial cells, and platelets (and other cells) by the action of phospholipase A_2. PAF acts directly on target cells through the effects of a specific G protein–coupled receptor. In addition to stimulating platelets, PAF causes bronchoconstriction and is 100 to 1000 times more potent than histamine in inducing vasodilation and increased vascular permeability. It also stimulates the synthesis of other mediators, such as eicosanoids and cytokines, from platelets and other cells. Thus, PAF can elicit many of the reactions of inflammation, including enhanced leukocyte adhesion, chemotaxis, leukocyte degranulation, and the respiratory burst.

Cytokines

Cytokines are polypeptide products of many cell types that function as mediators of inflammation and immune responses (Chapter 4). Different cytokines are involved in the earliest immune and inflammatory reactions to noxious stimuli and in the later adaptive (specific) immune responses to microbes. Some cytokines stimulate bone marrow precursors to produce more leukocytes, thus replacing the ones that are consumed during inflammation and immune responses. Molecularly characterized cytokines are called interleukins (abbreviated IL and numbered), referring to their ability to mediate communications between leukocytes. However, the nomenclature is imperfect—many interleukins act on cells other than leukocytes, and many cytokines that do act on leukocytes are not called interleukins, for historical reasons.

The major cytokines in acute inflammation are TNF, IL-1, IL-6, and a group of chemoattractant cytokines called chemokines. Other cytokines that are more important in chronic inflammation include interferon-γ (IFN-γ) and IL-12. A cytokine called IL-17, produced by T lymphocytes and other cells, plays an important role in recruiting neutrophils and is involved in host defense against infections and in inflammatory diseases.

Tumor Necrosis Factor and Interleukin-1. TNF and IL-1 are produced by activated macrophages, as well as mast cells, endothelial cells, and some other cell types (Fig. 2–17). Their secretion is stimulated by microbial products, such as bacterial endotoxin, immune complexes, and products of T lymphocytes generated during adaptive immune responses. As mentioned earlier, IL-1 is also the cytokine induced by activation of the inflammasome. The principal role of these cytokines in inflammation is in endothelial activation. Both TNF and IL-1 stimulate the expression of adhesion molecules on endothelial cells, resulting in increased leukocyte binding and recruitment, and enhance the production of additional cytokines (notably chemokines) and eicosanoids. TNF also increases the thrombogenicity of endothelium. IL-1 activates tissue fibroblasts, resulting in increased proliferation and production of ECM.

Although TNF and IL-1 are secreted by macrophages and other cells at sites of inflammation, they may enter the circulation and act at distant sites to induce the systemic acute-phase reaction that is often associated with infection and inflammatory diseases. Components of this reaction include fever, lethargy, hepatic synthesis of various acute-phase proteins (also stimulated by IL-6), metabolic wasting (cachexia), neutrophil release into the circulation, and fall in blood pressure. These systemic manifestations of inflammation are described later in the chapter.

Chemokines. The chemokines are a family of small (8 to 10 kDa), structurally related proteins that act primarily as chemoattractants for different subsets of leukocytes. The two main functions of chemokines are to recruit leukocytes to the site of inflammation and to control the normal anatomic organization of cells in lymphoid and other tissues. Combinations of chemokines that are produced transiently in response to inflammatory stimuli recruit particular cell

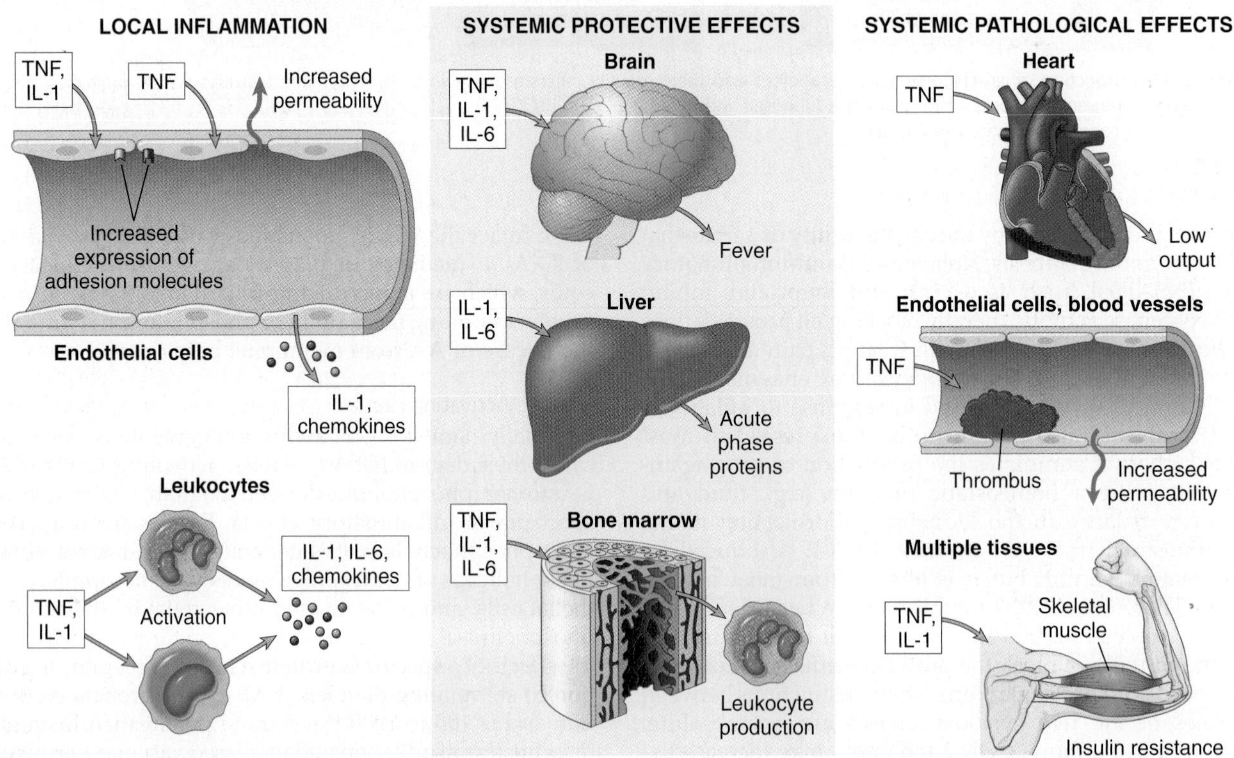

Figure 2–17 The roles of cytokines in acute inflammation. The cytokines TNF, IL-1, and IL-6 are key mediators of leukocyte recruitment in local inflammatory responses and also play important roles in the systemic reactions of inflammation.

populations (e.g., neutrophils, lymphocytes or eosinophils) to sites of inflammation. Chemokines also activate leukocytes; one consequence of such activation, as mentioned earlier, is increased affinity of leukocyte integrins for their ligands on endothelial cells. Some chemokines are produced constitutively in tissues and are responsible for the anatomic segregation of different cell populations in tissues (e.g., the segregation of T and B lymphocytes in different areas of lymph nodes and spleen). Chemokines mediate their activities by binding to specific G protein–coupled receptors on target cells; two of these chemokine receptors (called CXCR4 and CCR5) are important coreceptors for the binding and entry of the human immunodeficiency virus into lymphocytes (Chapter 4).

Chemokines are classified into four groups based on the arrangement of conserved cysteine residues. The two major groups are the CXC and CC chemokines:

- *CXC chemokines* have one amino acid separating the conserved cysteines and act primarily on neutrophils. IL-8 is typical of this group; it is produced by activated macrophages, endothelial cells, mast cells, and fibroblasts, mainly in response to microbial products and other cytokines such as IL-1 and TNF.
- *CC chemokines* have adjacent cysteine residues and include monocyte chemoattractant protein-1 (MCP-1) and macrophage inflammatory protein-1α (MIP-1α) (both chemotactic predominantly for monocytes), RANTES (*r*egulated on *a*ctivation, *n*ormal *T* cell–*e*xpressed and *s*ecreted) (chemotactic for memory CD4+ T cells and monocytes), and eotaxin (chemotactic for eosinophils).

Reactive Oxygen Species

ROS are synthesized via the NADPH oxidase (phagocyte oxidase) pathway and are released from neutrophils and macrophages that are activated by microbes, immune complexes, cytokines, and a variety of other inflammatory stimuli. The synthesis and regulation of these oxygen-derived free radicals have been described in Chapter 1, in the context of cell injury, and earlier in this chapter in the discussion of leukocyte activation. When the ROS are produced within lysosomes they function to destroy phagocytosed microbes and necrotic cells. When secreted at low levels, ROS can increase chemokine, cytokine, and adhesion molecule expression, thus amplifying the cascade of inflammatory mediators. At higher levels, these mediators are responsible for tissue injury by several mechanisms, including (1) endothelial damage, with thrombosis and increased permeability; (2) protease activation and antiprotease inactivation, with a net increase in breakdown of the ECM; and (3) direct injury to other cell types (e.g., tumor cells, red cells, parenchymal cells). Fortunately, various antioxidant protective mechanisms (e.g., mediated by catalase, superoxide dismutase, and glutathione) present in tissues and blood minimize the toxicity of the oxygen metabolites (Chapter 1).

Nitric Oxide

NO is a short-lived, soluble, free radical gas produced by many cell types and capable of mediating a variety of functions. In the central nervous system it regulates neurotransmitter release as well as blood flow. Macrophages use it as a cytotoxic agent for killing microbes and tumor cells. When produced by endothelial cells it relaxes vascular smooth muscle and causes vasodilation.

NO is synthesized de novo from L-arginine, molecular oxygen, and NADPH by the enzyme nitric oxide synthase (NOS). There are three isoforms of NOS, with different tissue distributions.

- Type I, neuronal NOS (nNOS), is constitutively expressed in neurons, and does not play a significant role in inflammation.
- Type II, inducible NOS (iNOS), is induced in macrophages and endothelial cells by a number of inflammatory cytokines and mediators, most notably by IL-1, TNF, and IFN-γ, and by bacterial endotoxin, and is responsible for production of NO in inflammatory reactions. This inducible form is also present in many other cell types, including hepatocytes, cardiac myocytes, and respiratory epithelial cells.
- Type III, endothelial NOS, (eNOS), is constitutively synthesized primarily (but not exclusively) in endothelium.

An important function of NO is as a microbicidal (cytotoxic) agent in activated macrophages. NO plays other roles in inflammation, including vasodilation, antagonism of all stages of platelet activation (adhesion, aggregation, and degranulation), and reduction of leukocyte recruitment at inflammatory sites.

Lysosomal Enzymes of Leukocytes

The lysosomal granules of neutrophils and monocytes contain many enzymes that destroy phagocytosed substances and are capable of causing tissue damage. Lysosomal granule contents also may be released from activated leukocytes, as described earlier. Acid proteases generally are active only in the low-pH environment of phagolysosomes, whereas neutral proteases, including elastase, collagenase, and cathepsin, are active in extracellular locations and cause tissue injury by degrading elastin, collagen, basement membrane, and other matrix proteins. Neutral proteases also can cleave the complement proteins C3 and C5 directly to generate the vasoactive mediators C3a and C5a and can generate bradykinin-like peptides from kininogen.

The potentially damaging effects of lysosomal enzymes are limited by antiproteases present in the plasma and tissue fluids. These include α_1-antitrypsin, the major inhibitor of neutrophil elastase, and α_2-macroglobulin. Deficiencies of these inhibitors may result in sustained activation of leukocyte proteases, resulting in tissue destruction at sites of leukocyte accumulation. For instance, α_1-antitrypsin deficiency in the lung can cause a severe panacinar emphysema (Chapter 12).

Neuropeptides

Like the vasoactive amines, neuropeptides can initiate inflammatory responses; these are small proteins, such as substance P, that transmit pain signals, regulate vessel tone, and modulate vascular permeability. Nerve fibers that secrete neuropeptides are especially prominent in the lung and gastrointestinal tract.

SUMMARY

Major Cell-Derived Mediators of Inflammation

- Vasoactive amines—histamine, serotonin: Their main effects are vasodilation and increased vascular permeability.
- Arachidonic acid metabolites—prostaglandins and leukotrienes: Several forms exist and are involved in vascular reactions, leukocyte chemotaxis, and other reactions of inflammation; they are antagonized by lipoxins.
- Cytokines: These proteins, produced by many cell types, usually act at short range; they mediate multiple effects, mainly in leukocyte recruitment and migration; principal ones in acute inflammation are TNF, IL-1, IL-6, and chemokines.
- ROS: Roles include microbial killing and tissue injury.
- NO: Effects are vasodilation and microbial killing.
- Lysosomal enzymes: Roles include microbial killing and tissue injury.

Plasma Protein–Derived Mediators

Circulating proteins of three interrelated systems—the complement, kinin, and coagulation systems—are involved in several aspects of the inflammatory reaction.

Complement

The *complement system* consists of plasma proteins that play an important role in host defense (immunity) and inflammation. Upon activation, different complement proteins coat (opsonize) particles, such as microbes, for phagocytosis and destruction, and contribute to the inflammatory response by increasing vascular permeability and leukocyte chemotaxis. Complement activation ultimately generates a porelike membrane attack complex (MAC) that punches holes in the membranes of invading microbes. Here we summarize the role of the complement system in inflammation.

- Complement components, numbered C1 to C9, are present in plasma in inactive forms, and many of them are activated by proteolysis to acquire their own proteolytic activity, thus setting up an enzymatic cascade.
- The critical step in the generation of biologically active complement products is the activation of the third component, C3 (Fig. 2–18). C3 cleavage occurs by three pathways: (1) the *classical pathway,* triggered by fixation of the first complement component C1 to antigen-antibody complexes; (2) the *alternative pathway,* triggered by bacterial polysaccharides (e.g., endotoxin) and other microbial cell wall components, and involving a distinct set of plasma proteins including properdin and factors B and D; and (3) the *lectin pathway,* in which a plasma lectin binds to mannose residues on microbes and activates an early component of the classical pathway (but in the absence of antibodies).
- All three pathways lead to the formation of a C3 convertase that cleaves C3 to C3a and C3b. C3b deposits on the cell or microbial surface where complement was activated and then binds to the C3 convertase complex to form C5 convertase; this complex cleaves C5 to generate C5a and C5b and initiate the final stages of assembly of C6 to C9.

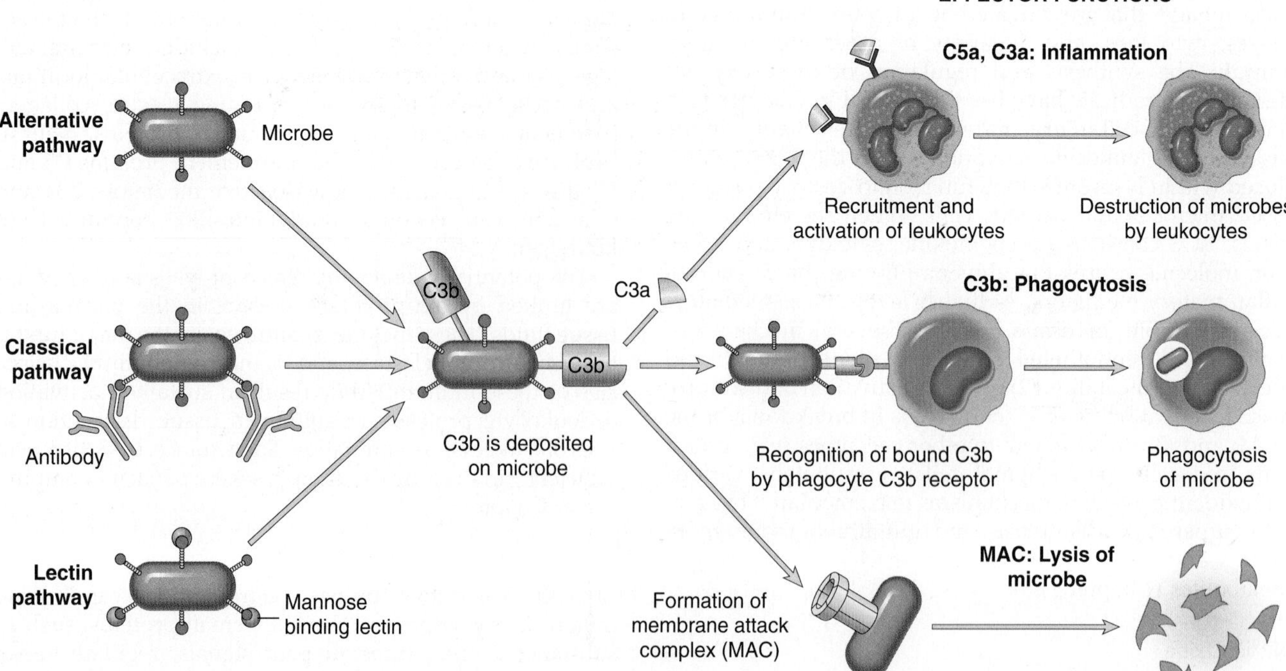

Figure 2–18 The activation and functions of the complement system. Activation of complement by different pathways leads to cleavage of C3. The functions of the complement system are mediated by breakdown products of C3 and other complement proteins, and by the membrane attack complex (MAC).

The complement-derived factors that are produced along the way contribute to a variety of phenomena in acute inflammation:

- *Vascular effects.* C3a and C5a increase vascular permeability and cause vasodilation by inducing mast cells to release histamine. These complement products are also called anaphylatoxins because their actions mimic those of mast cells, which are the main cellular effectors of the severe allergic reaction called anaphylaxis (Chapter 4). C5a also activates the lipoxygenase pathway of AA metabolism in neutrophils and macrophages, causing release of more inflammatory mediators.
- *Leukocyte activation, adhesion, and chemotaxis.* C5a, and to lesser extent, C3a and C4a, activate leukocytes, increasing their adhesion to endothelium, and is a potent chemotactic agent for neutrophils, monocytes, eosinophils, and basophils.
- *Phagocytosis.* When fixed to a microbial surface, C3b and its inactive proteolytic product iC3b act as opsonins, augmenting phagocytosis by neutrophils and macrophages, which express receptors for these complement products.
- The MAC, which is made up of multiple copies of the final component C9, kills some bacteria (especially thin-walled *Neisseria*) by creating pores that disrupt osmotic balance.

The activation of complement is tightly controlled by cell-associated and circulating regulatory proteins. The presence of these inhibitors in host cell membranes protects normal cells from inappropriate damage during protective reactions against microbes. Inherited deficiencies of these regulatory proteins lead to spontaneous complement activation:

- A protein called *C1 inhibitor* blocks activation of C1, and its inherited deficiency causes a disease called hereditary angioedema, in which excessive production of kinins secondary to complement activation results in edema in multiple tissues, including the larynx.
- Another protein called *decay-accelerating factor* (DAF) normally limits the formation of C3 and C5 convertases. In a disease called *paroxysmal nocturnal hemoglobinuria,* there is an acquired deficiency of DAF that results in complement-mediated lysis of red cells (which are more sensitive to lysis than most nucleated cells) (Chapter 11).
- *Factor H* is a plasma protein that also limits convertase formation; its deficiency is associated with a kidney disease called the *hemolytic uremic syndrome* (Chapter 13), as well as spontaneous vascular permeability in *macular degeneration* of the eye.

Even in the presence of regulatory proteins, inappropriate or excessive complement activation (e.g., in antibody-mediated diseases) can overwhelm the regulatory mechanisms; this is why complement activation is responsible for serious tissue injury in a variety of immunologic disorders (Chapter 4).

Coagulation and Kinin Systems

Some of the molecules activated during blood clotting are capable of triggering multiple aspects of the inflammatory response. *Hageman factor* (also known as *factor XII of the intrinsic coagulation cascade*) (Fig. 2–19) is a protein synthesized by the liver that circulates in an inactive form until it encounters collagen, basement membrane, or activated platelets (e.g., at a site of endothelial injury). Activated Hageman factor (factor XIIa) initiates four systems that may contribute to the inflammatory response: (1) the kinin system, producing vasoactive kinins; (2) the clotting

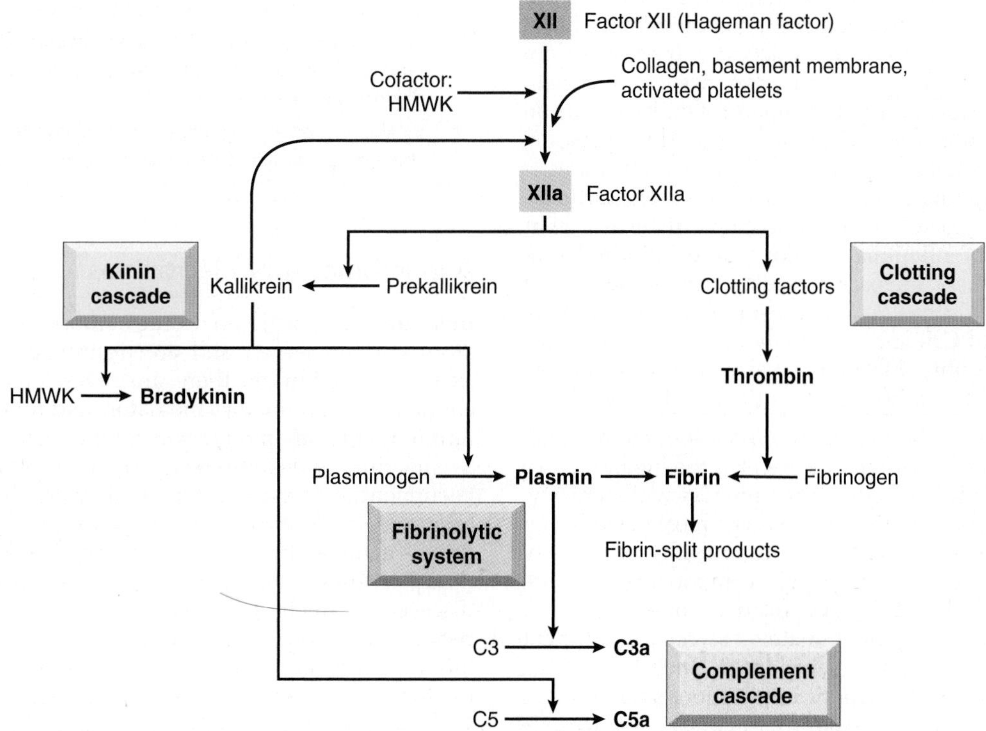

Figure 2–19 Interrelationships among the four plasma mediator systems triggered by activation of factor XII (Hageman factor). See text for details.

system, inducing the activation of thrombin, fibrinopeptides, and factor X, all with inflammatory properties; (3) the fibrinolytic system, producing plasmin and inactivating thrombin; and (4) the complement system, producing the anaphylatoxins C3a and C5a. These are described below.

- *Kinin system* activation leads ultimately to the formation of *bradykinin* from its circulating precursor, high-molecular-weight kininogen (HMWK) (Fig. 2–19). Like histamine, bradykinin causes increased vascular permeability, arteriolar dilation, and bronchial smooth muscle contraction. It also causes pain when injected into the skin. The actions of bradykinin are short-lived because it is rapidly degraded by kininases present in plasma and tissues. Of note, *kallikrein*, an intermediate in the kinin cascade with chemotactic activity, also is a potent activator of Hageman factor and thus constitutes another link between the kinin and clotting systems.
- In the *clotting system* (Chapter 3), the proteolytic cascade leads to activation of thrombin, which then cleaves circulating soluble fibrinogen to generate an insoluble *fibrin clot. Factor Xa,* an intermediate in the clotting cascade, causes increased vascular permeability and leukocyte emigration. Thrombin participates in inflammation by binding to protease-activated receptors that are expressed on platelets, endothelial cells, and many other cell types. Binding of thrombin to these receptors on endothelial cells leads to their activation and enhanced leukocyte adhesion. In addition, thrombin generates *fibrinopeptides* (during fibrinogen cleavage) that increase vascular permeability and are chemotactic for leukocytes. Thrombin also cleaves C5 to generate C5a, thus linking coagulation with complement activation.
- As a rule, whenever clotting is initiated (e.g., by activated Hageman factor), the *fibrinolytic system* is also activated concurrently. This mechanism serves to limit clotting by cleaving fibrin, thereby solubilizing the fibrin clot (Chapter 3). *Plasminogen activator* (released from endothelium, leukocytes, and other tissues) and *kallikrein* cleave *plasminogen,* a plasma protein bound up in the evolving fibrin clot. The resulting product, plasmin, is a multifunctional protease that cleaves fibrin and is therefore important in lysing clots. However, fibrinolysis also participates in multiple steps in the vascular phenomena of inflammation. For example, fibrin degradation products increase vascular permeability, and plasmin cleaves the C3 complement protein, resulting in production of C3a and vasodilation and increased vascular permeability. Plasmin can also activate Hageman factor, thereby amplifying the entire set of responses.

As is evident from the preceding discussion, many molecules are involved in different aspects of the inflammatory reaction, and these molecules often interact with, amplify, and antagonize one another. From this almost bewildering potpourri of chemical mediators, it is possible to identify the major contributors to various components of acute inflammation (Table 2–7). The relative contributions of individual mediators to inflammatory reactions to different stimuli have yet to be fully elucidated. Such knowledge would have obvious therapeutic implications since it might allow one to "custom design" antagonists for various inflammatory diseases.

Table 2–7 Role of Mediators in Different Reactions of Inflammation

Inflammatory Component	Mediators
Vasodilation	Prostaglandins Nitric oxide Histamine
Increased vascular permeability	Histamine and serotonin C3a and C5a (by liberating vasoactive amines from mast cells, other cells) Bradykinin Leukotrienes C_4, D_4, E_4 PAF Substance P
Chemotaxis, leukocyte recruitment and activation	TNF, IL-1 Chemokines C3a, C5a Leukotriene B_4 Bacterial products (e.g., *N*-formyl methyl peptides)
Fever	IL-1, TNF Prostaglandins
Pain	Prostaglandins Bradykinin
Tissue damage	Lysosomal enzymes of leukocytes Reactive oxygen species Nitric oxide

IL-1, interleukin-1; PAF, platelet-activating factor; TNF, tumor necrosis factor.

SUMMARY

Plasma Protein–Derived Mediators of Inflammation

- Complement proteins: Activation of the complement system by microbes or antibodies leads to the generation of multiple breakdown products, which are responsible for leukocyte chemotaxis, opsonization and phagocytosis of microbes and other particles, and cell killing.
- Coagulation proteins: Activated factor XII triggers the clotting, kinin, and complement cascades and activates the fibrinolytic system.
- Kinins: Produced by proteolytic cleavage of precursors, this group mediates vascular reaction and pain.

Anti-inflammatory Mechanisms

Inflammatory reactions subside because many of the mediators are short-lived and are destroyed by degradative *enzymes*. In addition, there are several mechanisms that counteract inflammatory mediators and function to limit or terminate the inflammatory response. Some of these, such as lipoxins, and complement regulatory proteins, have been mentioned earlier. Activated macrophages and other cells secrete a cytokine, IL-10, whose major function is to down-regulate the responses of activated macrophages, thus providing a negative feedback loop. In a rare inherited disease in which IL-10 receptors are mutated, affected patients develop severe colitis in infancy. Other anti-inflammatory cytokines include TGF-β, which is also a mediator of fibrosis in tissue repair after inflammation. Cells also express a number of intracellular proteins, such as tyrosine phosphatases, that inhibit pro-inflammatory signals triggered by receptors that recognize microbes and cytokines.

CHRONIC INFLAMMATION

Chronic inflammation is inflammation of prolonged duration (weeks to years) in which continuing inflammation, tissue injury, and healing, often by fibrosis, proceed simultaneously. In contrast with acute inflammation, which is distinguished by vascular changes, edema, and a predominantly neutrophilic infiltrate, chronic inflammation is characterized by a different set of reactions (Fig. 2–20; see also Table 2–1):

- *Infiltration with mononuclear cells,* including macrophages, lymphocytes, and plasma cells
- *Tissue destruction,* largely induced by the products of the inflammatory cells
- *Repair,* involving new vessel proliferation (angiogenesis) and fibrosis

Acute inflammation may progress to chronic inflammation if the acute response cannot be resolved, either because of the persistence of the injurious agent or because of interference with the normal process of healing. For example, a peptic ulcer of the duodenum initially shows acute inflammation followed by the beginning stages of resolution. However, recurrent bouts of duodenal epithelial injury interrupt this process, resulting in a lesion characterized by both acute and chronic inflammation (Chapter 14). Alternatively, some forms of injury (e.g., immunologic reactions, some viral infections) engender a chronic inflammatory response from the outset.

Chronic inflammation may arise in the following settings:

- *Persistent infections* by microbes that are difficult to eradicate. These include *Mycobacterium tuberculosis, Treponema pallidum* (the causative organism of syphilis), and certain viruses and fungi, all of which tend to establish persistent infections and elicit a T lymphocyte–mediated immune response called *delayed-type hypersensitivity* (Chapter 4).
- *Immune-mediated inflammatory diseases (hypersensitivity diseases).* Diseases that are caused by excessive and inappropriate activation of the immune system are increasingly recognized as being important health problems (Chapter 4). Under certain conditions, immune reactions develop against the affected person's own tissues, leading to *autoimmune diseases.* In such diseases, autoantigens evoke a self-perpetuating immune reaction that results in tissue damage and persistent inflammation. Autoimmunity plays an important role in several common and debilitating chronic inflammatory diseases, such as rheumatoid arthritis, inflammatory bowel disease, and psoriasis. Immune responses against common environmental substances are the cause of *allergic diseases,* such as bronchial asthma. Immune-mediated diseases may show morphologic patterns of mixed acute and chronic inflammation because they are characterized by repeated bouts of inflammation. Since, in most cases, the eliciting antigens cannot be eliminated, these disorders tend to be chronic and intractable.
- *Prolonged exposure to potentially toxic agents.* Examples are nondegradable exogenous materials such as inhaled particulate silica, which can induce a chronic inflammatory response in the lungs (silicosis, Chapter 12), and endogenous agents such as cholesterol crystals, which may contribute to atherosclerosis (Chapter 9).
- Mild forms of chronic inflammation may be important in the pathogenesis of many diseases that are not conventionally thought of as inflammatory disorders. Such diseases include neurodegenerative disorders such as Alzheimer disease, atherosclerosis, metabolic syndrome and the associated type 2 diabetes, and some forms of cancer in which inflammatory reactions promote tumor development. As mentioned earlier in the chapter, in many of these conditions the inflammation may be triggered by recognition of the initiating stimuli by the inflammasome. The role of inflammation in these conditions is discussed in the relevant chapters.

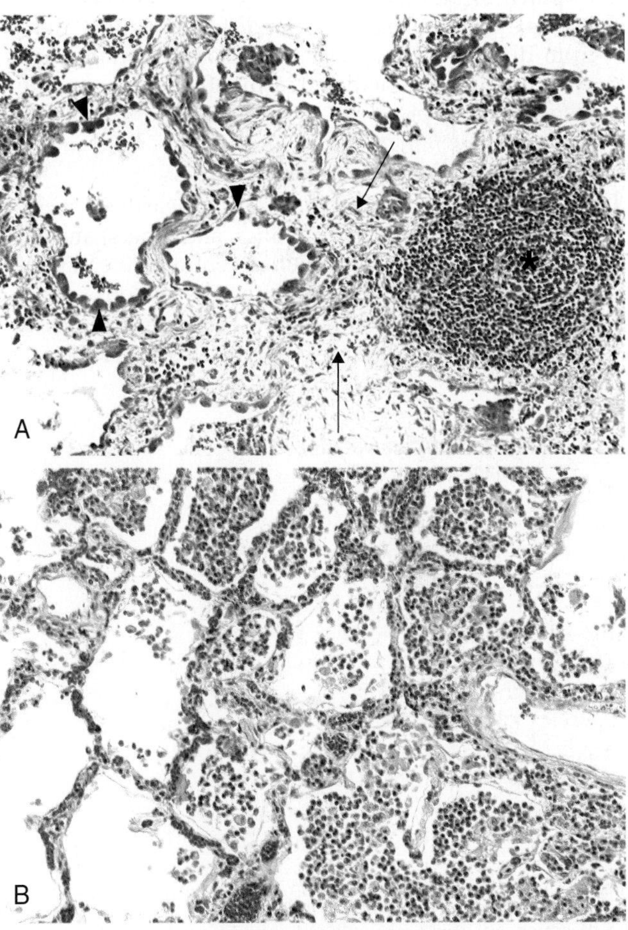

Figure 2–20 A, Chronic inflammation in the lung, showing the characteristic histologic features: collection of chronic inflammatory cells (*asterisk*); destruction of parenchyma, in which normal alveoli are replaced by spaces lined by cuboidal epithelium (*arrowheads*); and replacement by connective tissue, resulting in fibrosis (*arrows*). **B,** By contrast, in acute inflammation of the lung (acute bronchopneumonia), neutrophils fill the alveolar spaces and blood vessels are congested.

Chronic Inflammatory Cells and Mediators

The combination of prolonged and repeated inflammation, tissue destruction and fibrosis that characterizes chronic inflammation involves complex interactions between several cell populations and their secreted mediators. Understanding the pathogenesis of chronic inflammatory reactions requires an appreciation of these cells and their biologic responses and functions.

Macrophages

Macrophages, the dominant cells of chronic inflammation, are tissue cells derived from circulating blood monocytes after their emigration from the bloodstream. Macrophages are normally diffusely scattered in most connective tissues and are also found in organs such as the liver (where they are called Kupffer cells), spleen and lymph nodes (where they are called sinus histiocytes), central nervous system (microglial cells), and lungs (alveolar macrophages). Together these cells constitute the so-called *mononuclear phagocyte system,* also known by the older name of reticuloendothelial system. In all tissues, macrophages act as filters for particulate matter, microbes, and senescent cells, as well as the effector cells that eliminate microbes in cellular and humoral immune responses (Chapter 4).

Monocytes arise from precursors in the bone marrow and circulate in the blood for only about a day. Under the influence of adhesion molecules and chemokines, they migrate to a site of injury within 24 to 48 hours after the onset of acute inflammation, as described earlier. When monocytes reach the extravascular tissue, they undergo transformation into macrophages, which are somewhat larger and have a longer lifespan and a greater capacity for phagocytosis than do blood monocytes.

Tissue macrophages are activated by diverse stimuli to perform a range of functions. Two major pathways of macrophage activation, *classical* and *alternative,* have been described (Fig. 2–21):

- *Classical macrophage activation* is induced by microbial products such as endotoxin, by T cell–derived signals, importantly the cytokine IFN-γ, and by foreign substances including crystals and particulate matter. Classically activated macrophages produce lysosomal enzymes, NO, and ROS, all of which enhance their ability to kill ingested organisms, and secrete cytokines that stimulate inflammation. These macrophages are important in host defense against ingested microbes and in many chronic inflammatory reactions.
- *Alternative macrophage activation* is induced by cytokines other than IFN-γ, such as IL-4 and IL-13, produced by T lymphocytes and other cells, including mast cells and eosinophils. Alternatively activated macrophages are not actively microbicidal; instead, their principal role is in tissue repair. They secrete growth factors that promote angiogenesis, activate fibroblasts and stimulate collagen synthesis. It may be that in response to most injurious stimuli, macrophages are initially activated by the classical pathway, designed to destroy the offending agents, and this is followed by alternative activation, which initiates tissue repair. However, such a precise sequence is not well documented in most inflammatory reactions.

Macrophages have several critical roles in host defense and the inflammatory response.

- Macrophages, like the other type of phagocyte, the neutrophils, *ingest and eliminate microbes and dead tissues.* Because macrophages respond to activating signals from T lymphocytes, they are the most important phagocytes in the cell-mediated arm of adaptive immune responses (Chapter 4).
- Macrophages *initiate the process of tissue repair* and are involved in scar formation and fibrosis.
- Macrophages *secrete mediators of inflammation,* such as cytokines (TNF, IL-1, chemokines, and others) and eicosanoids. These cells are therefore central to the initiation and propagation of all inflammatory reactions.
- Macrophages *display antigens to T lymphocytes and respond to signals from T cells,* thus setting up a feedback loop that

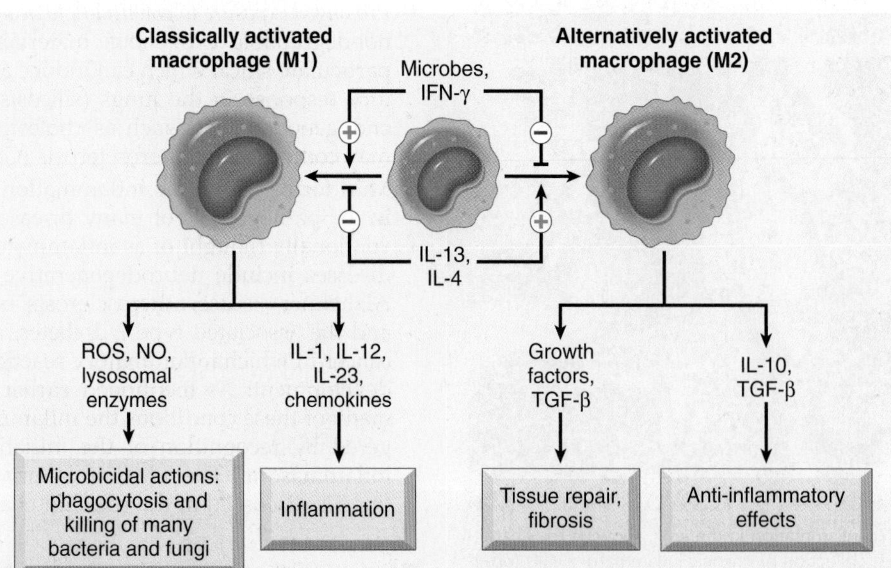

Figure 2–21 Pathways of macrophage activation. Different stimuli activate monocytes/macrophages to develop into functionally distinct populations. Classically activated macrophages are induced by microbial products and cytokines, particularly IFN-γ, and are microbicidal and involved in potentially harmful inflammation. Alternatively activated macrophages are induced by IL-4 and IL-13, produced by T_H2 cells (a helper T cell subset) and other leukocytes, and are important in tissue repair and fibrosis. IFN-γ, interferon-γ; IL-4, IL-13, interkeukin-4, -13.

is essential for defense against many microbes by cell-mediated immune responses. The same bidirectional interactions are central to the development of chronic inflammatory diseases. The roles of cytokines in these interactions are discussed later.

After the initiating stimulus is eliminated and the inflammatory reaction abates, macrophages eventually die or wander off into lymphatics. In chronic inflammatory sites, however, macrophage accumulation persists, because of continued recruitment from the blood and local proliferation. IFN-γ can also induce macrophages to fuse into large, multinucleate giant cells.

Lymphocytes

Lymphocytes are mobilized in the setting of any specific immune stimulus (i.e., infections) as well as non–immune-mediated inflammation (e.g., due to ischemic necrosis or trauma), and are the major drivers of inflammation in many autoimmune and other chronic inflammatory diseases. The activation of T and B lymphocytes is part of the adaptive immune response in infections and immunologic diseases (Chapter 4). Both classes of lymphocytes migrate into inflammatory sites using some of the same adhesion molecule pairs and chemokines that recruit other leukocytes. In the tissues, B lymphocytes may develop into *plasma cells,* which secrete antibodies, and CD4+ T lymphocytes are activated to secrete cytokines.

By virtue of cytokine secretion, CD4+ T lymphocytes promote inflammation and influence the nature of the inflammatory reaction. There are three subsets of CD4+ helper T cells that secrete different sets of cytokines and elicit different types of inflammation:

- T_H1 cells produce the cytokine IFN-γ, which activates macrophages in the classical pathway.
- T_H2 cells secrete IL-4, IL-5, and IL-13, which recruit and activate eosinophils and are responsible for the alternative pathway of macrophage activation.
- T_H17 cells secrete IL-17 and other cytokines that induce the secretion of chemokines responsible for recruiting neutrophils and monocytes into the reaction.

Both T_H1 and T_H17 cells are involved in defense against many types of bacteria and viruses and in autoimmune diseases. T_H2 cells are important in defense against helminthic parasites and in allergic inflammation. These T cell subsets and their functions are described in more detail in Chapter 4.

Lymphocytes and macrophages interact in a bidirectional way, and these interactions play an important role in propagating chronic inflammation (Fig. 2–22). Macrophages display antigens to T cells, express membrane molecules (called costimulators), and produce cytokines (IL-12 and others) that stimulate T cell responses (Chapter 4). Activated T lymphocytes, in turn, produce cytokines, described earlier, which recruit and activate macrophages and thus promote more antigen presentation and cytokine secretion. The result is a cycle of cellular reactions that fuel and sustain chronic inflammation. In some strong and prolonged inflammatory reactions, the accumulation of lymphocytes, antigen-presenting cells, and plasma cells may assume the morphologic features of lymphoid organs, and akin to lymph nodes, may even contain well-formed germinal centers. This pattern of lymphoid organogenesis is often seen in the synovium of patients with long-standing rheumatoid arthritis and the thyroid of patients with autoimmune thyroiditis.

Other Cells

Eosinophils are characteristically found in inflammatory sites around parasitic infections and as part of immune reactions mediated by IgE, typically associated with allergies. Their recruitment is driven by adhesion molecules similar to those used by neutrophils, and by specific chemokines (e.g., eotaxin) derived from leukocytes and epithelial cells. Eosinophil granules contain major basic protein, a highly charged cationic protein that is toxic to parasites but also causes epithelial cell necrosis.

Mast cells are sentinel cells widely distributed in connective tissues throughout the body, and they can participate in both acute and chronic inflammatory responses. In atopic persons (those prone to allergic reactions), mast cells are "armed" with IgE antibody specific for certain

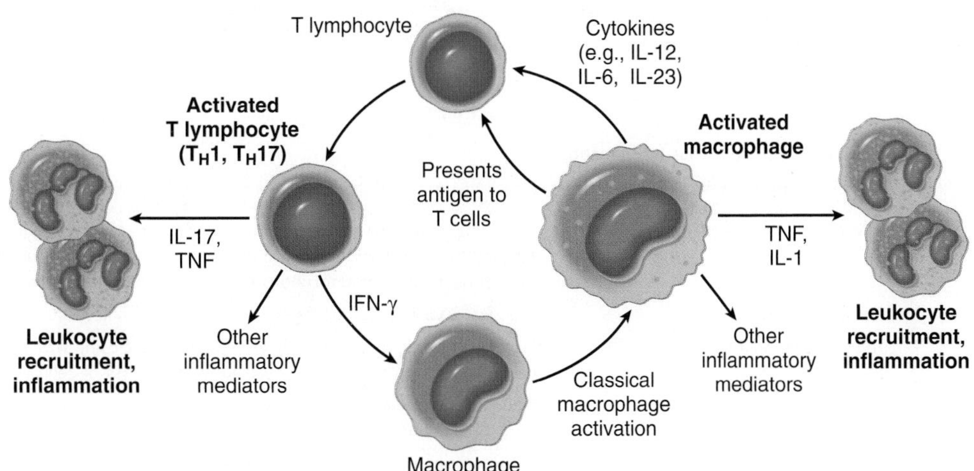

Figure 2–22 Macrophage–lymphocyte interactions in chronic inflammation. Activated lymphocytes and macrophages stimulate each other, and both cell types release inflammatory mediators that affect other cells. IFN-γ, interferon-γ; IL-1, interleukin-1; TNF, tumor necrosis factor.

environmental antigens. When these antigens are subsequently encountered, the IgE-coated mast cells are triggered to release histamines and AA metabolites that elicit the early vascular changes of acute inflammation. IgE-armed mast cells are central players in allergic reactions, including anaphylactic shock (Chapter 4). Mast cells can also elaborate cytokines such as TNF and chemokines and may play a beneficial role in combating some infections.

An important final point: *Although the presence of neutrophils is the hallmark of acute inflammation, many forms of chronic inflammation may continue to show extensive neutrophilic infiltrates,* as a result of either persistent microbes or necrotic cells, or mediators elaborated by macrophages. Such inflammatory lesions are sometimes called "acute on chronic"—for example, in inflammation of bones (osteomyelitis).

Granulomatous Inflammation

Granulomatous inflammation is a distinctive pattern of chronic inflammation characterized by aggregates of activated macrophages with scattered lymphocytes. Granulomas are characteristic of certain specific pathologic states; consequently, recognition of the granulomatous pattern is important because of the limited number of conditions (some life-threatening) that cause it (Table 2–8). Granulomas can form under three settings:

- With persistent T-cell responses to certain microbes (such as *Mycobacterium tuberculosis, T. pallidum,* or fungi), in which T cell–derived cytokines are responsible for chronic macrophage activation. *Tuberculosis is the prototype of a granulomatous disease caused by infection and should always be excluded as the cause when granulomas are identified.*
- Granulomas may also develop in some immune-mediated inflammatory diseases, notably Crohn disease, which is one type of inflammatory bowel disease and an important cause of granulomatous inflammation in the United States.
- They are also seen in a disease of unknown etiology called sarcoidosis, and they develop in response to relatively inert foreign bodies (e.g., suture or splinter), forming so-called *foreign body granulomas.*

The formation of a granuloma effectively "walls off" the offending agent and is therefore a useful defense mechanism. However, granuloma formation does not always lead to eradication of the causal agent, which is frequently resistant to killing or degradation, and granulomatous inflammation with subsequent fibrosis may even be the major cause of organ dysfunction in some diseases, such as tuberculosis.

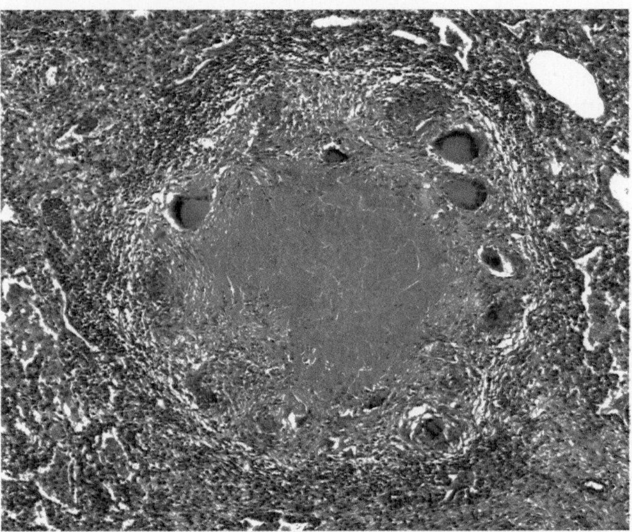

Figure 2–23 A typical granuloma resulting from infection with *Mycobacterium tuberculosis* showing central area of caseous necrosis, activated epithelioid macrophages, giant cells, and a peripheral accumulation of lymphocytes.

MORPHOLOGY

In the usual H&E preparations (Fig. 2–23), some of the activated macrophages in granulomas have pink, granular cytoplasm with indistinct cell boundaries; these are called **epithelioid cells** because of their resemblance to epithelia. Typically, the aggregates of epithelioid macrophages are surrounded by a collar of lymphocytes. Older granulomas may have a rim of fibroblasts and connective tissue. Frequently, but not invariably, multinucleate **giant cells** 40 to 50 μm in diameter are found in granulomas. Such cells consist of a large mass of cytoplasm and many nuclei, and they derive from the fusion of multiple activated macrophages. In granulomas

Table 2–8 Examples of Diseases with Granulomatous Inflammation

Disease	Cause	Tissue Reaction
Tuberculosis	*Mycobacterium tuberculosis*	Caseating granuloma (tubercle): focus of activated macrophages (epithelioid cells), rimmed by fibroblasts, lymphocytes, histiocytes, occasional Langhans giant cells; central necrosis with amorphous granular debris; acid-fast bacilli
Leprosy	*Mycobacterium leprae*	Acid-fast bacilli in macrophages; noncaseating granulomas
Syphilis	*Treponema pallidum*	Gumma: microscopic to grossly visible lesion, enclosing wall of histiocytes; plasma cell infiltrate; central cells are necrotic without loss of cellular outline
Cat-scratch disease	Gram-negative bacillus	Rounded or stellate granuloma containing central granular debris and neutrophils; giant cells uncommon
Sarcoidosis	Unknown etiology	Noncaseating granulomas with abundant activated macrophages
Crohn disease	Immune reaction against intestinal bacteria, self antigens	Occasional noncaseating granulomas in the wall of the intestine, with dense chronic inflammatory infiltrate

associated with certain infectious organisms (most classically the tubercle bacillus), a combination of hypoxia and free radical injury leads to a central zone of necrosis. On gross examination, this has a granular, cheesy appearance and is therefore called **caseous necrosis** (Chapters 1 and 13). On microscopic examination, this necrotic material appears as eosinophilic amorphous, structureless, granular debris, with complete loss of cellular details. The granulomas associated with Crohn disease, sarcoidosis, and foreign body reactions tend to not have necrotic centers and are said to be "non-caseating." Healing of granulomas is accompanied by fibrosis that may be quite extensive.

SUMMARY

Features of Chronic Inflammation

- Prolonged host response to persistent stimulus
- Caused by microbes that resist elimination, immune responses against self and environmental antigens, and some toxic substances (e.g., silica); underlies many important diseases
- Characterized by persistent inflammation, tissue injury, attempted repair by scarring, and immune response
- Cellular infiltrate consisting of activated macrophages, lymphocytes, and plasma cells, often with prominent fibrosis
- Mediated by cytokines produced by macrophages and lymphocytes (notably T lymphocytes), with a tendency to an amplified and prolonged inflammatory response owing to bidirectional interactions between these cells

SYSTEMIC EFFECTS OF INFLAMMATION

Anyone who has suffered a severe bout of viral illness (such as influenza) has experienced the systemic effects of inflammation, collectively called the *acute-phase reaction,* or the systemic inflammatory response syndrome. *The cytokines TNF, IL-1, and IL-6 are the most important mediators of the acute-phase reaction.* These cytokines are produced by leukocytes (and other cell types) in response to infection or in immune reactions and are released systemically. TNF and IL-1 have similar biologic actions, although these may differ in subtle ways (Fig. 2–17). IL-6 stimulates the hepatic synthesis of a number of plasma proteins, described further on.

The acute-phase response consists of several clinical and pathologic changes.

- *Fever,* characterized by an elevation of body temperature, is one of the most prominent manifestations of the acute-phase response. Fever is produced in response to substances called pyrogens that act by stimulating prostaglandin synthesis in the vascular and perivascular cells of the hypothalamus. Bacterial products, such as lipopolysaccharide (LPS) (called *exogenous pyrogens*), stimulate leukocytes to release cytokines such as IL-1 and TNF (called *endogenous pyrogens*), which increase the levels of cyclooxygenases that convert AA into prostaglandins. In the hypothalamus the prostaglandins, especially PGE_2, stimulate the production of neurotransmitters, which function to reset the temperature set point at a higher level. NSAIDs, including aspirin, reduce fever by inhibiting cyclooxygenase and thus blocking prostaglandin synthesis. Although fever was recognized as a sign of infection hundreds of years ago, it is still not clear what the purpose of this reaction may be. An elevated body temperature has been shown to help amphibians ward off microbial infections, and it is assumed that fever does the same for mammals, although the mechanism is unknown.
- *Elevated plasma levels of acute-phase proteins.* These plasma proteins are mostly synthesized in the liver, and in the setting of acute inflammation, their concentrations may increase several hundred-fold. Three of the best known of these proteins are C-reactive protein (CRP), fibrinogen, and serum amyloid A (SAA) protein. Synthesis of these molecules by hepatocytes is stimulated by cytokines, especially IL-6. Many acute-phase proteins, such as CRP and SAA, bind to microbial cell walls, and they may act as opsonins and fix complement, thus promoting the elimination of the microbes. Fibrinogen binds to erythrocytes and causes them to form stacks (rouleaux) that sediment more rapidly at unit gravity than individual erythrocytes. This is the basis for measuring the erythrocyte sedimentation rate (ESR) as a simple test for the systemic inflammatory response, caused by any number of stimuli, including LPS. Serial measurements of ESR and CRP are used to assess therapeutic responses in patients with inflammatory disorders such as rheumatoid arthritis. Elevated serum levels of CRP are now used as a marker for increased risk of myocardial infarction or stroke in patients with atherosclerotic vascular disease. It is believed that inflammation is involved in the development of atherosclerosis (Chapter 9), and increased CRP is a measure of inflammation.
- *Leukocytosis* is a common feature of inflammatory reactions, especially those induced by bacterial infection (see Table 11–6, Chapter 11). The leukocyte count usually climbs to 15,000 to 20,000 cells/mL, but in some extraordinary cases it may reach 40,000 to 100,000 cells/mL. These extreme elevations are referred to as *leukemoid reactions* because they are similar to those seen in leukemia. The leukocytosis occurs initially because of accelerated release of cells (under the influence of cytokines, including TNF and IL-1) from the bone marrow postmitotic reserve pool. Both mature and immature neutrophils may be seen in the blood; the presence of circulating immature cells is referred to as a "shift to the left." Prolonged infection also stimulates production of colony-stimulating factors (CSFs), which increase the bone marrow output of leukocytes, thus compensating for the consumption of these cells in the inflammatory reaction. Most bacterial infections induce an increase in the blood neutrophil count, called neutrophilia. Viral infections, such as infectious mononucleosis, mumps, and German measles, are associated with increased numbers of lymphocytes (lymphocytosis). Bronchial asthma, hay fever, and parasite infestations all involve an increase in the absolute number of eosinophils, creating an

eosinophilia. Certain infections (typhoid fever and infections caused by some viruses, rickettsiae, and certain protozoa) are paradoxically associated with a decreased number of circulating white cells (leukopenia), likely because of cytokine-induced sequestration of lymphocytes in lymph nodes.

- Other manifestations of the acute-phase response include increased heart rate and blood pressure; decreased sweating, mainly as a result of redirection of blood flow from cutaneous to deep vascular beds, to minimize heat loss through the skin; and rigors (shivering), chills (perception of being cold as the hypothalamus resets the body temperature), anorexia, somnolence, and malaise, probably secondary to the actions of cytokines on brain cells.
- In severe bacterial infections (sepsis), the large amounts of bacterial products in the blood or extravascular tissue stimulate the production of several cytokines, notably TNF, as well as IL-12 and IL-1. TNF can cause disseminated intravascular coagulation (DIC), metabolic disturbances including acidosis, and hypotensive shock. This clinical triad is described as *septic shock*; it is discussed in more detail in Chapter 3.

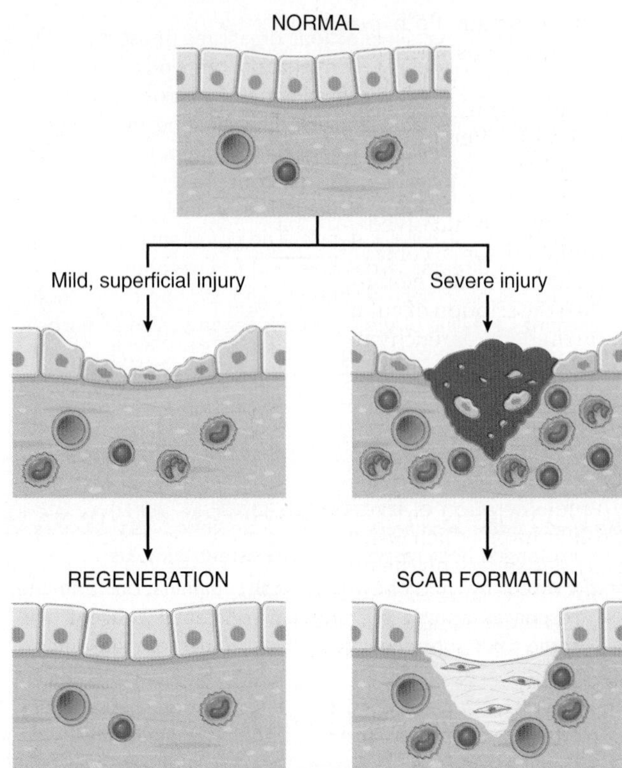

Figure 2–24 Mechanisms of tissue repair: regeneration and scar formation. After mild injury, which damages the epithelium but not the underlying tissue, resolution occurs by regeneration, but after more severe injury with damage to the connective tissue, repair is by scar formation.

SUMMARY
Systemic Effects of Inflammation

- Fever: cytokines (TNF, IL-1) stimulate production of prostaglandins in hypothalamus
- Production of acute-phase proteins: C-reactive protein, others; synthesis stimulated by cytokines (IL-6, others) acting on liver cells
- Leukocytosis: cytokines (CSFs) stimulate production of leukocytes from precursors in the bone marrow
- In some severe infections, septic shock: fall in blood pressure, disseminated intravascular coagulation, metabolic abnormalities; induced by high levels of TNF

Even before the inflammatory reaction ends, the body begins the process of healing the damage and restoring normal structure and function. This process is called repair, and it involves the proliferation and differentiation of several cell types and the deposition of connective tissue. Defects in tissue repair have serious consequences. Conversely, excessive connective tissue deposition (fibrosis) is also a cause of significant abnormalities. Therefore, the mechanisms and regulation of the repair process are of great physiologic and pathologic importance.

OVERVIEW OF TISSUE REPAIR

Critical to the survival of an organism is the ability to repair the damage caused by toxic insults and inflammation. The inflammatory response to microbes and injured tissues not only serves to eliminate these dangers but also sets into motion the process of repair. Repair, sometimes called healing, refers to the restoration of tissue architecture and function after an injury. It occurs by two types of reactions: regeneration of the injured tissue and scar formation by the deposition of connective tissue (Fig. 2–24).

- *Regeneration.* Some tissues are able to replace the damaged cells and essentially return to a normal state; this process is called regeneration. Regeneration occurs by proliferation of residual (uninjured) cells that retain the capacity to divide, and by replacement from tissue stem cells. It is the typical response to injury in the rapidly dividing epithelia of the skin and intestines, and some parenchymal organs, notably the liver.
- *Scar formation.* If the injured tissues are incapable of regeneration, or if the supporting structures of the tissue are severely damaged, repair occurs by the laying down of connective (fibrous) tissue, a process that results in scar formation. Although the fibrous scar cannot perform the function of lost parenchymal cells, it provides enough structural stability that the injured tissue is usually able to function. The term *fibrosis* is most often used to describe the extensive deposition of collagen that occurs in the lungs, liver, kidney, and other organs as a consequence of chronic inflammation, or in the myocardium after extensive ischemic necrosis (infarction). If fibrosis develops in a tissue space occupied by an inflammatory exudate, it is called organization (as in organizing pneumonia affecting the lung).

After many common types of injury, both regeneration and scar formation contribute in varying degrees to the ultimate repair. Both processes involve the proliferation of various cells and close interactions between cells and the ECM. The next section discusses the principles of cellular proliferation, the roles of growth factors in the proliferation of different cell types involved in repair, and the roles of stem cells in tissue homeostasis. This is followed by a summary of some important properties of the ECM and how it is involved in repair. These sections lay the foundation for a consideration of the salient features of regeneration and healing by scar formation, concluding with a description of cutaneous wound healing and fibrosis (scarring) in parenchymal organs as illustrations of the repair process.

CELL AND TISSUE REGENERATION

The regeneration of injured cells and tissues involves cell proliferation, which is driven by growth factors and is critically dependent on the integrity of the extracellular matrix. Before describing examples of repair by regeneration, we discuss the general principles of cell proliferation and the functions of the ECM in this process.

The Control of Cell Proliferation

Several cell types proliferate during tissue repair. These include the remnants of the injured tissue (which attempt to restore normal structure), vascular endothelial cells (to create new vessels that provide the nutrients needed for the repair process), and fibroblasts (the source of the fibrous tissue that forms the scar to fill defects that cannot be corrected by regeneration). The proliferation of these cell types is driven by proteins called *growth factors.* The production of polypeptide growth factors and the ability of cells to divide in response to these factors are important determinants of the adequacy of the repair process.

The normal size of cell populations is determined by a balance among cell proliferation, cell death by apoptosis, and emergence of new differentiated cells from stem cells (Fig. 2-25). The key processes in the proliferation of cells are DNA replication and mitosis. The sequence of events that control these two processes is known as the *cell cycle,* described in detail in Chapter 5 in the context of cancer. At this stage, it is sufficient to note that nondividing cells are in cell cycle arrest in the G_1 phase or have exited the cycle and are in the G_0 phase. Growth factors stimulate cells to transition from G_0 into the G_1 phase and beyond into DNA synthesis (S), G_2, and mitosis (M) phases. Progression is regulated by cyclins, whose activity is controlled by cyclin-dependent kinases. Once cells enter the S phase, their DNA is replicated and they progress through G_2 and mitosis.

Proliferative Capacities of Tissues

The ability of tissues to repair themselves is critically influenced by their intrinsic proliferative capacity. On the basis of this criterion, the tissues of the body are divided into three groups.

- *Labile (continuously dividing) tissues.* Cells of these tissues are continuously being lost and replaced by maturation from stem cells and by proliferation of mature cells.

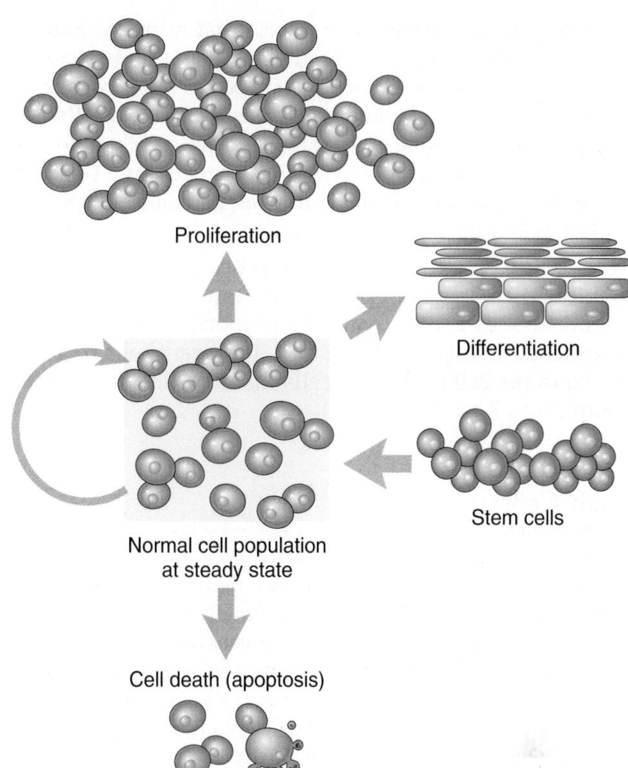

Figure 2–25 Mechanisms regulating cell populations. Cell numbers can be altered by increased or decreased rates of stem cell input, cell death by apoptosis, or changes in the rates of proliferation or differentiation. *(Modified from McCarthy NJ, et al: Apoptosis in the development of the immune system: growth factors, clonal selection and bcl-2. Cancer Metastasis Rev 11:157, 1992.)*

  Labile cells include hematopoietic cells in the bone marrow and the majority of surface epithelia, such as the stratified squamous surfaces of the skin, oral cavity, vagina, and cervix; the cuboidal epithelia of the ducts draining exocrine organs (e.g., salivary glands, pancreas, biliary tract); the columnar epithelium of the gastrointestinal tract, uterus, and fallopian tubes; and the transitional epithelium of the urinary tract. These tissues can readily regenerate after injury as long as the pool of stem cells is preserved.
- *Stable tissues.* Cells of these tissues are quiescent and have only minimal replicative activity in their normal state. However, these cells are capable of proliferating in response to injury or loss of tissue mass. Stable cells constitute the parenchyma of most solid tissues, such as liver, kidney, and pancreas. They also include endothelial cells, fibroblasts, and smooth muscle cells; the proliferation of these cells is particularly important in wound healing. With the exception of liver, stable tissues have a limited capacity to regenerate after injury.
- *Permanent tissues.* The cells of these tissues are considered to be terminally differentiated and nonproliferative in postnatal life. Most neurons and cardiac muscle cells belong to this category. Thus, injury to brain or heart is irreversible and results in a scar, because neurons and cardiac myocytes cannot regenerate. Limited stem cell replication and differentiation occur in some areas of the adult brain, and there is some evidence that cardiac stem

cells may proliferate after myocardial necrosis. Nevertheless, whatever proliferative capacity may exist in these tissues, it is insufficient to produce tissue regeneration after injury. Skeletal muscle is usually classified as a permanent tissue, but satellite cells attached to the endomysial sheath provide some regenerative capacity for this tissue. In permanent tissues, repair is typically dominated by scar formation.

With the exception of tissues composed primarily of nondividing permanent cells (e.g., cardiac muscle, nerve), most mature tissues contain variable proportions of three cell types: continuously dividing cells, quiescent cells that can return to the cell cycle, and cells that have lost replicative ability.

Stem Cells

In most dividing tissues the mature cells are terminally differentiated and short-lived. As mature cells die, the tissue is replenished by the differentiation of cells generated from stem cells. Thus, in these tissues there is a homeostatic equilibrium between the replication, self-renewal, and differentiation of stem cells and the death of the mature, fully differentiated cells. Such relationships are particularly evident in the continuously dividing epithelium of the skin and the gastrointestinal tract, in which stem cells live near the basal layer of the epithelium, and cells differentiate as they migrate to the upper layers of the epithelium before they die and are shed from the surface.

Stem cells are characterized by two important properties: self-renewal capacity and asymmetric replication. Asymmetric replication means that when a stem cell divides, one daughter cell enters a differentiation pathway and gives rise to mature cells, while the other remains an undifferentiated stem cell that retains its self-renewal capacity. Self-renewal enables stem cells to maintain a functional population of precursors for long periods of time. Although the scientific literature is replete with descriptions of various types of stem cells, fundamentally there are two kinds:

- *Embryonic stem cells (ES cells)* are the most undifferentiated stem cells. They are present in the inner cell mass of the blastocyst and have extensive cell renewal capacity. Hence they can be maintained in culture for over a year without differentiating. Under appropriate culture conditions, ES cells can be induced to form specialized cells of all three germ cell layers, including neurons, cardiac muscle, liver cells, and pancreatic islet cells.
- *Adult stem cells,* also called tissue stem cells, are less undifferentiated than ES cells and are found among differentiated cells within an organ or tissue. Although, like ES cells, they also have self-renewal capacity, this property is much more limited. In addition, their lineage potential (ability to give rise to specialized cells) is restricted to some or all of the differentiated cells of the tissue or organ in which they are found.

Whereas the normal function of ES cells is to give rise to all cells of the body, adult stem cells are involved in tissue homeostasis. They maintain the compartment size both in tissues with high turnover, such as skin, bone marrow, and gut epithelium, and in those with low cell turnover, such as heart and blood vessels. Although there is much interest in isolation and infusion of tissue stem cells for replenishment of specialized cells in organs such as the heart (after a myocardial infarct) and brain (after a stroke), tissue stem cells are rare and very difficult to isolate to purity. Furthermore, they occur in specialized microenvironments within the organ called *stem cell niches.* Apparently, signals from other cells in such niches keep the stem cells quiescent and undifferentiated. Stem cell niches have been identified in many organs. In the brain, neural stem cells occur in the subventricular zone and dentate gyrus; in the skin, tissue stem cells are found in the bulge region of the hair follicle; and in the cornea, they are found at the limbus.

Perhaps the most extensively studied tissue stem cells are hematopoietic stem cells found in the bone marrow. Although rare, they can be purified to virtual purity based on cell surface markers. Hematopoietic stem cells can be isolated from bone marrow as well as from the peripheral blood after mobilization by administration of certain cytokines such as granulocyte colony-stimulating factor (G-CSF). As is well known, they can give rise to all blood cell lineages and continuously replenish the formed elements of the blood as these are consumed in the periphery. In clinical practice, marrow stem cells are used for treatment of diseases such as leukemia and lymphomas (Chapter 11). In addition to hematopoietic stem cells, the bone marrow also contains a somewhat distinctive population of tissue stem cells, often called *mesenchymal stem cells.* These cells can give rise to a variety of mesenchymal cells, such as chondroblasts, osteoblasts, and myoblasts. Hence, there is great interest in their therapeutic potential.

The ability to identify and isolate stem cells has given rise to the new field of *regenerative medicine,* which has as its main goal the repopulation of damaged organs by using differentiated progeny of ES cells or adult stem cells. Since ES cells have extensive self-renewal capacity and can give rise to all cell lineages, they often are considered ideal for developing specialized cells for therapeutic purposes. However, since ES cells are derived from blastocysts (typically produced from in vitro fertilization), their progeny carry histocompatibility molecules (human leukocyte antigen [HLA] in people) (Chapter 4) of the donors of the egg and sperm. Thus, they are likely to evoke immunologically mediated rejection by the host, just as organs transplanted from genetically disparate hosts do. Hence, much effort has gone into producing cells with the potential of ES cells from patient tissues. To accomplish this goal, the expressed genes in ES cells and differentiated cells have been compared and a handful of genes that are critical for the "stem-cell-ness" of ES cells have been identified. Introduction of such genes into fully differentiated cells, such as fibroblasts or skin epithelial cells, leads, quite remarkably, to reprogramming of the somatic cell nucleus, such that the cells acquire many of the properties of ES cells. These cells are called *induced pluripotent stem cells (iPS cells)* (Fig. 2–26). Since iPS cells can be derived from each patient, their differentiated progeny should engraft successfully and restore or replace damaged or deficient cells in the patient—for example, insulin-secreting β cells in a patient with diabetes. Although iPS cells hold considerable promise, their clinical usefulness remains to be proved.

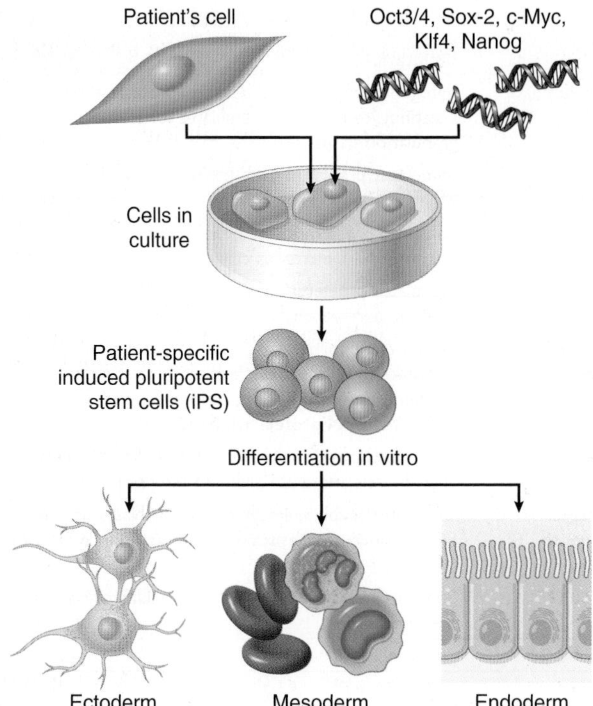

Figure 2–26 The production of induced pluripotent stem cells (iPS cells). Genes that confer stem cell properties are introduced into a patient's differentiated cells, giving rise to stem cells, which can be induced to differentiate into various lineages.

SUMMARY

Cell Proliferation, the Cell Cycle, and Stem Cells

- Regeneration of tissues is driven by proliferation of uninjured (residual) cells and replacement from stem cells.
- Cell proliferation occurs when quiescent cells enter the cell cycle. The cell cycle is tightly regulated by stimulators and inhibitors and contains intrinsic checkpoint controls to prevent replication of abnormal cells.
- Tissues are divided into labile, stable, and permanent, according to the proliferative capacity of their cells.
- Continuously dividing tissues (labile tissues) contain mature cells that are capable of dividing and stem cells that differentiate to replenish lost cells.
- Stem cells from embryos (ES cells) are pluripotent; adult tissues, particularly the bone marrow, contain adult stem cells capable of generating multiple cell lineages.
- Induced pluripotent stem cells (iPS cells) are derived by introducing into mature cells genes that are characteristic of ES cells. iPS cells acquire many characteristics of stem cells.

Growth Factors

Most growth factors are proteins that stimulate the survival and proliferation of particular cells, and may also promote migration, differentiation, and other cellular responses. They induce cell proliferation by binding to specific receptors and affecting the expression of genes whose products typically have several functions: They promote entry of cells into the cell cycle, they relieve blocks on cell cycle progression (thus promoting replication), they prevent apoptosis, and they enhance the synthesis of cellular proteins in preparation for mitosis. A major activity of growth factors is to stimulate the function of growth control genes, many of which are called *proto-oncogenes* because mutations in them lead to unrestrained cell proliferation characteristic of cancer (oncogenesis) (Chapter 5).

There is a huge (and ever-increasing) list of known growth factors. In the following discussion, rather than attempting an exhaustive cataloguing, we highlight only selected molecules that contribute to tissue repair (Table 2–9). Many of the growth factors that are involved in repair are produced by macrophages and lymphocytes that are recruited to the site of injury or are activated at this site, as part of the inflammatory process. Other growth factors are produced by parenchymal cells or stromal (connective tissue) cells in response to cell injury. We start the discussion by describing general principles of growth factor actions. We return to the roles of individual growth factors in the repair process later in the chapter.

Signaling Mechanisms of Growth Factor Receptors

Most growth factors function by binding to specific cell-surface receptors and triggering biochemical signals in cells. The major intracellular signaling pathways induced by growth factor receptors are similar to those of many other cellular receptors that recognize extracellular ligands. In general, these signals lead to the stimulation or repression of gene expression. Signaling may occur directly in the same cell that produces the factor (autocrine signaling), between adjacent cells (paracrine signaling), or over greater distances (endocrine signaling).

Receptor proteins are generally located on the cell surface, but they may be intracellular; in the latter case, the ligands must be sufficiently hydrophobic to enter the cell (e.g., vitamin D, or steroid and thyroid hormones). On the basis of their major signaling transduction pathways, plasma membrane receptors fall into three main types, listed in Table 2–10.

- *Receptors with intrinsic kinase activity.* Binding of ligand to the extracellular portion of the receptor causes dimerization and subsequent phosphorylation of the receptor subunits. Once phosphorylated, the receptors can bind and activate other intracellular proteins (e.g., RAS, phosphatidylinositol 3[PI3]-kinase, phospholipase Cγ [PLC-γ]) and stimulate downstream signals that lead to cell proliferation, or induction of various transcriptional programs.
- *G protein–coupled receptors.* These receptors contain seven-transmembrane α-helix segments and are also known as seven-transmembrane receptors. After ligand binding, the receptors associate with intracellular guanosine triphosphate (GTP)-binding proteins (G proteins) that contain guanosine diphosphate (GDP). Binding of the G proteins causes the exchange of GDP with GTP, resulting in activation of the proteins. Among the several signaling pathways activated through G protein–coupled receptors are those involving cyclic AMP (cAMP), and the generation of inositol 1,4,5-triphosphate (IP_3), which releases calcium from the endoplasmic

Table 2–9 Growth Factors Involved in Regeneration and Repair

Growth Factor	Sources	Functions
Epidermal growth factor (EGF)	Activated macrophages, salivary glands, keratinocytes, and many other cells	Mitogenic for keratinocytes and fibroblasts; stimulates keratinocyte migration; stimulates formation of granulation tissue
Transforming growth factor-α (TGF-α)	Activated macrophages, keratinocytes, many other cell types	Stimulates proliferation of hepatocytes and many other epithelial cells
Hepatocyte growth factor (HGF) (scatter factor)	Fibroblasts, stromal cells in the liver, endothelial cells	Enhances proliferation of hepatocytes and other epithelial cells; increases cell motility
Vascular endothelial growth factor (VEGF)	Mesenchymal cells	Stimulates proliferation of endothelial cells; increases vascular permeability
Platelet-derived growth factor (PDGF)	Platelets, macrophages, endothelial cells, smooth muscle cells, keratinocytes	Chemotactic for neutrophils, macrophages, fibroblasts, and smooth muscle cells; activates and stimulates proliferation of fibroblasts, endothelial, and other cells; stimulates ECM protein synthesis
Fibroblast growth factors (FGFs), including acidic (FGF-1) and basic (FGF-2)	Macrophages, mast cells, endothelial cells, many other cell types	Chemotactic and mitogenic for fibroblasts; stimulates angiogenesis and ECM protein synthesis
Transforming growth factor-β (TGF-β)	Platelets, T lymphocytes, macrophages, endothelial cells, keratinocytes, smooth muscle cells, fibroblasts	Chemotactic for leukocytes and fibroblasts; stimulates ECM protein synthesis; suppresses acute inflammation
Keratinocyte growth factor (KGF) (i.e., FGF-7)	Fibroblasts	Stimulates keratinocyte migration, proliferation, and differentiation

ECM, extracellular membrane.

reticulum. Receptors in this category constitute the largest family of plasma membrane receptors (more than 1500 members have been identified).

- *Receptors without intrinsic enzymatic activity.* These are usually monomeric transmembrane molecules with an extracellular ligand-binding domain; ligand interaction induces an intracellular conformational change that allows association with intracellular protein kinases called Janus kinases (JAKs). Phosphorylation of JAKs activates cytoplasmic transcription factors called STATs (signal transducers and activators of transcription), which shuttle into the nucleus and induce transcription of target genes.

SUMMARY

Growth Factors, Receptors, and Signal Transduction

- Polypeptide growth factors act in autocrine, paracrine, or endocrine manner.
- Growth factors are produced transiently in response to an external stimulus and act by binding to cellular receptors. Different classes of growth factor receptors include receptors with intrinsic kinase activity, G protein–coupled receptors and receptors without intrinsic kinase activity.
- Growth factors such as epidermal growth factor (EGF) and hepatocyte growth factor (HGF) bind to receptors with intrinsic kinase activity, triggering a cascade of phosphorylating events through MAP kinases, which culminate in transcription factor activation and DNA replication.
- G protein–coupled receptors produce multiple effects via the cAMP and Ca^{2+} pathways. Chemokines utilize such receptors.
- Cytokines generally bind to receptors without kinase activity; such receptors interact with cytoplasmic transcription factors that move into the nucleus.
- Most growth factors have multiple effects, such as cell migration, differentiation, stimulation of angiogenesis, and fibrogenesis, in addition to cell proliferation.

Table 2–10 Principal Signaling Pathways Used by Cell Surface Receptors

Receptor Class	Ligands	Signaling Mechanism(s)
Receptors with intrinsic tyrosine kinase activity	EGF, VEGF, FGF, HGF	Ligand binding to one chain of the receptor activates tyrosine kinase on the other chain, resulting in activation of multiple downstream signaling pathways (RAS-MAP kinase, PI-3 kinase, PLC-γ) and activation of various transcription factors.
G protein–coupled seven-transmembrane receptors (GPCRs)	Multiple inflammatory mediators, hormones, all chemokines	Ligand binding induces switch from GDP-bound inactive form of associated G protein to GTP-bound active form; activates cAMP; Ca^{2+} influx leading to increased cell motility; multiple other effects.
Receptors without intrinsic enzymatic activity	Many cytokines including interferons, growth hormone, CSFs, EPO	Ligand binding recruits kinases (e.g., Janus kinases [JAKs]) that phosphorylate and activate transcription factors (e.g., signal transducers and activators of transcription [STATs]).

cAMP, cyclic adenosine monophosphate; CSFs, colony-stimulating factors; EGF, epidermal growth factor; EPO, epopoietin; FGF, fibroblast growth factor; GDP, guanosine diphosphate; GTP, guanosine triphosphate; HGF, hepatocyte growth factor; PI3, phosphatidylinositol-3; PLC-γ, phospholipase Cγ; MAP, microtubule-associated protein; VEGF, vascular endothelial growth factor.

Role of the Extracellular Matrix in Tissue Repair

Tissue repair depends not only on growth factor activity but also on interactions between cells and ECM components. The ECM is a complex of several proteins that assembles into a network that surrounds cells and constitutes a significant proportion of any tissue. *ECM sequesters water, providing turgor to soft tissues, and minerals, giving rigidity to bone. It also regulates the proliferation, movement, and differentiation of the cells living within it, by supplying a substrate for cell adhesion and migration and serving as a reservoir for growth factors.* The ECM is constantly being remodeled; its synthesis and degradation accompany morphogenesis, wound healing, chronic fibrosis, and tumor invasion and metastasis.

ECM occurs in two basic forms: interstitial matrix and basement membrane (Fig. 2–27).

- *Interstitial matrix:* This form of ECM is present in the spaces between cells in connective tissue, and between epithelium and supportive vascular and smooth muscle structures. It is synthesized by mesenchymal cells (e.g., fibroblasts) and tends to form a three-dimensional, amorphous gel. Its major constituents are fibrillar and nonfibrillar collagens, as well as fibronectin, elastin, proteoglycans, hyaluronate, and other elements (described later).
- *Basement membrane:* The seemingly random array of interstitial matrix in connective tissues becomes highly organized around epithelial cells, endothelial cells, and smooth muscle cells, forming the specialized basement membrane. The basement membrane lies beneath the epithelium and is synthesized by overlying epithelium and underlying mesenchymal cells; it tends to form a platelike "chicken wire" mesh. Its major constituents are amorphous nonfibrillar type IV collagen and laminin (see later).

Components of the Extracellular Matrix

There are three basic components of ECM: (1) fibrous structural proteins such as collagens and elastins, which confer tensile strength and recoil; (2) water-hydrated gels such as proteoglycans and hyaluronan, which permit resilience and lubrication; and (3) adhesive glycoproteins that connect the matrix elements to one another and to cells (Fig. 2–27).

Collagen

The collagens are composed of three separate polypeptide chains braided into a ropelike triple helix. Approximately 30 collagen types have been identified, some of which are unique to specific cells and tissues. Some collagen types (e.g., types I, II, III, and V) form fibrils by virtue of lateral cross-linking of the triple helices. The fibrillar collagens form a major proportion of the connective tissue in healing wounds and particularly in scars. The tensile strength of the fibrillar collagens derives from their cross-linking, which is the result of covalent bonds catalyzed by the enzyme lysyl-oxidase. This process is dependent on vitamin C; therefore, individuals with vitamin C deficiency have skeletal deformities, bleed easily because of weak vascular wall basement membrane, and suffer from poor wound healing. Genetic defects in these collagens cause diseases such as osteogenesis imperfecta and Ehlers-Danlos syndrome. Other collagens are nonfibrillar and may form basement membrane (type IV) or be components of other structures such as intervertebral disks (type IX) or dermal–epidermal junctions (type VII).

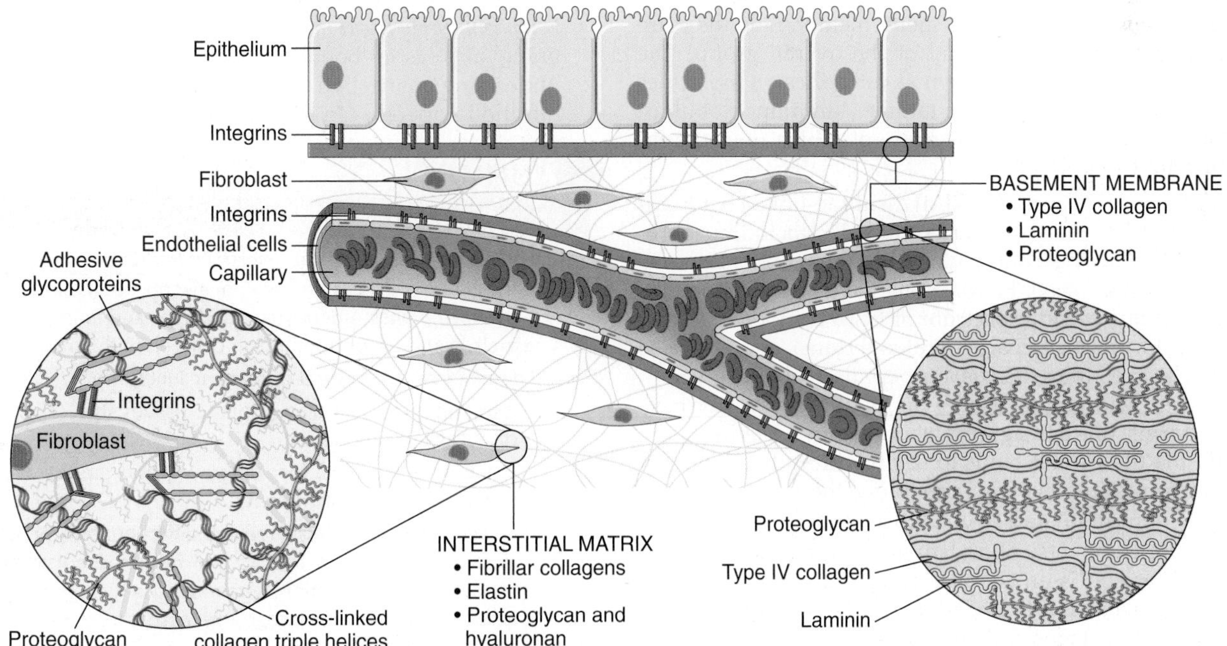

Figure 2–27 The major components of the extracellular matrix (ECM), including collagens, proteoglycans, and adhesive glycoproteins. Note that although there is some overlap in their constituents, basement membrane and interstitial ECM differ in general composition and architecture. Both epithelial and mesenchymal cells (e.g., fibroblasts) interact with ECM through integrins. For simplification, many ECM components have been left out (e.g., elastin, fibrillin, hyaluronan, syndecan).

Elastin

The ability of tissues to recoil and return to a baseline structure after physical stress is conferred by elastic tissue. This is especially important in the walls of large vessels (which must accommodate recurrent pulsatile flow), as well as in the uterus, skin, and ligaments. Morphologically, elastic fibers consist of a central core of elastin surrounded by a meshlike network of fibrillin glycoprotein. Defects in fibrillin synthesis lead to skeletal abnormalities and weakened aortic walls (as in Marfan syndrome, discussed in Chapter 6).

Proteoglycans and Hyaluronan

Proteoglycans form highly hydrated compressible gels conferring resilience and lubrication (such as in the cartilage in joints). They consist of long polysaccharides, called glycosaminoglycans or mucopolysaccharides (examples are dermatan sulfate and heparan sulfate), linked to a protein backbone. Hyaluronan (also called hyaluronic acid), a huge mucopolysaccharide without a protein core, is also an important constituent of the ECM that binds water, and forms a viscous, gelatin-like matrix. Besides providing compressibility to tissues, proteoglycans also serve as reservoirs for growth factors secreted into the ECM (e.g., fibroblast growth factor [FGF], HGF). Some proteoglycans are integral cell membrane proteins that have roles in cell proliferation, migration, and adhesion—for example, by binding growth factors and chemokines and providing high local concentrations of these mediators.

Adhesive Glycoproteins and Adhesion Receptors

Adhesive glycoproteins and adhesion receptors are structurally diverse molecules involved in cell-to-cell adhesion, the linkage of cells to the ECM, and binding between ECM components. The adhesive glycoproteins include fibronectin (a major component of the interstitial ECM) and laminin (a major constituent of basement membrane); they are described here as prototypical of the overall group. The adhesion receptors, also known as cell adhesion molecules (CAMs), are grouped into four families—immunoglobulins, cadherins, selectins, and integrins—of which only the integrins are discussed here.

- *Fibronectin* is a large (450-kDa) disulfide-linked heterodimer synthesized by a variety of cells, including fibroblasts, monocytes, and endothelium that exists in tissue and plasma forms. Fibronectins have specific domains that bind to a wide spectrum of ECM components (e.g., collagen, fibrin, heparin, proteoglycans) and can also attach to cell integrins via a tripeptide arginine-glycine-aspartic acid (abbreviated *RGD*) motif. Tissue fibronectin forms fibrillar aggregates at wound healing sites; plasma fibronectin binds to fibrin within the blood clot that forms in a wound, providing the substratum for ECM deposition and re-epithelialization.
- *Laminin* is the most abundant glycoprotein in basement membrane. It is an 820-kDa cross-shaped heterotrimer that connects cells to underlying ECM components such as type IV collagen and heparan sulfate. Besides mediating attachment to basement membrane, laminin can also modulate cell proliferation, differentiation, and motility.
- *Integrins* are a family of transmembrane heterodimeric glycoprotein chains that were introduced in the context of leukocyte adhesion to endothelium. They are also the main cellular receptors for ECM components, such as fibronectins and laminins. We have already discussed some of the integrins as leukocyte surface molecules that mediate firm adhesion and transmigration across endothelium at sites of inflammation, and we shall meet them again when we discuss platelet aggregation in Chapter 3. Integrins are present in the plasma membrane of most cells, with the exception of red blood cells. They bind to many ECM components through RGD motifs, initiating signaling cascades that can affect cell locomotion, proliferation, and differentiation. Their intracellular domains link to actin filaments, thereby affecting cell shape and mobility.

Functions of the Extracellular Matrix

The ECM is much more than a space filler around cells. Its various functions include

- *Mechanical support* for cell anchorage and cell migration, and maintenance of cell polarity
- *Control of cell proliferation* by binding and displaying growth factors and by signaling through cellular receptors of the integrin family. The type of ECM proteins can affect the degree of differentiation of the cells in the tissue, again acting largely through cell surface integrins.
- *Scaffolding for tissue renewal.* Because maintenance of normal tissue structure requires a basement membrane or stromal scaffold, the integrity of the basement membrane or the stroma of parenchymal cells is critical for the organized regeneration of tissues. Thus, although labile and stable cells are capable of regeneration, disruption of the ECM results in a failure of the tissues to regenerate and repair by scar formation (Fig. 2–24).
- *Establishment of tissue microenvironments.* Basement membrane acts as a boundary between epithelium and underlying connective tissue and also forms part of the filtration apparatus in the kidney.

SUMMARY

Extracellular Matrix and Tissue Repair

- The ECM consists of the *interstitial matrix* between cells, made up of collagens and several glycoproteins, and *basement membranes* underlying epithelia and surrounding vessels, made up of nonfibrillar collagen and laminin.
- The ECM serves several important functions:
  - It provides mechanical support to tissues; this is the role of collagens and elastin.
  - It acts as a substrate for cell growth and the formation of tissue microenvironments.
  - It regulates cell proliferation and differentiation; proteoglycans bind growth factors and display them at high concentration, and fibronectin and laminin stimulate cells through cellular integrin receptors.
- An intact ECM is required for tissue regeneration, and if the ECM is damaged, repair can be accomplished only by scar formation.

Having described the basic components of tissue repair, we now proceed to a discussion of repair by regeneration and by scar formation.

Role of Regeneration in Tissue Repair

The importance of regeneration in the replacement of injured tissues varies in different types of tissues and with the severity of injury.

- In labile tissues, such as the epithelia of the intestinal tract and skin, injured cells are rapidly replaced by proliferation of residual cells and differentiation of tissue stem cells provided the underlying basement membrane is intact. The growth factors involved in these processes are not defined. Loss of blood cells is corrected by proliferation of hematopoietic progenitors in the bone marrow and other tissues, driven by CSFs, which are produced in response to the reduced numbers of blood cells.
- Tissue regeneration can occur in parenchymal organs with stable cell populations, but with the exception of the liver, this is usually a limited process. Pancreas, adrenal, thyroid, and lung have some regenerative capacity. The surgical removal of a kidney elicits in the contralateral kidney a compensatory response that consists of both hypertrophy and hyperplasia of proximal duct cells. The mechanisms underlying this response are not understood.
- The regenerative response of the liver that occurs after surgical removal of hepatic tissue is remarkable and unique among all organs. As much as 40% to 60% of the liver may be removed in a procedure called living-donor transplantation, in which a portion of the liver is resected from a normal person and transplanted into a recipient with end-stage liver disease (Fig. 2–28), or after partial hepatectomy performed for tumor removal. In both situations, the removal of tissue triggers a proliferative response of the remaining hepatocytes (which are normally quiescent), and the subsequent replication of hepatic nonparenchymal cells. In experimental systems, hepatocyte replication after partial hepatectomy is initiated by cytokines (e.g., TNF, IL-6) that prepare the cells for replication by stimulating the transition from G_0 to G_1 in the cell cycle. Progression through the cell cycle is dependent on the activity of growth factors such as HGF (produced by fibroblasts, endothelial cells, and liver nonparenchymal cells) and the EGF family of factors, which includes transforming growth factor-α (TGF-α) (produced by many cell types).

A point worthy of emphasis is that *extensive regeneration or compensatory hyperplasia can occur only if the residual connective tissue framework is structurally intact, as after partial surgical resection. By contrast, if the entire tissue is damaged by infection or inflammation, regeneration is incomplete and is accompanied by scarring*. For example, extensive destruction of the liver with collapse of the reticulin framework, as occurs in a liver abscess, leads to scar formation even though the remaining liver cells have the capacity to regenerate.

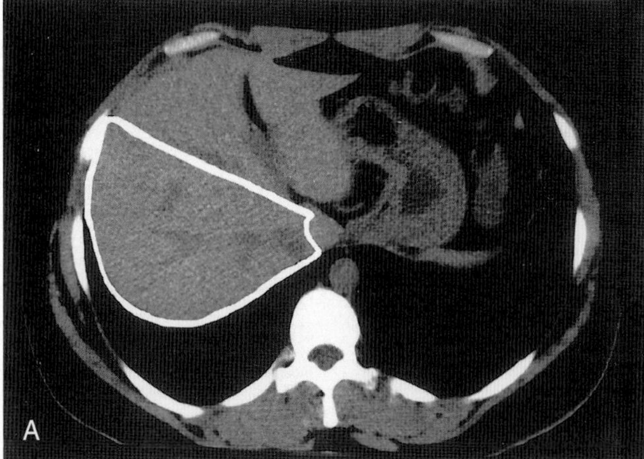

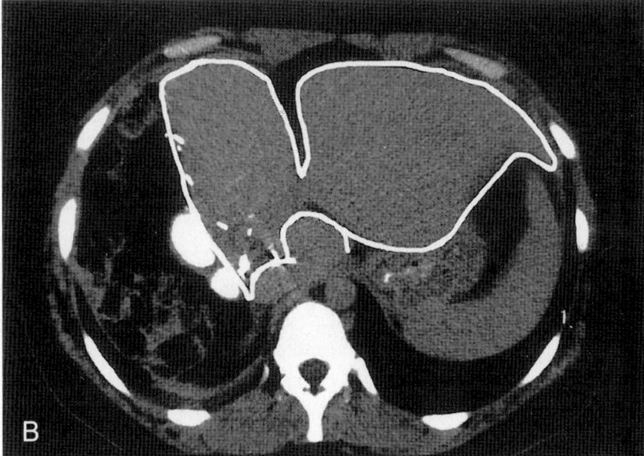

Figure 2–28 Regeneration of the liver. Computed tomography scans show a donor liver in living-donor liver transplantation. **A,** The donor liver before the operation. Note the right lobe (*outline*), which will be resected and used as a transplant. **B,** Scan of the same liver 1 week after resection of the right lobe; note the enlargement of the left lobe (*outline*) without regrowth of the right lobe.

(Courtesy of R. Troisi, MD, Ghent University, Flanders, Belgium.)

SCAR FORMATION

As discussed earlier, if tissue injury is severe or chronic and results in damage to parenchymal cells and epithelia as well as the connective tissue, or if nondividing cells are injured, repair cannot be accomplished by regeneration alone. Under these conditions, repair occurs by replacement of the nonregenerated cells with connective tissue, leading to the formation of a scar, or by a combination of regeneration of some cells and scar formation.

Steps in Scar Formation

Repair by connective tissue deposition consists of sequential processes that follow the inflammatory response (Fig. 2–29):

- Formation of new blood vessels (angiogenesis)
- Migration and proliferation of fibroblasts and deposition of connective tissue, which, together with abundant

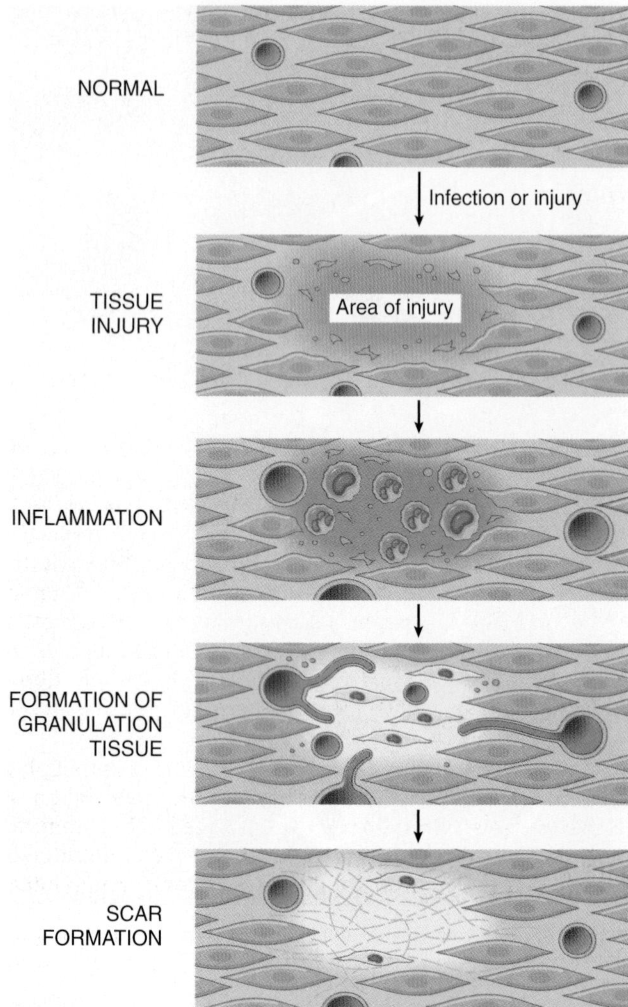

Figure 2–29 Steps in repair by scar formation. Injury to a tissue that has limited regenerative capacity first induces inflammation, which clears dead cells and microbes, if any. This is followed by formation of vascularized granulation tissue and then deposition of ECM to form the scar. ECM, extracellular matrix.

vessels and interspersed leukocytes, has a pink, granular appearance and hence is called *granulation tissue*

- Maturation and reorganization of the fibrous tissue (remodeling) to produce the stable fibrous scar

Repair begins within 24 hours of injury by the emigration of fibroblasts and the induction of fibroblast and endothelial cell proliferation. By 3 to 5 days, the specialized granulation tissue that is characteristic of healing is apparent. The term granulation tissue derives from the gross appearance, such as that beneath the scab of a skin wound. Its histologic appearance is characterized by proliferation of fibroblasts and new thin-walled, delicate capillaries (angiogenesis) in a loose ECM, often with admixed inflammatory cells, mainly macrophages (Fig. 2–30, *A*). Granulation tissue progressively accumulates more fibroblasts, which lay down collagen, eventually resulting in the formation of a scar (Fig. 2–30, *B*). Scars remodel over time. We next describe each of the steps in this process.

Angiogenesis

Angiogenesis is the process of new blood vessel development from existing vessels, primarily venules. It is critical in healing at sites of injury, in the development of collateral circulations at sites of ischemia, and in allowing tumors to increase in size beyond the constraints of their original blood supply. Much work has been done to understand the mechanisms underlying angiogenesis, and therapies to either augment the process (e.g., to improve blood flow to a heart ravaged by coronary atherosclerosis) or inhibit it (e.g., to frustrate tumor growth or block pathologic vessel growth such as in diabetic retinopathy) are being developed.

Angiogenesis involves sprouting of new vessels from existing ones and consists of the following steps (Fig. 2–31):

- Vasodilation occurring in response to NO and increased permeability induced by VEGF
- Separation of pericytes from the abluminal surface
- Migration of endothelial cells toward the area of tissue injury

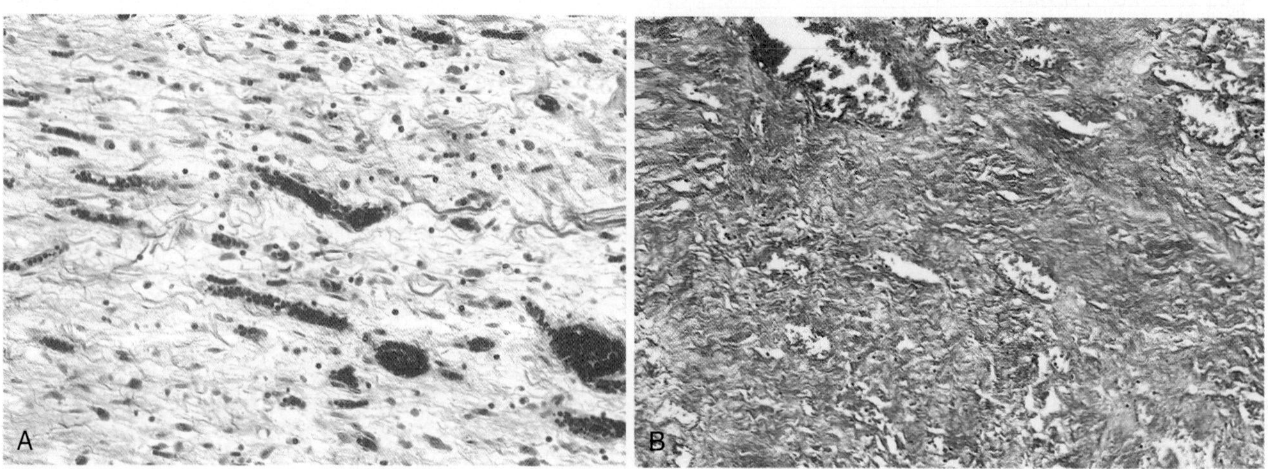

Figure 2–30 A, Granulation tissue showing numerous blood vessels, edema, and a loose ECM containing occasional inflammatory cells. Collagen is stained blue by the trichrome stain; minimal mature collagen can be seen at this point. **B,** Trichrome stain of mature scar, showing dense collagen with only scattered vascular channels. ECM, extracellular matrix.

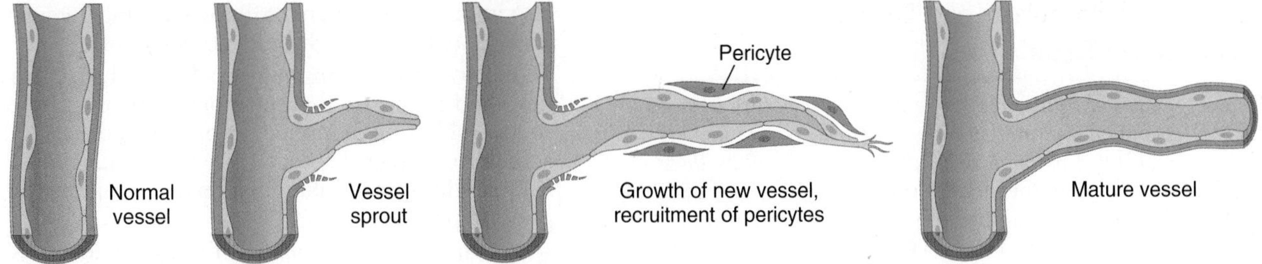

Figure 2–31 Mechanism of angiogenesis. In tissue repair, angiogenesis occurs mainly by growth factor–driven outgrowth of residual endothelium, sprouting of new vessels, and recruitment of pericytes to form new vessels.

- Proliferation of endothelial cells just behind the leading front of migrating cells
- Remodeling into capillary tubes
- Recruitment of periendothelial cells (pericytes for small capillaries and smooth muscle cells for larger vessels) to form the mature vessel
- Suppression of endothelial proliferation and migration and deposition of the basement membrane

The process of angiogenesis involves a variety of growth factors, cell–cell interactions, interactions with ECM proteins, and tissue enzymes.

Growth Factors Involved in Angiogenesis

Several growth factors contribute to angiogenesis; the most important are VEGF and basic fibroblast growth factor (FGF-2).

- The *VEGF family of growth factors* includes VEGF-A, -B, -C, -D, and -E and placental growth factor (PlGF). VEGF-A is generally referred to as VEGF and is the major inducer of angiogenesis after injury and in tumors; VEGF-B and PlGF are involved in vessel development in the embryo; and VEGF-C and -D stimulate both lymphangiogenesis and angiogenesis. VEGFs are expressed in most adult tissues, with the highest expression in epithelial cells adjacent to fenestrated epithelium (e.g., podocytes in the kidney, pigment epithelium in the retina). They bind to a family of tyrosine kinase receptors (VEGFR-1, -2, and -3). The most important of these receptors for angiogenesis is VEGFR-2, which is expressed by VEGF target cells, especially endothelial cells. Of the many inducers of VEGF, hypoxia is the most important; others are platelet-derived growth factor (PDGF), TGF-α, and TGF-β.

  VEGF stimulates both migration and proliferation of endothelial cells, thus initiating the process of capillary sprouting in angiogenesis. It promotes vasodilation by stimulating the production of NO, and contributes to the formation of the vascular lumen. Antibodies against VEGF are approved for the treatment of some tumors that depend on angiogenesis for their spread and growth. These antibodies are also used in the treatment of "wet" (neovascular) age-related macular degeneration, a major cause of visual impairment in adults older than 50 years of age, and is in clinical trials for the treatment of the angiogenesis associated with retinopathy of prematurity and the leaky vessels that lead to diabetic macular edema.
- The *FGF family of growth factors* has more than 20 members; the best characterized are FGF-1 (acidic FGF) and FGF-2 (basic FGF). These growth factors are produced by many cell types and bind to a family of plasma membrane receptors that have tyrosine kinase activity. Released FGF can bind to heparan sulfate and be stored in the ECM. FGF-2 participates in angiogenesis mostly by stimulating the proliferation of endothelial cells. It also promotes the migration of macrophages and fibroblasts to the damaged area, and stimulates epithelial cell migration to cover epidermal wounds.
- *Angiopoietins Ang1 and Ang2* are growth factors that play a role in angiogenesis and the structural maturation of new vessels. Newly formed vessels need to be stabilized by the recruitment of pericytes and smooth muscle cells and by the deposition of connective tissue. Ang1 interacts with a tyrosine kinase receptor on endothelial cells called Tie2. The growth factors PDGF and TGF-β also participate in the stabilization process—PDGF recruits smooth muscle cells and TGF-β suppresses endothelial proliferation and migration, and enhances the production of ECM proteins.

The growth of blood vessels during embryonic development is called *vasculogenesis.* In vasculogenesis, vessels are formed de novo by the coalescence of endothelial precursors called angioblasts. Angioblasts are derived from hemangioblasts, which also provide the precursors of the hematopoietic system. In addition, there are endothelial progenitors in the adult that are derived from bone marrow stem cells and circulate. The contribution of these cells to angiogenesis in adults is not definitely established.

ECM proteins participate in the process of vessel sprouting in angiogenesis, largely through interactions with integrin receptors in endothelial cells and by providing the scaffold for vessel growth. Enzymes in the ECM, notably the matrix metalloproteinases (MMPs), degrade the ECM to permit remodeling and extension of the vascular tube. Newly formed vessels are leaky because of incomplete interendothelial junctions and because VEGF increases vascular permeability. This leakiness explains why granulation tissue is often edematous and accounts in part for the edema that may persist in healing wounds long after the acute inflammatory response has resolved. Furthermore, it leads to high intratumoral pressure and is the basis for the edema that is so problematic in ocular angiogenesis in pathologic processes such as wet macular degeneration.

Activation of Fibroblasts and Deposition of Connective Tissue

The laying down of connective tissue in the scar occurs in two steps: (1) migration and proliferation of fibroblasts into the site of injury and (2) deposition of ECM proteins produced by these cells. The recruitment and activation of fibroblasts to synthesize connective tissue proteins are driven by many growth factors, including PDGF, FGF-2 (described earlier), and TGF-β. The major source of these factors is inflammatory cells, particularly macrophages, which are present at sites of injury and in granulation tissue. Sites of inflammation are also rich in mast cells, and in the appropriate chemotactic milieu, lymphocytes may be present as well. Each of these cell types can secrete cytokines and growth factors that contribute to fibroblast proliferation and activation.

As healing progresses, the number of proliferating fibroblasts and new vessels decreases; however, the fibroblasts progressively assume a more synthetic phenotype, so there is increased deposition of ECM. Collagen synthesis, in particular, is critical to the development of strength in a healing wound site. As described later, collagen synthesis by fibroblasts begins early in wound healing (days 3 to 5) and continues for several weeks, depending on the size of the wound. Net collagen accumulation, however, depends not only on increased synthesis but also on diminished collagen degradation (discussed later). Ultimately, the granulation tissue evolves into a scar composed of largely inactive, spindle-shaped fibroblasts, dense collagen, fragments of elastic tissue, and other ECM components (Fig. 2–30, *B*). As the scar matures, there is progressive vascular regression, which eventually transforms the highly vascularized granulation tissue into a pale, largely avascular scar.

Growth Factors Involved in ECM Deposition and Scar Formation

Many growth factors are involved in these processes, including TGF-β, PDGF, and FGF. Because FGF also is involved in angiogenesis, it was described earlier. Here we briefly describe the major properties of TGF-β and PDGF.

- *Transforming growth factor-β (TGF-β)* belongs to a family of homologous polypeptides (TGF-β1, -β2, and -β3) that includes other cytokines such as bone morphogenetic proteins. The TGF-β1 isoform is widely distributed and is usually referred to as TGF-β. The active factor binds to two cell surface receptors with serine-threonine kinase activity, triggering the phosphorylation of transcription factors called Smads. TGF-β has many and often opposite effects, depending on the cell type and the metabolic state of the tissue. In the context of inflammation and repair, TGF-β has two main functions:
  - TGF-β stimulates the production of collagen, fibronectin, and proteoglycans, and it inhibits collagen degradation by both decreasing proteinase activity and increasing the activity of tissue inhibitors of proteinases known as TIMPs (discussed later on). TGF-β is involved not only in scar formation after injury but also in the development of fibrosis in lung, liver, and kidneys that follows chronic inflammation.
  - TGF-β is an anti-inflammatory cytokine that serves to limit and terminate inflammatory responses. It does so by inhibiting lymphocyte proliferation and the activity of other leukocytes. Mice lacking TGF-β exhibit widespread inflammation and abundant lymphocyte proliferation.
- *Platelet-derived growth factor (PDGF)* belongs to a family of closely related proteins, each consisting of two chains, designated A and B. There are five main PDGF isoforms, of which the BB isoform is the prototype; it is often referred to simply as PDGF. PDGFs bind to receptors designated as PDGFRα and PDGFRβ. PDGF is stored in platelets and released on platelet activation and is also produced by endothelial cells, activated macrophages, smooth muscle cells, and many tumor cells. PDGF causes migration and proliferation of fibroblasts and smooth muscle cells and may contribute to the migration of macrophages.
- *Cytokines* (discussed earlier as mediators of inflammation, and in Chapter 4 in the context of immune responses) may also function as growth factors and participate in ECM deposition and scar formation. IL-1 and IL-13, for example, act on fibroblasts to stimulate collagen synthesis, and can also enhance the proliferation and migration of fibroblasts.

Remodeling of Connective Tissue

After its synthesis and deposition, the connective tissue in the scar continues to be modified and remodeled. Thus, the outcome of the repair process is a balance between synthesis and degradation of ECM proteins. We have already discussed the cells and factors that regulate ECM synthesis. *The degradation of collagens and other ECM components is accomplished by a family of matrix metalloproteinases (MMPs),* which are dependent on zinc ions for their activity. MMPs should be distinguished from neutrophil elastase, cathepsin G, plasmin, and other serine proteinases that can also degrade ECM but are not metalloenzymes. MMPs include interstitial collagenases, which cleave fibrillar collagen (MMP-1, -2, and -3); gelatinases (MMP-2 and -9), which degrade amorphous collagen and fibronectin; and stromelysins (MMP-3, -10, and -11), which degrade a variety of ECM constituents, including proteoglycans, laminin, fibronectin, and amorphous collagen.

MMPs are produced by a variety of cell types (fibroblasts, macrophages, neutrophils, synovial cells, and some epithelial cells), and their synthesis and secretion are regulated by growth factors, cytokines, and other agents. The activity of the MMPs is tightly controlled. They are produced as inactive precursors (zymogens) that must be first activated; this is accomplished by proteases (e.g., plasmin) likely to be present only at sites of injury. In addition, activated MMPs can be rapidly inhibited by specific tissue inhibitors of metalloproteinases (TIMPs), produced by most mesenchymal cells. Thus, during scarring, MMPs are activated to remodel the deposited ECM, and then their activity is shut down by the TIMPs.

SUMMARY

Repair by Scar Formation

- Tissues can be repaired by regeneration with complete restoration of form and function, or by replacement with connective tissue and scar formation.
- Repair by connective tissue deposition involves angiogenesis, migration and proliferation of fibroblasts, collagen synthesis, and connective tissue remodeling.
- Repair by connective tissue starts with the formation of granulation tissue and culminates in the laying down of fibrous tissue.
- Multiple growth factors stimulate the proliferation of the cell types involved in repair.
- TGF-β is a potent fibrogenic agent; ECM deposition depends on the balance among fibrogenic agents, the metalloproteinases (MMPs) that digest ECM, and the TIMPs.

FACTORS THAT INFLUENCE TISSUE REPAIR

Tissue repair may be altered by a variety of influences, frequently reducing the quality or adequacy of the reparative process. Variables that modify healing may be extrinsic (e.g., infection) or intrinsic to the injured tissue. Particularly important are infections and diabetes.

- *Infection* is clinically the most important cause of delay in healing; it prolongs inflammation and potentially increases the local tissue injury.
- *Nutrition* has profound effects on repair; protein deficiency, for example, and especially vitamin C deficiency inhibit collagen synthesis and retard healing.
- *Glucocorticoids* (steroids) have well-documented anti-inflammatory effects, and their administration may result in weakness of the scar because of inhibition of TGF-β production and diminished fibrosis. In some instances, however, the anti-inflammatory effects of glucocorticoids are desirable. For example, in corneal infections, glucocorticoids are sometimes prescribed (along with antibiotics) to reduce the likelihood of opacity that may result from collagen deposition.
- *Mechanical variables* such as increased local pressure or torsion may cause wounds to pull apart, or dehisce.
- *Poor perfusion,* due either to arteriosclerosis and diabetes or to obstructed venous drainage (e.g., in varicose veins), also impairs healing.
- *Foreign bodies* such as fragments of steel, glass, or even bone impede healing.
- The type and extent of tissue injury affects the subsequent repair. Complete restoration can occur only in tissues composed of stable and labile cells; injury to tissues composed of permanent cells must inevitably result in scarring, as in healing of a myocardial infarct.
- The *location of the injury* and the character of the tissue in which the injury occurs are also important. For example, inflammation arising in tissue spaces (e.g., pleural, peritoneal, or synovial cavities) develops extensive exudates. Subsequent repair may occur by digestion of the exudate, initiated by the proteolytic enzymes of leukocytes and resorption of the liquefied exudate. This is called resolution, and generally, in the absence of cellular necrosis, normal tissue architecture is restored. In the setting of larger accumulations, however, the exudate undergoes organization: Granulation tissue grows into the exudate, and a fibrous scar ultimately forms.
- *Aberrations of cell growth* and ECM production may occur even in what begins as normal wound healing. For example, the accumulation of exuberant amounts of collagen can give rise to prominent, raised scars known as *keloids* (Fig. 2–32). There appears to be a heritable predisposition to keloid formation, and the condition is more common in African-Americans. Healing wounds may also generate exuberant granulation tissue that protrudes above the level of the surrounding skin and hinders re-epithelialization. Such tissue is called "proud

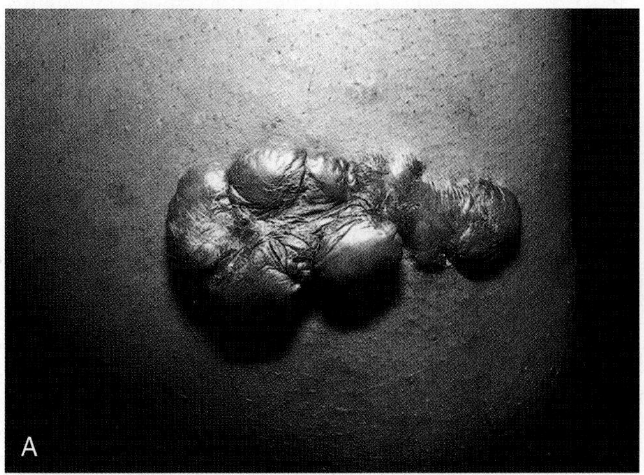

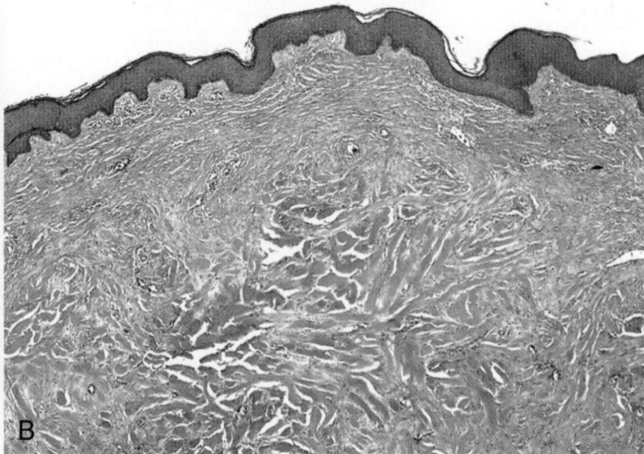

Figure 2–32 Keloid. **A,** Excess collagen deposition in the skin forming a raised scar known as a keloid. **B,** Thick connective tissue deposition in the dermis.

(A, From Murphy GF, Herzberg AJ: Atlas of Dermatology. Philadelphia, WB Saunders, 1996. B, Courtesy of Z. Argenyi, MD, University of Washington, Seattle, Washington.)

flesh" in old medical parlance, and restoration of epithelial continuity requires cautery or surgical resection of the granulation tissue.

SELECTED CLINICAL EXAMPLES OF TISSUE REPAIR AND FIBROSIS

Thus far we have discussed the general principles and mechanisms of repair by regeneration and scarring. In this section we describe two clinically significant types of repair—the healing of skin wounds (cutaneous wound healing) and fibrosis in injured parenchymal organs.

Healing of Skin Wounds

Cutaneous wound healing is a process that involves both epithelial regeneration and the formation of connective tissue scar and is thus illustrative of the general principles that apply to healing in all tissues.

Depending on the nature and size of the wound, the healing of skin wounds is said to occur by first or second intention.

Healing by First Intention

One of the simplest examples of wound repair is the healing of a clean, uninfected surgical incision approximated by surgical sutures (Fig. 2–33). This is referred to as primary

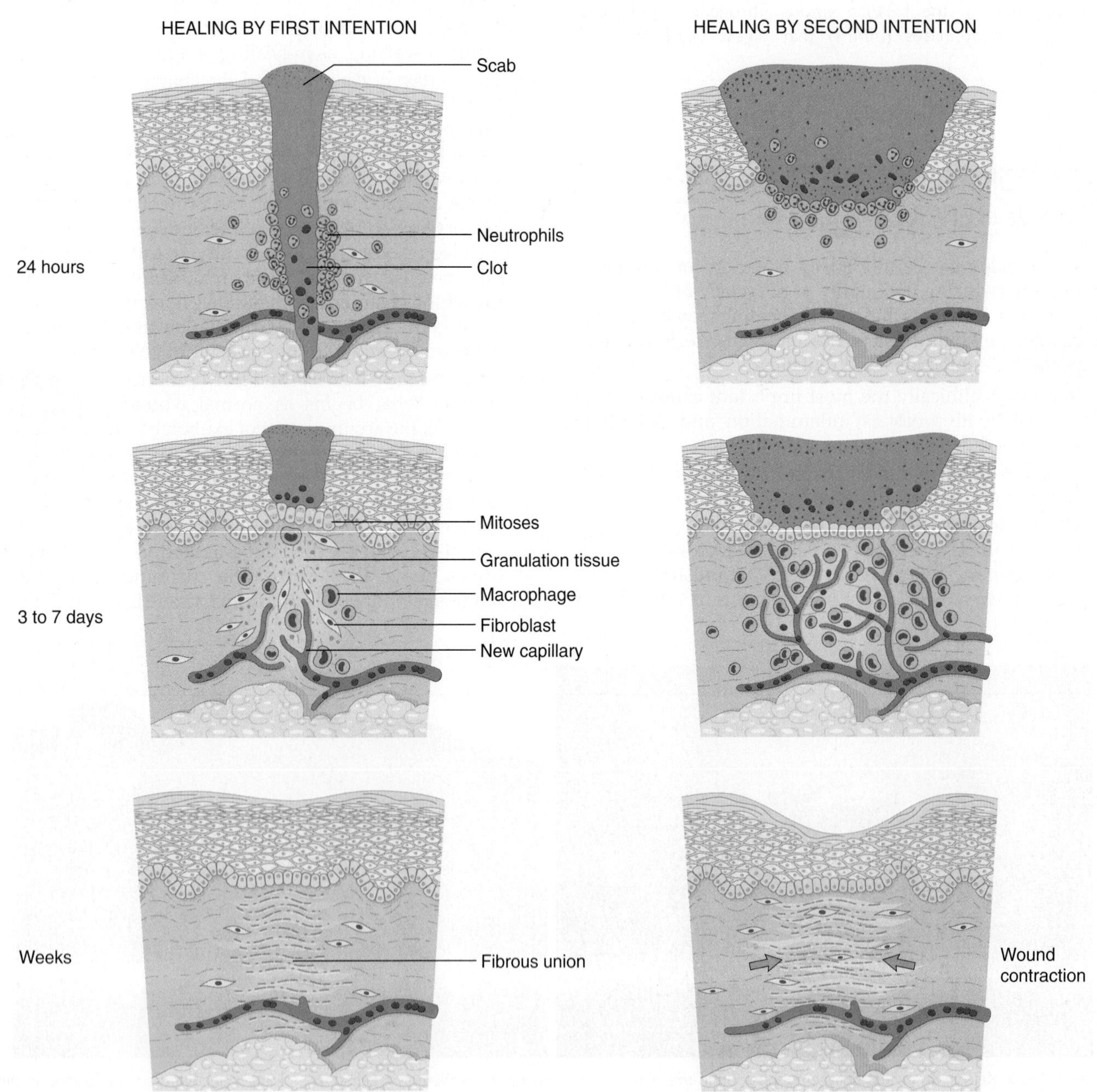

Figure 2–33 Steps in wound healing by first intention (*left*) and second intention (*right*). In the latter case, note the large amount of granulation tissue and wound contraction.

union, or healing by first intention. The incision causes only focal disruption of epithelial basement membrane continuity and death of relatively few epithelial and connective tissue cells. As a result, *epithelial regeneration is the principal mechanism of repair.* A small scar is formed, but there is minimal wound contraction. The narrow incisional space first fills with fibrin-clotted blood, which then is rapidly invaded by granulation tissue and covered by new epithelium. The steps in the process are well defined:

- Within 24 hours, neutrophils are seen at the incision margin, migrating toward the fibrin clot. Basal cells at the cut edge of the epidermis begin to show increased mitotic activity. Within 24 to 48 hours, epithelial cells from both edges have begun to migrate and proliferate along the dermis, depositing basement membrane components as they progress. The cells meet in the midline beneath the surface scab, yielding a thin but continuous epithelial layer.
- By day 3, neutrophils have been largely replaced by macrophages, and granulation tissue progressively invades the incision space. Collagen fibers are now evident at the incision margins, but these are vertically oriented and do not bridge the incision. Epithelial cell proliferation continues, yielding a thickened epidermal covering layer.
- By day 5, neovascularization reaches its peak as granulation tissue fills the incisional space. Collagen fibrils become more abundant and begin to bridge the incision. The epidermis recovers its normal thickness as differentiation of surface cells yields a mature epidermal architecture with surface keratinization.
- During the second week, there is continued collagen accumulation and fibroblast proliferation. The leukocyte infiltrate, edema, and increased vascularity are substantially diminished. The long process of "blanching" begins, accomplished by increasing collagen deposition within the incisional scar and the regression of vascular channels.
- By the end of the first month, the scar consists of a cellular connective tissue, largely devoid of inflammatory cells, covered by an essentially normal epidermis. However, the dermal appendages destroyed in the line of the incision are permanently lost. The tensile strength of the wound increases with time, as described later.

Healing by Second Intention

When cell or tissue loss is more extensive, such as in large wounds, at sites of abscess formation, ulceration, and ischemic necrosis (infarction) in parenchymal organs, the repair process is more complex and involves a combination of regeneration and scarring. In second intention healing of skin wounds, also known as healing by secondary union (Fig. 2–34; see also Fig. 2–33), the inflammatory reaction is

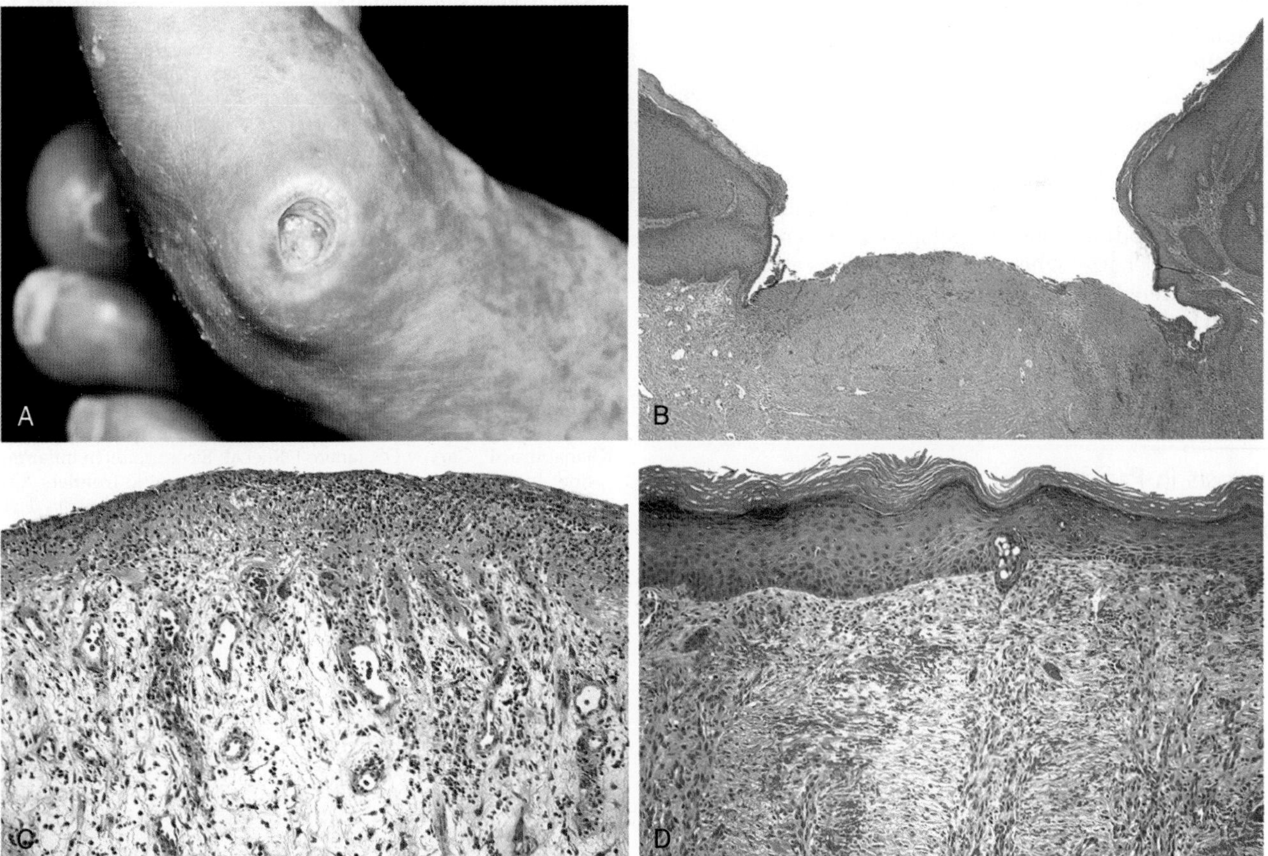

Figure 2–34 Healing of skin ulcers. **A,** Pressure ulcer of the skin, commonly found in diabetic patients. **B,** A skin ulcer with a large gap between the edges of the lesion. **C,** A thin layer of epidermal re-epithelialization, and extensive granulation tissue formation in the dermis. **D,** Continuing re-epithelialization of the epidermis and wound contraction.

(Courtesy of Z. Argenyi, MD, University of Washington, Seattle, Wash.)

more intense, and there is development of abundant granulation tissue, with accumulation of ECM and formation of a large scar, followed by wound contraction mediated by the action of myofibroblasts.

Secondary healing differs from primary healing in several respects:

- A larger clot or scab rich in fibrin and fibronectin forms at the surface of the wound.
- Inflammation is more intense because large tissue defects have a greater volume of necrotic debris, exudate, and fibrin that must be removed. Consequently, large defects have a greater potential for secondary, inflammation-mediated, injury.
- Larger defects require a greater volume of granulation tissue to fill in the gaps and provide the underlying framework for the regrowth of tissue epithelium. A greater volume of granulation tissue generally results in a greater mass of scar tissue.
- Secondary healing involves wound contraction. Within 6 weeks, for example, large skin defects may be reduced to 5% to 10% of their original size, largely by contraction. This process has been ascribed to the presence of myofibroblasts, which are modified fibroblasts exhibiting many of the ultrastructural and functional features of contractile smooth muscle cells.

Wound Strength

Carefully sutured wounds have approximately 70% of the strength of normal skin, largely because of the placement of sutures. When sutures are removed, usually at 1 week, wound strength is approximately 10% of that of unwounded skin, but this increases rapidly over the next 4 weeks. The recovery of tensile strength results from collagen synthesis exceeding degradation during the first 2 months, and from structural modifications of collagen (e.g., cross-linking, increased fiber size) when synthesis declines at later times. Wound strength reaches approximately 70% to 80% of normal by 3 months and usually does not improve substantially beyond that point.

Fibrosis in Parenchymal Organs

Deposition of collagen is part of normal wound healing. The term *fibrosis* is used to denote the excessive deposition of collagen and other ECM components in a tissue. As already mentioned, the terms *scar* and *fibrosis* are used interchangeably, but *fibrosis* most often refers to the deposition of collagen in chronic diseases.

The basic mechanisms of fibrosis are the same as those of scar formation during tissue repair. However, tissue repair typically occurs after a short-lived injurious stimulus and follows an orderly sequence of steps, whereas fibrosis is induced by persistent injurious stimuli such as infections, immunologic reactions, and other types of tissue injury. The fibrosis seen in chronic diseases such as pulmonary fibrosis is often responsible for organ dysfunction and even organ failure.

SUMMARY

Cutaneous Wound Healing and Pathologic Aspects of Repair

- Cutaneous wounds can heal by primary union (first intention) or secondary union (second intention); secondary healing involves more extensive scarring and wound contraction.
- Wound healing can be altered by many conditions, particularly infection and diabetes; the type, volume, and location of the injury are also important factors in healing.
- Excessive production of ECM can cause keloids in the skin.
- Persistent stimulation of collagen synthesis in chronic inflammatory diseases leads to fibrosis of the tissue.

BIBLIOGRAPHY

Bradley JR: TNF-mediated inflammatory disease. J Pathol 214:149, 2008. *[An overview of the biology of TNF and the clinical utility of TNF antagonists.]*

Carlson BM: Some principles of regeneration in mammalian systems. Anat Rec 287:4, 2005. *[A thoughtful review of the evolutionary aspects and general mechanisms of limb and organ regeneration.]*

Carmeliet P: Angiogenesis in life, disease and medicine. Nature 438:932, 2005. *[A review of the main aspects of normal and abnormal angiogenesis.]*

Charo IF, Ransohoff RM: The many roles of chemokines and chemokine receptors in inflammation. N Engl J Med 354:610, 2006. *[An overview of the functions of chemokines in inflammation.]*

Fausto N: Liver regeneration and repair: hepatocytes, progenitor cells and stem cells. Hepatology 39:1477, 2004. *[A review of the cellular and molecular mechanisms of liver regeneration.]*

Gabay C, Lamacchia C, Palmer G: IL-1 pathways in inflammation and human diseases. Nat Rev Rheumatol 6:232, 2010. *[An excellent review of the biology of IL-1 and the therapeutic targeting of this cytokine in inflammatory diseases.]*

Gurtner GC, Werner S, Barrandon Y, Longaker MT: Wound repair and regeneration. Nature 453:314, 2008. *[An excellent review of the principles of tissue regeneration and repair.]*

Hynes RO: Integrins: bidirectional, allosteric signaling machines. Cell 110:673, 2002. *[An excellent review of the molecular mechanisms of integrin signaling, linking ECM components to intracellular signal transduction pathways.]*

Jiang D, Liang J, Noble PW: Hyaluronans in tissue injury and repair. Annu Rev Cell Dev Biol 23:435, 2007. *[A discussion of the role of a major family of ECM proteins in tissue repair.]*

Khanapure SP, Garvey DS, Janero DR, et al: Eicosanoids in inflammation: biosynthesis, pharmacology, and therapeutic frontiers. Curr Top Med Chem 7:311, 2007. *[A summary of the properties of this important class of inflammatory mediators.]*

Lentsch AB, Ward PA: Regulation of inflammatory vascular damage. J Pathol 190:343, 2000. *[Discussion of the mechanisms of endothelial damage and increased vascular permeability.]*

Ley K, Laudanna C, Cybulsky MI, Nourshargh S: Getting to the site of inflammation: the leukocyte adhesion cascade updated. Nat Rev Immunol 7:678, 2007. *[A modern discussion of leukocyte recruitment to sites of inflammation.]*

Martin P, Leibovich SJ: Inflammatory cells during wound repair: the good, the bad, and the ugly. Trends Cell Biol 15:599, 2005. *[Good review on the multiple roles of inflammatory cells in repair.]*

Masters SL, Simon A, Aksentijevich I, Kastner DL: Horror autoinflammaticus: the molecular pathophysiology of autoinflammatory disease. Annu Rev Immunol 27:621, 2009. *[An excellent discussion of autoinflammatory syndromes caused by gain-of-function mutations in components of the inflammasome.]*

McAnully RJ: Fibroblasts and myofibroblasts: their source, function, and role in disease. Int J Biochem Cell Biol 39:666, 2007. *[A discussion of the two major types of stroma cells and their roles on tissue repair and fibrosis.]*

Muller WA: Mechanisms of leukocyte transendothelial migration. Annu Rev Pathol 6:323, 2011. *[A thoughtful review of the mechanisms by which leukocytes traverse the endothelium.]*

Nagy JA, Dvorak AM, Dvorak HF: VEGF-A and the induction of pathological angiogenesis. Annu Rev Pathol 2:251, 2007. *[A review of the VEGF family of growth factors and their role in angiogenesis in cancer, inflammation, and various disease states.]*

Nathan C, Ding A: Nonresolving inflammation. Cell 140:871, 2010. *[A discussion of the abnormalities that lead to chronic inflammation.]*

Page-McCaw A, Ewald AJ, Werb Z: Matrix metalloproteinases and the regulation of tissue remodelling. Nat Rev Mol Cell Biol 8:221, 2007. *[A review of the function of matrix modifying enzymes in tissue repair.]*

Papayannapoulos V, Zychlinsky A: NETs: a new strategy for using old weapons. Trends Immunol 30:513, 2009. *[A review of a newly discovered mechanism by which neutrophils destroy microbes.]*

Ricklin D, Hajishengallis G, Yang K, Lambris JD: Complement: a key system for immune surveillance and homeostasis. Nat Immunol 11:785, 2010. *[A current overview of the activation and functions of the complement system and its role in disease.]*

Rock KL, Kono H: The inflammatory response to cell death. Annu Rev Pathol 3:99, 2008. *[An excellent discussion of how the immune system recognizes necrotic cells.]*

Schultz GS, Wysocki A: Interactions between extracellular matrix and growth factors in wound healing. Wound Repair Regen 17:153, 2009. *[A discussion of the regulation of growth factors by the ECM.]*

Schroder K, Tschopp J: The inflammasomes. Cell 140:821, 2010. *[An excellent review of the cellular machinery that recognizes products of dead cells, many foreign and abnormal substances, and some microbes.]*

Segal AW: How neutrophils kill microbes. Annu Rev Immunol 23:197, 2005. *[An excellent discussion of the microbicidal mechanisms of neutrophils.]*

Stappenbeck TS, Miyoshi H: The role of stromal stem cells in tissue regeneration and wound repair. Science 324:1666, 2009. *[An excellent review of the role of tissue stem cells in repair.]*

Stearns-Kurosawa DJ, Osuchowski MF, Valentine C, et al: The pathogenesis of sepsis. Annu Rev Pathol 6:19, 2011. *[A discussion of the current concepts of pathogenic mechanisms in sepsis and septic shock.]*

Takeuchi O, Akira S: Pattern recognition receptors and inflammation. Cell 140:805, 2010. *[An excellent overview of Toll-like receptors and other pattern recognition receptor families, and their roles in host defense and inflammation.]*

Wynn TA: Cellular and molecular mechanisms of fibrosis. J Pathol 214:199, 2008. *[An overview of the cellular mechanisms of fibrosis, with an emphasis on the role of the immune system in fibrotic reactions to chronic infections.]*

Yamanaka S, Blau HM: Nuclear reprogramming to a pluripotent state by three approaches. Nature 465:704, 2010. *[A review of the exciting technology for generating iPS cells for regenerative medicine.]*

See Targeted Therapy available online at
studentconsult.com

CHAPTER 3

Hemodynamic Disorders, Thromboembolism, and Shock

CHAPTER CONTENTS

The health of cells and tissues depends on the circulation of blood, which delivers oxygen and nutrients and removes wastes generated by cellular metabolism. Under normal conditions, as blood passes through capillary beds, proteins in the plasma are retained within the vasculature and there is little net movement of water and electrolytes into the tissues. This balance is often disturbed by pathologic conditions that alter endothelial function, increase vascular pressure, or decrease plasma protein content, all of which promote *edema*—accumulation of fluid resulting from a net outward movement of water into extravascular spaces. Depending on its severity and location, edema may have minimal or profound effects. In the lower extremities, it may only make one's shoes feel snugger after a long sedentary day; in the lungs, however, edema fluid can fill alveoli, causing life-threatening hypoxia.

Our blood vessels are frequently subject to trauma of varying degrees. *Hemostasis* is the process of blood clotting that prevents excessive bleeding after blood vessel damage. Inadequate hemostasis may result in *hemorrhage,* which can compromise regional tissue perfusion and, if massive and rapid, may lead to *hypotension, shock,* and death. Conversely, inappropriate clotting (*thrombosis*) or migration of clots (*embolism*) can obstruct blood vessels, potentially causing ischemic cell death (*infarction*). Indeed, *thromboembolism* lies at the heart of three major causes of morbidity and death in developed countries: myocardial infarction, pulmonary embolism, and cerebrovascular accident (stroke).

HYPEREMIA AND CONGESTION

Hyperemia and congestion both refer to an increase in blood volume within a tissue but they have different underlying mechanisms. *Hyperemia is an active process* resulting from arteriolar dilation and increased blood inflow, as occurs at sites of inflammation or in exercising skeletal muscle. Hyperemic tissues are redder than normal because of engorgement with oxygenated blood. *Congestion is a passive process* resulting from impaired outflow of venous blood from a tissue. It can occur systemically, as in cardiac failure, or locally as a consequence of an isolated venous obstruction. Congested tissues have an abnormal blue-red color (*cyanosis*) that stems from the accumulation of deoxygenated hemoglobin in the affected area. In long-standing *chronic congestion,* inadequate tissue perfusion and persistent hypoxia may lead to parenchymal cell death and secondary tissue fibrosis, and the elevated intravascular pressures may cause edema or sometimes rupture capillaries, producing focal hemorrhages.

MORPHOLOGY

Cut surfaces of hyperemic or congested tissues feel wet and typically ooze blood. On microscopic examination, **acute pulmonary congestion** is marked by blood-engorged alveolar capillaries and variable degrees of alveolar septal edema and intra-alveolar hemorrhage. In **chronic pulmonary congestion,** the septa become thickened and fibrotic, and the alveolar spaces contain numerous macrophages laden with hemosiderin ("heart failure cells") derived from phagocytosed red cells. In **acute hepatic congestion,** the central vein and sinusoids are distended with blood, and there may even be central hepatocyte dropout due to necrosis. The periportal hepatocytes, better oxygenated because of their proximity to hepatic arterioles, experience less severe hypoxia and may develop only reversible fatty change. In **chronic passive congestion of the liver,** the central regions of the hepatic lobules, viewed on gross examination, are red-brown and slightly depressed (owing to cell loss) and are accentuated against the surrounding zones of uncongested tan, sometimes fatty, liver **(nutmeg liver)** (Fig. 3–1, A). Microscopic findings include centrilobular hepatocyte

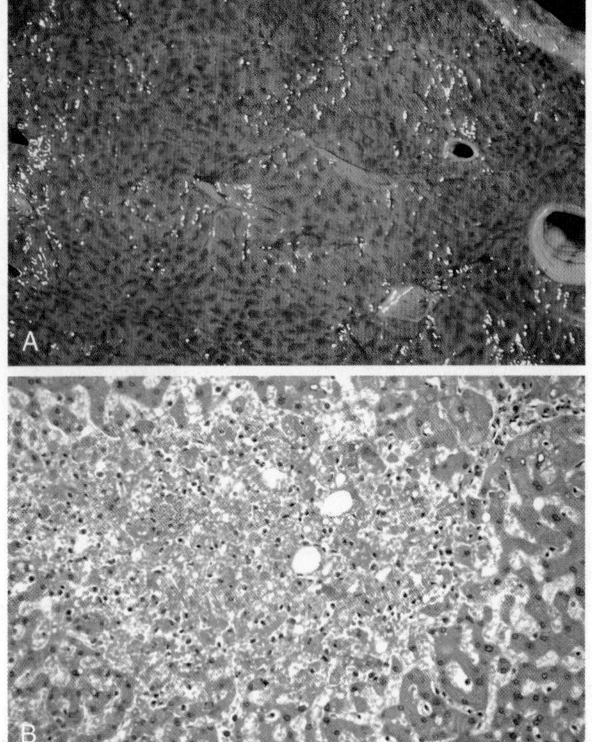

Figure 3–1 Liver with chronic passive congestion and hemorrhagic necrosis. **A,** In this autopsy specimen, central areas are red and slightly depressed compared with the surrounding tan viable parenchyma, creating "nutmeg liver" (so called because it resembles the cut surface of a nutmeg). **B,** Microscopic preparation shows centrilobular hepatic necrosis with hemorrhage and scattered inflammatory cells.

(Courtesy of Dr. James Crawford.)

necrosis, hemorrhage, and hemosiderin-laden macrophages (Fig. 3–1, *B*). In long-standing, severe hepatic congestion (most commonly associated with heart failure), hepatic fibrosis ("cardiac cirrhosis") can develop. Because the central portion of the hepatic lobule is the last to receive blood, centrilobular necrosis also can occur in any setting of reduced hepatic blood flow (including shock from any cause); there need not be previous hepatic congestion.

EDEMA

Approximately 60% of lean body weight is water, two thirds of which is intracellular. Most of the remaining water is found in extracellular compartments in the form of interstitial fluid; only 5% of the body's water is in blood plasma. As noted earlier, *edema* is an accumulation of interstitial fluid within tissues. Extravascular fluid can also collect in body cavities such as the pleural cavity (*hydrothorax*), the pericardial cavity (*hydropericardium*), or the peritoneal cavity (*hydroperitoneum*, or *ascites*). *Anasarca* is severe, generalized edema marked by profound swelling of subcutaneous tissues and accumulation of fluid in body cavities.

Table 3–1 Pathophysiologic Causes of Edema

Increased Hydrostatic Pressure
Impaired Venous Return

Congestive heart failure
Constrictive pericarditis
Ascites (liver cirrhosis)
Venous obstruction or compression
  Thrombosis
  External pressure (e.g., mass)
  Lower extremity inactivity with prolonged dependency

Arteriolar Dilation
Heat Neurohumoral dysregulation
Reduced Plasma Osmotic Pressure (Hypoproteinemia)
Protein-losing glomerulopathies (nephrotic syndrome) Liver cirrhosis (ascites) Malnutrition Protein-losing gastroenteropathy
Lymphatic Obstruction
Inflammatory Neoplastic Postsurgical Postirradiation
Sodium Retention

Excessive salt intake with renal insufficiency
Increased tubular reabsorption of sodium
  Renal hypoperfusion
  Increased renin-angiotensin-aldosterone secretion

Inflammation
Acute inflammation Chronic inflammation Angiogenesis

Data from Leaf A, Cotran RS: *Renal Pathophysiology*, 3rd ed. New York, Oxford University Press, 1985, p 146.

Table 3–1 lists the major causes of edema. The mechanisms of inflammatory edema are largely related to increased vascular permeability and are discussed in Chapter 2; the *noninflammatory causes* are detailed in the following discussion.

Fluid movement between the vascular and interstitial spaces is governed mainly by two opposing forces—the *vascular hydrostatic pressure* and the *colloid osmotic pressure* produced by plasma proteins. Normally, the outflow of fluid produced by hydrostatic pressure at the arteriolar end of the microcirculation is neatly balanced by inflow due to the slightly elevated osmotic pressure at the venular end; hence there is only a small net outflow of fluid into the interstitial space, which is drained by lymphatic vessels. Either increased hydrostatic pressure or diminished colloid osmotic pressure causes increased movement of water into the interstitium (Fig. 3–2). This in turn increases the tissue hydrostatic pressure, and eventually a new equilibrium is achieved. Excess edema fluid is removed by lymphatic drainage and returned to the bloodstream by way of the thoracic duct (Fig. 3–2).

The edema fluid that accumulates owing to increased hydrostatic pressure or reduced intravascular colloid typically is a protein-poor *transudate*; it has a specific gravity less than 1.012. By contrast, because of increased vascular permeability, inflammatory edema fluid is a protein-rich

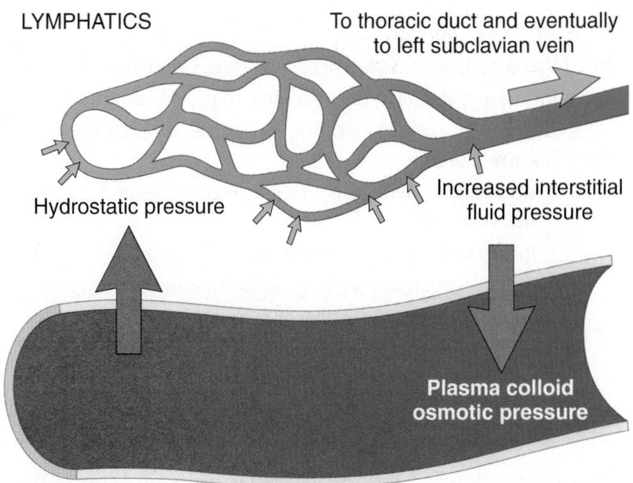

Figure 3–2 Factors influencing fluid movement across capillary walls. Capillary hydrostatic and osmotic forces are normally balanced so there is little net movement of fluid into the interstitium. However, *increased* hydrostatic pressure or *diminished* plasma osmotic pressure leads to extravascular fluid accumulation (edema). Tissue lymphatics drain much of the excess fluid back to the circulation by way of the thoracic duct; however, if the capacity for lymphatic drainage is exceeded, tissue edema results.

exudate with a specific gravity usually greater than 1.020 (see Chapter 2). We will now discuss the various causes of edema.

Increased Hydrostatic Pressure

Local increases in intravascular pressure can result from impaired venous return—for example, a deep venous thrombosis in the lower extremity can cause edema restricted to the distal portion of the affected leg. *Generalized* increases in venous pressure, with resultant systemic edema, occur most commonly in *congestive heart failure* (Chapter 10). Several factors increase venous hydrostatic pressure in patients with congestive heart failure (Fig. 3-3). The reduced cardiac output leads to hypoperfusion of the kidneys, triggering the renin-angiotensin-aldosterone axis and inducing sodium and water retention (*secondary hyperaldosteronism*). In patients with normal heart function, this adaptation increases cardiac filling and cardiac output, thereby improving renal perfusion. However, the failing heart often cannot increase its cardiac output in response to the compensatory increases in blood volume. Instead, a vicious circle of fluid retention, increased venous hydrostatic pressures, and worsening edema ensues. Unless cardiac output is restored or renal water retention is reduced (e.g., by salt restriction or treatment with diuretics or aldosterone antagonists) this downward spiral continues. Because secondary hyperaldosteronism is a common feature of generalized edema, salt restriction, diuretics, and aldosterone antagonists also are of value in the management of generalized edema resulting from other causes.

Reduced Plasma Osmotic Pressure

Under normal circumstances albumin accounts for almost half of the total plasma protein. Therefore conditions in which albumin is either lost from the circulation or synthesized in inadequate amounts are common causes of reduced plasma osmotic pressure. In *nephrotic syndrome* (Chapter 13), damaged glomerular capillaries become leaky, leading to the loss of albumin (and other plasma proteins) in the urine and the development of generalized edema. Reduced albumin synthesis occurs in the setting of severe liver disease (e.g., *cirrhosis*) (Chapter 15) and protein malnutrition (Chapter 7). Regardless of cause, low albumin levels lead in a stepwise fashion to edema, reduced intravascular volume, renal hypoperfusion, and secondary hyperaldosteronism. Unfortunately, increased salt and water retention by the kidney not only fails to correct the plasma volume deficit but also exacerbates the edema, since the primary defect—low serum protein—persists.

Lymphatic Obstruction

Impaired lymphatic drainage and consequent *lymphedema* usually result from a localized obstruction caused by an inflammatory or neoplastic condition. For example, the parasitic infection *filariasis* can cause massive edema of the lower extremity and external genitalia (so-called *elephantiasis*) by engendering inguinal lymphatic and lymph node fibrosis. Infiltration and obstruction of superficial lymphatics by breast cancer may cause edema of the overlying skin; the characteristic finely pitted appearance of the skin of the affected breast is called *peau d'orange* (orange peel). Lymphedema also may occur as a complication of therapy. One relatively common setting for this clinical entity is in women with breast cancer who undergo axillary lymph node resection and/or irradiation, both of which can disrupt and obstruct lymphatic drainage, resulting in severe lymphedema of the arm.

Sodium and Water Retention

Excessive retention of salt (and its obligate associated water) can lead to edema by increasing hydrostatic pressure (due to expansion of the intravascular volume) and

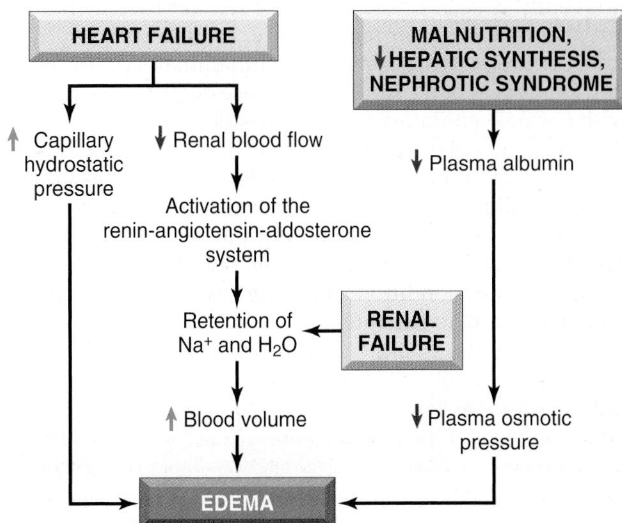

Figure 3–3 Pathways leading to systemic edema due to heart failure, renal failure, or reduced plasma osmotic pressure.

reducing plasma osmotic pressure. Excessive salt and water retention are seen in a wide variety of diseases that compromise renal function, including *poststreptococcal glomerulonephritis* and *acute renal failure* (Chapter 13).

MORPHOLOGY

Edema is easily recognized on gross inspection; microscopic examination shows clearing and separation of the extracellular matrix elements. Although any tissue can be involved, edema most commonly is encountered in subcutaneous tissues, lungs, and brain.

Subcutaneous edema can be diffuse but usually accumulates preferentially in parts of the body positioned the greatest distance below the heart where hydrostatic pressures are highest. Thus, edema typically is most pronounced in the legs with standing and the sacrum with recumbency, a relationship termed **dependent edema.** Finger pressure over edematous subcutaneous tissue displaces the interstitial fluid, leaving a finger-shaped depression; this appearance is called **pitting edema.** Edema due to **renal dysfunction** or **nephrotic syndrome** often manifests first in loose connective tissues (e.g., the eyelids, causing **periorbital edema**). With **pulmonary edema**, the lungs often are two to three times their normal weight, and sectioning reveals frothy, sometimes blood-tinged fluid consisting of a mixture of air, edema fluid, and extravasated red cells. **Brain edema** can be localized (e.g., due to abscess or tumor) or generalized, depending on the nature and extent of the pathologic process or injury. With generalized edema, the sulci are narrowed while the gyri are swollen and flattened against the skull.

Clinical Correlation

The effects of edema vary, ranging from merely annoying to rapidly fatal. Subcutaneous edema is important to recognize primarily because it signals potential underlying cardiac or renal disease; however, when significant, it also can impair wound healing or the clearance of infections. Pulmonary edema is a common clinical problem that most frequently is seen in the setting of left ventricular failure but also may occur in renal failure, acute respiratory distress syndrome (Chapter 11), and inflammatory and infectious disorders of the lung. It can cause death by interfering with normal ventilatory function; besides impeding oxygen diffusion, alveolar edema fluid also creates a favorable environment for infections. Brain edema is life-threatening; if the swelling is severe, the brain can *herniate* (extrude) through the foramen magnum. With increased intracranial pressure, the brain stem vascular supply can be compressed. Either condition can cause death by injuring the medullary centers (Chapter 22).

SUMMARY

Edema

- Edema is the result of the movement of fluid from the vasculature into the interstitial spaces; the fluid may be protein-poor (*transudate*) or protein-rich (*exudate*).
- Edema may be caused by:
  - increased hydrostatic pressure (e.g., heart failure)
  - increased vascular permeability (e.g., inflammation)
  - decreased colloid osmotic pressure, due to reduced plasma albumin
    - decreased synthesis (e.g., liver disease, protein malnutrition)
    - increased loss (e.g., nephrotic syndrome)
  - lymphatic obstruction (e.g., inflammation or neoplasia).
  - sodium retention (e.g., renal failure)

HEMORRHAGE

Hemorrhage, defined as the extravasation of blood from vessels, occurs in a variety of settings. As described earlier, capillary bleeding can occur in chronically congested tissues. The risk of hemorrhage (often after a seemingly insignificant injury) is increased in a wide variety of clinical disorders collectively called *hemorrhagic diatheses.* Trauma, atherosclerosis, or inflammatory or neoplastic erosion of a vessel wall also may lead to hemorrhage, which may be extensive if the affected vessel is a large vein or artery.

Hemorrhage may be manifested by different appearances and clinical consequences.

- Hemorrhage may be external or accumulate within a tissue as a *hematoma,* which ranges in significance from trivial (e.g., a bruise) to fatal (e.g., a massive retroperitoneal hematoma resulting from rupture of a dissecting aortic aneurysm) (Chapter 9).

  Large bleeds into body cavities are given various names according to location—*hemothorax, hemopericardium, hemoperitoneum,* or *hemarthrosis* (in joints). Extensive hemorrhages can occasionally result in jaundice from the massive breakdown of red cells and hemoglobin.
- *Petechiae* are minute (1 to 2 mm in diameter) hemorrhages into skin, mucous membranes, or serosal surfaces (Fig. 3–4, *A*); causes include low platelet counts (*thrombocytopenia*), defective platelet function, and loss of vascular wall support, as in vitamin C deficiency (Chapter 7).
- *Purpura* are slightly larger (3 to 5 mm) hemorrhages. Purpura can result from the same disorders that cause petechiae, as well as trauma, vascular inflammation (*vasculitis*), and increased vascular fragility.
- *Ecchymoses* are larger (1 to 2 cm) subcutaneous hematomas (colloquially called *bruises*). Extravasated red cells are phagocytosed and degraded by macrophages; the characteristic color changes of a bruise are due to the enzymatic conversion of hemoglobin (red-blue color) to bilirubin (blue-green color) and eventually hemosiderin (golden-brown).

The clinical significance of any particular hemorrhage depends on the volume of blood lost and the rate of bleeding. Rapid loss of up to 20% of the blood volume, or slow losses of even larger amounts, may have little impact in healthy adults; greater losses, however, can cause *hemorrhagic (hypovolemic) shock* (discussed later). The site of hemorrhage also is important; bleeding that would be trivial in

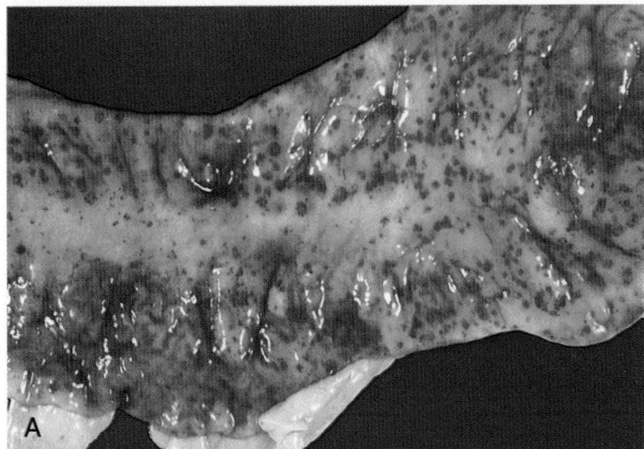

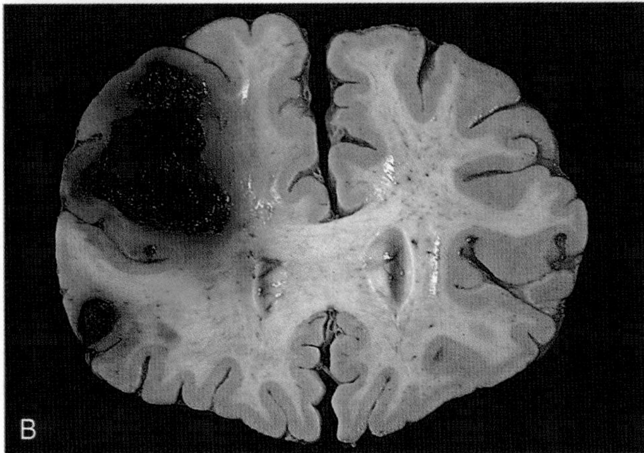

Figure 3–4 A, Punctate petechial hemorrhages of the colonic mucosa, a consequence of thrombocytopenia. **B,** Fatal intracerebral hemorrhage.

the subcutaneous tissues can cause death if located in the brain (Fig. 3–4, *B*). Finally, chronic or recurrent external blood loss (e.g., due to peptic ulcer or menstrual bleeding) frequently culminates in iron deficiency anemia as a consequence of loss of iron in hemoglobin. By contrast, iron is efficiently recycled from phagocytosed red cells, so internal bleeding (e.g., a hematoma) does not lead to iron deficiency.

HEMOSTASIS AND THROMBOSIS

Normal hemostasis comprises a series of regulated processes that maintain blood in a fluid, clot-free state in normal vessels while rapidly forming a localized *hemostatic plug* at the site of vascular injury. The pathologic counterpart of hemostasis is *thrombosis,* the formation of blood clot (*thrombus*) within intact vessels. Both hemostasis and thrombosis involve three elements: the *vascular wall, platelets,* and the *coagulation cascade.* The discussion here begins with normal hemostasis and its regulation.

Normal Hemostasis

The main steps in the process of hemostasis and its regulation are summarized below and shown in Figure 3–5.

- Vascular injury causes transient *arteriolar vasoconstriction* through reflex neurogenic mechanisms, augmented by local secretion of *endothelin* (a potent endothelium-derived vasoconstrictor) (Fig. 3–5, *A*). This effect is fleeting, however, and bleeding would quickly resume if not for the activation of platelets and coagulation factors.
- *Endothelial injury* exposes highly thrombogenic subendothelial extracellular matrix (ECM), facilitating *platelet adherence, activation, and aggregation.* The formation of the initial platelet plug is called *primary hemostasis* (Fig. 3–5, *B*).
- Endothelial injury also exposes *tissue factor* (also known as *factor III* or *thromboplastin*), a membrane-bound procoagulant glycoprotein synthesized by endothelial cells. Exposed tissue factor, acting in conjunction with factor VII (see later), is the major in vivo trigger of the coagulation cascade and its activation eventually culminates in the *activation of thrombin,* which has several roles in regulating coagulation.
- *Activated thrombin* promotes the formation of an insoluble *fibrin* clot by cleaving fibrinogen; thrombin also is a potent activator of additional platelets, which serve to reinforce the hemostatic plug. This sequence, termed secondary hemostasis, results in the formation of a stable clot capable of preventing further hemorrhage (Fig. 3–5, *C*).
- As bleeding is controlled, counterregulatory mechanisms (e.g., factors that produce fibrinolysis, such as *tissue-type plasminogen activator*) are set into motion to ensure that clot formation is limited to the site of injury (Fig. 3–5, *D*).

Discussed next in greater detail are the roles of endothelium, platelets, and the coagulation cascade.

Endothelium

Endothelial cells are central regulators of hemostasis; the balance between the anti- and prothrombotic activities of endothelium determines whether thrombus formation, propagation, or dissolution occurs. Normal endothelial cells express a variety of *anticoagulant* factors that inhibit platelet aggregation and coagulation and promote fibrinolysis; after injury or activation, however, this balance shifts, and endothelial cells acquire numerous *procoagulant* activities (Fig. 3–6). Besides trauma, endothelium can be activated by microbial pathogens, hemodynamic forces, and a number of pro-inflammatory mediators (Chapter 2).

Antithrombotic Properties of Normal Endothelium

Inhibitory Effects on Platelets. Intact endothelium prevents platelets (and plasma coagulation factors) from engaging the highly thrombogenic subendothelial ECM. Nonactivated platelets do not adhere to normal endothelium; even with activated platelets, prostacyclin (i.e., prostaglandin I_2 [PGI_2]) and nitric oxide produced by endothelium impede their adhesion. Both mediators also are potent vasodilators and inhibitors of platelet aggregation; their synthesis by endothelial cells is stimulated by a number of factors (e.g., thrombin, cytokines) produced during coagulation. Endothelial cells also produce adenosine diphosphatase, which degrades adenosine diphosphate (ADP) and further inhibits platelet aggregation (see later).

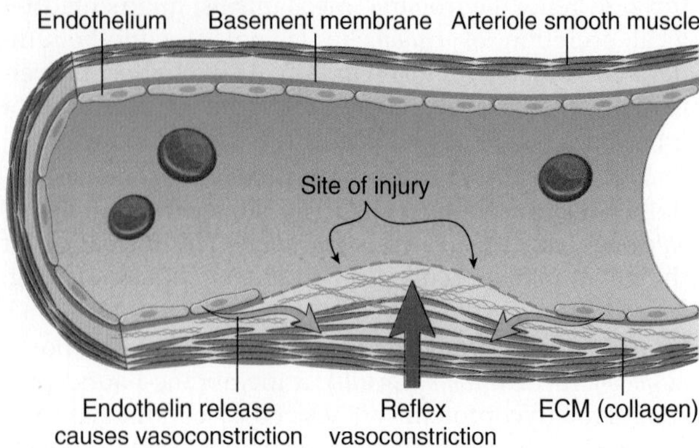

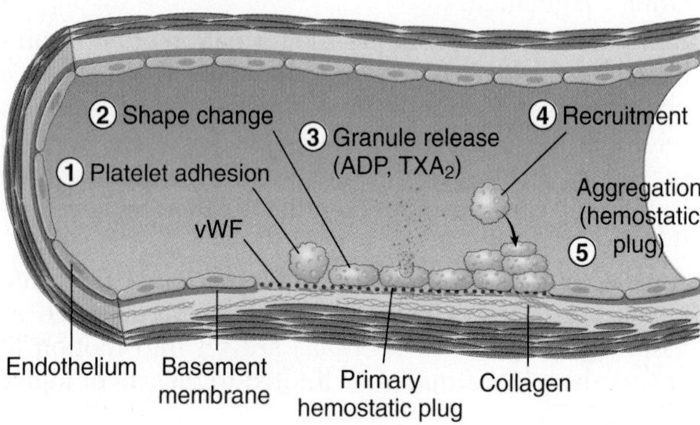

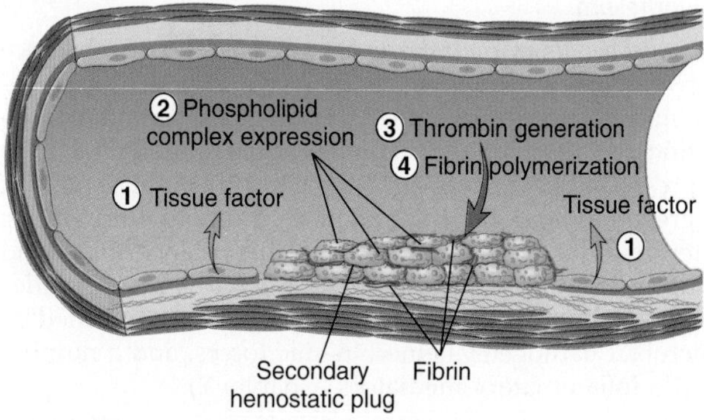

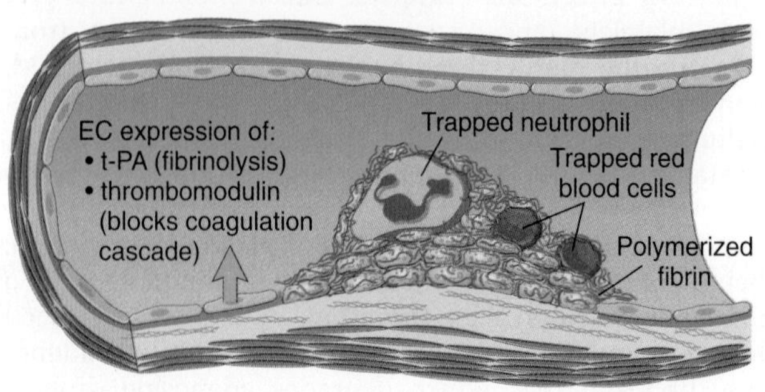

Figure 3–5 Normal hemostasis. **A,** After vascular injury, local neurohumoral factors induce a transient vasoconstriction. **B,** Platelets bind via glycoprotein Ib (GpIb) receptors to von Willebrand factor (vWF) on exposed extracellular matrix (ECM) and are activated, undergoing a shape change and granule release. Released adenosine diphosphate (ADP) and thromboxane A_2 (TxA_2) induce additional platelet aggregation through binding of platelet GpIIb-IIIa receptors to fibrinogen. This platelet aggregate fills the vascular defect, forming the *primary hemostatic plug.* **C,** Local activation of the coagulation cascade (involving tissue factor and platelet phospholipids) results in fibrin polymerization, "cementing" the platelets into a definitive *secondary hemostatic plug* that is larger and more stable than the primary plug and contains entrapped red cells and leukocytes. **D,** Counterregulatory mechanisms, such as release of t-PA (tissue plasminogen activator, a fibrinolytic product) and thrombomodulin (interfering with the coagulation cascade), limit the hemostatic process to the site of injury.

Inhibitory Effects on Coagulation Factors. These actions are mediated by factors expressed on endothelial surfaces, particularly heparin-like molecules, thrombomodulin, and tissue factor pathway inhibitor (Fig. 3–6). *The heparin-like molecules* act indirectly: They are cofactors that greatly enhance the inactivation of thrombin (and other coagulation factors) by the plasma protein *antithrombin III. Thrombomodulin* also acts indirectly: It binds to thrombin, thereby modifying the substrate specificity of thrombin, so that instead of cleaving fibrinogen, it instead cleaves and activates protein C, an anticoagulant. Activated protein C inhibits clotting by cleaving and inactivating two procoagulants, factor Va and factor VIIIa; it requires a cofactor, protein S, which is also synthesized by endothelial cells. Finally, tissue factor pathway inhibitor (TFPI) directly inhibits tissue factor–factor VIIa complex and factor Xa.

Fibrinolysis. Endothelial cells synthesize *tissue-type plasminogen activator,* a protease that cleaves plasminogen to plasmin; plasmin, in turn, cleaves fibrin to degrade thrombi.

Prothrombotic Properties of Injured or Activated Endothelium

Activation of Platelets. Endothelial injury brings platelets into contact with the subendothelial ECM, which includes among its constituents *von Willebrand factor (vWF),* a large multimeric protein that is synthesized by EC. vWF is held fast to the ECM through interactions with collagen and also binds tightly to Gp1b, a glycoprotein found on the surface of platelets. These interactions allow vWF to act as a sort of molecular glue that binds platelets tightly to denuded vessel walls (Fig. 3–7).

Activation of Clotting Factors. In response to cytokines (e.g., tumor necrosis factor [TNF] or interleukin-1 [IL-1]) or certain bacterial products including endotoxin, endothelial cells produce *tissue factor,* the major in vivo activator of coagulation, and downregulate the expression of thrombomodulin. Activated endothelial cells also bind coagulation factors IXa and Xa (see further on), which augments the catalytic activities of these factors.

Antifibrinolytic Effects. Activated endothelial cells secrete *plasminogen activator inhibitors (PAIs),* which limit fibrinolysis and thereby favor thrombosis.

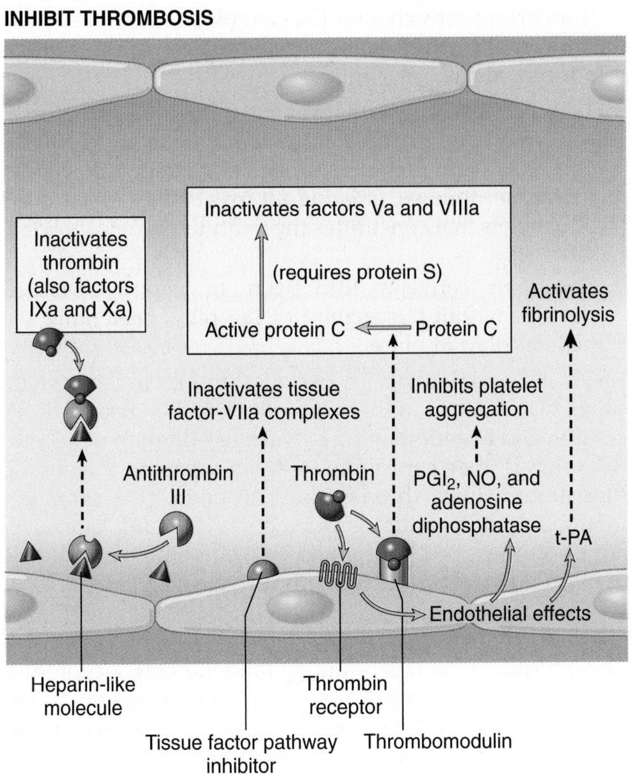

INHIBIT THROMBOSIS

Inactivates thrombin (also factors IXa and Xa)

Inactivates factors Va and VIIIa

(requires protein S)

Active protein C

Protein C

Activates fibrinolysis

Inactivates tissue factor-VIIa complexes

Inhibits platelet aggregation

Antithrombin III

Thrombin

PGI_2, NO, and adenosine diphosphatase

t-PA

Endothelial effects

Heparin-like molecule

Thrombin receptor

Tissue factor pathway inhibitor

Thrombomodulin

FAVOR THROMBOSIS

Extrinsic coagulation sequence

Platelet adhesion (held together by fibrinogen)

Exposure of membrane-bound tissue factor

vWF

Collagen

Figure 3–6 Anticoagulant properties of normal endothelium *(left)* and procoagulant properties of injured or activated endothelium *(right)*. NO, nitric oxide; PGI_2, prostaglandin I_2 (prostacyclin); t-PA, tissue plasminogen activator; vWF, von Willebrand factor. Thrombin receptors are also called protease-activated receptors (PARs).

SUMMARY

Endothelial Cells and Coagulation

- Intact, normal endothelial cells help to maintain blood flow by inhibiting the activation of platelets and coagulation factors.
- Endothelial cells stimulated by injury or inflammatory cytokines upregulate expression of procoagulant factors (e.g., tissue factor) that promote clotting, and downregulate expression of anticoagulant factors.
- Loss of endothelial integrity exposes subendothelial vWF and basement membrane collagen, stimulating platelet adhesion, platelet activation, and clot formation.

Platelets

Platelets are anucleate cell fragments shed into the bloodstream by marrow megakaryocytes. They play a critical role in normal hemostasis by forming a hemostatic plug that seals vascular defects, and by providing a surface that recruits and concentrates activated coagulation factors. Platelet function depends on several integrin family glycoprotein receptors, a contractile cytoskeleton, and two types of cytoplasmic granules:

- α *granules,* which express the adhesion molecule P-selectin on their membranes (Chapter 2) and contain

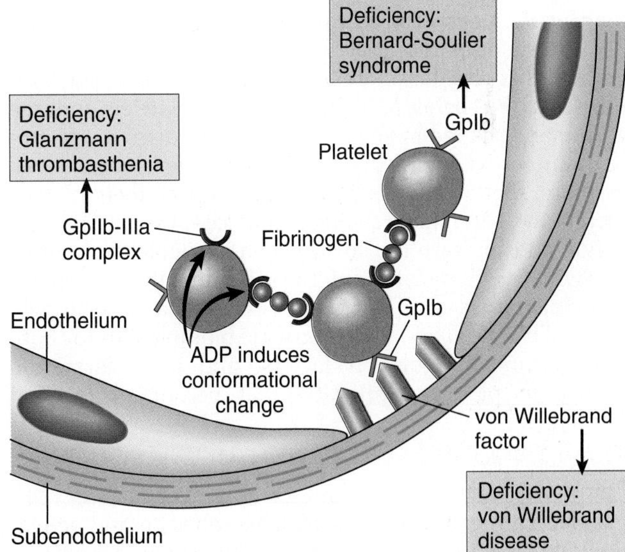

Figure 3–7 Platelet adhesion and aggregation. Von Willebrand factor functions as an *adhesion* bridge between subendothelial collagen and the glycoprotein Ib (GpIb) platelet receptor. Platelet *aggregation* is accomplished by fibrinogen binding to platelet GpIIb-IIIa receptors on different platelets. Congenital deficiencies in the various receptors or bridging molecules lead to the diseases indicated in the *colored boxes*. ADP, adenosine diphosphate.

fibrinogen, fibronectin, factors V and VIII, platelet factor-4 (a heparin-binding chemokine), platelet-derived growth factor (PDGF), and transforming growth factor-β (TGF-β)

- *Dense bodies* (δ granules), which contain adenine nucleotides (ADP and ATP), ionized calcium, histamine, serotonin, and epinephrine

After vascular injury, platelets encounter ECM constituents (collagen is most important) and adhesive glycoproteins such as vWF. This sets in motion a series of events that lead to (1) platelet adhesion, (2) platelet activation, and (3) platelet aggregation (Fig. 3–5, *B*).

Platelet Adhesion

Platelet adhesion initiates clot formation and depends on vWF and platelet glycoprotein Gp1b. Under shear stress (e.g., in flowing blood), vWF undergoes a conformational change, assuming an extended shape that allows it to bind simultaneously to collagen in the ECM and to platelet Gp1b (Fig. 3–7). The importance of this adhesive interaction is highlighted by genetic deficiencies of vWF and Gp1b, both of which result in bleeding disorders—von Willebrand disease (Chapter 11) and Bernard-Soulier disease (a rare condition), respectively.

Platelet Activation

Platelet adhesion leads to an irreversible shape change and secretion (release reaction) of both granule types—a process termed *platelet activation*. Calcium and ADP released from δ granules are especially important in subsequent events, since calcium is required by several coagulation factors and ADP is a potent activator of resting platelets. Activated platelets also synthesize thromboxane A_2 (TxA_2) (Chapter 2), a prostaglandin that activates additional nearby platelets and that also has an important role in platelet aggregation (described below). During activation, platelets undergo a dramatic change in shape from smooth discs to spheres with numerous long, spiky membrane extensions, as well as more subtle changes in the make-up of their plasma membranes. The shape changes enhance subsequent aggregation and increase the surface area available for interaction with coagulation factors. The subtle membrane changes include an increase in the surface expression of negatively charged *phospholipids,* which provide binding sites for both calcium and coagulation factors, and a conformation change in platelet GpIIb/IIIa that permits it to bind fibrinogen.

Platelet Aggregation

Platelet aggregation follows platelet adhesion and activation, and is stimulated by some of the same factors that induce platelet activation, such as TxA_2. Aggregation is promoted by bridging interactions between fibrinogen and GpIIb/IIIa receptors on adjacent platelets (Fig. 3–7). The importance of this interaction is emphasized by a rare inherited deficiency of GpIIb/IIIa (Glanzmann thrombasthenia), which is associated with bleeding and an inability of platelets to aggregate. Recognition of the central role of GpIIb-IIIa receptors in platelet aggregation has stimulated the development of antithrombotic agents that inhibit GpIIb-IIIa function.

Concurrent activation of the coagulation cascade generates thrombin, which stabilizes the platelet plug through two mechanisms:

- Thrombin activates a platelet surface receptor (protease-activated receptor [PAR]), which in concert with ADP and TxA_2 further enhances platelet aggregation. *Platelet contraction* follows, creating an irreversibly fused mass of platelets that constitutes the definitive *secondary hemostatic plug.*
- Thrombin converts fibrinogen to *fibrin* (discussed shortly) within the vicinity of the plug, cementing the platelet plug in place.

Red cells and leukocytes are also found in hemostatic plugs. Leukocytes adhere to platelets by means of P-selectin and to endothelium by various adhesion molecules (Chapter 2); they contribute to the inflammatory response that accompanies thrombosis. Thrombin also promotes inflammation by stimulating neutrophil and monocyte adhesion (described later) and by generating chemotactic *fibrin split products* during fibrinogen cleavage.

Platelet-Endothelial Interactions

The interplay of platelets and endothelium has a profound impact on clot formation. For example, prostaglandin PGI_2 (synthesized by normal endothelium) is a vasodilator and inhibits platelet aggregation, whereas TxA_2 (synthesized by activated platelets, as discussed above) is a potent vasoconstrictor. The balance between the opposing effects of PGI_2 and TxA_2 varies: In normal vessels, PGI_2 effects dominate and platelet aggregation is prevented, whereas endothelial injury decreases PGI_2 production and promotes platelet aggregation and TxA_2 production. The clinical utility of aspirin (an irreversible cyclooxygenase inhibitor) in lowering the risk of coronary thrombosis resides in its ability to permanently block TxA_2 production by platelets, which have no capacity for protein synthesis. Although endothelial PGI_2 production is also inhibited by aspirin, endothelial cells can resynthesize cyclooxygenase, thereby overcoming the blockade. In a manner similar to that for PGI_2, endothelium-derived nitric oxide also acts as a vasodilator and inhibitor of platelet aggregation (Fig. 3–6).

SUMMARY

Platelet Adhesion, Activation, and Aggregation

- Endothelial injury exposes the underlying basement membrane ECM; platelets adhere to the ECM primarily through binding of platelet GpIb receptors to vWF.
- Adhesion leads to platelet activation, an event associated with secretion of platelet granule contents, including calcium (a cofactor for several coagulation proteins) and ADP (a mediator of further platelet activation); dramatic changes in shape and membrane composition; and activation of GpIIb/IIIa receptors.
- The GpIIb/IIIa receptors on activated platelets form bridging crosslinks with fibrinogen, leading to platelet aggregation.
- Concomitant activation of thrombin promotes fibrin deposition, cementing the platelet plug in place.

Coagulation Cascade

The coagulation cascade constitutes the third arm of the hemostatic system. The pathways are schematically presented in Figure 3–8; only general principles are discussed here.

The coagulation cascade is a successive series of amplifying enzymatic reactions. At each step in the process, a proenzyme is proteolyzed to become an active enzyme, which in turn proteolyzes the next proenzyme in the series, eventually leading to the activation of thrombin and the formation of fibrin. *Thrombin has a key role,* as it acts at numerous points in the cascade (highlighted in Fig. 3–8). Thrombin proteolyzes *fibrinogen* into *fibrin* monomers that polymerize into an insoluble gel; this gel encases platelets and other circulating cells in the definitive secondary hemostatic plug. Fibrin polymers are stabilized by the cross-linking activity of factor XIIIa, which also is activated by thrombin.

Each reaction in the pathway depends on the assembly of a complex composed of an *enzyme* (an activated coagulation factor), a *substrate* (a proenzyme form of the next coagulation factor in the series), and a *cofactor* (a reaction accelerator). These components typically are assembled on a *phospholipid surface* (provided by endothelial cells or platelets) and are held together by interactions that depend on *calcium ions* (explaining why blood clotting is prevented

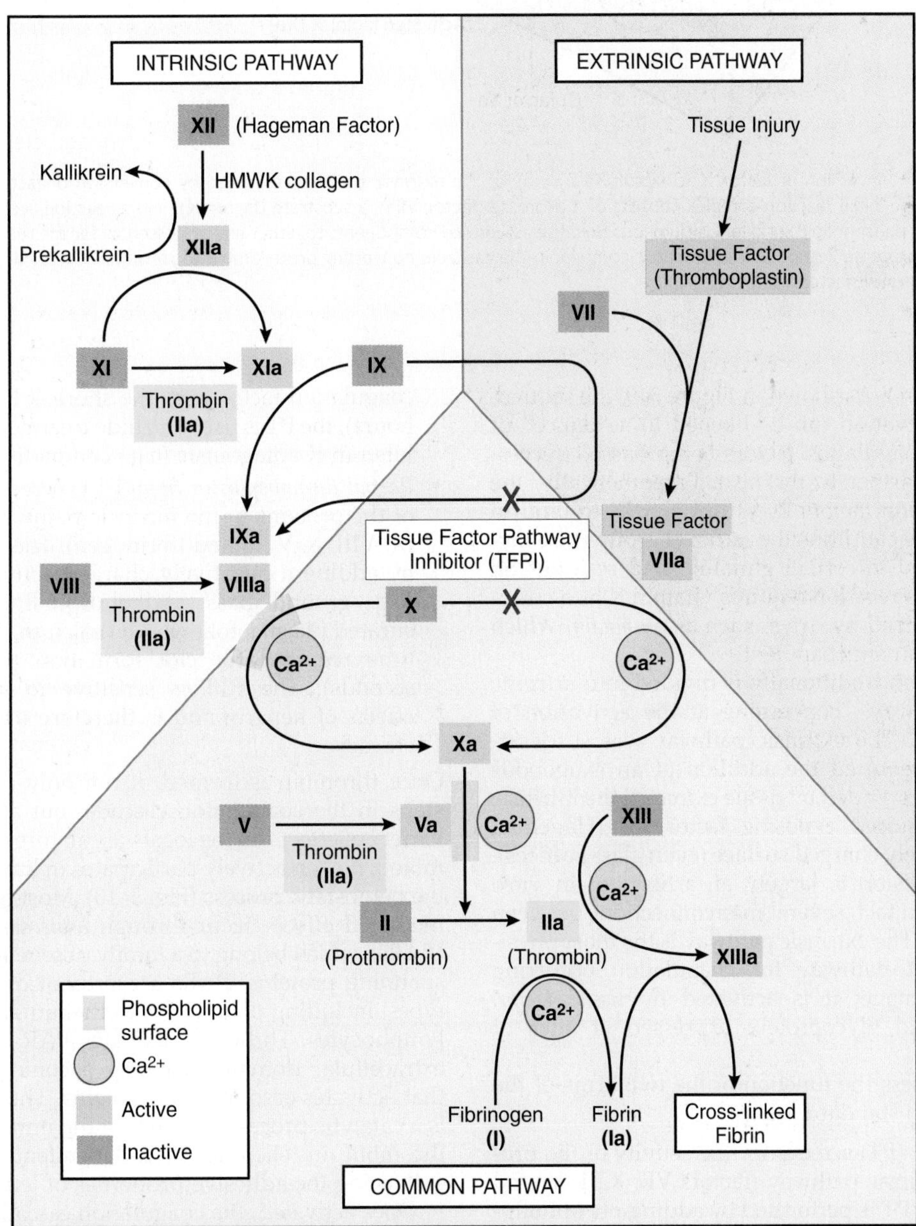

Figure 3–8 The coagulation cascade. Factor IX can be activated by either factor XIa or factor VIIa: In laboratory tests, activation is predominantly dependent on factor XIa, whereas in vivo, factor VIIa appears to be the predominant activator of factor IX. Factors in *red boxes* represent inactive molecules; activated factors, indicated with a lowercase *a*, are in *green boxes*. Note that thrombin (factor IIa) (in *light blue boxes*) contributes to coagulation through multiple positive feedback loops. The *red X's* denote points at which tissue factor pathway inhibitor (TFPI) inhibits activation of factor X and factor IX by factor VIIa. HMWK, high-molecular-weight kininogen; PL, phospholipid.

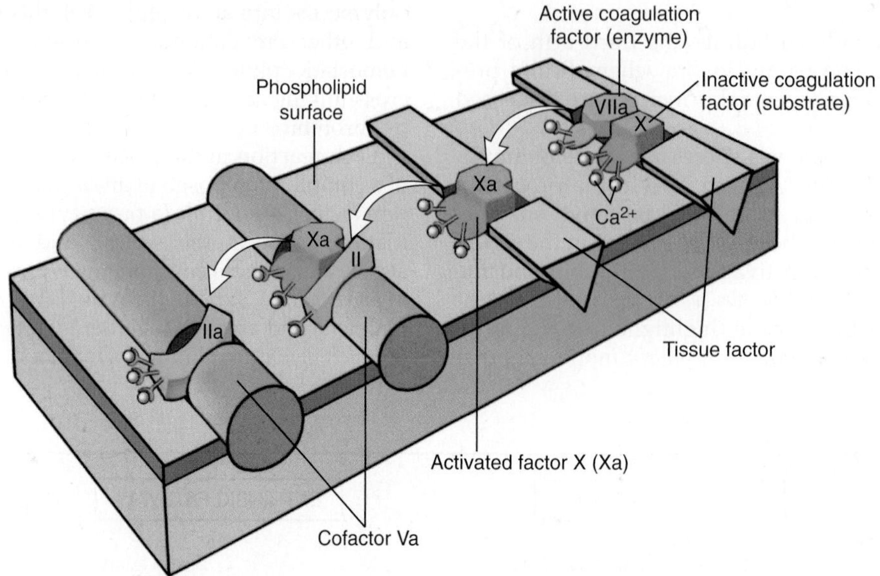

Figure 3–9 Sequential conversion of factor X to factor Xa by way of the extrinsic pathway, followed by conversion of factor II (prothrombin) to factor IIa (thrombin). The initial reaction complex consists of a protease (factor VIIa), a substrate (factor X), and a reaction accelerator (tissue factor) assembled on a platelet phospholipid surface. Calcium ions hold the assembled components together and are essential for the reaction. Activated factor Xa then becomes the protease component of the next complex in the cascade, converting prothrombin to thrombin (factor IIa) in the presence of a different reaction accelerator, factor Va.

by calcium chelators). As shown in Figure 3–9, the sequential cascade of activation can be likened to a "dance" of complexes, with coagulation factors being passed successively from one partner to the next. Parenthetically, the ability of coagulation factors II, VII, IX, and X to bind to calcium requires that additional γ-carboxyl groups be enzymatically appended to certain glutamic acid residues on these proteins. This reaction requires vitamin K as a cofactor and is antagonized by drugs such as *coumadin,* which is widely used as an anticoagulant.

Blood coagulation traditionally is divided into *extrinsic* and *intrinsic* pathways, converging at the activation of factor X (Fig. 3–8). The extrinsic pathway was so designated because it required the addition of an exogenous trigger (originally provided by tissue extracts); the intrinsic pathway only required exposing factor XII (Hageman factor) to a negatively charged surface (even glass suffices). However, this division is largely an artifact of in vitro testing; there are, in fact, several interconnections between the two pathways. The extrinsic pathway is the most physiologically relevant pathway for coagulation occurring after vascular damage; it is activated by *tissue factor,* a membrane-bound glycoprotein expressed at sites of injury.

Clinical labs assess the function of the two arms of the pathway using two standard assays.

- *Prothrombin time* (PT) screens for the activity of the proteins in the extrinsic pathway (factors VII, X, II, V, and fibrinogen). The PT is performed by adding phospholipids and tissue factor to a patient's citrated plasma (sodium citrate chelates calcium and prevents spontaneous clotting), followed by calcium, and the time to fibrin clot formation (usually 11 to 13 seconds) is recorded. Because factor VII is the vitamin K–dependent coagulation factor with the shortest half-life (roughly 7 hours), the PT is used to guide treatment of patients with vitamin K antagonists (e.g., coumadin).
- *Partial thromboplastin time* (PTT) screens for the activity of the proteins in the intrinsic pathway (factors XII, XI, IX, VIII, X, V, II, and fibrinogen). The PTT is performed by adding a negatively charged activator of factor XII (e.g., ground glass) and phospholipids to a patient's citrated plasma, followed by calcium, and recording the time required for clot formation (usually 28 to 35 seconds). The PTT is sensitive to the anticoagulant effects of heparin and is therefore used to monitor its efficacy.

Once thrombin is formed, it not only catalyzes the final steps in the coagulation cascade, but also exerts a wide variety of effects on the local vasculature and inflammatory milieu; it even actively participates in limiting the extent of the hemostatic process (Fig. 3–10). Most of these thrombin-mediated effects occur through *protease-activated receptors (PARs),* which belong to a family of seven-transmembrane-spanning proteins. PARs are present on a variety of cell types, including platelets, endothelium, monocytes, and T lymphocytes. Thrombin activates PARs by clipping their extracellular domains, causing a conformational change that activates associated G proteins. Thus, PAR activation is a catalytic process, explaining the impressive potency of thrombin in eliciting PAR-dependent effects, such as enhancing the adhesive properties of leukocytes.

Once activated, the coagulation cascade must be tightly restricted to the site of injury to prevent inappropriate and potentially dangerous clotting elsewhere in the vascular tree. Besides restricting factor activation to sites of exposed phospholipids, clotting also is controlled by three general categories of natural anticoagulants:

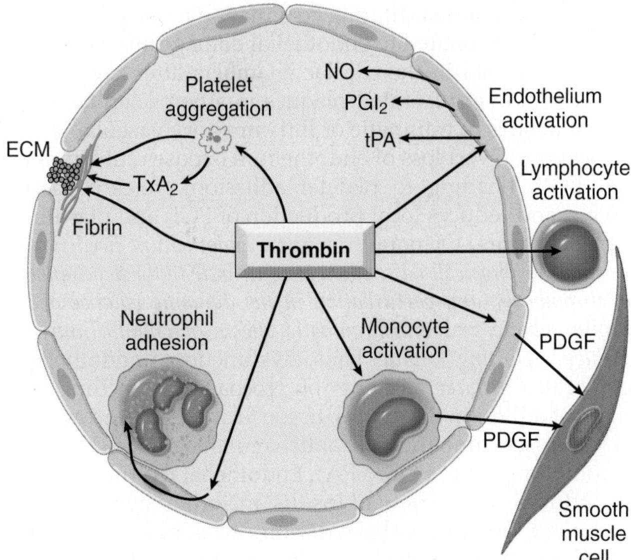

Figure 3–10 Role of thrombin in hemostasis and cellular activation. Thrombin generates fibrin by cleaving fibrinogen, activates factor XIII (which is responsible for cross-linking fibrin into an insoluble clot), and also activates several other coagulation factors, thereby amplifying the coagulation cascade (Fig. 3–8). Through protease-activated receptors (PARs), thrombin activates (1) platelet aggregation and TxA_2 secretion; (2) endothelium, which responds by generating leukocyte adhesion molecules and a variety of fibrinolytic (t-PA), vasoactive (NO, PGI_2), or cytokine (PDGF) mediators; and (3) leukocytes, increasing their adhesion to activated endothelium. ECM, extracellular matrix; NO, nitric oxide; PDGF, platelet-derived growth factor; PGI_2, prostaglandin I_2 (prostacyclin); TxA_2, thromboxane A_2; t-PA, tissue type plasminogen activator. See Figure 3–6 for anticoagulant activities mediated by thrombin via thrombomodulin.

(Courtesy of permission from Shaun Coughlin, MD, PhD, Cardiovascular Research Institute, University of California at San Francisco, San Francisco, California.)

- *Antithrombins* (e.g., antithrombin III) inhibit the activity of thrombin and other serine proteases, namely factors IXa, Xa, XIa, and XIIa. Antithrombin III is activated by binding to heparin-like molecules on endothelial cells—hence the clinical utility of heparin administration to limit thrombosis (Fig. 3–6).
- *Protein C and protein S* are two vitamin K-dependent proteins that act in a complex to proteolytically inactivate cofactors Va and VIIIa. Protein C activation by thrombomodulin was described earlier; protein S is a cofactor for protein C activity (Fig. 3–6).
- *Tissue factor pathway inhibitor (TFPI)* is a protein secreted by endothelium (and other cell types) that inactivates factor Xa and tissue factor–factor VIIa complexes (Fig. 3–8).

Clotting also sets into motion a *fibrinolytic cascade* that moderates the ultimate size of the clot. Fibrinolysis is largely carried out by *plasmin,* which breaks down fibrin and interferes with its polymerization (Fig. 3–11). The resulting *fibrin split products* (*FSPs* or *fibrin degradation products*) also can act as weak anticoagulants. Elevated levels of FSPs (most notably fibrin-derived *D-dimers*) can be used for diagnosing abnormal thrombotic states including disseminated intravascular coagulation (DIC) (Chapter 11), deep venous thrombosis, or pulmonary thromboembolism (described in detail later).

Plasmin is generated by proteolysis of *plasminogen*, an inactive plasma precursor, either by factor XII or by plasminogen activators (Fig. 3–11). The most important of the plasminogen activators is *tissue-type plasminogen activator (t-PA);* t-PA is synthesized principally by endothelial cells and is most active when attached to fibrin. The affinity for fibrin largely confines t-PA fibrinolytic activity to sites of recent thrombosis. *Urokinase-like plasminogen activator* (*u-PA*) is another plasminogen activator present in plasma and in various tissues; it can activate plasmin in the fluid phase. In addition, plasminogen can be cleaved to its active form by the bacterial product *streptokinase,* which is used clinically to lyse clots in some forms of thrombotic disease. As with any potent regulatory component, the activity of plasmin is tightly restricted. To prevent excess plasmin from lysing thrombi indiscriminately throughout the body, free plasmin rapidly complexes with circulating α_2-antiplasmin and is inactivated (Fig. 3–11).

Endothelial cells further modulate the coagulation-anticoagulation balance by releasing *plasminogen activator inhibitors (PAIs)*; these block fibrinolysis and confer an overall procoagulation effect (Fig. 3–11). PAI production

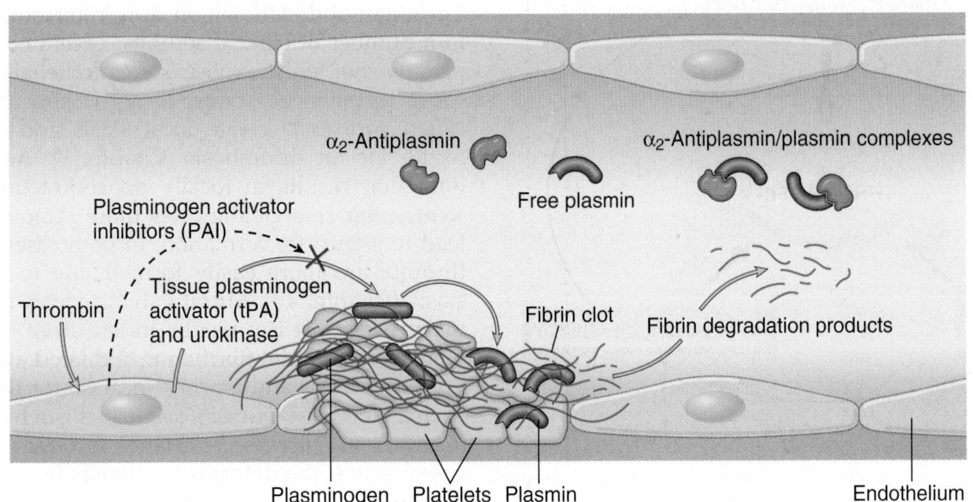

Figure 3–11 The fibrinolytic system, illustrating various plasminogen activators and inhibitors (see text).

is increased by inflammatory cytokines (in particular interferon-γ) and probably contributes to the intravascular thrombosis that accompanies severe inflammation.

SUMMARY

Coagulation Factors

- Coagulation occurs via the sequential enzymatic conversion of a cascade of circulating and locally synthesized proteins.
- Tissue factor elaborated at sites of injury is the most important initiator of the coagulation cascade in vivo.
- At the final stage of coagulation, thrombin converts fibrinogen into insoluble fibrin that contributes to formation of the definitive hemostatic plug.
- Coagulation normally is restricted to sites of vascular injury by
  - limiting enzymatic activation to phospholipid surfaces provided by activated platelets or endothelium
  - natural anticoagulants elaborated at sites of endothelial injury or during activation of the coagulation cascade
  - expression of thrombomodulin on normal endothelial cells, which binds thrombin and converts it into an anticoagulant
  - activation of fibrinolytic pathways (e.g., by association of tissue plasminogen activator with fibrin)

Thrombosis

Having reviewed the process of normal hemostasis, we now turn to the three primary *abnormalities that lead to thrombus formation (called Virchow's triad)*: (1) endothelial injury, (2) stasis or turbulent blood flow, and (3) hypercoagulability of the blood (Fig. 3–12).

Endothelial Injury

Endothelial injury is an important cause of thrombosis, particularly in the heart and the arteries, where high flow rates might otherwise impede clotting by preventing platelet adhesion or diluting coagulation factors. Examples of thrombosis related to endothelial damage are the formation of thrombi in the cardiac chambers after myocardial infarction, over ulcerated plaques in atherosclerotic arteries, or at sites of traumatic or inflammatory vascular injury (*vasculitis*). Overt loss of endothelium exposes subendothelial ECM (leading to platelet adhesion), releases tissue factor, and reduces local production of PGI_2 and plasminogen activators. Of note, however, *endothelium need not be denuded or physically disrupted to contribute to the development of thrombosis; any perturbation in the dynamic balance of the prothrombotic and antithrombotic effects of endothelium can influence clotting locally.* Thus, dysfunctional endothelium elaborates greater amounts of procoagulant factors (e.g., platelet adhesion molecules, tissue factor, PAI) and synthesizes lesser amounts of anticoagulant molecules (e.g., thrombomodulin, PGI_2, t-PA). Endothelial dysfunction can be induced by a variety of insults, including hypertension, turbulent blood flow, bacterial products, radiation injury, metabolic abnormalities such as homocystinuria and hypercholesterolemia, and toxins absorbed from cigarette smoke.

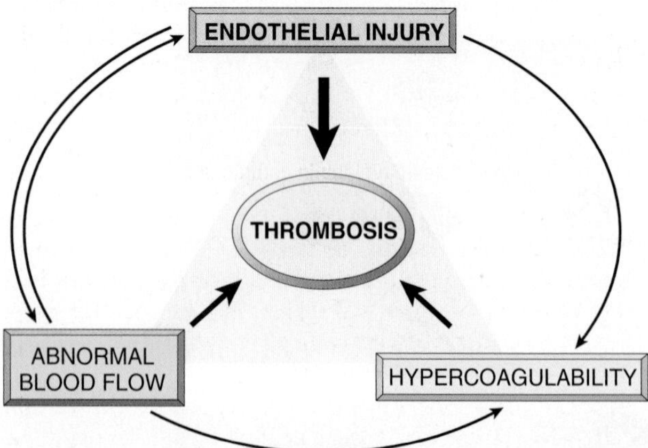

Figure 3–12 Virchow's triad in thrombosis. Endothelial integrity is the most important factor. Abnormalities of procoagulants or anticoagulants can tip the balance in favor of thrombosis. Abnormal blood flow (stasis or turbulence) can lead to hypercoagulability directly and also indirectly through endothelial dysfunction.

Abnormal Blood Flow

Turbulence contributes to arterial and cardiac thrombosis by causing endothelial injury or dysfunction, as well as by forming countercurrents and local pockets of stasis. *Stasis* is a major factor in the development of venous thrombi. Under conditions of normal *laminar* blood flow, platelets (and other blood cells) are found mainly in the center of the vessel lumen, separated from the endothelium by a slower-moving layer of plasma. By contrast, stasis and turbulent (chaotic) blood flow have the following deleterious effects:

- Both promote endothelial cell activation and enhanced procoagulant activity, in part through flow-induced changes in endothelial gene expression.
- Stasis allows platelets and leukocytes to come into contact with the endothelium when the flow is sluggish.
- Stasis also slows the washout of activated clotting factors and impedes the inflow of clotting factor inhibitors.

Turbulent and static blood flow contribute to thrombosis in a number of clinical settings. Ulcerated atherosclerotic plaques not only expose subendothelial ECM but also cause turbulence. Abnormal aortic and arterial dilations called *aneurysms* create local stasis and consequently a fertile site for thrombosis (Chapter 9). Acute myocardial infarction results in focally noncontractile myocardium. Ventricular remodeling after more remote infarction can lead to aneurysm formation. In both cases, cardiac mural thrombi are more easily formed due to the local blood stasis (Chapter 10). Mitral valve stenosis (e.g., after rheumatic heart disease) results in left atrial dilation. In conjunction with atrial fibrillation, a dilated atrium is a site of profound stasis and a prime location for the development of thrombi. *Hyperviscosity syndromes* (such as *polycythemia*) (Chapter 11) increase resistance to flow and cause small vessel stasis; the deformed red cells in sickle cell anemia (Chapter 11) cause vascular occlusions, and the resultant stasis also predisposes to thrombosis.

Hypercoagulability

Hypercoagulability contributes infrequently to arterial or intracardiac thrombosis but is an important underlying risk factor for venous thrombosis. It is loosely defined as any alteration of the coagulation pathways that predisposes affected persons to thrombosis, and can be divided into primary (genetic) and secondary (acquired) disorders (Table 3-2).

Primary (inherited) hypercoagulability most often is caused by mutations in the factor V and prothrombin genes:

- Approximately 2% to 15% of whites carry a specific factor V mutation (called the Leiden mutation, after the Dutch city where it was first described). The mutation alters an amino acid residue in factor V and renders it resistant to protein C. Thus, an important antithrombotic counter-regulatory mechanism is lost. Heterozygotes carry a 5-fold increased risk for venous thrombosis, with homozygotes having a 50-fold increased risk.
- A single-nucleotide substitution (G to A) in the 3′-untranslated region of the prothrombin gene is a fairly common allele (found in 1% to 2% of the general population). This variant results in increased prothrombin transcription and is associated with a nearly threefold increased risk for venous thromboses.

Table 3–2 Hypercoagulable States

Primary (Genetic)
Common (>1% of the Population)
Factor V mutation (G1691A mutation; factor V Leiden)
Prothrombin mutation (G20210A variant)
5,10-Methylene tetrahydrofolate reductase (homozygous C677T mutation)
Increased levels of factor VIII, IX, or XI or fibrinogen
Rare
Antithrombin III deficiency
Protein C deficiency
Protein S deficiency
Very Rare
Fibrinolysis defects
Homozygous homocystinuria (deficiency of cystathione β-synthetase)
Secondary (Acquired)
High Risk for Thrombosis
Prolonged bed rest or immobilization
Myocardial infarction
Atrial fibrillation
Tissue injury (surgery, fracture, burn)
Cancer
Prosthetic cardiac valves
Disseminated intravascular coagulation
Heparin-induced thrombocytopenia
Antiphospholipid antibody syndrome
Lower Risk for Thrombosis
Cardiomyopathy
Nephrotic syndrome
Hyperestrogenic states (pregnancy and postpartum)
Oral contraceptive use
Sickle cell anemia
Smoking

- Less common primary hypercoagulable states include inherited deficiencies of anticoagulants such as antithrombin III, protein C, or protein S; affected patients typically present with venous thrombosis and recurrent thromboembolism in adolescence or early adult life. Congenitally elevated levels of homocysteine contribute to arterial and venous thromboses (and indeed to the development of atherosclerosis) (Chapter 9).

Although the risk of thrombosis is only mildly increased in heterozygous carriers of factor V Leiden and the prothrombin gene variant, these genetic factors carry added significance for two reasons. First, both abnormal alleles are sufficiently frequent that homozygous and compound heterozygous persons are not uncommon, and these individuals are at much higher risk for thrombosis. More importantly, heterozygous individuals are at higher risk for venous thrombosis in the setting of other acquired risk factors, such as pregnancy, prolonged bed rest, and lengthy airplane flights. Consequently, *inherited causes of hypercoagulability should be considered in young patients (<50 years of age), even when other acquired risk factors are present.*

Secondary (acquired) hypercoagulability is seen in many settings (Table 3–2). In some situations (e.g., cardiac failure or trauma), stasis or vascular injury may be the most important factor. The hypercoagulability associated with oral contraceptive use and the hyperestrogenic state of pregnancy may be related to increased hepatic synthesis of coagulation factors and reduced synthesis of antithrombin III. In disseminated cancers, release of procoagulant tumor products (e.g., mucin from adenocarcinoma) predisposes to thrombosis. The hypercoagulability seen with advancing age has been attributed to increased platelet aggregation and reduced release of PGI_2 from endothelium. Smoking and obesity promote hypercoagulability by unknown mechanisms.

Among the acquired thrombophilic states, two are particularly important clinical problems and deserve special mention:

- *Heparin-induced thrombocytopenic (HIT) syndrome.* This syndrome occurs in up to 5% of patients treated with *unfractionated* heparin (for therapeutic anticoagulation). It is marked by the development of autoantibodies that bind complexes of heparin and platelet membrane protein (platelet factor-4) (Chapter 11). Although the mechanism is unclear, it appears that these antibodies may also bind similar complexes present on platelet and endothelial surfaces, resulting in platelet activation, aggregation, and consumption (hence *thrombocytopenia*), as well as causing endothelial cell injury. The overall result is a *prothrombotic state,* even in the face of heparin administration and low platelet counts. Newer low-molecular-weight *fractionated* heparin preparations induce autoantibodies less frequently but can still cause thrombosis if antibodies have already formed.
- *Antiphospholipid antibody syndrome.* This syndrome has protean manifestations, including recurrent thrombosis, repeated miscarriages, cardiac valve vegetations, and thrombocytopenia; it is associated with autoantibodies directed against anionic phospholipids (e.g., cardiolipin) or—more accurately—plasma protein antigens that are unveiled by binding to such phospholipids (e.g., prothrombin). In vivo, these antibodies induce a

hypercoagulable state, perhaps by inducing endothelial injury, by activating platelets or complement directly, or by interacting with the catalytic domains of certain coagulation factors. In vitro (in the absence of platelets and endothelium), however, the antibodies interfere with phospholipid complex assembly, thereby inhibiting coagulation (hence the designation *lupus anticoagulant*). In patients with anticardiolipin antibodies, serologic testing for syphilis will yield a false-positive result, because the antigen in the standard assays is embedded in cardiolipin.

Patients with antiphospholipid antibody syndrome fall into two categories. Many have *secondary antiphospholipid syndrome* due to a well-defined autoimmune disease, such as systemic lupus erythematosus (Chapter 4). The remainder of these patients exhibit only the manifestations of a hypercoagulable state without evidence of another autoimmune disorder (*primary antiphospholipid syndrome*). Although antiphospholipid antibodies are associated with thrombotic diatheses, they also occur in 5% to 15% of apparently normal persons; the implication is that their presence may be necessary but not sufficient to cause full-blown antiphospholipid antibody syndrome.

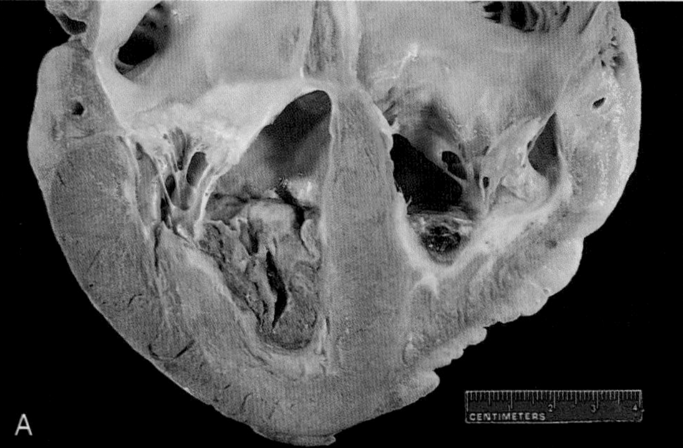

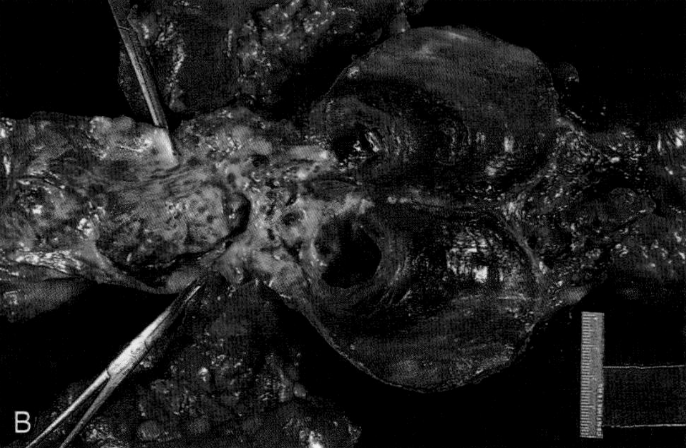

Figure 3–13 Mural thrombi. **A,** Thrombus in the left and right ventricular apices, overlying white fibrous scar. **B,** Laminated thrombus in a dilated abdominal aortic aneurysm. Numerous friable mural thrombi are also superimposed on advanced atherosclerotic lesions of the more proximal aorta (*left side of photograph*).

MORPHOLOGY

Thrombi can develop anywhere in the cardiovascular system. Arterial or cardiac thrombi typically arise at sites of endothelial injury or turbulence; venous thrombi characteristically occur at sites of stasis. Thrombi are focally attached to the underlying vascular surface and tend to propagate **toward** the heart; thus, arterial thrombi grow in a retrograde direction from the point of attachment, while venous thrombi extend in the direction of blood flow. The propagating portion of a thrombus tends to be poorly attached and therefore prone to fragmentation and migration through the blood as an **embolus.**

Thrombi can have grossly (and microscopically) apparent laminations called **lines of Zahn;** these represent pale platelet and fibrin layers alternating with darker red cell–rich layers. Such lines are significant in that they are only found in thrombi that form in flowing blood; their presence can therefore usually distinguish antemortem thrombosis from the bland nonlaminated clots that form in the postmortem state. Although thrombi formed in the "low-flow" venous system superficially resemble postmortem clots, careful evaluation generally reveals ill-defined laminations.

Thrombi occurring in heart chambers or in the aortic lumen are designated **mural thrombi.** Abnormal myocardial contraction (arrhythmias, dilated cardiomyopathy, or myocardial infarction) or endomyocardial injury (myocarditis, catheter trauma) promote cardiac mural thrombi (Fig. 3–13, *A*), while ulcerated atherosclerotic plaques and aneurysmal dilation promote aortic thrombosis (Fig. 3-13, *B*).

Arterial thrombi are typically relatively rich in platelets, as the processes underlying their development (e.g., endothelial injury) lead to platelet activation. Although usually superimposed on a ruptured atherosclerotic plaque, other vascular injuries (vasculitis, trauma) can also be causal. **Venous thrombi (phlebothrombosis)** frequently propagate some distance toward the heart, forming a long cast within the vessel lumen that is prone to give rise to emboli. An increase in the activity of coagulation factors is involved in the genesis of most venous thrombi, with platelet activation playing a secondary role. Because these thrombi form in the sluggish venous circulation, they tend to contain more enmeshed red cells, leading to the moniker **red,** or **stasis, thrombi.** The veins of the lower extremities are most commonly affected (90% of venous thromboses); however, venous thrombi also can occur in the upper extremities, periprostatic plexus, or ovarian and periuterine veins, and under special circumstances may be found in the dural sinuses, portal vein, or hepatic vein.

At autopsy, **postmortem clots** can sometimes be mistaken for venous thrombi. However, the former are gelatinous and due to red cell settling have a dark red dependent portion and a yellow "chicken fat" upper portion; they also are usually not attached to the underlying vessel wall. By contrast, red thrombi typically are firm, focally attached to vessel walls, and contain gray strands of deposited fibrin.

Thrombi on heart valves are called **vegetations.** Bacterial or fungal blood-borne infections can cause valve damage, leading to the development of large thrombotic masses **(infective endocarditis)** (Chapter 10). Sterile vegetations also can develop on noninfected valves in hypercoagulable states—the lesions of so-called **nonbacterial thrombotic endocarditis** (Chapter 10). Less commonly, sterile, **verrucous endocarditis (Libman-Sacks endocarditis)** can occur in the setting of systemic lupus erythematosus (Chapter 4).

Fate of the Thrombus

If a patient survives an initial thrombotic event, over the ensuing days to weeks the thrombus evolves through some combination of the following four processes:

- *Propagation.* The thrombus enlarges through the accretion of additional platelets and fibrin, increasing the odds of vascular occlusion or embolization.
- *Embolization.* Part or all of the thrombus is dislodged and transported elsewhere in the vasculature.
- *Dissolution.* If a thrombus is newly formed, activation of fibrinolytic factors may lead to its rapid shrinkage and complete dissolution. With older thrombi, extensive fibrin polymerization renders the thrombus substantially more resistant to plasmin-induced proteolysis, and lysis is ineffectual. This acquisition of resistance to lysis has clinical significance, as therapeutic administration of fibrinolytic agents (e.g., t-PA in the setting of acute coronary thrombosis) generally is not effective unless given within a few hours of thrombus formation.
- *Organization and recanalization.* Older thrombi become *organized* by the ingrowth of endothelial cells, smooth muscle cells, and fibroblasts into the fibrin-rich thrombus (Fig. 3–14). In time, capillary channels are formed that—to a limited extent—create conduits along the length of the thrombus, thereby reestablishing the continuity of the original lumen. Further recanalization can sometimes convert a thrombus into a vascularized mass of connective tissue that is eventually incorporated into the wall of the remodeled vessel. Occasionally, instead of organizing, the center of a thrombus undergoes enzymatic digestion, presumably because of the release of lysosomal enzymes from entrapped leukocytes. If bacterial seeding occurs, the contents of degraded thrombi serve as an ideal culture medium, and the resulting infection may weaken the vessel wall, leading to formation of a *mycotic aneurysm* (Chapter 9).

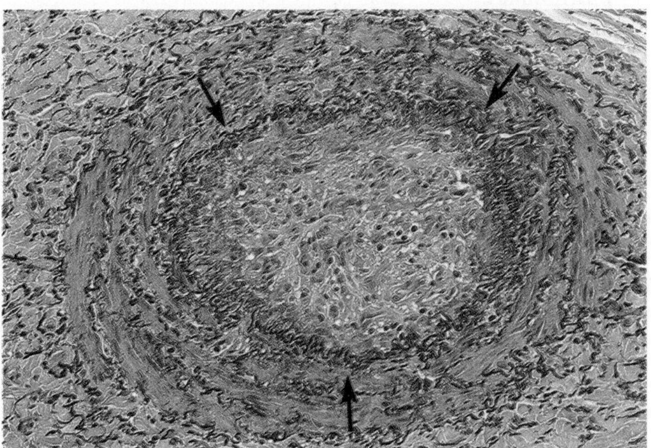

Figure 3–14 Low-power view of a thrombosed artery stained for elastic tissue. The original lumen is delineated by the internal elastic lamina *(arrows)* and is totally filled with organized thrombus.

Clinical Correlation

Thrombi are significant because *they cause obstruction of arteries and veins and may give rise to emboli.* Which effect is of greatest clinical importance depends on the site of thrombosis. Thus, while venous thrombi can cause congestion and edema in vascular beds distal to an obstruction, they are most worrisome because of their potential to embolize to the lungs and cause death. Conversely, while arterial thrombi can embolize and cause tissue infarction, their tendency to obstruct vessels (e.g., in coronary and cerebral vessels) is considerably more important.

Venous Thrombosis (Phlebothrombosis). Most venous thrombi occur in either the superficial or the deep veins of the leg. Superficial venous thrombi usually arise in the saphenous system, particularly in the setting of varicosities; these rarely embolize but can be painful and can cause local congestion and swelling from impaired venous outflow, predisposing the overlying skin to development of infections and *varicose ulcers.* Deep venous thromboses ("DVTs") in the *larger leg veins at or above the knee joint* (e.g., popliteal, femoral, and iliac veins) are more serious because they are prone to embolize. Although such DVTs may cause local pain and edema, the venous obstruction often is circumvented by collateral channels. Consequently, DVTs are entirely asymptomatic in *approximately 50% of patients* and are recognized only after they have embolized to the lungs.

Lower-extremity DVTs are associated with stasis and hypercoagulable states, as described earlier (Table 3–2); thus, common predisposing factors include congestive heart failure, bed rest and immobilization; the latter two factors reduce the milking action of leg muscles and thus slow venous return. Trauma, surgery, and burns not only immobilize a patient but are also associated with vascular injury, procoagulant release, increased hepatic synthesis of coagulation factors, and reduced t-PA production. Many factors contribute to the thrombotic diathesis of pregnancy; besides the potential for amniotic fluid infusion into the circulation at the time of delivery, pressure produced by the enlarging fetus and uterus can produce stasis in the veins of the legs, and late pregnancy and the postpartum period are associated with hypercoagulability. Tumor-associated procoagulant release is largely responsible for the increased risk of thromboembolic phenomena seen in disseminated cancers, which is sometimes referred to as *migratory thrombophlebitis* due to its tendency to transiently involve several different venous beds, or as *Trousseau syndrome,* for Armand Trousseau, who both described the disorder and suffered from it. Regardless of the specific clinical setting, the risk of DVT is increased in persons over age 50.

While the many conditions that predispose to thrombosis are well recognized, the phenomenon remains unpredictable. It occurs at a distressingly high frequency in otherwise healthy and ambulatory people without apparent provocation or underlying abnormality. Equally important is that asymptomatic thrombosis (and presumably subsequent resolution) occurs considerably more frequently than is generally appreciated.

SUMMARY

Thrombosis

- Thrombus development usually is related to one or more components of Virchow's triad:
  - endothelial injury (e.g., by toxins, hypertension, inflammation, or metabolic products)
  - abnormal blood flow, stasis or turbulence (e.g., due to aneurysms, atherosclerotic plaque)
  - hypercoagulability: either primary (e.g., factor V Leiden, increased prothrombin synthesis, antithrombin III deficiency) or secondary (e.g., bed rest, tissue damage, malignancy)
- Thrombi may propagate, resolve, become organized, or embolize.
- Thrombosis causes tissue injury by local vascular occlusion or by distal embolization.

Disseminated Intravascular Coagulation

Disseminated intravascular coagulation (DIC) is the sudden or insidious onset of widespread thrombosis within the microcirculation. It may be seen in disorders ranging from obstetric complications to advanced malignancy. The thrombi are generally microscopic in size, yet so numerous as to often cause circulatory insufficiency, particularly in the brain, lungs, heart, and kidneys. To complicate matters, the widespread microvascular thrombosis consumes platelets and coagulation proteins (hence the synonym *consumption coagulopathy*), and at the same time, fibrinolytic mechanisms are activated. Thus, an initially thrombotic disorder can evolve into a bleeding catastrophe. A point worthy of emphasis is that *DIC is not a primary disease but rather a potential complication of numerous conditions associated with widespread activation of thrombin.* It is discussed in greater detail along with other bleeding diatheses in Chapter 11.

EMBOLISM

An embolus is an intravascular solid, liquid, or gaseous mass that is carried by the blood to a site distant from its point of origin. The vast majority of emboli derive from a dislodged thrombus—hence the term *thromboembolism.* Less common types of emboli include fat droplets, bubbles of air or nitrogen, atherosclerotic debris (*cholesterol emboli*), tumor fragments, bits of bone marrow, and amniotic fluid. Inevitably, emboli lodge in vessels too small to permit further passage, resulting in partial or complete vascular occlusion; depending on the site of origin, emboli can lodge anywhere in the vascular tree. The primary consequence of systemic embolization is ischemic necrosis (*infarction*) of downstream tissues, while embolization in the pulmonary circulation leads to hypoxia, hypotension, and right-sided heart failure.

Pulmonary Thromboembolism

The incidence of pulmonary embolism is 2 to 4 per 1000 hospitalized patients. Although the rate of fatal pulmonary embolus (PE) has declined from 6% to 2% over the last quarter-century, pulmonary embolism still causes about 200,000 deaths per year in the United States. In greater than 95% of cases, venous emboli originate from thrombi within deep leg veins proximal to the popliteal fossa; embolization from lower leg thrombi is uncommon.

Fragmented thrombi from DVTs are carried through progressively larger channels and usually pass through the right side of the heart before arresting in the pulmonary vasculature. Depending on size, a PE can occlude the main pulmonary artery, lodge at the bifurcation of the right and left pulmonary arteries (*saddle embolus*), or pass into the smaller, branching arterioles (Fig. 3–15). Frequently, multiple emboli occur, either sequentially or as a shower of smaller emboli from a single large thrombus; *a patient who has had one pulmonary embolus is at increased risk for having more.* Rarely, an embolus passes through an atrial or ventricular defect and enters the systemic circulation (*paradoxical embolism*). A more complete discussion of PE is found in Chapter 12; the major clinical and pathologic features are the following:

- Most pulmonary emboli (60% to 80%) are small and clinically silent. With time, they undergo organization and become incorporated into the vascular wall; in some cases, organization of thromboemboli leaves behind bridging fibrous *webs.*
- At the other end of the spectrum, a large embolus that blocks a major pulmonary artery can cause sudden death.
- Embolic obstruction of medium-sized arteries and subsequent rupture of capillaries rendered anoxic can cause pulmonary hemorrhage. Such embolization does not usually cause pulmonary infarction since the area also receives blood through an intact bronchial circulation (dual circulation). However, a similar embolus in the setting of left-sided cardiac failure (and diminished bronchial artery perfusion) can lead to a pulmonary infarct.
- Embolism to small end-arteriolar pulmonary branches usually causes infarction.
- Multiple emboli occurring over time can cause pulmonary hypertension and right ventricular failure (cor pulmonale).

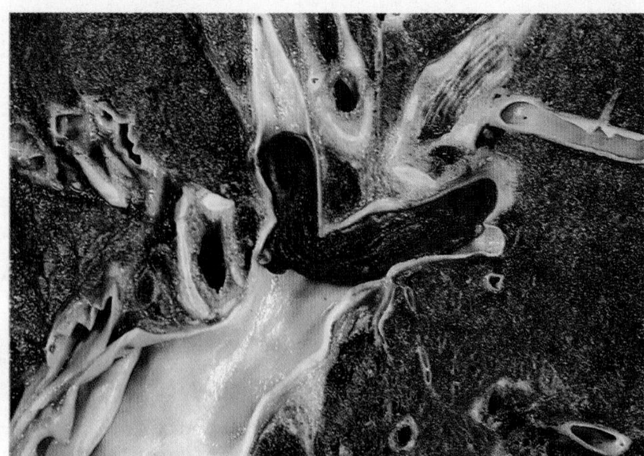

Figure 3–15 Embolus derived from a lower-extremity deep venous thrombus lodged in a pulmonary artery branch.

Systemic Thromboembolism

Most systemic emboli (80%) arise from intracardiac mural thrombi; two thirds are associated with left ventricular infarcts and another 25% with dilated left atria (e.g., secondary to mitral valve disease). The remainder originate from aortic aneurysms, thrombi overlying ulcerated atherosclerotic plaques, fragmented valvular vegetations (Chapter 10), or the venous system (*paradoxical emboli*); 10% to 15% of systemic emboli are of unknown origin.

By contrast with venous emboli, which lodge primarily in the lung, arterial emboli can travel virtually anywhere; their final resting place understandably depends on their point of origin and the relative flow rates of blood to the downstream tissues. Common arteriolar *embolization sites* include the lower extremities (75%) and central nervous system (10%); intestines, kidneys, and spleen are less common targets. The consequences of embolization depend on the caliber of the occluded vessel, the collateral supply, and the affected tissue's vulnerability to anoxia; arterial emboli often lodge in end arteries and cause infarction.

Fat Embolism

Soft tissue crush injury or rupture of marrow vascular sinusoids (long bone fracture) releases microscopic fat globules into the circulation. Fat and marrow emboli are common incidental findings after vigorous cardiopulmonary resuscitation but probably are of little clinical consequence. Similarily, although fat and marrow embolism occurs in some 90% of individuals with severe skeletal injuries (Fig. 3–16, *A*), less than 10% show any clinical findings. However, a minority of patients develop a symptomatic *fat embolism syndrome* characterized by *pulmonary insufficiency, neurologic symptoms, anemia, thrombocytopenia, and a diffuse petechial rash, which is fatal in 10% of cases.* Clinical signs and symptoms appear 1 to 3 days after injury as the sudden onset of tachypnea, dyspnea, tachycardia, irritability, and restlessness, which can progress rapidly to delirium or coma.

The pathogenesis of fat emboli syndrome involves both mechanical obstruction and biochemical injury. Fat microemboli occlude pulmonary and cerebral microvasculature, both directly and by triggering platelet aggregation. This deleterious effect is exacerbated by fatty acid release from lipid globules, which causes local toxic endothelial injury. Platelet activation and granulocyte recruitment (with free radical, protease, and eicosanoid release) (Chapter 2) complete the vascular assault. Because lipids are dissolved by the solvents used during tissue-processing, microscopic demonstration of fat microglobules (i.e., in the absence of accompanying marrow elements) requires specialized techniques (frozen sections and fat stains).

Amniotic Fluid Embolism

Amniotic fluid embolism is an uncommon, grave complication of labor and the immediate postpartum period (1 in 40,000 deliveries). The mortality rate approaches 80%, making it the most common cause of maternal death in the developed world; it accounts for 10% of maternal deaths in the United States, while 85% of survivors suffer some form of permanent neurologic deficit. Onset is characterized by sudden severe dyspnea, cyanosis, and hypotensive shock, followed by seizures and coma. If the patient survives the initial crisis, pulmonary edema typically develops, along with (in about half the patients) disseminated intravascular coagulation secondary to release of thrombogenic substances from amniotic fluid.

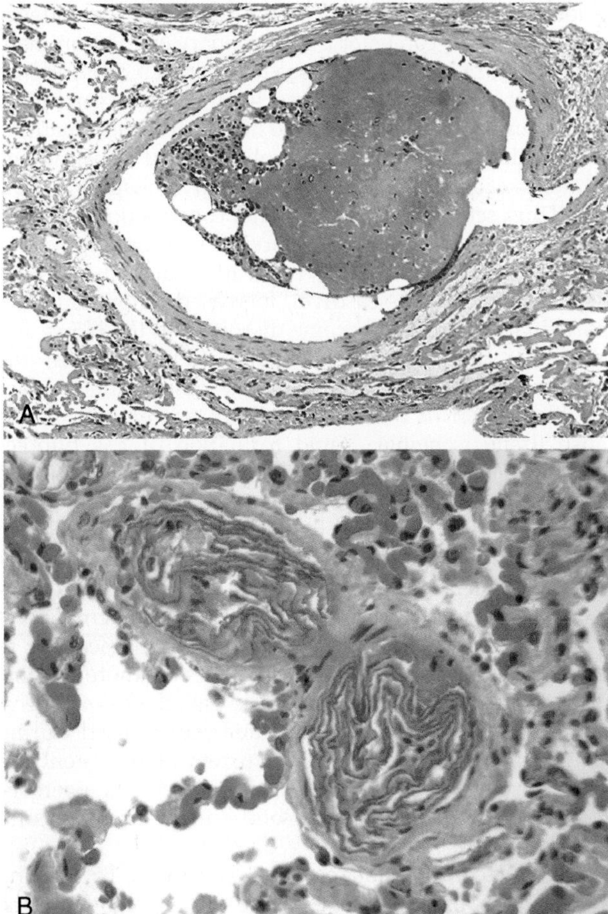

Figure 3–16 Unusual types of emboli. **A,** Bone marrow embolus. The embolus is composed of hematopoietic marrow and marrow fat cells (*clear spaces*) attached to a thrombus. **B,** Amniotic fluid emboli. Two small pulmonary arterioles are packed with laminated swirls of fetal squamous cells. The surrounding lung is edematous and congested.
(Courtesy of Dr. Beth Schwartz, Baltimore, Maryland.)

The underlying cause is entry of amniotic fluid (and its contents) into the maternal circulation via tears in the placental membranes and/or uterine vein rupture. Histologic analysis reveals squamous cells shed from fetal skin, lanugo hair, fat from vernix caseosa, and mucin derived from the fetal respiratory or gastrointestinal tracts in the maternal pulmonary microcirculation (Fig. 13-16, *B*). Other findings include marked pulmonary edema, diffuse alveolar damage (Chapter 12), and systemic fibrin thrombi generated by disseminated intravascular coagulation.

Air Embolism

Gas bubbles within the circulation can coalesce and obstruct vascular flow and cause distal ischemic injury. Thus, a small volume of air trapped in a coronary artery during bypass surgery or introduced into the cerebral arterial circulation by neurosurgery performed in an upright "sitting position" can occlude flow, with dire consequences. Small venous gas emboli generally have no deleterious effects, but sufficient air can enter the pulmonary circulation inadvertently during obstetric procedures or as a consequence of a chest wall injury to cause hypoxia, and very large venous emboli may arrest in the heart and cause death.

A particular form of gas embolism called *decompression sickness* is caused by sudden changes in atmospheric pressure. Thus, scuba divers, underwater construction workers, and persons in unpressurized aircraft who undergo rapid ascent are at risk. When air is breathed at high pressure (e.g., during a deep sea dive), increased amounts of gas (particularly nitrogen) become dissolved in the blood and tissues. If the diver then ascends (depressurizes) too rapidly, the nitrogen expands in the tissues and bubbles out of solution in the blood to form gas emboli, which cause tissue ischemia. Rapid formation of gas bubbles within skeletal muscles and supporting tissues in and about joints is responsible for the painful condition called "the bends" (so named in the 1880s because the afflicted person arches the back in a manner reminiscent of a then-popular women's fashion pose called the *Grecian bend*). Gas bubbles in the pulmonary vasculature cause edema, hemorrhages, and focal atelectasis or emphysema, leading to respiratory distress, the so-called *chokes.* A more chronic form of decompression sickness is called *caisson disease* (named for pressurized underwater vessels used during bridge construction) in which recurrent or persistent gas emboli in the bones lead to multifocal ischemic necrosis; the heads of the femurs, tibiae, and humeri are most commonly affected.

Acute decompression sickness is treated by placing affected persons in a high-pressure chamber, to force the gas back into solution. Subsequent slow decompression permits gradual gas resorption and exhalation so that obstructive bubbles do not re-form.

SUMMARY

Embolism

- An embolus is a solid, liquid, or gaseous mass carried by the blood to a site distant from its origin; most are dislodged thrombi.
- Pulmonary emboli derive primarily from lower-extremity deep vein thrombi; their effects depend mainly on the size of the embolus and the location in which it lodges. Consequences may include right-sided heart failure, pulmonary hemorrhage, pulmonary infarction, or sudden death.
- Systemic emboli derive primarily from cardiac mural or valvular thrombi, aortic aneurysms, or atherosclerotic plaques; whether an embolus causes tissue infarction depends on the site of embolization and the presence or absence of collateral circulation.

INFARCTION

An infarct is an area of ischemic necrosis caused by occlusion of the vascular supply to the affected tissue; the process by which such lesions form termed *infarction,* is a common and extremely important cause of clinical illness. Roughly 40% of all deaths in the United States are a consequence of cardiovascular disease, with most of these deaths stemming from myocardial or cerebral infarction. Pulmonary infarction is a common clinical complication, bowel infarction often is fatal, and ischemic necrosis of distal extremities (*gangrene*) causes substantial morbidity in the diabetic population.

Arterial thrombosis or arterial embolism underlies the vast majority of infarctions. Less common causes of arterial obstruction include vasospasm, expansion of an atheroma secondary to intraplaque hemorrhage, and extrinsic compression of a vessel, such as by tumor, a dissecting aortic aneurysm, or edema within a confined space (e.g., in *anterior tibial compartment syndrome*). Other uncommon causes of tissue infarction include vessel twisting (e.g., in testicular torsion or bowel volvulus), traumatic vascular rupture, and entrapment in a hernia sac. Although venous thrombosis can cause infarction, the more common outcome is simply congestion; typically, bypass channels rapidly open to provide sufficient outflow to restore the arterial inflow. Infarcts caused by venous thrombosis thus usually occur only in organs with a single efferent vein (e.g., testis or ovary).

MORPHOLOGY

Infarcts are classified on the basis of their color (reflecting the amount of hemorrhage) and the presence or absence of microbial infection. Thus, infarcts may be either **red (hemorrhagic)** or **white (anemic)** and may be either **septic** or **bland.**

Red infarcts (Fig. 3–17, *A*) occur (1) with venous occlusions (such as in ovarian torsion); (2) in loose tissues (e.g., lung) where blood can collect in infarcted zones; (3) in tissues with **dual circulations** such as lung and small intestine, where partial, inadequate perfusion by collateral arterial supplies is typical; (4) in previously congested tissues (as a consequence of sluggish venous outflow); and (5) when flow is reestablished after infarction has occurred (e.g., after angioplasty of an arterial obstruction).

White infarcts occur with arterial occlusions in solid organs with end-arterial circulations (e.g., heart, spleen, and kidney), and where tissue density limits the seepage of blood from adjoining patent vascular beds (Fig. 3–17, *B*). Infarcts tend to be wedge-shaped, with the occluded vessel at the apex and the organ periphery forming the base (Fig. 3–17); when the base is a serosal surface, there is often an overlying fibrinous exudate. Lateral margins may be irregular, reflecting flow from adjacent vessels. The margins of acute infarcts typically are indistinct and slightly hemorrhagic; with time, the edges become better defined by a narrow rim of hyperemia attributable to inflammation.

Infarcts resulting from arterial occlusions in organs without a dual circulation typically become progressively paler and sharply defined with time (Fig. 3–17, *B*). By comparison, hemorrhagic infarcts are the rule in the lung and other spongy organs (Fig. 3–17, *A*). Extravasated red cells in hemorrhagic infarcts are phagocytosed by macrophages, and the heme iron is converted to intracellular hemosiderin. Small amounts

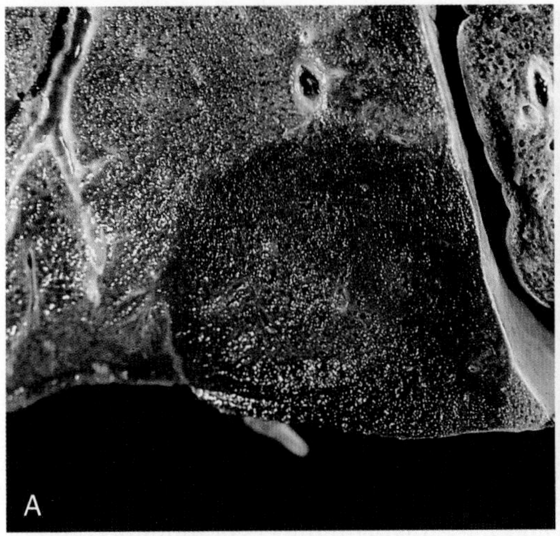

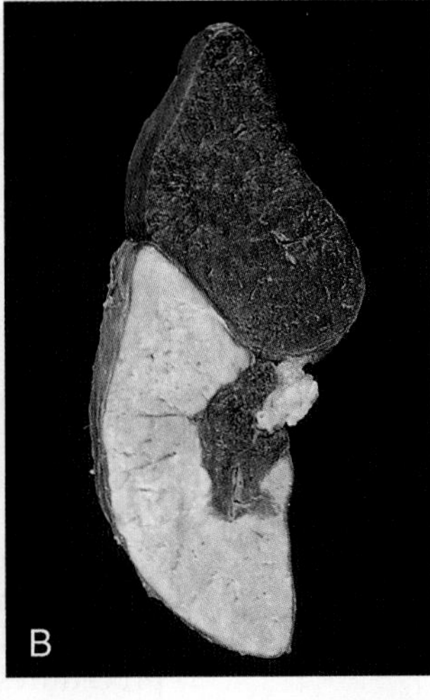

Figure 3–17 Red and white infarcts. **A,** Hemorrhagic, roughly wedge-shaped pulmonary infarct (red infarct). **B,** Sharply demarcated pale infarct in the spleen (white infarct).

do not impart any appreciable color to the tissue, but extensive hemorrhages leave a firm, brown residuum.

In most tissues, the main histologic finding associated with infarcts is **ischemic coagulative necrosis** (Chapter 1). An inflammatory response begins to develop along the margins of infarcts within a few hours and usually is well defined within 1 to 2 days. Eventually, inflammation is followed by repair, beginning in the preserved margins (Chapter 2). In some tissues, parenchymal regeneration can occur at the periphery of the infarct, where the underlying stromal architecture has been spared. Most infarcts, however, are ultimately replaced by scar (Fig. 3–18). The brain is an exception to these generalizations: Ischemic tissue injury in the central nervous system results in **liquefactive necrosis** (Chapter 1).

Septic infarctions occur when infected cardiac valve vegetations embolize, or when microbes seed necrotic tissue. In these cases the infarct is converted into an **abscess,** with a correspondingly greater inflammatory response (Chapter 2).

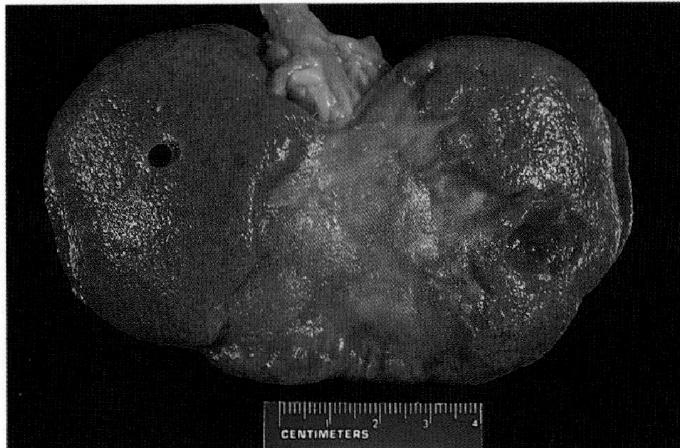

Figure 3–18 Remote kidney infarct, now replaced by a large fibrotic scar.

Factors That Influence Infarct Development. The effects of vascular occlusion range from inconsequential to tissue necrosis leading to organ dysfunction and sometimes death. The range of outcomes is influenced by (1) the anatomy of the vascular supply; (2) the time over which the occlusion develops; (3) the intrinsic vulnerability of the affected tissue to ischemic injury; and (4) the blood oxygen content.

- *Anatomy of the vascular supply.* The presence or absence of an alternative blood supply is the most important factor in determining whether occlusion of an individual vessel causes damage. The dual supply of the lung by the pulmonary and bronchial arteries means that obstruction of the pulmonary arterioles does not cause lung infarction unless the bronchial circulation also is compromised. Similarly, the liver, which receives blood from the hepatic artery and the portal vein, and the hand and forearm, with its parallel radial and ulnar arterial supply, are resistant to infarction. By contrast, the kidney and the spleen both have end-arterial circulations, and arterial obstruction generally leads to infarction in these tissues.
- *Rate of occlusion.* Slowly developing occlusions are less likely to cause infarction because they allow time for the development of collateral blood supplies. For example, small interarteriolar anastomoses, which normally carry minimal blood flow, interconnect the three major coronary arteries. If one coronary artery is slowly occluded (e.g., by encroaching atherosclerotic plaque), flow in this *collateral circulation* may increase sufficiently to prevent infarction—even if the original artery becomes completely occluded.
- *Tissue vulnerability to ischemia.* Neurons undergo irreversible damage when deprived of their blood supply for only 3 to 4 minutes. Myocardial cells, although hardier than neurons, still die after only 20 to 30 minutes of ischemia. By contrast, fibroblasts within myocardium remain viable after many hours of ischemia.
- *Hypoxemia.* Understandably, abnormally low blood O_2 content (regardless of cause) increases both the likelihood and extent of infarction.

SUMMARY

Infarction

- Infarcts are areas of ischemic necrosis most commonly caused by arterial occlusion (typically due to thrombosis or embolization); venous outflow obstruction is a less frequent cause.
- Infarcts caused by venous occlusion or occurring in spongy tissues typically are hemorrhagic (red); those caused by arterial occlusion in compact tissues typically are pale (white).
- Whether or not vascular occlusion causes tissue infarction is influenced by collateral blood supplies, the rate at which an obstruction develops, intrinsic tissue susceptibility to ischemic injury, and blood oxygenation.

SHOCK

Shock is the final common pathway for several potentially lethal events, including exsanguination, extensive trauma or burns, myocardial infarction, pulmonary embolism, and sepsis. Regardless of cause, *shock is characterized by systemic hypoperfusion of tissues; it can be caused by diminished cardiac output or by reduced effective circulating blood volume.* The consequences are *impaired tissue perfusion and cellular hypoxia.* Although shock initially is reversible, prolonged shock eventually leads to irreversible tissue injury that often proves fatal.

The most common forms of shock can be grouped into three pathogenic categories (Table 3–3):

- *Cardiogenic shock* results from low cardiac output due to myocardial pump failure. It may be caused by myocardial damage (infarction), ventricular arrhythmias, extrinsic compression (cardiac tamponade) (Chapter 10), or outflow obstruction (e.g., pulmonary embolism).
- *Hypovolemic shock* results from low cardiac output due to loss of blood or plasma volume (e.g., due to hemorrhage or fluid loss from severe burns).
- *Septic shock* results from arterial vasodilation and venous blood pooling that stems from the systemic immune response to microbial infection. Its complex pathogenesis is discussed in greater detail next.

Less commonly, shock can result from loss of vascular tone associated with anesthesia or secondary to a spinal cord injury (*neurogenic shock*). *Anaphylactic shock* results from systemic vasodilation and increased vascular permeability that is triggered by an immunoglobulin E–mediated hypersensitivity reaction (Chapter 4).

Pathogenesis of Septic Shock

Despite medical advances over the past several decades, septic shock remains a daunting clinical problem. Septic shock kills 20% of its victims, accounts for over 200,000 deaths annually in the United States, and is the number one cause of mortality in intensive care units. The incidence is rising, ironically, in part because of improved life support for critically ill patients, as well as an increase in invasive procedures and the growing numbers of immunocompromised patients (due to chemotherapy, immunosuppression, or HIV infection).

In septic shock, systemic arterial and venous dilation leads to tissue hypoperfusion, even though cardiac output is preserved or even initially increased. The decreased vascular tone is accompanied by widespread endothelial cell activation, often triggering a hypercoagulable state manifesting as disseminated intravascular coagulation. In addition, septic shock is associated with perturbations of metabolism that directly suppress cell and tissue function. *The net effect of these abnormalities is hypoperfusion and dysfunction of multiple organs.*

At present, gram-positive bacteria constitute the most common cause of septic shock, followed by gram-negative organisms and fungi. Although it was for a time thought that infections had to be disseminated to cause septic shock, infections localized to a specific tissue can trigger sepsis, even without detectable spread to the bloodstream. The ability of diverse flora to precipitate septic shock is consistent with the idea that several different microbial constituents can initiate the process. Most notably, macrophages, neutrophils, dendritic cells, endothelial cells, as well as soluble components of the innate immune system (e.g., complement) recognize and are activated by a variety of substances derived from microorganisms. Once activated, these cells and soluble factors initiate a number of inflammatory responses that interact in a complex, incompletely understood fashion to produce septic shock (Fig. 3–19). As an aside, a similar widespread inflammatory

Table 3–3 Three Major Types of Shock

Type of Shock	Clinical Examples	Principal Pathogenic Mechanisms
Cardiogenic	Myocardial infarction Ventricular rupture Arrhythmia Cardiac tamponade Pulmonary embolism	Failure of myocardial pump resulting from intrinsic myocardial damage, extrinsic pressure, or obstruction to outflow
Hypovolemic	Hemorrhage Fluid loss (e.g., vomiting, diarrhea, burns, trauma)	Inadequate blood or plasma volume
Septic	Overwhelming microbial infections Endotoxic shock Gram-positive septicemia Fungal sepsis Superantigens (e.g., toxic shock syndrome)	Peripheral vasodilation and pooling of blood; endothelial activation/injury; leukocyte-induced damage; disseminated intravascular coagulation; activation of cytokine cascades

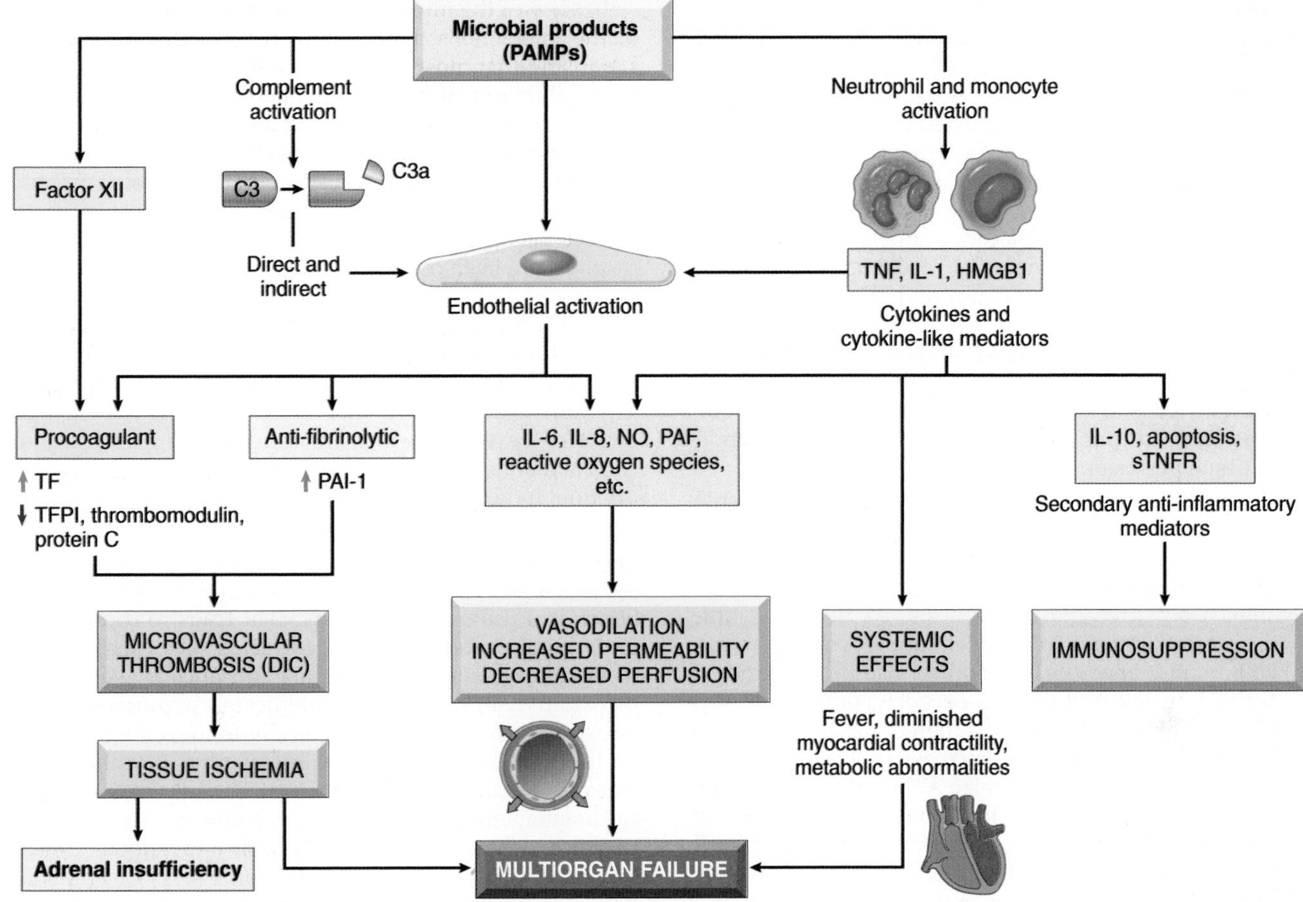

Figure 3–19 Major pathogenic pathways in septic shock. Microbial products activate endothelial cells and cellular and humoral elements of the innate immune system, initiating a cascade of events that lead to end-stage multiorgan failure. Additional details are given in the text. DIC, disseminated intravascular coagulation; HMGB1, high-mobility group box 1 protein; NO, nitric oxide; PAF, platelet-activating factor; PAI-1, plasminogen activator inhibitor-1; PAMP, pathogen-associated molecular pattern; STNFR, soluble tumor necrosis factor receptor; TF, tissue factor; TFPI, tissue factor pathway inhibitor.

response—the so-called *systemic inflammatory response syndrome (SIRS)*—can also be triggered in the absence of any apparent underlying infection; causes include extensive trauma or burns, pancreatitis, and diffuse ischemia.

Factors contributing to the pathophysiology of septic shock include the following:

- *Inflammatory mediators.* Cells of the innate immune system express receptors (e.g., Toll-like receptors [TLRs]) (Chapter 2) that recognize a host of microbe-derived substances containing so-called *pathogen-associated molecular patterns* (PAMPs). *Activation of pathogen recognition receptors by PAMPs triggers the innate immune responses that drive sepsis.* Upon activation, the inflammatory cells produce TNF and IL-1 (and other cytokines), plus cytokine-like mediators such as high-mobility group box 1 (HMGB1). Reactive oxygen species and lipid mediators such as prostaglandins and platelet-activating factor (PAF) also are elaborated (Chapter 2). These effector molecules activate endothelial cells, resulting in expression of adhesion molecules, a procoagulant phenotype, and secondary waves of cytokine production. The *complement cascade* also is activated by microbial components, both directly and through the proteolytic activity of plasmin (Chapter 2), resulting in the production of anaphylotoxins (C3a, C5a), chemotaxic fragments (C5a), and opsonins (C3b), all of which can contribute to the pro-inflammatory state.
- *Endothelial cell activation and injury.* Endothelial activation by microbial constituents or inflammatory cell mediators has three major sequelae: (1) thrombosis; (2) increased vascular permeability; and (3) vasodilation.

The derangement in coagulation is sufficient to produce the formidable complication of disseminated intravascular coagulation in up to half of septic patients. Sepsis alters the expression of many factors ultimately favoring coagulation. Pro-inflammatory cytokines result in increased tissue factor production, while at the same time dampening fibrinolysis by increasing PAI expression. The production of other endothelial anticoagulant factors, such as tissue factor pathway inhibitor, thrombomodulin, and protein C, is also diminished. The procoagulant tendency is further enhanced by decreased blood flow within small vessels, which produces stasis and diminishes the washout of activated coagulation factors. Acting in concert, these effects promote the systemic deposition of fibrin-rich thrombi in small vessels, thus exacerbating tissue hypoperfusion. In full-blown disseminated intravascular coagulation, there is also *consumption* of clotting factors and platelets, leading to concomitant bleeding and hemorrhage (Chapter 11).

The pro-inflammatory state associated with sepsis leads to widespread vascular leakage and tissue edema, with deleterious effects on both nutrient delivery and waste removal. It appears that inflammatory cytokines loosen endothelial cell tight junctions by causing the adhesion molecule VE-cadherin to be displaced from the junctions. The altered junctions become leaky, resulting in the accumulation of protein-rich exudates and edema throughout the body.

Expression of vasoactive inflammatory mediators (e.g., C3a, C5a, PAF), together with increased NO production, leads to systemic relaxation of vascular smooth muscle, producing hypotension and further reductions in tissue perfusion.

- *Metabolic abnormalities.* Septic patients exhibit insulin resistance and hyperglycemia. Cytokines such as TNF and IL-1, stress-induced hormones (such as glucagon, growth hormone, and glucocorticoid), and catecholamines all drive gluconeogenesis. At the same time, the pro-inflammatory cytokines suppress insulin release while simultaneously promoting insulin resistance in skeletal muscle and other tissues. Hyperglycemia suppresses neutrophil function—thereby decreasing bactericidal activity—and causes increased adhesion molecule expression on endothelial cells. Although sepsis initially is associated with a surge in glucocorticoid production, this increase is frequently followed by adrenal insufficiency and a relative glucocorticoid deficit. This effect may stem from depression of the synthetic capacity of adrenal glands or frank adrenal necrosis due to disseminated intravascular coagulation (*Waterhouse-Friderichsen syndrome*) (Chapter 19).
- *Immune suppression.* The hyperinflammatory state initiated by sepsis can paradoxically lead to a state of immunosuppression. Proposed mechanisms include production of anti-inflammatory mediators (e.g., soluble TNF receptor and IL-1 receptor antagonist), and widespread apoptosis of lymphocytes in the spleen and lymph nodes, the cause of which is uncertain. It is still debated whether immunosuppressive mediators are deleterious or protective in sepsis.
- *Organ dysfunction.* Systemic hypotension, increased vascular permeability, tissue edema, and small vessel thrombosis all decrease the delivery of oxygen and nutrients to the tissues and contribute to organ dysfunction. High levels of cytokines and secondary mediators can reduce myocardial contractility, thereby blunting cardiac output; increased vascular permeability and endothelial injury in the pulmonary circulation lead to the *acute respiratory distress syndrome* (ARDS) (Chapter 13). Ultimately, these factors conspire to cause multiorgan failure, particularly of the kidneys, liver, lungs, and heart, culminating in death.

Outcomes in patients with septic shock are difficult to predict; in general those with widespread infections and comorbid diseases have the highest mortality rates, but even young healthy individuals with virulent infections (e.g., meningococcal sepsis) can succumb within hours.

In view of the multiplicity of factors and the complexity of the interactions that underlie sepsis, it is perhaps not surprising that most attempts to intervene therapeutically with inhibitors of specific mediators have been of very modest benefit at best. The standard of care remains treatment with appropriate antibiotics, intensive insulin therapy for hyperglycemia, fluid resuscitation to maintain systemic pressures, and "physiologic doses" of corticosteroids to correct relative adrenal insufficiency. Some promising results have been observed in models of sepsis with treatments directed at restoring endothelial cell integrity.

An additional group of secreted bacterial proteins called *superantigens* also cause a syndrome similar to septic shock (e.g., *toxic shock syndrome*). Superantigens are polyclonal T-lymphocyte activators that induce T cells to release high levels of cytokines, which in turn results in a variety of clinical manifestations, ranging from a diffuse rash to vasodilation, hypotension, and death.

Stages of Shock

Shock is a progressive disorder that leads to death if the underlying problems are not corrected. The exact mechanisms of sepsis-related death are still unclear; aside from increased lymphocyte and enterocyte apoptosis, cellular necrosis is minimal. Death typically follows the failure of multiple organs, which usually offer no morphological clues to explain their dysfunction. For hypovolemic and cardiogenic shock, however, the pathways leading to a patient's demise are reasonably well understood. Unless the insult is massive and rapidly lethal (e.g., exsanguination from a ruptured aortic aneurysm), shock tends to evolve through three general (albeit somewhat artificial) stages. These stages have been documented most clearly in hypovolemic shock but are common to other forms as well:

- An initial *nonprogressive stage,* during which reflex compensatory mechanisms are activated and vital organ perfusion is maintained
- A *progressive stage,* characterized by tissue hypoperfusion and onset of worsening circulatory and metabolic derangement, including acidosis
- An *irreversible stage,* in which cellular and tissue injury is so severe that even if the hemodynamic defects are corrected, survival is not possible

In the early nonprogressive phase of shock, various *neurohumoral mechanisms* help maintain cardiac output and blood pressure. These mechanisms include baroreceptor reflexes, release of catecholamines and antidiuretic hormone, activation of the renin-angiotensin-aldersterone axis, and generalized sympathetic stimulation. The net effect is *tachycardia, peripheral vasoconstriction,* and *renal fluid conservation;* cutaneous vasoconstriction causes the characteristic "shocky" skin coolness and pallor (notably, septic shock can initially cause cutaneous *vasodilation,* so the patient may present with *warm, flushed skin*). Coronary and cerebral vessels are less sensitive to sympathetic signals and maintain relatively normal caliber, blood flow, and oxygen delivery. Thus, blood is shunted away from the skin to the vital organs such as the heart and the brain.

If the underlying causes are not corrected, shock passes imperceptibly to the progressive phase, which as noted is characterized by widespread tissue hypoxia. In the setting of persistent oxygen deficit, intracellular aerobic respiration is replaced by anaerobic glycolysis with excessive production of lactic acid. The resultant metabolic *lactic acidosis lowers the tissue pH, which blunts the vasomotor response*; arterioles dilate, and blood begins to pool in the microcirculation. Peripheral pooling not only worsens the cardiac output but also puts endothelial cells at risk for the development of anoxic injury with subsequent DIC. With widespread tissue hypoxia, vital organs are affected and begin to fail.

In the absence of appropriate intervention, the process eventually enters an irreversible stage. Widespread cell injury is reflected in lysosomal enzyme leakage, further aggravating the shock state. Myocardial contractile function worsens, in part because of increased nitric oxide synthesis. The ischemic bowel may allow intestinal flora to enter the circulation, and thus bacteremic shock may be superimposed. Commonly, further progression to renal failure occurs as a consequence of ischemic injury of the kidney (Chapter 13), and despite the best therapeutic interventions, the downward spiral frequently culminates in death.

MORPHOLOGY

The cellular and tissue effects of shock are essentially those of hypoxic injury (Chapter 1) and are caused by a combination of **hypoperfusion and microvascular thrombosis.** Although any organ can be affected, brain, heart, kidneys, adrenals, and gastrointestinal tract are most commonly involved. **Fibrin thrombi** can form in any tissue but typically are most readily visualized in kidney glomeruli. **Adrenal cortical cell lipid depletion** is akin to that seen in all forms of stress and reflects increased utilization of stored lipids for steroid synthesis. While the lungs are resistant to hypoxic injury in hypovolemic shock occurring after hemorrhage, sepsis or trauma can precipitate diffuse alveolar damage (Chapter 12), leading to so-called **shock lung.** Except for neuronal and cardiomyocyte loss, affected tissues can recover completely if the patient survives.

Clinical Course

The clinical manifestations of shock depend on the precipitating insult. In hypovolemic and cardiogenic shock, patients exhibit hypotension, a weak rapid pulse, tachypnea, and cool, clammy, cyanotic skin. As already noted, in septic shock, the skin may be warm and flushed owing to peripheral vasodilation. The primary threat to life is the underlying initiating event (e.g., myocardial infarction, severe hemorrhage, bacterial infection). However, the cardiac, cerebral, and pulmonary changes rapidly aggravate the situation. If patients survive the initial period, worsening renal function can provoke a phase dominated by progressive oliguria, acidosis, and electrolyte imbalances.

Prognosis varies with the origin of shock and its duration. Thus, more than 90% of young, otherwise healthy patients with hypovolemic shock survive with appropriate management; by comparison, septic or cardiogenic shock is associated with substantially worse outcomes, even with state-of-the-art care.

SUMMARY

Shock

- Shock is defined as a state of systemic tissue hypoperfusion due to reduced cardiac output and/or reduced effective circulating blood volume.
- The major types of shock are cardiogenic (e.g., myocardial infarction), hypovolemic (e.g., blood loss), and septic (e.g., infections).
- Shock of any form can lead to hypoxic tissue injury if not corrected.
- Septic shock is caused by the host response to bacterial or fungal infections; it is characterized by endothelial cell activation, vasodilation, edema, disseminated intravascular coagulation, and metabolic derangements.

BIBLIOGRAPHY

Akhtar S: Fat embolism. Anesthesiol Clin 27:533, 2009. *[Recent overview of the pathogenesis and clinical issues in fat embolism syndrome.]*

Coppola A, Tufano A, Cerbone AM, Di Minno G: Inherited thrombophilia: implications for prevention and treatment of venous thromboembolism. Semin Thromb Hemost 35:683, 2009. *[Review of the genetic underpinnings of hypercoagulable states in a volume of the journal devoted to various aspects of thrombophilia.]*

Crawley J et al: The central role of thrombin in hemostasis. J Thromb Haemost 5 (Suppl 1):95, 2007. *[Review of the various pathways impacted by thrombin activation.]*

Crawley J, Lane D: The haemostatic role of tissue factor pathway inhibitor. Arterioscler Thromb Vasc Biol 28:233, 2008. *[Summary of the physiologic roles of TFPI.]*

Cushman M: Epidemiology and risk factors for venous thrombosis. Semin Hematol 44:62, 2007. *[Overview of the risk factors and pathophysiology of venous clotting.]*

Dahlback B: Blood coagulation and its regulation by anticoagulant pathways: genetic pathogenesis of bleeding and thrombotic diseases. J Intern Med 257:209, 2005. *[Although slightly older, this is a good one-stop review on normal and abnormal hemostasis.]*

Esmon CT, Esmon NL: The link between vascular features and thrombosis. Annu Rev Physiol 2011. *[Up-to-date review of the interactions of endothelium, blood flow, and hemostasis/thrombosis.]*

Goldhaber SZ: Advanced treatment strategies for acute pulmonary embolism, including thrombolysis and embolectomy. J Thromb Haemost 7(Suppl 1):322, 2009. *[Up-to-date guide to the recognition and therapy of pulmonary embolism.]*

Holy EW, Tanner FC: Tissue factor in cardiovascular disease pathophysiology and pharmacological intervention. Adv Pharmacol 59:259, 2010. *[Comprehensive review of the roles of tissue factor in hemostasis and potential pathways to be exploited in preventing pathologic thrombosis.]*

Hong MS, Amanullah AM: Heparin-induced thrombocytopenia: a practical review. Rev Cardiovasc Med 11:13, 2010. *[As characterized by the title, a good, practical review of the mechanisms and therapies for heparin-induced thrombocytopenia.]*

Hotchkiss R, Karl I: The pathophysiology and treatment of sepsis. N Engl J Med 348:138, 2003. *[Although an older paper, this is extremely well-written, and lays a solid pathogenic foundation for the pathways underlying sepsis.]*

Jennings LK: Mechanisms of platelet activation: need for new strategies to protect against platelet-mediated atherothrombosis. Thromb Haemost 102:248, 2009. *[Excellent and current review of the roles played by platelets in thrombosis and inflammation, as well as possible targets for therapeutic intervention.]*

Kwaan HC, Samama MM: The significance of endothelial heterogeneity in thrombosis and hemostasis. Semin Thromb Hemost 36:286, 2010. *[Review with newer data regarding the influence of endothelium on hemostasis and thrombosis.]*

Mackman N, Tilley RE, Key NS: Role of the extrinsic pathway of blood coagulation in hemostasis and thrombosis. Arterioscler Thromb Vasc Biol 27:1687, 2007. *[Good general overview of fundamental pathways in coagulation.]*

Montagnana M, Franchi M, Danese E, et al: Disseminated intravascular coagulation in obstetric and gynecologic disorders. Semin Thromb Hemost 36:404, 2010. *[Review of the mechanisms of DIC, and a good discussion of the pathophysiology of amniotic fluid embolism.]*

Munford RS: Severe sepsis and septic shock: the role of gram-negative bacteremia. Annu Rev Pathol 1:467, 2006. *[An interesting and provocative view regarding the pathogenesis of septic shock.]*

Osinbowale O, Ali L, Chi YW: Venous thromboembolism: a clinical review. Postgrad Med 122:54, 2010. *[Good review at a medical student/house officer level.]*

Stearns-Kurosawa DJ, Osuchowski MF, Valentine C, et al: The pathogenesis of sepsis. Ann Rev Pathol Mech Dis 6:19, 2011. *[Good update on some of the newer approaches to understanding and therapeutically targeting sepsis.]*

Rijken DC, Lijnen HR: New insights into the molecular mechanisms of the fibrinolytic system. J Thromb Haemost 7:4, 2009. *[Excellent review of fibrinolytic pathways.]*

Ruiz-Irastorza G, Crowther M, Branch W, Khamashta MA: Antiphospholipid syndrome. Lancet 376:1498, 2010. *[Good summary of the anti-phospholipid syndrome with emphasis on diagnosis and therapeutics.]*

Wu KK, Matijevic-Aleksic N: Molecular aspects of thrombosis and antithrombotic drugs. Crit Rev Clin Lab Sci 42:249, 2005. *[Lengthy, thorough overview of the mechanisms of thrombus formation with emphasis on targets for therapeutic intervention.]*

Zwicker J, Furie BC, Furie B: Cancer-associated thrombosis. Crit Rev Oncol Hematol 62:126, 2007. *[Thorough review of the mechanisms underlying the hypercoagulable state of malignancy.]*

See Targeted Therapy available online at
studentconsult.com

CHAPTER 4

Diseases of the Immune System

CHAPTER CONTENTS

Immunity refers to protection against infections, and the immune system is the collection of cells and molecules that are responsible for defending the body against the countless pathogenic microbes in the environment. Deficiencies in immune defenses result in an increased susceptibility to infections, which can be life-threatening if the deficits are not corrected. On the other hand, the immune system is itself capable of causing great harm and is the root cause of some of the most vexing and intractable diseases of the modern world. Thus, diseases of immunity range from those caused by "too little" to those caused by "too much or inappropriate" immune activity.

This chapter starts with a brief review of some of the basic concepts of lymphocyte biology and normal immune responses, which establishes a foundation for the subsequent discussions of diseases caused by excessive or inappropriate immune responses, rejection of organ transplants and immune deficiency disorders. The chapter concludes with a discussion of amyloidosis, a disease characterized by the abnormal extracellular deposition of certain proteins (some of which are produced in the setting of immune responses).

INNATE AND ADAPTIVE IMMUNITY

Defense against microbes consists of two types of reactions (Fig. 4–1). *Innate immunity* (also called natural, or native, immunity) is mediated by cells and proteins that are always present and poised to fight against microbes, being called into action immediately in response to infection. The major components of innate immunity are epithelial barriers of the skin, gastrointestinal tract, and respiratory tract, which prevent microbe entry; phagocytic leukocytes (neutrophils and macrophages); a specialized cell type called the natural killer (NK) cell; and several circulating plasma proteins, the most important of which are the proteins of the complement system.

The innate immune response is able to prevent and control many infections. However, many pathogenic microbes have evolved to overcome the early defenses, and protection against these infections requires the more specialized and powerful mechanisms of *adaptive immunity* (also called acquired, or specific, immunity). Adaptive immunity is normally silent and responds (or "adapts") to

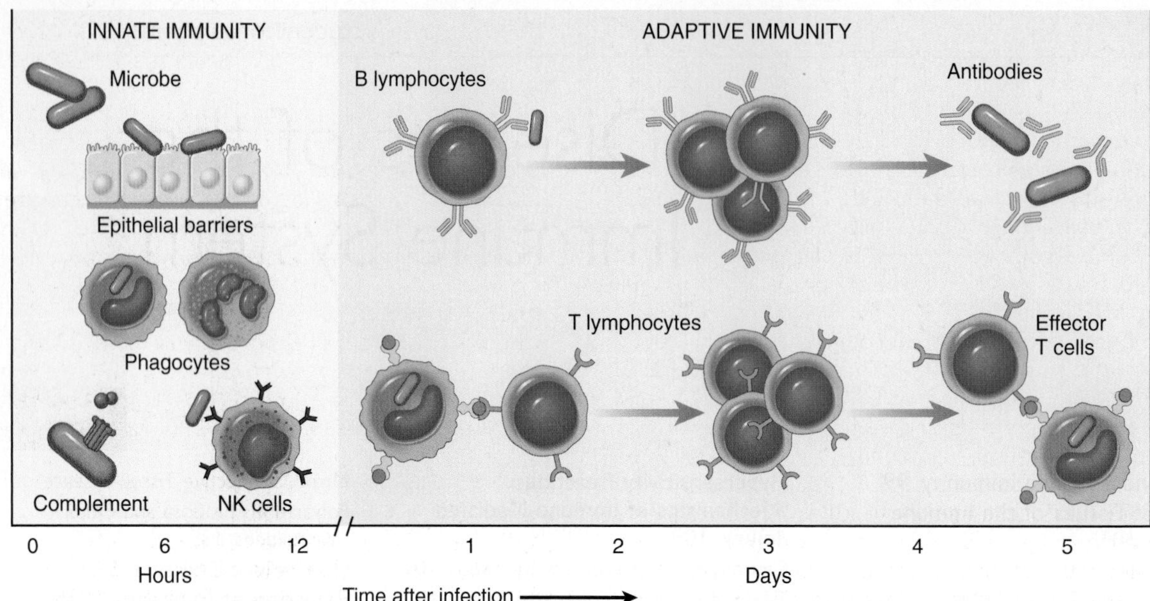

Figure 4–1 The principal mechanisms of innate immunity and adaptive immunity. NK, natural killer.

the presence of infectious microbes by becoming active, expanding, and generating potent mechanisms for neutralizing and eliminating the microbes. *The components of the adaptive immune system are lymphocytes and their products.* By convention, the terms "immune system" and "immune response" refer to adaptive immunity.

There are two types of adaptive immune responses: humoral immunity, mediated by soluble proteins called antibodies that are produced by B lymphocytes (also called B cells), and cell-mediated (or cellular) immunity, mediated by T lymphocytes (also called T cells). Antibodies provide protection against extracellular microbes in the blood, mucosal secretions, and tissues. T lymphocytes are important in defense against intracellular microbes. They work by either directly killing infected cells (accomplished by cytotoxic T lymphocytes) or by activating phagocytes to kill ingested microbes, via the production of soluble protein mediators called cytokines (made by helper T cells). The main properties and functions of the cells of the immune system are described in the next section.

When the immune system is inappropriately triggered or not properly controlled, the same mechanisms that are involved in host defense cause tissue injury and disease. The reaction of the cells of innate and adaptive immunity may be manifested as *inflammation.* As discussed in Chapter 2, inflammation is a beneficial process, but it is also the basis for many human diseases. Presented later in this chapter is an overview of the ways in which the adaptive immune response triggers pathologic inflammatory reactions.

CELLS AND TISSUES OF THE IMMUNE SYSTEM

The cells of the immune system consist of lymphocytes, which recognize antigens and mount adaptive immune responses; specialized antigen-presenting cells (APCs), which capture and display microbial and other antigens to the lymphocytes; and various effector cells, whose function is to eliminate microbes and other antigens. Two remarkable features of the immune system are the specialization of the cells to perform diverse functions, and the precise control mechanisms that permit useful responses when needed and prevent potentially harmful ones.

Lymphocytes

Lymphocytes are present in the circulation and in various lymphoid organs. Although all lymphocytes appear morphologically identical, there are actually several functionally and phenotypically distinct lymphocyte populations. Lymphocytes develop from precursors in the generative lymphoid organs; T lymphocytes are so called because they mature in the thymus, whereas B lymphocytes mature in the bone marrow. Each T or B lymphocyte expresses receptors for a single antigen, and the total population of lymphocytes (numbering about 10^{12} in humans) is capable of recognizing tens or hundreds of millions of antigens. This enormous diversity of antigen recognition is generated by the somatic rearrangement of antigen receptor genes during lymphocyte maturation, and variations that are introduced during the joining of different gene segments to form antigen receptors. These antigen receptors are rearranged and expressed in lymphocytes but not in any other cell. Therefore, the demonstration of antigen receptor gene rearrangements by molecular methods (e.g., polymerase chain reaction [PCR] assay) is a definitive marker of T or B lymphocytes. Because each lymphocyte has a unique DNA rearrangement (and hence a unique antigen receptor), molecular analysis of the rearrangements in cell populations can distinguish polyclonal (non-neoplastic) lymphocyte proliferations from monoclonal (neoplastic) expansions. Such analyses are used in the diagnosis of lymphoid malignancies (Chapter 11).

T Lymphocytes

Thymus-derived, or T, lymphocytes are the effector cells of cellular immunity and the "helper cells" for antibody responses to protein antigens. T cells constitute 60% to 70% of the lymphocytes in peripheral blood and are the major lymphocyte population in splenic periarteriolar sheaths and lymph node interfollicular zones. T cells do not detect free or circulating antigens. Instead, the vast majority (greater than 95%) of T cells recognize only peptide fragments of protein antigens bound to proteins of the major histocompatibility complex (MHC). The MHC was discovered on the basis of studies of graft rejection and acceptance (tissue, or "histo," compatibility). It is now known that *the normal function of MHC molecules is to display peptides for recognition by T lymphocytes.* By forcing T cells to see MHC-bound peptides on cell surfaces the system ensures that T cells can recognize antigens displayed by other cells. T cells function by interacting with other cells—either to kill infected cells or to activate phagocytes or B lymphocytes that have ingested protein antigens. In each person, T cells recognize only peptides displayed by that person's MHC molecules, which, of course, are the only MHC molecules that the T cells normally encounter. This phenomenon is called MHC restriction. Peptide antigens presented by self MHC molecules are recognized by the T cell receptor (TCR), which is a heterodimer composed of disulfide-linked α and β protein chains (Fig. 4–2, *A*); each chain has a variable region that participates in binding a particular peptide antigen and a constant region that interacts with associated signaling molecules.

TCRs are noncovalently linked to a cluster of five invariant polypeptide chains, the γ, δ, and ε proteins of the CD3 molecular complex and two ζ chains (Fig. 4-2, *A*). The CD3 proteins and ζ chains do not themselves bind antigens; instead, they are attached to the TCR and deliver intracellular biochemical signals after TCR recognition of antigen. In addition to these signaling proteins, T cells express a number of other invariant molecules that serve diverse functions. CD4 and CD8 are expressed on distinct T cell subsets and serve as coreceptors for T cell activation. During antigen recognition, CD4 molecules on T cells bind to invariant portions of class II MHC molecules (see later) on selected APCs; in an analogous fashion, CD8 binds to class I MHC molecules. CD4 is expressed on 50%–60% of mature T cells, whereas CD8 is expressed on about 40% of T cells. The CD4- and CD8-expressing T cells—called CD4+ and CD8+ cells, respectively—perform different but overlapping functions. CD4+ T cells are "helper" T cells because they secrete soluble molecules (cytokines) that help B cells to produce antibodies (the origin of the name "helper" cells) and also help macrophages to destroy phagocytosed microbes. The central role of CD4+ helper cells in immunity is highlighted by the severe compromise that results from the destruction of this subset by human immunodeficiency

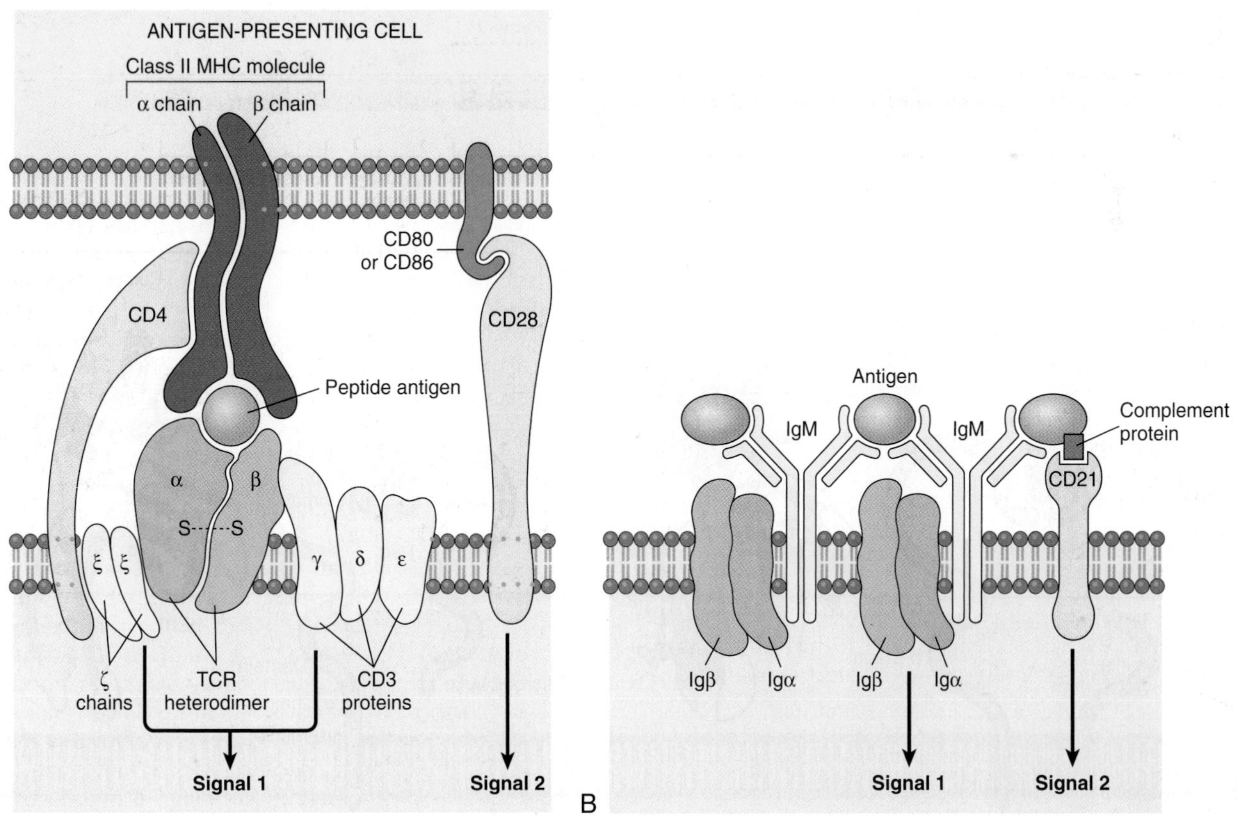

Figure 4–2 Lymphocyte antigen receptors. **A,** The T cell receptor (TCR) complex and other molecules involved in T cell activation. The TCRα and TCRβ chains recognize antigen (in the form of peptide–MHC complexes expressed on antigen-presenting cells), and the linked CD3 complex initiates activating signals. CD4 and CD28 are also involved in T cell activation. (Note that some T cells express CD8 and not CD4; these molecules serve analogous roles.) **B,** The B cell receptor complex is composed of membrane IgM (or IgD, *not shown*) and the associated signaling proteins Igα and Igβ. CD21 is a receptor for a complement component that promotes B cell activation. Ig, immunoglobulin; MHC, major histocompatibilty complex.

virus (HIV) infection. CD8+ T cells can also secrete cytokines, but they play a more important role in directly killing virus-infected or tumor cells, and hence are called "cytotoxic" T lymphocytes (CTLs). Other important invariant proteins on T cells include CD28, which functions as the receptor for molecules that are induced on APCs by microbes (and are called costimulators), and various adhesion molecules that strengthen the bond between the T cells and APCs and control the migration of the T cells to different tissues.

In a minority of peripheral blood T cells and in many of the T cells associated with mucosal surfaces (e.g., lung, gastrointestinal tract), the TCRs are heterodimers of γ and δ chains, which are similar but not identical to the α and β chains of most TCRs. Such γδ T cells, which do not express CD4 or CD8, recognize nonprotein molecules (e.g., bacterial lipoglycans), but their functional roles are not well understood. Another small population of T cells expresses markers of T cells and NK cells. These so-called NKT cells recognize microbial glycolipids, and may play a role in defense against some infections. The antigen receptors of NKT cells are much less diverse than the receptors of "conventional" T cells, suggesting that the former recognize conserved microbial structures.

Another population of T cells that functions to suppress immune responses is that of regulatory T lymphocytes. This cell type is described later, in the context of tolerance of self antigens.

Major Histocompatibility Complex Molecules: The Peptide Display System of Adaptive Immunity

Because MHC molecules are fundamental to T cell recognition of antigens, and because genetic variations in MHC molecules are associated with immunologic diseases, it is important to review the structure and function of these molecules. The human MHC, known as the human leukocyte antigen (HLA) complex, consists of a cluster of genes on chromosome 6 (Fig. 4–3). The HLA system is highly polymorphic; that is, there are several alternative forms (alleles) of a gene at each locus (estimated to number about 3500 for all HLA genes and about 1100 for HLA-B alleles alone). Such diversity provides a system whereby a vast range of peptides can be displayed by MHC molecules for recognition by T cells. As we shall see, this polymorphism also constitutes a formidable barrier to organ transplantation.

On the basis of their chemical structure, tissue distribution, and function, MHC gene products fall into two main categories:

- *Class I MHC* molecules are encoded by three closely linked loci, designated HLA-A, HLA-B, and HLA-C (Fig. 4–3). Each of these molecules is a heterodimer, consisting of a polymorphic 44-kDa α chain noncovalently associated with an invariant 12-kDa β_2-microglobulin polypeptide (encoded by a separate gene on chromosome 15). The extracellular portion of the α chain

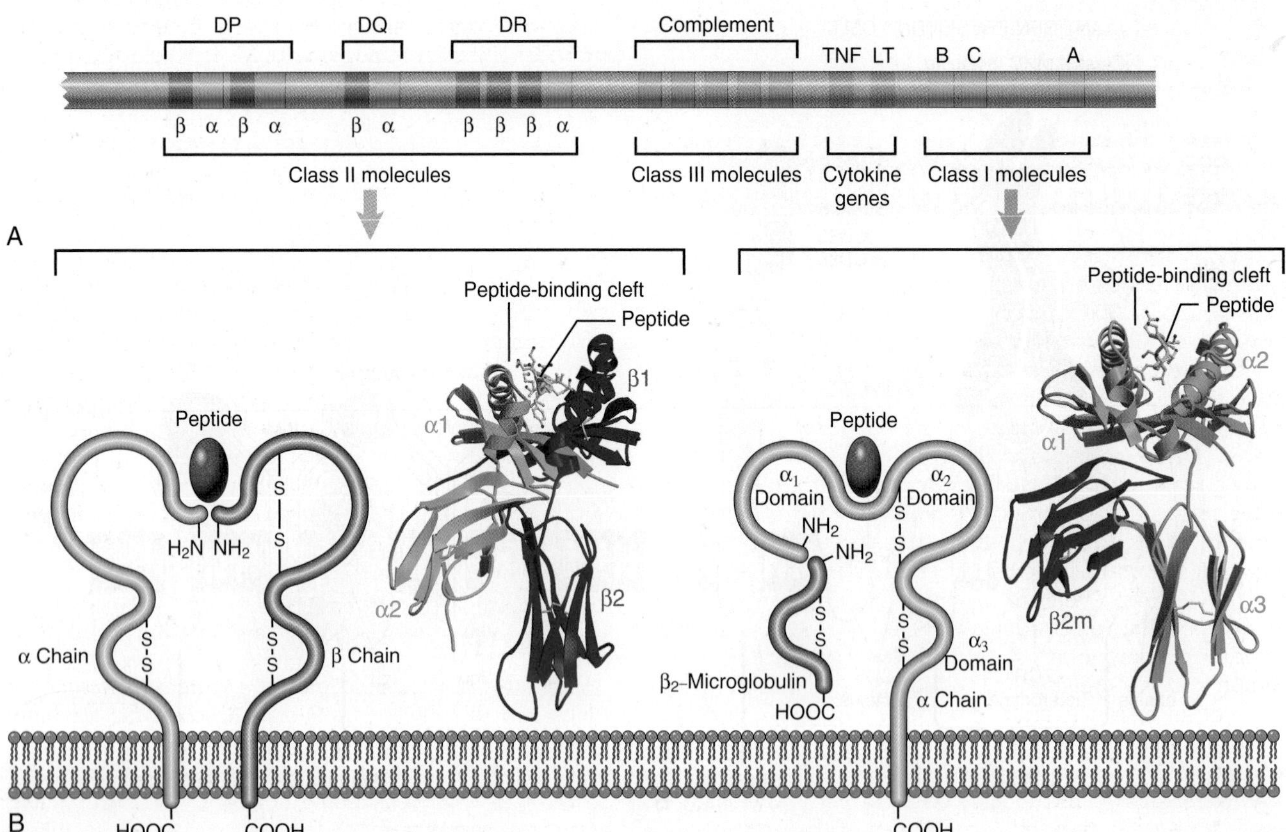

Figure 4–3 The human leukocyte antigen (HLA) complex and the structure of HLA molecules. **A,** The location of genes in the HLA complex. The sizes and distances between genes are not to scale. The class II region also contains genes that encode several proteins involved in antigen processing (not shown). **B,** Schematic diagrams and crystal structures of class I and class II HLA molecules. LT, lymphotoxin; TNF, tumor necrosis factor.

(Crystal structures are courtesy of Dr. P. Bjorkman, California Institute of Technology, Pasadena, California.)

contains a cleft where the polymorphic residues are located and where foreign peptides bind to MHC molecules for presentation to T cells, and a conserved region that binds CD8, ensuring that only CD8+ T cells can respond to peptides displayed by class I molecules. In general, class I MHC molecules bind and display peptides derived from proteins synthesized in the cytoplasm of the cell (e.g., viral antigens). Because class I MHC molecules are present on all nucleated cells, all virus-infected cells can be detected and eliminated by CD8+ CTLs.

- *Class II MHC* molecules are encoded by genes in the HLA-D region, which contains at least three subregions: DP, DQ, and DR. Class II MHC molecules are heterodimers of noncovalently linked polymorphic α and β subunits (Fig. 4–3). The extracellular portion of the class II MHC heterodimer contains a cleft for the binding of antigenic peptides and a region that binds CD4. Class II MHC expression is restricted to a few types of cells, mainly APCs (notably, dendritic cells [DCs]), macrophages, and B cells. In general, class II MHC molecules bind to peptides derived from proteins synthesized outside the cell (e.g., those derived from extracellular bacteria) and ingested into the cell. This property allows CD4+ T cells to recognize the presence of extracellular pathogens and to orchestrate a protective response.
- Several other proteins are encoded in the MHC locus, some of which have been called "class III molecules." These include complement components (C2, C3, and Bf) and the cytokines tumor necrosis factor (TNF) and lymphotoxin. These molecules do not form a part of the peptide display system and are not discussed further.

Each person inherits one HLA allele from each parent; typically, then, two different molecules are expressed for every HLA locus. Cells of a heterozygous person can therefore express six different class I HLA molecules: three of maternal origin and three of paternal origin. Similarly, a given individual expresses maternal and paternal alleles of the class II MHC loci; because some HLA-D α and β chains can mix and match with each other, each class II–expressing cell can have as many as 20 different class II MHC molecules. Different MHC alleles bind to different peptide fragments; *the expression of many different MHC molecules allows each cell to present a wide array of peptide antigens.*

As a result of the polymorphism at the major HLA loci in the population, a virtually infinite number of combinations of molecules exist, and each person expresses a unique MHC antigenic profile on his or her cells. The combination of HLA alleles for each person is called the HLA haplotype. The implications of HLA polymorphism are obvious in the context of transplantation—because each person has HLA alleles that differ to some extent from every other person's, grafts from virtually any donor will evoke immune responses in the recipient and be rejected (except, of course, for identical twins). In fact, HLA molecules were discovered in the course of early attempts at tissue transplantation. HLA molecules of the graft evoke both humoral and cell-mediated responses, eventually leading to graft destruction (as discussed later in this chapter). This ability of MHC molecules to trigger immune responses is the reason these molecules are often called "antigens." It is believed that the polymorphism of MHC genes arose to enable display of and response to any conceivable microbial peptide encountered in the environment.

The role of the MHC in T cell stimulation also has important implications for the genetic control of immune responses. The ability of any given MHC allele to bind the peptide antigens generated from a particular pathogen will determine whether a specific person's T cells can actually "see" and respond to that pathogen. The inheritance of particular alleles influences both protective and harmful immune responses. For example, if the antigen is ragweed pollen and the response is an allergic reaction, inheritance of some HLA genes may make individuals susceptible to "hay fever," the colloquial name for ragweed allergy. On the other hand, responsiveness to a viral antigen, determined by inheritance of certain HLA alleles, may be beneficial for the host.

Finally, *many autoimmune diseases are associated with particular HLA alleles.* We return to a discussion of HLA associations with diseases when we consider autoimmunity.

B Lymphocytes

Bone marrow–derived B lymphocytes are the cells that produce antibodies and are thus the effector cells of humoral immunity. B cells make up 10% to 20% of the circulating peripheral lymphocyte population. They also are present in bone marrow and in the follicles of peripheral lymphoid tissues (lymph nodes, spleen, tonsils, and other mucosal tissues).

B cells recognize antigen by means of membrane-bound antibody of the immunoglobulin M (IgM) class, expressed on the surface together with signaling molecules to form the B cell receptor (BCR) complex (Fig. 4–2, *B*). Whereas T cells can recognize only MHC-associated peptides, B cells can recognize and respond to many more chemical structures, including soluble or cell-associated proteins, lipids, polysaccharides, nucleic acids, and small chemicals; furthermore, B cells (and antibodies) recognize native (properly folded) forms of these antigens. As with TCRs, each antibody has a unique antigen specificity. The diversity of antibodies is generated during somatic rearrangements of immunoglobulin genes. B cells express several invariant molecules that are responsible for signal transduction and for activation of the cells (Fig. 4–2, *B*). Some are the signaling molecules attached to the BCR; another example is CD21 (also known as the type 2 complement receptor, or CR2), which recognizes a complement breakdown product that frequently is deposited on microbes and promotes B cell responses to microbial antigens. Interestingly, the ubiquitous Epstein-Barr virus has cleverly evolved to use CD21 as a receptor for binding to B cells and infecting them.

After stimulation, B cells differentiate into *plasma cells,* which secrete large amounts of antibodies, the mediators of humoral immunity. There are five classes, or isotypes, of immunoglobulins: IgG, IgM, and IgA constitute more than 95% of circulating antibodies. IgA is the major isotype in mucosal secretions; IgE is present in the circulation at very low concentrations and also is found attached to the surfaces of tissue mast cells; and IgD is expressed on the surfaces of B cells but is not secreted. As discussed later, each isotype has characteristic abilities to activate complement or recruit inflammatory cells and thus plays a different role in host defense and disease states.

Natural Killer Cells

Natural killer (NK) cells are lymphocytes that arise from the common lymphoid progenitor that gives rise to T and B lymphocytes. However, NK cells are cells of innate immunity and do not express highly variable and clonally distributed receptors for antigens. Therefore, *they do not have specificities as diverse as do T cells or B cells*. NK cells have two types of receptors—inhibitory and activating. The inhibitory receptors recognize self class I MHC molecules, which are expressed on all healthy cells, whereas the activating receptors recognize molecules that are expressed or upregulated on stressed or infected cells or cells with DNA damage. Normally, the effects of the inhibitory receptors dominate over those of the activating receptors, thereby preventing activation of the NK cells. Infections (especially viral infections) and stress are associated with reduced expression of class I MHC molecules, thus releasing the NK cells from inhibition. At the same time, there is increased engagement of the activating receptors. The net result is that the NK cells are activated and the infected or stressed cells are killed and eliminated.

Antigen-Presenting Cells

The immune system contains several cell types that are specialized to capture microbial antigens and display these to lymphocytes. Foremost among these APCs are dendritic cells (DCs), the major cells for displaying protein antigens to naive T cells to initiate immune responses. Several other cell types present antigens to different lymphocytes at various stages of immune responses.

Dendritic Cells

Cells with dendritic morphology (i.e., with fine dendritic cytoplasmic processes) occur as two functionally distinct types. *Dendritic cells (DCs)*, sometimes called interdigitating DCs, express high levels of class II MHC and T cell costimulatory molecules and function to capture and present antigens to T cells. DCs reside in and under epithelia, where they are strategically located to capture entering microbes; an example is the Langerhans cell of the epidermis. DCs also are present in the T cell zones of lymphoid tissues, where they present antigens to T cells circulating through these tissues, and in the interstitium of many nonlymphoid organs, such as the heart and lungs, where they are poised to capture the antigens of any invading microbes. One subset of DCs is called *plasmacytoid DCs* because of their resemblance to plasma cells. These cells are present in the blood and lymphoid organs, and are major sources of the antiviral cytokine type I interferon, produced in response to many viruses.

The second type of cells with dendritic morphology are *follicular dendritic cells (FDCs)*. These cells are located in the germinal centers of lymphoid follicles in the spleen and lymph nodes. FDCs bear receptors for the Fc tails of IgG molecules and for complement proteins and hence efficiently trap antigens bound to antibodies and complement. These cells display antigens to activated B lymphocytes in lymphoid follicles and promote secondary antibody responses, but are not involved in capturing antigens for display to T cells.

Other Antigen-Presenting Cells

Macrophages ingest microbes and other particulate antigens and display peptides for recognition by T lymphocytes. These T cells in turn activate the macrophages to kill the microbes, the central reaction of cell-mediated immunity. B cells present peptides to helper T cells and receive signals that stimulate antibody responses to protein antigens.

Effector Cells

Many different types of leukocytes perform the ultimate task of the immune response, which is to eliminate infections. NK cells are front-line effector cells in that they can rapidly react against "stressed" cells. Antibody-secreting plasma cells are the effector cells of humoral immunity. T lymphocytes, both CD4+ helper T cells and CD8+ CTLs, are effector cells of cell-mediated immunity. These lymphocytes often function in host defense together with other cells. Macrophages, as described in Chapter 2, bind microbes that are coated with antibodies or complement and then phagocytose and destroy these microbes, thus serving as effector cells of humoral immunity. Macrophages also respond to signals from helper T cells, which improves their ability to destroy phagocytosed microbes, thus serving as effector cells of cellular immunity. T lymphocytes secrete cytokines that recruit and activate other leukocytes, such as neutrophils and eosinophils, and together these cell types function in defense against various pathogens.

Lymphoid Tissues

The lymphoid tissues of the body are divided into generative (primary) organs, where lymphocytes express antigen receptors and mature, and peripheral (secondary) lymphoid organs, where adaptive immune responses develop. The generative organs are the thymus and bone marrow, and the peripheral organs are the lymph nodes, spleen, and mucosal and cutaneous lymphoid tissues. Mature lymphocytes recirculate through the peripheral organs, hunting for microbial antigens that they can respond to. An important characteristic of these organs is that T and B lymphocytes are anatomically organized in a manner that facilitates the adaptive immune response, a process that is described later.

SUMMARY

Cells and Tissues of the Immune System

- Lymphocytes are the mediators of adaptive immunity and the only cells that produce specific and diverse receptors for antigens.
- T (thymus-derived) lymphocytes express TCRs that recognize peptide antigens displayed by MHC molecules on the surface of APCs.

- B (bone marrow–derived) lymphocytes express membrane-bound antibodies that recognize a wide variety of antigens. B cells are activated to become plasma cells, which secrete antibodies.
- NK cells kill cells that are infected by some microbes or are stressed and damaged beyond repair. NK cells express inhibitory receptors that recognize MHC molecules that are normally expressed on healthy cells, and are thus prevented from killing normal cells.
- APCs capture microbes and other antigens, transport them to lymphoid organs, and display them for recognition by lymphocytes. The most efficient APCs are DCs, which are located in epithelia and most tissues.
- The cells of the immune system are organized in tissues. Some of these tissues are the sites of mature lymphocyte production (the generative lymphoid organs, the bone marrow and thymus), while others are the sites of immune responses (the peripheral lymphoid organs, including lymph nodes, spleen, and mucosal lymphoid tissues).

OVERVIEW OF NORMAL IMMUNE RESPONSES

The previous section described the major components of the immune system. This section summarizes the key features of normal immune responses. This overview will serve as a foundation for the subsequent discussions of diseases caused by deficient or uncontrolled immune responses.

The Early Innate Immune Response to Microbes

The principal barriers between hosts and their environment are the epithelia of the skin and the gastrointestinal and respiratory tracts. Infectious microbes usually enter through these routes and attempt to colonize the hosts. The mechanisms of innate immunity operate at every step in a microbe's attempt to invade. At the site of entry, epithelia serve as physical barriers to infections and eliminate microbes through production of peptide antibiotics and the actions of intraepithelial lymphocytes. If microbes are able to survive and traverse these epithelia, they encounter phagocytes, including neutrophils, which are rapidly recruited from the blood into tissues, and macrophages, which live in tissues under epithelia. The function of these phagocytic cells is to ingest microbes and destroy them by producing microbicidal substances. In response to recognition of microbes, phagocytes, DCs, and many other cell types secrete proteins called cytokines (described later), which promote inflammation and microbial killing and enhance protective immune responses. Cells use several receptors to sense microbes; foremost among these are the Toll-like receptors (TLRs), so named because of homology with the *Drosophila* Toll protein, that recognize bacterial and viral components (Chapter 2). NK cells kill virus-infected cells and produce the macrophage-activating cytokine IFN-γ. If the microbes enter the blood, many plasma proteins, including the proteins of the complement system, recognize the microbes and are activated, and their products kill microbes and coat (opsonize) the microbes for phagocytosis. In addition to combating infections, innate immune responses stimulate subsequent adaptive immunity, providing signals that are essential for initiating the responses of antigen-specific T and B lymphocytes.

The Capture and Display of Microbial Antigens

Microbes that enter through epithelia, along with their protein antigens, are captured by DCs that are resident in and under these epithelia. Antigen-bearing DCs then migrate to draining lymph nodes (Fig. 4–4). Protein antigens are proteolytically digested in the APCs to generate peptides that are displayed on the surface of the APCs bound to MHC molecules. Antigens in different cellular compartments are presented by different MHC molecules and are recognized by different subsets of T cells. Antigens that are ingested from the extracellular environment are processed in endosomal and lysosomal vesicles and then are displayed bound to class II MHC molecules. Because CD4 binds to class II MHC molecules, CD4+ helper T cells recognize class II–associated peptides. By contrast, antigens in the cytoplasm are displayed by class I MHC molecules and are recognized by CD8+ cytotoxic T cells, because CD8 binds to class I MHC. This segregation of different antigens is key to the specialized functions of CD4+ and CD8+ T cells; as we discuss below, the two classes of T cells are designed to combat microbes that are located in different cellular compartments. Protein antigens, as well as polysaccharides and other nonprotein antigens, can also be recognized directly by B lymphocytes in the lymphoid follicles of the peripheral lymphoid organs.

Before being recognized by B and T cells, the microbe elicits an innate immune response. This response activates APCs to express costimulatory molecules and secrete cytokines that stimulate the proliferation and differentiation of T lymphocytes. The principal costimulators for T cells are the B7 molecules (CD80 and CD86) that are expressed on APCs and recognized by the CD28 receptor on naive T cells. The innate immune response to some microbes and polysaccharides also results in the activation of complement, generating cleavage products that enhance the proliferation and differentiation of B lymphocytes. Thus, antigen (signal 1 in Fig. 4–2) and molecules produced during innate immune responses (signal 2 in Fig. 4–2) function cooperatively to activate antigen-specific lymphocytes. The requirement for microbe-triggered signal 2 ensures that the adaptive immune response is induced by microbes and not by harmless substances.

Cell-Mediated Immunity: Activation of T Lymphocytes and Elimination of Cell-Associated Microbes

Naive T lymphocytes are activated by antigen and costimulators in peripheral lymphoid organs, and proliferate and differentiate into effector cells, most of which migrate to any site where the antigen (microbe) is present (Fig. 4–4). Upon activation, T lymphocytes secrete soluble proteins called *cytokines,* which function as growth and

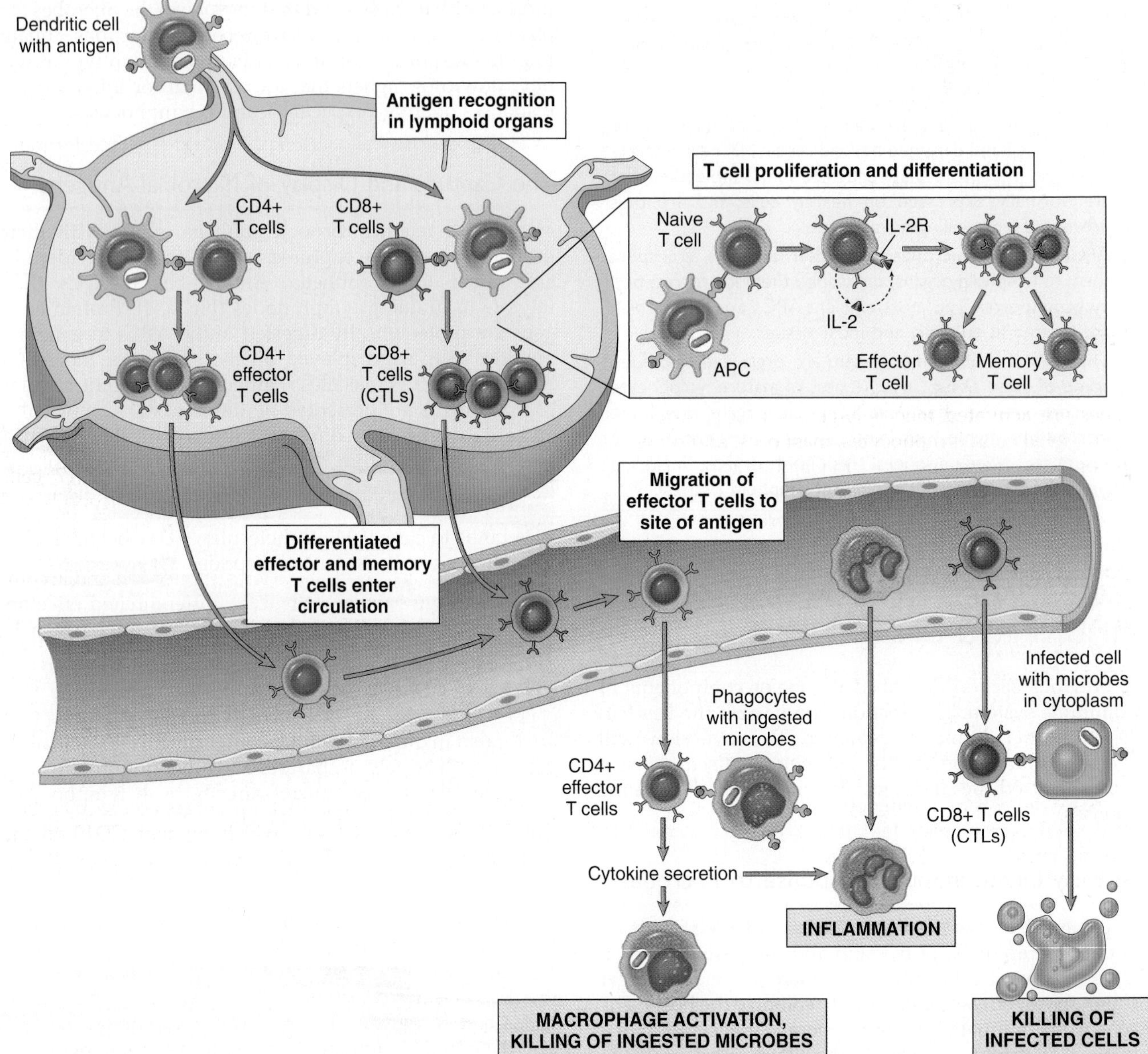

Figure 4–4 Cell-mediated immunity. Naive T cells recognize MHC-associated peptide antigens displayed on dendritic cells in lymph nodes. The T cells are activated to proliferate (under the influence of the cytokine IL-2) and to differentiate into effector and memory cells, which migrate to sites of infection and serve various functions in cell-mediated immunity. Effector CD4+ T cells of the T_H1 subset recognize the antigens of microbes ingested by phagocytes and activate the phagocytes to kill the microbes; T_H17 effector cells enhance leukocyte recruitment and stimulate inflammation; T_H2 cells activate eosinophils. CD8+ CTLs kill infected cells harboring microbes in the cytoplasm. Some activated T cells differentiate into long-lived memory cells. APC, antigen-presenting cell; CTLs, cytotoxic T lymphocytes.

differentiation factors for lymphocytes and other cells, and mediate communications between leukocytes. Because of the important roles of cytokines in both beneficial immune responses and in inflammatory diseases, it is important to understand their properties and actions.

Cytokines: Messenger Molecules of the Immune System

Cytokines are polypeptide products of many cell types (but principally activated lymphocytes and macrophages) that function as mediators of inflammation and immune responses. They were introduced in Chapter 2 in the context of inflammation; here we review their general properties and focus on those cytokines specifically involved in immunity.

Although different cytokines have diverse actions and functions, they all share some common features. Cytokines are synthesized and secreted in response to external stimuli, which may be microbial products, antigen recognition, or other cytokines. Their secretion typically is transient and is controlled by transcription and post-translational mechanisms. The actions of cytokines may be *autocrine* (on the cell that produces the cytokine), *paracrine* (on adjacent cells), and, less commonly, *endocrine* (at a distance from the site of production) (Chapter 2). The effects of cytokines tend to be pleiotropic (one cytokine can have diverse biologic activities, often on many cell types) and redundant (multiple cytokines may have the same activity). Molecularly defined cytokines are called interleukins, referring to their ability to mediate communications between leukocytes.

Cytokines may be grouped into several classes on the basis of their biologic activities and functions.

- *Cytokines involved in innate immunity and inflammation,* the earliest host response to microbes and dead cells. The major cytokines in this group are TNF and interleukin-1 (IL-1) and a group of chemoattractant cytokines called chemokines. IL-12, IFN-γ, IL-6, IL-23, and several other cytokines also participate in the early innate immune response. Major sources of these cytokines are activated macrophages and DCs, as well as endothelial cells, lymphocytes, mast cells, and other cell types. These were described in Chapter 2.
- *Cytokines that regulate lymphocyte responses and effector functions in adaptive immunity.* Different cytokines are involved in the proliferation and differentiation of lymphocytes (e.g., IL-2, IL-4), and in the activation of various effector cells (e.g., IFN-γ, which activates macrophages; IL-5, which activates eosinophils). The major sources of these cytokines are CD4+ helper T lymphocytes stimulated by antigens and costimulators. These cytokines are key participants in the induction and effector phases of adaptive cell-mediated immune responses (see later).
- *Cytokines that stimulate hematopoiesis.* Many of these are called colony-stimulating factors. They function to increase the output of leukocytes from the bone marrow and to thus replenish leukocytes that are consumed during immune and inflammatory reactions.

Effector Functions of T Lymphocytes

One of the earliest responses of CD4+ helper T cells is secretion of the cytokine IL-2 and expression of high-affinity receptors for IL-2. IL-2 is a growth factor that acts on these T lymphocytes and stimulates their proliferation, leading to an increase in the number of antigen-specific lymphocytes. Some of the progeny of the expanded pool of T cells differentiate into effector cells that can secrete different sets of cytokines and thus perform different functions. *The best-defined subsets of CD4+ helper cells are the T_H1, T_H2, and T_H17 subsets* (Fig. 4–5). T_H1 cells produce the cytokine IFN-γ, which activates macrophages and stimulates B cells to produce antibodies that activate complement and coat microbes for phagocytosis. T_H2 cells produce IL-4, which stimulates B cells to differentiate into IgE-secreting plasma cells; IL-5, which activates eosinophils; and IL-13, which activates mucosal epithelial cells to secrete mucus and expel microbes, and activates macrophages to secrete growth factors important for tissue repair. T_H17 cells produce the cytokine IL-17, which recruits neutrophils and thus promotes inflammation; T_H17 cells play an important role in some T cell–mediated inflammatory disorders. These effector cells migrate to sites of infection and accompanying tissue damage. When the differentiated effectors again encounter cell-associated microbes, they are activated to perform the functions that are responsible for elimination of the microbes. The key mediators of the functions of helper T cells are various cytokines and the surface molecule called CD40 ligand (CD40L), which binds to its receptor, CD40, on B cells and macrophages. Differentiated CD4+ effector T cells of the T_H1 subset recognize microbial peptides on macrophages that have ingested the microbes. The T cells express CD40L, which engages CD40 on the macrophages, and the T cells secrete the cytokine IFN-γ,

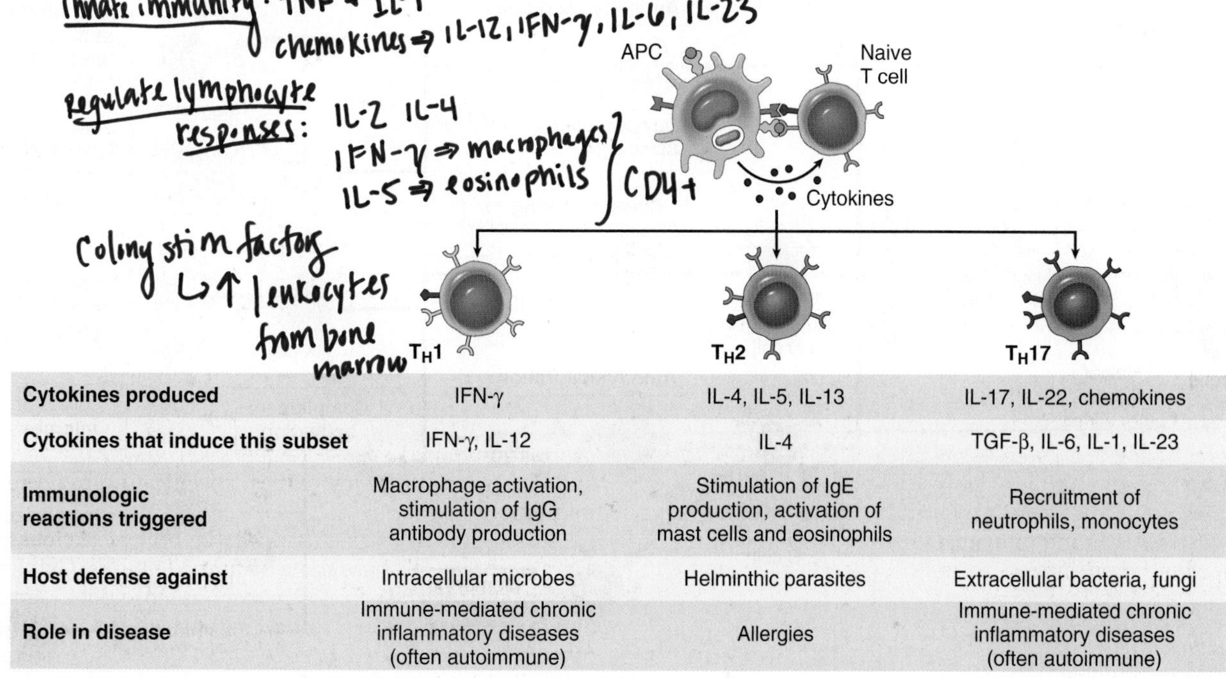

	T_H1	T_H2	T_H17
Cytokines produced	IFN-γ	IL-4, IL-5, IL-13	IL-17, IL-22, chemokines
Cytokines that induce this subset	IFN-γ, IL-12	IL-4	TGF-β, IL-6, IL-1, IL-23
Immunologic reactions triggered	Macrophage activation, stimulation of IgG antibody production	Stimulation of IgE production, activation of mast cells and eosinophils	Recruitment of neutrophils, monocytes
Host defense against	Intracellular microbes	Helminthic parasites	Extracellular bacteria, fungi
Role in disease	Immune-mediated chronic inflammatory diseases (often autoimmune)	Allergies	Immune-mediated chronic inflammatory diseases (often autoimmune)

Figure 4–5 Subsets of CD4+ effector T cells. In response to stimuli (mainly cytokines) present at the time of antigen recognition, naive CD4+ helper T cells may differentiate into populations of effector cells that produce distinct sets of cytokines and perform different functions. The types of immune reactions elicited by each subset, and its role in host defense and immunological diseases, are summarized. Two other populations of CD4+ T cells, regulatory cells and follicular helper cells, are not shown.

which is a potent macrophage activator. The combination of CD40- and IFN-γ-mediated activation results in the induction of potent microbicidal substances in the macrophages, including reactive oxygen species and nitric oxide, leading to the destruction of ingested microbes. T_H2 cells elicit cellular defense reactions that are dominated by eosinophils and not macrophages. As discussed later, CD4+ helper T cells also stimulate B cell responses by CD40L and cytokines. Some CD4+ T cells remain in the lymphoid organs in which they were activated and then migrate into follicles, where they stimulate antibody responses; these cells are called follicular helper T cells.

Activated CD8+ lymphocytes differentiate into CTLs, which kill cells harboring microbes in the cytoplasm. These microbes may be viruses that infect many cell types, or bacteria that are ingested by macrophages but have learned to escape from phagocytic vesicles into the cytoplasm (where they are inaccessible to the killing machinery of phagocytes, which is largely confined to vesicles). By destroying the infected cells, CTLs eliminate the reservoirs of infection.

Humoral Immunity: Activation of B Lymphocytes and Elimination of Extracellular Microbes

Upon activation, B lymphocytes proliferate and then differentiate into plasma cells that secrete different classes of antibodies with distinct functions (Fig. 4–6). There are two major mechanisms of B cell activation.

- *T cell–independent.* Many polysaccharide and lipid antigens have multiple identical antigenic determinants (epitopes) that are able to engage several antigen receptor molecules on each B cell and initiate the process of B cell activation.
- *T cell–dependent.* Typical globular protein antigens are not able to bind to many antigen receptors, and the full response of B cells to protein antigens requires help from CD4+ T cells. B cells also can act as APCs—they ingest protein antigens, degrade them, and display peptides bound to class II MHC molecules for recognition by helper T cells. The helper T cells express CD40L and secrete cytokines, which work together to activate the B cells.

Some of the progeny of the expanded B cell clones differentiate into antibody-secreting *plasma cells.* Each plasma cell secretes antibodies that have the same specificity as the cell surface antibodies (B cell receptors) that first recognized the antigen. Polysaccharides and lipids stimulate secretion mainly of IgM antibody. Protein antigens, by virtue of CD40L- and cytokine-mediated helper T cell actions, induce the production of antibodies of different classes (IgG, IgA, IgE). This production of functionally different antibodies, all with the same specificity, is called heavy-chain class (isotype) switching; it provides plasticity in the antibody response, allowing antibodies to serve many functions. Helper T cells also stimulate the production of antibodies with higher and higher affinity for the antigen. This process, called affinity maturation, improves the quality of the humoral immune response.

The humoral immune response combats microbes in numerous ways (Fig. 4–6).

- Antibodies bind to microbes and prevent them from infecting cells, thereby "neutralizing" the microbes.

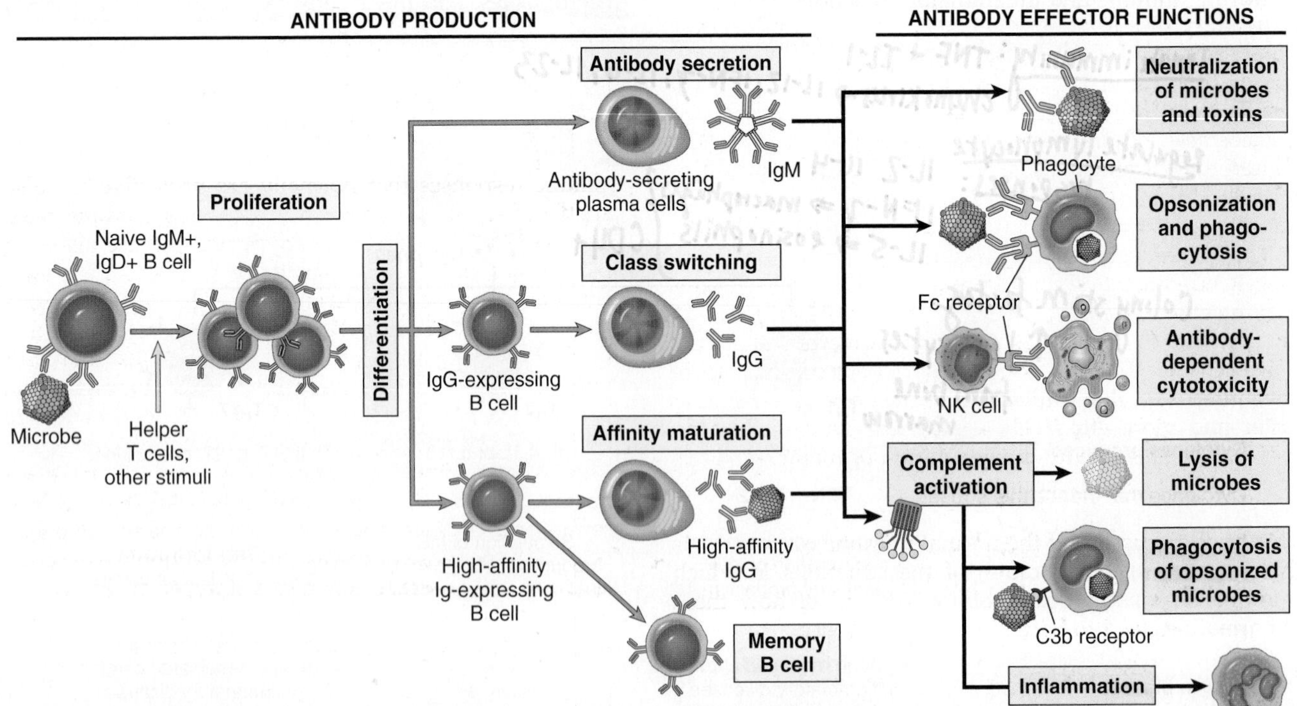

Figure 4–6 Humoral immunity. Naive B lymphocytes recognize antigens, and under the influence of helper T cells and other stimuli (not shown), the B cells are activated to proliferate and to differentiate into antibody-secreting plasma cells. Some of the activated B cells undergo heavy chain class switching and affinity maturation, and some become long-lived memory cells. Antibodies of different heavy chain isotypes (classes) perform different effector functions, shown on the right.

- IgG antibodies coat ("opsonize") microbes and target them for phagocytosis, since phagocytes (neutrophils and macrophages) express receptors for the Fc tails of IgG molecules.
- IgG and IgM activate the complement system by the classical pathway, and complement products promote phagocytosis and destruction of microbes. Production of most opsonizing and complement-fixing IgG antibodies is stimulated by IFN-γ, typically produced by T_H1 helper cells, which respond to many bacteria and viruses, and IgG antibodies are important mechanisms of defense against these microbes.
- IgA is secreted in mucosal tissues and neutralizes microbes in the lumens of the respiratory and gastrointestinal tracts (and other mucosal tissues).
- IgG is actively transported across the placenta and protects the newborn until the immune system becomes mature. This is called *passive immunity*.
- IgE coats helminthic parasites and functions with mast cells and eosinophils to kill them. As mentioned earlier, T_H2 helper cells secrete cytokines that stimulate the production of IgE and activate eosinophils, and thus the response to helminths is orchestrated by T_H2 cells.

Circulating IgG antibodies have half-lives of about 3 weeks, which is much longer than the half-lives of most blood proteins, as a consequence of special mechanisms for recycling IgG and reducing its catabolism. Some antibody-secreting plasma cells migrate to the bone marrow and live for years, continuing to produce low levels of antibodies.

Decline of Immune Responses and Immunologic Memory

A majority of effector lymphocytes induced by an infectious pathogen die by apoptosis after the microbe is eliminated, thus returning the immune system to its basal resting state. This return to a stable or steady state, called homeostasis, occurs because microbes provide essential stimuli for lymphocyte survival and activation, and effector cells are short-lived. Therefore, as the stimuli are eliminated, the activated lymphocytes are no longer kept alive.

The initial activation of lymphocytes also generates long-lived *memory cells*, which may survive for years after the infection. Memory cells are an expanded pool of antigen-specific lymphocytes (more numerous than the naive cells specific for any antigen that are present before encounter with that antigen), and memory cells respond faster and more effectively against the antigen than do naive cells. This is why the generation of memory cells is an important goal of vaccination.

This brief discussion of the normal immune response sets the stage for a consideration of the situations in which immune responses become abnormal, and of how these abnormalities lead to tissue injury and disease.

SUMMARY

Overview of Normal Immune Responses

- The physiologic function of the immune system is defense against infectious microbes.
- The early reaction to microbes is mediated by the mechanisms of innate immunity, which are ready to respond to microbes. These mechanisms include epithelial barriers, phagocytes, NK cells, and plasma proteins (e.g., of the complement system). The reaction of innate immunity is often manifested as inflammation.
- The defense reactions of adaptive immunity develop slowly, but are more potent and specialized.
- Microbes and other foreign antigens are captured by DCs and transported to lymph nodes, where the antigens are recognized by naive lymphocytes. The lymphocytes are activated to proliferate and differentiate into effector and memory cells.
- Cell-mediated immunity is the reaction of T lymphocytes, designed to combat cell-associated microbes (e.g., phagocytosed microbes and microbes in the cytoplasm of infected cells). Humoral immunity is mediated by antibodies and is effective against extracellular microbes (in the circulation and mucosal lumens).
- CD4+ helper T cells help B cells to make antibodies, activate macrophages to destroy ingested microbes, stimulate recruitment of leukocytes, and regulate all immune responses to protein antigens. The functions of CD4+ T cells are mediated by secreted proteins called cytokines. CD8+ CTLs kill cells that express antigens in the cytoplasm that are seen as foreign (e.g., virus-infected and tumor cells).
- Antibodies secreted by plasma cells neutralize microbes and block their infectivity, and promote the phagocytosis and destruction of pathogens. Antibodies also confer passive immunity to neonates.

HYPERSENSITIVITY REACTIONS: MECHANISMS OF IMMUNE-MEDIATED INJURY

Immune responses that normally are protective are also capable of causing tissue injury. Injurious immune reactions are grouped under *hypersensitivity*, and the resulting diseases are called hypersensitivity diseases. This term originated from the idea that persons who mount immune responses against an antigen are "sensitized" to that antigen, so pathologic or excessive reactions represent manifestations of a "hypersensitive" state. Normally, an exquisite system of checks and balances optimizes the eradication of infecting organisms without serious injury to host tissues. However, immune responses may be inadequately controlled or inappropriately targeted to host tissues, and in such situations, the normally beneficial response is the cause of disease. In this section we describe the causes and general mechanisms of hypersensitivity diseases and then discuss specific situations in which the immune response is responsible for the disease.

Causes of Hypersensitivity Reactions

Pathologic immune responses may be directed against different types of antigens and may result from various underlying abnormalities.

- *Autoimmunity: reactions against self antigens.* Normally, the immune system does not react against self-generated antigens. This phenomenon is called self tolerance, implying that the body "tolerates" its own antigens. On occasion, self-tolerance fails, resulting in reactions against the body's own cells and tissues; collectively, such reactions constitute autoimmunity. The diseases caused by autoimmunity are referred to as autoimmune diseases. We shall return to the mechanisms of self-tolerance and autoimmunity later in this chapter.
- *Reactions against microbes.* There are many types of reactions against microbial antigens that may cause disease. In some cases, the reaction appears to be excessive or the microbial antigen is unusually persistent. If antibodies are produced against such antigens, the antibodies may bind to the microbial antigens to produce immune complexes, which deposit in tissues and trigger inflammation; this is the underlying mechanism of poststreptococcal glomerulonephritis (Chapter 13). T cell responses against persistent microbes may give rise to severe inflammation, sometimes with the formation of granulomas (Chapter 2); this is the cause of tissue injury in tuberculosis and other infections. Rarely, antibodies or T cells reactive with a microbe cross-react with a host tissue; such cross-reactivity is believed to be the basis for rheumatic heart disease (Chapter 10). In some instances, the disease-causing immune response may be entirely normal, but in the process of eradicating the infection, host tissues are injured. In viral hepatitis, the virus that infects liver cells is not cytopathic, but it is recognized as foreign by the immune system. Cytotoxic T cells try to eliminate infected cells, and this normal immune response damages liver cells.
- *Reactions against environmental antigens.* Most healthy people do not react strongly against common environmental substances (e.g., pollens, animal danders, or dust mites), but almost 20% of the population are "allergic" to these substances. These individuals are genetically predisposed to make unusual immune responses to a variety of noninfectious, and otherwise harmless, antigens to which all persons are exposed but against which only some react.

In all of these conditions, tissue injury is caused by the same mechanisms that normally function to eliminate infectious pathogens—namely, antibodies, effector T lymphocytes, and various other effector cells. The problem in these diseases is that the response is triggered and maintained inappropriately. Because the stimuli for these abnormal immune responses are difficult or impossible to eliminate (e.g., self antigens, persistent microbes, or environmental antigens), and the immune system has many intrinsic positive feedback loops (amplification mechanisms), once a pathologic immune response starts it is difficult to control or terminate it. Therefore, these hypersensitivity diseases tend to be chronic and debilitating, and are therapeutic challenges. Since inflammation, typically chronic inflammation, is a major component of the pathology of these disorders, they are sometimes grouped under the rubric *immune-mediated inflammatory diseases.*

Types of Hypersensitivity Reactions

Hypersensitivity reactions are traditionally subdivided into four types based on the principal immune mechanism responsible for injury; three are variations on antibody-mediated injury, whereas the fourth is T cell–mediated (Table 4–1). The rationale for this classification is that the mechanism of immune injury is often a good predictor of the clinical manifestations and may even help to guide the therapy. However, this classification of immune-mediated diseases is not perfect, because several immune reactions may coexist in one disease.

- *Immediate (type I) hypersensitivity,* often called *allergy,* results from the activation of the T_H2 subset of CD4+ helper T cells by environmental antigens, leading to the production of IgE antibodies, which become attached to mast cells. When these IgE molecules bind the antigen (allergen), the mast cells are triggered to release mediators that transiently affect vascular permeability and

Table 4–1 Mechanisms of Hypersensitivity Reactions

Type	Immune Mechanisms	Histopathologic Lesions	Prototypical Disorders
Immediate (type I) hypersensitivity	Production of IgE antibody → immediate release of vasoactive amines and other mediators from mast cells; later recruitment of inflammatory cells	Vascular dilation, edema, smooth muscle contraction, mucus production, tissue injury, inflammation	Anaphylaxis; allergies; bronchial asthma (atopic forms)
Antibody-mediated (type II) hypersensitivity	Production of IgG, IgM → binds to antigen on target cell or tissue → phagocytosis or lysis of target cell by activated complement or Fc receptors; recruitment of leukocytes	Phagocytosis and lysis of cells; inflammation; in some diseases, functional derangements without cell or tissue injury	Autoimmune hemolytic anemia; Goodpasture syndrome
Immune complex–mediated (type III) hypersensitivity	Deposition of antigen–antibody complexes → complement activation → recruitment of leukocytes by complement products and Fc receptors → release of enzymes and other toxic molecules	Inflammation, necrotizing vasculitis (fibrinoid necrosis)	Systemic lupus erythematosus; some forms of glomerulonephritis; serum sickness; Arthus reaction
Cell-mediated (type IV) hypersensitivity	Activated T lymphocytes → (1) release of cytokines, inflammation and macrophage activation; (2) T cell–mediated cytotoxicity	Perivascular cellular infiltrates; edema; granuloma formation; cell destruction	Contact dermatitis; multiple sclerosis; type I diabetes; tuberculosis

IgE, IgG, IgM, immunoglobulins E, G, M.

induce smooth muscle contraction in various organs, and that also may stimulate more prolonged inflammation (the late-phase reaction). These diseases are commonly called allergic, or atopic, disorders.

- *Antibody-mediated (type II) hypersensitivity disorders* are caused by antibodies that bind to fixed tissue or cell surface antigens, promoting phagocytosis and destruction of the coated cells or triggering pathologic inflammation in tissues.
- *Immune complex–mediated (type III) hypersensitivity disorders* are caused by antibodies binding to antigens to form complexes that circulate and deposit in vascular beds and stimulate inflammation, typically as a consequence of complement activation. Tissue injury in these diseases is the result of the inflammation.
- *T cell–mediated (type IV) hypersensitivity disorders* are caused mainly by immune responses in which T lymphocytes of the T_H1 and T_H17 subsets produce cytokines that induce inflammation and activate neutrophils and macrophages, which are responsible for tissue injury. CD8+ CTLs also may contribute to injury by directly killing host cells.

Immediate (Type I) Hypersensitivity

Immediate hypersensitivity is a tissue reaction that occurs rapidly (typically within minutes) after the interaction of antigen with IgE antibody that is bound to the surface of mast cells in a sensitized host. The reaction is initiated by entry of an antigen, which is called an allergen because it triggers allergy. Many allergens are environmental substances that are harmless for most persons on exposure. Some people apparently inherit genes that make them susceptible to allergies. This susceptibility is manifested by the propensity of such persons to mount strong T_H2 responses and, subsequently, to produce IgE antibody against the allergens. The IgE is central to the activation of the mast cells and release of mediators that are responsible for the clinical and pathologic manifestations of the reaction. Immediate hypersensitivity may occur as a local reaction that is merely annoying (e.g., seasonal rhinitis, or hay fever), severely debilitating (asthma), or even fatal (anaphylaxis).

Sequence of Events in Immediate Hypersensitivity Reactions

Most hypersensitivity reactions follow the same sequence of cellular responses (Fig. 4–7):

- *Activation of T_H2 cells and production of IgE antibody.* Allergens may be introduced by inhalation, ingestion, or injection. Variables that probably contribute to the strong T_H2 responses to allergens include the route of entry, dose, and chronicity of antigen exposure, and the genetic makeup of the host. It is not clear if allergenic substances also have unique structural properties that endow them with the ability to elicit T_H2 responses. *Immediate hypersensitivity is the prototypical T_H2-mediated reaction.* The T_H2 cells that are induced secrete several cytokines, including IL-4, IL-5, and IL-13, which are responsible for essentially all the reactions of immediate hypersensitivity. IL-4 stimulates B cells specific for the allergen to undergo heavy-chain class switching to IgE and to secrete this immunoglobulin isotype. IL-5 activates eosinophils that are recruited to the reaction, and IL-13 acts on epithelial cells and stimulates mucus secretion. T_H2 cells often are recruited to the site of allergic reactions in response to chemokines that are produced locally; among these chemokines is eotaxin, which also recruits eosinophils to the same site.
- *Sensitization of mast cells by IgE antibody.* Mast cells are derived from precursors in the bone marrow, are widely distributed in tissues, and often reside near blood vessels and nerves and in subepithelial locations. Mast cells

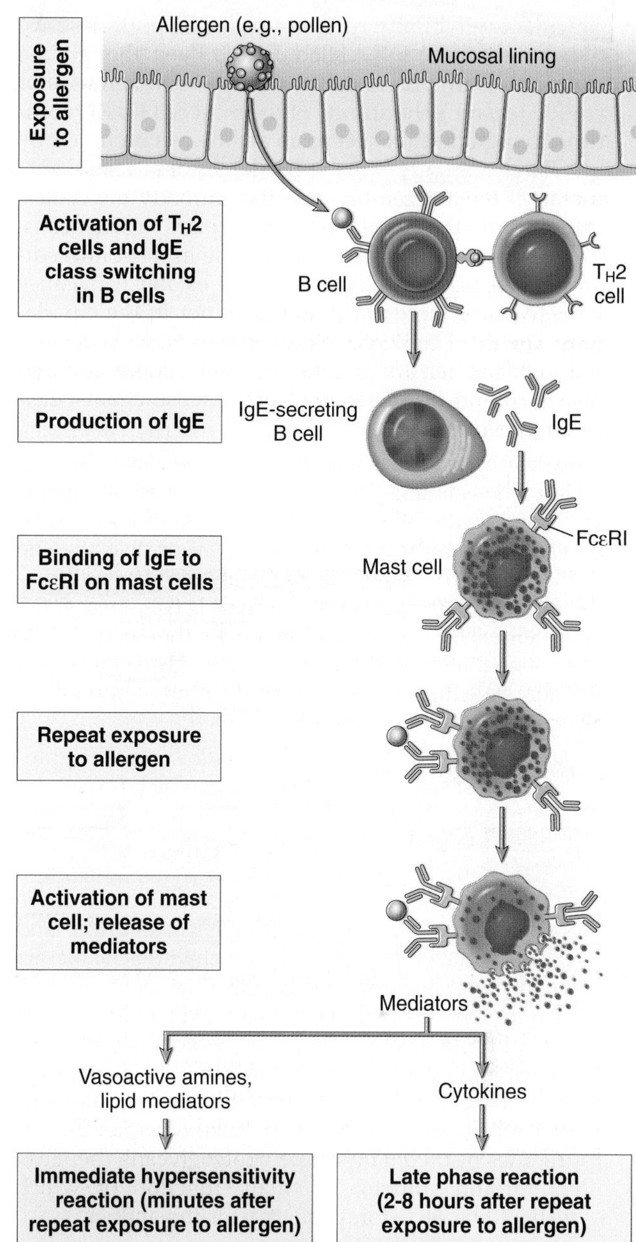

Figure 4–7 Sequence of events in immediate (type I) hypersensitivity. Immediate hypersensitivity reactions are initiated by the introduction of an allergen, which stimulates T_H2 responses and IgE production. IgE binds to Fc receptors (FcεRI) on mast cells, and subsequent exposure to the allergen activates the mast cells to secrete the mediators that are responsible for the pathologic manifestations of immediate hypersensitivity.

express a high-affinity receptor for the Fc portion of the ε heavy chain of IgE, called FcεRI. Even though the serum concentration of IgE is very low (in the range of 1 to 100 μg/mL), the affinity of the mast cell FcεRI receptor is so high that the receptors are always occupied by IgE. These antibody-bearing mast cells are "sensitized" to react if the antigen binds to the antibody molecules. Basophils are the circulating counterparts of mast cells. They also express FcεRI, but their role in most immediate hypersensitivity reactions is not established (since these reactions occur in tissues and not in the circulation). The third cell type that expresses FcεRI is eosinophils, which often are present in these reactions and also have a role in IgE-mediated host defense against helminth infections, described later.

- *Activation of mast cells and release of mediators.* When a person who was sensitized by exposure to an allergen is reexposed to the allergen, it binds to multiple specific IgE molecules on mast cells, usually at or near the site of allergen entry. When these IgE molecules are cross-linked, a series of biochemical signals is triggered in the mast cells. The signals culminate in the secretion of various mediators from the mast cells. Three groups of mediators are the most important in different immediate hypersensitivity reactions (Fig. 4–8):
  - *Vasoactive amines released from granule stores.* The granules of mast cells contain histamine, which is released within seconds or minutes of activation. Histamine causes vasodilation, increased vascular permeability, smooth muscle contraction, and increased secretion of mucus. Other rapidly released mediators include adenosine (which causes bronchoconstriction and inhibits platelet aggregation) and chemotactic factors for neutrophils and eosinophils. Other mast cell granule contents that may be secreted include several neutral proteases (e.g., tryptase), which may damage tissues and also generate kinins and cleave complement components to produce additional chemotactic and inflammatory factors (e.g., C3a) (Chapter 2). The granules also contain acidic proteoglycans (heparin, chondroitin sulfate), the main function of which seems to be as a storage matrix for the amines.
  - *Newly synthesized lipid mediators.* Mast cells synthesize and secrete prostaglandins and leukotrienes, by the same pathways as do other leukocytes (Chapter 2). These lipid mediators have several actions that are important in immediate hypersensitivity reactions. Prostaglandin D_2 (PGD_2) is the most abundant mediator generated by the cyclooxygenase pathway in mast cells. It causes intense bronchospasm as well as increased mucus secretion. The leukotrienes LTC_4 and LTD_4 are the most potent vasoactive and spasmogenic agents known; on a molar basis, they are several thousand times more active than histamine in increasing vascular permeability and in causing bronchial smooth muscle contraction. LTB_4 is highly chemotactic for neutrophils, eosinophils, and monocytes.
  - *Cytokines.* Activation of mast cells results in the synthesis and secretion of several cytokines that are important for the late-phase reaction. These include TNF and chemokines, which recruit and activate leukocytes (Chapter 2); IL-4 and IL-5, which amplify the T_H2-initiated immune reaction; and IL-13, which stimulates epithelial cell mucus secretion.

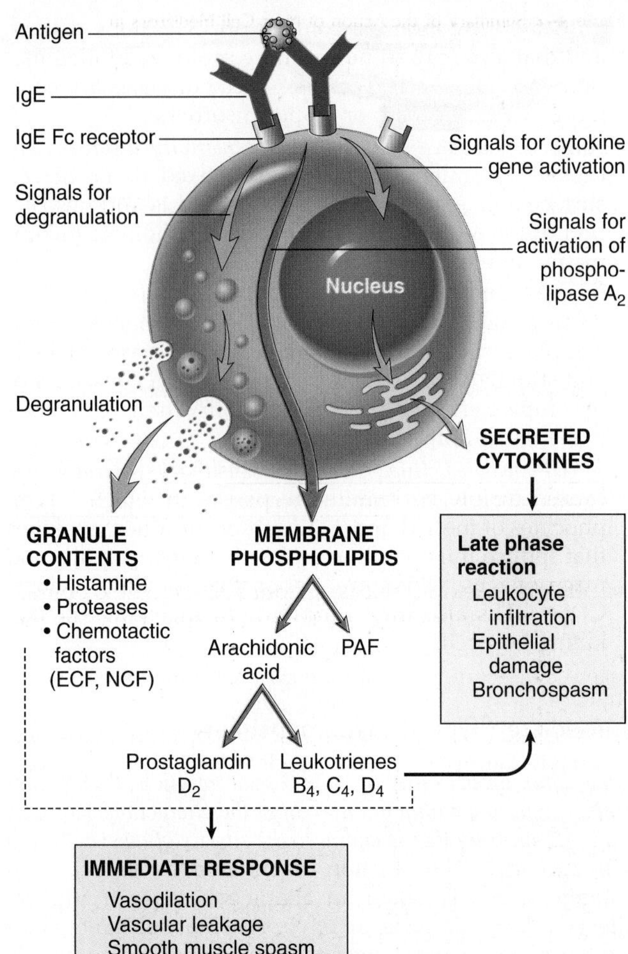

Figure 4–8 Mast cell mediators. Upon activation, mast cells release various classes of mediators that are responsible for the immediate and late-phase reactions. ECF, eosinophil chemotactic factor; NCF, neutrophil chemotactic factor (neither of these has been biochemically defined); PAF, platelet-activating factor.

In summary, a variety of compounds that act on blood vessels, smooth muscle, and leukocytes mediate type I hypersensitivity reactions (Table 4–2). Some of these compounds are released rapidly from sensitized mast cells and are responsible for the intense immediate reactions associated with conditions such as systemic anaphylaxis. Others, such as cytokines, are responsible for the inflammation seen in late-phase reactions.

Often, the IgE-triggered reaction has two well-defined phases (Fig. 4–9): (1) the *immediate response,* characterized by vasodilation, vascular leakage, and smooth muscle spasm, usually evident within 5 to 30 minutes after exposure to an allergen and subsiding by 60 minutes; and (2) a second, *late-phase reaction* that usually sets in 2 to 8 hours later and may last for several days and is characterized by inflammation as well as tissue destruction, such as mucosal epithelial cell damage. The dominant inflammatory cells in the late-phase reaction are neutrophils, eosinophils, and lymphocytes, especially T_H2 cells. Neutrophils are recruited by various chemokines; their roles in inflammation were described in Chapter 2. Eosinophils are recruited by eotaxin

Table 4–2 Summary of the Action of Mast Cell Mediators in Immediate (Type I) Hypersensitivity

Action	Mediators
Vasodilation, increased vascular permeability	Histamine PAF Leukotrienes C_4, D_4, E_4 Neutral proteases that activate complement and kinins Prostaglandin D_2
Smooth muscle spasm	Leukotrienes C_4, D_4, E_4 Histamine Prostaglandins PAF
Cellular infiltration	Cytokines (e.g., chemokines, TNF) Leukotriene B_4 Eosinophil and neutrophil chemotactic factors (not defined biochemically)

PAF, platelet-activating factor; TNF, tumor necrosis factor.

and other chemokines released from TNF-activated epithelium and are important effectors of tissue injury in the late-phase response. Eosinophils produce major basic protein and eosinophil cationic protein, which are toxic to epithelial cells, and LTC_4 and platelet-activating factor, which promote inflammation. T_H2 cells produce cytokines that have multiple actions, as described earlier. These recruited leukocytes can amplify and sustain the inflammatory response even in the absence of continuous allergen exposure. In addition, inflammatory leukocytes are responsible for much of the epithelial cell injury in immediate hypersensitivity. Because inflammation is a major component of many allergic diseases, notably asthma and atopic dermatitis, therapy usually includes anti-inflammatory drugs such as corticosteroids.

Clinical and Pathologic Manifestations

An immediate hypersensitivity reaction may occur as a systemic disorder or as a local reaction. The nature of the reaction is often determined by the route of antigen exposure. Systemic exposure to protein antigens (e.g., in bee venom) or drugs (e.g., penicillin) may result in systemic anaphylaxis. Within minutes of the exposure in a sensitized host, itching, urticaria (hives), and skin erythema appear, followed in short order by profound respiratory difficulty caused by pulmonary bronchoconstriction and accentuated by hypersecretion of mucus. Laryngeal edema may exacerbate matters by causing upper airway obstruction. In addition, the musculature of the entire gastrointestinal tract may be affected, with resultant vomiting, abdominal cramps, and diarrhea. Without immediate intervention, there may be systemic vasodilation with a fall in blood pressure (anaphylactic shock), and the patient may progress to circulatory collapse and death within minutes.

Local reactions generally occur when the antigen is confined to a particular site, such as skin (contact, causing urticaria), gastrointestinal tract (ingestion, causing diarrhea), or lung (inhalation, causing bronchoconstriction). The common forms of skin and food allergies, hay fever, and certain forms of asthma are examples of localized allergic reactions. However, ingestion or inhalation of allergens also can trigger systemic reactions.

Susceptibility to localized type I reactions has a strong genetic component, and the term *atopy* is used to imply familial predisposition to such localized reactions. Patients who suffer from nasobronchial allergy (including hay fever and some forms of asthma) often have a family history of similar conditions. Genes that are implicated in susceptibility to asthma and other atopic disorders include those encoding HLA molecules (which may confer immune responsiveness to particular allergens), cytokines (which may control T_H2 responses), a component of the FcεRI, and ADAM33, a metalloproteinase that may be involved in tissue remodeling in the airways.

The reactions of immediate hypersensitivity clearly did not evolve solely to cause human discomfort and disease. The immune response dependent on T_H2 cells and IgE—in particular, the late-phase inflammatory reaction—plays an important protective role in combating parasitic infections.

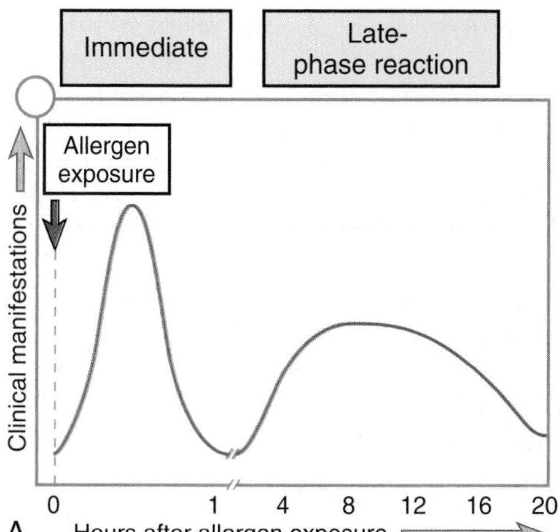

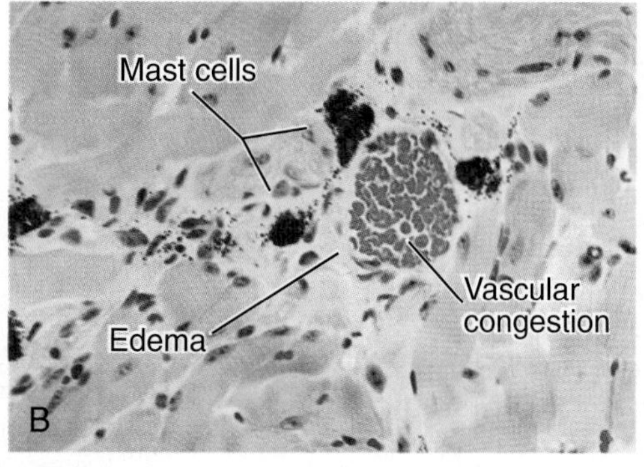

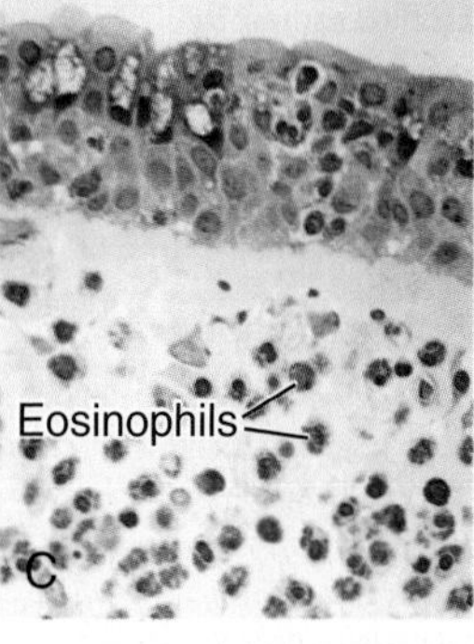

Figure 4–9 Immediate hypersensitivity. **A,** Kinetics of the immediate and late-phase reactions. The immediate vascular and smooth muscle reaction to allergen develops within minutes after challenge (allergen exposure in a previously sensitized person), and the late-phase reaction develops 2 to 24 hours later. **B–C,** Morphology: The immediate reaction **(B)** is characterized by vasodilation, congestion, and edema, and the late-phase reaction **(C)** is characterized by an inflammatory infiltrate rich in eosinophils, neutrophils, and T cells.

(B and C, Courtesy of Dr. Daniel Friend, Department of Pathology, Brigham and Women's Hospital, Boston, Massachusetts.)

IgE antibodies are produced in response to many helminthic infections, and their physiologic function is to target helminths for destruction by eosinophils and mast cells. Mast cells also are involved in defense against bacterial infections. And snake aficionados will be relieved to hear that their mast cells may protect them from some snake venoms by releasing granule proteases that degrade the toxins. Why these beneficial responses are inappropriately activated by harmless environmental antigens, giving rise to allergies, remains a puzzle.

SUMMARY

Immediate (Type I) Hypersensitivity

- Also called allergic reactions, or allergies
- Induced by environmental antigens (allergens) that stimulate strong T_H2 responses and IgE production in genetically susceptible individuals
- IgE coats mast cells by binding to Fcε receptors; reexposure to the allergen leads to cross-linking of the IgE and FcεRI, activation of mast cells, and release of mediators.
- Principal mediators are histamine, proteases, and other granule contents; prostaglandins and leukotrienes; and cytokines.
- Mediators are responsible for the immediate vascular and smooth muscle reactions and the late-phase reaction (inflammation).
- The clinical manifestations may be local or systemic, and range from mildly annoying rhinitis to fatal anaphylaxis.

Antibody-Mediated Diseases (Type II Hypersensitivity)

Antibody-mediated (type II) hypersensitivity disorders are caused by antibodies directed against target antigens on the surface of cells or other tissue components. The antigens may be normal molecules intrinsic to cell membranes or in the extracellular matrix, or they may be adsorbed exogenous antigens (e.g., a drug metabolite). Antibody-mediated abnormalities are the underlying cause of many human diseases; examples of these are listed in Table 4–3. In all of these disorders, the tissue damage or functional abnormalities result from a limited number of mechanisms.

Mechanisms of Antibody-Mediated Diseases

Antibodies cause disease by targeting cells for phagocytosis, by activating the complement system, and by interfering with normal cellular functions (Fig. 4–10). The antibodies that are responsible typically are high-affinity antibodies capable of activating complement and binding to the Fc receptors of phagocytes.

- *Opsonization and phagocytosis.* When circulating cells, such as erythrocytes or platelets, are coated (opsonized) with autoantibodies, with or without complement proteins, the cells become targets for phagocytosis by neutrophils and macrophages (Fig. 4–10, *A*). These phagocytes express receptors for the Fc tails of IgG antibodies and for breakdown products of the C3 complement protein, and use these receptors to bind and ingest opsonized particles. Opsonized cells are usually eliminated in the spleen, and this is why splenectomy is of

Table 4–3 Examples of Antibody-Mediated Diseases (Type II Hypersensitivity)

Disease	Target Antigen	Mechanisms of Disease	Clinicopathologic Manifestations
Autoimmune hemolytic anemia	Red cell membrane proteins (Rh blood group antigens, I antigen)	Opsonization and phagocytosis of erythrocytes	Hemolysis, anemia
Autoimmune thrombocytopenic purpura	Platelet membrane proteins (GpIIb/IIIa integrin)	Opsonization and phagocytosis of platelets	Bleeding
Pemphigus vulgaris	Proteins in intercellular junctions of epidermal cells (epidermal desmoglein)	Antibody-mediated activation of proteases, disruption of intercellular adhesions	Skin vesicles (bullae)
Vasculitis caused by ANCA	Neutrophil granule proteins, presumably released from activated neutrophils	Neutrophil degranulation and inflammation	Vasculitis
Goodpasture syndrome	Noncollagenous protein (NC1) in basement membranes of kidney glomeruli and lung alveoli	Complement- and Fc receptor–mediated inflammation	Nephritis, lung hemorrhage
Acute rheumatic fever	Streptococcal cell wall antigen; antibody cross-reacts with myocardial antigen	Inflammation, macrophage activation	Myocarditis
Myasthenia gravis	Acetylcholine receptor	Antibody inhibits acetylcholine binding, downmodulates receptors	Muscle weakness, paralysis
Graves disease (hyperthyroidism)	TSH receptor	Antibody-mediated stimulation of TSH receptors	Hyperthyroidism
Insulin-resistant diabetes	Insulin receptor	Antibody inhibits binding of insulin	Hyperglycemia, ketoacidosis
Pernicious anemia	Intrinsic factor of gastric parietal cells	Neutralization of intrinsic factor, decreased absorption of vitamin B_{12}	Abnormal myelopoiesis, anemia

ANCA, antineutrophil cytoplasmic antibodies; TSH, thyroid-stimulating hormone.

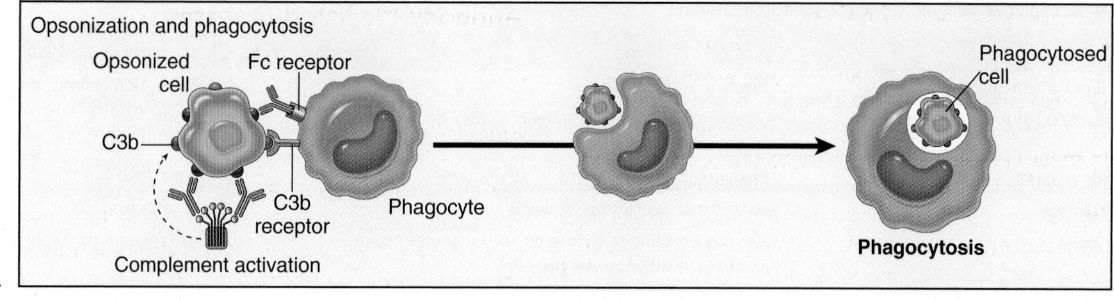

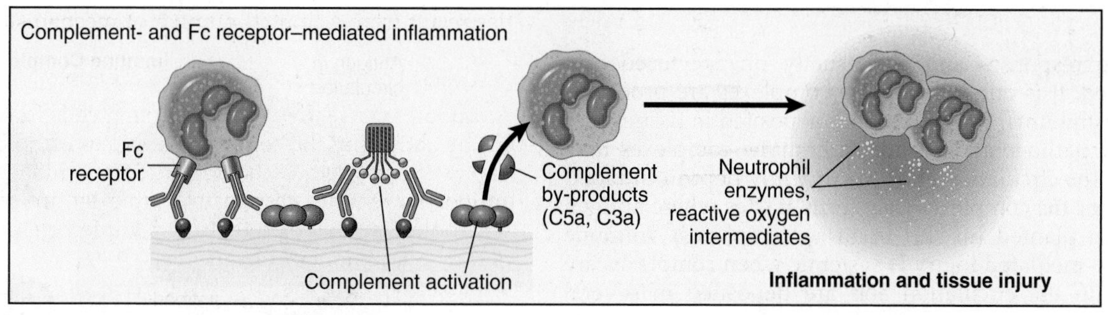

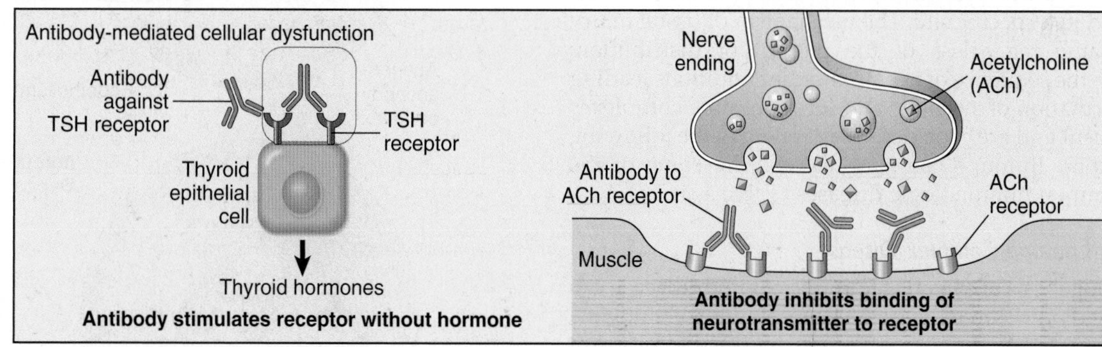

Figure 4–10 Mechanisms of antibody-mediated injury. **A,** Opsonization of cells by antibodies and complement components, and ingestion of opsonized cells by phagocytes. **B,** Inflammation induced by antibody binding to Fc receptors of leukocytes and by complement breakdown products. **C,** Antireceptor antibodies disturb the normal function of receptors. In these examples, antibodies against the thyroid-stimulating hormone (TSH) receptor activate thyroid cells in Graves disease, and acetylcholine (ACh) receptor antibodies impair neuromuscular transmission in myasthenia gravis.

clinical benefit in autoimmune thrombocytopenia and some forms of autoimmune hemolytic anemia.

- *Inflammation.* Antibodies bound to cellular or tissue antigens activate the complement system by the "classical" pathway (Fig. 4–10, *B*). Products of complement activation serve several functions (see Fig. 2–18, Chapter 2), one of which is to recruit neutrophils and monocytes, triggering inflammation in tissues. Leukocytes may also be activated by engagement of Fc receptors, which recognize the bound antibodies. This mechanism of injury is exemplified by Goodpasture syndrome and pemphigus vulgaris.
- *Antibody-mediated cellular dysfunction.* In some cases, antibodies directed against cell surface receptors impair or dysregulate cellular function without causing cell injury or inflammation (Fig. 4–10, *C*). In myasthenia gravis, antibodies against acetylcholine receptors in the motor end plates of skeletal muscles inhibit neuromuscular transmission, with resultant muscle weakness. Antibodies can also stimulate cellular responses excessively. In Graves disease, antibodies against the thyroid-stimulating hormone receptor stimulate thyroid epithelial cells to secrete thyroid hormones, resulting in hyperthyroidism. Antibodies against hormones and other essential proteins can neutralize and block the actions of these molecules, causing functional derangements.

Immune Complex Diseases (Type III Hypersensitivity)

Antigen–antibody (immune) complexes that are formed in the circulation may deposit in blood vessels, leading to complement activation and acute inflammation. The antigens in these complexes may be exogenous antigens, such as microbial proteins, or endogenous antigens, such as nucleoproteins. The mere formation of immune complexes does not equate with hypersensitivity disease; small amounts of antigen–antibody complexes may be produced during normal

Table 4–4 Examples of Immune Complex–Mediated Diseases

Disease	Antigen Involved	Clinicopathologic Manifestations
Systemic lupus erythematosus	Nuclear antigens	Nephritis, skin lesions, arthritis, others
Poststreptococcal glomerulonephritis	Streptococcal cell wall antigen(s); may be "planted" in glomerular basement membrane	Nephritis
Polyarteritis nodosa	Hepatitis B virus antigens in some cases	Systemic vasculitis
Reactive arthritis	Bacterial antigens (e.g., *Yersinia*)	Acute arthritis
Serum sickness	Various proteins (e.g., foreign serum protein such as horse antithymocyte globulin)	Arthritis, vasculitis, nephritis
Arthus reaction (experimental)	Various foreign proteins	Cutaneous vasculitis

immune responses and are usually phagocytosed and destroyed. It is only when these complexes are produced in large amounts, persist, and are deposited in tissues that they are pathogenic. Pathogenic immune complexes may form in the circulation and subsequently deposit in blood vessels, or the complexes may form at sites where antigen has been planted (in situ immune complexes). Immune complex–mediated injury is systemic when complexes are formed in the circulation and are deposited in several organs, or it may be localized to particular organs (e.g., kidneys, joints, or skin) if the complexes are formed and deposited in a specific site. The mechanism of tissue injury is the same regardless of the pattern of distribution; however, the sequence of events and the conditions leading to the formation of systemic and local immune complexes are different and are considered separately in the following descriptions. Immune complex diseases are some of the most common immunologic diseases (Table 4–4).

Systemic Immune Complex Disease

The pathogenesis of systemic immune complex disease can be divided into three phases: (1) formation of antigen-antibody complexes in the circulation and (2) deposition of the immune complexes in various tissues, thereby initiating (3) an inflammatory reaction in various sites throughout the body (Fig. 4–11).

Acute serum sickness is the prototype of a systemic immune complex disease. It was first described in humans when large amounts of foreign serum were administered for passive immunization (e.g., in persons receiving horse serum containing antidiphtheria antibody); it is now seen only rarely (e.g., in patients injected with rabbit or horse antithymocyte globulin for treatment of aplastic anemia or graft rejection, or patients with snakebite given anti-venom antibody made in animals). Although serum sickness is no longer common, the study of its pathogenesis sheds light on the mechanisms of human immune complex diseases. Approximately 5 days after the foreign protein is injected, specific antibodies are produced; these react with the antigen still present in the circulation to form antigen-antibody complexes. The complexes deposit in blood vessels in various tissue beds, triggering the subsequent injurious inflammatory reaction.

Several *variables determine whether immune complex formation leads to tissue deposition and disease.* Perhaps foremost among these factors is the size of the complexes. Very large complexes or complexes with many free IgG Fc regions (typically formed in antibody excess) are rapidly removed from the circulation by macrophages in the spleen and liver

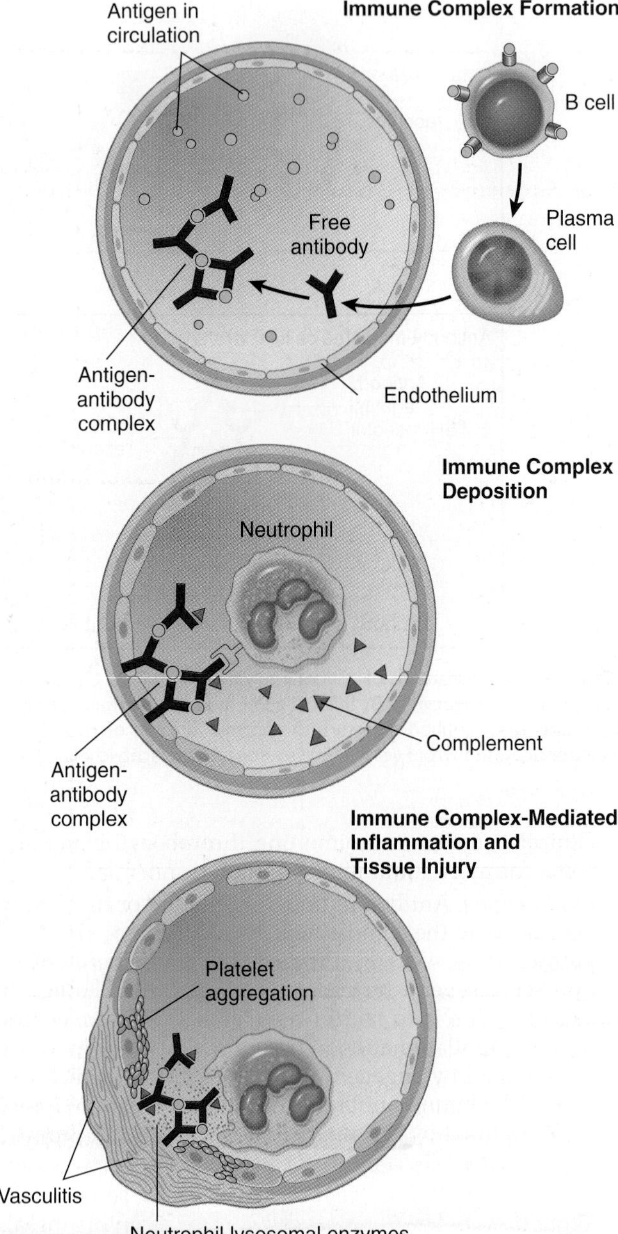

Figure 4–11 Immune complex disease: The sequential phases in the induction of systemic immune complex–mediated diseases (type III hypersensitivity).

and are therefore usually harmless. The most pathogenic complexes are formed during antigen excess and are small or intermediate in size and are cleared less effectively by phagocytes and therefore circulate longer. In addition, the charge of the complex, the valency of the antigen, the avidity of the antibody, and the hemodynamics of a given vascular bed all influence the tendency to develop disease. The favored sites of deposition are kidneys, joints, and small blood vessels in many tissues. Localization in the kidney and joints is explained in part by the high hemodynamic pressures associated with the filtration function of the glomerulus and the synovium. For complexes to leave the circulation and deposit within or outside the vessel wall, an increase in vascular permeability also must occur. This is probably triggered when immune complexes bind to leukocytes and mast cells by means of Fc and C3b receptors and stimulate release of mediators that increase vascular permeability.

Once complexes are deposited in the tissue, the third phase, the *inflammatory reaction*, ensues. During this phase (approximately 10 days after antigen administration), clinical features such as fever, urticaria, arthralgias, lymph node enlargement, and proteinuria appear. Wherever immune complexes deposit, characteristic tissue damage occurs. The immune complexes activate the complement system, leading to the release of biologically active fragments such as the anaphylatoxins (C3a and C5a), which increase vascular permeability and are chemotactic for neutrophils and monocytes (Chapter 2). The complexes also bind to Fcγ receptors on neutrophils and monocytes, activating these cells. Attempted phagocytosis of immune complexes by the leukocytes results in the secretion of a variety of additional pro-inflammatory substances, including prostaglandins, vasodilator peptides, and chemotactic substances, as well as lysosomal enzymes capable of digesting basement membrane, collagen, elastin, and cartilage, and reactive-oxygen species that damage tissues. Immune complexes can also cause platelet aggregation and activate Hageman factor; both of these reactions augment the inflammatory process and initiate formation of microthrombi, which contribute to the tissue injury by producing local ischemia (Fig. 4–11). The resultant pathologic lesion is termed *vasculitis* if it occurs in blood vessels, *glomerulonephritis* if it occurs in renal glomeruli, *arthritis* if it occurs in the joints, and so on.

Predictably, the antibody classes that induce such lesions are complement-fixing antibodies (i.e., IgG and IgM) and antibodies that bind to phagocyte Fc receptors (IgG). During the active phase of the disease, consumption of complement may result in decreased serum complement levels. The role of complement- and Fc receptor–dependent inflammation in the pathogenesis of the tissue injury is supported by the observation that experimental depletion of serum complement levels or knockout of Fc receptors in mice greatly reduces the severity of lesions, as does depletion of neutrophils.

MORPHOLOGY

The morphologic appearance of immune complex injury is dominated by acute **necrotizing vasculitis,** microthrombi, and superimposed ischemic necrosis accompanied by acute inflammation of the affected organs. The necrotic vessel wall takes on a smudgy eosinophilic appearance called **fibrinoid necrosis,** caused by protein deposition (see Fig. 1–13, Chapter 1). Immune complexes can be visualized in the tissues, usually in the vascular wall (examples of such deposits in the kidney in lupus are shown in Fig. 4–18, *E*). In due course, the lesions tend to resolve, especially when they were brought about by a single exposure to antigen (e.g., in acute serum sickness or acute poststreptococcal glomerulonephritis) (Chapter 13). However, chronic immune complex disease develops when there is persistent antigenemia or repeated exposure to an antigen. This occurs in some human diseases, such as systemic lupus erythematosus (SLE). Most often, even though the morphologic changes and other findings strongly implicate immune complex disease, the inciting antigens are unknown.

Local Immune Complex Disease

A model of local immune complex diseases is the *Arthus reaction,* in which an area of tissue necrosis appears as a result of acute immune complex vasculitis. The reaction is produced experimentally by injecting an antigen into the skin of a previously immunized animal (i.e., pre-formed antibodies against the antigen are already present in the circulation). Because of the initial antibody excess, immune complexes are formed as the antigen diffuses into the vascular wall; these are precipitated at the site of injection and trigger the same inflammatory reaction and histologic appearance as in systemic immune complex disease. Arthus lesions evolve over a few hours and reach a peak 4 to 10 hours after injection, when the injection site develops visible edema with severe hemorrhage, occasionally followed by ulceration.

SUMMARY

Pathogenesis of Diseases Caused by Antibodies and Immune Complexes

- Antibodies can coat (opsonize) cells, with or without complement proteins, and target these cells for phagocytosis by macrophages, which express receptors for the Fc tails of IgG molecules and for complement proteins. The result is depletion of the opsonized cells.
- Antibodies and immune complexes may deposit in tissues or blood vessels, and elicit an acute inflammatory reaction by activating complement, with release of breakdown products, or by engaging Fc receptors of leukocytes. The inflammatory reaction causes tissue injury.
- Antibodies can bind to cell surface receptors or essential molecules, and cause functional derangements (either inhibition or unregulated activation) without cell injury.

T Cell–Mediated (Type IV) Hypersensitivity

Several autoimmune disorders, as well as pathologic reactions to environmental chemicals and persistent microbes, are now known to be caused by T cells (Table 4–5). The occurrence and significance of T lymphocyte–mediated tissue injury

Table 4–5 T Cell–Mediated Diseases*

Disease	Specificity of Pathogenic T Cells	Principal Mechanisms of Tissue Injury	Clinicopathologic Manifestations
Rheumatoid arthritis	Collagen?; citrullinated self proteins?	Inflammation mediated by T_H17 (and T_H1?) cytokines; role of antibodies and immune complexes?	Chronic arthritis with inflammation, destruction of articular cartilage and bone
Multiple sclerosis	Protein antigens in myelin (e.g., myelin basic protein)	Inflammation mediated by T_H1 and T_H17 cytokines, myelin destruction by activated macrophages	Demyelination in CNS with perivascular inflammation; paralysis, ocular lesions
Type 1 diabetes mellitus	Antigens of pancreatic islet β cells (insulin, glutamic acid decarboxylase, others)	T cell–mediated inflammation, destruction of islet cells by CTLs	Insulitis (chronic inflammation in islets), destruction of β cells; diabetes
Hashimoto thyroiditis	Thyroglobulin, other thyroid proteins	Inflammation, CTL-mediated killing of thyroid epithelial cells	Hypothyroidism
Inflammatory bowel disease	Enteric bacteria; self antigens?	Inflammation mediated mainly by T_H17 cytokines	Chronic intestinal inflammation, ulceration, obstruction
Autoimmune myocarditis	Myosin heavy chain protein	CTL-mediated killing of myocardial cells; inflammation mediated by T_H1 cytokines	Cardiomyopathy
Contact sensitivity	Various environmental chemicals (e.g., urushiol from poison ivy or poison oak)	Inflammation mediated by T_H1 (and T_H17?) cytokines	Epidermal necrosis, dermal inflammation with skin rash and blisters

*Examples of human T cell–mediated diseases are listed. In many cases, the specificity of the T cells and the mechanisms of tissue injury are inferred on the basis of similarity to experimental animal models of the diseases.
CNS, central nervous system; CTL, cytotoxic T lymphocyte.

have been increasingly appreciated as the methods for detecting and purifying T cells from patients' circulation and lesions have improved. This group of diseases is of great clinical interest because many of the new, rationally designed biologic therapies for immune-mediated inflammatory diseases have been developed to target abnormal T cell reactions. Two types of T cell reactions are capable of causing tissue injury and disease: (1) cytokine-mediated inflammation, in which the cytokines are produced mainly by CD4+ T cells, and (2) direct cell cytotoxicity, mediated by CD8+ T cells (Fig. 4–12). In inflammation, exemplified by the delayed-type hypersensitivity (DTH) reaction, CD4+ T cells of the T_H1 and T_H17 subsets secrete cytokines, which recruit and activate other cells, especially macrophages, and these are the major effector cells of injury. In cell-mediated cytotoxicity, cytotoxic CD8+ T cells are responsible for tissue damage.

Inflammatory Reactions Elicited by CD4+ T Cells

The sequence of events in T cell–mediated inflammatory reactions begins with the first exposure to antigen and is essentially the same as the reactions of cell-mediated immunity (Fig. 4–4). Naive CD4+ T lymphocytes recognize peptide antigens of self or microbial proteins in association with class II MHC molecules on the surface of DCs (or macrophages) that have processed the antigens. If the DCs produce IL-12, the naive T cells differentiate into effector cells of the T_H1 type. The cytokine IFN-γ, made by NK cells and by the T_H1 cells themselves, further promotes T_H1 differentiation, providing a powerful positive feedback loop. If the APCs produce IL-1, IL-6, or IL-23 instead of IL-12, the CD4+ cells develop into T_H17 effectors. On subsequent exposure to the antigen, the previously generated effector cells are recruited to the site of antigen exposure and are activated by the antigen presented by local APCs. The T_H1 cells secrete IFN-γ, which is the most potent macrophage-activating cytokine known. Activated macrophages have increased phagocytic and microbicidal activity. Activated macrophages also express more class II MHC molecules and costimulators, leading to augmented antigen presentation capacity, and the cells secrete more IL-12, thus stimulating more T_H1 responses. Upon activation by antigen, T_H17 effector cells secrete IL-17 and several other cytokines, which promote the recruitment of neutrophils (and monocytes) and thus induce inflammation. Because the cytokines produced by the T cells enhance leukocyte recruitment and activation, these inflammatory reactions become chronic unless the offending agent is eliminated or the cycle is interrupted therapeutically. In fact, inflammation occurs as an early response to microbes and dead cells (Chapter 2), but it is greatly increased and prolonged when T cells are involved.

Delayed-type hypersensitivity (DTH), described next, is an illustrative model of T cell–mediated inflammation and tissue injury. The same reactions are the underlying basis for several diseases. *Contact dermatitis* is an example of tissue injury resulting from T cell–mediated inflammation. It is evoked by contact with pentadecylcatechol (also known as urushiol, the active component of poison ivy and poison oak, which probably becomes antigenic by binding to a host protein). On reexposure of a previously exposed person to the plants, sensitized T_H1 CD4+ cells accumulate in the dermis and migrate toward the antigen within the epidermis. Here they release cytokines that damage keratinocytes, causing separation of these cells and formation of an intraepidermal vesicle, and inflammation manifested as a vesicular dermatitis. It has long been thought that several *systemic diseases,* such as type 1 diabetes and multiple sclerosis, are caused by T_H1 and T_H17 reactions against self antigens, and Crohn disease may be caused by uncontrolled reactions involving the same T cells but directed against intestinal bacteria. T cell–mediated inflammation also plays a role in the rejection of transplants, described later in the chapter.

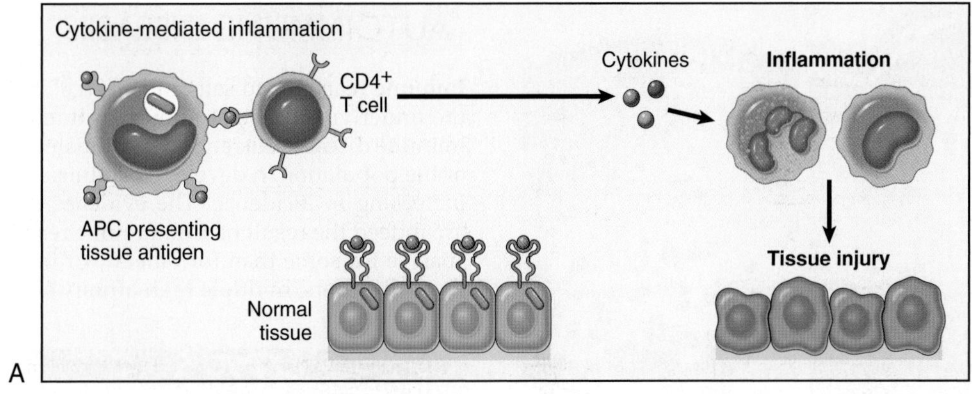

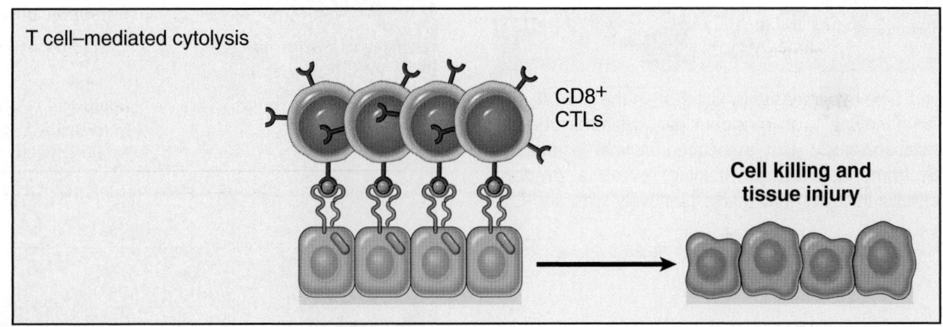

Figure 4–12 Mechanisms of T cell–mediated (type IV) hypersensitivity reactions. **A,** In cytokine-mediated inflammatory reactions, CD4+ T cells respond to tissue antigens by secreting cytokines that stimulate inflammation and activate phagocytes, leading to tissue injury. **B,** In some diseases, CD8+ CTLs directly kill tissue cells. APC, antigen-presenting cell; CTLs, cytotoxic T lymphocytes.

Delayed-Type Hypersensitivity

DTH is a T cell–mediated reaction that develops in response to antigen challenge in a previously sensitized individual. In contrast with immediate hypersensitivity, the DTH reaction is delayed for 12 to 48 hours, which is the time it takes for effector T cells to be recruited to the site of antigen challenge and to be activated to secrete cytokines. The classic example of DTH is the tuberculin reaction, elicited by challenge with a protein extract of *M. tuberculosis* (tuberculin) in a person who has previously been exposed to the tubercle bacillus. Between 8 and 12 hours after intracutaneous injection of tuberculin, a local area of erythema and induration appears, reaching a peak (typically 1 to 2 cm in diameter) in 24 to 72 hours and thereafter slowly subsiding. On histologic examination, the DTH reaction is characterized by perivascular accumulation ("cuffing") of CD4+ helper T cells and macrophages (Fig. 4–13). Local secretion of cytokines by these cells leads to increased microvascular permeability, giving rise to dermal edema and fibrin deposition; the latter is the main cause of the tissue induration in these responses. DTH reactions are mediated primarily by T_H1 cells; the contribution of T_H17 cells is unclear. The tuberculin response is used to screen populations for people who have had previous exposure to tuberculosis and therefore have circulating memory T cells specific for mycobacterial proteins. Notably, immunosuppression or loss of CD4+ T cells (e.g., resulting from HIV infection) may lead to a negative tuberculin response even in the presence of a severe infection.

Prolonged DTH reactions against persistent microbes or other stimuli may result in a special morphologic pattern of reaction called *granulomatous inflammation.* The initial perivascular CD4+ T cell infiltrate is progressively replaced by macrophages over a period of 2 to 3 weeks. These accumulated macrophages typically exhibit morphologic evidence of activation; that is, they become large, flat, and eosinophilic, and are called epithelioid cells. The epithelioid cells occasionally fuse under the influence of cytokines (e.g., IFN-γ) to form multinucleate giant cells. A microscopic aggregate of epithelioid cells, typically surrounded by a collar of lymphocytes, is called a granuloma (Fig. 4–14, *A*). The process is essentially a chronic form of T_H1-mediated inflammation and macrophage activation (Fig. 4–14, *B*). Older granulomas develop an enclosing rim of fibroblasts and connective tissue. Recognition of a granuloma is of diagnostic importance because of the limited number of conditions that can cause it (Chapter 2).

T Cell–Mediated Cytotoxicity

In this form of T cell–mediated tissue injury, CD8+ CTLs kill antigen-bearing target cells. As discussed earlier, class I MHC molecules bind to intracellular peptide antigens and present the peptides to CD8+ T lymphocytes, stimulating the differentiation of these T cells into effector cells called CTLs. CTLs play a critical role in resistance to virus infections and some tumors. The principal mechanism of killing by CTLs is dependent on the perforin–granzyme system. Perforin and granzymes are stored in the granules of CTLs and are rapidly released when CTLs engage their targets (cells bearing the appropriate class I MHC–bound peptides). Perforin binds to the plasma membrane of the

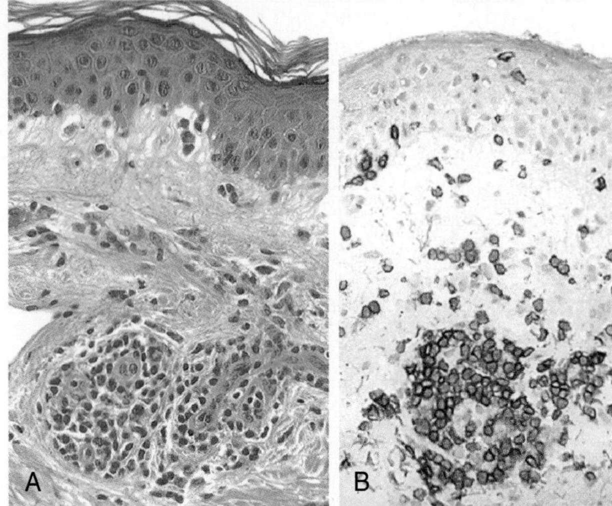

Figure 4–13 Delayed-type hypersensitivity reaction in the skin. **A,** Perivascular accumulation ("cuffing") of mononuclear inflammatory cells (lymphocytes and macrophages), with associated dermal edema and fibrin deposition. **B,** Immunoperoxidase staining reveals a predominantly perivascular cellular infiltrate that marks positively with anti-CD4 antibodies.

(B, Courtesy of Dr. Louis Picker, Department of Pathology, Oregon Health & Science University, Portland, Oregon.)

target cells and promotes the entry of granzymes, which are proteases that specifically cleave and thereby activate cellular caspases. These enzymes induce apoptotic death of the target cells (Chapter 1). CTLs play an important role in the rejection of solid-organ transplants and may contribute to many immunologic diseases, such as type 1 diabetes (in which insulin-producing β cells in pancreatic islets are destroyed by an autoimmune T cell reaction). CD8+ T cells may also secrete IFN-γ and contribute to cytokine-mediated inflammation, but less so than CD4+ cells.

SUMMARY

Mechanisms of T Cell–Mediated Hypersensitivity Reactions

- Cytokine-mediated inflammation: CD4+ T cells are activated by exposure to a protein antigen and differentiate into T_H1 and T_H17 effector cells. Subsequent exposure to the antigen results in the secretion of cytokines. IFN-γ activates macrophages to produce substances that cause tissue damage and promote fibrosis, and IL-17 and other cytokines recruit leukocytes, thus promoting inflammation.
- T cell–mediated cytotoxicity: CD8+ CTLs specific for an antigen recognize cells expressing the target antigen and kill these cells. CD8+ T cells also secrete IFN-γ.

With the basic mechanisms of pathologic immune reactions as background, we now proceed to a consideration of two categories of reactions that are of great clinical importance: autoimmunity and transplant rejection.

AUTOIMMUNE DISEASES

Immune reactions to self antigens (i.e., autoimmunity) are the underlying cause of numerous human diseases. Autoimmune diseases currently are estimated to affect 2% to 5% of the population in developed countries, and appear to be increasing in incidence. The evidence that these diseases are indeed the result of autoimmune reactions is more persuasive for some than for others. For instance, in many of these disorders, multiple high-affinity autoantibodies have

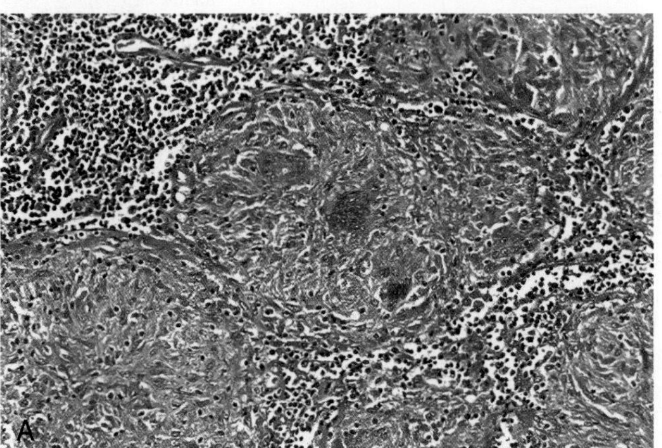

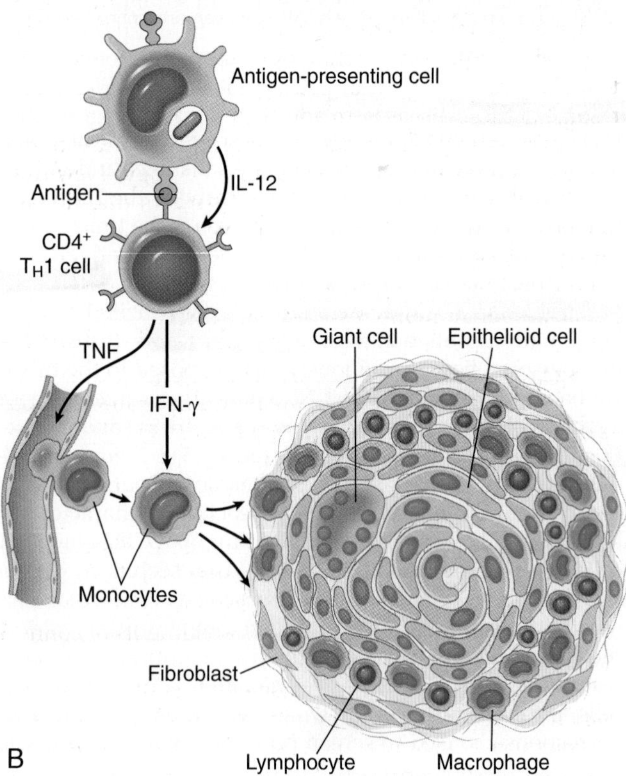

Figure 4–14 Granulomatous inflammation. **A,** A section of a lymph node shows several granulomas, each made up of an aggregate of epithelioid cells and surrounded by lymphocytes. The granuloma in the center shows several multinucleate giant cells. **B,** The events that give rise to the formation of granulomas in type IV hypersensitivity reactions. Note the role played by T cell–derived cytokines.

(A, Courtesy of Dr. Trace Worrell, Department of Pathology, University of Texas Southwestern Medical School, Dallas, Texas.)

Table 4–6 Autoimmune Diseases

Organ-Specific	Systemic
Diseases Mediated by Antibodies	
Autoimmune hemolytic anemia	Systemic lupus erythematosus
Autoimmune thrombocytopenia	
Autoimmune atrophic gastritis of pernicious anemia	
Myasthenia gravis	
Graves disease	
Goodpasture syndrome	
Diseases Mediated by T Cells*	
Type I diabetes mellitus	Rheumatoid arthritis
Multiple sclerosis	Systemic sclerosis (scleroderma)
Hashimoto thyroiditis	Sjögren syndrome
Crohn disease	
Diseases Postulated to Be of Autoimmune Origin†	
Primary biliary cirrhosis	Polyarteritis nodosa
Autoimmune (chronic active) hepatitis	Inflammatory myopathies

*A role for T cells has been demonstrated in these disorders, but antibodies also may be involved in tissue injury.
†An autoimmune basis for these disorders is suspected, but the supporting evidence is not strong.

been identified, and in some cases these antibodies are known to cause pathologic abnormalities (Table 4-6). Similarly, with improving technology, there is growing evidence for the activation of pathogenic self-reactive T cells in some of these diseases. In addition, experimental models have proved very informative, providing circumstantial evidence supporting an autoimmune etiology. Nevertheless, it is fair to say that for many disorders traditionally classified as autoimmune, this etiologic origin is suspected but not proved.

Presumed autoimmune diseases range from those in which specific immune responses are directed against one particular organ or cell type and result in localized tissue damage, to multisystem diseases characterized by lesions in many organs and associated with multiple autoantibodies or T cell–mediated reactions against numerous self antigens. In many of the systemic diseases that are caused by immune complexes and autoantibodies, the lesions affect principally the connective tissue and blood vessels of the various organs involved. Therefore, these diseases are often referred to as "collagen vascular" or "connective tissue" disorders, even though the immunologic reactions are not specifically directed against constituents of connective tissue or blood vessels.

Normal persons are unresponsive (tolerant) to their own (self) antigens, and autoimmunity results from a failure of self-tolerance. Therefore, understanding the pathogenesis of autoimmunity requires familiarity with the mechanisms of normal immunologic tolerance.

Immunologic Tolerance

Immunologic tolerance is unresponsiveness to an antigen that is induced by exposure of specific lymphocytes to that antigen. Self-tolerance refers to a lack of immune responsiveness to one's own tissue antigens. Billions of different antigen receptors are randomly generated in developing T and B lymphocytes, and it is not surprising that during this process, receptors are produced that can recognize self antigens. Since these antigens cannot all be concealed from the immune system, there must be means of eliminating or controlling self-reactive lymphocytes. Several mechanisms work in concert to select against self-reactivity and to thus prevent immune reactions against the body's own antigens. These mechanisms are broadly divided into two groups: central tolerance and peripheral tolerance (Fig. 4–15).

Central tolerance. The principal mechanism of central tolerance is the antigen-induced deletion (death) of self-reactive T and B lymphocytes during their maturation in central (generative) lymphoid organs (i.e., in the thymus for T cells and in the bone marrow for B cells). In the thymus, many autologous (self) protein antigens are processed and presented by thymic APCs in association with self MHC. Any immature T cell that encounters such a self antigen undergoes apoptosis (a process called deletion, or negative selection), and the T cells that complete their maturation are thereby depleted of self-reactive cells (Fig. 4–15). An exciting advance has been the identification of putative transcription factors that induce the expression of peripheral tissue antigens in the thymus, thus making the thymus an immunologic mirror of self. One such factor is called the autoimmune regulator (AIRE); mutations in the *AIRE* gene are responsible for an autoimmune polyendocrine syndrome in which T cells specific for multiple self antigens escape deletion (presumably because these self antigens are not expressed in the thymus), and attack tissues expressing the self antigens. Some T cells that encounter self antigens in the thymus are not killed but differentiate into regulatory T cells, as described later.

Immature B cells that recognize self antigens with high affinity in the bone marrow also may die by apoptosis. Some self-reactive B cells may not be deleted but may undergo a second round of rearrangement of antigen receptor genes and then express new receptors that are no longer self-reactive (a process called "receptor editing").

Unfortunately, the process of deletion of self-reactive lymphocytes is not perfect. Many self antigens may not be present in the thymus, so T cells bearing receptors for such autoantigens can escape into the periphery. There is similar "slippage" in the B cell system as well, and B cells that bear receptors for a variety of self antigens, including thyroglobulin, collagen, and DNA, can be found in healthy persons.

Peripheral tolerance. Self-reactive T cells that escape negative selection in the thymus can potentially wreak havoc unless they are deleted or effectively muzzled. Several mechanisms in the peripheral tissues that silence such potentially autoreactive T cells have been identified (Fig. 4–15):

- *Anergy*: This term refers to functional inactivation (rather than death) of lymphocytes induced by encounter with antigens under certain conditions. As described previously, activation of T cells requires two signals: recognition of peptide antigen in association with self MHC molecules on APCs, and a set of second costimulatory

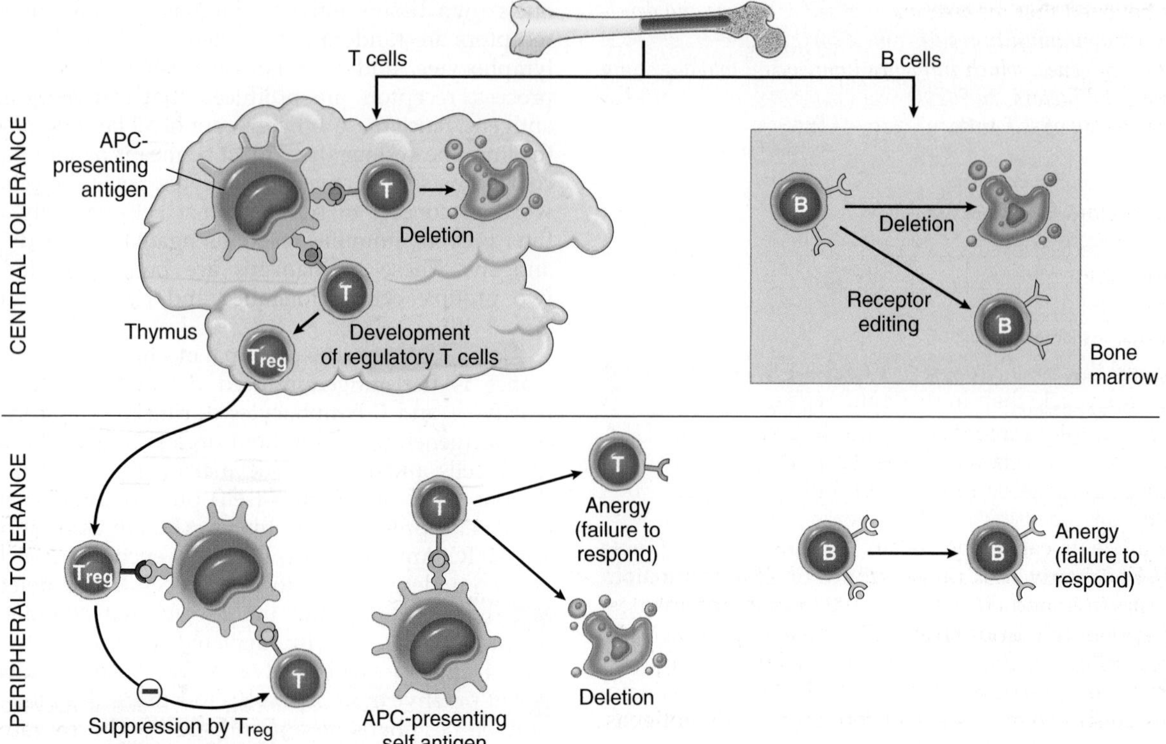

Figure 4–15 Immunologic self-tolerance: The principal mechanisms of central and peripheral self-tolerance in T and B cells.

signals (e.g., through B7 molecules) provided by the APCs. If the second costimulatory signals are not delivered, or if an inhibitory receptor on the T cell (rather than the costimulatory receptor) is engaged when the cell encounters self antigen, the T cell becomes anergic and cannot respond to the antigen (Fig. 4–15). Because costimulatory molecules are not strongly expressed on most normal tissues, the encounter between autoreactive T cells and self antigens in tissues may result in anergy. B cells can also become anergic if they encounter antigen in the absence of specific helper T cells.

- *Suppression by regulatory T cells*: The responses of T lymphocytes to self antigens may be actively suppressed by regulatory T cells. The best-defined populations of regulatory T cells express CD25, one of the chains of the receptor for IL-2, and require IL-2 for their generation and survival. These cells also express a unique transcription factor called FoxP3. This protein is necessary for the development of regulatory cells, and mutations in the *FOXP3* gene are responsible for a systemic autoimmune disease called IPEX (immune dysregulation, polyendocrinopathy, enteropathy, X-linked syndrome), which is associated with deficiency of regulatory T cells. Several mechanisms have been proposed to explain how regulatory T cells control immune responses, including secretion of immunosuppressive cytokines (e.g., IL-10, transforming growth factor-β [TGF-β]), which can dampen a variety of T cell responses, and competitive blocking of B7 molecules on APCs.
- *Activation-induced cell death*: Another mechanism of peripheral tolerance involves apoptosis of mature lymphocytes as a result of self-antigen recognition. One mechanism of apoptosis involves the death receptor Fas (a member of the TNF receptor family), which can be engaged by its ligand coexpressed on the same or neighboring cells. The same pathway is important for the deletion of self-reactive B cells by Fas ligand expressed on T cells. The importance of this pathway of self-tolerance is illustrated by the discovery that mutations in the *FAS* gene are responsible for an autoimmune disease called the autoimmune lymphoproliferative syndrome (ALPS), characterized by lymphadenopathy and multiple autoantibodies including anti-DNA. Defects in Fas and Fas ligand are also the cause of similar autoimmune diseases in mice. The mitochondrial pathway of apoptosis, which does not depend on death receptors, may also be involved in the elimination of self-reactive lymphocytes.

Mechanisms of Autoimmunity

Proceeding from the foregoing summary of the principal mechanisms of self-tolerance, we can ask how these mechanisms might break down to give rise to pathologic autoimmunity. Unfortunately, there are no simple answers to this question, and the underlying causes of most human autoimmune diseases remain to be determined. As mentioned earlier, certain mutations can compromise one or another pathway of self-tolerance and cause pathologic autoimmunity. Study of these single-gene mutations is extremely informative, and such research helps to establish the biologic significance of the various pathways of self-tolerance. The diseases caused by such mutations are rare, however, and most autoimmune diseases cannot be explained by defects in single genes.

It is believed that *the breakdown of self-tolerance and development of autoimmunity result from a combination of inherited susceptibility genes, which influence lymphocyte tolerance, and environmental factors, such as infections or tissue injury, that alter the display of self antigens* (Fig. 4–16).

Genetic Factors in Autoimmunity

There is abundant evidence that susceptibility genes play an important role in the development of autoimmune diseases.

- Autoimmune diseases have a tendency to run in families, and there is a greater incidence of the same disease in monozygotic than in dizygotic twins.
- Several autoimmune diseases are linked with the HLA locus, especially class II alleles (HLA-DR, -DQ). The frequency of a disease in a person with a particular HLA allele, compared with that in people who do not inherit that allele, is called the *odds ratio* or *relative risk* (Table 4-7). The relative risk ranges from 3 or 4 for rheumatoid arthritis (RA) and HLA-DR4 to 100 or more for ankylosing spondylitis and HLA-B27. However, how MHC genes influence the development of autoimmunity is still not clear, especially because MHC molecules do not distinguish between self and foreign peptide antigens. It is also worthy of note that most people with a susceptibility-related MHC allele never develop any disease, and, conversely, people without the relevant MHC gene can develop the disease. Expression of a particular MHC gene is therefore but one variable that can contribute to autoimmunity.
- Genome-wide association studies and linkage studies in families are revealing many genetic polymorphisms that are associated with different autoimmune diseases (Table 4–8). Some of these polymorphisms seem to be associated with several diseases, suggesting that the genes involved influence general mechanisms of self-tolerance and immune regulation. Others are disease-specific and may influence end-organ sensitivity or display of particular self antigens. There is great interest in elucidating how these genes contribute to autoimmunity, and many plausible hypotheses have been proposed (Table 4–8), but the actual role of these genes in the development of particular autoimmune diseases is not established.

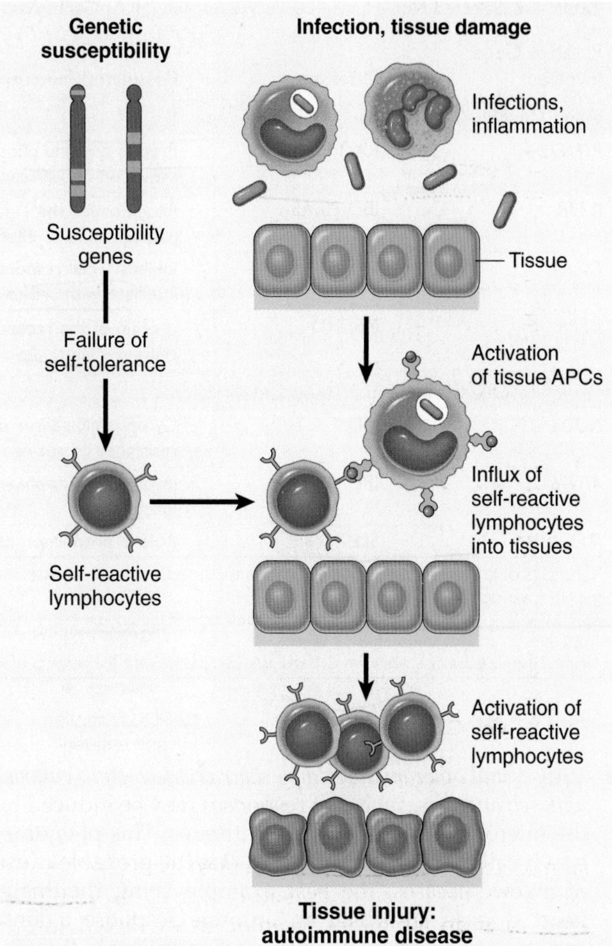

Figure 4–16 Pathogenesis of autoimmunity. Autoimmunity arises from the inheritance of susceptibility genes that may interfere with self-tolerance, in association with environmental triggers (infection, tissue injury, inflammation) that alter the display of self antigens, promote lymphocyte entry into tissues, and enhance the activation of self-reactive lymphocytes.

Role of Infections and Tissue Injury

A variety of microbes, including bacteria, mycoplasmas, and viruses, have been implicated as triggers for autoimmunity. Microbes may induce autoimmune reactions by several mechanisms:

Table 4–7 Association of Human Leukocyte Antigen (HLA) Alleles with Autoimmune Diseases

Disease	HLA Allele	Odds Ratio*
Rheumatoid arthritis (anti-CCP Ab–positive)†	DRB1	4–12
Type 1 diabetes	DRB1*0301-DQA1*0501-DQB1*0201 haplotype	4
	DRB1*0401- DQA1*0301-DQB1*0302 haplotype	8
	DRB1*0301/0401 haplotype heterozygotes	35
Multiple sclerosis	DRB1*1501	3
Systemic lupus erythematosus	DRB1*0301	2
	DRB1*1501	1.3
Ankylosing spondylitis	B*27 (mainly B*2705 and B*2702)	100–200
Celiac disease	DQA1*0501-DQB1*0201 haplotype	7

*The *odds ratio* (also called *relative risk*) is the approximate value of the increased risk of the disease associated with the inheritance of particular HLA alleles. The data are from European-derived populations.

†Anti-CCP Ab, antibodies directed against cyclic citrullinated peptides. Data are from patients who tested positive for these antibodies in serum.

Table courtesy of Dr. Michelle Fernando, Imperial College London.

Table 4–8 Selected Non–Human Leukocyte Antigen (HLA) Genes Associated with Autoimmune Diseases

Putative Gene Involved*	Diseases	Postulated Function of Encoded Protein and Role of Mutation/Polymorphism in Disease
Genes Involved in Immune Regulation		
PTPN22	RA, T1D, IBD	Protein tyrosine phosphatase, may affect signaling in lymphocytes and may alter negative selection or activation of self-reactive T cells
IL23R	IBD, PS, AS	Receptor for the T_H17-inducing cytokine IL-23; may alter differentiation of CD4+ T cells into pathogenic T_H17 effector cells
CTLA4	T1D, RA	Inhibits T cell responses by terminating activation and promoting activity of regulatory T cells; may interfere with self-tolerance
IL2RA	MS, T1D	α chain of the receptor for IL-2, which is a growth and survival factor for activated and regulatory T cells; may affect development of effector cells and/or regulation of immune responses
Genes Involved in Immune Responses to Microbes		
NOD2	IBD	Cytoplasmic sensor of bacteria expressed in Paneth and other intestinal epithelial cells; may control resistance to gut commensal bacteria
ATG16	IBD	Involved in autophagy; possible role in defense against microbes and maintenance of epithelial barrier function
IRF5, IFIH1	SLE	Role in production of type I IFN, involved in the pathogenesis of SLE (see text)

*The probable linkage of these genes with various autoimmune diseases has been defined by genome-wide association studies (GWAS) and other methods for studying disease-associated polymorphisms.

AS, ankylosing spondylitis; IBD, inflammatory bowel disease; IFN, interferon; MS, multiple sclerosis; PS, psoriasis; RA, rheumatoid arthritis; SLE, systemic lupus erythematosus; T1D, type 1 diabetes.

Adapted from Zenewicz L, Abraham C, Flavell RA, Cho J: Unraveling the genetics of autoimmunity. Cell 140:791, 2010.

- *Viruses and other microbes may share cross-reacting epitopes with self antigens,* such that responses may be induced by the microbe but may attack self tissues. This phenomenon is called molecular mimicry. It is the probable cause of a few diseases, the best example being rheumatic heart disease, in which an immune response against streptococci cross-reacts with cardiac antigens. It is not known if more subtle mimicry plays a role in other autoimmune diseases.
- *Microbial infections with resultant tissue necrosis and inflammation can cause upregulation of costimulatory molecules on APCs in the tissue,* thus favoring a breakdown of T cell anergy and subsequent T cell activation.

There is no lack of possible mechanisms to explain how infectious agents might participate in the pathogenesis of autoimmunity. At present, however, no evidence is available that clearly implicates any microbe in the causation of human autoimmune diseases. Adding to the complexity are recent suggestions (based largely on epidemiologic data) that infections may paradoxically protect affected persons from some autoimmune diseases, notably type 1 diabetes and multiple sclerosis. The possible mechanisms underlying this effect are not understood.

The display of tissue antigens may be altered by a variety of environmental insults, not only infections. As discussed later, ultraviolet (UV) radiation causes cell death and may lead to the exposure of nuclear antigens, which elicit pathologic immune responses in lupus; this mechanism is the proposed explanation for the association of lupus flares with exposure to sunlight. Smoking is a risk factor for RA, perhaps because it leads to chemical modification of self antigens. Local tissue injury for any reason may lead to the release of self antigens and autoimmune responses.

Finally, there is a strong gender bias of autoimmunity, with many of these diseases being more common in women than in men. The underlying mechanisms are still not well understood, and may include the effects of hormones and other factors.

An autoimmune response may itself promote further autoimmune attack. Tissue injury caused by an autoimmune response or any other cause may lead to exposure of self antigen epitopes that were previously concealed but are now presented to T cells in an immunogenic form. The activation of such autoreactive T cells is called "epitope spreading," because the immune response "spreads" to epitopes that were not recognized initially. This is one of the mechanisms that may contribute to the chronicity of autoimmune diseases.

SUMMARY

Immunologic Tolerance and Autoimmunity

- *Tolerance* (unresponsiveness) to self antigens is a fundamental property of the immune system, and breakdown of tolerance is the basis of autoimmune diseases.
- *Central tolerance*: Immature lymphocytes that recognize self antigens in the central (generative) lymphoid organs are killed by apoptosis; in the B cell lineage, some of the self-reactive lymphocytes switch to new antigen receptors that are not self-reactive.
- *Peripheral tolerance*: Mature lymphocytes that recognize self antigens in peripheral tissues become functionally inactive (anergic), or are suppressed by regulatory T lymphocytes, or die by apoptosis.
- The *factors that lead to a failure of self-tolerance and the development of autoimmunity* include (1) inheritance of susceptibility genes that may disrupt different tolerance pathways and (2) infections and tissue alterations that may expose self-antigens and activate APCs and lymphocytes in the tissues.

Having discussed the general principles of tolerance and autoimmunity, we proceed to a discussion of some of the most common and important autoimmune diseases. Although each disease is discussed separately, considerable overlap is apparent in their clinical, serologic, and morphologic features. Only the systemic autoimmune diseases are covered in this chapter; the autoimmune diseases that affect single organ systems are more appropriately discussed in the chapters that deal with the relevant organs.

Systemic Lupus Erythematosus

Systemic lupus erythematosus (SLE) is a multisystem autoimmune disease of protean manifestations and variable clinical behavior. Clinically, it is an unpredictable, remitting and relapsing disease of acute or insidious onset that may involve virtually any organ in the body; however, it affects principally the skin, kidneys, serosal membranes, joints, and heart. Immunologically, the disease is associated with an enormous array of autoantibodies, classically including antinuclear antibodies (ANAs). The clinical presentation of SLE is so variable, with so many overlapping features with those of other autoimmune diseases (RA, polymyositis, and others), that it has been necessary to develop diagnostic criteria for SLE (Table 4–9). The diagnosis is established by demonstration of four or more of the criteria during any interval of observation.

Incidence and prevalence estimates of SLE vary among racial and ethnic groups; some studies estimate the prevalence to be as high as 0.2% in certain groups. As with many autoimmune diseases, there is a strong (approximately 9:1) female preponderance, and the disease affects 1 in 700 women of childbearing age. SLE is more common and severe in black Americans, affecting 1 in 245 women in that group. Onset typically is in the second or third decade of life, but it may manifest at any age, including early childhood.

PATHOGENESIS

The fundamental defect in SLE is a failure to maintain self-tolerance, leading to the production of a large number of autoantibodies that can damage tissues either directly or in the form of immune complex deposits. As in other autoimmune diseases, the pathogenesis of SLE involves a combination of genetic and environmental factors. Recent studies have revealed interesting clues about the pathogenesis of this enigmatic disorder (Fig. 4–17).

Genetic Factors. Many lines of evidence support a genetic predisposition to SLE.

- **Familial association.** Family members have an increased risk for the development of SLE, and up to 20% of clinically unaffected first-degree relatives may have autoantibodies. There is a high rate of concordance in

Table 4–9 1997 Revised Criteria for Classification of Systemic Lupus Erythematosus*

Criterion	Definition
1. Malar rash	Fixed erythema, flat or raised, over the malar eminences, tending to spare the nasolabial folds
2. Discoid rash	Erythematous raised patches with adherent keratotic scaling and follicular plugging; atrophic scarring may occur in older lesions
3. Photosensitivity	Rash occurring as an unusual reaction to sunlight, reported in patient history or as physician observation
4. Oral ulcers	Oral or nasopharyngeal ulceration, usually painless, observed by a physician
5. Arthritis	Nonerosive arthritis involving two or more peripheral joints, characterized by tenderness, swelling, or effusion
6. Serositis	Pleuritis—convincing history of pleuritic pain or rub heard by a physician or evidence of pleural effusion *or* Pericarditis—documented by electrocardiogram or rub or evidence of pericardial effusion
7. Renal disorder	Persistent proteinuria >0.5 g/dL or >3+ if quantitation not performed *or* Cellular casts—may be red blood cell, hemoglobin, granular, tubular, or mixed
8. Neurologic disorder	Seizures—in the absence of offending drugs or known metabolic derangements, (e.g., uremia, ketoacidosis, or electrolyte imbalance) *or* Psychosis—in the absence of offending drugs or known metabolic derangements, (e.g., uremia, ketoacidosis, or electrolyte imbalance)
9. Hematologic disorder	Hemolytic anemia—with reticulocytosis *or* Leukopenia—$<4.0 \times 10^9$/L (4000/mm^3) total on two or more occasions *or* Lymphopenia—$<1.5 \times 10^9$/L (1500/mm^3) on two or more occasions *or* Thrombocytopenia—$<100 \times 10^9$/L (100×10^3/mm^3) in the absence of offending drugs
10. Immunologic disorder	Anti-DNA antibody to native DNA in abnormal titer or Anti-Sm—presence of antibody to Sm nuclear antigen or Positive finding of antiphospholipid antibodies based on (1) an abnormal serum level of IgG or IgM anticardiolipin antibodies, (2) a positive test for lupus anticoagulant using a standard test, or (3) a false-positive serologic test for syphilis known to be positive for at least 6 months and confirmed by negative *Treponema pallidum* immobilization or fluorescent treponemal antibody absorption test
11. Antinuclear antibody	An abnormal titer of antinuclear antibody by immunofluorescence or an equivalent assay at any point in time and in the absence of drugs known to be associated with drug-induced lupus syndrome

*The proposed classification is based on 11 criteria. For the purpose of identifying patients in clinical studies, a person is said to have systemic lupus erythematosus if any 4 or more of the 11 criteria are present, serially or simultaneously, during any period of observation.

From Tan EM, Cohen AS, Fries JF, et al: The revised criteria for the classification of systemic lupus erythematosus. Arthritis Rheum 25:1271, 1982; and Hochberg MC: Updating the American College of Rheumatology revised criteria for the classification of systemic lupus erythematosus. Arthritis Rheum 40:1725, 1997.

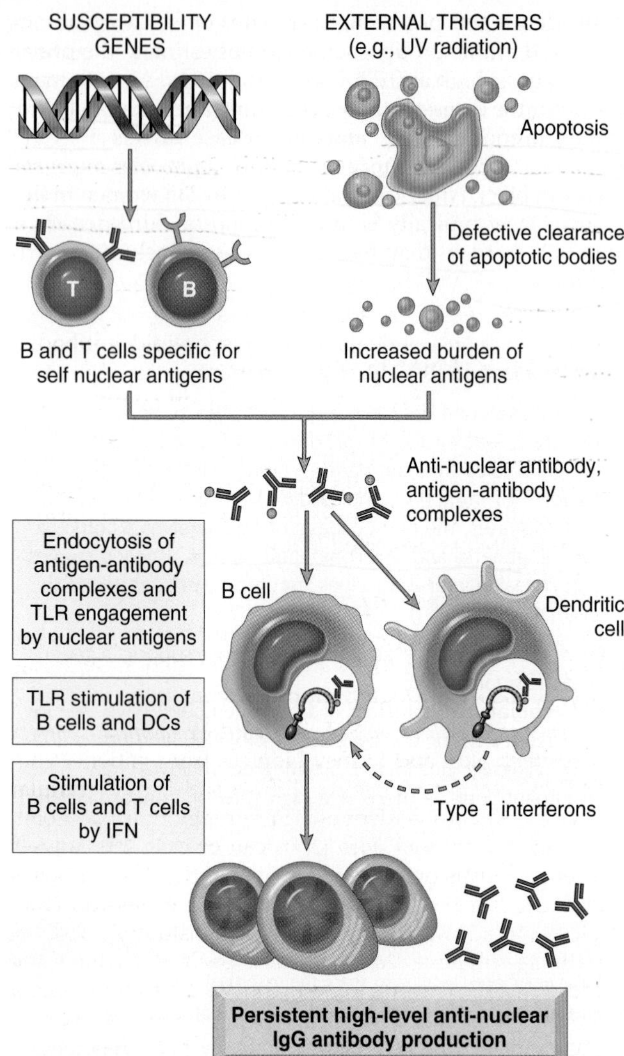

Figure 4–17 Model for the pathogenesis of systemic lupus erythematosus. Genetic susceptibility and exposure result in failure of self-tolerance and persistence of nuclear antigens. Autoantibodies serve to internalize nuclear components, which engage TLRs and stimulate IFN production. IFN may stimulate B and T cell responses to the nuclear antigens. IFN, interferon; IgG, immunoglobulin G; MHC, major histocompatibility complex; TLRs, Toll-like receptors; UV, ultraviolet.

monozygotic twins (25%) versus dizygotic twins (1% to 3%).

- **HLA association.** The odds ratio (relative risk) for persons with HLA-DR2 or HLA-DR3 is 2 to 3, and if both haplotypes are present, the risk is about 5.
- **Other genes.** Genetic deficiencies of classical pathway complement proteins, especially C1q, C2, or C4, are seen in about 10% of patients with SLE. The complement deficiencies may result in defective clearance of immune complexes and apoptotic cells, and failure of B cell tolerance. A polymorphism in the inhibitory Fc receptor, FcγRIIb, has been described in some patients; this may contribute to inadequate control of B cell activation. Many other genes have been detected by genome-wide association studies, but the role of each of these is not established and their contribution to the development of the disease remains unclear.

Environmental Factors. There are many indications that environmental factors are involved in the pathogenesis of SLE.

- **Ultraviolet (UV) radiation** (sun exposure) exacerbates the lesions of SLE. A postulated mechanism of this effect is that UV radiation causes apoptosis of host cells, leading to an increased burden of nuclear fragments and inflammatory responses to the products of dead cells.
- **Cigarette smoking** has been shown to be associated with the development of SLE. Although the mechanism of this is unknown, smoking tobacco may modulate the production of autoantibodies.
- **Sex hormones** had been thought to exert an important influence on the development of disease, because SLE is 10 times more common in women during reproductive years than in men of similar ages but only 2 to 3 times more common in women during childhood or after the age of 65. However, treatment of women with oral contraceptives containing high doses of estrogen and progesterone did not influence the frequency or severity of disease flares, suggesting that factors other than hormones may account for the increased risk of this disease in women.
- **Drugs** such as procainamide and hydralazine can induce an SLE-like disease, although typically glomerulonephritis does not develop. These drugs cause demethylation of DNA, which could influence the expression of a variety of genes involved in the development of autoimmunity, or the ability of DNA to activate host cells.

Immunologic Abnormalities in SLE. Studies have implicated several components of the innate and adaptive immune system in the pathogenesis of SLE.

- **Type I interferons.** Blood cells show a striking molecular signature that indicates exposure to interferon-α (IFN-α), a type I interferon that is produced mainly by plasmacytoid DCs. Some studies have shown that such cells from patients with SLE also produce abnormally large amounts of IFN-α.
- **TLR signals.** Studies in animal models have shown that TLRs that recognize DNA and RNA, notably the DNA-recognizing TLR9 and the RNA-recognizing TLR7, produce signals that activate B cells specific for self nuclear antigens.
- **Failure of B cell tolerance.** Studies with B cells from patients with SLE suggest the presence of defects in both central and peripheral tolerance, resulting in a higher frequency of autoreactive B cells than that typical for healthy people.

Based on these clues, a model for the pathogenesis of SLE has been proposed (Fig. 4–17). According to this model, UV irradiation and other environmental insults lead to the apoptosis of cells. Inadequate clearance of the nuclei of these cells, in part because of defects in clearance mechanisms such as complement proteins and receptors, results in a large burden of nuclear antigens. Polymorphisms in various genes, which are susceptibility genes for lupus, lead to defective ability to maintain self-tolerance in B and T lymphocytes, because of which self-reactive lymphocytes remain functional. The self-reactive B cells are stimulated by the self nuclear antigens, and antibodies are produced against the antigens. Complexes of the antigens and antibodies bind to

Fc receptors on B cells and DCs and may be internalized. The nucleic acid components engage TLRs and stimulate B cells to produce autoantibodies and activate DCs, particularly plasmacytoid DCs, to produce IFN-α, which further enhances the immune response and causes more apoptosis. The net result is a cycle of antigen release and immune activation resulting in the production of high-affinity autoantibodies.

Spectrum of Autoantibodies in SLE

Antibodies have been identified against a host of nuclear and cytoplasmic components of the cell that are specific to neither organs nor species. Another group of antibodies is directed against surface antigens of blood cells, while yet another is reactive with proteins in complex with phospholipids (antiphospholipid antibodies) (Chapter 3).

- *Antinuclear antibodies.* ANAs are directed against several nuclear antigens and can be grouped into four categories: (1) antibodies to DNA, (2) antibodies to histones, (3) antibodies to nonhistone proteins bound to RNA, and (4) antibodies to nucleolar antigens. Table 4–10 lists several autoantibodies, including ANAs, and their association with SLE as well as with other autoimmune diseases, to be discussed later. The most widely used method of detecting ANAs is the indirect immunofluorescence assay (IFA), which screens for autoantibodies that bind to a variety of nuclear antigens, including DNA, RNA, and proteins. Four staining patterns are seen with IFA: homogeneous or diffuse, rim or peripheral, speckled, and nucleolar. While each pattern can be suggestive of the presence of specific autoantibodies, the strength of these associations is limited and should not be relied on. *ANA testing by IFA is extremely sensitive, as more than 95% of patients with SLE will test positive, but the test's specificity is quite limited, because patients with other autoimmune diseases, chronic infections, and cancer will test positive as well.* Furthermore, ANAs are seen in approximately 5% to 15% of healthy people, and the incidence increases with age. Recently, the IFA has been replaced in many clinical laboratories by multiplex flow cytometry immunoassays that can simultaneously test for multiple specific autoantibodies, but these assays may lack the sensitivity of the IFA. *Antibodies to double-stranded DNA (dsDNA) and the so-called Smith (Sm) antigen can be detected by ELISA or multiplex flow methods and are specific for SLE.*
- *Other autoantibodies.* Antibodies against blood cells, including red cells, platelets, and lymphocytes, are found in many patients. Antiphospholipid antibodies are present in 40% to 50% of patients with lupus and react with a wide variety of proteins in complex with phospholipids. Some bind to cardiolipin antigen, used in serologic tests for syphilis, so patients with lupus may have a false-positive test result for syphilis. Antiphospholipid antibodies contribute to coagulation abnormalities, which are described below.

Mechanisms of Tissue Injury

Regardless of the exact sequence by which autoantibodies are formed, they are likely to be the mediators of tissue injury, probably through multiple mechanisms.

- *Most organ damage in SLE is caused by immune complex deposition.* Skin and kidney biopsies from patients with SLE typically demonstrate diffuse and heavy granular deposits of complement and immunoglobulin. Autoantibodies complexed with DNA can be detected as well. These deposits of immune complexes had been thought to cause tissue damage by activating the classical complement pathway (type III hypersensitivity); 75% of patients will have reduced serum levels of C3 and C4 at the time of SLE flares, presumably because complement is being activated and consumed faster than it can be produced. However, people and rodents deficient in C1q are not protected from SLE and actually can spontaneously develop SLE, raising the possibility that

Table 4–10 Selected Autoantibodies Associated with Presumed Autoimmune Diseases

Autoantibody (Specificity)	Major Disease Association(s)	Likely Role(s) in Disease
Anti-dsDNA (double-stranded DNA)	SLE*	Formation of immune complexes
Anti-Sm (ribonuclear core protein, Sm antigen)	SLE*	Formation of immune complexes
Anti-RNP U1 (ribonuclear protein)	SLE, mixed connective tissue disease	Formation of immune complexes
Anti–SS-A (Ro), anti–SS-B (La) (ribonucleoproteins)	Sjögren syndrome, SLE	Role in Sjögren syndrome not known
Anti–Scl-70 (DNA topoisomerase I)	Systemic sclerosis*	Unknown
Anti-histones (histone proteins)	SLE	Formation of immune complexes
Anti-centromere (centromere proteins)	Limited scleroderma, systemic sclerosis*	Unknown
Antiphospholipid (phospholipid–protein complexes involved in blood coagulation)	Antiphospholipid syndrome, SLE	Thrombotic episodes
Anti-Jo1 (histidyl tRNA ligase)	Inflammatory myopathies*	Unknown
Anti-mitochondrial	Primary biliary cirrhosis*	Unknown
Anti-eTg (transglutaminase)	Dermatitis herpetiformis	Unknown
Anti–neutrophil cytoplasmic antibody (ANCA) (proteins in neutrophil cytoplasm)	Various vasculitides*	Formation of immune complexes? Neutrophil degranulation?
Anti–smooth muscle	Chronic autoimmune hepatitis	Unknown

Each antibody specificity is detected in 30% to 90% of patients with a particular disease. Asterisks indicate high correlation between the antibody specificity and the disease.
SLE, systemic lupus erythematosus.

complement-independent mechanisms may also contribute to tissue damage.

- *Autoantibodies of different specificities contribute to the pathology and clinical manifestations of SLE* (type II hypersensitivity). *Autoantibodies against red cells, white cells, and platelets* opsonize these cells and lead to their phagocytosis, resulting in cytopenias. *Autoantibodies against various phospholipids* lead to increased thrombosis in patients, with varied clinical consequences, including recurrent spontaneous abortion and thrombotic episodes. These disorders are part of the *antiphospholipid syndrome.* Paradoxically, these antibodies interfere with clotting tests and are actually called "lupus anticoagulants." Autoantibodies are also produced against clotting factors such as thrombin, and these too may contribute to clotting disorders. *Autoantibodies against central nervous system receptors for various neurotransmitters* have been implicated in the neuropsychiatric complications of the disease.
- There is no evidence that ANAs can permeate intact cells. However, if cell nuclei are exposed, the ANAs can bind to them. In tissues, nuclei of damaged cells react with ANAs, lose their chromatin pattern, and become homogeneous, to produce so-called *LE bodies* or *hematoxylin bodies.* An in vitro correlate of this is the *LE cell,* a neutrophil or macrophage that has engulfed the denatured nucleus of another injured cell. When blood is withdrawn and agitated, a number of leukocytes are sufficiently damaged to expose their nuclei to ANAs, with secondary complement activation; these antibody- and complement-opsonized nuclei are then readily phagocytosed. Although the LE cell test is positive in as many as 70% of patients with SLE, it is now largely of historical interest.

MORPHOLOGY

SLE is a systemic disease with protean manifestations (Table 4–9). The morphologic changes in SLE are therefore extremely variable and depend on the nature of the autoantibodies, the tissue in which immune complexes deposit, and the course and duration of disease. The most characteristic morphologic changes result from the deposition of immune complexes in a variety of tissues.

Blood Vessels. An **acute necrotizing vasculitis** affecting small arteries and arterioles may be present in any tissue. The arteritis is characterized by necrosis and by fibrinoid deposits within vessel walls containing antibody, DNA, complement fragments, and fibrinogen; a transmural and perivascular leukocytic infiltrate is also frequently present. In chronic stages, vessels show fibrous thickening with luminal narrowing.

Kidneys. Kidney involvement is one of the most important clinical features of SLE, with renal failure being the most common cause of death. The focus here is on glomerular pathology, although interstitial and tubular lesions are also seen in SLE.

The pathogenesis of all forms of **glomerulonephritis** in SLE involves deposition of DNA–anti-DNA complexes within the glomeruli. These evoke an inflammatory response that may cause proliferation of the endothelial, mesangial, and/or epithelial cells and, in severe cases, necrosis of the glomeruli. Although the kidney appears normal by light microscopy in 25% to 30% of cases, almost all cases of SLE show some renal abnormality if examined by immunofluorescence and electron microscopy. According to the current International Society of Nephrology/Renal Pathology Society morphologic classification, there are six patterns of glomerular disease in SLE (none of which is specific to the disease): **class I,** minimal mesangial lupus nephritis; **class II,** mesangial proliferative lupus nephritis; **class III,** focal lupus nephritis; **class IV,** diffuse lupus nephritis; **class V,** membranous lupus nephritis; and **class VI,** advanced sclerosing lupus nephritis.

- **Minimal mesangial lupus nephritis (class I)** is rarely encountered in renal biopsies. Immune complexes are present in the mesangium, but there are no concomitant structural alterations detectable by light microscopy.
- **Mesangial proliferative lupus nephritis (class II)** is seen in 10% to 25% of cases and is associated with mild clinical symptoms. Immune complexes deposit in the mesangium, with a mild to moderate increase in the mesangial matrix and cellularity.
- **Focal lupus nephritis (class III)** is seen in 20% to 35% of cases. Lesions are visualized in fewer than half the glomeruli, and they may be segmentally or globally distributed within each glomerulus. Active lesions are characterized by swelling and proliferation of endothelial and mesangial cells, infiltration by neutrophils, and/or fibrinoid deposits with capillary thrombi (Fig. 4–18, *A*). The clinical presentation may range from only mild microscopic hematuria and proteinuria to a more active urinary sediment with red blood cell casts and acute, severe renal insufficiency.
- **Diffuse lupus nephritis (class IV)** is the most serious form of renal lesions in SLE and is also the most commonly encountered in renal biopsies, occurring in 35% to 60% of patients. It is distinguished from focal lupus nephritis (class III) by involvement of half or more of glomeruli. Most of the glomeruli show endothelial and mesangial proliferation, leading to diffuse hypercellularity of these structures (Fig. 4–18, *B*) and producing in some cases epithelial crescents that fill Bowman's space. When extensive, subendothelial immune complexes create a circumferential thickening of the capillary wall, resembling rigid "wire loops" on routine light microscopy (Fig. 4–18, *C*). Electron microscopy reveals prominent electron-dense subendothelial immune complexes (between endothelium and basement membrane) (Fig. 4–18, *D*), but immune complexes are also usually present in other parts of the capillary wall and in the mesangium. Immune complexes can be visualized by staining with fluorescent antibodies directed against immunoglobulins or complement, resulting in a granular fluorescent staining pattern (Fig. 4–18, *E*). In due course, glomerular injury may give rise to scarring (glomerulosclerosis). Most affected patients have hematuria with moderate to severe proteinuria, hypertension, and renal insufficiency.
- **Membranous lupus nephritis (class V)** occurs in 10% to 15% of cases and is the designation for glomerular disease characterized by widespread thickening of the capillary wall due to deposition of subepithelial immune complexes. Membranous glomerulonephritis associated

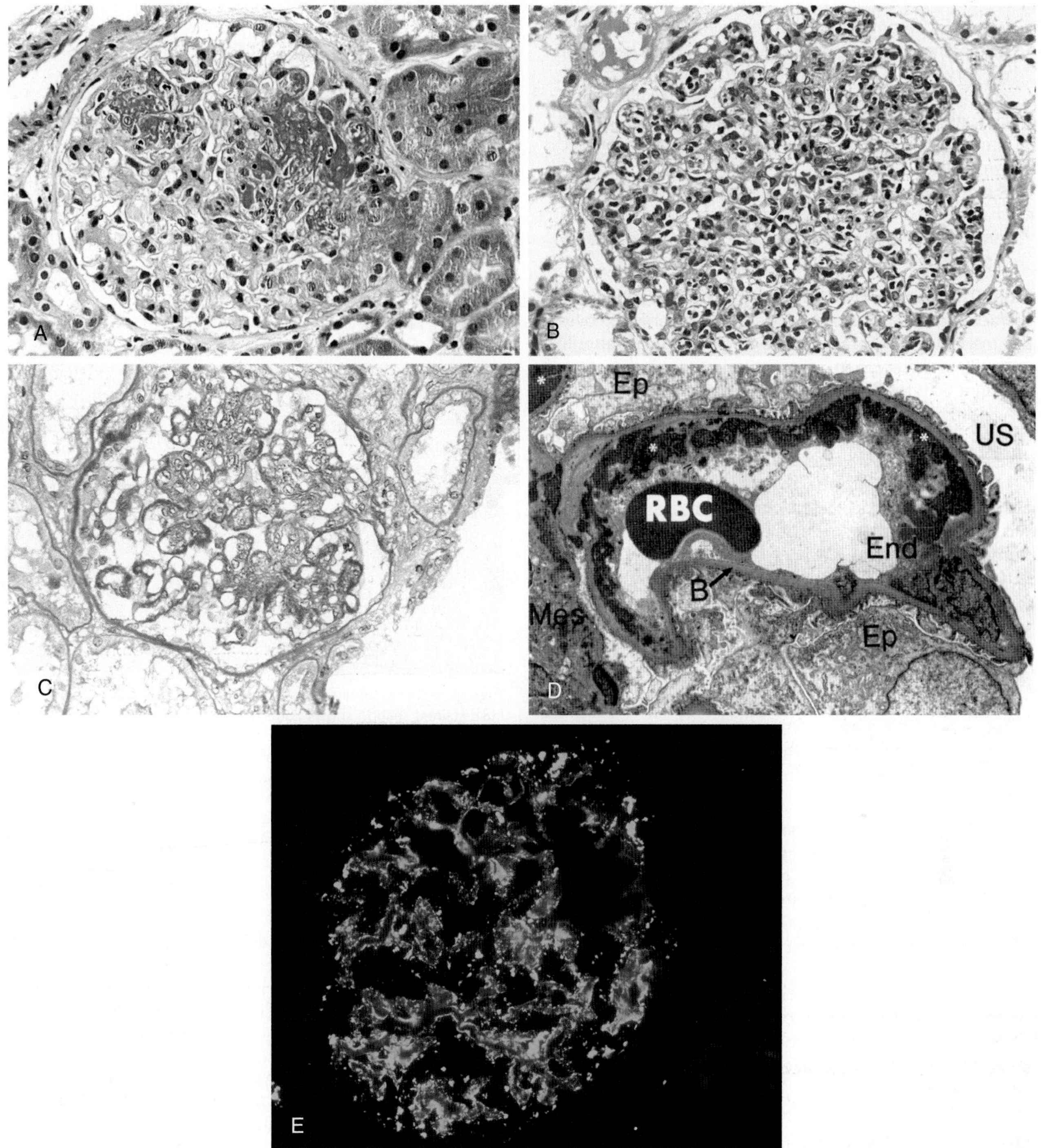

Figure 4–18 Lupus nephritis. **A,** Focal lupus nephritis, with two necrotizing lesions in a glomerulus (segmental distribution) (H&E stain). **B,** Diffuse lupus nephritis. Note the marked global increase in cellularity throughout the glomerulus (H&E stain). **C,** Lupus nephritis showing a glomerulus with several "wire loop" lesions representing extensive subendothelial deposits of immune complexes (periodic acid Schiff stain). **D,** Electron micrograph of a renal glomerular capillary loop from a patient with SLE nephritis. Confluent subendothelial dense deposits correspond to "wire loops" seen by light microscopy. **E,** Deposition of IgG antibody in a granular pattern, detected by immunofluorescence. B, basement membrane; End, endothelium; Ep, epithelial cell with foot processes; Mes, mesangium; RBC, red blood cell in capillary lumen; US, urinary space; *, electron-dense deposits in subendothelial location.

(A–C, courtesy of Dr. Helmut Rennke, Department of Pathology, Brigham and Women's Hospital, Boston, Massachusetts. D, Courtesy of Dr. Edwin Eigenbrodt, Department of Pathology, University of Texas Southwestern Medical School, Dallas. E, Courtesy of Dr. Jean Olson, Department of Pathology, University of California, San Francisco, California.)

with SLE is very similar to that encountered in idiopathic membranous nephropathy (Chapter 13). Thickening of capillary walls is caused by increased deposition of basement membrane–like material, as well as accumulation of immune complexes. Patients with this histologic change almost always have severe proteinuria with overt nephrotic syndrome (Chapter 13).

- **Advanced sclerosing lupus nephritis (class VI)** is characterized by **complete sclerosis** of greater than 90% of glomeruli and corresponds to clinical end stage renal disease.

Skin. The **skin** is involved in a majority of patients; a characteristic erythematous or maculopapular eruption over the malar eminences and bridge of the nose ("butterfly pattern") is observed in approximately half of the cases. Exposure to sunlight (UV light) exacerbates the erythema (so-called **photosensitivity**), and a similar rash may be present elsewhere on the extremities and trunk, frequently in sun-exposed areas. Histopathologic findings include liquefactive degeneration of the basal layer of the epidermis, edema at the dermoepidermal junction, and mononuclear infiltrates around blood vessels and skin appendages (Fig. 4–19, *A*). Immunofluorescence microscopy reveals deposition of immunoglobulin and complement at the dermoepidermal junction (Fig. 4–19, *B*); similar immunoglobulin and complement deposits may also be present in apparently uninvolved skin.

Joints. Joint involvement is frequent but usually is not associated with striking anatomic changes or with joint deformity. When present, it consists of swelling and a nonspecific mononuclear cell infiltration in the synovial membranes. Erosion of the membranes and destruction of articular cartilage, such as in RA, are exceedingly rare.

CNS. Central nervous system (CNS) involvement also is very common, with focal neurologic deficits and/or neuropsychiatric symptoms. CNS disease often is ascribed to vascular lesions causing ischemia or multifocal cerebral microinfarcts. Small vessel angiopathy with noninflammatory intimal proliferation is the most frequent pathological lesion; frank vasculitis is uncommon. The angiopathy may result from thrombosis caused by antiphospholipid antibodies. Premature atherosclerosis occurs and may contribute to CNS ischemia. Another postulated mechanism for CNS disease is injury from antineuronal antibodies with consequent neurologic dysfunction, but this hypothesis remains unproved.

Other Organs. The **spleen** may be moderately enlarged. Capsular fibrous thickening is common, as is follicular hyperplasia with numerous plasma cells in the red pulp. Central penicilliary arteries characteristically show thickening and perivascular fibrosis, producing **onion-skin lesions**.

Pericardium and pleura, in particular, are **serosal membranes** that show a variety of inflammatory changes in SLE ranging (in the acute phase) from serous effusions to fibrinous exudates that may progress to fibrous opacification in the chronic stage.

Involvement of the heart is manifested primarily in the form of pericarditis. Myocarditis, in the form of a nonspecific mononuclear cell infiltrate, and valvular lesions, called **Libman-Sacks endocarditis,** also occur but are less common in the current era of aggressive corticosteroid therapy. This **nonbacterial verrucous endocarditis** takes the form of irregular, 1- to 3-mm warty deposits, seen as distinctive lesions on either surface of the leaflets (i.e., on the surface exposed to the forward flow of the blood or on the underside of the leaflet) (see Chapter 10). An increasing number of patients also show clinical and anatomic manifestations of coronary artery disease. The basis of accelerated atherosclerosis is not fully understood, but the process seems to be multifactorial; certainly, immune complexes can deposit in the coronary vasculature, leading to endothelial damage by that pathway. Moreover, glucocorticoid treatment causes alterations in lipid metabolism, and renal disease (common in SLE) causes hypertension; both of these are risk factors for atherosclerosis (Chapter 9).

Many **other organs and tissues** may be involved. The changes consist essentially of acute vasculitis of the small vessels, foci of mononuclear infiltrations, and fibrinoid deposits. In addition, **lungs** may reveal interstitial fibrosis, along with pleural inflammation; the **liver** shows nonspecific inflammation of the portal tracts.

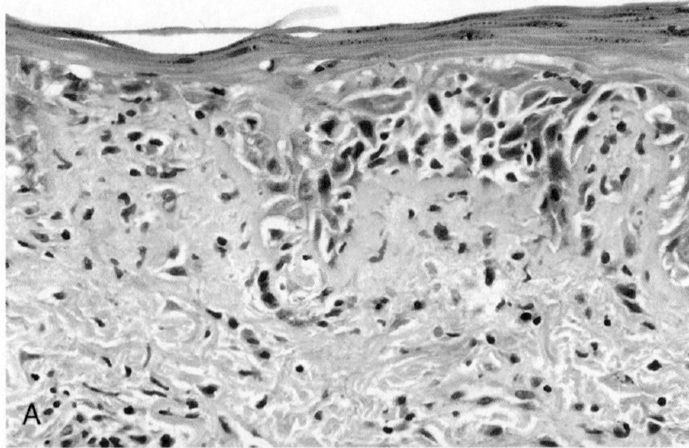

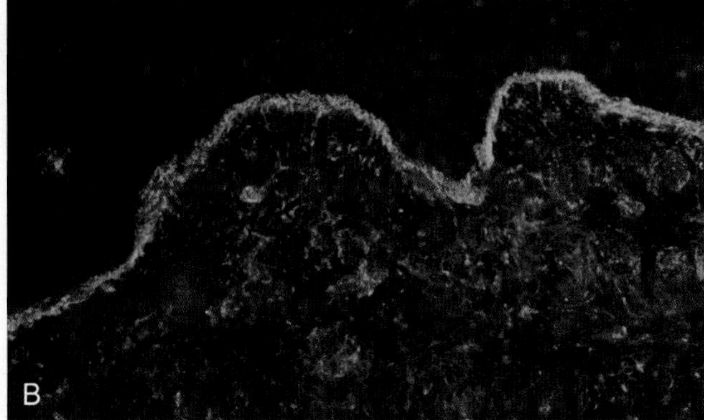

Figure 4–19 Systemic lupus erythematosus involving the skin. **A,** An H&E-stained section shows liquefactive degeneration of the basal layer of the epidermis and edema at the dermoepidermal junction. **B,** An immunofluorescence micrograph stained for IgG reveals deposits of immunoglobulin along the dermoepidermal junction. H&E, hematoxylin–eosin; IgG, immunoglobulin G.

(A, Courtesy of Dr. Jag Bhawan, Boston University School of Medicine, Boston, Massachusetts. B, Courtesy of Dr. Richard Sontheimer, Department of Dermatology, University of Texas Southwestern Medical School, Dallas, Texas.)

Clinical Manifestations

SLE is a multisystem disease that is highly variable in clinical presentation. Typically, the patient is a young woman with some, but rarely all, of the following features: a butterfly rash over the face, fever, pain and swelling in one or more peripheral joints (hands and wrists, knees, feet, ankles, elbows, shoulders), pleuritic chest pain, and photosensitivity. In many patients, however, the presentation of SLE is subtle and puzzling, taking forms such as a febrile illness of unknown origin, abnormal urinary findings, or joint disease masquerading as RA or rheumatic fever. ANAs are found in virtually 100% of patients, but an important point is that ANAs are not specific (Table 4–10). A variety of clinical findings may point toward renal involvement, including hematuria, red cell casts, proteinuria, and in some cases the classic nephrotic syndrome (Chapter 13). Laboratory evidence of some hematologic derangement is common, and in some patients anemia or thrombocytopenia may be the presenting manifestation as well as the dominant clinical problem. In still others, neuropsychiatric manifestations, including psychosis or convulsions, or coronary artery disease may be prominent clinical problems. Patients with SLE are also prone to infections, presumably because of their underlying immune dysfunction and treatment with immunosuppressive drugs. Recent strategies include B cell depletion with anti-CD20 antibody (Rituximab) and by blocking growth factors. The course of the disease is variable and unpredictable. Rare acute cases progress to death within weeks to months. More often, with appropriate therapy, the disease is characterized by flareups and remissions spanning a period of years or even decades. During acute flareups, increased deposition of immune complexes and the accompanying complement activation are thought to result in hypocomplementemia. Disease exacerbations usually are treated with corticosteroids or other immunosuppressive drugs. Even without therapy, in some patients the disease may run a benign course with only skin manifestations and mild hematuria for years. The outcome has improved significantly, and a 5-year survival can be expected in approximately 95% of patients. *The most common causes of death are renal failure, intercurrent infections, and cardiovascular disease.* The incidence of cancer also is increased, particularly B cell lymphomas, an association common to diseases marked by B cell hyperstimulation (e.g., Sjögren syndrome, discussed below). Patients treated with steroids and immunosuppressive drugs incur the usual risks associated with such therapy.

SUMMARY

Systemic Lupus Erythematosus

- SLE is a systemic autoimmune disease caused by autoantibodies produced against numerous self-antigens and the formation of immune complexes.
- The major autoantibodies, and the ones responsible for the formation of circulating immune complexes, are directed against nuclear antigens. Other autoantibodies react with erythrocytes, platelets, and various complexes of phospholipids with proteins.
- Disease manifestations include nephritis, skin lesions and arthritis (caused by the deposition of immune complexes), and hematologic and neurologic abnormalities.
- The underlying cause of the breakdown in self-tolerance in SLE is unknown; it may include excess or persistence of nuclear antigens, multiple inherited susceptibility genes, and environmental triggers (e.g., UV irradiation, which results in cellular apoptosis and release of nuclear proteins).

Rheumatoid Arthritis

Rheumatoid arthritis (RA) is a systemic, chronic inflammatory disease affecting many tissues but principally attacking the joints to produce a nonsuppurative proliferative synovitis that frequently progresses to destroy articular cartilage and underlying bone with resulting disabling arthritis. Because the principal lesions affect the joints and bones, this disease, as well as the juvenile form and other inflammatory diseases of joints, is discussed in Chapter 20.

Sjögren Syndrome

Sjögren syndrome is a clinicopathologic entity characterized by dry eyes (*keratoconjunctivitis sicca*) and dry mouth (*xerostomia*), resulting from immune-mediated destruction of the lacrimal and salivary glands. It occurs as an isolated disorder (primary form), also known as the *sicca syndrome,* or more often in association with another autoimmune disease (secondary form). Among the associated disorders, RA is the most common, but some patients have SLE, polymyositis, systemic sclerosis, vasculitis, or thyroiditis.

PATHOGENESIS

Several lines of evidence suggest that Sjögren syndrome is an autoimmune disease caused by CD4+ T cell reactions against unknown antigens in the ductal epithelial cells of the exocrine glands. There is also systemic B cell hyperactivity, as evidenced by the presence of ANAs and rheumatoid factor (RF) (even in the absence of associated RA). Most patients with primary Sjögren syndrome have autoantibodies to the ribonucleoprotein (RNP) antigens SS-A (Ro) and SS-B (La); note that these antibodies are also present in some SLE patients and are therefore not diagnostic for Sjögren syndrome (Table 4–10). Although patients with high-titer anti-SS-A antibodies are more likely to have systemic (extraglandular) manifestations, there is no evidence that the autoantibodies cause primary tissue injury. A viral trigger also has been suggested, but no causative virus has been identified conclusively. Genetic variables play a role in the pathogenesis of Sjögren syndrome. As with SLE, inheritance of certain class II MHC alleles predisposes to the development of specific RNP autoantibodies.

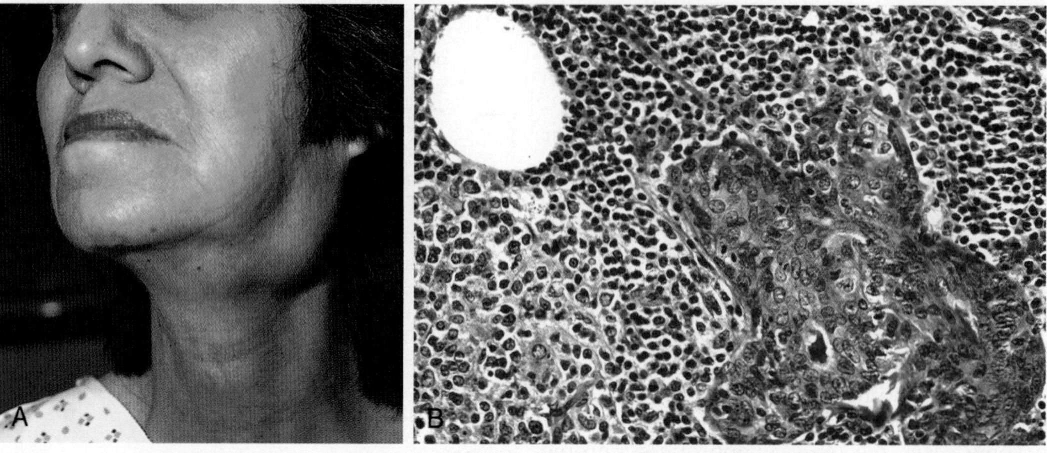

Figure 4–20 Sjögren syndrome. **A,** Enlargement of the salivary gland. **B,** Histopathologic findings include intense lymphocytic and plasma cell infiltration with ductal epithelial hyperplasia.

(A, Courtesy of Dr. Richard Sontheimer, Department of Dermatology, University of Texas Southwestern Medical School, Dallas, Texas. B, Courtesy of Dr. Dennis Burns, Department of Pathology, University of Texas Southwestern Medical School, Dallas, Texas.)

MORPHOLOGY

Lacrimal and salivary glands are the primary targets, but other secretory glands, including those in the nasopharynx, upper airway, and vagina, also may be involved. Histologic examination shows an intense lymphocyte (primarily activated CD4+ T cells) and plasma cell infiltrate, occasionally forming lymphoid follicles with germinal centers. There is associated destruction of the native architecture (Fig. 4–20).

Lacrimal gland destruction results in a lack of tears, leading to drying of the corneal epithelium, with subsequent inflammation, erosion, and ulceration **(keratoconjunctivitis).** Similar changes may occur in the oral mucosa as a result of loss of salivary gland output, giving rise to mucosal atrophy, with inflammatory fissuring and ulceration **(xerostomia).** Dryness and crusting of the nose may lead to ulcerations and even perforation of the nasal septum. When the respiratory passages are involved, secondary laryngitis, bronchitis, and pneumonitis may appear. Approximately 25% of the patients (especially those with anti-SS-A antibodies) acquire extraglandular disease involving the CNS, skin, kidneys, and muscles. Renal lesions take the form of mild interstitial nephritis associated with tubular transport defects; unlike in SLE, glomerulonephritis is rare.

Clinical Course

Approximately 90% of Sjögren syndrome cases occur in women between the ages of 35 and 45 years. Patients present with dry mouth, lack of tears, and the resultant complications described above. Salivary glands are often enlarged as a result of lymphocytic infiltrates (Fig. 4-20). Extraglandular manifestations include synovitis, pulmonary fibrosis, and peripheral neuropathy. About 60% of Sjögren patients have another accompanying autoimmune disorder such as RA. Notably, there is a 40-fold increased risk for developing a non-Hodgkin B cell lymphoma, arising in the setting of the initial robust polyclonal B cell proliferation. These so-called marginal zone lymphomas are discussed in Chapter 11.

SUMMARY

Sjögren Syndrome

- Sjögren syndrome is an inflammatory disease that affects primarily the salivary and lacrimal glands, causing dryness of the mouth and eyes.
- The disease is believed to be caused by an autoimmune T cell reaction against one or more unknown self antigens expressed in these glands, or immune reactions against the antigens of a virus that infects the tissues.

Systemic Sclerosis (Scleroderma)

Systemic sclerosis (SS) is an immunologic disorder characterized by excessive fibrosis in multiple tissues, obliterative vascular disease, and evidence of autoimmunity, mainly the production of multiple autoantibodies. It is commonly called scleroderma because the skin is a major target, but this disorder is better labeled "systemic" because lesions are present throughout the body. Cutaneous involvement is the usual presenting manifestation and eventually appears in approximately 95% of cases, but it is the visceral involvement—of the gastrointestinal tract, lungs, kidneys, heart, and skeletal muscles—that is responsible for most of the related morbidity and mortality.

SS can be classified into two groups on the basis of its clinical course:

- *Diffuse scleroderma,* characterized by initial widespread skin involvement, with rapid progression and early visceral involvement
- *Limited scleroderma,* with relatively mild skin involvement, often confined to the fingers and face. Involvement of the viscera occurs late, so the disease in these patients generally has a fairly benign course. This clinical presentation is also called the CREST syndrome because of its frequent features of calcinosis, Raynaud phenomenon, esophageal dysmotility, sclerodactyly, and telangiectasia.

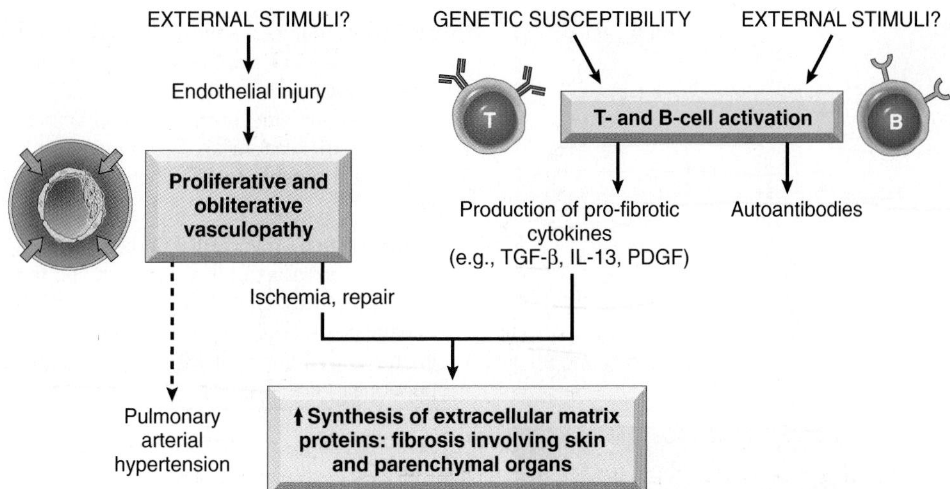

Figure 4–21 A model for the pathogenesis of systemic sclerosis. Unknown external stimuli cause vascular abnormalities and immune activation in genetically susceptible individuals, and both contribute to the excessive fibrosis.

PATHOGENESIS

The cause of the disease is not known, but genetic and environmental factors probably contribute. A postulated sequence of events is the following (Fig. 4–21).

- **Injury to endothelial cells** of small arteries by unknown mechanisms leads to endothelial activation, increased expression of adhesion molecules, and migration of activated T cells into the perivascular tissues. The local T cell reaction may cause further activation and injury to endothelial cells.
- **T cells** respond to some self antigen and produce cytokines. It has been suggested that the dominant T cells are T_H2 cells, and their cytokines induce alternative macrophage activation and collagen deposition. The activated T cells and macrophages produce **cytokines that activate fibroblasts and stimulate collagen production,** resulting in fibrosis. These cytokines include TGF-β, IL-13, platelet-derived growth factor (PDGF), and others.
- Repeated bouts of endothelial damage followed by platelet aggregation lead to **endothelial proliferation and intimal fibrosis,** which, together with periadventitial fibrosis, narrow the small vessels, with eventual **ischemic injury.** The subsequent repair reaction may lead to more fibrosis, thus setting up a self-perpetuating cycle.
- **B cell activation** also occurs, as indicated by the presence of hypergammaglobulinemia and ANAs. Although there is no evidence that humoral immunity plays a significant role in the pathogenesis of SS, two of the ANAs are virtually unique to this disease and are therefore useful in diagnosis (Table 4–10). One of these, directed **against DNA topoisomerase I** (anti-Scl 70), is highly specific; it is present in as many as 70% of patients with diffuse scleroderma (and in less than 1% of patients with other connective tissue diseases) and is a marker for the development of more aggressive disease with pulmonary fibrosis and peripheral vascular changes. The other ANA is an **anticentromere antibody,** found in as many as 90% of patients with limited scleroderma (i.e., the CREST syndrome); it indicates a relatively benign course.

MORPHOLOGY

Virtually any organ may be affected in SS, but the most prominent changes are found in the skin, musculoskeletal system, gastrointestinal tract, lungs, kidneys, and heart.

Skin. The vast majority of patients have diffuse, sclerotic atrophy of the skin, usually beginning in the fingers and distal regions of the upper extremities and extending proximally to involve the upper arms, shoulders, neck, and face. In the early stages, affected skin areas are somewhat edematous and have a doughy consistency. Histopathologic findings include edema and perivascular infiltrates containing CD4+ T cells. Capillaries and small arteries (as large as 500 μm in diameter) may show thickening of the basal lamina, endothelial cell damage, and partial occlusion. With progression, the edematous phase is replaced by progressive fibrosis of the dermis, which becomes tightly bound to the subcutaneous structures. There is marked increase of compact collagen in the dermis along with thinning of the epidermis, atrophy of the dermal appendages, and hyaline thickening of the walls of dermal arterioles and capillaries (Fig. 4–22, *A, B*). Focal and sometimes diffuse subcutaneous calcifications may develop, especially in patients with the CREST syndrome. In advanced stages, the fingers take on a tapered, clawlike appearance with limitation of motion in the joints (Fig. 4–22, *C*), and the face becomes a drawn mask. Loss of blood supply may lead to cutaneous ulcerations and to atrophic changes in the terminal phalanges, including autoamputation.

Gastrointestinal Tract. The gastrointestinal tract is affected in approximately 90% of patients. Progressive atrophy and collagenous fibrous replacement of the muscularis may develop at any level of the gut but are most severe in the esophagus, with the lower two thirds often demonstrating an inflexibility not unlike that typical of a rubber hose. The associated dysfunction of the lower esophageal sphincter gives rise to gastroesophageal reflux and its complications, including Barrett metaplasia (Chapter 14) and strictures. The mucosa is thinned and may be ulcerated, and there is excessive collagenization of the lamina propria and submucosa.

Since the emergence of AIDS in 1981, the concerted efforts of epidemiologists, immunologists, and molecular biologists have resulted in spectacular advances in our understanding of this disorder. Despite all this progress, however, the prognosis of patients with AIDS remains guarded. Although the mortality rate has declined as a result of the use of potent combinations of antiretroviral drugs, all treated patients still carry viral DNA in their lymphoid tissues. Can there be a cure with persistent virus? Despite the considerable effort that has been mounted to develop a vaccine, many hurdles remain to be crossed before vaccine-based prophylaxis or treatment becomes a reality. Molecular analyses have revealed an alarming degree of variation in viral isolates from different patients, rendering vaccine development even more difficult. A further complication to this task is that the nature of the protective immune response is not yet fully understood. Consequently, at present, prevention and effective public health measures, combined with antiretroviral therapy, are the mainstays in the fight against AIDS.

AMYLOIDOSIS

Amyloidosis is a condition associated with a number of inherited and inflammatory disorders in which extracellular deposits of fibrillar proteins are responsible for tissue damage and functional compromise. These abnormal fibrils are produced by the aggregation of misfolded proteins (which are soluble in their normal folded configuration) or protein fragments. The fibrillar deposits bind a wide variety of proteoglycans and glycosaminoglycans, including heparan sulfate and dermatan sulfate, and plasma proteins, notably serum amyloid P component (SAP). The presence of abundant charged sugar groups in these adsorbed proteins gives the deposits staining characteristics that were thought to resemble starch (amylose). Therefore, the deposits were called "amyloid," a name that is firmly entrenched despite the realization that the deposits are unrelated to starch.

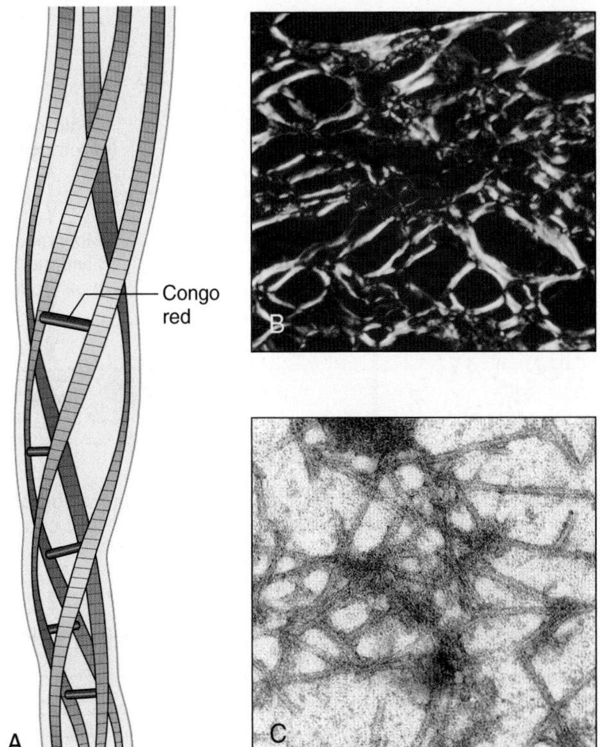

Figure 4–31 Structure of amyloid. **A,** Schematic diagram of an amyloid fiber showing fibrils (four are shown; as many as six may be present) wound around one another with regularly spaced binding of the Congo red dye. **B,** Congo red staining shows an apple-green birefringence under polarized light, a diagnostic feature of amyloid. **C,** Electron micrograph of 7.4- to 10-nm amyloid fibrils.

(Reproduced from Merlini G, Bellotti V: Molecular mechanisms of amyloidosis. N Engl J Med 349:583–596, 2003. Copyright 2003 Massachusetts Medical Society. All rights reserved.)

PATHOGENESIS OF AMYLOID DEPOSITION

Amyloidosis is fundamentally a disorder of protein misfolding. Amyloid is not a structurally homogeneous protein, although it always has the same morphologic appearance. In fact, more than 20 (at last count, 23) different proteins can aggregate to form fibrils with the appearance of amyloid. Regardless of their derivation, all amyloid deposits are composed of nonbranching fibrils, 7.5 to 10 nm in diameter, each formed of β-sheet polypeptide chains that are wound together (Fig. 4–31). The dye Congo red binds to these fibrils and produces a red–green dichroism (birefringence), which is commonly used to identify amyloid deposits in tissues.

Amyloidosis results from abnormal folding of proteins, which are deposited as fibrils in extracellular tissues and disrupt normal function. Normally, misfolded proteins are degraded intracellularly in proteasomes, or extracellularly by macrophages. It appears that in amyloidosis, these quality control mechanisms fail, allowing the misfolded protein to accumulate outside cells. Misfolded proteins often are unstable and self-associate, ultimately leading to the formation of oligomers and fibrils that are deposited in tissues. The diverse conditions that are associated with amyloidosis all are likely to result in excessive production of proteins that are prone to misfolding (Fig. 4–32). The proteins that form amyloid fall into two general categories: (1) normal proteins that have an inherent tendency to fold improperly, associate to form fibrils, and do so when they are produced in increased amounts and (2) mutant proteins that are prone to misfolding and subsequent aggregation. Of the many biochemically distinct forms of amyloid proteins that have been identified, three are most common:

- The **AL (amyloid light chain) protein** is produced by plasma cells and is made up of complete immunoglobulin light chains, the amino-terminal fragments of light chains, or both. For unknown reasons, only a few types of immunoglobulin light chains are prone to forming aggregates. As expected, the deposition of amyloid fibril protein of the AL type is associated with some form of monoclonal B cell proliferation. Defective degradation has also been invoked as the basis for fibril formation, and perhaps particular light chains are resistant to complete proteolysis. However, there are no sequence motifs peculiar to the immunoglobulin light chains found in amyloid deposits.
- The **AA (amyloid-associated) fibril** is a unique nonimmunoglobulin protein derived from a larger (12-kDa)

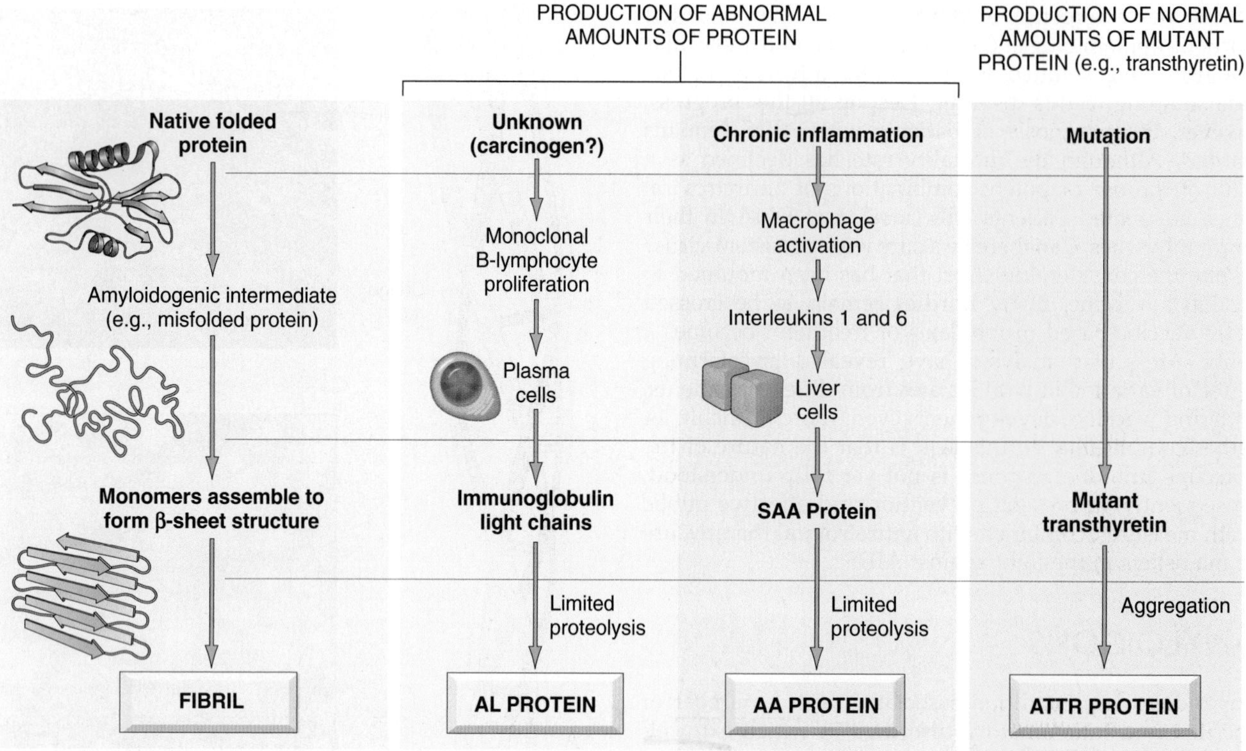

Figure 4–32 Pathogenesis of amyloidosis. The proposed mechanisms underlying deposition of the major forms of amyloid fibrils.

serum precursor called SAA (serum amyloid-associated) protein that is synthesized in the liver. SAA is synthesized by liver cells under the influence of cytokines such as IL-6 and IL-1 that are produced during inflammation; thus, long-standing inflammation leads to elevated SAA levels, and ultimately the AA form of amyloid deposits. However, increased production of SAA by itself is not sufficient for the deposition of amyloid. Elevation of serum SAA levels is common to inflammatory states but in most instances does not lead to amyloidosis. There are two possible explanations for this. According to one view, SAA normally is degraded to soluble end products by the action of monocyte-derived enzymes. Conceivably, people who develop amyloidosis have an enzyme defect that results in incomplete breakdown of SAA, thus generating insoluble AA molecules. Alternatively, a genetically determined structural abnormality in the SAA molecule itself renders it resistant to degradation by macrophages.

- **Aβ amyloid** is found in the cerebral lesions of Alzheimer disease. Aβ is a 4-kDa peptide that constitutes the core of cerebral plaques and the amyloid deposits in cerebral blood vessels in this disease. The Aβ protein is derived from a much larger transmembrane glycoprotein called amyloid precursor protein (APP) (Chapter 22).

Several other proteins have been found in amyloid deposits in a variety of clinical settings:

- **Transthyretin** (TTR) is a normal serum protein that binds and transports thyroxine and retinol, hence the name. Mutations in the gene encoding TTR may alter its structure, making the protein prone to misfolding and aggregation, and resistant to proteolysis. This leads to the formation of aggregates that deposit as amyloid. The resultant diseases are called familial amyloid polyneuropathies. TTR is also deposited in the heart of aged persons (senile systemic amyloidosis); in such cases the protein is structurally normal, but it accumulates at high concentrations. Some cases of familial amyloidosis are associated with deposits of mutant lysozyme.
- **β_2-Microglobulin,** a component of MHC class I molecules and a normal serum protein, has been identified as the amyloid fibril subunit (Aβ2m) in amyloidosis that complicates the course of patients on long-term hemodialysis. Aβ2m fibers are structurally similar to normal β2m protein. This protein is present in high concentrations in the serum of patients with renal disease and is retained in the circulation because it is not efficiently filtered through dialysis membranes. In some series, as many as 60% to 80% of patients on long-term dialysis developed amyloid deposits in the synovium, joints, and tendon sheaths.
- Amyloid deposits derived from diverse precursors such as hormones (procalcitonin) and keratin also have been reported.

Classification of Amyloidosis

Because a given biochemical form of amyloid (e.g., AA) may be associated with amyloid deposition in diverse clinical settings, a combined biochemical and clinical classification is followed for this discussion (Table 4–13). Amyloid may be systemic (generalized), involving several organ systems, or it may be localized, when deposits are limited to a single organ, such as the heart. On clinical grounds, the systemic, or generalized, pattern is subclassified into *primary amyloidosis* when associated with a monoclonal

Table 4–13 Classification of Amyloidosis

Clinicopathologic Category	Associated Disease(s)	Major Fibril Protein	Chemically Related Precursor Protein
Systemic (Generalized) Amyloidosis			
Immunocyte dyscrasias with amyloidosis (primary amyloidosis)	Multiple myeloma and other monoclonal plasma cell proliferations	AL	Immunoglobulin light chains, chiefly λ type
Reactive systemic amyloidosis (secondary amyloidosis)	Chronic inflammatory conditions	AA	SAA
Hemodialysis-associated amyloidosis	Chronic renal failure	$A\beta_2m$	β_2-Microglobulin
Hereditary Amyloidosis			
Familial Mediterranean fever		AA	SAA
Familial amyloidotic neuropathies (several types)		ATTR	Transthyretin
Systemic senile amyloidosis		ATTR	Transthyretin
Localized Amyloidosis			
Senile cerebral	Alzheimer disease	Aβ	APP
Endocrine			
Medullary carcinoma of thyroid		A Cal	Calcitonin
Islets of Langerhans	Type 2 diabetes	AIAPP	Islet amyloid peptide
Isolated atrial amyloidosis		AANF	Atrial natriuretic factor

plasma cell proliferation and *secondary amyloidosis* when it occurs as a complication of an underlying chronic inflammatory or tissue destructive process. Hereditary or familial amyloidosis constitutes a separate, albeit heterogeneous group, with several distinctive patterns of organ involvement.

Primary Amyloidosis: Immunocyte Dyscrasias with Amyloidosis

Amyloid in this category usually is systemic in distribution and is of the AL type. With approximately 3000 new cases each year in the United States, this is the most common form of amyloidosis. In some of these cases, there is a readily identifiable monoclonal plasma cell proliferation; best defined is the occurrence of systemic amyloidosis in 5% to 15% of patients with multiple myeloma, a plasma cell tumor characterized by multiple osteolytic lesions throughout the skeletal system (Chapter 11). The malignant plasma cells characteristically synthesize abnormal amounts of a single specific immunoglobulin (monoclonal gammopathy), producing an M (myeloma) protein spike on serum electrophoresis. In addition to the synthesis of whole immunoglobulin molecules, plasma cells also may synthesize and secrete either the λ or κ light chain, also known as Bence Jones proteins. By virtue of their small molecular size, these proteins frequently are also excreted in the urine. Almost all patients with myeloma who develop amyloidosis have Bence Jones proteins in the serum or urine, or both. However, amyloidosis develops in only 6% to 15% of patients with myeloma who have free light chains. Clearly, the presence of Bence Jones proteins, although necessary, is by itself not sufficient to produce amyloidosis. Other variables, such as the type of light chain produced and its catabolism, contribute to the "amyloidogenic potential" and influence the deposition of Bence Jones proteins.

The great majority of patients with AL amyloid do not have classic multiple myeloma or any other overt B cell neoplasm; such cases are nevertheless classified as primary amyloidosis because their clinical features derive from the effects of amyloid deposition without any other associated disease. In virtually all such cases, patients have a modest increase in the number of plasma cells in the bone marrow, and monoclonal immunoglobulins or free light chains can be found in the serum or urine. Clearly, these patients have an underlying monoclonal plasma cell proliferation in which production of an abnormal protein, rather than production of tumor masses, is the predominant manifestation.

Reactive Systemic Amyloidosis

The amyloid deposits in this pattern are systemic in distribution and are composed of AA protein. This category was previously referred to as secondary amyloidosis, because it is *secondary to an associated inflammatory condition.* In fact, the feature common to most cases of reactive systemic amyloidosis is chronic inflammation. Classically, tuberculosis, bronchiectasis, and chronic osteomyelitis were the most common causes; with the advent of effective antimicrobial therapies, reactive systemic amyloidosis is seen most frequently in the setting of chronic inflammation caused by autoimmune states (e.g., RA, ankylosing spondylitis, inflammatory bowel disease). Patients with RA are particularly prone to develop amyloidosis, with amyloid deposition seen in as many as 3% of RA cases. Chronic skin infections caused by "skin-popping" of narcotics are also associated with amyloid deposition. Finally, reactive systemic amyloidosis may also occur in association with tumors, the two most common being renal cell carcinoma and Hodgkin lymphoma.

Familial (Hereditary) Amyloidosis

A variety of familial forms of amyloidosis have been described; most are rare and occur in limited geographic areas. The best-characterized is an autosomal recessive condition called familial Mediterranean fever. This is a febrile disorder characterized by attacks of fever accompanied by inflammation of serosal surfaces, including peritoneum, pleura, and synovial membrane. This disorder is encountered largely in persons of Armenian, Sephardic Jewish, and Arabic origins. It is associated with widespread tissue involvement indistinguishable from reactive systemic amyloidosis. The amyloid fibril proteins are made up of AA proteins, suggesting that this form of amyloidosis is related to the recurrent bouts of inflammation that characterize this disease. The gene for familial Mediterranean fever is called *pyrin* and encodes a protein that is a component of the inflammasome (Chapter 2). Patients have gain-of-function mutations in *pyrin* that result in constitutive overproduction of the pro-inflammatory cytokine IL-1 and persistent inflammation.

In contrast with familial Mediterranean fever, a group of autosomal dominant familial disorders is characterized by deposition of amyloid predominantly in the peripheral and autonomic nerves. These familial amyloidotic polyneuropathies have been described in kindreds in different parts of the world—for example, in Portugal, Japan, Sweden, and the United States. As mentioned previously, the fibrils in these familial polyneuropathies are made up of mutant forms of transthyretin (ATTRs).

Localized Amyloidosis

Sometimes deposition of amyloid is limited to a single organ or tissue without involvement of any other site in the body. The deposits may produce grossly detectable nodular masses or be evident only on microscopic examination. Nodular (tumor-forming) deposits of amyloid are most often encountered in the lung, larynx, skin, urinary bladder, tongue, and the region about the eye. Frequently, there are infiltrates of lymphocytes and plasma cells in the periphery of these amyloid masses, raising the question of whether the mononuclear infiltrate is a response to the deposition of amyloid or instead is responsible for it. At least in some cases, the amyloid consists of AL protein and may therefore represent a localized form of plasma cell–derived amyloid.

Endocrine Amyloid

Microscopic deposits of localized amyloid may be found in certain endocrine tumors, such as medullary carcinoma of the thyroid gland, islet tumors of the pancreas, pheochromocytomas, and undifferentiated carcinomas of the stomach, as well as in the islets of Langerhans in patients with type 2 diabetes mellitus. In these settings, the amyloidogenic proteins seem to be derived either from polypeptide hormones (medullary carcinoma) or from unique proteins (e.g., islet amyloid polypeptide).

Amyloid of Aging

Several well-documented forms of amyloid deposition occur with aging. Senile systemic amyloidosis refers to the systemic deposition of amyloid in elderly persons (usually in their 70s and 80s). Because of the dominant involvement and related dysfunction of the heart (typically manifesting as a restrictive cardiomyopathy and arrhythmias), this form also is called *senile cardiac amyloidosis*. The amyloid in this form is composed of normal transthyretin. In addition, another form typically affecting only the heart results from the deposition of a mutant form of TTR. Approximately 4% of the black population in the United States are carriers of the mutant allele, and cardiomyopathy has been identified in both homozygous and heterozygous patients.

MORPHOLOGY

There are no consistent or distinctive patterns of organ or tissue distribution of amyloid deposits in any of the categories cited. Nonetheless, a few generalizations can be made. In amyloidosis secondary to chronic inflammatory disorders, kidneys, liver, spleen, lymph nodes, adrenals, and thyroid, as well as many other tissues, typically are affected. Although primary (AL) amyloidosis cannot reliably be distinguished from the secondary form by its organ distribution, it more often involves the heart, gastrointestinal tract, respiratory tract, peripheral nerves, skin, and tongue. However, the same organs affected by reactive systemic amyloidosis (secondary amyloidosis), including kidneys, liver, and spleen, also may contain deposits in the immunocyte-associated form of the disease. The localization of amyloid deposits in the hereditary syndromes is varied. In familial Mediterranean fever, the amyloidosis may be widespread, involving the kidneys, blood vessels, spleen, respiratory tract, and (rarely) liver. The localization of amyloid in the remaining hereditary syndromes can be inferred from the designation of these entities.

Whatever the clinical disorder, the amyloidosis may or may not be apparent grossly. Often small amounts are not recognized until the surface of the cut organ is painted with iodine and sulfuric acid. This yields mahogany brown staining of the amyloid deposits. When amyloid accumulates in larger amounts, the organ frequently is enlarged and the tissue typically appears gray with a waxy, firm consistency. **On histologic examination, the amyloid deposition is always extracellular and begins between cells,** often closely adjacent to basement membranes. As the amyloid accumulates, it encroaches on the cells, in time surrounding and destroying them. In the AL form, perivascular and vascular localizations are common.

The histologic diagnosis of amyloid is based almost entirely on its staining characteristics. The most commonly used staining technique uses the dye Congo red, which under ordinary light imparts a pink or red color to amyloid deposits. Under polarized light the Congo red–stained amyloid shows so-called apple-green birefringence (Fig. 4–33). This reaction is shared by all forms of amyloid and is caused by the crossed β-pleated configuration of amyloid fibrils. Confirmation can be obtained by electron microscopy, which reveals amorphous nonoriented thin fibrils. AA, AL, and ATTR types of amyloid also can be distinguished from one another by specific immunohistochemical staining.

Because the pattern of organ involvement in different clinical forms of amyloidosis is variable, each of the major organ involvements is described separately.

Kidney. Amyloidosis of the kidney is the most common and most serious feature of the disease. Grossly, the kidney may appear unchanged, or it may be abnormally large, pale, gray, and firm; in long-standing cases, the kidney may be reduced in size. Microscopically, the **amyloid deposits are found principally in the glomeruli,** but they also are present in the interstitial peritubular tissue as well as in the walls of the blood vessels. The glomerulus first develops focal deposits

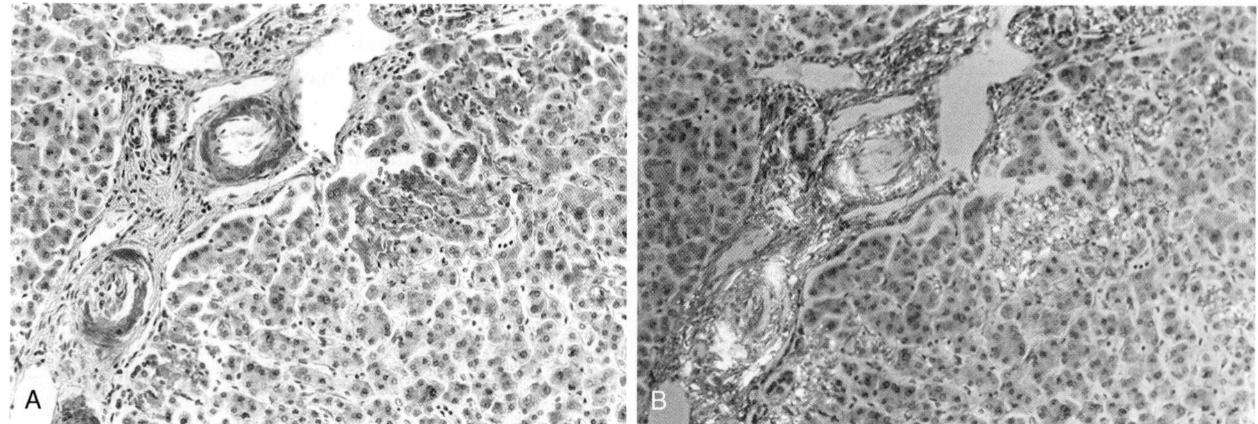

Figure 4–33 Amyloidosis: hepatic involvement. **A,** Staining of a section of the liver with Congo red reveals pink-red deposits of amyloid in the walls of blood vessels and along sinusoids. **B,** Note the yellow-green birefringence of the deposits when observed under the polarizing microscope. *(Courtesy of Dr. Trace Worrell and Sandy Hinton, Department of Pathology, University of Texas Southwestern Medical School, Dallas, Texas.)*

within the mesangial matrix and diffuse or nodular thickenings of the basement membranes of the capillary loops. With progression, the deposition encroaches on the capillary lumina and eventually leads to total obliteration of the vascular tuft (Fig. 4–34, *A*). The interstitial peritubular deposits frequently are associated with the appearance of amorphous pink casts within the tubular lumens, presumably of a proteinaceous nature. Amyloid deposits may develop in the walls of blood vessels of all sizes, often causing marked vascular narrowing.

Spleen. Amyloidosis of the spleen often causes moderate or even marked enlargement (200 to 800 gm). For obscure reasons, either of two patterns may develop. The deposits may be virtually limited to the splenic follicles, producing tapioca-like granules on gross examination ("sago spleen"), or the amyloidosis may principally involve the splenic sinuses, eventually extending to the splenic pulp, with formation of large, sheetlike deposits ("lardaceous spleen"). In both patterns, the spleen is firm in consistency. The presence of blood in splenic sinuses usually imparts a reddish color to the waxy, friable deposits.

Liver. Amyloidosis of the liver may cause massive enlargement (as much as 9000 gm). In such advanced cases, the liver is extremely pale, grayish, and waxy on both the external surface and the cut section. Histologic analysis shows that **amyloid deposits first appear in the space of Disse** and then progressively enlarge to encroach on the adjacent hepatic parenchyma and sinusoids (Fig. 4–33). The trapped liver cells undergo compression atrophy and are eventually replaced by sheets of amyloid; remarkably, normal liver function may be preserved even in the setting of severe involvement.

Heart. Amyloidosis of the heart may occur either as isolated organ involvement or as part of a systemic distribution. When accompanied by systemic involvement, it is usually of the AL form. The isolated form (senile amyloidosis) usually is confined to older persons. The deposits may not be evident on gross examination, or they may cause minimal to moderate cardiac enlargement. The most characteristic gross findings are gray-pink, dewdrop-like subendocardial elevations, particularly evident in the atrial chambers. On histologic examination, deposits typically are found throughout the myocardium, beginning **between myocardial fibers** and eventually causing their pressure atrophy (Fig. 4–34, *B*).

Other Organs. Amyloidosis of other organs generally is encountered in systemic disease. The adrenals, thyroid, and

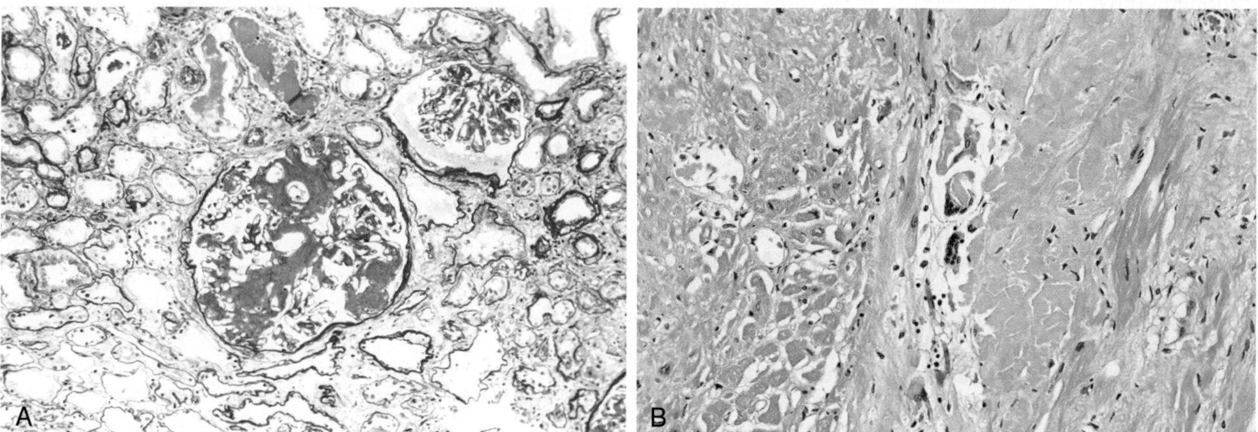

Figure 4–34 Amyloidosis: renal and cardiac involvement. **A,** Amyloidosis of the kidney. The glomerular architecture is almost totally obliterated by the massive accumulation of amyloid. **B,** Cardiac amyloidosis. The atrophic myocardial fibers are separated by structureless, pink-staining amyloid.

pituitary are common sites of involvement. In such cases as well, the amyloid deposition begins in relation to stromal and endothelial cells and progressively encroaches on the parenchymal cells. Surprisingly large amounts of amyloid may be present in any of these endocrine glands without apparent disturbance of function. In the gastrointestinal tract, a relatively favored site for deposition, amyloid may be found at all levels, sometimes producing tumorous masses that must be distinguished from neoplasms. Nodular depositions in the tongue may produce **macroglossia.** On the basis of the frequent involvement of the gastrointestinal tract in systemic cases, gingival, intestinal, and rectal biopsies serve in the diagnosis of suspected cases. Deposition of β_2-microglobulin amyloid in patients receiving long-term dialysis occurs most commonly in the **carpal ligaments of the wrist,** resulting in compression of the median nerve (leading to carpal tunnel syndrome).

Clinical Course

Amyloidosis may be an unsuspected finding at autopsy in a patient who has no apparent related clinical manifestations, or it may be responsible for serious clinical dysfunction and even death. The clinical course depends on the particular sites or organs affected and the severity of the involvement. Nonspecific complaints such as weakness, fatigue, and weight loss are the most common presenting manifestations. Later in the course, amyloidosis tends to manifest in one of several ways: by renal disease, hepatomegaly, splenomegaly, or cardiac abnormalities. Renal involvement giving rise to severe proteinuria (nephrotic syndrome) (Chapter 13) often is the major cause of symptoms in reactive systemic amyloidosis. Progression of the renal disease may lead to renal failure, which is an important cause of death in amyloidosis. The hepatosplenomegaly rarely causes significant clinical dysfunction, but it may be the presenting finding. Cardiac amyloidosis may manifest as conduction disturbances or as restrictive cardiomyopathy (Chapter 10). Cardiac arrhythmias are an important cause of death in cardiac amyloidosis. In one large series, 40% of the patients with AL amyloid died of cardiac disease.

The diagnosis of amyloidosis may be suspected from the clinical signs and symptoms and from some of the findings mentioned; however, more specific tests must often be done for definitive diagnosis. Biopsy and subsequent Congo red staining is the most important tool in the diagnosis of amyloidosis. In general, biopsy is taken from the organ suspected to be involved. For example, renal biopsy is useful in the presence of urinary abnormalities. Rectal and gingival biopsy specimens contain amyloid in as many as 75% of cases with generalized amyloidosis. Examination of abdominal fat aspirates stained with Congo red is a simple, low-risk method. In suspected cases of AL amyloidosis, serum and urinary protein electrophoresis and immunoelectrophoresis should be performed. Bone marrow examination in such cases usually shows plasmacytosis, even if skeletal lesions of multiple myeloma are not present. Proteomic analysis of affected tissue is now being widely used for detection of small amounts of amyloid (from fat aspirates) and for definitive identification of the type of amyloid.

The outlook for patients with generalized amyloidosis is poor, with the mean survival time after diagnosis ranging from 1 to 3 years. In AA amyloidosis, the prognosis depends to some extent on the control of the underlying condition. Patients with myeloma-associated amyloidosis have a poorer prognosis, although they may respond to cytotoxic drugs used to treat the underlying disorder. Resorption of amyloid after treatment of the associated condition has been reported, but this is a rare occurrence.

SUMMARY

Amyloidosis

- Amyloidosis is a disorder characterized by the extracellular deposits of misfolded proteins that aggregate to form insoluble fibrils.
- The deposition of these proteins may result from excessive production of proteins that are prone to misfolding and aggregation; mutations that produce proteins that cannot fold properly and tend to aggregate; or defective or incomplete proteolytic degradation of extracellular proteins.
- Amyloidosis may be localized or systemic. It is seen in association with a variety of primary disorders, including monoclonal plasma cell proliferations (in which the amyloid deposits consist of immunoglobulin light chains); chronic inflammatory diseases such as RA (deposits of amyloid A protein, derived from an acute-phase protein produced in inflammation); Alzheimer disease (amyloid B protein); familial conditions in which the amyloid deposits consist of mutants of normal proteins (e.g., transthyretin in familial amyloid polyneuropathies); amyloidosis associated with dialysis (deposits of β_2-microglobulin, whose clearance is defective).
- Amyloid deposits cause tissue injury and impair normal function by causing pressure on cells and tissues. They do not evoke an inflammatory response.

BIBLIOGRAPHY

Banchereau J, Pascual V: Type I interferon in systemic lupus erythematosus and other autoimmune diseases. Immunity 25:383, 2006. *[A review of the recently discovered role of interferons in SLE and other autoimmune diseases, and the potential for targeting this family of cytokines for therapy.]*

Campbell DJ, Koch MA: Phenotypic and functional specialization of FoxP3+ regulatory T cells. Nat Rev Immunol 11:119, 2011. *[A current review of the properties and functions of regulatory T cells.]*

Chervonsky A: Influence of microbial environment on autoimmunity. Nat Immunol 11:28, 2010. *[A summary of the role of microbes and other environmental factors in the development of autoimmunity.]*

Cunningham-Rundles C, Ponda PP: Molecular defects in T- and B-cell primary immunodeficiency diseases. Nat Rev Immunol 5:880, 2006. *[Excellent, up-to-date review of primary immunodeficiencies.]*

Davidson A, Diamond B: Autoimmune diseases. N Engl J Med 345:340, 2001. *[A readable overview of the etiology, pathogenesis, and therapy for autoimmune diseases.]*

Douek DC, Roederer M, Koup RA: Emerging concepts in the immunopathogenesis of AIDS. Annu Rev Med 60:471, 2009. *[A balanced discussion of the pathogenesis of AIDS, and the still unresolved issues.]*

Fairhurst AM, Wandstrat AE, Wakeland EK: Systemic lupus erythematosus: multiple immunological phenotypes in a complex genetic disease. Adv Immunol 92:1, 2006. *[A comprehensive review of the* balanced translocations, deletions, and cytogenetic manifestations of gene amplification.

- Balanced translocations contribute to carcinogenesis by overexpression of oncogenes or generation of novel fusion proteins with altered signaling capacity. Deletions frequently affect tumor suppressor genes, whereas gene amplification increases the expression of oncogenes.
- Overexpression of miRNAs can contribute to carcinogenesis by reducing the expression of tumor suppressors, while deletion or loss of expression of miRNAs can lead to overexpression of proto-oncogenes.
- Tumor suppressor genes and DNA repair genes also may be silenced by epigenetic changes, which involve reversible, heritable changes in gene expression that occur not by mutation but by methylation of the promoter.

CARCINOGENESIS: A MULTISTEP PROCESS

Carcinogenesis is a multistep process resulting from the accumulation of multiple genetic alterations that collectively give rise to the transformed phenotype. Many cancers arise from non-neoplastic precursor lesions, which molecular analyses have shown already possess some of the mutations needed to establish a full-blown cancer. Presumably these mutations provide the cells of the precursor lesion with a selective advantage. Once initiated, cancers continue to undergo darwinian selection.

As discussed earlier, malignant neoplasms have several phenotypic attributes, such as excessive growth, local invasiveness, and the ability to form distant metastases. Furthermore, it is well established that over a period of time, many tumors become more aggressive and acquire greater malignant potential. This phenomenon is referred to as *tumor progression* and is not represented simply by an increase in tumor size. Careful clinical and experimental studies reveal that increasing malignancy often is acquired in an incremental fashion. At the molecular level, tumor progression and associated heterogeneity are most likely to result from multiple mutations that accumulate independently in different cells, generating subclones with different characteristics (Fig. 5-17) such as ability to invade, rate of growth, metastatic ability, karyotype, hormonal responsiveness, and susceptibility to antineoplastic drugs. Some of the mutations may be lethal; others may spur cell growth by affecting proto-oncogenes or cancer suppressor genes. *Thus even though most malignant tumors are monoclonal in origin, by the time they become clinically evident their constituent cells may be extremely heterogeneous.*

During progression, tumor cells are subjected to immune and nonimmune selection pressures. For example, cells that are highly antigenic are destroyed by host defenses, whereas those with reduced growth factor requirements are positively selected. A growing tumor, therefore, tends to be enriched for subclones that "beat the odds" and are adept at survival, growth, invasion, and metastasis. Finally, experience has shown that when tumors recur after chemotherapy, the recurrent tumor is almost always resistant to the drug regimen if it is given again. This acquired resistance, too, is a manifestation of selection, as subclones that by chance bear mutations (or perhaps epigenetic alterations) imparting drug resistance survive and are responsible for tumor regrowth. Thus, *genetic evolution and selection can explain two of the most pernicious properties of cancers: the tendency for cancers to become (1) more aggressive and (2) less responsive to therapy over time.*

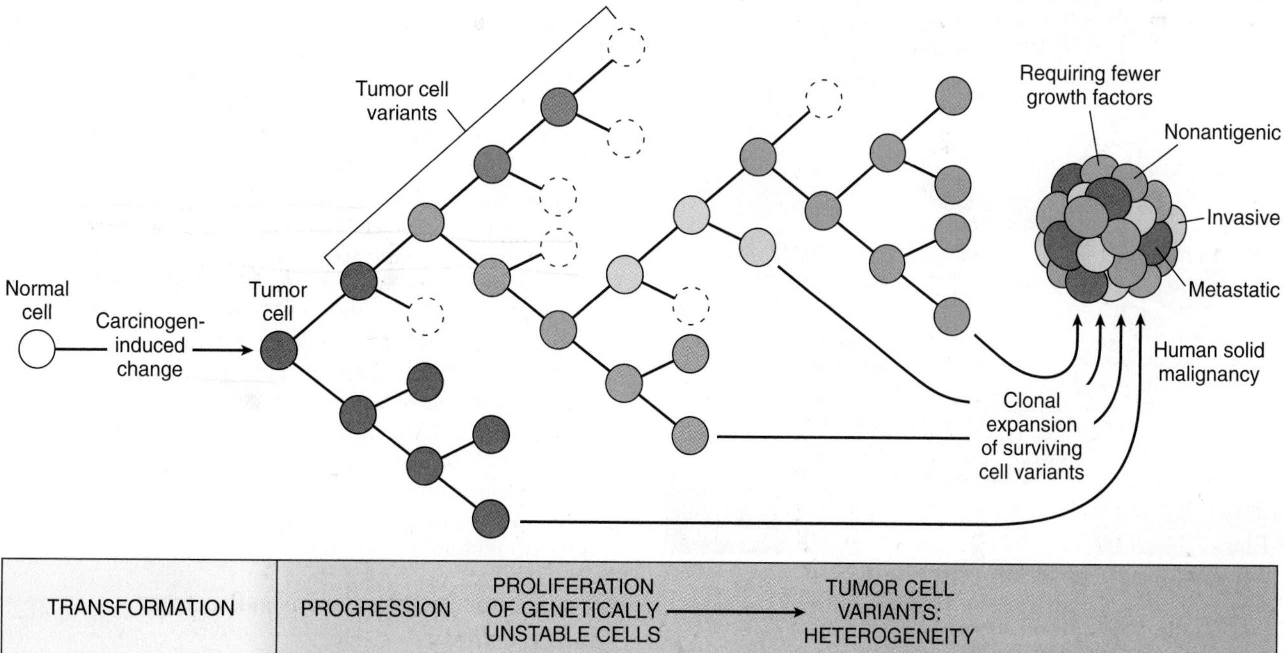

Figure 5–17 Tumor progression and generation of heterogeneity. New subclones arise from the descendants of the original transformed cell by multiple mutations. With progression, the tumor mass becomes enriched for variants that are more adept at evading host defenses and are likely to be more aggressive.

HALLMARKS OF CANCER

This overview serves as background for a more detailed consideration of the molecular pathogenesis of cancer and the carcinogenic agents that inflict genetic damage. In the past 30-some years, hundreds of cancer-associated genes have been discovered. Some, such as *TP53*, are commonly mutated; others, such as *ABL*, are affected only in certain leukemias. Each cancer gene has a specific function, the dysregulation of which contributes to the origin or progression of malignancy. It is best, therefore, to consider cancer-related genes in the context of several fundamental changes in cell physiology, the so-called hallmarks of cancer, which together dictate the malignant phenotype. Six of these are illustrated in Figure 5–18:

- Self-sufficiency in growth signals
- Insensitivity to growth inhibitory signals
- Evasion of cell death
- Limitless replicative potential
- Development of sustained angiogenesis
- Ability to invade and metastasize

To this list may be added two *"emerging" hallmarks* of cancer, reprogramming of energy metabolism and evasion of the immune system, and two *enabling characteristics*, genomic instability and tumor-promoting inflammation.

Mutations in genes that regulate some or all of these cellular traits are seen in every cancer; accordingly, these traits form the basis of the following discussion of the molecular origins of cancer. Of note, by convention, gene symbols are *italicized* but their protein products are not (e.g., *RB* gene and Rb protein, *TP53* and p53, *MYC* and MYC).

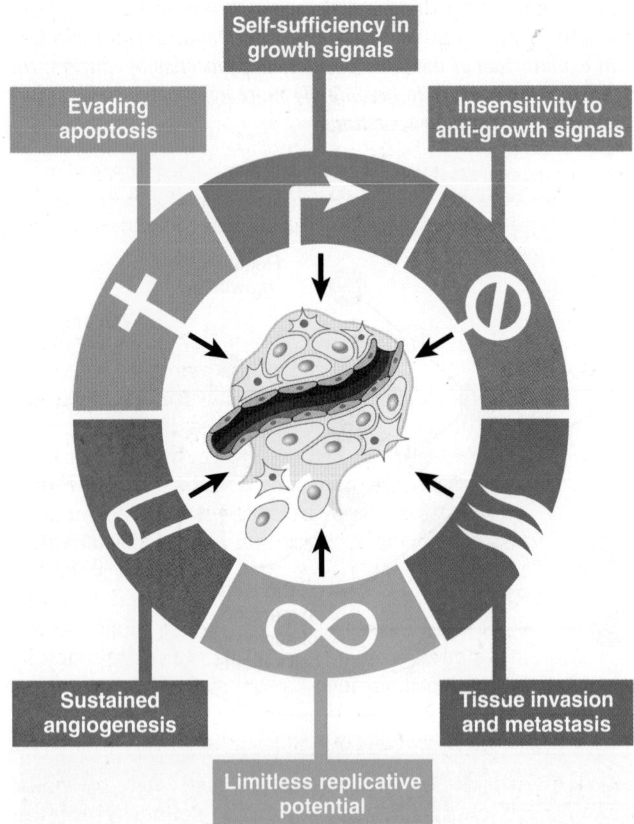

Figure 5–18 Six hallmarks of cancer. Most cancer cells acquire these properties during their development, typically by mutations in the relevant genes.
(From Hanahan D, Weinberg RA: The hallmarks of cancer. Cell 100:57, 2000.)

Self-Sufficiency in Growth Signals

Cancer cells use a number of strategies to drive their proliferation and become insensitive to normal growth regulators. To appreciate these phenomena, it is helpful to review briefly the sequence of events that characterize normal cell proliferation (introduced in Chapter 2). Under physiologic conditions, cell proliferation can be readily resolved into the following steps:

1. The binding of a growth factor to its specific receptor on the cell membrane
2. Transient and limited activation of the growth factor receptor, which in turn activates several signal-transducing proteins on the inner leaflet of the plasma membrane
3. Transmission of the transduced signal across the cytosol to the nucleus by second messengers or a cascade of signal transduction molecules
4. Induction and activation of nuclear regulatory factors that initiate and regulate DNA transcription
5. Entry and progression of the cell into the cell cycle, resulting ultimately in cell division

The mechanisms that endow cancer cells with the ability to proliferate can be grouped according to their role in the growth factor–induced signal transduction cascade and cell cycle regulation. Indeed, each one of the listed steps is susceptible to corruption in cancer cells.

Growth Factors

All normal cells require stimulation by growth factors to undergo proliferation. Most soluble growth factors are made by one cell type and act on a neighboring cell to stimulate proliferation (paracrine action). Normally, cells that produce the growth factor do not express the cognate receptor. This specificity prevents the formation of positive feedback loops within the same cell.

- Many cancer cells acquire growth self-sufficiency by acquiring the ability to synthesize the same growth factors to which they are responsive. For example, many glioblastomas secrete platelet-derived growth factor (PDGF) and express the PDGF receptor, and many sarcomas make both transforming growth factor-α (TGF-α) and its receptor. Similar autocrine loops are fairly common in many types of cancer.
- Another mechanism by which cancer cells acquire growth self-sufficiency is by interaction with stroma. In some cases, tumor cells send signals to activate normal cells in the supporting stroma, which in turn produce growth factors that promote tumor growth.

Growth Factor Receptors and Non-Receptor Tyrosine Kinases

The next group in the sequence of signal transduction is growth factor receptors, and several oncogenes that result from the overexpression or mutation of growth factor receptors have been identified. Mutant receptor proteins deliver continuous mitogenic signals to cells, even in the absence of the growth factor in the environment. More common than mutations is overexpression of growth factor receptors, which can render cancer cells hyperresponsive to levels of the growth factor that would not normally trigger proliferation. The best-documented examples of overexpression involve the epidermal growth factor (EGF) receptor family. ERBB1, the EGF receptor, is overexpressed in 80% of squamous cell carcinomas of the lung, 50% or more of glioblastomas, and 80% to 100% of epithelial tumors of the head and neck. The gene encoding a related receptor, *HER2/NEU* (*ERBB2*), is amplified in 25% to 30% of breast cancers and adenocarcinomas of the lung, ovary, and salivary glands. These tumors are exquisitely sensitive to the mitogenic effects of small amounts of growth factors, and a high level of HER2/NEU protein in breast cancer cells is a harbinger of poor prognosis. The significance of *HER2/NEU* in the pathogenesis of breast cancers is illustrated dramatically by the clinical benefit derived from blocking the extracellular domain of this receptor with anti-*HER2/NEU* antibodies. Treatment of breast cancer with anti-HER2/NEU antibody is an elegant example of "bench to bedside" medicine.

Downstream Signal-Transducing Proteins

A relatively common mechanism by which cancer cells acquire growth autonomy is mutations in genes that encode various components of the signaling pathways downstream of growth factor receptors. These signaling proteins couple growth factor receptors to their nuclear targets. They receive signals from activated growth factor receptors and transmit them to the nucleus, either through second messengers or through a cascade of phosphorylation and activation of signal transduction molecules. Two important members in this category are *RAS* and *ABL*. Each of these is discussed briefly next.

RAS Protein. *RAS* is the most commonly mutated proto-oncogene in human tumors. Indeed, approximately 30% of all human tumors contain mutated versions of the *RAS* gene, and the frequency is even higher in some specific cancers (e.g., colon and pancreatic adenocarcinomas).

- RAS is a member of a family of small G proteins that bind guanosine nucleotides (guanosine triphosphate [GTP] and guanosine diphosphate [GDP]), similar to the larger trimolecular G proteins.
- Normal RAS proteins flip back and forth between an excited signal-transmitting state and a quiescent state. RAS proteins are inactive when bound to GDP; stimulation of cells by growth factors such as EGF and PDGF leads to exchange of GDP for GTP and subsequent conformational changes that generate active RAS (Fig. 5–19). This excited signal-emitting state is short-lived, however, because the intrinsic guanosine triphosphatase (GTPase) activity of RAS hydrolyzes GTP to GDP, releasing a phosphate group and returning the protein to its quiescent GDP-bound state. The GTPase activity of activated RAS protein is magnified dramatically by a family of GTPase-activating proteins (GAPs), which act as molecular brakes that prevent uncontrolled RAS activation by favoring hydrolysis of GTP to GDP.

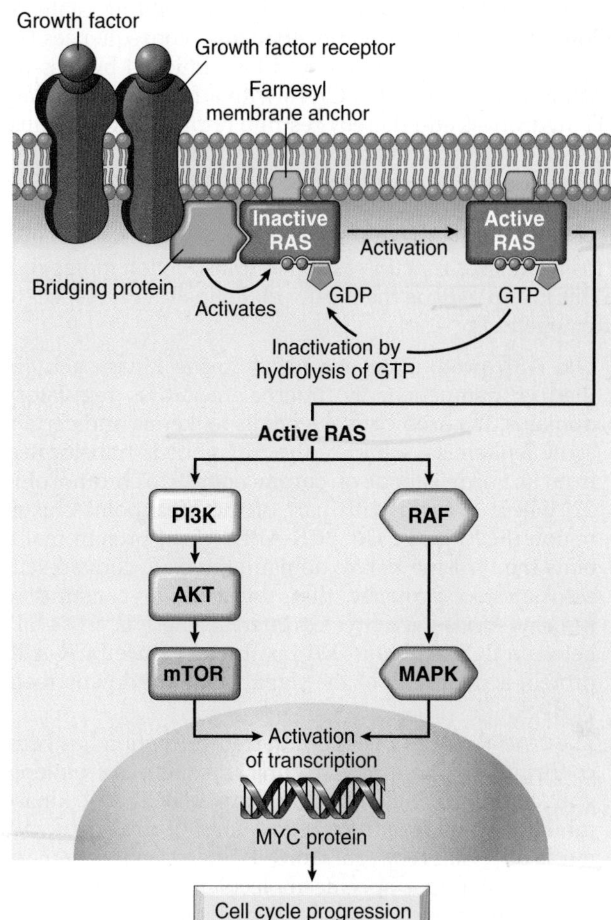

Figure 5–19 Model for action of *RAS* genes. When a normal cell is stimulated through a growth factor receptor, inactive (GDP-bound) RAS is activated to a GTP-bound state. Activated RAS transduces proliferative signals to the nucleus along two pathways: the so-called RAF/ERK/MAP kinase pathway and the PI3 kinase/AKT pathway. GDP, guanosine diphosphate; GTP, guanosine triphosphate; MAP, mitogen-activated protein; PI3, phosphatidylinositol-3.

- The activated RAS stimulates downstream regulators of proliferation by two distinct pathways that converge on the nucleus and flood it with signals for cell proliferation. While details of the signaling cascades (some of which are illustrated in Fig. 5–19) downstream of RAS are not discussed here, an important point is that mutational activation of these "messengers" to the nucleus can mimic the growth promoting effects of activated RAS. For example, BRAF, which lies in the so-called RAF/ERK/MAP kinase pathway, is mutated in more than 60% of melanomas. Mutations of PI3 kinase in the PI3K/AKT pathway also occur with high frequency in some tumor types. Indeed, it appears that activating mutations of RAS as well as its downstream signaling molecules are very common in a wide variety of tumors.

The RAS protein most commonly is activated by point mutations in amino acid residues that are either within the GTP-binding pocket or in the enzymatic region essential for GTP hydrolysis. Both kinds of mutations interfere with GTP hydrolysis, which is essential to inactivate RAS. RAS is thus trapped in its activated, GTP-bound form, and the cell is forced into a continuously proliferating state. It follows from this scenario that the consequences of mutations in RAS protein would be mimicked by loss-of-function mutations in the GAPs with a failure to simulate GTP hydrolysis and thereby restrain normal RAS proteins. Indeed, disabling mutation of neurofibromin-1 (NF-1), a GAP, is associated with familial neurofibromatosis type 1 (Chapter 22).

ABL. In addition to *RAS*, several non–receptor-associated tyrosine kinases function as signal transduction molecules. In this group, *ABL* is the most well defined with respect to carcinogenesis.

- The *ABL* proto-oncogene has tyrosine kinase activity that is dampened by internal negative regulatory domains. In chronic myelogenous leukemia and certain acute leukemias, a part of the *ABL* gene is translocated from its normal abode on chromosome 9 to chromosome 22, where it fuses with part of the breakpoint cluster region (*BCR*) gene. The BCR-ABL hybrid protein maintains the tyrosine kinase domain; the BCR domain self-associates, a property that unleashes a constitutive tyrosine kinase activity. Of interest, there is cross-talk between BCR-ABL and RAS pathways, since BCR-ABL protein activates all of the signals that are downstream of RAS.
- The crucial role of *BCR-ABL* in transformation has been confirmed by the dramatic clinical response of patients with chronic myelogenous leukemia to BCR-ABL kinase inhibitors. The prototype of this kind of drug, imatinib mesylate (Gleevec), galvanized interest in design of drugs that target specific molecular lesions found in various cancers (so-called *targeted therapy*). BCR-ABL also is an example of the concept of *oncogene addiction,* wherein a tumor is profoundly dependent on a single signaling molecule. BCR-ABL fusion gene formation is an early, perhaps initiating, event that drives leukemogenesis. Development of leukemia probably requires other collaborating mutations, but the transformed cell continues to depend on BCR-ABL for signals that mediate growth and survival. BCR-ABL signaling can be seen as the central lodgepole around which the structure is built. If the lodgepole is removed by inhibition of the BCR-ABL kinase, the structure collapses. In view of this level of dependency, it is not surprising that acquired resistance of tumors to BCR-ABL inhibitors often is due to the outgrowth of a subclone with a mutation in BCR-ABL that prevents binding of the drug to the BCR-ABL protein.

Nuclear Transcription Factors

Ultimately, all signal transduction pathways enter the nucleus and have an impact on a large bank of responder genes that orchestrate the cell's orderly advance through the mitotic cycle. Indeed, the ultimate consequence of signaling through oncoproteins such as RAS or ABL is inappropriate and continuous stimulation of nuclear transcription factors that drive the expression of growth-promoting genes. Growth autonomy may thus be a consequence of mutations affecting genes that regulate transcription of DNA. A host of oncoproteins, including products of the *MYC, MYB, JUN, FOS,* and *REL* oncogenes, function as transcription factors that regulate the expression of growth-promoting genes, such as cyclins. Of these, the *MYC* gene is involved most commonly in human tumors.

The MYC protein can either activate or repress the transcription of other genes. Those activated by MYC include several growth-promoting genes, including cyclin-dependent kinases (CDKs), whose products drive cells into the cell cycle (discussed next). Genes repressed by MYC include the CDK inhibitors (CDKIs). Thus, dysregulation of MYC promotes tumorigenesis by increasing expression of genes that promote progression through the cell cycle and repressing genes that slow or prevent progression through the cell cycle. MYC also is a key regulator of intermediate metabolism, upregulating genes that promote aerobic glycolysis (the so-called Warburg effect, described later) and the increased utilization of glutamine, two metabolic changes that are hallmarks of cancer cells. Dysregulation of the *MYC* gene resulting from a t(8;14) translocation occurs in Burkitt lymphoma, a B cell tumor. *MYC* also is amplified in breast, colon, lung, and many other cancers; the related *NMYC* and *LMYC* genes are amplified in neuroblastomas and small cell cancers of lung.

Cyclins and Cyclin-Dependent Kinases

The ultimate outcome of all growth-promoting stimuli is the entry of quiescent cells into the cell cycle. Cancers may become autonomous if the genes that drive the cell cycle become dysregulated by mutations or amplification. Before further consideration of this aspect of carcinogenesis, a brief review of the normal cell cycle is warranted (Fig. 5–20).

The Normal Cell Cycle

Cell proliferation is a tightly controlled process that involves a large number of molecules and interrelated pathways. The replication of cells is stimulated by growth factors or by signaling from ECM components through integrins. To achieve DNA replication and division, the cell goes through a tightly controlled sequence of events known as the cell cycle. The cell cycle consists of G_1 (presynthetic), S (DNA synthesis), G_2 (premitotic), and M (mitotic) phases. Quiescent cells that have not entered the cell cycle are in the G_0 state. Each cell cycle phase is dependent on the proper activation and completion of the previous ones and the cycle stops at a place at which an essential gene function is deficient. Because of its central role in maintaining tissue homeostasis and regulating physiologic growth processes such as regeneration and repair, the cell cycle has multiple checkpoints, particularly during emergence from G_0 into G_1 and the transition from G_1 to S phase.

Cells can enter G_1 either from G_0 (quiescent cells) or after completing mitosis (continuously replicating cells). Quiescent cells must first go through the transition from G_0 to G_1, the first decision step, which functions as a gateway to the cell cycle. Cells in G_1 progress through the cell cycle and reach a critical stage at the G_1-S transition, known as a restriction point, a rate-limiting step for replication. On passing this restriction point, normal cells become irreversibly committed to DNA replication. The cell cycle is tightly controlled by activators and inhibitors.

- Progression through the cell cycle, particularly at the G_1-S transition, is regulated by proteins called *cyclins,* so

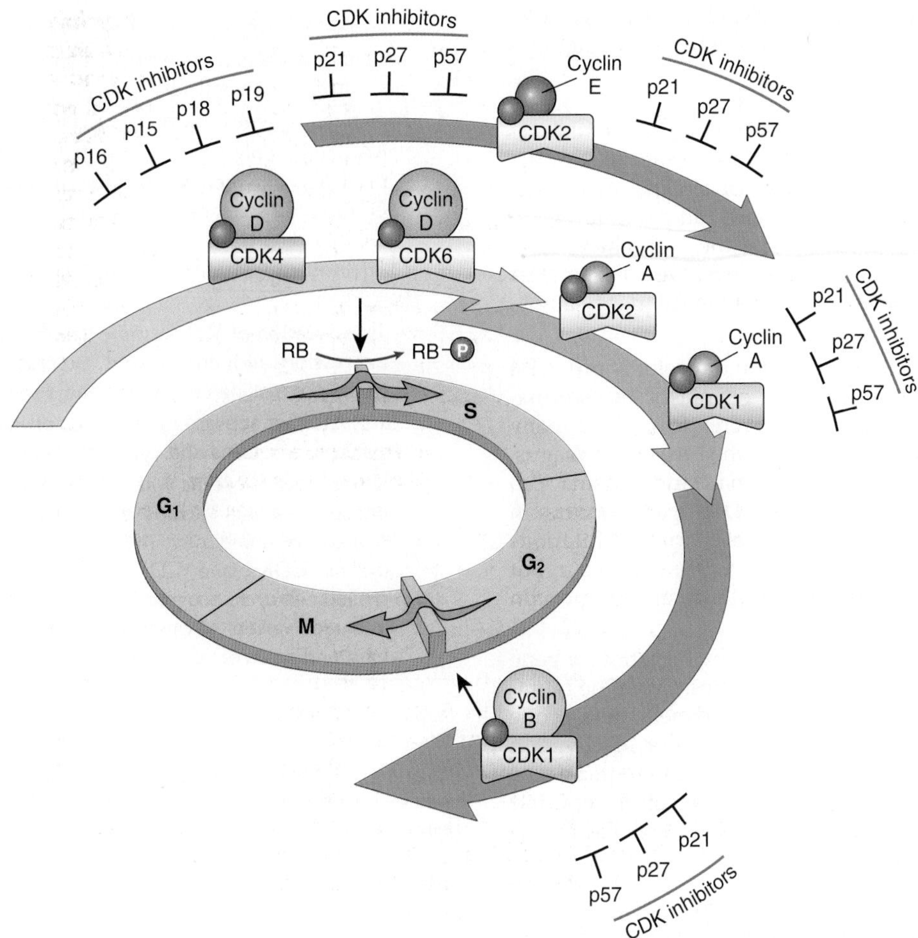

Figure 5–20 Role of cyclins, cyclin-dependent kinases (CDKs), and CDK inhibitors in regulating the cell cycle. The *shaded arrows* represent the phases of the cell cycle during which specific cyclin–CDK complexes are active. As illustrated, cyclin D–CDK4, cyclin D–CDK6, and cyclin E–CDK2 regulate the G_1-to-S transition by phosphorylating the Rb protein (pRb). Cyclin A–CDK2 and cyclin A–CDK1 are active in the S phase. Cyclin B–CDK1 is essential for the G_2-to-M transition. Two families of CDK inhibitors can block activity of CDKs and progression through the cell cycle. The so-called INK4 inhibitors, composed of p16, p15, p18, and p19, act on cyclin D–CDK4 and cyclin D–CDK6. The other family of three inhibitors, p21, p27, and p57, can inhibit all CDKs.

called because of the cyclic nature of their production and degradation, and associated enzymes, the *cyclin-dependent kinases* (CDKs). CDKs acquire catalytic activity by binding to and forming complexes with the cyclins. The orderly progression of cells through the various phases of the cell cycle is orchestrated by CDKs, which are activated by binding to the cyclins.

- The CDK–cyclin complexes phosphorylate crucial target proteins that drive the cell through the cell cycle. On completion of this task, cyclin levels decline rapidly. More than 15 cyclins have been identified; cyclins D, E, A, and B appear sequentially during the cell cycle and bind to one or more CDKs. The cell cycle may thus be seen as a relay race in which each leg is regulated by a distinct set of cyclins: As one set of cyclins leaves the track, the next set takes over (Fig. 5–20). Activated CDKs in these complexes drive the cell cycle by phosphorylating proteins that regulate cell cycle transitions. One such protein is the retinoblastoma protein (Rb), discussed later.
- The activity of CDK–cyclin complexes is regulated by CDK inhibitors (CDKIs), which enforce cell cycle checkpoints. Embedded in the cell cycle are surveillance mechanisms that are geared to sensing damage to DNA and chromosomes. These quality control checks are called *checkpoints;* they ensure that cells with damaged DNA or chromosomes do not complete replication. The G_1-S checkpoint monitors the integrity of DNA before DNA replication, whereas the G_2-M checkpoint checks DNA after replication and monitors whether the cell can safely enter mitosis. When cells sense DNA damage, checkpoint activation delays the cell cycle and triggers DNA repair mechanisms. If DNA damage is too severe to be repaired, the cells are eliminated by apoptosis, or enter a nonreplicative state called senescence, primarily through p53-dependent mechanisms, discussed later on. Mutations in genes regulating these checkpoints allow cells with damaged DNA to divide, producing daughter cells carrying mutations.
- There are several families of CDKIs. One family, composed of three proteins called p21 (CDKN1A), p27 (CDKN1B), and p57 (CDKN1C), inhibits the CDKs broadly, whereas the other family of CDKIs has selective effects on cyclin CDK4 and cyclin CDK6. The four

members of this family—p15 (CDKN2B), p16 (CDKN2A), p18 (CDKN2C), and p19 (CDKN2D)—are sometimes called INK4 (A to D) proteins.

Alterations in Cell Cycle Control Proteins in Cancer Cells

With this background it is easy to appreciate that mutations that dysregulate the activity of cyclins and CDKs would favor cell proliferation. Indeed, all cancers appear to have genetic lesions that disable the G_1-S checkpoint, causing cells to continually reenter the S phase. For unclear reasons, particular lesions vary widely in frequency across tumor types.

- Mishaps increasing the expression of cyclin D or CDK4 seem to be a common event in neoplastic transformation. The cyclin D genes are overexpressed in many cancers, including those affecting the breast, esophagus, liver, and a subset of lymphomas and plasma cell tumors. Amplification of the *CDK4* gene occurs in melanomas, sarcomas, and glioblastomas. Mutations affecting cyclins B and E and other CDKs also occur, but they are much less frequent than those affecting cyclin CDK4.
- The CDKIs frequently are disabled by mutation or gene silencing in many human malignancies. Germline mutations of *CDKN2A* are present in 25% of melanoma-prone kindreds. Somatically acquired deletion or inactivation of *CDKN2A* is seen in 75% of pancreatic carcinomas, 40% to 70% of glioblastomas, 50% of esophageal cancers, and 20% of non–small cell lung carcinomas, soft tissue sarcomas, and bladder cancers.

A final consideration of importance in a discussion of growth-promoting signals is that the increased production of oncoproteins does not by itself lead to sustained proliferation of cancer cells. There are two built-in mechanisms, cell senescence and apoptosis, that oppose oncogene-mediated cell growth. As discussed later, genes that regulate these two braking mechanisms must be disabled to allow unopposed action of oncogenes.

SUMMARY

Oncogenes That Promote Unregulated Proliferation (Self-Sufficiency in Growth Signals)

Proto-oncogenes: normal cellular genes whose products promote cell proliferation

Oncogenes: mutant or overexpressed versions of proto-oncogenes that function autonomously without a requirement for normal growth-promoting signals

Oncoproteins promote uncontrolled cell proliferation by several mechanisms:

- Stimulus-independent expression of growth factor and its receptor, setting up an autocrine loop of cell proliferation
  - PDGF–PDGF receptor in brain tumors
- Mutations in genes encoding growth factor receptors or tyrosine kinases leading to constitutive signaling
  - EGF receptor family members, including HER2/NEU (breast, lung, and other tumors)
  - Fusion of ABL tyrosine kinase with BCR protein in certain leukemias generates a hybrid protein with constitutive kinase activity.
- Mutations in genes encoding signaling molecules
  - RAS commonly is mutated in human cancers and normally flips between resting GDP-bound state and active GTP-bound state; mutations block hydrolysis of GTP to GDP, leading to unchecked signaling.
- Overproduction or unregulated activity of transcription factors
  - Translocation of *MYC* in some lymphomas leads to overexpression and unregulated expression of its target genes controlling cell cycling and survival.
- Mutations that activate cyclin genes or inactivate negative regulators of cyclins and cyclin-dependent kinases
  - Complexes of cyclins with CDKs drive the cell cycle by phosphorylating various substrates. CDKs are controlled by inhibitors; mutations in genes encoding cyclins, CDKs, and CDK inhibitors result in uncontrolled cell cycle progression. Such mutations are found in a wide variety of cancers including melanomas, brain, lung, and pancreatic cancer.

Insensitivity to Growth Inhibitory Signals

Isaac Newton theorized that every action has an equal and opposite reaction. Although Newton was not a cancer biologist, his formulation holds true for cell growth. Whereas oncogenes encode proteins that promote cell growth, the products of tumor suppressor genes apply brakes to cell proliferation. Disruption of such genes renders cells refractory to growth inhibition and mimics the growth-promoting effects of oncogenes. The following discussion describes tumor suppressor genes, their products, and possible mechanisms by which loss of their function contributes to unregulated cell growth.

RB *Gene: Governor of the Cell Cycle*

It is useful to begin with the retinoblastoma gene (*RB*), the first tumor suppressor gene to be discovered and, as it happens, a prototypical representative. As with many advances in medicine, the discovery of tumor suppressor genes was accomplished by the study of a rare disease—in this case, retinoblastoma, an uncommon childhood tumor. Approximately 60% of retinoblastomas are sporadic, and the remaining ones are familial, the predisposition to develop the tumor being transmitted as an autosomal dominant trait. To account for the sporadic and familial occurrence of an identical tumor, Knudson, in 1974, proposed his now famous *two-hit hypothesis*, which in molecular terms can be stated as follows:

- Two mutations (*hits*) are required to produce retinoblastoma. These involve the *RB* gene, which has been mapped to chromosomal locus 13q14. Both of the normal alleles of the *RB* locus must be inactivated (hence the two hits) for the development of retinoblastoma (Fig. 5–21).
- In familial cases, children inherit one defective copy of the *RB* gene in the germ line; the other copy is normal.

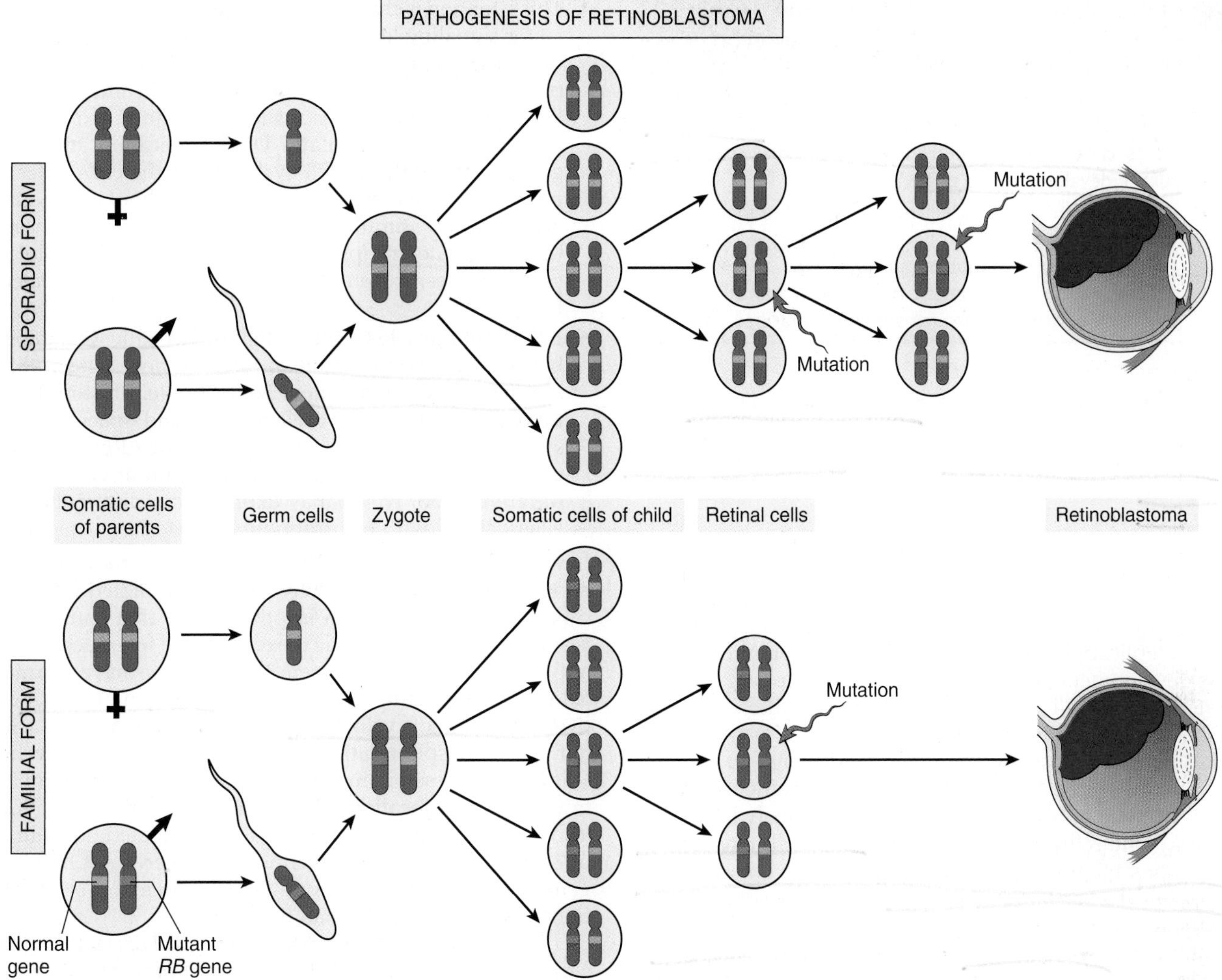

Figure 5–21 Pathogenesis of retinoblastoma. Two mutations of the *RB* chromosomal locus, on 13q14, lead to neoplastic proliferation of the retinal cells. In the familial form, all somatic cells inherit one mutant *RB* gene from a carrier parent. The second mutation affects the *RB* locus in one of the retinal cells after birth. In the sporadic form, both mutations at the *RB* locus are acquired by the retinal cells after birth.

Retinoblastoma develops when the normal *RB* gene is lost in retinoblasts as a result of somatic mutation. Because in retinoblastoma families only a single somatic mutation is required for expression of the disease, the familial transmission follows an autosomal dominant inheritance pattern.

- In sporadic cases, both normal *RB* alleles are lost by somatic mutation in one of the retinoblasts. The end result is the same: a retinal cell that has lost both of the normal copies of the *RB* gene becomes cancerous.

Although the loss of normal *RB* genes initially was discovered in retinoblastomas, it is now evident that homozygous loss of this gene is a fairly common feature of several tumors, including breast cancer, small cell cancer of the lung, and bladder cancer. Patients with familial retinoblastoma also are at greatly increased risk for development of osteosarcomas and some soft tissue sarcomas.

At this point, some clarification of terminology is in order: A cell heterozygous at the *RB* locus is not neoplastic. Tumors develop when the cell loses its normal *RB* gene copy and thus becomes *homozygous* for the mutant allele.

In principle, antigrowth signals can prevent cell proliferation by several complementary mechanisms. The signal may cause dividing cells to enter G_0 (quiescence), where they remain until external cues prod their reentry into the proliferative pool. Alternatively, the cells may enter a postmitotic, differentiated pool and lose replicative potential. Nonreplicative senescence, alluded to earlier, is another escape mechanism from sustained cell growth. And, as a last-ditch effort, the cells may be programmed for death by apoptosis. As we shall see, tumor suppressor genes have all these "tricks" in their toolbox designed to halt wayward cells from becoming malignant.

The subsequent discussion of growth inhibitory mechanisms and their evasion focuses initially on the prototypical tumor suppressor gene, the *RB* gene.

SUMMARY

Insensitivity to Growth Inhibitory Signals

- Tumor suppressor genes encode proteins that inhibit cellular proliferation by regulating the cell cycle. Unlike oncogenes, both copies of the gene must be dysfunctional for tumor development to occur.
- In cases with familial predisposition for development of tumors, affected persons inherit one defective (nonfunctional) copy of a tumor suppressor gene and lose the second one through somatic mutation. In sporadic cases, both copies are lost through somatic mutations.

The *RB* gene product is a DNA-binding protein that is expressed in every cell type examined, where it exists in an *active hypophosphorylated state* and an *inactive hyperphosphorylated state.* The importance of Rb lies in its regulation of the G_1/S checkpoint, the portal through which cells must pass before DNA replication commences.

As background for an understanding of how tumor suppressors function, it is useful to briefly revisit the cell cycle: In embryos, cell divisions proceed at an amazing clip, with DNA replication beginning immediately after mitosis ends. As development proceeds, however, two gaps are incorporated into the cell cycle: gap 1 (G_1) between mitosis (M) and DNA replication (S), and gap 2 (G_2) between DNA replication (S) and mitosis (M) (Fig. 5–20). Although each phase of the cell cycle circuitry is monitored carefully, the transition from G_1 to S is believed to be an extremely important checkpoint in the cell cycle "clock." Once cells cross the G_1 checkpoint they can pause the cell cycle for a time, but they are obligated to complete mitosis. In G_1, however, cells can remove themselves entirely from the cell cycle, either temporarily (quiescence, or G_0) or permanently (senescence). Indeed, during development, as cells become terminally differentiated, they exit the cell cycle and enter G_0. Cells in G_0 remain there until external cues, such as mitogenic signaling, push them back into the cell cycle. In G_1, therefore, diverse signals are integrated to determine whether the cell should progress through the cell cycle, or exit the cell cycle and differentiate, and Rb is a key hub integrating external mitogenic and differentiation signals to make this decision.

To appreciate this crucial role of Rb in the cell cycle, it is helpful to review the mechanisms that enforce the G_1/S transition.

- The initiation of DNA replication (S phase) requires the activity of cyclin E/CDK2 complexes, and expression of cyclin E is dependent on the E2F family of transcription factors. Early in G_1, Rb is in its hypophosphorylated active form, and it binds to and inhibits the E2F family of transcription factors, preventing transcription of cyclin E. Hypophosphorylated Rb blocks E2F-mediated transcription in at least two ways (Fig. 5–22). First, it sequesters E2F, preventing it from interacting with other transcriptional activators. Second, Rb recruits chromatin remodeling proteins, such as histone deacetylases and histone methyltransferases, which bind to the promoters of E2F-responsive genes such as cyclin E. These enzymes modify chromatin at the promoters to make DNA insensitive to transcription factors.
- This situation is changed on mitogenic signaling. Growth factor signaling leads to cyclin D expression and activation of cyclin D–CDK4/6 complexes. These complexes phosphorylate Rb, inactivating the protein and releasing E2F to induce target genes such as cyclin E. Expression of cyclin E then stimulates DNA replication and progression through the cell cycle. When the cells enter S phase, they are committed to divide without additional growth factor stimulation. During the ensuing M phase, the phosphate groups are removed from Rb by cellular phosphatases, regenerating the hypophosphorylated form of Rb.
- E2F is not the sole target of Rb. The versatile Rb protein binds to a variety of other transcription factors that regulate cell differentiation. For example, Rb stimulates myocyte-, adipocyte-, melanocyte-, and macrophage-specific transcription factors. Thus, the Rb pathway couples control of cell cycle progression at G_0-G_1 with differentiation, which may explain how differentiation is associated with exit from the cell cycle.

In view of the centrality of Rb to the control of the cell cycle, an interesting question is why *RB* is not mutated in every cancer. In fact, mutations in other genes that control Rb phosphorylation can mimic the effect of *RB* loss; such genes are mutated in many cancers that seem to have normal *RB* genes. For example, mutational activation of CDK4 or overexpression of cyclin D favors cell proliferation by facilitating Rb phosphorylation and inactivation. Indeed, cyclin D is overexpressed in many tumors because of gene amplification or translocation. Mutational inactivation of CDKIs also would drive the cell cycle by unregulated activation of cyclins and CDKs. As mentioned earlier, the *CDKN2A* gene is an extremely common target of deletion or mutational inactivation in human tumors.

The emerging paradigm is that loss of normal cell cycle control is central to malignant transformation and that at least one of the four key regulators of the cell cycle (CDKN2A, cyclin D, CDK4, Rb) is mutated in most human cancers. Furthermore, the transforming proteins of several oncogenic human DNA viruses act, in part, by neutralizing the growth inhibitory activities of Rb. For example, the human papillomavirus (HPV) E7 protein binds to the hypophosphorylated form of Rb, preventing it from inhibiting the E2F transcription factors. Thus, Rb is functionally deleted, leading to uncontrolled growth.

SUMMARY

***RB* Gene: Governor of the Cell Cycle**

- Rb exerts antiproliferative effects by controlling the G_1-to-S transition of the cell cycle. In its active form, Rb is hypophosphorylated and binds to E2F transcription factor. This interaction prevents transcription of genes like cyclin E that are needed for DNA replication, and so the cells are arrested in G_1.
- Growth factor signaling leads to cyclin D expression, activation of the cyclin D–CDK4/6 complexes, inactivation of Rb by phosphorylation, and thus release of E2F.
- Loss of cell cycle control is fundamental to malignant transformation. Almost all cancers have a disabled G_1

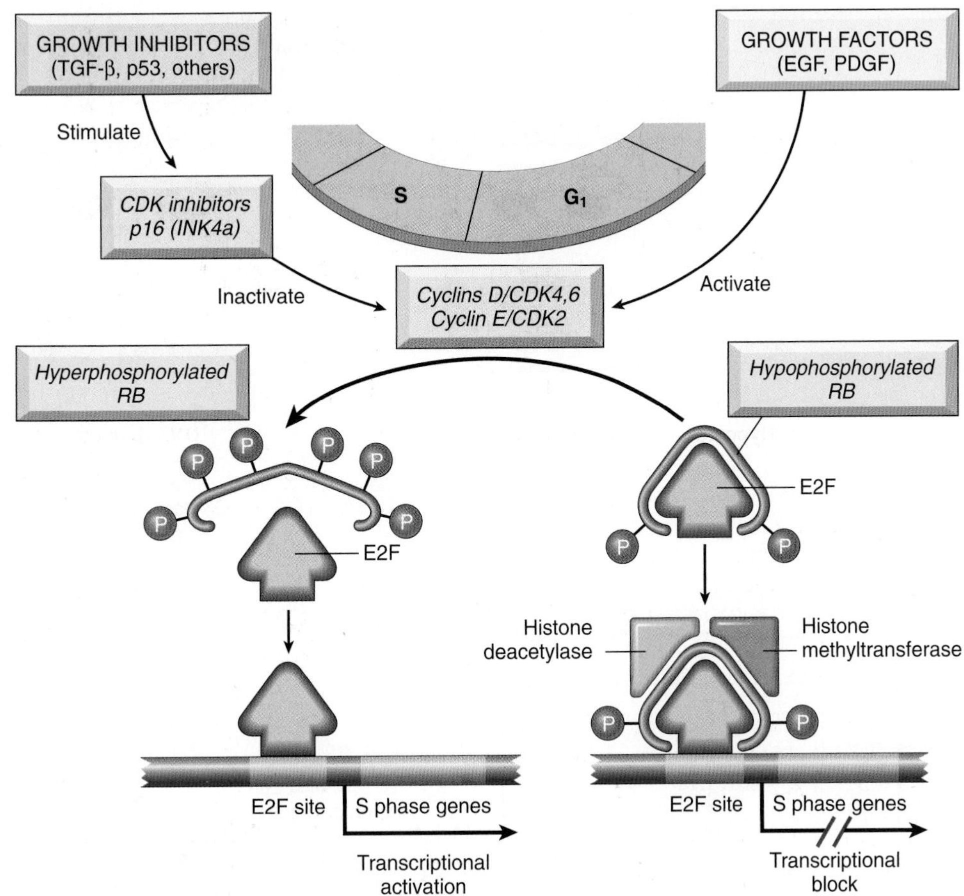

Figure 5–22 The role of Rb in regulating the G_1–S checkpoint of the cell cycle. Hypophosphorylated Rb in complex with the E2F transcription factors binds to DNA, recruits chromatin remodeling factors (histone deacetylases and histone methyltransferases), and inhibits transcription of genes whose products are required for the S phase of the cell cycle. When Rb is phosphorylated by the cyclin D–CDK4, cyclin D–CDK6, and cyclin E–CDK2 complexes, it releases E2F. The latter then activates transcription of S-phase genes. The phosphorylation of Rb is inhibited by CDKIs, because they inactivate cyclin-CDK complexes. Virtually all cancer cells show dysregulation of the G_1–S checkpoint as a result of mutation in one of four genes that regulate the phosphorylation of Rb; these genes are *RB, CDK4, cyclin D,* and *CDKN2A [p16]*. EGF, epidermal growth factor; PDGF, platelet-derived growth factor.

checkpoint due to mutation of either *RB* or genes that affect Rb function, such as cyclin D, CDK4, and CDKIs.

- Many oncogenic DNA viruses, like HPV, encode proteins (e.g., E7) that bind to Rb and render it nonfunctional.

TP53 *Gene: Guardian of the Genome*

The p53-encoding tumor suppressor gene, *TP53,* is one of the most commonly mutated genes in human cancers. The p53 protein thwarts neoplastic transformation by three interlocking mechanisms: activation of temporary cell cycle arrest (termed quiescence), induction of permanent cell cycle arrest (termed senescence), or triggering of programmed cell death (termed apoptosis). If Rb "senses" external signals, p53 can be viewed as a central monitor of internal stress, directing the stressed cells toward one of these three pathways.

A variety of stresses trigger the p53 response pathways, including anoxia, inappropriate oncoprotein activity (e.g., MYC or RAS), and damage to the integrity of DNA. By managing the DNA damage response, p53 plays a central role in maintaining the integrity of the genome, as described next.

In nonstressed, healthy cells, p53 has a short half-life (20 minutes) because of its association with MDM2, a protein that targets p53 for destruction. When the cell is stressed, for example, by an assault on its DNA, "sensors" that include protein kinases such as ATM (ataxia telangiectasia mutated) are activated. These activated complexes catalyze post-translational modifications in p53 that release it from MDM2 and increase its half-life and enhance its ability to drive the transcription of target genes. Hundreds of genes whose transcription is triggered by p53 have been found. These genes suppress neoplastic transformation by three mechanisms:

- *p53-mediated cell cycle arrest may be considered the primordial response to DNA damage* (Fig. 5–23). It occurs late in the G_1 phase and is caused mainly by p53-dependent transcription of the CDKI gene *CDKN1A (p21).* The p21 protein, as described earlier, inhibits cyclin–CDK complexes and prevents phosphorylation of Rb, thereby arresting cells in the G_1 phase. Such a pause in cell cycling is welcome, because it gives the cells "breathing time" to repair DNA damage. The p53 protein also

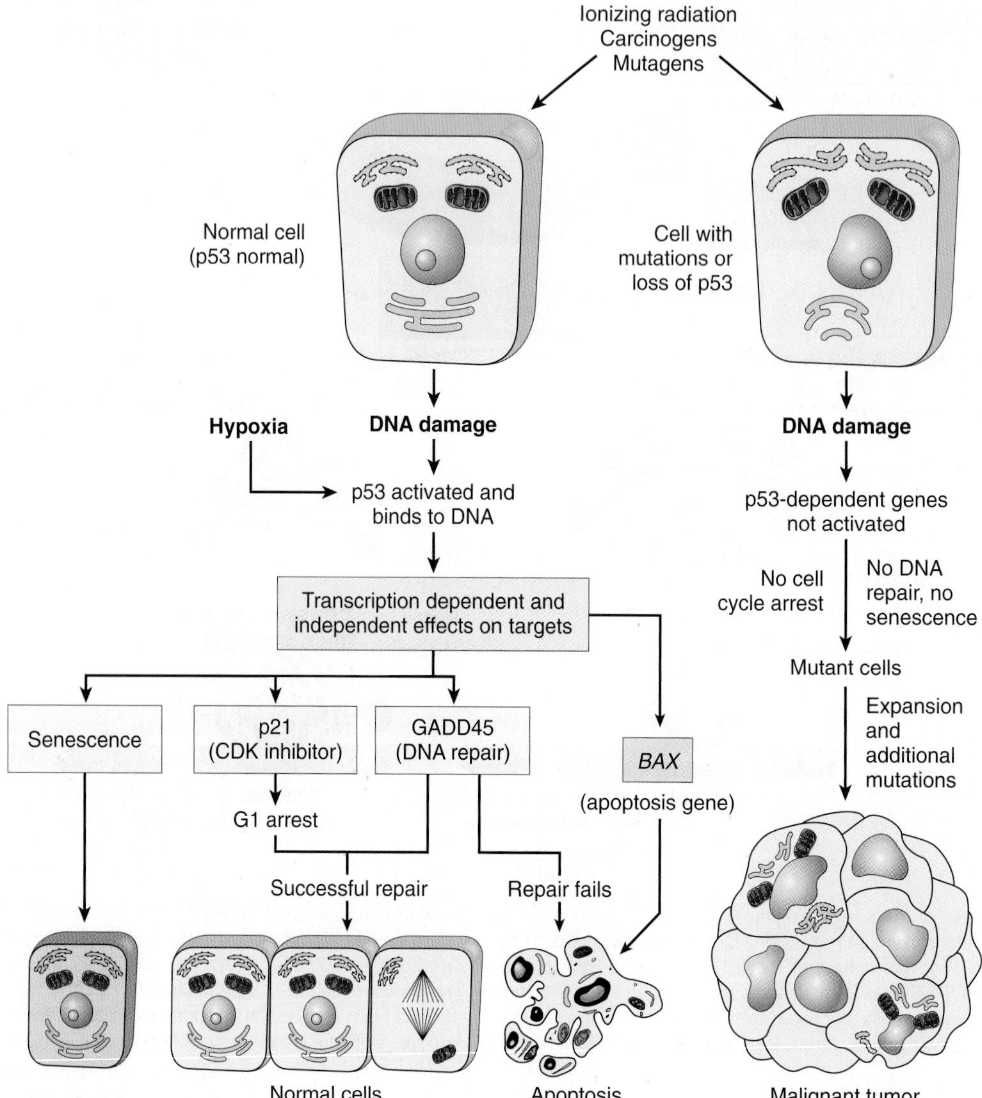

Figure 5–23 The role of p53 in maintaining the integrity of the genome. Activation of normal p53 by DNA-damaging agents or by hypoxia leads to cell cycle arrest in G_1 and induction of DNA repair, by transcriptional upregulation of the cyclin-dependent kinase inhibitor *CDKN1A* (p21) and the *GADD45* genes. Successful repair of DNA allows cells to proceed with the cell cycle; if DNA repair fails, p53 triggers either apoptosis or senescence. In cells with loss or mutations of *TP53*, DNA damage does not induce cell cycle arrest or DNA repair, and genetically damaged cells proliferate, giving rise eventually to malignant neoplasms.

induces expression of DNA damage repair genes. If DNA damage is repaired successfully, p53 upregulates transcription of MDM2, leading to destruction of p53 and relief of the cell cycle block. If the damage cannot be repaired, the cell may enter p53-induced senescence or undergo p53-directed apoptosis.

- *p53-induced senescence is a permanent cell cycle arrest* characterized by specific changes in morphology and gene expression that differentiate it from quiescence or reversible cell cycle arrest. Senescence requires activation of p53 and/or Rb and expression of their mediators, such as the CDKIs. The mechanisms of senescence are unclear but seem to involve global chromatin changes, which drastically and permanently alter gene expression.
- *p53-induced apoptosis of cells with irreversible DNA damage is the ultimate protective mechanism against neoplastic transformation.* It is mediated by several pro-apoptotic genes such as *BAX* and *PUMA* (described later).

Until recently it was thought that these functions of p53 were mediated exclusively by transcriptional activation of genes with antiproliferative, apoptotic, and senescence-inducing functions, as discussed earlier. But the waters were muddied when it was discovered that p53 represses a subset of pro-proliferative and anti-apoptotic genes as well. How could p53, a transcriptional activator, repress gene function? The answer came from the discovery that p53 can transcriptionally activate certain miRNAs (the "small guys with big clubs"). As discussed in Chapter 6, miRNAs can prevent translation of their target genes. The miRNAs activated by p53 can inhibit the translation of pro-proliferative genes such as cyclins and anti-apoptotic genes such as *BCL2*.

Li-Fraumeni syndrome – inherited bad p53 gene

To summarize, p53 is activated by stresses such as DNA damage and assists in DNA repair by causing G_1 arrest and inducing DNA repair genes. A cell with damaged DNA that cannot be repaired is directed by *p53 to either enter senescence or undergo apoptosis* (Fig. 5–25). In view of these activities, *p53 has been rightfully called the "guardian of the genome."* With homozygous loss of the *TP53* gene, DNA damage goes unrepaired, mutations become fixed in dividing cells, and the cell turns onto a one-way street leading to malignant transformation.

Confirming the importance of *TP53* in controlling carcinogenesis, more than 70% of human cancers have a defect in this gene, and the remaining malignant neoplasms have defects in genes upstream or downstream of *TP53*. Biallelic loss of the *TP53* gene is found in virtually every type of cancer, including carcinomas of the lung, colon, and breast—the three leading causes of cancer deaths. In most cases, inactivating mutations affecting both *TP53* alleles are acquired in somatic cells. Less commonly, some patients inherit a mutant *TP53* allele; the resulting disease is called the *Li-Fraumeni syndrome*. As with the *RB* gene, inheritance of one mutant allele predisposes affected persons to develop malignant tumors because only one additional hit is needed to inactivate the second, normal allele. Patients with the Li-Fraumeni syndrome have a 25-fold greater chance of developing a malignant tumor by age 50 compared with the general population. In contrast with tumors developing in patients who inherit a mutant *RB* allele, the spectrum of tumors that develop in patients with the Li-Fraumeni syndrome is varied; the most common types are sarcomas, breast cancer, leukemia, brain tumors, and carcinomas of the adrenal cortex. Compared with persons diagnosed with sporadic tumors, patients with Li-Fraumeni syndrome develop tumors at a younger age and may develop multiple primary tumors.

As with Rb protein, normal p53 also can be rendered nonfunctional by certain DNA viruses. Proteins encoded by oncogenic HPVs, hepatitis B virus (HBV), and possibly Epstein-Barr virus (EBV) can bind to normal p53 and nullify its protective function. Thus, DNA viruses can subvert two of the best-understood tumor suppressors, Rb and p53.

SUMMARY

TP53 Gene: Guardian of the Genome

- The p53 protein is the central monitor of stress in the cell and can be activated by anoxia, inappropriate oncogene signaling, or DNA damage. Activated p53 controls the expression and activity of genes involved in cell cycle arrest, DNA repair, cellular senescence, and apoptosis.
- DNA damage leads to activation of p53 by phosphorylation. Activated p53 drives transcription of *CDKN1A (p21)*, which prevents Rb phosphorylation, thereby causing a G_1-S block in the cell cycle. This pause allows the cells to repair DNA damage.
- If DNA damage cannot be repaired, p53 induces cellular senescence or apoptosis.
- Of human tumors, 70% demonstrate biallelic loss of *TP53*. Patients with the rare Li-Fraumeni syndrome inherit one defective copy in the germ line and lose the sec in somatic tissues; such persons develop a variety tumors.
- As with Rb, p53 can be incapacitated by binding to proteins encoded by oncogenic DNA viruses such as HPV.

Transforming Growth Factor-β Pathway

Although much is known about the circuitry that applies brakes to the cell cycle, the molecules that transmit antiproliferative signals to cells are less well characterized. Best-known is TGF-β, a member of a family of dimeric growth factors that includes bone morphogenetic proteins and activins. In most normal epithelial, endothelial, and hematopoietic cells, TGF-β is a potent inhibitor of proliferation. It regulates cellular processes by binding to a complex composed of TGF-β receptors I and II. Dimerization of the receptor upon ligand binding leads to a cascade of events that result in the transcriptional activation of CDKIs with growth-suppressing activity, as well as repression of growth-promoting genes such as *MYC, CDK2, CDK4,* and those encoding cyclins A and E.

In many forms of cancer, the growth-inhibiting effects of the TGF-β pathways are impaired by mutations affecting TGF-β signaling. These mutations may alter the type II TGF-β receptor or SMAD molecules that serve to transduce antiproliferative signals from the receptor to the nucleus. Mutations affecting the type II receptor are seen in cancers of the colon, stomach, and endometrium. Mutational inactivation of SMAD4, 1 of the 10 proteins known to be involved in TGF-β signaling, is common in pancreatic cancers. *In 100% of pancreatic cancers and 83% of colon cancers, at least one component of the TGF-β pathway is mutated.* In many cancers, however, loss of TGF-β–mediated growth control occurs at a level downstream of the core signaling pathway, for example, loss of p21 and/or persistent expression of MYC. These tumor cells can then use other elements of the TGF-β–induced program, including immune system suppression–evasion or promotion of angiogenesis, to facilitate tumor progression. Thus, TGF-β can function to prevent or promote tumor growth, depending on the state of other genes in the cell. Indeed, in many late-stage tumors, TGF-β signaling activates epithelial-to-mesenchymal transition (EMT), a process that promotes migration, invasion, and metastasis, as described later.

Contact Inhibition, NF2, *and* APC

When nontransformed cells are grown in culture, they proliferate until confluent monolayers are generated; cell–cell contacts formed in these monolayers suppress further cell proliferation. Of importance, "contact inhibition" is abolished in cancer cells, allowing them to pile on top of one another. The mechanisms that govern contact inhibition are only now being discovered. Cell–cell contacts in many tissues are mediated by homodimeric interactions between transmembrane proteins called cadherins. E-cadherin (E for epithelial) mediates cell–cell contact in epithelial layers. How E-cadherin maintains normal contact inhibition is not fully understood. One mechanism that sustains contact inhibition is mediated by the tumor suppressor gene *NF2*. Its product, neurofibromin-2, more commonly called merlin, facilitates E-cadherin mediated contact inhibition. Homozygous loss of *NF2* is known to cause a form of neural tumors associated with the condition called neurofibromatosis.

There are other mechanisms of E-cadherin regulation as well. One such mechanism is illustrated by the rare hereditary disease *adenomatous polyposis coli* (APC). This disorder is characterized by the development of numerous adenomatous polyps in the colon that have a very high incidence of transformation into colonic cancers. They consistently show loss of a tumor suppressor gene called *APC* (named for the disease). The *APC* gene exerts antiproliferative effects in an unusual manner. It encodes a cytoplasmic protein whose dominant function is to regulate the intracellular levels of β-catenin, a protein with many functions. On the one hand, β-catenin binds to the cytoplasmic portion of E-cadherin; on the other hand, it can translocate to the nucleus and activate cell proliferation. Here the focus is on the latter function of this protein. β-Catenin is an important component of the so-called WNT signaling pathway that regulates cell proliferation (illustrated in Fig. 5–24). WNT is a soluble factor that can induce cellular proliferation. It does so by binding to its receptor and transmitting signals that prevent the degradation of β-catenin, allowing it to translocate to the nucleus, where it acts as a transcriptional activator in conjunction with another molecule, called TcF (Fig. 5–24, *B*). In quiescent cells, which are not exposed to WNT, cytoplasmic β-catenin is degraded by a *destruction complex*, of which APC is an integral part (Fig. 5–24, *A*). With loss of APC (in malignant cells), β-catenin degradation is prevented, and the WNT signaling response is inappropriately activated in the absence of WNT (Fig. 5–24, *C*). This leads to transcription of growth-promoting genes, such as cyclin D1 and *MYC*, as well as transcriptional regulators, such as TWIST and SLUG, that repress E-cadherin expression and thus reduce contact inhibition.

APC behaves as a typical tumor suppressor gene. Persons born with one mutant allele typically are found to have hundreds to thousands of adenomatous polyps in the colon by their teens or 20s; these polyps show loss of the other *APC* allele. Almost invariably, one or more polyps undergo malignant transformation, as discussed later. *APC* mutations are seen in 70% to 80% of sporadic colon cancers. Colonic cancers that have normal *APC* genes show activating mutations of β-catenin that render them refractory to the degrading action of APC.

SUMMARY

Transforming Growth Factor-β and APC–β-Catenin Pathways

- **TGF-β inhibits proliferation of many cell types by activation of growth-inhibiting genes such as CDKIs and suppression of growth-promoting genes such as *MYC* and those encoding cyclins.**

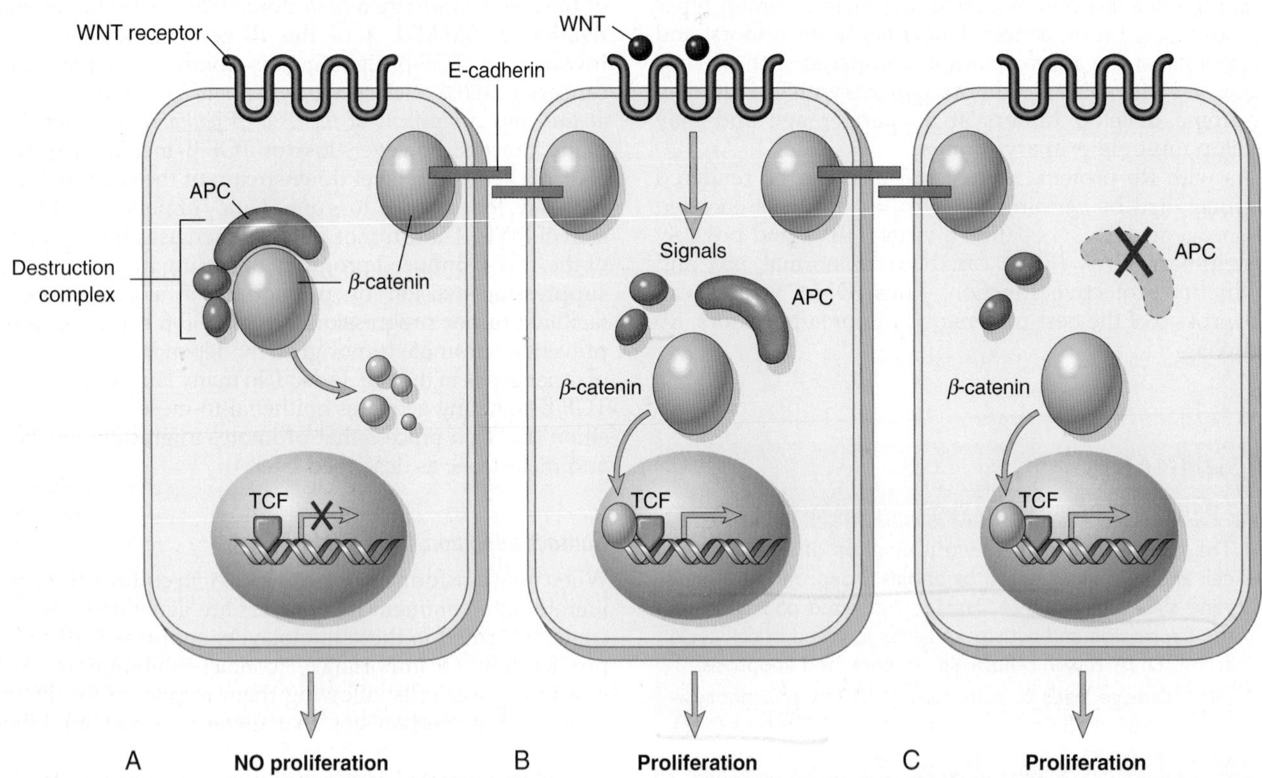

Figure 5–24 A–C, The role of APC in regulating the stability and function of β-catenin. APC and β-catenin are components of the WNT signaling pathway. In resting cells (not exposed to WNT), β-catenin forms a macromolecular complex containing the APC protein. This complex leads to the destruction of β-catenin, and intracellular levels of β-catenin are low. When cells are stimulated by secreted WNT molecules, the *destruction complex* is deactivated, β-catenin degradation does not occur, and cytoplasmic levels increase. β-Catenin translocates to the nucleus, where it binds to TCF, a transcription factor that activates several genes involved in the cell cycle. When APC is mutated or absent, the destruction of β-catenin cannot occur. β-Catenin translocates to the nucleus and coactivates genes that promote the cell cycle, and cells behave as if they are under constant stimulation by the WNT pathway.

- TGF-β function is compromised in many tumors by mutations in its receptors (colon, stomach, endometrium) or by mutational inactivation of *SMAD* genes that transduce TGF-β signaling (pancreas).
- E-cadherin maintains contact inhibition, which is lost in malignant cells.
- *APC* gene exerts antiproliferative actions by regulating the destruction of the cytoplasmic protein β-catenin. With a loss of *APC*, β-catenin is not destroyed, and it translocates to the nucleus, where it acts as a growth-promoting transcription factor.
- In familial adenomatous polyposis syndrome, inheritance of a germ line mutation in the *APC* gene and sporadic loss of the sole normal allele causes the development of hundreds of colonic polyps at a young age. Inevitably, one or more of these polyps evolves into a colonic cancer. Somatic loss of both alleles of the *APC* gene is seen in approximately 70% of sporadic colon cancers.

Evasion of Cell Death

As discussed in Chapter 1, apoptosis, or programmed cell death, refers to an orderly dismantling of cells into component pieces that can then be consumed and disposed of by neighboring cells. *It is now well established that accumulation of neoplastic cells may result not only from activation of growth-promoting oncogenes or inactivation of growth-suppressing tumor suppressor genes but also from mutations in the genes that regulate apoptosis.*

The apoptotic pathway can be divided into upstream regulators and downstream effectors. The regulators are divided into two major pathways, one interpreting extracellular or extrinsic signals and the other interpreting intracellular signals. Stimulation of either pathway results in activation of a normally inactive protease (caspase-8 or caspase-9, respectively), which initiates a proteolytic cascade involving "executioner" caspases that disassemble the cell in orderly fashion. The cellular remains are then efficiently consumed by the cellular neighbors and professional phagocytes, without stimulating inflammation. Figure 5–25 shows, in simplified form, the sequence of events that lead to apoptosis by signaling through death receptors, which are members of the TNF receptor family (extrinsic pathway), and by DNA damage and other stresses (intrinsic pathway).

- The extrinsic (death receptor) pathway is initiated when a TNF receptor, such as CD95 (Fas), is bound to its ligand, CD95L, leading to trimerization of the receptor and its cytoplasmic *death domains,* which attract the intracellular adaptor protein FADD. This protein recruits procaspase-8 to form the death-inducing signaling complex. Procaspase-8 is activated by cleavage into smaller subunits, generating caspase-8. Caspase-8 then activates downstream caspases such as caspase-3, an *executioner caspase* that cleaves DNA and other substrates to cause cell death.
- The intrinsic (mitochondrial) pathway of apoptosis is triggered by a variety of stimuli, including withdrawal of survival factors, stress, and injury. Activation of this pathway leads to permeabilization of the mitochondrial outer membrane and release of molecules, such as cytochrome c, that initiate apoptosis.

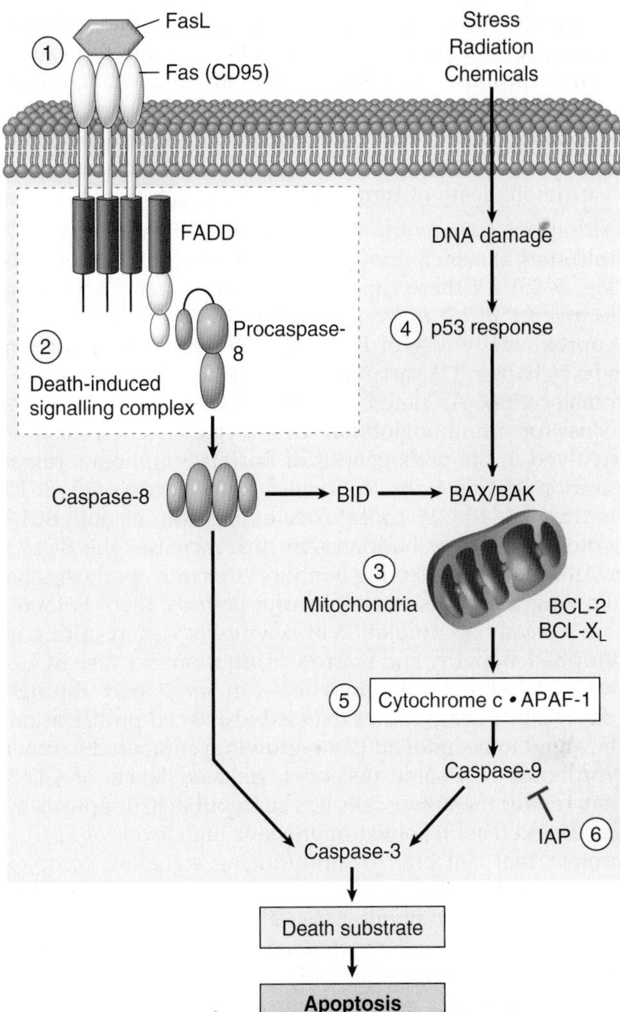

Figure 5–25 Simplified schema of CD95 receptor–induced and DNA damage–triggered pathways of apoptosis and mechanisms used by tumor cells to evade cell death: *1*, Reduced CD95 level. 2, Inactivation of death-induced signaling complex by FLICE protein. 3, Reduced egress of cytochrome c from mitochondrion as a result of upregulation of BCL2. 4, Reduced levels of pro-apoptotic BAX resulting from loss of p53. 5, Loss of APAF-1. 6, Upregulation of inhibitors of apoptosis.

The integrity of the mitochondrial outer membrane is regulated by pro-apoptotic and anti-apoptotic members of the BCL2 family of proteins. The pro-apoptotic proteins BAX and BAK are required for apoptosis and directly promote mitochondrial permeabilization. Their action is inhibited by the anti-apoptotic members of this family exemplified by BCL2 and BCL-X$_L$. A third set of proteins, the so-called BH3-only proteins, which include BAD, BID, and PUMA, regulate the balance between the pro- and anti-apoptotic members of the BCL2 family. The BH3-only proteins promote apoptosis by neutralizing the actions of anti-apoptotic proteins like BCL2 and BCL-X$_L$. When the sum total of all BH3 proteins expressed "overwhelms" the anti-apoptotic BCL2/BCLX$_L$ protein barrier, BAX and BAK are activated and form pores in the mitochondrial membrane. Cytochrome c leaks into the cytosol, where it binds to APAF-1 and activates caspase-9. Like caspase-8 of the extrinsic pathway, caspase-9 can cleave and activate the executioner caspases. Caspases can be inhibited by a family of proteins called inhibitor of apoptosis proteins (IAPs). Because of the pro-apoptotic effect of BH3 only proteins, efforts are underway to develop BH3 mimetic drugs to promote death of tumor cells.

Within this framework, it is possible to illustrate the multiple sites at which apoptosis is frustrated by cancer cells (Fig. 5-25). Of these candidates, perhaps *best-established is the role of BCL2 in protecting tumor cells from apoptosis.* Approximately 85% of B cell lymphomas of the follicular type (Chapter 11) carry a characteristic t(14;18) (q32;q21) translocation. As noted earlier, 14q32, the chromosomal locus for immunoglobulin heavy-chain genes, also is involved in the pathogenesis of Burkitt lymphoma. Juxtaposition of this transcriptionally active locus with *BCL2* (located at 18q21) causes overexpression of the BCL2 protein. This overabundance in turn increases the BCL2/ $BCL\text{-}X_L$ buffer, protecting lymphocytes from apoptosis and allowing them to survive for long periods; there is therefore a steady accumulation of B lymphocytes, resulting in lymphadenopathy and marrow infiltration. Because BCL2-overexpressing lymphomas arise in large part through reduced cell death rather than explosive cell proliferation, they tend to be indolent (slow-growing) compared to other lymphomas. In some instances, reduced levels of CD95 may render the tumor cells less susceptible to apoptosis by Fas ligand (FasL). Some tumors have high levels of FLIP, a protein that can bind death-inducing signaling complex and prevent activation of caspase 8.

As mentioned previously, *TP53 is an important pro-apoptotic gene that induces apoptosis in cells that are unable to repair DNA damage.* Similarly, unrestrained action of growth-promoting genes such as *MYC* also leads to apoptosis. Thus, both major oncogenic pathways—inability to repair DNA damage and inappropriate activation of oncogenes—converge on the apoptotic machinery, which, by causing cell death, acts as a major barrier to carcinogenesis.

Autophagy

As described in Chapter 1, autophagy is a key catabolic process that helps balance synthesis, degradation, and recycling of cellular products. During autophagy, cellular organelles, such as ribosomes and mitochondria, are sequestered from the rest of the cell by a membrane (autophagosome) and then fused to a lysosome, where they are degraded and utilized for cellular energy generation. The same process can signal cells to die if they cannot be rescued by the recycling of organelles. It is a tightly regulated process that plays an important role in normal cell function, and can help starving cells shift nutrients from unused cell processes to vital ones. Autophagy, like apoptosis, has regulatory and effector machinery. The effector components consist of proteins that lead to the formation of autophagosomes and direct their contents to lysosomes. Not surprisingly, the regulatory components of autophagy overlap with many of the signaling components that regulate apoptosis. For example, a protein, Beclin-1, required for autophagy, belongs to the BH3 domain containing proteins that regulate apoptosis. When cells sense internal stress (e.g., DNA damage), they may undergo apoptosis or Beclin-1–induced autophagy. Thus, autophagy, by analogy with apoptosis, appears to prevent the growth of tumor cells. Later in tumor growth, however, autophagy may be helpful to tumors. The metabolites generated by autophagy may supply crucial building blocks for growth and survival in the nutrient-poor environments that tumor cells inhabit. Indeed, autophagy may promote tumor survival in unfriendly climates or during therapy. Thus, autophagy may act as either a "friend" or a "foe," depending on other internal and external factors.

SUMMARY

Evasion of Apoptosis

- Apoptosis can be initiated through extrinsic or intrinsic pathways.
- Both pathways result in the activation of a proteolytic cascade of caspases that destroys the cell.
- Mitochondrial outer membrane permeabilization is regulated by the balance between pro-apoptotic (e.g., BAX, BAK) and anti-apoptotic molecules (BCL2, $BCL\text{-}X_L$). BH-3–only molecules activate apoptosis by tilting the balance in favor of the pro-apoptotic molecules.
- In 85% of follicular B cell lymphomas, the anti-apoptotic gene *BCL2* is activated by the t(14;18) translocation.
- Stress may also induce cells to consume their components in a process called autophagy. Cancer cells may accumulate mutations to avoid autophagy, or may corrupt the process to provide parts for continued growth.

Limitless Replicative Potential

As discussed previously in the context of cellular aging (Chapter 1), most normal human cells have a capacity of 60 to 70 doublings. Thereafter, the cells lose the capacity to divide and enter senescence. This phenomenon has been ascribed to progressive shortening of *telomeres* at the ends of chromosomes. The consequences of such shortening, when pronounced, are drastic:

- Short telomeres seem to be recognized by the DNA repair machinery as double-stranded DNA breaks, leading to cell cycle arrest and senescence, mediated by *TP53* and *RB*. In cells in which the checkpoints are disabled by *TP53* or *RB* mutations, the nonhomologous end-joining pathway is activated in a last-ditch effort to save the cell, joining the shortened ends of two chromosomes.
- Such an inappropriately activated repair system results in dicentric chromosomes that are pulled apart at anaphase, resulting in new double-stranded DNA breaks. The resulting genomic instability from the repeated bridge–fusion–breakage cycles eventually produces mitotic catastrophe, characterized by massive apoptosis.

It follows that for tumors to grow indefinitely, as they often do, loss of growth restraints is not enough. Tumor cells also must develop ways to avoid both cellular senescence and mitotic catastrophe (Fig. 5–26). If during crisis a cell manages to reactivate telomerase, the bridge–fusion–breakage cycles cease, and the cell is able to avoid death. However, during this period of genomic instability that precedes telomerase activation, numerous mutations could accumulate, helping the cell march toward malignancy. Telomerase, active in normal stem cells, normally is absent from, or present at very low levels in, most somatic cells. By contrast, telomere maintenance is seen in virtually all types of cancers. In 85% to 95% of cancers, this is due to upregulation of the enzyme telomerase. A few tumors use other mechanisms, termed alternative lengthening of telomeres, which probably depend on DNA recombination.

Of interest, in a study of the progression from colonic adenoma to colonic adenocarcinoma, early lesions had a high degree of genomic instability with low telomerase expression, whereas malignant lesions had complex karyotypes with high levels of telomerase activity, consistent with a model of telomere-driven tumorigenesis in human cancer. Thus, it appears that in this model, unregulated proliferation in incipient tumors leads to telomere shortening, followed by chromosomal instability and mutation accumulation. If telomerase is then reactivated in these cells, telomeres are extended and these mutations become fixed, contributing to tumor growth. Several other mechanisms of genomic instability are discussed later.

SUMMARY

Limitless Replicative Potential

- In normal cells, which lack expression of telomerase, the shortened telomeres generated by cell division eventually activate cell cycle checkpoints, leading to senescence and placing a limit on the number of divisions a cell may undergo.
- In cells that have disabled checkpoints, DNA repair pathways are inappropriately activated by shortened telomeres, leading to massive chromosomal instability and mitotic crisis.
- Tumor cells reactivate telomerase, thus staving off mitotic catastrophe and achieving immortality.

Development of Sustained Angiogenesis

Even with all the growth advantages, as described previously, tumors cannot enlarge beyond 1 to 2 mm in diameter unless they are vascularized. Like normal tissues, tumors require delivery of oxygen and nutrients and removal of waste products; the 1- to 2-mm zone presumably represents the maximal distance across which oxygen, nutrients, and waste can diffuse from blood vessels. Cancer

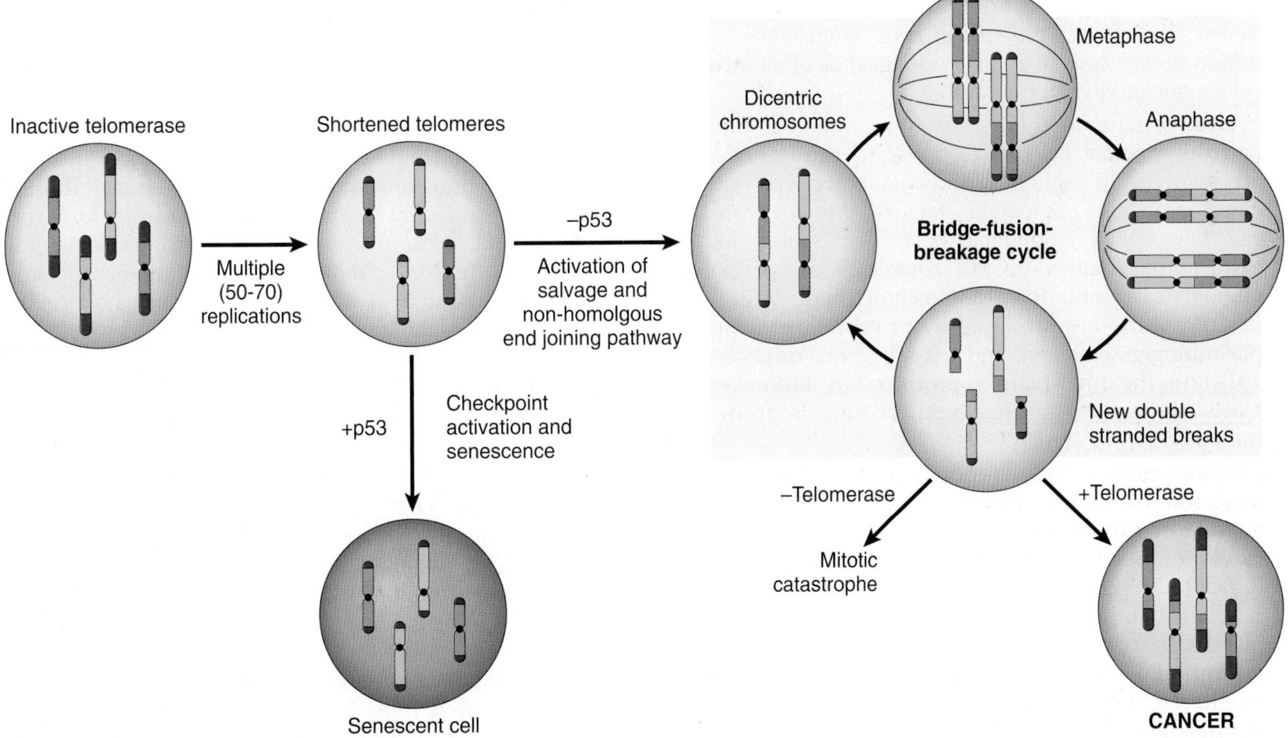

Figure 5–26 Sequence of events in the development of limitless replicative potential. Replication of somatic cells, which do not express telomerase, leads to shortened telomeres. In the presence of competent checkpoints, cells undergo arrest and enter nonreplicative senescence. In the absence of checkpoints, DNA repair pathways are inappropriately activated, leading to the formation of dicentric chromosomes. At mitosis, the dicentric chromosomes are pulled apart, generating random double-stranded breaks, which then activate DNA repair pathways, leading to the random association of double-stranded ends and the formation, again, of dicentric chromosomes. Cells undergo numerous rounds of this bridge–fusion–breakage cycle, which generates massive chromosomal instability and numerous mutations. If cells fail to reexpress telomerase, they eventually undergo mitotic catastrophe and death. Reexpression of telomerase allows the cells to escape the bridge–fusion–breakage cycle, thus promoting their survival and tumorigenesis.

cells (and large benign tumors) can stimulate neoangiogenesis, during which new vessels sprout from previously existing capillaries, or, in some cases, vasculogenesis, in which endothelial cells are recruited from the bone marrow. Tumor vasculature is abnormal, however. The vessels are leaky and dilated, with a haphazard pattern of connection. Neovascularization has a dual effect on tumor growth: Perfusion supplies needed nutrients and oxygen, and newly formed endothelial cells stimulate the growth of adjacent tumor cells by secreting growth factors, such as insulin-like growth factors, PDGF, and granulocyte-macrophage colony-stimulating factor. Angiogenesis is required not only for continued tumor growth but also for access to the vasculature and hence for metastasis. *Angiogenesis is thus a necessary biologic correlate of neoplasia, both benign and malignant.*

How do growing tumors develop a blood supply? The emerging paradigm is that tumor angiogenesis is controlled by a balance between pro-angiogenic and inhibitory factors.

- The prototypical angiogenesis inducer and inhibitor are vascular endothelial growth factor (VEGF) and thrombospondin-1 (TSP-1), respectively. Early in their growth, most human tumors do not induce angiogenesis. They remain small or in situ for years until the angiogenic switch terminates this stage of vascular quiescence. Normal p53 induces synthesis of TSP-1.
- The molecular basis of the angiogenic switch involves increased production of angiogenic factors and/or loss of angiogenesis inhibitors. These factors may be produced directly by the tumor cells themselves or by inflammatory cells (e.g., macrophages) or other stromal cells associated with the tumors.
- Proteases, elaborated either by the tumor cells directly or from stromal cells in response to the tumor, also are involved in regulating the balance between angiogenic and anti-angiogenic factors. Many proteases can release the angiogenic basic FGF stored in the extracellular matrix (ECM); conversely, three potent angiogenesis inhibitors—angiostatin, endostatin, and vasculostatin—are produced by proteolytic cleavage of plasminogen, collagen, and transthyretin, respectively. TSP-1, on the other hand, is produced by stromal fibroblasts themselves in response to signals from the tumor cells.
- The angiogenic switch is controlled by several physiologic stimuli, such as hypoxia. Relative lack of oxygen stimulates production of a variety of pro-angiogenic cytokines, such as vascular endothelial growth factor (VEGF), through activation of hypoxia-inducible factor-1α (HIF-1α), an oxygen-sensitive transcription factor. HIF-1α is continuously produced, but in normoxic settings the von Hippel–Lindau protein (VHL) binds to HIF-1α, leading to ubiquitination and destruction of HIF-1α.
- In hypoxic conditions, such as in a tumor that has reached a critical size, the lack of oxygen prevents HIF-1α recognition by VHL, and it is not destroyed. HIF-1α translocates to the nucleus and activates transcription of its target genes, such as VEGF. Because of these activities, *VHL* acts as a tumor suppressor gene, and germline mutations of the *VHL* gene are associated with hereditary renal cell cancers, pheochromocytomas, hemangiomas of the central nervous system, retinal angiomas, and renal cysts (*VHL syndrome*).
- VEGF also increases the expression of ligands that activate the Notch signaling pathway, which regulates the branching and density of the new vessels. Because of the crucial role of angiogenesis in tumor growth, much interest is focused on anti-angiogenesis therapy. Indeed, anti-VEGF antibody is now approved for the treatment of several types of cancers.

SUMMARY

Development of Sustained Angiogenesis

- Vascularization of tumors is essential for their growth and is controlled by the balance between angiogenic and anti-angiogenic factors that are produced by tumor and stromal cells.
- Hypoxia triggers angiogenesis through the actions of HIF-1α on the transcription of the pro-angiogenic factor VEGF. Because of its ability to degrade HIF-1α and thereby prevent angiogenesis, VHL acts as a tumor suppressor. Inheritance of germ line mutations of *VHL* causes VHL syndrome, characterized by the development of a variety of tumors.
- Many other factors regulate angiogenesis; for example, p53 induces synthesis of the angiogenesis inhibitor TSP-1.

Ability to Invade and Metastasize

The spread of tumors is a complex process involving a series of sequential steps called the invasion–metastasis cascade (Fig. 5–27). These steps consist of local invasion, intravasation into blood and lymph vessels, transit through the vasculature, extravasation from the vessels, formation of micrometastases, and growth of micrometastases into macroscopic tumors. Predictably, this sequence of steps may be interrupted at any stage by either host-related or tumor-related factors. For the purpose of discussion, the metastatic cascade can be subdivided into two phases: (1) invasion of ECM and (2) vascular dissemination and homing of tumor cells.

Invasion of Extracellular Matrix (ECM)

As is well recognized, human tissues are organized into a series of compartments separated from each other by two types of ECM: basement membranes and interstitial connective tissue (Chapter 2). Although organized differently, each type of ECM is composed of collagens, glycoproteins, and proteoglycans. Tumor cells must interact with the ECM at several stages in the metastatic cascade (Fig. 5–27). A carcinoma first must breach the underlying basement membrane, then traverse the interstitial connective tissue, and ultimately gain access to the circulation by penetrating the vascular basement membrane. This cycle is repeated when tumor cell emboli extravasate at a distant site. Thus, to metastasize, a tumor cell must cross several different basement membranes, as well as negotiate its way through at least two interstitial matrices. Invasion of the ECM is an active process that requires four steps (Fig. 5–28):

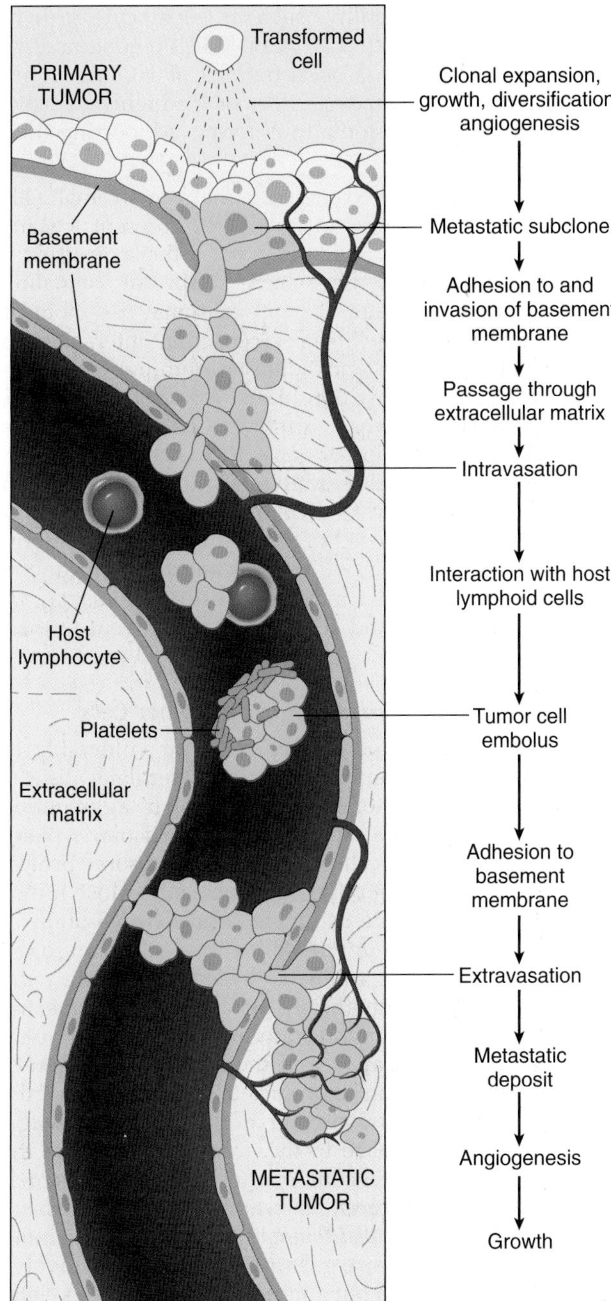

Figure 5–27 The metastatic cascade: The sequential steps involved in the hematogenous spread of a tumor.

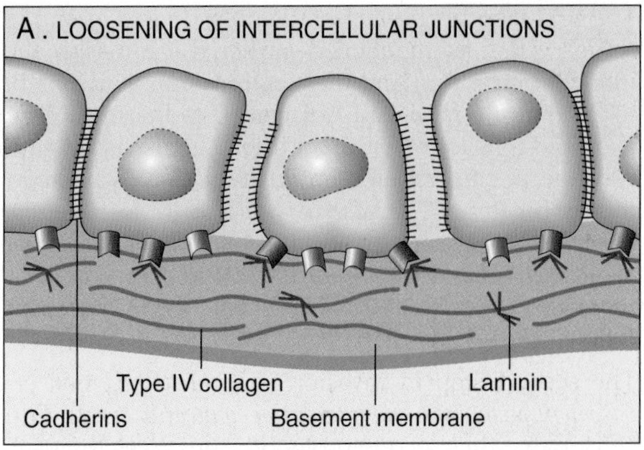

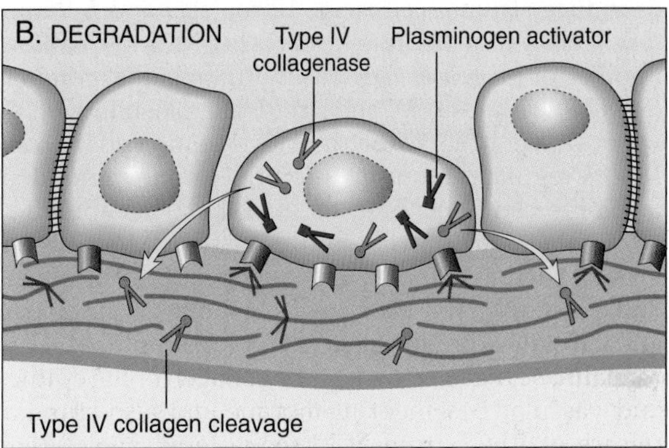

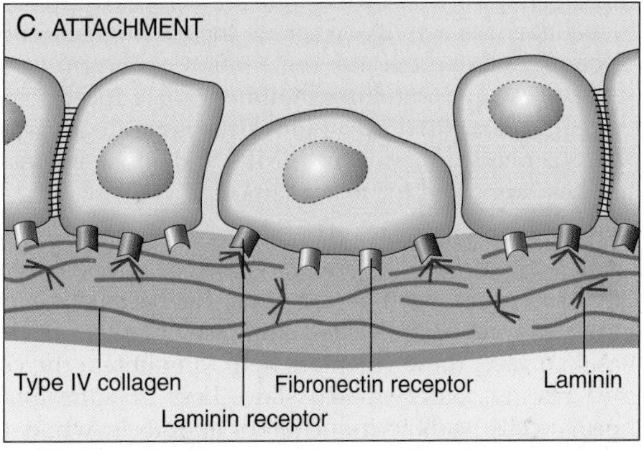

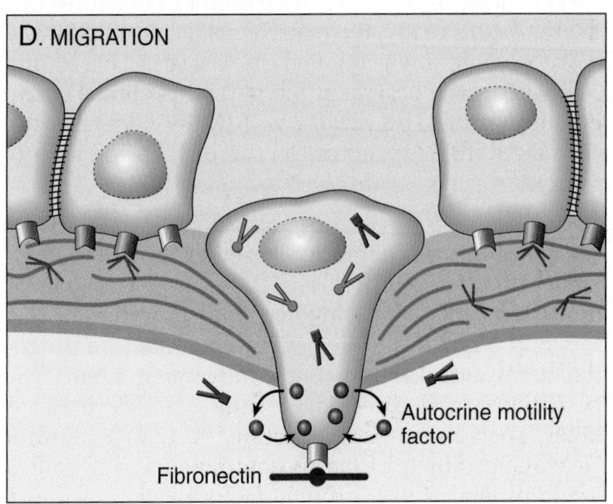

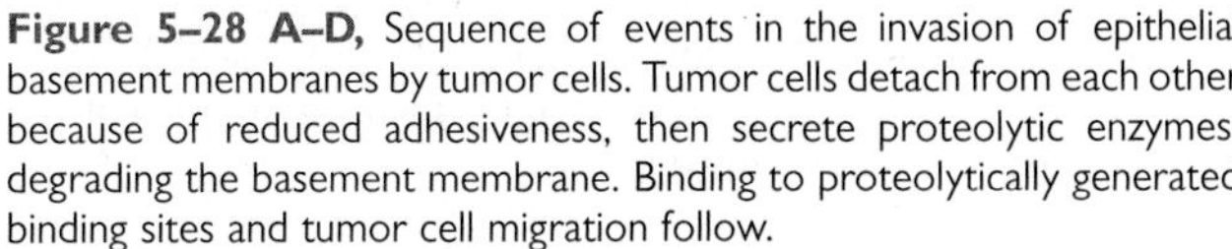
Figure 5–28 A–D, Sequence of events in the invasion of epithelial basement membranes by tumor cells. Tumor cells detach from each other because of reduced adhesiveness, then secrete proteolytic enzymes, degrading the basement membrane. Binding to proteolytically generated binding sites and tumor cell migration follow.

- The first step in the metastatic cascade is a *loosening* of tumor cells. As mentioned earlier, E-cadherins act as intercellular glues, and their cytoplasmic portions bind to β-catenin (Fig. 5–24). Adjacent E-cadherin molecules keep the cells together; in addition, as discussed earlier, E-cadherin can transmit antigrowth signals by sequestering β-catenin. *E-cadherin function is lost in almost all epithelial cancers, either by mutational inactivation of E-cadherin genes, by activation of β-catenin genes, or by inappropriate expression of the SNAIL and TWIST transcription factors, which suppress E-cadherin expression.*
- The second step in invasion is local *degradation of the basement membrane and interstitial connective tissue.* Tumor cells may either secrete proteolytic enzymes themselves or induce stromal cells (e.g., fibroblasts and inflammatory cells) to elaborate proteases. Multiple different families of proteases, such as matrix metalloproteinases (MMPs), cathepsin D, and urokinase plasminogen activator, have been implicated in tumor cell invasion. MMPs regulate tumor invasion not only by remodeling insoluble components of the basement membrane and interstitial matrix but also by releasing ECM-sequestered growth factors. Indeed, cleavage products of collagen and proteoglycans also have chemotactic, angiogenic, and growth-promoting effects. For example, MMP-9 is a gelatinase that cleaves type IV collagen of the epithelial and vascular basement membrane and also stimulates release of VEGF from ECM-sequestered pools. Benign tumors of the breast, colon, and stomach show little type IV collagenase activity, whereas their malignant counterparts overexpress this enzyme. Concurrently, the levels of metalloproteinase inhibitors are reduced so that the balance is tilted greatly toward tissue degradation. Indeed, overexpression of MMPs and other proteases has been reported for many tumors.
- The third step in invasion involves *changes in attachment of tumor cells to ECM proteins.* Normal epithelial cells have receptors, such as integrins, for basement membrane laminin and collagens that are polarized at their basal surface; these receptors help to maintain the cells in a resting, differentiated state. Loss of adhesion in normal cells leads to induction of apoptosis, while, not surprisingly, tumor cells are resistant to this form of cell death. Additionally, the matrix itself is modified in ways that promote invasion and metastasis. For example, cleavage of the basement membrane proteins, collagen IV and laminin, by MMP-2 or MMP-9 generates novel sites that bind to receptors on tumor cells and stimulate migration.
- *Locomotion* is the final step of invasion, propelling tumor cells through the degraded basement membranes and zones of matrix proteolysis. Migration is a complex, multistep process that involves many families of receptors and signaling proteins that eventually impinge on the actin cytoskeleton. Such movement seems to be potentiated and directed by tumor cell–derived cytokines, such as autocrine motility factors. In addition, cleavage products of matrix components (e.g., collagen, laminin) and some growth factors (e.g., insulin-like growth factors I and II) have chemotactic activity for tumor cells. Stromal cells also produce paracrine effectors of cell motility, such as hepatocyte growth factor/scatter factor (HGF/SCF), which binds to receptors on tumor cells. Concentrations of HGF/SCF are elevated at the advancing edges of the highly invasive brain tumor glioblastoma multiforme, supporting their role in motility.

More recently, it has become clear that the stromal cells surrounding tumor cells do not merely present a static barrier for tumor cells to traverse but rather constitute a variable environment in which reciprocal signaling between tumor cells and stromal cells may promote or prevent tumorigenesis. Stromal cells that interact with tumors include innate and adaptive immune cells (discussed later), as well as fibroblasts. A variety of studies have demonstrated that tumor-associated fibroblasts exhibit altered expression of genes that encode ECM molecules, proteases, protease inhibitors, and various growth factors. Thus, tumor cells live in a complex and ever-changing milieu composed of ECM, growth factors, fibroblasts, and immune cells, with significant cross-talk among all the components. The most successful tumors may be those that can co-opt and adapt this environment to their own nefarious ends.

Vascular Dissemination and Homing of Tumor Cells

When in the circulation, tumor cells are vulnerable to destruction by host immune cells (discussed later). In the bloodstream, some tumor cells form emboli by aggregating and adhering to circulating leukocytes, particularly platelets; aggregated tumor cells are thus afforded some protection from the antitumor host effector cells. Most tumor cells, however, circulate as single cells. Extravasation of free tumor cells or tumor emboli involves adhesion to the vascular endothelium, followed by egress through the basement membrane into the organ parenchyma by mechanisms similar to those involved in invasion.

The site of extravasation and the organ distribution of metastases generally can be predicted by the location of the primary tumor and its vascular or lymphatic drainage. Many tumors metastasize to the organ that presents the first capillary bed they encounter after entering the circulation. *In many cases, however, the natural pathways of drainage do not readily explain the distribution of metastases.* As pointed out earlier, some tumors (e.g., lung cancers) tend to involve the adrenals quite often but almost never spread to skeletal muscle. Such organ tropism may be related to the following mechanisms:

- Expression of adhesion molecules by tumor cells whose ligands are expressed preferentially on the endothelium of target organs
- Expression of chemokines and their receptors. As discussed in Chapter 2, chemokines participate in directed movement (chemotaxis) of leukocytes, and it seems that cancer cells use similar tricks to home in on specific tissues. Human breast cancer cells express high levels of the chemokine receptors *CXCR4* and *CCR7*. The ligands for these receptors (i.e., chemokines CXCL12 and CCL21) are highly expressed only in those organs to which breast cancer cells metastasize. On the basis of this observation, it is speculated that blockade of chemokine receptors may limit metastases.

- Once they reach a target, the tumor cells must be able to colonize the site. Factors that regulate colonization are not completely understood. However, it is known that after extravasation, tumor cells are dependent on a receptive stroma for growth. Thus, in some cases, the target tissue may be a nonpermissive environment—unfavorable soil, so to speak, for the growth of tumor seedlings. For example, although well vascularized, skeletal muscles are rarely the site of metastases.

Despite their "cleverness" in escaping their sites of origin, tumor cells are quite inefficient in colonizing of distant organs. Millions of tumor cells are shed daily from even small tumors. These cells can be detected in the bloodstream and in small foci in the bone marrow, even in patients in whom gross metastatic lesions never develop. Indeed, the concept of dormancy, referring to the prolonged survival of micrometastases without progression, is well described in melanoma and in breast and prostate cancer.

Although the molecular mechanisms of colonization are just beginning to be unraveled in mouse models, a consistent theme seems to be that tumor cells secrete cytokines, growth factors, and proteases that act on the resident stromal cells, which in turn make the metastatic site habitable for the cancer cell. With a better molecular understanding of the mechanisms of metastasis, the clinician's ability to target them therapeutically will be greatly enhanced. Despite the foregoing considerations, the precise localization of metastases cannot be predicted with any form of cancer. Evidently, many tumors have not read the relevant chapters of the pathology textbooks!

Molecular Genetics of Metastasis

A long-held theory of tumor progression suggests that as tumors grow, individual cells randomly accumulate mutations, creating subclones with distinct combinations of mutations. According to this hypothesis, only a small subpopulation of the tumor cells contains all of the mutations necessary for metastasis. Recent experiments, however, in which gene profiling was performed for primary tumors and for metastatic deposits, have challenged this hypothesis. For example, a subset of breast cancers has a gene expression signature similar to that found in metastases, although no clinical evidence for metastasis is apparent. In these tumors, most if not all cells apparently acquire a predilection for metastatic spread early on, during primary carcinogenesis. Metastasis, according to this view, is not dependent on the stochastic generation of metastatic subclones during tumor progression, but is an intrinsic property of the tumor developed during carcinogenesis. Of note, however, gene expression analyses like those just described would not detect a small subset of metastatic subclones within a large tumor. Perhaps both mechanisms are operative, with aggressive tumors acquiring a metastasis-permissive gene expression pattern early in tumorigenesis that requires some additional random mutations to complete the metastatic phenotype.

An open question in cancer biology is whether there are genes whose principal or sole contribution to tumorigenesis is to control metastases. This question is of more than academic interest, because if altered forms of certain genes promote or suppress the metastatic phenotype, their detection in a primary tumor would have both prognostic and therapeutic implications. Among candidates for such metastasis oncogenes are those encoding SNAIL and TWIST, transcription factors whose primary function is to promote epithelial-to-mesenchymal transition (EMT). In EMT, carcinoma cells downregulate certain epithelial markers (e.g., E-cadherin) and upregulate certain mesenchymal markers (e.g., vimentin, smooth muscle actin). These molecular changes are accompanied by phenotypic alterations such as morphologic change from polygonal epithelioid cell shape to a spindly mesenchymal shape, along with increased production of proteolytic enzymes that promote migration and invasion. These changes are believed to favor the development of a promigratory phenotype that is essential for metastasis. Loss of E-cadherin expression seems to be a key event in EMT, and SNAIL and TWIST are transcriptional repressors that promote EMT by downregulating E-cadherin expression. How expression of these master regulator transcription factors is stimulated in tumors is not clear; however, experimental models suggest that interactions of tumor cells with stromal cells are a key stimulus for this change. Thus, acquisition of a metastatic phenotype may not require a set of mutations but may be an emergent property arising from the interactions of tumor cells and stroma.

SUMMARY

Invasion and Metastasis

- Ability to invade tissues, a hallmark of malignancy, occurs in four steps: loosening of cell–cell contacts, degradation of ECM, attachment to novel ECM components, and migration of tumor cells.
- Cell–cell contacts are lost by the inactivation of E-cadherin through a variety of pathways.
- Basement membrane and interstitial matrix degradation is mediated by proteolytic enzymes secreted by tumor cells and stromal cells, such as MMPs and cathepsins.
- Proteolytic enzymes also release growth factors sequestered in the ECM and generate chemotactic and angiogenic fragments from cleavage of ECM glycoproteins.
- The metastatic site of many tumors can be predicted by the location of the primary tumor. Many tumors arrest in the first capillary bed they encounter (lung and liver, most commonly).
- Some tumors show organ tropism, probably due to activation of adhesion or chemokine receptors whose ligands are expressed by endothelial cells at the metastatic site.

Reprogramming Energy Metabolism

Reprogramming of energy metabolism is so common to tumors that it is now considered a hallmark of cancer. Even in the presence of ample oxygen, cancer cells shift their glucose metabolism away from the oxygen-hungry but efficient mitochondria to glycolysis. This phenomenon, called the Warburg effect and also known as aerobic glycolysis, has been recognized for many years (indeed, Otto Warburg received the Nobel prize for discovery of the effect that bears his name in 1931) but was largely neglected until recently.

As is well known, aerobic glycolysis is less efficient than mitochondrial oxidative phosphorylation, producing 2 molecules of ATP per molecule of glucose, versus 36. Yet tumors that adopt aerobic glycolysis, such as Burkitt lymphoma, are the most rapidly growing of human cancers. Indeed, in clinical practice, the "glucose hunger" of such tumors is used to visualize tumors by positron emission tomography (PET) scanning, in which the patient is injected with ^{18}F-fluorodeoxyglucose, a nonmetabolizable derivative of glucose. Most tumors are PET-positive, and rapidly growing ones are markedly so.

Importantly, it is now recognized that rapidly dividing normal cells, such as those in the embryo, also adopt Warburg metabolism, indicating that this mode of metabolism is favored when rapid growth is required. How can this be, given that aerobic glycolysis generates much less ATP per mole of glucose? In addition to doubling its DNA content before division, an actively dividing cell (whether normal or transformed) must also double all of its other components, including membranes, proteins, and organelles. This task requires increased uptake of nutrients, particularly glucose and amino acids. Studies of intermediate metabolism suggest that in rapidly growing cells glucose is the primary source of the carbons that are used for synthesis of lipids (needed for membrane assembly) as well as other metabolites needed for nucleic acid synthesis. This pattern of glucose carbon use is achieved by shunting pyruvate toward biosynthetic pathways at the expense of the oxidative phosphorylation pathway and ATP generation. Thus, the metabolism of cancer can also be viewed from a darwinian perspective; tumor cells that adapt this altered metabolism are able to divide more rapidly and outpace competing tumor cells that do not.

Since aerobic glycolysis continues in tumors in the face of adequate oxygen, it follows that the changes that promote the switch in metabolism must have become hard wired in the tumor cell. It is now becoming clear that oncogenes and tumor suppressors that favor cell growth, such as TP53, PTEN, and Akt (an intermediary in RAS signaling) stimulate glucose uptake by affecting glucose transporter proteins and favor aerobic glycolysis. Indeed the Warburg effect appears to be sufficiently central to the cancer phenotype that drugs that target this pathway are being developed for therapy.

Evasion of the Immune System

As mentioned at the outset, the ability of tumors to evade destruction by the immune system (like the reprogramming of the energy metabolism) is now considered a hallmark of cancer. Most tumors arise in immunocompetent hosts; accordingly, a likely strategy for success is to trick the immune system in such a way that the tumor fails to be recognized or eliminated despite the fact the affected person's body has an army of cells that are quite capable of thwarting a microbial infection or rejecting an allogeneic organ transplant. Discussion of this hallmark is postponed to a later section, since it is best understood in the context of the nature of tumor antigens and how they might be recognized.

Genomic Instability as an Enabler of Malignancy

The preceding section identified eight defining features of malignancy and the genetic alterations that are responsible for the phenotypic attributes of cancer cells. How do these mutations arise? Although humans are awash in environmental agents that are mutagenic (e.g., chemicals, radiation, sunlight), cancers are relatively rare outcomes of these encounters. This state of affairs results from the ability of normal cells to repair DNA damage. The importance of DNA repair in maintaining the integrity of the genome is highlighted by several inherited disorders in which genes that encode proteins involved in DNA repair are defective. *Persons born with such inherited defects in DNA repair proteins are at greatly increased risk for the development of cancer.* Typically, genomic instability occurs when both copies of the gene are lost; however, recent work has suggested that at least a subset of these genes may promote cancer in a haploinsufficient manner. Defects in three types of DNA repair systems—mismatch repair, nucleotide excision repair, and recombination repair—are presented next. While these discussions focus on inherited syndromes, a point worthy of emphasis is that sporadic cancers often incur mutations in these genes as well, which in turn enable the accumulation of mutations in other genes whose dysfunction contributes to the hallmarks of cancer.

Hereditary Nonpolyposis Colon Cancer Syndrome

The role of DNA repair genes in predisposition to cancer is illustrated dramatically by hereditary nonpolyposis colon carcinoma (HNPCC) syndrome. This disorder, characterized by familial carcinomas of the colon affecting predominantly the cecum and proximal colon (Chapter 14), results from defects in genes involved in DNA mismatch repair. When a strand of DNA is being repaired, these genes act as "spell checkers." For example, if there is an erroneous pairing of G with T, rather than the normal A with T, the mismatch repair genes correct the defect. Without these "proofreaders," errors accumulate at an increased rate, a so-called mutator phenotype. Mutations in at least four mismatch repair genes have been found to underlie HNPCC (Chapter 14). Each affected person inherits one defective copy of one of several DNA mismatch repair genes and acquires the second hit in colonic epithelial cells. Thus, DNA repair genes affect cell growth only indirectly—by allowing mutations in other genes during the process of normal cell division. A characteristic finding in the genome of patients with mismatch repair defects is microsatellite instability (MSI). Microsatellites are tandem repeats of one to six nucleotides found throughout the genome. In normal people, the length of these microsatellites remains constant. By contrast, in patients with HNPCC, these satellites are unstable and increase or decrease in length. Although HNPCC accounts for only 2% to 4% of all colonic cancers, MSI can be detected in about 15% of sporadic cancers. The growth-regulating genes that are mutated in HNPCC include those encoding TGF-β receptor type II, BAX, and other oncogenes and tumor suppressor genes.

Xeroderma Pigmentosum

Patients with another inherited disorder, xeroderma pigmentosum, are at increased risk for the development of cancers of sun-exposed skin. The basis for this disorder is defective DNA repair. Ultraviolet (UV) rays in sunlight cause cross-linking of pyrimidine residues, preventing normal DNA replication. Such DNA damage is repaired by the nucleotide excision repair system. Several proteins are involved in nucleotide excision repair, and an inherited loss of any one of these can give rise to xeroderma pigmentosum.

Diseases with Defects in DNA Repair by Homologous Recombination

A group of autosomal recessive disorders comprising Bloom syndrome, ataxia-telangiectasia, and Fanconi anemia is characterized by hypersensitivity to other DNA-damaging agents, such as ionizing radiation (in Bloom syndrome and ataxia-telangiectasia), or to DNA cross-linking agents, such as nitrogen mustard (in Fanconi anemia). Their phenotype is complex and includes, in addition to predisposition to cancer, features such as neural symptoms (in ataxia-telangiectasia), anemia (in Fanconi anemia), and developmental defects (in Bloom syndrome). The gene mutated in ataxia-telangiectasia is *ATM,* which encodes a protein kinase that is important in recognizing DNA damage caused by ionizing radiation and initiating p53 activation.

Evidence for the role of DNA repair genes in the origin of cancer also comes from the study of hereditary breast cancer. Mutations in two genes, *BRCA1* and *BRCA2,* account for 50% of cases of familial breast cancer. In addition to breast cancer, women with *BRCA1* mutations have a substantially higher risk of epithelial ovarian cancers, and men have a slightly higher risk of prostate cancer. Likewise, mutations in the *BRCA2* gene increase the risk of breast cancer in both men and women, as well as cancer of the ovary, prostate, pancreas, bile ducts, stomach, melanocytes, and B lymphocytes. Although the functions of these genes have not been elucidated fully, cells that lack these genes develop chromosomal breaks and severe aneuploidy. Indeed, both genes seem to function, at least in part, in the homologous recombination DNA repair pathway. For example, BRCA1 forms a complex with other proteins in the homologous recombination pathway and also is linked to the ATM kinase pathway. *BRCA2* was identified as one of several genes mutated in Fanconi anemia, and the BRCA2 protein has been shown to bind to RAD51, a protein required for homologous recombination. Similar to other tumor suppressor genes, both copies of *BRCA1* and *BRCA2* must be inactivated for cancer to develop. Although linkage of *BRCA1* and *BRCA2* to familial breast cancers is established, these genes are rarely inactivated in sporadic cases of breast cancer. In this regard, *BRCA1* and *BRCA2* are different from other tumor suppressor genes, such as *APC* and *TP53,* which are inactivated in both familial and sporadic cancers.

Cancers Resulting From Mutations Induced by Regulated Genomic Instability: Lymphoid Neoplasms

A special type of DNA damage plays a central role in the pathogenesis of tumors of B and T lymphocytes. As described earlier, adaptive immunity relies on the ability of B and T cells to diversify their antigen receptor genes. Early B and T cells both express a pair of gene products, RAG1 and RAG2, that carry out V(D)J segment recombination, permitting the assembling of functional antigen receptor genes. In addition, after encountering antigen, mature B cells express a specialized enzyme called activation-induced cytosine deaminase (AID), which catalyzes both immunoglobulin gene class switch recombination and somatic hypermutation. Errors during antigen receptor gene assembly and diversification are responsible for many of the mutations that cause lymphoid neoplasms, described in detail in Chapter 11.

SUMMARY

Genomic Instability as Enabler of Malignancy

- Persons with inherited mutations of genes involved in DNA repair systems are at greatly increased risk for the development of cancer.
- Patients with HNPCC syndrome have defects in the mismatch repair system, leading to development of carcinomas of the colon. These patients' genomes show MSI, characterized by changes in length of short tandem repeating sequences throughout the genome.
- Patients with xeroderma pigmentosum have a defect in the nucleotide excision repair pathway and are at increased risk for the development of cancers of the skin exposed to UV light, because of an inability to repair pyrimidine dimers.
- Syndromes involving defects in the homologous recombination DNA repair system constitute a group of disorders—Bloom syndrome, ataxia-telangiectasia, and Fanconi anemia—that are characterized by hypersensitivity to DNA-damaging agents, such as ionizing radiation. *BRCA1* and *BRCA2,* which are mutated in familial breast cancers, are involved in DNA repair.
- Mutations incurred in lymphoid cells expressing gene products that induce genomic instability (RAG1, RAG2, AID) are important causes of lymphoid neoplasms.

Tumor-Promoting Inflammation as Enabler of Malignancy

Accumulating evidence suggests that inflammation, often thought of as a protective response against tumors, can paradoxically also enable malignancy. This occurs in two different settings:

- *Persistent chronic inflammation in response to microbial infections or as part of an autoimmune reaction.* This is exemplified by the increased risk of cancer in patients affected by a variety of chronic inflammatory diseases of the gastrointestinal tract. These include Barrett esophagus, ulcerative colitis, *H. pylori* gastritis, hepatitis B and C, and chronic pancreatitis. As with any cause of chronic tissue injury, there is a compensatory proliferation of cells in an attempt to repair the damage. This regenerative process is aided and abetted by a plethora of growth factors, cytokines, chemokines, and other bioactive substances produced by activated immune cells collected at the site. Persistent cell replication and reduced apoptosis under these conditions place the cells at risk of acquiring mutations in one or more of the genes involved in carcinogenesis. In addition, inflammatory cells such as neutrophils can contribute to carcinogenesis by secretion of reactive oxygen species, which in turn can inflict additional DNA damage in rapidly dividing cells.

- *When inflammation occurs in response to tumors.* Pathologists have known for quite some time that many tumors are infiltrated by leukocytes. The degree of inflammation varies, but virtually every tumor contains cells of the adaptive and innate components of the immune system. The conventional wisdom has been that the inflammatory reaction is protective since it represents an attempt by the host to destroy the tumor. Indeed, that may well be the purpose of the inflammatory reaction, but these cells can exert tumor-promoting activity by producing growth factors and inflicting additional DNA damage as described above.

Whatever the precise mechanism, the link between inflammation and cancer has practical implications. For instance, expression of the enzyme cyclooxygenase-2 (COX-2), which brings about the conversion of arachidonic acid into prostaglandins (Chapter 2), is induced by inflammatory stimuli and is increased in colon cancers and other tumors. The use of COX-2 inhibitors for cancer prevention and treatment is an active area of research.

Important clinical considerations emerge from the principles presented in the foregoing discussion of the hallmarks of cancer: These hallmarks provide a road map for the development of new therapeutic agents for the treatment of cancer (Fig. 5–29).

Multistep Carcinogenesis and Cancer Progression

As described earlier, the acquisition of several fundamental abnormalities is a prerequisite to development of malignancy. It follows, then, that *each cancer must result from accumulation of multiple mutations.* A dramatic example of incremental acquisition of the malignant phenotype is documented by the study of colon carcinoma. These lesions are believed to evolve through a series of morphologically identifiable stages: colon epithelial hyperplasia followed by formation of adenomas that progressively enlarge and ultimately undergo malignant transformation (Chapter 14). The proposed molecular correlates of this adenoma-carcinoma sequence are illustrated in Figure 5–30. According to this scheme, inactivation of the *APC* tumor suppressor gene occurs first, followed by activation of *RAS* and, ultimately, loss of a tumor suppressor gene on 18q and loss of *TP53*. The precise temporal sequence of mutations may be different in different tumors.

ETIOLOGY OF CANCER: CARCINOGENIC AGENTS

Genetic damage lies at the heart of carcinogenesis. What extrinsic agents can inflict such damage? Three classes of carcinogenic agents have been identified: (1) chemicals, (2) radiant energy, and (3) microbial agents. Chemicals and radiant energy are documented causes of cancer in humans, and oncogenic viruses are involved in the pathogenesis of tumors in several animal models and some human tumors. In the following discussion, each class of agent is considered separately; of note, however, several may act in concert or sequentially to produce the multiple genetic abnormalities characteristic of neoplastic cells.

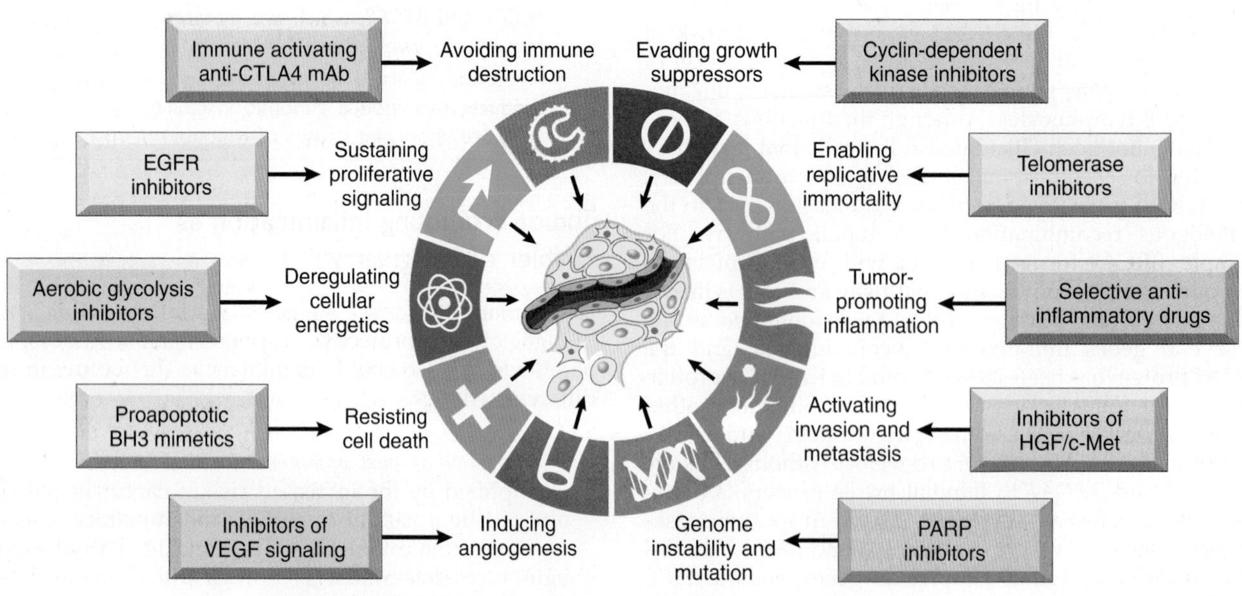

Figure 5–29 Therapeutic targeting of hallmarks of cancer.
(From Hanahan D, Weiberg RA: The hallmarks of cancer: the next generation. Cell 144:646, 2011.)

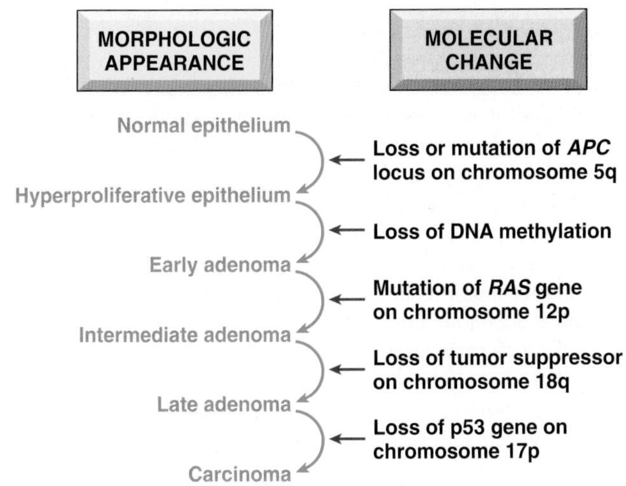

Figure 5–30 Molecular model for the evolution of colorectal cancers through the adenoma–carcinoma sequence.
(Data from studies by Fearon ER, Vogelstein B: A genetic model of colorectal carcinogenesis. Cell 61:759, 1990.)

Chemical Carcinogens

More than 200 years ago, the London surgeon Sir Percival Pott correctly attributed scrotal skin cancer in chimney sweeps to chronic exposure to soot. On the basis of this observation, the Danish Chimney Sweeps Guild ruled that its members must bathe daily. No public health measure since that time has achieved so much in the control of a form of cancer. Subsequently, hundreds of chemicals have been shown to be carcinogenic in animals.

Some of the major agents are presented in Table 5–4. A few comments on a handful of these are offered next.

Table 5–4 Major Chemical Carcinogens

Direct-Acting Carcinogens
Alkylating Agents
β-Propiolactone Dimethyl sulfate Diepoxybutane Anticancer drugs (cyclophosphamide, chlorambucil, nitrosoureas, and others)
Acylating Agents
1-Acetyl-imidazole Dimethylcarbamyl chloride
Procarcinogens That Require Metabolic Activation
Polycyclic and Heterocyclic Aromatic Hydrocarbons
Benz(*a*)anthracene Benzo(*a*)pyrene Dibenz(*a,h*)anthracene 3-Methylcholanthrene 7, 12-Dimethylbenz(*a*)anthracene
Aromatic Amines, Amides, Azo Dyes
2-Naphthylamine (β-naphthylamine) Benzidine 2-Acetylaminofluorene Dimethylaminoazobenzene (butter yellow)
Natural Plant and Microbial Products
Aflatoxin B_1 Griseofulvin Cycasin Safrole Betel nuts
Others
Nitrosamine and amides Vinyl chloride, nickel, chromium Insecticides, fungicides Polychlorinated biphenyls

Direct-Acting Agents

Direct-acting agents require no metabolic conversion to become carcinogenic. They are in general weak carcinogens but are important because some of them are cancer chemotherapy drugs (e.g., alkylating agents) used in regimens that may cure certain types of cancer (e.g., Hodgkin lymphoma), only to evoke a subsequent, second form of cancer, usually leukemia. This situation is even more tragic when the initial use of such agents has been for non-neoplastic disorders, such as rheumatoid arthritis or Wegener granulomatosis. The associated risk of induced cancer is low, but its existence dictates judicious use of such agents.

Indirect-Acting Agents

The designation *indirect-acting* refers to chemicals that require metabolic conversion to an *ultimate carcinogen.* Some of the most potent indirect chemical carcinogens are polycyclic hydrocarbons, present in fossil fuels. For example, benzo[*a*]pyrene and other carcinogens are formed in the high-temperature combustion of tobacco in cigarette smoking. *These products are implicated in the causation of lung cancer in cigarette smokers.* Polycyclic hydrocarbons also may be produced from animal fats during the process of broiling meats and are present in smoked meats and fish. The principal active products in many hydrocarbons are epoxides, which form covalent adducts (addition products) with molecules in the cell, principally DNA, but also with RNA and proteins.

The aromatic amines and azo dyes constitute another class of indirect-acting carcinogens. Before its carcinogenicity was recognized, β-naphthylamine was responsible for a 50-fold increased incidence of bladder cancers in heavily exposed workers in the aniline dye and rubber industries. Many other occupational carcinogens are listed in Table 5–2. Because indirect-acting carcinogens require metabolic activation for their conversion to DNA-damaging agents, much interest is focused on the enzymatic pathways that are involved, such as that mediated by the cytochrome P-450–dependent monooxygenases. The genes that encode these enzymes are polymorphic, and enzyme activity varies among different persons. It is widely believed that the susceptibility to chemical carcinogenesis depends at least in part on the specific allelic form of the enzyme inherited. Thus, it may be possible in the future to assess cancer risk in a given patient by genetic analysis of such enzyme polymorphisms.

A few other agents merit brief mention. Aflatoxin B_1 is of interest because it is a naturally occurring agent produced by some strains of *Aspergillus,* a mold that grows on improperly stored grains and nuts. A strong correlation has been found between the dietary level of this food contaminant and the incidence of hepatocellular carcinoma in some parts of Africa and the Far East. Additionally, vinyl chloride, arsenic, nickel, chromium, insecticides, fungicides, and polychlorinated biphenyls are potential carcinogens in the workplace and about the house. Finally, nitrites used as food preservatives have caused concern, since they cause nitrosylation of amines contained in the food. The nitrosamines thus formed are suspected to be carcinogenic.

Mechanisms of Action of Chemical Carcinogens

Because malignant transformation results from mutations, it should come as no surprise that most chemical carcinogens are mutagenic. Indeed, all direct and ultimate carcinogens contain highly reactive electrophile groups that form chemical adducts with DNA, as well as with proteins and RNA. Although any gene may be the target of chemical carcinogens, the commonly mutated oncogenes and tumor suppressors, such as *RAS* and *TP53,* are important targets of chemical carcinogens. Indeed, specific chemical carcinogens, such as aflatoxin B_1, produce characteristic mutations in the *TP53* gene, such that detection of the "*signature mutation*" within the *TP53* gene establishes aflatoxin as the causative agent. These associations are proving to be useful tools in epidemiologic studies of chemical carcinogenesis.

Carcinogenicity of some chemicals is augmented by subsequent administration of *promoters* (e.g., phorbol esters, hormones, phenols, certain drugs) that by themselves are nontumorigenic. To be effective, repeated or sustained exposure to the promoter must *follow* the application of the mutagenic chemical, or *initiator.* The initiation-promotion sequence of chemical carcinogenesis raises an important question: Since promoters are not mutagenic, how do they contribute to tumorigenesis? Although the effects of tumor promoters are pleiotropic, *induction of cell proliferation is a sine qua non of tumor promotion.* It seems most likely that while the application of an initiator may cause the mutational activation of an oncogene such as *RAS,* subsequent application of promoters leads to clonal expansion of initiated (mutated) cells. Forced to proliferate, the initiated clone of cells accumulates additional mutations, developing eventually into a malignant tumor. Indeed, the concept that sustained cell proliferation increases the risk of mutagenesis, and hence promotes neoplastic transformation, also is applicable to human carcinogenesis. For example, endometrial hyperplasia (Chapter 18) and increased regenerative activity that accompanies chronic liver cell injury are associated with the development of cancer in these organs. Were it not for the DNA repair mechanisms discussed earlier, the incidence of chemically induced cancers in all likelihood would be much higher. As mentioned previously, the rare hereditary disorders of DNA repair, including xeroderma pigmentosum, are associated with greatly increased risk of cancers induced by UV light and certain chemicals.

SUMMARY

Chemical Carcinogens

- Chemical carcinogens have highly reactive electrophile groups that directly damage DNA, leading to mutations and eventually cancer.
- Direct-acting agents do not require metabolic conversion to become carcinogenic, while indirect-acting agents are not active until converted to an ultimate carcinogen by endogenous metabolic pathways. Hence, polymorphisms of endogenous enzymes such as cytochrome P-450 may influence carcinogenesis.
- After exposure of a cell to a mutagen or an initiator, tumorigenesis can be enhanced by exposure to promoters, which stimulate proliferation of the mutated cells.
- Examples of human carcinogens are direct-acting agents (e.g., alkylating agents used for chemotherapy), indirect-acting agents (e.g., benzopyrene, azo dyes, aflatoxin), and promoters or agents that cause hyperplasia of endometrium or regenerative activity in the liver.

Radiation Carcinogenesis

Radiation, whatever its source (UV rays of sunlight, x-rays, nuclear fission, radionuclides) is an established carcinogen. Unprotected miners of radioactive elements have a 10-fold increased incidence of lung cancers. Follow-up study of survivors of the atomic bombs dropped on Hiroshima and Nagasaki disclosed a markedly increased incidence of leukemia—principally myelogenous leukemias—after an average latent period of about 7 years, as well as increased mortality rates for thyroid, breast, colon, and lung carcinomas. The nuclear power accident at Chernobyl in the former Soviet Union continues to exact its toll in the form of high cancer incidence in the surrounding areas. More recently, it is feared that radiation release from a nuclear power plant in Japan damaged by a massive earthquake and tsunami will result in significantly increased cancer incidence in the surrounding geographic areas.

Therapeutic irradiation of the head and neck can give rise to papillary thyroid cancers years later. The oncogenic properties of ionizing radiation are related to its mutagenic effects; it causes chromosome breakage, translocations, and, less frequently, point mutations. Biologically, double-stranded DNA breaks seem to be the most important form of DNA damage caused by radiation.

The oncogenic effect of UV rays merits special mention because it highlights the importance of DNA repair in carcinogenesis. Natural UV radiation derived from the sun can cause skin cancers (melanomas, squamous cell carcinomas, and basal cell carcinomas). At greatest risk are fair-skinned people who live in locales such as Australia and New Zealand that receive a great deal of sunlight. Nonmelanoma skin cancers are associated with total cumulative exposure to UV radiation, whereas melanomas are associated with intense intermittent exposure—as occurs with sunbathing. UV light has several biologic effects on cells. Of particular relevance to carcinogenesis is the ability to damage DNA by forming pyrimidine dimers.

This type of DNA damage is repaired by the nucleotide excision repair pathway. With extensive exposure to UV light, the repair systems may be overwhelmed, and skin cancer results. As mentioned earlier, patients with the inherited disease *xeroderma pigmentosum* have a defect in the nucleotide excision repair pathway. As expected, there is a greatly increased predisposition to skin cancers in this disorder.

SUMMARY

Radiation Carcinogenesis

- Ionizing radiation causes chromosome breakage, translocations, and, less frequently, point mutations, leading to genetic damage and carcinogenesis.
- UV rays induce the formation of pyrimidine dimers within DNA, leading to mutations. Therefore, UV rays can give rise to squamous cell carcinomas and melanomas of the skin.

Viral and Microbial Oncogenesis

Many DNA and RNA viruses have proved to be oncogenic in animals as disparate as frogs and primates. Despite intense scrutiny, however, only a few viruses have been linked with human cancer. The following discussion focuses on human oncogenic viruses. Also discussed is the emerging role of the bacterium *H. pylori* in gastric cancer.

Oncogenic RNA Viruses

The study of oncogenic retroviruses in animals has provided spectacular insights into the genetic basis of cancer. However, only one retrovirus, the human T cell lymphotropic virus-1 (HTLV-1), has been demonstrated to cause cancer in humans. HTLV-1 is associated with a form of T cell leukemia/lymphoma that is endemic in certain parts of Japan and the Caribbean basin but is found sporadically elsewhere, including the United States. Similar to the human immunodeficiency virus (HIV), HTLV-1 has tropism for CD4+ T cells, and this subset of T cells is the major target for neoplastic transformation. Human infection requires transmission of infected T cells through sexual intercourse, blood products, or breastfeeding. Leukemia develops only in about 3% to 5% of infected persons after a long latent period of 20 to 50 years.

There is little doubt that HTLV-1 infection of T lymphocytes is necessary for leukemogenesis, but the molecular mechanisms of transformation are not clear. The HTLV-1 genome does not contain a viral oncogene, and in contrast with certain animal retroviruses, no consistent integration site next to a cellular oncogene has been discovered. Indeed, the long latency period between initial infection and development of disease suggests a multistep process, during which many oncogenic mutations are accumulated.

The genome of HTLV-1 contains, in addition to the usual retroviral genes, a unique region called *pX*. This region contains several genes, including one called *TAX*. The TAX protein has been shown to be necessary and sufficient for cellular transformation. By interacting with several transcription factors, such as NF-κB, the TAX protein can transactivate the expression of genes that encode cytokines, cytokine receptors, and costimulatory molecules. This inappropriate gene expression leads to autocrine signaling loops and increased activation of promitogenic signaling cascades. Furthermore, TAX can drive progression through the cell cycle by directly binding to and activating cyclins. In addition, TAX can repress the function of several tumor suppressor genes that control the cell cycle, including *CDKN2A/p16* and *TP53*. From these and other observations, the following scenario is emerging (Fig. 5–31): The *TAX* gene turns on several cytokine genes and their receptors (e.g., the interleukins IL-2 and IL-2R and IL-15 and IL-15R), setting up an autocrine system that drives T cell proliferation. Of these cytokines, IL-15 seems to be more important, but much remains to be defined. Additionally, a parallel paracrine pathway is activated by increased production of granulocyte-macrophage colony-stimulating factor, which stimulates neighboring macrophages to produce other T cell mitogens. Initially, the T cell proliferation is polyclonal, because the virus infects many cells, but because of TAX-based inactivation of tumor suppressor genes such as *TP53*, the proliferating T cells are at increased risk for secondary transforming events (mutations), which lead ultimately to the outgrowth of a monoclonal neoplastic T cell population.

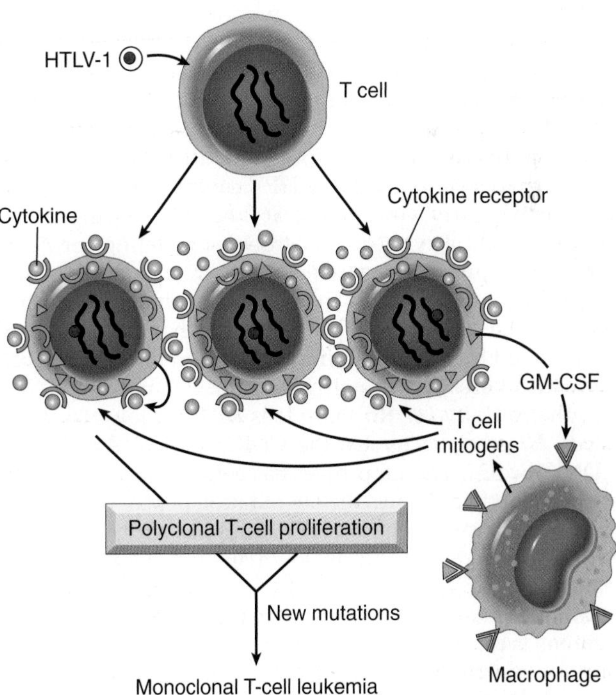

Figure 5–31 Pathogenesis of human T cell lymphotropic virus (HTLV-1)–induced T cell leukemia/lymphoma. HTLV-1 infects many T cells and initially causes polyclonal proliferation by autocrine and paracrine pathways triggered by the *TAX* gene. Simultaneously, TAX neutralizes growth inhibitory signals by affecting *TP53* and *CDKN2A/p16* genes. Ultimately, a monoclonal T cell leukemia/lymphoma results when one proliferating T cell suffers additional mutations.

SUMMARY

Oncogenic RNA Viruses

- HTLV-1 causes a T cell leukemia that is endemic in Japan and the Caribbean.
- The HTLV-1 genome encodes a viral TAX protein, which turns on genes for cytokines and their receptors in infected T cells. This sets up autocrine and paracrine signaling loops that stimulate T cell proliferation. Although this proliferation initially is polyclonal, the proliferating T cells are at increased risk for secondary mutations that lead to the outgrowth of a monoclonal leukemia.

Oncogenic DNA Viruses

As with RNA viruses, several oncogenic DNA viruses that cause tumors in animals have been identified. Four DNA viruses—HPV, Epstein-Barr virus (EBV), Kaposi sarcoma herpesvirus (KSHV, also called human herpesvirus-8 [HHV-8]), and hepatitis B virus (HBV)—are of special interest because they are strongly associated with human cancer. KSHV and Kaposi sarcoma are discussed in Chapter 4. The others are presented here.

Human Papillomavirus

Scores of genetically distinct types of HPV have been identified. Some types (e.g., 1, 2, 4, and 7) cause benign squamous papillomas (warts) in humans (Chapters 18 and 21). Genital warts have low malignant potential and are also associated with low-risk HPVs, predominantly HPV-6 and HPV-11. By contrast, high-risk HPVs (e.g., types 16 and 18) cause several cancers, particularly squamous cell carcinoma of the cervix and anogenital region. In addition, at least 20% of oropharyngeal cancers, particularly those arising in the tonsils, are associated with HPV.

The oncogenic potential of HPV can be related to products of two early viral genes, E6 and E7. Together, they interact with a variety of growth-regulating proteins encoded by proto-oncogenes and tumor suppressor genes. The E7 protein binds to the retinoblastoma protein and releases the E2F transcription factors that normally are sequestered by Rb, promoting progression through the cell cycle. Of interest, E7 protein from high-risk HPV types has a higher affinity for Rb than does E7 from low-risk HPV types. E7 also inactivates the CDKIs CDKN1A/p21 and CDNK1B/p27. The E6 protein has complementary effects. It binds to and mediates the degradation of p53. By analogy with E7, E6 from high-risk HPV types has a higher affinity for p53 than does E6 from low-risk HPV types. Also of interest, in benign warts the HPV genome is maintained in a nonintegrated episomal form, while in cancers the HPV genome is randomly integrated into the host genome. Integration interrupts the viral DNA, resulting in overexpression of the oncoproteins E6 and E7. Furthermore, cells in which the viral genome has integrated show significantly more genomic instability.

To summarize, infection with high-risk HPV types simulates the loss of tumor suppressor genes, activates cyclins, inhibits apoptosis, and combats cellular senescence. Thus, it is evident that many of the hallmarks of cancer discussed earlier are driven by HPV proteins. However, infection with HPV itself is not sufficient for carcinogenesis. For example, when human keratinocytes are transfected with DNA from HPV-16, -18, or -31 in vitro, they are immortalized, but they do not form tumors in experimental animals. Cotransfection with a mutated *RAS* gene results in full malignant transformation. These data strongly suggest that HPV, in all likelihood, acts in concert with other environmental factors (Chapter 18). However, the primacy of HPV infection in the causation of cervical cancer is attested to by the near-complete protection from this cancer by anti-HPV vaccines.

Epstein-Barr Virus

EBV was the first virus linked to a human tumor, Burkitt lymphoma. Over the last 40 years, however, EBV has been discovered with the cells of a surprisingly diverse list of tumors, including B cell lymphomas in patients with defective T cell immunity (e.g., those infected with HIV), a subset of Hodgkin lymphoma, nasopharyngeal carcinoma, a subset of T cell lymphomas, gastric carcinomas, NK cell lymphomas, and even, in rare instances, sarcomas, mainly in the immunosuppressed.

Burkitt lymphoma is endemic in certain parts of Africa and is sporadic elsewhere. In endemic areas, tumor cells in virtually all affected patients carry the EBV genome. The molecular basis for B cell proliferations induced by EBV is complex. EBV uses the complement receptor CD21 to attach to and infect B cells. In vitro, such infection leads to polyclonal B cell proliferation and generation of B lymphoblastoid cell lines. One of the EBV-encoded genes, called *LMP1* (latent membrane protein 1) acts as an oncogene, and its expression in transgenic mice induces B cell lymphomas. LMP1 promotes B cell proliferation by activating signaling pathways, such as NF-κB and JAK/STAT, which mimic B cell activation by the B cell surface molecule CD40. Concurrently, LMP1 prevents apoptosis by activating BCL2. Thus, the virus "borrows" a normal B cell activation pathway to promote its own replication by expanding the pool of cells susceptible to infection. Another EBV-encoded protein, EBNA2, transactivates several host genes, including cyclin D and the *src* family of proto-oncogenes. In addition, the EBV genome contains a viral cytokine, vIL-10, that was pirated from the host genome. This viral cytokine can prevent macrophages and monocytes from activating T cells and killing virally infected cells.

In immunologically normal persons, EBV-driven polyclonal B cell proliferation is readily controlled, and the affected patient either remains asymptomatic or experiences a self-limited episode of infectious mononucleosis (Chapter 11). Evasion of the immune system seems to be a key step in EBV-related oncogenesis. In regions of the world in which Burkitt lymphoma is endemic, concomitant (endemic) malaria (or other infections) impairs immune competence, allowing sustained B cell proliferation. Of interest, although *LMP1* is the primary transforming oncogene in the EBV genome, it is not expressed in EBV-associated Burkitt lymphoma, presumably because it also is one of the major viral antigens recognized by the immune system. Infected cells expressing viral antigens such as LMP-1 are kept in check by the immune system. Lymphoma cells may emerge only when translocations activate the *MYC* oncogene, a consistent feature of this tumor. MYC may substitute for LMP1 signaling, allowing the tumor cells to downregulate LMP1 and evade the immune system. Of note, in nonendemic areas, 80% of tumors are negative for EBV, but virtually all tumors possess *MYC* translocations. This observation suggests that although non-African Burkitt lymphomas are triggered by mechanisms other than EBV, these cancers develop by similar pathways.

In patients with deficient T cell function, including those with HIV and organ transplant recipients, EBV-infected B cells undergo polyclonal expansion, producing lymphoblastoid-like cells. In contrast with Burkitt lymphoma, the B lymphoblasts in immunosuppressed patients do express viral antigens, such as LMP-1, that are recognized by T cells. These potentially lethal proliferations can be subdued if T cell immunity can be restored, as may be achieved by withdrawal of immunosuppressive drugs in transplant recipients.

Nasopharyngeal carcinoma is endemic in southern China and some other locales, and the EBV genome is found in all tumors. LMP-1 is expressed in the carcinoma cells and, as in B cells, activates the NF-κB pathway. Furthermore, LMP1 induces the expression of pro-angiogenic factors such as VEGF, FGF-2, MMP-9, and COX-2, which may contribute to oncogenesis. How EBV enters epithelial cells is unclear, as these cells fail to express the CD21 protein that serves as the EBV receptor in B cells.

SUMMARY

Oncogenic DNA Viruses

- HPV is associated with benign warts, as well as cervical cancer.
- The oncogenicity of HPV is related to the expression of two viral oncoproteins, E6 and E7; they bind to p53 and Rb, respectively, neutralizing their function.
- E6 and E7 from high-risk strains of HPV (which give rise to cancers) have higher affinity for their targets than do E6 and E7 from low-risk strains of HPV (which give rise to benign warts).
- EBV is implicated in the pathogenesis of Burkitt lymphomas, lymphomas in immunosuppressed patients (HIV infection or organ transplant recipients), some forms of Hodgkin lymphoma, uncommon T cell and NK cell tumors, nasopharyngeal carcinoma, a subset of gastric carcinoma, and rarely sarcomas.
- Certain EBV gene products contribute to oncogenesis by stimulating a normal B cell proliferation pathway. Concomitant compromise of immune competence allows sustained B cell proliferation, leading eventually to development of lymphoma, with occurrence of additional mutations such as t(8;14) leading to activation of the *MYC* gene.

Hepatitis B and Hepatitis C Viruses

The epidemiologic evidence linking chronic HBV and hepatitis C virus (HCV) infection with hepatocellular carcinoma is strong (Chapter 15). It is estimated that 70% to 85% of hepatocellular carcinomas worldwide are due to infection with HBV or HCV. However, the mode of action of these viruses in tumorigenesis is not fully elucidated. The HBV and HCV genomes do not encode any viral oncoproteins, and although the HBV DNA is integrated within the human genome, there is no consistent pattern of integration in liver cells. Indeed, the oncogenic effects of HBV and HCV are multifactorial, but the dominant effect seems to be immunologically mediated chronic inflammation with hepatocyte death leading to regeneration and genomic damage. Although the immune system generally is thought to be protective, recent work has demonstrated that in the setting of unresolved chronic inflammation, as occurs in viral hepatitis or chronic gastritis caused by *H. pylori* (see further on), the immune response may become maladaptive, promoting tumorigenesis.

As with any cause of hepatocellular injury, chronic viral infection leads to the compensatory proliferation of hepatocytes. This regenerative process is aided and abetted by a plethora of growth factors, cytokines, chemokines, and other bioactive substances produced by activated immune cells that promote cell survival, tissue remodeling, and angiogenesis. The activated immune cells also produce other mediators, such as reactive oxygen species, that are genotoxic and mutagenic. A key molecular step seems to be activation of the nuclear factor-κB (NF-κB) pathway in hepatocytes caused by mediators derived from the activated immune cells. Activation of the NF-κB pathway within hepatocytes blocks apoptosis, allowing the dividing hepatocytes to incur genotoxic stress and to accumulate mutations. Although this seems to be the dominant mechanism in the pathogenesis of virus-induced hepatocellular carcinoma, both HBV and HCV also contain proteins within their genomes that may more directly promote the development of cancer. The HBV genome contains a gene known as *HBx*, and hepatocellular cancers develop in mice transgenic for this gene. *HBx* can directly or indirectly activate a variety of transcription factors and several signal transduction pathways. In addition, viral integration can cause secondary rearrangements of chromosomes, including multiple deletions that may harbor unknown tumor suppressor genes.

Although not a DNA virus, HCV also is strongly linked to the pathogenesis of liver cancer. The molecular mechanisms used by HCV are less well defined than those for HBV. In addition to chronic liver cell injury and compensatory regeneration, components of the HCV genome, such as the HCV core protein, may have a direct effect on tumorigenesis, possibly by activating a variety of growth-promoting signal transduction pathways.

SUMMARY

Hepatitis B and Hepatitis C Viruses

- Between 70% and 85% of hepatocellular carcinomas worldwide are due to infection with HBV or HCV.
- The oncogenic effects of HBV and HCV are multifactorial, but the dominant effect seems to be immunologically mediated chronic inflammation, with hepatocellular injury, stimulation of hepatocyte proliferation, and production of reactive oxygen species that can damage DNA.
- The HBx protein of HBV and the HCV core protein can activate a variety of signal transduction pathways that also may contribute to carcinogenesis.

acter pylori

criminated as a cause of peptic ulcers, *H. pylori* now quired the dubious distinction of being the first bacterium classified as a carcinogen. Indeed, *H. pylori* infection is implicated in the genesis of both gastric adenocarcinomas and gastric lymphomas.

The scenario for the development of gastric adenocarcinoma is similar to that for HBV- and HCV-induced liver cancer. It involves increased epithelial cell proliferation on a background of chronic inflammation. As in viral hepatitis, the inflammatory milieu contains numerous genotoxic agents, such as reactive oxygen species. The sequence of histopathologic changes consists of initial development of chronic inflammation/gastritis, followed by gastric atrophy, intestinal metaplasia of the lining cells, dysplasia, and cancer. This sequence takes decades to complete and occurs in only 3% of infected patients. Like those of HBV and HCV, the *H. pylori* genome also contains genes directly implicated in oncogenesis. Strains associated with gastric adenocarcinoma have been shown to contain a "pathogenicity island" that contains cytotoxin-associated A gene (*CagA*). Although *H. pylori* is noninvasive, *CagA* is injected into gastric epithelial cells, where it has a variety of effects, including the initiation of a signaling cascade that mimics unregulated growth factor stimulation.

As mentioned previously, *H. pylori* is associated with an increased risk for the development of gastric lymphomas as well. The gastric lymphomas are of B cell origin, and because the transformed B cells grow in a pattern resembling that of normal mucosa-associated lymphoid tissue (MALT), they also have been referred to as MALT lymphomas (Chapter 11). Their molecular pathogenesis is incompletely understood but seems to involve strain-specific *H. pylori* factors, as well as host genetic factors, such as polymorphisms in the promoters of inflammatory cytokines such as IL-1β and tumor necrosis factor (TNF). It is thought that *H. pylori* infection leads to the activation of *H. pylori*–reactive T cells, which in turn cause polyclonal B cell proliferation. In time, a monoclonal B cell tumor emerges in the proliferating B cells, perhaps as a result of accumulation of mutations in growth regulatory genes. In keeping with this model, early in the course of disease, eradication of *H. pylori* "cures" the lymphoma by removing antigenic stimulus for T cells.

SUMMARY

Helicobacter pylori

- *H. pylori* infection has been implicated in both gastric adenocarcinoma and MALT lymphoma.
- The mechanism of *H. pylori*–induced gastric cancers is multifactorial, including immunologically mediated chronic inflammation, stimulation of gastric cell proliferation, and production of reactive oxygen species that damage DNA. *H. pylori* pathogenicity genes, such as *CagA*, also may contribute by stimulating growth factor pathways.
- It is thought that *H. pylori* infection leads to polyclonal B cell proliferations and that eventually a monoclonal B cell tumor (MALT lymphoma) emerges as a result of accumulation of mutations.

HOST DEFENSE AGAINST TUMORS: TUMOR IMMUNITY

The idea that tumors are not entirely "self" was conceived by Ehrlich, who proposed that immune-mediated recognition of autologous tumor cells may be a "positive mechanism" capable of eliminating transformed cells. Subsequently, Lewis Thomas and Macfarlane Burnet formalized this concept by coining the term *immune surveillance* to refer to recognition and destruction of newly appearing tumor cells, which are seen as foreign by the host immune system. That cancers occur implies that immune surveillance is imperfect; the escape of some tumors from such policing, however, does not preclude the possibility that others may have been aborted. This section addresses certain questions about tumor immunity: What is the nature of tumor antigens? What host effector systems may recognize tumor cells? Is tumor immunity effective against spontaneous neoplasms?

Tumor Antigens

Antigens that elicit an immune response have been demonstrated in many experimentally induced tumors and in some human cancers. Initially, they were broadly classified into two categories based on their patterns of expression: *tumor-specific antigens,* which are present only on tumor cells and not on any normal cells, and *tumor-associated antigens,* which are present on tumor cells and also on some normal cells. This classification, however, is imperfect, because many antigens thought to be tumor-specific turned out to be expressed by some normal cells as well. The modern classification of tumor antigens is based on their molecular structure and source.

An important advance in the field of tumor immunology was the development of techniques for identifying tumor antigens that were recognized by cytotoxic T lymphocytes (CTLs), because CTLs are responsible for the major immune defense mechanism against tumors. As described in Chapter 4, CTLs recognize peptides derived from cytoplasmic proteins that are displayed bound to class I major histocompatibility complex (MHC) molecules.

Described next are the main classes of tumor antigens (Fig. 5–32).

Products of Mutated Oncogenes and Tumor Suppressor Genes

Neoplastic transformation, as discussed, results from genetic alterations, some of which may lead to the expression of cell surface antigens that are seen as non-self by the immune system. Antigens in this category are derived from mutant oncoproteins and tumor suppressor proteins. Unique tumor antigens arise from β-catenin, RAS, p53, and CDK4, for which the encoding genes frequently are mutated in tumors. Because the mutant genes are present only in tumors, their peptides are expressed only in tumor cells. Since many tumors may carry the same mutation, such antigens are shared by different tumors. Although CTLs can be induced against such antigens, they do not appear to elicit protective responses in vivo. In some cases, unmutated oncogenes are overexpressed in tumors. The best

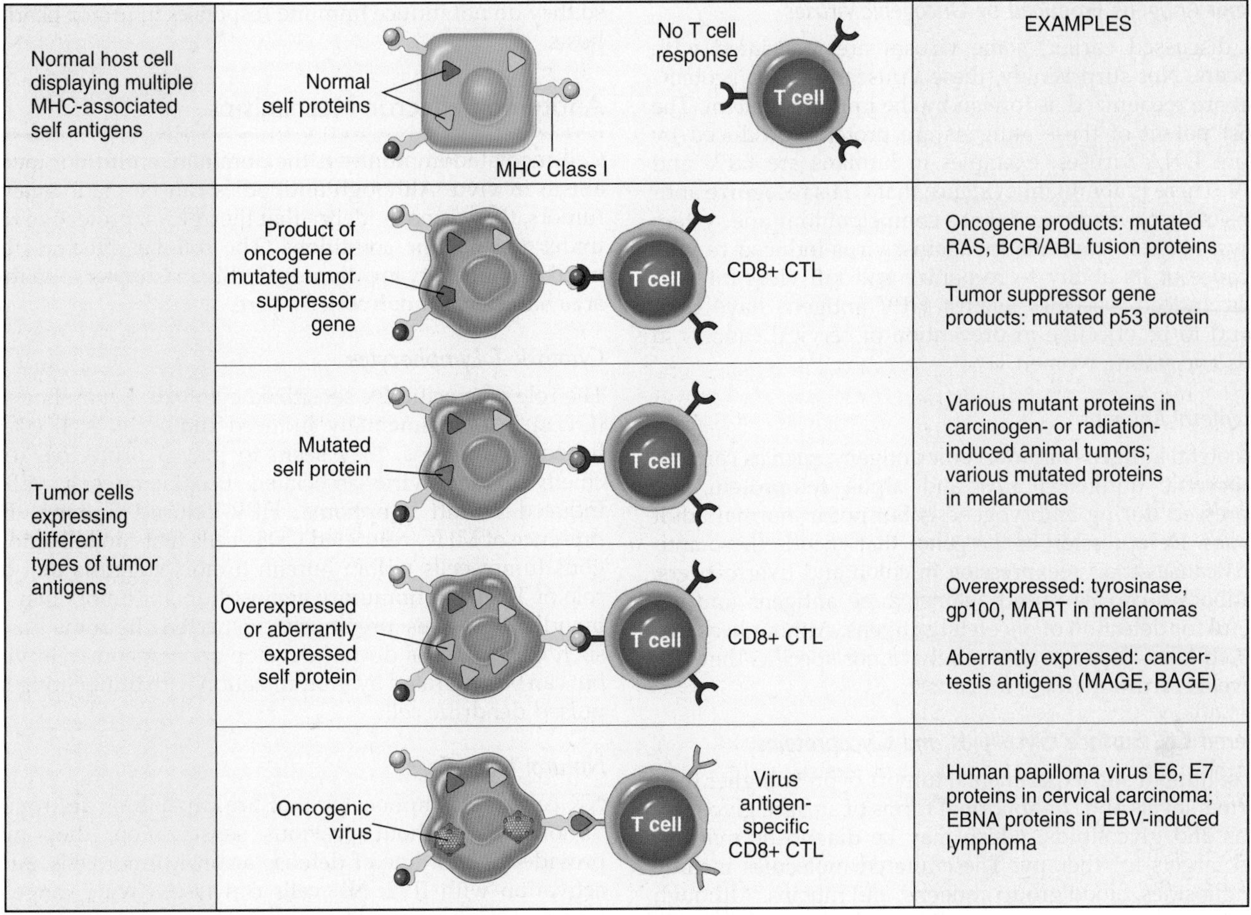

Figure 5–32 Tumor antigens recognized by CD8+ T cells.
(Modified from Abbas AK, Lichtman AH: Cellular and Molecular Immunology, 5th ed. Philadelphia, WB Saunders, 2003.)

example is that of the *HER2/NEU* oncogene, whose product is highly expressed in a subset of breast cancers. Antibodies targeted against Her2/Neu protein are used clinically for the treatment of breast cancers.

Products of Other Mutated Genes

Because of the genetic instability of tumor cells, many genes are mutated in these cells, including genes whose products are not related to the transformed phenotype and have no known function. Products of these mutated genes are potential tumor antigens. These antigens are extremely diverse, because the carcinogens that induce the tumors may randomly mutagenize virtually any host gene. Mutated cellular proteins are found more frequently in chemical carcinogen- or radiation-induced animal tumors than in spontaneous human cancers. They can be targeted by the immune system, since there is no self-tolerance against them.

Overexpressed or Aberrantly Expressed Cellular Proteins

Tumor antigens may be normal cellular proteins that are abnormally expressed in tumor cells and elicit immune responses. In a subset of human melanomas, some tumor antigens are structurally normal proteins that are produced at low levels in normal cells and overexpressed in tumor cells. One such antigen is tyrosinase, an enzyme involved in melanin biosynthesis that is expressed only in normal melanocytes and melanomas. T cells from patients with melanoma recognize peptides derived from tyrosinase, raising the possibility that tyrosinase vaccines may stimulate such responses to melanomas; clinical trials with these vaccines are ongoing. It is somewhat surprising that these patients are able to respond to a normal self-antigen. The probable explanation is that tyrosinase normally is produced in such small amounts and in so few cells that it is not recognized by the immune system and fails to induce tolerance.

Another group, the so-called cancer-testis antigens, are encoded by genes that are silent in all normal adult tissues except the testis, and are deregulated in cancer cells—hence their name. Although the protein is present in the testis, it is not expressed on the cell surface in an antigenic form, because sperm do not express MHC class I molecules. Thus, for all practical purposes, these antigens are tumor-specific. Prototypical of this group is the MAGE (*m*elanoma *a*ntigen *ge*ne) family of genes. Although they are tumor-specific, MAGE antigens are not unique for individual tumors. MAGE-1 is expressed on 37% of melanomas and a variable number of lung, liver, stomach, and esophageal carcinomas. Similar antigens called GAGE, BAGE, and RAGE have been detected in other tumors. Several antigens from this category are now being used in tumor vaccine trials.

Tumor Antigens Produced by Oncogenic Viruses

As discussed earlier, some viruses are associated with cancers. Not surprisingly, these viruses produce proteins that are recognized as foreign by the immune system. The most potent of these antigens are proteins produced by latent DNA viruses; examples in humans are HPV and EBV. There is abundant evidence that CTLs recognize antigens of these viruses and that a competent immune system plays a role in surveillance against virus-induced tumors because of its ability to recognize and kill virus-infected cells. Indeed, vaccines against HPV antigens have been found to be effective in prevention of cervical cancers in girls and young women.

Oncofetal Antigens

Oncofetal antigens or embryonic antigens, such as carcinoembryonic antigen (CEA) and alpha fetoprotein, are expressed during embryogenesis but not in normal adult tissues. Derepression of the genes that encode these antigens causes their reexpression in colon and liver cancers. Antibodies can be raised against these antigens and are useful for detection of oncofetal antigens. Although, as discussed later, they are not entirely tumor-specific, they can serve as serum markers for cancer.

Altered Cell Surface Glycolipids and Glycoproteins

Most human and experimental tumors express higher than normal levels and/or abnormal forms of surface glycoproteins and glycolipids, which may be diagnostic markers and targets for therapy. These altered molecules include gangliosides, blood group antigens, and mucins. Although most of the epitopes recognized by antibodies raised against such antigens are not specifically expressed on tumors, they are present at higher levels on cancer cells than on normal cells. This class of antigens is a target for cancer therapy with specific antibodies.

Several mucins are of special interest and have been the focus of diagnostic and therapeutic studies. These include CA-125 and CA-19-9, expressed on ovarian carcinomas, and MUC-1, expressed on breast carcinomas. Unlike many other types of mucins, MUC-1 is an integral membrane protein that normally is expressed only on the apical surface of breast ductal epithelium, a site that is relatively sequestered from the immune system. In ductal carcinomas of the breast, however, the molecule is expressed in an unpolarized fashion and contains new, tumor-specific carbohydrate and peptide epitopes. These epitopes induce both antibody and T cell responses in cancer patients and are therefore candidates for tumor vaccines.

Cell Type–Specific Differentiation Antigens

Tumors express molecules that normally are present on the cells of origin. These antigens are called *differentiation antigens,* because they are specific for particular lineages or differentiation stages of various cell types. Their importance is as potential targets for immunotherapy and in identifying the tissue of origin of tumors. For example, lymphomas may be diagnosed as B cell–derived tumors by the detection of surface markers characteristic of this lineage, such as CD20. Antibodies against CD20 are used for immunotherapy of certain B cell lymphomas. These differentiation antigens typically are normal self-antigens, so they do not induce immune responses in tumor-bearing hosts.

Antitumor Effector Mechanisms

Cell-mediated immunity is the dominant antitumor mechanism in vivo. Although antibodies can be made against tumors, there is no evidence that they play a protective role under physiologic conditions. The cellular effectors that mediate immunity are discussed fully in Chapter 4, so they are characterized only briefly here.

Cytotoxic T Lymphocytes

The role of specifically sensitized cytotoxic T lymphocytes (CTLs) in experimentally induced tumors is well established. In humans, they seem to play a protective role, chiefly against virus-associated neoplasms (e.g., EBV-induced Burkitt lymphoma, HPV-induced tumors). The presence of MHC-restricted CD8+ cells that can kill autologous tumor cells within human tumors suggests that the role of T cells in immunity against human tumors may be broader than was previously suspected. In some cases, such CD8+ T cells do not develop spontaneously in vivo but can be generated by immunization with tumor antigen–pulsed dendritic cells.

Natural Killer Cells

NK cells are lymphocytes that are capable of destroying tumor cells without previous sensitization; they may provide the first line of defense against tumor cells. After activation with IL-2, NK cells can lyse a wide range of human tumors, including many that seem to be nonimmunogenic for T cells. T cells and NK cells apparently provide complementary antitumor mechanisms. Tumors that fail to express MHC class I antigens cannot be recognized by T cells, but these tumors may trigger NK cells because the latter are inhibited by recognition of normal autologous class I molecules (Chapter 4). Thus, tumors may downregulate MHC class I molecules to avoid recognition by T cells, which then makes them prime targets for NK cells. The triggering receptors on NK cells are extremely diverse and belong to several gene families. NKG2D proteins expressed on NK cells and some T cells are important activating receptors. They recognize stress-induced antigens that are expressed on tumor cells and on cells that have incurred DNA damage and are at risk for neoplastic transformation.

Macrophages

Classically activated macrophages of the M1 type (Chapter 2) exhibit cytotoxicity against tumor cells in vitro. T cells, NK cells, and macrophages may collaborate in antitumor reactivity, because interferon-γ, a cytokine secreted by T cells and NK cells, is a potent activator of macrophages. Activated macrophages may kill tumors by mechanisms similar to those used to kill microbes (e.g., production of reactive oxygen metabolites) (Chapter 2) or by secretion of tumor necrosis factor (TNF).

Humoral Mechanisms

Although there is no evidence for the protective effects of antitumor antibodies against spontaneous tumors, administration of monoclonal antibodies against tumor cells can be therapeutically effective. A monoclonal antibody against CD20, a B cell surface antigen, is widely used for treatment of certain non-Hodgkin lymphomas.

Immune Surveillance and Immune Evasion by Tumors

In view of the host of possible and potential antitumor mechanisms, is there any evidence that they operate in vivo to prevent the emergence of neoplasms? The strongest argument for the existence of immune surveillance is the increased frequency of cancers in immunodeficient hosts. About 5% of persons with congenital immunodeficiencies develop cancers, a rate that is about 200 times reported rates for persons without such immunodeficiencies. By analogy, immunosuppressed transplant recipients and patients with acquired immunodeficiency syndrome have increased numbers of malignancies. Of note, most (but not all) of these neoplasms are lymphomas, often lymphomas of activated B cells. Particularly illustrative is X-linked lymphoproliferative disorder. When affected boys develop an EBV infection, such infection does not take the usual self-limited form of infectious mononucleosis but instead evolves into a fatal form of infectious mononucleosis or, even worse, malignant lymphoma.

Most cancers occur in persons who do not suffer from any overt immunodeficiency. If immune surveillance exists, how do cancers evade the immune system in immunocompetent hosts? Several escape mechanisms have been proposed:

- *Selective outgrowth of antigen-negative variants.* During tumor progression, strongly immunogenic subclones may be eliminated. This notion is supported by experiments in which tumors arising in immunocompromised mice express antigens that are recognized, with consequent elimination of the tumors by the immune system in normal mice, whereas similar tumors arising in immunocompetent mice are nonimmunogenic.
- *Loss or reduced expression of histocompatibility molecules.* Tumor cells may fail to express normal levels of human leukocyte antigen (HLA) class I, escaping attack by CTLs. Such cells, however, may trigger NK cells.
- *Immunosuppression.* Many oncogenic agents (e.g., chemicals, ionizing radiation) suppress host immune responses. Tumors or tumor products also may be immunosuppressive. For example, TGF-β, secreted in large quantities by many tumors, is a potent immunosuppressant. In some cases, the immune response induced by the tumor may inhibit tumor immunity. Several mechanisms of such inhibition have been described. For instance, recognition of tumor cells may lead to engagement of the T cell inhibitory receptor, CTLA-4, or activation of regulatory T cells that suppress immune responses. More insidiously, some tumors express FasL, which can engage Fas on immune cell surfaces and induce the immune cell to enter apoptosis!
- *Antigen masking.* Many tumor cells produce a thicker coat of external glycocalyx molecules, such as sialic acid–containing mucopolysaccharides, than normal cells. This thick coat may block access of immune cells to antigen-presenting molecules, thereby preventing antigen recognition and cell killing.
- *Downregulation of co-stimulatory molecules.* Costimulatory molecules are required to initiate strong T cell responses. Many tumors reduce expression of these costimulatory molecules.

SUMMARY

Immune Surveillance

- Tumor cells can be recognized by the immune system as non-self and destroyed.
- Antitumor activity is mediated by predominantly cell-mediated mechanisms. Tumor antigens are presented on the cell surface by MHC class I molecules and are recognized by CD8+ CTLs.
- The different classes of tumor antigens include products of mutated proto-oncogenes, tumor suppressor genes, overexpressed or aberrantly expressed proteins, tumor antigens produced by oncogenic viruses, oncofetal antigens, altered glycolipids and glycoproteins, and cell type–specific differentiation antigens.
- Immunosuppressed patients have an increased risk for development of cancer.
- In immunocompetent patients, tumors may avoid the immune system by several mechanisms, including selective outgrowth of antigen-negative variants, loss or reduced expression of histocompatibility antigens, and immunosuppression mediated by secretion of factors (e.g., TGF-β) from the tumor.

CLINICAL ASPECTS OF NEOPLASIA

The importance of neoplasms ultimately lies in their effects on patients. Although malignant tumors are of course more threatening than benign tumors, morbidity and mortality may be associated with any tumor, even a benign one. Indeed, both malignant and benign tumors may cause problems because of (1) location and impingement on adjacent structures, (2) functional activity such as hormone synthesis or the development of paraneoplastic syndromes, (3) bleeding and infections when the tumor ulcerates through adjacent surfaces, (4) symptoms that result from rupture or infarction, and (5) cachexia or wasting. The following discussion considers the effects of a tumor on the host, the grading and clinical staging of cancer, and the laboratory diagnosis of neoplasms.

Effects of Tumor on Host

Location is crucial in both benign and malignant tumors. A small (1-cm) pituitary adenoma can compress and destroy the surrounding normal gland, giving rise to hypopituitarism. A 0.5-cm leiomyoma in the wall of the renal artery may encroach on the blood supply, leading to renal ischemia and hypertension. A comparably small carcinoma within the common bile duct may induce fatal biliary tract obstruction.

Hormone production is seen with benign and malignant neoplasms arising in endocrine glands. Adenomas and carcinomas arising in the beta cells of the pancreatic islets of Langerhans can produce hyperinsulinism, sometimes fatal. By analogy, some adenomas and carcinomas of the adrenal cortex elaborate corticosteroids that affect the patient (e.g., aldosterone, which induces sodium retention, hypertension, and hypokalemia). Such hormonal activity is more likely with a well-differentiated benign tumor than with a corresponding carcinoma.

A tumor may ulcerate through a surface, with consequent bleeding or secondary infection. Benign or malignant neoplasms that protrude into the gut lumen may become caught in the peristaltic pull of the gut, causing intussusception (Chapter 14) and intestinal obstruction or infarction.

Cancer Cachexia

Many cancer patients suffer progressive loss of body fat and lean body mass, accompanied by profound weakness, anorexia, and anemia—a condition referred to as *cachexia.* There is some correlation between the size and extent of spread of the cancer and the severity of the cachexia. However, cachexia is not caused by the nutritional demands of the tumor. Although patients with cancer often are anorexic, current evidence indicates that cachexia results from the action of soluble factors such as cytokines produced by the tumor and the host, rather than reduced food intake. In patients with cancer, calorie expenditure remains high, and basal metabolic rate is increased, despite reduced food intake. This is in contrast with the lower metabolic rate that occurs as an adaptive response in starvation. The basis of these metabolic abnormalities is not fully understood. It is suspected that TNF produced by macrophages in response to tumor cells or by the tumor cells themselves mediates cachexia. TNF suppresses appetite and inhibits the action of lipoprotein lipase, inhibiting the release of free fatty acids from lipoproteins. Additionally, a protein-mobilizing factor called proteolysis-inducing factor, which causes breakdown of skeletal muscle proteins by the ubiquitin-proteosome pathway, has been detected in the serum of cancer patients. Other molecules with lipolytic action also have been found. There is no satisfactory treatment for cancer cachexia other than removal of the underlying cause, the tumor.

Paraneoplastic Syndromes

Symptom complexes that occur in patients with cancer and that cannot be readily explained by local or distant spread of the tumor or by the elaboration of hormones not indigenous to the tissue of origin of the tumor are referred to as *paraneoplastic syndromes.* They appear in 10% to 15% of patients with cancer, and their clinical recognition is important for several reasons:

- Such syndromes may represent the earliest manifestation of an occult neoplasm.
- In affected patients, the pathologic changes may be associated with significant clinical illness and may even be lethal.
- The symptom complex may mimic metastatic disease, thereby confounding treatment.

The paraneoplastic syndromes are diverse and are associated with many different tumors (Table 5–5). *The most common such syndromes are hypercalcemia, Cushing syndrome, and nonbacterial thrombotic endocarditis;* the neoplasms most often associated with these and other syndromes are lung and breast cancers and hematologic malignancies. Hypercalcemia in cancer patients is multifactorial, but the most important mechanism is the synthesis of a parathyroid hormone–related protein (PTHrP) by tumor cells. Also implicated are other tumor-derived factors, such as TGF-α, a polypeptide factor that activates osteoclasts, and the active form of vitamin D. Another possible mechanism for hypercalcemia is widespread osteolytic metastatic disease of bone; of note, however, *hypercalcemia resulting from skeletal metastases is not a paraneoplastic syndrome.* Cushing syndrome arising as a paraneoplastic phenomenon usually is related to ectopic production of ACTH or ACTH-like polypeptides by cancer cells, as occurs in small cell cancers of the lung. Sometimes one tumor induces several syndromes concurrently. For example, bronchogenic carcinomas may elaborate products identical to or having the effects of ACTH, antidiuretic hormone, parathyroid hormone, serotonin, human chorionic gonadotropin, and other bioactive substances.

Paraneoplastic syndromes also may manifest as hypercoagulability, leading to venous thrombosis and nonbacterial thrombotic endocarditis (Chapter 10). Other manifestations are clubbing of the fingers and hypertrophic osteoarthropathy in patients with lung carcinomas (Chapter 12). Still others are discussed in the consideration of cancers of the various organs of the body.

Grading and Staging of Cancer

Methods to quantify the probable clinical aggressiveness of a given neoplasm and its apparent extent and spread in the individual patient are necessary for making an accurate prognosis and for comparing end results of various treatment protocols. For instance, the results of treating extremely small, highly differentiated thyroid adenocarcinomas that are localized to the thyroid gland are likely to be different from those obtained from treating highly anaplastic thyroid cancers that have invaded the neck organs.

The *grading* of a cancer attempts to establish some estimate of its aggressiveness or level of malignancy based on the cytologic differentiation of tumor cells and the number of mitoses within the tumor. The cancer may be classified as grade I, II, III, or IV, in order of increasing anaplasia. Criteria for the individual grades vary with each form of neoplasia and are not detailed here. Difficulties in establishing clear-cut criteria have led in some instances to descriptive characterizations (e.g., "well-differentiated adenocarcinoma with no evidence of vascular or lymphatic invasion" or "highly anaplastic sarcoma with extensive vascular invasion").

Staging of cancers is based on the size of the primary lesion, its extent of spread to regional lymph nodes, and the presence or absence of metastases. This assessment usually is based on clinical and radiographic examination (computed tomography and magnetic resonance imaging) and in some cases surgical exploration. Two methods of

Table 5–5 Paraneoplastic Syndromes

Clinical Syndrome	Major Forms of Neoplasia	Causal Mechanism(s)/Agent(s)
Endocrinopathies		
Cushing syndrome	Small cell carcinoma of lung Pancreatic carcinoma Neural tumors	ACTH or ACTH-like substance
Syndrome of inappropriate antidiuretic hormone secretion	Small cell carcinoma of lung; intracranial neoplasms	Antidiuretic hormone or atrial natriuretic hormones
Hypercalcemia	Squamous cell carcinoma of lung Breast carcinoma Renal carcinoma Adult T cell leukemia/lymphoma Ovarian carcinoma	Parathyroid hormone–related protein, TGF-α, TNF, IL-1
Hypoglycemia	Fibrosarcoma Other mesenchymal sarcomas Hepatocellular carcinoma	Insulin or insulin-like substance
Carcinoid syndrome	Bronchial adenoma (carcinoid) Pancreatic carcinoma Gastric carcinoma	Serotonin, bradykinin
Polycythemia	Renal carcinoma Cerebellar hemangioma Hepatocellular carcinoma	Erythropoietin
Nerve and Muscle Syndrome		
Myasthenia	Bronchogenic carcinoma, thymoma	Immunologic
Disorders of the central and peripheral nervous systems	Breast carcinoma, teratoma	
Dermatologic Disorders		
Acanthosis nigricans	Gastric carcinoma Lung carcinoma Uterine carcinoma	Immunologic; secretion of epidermal growth factor
Dermatomyositis	Bronchogenic and breast carcinoma	Immunologic
Osseous, Articular, and Soft Tissue Changes		
Hypertrophic osteoarthropathy and clubbing of the fingers	Bronchogenic carcinoma	Unknown
Vascular and Hematologic Changes		
Venous thrombosis (Trousseau phenomenon)	Pancreatic carcinoma Bronchogenic carcinoma Other cancers	Tumor products (mucins that activate clotting)
Nonbacterial thrombotic endocarditis	Advanced cancers	Hypercoagulability
Anemia	Thymoma	Immunologic
Others		
Nephrotic syndrome	Various cancers	Tumor antigens, immune complexes

ACTH, adrenocorticotropic hormone; IL-1, interleukin-1; TGF-α, transforming growth factor-α; TNF, tumor necrosis factor.

staging are currently in use: the TNM system (*T,* primary tumor; *N,* regional lymph node involvement; *M,* metastases) and the AJC (American Joint Committee) system. In the *TNM system,* T1, T2, T3, and T4 describe the increasing size of the primary lesion; N0, N1, N2, and N3 indicate progressively advancing node involvement; and M0 and M1 reflect the absence and presence, respectively, of distant metastases. In the *AJC method,* the cancers are divided into stages 0 to IV, incorporating the size of primary lesions and the presence of nodal spread and of distant metastases. Examples of the application of these two staging systems are cited in subsequent chapters. Of note, *when compared with grading, staging has proved to be of greater clinical value.*

SUMMARY

Clinical Aspects of Tumors

- *Cachexia,* defined as progressive loss of body fat and lean body mass, accompanied by profound weakness, anorexia, and anemia, is caused by release of cytokines by the tumor or host.
- Paraneoplastic syndromes, defined as systemic symptoms that cannot be explained by tumor spread or by hormones appropriate to the tissue, are caused by the ectopic production and secretion of bioactive substances such as ACTH, PTHrP, or TGF-α.

- Grading of tumors is determined by cytologic appearance and is based on the idea that behavior and differentiation are related, with poorly differentiated tumors having more aggressive behavior.
- Staging, determined by surgical exploration or imaging, is based on size, local and regional lymph node spread, and distant metastases. Staging is of greater clinical value than grading.

Laboratory Diagnosis of Cancer

Morphologic Methods

In most instances, the laboratory diagnosis of cancer is not difficult. The two ends of the benign–malignant spectrum pose no problems; in the middle, however, lies a "no man's land" where the wise tread cautiously. Clinicians tend to underestimate the contributions they make to the diagnosis of a neoplasm. Clinical and radiologic data are invaluable for optimal pathologic diagnosis. Radiation-induced changes in the skin or mucosa can be similar to those of cancer. Sections taken from a healing fracture can mimic an osteosarcoma. The laboratory evaluation of a lesion can be only as good as the specimen submitted for examination. The specimen must be adequate, representative, and properly preserved.

Several sampling approaches are available, including excision or biopsy, fine-needle aspiration, and cytologic smears. When excision of a lesion is not possible, selection of an appropriate site for biopsy of a large mass requires awareness that the margins may not be representative and the center may be largely necrotic. Requesting *frozen section* diagnosis is sometimes desirable, as, for example, in determining the nature of a mass lesion or in evaluating the regional lymph nodes in a patient with cancer for metastasis. This method, in which a sample is quick-frozen and sectioned, permits histologic evaluation within minutes. In experienced, competent hands, frozen section diagnosis is accurate, but there are particular instances in which the better histologic detail provided by the more time-consuming routine methods is needed. In such instances, it is better to wait a few days, despite the drawbacks, than to perform inadequate or unnecessary surgery.

Fine needle aspiration of tumors is another approach that is widely used. It involves aspiration of cells from a mass, followed by cytologic examination of the smear. This procedure is used most commonly with readily palpable lesions affecting the breast, thyroid, lymph nodes, and salivary glands. Modern imaging techniques permit extension of the method to deeper structures, such as the liver, pancreas, and pelvic lymph nodes. Use of this diagnostic modality obviates surgery and its attendant risks. Although it entails some difficulties, such as small sample size and sampling errors, in experienced hands it can be reliable, rapid, and useful.

Cytologic (Papanicolaou) smears provide another method for the detection of cancer. Historically, this approach has been used widely for discovery of carcinoma of the cervix, often at an in situ stage, but now it is used to investigate many other forms of suspected malignancy, such as endometrial carcinoma, bronchogenic carcinoma, bladder and prostate tumors, and gastric carcinomas; for the identification of tumor cells in abdominal, pleural, joint, and cerebrospinal fluids; and, less commonly, for evaluation of other forms of neoplasia. Neoplastic cells are less cohesive than others and are therefore shed into fluids or secretions (Fig. 5–33). The shed cells are evaluated for features of anaplasia indicative of their origin from a tumor. The gratifying control of cervical cancer is the best testament to the value of the cytologic method.

Immunocytochemistry offers a powerful adjunct to routine histologic examination. Detection of cytokeratin by specific monoclonal antibodies labeled with peroxidase points to a diagnosis of undifferentiated carcinoma rather than large cell lymphoma. Similarly, detection of prostate-specific antigen (PSA) in metastatic deposits by immunohistochemical staining allows definitive diagnosis of a primary tumor in the prostate. Immunocytochemical detection of estrogen receptors allows prognostication and directs therapeutic intervention in breast cancers.

Flow cytometry is used routinely in the classification of leukemias and lymphomas. In this method, fluorescent antibodies against cell surface molecules and

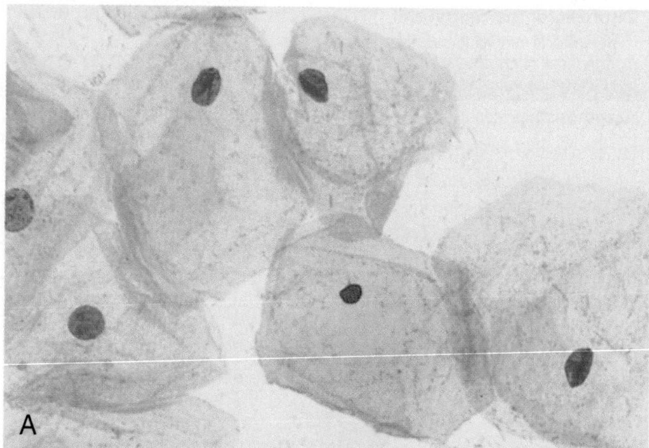

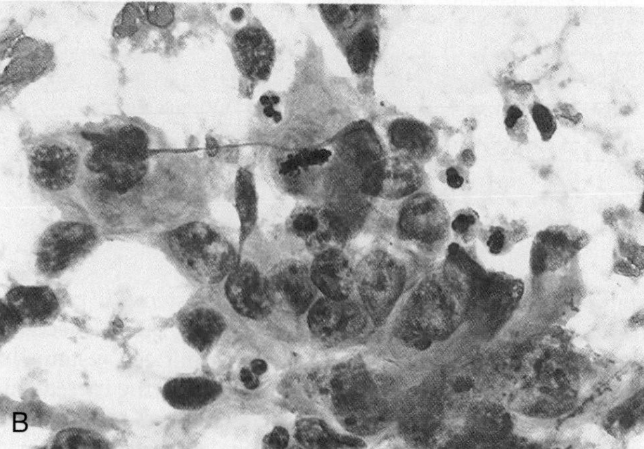

Figure 5–33 A, Normal Papanicolaou smear from the uterine cervix. Large, flat cells with small nuclei are typical. **B,** Abnormal smear containing a sheet of malignant cells with large hyperchromatic nuclei. Nuclear pleomorphism is evident, and one cell is in mitosis. A few interspersed neutrophils, much smaller in size and with compact, lobate nuclei, are seen.

(Courtesy of Dr. Richard M. DeMay, Department of Pathology, University of Chicago, Chicago, Illinois.)

differentiation antigens are used to obtain the phenotype of malignant cells.

Tumor Markers

Biochemical assays for tumor-associated enzymes, hormones, and other tumor markers in the blood cannot be utilized for definitive diagnosis of cancer; however, they can be useful screening tests and in some instances have utility in quantitating the response to therapy or detecting disease recurrence. The application of these assays is considered with many of the specific forms of neoplasia discussed in other chapters, so only a few examples suffice here. PSA, used to screen for prostatic adenocarcinoma, may be one of the most frequently and successfully used tumor markers in clinical practice. Prostatic carcinoma can be suspected when elevated levels of PSA are found in the blood. However, PSA screening also highlights problems encountered with use of virtually every tumor marker. Although PSA levels often are elevated in cancer, PSA levels also may be elevated in benign prostatic hyperplasia (Chapter 17). Furthermore, there is no PSA level that ensures that a patient does not have prostate cancer. *Thus, the PSA test suffers from both low sensitivity and low specificity.* PSA assay is extremely valuable, however, for detecting residual disease or recurrence following treatment for prostate cancer. Other tumor markers occasionally used in clinical practice include carcinoembryonic antigen (CEA), which is elaborated by carcinomas of the colon, pancreas, stomach, and breast, and alpha fetoprotein, which is produced by hepatocellular carcinomas, yolk sac remnants in the gonads, and occasionally teratocarcinomas and embryonal cell carcinomas. Unfortunately, like PSA, both of these markers can be produced in a variety of non-neoplastic conditions as well. Thus, CEA and alpha fetoprotein assays lack both specificity and sensitivity required for the early detection of cancers. As with PSA screening, they are still particularly useful in the detection of recurrences after excision. With successful resection of the tumor, these markers disappear from the serum; their reappearance almost always signifies the beginning of the end. CEA is further discussed in Chapter 14 and alpha fetoprotein in Chapter 15.

Molecular Diagnosis

An increasing number of molecular techniques are being used for the diagnosis of tumors and for predicting their behavior.

- *Diagnosis of malignancy*: Because each T and B cell exhibits its unique rearrangement of its antigen receptor genes, polymerase chain reaction (PCR)–based detection of T cell receptor or immunoglobulin genes allows distinction between monoclonal (neoplastic) and polyclonal (reactive) proliferations. Many hematopoietic neoplasms, as well as a few solid tumors, are defined by particular translocations, so the diagnosis can be made by detection of such translocations. For example, fluorescence in situ hybridization (FISH) or PCR analysis (Chapter 6) can be used to detect translocations characteristic of Ewing sarcoma and several leukemias and lymphomas. PCR-based detection of *BCR-ABL* transcripts provides the molecular diagnosis of chronic myeloid leukemia.
- *Prognosis and behavior*: Certain genetic alterations are associated with a poor prognosis, and thus the presence of these alterations determines the patient's subsequent therapy. FISH and PCR methods can be used to detect amplification of oncogenes such as *HER2/NEU* and *NMYC*, which provide prognostic and therapeutic information for breast cancers and neuroblastomas.
- *Detection of minimal residual disease*: Another emerging use of molecular techniques is for detection of minimal residual disease after treatment. For example, detection of *BCR-ABL* transcripts by PCR assay gives a measure of residual disease in patients treated for chronic myeloid leukemia. Recognition that virtually all advanced tumors are associated with both intact circulating tumor cells and products derived from tumors (e.g., tumor DNA) has led to interest in following tumor burden through sensitive blood tests.
- *Diagnosis of hereditary predisposition to cancer*: Germline mutation of several tumor suppressor genes, such as *BRCA1*, increases a patient's risk for development of certain types of cancer. Thus, detection of these mutated alleles may allow the patient and the physician to devise an aggressive screening protocol, as well as an opportunity for prophylactic surgery. In addition, such detection allows genetic counseling of relatives at risk.
- *Therapeutic decision-making*: Therapies that directly target specific mutations are increasingly being developed, and thus detection of such mutations in a tumor can guide the development of targeted therapy, as discussed later. It is now becoming evident that certain targetable mutations may transgress morphologic categories. For example, mutations of the ALK kinase, originally described in a subset of T cell lymphomas, also have been identified in a small percentage of non–small cell carcinomas and neuroblastomas. Clinical trials have shown that lung cancers with ALK mutations respond to ALK inhibitors, whereas other lung cancers do not, leading to recent FDA approval of ALK inhibitors for use in patients with "ALK-mutated" lung cancer. Another recent dramatic example of molecularly "tailored" therapy is seen in melanoma, in which tumors with a valine for glutamate substitution in amino acid 600 (V600E) of the serine/threonine kinase BRAF respond well to BRAF inhibition, whereas melanomas without this mutation show no response. Of some interest, the V600E mutation is also present in a subset of colon cancers, certain thyroid cancers, 100% of hairy cell leukemias, and Langerhans cell histiocytosis (Fig. 5–34). These tumors are morphologically diverse and have distinct cells of origin, but they share identical oncogenic lesions in a common pro-growth pathway.

Molecular Profiling of Tumors

Molecular profiling of tumors can be done both at the level of mRNA and by nucleotide sequencing. Each of these two is described next.

Expression Profiling

This technique allows simultaneous measurements of the expression levels of several thousand genes. The principle of this so-called gene chip technology is illustrated in Figure 5–35 and described briefly here.

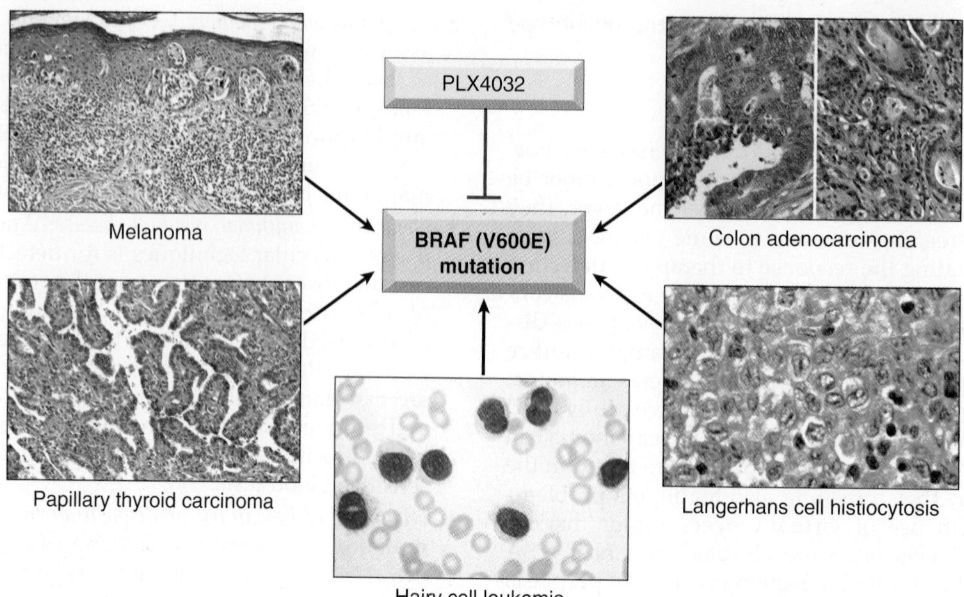

Figure 5–34 Diverse tumor types that share a common mutation, BRAF (V600E), may be candidates for treatments with the same drug, called PLX4032.

As can be seen, the process begins by extraction of mRNA from any two sources (e.g., normal and malignant, normal and preneoplastic, or two tumors of the same histologic type). Complementary DNA (cDNA) copies of the mRNA are synthesized in vitro with fluorescently labeled nucleotides. The fluorescence-labeled cDNA strands are hybridized to sequence-specific DNA probes linked to a solid support, such as a silicon chip. A 1-cm^2 chip can contain thousands of probes arranged in an array of columns and rows. After hybridization, high-resolution laser scanning detects fluorescent signals from each of the spots. The fluorescence intensity of each spot is proportional to the level of expression of the original mRNA used to synthesize the cDNA hybridized to that spot. For each sample, therefore, the expression level of thousands of genes is obtained, and by using bioinformatic tools, the relative levels of gene expression in different samples can be compared. In essence, a molecular profile is generated for each tissue analyzed.

Such analysis has revealed that phenotypically identical large B cell lymphomas (Chapter 11) from different patients are heterogeneous with respect to their gene expression and survival rates. Similar approaches are now being explored in other cancers, such as breast cancers and melanomas.

Whole Genome Sequencing

The progression and development of next-generation sequencing technologies promise even more in-depth analysis of tumors. The advances in such technologies are currently outpacing the famous Moore's law of microprocessors. Sequencing an entire tumor genome, which just a couple of years ago would have taken months and millions of dollars, now takes days and costs a few thousand dollars. Sequences of the entire tumor genomes, when compared with the normal genome from the same patient, can reveal all the somatic alterations present in a tumor.

Recent results from genomic analyses of tumors have revealed that individual tumors can contain from a handful of somatic mutations (certain childhood leukemias) to tens of thousands of mutations, with the highest mutational burden being found in cancers associated with mutagen exposure, such as lung cancer and skin cancer. Among these are two types of mutations: (1) those that subvert normal control of cell proliferation, differentiation, and homeostasis and (2) those that have no effect on cell phenotype. The first set of mutations is referred to as *driver mutations* because they may drive the neoplastic process and hence could be therapeutic targets. The other set of mutations, often much more numerous than driver mutations, most often fall in noncoding regions of the genome or have a neutral effect on growth, not conferring any advantage or disadvantage. Such mutations are called *passenger mutations*. They result from genomic instability of cancer cells and are merely "along for the ride."

In general, driver mutations are recurrent and are present in a substantial percentage of patients with a particular cancer. Thus, for example, *BCR-ABL* fusion genes are present in all cases of chronic myelogenous leukemia, and the fusion protein is an excellent drug target. However, driver mutations may be present in only a subset of tumors of a particular type. For example, approximately 4% of non–small cell lung cancers harbor an *EML4-ALK* tyrosine kinase fusion gene; as already mentioned, in these relatively rare instances, the patient responds well to ALK inhibitors. An additional complication is that some passenger mutations nevertheless have important roles in drug resistance. For example, the mutations in BCR-ABL that confer resistance to imatinib in chronic myelogenous leukemia are present as passenger mutations in rare clones before therapy begins. Because they confer a powerful selective advantage, these mutations are converted from passengers to drivers in the face of drug therapy; it is suspected that the genomic instability of cancer cells sows the seeds of resistance through similar scenarios in many kinds of tumors. Furthermore, in some instances, several distinct and relatively uncommon mutations all converge on the

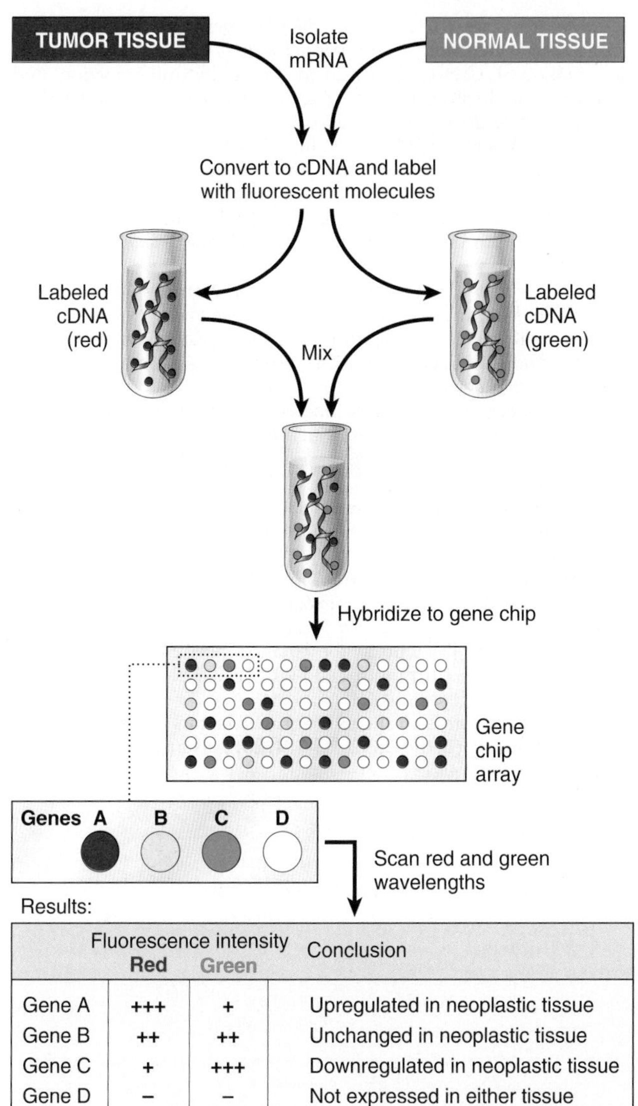

	Fluorescence intensity Red	Green	Conclusion
Gene A	+++	+	Upregulated in neoplastic tissue
Gene B	++	++	Unchanged in neoplastic tissue
Gene C	+	+++	Downregulated in neoplastic tissue
Gene D	–	–	Not expressed in either tissue

Figure 5–35 Complementary DNA (cDNA) microarray analysis. Messenger RNA (mRNA) is extracted from the samples, reverse transcribed to cDNA, and labeled with fluorescent molecules. In the case illustrated, *red* fluorescent molecules were used for normal cDNA, and *green* molecules were used for tumor cDNA. The labeled cDNAs are mixed and applied to a gene chip, which contains thousands of DNA probes representing known genes. The labeled cDNAs hybridize to spots that contain complementary sequences. The hybridization is detected by laser scanning of the chip, and the results are read in units of red or green fluorescence intensity. In the example shown, *spot A* has high red fluorescence, indicating that a greater number of cDNAs from neoplastic cells hybridized to gene A. Thus, gene A seems to be upregulated in tumor cells. *(Courtesy of Dr. Robert Anders, Department of Pathology, University of Chicago, Chicago, Illinois.)*

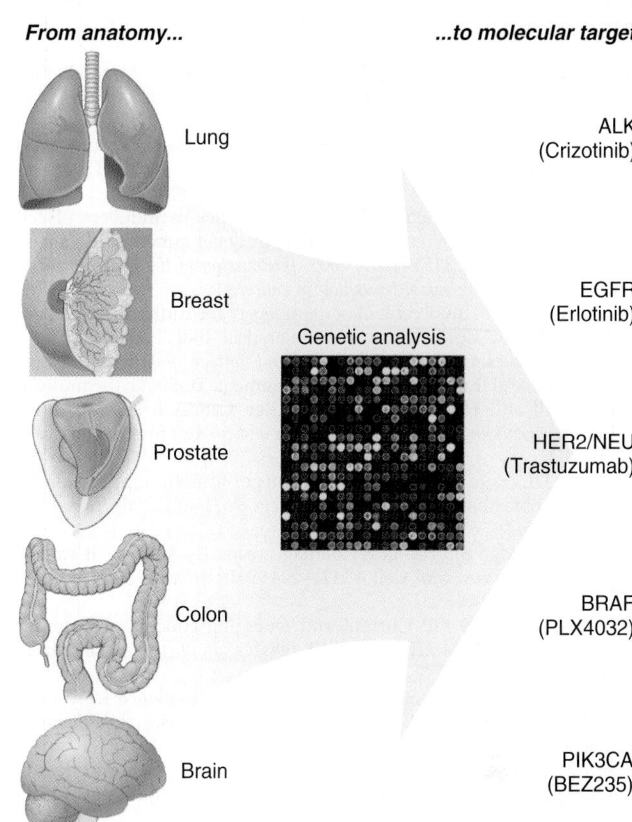

Figure 5–36 A paradigm shift: Classification of cancer according to therapeutic targets rather than cell of origin and morphology.

same pathway (such as resistance to apoptosis) and contribute to the cancer phenotype. It is therefore useful to categorize mutations on the basis of their ability to drive the cells along the "hallmarks of cancer" pathways.

It is hoped that identification of all potentially targetable mutations in each individual tumor will refocus the treatment of tumors from the tissue of origin to the molecular lesion, as drugs that target specific mutations are developed (Fig. 5–36). This approach represents a paradigm shift in the classification and therapy of tumors. Perhaps in the future the diverse group of tumors that bear a common mutation such as BRAF will be classified as BRAF-omas (Fig. 5–34), rather than individual types based on morphology or cell of origin!

SUMMARY

Laboratory Diagnosis of Cancer

- Several sampling approaches exist for the diagnosis of tumors, including excision, biopsy, fine-needle aspiration, and cytologic smears.
- Immunohistochemistry and flow cytometry studies help in the diagnosis and classification of tumors, because distinct protein expression patterns define different entities.
- Proteins released by tumors into the serum, such as PSA, can be used to screen populations for cancer and to monitor for recurrence after treatment.
- Molecular analyses are used to determine diagnosis, prognosis, the detection of minimal residual disease, and the diagnosis of hereditary predisposition to cancer.
- Molecular profiling of tumors by cDNA arrays and sequencing can determine expression of large segments of the genome and catalog all of the mutations in the tumor genome and thus may be useful in molecular stratification of otherwise identical tumors or those of distinct histogenesis that share a mutation for the purpose of treatment and prognostication.

BIBLIOGRAPHY

Ahmed Z, Bicknell R: Angiogenic signalling pathways. Methods Mol Biol 467:3–24, 2009. *[Discussion of many signaling pathways in angiogenesis.]*

Artandi SE, DePinho RA: Telomeres and telomerase in cancer. Carcinogenesis 31:9–18, 2010. *[Review discussing the importance of telomeres and telomerase.]*

Barrallo-Gimeno A, Nieto MA: The Snail genes as inducers of cell movement and survival: implications in development and cancer. Development 132:3151–3161, 2005. *[Discussion of the genes involved in epithelial-mesenchymal transition in cancer.]*

Berx G, van Roy F: Involvement of members of the cadherin superfamily in cancer. Cold Spring Harb Perspect Biol 1:a003129, 2009. *[Review discussing the role of cadherins and contact inhibition in cancer.]*

Bierie B, Moses HL: Tumour microenvironment: TGFbeta: the molecular Jekyll and Hyde of cancer. Nat Rev Cancer 6:506–520, 2006. *[Review discussing the tumor-suppressive and tumor-promoting effects of TGF-β.]*

Burkhart DL, Sage J: Cellular mechanisms of tumour suppression by the retinoblastoma gene. Nat Rev Cancer 8:671–682, 2008. *[Review of Rb function.]*

Ciccia A, Elledge SJ: The DNA damage response: making it safe to play with knives. Mol Cell 40:179–204, 2010. *[Review discussing the DNA damage response.]*

Coghlin C, Murray GI: Current and emerging concepts in tumour metastasis. J Pathol 222:1–15, 2010. *[Discussion of current concepts in metastasis.]*

Collado M, Serrano M: Senescence in tumours: evidence from mice and humans. Nat Rev Cancer 10:51–57, 2010. *[Update on mechanisms of senescence.]*

Feron O: Pyruvate into lactate and back: from the Warburg effect to symbiotic energy fuel exchange in cancer cells. Radiother Oncol 92:329–333, 2009. *[An account of the reemergence and molecular pathways of reprogramming of energy metabolism in cancer.]*

Grivennikov SI, Greten FR, Karin M: Immunity, inflammation, and cancer. Cell 140:883–899, 2010. *[A summary of the links between inflammation and the development of cancer.]*

Hanahan D, Weinberg RA: The hallmarks of cancer (2011): the next generation. Cell 144:646–674, 2011. *[Reexamination of the hallmarks of cancer.]*

Junttila MR, Evan GI: p53—a jack of all trades but master of none. Nat Rev Cancer 9:821–829, 2009. *[Update summarizing p53 function.]*

Kalluri R, Zeisberg M: Fibroblasts in cancer. Nat Rev Cancer 6:392–401, 2006. *[Review discussing the role of stroma in cancer.]*

Mathew R, Karantza-Wadsworth V, White E: Role of autophagy in cancer. Nat Rev Cancer 7:961–967, 2007. *[A discussion of the mechanisms of autophagy.]*

Negrini S, Gorgoulis VG, Halazonetis TD: Genomic instability—an evolving hallmark of cancer. Nat Rev Mol Cell Biol 11:220–228, 2010. *[Review on mechanisms of genomic instability, an enabler of malignancy.]*

Perona R: Cell signalling: growth factors and tyrosine kinase receptors. Clin Transl Oncol 8:77–82, 2006. *[Update on signaling pathways in cancer.]*

Stratton MR, Campbell PJ, Futreal PA: The cancer genome. Nature 458:719–724, 2009. *[Excellent summary of next-generation sequencing technologies and their application to cancer.]*

Willis SN, Adams JM: Life in the balance: how BH3-only proteins induce apoptosis. Curr Opin Cell Biol 17:617–625, 2005. *[A review of the mechanisms of apoptosis.]*

Witsch E, Sela M, Yarden Y: Roles for growth factors in cancer progression. Physiology (Bethesda) 25:85–101, 2010. *[An update on the role of growth factors in cancer.]*

See Targeted Therapy available online at **studentconsult.com**

CHAPTER 6

Genetic and Pediatric Diseases

CHAPTER CONTENTS

GENETIC DISEASES

The completion of the human genome project has been a landmark event in the study of human diseases. It has now been established that humans have only about 25,000 protein-coding genes, far fewer than the 100,000 previously estimated and almost half the number in the lowly rice plant (*Oryza sativa*)! The unraveling of this "genetic architecture" promises to unlock secrets of inherited as well as acquired human disease, since ultimately all diseases involve changes in gene structure or expression. Powerful technologies now allow applications of the human gene sequences to the analysis of human diseases. For example, the human genome project cost approximately 3 billion dollars and many years to complete; current high-throughput sequencing technologies can do the same work in a few weeks for less than $10,000. The speed and reduced costs of DNA sequencing are increasingly facilitating the application of "personalized medicine" to the treatment of cancer and other diseases with a genetic component.

Because several pediatric disorders are of genetic origin, developmental and pediatric diseases are discussed along with genetic diseases in this chapter. However, *it must be borne in mind that not all genetic disorders manifest in infancy and childhood, and conversely, many pediatric diseases are not of genetic origin.* To the latter category belong diseases resulting from immaturity of organ systems. In this context it is helpful to clarify three commonly used terms: hereditary, familial, and congenital. *Hereditary* disorders, by definition, are derived from one's parents, are transmitted in the gametes through the generations, and therefore are *familial.* The term *congenital* simply implies "present at birth." Of note, some congenital diseases are not genetic (e.g., congenital syphilis). On the other hand, not all genetic diseases are congenital; the expression of Huntington disease, for example, begins only after the third or fourth decade of life.

NATURE OF GENETIC ABNORMALITIES CONTRIBUTING TO HUMAN DISEASE

There are several types of genetic abnormalities that affect the structure and function of proteins, disrupting cellular homeostasis and contributing to disease.

Mutations in Protein-Coding Genes

As is well recognized, the term *mutation* refers to permanent changes in the DNA. Those that affect germ cells are transmitted to the progeny and may give rise to inherited diseases. Mutations in somatic cells are not transmitted to the progeny but are important in the causation of cancers and some congenital malformations.

Details of specific mutations and their effects are discussed along with the relevant disorders throughout this book. Cited here are some common examples of gene mutations and their effects:

- *Point mutations* result from the substitution of a single nucleotide base by a different base, resulting in the replacement of one amino acid by another in the protein product. The mutation in the β-globin chain of hemoglobin giving rise to sickle cell anemia is an excellent example of a point mutation that alters the meaning of the genetic code. Such mutations are sometimes called *missense mutations.*
- By contrast, certain point mutations may change an amino acid codon to a chain termination codon, or *stop codon.* Such "nonsense" mutations interrupt translation, and in most cases RNAs are rapidly degraded, a phenomenon called nonsense mediated decay, such that little or no protein is formed.
- *Frameshift mutations* occur when the insertion or deletion of one or two base pairs alters the reading frame of the DNA strand.
- *Trinucleotide repeat mutations* belong to a special category, because these mutations are characterized by amplification of a sequence of three nucleotides. Although the specific nucleotide sequence that undergoes amplification varies with different disorders, all affected sequences share the nucleotides guanine (G) and cytosine (C). For example, in fragile X syndrome, prototypical of this category of disorders, there are 200 to 4000 tandem repeats of the sequence CGG within a gene called *FMR1*. In normal populations, the number of repeats is small, averaging 29. The expansions of the trinucleotide sequences prevent normal expression of the *FMR1* gene, thus giving rise to mental retardation. Another distinguishing feature of trinucleotide repeat mutations is that they are dynamic (i.e., the degree of amplification increases during gametogenesis). These features, discussed in greater detail later in this chapter, influence the pattern of inheritance and the phenotypic manifestations of the diseases caused by this class of mutations.

Alterations in Protein-Coding Genes Other Than Mutations

In addition to alterations in DNA sequence, coding genes also can undergo structural variations, such as copy number changes (amplifications or deletions), or translocations, resulting in aberrant gain or loss of protein function. As with mutations, structural changes may occur in the germline, or be acquired in somatic tissues. In many instances, pathogenic germ line alterations can involve a contiguous portion of a chromosome rather than a single gene, such as in the 22q microdeletion syndrome, discussed later on. With the widespread availability of array technology for assessing genome-wide DNA copy number variation at very high resolution, pathogenic structural alterations have now been discovered in common disorders such as autism. Cancers often contain somatically acquired structural alterations, including amplifications, deletions, and translocations. The so-called Philadelphia chromosome—translocation t(9;22) between the *BCR* and *ABL* genes in chronic myelogenous leukemia (Chapter 11)—is a classic example.

Sequence and Copy Number Variations (Polymorphisms)

A surprising revelation from the recent progress in genomics is that, on average, any two individuals share greater than 99.5% of their DNA sequences. Thus, the remarkable diversity of humans is encoded in less than 0.5% of our DNA. Though small when compared to the total nucleotide sequences, this 0.5% represents about 15 million base pairs. The two most common forms of DNA variations (polymorphisms) in the human genome are single-nucleotide polymorphisms (SNPs) and copy number variations (CNVs).

- SNPs represent variation at single isolated nucleotide positions and are almost always biallelic (i.e., one of only two choices exist at a given site within the population, such as A or T). Much effort has been devoted to making SNP maps of the human genome. These efforts have identified over 6 million SNPs in the human population, many of which show wide variation in frequency in different populations. SNPs may occur anywhere in the genome—within exons, introns, or intergenic regions—but less than 1% of SNPs occurs in coding regions. These coding sequence variations are important, since they could alter the gene product and predispose to a phenotypic difference or to a disease. Much more commonly, however, the SNP is just a marker that is co-inherited with a disease-associated gene as a result of physical proximity. Another way of expressing this is to say that the SNP and the causative genetic factor are in linkage disequilibrium. There is optimism that groups of SNPs could serve as reliable markers of risk for multigenic complex diseases such as type II diabetes and hypertension, and that by identifying such variants, strategies for disease prevention could be developed (discussed later).
- CNVs are a recently identified form of genetic variation consisting of different numbers of large contiguous stretches of DNA from 1000 base pairs to millions of base pairs. In some instances these loci are, like SNPs, biallelic and simply duplicated or deleted in a subset of

the population. In other instances there are complex rearrangements of genomic material, with multiple alleles in the human population. Current estimates are that CNVs are responsible for between 5 and 24 million base pairs of sequence difference between any two individuals. Approximately 50% of CNVs involve gene-coding sequences; thus, CNVs may underlie a large portion of human phenotypic diversity. There is a significant overrepresentation of certain gene families in regions affected by CNVs; these include genes involved in the immune system and in the nervous system. It is assumed that copy number diversity in such gene families has been subject to strong evolutionary selection, since they would enhance human adaptation to changing environmental factors.

Epigenetic Changes

Epigenetic changes are those involving modulation of gene or protein expression in the absence of alterations in DNA sequence (i.e., mutation) or structure of the encoding gene. Epigenetic regulation is of critical importance during development, as well as in homeostasis of fully developed tissues. One central mechanism of epigenetic regulation is by alterations in the methylation of cytosine residues at gene promoters—heavily methylated promoters become inaccessible to RNA polymerase, leading to transcriptional silencing. Promoter methylation and silencing of tumor suppressor genes (Chapter 5) commonly are observed in many human cancers, leading to unchecked cell growth and proliferation. Another major player in epigenetic regulation of transcription involves the family of *histone proteins,* which are components of structures called nucleosomes, around which DNA is coiled. Histone proteins undergo a variety of reversible modifications (e.g., methylation, acetylation) that affect secondary and tertiary DNA structure, and hence, gene transcription. As expected, abnormalities of histone modification are observed in many acquired diseases such as cancer, leading to transcriptional deregulation. Physiologic epigenetic silencing during development is called *imprinting,* and disorders of imprinting are discussed later on.

Alterations in Non-Coding RNAs

It is worth noting that until recently the major focus of gene hunting has been discovery of genes that encode for proteins. Recent studies indicate, however, that a very large number of genes do not encode proteins. Instead, the non-encoded products of these genes—so-called "non-coding RNAs (ncRNAs)"—play important regulatory functions. Although many distinct families of ncRNAs exist, here we will only discuss two examples: small RNA molecules called *microRNAs (miRNAs),* and *long non-coding RNAs (lncRNAs)* (the latter encompasses ncRNAs >200 nucleotides in length). The miRNAs, unlike messenger RNAs, do not encode proteins but instead inhibit the translation of target mRNAs into their corresponding proteins. Posttranscriptional silencing of gene expression by miRNA is preserved in all living forms from plants to humans and is therefore a fundamental mechanism of gene regulation. Because of their profound influence on gene regulation, miRNAs are assuming central importance in efforts to elucidate normal developmental pathways, as well as pathologic conditions, such as cancer. Andrew Fire and Craig Mello were awarded the Nobel prize in physiology or medicine in 2006 for their work on miRNAs.

By current estimates, there are approximately 1000 genes in humans that encode miRNAs. Transcription of miRNA genes produces primary miRNA transcript (pri-miRNA), which is processed within the nucleus to form another structure called pre-miRNA (Fig. 6–1). With the

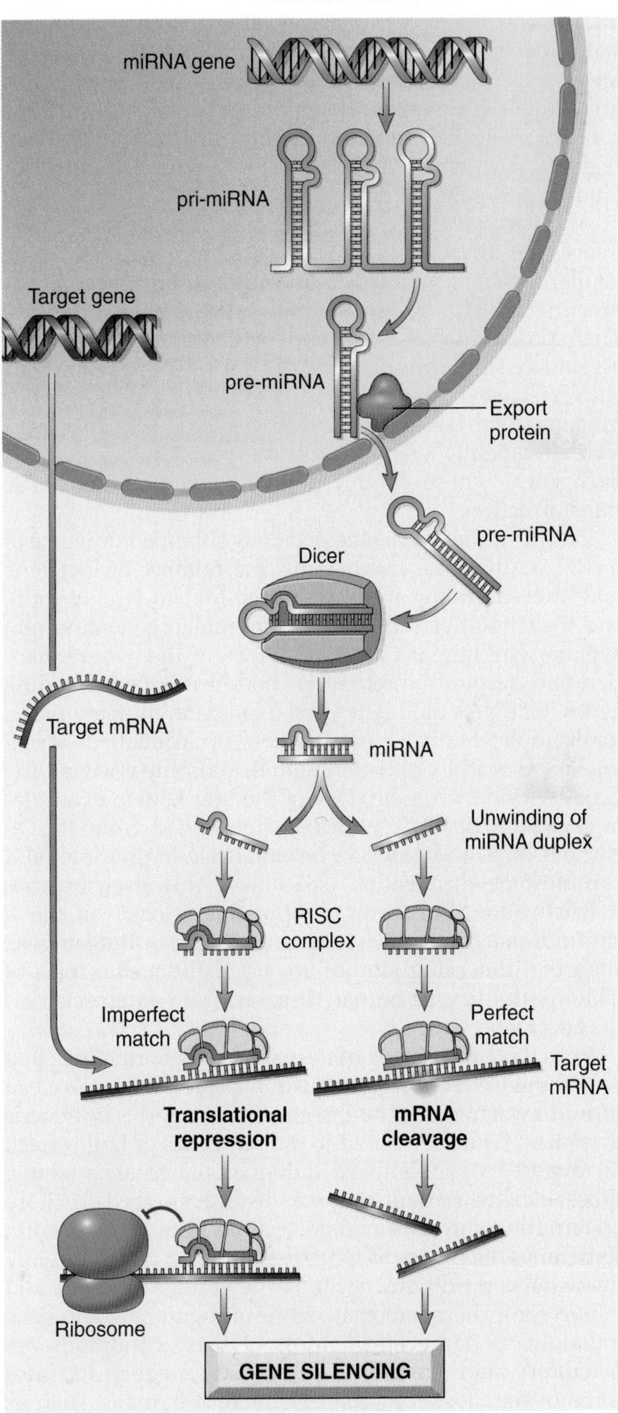

Figure 6–1 Generation of microRNAs and their mode of action in regulating gene function. pri-miRNA, primary microRNA transcript; pre-miRNA, precursor microRNA; RISC, RNA-induced silencing complex.

help of specific transporter proteins, pre-miRNA is exported to the cytoplasm. Additional "cutting" by an enzyme, appropriately called Dicer, generates mature miRNAs that are about 21 to 30 nucleotides in length (hence the designation *micro-*). At this stage the miRNA is still double-stranded. Next, the miRNA unwinds, and single strands of this duplex are incorporated into a multiprotein complex called RNA-induced silencing complex (RISC). Base pairing between the miRNA strand and its target mRNA directs the RISC to either cause mRNA cleavage or repress its translation. In this way, the gene from which the target mRNA was derived is silenced (at a post-transcriptional state). Given that the numbers of miRNA genes are far fewer than those that encode proteins, it follows that a given miRNA can silence many target genes. All mRNAs contain a so-called seed sequence in their 3′ untranslated region (UTR), which determines the specificity of miRNA binding and gene silencing.

Another species of gene-silencing RNA, called small interfering RNAs (siRNAs), works in a manner quite similar to that of miRNA. Unlike miRNA, however, siRNA precursors are introduced by investigators into the cell. Their processing by Dicer and functioning via RISC are essentially similar to that described for miRNA. Synthetic siRNAs have become powerful tools for studying gene function in the laboratory, and are being developed as possible therapeutic agents to silence specific genes, such as oncogenes, whose products are involved in neoplastic transformation.

Recent studies have elucidated an untapped universe of lncRNAs (by some calculations, the number of lncRNAs may exceed coding mRNAs by ten-fold to twenty-fold), and their putative functions in the human genome might explain why humans are at the apex of the evolutionary pyramid despite the relatively modest number of coding genes. lncRNAs modulate gene expression in many ways; for example, they can bind to regions of chromatin, restricting access of RNA polymerase to the encompassed coding genes within the region. One of the best known examples of lncRNAs is XIST, which is transcribed from the X-chromosome, and plays an essential role in physiologic X chromosome inactivation (see later). XIST itself escapes X inactivation, but forms a repressive "cloak" on the X chromosome from which it is transcribed, resulting in gene silencing. Emerging studies are highlighting the roles of lncRNAs in various human diseases, from atherosclerosis to cancer.

With this brief review of the nature of abnormalities that contribute to the pathogenesis of human diseases, we can turn our attention to the three major categories of genetic disorders: (1) those related to mutant genes of large effect, (2) diseases with complex multigenic inheritance (sometimes known as multifactorial disorders), and (3) those arising from chromosomal aberrations. The first category, sometimes referred to as *mendelian disorders,* includes many uncommon conditions, such as the storage diseases and inborn errors of metabolism, all resulting from single-gene mutations of large effect. Most of these conditions are hereditary and familial. The second category includes some of the most common disorders of humans, such as hypertension and diabetes mellitus. Multifactorial, or complex, inheritance implies that both genetic and environmental influences condition the expression of a phenotypic characteristic or disease. The third category includes disorders that are the consequence of numeric or structural abnormalities in the chromosomes.

To these three well-known categories, it is necessary to add a heterogeneous group of genetic disorders that, like mendelian disorders, involve single genes but do not follow simple mendelian rules of inheritance. These single-gene disorders with nonclassic inheritance patterns include those resulting from triplet repeat mutations, those arising from mutations in mitochondrial DNA, and those in which the transmission is influenced by an epigenetic phenomenon called *genomic imprinting.* Each of these four categories is discussed separately.

MENDELIAN DISORDERS: DISEASES CAUSED BY SINGLE-GENE DEFECTS

Single-gene defects (mutations) follow the well-known mendelian patterns of inheritance (Tables 6–1 and 6–2). Although individually each is rare, altogether they account for approximately 1% of all adult admissions to hospitals and about 6% to 8% of all pediatric hospital admissions. Listed next are a few important tenets and caveats of relevance in a consideration of mendelian disorders:

- Mutations involving single genes follow one of three patterns of inheritance: autosomal dominant, autosomal recessive, or X-linked.
- A single-gene mutation may lead to many phenotypic effects (*pleiotropy*), and conversely, mutations at several genetic loci may produce the same trait (*genetic heterogeneity*). For example, Marfan syndrome, which results from a basic defect in connective tissue, is associated

Table 6–1 Estimated Prevalence of Selected Mendelian Disorders Among Liveborn Infants

Disorder	Estimated Prevalence
Autosomal Dominant Inheritance	
Familial hypercholesterolemia	1 in 500
Polycystic kidney disease	1 in 1000
Hereditary spherocytosis	1 in 5000 (Northern Europe)
Marfan syndrome	1 in 5000
Huntington disease	1 in 10,000
Autosomal Recessive Inheritance	
Sickle cell anemia	1 in 500 (U.S. African Americans)*
Cystic fibrosis	1 in 3200 (U.S. Caucasians)
Tay-Sachs disease	1 in 3500 (U.S. Ashkenazi Jewish; French Canadians)
Phenylketonuria	1 in 10,000
Mucopolysaccharidoses—all types	1 in 25,000
Glycogen storage diseases—all types	1 in 50,000
Galactosemia	1 in 60,000
X-Linked Inheritance	
Duchenne muscular dystrophy	1 in 3500 (U.S. males)
Hemophilia	1 in 5000 (U.S. males)

*The prevalence of heterozygous sickle cell *trait* is 1 in 12 for U.S. African Americans.

Table 6–2 Biochemical Basis and Inheritance Pattern for Selected Mendelian Disorders

Disease	Abnormal Protein	Protein Type/Function
Autosomal Dominant Inheritance		
Familial hypercholesterolemia	Low-density lipoprotein receptor	Receptor transport
Marfan syndrome	Fibrillin	Structural support: extracellular matrix
Ehlers-Danlos syndrome*	Collagen	Structural support: extracellular matrix
Hereditary spherocytosis	Spectrin, ankyrin, or protein 4.1	Structural support: red blood cell membrane
Neurofibromatosis, type 1	Neurofibromin-1 (NF-1)	Growth regulation
Adult polycystic kidney disease	Polycystin-1 (PKD-1)	Cell–cell and cell–matrix interactions
Autosomal Recessive Inheritance		
Cystic fibrosis	Cystic fibrosis transmembrane regulator	Ion channel
Phenylketonuria	Phenylalanine hydroxylase	Enzyme
Tay-Sachs disease	Hexosaminidase	Enzyme
Severe combined immunodeficiency	Adenosine deaminase	Enzyme
α- and β-Thalassemias†	Hemoglobin	Oxygen transport
Sickle cell anemia†	Hemoglobin	Oxygen transport
X-linked Recessive Inheritance		
Hemophilia A	Factor VIII	Coagulation
Duchenne/Becker muscular dystrophy	Dystrophin	Structural support: cell membrane
Fragile X syndrome	FMRP	RNA translation

*Some variants of Ehlers-Danlos syndrome have an autosomal recessive inheritance pattern.
†Although full-blown symptoms require biallelic mutations, heterozygotes for thalassemia and sickle cell anemia may present with mild clinical disease. Thus, these disorders sometimes are categorized as "autosomal codominant" entities.

with widespread effects involving the skeleton, eye, and cardiovascular system, all of which stem from a mutation in the gene encoding fibrillin, a component of connective tissues. On the other hand, retinitis pigmentosa, an inherited disorder associated with abnormal retinal pigmentation and consequent visual impairment, can be caused by several different types of mutations. Recognition of genetic heterogeneity not only is important in genetic counseling but also facilitates understanding of the pathogenesis of common disorders such as diabetes mellitus (Chapter 19).

- It is now increasingly being recognized that even known "single-gene" diseases are influenced by inheritance at other genetic loci, which are called *modifier* genes. As discussed later in the section on cystic fibrosis, these modifier loci can affect the severity or extent of the disease.
- The use of proactive prenatal genetic screening in high-risk populations (e.g., persons of Ashkenazi Jewish descent) has significantly reduced the incidence (Table 6–1) of certain genetic disorders such as Tay-Sachs disease.

Transmission Patterns of Single-Gene Disorders

Disorders of Autosomal Dominant Inheritance

Disorders of autosomal dominant inheritance are manifested in the heterozygous state, so at least one parent in an index case usually is affected; both males and females are affected, and both can transmit the condition. When an affected person marries an unaffected one, every child has one chance in two of having the disease. The following features also pertain to autosomal dominant diseases:

- With any autosomal dominant disorder, some patients do not have affected parents. Such patients owe their disorder to new mutations involving either the egg or the sperm from which they were derived. Their siblings are neither affected nor at increased risk for development of the disease.
- Clinical features can be modified by reduced penetrance and variable expressivity. Some persons inherit the mutant gene but are phenotypically normal. This mode of expression is referred to as *reduced penetrance.* The variables that affect penetrance are not clearly understood. In contrast with penetrance, if a trait is consistently associated with a mutant gene but is expressed differently among persons carrying the gene, the phenomenon is called *variable expressivity.* For example, manifestations of neurofibromatosis 1 range from brownish spots on the skin to multiple tumors and skeletal deformities.
- In many conditions, the age at onset is delayed, and symptoms and signs do not appear until adulthood (as in Huntington disease).
- In autosomal dominant disorders, a 50% reduction in the normal gene product is associated with clinical signs and symptoms. Because a 50% loss of enzyme activity can be compensated for, involved genes in autosomal dominant disorders usually do not encode enzyme proteins, but instead fall into two other categories of proteins:
    - Those involved in regulation of complex metabolic pathways, often subject to feedback control (e.g., membrane receptors, transport proteins). An example of this mechanism of inheritance is familial hypercholesterolemia, which results from mutation in the

low-density lipoprotein (LDL) receptor gene (discussed later).
   - Key structural proteins, such as collagen and cytoskeletal components of the red cell membrane (e.g., spectrin, abnormalities of which result in hereditary spherocytosis)

The biochemical mechanisms by which a 50% reduction in the levels of such proteins results in an abnormal phenotype are not fully understood. In some cases, especially when the gene encodes one subunit of a multimeric protein, the product of the mutant allele can interfere with the assembly of a functionally normal multimer. For example, the collagen molecule is a trimer in which the three collagen chains are arranged in a helical configuration. Even with a single mutant collagen chain, normal collagen trimers cannot be formed, so there is a marked deficiency of collagen. In this instance the mutant allele is called *dominant negative,* because it impairs the function of a normal allele. This effect is illustrated in some forms of osteogenesis imperfecta (Chapter 20).

Disorders of Autosomal Recessive Inheritance

Disorders of autosomal recessive inheritance make up the largest group of mendelian disorders. They occur when both of the alleles at a given gene locus are mutants; therefore, such disorders are characterized by the following features: (1) The trait does not usually affect the parents, but siblings may show the disease; (2) siblings have one chance in four of being affected (i.e., the recurrence risk is 25% for each birth); and (3) if the mutant gene occurs with a low frequency in the population, there is a strong likelihood that the affected patient (the proband) is the product of a consanguineous marriage.

In contrast with the features of autosomal dominant diseases, the following features generally apply to most autosomal recessive disorders:

- The expression of the defect tends to be more uniform than in autosomal dominant disorders.
- Complete penetrance is common.
- Onset is frequently early in life.
- Although new mutations for recessive disorders do occur, they are rarely detected clinically. Because the affected person is an asymptomatic heterozygote, several generations may pass before the descendants of such a person mate with other heterozygotes and produce affected offspring.
- In many cases, enzyme proteins are affected by the mutation. In heterozygotes, equal amounts of normal and defective enzyme are synthesized. Usually the natural "margin of safety" ensures that cells with half of their complement of the enzyme function normally.

X-Linked Disorders

All sex-linked disorders are X-linked. No Y-linked diseases are known as yet. Save for determinants that dictate male differentiation, the only characteristic that may be located on the Y chromosome is the attribute of hairy ears, which is not altogether devastating. Most X-linked disorders are X-linked *recessive* and are characterized by the following features:

- They are transmitted by heterozygous female carriers only to sons, who of course are hemizygous for the X chromosome.
- Heterozygous females rarely express the full phenotypic change, because they have the paired normal allele; although one of the X chromosomes in females is inactivated (see further on), this process of inactivation is *random,* which typically allows sufficient numbers of cells with the normal expressed allele to emerge.
- An affected male does not transmit the disorder to sons, but all daughters are carriers. Sons of heterozygous women have one chance in two of receiving the mutant gene.

SUMMARY

Transmission Patterns of Single-Gene Disorders

- Autosomal dominant disorders are characterized by expression in heterozygous state; they affect males and females equally, and both sexes can transmit the disorder.
- Enzyme proteins are not affected in autosomal dominant disorders; instead, receptors and structural proteins are involved.
- Autosomal recessive diseases occur when both copies of a gene are mutated; enzyme proteins are frequently involved. Males and females are affected equally.
- X-linked disorders are transmitted by heterozygous females to their sons, who manifest the disease. Female carriers usually are protected because of random inactivation of one X chromosome.

Diseases Caused by Mutations in Genes Encoding Structural Proteins

Marfan Syndrome

In Marfan syndrome, a connective tissue disorder of autosomal dominant inheritance, the basic biochemical abnormality is a mutation affecting fibrillin. This glycoprotein, secreted by fibroblasts, is the major component of microfibrils found in the extracellular matrix. Microfibrils serve as scaffolding for the deposition of tropoelastin, an integral component of elastic fibers. Although microfibrils are widely distributed in the body, they are particularly abundant in the aorta, ligaments, and the ciliary zonules that support the ocular lens; these tissues are prominently affected in Marfan syndrome.

Fibrillin is encoded by the *FBN1* gene, which maps to chromosomal locus 15q21. Mutations in the *FBN1* gene are found in all patients with Marfan syndrome. However, molecular diagnosis of Marfan syndrome is not yet feasible, because more than 600 distinct causative mutations in the very large *FBN1* gene have been found. Since heterozygotes have clinical symptoms, it follows that the mutant fibrillin protein must act as a dominant negative by preventing the assembly of normal microfibrils. The prevalence of Marfan syndrome is estimated to be 1 per 5000. Approximately 70% to 85% of cases are familial, and the rest are sporadic, arising from de novo *FBN1* mutations in the germ cells of parents.

While many of the abnormalities in Marfan syndrome can be explained on the basis of structural failure of connective tissues, some, such as overgrowth of bones, are difficult to relate to simple loss of fibrillin. Recent studies indicate that loss of microfibrils gives rise to abnormal and excessive activation of transforming growth factor-β (TGF-β), since normal microfibrils sequester TGF-β, thereby controlling bioavailability of this cytokine. Excessive TGF-β signaling has deleterious effects on vascular smooth muscle development and the integrity of extracellular matrix. In support of this hypothesis, mutations in the TGF-β type II receptor give rise to a related syndrome, called Marfan syndrome type 2 (MFS2). Of note, angiotensin receptor blockers, which inhibit the activity of TGF-β, have been shown to improve aortic and cardiac function in mouse models of Marfan syndrome and currently are being evaluated in clinical trials.

MORPHOLOGY

Skeletal abnormalities are the most obvious feature of Marfan syndrome. Patients have a slender, elongated habitus with abnormally long legs, arms, and fingers (arachnodactyly); a high-arched palate; and hyperextensibility of joints. A variety of spinal deformities, such as severe kyphoscoliosis, may be present. The chest is deformed, exhibiting either pectus excavatum (i.e., deeply depressed sternum) or a pigeon-breast deformity. The most characteristic **ocular change** is bilateral dislocation, or subluxation, of the lens secondary to weakness of its suspensory ligaments **(ectopia lentis).** This abnormality is so uncommon in persons who do not have this genetic disease that the finding of bilateral ectopia lentis should raise the diagnostic possibility of Marfan syndrome. Most serious, however, is the involvement of the **cardiovascular system.** Fragmentation of the elastic fibers in the tunica media of the aorta predisposes affected patients to aneurysmal dilation and aortic dissection (Chapter 9). These changes, called **cystic medionecrosis,** are not specific for Marfan syndrome. Similar lesions occur in hypertension and with aging. Loss of medial support causes dilation of the aortic valve ring, giving rise to aortic incompetence. The cardiac valves, especially the mitral valve, may be excessively distensible and regurgitant **(floppy valve syndrome),** giving rise to mitral valve prolapse and congestive cardiac failure (Chapter 10). Death from aortic rupture may occur at any age, and aortic rupture is in fact the most common cause of death. Less commonly, cardiac failure is the terminal event.

Although the lesions described are typical of Marfan syndrome, they are not seen in all cases. There is much variation in clinical expression, and some patients may exhibit predominantly cardiovascular lesions with minimal skeletal and ocular changes. The variable expressivity is believed to be related to different allelic mutations in the *FBN1* gene.

Ehlers-Danlos Syndromes

Ehlers-Danlos syndromes (EDSs) are a group of diseases characterized by defects in collagen synthesis or structure. All are single-gene disorders, but the mode of inheritance encompasses both autosomal dominant and recessive patterns. There are approximately 30 distinct types of collagen; all have characteristic tissue distributions and are the products of different genes. To some extent, the clinical heterogeneity of EDS can be explained by mutations in different collagen genes.

At least six clinical and genetic variants of EDS are recognized. Because defective collagen is the basis for these disorders, certain clinical features are common to all variants.

As might be expected, tissues rich in collagen, such as skin, ligaments, and joints, frequently are involved in most variants of EDS. Because the abnormal collagen fibers lack adequate tensile strength, the *skin is hyperextensible and joints are hypermobile.* These features permit grotesque contortions, such as bending the thumb backward to touch the forearm and bending the knee upward to create almost a right angle. Indeed, it is believed that most contortionists have one of the EDSs; however, a predisposition to joint dislocation is one of the prices paid for this virtuosity. *The skin is extraordinarily stretchable, extremely fragile,* and *vulnerable to trauma.* Minor injuries produce gaping defects, and surgical repair or any surgical intervention is accomplished only with great difficulty because of the lack of normal tensile strength. The basic defect in connective tissue may lead to serious internal complications, including rupture of the colon and large arteries (vascular EDS); ocular fragility, with rupture of the cornea and retinal detachment (kyphoscoliotic EDS); and diaphragmatic hernias (classical EDS), among others.

The molecular bases for three of the more common variants are as follows:

- *Deficiency of the enzyme lysyl hydroxylase.* Decreased hydroxylation of lysyl residues in types I and III collagen interferes with the formation of cross-links among collagen molecules. As might be expected, this variant (kyphoscoliotic EDS), resulting from an enzyme deficiency, is inherited as an autosomal recessive disorder.
- *Deficient synthesis of type III collagen resulting from mutations affecting the COL3A1* gene. This variant, the vascular type, is inherited as an autosomal dominant disorder and is characterized by weakness of tissues rich in type III collagen (e.g., blood vessels, bowel wall), predisposing them to rupture.
- *Deficient synthesis of type V collagen* due to mutations in *COL5A1* and *COL5A2* is inherited as an autosomal dominant disorder and results in classical EDS.

SUMMARY

Marfan Syndrome

- Marfan syndrome is caused by a mutation in the *FBN1* gene encoding fibrillin, which is required for structural integrity of connective tissues.
- The major tissues affected are the skeleton, eyes, and cardiovascular system.
- Clinical features may include tall stature, long fingers, bilateral subluxation of lens, mitral valve prolapse, aortic aneurysm, and aortic dissection.
- Clinical trials with drugs that inhibit TGF-β signaling such as angiotensin receptor blockers are ongoing, as these have been shown to improve aortic and cardiac function in mouse models.

Ehlers-Danlos Syndromes

- There are six variants of Ehlers-Danlos syndromes, all characterized by defects in collagen synthesis or assembly. Each of the variants is caused by a distinct mutation.
- Clinical features may include fragile, hyperextensible skin vulnerable to trauma, hypermobile joints, and ruptures involving colon, cornea, or large arteries. Wound healing is poor.

Diseases Caused by Mutations in Genes Encoding Receptor Proteins or Channels

Familial Hypercholesterolemia

Familial hypercholesterolemia is among the most common mendelian disorders; the frequency of the heterozygous condition is 1 in 500 in the general population. It is caused by a mutation in the *LDLR* gene that encodes the receptor for low-density lipoprotein (LDL), the form in which 70% of total plasma cholesterol is transported. A brief review of the synthesis and transport of cholesterol follows.

Normal Cholesterol Metabolism. Cholesterol may be derived from the diet or from endogenous synthesis. Dietary triglycerides and cholesterol are incorporated into chylomicrons in the intestinal mucosa, which drain by way of the gut lymphatics into the blood. These chylomicrons are hydrolyzed by an endothelial lipoprotein lipase in the capillaries of muscle and fat. The chylomicron remnants, rich in cholesterol, are then delivered to the liver. Some of the cholesterol enters the metabolic pool (to be described), and some is excreted as free cholesterol or bile acids into the biliary tract. The endogenous synthesis of cholesterol and LDL begins in the liver (Fig. 6–2). The first step in the synthesis of LDL is the secretion of triglyceride-rich very-low-density lipoprotein (VLDL) by the liver into the blood. In the capillaries of adipose tissue and muscle, the VLDL particle undergoes lipolysis and is converted to intermediate-density lipoprotein (IDL). In comparison with VLDL, the content of triglyceride is reduced and that of cholesteryl esters enriched in intermediate-density lipoprotein (IDL), but IDL retains on its surface two of the three VLDL-associated apolipoproteins B-100 and E. Further metabolism of IDL occurs along two pathways: Most of the IDL particles are directly taken up by the liver through the LDL receptor described later; others are converted to cholesterol-rich LDL by a further loss of triglycerides and apolipoprotein E. In the liver cells, IDL is recycled to generate VLDL.

Two thirds of the resultant LDL particles are metabolized by the LDL receptor pathway, and the rest is metabolized by a receptor for oxidized LDL (scavenger receptor), to be described later. The LDL receptor binds to apolipoproteins B-100 and E and thus is involved in the transport of both LDL and IDL. *Although the LDL receptors are widely distributed, approximately 75% are located on hepatocytes, so the liver plays an extremely important role in LDL metabolism.* The first step in the receptor-mediated transport of LDL involves binding to the cell surface receptor, followed by endocytotic internalization inside so-called "clathrin-coated pits" (Fig. 6–3). Within the cell, the endocytic vesicles fuse with the lysosomes, and the LDL molecule is enzymatically degraded, resulting ultimately in the release of free cholesterol into the cytoplasm. *The cholesterol not only is used by the cell for membrane synthesis but also takes part in intracellular cholesterol homeostasis by a sophisticated system of feedback control*:

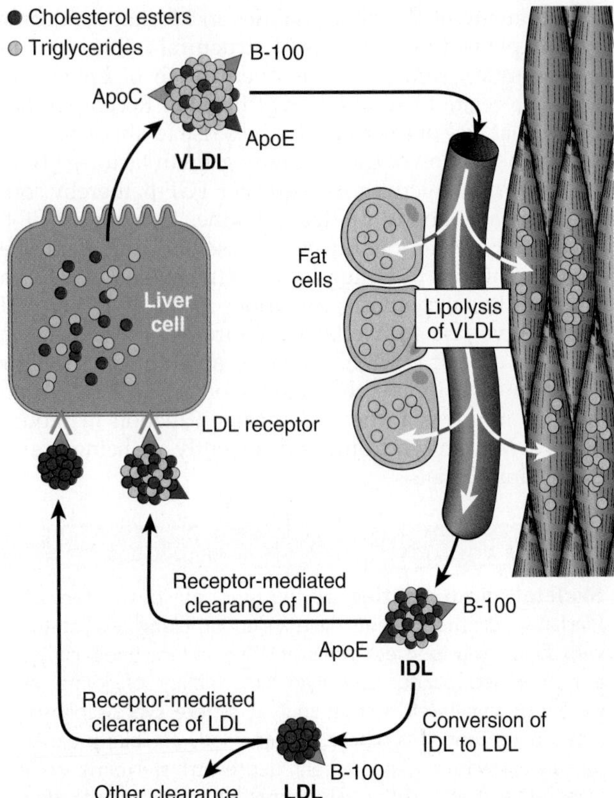

Figure 6–2 Low-density lipoprotein (LDL) metabolism and the role of the liver in its synthesis and clearance. Lipolysis of very-low-density lipoprotein (VLDL) by lipoprotein lipase in the capillaries releases triglycerides, which are then stored in fat cells and used as a source of energy in skeletal muscles. IDL (intermediate-density lipoprotein) remains in the blood and is taken up by the liver.

- It suppresses cholesterol synthesis by inhibiting the activity of the enzyme 3-hydroxy-3-methylglutaryl–coenzyme A reductase (HMG-CoA reductase), which is the rate-limiting enzyme in the synthetic pathway.
- It stimulates the formation of cholesterol esters for storage of excess cholesterol.
- It downregulates the synthesis of cell surface LDL receptors, thus protecting cells from excessive accumulation of cholesterol.

The transport of LDL by the scavenger receptors, alluded to earlier, seems to take place in cells of the mononuclear-phagocyte system and possibly in other cells as well. Monocytes and macrophages have receptors for chemically modified (e.g., acetylated or oxidized) LDLs. The amount catabolized by this "scavenger receptor" pathway is directly related to the plasma cholesterol level.

PATHOGENESIS OF FAMILIAL HYPERCHOLESTEROLEMIA

In familial hypercholesterolemia, mutations in the LDL receptor protein impair the intracellular transport and catabolism of LDL, resulting in accumulation of LDL cholesterol in the plasma. In addition, the absence of LDL receptors on liver cells also impairs the transport of IDL into the liver, so a greater proportion of plasma IDL is converted into LDL. Thus, patients with familial hypercholesterolemia develop excessive levels of serum cholesterol as a result of the combined effects of reduced catabolism and excessive biosynthesis (Fig. 6–2). In the presence of such hypercholesterolemia, there is a marked increase of cholesterol traffic into the monocyte-macrophages and vascular walls mediated by the scavenger receptor. This accounts for the appearance of skin xanthomas and premature atherosclerosis.

Familial hypercholesterolemia is an autosomal dominant disease. Heterozygotes have a two- to three-fold elevation of plasma cholesterol levels, whereas homozygotes may have in excess of a five-fold elevation. Although their cholesterol levels are elevated from birth, heterozygotes remain asymptomatic until adult life, when they develop cholesterol deposits (xanthomas) along tendon sheaths and premature atherosclerosis resulting in coronary artery disease. Homozygotes are much more severely affected, developing cutaneous xanthomas in childhood and often dying of myocardial infarction before the age of 20 years.

Analysis of the cloned LDL receptor gene has revealed that more than 900 different mutations can give rise to familial hypercholesterolemia. These can be divided into five categories. Class I mutations are uncommon, and they are associated with complete loss of receptor synthesis. With class II mutations, the most prevalent form, the receptor protein is synthesized, but its transport from the endoplasmic reticulum to the Golgi apparatus is impaired due to defects in protein folding. Class III mutations produce receptors that are transported to the cell surface but fail to bind LDL normally. Class IV mutations give rise to receptors that fail to internalize within clathrin pits after binding to LDL, while class V mutations encode receptors that can bind LDL and are internalized but are trapped in endosomes because dissociation of receptor and bound LDL does not occur.

The discovery of the critical role of LDL receptors in cholesterol homeostasis has led to the rational design of the statin family of drugs that are now widely used to lower plasma cholesterol. They inhibit the activity of HMG-CoA reductase and thus promote greater synthesis of LDL receptor (Fig. 6–3).

SUMMARY

Familial Hypercholesterolemia

- Familial hypercholesterolemia is an autosomal dominant disorder caused by mutations in the gene encoding the LDL receptor.
- Patients develop hypercholesterolemia as a consequence of impaired transport of LDL into the cells.
- In heterozygotes, elevated serum cholesterol greatly increases the risk of atherosclerosis and resultant coronary artery disease; homozygotes have an even greater increase in serum cholesterol and a higher frequency of ischemic heart disease. Cholesterol also deposits along tendon sheaths to produce xanthomas.

Cystic Fibrosis

With an incidence of 1 in 3200 live births in the United States, *cystic fibrosis (CF) is the most common lethal genetic disease that affects white populations.* It is uncommon among Asians (1 in 31,000 live births) and African Americans (1 in 15,000 live births). CF follows simple *autosomal recessive* transmission, and does not affect heterozygote carriers. There is, however, a bewildering compendium of phenotypic variation that results from diverse mutations in the CF-associated gene, the tissue-specific effects of loss of this gene's function, and the influence of newly recognized disease modifiers. It is, fundamentally, a *disorder of epithelial transport affecting fluid secretion in exocrine glands and the epithelial lining of the respiratory, gastrointestinal, and reproductive tracts.* Indeed, abnormally viscid mucous secretions that block the airways and the pancreatic ducts are responsible for the two most important clinical manifestations: recurrent and chronic pulmonary infections and pancreatic insufficiency. In addition, although the exocrine sweat glands are structurally normal (and remain so throughout the course of this disease), *a high level of sodium chloride in the sweat is a consistent and characteristic biochemical abnormality in CF.*

PATHOGENESIS

The primary defect in CF is abnormal function of an epithelial chloride channel protein encoded by the CF transmembrane conductance regulator (*CFTR*) gene at chromosomal locus 7q31.2. The changes in mucus are considered secondary to the disturbance in transport of chloride ions. In normal epithelia, the transport of chloride ions across the cell membrane occurs through transmembrane proteins, such as CFTR, that form chloride channels. Mutations in the *CFTR* gene render the epithelial membranes relatively impermeable to chloride ions (Fig. 6–4). However, the impact of this defect on transport function is tissue-specific. The major function of the CFTR protein in the sweat gland ducts is to reabsorb luminal chloride ions and augment sodium reabsorption through the epithelial sodium channel (ENaC). Therefore, in the sweat ducts, loss of CFTR function leads to decreased reabsorption of sodium chloride and production of hypertonic ("salty") sweat (Fig. 6–4, *top*). In contrast with that in the sweat glands, CFTR in the respiratory and intestinal epithelium forms one of the most important avenues for active luminal secretion of chloride. At these sites, *CFTR* mutations result in loss or reduction of chloride secretion into the lumen (Fig. 6–4, *bottom*). Active luminal sodium absorption through ENaCs also is increased, and both of these ion changes increase passive water reabsorption from the lumen, lowering the water content of the surface fluid layer coating mucosal cells. Thus, unlike the sweat ducts, there is no difference in the salt concentration of the surface fluid layer coating the respiratory and intestinal mucosal cells in normal persons and in those with CF. Instead, the pathogenesis of respiratory and intestinal complications in CF seems to stem from an isotonic but low-volume surface fluid layer. In the lungs, this dehydration leads to defective mucociliary action and the accumulation of concentrated, viscid secretions that obstruct the air passages and predispose to recurrent pulmonary infections.

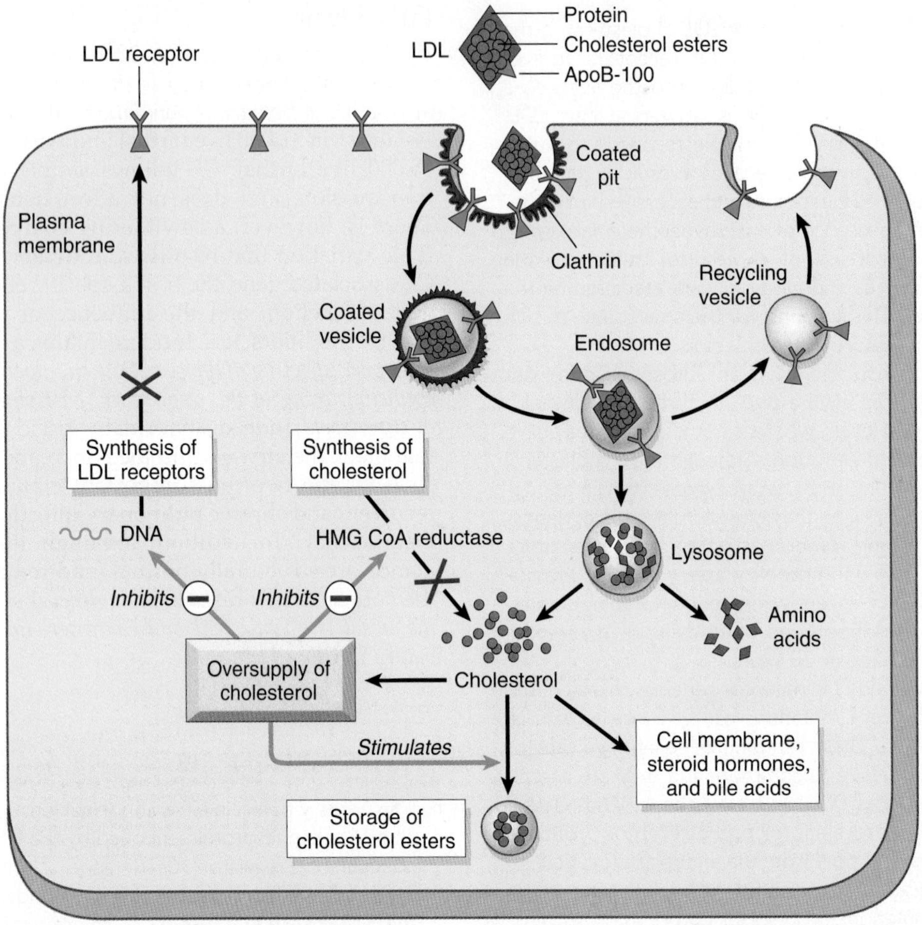

Figure 6–3 The LDL receptor pathway and regulation of cholesterol metabolism. The *yellow arrows* show three regulatory functions of free intracellular cholesterol: (1) suppression of cholesterol synthesis by inhibition of HMG-CoA reductase, (2) stimulating the storage of excess cholesterol as esters, and (3) inhibition of synthesis of LDL receptors. HMG-CoA reductase, 3-hydroxy-3-methylglutaryl–coenzyme A reductase; LDL, low-density lipoprotein.

Since the *CFTR* gene was cloned in 1989, more than 1300 disease-causing mutations have been identified. They can be classified as severe or mild, depending on the clinical phenotype: **Severe** mutations are associated with complete loss of CFTR protein function, whereas **mild** mutations allow some residual function. The most common severe *CFTR* mutation is a deletion of three nucleotides coding for phenylalanine at amino acid position 508 (*ΔF508*). This causes misfolding and total loss of the CFTR. Worldwide, *ΔF508* mutation is found in approximately 70% of patients with CF. Since CF is an autosomal recessive disease, affected persons harbor mutations on both alleles. As discussed later, the combination of mutations on the two alleles influences the overall phenotype, as well as organ-specific manifestations. Although CF remains one of the best-known examples of the "one gene–one disease" axiom, there is increasing evidence that other genes modify the frequency and severity of organ-specific manifestations. One example of a candidate genetic modifier is **mannose-binding lectin,** a key effector of innate immunity involved in phagocytosis of microorganisms. In the setting of CF, polymorphisms in one or both mannose-binding lectin alleles that produce lower circulating levels of the protein are associated with a three-fold higher risk of end-stage lung disease, due to chronic bacterial infections.

MORPHOLOGY

The anatomic changes are highly variable and depend on which glands are affected and on the severity of this involvement. **Pancreatic abnormalities** are present in 85% to 90% of patients with CF. In the milder cases, there may be only accumulations of mucus in the small ducts, with some dilation of the exocrine glands. In more advanced cases, usually seen in older children or adolescents, the ducts are totally plugged, causing atrophy of the exocrine glands and progressive fibrosis (Fig. 6–5). The total loss of pancreatic exocrine secretion impairs fat absorption, so avitaminosis A may contribute to squamous metaplasia of the lining epithelium of the ducts in the pancreas, which are already injured by the inspissated mucus secretions. Thick viscid plugs of mucus also may be found in the small intestine of infants. Sometimes these cause small bowel obstruction, known as **meconium ileus.**

The **pulmonary changes** are the most serious complications of this disease (Fig. 6–6). These changes stem from obstruction and infection of the air passages secondary to the viscous mucus secretions of the submucosal glands of the respiratory tree. The bronchioles often are distended with thick mucus, associated with marked hyperplasia and

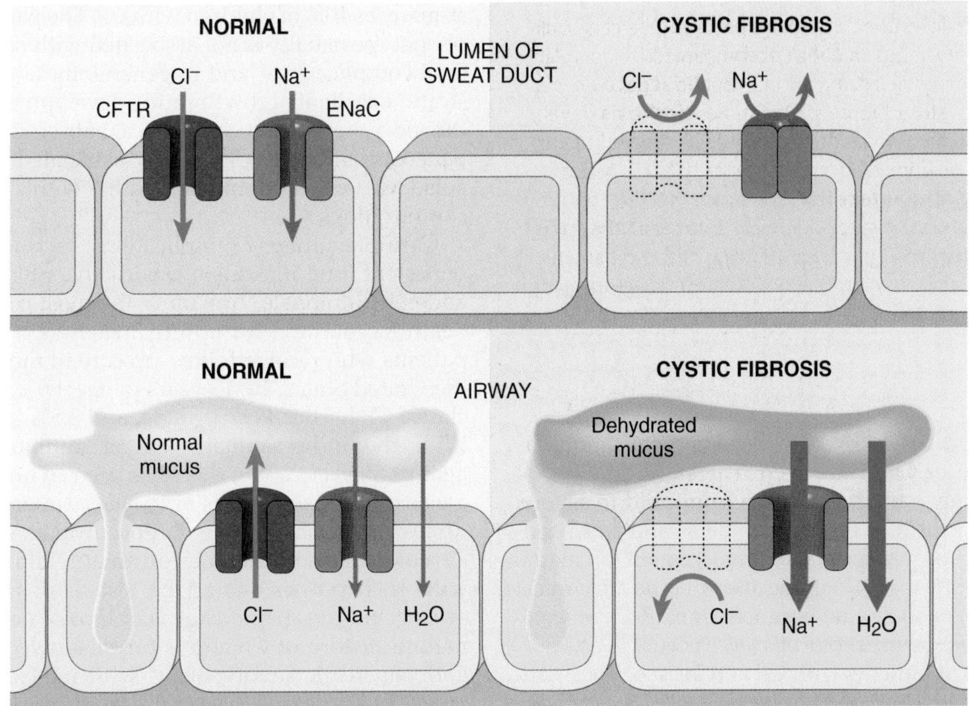

Figure 6–4 Top, In cystic fibrosis (CF), a chloride channel defect in the sweat duct causes increased chloride and sodium concentration in sweat. **Bottom,** Patients with CF have decreased chloride secretion and increased sodium and water reabsorption in the airways, leading to dehydration of the mucus layer coating epithelial cells, defective mucociliary action, and mucous plugging. CFTR, cystic fibrosis transmembrane conductance regulator; ENaC, epithelial sodium channel responsible for intracellular sodium conduction.

hypertrophy of the mucus-secreting cells. Superimposed infections give rise to severe chronic bronchitis and bronchiectasis. Development of lung abscesses is common. *Staphylococcus aureus, Haemophilus influenzae,* and *Pseudomonas aeruginosa* are the three most common organisms responsible for lung infections. Even more sinister is the increasing frequency of infection with another pseudomonad, *Burkholderia cepacia.* This opportunistic bacterium is particularly hardy, and infection with this organism has been associated with fulminant illness ("cepacia syndrome"). The **liver**

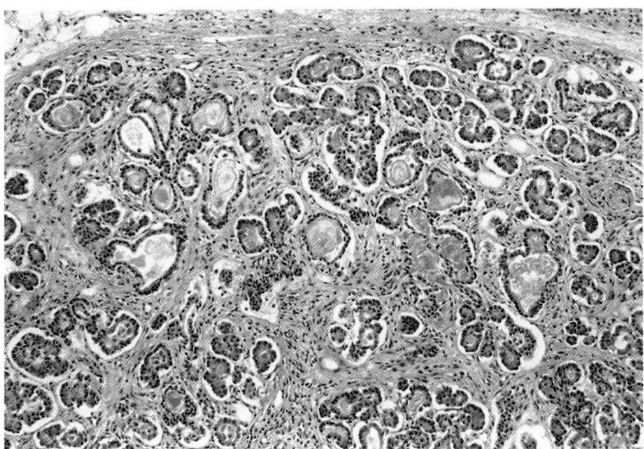

Figure 6–5 Mild to moderate changes of cystic fibrosis in the pancreas. The ducts are dilated and plugged with eosinophilic mucin, and the parenchymal glands are atrophic and replaced by fibrous tissue.

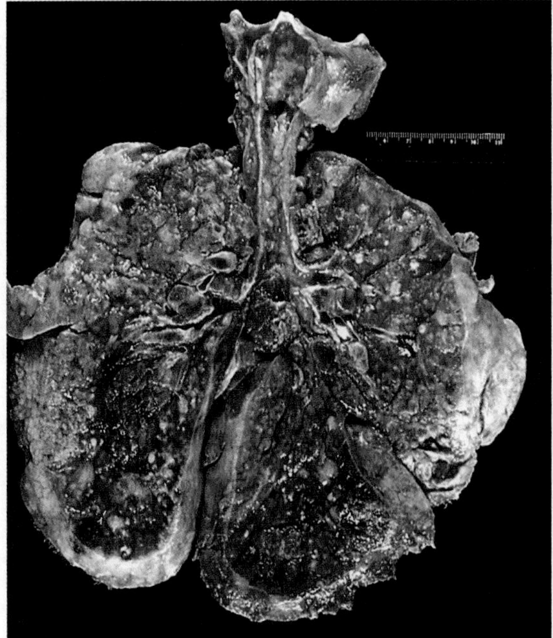

Figure 6–6 Lungs of a patient who died of cystic fibrosis. Extensive mucous plugging and dilation of the tracheobronchial tree are apparent. The pulmonary parenchyma is consolidated by a combination of both secretions and pneumonia; the *greenish* discoloration is the product of *Pseudomonas* infections.

(Courtesy of Dr. Eduardo Yunis, Children's Hospital of Pittsburgh, Pittsburgh, Pennsylvania.)

involvement follows the same basic pattern. Bile canaliculi are plugged by mucinous material, accompanied by ductular proliferation and portal inflammation. Hepatic **steatosis** is a common finding in liver biopsies. Over time, **cirrhosis** develops, resulting in diffuse hepatic nodularity. Such severe hepatic involvement is encountered in less than 10% of patients. **Azoospermia and infertility** are found in 95% of the affected males who survive to adulthood; **bilateral absence of the vas deferens** is a frequent finding in these patients. In some males, this may be the only feature suggesting an underlying *CFTR* mutation.

Clinical Course

In few childhood diseases are clinical manifestations as protean as those of CF (Table 6–3). The signs and symptoms are extremely varied and range from mild to severe, from presence at birth to onset years later, and from confinement to one organ system to involvement of many. Approximately 5% to 10% of the cases come to clinical attention at birth or soon after because of an attack of *meconium ileus. Exocrine pancreatic insufficiency* occurs in a majority (85% to 90%) of patients with CF and is associated with "severe" *CFTR* mutations on *both* alleles (e.g., *ΔF508/ΔF508*), whereas 10% to 15% of patients with one "severe" and one "mild" *CFTR* mutation, or two "mild" *CFTR* mutations, retain sufficient pancreatic exocrine function that enzyme supplementation is not required—the *pancreas-sufficient* phenotype. Pancreatic insufficiency is associated with malabsorption of protein and fat and increased fecal loss. Manifestations of malabsorption (e.g., large, foul-smelling stools; abdominal distention; poor weight gain) appear during the first year of life. The faulty fat absorption may induce deficiency states of the fat-soluble vitamins, resulting in manifestations of avitaminosis A, D, or K. Hypoproteinemia may be severe enough to cause generalized edema. Persistent diarrhea may result in rectal prolapse in as many as 10% of children with CF. The pancreas-sufficient phenotype usually is not associated with other gastrointestinal complications, and in general, these patients demonstrate excellent growth and development. *"Idiopathic" chronic pancreatitis* occurs in a subset of patients with pancreas-sufficient CF and is associated with recurring episodes of abdominal pain with life-threatening complications.

Cardiorespiratory complications, such as chronic cough, persistent lung infections, obstructive pulmonary disease, and cor pulmonale, constitute the most common cause of death (accounting for approximately 80% of fatalities) in patients who receive follow-up care in most CF centers in the United States. By 18 years of age, 80% of patients with classic CF harbor *P. aeruginosa,* and 3.5% harbor *B. cepacia.* With the indiscriminate use of antibiotic prophylaxis against *Staphylococcus,* there has been an unfortunate resurgence of resistant strains of *Pseudomonas* in many patients. *Recurrent sinonasal polyps* can occur in as many as 10% to 25% of patients with CF; accordingly, children who present with such polyps should be tested for abnormalities of sweat chloride. Significant *liver disease* occurs late in the natural history of CF and is foreshadowed by pulmonary and pancreatic involvement; with increasing life expectancy, liver disease is now the third most common cause of death in patients with CF (after cardiopulmonary and transplant-related complication).

In most cases, the diagnosis of CF is based on persistently elevated sweat electrolyte concentrations (often the mother makes the diagnosis because her infant "tastes salty"), characteristic clinical findings (sinopulmonary disease and gastrointestinal manifestations), or a family history. Sequencing the *CFTR* gene is, of course, the standard modality for diagnosis of CF. Therefore, in patients with clinical findings or family history (or both) suggestive of this disorder, genetic analysis may be warranted. Advances in management of CF have meant that more patients are now surviving to adulthood; the median life

Table 6–3 Clinical Features and Diagnostic Criteria for Cystic Fibrosis

Clinical Features of Cystic Fibrosis
1. Chronic sinopulmonary disease manifested by
a. Persistent colonization/infection with typical cystic fibrosis pathogens, including *Staphylococcus aureus*, nontypable *Haemophilus influenzae*, mucoid and nonmucoid *Pseudomonas aeruginosa*, *Burkholderia cepacia*
b. Chronic cough and sputum production
c. Persistent chest radiograph abnormalities (e.g., bronchiectasis, atelectasis, infiltrates, hyperinflation)
d. Airway obstruction manifested by wheezing and air trapping
e. Nasal polyps; radiographic or computed tomographic abnormalities of paranasal sinuses
f. Digital clubbing
2. Gastrointestinal and nutritional abnormalities, including
a. Intestinal: meconium ileus, distal intestinal obstruction syndrome, rectal prolapse
b. Pancreatic: pancreatic insufficiency, recurrent acute pancreatitis, chronic pancreatitis
c. Hepatic: chronic hepatic disease manifested by clinical or histologic evidence of focal biliary cirrhosis, or multilobular cirrhosis, prolonged neonatal jaundice
d. Nutritional: failure to thrive (protein–calorie malnutrition), hypoproteinemia, edema, complications secondary to fat-soluble vitamin deficiency
3. Salt loss syndromes: acute salt depletion, chronic metabolic alkalosis
4. Male urogenital abnormalities resulting in obstructive azoospermia (congenital bilateral absence of vas deferens)
Criteria for Diagnosis of Cystic Fibrosis
One or more characteristic phenotypic features, OR a history of cystic fibrosis in a sibling, OR a positive newborn screening test result
AND
An increased sweat chloride concentration on two or more occasions, OR identification of two cystic fibrosis mutations, OR demonstration of abnormal epithelial nasal ion transport

Adapted with permission from Rosenstein BJ, Cutting GR: The diagnosis of cystic fibrosis: a consensus statement. J Pediatr 132:589, 1998.

expectancy is now 36 years and continues to increase. Clinical trials with gene therapy in humans are still in their early stages but provide a source of encouragement for millions of patients with CF worldwide.

SUMMARY

Cystic Fibrosis

- CF is an autosomal recessive disease caused by mutations in the *CFTR* gene encoding the CF transmembrane regulator.
- The principal defect is of chloride ion transport, resulting in high salt concentrations in sweat and in viscous luminal secretions in respiratory and gastrointestinal tracts.
- *CFTR* mutations can be severe (*ΔF508*), resulting in multisystem disease, or mild, with limited disease extent and severity.
- Cardiopulmonary complications constitute the most common cause of death; pulmonary infections, especially with resistant pseudomonads, are frequent. Bronchiectasis and right-sided heart failure are long-term sequelae.
- Pancreatic insufficiency is extremely common; infertility caused by congenital bilateral absence of vas deferens is a characteristic finding in adult patients with CF.
- Liver disease, including cirrhosis, is increasing in frequency due to improved survival.

Diseases Caused by Mutations in Genes Encoding Enzyme Proteins

Phenylketonuria

There are several variants of phenylketonuria (PKU), an inborn error of metabolism that affects 1 in 10,000 live-born white infants. The most common form, referred to as *classic phenylketonuria,* is quite common in persons of Scandinavian descent and is distinctly uncommon in African American and Jewish populations.

Homozygotes with this autosomal recessive disorder classically have a severe lack of the enzyme phenylalanine hydroxylase (PAH), leading to hyperphenylalaninemia and PKU. Affected infants are normal at birth but within a few weeks exhibit a rising plasma phenylalanine level, which in some way impairs brain development. Usually, by 6 months of life, *severe mental retardation* becomes all too evident; less than 4% of untreated phenylketonuric children have intelligence quotients (IQs) greater than 50 or 60. About one third of these children are never able to walk, and two thirds cannot talk. *Seizures,* other neurologic abnormalities, *decreased pigmentation of hair and skin,* and *eczema* often accompany the *mental retardation* in untreated children. Hyperphenylalaninemia and the resultant mental retardation can be avoided by restriction of phenylalanine intake early in life. Hence, several screening procedures are routinely performed to detect PKU in the immediate postnatal period.

Many female patients with PKU who receive dietary treatment beginning early in life reach child-bearing age and are clinically normal. Most of them have marked hyperphenylalaninemia, because dietary treatment is discontinued after they reach adulthood. Between 75% and 90% of children born to such women are mentally retarded and microcephalic, and 15% have congenital heart disease, even though the infants themselves are heterozygotes. This syndrome, termed *maternal PKU,* results from the teratogenic effects of phenylalanine or its metabolites that cross the placenta and affect specific fetal organs during development. The presence and severity of the fetal anomalies directly correlate with the maternal phenylalanine level, so *it is imperative that maternal dietary restriction of phenylalanine be initiated before conception and continued throughout pregnancy.*

The biochemical abnormality in PKU is an inability to convert phenylalanine into tyrosine. In normal children, less than 50% of the dietary intake of phenylalanine is necessary for protein synthesis. The remainder is converted to tyrosine by the phenylalanine hydroxylase system (Fig. 6–7). When phenylalanine metabolism is blocked because of a lack of PAH enzyme, minor shunt pathways come into play, yielding several intermediates that are excreted in large amounts in the urine and in the sweat. These impart a *strong musty or mousy odor* to affected infants. It is believed that excess phenylalanine or its metabolites contribute to the brain damage in PKU. Concomitant lack of tyrosine (Fig. 6–7), a precursor of melanin, is responsible for the light color of hair and skin.

At the molecular level, approximately 500 mutant alleles of the *PAH* gene have been identified, only some of which cause a severe deficiency of the enzyme. Infants with mutations resulting in a lack of PAH activity present with the classic features of PKU, while those with approximately 6% residual activity present with milder disease. Moreover,

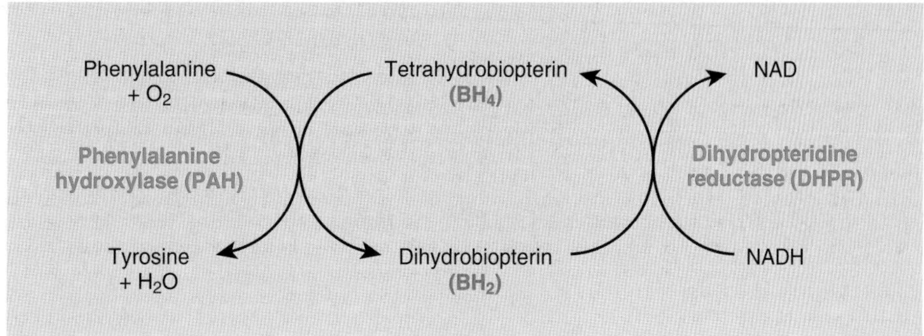

Figure 6–7 The phenylalanine hydroxylase system. NADH, nicotinamide adenine dinucleotide, reduced form.

some mutations result in only modest elevations of blood phenylalanine levels without associated neurologic damage. This latter condition, referred to as *benign hyperphenylalaninemia,* is important to recognize, because affected persons may well have positive screening tests but do not acquire the stigmata of PKU. Because of the numerous disease-causing alleles of the phenylalanine hydroxylase gene, molecular diagnosis is not feasible, and measurement of serum phenylalanine levels is necessary to differentiate benign hyperphenylalaninemia from PKU; the levels in the latter disorder typically are five times (or more) higher than normal. Once a biochemical diagnosis is established, the specific mutation causing PKU can be determined. With this information, carrier testing of at-risk family members can be performed.

While 98% of cases of PKU are attributable to mutations in PAH, approximately 2% arise from abnormalities in synthesis or recycling of the cofactor *tetrahydrobiopterin* (Fig. 6–7). *Clinical recognition of these variant forms of PKU is important to establish a prognosis, because the patients cannot be treated by dietary restriction of phenylalanine.*

Galactosemia

Galactosemia is an autosomal recessive disorder of galactose metabolism that affects 1 in 60,000 live-born infants. Normally, lactase splits lactose, the major carbohydrate of mammalian milk, into glucose and galactose in the intestinal microvilli. Galactose is then converted to glucose in several steps, in one of which the enzyme galactose-1-phosphate uridyltransferase (GALT) is required. Lack of this enzyme, due to homozygous mutations in the encoding gene *GALT*, is responsible for galactosemia. As a result of this transferase deficiency, galactose-1-phosphate and other metabolites, including galactitol, accumulate in many tissues, including the liver, spleen, lens of the eye, kidney, and cerebral cortex.

The liver, eyes, and brain bear the brunt of the damage. The early-onset hepatomegaly is due largely to fatty change, but in time widespread scarring that closely resembles the cirrhosis of alcohol abuse may supervene (Chapter 15). Opacification of the lens (cataract) develops, probably because the lens absorbs water and swells as galactitol, produced by alternative metabolic pathways, accumulates and increases its tonicity. Nonspecific alterations appear in the central nervous system (CNS), including loss of nerve cells, gliosis, and edema. There is still no clear understanding of the mechanism of injury to the liver and brain.

Almost from birth, affected infants fail to thrive. *Vomiting and diarrhea* appear within a few days of milk ingestion. *Jaundice* and *hepatomegaly* usually become evident during the first week of life. Accumulation of galactose and galactose-1-phosphate in the kidney impairs amino acid transport, resulting in aminoaciduria. Fulminant *Escherichia coli* septicemia occurs with increased frequency. The diagnosis of galactosemia can be suspected from demonstration in the urine of a reducing sugar other than glucose, but tests that directly identify the deficiency of the transferase in leukocytes and red cells are more reliable. Antenatal diagnosis is possible by assay of GALT activity in cultured amniotic fluid cells or determination of galactitol level in amniotic fluid supernatant.

Many of the clinical and morphologic changes of galactosemia can be prevented or ameliorated by early removal of galactose from the diet for at least the first 2 years of life. Control instituted soon after birth prevents the cataracts and liver damage and permits almost normal development. Even with dietary restrictions, however, it is now established that older patients frequently are affected by a speech disorder and gonadal failure (especially premature ovarian failure) and, less commonly, by an ataxic condition.

SUMMARY

Phenylketonuria

- PKU is a disorder of autosomal recessive inheritance caused by a lack of the enzyme phenylalanine hydroxylase and consequent inability to metabolize phenylalanine.
- Clinical features of untreated PKU may include severe mental retardation, seizures, and decreased pigmentation of skin, which can be avoided by restricting the intake of phenylalanine in the diet.
- Female patients with PKU who discontinue dietary treatment can give birth to children with malformations and neurologic impairment resulting from transplacental passage of phenylalanine metabolites.

Galactosemia

- Galactosemia is caused by an inherited lack of the GALT enzyme, leading to accumulation of galactose-1-phosphate and its metabolites in tissues.
- Clinical features may include jaundice, liver damage, cataracts, neural damage, vomiting and diarrhea, and *E. coli* sepsis. Dietary restriction of galactose can prevent at least some of the more severe complications.

Lysosomal Storage Diseases

Lysosomes, the digestive system of the cells, contain a variety of hydrolytic enzymes that are involved in the breakdown of complex substrates, such as sphingolipids and mucopolysaccharides, into soluble end products. These large molecules may be derived from the turnover of intracellular organelles that enter the lysosomes by autophagy, or they may be acquired from outside the cell by phagocytosis. With an inherited lack of a lysosomal enzyme, catabolism of its substrate remains incomplete, leading to accumulation of the partially degraded insoluble metabolites within the lysosomes (Fig. 6–8). Approximately 40 lysosomal storage diseases have been identified, each resulting from the functional absence of a specific lysosomal enzyme or proteins involved in their function. Traditionally, lysosomal storage disorders are divided into broad categories based on the biochemical nature of the substrates and the accumulated metabolites, but a more mechanistic classification is based on the underlying molecular defect (Table 6–4). Within each group are several entities, each resulting from the deficiency of a specific enzyme. Despite this complexity, certain features are common to most diseases in this group:

- Autosomal recessive transmission
- Patient population consisting of infants and young children

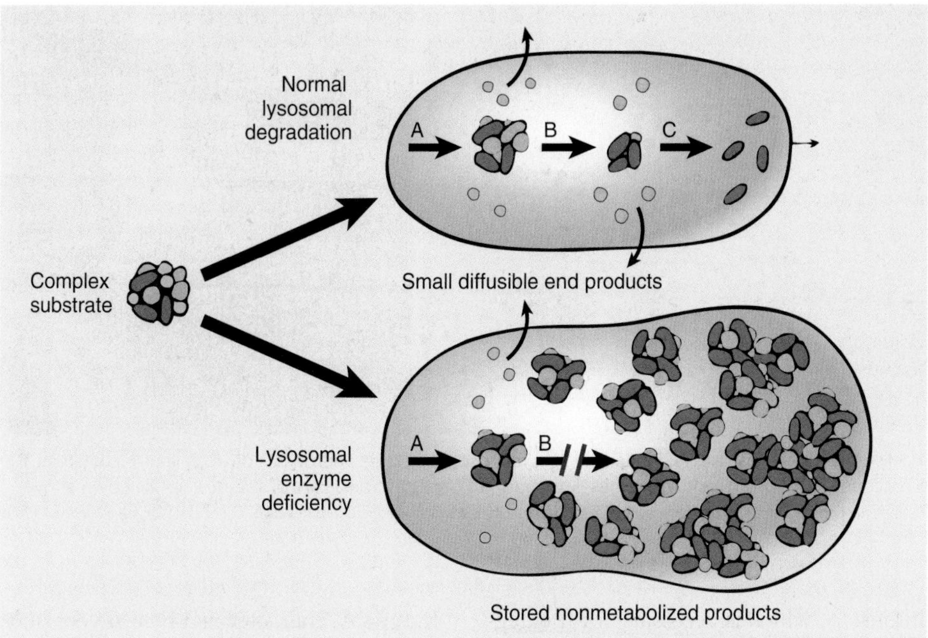

Figure 6–8 Pathogenesis of lysosomal storage diseases. In this example, a complex substrate is normally degraded by a series of lysosomal enzymes (*A*, *B*, and *C*) into soluble end products. If there is a deficiency or malfunction of one of the enzymes (e.g., *B*), catabolism is incomplete, and insoluble intermediates accumulate in the lysosomes.

- Storage of insoluble intermediates in the mononuclear phagocyte system, giving rise to hepatosplenomegaly
- Frequent CNS involvement with associated neuronal damage
- Cellular dysfunctions, caused not only by storage of undigested material but also by a cascade of secondary events triggered, for example, by macrophage activation and release of cytokines

Fortunately for the potential victims of the diseases, most of these conditions are very rare, and their detailed description is better relegated to specialized texts and reviews. Only a few of the more common conditions are considered here. Type II glycogen storage disease (Pompe disease), also a lysosomal disorder, is discussed later in the chapter.

Tay-Sachs Disease (G_{M2} Gangliosidosis: Deficiency in Hexosaminidase β Subunit)

Gangliosidoses are characterized by accumulation of gangliosides, principally in the brain, as a result of a deficiency of a catabolic lysosomal enzyme. Depending on the ganglioside involved, these disorders are subclassified into G_{M1} and G_{M2} categories. Tay-Sachs disease, by far the most common of all gangliosidoses, is characterized by a mutation in and consequent deficiency of the β subunit of the

Table 6–4 Lysosomal Storage Disorders

Disease Category	Disease	Deficiency
Primary lysosomal hydrolase defect	Gaucher disease G_{M1} gangliosidosis Tay-Sachs disease Sandhoff disease Fabry disease Krabbe disease Niemann-Pick disease types A and B	Glucocerebrosidase G_{M1}-β-galactosidase Hexosaminidase, α subunit Hexosaminidase, β subunit α-Galactosidase A Galactosylceramidase Sphingomyelinase
Posttranslational processing defect of lysosomal enzymes	Mucosulfatidosis (juvenile sulfatidosis)	Multiple sulfatases
Inefficient targeting of synthesized hydrolase to the lysosome	Mucolipidosis types II and III alpha/beta	*N*-acetyl glucosamine-1-phosphotransferase
Defect in lysosomal enzyme protection	Galactosialidosis	Protective protein cathepsin A (β-galactosidase and neuraminidase)
Defect in soluble nonenzymatic lysosomal proteins	G_{M2} activator protein deficiency, variant AB Sphingolipid activator protein deficiency	G_{M2} activator protein Sphingolipid activator protein
Transmembrane (nonenzymatic) protein deficiency	Niemann-Pick disease type C (NPC) Salla disease (free sialic acid storage)	*NPC1* and *NPC2* Sialin

Data from Jeyakumar M, Dwek RA, Butters TD, Platt FM: Storage solutions: treating lysosomal disorders of the brain. Nat Rev Neurosci 6:1, 2005.

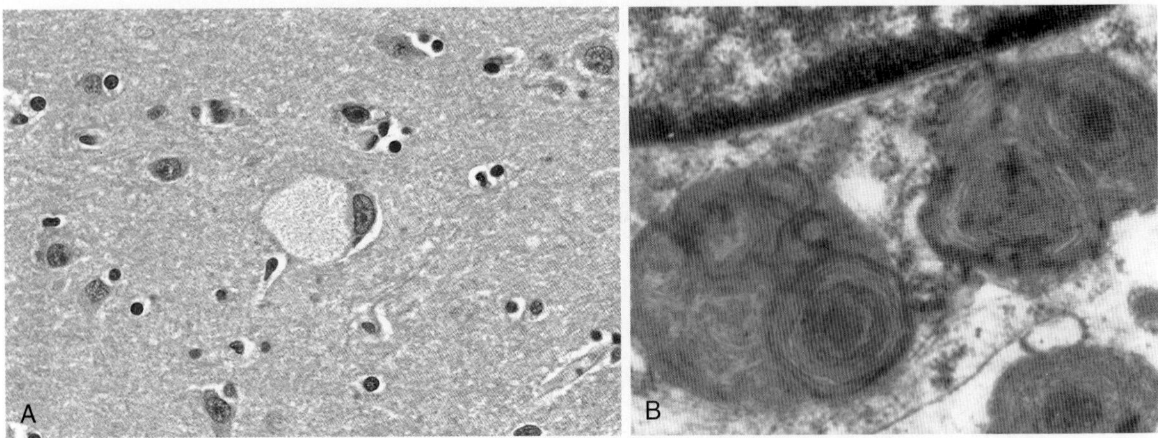

Figure 6–9 Ganglion cells in Tay-Sachs disease. **A,** Under the light microscope, a large neuron has obvious lipid vacuolation. **B,** A portion of a neuron under the electron microscope shows prominent lysosomes with whorled configurations. Part of the nucleus is shown above.

(A, Courtesy of Dr. Arthur Weinberg, Department of Pathology, University of Texas Southwestern Medical Center, Dallas, Texas. B, Courtesy of Dr. Joe Rutledge, Children's Regional Medical Center, Seattle, Washington.)

enzyme hexosaminidase A, which is necessary for the degradation of G_{M2}. More than 100 mutations have been described; most affect protein folding or intracellular transport. The brain is principally affected, because it is most involved in ganglioside metabolism. *The storage of G_{M2} occurs within neurons, axon cylinders of nerves, and glial cells throughout the CNS.* Affected cells appear swollen and sometimes foamy (Fig. 6–9, *A*). Electron microscopy reveals whorled configurations within lysosomes composed of onion-skin layers of membranes (Fig. 6–9, *B*). These pathologic changes are found throughout the CNS (including the spinal cord), peripheral nerves, and autonomic nervous system. The retina usually is involved as well, where the pallor produced by swollen ganglion cells in the peripheral retina results in a contrasting "cherry red" spot in the relatively unaffected central macula.

The molecular basis for neuronal injury is not fully understood. Because in many cases the mutant protein is misfolded, it induces the so-called "unfolded protein" response (Chapter 1). If such misfolded proteins are not stabilized by chaperones, they trigger apoptosis. These findings have spurred clinical trials of *molecular chaperone therapy* for this and similar lysosomal storage diseases. Such therapy involves use of small molecules that increase chaperone synthesis or reduce degradation of misfolded proteins by the proteosomes.

In the most common acute infantile variant of Tay-Sachs disease, infants appear normal at birth, but motor weakness begins at 3 to 6 months of age, followed by neurologic impairment, onset of blindness, and progressively more severe neurologic dysfunctions. Death occurs within 2 or 3 years. Tay-Sachs disease, like other lipidoses, is most common among Ashkenazi Jews, among whom the frequency of heterozygous carriers is estimated to be 1 in 30. Heterozygote carriers can be reliably detected by estimation of the level of hexosaminidase in the serum or by DNA analysis.

Niemann-Pick Disease Types A and B

Type A and type B Niemann-Pick disease are related entities characterized by a primary deficiency of acid sphingomyelinase and the resultant accumulation of sphingomyelin. In type A, characterized by a severe deficiency of sphingomyelinase, the breakdown of sphingomyelin into ceramide and phosphorylcholine is impaired, and excess sphingomyelin accumulates in all phagocytic cells and in the neurons. The macrophages become stuffed with droplets or particles of the complex lipid, imparting a fine vacuolation or foaminess to the cytoplasm (Fig. 6–10). Electron microscopy confirms that the vacuoles are engorged secondary lysosomes that often contain membranous cytoplasmic bodies resembling concentric lamellated myelin figures, sometimes called "zebra" bodies. Because of their high content of phagocytic cells, *the organs most severely affected are the spleen, liver, bone marrow, lymph nodes, and lungs.* The splenic enlargement may be striking. In addition, the entire CNS, including the spinal cord and ganglia, is involved in this tragic, inexorable process. The affected neurons are enlarged and vacuolated as a result of the storage of lipids. This variant manifests itself in infancy with *massive visceromegaly and severe neurologic deterioration.*

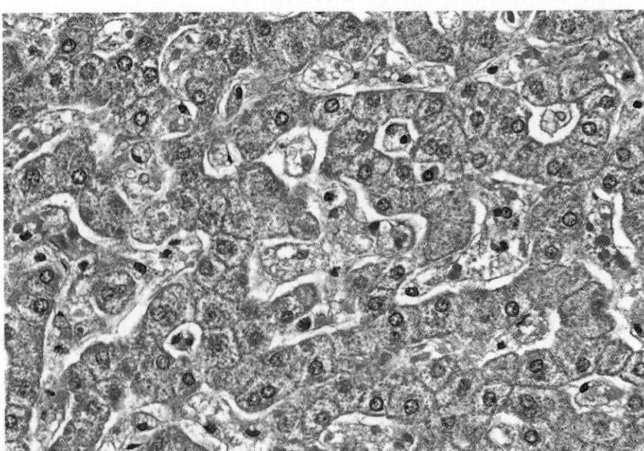

Figure 6–10 Niemann-Pick disease in liver. The hepatocytes and Kupffer cells have a foamy, vacuolated appearance resulting from deposition of lipids.

(Courtesy of Dr. Arthur Weinberg, Department of Pathology, University of Texas Southwestern Medical Center, Dallas, Texas.)

Death usually occurs within the first 3 years of life. By comparison, patients with the type B variant have organomegaly but no neurologic manifestations. Estimation of sphingomyelinase activity in the leukocytes or cultured fibroblasts can be used for diagnosis of suspected cases, as well as for detection of carriers. Antenatal diagnosis is possible by enzyme assays or DNA probe analysis.

Niemann-Pick Disease Type C

Although previously considered to be related to type A and type B Niemann-Pick disease, type C (NPC) is quite distinct at the biochemical and molecular levels and is more common than types A and B combined. Mutations in two related genes, *NPC1* and *NPC2*, can give rise to the disorder, with *NPC1* being responsible for a majority of cases. Unlike most other lysosomal storage diseases, NPC is due to a primary defect in lipid transport. Affected cells accumulate cholesterol as well as gangliosides such as G_{M1} and G_{M2}. Both NPC1 and NPC2 are involved in the transport of free cholesterol from the lysosomes to the cytoplasm. NPC is clinically heterogeneous: The most common form manifests in childhood and is marked by ataxia, vertical supranuclear gaze palsy, dystonia, dysarthria, and psychomotor regression.

Gaucher Disease

Gaucher disease results from mutation in the gene that encodes glucocerebrosidase. There are three autosomal recessive variants of Gaucher disease resulting from distinct allelic mutations. Common to all is variably deficient activity of a glucocerebrosidase that normally cleaves the glucose residue from ceramide. This deficit leads to an accumulation of glucocerebroside, an intermediate in glycolipid metabolism, in the mononuclear phagocytic cells and their transformation into so-called Gaucher cells. Normally the glycolipids derived from the breakdown of senescent blood cells are sequentially degraded by the phagocytic cells of the body particularly in the liver, spleen, and bone marrow. In Gaucher disease, the degradation stops at the level of glucocerebrosides, which accumulate in the phagocytes. These phagocytes—the Gaucher cells—become enlarged, with some reaching a diameter as great as 100 μm, because of the accumulation of distended lysosomes, and acquire a pathognomonic cytoplasmic appearance characterized as "wrinkled tissue paper" (Fig. 6–11). No distinct vacuolation is present. It is evident now that Gaucher disease is caused not just by the burden of storage material but also by activation of the macrophages. High levels of macrophage-derived cytokines, such as interleukins (IL-1, IL-6) and tumor necrosis factor (TNF), are found in affected tissues.

One variant, type I, also called the *chronic non-neuronopathic form,* accounts for 99% of cases of Gaucher disease. It is characterized by clinical or radiographic bone involvement (osteopenia, focal lytic lesions, and osteonecrosis) in 70% to 100% of cases. Additional features are hepatosplenomegaly and the absence of CNS involvement. The spleen often enlarges to massive proportions, filling the entire abdomen. Gaucher cells are found in the liver, spleen, lymph nodes, and bone marrow. Marrow replacement and cortical erosion may produce radiographically visible skeletal lesions, as well as a reduction in the formed elements of blood. Bone changes are believed to be caused by the aforementioned macrophage-derived cytokines. Type I is most common in Ashkenazi Jews; unlike other variants, it is compatible with long life. Types II and III variants are characterized by neurologic signs and symptoms. In type II, these manifestations appear during infancy (*acute infantile neuronopathic form*) and are more severe, whereas in type III, they emerge later and are milder (*chronic neuronopathic form*). Although the liver and spleen also are involved, the clinical features in types II and III are dominated by neurologic disturbances, including convulsions and progressive mental deterioration. The level of glucocerebrosides in leukocytes or cultured fibroblasts is helpful in diagnosis and in the detection of heterozygote carriers.

Current therapy is aimed at lifelong enzyme replacement by infusion of recombinant glucocerebrosidase. A newer form of therapy involves reducing the substrate (glucocerebroside) by oral administration of drugs that inhibit glucocerebroside synthase. Since glucosylceramide is reduced, its accumulation also is reduced. Recent clinical trials in humans have shown considerable promise for this

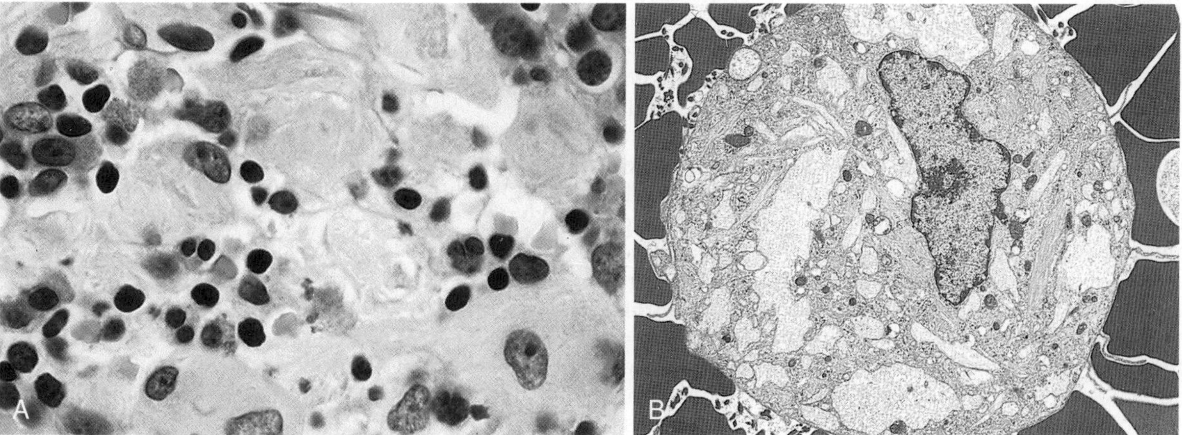

Figure 6–11 Gaucher disease involving the bone marrow. **A,** Gaucher cells with abundant lipid-laden granular cytoplasm. **B,** Electron micrograph of Gaucher cells with elongated distended lysosomes.

(Courtesy of Dr. Matthew Fries, Department of Pathology, University of Texas Southwestern Medical Center, Dallas, Texas.)

modality of therapy, with decrease in splenomegaly and improvements in skeletal disease. On the horizon is glucocerebrosidase gene therapy involving infusion of autologous hematopoietic stem cells transfected with the normal gene.

Mucopolysaccharidoses

Mucopolysaccharidoses (MPSs) are characterized by defective degradation (and therefore excessive storage) of mucopolysaccharides in various tissues. Recall that mucopolysaccharides form a part of ground substance and are synthesized by connective tissue fibroblasts. Most of the mucopolysaccharide is secreted into the ground substance, but a certain fraction is degraded within lysosomes. Multiple enzymes are involved in this catabolic pathway; it is the lack of these enzymes that leads to accumulation of mucopolysaccharides within the lysosomes. Several clinical variants of MPS, classified numerically from MPS I to MPS VII, have been described, each resulting from the deficiency of one specific enzyme. The mucopolysaccharides that accumulate within the tissues include dermatan sulfate, heparan sulfate, keratan sulfate, and (in some cases) chondroitin sulfate.

Hepatosplenomegaly, skeletal deformities, lesions of heart valves, and subendothelial arterial deposits, particularly in the coronary arteries, and lesions in the brain, are common threads that run through all of the MPSs. In many of the more protracted syndromes, coronary subendothelial lesions lead to myocardial ischemia. *Thus, myocardial infarction and cardiac decompensation are important causes of death.* Most cases are associated with *coarse facial features, clouding of the cornea, joint stiffness, and mental retardation.* Urinary excretion of the accumulated mucopolysaccharides often is increased. With all of these disorders except one, the mode of inheritance is autosomal recessive; the exception, Hunter syndrome, is an X-linked recessive disease. Of the seven recognized variants, only two well-characterized syndromes are discussed briefly here.

MPS type I, also known as *Hurler syndrome,* is caused by a deficiency of α-L-iduronidase. In Hurler syndrome, affected children have a life expectancy of 6 to 10 years, and death is often due to cardiac complications. Accumulation of dermatan sulfate and heparan sulfate is seen in cells of the mononuclear phagocyte system, in fibroblasts, and within endothelium and smooth muscle cells of the vascular wall. The affected cells are swollen and have clear cytoplasm, resulting from the accumulation of material positive for periodic acid–Schiff staining within engorged, vacuolated lysosomes. Lysosomal inclusions also are found in neurons, accounting for the mental retardation.

The other well-characterized variant, MPS type II or *Hunter syndrome,* differs from Hurler syndrome in its mode of inheritance (X-linked), the absence of corneal clouding, and often its milder clinical course. As in Hurler syndrome, the accumulated mucopolysaccharides in Hunter syndrome are heparan sulfate and dermatan sulfate, but this results from a deficiency of L-iduronate sulfatase. Despite the difference in enzyme deficiency, an accumulation of identical substrates occurs because breakdown of heparan sulfate and dermatan sulfate requires both α-L-iduronidase and the sulfatase; if either one is missing, further degradation is blocked.

SUMMARY

Lysosomal Storage Diseases

- *Tay-Sachs disease* is caused by an inability to metabolize G_{M2} gangliosides due to lack of the β subunit of lysosomal hexosaminidase. G_{M2} gangliosides accumulate in the CNS and cause severe mental retardation, blindness, motor weakness, and death by 2 to 3 years of age.
- *Niemann-Pick disease types A and B* are caused by a deficiency of sphingomyelinase. In the more severe, type A variant, accumulation of sphingomyelin in the nervous system results in neuronal damage. Lipid also is stored in phagocytes within the liver, spleen, bone marrow, and lymph nodes, causing their enlargement. In type B, neuronal damage is not present.
- *Niemann-Pick disease type C* is caused by a defect in cholesterol transport and resultant accumulation of cholesterol and gangliosides in the nervous system. Affected children exhibit ataxia, dysarthria, and psychomotor regression.
- *Gaucher disease* results from lack of the lysosomal enzyme glucocerebrosidase and accumulation of glucocerebroside in mononuclear phagocytic cells. In the most common, type I variant, affected phagocytes become enlarged (Gaucher cells) and accumulate in liver, spleen, and bone marrow, causing hepatosplenomegaly and bone erosion. Types II and III are characterized by variable neuronal involvement.
- *Mucopolysaccharidoses* result from accumulation of mucopolysaccharides in many tissues including liver, spleen, heart, blood vessels, brain, cornea, and joints. Affected patients in all forms have coarse facial features. Manifestations of Hurler syndrome include corneal clouding, coronary arterial and valvular deposits, and death in childhood. Hunter syndrome is associated with a milder clinical course.

Glycogen Storage Diseases (Glycogenoses)

An inherited deficiency of any one of the enzymes involved in glycogen synthesis or degradation can result in excessive accumulation of glycogen or some abnormal form of glycogen in various tissues. The type of glycogen stored, its intracellular location, and the tissue distribution of the affected cells vary depending on the specific enzyme deficiency. Regardless of the tissue or cells affected, the glycogen most often is stored within the cytoplasm, or sometimes within nuclei. One variant, Pompe disease, is a form of lysosomal storage disease, because the missing enzyme is localized to lysosomes. Most glycogenoses are inherited as autosomal recessive diseases, as is common with "missing enzyme" syndromes.

Approximately a dozen forms of glycogenoses have been described in association with specific enzyme deficiencies. On the basis of pathophysiologic findings, they can be grouped into three categories (Table 6–5):

- *Hepatic type.* Liver contains several enzymes that synthesize glycogen for storage and also break it down into free glucose. Hence, a deficiency of the hepatic enzymes involved in glycogen metabolism is associated with two major clinical effects: *enlargement of the liver due to storage*

Table 6–5 Principal Subgroups of Glycogenoses

Clinicopathologic Category	Specific Type	Enzyme Deficiency	Morphologic Changes	Clinical Features
Hepatic type	Hepatorenal (von Gierke disease, type I)	Glucose-6-phosphatase	*Hepatomegaly*: intracytoplasmic accumulations of glycogen and small amounts of lipid; intranuclear glycogen *Renomegaly*: intracytoplasmic accumulations of glycogen in cortical tubular epithelial cells	In untreated patients, failure to thrive, stunted growth, hepatomegaly, and renomegaly Hypoglycemia due to failure of glucose mobilization, often leading to convulsions Hyperlipidemia and hyperuricemia resulting from deranged glucose metabolism; many patients develop gout and skin xanthomas Bleeding tendency due to platelet dysfunction With treatment (providing continuous source of glucose), most patients survive and develop late complications (e.g., hepatic adenomas)
Myopathic type	McArdle syndrome (type V)	Muscle phosphorylase	*Skeletal muscle only*: accumulations of glycogen predominant in subsarcolemmal location	Painful cramps associated with strenuous exercise Myoglobinuria occurs in 50% of cases Onset in adulthood (>20 yr) Muscular exercise fails to raise lactate level in venous blood Compatible with normal longevity
Miscellaneous type	Generalized glycogenosis (Pompe disease, type II)	Lysosomal glucosidase (acid maltase)	*Mild hepatomegaly*: ballooning of lysosomes with glycogen creating lacy cytoplasmic pattern *Cardiomegaly*: glycogen within sarcoplasm as well as membrane-bound *Skeletal muscle*: similar to heart (see above under cardiomegaly)	Massive cardiomegaly, muscle hypotonia, and cardiorespiratory failure before age 2 Milder adult form with only skeletal muscle involvement manifests with chronic myopathy.

of glycogen and *hypoglycemia due to a failure of glucose production* (Fig. 6–12). *Von Gierke* disease (type I glycogenosis), resulting from a lack of glucose-6-phosphatase, is the most important example of the hepatic form of glycogenosis (Table 6–5).

- *Myopathic type.* In striated muscle, glycogen is an important source of energy. Not surprisingly, most forms of glycogen storage disease affect muscles. When enzymes that are involved in glycolysis are deficient, glycogen storage occurs in muscles and there is an associated muscle weakness due to impaired energy production. Typically, *the myopathic forms of glycogen storage diseases are marked by muscle cramps after exercise, myoglobinuria, and failure of exercise to induce an elevation in blood lactate levels because of a block in glycolysis.* McArdle disease (type V glycogenosis), resulting from a deficiency of muscle phosphorylase, is the prototype of myopathic glycogenoses.
- Type II glycogenosis (*Pompe disease*) is caused by a deficiency of lysosomal acid maltase and so is associated with deposition of glycogen in virtually every organ, but cardiomegaly is most prominent. Most affected patients die within 2 years of onset of cardiorespiratory failure. Therapy with the missing enzyme (glucosidase) can reverse cardiac muscle damage and modestly increase longevity.

SUMMARY

Glycogen Storage Diseases

- Inherited deficiency of enzymes involved in glycogen metabolism can result in storage of normal or abnormal forms of glycogen, predominantly in liver or muscles or in all tissues.
- In the *hepatic form* (von Gierke disease), liver cells store glycogen because of a lack of hepatic glucose-6-phosphatase. There are several *myopathic forms,* including McArdle disease, in which muscle phosphorylase lack gives rise to storage in skeletal muscles and cramps after exercise. In *Pompe disease* there is lack of lysosomal acid maltase, and all organs are affected, but heart involvement is predominant.

Diseases Caused by Mutations in Genes Encoding Proteins That Regulate Cell Growth

As detailed in Chapter 5, two classes of genes, proto-oncogenes and tumor suppressor genes, regulate normal cell growth and differentiation. Mutations affecting these genes, most often in somatic cells, are involved in the

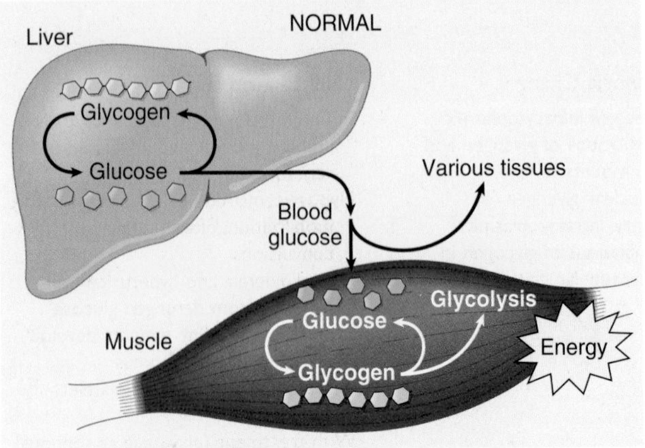

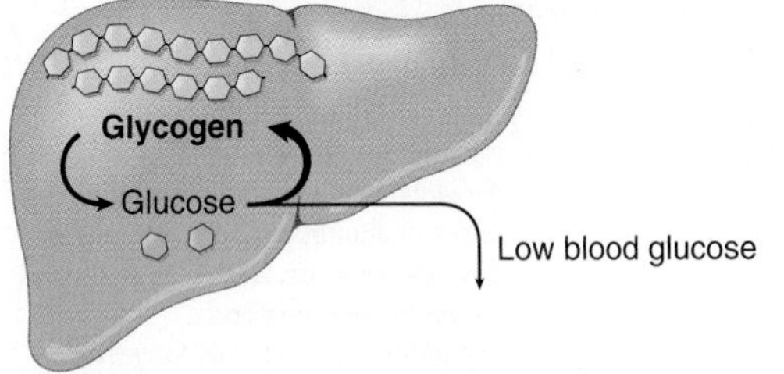

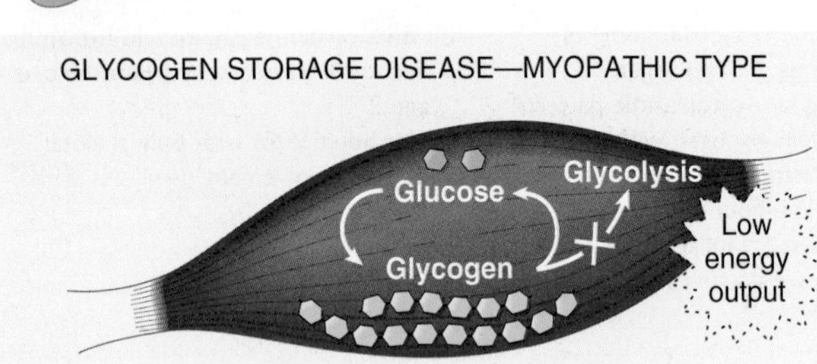

Figure 6–12 **Top,** A simplified scheme of normal glycogen metabolism in the liver and skeletal muscles. **Middle,** The effects of an inherited deficiency of hepatic enzymes involved in glycogen metabolism. **Bottom,** The consequences of a genetic deficiency in the enzymes that metabolize glycogen in skeletal muscles.

pathogenesis of tumors. In approximately 5% to 10% of all cancers, however, mutations affecting certain tumor suppressor genes are present in all cells of the body, including germ cells and hence can be transmitted to the offspring. These mutant genes predispose the offspring to hereditary tumors, a topic discussed in greater detail in Chapter 5.

COMPLEX MULTIGENIC DISORDERS

Complex multigenic disorders—so-called multifactorial or polygenic disorders—are caused by interactions between variant forms of genes and environmental factors. A genetic variant that has at least two alleles and occurs in at least 1% of the population is called a *polymorphism*. According to the common disease–common variant hypothesis, complex multigenic disorders occur when many polymorphisms, each with a modest effect and low penetrance, are co-inherited. Two additional important facts have emerged from studies of common complex disorders such as type 1 diabetes:

- While complex disorders result from the collective inheritance of many polymorphisms, different polymorphisms vary in significance. For example, of the 20 to 30 genes implicated in type 1 diabetes, 6 or 7 are most important, and a few HLA alleles contribute more than 50% of the risk (Chapter 19).
- Some polymorphisms are common to multiple diseases of the same type, while others are disease-specific. This observation is well illustrated in immune-mediated inflammatory diseases (Chapter 4).

Several normal phenotypic characteristics are governed by multigenic inheritance, such as hair color, eye color, skin color, height, and intelligence. These characteristics (also known as *quantitative trait loci* [QTLs]) show a continuous variation within, as well as across, all population groups. Environmental influences, however, significantly modify the phenotypic expression of complex traits. For example, type 2 diabetes mellitus has many of the features of a complex multigenic disorder. It is well recognized clinically that affected persons often first exhibit clinical manifestations of this disease after weight gain. Thus, obesity as well as other environmental influences, unmasks the diabetic genetic trait. Assigning a disease to this mode of inheritance must be done with caution. Such attribution depends on many factors but first on familial clustering and the exclusion of mendelian and chromosomal modes of transmission. A range of levels of severity of a disease is suggestive of a complex multigenic disorder, but as pointed out earlier, variable expressivity and reduced penetrance of single mutant genes also may account for this phenomenon. Because of these problems, sometimes it is difficult to distinguish between mendelian and multifactorial disorders.

CYTOGENETIC DISORDERS

Chromosomal abnormalities occur much more frequently than is generally appreciated. It is estimated that approximately 1 in 200 newborn infants has some form of chromosomal abnormality. The figure is much higher in fetuses that do not survive to term. It is estimated that in 50% of first-trimester spontaneous abortions, the fetus has a chromosomal abnormality. Cytogenetic disorders may result from alterations in the number or structure of chromosomes and may affect autosomes or sex chromosomes.

Before embarking on a discussion of chromosomal aberrations, it is appropriate to review karyotyping as the basic tool of the cytogeneticist. A *karyotype* is a photographic representation of a stained metaphase spread in which the chromosomes are arranged in order of decreasing length. A variety of techniques for staining chromosomes have been developed. With the widely used Giemsa stain (G banding) technique, each chromosome set can be seen to possess a distinctive pattern of alternating light and dark bands of variable widths (Fig. 6–13). The use of banding techniques allows identification of each chromosome, and can detect and localize structural abnormalities large enough to produce changes in banding pattern (described later).

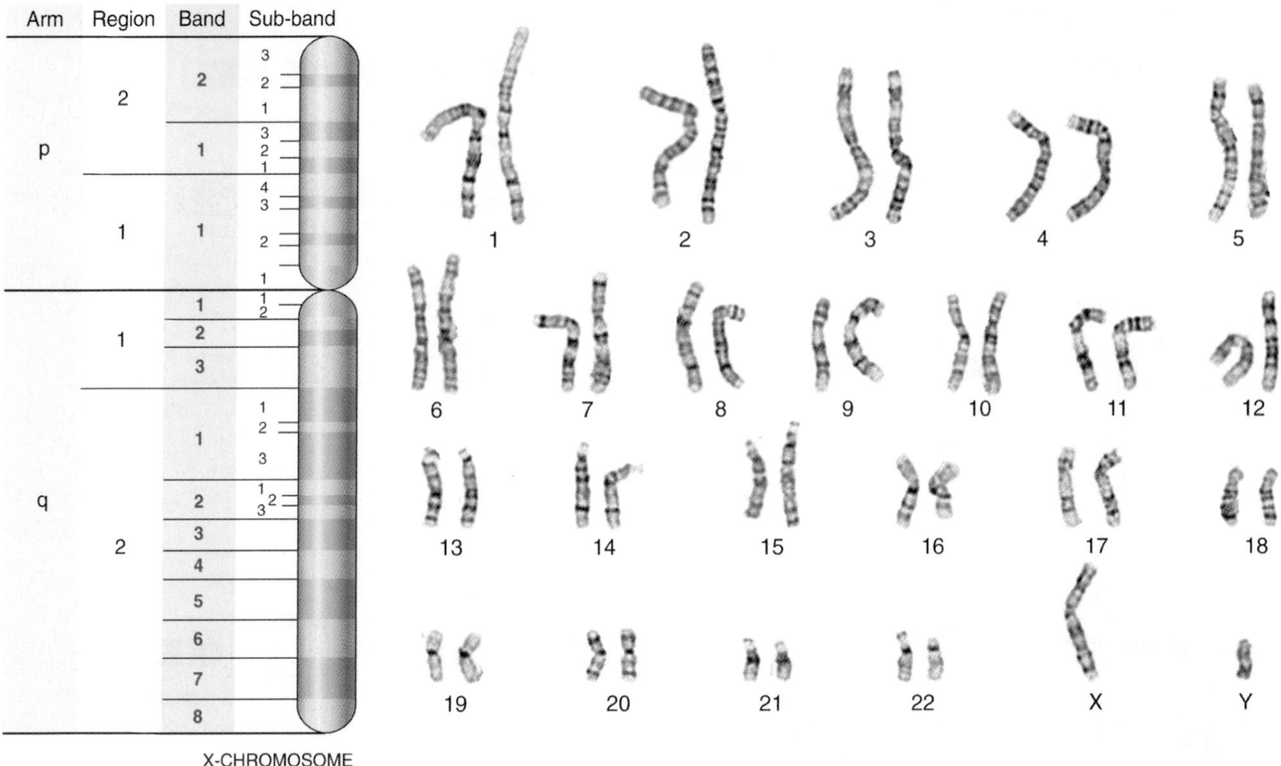

Figure 6–13 G-banded karyotype from a normal male (46,XY). Also shown is the banding pattern of the X-chromosome with nomenclature of arms, regions, bands, and sub-bands.

(Karyotype courtesy of Dr. Stuart Schwartz, Department of Pathology, University of Chicago, Chicago, Illinois.)

Numeric Abnormalities

In humans, the normal chromosome count is 46 (i.e., $2n = 46$). Any exact multiple of the haploid number (n) is called *euploid.* Chromosome numbers such as $3n$ and $4n$ are called *polyploid.* Polyploidy generally results in a spontaneous abortion. Any number that is not an exact multiple of n is called *aneuploid.* The chief cause of aneuploidy is nondisjunction of a homologous pair of chromosomes at the first meiotic division or a failure of sister chromatids to separate during the second meiotic division. The latter also may occur during mitosis in somatic cells, leading to the production of two aneuploid cells. Failure of pairing of homologous chromosomes followed by random assortment (anaphase lag) can also lead to aneuploidy. When nondisjunction occurs at the time of meiosis, the gametes formed have either an extra chromosome ($n + 1$) or one less chromosome ($n - 1$). Fertilization of such gametes by normal gametes would result in two types of zygotes: trisomic, with an extra chromosome ($2n + 1$), or monosomic ($2n - 1$). Monosomy involving an autosome is incompatible with life, whereas trisomies of certain autosomes and monosomy involving sex chromosomes are compatible with life. These, as we shall see, are associated with variable degrees of phenotypic abnormality. *Mosaicism* is a term used to describe the presence of two or more populations of cells with different complements of chromosomes in the same individual. In the context of chromosome numbers, postzygotic mitotic nondisjunction would result in the production of a trisomic and a monosomic daughter cell; the descendants of these cells would then produce a mosaic. As discussed later, mosaicism affecting sex chromosomes is common, whereas autosomal mosaicism is not.

Structural Abnormalities

Structural changes in the chromosomes usually result from chromosomal breakage followed by loss or rearrangement of material. Such changes usually are designated using a cytogenetic shorthand in which *p* (French, *petit*) denotes the short arm of a chromosome, and *q*, the long arm. Each arm is then divided into numbered regions (1, 2, 3, and so on) from centromere outward, and within each region the bands are numerically ordered (Fig. 6–13). Thus, 2q34 indicates chromosome 2, long arm, region 3, band 4. The patterns of chromosomal rearrangement after breakage (Fig. 6–14) are as follows:

- *Translocation* implies transfer of a part of one chromosome to another chromosome. The process is usually reciprocal (i.e., fragments are exchanged between two chromosomes). In genetic shorthand, translocations are indicated by *t* followed by the involved chromosomes in numeric order—for example, 46,XX,t(2;5)(q31;p14). This notation would indicate a reciprocal translocation involving the long arm (q) of chromosome 2 at region 3, band 1, and the short arm of chromosome 5, region 1, band 4. When the entire broken fragments are exchanged, the resulting balanced reciprocal translocation (Fig. 6–14) is not harmful to the carrier, who has the normal number of chromosomes and the full complement of genetic material. However, during gametogenesis,

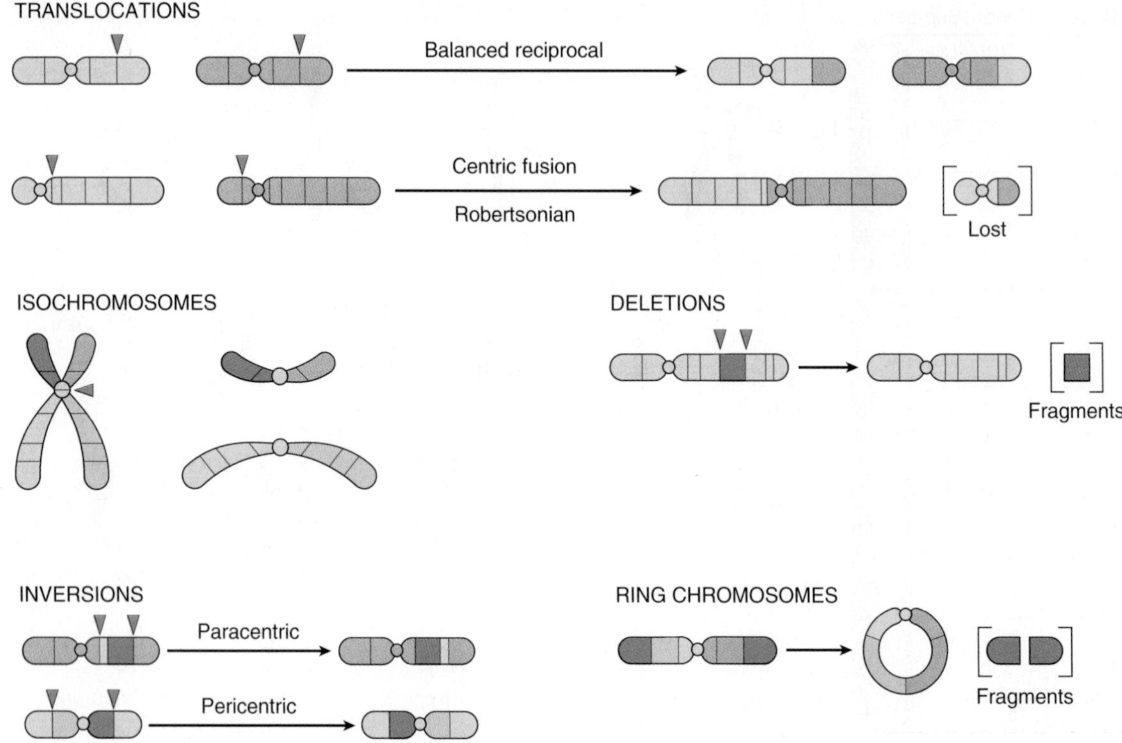

Figure 6–14 Types of chromosomal rearrangements.

abnormal (unbalanced) gametes are formed, resulting in abnormal zygotes. A special pattern of translocation involving two acrocentric chromosomes is called *centric fusion type,* or *robertsonian,* translocation. The breaks typically occur close to the centromere, affecting the short arms of both chromosomes. Transfer of the segments leads to one very large chromosome and one extremely small one (Fig. 6–14). The short fragments are lost, and the carrier has 45 chromosomes. Because the short arms of all acrocentric chromosomes carry highly redundant genes (e.g., ribosomal RNA genes), such loss is compatible with survival. However, difficulties arise during gametogenesis, resulting in the formation of unbalanced gametes that could lead to abnormal offspring.

- *Isochromosomes* result when the centromere divides horizontally rather than vertically. One of the two arms of the chromosome is then lost, and the remaining arm is duplicated, resulting in a chromosome with two short arms only or two long arms only. The most common isochromosome present in live births involves the long arm of the X chromosome and is designated *i(Xq)*. When fertilization occurs by a gamete that contains a normal X chromosome, the result is monosomy for genes on Xp and trisomy for genes on Xq.
- *Deletion* involves loss of a portion of a chromosome. A single break may delete a terminal segment. Two interstitial breaks, with reunion of the proximal and distal segments, may result in loss of an intermediate segment. The isolated fragment, which lacks a centromere, almost never survives, and thus many genes are lost.
- *Inversions* occur when there are two interstitial breaks in a chromosome, and the segment reunites after a complete turnaround.
- A *ring chromosome* is a variant of a deletion. After loss of segments from each end of the chromosome, the arms unite to form a ring.

General Features of Chromosomal Disorders

- Chromosomal disorders may be associated with absence (deletion, monosomy), excess (trisomy), or abnormal rearrangements (translocations) of chromosomes.
- In general, loss of chromosomal material produces more severe defects than does gain of chromosomal material.
- Excess chromosomal material may result from a complete chromosome (as in trisomy) or from part of a chromosome (as in robertsonian translocation).
- Imbalances of sex chromosomes (excess or loss) are tolerated much better than are similar imbalances of autosomes.
- Sex chromosomal disorders often produce subtle abnormalities, sometimes not detected at birth. Infertility, a common manifestation, cannot be diagnosed until adolescence.
- In most cases, chromosomal disorders result from de novo changes (i.e., parents are normal, and risk of recurrence in siblings is low). An uncommon but important exception to this principle is exhibited by the translocation form of Down syndrome (described later).

Some specific examples of diseases involving changes in the karyotype are presented next.

Cytogenetic Disorders Involving Autosomes

Three autosomal trisomies (21, 18, and 13) and one deletion syndrome (cri du chat syndrome), which results from partial deletion of the short arm of chromosome 5, were the first chromosomal abnormalities identified. More recently, several additional trisomies and deletion syndromes (such as that affecting 22q) have been described. Most of these disorders are quite uncommon, but their clinical features should permit ready recognition (Fig. 6–15).

Only trisomy 21 and 22q11.2 deletion occur with sufficient frequency to merit further consideration.

Trisomy 21 (Down Syndrome)

Down syndrome is the most common of the chromosomal disorders. About 95% of affected persons have trisomy 21, so their chromosome count is 47. As mentioned earlier, the most common cause of trisomy, and therefore of Down syndrome, is *meiotic nondisjunction.* The parents of such children have a normal karyotype and are normal in all respects. *Maternal age has a strong influence* on the incidence of Down syndrome. It occurs in 1 in 1550 live births in women younger than 20 years, in contrast with 1 in 25 live births in women older than 45 years. The correlation with maternal age suggests that in most cases the meiotic nondisjunction of chromosome 21 occurs in the ovum. Indeed, in 95% of cases the extra chromosome is of maternal origin. The reason for the increased susceptibility of the ovum to nondisjunction is not fully understood. No effect of paternal age has been found in those cases in which the extra chromosome is derived from the father.

In about 4% of all patients with trisomy 21, the extra chromosomal material is present not as an extra chromosome but as a translocation of the long arm of chromosome 21 to chromosome 22 or 14. Such cases frequently (but not always) are familial, and the translocated chromosome is inherited from one of the parents, who typically is a carrier of a robertsonian translocation. Approximately 1% of patients with trisomy 21 are mosaics, usually having a mixture of 46- and 47-chromosome cells. These cases result from mitotic nondisjunction of chromosome 21 during an early stage of embryogenesis. Clinical manifestations in such cases are variable and milder, depending on the proportion of abnormal cells.

The diagnostic clinical features of this condition—flat facial profile, oblique palpebral fissures, and epicanthic folds (Fig. 6–15) —are usually readily evident, even at birth. Down syndrome is a leading cause of severe mental retardation; approximately 80% of those afflicted have an IQ of 25 to 50. Ironically, these severely disadvantaged children may have a gentle, shy manner and may be more easily directed than their more fortunate normal siblings. Of interest, some mosaics with Down syndrome have mild phenotypic changes and often even have normal or near-normal intelligence. In addition to the phenotypic abnormalities and the mental retardation already noted, some other clinical features are worthy of mention:

- Approximately 40% of the patients have congenital heart disease, most commonly defects of the endocardial cushion, including atrial septal defects, atrioventricular valve malformations, and ventricular septal defects (Chapter 10). Cardiac problems are responsible for a majority of the deaths in infancy and early childhood. Several other congenital malformations, including atresias of the esophagus and small bowel, also are common.
- Children with trisomy 21 have a 10- to 20-fold increased risk of developing acute leukemia. Both acute lymphoblastic leukemias and acute myeloid leukemias occur (Chapter 11).
- Virtually all patients with trisomy 21 older than age 40 develop neuropathologic changes characteristic of Alzheimer disease, a degenerative disorder of the brain (Chapter 22).
- Patients with Down syndrome demonstrate abnormal immune responses that predispose them to serious infections, particularly of the lungs, and to thyroid autoimmunity (Chapter 19). Although several abnormalities, affecting mainly T cell functions, have been reported, the basis for the immunologic disturbances is not clear.

Despite all of these problems, improved medical care has increased the longevity of persons with trisomy 21. Currently the median age at death is 47 years (up from 25 years in 1983). Although the karyotype of Down syndrome has been known for decades, the molecular basis for this disease remains elusive. Data from the human genome project indicate that chromosome 21 carries about 500 annotated genes, including approximately 170 that are conserved protein-coding genes and 5 miRNAs. It is unclear whether the phenotype of Down syndrome arises as a consequence of increased gene dosage of protein coding genes on chromosome 21 itself or of the effects of deregulated miRNA expression on target genes located on other chromosomes (as described previously, miRNAs act through inhibition of target gene expression). Two chromosome 21 candidate genes, *DYRK1A,* which codes for a serine-threonine kinase, and *RCAN1* (*r*egulator of *ca*lci*n*eurin *1*), which codes for a protein that inhibits a critical cellular phosphatase enzyme called calcineurin, have emerged as the "top culprits" in the pathogenesis of Down syndrome.

22q11.2 Deletion Syndrome

The 22q11.2 deletion syndrome encompasses a spectrum of disorders that result from a small interstitial deletion of band 11 on the long arm of chromosome 22. The clinical features of this deletion syndrome include congenital heart disease affecting the outflow tracts, abnormalities of the palate, facial dysmorphism, developmental delay, thymic hypoplasia with impaired T cell immunity (Chapter 4), and parathyroid hypoplasia resulting in hypocalcemia (Chapter 19). Previously, these clinical features were believed to represent two different disorders: *DiGeorge syndrome* and *velocardiofacial syndrome.* However, it is now known that both are caused by 22q11.2 deletion. Variations in the size and position of the deletion are thought to be responsible for the differing clinical manifestations. When T cell immunodeficiency and hypocalcemia are the dominant features, the patients are said to have *DiGeorge syndrome,* whereas patients with the so-called *velocardiofacial syndrome* have mild immunodeficiency but pronounced dysmorphology

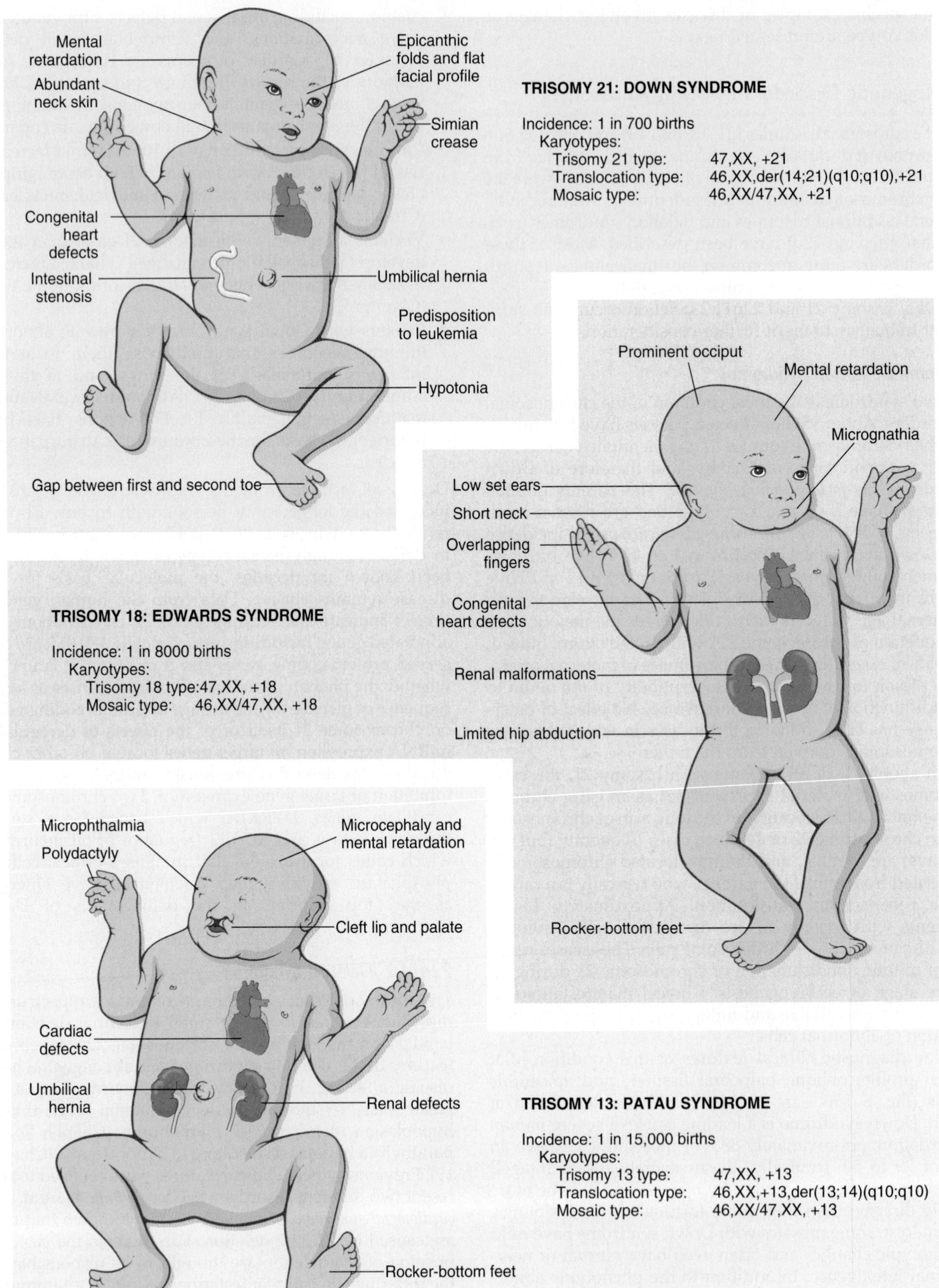

Figure 6–15 Clinical features and karyotypes of the three most common autosomal trisomies.

and cardiac defects. In addition to these malformations, patients with 22q11.2 deletion are at *particularly high risk for psychoses such as schizophrenia and bipolar disorder.* The molecular basis for this syndrome is not fully understood. The affected region of chromosome 11 encodes many genes. Among these, a transcription factor gene called *TBX1* is suspected to be responsible, since its loss seems to correlate with the occurrence of DiGeorge syndrome.

The diagnosis of this condition may be suspected on clinical grounds but can be established only by detection of the deletion by fluorescence in situ hybridization (FISH) (Fig. 6–37, *B*).

SUMMARY

Cytogenetic Disorders Involving Autosomes

- *Down syndrome* is associated with an extra copy of genes on chromosome 21, most commonly due to trisomy 21 and less frequently from translocation of extra chromosomal material from chromosome 21 to other chromosomes or from mosaicism.
- Patients with Down syndrome have severe mental retardation, flat facial profile, epicanthic folds, cardiac malformations, higher risk of leukemia and infections, and premature development of Alzheimer disease.
- Deletion of genes at chromosomal locus 22q11.2 gives rise to malformations affecting the face, heart, thymus, and parathyroids. The resulting disorders are recognized as (1) *DiGeorge syndrome* (thymic hypoplasia with diminished T cell immunity and parathyroid hypoplasia with hypocalcemia) and (2) *velocardiofacial syndrome* (congenital heart disease involving outflow tracts, facial dysmorphism, and developmental delay).

Cytogenetic Disorders Involving Sex Chromosomes

A number of abnormal karyotypes involving the sex chromosomes, ranging from 45,X to 49,XXXXY, are compatible with life. Indeed, phenotypically normal males with two and even three Y chromosomes have been identified. Such extreme karyotypic deviations are not encountered with the autosomes. In large part, this latitude relates to two factors: (1) lyonization of X chromosomes and (2) the small amount of genetic information carried by the Y chromosome. The consideration of lyonization must begin with Mary Lyon, who in 1962 proposed that in females, only one X chromosome is genetically active. X inactivation occurs early in fetal life, about 16 days after conception: Either the paternal or the maternal X chromosome is randomly inactivated in each of the primitive cells representing the developing embryo. Once inactivated, the same X chromosome remains genetically neutralized in all of the progeny of these cells. Moreover, all but one X chromosome is inactivated, and so a 48,XXXX female has only one active X chromosome. This phenomenon explains why normal females do not have a double dose (compared with males) of phenotypic attributes encoded on the X chromosome. The Lyon hypothesis also explains why normal females are in reality mosaics, containing two cell populations: one with an active maternal X, the other with an active paternal X.

Although essentially accurate, the Lyon hypothesis subsequently has been somewhat modified. Most important, the initial presumption that all of the genes on the inactive X are "switched off" has been revised as more recent studies suggest that 21% of genes on Xp, and a smaller number (3%) on Xq, escape X inactivation. This possibility has implications for monosomic X chromosome disorders, or Turner syndrome, as discussed later on.

Extra Y chromosomes are readily tolerated because the only information known to be carried on the Y chromosome seems to relate to male differentiation. Of note, whatever the number of X chromosomes, the presence of a Y invariably dictates the male phenotype. The gene for male differentiation (*SRY,* sex-determining region of Y chromosome) is located on the short arm of the Y.

Described briefly next are two disorders, Klinefelter syndrome and Turner syndrome, that result from aberrations of sex chromosomes.

Klinefelter Syndrome

Klinefelter syndrome is best defined as male hypogonadism that develops when there are at least two X chromosomes and one or more Y chromosomes. Most affected patients have a 47,XXY karyotype. This karyotype results from nondisjunction of sex chromosomes during meiosis. The extra X chromosome may be of either maternal or paternal origin. Advanced maternal age and a history of irradiation in either parent may contribute to the meiotic error resulting in this condition. Approximately 15% of the patients show mosaic patterns, including 46,XY/47,XXY, 47,XXY/48,XXXY, and variations on this theme. The presence of a 46,XY line in mosaics usually is associated with a milder clinical condition.

Klinefelter syndrome is associated with a wide range of clinical manifestations. In some persons it may be expressed only as hypogonadism, but most patients have a distinctive body habitus with an *increase in length between the soles and the pubic bone,* which creates the appearance of an elongated body. Also characteristic is eunuchoid body habitus. *Reduced facial, body, and pubic hair* and *gynecomastia* also are frequently seen. The testes are markedly reduced in size, sometimes to only 2 cm in greatest dimension. In keeping with the *testicular atrophy,* the serum testosterone levels are lower than normal, and urinary gonadotropin levels are elevated.

Klinefelter syndrome is the most common cause of hypogonadism in males. Only rarely are patients fertile, and presumably such persons are mosaics with a large proportion of 46,XY cells. The sterility is due to impaired spermatogenesis, sometimes to the extent of total azoospermia. Histologic examination reveals hyalinization of tubules, which appear as ghostlike structures on tissue section. By contrast, Leydig cells are prominent, as a result of either hyperplasia or an apparent increase related to loss of tubules. Although Klinefelter syndrome may be associated with mental retardation, the degree of intellectual impairment typically is mild, and in some cases, no deficit is detectable. The reduction in intelligence is correlated with the number of extra X chromosomes. Klinefelter syndrome is associated with a higher frequency of several disorders, including breast cancer (seen 20 times more commonly than in normal males), extragonadal germ cell tumors, and autoimmune diseases such as systemic lupus erythematosus.

Turner Syndrome

Turner syndrome, characterized by primary hypogonadism in phenotypic females, results from partial or complete monosomy of the short arm of the X chromosome. With routine cytogenetic methods, the entire X chromosome is found to be missing in 57% of patients, resulting in a 45,X karyotype. These patients are the most severely affected, and the diagnosis often can be made at birth or early in childhood. Typical clinical features associated with 45,X Turner syndrome include significant growth retardation, leading to abnormally short stature (below the third percentile); swelling of the nape of the neck due to distended lymphatic channels (in infancy) that is seen as webbing of the neck in older children; low posterior hairline; cubitus valgus (an increase in the carrying angle of the arms); shieldlike chest with widely spaced nipples; high-arched palate; lymphedema of the hands and feet; and a variety of congenital malformations such as horseshoe kidney, bicuspid aortic valve, and coarctation of the aorta (Fig. 6–16). Cardiovascular abnormalities are the most common cause of death in childhood. In adolescence, affected girls fail to develop normal secondary sex characteristics; the genitalia remain infantile, breast development is minimal, and little pubic hair appears. Most patients have primary amenorrhea, and morphologic examination reveals transformation of the ovaries into white streaks of fibrous stroma devoid of follicles. The mental status of these patients usually is normal, but subtle defects in nonverbal, visual-spatial information processing have been noted. Curiously, hypothyroidism caused by autoantibodies occurs, especially in women with isochromosome Xp. As many as 50% of these patients develop clinical hypothyroidism. In adult patients, *a combination of short stature and primary amenorrhea should prompt strong suspicion for Turner syndrome.* The diagnosis is established by karyotyping.

Approximately 43% of patients with Turner syndrome either are mosaics (one of the cell lines being 45,X) or have structural abnormalities of the X chromosome. The most common is deletion of the short arm, resulting in the formation of an isochromosome of the long arm, 46,X,i(X)(q10). The net effect of the associated structural abnormalities is to produce partial monosomy of the X chromosome. Combinations of deletions and mosaicism are reported. It is important to appreciate the karyotypic heterogeneity associated with Turner syndrome because it is responsible for significant variations in the phenotype. In contrast with the patients with monosomy X, *those who are mosaics or have deletion variants may have an almost normal appearance and may present only with primary amenorrhea.*

The molecular pathogenesis of Turner syndrome is not completely understood, but studies have begun to shed some light. As mentioned earlier, both X chromosomes are active during oogenesis and are essential for normal development of the ovaries. During normal fetal development, ovaries contain as many as 7 million oocytes. The oocytes gradually disappear so that by menarche their numbers have dwindled to a mere 400,000, and when menopause occurs fewer than 10,000 remain. In Turner syndrome, fetal ovaries develop normally early in embryogenesis, but the absence of the second X chromosome leads to an accelerated loss of oocytes, which is complete by age 2 years. In a sense, therefore, "menopause occurs before menarche," and the ovaries are reduced to atrophic fibrous strands, devoid of ova and follicles (*streak ovaries*). Because patients with Turner syndrome also have other (nongonadal) abnormalities, it follows that some genes for normal growth and development of somatic tissues also must reside on the X chromosome. Among the genes involved in the Turner phenotype is the short stature homeobox (*SHOX*) gene at Xp22.33. *This is one of the genes that remain active in both X chromosomes* and is unique in having an active homologue on the short arm of the Y chromosome. Thus, both normal males and females have two copies of this gene. One copy of *SHOX* gives rise to short stature. Indeed, deletions of the *SHOX* gene are noted in 2% to 5% of otherwise normal children with short stature. Whereas one copy of *SHOX* can explain growth deficit in Turner syndrome, it cannot explain other important clinical

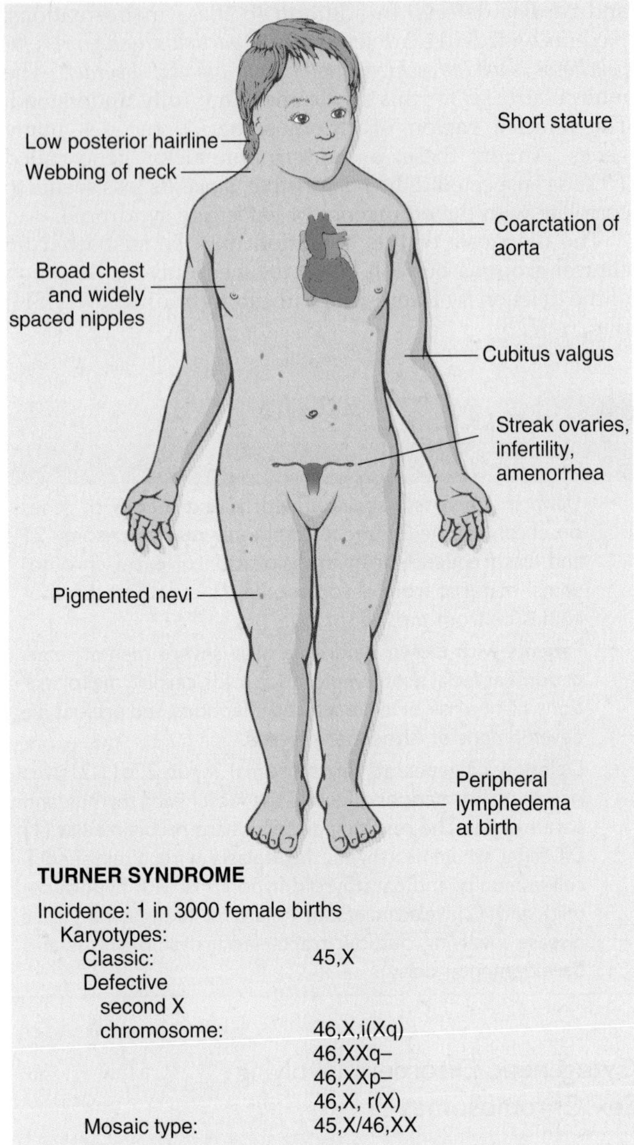

Figure 6–16 Clinical features and karyotypes of Turner syndrome.

features such as cardiac malformations and endocrine abnormalities. Clearly, several other genes located on the X chromosome also are involved.

SUMMARY

Cytogenetic Disorders Involving Sex Chromosomes

- In females, one X chromosome, maternal or paternal, is randomly inactivated during development (Lyon hypothesis).
- In *Klinefelter syndrome*, there are two or more X chromosomes with one Y chromosome as a result of nondisjunction of sex chromosomes. Patients have testicular atrophy, sterility, reduced body hair, gynecomastia, and eunuchoid body habitus. It is the most common cause of male sterility.
- In *Turner syndrome*, there is partial or complete monosomy of genes on the short arm of the X chromosome, most commonly due to absence of one X chromosome (45,X) and less commonly from mosaicism, or from deletions involving the short arm of the X chromosome. Short stature, webbing of the neck, cubitus valgus, cardiovascular malformations, amenorrhea, lack of secondary sex characteristics, and fibrotic ovaries are typical clinical features.

SINGLE-GENE DISORDERS WITH ATYPICAL PATTERNS OF INHERITANCE

Three groups of diseases resulting from mutations affecting single genes do not follow the mendelian rules of inheritance:

- Diseases caused by triplet repeat mutations
- Diseases caused by mutations in mitochondrial genes
- Diseases associated with alteration of imprinted regions of the genome

Triplet Repeat Mutations: Fragile X Syndrome

Fragile X syndrome is the prototype of diseases in which the causative mutation occurs in a long repeating sequence of three nucleotides. Other examples of diseases associated with trinucleotide repeat mutations are Huntington disease and myotonic dystrophy. About 40 diseases are now known to be caused by this type of mutation, and all disorders discovered so far are associated with neurodegenerative changes. In each of these conditions, *amplification of specific sets of three nucleotides within the gene disrupts its function.* Certain unique features of trinucleotide repeat mutations, described later, are responsible for the atypical pattern of inheritance of the associated diseases.

Fragile X syndrome results from a mutation in the *FMR1* gene, which maps to Xq27.3. The syndrome gets its name from the karyotypic appearance of the X chromosome in the original method of diagnosis: Culturing patient cells in a folate-deficient medium typically revealed a *discontinuity of staining or constriction in the long arm of the X chromosome.* This method has now been supplanted by DNA-based analysis of triplet repeat size as discussed later. With a frequency of 1 in 1550 for affected males and 1 in 8000 for affected females, *fragile X syndrome is the second most common genetic cause of mental retardation, after Down syndrome.* Clinically affected males have moderate to severe mental retardation. The characteristic physical phenotype includes a long face with a large mandible, large everted ears, and large testicles (*macroorchidism*). Although characteristic of fragile X syndrome, these abnormalities are not always present or may be quite subtle. The only distinctive physical abnormality that can be detected in at least 90% of postpubertal males with fragile X syndrome is macroorchidism.

As with all X-linked diseases, fragile X syndrome predominantly affects males. Analysis of several pedigrees, however, reveals some patterns of transmission not typically associated with other X-linked recessive disorders (Fig. 6–17). These include the following:

- *Carrier males*: Approximately 20% of males who, by pedigree analysis and by molecular tests, are known to carry a fragile X mutation are clinically and cytogenetically normal. Because carrier males transmit the trait through all their daughters (phenotypically normal) to affected grandchildren, they are called *normal transmitting males.*
- *Affected females*: From 30% to 50% of carrier females are affected (i.e., mentally retarded), a number much higher than that for other X-linked recessive disorders.
- *Anticipation*: This term refers to the phenomenon whereby clinical features of fragile X syndrome worsen with each successive generation, as if the mutation becomes increasingly deleterious as it is transmitted from a man to his grandsons and great-grandsons.

These unusual features have been related to the dynamic nature of the mutation. In the normal population, the number of repeats of the sequence CGG in the *FMR1* gene is small, averaging around 29, whereas affected persons have 200 to 4000 repeats. These so-called full mutations are believed to arise through an intermediate stage of *premutations* characterized by 52 to 200 CGG repeats. Carrier males and females have premutations. During oogenesis (but not spermatogenesis), the premutations can be converted to full mutations by further amplification of the CGG repeats, which can then be transmitted to both the sons and the daughters of the carrier female. These observations provide an explanation for why some carrier males are unaffected (they have premutations), and certain carrier females are affected (they inherit full mutations). Recent studies indicate that premutations are not so benign after all. *Approximately 30% of females carrying the premutation have premature ovarian failure (before the age of 40 years), and about one third of premutation-carrying males exhibit a progressive neurodegenerative syndrome starting in their sixth decade.* This syndrome, referred to as fragile X–associated tremor-ataxia, is characterized by intention tremors and cerebellar ataxia and may progress to parkinsonism. It is clear, however, that the abnormalities in permutation carriers are milder and occur later in life.

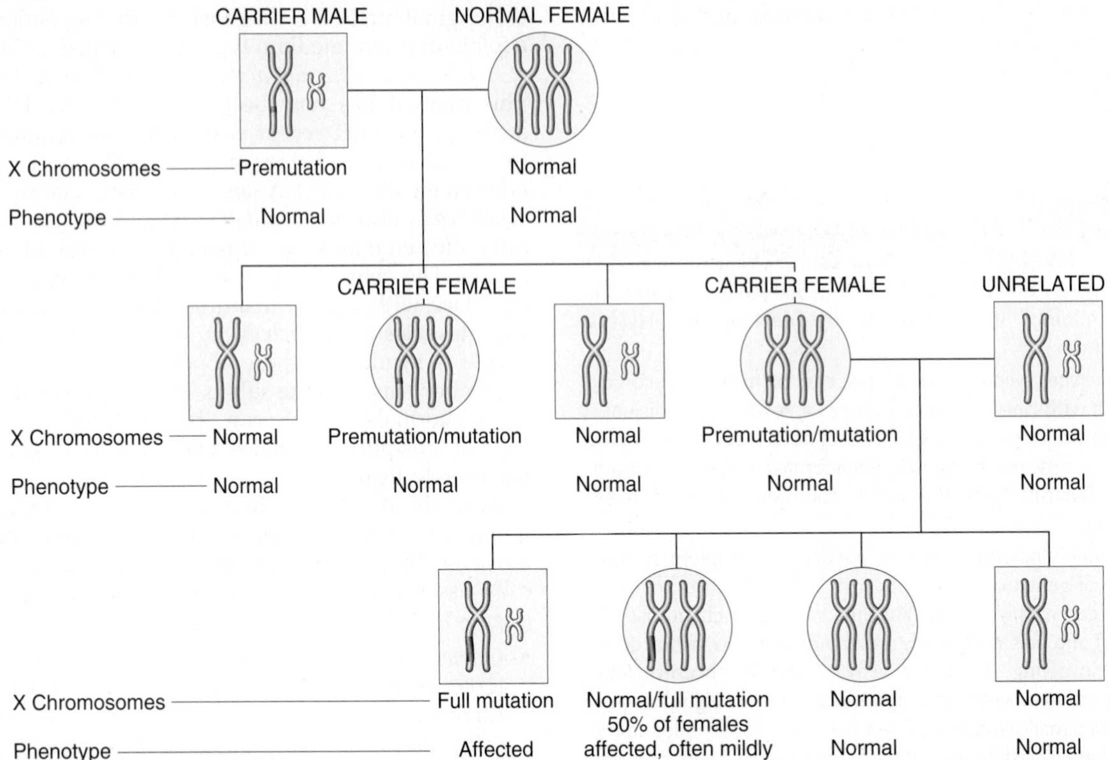

Figure 6–17 Fragile X pedigree. X and Y chromosomes are shown. Note that in the first generation, all sons are normal and all females are carriers. During oogenesis in the carrier female, premutation expands to full mutation; hence, in the next generation, all males who inherit the X with full mutation are affected. However, only 50% of females who inherit the full mutation are affected, and often only mildly.

(Based on an original sketch courtesy of Dr. Nancy Schneider, Department of Pathology, University of Texas Southwestern Medical School, Dallas, Texas.)

PATHOGENESIS

The molecular basis for fragile X syndrome is beginning to be understood and relates to silencing of the product of the *FMR1* gene, familial mental retardation protein (FMRP). The normal *FMR1* gene contains CGG repeats in its 5′ untranslated region. When the number of trinucleotide repeats in the *FMR1* gene exceeds approximately 230, the DNA of the entire 5′ region of the gene becomes abnormally methylated. Methylation also extends upstream into the promoter region of the gene, resulting in transcriptional suppression of *FMR1*. The resulting absence of FMRP is believed to cause the phenotypic changes. FMRP is widely expressed in normal tissues, but higher levels are found in the brain and the testis. Current evidence suggests that FMRP is an RNA-binding protein that is transported from the cytoplasm to the nucleus, where it binds specific mRNAs and transports them to the axons and dendrites (Fig. 6–18). It is in the synapses that FMRP–mRNA complexes perform critical roles in regulating the translation of specific mRNAs. The absence of this finely coordinated "shuttle" function seems to underlie the causation of fragile X syndrome.

As noted, in addition to fragile X syndrome, many other neurodegenerative diseases related to trinucleotide repeat expansions are recognized. Some general principles follow:

- In all cases, gene functions are altered by an expansion of the repeats, but the precise threshold at which

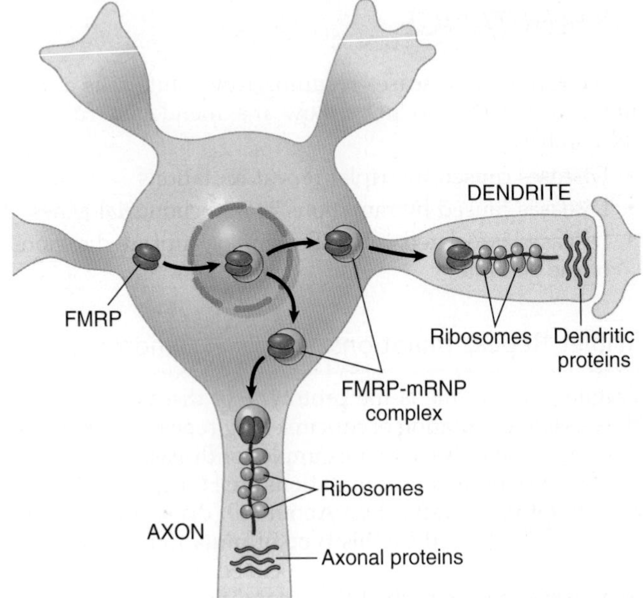

Figure 6–18 A model for the action of familial mental retardation protein (FMRP) in neurons. FMRP plays a critical role in regulating the translation of axonal proteins from bound RNAs. These locally produced proteins, in turn, play diverse roles in the microenvironment of the synapse.

(Adapted from Hin P, Warren ST: New insights into fragile X syndrome: from molecules to neurobehavior. Trends Biochem Sci 28:152, 2003.)

premutations are converted to full mutations differs with each disorder.

- While the expansion in fragile X syndrome occurs during oogenesis, in other disorders such as Huntington disease, premutations are converted to full mutations during spermatogenesis.
- The expansion may involve any part of the gene, and the range of possibilities can be divided into two broad categories: those that affect untranslated regions (as in fragile X syndrome) or coding regions (as in Huntington disease) (Fig. 6–19). When mutations affect noncoding regions, there is "loss of function," since protein synthesis is suppressed (e.g., FMRP). By contrast, mutations involving translated parts of the gene give rise to misfolded proteins that interfere with function of normal proteins (e.g., Huntington disease). Many of these so-called toxic gain-of-function mutations involve CAG repeats that encode polyglutamine tracts, and the resultant diseases are sometimes referred to as "polyglutamine diseases," affecting primarily the nervous system. Accumulation of misfolded proteins in aggregates within the cytoplasm is a common feature of such diseases.

SUMMARY

Fragile X Syndrome

- Pathologic amplification of trinucleotide repeats causes loss-of-function (fragile X syndrome) or gain-of-function mutations (Huntington disease). Most such mutations produce neurodegenerative disorders.
- Fragile X syndrome results from loss of *FMR1* gene function and is characterized by mental retardation, macro-orchidism, and abnormal facial features.
- In the normal population, there are about 29 CGG repeats in the *FMR1* gene. The genomes of carrier males and females contain premutations with 52 to 200 CGG repeats that can expand to 4000 repeats (full mutations) during oogenesis. When full mutations are transmitted to progeny, fragile X syndrome occurs.

Diseases Caused by Mutations in Mitochondrial Genes

Mitochondria contain several genes that encode enzymes involved in oxidative phosphorylation. Inheritance of mitochondrial DNA differs from that of nuclear DNA in that the former is associated with *maternal inheritance.* The reason for this peculiarity is that ova contain mitochondria within their abundant cytoplasm, whereas spermatozoa contain few, if any, mitochondria. The mitochondrial DNA complement of the zygote is therefore derived entirely from the ovum. Thus, only mothers transmit mitochondrial genes to all of their offspring, both male and female; however, daughters but not sons transmit the DNA further to their progeny.

Diseases caused by mutations in mitochondrial genes are rare. Because mitochondrial DNA encodes enzymes involved in oxidative phosphorylation, diseases caused by mutations in such genes affect organs most dependent on oxidative phosphorylation (skeletal muscle, heart, brain). Leber hereditary optic neuropathy is the prototypical disorder in this group. This neurodegenerative disease manifests itself as progressive bilateral loss of central vision that leads in due course to blindness.

Diseases Caused by Alterations of Imprinted Regions: Prader-Willi and Angelman Syndromes

All humans inherit two copies of each gene (except, of course, the sex chromosome genes in males), carried on homologous maternal and paternal chromosomes. It was long assumed that there was no difference between normal homologous genes derived from the mother and those from the father. Indeed, this is true for many genes. It has now been established, however, that functional differences exist between the paternal and the maternal copies of some genes. These differences arise from an epigenetic process called *genomic imprinting,* whereby certain genes are differentially "inactivated" during paternal and maternal gametogenesis. Thus, *maternal imprinting* refers to transcriptional silencing of the maternal allele, whereas *paternal imprinting* implies that the paternal allele is inactivated. At the molecular level, imprinting is associated with methylation of the gene promoter, as well as related events such as

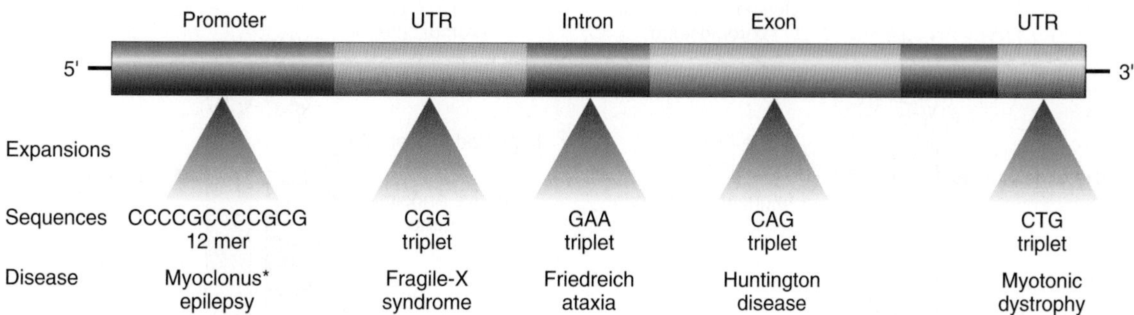

Figure 6–19 Sites of expansion and the affected sequence in selected diseases caused by nucleotide repeat mutations. UTR, untranslated region. *Though not strictly a trinucleotide-repeat disease, progressive myoclonus epilepsy is caused, like others in this group, by a heritable DNA expansion. The expanded segment is in the promoter region of the gene.

modification of DNA-binding histone proteins, the sum total effect of which is to silence the gene. Imprinting occurs in ovum or sperm and is then stably transmitted to all somatic cells derived from the zygote.

Genomic imprinting is best illustrated by considering two uncommon genetic disorders: Prader-Willi syndrome and Angelman syndrome.

Prader-Willi syndrome is characterized by mental retardation, short stature, hypotonia, obesity, small hands and feet, and hypogonadism. In 60% to 75% of cases, an interstitial deletion of band q12 in the long arm of chromosome 15—del(15)(q11;q13)—can be detected. In many patients without a detectable cytogenetic abnormality, FISH analysis reveals smaller deletions within the same region. *It is striking that in all cases, the deletion affects the paternally derived chromosome 15.* In contrast with Prader-Willi syndrome, patients with the phenotypically distinct *Angelman syndrome* are born with a deletion of the same chromosomal region derived from their mothers. Patients with Angelman syndrome also are mentally retarded, but in addition they present with ataxic gait, seizures, and inappropriate laughter. Because of the laughter and ataxia, this syndrome has been called the *happy puppet syndrome.* A comparison of these two syndromes clearly demonstrates the "parent-of-origin" effects on gene function. If all the paternal and maternal genes contained within chromosome 15 were expressed in an identical fashion, clinical features resulting from these deletions would be expected to be identical regardless of the parental origin of chromosome 15.

The molecular basis of these two syndromes can be understood in the context of imprinting (Fig. 6–20). A set of genes on the maternal chromosome at 15q12 is imprinted (and hence silenced), so the only functional alleles are provided by the paternal chromosome. When these are lost as a result of a deletion (in the paternal chromosome), the patient develops Prader-Willi syndrome. Conversely, a distinct gene that also maps to the same region of chromosome 15 is imprinted on the paternal chromosome. Only the maternally derived allele of the gene normally is active. Deletion of this maternal gene on chromosome 15 gives rise to the Angelman syndrome. Molecular studies of cytogenetically normal patients with Prader-Willi syndrome have revealed that in some cases, both of the structurally normal copies of chromosome 15 are derived from the mother. *Inheritance of both chromosomes of a pair from one parent is called uniparental disomy.* The net effect is the same (i.e., the patient does not have a functional set of genes from the [nonimprinted] paternal chromosome 15).

Angelman syndrome, as might be expected, also can result from uniparental disomy of parental chromosome 15. The Angelman syndrome gene (imprinted on the paternal chromosome) is now known to encode a ligase that has a role in the ubiquitin-proteasome proteolytic pathway (Chapter 1). This gene, called, somewhat laboriously, *UBE3A,* is expressed primarily from the maternal allele in specific regions of the normal brain. In Angelman syndrome, *UBE3A* is not expressed in these areas of the brain—hence the neurologic manifestations.

Prader-Willi syndrome, unlike Angelman syndrome, probably is caused by the loss of function of several genes located on chromosome 15 between q11 and q13. These genes are still being fully characterized.

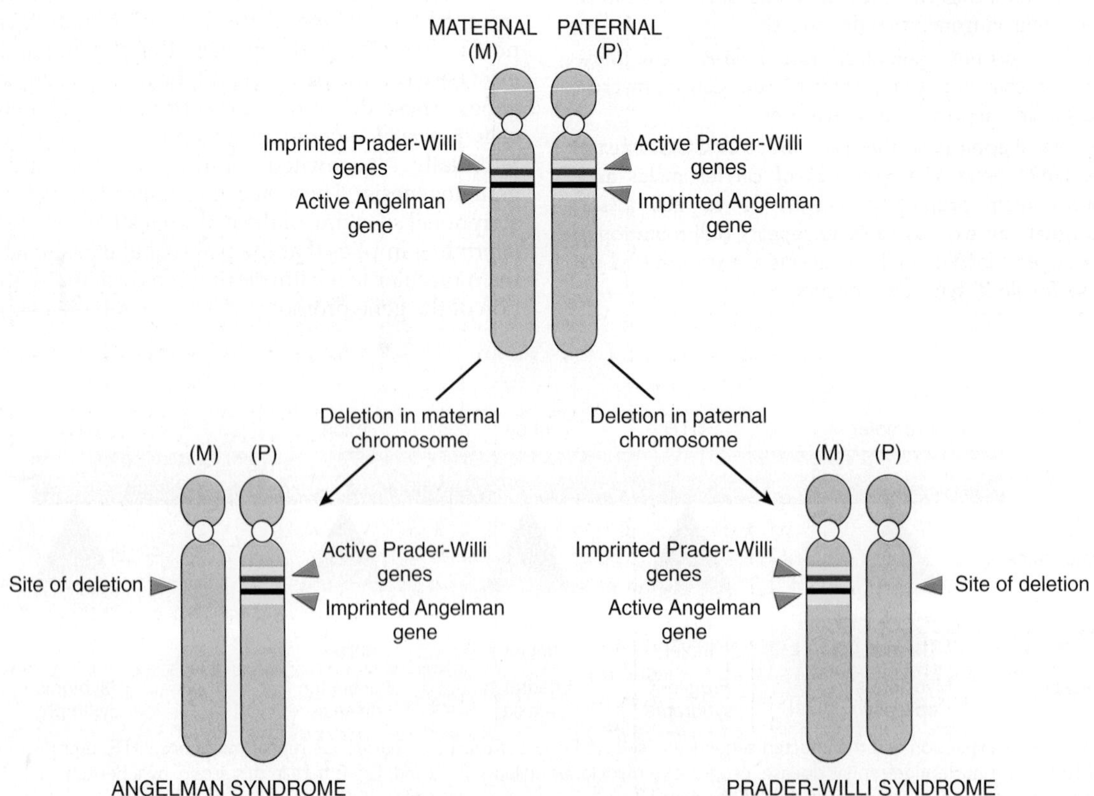

Figure 6–20 Genetics of Angelman and Prader-Willi syndromes.

SUMMARY
Genomic Imprinting

- Imprinting involves transcriptional silencing of the paternal or maternal copies of certain genes during gametogenesis. For such genes only one functional copy exists in the individual. Loss of the functional allele (not imprinted) by deletions gives rise to diseases.
- *Prader-Willi syndrome* results from deletion of paternal chromosomal region 15q12 and is characterized by mental retardation, short stature, hypotonia, obesity, and hypogonadism.
- *Angelman syndrome* results from deletion of maternal chromosomal region 15q12 and is characterized by mental retardation, ataxia, seizures, and inappropriate laughter.

PEDIATRIC DISEASES

As mentioned earlier and illustrated by several examples, many diseases of infancy and childhood are of genetic origin. Others, although not genetic, either are unique to children or take distinctive forms in this patient population and thus merit the designation *pediatric diseases.* During each stage of development, infants and children are prey to a somewhat different group of diseases (Table 6–6). Clearly, diseases of infancy (i.e., the first year of life) pose the highest risk of death. During this phase, the neonatal period (the first 4 weeks of life) is unquestionably the most hazardous time.

Once the infant survives the first year of life, the outlook brightens considerably. However, it is sobering to note that between 1 year and 14 years of age, injuries resulting from accidents are the leading cause of death. Not all conditions listed in Table 6–6 are described in this chapter; only a select few that are most common are considered here. Although general principles of neoplastic disease and specific tumors are discussed elsewhere, a few tumors of children are described, to highlight the differences between pediatric and adult neoplasms.

CONGENITAL ANOMALIES

Congenital anomalies are structural defects that are present at birth, although some, such as cardiac defects and renal anomalies, may not become clinically apparent until years later. As will be evident from the ensuing discussion, the term *congenital* does not imply or exclude a genetic basis for birth defects. It is estimated that about 120,000 babies are born with a birth defect each year in the United States, an incidence of 1 in 33. As indicated in Table 6–6, congenital anomalies constitute an important cause of infant mortality. Moreover, they continue to be a significant cause of illness, disability, and death throughout the early years of life.

Before consideration of the etiology and pathogenesis of congenital anomalies, it is essential to define some of the terms used to describe errors in morphogenesis.

- *Malformations* represent primary errors of morphogenesis. In other words, there is an *intrinsically abnormal developmental process.* Malformations usually are

Table 6–6 Causes of Death by Age

Cause*	Rate†
Under 1 Year	**677.3**
Congenital malformations, deformations, and chromosomal anomalies	
Disorders related to short gestation and low birth weight	
Sudden infant death syndrome (SIDS)	
Newborn affected by maternal complications of pregnancy	
Newborn affected by complications of placenta, cord, and membranes	
Respiratory distress syndrome of newborn	
Accidents (unintentional injuries)	
Bacterial sepsis of newborn	
Neonatal hemorrhage	
Diseases of the circulatory system	
1–4 Years	**28.2**
Accidents (unintentional injuries)	
Congenital malformations, deformations, and chromosomal abnormalities	
Assault (homicide)	
1–4 Years—cont'd	**28.2**
Malignant neoplasms	
Diseases of the heart‡	
5–9 Years	**13.6**
Accidents (unintentional injuries)	
Malignant neoplasms	
Congenital malformations, deformations, and chromosomal abnormalities	
Assault (homicide)	
Diseases of the heart	
10–14 Years	**16.7**
Accidents (unintentional injuries)	
Malignant neoplasms	
Assault (homicide)	
Intentional self-harm (suicide)	
Congenital malformations, deformations, and chromosomal abnormalities	

Data from Heron MP, Sutton PD, Xu J, et al: Annual Summary of Vital Statistics: 2007. Pediatrics 125:4, 2010.
*Causes are listed in decreasing order of frequency. All causes and rates are final 2007 statistics.
†Rates are expressed per 100,000 population from all causes within each age group.
‡Excludes congenital heart disease.

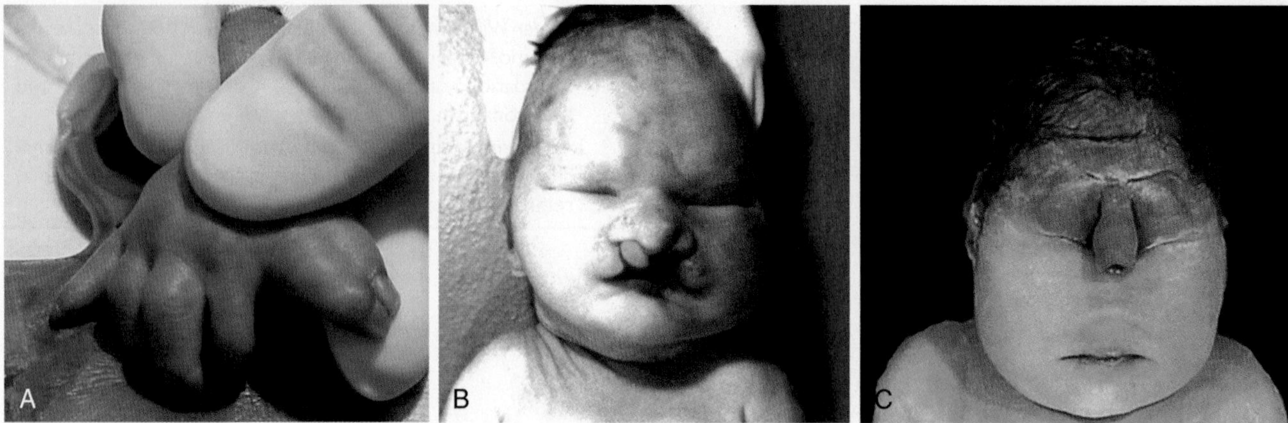

Figure 6–21 Human malformations can range in severity from the incidental to the lethal. **A,** *Polydactyly* (one or more extra digits) and *syndactyly* (fusion of digits), have little functional consequence when they occur in isolation. **B,** Similarly, *cleft lip,* with or without associated *cleft palate,* is compatible with life when it occurs as an isolated anomaly; in this case, however, the child had an underlying *malformation syndrome* (trisomy 13) and expired because of severe cardiac defects. **C,** Stillbirth representing a severe and essentially lethal malformation, in which the midface structures are fused or ill-formed; in almost all cases, this degree of external dysmorphogenesis is associated with severe internal anomalies such as maldevelopment of the brain and cardiac defects.

(A and C, Courtesy of Dr. Reade Quinton, Department of Pathology, University of Texas Southwestern Medical Center, Dallas, Texas. B, Courtesy of Dr. Beverly Rogers, Department of Pathology, University of Texas Southwestern Medical Center, Dallas, Texas.)

multifactorial, rather than the result of a single gene or chromosomal defect. They may manifest in any of several patterns. In some presentations, such as congenital heart diseases, single body systems may be involved, whereas in others, multiple malformations involving many organs and tissues may coexist (Fig. 6–21).

- *Disruptions* result from secondary destruction of an organ or body region that was previously normal in development; thus, in contrast with malformations, disruptions arise from an *extrinsic disturbance in morphogenesis. Amniotic bands,* denoting rupture of amnion with resultant formation of "bands" that encircle, compress, or attach to parts of the developing fetus, constitute the classic example of a disruption (Fig. 6–22). A variety of environmental agents may cause disruptions (see below). Disruptions are not heritable, of course, and thus are not associated with risk of recurrence in subsequent pregnancies.
- *Deformations,* like disruptions, also represent an *extrinsic disturbance of development* rather than an intrinsic error of morphogenesis. Deformations are common problems, affecting approximately 2% of newborn infants to various degrees. Fundamental to the pathogenesis of deformations is localized or generalized compression of the growing fetus by abnormal biomechanical forces, leading eventually to a variety of structural abnormalities. The most common cause of such deformations is uterine constraint. Between weeks 35 and 38 of gestation, rapid increase in the size of the fetus outpaces the growth of the uterus, and the relative amount of amniotic fluid (which normally acts as a cushion) also decreases. Thus, even the normal fetus is subjected to some degree of uterine constraint. However, several variables increase the likelihood of excessive compression of the fetus, including maternal conditions such as first pregnancy, small uterus, malformed (bicornuate) uterus, and leiomyomas. Causes relating to the fetus, such as presence of multiple fetuses, oligohydramnios, and abnormal fetal presentation, also may be involved.
- *Sequence* refers to multiple congenital anomalies that result from *secondary effects of a single localized aberration in organogenesis.* The initiating event may be a malformation, deformation, or disruption. An excellent example is the oligohydramnios (or Potter) sequence (Fig. 6–23, *A*). Oligohydramnios, denoting decreased amniotic fluid, may be caused by a variety of unrelated maternal, placental, or fetal abnormalities. Chronic leakage of amniotic fluid due to rupture of the amnion, uteroplacental insufficiency resulting from maternal hypertension or severe toxemia, and renal agenesis in the fetus

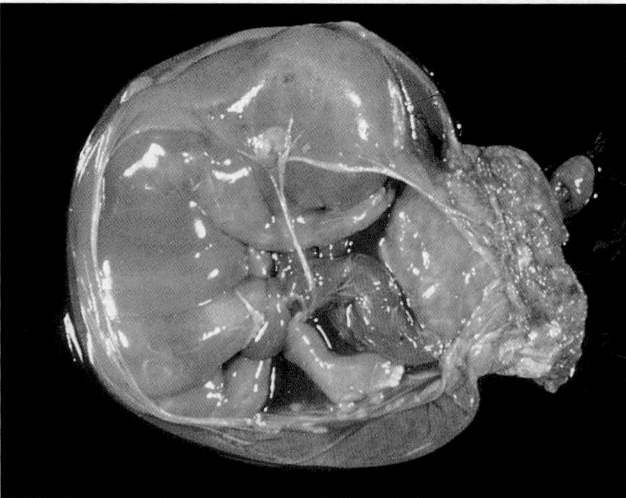

Figure 6–22 Disruptions occur in a developing organ because of an extrinsic abnormality that interferes with normal morphogenesis. *Amniotic bands* are a frequent cause of disruptions. In the gross specimen shown, the placenta is at the *right of the diagram,* and the band of amnion extends from the *top portion of the amniotic sac* to encircle the leg of the fetus.

(Courtesy of Dr. Theonia Boyd, Children's Hospital of Boston, Boston, Massachusetts.)

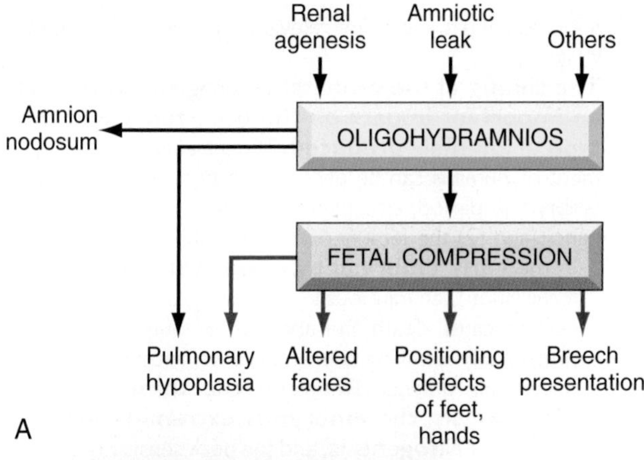

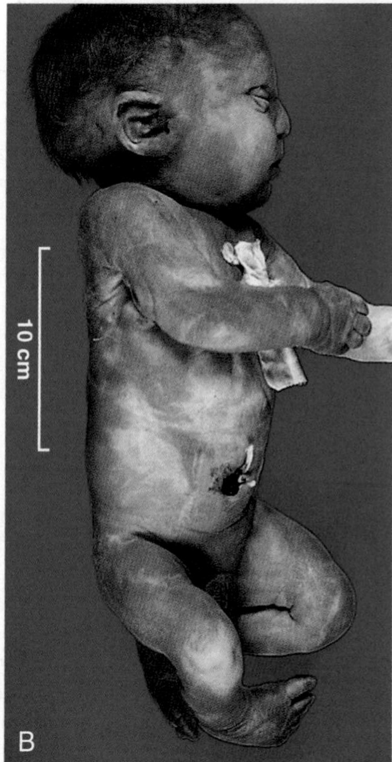

Figure 6–23 A, Pathogenesis of the oligohydramnios (Potter) sequence. **B,** Infant with oligohydramnios (Potter) sequence. Note flattened facial features and deformed foot (talipes equinovarus).

(because fetal urine is a major constituent of amniotic fluid) all are potential causes of oligohydramnios. The fetal compression associated with significant oligohydramnios in turn results in a classic phenotype in the newborn infant, including flattened facies and positional abnormalities of the hands and feet (Fig. 6–23, *B*). The hips may be dislocated. Growth of the chest wall and the contained lungs also is compromised, sometimes to such an extent that survival is not possible. If the embryologic connection between these defects and the initiating event is not recognized, a sequence may be mistaken for a malformation syndrome.

- *Malformation syndrome* refers to the presence of several defects that cannot be explained on the basis of a single localizing initiating error in morphogenesis. Syndromes most often arise from a single causative condition (e.g., viral infection or a specific chromosomal abnormality) that simultaneously affects several tissues.
- In addition to these global definitions, some general terms are applied to organ-specific malformations: *Agenesis* refers to the complete absence of an organ or its anlage, whereas *aplasia* and *hypoplasia* indicate incomplete development and underdevelopment, respectively, of an organ. *Atresia* describes the absence of an opening, usually of a hollow visceral organ or duct such as intestines and bile ducts.

Etiology

Known causes of errors in human malformations can be grouped into three major categories: *genetic, environmental,* and *multifactorial* (Table 6–7). *The cause has not been identified for almost half of the reported cases.*

Genetic causes of malformations include all of the previously discussed mechanisms of genetic disease. Virtually all chromosomal syndromes are associated with congenital malformations. Examples are Down syndrome and other trisomies, Turner syndrome, and Klinefelter syndrome. Most chromosomal disorders arise during gametogenesis and hence are not familial. Single-gene mutations, characterized by mendelian inheritance, may underlie major malformations. For example, holoprosencephaly is the most common developmental defect of the forebrain and midface in humans (see Chapter 22); the Hedgehog signaling

Table 6–7 Causes of Congenital Malformations in Humans

Cause	Frequency of Malformations* (%)
Genetic	
Chromosomal aberrations	10–15
Mendelian inheritance	2–10
Environmental	
Maternal/placental infections Rubella Toxoplasmosis Syphilis Cytomegalovirus infection Human immunodeficiency virus infection	2–3
Maternal disease states Diabetes Phenylketonuria Endocrinopathies	6–8
Drugs and chemicals Alcohol Folic acid antagonists Androgens Phenytoin Thalidomide Warfarin 13-*Cis*-retinoic acid Others	~1
Irradiation	~1
Multifactorial	20–25
Unknown	40–60

Data from Stevenson RE, Hall JG, Goodman RM (eds): Human Malformations and Related Anomalies. New York, Oxford University Press, 1993, p 115.
*Live births.

pathway plays a critical role in the morphogenesis of these structures, and loss-of-function mutations of individual components within this pathway are reported in families with a history of recurrent holoprosencephaly.

Environmental influences, such as viral infections, drugs, and radiation to which the mother was exposed during pregnancy, may cause fetal malformations (the appellation of "malformation" is used loosely in this context, since technically, these anomalies represent *disruptions*). Among the viral infections listed in Table 6–7, rubella was a major scourge of the 19th and early 20th centuries. Fortunately, maternal rubella and the resultant *rubella embryopathy* have been virtually eliminated in developed countries as a result of vaccination. A variety of drugs and chemicals have been suspected to be teratogenic, but perhaps less than 1% of congenital malformations are caused by these agents. The list includes thalidomide, alcohol, anticonvulsants, warfarin (oral anticoagulant), and 13-*cis*-retinoic acid, which is used in the treatment of severe acne. For example, *thalidomide,* once used as a tranquilizer in Europe and currently used for treatment of certain cancers, causes an extremely high incidence (50% to 80%) of limb malformations. *Alcohol,* perhaps the most widely used agent today, is an important environmental teratogen. Affected infants show prenatal and postnatal growth retardation, facial anomalies (microcephaly, short palpebral fissures, maxillary hypoplasia), and psychomotor disturbances. These features in combination are designated the *fetal alcohol syndrome.* While cigarette smoke–derived nicotine has not been convincingly demonstrated to be a teratogen, there is a high incidence of spontaneous abortions, premature labor, and placental abnormalities among pregnant smokers; babies born to mothers who smoke often have a low birth weight and may be prone to the sudden infant death syndrome (SIDS). *In light of these findings, it is best to avoid nicotine exposure altogether during pregnancy.* Among maternal conditions listed in Table 6–7, *diabetes mellitus* is a common entity, and despite advances in antenatal obstetric monitoring and glucose control, the incidence of major malformations in infants of diabetic mothers stands between 6% and 10% in most reported series. Maternal hyperglycemia–induced fetal hyperinsulinemia results in fetal macrosomia (organomegaly and increased body fat and muscle mass); cardiac anomalies, neural tube defects, and other CNS malformations are some of the major anomalies seen in *diabetic embryopathy.*

Multifactorial inheritance, which implies the interaction of environmental influences with two or more genes of small effect, is the most common genetic cause of congenital malformations. Included in this category are some relatively common malformations such as cleft lip and palate and neural tube defects. The importance of environmental contributions to multifactorial inheritance is underscored by the dramatic reduction in the incidence of neural tube defects by periconceptional intake of folic acid in the diet. The recurrence risks and mode of transmission of multifactorial disorders are described earlier in this chapter.

PATHOGENESIS

The pathogenesis of congenital anomalies is complex and still poorly understood, but two general principles of developmental pathology are relevant regardless of the etiologic agent:

1. **The timing of the prenatal teratogenic insult has an important impact on the occurrence and the type of anomaly produced.** The intrauterine development of humans can be divided into two phases: (1) the embryonic period, occupying the first 9 weeks of pregnancy, and (2) the fetal period, terminating at birth.
   - In the **early embryonic period** (first 3 weeks after fertilization), an injurious agent damages either enough cells to cause death and abortion or only a few cells, presumably allowing the embryo to recover without developing defects. **Between the third and the ninth weeks, the embryo is extremely susceptible to teratogenesis,** and the peak sensitivity during this period occurs between the fourth and the fifth weeks. During this period organs are being crafted out of the germ cell layers.
   - The **fetal period** that follows organogenesis is marked chiefly by the further growth and maturation of the organs, with greatly reduced susceptibility to teratogenic agents. Instead, the fetus is susceptible to growth retardation or injury to already formed organs. It is therefore possible for a given agent to produce different anomalies if exposure occurs at different times of gestation.
2. The complex interplay between environmental teratogens and intrinsic genetic defects is exemplified by the fact that features of dysmorphogenesis caused by environmental insults often can be recapitulated by genetic defects in the pathways targeted by these teratogens. Some representative examples follow:
   - **Cyclopamine** is a plant teratogen. Pregnant sheep who feed on plants containing cyclopamine give birth to lambs that have severe craniofacial abnormalities including holoprosencephaly and **cyclopia** (single fused eye—hence the origin of the moniker cyclopamine). This compound is a potent inhibitor of Hedgehog signaling in the embryo, and as stated previously, mutations of Hedgehog genes are present in subsets of fetuses with holoprosencephaly.
   - **Valproic acid** is an antiepileptic and a recognized teratogen. Valproic acid disrupts expression of a family of highly conserved developmentally critical transcription factors known as **homeobox (HOX)** proteins. In vertebrates, HOX proteins have been implicated in the patterning of limbs, vertebrae, and craniofacial structures. Not surprisingly, mutations in HOX family genes are responsible for congenital anomalies that mimic features observed in **valproic acid embryopathy.**
   - The vitamin A (retinol) derivative **all-trans-retinoic acid** is essential for normal development and differentiation, and its **absence** during embryogenesis results in a constellation of malformations affecting multiple organ systems, including the eyes, genitourinary system, cardiovascular system, diaphragm, and lungs (see Chapter 7 for vitamin A deficiency in the postnatal period). Conversely, **excessive exposure to retinoic acid also is teratogenic.** Infants born to mothers treated with retinoic acid for severe acne have a predictable phenotype **(retinoic acid embryopathy),** including CNS, cardiac, and craniofacial defects,

such as **cleft lip and cleft palate.** The last entity may stem from retinoic acid–mediated deregulation of components of the transforming growth factor-β (TGF-β) signaling pathway, which is involved in palatogenesis. Mice with knockout of the *Tgfb3* gene uniformly develop cleft palate, once again underscoring the functional relationship between teratogenic exposure and signaling pathways in the causation of congenital anomalies.

SUMMARY

Congenital Anomalies

- Congenital anomalies result from intrinsic abnormalities (malformations) as well as extrinsic disturbances (deformations, disruptions).
- Congenital anomalies can result from genetic (chromosomal abnormalities, gene mutations), environmental (infections, drugs, alcohol), and multifactorial causes.
- The timing of the in utero insult has profound influence on the extent of congenital anomalies, with earlier events usually demonstrating greater impact.
- The interplay between genetic and environmental causes of anomalies is demonstrated by the fact that teratogens often target signaling pathways in which mutations have been reported as a cause for the same anomalies.

PERINATAL INFECTIONS

Infections of the fetus and neonate may be acquired transcervically (ascending infections) or transplacentally (hematologic infections).

- *Transcervical, or ascending, infections* involve spread of infection from the cervicovaginal canal and may be acquired in utero or during birth. Most bacterial infections (e.g., α-hemolytic streptococcal infection) and a few viral infections (e.g., herpes simplex) are acquired in this manner. In general, the fetus acquires the infection by "inhaling" infected amniotic fluid into the lungs or by passing through an infected birth canal during delivery. Fetal infection usually is associated with inflammation of the placental membranes (chorioamnionitis) and inflammation of the umbilical cord (funisitis). This mode of spread is typical for pneumonia and, in severe cases, sepsis and meningitis.
- *Transplacental infections* gain access to the fetal bloodstream by crossing the placenta via the chorionic villi, and may occur at any time during gestation or occasionally, as may be the case with hepatitis B and human immunodeficiency virus, at the time of delivery via maternal-to-fetal transfusion. Most parasitic (e.g., toxoplasma, malaria) and viral infections and a few bacterial infections (i.e., from *Listeria* and *Treponema*) demonstrate this mode of hematogenous transmission. The clinical manifestations of these infections are highly variable, depending largely on the gestational timing and the microorganism involved. The most important transplacental infections can be conveniently remembered by the acronym *TORCH.* The elements of the TORCH complex are *Toxoplasma* (T), rubella virus (R), cytomegalovirus (C), herpesvirus (H), and any of a number of other (O) microbes such as *Treponema pallidum.* These agents are grouped together because they may evoke similar clinical and pathologic manifestations. TORCH infections occurring early in gestation may cause chronic sequelae in the child, including growth restriction, mental retardation, cataracts, and congenital cardiac anomalies, whereas infections later in pregnancy result primarily in tissue injury accompanied by inflammation (encephalitis, chorioretinitis, hepatosplenomegaly, pneumonia, and myocarditis).

PREMATURITY AND FETAL GROWTH RESTRICTION

Prematurity is the second most common cause of neonatal mortality (second only to congenital anomalies), and is defined by a gestational age less than 37 weeks. As might be expected, infants born before completion of gestation also weigh less than normal (below 2500 gm). The major risk factors for prematurity include premature rupture of membranes; intrauterine infection leading to inflammation of the placental membranes (chorioamnionitis); structural abnormalities of the uterus, cervix, and placenta; and multiple gestation (e.g., twin pregnancy). It is well established that children born before completion of the full period of gestation demonstrate higher morbidity and mortality rates than those reported for full-term infants. The immaturity of organ systems in preterm infants makes them especially vulnerable to several important complications:

- Respiratory distress syndrome (RDS), also called hyaline membrane disease
- Necrotizing enterocolitis (NEC)
- Sepsis
- Intraventricular and germinal matrix hemorrhage (Chapter 22)
- Long-term sequelae, including developmental delay

Although birth weight is low in preterm infants, it usually is appropriate once adjusted for gestational age. By contrast, as many as one third of infants who weigh less than 2500 gm are born at term and are therefore undergrown rather than immature. These small-for-gestational-age (SGA) infants suffer from fetal growth restriction. Fetal growth restriction may result from fetal, maternal, or placental abnormalities, although in many cases the specific cause is unknown.

- *Fetal factors*: This category consists of conditions that intrinsically reduce growth potential of the fetus despite an adequate supply of nutrients from the mother. Prominent among such fetal conditions are *chromosomal disorders, congenital anomalies,* and *congenital infections.* Chromosomal abnormalities may be detected in as many as 17% of fetuses evaluated for fetal growth restriction and in as many as 66% of fetuses with documented ultrasonographic malformations. *Fetal infection* should be considered in all growth-restricted neonates, with the TORCH group of infections (see earlier) being a common cause. When the causation is intrinsic to the fetus, growth retardation is *symmetric* (i.e., affects all organ systems equally).

- *Placental factors*: Placental causes include any factor that compromises the uteroplacental supply line. This may result from placenta previa (low implantation of the placenta), placental abruption (separation of placenta from the decidua by a retroplacental clot), or placental infarction. With placental (and maternal) causes of growth restriction, the growth retardation is *asymmetric* (i.e., the brain is spared relative to visceral organs such as the liver).
- *Maternal factors*: This category comprises by far the most common causes of the growth deficit in SGA infants. Important examples are vascular diseases such as preeclampsia ("toxemia of pregnancy") (Chapter 18) and chronic hypertension. The list of other maternal conditions associated with fetal growth restriction is long, but some of the avoidable influences are maternal narcotic abuse, alcohol intake, and heavy cigarette smoking (as noted previously, many of these same causes also are involved in the pathogenesis of congenital anomalies). Drugs causing fetal growth restriction in similar fashion include teratogens, such as the commonly administered anticonvulsant phenytoin (Dilantin), as well as nonteratogenic agents. Maternal malnutrition (in particular, prolonged hypoglycemia) also may affect fetal growth, but the association between growth restriction in infants and the nutritional status of the mother is complex.

Not only is the growth-restricted infant handicapped in the perinatal period, but the deficits also persist into childhood and adult life. Affected persons are thus more likely to have cerebral dysfunction, learning disabilities, and sensory (i.e., visual and hearing) impairment.

RESPIRATORY DISTRESS SYNDROME OF THE NEWBORN

There are many causes of respiratory distress in the newborn, including excessive sedation of the mother, fetal head injury during delivery, aspiration of blood or amniotic fluid, and intrauterine hypoxia secondary to compression from coiling of the umbilical cord about the neck. The most common cause, however, is *respiratory distress syndrome (RDS), also known as hyaline membrane disease* because of the formation of "membranes" in the peripheral air spaces observed in infants who succumb to this condition. An estimated 24,000 cases of RDS are reported annually in the United States, and improvements in management of this condition have sharply decreased deaths due to respiratory insufficiency from as many as 5000 per year a decade ago to less than 900 cases yearly.

PATHOGENESIS

RDS is basically a disease of premature infants. It occurs in about 60% of infants born at less than 28 weeks of gestation, 30% of those born between 28 to 34 weeks' gestation, and less than 5% of those born after 34 weeks' gestation. There are also strong though not invariable associations with **male gender, maternal diabetes,** and delivery by **cesarean section.**

The fundamental defect in RDS is the inability of the immature lung to synthesize sufficient surfactant. Surfactant is a complex of surface-active phospholipids, principally dipalmitoylphosphatidylcholine (lecithin) and at least two groups of **surfactant-associated proteins.** The importance of surfactant-associated proteins in normal lung function can be gauged by the occurrence of severe respiratory failure in neonates with congenital deficiency of surfactant caused by mutations in the corresponding genes. Surfactant is synthesized by type II pneumocytes and, with the healthy newborn's first breath, rapidly coats the surface of alveoli, reducing surface tension and thus decreasing the pressure required to keep alveoli open. In a lung deficient in surfactant, alveoli tend to collapse, and a relatively greater inspiratory effort is required with each breath to open the alveoli. The infant rapidly tires from breathing, and generalized atelectasis sets in. The resulting hypoxia sets into motion a sequence of events that lead to epithelial and endothelial damage and eventually to the formation of hyaline membranes (Fig. 6–24). As discussed later, this classical picture of surfactant deficiency is greatly modified by surfactant treatment.

Surfactant synthesis is regulated by hormones. Corticosteroids stimulate the formation of surfactant lipids

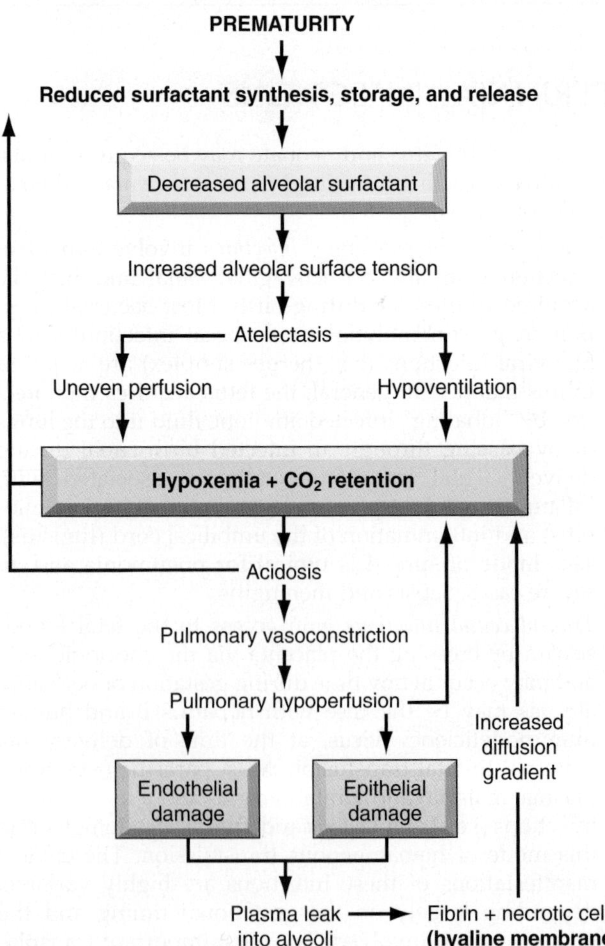

Figure 6–24 Pathophysiology of respiratory distress syndrome (see text).

and associated proteins. Therefore, conditions associated with intrauterine stress and fetal growth restriction that increase corticosteroid release lower the risk of developing RDS. Surfactant synthesis can be suppressed by the compensatory high blood levels of insulin in infants of diabetic mothers, which counteracts the effects of steroids. This may explain, in part, why infants of diabetic mothers are at higher risk for developing RDS. Labor is known to increase surfactant synthesis; accordingly, cesarean section performed before the onset of labor may be associated with increased risk for RDS.

MORPHOLOGY

The lungs in infants with RDS are of normal size but are heavy and relatively airless. They have a mottled purple color, and on microscopic examination the tissue appears solid, with poorly developed, generally collapsed (atelectatic) alveoli. If the infant dies within the first several hours of life, only necrotic cellular debris will be present in the terminal bronchioles and alveolar ducts. Later in the course, characteristic **eosinophilic hyaline membranes** line the respiratory bronchioles, alveolar ducts, and random alveoli (Fig. 6–25). These "membranes" contain necrotic epithelial cells admixed with extravasated plasma proteins. There is a remarkable paucity of neutrophilic inflammatory reaction associated with these membranes. The lesions of hyaline membrane disease are never seen in stillborn infants or in live-born infants who die within a few hours of birth. If the infant dies after several days, evidence of reparative changes, including proliferation of type II pneumocytes and interstitial fibrosis, is seen.

Clinical Features

The classic clinical presentation before the era of treatment with exogenous surfactant was described earlier. Currently, the actual clinical course and prognosis for neonatal RDS vary, depending on the maturity and birth weight of the infant and the promptness of institution of therapy. A major thrust in the control of RDS focuses on prevention, either by delaying labor until the fetal lung reaches maturity or by inducing maturation of the lung in the fetus at risk. Critical to these objectives is the ability to assess fetal lung maturity accurately. Because pulmonary secretions are discharged into the amniotic fluid, analysis of amniotic fluid phospholipids provides a good estimate of the level of surfactant in the alveolar lining. Prophylactic administration of exogenous surfactant at birth to extremely premature infants (born before a gestational age of 28 weeks) has been shown to be very beneficial, such that it is now uncommon for infants to die of acute RDS.

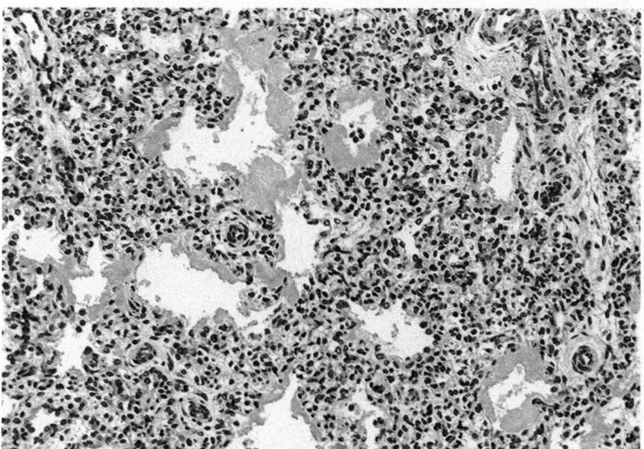

Figure 6–25 Hyaline membrane disease (hematoxylin-eosin stain). Alternating atelectasis and dilation of the alveoli can be seen. Note the eosinophilic thick hyaline membranes lining the dilated alveoli.

In uncomplicated cases, recovery begins to occur within 3 or 4 days. In affected infants, oxygen is required. Use of high concentrations of ventilator-administered oxygen for prolonged periods, however, is associated with two well-known complications: *retrolental fibroplasia* (also called *retinopathy of prematurity*) in the eyes and *bronchopulmonary dysplasia* (BPD):

- Retinopathy of prematurity has a two-phase pathogenesis. During the *hyperoxic* phase of RDS therapy (phase I), expression of the pro-angiogenic vascular endothelial growth factor (VEGF) is markedly decreased, causing endothelial cell apoptosis; VEGF levels rebound after return to relatively hypoxic room air ventilation (phase II), inducing retinal vessel proliferation (*neovascularization*) characteristic of the lesions in the retina.
- *The major abnormality in BPD is a striking decrease in alveolar septation* (manifested as large, simplified alveolar structures) and a dysmorphic capillary configuration. Thus, the current view is that BPD is caused by a potentially reversible impairment in the development of alveolar septation at the so-called saccular stage. Multiple factors—hyperoxemia, hyperventilation, prematurity, inflammatory cytokines, and vascular maldevelopment—contribute to BPD and probably act additively or synergistically to promote injury. The levels of a variety of pro-inflammatory cytokines (TNF and the interleukins IL-1β, IL-6, and IL-8) are increased in the alveoli of infants in whom BPD subsequently develops, suggesting a role for these cytokines in arresting pulmonary development.

Fortunately, both complications are now significantly less common as a result of gentler ventilation techniques, antenatal glucocorticoid therapy, and prophylactic surfactant treatments.

Infants who recover from RDS also are at increased risk for developing a variety of other complications associated with preterm birth; most important among these are *patent ductus arteriosus, intraventricular hemorrhage,* and *necrotizing enterocolitis* (NEC). Thus, although technologic advances help save the lives of many infants with RDS, they also bring to the surface the exquisite fragility of the immature neonate.

SUMMARY

Neonatal Respiratory Distress Syndrome

- Neonatal RDS (hyaline membrane disease) is a disease of prematurity; most cases occur in neonates born before 28 weeks of gestational age.

- The fundamental abnormality in RDS is insufficient pulmonary surfactant, which results in failure of lungs to inflate after birth.
- The characteristic morphologic pattern in RDS is the presence of hyaline membranes (consisting of necrotic epithelial cells and plasma proteins) lining the airways.
- RDS can be ameliorated by prophylactic administration of steroids, surfactant therapy, and by improved ventilation techniques.
- Long-term sequelae associated with RDS therapy include retinopathy of prematurity and BPD; the incidence of both complications has decreased with improvements in management of RDS.

NECROTIZING ENTEROCOLITIS

Necrotizing enterocolitis (NEC) most commonly occurs in premature infants, with the incidence of the disease being inversely proportional to the gestational age. It occurs in approximately 1 of 10 very-low-birth-weight infants (less than 1500 gm). In addition to *prematurity,* most cases are associated with *enteral feeding,* suggesting that some postnatal insult (such as introduction of bacteria) sets in motion the cascade culminating in tissue destruction. While *infectious agents* are likely to play a role in NEC pathogenesis, no single bacterial pathogen has been linked to the disease. A large number of *inflammatory mediators* have been associated with NEC. One particular mediator, platelet-activating factor (PAF), has been implicated in increasing mucosal permeability by promoting enterocyte apoptosis and compromising intercellular tight junctions, thereby "adding fuel to the fire."

NEC typically involves the terminal ileum, cecum, and right colon, although any part of the small or large intestine may be involved. The involved segment typically is distended, friable, and congested (Fig. 6–26), or it can be frankly gangrenous; intestinal perforation with accompanying peritonitis may be seen. On microscopic examination, mucosal or transmural coagulative necrosis, ulceration, bacterial colonization, and submucosal gas bubbles are all features associated with NEC. Evidence of reparative changes, such as granulation tissue and fibrosis, may be seen shortly after resolution of the acute episode.

The clinical course is fairly typical, with the onset of bloody stools, abdominal distention, and development of circulatory collapse. Abdominal radiographs often demonstrate gas within the intestinal wall (*pneumatosis intestinalis*). When detected early, NEC often can be managed conservatively, but many cases (20% to 60%) require operative intervention including resection of the necrotic segments of bowel. NEC is associated with high perinatal mortality; infants who survive often develop *post-NEC strictures* from fibrosis caused by the healing process.

SUDDEN INFANT DEATH SYNDROME

Sudden infant death syndrome (SIDS) is a disease of unknown cause. The National Institute of Child Health and Human Development defines *SIDS* as "the sudden death of an infant under 1 year of age which remains unexplained after a thorough case investigation, *including performance of a complete autopsy, examination of the death scene, and review of the clinical history.*" An aspect of SIDS that is not stressed in the definition is that the infant usually dies while asleep—hence the lay terms *crib death* and *cot death.* SIDS is the leading cause of death between the ages of 1 month and 1 year in U.S. infants, and the third leading cause of death overall in this age group, after congenital anomalies and diseases of prematurity and low birth weight. In 90% of cases, the infant is younger than 6 months; most are between the ages of 2 and 4 months.

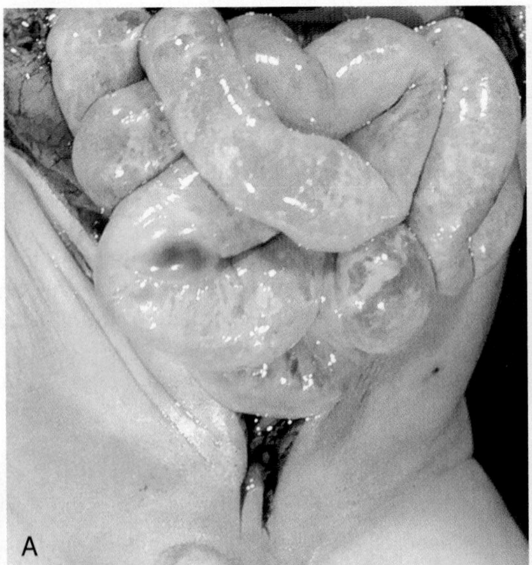

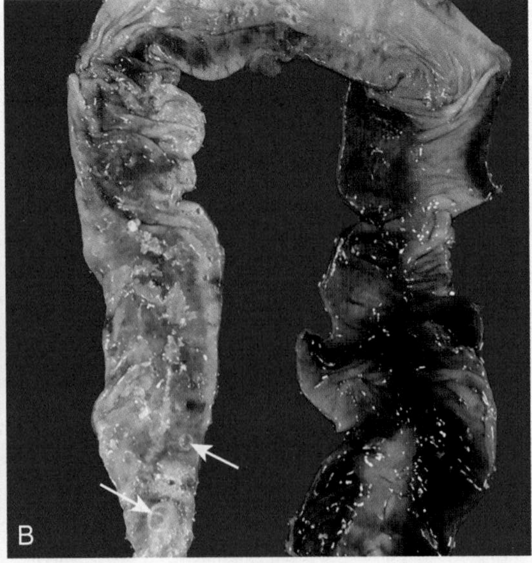

Figure 6–26 Necrotizing enterocolitis. **A,** At postmortem examination in a severe case, the entire small bowel was markedly distended with a perilously thin wall (usually this appearance implies impending perforation). **B,** The congested portion of the ileum corresponds to areas of hemorrhagic infarction and transmural necrosis seen on microscopy. Submucosal gas bubbles (*pneumatosis intestinalis*) can be seen in several areas (*arrows*).

PATHOGENESIS

The circumstances surrounding SIDS have been explored in great detail, and the general consensus is that it is a **multifactorial condition,** with a variable mixture of contributing causes in a given case. A proposed "triple-risk" model of SIDS postulates the intersection of three overlapping variables: (1) **a vulnerable infant,** (2) **a critical developmental period in homeostatic control,** and (3) **one or more exogenous stressors.** According to this model, several factors make the infant vulnerable to sudden death during the critical developmental period (i.e., 1 month to 1 year). These vulnerability factors may be specific to the parents or the infant, while the exogenous stressor(s) is attributable to the environment (Table 6–8). Although numerous factors have been proposed to account for a vulnerable infant, **the most compelling hypothesis is that SIDS reflects a delayed development of arousal and cardiorespiratory control.** Regions of the brain stem, particularly the **arcuate nucleus** located in the ventral medullary surface, play a critical role in the body's arousal response to noxious stimuli such as hypercarbia, hypoxia, and thermal stress encountered during sleep. In addition, these areas regulate breathing, heart rate, and body temperature. In certain infants, for as-yet inexplicable reasons, there may be a maldevelopment or delay in maturation of this region, compromising the arousal response to noxious stimuli. Certain polymorphic variants in genes related to **serotonergic signaling** and **autonomic innervation** have been identified at a higher frequency in SIDS babies than in the general population, suggesting that genetic factors may play a role in predisposing the infant to impaired arousal. Among the potential environmental causes, prone sleeping position, sleeping on soft surfaces, and thermal stress are possibly the most important modifiable risk factors for SIDS. The prone position increases the infant's vulnerability to one or more recognized noxious stimuli (hypoxia, hypercarbia, and thermal stress) during sleep. In addition, the prone position also is associated with decreased arousal responsiveness compared with the supine position. Results of studies from Europe, Australia, New Zealand, and the United States showed clearly increased risk for SIDS in infants who sleep in a prone position, prompting the American Academy of Pediatrics to recommend placing **healthy infants on their back** when laying them down to sleep. This "Back to Sleep" campaign has resulted in substantial decreases in SIDS-related deaths since its inception in 1994.

MORPHOLOGY

Anatomic studies of victims have yielded inconsistent histologic findings. **Multiple petechiae** are the most common finding in the typical SIDS autopsy (in approximately 80% of cases); these usually are present on the thymus, visceral and parietal pleura, and epicardium. On gross examination, the lungs usually are congested, and **vascular engorgement** with or without **pulmonary edema** is demonstrable on microscopic examination in a majority of cases. Sophisticated morphometric studies have revealed quantitative brain stem abnormalities such as **hypoplasia of the arcuate nucleus** or a subtle decrease in brain stem neuronal populations in several cases; these observations are not uniform, however, and use of such studies is not feasible in most "routine" autopsy procedures.

Table 6–8 Factors Associated with Sudden Infant Death Syndrome (SIDS)

Parental
Young maternal age (younger than 20 years)
Maternal smoking during pregnancy
Drug abuse in *either* parent—specifically, paternal marijuana and maternal opiate/cocaine use
Short intergestational intervals
Late or no prenatal care
Low socioeconomic group
African American and American Indian ethnicity (? socioeconomic factors)
Infant
Brain stem abnormalities associated with defective arousal and cardiorespiratory control
Prematurity and/or low birth weight
Male sex
Product of a multiple birth
SIDS in an earlier sibling
Antecedent respiratory infections
Germline polymorphisms in autonomic nervous system genes
Environment
Prone sleep position
Sleeping on a soft surface
Hyperthermia
Sleeping with parents in first 3 months of life
Postmortem Abnormalities Detected in Cases of Sudden Unexpected Infant Death*
Infections
Viral myocarditis
Bronchopneumonia
Unsuspected congenital anomaly
Congenital aortic stenosis
Anomalous origin of the left coronary artery from the pulmonary artery
Traumatic child abuse
Intentional suffocation (filicide)
Genetic and metabolic defects
Long QT syndrome (*SCN5A* and *KCNQ1* mutations)
Fatty acid oxidation disorders (*MCAD, LCHAD, SCHAD* mutations)
Histiocytoid cardiomyopathy (*MTCYB* mutations)
Abnormal inflammatory responsiveness (partial deletions in *C4a* and *C4b*)

*SIDS is not the only cause of sudden unexpected death in infancy; instead, it is a *diagnosis of exclusion*. Therefore, performance of an autopsy may reveal findings that would explain the cause of sudden unexpected death. These cases should *not*, strictly speaking, be designated SIDS.

C4, complement component 4; KCNQ1, potassium voltage-gated channel; LCHAD, long-chain 3-hydroxyacyl coenzyme A dehydrogenase; MCAD, medium-chain acyl coenzyme A dehydrogenase; MTCYB, mitochondrial cytochrome *b*; SCHAD, short-chain 3-hydroxyacyl coenzyme A dehydrogenase; SCN5A, sodium channel, voltage-gated.

Of note, SIDS is not the only cause of sudden unexpected death in infancy. In fact, SIDS is a diagnosis of exclusion, requiring careful examination of the death scene and a complete postmortem examination. The latter can reveal an unsuspected cause of sudden death in as many as 20% or more of babies presumed to have died of SIDS (Table 6–8). Infections (e.g., viral myocarditis or bronchopneumonia) are the most common causes of sudden "unexpected" death, followed by an unsuspected congenital anomaly. As a result of advancements in molecular diagnostics, several genetic causes of sudden "unexpected" infant death have emerged. For example, fatty acid oxidation disorders, characterized by defects in mitochondrial fatty acid oxidative enzymes, may be responsible for as many as 5% of sudden deaths in infancy; of these, a deficiency in medium-chain acyl-coenzyme A dehydrogenase is the most common. Retrospective analyses in cases of sudden infant death originally designated SIDS also have revealed mutations of cardiac sodium and potassium channels, which result in a form of cardiac arrhythmia characterized by prolonged QT intervals; these cases account for no more than 1% of SIDS deaths. SIDS in an earlier sibling is associated with a five-fold relative risk of recurrence; traumatic child abuse must be carefully excluded under these circumstances.

SUMMARY

Sudden Infant Death Syndrome

- SIDS is a disorder of *unknown cause*, defined as the sudden death of an infant younger than 1 year of age that remains unexplained after a thorough case investigation including performance of an autopsy. Most SIDS deaths occur between the ages of 2 and 4 months.
- The most likely basis for SIDS is a delayed development in arousal reflexes and cardiorespiratory control.
- Numerous risk factors have been proposed, of which the prone sleeping position is best recognized—hence the success of the "Back to Sleep" program in reducing the incidence of SIDS.

Table 6–9 Major Causes of Fetal Hydrops*

Cause
Cardiovascular
Malformations
Tachyarrhythmia
High-output failure
Chromosomal
Turner syndrome
Trisomy 21, trisomy 18
Thoracic
Cystic adenomatoid malformation
Diaphragmatic hernia
Fetal Anemia
Homozygous α-thalassemia
Parvovirus B19
Immune hydrops (Rh and ABO)
Twin Gestation
Twin-to-twin transfusion
Infection (excluding parvovirus)
Cytomegalovirus infection
Syphilis
Toxoplasmosis
Genitourinary tract malformations
Tumors
Genetic/metabolic disorder

*The cause of fetal hydrops may be "idiopathic" in as many as 20% of cases.
Modified from Machin GA: Hydrops, cystic hygroma, hydrothorax, pericardial effusions, and fetal ascites. In Gilbert-Barnes E (ed): Potter's pathology of fetus and infant. St. Louis, Mosby, 1997.

FETAL HYDROPS

Fetal hydrops refers to the accumulation of edema fluid in the fetus during intrauterine growth. The causes of fetal hydrops are manifold; the most important are listed in Table 6–9. In the past, hemolytic anemia caused by Rh blood group incompatibility between mother and fetus (immune hydrops) was the most common cause, but with the successful prophylaxis of this disorder during pregnancy, causes of nonimmune hydrops have emerged as the principal culprits. Notably, the intrauterine fluid accumulation can be quite variable, ranging in degree from progressive, generalized edema of the fetus (*hydrops fetalis*), a usually lethal condition, to more localized and less marked edematous processes, such as isolated pleural and peritoneal effusions or postnuchal fluid collections (*cystic hygroma*), that often are compatible with life (Fig. 6–27). The mechanism of immune hydrops is discussed first, followed by other important causes of fetal hydrops.

Immune Hydrops

Immune hydrops results from an antibody-induced *hemolytic disease in the newborn* that is caused by blood group incompatibility between mother and fetus. Such an incompatibility occurs only when the fetus inherits red cell antigenic determinants from the father that are foreign to the mother. The most common antigens to result in clinically significant hemolysis are the Rh and ABO blood group antigens. Of the numerous antigens included in the Rh system, only the D antigen is a major cause of Rh incompatibility. Fetal red cells may reach the maternal circulation during the last trimester of pregnancy, when the cytotrophoblast is no longer present as a barrier, or during childbirth itself (fetomaternal bleed). The mother then becomes sensitized to the foreign antigen and produces antibodies that can freely traverse the placenta to the fetus, in which they cause red cell destruction. With initiation of immune hemolysis, progressive anemia in the fetus leads to tissue ischemia, intrauterine cardiac failure, and peripheral pooling of fluid (edema). As discussed later, cardiac failure may be the final pathway by which edema occurs in many cases of nonimmune hydrops as well.

Several factors influence the immune response to Rh-positive fetal red cells that reach the maternal circulation:

- Concurrent ABO incompatibility protects the mother against Rh immunization, because the fetal red cells are promptly coated by isohemagglutinins (pre-formed anti-A or anti-B antibodies) and removed from the maternal circulation.
- The antibody response depends on the dose of immunizing antigen, so hemolytic disease develops only when the mother has experienced a significant transplacental bleed (more than 1 mL of Rh-positive red cells).
- The isotype of the antibody is important, because immunoglobulin G (IgG) (but not IgM) antibodies can cross the placenta. The initial exposure to Rh antigen evokes the formation of IgM antibodies, *so Rh disease is very uncommon with the first pregnancy*. Subsequent exposure

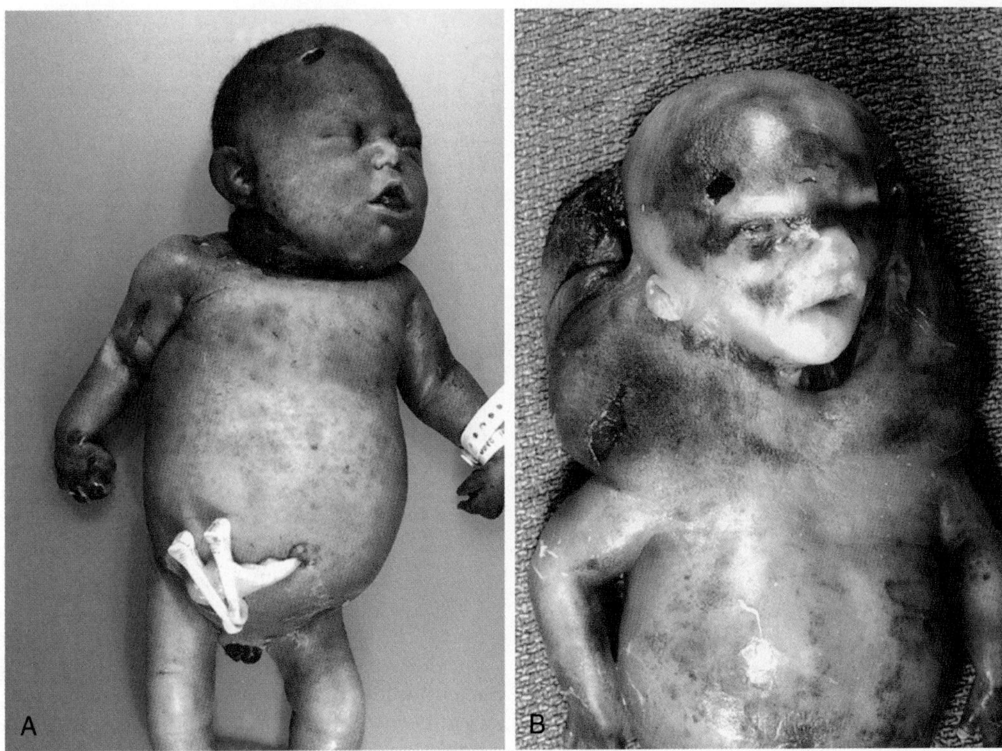

Figure 6–27 Hydrops fetalis. **A,** Generalized accumulation of fluid in the fetus. **B,** Fluid accumulation particularly prominent in the soft tissues of the neck. This condition has been termed *cystic hygroma.* Cystic hygromas are characteristically seen with, but not limited to, constitutional chromosomal anomalies such as 45,X karyotypes.

(Courtesy of Dr. Beverly Rogers, Department of Pathology, University of Texas Southwestern Medical Center, Dallas, Texas.)

during the second or third pregnancy generally leads to a brisk IgG antibody response.

Appreciation of the role of previous sensitization in the pathogenesis of Rh-hemolytic disease of the newborn has led to its therapeutic control. Currently, Rh-negative mothers are given anti-D globulin soon after the delivery of an Rh-positive baby. The anti-D antibodies mask the antigenic sites on the fetal red cells that may have leaked into the maternal circulation during childbirth, thus preventing long-lasting sensitization to Rh antigens.

As a result of the remarkable success achieved in prevention of Rh hemolysis, fetomaternal ABO incompatibility currently is the most common cause of immune hemolytic disease of the newborn. Although ABO incompatibility occurs in approximately 20% to 25% of pregnancies, hemolysis develops in only a small fraction of infants born subsequently, and in general the disease is much milder than Rh incompatibility. ABO hemolytic disease occurs almost exclusively in infants of blood group A or B who are born to mothers of blood group O. The normal anti-A and anti-B isohemagglutinins in group O mothers usually are of the IgM type and therefore do not cross the placenta. However, for reasons not well understood, certain group O women possess IgG antibodies directed against group A or B antigens (or both) even without previous sensitization. Therefore, the firstborn may be affected. Fortunately, even with transplacentally acquired antibodies, lysis of the infant's red cells is minimal. There is no effective method of preventing hemolytic disease resulting from ABO incompatibility.

Nonimmune Hydrops

The major causes of nonimmune hydrops include those disorders associated with *cardiovascular defects, chromosomal anomalies,* and *fetal anemia.* Both structural cardiovascular defects and functional abnormalities (i.e., arrhythmias) may result in intrauterine cardiac failure and hydrops. Among the chromosomal anomalies, 45,X karyotype (Turner syndrome) and trisomies 21 and 18 are associated with fetal hydrops; the basis for this disorder usually is the presence of underlying structural cardiac anomalies, although in Turner syndrome there may be an abnormality of lymphatic drainage from the neck leading to postnuchal fluid accumulation (resulting in *cystic hygromas*). Fetal anemias due to causes other than Rh or ABO incompatibility also may result in hydrops. In fact, in some parts of the world (e.g., Southeast Asia), severe fetal anemia caused by homozygous α-thalassemia probably is the most common cause of fetal hydrops. Transplacental infection by parvovirus B19 is increasingly recognized as an important cause of fetal hydrops. The virus gains entry into erythroid precursors (normoblasts), where it replicates. The ensuing cellular injury leads to the death of the normoblasts and aplastic anemia. Parvoviral intranuclear inclusions can be seen within circulating and marrow erythroid precursors (Fig. 6–28). The basis for fetal hydrops in fetal anemia of both immune and nonimmune cause is tissue ischemia with secondary myocardial dysfunction and circulatory failure. Additionally, secondary liver failure may occur, with loss of synthetic function contributing to

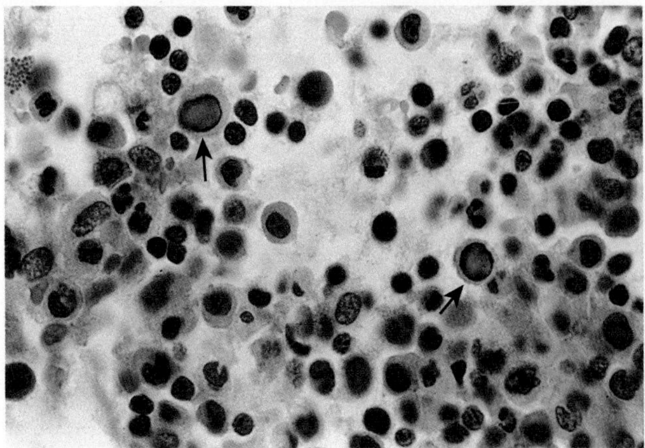

Figure 6–28 Bone marrow from an infant infected with parvovirus B19. The *arrows* point to two erythroid precursors with large homogeneous intranuclear inclusions and a surrounding peripheral rim of residual chromatin.

hypoalbuminemia, reduced plasma osmotic pressure, and edema.

MORPHOLOGY

The anatomic findings in fetuses with intrauterine fluid accumulation vary with both the severity of the disease and the underlying etiologic disorder. As previously noted, **hydrops fetalis** represents the most severe and generalized manifestation (Fig. 6–27), and lesser degrees of edema such as isolated pleural, peritoneal, or postnuchal fluid collections can occur. Accordingly, infants may be stillborn, die within the first few days, or recover completely. The presence of dysmorphic features suggests underlying constitutional chromosomal abnormalities; postmortem examination may reveal a cardiac anomaly. In hydrops associated with fetal anemia, both fetus and placenta are characteristically pale; in most cases, the liver and spleen are enlarged as a consequence of **cardiac failure** and congestion. Additionally, the bone marrow shows compensatory hyperplasia of erythroid precursors (parvovirus-associated aplastic anemia being a notable exception), and **extramedullary hematopoiesis** is present in the liver, the spleen, and possibly other tissues such as the kidneys, the lungs, the lymph nodes, and even the heart. The increased hematopoietic activity accounts for the presence in the peripheral circulation of large numbers of normoblasts, and even more immature erythroblasts (**erythroblastosis fetalis**) (Fig. 6–29).

The presence of hemolysis in Rh or ABO incompatibility is associated with the added complication of increased circulating bilirubin from the red cell breakdown. The CNS may be damaged when hyperbilirubinemia is marked (usually above 20 mg/dL in full-term infants, but often less in premature infants). The circulating unconjugated bilirubin is taken up by the brain tissue, on which it apparently exerts a toxic effect. The basal ganglia and brain stem are particularly prone to deposition of bilirubin pigment, which imparts a characteristic yellow hue to the parenchyma (**kernicterus**) (Fig. 6–30).

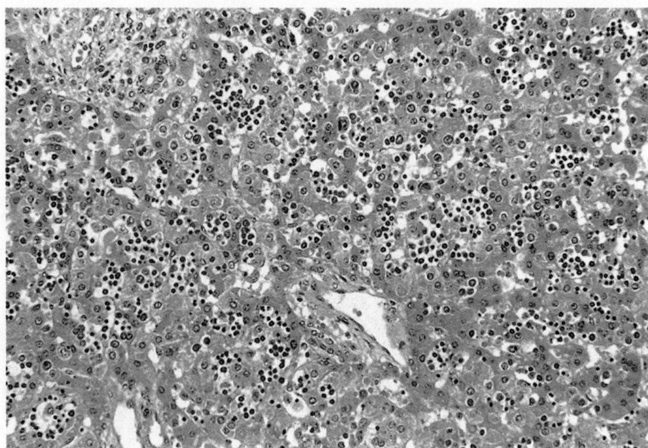

Figure 6–29 Numerous islands of extramedullary hematopoiesis *(small blue cells)* are scattered among mature hepatocytes in this histologic preparation from an infant with nonimmune hydrops fetalis.

Clinical Course

Early recognition of intrauterine fluid accumulation is imperative, since even severe cases can sometimes be salvaged with currently available therapy. Fetal hydrops that results from Rh incompatibility may be more or less accurately predicted, because severity correlates well with rapidly rising Rh antibody titers in the mother during pregnancy. Amniotic fluid obtained by amniocentesis may show high levels of bilirubin. The human anti-globulin test (Coombs test) (Chapter 11) using fetal cord blood yields a positive result if the red cells have been coated by maternal antibody. Antenatal exchange transfusion is an effective form of therapy. Postnatally, phototherapy is helpful, because visible light converts bilirubin to readily excreted

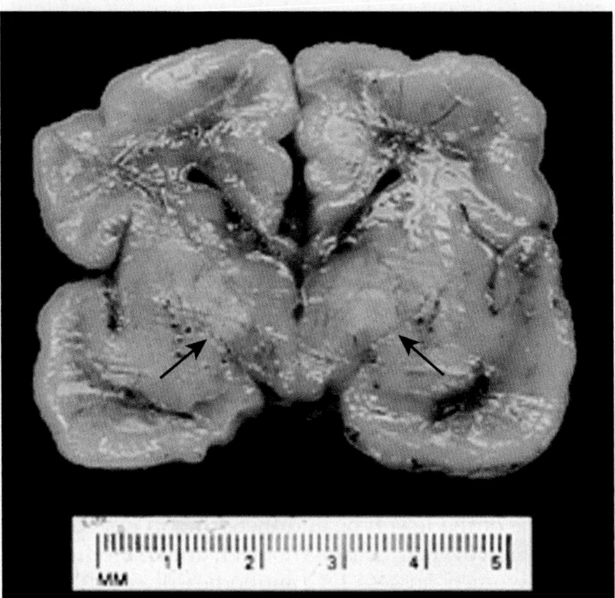

Figure 6–30 Kernicterus. Severe hyperbilirubinemia in the neonatal period—for example, secondary to immune hydrolysis—results in deposition of bilirubin pigment (*arrows*) in the brain parenchyma. This occurs because the blood–brain barrier is less well developed in the neonatal period than it is in adulthood. Infants who survive develop long-term neurologic sequelae.

dipyrroles. As already discussed, in an overwhelming majority of cases, administration of anti-D globulins to the mother can prevent the occurrence of immune hydrops in subsequent pregnancies. Group ABO hemolytic disease is more difficult to predict but is readily anticipated by awareness of the blood incompatibility between mother and father and by hemoglobin and bilirubin determinations in the vulnerable newborn infant. In fatal cases of fetal hydrops, a thorough postmortem examination is imperative to determine the cause and to exclude a potentially recurring cause such as a chromosomal abnormality.

SUMMARY

Fetal Hydrops

- Fetal hydrops refers to the accumulation of edema fluid in the fetus during intrauterine growth.
- The degree of fluid accumulation is variable, from generalized hydrops fetalis to localized cystic hygromas.
- The most common causes of fetal hydrops are *nonimmune* (chromosomal abnormalities, cardiovascular defects, and fetal anemia), while immune hydrops has become less frequent as a result of Rh antibody prophylaxis.
- Erythroblastosis fetalis (due to circulating immature erythroid precursors) is a characteristic finding of fetal anemia-associated hydrops.
- Hemolysis-induced hyperbilirubinemia can result in kernicterus in the basal ganglia and brain stem, particularly in premature infants.

TUMORS AND TUMOR-LIKE LESIONS OF INFANCY AND CHILDHOOD

Malignant neoplasms constitute the second most common cause of death in children between the ages of 4 and 14 years; only accidents exact a higher toll. Benign tumors are even more common than cancers.

It is difficult to segregate, on morphologic grounds, true tumors from tumor-like lesions in the infant and child. In this context, two special categories of tumor-like lesions should be recognized:

- *Heterotopia* or *choristoma* refers to microscopically normal cells or tissues that are present in abnormal locations. Examples are a pancreatic tissue "rest" found in the wall of the stomach or small intestine and a small mass of adrenal cells found in the kidney, lungs, ovaries, or elsewhere. Heterotopic rests usually are of little clinical significance, but on the basis of their appearance they can be confused with neoplasms.
- *Hamartoma* refers to an excessive but focal overgrowth of cells and tissues native to the organ in which it occurs. Although the cellular elements are mature and identical to those found in the remainder of the organ, they do not reproduce the normal architecture of the surrounding tissue. Hamartomas can be thought of as the linkage between malformations and neoplasms. The line of demarcation between a hamartoma and a benign neoplasm frequently is tenuous and is variously interpreted. Hemangiomas, lymphangiomas, rhabdomyomas of the heart, and adenomas of the liver are considered by some researchers to be hamartomas and by others to be true neoplasms.

Benign Tumors

Virtually any tumor may be encountered in the pediatric age group, but three—hemangiomas, lymphangiomas, and sacrococcygeal teratomas—deserve special mention here because they occur commonly in childhood.

Hemangiomas are the most common tumors of infancy. Both cavernous and capillary hemangiomas may be encountered (Chapter 9), although the latter often are more cellular than in adults and thus may be deceptively worrisome-appearing. In children, most hemangiomas are located in the skin, particularly on the face and scalp, where they produce flat to elevated, irregular, red-blue masses; the flat, larger lesions are referred to as *port wine stains*. Hemangiomas may enlarge as the child gets older, but in many instances they spontaneously regress (Fig. 6–31). The vast majority of superficial hemangiomas have no more than a cosmetic significance; rarely, they may be the manifestation of a hereditary disorder associated with disease within internal organs, such as the von

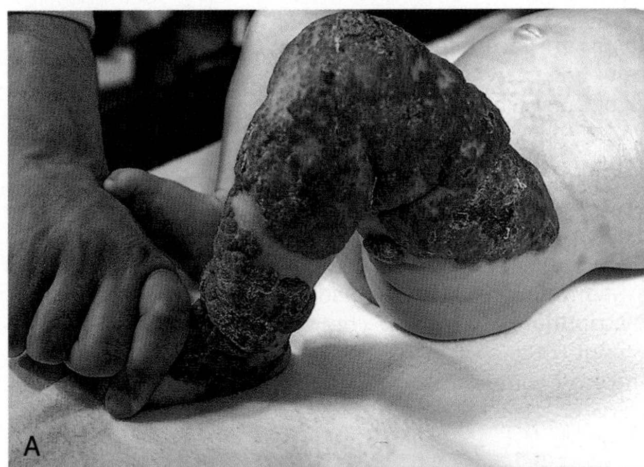

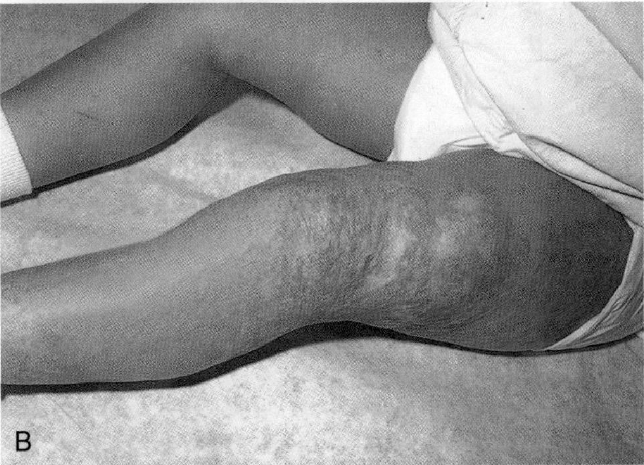

Figure 6–31 Congenital capillary hemangioma at birth (**A**) and at 2 years of age (**B**) after the lesion had undergone spontaneous regression.
(Courtesy of Dr. Eduardo Yunis, Children's Hospital of Pittsburgh, Pittsburgh, Pennsylvania.)

Hippel-Lindau and Sturge-Weber syndromes (Chapter 9). A subset of CNS cavernous hemangiomas can occur in the familial setting; affected families harbor mutations in one of three *cerebral cavernous malformation* (CCM) genes.

Lymphangiomas represent the lymphatic counterpart of hemangiomas. Microscopic examination shows cystic and cavernous spaces lined by endothelial cells and surrounded by lymphoid aggregates; the spaces usually contain pale fluid. They may occur on the skin but, more important, also are encountered in the deeper regions of the neck, axilla, mediastinum, and retroperitoneum. Although histologically benign, they tend to increase in size after birth and may encroach on mediastinal structures or nerve trunks in axilla.

Sacrococcygeal teratomas are the most common germ cell tumors of childhood, accounting for 40% or more of cases (Fig. 6–32). In view of the overlap in the mechanisms underlying teratogenesis and oncogenesis, it is interesting that approximately 10% of sacrococcygeal teratomas are associated with congenital anomalies, primarily defects of the hindgut and cloacal region and other midline defects (e.g., meningocele, spina bifida) not believed to result from local effects of the tumor. Approximately 75% of these tumors are histologically mature with a benign course, and about 12% are unmistakably malignant and lethal (Chapter 17). The remainder are designated *immature teratomas,* and their malignant potential correlates with the amount of immature tissue elements present. Most of the benign teratomas are encountered in younger infants (4 months of age or younger), whereas children with malignant lesions tend to be somewhat older.

Malignant Tumors

The organ systems involved most commonly by malignant neoplasms in infancy and childhood are the hematopoietic system, neural tissue, and soft tissues (Table 6–10). This distribution is in sharp contrast with that in adults, in whom tumors of the lung, heart, prostate, and colon are the most common forms. Malignant tumors of infancy and

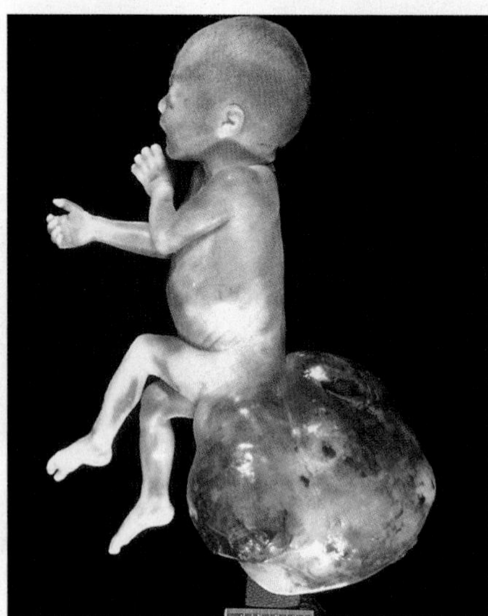

Figure 6–32 Sacrococcygeal teratoma. Note the size of the lesion compared with that of the infant.

Table 6–10 Common Malignant Neoplasms of Infancy and Childhood

0–4 Years of Age	5–9 Years of Age	10–14 Years of Age
Leukemia	Leukemia	Hepatocellular carcinoma
Retinoblastoma	Retinoblastoma	Soft tissue sarcoma
Neuroblastoma	Neuroblastoma	Osteogenic sarcoma
Wilms tumor	Hepatocellular carcinoma	Thyroid carcinoma
Hepatoblastoma	Soft tissue sarcoma	Hodgkin disease
Soft tissue sarcoma (especially rhabdomyosarcoma)	Ewing tumor	
Teratomas	CNS tumors	
CNS tumors	Lymphoma	

CNS, central nervous system.

childhood differ biologically and histologically from those in adults. The main differences are as follows:

- Relatively frequent demonstration of a close relationship between abnormal development (teratogenesis) and tumor induction (oncogenesis)
- Prevalence of constitutional genetic abnormalities or syndromes that predispose to cancer
- Tendency of fetal and neonatal malignancies to spontaneously regress or undergo "differentiation" into mature elements
- Improved survival or cure of many childhood tumors, so that more attention is now being paid to minimizing the adverse delayed effects of chemotherapy and radiotherapy in survivors, including the development of second malignancies

Many malignant pediatric neoplasms are histologically unique. In general, they tend to have a primitive (*embryonal*) rather than pleomorphic-anaplastic microscopic appearance, and frequently they exhibit features of organogenesis specific to the site of tumor origin. Because of their primitive histologic appearance, many childhood tumors have been collectively referred to as *small, round, blue cell tumors*. These are characterized by sheets of cells with small, round nuclei. The tumors in this category include neuroblastoma, lymphoma, rhabdomyosarcoma, Ewing sarcoma (peripheral neuroectodermal tumor), and some cases of Wilms tumor. Sufficient distinctive features usually are present to permit definitive diagnosis on the basis of histologic examination alone, but when necessary, clinical and radiographic findings, combined with ancillary studies (e.g., chromosome analysis, immunoperoxidase stains, electron microscopy) are used. Three common tumors—neuroblastoma, retinoblastoma, and Wilms tumor—are described here to highlight the differences between pediatric tumors and those in adults.

Neuroblastoma

The term *neuroblastic* includes tumors of the sympathetic ganglia and adrenal medulla that are derived from primordial neural crest cells populating these sites; neuroblastoma is the most important member of this family. It is the second most common solid malignancy of childhood after brain tumors, accounting for 7% to 10% of all pediatric neoplasms, and as many as 50% of malignancies diagnosed in infancy. Neuroblastomas demonstrate several unique features in their natural history, including *spontaneous regression* and *spontaneous or therapy-induced maturation.* Most occur sporadically, but 1% to 2% are familial, with autosomal dominant transmission, and in such cases the neoplasms may involve both of the adrenals or multiple primary autonomic sites. Germ line mutations in the *anaplastic lymphoma kinase* gene (*ALK*) recently have been identified as a major cause of familial predisposition to neuroblastoma. Somatic gain-of-function *ALK* mutations also are observed in a subset of sporadic neuroblastomas. It is envisioned that tumors harboring *ALK* mutations in either the germline or somatic setting will be amenable to treatment using drugs that target the activity of this kinase.

MORPHOLOGY

In childhood, about 40% of neuroblastomas arise in the **adrenal medulla.** The remainder occur anywhere along the sympathetic chain, with the most common locations being the paravertebral region of the abdomen (25%) and posterior mediastinum (15%). Macroscopically, neuroblastomas range in size from minute nodules (the in situ lesions) to large masses weighing more than 1 kg. In situ neuroblastomas are reported to be 40 times more frequent than overt tumors. The great preponderance of these silent lesions spontaneously regress, leaving only a focus of fibrosis or calcification in the adult. Some neuroblastomas are sharply demarcated with a fibrous pseudocapsule, but others are far more infiltrative and invade surrounding structures, including the kidneys, renal vein, and vena cava, and envelop the aorta. On transection, they are composed of soft, gray-tan, brainlike tissue. Larger tumors have areas of necrosis, cystic softening, and hemorrhage.

Histologically, classic neuroblastomas are composed of small, primitive-appearing cells with dark nuclei, scant cytoplasm, and poorly defined cell borders growing in solid sheets (Fig. 6–33, *A*). Mitotic activity, nuclear breakdown ("karyorrhexis"), and pleomorphism may be prominent. The background often demonstrates a faintly eosinophilic fibrillary material (neuropil) that corresponds to neuritic processes of the primitive neuroblasts. Typically, so-called **Homer-Wright pseudo-rosettes** can be found in which the tumor cells are concentrically arranged about a central space filled with neuropil (the absence of an actual central lumen garners the designation "pseudo-"). Other helpful features include immunochemical detection of **neuron-specific enolase** and demonstration on ultrastructural studies of small, membrane-bound, cytoplasmic catecholamine-containing secretory granules.

Some neoplasms show signs of **maturation**, either spontaneous or therapy-induced. Larger cells having more abundant cytoplasm with large vesicular nuclei and a prominent nucleolus, representing **ganglion cells** in various stages of maturation, may be found in tumors admixed with primitive neuroblasts **(ganglioneuroblastoma).** Even better-differentiated lesions contain many more large cells resembling mature ganglion cells in the absence of residual neuroblasts; such neoplasms merit the designation **ganglioneuroma** (Fig. 6–33, *B*). Maturation of neuroblasts into ganglion cells usually is accompanied by the appearance of Schwann cells. In fact, the presence of a "schwannian stroma" composed of organized fascicles of neuritic processes, mature **Schwann cells,** and fibroblasts is a histologic prerequisite for the designation of ganglioneuroblastoma and ganglioneuroma; ganglion cells in and of themselves do not fulfill the criteria for maturation.

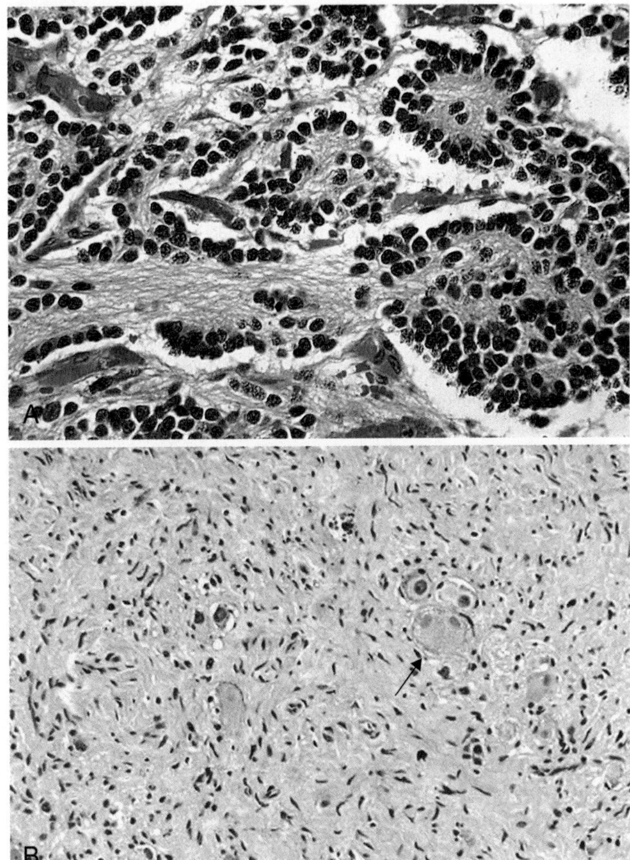

Figure 6–33 A, Neuroblastoma. This tumor is composed of small cells embedded in a finely fibrillar matrix (neuropil). A Homer-Wright pseudorosette (tumor cells arranged concentrically around a central core of neuropil) is seen in the upper right corner. **B,** Ganglioneuromas, arising from spontaneous or therapy-induced maturation of neuroblastomas, are characterized by clusters of large cells with vesicular nuclei and abundant eosinophilic cytoplasm (*arrow*), representing neoplastic ganglion cells. Spindle-shaped Schwann cells are present in the background stroma.

Clinical Course and Prognosis

Many factors influence prognosis, but the most important are the stage of the tumor and the age of the patient.

- Staging of neuroblastomas (Table 6–11) assumes great importance in establishing a prognosis. Special note should be taken of stage 4S (S means special), because the outlook for these patients is excellent, despite the spread of disease. As noted in Table 6–11, the primary tumor would be classified as stage 1 or 2 but for the presence of metastases, which are limited to liver, skin, and bone marrow, without bone involvement. Infants with 4S tumors have an excellent prognosis with minimal therapy, and it is not uncommon for the primary or metastatic tumors to undergo spontaneous regression. The biologic basis for this welcome behavior is not clear.

Table 6–11 Staging of Neuroblastomas

Stage 1	Localized tumor completely excised, with or without microscopic residual disease; representative ipsilateral nonadherent lymph nodes negative for tumor (nodes adherent to the primary tumor may be positive for tumor)
Stage 2A	Localized tumor resected incompletely grossly; representative ipsilateral nonadherent lymph nodes negative for tumor microscopically
Stage 2B	Localized tumor with or without complete gross excision, ipsilateral nonadherent lymph nodes positive for tumor; enlarged contralateral lymph nodes, which are negative for tumor microscopically
Stage 3	Unresectable unilateral tumor infiltrating across the midline with or without regional lymph node involvement; or localized unilateral tumor with contralateral regional lymph node involvement
Stage 4	Any primary tumor with dissemination to distant lymph nodes, bone, bone marrow, liver, skin, and/or other organs (*except as defined for stage 4S*)
Stage 4S*	Localized primary tumor (as defined for stage 1, 2A, or 2B) with dissemination limited to skin, liver, and/or bone marrow (<10% of nucleated cells are constituted by neoplastic cells; >10% involvement of bone marrow is considered as stage 4); *stage 4S limited to infants younger than 1 year of age*

*S, special.
Adapted from Brodeur GM, Pritchard J, Berthold F, et al: Revisions of the international neuroblastoma diagnosis, staging, and response to treatment. J Clin Oncol 11:1466, 1993.

- *Age is the other important determinant of outcome,* and the outlook for children younger than 18 months is much more favorable than for older children at a comparable stage of disease. Most neoplasms diagnosed in children during the first 18 months of life are stage 1 or 2, or stage 4S ("low" risk category in Table 6–11), while neoplasms in older children fall into the "intermediate" or "high" risk category.
- *Morphology* is an independent prognostic variable in neuroblastic tumors; evidence of schwannian stroma and gangliocytic differentiation is indicative of a favorable histologic pattern.
- *Amplification of the NMYC oncogene* in neuroblastomas is a molecular event that has profound impact on prognosis. *NMYC* amplification is present in about 25% to 30% of primary tumors, most in advanced-stage disease; the greater the number of copies, the worse the prognosis. *NMYC amplification is currently the most important genetic abnormality used in risk stratification of neuroblastic tumors and automatically renders a tumor as "high" risk, irrespective of stage or age.*
- Deletion of the distal short arm of chromosome 1, gain of the distal long arm of chromosome 17, and overexpression of telomerase all are adverse prognostic factors, while expression of TrkA, a high-affinity receptor for nerve growth factor that is indicative of differentiation toward sympathetic ganglia lineage, is associated with favorable prognosis.

Children younger than 2 years with neuroblastomas generally present with protuberant abdomen resulting from an abdominal mass, fever, and weight loss. In older children the neuroblastomas may remain unnoticed until metastases cause hepatomegaly, ascites, and bone pain. Neuroblastomas may metastasize widely through the hematogenous and lymphatic systems, particularly to liver, lungs, bones, and the bone marrow. In neonates, disseminated neuroblastomas may manifest with multiple cutaneous metastases associated with deep blue discoloration to the skin (earning the rather unfortunate moniker of "blueberry muffin baby"). As already noted, many variables can influence the prognosis of neuroblastomas, but as a rule of thumb, stage and age are the paramount determinants. Tumors of all stages diagnosed in the first 18 months of life, as well as low-stage tumors in older children, have a favorable prognosis, while high-stage tumors diagnosed in children younger than 18 months of age have the poorest outcome. About 90% of neuroblastomas, regardless of location, produce catecholamines (similar to the catecholamines associated with pheochromocytomas), which constitutes an important diagnostic feature (i.e., elevated blood levels of catecholamines and elevated urine levels of catecholamine metabolites such as vanillylmandelic acid [VMA] and homovanillic acid [HVA]). Despite the elaboration of catecholamines, hypertension is much less frequent with these neoplasms than with pheochromocytomas (Chapter 19).

SUMMARY

Neuroblastoma

- Neuroblastomas and related tumors arise from neural crest–derived cells in the sympathetic ganglia and adrenal medulla.
- Neuroblastomas are undifferentiated, whereas ganglioneuroblastomas and ganglioneuromas demonstrate evidence of differentiation (schwannian stroma and ganglion cells). Homer-Wright pseudo-rosettes are characteristic of neuroblastomas.
- Age, stage, and *NMYC* amplification are the most important prognostic features; children younger than 18 months usually have a better prognosis than older children, while children with higher-stage tumors or *NMYC* amplification fare worse.
- Neuroblastomas secrete catecholamines, whose metabolites (VMA/HVA) can be used for screening patients.

Retinoblastoma

Retinoblastoma is the most common primary intraocular malignancy of children. The molecular genetics of retinoblastoma has been discussed previously (Chapter 5). Approximately 40% of the tumors are associated with a germline mutation in the *RB1* gene and are therefore heritable. The remaining 60% of the tumors develop sporadically, and these have somatic *RB1* gene mutations. Although the name *retinoblastoma* might suggest origin from a primitive retinal cell that is capable of differentiation into both glial and neuronal cells, it is now clear that the cell of origin of retinoblastoma is neuronal. As noted earlier, in approximately 40% of cases, retinoblastoma occurs in persons who inherit a germ line mutation of one *RB* allele. *Familial cases typically are associated with development of multiple tumors that are bilateral,* although they may be unifocal and unilateral.

The metabolism of vitamin D can be outlined as follows (Fig. 7–20):

1. Absorption of vitamin D along with other fats in the gut or synthesis from precursors in the skin
2. Binding to plasma α_1-globulin (vitamin D–binding protein) and transport to liver
3. Conversion to 25-hydroxyvitamin D (25-OH-D) by 25-hydroxylase in the liver
4. Conversion of 25-OH-D to 1,25-dihydroxyvitamin D [1,25-$(OH)_2$-D] (biologically the most active form of vitamin D) by α_1-hydroxylase in the kidney

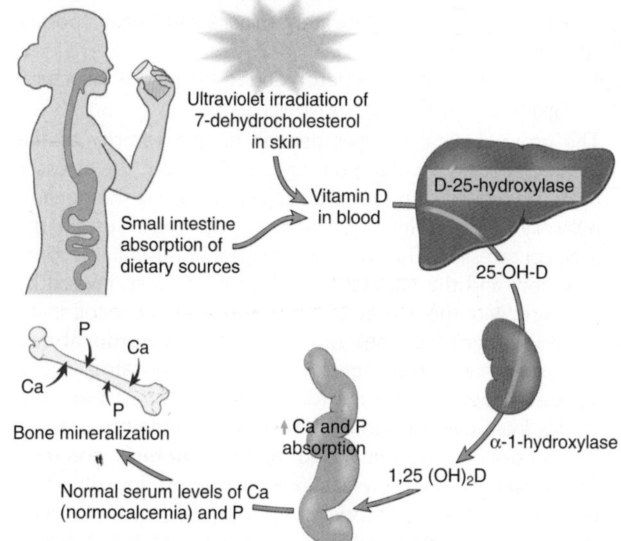

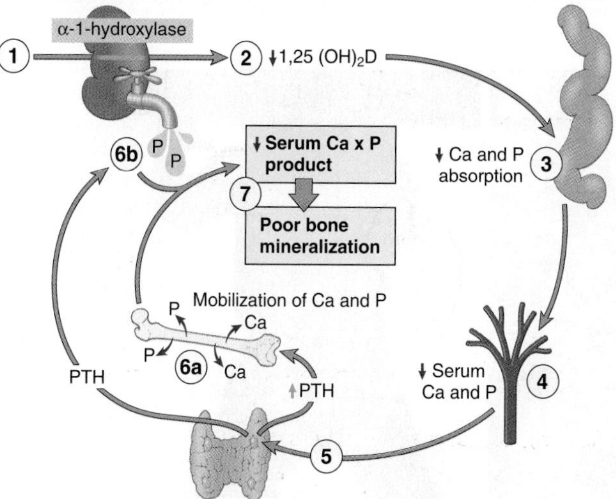

Figure 7–20 A, Normal vitamin D metabolism. **B,** Vitamin D deficiency. There is inadequate substrate for the renal hydroxylase (*1*), yielding a deficiency of 1,25-$(OH)_2$D (*2*), and deficient absorption of calcium and phosphorus from the gut (*3*), with consequent depressed serum levels of both (*4*). The hypocalcemia activates the parathyroid glands (*5*), causing mobilization of calcium and phosphorus from bone (*6a*). Simultaneously, parathyroid hormone (PTH) induces wasting of phosphate in the urine (*6b*) and calcium retention. Consequently, the serum levels of calcium are normal or nearly normal, but the phosphate is low; hence, mineralization is impaired (*7*).

Renal production of 1,25-$(OH)_2$-D is regulated by three mechanisms:

- *Hypocalcemia stimulates secretion of parathyroid hormone (PTH),* which in turn augments the conversion of 25-OH-D to 1,25-$(OH)_2$-D by activating α_1-hydroxylase.
- *Hypophosphatemia directly activates α_1-hydroxylase,* thereby increasing the formation of 1,25$(OH)_2$-D.
- In a feedback loop, increased levels of 1,25-$(OH)_2$-D downregulate the synthesis of this metabolite by inhibiting the action of α_1-hydroxylase (decreases in 1,25-$(OH)_2$-D have the opposite effect).

Functions. Like retinoids and steroid hormones, 1,25-$(OH)_2$-D acts by binding to a high-affinity nuclear receptor that in turn binds to regulatory DNA sequences, thereby inducing transcription of specific target genes. The receptors for 1,25-$(OH)_2$-D are present in most nucleated cells of the body, and they transduce signals that result in various biologic activities, beyond those involved in calcium and phosphorus homeostasis. Nevertheless, the best-understood functions of vitamin D relate to the maintenance of normal plasma levels of calcium and phosphorus, through action on the intestines, bones, and kidneys (Fig. 7–20).

The active form of vitamin D:

- *Stimulates intestinal absorption of calcium* through upregulation of calcium transport, in enterocytes
- *Stimulates calcium resorption in renal distal tubules.*
- *Collaborates with PTH to regulate blood calcium.* This occurs in part through upregulation of RANK ligand on osteoblasts, which in turn activates RANK receptors on osteoclast precursors. RANK activation produces signals that increase osteoclast differentiation and bone resorptive activities (Chapter 20).
- *Promotes the mineralization of bone.* Vitamin D is needed for the mineralization of osteoid matrix and epiphyseal cartilage during the formation of flat and long bones. It stimulates osteoblasts to synthesize the calcium-binding protein osteocalcin, which promotes calcium deposition.

Of note, effects of vitamin D on bone depend on the plasma levels of calcium: On the one hand, in hypocalcemic states 1,25-$(OH)_2$-D together with PTH increases the resorption of calcium and phosphorus from bone to support blood levels. On the other hand, in normocalcemic states vitamin D also is required for calcium deposition in epiphyseal cartilage and osteoid matrix.

Deficiency States

Rickets in growing children and *osteomalacia* in adults are skeletal diseases with worldwide distribution. They may result from diets deficient in calcium and vitamin D, but probably more important is limited exposure to sunlight (for instance, in heavily veiled women; children born to mothers who have frequent pregnancies followed by lactation, which leads to vitamin D deficiency; and inhabitants of northern climates with scant sunlight). Other, less common causes of rickets and osteomalacia include renal disorders causing decreased synthesis of 1,25-$(OH)_2$-D or phosphate depletion, and malabsorption disorders. Although rickets and osteomalacia rarely occur outside high-risk groups, milder forms of vitamin D deficiency (also called vitamin D insufficiency) leading to bone loss and hip fractures are common among elderly persons. Studies also suggest that vitamin D may be important for preventing demineralization of bones. It appears that certain genetically determined variants of the vitamin D receptor are associated with an accelerated loss of bone minerals with aging and certain familial forms of osteoporosis (Chapter 20).

Whatever the basis, a deficiency of vitamin D tends to cause hypocalcemia. This in turn stimulates PTH production, which (1) activates renal α_1-hydroxylase, increasing the amount of active vitamin D and calcium absorption; (2) mobilizes calcium from bone; (3) decreases renal calcium excretion; and (4) increases renal excretion of phosphate. Thus, the serum level of calcium is restored to near normal, but hypophosphatemia persists, so mineralization of bone is impaired or there is high bone turnover.

An understanding of the morphologic changes in rickets and *osteomalacia* is facilitated by a brief summary of normal bone development and maintenance. The development of flat bones in the skeleton involves intramembranous ossification, while the formation of long tubular bones proceeds by endochondral ossification. With intramembranous bone formation, mesenchymal cells differentiate directly into osteoblasts, which synthesize the collagenous osteoid matrix on which calcium is deposited. By contrast, with endochondral ossification, growing cartilage at the epiphyseal plates is provisionally mineralized and then progressively resorbed and replaced by osteoid matrix, which undergoes mineralization to create bone (Fig. 7–21, *A*).

MORPHOLOGY

The basic derangement in both rickets and osteomalacia is an excess of unmineralized bone matrix. The changes that occur in the growing bones of children with rickets, however, are complicated by inadequate provisional calcification of epiphyseal cartilage, deranging endochondral bone growth. The following sequence ensues in rickets:

- Overgrowth of epiphyseal cartilage due to inadequate provisional calcification and failure of the cartilage cells to mature and disintegrate
- Persistence of distorted, irregular masses of cartilage, many of which project into the marrow cavity
- Deposition of osteoid matrix on inadequately mineralized cartilaginous remnants
- Disruption of the orderly replacement of cartilage by osteoid matrix, with enlargement and lateral expansion of the osteochondral junction (Fig. 7–21, *B*)
- Abnormal overgrowth of capillaries and fibroblasts in the disorganized zone resulting from microfractures and stresses on the inadequately mineralized, weak, poorly formed bone
- Deformation of the skeleton due to the loss of structural rigidity of the developing bones

The gross skeletal changes depend on the severity of the rachitic process; its duration; and, in particular, the stresses to which individual bones are subjected. During the nonambulatory stage of infancy, the head and chest sustain the greatest stresses. The softened occipital bones may become flattened, and the parietal bones can be buckled inward by pressure; with the release of the pressure, elastic recoil snaps the bones back into their original positions **(craniotabes).** An excess of osteoid produces **frontal bossing** and a squared appearance to the head. Deformation of the chest results from overgrowth of cartilage or osteoid tissue at the costochondral junction, producing the "**rachitic rosary**." The weakened metaphyseal areas of the ribs are subject to the pull of the respiratory muscles, causing them to bend inward and creating anterior protrusion of the sternum **(pigeon breast deformity).** The inward pull at the margin of the diaphragm creates the **Harrison groove,** girdling the

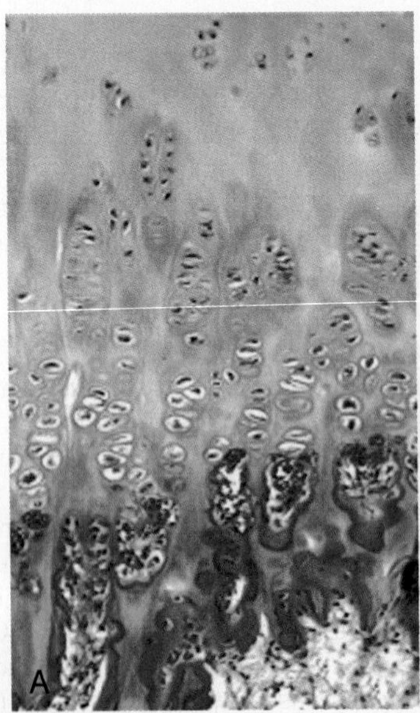

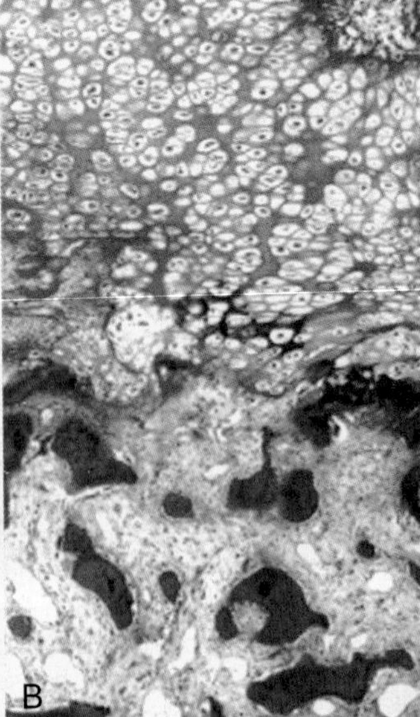

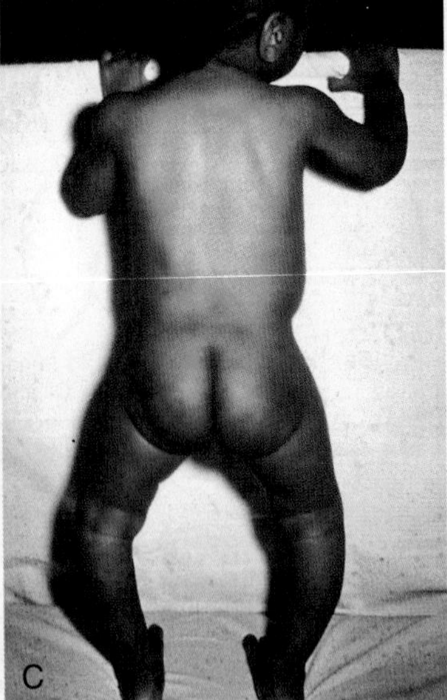

Figure 7–21 Rickets. **A,** Normal costochondral junction of a young child. Note cartilage palisade formation and orderly transition from cartilage to new bone. **B,** Rachitic costochondral junction in which the palisade of cartilage is absent. Darker trabeculae are well-formed bone; paler trabeculae consist of uncalcified osteoid. **C,** Note bowing of legs as a consequence of the formation of poorly mineralized bone in a child with rickets.

(B, Courtesy of Dr. Andrew E. Rosenberg, Massachusetts General Hospital, Boston, Massachusetts.)

thoracic cavity at the lower margin of the rib cage. The pelvis may become deformed. When an ambulating child develops rickets, deformities are likely to affect the spine, pelvis, and long bones (e.g., tibia), causing, most notably, **lumbar lordosis** and **bowing of the legs** (Fig. 7–21, *C*).

In adults, the lack of vitamin D deranges the normal bone remodeling that occurs throughout life. The newly formed osteoid matrix laid down by osteoblasts is inadequately mineralized, producing the excess of persistent osteoid that is characteristic of osteomalacia. Although the contours of the bone are not affected, the bone is weak and vulnerable to gross fractures or microfractures, which are most likely to affect vertebral bodies and femoral necks. On histologic examination, the unmineralized osteoid can be visualized as a thickened layer of matrix (which stains pink in hematoxylin and eosin preparations) arranged about the more basophilic, normally mineralized trabeculae.

Toxicity. Prolonged exposure to normal sunlight does not produce an excess of vitamin D, but megadoses of orally administered vitamin can lead to hypervitaminosis. In children, hypervitaminosis D may take the form of metastatic calcifications of soft tissues such as the kidney; in adults, it causes bone pain and hypercalcemia. As a point of some interest, the toxic potential of this vitamin is so great that in sufficiently large doses it is a potent rodenticide!

Vitamin C (Ascorbic Acid)

A deficiency of water-soluble vitamin C leads to the development of *scurvy,* characterized principally by *bone disease in growing children* and by *hemorrhages and healing defects in both children and adults.* Sailors of the British Royal Navy were nicknamed "limeys" because at the end of the 18th century the Navy began to provide lime and lemon juice to them to prevent scurvy during their long sojourn at sea. It was not until 1932 that ascorbic acid was identified and synthesized. Unlike vitamin D, ascorbic acid is not synthesized endogenously in humans, who therefore are entirely dependent on the diet for this nutrient. Vitamin C is present in milk and some animal products (liver, fish) and is abundant in a variety of fruits and vegetables. All but the most restricted diets provide adequate amounts of vitamin C.

Function. Ascorbic acid acts in a variety of biosynthetic pathways by accelerating hydroxylation and amidation reactions. The most clearly established function of vitamin C is the activation of prolyl and lysyl hydroxylases from inactive precursors, allowing for hydroxylation of procollagen. Inadequately hydroxylated procollagen cannot acquire a stable helical configuration or be adequately cross-linked, so it is poorly secreted from the fibroblasts. Those molecules that are secreted lack tensile strength, are more soluble, and are more vulnerable to enzymatic degradation. Collagen, which normally has the highest content of hydroxyproline, is most affected, particularly in blood vessels, accounting for the predisposition to hemorrhages in scurvy. In addition, a deficiency of vitamin C suppresses the synthesis of collagen polypeptides, independent of effects on proline hydroxylation.

Vitamin C also has antioxidant properties. These include an ability to scavenge free radicals directly and participation in metabolic reactions that regenerate the antioxidant form of vitamin E.

Deficiency States. Consequences of vitamin C deficiency are illustrated in Figure 7–22. Fortunately, because of the abundance of ascorbic acid in foods, scurvy has ceased to be a global problem. It is sometimes encountered even in affluent populations as a secondary deficiency, particularly among elderly persons, people who live alone, and chronic alcoholics—groups often characterized by erratic and inadequate eating patterns. Occasionally, scurvy appears in patients undergoing peritoneal dialysis and hemodialysis and among food faddists.

Toxicity. The popular notion that megadoses of vitamin C protect against the common cold or at least allay the

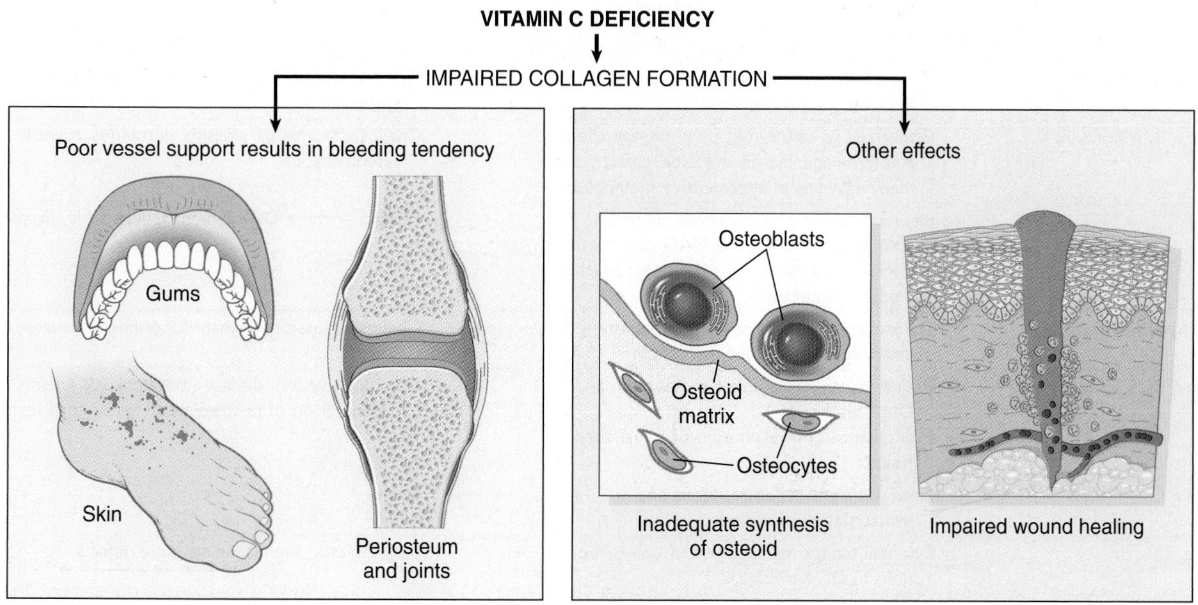

Figure 7–22 Major consequences of vitamin C deficiency caused by impaired formation of collagen. They include bleeding tendency due to poor vascular support, inadequate formation of osteoid matrix, and impaired wound healing.

symptoms has not been borne out by controlled clinical studies. Such slight relief as may be experienced probably is a result of the mild antihistamine action of ascorbic acid. The large excess of vitamin C is promptly excreted in the urine but may cause uricosuria and increased absorption of iron, with the potential for iron overload.

Other vitamins and some essential minerals are listed and briefly described in Tables 7-9 and 7-10. Folic acid and vitamin B_{12} are discussed in Chapter 11.

SUMMARY

Nutritional Diseases

- Primary PEM is a common cause of childhood deaths in poor countries. The two main primary PEM syndromes are marasmus and kwashiorkor. Secondary PEM occurs in the chronically ill and in patients with advanced cancer (as a result of cachexia).
- Kwashiorkor is characterized by hypoalbuminemia, generalized edema, fatty liver, skin changes, and defects in immunity. It is caused by diets low in protein but normal in calories.
- Marasmus is characterized by emaciation resulting from loss of muscle mass and fat with relative preservation of serum albumin. It is caused by diets severely lacking in calories—both protein and nonprotein.
- Anorexia nervosa is self-induced starvation; it is characterized by amenorrhea and multiple manifestations of low thyroid hormone levels. Bulimia is a condition in which food binges alternate with induced vomiting.
- Vitamins A and D are fat-soluble vitamins with a wide range of activities. Vitamin C and members of the vitamin B family are water-soluble (Table 7–9 lists vitamin functions and deficiency syndromes).

Obesity

In the United States, obesity has reached epidemic proportions. The prevalence of obesity increased from 13% to 34% between 1960 and 2008, and as of 2009, 68% of Americans between 20 and 75 years of age were overweight. Equally alarming, childhood obesity, a strong predictor of obesity in adults, also increased two- to three-fold over the same period. Recent studies suggest that the epidemic of obesity also is rapidly spreading in developing countries such as

Table 7–9 Vitamins: Major Functions and Deficiency Syndromes

Vitamin	Functions	Deficiency Syndromes
Fat-Soluble		
Vitamin A	A component of visual pigment Maintenance of specialized epithelia Maintenance of resistance to infection	Night blindness, xerophthalmia, blindness Squamous metaplasia Vulnerability to infection, particularly measles
Vitamin D	Facilitates intestinal absorption of calcium and phosphorus and mineralization of bone	Rickets in children Osteomalacia in adults
Vitamin E	Major antioxidant; scavenges free radicals	Spinocerebellar degeneration
Vitamin K	Cofactor in hepatic carboxylation of procoagulants—factors II (prothrombin), VII, IX, and X; and protein C and protein S	Bleeding diathesis
Water-Soluble		
Vitamin B_1 (thiamine)	As pyrophosphate, is coenzyme in decarboxylation reactions	Dry and wet beriberi, Wernicke syndrome, Korsakoff syndrome
Vitamin B_2 (riboflavin)	Converted to coenzymes flavin mononucleotide and flavin adenine dinucleotide, cofactors for many enzymes in intermediary metabolism	Cheilosis, stomatitis, glossitis, dermatitis, corneal vascularization
Niacin	Incorporated into nicotinamide adenine dinucleotide (NAD) and NAD phosphate; involved in a variety of oxidation–reduction (redox) reactions	Pellagra—"three Ds": dementia, dermatitis, diarrhea
Vitamin B_6 (pyridoxine)	Derivatives serve as coenzymes in many intermediary reactions	Cheilosis, glossitis, dermatitis, peripheral neuropathy
Vitamin B_{12}	Required for normal folate metabolism and DNA synthesis Maintenance of myelinization of spinal cord tracts	Combined system disease (megaloblastic anemia and degeneration of posterolateral spinal cord tracts)
Vitamin C	Serves in many redox reactions and hydroxylation of collagen	Scurvy
Folate	Essential for transfer and use of one-carbon units in DNA synthesis	Megaloblastic anemia, neural tube defects
Pantothenic acid	Incorporated in coenzyme A	No nonexperimental syndrome recognized
Biotin	Cofactor in carboxylation reactions	No clearly defined clinical syndrome

Table 7–10 Selected Trace Elements and Deficiency Syndromes

Element	Function	Basis of Deficiency	Clinical Features
Zinc	Component of enzymes, principally oxidases	Inadequate supplementation in artificial diets Interference with absorption by other dietary constituents Inborn error of metabolism	Rash around eyes, mouth, nose, and anus called acrodermatitis enteropathica Anorexia and diarrhea Growth retardation in children Depressed mental function Depressed wound healing and immune response Impaired night vision Infertility
Iron	Essential component of hemoglobin as well as several iron-containing metalloenzymes	Inadequate diet Chronic blood loss	Hypochromic, microcytic anemia
Iodine	Component of thyroid hormone	Inadequate supply in food and water	Goiter and hypothyroidism
Copper	Component of cytochrome *c* oxidase, dopamine β-hydroxylase, tyrosinase, lysyl oxidase, and unknown enzyme involved in cross-linking collagen	Inadequate supplementation in artificial diet Interference with absorption	Muscle weakness Neurologic defects Abnormal collagen cross-linking
Fluoride	Mechanism unknown	Inadequate supply in soil and water Inadequate supplementation	Dental caries
Selenium	Component of glutathione peroxidase Antioxidant with vitamin E	Inadequate amounts in soil and water	Myopathy Cardiomyopathy (Keshan disease)

India. Globally, the World Health Organization (WHO) estimates that by 2015, 700 million adults will be obese. The causes of this epidemic are complex but undoubtedly are related to societal changes in diet and levels of physical activity. *Obesity is associated with an increased risk of several important diseases (e.g., diabetes, hypertension),* making it a major public health concern. Indeed, in 2009 it was estimated that the health care cost of obesity had risen to $147 billion annually in the United States, a price tag that appears bound to rise as the nation's collective waistline expands.

Obesity is defined as a state of increased body weight, due to adipose tissue accumulation, that is of sufficient magnitude to produce adverse health effects. How does one measure fat accumulation? Several high-tech methods have been devised, but for practical purposes the following measures are commonly used:

- Some expression of weight in relation to height, such as the measurement referred to as the *body mass index* (BMI) = (weight in kilograms)/(height in meters)^2, or kg/m^2
- Skinfold measurements
- Various body circumferences, particularly the waist-to-hip circumference ratio

The BMI is closely correlated with body fat. BMIs in the range 18.5 to 25 kg/m^2 are considered normal, while BMIs between 25 and 30 kg/m^2 identify the overweight, and BMIs greater than 30 kg/m^2, the obese. It is generally agreed that a BMI higher than 30 kg/m^2 imparts a health risk. In the following discussion, for the sake of simplicity, the term obesity is applied to both the overweight and the truly obese.

The untoward effects of obesity are related not only to the total body weight but also to the distribution of the stored fat. *Central, or visceral, obesity,* in which fat accumulates in the trunk and in the abdominal cavity (in the mesentery and around viscera), is associated with a much higher risk for several diseases than is excess accumulation of fat in a diffuse distribution in subcutaneous tissue.

The etiology of obesity is complex and incompletely understood. Involved are genetic, environmental, and psychologic factors. However, simply put, obesity is a disorder of energy balance. The two sides of the energy equation, intake and expenditure, are finely regulated by neural and hormonal mechanisms, so that body weight is maintained within a narrow range for many years. Apparently, this fine balance is controlled by an internal set point, or "lipostat," that senses the quantity of energy stores (adipose tissue) and appropriately regulates food intake as well as energy expenditure. In recent years, several "obesity genes" have been identified. As might be expected, they encode the molecular components of the physiologic system that regulates energy balance. A key player in energy homeostasis is the *LEP* gene and its product, *leptin.* This unique member of the cytokine family, secreted by adipocytes, regulates both sides of the energy equation—intake of food and expenditure of energy. As discussed later, *the net effect of leptin is to reduce food intake and enhance the expenditure of energy.*

In a simplified way the neurohumoral mechanisms that regulate energy balance and body weight may be divided into three components (Fig. 7–23):

- *The peripheral or afferent system* generates signals from various sites. Its main components are *leptin and adiponectin* produced by fat cells, *insulin* from the pancreas, *ghrelin* from the stomach, and *peptide YY* from the ileum and colon. Leptin reduces food intake and is discussed in detail further on. Ghrelin secretion stimulates appetite, and it may function as a "meal-initiating" signal. Peptide YY, which is released postprandially by endocrine cells in the ileum and colon, is a satiety signal.
- *The arcuate nucleus in the hypothalamus,* which processes and integrates the peripheral signals and generates new signals that are transmitted by (1) POMC (pro-opiomelanocortin) and CART (cocaine- and amphetamine-regulated transcript) neurons; and (2)

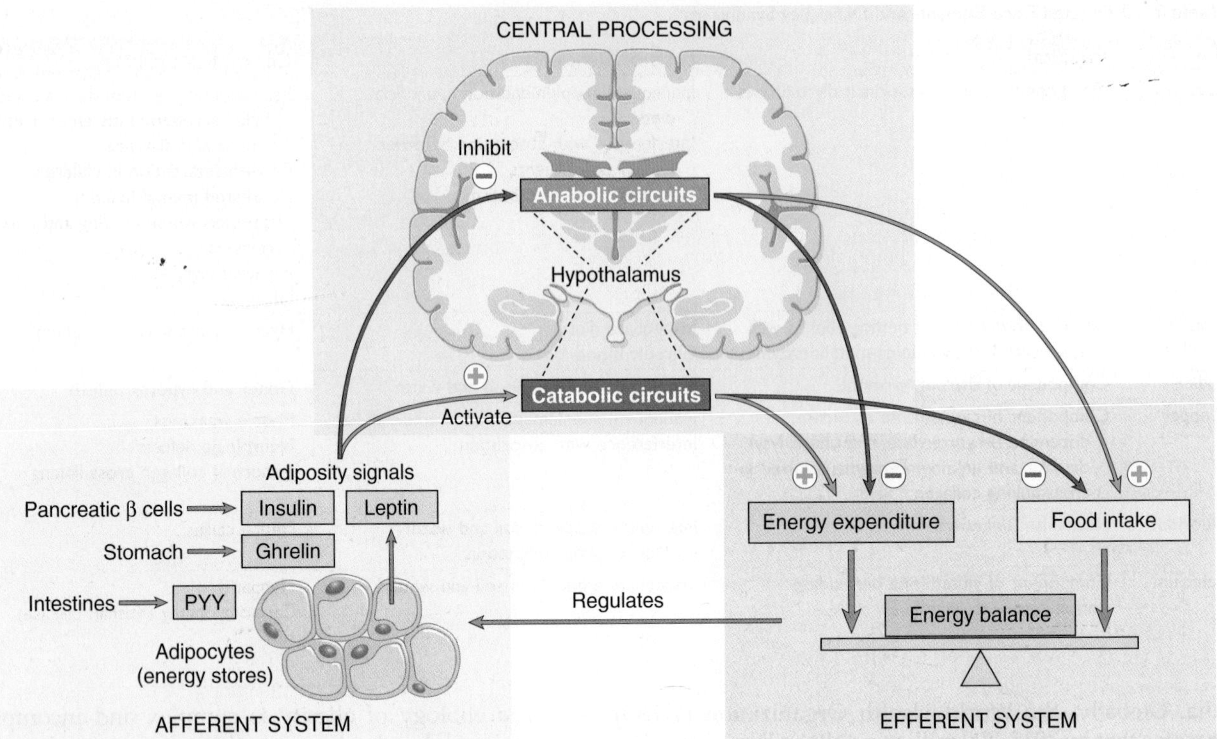

Figure 7–23 Energy balance regulatory circuitry. When sufficient energy is stored in adipose tissue and the individual is well fed, afferent adiposity signals (insulin, leptin, ghrelin, peptide YY) are delivered to the central neuronal processing units, in the hypothalamus. Here the adiposity signals inhibit anabolic circuits and activate catabolic circuits. The effector arms of these central circuits then influence energy balance by inhibiting food intake and promoting energy expenditure. This in turn reduces the energy stores, and pro-adiposity signals are blunted. Conversely, when energy stores are low, the available anabolic circuits take over, at the expense of catabolic circuits, to generate energy stores in the form of adipose tissue.

NPY (neuropeptide Y) and AgRP (agouti-related peptide) neurons.

- *The efferent system*, which consists of hypothalamic neurons regulated by the arcuate nucleus. POMC/CART neurons activate efferent neurons that enhance energy expenditure and weight loss, while NPY/AgRP neurons activate efferent neurons that promote food intake and weight gain. Signals transmitted by efferent neurons also communicate with forebrain and midbrain centers that control the autonomic nervous system.

Discussed next are three important components of the afferent system that regulate appetite and satiety: leptin, adipose tissue, and gut hormones.

Leptin

Through complex, incompletely understood mechanisms, the *output of leptin is regulated by the adequacy of fat stores.* With abundant adipose tissue, leptin secretion is stimulated, and the hormone travels to the hypothalamus, where it *reduces food intake by stimulating POMC/CART neurons and inhibiting NPY/AgRP neurons.* The opposite sequence of events occurs when there are inadequate stores of body fat: Leptin secretion is diminished and food intake is increased. In persons of stable weight, the activities of these pathways are balanced. Leptin also increases energy expenditure by stimulating physical activity, energy expenditure, and thermogenesis, which may be the most important catabolic effects mediated by leptin through the hypothalamus. Thermogenesis seems to be controlled in part by efferent hypothalamic signals that increase the release of norepinephrine from sympathetic nerve endings in adipose tissue. Fat cells express β_3-adrenergic receptors that, when stimulated by norepinephrine, cause fatty acid hydrolysis and also uncouple energy production from storage.

In rodents and humans, loss-of-function mutations affecting components of the leptin pathway give rise to massive obesity. Mice with mutations that disable the leptin gene or its receptor fail to sense the adequacy of fat stores, so they behave as if they are undernourished, eating ravenously. As in mice, mutations of the leptin gene or receptor in humans, although rare, may cause massive obesity. *More common are mutations in the melanocortin receptor-4 gene (MC4R) gene, found in 4% to 5% of patients with massive obesity.* These monogenic traits underscore the importance of the leptin pathway in the control of body weight, and it is possible that more common types of defects in this pathway will be discovered in the obese. For example, many obese persons have high blood leptin levels, suggesting that leptin resistance is prevalent among humans.

Adipose Tissue

In addition to leptin, adipose tissue produces other mediators, such as adiponectin, cytokines, chemokines, and steroid hormones, which allow adipose tissue to function as a link between lipid metabolism, nutrition, and inflammatory responses. *The total number of adipocytes is established by adolescence* and is higher in people who were obese as children, providing another reason for concern about childhood obesity. Although in adults about 10% of adipocytes turn over annually, the number of adipocytes remains constant, regardless of individual body mass. Diets fail in part because loss of fat from adipocytes causes leptin levels to fall, stimulating the appetite and diminishing energy expenditure.

Gut Hormones

Gut hormones are rapidly acting initiators and terminators of volitional eating. Prototypical examples are ghrelin and peptide YY (PYY). *Ghrelin* is produced in the stomach and is the only known gut peptide that increases food intake. It probably acts by stimulating the NPY/AgRP neurons in the hypothalamus. Ghrelin levels normally rise before meals and fall 1 to 2 hours afterward, but this drop is attenuated in obese persons. *PYY* is secreted from endocrine cells in the ileum and colon in response to consumption of food. It presumably acts by stimulating POMC/CART neurons in the hypothalamus, thereby decreasing food intake.

Clinical Consequences of Obesity

Obesity, particularly central obesity, is a known *risk factor for a number of conditions, including type 2 diabetes, cardiovascular disease, and cancer*. Central obesity also stands at the center of a cluster of alterations known as the metabolic syndrome, characterized by abnormalities of glucose and lipid metabolism coupled with hypertension and evidence of a systemic pro-inflammatory state. The mechanisms underlying these associations are complex and probably interrelated. The following associations are worthy of note:

- Obesity is associated with *insulin resistance* and hyperinsulinemia, important features of type 2 diabetes (formerly known as non–insulin-dependent diabetes). It has been speculated that excess insulin, in turn, may play a role in the retention of sodium, expansion of blood volume, production of excess norepinephrine, and smooth muscle proliferation that are the hallmarks of hypertension. Whatever the mechanism, *the risk of developing hypertension among previously normotensive persons increases proportionately with weight.*
- Obese persons generally have hypertriglyceridemia and low HDL cholesterol levels, factors that increase the risk of *coronary artery disease.* The association between obesity and heart disease is not straightforward, however, and such linkage as there is relates more to the associated diabetes and hypertension than to weight per se.
- *There is an increased incidence of certain cancers in the overweight,* including cancers of the esophagus, thyroid, colon, and kidney in men and cancers of the esophagus, endometrium, gallbladder, and kidney in women. Overall, obesity is associated with approximately 20% of cancer deaths in women and 14% of deaths in men. The underlying mechanisms are unknown and are likely to be multiple. One suspect is hyperinsulinemia. Insulin increases levels of insulin-like growth factor-1 (IGF-1), which can stimulate the growth and survival of many types of cancer cells by activating its cognate receptor, IGF1R. The association of obesity and endometrial cancer may be indirect: High estrogen levels are associated with an increased risk of endometrial cancer (Chapter 18), and obesity is known to raise estrogen levels. With breast cancer, the data are controversial.
- *Nonalcoholic steatohepatitis* is commonly associated with obesity and type 2 diabetes. This condition, also referred to as nonalcoholic fatty liver disease, can progress to fibrosis and cirrhosis (Chapter 15).
- *Cholelithiasis (gallstones)* is six times more common in obese than in lean subjects. The mechanism is mainly an increase in total body cholesterol, increased cholesterol turnover, and augmented biliary excretion of cholesterol in the bile, which in turn predisposes affected persons to the formation of cholesterol-rich gallstones (Chapter 15).
- *Hypoventilation syndrome* is a constellation of respiratory abnormalities in very obese persons. It has been called the *pickwickian syndrome,* after the fat lad who was constantly falling asleep in Charles Dickens' *The Pickwick Papers*. Hypersomnolence, both at night and during the day, is characteristic and is often associated with apneic pauses during sleep, polycythemia, and eventual right-sided heart failure.
- Marked adiposity is a predisposing factor for the development of degenerative joint disease (*osteoarthritis*). This form of arthritis, which typically appears in older persons, is attributed in large part to the cumulative effects of wear and tear on joints. The greater the body burden of fat, the greater the trauma to joints with passage of time.
- Markers of inflammation, such as C-reactive protein (CRP) and pro-inflammatory cytokines like TNF, are often elevated in obese persons. The basis for the inflammation is uncertain; both a direct pro-inflammatory effect of excess circulating lipids and increased release of cytokines from fat-laden adipocytes have been proposed. Whatever the cause, it is thought that chronic inflammation may contribute to many of the complications of obesity, including insulin resistance, metabolic abnormalities, thrombosis, cardiovascular disease, and cancer.

SUMMARY

Obesity

- Obesity is a disorder of energy regulation. It increases the risk for a number of important conditions such as insulin resistance, type 2 diabetes, hypertension, and hypertriglyceridemia, which are associated with the development of coronary artery disease.
- The regulation of energy balance is very complex. It has three main components: (1) afferent signals, provided mostly by insulin, leptin, ghrelin, and peptide YY; (2) the central hypothalamic system, which integrates afferent signals and triggers the efferent signals; and (3) efferent signals, which control energy balance.
- Leptin plays a key role in energy balance. Its output from adipose tissues is regulated by the abundance of fat stores. Leptin binding to its receptors in the hypothalamus reduces food intake by stimulating POMC/CART neurons and inhibiting NPY/AgRP neurons.
- In addition to diabetes and cardiovascular disease, obesity also is associated with increased risk for certain cancers, nonalcoholic fatty liver disease, and gallstones.

Diet and Systemic Diseases

The problems of under- and overnutrition, as well as specific nutrient deficiencies, have been discussed; however, the composition of the diet, even in the absence of any of these problems, may make a significant contribution to the causation and progression of a number of diseases. A few examples suffice here.

Currently, one of the most important and controversial issues is the contribution of diet to atherogenesis. The central question is whether dietary modification—specifically, reduction in the consumption of foods high in cholesterol and saturated animal fats (e.g., eggs, butter, beef)—can reduce serum cholesterol levels and prevent or retard the development of atherosclerosis (of most importance, coronary heart disease). The average adult in the United States consumes a large amount of fat and cholesterol daily, with a ratio of saturated fatty acids to polyunsaturated fatty acids of about 3:1. Lowering the level of saturates to the level of the polyunsaturates causes a 10% to 15% reduction in serum cholesterol level within a few weeks. Vegetable oils (e.g., corn and safflower oils) and fish oils contain polyunsaturated fatty acids and are good sources of such cholesterol-lowering lipids. Fish oil fatty acids belonging to the omega-3, or *n*-3, family have more double bonds than do the omega-6, or *n*-6, fatty acids found in vegetable oils. One study of Dutch men whose usual daily diet contained 30 gm of fish revealed a substantially lower frequency of death from coronary heart disease than that among comparable control subjects, providing some hope (but no definitive proof) that long-term supplementation of food with omega-3 fatty acids may reduce coronary artery disease.

Other specific effects of diet on disease have been recognized:

- Hypertension is reduced by restricting sodium intake.
- Dietary fiber, or roughage, resulting in increased fecal bulk, is thought by some investigators to have a preventive effect against diverticulosis of the colon.
- Caloric restriction has been convincingly demonstrated to increase life span in experimental animals, including monkeys. The basis for this striking observation is not clear (Chapter 1).
- Even lowly garlic has been touted to protect against heart disease (and also, alas, against kisses—and the devil), although research has yet to prove this effect unequivocally.

Diet and Cancer

With respect to carcinogenesis, three aspects of the diet are of concern: (1) the content of exogenous carcinogens, (2) the endogenous synthesis of carcinogens from dietary components, and (3) the lack of protective factors.

- An example of an exogenous carcinogen is *aflatoxin*, which is an important factor in the development of hepatocellular carcinomas in parts of Asia and Africa. Exposure to aflatoxin causes a specific mutation (codon 249) in the *P53* gene in tumor cells. The mutation can be used as a molecular signature for aflatoxin exposure in epidemiologic studies. Debate continues about the carcinogenicity of food additives, artificial sweeteners, and contaminating pesticides. Some artificial sweeteners (cyclamates and saccharin) have been implicated in the pathogenesis of bladder cancers, but convincing evidence is lacking.
- The concern about *endogenous* synthesis of carcinogens or promoters from components of the diet relates principally to gastric carcinomas. *Nitrosamines and nitrosamides* are suspected to generate these tumors in humans, as they induce gastric cancer in animals. These compounds are formed in the body from nitrites and amines or amides derived from digested proteins. Sources of nitrites include sodium nitrite, added to foods as a preservative, and nitrates, present in common vegetables, which are reduced in the gut by bacterial flora. There is, then, the potential for endogenous production of carcinogenic agents from dietary components, which might well have an effect on the stomach.
- High animal fat intake combined with low fiber intake has been implicated in the causation of colon cancer. The most convincing explanation for this association is as follows: High fat intake increases the level of bile acids in the gut, which in turn modifies intestinal flora, favoring the growth of microaerophilic bacteria. The bile acids or bile acid metabolites produced by these bacteria might serve as carcinogens or promoters. The protective effect of a high-fiber diet might relate to (1) increased stool bulk and decreased transit time, which decreases the exposure of mucosa to putative offenders, and (2) the capacity of certain fibers to bind carcinogens and thereby protect the mucosa. Attempts to document these theories in clinical and experimental studies have, on the whole, led to contradictory results.
- Vitamins C and E, β-carotenes, and selenium have been assumed to have anticarcinogenic effects because of their antioxidant properties. To date, however, no convincing evidence has emerged to show that these antioxidants act as chemopreventive agents. As already mentioned, retinoic acid promotes epithelial differentiation and is believed to reverse squamous metaplasia.

Thus, despite many tantalizing trends and proclamations by "diet gurus," to date there is no definite proof that diet in general can cause or protect against cancer. Nonetheless, concern persists that carcinogens lurk in things as pleasurable as a juicy steak and rich ice cream.

BIBLIOGRAPHY

Bellinger DC: Lead. Pediatrics 113:1016, 2004. *[An excellent overview of the subject.]*

Boffetta P, Hecht S, Gray N, et al: Smokeless tobacco and cancer. Lancet Oncol 9:667, 2009. *[A review of cancer risks associated with smokeless tobacco worldwide.]*

Centers for Disease Control and Prevention: Third National Report on Human Exposure to Environmental Chemicals, 2005. *[A very important survey of environmental chemicals, with comments on exposure and health risk trends.]*

Casals-Casas C, Desvergne B: Endocrine disruptors: from endocrine to metabolic disruption. Annu Rev Phys 73:135, 2011. *[An update discussing the scope and possible consequences of human exposure to this class of chemical.]*

Clarkson TW, Magos L, Myers GJ: The toxicology of mercury—current exposures and clinical manifestations. N Engl J Med 349:1731, 2003. *[An excellent overview of the subject.]*

Gregor MF, Hotamisligil GS: Inflammatory mechanisms in obesity. Annu Rev Immunol 29:445, 2011. *[A concise discussion of current views of the pro-inflammatory state associated with obesity.]*

Heiss G, Wallace R, Anderson GL, et al: Health risks and benefits 3 years after stopping randomized treatment with estrogen and progestin. JAMA 299:1036, 2008. *[A paper describing a persistently elevated risk of breast cancer in women 3 years after stopping HRT.]*

Hollick MF: Vitamin D deficiency. N Engl J Med 357:266, 2007. *[A comprehensive review of vitamin D deficiency.]*

Jornayvaz FR, Samuel VT, Shulman GI: The role of muscle insulin resistance in the pathogenesis of atherogenic dyslipidemia and nonalcoholic fatty liver disease associated with the metabolic syndrome. Annu Rev Nutr 30:273, 2010. *[An interesting perspective on the metabolic syndrome focused on the role of insulin resistance in skeletal muscle.]*

Manson JE, Hsia J, Johnson KC, et al: Estrogen plus progestin and the risk of coronary heart disease. N Engl J Med 349:523, 2003. *[A landmark study from the Women's Health Initiative.]*

Pope CA, Ezzati M, Dockery DW: Fine-particulate air pollution and life expectancy in the United States. N Engl J Med 360:376, 2009. *[An interesting paper correlating increases in life expectancy in major U.S. cities with decreases in fine-particulate air pollution.]*

Ravdin PM, Cronin KA, Howlader N, et al: The decrease in breast-cancer incidence in 2003 in the United States. N Engl J Med 356:1670, 2007. *[An important paper documenting the decrease in breast cancer that followed its linkage to HRT.]*

Roberts DL, Dive C, Renehan AG: Biological mechanisms linking obesity and cancer risk: new perspectives. Annu Rev Med 61:301, 2010. *[A discussion of the possible interactions between obesity and cancer risk.]*

Suzuki K, Simpson KA, Minnion JS, et al: The role of gut hormones and the hypothalamus in appetite regulation. Endocr J 57:359, 2010. *[An excellent review of the interplay between the gut and the hypothalamus in regulating food consumption.]*

Tang X-H, Gudas LJ: Retinoids, retinoic acid receptors, and cancer. Annu Rev Pathol 6:345, 2011. *[A review of the role of retinoids in cancer, with a focus on solid tumors.]*

See Targeted Therapy available online at
studentconsult.com

CHAPTER 8

General Pathology of Infectious Diseases

CHAPTER CONTENTS

This chapter reviews the general principles of the pathogenesis of infectious disease and describes the characteristic histopathologic changes for different disease categories. Infections that involve specific organs are discussed in other chapters of this book.

GENERAL PRINCIPLES OF MICROBIAL PATHOGENESIS

Infectious diseases remain an important health problem in the United States and worldwide despite the availability and use of effective vaccines and antibiotics. In the United States, 2 of the top 10 leading causes of death are attributable to infection (pneumonia and septicemia). Infectious diseases are particularly important causes of death among the elderly, people with the acquired immunodeficiency syndrome (AIDS), persons with chronic diseases, and patients receiving immunosuppressive drugs. In developing countries, unsanitary living conditions and malnutrition contribute to a massive burden of infectious diseases that kills more than 10 million people each year. Tragically, the most common victims are children with respiratory and diarrheal infections.

Categories of Infectious Agents

Infectious agents belong to a wide range of classes and vary greatly in size, ranging from prion protein aggregates of under 20 nm to 10-m tapeworms (Table 8–1).

Prions

Prions are composed of abnormal forms of a host protein termed *prion protein* (PrP). These agents cause transmissible spongiform encephalopathies, including kuru (associated with human cannibalism), Creutzfeldt-Jakob disease (CJD), bovine spongiform encephalopathy (BSE) (better known as "mad cow disease"), and variant Creutzfeldt-Jakob disease (vCJD) (probably transmitted to humans through consumption of meat from BSE-infected cattle). PrP is found normally in neurons. Diseases occur when the PrP undergoes a conformational change that confers resistance to proteases. The protease-resistant PrP promotes conversion of the normal protease-sensitive PrP to the abnormal form, explaining the infectious nature of these diseases. Accumulation of abnormal PrP leads to neuronal damage and distinctive spongiform pathologic changes in the brain. Spontaneous and inherited mutations in PrP that make it resistant to proteases have been observed in the sporadic and familial forms of CJD, respectively. CJD can be transmitted from person to person iatrogenically, by surgery, organ transplantation, or blood transfusion. These diseases are discussed in detail in Chapter 22.

Viruses

Viruses are obligate intracellular parasites that depend on the host cell's metabolic machinery for their replication. They consist of a nucleic acid genome surrounded by a protein coat (called a capsid) that is sometimes encased in a lipid membrane. Viruses are classified by their nucleic acid genome (DNA or RNA but not both), the shape of the capsid (icosahedral or helical), the presence or absence of

Table 8–1 Classes of Human Pathogens

Taxonomic Category	Size	Propagation Site(s)	Example(s)	Disease(s)
Prions	<20 nm	Intracellular	Prion protein	Creutzfeldt-Jacob disease
Viruses	20–300 nm	Obligate intracellular	Poliovirus	Poliomyelitis
Bacteria	0.2–15 μm	Obligate intracellular Extracellular Facultative intracellular	*Chlamydia trachomatis* *Streptococcus pneumoniae* *Mycobacterium tuberculosis*	Trachoma, urethritis Pneumonia Tuberculosis
Fungi	2–200 μm	Extracellular Facultative intracellular	*Candida albicans* *Histoplasma capsulatum*	Thrush Histoplasmosis
Protozoa	1–50 μm	Extracellular Facultative intracellular Obligate intracellular	*Trypanosoma gambiense* *Trypanosoma cruzi* *Leishmania donovani*	Sleeping sickness Chagas disease Kala-azar
Helminths	3 mm–10 m	Extracellular Intracellular	*Wuchereria bancrofti* *Trichinella spiralis*	Filariasis Trichinosis

a lipid envelope, their mode of replication, the preferred cell type for replication (called tropism), or the type of pathology they cause (Table 8–2). Some viral components and particles aggregate within infected cells and form characteristic inclusion bodies, which may be seen with the light microscope and are useful for diagnosis (Fig. 8–1). For example, cytomegalovirus (CMV)-infected cells are enlarged and show a large eosinophilic nuclear inclusion and smaller basophilic cytoplasmic inclusions; herpesviruses form a large nuclear inclusion surrounded by a clear halo; and both smallpox and rabies viruses form characteristic cytoplasmic inclusions. However, many viruses (e.g., poliovirus) do not produce inclusions.

Accounting for a large share of human infections, viruses can cause illnesses in several ways. Many viruses cause transient illnesses (e.g., colds, influenza). Other viruses are not eliminated from the body and persist within cells of the host for years, either continuing to multiply (e.g., chronic infection with hepatitis B virus [HBV]) or surviving in some nonreplicating form (termed *latent infection*) with the potential to be reactivated later. For example, herpes zoster virus, the cause of chickenpox, can enter dorsal root ganglia and establish latency there and later be periodically activated to cause shingles, a painful skin condition. Some viruses are involved in transformation of a host cell into a benign or malignant tumor (e.g., human papillomavirus [HPV]-induced benign warts and cervical carcinoma). Different species of viruses can produce the same clinical picture (e.g., upper respiratory infection); conversely, a single virus can cause different clinical manifestations depending on host age or immune status (e.g., CMV).

Table 8–2 Selected Human Viral Diseases and Their Pathogens

Organ System	Pathogen	Disease(s)
Respiratory	Adenovirus Rhinovirus Influenza viruses A, B Respiratory syncytial virus	Upper and lower respiratory tract infections, conjunctivitis Upper respiratory tract infection Influenza Bronchiolitis, pneumonia
Digestive	Mumps virus Rotavirus Norovirus Hepatitis A virus Hepatitis B virus Hepatitis D virus Hepatitis C virus Hepatitis E virus	Mumps, pancreatitis, orchitis Childhood gastroenteritis Gastroenteritis Acute viral hepatitis Acute or chronic hepatitis *With hepatitis B virus infection*: acute or chronic hepatitis Acute or chronic hepatitis Acute viral hepatitis
Systemic With skin eruptions	Measles virus Rubella virus Varicella-zoster virus Herpes simplex virus type 1 Herpes simplex virus type 2	Measles (rubeola) German measles (rubella) Chickenpox, shingles Oral herpes ("cold sore") Genital herpes
With hematopoietic disorders	Cytomegalovirus Epstein-Barr virus HIV-1 and HIV-2	Cytomegalic inclusion disease Infectious mononucleosis AIDS
Skin/genital warts	Papillomavirus	Condyloma; cervical carcinoma
Central nervous system	Poliovirus JC virus	Poliomyelitis Progressive multifocal leukoencephalopathy (opportunistic)

AIDS, acquired immunodeficiency syndrome; HIV, human immunodeficiency virus.

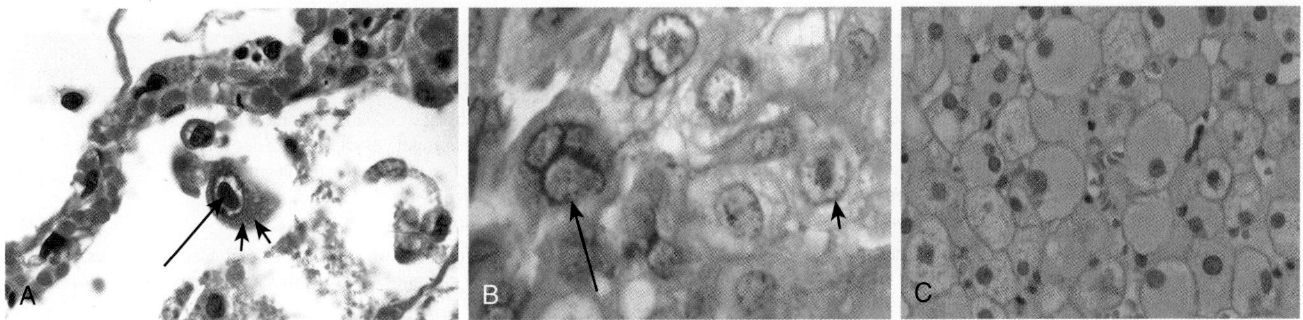

Figure 8–1 Examples of viral inclusions. **A,** Cytomegalovirus infection in the lung. Infected cells show distinct nuclear (*long arrow*) and ill-defined cytoplasmic (*short arrows*) inclusions. **B,** Varicella-zoster virus infection in the skin. Herpes simplex virus and varicella-zoster virus both cause characteristic cytopathologic changes, including fusion of epithelial cells, which produces multinucleate cells with molding of nuclei to one another (*long arrow*), and eosinophilic haloed nuclear inclusions (*short arrow*). **C,** Hepatitis B viral infection in liver. In chronic infections, infected hepatocytes show diffuse granular ("ground-glass") cytoplasm, reflecting accumulated hepatitis B surface antigen (HBsAg).

Bacteria

Bacterial infections are common causes of disease (Table 8-3). Bacteria are prokaryotes, meaning that they have a cell membrane but lack membrane-bound nuclei and other membrane-enclosed organelles. Most bacteria are bound by a cell wall consisting of peptidoglycan, a polymer of long sugar chains linked by peptide bridges surrounding the cell membrane. There are two common forms of cell wall structure: a thick wall that retains crystal-violet stain (gram-positive bacteria) and a thin cell wall surrounded by an outer membrane (gram-negative bacteria) (Fig. 8–2). Bacteria are classified by Gram staining (positive or negative), shape (spherical ones are cocci; rod-shaped ones are bacilli) (Fig. 8–3), and need for oxygen (aerobic or anaerobic). Motile bacteria have flagella, which are long helical filaments extending from the cell surface that rotate and move the bacteria. Some bacteria possess pili, another kind of surface projection that can attach bacteria to host cells or extracellular matrix. Bacteria synthesize their own DNA, RNA, and proteins, but they depend on the host for favorable growth conditions. Many bacteria remain extracellular when they grow in the host, while others survive and replicate either outside or inside of host cells (*facultative intracellular* bacteria) and some grow only inside host cells (*obligate intracellular* bacteria).

Normal healthy people can be colonized by as many as 10^{12} bacteria on the skin, 10^{10} bacteria in the mouth, and 10^{14} bacteria in the gastrointestinal tract. Bacteria colonizing the skin include *Staphylococcus epidermidis* and *Propionibacterium acnes,* the cause of acne. Aerobic and anaerobic bacteria in the mouth, particularly *Streptococcus mutans,* contribute to dental plaque, a major cause of tooth decay. There are over 3,000 taxa of bacteria in the normal intestinal flora of an individual human, but only a small subset, mainly anaerobes, account for the great majority.

Chlamydia and *Rickettsia* are obligate intracellular bacteria which replicate inside membrane-bound vacuoles in epithelial and endothelial cells, respectively. These bacteria get most or all of their energy source, ATP, from the host cell. *Chlamydia trachomatis* is the most frequent infectious cause of female sterility (by scarring and narrowing of the fallopian tubes) and blindness (by chronic inflammation of the conjunctiva that eventually causes scarring and opacification of the cornea). Rickettsiae injure the endothelial cells in which they grow, causing a hemorrhagic vasculitis, often visible as a rash, but they also may injure the central nervous system (CNS), with potentially fatal outcome, as in Rocky Mountain spotted fever and epidemic typhus. Rickettsiae are transmitted by arthropod vectors, including

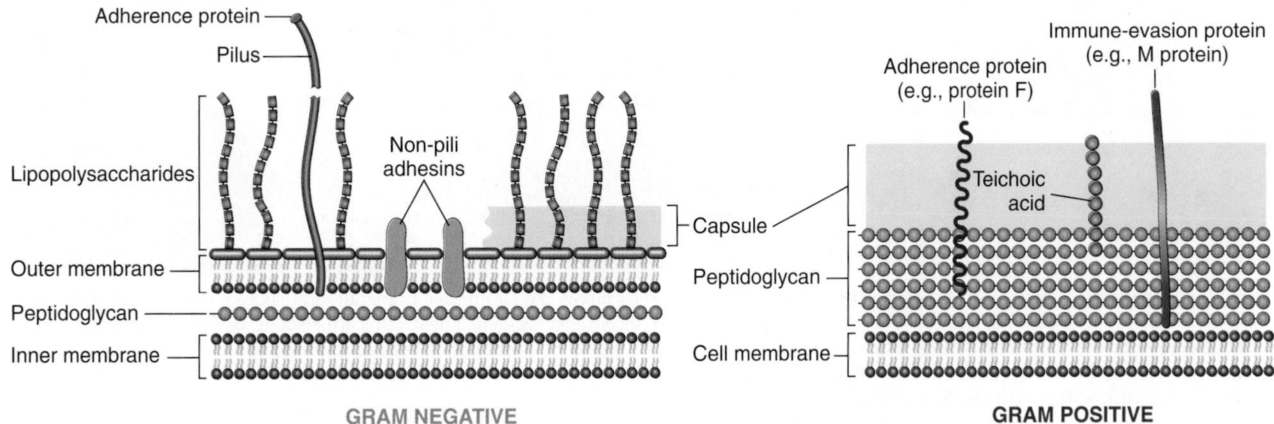

Figure 8–2 Molecules on the surface of gram-negative and gram-positive bacteria involved in the pathogenesis of infection.

Table 8–3 Selected Human Bacterial Diseases and Their Pathogens

Clinical/Microbiologic Category	Species	Frequent Disease Presentation(s)
Infections by pyogenic cocci	*Staphylococcus aureus, Staphylococcus epidermidis*	Abscess, cellulitis, pneumonia, sepsis
	Streptococcus pyogenes	Pharyngitis, erysipelas, scarlet fever
	Streptococcus pneumoniae (pneumococcus)	Lobar pneumonia, meningitis
	Neisseria meningitidis (meningococcus)	Meningitis
	Neisseria gonorrhoeae (gonococcus)	Gonorrhea
Gram-negative infections	*Escherichia coli,* Klebsiella pneumoniae**	Urinary tract infection, wound infection, abscess, pneumonia, sepsis, shock, endocarditis
	*Enterobacter (Aerobacter) aerogenes**	
	Proteus spp. (*Proteus mirabilis, Proteus morgagni*)*	
	Serratia marcescens, Pseudomonas* spp. (*Pseudomonas aeruginosa*),* *Bacteroides* spp. (*Bacteroides fragilis*)	
	Legionella spp. (*Legionella pneumophila*)	Legionnaires disease
Contagious childhood bacterial diseases	*Haemophilus influenzae*	Meningitis, upper and lower respiratory tract infections
	Bordetella pertussis	Whooping cough
	Corynebacterium diphtheriae	Diphtheria
Enteric infections	Enteropathogenic *E. coli, Shigella* spp., *Vibrio cholerae*	Invasive or noninvasive gastroenterocolitis
	Campylobacter jejuni, Campylobacter coli	
	Yersinia enterocolitica	
	Salmonella spp.	
	Salmonella typhi	Typhoid fever
Clostridial infections	*Clostridium tetani*	Tetanus (lockjaw)
	Clostridium botulinum	Botulism (paralytic food poisoning)
	Clostridium perfringens, Clostridium septicum	Gas gangrene, necrotizing cellulitis
	*Clostridium difficile**	Pseudomembranous colitis
Zoonotic bacterial infections	*Bacillus anthracis*	Anthrax
	Yersinia pestis	Bubonic plague
	Francisella tularensis	Tularemia
	Brucella melitensis, Brucella suis, Brucella abortus	Brucellosis (undulant fever)
	Borrelia recurrentis	Relapsing fever
	Borrelia burgdorferi	Lyme disease
Treponemal infections	*Treponema pallidum*	Syphilis
Mycobacterial infections	*Mycobacterium tuberculosis, M. bovis*	Tuberculosis
	Mycobacterium leprae	Leprosy
	Mycobacterium kansasii, Mycobacterium avium complex**	Atypical mycobacterial infections
Actinomycetal infections	*Nocardia asteroides**	Nocardiosis
	Actinomyces israelii	Actinomycosis

*Important opportunistic infections.

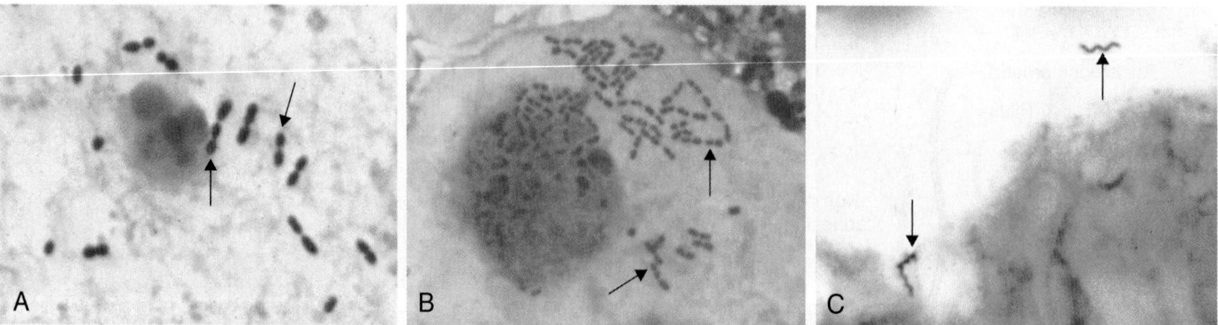

Figure 8–3 The variety of bacterial morphology. The bacteria are indicated by *arrows*. **A,** Gram stain preparation of sputum from a patient with pneumonia. Gram-positive, elongated cocci in pairs and short chains (*Streptococcus pneumoniae*) and a neutrophil are evident. **B,** Gram stain preparation of a bronchoalveolar lavage specimen showing gram-negative intracellular rods typical of members of Enterobacteriaceae such as *Klebsiella pneumoniae* or *Escherichia coli*. **C,** Silver stain preparation of brain tissue from a patient with Lyme disease meningoencephalitis. Two helical spirochetes (*Borrelia burgdorferi*) are indicated by *arrows*. **A, B,** and **C** are at different magnifications.

(B, Courtesy of Dr. Karen Krisher, Clinical Microbiology Institute, Wilsonville, Oregon. A and C, Courtesy of Dr. Kenneth Van Horn, Focus Diagnostics, Cypress, California.)

lice (in epidemic typhus), ticks (in Rocky Mountain spotted fever and ehrlichiosis), and mites (in scrub typhus).

Mycoplasma and the related genus *Ureaplasma* are unique among extracellular bacterial pathogens in that they do not have a cell wall. These are the tiniest free-living organisms known (125 to 300 nm).

Normal Microbiome. The intestinal tract and skin normally are colonized by a large number and diversity of bacterial species. Until recently, little was known about these species because most normal flora cannot be cultured. New techniques of microbial identification and speciation relying on ribosomal RNA sequencing have revealed normal microbial flora to be remarkably complex. This veritable ecosystem of microbes and their genes and products that humans live with is called the *microbiome*. In the intestinal tract, the microbiota are responsible not only for absorption of digested foods but also for maintaining the integrity of the epithelium and the normal functioning of the intestinal immune system, and for competitively inhibiting invasion and colonization by potentially pathogenic microbes. Depletion of the microbiome or change in its composition has been implicated in inflammatory bowel disease, the development of allergies, and increased incidence of various systemic autoimmune diseases.

Fungi

Fungi are eukaryotes that possess thick, chitin-containing cell walls and ergosterol-containing cell membranes. Fungi can grow either as rounded yeast cells or as slender, filamentous hyphae. Hyphae may be septate (with cell walls separating individual cells) or aseptate, which is an important distinguishing characteristic in clinical material. Some of the most important pathogenic fungi exhibit thermal dimorphism; that is, they grow as hyphal forms at room temperature but as yeast forms at body temperature. Fungi may produce sexual spores or, more commonly, asexual spores called *conidia*. The latter are produced on specialized structures or fruiting bodies arising along the hyphal filament.

Fungi may cause superficial or deep infections.

- Superficial infections involve the skin, hair, and nails. Fungal species that cause superficial infections are called *dermatophytes*. Infection of the skin is called *tinea*; thus, *tinea pedis* is "athlete's foot" and *tinea capitis* is scalp ringworm. Certain fungi invade the subcutaneous tissue, causing abscesses or granulomas sometimes called mycetomas.
- Deep fungal infections can spread systemically and invade tissues, destroying vital organs in immunocompromised hosts, but usually resolve or remain latent in otherwise normal hosts.

Fungi are divided into endemic and opportunistic species.

- Endemic fungi are invasive species that are limited to particular geographic regions (e.g., *Coccidioides* in the southwestern United States, *Histoplasma* in the Ohio River Valley).
- By contrast, opportunistic fungi (e.g., *Candida, Aspergillus, Mucor, Cryptococcus*) are ubiquitous organisms that either colonize individuals or are encountered from environmental sources. In immunodeficient individuals, opportunistic fungi give rise to life-threatening invasive infections characterized by tissue necrosis, hemorrhage, and vascular occlusion, with little or no inflammatory response (Fig. 8–4). Patients with AIDS often are infected by the opportunistic fungus *Pneumocystis jiroveci* (previously called *Pneumocystis carinii*).

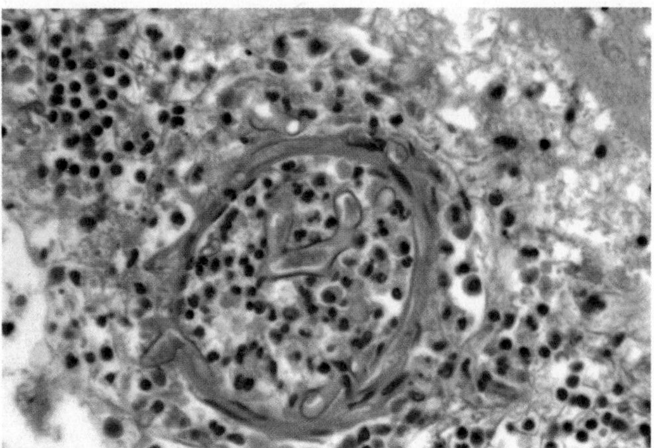

Figure 8–4 Meningeal blood vessels with angioinvasive *Mucor* species. Note the irregular width and near right-angle branching of the hyphae. *(Courtesy of Dr. Dan Milner, Department of Pathology, Brigham and Women's Hospital, Boston, Massachusetts.)*

Protozoa

Protozoa are single-celled eukaryotes that are major causes of disease and death in developing countries. Protozoa can replicate intracellularly within a variety of cells (e.g., *Plasmodium* in red cells, *Leishmania* in macrophages) or extracellularly in the urogenital system, intestine, or blood. *Trichomonas vaginalis* organisms are sexually transmitted flagellated protozoal parasites that often colonize the vagina and male urethra. The most prevalent intestinal protozoans, *Entamoeba histolytica* and *Giardia lamblia*, are ingested as nonmotile *cysts* in contaminated food or water and become motile *trophozoites* that attach to intestinal epithelial cells. Bloodborne protozoa (e.g., *Plasmodium, Trypanosoma, Leishmania*) are transmitted by insect vectors, in which they replicate before being passed to new human hosts. *Toxoplasma gondii* is acquired either through contact with oocyst-shedding kittens or by eating cyst-ridden, undercooked meat.

Helminths

Parasitic worms are highly differentiated multicellular organisms. Their life cycles are complex; most alternate between sexual reproduction in the definitive host and asexual multiplication in an intermediate host or vector. Thus, depending on the species, humans may harbor adult worms (e.g., *Ascaris lumbricoides*), immature stages (e.g., *Toxocara canis*), or asexual larval forms (e.g., *Echinococcus* spp.). Once adult worms take up residence in humans, they usually do not multiply but they produce eggs or larvae that are usually passed out in stool. Often, the severity of disease is in proportion to the number of infecting organisms. For example, a burden of 10 hookworms is associated with mild or no clinical disease, whereas 1000 hookworms consume enough blood to cause severe anemia. In some helminthic infections, such as schistosomiasis, disease is caused by inflammatory responses to the eggs or larvae, rather than to the adults.

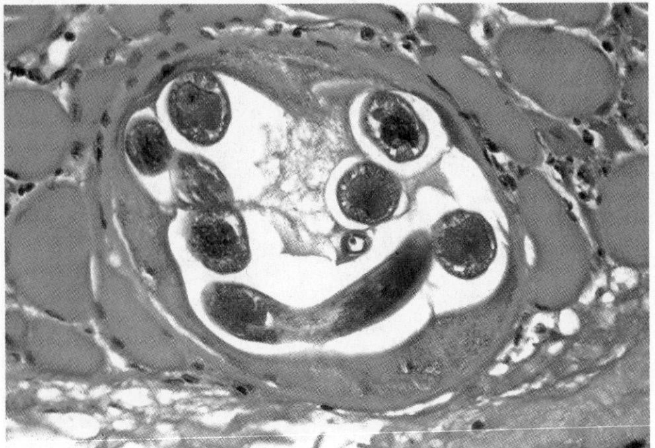

Figure 8–5 Coiled *Trichinella spiralis* larva within a skeletal muscle cell.

Helminths comprise three groups:

- *Roundworms* (*nematodes*) are circular in cross-section and nonsegmented. Intestinal nematodes include *Ascaris lumbricoides*, *Strongyloides stercoralis*, and hookworms. Nematodes that invade into tissue include the filariae and *Trichinella spiralis* (Fig. 8–5).
- *Tapeworms* (*cestodes*) have a head (scolex) and a ribbon of multiple flat segments (proglottids). They adsorb nutrition through their tegument and do not have a digestive tract. They include the fish, beef, and pork tapeworms, found in the human intestine. The larvae that develop after ingestion of eggs of certain tapeworms can cause cystic disease within tissues (*Echinoccus granulosus* larvae cause *hydatid* cysts; pork tapeworm larvae produce cysts called cysticerci in many organs).
- *Flukes* (*trematodes*) are leaf-shaped flatworms with prominent suckers that are used to attach to the host. They include liver and lung flukes and schistosomes.

Ectoparasites

Ectoparasites are insects (lice, bedbugs, fleas) or arachnids (mites, ticks, spiders) that attach to and live on or in the skin. Diseases caused directly by arthropods are characterized by itching and excoriations, such as pediculosis caused by lice attached to hairs, or scabies caused by mites burrowing into the stratum corneum. At the site of the bite, mouth parts may be found associated with a mixed infiltrate of lymphocytes, macrophages, and eosinophils. Arthropods also can serve as vectors for other pathogens, such as *Borrelia burgdorferi*, the agent of Lyme disease, which is transmitted by deer ticks.

SPECIAL TECHNIQUES FOR IDENTIFYING INFECTIOUS AGENTS

Some infectious agents can be seen in hematoxylin and eosin (H&E)–stained sections (e.g., the inclusion bodies formed by CMV and herpes simplex virus (HSV); bacterial clumps, which usually stain blue; *Candida* and *Mucor* among the fungi; most protozoans; all helminths). Many infectious agents, however, are best visualized by special stains that identify organisms on the basis of particular characteristics of their cell wall or coat—Gram, acid-fast, silver, mucicarmine, and Giemsa stains—or after labeling with specific antibodies (Table 8–4). Organisms are usually best visualized at the advancing edge of a lesion rather than at its center, particularly if there is necrosis.

Table 8–4 Special Techniques for Identifying Infectious Agents

Technique	Infectious Agent(s)
Gram stain	Most bacteria
Acid-fast stain	Mycobacteria, nocardiae (modified)
Silver stains	Fungi, legionellae, *Pneumocystis*
Periodic acid–Schiff	Fungi, amebae
Mucicarmine	Cryptococci
Giemsa	Leishmaniae, *Plasmodium*
Antibodies	All classes
Culture	All classes
DNA probes	All classes

Acute infections can be diagnosed serologically by detecting pathogen-specific antibodies in the serum. The presence of specific immunoglobulin M (IgM) antibody shortly after the onset of symptoms is often diagnostic. Alternatively, specific antibody titers can be measured early ("acute") and again at 4 to 6 weeks ("convalescent") after infection; a four-fold rise in titer usually is considered diagnostic. Assays for serum antibodies are very useful for the diagnosis of hepatitis caused by viruses.

Nucleic acid–based tests, collectively called *molecular diagnostics*, are used routinely to detect pathogens. Nucleic acid amplification techniques, such as polymerase chain reaction (PCR) and transcription-mediated amplification, are used for diagnosis of gonorrhea, chlamydial infection, tuberculosis, and herpes encephalitis. Molecular assays are much more sensitive than conventional testing for some pathogens. PCR testing of cerebrospinal fluid (CSF) for HSV encephalitis has a sensitivity of about 80%, whereas viral culture of CSF has a sensitivity of less than 10%. Similarly, nucleic acid tests for genital *Chlamydia* detect 10% to 30% more infections than does conventional *Chlamydia* culture. For other infections, such as gonorrhea, the sensitivity of nucleic acid testing is similar to that of culture. Quantitative nucleic acid amplification tests are used to guide the medical management of infections with human immunodeficiency virus (HIV), HBV and hepatitis C virus (HCV).

NEW AND EMERGING INFECTIOUS DISEASES

A surprising number of new infectious agents continue to be discovered. The infectious causes of some important diseases were previously unrecognized, because some of the infectious agents are difficult to culture; examples include *Helicobacter pylori* gastritis and peptic ulcer disease, HBV and HCV, and Legionnaires disease (pneumonia). Some infectious agents are relatively new to humans—for example, HIV, which causes AIDS, and *B. burgdorferi*, which causes Lyme disease. Other infections have become much more common because of immunosuppression caused by AIDS or therapy to prevent transplant rejection and for some cancers (e.g., Kaposi sarcoma, *Mycobacterium avium complex, P. jiroveci*). Finally, infectious diseases that are common in one geographic area may be introduced into a new area. For example, West Nile virus has been common in Europe, Asia, and Africa for years but was first described in the United States in 1999.

Several factors contribute to the emergence of infectious diseases:

- Human behavior affects the spread and demographics of infections. AIDS was first recognized in the United States as predominantly a disease of homosexual men and drug abusers, but heterosexual transmission is now more common. In sub-Saharan Africa, the area of the world with the highest number of AIDS cases, it is predominantly a heterosexual disease.
- Changes in the environment occasionally drive rates of infectious diseases. Deforestation of the eastern United States has led to massive increases in deer and mice, which carry the ticks that transmit Lyme disease, babesiosis, and ehrlichiosis. Global warming has also had an impact on the spread of infections. For example, the mosquitoes that carry Dengue fever, which used to be confined to the U.S.-Mexican border, are now found in 28 states.
- Pathogens adapt rapidly to selective pressures exerted by widespread use (and overuse) of antibiotics. Antibiotic resistance has developed and is now common in *Mycobacterium tuberculosis, Neisseria gonorrhoeae*, and *Staphylococcus aureus*. Similarly, development of drug-resistant parasites has dramatically increased the morbidity and mortality associated with *Plasmodium falciparum* infection in Asia, Africa, and Latin America.

Table 8–5 Potential Agents of Bioterrorism

Category A Diseases and Agents
Anthrax: *Bacillus anthracis*
Botulism: *Clostridium botulinum* toxin
Plague: *Yersinia pestis*
Smallpox: *Variola major* virus
Tularemia: *Francisella tularensis*
Viral hemorrhagic fevers: filoviruses (e.g., Ebola, Marburg) and arenaviruses (e.g., Lassa, Machupo)
Category B Diseases and Agents
Brucellosis: *Brucella* spp.
Epsilon toxin of *Clostridium perfringens*
Food safety threats: *Salmonella* spp., *Escherichia coli* O157:H7, *Shigella*, others
Glanders: *Burkholderia mallei*
Melioidosis: *Burkholderia pseudomallei*
Psittacosis: *Chlamydia psittaci*
Q fever: *Coxiella burnetii*
Ricin toxin from castor beans (*Ricinus communis*)
Staphylococcal enterotoxin B
Typhus fever: *Rickettsia prowazekii*
Viral encephalitis: alphaviruses (e.g., Venezuelan equine encephalitis, Eastern equine encephalitis, Western equine encephalitis)
Water safety threats: *Vibrio cholerae, Cryptosporidium parvum*, others
Category C Diseases and Agents
Emerging infectious disease threats: Nipah virus, hantavirus, possibly others

Adapted from Centers for Disease Control and Prevention Information (www.bt.cdc.gov/bioterrorism/2011).

AGENTS OF BIOTERRORISM

Sadly, the anthrax attacks in the United States in 2001 transformed the theoretical threat of bioterrorism into reality. The Centers for Disease Control and Prevention (CDC) has evaluated the microorganisms that pose the greatest danger as weapons on the basis of the efficiency with which disease can be transmitted, how difficult the microorganisms are to produce and distribute, what can be done to defend against them, and the extent to which they are likely to alarm the public and produce widespread fear. Based on these criteria, the CDC has ranked bioweapons into three categories, designated A, B, and C (Table 8–5).

The agents in the highest-risk category A can be readily disseminated or transmitted from person to person, typically cause diseases that can carry a high mortality rate with potential for major public health impact, may cause pandemics leading to public panic and social disruption, and are likely to require special action for public health preparedness. For example, the smallpox virus is a category A agent because of its high transmissibility, case mortality rates of 30% or greater, and the lack of effective antiviral therapy. Smallpox readily spreads from person to person, mainly through respiratory secretions and by direct contact with virus in skin lesions. After an incubation period of 7 to 17 days, the usual presenting manifestations are high fever, headache, and backache, followed by a rash, which first appears on the mucosa of the mouth and pharynx, face, and forearms and spreads to the trunk and legs. The rash initially is vesicular and later becomes pustular. Because affected persons are contagious during the incubation period, smallpox virus can rapidly spread throughout an unprotected population. Since routine smallpox vaccination ended in the United States in 1972, immunity has waned, leaving the population highly susceptible. Concern that smallpox could be used for bioterrorism has led to reinstitution of vaccination for some medical and military personnel.

Category B agents are moderately easy to disseminate, cause disease associated with moderate morbidity but low mortality, and require specific diagnostic and disease surveillance. Many of these agents can be spread in food or water. Category C agents include emerging pathogens that could be engineered for mass dissemination because of ease of availability, production, and dissemination; the potential for high morbidity and mortality; and great impact on health.

TRANSMISSION AND DISSEMINATION OF MICROBES

Routes of Entry of Microbes

Microbes can enter the host through breaches in the skin, inhalation, ingestion, or sexual transmission. The first defenses against infection are intact skin and mucosal surfaces, which provide physical barriers and produce antimicrobial substances. In general, respiratory, gastrointestinal, or genitourinary tract infections that occur in otherwise healthy persons are caused by relatively virulent microorganisms that are capable of damaging or penetrating intact epithelial barriers. By contrast, most skin infections in healthy persons are caused by less virulent organisms that enter the skin through damaged sites (cuts and burns).

Skin

The dense, keratinized outer layer of skin is a natural barrier to infection, and the low pH of the skin (less than 5.5) and the presence of fatty acids inhibit growth of microorganisms other than the normal flora. Skin normally is inhabited by bacteria and fungi, including potential opportunists, such as *S. aureus* and *Candida albicans.*

Most microorganisms penetrate through breaks in the skin, including superficial pricks (fungal infections), wounds (staphylococci), burns (*Pseudomonas aeruginosa*), and diabetic and pressure-related foot sores (multibacterial infections). Intravenous catheters in hospitalized patients provide portals for local or systemic infection. Needle sticks can expose the recipient to infected blood and transmit HBV, hepatitis C virus (HCV), or HIV. Some pathogens penetrate the skin via an insect or animal bite. Bites by fleas, ticks, mosquitoes, mites, and lice break the skin and transmit arboviruses (causes of yellow fever and encephalitis), bacteria (plague, Lyme disease, Rocky Mountain spotted fever), protozoa (malaria, leishmaniasis), and helminths (filariasis). Animal bites can lead to infections with bacteria or certain viruses, such as rabies. Only a few microorganisms are able to traverse the unbroken skin. For example, *Schistosoma* larvae released from freshwater snails penetrate swimmers' skin by releasing enzymes that dissolve the extracellular matrix. Certain fungi (dermatophytes) can infect intact stratum corneum, hair, and nails.

Gastrointestinal Tract

Gastrointestinal pathogens are transmitted by food or drink contaminated with fecal material. When hygiene fails, as may occur with natural disasters such as floods and earthquakes, diarrheal disease becomes rampant.

Acidic gastric secretions are important defenses and are lethal for many gastrointestinal pathogens. Healthy volunteers do not become infected by *Vibrio cholerae* unless they are fed 10^{11} organisms, but neutralizing the stomach acid reduces the infectious dose by 10,000-fold. By contrast, some ingested agents, such as *Shigella* and *Giardia* cysts, are relatively resistant to gastric acid, so fewer than 100 organisms of each can cause illness.

Other normal defenses within the gastrointestinal tract include (1) the layer of viscous mucus covering the intestinal epithelium, (2) lytic pancreatic enzymes and bile detergents, (3) mucosal antimicrobial peptides called defensins, (4) normal flora, and (5) secreted IgA antibodies. IgA antibodies are made by plasma cells located in mucosa-associated lymphoid tissue (MALT). These lymphoid aggregates are covered by a single layer of specialized epithelial cells called M cells, which are important for transport of antigens to MALT. Numerous gut pathogens use M cells to enter the host from the intestinal lumen, including poliovirus, enteropathic *Escherichia coli, V. cholerae, Salmonella typhi,* and *Shigella flexneri.*

Infection via the gastrointestinal tract occurs when local defenses are weakened or the organisms develop strategies to overcome these defenses. Host defenses are weakened by low gastric acidity, by antibiotics that alter the normal bacterial flora (e.g., in pseudomembranous colitis), or when there is stalled peristalsis or mechanical obstruction. Viruses that can enter the body through the intestinal tract (e.g., hepatitis A, rotavirus) are those that lack envelopes, because enveloped viruses are inactivated by bile and digestive enzymes.

Enteropathogenic bacteria cause gastrointestinal disease in several ways:

- *S. aureus* can contaminate and grow in food, where it releases powerful enterotoxins that, when ingested, cause food poisoning without any bacterial multiplication in the gut.
- *V. cholerae* and enterotoxigenic *E. coli* bind to the intestinal epithelium and multiply in the overlying mucous layer, where they release exotoxins that cause epithelial cells to secrete large volumes of fluid, resulting in watery diarrhea.
- *Shigella, Salmonella,* and *Campylobacter* invade locally and damage the intestinal mucosa and lamina propria, causing ulceration, inflammation, and hemorrhage—changes manifested clinically as dysentery.
- *Salmonella typhi* passes from the damaged mucosa through Peyer's patches and mesenteric lymph nodes and into the bloodstream, resulting in a systemic infection.

Fungal infection of the gastrointestinal tract occurs mainly in immunologically compromised persons. *Candida,* part of the normal gastrointestinal flora, shows a predilection for stratified squamous epithelium, causing oral thrush or membranous esophagitis, but also may spread to the stomach, lower gastrointestinal tract, and other organs.

Intestinal protozoa are transmitted as cysts, which resist stomach acid. In the gut, cysts convert to motile trophozoites and attach to sugars on the intestinal epithelia through surface lectins. What happens next differs among protozoa. *Giardia lamblia* attaches to the epithelial brush border, whereas cryptosporidia are taken up by enterocytes, in which they form gametes and oocysts. *E. histolytica* kills host cells by contact-mediated cytolysis through a channel-forming pore protein, with consequent ulceration and invasion of the colonic mucosa. *Intestinal helminths* cause disease when they are present in large numbers or by reaching ectopic sites, for example, by obstructing the gut or invading and damaging the bile ducts (*Ascaris lumbricoides*). Hookworms cause iron deficiency anemia by sucking blood from intestinal villi; *Diphyllobothrium,* the fish tapeworm, causes anemia by depriving the host of vitamin B_{12}. Finally, larvae of several helminths pass through the gut briefly on their way to another organ; for example, *Trichinella spiralis* larvae preferentially encyst in muscle, and *Echinococcus* larvae grow in the liver or lung.

Respiratory Tract

A large number of microorganisms, including viruses, bacteria, and fungi, are inhaled daily by every person. In many cases, the microbes are inhaled in dust or aerosol particles.

The distance these particles travel into the respiratory system is inversely proportional to their size. Large particles are trapped in the mucociliary blanket that lines the nose and the upper respiratory tract. Microorganisms trapped in the mucus secreted by goblet cells are transported by ciliary action to the back of the throat, where they are swallowed and cleared. Particles smaller than 5 μm travel directly to the alveoli, where they are phagocytosed by alveolar macrophages or by neutrophils recruited to the lung by cytokines.

Microorganisms that invade the normal healthy respiratory tract have developed specific mechanisms to overcome mucociliary defenses or to avoid destruction by alveolar macrophages. Some successful respiratory viruses evade these defenses by attaching to and entering epithelial cells in the lower respiratory tract and pharynx. For example, influenza viruses possess hemagglutinin proteins that project from the surface of the virus and bind to sialic acid on the surface of epithelial cells. This attachment induces the host cell to engulf the virus, leading to viral entry and replication within the host cell.

Certain bacterial respiratory pathogens, including *Haemophilus influenzae, Mycoplasma pneumoniae,* and *Bordetella pertussis,* release toxins that impair ciliary activity. Some bacteria lack the ability to overcome the defenses of the healthy lung and can cause respiratory infections only in compromised hosts. *S. pneumoniae* and *S. aureus* can cause pneumonia subsequent to influenza, because the viral infection causes loss of the protective ciliated epithelium. Chronic damage to mucociliary defense mechanisms occurs in smokers and people with cystic fibrosis, while acute injury occurs in intubated patients and in those who aspirate gastric acid.

Some respiratory pathogens avoid phagocytosis or destruction after phagocytosis. M. tuberculosis, for example, gains its foothold in alveoli because it escapes killing within the phagolysosomes of macrophages. Opportunistic fungi infect the lungs when cellular immunity is depressed or when leukocytes are reduced in number (e.g., *P. jiroveci* in patients with AIDS, *Aspergillus* spp. after chemotherapy).

Urogenital Tract

The urinary tract is almost always invaded from the exterior by way of the urethra. The regular flushing of the urinary tract with urine serves as a defense against invading microorganisms. Urine in the bladder is normally sterile, and successful pathogens (e.g., *N. gonorrhoeae, E. coli*) adhere to the urinary epithelium. Anatomy plays an important role in infection. Women have more than 10 times as many urinary tract infections as in men because the distance between the urinary bladder and skin (i.e., the length of the urethra) is 5 cm in women, in contrast with 20 cm in men. Obstruction of urinary flow or reflux can compromise normal defenses and increase susceptibility to urinary tract infections. Urinary tract infections often spread in retrograde fashion from the bladder to the kidney and cause acute and chronic pyelonephritis.

From puberty until menopause the vagina is protected from pathogens by a low pH resulting from catabolism of glycogen in the normal epithelium by lactobacilli. Antibiotics can kill the lactobacilli, allowing overgrowth of yeast, with resultant vaginal candidiasis.

Spread and Dissemination of Microbes Within the Body

Some microorganisms proliferate locally, at the site of initial infection, whereas others penetrate the epithelial barrier and spread to distant sites by way of the lymphatics, the blood, or nerves (Fig. 8–6). Pathogens that cause superficial infections stay confined to the lumen of hollow viscera (e.g., *Vibrio cholerae*) or adhere to or proliferate exclusively in or on epithelial cells (e.g., papillomaviruses, dermatophytes).

Microbes can spread within the body in several ways:

- Some extracellular bacteria, fungi, and helminths secrete lytic enzymes which destroy tissue and allow direct invasion. For example, *S. aureus* secretes hyaluronidase, which degrades the extracellular matrix between host cells. Invasive microbes initially follow tissue planes of least resistance and drain to regional lymphatics. *S. aureus* may travel from a localized abscess to the draining lymph nodes. This can sometimes lead to bacteremia and spread to deep organs (heart, bone).
- Microorganisms may be spread in the blood or lymph either free in extracellular fluid or within host cells. Some viruses (e.g., poliovirus, HBV), most bacteria and

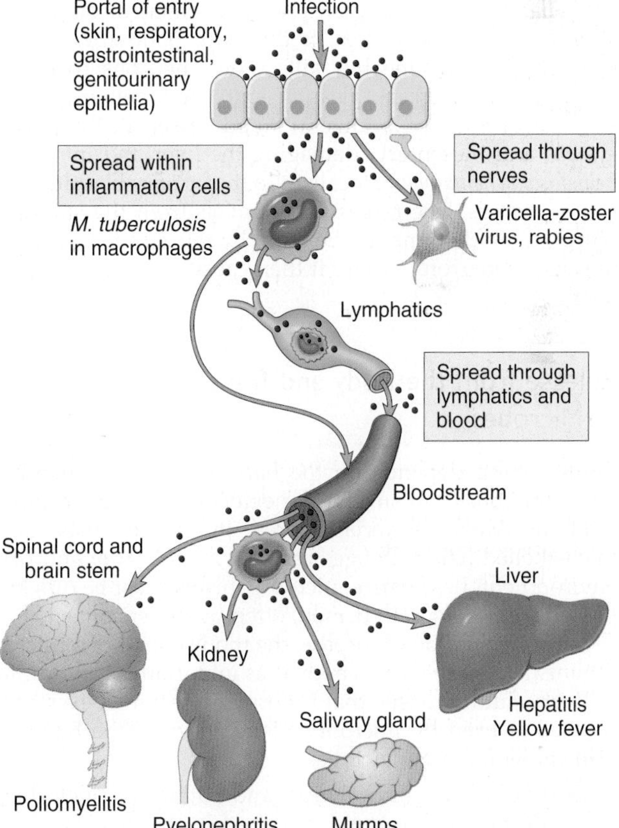

Figure 8–6 Routes of entry and dissemination of microbes. To enter the body, microbes penetrate epithelial or mucosal barriers. Infection may remain localized at the site of entry or spread to other sites in the body. Most common microbes (selected examples are shown) spread through the lymphatics or bloodstream (either freely or within inflammatory cells). However, certain viruses and bacterial toxins also may travel through nerves.

(Adapted from Mims CA: The Pathogenesis of Infectious Disease, 4th ed. San Diego, Academic Press, 1996.)

fungi, some protozoa (e.g., African trypanosomes), and all helminths are transported in blood, free in the plasma. Leukocytes can carry herpesviruses, HIV, mycobacteria, *Leishmania,* and *Toxoplasma.* The parasites *Plasmodium* and *Babesia* are carried within red blood cells.

- Most viruses spread locally from cell to cell by replication and release of infectious virions, but others may propagate from cell to cell by causing fusion of host cells, or by transport within nerves (as with rabies virus and varicella-zoster virus).

Spread of pathogens in the blood can have inconsequential or dire consequences. Infectious foci seeded by blood can be single and large (as with an abscess or tuberculoma) or multiple and tiny (as with miliary tuberculosis or *Candida* microabscesses). Sporadic bloodstream invasion by low-virulence or nonvirulent microbes (e.g., during brushing of teeth) is common but is quickly controlled by normal host defenses. By contrast, disseminated viremia, bacteremia, fungemia, or parasitemia by virulent pathogens is a serious danger and manifests as fever, low blood pressure, and multiple other systemic signs and symptoms of sepsis. Massive bloodstream invasion by bacteria can rapidly lead to fatal sepsis, even in previously healthy persons.

The major manifestations of infectious disease may appear at sites distant from the point of microbe entry. For example, varicella-zoster and measles viruses enter through the airways but cause rashes in the skin; poliovirus enters through the intestine but kills motor neurons to cause paralysis. *Schistosoma mansoni* parasites penetrate the skin but eventually localize in blood vessels of the portal system and mesentery, damaging the liver and intestine. *Schistosoma hematobium* localizes to the urinary bladder and causes cystitis. The rabies virus travels from the site of a bite by a rabid animal to the brain by retrograde transport in sensory neurons, where it then causes encephalitis and death.

Release from the Body and Transmission of Microbes

Transmission depends on the hardiness of the microbe. Some microbes can survive for extended periods in dust, food, or water. Bacterial spores, protozoan cysts, and thick-shelled helminth eggs can survive in a cool and dry environment. Less hardy microorganisms must be quickly passed from person to person, often by direct contact.

For transmission of disease, the mode of exit of a microorganism from the host's body is as important as entry into it. Every fluid or tissue that is normally secreted, excreted, or shed is used by microorganisms to leave the host for transmission to new victims.

- Skin flora, such as *S. aureus,* and pathogens, including the dermatophyte fungi, are shed in the desquamated skin. Some sexually transmitted pathogens are transmitted from genital skin lesions.
- Viruses that replicate in the salivary glands and are spread in saliva include mumps virus, cytomegalovirus, and rabies virus.
- Viruses and bacteria that are part of the normal respiratory flora or cause respiratory tract infections are shed in respiratory secretions during talking, coughing, and sneezing. Most respiratory pathogens, including influenza viruses, spread in large respiratory droplets, which travel no more than 3 feet. A few organisms, including *M. tuberculosis* and varicella-zoster virus, are spread from the respiratory tract by the airborne route in small respiratory droplets or within dust particles, which can travel long distances.
- Organisms shed in stool include many pathogens that replicate in the lumen or epithelium of the gut, such as *Shigella, Giardia lamblia,* and rotavirus. Pathogens that replicate in the liver (hepatitis A virus) or gallbladder (*Salmonella* serotype typhi) enter the intestine in bile and are shed in stool.
- Pathogens which exit the body in the blood are transmitted by invertebrate vectors, medical practices (blood transfusion, reuse of equipment) or sharing of needles by intravenous drug abusers. Bloodborne parasites, including *Plasmodium* spp. and arboviruses, are spread by biting insects.
- Urine is the usual mode of exodus from the human host by only a few organisms, including *Schistosoma haematobium,* which grows in the veins of the bladder and releases eggs that reach the urine.
- Sexually transmitted infections (STIs) infect and spread from the urethra, vagina, cervix, rectum, or oral pharynx. Organisms that cause STIs depend on direct contact for person-to-person spread because these pathogens do not survive in the environment. Transmission of STIs often is by asymptomatic people who do not realize that they are infected. Infection with one STI increases the risk for additional STIs, mainly because the risk factors are the same for all STIs. STIs are described in Chapters 17 and 18.
- Vertical transmission is from mother to fetus or newborn child, and occurs by three main anatomic routes. *Placental-fetal transmission* is most likely to occur when the mother has primary infection with a pathogen during pregnancy. The damage that occurs depends on the developmental stage of the fetus. For example, rubella infection during the first trimester can cause heart malformation, mental retardation, cataracts, or deafness in the infant, while little damage is caused by rubella infection during the third trimester. Vertical transmission also occurs during *passage of the neonate through the birth canal* (e.g., gonococcal or chlamydial conjunctivitis) or *through maternal milk* (e.g., CMV and HBV). Diagnosis of STIs in pregnant women is critical, because vertical transmission of STIs often can be prevented by treatment of the mother or newborn. For example, maternal transmission of HIV is the major cause of AIDS in children; it most often occurs prenatally, during delivery. Antiretroviral treatment of pregnant women with HIV infection and treatment of the newborn can reduce the rate of transmission of HIV to children from 25% to less than 2%.

Microbes also can be transmitted from animal to human (resulting in *zoonotic infections*), either through direct contact or consumption of animal products or indirectly by an invertebrate vector.

SUMMARY

Transmission of Microbes

- Transmission of infections can occur by contact (direct and indirect), respiratory droplets, fecal-oral route, sexual transmission, vertical transmission from mother to fetus or newborn, or insect/arthropod vectors.
- A pathogen can establish infection if it possesses virulence factors that overcome normal host defenses or if the host defenses are compromised.
- Host defenses against infection include:
  - *Skin:* tough keratinized barrier, low pH, fatty acids
  - *Respiratory system:* alveolar macrophages and mucociliary clearance by bronchial epithelium, IgA
  - *Gastrointestinal system:* acidic gastric pH, viscous mucus, pancreatic enzymes and bile, defensins, IgA, and normal flora
  - *Urogenital tract:* repeated flushing and acidic environment created by commensal vaginal flora

HOW MICROORGANISMS CAUSE DISEASE

Infectious agents establish infection and damage tissues by any of three mechanisms:

- They can contact or enter host cells and directly cause cell death.
- They may release toxins that kill cells at a distance, release enzymes that degrade tissue components, or damage blood vessels and cause ischemic necrosis.
- They can induce host immune responses that, although directed against the invader, cause additional tissue damage. Thus, as discussed in Chapters 2 and 4, the defensive responses of the host can be a mixed blessing. They are necessary to overcome the infection but at the same time may directly contribute to tissue damage.

Described next are some of the mechanisms whereby viruses and bacteria damage host tissues.

Mechanisms of Viral Injury

Viruses can directly damage host cells by entering them and replicating at the host's expense. The manifestations of viral infection are largely determined by the tropism of the virus for specific tissues and cell types.

- *A major determinant of tissue tropism is the presence of viral receptors on host cells.* Viruses possess specific cell surface proteins that bind to particular host cell surface proteins. Many viruses use normal cellular receptors of the host to enter cells. For example, HIV glycoprotein gp120 binds to CD4 on T cells and to the chemokine receptors CXCR4 (mainly on T cells) and CCR5 (mainly on macrophages) (Chapter 4). In some cases, host proteases are needed to enable binding of virus to host cells; for instance, a host protease cleaves and activates the influenza virus hemagglutinin.
- The ability of the virus to replicate inside some cells but not in others depends on the presence of cell type–specific transcription factors that recognize viral enhancer and promoter elements. For example, the JC virus, which causes leukoencephalopathy (Chapter 22), replicates specifically in oligodendroglia in the CNS, because the promoter and enhancer DNA sequences regulating viral gene expression are active in glial cells but not in neurons or endothelial cells.
- Physical circumstances, such as chemicals and temperature, contribute to tissue tropism. For example, enteroviruses replicate in the intestine in part because they can resist inactivation by acids, bile, and digestive enzymes. Rhinoviruses infect cells only within the upper respiratory tract because they replicate optimally at the lower temperatures characteristic of this site.

Once viruses are inside host cells, they can damage or kill the cells by a number of mechanisms (Fig. 8–7):

- *Direct cytopathic effects.* Viruses can kill cells by preventing synthesis of critical host macromolecules, by producing degradative enzymes and toxic proteins, or by inducing apoptosis. For example, poliovirus blocks synthesis of host proteins by inactivating cap-binding protein, which is essential for translation of host cell messenger RNAs (mRNAs) but leaves translation of poliovirus mRNAs unaffected. HSV produces proteins that inhibit synthesis of cellular DNA and mRNA and

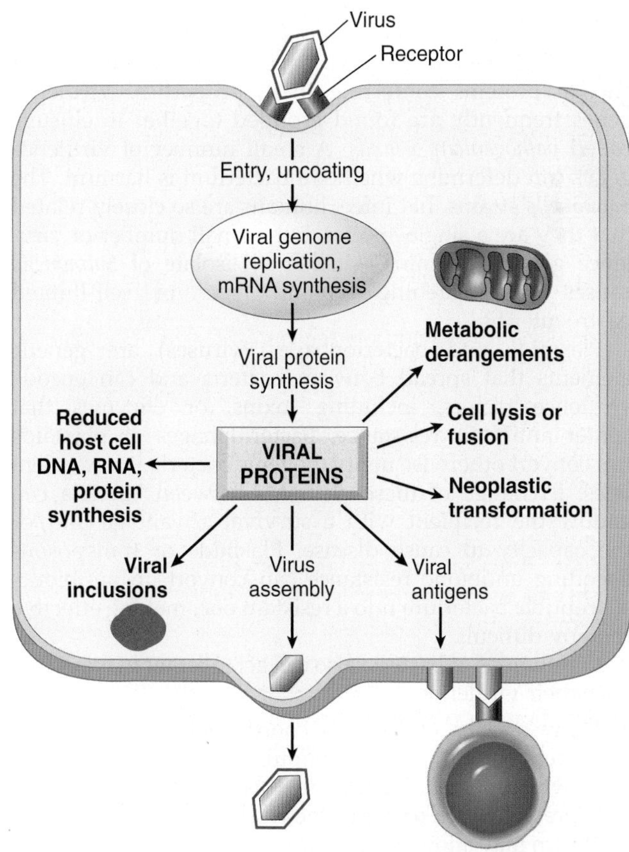

Figure 8–7 Mechanisms by which viruses cause injury to cells.

other proteins that degrade host DNA. Some viruses can stimulate apoptosis by production of proteins that are proapoptotic (e.g., HIV vpr protein). Viral replication also can trigger apoptosis of host cells by cell-intrinsic mechanisms, such as perturbations of the endoplasmic reticulum during virus assembly, which can activate proteases that mediate apoptosis (caspases).

- *Antiviral immune responses.* Viral proteins on the surface of host cells may be recognized by the immune system, and lymphocytes may attack virus-infected cells. Cytotoxic T lymphocytes (CTLs) are important for defense against viral infections, but CTLs also can be responsible for tissue injury. Acute liver failure during hepatitis B infection may be accelerated by CTL-mediated destruction of infected hepatocytes (a normal response to clear the infection).
- *Transformation of infected cells* into benign or malignant tumor cells. Different oncogenic viruses can stimulate cell growth and survival by a variety of mechanisms, including expression of virus-encoded oncogenes, anti-apoptotic strategies, and insertional mutagenesis (in which the insertion of viral DNA into the host genome alters the expression of nearby host genes). The mechanisms of viral transformation are numerous and are discussed in Chapter 5.

Mechanisms of Bacterial Injury

Bacterial Virulence

Bacterial damage to host tissues depends on the ability of the bacteria to adhere to host cells, invade cells and tissues, or deliver toxins. Pathogenic bacteria have virulence genes that encode proteins conferring these properties. Virulence genes frequently are found grouped together in clusters called *pathogenicity islands.* A small number of virulence genes can determine whether a bacterium is harmful. The *Salmonella* strains that infect humans are so closely related that they are a single species, but a small number of virulence genes determine whether an isolate of *Salmonella* causes life-threatening typhoid fever or self-limited gastroenteritis.

Plasmids and bacteriophages (viruses) are genetic elements that spread between bacteria and can encode virulence factors, including toxins, or enzymes that confer antibiotic resistance. Bacteriophages or plasmids can convert otherwise nonpathogenic bacteria into virulent ones. Exchange of these elements between bacteria can endow the recipient with a survival advantage and/or the capacity to cause disease. Plasmids or transposons encoding antibiotic resistance can convert an antibiotic-susceptible bacterium into a resistant one, making effective therapy difficult.

Populations of bacteria also can act together in ways that alter their virulence.

- Many species of bacteria coordinately regulate gene expression within a large population by *quorum sensing,* in which specific genes, such as virulence genes, are expressed when bacteria reach high concentrations. This in turn may allow bacteria growing in discrete host sites, such as an abscess or consolidated pneumonia, to overcome host defenses. *S. aureus* coordinately regulates virulence factors by secreting *autoinducer peptides.* As the bacteria grow to increasing concentrations, the level of the autoinducer peptide increases, stimulating exotoxin production.
- Communities of bacteria can form *biofilms* in which the organisms live within a viscous layer of extracellular polysaccharides that adhere to host tissues or devices such as intravascular catheters and artificial joints. Biofilms make bacteria inaccessible to immune effector mechanisms and increase their resistance to antimicrobial drugs. Biofilm formation seems to be important in the persistence and relapse of infections such as bacterial endocarditis, artificial joint infections, and respiratory infections in people with cystic fibrosis.

Bacterial Adherence to Host Cells

Bacterial surface molecules that bind to host cells or extracellular matrix are called *adhesins.* Diverse surface structures are involved in adhesion of various bacteria (Fig. 8–2). *Streptococcus pyogenes* has protein F and teichoic acid projecting from its cell wall that bind to fibronectin on the surface of host cells and in the extracellular matrix. Other bacteria have filamentous proteins called pili on their surfaces. Stalks of pili are structurally conserved, whereas amino acids on the tips of the pili vary and determine the binding specificity of the bacteria. Strains of *E. coli* that cause urinary tract infections uniquely express a specific P pilus, which binds to a gal(α1–4)gal moiety expressed on uroepithelial cells. Pili on *N. gonorrhoeae* bacteria mediate adherence of the bacteria to host cells and also are targets of the host antibody response. Variation in the type of pili expressed is an important mechanism by which *N. gonorrhoeae* escapes the immune response.

Virulence of Intracellular Bacteria

Facultative intracellular bacteria usually infect epithelial cells (*Shigella* and enteroinvasive *E. coli*), macrophages (*M. tuberculosis, M. leprae*), or both (*S. typhi*). The growth of bacteria in cells may allow them to escape from certain immune effector mechanisms, such as antibodies and complement, or may facilitate spread of the bacteria in the body, as when macrophages carry *M. tuberculosis* from the lung to other sites.

Bacteria have evolved a number of mechanisms for entering host cells. Some bacteria use the host immune response to enter macrophages. Coating of bacteria with antibodies or the complement protein C3b (opsonization) elicits phagocytosis of bacteria by macrophages. Like many bacteria, *M. tuberculosis* activates the alternative complement pathway, resulting in opsonization with C3b and uptake by host macrophages in which the mycobacteria live. Some gram-negative bacteria use a *type III secretion system* to enter epithelial cells. This system consists of needle-like structures projecting from the bacterial surface that bind and form pores in the host cell membrane through which proteins are injected that mediate rearrangement of the cell cytoskeleton and facilitate bacterial entry. Finally, bacteria such as *Listeria monocytogenes* can manipulate the cell cytoskeleton to spread directly from cell to cell, perhaps allowing the bacteria to evade immune defenses.

Intracellular bacteria have different strategies for interacting with the host cell. *Shigella* and *E. coli* inhibit host protein synthesis, replicate rapidly, and lyse the host cell within hours. Although most bacteria in macrophages are killed when the phagosome fuses with the acidic lysosome to form a phagolysosome, certain bacteria elude this host defense. For example, *M. tuberculosis* blocks fusion of the lysosome with the phagosome, allowing the bacteria to proliferate unchecked within the macrophage. Other bacteria avoid destruction in macrophages by escaping from the phagosome. *L. monocytogenes* produces a pore-forming protein called listeriolysin O and two phospholipases that degrade the phagosome membrane, allowing the bacteria to escape into the cytoplasm.

Bacterial Toxins

Any bacterial substance that contributes to illness can be considered a toxin. Toxins are classified as endotoxins, which are components of the bacterial cell, and exotoxins, which are proteins that are secreted by the bacterium.

Bacterial endotoxin is a lipopolysaccharide (LPS) that is a component of the outer membrane of gram-negative bacteria (Fig. 8–2). LPS is composed of a long-chain fatty acid anchor, termed lipid A, connected to a core sugar chain, both of which are very similar in all gram-negative bacteria. Attached to the core sugar is a variable carbohydrate chain (O antigen), which is used diagnostically to serotype strains of bacteria. Lipid A binds to CD14 on the surface of host leukocytes, and the complex then binds to Toll-like receptor 4 (TLR4), a pattern recognition receptor of the innate immune system that transmits signals that promote cell activation and inflammatory responses. Responses to LPS can be both beneficial and harmful to the host. The response is beneficial in that LPS activates protective immunity in several ways, including induction of important cytokines and chemoattractants (chemokines) of the immune system, as well as increased expression of costimulatory molecules, which enhance T lymphocyte activation. However, high levels of LPS play an important role in septic shock, disseminated intravascular coagulation (DIC), and acute respiratory distress syndrome, mainly through induction of excessive levels of cytokines such as TNF (Chapter 4).

Exotoxins are secreted proteins that cause cellular injury and disease. They can be classified into broad categories by their mechanism and site of action.

- *Enzymes.* Bacteria secrete a variety of enzymes (proteases, hyaluronidases, coagulases, fibrinolysins) that act on their respective substrates in vitro, but their role in disease is understood in only a few cases. For example, exfoliative toxins are proteases produced by *S. aureus* that cleave proteins known to hold keratinocytes together, causing the epidermis to detach from the deeper skin.
- *Toxins that alter intracellular signaling or regulatory pathways.* Most of these toxins have an active (A) component with enzymatic activity and a binding (B) component that binds cell surface receptors and delivers the A protein into the cell cytoplasm. The effect of these toxins depends on the binding specificity of the B domain and the cellular pathways affected by the A domain. A-B toxins are made by many bacteria including *Bacillus anthracis, V. cholerae,* and *Corynebacterium diphtheriae.* The mechanism of action of the A-B anthrax toxin is well understood (Fig. 8–8). Anthrax toxin has two alternate A components, edema factor (EF) and lethal factor (LF), which enter cells following binding to the B component and mediate different pathologic effects.
- *Superantigens* stimulate very large numbers of T lymphocytes by binding to conserved portions of the T cell receptor, leading to massive T lymphocyte proliferation and cytokine release. The high levels of cytokines lead to capillary leak and consequent shock. Superantigens made by *S. aureus* and *S. pyogenes* cause toxic shock syndrome (TSS).
- *Neurotoxins* produced by *Clostridium botulinum* and *Clostridium tetani* inhibit release of neurotransmitters, resulting in paralysis. These toxins do not kill neurons; instead, the A domains cleave proteins involved in secretion of neurotransmitters at the synaptic junction. Tetanus and botulism can result in death from respiratory failure due to paralysis of the chest and diaphragm muscles.
- Enterotoxins affect the gastrointestinal tract in different ways to cause varied effects, including nausea and vomiting (*S. aureus*), voluminous watery diarrhea (*V. cholerae*), or bloody diarrhea (*C. difficile*).

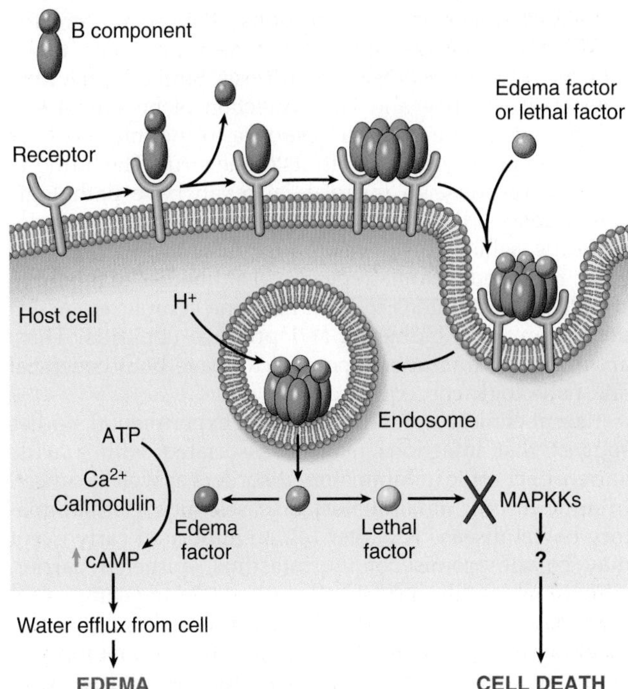

Figure 8–8 Mechanism of anthrax exotoxin action. The B component, also called "protective antigen," binds a cell-surface protein, is cleaved by a host protease, and forms a heptamer. Three A subunits of edema factor (EF) or lethal factor (LF) bind to the B heptamer, enter the cell, and are released into the cytoplasm. EF binds calcium and calmodulin to form an adenylate cyclase that increases intracellular cAMP, which causes efflux of water and interstitial edema. LF is a protease that destroys mitogen-activated protein kinase kinases (MAPKKs), leading to cell death. cAMP, cyclic adenosine monophosphate.

Injurious Effects of Host Immune Responses

As mentioned earlier, the host immune response to microbes can sometimes be the cause of tissue injury. The granulomatous inflammatory reaction to *M. tuberculosis* is a delayed hypersensitivity response that sequesters the bacilli and prevents spread, but also produces tissue damage (caseous necrosis) and fibrosis. Similarly, the liver damage from HBV and HCV infection of hepatocytes is due mainly to the immune response to the infected liver cells and not to cytopathic effects of the virus. The humoral immune response to microbes also can have pathologic consequences. For example, poststreptococcal glomerulonephritis, which can develop after infection with *S. pyogenes,* is caused by antistreptococcal antibodies that bind to streptococcal antigens to form immune complexes, which deposit in renal glomeruli and produce nephritis. Thus, antimicrobial immune responses can have both beneficial and pathologic consequences.

Recent clinical, epidemiologic, and experimental studies suggest that infections may be associated with a wide variety of chronic inflammatory disorders as well as cancer. In some chronic inflammatory diseases, such as inflammatory bowel disease (Chapter 14), an important early event may be compromise of the intestinal epithelial barrier, which enables the entry of both pathogenic and commensal microbes and their interactions with local immune cells, resulting in inflammation. The cycle of inflammation and epithelial injury may be the basis for the disease, with microbes playing the central role. Certain viruses (HBV, HCV) and bacteria (*H. pylori*) that are not known to carry or to activate oncogenes are associated with cancers, presumably because these microbes trigger chronic inflammation with subsequent repair, which provides fertile ground for the development of cancer (Chapter 5).

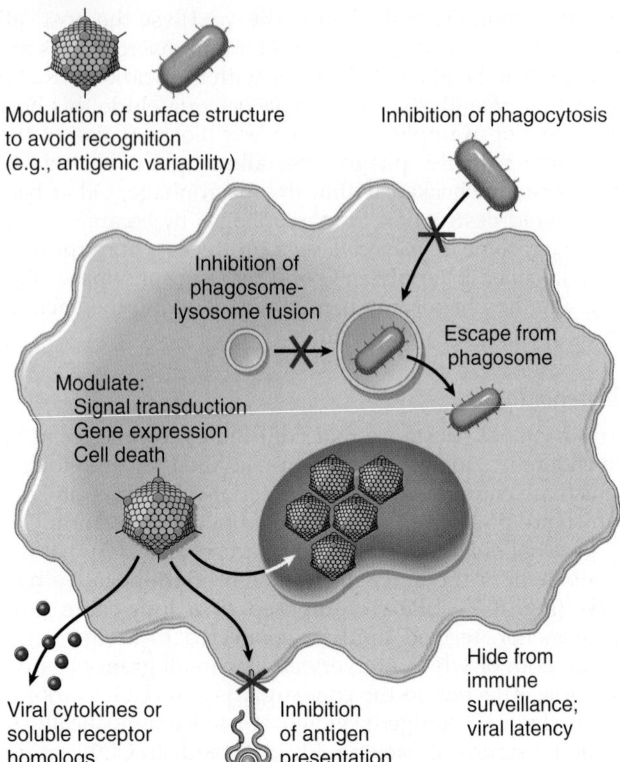

Figure 8–9 An overview of mechanisms used by viral and bacterial pathogens to evade innate and adaptive immunity.

(Modified with permission from Finlay B, McFadden G: Anti-immunology: evasion of the host immune system by bacterial and viral pathogens. Cell 124:767–782, 2006.)

SUMMARY

How Microorganisms Cause Disease

- Diseases caused by microbes involve an interplay of microbial virulence and host responses.
  - Infectious agents can cause cell death or dysfunction by directly interacting with the cell.
  - Injury may be due to local or systemic release of bacterial products, including endotoxins (LPS), exotoxins, or superantigens.
  - Pathogens can induce immune responses that cause tissue damage. Absence of an immune response may reduce the damage induced by some infections; conversely, immunocompromise can allow uncontrolled expansion of opportunistic agents or of microorganisms that can directly cause injury.

IMMUNE EVASION BY MICROBES

Humoral and cellular immune responses that protect the host from most infections are discussed in Chapter 4. Not surprisingly, microorganisms have developed many means to resist and evade the immune system (Fig. 8–9). These mechanisms, which are important determinants of microbial virulence and pathogenicity, include (1) antigenic variation, (2) resistance to innate immune defenses, and (3) impairment of effective T cell antimicrobial responses by specific or nonspecific immunosuppression.

Some microbes can evade immune responses by varying the antigens they express. Neutralizing antibodies block the ability of microbes to infect cells and recruit effector mechanisms to kill pathogens. To escape recognition, microbes use many strategies that involve genetic mechanisms for generating antigenic variation. The low fidelity of viral RNA polymerases (in HIV and many respiratory viruses including influenza virus) and reassortment of viral genomes (influenza viruses) create viral antigenic variation (Table 8–6). The spirochete *Borrelia recurrentis* repeatedly switches its surface antigens, and *Borrelia burgdorferi*, the

Table 8-6 Mechanisms of Antigenic Variation

Mechanism	Example	
	Agent(s)	Disease
High mutation rate	HIV Influenza virus	AIDS Influenza
Genetic reassortment	Influenza virus Rotavirus	Influenza Diarrhea
Genetic rearrangement (e.g., gene recombination, gene conversion, site-specific inversion)	*Borrelia burgdorferi* *Neisseria gonorrhoeae* *Trypanosoma* spp. *Plasmodium* spp.	Lyme disease Gonorrhea African sleeping sickness Malaria
Large diversity of serotypes	Rhinoviruses *Streptococcus pneumoniae*	Colds Pneumonia Meningitis

cause of Lyme disease, uses similar mechanisms to vary outer membrane proteins. *Trypanosoma* species have many genes for their major surface antigen, VSG, and can vary the expression of this surface protein. At least 80 different serotypes of *S. pneumoniae*, each with a different capsular polysaccharide, have been recognized.

Some microbes have devised methods for actively resisting immune defenses.

- Cationic antimicrobial peptides, including defensins, cathelicidins, and thrombocidins, provide important initial defenses against invading microbes. These peptides bind the bacterial membrane and form pores, killing the bacterium by hypoosmotic lysis. Bacterial pathogens (*Shigella* spp., *S. aureus*) avoid killing by making surface molecules that resist binding of antimicrobial peptides, or that inactivate or downregulate antimicrobial peptides by various mechanisms.
- Phagocytosis and killing of bacteria by polymorphonuclear leukocytes or neutrophils (PMNs) and monocytes constitute a critical host defense against extracellular bacteria. The carbohydrate capsule on the surface of many bacteria that cause pneumonia or meningitis (*S. pneumoniae, N. meningitidis, H. influenzae*) makes them more virulent by preventing phagocytosis of the organisms by neutrophils. Proteins on the surface of bacteria that inhibit phagocytosis include proteins A and M, expressed by *S. aureus* and *S. pyogenes,* respectively. Many bacteria make proteins that kill phagocytes, prevent their migration, or diminish their oxidative burst.
- *Viruses can produce molecules that inhibit innate immunity.* Viruses have developed a large number of strategies to combat interferons (IFNs), which are mediators of early host defense against viruses. Some viruses produce soluble homologues of IFN-α/β or IFN-γ receptors that bind to and inhibit actions of secreted IFNs, or produce proteins that inhibit intracellular JAK/STAT signaling downstream of IFN receptors. Viruses also may inactivate or inhibit double-stranded RNA–dependent protein kinase (PKR), a key mediator of the antiviral effects of IFN. Some viruses encode within their genomes homologues of cytokines, chemokines, or their receptors that act in various ways to inhibit immune responses. Finally, viruses have developed strategies to block apoptosis in the host cell, which may give the viruses time to replicate, persist or transform host cells.
- *Some microbes produce factors that decrease recognition of infected cells by CD4+ helper T cells and CD8+ cytotoxic T cells.* For example, several DNA viruses (e.g., herpesviruses, including HSV, CMV, and EBV) can bind to or alter localization of major histocompatibility complex (MHC) class I proteins, impairing peptide presentation to CD8+ cells. Downregulation of MHC class I molecules might make it likely that virus-infected cells would be targets for NK cells. However, herpesviruses also express MHC class I homologues that act as effective inhibitors of NK cells by engaging inhibitory receptors (Chapter 4). Herpesviruses can target MHC class II molecules for degradation, impairing antigen presentation to CD4+ T helper cells. Viruses also can infect leukocytes to directly compromise their function (e.g., HIV infects CD4+ T cells, macrophages, and dendritic cells).

SUMMARY

Immune Evasion by Microbes

After bypassing host tissue barriers, infectious microorganisms must also evade host innate and adaptive immunity mechanisms to successfully proliferate and be transmitted to the next host. Strategies include:

- Antigenic variation
- Inactivating antibodies or complement
- Resisting phagocytosis (e.g., by producing a capsule)
- Suppressing the host adaptive immune response (e.g., by inhibiting MHC expression and antigen presentation)

SPECTRUM OF INFLAMMATORY RESPONSES TO INFECTION

In contrast with the vast molecular diversity of microbes, the morphologic patterns of tissue responses to microbes are limited, as are the mechanisms directing these responses. Therefore, many pathogens produce similar reaction patterns, and few features are unique to or pathognomonic for a particular microorganism. It is the interaction between the microbe and the host that determines the histologic features of the inflammatory response.

There are five major histologic patterns of tissue reaction in infections: suppurative, mononuclear/granulomatous, cytopathic-cytoproliferative, necrosis, and chronic inflammation/scarring.

Suppurative (Purulent) Inflammation

This pattern is the reaction to acute tissue damage, characterized by increased vascular permeability and leukocytic infiltration, predominantly of neutrophils (Fig. 8–10). The neutrophils are attracted to the site of infection by release of chemoattractants from the "pyogenic" bacteria and host cells. Neutrophil enzymes cause liquefactive necrosis (Chapter 1).

MORPHOLOGY

Collections of neutrophils give rise to localized liquefactive necrosis, forming **abscesses.** The necrotic tissue and

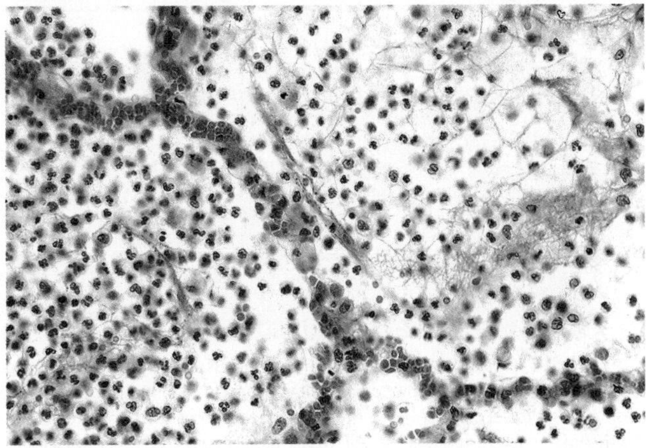

Figure 8–10 Pneumococcal pneumonia. Note the intra-alveolar polymorphonuclear exudate and intact alveolar septa.

inflammatory cells constitute pus, and bacteria that evoke pus formation are called "pyogenic." Typically, these are extracellular bacteria. The sizes of such lesions can vary from tiny microabscesses formed by bacteria seeding from an infected heart valve, to distended, pus-filled fallopian tubes caused by *N. gonorrhoeae*, to diffuse involvement of the meninges during *H. influenzae* infection, to entire lobes of the lung during pneumonia. The extent to which the lesions are destructive depends on their location and the organism involved. Thus, *S. pneumoniae* usually spares alveolar walls in the lung, and even lobar streptococcal pneumonias typically resolve completely without permanent damage (Fig. 8–10). On the other hand, *S. aureus* and *Klebsiella pneumoniae* destroy alveolar walls and form abscesses that heal with scar formation. Bacterial pharyngitis resolves without sequelae, whereas untreated acute bacterial infection can destroy a joint in a few days.

Mononuclear and Granulomatous Inflammation

Diffuse, predominantly mononuclear, interstitial infiltrates are a common feature of all chronic inflammatory processes, but development of such changes as an acute process often constitutes a response to viruses, intracellular bacteria, or intracellular parasites. In addition, spirochetes and some helminths provoke chronic mononuclear inflammatory responses.

MORPHOLOGY

Which mononuclear cell predominates within the inflammatory lesion depends on the host immune response to the organism. Thus, lymphocytes predominate in HBV infection (Fig. 8–11, *A*), whereas plasma cells are common in the primary and secondary lesions of syphilis (Fig. 8–11, *B*). The presence of these lymphoid cells reflects cell-mediated immune responses against the pathogen or pathogen-infected cells. Granulomatous inflammation is a distinctive form of mononuclear inflammation usually evoked by infectious agents that resist eradication (e.g., *M. tuberculosis, Histoplasma capsulatum*, schistosome eggs) but nevertheless are capable of stimulating strong T cell–mediated immunity. Granulomatous inflammation (Chapter 2) is characterized by accumulation of activated macrophages called "epithelioid" cells, which may fuse to form giant cells. In some cases, there is a central area of caseous necrosis (Fig. 8–11, *C*).

Cytopathic-Cytoproliferative Reaction

Cytopathic-cytoproliferative reactions usually are produced by viruses. The lesions are characterized by cell necrosis or cellular proliferation, usually with sparse inflammatory cells.

MORPHOLOGY

Some viruses replicate within cells and make viral aggregates that are visible as inclusion bodies (e.g., herpesviruses or adenovirus) or induce cells to fuse and form multinucleated cells called polykaryons (e.g., measles virus or herpesviruses) (Fig. 8–1). Focal cell damage in the skin may cause epithelial cells to become detached, forming blisters. Some viruses can cause epithelial cells to proliferate (e.g., venereal warts caused by HPV or the umbilicated papules of molluscum contagiosum caused by poxviruses). Finally, viruses can contribute to the development of malignant neoplasms (Chapter 5).

Tissue Necrosis

Clostridium perfringens and other organisms that secrete powerful toxins can cause such rapid and severe necrosis (gangrenous necrosis) that tissue damage is the dominant feature.

MORPHOLOGY

Because few inflammatory cells are present, necrotic lesions resemble infarcts with disruption or loss of basophilic nuclear staining and preservation of cellular outlines. Clostridia often are opportunistic pathogens that are introduced into muscle tissue by penetrating trauma or infection of the bowel in a neutropenic host. Similarly, the parasite *E. histolytica* causes colonic ulcers and liver abscesses characterized by extensive tissue destruction and liquefactive necrosis without a prominent inflammatory infiltrate. By entirely different mechanisms, viruses can cause widespread necrosis of host cells associated with inflammation, as exemplified by destruction of the temporal lobes of the brain by HSV or the liver by HBV.

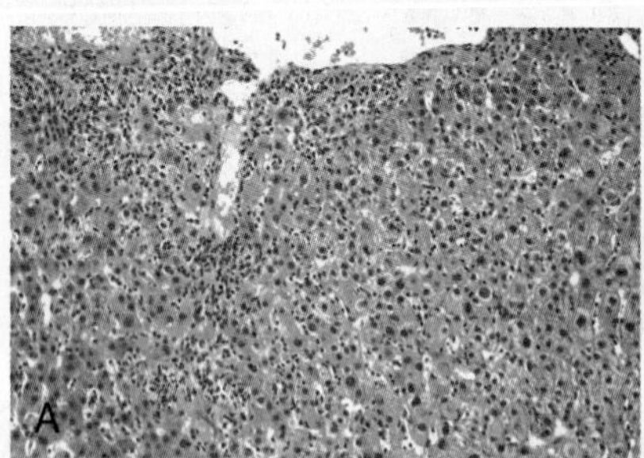

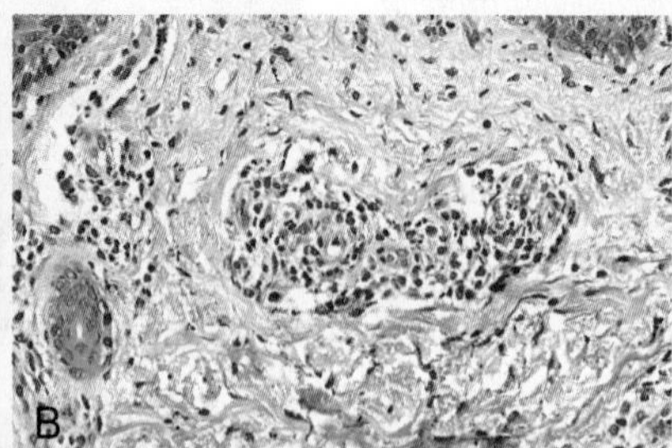

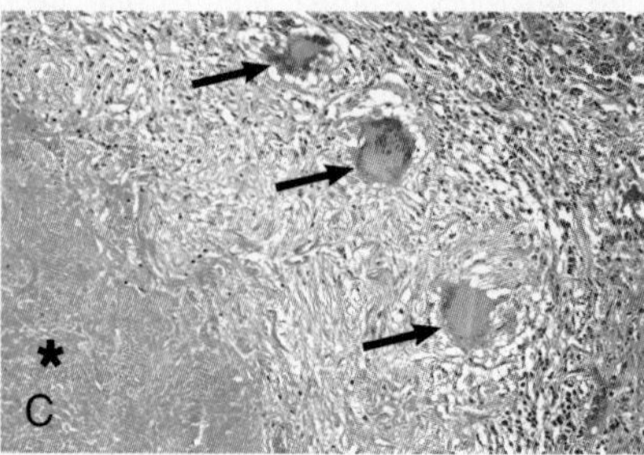

Figure 8–11 Mononuclear and granulomatous inflammation. **A,** Acute viral hepatitis characterized by a predominantly lymphocytic infiltrate. **B,** Secondary syphilis in the dermis with perivascular lymphoplasmacytic infiltrate and endothelial proliferation. **C,** Granulomatous inflammation in response to tuberculosis. Note the zone of caseation (*asterisk*), which normally forms the center of the granuloma, with a surrounding rim of activated epithelioid macrophages, some of which have fused to form giant cells (*arrows*); this in turn is surrounded by a zone of activated T lymphocytes. This high-magnification view highlights the histologic features; the granulomatous response typically takes the form of a three-dimensional sphere with the offending organism in the central area.

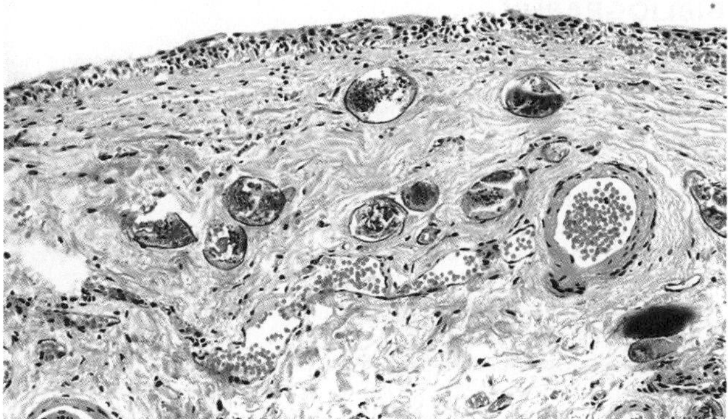

Figure 8–12 *Schistosoma haematobium* infection of the bladder with numerous calcified eggs and extensive scarring.

Chronic Inflammation and Scarring

Many infections elicit chronic inflammation, which can either resolve with complete healing or lead to extensive scarring.

MORPHOLOGY

Sometimes an exuberant scarring response is the major cause of dysfunction. For example, schistosome eggs cause "pipe-stem" fibrosis of the liver or fibrosis of the bladder wall (Fig. 8–12). *M. tuberculosis* causes constrictive fibrous pericarditis. Chronic HBV infection may cause cirrhosis of the liver, in which dense fibrous septa surround nodules of regenerating hepatocytes.

The patterns of tissue reactions described above are useful guidelines for analyzing microscopic features of infectious processes, but in practice it must be remembered that different types of host reactions often occur at the same time. For example, the lung of a patient with AIDS may be infected with CMV, which causes cytolytic changes, and, at the same time, by *Pneumocystis,* which causes interstitial inflammation. Similar patterns of inflammation also can be seen in tissue responses to physical or chemical agents and in inflammatory conditions of unknown cause (Chapter 2). Finally, in immunocompromised persons, the absence of a host inflammatory response frequently eliminates some of the histologic clues about the potential nature of infecting microorganism(s).

Infections in People with Immunodeficiencies

Inherited or acquired defects in immunity (Chapter 4) often impair only part of the immune system, rendering the affected persons susceptible to specific types of infections. Patients with antibody deficiency, as in X-linked agammaglobulinemia, contract severe bacterial infections by extracellular bacteria and a few viral infections (rotavirus and enteroviruses). Patients with T cell defects are susceptible to infections with intracellular pathogens, notably viruses and some parasites. Patients with deficiencies in early complement components are particularly susceptible to infections by encapsulated bacteria, such as *S. pneumoniae,* whereas deficiencies of the late components of complement are associated with *Neisseria* infections. Deficiencies in neutrophil function lead to increased infections with *S. aureus,* some gram-negative bacteria, and fungi. People with inherited deficiencies in mediators of innate and adaptive immunity sometimes show strikingly selective susceptibility to specific types of infections. These patterns reveal the essential roles of particular molecules in mediating protective immunity to specific microorganisms. For example, patients with mutations in signaling molecules downstream of several TLRs are prone to pyogenic bacterial diseases, particularly with *S. pneumoniae* infections. Impaired TLR3 responses are associated with childhood HSV encephalitis. Inherited defects in IL-17 immunity (such as mutations in STAT3, a transcription factor needed for T_H17 cell generation) are associated with chronic mucocutaneous candidiasis.

Acquired immunodeficiencies have a variety of causes, the most important being infection with HIV, which causes AIDS (Chapter 4). HIV infects and kills CD4+ helper T lymphocytes, leading to profound immunosuppression and a multitude of infections. Other causes of acquired immunodeficiency include infiltrative processes that suppress bone marrow function (e.g., leukemia), immunosuppressive drugs (such as those used to treat certain autoimmune diseases), and hemopoietic stem cell transplantation. Diseases of organ systems other than the immune system also can make patients susceptible to disease due to specific microorganisms. People with cystic fibrosis commonly get respiratory infections caused by *P. aeruginosa.* Lack of splenic function in persons with sickle cell disease makes them susceptible to infection with encapsulated bacteria such as *S. pneumoniae.* Burns destroy skin, removing this barrier to microbes, allowing infection with pathogens such as *P. aeruginosa.* Finally, malnutrition impairs immune defenses.

MORPHOLOGY

Patients with antibody, complement, or neutrophil defects may acquire severe local bacterial infections that do not elicit any significant neutrophilic infiltrate. In these patients, the identity of the causative organism may only be inferred by culture or appearance on special stains. Although many viral cytopathic effects (e.g., cell fusion or inclusions) (Fig. 8–1) may still be present, viral infections in immunocompromised hosts may not engender the anticipated mononuclear inflammatory response. In patients with AIDS who have no helper T cells and cannot mount normal cellular responses, organisms that would otherwise cause granulomatous inflammation (e.g., *M. avium complex*) fail to do so (Fig. 8–13).

SUMMARY

Patterns of Host Responses to Microbes

- In normal (immunocompetent) persons, the patterns of host responses are fairly stereotypical for different classes of microbes; these response patterns can be used to infer possible causal organisms.

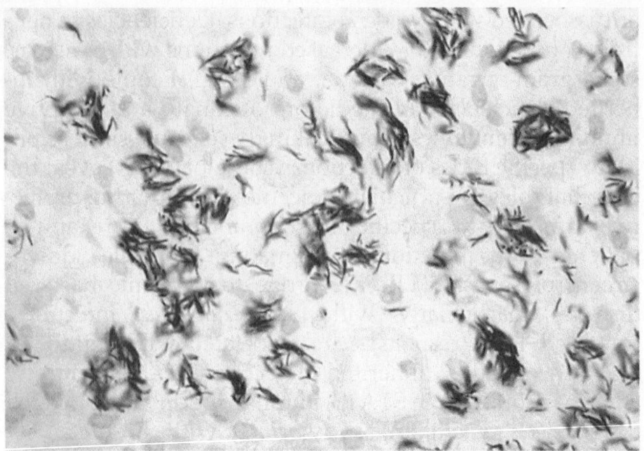

Figure 8–13 In the absence of appropriate T cell–mediated immunity, granulomatous host response does not occur. *Mycobacterium avium* infection in a patient with AIDS, showing massive intracellular macrophage infection with acid-fast organisms (filamentous and pink in this acid-fast stain preparation). The intracellular bacteria persist and even proliferate within macrophages, because there are inadequate T cells to mount a granulomatous response. AIDS, acquired immunodeficiency syndrome.

- Neutrophil-rich acute suppurative inflammation is typical of infections with many bacteria ("pyogenic" bacteria) and some fungi.
- Mononuclear cell infiltrates are common in many chronic infections and some acute viral infections.
- Granulomatous inflammation is the hallmark of infection with *Mycobacterium tuberculosis* and certain fungi.
- Cytopathic and proliferative lesions are caused by some viruses.
- Chronic inflammation and scarring represent the final common pathway of many infections.

BIBLIOGRAPHY

Aguzzi A: Prions: protein aggregation and infectious diseases. Physiol Rev 89:1105, 2009.

Coburn B, Sekirov I, Finlay BB: Type III secretion systems and disease. Clin Microbiol Rev 20:535, 2007.

Diacovich L, Gorvel JP: Bacterial manipulation of innate immunity to promote infection. Nat Rev Microbiol 8:117, 2010.

Haldar K, Murphy SC, Milner DA, Taylor TE: Malaria: mechanisms of erythrocytic infection and pathological correlates of severe disease. Annu Rev Pathol 2:217, 2007.

Irie RL: Diagnostic Pathology of Infectious Disease. Philadelphia, Saunders Elsevier, 2010.

Irie Y, Parsek MR: Quorum sensing and microbial biofilms. Curr Top Microbiol Immunol 322:67, 2008.

Lemichez E, Lecuit M, Nassif X, Bourdoulous S: Breaking the wall: targeting of the endothelium by pathogenic bacteria. Nat Rev Microbiol 8:93, 2010.

Lin PL, Flynn JL: Understanding latent tuberculosis: a moving target. J Immunol 185:15, 2010.

Mims CA: The Pathogenesis of Infectious Disease, 5th ed. San Diego, Academic Press, 2001.

O'Connor DH, Chandler FW, Schwartz DA, et al: Pathology of Infectious Diseases. Stamford, CT, Appleton & Lange, 1997.

Palmer GH, Brayton KA: Gene conversion is a convergent strategy for pathogen antigenic variation. Trends Parasitol 23:408, 2007.

Peleg AY, Hooper DC: Hospital-acquired infections due to gram-negative bacteria. N Engl J Med 362:1804, 2010.

Schmidt AC: Response to Dengue fever—the good, the bad and the ugly? N Engl J Med 363:484, 2010.

Segal BH: Aspergillosis. N Engl J Med 360:1870, 2009.

Speck SH, Ganem D: Viral latency and its regulation: lessons from the gamma-herpesviruses. Cell Host Microbe 8:100, 2010.

Writing Committee of the WHO Consultation on Clinical Aspects of Pandemic (H1N1) 2009 Influenza: Clinical aspects of pandemic 2009 influenza A(H1N1) virus infection. N Engl J Med 362:1708, 2010.

Young JA, Collier RJ: Anthrax toxin: receptor binding, internalization, pore formation, and translocation. Annu Rev Biochem 76:243, 2007.

See Targeted Therapy available online at **studentconsult.com**

CHAPTER 9

Blood Vessels

CHAPTER CONTENTS

Vascular maladies are of central importance in medicine, as they are responsible for some of the most common and lethal diseases afflicting mankind. Although most clinically significant vascular diseases are caused by arterial lesions, venous disorders also can wreak havoc. Vascular disease develops through two principal mechanisms:

- *Narrowing* or *complete obstruction of* vessel lumina, occurring either progressively (e.g., by atherosclerosis) or acutely (e.g., by thrombosis or embolism)
- *Weakening* of vessel walls, causing dilation and/or rupture

Presented next is an overview of vascular structure and function, as background for the diseases of blood vessels discussed later in the chapter.

STRUCTURE AND FUNCTION OF BLOOD VESSELS

In essence, all blood vessels consist of a tube with a luminal lining of endothelial cells surrounded by varying amounts of smooth muscle cells and extracellular matrix (ECM). However, the structure of each of these components varies in different parts of the vasculature according to functional needs (Fig. 9–1). To accommodate pulsatile flow and higher blood pressures, arterial walls are thicker than veins and invested with reinforcing layers of smooth muscle cells. As arteries narrow to arterioles, the ratio of wall thickness to lumen diameter increases, to allow more precise regulation of intravascular pressures. Veins, on the other hand, are distensible thin-walled vessels with high capacitance. In keeping with these specializations, certain pathologic lesions characteristically involve particular kinds of vessels. For example, atherosclerosis occurs mainly in larger, muscular arteries, while hypertension affects small arterioles, and specific forms of vasculitis selectively involve vessels of only a certain caliber.

Vessel walls are organized into three concentric layers: *intima, media,* and *adventitia* (see Fig. 9–1). These layers are present in all vessels but are most apparent in larger vessels and particularly arteries. The intima consists of an endothelial cell monolayer on a basement membrane with minimal underlying ECM; it is separated from the media by a dense elastic membrane called the *internal elastic lamina.* The media is composed predominantly of smooth muscle cells and ECM, surrounded by loose connective tissue, nerve fibers, and smaller vessels of the adventitia. An *external elastic lamina* is present in some arteries and defines the transition between media and adventitia. Diffusion of oxygen and nutrients from the lumen is adequate to sustain thin-walled vessels and the innermost smooth muscle cells of all vessels. In large and medium-sized vessels, however, small arterioles within the adventitia

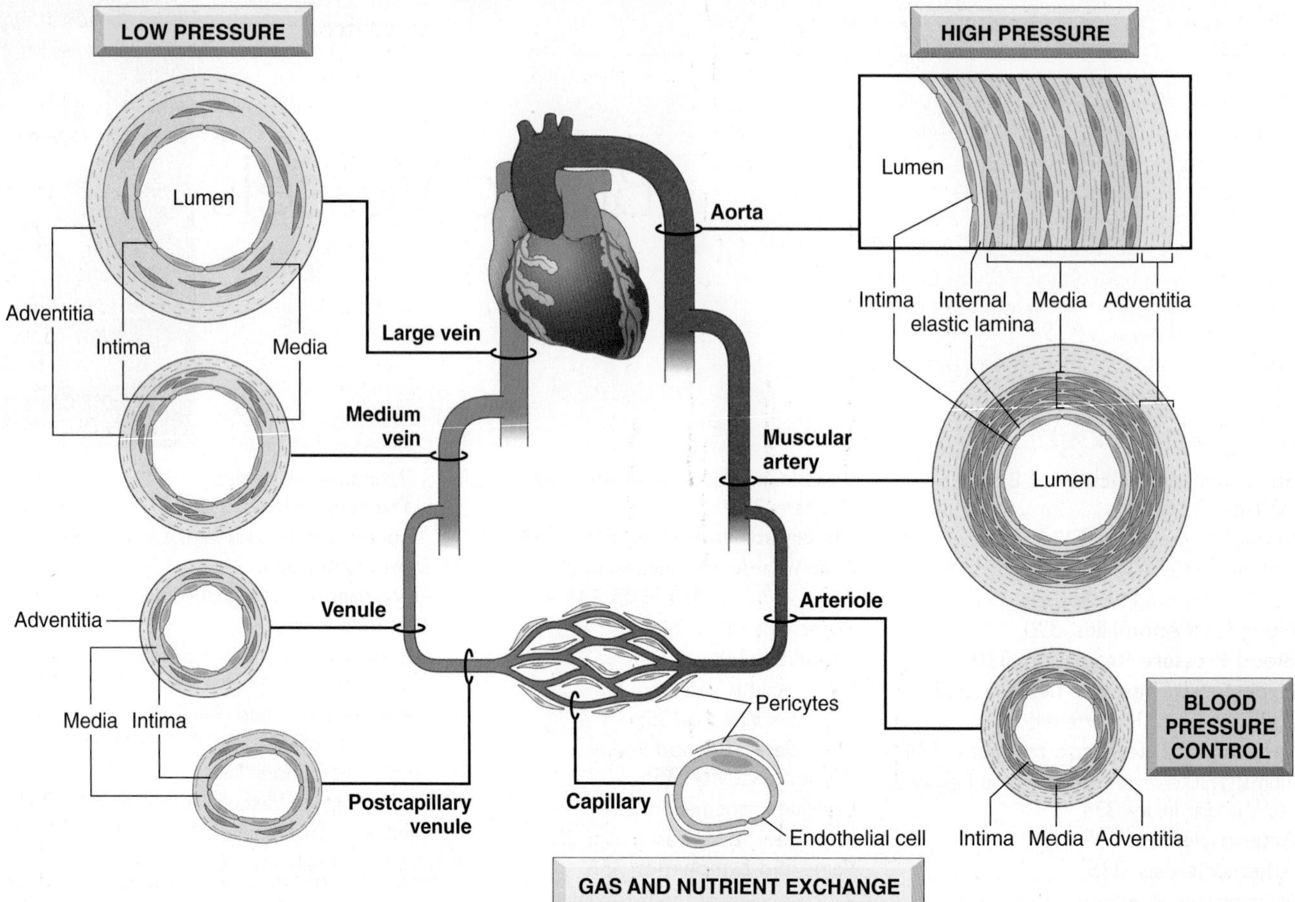

Figure 9–1 Regional vascular specializations. Although all vessels share the same general constituents, the thickness and composition of the various layers differ as a function of hemodynamic forces and tissue requirements.

(called *vasa vasorum*—literally, "vessels of the vessels") supply the outer half to two thirds of the media.

Vascular Organization

Arteries are divided into three types based on their size and structure:

- *Large elastic arteries* (e.g., aorta, arch vessels, iliac and pulmonary arteries). In these vessels, elastic fibers alternate with smooth muscle cells throughout the media, which expands during systole (storing some of the energy of each cardiac contraction), and recoils during diastole to propel blood distally. With age, the elasticity is lost, and vessels become "stiff pipes" that transmit high arterial pressures to distal organs, or dilated and tortuous (*ectatic*) conduits prone to rupture.
- *Medium-sized muscular arteries* (e.g., coronary and renal arteries). Here, the media is composed primarily of smooth muscle cells, with elastin limited to the internal and external elastic lamina. The medial smooth muscle cells are circularly or spirally arranged around the lumen, and regional blood flow is regulated by smooth muscle cell contraction (*vasoconstriction*) and relaxation (*vasodilation*) controlled by the autonomic nervous system and local metabolic factors (e.g., acidosis).
- *Small arteries* (2 mm or less in diameter) *and arterioles* (20 to 100 μm in diameter) *that lie within the connective tissue of organs.* The media in these vessels is mostly composed of smooth muscle cells. *Arterioles are where blood flow resistance is regulated.* As pressures drop during passage through arterioles, *the velocity of blood flow is sharply reduced, and flow becomes steady rather than pulsatile.* Because the resistance to fluid flow is inversely proportional to the fourth power of the diameter (i.e., halving the diameter increases resistance 16-fold), small changes in arteriolar lumen size have profound effects on blood pressure.

Capillaries have lumen diameters that approximate those of red cells (7 to 8 μm). These vessels are lined by endothelial cells and partially surrounded by smooth muscle cell–like cells called *pericytes.* Collectively, capillary beds have a very large total cross-sectional area and a low rate of blood flow. With their thin walls and slow flow, capillaries are ideally suited to the rapid exchange of diffusible substances between blood and tissue. The capillary network of most tissues is necessarily very rich, because diffusion of oxygen and nutrients is not efficient beyond 100 μm; metabolically active tissues (e.g., heart) have the highest capillary density.

Veins receive blood from the capillary beds as postcapillary venules, which anastomose to form collecting venules and progressively larger veins. The vascular leakage (edema) and leukocyte emigration characteristic of inflammation occurs preferentially in postcapillary venules (Chapter 2).

Compared with arteries at the same level of branching, veins have larger diameters, larger lumina, and thinner walls with less distinct layers, all adaptations to the low pressures found on the venous side of the circulation (see Fig. 9–1). Thus, *veins are more prone to dilation, external compression, and penetration by tumors or inflammatory processes.* In veins in which blood flows against gravity (e.g., those of the lower extremities), backflow is prevented by valves. Collectively, the venous system has a huge capacitance and normally contains approximately two thirds of the blood.

Lymphatics are thin-walled, endothelium-lined channels that drain fluid (lymph) from the interstitium of tissues, eventually returning it to the blood via the thoracic duct. Lymph also contains mononuclear inflammatory cells and a host of proteins. By delivering interstitial fluid to lymph nodes, lymphatics enable continuous monitoring of peripheral tissues for infection. *These channels can also disseminate disease by transporting microbes or tumor cells to distant sites.*

Endothelial Cells

Endothelium is a continuous sheet of cells lining the entire vascular tree that regulates many aspects of blood and blood vessel function (Table 9–1). Resting endothelial cells maintain a nonthrombogenic blood-tissue interface (Chapter 3), modulate inflammation (Chapter 2), and affect the growth of other cell types, particularly smooth muscle cells. Endothelial cells influence the vasoreactivity of the underlying smooth muscle cells by producing both relaxing factors (e.g., nitric oxide [NO]) and contracting factors (e.g., endothelin). In most regions, the interendothelial junctions normally are impermeable. However, these junctions open under the influence of hemodynamic stress (e.g., high blood pressure) and/or vasoactive agents (e.g., histamine in inflammation), flooding the adjacent tissues with electrolytes and protein. Vacuolar *transcytosis* also permits the movement of large amounts of solutes across intact endothelium. Endothelial cells also are active participants in the egress of leukocytes during inflammatory cell recruitment (Chapter 2).

Although endothelial cells throughout the vasculature share many attributes, they also show phenotypic variability depending on the anatomic site and adaptations to local environmental cues. Thus, endothelial cell populations from different parts of the vasculature (e.g., large vessels versus capillaries, or arteries versus veins) have distinct transcriptional programs and behaviors. *Fenestrations* (holes) in endothelial cells lining hepatocyte cords or renal glomeruli are specializations that facilitate filtration. Conversely, in the central nervous system, endothelial cells—in conjunction with astrocytes—collaborate to generate an impermeable *blood–brain barrier.*

Maintenance of a "normal," nonthrombogenic endothelial cell lining requires laminar flow, certain growth factors (e.g., vascular endothelial growth factor [VEGF]), and firm adhesion to the underlying basement membrane (Fig. 9–2). Trauma or other injuries that denude vessel walls of endothelial cells understandably tip the scales towards thrombosis and vasoconstriction. However, endothelial cells also respond to various physiologic and pathologic stimuli by modulating their usual (constitutive) functions and by expressing new (inducible) properties—a process called *endothelial activation.*

Inducers of endothelial activation include bacterial products, inflammatory cytokines, hemodynamic stresses

Table 9–1 Endothelial Cell Properties and Functions

Property/Function	Mediators/Products
Maintenance of permeability barrier	
Elaboration of anticoagulant, antithrombotic, fibrinolytic regulators	Prostacyclin Thrombomodulin Heparin-like molecules Plasminogen activator
Elaboration of prothrombotic molecules	Von Willebrand factor Tissue factor Plasminogen activator inhibitor
Extracellular matrix production	Collagen, proteoglycans
Modulation of blood flow and vascular reactivity	*Vasconstrictors*: endothelin, ACE *Vasodilators*: NO, prostacyclin
Regulation of inflammation and immunity	IL-1, IL-6, chemokines Adhesion molecules: VCAM-1, ICAM, E-selectin, P-selectin Histocompatibility antigens
Regulation of cell growth	*Growth stimulators*: PDGF, CSF, FGF *Growth inhibitors*: heparin, TGF-β
Oxidation of LDL	

ACE, angiotensin-converting enzyme; CSF, colony-stimulating factor; FGF, fibroblast growth factor; ICAM, intercelluar adhesion molecule; IL, interleukin; LDL, low-density lipoprotein; NO, nitric oxide; PDGF, platelet-derived growth factor; TGF-β, transforming growth factor-β; VCAM, vascular cell adhesion molecule.

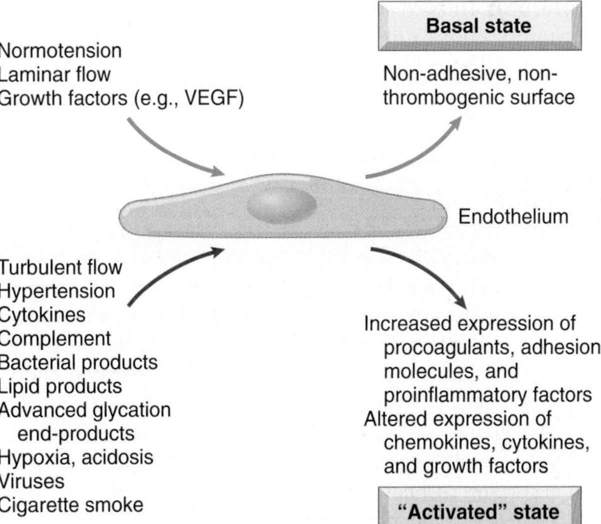

Figure 9–2 Basal and activated endothelial cell states. Normal blood pressure, laminar flow, and stable growth factor levels promote a basal endothelial cell state that maintains a nonthrombotic surface and appropriate vascular wall smooth muscle tone. Injury or exposure to certain mediators results in *endothelial activation,* a state in which endothelial cells have adhesive, procoagulant surfaces and release factors that lead to smooth muscle contraction and/or proliferation and matrix synthesis.

and lipid products (relevant to atherosclerosis, described later), advanced glycation end products (important in diabetic vascular injury), viruses, complement, and various metabolic insults (e.g., hypoxia) (see Fig. 9–2). Activated endothelial cells undergo shape changes, express adhesion molecules, and produce cytokines, chemokines, growth factors, pro- and anticoagulant factors, and a host of other biologically active products—all presumably intended to respond to the original stimulus. Some of these responses are rapid (occurring within minutes), reversible, and independent of new protein synthesis (e.g., endothelial contraction induced by histamines); others involve alterations in gene and protein expression, and may take days to develop or abate. Exposure of endothelial cells to inducers of activation in high amounts or for sustained periods may result in *endothelial dysfunction,* characterized by impaired endothelium-dependent vasodilation, hypercoagulable states, and increased oxygen free radical production. Dysfunctional endothelium can initiate thrombosis, promote atherosclerosis, or contribute to formation of the vascular lesions of hypertension and diabetes.

Vascular Smooth Muscle Cells

Smooth muscle cells participate in both normal vascular repair and pathologic processes such as atherosclerosis. When stimulated by various factors, smooth muscle cells can proliferate; upregulate ECM collagen, elastin, and proteoglycan production; and elaborate growth factors and cytokines. Smooth muscle cells also mediate the vasoconstriction or vasodilation that occurs in response to physiologic or pharmacologic stimuli.

The migratory and proliferative activities of smooth muscle cells are regulated by numerous factors. Among the most important pro-growth factors are platelet-derived growth factor (PDGF), endothelin, thrombin, fibroblast growth factors, and inflammatory mediators such as interferon-γ (IFN-γ) and interleukin-1 (IL-1). Factors that maintain smooth muscle cells in a quiescent state include heparan sulfate, NO, and transforming growth factor-α (TGF-α).

SUMMARY

Vascular Structure and Function

- All vessels are lined by endothelium; although all endothelial cells share certain homeostatic properties, endothelial cells in specific vascular beds have special features that allow for tissue-specific functions (e.g., fenestrated endothelial cells in renal glomeruli).
- The relative smooth muscle cell and matrix content of vessel walls (e.g., in arteries, veins, and capillaries) vary according to hemodynamic demands (e.g., pressure, pulsatility) and functional requirements.
- Endothelial cell function is tightly regulated in both the basal and activated states. Various physiologic and pathophysiologic stimuli induce endothelial activation and dysfunction that alter the endothelial cell phenotype (e.g., pro- versus anticoagulative, pro- versus anti-inflammatory, nonadhesive versus adhesive).

CONGENITAL ANOMALIES

Although rarely symptomatic, unusual anatomic variants in the vascular supply can cause complications during surgery, such as when a vessel in an unexpected location is injured. Cardiac surgeons and interventional cardiologists also must be familiar with coronary artery variants. Among the other congenital vascular anomalies, three deserve further mention:

- *Berry aneurysms* are thin-walled arterial outpouchings in cerebral vessels, classically at branch points around the circle of Willis; they occur where the arterial media is congenitally attenuated and can spontaneously rupture causing fatal intracerebral hemorrhage (see Chapter 22).
- *Arteriovenous (AV) fistulas* are abnormal connections between arteries and veins without an intervening capillary bed. They occur most commonly as developmental defects but can also result from rupture of arterial aneurysms into adjacent veins, from penetrating injuries that pierce arteries and veins, or from inflammatory necrosis of adjacent vessels. AV fistulas also are created surgically to provide vascular access for hemodialysis. Extensive AV fistulas can cause high-output cardiac failure by shunting large volumes of blood from the arterial to the venous circulation.
- *Fibromuscular dysplasia* is a focal irregular thickening of the walls of medium-sized and large muscular arteries due to a combination of medial and intimal hyperplasia and fibrosis. It can manifest at any age but occurs most frequently in young women. The focal wall thickening results in luminal stenosis or can be associated with abnormal vessel spasm that reduces vascular flow; *in the renal arteries, it can lead to renovascular hypertension.* Between the focal segments of thickened wall, the artery often also exhibits medial attenuation; vascular outpouchings can develop in these portions of the vessel and sometimes rupture.

BLOOD PRESSURE REGULATION

Systemic and local blood pressure must be maintained within a narrow range to prevent adverse outcomes. Low blood pressure (*hypotension*) results in inadequate organ perfusion, organ dysfunction, and sometimes tissue death. Conversely, high blood pressure (*hypertension*) causes vessel and end-organ damage and is one of the major risk factors for atherosclerosis (see later on).

Blood pressure is a function of *cardiac output* and *peripheral vascular resistance,* both of which are influenced by multiple genetic and environmental factors (Fig. 9–3). The integration of the various inputs ensures adequate systemic perfusion, despite regional demand differences.

- *Cardiac output* is a function of stroke volume and heart rate. The most important determinant of stroke volume is the filling pressure, which is regulated through sodium homeostasis and its effect on blood volume. Heart rate and myocardial contractility (a second factor affecting stroke volume) are both regulated by the α- and β-adrenergic systems (in addition to their effects on vascular tone).

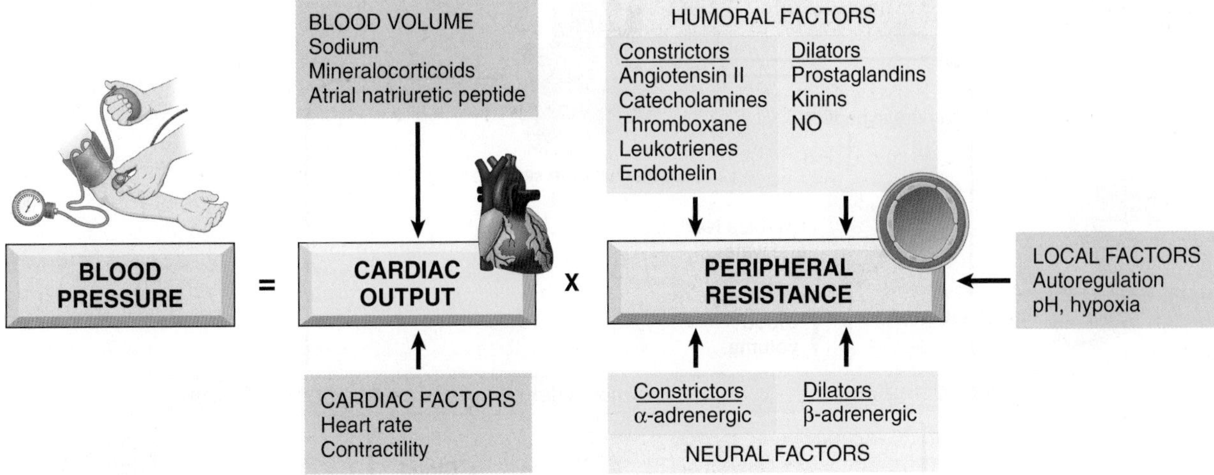

Figure 9–3 Blood pressure regulation.

- Peripheral resistance is regulated predominantly at the level of the arterioles by neural and hormonal inputs. Vascular tone reflects a balance between vasoconstrictors (including angiotensin II, catecholamines, and endothelin) and vasodilators (including kinins, prostaglandins, and NO). Resistance vessels also exhibit *autoregulation,* whereby increased blood flow induces vasoconstriction to protect tissues against hyperperfusion. Finally, blood pressure is fine-tuned by tissue pH and hypoxia to accommodate local metabolic demands.

Factors released from the kidneys, adrenals, and myocardium interact to influence vascular tone and to regulate blood volume by adjusting sodium balance (Fig. 9–4). The kidneys filter 170 liters of plasma containing 23 moles of salt daily. Thus, with a typical diet containing 100 mEq of sodium, 99.5% of the filtered salt must be reabsorbed to maintain total body sodium levels. About 98% of the filtered sodium is reabsorbed by several constitutively active transporters. Recovery of the remaining 2% of sodium occurs by way of the epithelial sodium channel (ENaC), which is tightly regulated by the renin–angiotensin system; it is this pathway that determines net sodium balance.

Kidneys influence peripheral resistance and sodium excretion/retention primarily through the renin-angiotensin system. The kidneys and heart contain cells that sense changes in blood pressure or blood volume. In response, these cells release several important regulators that act in concert to maintain normal blood pressure, as follows:

- *Renin* is a proteolytic enzyme produced by renal juxtaglomerular cells, myoepithelial cells that surround the glomerular afferent arterioles. Renin is released in response to low blood pressure in afferent arterioles, elevated levels of circulating catecholamines, or low sodium levels in the distal convoluted renal tubules. The latter occurs when the *glomerular filtration rate* falls (e.g., when the cardiac output is low), leading to increased sodium resorption by the proximal tubules and lower sodium levels more distally.
- Renin cleaves *plasma angiotensinogen* to *angiotensin I,* which in turn is converted to *angiotensin II* by angiotensin-converting enzyme (ACE) in the periphery. Angiotensin II raises blood pressure by (1) inducing vascular smooth muscle cell contraction, (2) stimulating aldosterone secretion by the adrenal gland, and (3) increasing tubular sodium resorption.
- The kidney also produces a variety of vascular relaxing substances (including prostaglandins and NO) that presumably counterbalance the vasopressor effects of angiotensin.
- *Adrenal aldosterone* increases blood pressure by its effect on blood volume; aldosterone increases sodium resorption (and thus water) in the distal convoluted tubule while also driving potassium excretion into the urine.
- *Myocardial natriuretic peptides* are released from atrial and ventricular myocardium in response to volume expansion; these inhibit sodium resorption in the distal renal tubules, thus leading to sodium excretion and diuresis. They also induce systemic vasodilation.

SUMMARY

Blood Pressure Regulation

- Blood pressure is determined by vascular resistance and cardiac output.
- Vascular resistance is regulated at the level of the arterioles, influenced by neural and hormonal inputs.
- Cardiac output is determined by heart rate and stroke volume, which is strongly influenced by blood volume. Blood volume in turn is regulated mainly by renal sodium excretion or resorption.
- Renin, a major regulator of blood pressure, is secreted by the kidneys in response to decreased blood pressure in afferent arterioles. In turn, renin cleaves angiotensinogen to angiotensin I; subsequent peripheral catabolism produces angiotensin II, which regulates blood pressure by increasing vascular smooth muscle cell tone and by increasing adrenal aldosterone secretion and, consequently, renal sodium resorption.

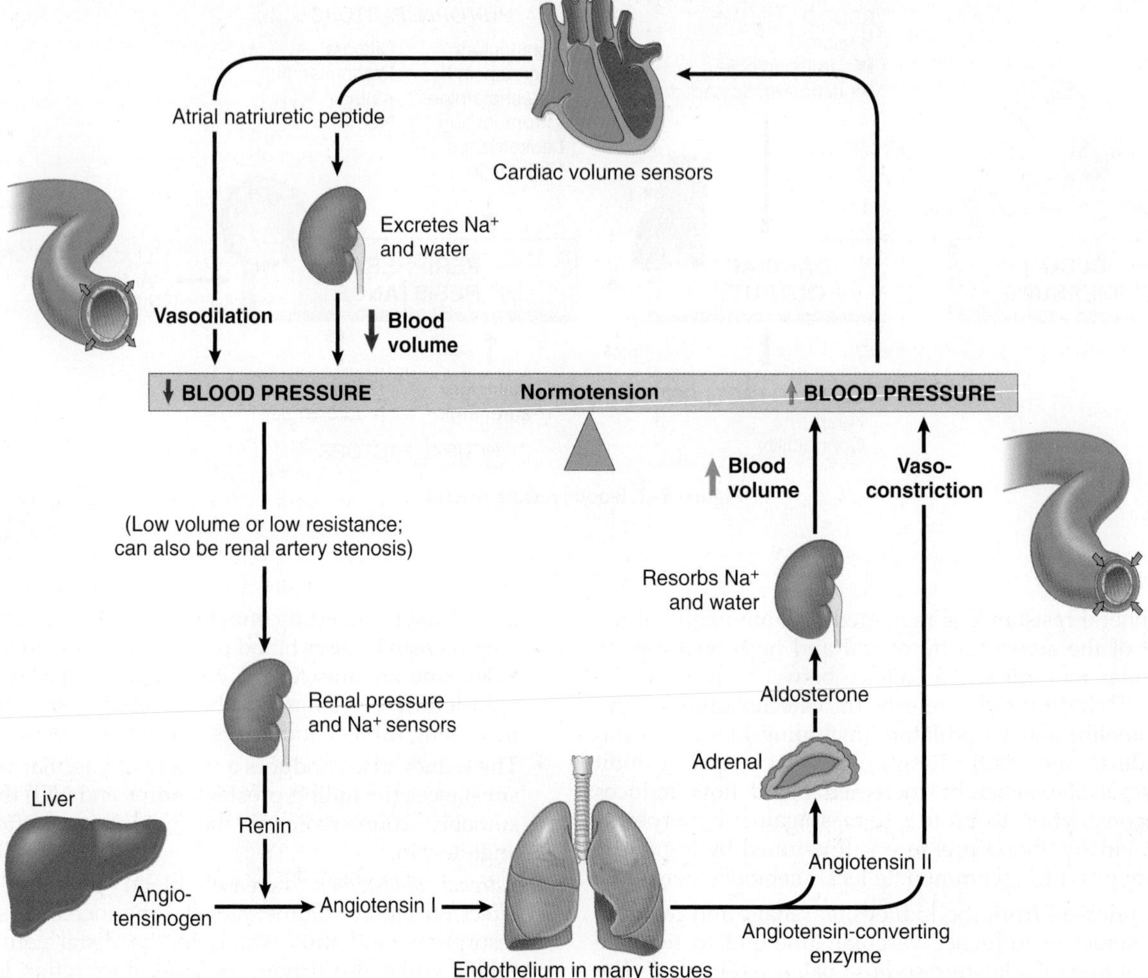

Figure 9–4 Interplay of renin, angiotensin, aldosterone, and atrial natriuretic peptide in blood pressure regulation (see text).

HYPERTENSIVE VASCULAR DISEASE

Hypertension is a major health problem in the developed world. Although it occasionally manifests in an acute aggressive form, high blood pressure is much more often asymptomatic for many years. This insidious condition is sometimes referred to as benign hypertension, but it is in fact far from harmless. Besides increasing the risk of stroke and atherosclerotic coronary heart disease, hypertension can lead to cardiac hypertrophy and heart failure (*hypertensive heart disease*), aortic dissection, multi-infarct dementia, and renal failure. While the molecular pathways of blood pressure regulation are reasonably well understood, the mechanisms leading to hypertension in the vast majority of affected persons remain unknown. The accepted wisdom is that such "essential hypertension" results from the interplay of genetic polymorphisms (which individually might be inconsequential) and environmental factors, which conspire to increase blood volume and/or peripheral resistance.

Epidemiology of Hypertension

Like height and weight, blood pressure is a continuously distributed variable, and the detrimental effects increase continuously as the pressure rises; no rigidly defined threshold reliably predicts who will suffer ill effects. Nevertheless, sustained diastolic pressures greater than 90 mm Hg, or sustained systolic pressures in excess of 140 mm Hg, are associated with an increased risk of atherosclerosis and are therefore used as cutoffs in diagnosing hypertension in clinical practice. By these criteria, some 25% of persons in the general population are hypertensive. As noted however, these values are somewhat arbitrary, and in patients with other cardiovascular risk factors (e.g., diabetes), lower thresholds may be applicable. The prevalence of pathologic effects of high blood pressure increases with age and is also higher in African Americans. Without appropriate treatment, some 50% of hypertensive patients die of ischemic heart disease (IHD) or congestive heart failure, and another third succumb to stroke. Reduction of blood pressure dramatically reduces the incidence and clinical sequelae (including death) of all forms of hypertension-related disease. Indeed, detection and treatment of asymptomatic hypertension constitute one of the few instances in which "preventive medicine" has a major demonstrated health benefit.

A small percentage of hypertensive patients (approximately 5%) present with a rapidly rising blood pressure that, if untreated, leads to death in within 1 to 2 years. Such *malignant hypertension* usually is severe (i.e., systolic pressures over 200 mm Hg or diastolic pressures over 120 mm Hg) and associated with renal failure and retinal hemorrhages, with or without papilledema. It can arise de novo but most commonly is superimposed on preexisting benign hypertension.

PATHOGENESIS

Table 9–2 lists the major causes of hypertension, but **most cases (95%) are idiopathic (essential hypertension).** This form is compatible with long life unless a myocardial infarction, stroke, or another complication supervenes. Most of the remaining cases **(secondary hypertension)** are due to primary renal disease, renal artery narrowing **(renovascular hypertension),** or adrenal disorders. Several relatively rare single-gene disorders cause hypertension (and hypotension) by affecting renal sodium resorption. Such disorders include

- **Gene defects in enzymes involved in aldosterone metabolism** (e.g., aldosterone synthase, 11β-hydroxylase, 17α-hydroxylase), leading to increased aldosterone secretion, increased salt and water resorption, and plasma volume expansion
- **Mutations in proteins that affect sodium resorption** (as in Liddle syndrome, which is caused by mutations in ENaC, leading to increased distal tubular resorption of sodium induced by aldosterone)

Table 9–2 Types and Causes of Hypertension (Systolic and Diastolic)

Essential Hypertension
Accounts for 90% to 95% of all cases
Secondary Hypertension
Renal
Acute glomerulonephritis
Chronic renal disease
Polycystic disease
Renal artery stenosis
Renal vasculitis
Renin-producing tumors
Endocrine
Adrenocortical hyperfunction (Cushing syndrome, primary aldosteronism, congenital adrenal hyperplasia, licorice ingestion)
Exogenous hormones (glucocorticoids, estrogen [including pregnancy-induced and oral contraceptives], sympathomimetics and tyramine-containing foods, monoamine oxidase inhibitors)
Pheochromocytoma
Acromegaly
Hypothyroidism (myxedema)
Hyperthyroidism (thyrotoxicosis)
Pregnancy-induced (pre-eclampsia)
Cardiovascular
Coarctation of aorta
Polyarteritis nodosa
Increased intravascular volume
Increased cardiac output
Rigidity of the aorta
Neurologic
Psychogenic
Increased intracranial pressure
Sleep apnea
Acute stress, including surgery

Mechanisms of Essential Hypertension

Although the specific triggers are unknown, it appears that both altered renal sodium handling and increased vascular resistance contribute to essential hypertension.

- **Reduced renal sodium excretion** in the presence of normal arterial pressure probably is a key pathogenic feature; indeed, this is a common etiologic factor in most forms of hypertension. Decreased sodium excretion causes an obligatory increase in fluid volume and increased cardiac output, thereby elevating blood pressure (Fig. 9–3). At the new higher blood pressure, the kidneys excrete additional sodium. Thus, a new steady state of sodium excretion is achieved, but at the expense of an elevated blood pressure.
- **Increased vascular resistance may stem from vasoconstriction or structural changes in vessel walls.** These are not necessarily independent factors, as chronic vasoconstriction may result in permanent thickening of the walls of affected vessels.
- **Genetic factors** play an important role in determining blood pressure, as shown by familial clustering of hypertension and by studies of monozygotic and dizygotic twins. Hypertension has been linked to specific angiotensinogen polymorphisms and angiotensin II receptor variants; polymorphisms of the renin-angiotensin system also may contribute to the known racial differences in blood pressure regulation. Susceptibility genes for essential hypertension in the larger population are currently unknown but probably include those that govern renal sodium handling, pressors, and smooth muscle cell growth.
- **Environmental factors,** such as stress, obesity, smoking, physical inactivity, and high levels of salt consumption, modify the impact of genetic determinants. Evidence linking dietary sodium intake with the prevalence of hypertension in different population groups is particularly strong.

MORPHOLOGY

Hypertension not only accelerates atherogenesis but also causes degenerative changes in the walls of large and medium-sized arteries that can lead to aortic dissection and cerebrovascular hemorrhage. Two forms of small blood vessel disease are hypertension-related: hyaline arteriolosclerosis and hyperplastic arteriolosclerosis (Fig. 9–5).

Hyaline arteriolosclerosis is associated with benign hypertension. It is marked by homogeneous, pink hyaline

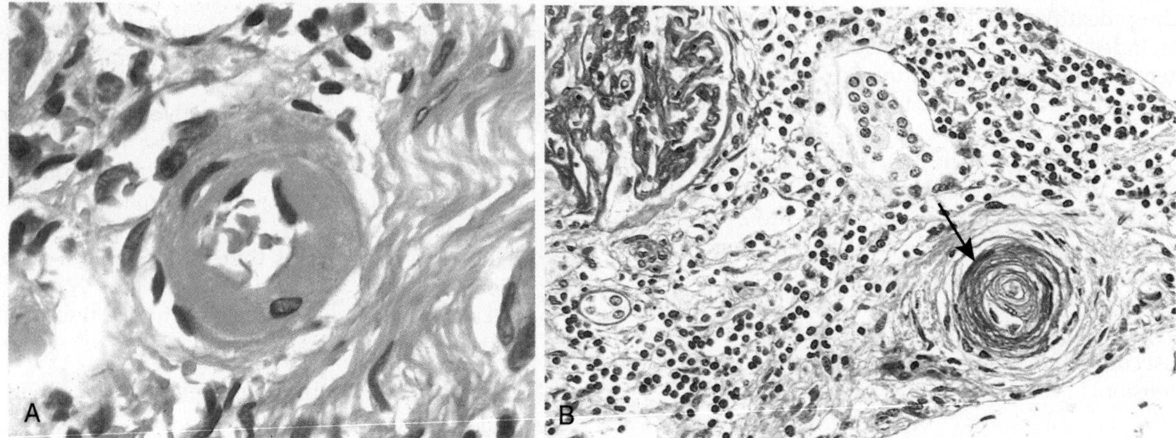

Figure 9–5 Hypertensive vascular disease. **A,** Hyaline arteriolosclerosis. The arteriolar wall is thickened with the deposition of amorphous proteinaceous material (hyalinized), and the lumen is markedly narrowed. **B,** Hyperplastic arteriolosclerosis ("onion-skinning") (*arrow*) causing luminal obliteration (periodic acid–Schiff stain).

(Courtesy of Helmut Rennke, MD, Brigham and Women's Hospital, Boston, Massachusetts.)

thickening of the arteriolar walls, with loss of underlying structural detail, and luminal narrowing (Fig. 9–5, *A*). The lesions stem from leakage of plasma components across injured endothelial cells, into vessel walls and increased ECM production by smooth muscle cells in response to chronic hemodynamic stress. In the kidneys, the arteriolar narrowing caused by hyaline arteriosclerosis leads to diffuse vascular compromise and **nephrosclerosis** (glomerular scarring). Although the vessels of elderly patients (normo- or hypertensive) show the same changes, hyaline arteriolosclerosis is more generalized and severe in patients with hypertension. The same lesions also are common in diabetic microangiopathy; in this disorder, the underlying etiology is hyperglycemia-associated endothelial cell dysfunction.

Hyperplastic arteriolosclerosis is more typical of severe hypertension. Vessels exhibit "onionskin," concentric, laminated thickening of arteriolar walls and luminal narrowing (Fig. 9–5, *B*). The laminations consist of smooth muscle cells and thickened, reduplicated basement membrane. In malignant hypertension these changes are accompanied by fibrinoid deposits and vessel wall necrosis **(necrotizing arteriolitis),** which are particularly prominent in the kidney.

SUMMARY

Hypertension

- Hypertension is a common disorder affecting 25% of the population; it is a major risk factor for atherosclerosis, congestive heart failure, and renal failure.
- Essential hypertension represents 95% of cases and is a complex, multifactorial disorder, involving both environmental influences and genetic polymorphisms that may influence sodium resorption, aldosterone pathways, and the renin–angiotensin system.
- Hypertension occasionally is caused by single-gene disorders or is secondary to diseases of the kidney, adrenal, or other endocrine organs.

VASCULAR WALL RESPONSE TO INJURY

Fundamental to a wide variety of vascular disorders is injury to the vessel wall, in particular endothelial cells. Such injurious stimuli may be biochemical, immunologic, or hemodynamic. As the main cellular components of the blood vessel walls, endothelial cells and smooth muscle cells play central roles in vascular pathology. The integrated function of these cells is critical for the vasculature to respond to various stimuli, and its responses can be adaptive or lead to pathologic lesions. Thus, endothelial injury or dysfunction (see earlier discussion) contributes to a host of pathologic processes including thrombosis, atherosclerosis, and hypertensive vascular lesions. Smooth muscle cell proliferation and matrix synthesis can help to repair a damaged vessel wall but also can lead to luminal occlusion.

Intimal Thickening: A Stereotypical Response to Vascular Injury

Vascular injury leading to endothelial cell loss or dysfunction *stimulates smooth muscle cell growth and associated matrix synthesis.* Healing of injured vessels involves the migration of smooth muscle cells or smooth muscle cell precursor cells into the intima. Here these cells proliferate, and synthesize ECM in much the same way that fibroblasts fill in a wound (Fig. 9-6), forming a neointima that typically is covered by an intact endothelial cell layer. This neointimal response occurs with any form of vascular damage or dysfunction, including infection, inflammation, immune injury, physical trauma (e.g., from a balloon catheter or hypertension), or toxic exposure (e.g. oxidized lipids or cigarette smoke). *Thus, intimal thickening is a stereotypical response of the vessel wall to any insult.*

Of note, the phenotype of neointimal smooth muscle cells is distinct from medial smooth muscle cells; neointimal smooth muscle cells lack the capacity to contract like

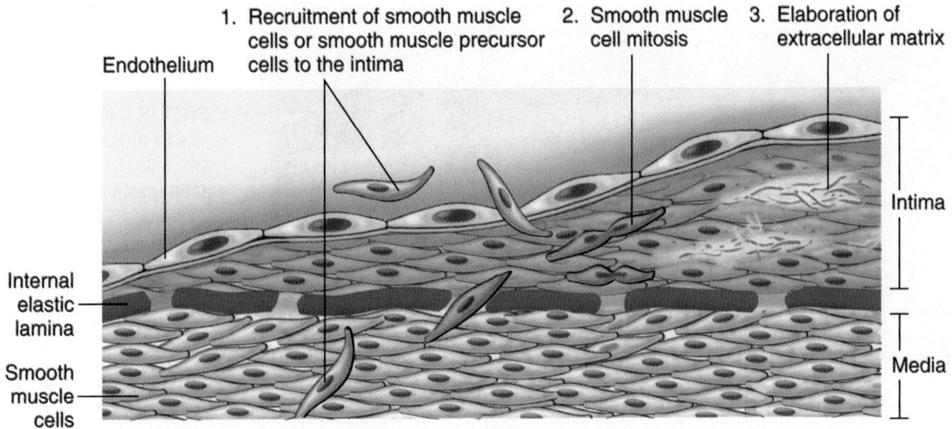

Figure 9–6 Stereotypical response to vascular injury. Schematic diagram of intimal thickening, emphasizing intimal smooth muscle cell migration and proliferation associated with extracellular matrix synthesis. Intimal smooth muscle cells may derive from the underlying media or may be recruited from circulating precursors; they are depicted in a color different from that of the medial smooth muscle cells, to emphasize their distinct phenotype.

medial smooth muscle cells, but do have the capacity to divide and have a considerably greater synthetic capacity than their medial colleagues. Although neointimal cells were previously thought to arise from dedifferentiated medial smooth muscle cells, increasing evidence suggests that at least a subset is derived from circulating precursor cells. The migratory, proliferative, and synthetic activities of the intimal smooth muscle cells are regulated by growth factors and cytokines produced by platelets, endothelial cells, and macrophages, as well as by activated coagulation and complement factors (as described previously).

With restoration and/or normalization of the endothelial cell layer, intimal smooth muscle cells can return to a nonproliferative state, but not before the healing response produces irreversible intimal thickening. With persistent or recurrent insults, further thickening can occur that leads to the stenosis of small and medium-sized blood vessels (e.g., as in atherosclerosis, discussed later). As a final note, it is also important to recognize that intimal thickening appears to be a part of normal aging. Such age-related intimal change typically is of no consequence, in part because compensatory outward remodeling of the vessel results in little net change in the luminal diameter.

ARTERIOSCLEROSIS

Arteriosclerosis literally means "hardening of the arteries"; it is a generic term reflecting arterial wall thickening and loss of elasticity. Three distinct types are recognized, each with different clinical and pathologic consequences:

- *Arteriolosclerosis* affects small arteries and arterioles and may cause downstream ischemic injury. The two variants, hyaline and hyperplastic arteriolosclerosis, were described above in relation to hypertension.
- *Mönckeberg medial sclerosis* is characterized by the presence of calcific deposits in muscular arteries, typically in persons older than 50. The lesions do not encroach on the vessel lumen and usually are not clinically significant.
- *Atherosclerosis,* from Greek root words for "gruel" and "hardening," is the most frequent and clinically important pattern and is the subject of the next section.

ATHEROSCLEROSIS

Atherosclerosis is characterized by the presence of intimal lesions called *atheromas* (or *atheromatous* or *atherosclerotic plaques*). Atheromatous plaques are raised lesions composed of soft grumous lipid cores (mainly cholesterol and cholesterol esters, with necrotic debris) covered by fibrous caps (Fig. 9–7). Atherosclerotic plaques can mechanically obstruct vascular lumina and are prone to rupture, resulting in catastrophic vessel thrombosis. Plaques also weaken the underlying media, sometimes leading to aneurysm formation. In the Western world, morbidity and mortality rates for atherosclerosis are higher than for any other disorder, with roughly half of all deaths attributable to this entity. Because coronary artery disease is an important manifestation of atherosclerosis, epidemiologic data related to atherosclerosis mortality typically reflect deaths caused by ischemic heart disease (IHD) (Chapter 10); indeed, myocardial infarction is responsible for almost one fourth of all deaths in the United States.

Epidemiology of Atherosclerosis

Atherosclerosis is virtually ubiquitous among most developed nations but is much less prevalent in Central and South America, Africa, and parts of Asia. The mortality rate for IHD in the United States is among the highest in the world, approximately five times higher than that in Japan. However, IHD is increasing in Japan, where it is now the second leading cause of death. Furthermore, Japanese emigrants who come to the United States and adopt American life styles and dietary customs acquire the same atherosclerosis risk as for U.S.-born persons, emphasizing the important etiologic role of environmental factors.

The prevalence and severity of atherosclerosis and IHD have been correlated with a number of risk factors in

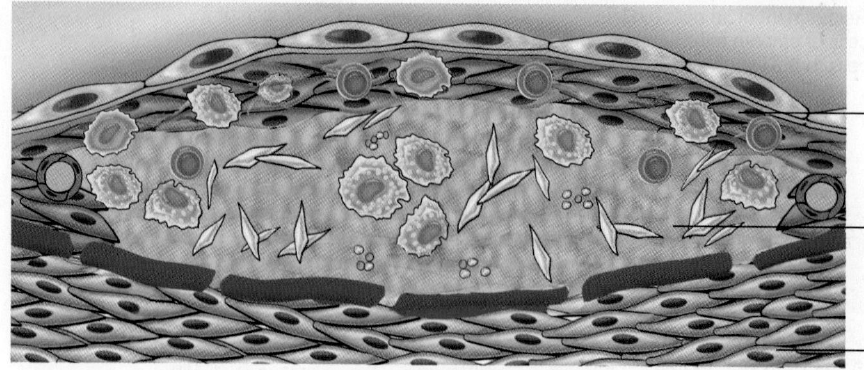

Figure 9–7 The basic structure of an atheromatous plaque.

several prospective analyses (e.g., the Framingham Heart Study); some of these risk factors are constitutional (and therefore less controllable) but others are acquired or related to modifiable behaviors (Table 9-3). *These risk factors have roughly multiplicative effects.* Thus, two factors increase the risk of myocardial infarction approximately four-fold, and three (i.e., hyperlipidemia, hypertension, and smoking), increase the rate by a factor of 7 (Fig. 9–8).

Constitutional Risk Factors

- *Genetics.* Family history is the most important independent risk factor for atherosclerosis. Certain mendelian disorders are strongly associated with atherosclerosis (e.g., familial hypercholesterolemia) (Chapter 6), but these account for only a small percentage of cases. Most familial risk is related to polygenic traits that go hand-in-hand with atherosclerosis, such as hypertension and diabetes, as well as other genetic polymorphisms.
- *Age.* Atherosclerosis usually remains clinically silent until lesions reach a critical threshold in middle age or later. Thus, the incidence of myocardial infarction increases five-fold between the ages of 40 and 60. Death rates from IHD continue to rise with each successive decade.
- *Gender.* All other factors being equal, premenopausal women are relatively protected against atherosclerosis (and its consequences) compared with age-matched men. Thus, myocardial infarction and other complications of atherosclerosis are uncommon in premenopausal women in the absence of other predisposing factors such as diabetes, hyperlipidemia, or severe hypertension. After menopause, however, the incidence of atherosclerosis-related diseases increases and, in old age, even exceeds that in men. Although a salutary effect of estrogen has long been proposed to explain this gender difference, clinical trials have shown no benefit of hormonal therapy for prevention of vascular disease. Indeed, postmenopausal estrogen replacement appears to *increase* cardiovascular risk. In addition to atherosclerosis, gender also influences other factors that can affect outcome in patients with IHD, such as hemostasis, infarct healing, and myocardial remodeling.

Table 9–3 Major Risk Factors for Atherosclerosis

Nonmodifiable (Constitutional)
Genetic abnormalities
Family history
Increasing age
Male gender
Modifiable
Hyperlipidemia
Hypertension
Cigarette smoking
Diabetes
Inflammation

Modifiable Major Risk Factors

- *Hyperlipidemia*—and, more specifically, *hypercholesterolemia*—is a major risk factor for development of atherosclerosis and is sufficient to induce lesions in the absence of other risk factors. The main cholesterol component associated with increased risk is low-density lipoprotein (LDL) cholesterol ("bad cholesterol"); LDL distributes cholesterol to peripheral tissues. By contrast, high-density lipoprotein (HDL) ("good cholesterol") mobilizes cholesterol from developing and existing vascular plaques and transports it to the liver for biliary excretion. Consequently, higher levels of HDL correlate with reduced risk.

  Recognition of these relationships has spurred the development of dietary and pharmacologic interventions that lower total serum cholesterol or LDL, and/or raise serum HDL, as follows:

  - High dietary intake of cholesterol and saturated fats (present in egg yolks, animal fats, and butter, for example) raises plasma cholesterol levels. Conversely, diets low in cholesterol, and/or containing higher ratios of polyunsaturated fats, lower plasma cholesterol levels.
  - Omega-3 fatty acids (abundant in fish oils) are beneficial, whereas (trans)-unsaturated fats produced by artificial hydrogenation of polyunsaturated oils (used in baked goods and margarine) adversely affect cholesterol profiles.
  - Exercise and moderate consumption of ethanol raise HDL levels, whereas obesity and smoking lower them.
  - *Statins* are a widely used class of drugs that lower circulating cholesterol levels by inhibiting

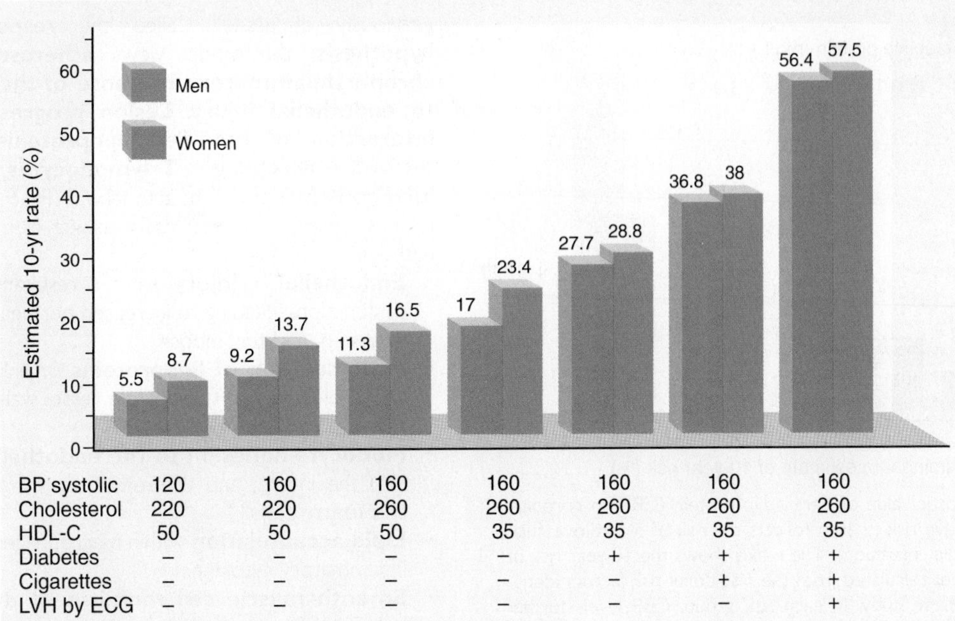

Figure 9–8 Estimated 10-year risk of coronary artery disease in 55-year-old men and women as a function of established risk factors—hyperlipidemia, hypertension, smoking, and diabetes. BP, blood pressure; ECG, electrocardiogram; HDL-C, high-density lipoprotein cholesterol; LVH, left ventricular hypertrophy.

(Data from O'Donnell CJ, Kannel WB: Cardiovascular risks of hypertension: lessons from observational studies. J Hypertension 16[Suppl 6]:3, 1998.)

hydroxymethylglutaryl coenzyme A (HMG-CoA) reductase, the rate-limiting enzyme in hepatic cholesterol biosynthesis.

- *Hypertension* (see earlier discussion) is another major risk factor for development of atherosclerosis. On its own, hypertension can increase the risk of IHD by approximately 60% (see Fig. 9–8). Hypertension also is the major cause of left ventricular hypertrophy (LVH), which also can contribute to myocardial ischemia (see Fig. 9–8).
- *Cigarette smoking* is a well-established risk factor in men and probably accounts for the increasing incidence and severity of atherosclerosis in women. Prolonged (years) smoking of one or more packs of cigarettes a day doubles the rate of IHD-related mortality, while smoking cessation reduces the risk.
- *Diabetes mellitus* is associated with raised circulating cholesterol levels and markedly increases the risk of atherosclerosis. Other factors being equal, the incidence of myocardial infarction is twice as high in diabetics as in nondiabetics. In addition, this disorder is associated with an increased risk of stroke and a 100-fold increase in atherosclerosis-induced gangrene of the lower extremities.

Additional Risk Factors

Roughly 20% of cardiovascular events occur in the absence of identifiable risk factors. For example, in previously healthy women more than 75% of cardiovascular events occur in those with LDL cholesterol levels below 160 mg/dL (a cut-off value generally considered to connote low risk). Other factors that contribute to risk include the following:

- *Inflammation.* Inflammatory cells are present during all stages of atheromatous plaque formation and are intimately linked with plaque progression and rupture (see following discussion). With increasing recognition of the role of inflammation, measures of systemic inflammation have become important in risk stratification. While several systemic markers of inflammation correlate with IHD risk, determination of *C-reactive protein* (CRP) has emerged as one of the simplest and most sensitive.
- *CRP levels.* CRP, a member of *pentraxin* family, is an acute-phase reactant synthesized primarily by the liver in response to a variety of inflammatory cytokines. Locally, CRP secreted by cells within atherosclerotic plaques can activate endothelial cells, increasing adhesiveness and inducing a prothrombotic state. Its clinical importance lies in its value as a circulating biomarker: *CRP levels strongly and independently predict the risk of myocardial infarction, stroke, peripheral arterial disease, and sudden cardiac death, even among apparently healthy persons* (Fig. 9–9). While there is no direct evidence that lowering CRP diminishes cardiovascular risk, it is of interest that CRP is reduced by smoking cessation, weight loss, and exercise. Moreover, statins reduce CRP levels independent of their LDL cholesterol-lowering effects, suggesting a possible anti-inflammatory action of these agents.
- *Hyperhomocysteinemia.* Serum homocysteine levels correlate with coronary atherosclerosis, peripheral vascular disease, stroke, and venous thrombosis. *Homocystinuria,* due to rare inborn errors of metabolism, causes elevated circulating homocysteine (greater than 100 μmol/L) and is associated with early-onset vascular disease. Although low folate and vitamin B_{12} levels can increase

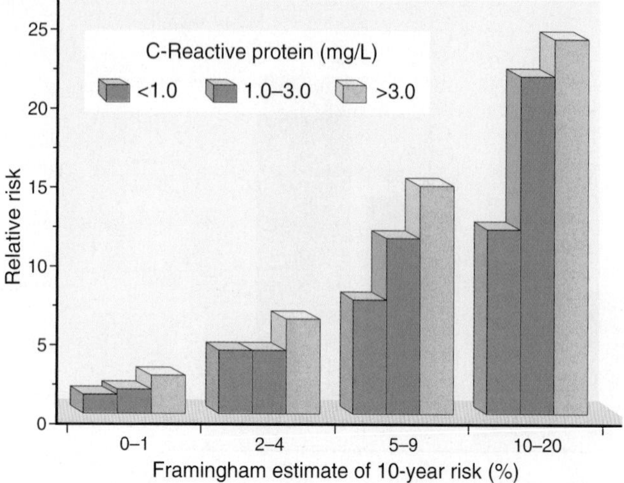

Figure 9–9 Prognostic value of C-reactive protein (CRP) in coronary artery disease. Relative risk (y-axis) reflects the risk of a cardiovascular event (e.g., myocardial infarction). The x-axis shows the 10-year risk of a cardiovascular event calculated from the traditional risk factors identified in the Framingham Study. In each risk group, CRP levels further stratify the patients.

(Data from Ridker PM, et al: Comparison of C-reactive protein and low-density lipoprotein cholesterol levels in the prediction of first cardiovascular events. N Engl J Med 347:1557, 2002.)

homocysteine levels, supplemental vitamin ingestion does not affect the incidence of cardiovascular disease.

- *Metabolic syndrome.* Associated with central obesity (Chapter 7), this clinical entity is characterized by insulin resistance, hypertension, dyslipidemia (elevated LDL and depressed HDL), hypercoagulability, and a pro-inflammatory state, which may be triggered by cytokines released from adipocytes. The dyslipidemia, hyperglycemia, and hypertension are all cardiac risk factors, while the systemic hypercoagulable and pro-inflammatory state may contribute to endothelial dysfunction and/or thrombosis.
- *Lipoprotein(a) levels.* Lipoprotein(a) is an LDL-like particle that contains apolipoprotein B-100 linked to apolipoprotein A. Lipoprotein(a) levels are correlated with coronary and cerebrovascular disease risk, independent of total cholesterol or LDL levels.
- *Elevated levels of procoagulants* are potent predictors of risk for major cardiovascular events. Excessive activation of thrombin, which you will recall initiates inflammation through cleavage of protease-activated receptors (PARs) on leukocytes, endothelium, and other cells, may be particularly atherogenic.
- *Other factors* associated with difficult-to-quantify risks include lack of exercise and living a competitive, stressful life style ("type A personality").

PATHOGENESIS

Historically, there have been two dominant theories regarding atherogenesis; one emphasizing intimal cellular proliferation in response to endothelial injury, and the other focusing on repeated formation and organization of thrombi. The contemporary view of atherogenesis incorporates elements of both theories and also integrates the risk factors previously discussed. Called the **response-to-injury hypothesis,** the model views **atherosclerosis as a chronic inflammatory response of the arterial wall to endothelial injury. Lesion progression involves interaction of modified lipoproteins, monocyte-derived macrophages, T lymphocytes, and the cellular constituents** of the arterial wall (Fig. 9–10). According to this model, atherosclerosis results from the following pathogenic events:

- **Endothelial injury**—and resultant endothelial dysfunction—leading to increased permeability, leukocyte adhesion, and thrombosis
- **Accumulation of lipoproteins** (mainly oxidized LDL and cholesterol crystals) in the vessel wall
- **Platelet adhesion**
- **Monocyte adhesion to the endothelium,** migration into the intima, and differentiation into **macrophages** and **foam cells**
- **Lipid accumulation** within macrophages, which release inflammatory cytokines
- **Smooth muscle cell recruitment due to factors released** from activated platelets, macrophages, and vascular wall cells
- **Smooth muscle cell proliferation and ECM production**

Some details of these steps are presented next.

Endothelial Injury. Endothelial cell injury is the cornerstone of the response to injury hypothesis. Endothelial cell loss due to any kind of injury—induced experimentally by mechanical denudation, hemodynamic forces, immune complex deposition, irradiation, or chemicals—results in intimal thickening; in the presence of high-lipid diets, typical atheromas ensue. However, **early human atherosclerotic lesions begin at sites of intact, but dysfunctional, endothelium.** These dysfunctional endothelial cells exhibit increased permeability, enhanced leukocyte adhesion, and altered gene expression, all of which may contribute to the development of atherosclerosis.

Suspected triggers of early atheromatous lesions include hypertension, hyperlipidemia, toxins from cigarette smoke, homocysteine, and even infectious agents. Inflammatory cytokines (e.g., tumor necrosis factor [TNF]) also can stimulate proatherogenic patterns of endothelial cell gene expression. Nevertheless, the two most important causes of endothelial dysfunction are hemodynamic disturbances and hypercholesterolemia.

Hemodynamic Disturbances. The importance of hemodynamic factors in atherogenesis is illustrated by the observation that plaques tend to occur at ostia of exiting vessels, at branch points, and along the posterior wall of the abdominal aorta, where there is turbulent blood flow. In vitro studies further demonstrate that nonturbulent laminar flow leads to the induction of endothelial genes whose products *protect* against atherosclerosis. Such "atheroprotective" genes could explain the nonrandom localization of early atherosclerotic lesions.

Lipids. Lipids typically are transported in the bloodstream bound to specific apoproteins (forming lipoprotein complexes). **Dyslipoproteinemias** can result from mutations in genes that encode apoproteins or lipoprotein receptors,

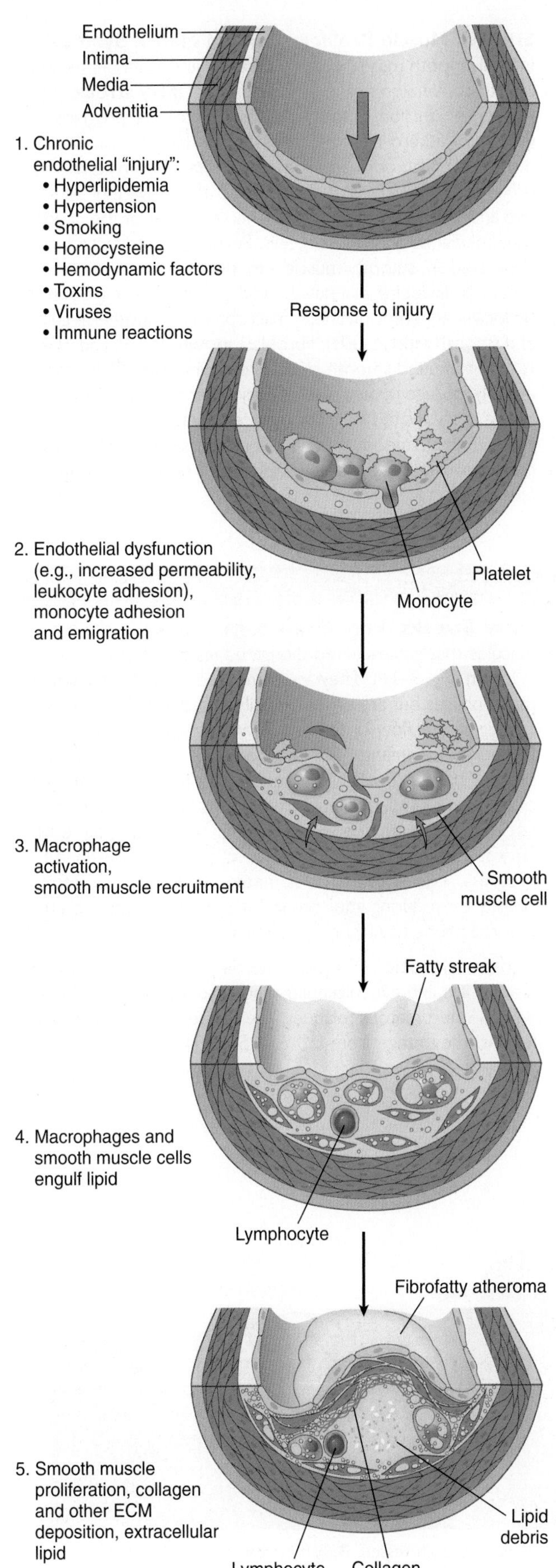

or from disorders that derange lipid metabolism, e.g., nephrotic syndrome, alcoholism, hypothyroidism, or diabetes mellitus. Common lipoprotein abnormalities in the general population (and indeed, present in many myocardial infarction survivors) include (1) increased LDL cholesterol levels, (2) decreased HDL cholesterol levels, and (3) increased levels of lipoprotein(a).

Several lines of evidence implicate hypercholesterolemia in atherogenesis:

- The dominant lipids in atheromatous plaques are cholesterol and cholesterol esters.
- Genetic defects in lipoprotein uptake and metabolism that cause hyperlipoproteinemia are associated with accelerated atherosclerosis. Thus, homozygous familial hypercholesterolemia, caused by defective LDL receptors and inadequate hepatic LDL uptake, can lead to myocardial infarction by age 20.
- Other genetic or acquired disorders (e.g., diabetes mellitus, hypothyroidism) that cause hypercholesterolemia lead to premature atherosclerosis.
- Epidemiologic analyses such as the famous Framingham study demonstrate a significant correlation between the severity of atherosclerosis and the levels of total plasma cholesterol or LDL.
- Lowering serum cholesterol by diet or drugs slows the rate of progression of atherosclerosis, causes regression of some plaques, and reduces the risk of cardiovascular events.

The mechanisms by which dyslipidemia contributes to atherogenesis include the following:

- Chronic hyperlipidemia, particularly hypercholesterolemia, can directly impair endothelial cell function by increasing local oxygen free radical production; among other things, oxygen free radicals accelerate NO decay, damping its vasodilator activity.
- With chronic hyperlipidemia, lipoproteins accumulate within the intima, where they are hypothesized to generate two pathogenic derivatives, **oxidized LDL and cholesterol crystals.** LDL is oxidized through the action of oxygen free radicals generated locally by macrophages or endothelial cells and ingested by macrophages through the **scavenger receptor,** resulting in **foam cell** formation. Oxidized LDL stimulates the local release of growth factors, cytokines, and chemokines, increasing monocyte recruitment, and also is cytotoxic to endothelial cells and smooth muscle cells. More recently, it has been shown that minute extracellular cholesterol crystals found in early atherosclerotic lesions serve as "danger" signals that activate innate immune cells such as monocytes and macrophages.

Inflammation. Inflammation contributes to the initiation, progression, and complications of atherosclerotic lesions. Normal vessels do not bind inflammatory cells. Early in atherogenesis, however, dysfunctional endothelial cells express

Figure 9–10 Response to injury in atherogenesis: **1,** Normal. **2,** Endothelial injury with monocyte and platelet adhesion. **3,** Monocyte and smooth muscle cell migration into the intima, with macrophage activation. **4,** Macrophage and smooth muscle cell uptake of modified lipids and further activation. **5,** Intimal smooth muscle cell proliferation with ECM elaboration, forming a well-developed plaque.

adhesion molecules that promote leukocyte adhesion; vascular cell adhesion molecule-1 (VCAM-1), in particular, binds monocytes and T cells. After these cells adhere to the endothelium, they migrate into the intima under the influence of locally produced chemokines.

- Monocytes differentiate into macrophages and avidly engulf lipoproteins, including oxidized LDL and small cholesterol crystals. Cholesterol crystals appear to be particularly important instigators of inflammation through activation of the inflammasome and subsequent release of IL-1 (Chapter 2). Activated macrophages also produce toxic oxygen species that drive LDL oxidation and elaborate growth factors that stimulate smooth muscle cell proliferation.
- T lymphocytes recruited to the intima interact with the macrophages and also contribute to a state of chronic inflammation. It is not clear whether the T cells are responding to specific antigens (e.g., bacterial or viral antigens, heat-shock proteins [see further on], or modified arterial wall constituents and lipoproteins) or are nonspecifically activated by the local inflammatory milieu. Nevertheless, activated T cells in the growing intimal lesions elaborate inflammatory cytokines (e.g., IFN-γ), which stimulate macrophages, endothelial cells, and smooth muscle cells.
- As a consequence of the chronic inflammatory state, activated leukocytes and vascular wall cells release growth factors that promote smooth muscle cell proliferation and matrix synthesis.

Infection. There is circumstantial evidence linking infections to atherosclerosis. Herpesvirus, cytomegalovirus, and *Chlamydia pneumoniae* all have been found in atherosclerotic plaque, and seroepidemiologic studies show increased antibody titers to *Chlamydia pneumoniae* in patients with more severe atherosclerosis. Infections with these organisms, however, are exceedingly common (as is atherosclerosis), making it difficult to draw conclusions about causality. It also is important to recognize that atherosclerosis can be induced in germ-free mice, indicating that there is no obligate role for infection in the disease process.

Smooth Muscle Proliferation and Matrix Synthesis. Intimal smooth muscle cell proliferation and ECM deposition lead to conversion of the earliest lesion, a **fatty streak,** into a mature atheroma, thus contributing to the progressive growth of atherosclerotic lesions (Fig. 9–10). Intimal smooth muscle cells can originate from the media or from circulating precursors; regardless of their source, they have a proliferative and synthetic phenotype distinct from that of the underlying medial smooth muscle cells. Several growth factors are implicated in smooth muscle cell proliferation and matrix synthesis, including platelet-derived growth factor (released by locally adherent platelets, macrophages, endothelial cells, and smooth muscle cells), fibroblast growth factor, and TGF-α. The recruited smooth muscle cells synthesize ECM (most notably collagen), which stabilizes atherosclerotic plaques. However, activated inflammatory cells in atheromas also can cause intimal smooth muscle cell apoptosis and breakdown of matrix, leading to the development of **unstable plaques** (see later).

MORPHOLOGY

Fatty Streaks. Fatty streaks begin as minute yellow, flat macules that coalesce into elongated lesions, 1 cm or more in length (Fig. 9–11). They are composed of lipid-filled foamy macrophages but are only minimally raised and do not cause any significant flow disturbance. Fatty streaks can appear in the aortas of infants younger than 1 year of age and are present in virtually all children older than 10 years, regardless of genetic, clinical, or dietary risk factors. The relationship of fatty streaks to atherosclerotic plaques is uncertain; although fatty streaks may evolve into plaques, not all are destined to progress. Nevertheless, it is notable that coronary fatty streaks form during adolescence at the same anatomic sites that are prone to plaques later in life.

Atherosclerotic Plaque. The key features of these lesions are intimal thickening and lipid accumulation (Fig. 9–7). Atheromatous plaques are white to yellow raised lesions; they range from 0.3 to 1.5 cm in diameter but can

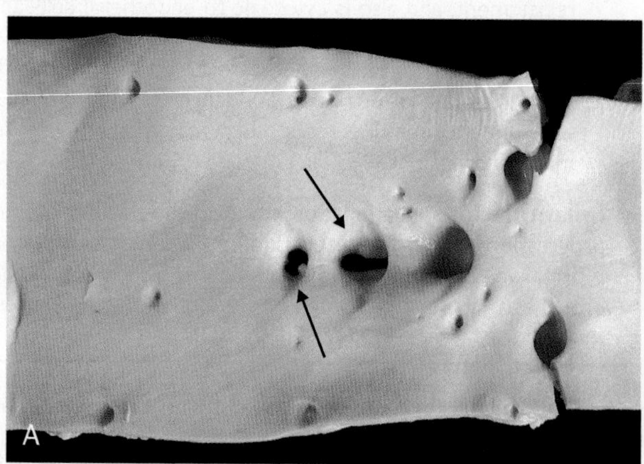

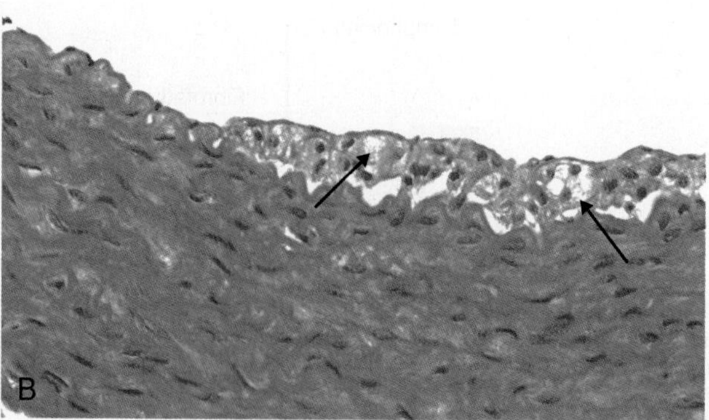

Figure 9–11 Fatty streaks. **A,** Aorta with fatty streaks (*arrows*), mainly near the ostia of branch vessels. **B,** Fatty streak in an experimental hypercholesterolemic rabbit, demonstrating intimal, macrophage-derived foam cells (*arrow*).

(B, Courtesy of Myron I. Cybulsky, MD, University of Toronto, Toronto, Ontario, Canada.)

25% of cases, granulomas and giant cells are absent, and lesions exhibit only a nonspecific panarteritis with a mixed infiltrate of acute and chronic inflammation. Healing is marked by medial and adventitial fibrosis and intimal thickening. Characteristically, lesions at different stages of development are seen within the same artery.

Clinical Features of Giant Cell Arteritis

Temporal arteritis is rare before the age of 50. Signs and symptoms may be vague and constitutional—fever, fatigue, weight loss—or take the form of facial pain or headache, most intense along the course of the superficial temporal artery, which is painful to palpation. Ocular symptoms (associated with involvement of the ophthalmic artery) abruptly appear in about 50% of patients; these range from diplopia to complete vision loss. Diagnosis depends on biopsy and histology; however, because involvement in temporal arteritis is patchy a negative biopsy result does not exclude the diagnosis. Corticosteroid or anti-TNF therapies are effective treatments.

Takayasu Arteritis

Takayasu arteritis is a granulomatous vasculitis of medium-sized and larger arteries *characterized principally by ocular disturbances and marked weakening of the pulses in the upper extremities* (hence the alternate name, *pulseless disease*). This disorder manifests with *transmural scarring and thickening of the aorta—particularly the aortic arch and great vessels—with severe luminal narrowing of the major branch vessels* (Fig. 9–24). Aortic lesions share many of the clinical and histologic features of giant cell aortitis. Indeed, the distinction between the two entities is made largely on the basis of a patient's age; those older than 50 years are designated giant cell aortitis, and those younger than 50 years, Takayasu aortitis. Although historically associated with Japanese ethnicity and certain HLA haplotypes, Takayasu aortitis has a global distribution. An autoimmune etiology is likely.

MORPHOLOGY

Takayasu arteritis classically affects the aortic arch and arch vessels; a third of cases also involve the remainder of the aorta and its branches. Occasionally, aortic root involvement causes dilation and aortic valve insufficiency. **Pulmonary arteries are involved in 50% of patients, and renal and coronary arteries also can be affected.** The takeoffs of the great vessels can be markedly narrowed and even obliterated (Fig. 9–24, *A* and *B*), explaining the upper extremity weakness and faint carotid pulses. The histologic picture (Fig. 9–24, *C*) encompasses a spectrum ranging from adventitial mononuclear infiltrates and perivascular cuffing of the vasa vasorum, to intense transmural mononuclear inflammation, to granulomatous inflammation, replete with giant cells and patchy medial necrosis. The inflammation is associated with irregular thickening of the vessel wall, intimal hyperplasia, and adventitial fibrosis.

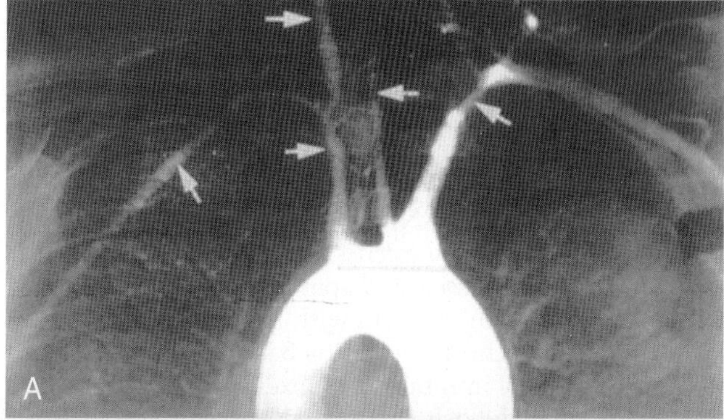

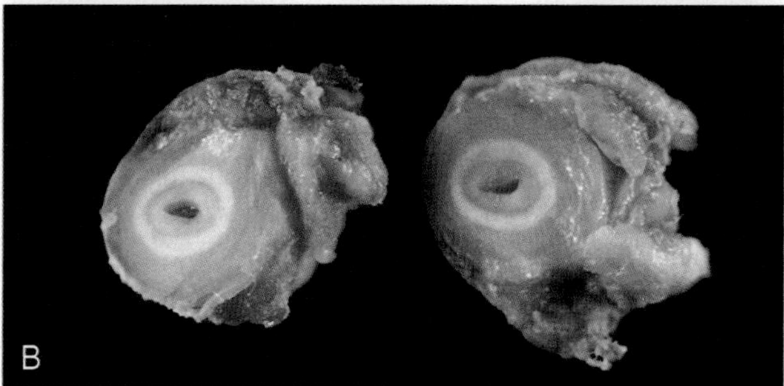

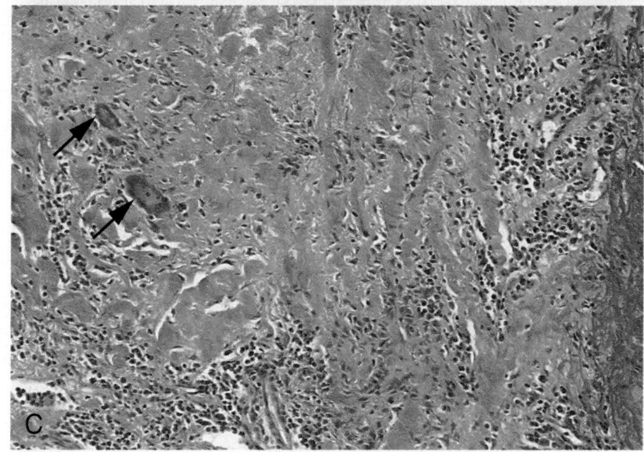

Figure 9–24 Takayasu arteritis. **A,** Aortic arch angiogram showing reduced flow of contrast material into the great vessels and narrowing of the brachiocephalic, carotid, and subclavian arteries (*arrows*). **B,** Cross-sections of the right carotid artery from the patient shown in **A** demonstrating marked intimal thickening and luminal narrowing. The *white circles* correspond to the original vessel wall; the inner core of tan tissue is the area of intimal hyperplasia. **C,** Histologic appearance in active Takayasu aortitis illustrating destruction and fibrosis of the arterial media associated with mononuclear infiltrates and inflammatory giant cells (*arrows*).

Clinical Features of Takayasu Aortitis

Initial signs and symptoms usually are nonspecific, including fatigue, weight loss, and fever. With progression, vascular signs and symptoms appear and dominate the clinical picture. These include reduced upper extremity blood pressure and pulse strength; neurologic deficits; and ocular disturbances, including visual field defects, retinal hemorrhages, and total blindness. Distal aorta disease can manifest as leg claudication, and pulmonary artery involvement can cause pulmonary hypertension. Narrowing of the coronary ostia can lead to myocardial infarction, and involvement of the renal arteries causes systemic hypertension in roughly half of the patients. The evolution of the disease is variable. Some cases rapidly progress, while others become quiescent after 1 to 2 years. In the latter scenario, long-term survival, albeit with visual or neurologic deficits, is possible.

Polyarteritis Nodosa

Polyarteritis nodosa (PAN) is a systemic vasculitis of *small or medium-sized muscular arteries* that typically involves the renal and visceral vessels and spares the pulmonary circulation. There is no association with ANCAs, but a third of the patients have chronic hepatitis B infection, which leads to the formation of immune complexes containing hepatitis B antigens that deposit in affected vessels. The cause is unknown in the remaining cases.

MORPHOLOGY

Classic PAN is a **segmental transmural necrotizing inflammation of small to medium-sized arteries,** often with superimposed thrombosis. Kidney, heart, liver, and gastrointestinal tract vessels are affected in descending order of frequency. Lesions usually involve only part of the vessel circumference and have a predilection for branch points. Impaired perfusion may lead to ulcerations, infarcts, ischemic atrophy, or hemorrhages in the distribution of affected vessels. The inflammatory process also weakens the arterial wall, leading to aneurysms and rupture.

In the acute phase, there is transmural mixed inflammatory infiltrate composed of neutrophils and mononuclear cells, frequently accompanied by **fibrinoid necrosis** and luminal thrombosis (Fig. 9–25). Older lesions show fibrous thickening of the vessel wall extending into the adventitia. Characteristically, **all stages of activity** (from early to late) **coexist** in different vessels or even within the same vessel, suggesting ongoing and recurrent pathogenic insults.

Clinical Features of PAN

PAN is primarily a disease of young adults but can occur in all age groups. The clinical course may range from acute to chronic but typically is episodic, with long symptom-free intervals. The systemic findings—malaise, fever, and weight loss—are nonspecific, and the vascular involvement is widely scattered, so that the clinical manifestations can be varied and puzzling. A "classic" presentation can involve some combination of rapidly accelerating hypertension due to renal artery involvement; abdominal pain and bloody stools caused by vascular gastrointestinal lesions; diffuse muscular aches and pains; and peripheral neuritis, predominantly affecting motor nerves. Renal involvement often is prominent and constitutes a major cause of death in these patients. Untreated, PAN typically is fatal; however, immunosuppression can yield remission or cure in 90% of the cases.

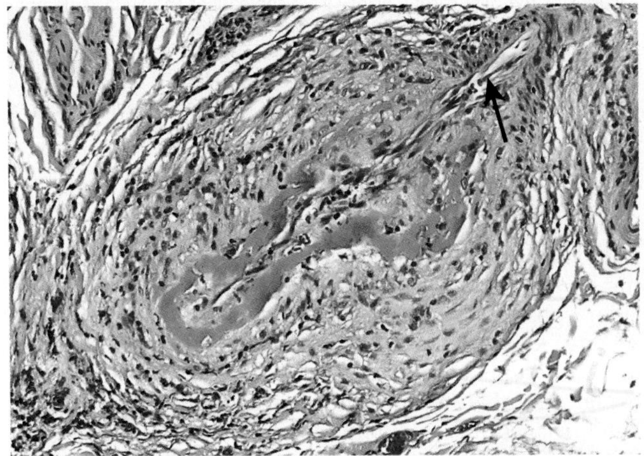

Figure 9–25 Polyarteritis nodosa, associated with segmental fibrinoid necrosis and thrombotic occlusion of a small artery. Note that part of the vessel (upper right, *arrow*) is uninvolved.

(Courtesy of Sidney Murphree, MD, Department of Pathology, University of Texas Southwestern Medical School, Dallas, Texas.)

Kawasaki Disease

Kawasaki disease is an acute, febrile, usually self-limited illness of infancy and childhood (80% of the patients are younger than 4 years of age) associated with an arteritis of mainly large to medium-sized vessels. *Its clinical significance stems from the involvement of coronary arteries.* Coronary arteritis can cause aneurysms that rupture or thrombose, resulting in myocardial infarction. Originally described in Japan, the disease is now recognized in the United States and elsewhere.

In genetically susceptible persons, a variety of infectious agents (mostly viral) have been posited to trigger the disease. The vasculitis may result from a delayed-type hypersensitivity response directed against cross-reactive or newly uncovered vascular antigen(s). Subsequent cytokine production and polyclonal B cell activation result in autoantibodies to endothelial cells and smooth muscle cells that precipitate the vasculitis.

MORPHOLOGY

The vasculitis resembles that seen in polyarteritis nodosa. There is a dense transmural inflammatory infiltrate, although the fibrinoid necrosis usually is less prominent than in polyarteritis nodosa. The acute vasculitis typically subsides spontaneously or in response to treatment, but aneurysm formation due to wall damage can supervene. As with other arteritides, healed lesions also can exhibit obstructive intimal thickening. Pathologic changes outside the cardiovascular system are rarely significant.

Clinical Features of Kawasaki Disease

Kawasaki disease typically manifests with conjunctival and oral erythema and blistering, edema of the hands and feet, erythema of the palms and soles, a desquamative rash, and cervical lymph node enlargement (hence its other name, *mucocutaneous lymph node syndrome*). Approximately 20% of untreated patients develop cardiovascular sequelae, ranging from asymptomatic coronary arteritis, to coronary artery ectasia, to large coronary artery aneurysms (7 to 8 mm in diameter) with rupture or thrombosis, myocardial infarction, and sudden death. With intravenous immunoglobulin therapy and aspirin, the rate of symptomatic coronary artery disease is reduced to about 4%.

Microscopic Polyangiitis

Microscopic polyangiitis is a *necrotizing vasculitis that generally affects capillaries, as well as small arterioles and venules.* It also is called *hypersensitivity vasculitis* or *leukocytoclastic vasculitis. Unlike in polyarteritis nodosa, all lesions of microscopic polyangiitis tend to be of the same age in any given patient.* The skin, mucous membranes, lungs, brain, heart, gastrointestinal tract, kidneys, and muscle all can be involved; *necrotizing glomerulonephritis* (seen in 90% of patients) *and pulmonary capillaritis are particularly common.* Microscopic angiitis can be a feature of a number of immune disorders, such as Henoch-Schönlein purpura, essential mixed cryoglobulinemia, or the vasculitis associated with connective tissue disorders.

In some cases, antibody responses to antigens such as drugs (e.g., penicillin), microorganisms (e.g., streptococci), heterologous proteins, or tumor proteins have been implicated. These reactions can either lead to immune complex deposition or trigger secondary immune responses (e.g., the development of ANCAs) that are pathogenic. Indeed, most cases are associated with MPO-ANCA. Recruitment and activation of neutrophils within affected vascular beds probably are responsible for the disease manifestations.

MORPHOLOGY

Microscopic polyangiitis is characterized by **segmental fibrinoid necrosis of the media with focal transmural necrotizing lesions**; granulomatous inflammation is absent. These lesions resemble those of polyarteritis nodosa but spare medium-sized and larger arteries, so that macroscopic infarcts are uncommon. In some areas (typically postcapillary venules), only infiltrating neutrophils that frequently undergo fragmentation are seen, giving rise to the term **leukocytoclastic vasculitis** (Fig. 9–26, *A*). Although immunoglobulins and complement components can be demonstrated in early skin lesions, most lesions are "pauci-immune" (i.e., show little or no antibody).

Clinical Features of Microscopic Polyangiitis

Depending on the vascular bed involved, major features include hemoptysis, hematuria, proteinuria, abdominal pain or bleeding, muscle pain or weakness, and palpable cutaneous purpura. With the exception of patients with widespread renal or CNS involvement, immunosuppression and removal of the offending agent induce durable remissions.

Wegener Granulomatosis

Wegener granulomatosis is a necrotizing vasculitis characterized by a specific triad of findings:

- *Granulomas* of the lung and/or the upper respiratory tract (ear, nose, sinuses, throat)
- *Vasculitis* of small to medium-sized vessels (capillaries, venules, arterioles, and arteries), most prominently in the lungs and upper respiratory tract
- *Glomerulonephritis*

"Limited" forms of disease can be restricted to the respiratory tract. Conversely, a widespread form of the disease can affect eyes, skin, and other organs, notably the heart; clinically, this resembles polyarteritis nodosa with the additional feature of respiratory involvement.

Wegener granulomatosis is likely to be initiated as a cell-mediated hypersensitivity response directed against inhaled infectious or environmental antigens. PR3-ANCAs are present in almost 95% of cases and probably drive the subsequent tissue injury; they also are useful markers of disease activity. After immunosuppressive therapy, ANCA levels fall dramatically, while rising titers are predictive of relapse.

MORPHOLOGY

Upper respiratory tract lesions range from granulomatous sinusitis to ulcerative lesions of the nose, palate, or pharynx;

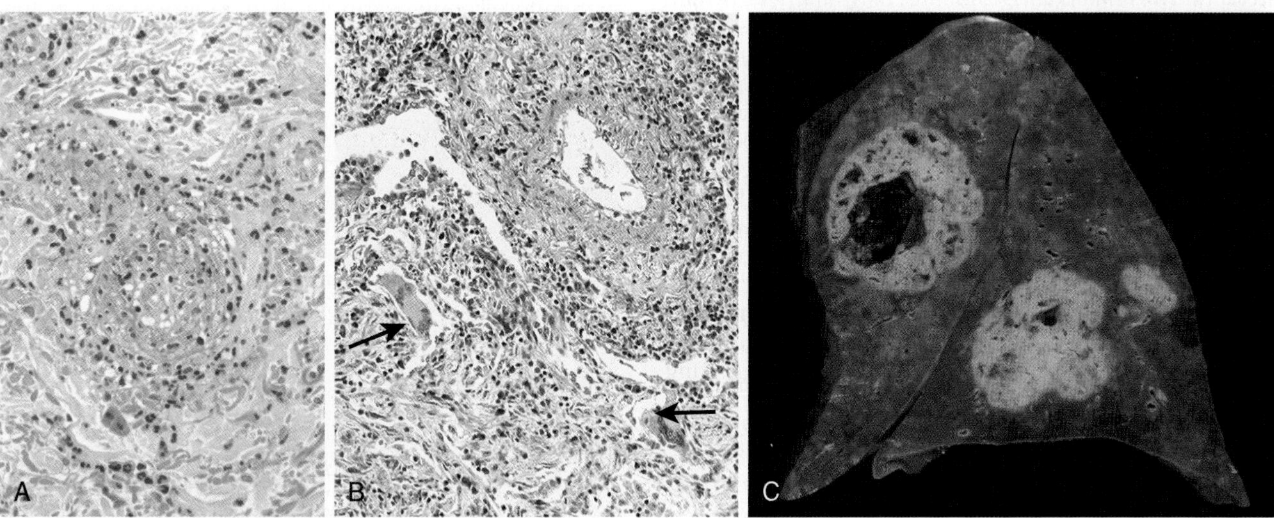

Figure 9–26 ANCA-associated small vessel vasculitis. **A,** Microscopic polyangiitis (leukocytoclastic vasculitis) with fragmented neutrophils in the thickened vessel wall. **B** and **C,** Wegener granulomatosis. **B,** Vasculitis of a small artery with adjacent granulomatous inflammation including giant cells (*arrows*). **C,** Lung from a patient with Wegener granulomatosis, demonstrating large nodular cavitating lesions.

(A, Courtesy of Scott Granter, MD, Brigham and Women's Hospital, Boston, Massachusetts. C, Courtesy of Sidney Murphree, MD, Department of Pathology, University of Texas Southwestern Medical School, Dallas, Texas.)

lung findings also vary, ranging from diffuse parenchymal infiltrates to granulomatous nodules. There is multifocal **necrotizing granulomatous vasculitis with a surrounding fibroblastic proliferation** (see Fig. 9–26, *B*). Multiple granulomata can coalesce to produce radiographically visible nodules with central cavitation (see Fig. 9–26, *B*). Destruction of vessels can lead to hemorrhage and hemoptysis. Lesions can ultimately undergo progressive fibrosis and organization.

The **renal lesions** range from mild, focal glomerular necrosis with thrombosis of isolated glomerular capillary loops **(focal and segmental necrotizing glomerulonephritis)** to more advanced glomerular lesions with diffuse necrosis and parietal cell proliferation forming epithelial crescents **(crescentic glomerulonephritis)** (Chapter 13).

Clinical Features of Wegener Granulomatosis

The typical patient is a 40-year old man, although women and persons of other ages can be affected. Classic presentations include bilateral pneumonitis with nodules and cavitary lesions (95%), chronic sinusitis (90%), mucosal ulcerations of the nasopharynx (75%), and renal disease (80%); patients with low-grade renal involvement may demonstrate only hematuria and proteinuria responsive to therapy, whereas more severe disease can portend rapidly progressive renal failure. Rash, myalgias, articular involvement, neuritis, and fever can also occur. If untreated, the mortality rate at 1 year is 80%. Treatment with steroids, cyclophosphamide, TNF inhibitors and anti–B cell antibodies (Rituximab) has improved this picture considerably. Most patients with Wegener granulomatosis now survive, but remain at high risk for relapses that can ultimately lead to renal failure.

Churg-Strauss Syndrome

Churg-Strauss syndrome (also called allergic granulomatosis and angiitis) is a *small vessel necrotizing vasculitis classically associated with asthma, allergic rhinitis, lung infiltrates, peripheral eosinophilia, extravascular necrotizing granulomas, and a striking infiltration of vessels and perivascular tissues by eosinophils.* It is a rare disorder, affecting 1 in 1 million people. Cutaneous involvement (with palpable purpura), gastrointestinal bleeding, and renal disease (primarily as focal and segmental glomerulosclerosis) are the major associations. Cytotoxicity produced by the myocardial eosinophilic infiltrates often leads to cardiomyopathy; cardiac involvement is seen in 60% of patients and is a major cause of morbidity and death.

Churg-Strauss syndrome may stem from "hyperresponsiveness" to some normally innocuous allergic stimulus. MPO-ANCAs are present in a minority of cases, suggesting that the disorder is pathogenically heterogeneous. The vascular lesions differ from those of polyarteritis nodosa or microscopic polyangiitis by virtue of the presence of *granulomas* and *eosinophils*.

Thromboangiitis Obliterans (Buerger Disease)

Thromboangiitis obliterans (Buerger disease) is a distinctive disorder that frequently results in severe vascular insufficiency and gangrene of the extremities. It is characterized by focal acute and chronic inflammation of medium-sized and small arteries, especially the tibial and radial arteries, associated with thrombosis; occasionally, secondary extension into adjacent veins and nerves may be seen. Buerger disease occurs almost exclusively in heavy tobacco smokers and usually develops before age 35.

The etiology is unknown. Direct endothelial cell toxicity caused by some component of tobacco is suspected; alternatively, a reactive compound in tobacco may modify vessel wall components and induce an immune response. Indeed, most patients with Buerger disease are hypersensitive to tobacco extracts. A genetic predilection is suggested by an increased prevalence in certain ethnic groups (Israeli, Indian subcontinent, Japanese) and an association with certain HLA haplotypes.

MORPHOLOGY

In thromboangiitis obliterans, there is a **sharply segmental acute and chronic transmural vasculitis of medium-sized and small arteries,** predominantly those of the extremities. In early stages, mixed inflammatory infiltrates are accompanied by luminal thrombosis; small **microabscesses,** occasionally rimmed by granulomatous inflammation, also may be present (Fig. 9–27). The inflammation often extends into contiguous veins and nerves (a feature that is rare in other forms of vasculitis). With time, thrombi can organize and recanalize, and eventually the artery and adjacent structures become encased in fibrous tissue.

Clinical Features of Buerger Disease

Early manifestations include cold-induced Raynaud phenomenon, instep foot pain induced by exercise (*instep claudication*), and a superficial nodular phlebitis (venous inflammation). The vascular insufficiency of Buerger disease tends to be accompanied by severe pain—even at rest—undoubtedly from the neural involvement. Chronic extremity ulcerations can develop, progressing over time (occasionally precipitously) to frank gangrene. Smoking

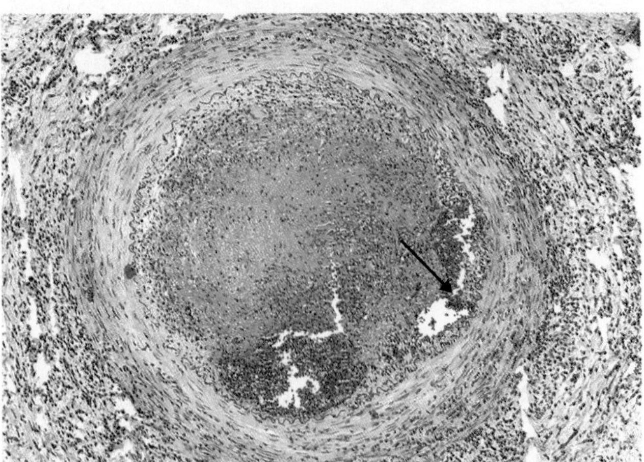

Figure 9–27 Thromboangiitis obliterans (Buerger disease). The lumen is occluded by thrombus containing abscesses (*arrow*) and the vessel wall is infiltrated with leukocytes.

abstinence in the early stages of the disease often can ameliorate further attacks; however, once established, the vascular lesions do not respond to smoking abstinence.

Vasculitis Associated with Other Noninfectious Disorders

Vasculitis resembling hypersensitivity angiitis or classic PAN can be associated with many other diseases, including malignancies and immunologic disorders such as rheumatoid arthritis, systemic lupus erythematosus, antiphospholipid antibody syndrome, and Henoch-Schönlein purpura. *Rheumatoid vasculitis* can occur in patients with severe, long-standing rheumatoid arthritis; it can cause a clinically significant aortitis but typically affects small and medium-sized arteries, leading to visceral infarction. Linking vasculitis to specific disorders may have important therapeutic implications. For example, although classic immune complex *lupus vasculitis* and antiphospholipid antibody syndrome can share morphologic features, the former requires anti-inflammatory therapy while anticoagulation is indicated in the latter.

Infectious Vasculitis

Localized arteritis may be caused by the direct invasion of arteries by infectious agents, usually bacteria or fungi, and in particular *Aspergillus* and *Mucor* spp. Vascular invasion can be part of a more general tissue infection (e.g., bacterial pneumonia or adjacent to abscesses), or—less commonly—arise from hematogenous spread of bacteria during septicemia or embolization from infective endocarditis.

Vascular infections can weaken arterial walls and culminate in *mycotic aneurysms* (see earlier), or can induce thrombosis and infarction. Thus, inflammation of vessels in bacterial meningitis can cause thrombosis and infarction, leading ultimately to extension of a subarachnoid infection into the brain parenchyma.

SUMMARY

Vasculitis

- Vasculitis is defined as inflammation of vessel walls; it frequently is associated with systemic manifestations (including fever, malaise, myalgias, and arthralgias) and organ dysfunction that depends on the pattern of vascular involvement.
- Vasculitis can result from infections but more commonly has an immunologic basis such as immune complex deposition, anti-neutrophil antibodies (ANCAs), or anti–endothelial cell antibodies.
- Different forms of vasculitis tend to specifically affect vessels of a particular caliber and location (see Fig. 9–22).

DISORDERS OF BLOOD VESSEL HYPERREACTIVITY

Several disorders are characterized by inappropriate or exaggerated vasoconstriction of blood vessels.

Raynaud Phenomenon

Raynaud phenomenon results from exaggerated vasoconstriction of arteries and arterioles in the extremities, particularly the fingers and toes, but also sometimes the nose, earlobes, or lips. The restricted blood flow induces paroxysmal pallor or cyanosis; involved digits characteristically show "red-white-and-blue" color changes from most proximal to most distal, reflecting proximal vasodilation, central vasoconstriction, and more distal cyanosis, respectively. Raynaud phenomenon can be a primary entity or may be secondary to other disorders.

Primary Raynaud phenomenon (previously called Raynaud disease) is caused by exaggerated central and local vasomotor responses to cold or emotion; it affects 3% to 5% of the general population and has a predilection for young women. Structural changes in the arterial walls are absent except late in the course, when intimal thickening may appear. The course usually is benign, but in chronic cases, atrophy of the skin, subcutaneous tissues, and muscles may occur. Ulceration and ischemic gangrene are rare.

Secondary Raynaud phenomenon refers to vascular insufficiency due to arterial disease caused by other entities including systemic lupus erythematosus, scleroderma, Buerger disease, or even atherosclerosis (see later). Indeed, since Raynaud phenomenon may be the first manifestation of such conditions, every patient with Raynaud phenomenon should be evaluated for these secondary causes.

Myocardial Vessel Vasospasm

Excessive constriction of arteries or arterioles may cause ischemia, and persistent vasospasm can even lead to tissue infarction. In addition to intrinsic hyperreactivity of medial smooth muscle cells, as described earlier for primary Raynaud disease, high levels of vasoactive mediators can precipitate prolonged vascular contraction. Such agents can be endogenous (e.g., epinephrine released by pheochromocytomas) or exogenous (cocaine or phenylephrine). Elevated thyroid hormone causes a similar effect by increasing the sensitivity of vessels to circulating catecholamines, while autoantibodies and T cells in scleroderma (Chapter 4) can cause vascular instability and vasospasm. In some susceptible persons, extreme psychological stress and the attendant release of catecholamines can lead to pathologic vasospasm.

When vasospasm of cardiac arterial or arteriolar beds (so-called *cardiac Raynaud*) is of sufficient duration (20 to 30 minutes), myocardial infarction occurs. Elevated levels of catechols also increase heart rate and myocardial contractility, exacerbating ischemia caused by the vasospasm. The outcome can be sudden cardiac death (probably caused by a fatal arrhythmia) or an ischemic dilated cardiomyopathy—so-called *Takotsubo cardiomyopathy* (also called "broken heart syndrome," because of the association with emotional duress). Histologic findings in acute cases may include microscopic areas of necrosis characterized by myocyte hypercontraction (*contraction band necrosis*) (Chapter 10); in subacute and chronic cases, microscopic foci of granulation tissue and/or scar may be present.

VEINS AND LYMPHATICS

Varicose veins and phlebothrombosis/thrombophlebitis account for at least 90% of cases of clinically relevant venous disease.

Varicose Veins of the Extremities

Varicose veins are abnormally dilated tortuous veins produced by chronically increased intraluminal pressures and weakened vessel wall support. The *superficial veins* of the upper and lower leg typically are involved. Up to 20% of men and a third of women develop lower extremity varicose veins. Obesity increases the risk, and the higher incidence in women probably reflects the prolonged elevation in venous pressure caused by compression of the inferior vena cava by the gravid uterus during pregnancy. There is also a familial tendency toward premature varicosities.

Clinical Features of Varicose Veins

Varicose dilation renders the venous valves incompetent and leads to lower extremity stasis, congestion, edema, pain, and thrombosis. The most disabling sequelae include persistent edema in the extremity and secondary ischemic skin changes, including *stasis dermatitis* and *ulcerations*. The latter can become chronic *varicose ulcers* as a consequence of poor wound healing and superimposed infections. Of note, *embolism from these superficial veins is very rare, in contrast with the relatively frequent emboli that arise from thrombosed deep veins* (Chapter 3).

Varicosities of Other Sites

Venous dilations in two other sites merit special attention:

- *Esophageal varices.* Liver cirrhosis (less frequently, portal vein obstruction or hepatic vein thrombosis) causes portal vein hypertension (Chapter 15). This in turn leads to the opening of porto-systemic shunts and increased blood flow into veins at the gastro-esophageal junction (forming *esophageal varices*), rectum (forming *hemorrhoids*), and periumbilical veins of the abdominal wall (forming a *caput medusae*). Esophageal varices are most important since they are prone to ruptures that can lead to massive (even fatal) upper gastrointestinal hemorrhage.
- *Hemorrhoids* are varicose dilations of the venous plexus at the anorectal junction that result from prolonged pelvic vascular congestion associated with pregnancy or straining to defecate. Hemorrhoids are a source of bleeding and prone to thrombosis and painful ulceration.

Thrombophlebitis and Phlebothrombosis

Thrombosis of deep leg veins accounts for more than 90% of cases of thrombophlebitis and phlebothrombosis. These two terms are largely interchangeable designations for venous thrombosis and inflammation. Other sites where venous thrombi may form are the periprostatic venous plexus in males and the pelvic venous plexus in females, as well as the large veins in the skull and the dural sinuses (especially in the setting of infection or inflammation). Peritoneal infections, including peritonitis, appendicitis, salpingitis, and pelvic abscesses, as well as certain conditions associated with hypercoagulability (e.g., polycythemia vera) (Chapter 11) can lead to portal vein thrombosis.

In deep venous thrombosis (DVT) of the legs, *prolonged immobilization resulting in venous stasis is the most important risk factor.* This can occur with extended bed rest or even just sitting during long plane or automobile trips. The postoperative state is another independent risk factor for DVT, as are congestive heart failure, pregnancy, oral contraceptive use, and obesity. Inherited defects in coagulation factors (Chapter 3) often predispose affected persons to development of thrombophlebitis. Venous thrombi may result from elaboration of procoagulant factors from malignant tumors (Chapter 5). The resulting hypercoagulable state can manifest as evanescent thromboses in different vascular beds at different times, resulting in so-called *migratory thrombophlebitis* or *Trousseau syndrome.*

Thrombi in the legs tend to produce few, if any, reliable signs or symptoms. When present, local manifestations include distal edema, cyanosis, superficial vein dilation, heat, tenderness, redness, swelling, and pain. In some cases, pain can be elicited by pressure over affected veins, squeezing the calf muscles, or forced dorsiflexion of the foot (*Homan sign*). However, symptoms often are absent, especially in bedridden patients, and *the absence of findings does not exclude DVT.*

Pulmonary embolism is a common and serious clinical complication of DVT (Chapter 3), resulting from fragmentation or detachment of the venous thrombus. In many cases, *the first manifestation of thrombophlebitis is a pulmonary embolus.* Depending on the size and number of emboli, the outcome can range from resolution with no symptoms to death.

Superior and Inferior Vena Cava Syndromes

The *superior vena cava syndrome* usually is caused by neoplasms that compress or invade the superior vena cava, such as bronchogenic carcinoma or mediastinal lymphoma. The resulting obstruction produces a characteristic clinical complex consisting of marked dilation of the veins of the head, neck, and arms associated with cyanosis. Pulmonary vessels also can be compressed, causing respiratory distress.

The *inferior vena cava syndrome* can be caused by neoplasms that compress or invade the inferior vena cava or by a thrombus from the hepatic, renal, or lower extremity veins that propagates upward. Certain neoplasms—particularly hepatocellular carcinoma and renal cell carcinoma—show a striking tendency to grow within veins, and these tumors may ultimately occlude the inferior vena cava. Obstruction of the inferior vena cava induces marked lower extremity edema, distention of the superficial collateral veins of the lower abdomen, and—with renal vein involvement—proteinuria of marked degree.

Lymphangitis and Lymphedema

Primary disorders of lymphatic vessels are extremely uncommon. Much more commonly, lymphatic vessels are involved by inflammatory, infectious, or malignant processes secondarily.

Lymphangitis refers to an acute inflammatory process caused by bacterial seeding of the lymphatic vessels and was discussed in Chapter 2. Clinically, the inflamed lymphatics appear as *red, painful subcutaneous streaks,* usually associated with tender enlargement of draining lymph nodes (*acute lymphadenitis*). If bacteria are not contained within the lymph nodes, they can pass into the venous circulation and cause bacteremia or sepsis.

Primary lymphedema can occur as an isolated congenital defect (simple congenital lymphedema) or as the familial *Milroy disease* (*heredofamilial congenital lymphedema*), resulting from agenesis or hypoplasia of lymphatics. *Secondary* or *obstructive lymphedema* stems from the accumulation of interstitial fluid behind an obstructed, previously normal lymphatic; such obstruction can result from various disorders or conditions:

- Tumors involving either the lymphatic channels or the regional lymph nodes
- Surgical procedures that sever lymphatic connections (e.g., axillary lymph nodes in radical mastectomy)
- Postradiation fibrosis
- Filariasis
- Postinflammatory thrombosis and scarring

Regardless of the cause, lymphedema increases the hydrostatic pressure in the lymphatics distal to the obstruction and causes edema. Chronic edema in turn may lead to deposition of ECM and fibrosis, producing *brawny induration* or a *peau d'orange* appearance of the overlying skin. Eventually, inadequate tissue perfusion can lead to skin ulceration. Rupture of dilated lymphatics, typically following obstruction by an infiltrating tumor mass, can lead to milky accumulations of lymph in various spaces designated *chylous ascites* (abdomen), *chylothorax,* and *chylopericardium.*

TUMORS

Tumors of blood vessels and lymphatics include common and benign hemangiomas, locally aggressive neoplasms that metastasize infrequently, and rare, highly malignant angiosarcomas (Table 9–4). Primary tumors of large vessels (aorta, pulmonary artery, and vena cava) are extremely rare and are mostly sarcomas. Congenital or developmental malformations and non-neoplastic reactive vascular proliferations (e.g., *bacillary angiomatosis*) also can manifest as tumor-like lesions.

Vascular neoplasms can arise from endothelium (e.g., hemangioma, lymphangioma, angiosarcoma) or cells that support or surround blood vessels (e.g., glomus tumor). Although a benign hemangioma usually can be distinguished with ease from an anaplastic high-grade angiosarcoma, on occasion the distinction between benign and malignant can be difficult. General rules of thumb are as follows:

- Benign tumors usually contain obvious vascular channels filled with blood cells or lymph that are lined by a monolayer of normal-appearing endothelial cells.
- Malignant tumors are more cellular, show cytologic atypia, are proliferative, and usually do not form well-organized vessels; confirmation of the endothelial derivation of such proliferations may require immunohistochemical detection of endothelial cell–specific markers, such as CD31 or von Willebrand factor.

Table 9–4 Classification of Vascular Tumors and Tumor-like Conditions

Benign Neoplasms, Developmental and Acquired Conditions
Hemangioma
Capillary hemangioma
Cavernous hemangioma
Pyogenic granuloma
Lymphangioma
Simple (capillary) lymphangioma
Cavernous lymphangioma (cystic hygroma)
Glomus tumor
Vascular ectasias
Nevus flammeus
Spider telangiectasia (arterial spider)
Hereditary hemorrhagic telangiectasis (Osler-Weber-Rendu disease)
Reactive vascular proliferations
Bacillary angiomatosis
Intermediate-Grade Neoplasms
Kaposi sarcoma
Hemangioendothelioma
Malignant Neoplasms
Angiosarcoma

Because these are tumors of dysregulated endothelial cells, the possibility of controlling their growth with inhibitors of blood vessel formation (antiangiogenic factors) is being explored.

Benign Tumors and Tumor-Like Conditions

Vascular Ectasias

Ectasia is a generic term for any local dilation of a structure, while *telangiectasia* is used to describe a permanent dilation of preexisting small vessels (capillaries, venules, and arterioles, usually in the skin or mucous membranes) that forms a discrete red lesion. These lesions can be congenital or acquired and *are not true neoplasms.*

- *Nevus flammeus* (a "birthmark"), the most common form of vascular ectasia, is a light pink to deep purple flat lesion on the head or neck composed of dilated vessels. Most ultimately regress spontaneously.
- The so-called *port wine stain* is a special form of nevus flammeus. These lesions tend to grow during childhood, thicken the skin surface, and do not fade with time. Such lesions occurring in the distribution of the trigeminal nerve are associated with the *Sturge-Weber syndrome* (also called *encephalotrigeminal angiomatosis*). This uncommon congenital disorder is associated with facial port wine nevi, ipsilateral venous angiomas in the cortical leptomeninges, mental retardation, seizures, hemiplegia, and radiopacities of the skull. Thus, *a large facial telangiectasia in a child with mental deficiency may indicate the presence of additional vascular malformations.*
- *Spider telangiectasias* are non-neoplastic vascular lesions with a general shape resembling that of a spider. These lesions manifest as radial, often pulsatile arrays of dilated subcutaneous arteries or arterioles (the "legs" of

the spider) about a central core (the spider's "body") that blanch with pressure. Spider telangiectasias commonly occur on the face, neck, or upper chest and most frequently are associated with hyperestrogenic states (e.g., in pregnant women or patients with cirrhosis).

- *Hereditary hemorrhagic telangiectasia (Osler-Weber-Rendu disease)* is an autosomal dominant disorder caused by mutations in genes that encode components of the TGF-β signaling pathway in endothelial cells. The telangiectasias are malformations composed of dilated capillaries and veins that are present at birth. They are widely distributed over the skin and oral mucous membranes, as well as in the respiratory, gastrointestinal, and urinary tracts. The lesions can spontaneously rupture, causing serious epistaxis (nosebleed), gastrointestinal bleeding, or hematuria.

Hemangiomas

Hemangiomas are very common tumors composed of blood-filled vessels (Fig. 9–28). These lesions constitute 7% of all benign tumors of infancy and childhood; most are present from birth and initially increase in size, but many eventually regress spontaneously. While hemangiomas typically are localized lesions confined to the head and neck, they occasionally may be more extensive (*angiomatosis*) and can arise internally. Nearly one third of these internal lesions are found in the liver. Malignant transformation is rare. Several histologic and clinical variants have been described:

- *Capillary hemangiomas* are the most common type; these occur in the skin, subcutaneous tissues, and mucous membranes of the oral cavities and lips, as well as in the liver, spleen, and kidneys (Fig. 9–28, *A*). Histologically, they are comprised of thin-walled capillaries with scant stroma (Fig. 9–28, *B*).
- *Juvenile hemangiomas* (so-called strawberry hemangiomas) of the newborn skin are extremely common (1 in 200 births) and can be multiple. These grow rapidly for a few months but then fade by the age of 1 to 3 years, with complete regression by age 7 in the vast majority of cases.
- *Pyogenic granulomas* are capillary hemangiomas that manifest as rapidly growing red pedunculated lesions on the skin, gingival, or oral mucosa. Microscopically they resemble exuberant granulation tissue. They bleed easily and are often ulcerated (Fig. 9–28, *C*). Roughly a quarter of the lesions develop after trauma, reaching a size of 1 to 2 cm within a few weeks. Curettage and cautery usually are curative. *Pregnancy tumor* (granuloma gravidarum) is a pyogenic granuloma that occurs infrequently (1% of patients) in the gingiva of pregnant women. These lesions may spontaneously regress (especially after pregnancy) or undergo fibrosis, but occasionally require surgical excision.

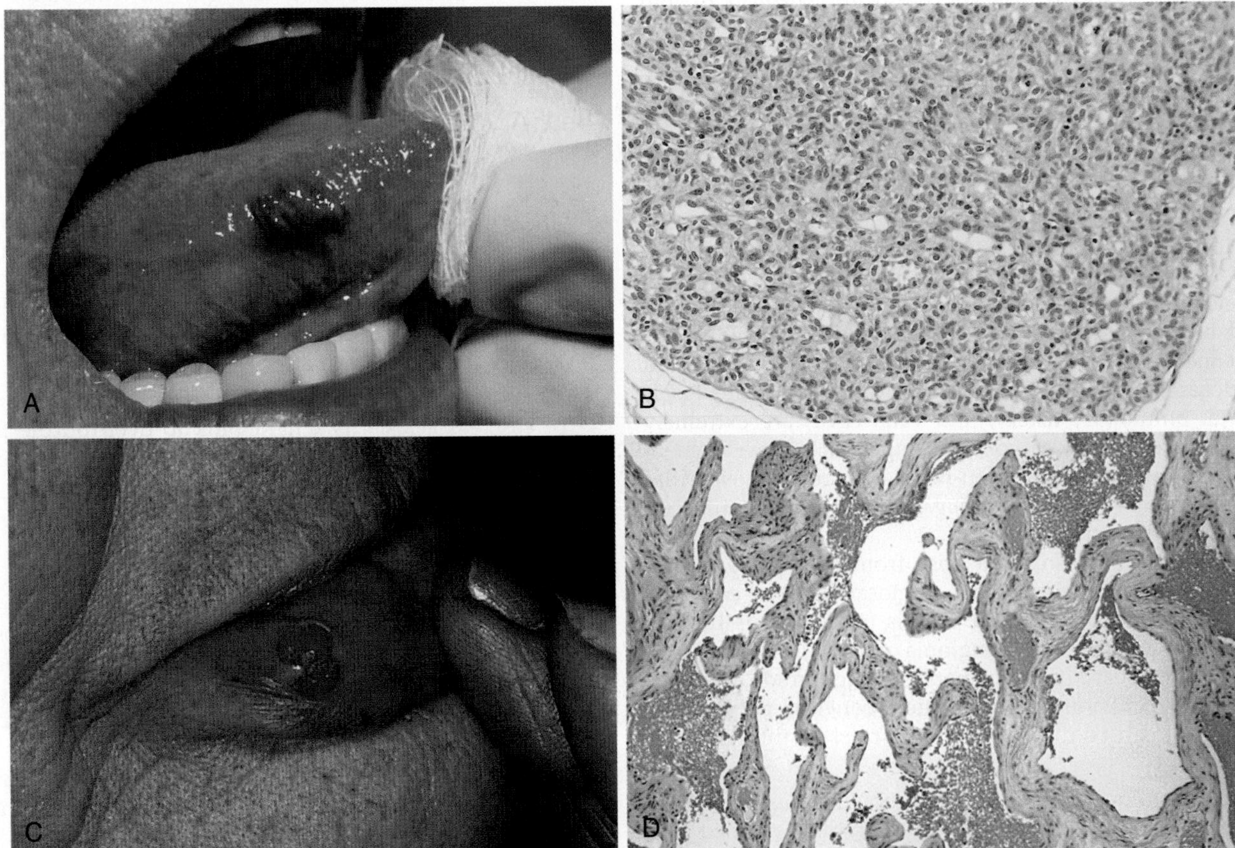

Figure 9–28 Hemangiomas. **A,** Hemangioma of the tongue. **B,** Histologic appearance in juvenile capillary hemangioma. **C,** Pyogenic granuloma of the lip. **D,** Histologic appearance in cavernous hemangioma.

(A and D, Courtesy of John Sexton, MD, Beth Israel Hospital, Boston, Massachusetts. B, Courtesy of Christopher D.M. Fletcher, MD, Brigham and Women's Hospital, Boston, Massachusetts. C, Courtesy of Thomas Rogers, MD, University of Texas Southwestern Medical School, Dallas, Texas.)

- *Cavernous hemangiomas* are composed of large, dilated vascular channels. Compared with capillary hemangiomas, *cavernous hemangiomas* are more infiltrative, frequently involve deep structures, and do not spontaneously regress. On histologic examination, the mass is sharply defined but unencapsulated and is composed of *large, cavernous blood-filled vascular spaces,* separated by connective tissue stroma (see Fig. 9–28, *D*). Intravascular thrombosis with associated dystrophic calcification is common. They may be locally destructive, so surgical excision may be required in some cases. More often the tumors are of little clinical significance, but they can be cosmetically troublesome and are vulnerable to traumatic ulceration and bleeding. Moreover, cavernous hemangiomas detected by imaging studies may be difficult to distinguish from their malignant counterparts. Brain hemangiomas also are problematic, as they can cause symptoms related to compression of adjacent tissue or rupture. Cavernous hemangiomas constitute one component of *von Hippel-Lindau disease* (Chapter 22), in which vascular lesions are commonly found in the cerebellum, brain stem, retina, pancreas, and liver.

Lymphangiomas

Lymphangiomas are the benign lymphatic counterpart of hemangiomas.

- *Simple (capillary) lymphangiomas* are slightly elevated or sometimes pedunculated lesions up to 1 to 2 cm in diameter that occur predominantly in the head, neck, and axillary subcutaneous tissues. Histologically, lymphangiomas are composed of networks of endothelium-lined spaces that can be *distinguished from capillary channels only by the absence of blood cells.*
- *Cavernous lymphangiomas (cystic hygromas)* typically are found in the neck or axilla of children, and more rarely in the retroperitoneum. Cavernous lymphangiomas can be large (up to 15 cm), filling the axilla or producing gross deformities of the neck. Of note, cavernous lymphangiomas of the neck are common in Turner syndrome. These lesions are composed of massively dilated lymphatic spaces lined by endothelial cells and separated by intervening connective tissue stroma containing lymphoid aggregates. The tumor margins are indistinct and unencapsulated, making definitive resection difficult.

Glomus Tumors (Glomangiomas)

Glomus tumors are benign, exquisitely painful tumors *arising from specialized smooth muscle cells of glomus bodies,* arteriovenous structures involved in thermoregulation. Although they may superficially resemble cavernous hemangiomas, glomangiomas arise from smooth muscle cells, rather than endothelial cells. They most commonly are found in the distal portion of the digits, especially under the fingernails. Excision is curative.

Bacillary Angiomatosis

Bacillary angiomatosis is a vascular proliferation in immunocompromised hosts (e.g., patients with AIDS) caused by opportunistic gram-negative bacilli of the *Bartonella* family. The lesions can involve the skin, bone, brain, and other organs. Two species have been implicated:

- *Bartonella henselae,* whose principal reservoir is the domestic cat; this organism causes *cat-scratch disease* (a necrotizing granulomatous disorder of lymph nodes) in immunocompetent hosts.
- *Bartonella quintana,* which is transmitted by human body lice; this microbe was the cause of "trench fever" in World War I.

Skin lesions are red papules and nodules, or rounded subcutaneous masses. Histologically, there is a proliferation of capillaries lined by prominent epithelioid endothelial cells, which exhibit nuclear atypia and mitoses (Fig. 9–29). Other features include infiltrating neutrophils, nuclear debris, and purplish granular collections of the causative bacteria.

The bacteria induce host tissues to produce hypoxia-inducible factor-1α (HIF-1α), which drives vascular endothelial growth factor (VEGF) production and vascular proliferation. The infections (and lesions) are cured by antibiotic treatment.

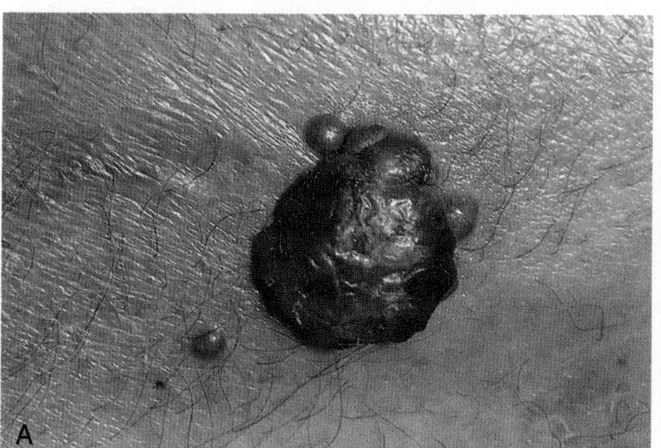

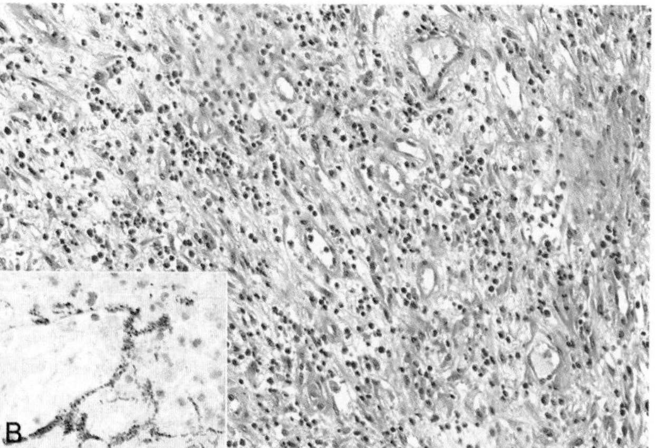

Figure 9–29 Bacillary angiomatosis. **A,** Characteristic cutaneous lesion. **B,** Histologic features are those of acute inflammation and capillary proliferation. **Inset,** Modified silver (Warthin-Starry) stain demonstrates clusters of tangled bacilli (*black*).

(A, Courtesy of Richard Johnson, MD, Beth Israel Deaconess Medical Center, Boston, Massachusetts. B and inset, courtesy of Scott Granter, MD, Brigham and Women's Hospital, Boston, Massachusetts.)

Intermediate-Grade (Borderline) Tumors

Kaposi Sarcoma

Kaposi sarcoma (KS) is a vascular neoplasm caused by Kaposi sarcoma herpesvirus (KSHV, also known as human herpesvirus-8, or HHV-8). Although it occurs in a number of contexts, *it is by far most common in patients with AIDS;* indeed, its presence is used as a criterion for the diagnosis. Four forms of KS, based on population demographics and risks, are recognized:

- *Classic KS* is a disorder of older men of Mediterranean, Middle Eastern, or Eastern European descent (especially Ashkenazic Jews); it is uncommon in the United States. It can be associated with malignancy or altered immunity but is not associated with HIV infection. Classic KS manifests as multiple red-purple skin plaques or nodules, usually on the distal lower extremities; these progressively increase in size and number and spread proximally. Although persistent, the tumors typically are asymptomatic and remain localized to the skin and subcutaneous tissue.
- *Endemic African KS* typically occurs in younger (under age 40) HIV-seronegative persons and can follow an indolent or aggressive course; it involves lymph nodes much more frequently than in the classic variant. In combination with AIDS-associated KS (see later), KS is now the most common tumor in central Africa. A particularly severe form, with prominent lymph node and visceral involvement, occurs in prepubertal children; the prognosis is poor, with an almost 100% mortality rate within 3 years.
- *Transplantation-associated KS* occurs in solid organ transplant recipients in the setting of T cell immunosuppression. The risk of KS is increased 100-fold in transplant recipients, in whom it pursues an aggressive course and often involves lymph nodes, mucosa, and viscera; cutaneous lesions may be absent. Lesions often regress with attenuation of immunosuppression, but at the risk of organ rejection.
- The incidence of KS has fallen more than 80% with the advent of antiretroviral therapy, but it continues to occur in HIV-infected persons with an incidence that is greater than 1000-fold higher than in the general population. *Worldwide, KS is the most common HIV-related malignancy.* AIDS-associated KS often involves lymph nodes and disseminates widely to viscera early in its course. Most patients eventually die of opportunistic infections rather than from KS.

PATHOGENESIS

Virtually all KS lesions are infected by KSHV. Like Epstein-Barr virus, KSHV is a γ-herpesvirus. It is transmitted both through sexual contact and by poorly understood nonsexual routes potentially including oral secretions and cutaneous exposures (of note, the prevalence of endemic African KS is inversely related to the wearing of shoes). KSHV and altered T cell immunity probably are required for KS development; in the elderly, diminished T cell immunity may be related to aging. It also is probable that acquired somatic mutations in the cells of origin contribute to tumor development and progression.

KSHV causes lytic and latent infections in endothelial cells, both of which probably are important in KS pathogenesis. A virally encoded G protein induces VEGF production, stimulating endothelial growth, and cytokines produced by inflammatory cells recruited to sites of lytic infection also create a local proliferative milieu. In latently infected cells, KSHV-encoded proteins disrupt normal cellular proliferation controls (e.g., through synthesis of a viral homologue of cyclin D) and prevent apoptosis by inhibiting p53. Thus, the local inflammatory environment favors cellular proliferation, and latently infected cells have a growth advantage. In its early stages, only a few cells are KSHV-infected, **but with time, virtually all of the proliferating cells carry the virus.**

MORPHOLOGY

In **classic KS** (and sometimes in other variants), the cutaneous lesions progress through three stages: patch, plaque, and nodule.

- **Patches** are pink, red, or purple macules, typically confined to the distal lower extremities (Fig. 9–30, *A*). Microscopic examination reveals dilated, irregular, and angulated blood vessels lined by endothelial cells and an interspersed infiltrate of chronic inflammatory cells, sometimes containing hemosiderin. These lesions can be difficult to distinguish from granulation tissue.
- With time, lesions spread proximally and become larger, violaceous, **raised plaques** (see Fig. 9–30, *A*) composed of dilated, jagged dermal vascular channels lined and surrounded by plump spindle cells. Other prominent features include extravasated erythrocytes, hemosiderin-laden macrophages, and other mononuclear cells.
- Eventually **nodular,** more overtly neoplastic, lesions appear. These are composed of plump, proliferating spindle cells, mostly located in the dermis or subcutaneous tissues (Fig. 9–30, *B*), often with interspersed slitlike spaces. The spindle cells express both endothelial cell and smooth muscle cell markers and often contain round, pink cytoplasmic globules that represent degenerating red blood cells within phagolysosomes. Hemorrhage and hemosiderin deposition is more pronounced, and mitotic figures are common. The nodular stage often is accompanied by nodal and visceral involvement, particularly in the African and AIDS-associated variants.

Clinical Features of KS

The course of disease varies widely according to the clinical setting. Most primary HHV-8 infections are asymptomatic. Classic KS is—at least initially—largely restricted to the surface of the body, and surgical resection usually is adequate for an excellent prognosis. Radiation therapy can be used for multiple lesions in a restricted area, and chemotherapy yields satisfactory results for more disseminated disease, including nodal involvement. In KS associated with immunosuppression, withdrawal of therapy (with or without adjunct chemotherapy or radiotherapy) often is effective. For AIDS-associated KS, HIV antiretroviral therapy generally is beneficial, with or without additional

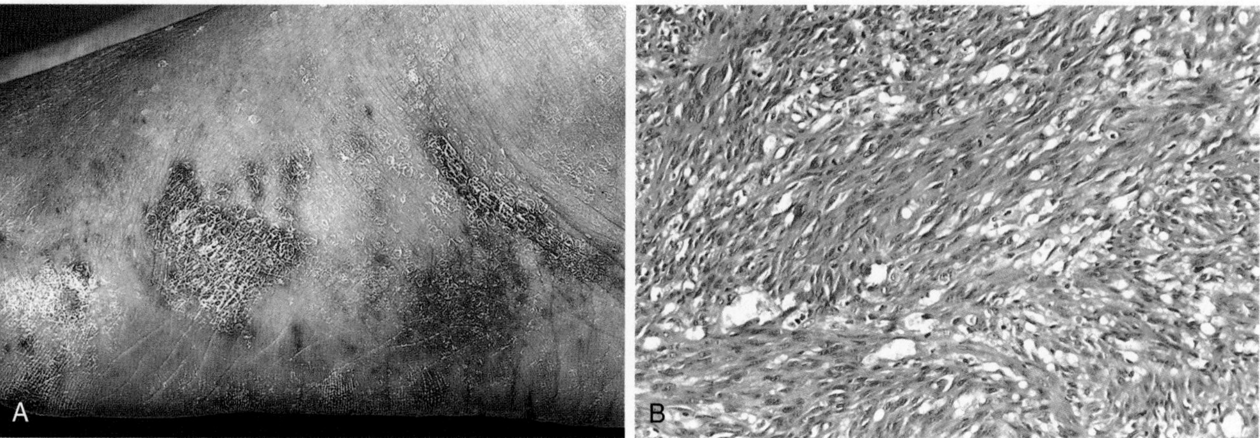

Figure 9–30 Kaposi sarcoma. **A,** Characteristic coalescent cutaneous red-purple macules and plaques. **B,** Histologic view of the nodular stage, demonstrating sheets of plump, proliferating spindle cells and slitlike vascular spaces.
(Courtesy of Christopher D.M. Fletcher, MD, Brigham and Women's Hospital, Boston, Massachusetts.)

therapy. Interferon-γ and angiogenesis inhibitors also have proved somewhat effective.

Hemangioendotheliomas

Hemangioendotheliomas comprise a wide spectrum of borderline vascular neoplasms with clinical behaviors *intermediate between those of benign, well-differentiated hemangiomas and aggressively malignant angiosarcomas.*

As an example, *epithelioid hemangioendothelioma* is a vascular tumor of adults arising in association with medium-sized to large veins. The clinical course is highly variable; while excision is curative in a majority of the cases, up to 40% of the tumors recur, and 20% to 30% eventually metastasize; perhaps 15% of patients die of their tumors. The tumor cells are plump and cuboidal and do not form well-defined vascular channels, so that they can be mistaken for metastatic epithelioid tumors or melanomas.

Malignant Tumors

Angiosarcomas

Angiosarcomas are malignant endothelial neoplasms (Fig. 9–31) that range from highly differentiated tumors resembling hemangiomas to wildly anaplastic lesions difficult to distinguish from carcinomas or melanomas. Older adults are more commonly affected. There is no gender bias, and lesions can occur at any site, but most often involve the skin, soft tissue, breast, and liver.

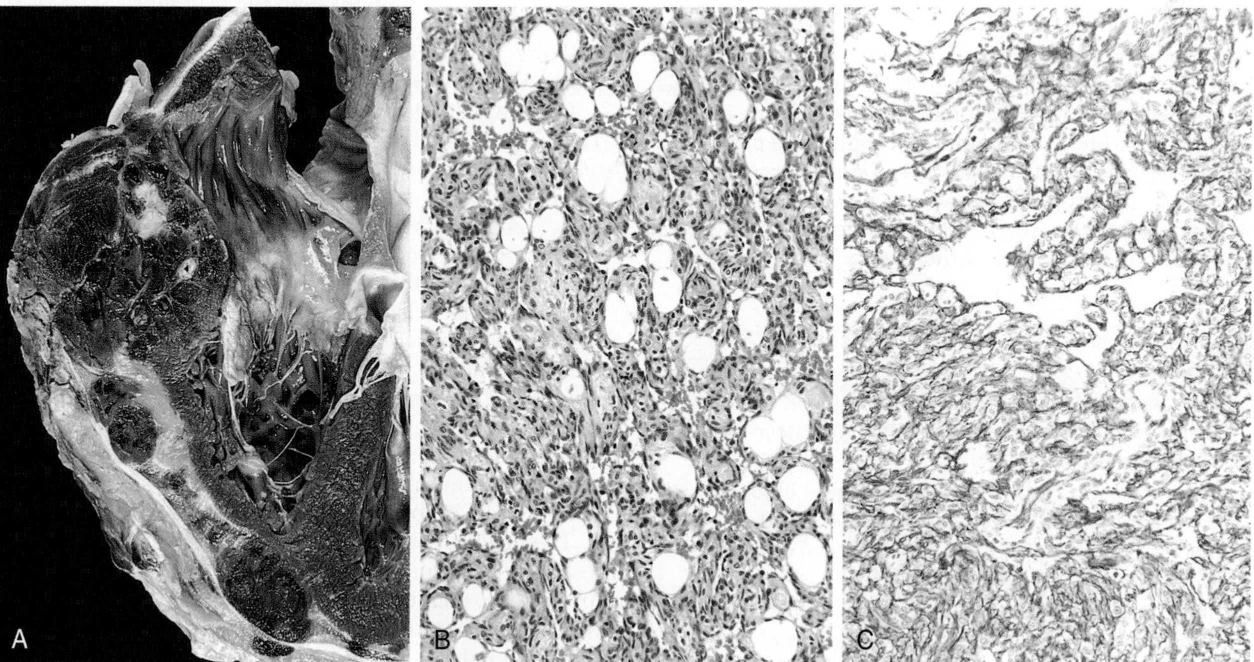

Figure 9–31 Angiosarcoma. **A,** Angiosarcoma of the right ventricle. **B,** Moderately differentiated angiosarcoma with dense clumps of atypical cells lining distinct vascular lumina. **C,** Immunohistochemical staining of angiosarcoma for the endothelial cell marker CD31.

Hepatic angiosarcomas are associated with certain carcinogens, including arsenical pesticides, Thorotrast (a radioactive contrast agent formerly used for radiologic imaging), and polyvinyl chloride (a widely used plastic, and one of the best known examples of human chemical carcinogenesis). A latent period of years between exposure and subsequent tumor development is typical.

Angiosarcomas also can arise in the setting of lymphedema, classically in the ipsilateral upper extremity several years after radical mastectomy (i.e., with lymph node resection) for breast cancer. In such instances, the tumor presumably arises from lymphatic vessels (*lymphangiosarcoma*). Angiosarcomas also can be induced by radiation and rarely are associated with long-term (years) indwelling foreign bodies (e.g., catheters).

MORPHOLOGY

In the skin, angiosarcomas begin as small, sharply demarcated, asymptomatic red nodules. More advanced lesions are large, fleshy red-tan to gray-white masses (Fig. 9–31, *A*) with margins that blend imperceptibly with surrounding structures. Necrosis and hemorrhage are common.

On microscopic examination, **the extent of differentiation is extremely variable,** ranging from plump atypical endothelial cells that form vascular channels (Fig. 9–31, *B*) to undifferentiated spindle cell tumors without discernible blood vessels. The endothelial cell origin can be demonstrated in the poorly differentiated tumors by staining for the endothelial cell markers CD31 and von Willebrand factor (Fig. 9–31, *C*).

Clinically, angiosarcomas are aggressive tumors that invade locally and metastasize. Current 5-year survival rates are only about 30%.

Hemangiopericytomas

These tumors derive their name from the cells of origin, the pericytes, myofibroblast-like cells that surround capillaries and venules. Recent studies indicate that tumors of pericytes are exceedingly rare and that most tumors previously assigned to this group have other cellular origins (e.g., fibroblasts). Accordingly, many are now placed in other diagnostic categories, such as solitary fibrous tumor, which often arises on the surface of the pleura.

SUMMARY

Vascular Tumors

- Vascular ectasias are not neoplasms, but rather dilations of existing vessels.
- Vascular neoplasms can derive from either blood vessels or lymphatics, and can be composed of endothelial cells (hemangioma, lymphangioma, angiosarcoma) or other cells of the vascular wall (e.g., glomus tumor)
- Most vascular tumors are benign (e.g., hemangiomas), some have an intermediate, locally aggressive behavior (e.g., Kaposi sarcoma), and others are highly malignant (e.g., angiosarcoma).
- Benign tumors typically form obvious vascular channels lined by normal-appearing endothelial cells. Malignant tumors more often are solid and cellular, exhibit cytologic aytpia, and lack well-defined vessels.

PATHOLOGY OF VASCULAR INTERVENTION

The morphologic changes that occur in vessels following therapeutic intervention—balloon angioplasty, stenting, or bypass surgery—recapitulate many of the changes that occur in the setting of other forms of vascular injury. Local trauma (due to stenting), vascular thrombosis (after angioplasty), and abnormal mechanical forces (e.g., a saphenous vein inserted into the arterial circulation as a coronary artery bypass graft) all induce the same stereotypical healing responses. Thus, just as with several risk factors for atherosclerosis, interventions that injure the endothelium also tend to induce intimal thickening by recruiting smooth muscle cells and promoting ECM deposition.

Endovascular Stenting

Arterial stenoses (especially those in coronary and carotid arteries) can be dilated by transiently inflating a balloon catheter to pressures sufficient to rupture the occluding plaque (*balloon angioplasty*); in doing so, a (hopefully) limited *arterial dissection* also is induced. Although most patients experience lessening of clinical signs and symptoms after angioplasty alone, *abrupt reclosure* can occur as a result of compression of the lumen by an extensive circumferential or longitudinal dissection, by vessel wall spasm, or by thrombosis. Thus, greater than 90% of endovascular coronary procedures now involve both angioplasty and concurrent *coronary stent* placement.

Coronary stents are expandable tubes of metallic mesh. They provide a larger and more regular lumen, "tack down" the intimal flaps and dissections that occur during angioplasty, and mechanically limit vascular spasm. Nevertheless, as a consequence of endothelial injury, *thrombosis* is an important immediate post-stenting complication, and patients must receive potent antithrombotic agents (primarily platelet antagonists) to prevent acute catastrophic thrombotic occlusions. The long-term success of angioplasty is limited by the development of *proliferative in-stent restenosis*. This intimal thickening is due to smooth muscle cell ingrowth, proliferation, and matrix synthesis, all driven by the initial vascular wall injury; it results in clinically significant luminal occlusion in 5% to 35% of patients within 6 to 12 months of stenting (Fig. 9–32).

The newest generation of *drug-eluting stents* is designed to avoid this complication by leaching antiproliferative drugs (e.g., paclitaxel, sirolimus) into the adjacent vessel wall to block smooth muscle cell activation. Although the duration of drug elution is short (on the order of days), use of these stents nevertheless reduces the incidence of restenosis at 1 year by 50% to 80%.

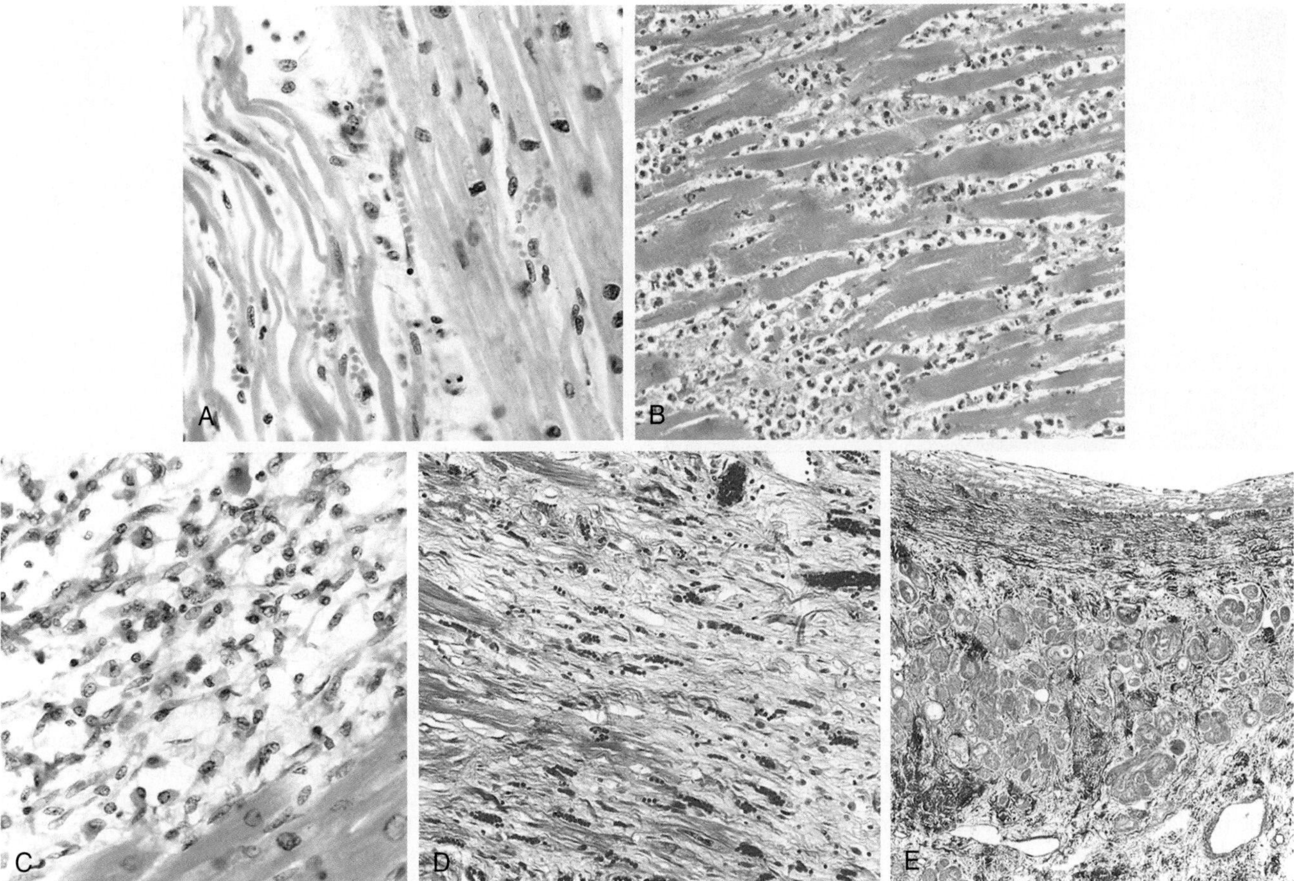

Figure 10–11 Microscopic features of myocardial infarction and its repair. **A,** One-day-old infarct showing coagulative necrosis and wavy fibers, compared with adjacent normal fibers (at *right*). Necrotic cells are separated by edema fluid. **B,** Dense neutrophilic infiltrate in the area of a 2- to 3-day-old infarct. **C,** Nearly complete removal of necrotic myocytes by phagocytic macrophages (7 to 10 days). **D,** Granulation tissue characterized by loose connective tissue and abundant capillaries. **E,** Healed myocardial infarct consisting of a dense collagenous scar. A few residual cardiac muscle cells are present. **D** and **E** are Masson's trichrome stain, which stains collagen blue.

inflammatory cells and ingrowth of new vessels from the infarct margins. Thus, an MI heals from its borders toward the center, and a large infarct may not heal as fast or as completely as a small one. Once an MI is completely healed, it is impossible to distinguish its age: Whether present for 8 weeks or 10 years, fibrous scars look the same.

Infarct Modification by Reperfusion

The therapeutic goal in acute MI is to salvage the maximal amount of ischemic myocardium; this is accomplished by restoration of tissue perfusion as quickly as possible (hence the adage "time is myocardium"). Such *reperfusion* is achieved by thrombolysis (dissolution of thrombus by tissue plasminogen activator), angioplasty, or coronary arterial bypass graft. Unfortunately, while preservation of viable (but at-risk) heart can improve both short- and long-term outcomes, reperfusion is not an unalloyed blessing. Indeed, restoration of blood flow into ischemic tissues can incite *greater* local damage than might otherwise have occurred—so-called *reperfusion injury.* The factors that contribute to reperfusion injury include: 1) Mitochondrial dysfunction: ischemia alters the mitochondrial membrane permeability, which allows proteins to move into the mitochondria. This leads to swelling and rupture of the outer membrane, releasing mitochondrial contents that promote apoptosis; 2) Myocyte hypercontracture: during periods of ischemia the intracellular levels of calcium are increased as a result of impaired calcium cycling and sarcolemmal damage. After reperfusion the contraction of myofibrils is augmented and uncontrolled, causing cytoskeletal damage and cell death; 3) Free radicals including superoxide anion (•O2), hydrogen peroxide (H_2O_2), hypochlorous acid (HOCl), nitric oxide–derived peroxynitrite, and hydroxyl radicals (•OH) are produced within minutes of reperfusion and cause damage to the myocytes by altering membrane proteins and phospholipids; 4) Leukocyte aggregation, which may occlude the microvasculature and contribute to the "no-reflow" phenomenon. Further, leukocytes elaborate proteases and elastases that cause cell death; 5) Platelet and complement activation also contribute to microvascular injury. Complement activation is thought to play a role in the no-reflow phenomenon by injuring the endothelium.

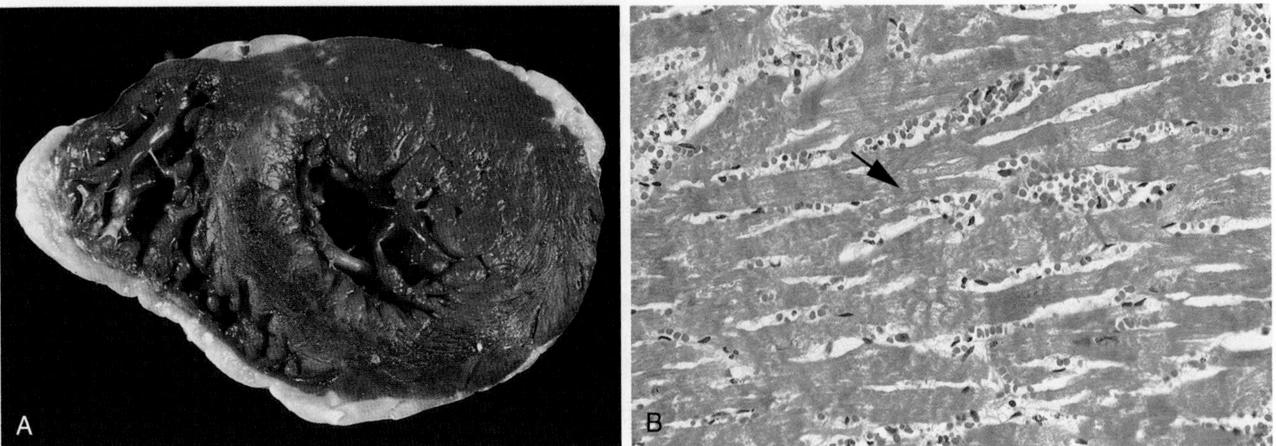

Figure 10–12 Reperfused myocardial infarction. **A,** The transverse heart slice (stained with triphenyl tetrazolium chloride) exhibits a large anterior wall myocardial infarction that is hemorrhagic because of bleeding from damaged vessels. Posterior wall is at *top*. **B,** Hemorrhage and contraction bands, visible as prominent hypereosinophilic cross-striations spanning myofibers (*arrow*), are seen microscopically.

The typical appearance of reperfused myocardium in the setting of an acute MI is shown in Figure 10–12. Such infarcts typically are hemorrhagic as a consequence of vascular injury and leakiness. Microscopically, irreversibly damaged myocytes subject to reperfusion show *contraction band necrosis;* in this pathologic process, intense eosinophilic bands of hypercontracted sarcomeres are created by an influx of calcium across plasma membranes that enhances actin-myosin interactions. In the absence of ATP, the sarcomeres cannot relax and get stuck in an agonal tetanic state. Thus, while *reperfusion can salvage reversibly injured cells, it also alters the morphology of irreversibly injured cells.*

Clinical Features

The classic MI is heralded by severe, crushing substernal chest pain (or pressure) that can radiate to the neck, jaw, epigastrium, or left arm. In contrast to angina pectoris, the associated pain typically lasts several minutes to hours, and is not relieved by nitroglycerin or rest. However, in a substantial minority of patients (10% to 15%), MIs have atypical signs and symptoms and may even be entirely asymptomatic. Such "silent" infarcts are particularly common in patients with underlying diabetes mellitus (in which autonomic neuropathies may prevent perception of pain) and in elderly persons.

The pulse generally is rapid and weak, and patients are often diaphoretic and nauseous (particularly with posterior wall MIs). Dyspnea is common, attributable to impaired myocardial contractility and dysfunction of the mitral valve apparatus, with resultant acute pulmonary congestion and edema. With massive MIs (involving more than 40% of the left ventricle), cardiogenic shock develops.

Electrocardiographic abnormalities are important for the diagnosis of MI; these include Q waves, ST segment changes, and T wave inversions (the latter two representing abnormalities in myocardial repolarization). Arrhythmias caused by electrical abnormalities in ischemic myocardium and conduction system are common; indeed, sudden cardiac death from a lethal arrhythmia accounts for the vast majority of MI-related deaths occurring before hospitalization.

The *laboratory evaluation* of MI is based on measuring blood levels of macromolecules that leak out of injured myocardial cells through damaged cell membranes (Fig. 10–13); these molecules include myoglobin, cardiac troponins T and I (TnT, TnI), creatine kinase (CK) (specifically the myocardial isoform, CK-MB), and lactate dehydrogenase. Troponins and CK-MB have high specificity and sensitivity for myocardial damage.

- CK-MB remains a valuable marker of myocardial injury, second only to the cardiac-specific troponins (see next entry). Total CK activity is not a reliable marker of cardiac injury since various isoforms of CK are also found in brain, myocardium, and skeletal muscle. However, the CK-MB isoform—principally derived

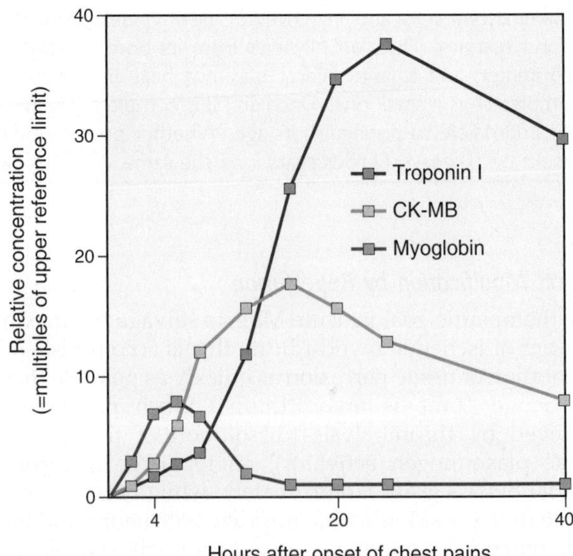

Figure 10-13 Multiple measurements of troponin I and myocardial form of creatine kinase (CK-MB) at different time points can be used to estimate the size and timing of MIs.

from myocardium, but also present at low levels in skeletal muscle—is the more specific indicator of heart damage. CK-MB activity begins to rise within 2 to 4 hours of MI, peaks at 24 to 48 hours, and returns to normal within approximately 72 hours.

- TnI and TnT normally are not found in the circulation; however, after acute MI, both are detectable within 2 to 4 hours, with levels peaking at 48 hours and remaining elevated for 7 to 10 days. Although cardiac troponin and CK-MB are equally sensitive markers of the early stages of an MI, persistence of elevated troponin levels for approximately 10 days allows the diagnosis of an acute MI long after CK-MB levels have returned to normal. With reperfusion, both troponin and CK-MB levels may peak earlier owing to more rapid washout of the enzyme from the necrotic tissue.

Consequences and Complications of Myocardial Infarction

Extraordinary progress has been made in improving patient outcomes after acute MI; the overall *in-hospital death rate* for MI is approximately 7%. Unfortunately, out-of-hospital mortality is substantially worse: A third of persons with ST elevation MIs (STEMIs) will die, usually of an arrhythmia within an hour of symptom onset, before they receive appropriate medical attention. Such statistics make the rising rate of coronary artery disease in developing countries with scarce hospital facilities all the more worrisome.

Nearly three fourths of patients experience one or more of the following complications after an acute MI (Fig. 10–14):

- *Contractile dysfunction.* In general, MIs affect left ventricular pump function in proportion to the volume of damage. In most cases, there is some degree of left ventricular failure manifested as hypotension, pulmonary congestion, and pulmonary edema. Severe "pump failure" (*cardiogenic shock*) occurs in roughly 10% of patients with transmural MIs and typically is associated with infarcts that damage 40% or more of the left ventricle.
- *Papillary muscle dysfunction.* Although papillary muscles rupture infrequently after MI, they often are dysfunctional and can be poorly contractile as a result of

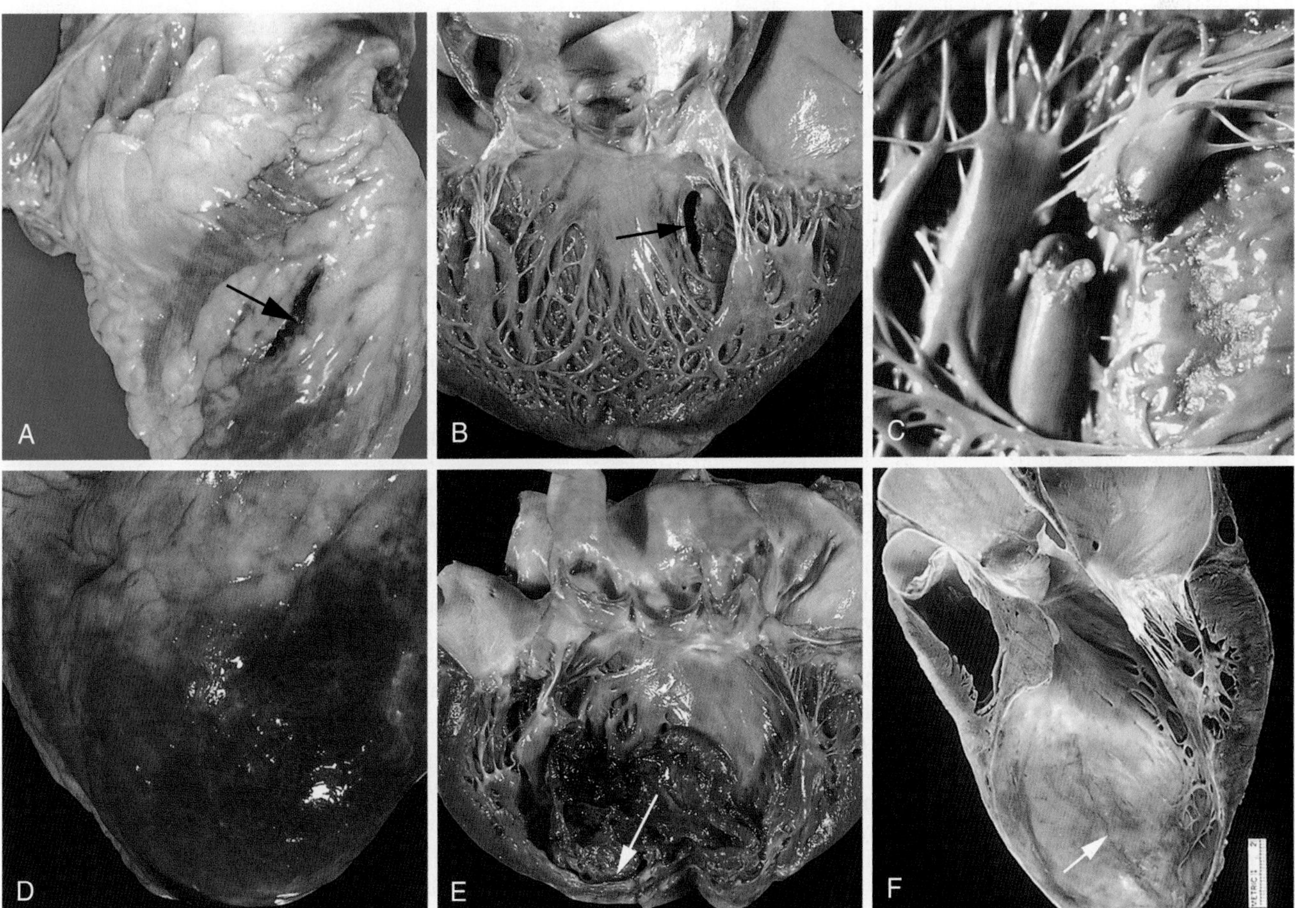

Figure 10–14 Complications of myocardial infarction. **A–C,** Cardiac rupture. **A,** Anterior free wall myocardial rupture (*arrow*). **B,** Ventricular septal rupture (*arrow*). **C,** Papillary muscle rupture. **D,** Fibrinous pericarditis, with a hemorrhagic, roughened epicardial surface overlying an acute infarct. **E,** Recent expansion of an anteroapical infarct with wall stretching and thinning (*arrow*) and mural thrombus. **F,** Large apical left ventricular aneurysm (*arrow*).

(A–E, Reproduced by permission from Schoen FJ: Interventional and Surgical Cardiovascular Pathology: Clinical Correlations and Basic Principles. Philadelphia, WB Saunders, 1989; F, Courtesy of William D. Edwards, MD, Mayo Clinic, Rochester, Minnesota.)

ischemia, leading to postinfarct mitral regurgitation. Much later, papillary muscle fibrosis and shortening or global ventricular dilation also can cause mitral valve insufficiency.

- *Right ventricular infarction.* Although isolated right ventricular infarction occurs in only 1% to 3% of MIs, the right ventricle frequently is injured in association with septal or left ventricular infarction. In either case, right-sided heart failure is a common outcome, leading to venous circulation pooling and systemic hypotension.
- *Myocardial rupture.* Rupture complicates only 1% to 5% of MIs but is frequently fatal when it occurs. Left ventricular free wall rupture is most common, usually resulting in rapidly fatal hemopericardium and cardiac tamponade (Fig. 10–14, *A*). Ventricular septal rupture creates a VSD with left-to-right shunting (Fig. 10–14, *B*), and papillary muscle rupture leads to severe mitral regurgitation (Fig. 10–14, *C*). Rupture occurs most commonly within 3 to 7 days after infarction—the time in the healing process when lysis of myocardial connective tissue is maximal and when much of the infarct has been converted to soft, friable granulation tissue. Risk factors for free wall rupture include age older than 60 years, anterior or lateral wall infarctions, female gender, lack of left ventricular hypertrophy, and first MI (as scarring associated with prior MIs tends to limit the risk of myocardial tearing).
- *Arrhythmias.* MIs lead to *myocardial irritability* and *conduction disturbances that can cause sudden death.* Approximately 90% of patients develop some form of rhythm disturbance, with the incidence being higher in STEMIs *versus* non-STEMIs. MI-associated arrhythmias include heart block of variable degree (including asystole), bradycardia, supraventricular tachyarrhythmias, ventricular premature contractions or ventricular tachycardia, and ventricular fibrillation. The risk of serious arrhythmias (e.g., ventricular fibrillation) is greatest in the first hour and declines thereafter.
- *Pericarditis.* Transmural MIs can elicit a fibrinohemorrhagic pericarditis; this is an epicardial manifestation of the underlying myocardial inflammation (Fig. 10–14, *D*). Heralded by anterior chest pain and a pericardial friction rub, pericarditis typically appears 2 to 3 days after infarction and then gradually resolves over the next few days. Extensive infarcts or severe pericardial inflammation occasionally can lead to large effusions or can organize to form dense adhesions that eventually manifest as a constrictive lesion.
- *Chamber dilation.* Because of the weakening of necrotic muscle, there may be disproportionate stretching, thinning, and dilation of the infarcted region (especially with anteroseptal infarcts).
- *Mural thrombus.* With any infarct, the combination of attenuated myocardial contractility (causing stasis) and endocardial damage (causing a thrombogenic surface) can foster *mural thrombosis* (Fig. 10–14, *E*), eventually leading to left-sided *thromboembolism.*
- *Ventricular aneurysm.* A late complication, aneurysms of the ventricle most commonly result from a large transmural anteroseptal infarct that heals with the formation of a thinned wall of scar tissue (Fig. 10–14, *F*). Although ventricular aneurysms frequently give rise to formation of mural thrombi, arrhythmias, and heart failure, they do not rupture.
- *Progressive late heart failure.* Discussed later on as "chronic IHD."

The risk of developing complications and the prognosis after MI depend on infarct size, site, and type (subendocardial versus transmural infarct). Thus, large transmural infarcts are associated with a higher probability of cardiogenic shock, arrhythmias, and late CHF, and patients with anterior transmural MIs are at greatest risk for free wall rupture, expansion, formation of mural thrombi, and aneurysm formation. By contrast, posterior transmural infarcts are more likely to be complicated by serious conduction blocks, right ventricular involvement, or both; when acute-onset VSDs occur in this area, they are more difficult to manage. Overall, patients with anterior infarcts have a much worse clinical course than those with posterior infarcts. With subendocardial infarcts, thrombi may form on the endocardial surface, but pericarditis, rupture, and aneurysms rarely occur.

In addition to the aforementioned scarring, the remaining viable myocardium attempts to compensate for the loss of contractile mass. Noninfarcted regions undergo hypertrophy and dilation; in combination with the scarring and thinning of the infarcted zones, the changes are collectively termed *ventricular remodeling.* The initial compensatory hypertrophy of noninfarcted myocardium is hemodynamically beneficial. The adaptive effect of remodeling can be overwhelmed, however, and ventricular function may decline in the setting of expansion and ventricular aneurysm formation.

Long-term prognosis after MI depends on many factors, the most important of which are left ventricular function and the severity of atherosclerotic narrowing of vessels perfusing the remaining viable myocardium. The overall mortality rate within the first year is about 30%, including deaths occurring before the patient reaches the hospital. Thereafter, the annual mortality rate is 3% to 4%.

Chronic Ischemic Heart Disease

Chronic IHD, also called *ischemic cardiomyopathy,* is essentially progressive heart failure secondary to ischemic myocardial damage. In most instances, there is a history of previous MI. In this setting, chronic IHD appears when the compensatory mechanisms (e.g., hypertrophy) of residual viable myocardium begin to fail. In other cases, severe obstructive CAD can cause diffuse myocardial dysfunction without frank infarction.

MORPHOLOGY

Patients with chronic IHD typically exhibit **left ventricular dilation and hypertrophy,** often with discrete areas of gray-white scarring from previous healed infarcts. Invariably, there is moderate to severe atherosclerosis of the coronary arteries, sometimes with total occlusion. The endocardium generally shows patchy, fibrous thickening, and mural thrombi may be present. Microscopic findings include myocardial hypertrophy, diffuse subendocardial myocyte vacuolization, and fibrosis from previous infarction.

Clinical Features

Severe, progressive heart failure characterizes chronic IHD, occasionally punctuated by new episodes of angina or infarction. Arrhythmias, CHF, and intercurrent MI account for most of the associated morbidity and mortality.

Cardiac Stem Cells

Because of the serious morbidity associated with IHD, there is much interest in exploring the possibility of using cardiac stem cells to replace the damaged myocardium. Although cardiac regeneration in metazoans (such as newts and zebrafish) is well described, the myocardium of higher-order animals is classically considered a postmitotic cell population without replicative potential. Increasing evidence, however, points to the presence of bone marrow-derived precursors—as well as a small resident stem cell population within the myocardium—capable of repopulating the mammalian heart. These cells are characterized by the expression of a cluster of cell surface markers that allow their isolation and purification. Besides self-renewal, these cardiac stem cells generate all cell lineages seen within the myocardium. Like all other tissue stem cells, they occur in very low frequency. They have a slow intrinsic rate of proliferation, which is greatest in neonates and decreases with age. Of interest, stem cell numbers and progeny increase after myocardial injury or hypertrophy, albeit to a limited extent, since hearts that suffer an MI clearly do not recover any significant function in the necrotic zone. Nevertheless, the potential for stimulating the proliferation of these cells in vivo is tantalizing because it could facilitate recovery of myocardial function after acute MI or chronic IHD. Conversely, ex vivo expansion and subsequent administration of such cells after an MI is another area of vigorous investigation. Unfortunately, results thus far have been less than exciting. Implanted stem cells may show some cardiomyocyte differentiation, but the durability of this benefit has been limited, and they do not contribute significantly to the restoration of contractile force; moreover, aberrant integration into the conducting system of the host heart carries the risk of formation of autonomous arrhythmic foci.

SUMMARY

Ischemic Heart Disease

- In the vast majority of cases, cardiac ischemia is due to coronary artery atherosclerosis; vasospasm, vasculitis, and embolism are less common causes.
- Cardiac ischemia results from a mismatch between coronary supply and myocardial demand and manifests as different, albeit overlapping syndromes:
  - *Angina pectoris* is exertional chest pain due to inadequate perfusion, and is typically due to atherosclerotic disease causing greater than 70% fixed stenosis (so-called critical stenosis).
  - *Unstable angina* results from a small fissure or rupture of atherosclerotic plaque triggering platelet aggregation, vasoconstriction, and formation of a mural thrombus that need not necessarily be occlusive.
  - *Acute myocardial infarction* typically results from acute thrombosis after plaque disruption; a majority occur in plaques that did not previously exhibit critical stenosis.
  - *Sudden cardiac death* usually results from a fatal arrhythmia, typically without significant acute myocardial damage.
  - *Ischemic cardiomyopathy* is progressive heart failure due to ischemic injury, either from previous infarction(s) or chronic ischemia.
- Myocardial ischemia leads to loss of myocyte function within 1 to 2 minutes but causes necrosis only after 20 to 40 minutes. Myocardial infarction is diagnosed on the basis of symptoms, electrocardiographic changes, and measurement of serum CK-MB and troponins. Gross and histologic changes of infarction require hours to days to develop.
- Infarction can be modified by therapeutic intervention (e.g., thrombolysis or stenting), which salvages myocardium at risk but may also induce reperfusion-related injury.
- Complications of infarction include ventricular rupture, papillary muscle rupture, aneurysm formation, mural thrombus, arrhythmia, pericarditis, and CHF.

ARRHYTHMIAS

As is well known, the heart contains specialized conduction system consisting of excitatory myocytes that regulate the rate and rhythm of cardiac contraction and are essential for normal cardiac function. This system is influenced by direct neural inputs (e.g., vagal stimulation), adrenergic agents (e.g., epinephrine [adrenaline]), hypoxia, and potassium concentrations (i.e., hyperkalemia can block signal transmission altogether). The components of the conduction system include (1) the *sinoatrial (SA) node* pacemaker (located at the junction of the right atrial appendage and superior vena cava), (2) the *atrioventricular (AV) node* (located in the right atrium along the atrial septum), (3) the *bundle of His*, connecting the right atrium to the ventricular septum, and the subsequent divisions into (4) the right and left bundle branches that stimulate their respective ventricles.

Abnormalities in myocardial conduction can be sustained or sporadic (*paroxysmal*). Aberrant rhythms can be initiated anywhere in the conduction system, from the SA node down to the level of an individual myocyte; they are typically designated as originating from the atrium (*supraventricular*) or within the ventricular myocardium. Arrhythmias can manifest as *tachycardia* (fast heart rate), *bradycardia* (slow heart rate), an irregular rhythm with normal ventricular contraction, chaotic depolarization without functional ventricular contraction (*ventricular fibrillation*), or no electrical activity at all (*asystole*). Patients may be unaware of a rhythm disorder or may note a "racing heart" or *palpitations;* loss of adequate cardiac output due to sustained arrhythmia can produce lightheadedness (near syncope), loss of consciousness (*syncope*), or *sudden cardiac death* (see further on).

Ischemic injury is the most common cause of rhythm disorders, because of direct damage or due to the dilation of heart chambers with consequent alteration in conduction system firing.

Far less common are inherited causes of arrhythmias. These are caused by mutations in genes that regulate various ion channels that regulate depolarization and repolarization of myocardial cells. Such *channelopathies* are important (but fortunately uncommon) substrates for fatal arrhythmias. They underlie some cases of sudden cardiac death, which is discussed next.

Sudden Cardiac Death

Sudden cardiac death (SCD) most commonly is defined as sudden death, typically due to sustained ventricular arrhythmias in individuals who have underlying structural heart disease which may or may not have been symptomatic in the past. Some 300,000 to 400,000 persons are victims of SCD each year in the United States alone. Coronary artery disease is the leading cause of death, being responsible for 80% to 90% of cases; unfortunately, SCD often is the first manifestation of IHD. Of interest, autopsy typically shows only chronic severe atherosclerotic disease; acute plaque disruption is found in only 10% to 20% of cases. Healed remote MIs are present in about 40% of the cases.

In younger victims of SCD, other, nonatherosclerotic causes are more common, including:

- Hereditary (channelopathies) or acquired abnormalities of the cardiac conduction system
- Congenital coronary arterial abnormalities
- Mitral valve prolapse
- Myocarditis or sarcoidosis
- Dilated or hypertrophic cardiomyopathy
- Pulmonary hypertension
- Myocardial hypertrophy. Increased cardiac mass is an independent risk factor for SCD; thus, in some young persons who die suddenly, including athletes, hypertensive hypertrophy or unexplained increased cardiac mass is the only pathologic finding.

The ultimate mechanism of SCD most often is a lethal arrhythmia (e.g., asystole or ventricular fibrillation). Of note, frank infarction need not occur; 80% to 90% of patients who suffer SCD but are successfully resuscitated do not show any enzymatic or ECG evidence of myocardial necrosis—even if the original cause was IHD! Although ischemic injury (and other pathologic conditions) can directly affect the major components of the conduction system, most cases of fatal arrhythmia are triggered by electrical irritability of myocardium distant from the conduction system.

The relationship of coronary artery disease to the various clinical end points discussed earlier is depicted in Figure 10–15.

The prognosis for patients vulnerable to SCD is markedly improved by medical intervention, particularly by implantation of automatic cardioverter-defibrillators that sense and electrically counteract episodes of ventricular fibrillation.

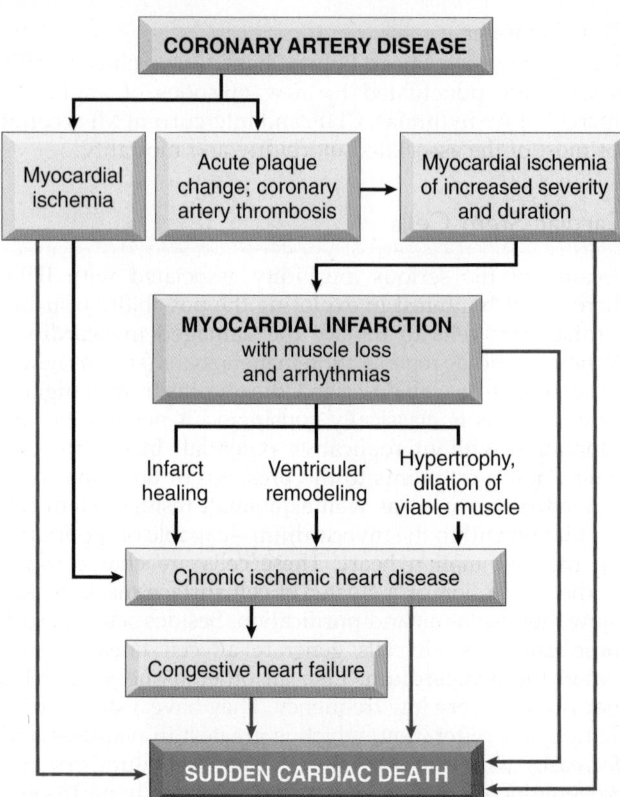

Figure 10–15 Pathways in the progression of ischemic heart disease showing the relationships among coronary artery disease and its major sequelae.

SUMMARY

Arrhythmias

- Arrhythmias can be caused by ischemic or structural changes in the conduction system or by myocyte electrical instability. In structurally normal hearts, arrhythmias more often are due to mutations in ion channels that cause aberrant repolarization or depolarization.
- SCD most frequently is due to coronary artery disease leading to ischemia. Myocardial irritability typically results from nonlethal ischemia or from preexisting fibrosis from previous myocardial injury. SCD less often is due to acute plaque rupture with thrombosis that induces a rapidly fatal arrhythmia.

HYPERTENSIVE HEART DISEASE

As discussed in Chapter 9, hypertension is a common disorder associated with considerable morbidity and affecting many organs, including the heart, brain, and kidneys. The comments here will focus specifically on the major cardiac complications of hypertension, which result from pressure overload and ventricular hypertrophy. Myocyte hypertrophy is an adaptive response to pressure overload; there are limits to myocardial adaptive capacity, however, and persistent hypertension eventually can culminate in dysfunction, cardiac dilation, CHF, and even sudden death. Although hypertensive heart disease most commonly affects the left side of the heart secondary to systemic hypertension, pulmonary hypertension also can cause right-sided hypertensive changes—so-called *cor pulmonale.*

Systemic (Left-Sided) Hypertensive Heart Disease

The criteria for the diagnosis of systemic hypertensive heart disease are (1) left ventricular hypertrophy in the absence of other cardiovascular pathology (e.g., valvular stenosis), and (2) a history or pathologic evidence of hypertension. The Framingham Heart Study established unequivocally that even mild hypertension (above 140/90 mm Hg), if sufficiently prolonged, induces left ventricular hypertrophy. Roughly 25% of the U.S. population suffers from at least this degree of hypertension.

MORPHOLOGY

As discussed earlier, systemic hypertension imposes pressure overload on the heart and is associated with gross and microscopic changes somewhat distinct from those caused by volume overload. The essential feature of systemic hypertensive heart disease is **left ventricular hypertrophy,** typically without ventricular dilation until very late in the process (Fig. 10–16, *A*). The heart weight can exceed 500 g (normal, 320 to 360 g), and the left ventricular wall thickness can exceed 2.0 cm (normal, 1.2 to 1.4 cm). With time, the increased left ventricular wall thickness imparts a stiffness that impairs diastolic filling and can result in left atrial dilation. In long-standing systemic hypertensive heart disease leading to congestive failure, the ventricle typically is dilated.

Microscopically, the transverse diameter of myocytes is increased and there is prominent nuclear enlargement and hyperchromasia ("boxcar nuclei"), as well as intercellular fibrosis.

Clinical Features

Compensated hypertensive heart disease typically is asymptomatic and is suspected only from discovery of elevated blood pressure on routine physical exams, or from ECG or echocardiographic findings of left ventricular hypertrophy. In some patients, the disease comes to attention with the onset of atrial fibrillation (secondary to left atrial enlargement) and/or CHF. The mechanisms by which hypertension leads to heart failure are incompletely understood; presumably the hypertrophic myocytes fail to contract efficiently, possibly due to structural abnormalities in newly assembled sarcomeres and because the vascular supply is inadequate to meet the demands of the increased muscle mass. Depending on the severity and duration of the condition, the underlying cause of hypertension, and the adequacy of therapeutic control, patients can (1) enjoy normal longevity and die of unrelated causes, (2) develop progressive IHD owing to the effects of hypertension in potentiating coronary atherosclerosis, (3) suffer progressive renal damage or cerebrovascular stroke, or (4) experience progressive heart failure. The risk of sudden cardiac death also is increased. Effective hypertension control can prevent or lead to the regression of cardiac hypertrophy and its attendant risks.

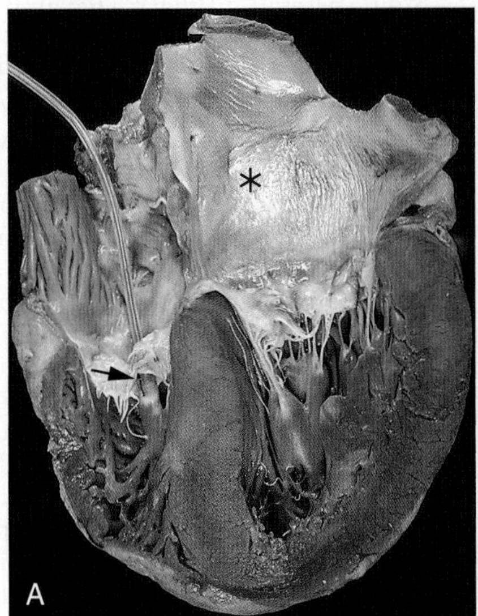

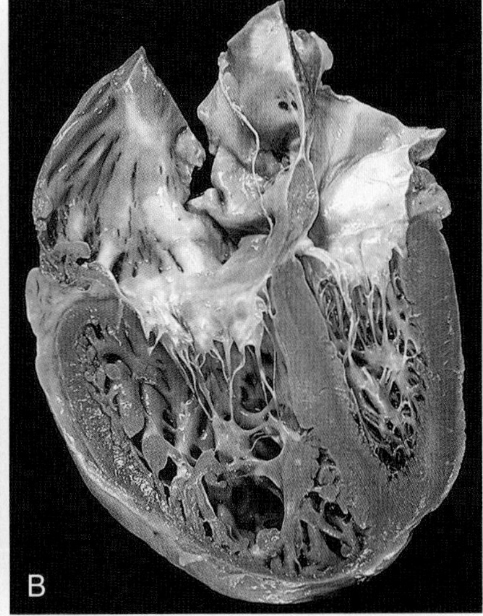

Figure 10–16 Hypertensive heart disease. **A,** Systemic (left-sided) hypertensive heart disease. There is marked concentric thickening of the left ventricular wall causing reduction in lumen size. The left ventricle and left atrium are on the right in this four-chamber view of the heart. A pacemaker is present incidentally in the right ventricle (*arrow*). Note also the left atrial dilation (*asterisk*) due to stiffening of the left ventricle and impaired diastolic relaxation, leading to atrial volume overload. **B,** Chronic cor pulmonale. The right ventricle (shown on the *left* side of this picture) is markedly dilated and hypertrophied with a thickened free wall and hypertrophied trabeculae. The shape and volume of the left ventricle have been distorted by the enlarged right ventricle.

Pulmonary Hypertensive Heart Disease—Cor Pulmonale

Cor pulmonale consists of right ventricular hypertrophy and dilation—frequently accompanied by right heart failure—caused by *pulmonary hypertension attributable to primary disorders of the lung parenchyma or pulmonary vasculature* (Table 10–4). Right ventricular dilation and hypertrophy caused by left ventricular failure (or by congenital heart disease) is substantially more common but is excluded by this definition.

Cor pulmonale can be acute in onset, as with pulmonary embolism, or can have a slow and insidious onset when due to prolonged pressure overloads in the setting of chronic lung and pulmonary vascular disease (Table 10–4).

MORPHOLOGY

In **acute cor pulmonale,** the right ventricle usually shows only dilation; if an embolism causes sudden death, the heart may even be of normal size. **Chronic cor pulmonale** is characterized by right ventricular (and often right atrial) hypertrophy. In extreme cases, the thickness of the right ventricular wall may be comparable with or even exceed that of the left ventricle (Fig. 10–16, *B*). When ventricular failure develops, the right ventricle and atrium often are dilated. Because chronic cor pulmonale occurs in the setting of pulmonary hypertension, the pulmonary arteries often contain atheromatous plaques and other lesions, reflecting long-standing pressure elevations.

Table 10–4 Disorders Predisposing to Cor Pulmonale

Diseases of the Pulmonary Parenchyma
Chronic obstructive pulmonary disease
Diffuse pulmonary interstitial fibrosis
Pneumoconiosis
Cystic fibrosis
Bronchiectasis
Diseases of the Pulmonary Vessels
Recurrent pulmonary thromboembolism
Primary pulmonary hypertension
Extensive pulmonary arteritis (e.g., Wegener granulomatosis)
Drug-, toxin-, or radiation-induced vascular obstruction
Extensive pulmonary tumor microembolism
Disorders Affecting Chest Movement
Kyphoscoliosis
Marked obesity (pickwickian syndrome)
Neuromuscular diseases
Disorders Inducing Pulmonary Arterial Constriction
Metabolic acidosis
Hypoxemia
Obstruction to major airways
Idiopathic alveolar hypoventilation

SUMMARY
Hypertensive Heart Disease

- Hypertensive heart disease can affect either the left ventricle or the right ventricle; in the latter case, the disorder is called cor pulmonale. Elevated pressures induce myocyte hypertrophy and interstitial fibrosis that increases wall thickness and stiffness.
- The chronic pressure overload of systemic hypertension causes left ventricular concentric hypertrophy, often associated with left atrial dilation due to impaired diastolic filling of the ventricle. Persistently elevated pressure overload can cause ventricular failure with dilation.
- Cor pulmonale results from pulmonary hypertension due to primary lung parenchymal or vascular disorders. Hypertrophy of both the right ventricle and the right atrium is characteristic; dilation also may be seen when failure supervenes.

VALVULAR HEART DISEASE

Valvular disease results in stenosis or insufficiency (regurgitation or incompetence), or both.

- *Stenosis is the failure of a valve to open completely, obstructing forward flow.* Valvular stenosis is almost always due to a primary cuspal abnormality and is virtually always a chronic process (e.g., calcification or valve scarring).
- *Insufficiency results from failure of a valve to close completely, thereby allowing regurgitation (backflow) of blood.* Valvular insufficiency can result from either intrinsic disease of the valve cusps (e.g., endocarditis) or disruption of the supporting structures (e.g., the aorta, mitral annulus, tendinous cords, papillary muscles, or ventricular free wall) without primary cuspal injury. It can appear abruptly, as with chordal rupture, or insidiously as a consequence of leaflet scarring and retraction.

Stenosis or regurgitation can occur alone or together in the same valve. Valvular disease can involve only one valve (the mitral valve being the most common target), or more than one valve. Abnormal flow through diseased valves typically produces abnormal heart sounds called *murmurs;* severe lesions can even be palpated as *thrills.* Depending on the valve involved, murmurs are best heard at different locations on the chest wall; moreover, the nature (regurgitation versus stenosis) and severity of the valvular disease determines the quality and timing of the murmur (e.g., harsh systolic or soft diastolic murmurs).

The outcome of valvular disease depends on the valve involved, the degree of impairment, the tempo of its development, and the effectiveness of compensatory mechanisms. For example, sudden destruction of an aortic valve cusp by infection can cause massive regurgitation and the abrupt onset of cardiac failure. By contrast, rheumatic mitral stenosis usually progresses over years, and its clinical effects can be well tolerated until late in the course.

Valvular abnormalities can be congenital or acquired. By far the most common congenital valvular lesion is a *bicuspid aortic valve,* containing only two functional cusps instead of the normal three; this malformation occurs with a frequency of 1% to 2% of all live births, and has been associated with a number of mutations including those affecting proteins of the Notch signaling pathway. The two cusps are of unequal size, with the larger cusp exhibiting a midline *raphe* resulting from incomplete cuspal separation (Fig. 10–17, *B*). Bicuspid aortic valves are generally neither stenotic nor incompetent through early life; however, they are more prone to early and progressive degenerative calcification (see further on).

The most important causes of acquired valvular diseases are summarized in Table 10–5; acquired stenoses of the aortic and mitral valves account for approximately two thirds of all valve disease.

Table 10–5 Etiology of Acquired Heart Valve Disease

Mitral Valve Disease	Aortic Valve Disease
Mitral Stenosis	**Aortic Stenosis**
Postinflammatory scarring (rheumatic heart disease)	Postinflammatory scarring (rheumatic heart disease) Senile calcific aortic stenosis Calcification of congenitally deformed valve
Mitral Regurgitation	**Aortic Regurgitation**
Abnormalities of leaflets and commissures Postinflammatory scarring Infective endocarditis Mitral valve prolapse "Fen-phen"–induced valvular fibrosis Abnormalities of tensor apparatus Rupture of papillary muscle Papillary muscle dysfunction (fibrosis) Rupture of chordae tendineae Abnormalities of left ventricular cavity and/or annulus Left ventricular enlargement (myocarditis, dilated cardiomyopathy) Calcification of mitral ring	Intrinsic valvular disease Postinflammatory scarring (rheumatic heart disease) Infective endocarditis Aortic disease Degenerative aortic dilation Syphilitic aortitis Ankylosing spondylitis Rheumatoid arthritis Marfan syndrome

Fen-phen, fenfluramine-phentermine. Data from Schoen FJ: Surgical pathology of removed natural and prosthetic valves. Hum Pathol 18:558, 1987.

Degenerative Valve Disease

Degenerative valve disease is a term used to describe changes that affect the integrity of valvular extracellular matrix (ECM). Degenerative changes include

- *Calcifications,* which can be cuspal (typically in the aortic valve) (Fig. 11–17, *A* and *B*) or annular (in the mitral valve) (Fig. 11–17, *C* and *D*). The mitral annular calcification usually is asymptomatic unless it encroaches on the adjacent conduction system.
- *Decreased numbers of valve fibroblasts and myofibroblasts*
- *Alterations in the ECM.* In some cases, changes consist of increased proteoglycan and diminished fibrillar collagen and elastin (*myxomatous degeneration*); in other cases, the valve becomes fibrotic and scarred.
- *Changes in the production of matrix metalloproteinases or their inhibitors*

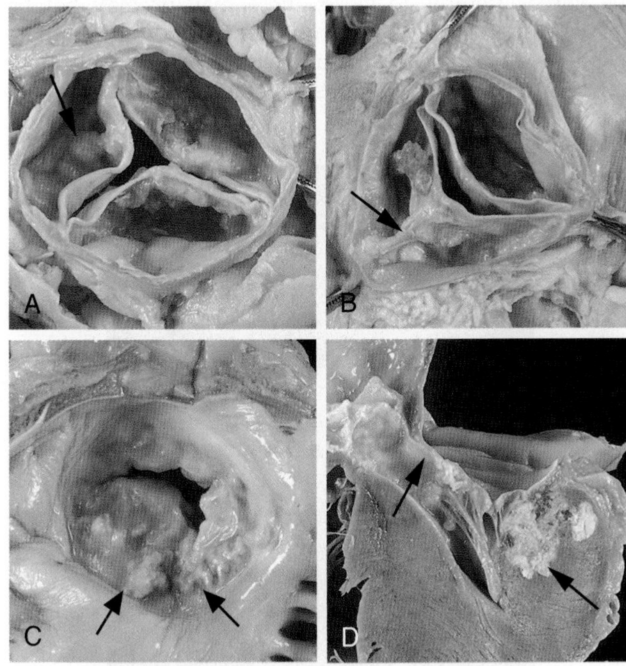

Figure 10–17 Calcific valvular degeneration. **A,** Calcific aortic stenosis of a previously normal valve (viewed from *above* the valve). Nodular masses of calcium are heaped up within the sinuses of Valsalva (*arrow*). Note that the commissures are not fused, as in rheumatic aortic valve stenosis (Fig. 10–19, *C*). **B,** Calcific aortic stenosis occurring on a congenitally bicuspid valve. One cusp has a partial fusion at its center, called a *raphe* (*arrow*). **C** and **D,** Mitral annular calcification, with calcific nodules within the annulus (attachment margin) of the mitral leaflets (*arrows*). **C,** Left atrial view. **D,** Cut section demonstrating the extension of the calcification into the underlying myocardium. Such involvement of adjacent structures near the interventricular septum can impinge on the conduction system.

Degenerative changes in the cardiac valves probably are an inevitable part of the aging process, because of the repetitive mechanical stresses to which valves are subjected—40 million beats per year, with each normal opening and closing requiring substantial valve deformation.

Calcific Aortic Stenosis

Calcific aortic degeneration is the most common cause of aortic stenosis. Although progressive age-associated "wear and tear" has been the pathologic mechanism most often proposed, cuspal fibrosis and calcification are increasingly viewed as the valvular counterparts to age-related arteriosclerosis. Thus, chronic injury due to hyperlipidemia, hypertension, inflammation, and other factors implicated in atherosclerosis probably play a significant role in the pathogenesis. In most cases, calcific degeneration is asymptomatic and is discovered only incidentally by viewing calcifications on a routine chest radiograph or at autopsy. In other patients, valvular sclerosis and/or calcification can be severe enough to cause stenosis, necessitating surgical intervention.

The incidence of calcific aortic stenosis is increasing with the rising average age for the U.S. population. In anatomically normal valves, it typically begins to manifest when patients reach their 70s and 80s; onset with bicuspid aortic valves is at a much earlier age (often 40 to 50 years).

MORPHOLOGY

The hallmark of calcific aortic stenosis is heaped-up calcified masses on the outflow side of the cusps; these protrude into the sinuses of Valsalva and mechanically impede valve opening (Fig. 10–17, *A* and *B*); commissural fusion (usually a sign of previous inflammation) is not a typical feature of degenerative aortic stenosis, although the cusps may become secondarily fibrosed and thickened. An earlier, hemodynamically inconsequential stage of the calcification process is called aortic valve sclerosis.

Clinical Features

In severe disease, valve orifices can be compromised by as much as 70% to 80% (from a normal area of approximately 4 cm^2 to as little as 0.5 to 1 cm^2). Cardiac output is maintained only by virtue of concentric left ventricular hypertrophy, and the chronic outflow obstruction can drive left ventricular pressures to 200 mm Hg or more. The hypertrophied myocardium is prone to ischemia, and angina can develop. Systolic and diastolic dysfunction collude to cause CHF, and cardiac decompensation eventually ensues. The development of angina, CHF, or syncope in aortic stenosis heralds the exhaustion of compensatory cardiac hyperfunction and carries a poor prognosis; without surgical intervention, 50% to 80% of patients die within 2 to 3 years of the onset of symptoms like CHF, angina, and syncope.

Myxomatous Mitral Valve

In *myxomatous degeneration of the mitral valve,* one or both mitral leaflets are "floppy" and *prolapse*—they balloon back into the left atrium during systole. *Mitral valve prolapse* is a primary form of myxomatous mitral degeneration affecting some 0.5% to 2.4% of adults; thus, it is one of the most common forms of valvular heart disease in the Western world. Men and women are equally affected. Secondary myxomatous mitral degeneration can occur in any one of a number of settings where mitral regurgitation is caused by some other entity (e.g., IHD).

PATHOGENESIS

The basis for **primary** myxomatous degeneration is unknown. Nevertheless, an underlying (possibly systemic) intrinsic defect of connective tissue synthesis or remodeling is likely. Thus, myxomatous degeneration of the mitral valve is a common feature of Marfan syndrome (due to fibrillin-1 mutations) (Chapter 6), and occasionally occurs in other connective tissue disorders. In some patients with primary disease, additional hints of structural abnormalities in the systemic connective tissue, including scoliosis and high-arched palate, may be found. Subtle defects in structural proteins (or the cells that make them) may cause hemodynamically stressed connective tissues rich in microfibrils and elastin (e.g., cardiac valves) to elaborate defective ECM. **Secondary** myxomatous change presumably results from injury to the valve myofibroblasts, imposed by chronically aberrant hemodynamic forces.

MORPHOLOGY

Myxomatous degeneration of the mitral valve is characterized by ballooning (hooding) of the mitral leaflets (Fig. 10–18). The affected leaflets are enlarged, redundant, thick, and rubbery; the tendinous cords also tend to be elongated, thinned, and occasionally rupture. In those with primary mitral desease, concomitant tricuspid valve involvement is frequent (20% to 40% of cases); less commonly aortic and pulmonic valves can also be affected. On histologic examination, the essential change is thinning of the valve layer known as the **fibrosa** layer of the valve, on which the structural integrity of the leaflet depends, accompanied by expansion of the middle **spongiosa** layer owing to increased deposition of myxomatous (mucoid) material. The same changes occur whether the myxomatous degeneration is due to an intrinsic ECM defect (primary), or is caused by regurgitation secondary to another etiologic process (e.g., ischemic dysfunction).

Clinical Features

Most patients are asymptomatic, and the valvular abnormality is discovered only incidentally on physical examination. In a minority of cases, patients may complain of palpitations, dyspnea, or atypical chest pain. Auscultation discloses a midsystolic click, caused by abrupt tension on the redundant valve leaflets and chordae tendineae as the valve attempts to close; there may or may not be an associated regurgitant murmur. Although in most instances the natural history and clinical course are benign, approximately 3% of patients develop complications such

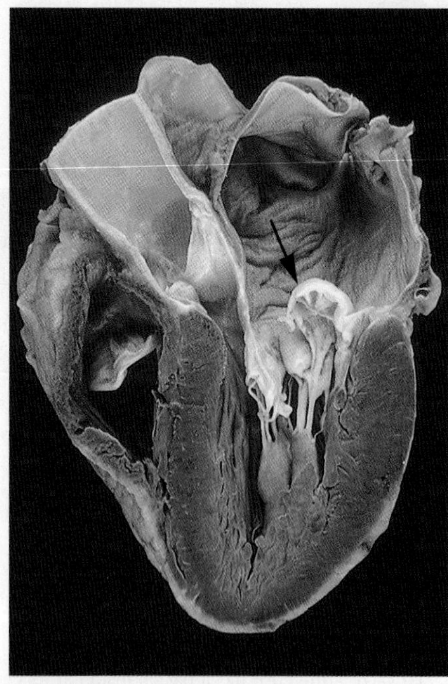

Figure 10–18 Myxomatous degeneration of the mitral valve. There is prominent hooding with prolapse of the posterior mitral leaflet (*arrow*) into the left atrium; the atrium also is dilated, reflecting long-standing valvular insufficiency and volume overload. The left ventricle is on the *right* in this four-chamber view.

(Courtesy of William D. Edwards, MD, Mayo Clinic, Rochester, Minnesota.)

as hemodynamically significant mitral regurgitation and congestive heart failure, particularly if the chordae or valve leaflets rupture. Patients with primary myxomatous degeneration also are at increased risk for the development of infective endocarditis (see later), as well as sudden cardiac death due to ventricular arrhythmias. Stroke or other systemic infarction may rarely occur from embolism of thrombi formed in the left atrium.

Rheumatic Valvular Disease

Rheumatic fever is an acute, immunologically mediated, multisystem inflammatory disease that occurs after group A β-hemolytic streptococcal infections (usually pharyngitis, but also rarely with infections at other sites such as skin). Rheumatic heart disease is the cardiac manifestation of rheumatic fever. *It is associated with inflammation of all parts of the heart, but valvular inflammation and scarring produces the most important clinical features.*

The valvular disease principally takes the form of deforming fibrotic mitral stenosis; indeed rheumatic heart disease is essentially the *only* cause of acquired mitral stenosis. The incidence of rheumatic fever (and thus rheumatic heart disease) has declined remarkably in many parts of the Western world over the past several decades; this is due to a combination of improved socioeconomic conditions, rapid diagnosis and treatment of streptococcal pharyngitis, and a fortuitous (and unexplained) decline in the virulence of many strains of group A streptococci. Nevertheless, in developing countries and economically depressed urban areas in the United States, rheumatic fever and rheumatic heart disease remain important public health problems.

PATHOGENESIS

Acute rheumatic fever is a hypersensitivity reaction classically attributed to antibodies directed against group A streptococcal molecules that also are cross-reactive with host antigens (see also Chapter 4). In particular, antibodies against M proteins of certain streptococcal strains bind to proteins in the myocardium and cardiac valves and cause injury through the activation of complement and Fc receptor–bearing cells (including macrophages). CD4+ T cells that recognize streptococcal peptides also can cross-react with host antigens and elicit cytokine-mediated inflammatory responses. The characteristic 2- to 3-week delay in symptom onset after infection is explained by the time needed to generate an immune response; streptococci are completely absent from the lesions. Since only a small minority of infected patients develop rheumatic fever (estimated at 3%), a genetic susceptibility is likely to influence the development of the cross-reactive immune responses. The chronic fibrotic lesions are the predictable consequence of healing and scarring associated with the resolution of the acute inflammation.

MORPHOLOGY

Acute rheumatic fever is characterized by discrete inflammatory foci within a variety of tissues. The myocardial inflammatory lesions—called **Aschoff bodies**—are pathognomonic for rheumatic fever (Fig. 10–19, *B*); these are collections of lymphocytes (primarily T cells), scattered plasma cells, and plump activated macrophages called **Anitschkow cells** occasionally punctuating zones of fibrinoid necrosis. The Anitschkow cells have abundant cytoplasm and central nuclei with chromatin condensed to form a slender, wavy ribbon (so-called caterpillar cells). During acute rheumatic fever, Aschoff bodies can be found in any of the three layers of the heart—pericardium, myocardium, or endocardium (including valves). Hence, rheumatic fever is said to cause **pancarditis,** with the following salient features:

- The pericardium exhibits a fibrinous exudate, which generally resolves without sequelae.
- The myocardial involvement—myocarditis—takes the form of scattered Aschoff bodies within the interstitial connective tissue.
- Valve involvement results in fibrinoid necrosis and fibrin deposition along the lines of closure (Fig. 10–19, *A*) forming 1- to 2-mm vegetations—**verrucae**—that cause little disturbance in cardiac function.

Chronic rheumatic heart disease is characterized by organization of the acute inflammation and subsequent scarring. Aschoff bodies are replaced by fibrous scar so that these lesions are rarely seen in chronic rheumatic heart disease. Most characteristically, valve cusps and leaflets become permanently thickened and retracted. Classically, the mitral valves exhibit **leaflet thickening, commissural fusion and shortening, and thickening and fusion of the chordae tendineae** (Fig. 10–19, *C-E*). Fibrous bridging across the valvular commissures and calcification create "fish-mouth" or "buttonhole" stenoses (Fig. 10–19, *C*). Microscopic examination shows neovascularization (grossly evident in Fig. 10–19, *D*) and diffuse fibrosis that obliterates the normal leaflet architecture.

The most important functional consequence of rheumatic heart disease is **valvular stenosis and regurgitation**; stenosis tends to predominate. The mitral valve alone is involved in 70% of cases, with combined mitral and aortic disease in another 25%; the tricuspid valve usually is less frequently (and less severely) involved; and the pulmonic valve almost always escapes injury. With tight mitral stenosis, the left atrium progressively dilates owing to pressure overload, precipitating atrial fibrillation. The combination of dilation and fibrillation is a fertile substrate for thrombosis, and formation of large mural thrombi is common. Long-standing passive venous congestion gives rise to pulmonary vascular and parenchymal changes typical of left-sided heart failure. In time, this leads to right ventricular hypertrophy and failure. With pure mitral stenosis, the left ventricle generally is normal.

Clinical Features

Acute rheumatic fever occurs most often in children; the principal clinical manifestation is carditis. Nevertheless, about 20% of first attacks occur in adults, with arthritis being the predominant feature. Symptoms in all age groups typically begin 2 to 3 weeks after streptococcal infection, and are heralded by fever and migratory polyarthritis—one large joint after another becomes painful and swollen for a period of days, followed by spontaneous resolution with no residual disability. Although cultures are negative for streptococci at the time of symptom onset, serum titers

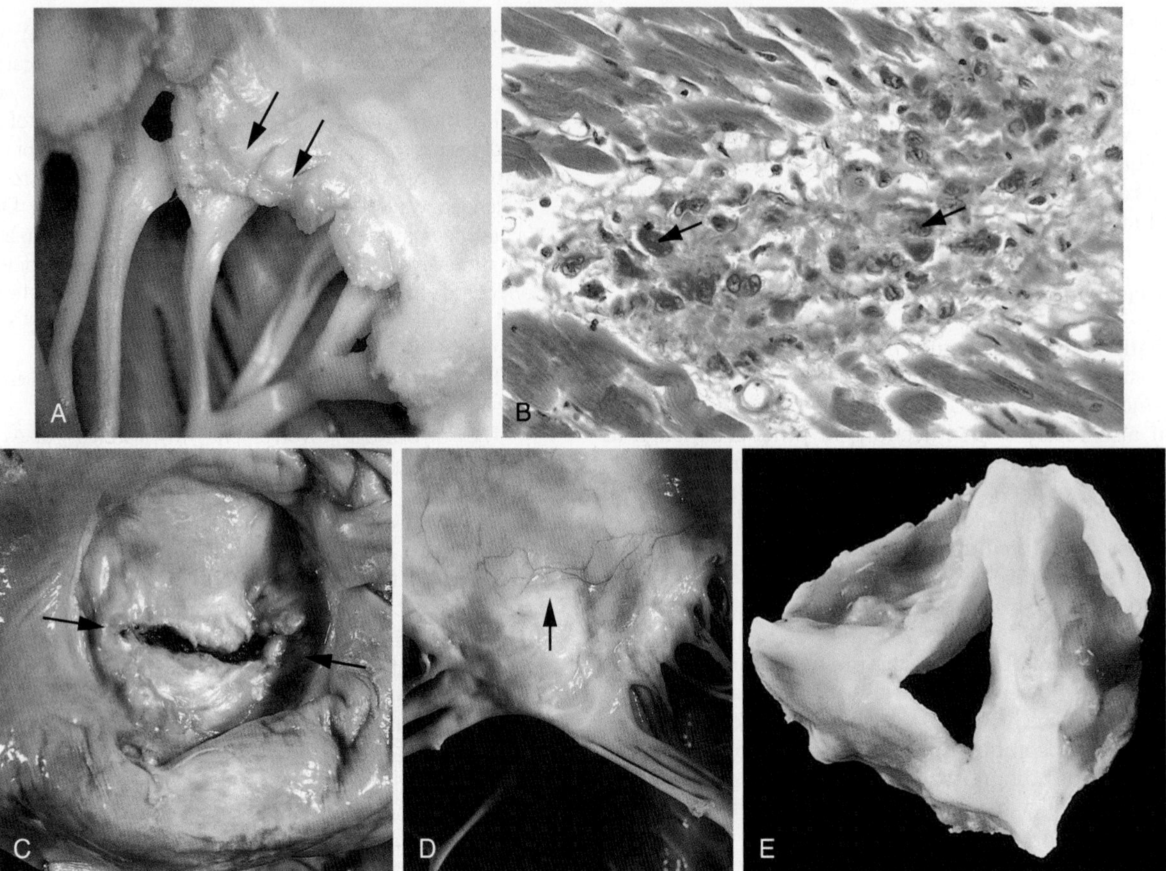

Figure 10–19 Acute and chronic rheumatic heart disease. **A,** Acute rheumatic mitral valvulitis superimposed on chronic rheumatic heart disease. Small vegetations (verrucae) are visible along the line of closure of the mitral valve leaflet (*arrows*). Previous episodes of rheumatic valvulitis have caused fibrous thickening and fusion of the chordae tendineae. **B,** Microscopic appearance of an Aschoff body in acute rheumatic carditis; there is central necrosis associated with a circumscribed collection of mononuclear inflammatory cells, including some activated macrophages with prominent nucleoli and central wavy (caterpillar) chromatin (*arrows*). **C** and **D,** Mitral stenosis with diffuse fibrous thickening and distortion of the valve leaflets, commissural fusion (*arrows*), and thickening and shortening of the chordae tendineae. There is marked left atrial dilation as seen from above the valve (**C**). **D,** Anterior leaflet of an opened rheumatic mitral valve; note the inflammatory neovascularization (*arrow*). **E,** Surgically removed specimen of rheumatic aortic stenosis, demonstrating thickening and distortion of the cusps with commissural fusion.

(E, From Schoen FJ, St John-Sutton M: Contemporary issues in the pathology of valvular heart disease. Hum Pathol 18:568, 1967.)

to one or more streptococcal antigens (e.g., streptolysin O or DNAase) usually are elevated. The clinical signs of carditis include pericardial friction rubs and arrhythmias; myocarditis can be sufficiently aggressive that cardiac dilation ensues, causing functional mitral insufficiency and CHF. Nevertheless, less than 1% of patients die of acute rheumatic fever.

The diagnosis of acute rheumatic fever is made based on serologic evidence of previous streptococcal infection in conjunction with two or more of the so-called *Jones criteria*: (1) carditis; (2) migratory polyarthritis of large joints; (3) subcutaneous nodules; (4) erythema marginatum skin rashes; and (5) Sydenham chorea, a neurologic disorder characterized by involuntary purposeless, rapid movements (also called *St. Vitus dance*). Minor criteria such as fever, arthralgias, ECG changes, or elevated acute phase reactants also can help support the diagnosis.

After an initial attack and the generation of immunologic memory, patients are increasingly vulnerable to disease reactivation with subsequent streptococcal infections. Carditis is likely to worsen with each recurrence, and the damage is cumulative. However, *chronic rheumatic carditis* usually does not manifest itself clinically until years or even decades after the initial episode of rheumatic fever. At that time, the signs and symptoms of valvular disease depend on which cardiac valve(s) are involved. In addition to various cardiac murmurs, cardiac hypertrophy and dilation, and CHF, patients with chronic rheumatic heart disease often have arrhythmias (particularly atrial fibrillation in the setting of mitral stenosis), and thromboembolic complications due to atrial mural thrombi. In addition, scarred and deformed valves are more susceptible to infective endocarditis. The long-term prognosis is highly variable. In some cases, a relentless cycle of valvular deformity ensues, yielding hemodynamic abnormality, which begets further deforming fibrosis. Surgical repair or replacement of diseased valves has greatly improved the outlook for patients with rheumatic heart disease.

Infective Endocarditis

Infective endocarditis is a serious infection mandating prompt diagnosis and intervention. Microbial invasion of heart valves or mural endocardium—often with destruction of the underlying cardiac tissues—characteristically results in bulky, friable *vegetations* composed of necrotic debris, thrombus, and organisms. The aorta, aneurysmal sacs, other blood vessels and prosthetic devices also can become infected. Although fungi, rickettsiae (agents of Q fever), and chlamydial species can cause endocarditis, the vast majority of cases are caused by extracellular bacteria.

Infective endocarditis can be classified into *acute* and *subacute* forms, based on the tempo and severity of the clinical course; the distinctions are attributable to the virulence of the responsible microbe and whether underlying cardiac disease is present. Of note, a clear delineation between acute and subacute endocarditis does not always exist, and many cases fall somewhere along the spectrum between the two forms.

- *Acute endocarditis* refers to tumultuous, destructive infections, frequently involving a highly virulent organism attacking a previously normal valve, and capable of causing substantial morbidity and mortality even with appropriate antibiotic therapy and/or surgery.
- *Subacute endocarditis* refers to infections by organisms of low virulence involving a previously abnormal heart, especially scarred or deformed valves. The disease typically appears insidiously and—even untreated—follows a protracted course of weeks to months; most patients recover after appropriate antibiotic therapy.

PATHOGENESIS

Infective endocarditis can develop on previously normal valves, but cardiac abnormalities predispose to such infections; rheumatic heart disease, mitral valve prolapse, bicuspid aortic valves, and calcific valvular stenosis are all common substrates. Prosthetic heart valves (discussed later) now account for 10% to 20% of all cases of infective endocarditis. Sterile platelet-fibrin deposits at sites of pacemaker lines, indwelling vascular catheters, or damaged endocardium due to jet streams caused by preexisting cardiac disease all can be foci for bacterial seeding with subsequent development of endocarditis. Host factors such as neutropenia, immunodeficiency, malignancy, diabetes mellitus, and alcohol or intravenous drug abuse also increase the risk of infective endocarditis, as well as adversely affecting outcomes.

The causative organisms differ depending on the underlying risk factors. Fifty percent to 60% of cases of endocarditis occurring on damaged or deformed valves are caused by *Streptococcus viridans*, a relatively banal group of normal oral flora. By contrast, the more virulent *S. aureus* (common to skin) can attack deformed **as well as healthy** valves and is responsible for 10% to 20% of cases overall; it also is the major offender in infections occurring in intravenous drug abusers. Additional bacterial agents include enterococci and the so-called HACEK group (*Haemophilus, Actinobacillus, Cardiobacterium, Eikenella,* and *Kingella*), all commensals in the oral cavity. More rarely, gram-negative bacilli and fungi are involved. In about 10% of all cases of endocarditis, no organism is isolated from the blood ("culture-negative" endocarditis) because of previous antibiotic therapy, difficulties in isolating the offending agent, or because deeply embedded organisms within the enlarging vegetation are not released into the blood.

Foremost among the factors predisposing to endocarditis is seeding of the blood with microbes. The mechanism or portal of entry of the agent into the bloodstream may be an obvious infection elsewhere, a dental or surgical procedure that causes a transient bacteremia, injection of contaminated material directly into the bloodstream by intravenous drug users, or an occult source from the gut, oral cavity, or trivial injuries. Recognition of predisposing anatomic substrates and clinical conditions causing bacteremia allows appropriate antibiotic prophylaxis.

MORPHOLOGY

In both acute and subacute forms of the disease, **friable, bulky, and potentially destructive vegetations** containing fibrin, inflammatory cells, and microorganisms are present on the heart valves (Figs. 10–20 and 10–21). The aortic and mitral valves are the most common sites of infection, although the tricuspid valve is a frequent target in the setting of intravenous drug abuse. Vegetations may be single or multiple and may involve more than one valve; they can sometimes erode into the underlying myocardium to produce an abscess cavity **(ring abscess)** (Fig. 10-21, *B*). Shedding of **emboli** is common because of the friable nature of the vegetations. Since the fragmented vegetations contain large numbers of organisms, abscesses often develop at the sites where emboli lodge, leading to development of **septic infarcts** and **mycotic aneurysms.**

Subacute endocarditis typically elicits less valvular destruction than that associated with acute endocarditis. On microscopic examination, the subacute vegetations of infective endocarditis often have granulation tissue at their bases (suggesting chronicity), promoting development of chronic inflammatory infiltrates, fibrosis, and calcification over time.

Clinical Features

Fever is the most consistent sign of infective endocarditis. However, in subacute disease (particularly in the elderly), fever may be absent, and the only manifestations may be nonspecific fatigue, weight loss, and a flulike syndrome; splenomegaly also is common in subacute cases. By contrast, acute endocarditis often manifests with a stormy onset including rapidly developing fever, chills, weakness, and lassitude. Murmurs are present in 90% of patients with left-sided lesions; microemboli can give rise to petechia, nail bed (*splinter*) hemorrhages, retinal hemorrhages (*Roth spots*), painless palm or sole erythematous lesions (*Janeway lesions*), or painful fingertip nodules (*Osler nodes*); diagnosis is confirmed by positive blood cultures and echocardiographic findings.

Prognosis depends on the infecting organism and on whether or not complications develop. Complications generally begin within the first weeks after onset of the infectious process and can include glomerulonephritis due to glomerular trapping of antigen-antibody complexes, with hematuria, albuminuria, or renal failure (Chapter 13). A septic pathophysiologic picture, arrhythmias (suggesting

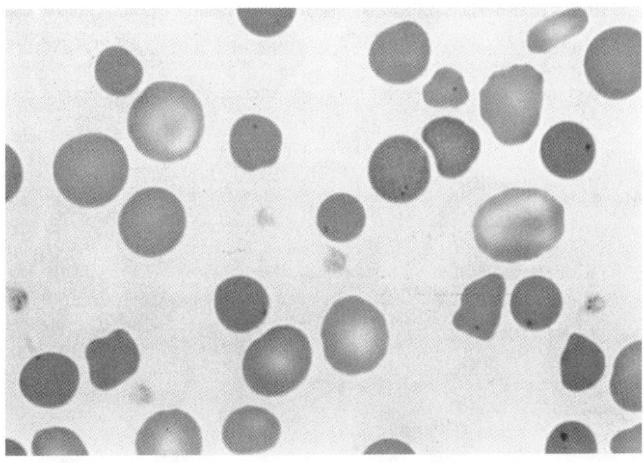

Figure 11–2 Hereditary spherocytosis—peripheral blood smear. Note the anisocytosis and several hyperchromic spherocytes. Howell-Jolly bodies (small nuclear remnants) are also present in the red cells of this asplenic patient.

(Courtesy of Dr. Robert W. McKenna, Department of Pathology, University of Texas Southwestern Medical School, Dallas, Texas.)

Clinical Features

The characteristic clinical features are *anemia, splenomegaly, and jaundice.* The anemia is highly variable in severity, ranging from subclinical to profound; most commonly it is of moderate degree. Because of their spherical shape, red cells in hereditary spherocytosis have *increased osmotic fragility* when placed in hypotonic salt solutions, a characteristic that can help establish the diagnosis.

The clinical course often is stable but may be punctuated by *aplastic crises.* The most severe crises are triggered by parvovirus B19, which infects and destroys erythroblasts in the bone marrow. Because red cells in hereditary spherocytosis have a shortened life span, a lack of red cell production for even a few days results in a rapid worsening of the anemia. Such episodes are self-limited, but some patients need supportive blood transfusions during the period of red cell aplasia.

There is no specific treatment for hereditary spherocytosis. *Splenectomy* provides relief for symptomatic patients by removing the major site of red cell destruction. The benefits of splenectomy must be weighed against the risk of increased susceptibility to infections, particularly in children. Partial splenectomy is gaining favor, because this approach may produce hematologic improvement while maintaining protection against sepsis.

Sickle Cell Anemia

The hemoglobinopathies are a group of hereditary disorders caused by inherited mutations that lead to structural abnormalities in hemoglobin. Sickle cell anemia, the prototypical (and most prevalent) hemoglobinopathy, stems from a mutation in the β-globin gene that creates sickle hemoglobin (HbS). Other hemoglobinopathies are infrequent and beyond the scope of this discussion.

Normal hemoglobins are tetramers composed of two pairs of similar chains. On average, the normal adult red cell contains 96% HbA ($\alpha 2\beta 2$), 3% HbA2 ($\alpha 2\delta 2$), and 1% fetal Hb (HbF, $\alpha 2\gamma 2$). *HbS is produced by the substitution of valine for glutamic acid at the sixth amino acid residue of β-globin.* In homozygotes, all HbA is replaced by HbS, whereas in heterozygotes, only about half is replaced.

Incidence

Sickle cell anemia is the most common familial hemolytic anemia in the world. In parts of Africa where malaria is endemic, the gene frequency approaches 30% as a result of a small but significant protective effect of HbS against *Plasmodium falciparum* malaria. In the United States, approximately 8% of blacks are heterozygous for HbS, and about 1 in 600 have sickle cell anemia.

PATHOGENESIS

On deoxygenation, HbS molecules form long polymers by means of intermolecular contacts that involve the abnormal valine residue at position 6. These polymers distort the red cell, which assumes an elongated crescentic, or sickle, shape (Fig. 11–3). The sickling of red cells initially is reversible upon reoxygenation. However, the distortion of the membrane that is produced by each sickling episode leads to an influx of calcium, which causes the loss of potassium and water and also damages the membrane skeleton. Over time, this cumulative damage creates **irreversibly sickled cells,** which are rapidly hemolyzed.

Many variables influence the sickling of red cells in vivo. The three most important factors are

- **The presence of hemoglobins other than HbS.** In heterozygotes approximately 40% of Hb is HbS and the remainder is HbA, which interacts only weakly with deoxygenated HbS. Because the presence of HbA greatly retards the polymerization of HbS, the red cells of heterozygotes have little tendency to sickle in vivo. Such persons are said to have **sickle cell trait.** HbC, another mutant β-globin, has a lysine residue instead of the normal glutamic acid residue at position 6. About 2.3% of American blacks are heterozygous carriers of HbC; as a result, about 1 in 1250 newborns are compound heterozygotes for HbC and HbS. Because HbC has a greater tendency to aggregate with HbS than does HbA, HbS/HbC compound heterozygotes have a symptomatic sickling disorder called **HbSC disease.** HbF interacts weakly with HbS, so newborns with sickle cell anemia do not manifest the disease until HbF falls to adult levels, generally around the age of 5 to 6 months.
- **The intracellular concentration of HbS.** The polymerization of deoxygenated HbS is strongly concentration-dependent. Thus, red cell dehydration, which increases the Hb concentration, facilitates sickling. Conversely, the coexistence of α-thalassemia (described later), which decreases the Hb concentration, reduces sickling. The relatively low concentration of HbS also contributes to the absence of sickling in heterozygotes with sickle cell trait.
- **The transit time for red cells through the microvasculature.** The normal transit times of red cells through capillaries are too short for significant polymerization of deoxygenated HbS to occur. Hence, sickling in microvascular beds is confined to areas of the body in which blood flow is sluggish. This is the normal situation

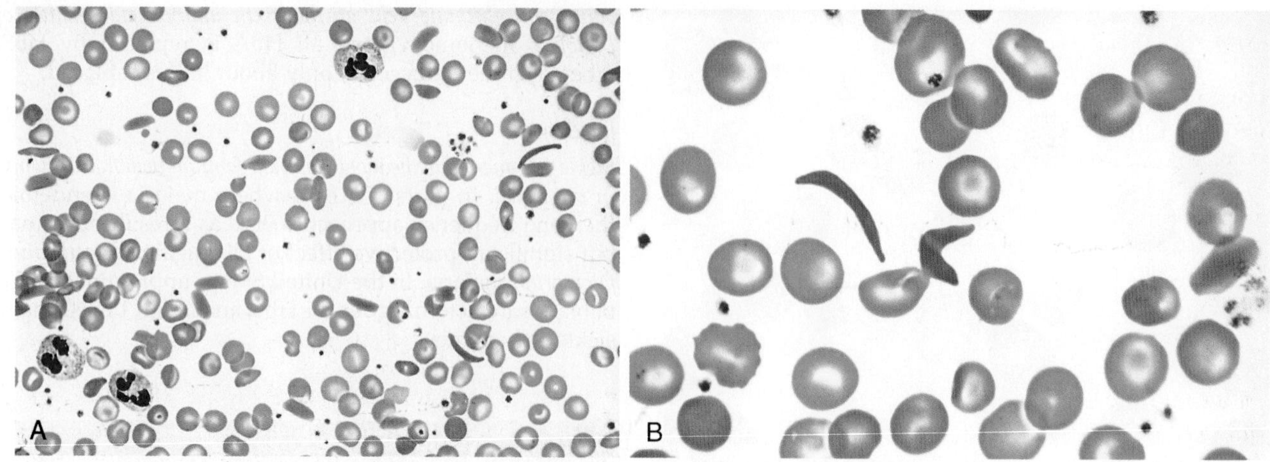

Figure 11–3 Sickle cell anemia—peripheral blood smear. **A,** Low magnification shows sickle cells, anisocytosis, poikilocytosis, and target cells. **B,** Higher magnification shows an irreversibly sickled cell in the center.
(Courtesy of Dr. Robert W. McKenna, Department of Pathology, University of Texas Southwestern Medical School, Dallas, Texas.)

in the spleen and the bone marrow, two tissues prominently affected by sickle cell disease. Sickling also can be triggered in other microvascular beds by acquired factors that retard the passage of red cells. As described previously, inflammation slows the flow of blood by increasing the adhesion of leukocytes and red cells to endothelium and by inducing the exudation of fluid through leaky vessels. In addition, sickle red cells have a greater tendency than normal red cells to adhere to endothelial cells, apparently because repeated bouts of sickling causes membrane damage that make them sticky. These factors conspire to prolong the transit times of sickle red cells, increasing the probability of clinically significant sickling.

Two major consequences arise from the sickling of red cells (Fig. 11–4). First, the red cell membrane damage and dehydration caused by repeated episodes of sickling produce a **chronic hemolytic anemia.** The mean life span of red cells in sickle cell anemia is only 20 days (one sixth of normal). Second, red cell sickling produces widespread **microvascular obstructions,** which result in ischemic tissue damage and pain crises. Vaso-occlusion does not correlate with the number of irreversibly sickled cells and therefore appears to result from factors such as infection, inflammation, dehydration, and acidosis that enhance the sickling of reversibly sickled cells.

MORPHOLOGY

The anatomic alterations in sickle cell anemia stem from (1) the severe chronic hemolytic anemia, (2) the increased breakdown of heme to bilirubin, and (3) microvascular obstructions, which provoke tissue ischemia and infarction. In peripheral smears, elongated, spindled, or boat-shaped irreversibly sickled red cells are evident (Fig. 11–3). Both the anemia and the vascular stasis lead to hypoxia-induced fatty changes in the heart, liver, and renal tubules. There is a compensatory hyperplasia of erythroid progenitors in the marrow. The cellular proliferation in the marrow often causes bone resorption and secondary new bone formation, resulting in prominent cheekbones and changes in the skull resembling a "crewcut" in radiographs. Extramedullary hematopoiesis may appear in the liver and spleen.

In children there is moderate **splenomegaly** (splenic weight up to 500 g) due to red pulp congestion caused by entrapment of sickled red cells. However, the chronic splenic erythrostasis produces hypoxic damage and infarcts, which over time reduce the spleen to a useless nubbin of fibrous

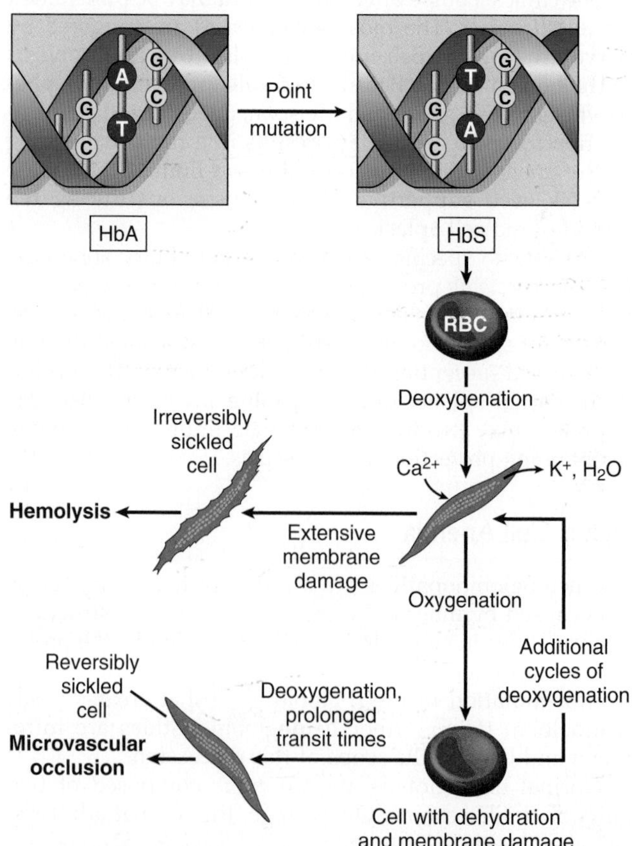

Figure 11–4 Pathophysiology of sickle cell disease.

tissue. This process, referred to as **autosplenectomy,** is complete by adulthood.

Vascular congestion, thrombosis, and infarction can affect any organ, including the bones, liver, kidney, retina, brain, lung, and skin. The bone marrow is particularly prone to ischemia because of its sluggish blood flow and high rate of metabolism. Priapism, another frequent problem, can lead to penile fibrosis and erectile dysfunction. As with the other hemolytic anemias, **hemosiderosis** and **gallstones** are common.

Clinical Course

Homozygous sickle cell disease usually is asymptomatic until 6 months of age when the shift from HbF to HbS is complete. The anemia is moderate to severe; most patients have hematocrits 18% to 30% (normal range, 36% to 48%). The chronic hemolysis is associated with hyperbilirubinemia and compensatory reticulocytosis. From its onset, the disease runs an unremitting course punctuated by sudden crises. The most serious of these are the *vaso-occlusive,* or *pain, crises.* The vaso-occlusion in these episodes can involve many sites but occurs most commonly in the bone marrow, where it often progresses to infarction.

A feared complication is the *acute chest syndrome,* which can be triggered by pulmonary infections or fat emboli from infarcted marrow. The blood flow in the inflamed, ischemic lung becomes sluggish and "spleenlike," leading to sickling within hypoxemic pulmonary beds. This exacerbates the underlying pulmonary dysfunction, creating a vicious circle of worsening pulmonary and systemic hypoxemia, sickling, and vaso-occlusion. Another major complication is *stroke,* which sometimes occurs in the setting of the acute chest syndrome. Although virtually any organ can be damaged by ischemic injury, *the acute chest syndrome and stroke are the two leading causes of ischemia-related death.*

A second acute event, *aplastic crisis,* is caused by a sudden decrease in red cell production. As in hereditary spherocytosis, this usually is triggered by the infection of erythroblasts by parvovirus B19 and, while severe, is self-limited.

In addition to these crises, patients with sickle cell disease are prone to *infections.* Both children and adults with sickle cell disease are functionally asplenic, making them susceptible to infections caused by encapsulated bacteria, such as pneumococci. In adults the basis for "hyposplenism" is autoinfarction. In the earlier childhood phase of splenic enlargement, congestion caused by trapped sickled red cells apparently interferes with bacterial sequestration and killing; hence, even children with enlarged spleens are at risk for development of fatal septicemia. Patients with sickle cell disease also are predisposed to *Salmonella* osteomyelitis, possibly in part because of poorly understood acquired defects in complement function.

In homozygous sickle cell disease, irreversibly sickled red cells are seen in routine peripheral blood smears. In sickle cell trait, sickling can be induced in vitro by exposing cells to marked hypoxia. The diagnosis is confirmed by electrophoretic demonstration of HbS. Prenatal diagnosis of sickle cell anemia can be performed by analyzing fetal DNA obtained by amniocentesis or biopsy of chorionic villi.

The clinical course is highly variable. As a result of improvements in supportive care, an increasing number of patients are surviving into adulthood and producing offspring. Of particular importance is prophylactic treatment with penicillin to prevent pneumococcal infections. Approximately 50% of patients survive beyond the fifth decade. By contrast, sickle cell trait causes symptoms rarely and only under extreme conditions, such as after vigorous exertion at high altitudes.

A mainstay of therapy is hydroxyurea, a "gentle" inhibitor of DNA synthesis. Hydroxyurea reduces pain crises and lessens the anemia through several beneficial intracorpuscular and extracorpuscular effects, including (1) an increase in red cell levels of HbF; (2) an anti-inflammatory effect due to the inhibition of white cell production; (3) an increase in red cell size, which lowers the mean cell hemoglobin concentration; and (4) its metabolism to NO, a potent vasodilator and inhibitor of platelet aggregation. Encouraging results also have been obtained with allogeneic bone marrow transplantation, which has the potential to be curative.

Thalassemia

The thalassemias are inherited disorders caused by mutations that decrease the synthesis of α- or β-globin chains. As a result, there is a deficiency of Hb and additional red cell changes due to the relative excess of the unaffected globin chain. The mutations that cause thalassemia are particularly common among populations in Mediterranean, African, and Asian regions in which malaria is endemic. As with HbS, it is hypothesized that globin mutations associated with thalassemia are protective against falciparum malaria.

PATHOGENESIS

A diverse collection of α-globin and β-globin mutations underlies the thalassemias, which are autosomal codominant conditions. As described previously, adult hemoglobin, or HbA, is a tetramer composed of two α chains and two β chains. The α chains are encoded by two α-globin genes, which lie in tandem on chromosome 16, while the β chains are encoded by a single β-globin gene located on chromosome 11. The clinical features vary widely depending on the specific combination of mutated alleles that are inherited by the patient (Table 11–3), as described next.

β-Thalassemia

The mutations associated with β-thalassemia fall into two categories: (1) β^0, in which no β-globin chains are produced; and (2) β^+, in which there is reduced (but detectable) β-globin synthesis. Sequencing of β-thalassemia genes has revealed more than 100 different causative mutations, a majority consisting of single-base changes. Persons inheriting one abnormal allele have **β-thalassemia minor** (also known as **β-thalassemia trait**), which is asymptomatic or mildly symptomatic. Most people inheriting any two β^0 and β^+ alleles have **β-thalassemia major;** occasionally, persons inheriting two β^+ alleles have a milder disease termed **β-thalassemia intermedia.** In contrast with α-thalassemias (described

Table 11–3 Clinical and Genetic Classification of Thalassemias

Clinical Syndrome	Genotype	Clinical Features	Molecular Genetics
β-Thalassemias			
β-Thalassemia major	Homozygous β-thalassemia (β^0/β^0, β^+/β^+, β^0/β^+)	Severe anemia; regular blood transfusions required	Mainly point mutations that lead to defects in the transcription, splicing, or translation of β-globin mRNA
β-Thalassemia intermedia	Variable (β^0/β^+, β^+/β^+, β^0/β, β^+/β)	Severe anemia, but regular blood transfusions not required	
β-Thalassemia minor	Heterozygous β-thalassemia (β^0/β, β^+/β)	Asymptomatic with mild or absent anemia; red cell abnormalities seen	
α-Thalassemias			
Silent carrier	–/α, α/α	Asymptomatic; no red cell abnormality	Mainly gene deletions
α-Thalassemia trait	–/–, α/α (Asian) –/α, –/α (black African, Asian)	Asymptomatic, like β-thalassemia minor	
HbH disease	–/–, –/α	Severe; resembles β-thalassemia intermedia	
Hydrops fetalis	–/–, –/–	Lethal in utero without transfusions	

HgH, hemoglobin H; mRNA, messenger ribonucleic acid.

later), **gene deletions rarely underlie β-thalassemias** (Table 11–3).

The mutations responsible for β-thalassemia disrupt β-globin synthesis in several different ways (Fig. 11–5):

- **Mutations leading to aberrant RNA splicing are the most common cause of β-thalassemia.** Some of these mutations disrupt the normal RNA splice junctions; as a result, no mature mRNA is made and there is a complete failure of β-globin production, creating β^0. Other mutations create new splice junctions in abnormal positions—within an intron, for example. Because the normal splice sites are intact, both normal and abnormal splicing occurs, and some normal β-globin mRNA is made. These alleles are designated β^+.
- Some mutations lie within the β-globin promoter and lower the rate of β-globin gene transcription. Because some normal β-globin is synthesized, these are β^+ alleles.
- Other mutations involve the coding regions of the β-globin gene, usually with severe consequences. For example, some single-nucleotide changes create termination ("stop") codons that interrupt the translation of β-globin mRNA and completely prevent the synthesis of β-globin.

Two mechanisms contribute to the anemia in β-thalassemia. The reduced synthesis of β-globin leads to inadequate HbA formation and results in the production of poorly hemoglobinized red cells that are pale **(hypochromic)** and small in size **(microcytic).** Even more important is the **imbalance in β-globin and α-globin chain synthesis,** as this creates an excess of unpaired α chains that aggregate into insoluble precipitates, which bind and severely damage the membranes of both red cells and erythroid precursors. A high fraction of the damaged erythroid precursors die by apoptosis (Fig. 11–6), a phenomenon termed **ineffective erythropoiesis,** and the few red cells that are produced have a shortened life span due to **extravascular hemolysis.** Ineffective hematopoiesis has another untoward effect: It is associated with an inappropriate increase in the absorption of dietary iron, which without medical intervention inevitably leads to **iron overload.** The increased iron absorption is caused by inappropriately low levels of hepcidin, which is a negative regulator of iron absorption (see later).

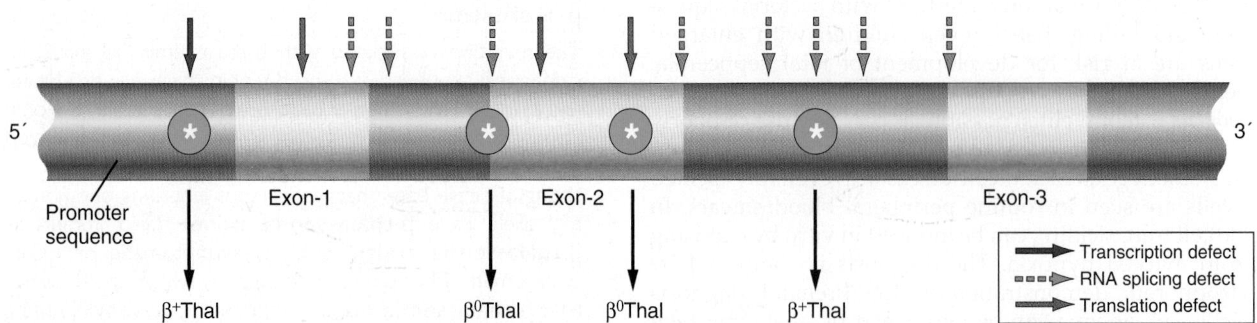

Figure 11–5 Distribution of β-globin gene mutations associated with β-thalassemia. *Arrows* denote sites at which point mutations giving rise to β^+ or β^0 thalassemia have been identified.

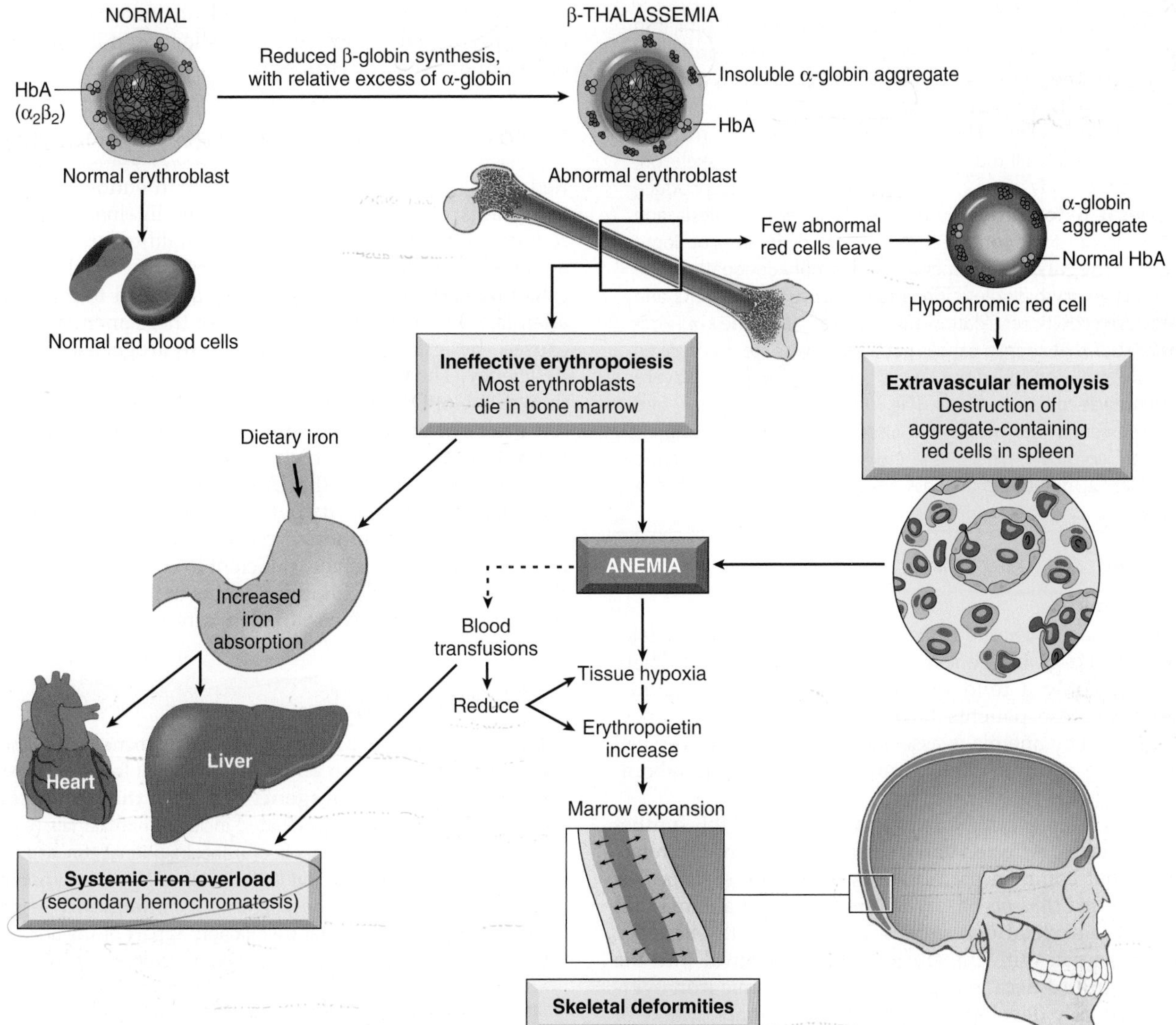

Figure 11–6 Pathogenesis of β-thalassemia major. Note that aggregates of excess α-globin are not visible on routine blood smears. Blood transfusions constitute a double-edged sword, diminishing the anemia and its attendant complications but also adding to the systemic iron overload.

α-Thalassemia

Unlike β-thalassemia, **α-thalassemia is caused mainly by deletions involving one or more of the α-globin genes.** The severity of the disease is proportional to the number of α-globin genes that are missing (Table 11–3). For example, the loss of a single α-globin gene produces a silent-carrier state, whereas the deletion of all four α-globin genes is lethal in utero because the red cells have virtually no oxygen-delivering capacity. With loss of three α-globin genes there is a relative excess of β-globin or (early in life) γ-globin chains. Excess β-globin and γ-globin chains form relatively stable β4 and γ4 tetramers known as HbH and Hb Bart, respectively, which cause less membrane damage than the free α-globin chains that are found in β-thalassemia; as a result, ineffective erythropoiesis is less pronounced in α-thalassemia. Unfortunately, both HbH and Hb Bart have an abnormally high affinity for oxygen, which renders them ineffective at delivering oxygen to the tissues.

MORPHOLOGY

A range of pathologic features are seen, depending on the specific underlying molecular lesion. On one end of the spectrum is β-thalassemia minor and α-thalassemia trait, in which the abnormalities are confined to the peripheral blood. In smears the red cells are small (microcytic) and pale (hypochromic), but regular in shape. Often seen are **target cells,** cells with an increased surface area-to-volume ratio that allows the cytoplasm to collect in a central, dark-red "puddle." On the other end of the spectrum, in β-thalassemia major, peripheral blood smears show marked **microcytosis, hypochromia, poikilocytosis** (variation in cell size), and **anisocytosis** (variation in cell shape). Nucleated red cells (normoblasts) are also seen that reflect the underlying erythropoietic drive. β-Thalassemia intermedia and HbH disease are associated with peripheral smear findings that lie between these two extremes.

The anatomic changes in β-thalassemia major are similar in kind to those seen in other hemolytic anemias but profound in degree. The ineffective erythropoiesis and hemolysis result in a striking hyperplasia of erythroid progenitors, with a shift toward early forms. The expanded erythropoietic marrow may completely fill the intramedullary space of the skeleton, invade the bony cortex, impair bone growth, and produce **skeletal deformities.** Extramedullary hematopoiesis and hyperplasia of mononuclear phagocytes result in prominent **splenomegaly,** hepatomegaly, and lymphadenopathy. The ineffective erythropoietic precursors consume nutrients and produce growth retardation and a degree of **cachexia** reminiscent of that seen in cancer patients. Unless steps are taken to prevent iron overload, over the span of years severe **hemosiderosis** develops (Fig. 11–6). HbH disease and β-thalassemia intermedia are also associated with splenomegaly, erythroid hyperplasia, and growth retardation related to anemia, but these are less severe than in β-thalassemia major.

Clinical Course

β-Thalassemia minor and α-thalassemia trait (caused by deletion of two α-globin genes) are often asymptomatic. There is usually only a mild microcytic hypochromic anemia; generally, these patients have a normal life expectancy. Iron deficiency anemia is associated with a similar red cell appearance and must be excluded by appropriate laboratory tests (described later).

β-Thalassemia major manifests postnatally as HbF synthesis diminishes. Affected children suffer from growth retardation that commences in infancy. They are *sustained by repeated blood transfusions,* which improve the anemia and reduce the skeletal deformities associated with excessive erythropoiesis. With transfusions alone, survival into the second or third decade is possible, but systemic iron overload gradually develops owing to inappropriate uptake of iron from the gut and the iron load in transfused red cells. Unless patients are treated aggressively with iron chelators, cardiac dysfunction from *secondary hemochromatosis* inevitably develops and often is fatal in the second or third decade of life. When feasible, bone marrow transplantation at an early age is the treatment of choice. HbH disease (caused by deletion of three α-globin genes) and β-thalassemia intermedia are not as severe as β-thalassemia major, since the imbalance in α- and β-globin chain synthesis is not as great and hematopoiesis is more effective. Anemia is of moderate severity and patients usually do not require transfusions. Thus, the iron overload that is so common in β-thalassemia major is rarely seen.

The diagnosis of β-thalassemia major can be strongly suspected on clinical grounds. *Hb electrophoresis* shows profound reduction or absence of HbA and increased levels of HbF. The HbA2 level may be normal or increased. Similar but less profound changes are noted in patients affected by β-thalassemia intermedia. *Prenatal diagnosis* of β-thalassemia is challenging due to the diversity of causative mutations, but can be made in specialized centers by DNA analysis. In fact, thalassemia was the first disease diagnosed by DNA-based tests, opening the way for the field of molecular diagnostics. The diagnosis of β-thalassemia minor is made by Hb electrophoresis, which typically reveals a reduced level of HbA (α2β2) and an increased level of HbA2 (α2δ2). HbH disease can be diagnosed by detection of β4 tetramers by electrophoresis.

Glucose-6-Phosphate Dehydrogenase Deficiency

Red cells are constantly exposed to both endogenous and exogenous oxidants, which are normally inactivated by reduced glutathione (GSH). Abnormalities affecting the enzymes responsible for the synthesis of GSH leave red cells vulnerable to oxidative injury and lead to hemolytic anemias. By far the most common of these anemias is that caused by glucose-6-phosphate dehydrogenase (G6PD) deficiency. The G6PD gene is on the X chromosome. More than 400 G6PD variants have been identified, but only a few are associated with disease. One of the most important variants is G6PD A⁻, which is carried by approximately 10% of black males in the United States. G6PD A⁻ has a normal enzymatic activity but a decreased half-life. Because red cells do not synthesize proteins, older G6PD A⁻ red cells become progressively deficient in enzyme activity and the reduced form of glutathione. This in turn renders older red cells more sensitive to oxidant stress.

PATHOGENESIS

G6PD deficiency produces no symptoms until the patient is exposed to an environmental factor (most commonly infectious agents or drugs) that produces oxidants. The drugs incriminated include antimalarials (e.g., primaquine), sulfonamides, nitrofurantoin, phenacetin, aspirin (in large doses), and vitamin K derivatives. More commonly, episodes of hemolysis are triggered by **infections,** which induce phagocytes to generate oxidants as part of the normal host response. These oxidants, such as hydrogen peroxide, are normally sopped up by GSH, which is converted to oxidized glutathione in the process. Because regeneration of GSH is impaired in G6PD-deficient cells, oxidants are free to "attack" other red cell components including globin chains, which have sulfhydryl groups that are susceptible to oxidation. Oxidized hemoglobin denatures and precipitates, forming intracellular inclusions called **Heinz bodies,** which can damage the cell membrane sufficiently to cause intravascular hemolysis. Other, less severely damaged cells lose their deformability and suffer further injury when splenic phagocytes attempt to "pluck out" the Heinz bodies, creating so-called **bite cells** (Fig. 11–7). Such cells become trapped upon recirculation to the spleen and are destroyed by phagocytes (extravascular hemolysis).

Clinical Features

Drug-induced hemolysis is acute and of variable severity. Typically, patients develop hemolysis after a lag of 2 or 3 days. Since G6PD is X-linked, the red cells of affected males are uniformly deficient and vulnerable to oxidant injury. By contrast, random inactivation of one X chromosome in heterozygous females (Chapter 6) creates two populations of red cells, one normal and the other G6PD-deficient. Most carrier females are unaffected except for those with a large proportion of deficient red cells (a chance situation known as *unfavorable lyonization*). In the case of the G6PD

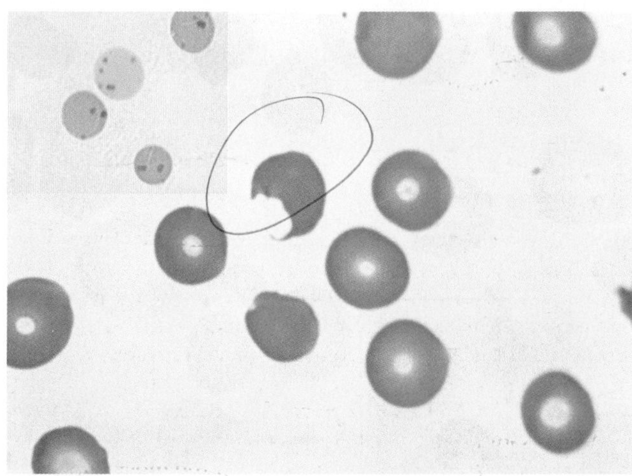

Figure 11–7 Glucose-6-phosphate dehydrogenase deficiency after oxidant drug exposure—peripheral blood smear. **Inset,** Red cells with precipitates of denatured globin (Heinz bodies) revealed by supravital staining. As the splenic macrophages pluck out these inclusions, "bite cells" like the one in this smear are produced.

(Courtesy of Dr. Robert W. McKenna, Department of Pathology, University of Texas Southwestern Medical School, Dallas, Texas.)

A^- variant, it is mainly older red cells that are susceptible to lysis. Since the marrow compensates for the anemia by producing new resistant red cells, the hemolysis abates even if the drug exposure continues. In other variants such as G6PD Mediterranean, found mainly in the Middle East, the enzyme deficiency and the hemolysis that occur on exposure to oxidants are more severe.

Paroxysmal Nocturnal Hemoglobinuria

Paroxysmal nocturnal hemoglobinuria (PNH) is a rare disorder worthy of mention because it is the only hemolytic anemia that results from an *acquired somatic mutation in myeloid stem cells.*

PATHOGENESIS

PNH stems from **acquired mutations in gene PIGA,** which is required for the synthesis of phosphatidylinositol glycan (PIG), a membrane anchor that is a component of many proteins. Without the "PIG-tail," these proteins cannot be expressed on the cell surface. The affected proteins include several that limit the activation of complement. As a result, PIGA-deficient precursors give rise to red cells that are **inordinately sensitive to complement-mediated lysis.** Leukocytes are also deficient in these protective proteins, but nucleated cells are generally less sensitive to complement than are red cells, and as a result the red cells take the brunt of the attack. The paroxysmal nocturnal hemolysis that gives the disorder its name occurs because the fixation of complement is enhanced by the slight decrease in blood pH that accompanies sleep (owing to CO_2 retention). However, most patients present less dramatically with anemia due to chronic low-level hemolysis. Another complication that is often serious and sometimes fatal is **venous thrombosis.** The etiopathogenesis of the prothrombotic state is somehow also related to the activity of the complement membrane attack complex, as inhibitors of this complex (described below) greatly lessen the incidence of thrombosis.

Because *PIGA* is X-linked, normal cells have only a single active *PIGA* gene, mutation of which is sufficient to give rise to PIGA deficiency. Because all myeloid lineages are affected in PNH, the responsible **mutations must occur in an early myeloid progenitor with self-renewal capacity.** Remarkably, many normal individuals harbor small numbers of bone marrow cells bearing *PIGA* mutations identical to those that cause PNH. It is believed that clinically evident PNH occurs only in rare instances in which the *PIGA* mutant clone has a survival advantage. One setting in which this may be true is in primary bone marrow failure (aplastic anemia), which most often appears to be caused by immune-mediated destruction or suppression of marrow stem cells. It is hypothesized that PIGA-deficient stem cells somehow escape the immune attack and eventually replace the normal marrow elements. Targeted therapy with an antibody that inhibits the C5b–C9 membrane attack complex is effective at diminishing both the hemolysis and the thrombotic complications, but also places patients at high risk for *Neisseria* infections, including meningococcal sepsis.

Immunohemolytic Anemias

Some individuals develop antibodies that recognize determinants on red cell membranes and cause hemolytic anemia. These antibodies may arise spontaneously or be induced by exogenous agents such as drugs or chemicals. Immunohemolytic anemias are uncommon and classified on the basis of (1) the nature of the antibody and (2) the presence of predisposing conditions (summarized in Table 11–4).

The diagnosis of immunohemolytic anemias depends on the detection of antibodies and/or complement on red cells. This is done with the *direct Coombs antiglobulin test,* in which the patient's red cells are incubated with antibodies against human immunoglobulin or complement. In a positive test result, these antibodies cause the patient's red cells to clump (agglutinate). The *indirect Coombs test,* which assesses the ability of the patient's serum to agglutinate test red cells bearing defined surface determinants, can then be used to characterize the target of the antibody.

Warm Antibody Immunohemolytic Anemias

Warm antibody immunohemolytic anemias are caused by immunoglobulin G (IgG) or, rarely, IgA antibodies that are active at 37°C. More than 60% of cases are idiopathic

Table 11–4 Classification of Immunohemolytic Anemias

Warm Antibody Type
Primary (idiopathic)
Secondary: B cell neoplasms (e.g., chronic lymphocytic leukemia), autoimmune disorders (e.g., systemic lupus erythematosus), drugs (e.g., α-methyldopa, penicillin, quinidine)
Cold Antibody Type
Acute: Mycoplasma infection, infectious mononucleosis
Chronic: idiopathic, B cell lymphoid neoplasms (e.g., lymphoplasmacytic lymphoma)

(primary), while another 25% are secondary to an underlying disease affecting the immune system (e.g., systemic lupus erythematosus) or are induced by drugs. *The hemolysis usually results from the opsonization of red cells by the autoantibodies,* which leads to erythrophagocytosis in the spleen and elsewhere. In addition, incomplete consumption ("nibbling") of antibody-coated red cells by macrophages removes membrane. With loss of cell membrane the red cells are transformed into *spherocytes,* which are rapidly destroyed in the spleen, as described earlier for hereditary spherocytosis. The clinical severity of immunohemolytic anemias is quite variable. Most patients have chronic mild anemia with moderate splenomegaly and require no treatment.

The mechanisms of hemolysis induced by drugs are varied and in some instances poorly understood. Drugs such as α-methyldopa induce autoantibodies against intrinsic red cell constituents, in particular Rh blood group antigens. Presumably, the drug somehow alters the immunogenicity of native epitopes and thereby circumvents T cell tolerance (Chapter 4). Other drugs such as penicillin act as haptens, inducing an antibody response by binding covalently to red cell membrane proteins. Sometimes antibodies recognize a drug in the circulation and form immune complexes that are deposited on red cell membranes. Here they may fix complement or act as opsonins, either of which can lead to hemolysis.

Cold Antibody Immunohemolytic Anemias

Cold antibody immunohemolytic anemias usually are caused by low-affinity IgM antibodies that bind to red cell membranes only at temperatures below 30°C, such as occur in distal parts of the body (e.g., ears, hands, and toes) in cold weather. Although bound IgM fixes complement well, the latter steps of the complement fixation cascade occur inefficiently at temperatures lower than 37°C. As a result, most cells with bound IgM pick up some C3b but are not lysed intravascularly. When these cells travel to warmer areas, the weakly bound IgM antibody is released, but the coating of C3b remains. Because C3b is an opsonin (Chapter 2), the cells are phagocytosed by macrophages, mainly in the spleen and liver; hence, the *hemolysis is extravascular.* Binding of pentavalent IgM also cross-links red cells and causes them to clump (agglutinate). *Sludging of blood in capillaries due to agglutination often produces Raynaud phenomenon* in the extremities of affected individuals. Cold agglutinins sometimes also appear transiently during recovery from pneumonia caused by *Mycoplasma* spp. and infectious mononucleosis, producing a mild anemia of little clinical importance. More important chronic forms of cold agglutinin hemolytic anemia occur in association with certain B cell neoplasms or as an idiopathic condition.

Hemolytic Anemias Resulting from Mechanical Trauma to Red Cells

Abnormal mechanical forces result in red cell hemolysis in a variety of circumstances. *Traumatic hemolysis* can occur incidentally during any activity involving repeated physical blows or their equivalent (e.g., marathon racing, karate chopping, bongo drumming) but is of little clinical importance. More significant mechanical hemolysis is sometimes produced by defective cardiac valve prostheses (the blender effect), which can create sufficiently turbulent blood flow to shear red cells. *Microangiopathic hemolytic anemia* is observed in pathologic states in which small vessels become partially obstructed or narrowed by lesions that predispose passing red cells to mechanical damage. The most frequent of these conditions is disseminated intravascular coagulation (DIC) (see later), in which vessels are narrowed by the intravascular deposition of fibrin. Other causes of microangiopathic hemolytic anemia include malignant hypertension, systemic lupus erythematosus, thrombotic thrombocytopenic purpura, hemolytic uremic syndrome, and disseminated cancer. The morphologic alterations in the injured red cells (*schistocytes*) are striking and quite characteristic; "burr cells," "helmet cells," and "triangle cells" may be seen (Fig. 11–8). While microangiopathic hemolysis is not usually in and of itself a major clinical problem, it often points to a serious underlying condition.

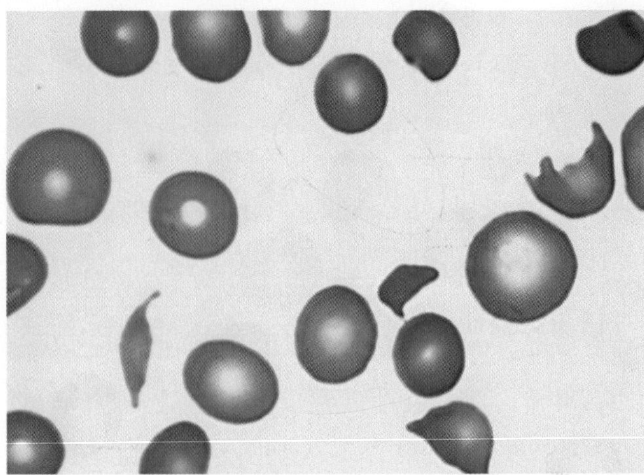

Figure 11–8 Microangiopathic hemolytic anemia—peripheral blood smear. This specimen from a patient with hemolytic uremic syndrome contains several fragmented red cells.

(Courtesy of Dr. Robert W. McKenna, Department of Pathology, University of Texas Southwestern Medical School, Dallas, Texas.)

Malaria

It is estimated that malaria affects 500 million and kills more than 1 million people per year, making it one of the most widespread afflictions of humans. Malaria is endemic in Asia and Africa, but with widespread jet travel cases are now seen all over the world. It is caused by one of four types of protozoa. Of these, the most important is *Plasmodium falciparum,* which causes tertian malaria (falciparum malaria), a serious disorder with a high fatality rate. The other three species of *Plasmodium* that infect humans—*Plasmodium malariae, Plasmodium vivax,* and *Plasmodium ovale*—cause relatively benign disease. All forms are transmitted by the bite of female *Anopheles* mosquitoes, and humans are the only natural reservoir.

PATHOGENESIS

The life cycle of plasmodia is complex. As mosquitoes feed on human blood, sporozoites are introduced from the saliva and within a few minutes infect liver cells. Here the parasites multiply rapidly to form a schizont containing thousands of merozoites. After a period of days to several weeks that varies with the *Plasmodium* species, the infected hepatocytes release the merozoites, which quickly infect red cells. Intraerythrocytic parasites either continue asexual reproduction to produce more merozoites or give rise to **gametocytes** capable of infecting the next hungry mosquito. During their asexual reproduction in red cells, each of the four forms of malaria develops into **trophozoites** with a somewhat distinctive appearance. Thus, **the species of malaria that is responsible for an infection can be identified in appropriately stained thick smears of peripheral blood.** The asexual phase is completed when the trophozoites give rise to new merozoites, which escape by lysing the red cells.

Clinical Features

The distinctive clinical and anatomic features of malaria are related to the following factors:

- Showers of new merozoites are released from the red cells at intervals of approximately 48 hours for *P. vivax, P. ovale,* and *P. falciparum* and 72 hours for *P. malariae.* The episodic shaking, chills, and fever coincide with this release.
- The parasites destroy large numbers of infected red cells, thereby causing a hemolytic anemia.
- A characteristic brown malarial pigment derived from hemoglobin called hematin is released from the ruptured red cells and produces discoloration of the spleen, liver, lymph nodes, and bone marrow.
- Activation of defense mechanisms in the host leads to a marked hyperplasia of mononuclear phagocytes, producing massive splenomegaly and occasional hepatomegaly.

Fatal falciparum malaria often involves the brain, a complication known as cerebral malaria. Normally, red cells bear negatively charged surfaces that interact poorly with endothelial cells. Infection of red cells with *P. falciparum* induces the appearance of positively charged surface knobs containing parasite-encoded proteins, which bind to adhesion molecules expressed on activated endothelium. Several endothelial cell adhesion molecules, including intercellular adhesion molecule-1 (ICAM-1), have been proposed to mediate this interaction, which leads to the trapping of red cells in postcapillary venules. In an unfortunate minority of patients, mainly children, this process involves cerebral vessels, which become engorged and occluded. *Cerebral malaria* is rapidly progressive; convulsions, coma, and death usually occur within days to weeks. Fortunately, falciparum malaria usually pursues a chronic course, which may be punctuated at any time by *blackwater fever.* The trigger is obscure for this uncommon complication, which is associated with massive intravascular hemolysis, hemoglobinemia, hemoglobinuria, and jaundice.

With appropriate chemotherapy, the prognosis for patients with most forms of malaria is good; however, treatment of falciparum malaria is becoming more difficult with the emergence of drug-resistant strains. Because of the potentially serious consequences of the disease, early diagnosis and treatment are important. The ultimate solution is an effective vaccine, which is long-sought but still elusive.

SUMMARY

Hemolytic Anemias

Hereditary Spherocytosis

- Autosomal dominant disorder caused by mutations that affect the red cell membrane skeleton, leading to loss of membrane and eventual conversion of red cells to spherocytes, which are phagocytosed and removed in the spleen
- Manifested by anemia, splenomegaly

Sickle Cell Anemia

- Autosomal recessive disorder resulting from a mutation in β-globin that causes deoxygenated hemoglobin to self-associate into long polymers that distort (sickle) the red cell
- Blockage of vessels by sickled cells causes pain crises and tissue infarction, particularly of the marrow and spleen
- Red cell membrane damage caused by repeated bouts of sickling results in a moderate to severe hemolytic anemia

Thalassemias

- Autosomal codominant disorders caused by mutations in α- or β-globin that reduce hemoglobin synthesis, resulting in a microcytic, hypochromic anemia. In β-thalassemia, unpaired α-globin chains form aggregates that damage red cell precursors and further impair erythropoiesis.

Glucose-6-Phosphate Dehydrogenase (G6PD) Deficiency

- X-linked disorder caused by mutations that destabilize G6PD, making red cells susceptible to oxidant damage

Immunohemolytic Anemias

- Caused by antibodies against either normal red cell constituents or antigens modified by haptens (such as drugs)
- Antibody binding results in either red cell opsonization and extravascular hemolysis or (uncommonly) complement fixation and intravascular hemolysis

Malaria

- Intracellular red cell parasite that causes chronic hemolysis of variable severity
- Falciparum malaria may be fatal due to the propensity of infected red cells to adhere to small vessels in the brain (cerebral malaria)

ANEMIAS OF DIMINISHED ERYTHROPOIESIS

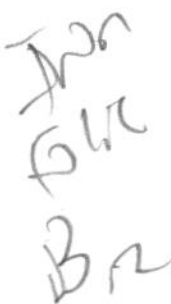

The category of anemias involving diminished erythropoiesis includes anemias that are caused by an inadequate dietary supply of nutrients, particularly iron, folic acid, and vitamin B_{12}. Other anemias of this type are those associated with bone marrow failure (aplastic anemia), systemic inflammation (anemia of chronic disease), or bone marrow infiltration by tumor or inflammatory cells (myelophthisic anemia). In this section, some common examples of anemias of these types are discussed individually.

Iron Deficiency Anemia

About 10% of people living in developed countries and 25% to 50% of those in developing countries are anemic. In both settings, *the most frequent cause of anemia is iron deficiency.* The factors responsible for iron deficiency differ in various populations and are best understood in the context of normal iron metabolism.

The normal total body iron mass is about 2.5 g for women and 3.5 g for men. Approximately 80% of functional body iron is present in hemoglobin, with the remainder being found in myoglobin and iron-containing enzymes (e.g., catalase, cytochromes). The iron storage pool, consisting of hemosiderin and ferritin-bound iron in the liver, spleen, bone marrow, and skeletal muscle, contains on average 15% to 20% of total body iron. Because *serum ferritin* is largely derived from this storage pool, the serum ferritin level is a good measure of iron stores. *Assessment of bone marrow iron* is another reliable but more invasive method for estimating iron stores. Iron is transported in the plasma bound to the protein *transferrin.* In normal persons, transferrin is about 33% saturated with iron, yielding serum iron levels that average 120 μg/dL in men and 100 μg/dL in women. Thus, the normal total iron-binding capacity of serum is 300 to 350 μg/dL.

In keeping with the high prevalence of iron deficiency, evolutionary pressures have yielded metabolic pathways that are strongly biased toward iron retention. There is no regulated pathway for iron excretion, which is limited to the 1 to 2 mg/day that is lost through the shedding of mucosal and skin epithelial cells. *Iron balance is maintained largely by regulating the absorption of dietary iron.* The normal daily Western diet contains 10 to 20 mg of iron. Most of this is found in heme within meat and poultry, with the remainder present as inorganic iron in vegetables. About 20% of heme iron and 1% to 2% of nonheme iron are absorbable; hence, the average Western diet contains sufficient iron to balance fixed daily losses.

Iron is absorbed in the duodenum (Fig. 11–9). Nonheme iron is carried across the apical and basolateral membranes of enterocytes by distinct transporters. After reduction by ferric reductase, ferrous iron (Fe^{2+}) is transported across the apical membrane by divalent metal transporter-1 (DMT1). A second transporter, ferroportin, then moves iron from the cytoplasm to the plasma across the basolateral membrane. The newly absorbed iron is next oxidized by hephaestin and ceruloplasmin to ferric iron (Fe^{3+}), the form of iron that binds to transferrin. Both DMT1 and ferroportin are widely distributed in the body and are involved in iron transport in other tissues as well. As depicted in Figure 11–9, only a fraction of the iron that enters enterocytes is delivered to transferrin by ferroportin. The remainder is incorporated into cytoplasmic ferritin and lost through the exfoliation of mucosal cells.

When the body is replete with iron, most iron entering duodenal cells is "handed off" to ferritin, whereas transfer to plasma transferrin is enhanced when iron is deficient or erythropoiesis is inefficient. This balance is regulated by hepcidin, a small hepatic peptide that is synthesized and secreted in an iron-dependent fashion. Plasma hepcidin binds ferroportin and induces its internalization and degradation; thus, when hepcidin concentrations are high, ferroportin levels fall and less iron is absorbed. Conversely, when hepcidin levels are low (as occurs in hemochromatosis) (Chapter 15), basolateral transport of iron is increased, eventually leading to systemic iron overload.

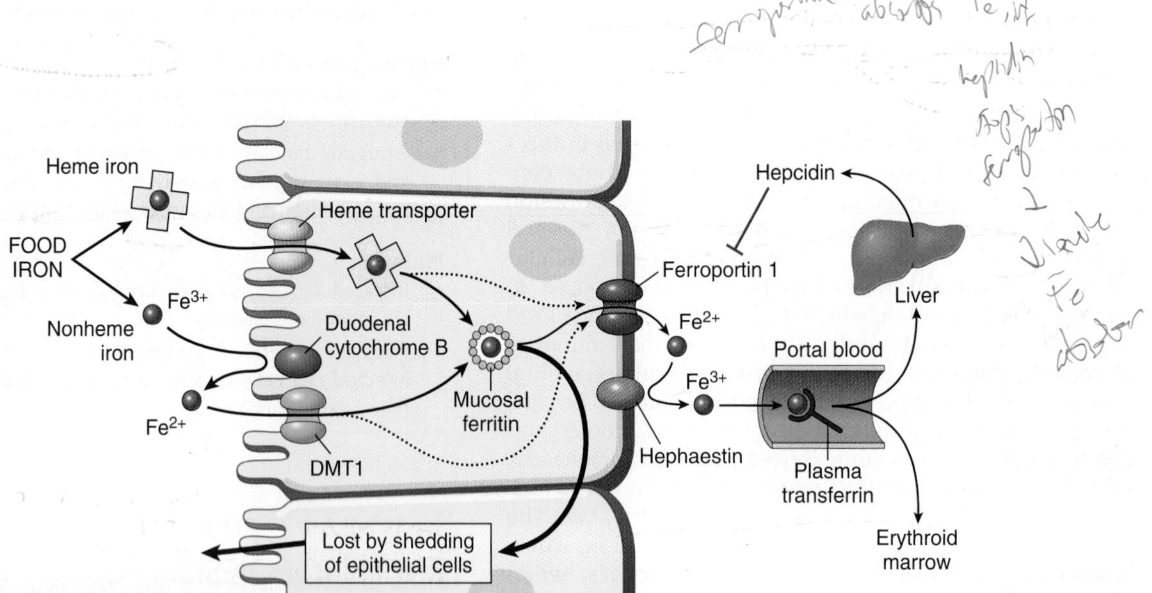

Figure 11–9 Regulation of iron absorption. Duodenal epithelial cell uptake of heme and nonheme iron discussed in the text is depicted. When the storage sites of the body are replete with iron and erythropoietic activity is normal, plasma hepcidin levels are high. This situation leads to downregulation of ferroportin and trapping of most of the absorbed iron, which is lost when duodenal epithelial cells are shed into the gut. Conversely, when body iron stores decrease or erythropoiesis is stimulated, hepcidin levels fall and ferroportin activity increases, allowing a greater fraction of the absorbed iron to be transferred into plasma transferrin. DMT1, divalent metal transporter-1.

PATHOGENESIS

Iron deficiency arises in a variety of settings:

- **Chronic blood loss is the most important cause of iron deficiency anemia in the Western world;** the most common sources of bleeding are the gastrointestinal tract (e.g., peptic ulcers, colonic cancer, hemorrhoids) and the female genital tract (e.g., menorrhagia, metrorrhagia, cancers).
- **In the developing world, low intake and poor bioavailability due to predominantly vegetarian diets are the most common causes of iron deficiency.** In the United States, low dietary intake is an infrequent culprit but is sometimes culpable in infants fed exclusively milk, the impoverished, the elderly, and teenagers subsisting predominantly on junk food.
- Increased demands not met by normal dietary intake occur worldwide during pregnancy and infancy.
- Malabsorption can occur with celiac disease or after gastrectomy (Chapter 14).

Regardless of the cause, iron deficiency develops insidiously. Iron stores are depleted first, marked by a decline in serum ferritin and the absence of stainable iron in the bone marrow. These changes are followed by a decrease in serum iron and a rise in the serum transferrin. Ultimately, the capacity to synthesize hemoglobin, myoglobin, and other iron-containing proteins is diminished, leading to microcytic anemia, impaired work and cognitive performance, and even reduced immunocompetence.

Clinical Features

In most instances, iron deficiency anemia is usually mild and asymptomatic. Nonspecific manifestations, such as weakness, listlessness, and pallor, may be present in severe cases. With long-standing anemia, abnormalities of the fingernails, including thinning, flattening, and "spooning," may appear. A curious but characteristic neurobehavioral complication is *pica,* the compunction to consume nonfoodstuffs such as dirt or clay.

In peripheral smears red cells are *microcytic* and *hypochromic* (Fig. 11–10). *Diagnostic criteria* include anemia, hypochromic and microcytic red cell indices, low serum ferritin and iron levels, low transferrin saturation, increased total iron-binding capacity, and, ultimately, response to iron therapy. For unclear reasons, the platelet count often is elevated. Erythropoietin levels are increased, but the marrow response is blunted by the iron deficiency; thus, marrow cellularity usually is only slightly increased.

Persons often die with iron deficiency anemia, but virtually never of it. An important point is that in well-nourished persons, microcytic hypochromic anemia is not a disease but rather a symptom of some underlying disorder.

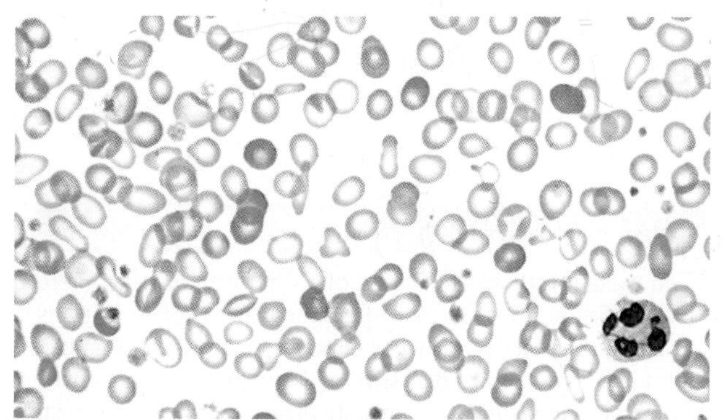

Figure 11–10 Iron deficiency anemia—peripheral blood smear. Note the increased central pallor of most of the red cells. Scattered, fully hemoglobinized cells, from a recent blood transfusion, stand out in contrast.

(Courtesy of Dr. Robert W. McKenna, Department of Pathology, University of Texas Southwestern Medical School, Dallas, Texas.)

Anemia of Chronic Disease

Anemia associated with chronic disease is the most common form of anemia in hospitalized patients. It superficially resembles the anemia of iron deficiency but arises instead from the suppression of erythropoiesis by systemic inflammation. It occurs in a variety of disorders associated with sustained inflammation, including:

- Chronic microbial infections, such as osteomyelitis, bacterial endocarditis, and lung abscess
- Chronic immune disorders, such as rheumatoid arthritis and regional enteritis
- Neoplasms, such as Hodgkin lymphoma and carcinomas of the lung and breast

PATHOGENESIS

The anemia of chronic disease stems from high levels of plasma hepcidin, which blocks the transfer of iron to erythroid precursors by downregulating ferroportin in macrophages. The elevated hepcidin levels are caused by pro-inflammatory cytokines such as IL-6, which increase hepatic hepcidin synthesis. In addition, chronic inflammation blunts erythropoietin synthesis by the kidney, lowering red cell production by the marrow. The functional advantages of these adaptations in the face of systemic inflammation are unclear; they may serve to inhibit the growth of iron-dependent microorganisms or to augment certain aspects of host immunity.

Clinical Features

As in anemia of iron deficiency, the serum iron levels usually are low in the anemia of chronic disease, and the red cells may even be slightly hypochromic and microcytic. Unlike iron deficiency anemia, however, *storage iron in the bone marrow is increased, the serum ferritin concentration is elevated, and the total iron-binding capacity is reduced.* Administration of erythropoietin and iron can improve the anemia, but only effective treatment of the underlying condition is curative.

Megaloblastic Anemias

The two principal causes of megaloblastic anemia are folate deficiency and vitamin B_{12} deficiency. Both vitamins are required for DNA synthesis and the effects of their deficiency on hematopoiesis are essentially identical. However, the causes and consequences of folate and vitamin B_{12} deficiency differ in important ways.

PATHOGENESIS

The morphologic hallmark of megaloblastic anemia is the presence of megaloblasts, enlarged erythroid precursors that give rise to abnormally large red cells (macrocytes). Granulocyte precursors are also increased in size. Underlying this **cellular gigantism** is a defect in DNA synthesis that impairs nuclear maturation and cell division. Because the synthesis of RNA and cytoplasmic elements proceeds at a normal rate and thus outpaces that of the nucleus, the hematopoietic precursors show **nuclear-cytoplasmic asynchrony.** This maturational derangement contributes to the anemia in several ways. Many megaloblasts are so defective in DNA synthesis that they undergo apoptosis in the marrow (**ineffective hematopoiesis**). Others mature into red cells but do so after fewer cell divisions, further diminishing the output of red cells. Granulocyte and platelet precursors are also affected (although not as severely) and most patients present with pancytopenia (anemia, thrombocytopenia, and granulocytopenia).

MORPHOLOGY

Certain morphologic features are common to all forms of megaloblastic anemia. The bone marrow is markedly hypercellular and contains numerous megaloblastic erythroid progenitors. **Megaloblasts** are larger than normal erythroid progenitors (normoblasts) and have delicate, finely reticulated nuclear chromatin (indicative of nuclear immaturity) (Fig. 11–11). As megaloblasts differentiate and acquire hemoglobin, the nucleus retains its finely distributed chromatin and fails to undergo the chromatin clumping typical of normoblasts. The granulocytic precursors also demonstrate nuclear-cytoplasmic asynchrony, yielding **giant metamyelocytes.** Megakaryocytes may also be abnormally large and have bizarre multilobed nuclei.

In the peripheral blood the earliest change is the appearance of **hypersegmented neutrophils,** which appear before the onset of anemia. Normal neutrophils have three or four nuclear lobes, but in megaloblastic anemias they often have five or more. The red cells typically include large, **egg-shaped macro-ovalocytes;** the mean cell volume often is greater than 110 fL (normal, 82 to 92 fL). Although macrocytes appear hyperchromic, in reality the mean cell hemoglobin concentration is normal. Large, misshapen platelets also may be seen. Morphologic changes in other systems, especially the gastrointestinal tract, also occur, giving rise to some of the clinical manifestations.

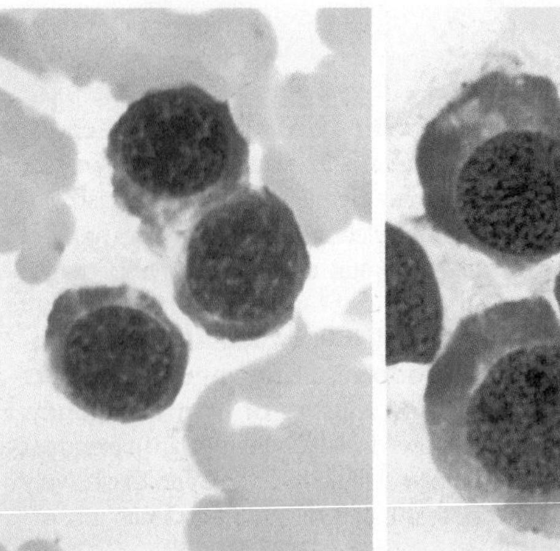

Figure 11–11 Comparison of normoblasts (*left*) and megaloblasts (*right*)—bone marrow aspirate. Megaloblasts are larger, have relatively immature nuclei with finely reticulated chromatin, and abundant basophilic cytoplasm.

(Courtesy of Dr. José Hernandez, Department of Pathology, University of Texas Southwestern Medical School, Dallas, Texas.)

Folate (Folic Acid) Deficiency Anemia

Megaloblastic anemia secondary to folate deficiency is not common, but marginal folate stores occur with surprising frequency even in apparently healthy persons. The risk of clinically significant folate deficiency is high in those with a poor diet (the economically deprived, the indigent, and the elderly) or increased metabolic needs (pregnant women and patients with chronic hemolytic anemias).

Folate is present in nearly all foods but is destroyed by 10 to 15 minutes of cooking. Thus, the best sources are fresh uncooked vegetables and fruits. Food folates are predominantly in polyglutamate form and must be split into monoglutamates for absorption, a conversion that is hampered by concurrent consumption of acidic foods and substances found in beans and other legumes. Phenytoin (dilantin) and a few other drugs also inhibit folate absorption, while others, such as methotrexate, inhibit folate metabolism. The principal site of intestinal absorption is the upper third of the small intestine; thus, malabsorptive disorders that affect this level of the gut, such as celiac disease and tropical sprue, can impair folate uptake.

PATHOGENESIS

The metabolism and functions of folate are complex. Here, it is sufficient to note that after absorption folate is transported in the blood mainly as a monoglutamate. Within cells it is further metabolized to several derivatives, but its conversion from dihydrofolate to tetrahydrofolate by dihydrofolate reductase is particularly important. **Tetrahydrofolate acts as an acceptor and donor of one-carbon units** in several reactions that are required for the synthesis of **purines and thymidylate,** the building blocks of DNA, and its deficiency accounts for the defect in DNA replication that underlies megaloblastic anemia.

Clinical Features

The onset of the anemia of folate deficiency is insidious, being associated with nonspecific symptoms such as weakness and easy fatigability. The clinical picture may be complicated by the coexistent deficiency of other vitamins, especially in alcoholics. Because the cells lining the gastrointestinal tract, like the hematopoietic system, turn over rapidly, symptoms referable to the alimentary tract, such as sore tongue, are common. *Unlike in vitamin B_{12} deficiency, neurologic abnormalities do not occur.*

The diagnosis of a megaloblastic anemia is readily made from examination of smears of peripheral blood and bone marrow. The anemia of folate deficiency is best distinguished from that of vitamin B_{12} deficiency by measuring serum and red cell folate and vitamin B_{12} levels.

Vitamin B_{12} (Cobalamin) Deficiency Anemia (Pernicious Anemia)

Inadequate levels of vitamin B_{12} (also known as cobalamin) result in a megaloblastic anemia identical to that seen with folate deficiency. However, vitamin B_{12} deficiency can also cause a demyelinating disorder of the peripheral nerves and the spinal cord. There are many causes of vitamin B_{12} deficiency. The term *pernicious anemia,* a relic of days when the cause and therapy of this condition were unknown, applies to vitamin B_{12} deficiency that results from defects involving intrinsic factor. Intrinsic factor plays a critical role in the absorption of vitamin B_{12}, a multistep process that proceeds as follows:

1. Peptic digestion releases dietary vitamin B_{12}, allowing it to bind a salivary protein called *haptocorrin.*
2. On entering the duodenum, haptocorrin–B_{12} complexes are processed by pancreatic proteases; this releases B_{12}, which attaches to *intrinsic factor* secreted from the parietal cells of the gastric fundic mucosa.
3. The intrinsic factor–B_{12} complexes pass to the distal ileum and attach to *cubulin,* a receptor for intrinsic factor, and are taken up into enterocytes.
4. The absorbed vitamin B_{12} is transferred across the basolateral membranes of enterocytes to plasma *transcobalamin,* which delivers vitamin B_{12} to the liver and other cells of the body.

PATHOGENESIS

Long-standing malabsorption underlies the vast majority of cases of vitamin B_{12} deficiency. Vitamin B_{12} is abundant in all food derived from animals, including eggs and dairy products, and is resistant to cooking and boiling. Even bacterial contamination of water and nonanimal foods can provide adequate amounts. As a result, deficiencies due to diet are rare, being confined to strict vegans. Once vitamin B_{12} is absorbed, the body handles it very efficiently. It is stored in the liver, which normally contains reserves sufficient to support bodily needs for 5 to 20 years.

Pernicious anemia is the most frequent cause of vitamin B_{12} deficiency. This disease seems to stem from an autoimmune reaction against parietal cells and intrinsic factor itself, which produces gastric mucosal atrophy (Chapter 14). Several associations favor an autoimmune basis:

- Autoantibodies are present in the serum and gastric juice of most patients. Three types of antibodies have been found: **parietal canalicular antibodies,** which bind to the mucosal parietal cells; **blocking antibodies,** which disrupt the binding of vitamin B_{12} to intrinsic factor; and **intrinsic factor–B_{12} complex antibodies,** which prevent the complex from binding to cubulin.
- Pernicious anemia frequently occurs concomitantly with other autoimmune diseases, such as Hashimoto thyroiditis, Addison disease, and type I diabetes mellitus.
- Serum antibodies to intrinsic factor are often present in patients with other autoimmune diseases.

Chronic vitamin B_{12} malabsorption is also seen after gastrectomy (owing to loss of intrinsic factor–producing cells) or ileal resection (owing to loss of intrinsic factor–B_{12} complex–absorbing cells), and in disorders that disrupt the function of the distal ileum (such as Crohn disease, tropical sprue, and Whipple disease). Particularly in older persons, gastric atrophy and achlorhydria may interfere with the production of acid and pepsin, which are needed to release the vitamin B_{12} from its bound form in food.

The metabolic defects responsible for the anemia are intertwined with folate metabolism. Vitamin B_{12} is required for recycling of tetrahydrofolate, the form of folate that is needed for DNA synthesis. In keeping with this relationship, the anemia of vitamin B_{12} deficiency is reversed with administration of folate. By contrast, folate administration does not prevent and may in fact worsen the neurologic symptoms. The main neurologic lesions associated with vitamin B_{12} deficiency are **demyelination of the posterior and lateral columns of the spinal cord,** sometimes beginning in the peripheral nerves. In time, axonal degeneration may supervene. The severity of the neurologic manifestations is not related to the degree of anemia. Indeed, the neurologic disease may occur in the absence of overt megaloblastic anemia.

Clinical Features

The manifestations of vitamin B_{12} deficiency are nonspecific. As with all anemias, findings include pallor, easy fatigability, and, in severe cases, dyspnea and even congestive heart failure. The increased destruction of erythroid progenitors may give rise to mild jaundice. Gastrointestinal signs and symptoms similar to those of folate deficiency are seen. The spinal cord disease begins with symmetric numbness, tingling, and burning in feet or hands, followed by unsteadiness of gait and loss of position sense, particularly in the toes. Although the anemia responds dramatically to parenteral vitamin B_{12}, the neurologic manifestations often fail to resolve. As discussed in Chapter 14, patients with pernicious anemia have an increased risk for the development of gastric carcinoma.

The diagnostic features of pernicious anemia include (1) low serum vitamin B_{12} levels, (2) normal or elevated serum folate levels, (3) serum antibodies to intrinsic factor, (4) moderate to severe megaloblastic anemia, (5) leukopenia with hypersegmented granulocytes, and (6) a dramatic reticulocytic response (within 2 to 3 days) to parenteral administration of vitamin B_{12}.

Aplastic Anemia

Aplastic anemia is a disorder in which *multipotent myeloid stem cells are suppressed, leading to bone marrow failure and pancytopenia.* It must be distinguished from pure red cell aplasia, in which only erythroid progenitors are affected and anemia is the only manifestation.

PATHOGENESIS

In more than half of the cases, aplastic anemia is **idiopathic.** In the remainder, an exposure to a **known myelotoxic agent,** such as a drug or a chemical, can be identified. With some agents, the marrow damage is predictable, dose-related, and reversible. Included in this category are antineoplastic drugs (e.g., alkylating agents, antimetabolites), benzene, and chloramphenicol. In other instances, marrow toxicity occurs as an "idiosyncratic" or hypersensitivity reaction to small doses of known myelotoxic drugs (e.g., chloramphenicol) or to drugs such as sulfonamides, which are not myelotoxic in other persons. Aplastic anemia sometimes arises after certain viral infections, most often community-acquired viral hepatitis. The specific virus responsible is not known; hepatitis viruses A, B, and C are not the culprits. Marrow aplasia develops insidiously several months after recovery from the hepatitis and follows a relentless course.

The pathogenic events leading to marrow failure remain vague, but it seems that **autoreactive T cells** play an important role. This is supported by a variety of experimental data and clinical experience showing that aplastic anemia responds to immunosuppressive therapy aimed at T cells in 70% to 80% of cases. Much less clear are the events that trigger the T cell attack on marrow stem cells; viral antigens, drug-derived haptens, and/or genetic damage may create neoantigens within stem cells that serve as targets for the immune system.

Rare but interesting genetic conditions also are associated with marrow failure. From 5% to 10% of patients with "acquired" aplastic anemia have inherited **defects in telomerase,** which as noted earlier is needed for the maintenance and stability of chromosomes. It is hypothesized that the defect in telomerase leads to premature senescence of hematopoietic stem cells. Of further interest, the bone marrow cells in up to 50% of sporadic cases have unusually short telomeres, possibly as a consequence of as-yet undiscovered defects in telomerase, or of excessive replication of hematopoietic stem cells, which may lead to premature senescence. Some children with Fanconi anemia, an inherited disorder of DNA repair, also develop marrow aplasia.

MORPHOLOGY

The bone marrow in aplastic anemia is markedly hypocellular, with greater than 90% of the intertrabecular space being occupied by fat. The limited cellularity often consists only of lymphocytes and plasma cells. Anemia may cause fatty change in the liver. Thrombocytopenia and granulocytopenia may result in hemorrhages and bacterial infections, respectively. The requirement for transfusions may eventually lead to hemosiderosis.

Clinical Course

Aplastic anemia affects persons of all ages and both sexes. The slowly progressive *anemia* causes the insidious development of weakness, pallor, and dyspnea. *Thrombocytopenia* often manifests with petechiae and ecchymoses. *Granulocytopenia* may be manifested by frequent and persistent minor infections or by the sudden onset of chills, fever, and prostration. It is important to separate aplastic anemia from anemias caused by marrow infiltration (myelophthisic anemia), "aleukemic leukemia," and granulomatous diseases, which may have similar clinical presentations but are easily distinguished on examination of the bone marrow. Aplastic anemia does not cause splenomegaly; if it is present, another diagnosis should be sought. Typically, the red cells are normochromic and normocytic or slightly macrocytic. *Reticulocytes are reduced* in number (reticulocytopenia).

The prognosis is unpredictable. Withdrawal of drugs sometimes leads to remission, but this is the exception rather than the rule. The idiopathic form carries a poor prognosis if left untreated. Bone marrow transplantation often is curative, particularly in nontransfused patients younger than 40 years of age. Transfusions sensitize patients to alloantigens, producing a high rate of engraftment failure; thus, they must be minimized in persons eligible for bone marrow transplantation. Successful transplantation requires "conditioning" with high doses of immunosuppressive radiation or chemotherapy, reinforcing the notion that autoimmunity has an important role in the disease. As mentioned earlier, patients who are poor transplantation candidates often benefit from immunosuppressive therapy.

Myelophthisic Anemia

Myelophthisic anemia is caused by *extensive infiltration of the marrow by tumors or other lesions.* It most commonly is associated with metastatic breast, lung, or prostate cancer. Other tumors, advanced tuberculosis, lipid storage disorders, and osteosclerosis can produce a similar clinical picture. The principal manifestations include anemia and thrombocytopenia; in general, the white cell series is less affected. Characteristically misshapen red cells, some *resembling teardrops,* are seen in the peripheral blood. Immature granulocytic and erythrocytic precursors also may be present (*leukoerythroblastosis*) along with mild leukocytosis. Treatment is directed at the underlying condition.

SUMMARY

Anemias of Diminished Erythropoiesis

Iron Deficiency Anemia

- Caused by chronic bleeding or inadequate iron intake; results in insufficient hemoglobin synthesis and hypochromic, microcytic red cells

Anemia of Chronic Disease

- Caused by inflammatory cytokines, which increase hepcidin levels and thereby sequester iron in macrophages, and also suppress erythropoietin production

Megaloblastic Anemia
- Caused by deficiencies of folate or vitamin B_{12} that lead to inadequate synthesis of thymidine and defective DNA replication
- Results in enlarged abnormal hematopoietic precursors (megaloblasts), ineffective hematopoiesis, macrocytic anemia, and (in most cases) pancytopenia

Aplastic Anemia
- Caused by bone marrow failure (hypocellularity) due to diverse causes, including exposures to toxins and radiation, idiosyncratic reactions to drugs and viruses, and inherited defects in telomerase and DNA repair

Myelophthisic Anemia
- Caused by replacement of the bone marrow by infiltrative processes such as metastatic carcinoma and granulomatous disease
- Leads to the appearance of early erythroid and granulocytic precursors (leukoerythroblastosis) and teardrop-shaped red cells in the peripheral blood

POLYCYTHEMIA

Polycythemia, or *erythrocytosis,* denotes an increase in red cells per unit volume of peripheral blood, usually in association with an increase in hemoglobin concentration. Polycythemia may be *absolute* (defined as an increase in total red cell mass) or *relative.* Relative polycythemia results from dehydration, such as occurs with water deprivation, prolonged vomiting, diarrhea, or the excessive use of diuretics. Absolute polycythemia is described as *primary* when the increased red cell mass results from an autonomous proliferation of erythroid progenitors, and *secondary* when the excessive proliferation stems from elevated levels of erythropoietin. Primary polycythemia (polycythemia vera) is a clonal, neoplastic myeloproliferative disorder considered later in this chapter. The increases in erythropoietin that cause secondary forms of absolute polycythemia have a variety of causes (Table 11–5).

Table 11–5 Pathophysiologic Classification of Polycythemia

Relative
Reduced plasma volume (hemoconcentration)
Absolute
Primary
Abnormal proliferation of myeloid stem cells, normal or low erythropoietin levels (polycythemia vera); inherited activating mutations in the erythropoietin receptor (rare)
Secondary
Increased erythropoietin levels
Adaptive: lung disease, high-altitude living, cyanotic heart disease
Paraneoplastic: erythropoietin-secreting tumors (e.g., renal cell carcinoma, hepatomacellular carcinoma, cerebellar hemangioblastoma)
Surreptitious: endurance athletes

WHITE CELL DISORDERS

Disorders of white cells include deficiencies (leukopenias) and proliferations, which may be reactive or neoplastic. Reactive proliferation in response to a primary, often microbial, disease is common. Neoplastic disorders, though less common, are more ominous: They cause approximately 9% of all cancer deaths in adults and a staggering 40% in children younger than 15 years of age.

Presented next are brief descriptions of some non-neoplastic conditions, followed by more detailed considerations of the malignant proliferations of white cells.

NON-NEOPLASTIC DISORDERS OF WHITE CELLS

Leukopenia

Leukopenia results most commonly from a decrease in granulocytes, the most numerous circulating white cells. Lymphopenia is much less common; it is associated with rare congenital immunodeficiency diseases, advanced human immunodeficiency virus (HIV) infection, and treatment with high doses of corticosteroids. Only the more common leukopenias of granulocytes are discussed here.

Neutropenia/Agranulocytosis

A reduction in the number of granulocytes in blood is known as *neutropenia* or, when severe, *agranulocytosis.* Neutropenic persons are susceptible to bacterial and fungal infections, in whom they can be fatal. The risk of infection rises sharply as the neutrophil count falls below 500 cells/μL.

PATHOGENESIS

The mechanisms underlying neutropenia can be divided into two broad categories:
- **Decreased granulocyte production.** Clinically important reductions in granulopoiesis are most often caused by marrow failure (as occurs in aplastic anemia), extensive replacement of the marrow by tumor (such as in leukemias), or cancer chemotherapy. Alternatively, some neutropenias are isolated, with only the differentiation of committed granulocytic precursors being affected. The forms of neutropenia are most often caused by certain drugs or, less commonly, by neoplastic proliferations of cytotoxic T cells and natural killer (NK) cells.

- **Increased granulocyte destruction.** This can be encountered with immune-mediated injury (triggered in some cases by drugs) or in overwhelming bacterial, fungal, or rickettsial infections due to increased peripheral utilization. Splenomegaly also can lead to the sequestration and accelerated removal of neutrophils.

MORPHOLOGY

The alterations in the bone marrow depend on the underlying cause of the neutropenia. **Marrow hypercellularity** is seen when there is excessive neutrophil destruction or ineffective granulopoiesis, such as occurs in megaloblastic anemia. By contrast, **agents such as drugs that cause neutropenia do so by suppressing granulocytopoiesis,** thus decreasing the numbers of granulocytic precursors. Erythropoiesis and megakaryopoiesis can be normal if the responsible agent specifically affects granulocytes, but most myelotoxic drugs reduce marrow elements from all lineages.

Clinical Features

The initial symptoms often are malaise, chills, and fever, with subsequent marked weakness and fatigability. Infections constitute the major problem. They commonly take the form of ulcerating, necrotizing lesions of the gingiva, floor of the mouth, buccal mucosa, pharynx, or other sites within the oral cavity (agranulocytic angina). Owing to the lack of leukocytes, such lesions often contain large masses or sheets of microorganisms. In addition to removal of the offending drug and control of infection, treatment efforts may also include granulocyte colony-stimulating factor, which stimulates neutrophil production by the bone marrow.

Reactive Leukocytosis

An increase in the number of white cells in the blood is common in a variety of inflammatory states caused by microbial and nonmicrobial stimuli. Leukocytoses are relatively nonspecific and are classified according to the particular white cell series that is affected (Table 11-6). As discussed later on, in some cases reactive leukocytosis may mimic leukemia. Such *"leukemoid" reactions* must be distinguished from true white cell malignancies. Infectious mononucleosis merits separate consideration because it gives rise to a distinctive syndrome associated with lymphocytosis.

Infectious Mononucleosis

Infectious mononucleosis is an acute, self-limited disease of adolescents and young adults that is caused by Epstein-Barr virus (EBV), a member of the herpesvirus family. The infection is characterized by (1) fever, sore throat, and generalized lymphadenitis and (2) a lymphocytosis of activated, CD8+ T cells. Of note, cytomegalovirus infection induces a similar syndrome that can be differentiated only by serologic methods.

EBV is ubiquitous in all human populations. In the developing world, EBV infection in early childhood is nearly universal. At this age, symptomatic disease is uncommon, and even though infected hosts mount an immune response (described later), more than half continue to shed virus. By contrast, in developed countries with better standards of hygiene, infection usually is delayed until adolescence or young adulthood. For unclear reasons, only about 20% of healthy seropositive persons in developed countries shed the virus, and only about 50% of those who are exposed to the virus acquire the infection.

Table 11–6 Causes of Leukocytosis

Neutrophilic Leukocytosis
Acute bacterial infections (especially those caused by pyogenic organisms); sterile inflammation caused by, for example, tissue necrosis (myocardial infarction, burns)
Eosinophilic Leukocytosis (Eosinophilia)
Allergic disorders such as asthma, hay fever, allergic skin diseases (e.g., pemphigus, dermatitis herpetiformis); parasitic infestations; drug reactions; certain malignancies (e.g., Hodgkin lymphoma and some non-Hodgkin lymphomas); collagen-vascular disorders and some vasculitides; atheroembolic disease (transient)
Basophilic Leukocytosis (Basophilia)
Rare, often indicative of a myeloproliferative disease (e.g., chronic myelogenous leukemia)
Monocytosis
Chronic infections (e.g., tuberculosis), bacterial endocarditis, rickettsiosis, and malaria; collagen vascular diseases (e.g., systemic lupus erythematosus); and inflammatory bowel diseases (e.g., ulcerative colitis)
Lymphocytosis
Accompanies monocytosis in many disorders associated with chronic immunologic stimulation (e.g., tuberculosis, brucellosis); viral infections (e.g., hepatitis A, cytomegalovirus, Epstein-Barr virus); *Bordetella pertussis* infection

PATHOGENESIS

Transmission to a seronegative "kissing cousin" usually involves direct oral contact. It is hypothesized (but has not been proved) that the virus initially infects oropharyngeal epithelial cells and then spreads to underlying lymphoid tissue (tonsils and adenoids), where mature B cells are infected. The infection of B cells takes one of two forms. In a minority of cells, the infection is lytic, leading to viral replication and eventual cell lysis accompanied by the release of virions. In most cells, however, the infection is nonproductive, and the virus persists in latent form as an extrachromosomal episome. **B cells that are latently infected with EBV undergo polyclonal activation and proliferation,** as a result of the action of several EBV proteins (Chapter 5). These cells disseminate in the circulation and secrete antibodies with several specificities, including the well-known heterophil anti-sheep red cell antibodies that are detected in diagnostic tests for mononucleosis. During acute infections, EBV is shed in the saliva; it is not known if the source of these virions is oropharyngeal epithelial cells or B cells.

A normal immune response is extremely important in controlling the proliferation of EBV-infected B cells and the spread of the virus. Early in the course of the infection, IgM antibodies are formed against viral capsid antigens. Later the serologic response shifts to IgG antibodies, which persist for life. More important in the control of the EBV-positive B cell proliferation are cytotoxic CD8+ T cells and NK cells. **Virus-specific CD8+ T cells appear in the circulation as atypical lymphocytes, a finding that is characteristic of mononucleosis.** In otherwise healthy persons, the fully developed humoral and cellular responses to EBV act as brakes on viral shedding. In most cases, however, a small number of latently infected EBV-positive B cells escape the immune response and persist for the life of the patient. As described later, impaired T cell immunity in the host can have disastrous consequences.

MORPHOLOGY

The major alterations involve the blood, lymph nodes, spleen, liver, central nervous system, and occasionally other organs. There is peripheral blood **leukocytosis**; the white cell count is usually between 12,000 and 18,000 cells/μL. Typically more than half of these cells are large **atypical lymphocytes,** 12 to 16 μm in diameter, with an oval, indented, or folded nucleus and abundant cytoplasm with a few azurophilic granules (Fig. 11–12). These atypical lymphocytes, which are sufficiently distinctive to suggest the diagnosis, are mainly CD8+ T cells.

Lymphadenopathy is common and is most prominent in the posterior cervical, axillary, and groin regions. On histologic examination, the enlarged nodes are flooded by atypical lymphocytes, which occupy the paracortical (T cell) areas. A few cells resembling Reed-Sternberg cells, the hallmark of Hodgkin lymphoma, often are seen. Because of these atypical features, special tests are sometimes needed to distinguish the reactive changes of mononucleosis from lymphoma.

The **spleen** is enlarged in most cases, weighing between 300 and 500 g, and exhibits a heavy infiltration of atypical lymphocytes. As a result of the rapid increase in splenic size and the infiltration of the trabeculae and capsule by the lymphocytes, such spleens are fragile and prone to rupture after even minor trauma.

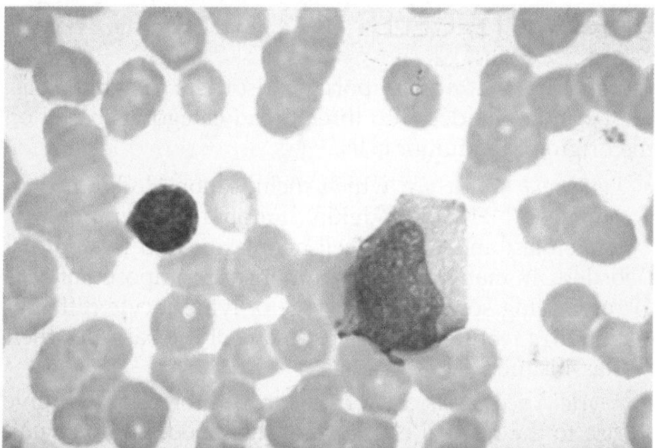

Figure 11–12 Atypical lymphocytes in infectious mononucleosis—peripheral blood smear. The cell on the *left* is a normal small resting lymphocyte with a compact nucleus and scant cytoplasm. By contrast, the atypical lymphocyte on the *right* has abundant cytoplasm and a large nucleus with dispersed chromatin.

Atypical lymphocytes usually also infiltrate the portal areas and sinusoids of the **liver.** Scattered apoptotic cells or foci of parenchymal necrosis associated with a lymphocytic infiltrate also may be present—a picture that can be difficult to distinguish from that in other forms of viral hepatitis.

Clinical Features

Although mononucleosis classically manifests with fever, sore throat, lymphadenitis, and the other features mentioned earlier, atypical presentations are not unusual. Sometimes there is little or no fever and only fatigue and lymphadenopathy, raising the specter of lymphoma; fever of unknown origin, unassociated with lymphadenopathy or other localized findings; hepatitis that is difficult to differentiate from one of the hepatotropic viral syndromes (Chapter 15); or a febrile rash resembling rubella. Ultimately, the diagnosis depends on the following findings, in increasing order of specificity: (1) lymphocytosis with the characteristic atypical lymphocytes in the peripheral blood, (2) a positive heterophil reaction (Monospot test), and (3) a rising titer of antibodies specific for EBV antigens (viral capsid antigens, early antigens, or Epstein-Barr nuclear antigen). In most patients, mononucleosis resolves within 4 to 6 weeks, but sometimes the fatigue lasts longer. Occasionally, one or more complications supervene. Perhaps the most common of these is hepatic dysfunction, associated with jaundice, elevated hepatic enzyme levels, disturbed appetite, and, rarely, even liver failure. Other complications involve the nervous system, kidneys, bone marrow, lungs, eyes, heart, and spleen (including fatal splenic rupture).

EBV is a potent transforming virus that plays a role in the pathogenesis of a number of human malignancies, including several types of B cell lymphoma (Chapter 5). A serious complication in those lacking T cell immunity (such as organ and bone marrow transplant recipients and HIV-infected individuals) is unimpeded EBV-driven B cell proliferation. This process can be initiated by an acute infection or the reactivation of a latent B cell infection and generally begins as a polyclonal proliferation that transforms to overt monoclonal B cell lymphoma over time. Reconstitution of immunity (e.g., by cessation of immunosuppressive drugs) is sometimes sufficient to cause complete regression of the B cell proliferation, which is uniformly fatal if left untreated.

The importance of T cells and NK cells in the control of EBV infection is driven home by X-linked lymphoproliferative syndrome, a rare inherited immunodeficiency characterized by an ineffective immune response to EBV. Most affected boys have mutations in the *SH2D1A* gene, which encodes a signaling protein that participates in the activation of T cells and NK cells and in antibody production. In more than 50% of cases, EBV causes an acute overwhelming infection that is usually fatal. Others succumb to lymphoma or infections related to hypogammaglobulinemia, the basis of which is not understood.

Reactive Lymphadenitis

Infections and nonmicrobial inflammatory stimuli often activate immune cells residing in lymph nodes, which act as defensive barriers. Any immune response against foreign antigens can lead to lymph node enlargement (lymphadenopathy). The infections causing lymphadenitis are varied and numerous, and may be acute or chronic. In most instances the histologic appearance of the lymph node reaction is nonspecific. A somewhat distinctive form of lymphadenitis that occurs with cat-scratch disease is described separately later.

Acute Nonspecific Lymphadenitis

This form of lymphadenitis may be isolated to a group of nodes draining a local infection, or be generalized, as in systemic infectious and inflammatory conditions.

MORPHOLOGY

Inflamed nodes in acute nonspecific lymphadenitis are swollen, gray-red, and engorged. Histologically, there are **large germinal centers** containing numerous mitotic figures. When the cause is a pyogenic organism, a neutrophilic infiltrate is seen around the follicles and within the lymphoid sinuses. With severe infections, the centers of follicles can undergo necrosis, leading to the formation of an abscess.

Affected nodes are tender and may become fluctuant if abscess formation is extensive. The overlying skin is frequently red and may develop draining sinuses. With control of the infection the lymph nodes may revert to a normal "resting" appearance or if damaged undergo scarring.

Chronic Nonspecific Lymphadenitis

Depending on the causative agent, chronic nonspecific lymphadenitis can assume one of three patterns: follicular hyperplasia, paracortical hyperplasia, or sinus histiocytosis.

MORPHOLOGY

Follicular Hyperplasia. This pattern occurs with infections or inflammatory processes that activate B cells, which migrate into B cell follicles and create the **follicular (or germinal center) reaction.** The reactive follicles contain numerous activated B cells, scattered T cells, and phagocytic macrophages containing nuclear debris (tingible body macrophages), and a meshwork of antigen-presenting follicular dendritic cells. Causes of follicular hyperplasia include **rheumatoid arthritis, toxoplasmosis,** and early **HIV infection.** This form of lymphadenitis can be confused morphologically with follicular lymphoma (discussed later). Findings that favor follicular hyperplasia are (1) the preservation of the lymph node architecture; (2) variation in the shape and size of the germinal centers; (3) the presence of a mixture of germinal center lymphocytes of varying shape and size; and (4) prominent phagocytic and mitotic activity in germinal centers.

Paracortical Hyperplasia. This pattern is caused by immune reactions involving the **T cell regions** of the lymph node. When activated, parafollicular T cells transform into large proliferating immunoblasts that can efface the B cell follicles. Paracortical hyperplasia is encountered in **viral infections** (such as EBV), after certain **vaccinations** (e.g., smallpox), and in immune reactions induced by **drugs** (especially phenytoin).

Sinus Histiocytosis. This reactive pattern is characterized by distention and prominence of the lymphatic sinusoids, owing to a marked **hypertrophy of lining endothelial cells** and an **infiltrate of macrophages (histiocytes).** It often is encountered in lymph nodes draining cancers and may represent an immune response to the tumor or its products.

Cat-Scratch Disease

Cat-scratch disease is a self-limited lymphadenitis caused by the bacterium *Bartonella henselae.* It is primarily a disease of childhood; 90% of the patients are younger than 18 years of age. It manifests with regional lymphadenopathy, most frequently in the axilla and the neck. The nodal enlargement appears approximately 2 weeks after a feline scratch or, less commonly, after a splinter or thorn injury. An inflammatory nodule, vesicle, or eschar is sometimes visible at the site of the skin injury. In most patients the lymph node enlargement regresses over a period of 2 to 4 months. Encephalitis, osteomyelitis, or thrombocytopenia may develop in rare patients.

MORPHOLOGY

The nodal changes in cat-scratch disease are quite characteristic. Initially sarcoid-like granulomas form, but these then undergo central necrosis associated with an infiltrate of neutrophils. These **irregular stellate necrotizing granulomas** are similar in appearance to those seen in a limited number of other infections, such as lymphogranuloma venereum. The microbe is extracellular and can be visualized with silver stains. The diagnosis is based on a history of exposure to cats, the characteristic clinical findings, a positive result on serologic testing for antibodies to *Bartonella*, and the distinctive morphologic changes in the lymph nodes.

NEOPLASTIC PROLIFERATIONS OF WHITE CELLS

Tumors are the most important disorders of white cells. They can be divided into three broad categories based on the origin of the tumor cells:

- *Lymphoid neoplasms,* which include non-Hodgkin lymphomas (NHLs), Hodgkin lymphomas, lymphocytic leukemias, and plasma cell neoplasms and related disorders. In many instances tumors are composed of cells resembling some normal stage of lymphocyte differentiation, a feature that serves as one of the bases for their classification.
- *Myeloid neoplasms* arise from progenitor cells that give rise to the formed elements of the blood: granulocytes, red cells, and platelets. The myeloid neoplasms fall into three fairly distinct subcategories: *acute myeloid leukemias,* in which immature progenitor cells accumulate in the bone marrow; *myeloproliferative disorders,* in which an inappropriate increase in the production of formed

blood elements leads to elevated blood cell counts; and *myelodysplastic syndromes,* which are characteristically associated with ineffective hematopoiesis and cytopenias.

- *Histiocytic neoplasms* include proliferative lesions of macrophages and dendritic cells. Of special interest is a spectrum of proliferations of Langerhans cells (*Langerhans cell histiocytoses*).

Lymphoid Neoplasms

The numerous lymphoid neoplasms vary widely in their clinical presentation and behavior, and thus present challenges to students and clinicians alike. Some characteristically manifest as *leukemias,* with involvement of the bone marrow and the peripheral blood. Others tend to manifest as *lymphomas,* tumors that produce masses in lymph nodes or other tissues. *Plasma cell tumors* usually arise within the bones and manifest as discrete masses, causing systemic symptoms related to the production of a complete or partial monoclonal immunoglobulin. While these tendencies are reflected in the names given to these entities, in reality all lymphoid neoplasms have the potential to spread to lymph nodes and various tissues throughout the body, especially the liver, spleen, bone marrow, and peripheral blood. *Because of their overlapping clinical behavior, the various lymphoid neoplasms can be distinguished with certainty only by the morphologic and molecular characteristics of the tumor cells.* Stated another way, for purposes of diagnosis and prognostication, it is most important to focus on what the tumor cell is, not where it resides in the patient.

Two groups of lymphomas are recognized: *Hodgkin lymphomas* and *non-Hodgkin lymphomas.* Although both arise most commonly in lymphoid tissues, Hodgkin lymphoma is set apart by the presence of distinctive neoplastic Reed-Sternberg giant cells (see later), which usually are greatly outnumbered by non-neoplastic inflammatory cells. The biologic behavior and clinical treatment of Hodgkin lymphoma also are different from those of NHLs, making the distinction of practical importance.

Historically, few areas of pathology evoked as much controversy and confusion as the classification of lymphoid neoplasms, which is perhaps inevitable in view of the intrinsic complexity of the immune system, from which they arise. Great progress has been made over the past several decades, however, and an international working group of pathologists, molecular biologists, and clinicians working on behalf of the World Health Organization (WHO) has formulated a widely accepted classification scheme that relies on a combination of morphologic, phenotypic, genotypic, and clinical features. As background for the subsequent discussion of this classification, certain important principles warrant consideration:

- B and T cell tumors often are composed of cells that are arrested at or derived from a specific stage of their normal differentiation (Fig. 11–13). The diagnosis and classification of these tumors rely heavily on tests (either immunohistochemistry or flow cytometry) that detect lineage-specific antigens (e.g., B cell, T cell, and NK cell markers) and markers of maturity. By convention, many such markers are identified by their cluster of differentiation (CD) number.
- The most common lymphomas are derived from germinal center or post–germinal center B cells. This conclusion is drawn from molecular analyses showing that most B cell lymphomas have undergone somatic hypermutation, an event confined to germinal center B cells. Normal germinal center B cells also undergo immunoglobulin class switching, an event that allows B cells to express immunoglobulins other than IgM. Class switching and somatic hypermutation are mistake-prone forms of regulated genomic instability, which places germinal center B cells at high risk for potentially transforming mutations. In fact, many of the recurrent chromosomal translocations found in mature B cell malignancies involve the immunoglobulin loci and appear to stem from "accidents" during attempted diversification of the immunoglobulin genes. In this regard, it is interesting that mature T cells, which are genomically stable, give rise to lymphomas infrequently and only very rarely have chromosomal translocations involving the T cell receptor loci.
- All lymphoid neoplasms are derived from a single transformed cell and are therefore clonal. As described in Chapter 4, differentiating precursor B and T cells rearrange their antigen receptor genes, thereby ensuring that each lymphocyte makes a single, unique antigen receptor. Because antigen receptor gene rearrangement virtually always precedes transformation, the daughter cells derived from a given malignant progenitor share the same antigen receptor gene configuration and synthesize identical antigen receptor proteins (either immunoglobulins or T cell receptors). Thus, analyses of antigen receptor genes and their protein products can be used to differentiate clonal neoplasms from polyclonal, reactive processes.
- Lymphoid neoplasms often disrupt normal immune function. Both immunodeficiency (as evident by increased susceptibility to infection) and autoimmunity may be seen, sometimes in the same patient. Ironically, patients with inherited or acquired immunodeficiency are themselves at high risk for the development of certain lymphoid neoplasms, particularly those associated with EBV infection.
- Although NHLs often manifest at a particular tissue site, sensitive molecular assays usually show the tumor to be widely disseminated at diagnosis. As a result, with few exceptions, only systemic therapies are curative. By contrast, Hodgkin lymphoma often arises at a single site and spreads in a predictable fashion to contiguous lymph node groups. For this reason, early in its course, it is sometimes treated with local therapy alone.

The WHO classification of lymphoid neoplasms considers the morphology, cell of origin (determined by immunophenotyping), clinical features, and genotype (e.g., karyotype, presence of viral genomes) of each entity. It encompasses all lymphoid neoplasms, including leukemias and multiple myeloma, and separates them on the basis of origin into three major categories: (1) tumors of B cells, (2) tumors of T cells and NK cells, and (3) Hodgkin lymphoma.

An updated version of the WHO classification of lymphoid neoplasms is presented in Table 11–7. As is evident, the diagnostic entities are numerous. The focus here is on the following subsets of neoplasms:

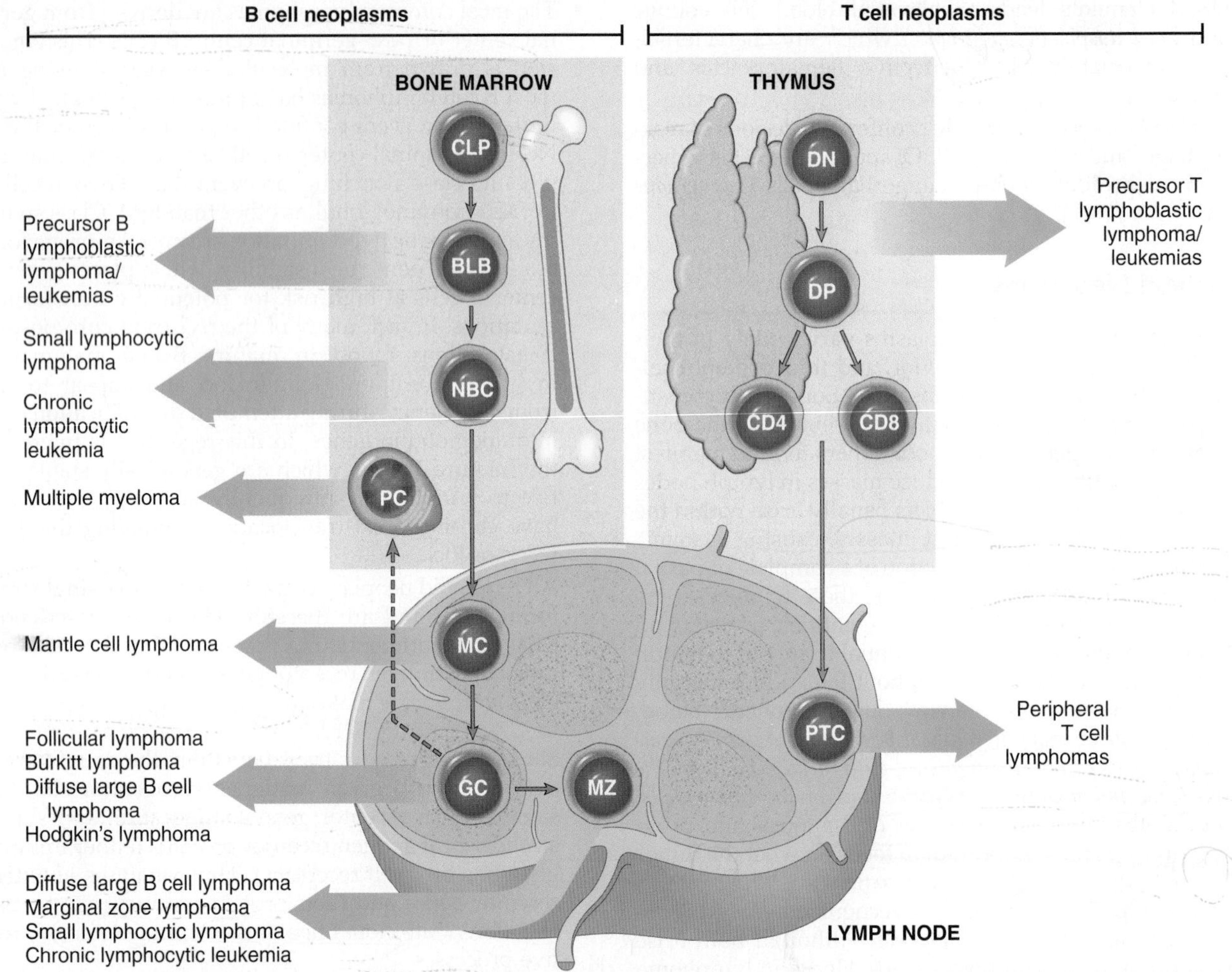

Figure 11–13 Origin of lymphoid neoplasms. Stages of B and T cell differentiation from which specific lymphoid and tumors emerge are shown. BLB, pre-B lymphoblast; CLP, common lymphoid progenitor; DN, CD4–/CD8– (double-negative) pro-T cell; DP, CD4+/CD8+ (double-positive) pre-T cell; GC, germinal center B cell; MC, mantle zone B cell; MZ, marginal zone B cell; NBC, naive B cell; PC, plasma cell; PTC, peripheral T cell.

- Precursor B and T cell lymphoblastic lymphoma/ leukemia—commonly called acute lymphoblastic leukemia (ALL)
- Chronic lymphocytic leukemia/small lymphocytic lymphoma
- Follicular lymphoma
- Mantle cell lymphoma
- Diffuse large B cell lymphomas
- Burkitt lymphoma
- Multiple myeloma and related plasma cell tumors
- Hodgkin lymphoma

Together these neoplasms constitute more than 90% of the lymphoid tumors seen in the United States.

The salient features of the more common lymphoid leukemias, non-Hodgkin lymphomas, and plasma cell tumors are summarized in Table 11–8. Hodgkin lymphomas will be discussed later. Also included in the following discussion are a few of the uncommon entities with distinctive clinicopathologic features.

Acute Lymphoblastic Leukemia/Lymphoblastic Lymphoma

Acute lymphoblastic leukemia (ALL) and lymphoblastic lymphoma are aggressive tumors, composed of immature lymphocytes (lymphoblasts), that occur predominantly in children and young adults. The various lymphoblastic tumors are morphologically indistinguishable, often cause similar signs and symptoms, and are treated similarly. These tumors are therefore considered together here.

Just as B cell precursors normally develop within the bone marrow, pre-B cell tumors usually manifest in the bone marrow and peripheral blood as leukemias. Similarly, pre-T cell tumors commonly manifest as masses involving the thymus, the normal site of early T cell differentiation. However, pre-T cell "lymphomas" often progress rapidly to a leukemic phase, and other pre-T cell tumors seem to involve only the marrow at presentation. Hence, *both pre-B and pre-T cell tumors usually take on the clinical appearance of ALL at some time during their course.* As a group, ALLs constitute 80% of childhood leukemia, peaking in incidence at age 4, with most cases being of pre-B cell origin. The pre-T cell tumors are most common in male patients between 15 and 20 years of age.

Table 11–7 WHO Classification of Lymphoid Neoplasms*

Precursor B Cell Neoplasms
Precursor B cell leukemia/lymphoma (B-ALL)
Peripheral B Cell Neoplasms
B cell chronic lymphocytic leukemia (CLL)/small lymphocytic lymphoma (SLL)
B cell prolymphocytic leukemia
Lymphoplasmacytic lymphoma
Mantle cell lymphoma
Follicular lymphoma
Extranodal marginal zone lymphoma
Splenic and nodal marginal zone lymphoma
Hairy cell leukemia
Plasmacytoma/plasma cell myeloma
Diffuse large B cell lymphoma (multiple subtypes)
Burkitt lymphoma
Precursor T Cell Neoplasms
Precursor T cell leukemia/lymphoma (T-ALL)
Peripheral T/NK Cell Neoplasms
T cell prolymphocytic leukemia
T cell granular lymphocytic leukemia
Mycosis fungoides/Sézary syndrome
Peripheral T cell lymphoma, unspecified
Angioimmunoblastic T cell lymphoma
Anaplastic large cell lymphoma
Enteropathy-type T cell lymphoma
Panniculitis-like T cell lymphoma
Hepatosplenic $\gamma\delta$ T cell lymphoma
Adult T cell lymphoma/leukemia
Extranodal NK/T cell lymphoma
Aggressive NK cell leukemia
Hodgkin Lymphoma
Nodular sclerosis
Mixed cellularity
Lymphocyte-rich
Lymphocyte-depletion
Lymphocyte predominance, nodular

*Entries in *italics* are among the most common lymphoid tumors.
NK, natural killer; WHO, World Health Organization.

The pathogenesis, laboratory findings, and clinical features of ALL closely resemble those of acute myeloid leukemia (AML), the other major type of acute leukemia. Because of these similarities, the features common to the acute leukemias are reviewed first, followed by a discussion of those specific to ALL.

PATHOGENESIS

The principal pathogenic defect in acute leukemia and lymphoblastic lymphoma is a block in differentiation. This "maturation arrest" stems from **acquired mutations in specific transcription factors that regulate the differentiation of immature lymphoid or myeloid progenitors.** Normal B cell, T cell, and myeloid differentiation are regulated by different lineage-specific transcription factors; accordingly, the mutated transcription factor genes found in acute leukemias derived from each of these lineages also are distinct. The most commonly mutated transcription factor genes are *TEL1*, *AML1*, *E2A*, *PAX5*, and *EBF* in ALLs of B cell origin (B-ALLs) and *TAL1* and *NOTCH1* in T cell ALLs (T-ALLs).

Acute leukemias also are associated with complementary acquired mutations that allow the tumor cells to proliferate in a growth factor–independent fashion. In B-ALL, one of the most important mutations of this type is a *BCR-ABL* fusion gene created by a (9;22) translocation (the so-called Philadelphia chromosome, for the city of its discovery). As discussed later on, the same translocation also is found in chronic myelogenous leukemia (CML). The *BCR-ABL* fusion gene encodes a BCR-ABL tyrosine kinase that constitutively activates the same pathways that are normally stimulated by growth factors. Some T-ALLs are associated with a different ABL fusion gene, *NUP214-ABL*, which has functional consequences similar to those of *BCR-ABL*.

In tumors manifesting as "leukemias," blasts accumulating in the marrow suppress the growth of normal hematopoietic cells by physical displacement and by other, poorly understood mechanisms. Eventually this suppression produces bone marrow failure, which accounts for the major clinical manifestations. The therapeutic goal, therefore, is to reduce the leukemic clone sufficiently to allow normal hematopoiesis to resume.

Clinical Features of Acute Leukemias

Acute leukemias have the following characteristics:

- *Abrupt, stormy onset.* Most patients present for medical attention within 3 months of the onset of symptoms.
- *Clinical signs and symptoms related to suppressed marrow function,* including fatigue (due to anemia), fever (reflecting infections resulting from neutropenia), and bleeding (petechiae, ecchymoses, epistaxis, gum bleeding) secondary to thrombocytopenia
- *Bone pain and tenderness,* resulting from marrow expansion and infiltration of the subperiosteum
- *Generalized lymphadenopathy, splenomegaly, and hepatomegaly due to dissemination of the leukemic cells.* These are more pronounced in ALL than in AML.
- *Central nervous system manifestations,* including headache, vomiting, and nerve palsies resulting from meningeal spread. These are more common in children than in adults and in ALL than in AML.

Laboratory Findings in Acute Leukemias

The diagnosis of acute leukemia rests on the identification of blasts. The peripheral blood sometimes contains no blasts (aleukemic leukemia); in such cases the diagnosis can be established only by marrow examination.

The white cell count is variable; it may be greater than 100,000 cells/μL but in about half of the patients is less than 10,000 cells/μL. Anemia is almost always present, and the platelet count usually is below 100,000/μL. Neutropenia is another common finding.

MORPHOLOGY

Because of differing responses to therapy, it is of great practical importance to distinguish ALL from AML. By definition, in ALL blasts compose more than 25% of the marrow cellularity. In Wright-Giemsa–stained preparations, lymphoblasts have coarse, clumped chromatin, one or

Table 11–8 Characteristics of the More Common Lymphoid Leukemias, Non-Hodgkin Lymphomas, and Plasma Cell Tumors

Clinical Entity	Frequency	Salient Morphology	Immunophenotype	Comments
Precursor B cell lymphoblastic leukemia/ lymphoma	85% of childhood acute leukemias	Lymphoblasts with irregular nuclear contours, condensed chromatin, small nucleoli, and scant, agranular cytoplasm	TdT+ immature B cells (CD19+, variable expression of other B cell markers)	Usually manifests as acute leukemia; less common in adults; prognosis is predicted by karyotype
Precursor T cell leukemia/ lymphoma	15% of childhood acute leukemias; 40% of childhood lymphomas	Identical to precursor B cell lymphoblastic leukemia/ lymphoma	TdT+ immature T cells (CD2+, CD7+, variable expression of other T cell markers)	Most common in adolescent males; often manifests as a mediastinal mass associated with *NOTCH1* mutations
Small lymphocytic lymphoma/chronic lymphocytic leukemia	3–4% of adult lymphomas; 30% of all leukemias	Small resting lymphocytes mixed with variable numbers of large activated cells; lymph nodes diffusely effaced	CD5+ B cell expressing surface immunoglobulin	Occurs in older adults; usually involves nodes, marrow, and spleen; most patients have peripheral blood involvement; indolent
Follicular lymphoma	40% of adult lymphomas	Frequent small "cleaved" cells mixed with large cells; growth pattern usually is nodular (follicular)	CD10+, BCL2+ mature B cells that express surface immunoglobulin	Occurs in older adults; usually involves nodes, marrow, and spleen; associated with t(14;18); indolent
Mantle cell lymphoma	3–4% of adult lymphomas	Small to intermediate-sized irregular lymphocytes growing in a diffuse pattern	CD5+ mature B cells that express cyclin D1 and have surface Ig	Occurs mainly in older males; usually involves nodes, marrow, spleen, and GI tract; t(11;14) is characteristic; moderately aggressive
Extranodal marginal zone lymphoma	~5% of adult lymphomas	Malignant B cells home to epithelium, creating "lymphoepithelial lesions"	CD5–, CD10– mature B cells with surface immunoglobulin	Frequently occurs at extranodal sites involved by chronic inflammation; very indolent; may be cured by local excision
Diffuse large B cell lymphoma	40–50% of adult lymphomas	Variable; most resemble large germinal center B cells; diffuse growth pattern	Mature B cells with variable expression of CD10 and surface immunoglobulin	Occurs in all age groups but most common in older adults; often arises at extranodal sites; aggressive
Burkitt lymphoma	<1% of lymphomas in the United States	Intermediate-sized round lymphoid cells with several nucleoli; diffuse growth pattern associated with apoptosis produces a "starry sky" appearance	Mature CD10+ B cells expressing surface immunoglobulin	Endemic in Africa, sporadic elsewhere; associated with immunosuppression and EBV (subset of cases); predominantly affects children; often manifests with visceral involvement; highly aggressive
Plasmacytoma/plasma cell myeloma	Most common lymphoid neoplasm in older adults	Plasma cells in sheets, sometimes with prominent nucleoli or inclusions containing immunoglobulins	Terminally differentiated plasma cells containing cytoplasmic immunoglobulins	Myeloma manifests as disseminated bone disease, often with destructive lytic lesions; hypercalcemia, renal insufficiency, and bacterial infections are common
Mycosis fungoides	Most common cutaneous lymphoid malignancy	In most cases, small lymphoid cells with markedly convoluted nuclei; cells often infiltrate the epidermis (Pautrier microabscesses)	CD4+ mature T cells	Manifests with localized or more generalized skin involvement; generally indolent *Sézary syndrome*: a more aggressive variant characterized by diffuse skin erythema and peripheral blood involvement
Peripheral T cell lymphoma, not otherwise specified (NOS)	Most common adult T cell lymphoma	Variable; usually a spectrum of small to large lymphoid cells	Mature T cell phenotype (CD3+)	Probably spans a diverse collection of rare tumors; often disseminated, generally aggressive

EBV, Epstein-Barr virus; GI, gastrointestinal; TdT, terminal deoxynucleotidyl transferase.

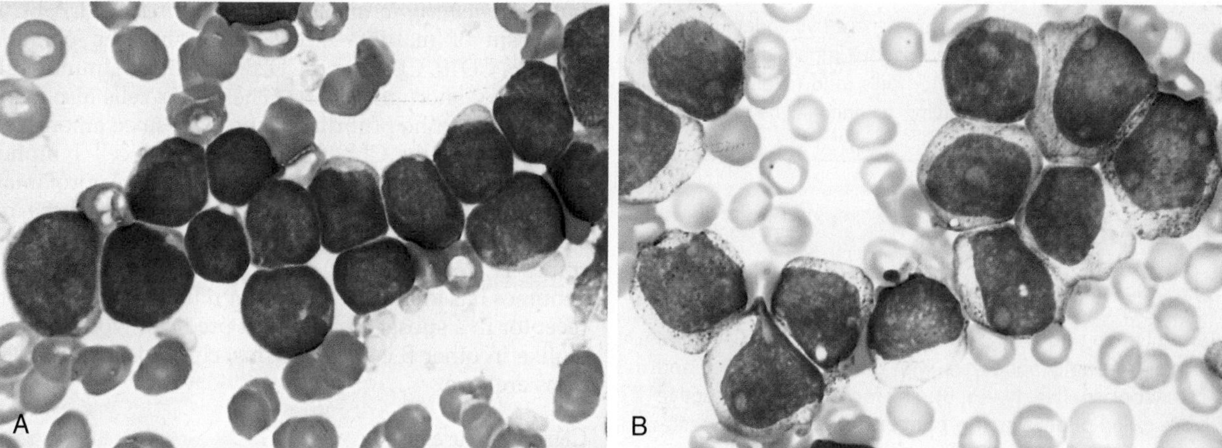

Figure 11–14 Morphologic comparison of lymphoblasts and myeloblasts. **A,** Lymphoblastic leukemia/lymphoma. Lymphoblasts have condensed nuclear chromatin, small nucleoli, and scant agranular cytoplasm. **B,** Acute myeloid leukemia. Myeloblasts have delicate nuclear chromatin, prominent nucleoli, and fine azurophilic cytoplasmic granules.
(Courtesy of Dr. Robert W. McKenna, Department of Pathology, University of Texas Southwestern Medical School, Dallas, Texas.)

two nucleoli, and scant agranular cytoplasm (Fig. 11–14, *A*), whereas myeloblasts have nuclei with finer chromatin and more cytoplasm, which often contains granules (Fig. 11–14, *B*). Lymphoblasts also often contain cytoplasmic glycogen granules that are periodic acid–Schiff–positive, whereas myeloblasts are often peroxidase-positive.

With completion of the foregoing "short course" in acute leukemia, our focus now returns to the ALLs; the AMLs are discussed later.

Genetic Features. Approximately 90% of ALLs have nonrandom karyotypic abnormalities. Most common in childhood pre-B cell tumors are hyperdiploidy (more than 50 chromosomes/cell) and the presence of a cryptic (12;21) translocation involving the *TEL1* and *AML1* genes, while about 25% of adult pre-B cell tumors harbor the (9;22) translocation involving the *ABL* and *BCR* genes. Pre-T cell tumors are associated with diverse chromosomal aberrations, including frequent translocations involving the T cell receptor loci and transcription factor genes such as *TAL1*.

Immunophenotypic Features. Immunophenotyping is very useful in subtyping lymphoblastic tumors and distinguishing them from AML. Terminal deoxynucleotidyl transferase (TdT), an enzyme specifically expressed in pre-B and pre-T cells, is present in more than 95% of cases. Further subtyping of ALL into pre-B and pre-T cell types relies on stains for lineage-specific markers, such as CD19 (B cell) and CD3 (T cell).

Prognosis

Treatment of childhood ALL is one of the great success stories in oncology. Children 2 to 10 years of age have the best prognosis; with intensive chemotherapy up to 80% are cured. Other groups of patients do less well. Variables correlated with worse outcomes include male gender; age younger than 2 or older than 10 years; a high leukocyte count at diagnosis; and molecular evidence of persistent disease on day 28 of treatment. Age-dependent differences in the frequencies of various karyotypic abnormalities largely explain the relationship of age to outcome. Tumors with "good prognosis" chromosomal aberrations (such as the t[12;21] and hyperdiploidy) are common in the 2- to 10-year age group. By contrast, rearrangements of the gene *MLL* or the presence of a *BCR-ABL* fusion gene, both associated with poor outcomes in B cell tumors, are most common in children younger than 2 years of age and adults, respectively. None of the chromosomal rearrangements found in pre-T cell tumors is predictive of outcome.

Chronic Lymphocytic Leukemia/Small Lymphocytic Lymphoma

Chronic lymphocytic leukemia (CLL) and small lymphocytic lymphoma (SLL) are essentially identical, differing only in the extent of peripheral blood involvement. Somewhat arbitrarily, if the peripheral blood lymphocyte count exceeds 4000 cells/μL, the patient is diagnosed with CLL; if it does not, a diagnosis of SLL is made. Most patients with lymphoid neoplasms fit the diagnostic criteria for CLL, which is the most common leukemia of adults in the Western world. By contrast, SLL constitutes only 4% of NHLs. For unclear reasons, CLL/SLL is much less common in Asia.

PATHOGENESIS

CLL/SLL is an indolent, slowly growing tumor, suggesting that increased tumor cell survival is more important than tumor cell proliferation in this disease. In line with this idea, the **tumor cells contain high levels of BCL2,** a protein that inhibits apoptosis (Chapters 1 and 5). Unlike in follicular lymphoma (discussed later), the *BCL2* gene is not rearranged. Some evidence suggests that *BCL2* is upregulated in the tumor cells as a consequence of the loss of several regulatory micro-RNAs that are encoded on chromosome 13.

Another important pathogenic aspect of CLL/SLL is **immune dysregulation.** Through unclear mechanisms, the accumulation of CLL/SLL cells suppresses normal B cell function, often resulting in **hypogammaglobulinemia.** Paradoxically, approximately 15% of patients have autoantibodies against their own red cells or platelets. When present, the autoantibodies are made by nonmalignant bystander B cells, indicating that the tumor cells somehow impair immune tolerance. As time passes the tumor cells tend to displace the normal marrow elements, leading to anemia, neutropenia, and eventual thrombocytopenia.

MORPHOLOGY

In SLL/CLL, sheets of small lymphocytes and scattered ill-defined foci of larger, actively dividing cells diffusely efface involved lymph nodes (Fig. 11–15, *A*). The predominant cells are small, resting lymphocytes with dark, round nuclei, and scanty cytoplasm (Fig. 11–15, *B*). The foci of mitotically active cells are called **proliferation centers,** which are pathognomonic for CLL/SLL. In addition to the lymph nodes, the bone marrow, spleen, and liver are involved in almost all cases. In most patients there is an absolute **lymphocytosis** featuring small, mature-looking lymphocytes. The circulating tumor cells are fragile and during the preparation of smears frequently are disrupted, producing characteristic **smudge cells.** Variable numbers of larger activated lymphocytes are also usually present in the blood smear.

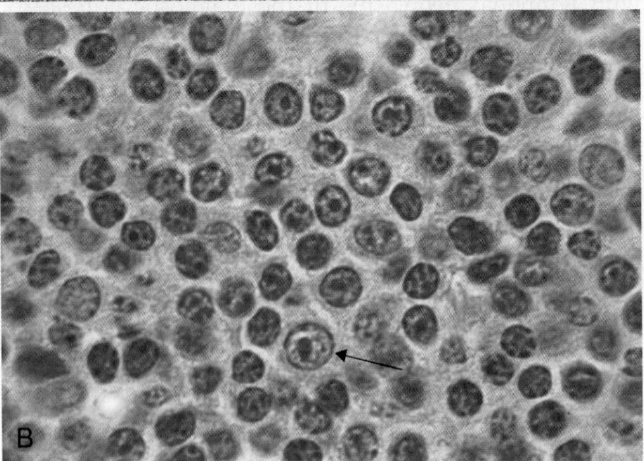

Figure 11–15 Small lymphocytic lymphoma/chronic lymphocytic leukemia—lymph node. **A,** Low-power view shows diffuse effacement of nodal architecture. **B,** At high power, a majority of the tumor cells have the appearance of small, round lymphocytes. A "prolymphocyte," a larger cell with a centrally placed nucleolus, also is present in this field (*arrow*).

(A, Courtesy of Dr. José Hernandez, Department of Pathology, University of Texas Southwestern Medical School, Dallas, Texas.)

Immunophenotypic and Genetic Features. CLL/SLL is a neoplasm of mature B cells expressing the pan-B cell markers CD19, CD20, and CD23 and surface immunoglobulin heavy and light chains. The tumor cells also express CD5. This is a helpful diagnostic clue, since among B cell lymphomas only CLL/SLL and mantle cell lymphoma (discussed later) commonly express CD5. Approximately 50% of tumors have karyotypic abnormalities, the most common of which are trisomy 12 and deletions of chromosomes 11, 13, and 17. "Deep sequencing" of CLL/SLL cell genomes has identified activating mutations in the Notch1 receptor in a subset of cases that predict a worse outcome. Unlike in other B cell neoplasms, chromosomal translocations are rare.

Clinical Features

When first detected, CLL/SLL is often asymptomatic. The most common clinical signs and symptoms are nonspecific and include easy fatigability, weight loss, and anorexia. Generalized *lymphadenopathy* and *hepatosplenomegaly* are present in 50% to 60% of patients. The leukocyte count may be increased only slightly (in SLL) or may exceed 200,000 cells/μL. *Hypogammaglobulinemia* develops in more than 50% of the patients, usually late in the course, and leads to an increased susceptibility to bacterial infections. Less commonly *autoimmune hemolytic anemia* and *thrombocytopenia* are seen. The course and prognosis are extremely variable. Many patients live more than 10 years after diagnosis and die of unrelated causes. The median survival is 4 to 6 years, however, and as time passes, CLL/SLL tends to transform to more aggressive tumors that resemble either prolymphocytic leukemia or diffuse large B cell lymphoma. Once transformation occurs, the median survival is less than 1 year.

Follicular Lymphoma

This relatively common tumor constitutes 40% of the adult NHLs in the United States. Like CLL/SLL, it occurs much less frequently in Asian populations.

PATHOGENESIS

As in CLL/SLL, the neoplastic cells characteristically express BCL2, a protein that is absent from normal germinal center B cells. **Greater than 85% of tumors have a characteristic (14;18) translocation** that fuses the *BCL2* gene on chromosome 18 to the *IgH* locus on chromosome 14. This chromosomal rearrangement explains the inappropriate "overexpression" of BCL2 protein in the tumor cells and contributes to tumor cell survival. Whole genome sequencing of follicular lymphomas has identified loss-of-function mutations in several genes encoding histone acetyl transferases in about a third of cases, suggesting that epigenetic changes also contribute to the genesis of these tumors.

MORPHOLOGY

Lymph nodes usually are effaced by a distinctly **nodular proliferation** (Fig 11–16, *A*). The tumor cells resemble

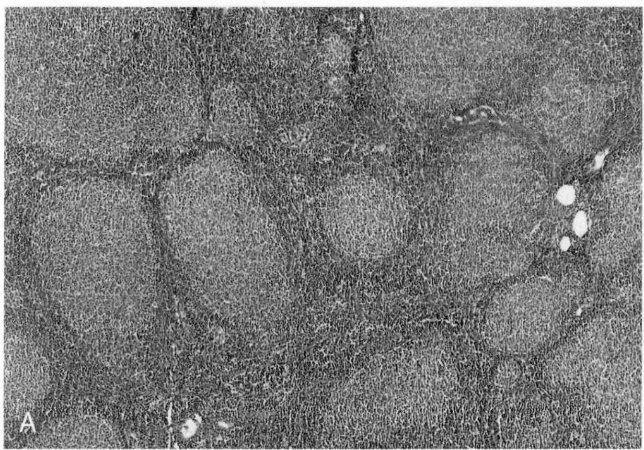
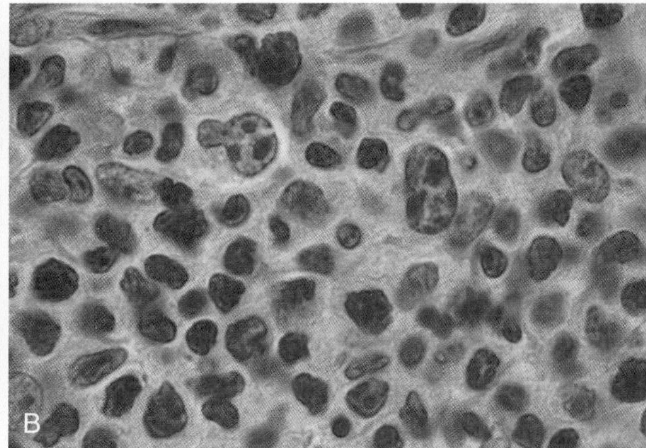

Figure 11–16 Follicular lymphoma—lymph node. **A,** Nodular aggregates of lymphoma cells are present throughout. **B,** At high magnification, small lymphoid cells with condensed chromatin and irregular or cleaved nuclear outlines (centrocytes) are mixed with a population of larger cells with nucleoli (centroblasts).

(A, Courtesy of Dr. Robert W. McKenna, Department of Pathology, University of Texas Southwestern Medical School, Dallas, Texas.)

normal germinal center B cells. Most commonly the predominant neoplastic cells are slightly larger than resting lymphocytes that have angular "cleaved" nuclei with prominent indentations and linear infoldings (Fig. 11–16, *B*). The nuclear chromatin is coarse and condensed, and nucleoli are indistinct. These small, cleaved cells are mixed with variable numbers of larger cells with vesicular chromatin, several nucleoli, and modest amounts of cytoplasm. In most tumors, large cells are a minor component of the overall cellularity, mitoses are infrequent, and single necrotic cells (cells undergoing apoptosis) are not seen. These features help to distinguish follicular lymphoma from follicular hyperplasia, in which mitoses and apoptosis are prominent. Uncommonly, large cells predominate, a histologic pattern that correlates with a more aggressive clinical behavior.

Immunophenotypic Features. These tumors express pan-B cell markers (CD19 and CD20), CD10, and BCL6, a transcription factor required for the generation of germinal center B cells.

Clinical Features

Follicular lymphoma mainly occurs in adults older than 50 years of age and affects males and females equally. It usually manifests as *painless, generalized lymphadenopathy.* The bone marrow is almost always involved at diagnosis, while visceral disease is uncommon. While the natural history is prolonged (median survival, 7 to 9 years), *follicular lymphoma is not curable,* an unfortunate feature shared with most other relatively indolent lymphoid malignancies. As a result, therapy with cytotoxic drugs and rituximab (anti-CD20 antibody) is reserved for those with bulky, symptomatic disease. In about 40% of patients, follicular lymphoma progresses to diffuse large B cell lymphoma. This transformation is an ominous event, as tumors arising from such conversions are much less curable than de novo diffuse large B cell lymphomas, described later.

Mantle Cell Lymphoma

Mantle cell lymphoma is composed of cells resembling the naive B cells found in the mantle zones of normal lymphoid follicles. It constitutes approximately 4% of all NHLs and occurs mainly in men older than 50 years of age.

MORPHOLOGY

Mantle cell lymphoma may involve lymph nodes in a diffuse or vaguely nodular pattern. The tumor cells usually are slightly larger than normal lymphocytes and have an irregular nucleus, inconspicuous nucleoli, and scant cytoplasm. Less commonly, the cells are larger and morphologically resemble lymphoblasts. The bone marrow is involved in most cases and the peripheral blood in about 20% of cases. The tumor sometimes arises in the gastrointestinal tract, often manifesting as multifocal submucosal nodules that grossly resemble polyps (lymphomatoid polyposis).

Immunophenotypic and Genetic Features. *Almost all tumors have an (11;14) translocation that fuses the cyclin D1 gene to the IgH locus.* This translocation dysregulates the expression of cyclin D1, a cell cycle regulator (Chapter 5), and is believed to be an important mediator of uncontrolled tumor cell growth. The tumor cells usually coexpress surface IgM and IgD, pan-B cell antigens (CD19 and CD20), and CD5. Mantle cell lymphoma is most readily distinguished from CLL/SLL by the absence of proliferation centers and the presence of cyclin D1 protein.

Clinical Features

Most patients present with fatigue and lymphadenopathy and are found to have generalized disease involving the bone marrow, spleen, liver, and (often) the gastrointestinal tract. These tumors are moderately aggressive and incurable. The median survival is 3 to 5 years.

Diffuse Large B Cell Lymphoma

Diffuse large B cell lymphoma is the *most common type of lymphoma in adults, accounting for approximately 50% of adult NHLs.* It includes several subtypes that share an aggressive natural history.

PATHOGENESIS

About one third of tumors have rearrangements of the *BCL6* gene, located on 3q27, and an even higher fraction of tumors have activating point mutations in the BCL6 promoter. Both aberrations result in increased levels of BCL6 protein, an important transcriptional regulator of gene expression in germinal center B cells. Another 30% of tumors have a (14;18) translocation involving the *BCL2* gene that results in overexpression of BCL2 protein. Some of these tumors may represent "transformed" follicular lymphomas. Indeed, like follicular lymphoma, about a third of diffuse large B cell lymphomas have loss-of-function mutations in genes encoding histone acetyl transferases, pointing to a potential role for epigenetic alterations in this tumor.

MORPHOLOGY

The neoplastic B cells are large (at least three to four times the size of resting lymphocytes) and vary in appearance from tumor to tumor. In many tumors, cells with round or oval nuclear contours, dispersed chromatin, several distinct nucleoli, and modest amounts of pale cytoplasm predominate (Fig. 11–17). In other tumors, the cells have a round or multilobate vesicular nucleus, one or two prominent centrally placed nucleoli, and abundant pale or basophilic cytoplasm. Occasionally, the tumor cells are highly anaplastic and include tumor giant cells resembling Reed-Sternberg cells, the malignant cells of Hodgkin lymphoma.

Immunophenotypic Features. These mature B cell tumors express pan-B cell antigens, such as CD19 and CD20. Many also express surface IgM and/or IgG. Other antigens (e.g., CD10, BCL2) are variably expressed.

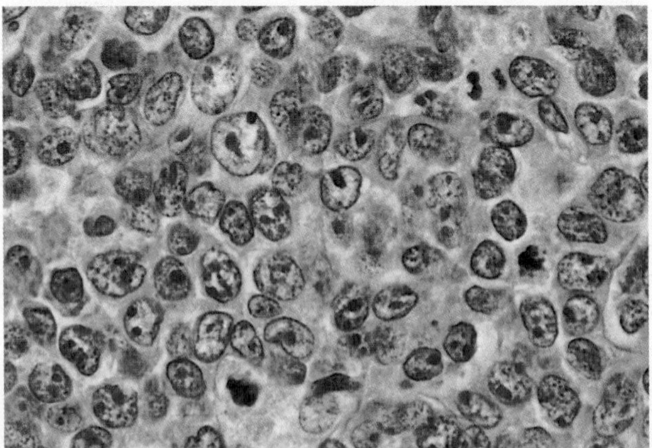

Figure 11–17 Diffuse large B cell lymphoma—lymph node. The tumor cells have large nuclei with open chromatin and prominent nucleoli. *(Courtesy of Dr. Robert W. McKenna, Department of Pathology, University of Texas Southwestern Medical School, Dallas, Texas.)*

Subtypes of Diffuse Large B Cell Lymphoma. Several distinctive clinicopathologic subtypes are included in the category of diffuse large B cell lymphoma. *EBV-associated diffuse large B cell lymphomas* arise in the setting of the acquired immunodeficiency syndrome (AIDS), iatrogenic immunosuppression (e.g., in transplant recipients), and the elderly. In the post-transplantation setting, these tumors often begin as EBV-driven polyclonal B cell proliferations that may regress if immune function is restored. Otherwise, transformation to clonal large B cell lymphoma is observed over weeks to months. *Kaposi sarcoma herpesvirus* (KSHV), also called *human herpesvirus type 8* (HHV-8), is associated with rare *primary effusion lymphomas,* which may arise within the pleural cavity, pericardium, or peritoneum. These lymphomas are latently infected with KSHV, which encodes proteins homologous to several known oncoproteins, including cyclin D1, and are confined to immunosuppressed hosts. Of note, KSHV also is associated with Kaposi sarcoma in patients with AIDS (Chapters 4 and 9). *Mediastinal large B cell lymphoma* occurs most often in young women and shows a predilection for spread to abdominal viscera and the central nervous system.

Clinical Features

Although the median age at presentation is about 60 years, diffuse large B cell lymphomas can occur at any age; they constitute about 15% of childhood lymphomas. Patients typically present with a rapidly enlarging, often symptomatic mass at one or several sites. *Extranodal presentations are common.* Although the gastrointestinal tract and the brain are among the more frequent extranodal sites, tumors can appear in virtually any organ or tissue. Unlike the more indolent lymphomas (e.g., follicular lymphoma), involvement of the liver, spleen, and bone marrow is not common at diagnosis.

Without treatment, diffuse large cell B cell lymphomas are aggressive and rapidly fatal. With intensive combination chemotherapy and anti-CD20 immunotherapy, complete remissions are achieved in 60% to 80% of the patients; of these, approximately 50% remain free of disease and appear to be cured. For those not so fortunate, other aggressive treatments (e.g., high-dose chemotherapy and hematopoietic stem cell transplantation) offer some hope. Microarray-based molecular profiling of these tumors can predict response to current therapies and is being used to identify new, targeted therapy approaches.

Burkitt Lymphoma

Burkitt lymphoma is endemic in parts of Africa and occurs sporadically in other geographic areas, including the United States. Histologically, the African and nonendemic diseases are identical, although there are clinical and virologic differences.

PATHOGENESIS

Burkitt lymphoma is highly associated with translocations involving the *MYC* gene on chromosome 8. Most translocations fuse *MYC* with the *IgH* gene on chromosome 14, but variant translocations involving the κ and λ light chain loci on chromosomes 2 and 22, respectively, are also observed. The net result of each is the same—the dysregulation and overexpression of MYC protein. The role of MYC in transformation is discussed in Chapter 5. In most endemic cases and about 20% of sporadic cases, the tumor cells are latently infected with EBV, but the role of EBV in the genesis of this tumor remains uncertain.

MORPHOLOGY

The tumor cells are intermediate in size and typically have round or oval nuclei and two to five distinct nucleoli (Fig. 11–18). There is a moderate amount of basophilic or amphophilic cytoplasm that often contains small, lipid-filled vacuoles (a feature appreciated only on smears). **Very high rates of proliferation and apoptosis are characteristic,** the latter accounting for the presence of numerous tissue macrophages containing ingested nuclear debris. These benign macrophages often are surrounded by a clear space, creating a **"starry sky" pattern.**

Immunophenotypic Features

These B cell tumors express surface IgM, the pan-B cell markers CD19 and CD20, and the germinal center B cell markers CD10 and BCL6.

Clinical Features

Both the endemic and nonendemic sporadic forms affect mainly children and young adults. Burkitt lymphoma accounts for approximately 30% of childhood NHLs in the United States. In both settings, the disease usually arises at extranodal sites. Endemic tumors often manifest as maxillary or mandibular masses, whereas abdominal tumors involving the bowel, retroperitoneum, and ovaries are more common in North America. Leukemic presentations are uncommon but do occur and must be distinguished from ALL, which is treated with different drug regimens. Burkitt lymphoma is among the fastest-growing human neoplasms; however, with very aggressive chemotherapy regimens, a majority of patients can be cured.

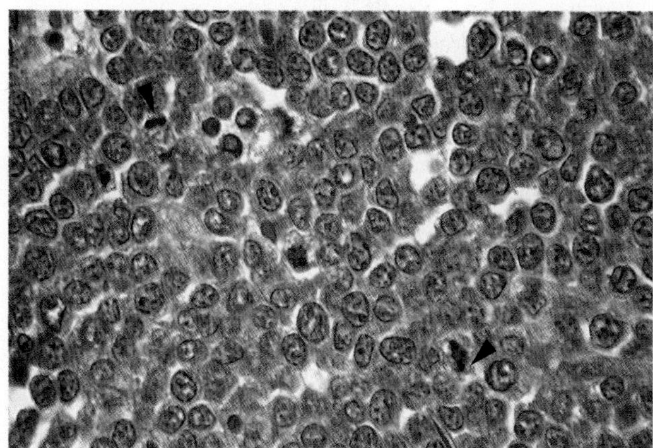

Figure 11–18 Burkitt lymphoma—lymph node. The tumor cells and their nuclei are fairly uniform, giving a monotonous appearance. Note the high level of mitotic activity (*arrowheads*) and prominent nucleoli. The "starry sky" pattern produced by interspersed, lightly staining, normal macrophages is better appreciated at a lower magnification.

(Courtesy of Dr. Robert W. McKenna, Department of Pathology, University of Texas Southwestern Medical School, Dallas, Texas.)

Multiple Myeloma and Related Plasma Cell Tumors

In virtually all cases, multiple myelomas and related plasma cell tumors secrete a single complete or partial immunoglobulin. Because these immunoglobulins can be detected in the serum, these disorders are also referred to as *monoclonal gammopathies,* and the associated immunoglobulin is often referred to as an *M protein.* Although M proteins may be indicative of overt malignancy, they also are found surprisingly often in otherwise normal elderly persons—a condition called monoclonal gammopathy of undetermined significance (MGUS), described later. Collectively, these disorders account for approximately 15% of the deaths that are caused by tumors of white blood cells. They are most common in middle-aged and elderly persons.

The plasma cell neoplasms can be divided into six major variants: (1) multiple myeloma, (2) solitary plasmacytoma, (3) lymphoplasmacytic lymphoma, (4) heavy-chain disease, (5) primary amyloidosis, and (6) MGUS. The focus here is on the most important of these disorders, multiple myeloma and lymphoplasmacytic lymphoma, with a brief discussion of the other disorders.

Multiple Myeloma

Multiple myeloma is one of the most common lymphoid malignancies; approximately 20,000 new cases are diagnosed in the United States each year. The median age at diagnosis is 70 years of age, and it is more common in males and in people of African origin. *It principally involves the bone marrow and usually is associated with lytic lesions throughout the skeletal system.*

The most frequent M protein produced by myeloma cells is IgG (60%), followed by IgA (20% to 25%); only rarely are IgM, IgD, or IgE M proteins observed. In the remaining 15% to 20% of cases, the plasma cells produce *only* κ or λ light chains. Because of their low molecular weight, free light chains are excreted in the urine, where they are termed Bence Jones proteins. Even more commonly, malignant plasma cells secrete both complete immunoglobulins and free light chains and thus produce both M proteins and Bence Jones proteins. As described later on, the excess light chains have important pathogenic effects.

Solitary Plasmacytoma

Sometimes plasma tumors manifest as *solitary plasmacytomas* involving the skeleton or the soft tissues. Solitary skeletal plasmacytomas tend to occur in the same locations as does multiple myeloma and usually progress to full-blown multiple myeloma over a period of 5 to 10 years; these tumors probably are best thought of as an early stage of multiple myeloma. Modestly elevated M proteins are present in some cases at diagnosis. By contrast, plasmacytomas that occur in soft tissues (most often the upper respiratory tract) spread infrequently and often are cured by local resection.

Table 11–13 Causes of Thrombocytopenia

Decreased Production of Platelets
Generalized Bone Marrow Dysfunction
Aplastic anemia: congenital and acquired Marrow infiltration: leukemia, disseminated cancer
Selective Impairment of Platelet Production
Drug-induced: alcohol, thiazides, cytotoxic drugs Infections: measles, HIV infection
Ineffective Megakaryopoiesis
Megaloblastic anemia Paroxysmal nocturnal hemoglobinuria
Decreased Platelet Survival
Immunologic Destruction
Autoimmune: immune thrombocytopenic purpura, systemic lupus erythematosus Isoimmune: post-transfusion and neonatal Drug-associated: quinidine, heparin, sulfa compounds Infections: infectious mononucleosis, HIV infection, cytomegalovirus infection
Nonimmunologic Destruction
Disseminated intravascular coagulation Thrombotic thrombocytopenic purpura Giant hemangiomas Microangiopathic hemolytic anemias
Sequestration
Hypersplenism
Dilutional
Multiple transfusions (e.g., for massive blood loss)

HIV, human immunodeficiency virus.

cases of chronic ITP. The spleen is an important site of antiplatelet antibody production and the major site of destruction of the IgG-coated platelets. Although splenomegaly is not a feature of uncomplicated chronic ITP, the importance of the spleen in the premature destruction of platelets is proved by the benefits of splenectomy, which normalizes the platelet count and induces a complete remission in more than two thirds of patients. The bone marrow usually contains increased numbers of megakaryocytes, a finding common to all forms of thrombocytopenia caused by accelerated platelet destruction.

The onset of chronic ITP is insidious. Common findings include petechiae, easy bruising, epistaxis, gum bleeding, and hemorrhages after minor trauma. Fortunately, more serious intracerebral or subarachnoid hemorrhages are uncommon. The diagnosis rests on the clinical features, the presence of thrombocytopenia, examination of the marrow, and the exclusion of secondary ITP. Reliable clinical tests for antiplatelet antibodies are not available.

Heparin-Induced Thrombocytopenia

This special type of drug-induced thrombocytopenia (discussed in more detail in Chapter 3) merits brief mention because of its clinical importance. Moderate to severe thrombocytopenia develops in 3% to 5% of patients after 1 to 2 weeks of treatment with unfractionated heparin. The disorder is caused by IgG antibodies that bind to platelet factor 4 on platelet membranes in a heparin-dependent fashion. Resultant activation of the platelets induces their aggregation, thereby exacerbating the condition that heparin is used to treat—thrombosis. Both venous and arterial thromboses occur, even in the setting of marked thrombocytopenia, and can cause severe morbidity (e.g., loss of limbs) and death. Cessation of heparin therapy breaks the cycle of platelet activation and consumption. The risk of this complication is lowered (but not prevented entirely) by use of low-molecular-weight heparin preparations.

Thrombotic Microangiopathies: Thrombotic Thrombocytopenic Purpura and Hemolytic Uremic Syndrome

The term *thrombotic microangiopathies* encompasses a spectrum of clinical syndromes that include thrombotic thrombocytopenic purpura (TTP) and hemolytic uremic syndrome (HUS). As originally defined, TTP is associated with the pentad of fever, thrombocytopenia, microangiopathic hemolytic anemia, transient neurologic deficits, and renal failure. HUS also is associated with microangiopathic hemolytic anemia and thrombocytopenia but is distinguished from TTP by the absence of neurologic symptoms, the dominance of acute renal failure, and frequent occurrence in children (Chapter 13). Clinical experience has blurred these distinctions, as many adults with TTP lack one or more of the five criteria, and some patients with HUS have fever and neurologic dysfunction. *Fundamental to both conditions is the widespread formation of platelet-rich thrombi in the microcirculation.* The consumption of platelets leads to thrombocytopenia, and the narrowing of blood vessels by the platelet-rich thrombi results in a microangiopathic hemolytic anemia.

PATHOGENESIS

For many years the pathogenesis of TTP was enigmatic, although treatment with plasma exchange (initiated in the early 1970s) converted a disease that was almost uniformly fatal to one that is now successfully treated in more than 80% of affected persons. The underlying cause of most cases of TTP has now been elucidated. In brief, **symptomatic patients are deficient in the metalloprotease ADAMTS 13.** This enzyme degrades very-high-molecular-weight multimers of von Willebrand factor (vWF); hence, a deficiency of ADAMTS 13 allows abnormally large vWF multimers to accumulate in plasma. Under some circumstances, these colossal vWF multimers promote the formation of platelet microaggregates throughout the circulation. The superimposition of an endothelial cell injury (caused by some other condition) can further promote microaggregate formation, thus initiating or exacerbating clinically evident TTP.

ADAMTS 13 deficiency can be inherited or acquired, the latter by way of autoantibodies that bind and inhibit the metalloprotease. TTP must be considered in any patient with unexplained thrombocytopenia and microangiopathic hemolytic anemia, as any delay in diagnosis can be fatal.

Although clinically similar to TTP, HUS has a different pathogenesis. Most cases in children and elderly persons are triggered by infectious gastroenteritis caused by *E. coli* strain O157:H7. This organism elaborates a Shiga-like toxin that damages endothelial cells, which initiates platelet activation and aggregation. Affected persons often present with bloody diarrhea, followed a few days later by acute renal failure and microangiopathic anemia. Recovery is possible with supportive care and plasma exchange, but irreversible renal damage and death can occur in more severe cases. About 10% of cases of HUS are caused by inherited mutations or autoantibodies that lead to deficiency of factor H, factor I, or CD46, each of which is a negative regulator of the alternative complement cascade. The absence of these factors leads to uncontrolled complement activation after minor endothelial injury, resulting in thrombosis. HUS also can be seen after other exposures (e.g., to certain drugs or radiation) that damage endothelial cells. Here the prognosis is more guarded, as the underlying conditions that trigger these forms of HUS are often chronic or life-threatening.

Although DIC and the thrombotic microangiopathies share features such as microvascular occlusion and microangiopathic hemolytic anemia, they are pathogenically distinct. Unlike in DIC, in TTP and HUS activation of the coagulation cascade is not of primary importance, so results of laboratory tests of coagulation (such as the PT and the PTT) usually are normal.

COAGULATION DISORDERS

Coagulation disorders result from either congenital or acquired deficiencies of clotting factors. *Acquired deficiencies are most common* and often involve several factors simultaneously. As discussed in Chapter 7, *vitamin K* is required for the synthesis of prothrombin and clotting factors VII, IX, and X, and its deficiency causes a severe coagulation defect. The liver synthesizes several coagulation factors and also removes many activated coagulation factors from the circulation; thus, *hepatic parenchymal diseases are common causes* of complex hemorrhagic diatheses. As already discussed, DIC also may lead to multiple concomitant factor deficiencies. Rarely, autoantibodies may cause acquired deficiencies limited to a single factor.

Hereditary deficiencies of each of the coagulation factors have been identified. Hemophilia A (a deficiency of factor VIII) and hemophilia B (Christmas disease, a deficiency of factor IX) are X-linked traits, whereas most deficiencies are autosomal recessive disorders. Of the inherited deficiencies, only von Willebrand disease, hemophilia A, and hemophilia B are sufficiently common to warrant further consideration.

Deficiencies of Factor VIII–von Willebrand Factor Complex

Hemophilia A and von Willebrand disease are caused by qualitative or quantitative defects involving the factor VIII–von Willebrand factor (vWF) complex. As background for subsequent discussion of these disorders, it is useful to review the structure and function of these two proteins (Fig. 11–29).

As described earlier, factor VIII is an essential cofactor for factor IX, which activates factor X in the intrinsic coagulation pathway. *Circulating factor VIII binds noncovalently to vWF,* which exists as multimers of up to 20 MDa in weight. These two proteins are encoded by separate genes and are synthesized by different cells. Endothelial cells are the major source of plasma vWF, whereas most factor VIII is synthesized in the liver. vWF is found in the plasma (in association with factor VIII), in platelet granules, in endothelial cells within cytoplasmic vesicles called Weibel-Palade bodies, and in the subendothelium, where it binds to collagen.

When endothelial cells are stripped away by trauma or injury, subendothelial vWF is exposed and binds to platelets, mainly through glycoprotein Ib and to a lesser degree through glycoprotein IIb/IIIa (Fig. 11–29). *The most*

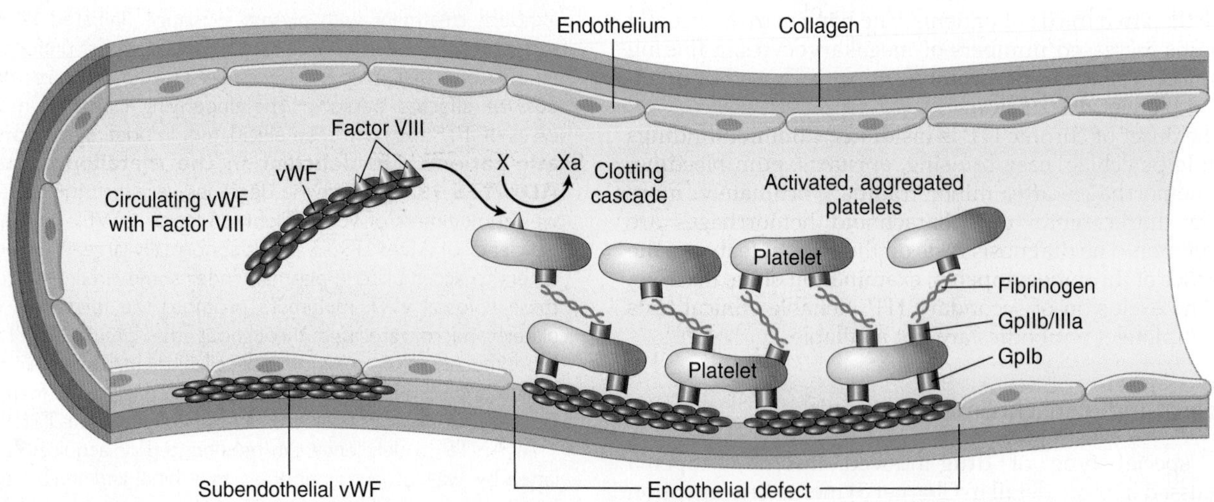

Figure 11–29 Structure and function of factor VIII–von Willebrand factor (vWF) complex. Factor VIII and vWF circulate as a complex. vWF also is present in the subendothelial matrix of normal blood vessels. Factor VIII takes part in the coagulation cascade by activating factor X by means of factor IX (*not shown*). vWF causes adhesion of platelets to subendothelial collagen, primarily through the glycoprotein Ib (GpIb) platelet receptor.

important function of vWF is to facilitate the adhesion of platelets to damaged blood vessel walls, a crucial early event in the formation of a hemostatic plug. Inadequate platelet adhesion is believed to underlie the bleeding tendency in von Willebrand disease. In addition to its role in platelet adhesion, vWF also stabilizes factor VIII; thus, vWF deficiency leads to a secondary deficiency of factor VIII.

The various forms of von Willebrand disease are diagnosed by measuring the quantity, size, and function of vWF. vWF function is assessed using the ristocetin platelet agglutination test. Ristocetin somehow "activates" the bivalent binding of vWF and platelet membrane glycoprotein Ib, creating interplatelet "bridges" that cause platelets to clump (agglutination), an event that can be measured easily. Thus, ristocetin-dependent platelet agglutination serves as a useful bioassay for vWF.

With this background we now turn to the discussion of diseases resulting from deficiencies of factor VIII–vWF complex.

von Willebrand Disease

von Willebrand disease is transmitted as an autosomal dominant disorder. It usually presents as *spontaneous bleeding from mucous membranes, excessive bleeding from wounds, and menorrhagia.* It is underrecognized, as the diagnosis requires sophisticated tests and the clinical manifestations often are quite mild. Actually, this disease is surprisingly prevalent, particularly in persons of European descent. *It is estimated that approximately 1% of people in the United States have von Willebrand disease, making it the most common inherited bleeding disorder.*

People with von Willebrand disease have compound defects in platelet function and coagulation, but in most cases only the platelet defect produces clinical findings. The exceptions are rare patients with homozygous von Willebrand disease, in whom there is a concomitant deficiency of factor VIII severe enough to produce features resembling those of hemophilia (described later on).

The classic and most common variant of von Willebrand disease (type I) is an autosomal dominant disorder in which the quantity of circulating vWF is reduced. There is also a measurable but clinically insignificant decrease in factor VIII levels. The other, less common varieties of von Willebrand disease are caused by mutations that produce both qualitative and quantitative defects in vWF. *Type II* is divided into several subtypes *characterized by the selective loss of high-molecular-weight multimers of vWF.* Because these large multimers are the most active form, there is a functional deficiency of vWF. In type IIA, the high-molecular-weight multimers are not synthesized, leading to a true deficiency. In type IIB, abnormal "hyperfunctional" high-molecular-weight multimers are synthesized that are rapidly removed from the circulation. These high-molecular-weight multimers cause spontaneous platelet aggregation (a situation reminiscent of the very-high-molecular-weight multimer aggregates seen in TTP); indeed, some people with type IIB von Willebrand disease have mild chronic thrombocytopenia, presumably due to platelet consumption.

Hemophilia A—Factor VIII Deficiency

Hemophilia A is the most common hereditary cause of serious bleeding. It is an X-linked recessive disorder caused by reduced factor VIII activity. It primarily affects males. Much less commonly excessive bleeding occurs in heterozygous females, presumably due to preferential inactivation of the X chromosome carrying the normal factor VIII gene (unfavorable lyonization). *Approximately 30% of cases are caused by new mutations;* in the remainder, there is a positive family history. Severe hemophilia A is observed in people with marked deficiencies of factor VIII (activity levels less than 1% of normal). Milder deficiencies may only become apparent when other predisposing conditions, such as trauma, are also present. The varying degrees of factor VIII deficiency are explained by the existence of many different causative mutations. As in the thalassemias, several types of genetic lesions (e.g., deletions, inversions, splice junction mutations) have been identified. In about 10% of patients, the factor VIII concentration is normal by immunoassay, but the coagulant activity is low because of a mutation in factor VIII that causes a loss of function.

In symptomatic cases there is a tendency toward *easy bruising and massive hemorrhage after trauma or operative procedures.* In addition, "spontaneous" hemorrhages frequently are encountered in tissues that normally are subject to mechanical stress, particularly the joints, where recurrent bleeds (*hemarthroses*) lead to progressive deformities that can be crippling. *Petechiae are characteristically absent.* Specific assays for factor VIII are used to confirm the diagnosis of hemophilia A. Typically, patients with hemophilia A have a prolonged PTT that is corrected by mixing the patient's plasma with normal plasma. Specific factor assays are then used to confirm the deficiency of factor VIII. In approximately 15% of those with severe hemophilia A replacement therapy is complicated by the development of neutralizing antibodies against factor VIII, probably because factor VIII is seen by the immune system as a "foreign" antigen. In these persons, the PTT fails to correct in mixing studies.

Hemophilia A is treated with factor VIII infusions. Historically, factor VIII was prepared from human plasma, carrying with it the risk of transmission of viral diseases. As mentioned in Chapter 4, before 1985 thousands of hemophiliacs received factor VIII preparations contaminated with HIV. Subsequently, many became seropositive and developed AIDS. The availability and widespread use of recombinant factor VIII and more highly purified factor VIII concentrates have now eliminated the infectious risk of factor VIII replacement therapy.

Hemophilia B—Factor IX Deficiency

Severe factor IX deficiency is an X-linked disorder that is indistinguishable clinically from hemophilia A but much less common. The PTT is prolonged. The diagnosis is made using specific assays of factor IX. It is treated by infusion of recombinant factor IX.

SUMMARY

Bleeding Disorders

Disseminated Intravascular Coagulation

- Syndrome in which systemic activation of the coagulation leads to consumption of coagulation factors and platelets
- Can be dominated by bleeding, vascular occlusion and tissue hypoxemia, or both
- Common triggers: sepsis, major trauma, certain cancers, obstetric complications

Immune Thrombocytopenic Purpura

- Caused by autoantibodies against platelet antigens
- May be triggered by drugs, infections, or lymphomas, or may be idiopathic

Thrombotic Thrombocytopenic Purpura and Hemolytic Uremic Syndrome

- Both manifest with thrombocytopenia, microangiopathic hemolytic anemia, and renal failure; fever and CNS involvement are more typical of TTP.
- *TTP*: Caused by acquired or inherited deficiencies of ADAMTS 13, a plasma metalloprotease that cleaves very-high-molecular-weight multimers of von Willebrand factor (vWF). Deficiency of ADAMTS 13 results in abnormally large vWF multimers that activate platelets.
- *Hemolytic uremic syndrome*: caused by deficiencies of complement regulatory proteins or agents that damage endothelial cells, such as a Shiga-like toxin elaborated by *E. coli* strain O157:H7. The endothelial injury initiates platelet activation, platelet aggregation, and microvascular thrombosis.

von Willebrand Disease

- Autosomal dominant disorder caused by mutations in vWF, a large protein that promotes the adhesion of platelets to subendothelial collagen
- Typically causes a mild to moderate bleeding disorder resembling that associated with thrombocytopenia

Hemophilia

- *Hemophilia A*: X-linked disorder caused by mutations in factor VIII. Affected males typically present with severe bleeding into soft tissues and joints and have a PTT.
- *Hemophilia B*: X-linked disorder caused by mutations in coagulation factor IX. It is clinically identical to hemophilia A.

DISORDERS THAT AFFECT THE SPLEEN AND THYMUS

SPLENOMEGALY

The spleen is frequently involved in a wide variety of systemic diseases. In virtually all instances, the spleen responds by enlarging (splenomegaly), an alteration that produces a set of stereotypical signs and symptoms. Evaluation of splenic enlargement is aided by recognition of the usual limits of splenomegaly produced by specific disorders. It would be erroneous to attribute an enlarged spleen pushing into the pelvis to vitamin B_{12} deficiency, or to entertain a diagnosis of CML in the absence of splenomegaly. In the following list, disorders are grouped according to the degree of splenomegaly that they characteristically produce:

A. *Massive splenomegaly* (weight more than 1000 g)
   - Myeloproliferative disorders (chronic myelogenous leukemia, primary myelofibrosis)
   - Chronic lymphocytic leukemia and hairy cell leukemia
   - Lymphomas
   - Malaria
   - Gaucher disease
   - Primary tumors of the spleen (rare)

B. *Moderate splenomegaly* (weight 500 to 1000 g)
   - Chronic congestive splenomegaly (portal hypertension or splenic vein obstruction)
   - Acute leukemias (variable)
   - Hereditary spherocytosis
   - Thalassemia major
   - Autoimmune hemolytic anemia
   - Amyloidosis
   - Niemann-Pick disease
   - Chronic splenitis (especially with infective endocarditis)
   - Tuberculosis, sarcoidosis, typhoid
   - Metastatic carcinoma or sarcoma

C. *Mild splenomegaly* (weight less than 500 g)
   - Acute splenitis
   - Acute splenic congestion
   - Infectious mononucleosis
   - Miscellaneous disorders, including septicemia, systemic lupus erythematosus, and intra-abdominal infections

The microscopic changes associated with these diseases are discussed in the relevant sections of this and other chapters.

A chronically enlarged spleen often removes excessive numbers of one or more of the formed elements of blood, resulting in anemia, leukopenia, or thrombocytopenia. This is referred to as *hypersplenism,* a state that can be associated with many of the diseases listed previously. In addition, platelets are particularly susceptible to sequestration in the interstices of the red pulp; as a result, thrombocytopenia is more prevalent and severe in persons with splenomegaly than is anemia or neutropenia.

DISORDERS OF THE THYMUS

As is well known, the thymus has a crucial role in T cell differentiation. It is not surprising, therefore, that the thymus can be involved by lymphomas, particularly those of T cell lineage (discussed earlier in this chapter). The focus here is on the two most frequent (albeit still uncommon) disorders of the thymus: thymic hyperplasia and thymoma.

Thymic Hyperplasia

Thymic enlargement often is associated with the presence of lymphoid follicles, or germinal centers, within the medulla. These germinal centers contain reactive B cells, which are only present in small numbers in normal thymuses. Thymic follicular hyperplasia is found in most patients with myasthenia gravis and sometimes also occurs in other autoimmune diseases, such as systemic lupus erythematosus and rheumatoid arthritis. The relationship between the thymus and myasthenia gravis is discussed in Chapter 21. Of significance, removal of the hyperplastic thymus is often beneficial early in the disease.

Thymoma

Thymomas are tumors of thymic epithelial cells. Several classification systems for thymoma based on cytologic and biologic criteria have been proposed. One simple and clinically useful classification is as follows:

- Benign or encapsulated thymoma: cytologically and biologically benign
- Malignant thymoma
  - *Type I*: cytologically benign but infiltrative and locally aggressive
  - *Type II* (thymic carcinoma): cytologically and biologically malignant

MORPHOLOGY

Macroscopically, thymomas are lobulated, firm, gray-white masses up to 15 to 20 cm in dimension. Most appear encapsulated, but in 20% to 25%, penetration of the capsule and infiltration of perithymic tissues and structures are seen. Microscopically, virtually all thymomas are made up of a mixture of epithelial tumor cells and non-neoplastic thymocytes (immature T cells). In **benign thymomas,** the epithelial cells are spindled or elongated and resemble those that normally populate the medulla. As a result, these are sometimes referred to as **medullary thymomas.** In other tumors, there is an admixture of the plumper, rounder, cortical-type epithelial cells; this pattern is sometimes referred to as a mixed thymoma. The medullary and mixed patterns account for 60% to 70% of all thymomas.

Malignant thymoma type I is cytologically bland but locally invasive; it accounts for 20% to 25% of all thymomas. These tumors also occasionally (and unpredictably) metastasize. They are composed of varying proportions of epithelial cells and reactive thymocytes. The epithelial cells usually have abundant cytoplasm and rounded vesicular nuclei, an appearance similar to normal thymic cortical epithelial cells; spindled epithelial cells are sometimes present as well. The epithelial cells often palisade around blood vessels. **The critical distinguishing feature is the penetration of the capsule with the invasion of surrounding structures.**

Malignant thymoma type II is perhaps better thought of as a form of **thymic carcinoma.** These tumors account for about 5% of thymomas. Macroscopically, they usually are fleshy, obviously invasive masses that often metastasize to such sites as the lungs. Microscopically, most resemble **squamous cell carcinoma.** The next most common type is **lymphoepithelioma-like carcinoma,** a tumor composed of anaplastic cortical-type epithelial cells mixed with large numbers of thymocytes. Tumors of this type are more common in Asian populations and sometimes contain the EBV genome.

Clinical Features

Thymomas are rare. They may arise at any age, but most occur in middle-aged adults. In a large series about 30% were asymptomatic; 30% to 40% produced local manifestations such as cough, dyspnea, and superior vena cava syndrome; and the remainder were associated with a systemic disease, most commonly myasthenia gravis, in which a concomitant thymoma was discovered in 15% to 20% of patients. Removal of the tumor often leads to improvement of the neuromuscular disorder. Additional associations with thymoma include hypogammaglobulinemia, systemic lupus erythematosus, pure red cell aplasia, and nonthymic cancers.

BIBLIOGRAPHY

RED CELL DISORDERS

An X, Mohandas N: Disorders of the red cell membrane. Br J Haematol 141:367, 2008. *[An excellent overview of inherited red cell membrane defects.]*

Brodsky RA: Advances in the diagnosis and treatment of paroxysmal nocturnal hemoglobinuria. Blood Rev 22:65, 2008. *[Discussion of the advantages and limitations of treatment of PNH with antibodies that inhibit the C5b–C9 membrane attack complex.]*

Ganz T, Nemeth E: Iron sequestration and the anemia of inflammation. Semin Hematol 46:387, 2009. *[An update focused on how inflammation alters iron metabolism via effects on hepcidin production.]*

Haldar K, Murphy SC, Milner DA, Taylor TE: Malaria: mechanisms of erythrocytic infection and pathological correlates of severe disease. Annu Rev Pathol 2:217, 2007. *[A review of the proposed mechanisms underlying red cell infection by malarial parasites and the events leading to cerebral malaria.]*

Platt OS: Hydroxyurea for the treatment of sickle cell disease. N Engl J Med 358:1362, 2008. *[A review focused on the beneficial effects of hydroxyurea in sickle cell disease.]*

Young NS, Scheinberg P, Calado RT: Aplastic anemia. Curr Opin Hematol 15:162, 2008. *[An updated perspective on the role of the immune system in aplastic anemia.]*

WHITE CELL DISORDERS

Anderson KC, Carrasco RD: Pathogenesis of myeloma. Annu Rev Pathol 6:249, 2011. *[A review of recent advances in understanding the molecular pathogenesis of multiple myeloma.]*

Jaffe ES, Harris NL, Stein H, Isaacson PG: Classification of lymphoid neoplasms: the microscope as a tool for disease discovery. Blood 112:4384, 2008. *[An overview of the origins and utility of the most recent WHO classification of lymphoid neoplasms.]*

Lenz G, Staudt LM: Aggressive lymphomas. N Engl J Med 362:1417, 2010. *[An excellent brief review of the molecular origins of aggressive B cell lymphomas.]*

Marcucci G, Haferlach T, Dohner H: Molecular genetics of adult acute myeloid leukemia: prognostic and therapeutic implications. J Clin Oncol 29:475, 2011. *[A current view of the clinical role of molecular genetics in AML.]*

Pui CH, Robison LL, Look AT: Acute lymphoblastic leukemia. Lancet 371:1030, 2008. *[A review of the molecular pathogenesis, diagnosis, and treatment of ALL.]*

Schmitz R, Stanelle J, Hansmann ML, Kuppers R: Pathogenesis of classical and lymphocyte-predominant Hodgkin lymphoma. Annu Rev Pathol 4:151, 2009. *[A concise review of Hodgkin lymphoma pathogenesis.]*

Vardiman JW, Thiele J, Arber DA, et al: The 2008 revision of the World Health Organization (WHO) classification of myeloid neoplasms and acute leukemia. Blood 114:937, 2008. *[A report providing the rationale for revision of the the WHO classification of myeloid neoplasms.]*

BLEEDING DISORDERS

Arepally GM, Ortel TL: Heparin-induced thrombocytopenia. Annu Rev Med 61:77, 2010. *[A discussion of pathogenesis, clinical features, diagnostic criteria, and therapeutic approaches in HIT.]*

De Meyer SF, Deckmyn H, Vanhoorelbeke K: von Willebrand factor to the rescue. Blood 113:5049, 2009. *[An update on the molecular pathogenesis and treatment of vWD.]*

Noris M, Remuzzi G: Atypical hemolytic uremic syndrome. N Engl J Med 361:1676, 2009. *[An article focused on the role of excessive activation of the alternative complement pathway in some forms of HUS.]*

Pawlinski R, Mackman N: Cellular sources of tissue factor in endotoxemia and sepsis. Thromb Res 125(S1):S70, 2010. *[An overview of the role of cellular procoagulants in DIC associated with bacterial infection.]*

Zhou Z, Nguyen TC, Guchhait P, Dong JF: Von Willebrand factor, ADAMTS-13, and thrombotic thrombocytopenia purpura. Semin Thromb Hemost 36:71, 2010. *[A review focused on the role of vWF deregulation and ADAMTS 13 deficiency in TTP.]*

DISORDERS THAT AFFECT THE SPLEEN AND THYMUS

Choi SS, Kim KD, Chung KY: Prognostic and clinical relevance of the World Health Organization schema for the classification of thymic epithelial tumors: a clinicopathologic study of 108 patients and literature review. Chest 127:755, 2005. *[A large clinicopathologic series that shows that stage is the best predictor of outcome in thymoma.]*

Asbestosis and Asbestos-Related Diseases

Asbestos is a family of crystalline hydrated silicates with a fibrous geometry. On the basis of epidemiologic studies, occupational exposure to asbestos is linked to (1) parenchymal interstitial fibrosis (*asbestosis*); (2) localized fibrous plaques or, rarely, diffuse fibrosis in the pleura; (3) pleural effusions; (4) lung carcinomas; (5) malignant pleural and peritoneal mesotheliomas; and (6) laryngeal carcinoma. An increased incidence of asbestos-related cancers in family members of asbestos workers has alerted the general public to the potential hazards of asbestos in the environment.

PATHOGENESIS

Concentration, size, shape, and solubility of the different forms of asbestos dictate whether inhalation of the material will cause disease. There are two distinct forms of asbestos: **serpentine,** in which the fiber is curly and flexible, and **amphibole,** in which the fiber is straight, stiff, and brittle. Several subtypes of curly and straight asbestos fibers are recognized. The serpentine **chrysotile** accounts for most of the asbestos used in industry. Amphiboles, even though less prevalent, are more pathogenic than the serpentine chrysotile, but both types can produce asbestosis, lung cancer, and mesothelioma. The greater pathogenicity of straight and stiff amphiboles is apparently related to their structure. The serpentine chrysotiles, with their more flexible, curled structure, are likely to become impacted in the upper respiratory passages and removed by the mucociliary elevator. Those that are trapped in the lungs are gradually leached from the tissues, because they are more soluble than amphiboles. The straight, stiff amphiboles, in contrast, align themselves in the airstream and are hence delivered deeper into the lungs, where they may penetrate epithelial cells to reach the interstitium. Despite these differences, both asbestos forms are fibrogenic, and increasing exposure to either is associated with a higher incidence of all asbestos-related diseases. Asbestosis, like other pneumoconioses, causes fibrosis by a process involving interaction of particulates with lung macrophages.

In addition to cellular and fibrotic lung reactions, asbestos probably also functions as both a tumor initiator and a promoter. Some of the oncogenic effects of asbestos on the mesothelium are mediated by reactive free radicals generated by asbestos fibers, which preferentially localize in the distal lung close to the mesothelial layer. However, potentially toxic chemicals adsorbed onto the asbestos fibers undoubtedly contribute to the pathogenicity of the fibers. For example, **the adsorption of carcinogens in tobacco smoke onto asbestos fibers may well be important to the remarkable synergy between tobacco smoking and the development of lung carcinoma in asbestos workers.**

MORPHOLOGY

Asbestosis is marked by diffuse pulmonary interstitial fibrosis. These changes are indistinguishable from UIP, except for the presence of **asbestos bodies,** which are seen as golden brown, fusiform or beaded rods with a translucent center.

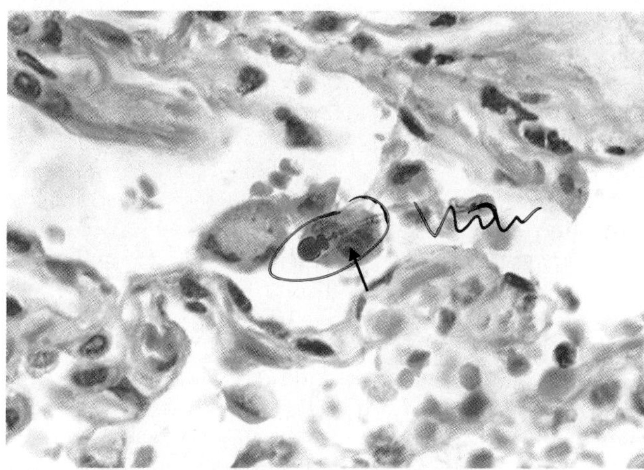

Figure 12–21 High-power detail of an asbestos body, revealing the typical beading and knobbed ends *(arrow)*.

They consist of asbestos fibers coated with an iron-containing proteinaceous material (Fig. 12–21). Asbestos bodies apparently are formed when macrophages attempt to phagocytose asbestos fibers; the iron is derived from phagocyte ferritin. Asbestos bodies sometimes can be found in the lungs of normal persons, but usually in much lower concentrations and without an accompanying interstitial fibrosis.

In contrast with CWP and silicosis, asbestosis begins in the lower lobes and subpleurally, but the middle and upper lobes of the lungs become affected as fibrosis progresses. Contraction of the fibrous tissue distorts the normal architecture, creating enlarged air spaces enclosed within thick fibrous walls. In this way the affected regions become honeycombed. Simultaneously, fibrosis develops in the visceral pleura, causing adhesions between the lungs and the chest wall. The scarring may trap and narrow pulmonary arteries and arterioles, causing pulmonary hypertension and cor pulmonale.

Pleural plaques are the most common manifestation of asbestos exposure and are well-circumscribed plaques of dense collagen (Fig. 12–22), often containing calcium. They develop most frequently on the anterior and posterolateral aspects of the **parietal pleura** and over the domes of the diaphragm. They do not contain asbestos bodies, and only rarely do they occur in persons with no history or evidence of asbestos exposure. Uncommonly, asbestos exposure induces pleural effusion or diffuse pleural fibrosis.

Clinical Features

The clinical findings in asbestosis are indistinguishable from those of any other chronic interstitial lung disease. Typically, progressively worsening dyspnea appears 10 to 20 years after exposure. The dyspnea is usually accompanied by a cough associated with production of sputum. The disease may remain static or progress to congestive heart failure, cor pulmonale, and death. Pleural plaques are usually asymptomatic and are detected on radiographs as circumscribed densities. *Both lung carcinoma and malignant mesothelioma develop in workers exposed to asbestos.* The risk of lung carcinoma is increased about five-fold for asbestos workers; the relative risk for mesothelioma, normally a very rare tumor (2 to 17 cases per 1 million persons), is more than 1000 times greater. Concomitant cigarette

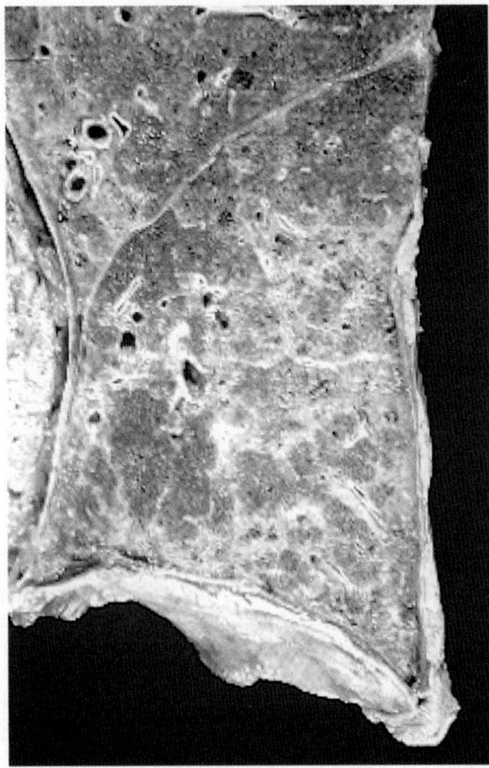

Figure 12–22 Asbestosis. Markedly thickened visceral pleura covers the lateral and diaphragmatic surface of lung. Note also severe interstitial fibrosis diffusely affecting the lower lobe of the lung.

smoking greatly increases the risk of lung carcinoma but not that of mesothelioma. Lung or pleural cancer associated with asbestos exposure carries a particularly grim prognosis.

SUMMARY

Pneumoconioses

- Pneumoconioses encompass a group of chronic fibrosing diseases of the lung resulting from exposure to organic and inorganic particulates, most commonly mineral dust.
- Pulmonary alveolar macrophages play a central role in the pathogenesis of lung injury by promoting inflammation and producing reactive oxygen species and fibrogenic cytokines.
- Coal dust–induced disease varies from *asymptomatic anthracosis*, to *simple coal worker's pneumoconiosis* (coal macules or nodules, and centrilobular emphysema), to progressive massive fibrosis (PMF), manifested by increasing pulmonary dysfunction, pulmonary hypertension, and cor pulmonale.
- Silicosis is the most common pneumoconiosis in the world, and crystalline silica (e.g., quartz) is the usual culprit.
- The manifestations of silicosis can range from asymptomatic silicotic nodules to PMF; persons with silicosis also have an increased susceptibility to tuberculosis. The relationship between silica exposure and subsequent lung cancer is controversial.
- Asbestos fibers come in two forms; the stiff *amphiboles* have a greater fibrogenic and carcinogenic potential than the serpentine *chrysotiles*.
- Asbestos exposure is linked with six disease processes: (1) parenchymal interstitial fibrosis (*asbestosis*); (2) localized fibrous plaques or, rarely, diffuse pleural fibrosis; (3) pleural effusions; (4) lung cancer; (5) malignant pleural and peritoneal mesotheliomas; and (6) laryngeal cancer.
- Cigarette smoking increases the risk of lung cancer in the setting of asbestos exposure; moreover, even family members of workers exposed to asbestos are at increased risk for cancer.

Drug- and Radiation-Induced Pulmonary Diseases

Drugs can cause a variety of both acute and chronic alterations in respiratory structure and function. For example, *bleomycin*, an anticancer agent, causes pneumonitis and interstitial fibrosis, as a result of direct toxicity of the drug and by stimulating the influx of inflammatory cells into the alveoli. Similarly, *amiodarone*, an antiarrhythmic agent, also is associated with risk for pneumonitis and fibrosis. *Radiation pneumonitis* is a well-known complication of therapeutic irradiation of pulmonary and other thoracic tumors. *Acute radiation pneumonitis,* which typically occurs 1 to 6 months after therapy in as many as 20% of the patients, is manifested by fever, dyspnea out of proportion to the volume of irradiated lung, pleural effusion, and development of pulmonary infiltrates corresponding to the area of radiation. These signs and symptoms may resolve with corticosteroid therapy or progress to *chronic radiation pneumonitis,* associated with pulmonary fibrosis.

Granulomatous Diseases

Sarcoidosis

Although sarcoidosis is considered here as an example of a restrictive lung disease, it is important to note that sarcoidosis is a *multisystem disease of unknown etiology characterized by noncaseating granulomas in many tissues and organs.* Other diseases, including mycobacterial or fungal infections and berylliosis, sometimes also produce noncaseating granulomas; therefore, the histologic *diagnosis of sarcoidosis is one of exclusion.* Although the multisystem involvement of sarcoidosis can manifest in many clinical guises, bilateral hilar lymphadenopathy or lung involvement (or both), visible on chest radiographs, is the major presenting manifestation in most cases. Eye and skin involvement each occurs in about 25% of cases, and either may occasionally be the presenting feature of the disease.

Epidemiology

Sarcoidosis occurs throughout the world, affecting both genders and all races and age groups. There are, however, certain interesting epidemiologic trends, including:

- There is a consistent predilection for adults younger than 40 years of age.
- A high incidence has been noted in Danish and Swedish populations, and in the United States among African

Americans (in whom the frequency of involvement is 10 times greater than in whites).

- Sarcoidosis is one of the few pulmonary diseases with a higher prevalence among *nonsmokers*.

ETIOLOGY AND PATHOGENESIS

Although the etiology of sarcoidosis remains unknown, several lines of evidence suggest that it is a disease of disordered immune regulation in genetically predisposed persons exposed to certain environmental agents. The role of each of these contributory influences is summarized in the following discussion.

Several **immunologic abnormalities** in sarcoidosis suggest the development of a cell-mediated response to an unidentified antigen. The process is driven by CD4+ helper T cells. These abnormalities include:

- Intra-alveolar and interstitial accumulation of CD4+ T_H1 cells
- Oligoclonal expansion of T cell subsets as determined by analysis of T cell receptor rearrangement
- Increases in T cell–derived T_H1 cytokines such as IL-2 and IFN-γ, resulting in T cell expansion and macrophage activation, respectively
- Increases in several cytokines in the local environment (IL-8, TNF, macrophage inflammatory protein-1α) that favor recruitment of additional T cells and monocytes and contribute to the formation of granulomas
- Anergy to common skin test antigens such as *Candida* or purified protein derivative (PPD), that may result from pulmonary recruitment of CD4+ T cells and consequent peripheral depletion
- Polyclonal hypergammaglobulinemia, another manifestation of T_H cell dysregulation
- The role of genetic factors is suggested by familial and racial clustering of cases and association with certain human leukocyte antigen (HLA) genotypes (e.g., class I HLA-A1 and HLA-B8)

After lung transplantation, sarcoidosis recurs in the new lungs in 75% of patients. Finally, several putative "antigens" have been proposed as the inciting agent for sarcoidosis (e.g., viruses, mycobacteria, *Borrelia,* pollen), but thus far **there is no unequivocal evidence to suggest that sarcoidosis is caused by an infectious agent.**

MORPHOLOGY

The diagnostic histopathologic feature of sarcoidosis is the **noncaseating epithelioid granuloma,** irrespective of the organ involved (Fig. 12–23). This is a discrete, compact collection of epithelioid cells rimmed by an outer zone of largely CD4+ T cells. The epithelioid cells are derived from macrophages and are characterized by abundant eosinophilic cytoplasm and vesicular nuclei. It is not uncommon to see intermixed multinucleate giant cells formed by fusion of macrophages. A thin layer of laminated fibroblasts is present peripheral to the granuloma; over time, these proliferate and lay down collagen that replaces the entire granuloma with a hyalinized scar. Two other microscopic features are sometimes seen in the granulomas: (1) **Schaumann bodies,** laminated concretions composed of calcium and proteins; and (2) **asteroid bodies,** stellate inclusions enclosed within giant cells. Their presence is not required for diagnosis of sarcoidosis—they also may occur in granulomas of other origins. Rarely, foci of central necrosis may be present in sarcoid granulomas, suggesting an infectious process. Caseation necrosis typical of tuberculosis is absent.

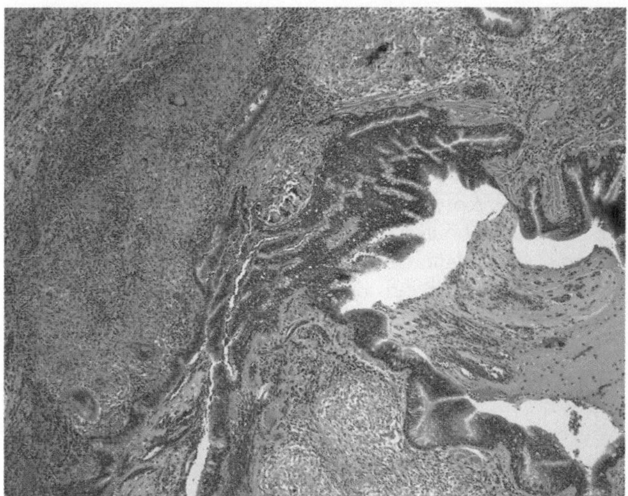

Figure 12–23 Sarcoid. Characteristic peribronchial noncaseating granulomas with many giant cells.

The **lungs** are involved at some stage of the disease in 90% of patients. The granulomas predominantly involve the interstitium rather than air spaces, with some tendency to localize in the connective tissue around bronchioles and pulmonary venules and in the pleura ("lymphangitic" distribution). The bronchoalveolar lavage fluid contains abundant CD4+ T cells. In 5% to 15% of patients, the granulomas eventually are replaced by **diffuse interstitial fibrosis,** resulting in a so-called honeycomb lung.

Intrathoracic **hilar and paratracheal lymph nodes** are enlarged in 75% to 90% of patients, while a third present with peripheral lymphadenopathy. The nodes are characteristically painless and have a firm, rubbery texture. Unlike in tuberculosis, lymph nodes in sarcoidosis are "nonmatted" (nonadherent) and do not ulcerate.

Skin lesions are encountered in approximately 25% of patients. **Erythema nodosum,** the hallmark of acute sarcoidosis, consists of raised, red, tender nodules on the anterior aspects of the legs. Sarcoidal granulomas are uncommon in these lesions. By contrast, discrete painless subcutaneous nodules can also occur in sarcoidosis, and these usually reveal abundant noncaseating granulomas.

Involvement of the eye and lacrimal glands occurs in about one fifth to one half of patients. The ocular involvement takes the form of iritis or iridocyclitis and may be unilateral or bilateral. As a consequence, corneal opacities, glaucoma, and (less commonly) total loss of vision may develop. The posterior uveal tract also is affected, with resultant **choroiditis, retinitis,** and **optic nerve involvement.** These ocular lesions are frequently accompanied by inflammation in the lacrimal glands, with suppression of lacrimation **(sicca syndrome). Unilateral or bilateral parotitis with painful enlargement of the parotid glands**

occurs in less than 10% of patients with sarcoidosis; some go on to develop xerostomia (dry mouth). Combined uveoparotid involvement is designated **Mikulicz syndrome.**

The spleen may appear unaffected grossly, but in about three fourths of cases, it contains granulomas. In approximately 10%, it becomes clinically enlarged. **The liver** demonstrates microscopic granulomatous lesions, usually in the portal triads, about as often as the spleen, but only about one third of the patients demonstrate hepatomegaly or abnormal liver function. Sarcoid involvement of **bone marrow** is reported in as many as 40% of patients, although it rarely causes severe manifestations. Other findings may include hypercalcemia and hypercalciuria. These changes are not related to bone destruction but rather are caused by increased calcium absorption secondary to production of active vitamin D by the mononuclear phagocytes in the granulomas.

Clinical Features

In many affected persons the disease is entirely asymptomatic, discovered on routine chest films as bilateral hilar adenopathy or as an incidental finding at autopsy. In others, peripheral lymphadenopathy, cutaneous lesions, eye involvement, splenomegaly, or hepatomegaly may be presenting manifestations. In about two thirds of symptomatic cases, there is gradual appearance of respiratory symptoms (shortness of breath, dry cough, or vague substernal discomfort) or constitutional signs and symptoms (fever, fatigue, weight loss, anorexia, night sweats). Because of the variable and nondiagnostic clinical features, resort is frequently made to lung or lymph node biopsies. *The presence of noncaseating granulomas is suggestive of sarcoidosis, but other identifiable causes of granulomatous inflammation must be excluded.*

Sarcoidosis follows an unpredictable course characterized by either progressive chronicity or periods of activity interspersed with remissions. The remissions may be spontaneous or initiated by steroid therapy and often are permanent. Overall, 65% to 70% of affected persons recover with minimal or no residual manifestations. Another 20% develop permanent lung dysfunction or visual impairment. Of the remaining 10% to 15%, most succumb to progressive pulmonary fibrosis and cor pulmonale.

SUMMARY

Sarcoidosis

- Sarcoidosis is a multisystem disease of unknown etiology; the diagnostic histopathologic feature is the presence of noncaseating granulomas in various tissues.
- Immunologic abnormalities include high levels of CD4+ T cells in the lung that secrete T_H1-dependent cytokines such as IFN-γ and IL-2 locally.
- Clinical manifestations include lymph node enlargement, eye involvement (sicca syndrome [dry eyes], iritis, or iridocyclitis), skin lesions (erythema nodosum, painless subcutaneous nodules), and visceral (liver, skin, marrow) involvement. Lung involvement occurs in 90% of cases, with formation of granulomas and interstitial fibrosis.

Hypersensitivity Pneumonitis

Hypersensitivity pneumonitis is an immunologically mediated inflammatory lung disease that primarily affects the alveoli and is therefore often called *allergic alveolitis.* Most often it is an occupational disease that results from heightened sensitivity to inhaled antigens such as in moldy hay (Table 12–5). Unlike bronchial asthma, in which *bronchi are the focus of immunologically mediated injury, the damage in hypersensitivity pneumonitis occurs at the level of alveoli.* Hence, it manifests as a predominantly restrictive lung disease with decreased diffusion capacity, lung compliance, and total lung volume. The occupational exposures are diverse, but the syndromes share common clinical and pathologic findings and probably have a very similar pathophysiologic basis.

Several lines of evidence suggest that hypersensitivity pneumonitis is an immunologically mediated disease:

- Bronchoalveolar lavage specimens consistently demonstrate increased numbers of T lymphocytes of both CD4+ and CD8+ phenotype.

Table 12–5 Selected Causes of Hypersensitivity Pneumonitis

Syndrome	Exposure	Antigens
Fungal and Bacterial Antigens		
Farmer's lung	Moldy hay	*Micropolyspora faeni*
Bagassosis	Moldy pressed sugar cane (bagasse)	Thermophilic actinomycetes
Maple bark disease	Moldy maple bark	*Cryptostroma corticale*
Humidifier lung	Cool-mist humidifier	Thermophilic actinomycetes, *Aureobasidium pullulans*
Malt worker's lung	Moldy barley	*Aspergillus clavatus*
Cheese washer's lung	Moldy cheese	*Penicillium casei*
Insect Products		
Miller's lung	Dust-contaminated grain	*Sitophilus granarius* (wheat weevil)
Animal Products		
Pigeon breeder's lung	Pigeon droppings	Pigeon serum proteins in droppings
Chemicals		
Chemical worker's lung	Chemical industry	Trimellitic anhydride, isocyanates

- Most patients with hypersensitivity pneumonitis have specific precipitating antibodies in their serum, and complement and immunoglobulins have been demonstrated within vessel walls by immunofluorescence, indicating type III hypersensitivity. The presence of noncaseating granulomas in two thirds of patients with this disorder suggests a role for type IV hypersensitivity as well.

In summary, hypersensitivity pneumonitis is an immunologically mediated response to an extrinsic antigen that involves both immune complex and delayed-type hypersensitivity reactions.

MORPHOLOGY

The histopathologic picture in both acute and chronic forms of hypersensitivity pneumonitis includes patchy mononuclear cell infiltrates in the pulmonary interstitium, with a characteristic peribronchiolar accentuation. Lymphocytes predominate, but plasma cells and epithelioid cells also are present. In acute forms of the disease, variable numbers of neutrophils may also be seen. **Interstitial noncaseating granulomas** are present in more than two thirds of cases, usually in a peribronchiolar location (Fig. 12–24). In advanced chronic cases, diffuse interstitial fibrosis occurs.

Clinical Features

Hypersensitivity pneumonitis may manifest either as an *acute reaction,* with fever, cough, dyspnea, and constitutional signs and symptoms arising 4 to 8 hours after exposure, or as a *chronic disease* characterized by insidious onset of cough, dyspnea, malaise, and weight loss. With the acute form of this disease, the diagnosis is usually obvious because of the temporal relationship of symptom onset to exposure to the incriminating antigen. *If antigenic exposure is terminated after acute attacks of the disease,* complete resolution of pulmonary symptoms occurs within days. Failure to remove the inciting agent from the environment eventually results in an irreversible chronic interstitial pulmonary disease.

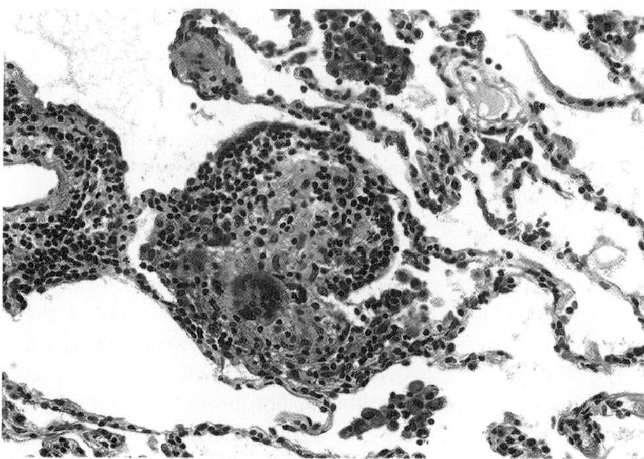

Figure 12–24 Hypersensitivity pneumonitis, histologic appearance. Loosely formed interstitial granulomas and chronic inflammation are characteristic.

Pulmonary Eosinophilia

A number of clinical and pathologic pulmonary entities are characterized by an infiltration and activation of eosinophils, the latter by elevated levels of alveolar IL-5. These diverse diseases generally are of immunologic origin, but the etiology is not understood. Pulmonary eosinophilia is divided into the following categories:

- *Acute eosinophilic pneumonia with respiratory failure,* characterized by rapid onset of fever, dyspnea, hypoxia, and diffuse pulmonary infiltrates on chest radiographs. The bronchoalveolar lavage fluid typically contains more than 25% eosinophils. There is prompt response to corticosteroids.
- *Simple pulmonary eosinophilia* (Loeffler syndrome), characterized by transient pulmonary lesions, eosinophilia in the blood, and a benign clinical course. The alveolar septa are thickened by an infiltrate containing eosinophils and occasional giant cells.
- *Tropical eosinophilia,* caused by infection with microfilariae and helminthic parasites
- *Secondary eosinophilia,* seen, for example, in association with asthma, drug allergies, and certain forms of vasculitis
- *Idiopathic chronic eosinophilic pneumonia,* characterized by aggregates of lymphocytes and eosinophils within the septal walls and the alveolar spaces, typically in the periphery of the lung fields, and accompanied by high fever, night sweats, and dyspnea. This is a disease of exclusion, once other causes of pulmonary eosinophilia have been ruled out.

Smoking-Related Interstitial Diseases

The role of cigarette smoking in causing obstructive pulmonary disease (emphysema and chronic bronchitis) has been discussed. Smoking also is associated with restrictive or interstitial lung diseases. *Desquamative interstitial pneumonia* (DIP) and *respiratory bronchiolitis* are the two related examples of smoking-associated interstitial lung disease. The most striking histologic feature of DIP is the accumulation of large numbers of macrophages with abundant cytoplasm containing dusty-brown pigment (*smoker's macrophages*) in the air spaces (Fig. 12–25). The alveolar septa are thickened by a sparse inflammatory infiltrate (usually lymphocytes), and interstitial fibrosis, when present, is mild. Pulmonary functions usually show a mild restrictive abnormality, and patients with DIP typically have a good prognosis with excellent response to steroid therapy and smoking cessation. Respiratory bronchiolitis is a common histologic lesion found in smokers, characterized by the presence of pigmented intraluminal macrophages akin to those in DIP, but in a "bronchiolocentric" distribution (first- and second-order respiratory bronchioles). Mild peribronchiolar fibrosis also is seen. As with DIP, affected patients present with gradual onset of dyspnea and dry cough, and the symptoms recede with cessation of smoking.

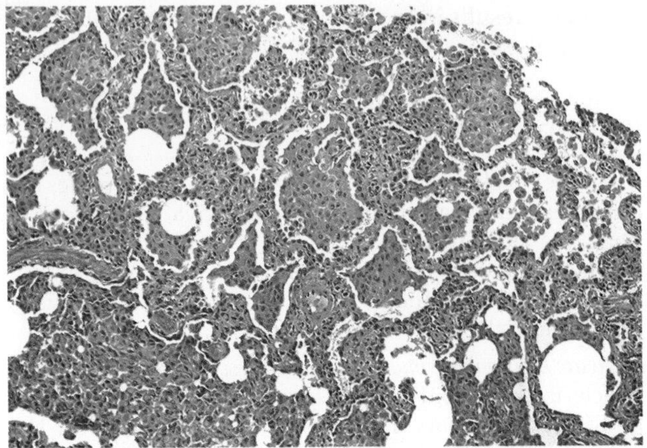

Figure 12–25 Desquamative interstitial pneumonia. There is accumulation of large numbers of macrophages within the alveolar spaces with only slight fibrous thickening of the alveolar walls.

PULMONARY DISEASES OF VASCULAR ORIGIN

Pulmonary Embolism, Hemorrhage, and Infarction

Blood clots that occlude the large pulmonary arteries are almost always embolic in origin. More than 95% of all pulmonary emboli arise from thrombi within the large deep veins of the lower legs, typically originating in the popliteal vein and larger veins above it. Thromboembolism causes approximately 50,000 deaths per year in the United States. Even when not directly fatal, it can complicate the course of other diseases. The true incidence of nonfatal pulmonary embolism is not known. Some cases of embolism undoubtedly occur outside the hospital in ambulatory patients, in whom the emboli are small and clinically silent. Even among hospitalized patients, no more than one third are diagnosed before death. Autopsy data on the incidence of pulmonary embolism vary widely, ranging from 1% in the general hospitalized population, to 30% in persons dying after severe burns, trauma, or fractures.

The influences that predispose the patient to venous thrombosis in the legs are discussed in Chapter 3, but the following risk factors are paramount: (1) prolonged bedrest (particularly with immobilization of the legs); (2) surgery, especially orthopedic surgery, of knee and hip; (3) severe trauma (including burns or multiple fractures); (4) congestive heart failure; (5) in women, the period around parturition or oral contraception using birth control pills with high estrogen content; (6) disseminated cancer; and (7) primary disorders of hypercoagulability (e.g., factor V Leiden) (Chapter 3).

The pathophysiologic consequences of thromboembolism in the lung depend largely on the size of the embolus, which in turn dictates the size of the occluded pulmonary artery, and on the cardiopulmonary status of the patient. There are two important consequences of embolic pulmonary arterial occlusion: (1) an increase in pulmonary artery pressure from blockage of flow and, possibly, vasospasm caused by neurogenic mechanisms and/or release of mediators (e.g., thromboxane A_2, serotonin); and (2) ischemia of the downstream pulmonary parenchyma. Thus, occlusion of a *major vessel* results in a sudden increase in pulmonary artery pressure, diminished cardiac output, right-sided heart failure (*acute cor pulmonale*), or even death. Usually hypoxemia also develops, as a result of multiple mechanisms:

- *Perfusion of lung zones that have become atelectatic.* The alveolar collapse occurs in the ischemic areas because of a reduction in surfactant production and because pain associated with embolism leads to reduced movement of the chest wall; in addition, some of the pulmonary blood flow is redirected through areas of the lung that normally are hypoventilated.
- The decrease in cardiac output causes a *widening of the difference in arterial-venous oxygen saturation.*
- *Right-to-left shunting* of blood may occur through a patent foramen ovale, present in 30% of normal persons.
- If *smaller vessels* are occluded, the result is less catastrophic, and the event may even be clinically silent.

Recall that the lungs are oxygenated not only by the pulmonary arteries but also by bronchial arteries and directly from air in the alveoli. Thus, ischemic necrosis (infarction) is the exception rather than the rule, occurring in as few as 10% of patients with thromboemboli. It occurs only if there is compromise in cardiac function or bronchial circulation, or if the region of the lung at risk is underventilated as a result of underlying pulmonary disease.

MORPHOLOGY

The morphologic consequences of pulmonary embolism, as noted, depend on the size of the embolic mass and the general state of the circulation. A large embolus may embed in the main pulmonary artery or its major branches or lodge astride the bifurcation as a **saddle embolus** (Fig. 12–26). Death usually follows so suddenly from hypoxia or acute failure of the right side of the heart (acute cor pulmonale) that there is no time for morphologic alterations in the lung. Smaller emboli become impacted in medium-sized and small pulmonary arteries. With adequate circulation and bronchial arterial flow, the vitality of the lung parenchyma is maintained, but alveolar hemorrhage may occur as a result of ischemic damage to the endothelial cells.

With compromised cardiovascular status, as may occur with congestive heart failure, **infarction** results. The more peripheral the embolic occlusion, the higher the risk of infarction. About three fourths of all infarcts affect the lower lobes, and more than half are multiple. Characteristically, they are wedge-shaped, with their base at the pleural surface and the apex pointing toward the hilus of the lung. Pulmonary infarcts typically are hemorrhagic and appear as raised, red-blue areas in the early stages (Fig. 12–27). The adjacent pleural surface often is covered by a fibrinous exudate. If the occluded vessel can be identified, it usually is found near the apex of the infarcted area. The red cells begin to lyse within 48 hours, and the infarct pales, eventually becoming red-brown as hemosiderin is produced. In time, fibrous replacement begins at the margins as a gray-white peripheral zone and eventually converts the infarct into a scar. On histologic examination, the hallmark of fresh infarcts is coagulative necrosis of the lung parenchyma and hemorrhage.

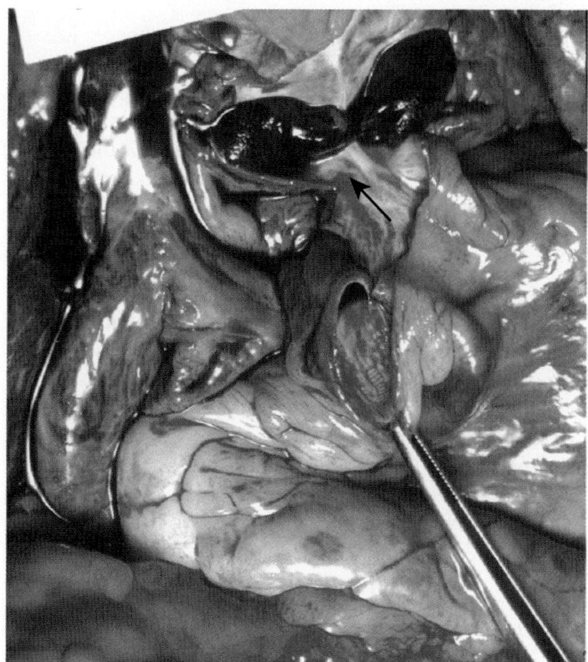

Figure 12–26 Large saddle embolus from the femoral vein lying astride the main left and right pulmonary arteries.
(Courtesy of Dr. Linda Margraf, Department of Pathology, University of Texas Southwestern Medical School, Dallas, Texas.)

Clinical Features

The clinical consequences of pulmonary thromboembolism are summarized as follows:

- Most pulmonary emboli (60% to 80%) are clinically silent because they are small; the embolic mass is rapidly removed by fibrinolytic activity, and the bronchial circulation sustains the viability of the affected lung parenchyma until this is accomplished.
- In 5% of cases, sudden death, acute right-sided heart failure (acute cor pulmonale), or cardiovascular collapse (shock) may occur typically when more than 60% of the total pulmonary vasculature is obstructed by a large embolus or multiple simultaneous small emboli. Massive pulmonary embolism is one of the few causes of literally instantaneous death, even before the person experiences chest pain or dyspnea.
- Obstruction of relatively small to medium pulmonary branches (10% to 15% of cases) that behave as end arteries causes pulmonary infarction when some element of circulatory insufficiency is present. Typically, persons who sustain such infarction manifest dyspnea.
- In a small but significant subset of patients (accounting for less than 3% of cases), recurrent multiple emboli lead to pulmonary hypertension, chronic right-sided heart strain (chronic cor pulmonale), and, in time, pulmonary vascular sclerosis with progressively worsening dyspnea.

Emboli usually resolve after the initial acute event. They contract, and endogenous fibrinolytic activity may cause total lysis of the thrombus. However, in the presence of an underlying predisposing factor, a small, innocuous embolus may presage a larger one, and *patients who have experienced one pulmonary embolism have a 30% chance of developing a second.* Prophylactic therapy may include anticoagulation, early ambulation for postoperative and postparturient patients, application of elastic stockings, intermittent pneumatic calf compression, and isometric leg exercises for bedridden patients. Patients with pulmonary embolism are given anticoagulation therapy. Patients with massive pulmonary embolism are candidates for thrombolytic therapy.

Nonthrombotic forms of pulmonary embolism include several uncommon but potentially lethal forms, such as air, fat, and amniotic fluid embolism (Chapter 3). Intravenous drug abuse often is associated with foreign body embolism in the pulmonary microvasculature; the presence of magnesium trisilicate (talc) in the intravenous mixture elicits a granulomatous response within the interstitium or pulmonary arteries. Involvement of the interstitium may lead to fibrosis, while the latter leads to pulmonary hypertension. Residual talc crystals can be demonstrated within the granulomas using polarized light. Bone marrow embolism (presence of hematopoietic and fat elements within pulmonary circulation) can occur after massive trauma and in patients with bone infarction secondary to sickle cell anemia.

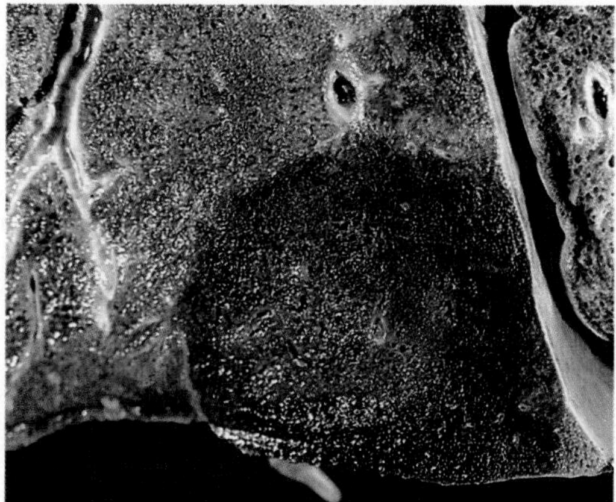

Figure 12–27 A small, roughly wedge-shaped hemorrhagic pulmonary infarct of recent occurrence.

SUMMARY
Pulmonary Embolism

- Almost all large pulmonary artery thrombi are embolic in origin, usually arising from the deep veins of the lower leg.
- Risk factors include prolonged bedrest, leg surgery, severe trauma, CHF, use of oral contraceptives (especially those with high estrogen content), disseminated cancer, and genetic causes of hypercoagulability.
- The vast majority (60% to 80%) of emboli are clinically silent, a minority (5%) cause acute cor pulmonale, shock, or death (typically from large "saddle emboli"), and the remaining cause pulmonary infarction.
- Risk of recurrence is high.

Pulmonary Hypertension

The pulmonary circulation normally is one of low resistance; pulmonary blood pressures are only about one eighth of systemic pressures. Pulmonary hypertension (when mean pulmonary pressures reach one fourth or more of systemic levels) is most often *secondary* to a decrease in the cross-sectional area of the pulmonary vascular bed, or to increased pulmonary vascular blood flow. The causes of secondary pulmonary hypertension include:

- *Chronic obstructive or interstitial lung disease,* which is accompanied by destruction of lung parenchyma and consequent reduction in alveolar capillaries. This causes increased pulmonary arterial resistance and secondarily, elevated arterial pressure.
- *Recurrent pulmonary emboli.* Presence of these emboli leads to a reduction in the functional cross-sectional area of the pulmonary vascular bed, leading in turn to increased vascular resistance.
- *Antecedent heart disease,* for example, *mitral stenosis,* which increases left atrial pressure, leading to higher pulmonary venous pressures, and ultimately pulmonary arterial hypertension. *Congenital left-to-right shunts* are another cause of secondary pulmonary hypertension.

Uncommonly, pulmonary hypertension exists even though all known causes of increased pulmonary pressure have been excluded; this is referred to as *primary,* or *idiopathic, pulmonary arterial hypertension.* Of these, the vast majority of cases are sporadic, and only 6% are familial with an autosomal dominant mode of inheritance.

PATHOGENESIS

According to current thinking, **pulmonary endothelial cell and/or vascular smooth muscle dysfunction** is the probable underlying basis for most forms of pulmonary hypertension.

- In states of **secondary pulmonary hypertension,** endothelial cell dysfunction arises as a consequence of the underlying disorder (e.g., shear and mechanical injury due to increased blood flow in left-to-right shunts, or biochemical injury produced by fibrin in recurrent thromboembolism). Endothelial cell dysfunction reduces production of vasodilatory agents (e.g., nitric oxide, prostacyclin) while increasing synthesis of vasoconstrictive mediators like endothelin. In addition, there is production of growth factors and cytokines that induce the migration and replication of vascular smooth muscle and elaboration of extracellular matrix.
- In **primary pulmonary hypertension,** especially in the uncommon **familial form,** the TGF-β signaling pathway has emerged as a key mediator of endothelial and smooth muscle dysfunction. Specifically, germline mutations of **bone morphogenetic protein receptor type 2** (BMPR-2), a cell surface molecule that binds to a variety of TGF-β pathway ligands, have been demonstrated in 50% of familial cases. The *BMPR2* gene product is inhibitory in its effects on proliferation; hence, loss-of-function mutations of this gene result in abnormal vascular endothelial and pulmonary smooth muscle proliferation. The endothelial proliferations in these instances usually are **monoclonal,** reiterating the genetic basis of their origin. However, not all persons with germline mutations of *BMPR2* develop primary pulmonary hypertension, suggesting the existence of **modifier genes** that probably affect penetrance of this particular phenotype.
- Studies on sporadic forms of primary pulmonary hypertension point to a possible role for the **serotonin transporter gene** (*5HTT*). Specifically, pulmonary smooth muscle cells from some patients with primary pulmonary hypertension demonstrate increased proliferation on exposure to serotonin or serum. Genetic polymorphisms of *5HTT* that lead to enhanced expression of the transporter protein on vascular smooth muscle are postulated to cause their proliferation.

MORPHOLOGY

Vascular alterations in all forms of pulmonary hypertension (primary and secondary) involve the entire arterial tree (Fig. 12–28) and include (1) in the **main elastic arteries,** atheromas similar to those in systemic atherosclerosis; (2) **in medium-sized muscular arteries,** proliferation of myointimal cells and smooth muscle cells, causing thickening of the intima and media with narrowing of the lumina; and (3) in **smaller arteries and arterioles,** thickening, medial hypertrophy, and reduplication of the internal and external elastic membranes. In these vessels, the wall thickness may exceed the diameter of the lumen, which is sometimes narrowed to the point of near-obliteration. Persons with idiopathic pulmonary arterial hypertension have characteristic **plexiform lesions,** in which endothelial proliferation forms multiple lumina within small arteries where they branch from a medium-sized artery.

Clinical Features

Secondary pulmonary hypertension may develop at any age. The clinical features reflect the underlying disease, usually pulmonary or cardiac, with accentuation of respiratory insufficiency and right-sided heart strain. Primary pulmonary hypertension, on the other hand, is almost always encountered in young adults, more commonly women, and is marked by fatigue, syncope (particularly on exercise), dyspnea on exertion, and sometimes chest pain. Eventually severe respiratory insufficiency and cyanosis develop, and death usually results from right-sided heart failure (decompensated cor pulmonale) within 2 to 5 years of diagnosis. Some amelioration of the respiratory distress can be achieved by vasodilators and antithrombotic agents, and continuous prostacyclin infusions may prolong life (months to years), but without lung transplantation the prognosis is still grim.

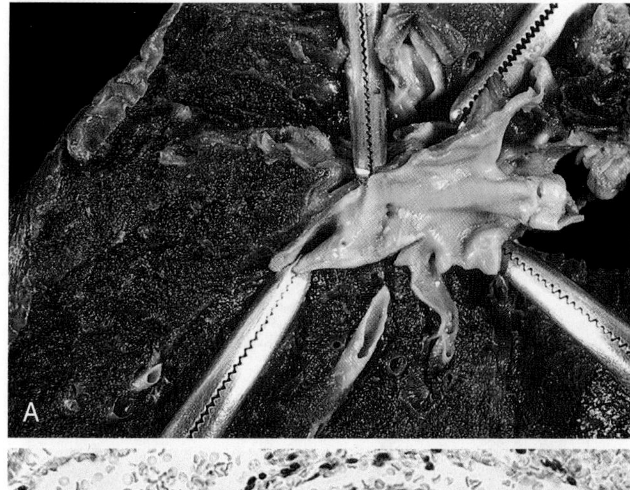

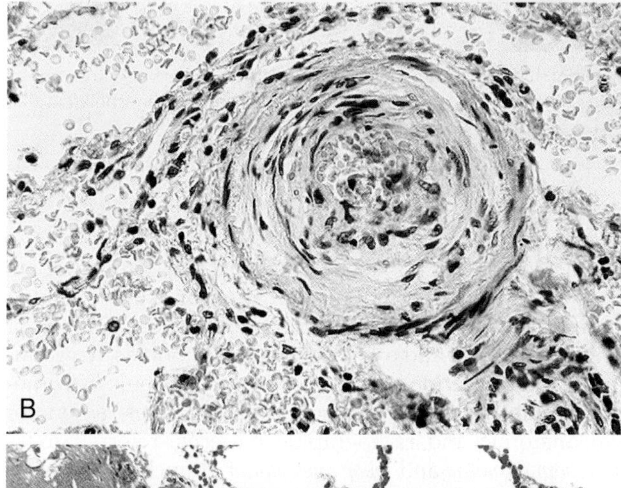

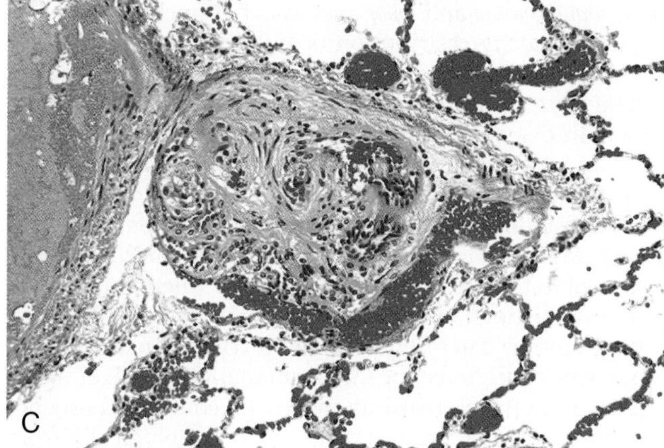

Figure 12–28 Vascular changes in pulmonary hypertension. **A,** Gross photograph of atheroma, a finding usually limited to large vessels. **B,** Marked medial hypertrophy. **C,** Plexiform lesion characteristic of advanced pulmonary hypertension seen in small arteries.

Diffuse Alveolar Hemorrhage Syndromes

While there may be several "secondary" causes of pulmonary hemorrhage (necrotizing bacterial pneumonia, passive venous congestion, bleeding diathesis), the diffuse alveolar hemorrhage syndromes constitute a group of "primary" immune-mediated diseases that manifest as the *triad of hemoptysis, anemia, and diffuse pulmonary infiltrates.*

Goodpasture Syndrome

Goodpasture syndrome, the prototype disorder of this group, is an uncommon but intriguing condition characterized by a *proliferative, usually rapidly progressive, glomerulonephritis* (Chapter 13) and *hemorrhagic interstitial pneumonitis.* Both the renal and the pulmonary lesions are caused by antibodies targeted against the noncollagenous domain of the α3 chain of collagen IV. These antibodies can be detected in the serum of more than 90% of persons with Goodpasture syndrome.

MORPHOLOGY

The lungs are heavy, with areas of red-brown consolidation, due to **diffuse alveolar hemorrhage.** Microscopic examination demonstrates focal necrosis of alveolar walls associated with intra-alveolar hemorrhages, fibrous thickening of the septa, and hypertrophic type II pneumocytes. Presence of **hemosiderin,** both within macrophages and extracellularly, is characteristic, indicating earlier episode(s) of hemorrhage (Fig. 12–29). The characteristic **linear pattern of immunoglobulin deposition** (usually IgG, sometimes IgA or IgM) that is the hallmark diagnostic finding in renal biopsy specimens (Chapter 13) also may be seen along the alveolar septa.

Plasmapheresis and immunosuppressive therapy have markedly improved the once-dismal prognosis for this disease. Plasma exchange removes offending antibodies, and immunosuppressive drugs inhibit antibody production. With severe renal disease, renal transplantation is eventually required.

Idiopathic Pulmonary Hemosiderosis

Idiopathic pulmonary hemosiderosis is a rare disease of uncertain etiology that has pulmonary manifestations and histologic features similar to those of Goodpasture syndrome, but there is no associated renal disease or circulating anti-basement membrane antibody. Most cases occur in children, although the disease is reported in adults as well, who have a better prognosis. With steroid and immunosuppressive therapy, survival has markedly improved from the historical 2.5 years; thus, an immune-mediated etiology is postulated.

Pulmonary Angiitis and Granulomatosis (Wegener Granulomatosis)

More than 80% of patients with Wegener granulomatosis (WG) develop upper respiratory or pulmonary manifestations at some time in the course of their disease. It is described in Chapter 9. Here we list the salient pulmonary features. The lung lesions are characterized by a combination of necrotizing vasculitis ("angiitis") and parenchymal necrotizing granulomatous inflammation. The manifestations of WG can include both upper respiratory symptoms (chronic sinusitis, epistaxis, nasal perforation) and pulmonary signs and symptoms (cough, hemoptysis, chest pain). PR3-ANCAs are present in close to 95% of cases (Chapter 9).

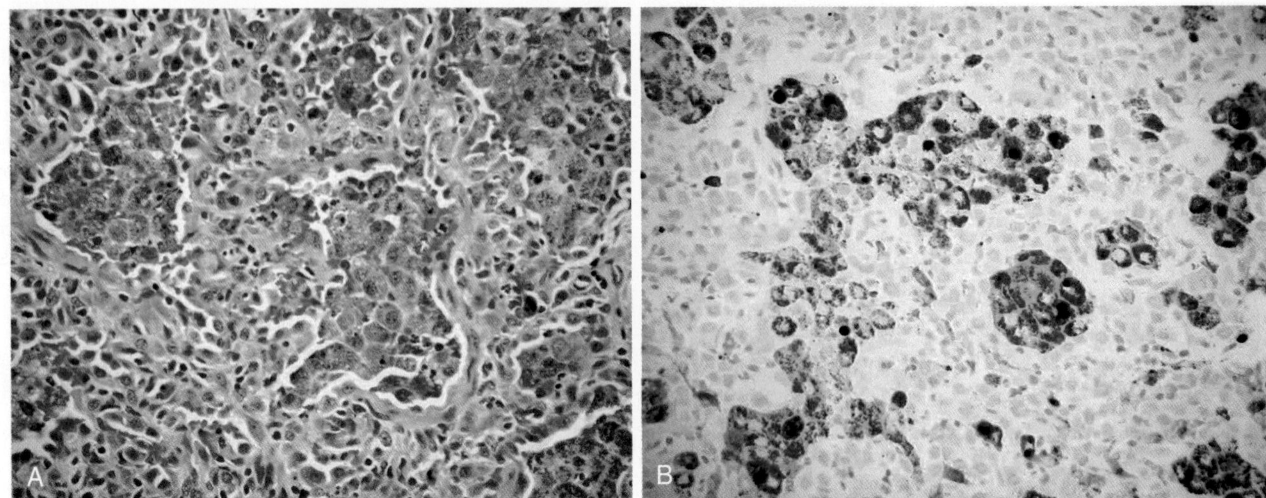

Figure 12–29 A, Lung biopsy specimen from a person with a diffuse alveolar hemorrhage syndrome demonstrates large numbers of intra-alveolar hemosiderin-laden macrophages on a background of thickened fibrous septa. **B,** The tissue has been stained with Prussian blue, an iron stain that highlights the abundant intracellular hemosiderin.

(From the Teaching Collection of the Department of Pathology, Children's Medical Center, Dallas, Texas.)

PULMONARY INFECTIONS

Pulmonary infections in the form of pneumonia are responsible for one sixth of all deaths in the United States. This is not surprising because (1) the epithelial surfaces of the lung are constantly exposed to many liters of air containing various levels of microbial contaminants; (2) nasopharyngeal flora are regularly aspirated during sleep, even by healthy persons; and (3) other common lung diseases render the lung parenchyma vulnerable to virulent organisms. The normal lung parenchyma remains sterile because of the efficiency of a number of immune and nonimmune defense mechanisms in the respiratory system, extending from the nasopharynx all the way into the alveolar air spaces (Fig. 12–30).

Despite the multitude of defense mechanisms, "chinks in the armor" do exist, predisposing even healthy persons to infections. Defects in innate immunity (including neutrophil and complement defects) and humoral immunodeficiency typically lead to an increased incidence of infections with pyogenic bacteria. For example, it has been shown that patients with mutations in MyD88, the adaptor protein downstream of many Toll-like receptors (microbial sensors in innate immunity), are extremely susceptible to severe necrotizing pneumococcal infections (and not most other infections). On the other hand, defects in T_H1 cell–mediated immunity lead mainly to increased infections with intracellular microbes such as atypical mycobacteria. In addition to inherited anomalies, several aspects of lifestyle interfere with host immune defense mechanisms and facilitate infections. For example, cigarette smoke compromises mucociliary clearance and pulmonary macrophage activity, and alcohol not only impairs cough and epiglottic reflexes, thereby increasing the risk of aspiration, but also interferes with neutrophil mobilization and chemotaxis.

Pneumonia can be very broadly defined as any infection in the lung. The clinical presentation may be as an acute, fulminant clinical disease or as a chronic disease with a more protracted course. The histologic spectrum of pneumonia may range from a fibrinopurulent alveolar exudate seen in acute bacterial pneumonias, to mononuclear interstitial infiltrates in viral and other atypical pneumonias, to granulomas and cavitation seen in many of the chronic pneumonias. Acute bacterial pneumonias can manifest as one of two anatomic and radiographic patterns, referred to as *bronchopneumonia* and *lobar pneumonia.* Bronchopneumonia implies a patchy distribution of inflammation that generally involves more than one lobe (Fig. 12–31). This pattern results from an initial infection of the bronchi and bronchioles with extension into the adjacent alveoli. By contrast, in lobar pneumonia the contiguous air spaces of part or all of a lobe are homogeneously filled with an exudate that can be visualized on radiographs as a lobar or segmental consolidation (Fig. 12–31). *Streptococcus pneumoniae* is responsible for more than 90% of lobar pneumonias. The anatomic distinction between lobar pneumonia and bronchopneumonia can often become blurry, because (1) many organisms cause infections that can manifest with either of the two patterns of distribution, and (2) confluent bronchopneumonia can be hard to distinguish radiologically from lobar pneumonia. *Therefore, it is best to classify pneumonias either by the specific etiologic agent or, if no pathogen can be isolated, by the clinical setting in which infection occurs.* The latter approach considerably narrows the list of suspected pathogens for administering empirical antimicrobial therapy. Pneumonia can arise in seven distinct clinical settings, and the implicated pathogens are reasonably specific to each category, as summarized in Table 12–6.

Community-Acquired Acute Pneumonias

Most community-acquired acute pneumonias are bacterial in origin. Not uncommonly, the infection follows a viral upper respiratory tract infection. The onset usually is abrupt, with high fever, shaking chills, pleuritic chest pain,

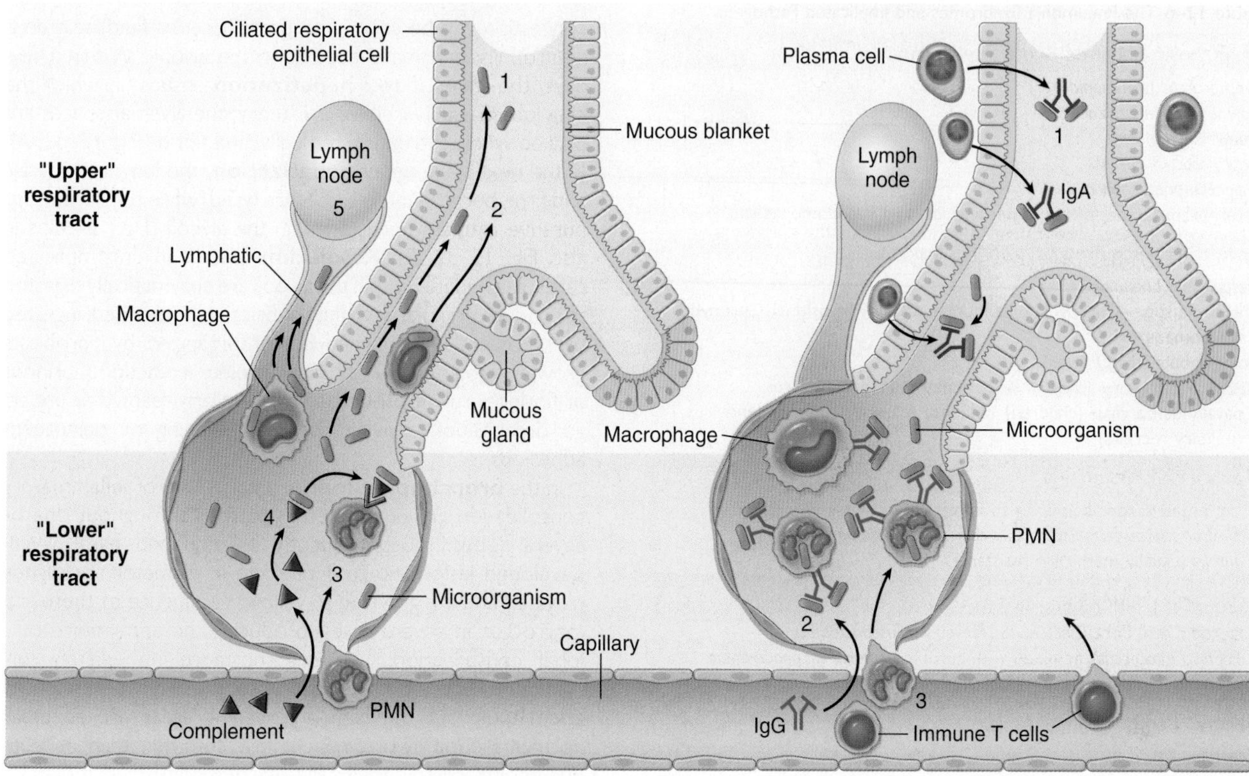

Figure 12–30 Lung defense mechanisms. **A,** Innate defenses against infection: *1,* In the normal lung, removal of microbial organisms depends on entrapment in the mucous blanket and removal by means of the mucociliary elevator; *2,* phagocytosis by alveolar macrophages that can kill and degrade organisms and remove them from the air spaces by migrating onto the mucociliary elevator; or *3,* phagocytosis and killing by neutrophils recruited by macrophage factors. *4,* Serum complement may enter the alveoli and be activated by the alternative pathway to provide the opsonin C3b, which enhances phagocytosis. *5,* Organisms, including those ingested by phagocytes, may reach the draining lymph nodes to initiate immune responses. **B,** Additional mechanisms operate after development of adaptive immunity. *1,* Secreted IgA can block attachment of the microorganism to epithelium in the upper respiratory tract. *2,* In the lower respiratory tract, serum antibodies (IgM, IgG) are present in the alveolar lining fluid. They activate complement more efficiently by the classic pathway, yielding C3b *(not shown).* In addition, IgG is opsonic. *3,* The accumulation of immune T cells is important for controlling infections by viruses and other intracellular microorganisms. PMN, polymorphonuclear cell.

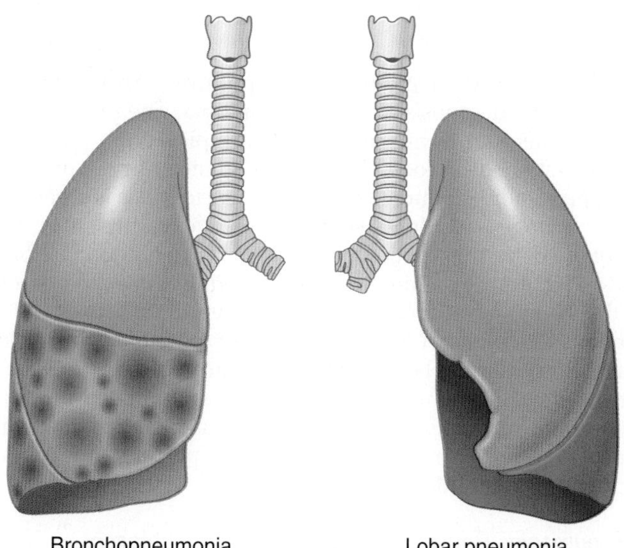

Figure 12–31 The anatomic distribution of bronchopneumonia and lobar pneumonia.

and a productive mucopurulent cough; occasional patients may have hemoptysis. *S. pneumoniae* (i.e., the pneumococcus) is the most common cause of community-acquired acute pneumonia; hence, pneumococcal pneumonia is discussed as the prototype for this subgroup.

Streptococcus pneumoniae *Infections*

Pneumococcal infections occur with increased frequency in three subsets of patients: (1) those with underlying chronic diseases such as CHF, COPD, or diabetes; (2) those with either congenital or acquired immunoglobulin defects (e.g., with the acquired immune deficiency syndrome [AIDS]); and (3) those with decreased or absent splenic function (e.g., sickle cell disease or after splenectomy). In the last group, such infections are more likely because the spleen contains the largest collection of phagocytes and is therefore the major organ responsible for removing pneumococci from the blood. The spleen is also an important organ for production of antibodies against polysaccharides, which are the dominant protective antibodies against encapsulated bacteria.

Table 12–6 The Pneumonia Syndromes and Implicated Pathogens

Community-Acquired Acute Pneumonia
Streptococcus pneumoniae
Haemophilus influenzae
Moraxella catarrhalis
Staphylococcus aureus
Legionella pneumophila
Enterobacteriaceae *(Klebsiella pneumoniae)* and Pseudomonas spp.
Community-Acquired Atypical Pneumonia
Mycoplasma pneumoniae
Chlamydia spp.—Chlamydia pneumoniae, Chlamydia psittaci, Chlamydia trachomatis
Coxiella burnetii (Q fever)
Viruses: respiratory syncytial virus, human metapneumovirus, parainfluenza virus (children); influenza A and B (adults); adenovirus (military recruits)
Nosocomial Pneumonia
Gram-negative rods belonging to Enterobacteriaceae (*Klebsiella* spp., *Serratia marcescens, Escherichia coli*) and *Pseudomonas* spp.
S. aureus (usually methicillin-resistant)
Aspiration Pneumonia
Anaerobic oral flora (*Bacteroides, Prevotella, Fusobacterium, Peptostreptococcus*), admixed with aerobic bacteria (*S. pneumoniae, S. aureus, H. influenzae,* and *Pseudomonas aeruginosa*)
Chronic Pneumonia
Nocardia
Actinomyces
Granulomatous: *Mycobacterium tuberculosis* and atypical mycobacteria, *Histoplasma capsulatum, Coccidioides immitis, Blastomyces dermatitidis*
Necrotizing Pneumonia and Lung Abscess
Anaerobic bacteria (extremely common), with or without mixed aerobic infection
S. aureus, K. pneumoniae, Streptococcus pyogenes, and type 3 pneumococcus (uncommon)
Pneumonia in the Immunocompromised Host
Cytomegalovirus
Pneumocystis jiroveci
Mycobacterium avium complex (MAC)
Invasive aspergillosis
Invasive candidiasis
"Usual" bacterial, viral, and fungal organisms (listed above)

MORPHOLOGY

With pneumococcal lung infection, either pattern of pneumonia, lobar or bronchopneumonia, may occur; the latter is much more prevalent at the extremes of age. Regardless of the distribution of the pneumonia, because pneumococcal lung infections usually are acquired by aspiration of pharyngeal flora (20% of adults harbor *S. pneumoniae* in the throat), the lower lobes or the right middle lobe is most frequently involved.

In the era before antibiotics, pneumococcal pneumonia involved entire or almost entire lobes and evolved through four stages: **congestion, red hepatization, gray hepatization,** and **resolution.** Early antibiotic therapy alters or halts this typical progression.

During the first stage, that of **congestion,** the affected lobe(s) is (are) heavy, red, and boggy; histologically, vascular congestion can be seen, with proteinaceous fluid, scattered neutrophils, and many bacteria in the alveoli. Within a few days, the stage of **red hepatization** ensues, in which the lung lobe has a liver-like consistency; the alveolar spaces are packed with neutrophils, red cells, and fibrin (Fig. 12–32, *A*). In the next stage, **gray hepatization,** the lung is dry, gray, and firm, because the red cells are lysed, while the fibrinosuppurative exudate persists within the alveoli (Fig. 12–33; see also Fig. 12–32, *B*). **Resolution** follows in uncomplicated cases, as exudates within the alveoli are enzymatically digested to produce granular, semifluid debris that is resorbed, ingested by macrophages, coughed up, or organized by fibroblasts growing into it (Fig. 12–32, *C*). The pleural reaction (fibrinous or fibrinopurulent **pleuritis**) may similarly resolve or undergo organization, leaving fibrous thickening or permanent adhesions.

In the **bronchopneumonic** pattern, foci of inflammatory consolidation are distributed in patches throughout one or several lobes, most frequently bilateral and basal. Well-developed lesions up to 3 or 4 cm in diameter are slightly elevated and are gray-red to yellow; confluence of these foci may occur in severe cases, producing the appearance of a lobar consolidation. The lung substance immediately surrounding areas of consolidation is usually hyperemic and edematous, but the large intervening areas are generally normal. Pleural involvement is less common than in lobar pneumonia. Histologically, the reaction consists of focal suppurative exudate that fills the bronchi, bronchioles, and adjacent alveolar spaces.

With appropriate therapy, complete restitution of the lung is the rule for both forms of pneumococcal pneumonia, but in occasional cases complications may occur: (1) tissue destruction and necrosis may lead to **abscess** formation; (2) suppurative material may accumulate in the pleural cavity, producing an **empyema;** (3) organization of the intra-alveolar exudate may convert areas of the lung into solid fibrous tissue; and (4) bacteremic dissemination may lead to **meningitis, arthritis,** or **infective endocarditis.** Complications are much more likely with serotype 3 pneumococci.

Examination of gram-stained sputum is an important step in the diagnosis of acute pneumonia. The presence of numerous neutrophils containing the typical gram-positive, lancet-shaped diplococci is good evidence of pneumococcal pneumonia; of note, however, *S. pneumoniae* is a part of the endogenous flora, so false-positive results may be obtained by this method. Isolation of pneumococci from blood cultures is more specific. During early phases of illness, blood cultures may be positive in 20% to 30% of persons with pneumonia. Whenever possible, antibiotic sensitivity should be determined. Commercial pneumococcal vaccines containing capsular polysaccharides from the common serotypes of the bacteria are available, and their proven efficacy mandates their use in persons at risk for pneumococcal infections (see earlier).

Pneumonias Caused by Other Important Pathogens

Other organisms commonly implicated in community-acquired acute pneumonias include the following.

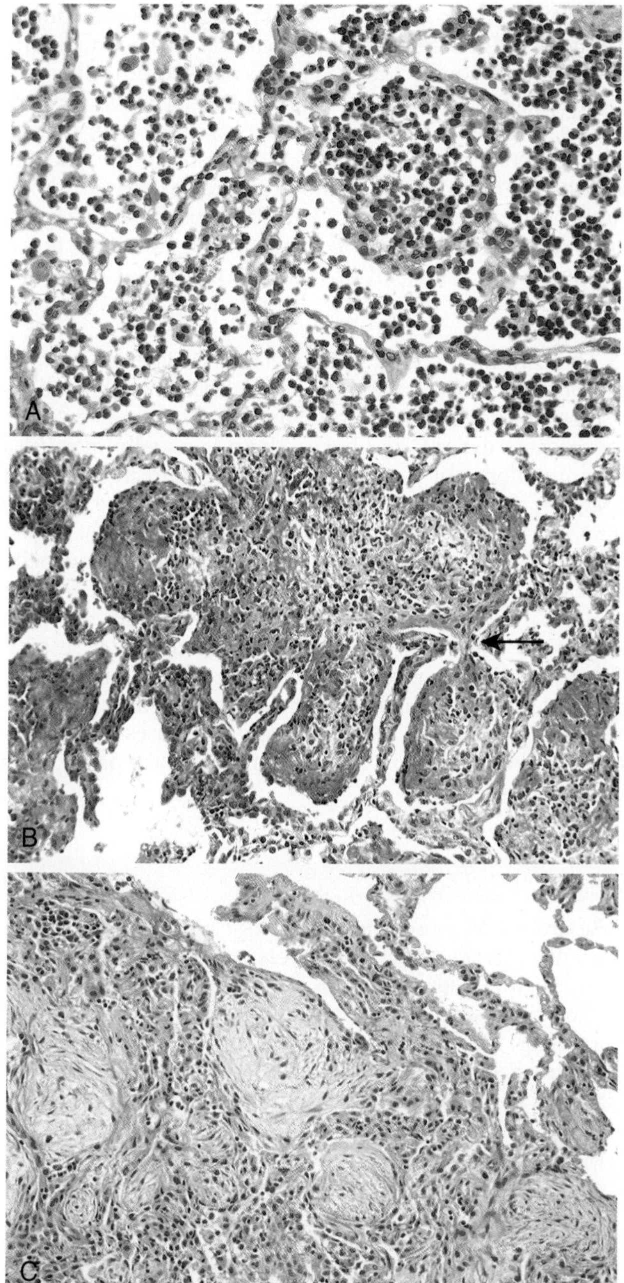

Figure 12–32 A, Acute pneumonia. The congested septal capillaries and extensive neutrophil exudation into alveoli correspond to early red hepatization. Fibrin nets have not yet formed. **B,** Early organization of intra-alveolar exudates, seen in areas to be streaming through the pores of Kohn (*arrow*). **C,** Advanced organizing pneumonia, featuring transformation of exudates to fibromyxoid masses richly infiltrated by macrophages and fibroblasts.

Haemophilus influenzae

- Both *encapsulated* and *unencapsulated* forms are important causes of community-acquired pneumonias. The former can cause a particularly life-threatening form of pneumonia in children, often after a respiratory viral infection.
- Adults at risk for developing infections include those with chronic pulmonary diseases such as chronic bronchitis, cystic fibrosis, and bronchiectasis. *H. influenzae is the most common bacterial cause of acute exacerbation of COPD.*
- Encapsulated *H. influenzae* type b was formerly an important cause of epiglottitis and suppurative meningitis in children, but vaccination against this organism in infancy has significantly reduced the risk.

Moraxella catarrhalis

- *M. catarrhalis* is being increasingly recognized as a cause of bacterial pneumonia, especially in elderly persons.
- It is the second most common bacterial cause of acute exacerbation of COPD in adults.
- Along with *S. pneumoniae* and *H. influenzae, M. catarrhalis* constitutes one of the three most common causes of otitis media (infection of the middle ear) in children.

Staphylococcus aureus

- *S. aureus* is an important cause of secondary bacterial pneumonia in children and healthy adults after viral respiratory illnesses (e.g., measles in children and influenza in both children and adults).
- Staphylococcal pneumonia is associated with a high incidence of complications, such as lung abscess and empyema.
- Staphylococcal pneumonia occurring in association with right-sided staphylococcal endocarditis is a serious complication of *intravenous drug abuse.*
- It is also an important cause of nosocomial pneumonia (discussed later).

Klebsiella pneumoniae

- *K. pneumoniae* is the most frequent cause of gram-negative bacterial pneumonia.

Figure 12–33 Gross view of lobar pneumonia with gray hepatization. The lower lobe is uniformly consolidated.

- *Klebsiella*-related pneumonia frequently afflicts debilitated and malnourished persons, particularly *chronic alcoholics.*
- Thick and gelatinous sputum is characteristic, because the organism produces an abundant viscid capsular polysaccharide, which the patient may have difficulty coughing up.

Pseudomonas aeruginosa

- Although discussed here with community-acquired pathogens because of its association with infections in cystic fibrosis, *P. aeruginosa* most commonly is seen in nosocomial settings (discussed later).
- *Pseudomonas* pneumonia also is common in persons who are neutropenic, usually secondary to chemotherapy; in victims of extensive burns; and in patients requiring mechanical ventilation.
- *P. aeruginosa* has a propensity to invade blood vessels at the site of infection, with consequent extrapulmonary spread; *Pseudomonas* bacteremia is a fulminant disease, with death often occurring within a matter of days.
- Histologic examination reveals coagulative necrosis of the pulmonary parenchyma with organisms invading the walls of necrotic blood vessels (*Pseudomonas* vasculitis).

Legionella pneumophila

- *L. pneumophila* is the agent of Legionnaire disease, an eponym for the epidemic and sporadic forms of pneumonia caused by this organism. Pontiac fever is a related self-limited upper respiratory tract infection caused by *L. pneumophila,* without pneumonic symptoms.
- *L. pneumophila* flourishes in artificial aquatic environments, such as water-cooling towers and within the tubing system of domestic (potable) water supplies. The mode of transmission is thought to be either inhalation of aerosolized organisms or aspiration of contaminated drinking water.
- *Legionella* pneumonia is common in persons with some predisposing condition such as cardiac, renal, immunologic, or hematologic disease. *Organ transplant recipients are particularly susceptible.*
- *Legionella* pneumonia can be quite severe, frequently requiring hospitalization, and immunosuppressed persons may have a fatality rate of 30% to 50%.
- Rapid diagnosis is facilitated by demonstration of *Legionella* antigens in the urine or by a positive fluorescent antibody test on sputum samples; culture remains the standard diagnostic modality. PCR-based tests can be used on bronchial secretions in atypical cases.

Community-Acquired Atypical Pneumonias

The term *primary atypical pneumonia* initially was applied to an acute febrile respiratory disease characterized by patchy inflammatory changes in the lungs, largely confined to the alveolar septa and pulmonary interstitium. The designation *atypical* denotes the moderate amounts of sputum, absence of physical findings of consolidation, only moderate elevation of white cell count, and lack of alveolar exudates. Atypical pneumonia is caused by a variety of organisms, *Mycoplasma pneumoniae* being the most common. *Mycoplasma* infections are particularly common among children and young adults. They occur sporadically or as local epidemics in closed communities (schools, military camps, prisons). Other etiologic agents are *viruses,* including influenza types A and B, the respiratory syncytial viruses, human metapneumovirus, adenovirus, rhinoviruses, rubeola virus, and varicella virus, and *Chlamydia pneumoniae* and *Coxiella burnetii* (the agent of Q fever) (Table 12–6). Nearly all of these agents can also cause a primarily upper respiratory tract infection ("common cold").

The common pathogenetic mechanism is attachment of the organisms to the respiratory epithelium followed by necrosis of the cells and an inflammatory response. When the process extends to alveoli, there is usually *interstitial* inflammation, but some outpouring of fluid into alveolar spaces may also occur, so that on chest films the changes may mimic those of bacterial pneumonia. Damage to and denudation of the respiratory epithelium inhibits mucociliary clearance and predisposes to secondary bacterial infections. Viral infections of the respiratory tract are well known for this complication. More serious lower respiratory tract infection is more likely to occur in infants, elderly persons, malnourished patients, alcoholics, and immunosuppressed persons. Not surprisingly, viruses and mycoplasmas frequently are involved in outbreaks of infection in hospitals.

MORPHOLOGY

Regardless of cause, the morphologic patterns in atypical pneumonias are similar. The process may be patchy, or it may involve whole lobes bilaterally or unilaterally. Macroscopically, the affected areas are red-blue, congested, and subcrepitant. On histologic examination, the **inflammatory reaction is largely confined within the walls of the alveoli** (Fig. 12–34). The septa are widened and edematous; they usually contain a mononuclear inflammatory infiltrate of lymphocytes, histiocytes, and, occasionally, plasma cells. In contrast with bacterial pneumonias, alveolar spaces in atypical pneumonias are remarkably free of cellular exudate. In severe cases, however, full-blown diffuse alveolar damage with hyaline membranes may develop. In less severe, uncomplicated cases, subsidence of the disease is followed by reconstitution of the native architecture. Superimposed bacterial infection, as expected, results in a mixed histologic picture.

Clinical Features

The clinical course of primary atypical pneumonia is extremely varied. It may masquerade as a severe upper respiratory tract infection or "chest cold" that goes undiagnosed, or it may manifest as a fulminant, life-threatening infection in immunocompromised patients. The initial presentation usually is that of an acute, nonspecific febrile illness characterized by fever, headache, and malaise and, later, cough with minimal sputum. Because the edema and exudation are both in a strategic position to cause an alveolocapillary block, there may be *respiratory distress seemingly out of proportion to the physical and radiographic findings.*

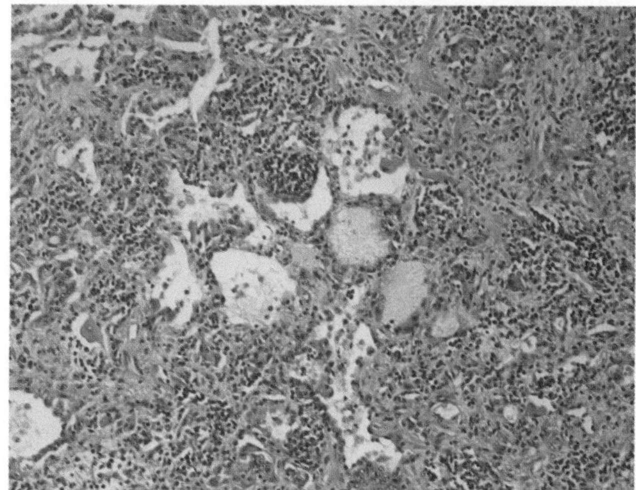

Figure 12–34 Viral pneumonia. The thickened alveolar walls are infiltrated with lymphocytes and some plasma cells, which are spilling over into alveolar spaces. Note focal alveolar edema in the *center* and early fibrosis at *upper right*.

Identifying the causative agent can be difficult. Tests for *Mycoplasma* antigens and polymerase chain reaction (PCR) testing for *Mycoplasma* DNA are available. As a practical matter, patients with community-acquired pneumonia for which a bacterial agent seems unlikely are treated with a macrolide antibiotic effective against *Mycoplasma* and *Chlamydia pneumoniae,* because these are the most common pathogens producing treatable disease.

Influenza Infections

Perhaps no other communicable disorder causes as much public distress in the developed world as the threat of an influenza epidemic. The influenza virus is a single-stranded RNA virus, bound by a nucleoprotein that determines the virus type—A, B, or C. The spherical surface of the virus is a lipid bilayer containing the viral hemagglutinin and neuraminidase, which determine the subtype (e.g., H1N1, H3N2). Host antibodies to the hemagglutinin and neuraminidase prevent and ameliorate, respectively, future infection with the influenza virus. The type A viruses infect humans, pigs, horses, and birds and are the major cause of *pandemic* and *epidemic* influenza infections. Epidemics of influenza occur through mutations of the hemagglutinin and neuraminidase antigens that allow the virus to escape most host antibodies (*antigenic drift*). Pandemics, which last longer and are more widespread than epidemics, may occur when both the hemagglutinin and neuraminidase are replaced through recombination of RNA segments with those of animal viruses, making all animals susceptible to the new influenza virus (*antigenic shift*). Commercially available influenza vaccines provide reasonable protection against the disease, especially in vulnerable infants and elderly persons. A particular subtype of avian influenza—"bird flu," caused by strain H5N1—has caused massive outbreaks in domesticated poultry in parts of Southeast Asia in the last several years; this strain is particularly dangerous, since it has the potential to "jump" to humans and thereby cause a worldwide influenza pandemic.

Influenza Virus Type A/H1N1 Infection

In March 2009, a novel swine-origin influenza A virus, strain H1N1, was identified, which spread in the United States and worldwide, leading to a pandemic affecting more than half a million patients, with more than 6200 deaths by November 2009.

Most patients have only a self-limiting illness, with viral replication limited to pharynx and tracheobronchial tree. Pneumonia occurs in severe disease. Comorbid conditions such as obesity, heart disease, and COPD are seen in fatal cases. Unlike the usual seasonal influenza in which older patients are more at risk of dying, the H1N1 pandemic killed only a few patients over 60 years of age, suggesting that immunity is achieved with previous exposure. Pathologic findings at autopsy include acute tracheobronchitis, bronchiolitis, diffuse alveolar damage, pulmonary thrombosis, and alveolar hemorrhage. In addition, approximately half have bacterial superinfection.

SUMMARY

Acute Pneumonias

- *S. pneumoniae* (the pneumococcus) is the most common cause of community-acquired acute pneumonia, and the distribution of inflammation is usually lobar.
- Morphologically, lobar pneumonias evolve through four stages: congestion, red hepatization, gray hepatization, and resolution.
- Other common causes of acute pneumonias in the community include *H. influenzae* and *M. catarrhalis* (both associated with acute exacerbations of COPD), *S. aureus* (usually secondary to viral respiratory infections), *K. pneumoniae* (observed in patients who are chronic alcoholics), *P. aeruginosa* (seen in persons with cystic fibrosis, in burn victims, and in patients with neutropenia), and *L. pneumophila,* seen particularly in organ transplant recipients.
- In contrast with acute pneumonias, *atypical pneumonias* are characterized by respiratory distress out of proportion to the clinical and radiologic signs, and by inflammation that is predominantly confined to alveolar septa, with generally clear alveoli.
- The most common causes of atypical pneumonias include those caused by *M. pneumoniae,* viruses including influenza viruses types A and B, human metapneumovirus, *C. pneumoniae,* and *C. burnetii* (agent of Q fever).

Hospital-Acquired Pneumonias

Nosocomial, or hospital-acquired, pneumonias are defined as pulmonary infections acquired in the course of a hospital stay. The specter of nosocomial pneumonia places an immense burden on the burgeoning costs of health care, in addition to the expected adverse impact on illness outcome. Nosocomial infections are common in hospitalized persons with severe underlying disease, those who are immunosuppressed, or those on prolonged antibiotic regimens. Those on mechanical ventilation represent a particularly high-risk group, and infections acquired in this setting are given the distinctive designation *ventilator-associated pneumonia.* Gram-negative rods (members of Enterobacteriaceae and *Pseudomonas* spp.) and *S. aureus* are the most common isolates; unlike with community-acquired pneumonias, *S. pneumoniae* is not a major pathogen in nosocomial infections.

Aspiration Pneumonia

Aspiration pneumonia occurs in debilitated patients or those who aspirate gastric contents either while unconscious (e.g., after a stroke) or during repeated vomiting. These patients have abnormal gag and swallowing reflexes that facilitate aspiration. The resultant pneumonia is partly chemical, resulting from the extremely irritating effects of the gastric acid, and partly bacterial. Although it is commonly assumed that anaerobic bacteria predominate, more recent studies implicate aerobes more commonly than anaerobes (Table 12–6). This type of pneumonia is often necrotizing, pursues a fulminant clinical course, and is a frequent cause of death in persons predisposed to aspiration. In those who survive, abscess formation is a common complication. Microaspiration, by contrast, occurs in many people, especially those with gastro-esophageal reflux, and may exacerbate other lung diseases but does not lead to pneumonia.

Lung Abscess

Lung abscess refers to a localized area of suppurative necrosis within the pulmonary parenchyma, resulting in the formation of one or more large cavities. The term *necrotizing pneumonia* has been used to describe a similar process resulting in multiple small cavitations; necrotizing pneumonia often coexists or evolves into lung abscess, making this distinction somewhat arbitrary. The causative organism may be introduced into the lung by any of the following mechanisms:

- *Aspiration of infective material* from carious teeth or infected sinuses or tonsils, particularly likely during oral surgery, anesthesia, coma, or alcoholic intoxication and in debilitated patients with depressed cough reflexes
- *Aspiration of gastric contents,* usually accompanied by infectious organisms from the oropharynx
- *As a complication of necrotizing bacterial pneumonias,* particularly those caused by *S. aureus, Streptococcus pyogenes, K. pneumoniae, Pseudomonas* spp., and, rarely, type 3 pneumococci. Mycotic infections and bronchiectasis may also lead to lung abscesses.
- *Bronchial obstruction,* particularly with bronchogenic carcinoma obstructing a bronchus or bronchiole. Impaired drainage, distal atelectasis, and aspiration of blood and tumor fragments all contribute to the development of abscesses. An abscess may also form within an excavated necrotic portion of a tumor.
- *Septic embolism,* from septic thrombophlebitis or from infective endocarditis of the right side of the heart
- In addition, lung abscesses may result from *hematogenous spread of bacteria* in disseminated pyogenic infection. This occurs most characteristically in staphylococcal bacteremia and often results in multiple lung abscesses.

Anaerobic bacteria are present in almost all lung abscesses, sometimes in vast numbers, and they are the exclusive isolates in one third to two thirds of cases. The most frequently encountered anaerobes are commensals normally found in the oral cavity, principally species of *Prevotella, Fusobacterium, Bacteroides, Peptostreptococcus,* and microaerophilic streptococci.

MORPHOLOGY

Abscesses range in diameter from a few millimeters to large cavities 5 to 6 cm across. The localization and number of abscesses depend on their mode of development. Pulmonary abscesses resulting from aspiration of infective material are much **more common on the right side** (with its more vertical airways) than on the left, and most are single. On the right side, they tend to occur in the posterior segment of the upper lobe and in the apical segments of the lower lobe, because these locations reflect the probable course of aspirated material when the patient is recumbent. Abscesses that develop in the course of pneumonia or bronchiectasis commonly are multiple, basal, and diffusely scattered. Septic emboli and abscesses arising from hematogenous seeding are commonly multiple and may affect any region of the lungs.

As the focus of suppuration enlarges, it almost inevitably ruptures into airways. Thus, the contained exudate may be partially drained, producing an air-fluid level on radiographic examination. Occasionally, abscesses rupture into the pleural cavity and produce bronchopleural fistulas, the consequence of which is **pneumothorax** or **empyema.** Other complications arise from embolization of septic material to the brain, giving rise to meningitis or brain abscess. On histologic examination, as expected with any abscess, the suppurative focus is surrounded by variable amounts of fibrous scarring and mononuclear infiltration (lymphocytes, plasma cells, macrophages), depending on the chronicity of the lesion.

Clinical Features

The manifestations of a lung abscess are much like those of bronchiectasis and include a prominent cough that usually yields copious amounts of foul-smelling, purulent, or sanguineous sputum; occasionally, hemoptysis occurs. Spiking fever and malaise are common. Clubbing of the fingers, weight loss, and anemia may all occur. Infective abscesses occur in 10% to 15% of patients with bronchogenic carcinoma; thus, when a lung abscess is suspected in an older person, underlying carcinoma must be considered. Secondary amyloidosis (Chapter 4) may develop in chronic cases. Treatment includes antibiotic therapy and, if needed, surgical drainage. Overall, the mortality rate is in the range of 10%.

Chronic Pneumonias

Chronic pneumonia most often is a localized lesion in an immunocompetent person, with or without regional lymph node involvement. There is typically granulomatous inflammation, which may be due to bacteria (e.g., *M. tuberculosis*) or fungi. In immunocompromised patients, such as those with debilitating illness, on immunosuppressive regimens, or with human immunodeficiency virus (HIV) infection (see below), systemic dissemination of the causative organism, accompanied by widespread disease, is the usual presentation. Tuberculosis is by far the most important entity within the spectrum of chronic pneumonias; the World Health Organization (WHO) estimates that tuberculosis causes 6% of all deaths worldwide, *making it the most common cause of death resulting from a single infectious agent.*

Tuberculosis

Tuberculosis is a communicable chronic granulomatous disease caused by *Mycobacterium tuberculosis.* It usually involves the lungs but may affect any organ or tissue in the body. Typically, the centers of tubercular granulomas undergo *caseous necrosis.*

Epidemiology

Among medically and economically deprived persons throughout the world, tuberculosis remains a leading cause of death. It is estimated that 1.7 billion people are infected worldwide, with 8 to 10 million new cases and 3 million deaths per year. In the Western world, deaths from tuberculosis peaked in 1800 and steadily declined throughout the 1800s and 1900s. However, in 1984 the decline in new cases stopped abruptly, a change that resulted from the increased incidence of tuberculosis in HIV-infected persons. As a consequence of intensive public health surveillance and tuberculosis prophylaxis among immunosuppressed persons, the incidence of tuberculosis in U.S.-born persons has declined since 1992. Currently, it is estimated that about 25,000 new cases with active tuberculosis arise in the United States annually, and nearly 40% of these are in immigrants from countries where tuberculosis is highly prevalent.

Tuberculosis flourishes under conditions of poverty, crowding, and chronic debilitating illness. Similarly, elderly persons, with their weakened defenses, are vulnerable. In the United States, tuberculosis is a disease of the elderly, the urban poor, patients with AIDS, and members of minority communities. African Americans, Native Americans, the Inuit (from Alaska), Hispanics, and immigrants from Southeast Asia have higher attack rates than those typical for other segments of the population. *Certain disease states also increase the risk:* diabetes mellitus, Hodgkin lymphoma, chronic lung disease (particularly silicosis), chronic renal failure, malnutrition, alcoholism, and immunosuppression. In areas of the world where HIV infection is prevalent, *it has become the single most important risk factor for the development of tuberculosis.*

It is important that *infection* be differentiated from *disease.* Infection implies seeding of a focus with organisms, which may or may not cause clinically significant tissue damage (i.e., disease). Although other routes may be involved, most infections are acquired by direct person-to-person transmission of airborne droplets of organisms from an active case to a susceptible host. In most persons, an asymptomatic focus of pulmonary infection appears that is self-limited, although uncommonly, primary tuberculosis may result in the development of fever and pleural effusions. Generally, the only evidence of infection, if any remains, is a tiny, telltale fibrocalcific nodule at the site of the infection. Viable organisms may remain dormant in such loci for decades, and possibly for the life of the host. Such persons are infected but do not have active disease and therefore cannot transmit organisms to others. Yet when their immune defenses are lowered, the infection may reactivate to produce communicable and potentially life-threatening disease.

Infection with *M. tuberculosis* typically leads to the development of delayed hypersensitivity, which can be detected by the tuberculin (Mantoux) test. About 2 to 4 weeks after the infection has begun, intracutaneous injection of 0.1 mL of PPD induces a visible and palpable induration (at least 5 mm in diameter) that peaks in 48 to 72 hours. Sometimes, more PPD is required to elicit the reaction, and unfortunately, in some responders, the standard dose may produce a large, necrotizing lesion. *A positive tuberculin skin test result* signifies cell-mediated hypersensitivity to tubercular antigens. It does not differentiate between infection and disease. A well-recognized limitation of this test is that *false-negative reactions (or skin test anergy) may be produced by certain viral infections, sarcoidosis, malnutrition, Hodgkin lymphoma, immunosuppression, and (notably) overwhelming active tuberculous disease.* False-positive reactions may result from infection by atypical mycobacteria.

About 80% of the population in certain Asian and African countries is tuberculin-positive. In contrast, in 1980, 5% to 10% of the U.S. population was positive, indicating the marked difference in rates of exposure to the tubercle bacillus. In general, 3% to 4% of previously unexposed persons acquire active tuberculosis during the first year after "tuberculin conversion," and no more than 15% do so thereafter. Thus, *only a small fraction of those who contract an infection develop active disease.*

Etiology

Mycobacteria are slender rods that are acid-fast (i.e., they have a high content of complex lipids that readily bind the Ziehl-Neelsen [carbol fuchsin] stain and subsequently stubbornly resist decolorization). *M. tuberculosis hominis* is responsible for most cases of tuberculosis; the reservoir of infection typically is found in persons with active pulmonary disease. Transmission usually is direct, by inhalation of airborne organisms in aerosols generated by expectoration or by exposure to contaminated secretions of infected persons. Oropharyngeal and intestinal tuberculosis contracted by drinking milk contaminated with *Mycobacterium bovis* infection is now rare in developed nations, but it is still seen in countries with tuberculous dairy cows and sales of unpasteurized milk. Other mycobacteria, particularly *Mycobacterium avium complex,* are much less virulent than *M. tuberculosis* and rarely cause disease in immunocompetent persons. However, they cause disease in 10% to 30% of patients with AIDS.

PATHOGENESIS

The pathogenesis of tuberculosis in the previously **unexposed immunocompetent** person is centered on the development of a targeted cell-mediated immunity that confers **resistance** to the organism and results in development of **tissue hypersensitivity** to tubercular antigens. The pathologic features of tuberculosis, such as caseating granulomas and cavitation, are the result of the destructive tissue hypersensitivity that is part and parcel of the host immune response. Because the effector cells for both processes are the same, the appearance of tissue hypersensitivity also signals the acquisition of immunity to the organism. The sequence of events from inhalation of the infectious inoculum to containment of the primary focus is illustrated in Fig. 12–35, A and B and is outlined next:

- Once a virulent strain of mycobacteria gains entry into the macrophage endosomes (a process mediated by several macrophage receptors, including the macrophage mannose receptor and complement receptors that recognize several components of the mycobacterial cell walls), the organisms are able to inhibit normal microbicidal responses by preventing the fusion of the lysosomes with the phagocytic vacuole. The prevention of phagolysosome formation allows unchecked mycobacterial proliferation. Thus, the earliest phase of primary tuberculosis (in the first 3 weeks) in the nonsensitized patient is characterized by bacillary proliferation within the pulmonary alveolar macrophages and air spaces, with resulting bacteremia and seeding of multiple sites. **Despite the bacteremia, most persons at this stage are asymptomatic or have a mild flu-like illness.**
- The genetic makeup of the patient may influence the course of the disease. In some people with polymorphisms of the **NRAMP1** (**n**atural **r**esistance–**a**ssociated **m**acrophage **p**rotein **1**) gene, the disease may progress from this point without development of an effective immune response. NRAMP1 is a transmembrane ion transport protein found in endosomes and lysosomes that is believed to contribute to microbial killing.
- The development of **cell-mediated immunity** occurs approximately 3 weeks after exposure. Processed mycobacterial antigens reach the draining lymph nodes and are presented to CD4 T cells by dendritic cells and macrophages. Under the influence of macrophage-secreted IL-12, CD4+ T cells of the T_H1 subset are generated that are capable of secreting IFN-γ.
- **IFN-γ released by the CD4+ T cells of the T_H1 subset is crucial in activating macrophages.** Activated macrophages, in turn, release a variety of mediators and upregulate expression of genes with important downstream effects, including (1) TNF, which is responsible for recruitment of monocytes, which in turn undergo activation and differentiation into the "epithelioid histiocytes"

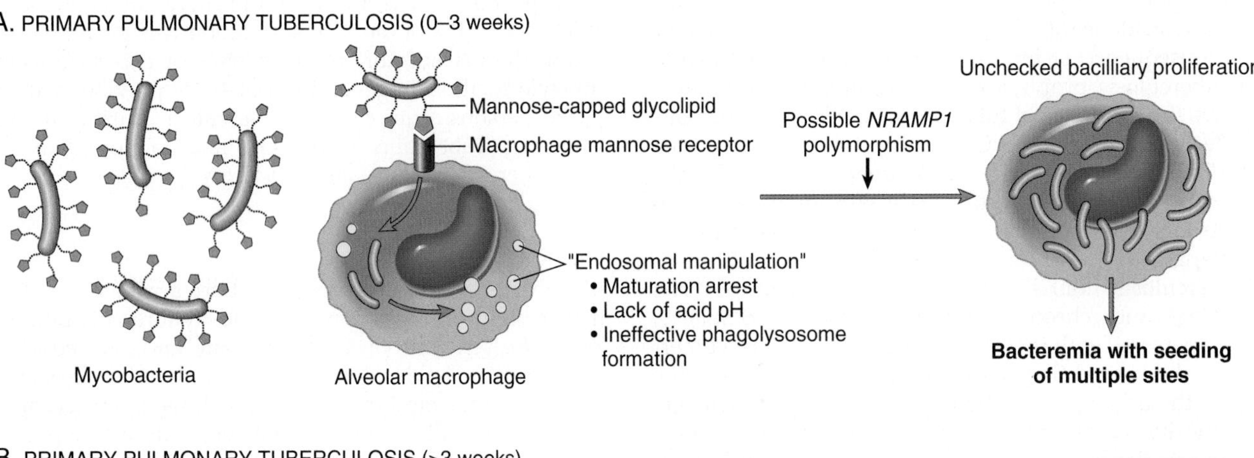

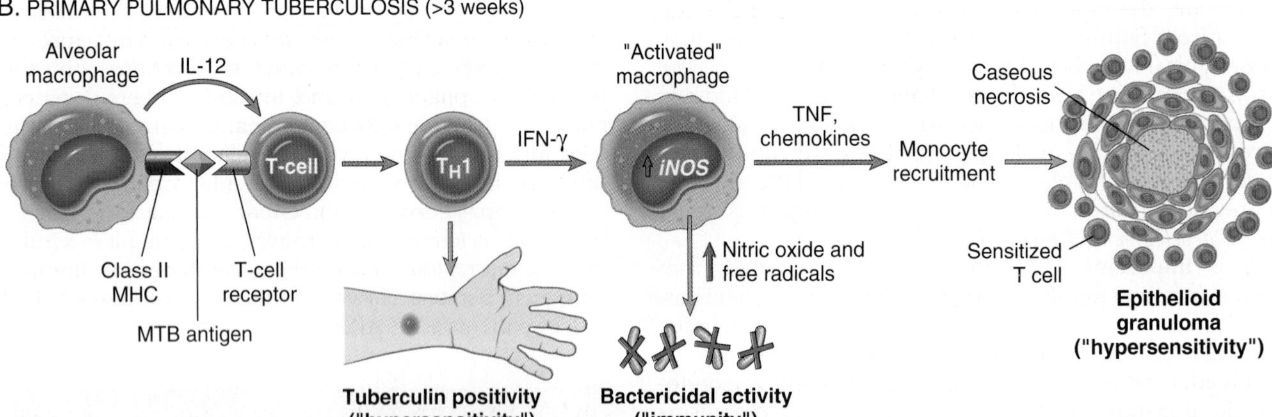

Figure 12–35 Sequence of events in the natural history of primary pulmonary tuberculosis. This sequence commences with inhalation of virulent strains of *Mycobacterium* and culminates in the development of immunity and delayed hypersensitivity to the organism. **A,** Events occurring in the first 3 weeks after exposure. **B,** Events thereafter. The development of resistance to the organism is accompanied by conversion to a positive result on tuberculin skin testing. Cells and bacteria are not drawn to scale. IFN-γ, interferon γ; iNOS, inducible nitric oxide synthase; MHC, major histocompatibility complex; MTB, *Mycobacterium tuberculosis*; *NRAMP1*, gene encoding natural resistance–associated macrophage protein 1; TNF, tumor necrosis factor.

that characterize the granulomatous response; (2) expression of the **inducible nitric oxide synthase** *(iNOS)* gene, which results in elevated **nitric oxide** levels at the site of infection, with excellent antibacterial activity; and (3) generation of reactive oxygen species, which can have antibacterial activity. You will recall that nitric oxide is a powerful oxidizing agent that results in generation of reactive nitrogen intermediates and other free radicals capable of oxidative destruction of several mycobacterial constituents, from cell wall to DNA.

- Defects in any of the steps of a T_H1 response (including IL-12, IFN-γ, TNF, or nitric oxide production) result in poorly formed granulomas, absence of resistance, and disease progression. Persons with inherited mutations in any component of the T_H1 pathway are extremely susceptible to infections with mycobacteria.

In summary, immunity to a tubercular infection is primarily mediated by T_H1 cells, which stimulate macrophages to kill bacteria. This immune response, while largely effective, comes at the cost of hypersensitivity and the accompanying tissue destruction. Reactivation of the infection or reexposure to the bacilli in a previously sensitized host results in rapid mobilization of a defensive reaction but also increased tissue necrosis. Just as hypersensitivity and resistance appear in parallel, so, too, the loss of hypersensitivity (indicated by tuberculin negativity in a tuberculin-positive patient) may be an ominous sign that resistance to the organism has faded.

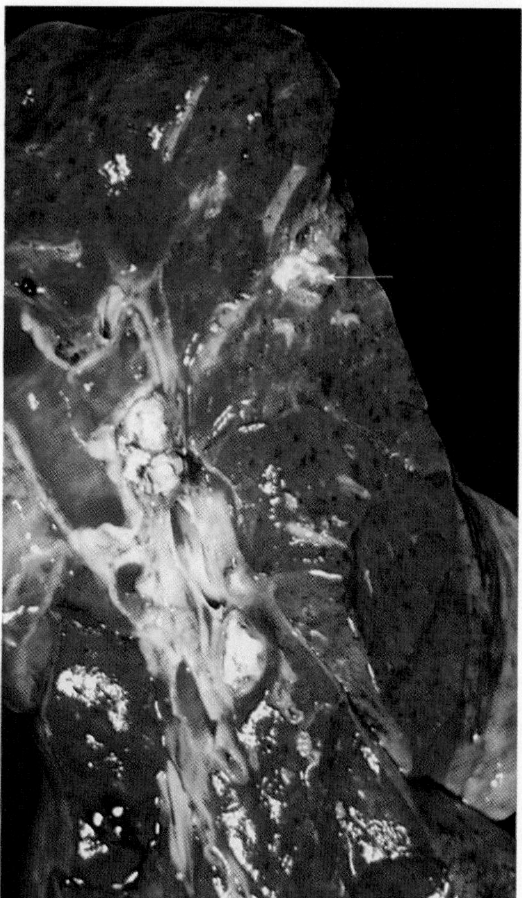

Figure 12–36 Primary pulmonary tuberculosis, Ghon complex. The gray-white parenchymal focus *(arrow)* is under the pleura in the *lower part* of the upper lobe. Hilar lymph nodes with caseation are seen on the *left.*

Primary Tuberculosis

Primary tuberculosis is the form of disease that develops in a previously unexposed and therefore unsensitized patient. Elderly persons and profoundly immunosuppressed patients may lose their sensitivity to the tubercle bacillus, so they may develop primary tuberculosis more than once. About 5% of those newly infected acquire significant disease.

MORPHOLOGY

In countries in which bovine tuberculosis and infected milk have largely disappeared, primary tuberculosis almost always begins in the lungs. Typically, the inhaled bacilli implant in the distal air spaces of the lower part of the upper lobe or the upper part of the lower lobe, usually close to the pleura. As sensitization develops, a 1- to 1.5-cm area of gray-white inflammatory consolidation emerges, the **Ghon focus.** In most cases the center of this focus undergoes caseous necrosis. Tubercle bacilli, either free or within phagocytes, travel in lymph drainage to the regional nodes, which also often caseate. **This combination of parenchymal lesion and nodal involvement** is referred to as the Ghon complex (Fig. 12–36). During the first few weeks, there is also lymphatic and hematogenous dissemination to other parts of the body. In approximately 95% of cases, development of cell-mediated immunity controls the infection. Hence, the Ghon complex undergoes progressive fibrosis, often followed by radiologically detectable calcification **(Ranke complex),** and despite seeding of other organs, no lesions develop.

On histologic examination, sites of active involvement are marked by a characteristic granulomatous inflammatory reaction that forms both caseating and noncaseating granulomas (Fig. 12–37, *A* to *C*), which consist of epithelioid histiocytes and multinucleate giant cells.

The major consequences of primary tuberculosis are that (1) it induces hypersensitivity and increased resistance; (2) the foci of scarring may harbor viable bacilli for years, perhaps for life, and thus be the nidus for *reactivation* at a later time when host defenses are compromised; and (3) uncommonly, it may lead to *progressive primary tuberculosis.* This complication occurs in patients who are immunocompromised or have nonspecific impairment of host defenses, as characteristic in malnourished children or in elderly persons. Certain racial groups, such as the Inuit, also are more prone to the development of progressive primary tuberculosis. The incidence of progressive primary tuberculosis is particularly high in HIV-positive patients with an advanced degree of immunosuppression (i.e., CD4+ counts below 200 cells/μL). Immunosuppression results in an inability to mount a CD4+ T cell–mediated immunologic reaction that would contain the primary focus; because hypersensitivity and resistance are most often concomitant factors, the lack of a tissue hypersensitivity reaction results

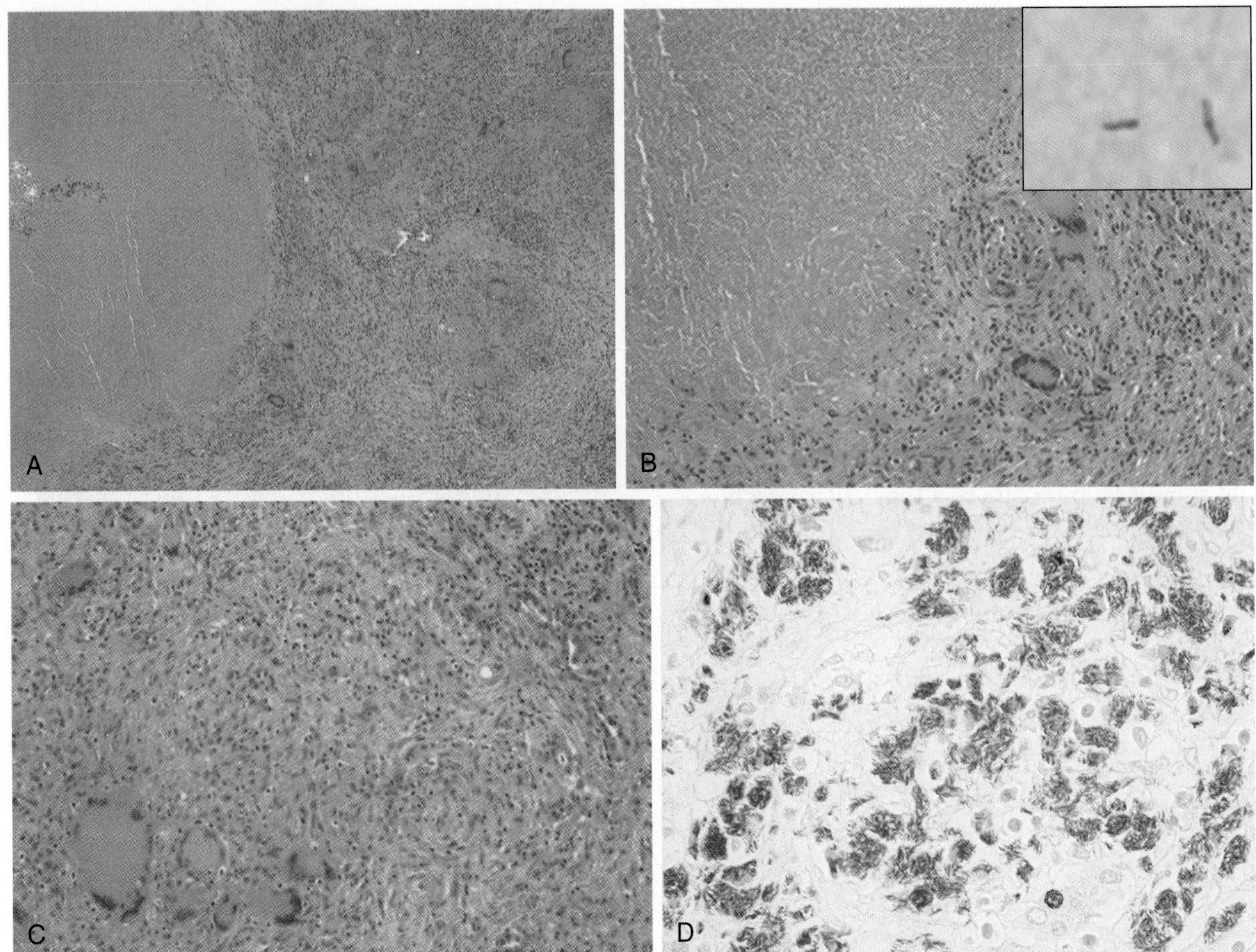

Figure 12–37 The morphologic spectrum of tuberculosis. **A** and **B,** A characteristic tubercle at low magnification **(A)** and at higher power **(B)** shows central granular caseation surrounded by epithelioid and multinucleate giant cells. This is the usual response seen in persons who have developed cell-mediated immunity to the organism. *Inset:* Acid-fast stain shows rare positive organisms. **C,** Occasionally, even in immunocompetent patients, tubercular granulomas may not show central caseation; hence, irrespective of the presence or absence of caseous necrosis, use of special stains for acid-fast organisms is indicated when granulomas are present. **D,** In this specimen from an immunosuppressed patient, sheets of foamy macrophages packed with mycobacteria are seen (acid-fast stain).

in the absence of the characteristic caseating granulomas (*nonreactive tuberculosis*) (Fig. 12–37, *D*).

Secondary Tuberculosis (Reactivation Tuberculosis)

Secondary tuberculosis is the pattern of disease that arises in a previously sensitized host. It may follow shortly after primary tuberculosis, but more commonly it arises from reactivation of dormant primary lesions many decades after initial infection, particularly when host resistance is weakened. It also may result from exogenous reinfection because of waning of the protection afforded by the primary disease or because of a large inoculum of virulent bacilli. Whatever the source of the organism, only a few patients (less than 5%) with primary disease subsequently develop secondary tuberculosis.

Secondary pulmonary tuberculosis is classically localized to the apex of one or both upper lobes. The reason is obscure but may relate to high oxygen tension in the apices. Because of the preexistence of hypersensitivity, the bacilli excite a prompt and marked tissue response that tends to wall off the focus. As a result of this localization, the regional lymph nodes are less prominently involved early in the disease than they are in primary tuberculosis. On the other hand, *cavitation occurs readily in the secondary form,* leading to erosion into and dissemination along airways. Such changes become an important source of infectivity, because the patient now produces sputum containing bacilli.

Secondary tuberculosis should always be an important consideration in HIV-positive patients who present with pulmonary disease. Of note, *although an increased risk of tuberculosis exists at all stages of HIV disease, the manifestations differ depending on the degree of immunosuppression.* For example, patients with less severe immunosuppression (CD4+ counts greater than 300 cells/mm^3) present with "usual" secondary tuberculosis (apical disease with cavitation) while those with more advanced immunosuppression (CD4+ counts below 200 cells/mm^3) present with a clinical picture that resembles progressive primary tuberculosis (lower and middle lobe consolidation, hilar lymphadenopathy, and noncavitary disease). The extent of immunosuppression also determines the frequency of extrapulmonary involvement, rising from 10% to 15% in mildly immunosuppressed patients to greater than 50% in those with severe immune deficiency.

MORPHOLOGY

The initial lesion usually is a small focus of consolidation, less than 2 cm in diameter, within 1 to 2 cm of the **apical pleura.** Such foci are sharply circumscribed, firm, gray-white to yellow areas that have a variable amount of central caseation and peripheral fibrosis. In favorable cases, the initial parenchymal focus undergoes progressive fibrous encapsulation, leaving only fibrocalcific scars. Histologically, the active lesions show characteristic coalescent tubercles with central caseation. Although tubercle bacilli can be demonstrated by appropriate methods in early exudative and caseous phases of granuloma formation, it is usually impossible to find them in the late, fibrocalcific stages. Localized, apical, secondary pulmonary tuberculosis may heal with fibrosis either spontaneously or after therapy, or the disease may progress and extend along several different pathways.

Progressive pulmonary tuberculosis may ensue. The apical lesion enlarges with expansion of the area of caseation. Erosion into a bronchus evacuates the caseous center, creating a ragged, **irregular cavity lined by caseous material** that is poorly walled off by fibrous tissue (Fig. 12–38). Erosion of blood vessels results in hemoptysis. With adequate treatment, the process may be arrested, although healing by fibrosis often distorts the pulmonary architecture. Irregular cavities, now free of caseation necrosis, may remain or collapse in the surrounding fibrosis. If the treatment is inadequate, or if host defenses are impaired, the infection may spread by direct expansion, by means of dissemination through airways, lymphatic channels, or within the vascular system. **Miliary pulmonary disease** occurs when organisms drain through lymphatics into the lymphatic ducts, which empty into the venous return to the right side of the heart and thence into the pulmonary arteries. Individual lesions are either microscopic or small, visible (2 mm) foci of yellow-white consolidation scattered through the lung parenchyma (the word *miliary* is derived from the resemblance of these foci to millet seeds). With progressive pulmonary tuberculosis, the pleural cavity is invariably involved and serous **pleural effusions, tuberculous empyema,** or **obliterative fibrous pleuritis** may develop.

Endobronchial, endotracheal, and **laryngeal tuberculosis** may develop when infective material is spread either through lymphatic channels or from expectorated infectious material. The mucosal lining may be studded with minute granulomatous lesions, sometimes apparent only on microscopic examination.

Systemic miliary tuberculosis ensues when the organisms disseminate through the systemic arterial system to almost every organ in the body. Granulomas are the same as in the lung. Miliary tuberculosis is most prominent in the liver, bone marrow, spleen, adrenals, meninges, kidneys, fallopian tubes, and epididymis (Fig. 12–39).

Isolated-organ tuberculosis may appear in any one of the organs or tissues seeded hematogenously and may be the presenting manifestation of tuberculosis. Organs typically involved include the meninges (tuberculous meningitis), kidneys (renal tuberculosis), adrenals, bones (osteomyelitis), and fallopian tubes (salpingitis). When the vertebrae are affected, the condition is referred to as Pott disease. Paraspinal "cold" abscesses may track along the tissue planes to present as an abdominal or pelvic mass.

Lymphadenitis is the most frequent form of extrapulmonary tuberculosis, usually occurring in the cervical region ("scrofula"). Lymphadenopathy tends to be unifocal, and most patients do not have concurrent extranodal disease. HIV-positive patients, on the other hand, almost always have multifocal disease, systemic symptoms, and either pulmonary or other organ involvement by active tuberculosis.

In years past, **intestinal tuberculosis** contracted by the drinking of contaminated milk was fairly common as a primary focus of tuberculosis. In developed countries today, intestinal tuberculosis is more often a complication of protracted advanced secondary tuberculosis, secondary to the swallowing of coughed-up infective material. Typically, the organisms are trapped in mucosal lymphoid aggregates of the small and large bowel, which then undergo inflammatory enlargement with ulceration of the overlying mucosa, particularly in the ileum.

The many patterns of tuberculosis are depicted in Figure 12–40.

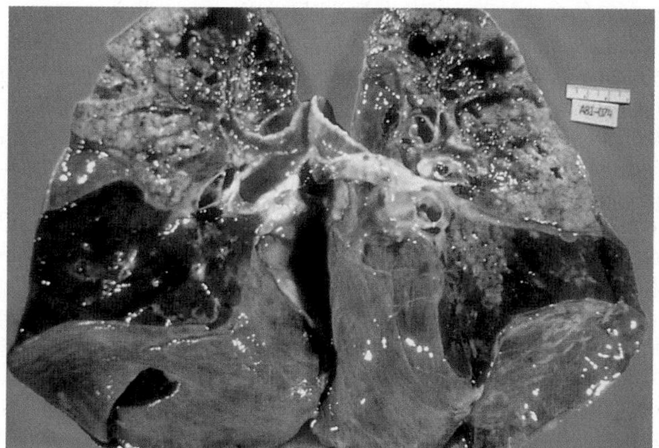

Figure 12–38 Secondary pulmonary tuberculosis. The upper parts of both lungs are riddled with gray-white areas of caseation and multiple areas of softening and cavitation.

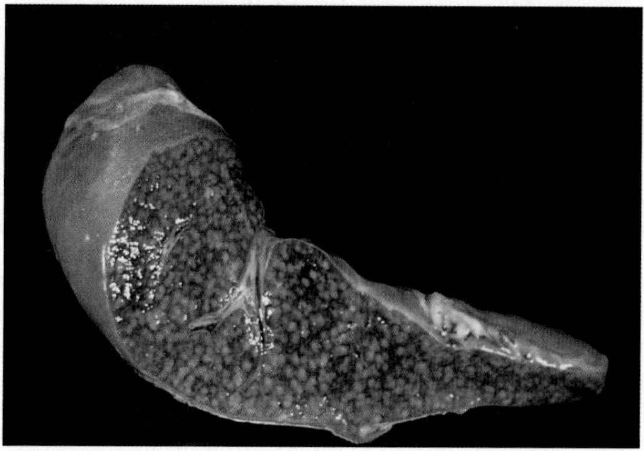

Figure 12–39 Miliary tuberculosis of the spleen. The cut surface shows numerous gray-white granulomas.

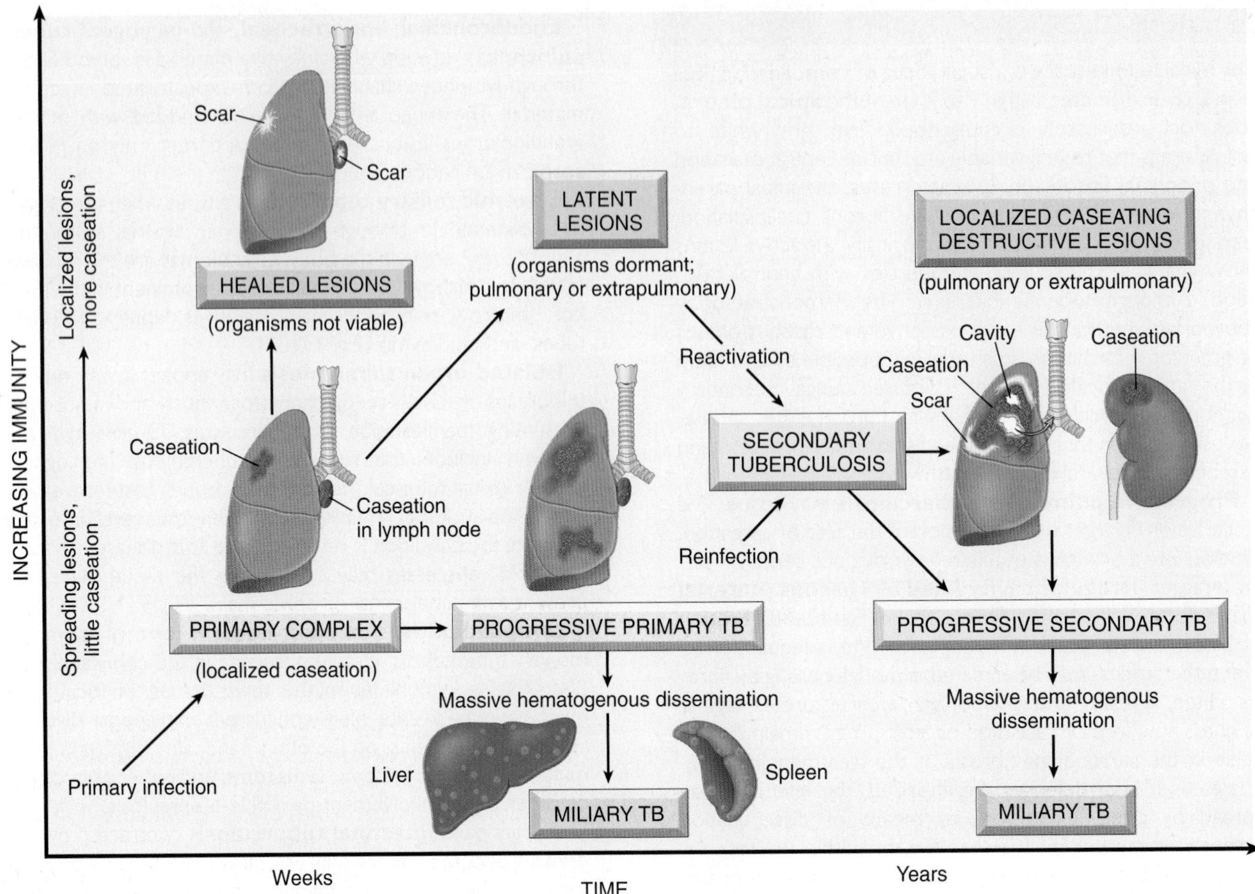

Figure 12–40 The natural history and spectrum of tuberculosis.
(Adapted from a sketch provided by Dr. R.K. Kumar, The University of New South Wales, School of Pathology, Sydney, Australia.)

Clinical Features

Localized secondary tuberculosis may be asymptomatic. When manifestations appear, they are usually *insidious* in onset, with gradual development of both systemic and localizing symptoms and signs. Systemic manifestations, probably related to the release of cytokines by activated macrophages (e.g., TNF and IL-1), often appear early in the disease course and include malaise, anorexia, weight loss, and fever. Commonly, the *fever is low grade* and remittent (appearing late each afternoon and then subsiding), and *night sweats* occur. With progressive pulmonary involvement, increasing amounts of sputum, at first mucoid and later purulent, appear. When cavitation is present, the sputum contains tubercle bacilli. Some degree of *hemoptysis* is present in about half of all cases of pulmonary tuberculosis. *Pleuritic pain* may result from extension of the infection to the pleural surfaces. Extrapulmonary manifestations of tuberculosis are legion and depend on the organ system involved (for example, tuberculous salpingitis may present as infertility, tuberculous meningitis with headache and neurologic deficits, Pott disease with back pain and paraplegia). The diagnosis of pulmonary disease is based in part on the history and on physical and radiographic findings of *consolidation or cavitation in the apices of the lungs.* Ultimately, however, *tubercle bacilli must be identified.*

The most common methodology for diagnosis of tuberculosis remains demonstration of acid-fast organisms in sputum by acid-fast stains or by use of fluorescent auramine rhodamine. Conventional cultures for mycobacteria require up to 10 weeks, but liquid media–based radiometric assays that detect mycobacterial metabolism are able to provide an answer within 2 weeks. PCR amplification can be performed on positive liquid media, as well as on tissue sections, to identify the mycobacterium. However, culture remains the standard diagnostic modality because it can identify the occasional PCR-negative case and also allows testing of drug susceptibility. Multidrug resistance (MDR), defined as resistance of mycobacteria to two or more of the primary drugs used for treatment of tuberculosis, is now seen more commonly, and the WHO estimates that 50 million people worldwide may be infected with multidrug-resistant tuberculosis.

The prognosis with tuberculosis generally is favorable if infection is localized to the lungs, but it worsens significantly when the disease occurs in aged, debilitated, or immunosuppressed persons, who are at high risk for the development of miliary tuberculosis, and in those with multidrug-resistant tuberculosis. Amyloidosis may develop in persistent cases.

SUMMARY

Tuberculosis

- Tuberculosis is a chronic granulomatous disease caused by *M. tuberculosis*, usually affecting the lungs, but virtually any extrapulmonary organ can be involved in isolated infection.
- Initial exposure to mycobacteria results in development of an immune response that confers resistance but also leads to hypersensitivity (as determined by a positive result on the *tuberculin skin test*).
- CD4+ T cells of the T_H1 subset have a crucial role in cell-mediated immunity against mycobacteria; mediators of inflammation and bacterial containment include IFN-γ, TNF, and nitric oxide.
- The histopathologic hallmark of host reaction to tuberculosis in immunocompetent persons is the presence of *granulomas*, usually with central caseating necrosis.
- Secondary (reactivation) tuberculosis arises in previously exposed persons when host immune defenses are compromised, and usually manifests as cavitary lesions in the lung apices.
- Both progressive primary tuberculosis and secondary tuberculosis can result in systemic seeding, causing life-threatening forms of disease such as miliary tuberculosis and tuberculous meningitis.
- HIV-seropositive status is a well-known risk factor for development or recrudescence of active tuberculosis.

Nontuberculous Mycobacterial Disease

Nontuberculous mycobacteria most commonly cause chronic but clinically localized pulmonary disease in immunocompetent persons. In the United States, strains implicated most frequently include *Mycobacterium avium-intracellulare* (also called *M. avium* complex), *Mycobacterium kansasii*, and *Mycobacterium abscessus*. It is not uncommon for nontuberculous mycobacterial infection to manifest as upper lobe cavitary disease, mimicking tuberculosis, especially in patients with a long history of smoking or alcohol abuse. Concomitant chronic pulmonary disease (COPD, cystic fibrosis, pneumoconiosis) is often present.

In *immunosuppressed persons* (primarily HIV-seropositive patients), *M. avium* complex infection manifests as disseminated disease, associated with systemic signs and symptoms (fever, night sweats, weight loss). Hepatosplenomegaly and lymphadenopathy, signifying involvement of the mononuclear phagocyte system by the opportunistic pathogen, is common, as are gastrointestinal symptoms such as diarrhea and malabsorption. Pulmonary involvement is often indistinguishable from tuberculosis in patients with AIDS. Disseminated *M. avium* complex infection in patients with AIDS tends to occur late in the clinical course, when CD4+ counts have fallen below 100 cells/μL. Hence, tissue examination usually does not reveal granulomas; instead, foamy histiocytes "stuffed" with atypical mycobacteria typically are seen.

Histoplasmosis, Coccidioidomycosis, and Blastomycosis

Infections caused by the dimorphic fungi, which include *Histoplasma capsulatum, Coccidioides immitis,* and *Blastomyces dermatitidis,* manifest either with isolated pulmonary involvement, as commonly seen in infected immunocompetent persons, or with disseminated disease in immunocompromised persons. T cell–mediated immune responses are critical for containing the infection, so persons with compromised cell-mediated immunity, such as those with HIV, are more prone to systemic disease. In part because of the overlap in clinical presentations, infectious diseases due to all three dimorphic fungi are considered together in this section.

Epidemiology

Each of the dimorphic fungi has a typical geographic distribution, as follows:

- *H. capsulatum*: This fungus is endemic in the Ohio and central Mississippi River valleys and along the Appalachian mountains in the southeastern United States. Warm, moist soil, enriched by droppings from bats and birds, provides the ideal medium for the growth of the mycelial form, which produces infectious spores.
- *C. immitis*: This organism is endemic in the southwestern and far western regions of the United States, particularly in California's San Joaquin Valley, where coccidial infection is known as "valley fever."
- *B. dermatitidis*: The endemic area is confined in the United States to areas overlapping with those in which histoplasmosis is found.

MORPHOLOGY

The yeast forms are fairly distinctive, which helps in the identification of individual fungi in tissue sections:

- *H. capsulatum*: round to oval, small yeast forms measuring 2 to 5 μm in diameter (Fig. 12–41, *A*)
- *C. immitis*: thick-walled, nonbudding spherules, 20 to 60 μm in diameter, often filled with small endospores (Fig. 12–41, *B*)
- *B. dermatitidis*: round to oval and larger than *Histoplasma* (5 to 25 μm in diameter); reproduce by characteristic broad-based budding (Fig. 12–41, *C* and *D*)

Clinical Features

Clinical manifestations may take the form of (1) *acute (primary) pulmonary infection,* (2) *chronic (granulomatous) pulmonary disease,* or (3) *disseminated miliary disease.* The primary pulmonary nodules, composed of aggregates of macrophages stuffed with organisms, are associated with similar lesions in the regional lymph nodes. These lesions evolve into small granulomas complete with giant cells and may develop central necrosis and later fibrosis and calcification. *The similarity to primary tuberculosis is striking,* and differentiation requires identification of the

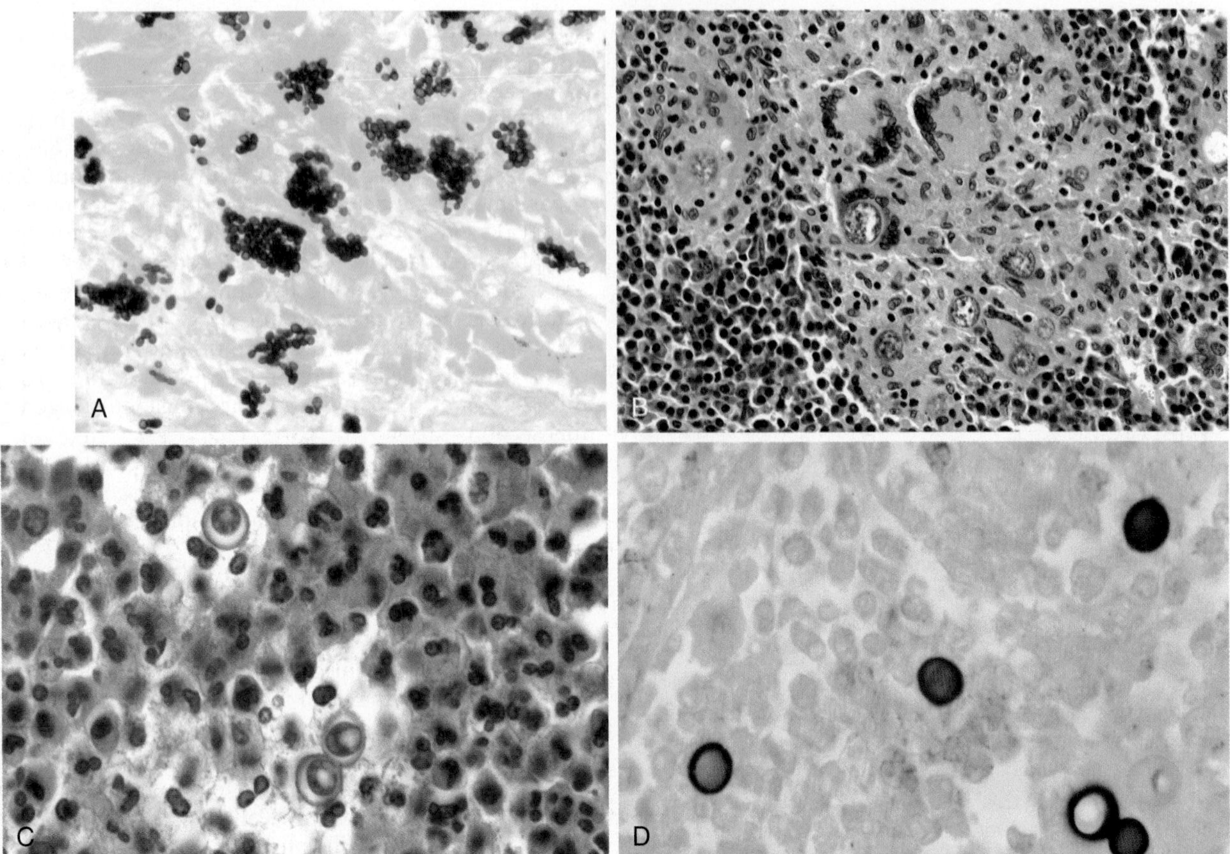

Figure 12–41 **A,** *Histoplasma capsulatum* yeast forms fill phagocytes in a lymph node of a patient with disseminated histoplasmosis (silver stain). **B,** Coccidioidomycosis with intact spherules within multinucleated giant cells. **C,** Blastomycosis, with rounded budding yeasts, larger than neutrophils. Note the characteristic thick wall and nuclei (not seen in other fungi). **D,** Silver stain highlights the broad-based budding seen in *Blastomyces immitis* organisms.

yeast forms (best seen with silver stains). The clinical symptoms and signs resemble those of a "flulike" syndrome, most often self-limited. In the vulnerable host, chronic cavitary pulmonary disease develops, with a predilection for the upper lobe, resembling the secondary form of tuberculosis. It is not uncommon for these fungi to give rise to perihilar mass lesions that resemble bronchogenic carcinoma radiologically. At this stage, manifestations may include cough, hemoptysis, and even dyspnea and chest pain.

In infants or immunocompromised adults, particularly those with HIV infection, disseminated disease (analogous to miliary tuberculosis) may develop. Under these circumstances there are no well-formed granulomas. Instead, focal collections of phagocytes stuffed with yeast forms are seen within cells of the mononuclear phagocyte system, including in the liver, spleen, lymph nodes, lymphoid tissue of the gastrointestinal tract, and bone marrow. The adrenals and meninges may also be involved, and in a minority of cases, ulcers form in the nose and mouth, on the tongue, or in the larynx. Disseminated disease is a hectic, febrile illness marked by hepatosplenomegaly, anemia, leukopenia, and thrombocytopenia. Cutaneous infections with disseminated *Blastomyces* organisms frequently induce striking epithelial hyperplasia, which may be mistaken for squamous cell carcinoma.

Pneumonia in the Immunocompromised Host

The appearance of a pulmonary infiltrate and signs of infection (e.g., fever) are some of the most common and serious complications in a person in whom the immune and defense systems are suppressed by disease, by immunosuppression for organ transplantation and antitumor therapy, or by irradiation. A wide variety of so-called opportunistic pathogens, many of which rarely cause infection in normal persons, can be the infecting agents with these pneumonias, and often more than one agent is involved. Some of the more common pulmonary pathogens are (1) the bacterial agents *P. aeruginosa*, *Mycobacterium* spp., *L. pneumophila,* and *Listeria monocytogenes;* (2) the viral agents cytomegalovirus and herpesvirus; and (3) the fungal agents *P. jiroveci*, *Candida* spp., *Aspergillus* spp., and *Cryptococcus neoformans.*

Cytomegalovirus Infections

Cytomegalovirus (CMV), a member of the herpesvirus family, may produce a variety of disease manifestations, depending partly on the age of the infected host but even more on the host's immune status. Cells infected by the virus exhibit gigantism of both the entire cell and its nucleus. Within the nucleus is an enlarged inclusion surrounded by a clear halo ("owl's eye"), which gives the name to the classic form of symptomatic disease that occurs in neonates—cytomegalic inclusion disease. Although classic cytomegalic inclusion disease involves many organs, CMV infections are discussed here because in immunosuppressed adults, particularly patients with AIDS and recipients of allogeneic bone marrow transplants, CMV pneumonitis is a serious problem.

Transmission of CMV can occur by several mechanisms, depending on the age group affected:

- A fetus can be infected transplacentally from a newly acquired or reactivated infection in the mother (*congenital* CMV infection).
- The virus can be transmitted to the baby through cervical or vaginal secretions at birth, or, later, through breast milk from a mother who has active infection (*perinatal* CMV infection).
- Preschool children, especially in day care centers, can acquire it through saliva. Toddlers thus infected readily transmit the virus to their parents.
- In patients older than 15 years of age, the venereal route is the dominant mode of transmission, but spread also may occur through contact with respiratory secretions and by the fecal-oral route.
- Iatrogenic transmission can occur at any age through organ transplantation or blood transfusions.

MORPHOLOGY

Histologically, the characteristic enlargement of cells can be appreciated. In the glandular organs, the parenchymal epithelial cells are affected; in the brain, the neurons; in the lungs, the alveolar macrophages and epithelial and endothelial cells; and in the kidneys, the tubular epithelial and glomerular endothelial cells. **Affected cells are strikingly enlarged, often to a diameter of 40 μm, and exhibit cellular and nuclear polymorphism.** Prominent intranuclear basophilic inclusions spanning half the nuclear diameter are usually set off from the nuclear membrane by a clear halo (Fig. 12–42). Within the cytoplasm of these cells, smaller basophilic inclusions may also be seen.

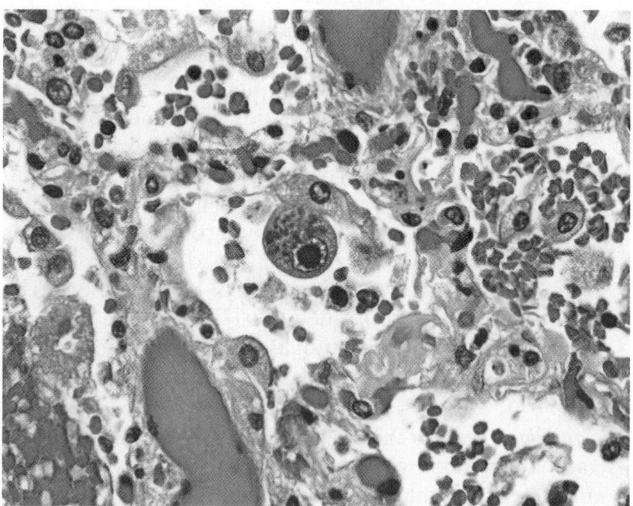

Figure 12–42 Cytomegalovirus infection of the lung. A typical distinct nuclear and multiple cytoplasmic inclusions are seen in an enlarged cell.

Cytomegalovirus Mononucleosis

In healthy young children and adults, the disease is nearly always asymptomatic. In surveys around the world, 50% to 100% of adults demonstrate anti-CMV antibodies in the serum, indicating previous exposure. The most common *clinical manifestation of CMV infection* in immunocompetent hosts beyond the neonatal period is an infectious mononucleosis–like illness, with fever, atypical lymphocytosis, lymphadenopathy, and hepatomegaly accompanied by abnormal liver function test results, suggesting mild hepatitis. Most patients recover from CMV mononucleosis without any sequelae, although excretion of the virus may occur in body fluids for months to years. Irrespective of the presence or absence of symptoms after infection, a person once infected becomes seropositive for life. The virus remains latent within leukocytes, which are the major reservoirs.

Cytomegalovirus Infection in Immunosuppressed Persons

Immunosuppression-related CMV infection occurs most commonly in recipients of transplants (such as heart, liver, kidney, lung, or allogeneic stem cell) and in patients with AIDS. This can be either primary infection or reactivation of a latent infection. CMV is the most common opportunistic viral pathogen in AIDS.

In all of these settings, serious, life-threatening disseminated CMV infections primarily affect the lungs (pneumonitis), gastrointestinal tract (colitis), and retina (retinitis); the central nervous system usually is spared. In pneumonitis, an interstitial mononuclear infiltrate with foci of necrosis develops, accompanied by the typical enlarged cells with inclusions, which can progress to ARDS. Intestinal necrosis and ulceration can develop and be extensive, leading to the formation of "pseudomembranes" (Chapter 14) and debilitating diarrhea. CMV retinitis, by far the most common form of opportunistic CMV disease, can occur either alone or in combination with involvement of the lungs and intestinal tract. Diagnosis of CMV infection is made by demonstration of characteristic viral inclusions in tissue sections, successful viral culture, rising antiviral antibody titer, and qualitative or quantitative PCR assay–based detection of CMV DNA. The latter has revolutionized the approach to monitoring patients after transplantation.

Pneumocystis *Pneumonia*

P. jiroveci (formerly known as *P. carinii*), an opportunistic infectious agent formerly considered to be a protozoan, is now classified as a fungus. Serologic evidence indicates that virtually all persons are exposed to *Pneumocystis* during the first few years of life, but in most the infection remains latent. Reactivation with development of clinical disease occurs almost exclusively in persons who are immunocompromised. Indeed, *P. jiroveci* is an extremely common cause of infection in patients with AIDS, and it also may infect severely malnourished infants and immunosuppressed persons (especially after organ transplantation or in persons receiving cytotoxic chemotherapy or corticosteroids). In patients with AIDS, the risk of acquiring *P. jiroveci* infections increases in inverse proportion to the CD4+ count, with counts less than 200 cells/μL having

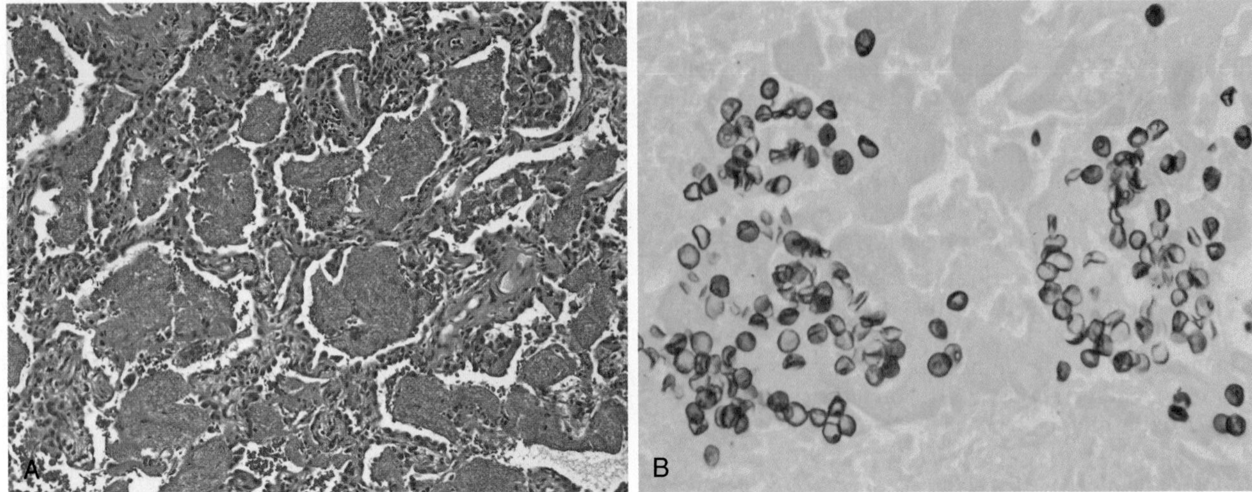

Figure 12–43 *Pneumocystis* pneumonia. **A,** The alveoli are filled with a characteristic foamy acellular exudate. **B,** Silver stain demonstrates cup-shaped and round cysts within the exudate.

a strong predictive value. *Pneumocystis* infection is largely confined to the lung, where it produces an interstitial pneumonitis.

MORPHOLOGY

Microscopically, involved areas of the lung demonstrate a characteristic **intra-alveolar foamy, pink-staining exudate** with hematoxylin-eosin (H&E) stain ("cotton candy" exudate) (Fig. 12–43, *A*). The septa are thickened by edema and a minimal mononuclear infiltrate. Special stains are required to visualize the organism. Silver stain of tissue sections reveals **round to cup-shaped cysts** (4 to 10 μm in diameter), often with intracystic bodies but without budding, in the alveolar exudates (Fig. 12–43, *B*).

The diagnosis of *Pneumocystis* pneumonia should be considered in any immunocompromised patient with respiratory symptoms and abnormal findings on the chest radiograph. Fever, dry cough, and dyspnea occur in 90% to 95% of patients, in whom radiographic evidence of bilateral perihilar and basilar infiltrates is typical. Hypoxia is frequent; pulmonary function studies show a restrictive lung defect. The most sensitive and effective method of diagnosis is to identify the organism in induced sputum or bronchoalveolar lavage fluid using immunofluorescence. If treatment is initiated before widespread involvement, the outlook for recovery is good; however, because residual organisms are likely to persist, particularly in patients with AIDS, relapses are common unless the underlying immunodeficiency is corrected or prophylactic therapy is given.

Opportunistic Fungal Infections

Candidiasis

Candida albicans is the most common disease-causing fungus. It is a normal inhabitant of the oral cavity, gastrointestinal tract, and vagina in many people. Even though systemic candidiasis (with associated pneumonia) is a disease that is restricted to immunocompromised patients, the protean manifestations of infections caused by *Candida* spp. are described in this section.

MORPHOLOGY

In tissue sections, *C. albicans* demonstrates yeastlike forms (blastoconidia), pseudohyphae, and true hyphae (Fig. 12–44, *A*). Pseudohyphae are an important diagnostic clue for *C. albicans* and represent budding yeast cells joined end to end at constrictions, thus simulating true fungal hyphae. The organisms may be visible with routine H&E stains, but a variety of special "fungal" stains (Gomori methenamine-silver, periodic acid–Schiff) commonly are used to better highlight the pathogens.

Clinical Features

Candidiasis can involve the mucous membranes, skin, and deep organs (invasive candidiasis).

- The most common presentation with candidiasis is that of a superficial infection on mucosal surfaces of the oral cavity (thrush). Florid proliferation of the fungi creates gray-white, dirty-looking pseudomembranes composed of matted organisms and inflammatory debris. Deep to the surface, there is mucosal hyperemia and inflammation. This form of candidiasis is seen in newborns, debilitated patients, and children receiving oral corticosteroids for asthma, and after a course of broad-spectrum antibiotics that destroy competing normal bacterial flora. The other major risk group includes HIV-positive patients; patients with oral thrush not associated with an obvious underlying condition should be evaluated for HIV infection.
- *Candida* vaginitis is an extremely common form of vaginal infection in women, especially those who are diabetic or pregnant or on oral contraceptive pills.
- *Candida* esophagitis is common in patients with AIDS and in those with hematolymphoid malignancies. These

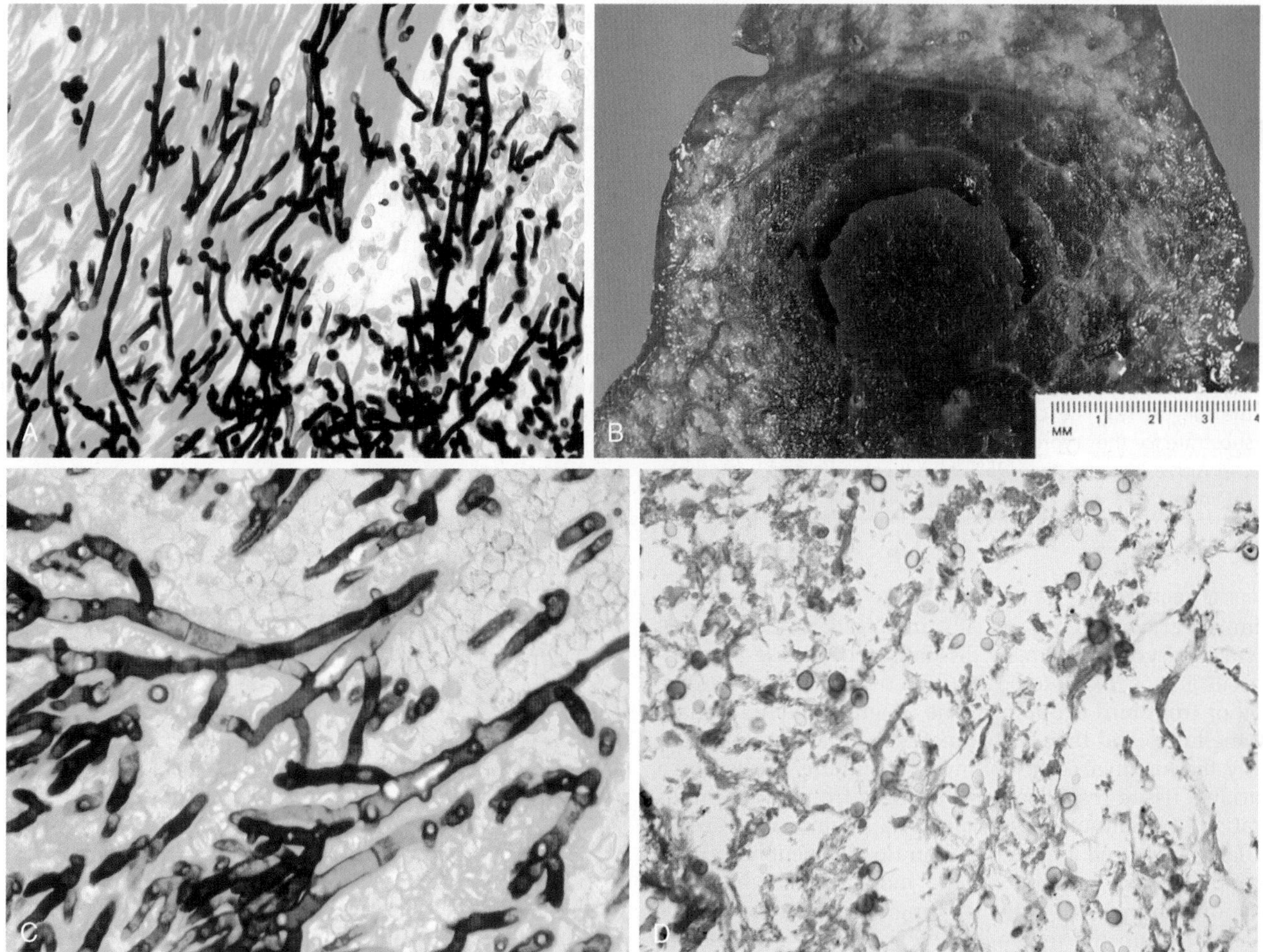

Figure 12–44 The morphology of fungal infections. **A,** *Candida* organism has pseudohyphae and budding yeasts (silver stain). **B,** Invasive aspergillosis (gross appearance) of the lung in a bone marrow transplant recipient. **C,** Gomori methenamine-silver (GMS) stain shows septate hyphae with acute-angle branching, consistent with *Aspergillus.* **D,** Cryptococcosis of the lung in a patient with AIDS. The organisms are somewhat variable in size.

(B, Courtesy of Dr. Dominick Cavuoti, Department of Pathology, University of Texas Southwestern Medical School, Dallas, Texas.)

patients present with dysphagia (painful swallowing) and retrosternal pain; endoscopy demonstrates white plaques and pseudomembranes resembling the changes of oral thrush on the esophageal mucosa.

- Cutaneous candidiasis can manifest in many different forms, including infection of the nail proper (*onychomycosis*), nail folds (*paronychia*), hair follicles (*folliculitis*), moist, intertriginous skin such as armpits or webs of the fingers and toes (*intertrigo*), and penile skin (*balanitis*). *Diaper rash* often is a cutaneous candidal infection seen in the perineum of infants, in the region of contact of wet diapers.
- Chronic mucocutaneous candidiasis is a chronic refractory disease afflicting the mucous membranes, skin, hair, and nails; it is associated with underlying T cell defects. Associated conditions include endocrinopathies (most commonly hypoparathyroidism and Addison disease) and the presence of autoantibodies. Disseminated candidiasis is rare in this disease. A recent finding is that the T_H17 subset of CD4+ T cells plays an especially important role in defense against *Candida* and a few other fungi. Patients with mutations affecting T_H17 responses are highly susceptible to severe mucocutaneous candidiasis (e.g., "Job syndrome").
- Invasive candidiasis implies blood-borne dissemination of organisms to various tissues or organs. Common patterns include (1) renal abscesses, (2) myocardial abscesses and endocarditis, (3) brain involvement (most commonly meningitis, but parenchymal microabscesses occur), (4) endophthalmitis (virtually any eye structure can be involved), (5) hepatic abscesses, and (6) *Candida* pneumonia, usually manifesting as bilateral nodular infiltrates, resembling *Pneumocystis* pneumonia (see earlier). Patients with acute leukemias who are profoundly neutropenic after chemotherapy are particularly prone to the development of systemic disease. *Candida* endocarditis is the most common fungal endocarditis, usually occurring in patients with prosthetic heart valves or in intravenous drug abusers.

Cryptococcosis

Cryptococcosis, caused by *C. neoformans,* rarely occurs in healthy persons. It almost exclusively manifests as an opportunistic infection in immunocompromised hosts, particularly patients with AIDS or hematolymphoid malignancies.

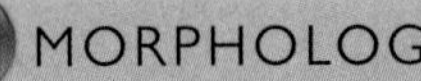

MORPHOLOGY

The fungus, a 5- to 10-μm yeast, has a thick, gelatinous capsule and reproduces by budding (Fig. 12–44, *D*). Unlike in *Candida* infections, however, pseudohyphal or true hyphal forms are not seen. **The capsule is invaluable to diagnosis:** (1) In routine H&E stains, the capsule is not directly visible, but often a clear "halo" can be seen surrounding the individual fungi representing the area occupied by the capsule. India ink or periodic acid–Schiff staining effectively highlights the fungus. (2) The capsular polysaccharide antigen is the substrate for the cryptococcal latex agglutination assay, which is positive in more than 95% of patients infected with the organism.

Clinical Features

Human cryptococcosis usually manifests as pulmonary, central nervous system, or disseminated disease. Cryptococcus is most likely to be acquired by inhalation from the soil or from bird droppings. The fungus initially localizes in the lungs and then disseminates to other sites, particularly the meninges. Sites of involvement are marked by a variable tissue response, which ranges from florid proliferation of gelatinous organisms with a minimal or absent inflammatory cell infiltrate (in immunodeficient hosts) to a granulomatous reaction (in the more reactive host). In immunosuppressed patients, fungi grow in gelatinous masses within the meninges or expand the perivascular Virchow-Robin spaces, producing the so-called soap-bubble lesions.

The Opportunistic Molds

Mucormycosis and *invasive aspergillosis* are uncommon infections almost always limited to immunocompromised hosts, particularly those with hematolymphoid malignancies or profound neutropenia, those undergoing corticosteroid therapy, or allogeneic stem cell transplant recipients.

MORPHOLOGY

Mucormycosis is caused by the class of fungi known as Zygomycetes. Their hyphae are **nonseptate** and branch at right angles; by contrast, the hyphae of *Aspergillus* organisms are **septate** and branch at more acute angles (Fig. 12–44, *C*). *Rhizopus* and *Mucor* are the two fungi of medical importance within the Zygomycetes class. Both zygomycetes and *Aspergillus* cause a nondistinctive, suppurative, sometimes granulomatous reaction with a **predilection for invading blood vessel walls, causing vascular necrosis and infarction.**

Clinical Features

In *rhinocerebral* and *pulmonary mucormycosis,* zygomycetes have a propensity to colonize the nasal cavity or sinuses and then spread by direct extension into the brain, orbit, and other head and neck structures. Patients with diabetic ketoacidosis are most likely to develop a fulminant invasive form of rhinocerebral mucormycosis. Pulmonary disease can be localized (e.g., cavitary lesions) or may manifest radiologically with diffuse "miliary" involvement.

Invasive aspergillosis occurs almost exclusively in patients who are immunosuppressed. The fungus preferentially localizes to the lungs, and infection most often manifests as a necrotizing pneumonia (Fig. 12–44, *B*). Systemic dissemination, especially to the brain, is an often fatal complication.

Allergic bronchopulmonary aspergillosis occurs in patients with asthma who develop an exacerbation of symptoms caused by a type I hypersensitivity against the fungus growing in the bronchi. Such patients often have circulating IgE antibodies against *Aspergillus* and peripheral eosinophilia.

Aspergilloma ("fungus ball") formation occurs by colonization of preexisting pulmonary cavities (e.g., ectatic bronchi or lung cysts, posttuberculosis cavitary lesions) by the fungus. These masses may act as ball valves to occlude the cavity, thereby predisposing the patient to infection and hemoptysis.

Pulmonary Disease in Human Immunodeficiency Virus Infection

Pulmonary disease continues to be the leading contributor to morbidity and mortality in HIV-infected persons. Although the use of potent antiretroviral agents and effective chemoprophylaxis has markedly decreased incidence and improved outcome, the plethora of entities involved makes diagnosis and treatment a distinct challenge.

- Despite the emphasis on "opportunistic" infections, it should be recognized that bacterial lower respiratory tract infection caused by the "usual" pathogens is one of the most serious pulmonary disorders in HIV infection. The implicated organisms include *S. pneumoniae, S. aureus, H. influenzae,* and gram-negative rods. Bacterial pneumonias in HIV-infected persons are more common, more severe, and more often associated with bacteremia than in those without HIV infection.
- Not all pulmonary infiltrates in HIV-infected persons are infectious. A host of noninfectious diseases, including Kaposi sarcoma (Chapters 4 and 9), pulmonary non-Hodgkin lymphoma (Chapter 11), and primary lung cancer, occur with increased frequency and must be excluded.
- *The CD4+ T cell count often is useful in narrowing the differential diagnosis.* As a rule of thumb, bacterial and tubercular infections are more likely at higher CD4+ counts (more than 200 cells/mm^3); *Pneumocystis* pneumonia usually occurs at CD4+ counts below 200 cells/mm^3, while CMV and *M. avium* complex infections are uncommon until the very late stages of immunosuppression (CD4+ counts below 50 cells/mm^3).

Finally, an important point is that pulmonary disease in HIV-infected persons may result from more than one cause, and that even common pathogens may be responsible for disease with atypical manifestations.

LUNG TUMORS

Although lungs frequently are the site of metastases from cancers arising in extrathoracic organs, primary lung cancer is also a common disease. Roughly 95% of primary lung tumors are carcinomas; the remaining 5% constitute a miscellaneous group that includes carcinoids, mesenchymal malignancies (e.g., fibrosarcomas, leiomyomas), lymphomas, and a few benign lesions. The most common benign tumor is a spherical, small (3 to 4 cm), discrete "hamartoma" that often shows up as a so-called coin lesion on chest radiographs. It consists mainly of mature cartilage, but this is often admixed with fat, fibrous tissue, and blood vessels in various proportions. Clonal cytogenic abnormalities have been demonstrated, indicating that it is a benign neoplasm, although still commonly referred to as hamartoma.

Carcinomas

Carcinoma of the lung (also known as "lung cancer") is without doubt the single most important cause of cancer-related deaths in industrialized countries. It has long held this position among males in the United States, accounting for about one third of cancer deaths in men, and has become the leading cause of cancer deaths in women as well. American Cancer Society estimates for 2011 included approximately 221,100 new cases of lung cancer and 156,900 deaths. The incidence among males is gradually decreasing, but it continues to increase among females, with more women dying each year from lung cancer than from breast cancers, since 1987. These statistics undoubtedly reflect the causal relationship of cigarette smoking and lung cancer. The peak incidence of lung cancer is in persons in their 50s and 60s. At diagnosis, more than 50% of patients already have distant metastatic disease, while a fourth have disease in the regional lymph nodes. The prognosis with lung cancer is dismal: The 5-year survival rate for all stages of lung cancer combined is about 16%, a figure that has not changed much over the last 30 years; even with disease localized to the lung, a 5-year survival rate of only 45% is typical.

The four major histologic types of carcinomas of the lung are adenocarcinoma, squamous cell carcinoma, small cell carcinoma, and large cell carcinoma (Table 12–7). In some cases there is a combination of histologic patterns (e.g., small cell carcinoma and adenocarcinoma). Of these, squamous cell and small cell carcinomas show the strongest association with smoking. Possibly because of changes in smoking patterns in the U.S., adenocarcinoma has replaced squamous cell carcinoma as the most common primary lung tumor in recent years. Adenocarcinomas also are by far the most common primary tumors arising in women, in never-smokers, and in persons younger than 45 years.

- Until recently, carcinomas of the lung were classified into two broad groups: small cell lung cancer (SCLC) and non–small cell lung cancer (NSCLC), with the latter including adenocarcinomas and squamous and large cell carcinomas.
- *The key reason for this historical distinction was that virtually all SCLCs have metastasized by the time of diagnosis and hence are not curable by surgery. Therefore, they are best treated by chemotherapy, with or without radiation therapy.* By contrast, NSCLCs were more likely to be resectable and usually responded poorly to chemotherapy; however, now therapies are available that target specific mutated gene products present in the various subtypes of NSCLC, mainly in adenocarcinomas. Thus, NSCLC must be subclassified into histologic and molecular subtypes.

Table 12–7 Histologic Classification of Malignant Epithelial Lung Tumors

Adenocarcinoma*
- Acinar, papillary, micropapillary, solid, lepidic predominant, mucinous subtypes

Squamous cell carcinoma

Large cell carcinoma
- Large cell neuroendocrine carcinoma

Small cell carcinoma
- Combined small cell carcinoma

Adenosquamous carcinoma

Carcinomas with pleomorphic, sarcomatoid, or sarcomatous elements
- Spindle cell carcinoma
- Giant cell carcinoma

Carcinoid tumor
- Typical, atypical

Carcinomas of salivary gland type

Unclassified carcinoma

*Adenocarcinoma and squamous cell and large cell carcinoma are collectively referred to as non–small cell lung carcinoma (NSCLC).

ETIOLOGY AND PATHOGENESIS

Smoking-related carcinomas of the lung arise by a stepwise accumulation of a multitude of genetic abnormalities (estimated to be in the thousands for small cell carcinoma) that result in transformation of benign progenitor cells in the lung into neoplastic cells.

The sequence of molecular changes is not random but follows a predictable sequence that parallels the histologic progression toward cancer. Thus, inactivation of the putative tumor suppressor genes located on the short arm of chromosome 3 (3p) is a very early event, whereas *TP53* mutations or activation of the *KRAS* oncogene occurs relatively late. More important, it seems that certain genetic changes, such as loss of chromosomal material on 3p, can be found even in benign bronchial epithelium of persons with lung cancer, as well as in the respiratory epithelium of smokers **without** lung cancer, suggesting that large areas of the respiratory mucosa are mutagenized after exposure to carcinogens ("field effect"). On this fertile soil, those cells that accumulate additional mutations ultimately develop into cancer.

A subset of adenocarcinomas, particularly those arising in nonsmoking women of Far Eastern origin, harbor activating mutations of the **epidermal growth factor receptor (EGFR).** Of note, these tumors are sensitive to a class of agents that inhibit EGFR signaling, although the response often is short-lived. EGFR and K-RAS mutations (in 30% of adenocarcinomas) are mutually exclusive. Other mutations occurring in 4% to 6% of adenocarcinomas are EML4-ALK tyrosine kinase fusion genes and c-MET tyrosine kinase gene amplifications. These abnormalities, while rare, are important because of their therapeutic implications, as they can be targeted with tyrosine kinase inhibitors. Indeed, the identification of genetic alterations producing overactive EGFR, ALK, and MET has opened up a new era of "personalized" lung cancer therapy, in which the genetics of the tumor guides the selection of drugs.

With regard to carcinogenic influences, there is strong evidence that **cigarette smoking** and, to a much lesser extent, other environmental insults are the main culprits responsible for the genetic changes that give rise to lung cancers.

About 90% of lung cancers occur in active smokers or those who stopped recently. A nearly linear correlation has been recognized between the frequency of lung cancer and pack-years of cigarette smoking. The increased risk becomes 60 times greater among habitual heavy smokers (two packs a day for 20 years) than among nonsmokers. Since only 11% of heavy smokers develop lung cancer, however, other predisposing factors must be operative in the pathogenesis of this deadly disease. For reasons not entirely clear, women have a higher susceptibility to carcinogens in tobacco than men. Although cessation of smoking decreases the risk of developing lung cancer over time, it may never return to baseline levels. In fact, genetic changes that predate lung cancer can persist for many years in the bronchial epithelium of former smokers. Passive smoking (proximity to cigarette smokers) increases the risk of developing lung cancer to approximately twice that of nonsmokers. The smoking of pipes and cigars also increases the risk, but only modestly.

Other influences may act in concert with smoking or may by themselves be responsible for some lung cancers; witness the increased incidence of this form of neoplasia in miners of radioactive ores; asbestos workers; and workers exposed to dusts containing arsenic, chromium, uranium, nickel, vinyl chloride, and mustard gas. Exposure to asbestos increases the risk of lung cancer fivefold in nonsmokers. By contrast, **heavy smokers exposed to asbestos have an approximately 55 times greater risk for development of lung cancer than that for nonsmokers not exposed to asbestos.**

Even though smoking and other environmental influences are paramount in the causation of lung cancer, it is well known that all persons exposed to tobacco smoke do not develop cancer. It is very likely that the mutagenic effect of carcinogens is conditioned by hereditary (genetic) factors. Recall that many chemicals (procarcinogens) require metabolic activation via the P-450 monooxygenase enzyme system for conversion into ultimate carcinogens (Chapter 5). There is evidence that persons with specific genetic polymorphisms involving the P-450 genes have an increased capacity to metabolize procarcinogens derived from cigarette smoke, and thus conceivably incur the greatest risk for development of lung cancer. Similarly, persons whose peripheral blood lymphocytes undergo chromosomal breakages after exposure to tobacco-related carcinogens (mutagen sensitivity genotype) have a greater than 10-fold risk of developing lung cancer over that of control subjects.

The sequential changes leading to cancer have been best documented for squamous cell carcinomas, but they also are present in other histologic subtypes. In essence, there is a linear correlation between the intensity of exposure to cigarette smoke and the appearance of ever more worrisome epithelial changes that begin with rather innocuous basal cell hyperplasia and squamous metaplasia and progress to squamous dysplasia and carcinoma in situ, before culminating in invasive cancer. **Among the major histologic subtypes of lung cancer, squamous and small-cell carcinomas show the strongest association with tobacco exposure.**

MORPHOLOGY

Carcinomas of the lung begin as small mucosal lesions that typically are firm and gray-white. They may arise as intraluminal masses, invade the bronchial mucosa, or form large bulky masses pushing into adjacent lung parenchyma. Some large masses undergo cavitation secondary to central necrosis or develop focal areas of hemorrhage. Finally, these tumors may extend to the pleura, invade the pleural cavity and chest wall, and spread to adjacent intrathoracic structures. More distant spread can occur by way of the lymphatics or the hematogenous route.

Squamous cell carcinomas are more common in men than in women and are closely correlated with a smoking history; they tend to **arise centrally in major bronchi** and eventually spread to local hilar nodes, but they disseminate outside the thorax later than do other histologic types. Large lesions may undergo central necrosis, giving rise to **cavitation.** The preneoplastic lesions that antedate, and usually accompany, invasive squamous cell carcinoma are well characterized. Squamous cell carcinomas often are preceded by the development, over years, of **squamous metaplasia or dysplasia** in the bronchial epithelium, which then transforms to **carcinoma in situ,** a phase that may last for several years (Fig. 12–45). By this time, atypical cells may be identified in cytologic smears of sputum or in bronchial lavage fluids or brushings, although the lesion is asymptomatic and undetectable on radiographs. Eventually, the small neoplasm reaches a symptomatic stage, when a well-defined tumor mass begins to obstruct the lumen of a major bronchus, often producing distal atelectasis and infection. Simultaneously, the lesion invades surrounding pulmonary substance (Fig. 12–46, *A*). On histologic examination, these tumors range from well-differentiated squamous cell neoplasms showing keratin pearls (Fig. 12–46, *B*) and intercellular bridges to poorly differentiated neoplasms exhibiting only minimal residual squamous cell features.

Adenocarcinomas may occur as central lesions like the squamous cell variant but usually are more **peripherally located,** many with a central scar. Adenocarcinomas are the most common type of lung cancer in women and nonsmokers. In general, adenocarcinomas grow slowly and form smaller masses than do the other subtypes, but they tend to metastasize widely at an early stage. On histologic examination, they may assume a variety of forms, including **acinar (gland-forming)** (Fig. 12–47, *C*), **papillary, mucinous** (formerly mucinous bronchioloalveolar carcinoma, which often is multifocal and may manifest as pneumonia-like consolidation), and **solid types.** The solid variant often requires demonstration of intracellular mucin production by special stains to establish its adenocarcinomatous lineage.

Although foci of squamous metaplasia and dysplasia may be present in the epithelium proximal to resected adenocarcinomas, these are not the precursor lesions for this tumor. The putative precursor of peripheral adenocarcinomas is thought to be **atypical adenomatous hyperplasia** (AAH) (Fig. 12–47, *A*) which progresses to adenocarcinoma in situ (formerly bronchioloalveolar carcinoma), minimally invasive adenocarcinoma (tumor less than 3 cm and invasive component measuring 5 mm or less), and invasive adenocarcinoma (tumor of any size that has invaded to depths greater than 5 mm). On microscopic examination, AAH is recognized as a

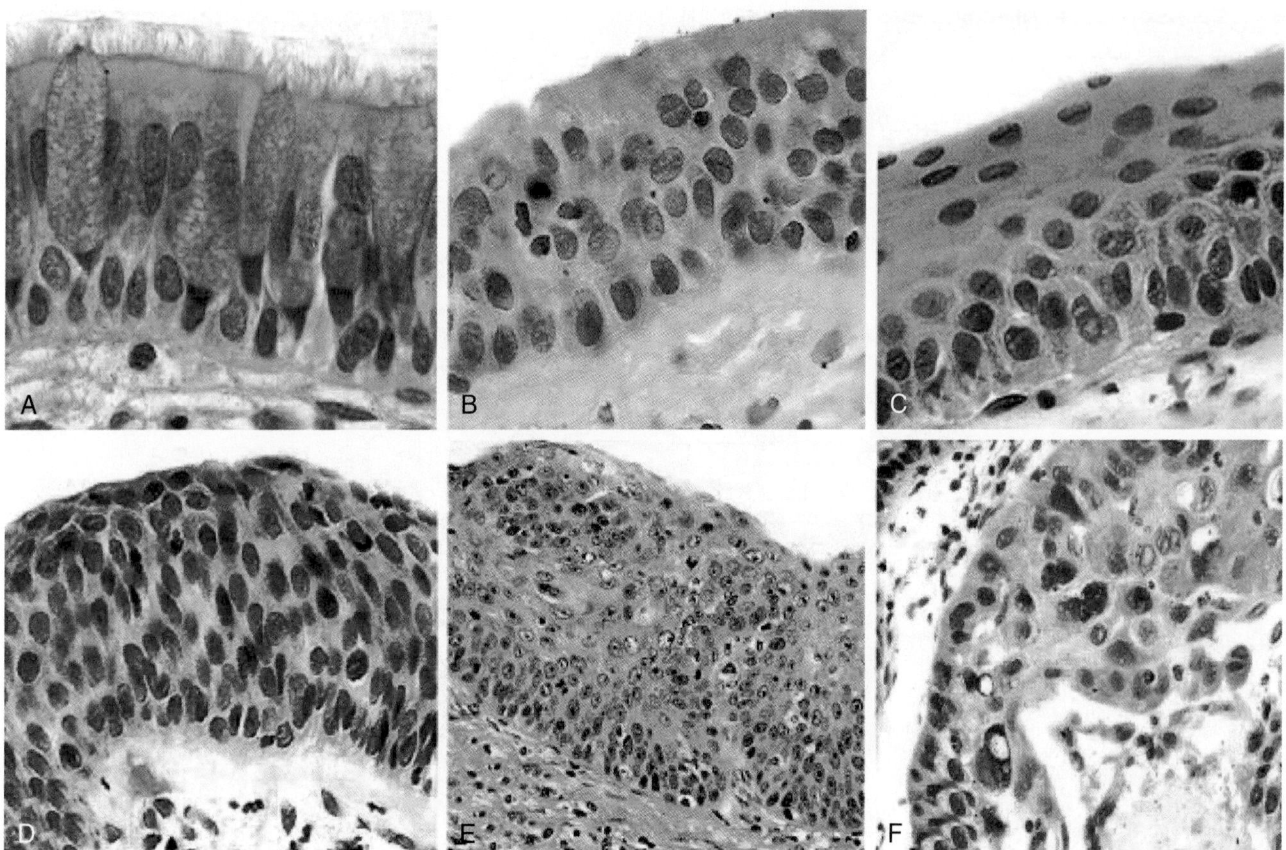

Figure 12–45 Precursor lesions of squamous cell carcinomas that may antedate the appearance of invasive tumor by years. **A–C,** Some of the earliest (and "mild") changes in smoking-damaged respiratory epithelium include goblet cell hyperplasia (**A**), basal cell (or reserve cell) hyperplasia (**B**), and squamous metaplasia (**C**). **D,** More ominous changes include the appearance of squamous dysplasia, characterized by the presence of disordered squamous epithelium, with loss of nuclear polarity, nuclear hyperchromasia, pleomorphism, and mitotic figures. **E** and **F,** Squamous dysplasia may, in turn, progress through the stages of mild, moderate, and severe dysplasia. Carcinoma in situ (CIS) (**E**) is the stage that immediately precedes invasive squamous carcinoma (**F**). Apart from the lack of basement membrane disruption in CIS, the cytologic features of CIS are similar to those in frank carcinoma. Unless treated, CIS eventually progresses to invasive cancer.

(A–E, Courtesy of Dr. Adi Gazdar, Department of Pathology, University of Texas Southwestern Medical School, Dallas. F, Reproduced with permission from Travis WD, Colby TV, Corrin B, et al [eds]: World Health Organization Histological Typing of Lung and Pleural Tumours. Heidelberg, Springer, 1999.)

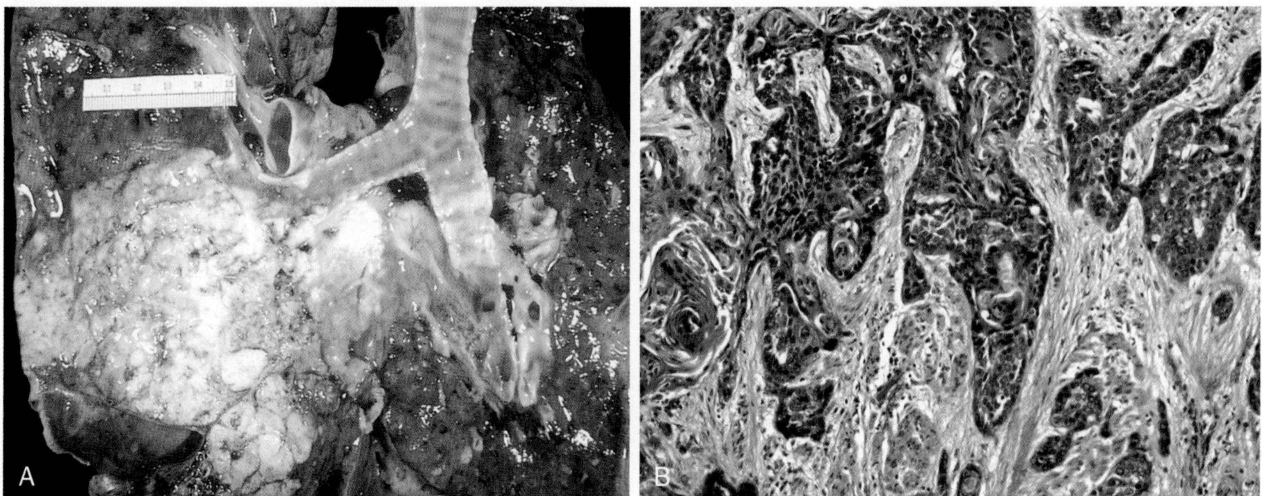

Figure 12–46 A, Squamous cell carcinoma usually begins as a central (hilar) mass and grows contiguously into the peripheral parenchyma as seen here. **B,** Well-differentiated squamous cell carcinoma showing keratinization and pearls.

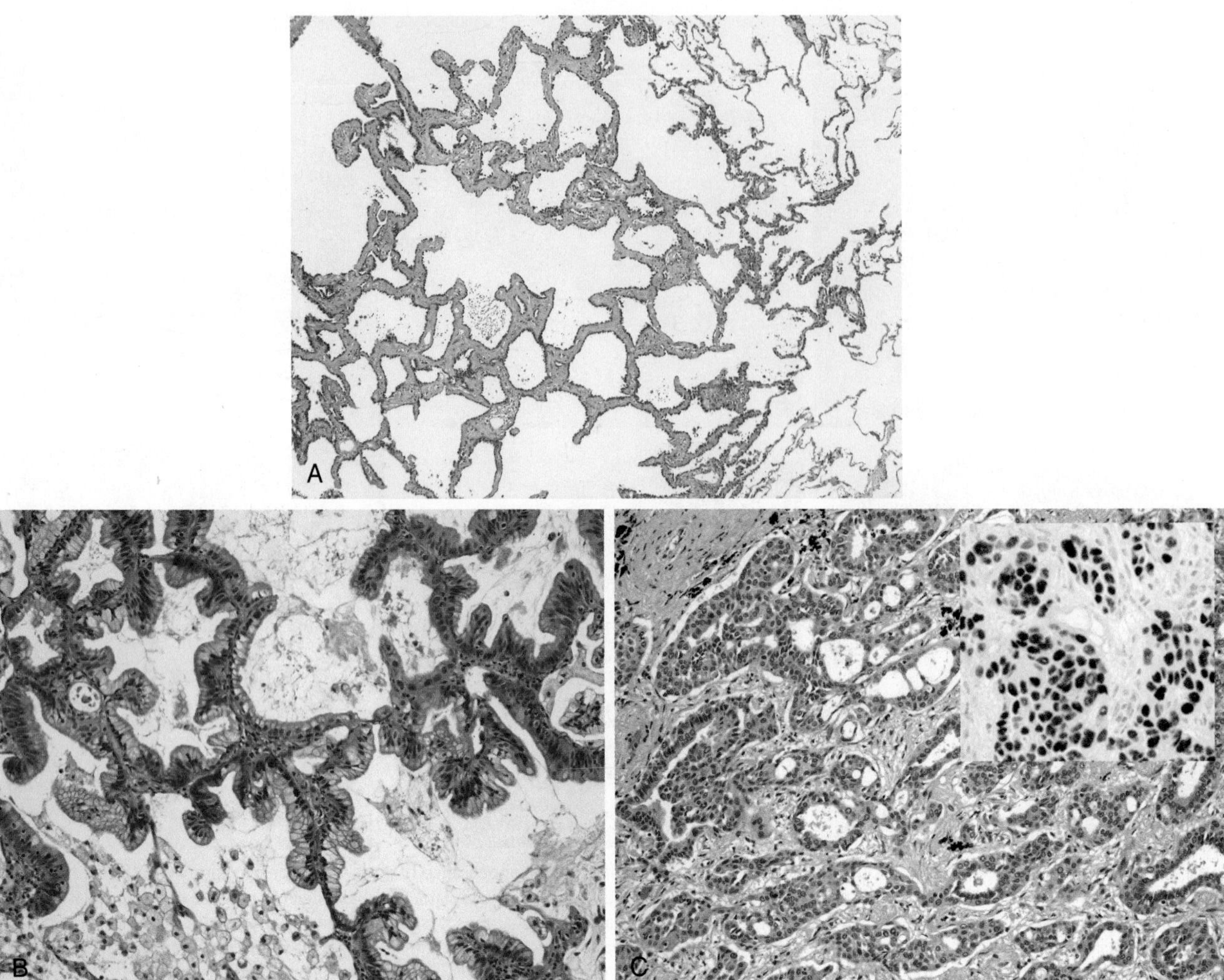

Figure 12–47 Glandular lesions of the lung. **A,** Atypical adenomatous hyperplasia with cuboidal epithelium and mild interstitial fibrosis. **B,** Adenocarcinoma in situ, mucinous subtype, with characteristic growth along preexisting alveolar septa, without invasion. **C,** Gland-forming adenocarcinoma; inset shows thyroid transcription factor 1 (TTF-1) positivity, which is seen in a majority of pulmonary adenocarcinomas.

well-demarcated focus of epithelial proliferation (with a thickness of 5 mm or less) composed of cuboidal to low-columnar cells, which demonstrate cytologic atypia of variable degree such as nuclear hyperchromasia, pleomorphism, prominent nucleoli, but not to the extent seen in adenocarcinoma. Genetic analyses have shown that lesions of AAH are monoclonal, and they share many of the molecular aberrations associated with adenocarcinomas (e.g., *K-RAS* mutations).

Adenocarcinoma in situ (AIS), formerly called bronchioloalveolar carcinoma, often involves peripheral parts of the lung, as a single nodule. **The key features of AIS are diameter of 3 cm or less, growth along preexisting structures, and preservation of alveolar architecture** (Fig. 12–47, *B*). The tumor cells, which may be nonmucinous, mucinous, or mixed, grow in a monolayer along the alveolar septa, which serve as a scaffold (this has been termed a "lepidic" growth pattern, an allusion to the resemblance of neoplastic cells to butterflies sitting on a fence). By definition, AIS does not demonstrate destruction of alveolar architecture or stromal invasion with desmoplasia, features that would merit the diagnosis of frank adenocarcinoma. By analogy to the adenoma–carcinoma sequence in the colon, it is proposed that some invasive adenocarcinomas of the lung may arise through an atypical adenomatous hyperplasia–adenocarcinoma in situ–invasive adenocarcinoma sequence. Studies of lung injury models in mice have now identified a population of multipotent cells at the bronchioloalveolar duct junction, termed bronchioalveolar stem cells (BASCs). After peripheral lung injury, the multipotent BASCs undergo expansion, replenishing the normal cell types (bronchiolar Clara cells and alveolar cells) found in this location, thereby facilitating epithelial regeneration. It is postulated that BASCs incur the initiating oncogenic event (for example, a somatic *K-RAS* mutation) that enables these cells to escape normal "checkpoint" mechanisms and results in pulmonary adenocarcinomas.

Large cell carcinomas are undifferentiated malignant epithelial tumors that lack the cytologic features of small cell carcinoma and have no glandular or squamous differentiation. The cells typically have large nuclei, prominent nucleoli, and a moderate amount of cytoplasm. Large cell carcinomas probably represent squamous cell or adenocarcinomas that are so undifferentiated that they can no longer be recognized by means of light microscopy. On ultrastructural examination, however, minimal glandular or squamous differentiation is common.

Small cell lung carcinomas (SCLCs) generally appear as pale gray, **centrally located masses** with extension into the lung parenchyma and early involvement of the hilar and mediastinal nodes. These cancers are composed of tumor cells with a round to fusiform shape, scant cytoplasm, and finely granular chromatin. Mitotic figures frequently are seen (Fig. 12–48). Despite the appellation of **small,** the neoplastic cells are usually twice the size of resting lymphocytes. Necrosis is invariably present and may be extensive. The tumor cells are markedly fragile and often show fragmentation and "crush artifact" in small biopsy specimens. Another feature of small cell carcinomas, best appreciated in cytologic specimens, is nuclear molding resulting from close apposition of tumor cells that have scant cytoplasm. These tumors often express a variety of neuroendocrine markers (Table 12–8) in addition to secreting a host of polypeptide hormones that may result in paraneoplastic syndromes (see below).

Combined patterns require no further comment. Of note, however, a significant minority of lung carcinomas reveal more than one line of cellular differentiation, sometimes several (Table 12–7), suggesting that all are derived from a multipotential progenitor cell.

For all of these neoplasms, it is possible to trace involvement of successive chains of nodes about the carina, in the mediastinum, and in the neck (scalene nodes) and clavicular regions and, sooner or later, distant metastases. Involvement of the left supraclavicular node (Virchow node) is particularly characteristic and sometimes calls attention to an occult primary tumor. These cancers, when advanced, often extend into the pleural or pericardial space, leading to inflammation and effusion. They may compress or infiltrate the superior vena cava to cause either venous congestion or the vena caval syndrome (Chapter 9). Apical neoplasms may invade the brachial or cervical sympathetic plexus to cause severe pain in the distribution of the ulnar nerve or to produce Horner syndrome (ipsilateral enophthalmos, ptosis, miosis, and anhidrosis). Such apical neoplasms sometimes are called **Pancoast tumors,** and the combination of clinical findings is known as Pancoast syndrome. Pancoast tumor often is accompanied by destruction of the first and second ribs and sometimes thoracic vertebrae. As with other cancers, tumor-node-metastasis (TNM) categories have been established to indicate the size and spread of the primary neoplasm.

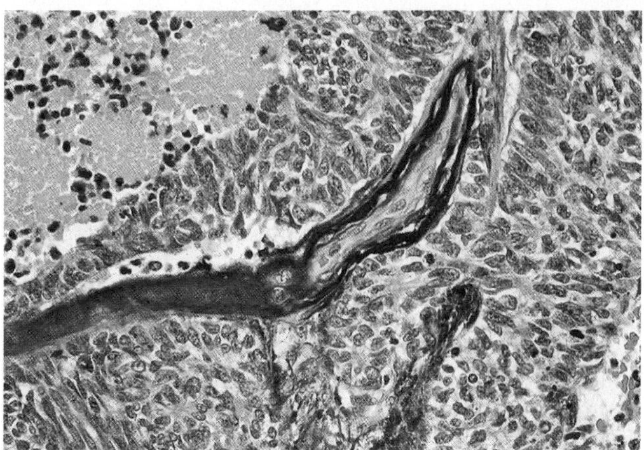

Figure 12–48 Small cell carcinoma with small deeply basophilic cells and areas of necrosis (*top left*). Note basophilic staining of vascular walls due to encrustation by DNA from necrotic tumor cells (Azzopardi effect).

Table 12–8 Comparison of Small Cell Lung Carcinoma (SCLC) and Non–Small Cell Lung Carcinoma (NSCLC)

Feature	SCLC	NSCLC
Histology	Scant cytoplasm; small, hyperchromatic nuclei with fine chromatin pattern; nucleoli indistinct; diffuse sheets of cells	Abundant cytoplasm; pleomorphic nuclei with coarse chromatin pattern; nucleoli often prominent; glandular or squamous architecture
Neuroendocrine markers	Usually present	Usually absent
For example, dense core granules on electron microscopy; expression of chromogranin, neuron-specific enolase, and synaptophysin		
Epithelial markers	Present	Present
Epithelial membrane antigen, carcinoembryonic antigen, and cytokeratin intermediate filaments		
Mucin	Absent	Present in adenocarcinomas
Peptide hormone production	Adrenocorticotropic hormone, antidiuretic hormone, gastrin-releasing peptide, calcitonin	Parathyroid hormone–related peptide (PTH-rp) in squamous cell carcinoma
Tumor suppressor gene abnormalities		
3p deletions	>90%	>80%
Rb mutations	~90%	~20%
p16/CDKN2A mutations	~10%	>50%
P53 mutations	>90%	>50%
Dominant oncogene abnormalities		
KRAS mutations	Rare	~30% (adenocarcinomas)
EGFR mutations	Absent	~20% (adenocarcinomas, nonsmokers, women)
ALK rearrangements	Absent	4%–6% adenocarcinomas, nonsmokers, often have signet ring morphology
Response to chemotherapy and radiotherapy	Often complete response but recur invariably	Uncommonly, complete response

Clinical Course

Carcinomas of the lung are silent, insidious lesions that in many cases have spread so as to be unresectable before they produce symptoms. In some instances, chronic cough and expectoration call attention to still localized, resectable disease. By the time hoarseness, chest pain, superior vena cava syndrome, pericardial or pleural effusion, or persistent segmental atelectasis or pneumonitis makes its appearance, the prognosis is grim. Too often, the tumor presents with symptoms emanating from metastatic spread to the brain (mental or neurologic changes), liver (hepatomegaly), or bones (pain). Although the adrenals may be nearly obliterated by metastatic disease, adrenal insufficiency (Addison disease) is uncommon, because islands of cortical cells sufficient to maintain adrenal function usually persist.

Overall, NSCLCs carry a better prognosis than SCLCs. When NSCLCs (squamous cell carcinomas or adenocarcinomas) are detected before metastasis or local spread, cure is possible by lobectomy or pneumonectomy. SCLCs, on the other hand, have invariably spread by the time they are first detected, even if the primary tumor appears small and localized. Thus, surgical resection is not a viable treatment. They are very sensitive to chemotherapy but invariably recur. Median survival even with treatment is 1 year.

It is variously estimated that 3% to 10% of all patients with lung cancer develop clinically overt *paraneoplastic syndromes.* These include (1) hypercalcemia caused by secretion of a parathyroid hormone–related peptide (osteolytic lesions may also cause hypercalcemia, but this would not be a paraneoplastic syndrome [Chapter 5]); (2) Cushing syndrome (from increased production of adrenocorticotropic hormone); (3) syndrome of inappropriate secretion of antidiuretic hormone; (4) neuromuscular syndromes, including a myasthenic syndrome, peripheral neuropathy, and polymyositis; (5) clubbing of the fingers and hypertrophic pulmonary osteoarthropathy; and (6) coagulation abnormalities, including migratory thrombophlebitis, nonbacterial endocarditis, and disseminated intravascular coagulation. Secretion of calcitonin and other ectopic hormones also has been documented by assays, but these products usually do not provoke distinctive syndromes. Hypercalcemia most often is encountered with squamous cell neoplasms, the hematologic syndromes with adenocarcinomas. The remaining syndromes are much more common with small cell neoplasms, but exceptions abound.

SUMMARY

Carcinomas of the Lung

- The four major histologic subtypes are adenocarcinomas (most common), squamous cell carcinoma, large cell carcinoma, and small cell carcinoma.
- Each of these is clinically and genetically distinct. SCLCs are best treated by chemotherapy, because almost all are metastatic at presentation. The other carcinomas may be curable by surgery if limited to the lung. Combination chemotherapy also is available along with anti-EGFR therapy for those adenocarcinomas with EGFR mutations, and ALK inhibitors for those with ALK mutations.
- Smoking is the most important risk factor for lung cancer; in women and nonsmokers, adenocarcinomas are the most common cancers.
- Precursor lesions include squamous dysplasia (for squamous cancer) and atypical adenomatous hyperplasia and adenocarcinoma in situ (formerly bronchioloalveolar carcinoma) (for some adenocarcinomas).
- Tumors 3 cm or less in diameter characterized by pure growth along preexisting structures (lepidic pattern) without stromal invasion are now called adenocarcinoma in situ.
- Lung cancers, particularly SCLCs, can cause *paraneoplastic syndromes*.

Carcinoid Tumors

Carcinoid tumors are malignant tumors composed of cells that contain dense-core neurosecretory granules in their cytoplasm and, rarely, may secrete hormonally active polypeptides. They are classified into typical (low-grade) and atypical (intermediate-grade) carcinoids; both are often resectable and curable. They occasionally occur as part of the multiple endocrine neoplasia syndrome (Chapter 19). Bronchial carcinoids occur at an early age (mean 40 years) and represent about 5% of all pulmonary neoplasms.

MORPHOLOGY

Most carcinoids originate in main bronchi and grow in one of two patterns: (1) an obstructing polypoid, spherical, intraluminal mass (Fig. 12–49, *A*); or (2) a mucosal plaque penetrating the bronchial wall to fan out in the peribronchial tissue—the so-called collar-button lesion. Even these penetrating lesions push into the lung substance along a broad front and are therefore reasonably well demarcated. Peripheral carcinoids are less common. Although 5% to 15% of carcinoids have metastasized to the hilar nodes at presentation, distant metastases are rare. Histologically, **typical carcinoids,** like their counterparts in the intestinal tract, are composed of nests of uniform cells that have regular round nuclei with "salt-and-pepper" chromatin, absent or rare mitoses, and little pleomorphism (Fig. 12–49, *B*). **Atypical carcinoid** tumors display a higher mitotic rate (but less than small or large cell carcinomas) and focal necrosis. The atypical tumors have a higher incidence of lymph node and distant metastasis than typical carcinoids. Unlike typical carcinoids, the atypical subset demonstrates *TP53* mutations in 20% to 40% of cases. **Typical carcinoid, atypical carcinoid, and small cell carcinoma can be considered to represent a continuum of increasing histologic aggressiveness and malignant potential within the spectrum of pulmonary neuroendocrine neoplasms.**

Most carcinoid tumors manifest with signs and symptoms related to their intraluminal growth (i.e., they cause cough, hemoptysis, and recurrent bronchial and pulmonary infections). Peripheral tumors are often asymptomatic, being discovered incidentally on chest radiographs.

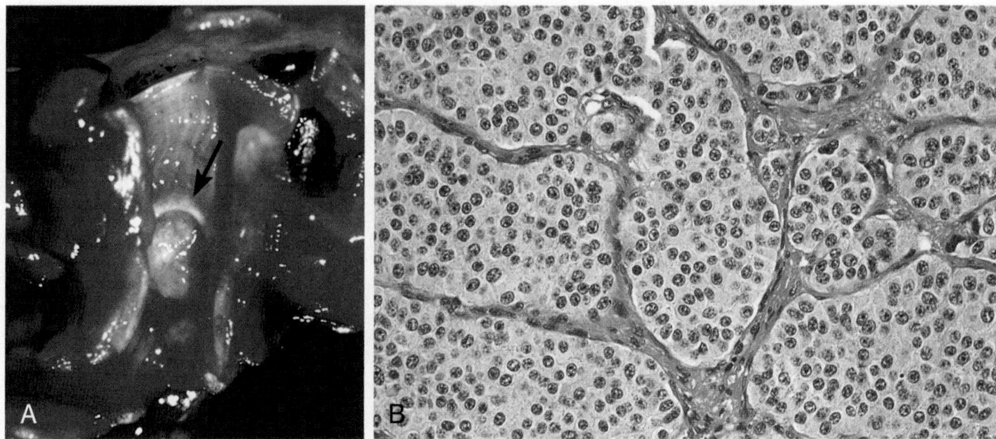

Figure 12-49 Bronchial carcinoid. **A,** Carcinoid growing as a spherical, pale mass *(arrow)* protruding into the lumen of the bronchus. **B,** Histologic appearance demonstrating small, rounded, uniform nuclei and moderate cytoplasm.
(Courtesy of Dr. Thomas Krausz, Department of Pathology, University of Chicago Pritzker School of Medicine, Chicago, Illinois.)

Only rarely do they induce the *carcinoid syndrome,* characterized by intermittent attacks of diarrhea, flushing, and cyanosis. The reported 5- and 10-year survival rates for typical carcinoids are above 85%, while these rates drop to 56% and 35%, respectively, for atypical carcinoids. Only 5% of patients with the most aggressive neuroendocrine lung tumor—SCLC—are alive at 10 years.

PLEURAL LESIONS

Pathologic involvement of the pleura is, with rare exceptions, a secondary complication of an underlying pulmonary disease. Evidence of secondary infection and pleural adhesions are particularly common findings at autopsy. Important primary disorders are (1) primary intrapleural bacterial infections and (2) a primary neoplasm of the pleura known as *malignant mesothelioma.*

Pleural Effusion and Pleuritis

In pleural effusion (the presence of fluid in the pleural space) the fluid can be either a transudate or an exudate. When the pleural fluid is a transudate, the condition is termed *hydrothorax.* Hydrothorax from CHF probably is the most common cause of fluid accumulation in the pleural cavity. An exudate, characterized by protein content greater than 2.9gm/dL and, often, inflammatory cells, suggests pleuritis. The four principal causes of *pleural exudate* formation are (1) microbial invasion through either direct extension of a pulmonary infection or blood-borne seeding (*suppurative pleuritis* or *empyema*); (2) cancer (lung carcinoma, metastatic neoplasms to the lung or pleural surface, mesothelioma); (3) pulmonary infarction; and (4) viral pleuritis. Other, less common causes of exudative pleural effusions are systemic lupus erythematosus, rheumatoid arthritis, and uremia, as well as previous thoracic surgery. Malignant effusions characteristically are large and frequently bloody (*hemorrhagic pleuritis*). Cytologic examination may reveal malignant and inflammatory cells.

Whatever the cause, transudates and serous exudates usually are resorbed without residual effects if the inciting cause is controlled or remits. By contrast, fibrinous, hemorrhagic, and suppurative exudates may lead to fibrous organization, yielding adhesions or fibrous pleural thickening, and sometimes minimal to massive calcifications.

Pneumothorax, Hemothorax, and Chylothorax

Pneumothorax refers to presence of air or other gas in the pleural sac. It may occur in young, apparently healthy adults, usually men without any known pulmonary disease (simple or spontaneous pneumothorax), or as a result of some thoracic or lung disorder (secondary pneumothorax), such as emphysema or a fractured rib. Secondary pneumothorax is the consequence of rupture of any pulmonary lesion situated close to the pleural surface that allows inspired air to gain access to the pleural cavity. Such pulmonary lesions include emphysema, lung abscess, tuberculosis, carcinoma, and many other, less common processes. Mechanical ventilatory support with high pressure also may trigger secondary pneumothorax.

There are several possible complications of pneumothorax. A ball-valve leak may create a tension pneumothorax that shifts the mediastinum. Compromise of the pulmonary circulation may follow and may even be fatal. If the leak seals and the lung is not reexpanded within a few weeks (either spontaneously or through medical or surgical intervention), so much scarring may occur that it can never be fully reexpanded. In these cases, serous fluid collects in the pleural cavity, creating hydropneumothorax. With prolonged collapse, the lung becomes vulnerable to infection, as does the pleural cavity when communication between it and the lung persists. Empyema is thus an important complication of pneumothorax (pyopneumothorax).

Hemothorax, the collection of whole blood (in contrast with bloody effusion) in the pleural cavity, is a complication of a ruptured intrathoracic aortic aneurysm that is almost always fatal. With hemothorax, in contrast with bloody pleural effusions, the blood clots within the pleural cavity.

Chylothorax is a pleural collection of a milky lymphatic fluid containing microglobules of lipid. The total volume of fluid may not be large, but chylothorax is always significant because it implies obstruction of the major lymph ducts, usually by an intrathoracic cancer (e.g., a primary or secondary mediastinal neoplasm, such as a lymphoma).

Malignant Mesothelioma

Malignant mesothelioma is a rare cancer of mesothelial cells, usually arising in the parietal or visceral pleura, although it also occurs, much less commonly, in the peritoneum and pericardium. It has assumed great importance because it is related to occupational exposure to asbestos in the air. Approximately 50% of persons with this cancer have a history of exposure to asbestos. Those who work directly with asbestos (shipyard workers, miners, insulators) are at greatest risk, but malignant mesotheliomas have appeared in persons whose only exposure was living in proximity to an asbestos factory or being a relative of an asbestos worker. The latent period for developing malignant mesothelioma is long, often 25 to 40 years after initial asbestos exposure, suggesting that multiple somatic genetic events are required for neoplastic conversion of a mesothelial cell. As stated earlier, *the combination of cigarette smoking and asbestos exposure greatly increases the risk of lung carcinoma, but it does not increase the risk of developing malignant mesothelioma.*

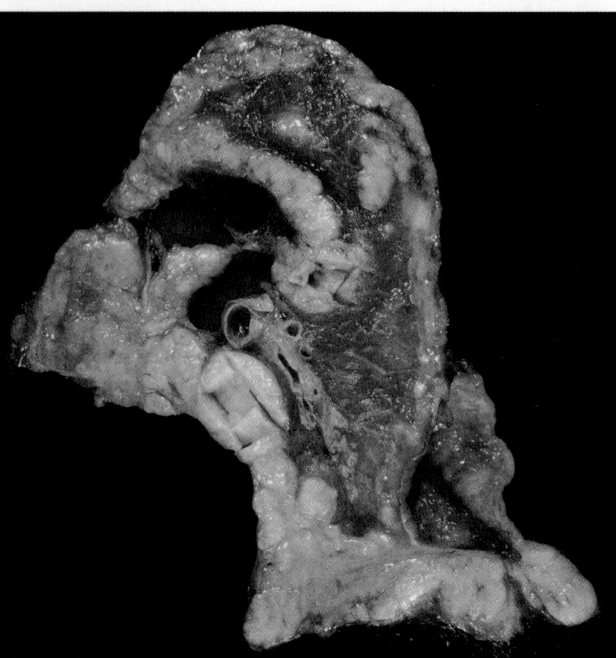

Figure 12–50 Malignant mesothelioma. Note the thick, firm, white pleural tumor that ensheathes this bisected lung.

MORPHOLOGY

Malignant mesotheliomas are often preceded by extensive **pleural fibrosis and plaque formation,** readily seen on computed tomography scans. These tumors begin in a localized area and over time spread widely, either by contiguous growth or by diffusely seeding the pleural surfaces. At autopsy, the affected lung **typically is ensheathed by a yellow-white, firm, sometimes gelatinous layer of tumor** that obliterates the pleural space (Fig. 12–50). Distant metastases are rare. The neoplasm may directly invade the thoracic wall or the subpleural lung tissue. Normal mesothelial cells are biphasic, giving rise to pleural lining cells as well as the underlying fibrous tissue. Therefore, histologically, mesotheliomas conform to one of three patterns: (1) **epithelial,** in which cuboidal cells line tubular and microcystic spaces, into which small papillary buds project; this is the most common pattern and also the one most likely to be confused with a pulmonary adenocarcinoma; (2) **sarcomatous,** in which spindled and sometimes fibroblastic-appearing cells grow in nondistinctive sheets; and (3) **biphasic,** having both sarcomatous and epithelial areas.

Asbestos is not removed or metabolized from the lung, so the fibers remain in the body for life. Thus, the lifetime risk after exposure does not diminish over time (unlike with smoking, in which the risk decreases after cessation). It has been hypothesized that asbestos fibers preferentially gather near the mesothelial cell layer, where they generate reactive oxygen species, which cause DNA damage with potentially oncogenic mutations. Somatic mutations of two tumor suppressor genes (*p16/CDKN2A*, at chromosomal locus 9p21, and *NF2*, at chromosomal locus 22q12) have been observed in malignant mesotheliomas.

LESIONS OF THE UPPER RESPIRATORY TRACT

Acute Infections

Acute infections of the upper respiratory tract are among the most common afflictions of humans, most frequently manifesting as the "common cold." The clinical features are well known: nasal congestion accompanied by watery discharge; sneezing; scratchy, dry sore throat; and a slight increase in temperature that is more pronounced in young children. The most common pathogens are rhinoviruses, but coronaviruses, respiratory syncytial viruses, parainfluenza and influenza viruses, adenoviruses, enteroviruses, and sometimes even group A β-hemolytic streptococci have been implicated. In a significant number of cases (around 40%) the cause cannot be determined; perhaps new viruses will be discovered. Most of these infections occur in the fall and winter and are self-limiting (usually lasting for a week or less). In a minority of cases, colds may be complicated by the development of bacterial otitis media or sinusitis.

In addition to the common cold, infections of the upper respiratory tract may produce signs and symptoms localized to the pharynx, epiglottis, or larynx. *Acute pharyngitis,* manifesting as a sore throat, may be caused by a host of agents. Mild pharyngitis with minimal physical findings frequently accompanies a cold and is the most common form of pharyngitis. More severe forms with tonsillitis, associated with marked hyperemia and exudates, occur with β-hemolytic streptococcal and adenovirus infections. Streptococcal tonsillitis is important to recognize and treat early, because of the associated potential for development of peritonsillar abscesses ("quinsy") or for progression to poststreptococcal glomerulonephritis and acute rheumatic fever. Coxsackievirus A infection may produce pharyngeal vesicles and ulcers (herpangina). Infectious mononucleosis, caused by Epstein-Barr virus (EBV), is an important cause of pharyngitis and bears the moniker of "kissing disease"—reflecting the common mode of transmission in previously nonexposed persons.

Acute *bacterial epiglottitis* is a syndrome predominantly affecting young children who have an infection of the epiglottis caused by *H. influenzae*, in which pain and airway obstruction are the major findings. The onset is abrupt. Failure to appreciate the need to maintain an open airway for a child with this condition can have fatal consequences. The advent of vaccination against *H. influenzae* has greatly decreased the incidence of this disease.

Acute laryngitis can result from inhalation of irritants or may be caused by allergic reactions. It may also be caused by the agents that produce the common cold and usually involve the pharynx and nasal passages as well as the larynx. Brief mention should be made of two uncommon but important forms of laryngitis: *tuberculous* and *diphtheritic.* The former is almost always a consequence of protracted active tuberculosis, during which infected sputum is coughed up. Diphtheritic laryngitis has fortunately become uncommon because of the widespread immunization of young children against diphtheria toxin. After it is inhaled, *Corynebacterium diphtheriae* implants on the mucosa of the upper airways, where it elaborates a powerful exotoxin that causes necrosis of the mucosal epithelium, accompanied by a dense fibrinopurulent exudate, to create the classic superficial, dirty-gray pseudomembrane of diphtheria. The major hazards of this infection are sloughing and aspiration of the pseudomembrane (causing obstruction of major airways) and absorption of bacterial exotoxins (producing myocarditis, peripheral neuropathy, or other tissue injury).

In children, parainfluenza virus is the most common cause of laryngotracheobronchitis, more commonly known as *croup,* but other agents such as respiratory syncytial virus also may precipitate this condition. Although self-limited, croup may cause frightening inspiratory stridor and harsh, persistent cough. In occasional cases, the laryngeal inflammatory reaction may narrow the airway sufficiently to result in respiratory failure. Viral infections in the upper respiratory tract predispose the patient to secondary bacterial infection, particularly by staphylococci, streptococci, and *H. influenzae.*

Nasopharyngeal Carcinoma

Nasopharyngeal carcinoma is a rare neoplasm that merits comment because of (1) the strong epidemiologic links to EBV and (2) the high frequency of this form of cancer among the Chinese, which raises the possibility of viral oncogenesis on a background of genetic susceptibility. It is thought that EBV infects the host by first replicating in the nasopharyngeal epithelium and then infecting nearby tonsillar B lymphocytes. In some persons this leads to transformation of the epithelial cells. Unlike the case with Burkitt lymphoma (Chapter 11), another EBV-associated tumor, the EBV genome is found in virtually all nasopharyngeal carcinomas, including those that occur outside the endemic areas in Asia.

The three histologic variants are keratinizing squamous cell carcinoma, nonkeratinizing squamous cell carcinoma, and undifferentiated carcinoma; the last-mentioned is the most common and the one most closely linked with EBV. The undifferentiated neoplasm is characterized by large epithelial cells with indistinct cell borders (reflecting "syncytial" growth) and prominent eosinophilic nucleoli. As described in Chapter 11, in infectious mononucleosis, EBV directly infects B lymphocytes, after which a marked proliferation of reactive T lymphocytes causes atypical lymphocytosis, seen in the peripheral blood, and enlarged lymph nodes. Similarly, in nasopharyngeal carcinomas, a striking influx of mature lymphocytes often can be seen. These neoplasms are therefore referred to as "lymphoepitheliomas"—a misnomer, because the lymphocytes are not part of the neoplastic process, nor are the tumors benign. The presence of large neoplastic cells in a background of reactive lymphocytes may give rise to an appearance similar to that in non-Hodgkin lymphomas, and immunohistochemical stains may be required to prove the epithelial nature of the malignant cells. Nasopharyngeal carcinomas invade locally, spread to cervical lymph nodes, and then metastasize to distant sites. They tend to be radiosensitive, and 5-year survival rates of 50% are reported even for patients with advanced cancers.

Laryngeal Tumors

A variety of non-neoplastic, benign, and malignant neoplasms of epithelial and mesenchymal origin may arise in the larynx, but only vocal cord nodules, papillomas, and squamous cell carcinomas are sufficiently common to merit comment. In all of these conditions, the most common presenting feature is hoarseness.

Nonmalignant Lesions

Vocal cord nodules ("polyps") are smooth, hemispherical protrusions (usually less than 0.5 cm in diameter) located, most often, on the true vocal cords. The nodules are composed of fibrous tissue and covered by stratified squamous mucosa that usually is intact but can be ulcerated from contact trauma with the other vocal cord. These lesions occur chiefly in heavy smokers or singers (singer's nodes), suggesting that they are the result of chronic irritation or abuse.

Laryngeal papilloma or *squamous papilloma* of the larynx is a benign neoplasm, usually located on the true vocal cords, that forms a soft, raspberry-like excrescence rarely more than 1 cm in diameter. Histologically, it consists of multiple, slender, finger-like projections supported by central fibrovascular cores and covered by an orderly, typical, stratified squamous epithelium. When the papilloma is on the free edge of the vocal cord, trauma may lead to ulceration that can be accompanied by hemoptysis.

Papillomas usually are single in adults but often are multiple in children, in whom the condition is referred to as *recurrent respiratory papillomatosis* (RRP), since they typically tend to recur after excision. These lesions are caused by human papillomavirus (HPV) types 6 and 11, do not become malignant, and often spontaneously regress at puberty. Cancerous transformation is rare. The most likely cause for their occurrence in children is vertical transmission from an infected mother during delivery. Therefore, the recent availability of an HPV vaccine that can protect women of reproductive age against infection with types 6 and 11 provides an opportunity for prevention of RRP in children.

Carcinoma of the Larynx

Carcinoma of the larynx represents only 2% of all cancers. It most commonly occurs after age 40 years and is more common in men than in women (with a gender ratio of 7:1). Environmental influences are very important in its causation; nearly all cases occur in smokers, and alcohol and asbestos exposure may also play roles. Human papillomavirus sequences have been detected in about 15% of tumors, which tend to have a better prognosis than other carcinomas.

About 95% of laryngeal cancers are typical squamous cell carcinomas. Rarely, adenocarcinomas are seen, presumably arising from mucous glands. The tumor develops directly on the vocal cords (glottic tumors) in 60% to 75% of cases, but it may arise above the cords (supraglottic; 25% to 40%) or below the cords (subglottic; less than 5%). Squamous cell carcinomas of the larynx begin as in situ lesions that later appear as pearly gray, wrinkled plaques on the mucosal surface, ultimately ulcerating and fungating (Fig. 12–51). The glottic tumors are usually keratinizing, well- to moderately differentiated squamous cell carcinomas, although nonkeratinizing, poorly differentiated carcinomas may also be seen. As expected with lesions arising from recurrent exposure to environmental carcinogens, adjacent mucosa may demonstrate squamous cell hyperplasia with foci of dysplasia, or even carcinoma in situ.

Carcinoma of the larynx manifests itself clinically with persistent hoarseness. The location of the tumor within the larynx has a significant bearing on prognosis. For example, about 90% of glottic tumors are confined to the larynx at diagnosis. First, as a result of interference with vocal cord mobility, they develop symptoms early in the course of disease; second, the glottic region has a sparse lymphatic supply, and spread beyond the larynx is uncommon. By contrast, the supraglottic larynx is rich in lymphatic spaces, and nearly a third of these tumors metastasize to regional (cervical) lymph nodes. The subglottic tumors tend to remain clinically quiescent, usually manifesting as advanced disease. With surgery, radiation therapy, or combination treatment, many patients can be cured, but about one third die of the disease. The usual cause of death is infection of the distal respiratory passages or widespread metastases and cachexia.

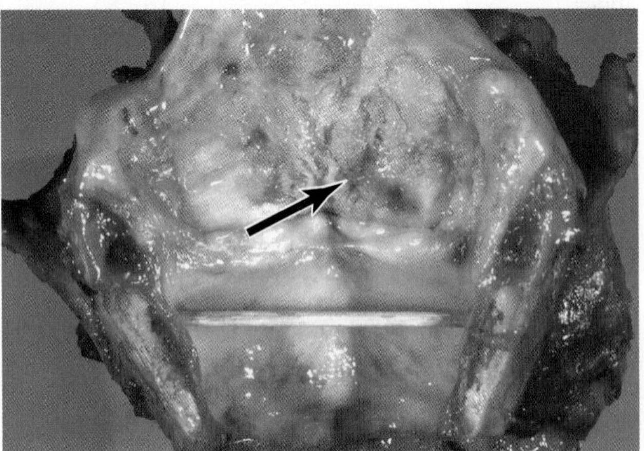

Figure 12–51 Laryngeal squamous cell carcinoma *(arrow)* arising in a supraglottic location (above the true vocal cord).

ACKNOWLEDGMENT

The contributions of Anirban Maitra, MD, to this chapter are gratefully acknowledged.

BIBLIOGRAPHY

American Thoracic Society; European Respiratory Society: International Multidisciplinary Consensus Classification of the Idiopathic Interstitial Pneumonias. This joint statement of the American Thoracic Society (ATS) and the European Respiratory Society (ERS) was adopted by the ATS board of directors, June 2001 and by the ERS Executive Committee, June 2001. Am J Respir Crit Care Med 165:277, 2002. *[The authoritative classification of interstitial pneumonias from the two major trans-Atlantic pulmonary societies.]*

Baughman RP, Lower EE, du Bois RM: Sarcoidosis. Lancet 361:1111, 2003. *[A good review of this subject, including evidence on the role of genetic polymorphisms that determine susceptibility to sarcoidosis, and treatment options.]*

Beasley MB: Smoking-related small airway disease—a review and update. Adv Anat Pathol 17:270, 2010. *[Review of histologic findings and pathogenesis of small airway disease in smoking-related diseases.]*

Collard HR, King TE Jr: Demystifying idiopathic interstitial pneumonia. Arch Intern Med 163:17, 2003. *[A review on the histopathologic and clinical features distinguishing interstitial pneumonias from other causes of pulmonary fibrosis, with particular emphasis on idiopathic pulmonary fibrosis and the importance of recognizing this pattern.]*

Cosio MG, Saetta M, Agusti A: Immunologic aspects of chronic obstructive pulmonary disease. N Engl J Med 360:2445, 2009. *[An excellent review of mechanisms leading to COPD.]*

Davies D, Wicks J, Powell RM, et al: Airway remodeling in asthma: new insights. J Allergy Clin Immunol 111:215, 2003. *[A review on the structural changes involved in asthma pathogenesis, and the role of candidate gene polymorphisms that may confer potential susceptibility to airway remodeling and asthma.]*

Eramo A, Haas TL, De Maria R: Lung cancer stem cells: tools and targets to fight lung cancer. Oncogene 29:4625, 2010. *[Review of what is currently known about lung cancer stem cells and their diagnostic, prognostic, and therapeutic implications.]*

Frieden TR, Sterling TR, Munsiff SS, et al: Tuberculosis. Lancet 362:887, 2003. *[A clinical review on global trends in tuberculosis, emergence of multidrug resistance, and measures for primary prevention of this disease from a public health perspective.]*

Hogg JC, Timens W: The pathology of chronic obstructive pulmonary disease. Annu Rev Pathol 4:435, 2009. *[A comprehensive review on the pathogenesis of COPD, stressing the roles of inflammation, tissue repair and remodeling, and small airway disease in COPD.]*

Horowitz JC, Martinez FJ, Thannickal VJ: Mesenchymal cell fate and phenotypes in the pathogenesis of emphysema. COPD 6:201, 2009. *[An excellent discussion of the emerging evidence supporting that genetic factors, inflammation and environmental factors, including cigarette smoke itself, collectively contribute to the pathogenesis of emphysema.]*

Jones KD: An update on lung cancer staging. Adv Anat Pathol 17:33, 2010. *[Review of the tumor-node-metastasis (TNM) criteria for lung cancer staging.]*

King PT: The pathophysiology of bronchiectasis. Int J Chron Obstruct Pulmon Dis 4:411, 2009. *[A review of the pathology, associated conditions, and microbiology of bronchiectasis.]*

Meyers DA: Genetics of asthma and allergy: what have we learned? J Allergy Clin Immunol 126:439, 2010. *[An update on genetic approaches to understanding the susceptibility and severity of asthma and allergy.]*

Noguchi M: Stepwise progression of pulmonary adenocarcinoma—clinical and molecular implications. Cancer Metastasis Rev 29:15, 2010. *[Correlates the progression of adenocarcinoma with molecular changes.]*

Rabinovitch M: Pathobiology of pulmonary hypertension. Annu Rev Pathol 2:369, 2007. *[Current concepts in the causation of pulmonary hypertension.]*

Rimal B, Greenberg AK, Rom WN: Basic pathogenetic mechanisms in silicosis: current understanding. Curr Opin Pulm Med 11:169; 2005. *[A review on how silica exposure leads to pulmonary disease, including discussions on the controversy surrounding the potential carcinogenic role of this mineral dust.]*

Runo J, Loyd J: Primary pulmonary hypertension. Lancet 361:1533, 2003. *[A comprehensive review on the genetics, pathophysiology, clinical manifestations, and treatment options for this entity.]*

Sekido Y, Fong KM, Minna JD: Molecular genetics of lung cancer. Annu Rev Med 54:73, 2003. *[An outstanding review on the molecular abnormalities underlying lung cancers, particularly those differentiating SCLCs from NSCLCs.]*

Simonneau G, Robbins IM, Beghetti M, et al: Updated clinical classification of pulmonary hypertension. J Am Coll Cardiol 30:54, 2009. *[This is a clinical classification based on pathophysiologic mechanisms, clinical presentation, and therapeutic approaches.]*

Stewart S, Rassi D: Advances in the understanding and classification of pulmonary hypertension. Histopathology 54:104, 2009. *[Describes recent advances in genetic and molecular mechanisms and histopathologic findings in pulmonary hypertension.]*

Travis WD, Brambilla E, Noguchi M, et al: International Association for the Study of Lung Cancer/American Thoracic Society/European Respiratory Society international multidisciplinary classification of lung adenocarcinoma. J Thorac Oncol 6:244, 2011. *[New classification of adenocarcinoma that incorporates clinical, radiologic, histologic, molecular, and prognostic features.]*

Tsushima K, King LS, Aggarwal NR, et al: Acute lung injury review. Intern Med 48:621, 2009. *[Includes definition, incidence, outcome, pathogenesis, and therapy of acute lung injury/acute respiratory distress syndrome.]*

Varella-Garcia M: Chromosomal and genomic changes in lung cancer. Cell Adh Migr 4:1, 2010. *[Comprehensive review of recurrent genomic changes affecting cell growth and differentiation and apoptotic pathways in lung cancer and their application to targeted therapy.]*

Walter MJ, Holtzmann MJ: A centennial history of research on asthma pathogenesis. Am J Respir Cell Mol Biol 32:483, 2005. *[An excellent summary paper describing important milestones in 100 years of research on the pathogenesis of asthma.]*

Ware LB: Pathophysiology of acute lung injury and the acute respiratory distress syndrome. Semin Respir Crit Care Med 27:337, 2006. *[An excellent discussion of the pathogenesis of ARDS.]*

See Targeted Therapy available online at **studentconsult.com**

CHAPTER 13

Kidney and Its Collecting System

CHAPTER CONTENTS

The kidney is a structurally complex organ that has evolved to carry out a number of important functions: excretion of the waste products of metabolism, regulation of body water and salt, maintenance of acid balance, and secretion of a variety of hormones and prostaglandins. Diseases of the kidney are as complex as its structure, but their study is facilitated by dividing them into those that affect its four components: glomeruli, tubules, interstitium, and blood vessels. This traditional approach is useful because the early manifestations of diseases that affect each of these components tend to be distinctive. Furthermore, some structures seem to be more vulnerable to specific forms of renal injury; for example, glomerular diseases are often immunologically mediated, whereas tubular and interstitial disorders are more likely to be caused by toxic or infectious agents. However, some disorders affect more than one structure, and functional interdependence of structures in the kidney means that damage to one component almost always secondarily affects the others. Thus, severe glomerular damage impairs the flow through the peritubular vascular system; conversely, tubular destruction, by increasing intraglomerular pressure and inducing cytokines and chemokines, may induce glomerular sclerosis. Whatever the origin, there is a tendency for chronic renal disease ultimately to damage all four components of the kidney, culminating in *end-stage kidney disease.* For these reasons, the early signs and symptoms of renal disease are particularly important in discerning the initiating cause of the disease, and therefore are referred to in the discussion of individual diseases. The functional reserve of the kidney is large, and much damage may occur before renal dysfunction becomes evident.

CLINICAL MANIFESTATIONS OF RENAL DISEASES

The clinical manifestations of renal disease can be grouped into reasonably well-defined syndromes. Some are peculiar to glomerular diseases and others are shared by several renal disorders. Before we list the syndromes, a few terms must be defined.

Azotemia is an elevation of blood urea nitrogen and creatinine levels and usually reflects a decreased glomerular filtration rate (GFR). GFR may be decreased as a consequence of intrinsic renal disease or extrarenal causes. *Prerenal azotemia* is encountered when there is hypoperfusion of the kidneys, which decreases GFR *in the absence of parenchymal damage. Postrenal azotemia* results when urine flow is obstructed below the level of the kidney. Relief of the obstruction is followed by correction of the azotemia.

When azotemia gives rise to clinical manifestations and systemic biochemical abnormalities, it is termed *uremia.* Uremia is characterized not only by failure of renal excretory function but also by a host of metabolic and endocrine alterations incident to renal damage. There is, in addition, secondary gastrointestinal (e.g., uremic gastroenteritis); neuromuscular (e.g., peripheral neuropathy); and cardiovascular (e.g., uremic fibrinous pericarditis) involvement.

We now turn to a brief description of the major renal syndromes:

- *Nephritic syndrome* results from glomerular injury and is dominated by the acute onset of usually grossly visible hematuria (red blood cells and red cell casts in urine), proteinuria of mild to moderate degree, azotemia, edema, and hypertension; it is the classic presentation of acute poststreptococcal glomerulonephritis.

- *Nephrotic syndrome* is a glomerular syndrome characterized by heavy proteinuria (excretion of greater than 3.5 g of protein/day in adults), hypoalbuminemia, severe edema, hyperlipidemia, and lipiduria (lipid in the urine).
- *Asymptomatic hematuria* or non-nephrotic *proteinuria,* or a combination of these two, is usually a manifestation of subtle or mild glomerular abnormalities.
- *Rapidly progressive glomerulonephritis* is associated with severe glomerular injury and results in loss of renal function in a few days or weeks. It is manifested by microscopic hematuria, dysmorphic red blood cells and red cell casts in the urine sediment, and mild to moderate proteinuria.
- *Acute kidney injury* is dominated by oliguria or anuria (no urine flow), and recent onset of azotemia. It can result from glomerular injury (such as rapidly progessive glomerulonephritis), interstitial injury, vascular injury (such as thrombotic microangiopathy), or acute tubular injury.
- *Chronic kidney disease,* characterized by prolonged symptoms and signs of uremia, is the result of progressive scarring in the kidney from any cause and may culminate in end-stage kidney disease, requiring dialysis or transplantation.
- *Urinary tract infection* is characterized by bacteriuria and pyuria (bacteria and leukocytes in the urine). The infection may be symptomatic or asymptomatic, and it may affect the kidney (*pyelonephritis*) or the bladder (*cystitis*) only.
- *Nephrolithiasis* (renal stones) is manifested by renal colic, hematuria (without red cell casts), and recurrent stone formation.

In addition to these renal syndromes, *urinary tract obstruction* and *renal tumors* also commonly present with signs and symptoms related to renal dysfunction and are discussed later.

GLOMERULAR DISEASES

Disorders affecting the glomerulus encompass a clinically important category of renal disease. The glomerulus consists of an anastomosing network of capillaries invested by two layers of epithelium. The visceral epithelium (composed of podocytes) is an intrinsic part of the capillary wall, whereas the parietal epithelium lines Bowman space (urinary space), the cavity in which plasma ultrafiltrate first collects. The glomerular capillary wall is the filtration unit and consists of the following structures (Figs. 13–1 and 13–2):

- A thin layer of fenestrated *endothelial cells,* each fenestra being 70 to 100 nm in diameter.
- A *glomerular basement membrane* (GBM) with a thick, electron-dense central layer, the *lamina densa,* and thinner, electron-lucent peripheral layers, the *lamina rara interna* and *lamina rara externa.* The GBM consists of collagen (mostly type IV), laminin, polyanionic proteoglycans, fibronectin, and several other glycoproteins.
- *Podocytes,* which are structurally complex cells that possess interdigitating processes embedded in and adherent to the lamina rara externa of the basement membrane. Adjacent *foot processes* are separated by 20- to 30-nm-wide *filtration slits,* which are bridged by a thin slit diaphragm composed in large part of nephrin (see further on).
- The glomerular tuft is supported by *mesangial cells* lying between the capillaries. Basement membrane–like mesangial matrix forms a meshwork through which the mesangial cells are scattered. These cells, of mesenchymal origin, are contractile and are capable of proliferation, of laying down collagen and other matrix components, and of secreting a number of biologically active mediators.

Normally, the glomerular filtration system is extraordinarily permeable to water and small solutes and almost completely impermeable to molecules of the size and molecular charge of albumin (a 70,000-kDa protein). This selective permeability, called glomerular barrier function, discriminates among protein molecules according to their size (the larger, the less permeable), their charge (the more cationic, the more permeable), and their configuration. The characteristics of the normal barrier depend on the complex structure of the capillary wall, the integrity of the GBM, and the many anionic molecules present within the wall, including the acidic proteoglycans of the GBM and the sialoglycoproteins of epithelial and endothelial cell coats. *The podocyte is also crucial to the maintenance of glomerular barrier function.* Podocyte slit diaphragms are important diffusion barriers for plasma proteins, and podocytes are also largely responsible for synthesis of GBM components.

In the past few years, much has been learned about the molecular architecture of the glomerular filtration barrier. *Nephrin,* a transmembrane glycoprotein, is the major component of the slit diaphragms between adjacent foot processes. Nephrin molecules from adjacent foot processes bind to each other through disulfide bridges at the center of the slit diaphragm. The intracellular part of nephrin interacts with several cytoskeletal and signaling proteins (Fig. 13–1). Nephrin and its associated proteins, including *podocin,* have a crucial role in maintaining the selective permeability of the glomerular filtration barrier. This role is dramatically illustrated by rare hereditary diseases in which mutations of nephrin or its partner proteins are associated with abnormal leakage into the urine of plasma proteins, giving rise to the nephrotic syndrome (discussed later). This observation suggests that acquired defects in the function or structure of slit diaphragms constitute an important mechanism of proteinuria, the hallmark of the nephrotic syndrome.

Glomeruli may be injured by diverse mechanisms and in the course of a number of systemic diseases (Table 13–1). Immunologically mediated diseases such as systemic lupus erythematosus, vascular disorders such as hypertension and hemolytic uremic syndrome, metabolic diseases such as diabetes mellitus, and some purely hereditary conditions such as Alport syndrome often affect the glomerulus. These are termed *secondary glomerular diseases* to differentiate them from those in which the kidney is the only or predominant organ involved. The latter constitute

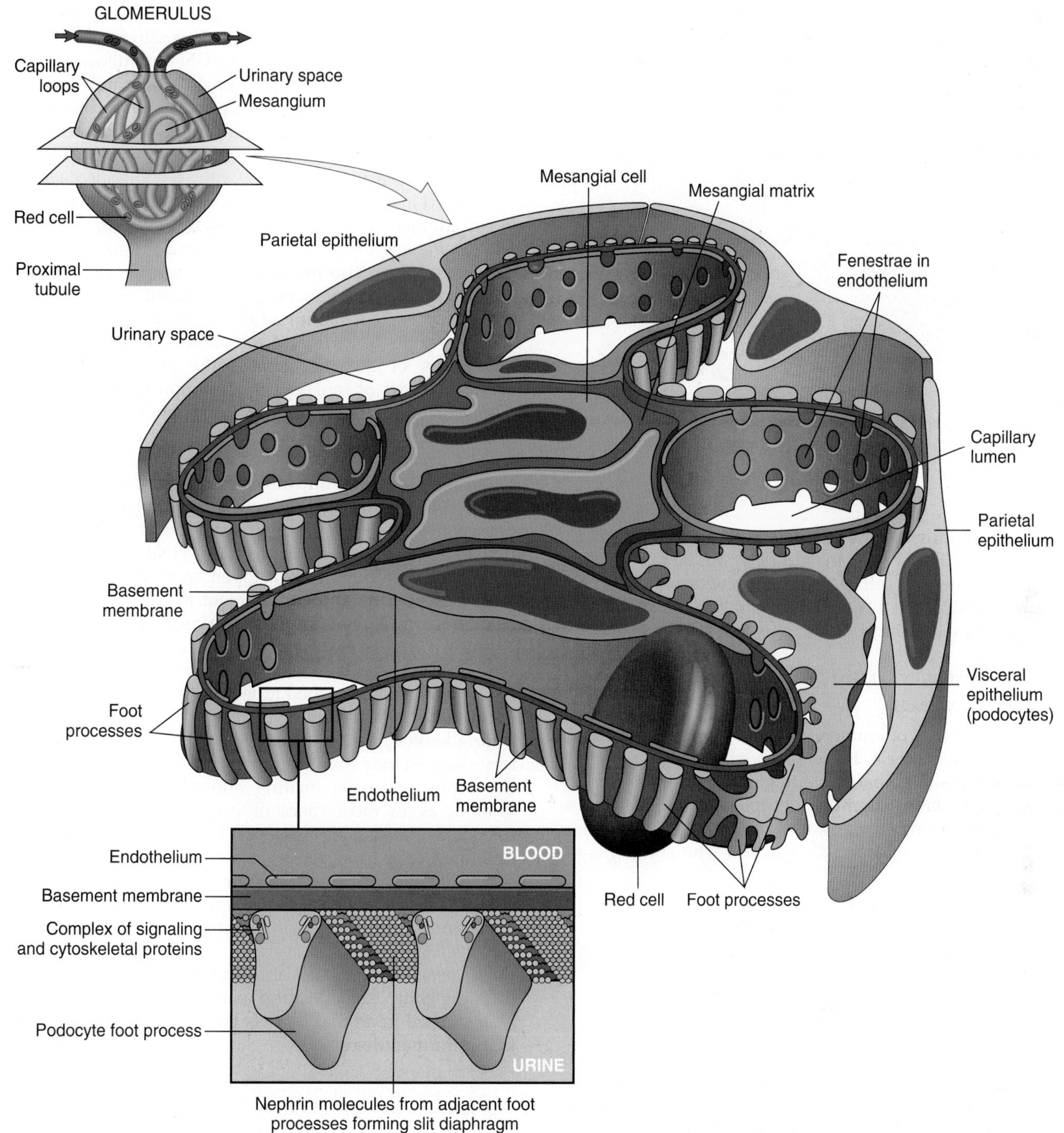

Figure 13–1 Schematic diagram of a lobe of a normal glomerulus.

the various types of *primary glomerular diseases,* which are discussed later in this section. The glomerular alterations in systemic diseases are discussed elsewhere.

Mechanisms of Glomerular Injury and Disease

Although little is known about the etiologic agents or triggering events, it is clear that immune mechanisms underlie most types of primary glomerular diseases and many of the secondary glomerular diseases. Under experimental conditions, glomerulonephritis (GN) can be readily induced by antibodies, and deposits of immunoglobulins, often with various components of complement, are found frequently in patients with GN. Cell-mediated immune mechanisms may also play a role in certain glomerular diseases.

Two forms of antibody-associated injury have been established: (1) injury resulting from deposition of soluble circulating antigen-antibody complexes in the glomerulus and (2) injury by antibodies reacting in situ within the glomerulus, either with insoluble fixed (intrinsic)

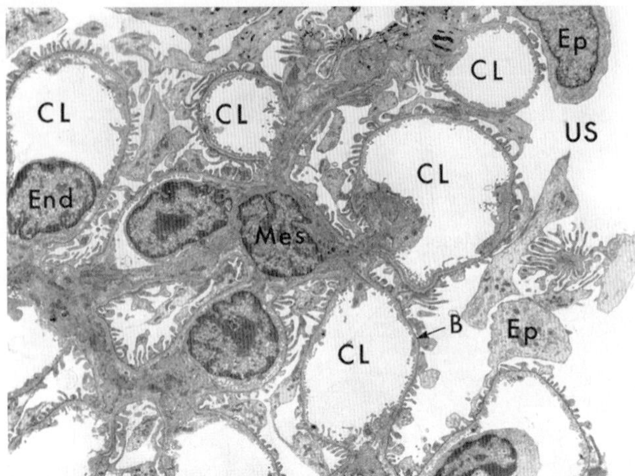

Figure 13–2 Low-power electron micrograph of rat glomerulus. B, basement membrane; CL, capillary lumen; End, endothelium; Ep, visceral epithelial cells (podocytes) with foot processes; Mes, mesangium; US, urinary space.

glomerular antigens or with molecules planted within the glomerulus (Fig. 13–3). In addition, antibodies directed against glomerular cell components may cause glomerular injury. These pathways are not mutually exclusive, and in humans all may contribute to injury.

Glomerulonephritis Caused by Circulating Immune Complexes

The pathogenesis of immune complex diseases is discussed in detail in Chapter 4. Presented here is a brief review of the salient features that relate to glomerular injury in GN.

With circulating immune complex–mediated disease, the glomerulus may be considered an "innocent bystander" because it does not incite the reaction. The antigen is not of glomerular origin. It may be endogenous, as in the GN associated with systemic lupus erythematosus, or it may be exogenous, as is probable in the GN that follows certain bacterial (streptococcal), viral (hepatitis B), parasitic (*Plasmodium falciparum* malaria), and spirochetal (*Treponema pallidum*) infections. Often the inciting antigen is unknown, as in most cases of membranoproliferative GN (MPGN).

Whatever the antigen may be, *antigen–antibody complexes* are formed in situ or in the circulation and are then trapped in the glomeruli, where they *produce injury, in large part through the activation of complement and the recruitment of leukocytes*. Injury also may occur through the engagement of Fc receptors on leukocytes independent of complement activation, as cross-linking of Fc receptors by IgG antibodies also results in leukocyte activation and degranulation. Regardless of the mechanism, the glomerular lesions usually consist of leukocytic infiltration (exudation) into glomeruli and variable proliferation of endothelial, mesangial, and parietal epithelial cells. Electron microscopy reveals the immune complexes as electron-dense deposits or clumps that lie at one of three sites: in the mesangium, between the endothelial cells and the GBM (subendothelial deposits), or between the outer surface of the GBM and the podocytes (subepithelial deposits). Deposits may be located at more than one site in a given case. The presence of immunoglobulins and complement in these deposits can be demonstrated by immunofluorescence microscopy (Fig. 13–4, *A*). *The pattern and location of immune complex deposition are helpful in distinguishing among various types of GN.*

Once deposited in the kidney, immune complexes may eventually be degraded or phagocytosed, mostly by infiltrating leukocytes and mesangial cells, and the inflammatory changes may then subside. Such a course occurs when the exposure to the inciting antigen is short-lived and limited, as in most cases of poststreptococcal or acute infection-related GN. However, if exposure to antigen is sustained over time, repeated cycles of immune complex formation, deposition, and injury may occur, leading to chronic GN. In some cases the source of chronic antigenic exposure is clear, such as in hepatitis B virus infection and self nuclear antigens in systemic lupus erythematosus. In other cases, however, the antigen is unknown. Circulating immune complex deposition as a mechanism of injury is well studied in animal models but is uncommonly identified in human disease.

Table 13–1 Glomerular Diseases

Primary Glomerular Diseases
Minimal-change disease
Focal segmental glomerulosclerosis
Membranous nephropathy
Acute postinfectious GN
Membranoproliferative GN
IgA nephropathy
Glomerulopathies Secondary to Systemic Diseases
Lupus nephritis (systemic lupus erythematosus)
Diabetic nephropathy
Amyloidosis
GN secondary to multiple myeloma
Goodpasture syndrome
Microscopic polyangiitis
Wegener granulomatosis
Henoch-Schönlein purpura
Bacterial endocarditis–related GN
Thrombotic microangiopathy
Hereditary Disorders
Alport syndrome
Fabry disease
Podocyte/slit-diaphragm protein mutations

GN, glomerulonephritis; IgA, immunoglobulin A.

Glomerulonephritis Caused by In Situ Immune Complexes

Antibody deposition in the glomerulus is a major pathway of glomerular injury. As noted, antibodies in this form of injury react directly with fixed or planted antigens in the glomerulus. Immune reactions in situ, trapping of circulating complexes, interactions between these two events, and local hemodynamic and structural determinants in the glomerulus all contribute to the morphologic and functional alterations in GN. Antibodies also may react in situ with previously "planted" nonglomerular antigens, which may localize in the kidney by interacting with various intrinsic components of the glomerulus. Planted antigens include nucleosomal complexes (in patients with systemic lupus erythematosus); bacterial products, such as endostroptosin, a protein expressed by group A streptococci; large aggregated proteins (e.g., aggregated

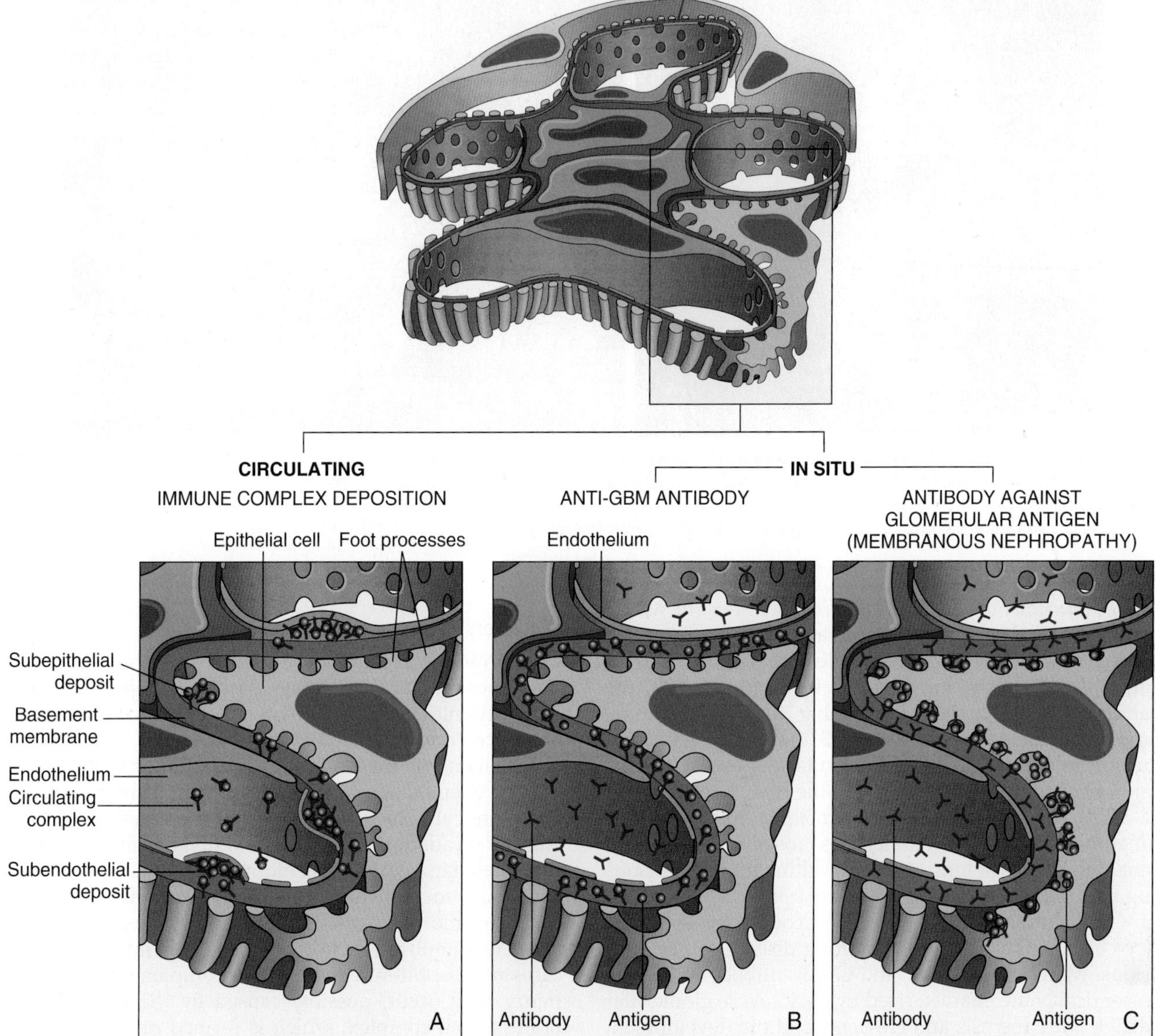

Figure 13–3 Antibody-mediated glomerular injury. Injury can result either from the deposition of circulating immune complexes or from formation of complexes in situ. **A,** Deposition of circulating immune complexes gives a granular immunofluorescence pattern. **B,** Anti-glomerular basement membrane (anti-GBM) antibody glomerulonephritis is characterized by a linear immunofluorescence pattern. **C,** Antibodies against some glomerular components deposit in a granular pattern.

immunoglobulin G [IgG]), which tend to deposit in the mesangium; and immune complexes themselves, because they contain reactive sites for further interactions with free antibody, free antigen, or complement. Most of these planted antigens induce a granular pattern of immunoglobulin deposition as seen by immunofluorescence microscopy.

The following factors affect glomerular localization of antigen, antibody, or immune complexes: the molecular charge and size of the reactants; glomerular hemodynamics; mesangial function; and the integrity of the charge-selective glomerular barrier. The localization of antigen, antibody, or immune complexes in turn determines the glomerular injury response. Studies in experimental models have shown that complexes deposited in the endothelium or subendothelium elicit an inflammatory reaction in the glomerulus with infiltration of leukocytes and exuberant proliferation of glomerular resident cells. By contrast, antibodies directed to the subepithelial region of glomerular capillaries are largely noninflammatory and elicit lesions similar to those of Heymann nephritis or membranous nephropathy (discussed later).

Anti-Glomerular Basement Membrane Antibody–Mediated Glomerulonephritis

The best-characterized disease in this group is classic anti-GBM antibody–mediated crescentic GN (Fig. 13-3, *B*). In this type of injury, antibodies are directed against fixed antigens in the GBM. It has its experimental counterpart in the nephritis of rodents called *nephrotoxic serum nephritis.* This is produced by injecting rats with anti-GBM antibodies produced by immunization of rabbits or other species with rat kidney. *Antibody–mediated GN in humans results*

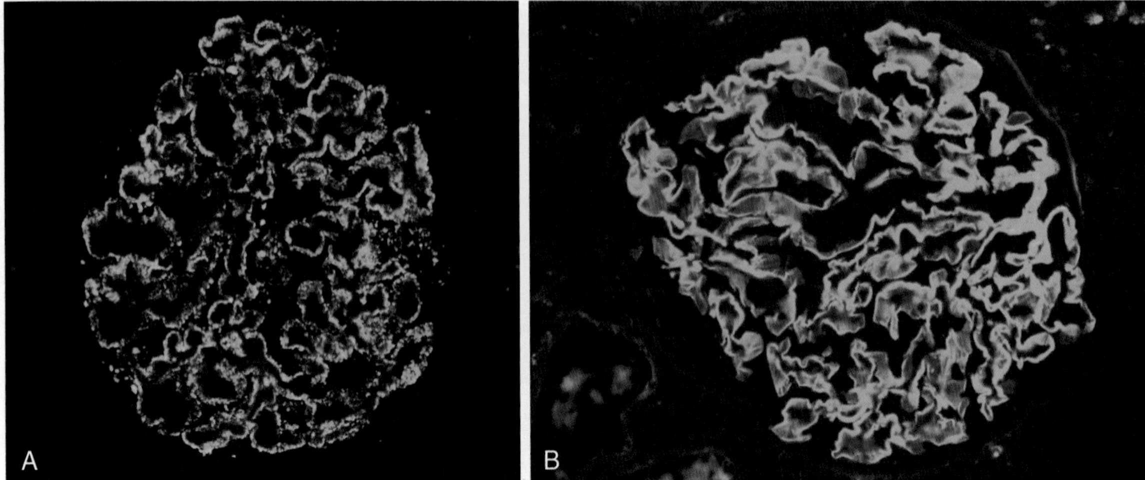

Figure 13–4 Two patterns of deposition of immune complexes as seen by immunofluorescence microscopy. **A,** Granular, characteristic of circulating and in situ immune complex deposition. **B,** Linear, characteristic of classic anti-glomerular basement membrane (anti-GBM) antibody glomerulonephritis.
(A, Courtesy of Dr. J. Kowalewska, Department of Pathology, University of Washington, Seattle, Washington.)

from the formation of autoantibodies directed against the GBM. Deposition of these antibodies creates a *linear pattern* of staining when the bound antibodies are visualized with immunofluorescence microscopy, in contrast with the granular pattern described for other forms of immune complex–mediated nephritis (Fig. 13–4, *B*). This distinction is useful in the diagnosis of glomerular disease. A conformational change in the α3 chain of the type IV collagen of the GBM appears to be key in inciting autoimmunity. Sometimes the anti-GBM antibodies cross-react with basement membranes of lung alveoli, resulting in simultaneous lung and kidney lesions (*Goodpasture syndrome*). Although anti-GBM antibody–mediated GN accounts for less than 1% of human GN cases, the resulting disease can be very serious. Many instances of anti-GBM antibody–mediated crescentic GN are characterized by very severe glomerular damage with necrosis and crescents and the development of the clinical syndrome of rapidly progressive GN (see below).

Mediators of Immune Injury

Once immune reactants are localized in the glomerulus, how does glomerular damage ensue? A major pathway of antibody-initiated injury involves complement activation and recruitment of leukocytes (Fig. 13–5). Activation of complement via the classical pathway leads to the generation of chemotactic agents (mainly C5a) for neutrophils and monocytes. Neutrophils release proteases, which cause GBM degradation; oxygen-derived free radicals, which cause cell damage; and arachidonic acid metabolites, which contribute to reduction in GFR. This mechanism applies only to some types of GN, however, because many types show few neutrophils in the damaged glomeruli. In these cases neutrophil-independent but complement-dependent injury may occur, possibly caused by the C5b-C9 membrane attack complex, which is formed on the GBM and may induce sublytic epithelial cell injury and stimulate the secretion of various inflammatory mediators from

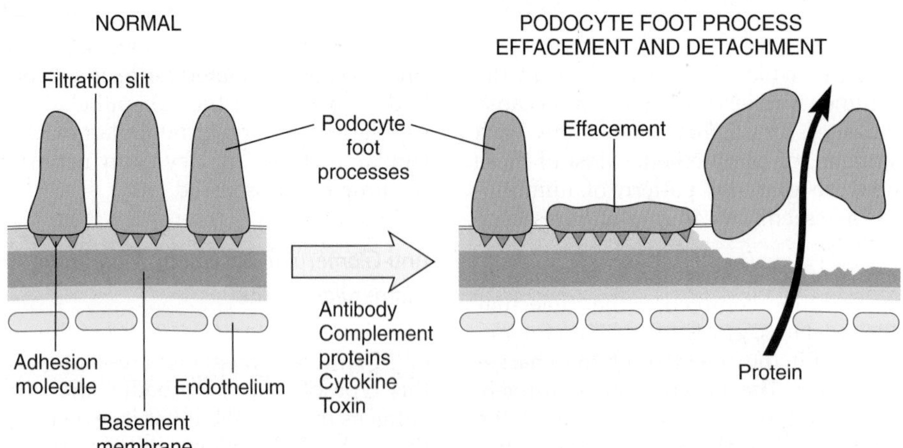

Figure 13–5 Podocyte injury. The postulated sequence may be initiated by antibodies to podocyte antigens, toxins, cytokines, or other factors. The common features are podocyte injury leading to foot process effacement and variable degrees of podocyte detachment, and degradation of the basement membrane. These defects permit plasma proteins to be lost into the urinary space.

mesangial and epithelial cells. The alternative and mannose-binding lectin pathways of complement can be activated by cell injury or apoptosis, also leading to glomerular injury (Fig. 13–5).

Antibodies against glomerular cell antigens also may directly damage glomerular cells or slit diaphragms. Such antibodies are suspected of being involved in certain disorders in which immune complexes are not found. Other mediators of glomerular damage include the following:

- *Monocytes and macrophages,* which infiltrate the glomerulus in antibody- and cell-mediated reactions and, when activated, release diverse mediators
- Sensitized T cells, formed during the course of a cell-mediated immune reaction, can cause experimental glomerular injury. In some forms of experimental GN, the disease can be induced by transfer of sensitized T cells. T cell–mediated injury may account for the instances of GN in which either there are no deposits of antibodies or immune complexes or the deposits do not correlate with the severity of damage. However, it has been difficult to establish a causal role for T cells or cell-mediated immune responses in human GN.
- *Platelets,* which aggregate in the glomerulus during immune-mediated injury and release prostaglandins and growth factors
- *Resident glomerular cells* (epithelial, mesangial, and endothelial), which can be stimulated to secrete mediators such as cytokines (interleukin-1), arachidonic acid metabolites, growth factors, nitric oxide, and endothelin
- *Thrombin,* produced as a consequence of intraglomerular thrombosis, which causes leukocyte infiltration and glomerular cell proliferation by triggering protease-activated receptors (PARs)

In essence, virtually all of the mediators described in the discussion of inflammation in Chapter 2 may contribute to glomerular injury.

Other Mechanisms of Glomerular Injury

Other mechanisms contribute to glomerular damage in certain primary renal disorders. Two that deserve special mention due to their importance are podocyte injury and nephron loss.

Podocyte Injury

Podocyte injury can be induced by antibodies to podocyte antigens; by toxins, as in an experimental model of proteinuria induced by the ribosome poison puromycin; conceivably by certain cytokines; or by still poorly characterized circulating factors, as in some cases of focal segmental glomerulosclerosis (see later). Podocyte injury is reflected by morphologic changes, which include effacement of foot processes, vacuolization, and retraction and detachment of cells from the GBM, and clinically by proteinuria. In most forms of glomerular injury, loss of normal slit diaphragms is key in the development of proteinuria (Fig. 13–5). Functional abnormalities of the slit diaphragm also may result from mutations in its structural components, such as nephrin and the associated podocin. Such mutations cause rare hereditary forms of the nephrotic syndrome.

Nephron Loss

Once renal disease, glomerular or otherwise, destroys sufficient nephrons to reduce the GFR to 30% to 50% of normal, progression to end-stage kidney disease proceeds inexorably at varying rates. Affected persons have proteinuria, and their kidneys show widespread *glomerulosclerosis.* Such progressive sclerosis may be initiated, at least in part, by the adaptive changes that occur in the remaining glomeruli not destroyed by the initial disease. These remaining glomeruli undergo hypertrophy to maintain renal function. This hypertrophy is associated with hemodynamic changes, including increases in single-nephron GFR, blood flow, and transcapillary pressure (capillary hypertension). These alterations ultimately become "maladaptive" and lead to further endothelial and podocyte injury, increased glomerular permeability to proteins, and accumulation of proteins and lipids in the mesangial matrix. This is followed by capillary obliteration, increased deposition of mesangial matrix and plasma proteins, and ultimately by segmental (affecting a portion) or global (complete) sclerosis of glomeruli. The latter results in further reductions in nephron mass and a vicious circle of progressive glomerulosclerosis.

SUMMARY

Glomerular Injury

- Antibody-mediated immune injury is an important mechanism of glomerular damage, mainly by way of complement- and leukocyte-mediated pathways. Antibodies also may be directly cytotoxic to cells in the glomerulus.
- The most common forms of antibody-mediated GN are caused by the formation of immune complexes, whether occurring in situ or by deposition of circulating immune complexes. These immune complexes may contain exogenous (e.g. microbial) circulating antigens or endogenous antigens (e.g. in membranous nephropathy). Immune complexes show a granular pattern of deposition.
- Autoantibodies against components of the GBM are the cause of anti-GBM-antibody–mediated disease, often associated with severe injury. The pattern of antibody deposition is linear.
- Immune complexes and antibodies cause injury by complement activation and leukocyte recruitment, with release of various mediators, and sometimes by direct podocyte damage.

We now turn to a consideration of specific types of GN and the glomerular syndromes they produce.

The Nephrotic Syndrome

The nephrotic syndrome refers to a clinical complex that includes

- *Massive proteinuria,* with daily protein loss in the urine of 3.5 g or more in adults
- *Hypoalbuminemia,* with plasma albumin levels less than 3 g/dL

- *Generalized edema,* the most obvious clinical manifestation
- *Hyperlipidemia and lipiduria.*

The nephrotic syndrome has diverse causes that share a common pathophysiology (Table 13–2). In all there is a derangement in the capillary walls of the glomeruli that results in increased permeability to plasma proteins. Any increased permeability resulting from either structural or physicochemical alterations in the GBM allows protein to escape from the plasma into the glomerular filtrate. With long-standing or extremely heavy proteinuria, serum albumin is decreased, resulting in hypoalbuminemia and a drop in plasma colloid osmotic pressure. As discussed in Chapter 3, the resulting decrease in intravascular volume and renal blood flow triggers increased release of renin from renal juxtaglomerular cells. Renin in turn stimulates the angiotensin-aldosterone axis, which promotes the retention of salt and water by the kidney. This tendency is exacerbated by reductions in the cardiac secretion of natriuretic factors. In the face of continuing proteinuria, these alterations further aggravate the edema and if unchecked may lead to the development of generalized edema (termed *anasarca*). At the onset, there is little or no azotemia, hematuria, or hypertension.

The genesis of the hyperlipidemia is more obscure. Presumably, hypoalbuminemia triggers increased synthesis of lipoproteins in the liver or massive proteinuria causes loss of an inhibitor of their synthesis. There is also abnormal transport of circulating lipid particles and impairment of peripheral breakdown of lipoproteins. The lipiduria, in turn, reflects the increased permeability of the GBM to lipoproteins.

Table 13–2 Causes of Nephrotic Syndrome

Cause	Prevalence (%)*	
	Children	Adults
Primary Glomerular Disease		
Membranous nephropathy	5	30
Minimal-change disease	65	10
Focal segmental glomerulosclerosis	10	35
Membranoproliferative glomerulonephritis	10	10
IgA nephropathy and others	10	15
Systemic Diseases with Renal Manifestations		
Diabetes mellitus		
Amyloidosis		
Systemic lupus erythematosus		
Ingestion of drugs (gold, penicillamine, "street heroin")		
Infections (malaria, syphilis, hepatitis B, HIV infection)		
Malignancy (carcinoma, melanoma)		
Miscellaneous (bee sting allergy, hereditary nephritis)		

*Approximate prevalence of primary disease is 95% of the cases in children, 60% in adults. Approximate prevalence of systemic disease is 5% of the cases in children, 40% in adults.
HIV, human immunodeficiency virus.

The relative frequencies of the several causes of the nephrotic syndrome vary according to age (Table 13–2). In children 1 to 7 years of age, for example, the nephrotic syndrome is almost always caused by a lesion primary to the kidney, whereas among adults it often is due to renal manifestations of a systemic disease. The most frequent systemic causes of the nephrotic syndrome in adults are diabetes, amyloidosis, and systemic lupus erythematosus. The renal lesions produced by these disorders are described in Chapter 4. The most important of the primary glomerular lesions that characteristically lead to the nephrotic syndrome are focal and segmental glomerulosclerosis and minimal-change disease. The latter is more important in children; the former, in adults. Two other primary lesions, membranous nephropathy and membranoproliferative glomerulonephritis, also commonly produce the nephrotic syndrome. These four lesions are discussed individually next.

Minimal-Change Disease

Minimal-change disease, a relatively benign disorder, is the most frequent cause of the nephrotic syndrome in children. Characteristically, the *glomeruli have a normal appearance by light microscopy but show diffuse effacement of podocyte foot processes when viewed with the electron microscope.* Although it may develop at any age, this condition is most common between the ages of 1 and 7 years.

The pathogenesis of proteinuria in minimal-change disease remains to be elucidated. On the basis of some experimental studies, the proteinuria has been attributed to a circulating, possibly T cell–derived, factor that causes podocyte damage and effacement of foot processes. Neither the nature of such a putative factor nor a causal role of T cells, however, is established in the human disease.

MORPHOLOGY

Under the light microscope, the glomeruli appear normal, thus giving rise to the name "minimal-change disease" (Fig. 13–6, *A*). The cells of the proximal convoluted tubules often are heavily laden with protein droplets and lipids, but this feature is secondary to tubular reabsorption of the lipoproteins passing through the diseased glomeruli. Even under the electron microscope, the GBM appears normal. The only obvious glomerular abnormality is the **uniform and diffuse effacement of the foot processes of the podocytes** (Fig. 13–6, *B*). The cytoplasm of the podocytes thus appears flattened over the external aspect of the GBM, obliterating the network of arcades between the podocytes and the GBM. There are also epithelial cell vacuolization, microvillus formation, and occasional focal detachments, suggesting some form of podocyte injury. With reversal of the changes in the podocytes (e.g., in response to corticosteroids), the proteinuria remits.

Clinical Course

The disease manifests with the insidious development of the nephrotic syndrome in an otherwise healthy child. There is no hypertension, and renal function is preserved in most of these patients. The protein loss usually is

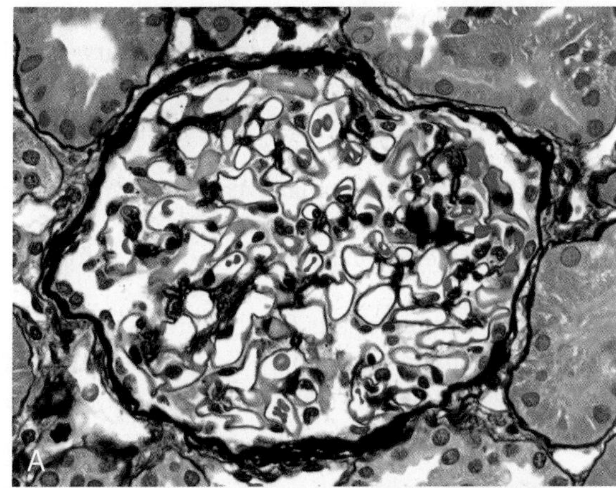

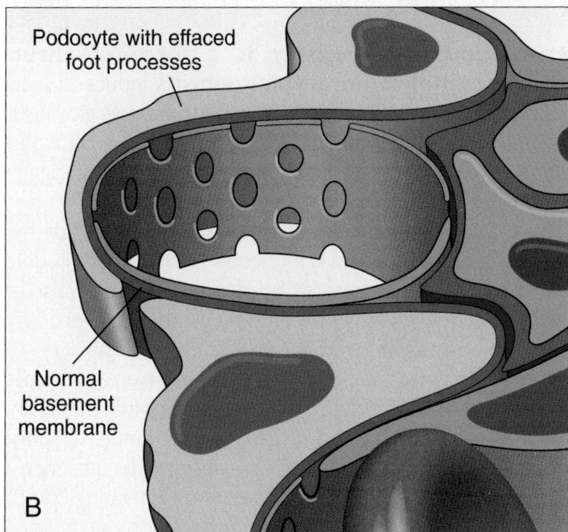

Figure 13–6 Minimal-change disease. **A,** Under the light microscope the silver methenamine–stained glomerulus appears normal, with a delicate basement membrane. **B,** Schematic diagram illustrating diffuse effacement of foot processes of podocytes with no immune deposits.

confined to the smaller plasma proteins, chiefly albumin (selective proteinuria). The prognosis for children with this disorder is good. *More than 90% of children respond to a short course of corticosteroid therapy;* however, proteinuria recurs in more than two thirds of the initial responders, some of whom become steroid-dependent. Less than 5% develop chronic kidney disease after 25 years, and it is likely that most persons in this subgroup had nephrotic syndrome caused by focal and segmental glomerulosclerosis not detected by biopsy. Because of its responsiveness to therapy in children, minimal-change disease must be differentiated from other causes of the nephrotic syndrome in nonresponders. Adults with this disease also respond to steroid therapy, but the response is slower and relapses are more common.

Focal Segmental Glomerulosclerosis

Focal segmental glomerulosclerosis (FSGS) is characterized histologically by sclerosis affecting some but not all glomeruli (*focal involvement*) and involving only segments of each affected glomerulus (*segmental involvement*). This histologic picture often is associated with the nephrotic syndrome. FSGS may be primary (idiopathic) or secondary to one of the following conditions:

- In association with other conditions, such as HIV infection (HIV nephropathy) or heroin abuse (heroin nephropathy)
- As a secondary event in other forms of GN (e.g., IgA nephropathy)
- As a maladaptation to nephron loss (as described earlier)
- In inherited or congenital forms. Autosomal dominant forms are associated with mutations in cytoskeletal proteins and podocin, both of which are required for the integrity of podocytes. In addition, a sequence variant in the apolipoprotein L1 gene (*APOL1*) on chromosome 22 appears to be strongly associated with an increased risk of FSGS and renal failure in individuals of African descent.

Primary FSGS accounts for approximately 20% to 30% of all cases of the nephrotic syndrome. It is an increasingly common cause of nephrotic syndrome in adults and remains a frequent cause in children.

PATHOGENESIS

The pathogenesis of primary FSGS is unknown. Some investigators have suggested that FSGS and minimal-change disease are part of a continuum and that minimal-change disease may transform into FSGS. Others believe them to be distinct clinicopathologic entities from the outset. In any case, **injury to the podocytes is thought to represent the initiating event of primary FSGS.** As with minimal-change disease, permeability-increasing factors produced by lymphocytes have been proposed. The deposition of hyaline masses in the glomeruli represents the entrapment of plasma proteins and lipids in foci of injury where sclerosis develops. IgM and complement proteins commonly seen in the lesion are also believed to result from nonspecific entrapment in damaged glomeruli. The recurrence of proteinuria and subsequent FSGS in a renal transplant in some patients who had FSGS, sometimes within 24 hours of transplantation, supports the idea that a circulating mediator is the cause of the podocyte damage in some cases.

MORPHOLOGY

In FSGS, the disease first affects only some of the glomeruli (hence the term ***focal***) and, in the case of primary FSGS, initially only the juxtamedullary glomeruli. With progression, eventually all levels of the cortex are affected. On histologic examination, FSGS is characterized by lesions occurring in some tufts within a glomerulus and sparing of the others (hence the term ***segmental***). Thus, the involvement is both focal and segmental (Fig. 13–7). The affected glomeruli exhibit **increased mesangial matrix, obliterated capillary lumina, and deposition of hyaline masses (hyalinosis) and lipid droplets.** In affected glomeruli, immunofluorescence microscopy often reveals nonspecific trapping of immunoglobulins, usually IgM, and complement

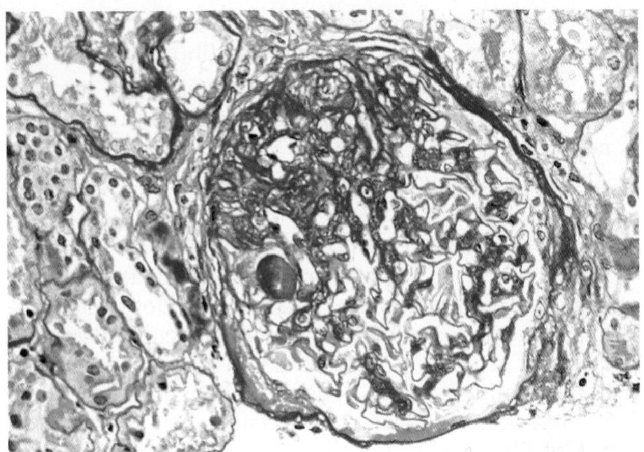

Figure 13–7 High-power view of focal and segmental glomerulosclerosis (periodic acid–Schiff stain), seen as a mass of scarred, obliterated capillary lumens with accumulations of matrix material that has replaced a portion of the glomerulus.

(Courtesy of Dr. H. Rennke, Department of Pathology, Brigham and Women's Hospital, Boston, Massachusetts.)

in the areas of hyalinosis. On electron microscopy, the podocytes exhibit **effacement of foot processes,** as in minimal-change disease.

In time, progression of the disease leads to global sclerosis of the glomeruli with pronounced tubular atrophy and interstitial fibrosis. This advanced picture is difficult to differentiate from other forms of chronic glomerular disease, described later on.

A morphologic variant called **collapsing glomerulopathy** is being increasingly reported. It is characterized by collapse of the glomerular tuft and podocyte hyperplasia. This is a more severe manifestation of FSGS that may be idiopathic or associated with HIV infection, drug-induced toxicities, and some microvascular injuries. It carries a particularly poor prognosis.

Clinical Course

In children it is important to distinguish FSGS as a cause of the nephrotic syndrome from minimal-change disease, because the clinical courses are markedly different. The incidence of hematuria and hypertension is higher in persons with FSGS than in those with minimal-change disease; the FSGS-associated proteinuria is nonselective; and in general the response to corticosteroid therapy is poor. At least 50% of patients with FSGS develop end-stage kidney disease within 10 years of diagnosis. Adults typically fare even less well than children.

Membranous Nephropathy

Membranous nephropathy is a slowly progressive disease, most common between 30 and 60 years of age. *It is characterized morphologically by the presence of subepithelial immunoglobulin-containing deposits along the GBM.* Early in the disease, the glomeruli may appear normal by light microscopy, but well-developed cases show *diffuse thickening of the capillary wall.*

In about 85% of cases, membranous nephropathy is caused by autoantibodies that cross-react with antigens expressed by podocytes. In the remainder (secondary membranous nephropathy), it occurs secondary to other disorders, including

- Infections (chronic hepatitis B, syphilis, schistosomiasis, malaria)
- Malignant tumors, particularly carcinoma of the lung and colon and melanoma
- Systemic lupus erythematosus and other autoimmune conditions
- Exposure to inorganic salts (gold, mercury)
- Drugs (penicillamine, captopril, nonsteroidal anti-inflammatory agents)

PATHOGENESIS

Membranous nephropathy is a form of chronic immune complex glomerulonephritis induced by antibodies reacting in situ to endogenous or planted glomerular antigens. An endogenous podocyte antigen, the phospholipase A_2 receptor, is the antigen that is most often recognized by the causative autoantibodies.

The experimental model of membranous nephropathy is Heymann nephritis, which is induced in animals by immunization with renal tubular brush border proteins that also are present on podocytes. The antibodies that are produced react with an antigen located in the glomerular capillary wall, resulting in granular deposits **(in situ immune complex formation)** and proteinuria without severe inflammation.

A puzzling aspect of the disease is how antigen-antibody complexes cause capillary damage despite the absence of inflammatory cells. The likely answer is by activating complement, which is uniformly present in the lesions of membranous nephropathy. It is hypothesized that complement activation leads to assembly of the C5b-C9 membrane attack complex, which damages mesangial cells and podocytes directly, setting in motion events that cause the loss of slit filter integrity and proteinuria.

MORPHOLOGY

Histologically, the main feature in membranous nephropathy is **diffuse thickening of the capillary wall** (Fig. 13–8, *A*). Electron microscopy reveals that this thickening is caused in part by **subepithelial deposits,** which nestle against the GBM and are separated from each other by small, spikelike protrusions of GBM matrix that form in reaction to the deposits **(spike and dome pattern)** (Fig. 13–8, *B*). As the disease progresses, these spikes close over the deposits, incorporating them into the GBM. In addition, as in other causes of nephrotic syndrome, the podocytes show **effacement of foot processes.** Later in the disease, the incorporated deposits may be broken down and eventually disappear, leaving cavities within the GBM. Continued deposition of basement membrane matrix leads to progressive thickening of basement membranes. With further progression, the glomeruli can become sclerosed. Immunofluorescence microscopy shows typical **granular deposits** of immunoglobulins and complement along the GBM (Fig. 13–4, *A*).

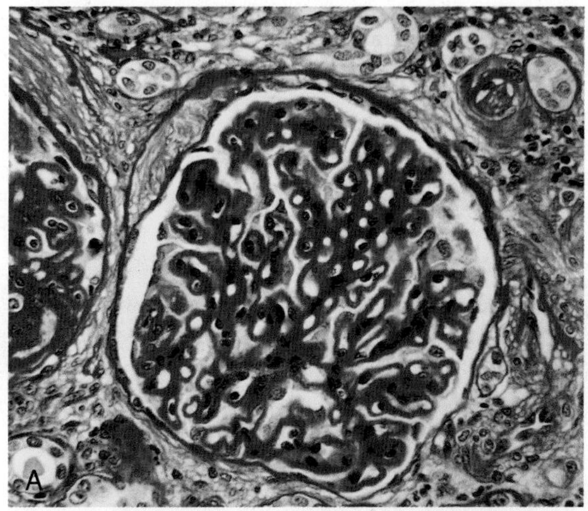

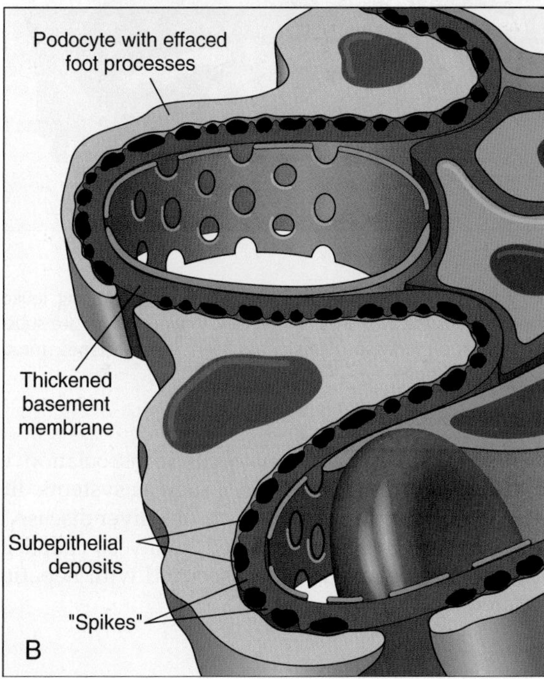

Figure 13–8 Membranous nephropathy. **A,** Diffuse thickening of the glomerular basement membrane (periodic acid–Schiff stain). **B,** Schematic diagram illustrating subepithelial deposits, effacement of foot processes, and the presence of *spikes* of basement membrane material between the immune deposits.

Clinical Course

Most cases of membranous nephropathy present as full-blown nephrotic syndrome, usually without antecedent illness; other individuals may have lesser degrees of proteinuria. In contrast with minimal-change disease, the proteinuria is nonselective, with urinary loss of globulins as well as smaller albumin molecules, and does not usually respond to corticosteroid therapy. Secondary causes of membranous nephropathy should be ruled out. Membranous nephropathy follows a notoriously variable and often indolent course. Overall, although proteinuria persists in greater than 60% of patients with membranous nephropathy, only about 40% suffer progressive disease terminating in renal failure after 2 to 20 years. An additional 10% to 30% have a more benign course with partial or complete remission of proteinuria.

Membranoproliferative Glomerulonephritis and Dense Deposit Disease

Membranoproliferative GN (MPGN) is manifested histologically by alterations in the GBM and mesangium and by proliferation of glomerular cells. It accounts for 5% to 10% of cases of idiopathic nephrotic syndrome in children and adults. Some patients present only with hematuria or proteinuria in the non-nephrotic range; others exhibit a combined nephrotic–nephritic picture. Two major types of MPGN (I and II) have traditionally been recognized on the basis of distinct ultrastructural, immunofluorescence, microscopic, and pathogenic findings, but these are now recognized to be separate entities, termed MPGN type I and dense deposit disease (formerly MPGN type II). Of the two types of disease, MPGN type I is far more common (about 80% of cases).

PATHOGENESIS

Different pathogenic mechanisms are involved in the development of MPGN and dense deposit disease.

- **Some cases of type I MPGN may be caused by circulating immune complexes,** akin to chronic serum sickness, or may be due to a planted antigen with subsequent *in situ* immune complex formation. In either case, the inciting antigen is not known. Type I MPGN also occurs in association with hepatitis B and C antigenemia, systemic lupus erythematosus, infected atrioventricular shunts, and extrarenal infections with persistent or episodic antigenemia.
- The pathogenesis of **dense deposit disease** is less clear. **The fundamental abnormality in dense deposit disease appears to be excessive complement activation.** Some patients have an autoantibody against C3 convertase, called **C3 nephritic factor,** which is believed to stabilize the enzyme and lead to uncontrolled cleavage of C3 and activation of the alternative complement pathway. Mutations in the gene encoding the complement regulatory protein **factor H** or autoantibodies to factor H have been described in some patients. These abnormalities result in excessive complement activation. Hypocomplementemia, more marked in dense deposit disease, is produced in part by excessive consumption of C3 and in part by reduced synthesis of C3 by the liver. It is still not clear how the complement abnormality induces the glomerular changes.

MORPHOLOGY

By light microscopy, type I MPGN and many cases of dense deposit disease are similar. The glomeruli are large, with an accentuated **lobular appearance,** and show **proliferation of mesangial and endothelial cells** as well as infiltrating leukocytes (Fig. 13–9, *A*). The **GBM is thickened,** and the glomerular capillary wall often shows a double contour, or "tram track," appearance, especially evident with use of silver or periodic acid–Schiff (PAS) stains. This **"splitting" of the GBM** is due to extension of processes of mesangial and inflammatory cells into the peripheral capillary loops and deposition of mesangial matrix (Fig. 13–9, *B*).

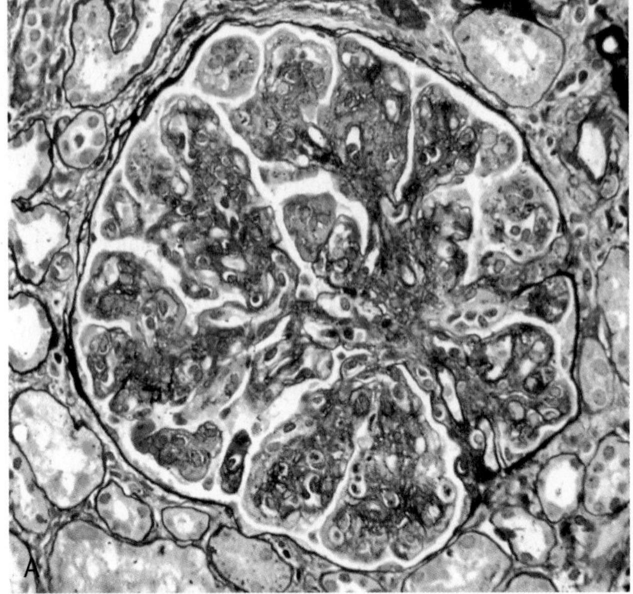

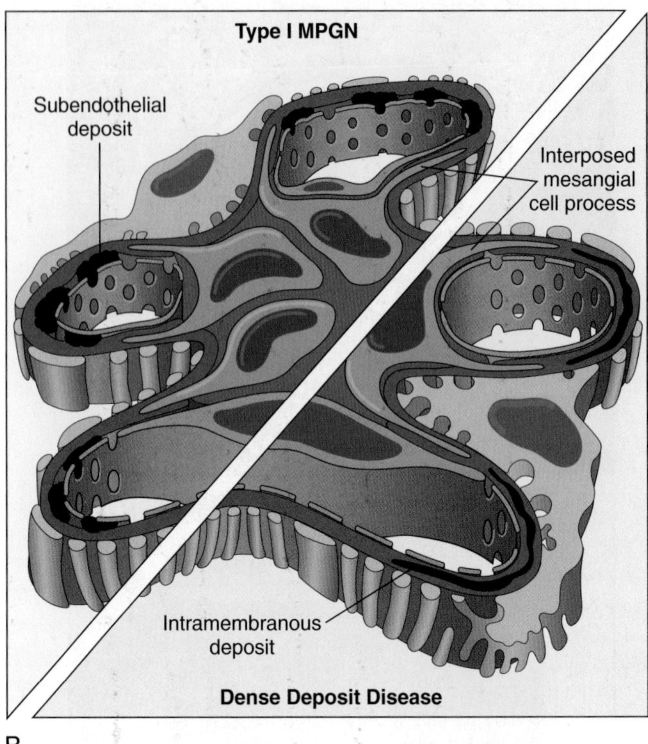

Figure 13–9 A, Membranoproliferative glomerulonephritis (MPGN), showing mesangial cell proliferation, basement membrane thickening, leukocyte infiltration, and accentuation of lobular architecture. **B,** Schematic representation of patterns in the two types of MPGN. In type I there are subendothelial deposits; in type II, now called dense deposit disease, intramembranous characteristically dense deposits are seen. In both types, mesangial interposition gives the appearance of split basement membranes when viewed by light microscopy.

Type I MPGN is characterized by discrete **subendothelial electron-dense deposits** (Fig. 13–9, *B*). By immunofluorescence microscopy, C3 is deposited in an irregular granular pattern, and IgG and early complement components (C1q and C4) often are also present, indicative of an immune complex pathogenesis.

By contrast, in the aptly named **dense deposit disease** the lamina densa and the subendothelial space of the GBM are transformed into an irregular, ribbon-like, extremely electron-dense structure, resulting from the deposition of material of unknown composition. C3 is present in irregular chunky and segmental linear foci in the basement membranes and in the mesangium. IgG and the early components of the classical complement pathway (C1q and C4) are usually absent.

Clinical Course

The principal mode of presentation (in approximately 50% of cases) is the nephrotic syndrome, although MPGN or dense deposit disease may begin as acute nephritis or mild proteinuria. The prognosis of MPGN type I generally is poor. In one study, none of the 60 patients followed for 1 to 20 years showed complete remission. Forty percent progressed to end-stage renal failure, 30% had variable degrees of renal insufficiency, and the remaining 30% had persistent nephrotic syndrome without renal failure. Dense deposit disease carries an even worse prognosis, and it tends to recur more frequently in renal transplant recipients. MPGN type I may occur in association with other disorders (*secondary MPGN*), such as systemic lupus erythematosus, hepatitis B and C, chronic liver disease, and chronic bacterial infections. Indeed, many so-called idiopathic cases are believed to be associated with hepatitis C and related cryoglobulinemia.

SUMMARY

The Nephrotic Syndrome

- The nephrotic syndrome is characterized by proteinuria, which results in hypoalbuminemia and edema.
- Podocyte injury is an underlying mechanism of proteinuria, and may be the result of nonimmune causes (as in minimal-change disease and FSGS) or immune mechanisms (as in membranous nephropathy).
- *Minimal-change disease* is the most frequent cause of nephrotic syndrome in children; it is manifested by proteinuria and effacement of glomerular foot processes without antibody deposits; the pathogenesis is unknown; the disease responds well to steroid therapy.
- *FSGS* may be primary (podocyte injury by unknown mechanisms) or secondary (e.g., as a consequence of previous glomerulonephritis, hypertension, or infection such as with HIV); glomeruli show focal and segmental obliteration of capillary lumina, and loss of foot processes; the disease often is resistant to therapy and may progress to end-stage renal disease.

- *Membranous nephropathy* is caused by an autoimmune response, most often directed against the phospholipase A_2 receptor on podocytes; it is characterized by granular subepithelial deposits of antibodies with GBM thickening and loss of foot processes but little or no inflammation; the disease often is resistant to steroid therapy.
- MPGN and dense deposit disease are now recognized to be distinct entities. MPGN is caused by immune complex deposition; dense deposit disease is a consequence of complement dysregulation. Both may present with nephrotic and/or nephritic features.

The Nephritic Syndrome

The nephritic syndrome is a clinical complex, usually of acute onset, characterized by (1) *hematuria* with dysmorphic red cells and red cell casts in the urine; (2) some degree of *oliguria and azotemia;* and (3) *hypertension.*

Although proteinuria and even edema also may be present, these usually are not as severe as in the nephrotic syndrome. The lesions that cause the nephritic syndrome have in common proliferation of the cells within the glomeruli, often accompanied by an inflammatory leukocytic infiltrate. This inflammatory reaction severely injures the capillary walls, permitting blood to pass into the urine and inducing hemodynamic changes that lead to a reduction in the GFR. The reduced GFR is manifested clinically by oliguria, fluid retention, and azotemia. Hypertension probably is a result of both the fluid retention and some augmented renin release from the ischemic kidneys.

The acute nephritic syndrome may be produced by systemic disorders such as systemic lupus erythematosus, or it may be secondary to primary glomerular disease. The latter is exemplified by acute postinfectious GN.

Acute Postinfectious (Poststreptococcal) Glomerulonephritis

Acute postinfectious GN, one of the more frequently occurring glomerular disorders, is caused by glomerular deposition of immune complexes resulting in proliferation of and damage to glomerular cells and infiltration of leukocytes, especially neutrophils. The inciting antigen may be exogenous or endogenous. The prototypic exogenous pattern is seen in poststreptococcal GN. Infections by organisms other than streptococci may also be associated with postinfectious GN. These include certain pneumococcal and staphylococcal infections as well as several common viral diseases such as mumps, measles, chickenpox, and hepatitis B and C. Endogenous antigens, as occur in systemic lupus erythematosus, also may cause a proliferative GN but more commonly result in a membranous nephropathy (see earlier) lacking the neutrophil infiltrates that are characteristic of postinfectious GN.

The classic case of poststreptococcal GN develops in a child 1 to 4 weeks after they recover from a group A streptococcal infection. Only certain "nephritogenic" strains of β-hemolytic streptococci evoke glomerular disease. In most cases, the initial infection is localized to the pharynx or skin.

PATHOGENESIS

Poststreptococcal GN is an immune complex disease in which tissue injury is primarily caused by complement activation by the classical pathway. Typical features of immune complex disease, such as hypocomplementemia and granular deposits of IgG and complement on the GBM, are seen. The relevant antigens probably are streptococcal proteins. Specific antigens implicated in pathogenesis include streptococcal exotoxin B (Spe B) and streptococcal GAPDH. Both activate the alternative complement pathway and have affinity for glomerular proteins and plasmin. It is not clear if immune complexes are formed mainly in the circulation or in situ (the latter by binding of antibodies to bacterial antigens "planted" in the GBM).

MORPHOLOGY

By light microscopy, the most characteristic change in postinfectious GN is **increased cellularity** of the glomerular tufts that affects nearly all glomeruli—hence the term **diffuse** (Fig. 13–10, *A*). The increased cellularity is caused both by proliferation and swelling of endothelial and mesangial cells and by infiltrating neutrophils and monocytes. Sometimes there is necrosis of the capillary walls. In a few cases, "crescents" (described later) may be observed within the urinary space, formed in response to the severe inflammatory injury. Electron microscopy shows deposited immune complexes arrayed as subendothelial, intramembranous, or, most often, **subepithelial "humps"** nestled against the GBM (Fig. 13–10, *B*). Mesangial deposits also are occasionally present. Immunofluorescence studies reveal scattered **granular deposits of IgG and complement** within the capillary walls and some mesangial areas, corresponding to the deposits visualized by electron microscopy. These deposits usually are cleared over a period of about 2 months.

Clinical Course

The onset of the kidney disease tends to be abrupt, heralded by malaise, a slight fever, nausea, and the nephritic syndrome. In the usual case, oliguria, azotemia, and hypertension are only mild to moderate. Characteristically, there is gross hematuria, the urine appearing smoky brown rather than bright red. Some degree of proteinuria is a constant feature of the disease, and as mentioned earlier it occasionally may be severe enough to produce the nephrotic syndrome. Serum complement levels are low during the active phase of the disease, and serum anti–streptolysin O antibody titers are elevated in poststreptococcal cases.

Recovery occurs in most children in epidemic cases. Some children develop rapidly progressive GN owing to severe injury with formation of crescents, or chronic renal disease from secondary scarring. The prognosis in sporadic cases is less clear. In adults, 15% to 50% of affected persons develop end-stage renal disease over the ensuing few years or 1 to 2 decades, depending on the clinical and histologic severity. By contrast, in children, the prevalence of chronicity after sporadic cases of acute postinfectious GN is much lower.

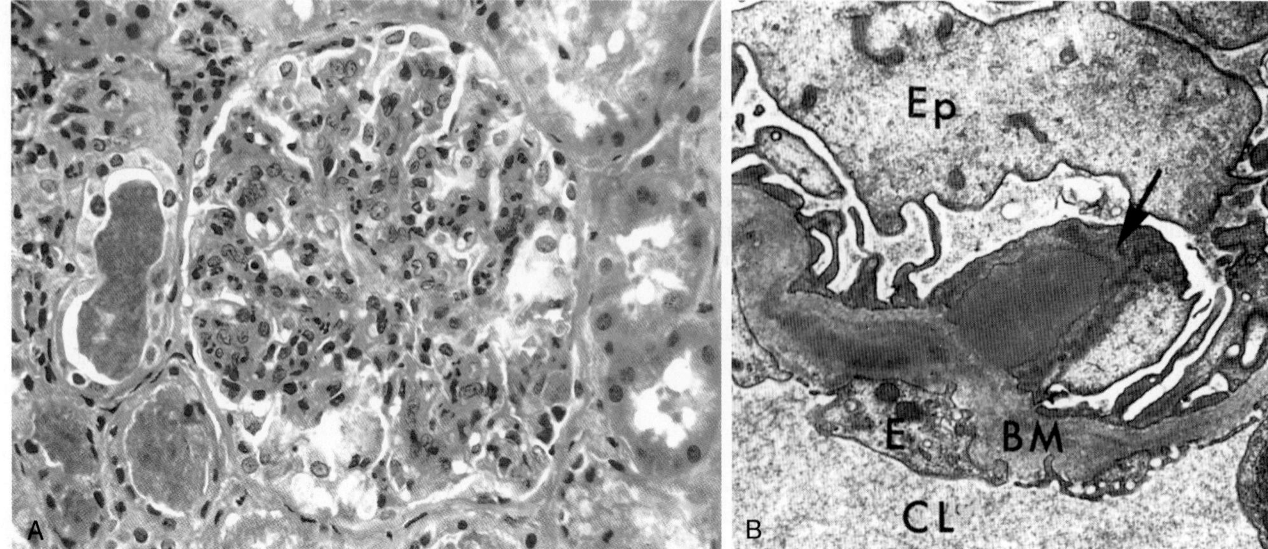

Figure 13–10 Poststreptococcal glomerulonephritis. **A,** Glomerular hypercellularity is caused by intracapillary leukocytes and proliferation of intrinsic glomerular cells. Note the red cell casts in the tubules. **B,** Typical electron-dense subepithelial "hump" (*arrow*) and intramembranous deposits. BM, basement membrane; CL, capillary lumen; E, endothelial cell; Ep, visceral epithelial cells (podocytes).

IgA Nephropathy

This condition usually affects children and young adults and begins as an episode of gross hematuria that occurs within 1 or 2 days of a nonspecific upper respiratory tract infection. Typically, the hematuria lasts several days and then subsides, only to recur every few months. It may be associated with local pain. *IgA nephropathy is one of the most common causes of recurrent microscopic or gross hematuria and is the most common glomerular disease revealed by renal biopsy worldwide.*

The hallmark of the disease is the deposition of IgA in the mesangium. Some workers have considered IgA nephropathy to be a localized variant of *Henoch-Schönlein purpura,* also characterized by IgA deposition in the mesangium. In contrast with IgA nephropathy, which is purely a renal disorder, Henoch-Schönlein purpura is a systemic syndrome involving the skin (purpuric rash), gastrointestinal tract (abdominal pain), joints (arthritis), and kidneys.

PATHOGENESIS

Accumulating evidence suggests that IgA nephropathy is associated with an abnormality in IgA production and clearance, as well as antibodies against abnormally glycosylated IgA. IgA, the main immunoglobulin in mucosal secretions, is increased in 50% of patients with IgA nephropathy owing to increased production of the IgA1 subtype by plasma cells in the bone marrow. In addition, circulating IgA-containing immune complexes are present in some cases. A genetic influence is suggested by the occurrence of this condition in families and in HLA–identical siblings, and by the increased frequency of certain HLA and complement genotypes in some populations. Studies also suggest an abnormality in glycosylation of the IgA1 immunoglobulin that reduces plasma clearance and favors deposition in the mesangium. This abnormal IgA1 may also elicit glycan-specific IgG antibodies. The prominent mesangial deposition of IgA may stem from entrapment of IgA immune complexes, and the absence of C1q and C4 in glomeruli points to activation of the alternative complement pathway. Taken together, these clues suggest that in genetically susceptible individuals, respiratory or gastrointestinal exposure to microbial or other antigens (e.g., viruses, bacteria, food proteins) may lead to increased IgA synthesis, some of which is abnormally glycosylated, and deposition of IgA and IgA-containing immune complexes in the mesangium, where they activate the alternative complement pathway and initiate glomerular injury. In support of this scenario, IgA nephropathy occurs with increased frequency in individuals with celiac disease, in whom intestinal mucosal defects are seen, and in liver disease, in which there is defective hepatobiliary clearance of IgA complexes **(secondary IgA nephropathy).**

MORPHOLOGY

Histologically, the lesions in IgA nephropathy vary considerably. The glomeruli may be normal or may show mesangial widening and segmental inflammation confined to some glomeruli (focal proliferative GN); diffuse mesangial proliferation (mesangioproliferative GN); or (rarely) overt crescentic GN. The characteristic immunofluorescence picture is of **mesangial deposition of IgA,** often with C3 and properdin and smaller amounts of IgG or IgM (Fig. 13–11). Early components of the classical complement pathway usually are absent. Electron microscopy confirms the presence of electron-dense deposits in the mesangium. The deposits may extend to the subendothelial area of adjacent capillary walls in a minority of cases, usually those with focal proliferation. Biopsy findings may help predict whether progression or response to intervention is likely.

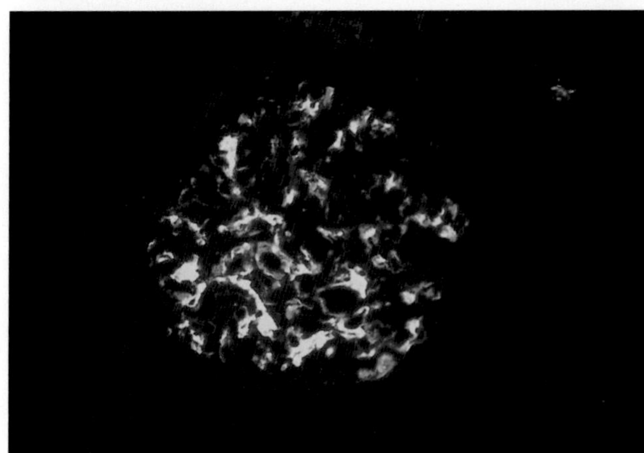

Figure 13–11 IgA nephropathy. Characteristic immunofluorescence deposition of IgA, principally in mesangial regions, is evident. IgA, immunoglobulin A.

Clinical Course

The disease most often affects children and young adults. More than half of those with IgA nephropathy present with gross hematuria after an infection of the respiratory or, less commonly, gastrointestinal or urinary tract; 30% to 40% have only microscopic hematuria, with or without proteinuria, and 5% to 10% develop a typical acute nephritic syndrome. The hematuria typically lasts for several days and then subsides, only to return every few months. The subsequent course is highly variable. Many patients maintain normal renal function for decades. Slow progression to chronic renal failure occurs in 25% to 50% of cases over a period of 20 years. Renal biopsy findings may help identify those with worse prognosis, as indicated by diffuse mesangial proliferation, segmental sclerosis, endocapillary proliferation, or tubulointerstitial fibrosis.

Hereditary Nephritis

Hereditary nephritis refers to a group of hereditary glomerular diseases caused by *mutations in genes encoding GBM proteins*. The best-studied entity is *Alport syndrome*, in which nephritis is accompanied by nerve deafness and various eye disorders, including lens dislocation, posterior cataracts, and corneal dystrophy.

PATHOGENESIS

The GBM is composed largely of type IV collagen, which is made up of heterotrimers of α3, α4, and α5 type IV collagen. This form of type IV collagen is crucial for normal function of the lens, cochlea, and glomerulus. Mutation of any one of the α chains results in defective heterotrimer assembly and, consequently, the disease manifestations of Alport syndrome.

MORPHOLOGY

On histologic examination, glomeruli in hereditary nephritis appear unremarkable until late in the course, when secondary sclerosis may occur. In some kidneys, interstitial cells take on a foamy appearance as a result of accumulation of neutral fats and mucopolysaccharides **(foam cells)** as a reaction to marked proteinuria. With progression, increasing glomerulosclerosis, vascular sclerosis, tubular atrophy, and interstitial fibrosis are typical changes. Under the electron microscope, the **basement membrane of glomeruli is thin** and attenuated early in the course. Late in the course, the GBM develops irregular foci of thickening or attenuation with pronounced splitting and lamination of the lamina densa, yielding a **"basketweave"** appearance.

Clinical Course

The inheritance is heterogeneous, being most commonly X-linked as a result of mutation of the gene encoding α5 type IV collagen. Males therefore tend to be affected more frequently and more severely than females and are more likely to develop renal failure. Rarely, inheritance is autosomal recessive or dominant, linked to defects in the genes that encode α3 or α4 type IV collagen. Persons with hereditary nephritis present at age 5 to 20 years with gross or microscopic hematuria and proteinuria, and overt renal failure occurs between 20 and 50 years of age.

Female carriers of X-linked Alport syndrome or carriers of either gender of the autosomal forms usually present with persistent hematuria, which most often is asymptomatic and is associated with a benign clinical course. In these patients, biopsy specimens show only thinning of the GBM.

SUMMARY

The Nephritic Syndrome

- The nephritic syndrome is characterized by hematuria, oliguria with azotemia, proteinuria, and hypertension.
- The most common cause is immunologically mediated glomerular injury; lesions are characterized by proliferative changes and leukocyte infiltration.
- *Acute postinfectious glomerulonephritis* typically occurs after streptococcal infection in children and young adults but may occur following infection with many other organisms; it is caused by deposition of immune complexes, mainly in the subepithelial spaces, with abundant neutrophils and proliferation of glomerular cells. Most affected children recover; the prognosis is worse in adults.
- *IgA nephropathy,* characterized by mesangial deposits of IgA-containing immune complexes, is the most common cause of the nephritic syndrome worldwide; it is also a common cause of recurrent hematuria; it commonly affects children and young adults and has a variable course.
- *Hereditary nephritis* (*Alport syndrome*) is caused by mutations in genes encoding GBM collagen; it manifests as hematuria and slowly progressing proteinuria and declining renal function; glomeruli appear normal by light microscopy until late in the disease course.

Rapidly Progressive Glomerulonephritis

Rapidly progressive glomerulonephritis (RPGN) is a clinical syndrome and not a specific etiologic form of GN. It is characterized by progressive loss of renal function, laboratory findings typical of the nephritic syndrome, and often severe oliguria. If untreated, it leads to death from renal failure within a period of weeks to months. *The characteristic histologic finding associated with RPGN is the presence of crescents* (crescentic GN).

PATHOGENESIS

Crescentic GN may be caused by a number of different diseases, some restricted to the kidney and others systemic. Although no single mechanism can explain all cases, there is little doubt that in most cases the glomerular injury is immunologically mediated. The diseases causing crescentic GN may be associated with a known disorder or it may be idiopathic. When the cause can be identified, about 12% of the patients have anti-GBM antibody–mediated crescentic GN with or without lung involvement; 44% have immune complex GN with crescents; and the remaining 44% have pauci-immune crescentic GN. All have severe glomerular injury.

Anti-Glomerular Basement Membrane Antibody–Mediated Crescentic Glomerulonephritis

Anti-GBM antibody–mediated crescentic GN is characterized by linear deposits of IgG and, in many cases, C3 on the GBM, as described earlier. In some patients, the anti-GBM antibodies also bind to pulmonary alveolar capillary basement membranes to produce the clinical picture of pulmonary hemorrhages associated with renal failure. These patients are said to have *Goodpasture syndrome,* to distinguish their condition from so-called idiopathic cases, in which renal involvement occurs in the absence of pulmonary disease. Anti-GBM antibodies are present in the serum and are helpful in diagnosis. It is important to recognize anti-GBM antibody–mediated crescentic GN, because affected persons benefit from plasmapheresis, which removes pathogenic antibodies from the circulation.

MORPHOLOGY

The kidneys are enlarged and pale, often with **petechial hemorrhages** on the cortical surfaces. Glomeruli show segmental necrosis and GBM breaks, with resulting proliferation of the parietal epithelial cells in response to the exudation of plasma proteins and the deposition of fibrin in Bowman's space. These distinctive lesions of proliferation are called **crescents** owing to their shape as they fill Bowman's space. Crescents are formed both by proliferation of parietal cells and by migration of monocytes/macrophages into Bowman's space (Fig. 13–12). Smaller numbers of other types of leukocytes also may be present. The uninvolved portion of the glomerulus shows no proliferation. Immunofluorescence studies characteristically show strong staining of linear IgG and C3 deposits along the GBM (Fig. 13–4, *B*). These antibodies typically recognize type IV collagen. Because of the diffuse distribution of type IV collagen in the glomerulus, the density of antibody : antigen complexes is not high enough for them to be seen by electron microscopy. Electron microscopy may show distinct ruptures in the GBM. The crescents eventually obliterate Bowman's space and compress the glomeruli. In time, crescents may undergo scarring, and glomerulosclerosis develops.

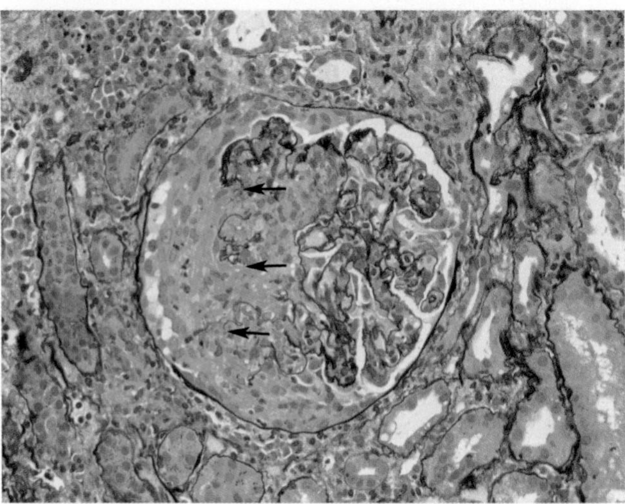

Figure 13–12 Crescentic glomerulonephritis (GN) (Jones silver methenamine stain). Note the areas of necrosis with rupture of capillary loops (*arrows*) and destruction of normal glomerular structures, and the adjacent crescent-shaped mass of proliferating cells and leukocytes filling the urinary space. The segmental distribution of the necrotizing and crescentic GN is typical of ANCA (antineutrophil cytoplasmic antibody)-associated crescentic GN.

Immune Complex–Mediated Crescentic Glomerulonephritis

Crescents can be a complication of any of the immune complex nephritides, including poststreptococcal GN, systemic lupus erythematosus, IgA nephropathy, and Henoch-Schönlein purpura. In some cases, immune complexes can be demonstrated but the underlying cause is undetermined. A consistent finding in this form of GN of any cause is the characteristic granular ("lumpy bumpy") pattern of staining of the GBM and/or mesangium for immunoglobulin and/or complement on immunofluorescence studies. This disorder usually does not respond to plasmapheresis.

MORPHOLOGY

There is severe injury in the form of **segmental necrosis** and GBM breaks with resultant crescent formation, as described earlier. However, in contrast with crescentic GN associated with anti-GBM antibodies, segments of glomeruli without necrosis show evidence of the underlying immune complex GN (e.g., diffuse proliferation and leukocyte exudation in postinfectious GN or systemic lupus erythematosus; mesangial proliferation in IgA nephropathy or Henoch-Schönlein purpura). Immunofluorescence shows the characteristic **granular pattern** of immune complex disease, and electron microscopy demonstrates discrete deposits.

Pauci-Immune Crescentic Glomerulonephritis

Pauci-immune type crescentic GN is defined by the lack of anti-GBM antibodies or of significant immune complex deposition detectable by immunofluorescence and electron microscopy. Antineutrophil cytoplasmic antibodies (ANCA) typically are found in the serum, which, as described in Chapter 9, have an etiopathogenic role in some vasculitides. In some instances, therefore, crescentic GN is a component of a systemic vasculitis such as microscopic polyangiitis or Wegener granulomatosis. In many cases, however, pauci-immune crescentic GN is limited to the kidney and is thus called idiopathic.

MORPHOLOGY

Glomeruli show **segmental necrosis** and GBM breaks with resulting crescent formation (see earlier). Uninvolved segments of glomeruli appear normal without proliferation or prominent inflammatory cell influx. In contrast with anti-GBM antibody disease, however, results of immunofluorescence studies for immunoglobulin and complement are negative or nearly so, and no deposits are detectable by electron microscopy.

Clinical Course

The onset of RPGN is much like that of the nephritic syndrome, except that the oliguria and azotemia are more pronounced. Proteinuria sometimes approaching nephrotic range may occur. Some affected persons become anuric and require long-term dialysis or transplantation. The prognosis can be roughly related to the fraction of involved glomeruli: Patients in whom crescents are present in less than 80% of the glomeruli have a better prognosis than those in whom the percentages of crescents are higher. Plasma exchange is of benefit in those with anti-GBM antibody GN and Goodpasture disease, as well as in some patients with ANCA-related pauci-immune crescentic GN.

SUMMARY

Rapidly Progressive Glomerulonephritis

- RPGN is a clinical entity with features of the nephritic syndrome and rapid loss of renal function.
- RPGN is commonly associated with severe glomerular injury with necrosis and GBM breaks and subsequent proliferation of parietal epithelium (crescents).
- RPGN may be immune-mediated, as when autoantibodies to the GBM develop in anti-GBM antibody disease or when it arises consequent to immune complex deposition; it also can be pauci-immune, associated with antineutrophil cytoplasmic antibodies.

DISEASES AFFECTING TUBULES AND INTERSTITIUM

Most forms of tubular injury also involve the interstitium, so the two are discussed together. Presented under this heading are diseases characterized by (1) inflammatory involvement of the tubules and interstitium (interstitial nephritis) or (2) ischemic or toxic tubular injury, leading to the morphologic appearance of *acute tubular injury* and the clinical syndrome of *acute kidney injury*.

Tubulointerstitial Nephritis

Tubulointerstitial nephritis (TIN) refers to a group of inflammatory diseases of the kidneys that primarily involve the interstitium and tubules. The glomeruli may be spared altogether or affected only late in the course. In most cases of TIN caused by bacterial infection, the renal pelvis is prominently involved—hence the more descriptive term *pyelonephritis* (from *pyelo,* "pelvis"). The term *interstitial nephritis* generally is reserved for cases of TIN that are nonbacterial in origin. These include tubular injury resulting from drugs, metabolic disorders such as hypokalemia, physical injury such as irradiation, viral infections, and immune reactions. On the basis of clinical features and the character of the inflammatory exudate, TIN, regardless of the etiologic agent, can be divided into acute and chronic categories. Discussed next is acute pyelonephritis, which is always of bacterial origin, followed by consideration of other, nonbacterial forms of interstitial nephritis.

Acute Pyelonephritis

Acute pyelonephritis, a common suppurative inflammation of the kidney and the renal pelvis, is caused by bacterial infection. It is an important manifestation of urinary tract infection (UTI), which can involve the lower (cystitis, prostatitis, urethritis) or upper (pyelonephritis) urinary tract, or both. As we shall see, the great majority of cases of pyelonephritis are associated with infection of the lower urinary tract. Such infection, however, may remain localized without extending to involve the kidney. UTIs constitute an extremely common clinical problem.

PATHOGENESIS

The principal causative organisms in acute pyelonephritis are the enteric gram-negative rods. *Escherichia coli* is by far the most common one. Other important organisms are *Proteus, Klebsiella, Enterobacter,* and *Pseudomonas;* these usually are associated with recurrent infections, especially in persons who undergo urinary tract manipulations or have congenital or acquired anomalies of the lower urinary tract (see later). Staphylococci and *Streptococcus faecalis* also may cause pyelonephritis, but they are uncommon pathogens in this setting.

Bacteria can reach the kidneys from the lower urinary tract (ascending infection) or through the bloodstream (hematogenous infection) (Fig. 13–13). **Ascending infection from the lower urinary tract is the most important and common route by which the bacteria reach the kidney.** Adhesion of bacteria to mucosal surfaces is followed by colonization of the distal urethra (and the introitus in females). Genetically determined properties of both the urothelium and the bacterial pathogens may facilitate adhesion to the urothelial lining by bacterial fimbriae (proteins that attach to receptors on the surface of urothelial cells), conferring susceptibility to infection. The organisms then reach the bladder, by expansive growth of the colonies and by moving against the flow of urine. This may occur during urethral instrumentation, including catheterization and cystoscopy. Although **hematogenous spread** is the far less

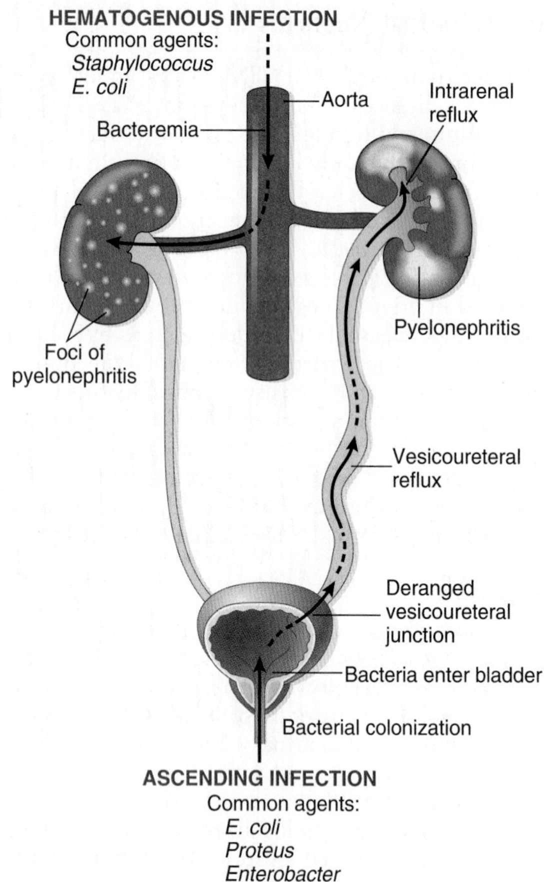

Figure 13–13 Pathways of renal infection. Hematogenous infection results from bacteremic spread. More common is ascending infection, which results from a combination of urinary bladder infection, vesicoureteral reflux, and intrarenal reflux.

common of the two, acute pyelonephritis may result from seeding of the kidneys by bacteria in the course of septicemia or infective endocarditis.

In the absence of instrumentation, UTI most commonly affects females. Because of the close proximity of the female urethra to the rectum, colonization by enteric bacteria is favored. Furthermore, the short urethra, and trauma to the urethra during sexual intercourse, facilitate the entry of bacteria into the urinary bladder. Ordinarily, bladder urine is sterile, as a result of the antimicrobial properties of the bladder mucosa and the flushing mechanism associated with periodic voiding of urine. With outflow obstruction or bladder dysfunction, however, the natural defense mechanisms of the bladder are overwhelmed, setting the stage for UTI. In the presence of stasis, bacteria introduced into the bladder can multiply undisturbed, without being flushed out or destroyed by the bladder wall. From the contaminated bladder urine, the bacteria ascend along the ureters to infect the renal pelvis and parenchyma. Accordingly, UTI is particularly frequent among patients with urinary tract obstruction, as may occur with benign prostatic hyperplasia and uterine prolapse. UTI frequency also is increased in diabetes because of the increased susceptibility to infection and neurogenic bladder dysfunction, which in turn predisposes to stasis.

Incompetence of the vesicoureteral orifice, resulting in **vesicoureteral reflux** (VUR), is an important cause of ascending infection. The reflux allows bacteria to ascend the ureter into the pelvis. VUR is present in 20% to 40% of young children with UTI, usually as a consequence of a congenital defect that results in incompetence of the ureterovesical valve. VUR also can be acquired in persons with a flaccid bladder resulting from spinal cord injury or with neurogenic bladder dysfunction secondary to diabetes. VUR results in residual urine after voiding in the urinary tract, which favors bacterial growth. Furthermore, VUR affords a ready mechanism by which the infected bladder urine can be propelled up to the renal pelvis and farther into the renal parenchyma through open ducts at the tips of the papillae **(intrarenal reflux).**

MORPHOLOGY

One or both kidneys may be involved. The affected kidney may be normal in size or enlarged. **Characteristically, discrete, yellowish, raised abscesses are grossly apparent on the renal surface** (Fig. 13–14). They may be widely scattered or limited to one region of the kidney, or they may coalesce to form a single large area of suppuration.

The characteristic histologic feature of acute pyelonephritis is liquefactive necrosis with abscess formation within the renal parenchyma. In the early stages pus formation (suppuration) is limited to the interstitial tissue, but later abscesses rupture into tubules. Large masses of intratubular neutrophils frequently extend within involved nephrons into the collecting ducts, giving rise to the characteristic white cell casts found in the urine. Typically, the glomeruli are not affected.

When obstruction is prominent, the pus may not drain and then fills the renal pelvis, calyces, and ureter, producing pyonephrosis.

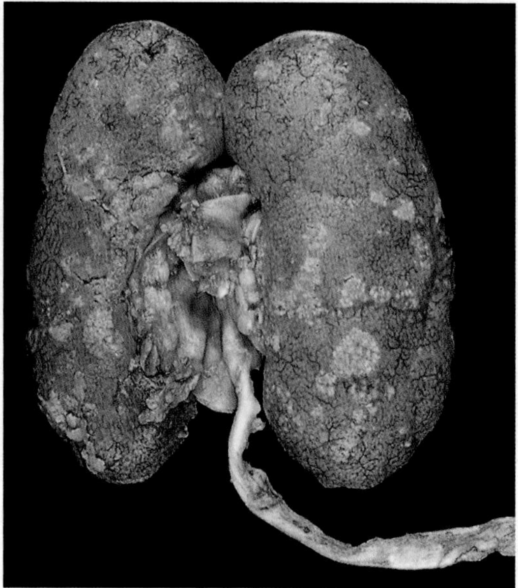

Figure 13–14 Acute pyelonephritis. The cortical surface is studded with focal pale abscesses, more numerous in the upper pole and middle region of the kidney; the lower pole is relatively unaffected. Between the abscesses there is dark congestion of the renal surface.

A second (and fortunately infrequent) form of pyelonephritis is necrosis of the renal papillae, known as **papillary necrosis.** There are three predisposing conditions for this: diabetes, urinary tract obstruction, and analgesic abuse. This lesion consists of a combination of ischemic and suppurative necrosis of the tips of the renal pyramids (renal papillae). The pathognomonic gross feature of papillary necrosis is sharply defined gray-white to yellow necrosis of the apical two thirds of the pyramids. One papilla or several or all papillae may be affected. Microscopically, the papillary tips show characteristic coagulative necrosis, with surrounding neutrophilic infiltrate.

When the bladder is involved in a UTI, as is often the case, **acute** or **chronic cystitis** results. In long-standing cases associated with obstruction, the bladder may be grossly hypertrophic, with trabeculation of its walls, or it may be thinned and markedly distended from retention of urine.

Clinical Course

Acute pyelonephritis often is associated with predisposing conditions, as described previously in the discussion of pathogenetic mechanisms. These factors include

- *Urinary obstruction,* either congenital or acquired
- *Instrumentation* of the urinary tract, most commonly catheterization
- *Vesicoureteral reflux*
- *Pregnancy*—4% to 6% of pregnant women develop bacteriuria sometime during pregnancy, and 20% to 40% of these eventually develop symptomatic urinary infection if not treated.
- *Female gender and patient age.* After the first year of life (an age by which congenital anomalies in males commonly become evident) and up to approximate age 40 years, infections are much more frequent in females. With increasing age, the incidence in males rises as a result of the development of prostatic hyperplasia, which causes urinary outflow obstruction.
- *Preexisting renal lesions,* causing intrarenal scarring and obstruction
- *Diabetes mellitus,* in which common predisposing factors are infection and bladder dysfunction
- *Immunosuppression and immunodeficiency*

The onset of uncomplicated acute pyelonephritis usually is sudden, with pain at the costovertebral angle and systemic evidence of infection, such as chills, fever, and malaise, and localizing urinary tract signs of dysuria, frequency, and urgency. The urine appears turgid due to the contained pus (pyuria). Even without antibiotic treatment, the disease tends to be benign and self-limited. The symptomatic phase of the disease typically lasts no longer than a week, although bacteriuria may persist much longer. The disease usually is unilateral, and affected persons thus do not develop renal failure because they still have one unaffected kidney. In cases in which predisposing factors are present, the disease may become recurrent or chronic, particularly when involvement is bilateral. The development of papillary necrosis is associated with a much poorer prognosis.

Chronic Pyelonephritis and Reflux Nephropathy

Chronic pyelonephritis is defined here as a morphologic entity in which predominantly interstitial inflammation and scarring of the renal parenchyma are associated with grossly visible scarring and deformity of the pelvicalyceal system. Chronic pyelonephritis is an important cause of chronic renal failure. It can be divided into two forms: chronic obstructive pyelonephritis and chronic reflux-associated pyelonephritis.

Chronic Obstructive Pyelonephritis

As noted, obstruction predisposes the kidney to infection. Recurrent infections superimposed on diffuse or localized obstructive lesions lead to recurrent bouts of renal inflammation and scarring, which eventually cause chronic pyelonephritis. The disease can be bilateral, as with congenital anomalies of the urethra (e.g., posterior urethral valves), resulting in fatal renal insufficiency unless the anomaly is corrected, or unilateral, such as occurs with calculi and unilateral obstructive lesions of the ureter.

Chronic Reflux–Associated Pyelonephritis (Reflux Nephropathy)

This is the more common form of chronic pyelonephritic scarring and results from superimposition of a UTI on congenital vesicoureteral reflux and intrarenal reflux. Reflux may be unilateral or bilateral; thus, the resultant renal damage either may cause scarring and atrophy of one kidney or may involve both, potentially leading to chronic renal insufficiency.

MORPHOLOGY

One or both kidneys may be involved, either diffusely or in patches. Even when involvement is bilateral, the kidneys are not equally damaged and therefore are not equally contracted. This **uneven scarring** is useful in differentiating chronic pyelonephritis from the more symmetrically contracted kidneys associated with vascular sclerosis (often referred to as "benign nephrosclerosis") and chronic GN. The hallmark of chronic pyelonephritis is **scarring involving the pelvis or calyces,** or both, leading to papillary blunting and marked **calyceal deformities** (Fig. 13–15).

The microscopic changes are largely nonspecific, and similar alterations may be seen with other chronic tubulointerstitial disorders such as analgesic nephropathy. The parenchyma shows the following features:

- Uneven interstitial fibrosis and an inflammatory infiltrate of lymphocytes, plasma cells, and occasionally neutrophils
- Dilation or contraction of tubules, with atrophy of the lining epithelium. Many of the dilated tubules contain pink to blue, glassy-appearing PAS-positive casts, known as colloid casts, that suggest the appearance of thyroid tissue—hence the descriptive term thyroidization. Often, neutrophils are seen within tubules.
- Chronic inflammatory cell infiltration and fibrosis involving the calyceal mucosa and wall
- Arteriolosclerosis caused by the frequently associated hypertension
- Glomerulosclerosis that usually develops as a secondary process caused by nephron loss (a maladaptation discussed earlier).

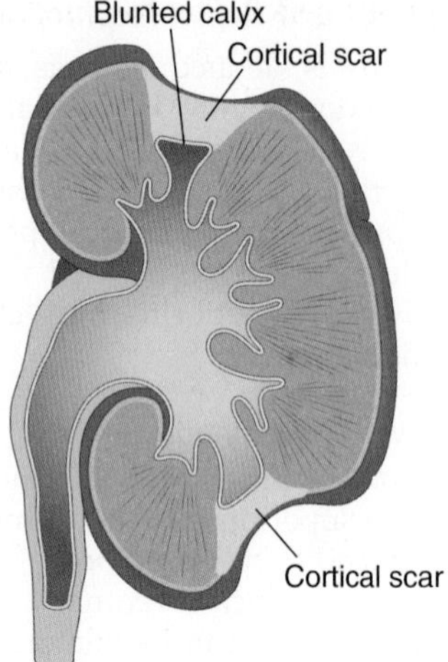

Figure 13–15 Typical coarse scars of chronic pyelonephritis associated with vesicoureteral reflux. The scars are usually located at the upper or lower poles of the kidney and are associated with underlying blunted calyces.

Clinical Course

Many persons with chronic pyelonephritis come to medical attention relatively late in the course of the disease, because of the gradual onset of renal insufficiency or because signs of kidney disease are noticed on routine laboratory tests. In other cases, the renal disease is heralded by the development of hypertension. The radiologic image is characteristic: The affected kidney is asymmetrically contracted, with some degree of blunting and deformity of the calyceal system (caliectasis). The presence or absence of significant bacteriuria is not particularly helpful diagnostically; its absence certainly should not rule out chronic pyelonephritis. If the disease is bilateral and progressive, tubular dysfunction occurs with loss of concentrating ability, manifested by polyuria and nocturia.

As noted earlier, some persons with chronic pyelonephritis or reflux nephropathy ultimately develop secondary glomerulosclerosis, associated with proteinuria; eventually, these injuries all contribute to progressive chronic kidney disease.

Drug-Induced Interstitial Nephritis

In this era of widespread antibiotic and analgesic use, drugs have emerged as an important cause of renal injury. Acute drug-induced tubulointerstitial nephritis (TIN) occurs as an adverse reaction to any of an increasing number of drugs. Acute drug-induced TIN is associated most frequently with synthetic penicillins (methicillin, ampicillin), other synthetic antibiotics (rifampin), diuretics (thiazides), nonsteroidal anti-inflammatory agents, and numerous other drugs (phenindione, cimetidine).

PATHOGENESIS

Many features of the disease suggest an immune mechanism. Clinical evidence of hypersensitivity includes latent period, eosinophilia and rash, the idiosyncratic nature of the drug reaction (i.e., the lack of dose dependency), and the recurrence of hypersensitivity after reexposure to the same drug or others that are similar in structure. Serum IgE levels are increased in some persons, suggesting type I hypersensitivity. In other cases the nature of the inflammatory infiltrate (discussed below) and the presence of positive skin tests to drugs suggest a T cell–mediated (type IV) hypersensitivity reaction.

The most likely sequence of pathogenic events is as follows: The drugs act as haptens that, during secretion by tubules, covalently bind to some cytoplasmic or extracellular component of tubular cells and become immunogenic. The resultant tubulointerstitial injury is then caused by IgE- and cell-mediated immune reactions to tubular cells or their basement membranes.

MORPHOLOGY

The abnormalities in acute drug-induced nephritis are in the interstitium, which shows pronounced edema and infiltration by mononuclear cells, principally lymphocytes and macrophages (Fig. 13–16). Eosinophils and neutrophils may be present, often in large numbers. With some drugs (e.g., methicillin, thiazides, rifampin), interstitial non-necrotizing granulomas with giant cells may be seen. The glomeruli are normal except in some cases caused by nonsteroidal anti-inflammatory agents, in which the hypersensitivity reaction also leads to podocyte foot process effacement and the nephrotic syndrome.

Clinical Course

The disease begins about 15 days (range, 2 to 40 days) after exposure to the drug and is characterized by *fever, eosinophilia* (which may be transient), *a rash* (in about 25% of persons), and *renal abnormalities.* Urinary findings include hematuria, minimal or no proteinuria, and leukocyturia (sometimes including eosinophils). A rising serum creatinine or acute kidney injury with oliguria develops in about 50% of cases, particularly in older patients. Clinical recognition of drug-induced kidney injury is imperative, because withdrawal of the offending drug is followed by recovery,

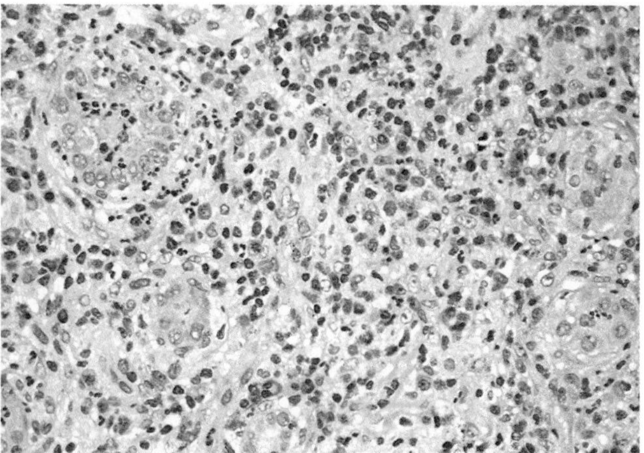

Figure 13–16 Drug-induced interstitial nephritis, with prominent eosinophilic and mononuclear infiltrate.

(Courtesy of Dr. H. Rennke, Department of Pathology, Brigham and Women's Hospital, Boston, Massachusetts.)

although it may take several months for renal function to return to normal.

SUMMARY

Tubulointerstitial Nephritis

- TIN consists of inflammatory disease primarily involving the renal tubules and interstitium.
- *Acute pyelonephritis* is a bacterial infection caused either by ascending infection as a result of reflux, obstruction, or other abnormality of the urinary tract, or by hematogenous spread of bacteria; characterized by abscess formation in the kidneys, sometimes with papillary necrosis.
- *Chronic pyelonephritis* usually is associated with urinary obstruction or reflux; results in scarring of the involved kidney, and gradual renal insufficiency.
- *Drug-induced interstitial nephritis* is an IgE- and T cell–mediated immune reaction to a drug; characterized by interstitial inflammation, often with abundant eosinophils, and edema.

Acute Tubular Injury

Acute tubular injury (ATI) is a clinicopathologic entity characterized morphologically by damaged tubular epithelial cells and clinically by acute decline of renal function, with granular casts and tubular cells observed in the urine. *This constellation of changes, termed acute kidney injury, manifests clinically as decreased GFR.* When ATI is caused by acute kidney injury, there may be oliguria (defined as urine output of less than 400 mL/day). Other causes of acute kidney injury include (1) severe glomerular diseases manifesting clinically as RPGN; (2) acute tubular injury caused by diffuse renal vascular diseases, such as microscopic polyangiitis and thrombotic microangiopathies; and (3) acute drug-induced allergic interstitial nephritis, which often is not associated with tubular injury. These other disorders involving acute kidney injury are discussed elsewhere in this chapter.

ATI arises in a variety of clinical settings, so it occurs relatively frequently. Most of these clinical conditions, ranging from severe trauma to acute pancreatitis to septicemia, have in common a period of inadequate blood flow to all or regions of peripheral organs such as the kidney, sometimes in the setting of marked hypotension and shock. The pattern of ATI associated with generalized or localized reduction in blood flow is called *ischemic ATI*. Mismatched blood transfusions and other hemolytic crises, as well as myoglobinuria, also produce a clinical picture resembling that in ischemic ATI. A second pattern, called *nephrotoxic ATI*, is caused by a variety of poisons, including heavy metals (e.g., mercury); organic solvents (e.g., carbon tetrachloride); and a multitude of drugs such as gentamicin and other antibiotics, and radiographic contrast agents. ATI is often reversible, and proper recognition and management can mean the difference between full recovery and death.

PATHOGENESIS

The decisive events in both ischemic and nephrotoxic ATI are believed to be

- Tubular injury. Tubular epithelial cells are particularly sensitive to anoxia and are also vulnerable to toxins (Fig. 13–17). Several factors predispose the tubules to toxic injury, including elevated intracellular concentrations of various molecules that are resorbed or secreted across the proximal tubule, as well as exposure to high concentrations of luminal solutes that are concentrated by the resorption of water from the glomerular filtrate.
- Persistent and severe disturbances in blood flow resulting in diminished oxygen and substrate delivery to tubular

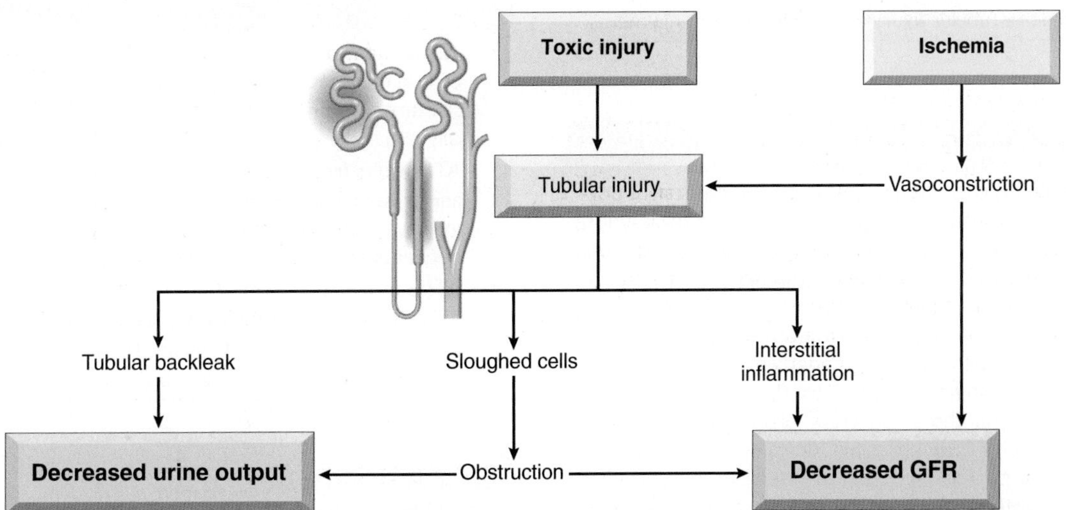

Figure 13–17 Pathophysiologic mechanisms of acute kidney injury. Various toxic injuries can directly damage tubules, which in turn directly decreases GFR and lowers urine output through multiple mechanisms. Ischemia and consequent vasoconstriction contribute directly to diminished GFR, and further contribute indirectly through injury to the tubules. Tubular cells, which are highly metabolically active and uniquely sensitive to diminished blood supply within the kidney, release several vasoconstrictor substances as part of the response to hypoxia, which then further exacerbates the overall injury.

cells. Ischemia causes numerous structural alterations in epithelial cells. **Loss of cell polarity** is an early reversible event. It leads to the redistribution of membrane proteins (e.g., Na^+,K^+-ATPase) from the basolateral to the luminal surface of tubular cells, resulting in decreased sodium reabsorption by proximal tubules and hence increased sodium delivery to distal tubules. The latter, through a tubuloglomerular feedback system, contributes to preglomerular arteriolar vasoconstriction. Redistribution or alteration of integrins that anchor tubular cells results in their detachment from the basement membranes and their shedding into the urine. If sufficient tubular debris builds up it can block the outflow of urine (obstruction by casts), increasing intratubular pressure and thereby decreasing the GFR. Additionally, fluid from the damaged tubules may leak into the interstitium (backleak), resulting in increased interstitial pressure and collapse of the tubules. Ischemic tubular cells also express chemokines, cytokines, and adhesion molecules such as P-selectin that recruit leukocytes and can participate in tissue injury (interstitial inflammation).

Ischemic renal injury also is characterized by severe hemodynamic alterations that cause reduced GFR. The major one is intrarenal **vasoconstriction,** which results in both reduced glomerular plasma flow and reduced oxygen delivery to the tubules in the outer medulla (thick ascending limb and straight segment of the proximal tubule) (Fig. 13–17). Although a number of vasoconstrictor pathways have been implicated in this phenomenon (e.g., renin-angiotensin, thromboxane A_2, sympathetic nerve activity), the current opinion is that vasoconstriction is mediated by **sublethal endothelial injury,** leading to increased release of the endothelial vasoconstrictor **endothelin** and decreased production of vasodilatory **nitric oxide and prostaglandins.** Finally, some evidence points to a direct effect of ischemia or toxins on the glomerulus, causing a reduced effective glomerular filtration surface.

In addition to vasoconstriction, the pathogenesis of ATI may involve apoptosis and necrosis of tubular cells. Dead cells may elicit an inflammatory reaction (Chapter 2) that exacerbates the tubular injury and functional derangements.

MORPHOLOGY

Ischemic ATI is characterized by lesions in the straight portions of the proximal tubule and the ascending thick limbs, but no segment of the proximal or distal tubules is spared. There is often a variety of **tubular injuries,** including attenuation of proximal tubular brush borders, blebbing and sloughing of brush borders, vacuolization of cells, and detachment of tubular cells from their underlying basement membranes with sloughing of cells into the urine. A striking additional finding is the presence of proteinaceous casts in the distal tubules and collecting ducts, which consist of Tamm-Horsfall protein (normally secreted by tubular epithelium) along with hemoglobin and other plasma proteins. When crush injuries have produced ATI, the casts also contain myoglobin. The interstitium usually shows generalized edema along with a mild inflammatory infiltrate consisting of polymorphonuclear leukocytes, lymphocytes, and plasma cells. The histologic picture in **toxic ATI** is basically similar, with some differences. Overt necrosis is most prominent in the proximal tubule, and the tubular basement membranes generally are spared.

If the patient survives for a week, epithelial regeneration becomes apparent in the form of a low cuboidal epithelial covering and mitotic activity in the surviving tubular epithelial cells. Acute kidney injury with underlying acute tubular injury as its cause may result in fibrosis rather than repair if the proximal tubular cells are arrested at G_2/M stage of the cell cycle after injury, as this arrest amplifies profibrotic mediators.

Clinical Course

The clinical course of ischemic ATI initially is dominated by the inciting medical, surgical or obstetric event. Affected patients often present with manifestations of acute kidney injury, including *oliguria and decreased GFR*. Not all patients may manifest oliguria; some will have anuria, while in others, particularly if the injury is milder, the ATI may be nonoliguric. During acute kidney injury, the clinical picture is dominated by electrolyte abnormalities, acidosis and the signs and symptoms of uremia and fluid overload. Depending upon the severity and nature of the underlying injury and comorbid conditions, the prognosis varies. In the absence of careful supportive treatment or dialysis, patients may die. When the cause of acute kidney injury is ATI, repair and tubular regeneration lead to gradual clinical improvement. With supportive care, patients who do not die from the underlying precipitating problem have a good chance of recovering renal function unless kidney disease was present at the time of the acute insult. In those with preexisting kidney disease complete recovery is less certain, and progression over time to end-stage renal disease is unfortunately too frequent.

SUMMARY

Acute Tubular Injury

- ATI is the most common cause of acute kidney injury; its clinical manifestations are electrolyte abnormalities, acidosis, uremia, and signs of fluid overload, often with oliguria.
- ATI results from ischemic or toxic injury to renal tubules, and is associated with intrarenal vasoconstriction resulting in reduced GFR and diminished delivery of oxygen and nutrients to tubular epithelial cells.
- ATI is characterized morphologically by injury or necrosis of segments of the tubules (typically the proximal tubules), proteinaceous casts in distal tubules, and interstitial edema.

DISEASES INVOLVING BLOOD VESSELS

Nearly all diseases of the kidney involve the renal blood vessels secondarily. Systemic vascular diseases, such as various forms of vasculitis, also involve renal blood vessels, and often the effects on the kidney are clinically important (Chapter 9). The kidney is intimately involved in the pathogenesis of both essential and secondary hypertension. This section covers the renal lesions associated with benign and malignant hypertension.

Arterionephrosclerosis

Arterionephrosclerosis is the term used for the thickening and sclerosis of arterial walls and the renal changes associated with benign hypertension. The characteristic morphologic alterations involve small arterioles and are called *hyaline arteriolosclerosis.* Some degree of arterionephrosclerosis, albeit mild, is present at autopsy in many persons older than 60 years of age. The frequency and severity of the lesions are increased at any age when hypertension is present.

PATHOGENESIS

Of note, many renal diseases cause hypertension, which in turn is associated with arterionephrosclerosis. Thus, this renal lesion often is superimposed on other primary kidney diseases. Similar changes in arteries and arterioles are seen in individuals with chronic thrombotic microangiopathies. Whether hypertension causes the arterionephrosclerosis, or a subtle primary microvascular renal injury causes the hypertension, which in turn accelerates the sclerosis, is unknown. Recent studies implicate mutation in the apolipoprotein L1 gene (the same gene implicated in increased risk for FSGS) as tightly linked to the high incidence of arterionephrosclerosis observed in African Americans. The mechanisms of increased risk of kidney disease are unknown, but this mutation confers protection against trypanosomal disease, so its prevalence may have been influenced by natural selection.

MORPHOLOGY

Grossly, the kidneys are **symmetrically atrophic,** each weighing 110 to 130 g. Typically the renal surface shows diffuse, fine granularity that resembles grain leather. Microscopically, the basic anatomic change is hyaline thickening of the walls of the small arteries and arterioles, known as **hyaline arteriolosclerosis.** This appears as a homogeneous, pink hyaline thickening, at the expense of the vessel lumina, with loss of underlying cellular detail (Fig. 13–18). The narrowing of the lumen results in markedly decreased blood flow through the affected vessels, with consequent ischemia in the organ served. All structures of the kidney show ischemic atrophy. In advanced cases of arterionephrosclerosis, the glomerular tufts may become sclerosed. Diffuse tubular atrophy and interstitial fibrosis are present. Often there is a scant interstitial lymphocytic infiltrate. The larger blood vessels (interlobar and arcuate arteries) show reduplication of internal elastic lamina along with fibrous thickening of the media **(fibroelastic hyperplasia)** and the subintima.

Clinical Course

This renal lesion alone rarely causes severe damage to the kidney except in persons with genetic susceptibility, such as African Americans, in whom it may lead to uremia and death. However, all patients with this lesion usually show some functional impairment, such as loss of concentrating ability or a variably diminished GFR. A mild degree of proteinuria is a frequent finding.

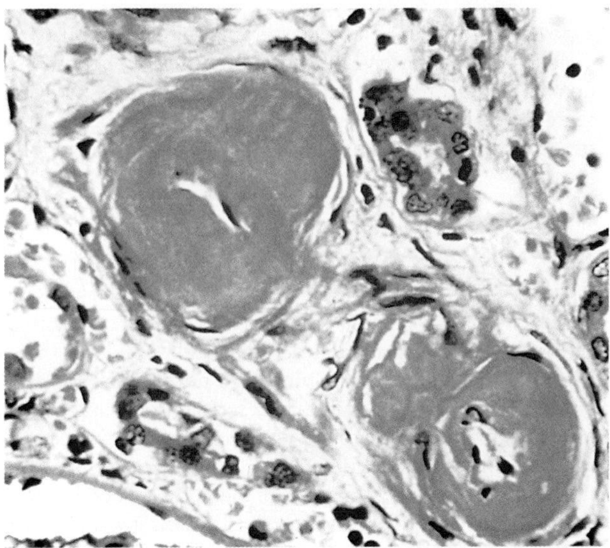

Figure 13–18 Benign nephrosclerosis. High-power view of two arterioles with hyaline deposition, marked thickening of the walls, and a narrowed lumen.

(Courtesy of Dr. M. A. Venkatachalam, Department of Pathology, University of Texas Health Sciences Center, San Antonio, Texas.)

Malignant Hypertension

Malignant hypertension, defined as blood pressure usually greater than 200/120 mm Hg, is far less common in the United States than so-called "benign" hypertension and occurs in only about 5% of persons with elevated blood pressure. It may arise de novo (i.e., without preexisting hypertension), or it may appear suddenly in a person who had mild hypertension. The prevalence of malignant hypertension is higher in less developed countries.

PATHOGENESIS

The basis for this turn for the worse in hypertensive subjects is unclear, but the following sequence is suggested: The initial event seems to be some form of vascular damage to the kidneys. This most commonly results from long-standing hypertension, with eventual injury to the arteriolar walls. The result is increased permeability of the small vessels to fibrinogen and other plasma proteins, endothelial injury, and platelet deposition. This leads to the appearance of **fibrinoid necrosis** of arterioles and small arteries and intravascular thrombosis. Mitogenic factors from platelets (e.g., platelet-derived growth factor) and plasma cause intimal hyperplasia of vessels, resulting in the **hyperplastic arteriolosclerosis** typical of organizing injury of malignant hypertension and of morphologically similar thrombotic microangiopathies (see later) and further narrowing of the lumina. The kidneys become markedly ischemic. With severe involvement of the renal afferent arterioles, the renin-angiotensin system receives a powerful stimulus. This then sets up a self-perpetuating cycle in which angiotensin II causes intrarenal vasoconstriction and the attendant renal ischemia perpetuates renin secretion. Aldosterone levels also are elevated, and the resultant salt retention exacerbates the elevation of blood pressure.

MORPHOLOGY

The kidney may be essentially normal in size or slightly shrunken, depending on the duration and severity of the hypertensive disease. Small, **pinpoint petechial hemorrhages** may appear on the cortical surface from rupture of arterioles or glomerular capillaries, giving the kidney a peculiar, **flea-bitten appearance.**

The microscopic changes reflect the pathogenetic events described earlier. Damage to the small vessels is manifested as **fibrinoid necrosis** of the arterioles (Fig. 13–19, *A*). The vessel walls show a homogeneous, granular eosinophilic appearance masking underlying detail. In the interlobular arteries and larger arterioles, proliferation of intimal cells after acute injury produces an onion-skin appearance (Fig. 13–19, *B*). This name is derived from the concentric arrangement of cells whose origin is believed to be intimal smooth muscle, although this issue has not been finally settled. This lesion, called **hyperplastic arteriolosclerosis,** causes marked narrowing of arterioles and small arteries, to the point of total obliteration. Necrosis also may involve glomeruli, with microthrombi within the glomeruli as well as necrotic arterioles. Similar lesions are seen in persons with acute thrombotic microangiopathies (described later), and in patients with scleroderma in renal crisis.

Clinical Course

The full-blown syndrome of malignant hypertension is characterized by papilledema, encephalopathy, cardiovascular abnormalities, and renal failure. Most often, the early symptoms are related to *increased intracranial pressure* and include headache, nausea, vomiting, and visual impairment, particularly the development of scotomas, or "spots" before the eyes. At the onset of rapidly mounting blood pressure there is marked proteinuria and microscopic, or sometimes macroscopic, hematuria but no significant alteration in renal function. Soon, however, *acute kidney injury develops.* The syndrome represents a true medical emergency that requires prompt and aggressive antihypertensive therapy before irreversible renal lesions develop. About 50% of patients survive at least 5 years, and further progress is still being made. Ninety percent of deaths are caused by uremia and the other 10% by cerebral hemorrhage or cardiac failure.

Thrombotic Microangiopathies

As described in Chapter 11, the term *thrombotic microangiopathy* refers to lesions seen in various clinical syndromes characterized morphologically by *widespread thrombosis in the microcirculation* and clinically by *microangiopathic hemolytic anemia, thrombocytopenia,* and, in certain instances, *renal failure.* Common causes of thrombotic microangiopathy include

- Childhood hemolytic uremic syndrome (HUS)
- Various forms of adult HUS
- Thrombotic thrombocytopenic purpura (TTP)
- Various drugs
- Malignant hypertension or scleroderma

PATHOGENESIS

The major pathogenetic factors in the thrombotic microangiopathies are endothelial activation (the dominant abnormality in HUS) and platelet activation and aggregation (which is dominant in TTP). Both may be caused by a number of external insults and inherited mutations, and together they lead to excessive small vessel thrombosis, the hallmark of these diseases.

- **Childhood HUS** is the best-characterized of the renal syndromes associated with thrombotic microangiopathy. As many as 75% of cases follow intestinal infection with Shiga toxin–producing *E. coli,* such as occurs in epidemics

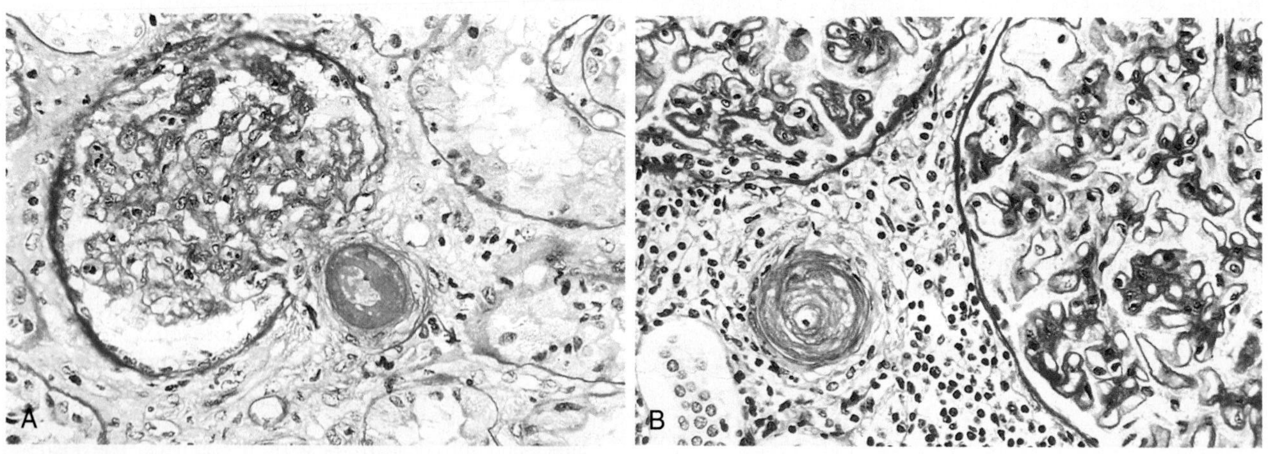

Figure 13–19 Malignant hypertension. **A,** Fibrinoid necrosis of afferent arteriole (periodic acid–Schiff stain). **B,** Hyperplastic arteriolosclerosis (onion-skin lesion).

(Courtesy of Dr. H. Rennke, Department of Pathology, Brigham and Women's Hospital, Boston, Massachusetts.)

caused by ingestion of infected ground meat (e.g., in hamburgers) and infections with *Shigella dysenteriae* type I. The pathogenesis of this syndrome is related to the effects of Shiga toxin, which is carried by neutrophils in the circulation. Renal glomerular endothelial cells are targets because the cells express the membrane receptor for the toxin. The toxin has multiple effects on the endothelium, including increased adhesion of leukocytes, increased endothelin production, and loss of endothelial nitric oxide (both favoring vasoconstriction), and (in the presence of cytokines, such as tumor necrosis factor) endothelial damage. The toxin also gains entry to the cells and directly causes cell death. The resultant endothelial damage leads to thrombosis, which is most prominent in glomerular capillaries, afferent arterioles, and interlobular arteries, as well as vasoconstriction, resulting in the characteristic thrombotic microangiopathy.

Approximately 10% of the cases of HUS in children are not preceded by diarrhea caused by Shiga toxin–producing bacteria. In a subset of these patients, mutational inactivation of complement regulatory proteins (e.g., factor H) allows uncontrolled complement activation after minor vascular injuries. These conditions promote the formation of thrombi.

- **Adult HUS.** In typical (epidemic, classic, diarrhea-positive) HUS, the trigger for endothelial injury and activation usually is a Shiga-like toxin, while in inherited forms of atypical HUS, the cause of endothelial injury appears to be excessive, inappropriate activation of complement. Many other forms of exposures and conditions, including drug toxicities, can occasionally precipitate a HUS-like picture, presumably also by injuring the endothelium.
- **TTP** often is caused by an acquired defect in proteolytic cleavage of von Willebrand factor (vWF) multimers due to autoantibodies, or more rarely, an inherited defect as seen in familial TTP (Chapter 11). Pathogenic autoantibodies, whether arising in a context of autoimmunity or drug-induced, typically are directed against ADAMTS 13 (a disintegrin and metalloprotease with thrombospondin-like motifs), a plasma protease that cleaves vWF multimers into smaller sizes. Autoantibody binding to ADAMTS 13 results in loss of function and increased levels of large vWF multimers in the circulation, which in turn can activate platelets spontaneously, leading to platelet aggregation and thrombosis. Genetic defects in ADAMTS 13 lead to a similar pattern of disease.

MORPHOLOGY

In childhood HUS, there are lesions of classic **thrombotic microangiopathy** with fibrin thrombi predominantly involving glomeruli, and extending into arterioles and larger arteries in severe cases. Cortical necrosis may be present. Morphologic changes in glomeruli resulting from endothelial injury include widening of the subendothelial space in glomerular capillaries, duplication or splitting of GBMs, and lysis of mesangial cells with mesangial disintegration. Chronically, scarring of glomeruli may develop.

Clinical Course

Typically, childhood HUS is characterized by the sudden onset, usually after a gastrointestinal or flulike prodromal episode, of bleeding manifestations (especially hematemesis and melena), severe oliguria, hematuria, microangiopathic hemolytic anemia, and (in some persons) prominent neurologic changes. *This disease is one of the main causes of acute kidney injury in children.* If the acute kidney injury is managed properly with dialysis, most patients recover in a matter of weeks. The long-term prognosis (over 15 to 25 years), however, is not uniformly favorable, because in about 25% of these children, renal insufficiency eventually develops as a consequence of the secondary scarring. Although HUS and TTP have some overlapping clinical features, such as microangiopathic hemolytic anemia and thrombocytopenia, TTP more often has dominant involvement of the central nervous system and the kidneys are less commonly involved compared to HUS.

SUMMARY

Vascular Diseases of the Kidney

- *Arterionephrosclerosis*: Progressive, chronic renal damage associated with hypertension. Characteristic features are hyaline arteriolosclerosis and narrowing of vascular lumina with resultant cortical atrophy.
- *Malignant hypertension*: Acute kidney injury associated with severe elevation of blood pressure. Arteries and arterioles show fibrinoid necrosis and hyperplasia of smooth muscle cells; petechial hemorrhages on the cortical surface.
- *Thrombotic microangiopathies*: Disorders characterized by fibrin thrombi in glomeruli and small vessels resulting in acute kidney injury. Childhood HUS is usually caused by endothelial injury by an *E. coli* toxin; TTP is often caused by defects in von Willebrand factor leading to excessive thrombosis, with platelet consumption.

CHRONIC KIDNEY DISEASE

Chronic kidney disease is the result of progressive scarring resulting from any type of kidney disease. Alterations in the function of remaining initially intact nephrons are ultimately maladaptive and cause further scarring. This eventually results in an end-stage kidney where glomeruli, tubules, interstitium and vessels are sclerosed, regardless of the primary site of injury. Unless the disorder is treated with dialysis or transplantation, death from uremia results.

MORPHOLOGY

Classically, the kidneys are **symmetrically contracted,** and their surfaces are red-brown and **diffusely granular** when the underlying disorder affects blood vessels or glomeruli. Kidneys damaged by chronic pyelonephritis are typically unevenly involved and have deep scars. Microscopically, the feature common to all cases is advanced scarring of the glomeruli, sometimes to the point of complete sclerosis (Fig. 13–20). This **obliteration of the glomeruli** is the end point of many diseases, and it is impossible to ascertain from

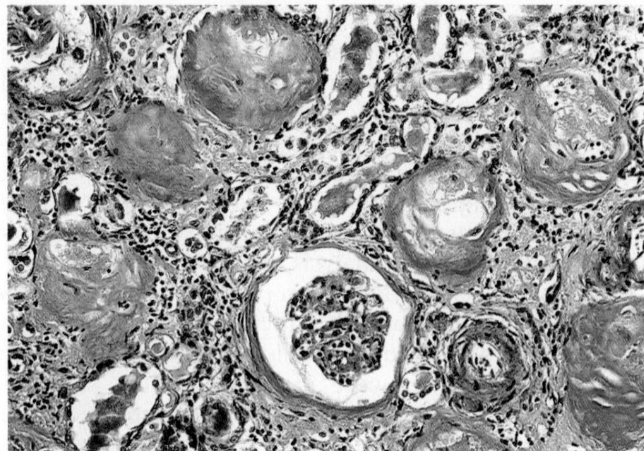

Figure 13–20 Chronic glomerulonephritis. A Masson trichrome preparation shows complete replacement of virtually all glomeruli by blue-staining collagen.

(Courtesy of Dr. M.A. Venkatachalam, Department of Pathology, University of Texas Health Sciences Center, San Antonio, Texas.)

such kidneys the nature of the initial lesion. There is also marked **interstitial fibrosis,** associated with atrophy and dropout of many of the tubules in the cortex, and diminution and loss of portions of the peritubular capillary network. The small and medium-sized arteries frequently are thick-walled, with narrowed lumina, secondary to hypertension. Lymphocytic (and, rarely, plasma cell) infiltrates are present in the fibrotic interstitial tissue. As damage to all structures progresses, it may become difficult to ascertain whether the primary lesion was glomerular, vascular, tubular, or interstitial. Such markedly damaged kidneys have been designated **end-stage kidneys.**

Clinical Course

Chronic kidney disease may sometimes develop insidiously and be discovered only late in its course, after the onset of renal insufficiency. Frequently, renal disease is first detected with the discovery of proteinuria, hypertension, or azotemia on routine medical examination. Disease-specific findings may precede development of chronic kidney disease. In patients with glomerular disease resulting in nephrotic syndrome, as the glomeruli undergo sclerotic changes, the avenue for protein loss is progressively closed, and the nephrotic syndrome thus becomes less severe with more advanced disease. Some degree of proteinuria, however, is present in almost all cases. Hypertension is very common, and its effects may dominate the clinical picture. Although microscopic hematuria is usually present, grossly bloody urine is infrequent at this late stage.

Without treatment, the prognosis is poor; relentless progression to uremia and death is the rule. The rate of progression is extremely variable.

CYSTIC DISEASES OF THE KIDNEY

Cystic diseases of the kidney are a heterogeneous group comprising hereditary, developmental, and acquired disorders. These diseases are important for several reasons:

- They are reasonably common and often present diagnostic problems for clinicians, radiologists, and pathologists.
- Some forms, such as adult polycystic disease, constitute major causes of chronic renal failure.
- Simple cysts can occasionally be confused with malignant tumors.

An emerging theme in the pathophysiology of the hereditary cystic diseases is that the underlying defect is in the cilia-centrosome complex of tubular epithelial cells. Such defects may interfere with fluid absorption or cellular maturation, resulting in cyst formation. A brief overview of simple cysts, the most common form, is presented next, followed by a more detailed discussion of polycystic kidney disease.

Simple Cysts

Simple cysts are generally innocuous lesions that occur as multiple or single cystic spaces of variable size. Commonly, they are 1 to 5 cm in diameter; translucent; lined by a gray, glistening, smooth membrane; and filled with clear fluid. On microscopic examination, these membranes are seen to be composed of a single layer of cuboidal or flattened cuboidal epithelium, which in many instances may be completely atrophic. The cysts usually are confined to the cortex. Rarely, massive cysts as large as 10 cm in diameter are encountered.

Simple cysts constitute a common postmortem finding that has no clinical significance. The main importance of cysts lies in their differentiation from kidney tumors, when they are discovered either incidentally or during evaluation of hemorrhage and pain. Radiographic studies show that in contrast with renal tumors, renal cysts have smooth contours, are almost always avascular, and produce fluid rather than solid tissue signals on ultrasonography.

Dialysis-associated acquired cysts occur in the kidneys of patients with end-stage kidney disease who have undergone prolonged dialysis. They are present in both the cortex and the medulla and may bleed, causing hematuria. Occasionally, renal adenomas or even papillary adenocarcinomas arise in the walls of these cysts.

Autosomal Dominant (Adult) Polycystic Kidney Disease

Adult polycystic kidney disease is characterized by multiple expanding cysts affecting both kidneys that ultimately destroy the intervening parenchyma. It is seen in approximately 1 in 500 to 1000 persons and accounts for 10% of cases of chronic kidney disease. This disease is genetically heterogeneous. It can be caused by inheritance of one of at least two autosomal dominant genes of very high penetrance. In 85% to 90% of families, *PKD1,* on the short arm of chromosome 16, is the defective gene. This gene encodes a large (460-kDa) and complex cell membrane-associated protein, called polycystin-1.

PATHOGENESIS

The polycystin molecule is mainly extracellular and has regions of homology with proteins involved in cell–cell or cell–matrix adhesion (e.g., domains that bind collagen, laminin, and fibronectin). It also has several other domains including those that can bind receptor tyrosine phosphatases. The polycystins have been localized to the primary cilium of tubular cells, like the nephrocystins linked to medullary cystic disease that are discussed later on, giving rise to the concept of renal cystic diseases as a type of **ciliopathy.** Cilia are hairlike organelles that project into the lumina from the apical surface of tubular cells, where they serve as mechanosensors of fluid flow. Current evidence suggests that polycystin mutations produce defects in mechanosensing. This in turn alters downstream signaling events involving calcium influx, leading to dysregulation of cell polarity, proliferation, and cell-cell and cell-matrix adhesion. It is interesting to note that whereas germline mutations of the *PKD1* gene are present in all renal tubular cells of affected persons, cysts develop in only some tubules. This is most likely due to loss of both alleles of *PKD1*. Thus, as with tumor suppressor genes, a second "somatic hit" is required for expression of the disease. The *PKD2* gene, implicated in 10% to 15% of cases, resides on chromosome 4 and encodes **polycystin 2,** a smaller, 110-kD protein. Polycystin 2 is thought to function as a calcium-permeable membrane channel, and is also expressed in cilia. Although structurally distinct, polycystins 1 and 2 are believed to act together by forming heterodimers. Thus, mutation in either gene gives rise to essentially the same phenotype, although patients with *PKD2* mutations have a slower rate of disease progression as compared with patients with *PKD1* mutations.

MORPHOLOGY

In autosomal dominant adult polycystic kidney disease, the kidney may reach enormous size, and weights of up to 4 kg for each kidney have been recorded. These **very large kidneys** are readily palpable abdominally as masses extending into the pelvis. On gross examination the kidney seems to be composed solely of a mass of cysts of various sizes up to 3 or 4 cm in diameter with no intervening parenchyma. The cysts are filled with fluid, which may be clear, turbid, or hemorrhagic (Fig. 13–21).

Cysts may arise at any level of the nephron, from tubules to collecting ducts, and therefore they have a variable, often atrophic, lining. Occasionally, Bowman's capsules are involved in the cyst formation, and in these cases glomerular tufts may be seen within the cystic space. The pressure of the expanding cysts leads to ischemic atrophy of the intervening renal substance. Some normal parenchyma may be dispersed among the cysts. Evidence of superimposed hypertension or infection is common. Asymptomatic liver cysts occur in one third of the patients.

Clinical Course

Polycystic kidney disease in adults usually *does not produce symptoms until the fourth decade of life,* by which time the kidneys are quite large, although small cysts start to develop in adolescence. The most common presenting complaint is *flank pain* or a heavy, dragging sensation. Acute distention of a cyst, either by intracystic hemorrhage or by obstruction, may cause excruciating pain. Sometimes attention is first drawn to the lesion on palpation of an abdominal mass. *Intermittent gross hematuria* commonly occurs. The most important complications, because of their deleterious effect on already marginal renal function, are *hypertension and urinary infection.* Hypertension of variable severity develops in about 75% of persons with this disorder. Saccular aneurysms of the circle of Willis (Chapter 22) are present in 10% to 30% of patients and are associated with a high incidence of subarachnoid hemorrhage.

Although the disease is ultimately fatal, the outlook is generally better than with most chronic kidney diseases. The condition tends to be relatively stable and progresses

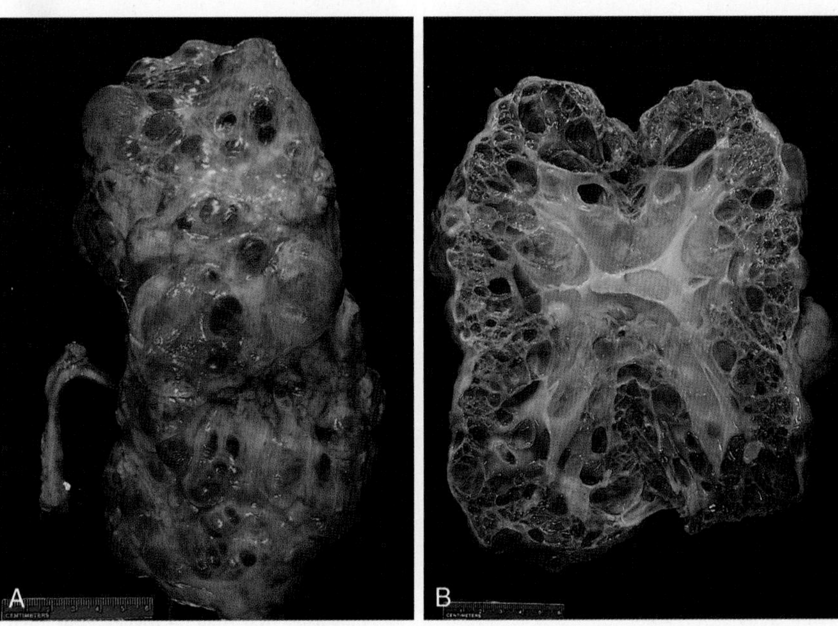

Figure 13–21 Autosomal dominant adult polycystic kidney, viewed from the external surface (**A**) and bisected (**B**). The kidney is markedly enlarged (centimeter rule is shown for scale), with numerous dilated cysts.

very slowly. End-stage kidney disease occurs at about age 50, but there is wide variation in the course of this disorder, and nearly normal life spans are reported. Patients in whom the disease progresses to renal failure are treated by renal transplantation. Death usually results from uremia or hypertensive complications.

Autosomal Recessive (Childhood) Polycystic Kidney Disease

The childhood form of polycystic kidney disease is a rare autosomal recessive disorder that is genetically distinct from adult polycystic kidney disease. It occurs in approximately 1 in 20,000 live births. Perinatal, neonatal, infantile, and juvenile subcategories have been defined, depending on age at presentation and the presence of associated hepatic lesions. All types result from mutations in the *PKHD1* gene, coding for a putative membrane receptor protein called *fibrocystin,* localized to the short arm of chromosome 6 (6p). Fibrocystin is found in cilia in tubular epithelial cells, but its function remains unknown.

MORPHOLOGY

In autosomal recessive polycystic kidney disease, **numerous small cysts** in the cortex and medulla give the kidney a spongelike appearance. Dilated, elongated channels at right angles to the cortical surface completely replace the medulla and cortex. The cysts have a uniform lining of cuboidal cells, reflecting their origin from the collecting tubules. The disease is invariably bilateral. In almost all cases, findings include multiple epithelium-lined **cysts in the liver** and proliferation of portal bile ducts.

Clinical Course

Perinatal and neonatal forms are most common; serious manifestations usually are present at birth, and young infants may die quickly from hepatic or renal failure. Patients who survive infancy develop liver cirrhosis (congenital hepatic fibrosis).

Medullary Diseases with Cysts

There are two major types of cystic disease affecting the medulla: *medullary sponge kidney,* a relatively common and usually innocuous condition, occasionally associated with nephrolithiasis, which will not be discussed further, and *nephronophthisis-medullary cystic disease complex,* which is almost always associated with renal dysfunction.

Nephronophthisis–medullary cystic disease complex is an under-appreciated cause of chronic kidney disease that usually begins in childhood. Four variants of this disease complex are recognized on the basis of the timing of onset: infantile, juvenile, and adolescent nephronophthisis and medullary cystic disease developing later in adult life. The juvenile form is the most common. Approximately 15% to 20% of children with juvenile nephronophthisis have extrarenal manifestations, which most often appear as retinal abnormalities, including retinitis pigmentosa, and even early-onset blindness in the most severe form. Other abnormalities found in some persons include oculomotor apraxia, mental retardation, cerebellar malformations, and liver fibrosis. In aggregate, the various forms of nephronophthisis are now thought to be the most common genetic cause of end-stage renal disease in children and young adults.

At least nine gene loci (NHP1-NHP9) have been identified for the autosomal recessive forms of the nephronophthisis complex. The majority of these genes encode proteins that are components of epithelial cilia, as is the case with other types of polycystic disease. Two autosomal forms cause disease in adults; these are far less common.

MORPHOLOGY

Pathologic features of medullary cystic disease include **small contracted kidneys.** Numerous small cysts lined by flattened or cuboidal epithelium are present, typically at the corticomedullary junction. Other pathologic changes are nonspecific, but most notably they include a chronic tubulointerstitial nephritis with tubular atrophy and thickened tubular basement membranes and progressive interstitial fibrosis.

Clinical Course

The initial manifestations are usually polyuria and polydipsia, a consequence of diminished tubular function. Progression to end-stage kidney disease ensues over a 5- to 10-year period. The disease is difficult to diagnose, since there are no serologic markers and the cysts may be too small to be seen with radiologic imaging. Adding to this difficulty, cysts may not be apparent on renal biopsy if the corticomedullary junction is not well sampled. A positive family history and unexplained chronic renal failure in young patients should lead to suspicion of nephronophthisis.

SUMMARY

Cystic Diseases

- *Adult polycystic kidney disease* is a disease of autosomal dominant inheritance caused by mutations in the genes encoding polycystin-1 or -2. It accounts for about 10% of cases of chronic renal failure; kidneys may be very large and contain many cysts.
- *Autosomal recessive (childhood) polycystic kidney disease* is caused by mutations in the gene encoding fibrocystin. It is less common than the adult form and strongly associated with liver abnormalities; kidneys contain numerous small cysts.
- *Nephronophthisis–medullary cystic disease complex* is being increasingly recognized as a cause of chronic kidney disease in children and young adults. Of autosomal recessive inheritance, it is associated with mutations in several genes that encode epithelial cell proteins called nephrocystins that may be involved in ciliary function; kidneys are contracted and contain multiple small cysts.

URINARY OUTFLOW OBSTRUCTION

Renal Stones

Urolithiasis is calculus formation at any level in the urinary collecting system, but most often the calculi arise in the kidney. They occur frequently, and it is estimated that by the age of 70 years, 11% of men and 5.6% of women in the United States will have experienced a symptomatic kidney stone. Symptomatic urolithiasis is more common in men than in women. A familial tendency toward stone formation has long been recognized.

PATHOGENESIS

There are three major types of stones.

- About 80% of renal stones are composed of either calcium oxalate or calcium oxalate mixed with calcium phosphate.
- Ten percent are composed of magnesium ammonium phosphate.
- Six percent to 9% are either uric acid or cystine stones.

In all cases, an organic matrix of mucoprotein is present that makes up about 2.5% of the stone by weight (Table 13–3).

The cause of stone formation is often obscure, particularly in the case of calcium-containing stones. Probably involved is a confluence of predisposing conditions, including the concentration of the solute, changes in urine pH, and bacterial infections. The **most important cause is increased urinary concentration of the stone's constituents, so that it exceeds their solubility in urine (supersaturation).** As shown in Table 13–3, 50% of patients who develop **calcium stones** have hypercalciuria that is not associated with hypercalcemia. Most in this group absorb calcium from the gut in excessive amounts **(absorptive hypercalciuria)** and promptly excrete it in the urine, and some have a primary renal defect of calcium reabsorption **(renal hypercalciuria).**

The causes of the other types of renal stones are better understood. **Magnesium ammonium phosphate (struvite) stones** almost always occur in persons with a persistently alkaline urine resulting from UTIs. In particular, infections with urea-splitting bacteria, such as *Proteus vulgaris* and staphylococci, predispose individuals to urolithiasis. Moreover, bacteria may serve as particulate nidi for the formation of any kind of stone. In avitaminosis A, desquamated cells from the metaplastic epithelium of the collecting system act as nidi.

Gout and diseases involving rapid cell turnover, such as the leukemias, lead to high uric acid levels in the urine and the possibility of **uric acid stones.** About half of people with uric acid stones, however, have neither hyperuricemia nor increased urine urate but demonstrate an unexplained tendency to excrete a persistently acid urine (with a pH less than 5.5). This low pH favors uric acid stone formation—in contrast with the high pH that favors formation of stones containing calcium phosphate. **Cystine stones** are almost invariably associated with a genetically determined defect in the renal transport of certain amino acids, including cystine. Like uric acid stones, cystine stones are more likely to form when the urine is relatively acidic.

Urolithiasis also may result from the lack of substances that normally inhibit mineral precipitation. Inhibitors of crystal formation in urine include Tamm-Horsfall protein, osteopontin, pyrophosphate, mucopolysaccharides, diphosphonates, and a glycoprotein called nephrocalcin, but no deficiency of any of these substances has been consistently demonstrated in persons with urolithiasis.

Table 13–3 Prevalence of Various Types of Renal Stones

Stone	Distribution (%)
Calcium oxalate and/or calcium phosphate	80
Idiopathic hypercalciuria (50%)	
Hypercalcemia and hypercalciuria (10%)	
Hyperoxaluria (5%)	
Enteric (4.5%)	
Primary (0.5%)	
Hyperuricosuria (20%)	
No known metabolic abnormality (15% to 20%)	
Struvite (Mg, NH_3, PO_4)	10
Renal infection	
Uric acid	6–7
Associated with hyperuricemia	
Associated with hyperuricosuria	
Idiopathic (50% of uric acid stones)	
Cystine	1–2
Others or unknown	±1–2

MORPHOLOGY

Stones are unilateral in about 80% of patients. Common sites of formation are renal pelves and calyces and the bladder. Often, many stones are found in one kidney. They tend to be small (average diameter, 2 to 3 mm) and may be smooth or jagged. Occasionally, progressive accretion of salts leads to the development of branching structures known as **staghorn calculi,** which create a cast of the renal pelvis and calyceal system. These massive stones usually are composed of magnesium ammonium phosphate.

Clinical Course

Stones may be present without producing either symptoms or significant renal damage. This is particularly true with large stones lodged in the renal pelvis. Smaller stones may pass into the ureter, where they may lodge, producing a typical intense pain known as *renal or ureteral colic,* characterized by paroxysms of flank pain radiating toward the groin. Often at this time there is *gross hematuria.* The clinical significance of stones lies in their capacity to obstruct urine flow or to produce sufficient trauma to cause ulceration and bleeding. In either case, they *predispose the sufferer to bacterial infection.* Fortunately, in most cases the diagnosis is readily made radiologically.

Hydronephrosis

Hydronephrosis refers to dilation of the renal pelvis and calyces, with accompanying atrophy of the parenchyma, caused by obstruction to the outflow of urine. The obstruction may be sudden or insidious, and it may occur at any level of the urinary tract, from the urethra to the renal pelvis. The most common causes are categorized as follows:

- *Congenital*: atresia of the urethra, valve formations in either ureter or urethra, aberrant renal artery compressing the ureter, renal ptosis with torsion, or kinking of the ureter
- *Acquired*
  - *Foreign bodies*: calculi, sloughed necrotic papillae
  - *Proliferative lesions*: benign prostatic hyperplasia, carcinoma of the prostate, bladder tumors (papilloma and carcinoma), contiguous malignant disease (retroperitoneal lymphoma, carcinoma of the cervix or uterus)
  - *Inflammation*: prostatitis, ureteritis, urethritis, retroperitoneal fibrosis
  - *Neurogenic*: spinal cord damage with paralysis of the bladder
  - *Normal pregnancy*: mild and reversible

Bilateral hydronephrosis occurs only when the obstruction is below the level of the ureters. If blockage is at the ureters or above, the lesion is unilateral. Sometimes obstruction is complete, allowing no urine to pass; usually it is only partial.

PATHOGENESIS

Even with complete obstruction, glomerular filtration persists for some time, and the filtrate subsequently diffuses back into the renal interstitium and perirenal spaces, whence it ultimately returns to the lymphatic and venous systems. Because of the continued filtration, the **affected calyces and pelvis become dilated,** often markedly so. The unusually high pressure thus generated in the renal pelvis, as well as that transmitted back through the collecting ducts, causes compression of the renal vasculature. Both arterial insufficiency and venous stasis result, although the latter probably is more important. The most severe effects are seen in the papillae, because they are subjected to the greatest increases in pressure. Accordingly, **the initial functional disturbances are largely tubular, manifested primarily by impaired concentrating ability.** Only later does glomerular filtration begin to diminish. Experimental studies indicate that serious irreversible damage occurs in about 3 weeks with complete obstruction, and in 3 months with incomplete obstruction. In addition to functional changes, the obstruction also triggers an interstitial inflammatory reaction, leading eventually to interstitial fibrosis.

MORPHOLOGY

Bilateral hydronephrosis (as well as unilateral hydronephrosis when the other kidney is already damaged or absent) leads to renal failure, and the onset of uremia tends to abort the natural course of the lesion. By contrast, **unilateral** involvement is associated with the full range of morphologic changes, which vary with the degree and speed of obstruction. With subtotal or intermittent obstruction, the kidney may be massively enlarged (lengths in the range of 20 cm), and the organ may consist almost entirely of the greatly distended pelvicalyceal system. The renal parenchyma itself is compressed and atrophied, with obliteration of the papillae and flattening of the pyramids (Fig. 13–22). On the other hand, when obstruction is sudden and complete, glomerular filtration is compromised relatively early, and as a consequence, renal function may cease while dilation is still comparatively slight. Depending on the level of the obstruction, one or both ureters may be dilated **(hydroureter).**

On microscopic examination the early lesions show tubular dilation, followed by atrophy and fibrous replacement of the tubular epithelium with relative sparing of the glomeruli. Eventually, in severe cases the glomeruli also become atrophic and disappear, converting the entire kidney into a thin shell of fibrous tissue. With sudden and complete obstruction, there may be coagulative necrosis of the renal papillae, similar to the changes of papillary necrosis. In uncomplicated cases the accompanying inflammatory reaction is minimal. Superimposed pyelonephritis, however, is common.

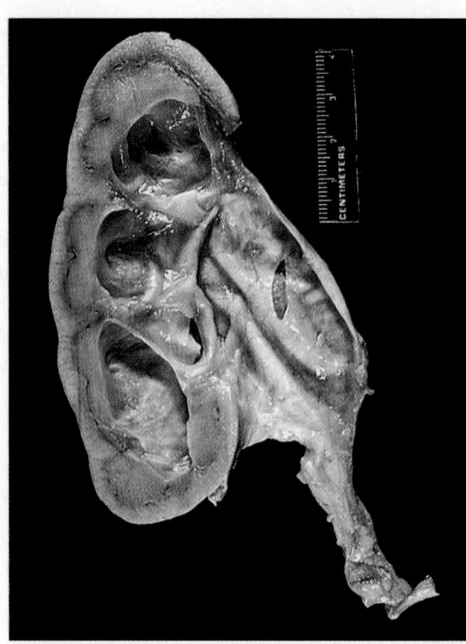

Figure 13–22 Hydronephrosis of the kidney, with marked dilation of the pelvis and calyces and thinning of renal parenchyma.

Clinical Course

Bilateral complete obstruction produces anuria, which is soon brought to medical attention. When the obstruction is below the bladder, the dominant symptoms are those of bladder distention. Paradoxically, incomplete bilateral obstruction causes polyuria rather than oliguria, as a result of defects in tubular concentrating mechanisms, and this may obscure the true nature of the disturbance. Unfortunately, *unilateral* hydronephrosis may remain completely silent for long periods unless the other kidney is for some reason not functioning. Often the enlarged kidney is discovered on routine physical examination. Sometimes the basic cause of the hydronephrosis, such as renal calculi or an obstructing tumor, produces symptoms that indirectly draw attention to the hydronephrosis. Removal of obstruction within a few weeks usually permits full return of function; however, with time the changes become irreversible.

TUMORS

Many types of benign and malignant tumors occur in the urinary tract. In general, benign tumors such as small (less than 0.5 cm in diameter) cortical papillary adenomas, which are found in 40% of adults, have no clinical significance. The most common malignant tumor of the kidney is renal cell carcinoma, followed in frequency by nephroblastoma (Wilms tumor) and by primary tumors of the calyces and pelvis. Other types of renal cancer are rare and need not be discussed here. *Tumors of the lower urinary tract are about twice as common as renal cell carcinomas.* They are described at the end of this section.

Tumors of the Kidney

Oncocytoma

Oncocytoma, a benign tumor that arises from the intercalated cells of collecting ducts, represents about 10% of renal tumors. These tumors are associated with genetic changes—loss of chromosomes 1, 14, and Y—that distinguish them from other renal neoplasms. Oncocytomas are histologically characterized by a plethora of mitochondria, providing the basis for their tan color and their finely granular eosinophilic cytoplasm that is seen histologically. A central stellate scar, which is another feature of oncocytomas, provides a characteristic appearance on imaging studies. Owing to their large size and clinical and radiologic similarity to some renal cell carcinomas, however, they are removed by nephrectomy, both to prevent such complications as spontaneous hemorrhage and to make a definitive diagnosis.

Renal Cell Carcinoma

Renal cell carcinomas are derived from the renal tubular epithelium and hence they are located predominantly in the cortex. These tumors represent 80% to 85% of all primary malignant tumors of the kidney and 2% to 3% of all cancers in adults. These data translate into about 58,000 cases per year in the United States; 40% of patients die of the disease. Carcinomas of the kidney are most common from the sixth to seventh decades, and men are affected about twice as commonly as women. The risk of developing these tumors is higher in smokers, hypertensive or obese patients, and those who have had occupational exposure to cadmium. The risk of developing renal cell cancer is increased 30-fold in persons who acquire polycystic disease as a complication of chronic dialysis. The role of genetic factors in the causation of these cancers is discussed later on.

Renal cell cancers are classified on the basis of morphology and growth patterns. However, recent advances in the understanding of the genetic basis of renal carcinomas have led to a new classification that takes into account the molecular origins of these tumors. The three most common forms, discussed next, are clear cell carcinoma, papillary renal cell carcinoma, and chromophobe renal carcinoma.

Clear Cell Carcinomas

Clear cell carcinomas are the most common type, accounting for 65% of renal cell cancers. Histologically, they are composed of cells with clear cytoplasm. Although most are sporadic, they also occur in familial forms or in association with von Hippel-Lindau (VHL) disease. It is the study of VHL disease that has provided molecular insights into the causation of clear cell carcinomas. VHL disease is inherited as an autosomal dominant trait and is characterized by predisposition to a variety of neoplasms, but particularly to hemangioblastomas of the cerebellum and retina. Hundreds of bilateral renal cysts and bilateral, often multiple, clear cell carcinomas develop in 40% to 60% of affected persons. Those with VHL syndrome inherit a germline mutation of the *VHL* gene on chromosomal band 3p25 and lose the second allele by somatic mutation. Thus, the loss of both copies of this tumor suppressor gene is a key step in the development of clear cell carcinoma. The *VHL* gene is also involved in the majority of sporadic clear cell carcinomas. Cytogenetic abnormalities giving rise to loss of chromosomal segment 3p14 to 3p26 are often seen in sporadic renal cell cancers. This region harbors the *VHL* gene (3p25.3). The second, nondeleted allele is inactivated by a somatic mutation or hypermethylation in 60% of sporadic cases. Thus, homozygous loss of the *VHL* gene seems to be the common underlying molecular abnormality in both sporadic and familial forms of clear cell carcinomas. The VHL protein causes the degradation of hypoxia-induced factors (HIFs), and in the absence of VHL, HIFs are stabilized. HIFs are transcription factors that contribute to carcinogenesis by stimulating the expression of vascular endothelial growth factor (VEGF), an important angiogenic factor, as well as a number of other genes that drive tumor cell growth (Chapter 5). An uncommon familial form of clear cell carcinoma unrelated to VHL disease also is associated with cytogenetic abnormalities involving the short arm of chromosome 3 (3p). In addition, recent deep sequencing of clear cell carcinoma genomes has revealed frequent loss-of-function mutations in *SETD2*, *JARID1C*, and *UTX*, all of which encode proteins that regulate histone methylation, suggesting that changes in the "epigenome" have a central role in the genesis of this subtype of renal carcinoma.

Papillary Renal Cell Carcinomas

Papillary renal cell carcinomas account for 10% to 15% of all renal cancers. As the name indicates, they show a papillary growth pattern. These tumors are frequently multifocal and bilateral and appear as early-stage tumors. Like clear cell carcinomas, they occur in familial and sporadic forms, but unlike these tumors, papillary renal cancers are not associated with abnormalities of chromosome 3. The culprit in most cases of hereditary papillary renal cell cancers is the *MET* proto-oncogene, located on chromosomal sub-band 7q31. The *MET* gene is a tyrosine kinase receptor for the growth factor called hepatocyte growth factor. The increased dosage of the *MET* gene due to duplications of chromosome 7 seems to spur abnormal growth in the proximal tubular epithelial cell precursors of papillary carcinomas. In familial cases, genetic analysis shows activating mutations of *MET* in the germline, along with increased gene dosage in the cancers. Activating mutations of the *MET* gene also are found in a subset of patients with sporadic forms of papillary renal cell carcinoma.

Chromophobe Renal Carcinomas

Chromophobe renal carcinomas are the least common, representing 5% of all renal cell carcinomas. They arise from intercalated cells of collecting ducts. Their name derives from the observation that the tumor cells stain more darkly (i.e., they are less clear) than cells in clear cell carcinomas. These tumors are unique in having multiple losses of entire chromosomes, including chromosomes 1, 2, 6, 10, 13, 17, and 21. Thus, they show extreme hypodiploidy. Because of multiple losses, the "critical hit" has not been determined. In general, chromophobe renal cancers have a good prognosis.

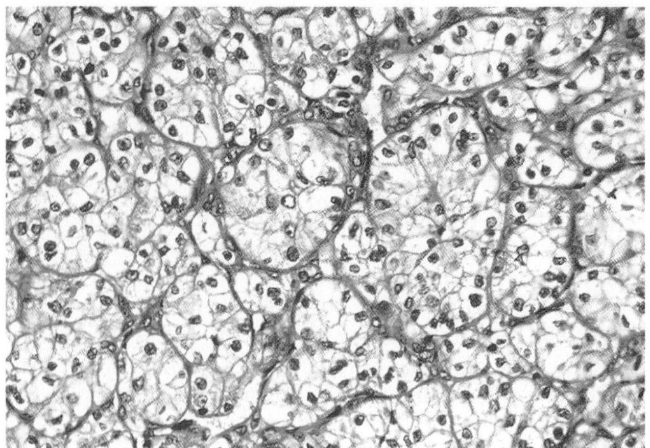

Figure 13–24 High-power detail of the clear cell pattern of renal cell carcinoma.

MORPHOLOGY

Clear cell cancers (the most common form of these renal carcinomas) usually are solitary and large when symptomatic (spherical masses 3 to 15 cm in diameter), but high-resolution radiographic techniques for investigation of unrelated problems sometimes detect smaller lesions incidentally. They may arise anywhere in the cortex. The cut surface of clear cell renal cell carcinomas is **yellow to orange to gray-white, with prominent areas of cystic softening or of hemorrhage,** either fresh or old (Fig. 13–23). The margins of the tumor are well defined. However, at times small processes project into the surrounding parenchyma and small satellite nodules are found, providing clear evidence of the aggressiveness of these lesions. As the tumor enlarges, it may fungate through the walls of the collecting system, extending through the calyces and pelvis as far as the ureter. Even more frequently, the **tumor invades the renal vein** and grows as a solid column within this vessel, sometimes extending in serpentine fashion as far as the inferior vena cava and even into the right side of the heart. Occasionally, direct invasion into the perinephric fat and adrenal gland may be seen.

Depending on the amounts of lipid and glycogen present, **the tumor cells of clear cell renal cell carcinoma may appear almost vacuolated or may be solid.** The classic vacuolated (lipid-laden), or clear cells are demarcated only by their cell membranes. The nuclei are usually small and round (Fig. 13–24). At the other extreme are granular cells, resembling the tubular epithelium, which have small, round, regular nuclei enclosed within granular pink cytoplasm. Some tumors are highly anaplastic, with numerous mitotic figures and markedly enlarged, hyperchromatic, pleomorphic nuclei. Between the extremes of clear cells and solid, granular cells, all intergradations may be found. The cellular arrangement, too, varies widely. The cells may form abortive tubules or may cluster in cords or disorganized masses. The stroma is usually scant but highly vascularized.

Papillary renal cell carcinomas exhibit various degrees of papilla formation with fibrovascular cores. They tend to be bilateral and multiple. They also may show gross evidence of necrosis, hemorrhage, and cystic degeneration, but they are less vibrantly orange-yellow because of their lower lipid content. The cells may have clear or, more commonly, pink cytoplasm. **Chromophobe-type renal cell carcinoma** tends to be grossly tan-brown. The cells usually have clear, flocculent cytoplasm with very prominent, distinct cell membranes. The nuclei are surrounded by halos of clear cytoplasm. Ultrastructurally, large numbers of characteristic macrovesicles are seen.

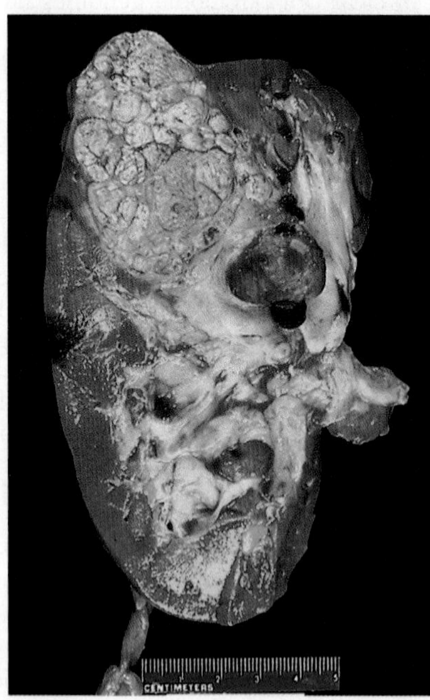

Figure 13–23 Renal cell carcinoma: Representative cross-section showing yellowish, spherical neoplasm in one pole of the kidney. Note the tumor in the dilated, thrombosed renal vein.

Clinical Course

Renal cell carcinomas have several peculiar clinical characteristics that create especially difficult and challenging diagnostic problems. The signs and symptoms vary, but the *most frequent presenting manifestation is hematuria, occurring in more than 50% of cases.* Macroscopic hematuria tends to be intermittent and fleeting, superimposed on a steady microscopic hematuria. Less commonly the tumor may declare itself simply by virtue of its size, when it has grown large enough to produce flank pain and a *palpable mass.* Because of the widespread use of imaging studies for unrelated conditions, even smaller tumors are detected. Extra-renal effects are *fever* and *polycythemia,* which, because they are nonspecific, may be misinterpreted for some time before their association with the renal tumor is appreciated. Polycythemia affects 5% to 10% of persons with this disease. It results from elaboration of erythropoietin by the cancer cells. Uncommonly, these tumors produce other hormone-like substances, resulting in hypercalcemia, hypertension, Cushing syndrome, or feminization or masculinization. These, as noted in Chapter 5, are *paraneoplastic syndromes*. In many patients, the primary tumor remains silent and is discovered only after its metastases have produced symptoms. The prevalent locations for metastases are the lungs and the bones. It must be apparent that renal cell carcinoma manifests in many ways, some quite devious, *but the triad of painless hematuria, a palpable abdominal mass, and dull flank pain is characteristic.*

SUMMARY

Renal Cell Carcinoma

Renal cell carcinomas account for 2% to 3% of all cancers in adults and are classified into three types:

- *Clear cell carcinomas* are the most common and are associated with homozygous loss of the VHL tumor suppressor protein; tumors frequently invade the renal vein.
- *Papillary renal cell carcinomas* frequently are associated with increased expression and activating mutations of the *MET* oncogene; they tend to be bilateral and multiple and show variable papilla formation.
- *Chromophobe renal cell carcinomas* are less common; tumor cells are not as clear as in the other renal cell carcinomas.

Wilms Tumor

Although Wilms tumor occurs infrequently in adults, it is the third most common organ cancer in children younger than 10 years of age. These tumors contain a variety of cell and tissue components, all derived from the mesoderm. Wilms tumor, like retinoblastoma, may arise sporadically or be familial, with the susceptibility to tumorigenesis inherited as an autosomal dominant trait. This tumor is discussed in greater detail in Chapter 6 along with other tumors of childhood.

Tumors and other lesions of the lower urinary tract (ureters, bladder, and urethra) are described in Chapter 17.

BIBLIOGRAPHY

Barratt J, Feehally J: IgA nephropathy. J Am Soc Nephrol 16:2088, 2005. *[A comprehensive update on the pathogenesis, clinical manifestations, and treatment of this disease.]*

Beck LH Jr, Bonegio RG, Lambeau G, et al: M-type phospholipase A_2 receptor as target antigen in idiopathic membranous nephropathy. N Engl J Med 361:11, 2009. *[A landmark study describing the discovery of the antigen in idiopathic membranous nephropathy.]*

D'Agati VD: The spectrum of focal segmental glomerulosclerosis: new insights. Curr Opin Nephrol Hypertens 17:271, 2008. *[A comprehensive review of mechanisms contributing to various forms of FSGS.]*

Genovese G, Friedman DJ, Ross MD, et al: Association of trypanolytic ApoL1 variants with kidney disease in African Americans. Science 329:841, 2010. *[A landmark study of natural selection, linking a genetic variant of apolipoprotein L1 in African Americans to protection against sleeping sickness, and risk for kidney disease.]*

Guay-Woodford LM: Renal cystic diseases: diverse phenotypes converge on the cilium/centrosome complex. Pediatr Nephrol 21:1369, 2006. *[An excellent review on the pathophysiology of renal cystic diseases, with emphasis on the role of ciliary dysfunction in tubular epithelial cells.]*

Gubler MC: Inherited diseases of the glomerular basement membrane. Nat Clin Pract Nephrol 4:24, 2008. *[A superb review of the pathophysiology, clinical presentations and diagnostic testing strategies for Alport syndrome, thin basement membrane disease, and other types of hereditary nephritis.]*

Harris PC: 2008 Homer W. Smith Award: Insights into the pathogenesis of polycystic kidney disease from gene discovery. J Am Soc Nephrol 20:1188, 2009. *[A review of the discovery of the major genes leading to polycystic kidney disease, along with their phenotypic manifestations.]*

Knowles MA: Molecular subtypes of bladder cancer: Jekyll and Hyde or chalk and cheese. Carcinogenesis 27:371, 2006. *[Comprehensive review of molecular changes in different types of bladder cancer.]*

Lionaki S, Jennette JC, Falk RJ: Anti-neutrophil cytoplasmic (ANCA) and anti-glomerular basement membrane (GBM) autoantibodies in necrotizing and crescentic glomerulonephritis. Semin Immunopathol 29:459, 2007. *[A good summary of mechanisms of injury and clinical manifestations in ANCA and anti-GBM antibody–mediated disease.]*

Mathieson PW: Minimal change nephropathy and focal segmental glomerulosclerosis. Semin Immunopathol 29:415, 2007. *[An excellent overview of new insights into the pathogenesis and diagnosis of MCD versus FSGS.]*

Miller O, Hemphill RR: Urinary tract infection and pyelonephritis. Emerg Med Clin North Am 19:655, 2001. *[An excellent review of acute urinary tract infections.]*

Murray PT, Devarajan P, Levey AS, et al: A framework and key research questions in AKI diagnosis and staging in different environments. Clin J Am Soc Nephrol 3:864, 2008. *[An excellent review outlining recent advances in early diagnosis and consequences of acute kidney injury.]*

Nsar SH, Markowitz GS, Stokes MB, et al: Acute postinfectious glomerulonephritis in modern era: experience with 86 adults and review of the literature. Medicine 87:21, 2008. *[A contemporary review of postinfectious glomerulonephritis with an emphasis on clinicopathologic correlations and epidemiologic associations.]*

Ronco P, Debiec H: Membranous glomerulopathy: the evolving story. Curr Opin Nephrol Hypertens 19:254, 2010. *[An excellent review of recent insights into the etiology of membranous nephropathy.]*

Schrier RW, Wang W, Poole B, et al: Acute renal failure: definitions, diagnosis, pathogenesis, and therapy. J Clin Invest 114:5, 2004. *[An insightful review covering all aspects of acute renal failure.]*

Tryggvason K, Patrakka J, Wartiovaava J: Hereditary proteinuria syndromes and mechanisms of proteinuria. N Engl J Med 354:1387, 2006. *[An excellent review of the pathophysiology of defects in glomerular permeability.]*

Tsai HM: The molecular biology of thrombotic microangiopathy. Kidney Int 70:16, 2006. *[An excellent review of the pathogenesis of HUS and TTP.]*

Wilson PD, Goilav B: Cystic disease of the kidney. Annu Rev Pathol 2:341, 2007. *[Pathobiology of a common condition affecting the kidney.]*

Worcester EM, Coe FL: Calcium kidney stones. N Engl J Med 363:954, 2010. *[A comprehensive review of the pathophysiology and management of the most common types of kidney stones.]*

See Targeted Therapy available online at **studentconsult.com**

CHAPTER 14

Oral Cavity and Gastrointestinal Tract

CHAPTER CONTENTS

The gastrointestinal tract is a hollow tube consisting of the esophagus, stomach, small intestine, colon, rectum, and anus. Each region has unique, complementary, and highly integrated functions that together serve to regulate the intake, processing, and absorption of ingested nutrients and the disposal of waste products. The intestines also are the principal site at which the immune system interfaces with a diverse array of antigens present in food and gut microbes. Thus, it is not surprising that the small intestine and colon frequently are involved by infectious and inflammatory processes. Finally, the colon is the most common site of gastrointestinal neoplasia in Western populations. In this chapter we discuss the diseases that affect each section of the gastrointestinal tract. Disorders that typically involve more than one segment, such as Crohn disease, are considered with the most frequently involved region.

ORAL CAVITY

Pathologic conditions of the oral cavity can be broadly divided into diseases affecting the oral mucosa, salivary glands, and jaws. Discussed next are the more common conditions affecting these sites. Although common, disorders affecting the teeth and supporting structures are not considered here. Reference should be made to specialized texts. Odontogenic cysts and tumors (benign and malignant), which are derived from the epithelial and/or mesenchymal tissues associated with tooth development, also are discussed briefly.

ORAL INFLAMMATORY LESIONS

Aphthous Ulcers (Canker Sores)

These common superficial mucosal ulcerations affect up to 40% of the population. They are more common in the first two decades of life, extremely painful, and recurrent. Although the cause of aphthous ulcers is not known, they do tend to be more prevalent within some families and may be associated with celiac disease, inflammatory bowel disease (IBD), and Behçet disease. Lesions can be solitary or multiple; typically, they are shallow, hyperemic ulcerations covered by a thin exudate and rimmed by a narrow zone of erythema (Fig. 14–1). In most cases they resolve spontaneously in 7 to 10 days but can recur.

Herpes Simplex Virus Infections

Most orofacial herpetic infections are caused by herpes simplex virus type 1 (HSV-1), with the remainder being caused by HSV-2 (genital herpes). With changing sexual practices, oral HSV-2 is increasingly common. Primary infections typically occur in children between 2 and 4 years of age and are often asymptomatic. However, in 10% to 20% of cases the primary infection manifests as *acute herpetic gingivostomatitis,* with abrupt onset of vesicles and ulcerations throughout the oral cavity. Most adults harbor latent HSV-1, and the virus can be reactivated, resulting in a so-called "cold sore" or *recurrent herpetic stomatitis.* Factors associated with HSV reactivation include trauma, allergies, exposure to ultraviolet light, upper respiratory tract infections, pregnancy, menstruation, immunosuppression, and exposure to extremes of temperature. These recurrent lesions, which occur at the site of primary inoculation or in adjacent mucosa innervated by the same ganglion, typically appear as groups of small (1 to 3 mm) vesicles. The lips (herpes labialis), nasal orifices, buccal mucosa, gingiva, and hard palate are the most common locations. Although lesions typically resolve within 7 to 10 days, they can persist in immunocompromised patients, who may require systemic antiviral therapy. Morphologically, the lesions resemble those seen in esophageal herpes (see Fig. 14–8) and genital herpes (Chapter 17). The infected cells become ballooned and have large eosinophilic intranuclear inclusions. Adjacent cells commonly fuse to form large multinucleated polykaryons.

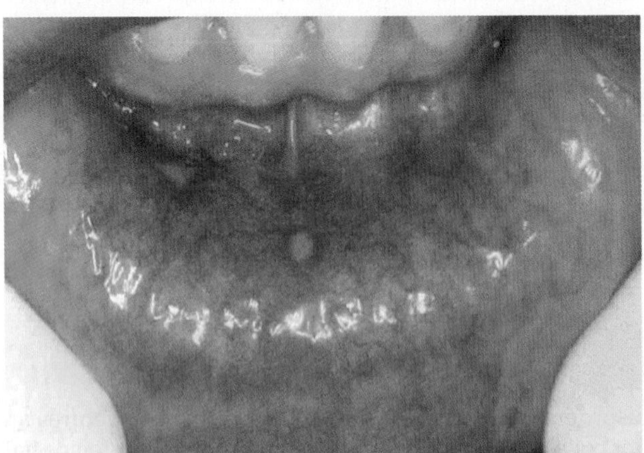

Figure 14–1 Aphthous ulcer. Single ulceration with an erythematous halo surrounding a yellowish fibrinopurulent membrane.

Oral Candidiasis (Thrush)

Candidiasis is the most common fungal infection of the oral cavity. *Candida albicans* is a normal component of the oral flora and only produces disease under unusual circumstances. Modifying factors include:

- Immunosuppression
- The strain of *C. albicans*
- The composition of the oral microbial flora (microbiota)

Broad-spectrum antibiotics that alter the normal microbiota can also promote oral candidiasis. The three major clinical forms of oral candidiasis are pseudomembranous, erythematous, and hyperplastic. The pseudomembranous form is most common and is known as *thrush.* This condition is characterized by a superficial, curdlike, gray to white inflammatory membrane composed of matted organisms enmeshed in a fibrinosuppurative exudate that can be readily scraped off to reveal an underlying erythematous base. In mildly immunosuppressed or debilitated individuals, such as diabetics, the infection usually remains superficial, but can spread to deep sites in association with more severe immunosuppression, including that seen in organ or hematopoietic stem cell transplant recipients, as well as patients with neutropenia, chemotherapy-induced immunosuppression, or AIDS.

SUMMARY

Oral Inflammatory Lesions

- *Aphthous ulcers* are painful superficial ulcers of unknown etiology that may be associated with systemic diseases.
- *Herpes simplex virus* causes a self-limited infection that presents with vesicles (cold sores, fever blisters) that rupture and heal, without scarring, and often leave latent virus in nerve ganglia. Reactivation can occur.
- *Oral candidiasis* may occur when the oral microbiota is altered (e.g., after antibiotic use). Invasive disease may occur in immunosuppressed individuals.

PROLIFERATIVE AND NEOPLASTIC LESIONS OF THE ORAL CAVITY

Fibrous Proliferative Lesions

Fibromas (Fig. 14–2, *A*) are submucosal nodular fibrous tissue masses that are formed when chronic irritation results in reactive connective tissue hyperplasia. They

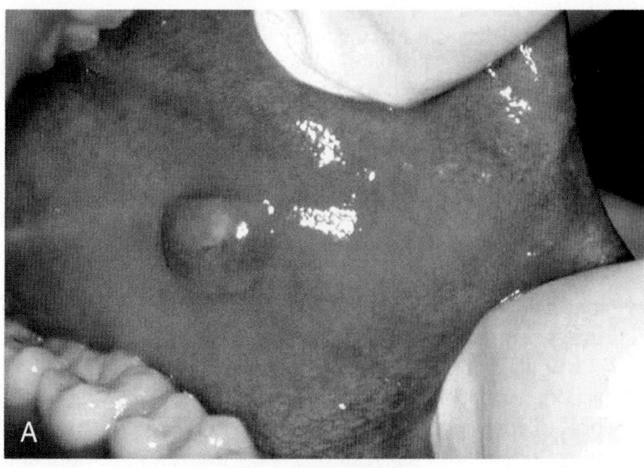

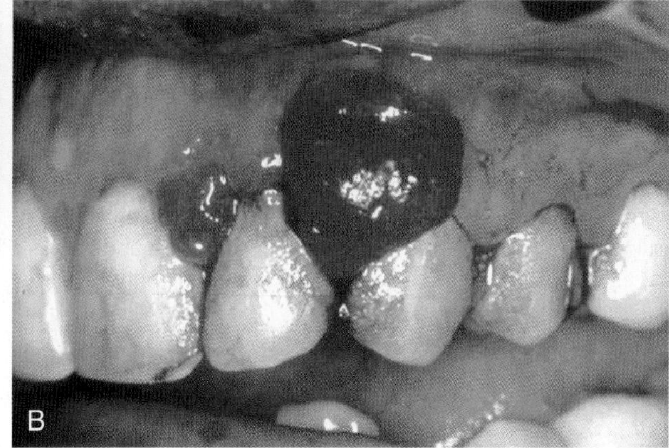

Figure 14–2 Fibrous proliferations. **A,** Fibroma. Smooth pink exophytic nodule on the buccal mucosa. **B,** Pyogenic granuloma. Erythematous hemorrhagic exophytic mass arising from the gingival mucosa.

occur most often on the buccal mucosa along the bite line and are thought to be reactions to chronic irritation. Treatment is complete surgical excision and removal of the source of irritation.

Pyogenic granulomas (Fig. 14–2, *B*) are pedunculated masses usually found on the gingiva of children, young adults, and pregnant women. These lesions are richly vascular and typically are ulcerated, which gives them a red to purple color. In some cases, growth can be rapid and raise fear of a malignant neoplasm. However, histologic examination demonstrates a dense proliferation of immature vessels similar to that seen in granulation tissue. Pyogenic granulomas can regress, mature into dense fibrous masses, or develop into a peripheral ossifying fibroma. Complete surgical excision is definitive treatment.

Leukoplakia and Erythroplakia

Leukoplakia is defined by the World Health Organization as "a white patch or plaque that cannot be scraped off and cannot be characterized clinically or pathologically as any other disease." This clinical term is reserved for lesions that arise in the oral cavity in the absence of any known etiologic factor (Fig. 14–3, *A*). Accordingly, white patches caused by obvious irritation or entities such as lichen planus and candidiasis are not considered leukoplakia. Approximately 3% of the world's population has leukoplakic lesions, of which 5% to 25% are premalignant and may progress to squamous cell carcinoma. *Thus, until proved otherwise by means of histologic evaluation, all leukoplakias must be considered precancerous.* A related but less common lesion, *erythroplakia,* is a red, velvety, possibly eroded area that is flat or slightly depressed relative to the surrounding mucosa. Erythroplakia is associated with a much greater risk of malignant transformation than leukoplakia. While leukoplakia and erythroplakia may be seen in adults at any age, they typically affect persons between the ages of 40 and 70 years, with a 2:1 male preponderance. *Although the etiology is multifactorial, tobacco use (cigarettes, pipes, cigars, and chewing tobacco) is the most common risk factor for leukoplakia and erythroplakia.*

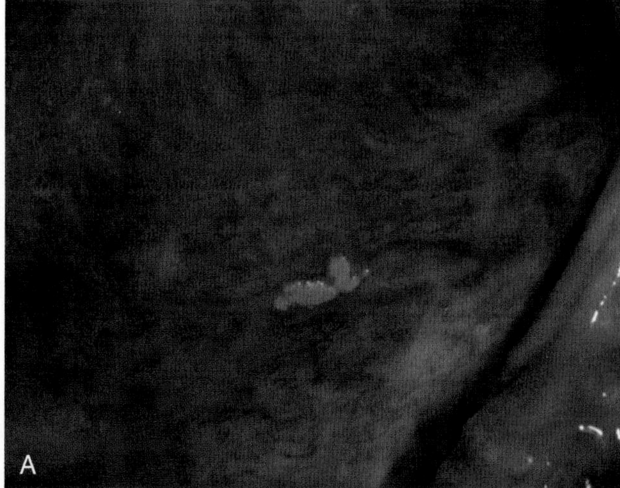

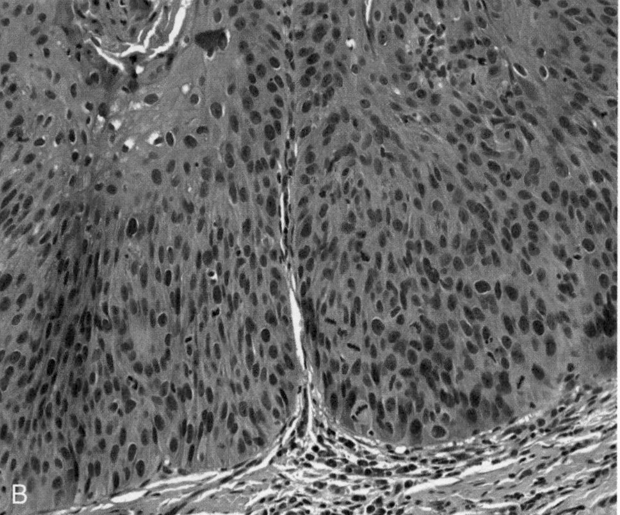

Figure 14–3 Leukoplakia. **A,** Clinical appearance of leukoplakia is highly variable. In this example, the lesion is smooth with well-demarcated borders and minimal elevation. **B,** Histologic appearance of leukoplakia showing dysplasia, characterized by nuclear and cellular pleomorphism and loss of normal maturation.

MORPHOLOGY

Leukoplakia includes a spectrum of histologic features ranging from **hyperkeratosis** overlying a thickened, acanthotic, but orderly mucosal lesions with marked **dysplasia** that sometimes merges with **carcinoma in situ** (Fig. 14–3, *B*). The most severe dysplastic changes are associated with erythroplakia, and more than 50% of these cases undergo malignant transformation. With increasing dysplasia and anaplasia, a subjacent inflammatory cell infiltrate of lymphocytes and macrophages is often present.

Squamous Cell Carcinoma

Approximately 95% of cancers of the oral cavity are squamous cell carcinomas, with the remainder largely consisting of adenocarcinomas of salivary glands, as discussed later. This aggressive epithelial malignancy is the sixth most common neoplasm in the world today. Despite numerous advances in treatment, the overall long-term survival rate has been less than 50% for the past 50 years. This dismal outlook is due to several factors, most notably the fact that oral cancer often is diagnosed at an advanced stage.

Multiple primary tumors may be present at initial diagnosis but more often are detected later, at an estimated rate of 3% to 7% per year; patients who survive 5 years after diagnosis of the initial tumor have up to a 35% chance of developing at least one new primary tumor within that interval. The development of these secondary tumors can be particularly devastating for persons whose initial lesions were small. Thus, despite a 5-year survival rate greater than 50% for patients with small tumors, these patients often die of second primary tumors. Therefore, surveillance and early detection of new premalignant lesions are critical for the long-term survival of patients with oral squamous cell carcinoma.

The elevated risk of additional primary tumors in these patients has led to the concept of "field cancerization." This hypothesis suggests that multiple primary tumors develop independently as a result of years of chronic mucosal exposure to carcinogens such as alcohol or tobacco (described next).

PATHOGENESIS

Squamous cancers of the oropharynx arise through two distinct pathogenic pathways. One group of tumors in the oral cavity occurs mainly in persons who are chronic alcohol and tobacco (both smoked and chewed) users. Deep sequencing of these cancers has revealed frequent mutations that bear a molecular signature consistent with exposure to carcinogens in tobacco. These mutations frequently involve *TP53* and genes that regulate the differentiation of squamous cells, such as *p63* and *NOTCH1*. The second group of tumors tends to occur in the tonsillar crypts or the base of the tongue and harbor oncogenic variants of human papillomavirus (HPV), particularly HPV-16. These tumors carry far fewer mutations than those associated with tobacco exposure and often overexpress p16, a cyclin-dependent kinase inhibitor. It is predicted that the incidence of HPV-associated oropharyngeal squamous cell carcinoma will surpass that of cervical cancer in the next decade, in part because the anatomic sites of origin—tonsillar crypts, base of tongue, and oropharynx—are not readily accessible or amenable to cytologic screening (unlike the cervix). Notably, the **prognosis for patients with HPV-positive tumors is better than for those with HPV-negative tumors.** The HPV vaccine, which is protective against cervical cancer, offers hope to limit the increasing frequency of HPV-associated oropharyngeal squamous cell carcinoma.

In India and southeast Asia, chewing of betel quid and paan are important predisposing factors. Betel quid is a "witch's brew" containing araca nut, slaked lime, and tobacco, all wrapped in betel nut leaf. It is likely that these tumors arise by a pathway similar to that characterized for tobacco use–associated tumors in the West.

MORPHOLOGY

Squamous cell carcinoma may arise anywhere in the oral cavity. However, **the most common locations are the ventral surface of the tongue, floor of the mouth, lower lip, soft palate, and gingiva** (Fig. 14–4, *A*). In early stages, these cancers can appear as raised, firm, pearly plaques or as irregular, roughened, or verrucous mucosal thickenings. Either pattern may be superimposed on a background of a leukoplakia or erythroplakia. As these lesions enlarge, they typically form ulcerated and protruding masses that have irregular and indurated or rolled borders. Histopathologic analysis has shown that **squamous cell carcinoma develops from dysplastic precursor lesions.** Histologic patterns **range from well-differentiated keratinizing neoplasms** (Fig. 14–4, *B*) **to anaplastic, sometimes sarcomatoid tumors.** However, the degree of histologic differentiation, as determined by the relative degree of keratinization, does not necessarily correlate with biologic behavior. Typically, oral squamous cell carcinoma infiltrates locally before it metastasizes. The cervical lymph nodes are the most common sites of regional metastasis; frequent sites of distant metastases include the mediastinal lymph nodes, lungs, and liver.

SUMMARY

Lesions of the Oral Cavity

- *Fibromas* and *pyogenic granulomas* are common reactive lesions of the oral mucosa.
- *Leukoplakias* are mucosal plaques that may undergo malignant transformation.
- The risk of malignant transformation is greater in *erythroplakia* (relative to leukoplakia).
- A majority of oral cavity cancers are *squamous cell carcinomas*.
- Oral squamous cell carcinomas are classically linked to tobacco and alcohol use, but the incidence of HPV-associated lesions is rising.

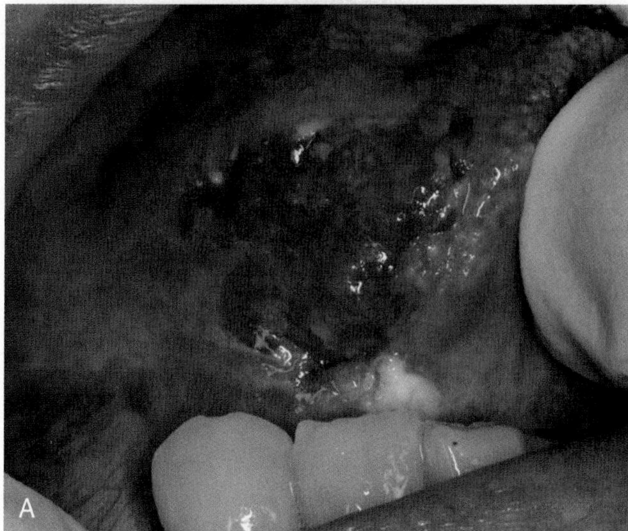

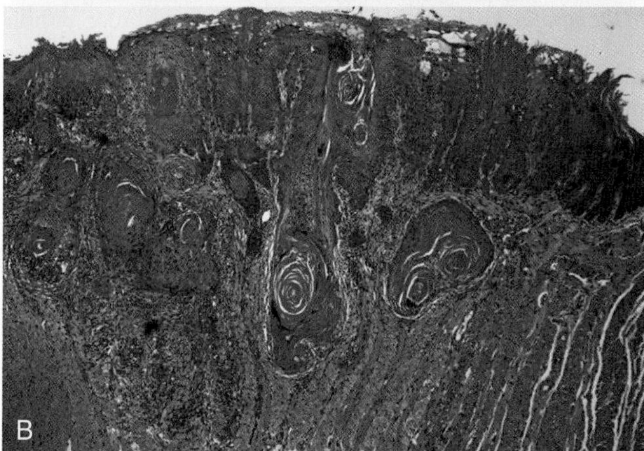

Figure 14–4 Oral squamous cell carcinoma. **A,** Clinical appearance demonstrating ulceration and induration of the oral mucosa. **B,** Histologic appearance demonstrating numerous nests and islands of malignant keratinocytes invading the underlying connective tissue stroma.

DISEASES OF SALIVARY GLANDS

There are three major salivary glands—parotid, submandibular, and sublingual—as well as innumerable minor salivary glands distributed throughout the oral mucosa. Inflammatory or neoplastic disease may develop within any of these.

Xerostomia

Xerostomia is defined as a *dry mouth* resulting from a decrease in the production of saliva. Its incidence varies among populations, but has been reported in more than 20% of individuals above the age of 70 years. It is a major feature of the autoimmune disorder Sjögren syndrome, in which it usually is accompanied by dry eyes (Chapter 4). A lack of salivary secretions is also a major complication of radiation therapy. However, xerostomia is most frequently observed as a result of many commonly prescribed classes of medications including anticholinergic, antidepressant/antipsychotic, diuretic, antihypertensive, sedative, muscle relaxant, analgesic, and antihistaminic agents. The oral cavity may merely reveal dry mucosa and/or atrophy of the papillae of the tongue, with fissuring and ulcerations, or, in Sjögren syndrome, concomitant inflammatory enlargement of the salivary glands. Complications of xerostomia include increased rates of dental caries and candidiasis, as well as difficulty in swallowing and speaking.

Sialadenitis

Sialadenitis, or inflammation of the salivary glands, may be induced by trauma, viral or bacterial infection, or autoimmune disease. The most common form of *viral sialadenitis is mumps,* which may produce enlargement of all salivary glands but predominantly involves the parotids. The mumps virus is a paramyxovirus related to the influenza and parainfluenza viruses. Mumps produces interstitial inflammation marked by a mononuclear inflammatory infiltrate. While mumps in children is most often a self-limited benign condition, in adults it can cause pancreatitis or orchitis; the latter sometimes causes sterility.

The *mucocele* is the most common inflammatory lesion of the salivary glands, and results from either blockage or rupture of a salivary gland duct, with consequent leakage of saliva into the surrounding connective tissue stroma. Mucocele occurs most often in toddlers, young adults, and the aged, and typically manifests as a fluctuant swelling of the lower lip that may change in size, particularly in association with meals (Fig. 14–5, *A*). Histologic examination demonstrates a cystlike space lined by inflammatory granulation tissue or fibrous connective tissue that is filled with mucin and inflammatory cells, particularly macrophages (Fig. 14–5, *B*). Complete excision of the cyst and the minor salivary gland lobule constitutes definitive treatment.

Bacterial sialadenitis is a common infection that most often involves the major salivary glands, particularly the submandibular glands. The most frequent pathogens are *Staphylococcus aureus* and *Streptococcus viridans.* Duct obstruction by stones (*sialolithiasis*) is a common antecedent to infection; it may also be induced by impacted food debris or by edema consequent to injury. Dehydration and decreased secretory function also may predispose to bacterial invasion and sometimes are associated with long-term phenothiazine therapy, which suppresses salivary secretion. Systemic dehydration, with decreased salivary secretions, may predispose to suppurative bacterial parotitis in elderly patients following major thoracic or abdominal surgery. This obstructive process and bacterial invasion lead to a nonspecific inflammation of the affected glands that may be largely interstitial or, when induced by staphylococcal or other pyogens, may be associated with overt suppurative necrosis and abscess formation.

Autoimmune sialadenitis, also called Sjögren syndrome, is discussed in Chapter 4.

Neoplasms

Despite their relatively simple morphology, the salivary glands give rise to at least 30 histologically distinct tumors. As indicated in Table 14-1, a small number of these neoplasms account for more than 90% of tumors. Overall, salivary gland tumors are relatively uncommon and represent less than 2% of all human tumors. Approximately 65% to 80% arise within the parotid, 10% in the submandibular gland, and the remainder in the minor salivary glands, including the sublingual glands. Approximately 15% to 30% of tumors in the parotid glands are malignant. By contrast, approximately 40% of submandibular, 50% of minor salivary gland, and 70% to 90% of sublingual tumors are cancerous. *Thus, the likelihood that a salivary gland tumor is malignant is inversely proportional, roughly, to the size of the gland.*

Salivary gland tumors usually occur in adults, with a slight female predominance, but about 5% occur in children younger than 16 years of age. Whatever the histologic pattern, parotid gland neoplasms produce swelling in front of and below the ear. In general, when they are first diagnosed, both benign and malignant lesions are usually 4 to 6 cm in diameter and are mobile on palpation except in the case of neglected malignant tumors. Benign tumors may be present for months to several years before coming to clinical attention, while cancers more often come to attention promptly, probably because of their more rapid growth. However, there are no reliable criteria to differentiate benign from malignant lesions on clinical grounds, and histopathologic evaluation is essential.

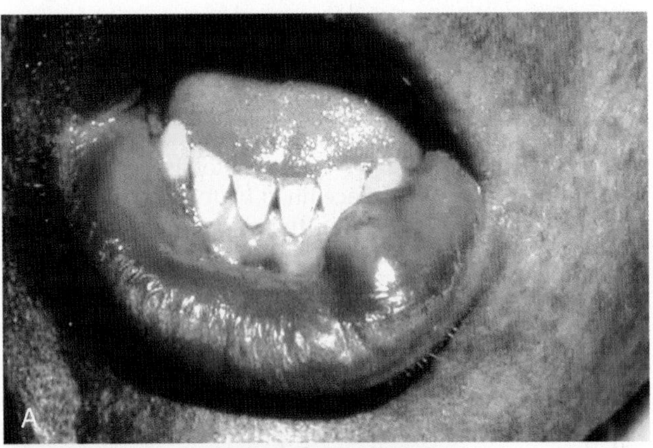

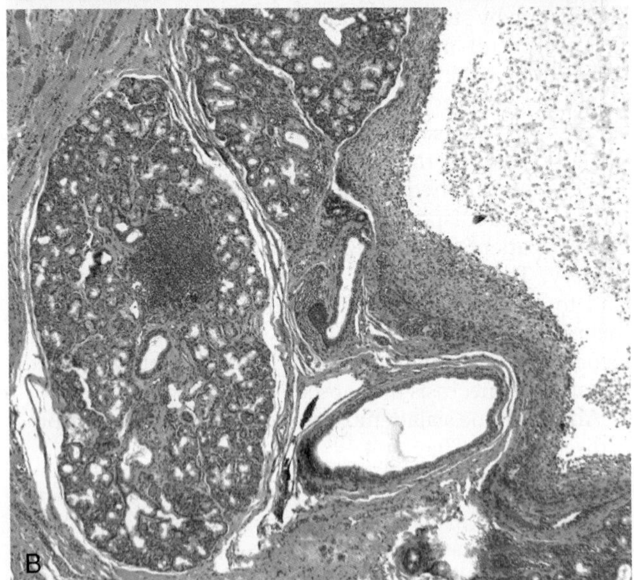

Figure 14–5 Mucocele. **A,** Fluctuant fluid-filled lesion on the lower lip subsequent to trauma. **B,** Cystlike cavity *(right)* filled with mucinous material and lined by organizing granulation tissue.

Table 14–1 Histopathologic Classification and Prevalence of the Most Common Benign and Malignant Salivary Gland Tumors

Benign	Malignant
Pleomorphic adenoma (50%)	Mucoepidermoid carcinoma (15%)
Warthin tumor (5%)	Acinic cell carcinoma (6%)
Oncocytoma (2%)	Adenocarcinoma NOS (6%)
Cystadenoma (2%)	Adenoid cystic carcinoma (4%)
Basal cell adenoma (2%)	Malignant mixed tumor (3%)

NOS, not otherwise specified.
Data from Ellis GL, Auclair PL, Gnepp DR: Surgical Pathology of the Salivary Glands, Vol 25: Major Problems in Pathology, Philadelphia, WB Saunders, 1991.

Pleomorphic Adenoma

Pleomorphic adenomas present as painless, slow-growing, mobile discrete masses. They represent about *60% of tumors in the parotid,* are less common in the submandibular glands, and are relatively rare in the minor salivary glands. Pleomorphic adenomas are benign tumors that consist of a mixture of ductal (epithelial) and myoepithelial cells, so they exhibit both epithelial and mesenchymal differentiation. Epithelial elements are dispersed throughout the matrix, which may contain variable mixtures of myxoid, hyaline, chondroid (cartilaginous), and even osseous tissue. In some pleomorphic adenomas, the epithelial elements predominate; in others, they are present only in widely dispersed foci. This histologic diversity has given rise to the alternative, albeit less preferred name *mixed tumor.* The tumors consistently overexpress the transcription factor PLAG1, often because of chromosomal rearrangements involving the *PLAG1* gene, but how PLAG1 contributes to tumor development is unknown.

Pleomorphic adenomas recur if incompletely excised: Recurrence rates approach 25% after simple enucleation of the tumor, but are only 4% after wider resection. In both settings, recurrence stems from a failure to recognize minute extensions of tumor into surrounding soft tissues.

Carcinoma arising in a pleomorphic adenoma is referred to variously as a *carcinoma ex pleomorphic adenoma* or *malignant mixed tumor.* The incidence of malignant transformation increases with time from 2% of tumors present for less than 5 years to almost 10% for those present for more than 15 years. The cancer usually takes the form of an adenocarcinoma or undifferentiated carcinoma. Unfortunately, these are among the most aggressive malignant neoplasms of salivary glands, with mortality rates of 30% to 50% at 5 years.

MORPHOLOGY

Pleomorphic adenomas typically manifest as rounded, well-demarcated masses rarely exceeding 6 cm in the greatest dimension. Although they are encapsulated, in some locations (particularly the palate), the capsule is not fully developed, and expansile growth produces protrusions into the surrounding tissues. The cut surface is gray-white and typically contains myxoid and blue translucent chondroid (cartilage-like) areas. **The most striking histologic feature is their characteristic heterogeneity.** Epithelial

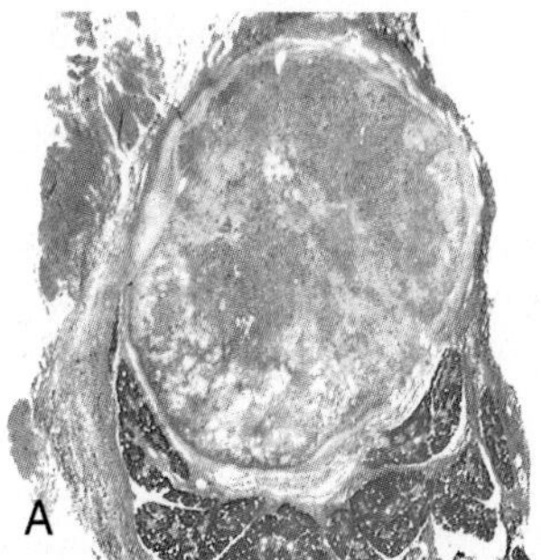

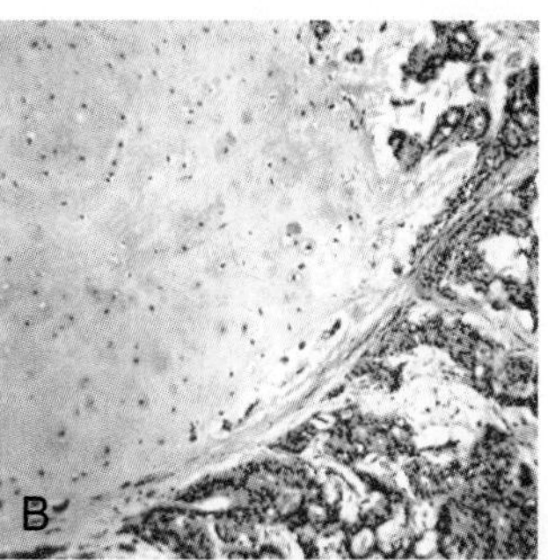

Figure 14–6 Pleomorphic adenoma. **A,** Low-power view showing a well-demarcated tumor with adjacent normal salivary gland parenchyma. **B,** High-power view showing epithelial cells as well as myoepithelial cells within chondroid matrix material.

elements resembling ductal or myoepithelial cells are arranged in **ducts, acini, irregular tubules, strands, or even sheets.** These typically are dispersed within a **mesenchyme-like background of loose myxoid tissue** containing **islands of chondroid** and, rarely, foci of bone (Fig. 14–6). Sometimes the epithelial cells form well-developed ducts lined by cuboidal to columnar cells with an underlying layer of deeply chromatic, small myoepithelial cells. In other instances there may be strands or sheets of myoepithelial cells. Islands of well-differentiated squamous epithelium also may be present. In most cases, no epithelial dysplasia or mitotic activity is evident. No difference in biologic behavior has been observed between the tumors composed largely of epithelial elements and those composed largely of mesenchymal elements.

Mucoepidermoid Carcinoma

Mucoepidermoid carcinomas are composed of variable mixtures of squamous cells, mucus-secreting cells, and intermediate cells. These neoplasms represent about 15% of all salivary gland tumors, and while they occur mainly (60% to 70%) in the parotids, they account for a large fraction of salivary gland neoplasms in the other glands, particularly the minor salivary glands. Overall, mucoepidermoid carcinoma is the most common form of primary *malignant* tumor of the salivary glands. It is commonly associated with chromosome rearrangements involving *MAML2,* a gene that encodes a signaling protein in the Notch pathway.

MORPHOLOGY

Mucoepidermoid carcinomas can grow as large as 8 cm in diameter and, although they are apparently circumscribed, they lack well-defined capsules and often are infiltrative. The cut surface is pale gray to white and frequently demonstrates small, mucinous cysts. On histologic examination, these tumors contain **cords, sheets, or cysts lined by squamous, mucous, or intermediate cells.** The latter is a hybrid cell type with both squamous features and mucus-filled vacuoles, which are most easily detected with mucin stains. Cytologically, tumor cells may be benign-appearing or highly anaplastic and unmistakably malignant. On this basis, mucoepidermoid carcinomas are subclassified as low-, intermediate-, or high-grade.

Clinical course and prognosis depend on histologic grade. Low-grade tumors may invade locally and recur in about 15% of cases but metastasize only rarely and afford a 5-year survival rate over 90%. By contrast, high-grade neoplasms and, to a lesser extent, intermediate-grade tumors are invasive and difficult to excise. As a result, they recur in 25% to 30% of cases, and about 30% metastasize to distant sites. The 5-year survival rate is only 50%.

SUMMARY

Diseases of Salivary Glands

- *Sialadenitis* (inflammation of the salivary glands) can be caused by trauma, infection (such as mumps), or an autoimmune reaction.
- *Pleomorphic adenoma* is a slow-growing neoplasm composed of a heterogeneous mixture of epithelial and mesenchymal cells.
- *Mucoepidermoid carcinoma* is a malignant neoplasm of variable biologic aggressiveness that is composed of a mixture of squamous and mucous cells.

ODONTOGENIC CYSTS AND TUMORS

In contrast with other skeletal sites, epithelium-lined cysts are common in the jaws. A majority of these cysts are derived from remnants of odontogenic epithelium. In general, these cysts are subclassified as either inflammatory or developmental. Only the most common of these lesions are considered here.

The *dentigerous cyst* originates around the crown of an unerupted tooth and is thought to be the result of a degeneration of the dental follicle (primordial tissue that makes the enamel surface of teeth). On radiographic evaluation, these unilocular lesions most often are associated with impacted third molar (wisdom) teeth. They are lined by a thin, stratified squamous epithelium that typically is associated with a dense chronic inflammatory infiltrate within the underlying connective tissue. Complete removal is curative.

Odontogenic keratocysts can occur at any age but are most frequent in persons between 10 and 40 years of age, have a male predominance, and typically are located within the posterior mandible. Differentiation of the *odontogenic keratocyst* from other odontogenic cysts is important because it is locally aggressive and has a high recurrence rate. On radiographic evaluation, odontogenic keratocysts are seen as well-defined unilocular or multilocular radiolucencies. On histologic examination, the cyst lining consists of a thin layer of parakeratinized or orthokeratinized stratified squamous epithelium with a prominent basal cell layer and a corrugated luminal epithelial surface. Treatment requires aggressive and complete removal; recurrence rates of up to 60% are associated with inadequate resection. Multiple odontogenic keratocysts may occur, particularly in patients with the nevoid basal cell carcinoma syndrome (Gorlin syndrome).

In contrast with the developmental cysts just described, the *periapical cyst* has an inflammatory etiology. These extremely common lesions occur at the tooth apex as a result of long-standing pulpitis, which may be caused by advanced caries or trauma. Necrosis of the pulpal tissue, which can traverse the length of the root and exit the apex of the tooth into the surrounding alveolar bone, can lead to a periapical abscess. Over time, granulation tissue (with or without an epithelial lining) may develop. These are often designated *periapical granuloma.* Although the lesion does not show true granulomatous inflammation, old terminology, like bad habits, is difficult to shed. Periapical inflammatory lesions persist as a result of bacteria or other offensive agents in the area. Successful treatment, therefore, necessitates the complete removal of the offending material followed by restoration or extraction of the tooth.

Odontogenic tumors are a complex group of lesions with diverse histologic appearances and clinical behaviors. Some are true neoplasms, either benign or malignant, while others are thought to be hamartomatous. Odontogenic tumors are derived from odontogenic epithelium, ectomesenchyme, or both. The two most common and clinically significant tumors are ameloblastoma and odontoma.

Ameloblastomas arise from odontogenic epithelium and do not demonstrate chondroid or osseous differentiation. These typically cystic lesions are slow-growing and, despite being locally invasive, have an indolent course.

Odontoma, the most common type of odontogenic tumor, arises from epithelium but shows extensive deposition of enamel and dentin. Odontomas are cured by local excision.

SUMMARY

Odontogenic Cysts and Tumors

- The jaws are a common site of epithelium-lined cysts derived from odontogenic remnants.
- The *odontogenic keratocyst* is locally aggressive, with a high recurrence rate.
- The *periapical cyst* is a reactive, inflammatory lesion associated with caries or dental trauma.
- The most common *odontogenic tumors* are *ameloblastoma* and *odontoma.*

ESOPHAGUS

The esophagus develops from the cranial portion of the foregut. It is a hollow, highly distensible muscular tube that extends from the epiglottis to the gastroesophageal junction, located just above the diaphragm. Acquired diseases of the esophagus run the gamut from lethal cancers to "heartburn," with clinical manifestations ranging from chronic and incapacitating disease to mere annoyance.

OBSTRUCTIVE AND VASCULAR DISEASES

Mechanical Obstruction

Atresia, fistulas, and duplications may occur in any part of the gastrointestinal tract. When they involve the esophagus, they are discovered shortly after birth, usually because of regurgitation during feeding, and must be corrected promptly. Absence, or *agenesis,* of the esophagus is extremely rare. *Atresia,* in which a thin, noncanalized cord replaces a segment of esophagus, is more common. Atresia occurs most commonly at or near the tracheal bifurcation and usually is associated with a *fistula* connecting the upper or lower esophageal pouches to a bronchus or the trachea. This abnormal connection can result in aspiration, suffocation, pneumonia, or severe fluid and electrolyte imbalances.

Passage of food can be impeded by esophageal *stenosis.* The narrowing generally is caused by fibrous thickening of the submucosa, atrophy of the muscularis propria, and secondary epithelial damage. *Stenosis most often is due to inflammation and scarring, which may be caused by chronic gastroesophageal reflux, irradiation, or caustic injury.* Stenosis-associated dysphagia usually is progressive; difficulty eating solids typically occurs long before problems with liquids.

Functional Obstruction

Efficient delivery of food and fluids to the stomach requires a coordinated wave of peristaltic contractions. Esophageal dysmotility interferes with this process and can take several forms, all of which are characterized by discoordinated contraction or spasm of the muscularis. Because it increases esophageal wall stress, spasm also can cause small *diverticula* to form.

Increased *lower esophageal sphincter* (LES) tone can result from impaired smooth muscle relaxation with consequent functional esophageal obstruction. *Achalasia is characterized by the triad of incomplete LES relaxation, increased LES tone, and esophageal aperistalsis.* Primary achalasia is caused by failure of distal esophageal inhibitory neurons and is, by definition, idiopathic. Degenerative changes in neural innervation, either intrinsic to the esophagus or within the extraesophageal vagus nerve or the dorsal motor nucleus of the vagus, also may occur. Secondary achalasia may arise in Chagas disease, in which *Trypanosoma cruzi* infection causes destruction of the myenteric plexus, failure of LES relaxation, and esophageal dilatation. Duodenal, colonic, and ureteric myenteric plexuses also can be affected in Chagas disease. Achalasia-like disease may be caused by diabetic autonomic neuropathy; infiltrative disorders such as malignancy, amyloidosis, or sarcoidosis; and lesions of dorsal motor nuclei, which may be produced by polio or surgical ablation.

Ectopia

Ectopic tissues (*developmental rests*) are common in the gastrointestinal tract. The most frequent site of *ectopic gastric mucosa* is the upper third of the esophagus, where it is referred to as an *inlet patch.* Although the presence of such tissue generally is asymptomatic, acid released by gastric mucosa within the esophagus can result in dysphagia, esophagitis, Barrett esophagus, or, rarely, adenocarcinoma. *Gastric heterotopia,* small patches of ectopic gastric mucosa in the small bowel or colon, may manifest with occult blood loss secondary to peptic ulceration of adjacent mucosa.

Esophageal Varices

Instead of returning directly to the heart, venous blood from the gastrointestinal tract is delivered to the liver via the portal vein before reaching the inferior vena cava. This circulatory pattern is responsible for the *first-pass effect,* in which drugs and other materials absorbed in the intestines are processed by the liver before entering the systemic circulation. Diseases that impede this flow cause portal hypertension, which can lead to the development of esophageal varices, an important cause of esophageal bleeding.

PATHOGENESIS

One of the few sites where the splanchnic and systemic venous circulations can communicate is the esophagus. Thus, portal hypertension induces development of collateral channels that allow portal blood to shunt into the caval system. However, these collateral veins enlarge the subepithelial and submucosal venous plexi within the distal esophagus. These vessels, termed **varices,** develop in 90% of cirrhotic patients, most commonly in association with alcoholic liver disease. Worldwide, hepatic schistosomiasis is the second most common cause of varices. A more detailed consideration of portal hypertension is given in Chapter 15.

MORPHOLOGY

Varices can be detected by angiography (Fig. 14–7, *A*) and appear as tortuous dilated veins lying primarily within the submucosa of the distal esophagus and proximal stomach. Varices may not be obvious on gross inspection of surgical or postmortem specimens, because they collapse in the absence of blood flow (Fig. 14–7, *B*). The overlying mucosa can be intact (Fig. 14–7, *C*) but is ulcerated and necrotic if rupture has occurred.

Clinical Features

Varices often are asymptomatic, but their rupture can lead to massive hematemesis and death. Variceal rupture therefore constitutes a medical emergency. Despite intervention, as many as half of the patients die from the first bleeding episode, either as a direct consequence of hemorrhage or due to hepatic coma triggered by the protein load that results from intraluminal bleeding and hypovolemic shock. Among those who survive, additional episodes of hemorrhage, each potentially fatal, occur in more than 50% of cases. As a result, greater than half of the deaths associated with advanced cirrhosis result from variceal rupture.

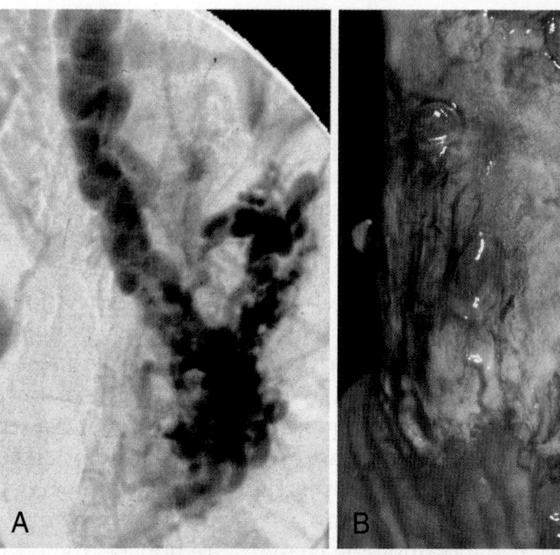

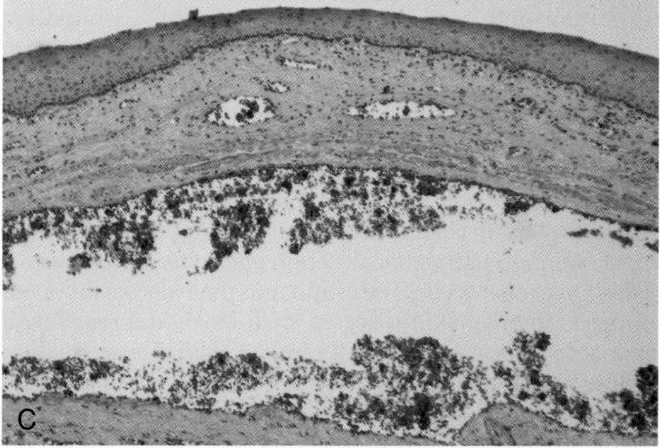

Figure 14–7 Esophageal varices. **A,** Angiogram showing several tortuous esophageal varices. Although the angiogram is striking, endoscopy is more commonly used to identify varices. **B,** Collapsed varices are present in this postmortem specimen corresponding to the angiogram in **A.** The polypoid areas are sites of variceal hemorrhage that were ligated with bands. **C,** Dilated varices beneath intact squamous mucosa.

ESOPHAGITIS

Lacerations

The most common esophageal lacerations are *Mallory-Weiss tears,* which are often associated with severe retching or vomiting, as may occur with acute alcohol intoxication. Normally, a reflex relaxation of the gastroesophageal musculature precedes the antiperistaltic contractile wave associated with vomiting. This relaxation is thought to fail during prolonged vomiting, with the result that refluxing gastric contents overwhelm the gastric inlet and cause the esophageal wall to stretch and tear. Patients often present with hematemesis.

The roughly linear lacerations of *Mallory-Weiss syndrome* are longitudinally oriented, range in length from millimeters to several centimeters, and usually cross the gastroesophageal junction. These tears are superficial and do not generally require surgical intervention; healing tends to be rapid and complete. By contrast, *Boerhaave syndrome,* characterized by transmural esophageal tears and mediastinitis, occurs rarely and is a catastrophic event. The factors giving rise to this syndrome are similar to those for Mallory-Weiss tears, but more severe.

Chemical and Infectious Esophagitis

The stratified squamous mucosa of the esophagus may be damaged by a variety of irritants including alcohol, corrosive acids or alkalis, excessively hot fluids, and heavy smoking. Medicinal pills may lodge and dissolve in the esophagus, rather than passing into the stomach intact, resulting in a condition termed *pill-induced esophagitis.* Esophagitis due to chemical injury generally causes only self-limited pain, particularly *odynophagia* (pain with swallowing). Hemorrhage, stricture, or perforation may occur in severe cases. Iatrogenic esophageal injury may be caused by cytotoxic *chemotherapy, radiation therapy,* or *graft-versus-host disease.* The morphologic changes are nonspecific with ulceration and accumulation of neutrophils. Irradiation causes blood vessel thickening adding some element of ischemic injury.

Infectious esophagitis may occur in otherwise healthy persons but is most frequent in those who are debilitated or immunosuppressed. In these patients, esophageal infection by *herpes simplex viruses, cytomegalovirus* (CMV), or *fungal organisms* is common. Among fungi, *Candida* is the most common pathogen, although *mucormycosis* and *aspergillosis* may also occur. The esophagus may also be involved in desquamative skin diseases such as *bullous pemphigoid* and *epidermolysis bullosa* and, rarely, *Crohn disease.*

Infection by fungi or bacteria can be primary or complicate a preexisting ulcer. Nonpathogenic oral bacteria frequently are found in ulcer beds, while pathogenic organisms, which account for about 10% of infectious esophagitis cases, may invade the lamina propria and cause necrosis of overlying mucosa. Candidiasis, in its most advanced form, is characterized by adherent, gray-white pseudomembranes composed of densely matted fungal hyphae and inflammatory cells covering the esophageal mucosa.

The endoscopic appearance often provides a clue to the identity of the infectious agent in viral esophagitis. Herpesviruses typically cause punched-out ulcers (Fig. 14–8, *A*), and histopathologic analysis demonstrates nuclear viral inclusions within a rim of degenerating epithelial cells at the ulcer edge (Fig. 14–8, *B*). By contrast, CMV causes shallower ulcerations and characteristic nuclear and cytoplasmic inclusions within capillary endothelium and stromal cells (Fig. 14–8, *C*). Immunohistochemical staining for viral antigens can be used as an ancillary diagnostic tool.

Reflux Esophagitis

The stratified squamous epithelium of the esophagus is resistant to abrasion from foods but is sensitive to acid. The submucosal glands of the proximal and distal esophagus contribute to mucosal protection by secreting mucin and bicarbonate. More important, constant LES tone prevents reflux of acidic gastric contents, which are under positive pressure. Reflux of gastric contents into the lower esophagus is the most frequent cause of esophagitis and the most common outpatient gastrointestinal diagnosis in the United States. The associated clinical condition is termed *gastroesophageal reflux disease* (GERD).

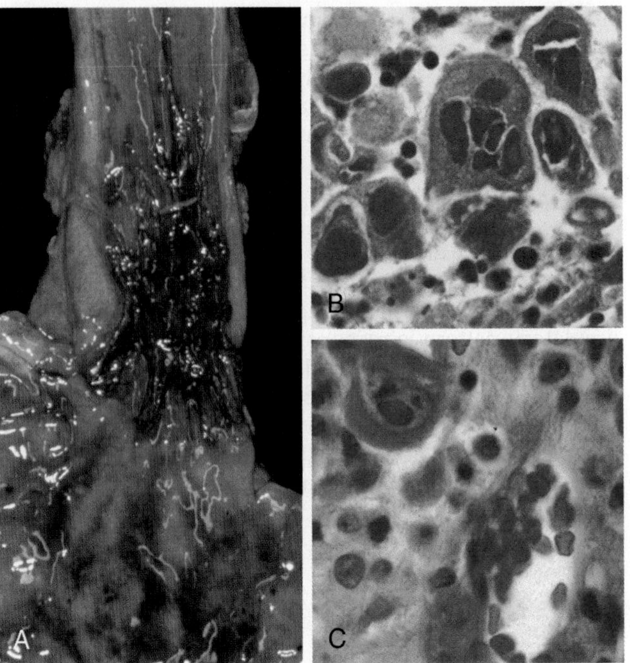

Figure 14–8 Viral esophagitis. **A,** Postmortem specimen with multiple herpetic ulcers in the distal esophagus. **B,** Multinucleate squamous cells containing herpesvirus nuclear inclusions. **C,** Cytomegalovirus-infected endothelial cells with nuclear and cytoplasmic inclusions.

PATHOGENESIS

Reflux of gastric juices is central to the development of mucosal injury in GERD. In severe cases, duodenal bile reflux may exacerbate the damage. Conditions that decrease LES tone or increase abdominal pressure contribute to GERD and include alcohol and tobacco use, obesity, central nervous system depressants, pregnancy, hiatal hernia (discussed later), delayed gastric emptying, and increased gastric volume. In many cases, no definitive cause is identified.

MORPHOLOGY

Simple **hyperemia,** evident to the endoscopist as redness, may be the only alteration. In mild GERD the mucosal histology is often unremarkable. With more significant disease, **eosinophils** are recruited into the squamous mucosa, followed by neutrophils, which usually are associated with more severe injury (Fig. 14–9, *A*). **Basal zone hyperplasia** exceeding 20% of the total epithelial thickness and elongation of lamina propria papillae, such that they extend into the upper third of the epithelium, also may be present.

Clinical Features

GERD is most common in adults older than 40 years of age but also occurs in infants and children. The most frequently reported symptoms are heartburn, dysphagia, and, less often, noticeable regurgitation of sour-tasting gastric contents. Rarely, chronic GERD is punctuated by attacks of

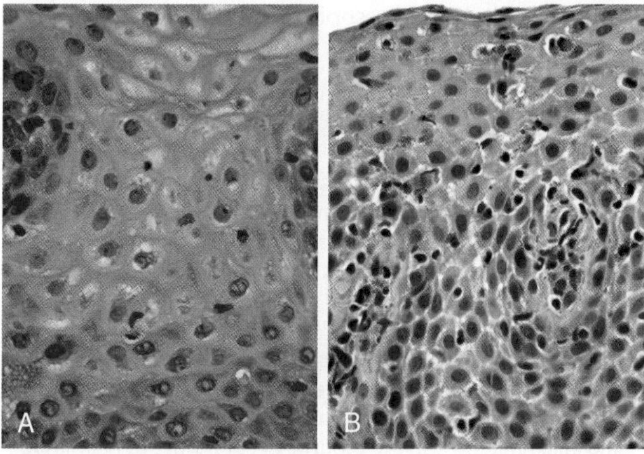

Figure 14–9 Esophagitis. **A,** Reflux esophagitis with scattered intraepithelial eosinophils. **B,** Eosinophilic esophagitis with numerous intraepithelial eosinophils.

severe chest pain that may be mistaken for heart disease. Treatment with proton pump inhibitors reduces gastric acidity and typically provides symptomatic relief. While the severity of symptoms is not closely related to the degree of histologic damage, the latter tends to increase with disease duration. Complications of reflux esophagitis include esophageal ulceration, hematemesis, melena, stricture development, and Barrett esophagus.

Hiatal hernia is characterized by separation of the diaphragmatic crura and protrusion of the stomach into the thorax through the resulting gap. Congenital hiatal hernias are recognized in infants and children, but many are acquired in later life. Hiatal hernia is asymptomatic in more than 90% of adult cases. Thus, symptoms, which are similar to GERD, are often associated with other causes of LES incompetence.

Eosinophilic Esophagitis

The incidence of eosinophilic esophagitis is increasing markedly. Symptoms include food impaction and dysphagia in adults and feeding intolerance or GERD-like symptoms in children. The cardinal histologic feature is epithelial infiltration by large numbers of eosinophils, particularly superficially (Fig. 14–9, *B*) and at sites far from the gastroesophageal junction. Their abundance can help to differentiate eosinophilic esophagitis from GERD, Crohn disease, and other causes of esophagitis. Certain clinical characteristics, particularly failure of high-dose proton pump inhibitor treatment and the absence of acid reflux, are also typical. A majority of persons with eosinophilic esophagitis are atopic, and many have atopic dermatitis, allergic rhinitis, asthma, or modest peripheral eosinophilia. Treatments include dietary restrictions to prevent exposure to food allergens, such as cow milk and soy products, and topical or systemic corticosteroids.

Barrett Esophagus

Barrett esophagus is a complication of chronic GERD that is characterized by *intestinal metaplasia within the esophageal squamous mucosa.* The incidence of Barrett esophagus is rising; it is estimated to occur in as many as 10% of persons with symptomatic GERD. White males are affected most often and typically present between 40 and 60 years of age. The greatest concern in Barrett esophagus is that *it confers an increased risk of esophageal adenocarcinoma.* Molecular studies suggest that Barrett epithelium may be more similar to adenocarcinoma than to normal esophageal epithelium, consistent with the view that Barrett esophagus is a premalignant condition. In keeping with this, epithelial *dysplasia,* considered to be a preinvasive lesion, develops in 0.2% to 1.0% of persons with Barrett esophagus each year; its incidence increases with duration of symptoms and increasing patient age. Although the vast majority of esophageal adenocarcinomas are associated with Barrett esophagus, it should be noted that most persons with Barrett esophagus do not develop esophageal cancer.

MORPHOLOGY

Barrett esophagus is recognized endoscopically as tongues or patches of red, velvety mucosa extending upward from the gastroesophageal junction. This metaplastic mucosa alternates with residual smooth, pale squamous (esophageal) mucosa proximally and interfaces with light-brown columnar (gastric) mucosa distally (Fig. 14–10, *A* and *B*). High-resolution endoscopes have increased the sensitivity of Barrett esophagus detection.

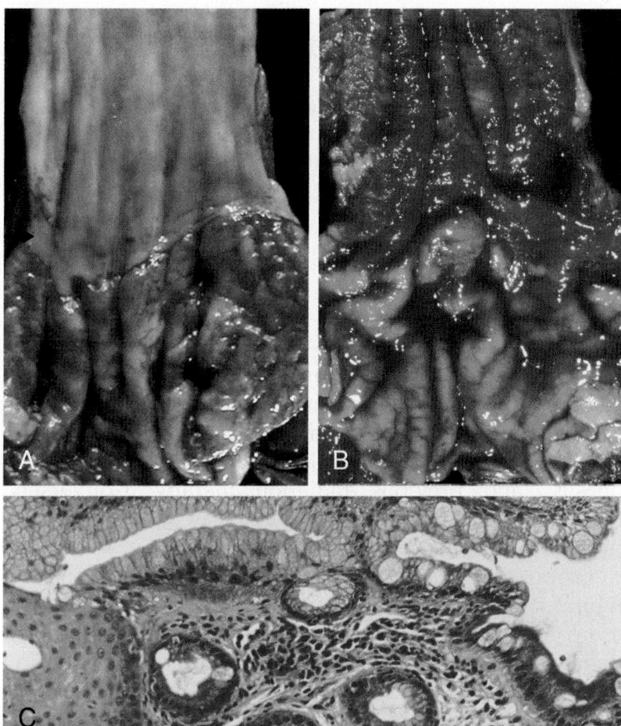

Figure 14–10 Barrett esophagus. **A,** Normal gastroesophageal junction. **B,** Barrett esophagus. Note the small islands of paler squamous mucosa within the Barrett mucosa. **C,** Histologic appearance of the gastroesophageal junction in Barrett esophagus. Note the transition between esophageal squamous mucosa (*left*) and metaplastic mucosa containing goblet cells (*right*).

Most authors require both endoscopic evidence of abnormal mucosa above the gastroesophageal junction and histologically documented gastric or intestinal metaplasia for diagnosis of Barrett esophagus. **Goblet cells**, which have distinct mucous vacuoles that stain pale blue by H&E and impart the shape of a wine goblet to the remaining cytoplasm, define intestinal metaplasia and are a feature of Barrett esophagus (Fig. 14–10, *C*). Dysplasia is classified as low-grade or high-grade on the basis of morphologic criteria. Intramucosal carcinoma is characterized by invasion of neoplastic epithelial cells into the lamina propria.

Clinical Features

Diagnosis of Barrett esophagus requires endoscopy and biopsy, usually prompted by GERD symptoms. The best course of management is a matter of debate. While many investigators agree that periodic endoscopy with biopsy, for detection of dysplasia, is reasonable, uncertainties about the frequency with which dysplasia occurs and whether it can regress spontaneously complicate clinical decision making. By contrast, intramucosal carcinoma requires therapeutic intervention. Treatment options include surgical resection (*esophagectomy*), and newer modalities such as photodynamic therapy, laser ablation, and endoscopic mucosectomy. Multifocal high-grade dysplasia, which carries a significant risk of progression to intramucosal or invasive carcinoma, may be treated in a fashion similar to intramucosal carcinoma.

ESOPHAGEAL TUMORS

Two morphologic variants account for a majority of esophageal cancers: adenocarcinoma and squamous cell carcinoma. Worldwide, squamous cell carcinoma is more common, but in the United States and other Western countries adenocarcinoma is on the rise. Other rare tumors occur but are not discussed here.

Adenocarcinoma

Esophageal adenocarcinoma typically arises in a background of Barrett esophagus and long-standing GERD. Risk of adenocarcinoma is greater in patients with documented dysplasia and is further increased by tobacco use, obesity, and previous radiation therapy. Conversely, reduced adenocarcinoma risk is associated with diets rich in fresh fruits and vegetables.

Esophageal adenocarcinoma occurs most frequently in whites and shows a strong gender bias, being seven times more common in men than in women. However, the incidence varies by a factor of 60 worldwide, with rates being highest in developed Western countries, including the United States, the United Kingdom, Canada, Australia, and the Netherlands, and lowest in Korea, Thailand, Japan, and Ecuador. In countries where esophageal adenocarcinoma is more common, the incidence has increased markedly since 1970, more rapidly than for almost any other cancer. As a result, esophageal adenocarcinoma, which represented less than 5% of esophageal cancers before 1970, now accounts for half of all esophageal cancers in the United States.

PATHOGENESIS

Molecular studies suggest that the progression of Barrett esophagus to adenocarcinoma occurs over an extended period through the stepwise acquisition of genetic and epigenetic changes. This model is supported by the observation that epithelial clones identified in nondysplastic Barrett metaplasia persist and accumulate mutations during progression to dysplasia and invasive carcinoma. Chromosomal abnormalities and *TP53* mutation are often present at early stages of esophageal adenocarcinoma. Additional genetic changes and inflammation also are thought to contribute to neoplastic progression.

MORPHOLOGY

Esophageal adenocarcinoma usually occurs in the distal third of the esophagus and may invade the adjacent gastric cardia (Fig. 14–11, *A*). While early lesions may appear as flat or raised patches in otherwise intact mucosa, tumors may form large exophytic masses, infiltrate diffusely, or ulcerate and invade deeply. On microscopic examination, Barrett esophagus frequently is present adjacent to the tumor. Tumors typically produce mucin and form glands (Fig. 14–11, *B*).

Clinical Features

Although esophageal adenocarcinomas are occasionally discovered during evaluation of GERD or surveillance of Barrett esophagus, they more commonly manifest with

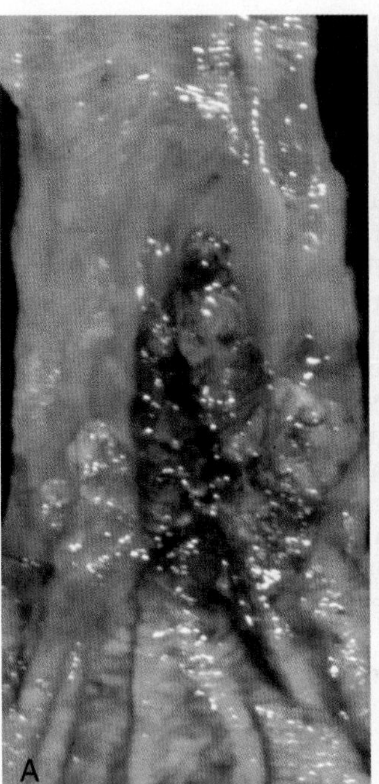

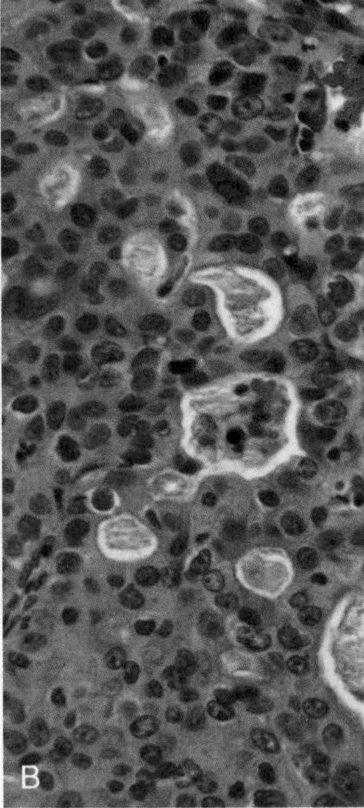

Figure 14–11 Esophageal adenocarcinoma. **A,** Adenocarcinoma usually occurs distally and, as in this case, often involves the gastric cardia. **B,** Esophageal adenocarcinoma growing as back-to-back glands.

pain or difficulty in swallowing, progressive weight loss, chest pain, or vomiting. By the time symptoms and signs appear, the tumor usually has spread to submucosal lymphatic vessels. As a result of the advanced stage at diagnosis, the overall 5-year survival rate is less than 25%. By contrast, 5-year survival approximates 80% in the few patients with adenocarcinoma limited to the mucosa or submucosa.

Squamous Cell Carcinoma

In the United States, esophageal squamous cell carcinoma typically occurs in adults older than 45 years of age and affects males four times more frequently than females. Risk factors include alcohol and tobacco use, poverty, caustic esophageal injury, achalasia, Plummer-Vinson syndrome, frequent consumption of very hot beverages, and previous radiation therapy to the mediastinum. It is nearly 6 times more common in African Americans than in whites—a striking risk disparity that cannot be accounted for by differences in rates of alcohol and tobacco use. The incidence of esophageal squamous cell carcinoma can vary by more than 100-fold between and within countries, being more common in rural and underdeveloped areas. The countries with highest incidences are Iran, central China, Hong Kong, Argentina, Brazil, and South Africa.

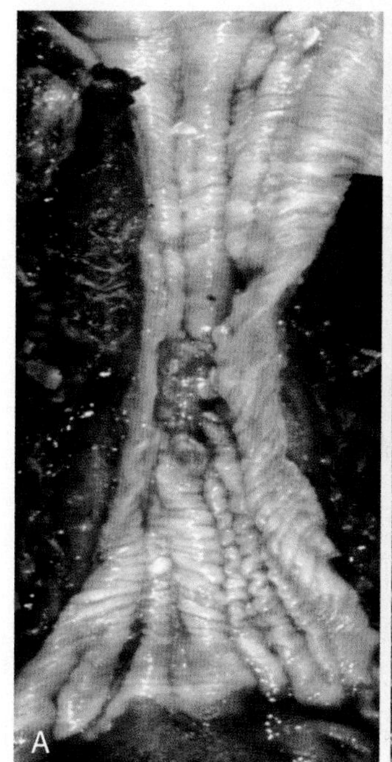

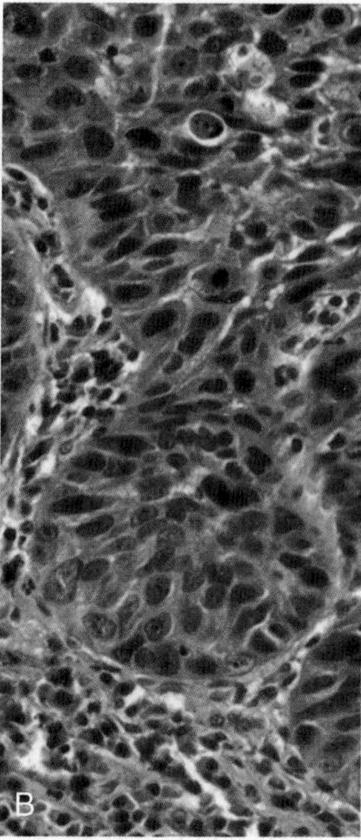

Figure 14–12 Esophageal squamous cell carcinoma. **A,** Squamous cell carcinoma most frequently is found in the midesophagus, where it commonly causes strictures. **B,** Squamous cell carcinoma composed of nests of malignant cells that partially recapitulate the stratified organization of squamous epithelium.

PATHOGENESIS

A majority of esophageal squamous cell carcinomas in Europe and the United States are at least partially attributable to the use of alcohol and tobacco, the effects of which synergize to increase risk. However, esophageal squamous cell carcinoma also is common in some regions where alcohol and tobacco use is uncommon. Thus, nutritional deficiencies, as well as polycyclic hydrocarbons, nitrosamines, and other mutagenic compounds, such as those found in fungus-contaminated foods, have been considered as possible risk factors. HPV infection also has been implicated in esophageal squamous cell carcinoma in high-risk but not in low-risk regions. The molecular pathogenesis of esophageal squamous cell carcinoma remains incompletely defined.

MORPHOLOGY

In contrast to the distal location of most adenocarcinomas, half of squamous cell carcinomas occur in the middle third of the esophagus (Fig. 14–12, *A*). Squamous cell carcinoma begins as an in situ lesion in the form of **squamous dysplasia.** Early lesions appear as small, gray-white plaquelike thickenings. Over months to years they grow into tumor masses that may be polypoid and protrude into and obstruct the lumen. Other tumors are either ulcerated or diffusely infiltrative lesions that spread within the esophageal wall, where they cause thickening, rigidity, and luminal narrowing. These cancers may invade surrounding structures including the respiratory tree, causing pneumonia; the aorta, causing catastrophic exsanguination; or the mediastinum and pericardium.

Most squamous cell carcinomas are moderately to well differentiated (Fig. 14–12, *B*). Less common histologic variants include verrucous squamous cell carcinoma, spindle cell carcinoma, and basaloid squamous cell carcinoma. Regardless of histologic type, symptomatic tumors are generally very large at diagnosis and have already invaded the esophageal wall. The rich submucosal lymphatic network promotes circumferential and longitudinal spread, and intramural tumor nodules may be present several centimeters away from the principal mass. The sites of lymph node metastases vary with tumor location: Cancers in the upper third of the esophagus favor cervical lymph nodes; those in the middle third favor mediastinal, paratracheal, and tracheobronchial nodes; and those in the lower third spread to gastric and celiac nodes.

Clinical Features

Clinical manifestations of squamous cell carcinoma of the esophagus begin insidiously and include dysphagia, odynophagia (pain on swallowing), and obstruction. As with other forms of esophageal obstruction, patients may unwittingly adjust to the progressively increasing obstruction by altering their diet from solid to liquid foods. Extreme weight loss and debilitation result from both impaired nutrition and effects of the tumor itself. Hemorrhage and sepsis may accompany tumor ulceration. Occasionally, the first symptoms are caused by aspiration of food through a tracheoesophageal fistula.

Increased use of endoscopic screening has led to earlier detection of esophageal squamous cell carcinoma. The timing is critical, because 5-year survival rates are 75% for patients with superficial esophageal carcinoma but much lower for patients with more advanced tumors. Lymph node metastases, which are common, are associated with poor prognosis. The overall 5-year survival rate remains a dismal 9%.

SUMMARY

Diseases of the Esophagus

- *Esophageal obstruction* may occur as a result of mechanical or functional anomalies. Mechanical causes include developmental defects, fibrotic strictures, and tumors.
- *Achalasia,* characterized by incomplete LES relaxation, increased LES tone, and esophageal aperistalsis, is a common form of *functional esophageal obstruction.*
- *Esophagitis* can result from chemical or infectious mucosal injury. Infections are most frequent in immunocompromised persons.
- The most common cause of esophagitis is *gastroesophageal reflux disease* (GERD), which must be differentiated from *eosinophilic esophagitis.*
- *Barrett esophagus,* which may develop in patients with chronic GERD, is associated with increased risk of esophageal adenocarcinoma.
- *Esophageal squamous cell carcinoma* is associated with alcohol and tobacco use, poverty, caustic esophageal injury, achalasia, tylosis, and Plummer-Vinson syndrome.

STOMACH

Disorders of the stomach are a frequent cause of clinical disease, with inflammatory and neoplastic lesions being particularly common. In the United States, symptoms related to gastric acid account for nearly one third of all health care spending on gastrointestinal disease. In addition, despite a decreasing incidence in certain locales, including the United States, gastric cancer remains a leading cause of death worldwide.

The stomach is divided into four major anatomic regions: the cardia, fundus, body, and antrum. The cardia is lined mainly by mucin-secreting *foveolar cells* that form shallow glands. The antral glands are similar but also contain endocrine cells, such as *G cells,* that release gastrin to stimulate luminal acid secretion by *parietal cells* within the gastric fundus and body. The well-developed glands of the body and fundus also contain *chief cells* that produce and secrete digestive enzymes such as pepsin.

INFLAMMATORY DISEASE OF THE STOMACH

Acute Gastritis

Acute gastritis is a transient mucosal inflammatory process that may be asymptomatic or cause variable degrees of epigastric pain, nausea, and vomiting. In more severe cases there may be mucosal erosion, ulceration, hemorrhage, hematemesis, melena, or, rarely, massive blood loss.

PATHOGENESIS

The gastric lumen is strongly acidic, with a pH close to one—more than a million times more acidic than the blood. This harsh environment contributes to digestion but also has the potential to damage the mucosa. Multiple mechanisms have evolved to protect the gastric mucosa (Fig. 14–13). Mucin secreted by surface **foveolar cells** forms a thin layer of mucus that prevents large food particles from directly touching the epithelium. The mucus layer also promotes formation of an "unstirred" layer of fluid over the epithelium that protects the mucosa and has a neutral pH as a result of bicarbonate ion secretion by surface epithelial cells. Finally, the rich vascular supply to the gastric mucosa delivers oxygen, bicarbonate, and nutrients while washing away acid that has back-diffused into the lamina propria. Acute or chronic gastritis can occur after disruption of any of these protective mechanisms. For example, reduced mucin synthesis in elderly persons is suggested to be one factor that explains their increased susceptibility to gastritis. Nonsteroidal anti-inflammatory drugs (NSAIDs) may interfere with cytoprotection normally provided by prostaglandins or reduce bicarbonate secretion, both of which increase the susceptibility of the gastric mucosa to injury. Ingestion of harsh chemicals, particularly acids or bases, either accidentally or as a suicide attempt, also results in severe gastric injury, predominantly as a consequence of direct damage to mucosal epithelial and stromal cells. Direct cellular injury also is implicated in gastritis due to excessive alcohol consumption, NSAIDs, radiation therapy, and chemotherapy.

MORPHOLOGY

On histologic examination, mild acute gastritis may be difficult to recognize, since the lamina propria shows only moderate edema and slight vascular congestion. The **surface epithelium is intact,** although scattered neutrophils may be present. Lamina propria lymphocytes and plasma cells are not prominent. The presence of neutrophils above the basement membrane—specifically, in direct contact with epithelial cells—is abnormal in all parts of the gastrointestinal tract and signifies **active inflammation.** With more severe mucosal damage, *erosion,* or loss of the superficial epithelium, may occur, leading to formation of mucosal neutrophilic infiltrates and purulent exudates. Hemorrhage also may occur, manifesting as dark puncta in an otherwise hyperemic mucosa. Concurrent presence of erosion and hemorrhage is termed **acute erosive hemorrhagic gastritis.**

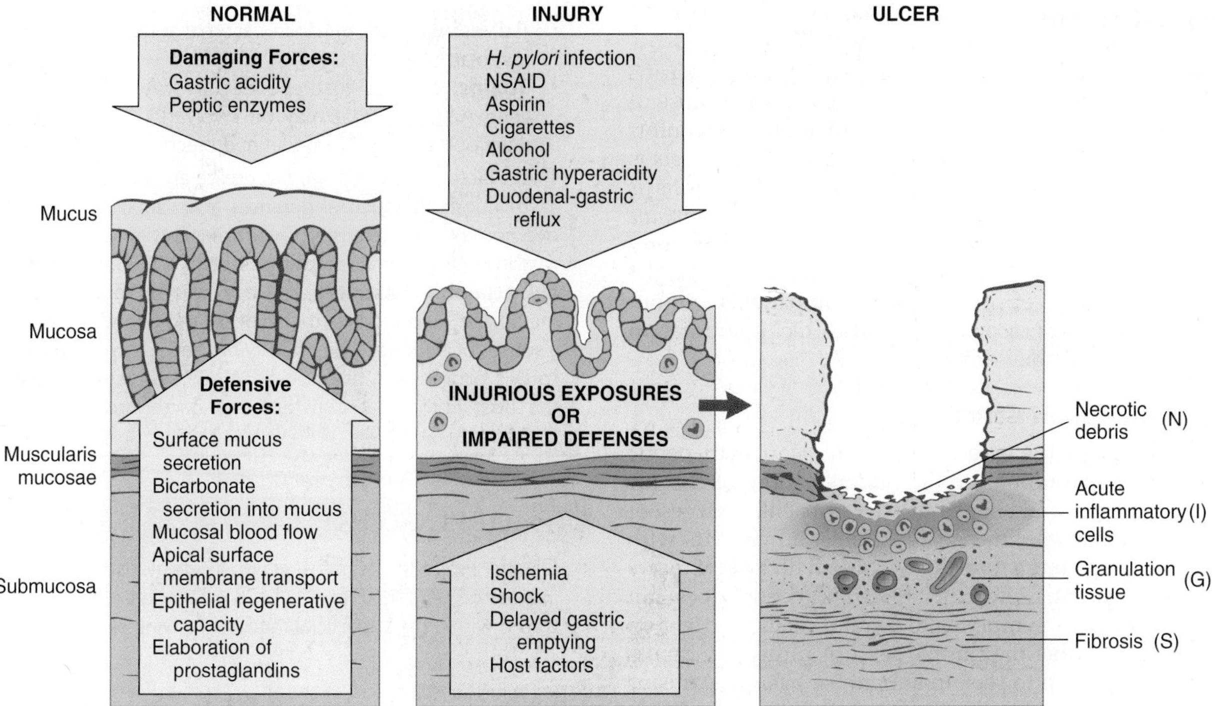

Figure 14–13 Mechanisms of gastric injury and protection. This diagram illustrates the progression from more mild forms of injury to ulceration that may occur with acute or chronic gastritis. Ulcers include layers of necrotic debris *(N)*, inflammation *(I)*, and granulation tissue *(G)*; a fibrotic scar *(S)*, which develops over time, is present only in chronic lesions.

Acute Peptic Ulceration

Focal, acute peptic injury is a well-known complication of therapy with NSAIDs as well as severe physiologic stress. Such lesions include

- *Stress ulcers,* most commonly affecting critically ill patients with shock, sepsis, or severe trauma
- *Curling ulcers,* occurring in the proximal duodenum and associated with severe burns or trauma
- *Cushing ulcers,* arising in the stomach, duodenum, or esophagus of persons with intracranial disease, have a high incidence of perforation

PATHOGENESIS

The pathogenesis of acute ulceration is complex and incompletely understood. NSAID-induced ulcers are caused by direct chemical irritation as well as cyclooxygenase inhibition, which prevents prostaglandin synthesis. This eliminates the protective effects of prostaglandins, which include enhanced bicarbonate secretion and increased vascular perfusion. Lesions associated with intracranial injury are thought to be caused by direct stimulation of vagal nuclei, which causes gastric acid hypersecretion. Systemic acidosis, a frequent finding in critically ill patients, also may contribute to mucosal injury by lowering the intracellular pH of mucosal cells. Hypoxia and reduced blood flow caused by stress-induced splanchnic vasoconstriction also contribute to acute ulcer pathogenesis.

MORPHOLOGY

Lesions described as acute gastric ulcers range in depth from shallow erosions caused by superficial epithelial damage to deeper lesions that penetrate the mucosa. Acute ulcers are rounded and typically are less than 1 cm in diameter. The ulcer base frequently is stained brown to black by acid-digested extravasated red cells, in some cases associated with transmural inflammation and local serositis. While these lesions may occur singly, more often multiple ulcers are present within the stomach and duodenum. Acute stress ulcers are sharply demarcated, with essentially normal adjacent mucosa, although there may be suffusion of blood into the mucosa and submucosa and some inflammatory reaction. The scarring and thickening of blood vessels that characterize chronic peptic ulcers are absent. Healing with complete reepithelialization occurs days or weeks after the injurious factors are removed.

Clinical Features

Symptoms of gastric ulcers include nausea, vomiting, and coffee-ground hematemesis. Bleeding from superficial gastric erosions or ulcers that may require transfusion develops in 1% to 4% of these patients. Other complications, including perforation, can also occur. Proton pump inhibitors, or the less frequently used histamine H_2 receptor antagonists, may blunt the impact of stress ulceration, but the most important determinant of outcome is the severity of the underlying condition.

Chronic Gastritis

The symptoms and signs associated with chronic gastritis typically are less severe but more persistent than those of acute gastritis. Nausea and upper abdominal discomfort may occur, sometimes with vomiting, but hematemesis is uncommon. *The most common cause of chronic gastritis is infection with the bacillus* Helicobacter pylori. *Autoimmune gastritis,* the most common cause of *atrophic gastritis,* represents less than 10% of cases of chronic gastritis and is the most common form of chronic gastritis in patients without *H. pylori* infection. Less common causes include radiation injury and chronic bile reflux.

Helicobacter pylori *Gastritis*

The discovery of the association of *H. pylori* with peptic ulcer disease revolutionized the understanding of chronic gastritis. These spiral-shaped or curved bacilli are present in gastric biopsy specimens from almost all patients with duodenal ulcers and a majority of those with gastric ulcers or chronic gastritis. Acute *H. pylori* infection does not produce sufficient symptoms to require medical attention in most cases; rather the chronic gastritis ultimately causes the afflicted person to seek treatment. *H. pylori* organisms are present in 90% of patients with chronic gastritis affecting the antrum. In addition, the increased acid secretion that occurs in *H. pylori* gastritis may result in peptic ulcer disease of the stomach or duodenum; *H. pylori* infection also confers increased risk of gastric cancer.

Epidemiology

In the United States, *H. pylori* infection is associated with poverty, household crowding, limited education, African American or Mexican American ethnicity, residence in areas with poor sanitation, and birth outside of the United States. Colonization rates exceed 70% in some groups and range from less than 10% to more than 80% worldwide. In high-prevalence areas, infection often is acquired in childhood and then persists for decades. Thus, the incidence of *H. pylori* infection correlates most closely with sanitation and hygiene during an individual's childhood.

PATHOGENESIS

H. pylori infection most often manifests as a **predominantly antral gastritis with high acid production, despite hypogastrinemia.** The risk of duodenal ulcer is increased in these patients, and in most cases, gastritis is limited to the antrum.

H. pylori organisms have adapted to the ecologic niche provided by gastric mucus. Although *H. pylori* may invade the gastric mucosa, the contribution of invasion to disease pathogenesis is not known. Four features are linked to *H. pylori* virulence:

- **Flagella,** which allow the bacteria to be motile in viscous mucus
- **Urease,** which generates ammonia from endogenous urea, thereby elevating local gastric pH around the organisms and protecting the bacteria from the acidic pH of the stomach
- **Adhesins,** which enhance bacterial adherence to surface foveolar cells
- **Toxins,** such as that encoded by cytotoxin-associated gene A (*CagA*), that may be involved in ulcer or cancer development by poorly defined mechanisms

These factors allow *H. pylori* to create an imbalance between gastroduodenal mucosal defenses and damaging forces that overcome those defenses. Over time, chronic antral *H. pylori* gastritis may progress to **pangastritis,** resulting in **multifocal atrophic gastritis,** reduced acid secretion, intestinal metaplasia, and increased risk of gastric adenocarcinoma in a subset of patients. The underlying mechanisms contributing to this progression are not clear, but interactions between the host immune system and the bacterium seem to be critical.

MORPHOLOGY

Gastric biopsy specimens generally demonstrate *H. pylori* in infected persons (Fig. 14–14, *A*). The organism is concentrated within the superficial mucus overlying epithelial cells in

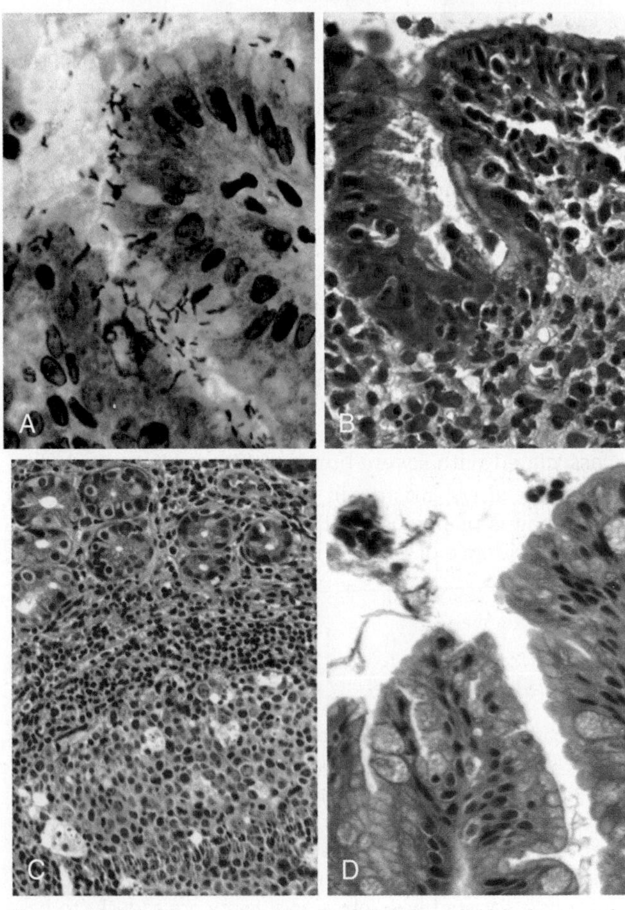

Figure 14–14 Chronic gastritis. **A,** Spiral-shaped *Helicobacter pylori* bacilli are highlighted in this Warthin-Starry silver stain. Organisms are abundant within surface mucus. **B,** Intraepithelial and lamina propria neutrophils are prominent. **C,** Lymphoid aggregates with germinal centers and abundant subepithelial plasma cells within the superficial lamina propria are characteristic of *H. pylori* gastritis. **D,** Intestinal metaplasia, recognizable as the presence of goblet cells admixed with gastric foveolar epithelium, can develop and is a risk factor for development of gastric adenocarcinoma.

the surface and neck regions. The inflammatory reaction includes a variable number of neutrophils within the lamina propria, including some that cross the basement membrane to assume an intraepithelial location (Fig. 14–14, *B*) and accumulate in the lumen of gastric pits to create pit abscesses. The superficial lamina propria includes large numbers of plasma cells, often in clusters or sheets, as well as increased numbers of lymphocytes and macrophages. When intense, inflammatory infiltrates may create thickened rugal folds, mimicking infiltrative lesions. Lymphoid aggregates, some with germinal centers, frequently are present (Fig. 14–14, *C*) and represent an induced form of **mucosa-associated lymphoid tissue** (MALT) that has the potential to transform into lymphoma. **Intestinal metaplasia,** characterized by the presence of goblet cells and columnar absorptive cells (Fig. 14–14, *D*), also may be present and is associated with increased risk of gastric adenocarcinoma. *H. pylori* shows tropism for gastric foveolar epitheleum and generally is not found in areas of intestinal metaplasia, acid-producing mucosa of the gastric body, or duodenal epithelium. Thus, an antral biopsy is preferred for evaluation of *H. pylori* gastritis.

Clinical Features

In addition to histologic identification of the organism, several diagnostic tests have been developed including a noninvasive serologic test for anti–*H. pylori* antibodies, fecal bacterial detection, and the urea breath test based on the generation of ammonia by bacterial urease. Gastric biopsy specimens also can be analyzed by the rapid urease test, bacterial culture, or polymerase chain reaction (PCR) assay for bacterial DNA. Effective treatments include combinations of antibiotics and proton pump inhibitors. Patients with *H. pylori* gastritis usually improve after treatment, although relapses can follow incomplete eradication or reinfection.

Autoimmune Gastritis

Autoimmune gastritis accounts for less than 10% of cases of chronic gastritis. In contrast with that caused by *H. pylori,* autoimmune gastritis typically spares the antrum and induces *hypergastrinemia* (Table 14–2). Autoimmune gastritis is characterized by

- Antibodies to parietal cells and intrinsic factor that can be detected in serum and gastric secretions
- Reduced serum pepsinogen I levels
- Antral endocrine cell hyperplasia
- Vitamin B_{12} deficiency
- Defective gastric acid secretion (*achlorhydria*)

PATHOGENESIS

Autoimmune gastritis is associated with loss of parietal cells, which secrete acid and intrinsic factor. Deficient acid production stimulates gastrin release, resulting in hypergastrinemia and hyperplasia of antral gastrin-producing G cells. Lack of intrinsic factor disables ileal vitamin B_{12} absorption, leading to B_{12} deficiency and megaloblastic anemia **(pernicious anemia);** reduced serum concentration of pepsinogen I reflects chief cell loss. Although *H. pylori* can cause hypochlorhydria, it is not associated with achlorhydria or pernicious anemia, because the parietal and chief cell damage is not as severe as in autoimmune gastritis.

MORPHOLOGY

Autoimmune gastritis is characterized by diffuse **damage of the oxyntic** (acid-producing) **mucosa** within the body and fundus. Damage to the antrum and cardia typically is absent or mild. With **diffuse atrophy,** the oxyntic mucosa of the body and fundus appears markedly thinned, and rugal folds are lost. Neutrophils may be present, but the inflammatory infiltrate more commonly is composed of lymphocytes, macrophages, and plasma cells; in contrast with ***H. pylori* gastritis,** the inflammatory reaction most often is deep and centered on the gastric glands. **Parietal and chief cell loss** can be extensive, and **intestinal metaplasia** may develop.

Clinical Features

Antibodies to parietal cells and intrinsic factor are present early in disease, but pernicious anemia develops in only a minority of patients. The median age at diagnosis is 60 years, and there is a slight female predominance. Autoimmune gastritis often is associated with other autoimmune diseases but is not linked to specific human leukocyte antigen (HLA) alleles.

Table 14–2 Characteristics of *Helicobacter pylori*–Associated and Autoimmune Gastritis

Feature	Location	
	H. pylori–Associated: Antrum	Autoimmune: Body
Inflammatory infiltrate	Neutrophils, subepithelial plasma cells	Lymphocytes, macrophages
Acid production	Increased to slightly decreased	Decreased
Gastrin	Normal to decreased	Increased
Other lesions	Hyperplastic/inflammatory polyps	Neuroendocrine hyperplasia
Serology	Antibodies to *H. pylori*	Antibodies to parietal cells (H^+,K^+-ATPase, intrinsic factor)
Sequelae	Peptic ulcer, adenocarcinoma, lymphoma	Atrophy, pernicious anemia, adenocarcinoma, carcinoid tumor
Associations	Low socioeconomic status, poverty, residence in rural areas	Autoimmune disease; thyroiditis, diabetes mellitus, Graves disease

Peptic Ulcer Disease

Peptic ulcer disease (PUD) most often is associated with *H. pylori* infection or NSAID use. In the US, the latter is becoming the most common cause of gastric ulcers as *H. pylori* infection rates fall and low-dose aspirin use in the aging population increases. PUD may occur in any portion of the gastrointestinal tract exposed to acidic gastric juices but is most common in the gastric antrum and first portion of the duodenum. PUD also may occur in the esophagus as a result of GERD or acid secretion by ectopic gastric mucosa, and in the small intestine secondary to gastric heteropia within a Meckel diverticulum.

Epidemiology

PUD is common and is a frequent cause of physician visits worldwide. It leads to treatment of over 3 million people, 190,000 hospitalizations, and 5000 deaths in the United States each year. The lifetime risk of developing an ulcer is approximately 10% for males and 4% for females.

PATHOGENESIS

H. pylori infection and NSAID use are the primary underlying causes of PUD. **The imbalances of mucosal defenses and damaging forces that cause chronic gastritis (Fig. 14–13) are also responsible for PUD.** Thus, PUD generally develops on a background of chronic gastritis. Although more than 70% of PUD cases are associated with *H. pylori* infection, only 5% to 10% of *H. pylori*–infected persons develop ulcers. It is probable that host factors as well as variation among *H. pylori* strains determine the clinical outcomes.

Gastric hyperacidity is fundamental to the pathogenesis of PUD. The acidity that drives PUD may be caused by *H. pylori* infection, parietal cell hyperplasia, excessive secretory responses, or impaired inhibition of stimulatory mechanisms such as gastrin release. For example, **Zollinger-Ellison syndrome,** characterized by multiple peptic ulcerations in the stomach, duodenum, and even jejunum, is caused by uncontrolled release of gastrin by a tumor and the resulting massive acid production. Cofactors in peptic ulcerogenesis include chronic NSAID use, as noted; cigarette smoking, which impairs mucosal blood flow and healing; and high-dose corticosteroids, which suppress prostaglandin synthesis and impair healing. Peptic ulcers are more frequent in persons with alcoholic cirrhosis, chronic obstructive pulmonary disease, chronic renal failure, and hyperparathyroidism. In the latter two conditions, hypercalcemia stimulates gastrin production and therefore increases acid secretion. Finally, psychologic stress may increase gastric acid production and exacerbate PUD.

MORPHOLOGY

Peptic ulcers are four times more common in the proximal duodenum than in the stomach. Duodenal ulcers usually occur within a few centimeters of the pyloric valve and involve the anterior duodenal wall. Gastric peptic ulcers are predominantly located near the interface of the body and antrum.

Peptic ulcers are solitary in more than 80% of patients. Lesions less than 0.3 cm in diameter tend to be shallow, whereas those over 0.6 cm are likely to be deeper. The classic peptic ulcer is a round to oval, **sharply punched-out defect** (Fig. 14–15, *A*). The base of peptic ulcers is smooth and clean as a result of peptic digestion of exudate and on histologic examination is composed of richly vascular granulation tissue (Fig. 14–15, *B*). Ongoing bleeding within the ulcer base may cause life-threatening hemorrhage. **Perforation** is a complication that demands emergent surgical intervention.

Clinical Features

Peptic ulcers are chronic, recurring lesions that occur most often in middle-aged to older adults without obvious precipitating conditions, other than chronic gastritis. A majority of peptic ulcers come to clinical attention after patient complaints of *epigastric burning or aching pain,* although a significant fraction manifest with complications such as *iron deficiency anemia, frank hemorrhage,* or *perforation.* The pain tends to occur 1 to 3 hours after meals during the day, is worse at night, and is relieved by alkali or food. Nausea,

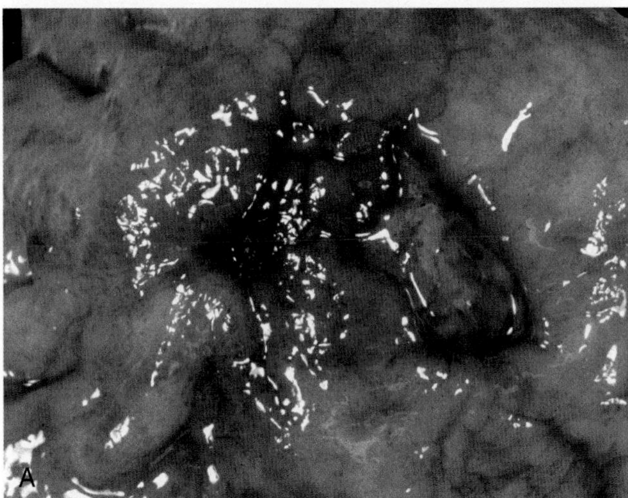

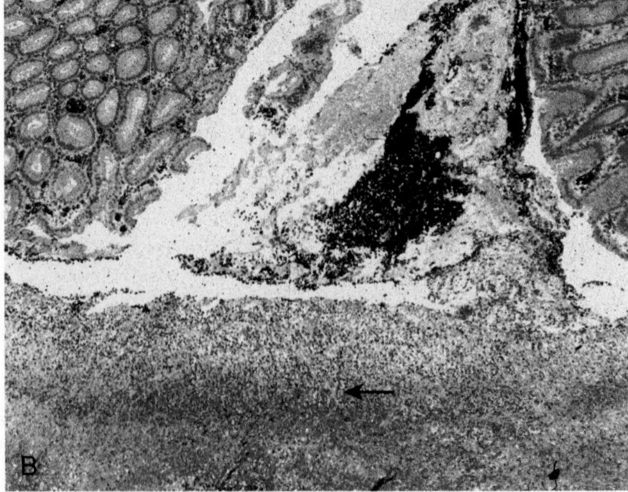

Figure 14–15 Acute gastric perforation in a patient presenting with free air under the diaphragm. **A,** Mucosal defect with clean edges. **B,** The necrotic ulcer base *(arrow)* is composed of granulation tissue.

vomiting, bloating, and belching may be present. Healing may occur with or without therapy, but the tendency to develop ulcers later remains.

A variety of surgical approaches formerly were used to treat PUD, but current therapies are aimed at *H. pylori* eradication with antibiotics and neutralization of gastric acid, usually through use of proton pump inhibitors. These efforts have markedly reduced the need for surgical management, which is reserved primarily for treatment of bleeding or perforated ulcers. PUD causes much more morbidity than mortality.

SUMMARY

Acute and Chronic Gastritis

- The spectrum of *acute gastritis* ranges from asymptomatic disease to mild epigastric pain, nausea, and vomiting. Causative factors include any agent or disease that interferes with gastric mucosal protection. Acute gastritis can progress to *acute gastric ulceration.*
- The most common cause of chronic gastritis is *H. pylori infection*; most remaining cases are caused by *autoimmune gastritis.*
- *H. pylori* gastritis typically affects the antrum and is associated with increased gastric acid production. The induced mucosa-associated lymphoid tissue (MALT) can transform into lymphoma.
- *Autoimmune gastritis* causes atrophy of the gastric body oxyntic glands, which results in decreased gastric acid production, antral G cell hyperplasia, achlorhydria, and vitamin B_{12} deficiency. Anti-parietal cell and anti–intrinsic factor antibodies typically are present.
- *Intestinal metaplasia* develops in both forms of chronic gastritis and is a risk factor for development of gastric adenocarcinoma.
- Peptic ulcer disease can be caused by *H. pylori* chronic gastritis and the resultant hyperchlorhydria or NSAID use. Ulcers can develop in the stomach or duodenum and usually heal after suppression of gastric acid production and, if present, eradication of the *H. pylori.*

NEOPLASTIC DISEASE OF THE STOMACH

Gastric Polyps

Polyps, nodules or masses that project above the level of the surrounding mucosa, are identified in up to 5% of upper gastrointestinal tract endoscopies. Polyps may develop as a result of epithelial or stromal cell hyperplasia, inflammation, ectopia, or neoplasia. Although many different types of polyps can occur in the stomach, only hyperplastic and inflammatory polyps, fundic gland polyps, and adenomas are considered here.

Inflammatory and Hyperplastic Polyps

Approximately 75% of all gastric polyps are *inflammatory* or *hyperplastic polyps.* They most commonly affect persons between 50 and 60 years of age, usually arising in a background of chronic gastritis that initiates the injury and reactive hyperplasia that cause polyp growth. If associated with *H. pylori* gastritis, polyps may regress after bacterial eradication.

MORPHOLOGY

In the stomach, inflammatory and hyperplastic polyps are essentially the same entity, with the distinction based solely on the degree of inflammation. The polyps frequently are multiple and characteristically are ovoid in shape, less than 1 cm in diameter, and covered by a smooth surface. On microscopic examination, polyps have irregular, cystically dilated, and elongated foveolar glands. The lamina propria typically is edematous with variable degrees of acute and chronic inflammation, and surface erosions may be present.

The frequency with which **dysplasia,** a precancerous in situ lesion, develops in inflammatory or hyperplastic polyps correlates with size; there is a significant increase in risk in polyps larger than 1.5 cm.

Fundic Gland Polyps

Fundic gland polyps occur sporadically and in persons with familial adenomatous polyposis (FAP) but do not have neoplastic potential. They are, however, worth mentioning here because their incidence has increased markedly as a result of the use of proton pump inhibitors. This likely results from increased gastrin secretion, in response to reduced acidity, and glandular hyperplasia driven by gastrin. Fundic gland polyps may be asymptomatic or associated with nausea, vomiting, or epigastric pain. These well-circumscribed polyps occur in the gastric body and fundus, often are multiple, and are composed of cystically dilated, irregular glands lined by flattened parietal and chief cells.

Gastric Adenoma

Gastric adenomas represent as many as 10% of all gastric polyps. Their incidence increases with age and varies among different populations in parallel with that of gastric adenocarcinoma. Patients usually are between 50 and 60 years of age, and males are affected three times more often than females. Similar to other forms of gastric dysplasia, adenomas almost always occur on a background of chronic gastritis with atrophy and intestinal metaplasia. The risk for development of adenocarcinoma in gastric adenomas is related to the size of the lesion and is particularly elevated with lesions greater than 2 cm in diameter. Overall, carcinoma may be present in up to 30% of gastric adenomas.

MORPHOLOGY

Gastric adenomas are most commonly located in the antrum and typically are composed of intestinal-type columnar epithelium. By definition, all gastrointestinal adenomas exhibit epithelial dysplasia, which can be classified as low- or high-grade. Both grades may include enlargement, elongation, and hyperchromasia of epithelial cell nuclei, epithelial crowding, and pseudostratification. High-grade dysplasia is characterized by more severe cytologic atypia and irregular architecture, including glandular budding and gland-within-gland, or cribriform, structures.

Gastric Adenocarcinoma

Adenocarcinoma is the most common malignancy of the stomach, comprising more than 90% of all gastric cancers. Early symptoms resemble those of chronic gastritis, including dyspepsia, dysphagia, and nausea. As a result, in low-incidence regions such as the United States, the cancer is often at advanced stages when clinical manifestations such as weight loss, anorexia, altered bowel habits, anemia, and hemorrhage trigger diagnostic evaluation.

Epidemiology

Gastric cancer rates vary markedly with geography. The incidence is up to 20 times higher in Japan, Chile, Costa Rica, and Eastern Europe than in North America, northern Europe, Africa, and Southeast Asia. Mass endoscopic screening programs can be successful in regions of high incidence, such as Japan, where 35% of newly detected cases are *early gastric cancer,* or tumors limited to the mucosa and submucosa. Unfortunately, mass screening programs are not cost-effective in regions in which the incidence is low, and less than 20% of cases are detected at an early stage in North America and northern Europe.

Gastric cancer is more common in lower socioeconomic groups and in persons with *multifocal mucosal atrophy and intestinal metaplasia.* PUD does not impart an increased risk of gastric cancer, but patients who have had *partial gastrectomies* for PUD have a slightly higher risk of developing cancer in the residual gastric stump as a result of hypochlorhydria, bile reflux, and chronic gastritis.

In the United States, *gastric cancer rates dropped by more than 85% during the 20th century.* Similar declines have been reported in many other Western countries, reflecting the importance of environmental and dietary factors. Despite this decrease in overall gastric adenocarcinoma incidence, *cancer of the gastric cardia is on the rise.* This trend probably is related to increased rates of Barrett esophagus and may reflect the growing prevalence of chronic GERD and obesity.

PATHOGENESIS

Gastric cancers are genetically heterogeneous but certain molecular alterations are common. We will consider these first to be followed by the role of *H. pylori*–induced chronic inflammation and the association of a subset of gastric cancers with EBV infection.

- **Mutations:** While the majority of gastric cancers are not hereditary, mutations identified in familial gastric cancer have provided important insights into mechanisms of carcinogenesis in sporadic cases. Germline mutations in *CDH1*, which encodes E-cadherin, a protein that contributes to epithelial intercellular adhesion, are associated with familial gastric cancers, usually of the diffuse type. Mutations in *CDH1* are present in about 50% of diffuse gastric tumors, while E-cadherin expression is drastically decreased in the rest, often by methylation of the *CDH1* promoter. **Thus, the loss of E-cadherin function seems to be a key step in the development of diffuse gastric cancer.**

  In contrast to *CDH1*, patients with familial adenomatous polyposis (FAP) who have germline mutations in **adenomatous polyposis coli (*APC*) genes** have an increased risk of intestinal-type gastric cancer. Sporadic intestinal-type gastric cancer is associated with several genetic abnormalities including acquired mutations of β-catenin, a protein that binds to both E-cadherin and APC protein; microsatellite instability; and hypermethylation of genes including *TGFβRII, BAX, IGFRII,* and *p16/INK4a. TP53* mutations are present in a majority of sporadic gastric cancers of both histologic types.
- ***H. pylori:*** Chronic gastritis, most commonly due to *H. pylori* infection, promotes the development and progression of cancers that may be induced by diverse genetic alterations (Chapter 5). As is the case with many forms of chronic inflammation, *H. pylori*–induced chronic gastritis is associated with increased production of proinflammatory proteins, such as interleukin-1β (IL-1β) and tumor necrosis factor (TNF). It is therefore not surprising that polymorphisms associated with enhanced production of these cytokines confer increased risk of chronic gastritis-associated intestinal-type gastric cancer in those with co-existing *H. pylori* infection.
- **EBV:** While *H. pylori* is most commonly associated with gastric cancer, approximately 10% of gastric adenocarcinomas are associated with Epstein-Barr virus (EBV) infection. Although the precise role of EBV in the development of gastric adenocarcinomas remains to be defined, it is notable that EBV episomes in these tumors frequently are clonal, suggesting that infection preceded neoplastic transformation. Further, *TP53* mutations are uncommon in the EBV-positive gastric tumors, suggesting that the molecular pathogenesis of these cancers is distinct from that of other gastric adenocarcinomas. Morphologically, EBV-positive tumors tend to occur in the proximal stomach and most commonly have a diffuse morphology with a marked lymphocytic infiltrate.

MORPHOLOGY

Gastric adenocarcinomas are classified according to their location in the stomach as well as gross and histologic morphology. The **Lauren classification** that separates gastric cancers into **intestinal** and **diffuse** types correlates with distinct patterns of molecular alterations, as discussed above. Intestinal-type cancers tend to be bulky (Fig. 14–16, *A*) and are composed of glandular structures similar to esophageal and colonic adenocarcinoma. Intestinal-type adenocarcinomas typically grow along broad cohesive fronts to form either an exophytic mass or an ulcerated tumor. The neoplastic cells often contain apical mucin vacuoles, and abundant mucin may be present in gland lumina.

Diffuse gastric cancers display an infiltrative growth pattern (Fig. 14–16, *B*) and are composed of discohesive cells with large mucin vacuoles that expand the cytoplasm and push the nucleus to the periphery, creating a **signet ring cell** morphology (Fig. 14–16, *C*). These cells permeate the mucosa and stomach wall individually or in small clusters. A mass may be difficult to appreciate in diffuse gastric cancer, but these infiltrative tumors often evoke a **desmoplastic** reaction that stiffens the gastric wall and may cause diffuse rugal flattening and a rigid, thickened wall that imparts a "leather bottle" appearance termed **linitis plastica.**

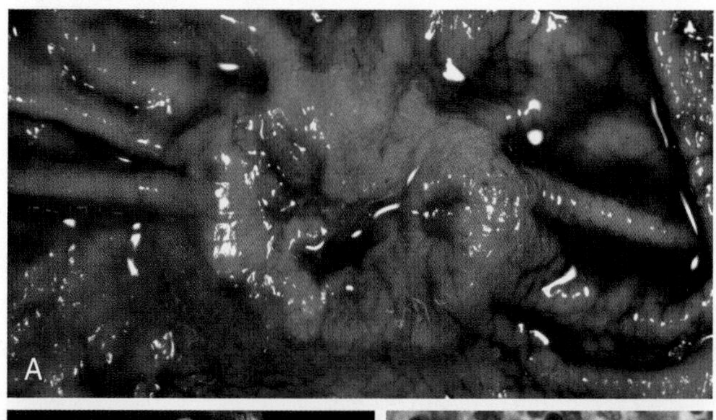

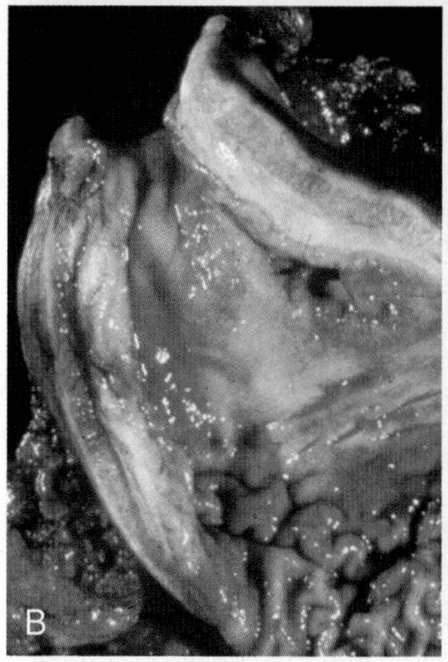

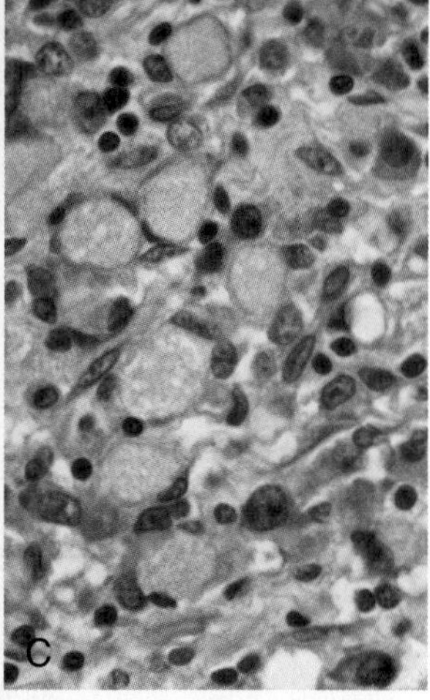

Figure 14–16 Gastric adenocarcinoma. **A,** Intestinal-type adenocarcinoma consisting of an elevated mass with heaped-up borders and central ulceration. Compare with the peptic ulcer in Figure 14-15, A. **B,** Linitis plastica. The gastric wall is markedly thickened, and rugal folds are partially lost. **C,** Signet ring cells with large cytoplasmic mucin vacuoles and peripherally displaced, crescent-shaped nuclei.

Clinical Features

Intestinal-type gastric cancer predominates in high-risk areas and develops from precursor lesions including flat dysplasia and adenomas. The mean age at presentation is 55 years, and the male-to-female ratio is 2:1. By contrast, the incidence of diffuse gastric cancer is relatively uniform across countries, there are no identified precursor lesions, and the disease occurs at similar frequencies in males and females. Of note, *the remarkable decrease in gastric cancer incidence applies only to the intestinal type,* which is most closely associated with atrophic gastritis and intestinal metaplasia. As a result, the incidences of intestinal and diffuse types of gastric cancers are now similar in some regions.

The depth of invasion and the extent of nodal and distant metastasis at the time of diagnosis remain the most powerful prognostic indicators for gastric cancer. Local invasion into the duodenum, pancreas, and retroperitoneum also is characteristic. When possible, surgical resection remains the preferred treatment for gastric adenocarcinoma. After surgical resection, the 5-year survival rate for early gastric cancer can exceed 90%, even if lymph node metastases are present. By contrast, the 5-year survival rate for advanced gastric cancer remains below 20%, in large part because current chemotherapy regimens are minimally effective. Because of the advanced stage at which most gastric cancers are discovered in the United States, the overall 5-year survival is less than 30%.

Lymphoma

Although extranodal lymphomas can arise in virtually any tissue, they do so most commonly in the gastrointestinal tract, particularly the stomach. In allogeneic hematopoietic stem cell and organ transplant recipients, the bowel also is the most frequent site for Epstein-Barr virus–positive B cell lymphoproliferations. Nearly 5% of all gastric malignancies are primary lymphomas, the most common of which are indolent extranodal marginal zone B cell lymphomas. In the gut, these tumors often are referred to as lymphomas of *mucosa-associated lymphoid tissue* (MALT), or *MALTomas.* This entity and the second most common primary lymphoma of the gut, diffuse large B cell lymphoma, are discussed in Chapter 11.

Carcinoid Tumor

Carcinoid tumors arise from neuroendocrine organs (e.g., the endocrine pancreas) and neuroendocrine-differentiated gastrointestinal epithelia (e.g., G-cells). A majority are found in the gastrointestinal tract, and more than 40% occur in the small intestine. The tracheobronchial tree and lungs are the next most commonly involved sites. Gastric carcinoids may be associated with endocrine cell hyperplasia, chronic atrophic gastritis, and Zollinger-Ellison syndrome. These tumors were called "carcinoid" because they are slower growing than carcinomas. The most current WHO classification describes these as low- or intermediate grade neuroendocrine tumors. The grade is based on mitotic activity and the fraction of cells immunohistochemically positive for Ki67, a mitotic marker. However, it is important to recognize that site within the GI tract and extent of local invasion are also important prognostic indicators (see later). High-grade neuroendocrine tumors, termed *neuroendocrine carcinoma,* frequently display necrosis and, in the GI tract, are most common in the jejunum.

MORPHOLOGY

Carcinoid tumors are intramural or submucosal masses that create small polypoid lesions (Fig. 14–17, *A*). The tumors are yellow or tan in appearance and elicit an intense desmoplastic reaction that may cause kinking of the bowel and obstruction. On histologic examination, carcinoid tumors are composed of islands, trabeculae, strands, glands, or sheets of uniform cells with scant, pink granular cytoplasm and a round to oval stippled nucleus (Fig. 14–17, *B*).

Clinical Features

The peak incidence of carcinoid tumors is in the sixth decade, but they may appear at any age. Symptoms are determined by the hormones produced. For example, the *carcinoid syndrome* is caused by vasoactive substances secreted by the tumor that cause cutaneous flushing, sweating, bronchospasm, colicky abdominal pain, diarrhea, and right-sided cardiac valvular fibrosis. When tumors are

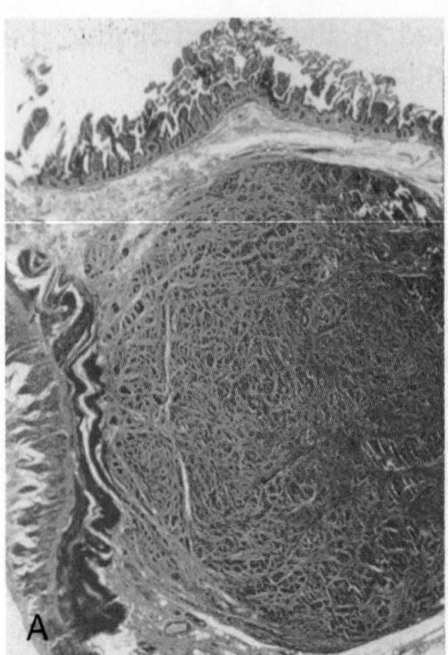

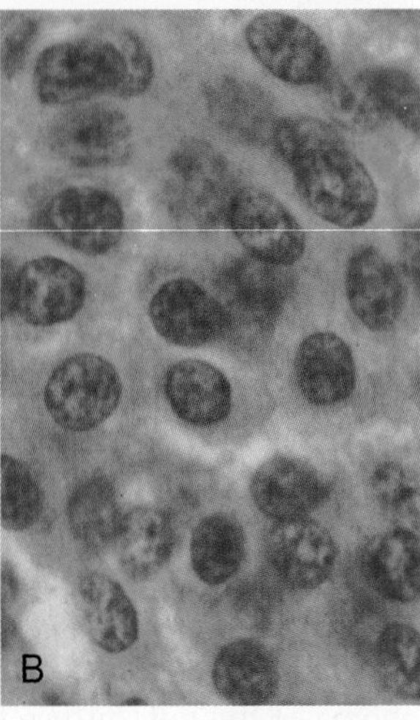

Figure 14–17 Gastrointestinal carcinoid tumor (neuroendocrine tumor). **A,** Carcinoid tumors often form a submucosal nodule composed of tumor cells embedded in dense fibrous tissue. **B,** High magnification shows the bland cytology that typifies carcinoid tumors. The chromatin texture, with fine and coarse clumps, frequently assumes a "salt and pepper" pattern. Despite their innocuous appearance, carcinoids can be aggressive.

confined to the intestine, the vasoactive substances released are metabolized to inactive forms by the liver—a "first-pass" effect similar to that seen with oral drugs. Thus, carcinoid syndrome occurs in less than 10% of patients and is *strongly associated with metastatic disease.*

The most important prognostic factor for gastrointestinal carcinoid tumors is location:

- *Foregut carcinoid tumors,* those found within the stomach, duodenum proximal to the ligament of Treitz, and esophagus, rarely metastasize and generally are cured by resection. Although rare, duodenal gastrin-producing carcinoid tumors, *gastrinomas,* have been associated with proton pump inhibitor therapy.
- *Midgut carcinoid tumors* that arise in the jejunum and ileum often are multiple and tend to be aggressive. In these tumors, greater depth of local invasion, increased size, and presence of necrosis and mitosis are associated with poor outcome.
- *Hindgut carcinoids* arising in the appendix and colorectum typically are discovered incidentally. Those in the appendix occur at any age and are almost uniformly benign. Rectal carcinoid tumors tend to produce polypeptide hormones and may manifest with abdominal pain and weight loss; they only occasionally metastasize.

Gastrointestinal Stromal Tumor

A wide variety of mesenchymal neoplasms may arise in the stomach. Many are named according to the cell type they most resemble; for example, smooth muscle tumors are called *leiomyomas* or *leiomyosarcomas,* nerve sheath tumors are termed *schwannomas,* and those resembling glomus bodies in the nail beds and at other sites are termed *glomus tumors.* These tumors are all rare and are not discussed here. *Gastrointestinal stromal tumor (GIST)* is the most common mesenchymal tumor of the abdomen, and more than half of these tumors occur in the stomach.

Epidemiology

Overall, GISTs are slightly more common in males. The peak incidence of gastric GIST is around 60 years of age, with less than 10% occurring in persons younger than 40 years of age.

PATHOGENESIS

Approximately **75% to 80% of all GISTs have oncogenic, gain-of-function mutations of the gene encoding the tyrosine kinase c-KIT,** which is the receptor for stem cell factor. Another 8% of GISTs have mutations that activate a related tyrosine kinase, platelet-derived growth factor receptor A (PDGFRA); thus activating mutations in tyrosine kinases are found in virtually all GISTs. However, either mutation is sufficient for tumorigenesis, and *c-KIT* and *PDGFRA* mutations are almost never found in a single tumor. GISTs appear to arise from, or share a common stem cell with, the interstitial cells of Cajal, which express c-KIT, are located in the muscularis propria, and serve as pacemaker cells for gut peristalsis.

MORPHOLOGY

Primary gastric GISTs usually form a solitary, well-circumscribed, fleshy, submucosal mass. Metastases may form multiple small serosal nodules or fewer large nodules in the liver; spread outside of the abdomen is uncommon. GISTs can be composed of thin, elongated **spindle cells** or plumper **epithelioid cells.** The most useful diagnostic marker is c-KIT, consistent with the relationship between GISTs and interstitial cells of Cajal, which is immunohistochemically detectable in 95% of these tumors.

Clinical Features

Symptoms of GISTs at presentation may be related to mass effects or mucosal ulceration. Complete surgical resection is the primary treatment for localized gastric GIST. The prognosis correlates with tumor size, mitotic index, and location, *with gastric GISTs being somewhat less aggressive than those arising in the small intestine.* Recurrence or metastasis is rare for gastric GISTs less than 5 cm across but common for mitotically active tumors larger than 10 cm. Patients with unresectable, recurrent, or metastatic disease often respond to *imatinib,* an inhibitor of the tyrosine kinase activity of c-KIT and PDGFRA that is also effective in suppressing BCR-ABL kinase activity in chronic myelogenous leukemia (Chapter 11). Unfortunately, GISTs eventually become resistant to imatinib, and other kinase inhibitors are now being evaluated in imatinib-resistant disease.

SUMMARY

Gastric Polyps and Tumors

- *Inflammatory and hyperplastic gastric polyps* are reactive lesions associated with chronic gastritis. Risk of dysplasia increases with polyp size.

- *Gastric adenomas* develop in a background of chronic gastritis and are particularly associated with intestinal metaplasia and mucosal (glandular) atrophy. Adenocarcinoma frequently arises in gastric adenomas, which therefore require complete excision and surveillance to detect recurrence.
- Gastric adenocarcinoma incidence varies markedly with geography and also is more common in lower socioeconomic groups.
- Gastric adenocarcinomas are classified according to location and gross and histologic morphology. Those with an *intestinal* histologic pattern tend to form bulky tumors and may be ulcerated, whereas those composed of *signet ring cells* typically display a diffuse infiltrative growth pattern that may thicken the gastric wall (*linitis plastica*) without forming a discrete mass.
- *H. pylori* infection is the most common etiologic agent for gastric adenocarcinoma, but other associations, including chronic atrophic gastritis and EBV infection, suggest several pathways of neoplastic transformation are operative.
- *Primary gastric lymphomas* most often are derived from the mucosa-associated lymphoid tissue whose development is induced by chronic gastritis.
- *Carcinoid tumors* arise from the diffuse components of the endocrine system, and are most common in the gastrointestinal tract, particularly the small intestine. The single most important prognostic factor is location: Tumors of the small intestine tend to be most aggressive, while those of the appendix are almost always benign.
- *Gastrointestinal stromal tumor* (GIST) is the most common mesenchymal tumor of the abdomen, occurs most often in the stomach; it arises from benign pacemaker cells, also known as the interstitial cells of Cajal. A majority of tumors have activating mutations in either the c-KIT or the PDGFRA tyrosine kinases and respond to kinase inhibitors.

SMALL AND LARGE INTESTINES

The small intestine and colon account for most of the length of the gastrointestinal tract and are the sites of a wide variety of diseases, many of which affect nutrient and water transport. Perturbation of these processes can cause malabsorption and diarrhea. The intestines are also the principal site where the immune system interfaces with a diverse array of antigens present in food and gut microbes. Indeed, intestinal bacteria outnumber eukaryotic cells in the human body by ten-fold. Thus, it is not surprising that the small intestine and colon frequently are involved by infectious and inflammatory processes. Finally, the colon is the most common site of gastrointestinal neoplasia in Western populations.

INTESTINAL OBSTRUCTION

Obstruction of the gastrointestinal tract may occur at any level, but the small intestine is most often involved because of its relatively narrow lumen. Collectively, *hernias, intestinal adhesions, intussusception,* and *volvulus* account for 80% of mechanical obstructions (Fig. 14–18), while tumors and infarction account for most of the remainder. The clinical manifestations of intestinal obstruction include abdominal pain and distention, vomiting, and constipation. Surgical intervention usually is required in cases involving mechanical obstruction or severe infarction.

Hirschsprung Disease

Hirschsprung disease occurs in approximately 1 of 5000 live births and stems from a congenital defect in colonic innervation. It may be isolated or occur in combination with other developmental abnormalities. It is more common in males but tends to be more severe in females. Siblings of patients have an increased risk of Hirschsprung disease.

Patients typically present as neonates with failure to pass meconium in the immediate postnatal period followed by obstructive constipation. The major threats to life

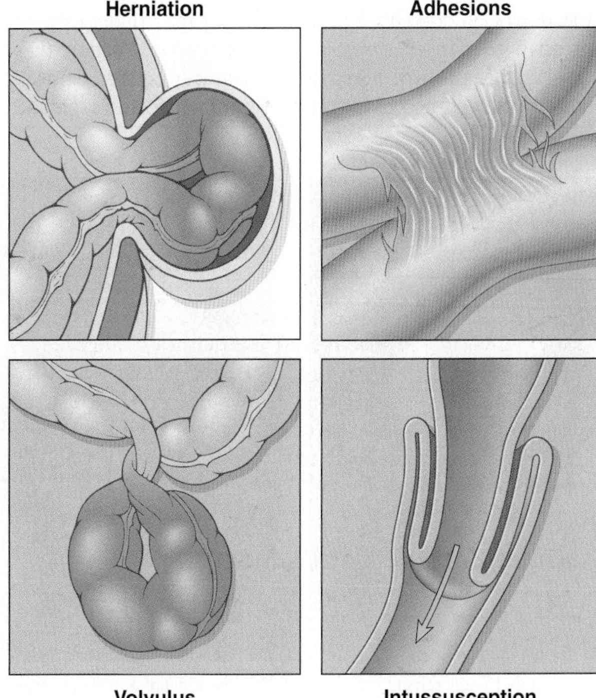

Figure 14–18 Intestinal obstruction. The four major mechanical causes of intestinal obstruction are (1) herniation of a segment in the umbilical or inguinal regions, (2) adhesion between loops of intestine, (3) volvulus, and (4) intussusception.

are enterocolitis, fluid and electrolyte disturbances, perforation, and peritonitis. Surgical resection of the aganglionic segment with anastomosis of the normal colon to the rectum is effective, although it may take years for patients to attain normal bowel function and continence.

PATHOGENESIS

The enteric neuronal plexus develops from neural crest cells that migrate into the bowel wall during embryogenesis. Hirschsprung disease, also known as **congenital aganglionic megacolon,** results when the normal migration of neural crest cells from cecum to rectum is disrupted. This produces a distal intestinal segment that lacks both the Meissner submucosal plexus and the Auerbach myenteric plexus ("aganglionosis"). Coordinated peristaltic contractions are absent and the subsequent functional obstruction results in dilation proximal to the affected segment. While the mechanisms underlying this defective neural crest cell migration are unknown, **heterozygous loss-of-function mutations in the receptor tyrosine kinase RET account for a majority of familial cases** and approximately 15% of sporadic cases. However, mutations also occur in other genes, only some of which have been identified, and modifying genes or environmental factors also play a role.

MORPHOLOGY

Hirschsprung disease always affects the rectum, but the length of the additional involved segments varies. Most cases are limited to the rectum and sigmoid colon, but severe disease can involve the entire colon. The aganglionic region may have a grossly normal or contracted appearance, while the normally innervated proximal colon may undergo progressive dilation as a result of the distal obstruction (Fig. 14–19). Diagnosis of Hirschsprung disease requires demonstrating the absence of ganglion cells in the affected segment.

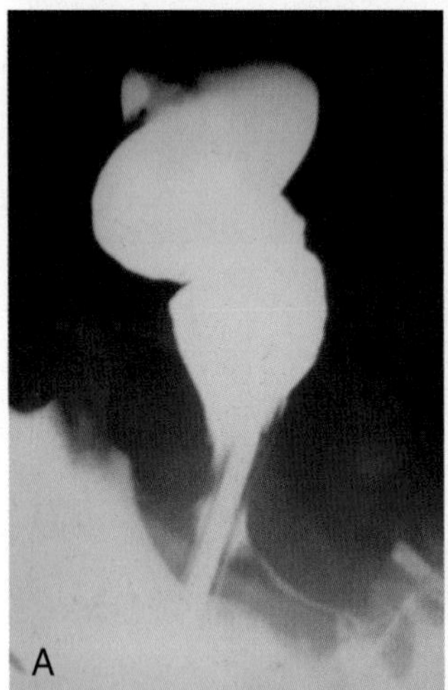

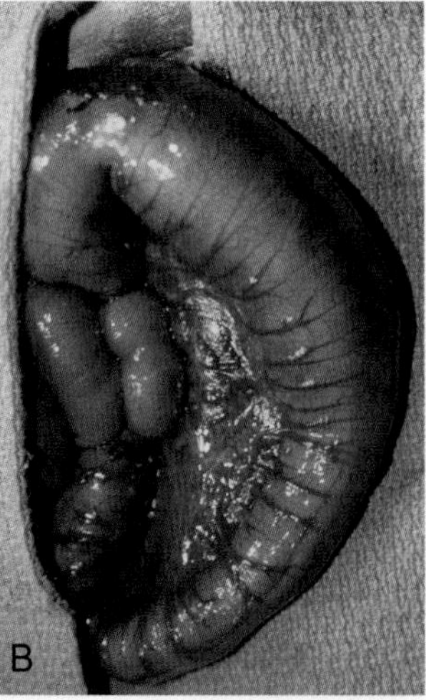

Figure 14–19 Hirschsprung disease. **A,** Preoperative barium enema study showing constricted rectum (*bottom of the image*) and dilated sigmoid colon. Ganglion cells were absent in the rectum, but present in the sigmoid colon. **B,** Corresponding intraoperative appearance of the dilated sigmoid colon.

(Courtesy of Dr. Aliya Husain, The University of Chicago, Chicago, Illinois.)

Abdominal Hernia

Any weakness or defect in the wall of the peritoneal cavity may permit protrusion of a serosa-lined pouch of peritoneum called a *hernia sac.* Acquired hernias most commonly occur anteriorly, through the inguinal and femoral canals or umbilicus, or at sites of surgical scars. These are of concern because of visceral protrusion (*external herniation*). This is particularly true of inguinal hernias, which tend to have narrow orifices and large sacs. Small bowel loops are herniated most often, but portions of omentum or large bowel also protrude, and any of these may become entrapped. Pressure at the neck of the pouch may impair venous drainage, leading to stasis and edema. These changes increase the bulk of the herniated loop, leading to permanent entrapment, or *incarceration,* and over time, arterial and venous compromise, or *strangulation,* can result in infarction.

SUMMARY

Intestinal Obstruction

- *Hirschsprung disease* is the result of defective neural crest cell migration from cecum to rectum. It gives rise to functional obstruction.
- *Abdominal herniation* may occur through any weakness or defect in the wall of the peritoneal cavity, including inguinal and femoral canals, umbilicus, and sites of surgical scarring.

VASCULAR DISORDERS OF BOWEL

The greater portion of the gastrointestinal tract is supplied by the celiac, superior mesenteric, and inferior mesenteric arteries. As they approach the intestinal wall, the superior and inferior mesenteric arteries fan out to form the mesenteric arcades. Interconnections between arcades, as well as collateral supplies from the proximal celiac and distal pudendal and iliac circulations, make it possible for the small intestine and colon to tolerate slowly progressive loss of the blood supply from one artery. By contrast, acute compromise of any major vessel can lead to infarction of several meters of intestine.

Ischemic Bowel Disease

Ischemic damage to the bowel wall can range from *mucosal infarction,* extending no deeper than the muscularis mucosa; to *mural infarction* of mucosa and submucosa; to *transmural infarction* involving all three layers of the wall. While mucosal or mural infarctions often are secondary to acute or chronic *hypoperfusion,* transmural infarction is generally caused by acute vascular obstruction. Important causes of acute arterial obstruction include severe *atherosclerosis* (which is often prominent at the origin of mesenteric vessels), *aortic aneurysm, hypercoagulable states, oral contraceptive use,* and *embolization of cardiac vegetations or aortic atheromas.* Intestinal hypoperfusion can also be associated with *cardiac failure, shock, dehydration,* or *vasoconstrictive drugs.* Systemic *vasculitides,* such as polyarteritis nodosum, Henoch-Schönlein purpura, or Wegener granulomatosis, also may damage intestinal arteries. Mesenteric venous thrombosis can also lead to ischemic disease, but is uncommon. Other causes include invasive neoplasms, cirrhosis, portal hypertension, trauma, or abdominal masses that compress the portal drainage.

PATHOGENESIS

Intestinal responses to ischemia occur in two phases. The initial hypoxic injury occurs at the onset of vascular compromise and, although some damage occurs, intestinal epithelial cells are relatively resistant to transient hypoxia. The second phase, reperfusion injury, is initiated by restoration of the blood supply and associated with the greatest damage. In severe cases multiorgan failure may occur. While the underlying mechanisms of reperfusion injury are incompletely understood, they involve free radical production, neutrophil infiltration, and release of inflammatory mediators, such as complement proteins and cytokines (Chapter 10). **The severity of vascular compromise, time frame during which it develops, and vessels affected are the major variables that determine severity of ischemic bowel disease.** Two aspects of intestinal vascular anatomy also contribute to the distribution of ischemic damage:

- Intestinal segments at the end of their respective arterial supplies are particularly susceptible to ischemia. These **watershed zones** include the splenic flexure, where the superior and inferior mesenteric arterial circulations terminate, and, to a lesser extent, the sigmoid colon and rectum where inferior mesenteric, pudendal, and iliac arterial circulations end. Generalized hypotension or hypoxemia can therefore cause localized injury, and ischemic disease should be considered in the differential diagnosis for focal colitis of the splenic flexure or rectosigmoid colon.
- Intestinal capillaries run alongside the glands, from crypt to surface, before making a hairpin turn at the surface to empty into the postcapillary venules. This configuration allows oxygenated blood to supply crypts but leaves the surface epithelium vulnerable to ischemic injury. This anatomy protects the crypts, which contain the epithelial stem cells that are necessary to repopulate the surface. Thus, surface epithelial atrophy, or even necrosis with consequent sloughing, with normal or hyperproliferative crypts constitutes a morphologic signature of ischemic intestinal disease.

MORPHOLOGY

Despite the increased susceptibility of watershed zones, **mucosal and mural infarction** may involve any level of the gut from stomach to anus. Disease frequently is segmental and patchy in distribution, and the mucosa is hemorrhagic and often ulcerated. The bowel wall is thickened by edema that may involve the mucosa or extend into the submucosa and muscularis propria. With severe disease, pathologic changes include extensive mucosal and submucosal hemorrhage and necrosis, but serosal hemorrhage and serositis generally are absent. Damage is more pronounced in acute arterial thrombosis and **transmural infarction.** Blood-tinged mucus or blood accumulates within the lumen. Coagulative necrosis of the muscularis propria occurs within 1 to 4 days and may be associated with purulent serositis and perforation.

In **mesenteric venous thrombosis,** arterial blood continues to flow for a time, resulting in a less abrupt transition from affected to normal bowel. However, propagation of the thrombus may lead to secondary involvement of the splanchnic bed. The ultimate result is similar to that produced by acute arterial obstruction, because impaired venous drainage eventually prevents entry of oxygenated arterial blood.

Microscopic examination of ischemic intestine demonstrates **atrophy or sloughing of surface epithelium** (Fig. 14–20, *A*). By contrast, crypts may be hyperproliferative. Inflammatory infiltrates initially are absent in acute ischemia, but neutrophils are recruited within hours of reperfusion. Chronic ischemia is accompanied by fibrous scarring of the lamina propria (Fig. 14–20, *B*) and, uncommonly, stricture formation. In acute phases of ischemic damage, bacterial superinfection and enterotoxin release may induce pseudomembrane formation that can resemble *Clostridium difficile*–associated pseudomembranous colitis (discussed later).

Clinical Features

Ischemic bowel disease tends to occur in older persons with coexisting cardiac or vascular disease. Acute transmural infarction typically manifests with sudden, severe abdominal pain and tenderness, sometimes accompanied by nausea, vomiting, bloody diarrhea, or grossly melanotic stool. This presentation may progress to shock and vascular collapse within hours as a result of blood loss. Peristaltic sounds diminish or disappear, and muscular spasm creates boardlike rigidity of the abdominal wall. Because these physical signs overlap with those of other abdominal emergencies, including acute appendicitis, perforated ulcer, and acute cholecystitis, the diagnosis of intestinal infarction may be delayed or missed, with disastrous consequences. As the mucosal barrier breaks down, bacteria enter the circulation and sepsis can develop; the mortality rate may exceed 50%.

The overall progression of ischemic enteritis depends on the underlying cause and severity of injury:

- *Mucosal and mural infarctions* by themselves may not be fatal. However, these may progress to more extensive,

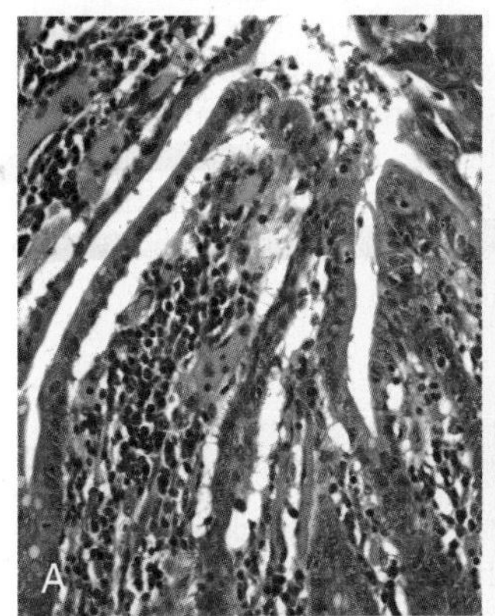

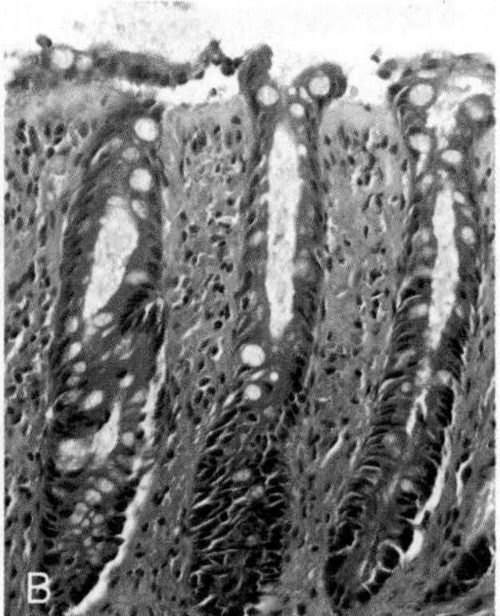

Figure 14–20 Ischemia. **A,** Characteristic attenuated and partially detached villous epithelium in acute jejunal ischemia. Note the hyperchromatic nuclei of proliferating crypt cells. **B,** Chronic colonic ischemia with atrophic surface epithelium and fibrotic lamina propria.

transmural infarction if the vascular supply is not restored by correction of the insult or, in chronic disease, by development of adequate collateral supplies.

- *Chronic ischemia* may masquerade as inflammatory bowel disease, with episodes of bloody diarrhea interspersed with periods of healing.
- *CMV infection* causes ischemic gastrointestinal disease as a consequence of the viral tropism for and infection of endothelial cells. CMV infection can be a complication of immunosuppressive therapy (Chapter 8).
- *Radiation enterocolitis* occurs when the gastrointestinal tract is irradiated. In addition to epithelial damage, radiation-induced vascular injury may be significant and produce changes that are similar to ischemic disease. In addition to clinical history, the presence of bizarre "radiation fibroblasts" within the stroma may provide an important clue to the etiology. Acute radiation enteritis manifests as anorexia, abdominal cramps, and a malabsorptive diarrhea, while chronic radiation enteritis or colitis often is more indolent and may present as an inflammatory colitis.
- *Necrotizing enterocolitis* is an acute disorder of the small and large intestines that can result in transmural necrosis. It is the most common acquired gastrointestinal emergency of neonates, particularly those who are premature or of low birth weight, and occurs most often when oral feeding is initiated (Chapter 6). Ischemic injury generally is considered to contribute to its pathogenesis.
- *Angiodysplasia* is characterized by malformed submucosal and mucosal blood vessels. It occurs *most often in the cecum or right colon,* and usually presents after the sixth decade of life. Although the prevalence of angiodysplasia is less than 1% in the adult population, *it accounts for 20% of major episodes of lower intestinal bleeding; intestinal hemorrhage may be chronic and intermittent or acute and massive.* The pathogenesis is unknown.

Hemorrhoids

Hemorrhoids affect about 5% of the general population. Simply put, hemorrhoids are dilated anal and perianal collateral vessels that connect the portal and caval venous systems to relieve elevated venous pressure within the hemorrhoid plexus. Thus, although hemorrhoids are both more common and less serious than esophageal varices, the pathogenesis of these lesions is similar. Common factors that predispose to hemorrhoids are constipation and associated straining, which increase intra-abdominal and venous pressures, venous stasis of pregnancy, and portal hypertension.

MORPHOLOGY

Collateral vessels within the inferior hemorrhoidal plexus are located below the anorectal line and are termed **external hemorrhoids,** while those that result from dilation of the superior hemorrhoidal plexus within the distal rectum are referred to as **internal hemorrhoids.** On histologic examination, hemorrhoids consist of thin-walled, dilated, submucosal vessels that protrude beneath the anal or rectal mucosa. In their exposed position, they are subject to trauma and tend to become inflamed, thrombosed, and, in the course of time, recanalized. Superficial ulceration may occur.

Clinical Features

Hemorrhoids often manifest with pain and rectal bleeding, particularly bright red blood seen on toilet tissue. Except in pregnant women, hemorrhoids are rarely encountered in persons younger than 30 years of age. Hemorrhoids also may develop as a result of portal hypertension, where the implications are more ominous. Hemorrhoidal bleeding generally is not a medical emergency; treatment options include sclerotherapy, rubber band ligation, and infrared coagulation. In severe cases, hemorrhoids may be removed surgically by *hemorrhoidectomy.*

SUMMARY

Vascular Disorders of Bowel

- Intestinal ischemia can occur as a result of either *arterial or venous obstruction.*
- *Ischemic bowel disease* resulting from hypoperfusion is most common at the splenic flexure, sigmoid colon, and rectum; these are *watershed zones* where two arterial circulations terminate.
- *Systemic vasculitides and infectious diseases* (e.g., CMV infection) can cause vascular disease that is not confined to the gastrointestinal tract.
- *Angiodysplasia* is a common cause of major lower gastrointestinal bleeding in the elderly.
- *Hemorrhoids* are collateral vessels that form to allow resolution of venous hypertension.

DIARRHEAL DISEASE

Malabsorptive Diarrhea

Diarrhea is a common symptom of many intestinal diseases, including those due to infection, inflammation, ischemia, malabsorption, and nutritional deficiency. This section focuses primarily on *malabsorption,* which manifests most commonly as *chronic diarrhea* and is characterized by defective absorption of fats, fat- and water-soluble vitamins, proteins, carbohydrates, electrolytes and minerals, and water. Other disorders associated with *secretory* and *exudative* types of diarrhea (e.g., cholera and inflammatory bowel disease, respectively) are addressed in separate sections.

Chronic malabsorption causes weight loss, anorexia, abdominal distention, borborygmi, and muscle wasting. A hallmark of malabsorption is *steatorrhea,* characterized by excessive fecal fat and bulky, frothy, greasy, yellow or clay-colored stools. *The chronic malabsorptive disorders most commonly encountered in the United States are pancreatic insufficiency, celiac disease, and Crohn disease.* Intestinal graft-versus-host disease is an important cause of both malabsorption and diarrhea after allogeneic hematopoietic stem cell transplantation. Environmental enteropathy (previously known as tropical sprue) is pervasive in some communities within developing countries.

Diarrhea is defined as an increase in stool mass, frequency, or fluidity, typically to volumes greater than 200 mL per day. In severe cases stool volume can exceed 14 L per day and, without fluid resuscitation, result in death. Painful, bloody, small-volume diarrhea is known as *dysentery*. Diarrhea can be classified into four major categories:

- *Secretory diarrhea* is characterized by isotonic stool and persists during fasting.
- *Osmotic diarrhea,* such as that occurring with lactase deficiency, is due to osmotic forces exerted by unabsorbed luminal solutes. The diarrheal fluid is more than 50 mOsm more concentrated than plasma, and the condition abates with fasting.
- *Malabsorptive diarrhea* caused by inadequate nutrient absorption is associated with steatorrhea and is relieved by fasting.
- *Exudative diarrhea* is due to inflammatory disease and characterized by purulent, bloody stools that continue during fasting.

Malabsorption results from disturbance in at least one of the four phases of nutrient absorption: (1) *intraluminal digestion,* in which proteins, carbohydrates, and fats are broken down into absorbable forms; (2) *terminal digestion,* which involves the hydrolysis of carbohydrates and peptides by disaccharidases and peptidases, respectively, in the brush border of the small intestinal mucosa; (3) *transepithelial transport,* in which nutrients, fluid, and electrolytes are transported across and processed within the small intestinal epithelium; and (4) *lymphatic transport* of absorbed lipids.

In many malabsorptive disorders, a defect in one of these processes predominates, but more than one usually contributes (Table 14–3). As a result, malabsorption syndromes resemble each other more than they differ. Symptoms and signs include *diarrhea* (from nutrient malabsorption and excessive intestinal secretion), *flatus, abdominal pain,* and *weight loss.* Inadequate absorption of vitamins and minerals can result in anemia and mucositis due to pyridoxine, folate, or vitamin B_{12} deficiency; bleeding due to vitamin K deficiency; osteopenia and tetany due to calcium, magnesium, or vitamin D deficiency; or neuropathy due to vitamin A or B_{12} deficiency. A variety of endocrine and skin disturbances also may occur.

Cystic Fibrosis

Cystic fibrosis is discussed in greater detail elsewhere (Chapter 6). Only the malabsorption associated with cystic fibrosis is considered here. Owing to the absence of the epithelial cystic fibrosis transmembrane conductance regulator (CFTR), persons with cystic fibrosis have defects in intestinal and pancreatic ductal chloride ion secretion. This abnormality leads to interference with bicarbonate, sodium, and water secretion, ultimately resulting in defective luminal hydration. This failure of hydration can result in meconium ileus, which is present in up to 10% of newborns with cystic fibrosis. In the pancreas, intraductal concretions can begin to form in utero. This leads to obstruction, low-grade chronic autodigestion of the pancreas, and eventual *exocrine pancreatic insufficiency in more than 80% of patients.* The result is failure of the intraluminal phase of nutrient absorption, which can be effectively treated in most patients with oral enzyme supplementation.

Celiac Disease

Celiac disease, also known as *celiac sprue* or *gluten-sensitive enteropathy,* is an immune-mediated enteropathy triggered by the ingestion of gluten-containing cereals, such as wheat, rye, or barley, in genetically predisposed persons. In countries whose populations consist predominantly of white people of European ancestry, celiac disease is a common disorder, with an estimated prevalence of 0.5%

Table 14–3 Defects in Malabsorptive and Diarrheal Disease

Disease	Intraluminal Digestion	Terminal Digestion	Transepithelial Transport	Lymphatic Transport
Celiac disease		+	+	
Tropical sprue		+	+	
Chronic pancreatitis	+			
Cystic fibrosis	+			
Primary bile acid malabsorption	+		+	
Carcinoid syndrome			+	
Autoimmune enteropathy		+	+	
Disaccharidase deficiency		+		
Whipple disease				+
Abetalipoproteinemia			+	
Viral gastroenteritis		+	+	
Bacterial gastroenteritis		+	+	
Parasitic gastroenteritis		+	+	
Inflammatory bowel disease	+	+	+	

+ indicates that the process is abnormal in the disease indicated. Other processes are not affected.

to 1%. The primary treatment for celiac disease is a *gluten-free diet.* Despite the challenges of adhering to such a diet, it does result in symptomatic improvement for most patients.

PATHOGENESIS

Celiac disease is an intestinal immune reaction to gluten, the major storage protein of wheat and similar grains. Gluten is digested by luminal and brush border enzymes into amino acids and peptides, including a 33–amino acid gliadin peptide that is resistant to degradation by gastric, pancreatic, and small intestinal proteases (Fig. 14–21). Gliadin is deamidated by tissue transglutaminase and is then able to interact with HLA-DQ2 or HLA-DQ8 on antigen-presenting cells and be presented to CD4+ T cells. These T cells produce cytokines that are likely to contribute to the tissue damage and characteristic mucosal histopathology. A characteristic B cell response follows: this includes production of anti-tissue transglutaminase, anti-deamidated gliadin, and, perhaps as a result of cross-reactive epitopes, anti-endomysial antibodies, which are diagnostically useful (see below). However, whether these antibodies contribute to celiac disease pathogenesis or are merely markers remains controversial. In addition to CD4+ cells, there is accumulation of CD8+ cells that are not specific for gliadin. These CD8+ cells may play an ancillary role in causing tissue damage. It is thought that deamidated gliadin peptides induce epithelial cells to produce the cytokine IL-15, which in turn triggers activation and proliferation of CD8+ intraepithelial lymphocytes that can express the MIC-A receptor NKG2D. These lymphocytes become cytotoxic and kill enterocytes that have been induced by various stressors to express surface MIC-A, an HLA class I–like protein that is recognized by NKG2D and, possibly, other epithelial proteins. The damage caused by these immune mechanisms may increase the movement of gliadin peptides across the epithelium, which are deamidated by tissue transglutaminase, thus perpetuating the cycle of disease.

While nearly all people eat grain and are exposed to gluten and gliadin, most do not develop celiac disease. Thus, host factors determine whether disease develops. Among these, HLA proteins seem to be critical, since almost all people with celiac disease carry the class II HLA-DQ2 or HLA-DQ8 alleles. However, the HLA locus accounts for less than half of the genetic component of celiac disease. Other genetic contributors are not fully defined. There is also an association of celiac disease with other immune diseases including type I diabetes, thyroiditis, and Sjögren syndrome.

MORPHOLOGY

Biopsy specimens from the second portion of the duodenum or proximal jejunum, which are exposed to the highest concentrations of dietary gluten, generally are diagnostic in celiac disease. The histopathologic picture is characterized by increased numbers of intraepithelial CD8+ T lymphocytes, with **intraepithelial lymphocytosis, crypt hyperplasia, and villous atrophy** (Fig. 14–22). This loss of mucosal and brush border surface area probably accounts for the malabsorption. In addition, increased rates of epithelial turnover, reflected in increased crypt mitotic activity, may limit the ability of absorptive enterocytes to fully differentiate and contribute to defects in terminal digestion and transepithelial transport. Other features of fully developed celiac disease include increased numbers of plasma cells, mast cells, and eosinophils, especially within the upper part of the lamina propria. With increased serologic screening and early detection of disease-associated antibodies, it is now appreciated that an increase in the number of intraepithelial lymphocytes,

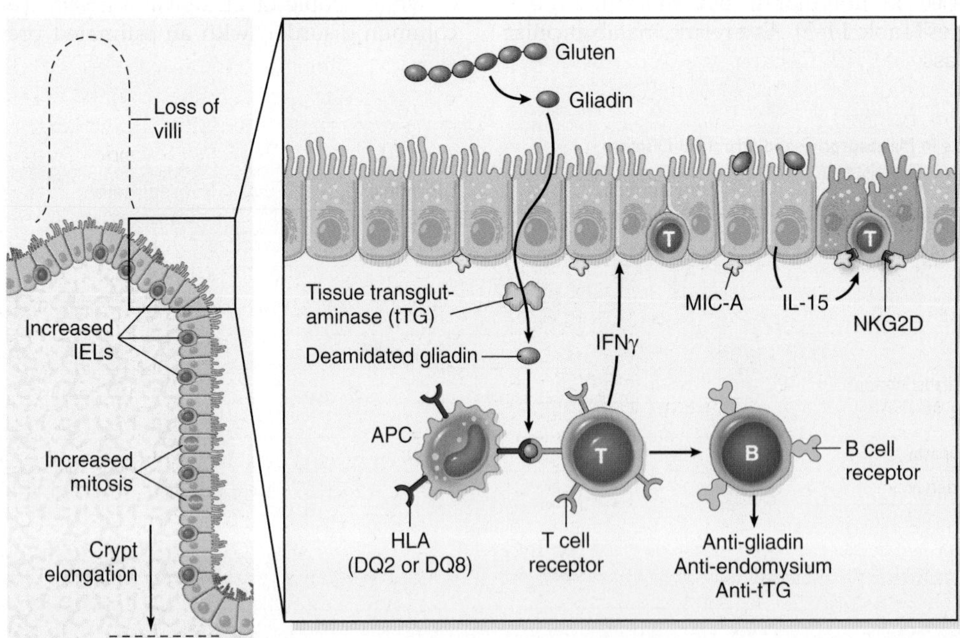

Figure 14–21 *Left panel,* The morphologic alterations that may be present in celiac disease, including villous atrophy, increased numbers of intraepithelial lymphocytes (IELs), and epithelial proliferation with crypt elongation. *Right panel,* A model for the pathogenesis of celiac disease. Note that both innate and adaptive immune mechanisms are involved in the tissue responses to gliadin.

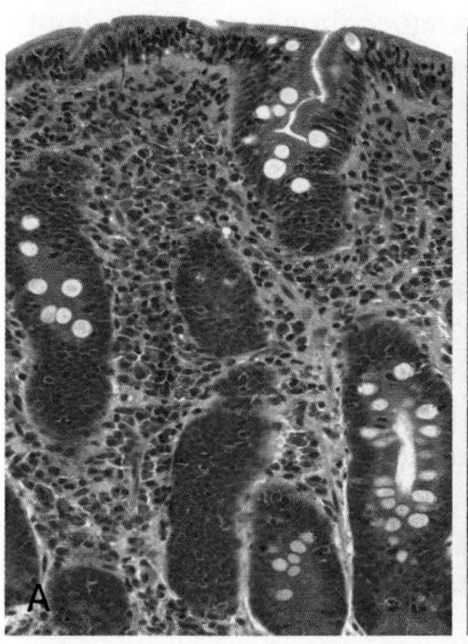

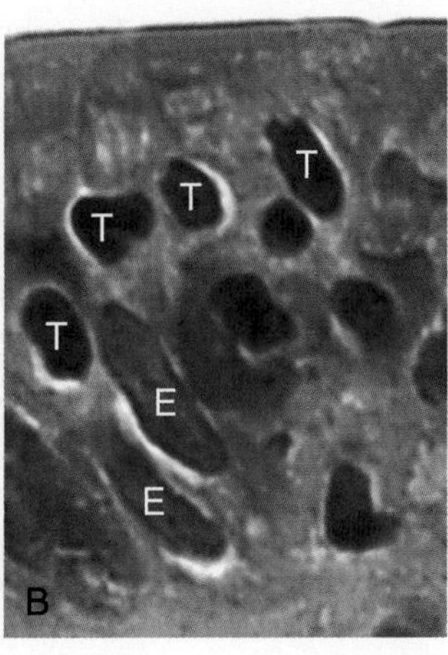

Figure 14–22 Celiac disease. **A,** Advanced cases of celiac disease show complete loss of villi, or total villous atrophy. Note the dense plasma cell infiltrates in the lamina propria. **B,** Infiltration of the surface epithelium by T lymphocytes, which can be recognized by their densely stained nuclei (labeled *T*). Compare with elongated, pale-staining epithelial nuclei (labeled *E*).

particularly within the villus, is a marker of mild forms of celiac disease. Intraepithelial lymphocytosis and villous atrophy are not specific for celiac disease, however, and can be a feature of other disorders, including viral enteritis. The combination of histologic and serologic findings is most specific for diagnosis of celiac disease.

Clinical Features

In adults, celiac disease manifests most commonly between the ages of 30 and 60. However, many cases escape clinical attention for extended periods because of atypical presentations. Some patients have *silent* celiac disease, defined as positive serology and villous atrophy without symptoms, or *latent* celiac disease, in which positive serology is not accompanied by villous atrophy. Symptomatic adult celiac disease is often associated with anemia (due to iron deficiency and, less commonly, B_{12} and folate deficiency), diarrhea, bloating, and fatigue.

Pediatric celiac disease, which affects male and female children equally, may manifest with *classic symptoms,* typically between the ages of 6 and 24 months (after introduction of gluten to the diet) with irritability, abdominal distention, anorexia, diarrhea, failure to thrive, weight loss, or muscle wasting. Children with *nonclassic symptoms* tend to present at older ages with complaints of abdominal pain, nausea, vomiting, bloating, or constipation. A characteristic pruritic, blistering skin lesion, *dermatitis herpetiformis,* also is present in as many as 10% of patients, and the incidence of *lymphocytic gastritis* and *lymphocytic colitis* also is increased.

Noninvasive serologic tests generally are performed before biopsy. The most sensitive tests are the presence of IgA antibodies to tissue transglutaminase or IgA or IgG antibodies to deamidated gliadin. Antiendomysial antibodies are highly specific but less sensitive than other antibodies. The absence of HLA-DQ2 or HLA-DQ8 is useful for its high negative predictive value, but the presence of these common alleles is not helpful in confirming the diagnosis.

Patients with celiac disease exhibit a higher than normal rate of malignancy. The most common celiac disease–associated cancer is *enteropathy-associated T cell lymphoma,* an aggressive tumor of intraepithelial T lymphocytes. *Small intestinal adenocarcinoma* also is more frequent in persons with celiac disease. Thus, when symptoms such as abdominal pain, diarrhea, and weight loss develop despite a strict gluten-free diet, cancer or *refractory sprue,* in which the response to a gluten-free diet is lost, must be considered. It is, however, important to recognize that failure to adhere to a gluten-free diet is the most common cause of recurrent symptoms, and that most people with celiac disease do well with dietary restrictions and die of unrelated causes.

Environmental (Tropical) Enteropathy

The term *environmental enteropathy* refers to a syndrome of stunted growth and impaired intestinal function that is common in developing countries, including many parts of sub-Saharan Africa, such as Gambia; aboriginal populations within northern Australia; and some groups within South America and Asia, such as residents of impoverished communities within Brazil, Guatemala, India, and Pakistan. The impact of environmental enteropathy, which was previously called *tropical enteropathy* or *tropical sprue,* cannot be overstated, as it is estimated to affect over 150 million children worldwide. Although malnutrition must contribute to the pathogenesis of this disorder, also referred to as *tropical enteropathy,* neither supplementary feeding nor vitamin and mineral supplementation are able to fully reverse the syndrome. Repeated bouts of diarrhea suffered within the first 2 or 3 years of life are most closely linked to environmental enteropathy. Many pathogens are endemic in these communities, but no single infectious agent has been linked to these diarrheal episodes. Intestinal biopsy specimens have been examined in only a small number of cases, and reported histologic features are more similar to those of severe celiac disease than to those of infectious enteritis. One hypothesis is that recurrent diarrhea establishes a cycle of mucosal injury, malnutrition, infection, and inflammation. However, this has not been established in part because accepted diagnostic criteria for environmental enteropathy are lacking, as the entity has been defined primarily by epidemiologic assessment of physical and cognitive growth and development.

Lactase (Disaccharidase) Deficiency

The disaccharidases, including lactase, are located in the apical brush border membrane of the villous absorptive epithelial cells. Because the defect is biochemical, biopsies are generally unremarkable. Lactase deficiency is of two types:

- *Congenital lactase deficiency* is an autosomal recessive disorder caused by a mutation in the gene encoding lactase. The disease is rare and manifests as explosive diarrhea with watery, frothy stools and abdominal distention after milk ingestion. Symptoms abate when exposure to milk and milk products is terminated, thus removing the osmotically active but unabsorbable lactose from the lumen.
- *Acquired lactase deficiency* is caused by downregulation of lactase gene expression and is particularly common among Native Americans, African Americans, and

Chinese populations. Downregulation of lactase occurs in the gut after childhood, perhaps reflecting the fact that, before farming of dairy animals, lactase was unnecessary after children stopped drinking mother's milk. Onset of acquired lactase deficiency is sometimes associated with enteric viral or bacterial infections.

Abetalipoproteinemia

Abetalipoproteinemia is an autosomal recessive disease characterized by an inability to secrete triglyceride-rich lipoproteins. Although it is rare, it is included here as an example of a transepithelial transport defect that leads to malabsorption. Mutation in the *microsomal triglyceride transfer protein* renders enterocytes unable to export lipoproteins and free fatty acids. As a result, monoglycerides and triglycerides accumulate within the epithelial cells. Lipid vacuoles in small intestinal epithelial cells are evident by light microscopy and can be highlighted by special stains, such as oil red O, particularly after a fatty meal. Abetalipoproteinemia manifests in infancy, and the clinical picture is dominated by failure to thrive, diarrhea, and steatorrhea. Failure to absorb essential fatty acids leads to deficiencies of fat-soluble vitamins, and lipid defects in plasma membranes often produce acanthocytic red cells (spur cells) in peripheral blood smears.

Irritable Bowel Syndrome

Irritable bowel syndrome (IBS) is characterized by chronic and relapsing abdominal pain, bloating, and changes in bowel habits including diarrhea and constipation. The pathogenesis is poorly defined but involves psychologic stressors, diet, and abnormal gastrointestinal motility. Despite very real symptoms, no gross or microscopic abnormalities are found in most IBS patients. Thus, the diagnosis depends on clinical symptoms. IBS typically manifests between 20 and 40 years of age, and there is a significant female predominance. Variability in diagnostic criteria makes it difficult to establish the incidence, but *reported prevalence rates in developed countries typically are between 5% and 10%*. In patients with diarrhea, microscopic colitis, celiac disease, giardiasis, lactose intolerance, small bowel bacterial overgrowth, bile salt malabsorption, colon cancer, and inflammatory bowel disease must be excluded (although IBS is common in patients with inflammatory bowel disease). The prognosis for IBS is most closely related to symptom duration, with longer duration correlating with reduced likelihood of improvement.

Microscopic Colitis

Microscopic colitis encompasses two entities, *collagenous colitis* and *lymphocytic colitis*. Both of these idiopathic diseases manifest with chronic, nonbloody, watery diarrhea without weight loss. Findings on radiologic and endoscopic studies typically are normal. Collagenous colitis, which occurs primarily in middle-aged and older women, is characterized by the presence of a dense subepithelial collagen layer, increased numbers of intraepithelial lymphocytes, and a mixed inflammatory infiltrate within the lamina propria. Lymphocytic colitis is histologically similar, but the subepithelial collagen layer is of normal thickness and the increase in intraepithelial lymphocytes may be greater, frequently exceeding one T lymphocyte per five colonocytes. Lymphocytic colitis is associated with celiac and autoimmune diseases, including thyroiditis, arthritis, and autoimmune or lymphocytic gastritis.

Graft-Versus-Host Disease

Graft-versus-host disease occurs after allogeneic hematopoietic stem cell transplantation. The small bowel and colon are involved in most cases. Although graft-versus-host disease is secondary to the targeting of antigens on the recipient's epithelial cells by donor T cells, the lymphocytic infiltrate in the lamina propria is typically sparse. Epithelial apoptosis, particularly of crypt cells, is the most common histologic finding. Intestinal graft-versus-host disease often manifests as a watery diarrhea.

SUMMARY

Malabsorptive Diarrhea

- Diarrhea can be characterized as *secretory, osmotic, malabsorptive*, or *exudative*.
- The malabsorption associated with cystic fibrosis is the result of *pancreatic insufficiency* (i.e., inadequate pancreatic digestive enzymes) and *deficient luminal breakdown* of nutrients.
- *Celiac disease* is an immune-mediated enteropathy triggered by the ingestion of gluten-containing grains. The malabsorptive diarrhea in celiac disease is due to *loss of brush border surface area* and, possibly, deficient enterocyte maturation as a result of immune-mediated epithelial damage.
- *Lactase deficiency* causes an *osmotic diarrhea* owing to the inability to break down or absorb lactose.
- *Irritable bowel syndrome* (IBS) is characterized by chronic, relapsing abdominal pain, bloating, and changes in bowel habits. The pathogenesis is poorly defined.
- The two forms of microscopic colitis, *collagenous colitis* and *lymphocytic colitis*, both cause chronic watery diarrhea. The intestines are grossly normal, and the diseases are identified by their characteristic histologic features.

Infectious Enterocolitis

Enterocolitis can manifest with a broad range of signs and symptoms including diarrhea, abdominal pain, urgency, perianal discomfort, incontinence, and hemorrhage. This global problem is responsible for more than 12,000 deaths per day among children in developing countries and half of all deaths before age 5 worldwide. Bacterial infections, such as enterotoxigenic *Escherichia coli*, frequently are responsible, but the most common pathogens vary with age, nutrition, and host immune status, as well as environmental influences (Table 14–4). For example, epidemics of cholera are common in areas with poor sanitation, as a result of inadequate public health measures, or as a consequence of natural disasters (e.g., the Haiti earthquake of 2010) or war. Pediatric infectious diarrhea, which may result in severe dehydration and metabolic acidosis, commonly is caused by enteric viruses. A summary of the epidemiology and clinical features of selected causes of bacterial enterocolitis is presented in

Table 14–4 Features of Bacterial Enterocolitides

Infection Type	Geography	Reservoir	Transmission	Epidemiology	Affected GI Sites	Symptoms	Complications
Cholera	India, Africa	Shellfish	Fecal-oral, water	Sporadic, endemic, epidemic	Small intestine	Severe watery diarrhea	Dehydration, electrolyte imbalances
Campylobacter spp.	Developed countries	Chickens, sheep, pigs, cattle	Poultry, milk, other foods	Sporadic; children, travelers	Colon	Watery or bloody diarrhea	Arthritis, Guillain-Barré syndrome
Shigellosis	Developing countries	Humans	Fecal-oral, food, water	Children	Left colon, ileum	Bloody diarrhea	Reactive arthritis hemolytic-uremic syndrome
Salmonellosis	Worldwide	Poultry, farm animals, reptiles	Meat, poultry, eggs, milk	Children, elderly	Colon and small intestine	Watery or bloody diarrhea	Sepsis
Enteric (typhoid) fever	India, Mexico, Philippines	Humans	Fecal-oral, water	Children. adolescents, travelers	Small intestine	Bloody diarrhea, fever	Chronic infection, carrier state, encephalopathy, myocarditis
Yersinia spp.	Northern and central Europe	Pigs	Pork, milk, water	Clustered cases	Ileum, appendix, right colon	Abdominal pain, fever, diarrhea	Autoimmune, e.g., reactive arthritis
Escherichia coli							
Enterotoxigenic (ETEC)	Developing countries	Unknown	Food, fecal-oral	Infants, adolescents, travelers	Small intestine	Severe watery diarrhea	Dehydration, electrolyte imbalances
Enterohemorrhagic (EHEC)	Worldwide	Widespread, includes cattle	Beef, milk, produce	Sporadic and epidemic	Colon	Bloody diarrhea	Hemolytic-uremic syndrome
Enteroinvasive (EIEC)	Developing countries	Unknown	Cheese, other foods, water	Young children	Colon	Bloody diarrhea	Unknown
Enteroaggregative (EAEC)	Worldwide	Unknown	Unknown	Children, adults, travelers	Colon	Nonbloody diarrhea, afebrile	Poorly defined
Pseudomembranous colitis (*C. difficile*)	Worldwide	Humans, hospitals	Antibiotics allow emergence	Immunosuppressed, antibiotic-treated	Colon	Watery diarrhea, fever	Relapse, toxic megacolon
Whipple disease	Rural > urban	Unknown	Unknown	Rare	Small intestine	Malabsorption	Arthritis, CNS disease
Mycobacterial infection	Worldwide	Unknown	Unknown	Immunosuppressed	Small intestine	Malabsorption, diarrhea, fever	Pneumonia, infection at other sites

CNS, central nervous system; GI, gastrointestinal.

Table 14–4. Representative bacterial, viral, and parasitic enterocolitides are discussed below.

Cholera

Vibrio cholerae organisms are comma-shaped, gram-negative bacteria that cause cholera, a disease that has been endemic in the Ganges Valley of India and Bangladesh for all of recorded history. *V. cholerae* is transmitted primarily by contaminated drinking water. However, it also can be present in food and causes rare cases of seafood-associated disease. There is a marked seasonal variation in most climates due to rapid growth of *Vibrio* bacteria at warm temperatures; the only animal reservoirs are shellfish and plankton. Relatively few *V. cholerae* serotypes are pathogenic, but other species of *Vibrio* also can cause disease.

PATHOGENESIS

Despite the severe diarrhea, *Vibrio* organisms are noninvasive and remain within the intestinal lumen. Flagellar proteins, which are involved in motility and attachment, are necessary for efficient bacterial colonization, and a secreted metalloproteinase that also has hemagglutinin activity is important for bacterial detachment and shedding in the stool. However, it is the **preformed enterotoxin,** cholera toxin, which causes disease. The toxin, which is composed of five B subunits that direct endocytosis and a single active A subunit, is delivered to the endoplasmic reticulum by **retrograde transport.** A fragment of the A subunit is transported from the endoplasmic reticulum lumen into the cytosol, where it interacts with cytosolic ADP ribosylation factors to ribosylate and activate the G protein $G_{s\alpha}$. This stimulates adenylate cyclase and the resulting increases in intracellular cyclic adenosine monophosphate (cAMP) open the cystic fibrosis transmembrane conductance regulator (CFTR), which releases chloride ions into the lumen. Sodium and bicarbonate absorption are also reduced. Accumulation of these ions creates an osmotic gradient that draws water into the lumen, leading to massive **secretory diarrhea.** Remarkably, mucosal biopsy specimens show only minimal morphologic alterations.

Clinical Features

Most exposed persons are asymptomatic or suffer only mild diarrhea. Those with severe disease have an abrupt onset of watery diarrhea and vomiting after an incubation period of 1 to 5 days. The rate of diarrheal stool production may reach 1 L per hour, leading to dehydration, hypotension, electrolyte imbalances, muscular cramping, anuria, shock, loss of consciousness, and death. Most deaths occur within the first 24 hours after presentation. Although the mortality rate for severe cholera is 50% to 70% without treatment, fluid replacement can save more than 99% of patients.

Campylobacter *Enterocolitis*

Campylobacter jejuni is the most common bacterial enteric pathogen in developed countries and is an important cause of traveler's diarrhea. Most infections are associated with ingestion of improperly cooked chicken, but outbreaks also can be caused by unpasteurized milk or contaminated water.

PATHOGENESIS

The pathogenesis of *Campylobacter* infection remains poorly defined, but four major virulence properties contribute: motility, adherence, toxin production, and invasion. Flagella allow *Campylobacter* to be motile. This facilitates adherence and colonization, which are also necessary for mucosal invasion. Cytotoxins that cause epithelial damage and a cholera toxin–like enterotoxin are also released by some *C. jejuni* isolates. **Dysentery** generally is associated with invasion and only occurs with a small minority of *Campylobacter* strains. **Enteric fever** occurs when bacteria proliferate within the lamina propria and mesenteric lymph nodes.

Campylobacter infection can result in reactive arthritis, primarily in patients with HLA-B27. Other extraintestinal complications, including erythema nodosum and Guillain-Barré syndrome, a flaccid paralysis caused by autoimmune-induced inflammation of peripheral nerves, are not HLA-linked. Fortunately, Guillain-Barré syndrome develops in 0.1% or less of persons infected with *Campylobacter.*

MORPHOLOGY

Campylobacter, Shigella, Salmonella, and many other bacterial infections, including ***Yersinia*** and ***E. coli,*** all induce a similar histopathology, termed **acute self-limited colitis,** and these pathogens cannot be reliably distinguished by tissue biopsy. Thus, specific diagnosis is primarily by stool culture. The histology of acute self-limited colitis includes prominent lamina propria and intraepithelial neutrophil infiltrates (Fig. 14–23, *A*); **cryptitis** (neutrophil infiltration of the crypts) and **crypt abscesses** (crypts with accumulations of luminal neutrophils) also may be present. The preservation of crypt architecture in most cases of acute self-limited colitis is helpful in distinguishing these infections from inflammatory bowel disease (Fig. 14–23, *B*).

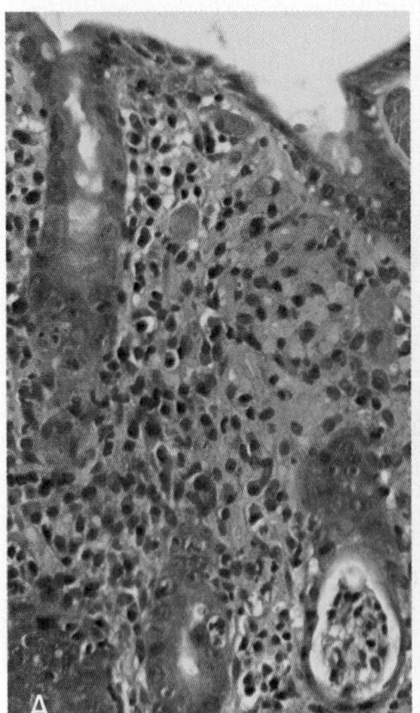

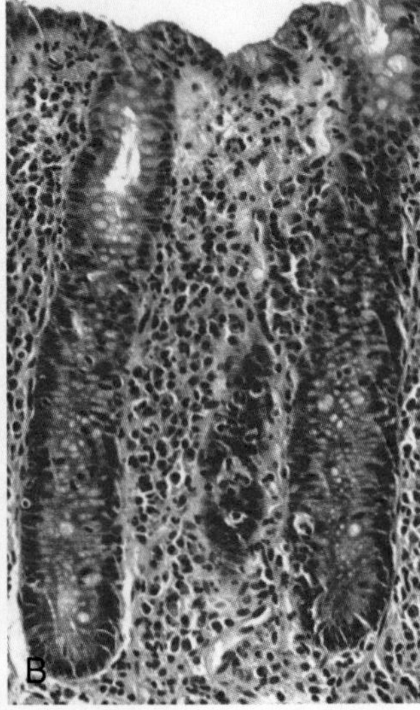

Figure 14–23 Bacterial enterocolitis. **A,** *Campylobacter jejuni* infection produces acute, self-limited colitis. Neutrophils can be seen within surface and crypt epithelium and a crypt abscess is present at the *lower right.* **B,** Enteroinvasive *Escherichia coli* infection is similar to other acute, self-limited colitides. Note the maintenance of normal crypt architecture and spacing, despite abundant intraepithelial neutrophils.

Clinical Features

Ingestion of as few as 500 *C. jejuni* organisms can cause disease after an incubation period of up to 8 days. Watery diarrhea, either acute or with onset after an influenza-like prodrome, is the primary manifestation, and dysentery develops in 15% to 50% of patients. Patients may shed bacteria for 1 month or more after clinical resolution. The disease is self limited and therefore antibiotic therapy generally is not required. Diagnosis is primarily by stool culture since the histologic changes are not specific for *Campylobacter* colitis.

Shigellosis

Shigella organisms are gram-negative bacilli that are unencapsulated, nonmotile, facultative anaerobes. Although humans are the only known reservoir, *Shigella* remains one of the most common causes of bloody diarrhea. It is estimated that 165 million cases occur worldwide each year. Shigellae are highly transmissible by the fecal-oral route or through ingestion of contaminated water and food; the *infective dose is fewer than 100 organisms* and each gram of stool contains as many as 10^9 organisms during acute phases of the disease.

In the United States and Europe, children in day care centers, migrant workers, travelers to developing countries, and residents of nursing homes are most commonly affected. Most *Shigella*-associated infections and deaths occur in children younger than 5 years of age; in countries in which *Shigella* is endemic, it is responsible for approximately 10% of all cases of pediatric diarrheal disease and as many as 75% of diarrheal deaths.

PATHOGENESIS

Shigella organisms are resistant to the harsh acidic environment of the stomach, which partially explains the very low infective dose. Once in the intestine, organisms are taken up by M (microfold) epithelial cells, which are specialized for sampling and uptake of luminal antigens. After intracellular proliferation, the bacteria escape into the lamina propria. These bacteria then infect small intestinal and colonic epithelial cells through the basolateral membranes, which express bacterial receptors. Alternatively, luminal shigellae can directly modulate epithelial tight junctions to expose basolateral bacterial receptors. The latter is partly mediated by virulence proteins, some of which are directly injected into the host cytoplasm by a type III secretion system. Some *Shigella dysenteriae* serotypes also release the Shiga toxin Stx, which inhibits eukaryotic protein synthesis and causes host cell death.

MORPHOLOGY

Shigella infections are most prominent in the left colon, but the ileum may also be involved, perhaps reflecting the abundance of M cells in the epithelium overlying the Peyer's patches. The histologic appearance in early cases is similar to that in other acute self-limited colitides. In more severe cases, the mucosa is hemorrhagic and ulcerated, and pseudomembranes may be present. Perhaps because of the tropism for M cells, aphthous-appearing ulcers similar to those seen in Crohn disease also may occur. The potential for confusion with chronic inflammatory bowel disease is substantial, particularly if there is distortion of crypt architecture. Confirmation of *Shigella* infection requires stool culture.

Clinical Features

After an incubation period of 1 to 7 days, *Shigella* causes self-limited disease characterized by about 6 days of diarrhea, fever, and abdominal pain. The initially watery diarrhea progresses to a dysenteric phase in approximately 50% of patients, and constitutional symptoms can persist for as long as 1 month. A subacute presentation also can develop in a minority of adults. Antibiotic treatment shortens the clinical course and reduces the duration over which organisms are shed in the stool, but antidiarrheal medications are contraindicated because they can prolong symptoms by delaying bacterial clearance.

Complications of *Shigella* infection are uncommon and include *reactive arthritis,* a triad of sterile arthritis, urethritis, and conjunctivitis that preferentially affects HLA-B27–positive men between 20 and 40 years of age. Hemolytic uremic syndrome, which typically is associated with *enterohemorrhagic Escherichia coli* (EHEC), also may occur after infection with shigellae that secrete Shiga toxin.

Escherichia coli

Escherichia coli are gram-negative bacilli that colonize the healthy GI tract; most are nonpathogenic, but a subset cause human disease. The latter are classified according to morphology, mechanism of pathogenesis, and in vitro behavior (Table 14–4). Here we summarize their pathogenic mechanisms:

- **Enterotoxigenic *E. coli* (ETEC) organisms** are the principal cause of traveler's diarrhea, and are spread by the fecal-oral route. They express a heat labile toxin (LT) that is similar to cholera toxin and a heat-stable toxin (ST) that increases intracellular cGMP with effects similar to the cAMP elevations caused by LT.
- **Enterohemorrhagic *E. coli* (EHEC) organisms** are categorized as O157:H7 and non-O157:H7 serotypes. Outbreaks of *E. coli* O157:H7 in developed countries have been associated with the consumption of inadequately cooked ground beef, milk, and vegetables. Both O157:H7 and non-O157:H7 serotypes produce Shiga-like toxins and can cause dysentery. They can also give rise to hemolytic-uremic syndrome (Chapter 13).
- **Enteroinvasive *E. coli* (EIEC) organisms** resemble *Shigella* bacteriologically but do not produce toxins. They invade the gut epithelial cells and produce a bloody diarrhea.
- **Enteroaggregative *E. coli* (EAEC) organisms** attach to enterocytes by adherence fimbriae. Although they produce LT and Shiga-like toxins, histologic damage is minimal.

Salmonellosis

Salmonella species, which are members of the Enterobacteriaceae family of gram-negative bacilli, are divided into

Salmonella typhi, the causative agent of typhoid fever (discussed in the next section) and nontyphoid *Salmonella* strains that cause gastroenteritis. Nontyphoid *Salmonella* infection usually is due to *Salmonella enteritidis;* more than 1 million cases occur each year in the United States, which result in 2000 deaths; the prevalence is even greater in many other countries. Infection is most common in young children and elderly persons, with peak incidence in summer and fall. Transmission usually is through contaminated food, particularly raw or undercooked meat, poultry, eggs, and milk.

PATHOGENESIS

Very few viable *Salmonella* organisms are necessary to cause infection, and the absence of gastric acid, as in persons with atrophic gastritis or those on acid-suppressive therapy, further reduces the required inoculum. Salmonellae possess **virulence genes that encode a type III secretion system** capable of transferring bacterial proteins into M cells and enterocytes. The transferred proteins activate host cell Rho GTPases, thereby triggering actin rearrangement and bacterial uptake into phagosomes where the bacteria can grow. Salmonellae also secrete a molecule that induces epithelial release of a chemoattractant eicosanoid that draws neutrophils into the lumen and potentiates mucosal damage. Stool cultures are essential for diagnosis.

Typhoid Fever

Typhoid fever, also referred to as enteric fever, is caused by *Salmonella typhi* and *Salmonella paratyphi*. It affects up to 30 million individuals worldwide each year. Infection by *S. typhi* is more common in endemic areas, where children and adolescents are most often affected. By contrast, *S. paratyphi* predominates in travelers and those living in developed countries. Humans are the sole reservoir for *S. typhi* and *S. paratyphi* and transmission occurs from person to person or via contaminated food or water. Gallbladder colonization may be associated with gallstones and a chronic carrier state. Acute infection is associated with anorexia, abdominal pain, bloating, nausea, vomiting, and bloody diarrhea followed by a short asymptomatic phase that gives way to bacteremia and fever with flu-like symptoms. It is during this phase that detection of organisms by blood culture may prompt antibiotic treatment and prevent further disease progression. Without such treatment, the febrile phase is followed by up to 2 weeks of sustained high fevers with abdominal tenderness that may mimic appendicitis. *Rose spots,* small erythematous maculopapular lesions, are seen on the chest and abdomen. Systemic dissemination may cause *extraintestinal complications* including encephalopathy, meningitis, seizures, endocarditis, myocarditis, pneumonia, and cholecystitis. Patients with sickle cell disease are particularly susceptible to *Salmonella* osteomyelitis.

Like *S. enteritidis, S. typhi* and *S. paratyphi* are taken up by M cells and then engulfed by mononuclear cells in the underlying lymphoid tissue. Thus, infection causes Peyer's patches in the terminal ileum to enlarge into plateau-like elevations up to 8 cm in diameter. Mucosal shedding creates oval ulcers oriented along the long axis of the ileum. However, unlike *S. enteritidis, S. typhi* and *S. paratyphi* can disseminate via lymphatic and blood vessels. This causes reactive hyperplasia of draining lymph nodes, in which bacteria-containing phagocytes accumulate. In addition, the spleen is enlarged and soft with pale red pulp, obliterated follicular markings, and prominent phagocyte hyperplasia. Randomly scattered small foci of parenchymal necrosis with macrophage aggregates, termed *typhoid nodules,* are also present in the liver, bone marrow, and lymph nodes.

Pseudomembranous Colitis

Pseudomembranous colitis, generally caused by *Clostridium difficile,* is also known as antibiotic-associated colitis or antibiotic-associated diarrhea. The latter terms apply to diarrhea developing during or after a course of antibiotic therapy and may be due to *C. difficile* as well as *Salmonella, C. perfringens* type A, or *S. aureus*. However, the latter two organisms produce enterotoxins and are common agents of food poisoning. They do not cause pseudomembranes. Disruption of the normal colonic microbiota by antibiotics allows *C. difficile* overgrowth. Toxins released by *C. difficile* cause the ribosylation of small GTPases, such as Rho, and lead to disruption of the epithelial cytoskeleton, tight junction barrier loss, cytokine release, and apoptosis.

MORPHOLOGY

Fully developed *C. difficile*–associated colitis is accompanied by formation of **pseudomembranes** (Fig. 14–24, *A*), made up of an adherent layer of inflammatory cells and debris at sites of colonic mucosal injury. The surface epithelium is denuded, and the superficial lamina propria contains a dense infiltrate of neutrophils and occasional fibrin thrombi within capillaries. Damaged crypts are distended by a mucopurulent exudate that "erupts" to the surface in a fashion reminiscent of a volcano (Fig. 14–24, *B*).

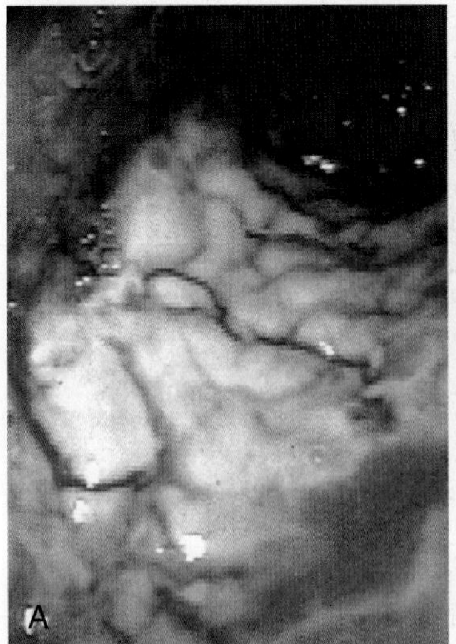

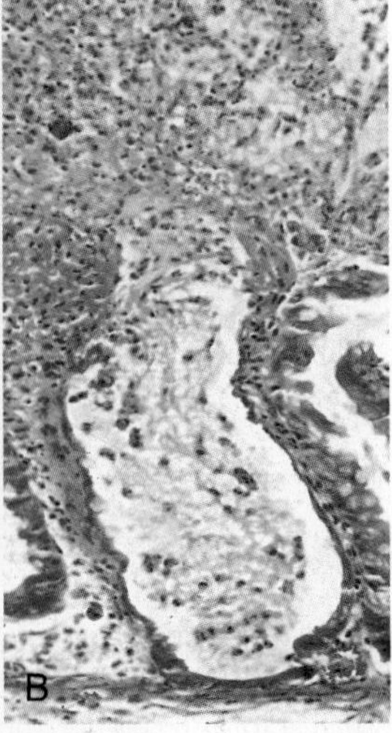

Figure 14–24 *Clostridium difficile* colitis. **A,** The colon is coated by tan pseudomembranes composed of neutrophils, dead epithelial cells, and inflammatory debris (endoscopic view). **B,** Typical pattern of neutrophils emanating from a crypt is reminiscent of a volcanic eruption.

Clinical Features

In addition to antibiotic exposure, risk factors for *C. difficile*–associated colitis include advanced age, hospitalization, and immunosuppression. The organism is particularly prevalent in hospitals; as many as 20% of hospitalized adults are colonized with *C. difficile* (a rate 10 times higher than in the general population), but most colonized patients are free of disease. Persons with *C. difficile*–associated colitis present with fever, leukocytosis, abdominal pain, cramps, hypoalbuminemia, watery diarrhea, and dehydration. Fecal leukocytes and occult blood may be present, but grossly bloody diarrhea is rare. Diagnosis of *C. difficile*–associated colitis usually is accomplished by detection of *C. difficile* toxin, rather than culture, and is supported by the characteristic histopathologic findings. Regimens of metronidazole or vancomycin are generally effective treatments, but antibiotic-resistant and hypervirulent *C. difficile* strains are increasingly common, and the infection may recur in at-risk patients.

Norovirus

Norovirus, previously known as Norwalk-like virus, is a common agent of nonbacterial infectious gastroenteritis. Norovirus causes approximately half of all gastroenteritis outbreaks worldwide and is a common cause of sporadic gastroenteritis in developed countries. Local outbreaks usually are related to contaminated food or water, but person-to-person transmission underlies most sporadic cases. Infections spread easily within schools, hospitals, and nursing homes and, most recently, on cruise ships. After a short incubation period, affected persons develop nausea, vomiting, watery diarrhea, and abdominal pain. Biopsy morphology is nonspecific. The disease is self-limited.

Rotavirus

The encapsulated rotavirus infects 140 million people and causes 1 million deaths each year, making rotavirus *the most common cause of severe childhood diarrhea and diarrhea-related deaths worldwide.* Children between 6 and 24 months of age are most vulnerable. Protection in the first 6 months of life is probably due to the presence of antibodies to rotavirus in breast milk, while protection beyond 2 years is due to immunity that develops after the first infection. Outbreaks in hospitals and day care centers are common, and infection spreads easily; the estimated minimal infective inoculum is only 10 viral particles. *Rotavirus selectively infects and destroys mature (absorptive) enterocytes in the small intestine, and the villus surface is repopulated by immature secretory cells.* This change in functional capacity results in loss of absorptive function and net secretion of water and electrolytes that is compounded by an osmotic diarrhea from incompletely absorbed nutrients. Like norovirus, rotavirus produces clinically apparent infection after a short incubation period, manifested by vomiting and watery diarrhea for several days. Vaccines are now available, and their use is beginning to change the epidemiology of rotavirus infection. For unknown reasons, oral rotavirus vaccines have been less effective in developing countries where they are most needed.

Parasitic Disease

Although viruses and bacteria are the predominant enteric pathogens in the United States, parasitic disease and protozoal infections affect over half of the world's population on a chronic or recurrent basis. The small intestine can harbor as many as 20 species of parasites, including nematodes, such as the roundworms *Ascaris* and *Strongyloides*; hookworms and pinworms; cestodes, including flatworms and tapeworms; trematodes, or flukes; and protozoa.

- *Ascaris lumbricoides.* This nematode infects more than 1 billion people worldwide as a result of human fecal-oral contamination. Ingested eggs hatch in the intestine and larvae penetrate the intestinal mucosa. From here the larvae migrate via the splanchnic circulation to the liver, creating hepatic abscesses, and then through the systemic circulation to the lung, where they can cause *Ascaris* pneumonitis. In the latter case, larvae migrate up the trachea, are swallowed, and arrive again in the intestine to mature into adult worms.
- *Strongyloides.* The larvae of *Strongyloides* live in fecally contaminated ground soil and can penetrate unbroken skin. They migrate through the lungs to the trachea from where they are swallowed and then mature into adult worms in the intestines. Unlike other intestinal worms, which require an ovum or larval stage outside the human, the eggs of *Strongyloides* can hatch within the intestine and release larvae that penetrate the mucosa, creating a vicious cycle referred to as autoinfection. Hence, *Strongyloides* infection can persist for life, and immunosuppressed individuals can develop overwhelming infections.
- *Necator americanus* and *Ancylostoma duodenale.* These hookworms infect 1 billion people worldwide and cause significant morbidity. Infection is initiated by larval penetration through the skin. After further development in the lungs, the larvae migrate up the trachea and are swallowed. Once in the duodenum, the larvae mature and the adult worms attach to the mucosa, suck blood, and reproduce. Hookworms are the leading cause of iron deficiency anemia in the developing world.
- *Giardia lamblia.* This flagellated protozoan, also referred to as *Giardia duodenalis* or *Giardia intestinalis*, is responsible for the *most common pathogenic parasitic infection in humans* and is spread by fecally contaminated water or food. Infection may occur after ingestion of as few as 10 cysts. Because cysts are resistant to chlorine, *Giardia* organisms are endemic in unfiltered public and rural water supplies. In the acid environment of the stomach excystation occurs and trophozoites are released. Secretory IgA and mucosal IL-6 responses are important for clearance of *Giardia* infections, and immunosuppressed, agammaglobulinemic, or malnourished persons often are severely affected. *Giardia* evade immune clearance through continuous modification of the major surface antigen, variant surface protein, and can persist for months or years while causing intermittent symptoms. *Giardia* infection decreases the expression of brush border enzymes, including lactase, and causes microvillous damage and apoptosis of small intestinal epithelial cells. *Giardia* trophozoites are noninvasive and can be identified in duodenal biopsy specimens by their

characteristic pear shape. Giardiasis is clinically characterized by acute or chronic diarrhea and can result in malabsorption.

SUMMARY

Infectious Enterocolitis

- *Vibrio cholerae* secretes a pre-formed toxin that causes massive chloride secretion. Water follows the resulting osmotic gradient, leading to *secretory diarrhea.*
- *Campylobacter jejuni* is the most common bacterial enteric pathogen in developed countries and also causes traveler's diarrhea. Most isolates are noninvasive. *Salmonella* and *Shigella* spp. are invasive and associated with exudative bloody diarrhea (dysentery). *Salmonella* infection is a common cause of food poisoning. *S. typhi* can cause systemic disease (typhoid fever).
- Pseudomembranous colitis is often triggered by antibiotic therapy that disrupts the normal microbiota and allows *C. difficile* to colonize and grow. The organism releases toxins that disrupt epithelial function. The associated inflammatory response includes characteristic volcano-like eruptions of neutrophils from colonic crypts that spread to form mucopurulent pseudomembranes.
- *Rotavirus* is the most common cause of severe childhood diarrhea and diarrheal mortality worldwide. The diarrhea is secondary to loss of mature enterocytes, resulting in malabsorption as well as secretion.
- *Parasitic* and *protozoal* infections affect over half of the world's population on a chronic or recurrent basis.

INFLAMMATORY INTESTINAL DISEASE

Sigmoid Diverticulitis

In general, diverticular disease refers to acquired pseudodiverticular outpouchings of the colonic mucosa and submucosa. Such *colonic diverticula* are rare in persons younger than 30 years of age, but the prevalence approaches 50% in Western adult populations beyond the age of 60. Diverticula generally are multiple, and the condition is referred to as *diverticulosis.* This disease is much less common in Japan and nonindustrialized countries, probably because of dietary differences.

PATHOGENESIS

Colonic diverticula tend to develop under conditions of elevated intraluminal pressure in the sigmoid colon. This is facilitated by the unique structure of the colonic muscularis propria, where nerves, arterial vasa recta, and their connective tissue sheaths penetrate the inner circular muscle coat to create discontinuities in the muscle wall. In other parts of the intestine, these gaps are reinforced by the external longitudinal layer of the muscularis propria, but in the colon, this muscle layer is discontinuous, being gathered into the three bands termed **taeniae coli.** High luminal pressures may be generated by exaggerated peristaltic contractions, with spasmodic sequestration of bowel segments that may be exacerbated by diets low in fiber, which reduce stool bulk.

MORPHOLOGY

Anatomically, colonic diverticula are small, flask-like outpouchings, usually 0.5 to 1 cm in diameter, that occur in a regular distribution in between the taeniae coli (Fig. 14–25, *A*). They are most common in the sigmoid colon, but other regions of the colon may be affected in severe cases. Because diverticula are compressible, easily emptied of fecal contents, and often surrounded by the fat-containing **epiploic appendices** on the surface of the colon, they may be missed on casual inspection. Colonic diverticula have a thin wall composed of a flattened or atrophic mucosa, compressed submucosa, and attenuated muscularis propria—often, this last component is totally absent (Fig. 14–30, *B* and *C*). Hypertrophy of the circular layer of the muscularis propria in the affected bowel segment is common. Obstruction of diverticula leads to inflammatory changes, producing **diverticulitis** and peridiverticulitis. Because the wall of the diverticulum is supported only by the muscularis mucosa and a thin layer of subserosal adipose tissue, inflammation and increased pressure within an obstructed diverticulum can lead to **perforation.** With or without perforation, recurrent diverticulitis may cause segmental colitis, fibrotic thickening in and around the colonic wall, or stricture formation. Perforation can lead to formation of pericolonic abscesses, development of sinus tracts, and, occasionally, peritonitis.

Clinical Features

Most persons with diverticular disease remain asymptomatic throughout their lives. About 20% of those affected develop complaints including intermittent cramping, continuous lower abdominal discomfort, constipation, and

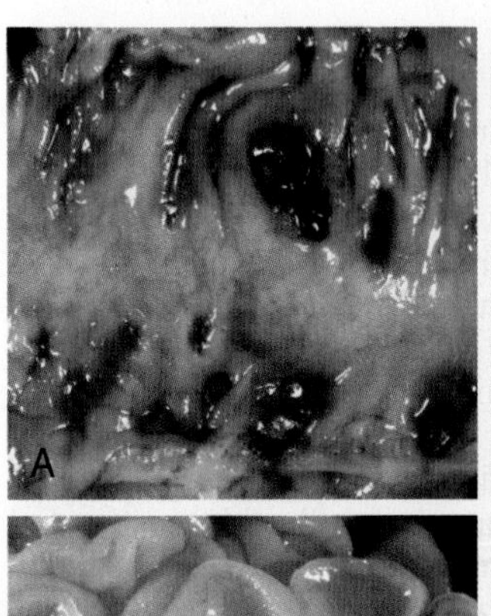

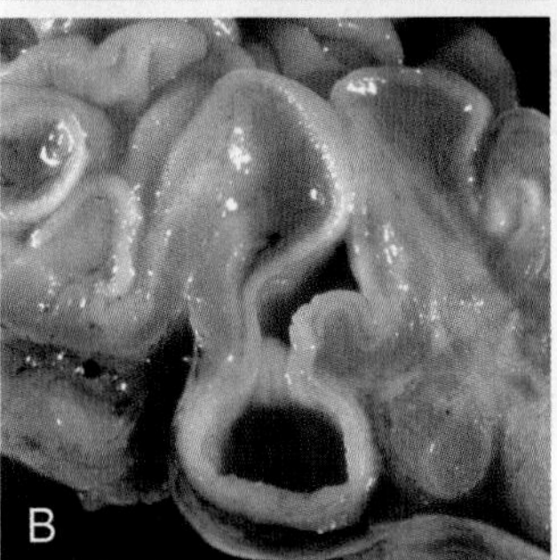

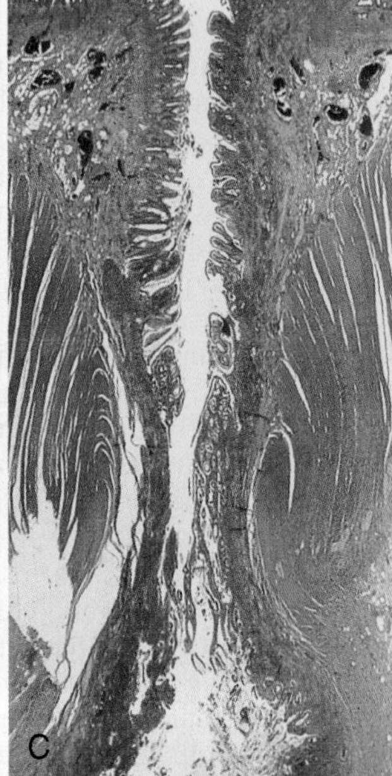

Figure 14–25 Sigmoid diverticular disease. **A,** Stool-filled diverticula are regularly arranged. **B,** Cross-section showing the outpouching of mucosa beneath the muscularis propria. **C,** Low-power photomicrograph of a sigmoid diverticulum showing protrusion of the mucosa and submucosa through the muscularis propria.

diarrhea. Longitudinal studies have shown that while diverticula can regress early in their development they often become more numerous and larger over time. Whether a high-fiber diet prevents such progression or protects against diverticulitis is unclear. Even when diverticulitis occurs, it most often resolves spontaneously or after antibiotic treatment, and relatively few patients require surgical intervention.

SUMMARY

Sigmoid Diverticulitis

- *Diverticular disease* of the sigmoid colon is common in Western populations over the age of 60. Contributing etiologic factors include low-fiber diets, colonic spasm, and the unique anatomy of the colon. Inflammation of diverticula, *diverticulitis,* affects a minority of persons with *diverticulosis* but can cause perforation in its most severe form.

Inflammatory Bowel Disease

Inflammatory bowel disease (IBD) is a chronic condition resulting from inappropriate mucosal immune activation. IBD encompasses two major entities, *Crohn disease* and *ulcerative colitis.* The distinction between ulcerative colitis and Crohn disease is based, in large part, on the distribution of affected sites and the morphologic expression of disease at those sites (Fig. 14–26; Table 14–5). *Ulcerative colitis is limited to the colon and rectum and extends only into the mucosa and submucosa.* By contrast, *Crohn disease, which also has been referred to as regional enteritis (because of frequent ileal involvement), may involve any area of the gastrointestinal tract and frequently is transmural.*

Table 14–5 Features That Differ Betwee Ulcerative Colitis

Feature	Crohn Dise	
Macroscopic		
Bowel region affected	Ileum ± co	
Rectal involvement	Sometime	
Distribution	Skip lesic	
Stricture	Yes	
Bowel wall appearance	Thick	Thin
Inflammation	Transmural	Limited to mucosa and submucosa
Pseudopolyps	Moderate	Marked
Ulcers	Deep, knifelike	Superficial, broad-based
Lymphoid reaction	Marked	Moderate
Fibrosis	Marked	Mild to none
Serositis	Marked	No
Granulomas	Yes (~35%)	No
Fistulas/sinuses	Yes	No
Clinical		
Perianal fistula	Yes (in colonic disease)	No
Fat/vitamin malabsorption	Yes	No
Malignant potential	With colonic involvement	Yes
Recurrence after surgery	Common	No
Toxic megacolon	No	Yes

NOTE: Not all features may be present in a single case.

Figure 14–26 Distribution of lesions in inflammatory bowel disease. The distinction between Crohn disease and ulcerative colitis is based primarily on morphology.

Epidemiology

Both Crohn disease and ulcerative colitis are more common in females and frequently present during adolescence or in young adults. In Western industrialized nations, IBD is most common among whites and, in the United States, occurs 3 to 5 times more often among eastern European (Ashkenazi) Jews. This predilection is at least partly due to genetic factors, as discussed next under "Pathogenesis." The geographic distribution of IBD is highly variable, but it is most prevalent in North America, northern Europe, and Australia. IBD incidence worldwide is on the rise and is becoming more common in regions in which the prevalence was historically low. The *hygiene hypothesis* suggests that these changes in incidence are related to improved food storage conditions and decreased food contamination. Specifically, it proposes that a reduced frequency of enteric infections due to improved hygiene has resulted in inadequate development of regulatory processes that limit mucosal immune responses early in life. As a result, exposure of susceptible individuals to normally innocuous microbes later in life triggers inappropriate immune responses that may be self-sustaining due to loss of intestinal epithelial barrier function. Although many details are ome data, including some from animal models observation in humans that an episode of acute ous gastroenteritis increases the risk of developing , are consistent with the hygiene hypothesis.

PATHOGENESIS

The cause(s) of IBD remains uncertain. However, **most investigators believe that IBD results from a combination of errant host interactions with intestinal microbiota, intestinal epithelial dysfunction, and aberrant mucosal immune responses.** This view is supported by epidemiologic, genetic, and clinical studies as well as data from laboratory models of IBD (Fig. 14–27).

- **Genetics.** Risk of disease is increased when there is an affected family member, and in Crohn disease, the concordance rate for monozygotic twins is approximately 50%. By contrast, concordance of monozygotic twins for ulcerative colitis is only 16%, suggesting that genetic factors are less dominant in this form of IBD.

  Molecular linkage analyses of affected families have identified *NOD2* (nucleotide oligomerization binding domain 2) as a susceptibility gene in Crohn disease. *NOD2* encodes a protein that binds to intracellular bacterial peptidoglycans and subsequently activates NF-κB. It has been postulated that disease-associated *NOD2* variants are less effective at recognizing and combating luminal microbes, which are then able to enter the lamina propria and trigger inflammatory reactions. Other data suggest that *NOD2* may regulate immune responses to prevent excessive activation by luminal microbes. Whatever the mechanism by which *NOD2* polymorphisms contribute to the pathogenesis of Crohn disease, it should be recognized that disease develops in less than 10% of persons carrying *NOD2* mutations, and *NOD2* mutations are uncommon in African and Asian patients with Crohn disease.

  In recent years, genome-wide association studies (GWAS) that assess single-nucleotide polymorphisms have been used to broaden the search for IBD-associated genes. The number of genes identified by GWAS is increasing rapidly (already numbering more than 30), but along with *NOD2*, two Crohn disease–related genes of particular interest are *ATG16L1* (autophagy-related 16–like-1), a part of the autophagosome pathway that is critical to host cell responses to intracellular bacteria, and *IRGM* (immunity-related GTPase M), which also is involved in autophagy and clearance of intracellular bacteria. *NOD2, ATG16L1,* and *IRGM* are expressed in multiple cell types, and their precise roles in the pathogenesis of Crohn disease have yet to be defined. Like *NOD2,* however, *ATG16L1* and *IRGM* are related to recognition and response to intracellular pathogens, supporting the hypothesis that inappropriate immune reactions to luminal bacteria are important in pathogenesis of IBD. None of these genes are associated with ulcerative colitis.
- **Mucosal immune responses.** Although the mechanisms by which mucosal immunity contributes to the pathogenesis of ulcerative colitis and Crohn disease are still being deciphered, immunosuppressive and immunomodulatory agents remain mainstays of IBD therapy. Polarization of helper T cells to the T_H1 type is well recognized in Crohn disease, and emerging data suggest that T_H17 T cells also contribute to disease pathogenesis. Consistent with this, certain polymorphisms of the IL-23 receptor confer protection from Crohn disease and ulcerative colitis (IL-23 is involved in the development and maintenance of T_H17 cells). The protection afforded by IL-23 receptor polymorphisms, together with the recognized effectiveness of anti-TNF therapy in some patients with ulcerative colitis, seems to support roles for T_H1 and T_H17 cells.

  Some data suggest that the pathogenic immune response in ulcerative colitis includes a significant T_H2 component. For example, mucosal IL-13 production is increased in ulcerative colitis, and, to a lesser degree, Crohn disease. However, the pathogenic role of T_H2 cells in IBD pathogenesis remains controversial. Polymorphisms of the *IL-10* gene as well as *IL-10R*, the IL10 receptor gene, have been linked to ulcerative colitis but not Crohn disease, further emphasizing the importance of immunoregulatory signals in IBD pathogenesis.

  Overall, it is likely that some combination of derangements that activate mucosal immunity and suppress immunoregulation contribute to the development of both ulcerative colitis and Crohn disease. The relative roles of the innate and adaptive arms of the immune system are the subject of ongoing intense scrutiny.
- **Epithelial defects.** A variety of epithelial defects have been described in Crohn disease, ulcerative colitis, or both. For example, defects in intestinal epithelial tight junction barrier function are present in patients with Crohn disease and a subset of their healthy first-degree relatives. This barrier dysfunction cosegregates with specific disease-associated *NOD2* polymorphisms, and experimental models demonstrate that barrier dysfunction can activate

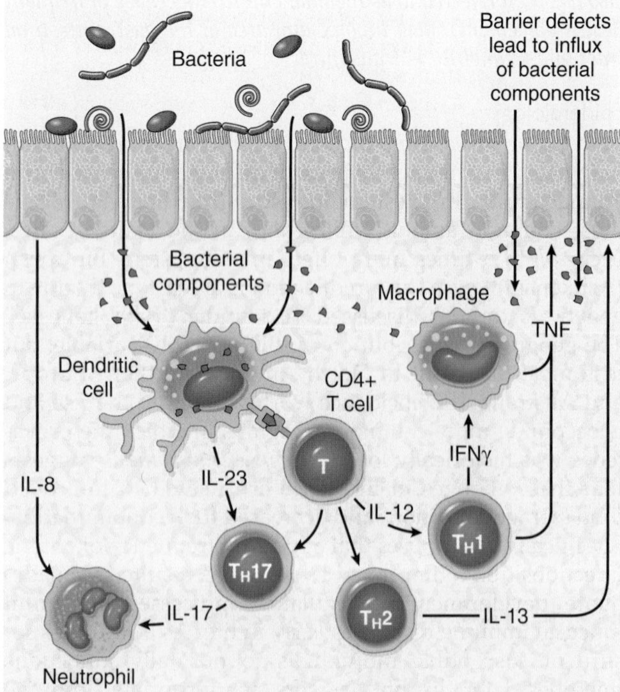

Figure 14–27 A model of pathogenesis of inflammatory bowel disease (IBD). Aspects of both Crohn disease and ulcerative colitis are shown.

innate and adaptive mucosal immunity and sensitize subjects to disease. Interestingly, the Paneth cell granules, which contain antimicrobial peptides that can affect composition of the luminal microbiota, are abnormal in patients with Crohn disease carrying *ATG16L1* mutations, thus providing one potential mechanism where a defective feedback loop between the epithelium and microbiota could contribute to disease pathogenesis.

- **Microbiota.** The quantity of microbial organisms in the gastrointestinal lumen is enormous, amounting to as many as 10^{12} organisms/mL of fecal material in the colon (50% of fecal mass). This abundance means that, on a per cell level, we are only about 10% human. There is significant inter-individual variation in the composition of this microbial population, which is modified by diet and disease. Despite a growing body of data that suggest that intestinal microbiota contribute to IBD pathogenesis, their precise role remains to be defined. In keeping with this, some antibiotics, such as metronidazole, can be helpful in maintenance of remission in Crohn disease. Ongoing studies suggest that ill-defined mixtures containing probiotic, or beneficial, bacteria also may combat disease in experimental models, as well as in some patients with IBD, although the mechanisms responsible are not well understood.

One model that unifies the roles of intestinal microbiota, epithelial function, and mucosal immunity suggests a cycle by which transepithelial flux of luminal bacterial components activates innate and adaptive immune responses. In a genetically susceptible host, the subsequent release of TNF and other immune-mediated signals direct epithelia to increase tight junction permeability, which further increases the flux of luminal material. These events may establish a self-amplifying cycle in which a stimulus at any site may be sufficient to initiate IBD. Although this model is helpful in advancing the current understanding of IBD pathogenesis, a variety of factors are associated with disease for unknown reasons. For example, a single episode of appendicitis is associated with reduced risk of developing ulcerative colitis. Tobacco use also modifies the risk of IBD. Somewhat surprisingly, the risk of Crohn disease is increased by smoking, whereas that of ulcerative colitis is reduced.

Crohn Disease

Crohn disease, also known as regional enteritis, may occur in any area of the gastrointestinal tract.

MORPHOLOGY

The most common sites involved by Crohn disease at presentation are the **terminal ileum, ileocecal valve,** and **cecum.** Disease is limited to the small intestine alone in about 40% of cases; the small intestine and the colon both are involved in 30% of patients; and the remainder of cases are characterized by colonic involvement only. The presence of multiple, separate, sharply delineated areas of disease, resulting in **skip lesions,** is characteristic of Crohn disease and may help in differentiation from ulcerative colitis. Strictures are common (Fig. 14–28, *A*).

The earliest lesion, the **aphthous ulcer,** may progress, and multiple lesions often coalesce into elongated, serpentine ulcers oriented along the axis of the bowel. Edema and loss of normal mucosal folds are common. Sparing of interspersed mucosa results in a coarsely textured, **cobblestone** appearance in which diseased tissue is depressed below the level of normal mucosa (Fig. 14–28, *B*). **Fissures** frequently develop between mucosal folds and may extend deeply to become sites of perforation or fistula tracts. The intestinal wall is thickened as a consequence of transmural edema, inflammation, submucosal fibrosis, and hypertrophy of the muscularis propria, all of which contribute to stricture formation. In cases with extensive transmural disease, mesenteric fat frequently extends around the serosal surface **(creeping fat)** (Fig. 14–28, *C*).

The microscopic features of active Crohn disease include abundant neutrophils that infiltrate and damage crypt epithelium. Clusters of neutrophils within a crypt are referred to as a **crypt abscess** and often are associated with crypt destruction. Ulceration is common in Crohn disease, and there may be an abrupt transition between ulcerated and normal mucosa. Repeated cycles of crypt destruction and regeneration lead to **distortion of mucosal architecture;** the normally straight and parallel crypts take on bizarre branching shapes and unusual orientations to one another (Fig. 14–29,

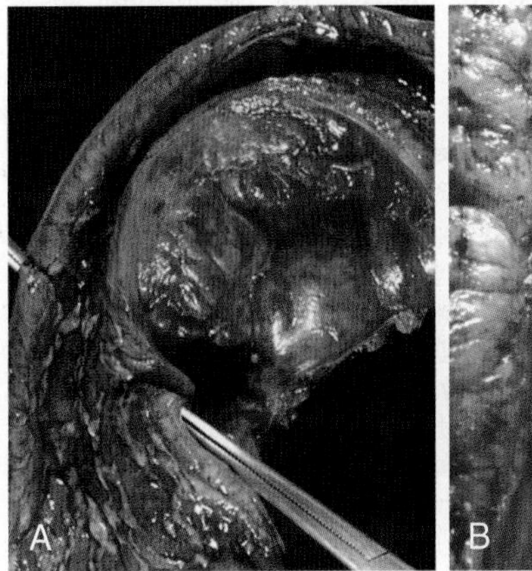

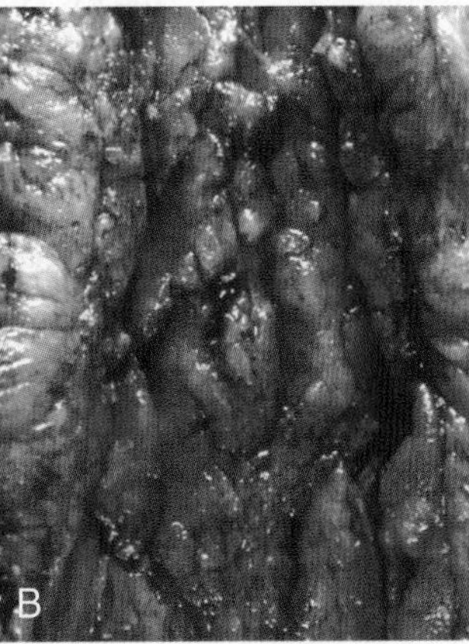

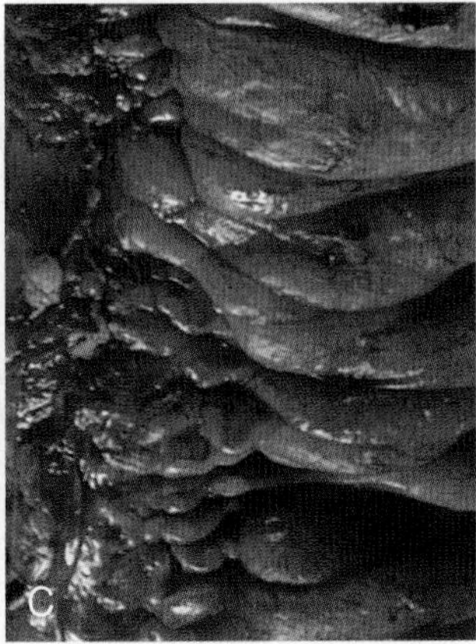

Figure 14–28 Gross pathology of Crohn disease. **A,** Small intestinal stricture. **B,** Linear mucosal ulcers and thickened intestinal wall. **C,** Creeping fat.

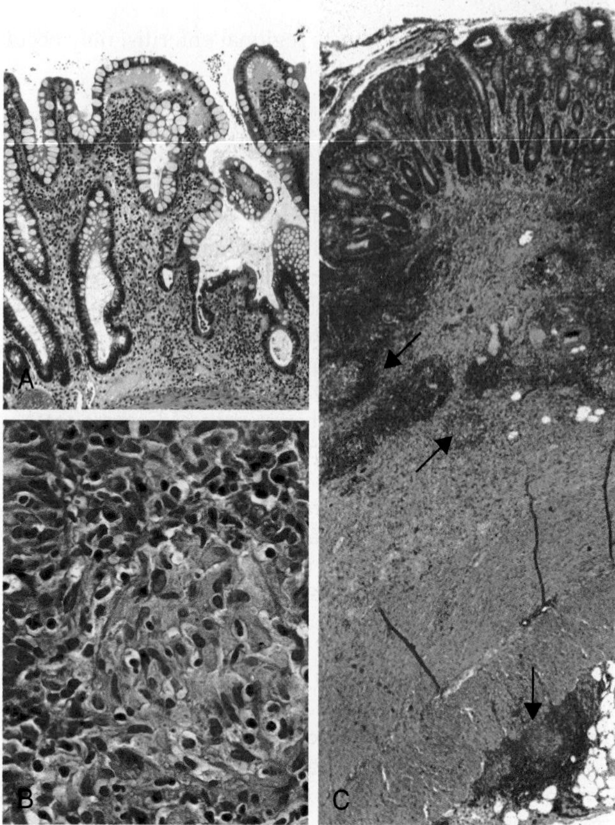

Figure 14–29 Microscopic pathology of Crohn disease. **A,** Haphazard crypt organization results from repeated injury and regeneration. **B,** Noncaseating granuloma. **C,** Transmural Crohn disease with submucosal and serosal granulomas (*arrows*).

A). Epithelial metaplasia, another consequence of chronic relapsing injury, often takes the form of gastric antral-appearing glands (pseudopyloric metaplasia). **Paneth cell metaplasia** also may occur in the left colon, where Paneth cells normally are absent. These architectural and metaplastic changes may persist even when active inflammation has resolved. Mucosal atrophy, with loss of crypts, may result after years of disease. **Noncaseating granulomas** (Fig. 14–29, *B*), a hallmark of Crohn disease, are found in approximately 35% of cases and may arise in areas of active disease or uninvolved regions in any layer of the intestinal wall (Fig. 14–29, *C*). Granulomas also may be found in mesenteric lymph nodes. Cutaneous granulomas form nodules that are referred to (misleadingly) as **metastatic Crohn disease. The absence of granulomas does not preclude a diagnosis of Crohn disease.**

Clinical Features

The clinical manifestations of Crohn disease are extremely variable. *In most patients, disease begins with intermittent attacks of relatively mild diarrhea, fever, and abdominal pain.* Approximately 20% of patients present acutely with right lower quadrant pain, fever, and bloody diarrhea that may mimic acute appendicitis or bowel perforation. Periods of active disease typically are interrupted by asymptomatic intervals that last for weeks to many months. Disease reactivation can be associated with a variety of external triggers, including physical or emotional stress, specific dietary items, and cigarette smoking.

Iron deficiency anemia may develop in persons with colonic disease, while extensive small bowel disease may result in serum protein loss and hypoalbuminemia, generalized nutrient malabsorption, or malabsorption of vitamin B_{12} and bile salts. Fibrosing strictures, particularly of the terminal ileum, are common and require surgical resection. Disease often recurs at the site of anastomosis, and as many as 40% of patients require additional resections within 10 years. Fistulas develop between loops of bowel and may also involve the urinary bladder, vagina, and abdominal or perianal skin. Perforations and peritoneal abscesses are common.

Extraintestinal manifestations of Crohn disease include uveitis, migratory polyarthritis, sacroiliitis, ankylosing spondylitis, erythema nodosum, and clubbing of the fingertips, any of which may develop before intestinal disease is recognized. Pericholangitis and primary sclerosing cholangitis also occur in Crohn disease but are more common in ulcerative colitis. As discussed later on, risk of colonic adenocarcinoma is increased in patients with long-standing colonic Crohn disease.

Ulcerative Colitis

Ulcerative colitis is closely related to Crohn disease. However, ulcerative colitis is limited to the colon and rectum. Some extraintestinal manifestations of ulcerative colitis overlap with those of Crohn disease, including migratory polyarthritis, sacroiliitis, ankylosing spondylitis, uveitis, skin lesions, pericholangitis, and primary sclerosing cholangitis.

MORPHOLOGY

Ulcerative colitis always involves the rectum and extends proximally in a continuous fashion to involve part or all of the colon. Skip lesions are not seen (although focal appendiceal or cecal inflammation occasionally may be present). Disease of the entire colon is termed **pancolitis** (Fig. 14–30, *A*). Disease limited to the rectum or rectosigmoid may be referred to descriptively as **ulcerative proctitis** or **ulcerative proctosigmoiditis.** The small intestine is normal, although mild mucosal inflammation of the distal ileum, **backwash ileitis,** may be present in severe cases of pancolitis.

On gross evaluation, involved colonic mucosa may be slightly red and granular-appearing or exhibit extensive **broad-based ulcers.** The transition between diseased and uninvolved colon can be abrupt (Fig. 14–30, *B*). Ulcers are aligned along the long axis of the colon but typically do not replicate the serpentine ulcers of Crohn disease. Isolated islands of regenerating mucosa often bulge into the lumen to create small elevations, termed **pseudopolyps.** Chronic disease may lead to **mucosal atrophy** and a flat, smooth mucosal surface lacking normal folds. Unlike in Crohn disease, **mural thickening is absent, the serosal surface is normal, and strictures do not occur.** However, inflammation and inflammatory mediators can damage the muscularis propria and disturb neuromuscular function leading to colonic dilation and **toxic megacolon,** which carries a significant risk of perforation.

Histologic features of mucosal disease in ulcerative colitis are similar to those in colonic Crohn disease and include inflammatory infiltrates, crypt abscesses, crypt distortion, and epithelial metaplasia. However, **skip lesions are absent and inflammation generally is limited to the mucosa and superficial submucosa** (Fig. 14–30, *C*). In severe cases, mucosal damage may be accompanied by ulcers that extend more deeply into the submucosa, but the muscularis propria is rarely involved. Submucosal fibrosis, mucosal atrophy, and distorted mucosal architecture remain as residua of healed disease, but the histologic pattern also may revert to near normal after prolonged remission. **Granulomas are not present.**

Clinical Features

Ulcerative colitis is a relapsing disorder characterized by attacks of bloody diarrhea with expulsion of stringy, mucoid material and lower abdominal pain and cramps that are temporarily relieved by defecation. These symptoms may persist for days, weeks, or months before they subside, and occasionally the initial attack may be severe enough to constitute a medical or surgical emergency. More than half of the patients have mild disease, and almost all experience at least one relapse during a 10-year period. Colectomy cures intestinal disease, but extraintestinal manifestations may persist.

The factors that trigger ulcerative colitis are not known, but as noted previously, infectious enteritis precedes disease onset in some cases. In other cases the first attack is preceded by psychologic stress, which also may be linked to relapse during remission. The initial onset of symptoms also has been reported to occur shortly after smoking cessation in some patients, and smoking may partially relieve symptoms. Unfortunately, studies of nicotine as a therapeutic agent have been disappointing.

Indeterminate Colitis

Histopathologic and clinical overlap between ulcerative colitis and Crohn disease is common, and it is not possible to make a distinction in up to 10% of patients with IBD. In such cases, termed *indeterminate colitis,* the small bowel is not involved, and the continuous pattern of colonic disease typically would indicate ulcerative colitis. However, patchy disease, fissures, a family history of Crohn disease, perianal lesions, onset after initiation of cigarette smoking, or findings that are not typical of ulcerative colitis may create uncertainty. Because of extensive overlap in medical management of ulcerative colitis and Crohn disease, patients carrying a diagnosis of indeterminate colitis can be treated effectively. Nevertheless, it is preferable, when possible, to definitively categorize patients, because evolving medical therapies and surgical management differ for ulcerative colitis and for Crohn disease.

Colitis-Associated Neoplasia

One of the most feared long-term complications of ulcerative colitis and colonic Crohn disease is the development of neoplasia. This process begins as dysplasia, which, just as in Barrett esophagus and chronic gastritis, is a step along the road to full-blown carcinoma. The risk of dysplasia is related to several factors:

- Risk increases sharply 8 to 10 years after disease initiation.
- Patients with pancolitis are at greater risk than those with only left-sided disease.
- Greater frequency and severity of active inflammation (characterized by the presence of neutrophils) may increase risk. This is another example of the enabling effect of inflammation on carcinogenesis (Chapter 5).

To facilitate early detection of neoplasia, patients typically are enrolled in surveillance programs approximately 8 years after diagnosis of IBD. The primary exception to this approach is in patients with primary sclerosing cholangitis,

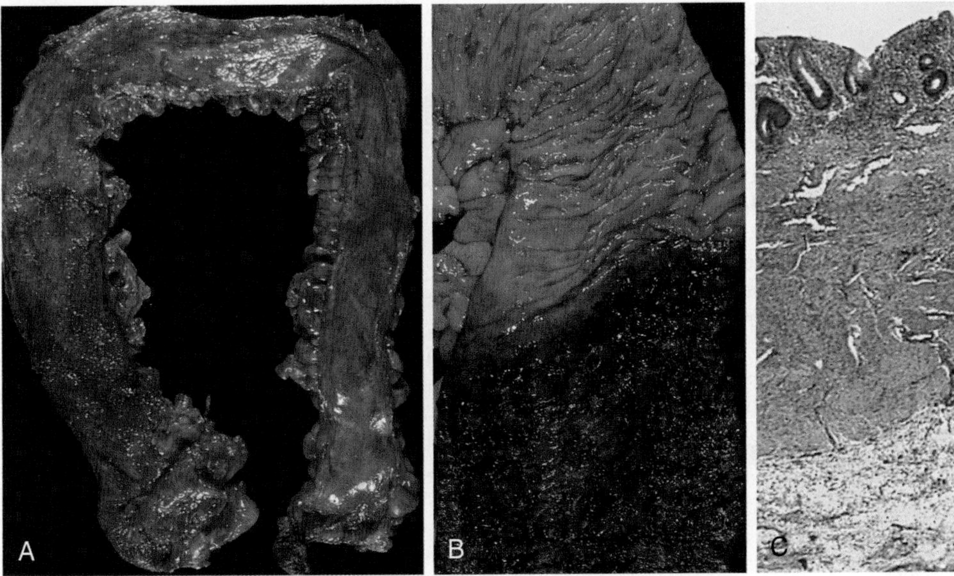

Figure 14–30 Pathology of ulcerative colitis. **A,** Total colectomy with pancolitis showing active disease, with red, granular mucosa in the cecum (*left*) and smooth, atrophic mucosa distally (*right*). **B,** Sharp demarcation between active ulcerative colitis (*bottom*) and normal (*top*). **C,** This full-thickness histologic section shows that disease is limited to the mucosa. Compare with Figures 14–28 and 14–29.

who are at markedly greater risk for development of dysplasia and generally are enrolled for surveillance at the time of diagnosis. Surveillance requires regular and extensive mucosal biopsy, making it a costly practice. In many cases, dysplasia occurs in flat areas of mucosa that are not recognized as abnormal on gross evaluation. Thus, advanced endoscopic imaging techniques are beginning to be used experimentally to increase sensitivity of detection in normal-looking tissue.

IBD-associated dysplasia is classified histologically as low-grade or high-grade. High-grade dysplasia can be associated with invasive carcinoma at the same site or elsewhere in the colon and therefore often prompts colectomy, particularly when the changes are multifocal. Low-grade dysplasia may be treated with colectomy or monitored closely, depending on a variety of clinical factors. Colonic adenomas (discussed later on) also occur in patients with IBD, and in some cases these may be difficult to differentiate from a polypoid focus of IBD-associated dysplasia.

SUMMARY

Inflammatory Bowel Disease

- Inflammatory bowel disease (IBD) is an umbrella term for Crohn disease and ulcerative colitis.
- Crohn disease most commonly affects the terminal ileum and cecum, but any site within the gastrointestinal tract can be involved; skip lesions and noncaseating granulomas are common.
- Ulcerative colitis is limited to the colon, is continuous from the rectum, and ranges in extent from only rectal disease to pancolitis; neither skip lesions nor granulomas are present.
- Both Crohn disease and ulcerative colitis can have extra-intestinal manifestations.
- The risk of colonic epithelial dysplasia and adenocarcinoma is increased in patients who have had IBD for more than 8 to 10 years.

COLONIC POLYPS AND NEOPLASTIC DISEASE

Polyps are most common in the colon but may occur in the esophagus, stomach, or small intestine. Those without stalks are referred to as *sessile*. As sessile polyps enlarge, proliferation of cells adjacent to the polyp and the effects of traction on the luminal protrusion, may combine to create a stalk. Polyps with stalks are termed *pedunculated*. In general, intestinal polyps can be classified as non-neoplastic or neoplastic. The most common neoplastic polyp is the adenoma, which has the potential to progress to cancer. Non-neoplastic colonic polyps can be further classified as inflammatory, hamartomatous, or hyperplastic.

Inflammatory Polyps

The polyp that forms as part of the *solitary rectal ulcer syndrome* is an example of the purely inflammatory lesion. Patients present with the clinical triad of rectal bleeding, mucus discharge, and an inflammatory lesion of the anterior rectal wall. The underlying cause is impaired relaxation of the anorectal sphincter, creating a sharp angle at the anterior rectal shelf. This leads to recurrent abrasion and ulceration of the overlying rectal mucosa. Chronic cycles of injury and healing produce a polypoid mass made up of inflamed and reactive mucosal tissue.

Hamartomatous Polyps

Hamartomatous polyps occur sporadically and as components of various genetically determined or acquired syndromes (Table 14–6). As described previously, hamartomas are disorganized, tumor-like growths composed of mature cell types normally present at the site at which the polyp develops. Hamartomatous polyposis syndromes are rare, but they are important to recognize because of associated intestinal and extraintestinal manifestations and the need to screen family members.

Juvenile Polyps

Juvenile polyps are the most common type of hamartomatous polyp. They may be *sporadic or syndromic.* In adults, the sporadic form sometimes is also referred to as an *inflammatory polyp*, particularly when dense inflammatory infiltrates are present. The vast majority of juvenile polyps occur in children younger than 5 years of age. *Juvenile polyps characteristically are located in the rectum,* and most manifest with rectal bleeding. In some cases, prolapse occurs and the polyp protrudes through the anal sphincter. Sporadic juvenile polyps are usually solitary but in persons with the autosomal dominant syndrome of juvenile polyposis the number varies from 3 to as many as 100. Colectomy may be required to limit the hemorrhage associated with polyp ulceration in juvenile polyposis. Dysplasia occurs in a small proportion of (mostly syndrome-associated) juvenile polyps, and the juvenile polyposis syndrome is associated with increased risk for the development of colonic adenocarcinoma.

MORPHOLOGY

Individual sporadic and syndromic juvenile polyps often are indistinguishable. They typically are pedunculated, smooth-surfaced, reddish lesions that are less than 3 cm in diameter and display characteristic cystic spaces on cut sections. Microscopic examination shows the spaces to be dilated glands filled with mucin and inflammatory debris (Fig. 14–31, A). Some data suggest that mucosal hyperplasia is the initiating event in polyp development, and this mechanism is consistent with the discovery that mutations in pathways that regulate cellular growth, such as transforming growth factor-β (TGF-β) signaling, are associated with autosomal dominant juvenile polyposis.

Peutz-Jeghers Syndrome

Peutz-Jeghers syndrome is a rare autosomal dominant disorder defined by the presence of multiple gastrointestinal

Table 14–6 Gastrointestinal (GI) Polyposis Syndromes

Syndrome	Mean Age at Presentation (years)	Mutated Gene(s)	GI Lesions	Selected Extragastrointestinal Manifestations
Peutz-Jeghers syndrome	10–15	*LKB1/STK11*	Arborizing polyps—small intestine > colon > stomach; colonic adenocarcinoma	Mucocutaneous pigmentation; increased risk of thyroid, breast, lung, pancreas, gonadal, and bladder cancers
Juvenile polyposis	<5	*SMAD4, BMPR1A*	Juvenile polyps; increased risk of gastric, small intestinal, colonic, and pancreatic adenocarcinoma	Pulmonary arteriovenous malformations, digital clubbing
Cowden syndrome, Bannayan-Ruvalcaba-Riley syndrome	<15	*PTEN*	Hamartomatous polyps, lipomas, ganglioneuromas, inflammatory polyps; increased risk of colon cancer	Benign skin tumors, benign and malignant thyroid and breast lesions
Cronkhite-Canada syndrome	>50	Nonhereditary	Hamartomatous colon polyps, crypt dilatation and edema in nonpolypoid mucosa	Nail atrophy, hair loss, abnormal skin pigmentation, cachexia, anemia
Tuberous sclerosis	Infancy to adulthood	*TSC1, TSC2*	Hamartomatous polyps (rectal)	Facial angiofibroma, cortical tubers, renal angiomyolipoma
Familial adenomatous polyposis (FAP)				
Classic FAP	10–15	*APC, MUTYH*	Multiple adenomas	Congenital RPE hypertrophy
Attenuated FAP	40–50	*APC, MUTYH*	Multiple adenomas	
Gardner syndrome	10–15	*APC, MUTYH*	Multiple adenomas	Osteomas, desmoids, skin cysts
Turcot syndrome	10–15	*APC, MUTYH*	Multiple adenomas	CNS tumors, medulloblastoma

CNS, central nervous system; RPE, retinal pigment epithelium.

hamartomatous polyps and mucocutaneous hyperpigmentation that carries an increased risk of several malignancies, including cancers of the colon, pancreas, breast, lung, ovaries, uterus, and testes, as well as other unusual neoplasms. Germ line heterozygous loss-of-function mutations in the gene *LKB1/STK11* are present in approximately half of the patients with the familial form of Peutz-Jeghers syndrome, as well as a subset of patients with the sporadic form. Intestinal polyps are most common in the small intestine, although they may also occur in the stomach and colon and, rarely, in the bladder and lungs. On gross evaluation, the polyps are large and pedunculated with a lobulated contour. Histologic examination demonstrates a characteristic arborizing network of connective tissue, smooth muscle, lamina propria, and glands lined by normal-appearing intestinal epithelium (Fig. 14–31, *B*).

Hyperplastic Polyps

Colonic hyperplastic polyps are common epithelial proliferations that typically are discovered in the sixth and seventh decades of life. The pathogenesis of hyperplastic polyps is incompletely understood, but formation of these lesions is thought to result from decreased epithelial cell turnover and delayed shedding of surface epithelial cells, leading to a "pileup" of goblet cells.

Although these lesions have no malignant potential, they must be distinguished from sessile serrated adenomas, histologically similar lesions that have malignant potential, as described later.

MORPHOLOGY

Hyperplastic polyps are most commonly found in the left colon and typically are less than 5 mm in diameter. They are smooth, nodular protrusions of the mucosa, often on the crests of mucosal folds. They may occur singly but more frequently are multiple, particularly in the sigmoid colon and rectum. Histologically, hyperplastic polyps are composed of mature goblet and absorptive cells. The delayed shedding of these cells leads to crowding that creates the serrated surface architecture that is the morphologic hallmark of these lesions (Fig. 14–32).

Adenomas

Any neoplastic mass lesion in the gastrointestinal tract may produce a mucosal protrusion, or polyp. The most common and clinically important neoplastic polyps are *colonic adenomas, benign polyps that give rise to a majority of colorectal adenocarcinomas*. Most adenomas, however, do not progress to adenocarcinoma.

Colorectal adenomas are characterized by the presence of epithelial dysplasia. These growths range from small, often pedunculated polyps to large sessile lesions. There is no gender predilection, and they are present in nearly 50% of adults living in the Western world beginning age 50. Because these polyps are precursors to colorectal cancer, current recommendations are that all adults in the United States undergo surveillance colonoscopy starting at age 50. Because persons with a family history are at risk for

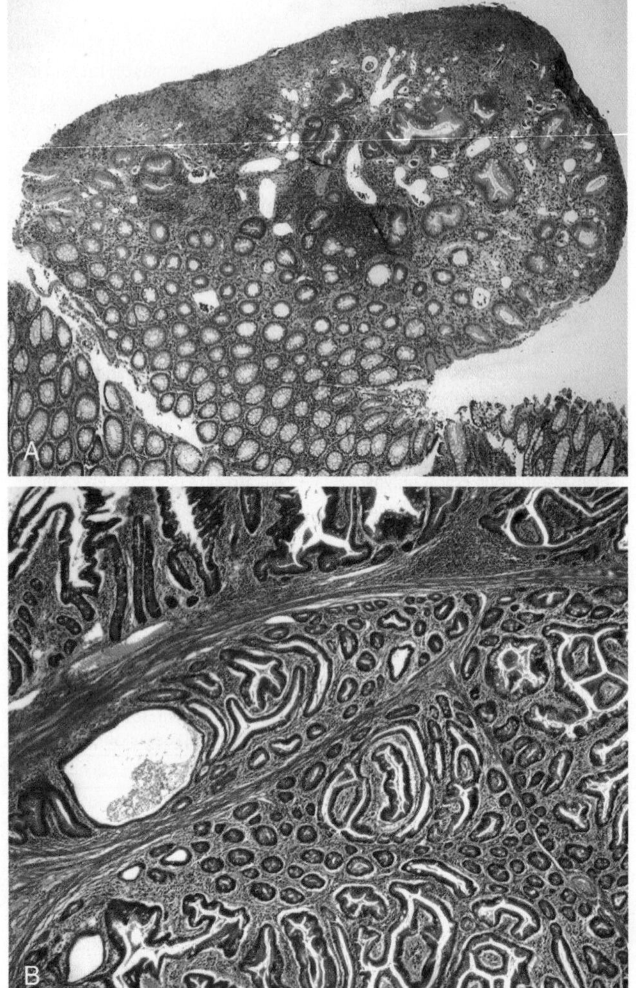

Figure 14–31 Hamartomatous polyps. **A,** Juvenile polyp. Note the surface erosion and cystically dilated crypts filled with mucus, neutrophils, and debris. **B,** Peutz-Jeghers polyp. Complex glandular architecture and bundles of smooth muscle help to distinguish Peutz-Jeghers polyps from juvenile polyps.

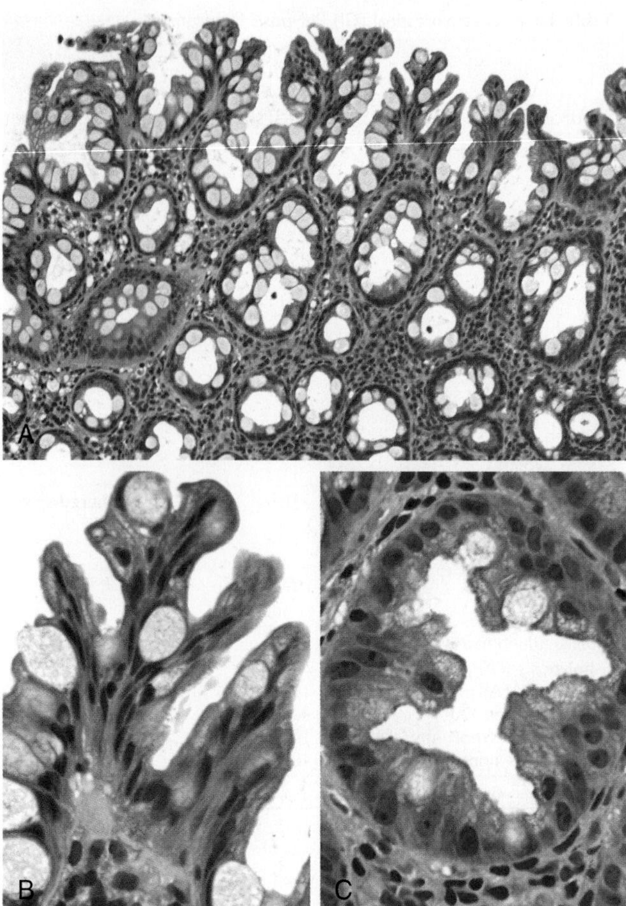

Figure 14–32 Hyperplastic polyp. **A,** Polyp surface with irregular tufting of epithelial cells. **B,** Tufting results from epithelial overcrowding. **C,** Epithelial crowding produces a serrated architecture when glands are cut in cross-section.

developing colon cancer earlier in life, they typically are screened at least 10 years before the youngest age at which a relative was diagnosed. While adenomas are less common in Asia, their frequency has risen (in parallel with an increasing incidence of colorectal adenocarcinoma) as Western diets and lifestyles become more common.

MORPHOLOGY

Typical adenomas range from 0.3 to 10 cm in diameter and can be **pedunculated** (Fig. 14–33, *A*) or **sessile,** with the surface of both types having a texture resembling velvet (Fig. 14–33, *B*) or a raspberry, due to the abnormal epithelial growth pattern. Histologically, the cytologic hallmark of **epithelial dysplasia** (Fig. 14–34, *C*) is nuclear hyperchromasia, elongation, and stratification. These changes are most easily appreciated at the surface of the adenoma, because the epithelium fails to mature as cells migrate out of the crypt. Pedunculated adenomas have slender fibromuscular stalks (Fig. 14–33, *C*) containing prominent blood vessels derived from the submucosa. The stalk usually is covered by non-neoplastic epithelium, but dysplastic epithelium is sometimes present.

Adenomas can be classified as **tubular, tubulovillous, or villous** on the basis of their architecture. These categories, however, have little clinical significance in isolation. Tubular adenomas tend to be small, pedunculated polyps composed of small, rounded or tubular glands (Fig. 14–34, *A*). By contrast, villous adenomas, which often are larger and sessile, are covered by slender villi (Fig. 14–34, *B*). Tubulovillous adenomas have a mixture of tubular and villous elements. Although foci of invasion are more frequent in villous adenomas than in tubular adenomas, villous architecture alone does not increase cancer risk when polyp size is considered.

The histologic features of **sessile serrated adenomas** overlap with those of hyperplastic polyps and the typical cytologic features of dysplasia are lacking (Fig. 14–34, *D*). However, these lesions, which are most common in the right colon, have a malignant potential similar to that of traditional adenomas. The most useful histologic feature that distinguishes sessile serrated adenomas and hyperplastic polyps is the presence of serrated architecture throughout the full length of the glands, including the crypt base, associated with crypt dilation and lateral growth, in the former (Fig. 14–34,

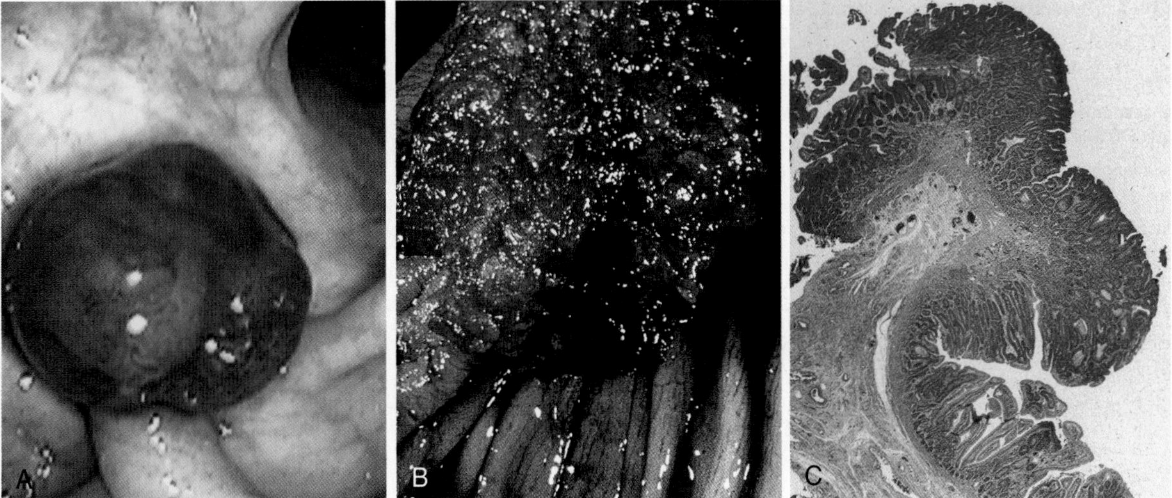

Figure 14–33 Colonic adenomas. **A,** Pedunculated adenoma (endoscopic view). **B,** Adenoma with a velvety surface. **C,** Low-magnification photomicrograph of a pedunculated tubular adenoma.

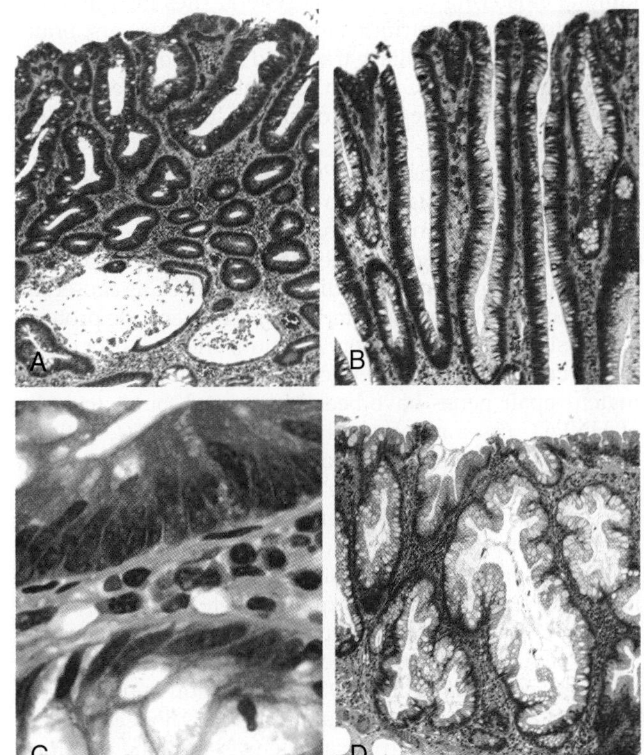

Figure 14–34 Histologic appearance of colonic adenomas. **A,** Tubular adenoma with a smooth surface and rounded glands. In this case, crypt dilation and rupture, with associated reactive inflammation, can be seen at the bottom of the field. **B,** Villous adenoma with long, slender projections that are reminiscent of small intestinal villi. **C,** Dysplastic epithelial cells (*top*) with an increased nuclear-to-cytoplasmic ratio, hyperchromatic and elongated nuclei, and nuclear pseudostratification. Compare with the nondysplastic epithelium below. **D,** Sessile serrated adenoma lined by goblet cells without typical cytologic features of dysplasia. This lesion is distinguished from a hyperplastic polyp by involvement of the crypts. Compare with the hyperplastic polyp in Figure 14–32.

D). By contrast, serrated architecture typically is confined to the surface of hyperplastic polyps.

Although most colorectal adenomas are benign lesions, a small proportion may harbor invasive cancer at the time of detection. **Size is the most important characteristic that correlates with risk of malignancy.** For example, while cancer is extremely rare in adenomas less than 1 cm in diameter, some studies suggest that nearly 40% of lesions larger than 4 cm in diameter contain foci of cancer. In addition to size, high-grade dysplasia is a risk factor for cancer in an individual polyp (but not other polyps in the same patient).

Familial Syndromes

Several syndromes associated with colonic polyps and increased rates of colon cancer have been described. The genetic basis of these disorders has been established and has greatly enhanced the current understanding of sporadic colon cancer (Table 14–7).

Familial Adenomatous Polyps

Familial adenomatous polyposis (FAP) is an autosomal dominant disorder marked by the appearance of numerous colorectal adenomas by the teenage years. It is caused by mutations of the *adenomatous polyposis coli* gene (*APC*). *A count of at least 100 polyps is necessary for a diagnosis* of classic FAP, and as many as several thousand may be present (Fig. 14–35). Except for their remarkable numbers, these growths are *morphologically indistinguishable from sporadic adenomas.* Colorectal adenocarcinoma develops in 100% of patients with untreated FAP, often before age 30. As a result, prophylactic colectomy is standard therapy for persons carrying *APC* mutations. However, patients remain at risk for *extraintestinal manifestations,* including neoplasia at other sites. Specific *APC* mutations are also associated with the development of other manifestations of FAP and explain variants such as Gardner syndrome and Turcot syndrome. In addition to intestinal polyps, clinical features of *Gardner syndrome,* a variant of FAP, may include osteomas of

Table 14–7 Common Patterns of Sporadic and Familial Colorectal Neoplasia

Etiology	Molecular Defect	Target Gene(s)	Transmission	Predominant Site(s)	Histology
Familial adenomatous polyposis (70% of FAP)	APC/WNT pathway	*APC*	Autosomal dominant	None	Tubular, villous; typical adenocarcinoma
Familial adenomatous polyposis (<10% of FAP)	DNA mismatch repair	*MUTYH*	None, recessive	None	Sessile serrated adenoma; mucinous adenocarcinoma
Hereditary nonpolyposis colorectal cancer	DNA mismatch repair	*MSH2, MLH1*	Autosomal dominant	Right side	Sessile serrated adenoma; mucinous adenocarcinoma
Sporadic colon cancer (80%)	APC/WNT pathway	*APC*	None	Left side	Tubular, villous; typical adenocarcinoma
Sporadic colon cancer (10% to 15%)	DNA mismatch repair	*MSH2, MLH1*	None	Right side	Sessile serrated adenoma; mucinous adenocarcinoma

mandible, skull, and long bones; epidermal cysts; desmoid and thyroid tumors; and dental abnormalities, including unerupted and supernumerary teeth. *Turcot syndrome* is rarer and is characterized by intestinal adenomas and tumors of the central nervous system. Two thirds of patients with Turcot syndrome have *APC* gene mutations and develop medulloblastomas. The remaining one third have mutations in one of several genes involved in DNA repair and develop glioblastomas. Some patients who have FAP without *APC* loss have mutations of the base excision repair gene *MUTYH*. The role of these genes in tumor development is discussed below.

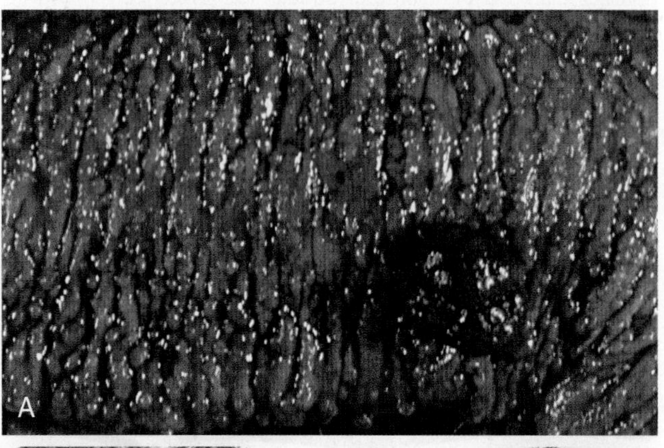

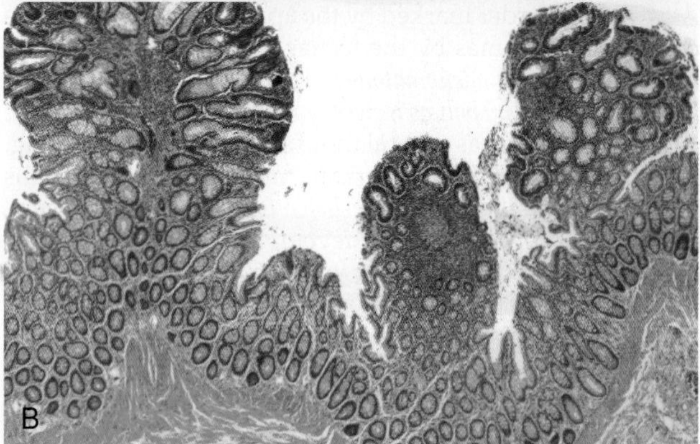

Figure 14–35 Familial adenomatous polyposis. **A,** Hundreds of small colonic polyps are present along with a dominant polyp (*right*). **B,** Three tubular adenomas are present in this single microscopic field.

Hereditary Nonpolyposis Colorectal Cancer

Hereditary nonpolyposis colorectal cancer (HNPCC), also known as Lynch syndrome, originally was described as familial clustering of cancers at several sites including the colorectum, endometrium, stomach, ovary, ureters, brain, small bowel, hepatobiliary tract, and skin. Colon cancers in patients with HNPCC tend to occur at *younger ages* than for sporadic colon cancers and often are located in the *right colon* (Table 14–7).

Just as identification of *APC* mutations in FAP has provided molecular insights into the pathogenesis of a majority of sporadic colon cancers, dissection of the defects in HNPCC has shed light on the mechanisms responsible for most of the remaining sporadic cases. HNPCC is caused by inherited germline mutations in genes that encode proteins responsible for the detection, excision, and repair of errors that occur during DNA replication. At least five such mismatch repair genes have been recognized, but a majority of HNPCC cases involve either *MSH2* or *MLH1.* Patients with HNPCC inherit one mutated DNA repair gene and one normal allele. When the second copy is lost through mutation or epigenetic silencing, defects in mismatch repair lead to the accumulation of mutations at rates up to 1000 times higher than normal, mostly in regions containing short repeating DNA sequences referred to as microsatellite DNA. The human genome contains approximately 50,000 to 100,000 microsatellites, which are prone to undergo expansion during DNA replication and represent the most frequent sites of mutations in HNPCC. The consequences of mismatch repair defects and the resulting *microsatellite instability* are discussed next in the context of colonic adenocarcinoma.

Adenocarcinoma

Adenocarcinoma of the colon is the most common malignancy of the gastrointestinal tract and is a major contributor to morbidity and mortality worldwide. By contrast, the small intestine, which accounts for 75% of the overall length of the gastrointestinal tract, is an uncommon site for benign and malignant tumors. Among malignant small intestinal tumors, adenocarcinomas and carcinoid tumors have roughly equal rates of occurrence, followed by lymphomas and sarcomas.

Epidemiology

Each year in the United States there are more than 130,000 new cases and 55,000 deaths from colorectal adenocarcinoma. This represents nearly 15% of all cancer-related deaths, second only to lung cancer. Colorectal cancer incidence peaks at 60 to 70 years of age, and less than 20% of cases occur before age 50. Males are affected slightly more often than females. Colorectal carcinoma is most prevalent in the United States, Canada, Australia, New Zealand, Denmark, Sweden, and other developed countries. The incidence of this cancer is as much as 30-fold lower in India, South America, and Africa. In Japan, where incidence was previously very low, rates have now risen to intermediate levels (similar to those in the United Kingdom), presumably as a result of changes in lifestyle and diet.

The dietary factors most closely associated with increased colorectal cancer rates are low intake of unabsorbable vegetable fiber and high intake of refined carbohydrates and fat.

In addition to dietary modification, pharmacologic chemoprevention has become an area of great interest. Several epidemiologic studies suggest that aspirin or other NSAIDs have a protective effect. This is consistent with studies showing that some NSAIDs cause polyp regression in patients with FAP in whom the rectum was left in place after colectomy. It is suspected that this effect is mediated by inhibition of the enzyme cyclooxygenase-2 (COX-2), which is highly expressed in 90% of colorectal carcinomas and 40% to 90% of adenomas and is known to promote epithelial proliferation, particularly in response to injury.

PATHOGENESIS

Studies of colorectal carcinogenesis have provided fundamental insights into the general mechanisms of cancer evolution. The combination of molecular events that lead to colonic adenocarcinoma is heterogeneous and includes genetic and epigenetic abnormalities. At least two distinct genetic pathways APC/β-catenin pathway, have been described. In simplest terms, these are the disturbances of which lead to increased WNT signaling, and the microsatellite instability pathway, which is associated with defects in DNA mismatch repair (see Table 14–7). Both pathways involve the stepwise accumulation of multiple mutations, but the genes involved and the mechanisms by which the mutations accumulate differ. Epigenetic events, the most common of which is methylation-induced gene silencing, may enhance progression along both pathways.

- The **APC/β-catenin pathway.** The classic **adenoma-carcinoma sequence,** which accounts for as much as 80% of sporadic colon tumors, typically involves mutation of the *APC* tumor suppressor early in the neoplastic process (Fig. 14–36). Both copies of the *APC* gene must be functionally inactivated, either by mutation or epigenetic events, for adenomas to develop. **APC is a key negative regulator of β-catenin, a component of the WNT signaling pathway** (Chapter 5). The APC protein normally binds to and promotes degradation of β-catenin. With loss of APC function, β-catenin accumulates and translocates to the nucleus, where it activates the transcription of genes, such as those encoding MYC and cyclin D1, which promote proliferation. This is followed by additional mutations, including activating mutations in *KRAS*, which also promote growth and prevent apoptosis. The conclusion that mutation of *KRAS* is a late event is supported by the observation that mutations are present in fewer than 10% of adenomas less than 1 cm in diameter, in 50% of adenomas greater than 1 cm in diameter, and in 50% of invasive adenocarcinomas. Neoplastic progression also is associated with mutations in other

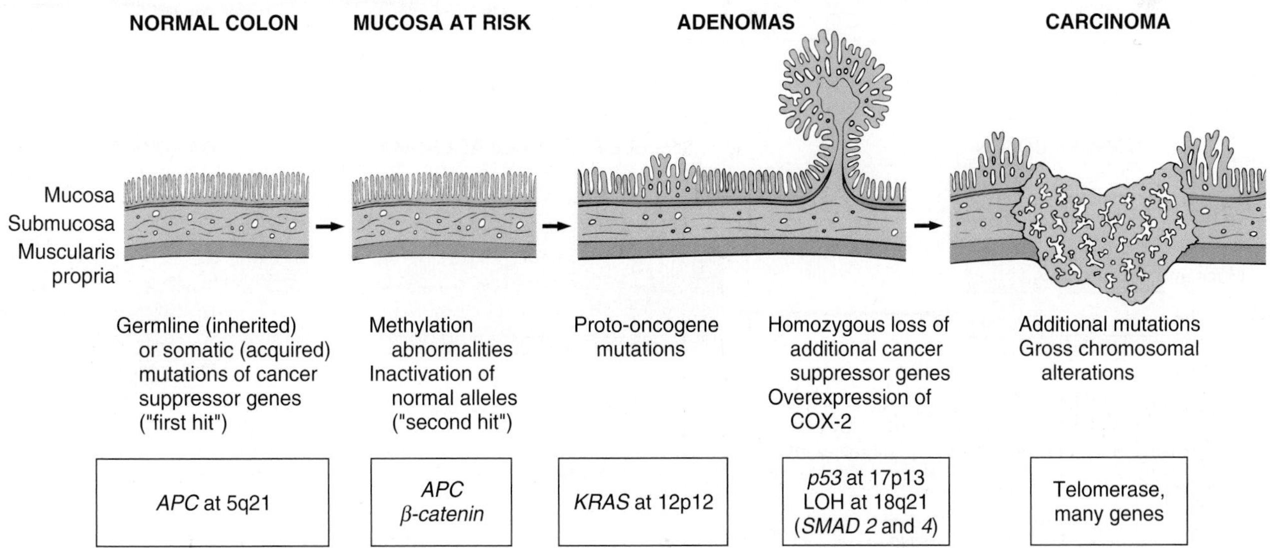

Figure 14–36 Morphologic and molecular changes in the adenoma-carcinoma sequence. It is postulated that loss of one normal copy of the tumor suppressor gene *APC* occurs early. Persons may be born with one mutant allele, making them extremely prone to the development of colon cancer, or inactivation of *APC* may occur later in life. This is the "first hit" according to Knudson's hypothesis. The loss of the intact copy of *APC* follows ("second hit"). Other mutations involving *KRAS*, *SMAD2*, and *SMAD4*, and the tumor suppressor gene *TP53*, lead to the emergence of carcinoma, in which additional mutations occur. Although there may be a preferred temporal sequence for these changes, it is the aggregate effect of the mutations, rather than their order of occurrence, that appears most critical.

tumor suppressor genes such as those encoding SMAD2 and SMAD4, which are effectors of TGF-β signaling. Because TGF-β signaling normally inhibits the cell cycle, loss of these genes may allow unrestrained cell growth. The tumor suppressor gene *TP53* is mutated in 70% to 80% of colon cancers but is uncommonly affected in adenomas, suggesting that *TP53* mutations also occur at late stages of tumor progression. "Loss of function" of *TP53* and other tumor suppressor genes often is caused by chromosomal deletions, highlighting chromosomal instability as a hallmark of the APC/β-catenin pathway. Alternatively, tumor suppressor genes may be silenced by methylation of CpG islands, a 5′ region of some genes that frequently includes the promoter and transcriptional start site. Expression of telomerase also increases as lesions become more advanced.

- **The microsatellite instability pathway.** In patients with DNA mismatch repair deficiency (due to loss of mismatch repair genes, as discussed earlier) mutations accumulate in microsatellite repeats, a condition referred to as **microsatellite instability.** These mutations generally are silent, because microsatellites typically are located in noncoding regions, but other microsatellite sequences are located in the coding or promoter regions of genes involved in regulation of cell growth, such as those encoding the type II TGF-β receptor and the pro-apoptotic protein BAX (Fig. 14–37). Because TGF-β inhibits colonic epithelial cell proliferation, type II TGF-β receptor mutants can contribute to uncontrolled cell growth, while loss of *BAX* may enhance the survival of genetically abnormal clones. Mutations in the oncogene *BRAF* and silencing of distinct groups of genes due to CpG island hypermethylation also are common in cancers that develop through DNA mismatch repair defects. By contrast, *KRAS* and *TP53* typically are not mutated. Thus, the combination of microsatellite instability, *BRAF* mutation, and methylation of specific targets, such as *MLH1*, is the signature of this pathway of carcinogenesis.

MORPHOLOGY

Overall, adenocarcinomas are distributed approximately equally over the entire length of the colon. **Tumors in the proximal colon often grow as polypoid, exophytic masses** that extend along one wall of the large-caliber cecum and ascending colon; these tumors rarely cause obstruction. By contrast, **carcinomas in the distal colon tend to be annular lesions that produce "napkin ring"** constrictions and luminal narrowing (Fig. 14–38), sometimes to the point of obstruction. Both forms grow into the bowel wall over time and may be palpable as firm masses. The general microscopic characteristics of right- and left-sided colonic adenocarcinomas are similar. Most tumors are composed of tall columnar cells that resemble dysplastic epithelium found in adenomas (Fig. 14–39, *A*). The invasive component of these tumors elicits a strong stromal desmoplastic response, which is responsible for their characteristic firm consistency. Some poorly differentiated tumors form few glands (Fig. 14–39, *B*). Others may produce abundant mucin that accumulates within the intestinal wall, and these carry a poor prognosis. Tumors also may be composed of signet ring cells that are similar to those in gastric cancer (Fig. 14–39, *C*).

Clinical Features

The availability of endoscopic screening combined with the recognition that most carcinomas arise within adenomas presents a unique opportunity for cancer prevention. Unfortunately, colorectal cancers develop insidiously and may therefore go undetected for long periods. Cecal and other *right-sided colon cancers* most often are called to clinical attention by the appearance of *fatigue and weakness due to iron deficiency anemia.* Thus, it is a clinical maxim that the underlying cause of iron deficiency anemia in an older man or postmenopausal woman is gastrointestinal cancer until proven otherwise. *Left-sided colorectal adenocarcinomas* may produce *occult bleeding, changes in bowel habits, or cramping* left lower quadrant discomfort.

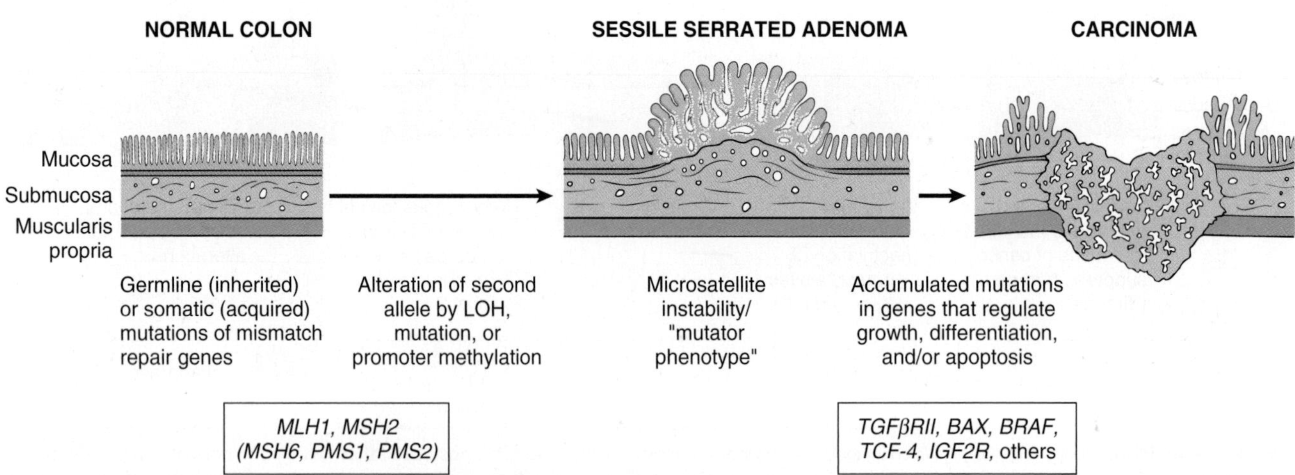

Figure 14–37 Morphologic and molecular changes in the mismatch repair pathway of colon carcinogenesis. Defects in mismatch repair genes result in microsatellite instability and permit accumulation of mutations in numerous genes. If these mutations affect genes involved in cell survival and proliferation, cancer may develop. LOH, loss of heterozygosity.

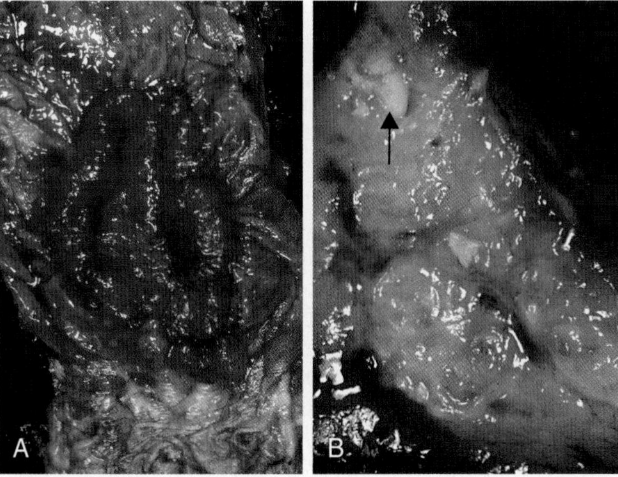

Figure 14–38 Colorectal carcinoma. **A,** Circumferential, ulcerated rectal cancer. Note the anal mucosa at the bottom of the image. **B,** Cancer of the sigmoid colon that has invaded through the muscularis propria and is present within subserosal adipose tissue (*left*). Areas of chalky necrosis are present within the colon wall (*arrow*).

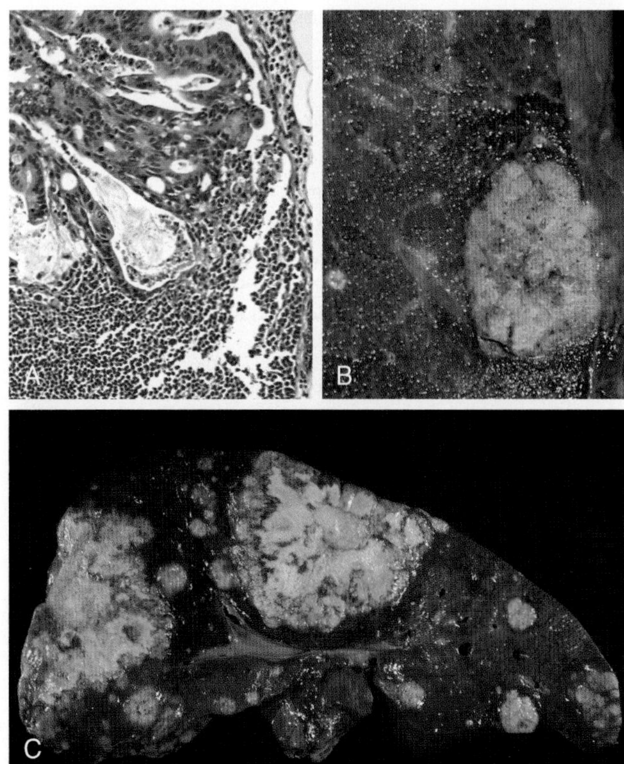

Figure 14–40 Metastatic colorectal carcinoma. **A,** Lymph node metastasis. Note the glandular structures within the subcapsular sinus. **B,** Solitary subpleural nodule of colorectal carcinoma metastatic to the lung. **C,** Liver containing two large and many smaller metastases. Note the central necrosis within metastases.

Although poorly differentiated and mucinous histologic patterns are associated with poor prognosis, *the two most important prognostic factors are depth of invasion and the presence or absence of lymph node metastases.* Invasion into the muscularis propria imparts significantly reduced survival that is decreased further by the presence of lymph node metastases (Fig. 14–40, *A*). These factors were originally recognized by Dukes and Kirklin and form the core of the TNM (tumor-node-metastasis) classification (Table 14–8) and staging system (Table 14–9) from the American Joint Committee on Cancer. Regardless of stage, however, some patients with small numbers of metastases do well for years after resection of distant tumor nodules. This observation once again emphasizes the clinical and molecular heterogeneity of colorectal carcinomas. Metastases may involve regional lymph nodes, lungs (Fig. 14–40, *B*), and bones, but because of the portal drainage, the liver is the most common site of metastatic lesions (Fig. 14–40, *C*). The rectum does not drain by way of the portal circulation, and metastases from carcinomas of the anal region often circumvent the liver.

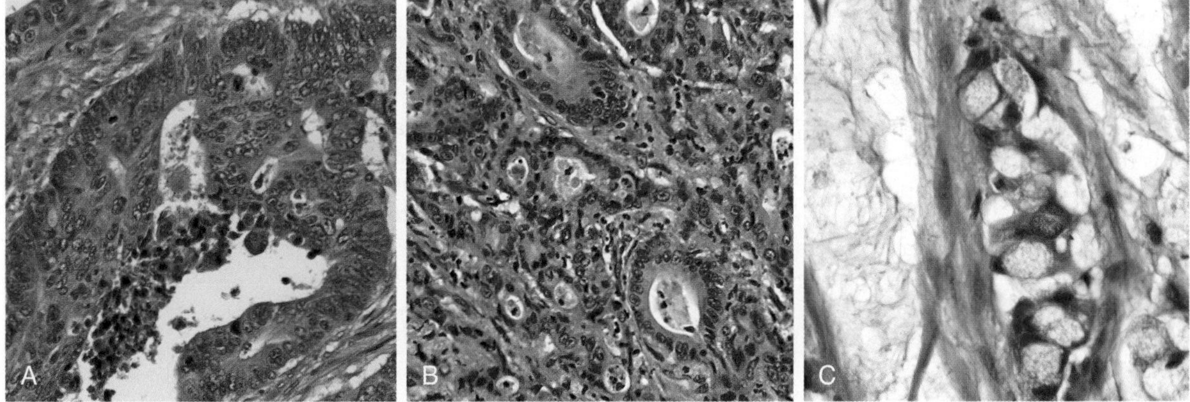

Figure 14–39 Histologic appearance of colorectal carcinoma. **A,** Well-differentiated adenocarcinoma. Note the elongated, hyperchromatic nuclei. Necrotic debris, present in the gland lumen, is typical. **B,** Poorly differentiated adenocarcinoma forms a few glands but is largely composed of infiltrating nests of tumor cells. **C,** Mucinous adenocarcinoma with signet ring cells and extracellular mucin pools.

Table 14–8 AJCC Tumor-Node-Metastasis (TNM) Classification of Colorectal Carcinoma

Designation	Description
Tumor	
Tis	In situ dysplasia or intramucosal carcinoma
T1	Tumor invades submucosa
T2	Tumor invades into, but not through, muscularis propria
T3	Tumor invades through muscularis propria
T4	Tumor invades adjacent organs or visceral peritoneum
Regional Lymph Nodes	
NX	Lymph nodes cannot be assessed
N0	No regional lymph node metastasis
N1	Metastasis in one to three regional lymph nodes
N2	Metastasis in four or more regional lymph nodes
Distant Metastasis	
MX	Distant metastasis cannot be assessed
M0	No distant metastasis
M1	Distant metastasis or seeding of abdominal organs

AJCC, American Joint Committee on Cancer.

Table 14–9 AJCC Colorectal Cancer Staging and Survival

Stage*	Tumor-Node-Metastasis (TNM) Criteria			5-Year Survival (%)
	T	N	M	
I	T1, T2	N0	M0	74
II				
IIA	T3	N0	M0	67
IIB	T4	N0	M0	59
III				
IIIA	T1, T2	N1	M0	73
IIIB	T3, T4	N1	M0	46
IIIC	Any T	N2	M0	28
IV	Any T	Any N	M1	6

*Colorectal cancer staging is based on the TNM classification (Table 14–8). For example, a T3 tumor without nodal or distant metastases is classified as stage IIA and is associated with a 5-year survival rate of 67%.
AJCC, American Joint Committee on Cancer.

SUMMARY

Colonic Polyps, Adenomas, and Adenocarcinomas

- *Intestinal polyps* can be classified as non-neoplastic or neoplastic. The non-neoplastic polyps can be further defined as inflammatory, hamartomatous, or hyperplastic.
- *Inflammatory polyps* form as a result of chronic cycles of injury and healing.
- *Hamartomatous polyps* occur sporadically or as a part of genetic diseases. In the latter case, they often are associated with increased risk of malignancy.
- Hyperplastic polyps are benign epithelial proliferations most commonly found in the left colon and rectum. They are not reactive in origin, in contrast with gastric hyperplastic polyps; have no malignant potential; and must be distinguished from *sessile serrated adenomas*.
- Benign epithelial neoplastic polyps of the intestines are termed *adenomas*. The hallmark feature of these lesions, which are the precursors of colonic adenocarcinomas, is cytologic dysplasia.
- In contrast with traditional adenomas, *sessile serrated adenomas* lack cytologic dysplasia and share morphologic features with hyperplastic polyps.
- *Familial adenomatous polyposis* (FAP) and *hereditary nonpolyposis colorectal cancer* (HNPCC) are the most common forms of familial colon cancer. FAP is caused by *APC* mutations, and patients typically have over 100 adenomas and develop colon cancer before the age of 30.
- HNPCC is caused by mutations in DNA mismatch repair genes. Patients with HNPCC have far fewer polyps and develop cancer at an older age than that typical for patients with FAP but at a younger age than in patients with sporadic colon cancer.
- FAP and HNPCC are examples of two distinct pathways of neoplastic transformation, both of which contribute to sporadic colon cancer.
- The vast majority of colonic cancers are adenocarcinomas. The two most important prognostic factors are *depth of invasion* and the presence or absence of *lymph node metastases*.

APPENDIX

The appendix is a normal true diverticulum of the cecum. Like any diverticulum, it is prone to acute and chronic inflammation, and acute appendicitis is a relatively common entity. Other lesions, including tumors, can also occur in the appendix but are far less common.

ACUTE APPENDICITIS

Acute appendicitis is most common in adolescents and young adults but may occur in any age group. The lifetime risk for appendicitis is 7%; males are affected slightly more often than females. Despite the prevalence of acute appendicitis, the diagnosis can be difficult to confirm preoperatively, and the condition may be confused with mesenteric lymphadenitis (often secondary to unrecognized *Yersinia* infection or viral enterocolitis), acute salpingitis, ectopic pregnancy, mittelschmerz (pain associated with ovulation), and Meckel diverticulitis.

PATHOGENESIS

Acute appendicitis is thought to be initiated by progressive increases in intraluminal pressure that compromises venous outflow. In 50% to 80% of cases, acute appendicitis is associated with overt luminal obstruction, usually by a small, stone-like mass of stool, or **fecalith,** or, less commonly, a gallstone, tumor, or mass of worms. Ischemic injury and stasis of luminal contents, which favor bacterial proliferation, trigger inflammatory responses including tissue edema and neutrophilic infiltration of the lumen, muscular wall, and periappendiceal soft tissues.

MORPHOLOGY

In early acute appendicitis, subserosal vessels are congested, and a modest perivascular neutrophilic infiltrate is present within all layers of the wall. The inflammatory reaction transforms the normal glistening serosa into a dull, granular-appearing, erythematous surface. Although mucosal neutrophils and focal superficial ulceration often are present, these findings are not specific, and diagnosis of acute appendicitis requires neutrophilic infiltration of the muscularis propria. In more severe cases, focal abscesses may form within the wall **(acute suppurative appendicitis),** and these may even progress to large areas of hemorrhagic ulceration and gangrenous necrosis that extend to the serosa, creating **acute gangrenous appendicitis,** which often is followed by rupture and suppurative peritonitis.

Clinical Features

Typically, early acute appendicitis produces periumbilical pain that ultimately localizes to the right lower quadrant, followed by nausea, vomiting, low-grade fever, and a mildly elevated peripheral white cell count. A classic physical finding is *McBurney's sign,* deep tenderness noted at a location two thirds of the distance from the umbilicus to the right anterior superior iliac spine (McBurney's point). These signs and symptoms often are absent, however, creating difficulty in clinical diagnosis.

TUMORS OF THE APPENDIX

The most common tumor of the appendix is the *carcinoid.* It usually is discovered incidentally at the time of surgery or on examination of a resected appendix. This neoplasm most frequently involves the distal tip of the appendix, where it produces a solid bulbous swelling up to 2 to 3 cm in diameter. Although intramural and transmural extension may be evident, nodal metastases are very infrequent, and distant spread is exceptionally rare. Conventional *adenomas* or *non–mucin-producing adenocarcinomas* also occur in the appendix and may cause obstruction and enlargement that mimics the changes of acute appendicitis. *Mucocele,* a dilated appendix filled with mucin, may simply stem from an obstructed appendix containing inspissated mucin or may be a consequence of *mucinous cystadenoma* or *mucinous cystadenocarcinoma.* In the latter instance, invasion through the appendiceal wall can lead to intraperitoneal seeding and spread. In women, the resulting peritoneal implants may be mistaken for mucinous ovarian tumors. In the most advanced cases, the abdomen fills with tenacious, semisolid mucin, a condition called *pseudomyxoma peritonei.* This disseminated intraperitoneal disease may be held in check for years by repeated debulking but in most instances is ultimately fatal.

SUMMARY

Appendix

- *Acute appendicitis* is most common in children and adolescents. It is thought to be initiated by increased intraluminal pressure consequent to obstruction of the appendiceal lumen, which compromises venous outflow.
- The most common tumor of the appendix is the *carcinoid.*
- The clinical presentation with *appendiceal adenocarcinoma* can be indistinguishable from that with acute appendicitis.

BIBLIOGRAPHY

ORAL CAVITY

Hennessey PT, Westra WH, Califano JA: Human papillomavirus and head and neck squamous cell carcinoma: recent evidence and clinical implications. J Dent Res 88:300, 2009. *[Discussion of head and neck cancers associated with HPV.]*

Leemans CR, Braakhuis BJ, Brakenhoff RH: The molecular biology of head and neck cancer. Nat Rev Cancer 11:9, 2011. *[An up to date discussion of the molecular biology of head and neck cancer.]*

Leivo I: Insights into a complex group of neoplastic disease: advances in histopathologic classification and molecular pathology of salivary gland cancer. Acta Oncol 45:662, 2006. *[A good review of the histologic spectrum of salivary gland tumors.]*

ESOPHAGUS

Liacouras CA, Furuta GT, Hirano I, et al: Eosinophilic esophagitis: updated consensus recommendations for children and adults. J Allergy Clin Immunol 128:3, 2011. *[The most current diagnostic definition of and therapeutic recommendations for eosinophilic esophagitis.]*

Sharma P: Clinical practice. Barrett's esophagus. N Engl J Med 361:2548, 2009. *[A comprehensive discussion of Barrett esophagus.]*

INFLAMMATORY DISEASE OF THE STOMACH

Malfertheiner P, Chan FK, McColl KE: Peptic ulcer disease. Lancet 374:1449, 2009. *[Summary of current understanding of peptic ulcer disease.]*

Mills JC, Shivdasani RA: Gastric epithelial stem cells. Gastroenterology 140:412, 2011. *[A good discussion of cell lineages and differentiation pathways in the gastric epithelium.]*

Polk DB, Peek RM, Jr: *Helicobacter pylori:* gastric cancer and beyond. Nat Rev Cancer 10:403, 2010. *[A good review of* H. pylori *and mechanisms by which it is linked to gastric cancer.]*

NEOPLASTIC DISEASE OF THE STOMACH

Murphy G, Pfeiffer R, Camargo MC, Rabkin CS: Meta-analysis shows that prevalence of Epstein-Barr virus-positive gastric cancer differs based on sex and anatomic location. Gastroenterology 137:824, 2009. *[A meta-analysis of over 15,000 gastric cancer cases tested for EBV RNA.]*

Polk DB, Peek RM Jr: *Helicobacter pylori:* gastric cancer and beyond. Nat Rev Cancer 10:403, 2010. *[A good review of* H. pylori *and mechanisms by which it is linked to gastric cancer.]*

Sagaert X, Van Cutsem E, De Hertogh G, et al: Gastric MALT lymphoma: a model of chronic inflammation-induced tumor development. Nat Rev Gastroenterol Hepatol 7:336, 2010. *[A discussion of gastric MALT lymphoma pathogenesis.]*

INTESTINAL OBSTRUCTION

Kapur RP: Practical pathology and genetics of Hirschsprung's disease. Semin Pediatr Surg 18:212, 2009. *[A review of Hirschsprung disease etiology and diagnosis.]*

Muysoms FE, Miserez M, Berrevoet F, et al: Classification of primary and incisional abdominal wall hernias. Hernia 13:407, 2009. *[An explanation of abdominal hernia classification.]*

VASCULAR DISORDERS

Barnert J, Messmann H: Diagnosis and management of lower gastrointestinal bleeding. Nat Rev Gastroenterol Hepatol 6:637, 2009. *[A good discussion of clinical approaches to lower GI bleeding.]*

Colgan SP, Taylor CT: Hypoxia: an alarm signal during intestinal inflammation. Nat Rev Gastroenterol Hepatol 7:281, 2010. *[A review of signaling events activated by intestinal hypoxia.]*

Sneider EB, Maykel JA: Diagnosis and management of symptomatic hemorrhoids. Surg Clin North Am 90:17, 2010. *[A clinically oriented review of hemorrhoids.]*

MALABSORPTIVE DIARRHEA

Khan S, Chang L: Diagnosis and management of IBS. Nat Rev Gastroenterol Hepatol 7:565, 2010. *[A recent review of IBS.]*

Moore SR, Lima NL, Soares AM, et al: Prolonged episodes of acute diarrhea reduce growth and increase risk of persistent diarrhea in children. Gastroenterology 139:1156, 2010. *[A detailed study of environmental enteropathy.]*

Pardi DS, Kelly CP: Microscopic colitis. Gastroenterology 140:1155, 2011. *[A review of collagenous and lymphocytic colitis.]*

Schuppan D, Junker Y, Barisani D: Celiac disease: from pathogenesis to novel therapies. Gastroenterology 137:1912, 2009. *[A recent review of celiac disease.]*

Suchy FJ, Brannon PM, Carpenter TO, et al: National Institutes of Health Consensus Development Conference: lactose intolerance and health. Ann Intern Med 152:792, 2010. *[A consensus conference on lactose intolerance.]*

INFECTIOUS ENTEROCOLITIS

Barton Behravesh C, Mody RK, Jungk J, et al: 2008 outbreak of *Salmonella* Saintpaul infections associated with raw produce. N Engl J Med 364:918, 2011. *[Analysis of a* Salmonella *epidemic.]*

John TJ, Dandona L, Sharma VP, Kakkar M: Continuing challenge of infectious diseases in India. Lancet 377:252, 2011. *[Review of enteric infections in India.]*

Kirkpatrick BD, Tribble DR: Update on human *Campylobacter jejuni* infections. Curr Opin Gastroenterol 27:1, 2011. *[Recent verview of* Campylobacter *gastroenteritis.]*

Kuehne SA, Cartman ST, Heap JT, et al: The role of toxin A and toxin B in *Clostridium difficile* infection. Nature 467:711, 2010. *[A detailed analysis of toxin function in* C. difficile *pathogenesis.]*

Navaneethan U, Giannella RA: Infectious colitis. Curr Opin Gastroenterol 27:66, 2011. *[Good overview of infectious colitis.]*

Prince Christopher RH, David KV, John SM, Sankarapandian V: Antibiotic therapy for *Shigella* dysentery. Cochrane Database Syst Rev 1:CD006784, 2010. *[A meta-analysis of antibiotic effectiveness in dysentery.]*

van Lieshout L, Verweij JJ: Newer diagnostic approaches to intestinal protozoa. Curr Opin Infect Dis 23:488, 2010. *[Recent review of evolving diagnostic tools.]*

SIGMOID DIVERTICULITIS

Eglinton T, Nguyen T, Raniga S, et al: Patterns of recurrence in patients with acute diverticulitis. Br J Surg 97:952, 2010. *[Evaluation of outcome following acute episodes of diverticulitis.]*

Hall J, Hammerich K, Roberts P: New paradigms in the management of diverticular disease. Curr Probl Surg 47:680, 2010. *[A recent review of approaches to diverticulosis and diverticulitis management.]*

INFLAMMATORY BOWEL DISEASE

Abraham C, Cho JH: Inflammatory bowel disease. N Engl J Med 361:2066, 2009. *[A complete review of IBD mechanisms and genomics.]*

Glocker EO, Kotlarz D, Boztug K, et al: Inflammatory bowel disease and mutations affecting the interleukin-10 receptor. N Engl J Med 361:2033, 2009. *[Identification of IL-10 receptor mutations in a subset of ulcerative colitis patients.]*

Goel GA, Kandiel A, Achkar JP, Lashner B: Molecular pathways underlying IBD-associated colorectal neoplasia: therapeutic implications. Am J Gastroenterol 106:719, 2011. *[A good review of colitis-associated cancer.]*

Kaser A, Zeissig S, Blumberg RS: Inflammatory bowel disease. Annu Rev Immunol 28:573, 2010. *[A review of immune mechanisms in IBD.]*

Marchiando AM, Graham WV, Turner JR: Epithelial barriers in homeostasis and disease. Annu Rev Pathol 5:119, 2010. *[A review of intestinal epithelial barrier function and its implications in IBD and other disorders.]*

Molodecky NA, Panaccione R, Ghosh S, et al: Challenges associated with identifying the environmental determinants of the inflammatory bowel diseases. Inflamm Bowel Dis 17:1792, 2011. *[A good discussion of environmental IBD triggers.]*

Turner JR: Intestinal mucosal barrier function in health and disease. Nat Rev Immunol 9:799, 2009. *[An analysis of epithelial-immune interactions in gastrointestinal disease.]*

COLONIC POLYPS AND NEOPLASTIC DISEASE

Beggs AD, Latchford AR, Vasen HF, et al: Peutz-Jeghers syndrome: a systematic review and recommendations for management. Gut 59:975, 2010. *[A review of Peutz-Jeghers disease etiology and management.]*

Boland CR, Goel A: Microsatellite instability in colorectal cancer. Gastroenterology 138:2073, 2010. *[A discussion of the microsatellite instability pathway of colon cancer.]*

Hardwick JC, Kodach LL, Offerhaus GJ, van den Brink GR: Bone morphogenetic protein signalling in colorectal cancer. Nat Rev Cancer 8:806, 2008. *[A good review of signaling pathways in colon cancer.]*

Jasperson KW, Tuohy TM, Neklason DW, Burt RW: Hereditary and familial colon cancer. Gastroenterology 138:2044, 2010. *[A comprehensive review of colon cancer syndromes.]*

Jass JR: Colorectal polyposes: from phenotype to diagnosis. Pathol Res Pract 204:431, 2008. *[A morphology-focused review of polyposis syndromes.]*

Noffsinger AE: Serrated polyps and colorectal cancer: new pathway to malignancy. Annu Rev Pathol 4:343, 2009. *[A detailed review of sessile serrated adenomas and the mechanisms by which they develop and progress.]*

Pino MS, Chung DC: The chromosomal instability pathway in colon cancer. Gastroenterology 138:2059, 2010. *[A review of colon cancer genetics.]*

APPENDIX

Cartwright SL, Knudson MP: Evaluation of acute abdominal pain in adults. Am Fam Physician 77:971, 2008. *[A clinically oriented approach to the acute abdomen.]*

Deschamps L, Couvelard A: Endocrine tumors of the appendix: a pathologic review. Arch Pathol Lab Med 134:871, 2010. *[A pathology-focused review of appendiceal carcinoid tumors.]*

Tang LH: Epithelial neoplasms of the appendix. Arch Pathol Lab Med 134:1612, 2010. *[A review of appendiceal cancers.]*

See Targeted Therapy available online at **studentconsult.com**

CHAPTER 15

Liver, Gallbladder, and Biliary Tract

CHAPTER CONTENTS

THE LIVER

The liver and its companion biliary tree and gallbladder are considered together because of their anatomic proximity and interrelated functions and the overlapping features of some diseases that affect these organs. This chapter focuses primarily on the liver, because it has by far the greater role in normal physiology and is the site of a wide variety of diseases.

Residing at the crossroads between the digestive tract and the rest of the body, the liver has the enormous task of maintaining the body's metabolic homeostasis. This task includes the processing of dietary amino acids, carbohydrates, lipids, and vitamins; synthesis of serum proteins; and detoxification and excretion into bile of endogenous waste products and xenobiotics. Thus, it is not surprising that the liver is vulnerable to a wide variety of metabolic, toxic, microbial, and circulatory insults. In some instances the disease process is primary to the liver. In others the hepatic involvement is secondary, often to some of the most common diseases in humans, such as heart failure, diabetes, and extrahepatic infections.

The liver has enormous functional reserve, and regeneration occurs in all but the most fulminant of hepatic diseases. Surgical removal of 60% of the liver in a normal person is followed by minimal and transient hepatic impairment, with restoration of most of its mass by regeneration within 4 to 6 weeks. In persons who have sustained massive hepatic necrosis, almost perfect restoration may occur if the patient can survive the metabolic insult of liver failure. The functional reserve and the regenerative capacity of the liver mask to some extent the clinical impact of early liver damage. However, with progression of diffuse disease or disruption of the circulation or bile flow, the consequences of deranged liver function become severe and even life-threatening.

Contributions of Drs. Jim Crawford and Nelson Fausto to this chapter in earlier editions are gratefully acknowledged.

Table 15–1 Clinical Consequences of Liver Disease

Characteristic Signs of Severe Hepatic Dysfunction
Jaundice and cholestasis
Hypoalbuminemia
Hyperammonemia
Hypoglycemia
Palmar erythema
Spider angiomas
Hypogonadism
Gynecomastia
Weight loss
Muscle wasting
Portal Hypertension Associated with Cirrhosis
Ascites with or without spontaneous bacterial peritonitis
Splenomegaly
Esophageal varices
Hemorrhoids
Caput medusae—abdominal skin
Complications of Hepatic Failure
Coagulopathy
Hepatic encephalopathy
Hepatorenal syndrome
Portopulmonary hypertension
Hepatopulmonary syndrome

CLINICAL SYNDROMES

The major clinical syndromes of liver disease are hepatic failure, cirrhosis, portal hypertension, and cholestasis. These conditions have characteristic clinical manifestations (Table 15–1), and a battery of laboratory tests for their evaluation (Table 15–2), with liver biopsy representing the gold standard for diagnosis.

Table 15–2 Laboratory Evaluation of Liver Disease

Test Category	Serum Measurement*
Hepatocyte integrity	Cytosolic hepatocellular enzymes† *Serum aspartate aminotransferase* (AST) *Serum alanine aminotransferase* (ALT) *Serum lactate dehydrogenase* (LDH)
Biliary excretory function	Substances secreted in bile† *Serum bilirubin* *Total:* unconjugated plus conjugated *Direct:* conjugated only *Delta:* covalently linked to albumin Urine bilirubin Serum bile acids Plasma membrane enzymes† (from damage to bile canaliculi) *Serum alkaline phosphatase* *Serum γ-glutamyl transpeptidase* Serum 5′-nucleotidase
Hepatocyte function	Proteins secreted into the blood *Serum albumin*‡ *Prothrombin time*† (factors V, VII, X, prothrombin, fibrinogen) Hepatocyte metabolism Serum ammonia† Aminopyrine breath test (hepatic demethylation) Galactose elimination (intravenous injection)

*The most commonly performed tests are in *italics*.
†An elevation indicates liver disease.
‡A decrease indicates liver disease.

Hepatic Failure

The most severe clinical consequence of liver disease is hepatic failure. It generally develops as the end point of progressive damage to the liver, either through insidious piecemeal destruction of hepatocytes or by repetitive waves of symptomatic parenchymal damage. Less commonly, hepatic failure is the result of sudden, massive destruction. Whatever the sequence, 80% to 90% of hepatic function must be lost before hepatic failure ensues. In many cases, the balance is tipped toward decompensation by intercurrent conditions or events that place demands on the liver. These include systemic infections, electrolyte disturbances, major surgery, heart failure, and gastrointestinal bleeding.

The patterns of injury that cause liver failure fall into three categories:

- *Acute liver failure with massive hepatic necrosis.* Most often caused by *drugs* or *viral hepatitis,* acute liver failure denotes clinical hepatic insufficiency that progresses from onset of symptoms to hepatic encephalopathy within 2 to 3 weeks. A course extending as long as 3 months is called subacute failure. *The histologic correlate of acute liver failure is massive hepatic necrosis,* whatever the underlying cause. It is an uncommon but life-threatening condition that often necessitates liver transplantation.
- *Chronic liver disease.* This is the most common route to hepatic failure and is the end point of relentless chronic liver damage. While all structural components of the liver are involved in end-stage chronic liver disease, the processes that initiate and drive chronic damage to the liver can usually be classified as either primarily hepatocytic (or *parenchymal*), biliary, or vascular. Regardless of the initiating factors, chronic damage to the liver often ends in cirrhosis, as described later.
- *Hepatic dysfunction without overt necrosis.* Less commonly than the forms described above, hepatocytes may be viable but unable to perform their normal metabolic function. Settings where this is seen most often are mitochondrial injury in Reye syndrome, acute fatty liver of pregnancy, and some drug- or toxin-mediated injuries.

Clinical Features

The clinical manifestations of hepatic failure from chronic liver disease are much the same regardless of the cause of the disease. *Jaundice* is an almost invariable finding. Impaired hepatic synthesis and secretion of albumin lead to *hypoalbuminemia,* which predisposes to peripheral edema. *Hyperammonemia* is attributable to defective hepatic urea cycle function. Signs and symptoms of chronic disease include *palmar erythema* (a reflection of local vasodilatation) and *spider angiomas* of the skin. Each angioma is a central, pulsating, dilated arteriole from which small vessels radiate. There may also be impaired estrogen metabolism and consequent hyperestrogenemia, which leads to *hypogonadism* and *gynecomastia* in men. Acute liver failure may manifest as jaundice or encephalopathy, but notably absent on physical examination are the other stigmata of chronic liver disease.

Hepatic failure is life-threatening for several reasons. The accumulation of toxic metabolites may have widespread effects and patients are highly susceptible to failure of multiple organ systems. Thus, respiratory failure with pneumonia and sepsis can give rise to renal failure and thus claim the lives of many individuals with hepatic failure. A *coagulopathy* develops, attributable to impaired hepatic synthesis of blood clotting factors. The resultant bleeding tendency may lead to massive gastrointestinal hemorrhage as well as bleeding elsewhere. Intestinal absorption of blood places a metabolic load on the liver that worsens the severity of hepatic failure.

The outlook with full-blown hepatic failure is particularly grave for persons with chronic liver disease. A rapid downhill course is usual, with death occurring within weeks to a few months in about 80% of cases. About 40% of patients with acute liver failure may recover spontaneously. Liver transplantation in acute or chronic liver failure can be curative, however. Conditions contributing to the extraordinary morbidity and eventual mortality associated with severe liver disease are discussed next.

Jaundice and Cholestasis

Jaundice results from the retention of bile. Hepatic bile formation serves two major functions. First, bile constitutes the primary pathway for the elimination of bilirubin, excess cholesterol, and xenobiotics that are insufficiently water-soluble to be excreted in the urine. Second, secreted bile salts and phospholipid molecules promote emulsification of dietary fat in the lumen of the gut. Bile formation is a complex process and is readily disrupted by a variety of hepatic insults. Thus, *jaundice,* a yellow discoloration of skin and sclerae (*icterus*), occurs when systemic retention of bilirubin produces serum levels above 2.0 mg/dL (the normal level in adults is below 1.2 mg/dL). *Cholestasis* is defined as systemic retention of not only bilirubin but also other solutes eliminated in bile (particularly bile salts and cholesterol).

Bilirubin and Bile Acids

Bilirubin is the end product of heme degradation (Fig. 15–1). Most of the daily production (0.2 to 0.3 g) is derived from breakdown of senescent red cells within mononuclear phagocytes, with the remainder derived primarily from the turnover of hepatic hemoproteins. Excessive destruction of erythroid progenitors in the bone marrow due to intramedullary apoptosis (ineffective erythropoiesis) is an important cause of jaundice in hematologic disorders (Chapter 11). Whatever the source, heme oxygenase oxidizes heme to biliverdin, which is then reduced to bilirubin by biliverdin reductase. Bilirubin thus formed outside the liver in cells of the mononuclear phagocyte system (including the spleen) is released and bound to serum albumin. Hepatocellular processing of bilirubin involves the following sequence:

1. Carrier-mediated uptake at the sinusoidal membrane
2. Cytosolic protein binding and delivery to the endoplasmic reticulum
3. Conjugation with one or two molecules of glucuronic acid by bilirubin uridine diphosphate–glucuronosyltransferase
4. Excretion of the water-soluble, nontoxic bilirubin glucuronides into bile. Most bilirubin glucuronides are deconjugated by gut bacterial β-glucuronidases and degraded to colorless urobilinogens. The urobilinogens and the residue of intact pigment are largely excreted in feces. Approximately 20% of the urobilinogens are reabsorbed in the ileum and colon, returned to the liver, and promptly reexcreted into bile. Conjugated and unconjugated bile acids also are reabsorbed in the ileum and returned to the liver by the *enterohepatic circulation.*

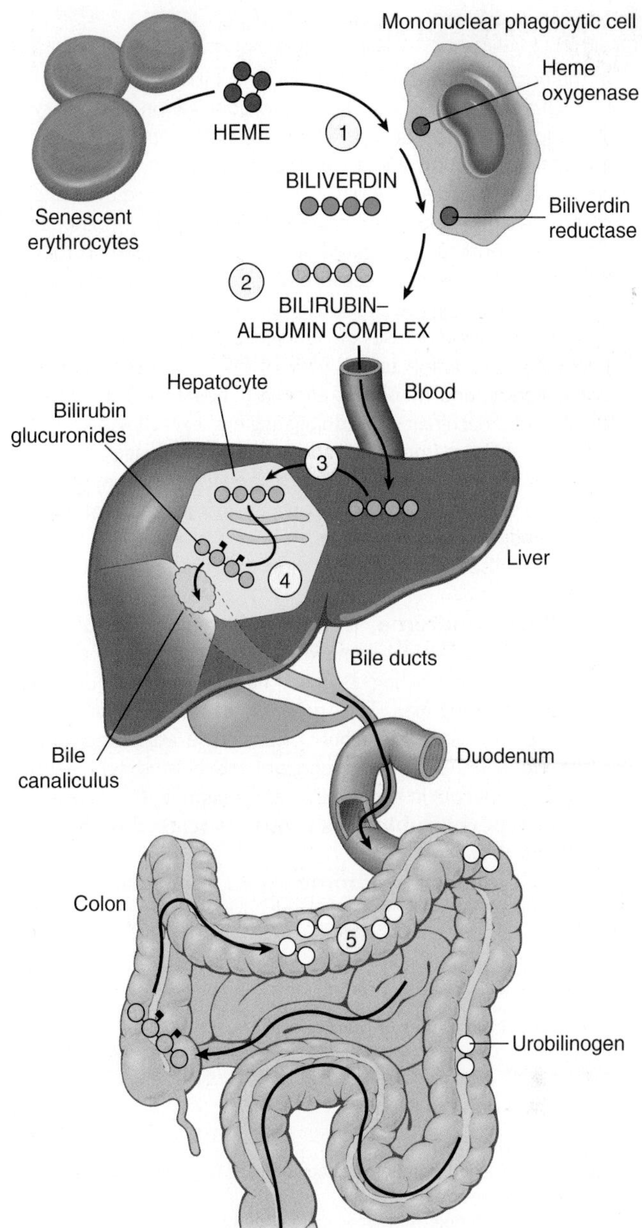

Figure 15–1 Bilirubin metabolism and elimination. *1,* Normal bilirubin production (0.2 to 0.3 g/day) is derived primarily from the breakdown of senescent circulating red cells, with a minor contribution from degradation of tissue heme-containing proteins. 2, Extrahepatic bilirubin is bound to serum albumin and delivered to the liver. *3* and *4,* Hepatocellular uptake (*3*) and glucuronidation (*4*) by glucuronosyltransferase in the hepatocytes generate bilirubin monoglucuronides and diglucuronides, which are water-soluble and readily excreted into bile. *5,* Gut bacteria deconjugate the bilirubin and degrade it to colorless urobilinogens. The urobilinogens and the residue of intact pigments are excreted in the feces, with some reabsorption and reexcretion into bile.

PATHOGENESIS

In the normal adult, the rate of systemic bilirubin production is equal to the rates of hepatic uptake, conjugation, and biliary excretion. Jaundice occurs when the equilibrium between bilirubin production and clearance is disrupted; the major responsible disorders are listed in Table 15–3. More than one mechanism may operate to cause jaundice, especially in hepatitis, when both unconjugated and conjugated bilirubin may be produced in excess. In severe disease, bilirubin levels may reach 30 to 40 mg/dL.

Of these various causes of jaundice, the most common are hepatitis, obstruction to the flow of bile (discussed later in this chapter), and hemolytic anemia (Chapter 11). Because the hepatic machinery for conjugating and excreting bilirubin does not fully mature until about 2 weeks of age, almost every newborn develops transient and mild unconjugated hyperbilirubinemia, termed **neonatal jaundice** or physiologic jaundice of the newborn.

Jaundice also may result from inborn errors of metabolism, including

- **Gilbert syndrome,** a relatively common (7% of the population), benign, somewhat heterogeneous inherited condition manifesting as mild, fluctuating unconjugated hyperbilirubinemia. The primary cause is decreased hepatic levels of glucuronosyltransferase attributed to a mutation in the encoding gene; polymorphisms in the gene may play a role in the variable expression of this disease. **The hyperbilirubinemia is not associated with any morbidity.**
- **Dubin-Johnson syndrome** results from an autosomal recessive defect in the transport protein responsible for hepatocellular excretion of bilirubin glucuronides across the canalicular membrane. Affected persons exhibit conjugated hyperbilirubinemia. Other than having a darkly pigmented liver (from polymerized epinephrine metabolites, not bilirubin) and hepatomegaly, patients are otherwise without functional problems.

Cholestasis, which results from impaired bile flow due to hepatocellular dysfunction or intrahepatic or extrahepatic biliary obstruction, also may manifest as jaundice. However, sometimes *pruritus* is the presenting symptom, the pathogenesis of which remains obscure. *Skin xanthomas* (focal accumulations of cholesterol) sometimes appear, the result of hyperlipidemia and impaired excretion of cholesterol. A *characteristic laboratory finding is elevated serum alkaline phosphatase,* an enzyme present in bile duct epithelium and in the canalicular membrane of hepatocytes. A different alkaline phosphatase isozyme normally is expressed in many other tissues such as bone, and so hepatic origin must be verified. Reduced bile flow also causes intestinal malabsorption including inadequate absorption of the fat-soluble vitamins A, D, and K.

Extrahepatic biliary obstruction frequently is amenable to surgical correction. By contrast, cholestasis caused by diseases of the intrahepatic biliary tree or hepatocellular secretory failure (collectively termed *intrahepatic cholestasis*) cannot be treated surgically (short of transplantation), and the patient's condition may be worsened by an operative procedure. Thus, *there is some urgency in identifying the cause of jaundice and cholestasis.*

Table 15–3 Main Causes of Jaundice

Predominantly Unconjugated Hyperbilirubinemia
Excess Production of Bilirubin
Hemolytic anemias Resorption of blood from internal hemorrhage (e.g., alimentary tract bleeding, hematomas) Ineffective erythropoiesis syndromes (e.g., pernicious anemia, thalassemia)
Reduced Hepatic Uptake
Drug interference with membrane carrier systems Diffuse hepatocellular disease (e.g., viral or drug-induced hepatitis, cirrhosis)
Impaired Bilirubin Conjugation
Physiologic jaundice of the newborn
Predominantly Conjugated Hyperbilirubinemia
Decreased Hepatocellular Excretion
Deficiency in canalicular membrane transporters Drug-induced canalicular membrane dysfunction (e.g., oral contraceptives, cyclosporine) Hepatocellular damage or toxicity (e.g., viral or drug-induced hepatitis, total parenteral nutrition, systemic infection)
Impaired Intra- or Extrahepatic Bile Flow
Inflammatory destruction of intrahepatic bile ducts (e.g., primary biliary cirrhosis, primary sclerosing cholangitis, graft-versus-host disease, liver transplantation); gall stones, carcinoma of the pancreas

SUMMARY

Jaundice and Cholestasis

- Jaundice occurs when retention of bilirubin leads to serum levels above 2.0 mg/dL.
- Hepatitis and intra- or extrahepatic obstruction of bile flow are the most common causes of jaundice involving the accumulation of conjugated bilirubin.
- Hemolytic anemias are the most common cause of jaundice involving the accumulation of unconjugated bilirubin.
- Cholestasis is the impairment of bile flow resulting in the retention of bilirubin, bile acids, and cholesterol.
- Serum alkaline phosphatase usually is elevated in cholestatic conditions.

Hepatic Encephalopathy

Hepatic encephalopathy may develop rapidly in acute liver failure or insidiously with gradually evolving chronic liver failure from cirrhosis. In either setting, patients with hepatic encephalopathy show a spectrum of brain dysfunction ranging from subtle behavioral abnormalities to marked confusion and stupor, to deep coma and death. These changes may progress over hours or days as, for example, in fulminant hepatic failure or gradually in a person with marginal hepatic function from chronic liver disease. Associated fluctuating neurologic signs include rigidity, hyperreflexia, nonspecific electroencephalographic changes, and, rarely, seizures. Particularly characteristic is *asterixis* (also called flapping tremor), which is a pattern of nonrhythmic, rapid extension-flexion movements of the head and extremities, best seen when the arms are held in extension with dorsiflexed wrists.

In most instances there are only minor morphologic changes in the brain, such as edema and an astrocytic reaction. Two factors seem to be important in the genesis of this disorder:

- Severe loss of hepatocellular function
- Shunting of blood from portal to systemic circulation around the chronically diseased liver

In the acute setting, an elevation in blood ammonia, which impairs neuronal function and promotes generalized brain edema, seems to be key. In the chronic setting, deranged neurotransmitter production, particularly in monoaminergic, opioidergic, γ-aminobutyric acid (GABA)-ergic, and endocannabanoid systems, leads to neuronal dysfunction.

Cirrhosis

Cirrhosis is among the top 10 causes of death in the Western world. Its major causes include chronic viral infections, alcoholic or nonalcoholic steatohepatitis (NASH), autoimmune diseases affecting hepatocytes and/or bile ducts, and iron overload. *Cirrhosis* is defined as a *diffuse process characterized by fibrosis and the conversion of normal liver architecture into structurally abnormal nodules.* Its main characteristics by definition are not focal but rather involve most (if not all) of the diseased liver and include

- *Fibrous septa* in the form of delicate bands or broad scars around multiple adjacent lobules. Long-standing fibrosis generally is irreversible so long as disease persists or if disease-associated vascular shunts are widespread, although regression is possible if the underlying cause of liver disease is reversed.
- *Parenchymal nodules,* ranging in size from very small (less than 3 mm in diameter—micronodules) to large (over 1 cm—macronodules), encircled by these fibrous bands. Hepatocytes in these nodules derive from two sources: (1) preexistent, long-lived hepatocytes that, by the time cirrhosis is established, display features of replicative senescence; and (2) newly formed hepatocytes capable of replication that are derived from stem/progenitor cells found adjacent to the canals of Hering and small bile ductules—the hepatobiliary stem cell niche. These stem/progenitor cells also give rise to the *ductular reactions* found at the periphery of most cirrhotic nodules, where parenchyma meets stromal scar, and are accompanied by proliferating endothelial cells, myofibroblasts, and inflammatory cells.

There is no satisfactory classification of cirrhosis save for specification of the presumed underlying etiology. After all known causes have been excluded, about 10% of cases remain, referred to as cryptogenic cirrhosis, although in recent years most of these are recognized as probable "burned-out" NASH. General principles are presented next; the distinguishing features of each form of cirrhosis are discussed subsequently in the relevant disease overview.

PATHOGENESIS

Three processes are central to the pathogenesis of cirrhosis: death of hepatocytes, extracellular matrix deposition, and vascular reorganization.

Changes in the connective tissue and extracellular matrix (ECM) are common to all forms of cirrhosis. In the normal liver, ECM consisting of interstitial collagens (fibril-forming collagen types I, III, V, and XI) is present only in the liver capsule, in portal tracts, and around central veins. The hepatocytes have no true basement membrane; instead, a delicate framework containing type IV collagen and other proteins lies in the space between sinusoidal endothelial cells and hepatocytes (the space of Disse). By contrast, in cirrhosis, types I and III collagen and other ECM components are deposited in the space of Disse (Fig. 15–2).

The major source of excess collagen in cirrhosis are the perisinusoidal stellate cells (formerly known as Ito cells), which lie in the space of Disse. Although they normally function as storage cells for vitamin A, during the development of fibrosis they activate and transform into myofibroblasts. The stimuli for the activation of stellate cells and production of collagen are believed to include reactive oxygen species, growth factors, and cytokines such as tumor necrosis factor (TNF), interleukin-1 (IL-1), and lymphotoxins, which can be produced by damaged hepatocytes or by stimulated Kupffer cells and sinusoidal endothelial cells. Activated stellate cells themselves produce growth factors, cytokines, and chemokines that cause their further proliferation and collagen synthesis—in particular, transforming growth factor-β (TGF-β). Portal fibroblasts probably also participate in some forms of cirrhosis. During the course of chronic liver disease, fibrosis is a dynamic process that involves the synthesis, deposition, and resorption of ECM components, modulated by changing balances between metalloproteases and tissue inhibitors of metalloproteases (Chapter 2). Thus, even in late-stage disease, if the disease process is halted or eliminated, significant remodeling and even restoration of liver function **(cirrhotic regression)** is possible.

Vascular injuries and changes also play significant roles in remodeling of the liver into a cirrhotic state. Inflammation and thrombosis of portal veins, hepatic arteries, and/or central veins may lead to alternating zones of parenchymal hypoperfusion, with resulting parenchymal atrophy, and hyperperfusion, with overcompensating regeneration. The major vascular lesions that contribute to defects in liver function are loss of sinusoidal endothelial cell fenestrations (Fig. 15–2) and the development of portal vein–hepatic vein and hepatic artery–portal vein vascular shunts. While normal sinusoids have fenestrated endothelial cells that allow free exchange of solutes between plasma and hepatocytes, loss of fenestrations and increased basement membrane

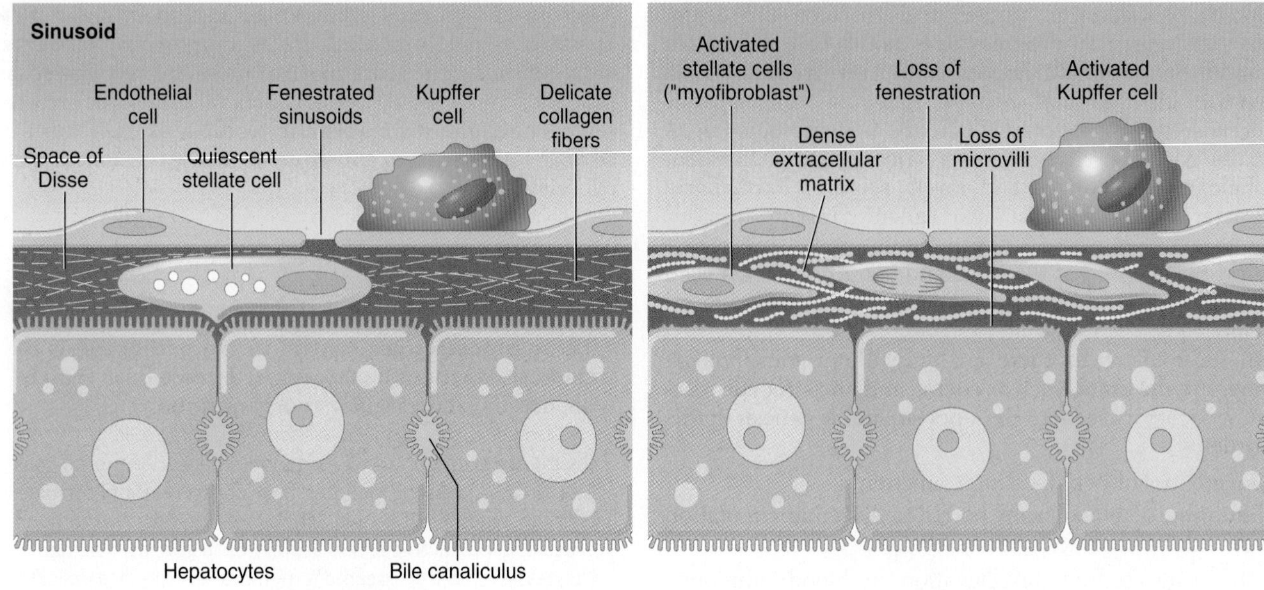

Figure 15–2 Liver fibrosis. In the normal liver, the perisinusoidal space (space of Disse) contains a delicate framework of extracellular matrix components. In liver fibrosis, stellate cells are activated to produce a dense layer of matrix material that is deposited in the perisinusoidal space. Collagen deposition blocks the endothelial fenestrations and prevents the free exchange of materials from the blood. Kupffer cells also are activated and produce cytokines that are involved in fibrosis. Note that this illustration is not to scale; the space of Disse is actually much narrower than shown.

formation convert thin-walled sinusoids into higher pressure, fast-flowing vascular channels without such solute exchange. In particular, the movement of proteins (e.g., albumin, clotting factors, lipoproteins) between hepatocytes and the plasma is markedly impaired. These functional changes are aggravated by the loss of microvilli from the hepatocyte surface, further diminishing its transport capacity. Vascular shunts mentioned earlier lead to abnormal vascular pressures in the liver and contribute to hepatic dysfunction and portal hypertension, described later.

The causes of liver cell injury that give rise to cirrhosis are varied and depend on the etiology (viral, alcoholic, drugs). As described earlier, the normal liver cells are replaced by parenchymal nodules derived from long-lived surviving hepatocytes and new cells generated from stem cells. The regenerating liver cells form spherical nodules confined by fibrous septa.

SUMMARY

Cirrhosis

- The three main characteristics of cirrhosis are (1) involvement of most or all of the liver, (2) bridging fibrous septa, and (3) parenchymal nodules containing a mix of senescent and replicating (often stem/progenitor cell-derived) hepatocytes.
- Cirrhosis usually is an end-stage process that may have multiple causes. The most frequent are chronic hepatitis B and C and alcoholic and nonalcoholic steatohepatitis. Less frequent causes are autoimmune and biliary diseases and metabolic conditions such as hemochromatosis.
- The main complications of cirrhosis are related to decreased liver function, portal hypertension, and increased risk for development of hepatocellular carcinoma.

Clinical Features

All forms of cirrhosis may be clinically silent. When symptoms appear, they typically are nonspecific and include anorexia, weight loss, weakness, and, in advanced disease, frank debilitation. Incipient or overt hepatic failure may develop, usually precipitated by imposition of a metabolic load on the liver, as from systemic infection or a gastrointestinal hemorrhage. Most cases of ultimately fatal cirrhosis involve one of the following mechanisms:

- Progressive liver failure
- A complication related to portal hypertension
- The development of hepatocellular carcinoma

Portal Hypertension

Increased resistance to portal blood flow may develop from prehepatic, intrahepatic, and posthepatic causes (described later). *The dominant intrahepatic cause is cirrhosis, accounting for most cases of portal hypertension.* Far less frequent are instances of *noncirrhotic portal hypertension*, such as from schistosomiasis, massive fatty change, diffuse granulomatous diseases (e.g., sarcoidosis, miliary tuberculosis), and diseases affecting the portal microcirculation, exemplified by *nodular regenerative hyperplasia*.

Portal hypertension in cirrhosis results from increased resistance to portal flow at the level of the sinusoids and compression of central veins by perivenular fibrosis and expanded parenchymal nodules. Anastomoses between the arterial and portal systems in the fibrous bands also contribute to portal hypertension by imposing arterial pressure on the normally low-pressure portal venous system. Another major factor in the causation of portal hypertension is an increase in portal venous blood flow resulting from a hyperdynamic circulation. This is caused by arterial vasodilation in the splanchnic circulation, resulting primarily from increased production of nitric oxide (NO) in the vascular bed. This occurs in response to reduced clearance of bacterial DNA absorbed from the gut that bypasses the Kupffer cells due to intrahepatic shunting of blood from portal to systemic circulation. Bacterial DNA causes increased production of NO. The major clinical consequences are discussed next (Fig. 15-3).

Ascites

Ascites refers to the collection of excess fluid in the peritoneal cavity. It usually becomes clinically detectable when at least 500 mL have accumulated, but many liters may collect, causing massive abdominal distention. Ascites generally is a serous fluid containing as much as 3 g/dL of protein (largely albumin). More importantly, the serum to ascites albumin gradient is ≥1.1 g/dL. The fluid may contain a scant number of mesothelial cells and mononuclear leukocytes. Influx of neutrophils suggests secondary infection, whereas presence of red cells points to possible disseminated intraabdominal cancer. With long-standing ascites, seepage of peritoneal fluid through transdiaphragmatic lymphatics may produce hydrothorax, more often on the right side.

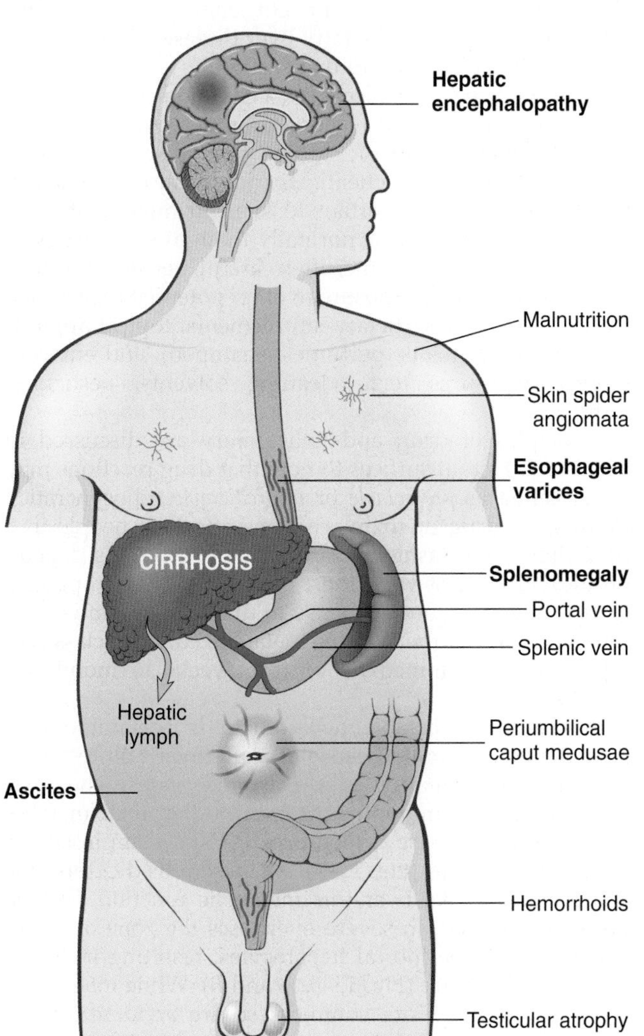

Figure 15-3 Some clinical consequences of portal hypertension in the setting of cirrhosis. The most important manifestations are in **bold** type.

PATHOGENESIS

The pathogenesis of ascites is complex, involving one or more of the following mechanisms:

- Increased movement of intravascular fluid into the extravascular space of Disse, caused by sinusoidal hypertension and hypoalbuminemia.
- Leakage of fluid from the hepatic interstitium into the peritoneal cavity. Normal thoracic duct lymph flow is 800 to 1000 mL/day. With cirrhosis, hepatic lymphatic flow may approach 20 L/day, exceeding thoracic duct capacity. Hepatic lymph is rich in proteins and low in triglycerides, as reflected in the protein-rich ascitic fluid.
- Renal retention of sodium and water due to secondary hyperaldosteronism (Chapter 3), despite a total body sodium mass greater than normal.

Portosystemic Shunt

With the rise in portal venous pressure, shunts develop wherever the systemic and portal circulations share capillary beds. Principal sites are veins around and within the rectum (manifest as hemorrhoids), the cardioesophageal junction (producing esophagogastric varices), the retroperitoneum, and the falciform ligament of the liver (involving periumbilical and abdominal wall collaterals). Although hemorrhoidal bleeding may occur, it is rarely massive or life-threatening. Much more important are the *esophagogastric varices* that appear in about 65% of persons with advanced cirrhosis of the liver, causing massive hematemesis and death in some instances (Chapter 14). Rarely, abdominal wall collaterals appear as dilated subcutaneous veins extending outward from the umbilicus (*caput medusae*).

Splenomegaly

Long-standing congestion may cause congestive splenomegaly. The degree of enlargement varies widely (usually 1000 g or less) and is not necessarily correlated with other features of portal hypertension. Massive splenomegaly may secondarily induce a variety of hematologic abnormalities attributable to hypersplenism (Chapter 11).

Hepatorenal Syndrome

Hepatorenal syndrome generally appears only with severe liver disease and is marked by the development of renal failure without primary abnormalities of the kidneys themselves. Excluded by this definition are concomitant toxic damage to both the liver and the kidney, as may occur in carbon tetrachloride and mushroom poisoning and the copper toxicity of Wilson disease. Also excluded are instances of advanced hepatic failure in which circulatory collapse leads to acute tubular necrosis and renal failure. Kidney function promptly improves if hepatic failure is reversed. Although the exact cause is unknown, evidence points to splanchnic vasodilatation and systemic vasoconstriction, leading to a severe reduction in renal blood flow, particularly to the cortex.

The syndrome is heralded by a drop in urine output and rising blood urea nitrogen and creatinine values. The ability to concentrate urine is retained, producing a hyperosmolar urine devoid of proteins and abnormal sediment that is surprisingly low in sodium (unlike renal tubular necrosis). Renal dialysis or other treatments are at best bridges to the only cure, liver transplantation; however, transplantation recipients with hepatorenal syndrome have a high mortality in the months after the operation.

Portopulmonary Hypertension and Hepatopulmonary Syndrome

Pulmonary dysfunction in chronic liver disease is common and may be life-threatening. Causes of liver injury also may damage the lungs (e.g., α_1-antitrypsin deficiency leading to both cirrhosis and emphysema). Ascites, pressing upward on the diaphragm, and pleural effusions associated with portal hypertension can compromise lung capacity. Finally, changes in pulmonary blood flow occurring secondary to hepatic failure may lead to *portopulmonary hypertension* or *hepatopulmonary syndrome.*

Portopulmonary hypertension is defined as pulmonary arterial hypertension associated with liver disease or portal hypertension. Although the mechanisms underlying this condition remain obscure, they seem to involve portal hypertension of any cause (cirrhotic or non-cirrhotic) and excessive pulmonary vasoconstriction and vascular remodeling, which eventually lead to right-sided heart failure; *the most common clinical manifestations are dyspnea on exertion* and clubbing of the fingers, followed by palpitations and chest pain.

Hepatopulmonary syndrome is associated with abnormal intrapulmonary vascular dilatation in combination with increased pulmonary blood flow. Shunting of blood through such dilatations leads to ventilation-perfusion mismatch and reduced oxygen diffusion, thus giving rise to *severe arterial hypoxemia with dyspnea and cyanosis.* Oxygen supplementation can alleviate these problems early on, though the most severe intrapulmonary vascular dilatation or formation of arteriovenous malformations causes right-to-left shunting that is only partially correctable. Platypnea (easier breathing while lying down as compared to when sitting or standing) and orthodeoxia (fall of arterial blood oxygen with upright posture) are pathognomonic of hepatopulmonary syndrome.

Selected patients with portopulmonary hypertension experience some degree of reversal of disturbed pulmonary function with liver transplantation.

DRUG- OR TOXIN-INDUCED LIVER DISEASE

As the major drug metabolizing and detoxifying organ in the body, the liver is subject to injury from an enormous array of therapeutic and environmental chemicals. Injury may result from direct toxicity, through hepatic conversion of a xenobiotic to an active toxin, or by immune mechanisms, such as by a drug or a metabolite acting as a hapten to convert a cellular protein into an immunogen.

A diagnosis of drug- or toxin-induced liver disease may be made on the basis of a temporal association of liver damage with drug or toxin exposure and, it is hoped, recovery on removal of the compound(s), combined with exclusion of other potential causes. *Exposure to a toxin or therapeutic agent should always be included in the differential diagnosis of any form of liver disease.* By far the most important agent that produces toxic liver injury is alcohol; its characteristic histologic (but not clinical) features are shared with nonalcoholic fatty liver disease (NAFLD) and therefore it is discussed in that section.

Drug-induced liver disease is a common condition that may manifest as a mild reaction or, much more seriously, as acute liver failure or chronic liver disease. A large number of drugs and chemicals can produce liver injury (Table 15–4). It is important to keep in mind that compounds other than those normally thought of as drugs or medicines may be to blame; often careful, persistent history taking will uncover exposure to other potential toxins such as herbal remedies, dietary supplements, topical applications (e.g., ointments, perfumes, shampoo), and environmental exposures (e.g., cleaning solvents, pesticides, fertilizers).

Principles of drug and toxic injury are discussed in Chapter 7. Here it suffices to note that drug reactions may be classified as *predictable* or *unpredictable* (idiosyncratic). Predictable drug or toxin reactions affect all people in a dose-dependent fashion. Unpredictable reactions depend on individual host variations, particularly the propensity to mount an immune response to drug-related antigen or the rate at which the agent is metabolized. Both classes of injury may be immediate or take weeks to months to develop.

A classic predictable hepatotoxin is acetaminophen, now the most common cause of acute liver failure necessitating transplantation in the United States. The toxic agent is not acetaminophen itself but rather toxic metabolites produced by the cytochrome P-450 system in acinus zone 3 hepatocytes (Fig. 15–4). As these cells die, the zone 2 hepatocytes take over this metabolic function, in turn becoming injured. In severe overdoses the zone of injury extends to the periportal hepatocytes, resulting in fulminant hepatic failure (Fig. 15–5, *A* and *B*). While intentional suicidal overdoses are common, so are accidental overdoses. This is because the cytotoxicity is dependent on the activity of the cytochrome P-450 system, which may be

Table 15–4 Different Forms of Drug- or Toxin-Induced Hepatic Injury

Pattern of Injury	Morphologic Findings	Examples of Associated Agents
Cholestatic	Bland hepatocellular cholestasis, without inflammation	Contraceptive and anabolic steroids; estrogen replacement therapy
Cholestatic hepatitis	Cholestasis with lobular inflammation and necrosis; may show bile duct destruction	Numerous antibiotics; phenothiazines
Hepatocellular necrosis	Spotty hepatocyte necrosis Submassive necrosis, zone 3 Massive necrosis	Methyldopa, phenytoin Acetaminophen, halothane Isoniazid, phenytoin
Steatosis	Macrovesicular	Ethanol, methotrexate, corticosteroids, total parenteral nutrition
Steatohepatitis	Microvesicular, Mallory bodies	Amiodarone, ethanol
Fibrosis and cirrhosis	Periportal and pericellular fibrosis	Methotrexate, isoniazid, enalapril
Granulomas	Noncaseating epithelioid granulomas	Sulfonamides, numerous other agents
Vascular lesions	Sinusoidal obstruction syndrome (venoocclusive disease): obliteration of central veins Budd-Chiari syndrome Sinusoidal dilatation Peliosis hepatis: blood-filled cavities, not lined by endothelial cells	High-dose chemotherapy, bush teas Oral contraceptives Oral contraceptives, numerous other agents Anabolic steroids, tamoxifen
Neoplasms	Hepatic adenoma Hepatocellular carcinoma Cholangiocarcinoma Angiosarcoma	Oral contraceptives, anabolic steroids Thorotrast Thorotrast Thorotrast, vinyl chloride

From Washington K: Metabolic and toxic conditions of the liver. In Iacobuzio-Donahue CA, Montgomery EA (eds): Gastrointestinal and Liver Pathology. Philadelphia, Churchill Livingstone, 2005.

upregulated by other agents taken in combination with acetaminophen, such as alcohol (beware acetaminophen as a hangover prophylactic) or codeine in acetaminophen compound tablets.

Examples of drugs that can cause idiosyncratic reactions are chlorpromazine (an agent that causes cholestasis in individuals who metabolize it slowly), halothane (which can cause a fatal immune-mediated hepatitis in some persons exposed to this anesthetic on several occasions), and other drugs such as sulfonamides, α-methyldopa, and allopurinol. Often, idiosyncratic drug or toxin reactions involve a variable combination of direct cytotoxicity and immune-mediated hepatocyte or bile duct destruction. Examples of hepatotoxins are given in each disease-specific category described later.

SUMMARY

Drug- or Toxin-Induced Liver Disease

- Drug- and toxin-induced liver disease may be predictable (intrinsic) or unpredictable (idiosyncratic).
- Predictable hepatotoxins affect most individuals in a dose-dependent fashion.
- Unpredictable hepatotoxins affect rare persons in an idiosyncratic way, often involving a combination of direct cytotoxicity and immune-mediated injury.
- Every pattern of liver injury can be caused by some toxin or drug; therefore, exposures involving these agents must always be considered in the differential diagnosis.
- In addition to prescription and over-the-counter medications, herbal remedies, dietary supplements, topical applications, and environmental exposures may be responsible for hepatotoxicity.

ACUTE AND CHRONIC HEPATITIS

The terminology of acute and chronic hepatitis can be confusing, since the term *hepatitis* is applied to a number of different diseases and different forms of liver injury. For example, *hepatitis* is a descriptor for specific histopathologic patterns of hepatocyte injury associated with inflammation and, when chronic, with scarring. Acute and chronic forms of hepatitis are distinguished in part by duration and in part by the pattern of cell injury. Viral hepatitides are also classified on the basis of the causative hepatotropic virus such as hepatitis types A, B, C, D, and E. Because all forms of hepatitis, including those due to the hepatitis viruses as well as autoimmune and drug- and toxin-induced hepatitides, share the same patterns of injury, the general descriptions are presented first, followed by clinicopathologic correlations specific to each cause.

MORPHOLOGY

On gross inspection, liver involved by mild acute hepatitis appears normal or slightly mottled. At the other end of the spectrum, in massive hepatic necrosis the liver may shrink to 500 to 700 g and become transformed into a limp, red organ covered by a wrinkled, baggy capsule. The distribution of liver destruction is extremely capricious: **The entire liver may be involved, or only patchy areas affected.** On sectioning (Fig. 15–5, *A*), necrotic areas have a muddy-red, mushy appearance with blotchy bile staining.

If patients survive for more than a week, surviving hepatocytes begin to regenerate (Chapter 2). If the parenchymal framework is preserved, regeneration is orderly and liver architecture is restored. With more massive destruction,

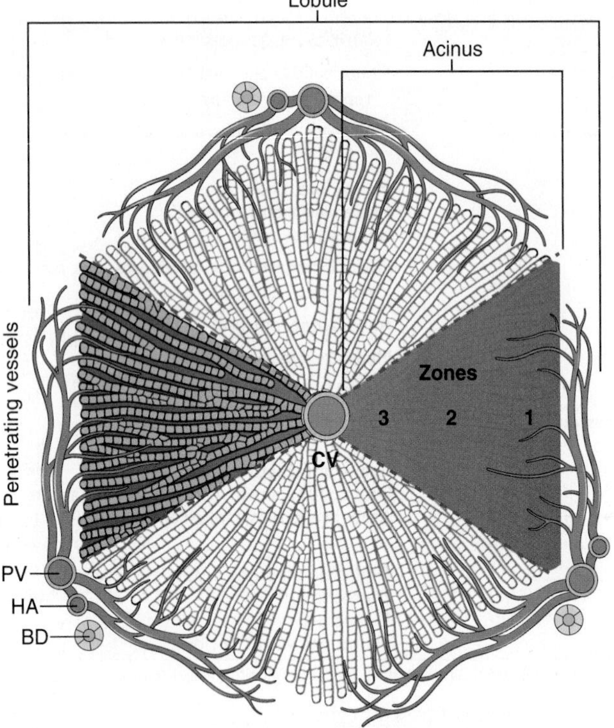

Figure 15–4 Microscopic architecture of the liver parenchyma. Both a lobule and an acinus are represented. The idealized classic lobule is represented as hexagonal centered on a central vein (CV), also known as terminal hepatic venule, and has portal tracts at three of its apices. The portal tracts contain branches of the portal vein (PV), hepatic artery (HA), and the bile duct (BD) system. Regions of the lobule generally are referred to as *periportal, midzonal,* and *centrilobular,* according to their proximity to portal spaces and central vein. Another useful way to subdivide the liver architecture is to use the blood supply as a point of reference. Using this approach, triangular acini can be recognized. Acini have at their base branches of portal vessels that penetrate the parenchyma ("penetrating vessels"). On the basis of the distance from the blood supply, the acinus is divided into zones 1 (closest to blood source), 2, and 3 (farthest from blood source).

Both hepatocyte injury and inflammation, while related, can be highly variable depending on etiology and host factors. The hepatocyte injury takes two forms. The first is swelling **(ballooning degeneration),** producing cells with empty-appearing pale cytoplasm that subsequently rupture and undergo **necrosis (cytolysis).** The necrotic cells appear to have **dropped out,** leaving collapsing sinusoidal collagen reticulin framework behind; scavenger macrophages mark sites of dropout. The second pattern of cell death is **apoptosis,** in which hepatocytes shrink, become intensely eosinophilic, and have fragmented nuclei; effector T cells may be present in the immediate vicinity. When located in the parenchyma away from portal tracts, these features are called **lobular hepatitis** (Fig. 15–6).

In severe cases, confluent necrosis of hepatocytes is seen around central veins (Fig. 15–5, *B*). In these areas there may be cellular debris, collapsed reticulin fibers, congestion/hemorrhage, and variable inflammation. With increasing severity, **central-portal bridging necrosis** develops, followed by, even worse, **parenchymal collapse.** When the injury is overwhelming, massive hepatic necrosis and fulminant liver failure ensue. In occasional cases, the injury is not regeneration is disorderly, yielding nodular masses of liver cells separated by granulation tissue and, eventually, scar, particularly in patients with a protracted course of submassive necrosis.

The gross appearance of the liver in chronic hepatitis may be normal or include grossly evident focal scarring or, as cirrhosis develops, may feature widespread nodularity surrounded by extensive scarring.

The general microscopic features of acute and chronic hepatitis of all causes are listed in Table 15–5. Unlike most other organ systems in which the distinction between acute and chronic inflammation depends on the predominant type of inflammatory cell—neutrophilic in acute injury, mononuclear in chronic phases—mononuclear infiltrates predominate in all phases of most hepatic diseases because they all invoke T cell–mediated immunity. Thus, **the distinction between acute and chronic hepatitis is based on the pattern of cell injury and severity of inflammation, with acute hepatitis often showing less inflammation and more hepatocyte death than chronic hepatitis.**

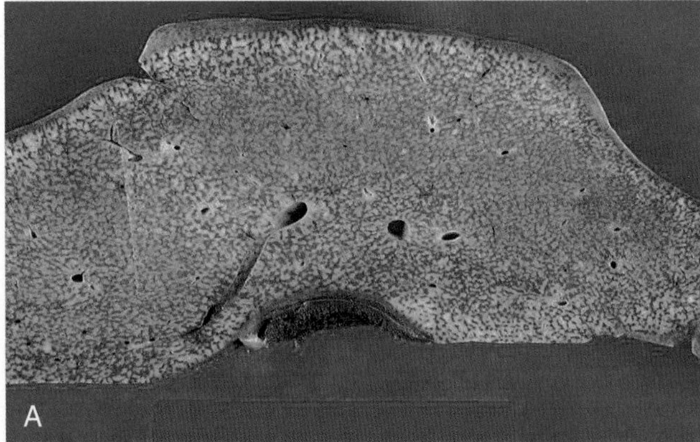

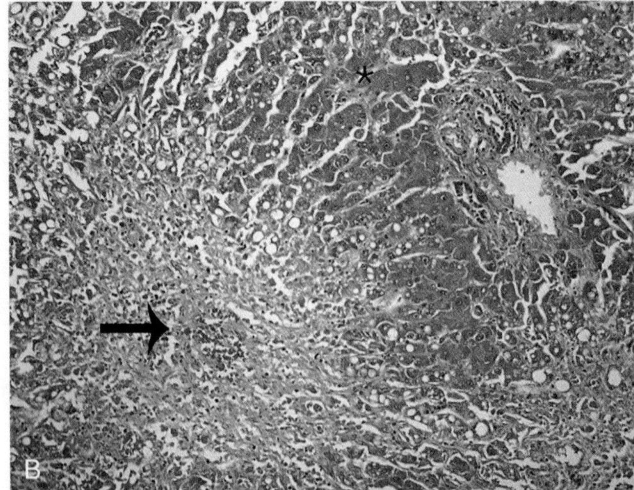

Figure 15–5 **A,** Massive necrosis, cut section of liver. The liver is small (700 g), bile-stained, soft, and congested. **B,** Hepatocellular necrosis caused by acetaminophen overdose. Confluent necrosis is seen in the perivenular region (zone 3) (*large arrow*). There is little inflammation. The residual normal tissue is indicated by the *asterisk*.

(Courtesy of Dr. Matthew Yeh, University of Washington, Seattle, Washington.)

Table 15–5 Main Morphologic Features of Acute and Chronic Viral Hepatitis

Acute Hepatitis
Gross Changes
Enlarged, reddened liver; greenish if cholestatic
Parenchymal Changes (Microscopic)
Hepatocyte injury: swelling (ballooning degeneration)
Cholestasis: canalicular bile plugs
HCV: mild fatty change of hepatocytes
Hepatocyte necrosis: isolated cells or clusters
Cytolysis (rupture) or apoptosis (shrinkage)
If severe: bridging necrosis (portal-portal, central-central, portal-central)
Lobular disarray: loss of normal architecture
Regenerative changes: hepatocyte proliferation
Sinusoidal cell reactive changes
Accumulation of phagocytosed cellular debris in Kupffer cells
Influx of mononuclear cells into sinusoids
Portal tracts
Inflammation: predominantly mononuclear
Inflammatory spillover into adjacent parenchyma, with hepatocyte necrosis
Chronic Hepatitis
Changes shared with acute hepatitis
Hepatocyte injury, necrosis, apoptosis, and regeneration
Sinusoidal cell reactive changes
Portal tracts
Inflammation
Confined to portal tracts, *or*
Spillover into adjacent parenchyma, with necrosis of hepatocytes ("interface hepatitis"), *or*
Bridging inflammation and necrosis
Fibrosis
Portal deposition, *or*
Portal and periportal deposition, *or*
Formation of bridging fibrous septa
HBV: ground-glass hepatocytes (accumulation of HBsAg)
HCV: bile duct epithelial cell proliferation, lymphoid aggregate formation

HBsAg, hepatitis B surface antigen; HBV, hepatitis B virus; HCV, hepatitis C virus.

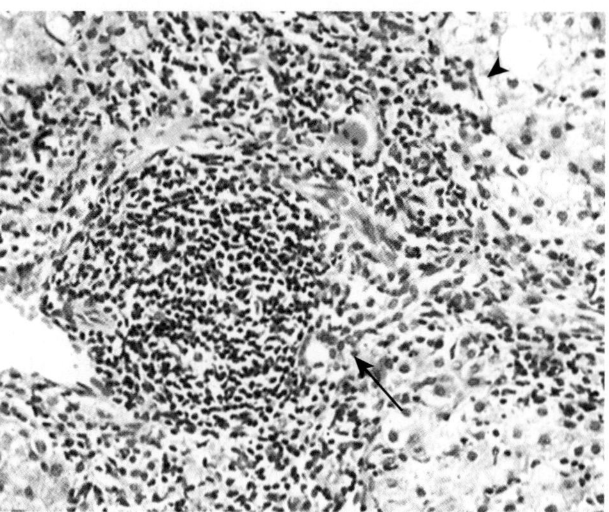

Figure 15–7 Chronic hepatitis showing portal tract expansion by a dense infiltrate of mononuclear cells (*arrow*) and interface hepatitis with spillover of inflammation into the parenchyma (*arrowhead*). The prominent lymphoid infiltrate is typical of the cause of disease in this biopsy: chronic hepatitis C.

severe enough to cause death (or necessitate transplantation), and the liver survives, although with abundant scarring that replaces areas of confluent necrosis. In such cases, some patients rapidly develop **posthepatitic cirrhosis.**

Portal inflammation in acute hepatitis is minimal or absent; dense **mononuclear portal infiltrates** of variable prominence are the defining lesion of **chronic hepatitis** (Fig. 15–7). There is often **interface hepatitis** as well, distinguished from lobular hepatitis by its location at the interface between hepatocellular parenchyma and portal stroma (or scars, when present). The hallmark of severe chronic liver damage is scarring. At first, only portal tracts exhibit fibrosis, but in some patients, with time, **fibrous septa**—bands of dense scar—will extend between portal tracts. In the most severe cases, continued scarring and nodule formation leads to the development of **cirrhosis** (Fig 15–8).

Clinical assessment of chronic hepatitis often requires liver biopsy in addition to clinical and serologic data. Liver biopsy is helpful in confirming the clinical diagnosis, excluding common concomitant conditions (e.g., fatty liver disease, hemochromatosis), assessing histologic features associated

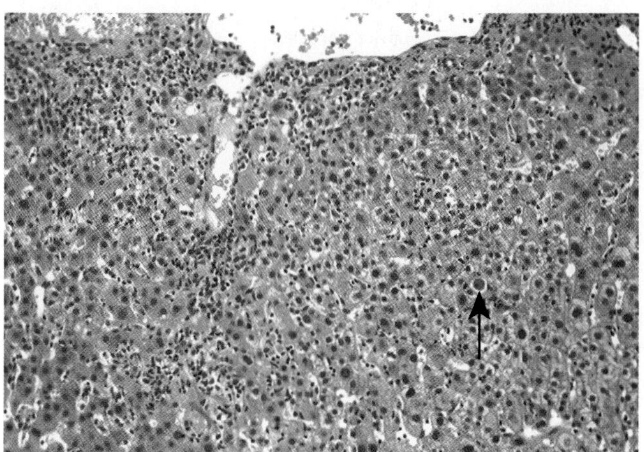

Figure 15–6 Acute viral hepatitis showing disruption of lobular architecture, inflammatory cells in sinusoids, and apoptotic cells (*arrow*).

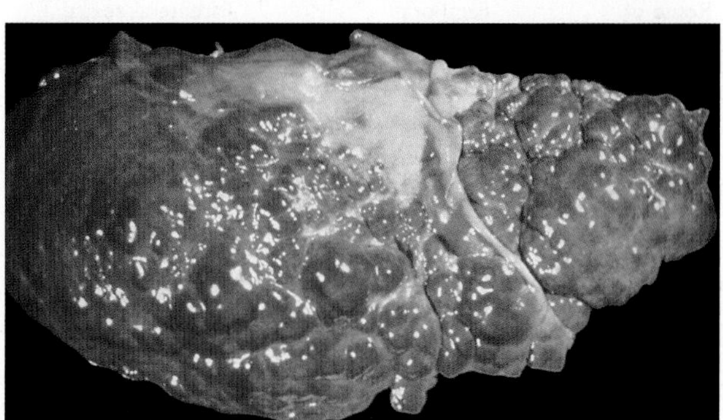

Figure 15–8 Cirrhosis resulting from chronic viral hepatitis. Note the irregular nodularity of the liver surface.

with an increased risk of malignancy (e.g., small and large cell change, described later), **grading the extent of hepatocyte injury and inflammation, and staging the progression of scarring.** Such grading and staging are useful for assessing prognosis and therapeutic options.

Viral Hepatitis

Viral hepatitis is caused mainly by hepatitis viruses A (HAV), B (HBV), C (HCV), D (HDV), and E (HEV). These viruses and their infections have distinct features, which are summarized in Table 15–6.

Hepatitis A Virus

Hepatitis A usually is a benign, self-limited disease with an incubation period of 2 to 6 weeks (average 28 days). HAV does not cause chronic hepatitis or a carrier state. Rarely there is fulminant hepatitis; fatalities occur at a rate of only 0.1%. HAV occurs throughout the world and is endemic in countries with poor hygiene and sanitation, so that most natives of such countries have detectable antibodies to HAV by the age of 10 years. Epidemics are not unusual. The disease tends to be mild or asymptomatic in children, with severe HAV infections occurring mainly in adults.

HAV is spread by ingestion of contaminated water and foods and is shed in the stool for 2 to 3 weeks before and 1 week after the onset of jaundice. HAV is not shed in any significant quantities in saliva, urine, or semen. Close personal contact with an infected person during the period of fecal shedding, with fecal-oral contamination, accounts for most cases and explains the outbreaks in institutional settings such as schools and nurseries. *Because HAV viremia is transient, blood-borne transmission of HAV occurs only rarely; therefore, donated blood is not routinely screened for this virus.* Waterborne epidemics may occur in developing countries where people live in overcrowded, unsanitary conditions. Among developed countries, sporadic infections may be contracted by the consumption of raw or steamed shellfish (oysters, mussels, clams), which concentrate the virus from seawater contaminated with human sewage.

HAV is a small, nonenveloped, single-stranded RNA picornavirus. It reaches the liver from the intestinal tract after ingestion, replicates in hepatocytes, and is shed in the bile and feces. The virus itself does not seem to be toxic to hepatocytes, and hence the liver injury seems to result from T cell–mediated damage of infected hepatocytes. As depicted in Figure 15–9, immunoglobulin M (IgM) antibodies against HAV appear in blood at the onset of symptoms. Detection of anti-HAV IgM antibody is the best diagnostic marker for the disease; IgG antibody persists beyond convalescence and is the primary defense against reinfection. In the United States, the prevalence of seropositivity increases gradually with age, reaching 40% by the age of 50 years.

Measures for the prevention and management of hepatitis A include (1) hygienic practices focused on the disposal of human wastes and personal hygiene; (2) passive immunization with immune serum globulin for persons at high risk for infection (very young, very old, or immunocompromised) after exposure to the virus; and (3) administration of inactivated-virus vaccine given either before exposure (e.g., before travel to endemic areas) or very early after exposure.

Hepatitis B Virus

HBV can produce various clinical syndromes:

- Acute hepatitis with recovery and clearance of the virus
- Fulminant hepatitis with massive liver necrosis
- Nonprogressive chronic hepatitis
- Progressive chronic disease sometimes ending in cirrhosis
- An asymptomatic carrier state

Table 15–6 The Hepatitis Viruses

Virus	Hepatitis A	Hepatitis B	Hepatitis C	Hepatitis D	Hepatitis E
Type of virus	ssRNA	Partially dsDNA	ssRNA	Circular defective ssRNA	ssRNA
Viral family	Hepatovirus; related to picornavirus	Hepadnavirus	Flaviridae	Subviral particle in Deltaviridae family	Hepevirus
Route of transmission	Fecal-oral (contaminated food or water)	Parenteral, sexual contact, perinatal	Parenteral; intranasal cocaine use is a risk factor	Parenteral	Fecal-oral
Incubation period	2–6 weeks	4–26 weeks	2–26 weeks	Same as for HBV	2–8 weeks
Frequency of chronic liver disease	Never	10%	~80%	5% (coinfection); ≤70% for superinfection	Never
Laboratory diagnosis	Detection of serum IgM antibodies	Detection of HBsAg or antibody to HBcAg	PCR assay for HCV RNA; 3rd-generation ELISA for antibody detection	Detection of IgM and IgG antibodies; HDV RNA serum; HDAg in liver	PCR assay for HEV RNA; detection of serum IgM and IgG antibodies

dsDNA, double-stranded DNA; ELISA, enzyme-linked immunosorbent assay; HBcAg, hepatitis B core antigen; HBsAg, hepatitis B surface antigen; HBV, hepatitis B virus; HCV, hepatitis C virus; HDAg, hepatitis D antigen; HDV, hepatitis D virus; HEV, hepatitis E virus; IgG, IgM, immunoglobulins G and M; PCR, polymerase chain reaction; ssRNA, single-stranded RNA.
From Washington K: Inflammatory and infectious diseases of the liver. In Iacobuzio-Donahue CA, Montgomery EA (eds): Gastrointestinal and Liver Pathology. Philadelphia, Churchill Livingstone, 2005.

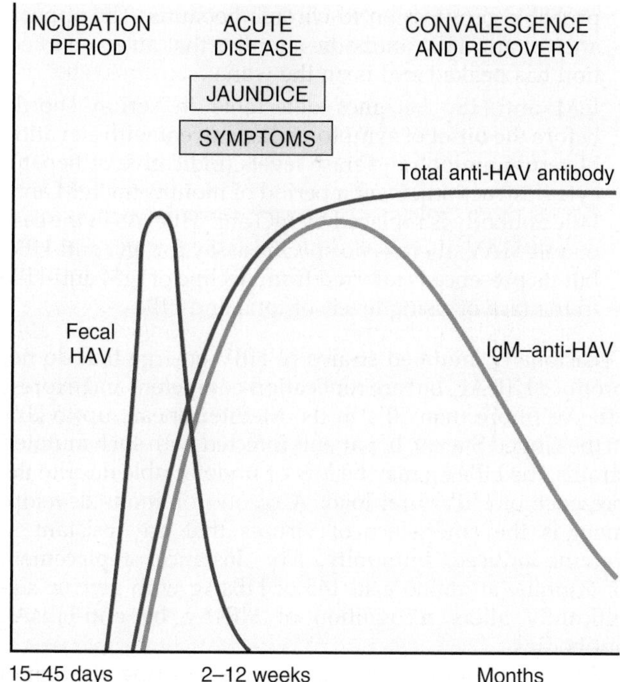

Figure 15–9 The sequence of serologic markers in acute hepatitis A infection. HAV, hepatitis A virus. There are no routinely available tests for IgG anti-HAV; therefore the presence of this antibody is inferred from the difference between total and IgM-HAV.

HBV-induced chronic liver disease is an important precursor for the development of hepatocellular carcinoma. Figure 15–10 depicts the approximate frequencies of these outcomes.

Epidemiology and Transmission. Globally, liver disease caused by HBV is an enormous problem, with an estimated 400 million people who are carriers of the virus. It is estimated that HBV will infect more than 2 billion people alive today at some point in their lives. About 80% of all chronic carriers live in Asia and the Western Pacific Rim region, where the prevalence of chronic hepatitis B is more than 10%. In the United States there are approximately 185,000 new infections per year. HBV is found in the blood during the last stages of a prolonged incubation period (4 to 26 weeks) and during active episodes of acute and chronic hepatitis. It also is present in all physiologic and pathologic body fluids, with the exception of stool. HBV is a hardy virus and can withstand extremes of temperature and humidity. Thus, whereas blood and body fluids are the primary vehicles of transmission, virus also may be spread by contact with body secretions such as semen, saliva, sweat, tears, breast milk, and pathologic effusions. In endemic regions, vertical transmission from mother to child during birth constitutes the main mode of transmission. In areas of low prevalence, horizontal transmission via transfusion, blood products, dialysis, needlestick accidents among health care workers, sharing of needles in intravenous drug use, and sexual transmission (homosexual or heterosexual) constitute the primary mechanisms for HBV infection. In one third of patients, the source of infection is unknown. Most HBV infections in adults are cleared, but vertical transmission produces a high rate of persistent infection since infants cannot readily clear the infection. Chronically infected persons are at significantly increased risk for development of hepatocellular carcinoma, explaining the high rate of that malignancy in Asia and Pacific Rim nations.

HBV Structure and Genome. HBV is a member of the Hepadnaviridae, a group of DNA-containing viruses that cause hepatitis in many animal species. HBV replication does not involve the integration of the virus in the DNA of the host cell, but integrated HBV frequently is found in cells. The integrated viruses generally have large deletions and rearrangements and usually become inactive. The genome of HBV is a partially double-stranded circular DNA molecule of 3200 nucleotides that encodes

- The precore/core region of a nucleocapsid "core" protein, the *hepatitis B core antigen (HBcAg)*, and a precore

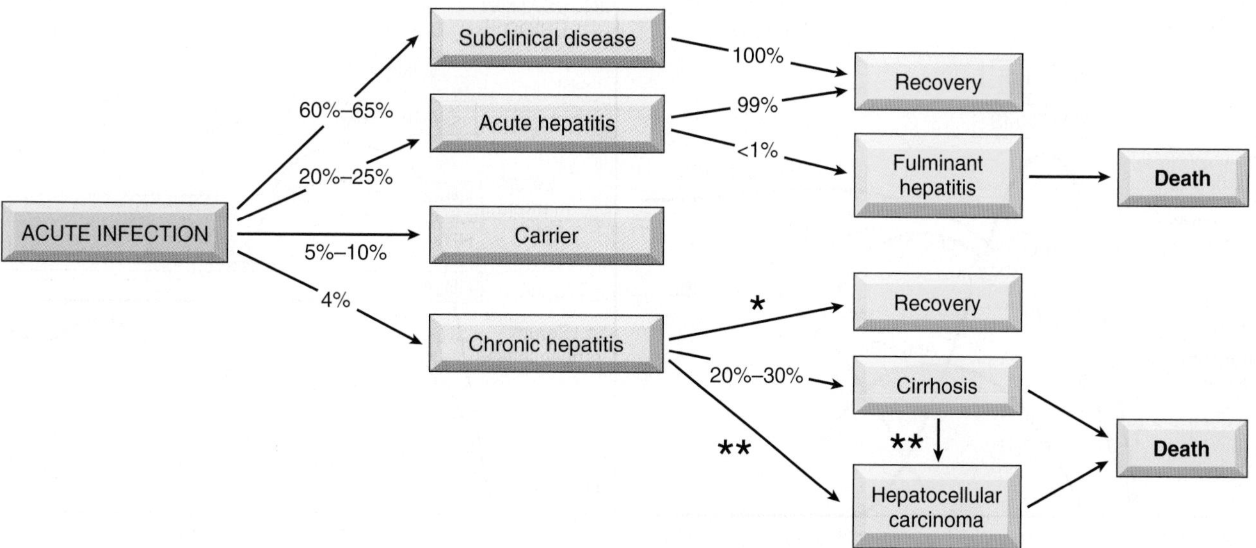

Figure 15–10 The potential outcomes with hepatitis B infection in adults, with their approximate annual frequencies in the United States. *Estimated rate of recovery from chronic hepatitis is 0.5% to 1% per year. **The risk of hepatocellular carcinoma is 0.02% per year for chronic hepatitis B and 2.5% per year when cirrhosis has developed.

protein designated hepatitis Be antigen (HBeAg). HBcAg is retained in the infected hepatocyte; HBeAg is secreted into blood and is essential for the establishment of persistent infection.

- Envelope glycoprotein, the *hepatitis B surface antigen (HBsAg),* which may be produced and secreted into the blood in massive amounts. Blood HBsAg is immunogenic.
- A *DNA polymerase* with an error-prone reverse transcriptase activity that generates mutations in the genomes of replicating virus at a high rate.
- *HBV-X* protein, which acts as a transcriptional transactivator for many viral and host genes through interaction with various transcription factors. HBV-X is required for viral infectivity and may have a role in the development of hepatocellular carcinoma by regulating p53 degradation and expression (Chapter 6).

Clinical Course

After exposure to the virus, there is a long, asymptomatic incubation period, which may be followed by acute disease (described later) lasting many weeks to months. The natural course of acute disease can be tracked using serum markers (Fig. 15–11):

- HBsAg appears before the onset of symptoms, peaks during overt disease, and then declines to undetectable levels in 3 to 6 months.
- Anti-HBs antibody does not rise until the acute disease is over and usually is not detectable for a few weeks to several months after the disappearance of HBsAg. Anti-HBs may persist for life, conferring immunity; this is the basis for current vaccination strategies using noninfectious HBsAg.
- HBeAg, HBV-DNA, and DNA polymerase appear in serum soon after HBsAg, and all signify active viral replication. Persistence of HBeAg is an important indicator of continued viral replication, infectivity, and probable progression to chronic hepatitis. The appearance of anti-HBe antibodies implies that an acute infection has peaked and is on the wane.
- IgM anti-HBc becomes detectable in serum shortly before the onset of symptoms, concurrent with elevation of serum aminotransferase levels (indicative of hepatocyte destruction). Over a period of months the IgM anti-HBc antibody is replaced by IgG anti-HBc. As in the case of anti-HAV, there is no specific assay for IgG anti-HBc, but its presence is inferred from decline of IgM anti-HBc in the face of rising levels of total anti-HBc.

Occasionally, mutated strains of HBV emerge that do not produce HBeAg, but are replication-competent and express HBcAg (more than 30% in the Mediterranean, up to 20% in the United States). In patients infected with such mutated strains, the HBeAg may be low or undetectable despite the presence of HBV viral load. A second ominous development is the emergence of viruses that are resistant to vaccine-induced immunity. For instance, replacement of arginine at amino acid 145 of HBsAg with glycine significantly alters recognition of HBsAg by anti-HBsAg antibodies.

Innate immunity protects the host during the initial phases of the infection, and a strong response by virus-specific CD4+ and CD8+ interferon γ-producing cells is associated with the resolution of acute infection. Current evidence suggests that HBV does not cause direct hepatocyte injury, and hepatocyte damage results from killing of the virus-infected cells by CD8+ cytotoxic T cells.

Hepatitis B can largely be prevented by vaccination and by the screening of donor blood, organs, and tissues. The vaccine is prepared from purified HBsAg produced in yeast. Vaccination induces a protective anti-HBs antibody response in 95% of infants, children, and adolescents. Universal vaccination has been a notable success in countries such as Taiwan and Gambia but unfortunately has not been adopted worldwide.

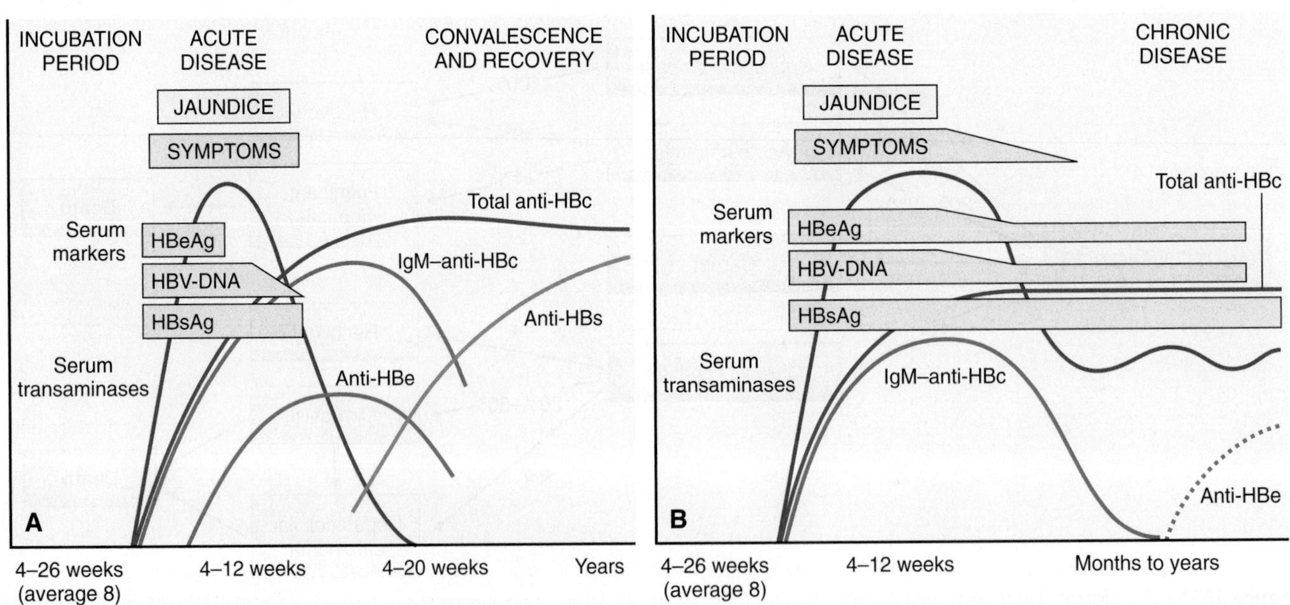

Figure 15–11 The sequence of serologic markers in acute hepatitis B infection. **A,** Resolution of active infection. **B,** Progression to chronic infection. See text for abbreviations.

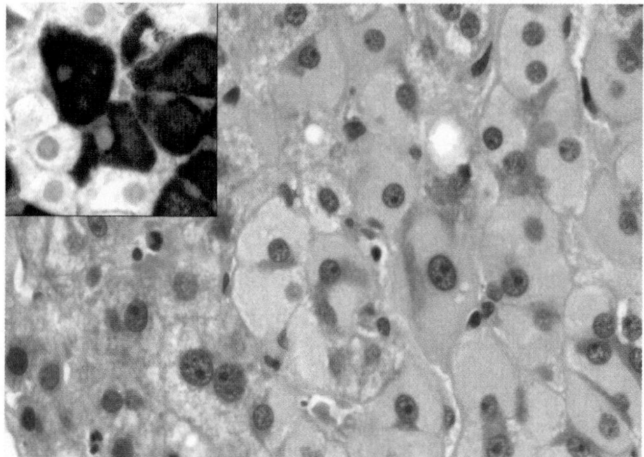

Figure 15-12 Ground-glass hepatocytes in chronic hepatitis B, caused by accumulation of HBsAg in cytoplasm, have large, pale, finely granular, pink cytoplasmic inclusions on hematoxylin-eosin staining; immunostaining (*inset*) confirms that the endoplasmic reticulum is ballooned with surface antigen (*brown*). HBsAg, hepatitis B surface antigen.

MORPHOLOGY

Microscopically, hepatitis B can produce all of the histologic features of acute and chronic hepatitis described earlier, but some liver biopsy specimens also display a particular morphologic feature that is nearly diagnostic, the **ground glass cell** (Fig. 15–12). In chronic HBV infection, some hepatocytes may have viral genomes integrated into the host genome. If, by chance, the surface antigen gene integrates into a host genomic site adjacent to an active promoter, then the cell is converted into a factory for surface antigen production. Usually in such cells full viral replication does not take place. Since surface antigen can only exit the cell as part of intact viral particles, the antigen just accumulates in these cells, creating a large cytoplasmic inclusion consisting of endoplasmic reticulum stuffed with surface antigen that has a fine, smoothly granular appearance similar to that of ground glass.

Hepatitis C Virus

Epidemiology and Transmission. HCV also is a major cause of liver disease. The worldwide carrier rate is estimated at 175 million persons (a 3% prevalence rate, ranging widely from 0.1% to 12%, depending on the country). Persistent chronic infection exists in 3 to 4 million persons in the United States, where the number of newly acquired HCV infections per year dropped from 180,000 in the mid-1980s to about 19,000 in 2006. This welcome change resulted from the marked reduction in transfusion-associated hepatitis C (as a result of screening procedures) and a decline of infections in intravenous drug abusers (related to practices motivated by fear of human immunodeficiency virus infection). However, the death rate from HCV will continue to climb for 20 to 25 years, because of the decades-long lag time between acute infection and liver failure. *The major route of transmission is through blood inoculation, with intravenous drug use accounting for at least 60% of cases in the United States.* Transmission by blood products is now fortunately rare, accounting for only 4% of all acute HCV infections. Occupational exposure among health care workers accounts for another 4% of cases. The rates of sexual transmission and vertical transmission are low. Infections of unknown origin account for 9% to 27% of cases. *HCV infection has a much higher rate than HBV of progression* to *chronic disease and eventual cirrhosis* (Fig. 15–13). In fact, hepatitis C is the condition that most frequently necessitates liver transplantation in the United States.

Viral Structure and Genome. HCV is a positive-sense single-stranded RNA virus belonging to the family Flaviviridae. It contains highly conserved 5′- and 3′-terminal regions that flank a single open reading frame of nearly 9500 nucleotides that encode structural and nonstructural proteins. HCV is subclassified into six genotypes, based on the genetic sequence. Moreover, because of the poor fidelity of RNA replication, an infected person may carry many HCV variants, called *quasispecies.* The relationships between quasispecies and disease progression are being investigated, but it seems that high multiplicity of quasispecies is associated with worse prognosis. In addition, this variability seriously hampers efforts to develop an HCV vaccine.

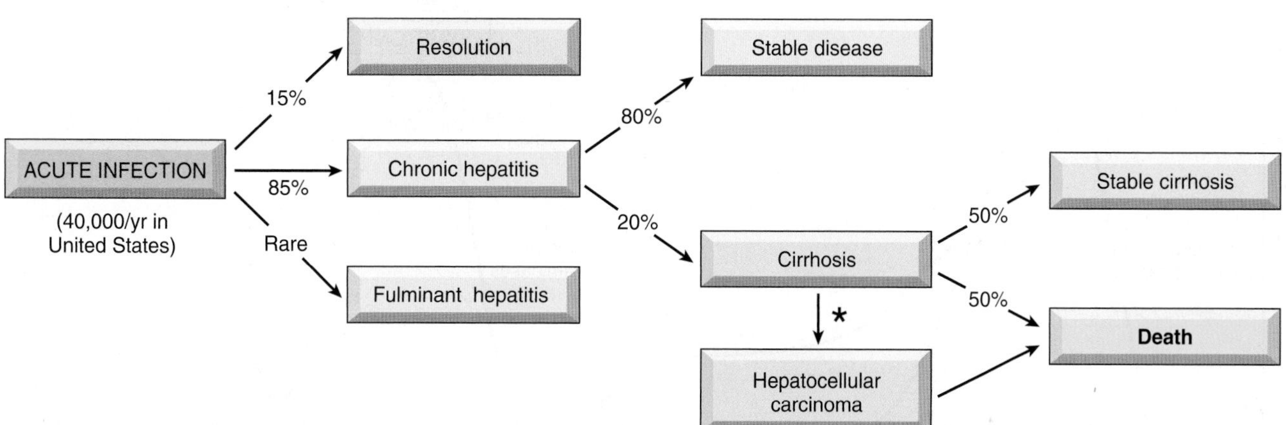

Figure 15–13 The potential outcomes of hepatitis C infection in adults, with their approximate annual frequencies in the United States. The population estimates are for newly detected infection; because of the decades-long lag time for progression from acute infection to cirrhosis, the actual annual death rate from hepatitis C is about 10,000 per year and exceeded 22,000 deaths per year by 2008. *The risk of hepatocellular carcinoma is 1% to 4% per year.

Clinical Course

The incubation period for hepatitis C ranges from 2 to 26 weeks, with a mean of 6 to 12 weeks. *Acute hepatitis C is asymptomatic in 75% of affected persons and is easily missed.* Thus, not much is known about this phase of the disease. HCV RNA can be detected in blood within days to 8 weeks depending on the inoculum size. Elevations of serum aminotransferases occur in 2 to 12 weeks. Although neutralizing anti-HCV antibodies develop within weeks to a few months, they *do not confer effective immunity* (Fig. 15–14). Strong immune responses involving CD4+ and CD8+ cells are associated with self-limited HCV infections, but it is not known why only a minority of persons are capable of clearing HCV infection.

In persistent infection, circulating HCV-RNA is detectable, and aminotransferases show episodic elevations, or continuous elevation with fluctuating levels. In a small percentage of affected persons, aminotransferase levels are normal even though abnormal liver histology persists. Increased enzyme activity may occur in the absence of clinical symptoms, presumably reflecting recurrent bouts of hepatocyte necrosis. *Persistent infection is the hallmark of HCV infection, occurring in 80% to 85% of patients with subclinical or asymptomatic acute infection* (Fig. 15–13). Cirrhosis develops in 20% of persistently infected persons: It can be present at the time of diagnosis or may take up to 20 years to develop. Alternatively, patients may have documented chronic HCV infection for decades, without progressing to cirrhosis. Fulminant hepatitis is rare. *Hepatitis C confers a significantly increased risk for hepatocellular carcinoma.*

MORPHOLOGY

Microscopically, chronic hepatitis C displays the typical features of chronic hepatitis described above, but has some distinctive, common associated findings: (1) **fatty change,** resulting either from altered lipid metabolism in infected hepatocytes, or insulin resistance and the so-called metabolic syndrome (described later); (2) **lymphoid infiltrates** in portal tracts, sometimes with fully formed lymphoid follicles (Fig. 15–7); and (3) **bile duct injury,** which may be related to direct infection of cholangiocytes by the virus.

Hepatitis D Virus

Also called *delta hepatitis virus,* HDV is a unique RNA virus that is replication-defective, causing infection only when it is encapsulated by HBsAg. Thus, *although taxonomically distinct from HBV, HDV is absolutely dependent on HBV coinfection for multiplication.* Delta hepatitis arises in two settings: (1) acute coinfection after exposure to serum containing both HDV and HBV and (2) superinfection of a chronic carrier of HBV with a new inoculum of HDV. In coinfections, HBV infection must first be established before HBsAg is made in sufficient amounts for production of HDV virions. Most coinfected persons clear the viruses and recover completely. By contrast, in most superinfected persons there is an acceleration of hepatitis, progressing to more severe chronic hepatitis 4 to 7 weeks later.

Infection by HDV is worldwide, with prevalence rates ranging from 8% among HBsAg carriers in southern Italy to as high as 40% in Africa and the Middle East. Surprisingly, HDV infection is uncommon in Southeast Asia and China, areas in which HBV infection is endemic. Periodic epidemic outbreaks have occurred in subtropical areas of Peru, Colombia, and Venezuela. In the United States, HDV infection is largely restricted to drug addicts and persons receiving multiple transfusions (e.g., hemophiliacs), who have prevalence rates of 1% to 10%.

HDV RNA and the HDV antigen (HDV Ag) are detectable in the blood and liver just before and in the early days of acute symptomatic disease. *IgM anti-HDV antibody is the most reliable indicator of recent HDV exposure,* as it is present at high titers only transiently in the immediate post-infection period. Acute coinfection by HDV and HBV

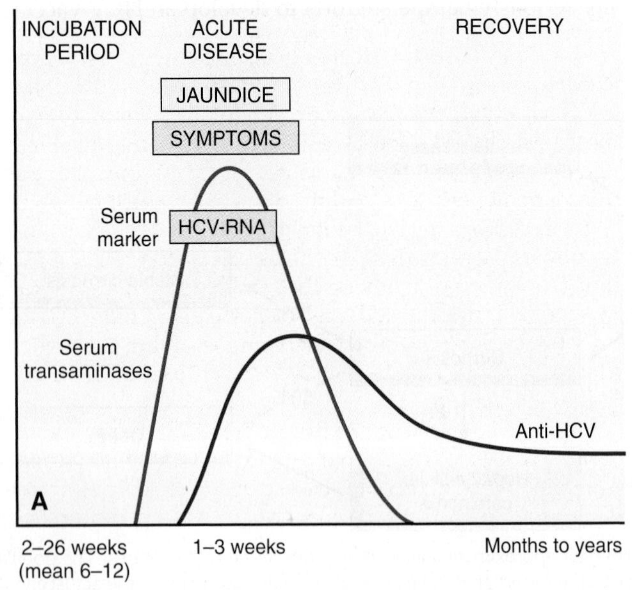

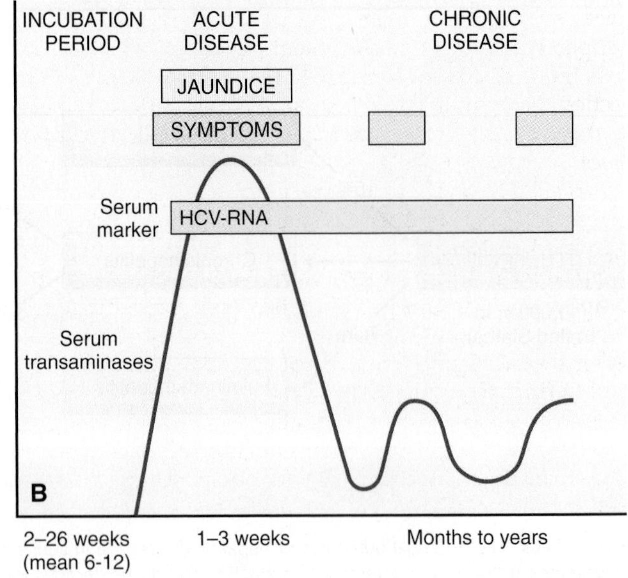

Figure 15–14 Sequence of serologic markers for hepatitis C. **A,** Acute infection with resolution. **B,** Progression to chronic infection. See text for abbreviations.

is best indicated by detection of IgM against both HDV Ag and HBcAg (denoting new infection with HBV). With chronic delta hepatitis arising from HDV superinfection, HBsAg is present in serum, and anti-HDV antibodies (IgM and IgG) persist in low titer for months or longer.

Hepatitis E Virus

HEV hepatitis is an enterically transmitted, waterborne infection occurring primarily beyond the years of infancy. HEV is endemic in India where it is caused by fecal contamination of drinking water. Prevalence rates of anti-HEV IgG antibodies approach 40% in the Indian population. Epidemics have been reported from Asia, sub-Saharan Africa, and Mexico. Sporadic infection seems to be uncommon; it is seen mainly in travelers and accounts for more than 50% of cases of sporadic acute viral hepatitis in India. *In most cases, the disease is self-limited; HEV is not associated with chronic liver disease or persistent viremia. A characteristic feature of the infection is the high mortality rate among pregnant women, approaching 20%.* The average incubation period after exposure is 6 weeks (range, 2 to 8 weeks).

HEV is a nonenveloped, single-stranded RNA hepevirus. A specific antigen, HEV Ag, can be identified in the cytoplasm of hepatocytes during active infection. Virus can be detected in stools, and anti-HEV IgG and IgM antibodies are detectable in serum.

Clinical Features and Outcomes for Viral Hepatitis

A number of clinical syndromes may develop after exposure to hepatitis viruses:

- *Asymptomatic acute infection*: serologic evidence only
- *Acute hepatitis*: anicteric or icteric
- *Fulminant hepatitis*: submassive to massive hepatic necrosis with acute liver failure
- *Chronic hepatitis*: with or without progression to cirrhosis
- *Chronic carrier state*: asymptomatic without apparent disease

Not all of the hepatotropic viruses provoke each of these clinical syndromes (Table 15–6). As already mentioned, viral persistence and development of chronic disease are much more common after HCV infection than for HBV infection. *Because other infectious or noninfectious causes, particularly drugs and toxins, can lead to essentially identical syndromes, serologic studies are critical for the diagnosis of viral hepatitis and identification of virus types.*

Presented next are brief summaries of clinical outcomes with viral hepatitis.

Asymptomatic Infection. Not surprisingly, patients with asymptomatic infection are identified only incidentally on the basis of minimally elevated serum aminotransferases or after the fact by the presence of antiviral antibodies.

Acute Viral Hepatitis. Any one of the hepatotropic viruses can cause acute viral hepatitis. Acute infections are easily detected for HBV infections but are only rarely diagnosed for HCV. Although the following description is based mostly on HBV infections, *acute viral hepatitis, whatever the agent, can be divided into four phases:* (1) *incubation period,* (2) *symptomatic preicteric phase,* (3) *symptomatic icteric phase (with jaundice and scleral icterus),* and (4) *convalescence.*

Peak infectivity, attributed to the presence of circulating infectious viral particles, occurs during the last asymptomatic days of the incubation period and the early days of acute symptoms. The preicteric phase is marked by nonspecific, constitutional symptoms. Malaise is followed in a few days by general fatigability, nausea, and loss of appetite. Weight loss, low-grade fever, headaches, muscle and joint aches, vomiting, and diarrhea are inconstant symptoms. About 10% of patients with acute hepatitis B develop a serum sickness–like syndrome consisting of fever, rash, and arthralgias, attributed to circulating immune complexes. The hepatitis-related origin of all of these symptoms is suggested by elevated serum aminotransferase levels. Physical examination reveals a mildly enlarged, tender liver. In some patients the nonspecific symptoms are more severe, with higher fever, shaking chills, and headache, sometimes accompanied by right upper quadrant pain and tender liver enlargement. Surprisingly, as jaundice appears and these patients enter the icteric phase, other symptoms abate. The jaundice is caused predominantly by conjugated hyperbilirubinemia, which produces dark-colored urine. With hepatocellular damage and consequent defect in bilirubin conjugation, unconjugated hyperbilirubinemia also can occur. The stools may become light-colored, and the retention of bile salts may cause pruritus. An icteric phase is usual in adults (but not children) infected with HAV, present in about half of the cases involving HBV, and absent in most cases of HCV infection. In a few weeks to perhaps several months, the jaundice and most of the other systemic symptoms clear as convalescence begins.

Fulminant Hepatitis. In a very small proportion of patients with acute hepatitis A, B, D, or E, acute liver failure may result from massive hepatic necrosis. (With the exception of immunosuppressed individuals, HCV almost never causes acute liver failure). Cases with a more protracted course of several weeks or months usually are referred to as "subacute hepatic necrosis"; the liver shows both massive necrosis and regenerative hyperplasia. As discussed later, drugs and chemicals also may cause massive hepatic necrosis.

Chronic Hepatitis. *Chronic hepatitis* is defined by the presence of symptomatic, biochemical, or serologic evidence of continuing or relapsing hepatic disease for more than 6 months, with histologically documented inflammation and necrosis. Although the hepatitis viruses are responsible for most cases, there are many causes of chronic hepatitis (described later), such as autoimmunity, drugs and toxins, Wilson disease, and α_1-antitrypsin (AAT) deficiency.

Etiology rather than the histologic pattern is the most important determinant of the probability of developing progressive chronic hepatitis. In particular, HCV is notorious for causing a chronic hepatitis evolving to cirrhosis (Fig. 15–13), regardless of histologic features at the time of initial evaluation.

The clinical features of chronic hepatitis are highly variable and are not predictive of outcome. In some patients, the only signs of chronic disease are persistent elevations of serum aminotransferase levels. The most common overt symptoms are fatigue and, less commonly, malaise, loss of appetite, and bouts of mild jaundice. Physical findings are few, the most common being spider angiomas, palmar erythema, mild hepatomegaly, and hepatic tenderness.

Laboratory studies may reveal prolongation of the prothrombin time and, in some instances, hypergammaglobulinemia, hyperbilirubinemia, and mildly elevated alkaline phosphatase levels. Occasionally in cases of HBV and HCV infection, circulating antibody-antigen complexes produce immune-complex disease in the form of vasculitis (subcutaneous or visceral) (Chapter 9) and glomerulonephritis (Chapter 13). Cryoglobulinemia is found in as many as 50% of patients with hepatitis C.

The clinical course is highly variable. Persons with hepatitis C may experience spontaneous remission or may have indolent disease without progression for years. Conversely, some patients have rapidly progressive disease and develop cirrhosis within a few years. The major causes of death in patients with chronic hepatitis relate to cirrhosis—namely, liver failure, hepatic encephalopathy, massive hematemesis from esophageal varices, and hepatocellular carcinoma.

The Carrier State. A *carrier* is an asymptomatic person who harbors and therefore can transmit an organism. With hepatotropic viruses, carriers are those who

- Harbor one of the viruses but are free of symptoms or of significant histologic hepatitis on liver biopsy
- Have liver damage evident on biopsy (e.g., only mild necroinflammatory activity and scarring that remains in the early, noncirrhotic stages) but are essentially free of symptoms or disability

Both types of carriers constitute reservoirs of infection. HBV infection early in life, particularly through vertical transmission during childbirth, produces a carrier state 90% to 95% of the time. By contrast, only 1% to 10% of HBV infections acquired in adulthood yield a carrier state. Persons with impaired immunity are particularly likely to become carriers. The situation is less clear with HDV, although there is a well-defined low risk of posttransfusion hepatitis D, indicative of a carrier state in conjunction with HBV infection. From 0.2% to 0.6% of the general U.S. population is estimated to carry HCV.

Other Viral Infections of the Liver

- *Epstein-Barr virus (EBV) infection* may cause a mild hepatitis during the acute phase of infectious mononucleosis.
- *Cytomegalovirus infection,* particularly in the newborn or immunocompromised, can cause the typical cytomegalic changes of that virus in almost any cell of the liver, including hepatocytes, cholangiocytes, and endothelial cells.
- *Herpes simplex* may infect hepatocytes in newborns or the immunosuppressed, leading to the appearance of the characteristic cytopathic changes and hepatic necrosis.
- *Yellow fever,* which has been a major and serious cause of hepatitis in tropical countries, causes hepatocyte apoptosis, which can be extensive. The apoptotic hepatocytes are intensely eosinophilic and are referred to as *Councilman bodies* after the pathologist who first described them. Infrequently, in children and immunosuppressed persons, hepatitis may be caused by rubella virus, adenovirus, or enterovirus infections.

SUMMARY
Viral Hepatitis

- In the alphabet of hepatotropic viruses, some easy mnemonic devices may be useful:
  - The vowels (hepatitis A and E) never cause chronic hepatitis, only acute hepatitis.
  - Only the consonants (hepatitis B, C, D) have the potential to cause chronic disease (C for consonant and for chronic).
  - Hepatitis B can be transmitted by blood, birthing, and "bonking" (as they say in the United Kingdom).
  - Hepatitis C is the single virus that is more often chronic than not (almost never detected acutely; 85% or more of patients develop chronic hepatitis, 20% of whom will develop cirrhosis).
  - Hepatitis D, the delta agent, is a defective virus, requiring hepatitis B coinfection for its own capacity to infect and replicate.
  - Hepatitis E is endemic in equatorial regions and frequently epidemic.
- The inflammatory cells in both acute and chronic viral hepatitis are mainly T cells; it is the pattern of injury that is different, not the nature of the infiltrate.
- Biopsy assessment in chronic viral hepatitis is most important for grading and staging of disease, which are used to decide whether a patient undergoes often arduous antiviral treatments.
- Patients with long-standing HBV or HCV infections are at increased risk for the development of hepatocellular carcinomas, even in the absence of established cirrhosis.

Autoimmune Hepatitis

Autoimmune hepatitis is a chronic disorder associated with histologic features that may be indistinguishable from chronic viral hepatitis. This disease may run an indolent or a severe course and typically responds dramatically to immunosuppressive therapy. Salient features include

- Female predominance (70%)
- Absence of serologic evidence of viral infection
- Elevated serum IgG (levels greater than 2.5 g/dL)
- High titers of autoantibodies in 80% of cases
- The presence of other forms of autoimmune diseases, seen in up to 60% of patients, including rheumatoid arthritis, thyroiditis, Sjögren syndrome, and ulcerative colitis

Autoimmune hepatitis can be divided into subtypes on the basis of the autoantibodies produced, but the relevance of this classification to clinical management is unclear. Most patients are found to have circulating antinuclear antibodies, anti–smooth muscle antibodies, liver/kidney microsomal antibody, and/or anti–soluble liver/pancreas antigen. These antibodies can be detected by immunofluorescence or enzyme-linked immunosorbent assays. The main effectors of cell damage in autoimmune hepatitis are believed to be CD4+ helper cells. Autoimmune hepatitis may manifest as mild to severe chronic hepatitis. Response to immunosuppressive therapy usually is dramatic, although a full remission of disease is unusual. The overall risk of cirrhosis, the main cause of death, is 5%.

MORPHOLOGY

Although autoimmune hepatitis shares patterns of injury with acute or chronic viral hepatitis, the time course of histologic progression differs. In viral hepatitis, fibrosis typically follows years or decades of slowly accumulating parenchymal injury, whereas in autoimmune hepatitis, there appears to be an early phase of severe cell injury and inflammation followed by rapid scarring. Of interest, and for unclear reasons, this early wave of hepatocyte damage and necrosis usually is subclinical. Clinical evolution correlates with a limited number of histologic patterns:

- Very severe hepatocyte injury associated with widespread **confluent necrosis**
- Marked inflammation concurrent with advanced scarring
- **Burned-out cirrhosis,** associated with little ongoing cell injury or inflammation. This last category was once the most common finding at diagnosis, but heightened clinical awareness of autoimmune hepatitis specifically has led to increasingly earlier diagnosis. Of note, the mononuclear infiltrate in autoimmune hepatitis frequently has **abundant plasma cells.**

Drug/Toxin-Mediated Injury Mimicking Hepatitis

Many drugs have effects that can mimic the features of acute or chronic viral or autoimmune hepatitis.

- As already described, *acetaminophen toxicity* is one of the leading causes of acute failure leading to liver transplantation. The histologic features may be indistinguishable from those of fulminant acute hepatitis A or hepatitis B.
- *Isoniazid* is an example of an idiosyncratic hepatotoxin that can cause a chronic hepatitis precisely mimicking chronic viral hepatitis that may or may not resolve on removal of the instigating agent.
- Other drugs (e.g., minocyclin and nitrofurantoin) or toxins can induce an autoimmune hepatitis with all of the clinical and histologic features typical of that disease: autoantibodies, elevated IgG, and plasma cell–rich hepatic infiltrates. Such cases sometimes respond to treatment with immunosuppression but occasionally do not, progressing to cirrhosis despite withdrawal of the inciting agent.

ALCOHOLIC AND NONALCOHOLIC FATTY LIVER DISEASE

Alcohol is a well-known cause of fatty liver disease in adults, and can manifest histologically as steatosis, steatohepatitis, and cirrhosis. In recent years it has become evident that another entity, the so-called nonalcoholic fatty liver disease (NAFLD), can mimic the entire spectrum of hepatic changes typically associated with alcohol abuse. NAFLD (described in more detail later) is associated with insulin resistance, obesity, diabetes mellitus, hypertension, and dyslipidemias, collectively called the metabolic syndrome. Since the morphologic changes of alcoholic and nonalcoholic fatty liver disease are indistinguishable, they are described together, followed by the distinctive clinical features of each of the entities.

MORPHOLOGY

Three categories of liver alterations are observed in fatty liver disease. They can be present in any combination: steatosis (fatty change), hepatitis (alcoholic or steatohepatitis), and fibrosis.

Hepatocellular Steatosis. Hepatocellular fat accumulation typically begins in centrilobular hepatocytes. The lipid droplets range from small (microvesicular) to large (macrovesicular), the largest filling and expanding the cell and displacing the nucleus. As steatosis becomes more extensive, the lipid accumulation spreads outward from the central vein to hepatocytes in the midlobule and then the periportal regions (Fig. 15–15). Macroscopically, the fatty liver with widespread steatosis is large (weighing 4 to 6 kg or more), soft, yellow, and greasy.

Steatohepatitis. These changes typically are more pronounced with alcohol use than in NAFLD, but can be seen with variable degrees of prominence in fatty liver disease of any cause:

- **Hepatocyte ballooning.** Single or scattered foci of cells undergo swelling and necrosis; as with steatosis, these features are most prominent in the centrilobular regions.
- **Mallory-Denk bodies.** These consist of tangled skeins of intermediate filaments (including ubiquitinated keratins 8 and 18) and are visible as eosinophilic cytoplasmic inclusions in degenerating hepatocytes (Fig. 15–16).
- **Neutrophil infiltration.** Predominantly neutrophilic infiltration may permeate the lobule and accumulate around degenerating hepatocytes, particularly those containing Mallory-Denk bodies. Lymphocytes and macrophages also may be seen in portal tracts or parenchyma (Fig. 15–16, *A* and *B*).

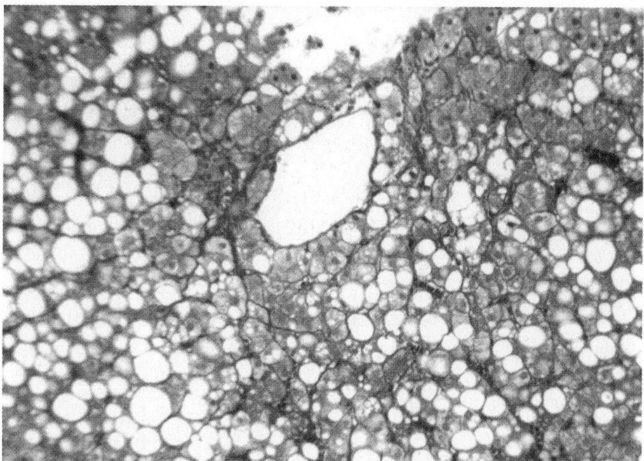

Figure 15–15 Fatty liver disease. Macrovesicular steatosis is most prominent around the central vein and extends outward to the portal tracts with increasing severity. The intracytoplasmic fat is seen as clear vacuoles. Some fibrosis (stained *blue*) is present in a characteristic perisinusoidal "chicken wire fence" pattern. (Masson trichrome stain.) *(Courtesy of Dr. Elizabeth Brunt, Washington University in St. Louis, St. Louis, Missouri.)*

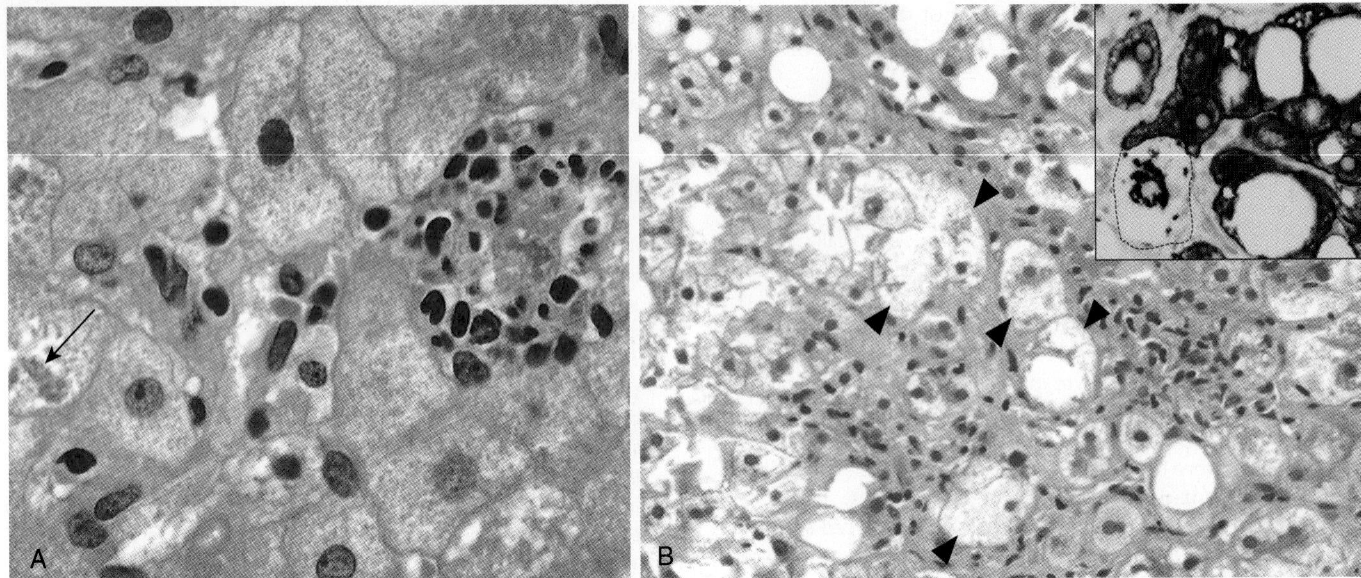

Figure 15-16 A, Alcoholic hepatitis with clustered inflammatory cells marking the site of a necrotic hepatocyte. A Mallory-Denk body is present in another hepatocyte (*arrow*). **B,** Steatohepatitis with many ballooned hepatocytes (*arrowheads*) containing prominent Mallory-Denk bodies; clusters of inflammatory cells are also seen; *inset* shows immunostaining for keratins 8 and 18 (*brown*), with most hepatocytes, including those with fat vacuoles, showing normal cytoplasmic staining, but in the ballooned cell (*dotted line*), the keratins are collapsed into the Mallory-Denk body, leaving the cytoplasm "empty."

(Courtesy of Dr. Elizabeth Brunt, Washington University in St. Louis, St. Louis, Missouri.)

Steatohepatitis with fibrosis. Fatty liver disease of all kinds has a distinctive pattern of scarring. Like the other changes, fibrosis appears first in the centrilobular region as **central vein sclerosis.** Perisinusoidal scar appears next in the space of Disse of the centrilobular region and then spreads outward, encircling individual or small clusters of hepatocytes in a **chicken wire fence pattern** (Fig. 15–15). These tendrils of fibrosis eventually link to portal tracts and then begin to condense to create **central-portal fibrous septa.** As these become more prominent, the liver takes on a nodular, cirrhotic appearance. Because in most cases of fatty liver disease the underlying cause persists, the continual subdivision of established nodules by new, perisinusoidal scarring leads to a classic **micronodular** or **Laennec cirrhosis.** Early in the course, the liver is yellow-tan, fatty, and enlarged. However, with persistent damage, over the course of years the liver is transformed into a brown, shrunken, nonfatty organ composed of cirrhotic nodules that are usually less than 0.3 cm in diameter—smaller than is typical for most chronic viral hepatitis (Fig. 15–17). The end-stage cirrhotic liver may enter into a "burned-out" phase devoid of fatty change and other typical features (Fig. 15–18). A majority of cases of **cryptogenic cirrhosis,** without clear etiology, are now recognized as "burned-out" NASH.

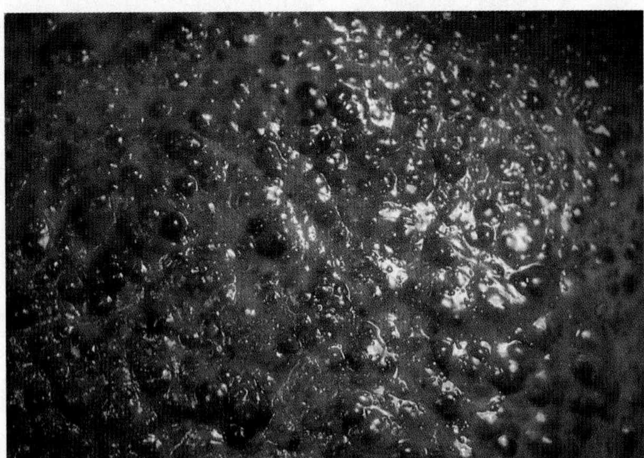

Figure 15–17 Alcoholic cirrhosis. The characteristic diffuse nodularity of the surface is induced by the underlying fibrous scarring. The average nodule size is 3 mm in this close-up view. The *greenish* tint is caused by bile stasis.

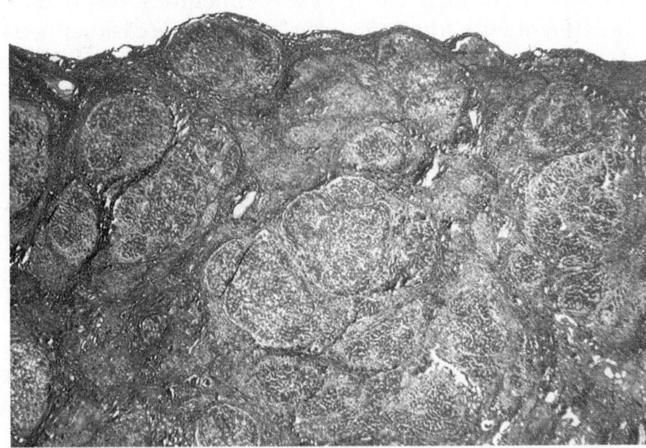

Figure 15–18 Steatohepatitis leading to cirrhosis. Small nodules are entrapped in *blue*-staining fibrous tissue; fatty accumulation is no longer seen in this "burned-out" stage. (Masson trichrome stain.)

Clinical Features

70% to 80% of individuals with gallstones remain asymptomatic throughout life, with the risk of symptoms diminishing over time. In the unfortunate minority, however, the symptoms are striking. There is usually pain, often excruciating, which typically localizes to the right upper quadrant or epigastric region and can be constant or, less commonly, spasmodic. Such "biliary" pain is caused by gallbladder or biliary tree obstruction, or by inflammation of the gallbladder itself. More severe complications include empyema, perforation, fistulas, inflammation of the biliary tree, and obstructive cholestasis or pancreatitis. The larger the calculi, the less likely they are to enter the cystic or common ducts to produce obstruction; it is the very small stones, or "gravel," that are more dangerous. Occasionally a large stone may erode directly into an adjacent loop of small bowel, generating intestinal obstruction (*gallstone ileus*).

Cholecystitis

Inflammation of the gallbladder may be acute, chronic, or acute superimposed on chronic, and almost always occurs in association with gallstones. In the United States, cholecystitis is one of the most common indications for abdominal surgery. Its epidemiologic distribution closely parallels that of gallstones.

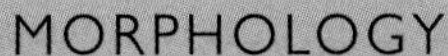

MORPHOLOGY

In **acute cholecystitis,** the gallbladder usually is enlarged and tense, and it assumes a bright red or blotchy, violaceous color, the latter imparted by subserosal hemorrhages. The serosa frequently is covered by a fibrinous, or in severe cases, fibrinopurulent exudate. In 90% of cases, stones are present, often obstructing the neck of the gallbladder or the cystic duct. The gallbladder lumen is filled with cloudy or turbid bile that may contain fibrin, blood, and frank pus. When the contained exudate is mostly pus, the condition is referred to as **empyema of the gallbladder.** In mild cases the gallbladder wall is thickened, edematous, and hyperemic. In more severe cases the gallbladder is transformed into a green-black necrotic organ—a condition termed **gangrenous cholecystitis.** On histologic examination, the inflammatory reactions are not distinctive and consist of the usual patterns of acute inflammation (i.e., edema, leukocytic infiltration, vascular congestion, frank abscess formation, or gangrenous necrosis).

The morphologic changes in **chronic cholecystitis** are extremely variable and sometimes subtle. The mere presence of stones within the gallbladder, even in the absence of acute inflammation, often is taken as sufficient justification for the diagnosis. The gallbladder may be contracted, of normal size, or enlarged. Mucosal ulcerations are infrequent; the submucosa and subserosa often are thickened from fibrosis. In the absence of superimposed acute cholecystitis, mural lymphocytes are the only signs of inflammation.

Acute Calculous Cholecystitis

Acute inflammation of a gallbladder that contains stones is termed *acute calculous cholecystitis* and is precipitated by obstruction of the gallbladder neck or cystic duct. *It is the most common major complication of gallstones and the most common reason for emergency cholecystectomy.* Manifestations of obstruction may appear with remarkable suddenness and constitute a surgical emergency. In some cases, however, symptoms may be mild and resolve without medical intervention.

Acute calculous cholecystitis is initially the result of chemical irritation and inflammation of the gallbladder wall in the setting of obstruction to bile outflow. The action of phospholipases derived from the mucosa hydrolyzes biliary lecithin to lysolecithin, which is toxic to the mucosa. The normally protective glycoprotein mucous layer is disrupted, exposing the mucosal epithelium to the direct detergent action of bile salts. Prostaglandins released within the wall of the distended gallbladder contribute to mucosal and mural inflammation. Distention and increased intraluminal pressure also may compromise blood flow to the mucosa. These events occur in the absence of bacterial infection; only later may bacterial contamination develop.

Acute Acalculous Cholecystitis

Between 5% and 12% of gallbladders removed for acute cholecystitis contain no gallstones. Most cases occur in seriously ill patients. Some of the most common predisposing insults are

- Major, nonbiliary surgery
- Severe trauma (e.g., from motor vehicle crashes)
- Severe burns
- Sepsis

Other contributing factors include dehydration, gallbladder stasis and sludging, vascular compromise, and, ultimately, bacterial contamination.

Chronic Cholecystitis

Chronic cholecystitis may be the sequel to repeated bouts of acute cholecystitis, but in most instances it develops without any history of acute attacks. Like acute cholecystitis it is almost always associated with gallstones. However, gallstones do not seem to have a direct role in the initiation of inflammation or the development of pain, because chronic acalculous cholecystitis causes symptoms and morphologic alterations similar to those seen in the calculous form. Rather, supersaturation of bile predisposes the patient to both chronic inflammation and, in most instances, stone formation. Microorganisms, usually *E. coli* and enterococci, can be cultured from the bile in only about one third of cases. Unlike acute calculous cholecystitis, stone obstruction of gallbladder outflow in chronic cholecystitis is not a requisite. Most gallbladders removed at elective surgery for gallstones show features of chronic cholecystitis, making it likely that biliary symptoms emerge after long-term coexistence of gallstones and low-grade inflammation.

Clinical Features

Acute calculous cholecystitis presents with biliary pain that lasts for more than 6 hours. The pain is severe, usually steady, upper abdominal in location, and often radiates to the right shoulder. Fever, nausea, leukocytosis, and prostration are classic; the presence of conjugated hyperbilirubinemia suggests obstruction of the common bile duct. The right subcostal region is markedly tender and rigid as a result of spasm of the abdominal muscles; occasionally a tender, distended gallbladder can be palpated. Mild attacks usually subside spontaneously over 1 to 10 days; however, recurrence is common. Approximately 25% of symptomatic patients are sufficiently ill to require surgical intervention.

Symptoms arising from *acute acalculous cholecystitis* usually are obscured by the generally severe clinical condition of the patient. The diagnosis therefore rests on keeping this possibility in mind.

Chronic cholecystitis does not have the striking manifestations of the acute forms and is usually characterized by recurrent attacks of steady epigastric or right upper quadrant pain. Nausea, vomiting, and intolerance for fatty foods are frequent accompaniments.

The diagnosis of acute cholecystitis usually is based on the detection of gallstones by ultrasonography, typically accompanied by evidence of a thickened gallbladder wall. Chronic cholecystitis, on the other hand, is a pathologic diagnosis based on the examination of the resected gallbladder. Attention to this disorder is important because of the potential for the following serious complications:

- Bacterial superinfection with cholangitis or sepsis
- Gallbladder perforation and local abscess formation
- Gallbladder rupture with diffuse peritonitis
- Biliary enteric (cholecystenteric) fistula, with drainage of bile into adjacent organs, entry of air and bacteria into the biliary tree, and potentially gallstone-induced intestinal obstruction (ileus)
- Aggravation of preexisting medical illness, with cardiac, pulmonary, renal, or liver decompensation

DISORDERS OF EXTRAHEPATIC BILE DUCTS

Choledocholithiasis and Cholangitis

Choledocholithiasis and cholangitis are considered together because these conditions frequently go hand in hand. *Choledocholithiasis* is the presence of stones within the biliary tree. In Western nations, almost all stones are derived from the gallbladder; in Asia, there is a much higher incidence of primary ductal and intrahepatic, usually pigmented, stone formation. Choledocholithiasis may not immediately obstruct major bile ducts; asymptomatic stones are found in about 10% of patients at the time of surgical cholecystectomy. Symptoms may develop because of (1) biliary obstruction, (2) cholangitis, (3) hepatic abscess, (4) chronic liver disease with secondary biliary cirrhosis, or (5) acute calculous cholecystitis.

Cholangitis is the term used for acute inflammation of the wall of bile ducts, almost always caused by bacterial infection of the normally sterile lumen. It can result from any lesion obstructing bile flow, most commonly choledocholithiasis, and also from surgery involving the biliary tree. Other causes include tumors, indwelling stents or catheters, acute pancreatitis, and benign strictures. Bacteria most likely enter the biliary tract through the sphincter of Oddi, rather than by the hematogenous route. *Ascending cholangitis* refers to the propensity of bacteria, once within the biliary tree, to infect intrahepatic biliary ducts. The usual pathogens are *E. coli, Klebsiella, Enterococci, Clostridium,* and *Bacteroides*. Two or more organisms are found in half of the cases. In some world populations, parasitic cholangitis is a significant problem. Causative organisms include *Fasciola hepatica* or schistosomiasis in Latin America and the Near East, *Clonorchis sinensis* or *Opisthorchis viverrini* in the Far East, and cryptosporidiosis in persons with acquired immunodeficiency syndrome.

Bacterial cholangitis usually produces fever, chills, abdominal pain, and jaundice. The most severe form of cholangitis is suppurative cholangitis, in which purulent bile fills and distends bile ducts, with an attendant risk of liver abscess formation. Because sepsis rather than cholestasis is the predominant risk in cholangitic patients, prompt diagnosis and intervention are imperative.

Secondary Biliary Cirrhosis

Prolonged obstruction of the extrahepatic biliary tree results in profound damage to the liver itself. The most common cause of obstruction is extrahepatic cholelithiasis. Other obstructive conditions include biliary atresia (discussed later on), malignancies of the biliary tree and head of the pancreas, and strictures resulting from previous surgical procedures. The initial morphologic features of cholestasis were described earlier and are entirely reversible with correction of the obstruction. However, secondary inflammation resulting from biliary obstruction initiates periportal fibrogenesis, which eventually leads to scarring and nodule formation, generating secondary biliary cirrhosis.

Biliary Atresia

Biliary atresia is a major cause of neonatal cholestasis, accounting for one third of the cases of cholestasis in infants and occurring in approximately 1 in 10,000 live births. *Biliary atresia is defined as a complete obstruction of bile flow caused by destruction or absence of all or part of the extrahepatic bile ducts.* It is the most frequent cause of death from liver disease in early childhood and accounts for more than half of the referrals of children for liver transplantation.

The salient features of biliary atresia include

- Inflammation and fibrosing stricture of the hepatic or common bile ducts
- Inflammation of major intrahepatic bile ducts, with progressive destruction of the intrahepatic biliary tree
- Florid features of biliary obstruction on liver biopsy (i.e., ductular reaction, portal tract edema and fibrosis, and parenchymal cholestasis)
- Periportal fibrosis and cirrhosis within 3 to 6 months of birth

Clinical Course

Infants with biliary atresia present with neonatal cholestasis; there is a slight female predominance. Affected infants have normal birth weights and postnatal weight gain. Stools become acholic as the disease evolves. Laboratory findings do not distinguish between biliary atresia and intrahepatic cholestasis, but a liver biopsy provides evidence of bile duct obstruction in 90% of cases of biliary atresia. Liver transplantation is the definitive treatment. Without surgical intervention, death usually occurs within 2 years of birth.

SUMMARY

Diseases of the Gallbladder and Extrahepatic Bile Ducts

- Gallbladder diseases include cholelithiasis and acute and chronic cholecystitis.
- Gallstone formation is a common condition in Western countries. The great majority of the gallstones are cholesterol stones. Pigmented stones containing bilirubin and calcium are most common in Asian countries.
- Risk factors for the development of cholesterol stones are advancing age, female gender, estrogen use, obesity, and heredity.
- Cholecystitis almost always occurs in association with cholelithiasis, although in about 10% of cases it occurs in the absence of gallstones.
- Acute calculous cholecystitis is the most common reason for emergency cholecystectomy.
- Obstructive lesions of the extrahepatic bile ducts in adults can give rise to ascending infection (cholangitis) and secondary biliary cirrhosis.
- Infants born with congenital biliary atresia present with neonatal cholestasis and require liver transplantation for cure.

TUMORS

Carcinoma of the Gallbladder

Although uncommon, carcinoma of the gallbladder is the most frequent malignant tumor of the biliary tract. It is 2 to 6 times more common in women and occurs most frequently in the seventh decade of life. Carcinoma of the gallbladder is more frequent in the populations of Mexico and Chile, presumably due to the higher incidence of gallstone disease in these regions. In the United States the incidence is highest in Hispanics and Native Americans. Only rarely is it discovered at a resectable stage, and the mean 5-year survival rate is a dismal 5%. Gallstones are present in 60% to 90% of cases. In Asia, where pyogenic and parasitic diseases of the biliary tree are more common, gallstones are less important. Presumably, gallbladders containing stones or infectious agents develop cancer as a result of recurrent trauma and chronic inflammation. The role of carcinogenic derivatives of bile acids is unclear.

MORPHOLOGY

Cancers of the gallbladder may exhibit **exophytic** or **infiltrating** growth patterns. The infiltrating pattern is more common and usually appears as a poorly defined area of diffuse thickening and induration of the gallbladder wall that may cover several square centimeters or involve the entire gallbladder. These tumors are scirrhous and very firm. The exophytic pattern grows into the lumen as an irregular, cauliflower-like mass but at the same time also invades the underlying wall (Fig. 15–37). **Most are adenocarcinomas,** which may be papillary or poorly differentiated. About 5% are squamous cell carcinomas or demonstrate adenosquamous differentiation, and rare neuroendocrine tumors also occur. By the time gallbladder cancers are discovered, most have invaded the liver or have spread to the bile ducts or to the portal hepatic lymph nodes.

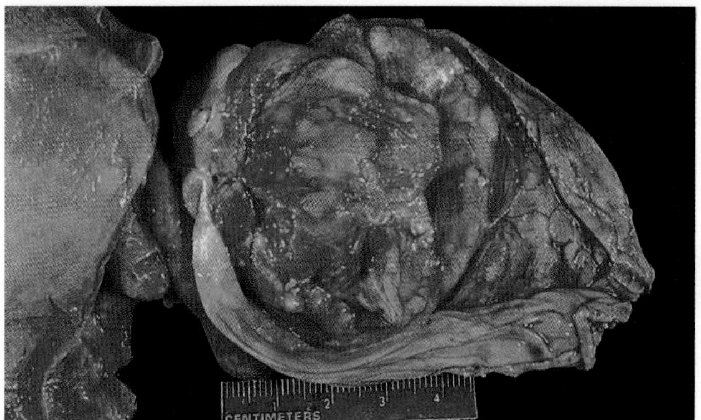

Figure 15–37 Adenocarcinoma of the gallbladder. The opened gallbladder contains a large, exophytic tumor that virtually fills the lumen.

Clinical Features

Preoperative diagnosis of carcinoma of the gallbladder is the exception, being reported in less than 20% of patients. Onset of symptoms is insidious, and presenting manifestations typically are indistinguishable from those associated with cholelithiasis: abdominal pain, jaundice, anorexia, and nausea and vomiting. The fortunate person develops early obstruction and acute cholecystitis or undergoes cholecystectomy for coexistent symptomatic gallstones before the tumor spreads to other sites.

Cholangiocarcinomas

Cholangiocarcinomas are adenocarcinomas that arise from cholangiocytes lining the intrahepatic and extrahepatic biliary ducts. Extrahepatic cholangiocarcinomas constitute approximately two thirds of these tumors and may develop at the hilum (known as Klatskin tumors) or more distally in the biliary tree. Cholangiocarcinomas occur mostly in persons of 50 to 70 years of age. Because both intra- and extrahepatic cholangiocarcinomas generally are asymptomatic until they reach an advanced stage, the prognosis is poor, and most patients have unresectable tumors. Risk factors include primary sclerosing cholangitis, fibropolycystic diseases of the biliary tree, and infestation by *Clonorchis sinensis* or *Opisthorchis viverrini*.

All risk factors for cholangiocarcinomas cause chronic cholestasis and inflammation, which presumably promote the occurrence of somatic mutations in cholangiocytes.

Several consistent genetic changes have been noted in these tumors, including activating mutations in the *KRAS* and *BRAF* oncogenes and loss-of-function mutations in the *TP53* tumor suppressor gene.

MORPHOLOGY

Cholangiocarcinomas are typical adenocarcinomas with more or less well-formed glands often accompanied by abundant fibrous stroma (desmoplasia) yielding a firm, gritty consistency (Fig. 15–38). Bile pigment and hyaline inclusions are absent from the tumor cells, while intracellular mucin may be prominent.

Because partial or complete obstruction of bile ducts rapidly leads to jaundice, extrahepatic biliary tumors tend to be relatively small at the time of diagnosis, whereas intrahepatic tumors may cause symptoms only when much of the liver is replaced by tumor. Cholangiocarcinomas may spread to extrahepatic sites such as regional lymph nodes, lungs, bones, and adrenal glands. Invasion along peribiliary nerves is another route of spread to the abdomen. Cholangiocarcinoma has a greater propensity for extrahepatic spread than does hepatocellular carcinoma.

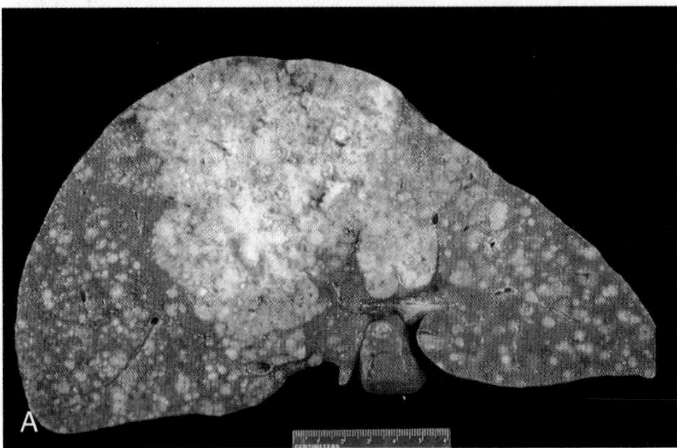

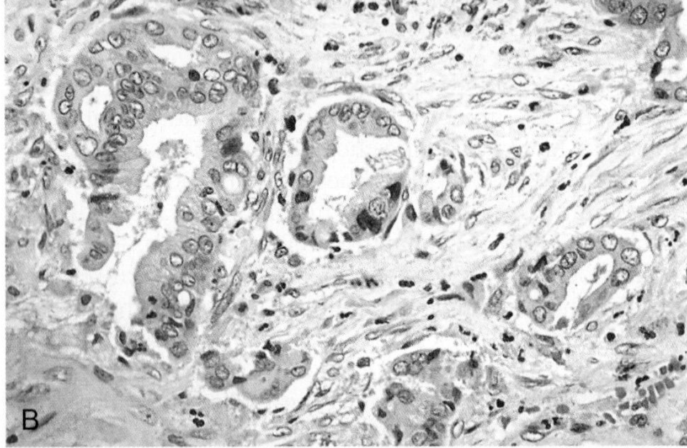

Figure 15–38 Cholangiocarcinoma. **A,** Massive neoplasm in the right lobe and widespread intrahepatic metastases. **B,** Tumor cells forming glandular structures surrounded by dense sclerotic stroma.

Clinical Features

Intrahepatic cholangiocarcinoma may be manifested by the presence of a liver mass and nonspecific signs and symptoms such as weight loss, pain, anorexia, and ascites. Symptoms and signs arising from *extrahepatic* cholangiocarcinomas (jaundice, acholic stools, nausea and vomiting, and weight loss) result from biliary obstruction. Commonly associated findings include elevated serum levels of alkaline phosphatase and aminotransferases. Surgical resection is the only treatment available, but in a large majority of cases is not curative. Transplantation is contraindicated. Mean survival times range from 6 to 18 months, regardless of whether aggressive resection or palliative surgery is performed.

BIBLIOGRAPHY

Beier JI, Arteel GE, McClain CJ: Advances in alcoholic liver disease. Curr Gastroenterol Rep 13:56, 2011.

Bernal W, Auzinger G, Dhawan A, et al: Acute liver failure. Lancet 376:190, 2010.

Bioulac-Sage P, Balabaud C, Zucman-Rossi J: Focal nodular hyperplasia, hepatocellular adenomas: past, present, future. Gastroenterol Clin Biol 34:355, 2010. *[From the pioneers of the new, molecular diagnostics of benign liver tumors.]*

Brunt EM: Pathology of nonalcoholic fatty liver disease. Nat Rev Gastroenterol Hepatol 7:195, 2010. *[As authoritative as one can be on the topic.]*

Chun LJ, Tong MJ, Busuttil RW, et al: Acetaminophen hepatotoxicity and acute liver failure. J Clin Gastroenterol 43:342, 2009. *[About the most common cause of acute liver failure leading to transplantation.]*

Czaja AJ, Manns MP: Advances in the diagnosis, pathogenesis, and management of autoimmune hepatitis. Gastroenterology 139:58, 2010.

Friedman SL: Mechanisms of hepatic fibrogenesis. Gastroenterology 134:1655, 2008. *[As authoritative as one can be on the topic.]*

Gatto M, Alvaro D: New insights on cholangiocarcinoma. World J Gastrointest Oncol 2:136, 2010.

Gouw ASW, Clouston AD, Theise ND: Ductular reactions in human livers: diversity at the interface. Hepatology 54:1853, 2011. *[A review of ductular reactions, the stem cell response of human livers in all liver diseases, that are related to mechanisms of regeneration, fibrogenesis and neoplasia.]*

Hirschfield GM, Heathcote EJ, Gershwin ME: Pathogenesis of cholestatic liver disease and therapeutic approaches. Gastroenterology 139:1481, 2010.

International Consensus Group for Hepatocellular Neoplasia: Pathologic diagnosis of early hepatocellular carcinoma. Hepatology 49:658, 2009. *[A good example of how change comes to medicine, individual efforts combining, over years, to achieve a new consensus.]*

Joyce MA, Tyrrell DL: The cell biology of hepatitis C virus. Microbes Infect 12:263, 2010.

Lai M, Liaw YF: Chronic hepatitis B: past, present, and future. Clin Liver Dis 14:531, 2010.

Lagana SM, Moreira RK, Lefkowitch JH: Hepatic granulomas: pathogenesis and differential diagnosis. Clin Liver Dis 14:605, 2010.

Paumgartner G: Biliary physiology and disease: reflections of a physician-scientist. Hepatology 51:1095, 2010. *[How bench top work comes to exert an impact on clinical medicine, sometimes, slowly, over decades.]*

Perrault M, Pécheur EI: The hepatitis C virus and its hepatic environment: a toxic but finely tuned partnership. Biochem J 423:303, 2009.

Pietrangelo A: Hereditary hemochromatosis: pathogenesis, diagnosis, and treatment. Gastroenterology 139:393, 2010.

Poupon R: Primary biliary cirrhosis: a 2010 update. J Hepatol 52:745, 2010.

Schilsky ML: Wilson disease: current status and the future. Biochimie 91:1278, 2009.

See Targeted Therapy available online at
studentconsult.com

Pancreas

CHAPTER CONTENTS

The pancreas has critical endocrine functions, and the exocrine portion of the pancreas is a major source of potent enzymes that are essential for digestion. Diseases affecting the pancreas can be the source of significant morbidity and mortality. Unfortunately, despite its physiologic importance, the retroperitoneal location of the pancreas and the generally vague nature of signs and symptoms associated with its injury or dysfunction allow many pancreatic diseases to progress undiagnosed for extended periods of time; thus, recognition of pancreatic disorders often requires a high degree of suspicion.

The pancreas is a transversely oriented retroperitoneal organ extending from the so-called C loop of the duodenum to the hilum of the spleen. Although the pancreas does not have well-defined anatomic subdivisions, adjacent vessels and ligaments serve to demarcate the organ into a head, body, and tail.

The pancreas gets its name from the Greek *pankreas,* meaning "all flesh," and is a complex lobulated organ with distinct endocrine and exocrine elements. The endocrine portion constitutes only 1% to 2% of the pancreas and is composed of about 1 million cell clusters, the islets of Langerhans; these cells secrete insulin, glucagon, and somatostatin. The most significant disorders of the *endocrine pancreas* are diabetes mellitus and neoplasms; these are described in detail in Chapter 19 and are not discussed further here.

The *exocrine pancreas* is composed of *acinar cells* that produce the digestive enzymes, and the ductules and ducts that convey them to the duodenum. The acinar cells are responsible for the synthesis of digestive enzymes, which are mostly made as inactive pro-enzymes that are stored in *zymogen granules.* When acinar cells are stimulated to secrete, the granules fuse with the apical plasma membrane and release their contents into the central acinar lumen. These secretions are transported to the duodenum through a series of anastomosing ducts.

The epithelial cells lining the ducts also are active participants in pancreatic secretion: The cuboidal cells lining the smaller ductules secrete bicarbonate-rich fluid, while the columnar cells lining the larger ducts produce mucin. The epithelial cells of the larger ducts also express the *cystic fibrosis transmembrane conductance regulator* (CFTR); aberrant function of this membrane protein affects the viscosity of the pancreatic secretions and has a fundamental role in the pathophysiology of pancreatic disease in persons with cystic fibrosis (Chapter 6).

As described later, autodigestion of the pancreas (e.g., in pancreatitis) can be a catastrophic event. A number of "fail-safe" mechanisms have evolved to minimize the risk of occurrence of this phenomenon:

- A majority of pancreatic enzymes are synthesized as inactive proenzymes and sequestered in membrane-bound zymogen granules, as mentioned above.
- Activation of proenzymes requires conversion of trypsinogen to trypsin by duodenal enteropeptidase (also called enterokinase).
- Trypsin inhibitors (e.g., SPINK1, also known as pancreatic secretory trypsin inhibitor) also are secreted by acinar and ductal cells.
- Trypsin cleaves and inactivates itself, a negative feedback mechanism that normally puts a limit on local levels of activated trypsin.
- Acinar cells are remarkably resistant to the action of activated enzymes such as trypsin, chymotrypsin, and phospholipase A_2.

Diseases of the exocrine pancreas include cystic fibrosis, congenital anomalies, acute and chronic pancreatitis, and neoplasms. Cystic fibrosis is discussed in detail in Chapter 6; the other pathologic processes are discussed in the remainder of this chapter.

The contributions of those who authored this chapter in previous editions of this book are gratefully acknowledged.

ONGENITAL ANOMALIES

Pancreatic development is a complex process involving fusion of dorsal and ventral primordia; subtle deviations in this process frequently give rise to congenital variations in pancreatic anatomy. While most of these do not cause disease per se, variants (especially in ductal anatomy) can present challenges to the endoscopist and the surgeon. For example, failure to recognize idiosyncratic anatomy could result in inadvertent severing of a pancreatic duct during surgery, resulting in pancreatitis.

Agenesis

Very rarely, the pancreas may be totally absent, a condition usually (but not invariably) associated with additional severe malformations that are incompatible with life. *Pancreatic duodenal homeobox 1* is a homeodomain transcription factor critical for normal pancreatic development, and mutations of the *PDX1* gene, located on chromosomal locus 13q12.1, have been associated with pancreatic agenesis.

Pancreas Divisum

Pancreas divisum is the most common clinically significant congenital pancreatic anomaly, with an incidence of 3% to 10% in autopsy series. It occurs when the duct systems of the fetal pancreatic primordia fail to fuse. As a result, the main pancreatic duct drains only a small portion of the head of the gland, while the bulk of the pancreas (from the dorsal pancreatic primordium) drains through the minor sphincter, which has a narrow opening. As a result of this defect in drainage, persons with pancreas divisum have elevated intraductal pressures throughout most of the pancreas and are at increased risk for chronic pancreatitis.

Annular Pancreas

Annular pancreas is a relatively uncommon variant of pancreatic fusion in which a ring of pancreatic tissue completely encircles the duodenum. It can manifest with signs and symptoms of duodenal obstruction such as gastric distention and vomiting.

Ectopic Pancreas

Aberrantly situated, or *ectopic,* pancreatic tissue occurs in about 2% of the population; favored sites are the stomach and duodenum, followed by the jejunum, Meckel diverticulum, and ileum. These embryologic rests typically are small (ranging from millimeters to centimeters in diameter) and are located in the submucosa; they are composed of normal pancreatic acini with occasional islets. Though usually incidental and asymptomatic, ectopic pancreas can cause pain from localized inflammation, or—rarely—can cause mucosal bleeding. Approximately 2% of pancreatic neuroendocrine tumors (Chapter 19) arise in ectopic pancreatic tissue.

Congenital Cysts

Congenital cysts probably result from anomalous development of the pancreatic ducts. In *polycystic disease,* the kidneys, liver, and pancreas can all contain cysts (Chapter 13). Congenital cysts generally are unilocular and range from microscopic to 5 cm in diameter. They are lined by either uniform cuboidal or flattened epithelium and are enclosed in a thin, fibrous capsule. These benign cysts contain clear serous fluid—an important point of distinction from pancreatic cystic neoplasms, which often are mucinous (see further on).

PANCREATITIS

Inflammatory disorders of the pancreas range in severity from mild, self-limited disease to life-threatening, widely destructive process, and are accordingly associated with deficits that may be trivial and transient or serious and permanent. In *acute pancreatitis,* function can return to normal if the underlying cause of inflammation is removed. By contrast, *chronic pancreatitis* is defined by irreversible destruction of exocrine pancreatic parenchyma.

Acute Pancreatitis

Acute pancreatitis is a reversible inflammatory disorder that varies in severity, ranging from focal edema and fat necrosis to widespread hemorrhagic parenchymal necrosis. Acute pancreatitis is relatively common, with an annual incidence of 10 to 20 per 100,000 people in the Western world. *Approximately 80% of cases are attributable to either biliary tract disease or alcoholism* (Table 16–1). Roughly 5% of patients with gallstones develop acute pancreatitis, and gallstones are implicated in 35% to 60% of cases overall.

Table 16–1 Etiologic Factors in Acute Pancreatitis

Metabolic
Alcoholism*
Hyperlipoproteinemia
Hypercalcemia
Drugs (e.g., azathioprine)
Genetic
Mutations in the cationic trypsinogen (*PRSS1*) and trypsin inhibitor (*SPINK1*) genes
Mechanical
Gallstones*
Trauma
Iatrogenic injury
Perioperative injury
Endoscopic procedures with dye injection
Vascular
Shock
Atheroembolism
Polyarteritis nodosa
Infectious
Mumps
Coxsackievirus

*Most common causes in the United States.

Excessive alcohol intake has been reported as a cause of acute pancreatitis at variable rates, from 65% of cases in the United States to 5% or less in the United Kingdom.

Other causes of acute pancreatitis include

- Non–gallstone-related obstruction of the pancreatic ducts (e.g., due to periampullary neoplasms such as pancreatic cancer, pancreas divisum, biliary "sludge," or parasites, particularly *Ascaris lumbricoides* and *Clonorchis sinensis*)
- Medications including anticonvulsants, cancer chemotherapeutic agents, thiazide diuretics, estrogens, and more than 85 others in clinical use
- Infections with mumps virus or coxsackievirus
- Metabolic disorders, including hypertriglyceridemia, hyperparathyroidism, and other hypercalcemic states
- Ischemia due to vascular thrombosis, embolism, vasculitis, or shock
- Trauma, both blunt force and iatrogenic during surgery or endoscopy
- Inherited mutations in genes encoding pancreatic enzymes or their inhibitors (e.g., *SPINK1*). For example, *hereditary pancreatitis* is an autosomal dominant disease with 80% penetrance that is characterized by recurrent attacks of severe pancreatitis, usually beginning in childhood. It is caused by mutations in the gene *PRSS1*, which encodes trypsinogen, the proenzyme of pancreatic trypsin. The pathogenic mutations alter the site through which trypsin cleaves and inactivates itself, abrogating an important negative feedback mechanism. This defect leads not only to the hyperactivation of trypsin, but also to the hyperactivation of many other digestive enzymes that require trypsin cleavage for their activation. As a result of this unbridled protease activity, the pancreas is prone to autodigestion and injury.

Of note, 10% to 20% of cases of acute pancreatitis have no identifiable cause (*idiopathic pancreatitis*), although a growing body of evidence suggests that many may have an underlying genetic basis.

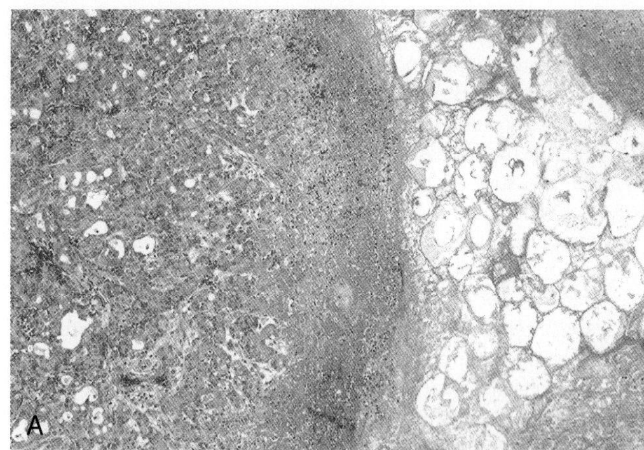

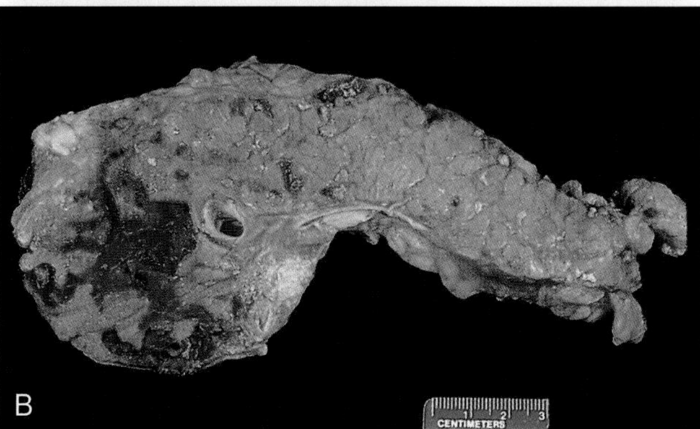

Figure 16–1 Acute pancreatitis. **A,** The microscopic field shows a region of fat necrosis (*right*) and focal pancreatic parenchymal necrosis (*center*). **B,** The pancreas has been sectioned longitudinally to reveal dark areas of hemorrhage in the pancreatic substance and a focal area of pale fat necrosis in the peripancreatic fat (*upper left*).

MORPHOLOGY

The basic alterations in acute pancreatitis are **(1) microvascular leakage causing edema, (2) necrosis of fat by lipases, (3) an acute inflammatory reaction, (4) proteolytic destruction of pancreatic parenchyma, and (5) destruction of blood vessels leading to interstitial hemorrhage.**

In milder forms, histologic alterations include interstitial edema and focal areas of fat necrosis in the pancreatic substance and peripancreatic fat (Fig. 16–1, *A*). Fat necrosis results from enzymatic destruction of fat cells; the released fatty acids combine with calcium to form insoluble salts that precipitate in situ.

In more severe forms, such as **acute necrotizing pancreatitis,** necrosis of pancreatic tissue affects acinar and ductal tissues as well as the islets of Langerhans; vascular damage causes hemorrhage into the parenchyma of the pancreas. Macroscopically, the pancreas exhibits red-black hemorrhagic areas interspersed with foci of yellow-white, chalky fat necrosis (Fig. 16–1, *B*). Fat necrosis also can occur in extrapancreatic fat, including the omentum and bowel mesentery, and even outside the abdominal cavity (e.g., in subcutaneous fat). In most cases the peritoneum contains a serous, slightly turbid, brown-tinged fluid with globules of fat (derived from enzymatically digested adipose tissue). In the most severe form, **hemorrhagic pancreatitis,** extensive parenchymal necrosis is accompanied by diffuse hemorrhage within the substance of the gland.

PATHOGENESIS

The histologic changes seen in acute pancreatitis strongly suggest **autodigestion of the pancreatic substance by inappropriately activated pancreatic enzymes.** As described previously, the zymogen forms of pancreatic enzymes must be enzymatically cleaved to be activated; trypsin is central in this process, so **activation of trypsin is a critical triggering event in acute pancreatitis.** If trypsin is inappropriately generated from its proenzyme trypsinogen, it can activate itself as well as other proenzymes (e.g., phospholipases and elastases) that can then take part in the process of autodigestion. Trypsin also converts prekallikrein to its activated form, thus sparking the kinin system, and, by activation of factor XII (Hageman factor), also sets in motion the clotting and complement systems (Chapter 2).

Three pathways can incite the initial enzyme activation that may lead to acute pancreatitis (Fig. 16–2):

- **Pancreatic duct obstruction.** Impaction of a gallstone or biliary sludge, or extrinsic compression of the ductal system by a mass blocks ductal flow, increases intraductal pressure, and allows accumulation of an enzyme-rich interstitial fluid. Since lipase is secreted in an active form, local fat necrosis may result. Injured tissues, periacinar myofibroblasts, and leukocytes then release pro-inflammatory cytokines that promote local inflammation and interstitial edema through a leaky microvasculature. Edema further compromises local blood flow, causing vascular insufficiency and ischemic injury to acinar cells.
- **Primary acinar cell injury.** This pathogenic mechanism comes into play in acute pancreatitis caused by ischemia, viral infections (e.g., mumps), drugs, and direct trauma to the pancreas.
- **Defective intracellular transport of proenzymes within acinar cells.** In normal acinar cells, digestive enzymes intended for zymogen granules (and eventually extracellular release) and hydrolytic enzymes destined for lysosomes are transported in discrete pathways after synthesis in the endoplasmic reticulum. However, at least in some animal models of metabolic injury, pancreatic proenzymes and lysosomal hydrolases become packaged together. This results in proenzyme activation, lysosomal rupture (action of phospholipases), and local release of activated enzymes. The role of this mechanism in human acute pancreatitis is not clear.

Alcohol consumption may cause pancreatitis by several mechanisms. Alcohol transiently increases pancreatic exocrine secretion and contraction of the sphincter of Oddi (the muscle regulating the tone at the ampulla of Vater). Alcohol also has direct toxic effects on acinar cells, including induction of oxidative stress in acinar cells, which leads to membrane damage (see below). Finally, chronic alcohol ingestion results in the secretion of protein-rich pancreatic fluid, which leads to the deposition of inspissated protein plugs and obstruction of small pancreatic ducts.

Clinical Features

Abdominal pain is the cardinal manifestation of acute pancreatitis. Its severity varies from mild and uncomfortable to severe and incapacitating. Suspected acute pancreatitis is diagnosed primarily by the presence of elevated plasma

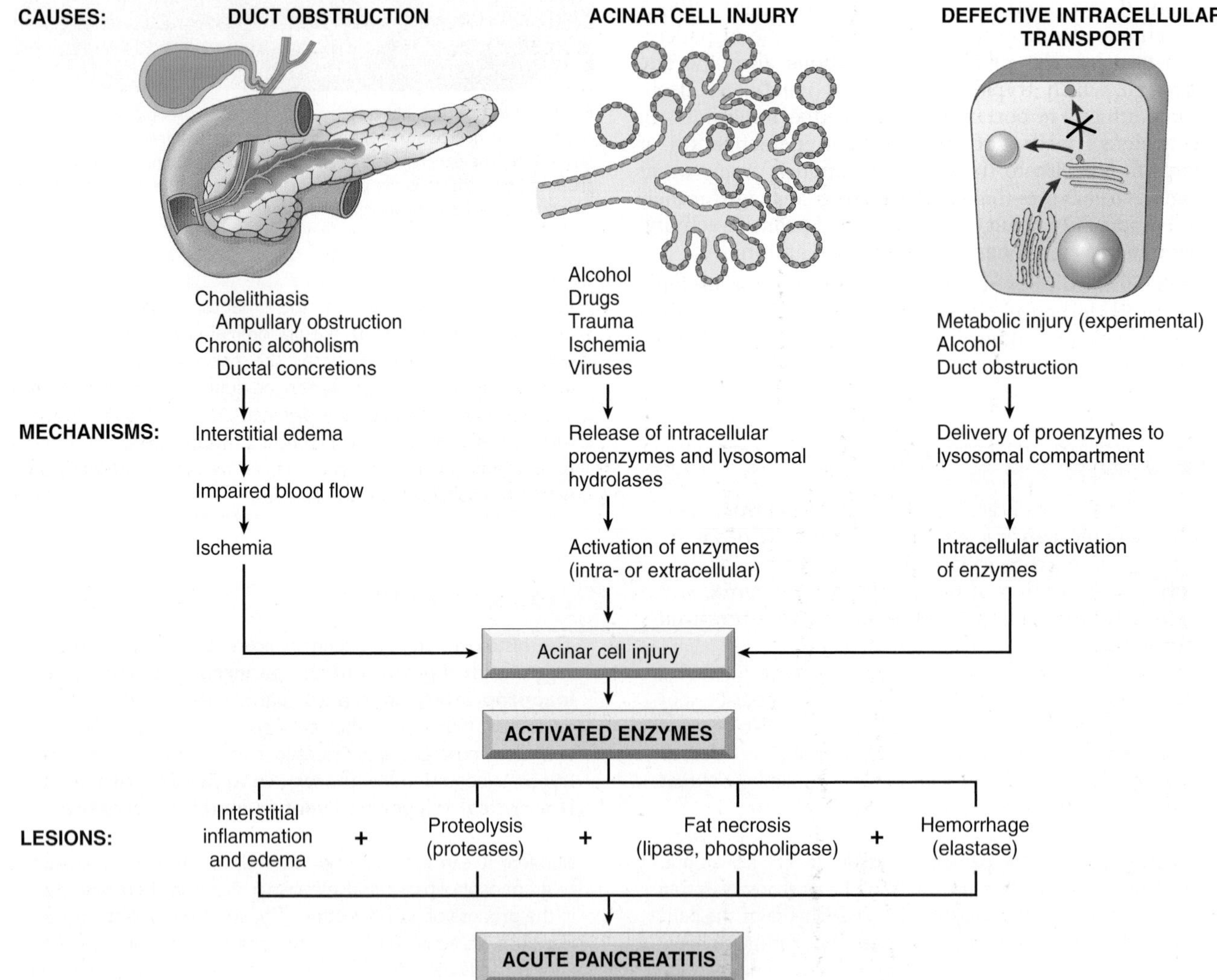

Figure 16–2 Proposed pathogenesis of acute pancreatitis.

levels of amylase and lipase and the exclusion of other causes of abdominal pain. In 80% of cases acute pancreatitis is mild and self limiting; the remaining 20% develop severe disease.

Full-blown acute pancreatitis constitutes a medical emergency of the first magnitude. Affected persons usually experience the sudden calamitous onset of an "acute abdomen" with pain, abdominal guarding, and the ominous absence of bowel sounds. Characteristically, the pain is constant and intense and often is referred to the upper back; it must be differentiated from pain of other causes such as perforated peptic ulcer, biliary colic, acute cholecystitis with rupture, and occlusion of mesenteric vessels with infarction of the bowel.

The manifestations of severe acute pancreatitis are attributable to systemic release of digestive enzymes and explosive activation of the inflammatory response. The initial clinical evaluation may reveal leukocytosis, disseminated intravascular coagulation (Chapter 11), acute respiratory distress syndrome (due to alveolar capillary injury) (Chapter 12), and diffuse fat necrosis. Peripheral vascular collapse (shock) can rapidly ensue as a result of increased microvascular permeability and resultant hypovolemia, compounded by endotoxemia (from breakdown of the barriers between gastrointestinal flora and the bloodstream), and renal failure due to acute tubular necrosis (Chapter 13).

Laboratory findings include markedly elevated serum amylase during the first 24 hours, followed (within 72 to 96 hours) by rising serum lipase levels. Hypocalcemia can result from precipitation of calcium in areas of fat necrosis; if persistent, it is a poor prognostic sign. The enlarged inflamed pancreas can be visualized by computed tomography (CT) or magnetic resonance imaging (MRI).

The crux of the management of acute pancreatitis is supportive therapy (e.g., maintaining blood pressure and alleviating pain) and "resting" the pancreas by total restriction of food and fluids. In 40% to 60% of cases of acute necrotizing pancreatitis, the necrotic debris becomes infected, usually by gram-negative organisms from the alimentary tract, further complicating the clinical course. Although most persons with acute pancreatitis eventually recover, some 5% die from shock during the first week of illness; acute respiratory distress syndrome and acute renal failure are ominous complications. In surviving patients, sequelae include sterile or infected *pancreatic "abscesses"* or *pancreatic pseudocysts.*

Pancreatic Pseudocysts

A common sequela of acute pancreatitis (and in particular, alcoholic pancreatitis) is a *pancreatic pseudocyst.* Liquefied areas of necrotic pancreatic tissue become walled off by fibrous tissue to form a cystic space, lacking an epithelial lining (hence the designation *pseudo*). The cyst contents are rich in pancreatic enzymes, and a laboratory assessment of the cyst aspirate can be diagnostic. Pseudocysts account for approximately 75% of all pancreatic cysts. While many pseudocysts spontaneously resolve, they can become secondarily infected, and larger pseudocysts can compress or even perforate into adjacent structures.

MORPHOLOGY

Pseudocysts usually are solitary; they commonly are attached to the surface of the gland and involve peripancreatic tissues such as the lesser omental sac or the retroperitoneum between the stomach and transverse colon or liver (Fig. 16–3, *A*). They can range in diameter from 2 cm to 30 cm. Since pseudocysts form by walling off areas of hemorrhagic fat necrosis, they typically are composed of necrotic debris encased by fibrous walls of granulation tissue lacking an epithelial lining (Fig. 16–3, *B*).

Chronic Pancreatitis

Chronic pancreatitis is characterized by long-standing inflammation, fibrosis, and destruction of the exocrine pancreas; in its late stages, the endocrine parenchyma also is lost. Although chronic pancreatitis can result from recurrent bouts of acute pancreatitis, *the chief distinction between acute and chronic pancreatitis is the irreversible impairment in pancreatic function in the latter.* The prevalence of chronic pancreatitis is difficult to determine but probably ranges between 0.04% and 5% of the U.S. population. By far *the most common cause of chronic pancreatitis is long-term alcohol abuse;* middle-aged men constitute the bulk of patients in

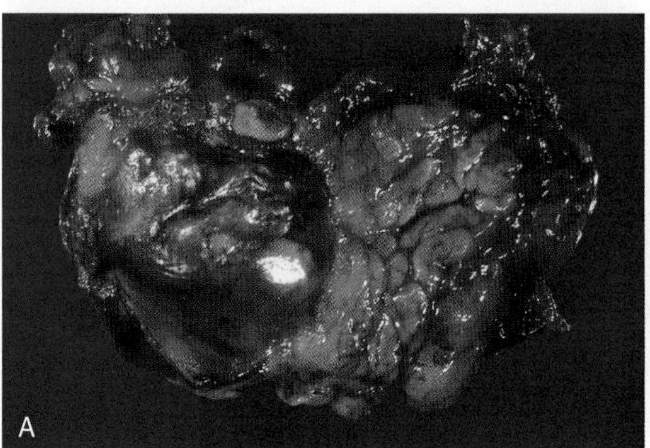

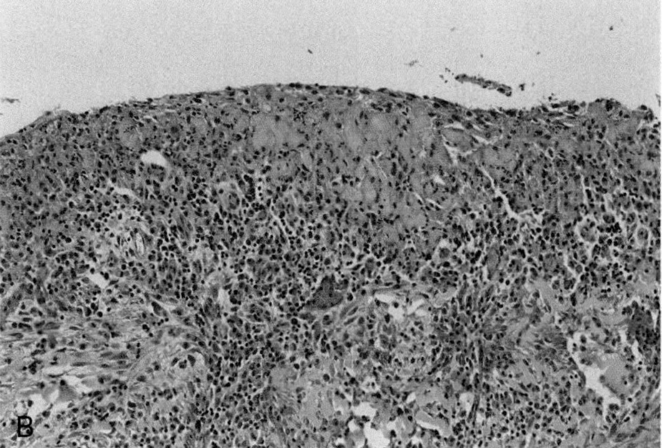

Figure 16–3 Pancreatic pseudocyst. **A,** Cross-section revealing a poorly defined cyst with a necrotic brownish wall. **B,** Histologically, the cyst lacks a true epithelial lining and instead is lined by fibrin and granulation tissue, with typical changes of chronic inflammation.

this etiologic group. Less common causes of chronic pancreatitis include

- Long-standing pancreatic duct *obstruction* (e.g., by pseudocysts, calculi, neoplasms, or pancreas divisum)
- *Tropical pancreatitis,* a poorly characterized heterogeneous disorder seen in Africa and Asia, with a subset of cases having a genetic basis
- *Hereditary pancreatitis* due to mutations in the pancreatic trypsinogen gene (*PRRS1*) (see Table 16–1 earlier), or the *SPINK1* gene encoding a trypsin inhibitor
- *Chronic pancreatitis associated with CFTR mutations.* As discussed in detail in Chapter 6, cystic fibrosis is caused by mutations in the *CFTR* gene; the CFTR protein also is expressed in pancreatic ductal epithelium, and *CFTR* mutations decrease bicarbonate secretion and increase the viscosity of the secretions, thereby promoting protein plugging.

As many as 40% of persons with chronic pancreatitis have no recognizable predisposing factors. As with acute pancreatitis, however, a growing number of these "idiopathic" cases are associated with inherited mutations in genes important for normal pancreatic exocrine function. For example, genetic testing reveals that 25% to 30% of patients with "idiopathic" pancreatitis harbor germline mutations in the *CFTR* gene, albeit distinct from the ones that lead to classic multisystem cystic fibrosis (Chapter 6).

MORPHOLOGY

Chronic pancreatitis is characterized by **parenchymal fibrosis, reduced number and size of acini, and variable dilation of the pancreatic ducts;** there is a relative sparing of the islets of Langerhans (Fig. 16–4, *A*). **Acinar loss** is a constant feature, usually with a chronic inflammatory infiltrate around remaining lobules and ducts. The ductal epithelium may be atrophied or hyperplastic or exhibit squamous metaplasia, and ductal concretions may be noted (Fig. 16–4, *B*). The remaining islets of Langerhans become embedded in the sclerotic tissue and may fuse and appear enlarged; eventually they also disappear. On gross evaluation, the gland is hard, sometimes with extremely dilated ducts and visible calcified concretions.

Autoimmune pancreatitis (AIP) is a distinct form of chronic pancreatitis that is characterized by one of two morphologic patterns: (1) striking infiltration of the pancreas by lymphoplasmacytic cells, many of which are positive for IgG4, accompanied by a "swirling" fibrosis and venulitis **(lymphoplasmacytic sclerosing pancreatitis),** or (2) a duct-centric mixed infiltrate composed of neutrophils, lymphocytes and plasma cells, often obliterating the ductal epithelium **(idiopathic duct centric pancreatitis).** IgG4-related autoimmune pancreatitis is a multisystem disease and may be one manifestation of IgG4-associated fibrosing disorders (Chapter 4). Recognition of autoimmune pancreatitis in both its forms is important, because it can mimic pancreatic cancer and also because it responds to steroid therapy.

PATHOGENESIS

Although the pathogenesis of chronic pancreatitis is not well defined, several hypotheses are proposed:

- **Ductal obstruction by concretions.** Many of the inciting agents in chronic pancreatitis (e.g., alcohol) increase the protein concentration of pancreatic secretions, and these proteins can form ductal plugs.
- **Toxic-metabolic.** Toxins, including alcohol and its metabolites, can exert a direct toxic effect on acinar cells, leading to lipid accumulation, acinar cell loss, and eventually parenchymal fibrosis.
- **Oxidative stress.** Alcohol-induced oxidative stress may generate free radicals in acinar cells, leading to membrane damage (Chapter 1), and subsequent expression of chemokines like interleukin-8 (IL-8), which recruits mononuclear inflammatory cells. Oxidative stress also promotes the fusion of lysosomes and zymogen granules with resulting acinar cell necrosis, inflammation, and fibrosis.

In contrast with acute pancreatitis, a variety of profibrogenic cytokines, such as transforming growth factor-β (TGF-β), connective tissue growth factor, and platelet-derived growth factor, are secreted in chronic pancreatitis. These cytokines induce the activation and proliferation of periacinar myofibroblasts ("pancreatic stellate cells"), which deposit collagen and are instrumental in the pathogenesis of fibrosis.

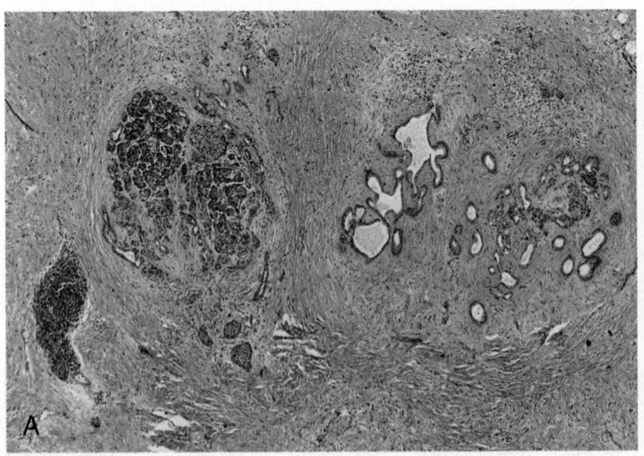

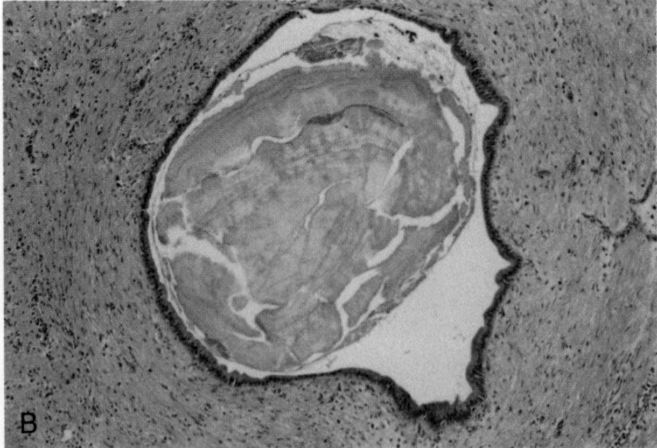

Figure 16–4 Chronic pancreatitis. **A,** Extensive fibrosis and atrophy has left only residual islets (*left*) and ducts (*right*), with a sprinkling of chronic inflammatory cells and acinar tissue. **B,** A higher-power view demonstrating dilated ducts with inspissated eosinophilic concretions in a patient with alcoholic chronic pancreatitis.

Clinical Features

Chronic pancreatitis manifests in several different ways. It may announce itself with repeated bouts of jaundice, vague indigestion, or persistent or recurrent abdominal and back pain, or it may be entirely silent until pancreatic insufficiency and diabetes mellitus develop (the latter as a consequence of islet destruction). Attacks can be precipitated by alcohol abuse, overeating (increases demand on pancreatic secretions), or opiates or other drugs that increase the muscle tone of the sphincter of Oddi.

The diagnosis of chronic pancreatitis requires a high degree of clinical suspicion. During an attack of abdominal pain, there may be mild fever and modest elevations of serum amylase. In end-stage disease, however, acinar destruction may be so advanced that enzyme elevations are absent. Gallstone-induced obstruction may manifest as jaundice or elevated levels of serum alkaline phosphatase. A very helpful finding is visualization of calcifications within the pancreas by CT or ultrasonography. Weight loss and hypoalbuminemic edema from malabsorption caused by pancreatic exocrine insufficiency also can point to the disease.

Although chronic pancreatitis is usually not acutely life-threatening, the long-term outlook is poor, with a 50% mortality rate over 20 to 25 years. Severe *pancreatic exocrine insufficiency* and chronic malabsorption may develop, as can *diabetes mellitus.* In other patients, *severe chronic pain* may dominate the clinical picture. *Pancreatic pseudocysts* (described earlier) develop in about 10% of patients. Persons with hereditary pancreatitis have a 40% lifetime risk of developing pancreatic cancer. The degree to which other forms of chronic pancreatitis contribute to cancer development is unclear.

SUMMARY

Pancreatitis

- *Acute pancreatitis* is characterized by inflammation and reversible parenchymal damage that ranges from focal edema and fat necrosis to widespread parenchymal necrosis and hemorrhage; the clinical presentation varies widely, from mild abdominal pain to rapidly fatal vascular collapse.
- *Chronic pancreatitis* is characterized by irreversible parenchymal damage and scar formation; clinical presentations include chronic malabsorption (due to pancreatic exocrine insufficiency) and diabetes mellitus (due to islet cell loss).
- Both entities share similar pathogenic mechanisms, and indeed recurrent acute pancreatitis can result in chronic pancreatitis. *Ductal obstruction* and *long-term alcohol abuse* are the most common causes in both forms. Inappropriate activation of pancreatic digestive enzymes (due to mutations in genes encoding trypsinogen or trypsin inhibitors) and primary acinar injury (due to toxins, infections, ischemia, or trauma) also cause pancreatitis.

PANCREATIC NEOPLASMS

Pancreatic exocrine neoplasms can be cystic or solid. Some tumors are benign, while others are among the most lethal of all malignancies.

Cystic Neoplasms

Only 5% to 15% of all pancreatic cysts are neoplastic; these constitute less than 5% of all pancreatic neoplasms. Some of these are entirely benign (e.g., serous cystadenoma); others, such as mucinous cystic neoplasms, can be benign or malignant.

Serous Cystadenomas

Serous cystadenomas account for approximately 25% of all pancreatic cystic neoplasms; they are composed of glycogen-rich cuboidal cells surrounding small cysts containing clear, straw-colored fluid (Fig. 16–5). The tumors typically manifest in the seventh decade of life with nonspecific symptoms such as abdominal pain; the female-to-male ratio is 2:1. These tumors are almost uniformly benign, and surgical resection is curative in the vast majority of patients. Most serous cystadenomas carry somatic mutations of the von Hippel-Lindau (*VHL*) tumor suppressor gene, the product of which binds to hypoxia-inducible factor 1 alpha (HIF1alpha) and results in its degradation (Chapter 5).

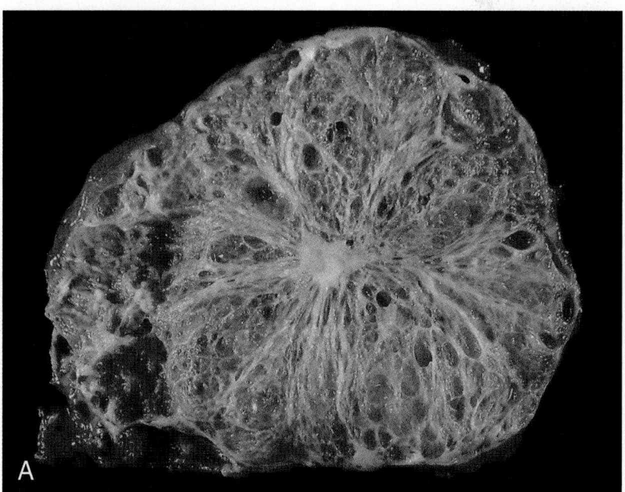

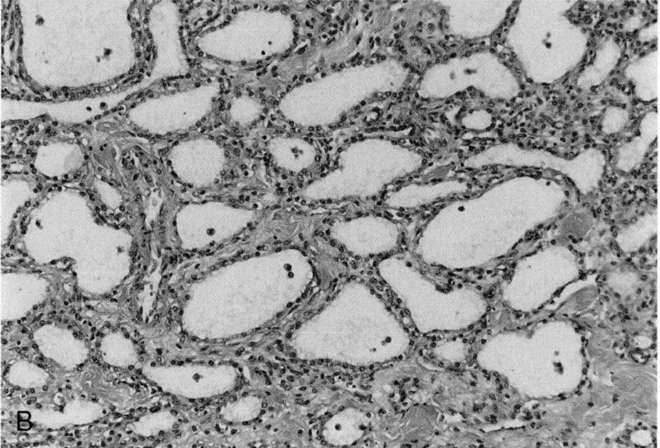

Figure 16–5 Serous cystadenoma. **A,** Cross-section through a serous cystadenoma. Only a thin rim of normal pancreatic parenchyma remains. The cysts are relatively small and contain clear, straw-colored fluid. **B,** The cysts are lined by cuboidal epithelium without atypia.

Mucinous Cystic Neoplasms

Close to 95% of mucinous cystic neoplasms arise in women, usually in the body or tail of the pancreas, and manifest as painless, slow-growing masses. The cystic spaces are filled with thick, tenacious mucin, and the cysts are lined by a columnar mucinous epithelium with an associated densely cellular stroma resembling that of the ovary (Fig. 16–6). Based on the degree of cytologic and architectural atypia in the lining epithelium, noninvasive mucinous cystic neoplasms are classified as harboring *low-grade, moderate,* or *severe* dysplasia. Up to one third of these cysts can be associated with an invasive adenocarcinoma. Distal pancreatectomy for noninvasive cysts typically is curative, even in the setting of severe dysplasia.

Intraductal Papillary Mucinous Neoplasms

Intraductal papillary mucinous neoplasms (IPMNs) are mucin-producing intraductal neoplasms. In contrast with mucinous cystic neoplasms, IPMNs occur more frequently in men than in women and more frequently involve the head of the pancreas. IPMNs arise in the main pancreatic ducts, or one of its major branch ducts, and lack the cellular stroma seen in mucinous cystic neoplasms (Fig. 16–7). As with mucinous cystic neoplasms, the epithelia of noninvasive IPMNs harbor various grades of dysplasia, and a subset of lesions is associated with an invasive adenocarcinoma component. Notably, up to two thirds of IPMNs harbor oncogenic mutations of *GNAS* on chromosome 20q13, which encodes the alpha subunit of a stimulatory G-protein, G_s (Chapter 19). Constitutive activation of this G-protein is predicted to result in an intracellular cascade that promotes cell proliferation.

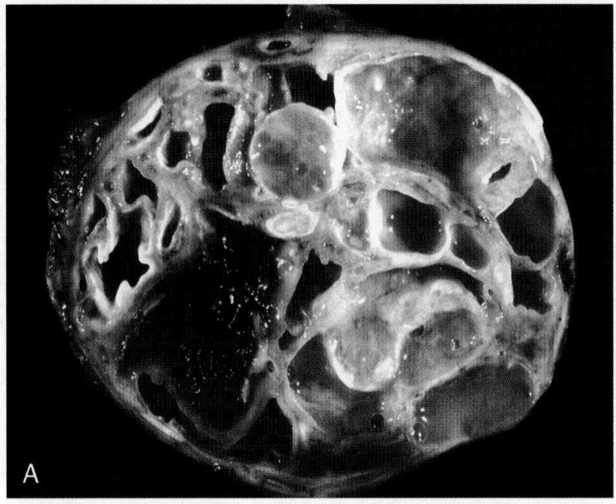

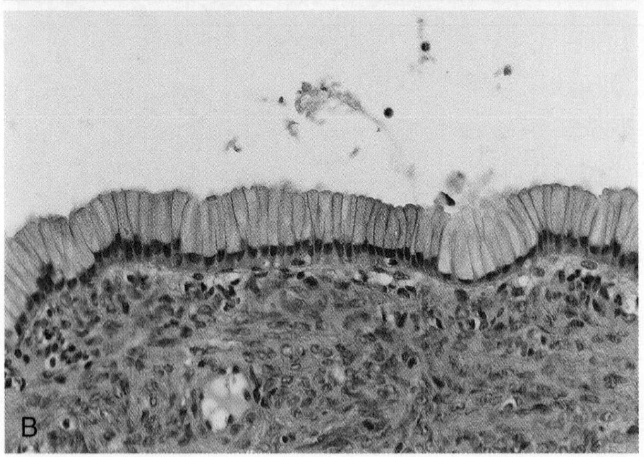

Figure 16–6 Mucinous cystic neoplasm. **A,** Cross-section through a mucinous multiloculated cyst in the tail of the pancreas. The cysts are large and filled with tenacious mucin. **B,** The cysts are lined by columnar mucinous epithelium, with a densely cellular "ovarian" stroma.

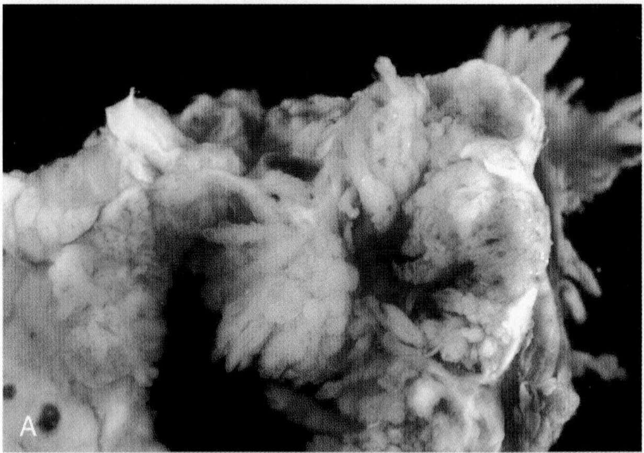

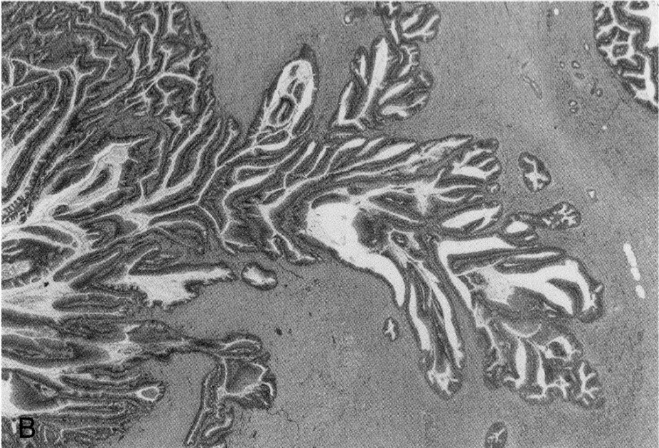

Figure 16–7 Intraductal papillary mucinous neoplasm. **A,** Cross-section through the head of the pancreas showing a prominent papillary neoplasm distending the main pancreatic duct. **B,** The papillary mucinous neoplasm involved the main pancreatic duct (*left*) and is extending down into the smaller ducts and ductules (*right*).

Pancreatic Carcinoma

Infiltrating ductal adenocarcinoma of the pancreas (more commonly referred to as "pancreatic cancer") is the fourth leading cause of cancer death in the United States, preceded only by lung, colon, and breast cancers. Although it is substantially less common than the other three malignancies, pancreatic carcinoma is near the top of the list of killers because it carries one of the highest mortality rates. Over 44,000 Americans were diagnosed with pancreatic cancer in 2010, and virtually all will die of it; the 5-year survival rate is dismal—less than 5%. Sadly, Ralph Steinman, one of the 2011 Nobel Laureates in physiology or medicine died of pancreatic cancer, three days before the announcement of his award.

PATHOGENESIS

Like all cancers, pancreatic cancer arises as a consequence of inherited and acquired mutations in cancer-associated genes. In a pattern analogous to that seen in the multistep progression of colon cancer (Chapter 5), there is a progressive accumulation of genetic changes in pancreatic epithelium as it proceeds from non-neoplastic, to noninvasive precursor lesions, to invasive carcinoma (Fig. 16–8). While both intraductal papillary mucinous neoplasms and mucinous cystic neoplasms can progress to invasive adenocarcinoma and are thus considered bona fide precursors of cancer (as noted earlier), the most common antecedent lesions of pancreatic cancer arise in small ducts and ductules, and are called **pancreatic intraepithelial neoplasias (PanINs).** Evidence in favor of the precursor relationship of PanINs to frank malignancy includes the fact that these microscopic lesions often are found adjacent to infiltrating carcinomas and the two share a number of genetic alterations. Moreover, the epithelial cells in PanINs show dramatic telomere shortening, potentially predisposing these lesions to accumulating additional chromosomal abnormalities on their way to becoming invasive carcinoma.

The recent sequencing of the pancreatic cancer genome has confirmed that four genes are most commonly affected by somatic mutations in this neoplasm: *KRAS, CDKNA2A/p16, SMAD4,* and *TP53*:

- *KRAS* is the most frequently altered oncogene in pancreatic cancer; it is activated by a point mutation in 80% to 90% of cases. These mutations impair the intrinsic GTPase activity of the Kras protein so that it is constitutively active. In turn, Kras activates a number of intracellular signaling pathways ("Kras effectors") that promote carcinogenesis (Chapter 5).
- The *p16 (CDKN2A)* gene is the most frequently inactivated tumor suppressor gene in pancreatic cancer, being turned off in 95% of cases. The p16 protein has a critical role in cell cycle control; inactivation removes an important checkpoint.
- The *SMAD4* tumor suppressor gene is inactivated in 55% of pancreatic cancers and only rarely in other tumors; it codes for a protein that plays an important role in signal transduction downstream of the transforming growth factor-β receptor.
- Inactivation of the *TP53* tumor suppressor gene occurs in 50% to 70% of pancreatic cancers. Its gene product, p53, acts both to enforce cell cycle checkpoints and as an inducer of apoptosis or senescence (Chapter 5).
- Mutations of *VHL* or *GNAS,* found in aforementioned pancreatic cysts, have not been described in ductal adenocarcinomas, and provide a likely basis for the widely different histopathology and natural history of these lesions.

What causes these molecular changes is unknown. Pancreatic cancer is primarily a disease of the elderly population, with 80% of cases occurring between the ages of 60 and 80. The strongest environmental influence is **smoking,** which doubles the risk. Chronic pancreatitis and diabetes mellitus are also both associated with an increased risk of pancreatic cancer. It is difficult to sort out whether chronic pancreatitis is the cause of pancreatic cancer or an effect of the disease, since small pancreatic cancers can block the pancreatic duct and thereby produce chronic pancreatitis. On the other hand, as discussed in Chapter 5, chronic inflammation is now considered an enabler of malignancy. Likewise, the basis of the association of diabetes mellitus with pancreatic cancer is also unclear, since diabetes can occur as a consequence of pancreatic cancer, and in fact, new-onset diabetes in an elderly patient may be the first sign of this malignancy. Familial clustering of pancreatic cancer has been reported, and a growing number of inherited genetic defects are now recognized that increase pancreatic cancer risk. For example, germline mutations of the familial breast/ovarian cancer gene *BRCA2* are seen in approximately 10% of cases arising in persons of Ashkenazi Jewish heritage.

MORPHOLOGY

Approximately 60% of pancreatic cancers arise in the head of the gland, 15% in the body, and 5% in the tail; in the remaining 20%, the neoplasm diffusely involves the entire

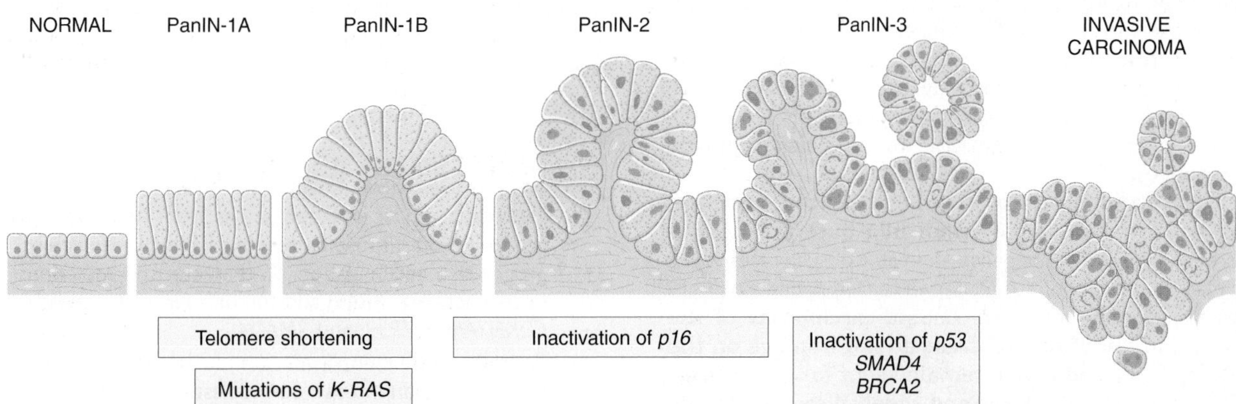

Figure 16–8 Progression model for the development of pancreatic cancer. It is postulated that telomere shortening and mutations of the oncogene *K-RAS* occur at early stages, inactivation of the *p16* tumor suppressor gene occurs at intermediate stages, and the inactivation of the *TP53, SMAD4,* and *BRCA2* tumor suppressor genes occurs at late stages. Note that while there is a general temporal sequence of changes, the accumulation of multiple mutations is more important than their occurrence in a specific order. PanIN, pancreatic intraepithelial neoplasm. The numbers following the labels on the top refer to stages in the development of PanINs.

(Modified from Maitra A, Hruban RH: Pancreatic cancer. Annu Rev Pathol Mech Dis 3:157, 2008.)

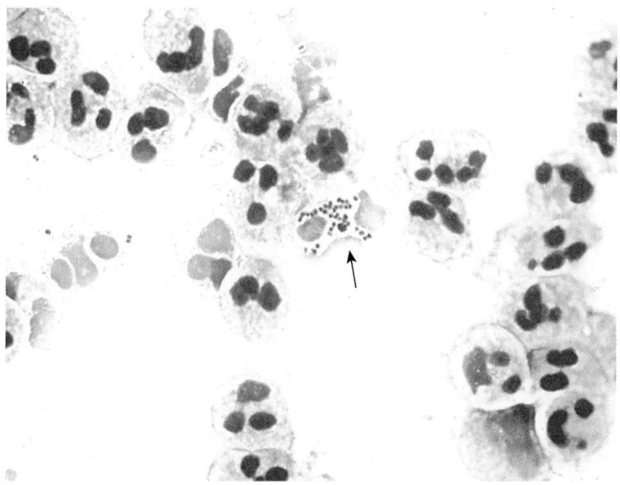

Figure 17–21 *Neisseria gonorrhoeae.* Gram stain of urethral discharge demonstrates characteristic gram-negative, intracellular diplococci (*arrow*).
(Courtesy of Dr. Rita Gander, Department of Pathology, University of Texas Southwestern Medical School, Dallas, Texas.)

MORPHOLOGY

N. gonorrhoeae provokes an intense, suppurative inflammatory reaction. In males this manifests most often as a **purulent urethral discharge,** associated with an edematous, congested urethral meatus. Gram-negative diplococci, many within the cytoplasm of neutrophils, are readily identified in Gram stains of the purulent exudate (Fig. 17–21). Ascending infection may result in the development of **acute prostatitis, epididymitis** (Fig. 17–22), or **orchitis.** Abscesses may complicate severe cases. Urethral and endocervical exudates tend to be less conspicuous in females, although acute inflammation of adjacent structures, such as the Bartholin glands, is fairly common. Ascending infection involving the uterus, fallopian tubes, and ovaries results in **acute salpingitis,** sometimes complicated by tuboovarian abscesses. The acute inflammatory process is followed by the development of granulation tissue and scarring, with resultant strictures and other permanent deformities of the involved structures, giving rise to **pelvic inflammatory disease** (Chapter 18).

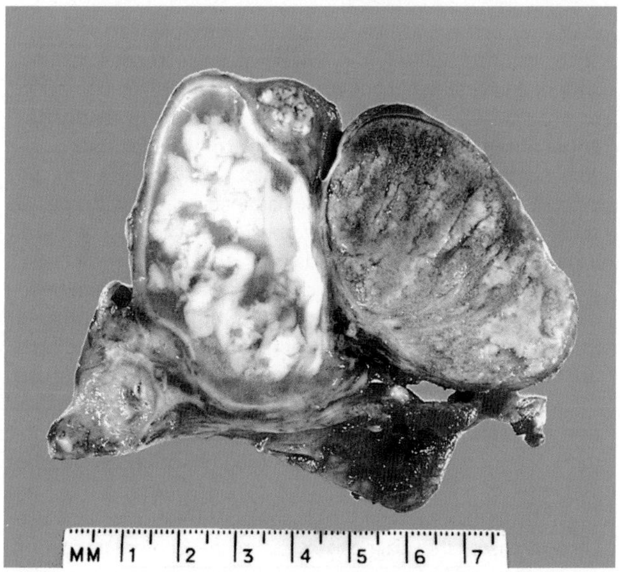

Figure 17–22 Acute epididymitis caused by gonococcal infection. The epididymis is involved by an abscess. Normal testis is seen on the *right.*

Clinical Features

In most infected males, gonorrhea is manifested by the presence of *dysuria, urinary frequency, and a mucopurulent urethral exudate* within 2 to 7 days of the time of initial infection. Treatment with appropriate antimicrobial therapy results in eradication of the organism and prompt resolution of symptoms. Untreated infections may ascend to involve the prostate, seminal vesicles, epididymis, and testis. Neglected cases may be complicated by chronic urethral stricture and, in more advanced cases, by permanent sterility. Untreated men also may become chronic carriers of *N. gonorrhoeae.*

Among female patients, acute infections acquired by vaginal intercourse may be asymptomatic or associated with *dysuria, lower pelvic pain, and vaginal discharge.* Untreated cases may be complicated by ascending infection, leading to acute inflammation of the fallopian tubes (salpingitis) and ovaries. Scarring of the fallopian tubes may occur, with resultant infertility and an increased risk of ectopic pregnancy. Gonococcal infection of the upper genital tract may spread to the peritoneal cavity, where the exudate may extend up the right paracolic gutter to the dome of the liver, resulting in gonococcal perihepatitis. Depending on sexual practices, other sites of primary infection in both males and females include the oropharynx and the anorectal area, with resultant acute pharyngitis and proctitis, respectively.

Disseminated infection is much less common than local infection, occurring in 0.5% to 3% of cases of gonorrhea. It is more common in females than in males. Manifestations include, most commonly, tenosynovitis, arthritis, and pustular or hemorrhagic skin lesions. Endocarditis and meningitis are rare presentations. Strains that cause disseminated infection usually are resistant to the lytic action of complement, but rare patients with inherited complement deficiencies are susceptible to systemic spread regardless of the infecting strain.

Gonococcal infection may be transmitted to infants during passage through the birth canal. The affected neonate may develop purulent infection of the eyes (ophthalmia neonatorum), an important cause of blindness in the past. The routine application of antibiotic ointment to the eyes of newborns has markedly reduced this disorder.

Both culture and a variety of tests that detect organism-specific nucleic acids can be used to diagnose gonococcal infections. The advantage of culture is that it permits determination of antibiotic sensitivity. Nucleic acid–based tests are more rapid and somewhat more sensitive than culture, and are being used increasingly.

SUMMARY

Gonorrhea

- Gonorrhea is a common STD affecting the genitourinary tract. Control of dissemination requires an effective complement-mediated immune response.
- In males there is a severe, symptomatic urethritis that can spread to the prostate, epididymis, and testis. In females the initial lesions on the cervix and urethra are less prominent than corresponding lesions in males, but ascending infection to fallopian tubes and ovaries can cause scarring and deformity with resultant sterility.
- Pregnant women can transmit gonorrhea to newborns during passage through the birth canal.
- Diagnosis can be made by culture of the exudates as well as by nucleic acid amplification techniques.

Nongonococcal Urethritis and Cervicitis

Nongonococcal urethritis (NGU) and cervicitis are the most common forms of STD. A variety of organisms has been implicated in the pathogenesis of NGU and cervicitis, including *C. trachomatis, Trichomonas vaginalis, U. urealyticum,* and *Mycoplasma genitalium. Most cases are apparently caused by C. trachomatis, and this organism is believed to be the most common bacterial cause of STD in the United States. U. urealyticum* is the next most common cause of NGU. Gonorrhea infection frequently is accompanied by chlamydial infection.

C. trachomatis is a small gram-negative bacterium that is an obligate intracellular pathogen. It exists in two forms. The infectious form, the *elementary body,* is capable of at least limited survival in the extracellular environment. The elementary body is taken up by host cells, primarily through a process of receptor-mediated endocytosis. Once inside the cell, the elementary body differentiates into a metabolically active form, termed the *reticulate body.* Using energy sources from the host cell, the reticulate body replicates and ultimately forms new elementary bodies capable of infecting additional cells. They preferentially infect columnar epithelial cells.

C. trachomatis infections may be associated with a wide range of clinical features that are virtually indistinguishable from those caused by *N. gonorrhoeae.* Thus, patients may develop epididymitis, prostatitis, pelvic inflammatory disease, pharyngitis, conjunctivitis, perihepatic inflammation, and, among persons engaging in anal sex, proctitis. *C. trachomatis* also causes lymphogranuloma venereum (LGV), discussed in the next section.

The morphologic and clinical features of chlamydial infection, with the exception of lymphogranuloma venereum, are virtually identical to those of gonorrhea. The primary infection is characterized by a *mucopurulent discharge containing a predominance of neutrophils.* Organisms are not visible in Gram-stained sections. In contrast with the gonococcus, *C. trachomatis* cannot be isolated with the use of conventional culture media. The diagnosis is best made by nucleic acid amplification tests on voided urine. Although culture can be done from genital swabs, it is not possible from urine. Molecular tests also are more sensitive than culture. Another important manifestation of chlamydial infection is *reactive arthritis* (formerly known as Reiter syndrome), predominantly in patients who are HLA-B27–positive. This condition typically manifests as a combination of urethritis, conjunctivitis, arthritis, and generalized mucocutaneous lesions.

SUMMARY

Nongonococcal Urethritis and Cervicitis

- NGU and cervicitis are the most common forms of STD. A majority of the cases are caused by *C. trachomatis,* and the rest by *T. vaginalis, U. urealyticum,* and *M. genitalium.*
- *C. trachomatis* is a gram-negative intracellular bacterium that causes a disease that is clinically indistinguishable from gonorrhea in both men and in women. Diagnosis requires detection of the bacteria by molecular methods. Culture from genital swabs is possible but requires special methods.
- In patients who are HLA-B27–positive, *C. trachomatis* infection can cause reactive arthritis along with conjunctivitis, and generalized mucocutaneous lesions.

Lymphogranuloma Venereum

Lymphogranuloma venereum (LGV) is a chronic, ulcerative disease caused by certain strains of *C. trachomatis,* which are distinct from those causing the more common NGU or cervicitis discussed earlier. It is a sporadic disease in the United States and western Europe but is endemic in parts of Asia, Africa, the Caribbean region, and South America. As in the case of granuloma inguinale (discussed later), sporadic cases of LGV are seen most often among persons with multiple sexual partners.

MORPHOLOGY

LGV may present as nonspecific urethritis, papular or ulcerative lesions involving the lower genitalia, tender inguinal and/or femoral lymphadenopathy that typically is unilateral, or proctocolitis. The lesions contain a **mixed granulomatous and neutrophilic inflammatory response;** variable numbers of chlamydial inclusions may be seen in the cytoplasm of epithelial cells or inflammatory cells with special staining methods. Regional lymphadenopathy is common, usually appearing within 30 days of the time of infection. Lymph node involvement is characterized by a granulomatous inflammatory reaction associated with irregularly shaped foci of necrosis and neutrophilic infiltration **(stellate abscesses).** With time, the inflammatory reaction gives rise to extensive fibrosis that can cause local lymphatic obstruction and strictures, producing **lymphedema.** Rectal strictures also occur, particularly in women. In active lesions, the diagnosis of LGV may be made by demonstration of the organism in biopsy sections or smears of exudate. In more chronic cases, the diagnosis rests on the demonstration of antibodies to the appropriate chlamydial serotypes in the patient's serum. Nucleic acid amplification tests have also been developed.

Chancroid (Soft Chancre)

Chancroid, sometimes called the "third" venereal disease (after syphilis and gonorrhea), is an acute, ulcerative infection caused by *Haemophilus ducreyi,* a small, gram-negative coccobacillus. The disease is most common in tropical and subtropical areas and is more prevalent in lower socioeconomic groups, particularly among men who have regular contact with prostitutes. *Chancroid is one of the most common causes of genital ulcers in Africa and Southeast Asia,* where it serves as an important cofactor in the transmission of HIV infection. Chancroid probably is underdiagnosed in the United States, because most STD clinics do not have facilities for isolating *H. ducreyi* and PCR-based tests are not widely available.

MORPHOLOGY

At 4 to 7 days after inoculation, a tender, **erythematous papule** develops on the external genitalia. In male patients, the primary lesion is usually on the penis; in female patients, most lesions occur in the vagina or periurethral area. Over the course of several days the surface of the primary lesion erodes to produce an **irregular ulcer,** which is more likely to be painful in males than in females. In contrast with the primary chancre of syphilis, the ulcer of chancroid is not indurated, and multiple lesions may be present. The base of the ulcer is covered by shaggy, yellow-gray exudate. The regional **lymph nodes,** particularly in the inguinal region, become enlarged and tender in about 50% of cases within 1 to 2 weeks of the primary inoculation. In untreated cases, the inflamed and enlarged nodes (buboes) may erode the overlying skin to produce chronic, draining ulcers.

On microscopic examination, the ulcer of chancroid contains a superficial zone of neutrophilic debris and fibrin, with an underlying zone of granulation tissue containing areas of necrosis and thrombosed vessels. A dense, lymphoplasmacytic inflammatory infiltrate is present beneath the layer of granulation tissue. Coccobacillary organisms sometimes are demonstrable in Gram- or silver-stained preparations, but they often are obscured by the mixed bacterial growth frequently present at the ulcer base. A definitive diagnosis of chancroid requires the identification of *H. ducreyi* on special culture media that are not widely available from commercial sources; even when such media are used, sensitivity is less than 80%. Therefore, the diagnosis often is based on clinical grounds alone.

Granuloma Inguinale

Granuloma inguinale is a chronic inflammatory disease caused by *Calymmatobacterium granulomatis,* a minute, encapsulated coccobacillus related to the *Klebsiella* genus. This disease is uncommon in the United States and western Europe but is endemic in rural areas in certain tropical and subtropical regions. When it occurs in urban settings, transmission of *C. granulomatis* typically is associated with a history of multiple sexual partners. Untreated cases are characterized by extensive scarring, often associated with lymphatic obstruction and lymphedema (elephantiasis) of the external genitalia. Culture of the organism is difficult, and PCR-based assays are not widely available.

MORPHOLOGY

Granuloma inguinale begins as a raised, papular lesion involving the moist, stratified squamous epithelium of the genitalia. The lesion eventually undergoes ulceration, accompanied by the development of abundant granulation tissue, which takes the form of a protuberant, soft, painless mass. As the lesion enlarges, its borders become raised and indurated. Disfiguring scars may develop in untreated cases, sometimes associated with formation of urethral, vulvar, or anal strictures. Regional lymph nodes typically are spared or show only nonspecific reactive changes, in contrast with chancroid.

Microscopic examination of active lesions reveals marked epithelial hyperplasia at the borders of the ulcer, sometimes mimicking carcinoma **(pseudoepitheliomatous hyperplasia).** A mixture of neutrophils and mononuclear inflammatory cells is present at the base of the ulcer and beneath the surrounding epithelium. The organisms are demonstrable in Giemsa-stained smears of the exudate as minute coccobacilli within vacuoles in macrophages (Donovan bodies). Silver stains (e.g., the Warthin-Starry stain) also may be used to demonstrate the organism.

SUMMARY

Lymphogranuloma Venereum, Chancroid, and Granuloma Inguinale

- LGV is caused by *C. trachomatis* serotypes that are distinct from those that cause NGU. LGV is associated with urethritis, ulcerative genital lesions, lymphadenopathy, and involvement of the rectum. The lesions show both acute and chronic inflammation; they progress to fibrosis, with consequent lymphedema and formation of rectal strictures.
- *H. ducreyi* infection causes an acute painful ulcerative genital infection called *chancroid.* Inguinal node involvement occurs in many cases and leads to their enlargement and ulceration. Ulcers show a superficial area of acute inflammation and necrosis, with an underlying zone of granulation tissue and mononuclear infiltrate. Diagnosis is possible by culture of the organism.
- *Granuloma inguinale* is a chronic fibrosing STD caused by *C. granulomatis.* The initial papular lesion on the genitalia expands and ulcerates, with formation of urethral, vulvar, or anal strictures in some cases. Microscopic examination reveals granulation tissue and intense epithelial hyperplasia that can mimic the histologic pattern in squamous cell carcinoma. Organisms are visible as small intracellular coccobacilli within vacuolated macrophages (Donovan bodies).

Trichomoniasis

T. vaginalis is a sexually transmitted protozoan that is a frequent cause of vaginitis. The trophozoite form adheres to the mucosa, where it causes superficial lesions. In females, *T. vaginalis* infection often is associated with loss of acid-producing Döderlein bacilli. It may be asymptomatic or be associated with pruritus and a profuse, frothy, yellow vaginal discharge. Urethral colonization may cause urinary frequency and dysuria. *T. vaginalis* infection typically is asymptomatic in males but in some cases may manifest as NGU. The organism usually is demonstrable in smears of vaginal scrapings.

Genital Herpes Simplex

Genital herpes infection, or herpes genitalis, is a common STD that affects an estimated 50 million people in the United States. Although both herpes simplex virus 1 (HSV-1) and HSV-2 can cause anogenital or oral infections, most cases of anogenital herpes are caused by HSV-2. However, *recent years have seen a rise in the number of genital infections caused by HSV-1, in part due to the increasing practice of oral sex.* Genital HSV infection may occur in any sexually active population. As with other STDs, the risk of infection is directly related to the number of sexual contacts. Up to 95% of HIV-positive men who have sex with men are seropositive for HSV-1 and/or HSV-2. HSV is transmitted when the virus comes into contact with a mucosal surface or broken skin of a susceptible host. Such transmission requires direct contact with an infected person, because the virus is readily inactivated at room temperature, particularly if dried.

MORPHOLOGY

The initial lesions of genital HSV infection are **painful, erythematous vesicles** on the mucosa or skin of the lower genitalia and adjacent extragenital sites. The anorectal area is a particularly common site of primary infection among men who have sex with men. Histologic changes include the presence of **intraepithelial vesicles** accompanied by necrotic cellular debris, neutrophils, and cells harboring characteristic intranuclear viral inclusions. The classic **Cowdry type A inclusion** appears as a light purple, homogeneous intranuclear structure surrounded by a clear halo. Infected cells commonly fuse to form multinucleate syncytia. The inclusions readily stain with antibodies to HSV, permitting a rapid, specific diagnosis of HSV infection in histologic sections or smears. Immunohistochemical tests have largely replaced detection of HSV infection by cytologic examination, which is less sensitive and prone to false-positive results.

Clinical Features

As mentioned earlier, both HSV-1 and HSV-2 can cause genital or oral infection, and both can produce primary or recurrent mucocutaneous lesions that are clinically indistinguishable. The manifestations of HSV infection vary considerably, depending on whether the infection is primary or recurrent. Primary infection with HSV-2 often is mildly symptomatic. In persons experiencing their first episode, locally painful vesicular lesions are often accompanied by dysuria, urethral discharge, local lymph node enlargement and tenderness, and systemic manifestations, such as fever, muscle aches, and headache. HSV is actively shed during this period and continues to be shed until the mucosal lesions have completely healed. Signs and symptoms may last for several weeks during the primary phase of disease. Recurrences are much more common with HSV-1 than with HSV-2 and typically are milder and of shorter duration than in the primary episode. As with primary infection, HSV is shed while active lesions are present.

In immunocompetent adults, herpes genitalis generally is not life-threatening. However, HSV does pose a major threat to immunosuppressed patients, in whom fatal, disseminated disease may develop. Also life-threatening is *neonatal herpes infection,* which occurs in about half of infants delivered vaginally of mothers suffering from either primary or recurrent genital HSV infection. The viral infection is acquired during passage through the birth canal. Its incidence has risen in parallel with the rise in genital HSV infection. *The manifestations of neonatal herpes, which typically develop during the second week of life, include rash, encephalitis, pneumonitis, and hepatic necrosis.* Approximately 60% of affected infants die of the disease, with significant morbidity occurring in about half of the survivors. The laboratory diagnosis of genital herpes relies on viral culture. Of note, however, the sensitivity of culture is low, especially for recurrent lesions, and declines rapidly as lesions begin to heal. Molecular diagnostic tests also are available but are used mostly in diagnosis of extragenital herpes, particularly with central nervous system infections.

Human Papillomavirus Infection

HPV causes a number of squamous proliferations in the genital tract, including condyloma acuminatum, as well as several precancerous lesions that commonly undergo transformation to carcinomas; these most commonly involve the cervix (Chapter 18), but also occur in the penis, vulva, and oropharyngeal tonsils. *Condylomata acuminata,* also known as venereal warts, are caused by HPV types 6 and 11. These lesions occur on the penis as well as on the female genitalia. They should not be confused with the condylomata lata of secondary syphilis. Genital HPV infection may be transmitted to neonates during vaginal delivery. Recurrent and potentially life-threatening papillomas of the upper respiratory tract may develop subsequently in affected infants.

MORPHOLOGY

In males, condylomata acuminata usually occur on the coronal sulcus or inner surface of the prepuce, where they range in size from small, sessile lesions to large, papillary proliferations measuring several centimeters in diameter. In females, they commonly occur on the vulva. Examples of the microscopic appearance of these lesions are presented in Chapter 18.

SUMMARY

Herpes Simplex Virus and Human Papillomavirus Infections

- HSV-2 and, less commonly, HSV-1 can cause genital infections. Initial (primary) infection causes painful, erythematous, intraepithelial vesicles on the mucosa and skin of external genitalia, along with regional lymph node enlargement. Recurrent lesions are more common with HSV-1 than with HSV-2 infection, and in general are less painful and less extensive than primary lesions.

- On histologic examination the vesicles of HSV infection contain necrotic cells and fused multinucleate giant cells with intranuclear inclusions (Cowdry type A) that stain with antibodies to the virus.
- Neonatal herpes can be life-threatening and occurs in children born to mothers with genital herpes. Affected infants have generalized herpes, often associated with encephalitis and consequent high mortality.
- HPV causes many proliferative lesions of the genital mucosa, including condyloma acuminatum, precancerous lesions, and invasive cancers.

BIBLIOGRAPHY

Bahrami A, Ro JY, Ayala AG: An overview of testicular germ cell tumors. Arch Pathol Lab Med 131:1267, 2007.

Bleeker MC, Heideman DA, Snijders PJ, et al: Penile cancer: epidemiology, pathogenesis, and prevention. World J Urol 27:141, 2009. *[A systematic review of the literature evaluating penile carcinogenesis, risk factors, and molecular mechanisms involved.]*

Bushman W: Etiology, epidemiology, and natural history of benign prostatic hyperplasia. Urol Clin N Am 36:403, 2009.

Centers for Disease Control and Prevention, Workowski KA, Berman SM: Sexually transmitted diseases treatment guidelines, 2006. MMWR Recomm Rep 55:1, 2006. *[An excellent updated review along with treatment recommendations.]*

Clark PE: Bladder cancer. Curr Opin Oncol 19:241, 2007. *[Reviews the diagnosis and management of both more superficial and advanced bladder cancer.]*

Donovan B: Sexually transmitted infections other than HIV. Lancet 363:545, 2004. *[A clinical review of STDs.]*

Epstein JI: An update of the Gleason grading system. J Urol 183:433, 2010.

Gori S, Porrozzi S, Roila F, et al: Germ cell tumours of the testis. Crit Rev Oncol Hematol 53:141, 2005. *[An informative review of the predisposing factors, clinical features, and treatment of testicular neoplasms.]*

Hsing AW, Chokkalingam AP: Prostate cancer epidemiology. Front Biosci 11:1388, 2006.

Loeb SA, Catalona WJ: Prostate-specific antigen in clinical practice. Cancer Lett 249:30, 2007. *[An excellent summary of clinical use of PSA.]*

Le BV, Schaeffer AJ: Genitourinary pain syndromes, prostatitis and lower urinary tract symptoms. Urol Clin North Am 36:527, 2009. *[A recent review of the etiology, diagnosis, symptoms, and treatment of prostatitis and interstitial cystitis along with pelvic pain syndromes.]*

Lee PK, Wilkins KB: Condyloma and other infections including human immunodeficiency virus. Surg Clin North Am 90:99, 2010.

Makorov DV, Loeb S, Getzenberg RH, Partin AW: Biomarkers for prostate cancer. Annu Rev Med 60:139, 2009. *[A review covering PSA and possible new prostate cancer biomarkers that are under evaluation.]*

Mitra AP, Cole RJ: Molecular pathogenesis and diagnostics of bladder cancer. Annu Rev Pathol 4:251, 2008.

Nelson WG, De Marzo AM, Yegnasubramanian S: Epigenetic alterations in human prostate cancers. Endocrinology 150:3991, 2009.

Patel AK, Chapple CR: Medical management of lower urinary tract symptoms in men: current treatment and future approaches. Nat Clin Pract Urol 5:211, 2008. *[This article also clarifies the terminology used to evaluate men with lower urinary tract symptoms.]*

Rapley EA, Nathanson KL: Predisposition alleles for testicular germ cell tumour. Curr Opin Genes Dev 20:225, 2010. *[An update on inherited risk factors in germ cell tumors.]*

Shand RL, Gelmann EP: Molecular biology of prostate-cancer pathogenesis. Curr Opin Urol 16:123, 2006.

Sulak PJ: Sexually transmitted diseases. Semin Reprod Med 21:399, 2003. *[An exhaustive review of STDs.]*

See Targeted Therapy available online at **studentconsult.com**

CHAPTER 18

Female Genital System and Breast

CHAPTER CONTENTS

VULVA

The *vulva* is the external female genitalia and includes the moist hair-bearing skin and mucosa in that region. Disorders of the vulva most frequently are inflammatory, rendering them more uncomfortable than serious. Malignant tumors of the vulva, although life-threatening, are rare.

VULVITIS

One of the most common causes of vulvitis is reactive inflammation in response to an exogenous stimulus, whether an irritant (contact irritant dermatitis) or an allergen (contact allergic dermatitis). Scratching-induced trauma secondary to associated intense "itching" (pruritus) often exacerbates the primary condition.

Contact irritant eczymatous dermatitis manifests as well-defined erythematous weeping and crusting papules and plaques (Chapter 23) and may be a reaction to urine, soaps, detergents, antiseptics, deodorants, or alcohol. Allergic dermatitis has a similar clinical appearance and may result from allergy to perfumes; additives in creams, lotions, and soaps; chemical treatments on clothing; and other antigens.

Vulvitis also may be caused by infections, which in this setting often are sexually transmitted (Chapter 17). The most important of these infectious agents in North America are human papillomavirus (HPV), the causative agent of condyloma acuminatum and vulvar intraepithelial neoplasia (VIN) (discussed later); herpes simplex virus (HSV-1 or -2), the agent of genital herpes with its characteristic

The contributions of Drs. Susan Lester (Diseases of Breast) and Anthony Montag (Diseases of Female Genital System) are gratefully acknowledged.

vesicular eruption; *N. gonorrhoeae,* a cause of suppurative infection of the vulvovaginal glands; *Treponema pallidum,* the syphilis pathogen, in association with the primary chancre at a vulvar site of inoculation; and *Candida,* also a potential cause of vulvitis.

An important complication of vulvitis is obstruction of the excretory ducts of Bartholin glands. This blockage may result in painful dilation of the glands (a Bartholin cyst) and abscess formation.

NON-NEOPLASTIC EPITHELIAL DISORDERS

The epithelium of the vulvar mucosa may undergo both atrophic thinning and hyperplastic thickening, often in the form of lichen sclerosus and lichen simplex chronicus, respectively.

Lichen Sclerosus

Lichen sclerosus is characterized by thinning of the epidermis, disappearance of rete pegs, hydropic degeneration of the basal cells, dermal fibrosis, and a scant perivascular, mononuclear inflammatory cell infiltrate (Fig. 18–1). It appears as smooth, white plaques (termed *leukoplakia*) or papules that in time may extend and coalesce. When the entire vulva is affected, the labia become somewhat atrophic and stiffened, and the vaginal orifice is constricted. Lichen sclerosus occurs in all age groups but most commonly affects postmenopausal women. The pathogenesis is uncertain, but the presence of activated T cells in the subepithelial inflammatory infiltrate and the increased frequency of autoimmune disorders in affected women suggest an autoimmune etiology. Lichen sclerosus is benign; however, a small percentage of women (1% to 5%) with symptomatic lichen sclerosus develop squamous cell carcinoma of the vulva.

Lichen Simplex Chronicus

Lichen simplex chronicus is marked by epithelial thickening (particularly of the stratum granulosum) and hyperkeratosis. Increased mitotic activity is seen in the basal and suprabasal layers; however, there is no epithelial atypia (Fig. 18–1). Leukocytic infiltration of the dermis is sometimes pronounced. These nonspecific changes are a consequence of chronic irritation, often caused by pruritus related to an underlying inflammatory dermatosis. Lichen simplex chronicus appears as an area of leukoplakia. With isolated lesions, no increased predisposition to cancer has been found, but lichen simplex chronicus often is present at the margins of established vulvar cancer, raising the possibility of an association with neoplastic disease.

Lichen sclerosus and lichen simplex chronicus may coexist in different areas of the body in the same person, and both lesions may take the form of leukoplakia. Similar white patches or plaques also are seen in a variety of other benign dermatoses, such as psoriasis and lichen planus (Chapter 23), as well as in malignant lesions of the vulva, such as squamous cell carcinoma in situ and invasive squamous cell carcinoma. Thus, biopsy and microscopic examination are needed to differentiate these clinically similar-appearing lesions.

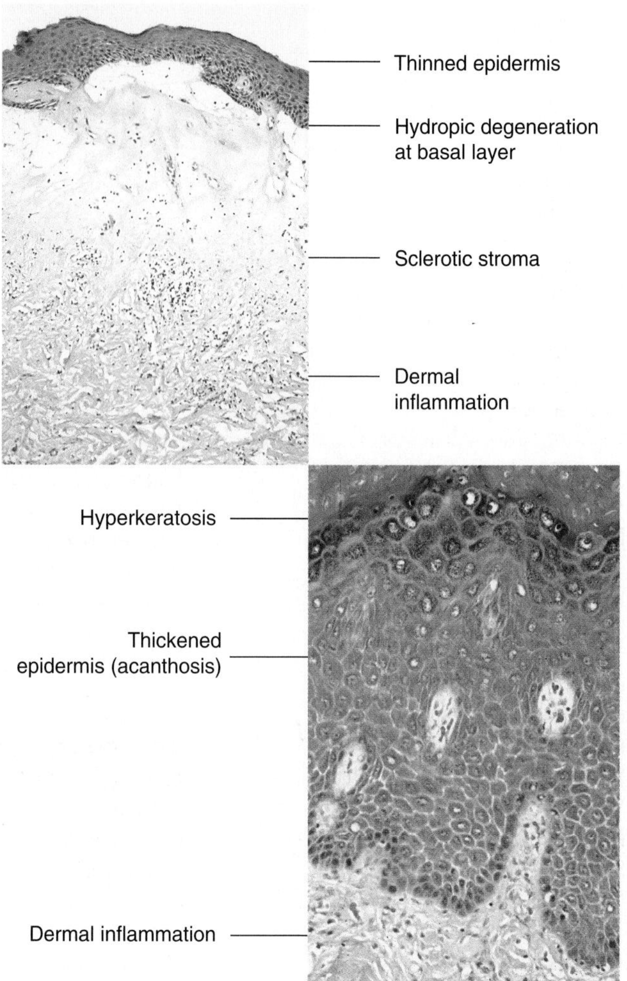

Figure 18–1 *Upper panel,* Lichen sclerosus. *Lower panel,* Lichen simplex chronicus. The main features of the lesions are labeled.

SUMMARY

Non-neoplastic Epithelial Disorders

- Lichen sclerosus is characterized by atrophic epithelium, usually with dermal fibrosis.
- Lichen sclerosus carries a slightly increased risk for development of squamous cell carcinoma.
- Lichen simplex chronicus is characterized by thickened epithelium (hyperplasia), usually with an inflammatory infiltrate.
- The lesions of lichen sclerosus and lichen simplex chronicus must be biopsied to definitively distinguish them from other causes of leukoplakia, such as squamous cell carcinoma of the vulva.

TUMORS

Condylomas

Condyloma is the name given to any warty lesion of the vulva. Most such lesions can be assigned to one of two distinctive forms. *Condylomata lata,* not commonly seen today, are flat, moist, minimally elevated lesions that occur in secondary syphilis (Chapter 17). The more common *condylomata acuminata* may be papillary and distinctly elevated or somewhat flat and rugose. They can occur anywhere on the anogenital surface, sometimes as single but more often as multiple lesions. When located on the vulva, they range from a few millimeters to many centimeters in diameter and are red-pink to pink-brown (Fig. 18–2). On histologic examination, the characteristic cellular feature is koilocytosis, a cytopathic change characterized by perinuclear cytoplasmic vacuolization and wrinkled nuclear contours that is a hallmark of HPV infection (Fig. 18–2; see also Chapter 17). Indeed, condylomata acuminata are strongly associated with HPV subtypes 6 and 11. HPV can be transmitted venereally, and identical lesions occur in men on the penis and around the anus. HPV 6 and 11 infections carry a low risk of malignant transformation, and hence, vulvar condylomas do not commonly progress to cancer.

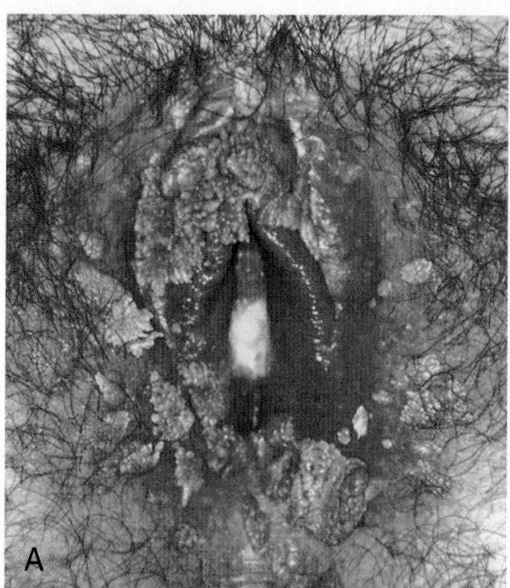

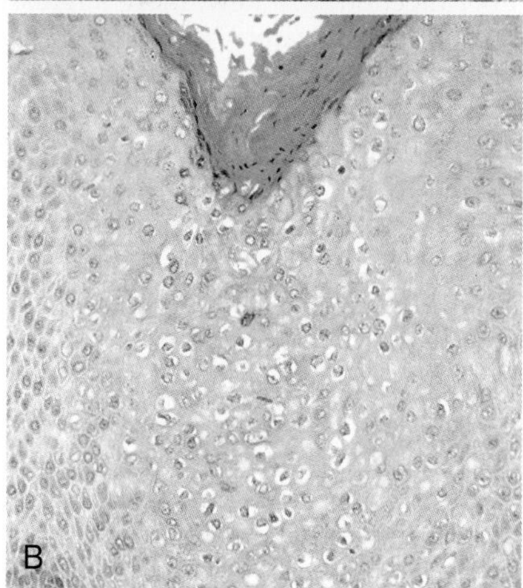

Figure 18–2 A, Numerous condylomas of the vulva. **B,** Histopathologic features of condyloma acuminatum include acanthosis, hyperkeratosis, and cytoplasmic vacuolation (koilocytosis, *center*).

(A, Courtesy of Dr. Alex Ferenczy, McGill University, Montreal, Quebec, Canada.)

Carcinoma of the Vulva

Carcinoma of the vulva represents about 3% of all female genital tract cancers, occurring mostly in women older than age 60. Approximately 90% of carcinomas are squamous cell carcinomas; the other tumors are mainly adenocarcinomas or basal cell carcinomas.

There appear to be two distinct forms of vulvar squamous cell carcinoma. The less common form is related to high-risk HPV strains (especially HPV subtypes 16 and 18) and occurs in middle-aged women, particularly cigarette smokers. In this form, the onset of carcinoma often is preceded by precancerous changes in the epithelium termed *vulvar intraepithelial neoplasia* (VIN). VIN progresses in most patients to greater degrees of atypia and eventually undergoes transformation to carcinoma in situ; however, progression to invasive carcinoma is not inevitable and often occurs after many years. Environmental factors such as cigarette smoking and immunodeficiency appear to increase the risk of such progression.

A second form of vulvar carcinoma occurs in older women. It is not associated with HPV but often is preceded by years of reactive epithelial changes, principally lichen sclerosus. The overlying epithelium frequently lacks the typical cytologic changes of VIN, but it may display subtle atypia of the basal layer and basal keratinization. Invasive tumors of this form tend to be well differentiated and highly keratinizing.

MORPHOLOGY

VIN and early vulvar carcinomas manifest as areas of **leukoplakia** in the form of whitish patches of epithelial thickening. In about one fourth of the cases, the lesions are pigmented owing to the presence of melanin. Over time, these areas are transformed into overt **exophytic** or ulcerative **endophytic tumors.** HPV-positive tumors often are multifocal and warty and tend to be poorly differentiated **squamous cell carcinomas,** whereas HPV-negative tumors usually are unifocal and typically manifest as well-differentiated keratinizing squamous cell carcinomas.

Both forms of vulvar carcinoma tend to remain confined to their site of origin for a few years but ultimately invade and spread, usually first to regional nodes. The risk of metastasis correlates with the size of the tumor and the depth of invasion. Women with tumors less than 2 cm in diameter have about a 90% 5-year survival rate after radical excision, whereas only 20% of those with advanced-stage lesions survive for 10 years.

Extramammary Paget Disease

Paget disease is an intraepidermal proliferation of malignant epithelial cells that can occur in the skin of the vulva or nipple of the breast. However, unlike in the breast, where Paget disease is virtually always associated with an

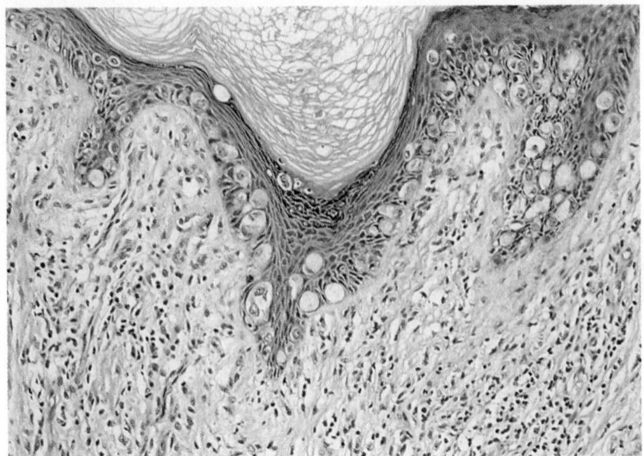

Figure 18–3 Paget disease of the vulva, with large tumor cells with abundant clear cytoplasm scattered throughout the epidermis.

underlying carcinoma, a majority of cases of vulvar (extramammary) Paget disease have no demonstrable underlying tumor. Instead, vulvar Paget cells most commonly appear to arise from epidermal progenitor cells. Only occasionally, Paget disease in this location is accompanied by a subepithelial or submucosal tumor arising in an adnexal structure, typically sweat glands.

Paget disease manifests as a red, scaly, crusted plaque that may mimic the appearance of an inflammatory dermatitis. On histologic examination, large epithelioid cells with abundant pale, finely granular cytoplasm and occasional cytoplasmic vacuoles infiltrate the epidermis, singly and in groups (Fig. 18–3). The presence of mucin, as detected by periodic acid–Schiff (PAS) staining, is useful in distinguishing Paget disease from vulvar melanoma, which lacks mucin.

Intraepidermal Paget disease may persist for years or even decades without evidence of invasion. However, when there is an associated tumor involving skin appendages, the Paget cells may invade locally, and ultimately metastasize. Once metastasis occurs, the prognosis is poor.

SUMMARY

Squamous Cell Carcinoma of the Vulva

- HPV-related vulvar squamous cell carcinomas usually are poorly differentiated lesions and sometimes are multifocal. They often evolve from vulvar intraepithelial neoplasia (VIN).
- Non–HPV-related vulvar squamous cell carcinomas occur in older women, usually are well differentiated and unifocal, and often are associated with lichen sclerosus or other inflammatory conditions.

Paget Disease of the Vulva

- Vulvar Paget disease is characterized by a red, scaly plaque caused by proliferation of malignant epithelial cells within the epidermis; usually, there is no underlying carcinoma, unlike Paget disease of nipple.
- Positive staining for PAS distinguishes Paget disease cells from melanoma.

VAGINA

In adult females, the vagina is seldom a site of primary disease. More often, it is involved secondarily by cancer or infections arising in adjacent organs (e.g., cervix, vulva, bladder, rectum).

Congenital anomalies of the vagina fortunately are uncommon and include entities such as total absence of the vagina, a septate or double vagina (usually associated with a septate cervix and, sometimes, septate uterus), and congenital, lateral Gartner duct cysts arising from persistent wolffian duct rests.

VAGINITIS

Vaginitis is a relatively common condition that is usually transient and of no clinical consequence. It is associated with production of a vaginal discharge (leukorrhea). A large variety of organisms have been implicated, including bacteria, fungi, and parasites. Many are normal commensals that become pathogenic only in the setting of diabetes, systemic antibiotic therapy (which causes disruption of normal microbial flora), immunodeficiency, pregnancy, or recent abortion. In adults, primary gonorrheal infection of the vagina is uncommon. The only other organisms worthy of mention, because they are frequent offenders, are *Candida albicans* and *Trichomonas vaginalis*. Candidal (monilial) vaginitis is characterized by a curdy white discharge. This organism is part of the normal vaginal flora in about 5% of women, so the appearance of symptomatic infection almost always involves one of the predisposing influences cited above or superinfection by a new, more aggressive strain. *T. vaginalis* produces a watery, copious gray-green discharge in which parasites can be identified by microscopy. *Trichomonas* also can be identified in about 10% of asymptomatic women; thus, active infection usually stems from sexual transmission of a new strain.

MALIGNANT NEOPLASMS

Squamous Cell Carcinoma

Squamous cell carcinoma of the vagina is an extremely uncommon cancer that usually occurs in women older than 60 years of age in the setting of risk factors similar to those associated with carcinoma of the cervix (discussed later). Vaginal intraepithelial neoplasia is a precursor lesion that is nearly always associated with HPV infection. Invasive squamous cell carcinoma of the vagina is associated with the presence of HPV DNA in more than half of the cases, presumably derived from HPV-positive VIN.

Clear Cell Adenocarcinoma

In 1970, clear cell adenocarcinoma, a very rare tumor, was identified in a cluster of young women whose mothers took diethylstilbestrol during pregnancy to prevent threatened abortion. Follow-up studies determined that the incidence of this tumor in persons exposed to diethylstilbestrol in utero was low (less than 1 per 1000, albeit about 40 times greater than in the unexposed population). However, since this agent was in wide use at the time it appears to be associated with a persistently elevated risk of cancer in those exposed. In about one third of exposed women, small glandular or microcystic inclusions appear in the vaginal mucosa. These benign lesions are seen as red, granular-appearing foci that on histologic examination are lined by mucus-secreting or ciliated columnar cells. This clinical condition is called *vaginal adenosis*, and it is from such precursor lesions that clear cell adenocarcinoma arises.

Sarcoma Botryoides

Sarcoma botryoides (embryonal rhabdomyosarcoma) is a rare form of primary vaginal cancer that manifests as soft polypoid masses. It usually is encountered in infants and children younger than 5 years of age. It also may occur in other sites, such as the urinary bladder and bile ducts. These lesions are described in further detail in Chapter 20.

CERVIX

Most cervical lesions are relatively banal inflammations (cervicitis), but the cervix also is the site of one of the most common cancers in women worldwide.

CERVICITIS

Inflammatory conditions of the cervix are extremely common and are associated with a purulent vaginal discharge. Cervicitis can be subclassified as infectious or noninfectious, although differentiation is difficult owing to the presence of normal vaginal flora including incidental vaginal aerobes and anaerobes, streptococci, staphylococci, enterococci, and *Escherichia coli.*

Much more important are *Chlamydia trachomatis, Ureaplasma urealyticum, T. vaginalis, Candida* spp., *Neisseria gonorrhoeae,* HSV-2 (the agent of herpes genitalis), and certain types of HPV, all of which are often sexually transmitted. *C. trachomatis* is by far the most common of these pathogens, accounting for as many as 40% of cases of cervicitis encountered in sexually transmitted disease (STD) clinics. Although less common, herpetic infections are noteworthy because maternal-infant transmission during childbirth may result in serious, sometimes fatal systemic herpetic infection in the newborn.

MORPHOLOGY

Nonspecific cervicitis may be either **acute** or **chronic.** The relatively uncommon **acute form** is limited to women in the postpartum period and usually is caused by staphylococci or streptococci. Chronic cervicitis consists of inflammation and epithelial regeneration, some degree of which is common in all women of reproductive age. The cervical epithelium may show hyperplasia and reactive changes in both squamous and columnar mucosae. Eventually, the columnar epithelium undergoes squamous metaplasia.

Cervicitis commonly comes to attention on routine examination or because of leukorrhea. Culture of the discharge must be interpreted cautiously, because (as mentioned previously) commensal organisms are virtually always present. Only the identification of known pathogens is helpful.

NEOPLASIA OF THE CERVIX

Most tumors of the cervix are of epithelial origin and are caused by oncogenic strains of human papillomavirus (HPV). During development, the columnar, mucus-secreting epithelium of the endocervix is joined to the squamous epithelial covering of the exocervix at the cervical os. With the onset of puberty, the squamocolumnar junction undergoes eversion, causing columnar epithelium to become visible on the exocervix. The exposed columnar cells, however, eventually undergo squamous metaplasia, forming a region called the *transformation zone* (Fig. 18–4).

PATHOGENESIS

HPV, the causative agent of cervical neoplasia, has a tropism for the immature squamous cells of the transformation zone. Most HPV infections are transient and are eliminated within months by an acute and chronic inflammatory response. A subset of infections persists, however, and some of these progress to cervical intraepithelial neoplasia (CIN), a

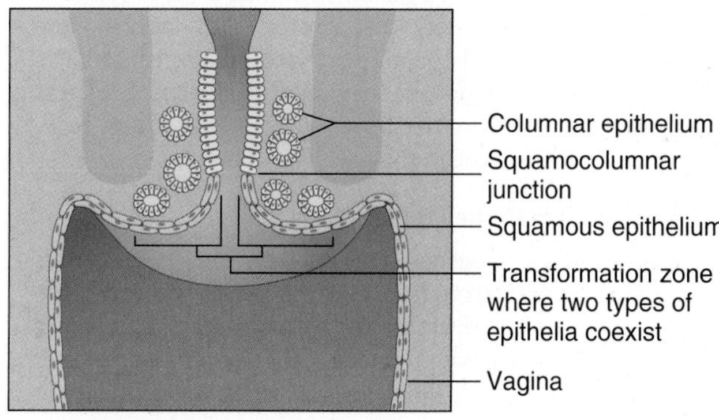

Figure 18–4 Development of the cervical transformation zone.

precursor lesion from which most invasive cervical carcinomas develop.

HPV is detectable by molecular methods in nearly all cases of CIN and cervical carcinoma. Important risk factors for the development of CIN and invasive carcinoma thus are directly related to HPV exposure and include

- Early age at first intercourse
- Multiple sexual partners
- Male partner with multiple previous sexual partners
- Persistent infection by high-risk strains of papillomavirus

Although HPV infection occurs in the most immature squamous cells of the basal layer, replication of HPV DNA takes place in more differentiated overlying squamous cells. Squamous cells at this stage of maturation do not normally replicate DNA, but HPV-infected squamous cells do, as a consequence of expression of two potent oncoproteins encoded in the HPV genome called E6 and E7. The E6 and E7 proteins bind and inactivate two critical tumor suppressors, p53 and Rb, respectively (Chapter 5), and in doing so promote growth and increased susceptibility to additional mutations that may eventually lead to carcinogenesis.

Recognized serotypes of HPV can be classified as high-risk or low-risk types based on their propensity to induce carcinogenesis. High-risk HPV infection is the most important risk factor for the development of CIN and carcinoma. Two high-risk HPV strains, types 16 and 18, account for approximately 70% of cases of CIN and cervical carcinoma. In general, infections with high-risk HPV serotypes are more likely to persist, which is a risk factor for progression to carcinoma. These HPV subtypes also show a propensity to integrate into the host cell genome, an event that is linked to progression. Low-risk HPV strains (e.g., types 6 and 11), on the other hand, are associated with development of condylomas of the lower genital tract (Fig. 18–5) and do not integrate into the host genome, remaining instead as free episomal viral DNA. Despite the strong association of HPV infection with cancer of the cervix, HPV is not sufficient to drive the neoplastic process. As mentioned below, several HPV-infected high-grade precursor lesions do not progress to invasive cancer. The progression of cervical dysplasias to cervical cancers has been attributed to diverse factors such as immune and hormonal status, or co-infection with other sexually transmitted agents. More recently, somatically acquired mutations in the tumor suppressor gene *LKB1* were identified in more than 20% of cervical cancers. *LKB1* was first identified as the gene mutated in Peutz-Jeghers syndrome, an autosomal dominant condition characterized by hamartomatous polyps of the GI tract (Chapter 14) and a significantly elevated risk of epithelial malignancies at a variety of anatomic sites including the cervix. *LKB1* is also frequently inactivated in lung cancer. The LKB1 protein is a serine-threonine kinase that phosphorylates and activates AMPK, a metabolic sensor. AMPK in turn regulates cell growth through the mTOR complex.

Cervical Intraepithelial Neoplasia (CIN)

HPV-related carcinogenesis begins with the precancerous epithelial change termed CIN, which usually precedes the development of an overt cancer by many years, sometimes decades. In keeping with this idea, CIN peaks in incidence at about 30 years of age, whereas invasive carcinoma peaks at about 45 years of age.

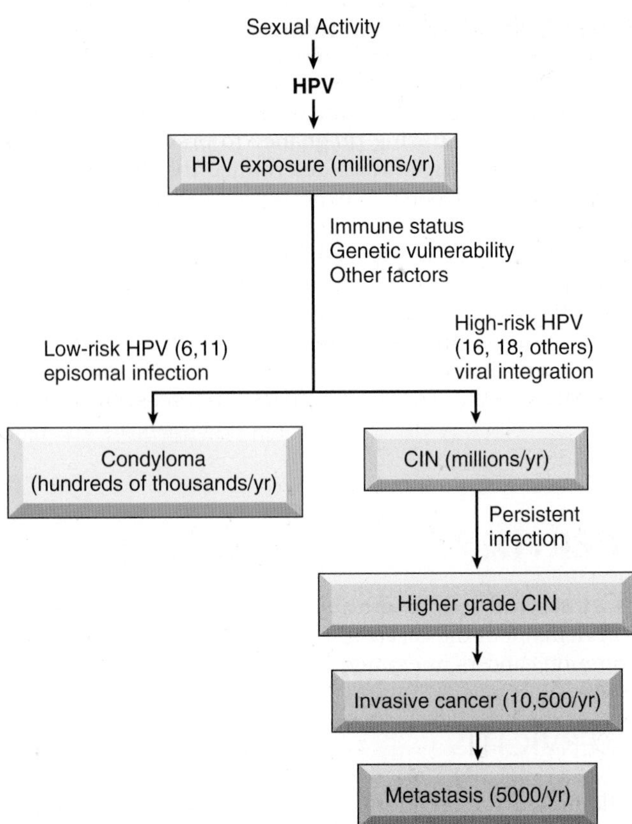

Figure 18–5 Possible consequences of human papillomavirus (HPV) infection. Progression is associated with integration of virus and acquisition of additional mutations as discussed in the text. CIN, cervical intraepithelial neoplasia.

CIN usually starts as low-grade dysplasia (CIN I) and progresses to moderate (CIN II) and then severe dysplasia (CIN III) over time; exceptions have been reported, however, and some patients already have CIN III when the condition is first diagnosed. Generally speaking, the higher the grade of CIN, the greater the likelihood of progression; of note, however, in many cases, even high-grade lesions fail to progress to cancer and may even regress. Because decisions about patient management are two-tiered (i.e., observation versus surgical treatment), this three-tiered grading system has recently been simplified to a two-tiered system, with CIN I renamed **low-grade squamous intraepithelial lesion** (LSIL) and CIN II and CIN III combined into one category referred to as **high-grade squamous intraepithelial lesion** (HSIL). As shown in Table 18–1, the decision to treat HSIL and to observe LSIL is based on differences in the natural histories of these two groups of lesions.

Table 18–1 Natural History of Squamous Intraepithelial Lesions (SILs)

Lesion	Regress	Persist	Progress
LSIL (CIN I)	60%	30%	10% (to HSIL)
HSIL (CIN II, III)	30%	60%	10% (to carcinoma)*

LSIL, low-grade SIL; HSIL, high-grade SIL.
*Progression within 10 years.

Cervical precancerous lesions are associated with abnormalities in cytologic preparations (Pap smears) that can be detected long before any abnormality is visible on gross inspection. Early detection of dysplastic changes is the rationale for the Papanicolaou (Pap) test, in which cells are scraped from the transformation zone and examined microscopically. To date, the Pap smear remains the most successful cancer screening test ever developed. In the United States, Pap screening has dramatically lowered the incidence of invasive cervical tumors to about 12,000 cases annually with a mortality of about 4000 per year; in fact, cervical cancer no longer ranks among the top 10 causes of cancer deaths in U.S. women. Paradoxically, the incidence of CIN has increased to its present level of more than 50,000 cases annually. Increased detection has certainly contributed to this.

The recently introduced quadrivalent HPV vaccine for types 6, 11, 16, and 18 is very effective in preventing HPV infections, which is expected to greatly lower the frequency of genital warts and cervical cancers associated with these HPV serotypes. Despite its efficacy, the vaccine does not supplant the need for routine cervical cancer screening—many at-risk women are already infected, and the vaccine protects against only some of the many oncogenic HPV serotypes.

MORPHOLOGY

Figure 18–6 illustrates the three stages of CIN. **CIN I** is characterized by dyplastic changes in the lower third of the squamous epithelium and koilocytotic change in the superficial layers of the epithelium. In **CIN II,** dysplasia extends to the middle third of the epithelium and takes the form of delayed keratinocyte maturation. It also is associated with some variation in cell and nuclear size, heterogeneity of nuclear chromatin, and presence of mitoses above the basal layer extending into the middle third of the epithelium. The superficial layer of cells shows some differentiation and occasionally demonstrates the koilocytotic changes described. The next stage, **CIN III,** is marked by almost complete loss of maturation, even greater variation in cell and nuclear size, chromatin heterogeneity, disorderly orientation of the cells, and normal or abnormal mitoses; these changes affect virtually all layers of the epithelium. Koilocytotic change usually is absent. These histologic features correlate with the cytologic appearances shown in Figure 18–7. As mentioned previously, for clinical purposes CIN is divided into LSIL (CIN I) and HSIL (CIN II and CIN III).

CIN is asymptomatic and comes to clinical attention through an abnormal Pap smear result. These cases are followed up by colposcopy, during which acetic acid is used to highlight the location of lesions and the areas to be biopsied. Women with biopsy-documented LSIL are managed conservatively with careful observation, whereas HSILs are treated with surgical excision (cone biopsy). Follow-up smears and clinical examination are mandated for life in patients with HSIL, as these women remain at risk for HPV-associated cervical, vulvar, and vaginal cancers.

Invasive Carcinoma of the Cervix

The most common cervical carcinomas are squamous cell carcinomas (75%), followed by adenocarcinomas and mixed adenosquamous carcinomas (20%) and small cell neuroendocrine carcinomas (less than 5%). All of these types of carcinomas are caused by HPV. Of interest, the relative proportion of adenocarcinomas has been increasing in recent decades owing to the decreasing incidence of invasive squamous carcinoma and suboptimal detection of glandular lesions by Pap smear.

Squamous cell carcinoma has a peak incidence at the age of about 45 years, some 10 to 15 years after detection of precursor CIN. As already discussed, progression of CIN to invasive carcinoma is variable and unpredictable and requires HPV infection as well as mutations in genes such as *LKB*. Risk factors for progression include cigarette smoking and human immunodeficiency virus

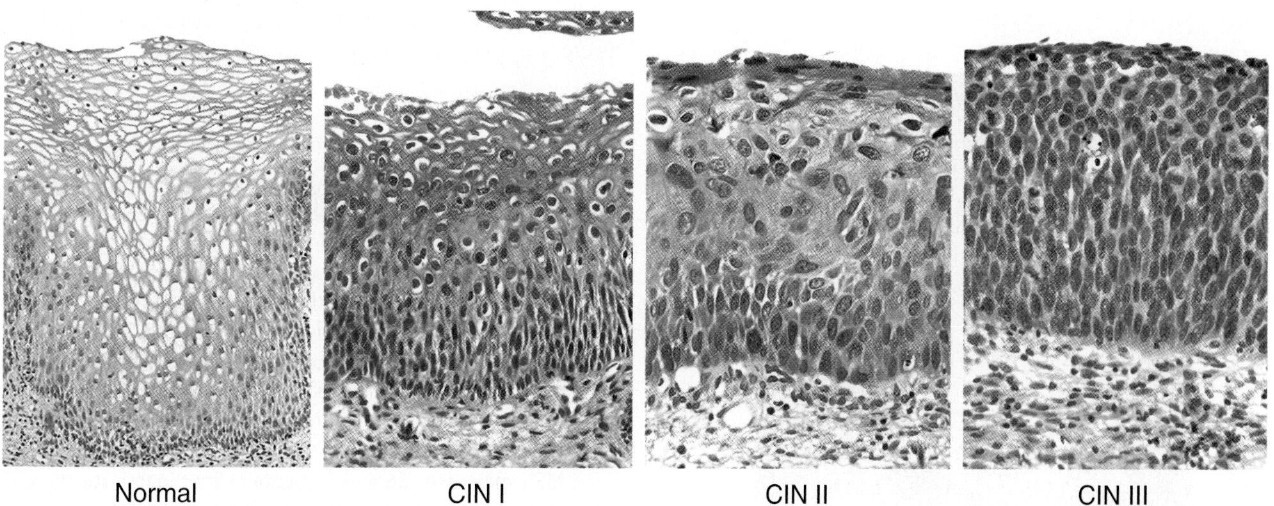

Figure 18–6 Spectrum of cervical intraepithelial neoplasia (CIN), with normal squamous epithelium for comparison: CIN I with koilocytotic atypia; CIN II with progressive atypia in all layers of the epithelium; and CIN III (carcinoma in situ) with diffuse atypia and loss of maturation.

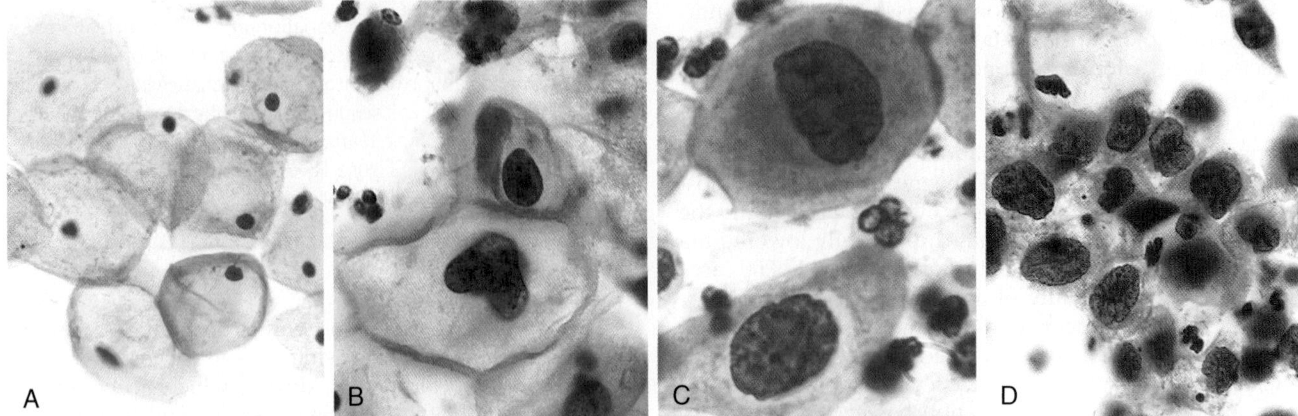

Figure 18–7 Cytologic features of cervical intraepithelial neoplasia (CIN) in a Papanicolaou smear. Superficial squamous cells may stain either red or blue. **A,** Normal exfoliated superficial squamous epithelial cells. **B,** CIN I—low-grade squamous intraepithelial lesion (LSIL). **C** and **D,** CIN II and CIN III, respectively—both high-grade squamous intraepithelial lesions (HSILs). Note the reduction in cytoplasm and the increase in the nucleus-to-cytoplasm ratio as the grade of the lesion increases. This observation reflects the progressive loss of cellular differentiation on the surface of the cervical lesions from which these cells are exfoliated (Figure 18–6).

(Courtesy of Dr. Edmund S. Cibas, Brigham and Women's Hospital, Boston, Massachusetts.)

(HIV) infection, the latter finding suggesting that immune surveillance has a role in holding CIN in check. Although risk factors may help stratify patients who are likely to progress from CIN to carcinoma, the only reliable way to monitor the disease course is with frequent physical examinations coupled with biopsy of suspicious lesions.

MORPHOLOGY

Invasive carcinomas of the cervix develop in the **transformation zone** and range from microscopic foci of stromal invasion to grossly conspicuous exophytic tumors (Fig. 18–8). Tumors encircling the cervix and penetrating into the underlying stroma produce a **barrel cervix,** which can be identified by direct palpation. Extension into the parametrial soft tissues can affix the uterus to the surrounding pelvic structures. The likelihood of spread to pelvic lymph nodes correlates with the depth of tumor invasion and the presence of tumor cells in vascular spaces. The risk of metastasis increases from less than 1% for tumors under 3 mm in depth to over 10% once invasion exceeds 3 mm. With the exception of unusual tumors exhibiting neuroendocrine differentiation, which are uniformly aggressive in their behavior, cervical carcinomas are graded based on their degree of squamous differentiation.

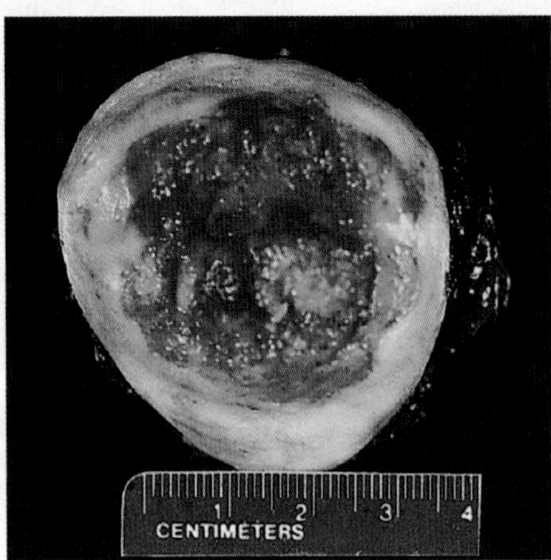

Figure 18–8 Cervical os with surrounding, invasive, exophytic cervical carcinoma.

Clinical Course

Invasive cervical cancer most often is seen in women who have never had a Pap smear or who have not been screened for many years. In such cases, cervical cancer often is symptomatic, with patients coming to medical attention for unexpected vaginal bleeding, leukorrhea, painful coitus (dyspareunia), or dysuria. Treatment is surgical by hysterectomy and lymph node dissection; small microinvasive carcinomas may be treated with cone biopsy. Mortality is most strongly related to tumor stage and, in the case of neuroendocrine carcinomas, to cell type. Most patients with advanced disease die as a result of local invasion rather than distant metastasis. In particular, renal failure stemming from obstruction of the urinary bladder and ureters is a common cause of death.

SUMMARY

Cervical Neoplasia

- Risk factors for cervical carcinoma are related to HPV exposure, such as early age at first intercourse, multiple sexual partners, and other factors including cigarette smoking and immunodeficiency.
- Nearly all cervical carcinomas are caused by HPV infections, particularly high-risk HPV types 16, 18, 31, and 33; the HPV vaccine is effective in preventing infection due to HPV types 16 and 18.
- HPV expresses E6 and E7 proteins that inactivate the p53 and Rb tumor suppressors, respectively, resulting in increased cell proliferation and suppression of DNA

embryonic ridge (milk line). Besides being curiosities, these congenital anomalies are subject to the same diseases that affect the normal breast. *Congenital inversion of the nipple* is of clinical significance because similar changes may be produced by an underlying cancer. *Galactocele* arises during lactation from cystic dilation of an obstructed duct. Besides being painful "lumps," these cysts may rupture, inciting a local inflammatory reaction, with production of an indurated focus falsely suggestive of malignancy.

FIBROCYSTIC CHANGES

The designation *fibrocystic* is applied to a miscellany of changes in the female breast that consist predominantly of cyst formation and fibrosis. In the past, these lesions were called *fibrocystic disease*. However, since most of these changes have little clinical significance beyond the need to distinguish them from cancer, the term *fibrocystic change* is preferred.

Overall, fibrocystic changes are the most common breast abnormality seen in premenopausal women. The changes tend to arise during reproductive age and are most likely a consequence of the *cyclic breast changes that occur normally in the menstrual cycle*. Estrogenic therapy and oral contraceptives do not seem to increase the incidence of these alterations, and oral contraceptives may, in fact, *decrease* the risk.

Fibrocystic changes can be subdivided into nonproliferative and proliferative patterns, as described next.

Nonproliferative Changes

Cysts and Fibrosis

Nonproliferative changes are the most common type of fibrocystic lesions, characterized by an increase in fibrous stroma associated with dilation of ducts and formation of variably sized cysts.

MORPHOLOGY

A single, large cyst may form within one breast, but changes usually are multifocal and often bilateral. The involved areas appear as ill-defined, diffusely increased densities and discrete nodularities on mammography. The cysts range from less than 1 cm and up to 5 cm in diameter. Unopened, they are brown to blue **(blue dome cysts)** and are filled with watery, turbid fluid (Fig. 18–23). The secretions within the cysts may calcify, producing microcalcifications on mammograms. Histologic examination reveals an epithelial lining that in larger cysts may be flattened or even totally atrophic (Fig. 18–24). Frequently, the lining cells are large and polygonal with abundant granular, eosinophilic cytoplasm and small, round, deeply chromatic nuclei. Such morphology is called **apocrine metaplasia** and virtually always is benign.

The stroma surrounding all types of cysts usually consists of compressed fibrous tissue that has lost the delicate, myxomatous appearance of normal breast stroma. A stromal lymphocytic infiltrate is common in this and all other variants of fibrocystic change.

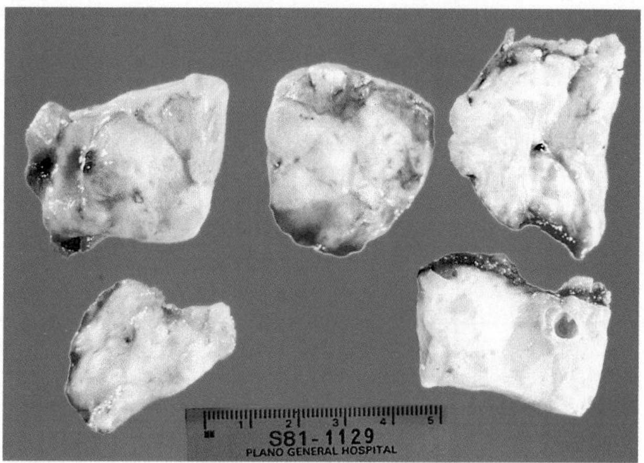

Figure 18–23 Fibrocystic change seen in breast biopsy specimens. The scattered, poorly demarcated white areas represent foci of fibrosis. In the specimen at the *lower right*, a transected empty cyst is evident; in the two specimens on the *left*, unopened blue dome cysts are seen.
(Courtesy of Dr. Kyle Molberg, Department of Pathology, University of Texas Southwestern Medical School, Dallas, Texas.)

Proliferative Change

Epithelial Hyperplasia

Normal ducts and lobules of the breast are lined by two layers of cells—a layer of luminal cells overlying a second layer of myoepithelial cells. *Epithelial hyperplasia* is recognized by the presence of more than two cell layers. The spectrum of epithelial hyperplasia ranges from mild and orderly to atypical hyperplasias with features that resemble those of in situ carcinoma.

MORPHOLOGY

The gross appearance of epithelial hyperplasia is not distinctive and is dominated by coexisting fibrous or cystic changes. Histologic examination shows an almost infinite spectrum of proliferative alterations. The ducts, ductules, or lobules may be filled with orderly cuboidal cells within which small gland

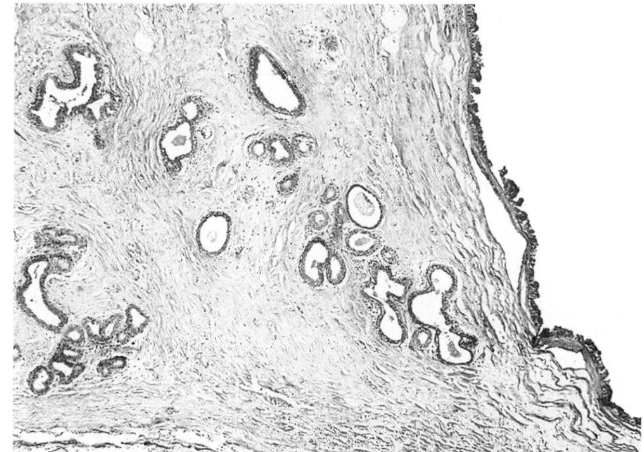

Figure 18–24 Fibrocystic change of the nonproliferative type in a breast biopsy specimen. Visible in this field are dilated ducts, producing microcysts and, at *right*, the wall of a large cyst lined with epithelial cells.
(Courtesy of Dr. Kyle Molberg, Department of Pathology, University of Texas Southwestern Medical School, Dallas, Texas.)

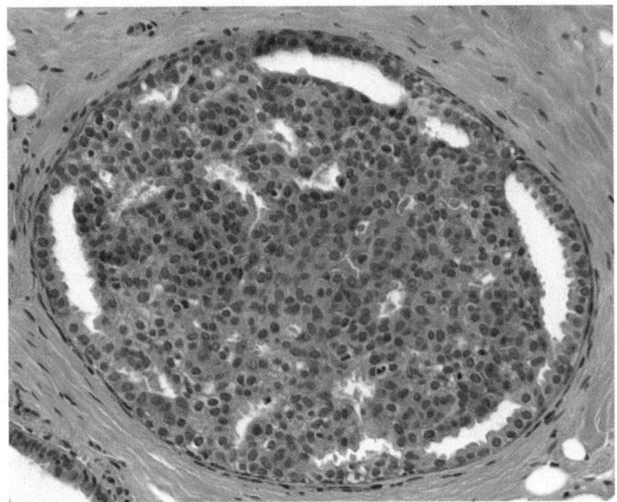

Figure 18–25 Epithelial hyperplasia in a breast biopsy specimen. The duct lumen is filled with a heterogeneous population of cells of differing morphology. Irregular slitlike fenestrations are prominent at the periphery.

patterns (called **fenestrations**) can be discerned (Fig. 18–25). Sometimes, the proliferating epithelium projects as multiple small papillary excrescences into the ductal lumen **(ductal papillomatosis).** The degree of hyperplasia, judged in part by the number of layers of intraductal epithelium, can be mild, moderate, or marked. Occasionally, hyperplasia produces microcalcifications on mammography, raising concern for cancer.

In some instances the hyperplastic cells have features bearing some resemblance to ductal carcinoma in situ (described later). Such hyperplasia is called **atypical ductal hyperplasia. Atypical lobular hyperplasia** is used to describe hyperplasias that exhibit changes that approach but do not meet diagnostic criteria for lobular carcinoma in situ. Both atypical ductal and lobular hyperplasia are associated with an increased risk of invasive carcinoma.

Sclerosing Adenosis

The type of fibrocystic change termed *sclerosing adenosis* is less common than cysts and hyperplasia but is significant because its clinical and morphologic features may mimic those of carcinoma. These lesions contain marked intralobular fibrosis and proliferation of small ductules and acini.

MORPHOLOGY

Grossly, the lesion has a hard, rubbery consistency, similar to that of breast cancer. Histologic examination shows a characteristic **proliferation of luminal spaces (adenosis) lined by epithelial cells and myoepithelial cells,** yielding masses of small glands within a fibrous stroma (Fig. 18–26). Aggregated glands may be virtually back to back, with single or multiple layers of cells in contact with one another. Marked stromal fibrosis, which may compress and distort the proliferating epithelium, is always associated with the adenosis—hence the designation **sclerosing adenosis.** This overgrowth of fibrous tissue may completely compress the lumina of the acini and ducts, so that they appear as solid cords of cells—a pattern that is difficult to distinguish histologically from invasive ductal carcinoma. The presence of double layers of epithelium and the identification of myoepithelial elements are helpful in arriving at the correct diagnosis.

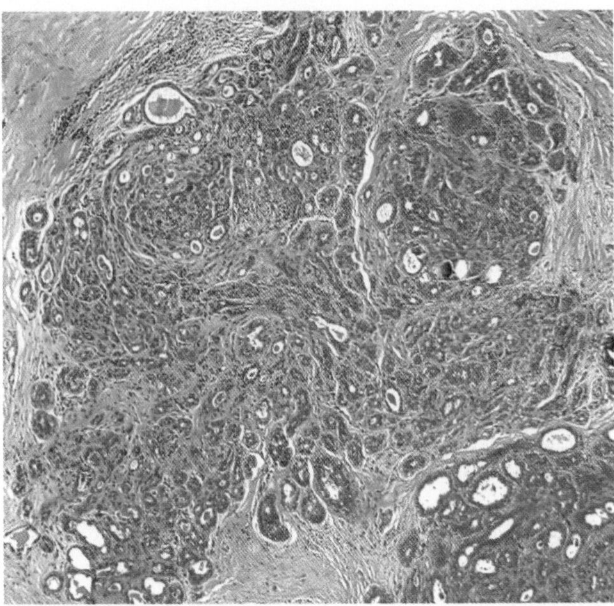

Figure 18–26 Sclerosing adenosis, breast biopsy. The involved terminal duct lobular unit is enlarged, and the acini are compressed and distorted by surrounding dense stroma. Unlike in breast carcinoma, the acini are arranged in a swirling pattern, and the outer border is well circumscribed.

Relationship of Fibrocystic Changes to Breast Carcinoma

Certain clinical features of fibrocystic change tend to distinguish it from cancer, but the only certain way of making this distinction is through biopsy and histologic examination. Although fibrocystic changes are benign, some features may confer an increased risk for development of cancer:

- *Minimal or no increased risk of breast carcinoma*: fibrosis, cystic changes, apocrine metaplasia, mild hyperplasia
- *Slightly increased risk* (1.5- to 2-fold): moderate to florid hyperplasia (without atypia), ductal papillomatosis, sclerosing adenosis
- *Significantly increased risk* (5-fold): atypical hyperplasia, whether ductular or lobular

Proliferative fibrocystic changes usually are bilateral and multifocal and are associated with increased risk of subsequent carcinoma in both breasts.

SUMMARY

Fibrocystic Changes

- Fibrocystic changes may be classified as nonproliferative (cystic) or proliferative.
- Proliferative lesions include epithelial proliferations of ducts and lobules (with or without features of atypia) and adenosis (proliferation of terminal ducts), sometimes associated with fibrosis (sclerosing adenosis).
- Atypical hyperplasia (whether ductal or lobular) is associated with a five-fold increase in the risk of developing carcinoma.

INFLAMMATORY PROCESSES

Inflammatory processes involving the breast are uncommon and are usually associated with pain and tenderness in the affected areas. Included in this category are several forms of mastitis and traumatic fat necrosis, none of which increase the risk of cancer.

Acute mastitis develops when bacteria, usually *Staphylococcus aureus,* gain access to the breast tissue through the ducts. The vast majority of cases arise during the early weeks of nursing, when the skin of the nipple is vulnerable to the development of fissures. Clinically, staphylococcal infections induce typical acute inflammatory changes, which can progress to form single or multiple abscesses.

Mammary duct ectasia (plasma cell mastitis) is a nonbacterial chronic inflammation of the breast associated with inspissation of breast secretions in the main excretory ducts. Ductal dilation and eventual rupture leads to reactive changes in the surrounding tissue that may present as a poorly defined periareolar mass with nipple retraction, mimicking the changes caused by some cancers. It is an uncommon condition usually encountered in parous women between 40 and 60 years of age.

MORPHOLOGY

Usually the inflammatory changes are confined to an area drained by one or more of the major excretory ducts of the nipple. On histologic examination, the ducts are filled with granular debris, sometimes containing leukocytes and lipid-laden macrophages. The lining epithelium generally is destroyed. **The most distinguishing features consist of a prominent lymphoplasmacytic infiltrate and occasional granulomas in the periductal stroma.**

Fat necrosis is an uncommon, innocuous lesion that is significant only because it often produces a mass. Most women with this condition report some antecedent trauma to the breast.

MORPHOLOGY

During the early stage of traumatic fat necrosis, the lesion is small, often tender, rarely more than 2 cm in diameter, and sharply localized. It consists of a central focus of necrotic fat cells surrounded by neutrophils and lipid-laden macrophages, sometimes with giant cells. This lesion later becomes enclosed by fibrous tissue and mononuclear leukocytes and eventually is replaced by scar tissue or a cyst consisting of necrotic debris. Calcifications may develop in either the scar or the cyst wall.

TUMORS OF THE BREAST

Tumors are the most important lesions of the female breast. Although they may arise from connective tissue or epithelial structures, it is the latter that give rise to the common breast neoplasms.

Fibroadenoma

Fibroadenoma is by far the most common benign neoplasm of the female breast. It is a biphasic tumor composed of fibroblastic stroma and epithelium-lined glands; however, only the stromal cells are clonal and truly neoplastic. Fibroadenomas typically appear in young women with a peak incidence in the third decade of life. They usually manifest as solitary, discrete, mobile masses. An absolute or relative increase in estrogen is thought to contribute to their development. In addition, fibroadenomas may enlarge late in the menstrual cycle and during pregnancy; after menopause, they may regress and calcify.

MORPHOLOGY

The fibroadenomas form discrete masses, 1 cm to 10 cm in diameter and of firm consistency (Fig. 18–27). A cut section shows a uniform tan-white color, punctuated by softer yellow-pink specks representing the glandular areas. Histologic examination shows a loose fibroblastic stroma containing ductlike, epithelium-lined spaces of various shapes and sizes. As in normal breast tissue, these glandular spaces are lined by luminal and myoepithelial cells with a well-defined, intact basement membrane.

Phyllodes Tumor

Like fibroadenomas, phyllodes tumors are biphasic, being composed of neoplastic stromal cells and epithelium-lined glands. However, the stromal element of these tumors is more cellular and abundant, often forming epithelium-lined leaflike projections (*phyllodes* is Greek for "leaflike"). These tumors are much less common than fibroadenomas and arise de novo, not from preexisting fibroadenomas. In the past, they had the tongue-tangling name *cystosarcoma phyllodes*—an unfortunate term because these tumors usually are benign. Ominous changes suggesting malignancy include increased stromal cellularity, anaplasia, high mitotic activity, rapid increase in size, and infiltrative margins. Fortunately, most phyllodes tumors remain localized and are cured by excision; malignant lesions may recur, but they also tend to remain localized. Only 15% of all cases are fully malignant, metastasizing to distant sites.

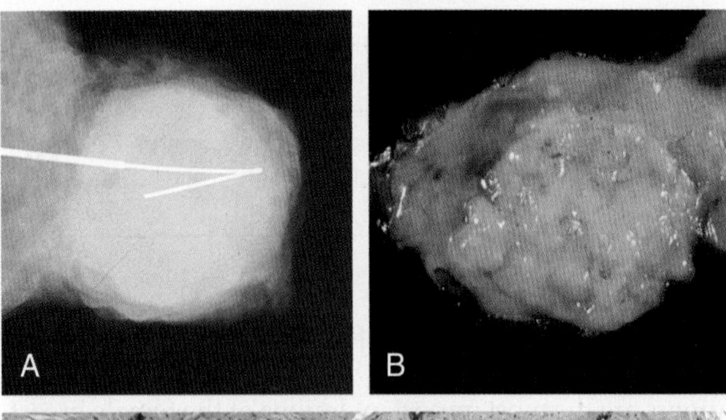

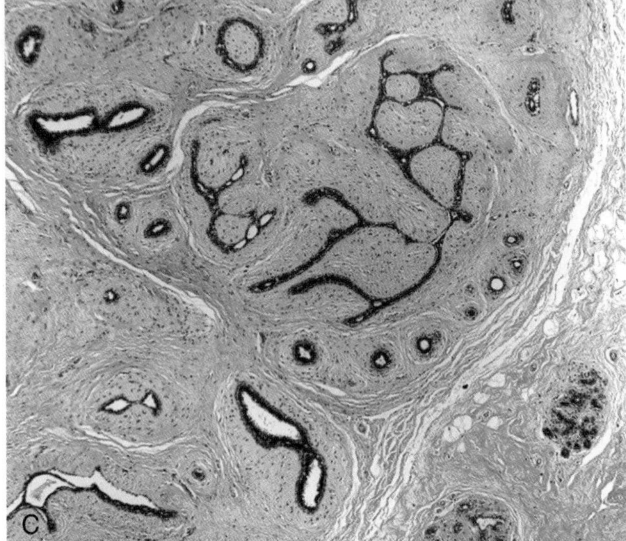

Figure 18–27 Fibroadenoma. **A,** The radiograph shows a characteristic well-circumscribed mass. **B,** In this gross specimen, a rubbery well-circumscribed mass is clearly demarcated from the surrounding adipose tissue. **C,** In this micrograph, the proliferation of intralobular stroma can be seen to compress the entrapped glands, creating a "pushing" border that is sharply delineated from the surrounding normal tissue.

Intraductal Papilloma

Intraductal papilloma is a benign neoplastic papillary growth. It is most often seen in premenopausal women. These lesions typically are solitary and found within the principal lactiferous ducts or sinuses. The clinical presentation may include

- Serous or bloody nipple discharge
- The presence of a *small subareolar tumor* a few millimeters in diameter
- *Nipple retraction,* in rare instances

MORPHOLOGY

The tumors usually are solitary and less than 1 cm in diameter, consisting of delicate, branching growths within a dilated duct. On histologic examination, they are composed of multiple papillae, each having a connective tissue core covered by epithelial cells that are double-layered, with an outer luminal layer overlying a myoepithelial layer. The presence of a double-layered epithelium helps to distinguish intraductal papilloma from intraductal papillary carcinoma, which can present with clinical features similar to benign papilloma.

Carcinoma

In 2010, more than 200,000 invasive breast cancers were diagnosed in women in the United States, and around 40,000 women died of this disease, making this scourge second only to lung cancer as a cause of cancer-related death in women. The lifetime risk of developing breast cancer is 1 in 8 for women in the United States. During the past 3 decades, the mortality rate among those diagnosed with breast cancer has dropped from 30% to 20%, mostly as a result of improved screening and treatment.

Epidemiology and Risk Factors

A large number of risk factors for breast cancer have been identified. Table 18–5 divides these into well-established and less well-established groups and indicates, when possible, the relative risk posed by each. Some of the more important risk factors are summarized next.

Age. Risk steadily increases throughout life, especially after menopause, peaking at roughly 80 years of age; 75% of women with breast cancer are older than 50 years of age, and only 5% are younger than 40.

Geographic Variations. Surprising differences in the incidence and mortality rates of breast cancer have been reported for various countries. The risk for development of this disease is significantly higher in North America and northern Europe than in Asia and Africa. For example, the incidence and mortality rates are five times higher in the

Table 18–5 Breast Cancer Risk Factors

Factor	Relative Risk
Well-Established Factors	
Geography	Varies in different areas
Age	Increases after age 30
Family history	
First-degree relative with breast cancer	1.2–3.0
Premenopausal	3.1
Premenopausal and bilateral	8.5–9.0
Postmenopausal	1.5
Postmenopausal and bilateral	4.0–5.4
Menstrual history	
Age at menarche <12 years	1.3
Age at menopause >55 years	1.5–2.0
Pregnancy	
First live birth from ages 25 to 29 years	1.5
First live birth after age 30 years	1.9
First live birth after age 35 years	2.0–3.0
Nulliparous	3.0
Benign breast disease	
Proliferative disease without atypia	1.6
Proliferative disease with atypical hyperplasia	>2.0
Lobular carcinoma in situ	6.9–12.0
Other Possible Factors	
Exogenous estrogens	
Oral contraceptives	
Obesity	
High-fat diet	
Alcohol consumption	
Cigarette smoking	

Data from Bilimoria MM, Morrow M: The women at increased risk for breast cancer: evaluation and management strategies. CA Cancer J Clin 46:263, 1995.

United States than in Japan. These differences seem to be environmental rather than genetic in origin, because migrants from low-incidence to high-incidence areas tend to acquire the rates of their adoptive countries, and vice versa. Diet, reproductive patterns, and nursing habits are thought to be involved.

Race/Ethnicity. The highest rate of breast cancer is in non-Hispanic white women. However, Hispanic and African American women tend to develop cancer at a younger age and are more likely to develop aggressive tumors that present at an advanced stage. Such disparities between ethnicities are an area of intense study and currently are thought to be due to a combination of genetic differences and social factors, such as lifestyle choices and access to health care.

Other Risk Factors. *Prolonged exposure to exogenous estrogens* postmenopausally, as occurs with hormone replacement therapy, has been proved to be useful for the prevention of osteoporosis. However, according to recent studies, relatively short-term use of combined estrogen plus progestin hormone therapy is associated with an increased risk of breast cancer, diagnosis at a more advanced stage of breast cancer, and higher incidence of abnormal mammograms. Because the 2002 Women's Health Initiative report suggested greater harm than benefit of combined estrogen plus a progestin, a precipitous decline has occurred in estrogen and progestin use, along with a serious reevaluation of perimenopausal hormone therapy.

Oral contraceptives have not been shown to affect the risk of breast cancer, even in women who have taken the pill for a long time or in women with a family history of breast cancer.

Ionizing radiation to the chest increases the risk of breast cancer. The magnitude of the risk depends on the radiation dose, the time since exposure, and age. Only women in whom irradiation occurred before age 30, during breast development, seem to be affected. For example, breast cancer develops in 20% to 30% of women who underwent irradiation for Hodgkin lymphoma in their teens and 20s, but the risk for women treated later in life is not elevated. Of import, the low doses of radiation associated with mammographic screening have no significant effect on the incidence of breast cancer.

Many other, less well-established risk factors, such as obesity, alcohol consumption, and a diet high in fat, have been implicated in the development of breast cancer by analysis of population studies. The risk associated with obesity probably is due to exposure of the breast to estrogen produced by adipose tissue.

PATHOGENESIS

The causes of breast cancer remain incompletely understood. However, three sets of influences seem to be important: (1) genetic changes, (2) hormonal influences, and (3) environmental variables.

Genetic Changes. As with all cancers, mutations affecting proto-oncogenes and tumor suppressor genes in breast epithelium underlie oncogenesis. Among the best-characterized is **overexpression of the *HER2/NEU* proto-oncogene,** which undergoes amplification in up to 30% of invasive breast cancers. This gene is a member of the epidermal growth factor receptor family, and its overexpression is associated with a poor prognosis. **Amplification of *RAS* and *MYC* genes also has been reported in some human breast cancers.** Mutations of the well-known tumor suppressor genes *RB* and *TP53* also may be present. A large number of genes including the estrogen receptor gene may be inactivated by promoter hypermethylation. Undoubtedly, the transformation process involves multiple acquired genetic alterations, which can occur in various combinations, thereby giving rise to different subtypes of breast cancer. **Gene expression profiling can separate breast cancer into four molecular subtypes:** (1) luminal A (estrogen receptor–positive, *HER2/NEU*-negative); (2) luminal B (estrogen receptor–positive, *HER2/NEU* overexpressing); (3) *HER2/NEU* positive (*HER2/NEU* over expressing, estrogen receptor–negative); and (4) basal-like (estrogen receptor–negative and *HER2/NEU*-negative). These subtypes are associated with different outcomes and, in some instances, different therapies.

Approximately 10% of breast cancers are related to specific inherited mutations. Women who carry a breast cancer susceptibility gene are more likely to have bilateral cancer, to have other familial forms of cancer (e.g., ovarian cancer), to have a positive family history (i.e., multiple first-degree relatives affected before menopause), to develop breast cancer before menopause, and to belong to certain ethnic groups (e.g., people of Ashkenazi Jewish descent). **Roughly one third of women with hereditary breast cancer have mutations in *BRCA1* (at chromosomal locus 17q21.3) or *BRCA2* (located on chromosomal band 13q12-13).** These genes encode large, complex proteins that do not exhibit close homology to each other or other proteins. Although the molecular basis for their strong association with breast cancer risk is still being elucidated, both BRCA1 and BRCA2 are believed to function in a common DNA repair pathway (Chapter 5).

Genetically, *BRCA1* and *BRCA2* are classic tumor suppressor genes, in that cancer arises only when both alleles are inactivated or defective—the first genetic lesion caused by a germline mutation and the second by a subsequent somatic mutation. Genetic testing is available, but its utility is complicated by the existence of hundreds of different mutant alleles, only some of which confer cancer susceptibility. The degree of penetrance, age at cancer onset, and susceptibility to other types of cancers differ among the specific mutations. Most carriers, however, develop breast cancer by the age of 70 years, as compared with only 7% of women who do not carry a mutation. The role of these genes in nonhereditary sporadic breast cancer is less clear, as mutations affecting *BRCA1* and *BRCA2* are infrequent in sporadic tumors. Less common genetic diseases associated with breast cancer are the Li-Fraumeni syndrome (caused by germline mutations in *TP53*) (Chapter 5), Cowden syndrome (caused by germline mutations in *PTEN*—mentioned earlier under endometrial carcinoma) (see also Chapter 14), and the ataxia-telangiectasia gene carriers (Chapter 5).

Hormonal Influences. Endogenous estrogen excess, or more accurately, hormonal imbalance, clearly has a significant role. Many of the risk factors mentioned (long duration of reproductive life, nulliparity, and late age at birth of first child) involve increased exposure to estrogen unopposed by progesterone (Table 18–5). Functioning ovarian tumors that elaborate estrogens are associated with breast cancer in postmenopausal women. Estrogens stimulate the production of growth factors, such as transforming growth factor-α, platelet-derived growth factor, and fibroblast growth factor and others, which may promote tumor development through paracrine and autocrine mechanisms.

Environmental Variables. Environmental influences are suggested by the variable incidence of breast cancer in genetically homogeneous groups and the geographic differences in prevalence, as discussed earlier.

MORPHOLOGY

The most common location of tumors within the breast is in the upper outer quadrant (50%), followed by the central portion (20%). About 4% of women with breast cancer have bilateral primary tumors or sequential lesions in the same breast.

Breast cancers are classified according to whether they have or have not penetrated the limiting basement membrane: Those that remain within this boundary are termed in situ carcinomas, and those that have spread beyond it are designated invasive or infiltrating carcinomas. In this classification, the main forms of breast carcinoma are as follows:

A. Noninvasive
   1. Ductal carcinoma in situ (DCIS)
   2. Lobular carcinoma in situ (LCIS)
B. Invasive (infiltrating)
   1. Invasive ductal carcinoma ("not otherwise specified"), the most common subtype of invasive carcinoma
   2. Invasive lobular carcinoma
   3. Medullary carcinoma
   4. Colloid carcinoma (mucinous carcinoma)
   5. Tubular carcinoma
   6. Other types

Noninvasive (in situ) Carcinoma

There are two types of noninvasive breast carcinoma: DCIS and LCIS. Morphologic studies have shown that both types usually arise from cells in the terminal duct lobular unit. DCIS tends to fill and distort ductlike spaces. By contrast, LCIS usually expands but does not alter the acini of lobules. Both are confined by a basement membrane and do not invade into stroma or lymphovascular channels.

DCIS has a wide variety of histologic appearances. Architectural patterns often are mixed and include solid, comedo, cribriform, papillary, micropapillary, and "clinging" types. Necrosis may be present in any of these types. Nuclear appearance tends to be uniform in a given case and ranges from bland and monotonous (low nuclear grade) to pleomorphic (high nuclear grade). The **comedo** subtype is distinctive and is characterized by cells with high-grade nuclei with extensive central necrosis (Fig. 18–28). The name derives from the toothpaste-like necrotic tissue that extrudes from transected ducts on application of gentle pressure. **Calcifications frequently are associated with DCIS,** originating as either calcified necrotic debris or calcified secretory material. The proportion of breast cancers that are diagnosed at the DCIS stage is only 5% in unscreened populations but up to 40% in screened populations, largely because of the ability of mammography to detect calcifications. DCIS only rarely manifests as a palpable or radiologically detectable mass. The prognosis with DCIS is excellent, with greater than 97% long-term survival after simple mastectomy. In some women, distant metastases develop without local recurrence; these patients usually are found to have extensive high-nuclear-grade DCIS, probably with small, undetected areas of invasion. At least one third of women with small areas of untreated DCIS of low nuclear grade will eventually develop invasive carcinoma. When invasive cancer does develop, it usually is in the same breast and quadrant as the earlier DCIS. Current treatment strategies attempt to eradicate the DCIS by surgery and irradiation. Treatment with antiestrogenic agents such as tamoxifen and aromatase also may decrease the risk of recurrence.

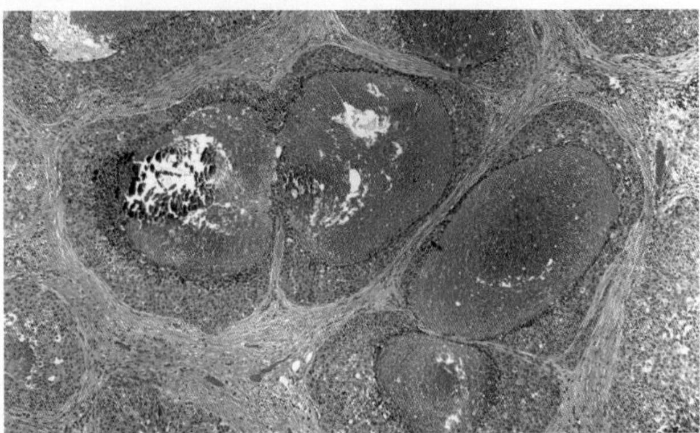

Figure 18–28 Comedo ductal carcinoma in situ (DCIS). Several adjacent ducts are filled by tumor associated with large central zones of necrosis and calcified debris. This type of DCIS most frequently is detected as radiologic calcifications.

Paget disease of the nipple is caused by the extension of DCIS up the lactiferous ducts and into the contiguous skin of the nipple, producing a unilateral crusting exudate over the nipple and areolar skin. In almost all cases, an underlying carcinoma is present, and approximately 50% of the time this carcinoma is invasive. Prognosis is based on the underlying carcinoma and is not affected by the presence of Paget disease.

LCIS has a uniform appearance. The cells are monomorphic with bland, round nuclei and occur in loosely cohesive clusters within the lobules (Fig. 18–29). Intracellular mucin vacuoles (sometimes forming signet ring cells) are common. LCIS is virtually always an incidental finding, because unlike DCIS, it is only rarely associated with calcifications. Therefore, the incidence of LCIS has remained unchanged in mammographically screened populations. Approximately one third of women with LCIS will eventually develop invasive carcinoma. Unlike with DCIS, **subsequent invasive carcinomas may arise in either breast.** Most of these cancers are invasive lobular carcinomas; however, invasive ductal carcinomas also arise from LCIS. Thus, **LCIS is both a marker of an increased risk of carcinoma in both breasts and a direct precursor of some cancers.** Current treatment involves either chemoprevention with tamoxifen along with close clinical and radiologic follow-up evaluation or, less commonly, bilateral prophylactic mastectomy.

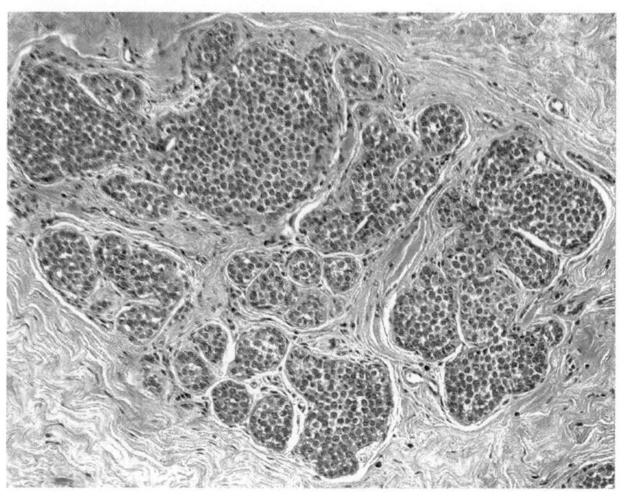

Figure 18–29 Lobular carcinoma in situ. A monomorphic population of small, rounded, loosely cohesive cells fills and expands the acini of a lobule. The underlying lobular architecture is intact.

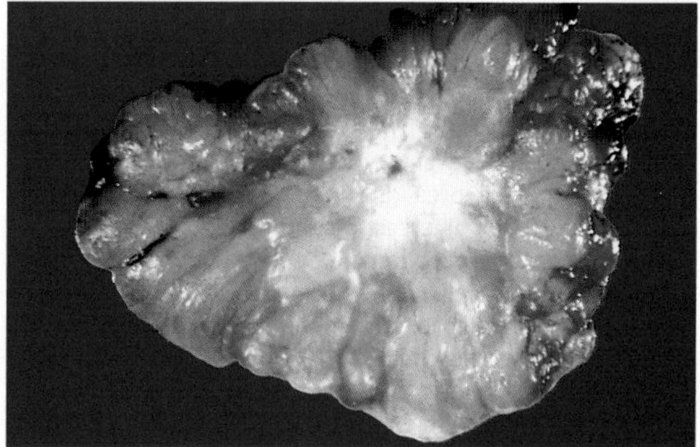

Figure 18–30 Invasive ductal carcinoma is evident in this breast biopsy specimen. The hard, fibrotic lesion infiltrates the surrounding tissue, causing retraction.

Invasive (Infiltrating) Carcinoma

The distinctive histologic patterns of the subtypes of invasive carcinoma are described first, followed by the gross features common to all.

Invasive ductal carcinoma is a term used for all carcinomas that cannot be subclassified into one of the specialized types described below. A majority (70% to 80%) of cancers fall into this group. This type of cancer usually is associated with DCIS and, rarely, LCIS. Most ductal carcinomas produce a desmoplastic response, which replaces normal breast fat (resulting in a mammographic density) and forms a hard, palpable mass (Fig. 18–30). The microscopic appearance is quite heterogeneous, ranging from tumors with well-developed tubule formation and low-grade nuclei to tumors consisting of sheets of anaplastic cells (Fig. 18–31). The tumor margins typically are irregular. Invasion of lymphovascular spaces may be seen. About two thirds express estrogen or progesterone receptors, and about one third overexpress HER2/NEU.

Invasive lobular carcinoma consists of cells morphologically identical to the cells of LCIS. Two thirds of the cases are associated with adjacent LCIS. The cells invade individually into stroma and are often aligned in "single-file" strands or chains. This growth pattern correlates with the presence of mutations that abrogate the function of E-cadherin, a surface protein that contributes to the cohesion of normal breast epithelial cells. Although most manifest as palpable masses or mammographic densities, a significant subgroup may exhibit a diffusely invasive pattern without a desmoplastic response and may be clinically occult. Lobular carcinomas have a unique pattern of metastases among breast cancers;

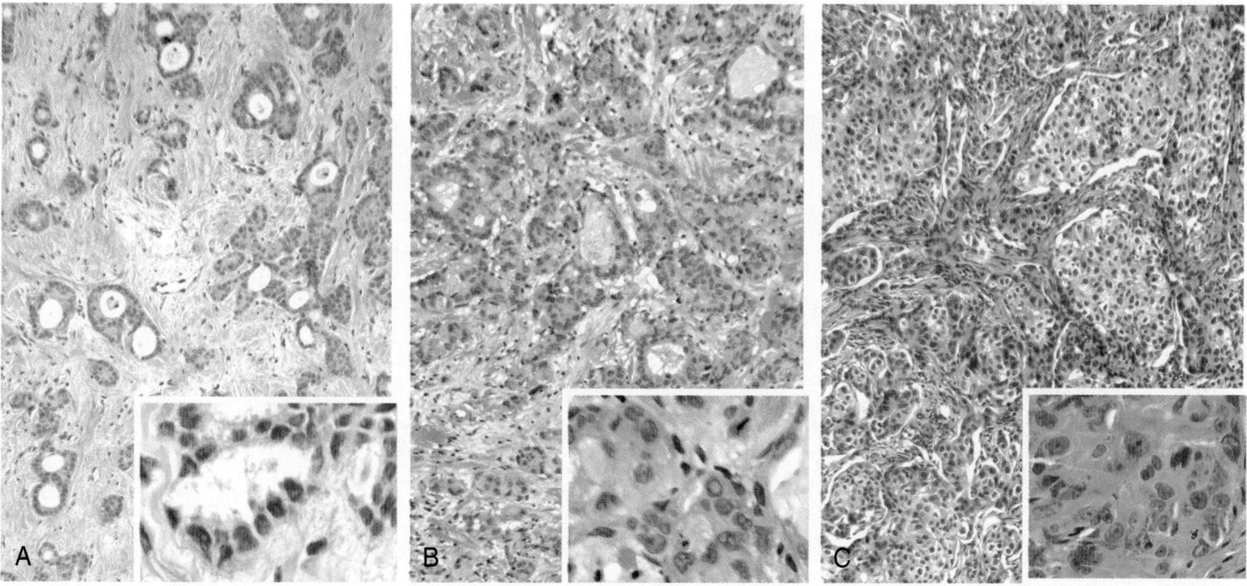

Figure 18–31 Invasive breast carcinomas of no special type (*insets* show each tumor at higher magnification). **A,** Well-differentiated carcinoma consists of tubular or cribriform glands containing cells with small monomorphic nuclei within a desmoplastic response. **B,** Moderately differentiated carcinoma demonstrates less tubule formation and more solid nests of cells with pleomorphic nuclei. **C,** Poorly differentiated carcinoma infiltrates as ragged sheets of pleomorphic cells containing numerous mitotic figures and areas of tumor necrosis.

they more frequently spread to cerebrospinal fluid, serosal surfaces, gastrointestinal tract, ovary, uterus, and bone marrow. Lobular carcinomas also are more frequently multicentric and bilateral (in 10% to 20% of cases). Almost all of these carcinomas express hormone receptors, whereas HER2/NEU overexpression is rare. These tumors comprise fewer than 20% of all breast carcinomas.

Inflammatory carcinoma is defined by the clinical presentation of an enlarged, swollen, erythematous breast, usually without a palpable mass. The underlying carcinoma is generally poorly differentiated and diffusely infiltrative. Characteristically, carcinoma involves dermal lymphatic spaces. The resultant blockage of these channels leads to edema, resulting in the characteristic "inflamed" clinical appearance; true inflammation is minimal to absent. Many of these tumors metastasize to distant sites; the overall 5-year survival is under 50%, and understandably even lower in those with metastatic disease at diagnosis.

Medullary carcinoma is a rare subtype of carcinoma, accounting for less than 1% of breast cancers. These cancers consist of sheets of large anaplastic cells with well-circumscribed, "pushing" borders (Fig. 18–32, *A*). Clinically, they can be mistaken for fibroadenomas. There is invariably a pronounced lymphoplasmacytic infiltrate. DCIS usually is absent or minimal. Medullary carcinomas occur with increased frequency in women with *BRCA1* mutations, although most women with medullary carcinoma are not carriers. These carcinomas uniformly lack the estrogen and progesterone receptors and do not overexpress HER2/NEU (a combination that often is referred to as **triple-negative**).

Colloid (mucinous) carcinoma also is a rare subtype. The tumor cells produce abundant quantities of extracellular mucin, which dissects into the surrounding stroma (Fig. 18–32, *B*). Like medullary carcinomas, they often present as well-circumscribed masses and can be mistaken for fibroadenomas. On gross evaluation, the tumors usually are soft and gelatinous. Most express hormone receptors but do not overexpress HER2/NEU.

Tubular carcinomas rarely present as palpable masses but account for 10% of invasive carcinomas smaller than 1 cm found with mammographic screening. They usually are detected as irregular mammographic densities. On microscopic examination, the carcinomas consist of well-formed tubules with low-grade nuclei. Lymph node metastases are rare, and prognosis is excellent. Virtually all tubular carcinomas express hormone receptors and do not show HER2/NEU overexpression.

Common Features of Invasive Cancers

In all forms of breast cancer, local disease progression leads to similar physical findings. Invasive cancers tend to become adherent and fixed to the pectoral muscles or deep fascia of the chest wall and the overlying skin, with consequent retraction or dimpling of the skin or nipple. The latter is an important sign because it may be the first indication of malignancy. Involvement of the lymphatic pathways may result in localized lymphedema. In such cases, the skin becomes thickened around exaggerated hair follicles, giving an appearance known as peau d'orange ("orange peel").

Clinical Course

Breast cancer often is discovered by the patient or her physician as a deceptively discrete, solitary, painless, and movable mass. At the time of clinical detection, the carcinoma typically is 2 to 3 cm in size, and involvement of the regional lymph nodes (most often axillary) is already present in about 50% of patients. With mammographic screening, carcinomas frequently are detected even before they become palpable. The average invasive carcinoma found by mammographic screening is around 1 cm in size, and only 15% of these have produced nodal metastases. In addition, DCIS often is detected before the development of invasive carcinoma during screening. As women age, fibrous breast tissue is replaced by fat, and screening becomes more sensitive as a result of the increased radiolucency of the breast and the increased incidence of malignancy. The current controversy over the best time to begin mammographic screening arises from efforts to balance the benefits of early cancer detection in some women with the

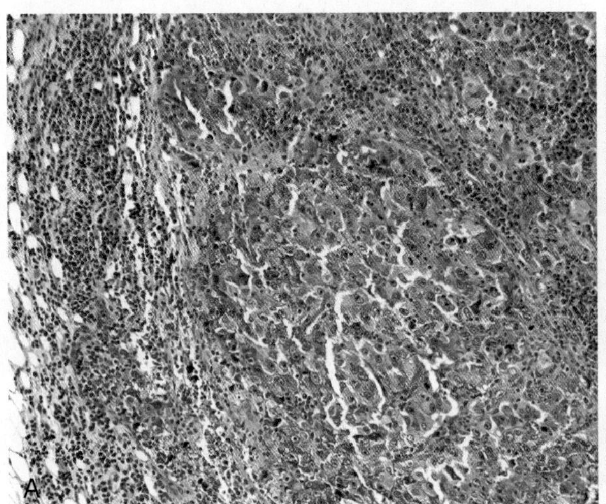

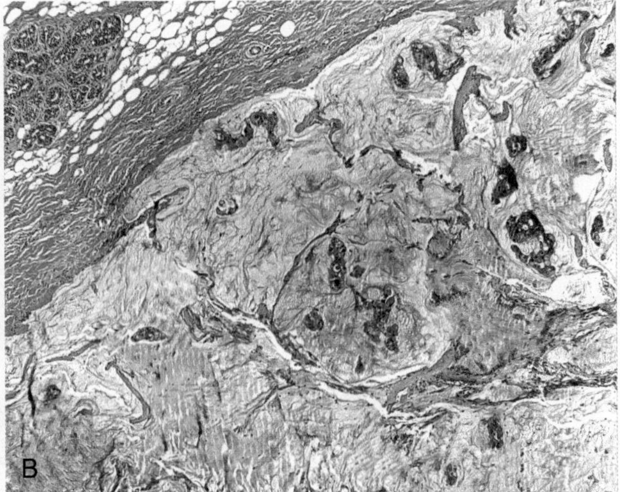

Figure 18–32 Special types of breast carcinoma. **A,** Medullary carcinoma. The highly pleomorphic tumor cells grow in cohesive sheets and are associated with a prominent reactive infiltrate of lymphocytes and plasma cells. **B,** Mucinous (colloid) carcinoma. The tumor cells are present in small clusters within large pools of mucin. Note the characteristic well-circumscribed border, which mimics the appearance of benign masses.

PATHOGENESIS

Both genetic and environmental factors are implicated in the pathogenesis of thyroid cancers.

Genetic Factors. Distinct molecular events are involved in the pathogenesis of the four major variants of thyroid cancer. As stated, medullary carcinomas do not arise from the follicular epithelium. Genetic alterations in the three follicular cell–derived malignancies are clustered along two oncogenic pathways—the mitogen-activated protein (MAP) kinase pathway and the phosphatidylinositol-3-kinase (PI-3K)/AKT pathway (Fig. 19–13). In normal cells, these pathways are transiently activated by binding of soluble growth factor ligands to the extracellular domain of receptor tyrosine kinases, which results in autophosphorylation of the cytoplasmic domain of the receptor, permitting intracellular signal transduction. In thyroid carcinomas, as with many solid cancers (Chapter 5), gain-of-function mutations along components of these pathways lead to constitutive activation even in the absence of ligand, thus promoting carcinogenesis.

- **Papillary thyroid carcinomas: Activation of the MAP kinase pathway is a feature of most papillary carcinomas** and can occur by one of two major mechanisms. The first mechanism involves rearrangements of *RET* or *NTRK1* (neurotrophic tyrosine kinase receptor 1), both of which encode transmembrane receptor tyrosine kinases, and the second mechanism involves activating point mutations in *BRAF*, whose product is an intermediate signaling component in the MAP kinase pathway (Fig. 19–13). The *RET* gene is not normally expressed in thyroid follicular cells. In papillary cancers, chromosomal rearrangements place the tyrosine kinase domain of *RET* under the transcriptional control of genes that are constitutively expressed in the thyroid epithelium. The novel fusion proteins that are so formed are known as RET/PTC (papillary thyroid carcinoma) and are present in approximately 20% to 40% of papillary thyroid cancers. The frequency of *RET/PTC* rearrangements is significantly higher in papillary cancers arising in the backdrop of radiation exposure. Similarly, rearrangements of *NTRK1* are present in 5% to 10% of papillary thyroid cancers, and the resultant fusion proteins are constitutively expressed in thyroid cells, leading to activation of MAP kinase pathways. One third to one half of papillary thyroid carcinomas harbor a gain-of-function mutation in the *BRAF* gene, which most commonly is a valine-to-glutamate change on codon 600 ($BRAF^{V600E}$). Since chromosomal rearrangements of the *RET* or *NTRK1* genes and mutations of *BRAF* have redundant effects on the thyroid epithelium (both mechanisms result in activation of the MAP kinase signaling pathway), papillary thyroid carcinomas demonstrate either one or the other molecular abnormality, but not both. *RET/PTC* rearrangements and *BRAF* point mutations are not observed in follicular adenomas or carcinomas.

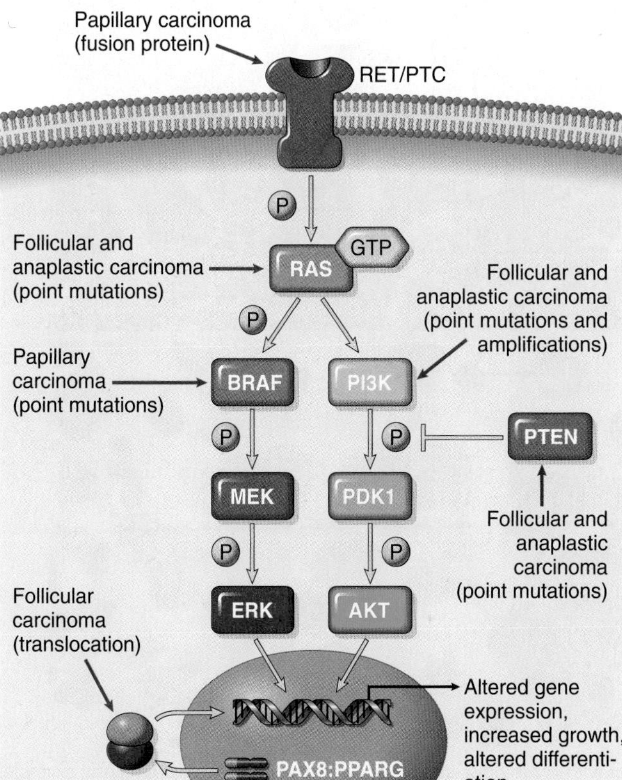

Figure 19–13 Genetic alterations in follicular cell–derived malignancies of the thyroid gland.

- **Follicular thyroid carcinomas:** Approximately one third to one half of follicular thyroid carcinomas harbor **mutations in the PI-3K/AKT signaling pathway,** resulting in constitutive activation of this oncogenic pathway. This subset of tumors includes those with gain-of-function point mutations of *RAS* and *PIK3CA*, those with amplification of *PIK3CA*, and those with loss-of-function mutations of *PTEN*, a tumor suppressor gene and negative regulator of this pathway. The progressive increase in the prevalence of *RAS* and *PIK3CA* mutations from benign follicular adenomas to follicular carcinomas to anaplastic carcinomas (see next) suggests a shared histogenesis and molecular evolution among these follicular cell–derived tumors. A unique (2;3)(q13;p25) translocation has been described in one third to one half of follicular carcinomas. This translocation creates a fusion gene composed of portions of *PAX8*, a paired homeobox gene that is important in thyroid development, and the peroxisome proliferator–activated receptor gene (*PPARG*), whose gene product is a nuclear hormone receptor implicated in terminal differentiation of cells. Less than 10% of follicular adenomas harbor ***PAX8/PPARG* fusion genes,** and thus far these have not been documented in other thyroid neoplasms.
- **Anaplastic carcinomas:** These highly aggressive and lethal tumors can arise de novo or, more commonly, by **dedifferentiation** of a well-differentiated papillary or follicular carcinoma. Molecular alterations present in anaplastic carcinomas include those also seen in well-differentiated carcinomas (e.g., *RAS* or *PIK3CA* mutations), albeit at a significantly higher rate, suggesting that the presence of these mutations might predispose existing thyroid neoplasms to transform. Other genetic *hits,* such as inactivation of *TP53*, are essentially restricted to anaplastic carcinomas and may also relate to their aggressive behavior.
- **Medullary thyroid carcinomas:** In contrast with the subtypes described earlier, these neoplasms arise from the

parafollicular C cells, rather than the follicular epithelium. Familial medullary thyroid carcinomas occur in multiple endocrine neoplasia type 2 (MEN-2) (see later) and are associated with germline ***RET* proto-oncogene mutations** that lead to constitutive activation of the receptor. *RET* mutations are also seen in approximately one half of nonfamilial (sporadic) medullary thyroid cancers. Chromosomal rearrangements involving *RET*, such as the *RET/PTC* translocations reported in papillary cancers, are not seen in medullary carcinomas.

Environmental Factors. The major risk factor predisposing to thyroid cancer is exposure to **ionizing radiation,** particularly during the first 2 decades of life. In keeping with this finding, there was a marked increase in the incidence of papillary carcinomas among children exposed to ionizing radiation after the Chernobyl nuclear disaster in 1986. **Deficiency of dietary iodine** (and by extension, an association with goiter) is linked with a higher frequency of follicular carcinomas.

Papillary Carcinoma

As mentioned earlier, papillary carcinomas represent the most common form of thyroid cancer. These tumors may occur at any age, and they account for the vast majority of thyroid carcinomas associated with previous exposure to ionizing radiation.

MORPHOLOGY

Papillary carcinomas may manifest as solitary or multifocal lesions within the thyroid. In some cases, they may be well circumscribed and even encapsulated; in other instances, they infiltrate the adjacent parenchyma with ill-defined margins. The lesions may contain areas of fibrosis and calcification and often are cystic. On cut surface, they may appear granular and sometimes contain grossly discernible papillary foci (Fig. 19–14, *A*). The definitive diagnosis of papillary carcinoma can be made only after microscopic examination. In current practice, **the diagnosis of papillary carcinoma is based on nuclear features** even in the absence of a papillary architecture. The nuclei of papillary carcinoma cells contain very finely dispersed chromatin, which imparts an **optically clear** appearance, giving rise to the designation **ground glass** or "Orphan Annie eye" nuclei (Fig. 19–14, *C* and *D*). In addition, invaginations of the cytoplasm may give the appearance of intranuclear inclusions (hence the designation **pseudoinclusions**) in cross-sections. A **papillary architecture** is common (Fig. 19–14, *B*); unlike hyperplastic papillary lesions seen in Graves disease, the neoplastic papillae have dense fibrovascular cores. Concentrically calcified structures termed **psammoma bodies** often are present within the papillae. Foci of lymphatic permeation by tumor cells are often present, but invasion of blood vessels is relatively uncommon, particularly in smaller lesions. Metastases to adjacent cervical lymph nodes are estimated to occur in about half of

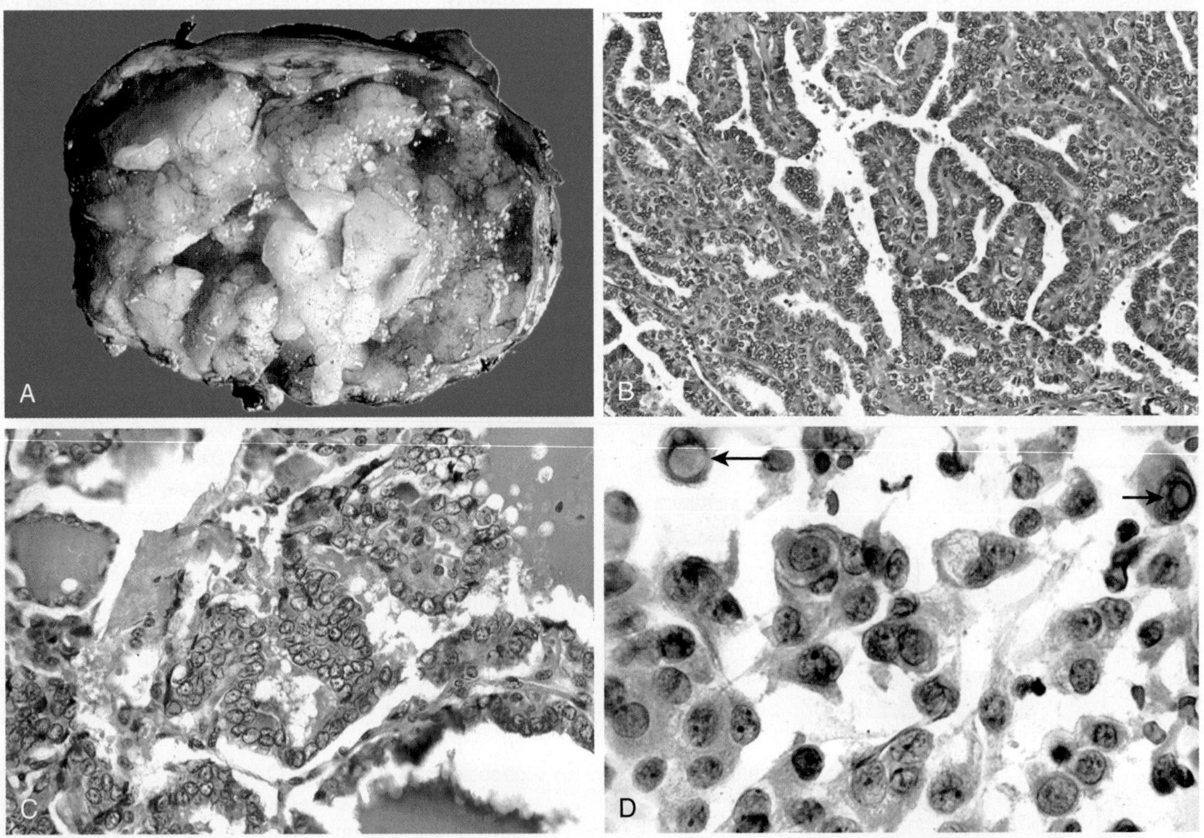

Figure 19–14 Papillary carcinoma of the thyroid. **A–C,** A papillary carcinoma with grossly discernible papillary structures. In this particular example, well-formed papillae (**B**) are lined by cells with characteristic empty-appearing nuclei, sometimes termed "Orphan Annie eye" nuclei (**C**). **D,** Cells obtained by fine-needle aspiration of a papillary carcinoma. Characteristic intranuclear inclusions are visible in some of the aspirated cells (*arrows*).
(Courtesy of Dr. S. Gokasalan, Department of Pathology, University of Texas Southwestern Medical School, Dallas, Texas.)

cases. There are over a dozen variants of papillary thyroid carcinoma, but the most common is one composed predominantly or exclusively of follicles (**follicular variant** of papillary thyroid carcinoma). The follicular variant more frequently is encapsulated and is associated with a lower incidence of lymph node metastases and extrathyroidal extension than that typical for conventional papillary carcinomas.

Clinical Features

Papillary carcinomas are nonfunctional tumors, so they manifest most often as a painless mass in the neck, either within the thyroid or as metastasis in a cervical lymph node. A preoperative diagnosis usually can be established by fine-needle aspiration on the basis of the characteristic nuclear features described earlier. Papillary carcinomas are indolent lesions, with 10-year survival rates in excess of 95%. Of interest, the presence of isolated cervical nodal metastases does not seem to have a significant influence on the generally good prognosis of these lesions. In a minority of patients, hematogenous metastases are present at the time of diagnosis, most commonly to the lung. The long-term survival of patients with papillary thyroid cancer is dependent on several factors, including age (in general, the prognosis is less favorable among patients older than 40 years), the presence of extrathyroidal extension, and presence of distant metastases (stage).

Follicular Carcinoma

Follicular carcinomas account for 5% to 15% of primary thyroid cancers. They are more common in women (occurring in a ratio of 3:1) and manifest at an older age than that typical for papillary carcinomas, with a peak incidence between the ages of 40 and 60 years. Follicular carcinoma is more frequent in areas with dietary iodine deficiency (accounting for 25% to 40% of thyroid cancers), while its incidence has either decreased or remained stable in iodine-sufficient areas of the world.

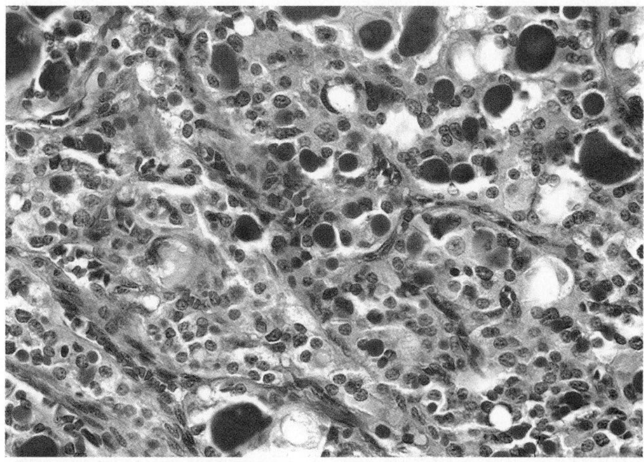

Figure 19–15 Follicular carcinoma of the thyroid. A few of the glandular lumina contain recognizable colloid.

MORPHOLOGY

On microscopic examination, most follicular carcinomas are composed of fairly uniform cells forming small follicles, reminiscent of normal thyroid (Fig. 19–15); in other cases, follicular differentiation may be less apparent. As with follicular adenomas, Hürthle cell variants of follicular carcinomas may be seen. Follicular carcinomas may be **widely invasive,** infiltrating the thyroid parenchyma and extrathyroidal soft tissues, or **minimally invasive.** The latter type are sharply demarcated lesions that may be impossible to distinguish from follicular adenomas on gross examination. **This distinction requires extensive histologic sampling of the tumor capsule–thyroid interface, to exclude capsular and/or vascular invasion** (Fig. 19–16). As mentioned earlier, follicular lesions in which the nuclear features are typical of papillary carcinomas should be regarded as follicular variants of papillary cancers.

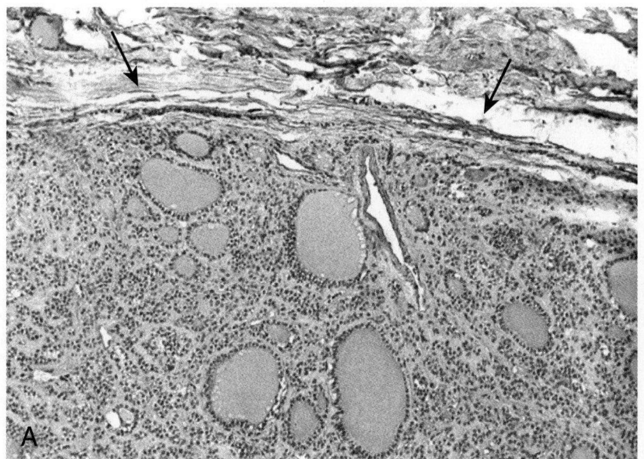

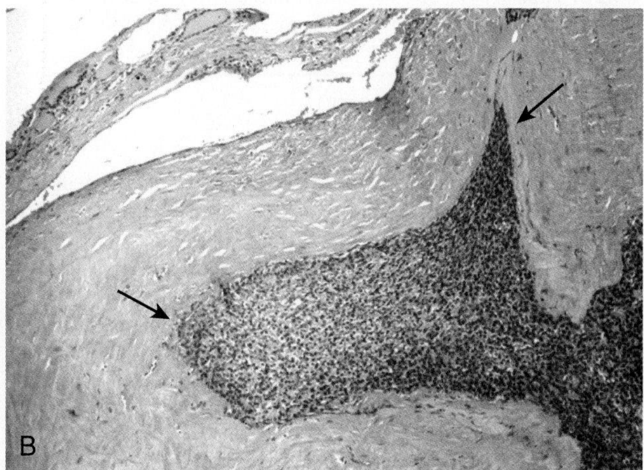

Figure 19–16 Capsular invasion in follicular carcinoma. Evaluating the integrity of the capsule is critical in distinguishing follicular adenomas from follicular carcinomas. **A,** In adenomas, a fibrous capsule, usually thin but occasionally more prominent, surrounds the neoplastic follicles and no capsular invasion is seen (*arrows*); compressed normal thyroid parenchyma usually is present external to the capsule (*top*). **B,** By contrast, follicular carcinomas demonstrate capsular invasion (*arrows*) that may be minimal, as in this case, or widespread, with extension into local structures of the neck.

Clinical Features

Follicular carcinomas manifest most frequently as solitary *cold thyroid nodules.* In rare cases, they may be hyperfunctional. These neoplasms tend to metastasize through the bloodstream (*hematogenous dissemination*) to the lungs, bone, and liver. In contrast with papillary carcinomas, regional nodal metastases are uncommon. As many as half of patients with widely invasive carcinomas succumb to their disease within 10 years, while less than 10% of patients with minimally invasive follicular carcinomas die within the same time span. Follicular carcinomas are treated with surgical excision. Well-differentiated metastases may take up radioactive iodine, which can be used to identify and also ablate such lesions. Because better-differentiated lesions may be stimulated by TSH, patients usually are placed on a thyroid hormone regimen after surgery to suppress endogenous TSH.

Anaplastic Carcinoma

Anaplastic carcinomas are undifferentiated tumors of the thyroid follicular epithelium, accounting for less than 5% of thyroid tumors. They are aggressive, with a mortality rate approaching 100%. Patients with anaplastic carcinoma are older than those with other types of thyroid cancer, with a mean age of 65 years. Approximately a quarter of patients with anaplastic thyroid carcinomas have a past history of a well-differentiated thyroid carcinoma, and another quarter harbor a concurrent well-differentiated tumor in the resected specimen.

MORPHOLOGY

Anaplastic carcinomas manifest as bulky masses that typically grow rapidly beyond the thyroid capsule into adjacent neck structures. On microscopic examination, these neoplasms are composed of highly anaplastic cells, which may take on any of several histologic patterns, including those populated by

- Large, pleomorphic giant cells
- Spindle cells with a sarcomatous appearance
- Mixed spindle and giant cell lesions

Foci of papillary or follicular differentiation may be present in some tumors, suggesting origin from a better-differentiated carcinoma.

Clinical Features

Anaplastic carcinomas grow with wild abandon despite therapy. Metastases to distant sites are common, but in most cases death occurs in less than 1 year as a result of aggressive local growth and compromise of vital structures in the neck.

Medullary Carcinoma

Medullary carcinomas of the thyroid are neuroendocrine neoplasms derived from the parafollicular cells, or C cells, of the thyroid. Like normal C cells, medullary carcinomas secrete calcitonin, the measurement of which plays an important role in the diagnosis and postoperative follow-up evaluation of patients. In some cases, the tumor cells elaborate other polypeptide hormones such as somatostatin, serotonin, and vasoactive intestinal peptide (VIP). Medullary carcinomas arise *sporadically* in about 70% of cases. The remaining 30% are *familial* cases occurring in the setting of MEN syndrome 2A or 2B, or familial medullary thyroid carcinoma without an associated MEN syndrome, as discussed later. Of note, both familial and sporadic medullary forms demonstrate activating *RET* mutations. Sporadic medullary carcinomas, as well as familial cases without an associated MEN syndrome, occur in adults, with a peak incidence in the fifth and sixth decades. Cases associated with MEN-2A or MEN-2B, by contrast, have been reported in younger patients, including children.

MORPHOLOGY

Medullary carcinomas may arise as a solitary nodule or may manifest as multiple lesions involving both lobes of the thyroid. **Multicentricity** is particularly common in familial cases. Larger lesions often contain areas of necrosis and hemorrhage and may extend through the capsule of the thyroid. On microscopic examination, medullary carcinomas are composed of polygonal to spindle-shaped cells, which may form nests, trabeculae, and even follicles. **Amyloid deposits,** derived from altered calcitonin molecules, are present in the adjacent stroma in many cases (Fig. 19–17) and are a distinctive feature. Calcitonin is readily demonstrable both within the cytoplasm of the tumor cells and in the stromal amyloid by immunohistochemical methods. Electron microscopy reveals variable numbers of intracytoplasmic membrane-bound, electron-dense granules (Fig. 19–18). One of the peculiar features of familial medullary carcinomas is the presence of **multicentric C cell hyperplasia** in the surrounding thyroid parenchyma, a feature usually absent in sporadic lesions. Foci of C cell hyperplasia are believed to represent the precursor lesions from which medullary carcinomas arise.

Clinical Features

In the sporadic cases, medullary carcinoma manifests most often as a mass in the neck, sometimes associated with compression effects such as dysphagia or hoarseness. In

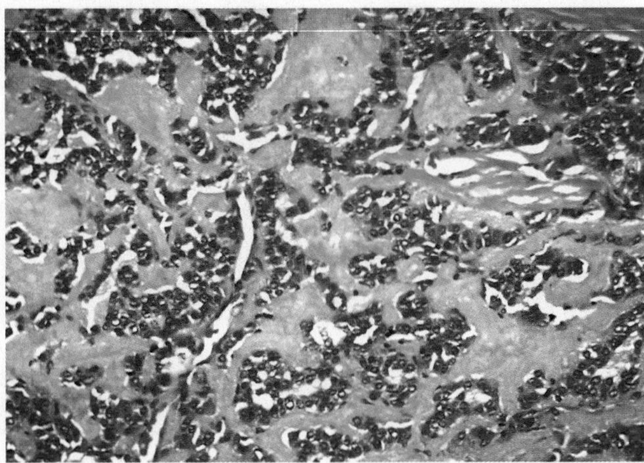

Figure 19–17 Medullary carcinoma of the thyroid. These tumors typically contain amyloid, visible here as homogeneous extracellular material, derived from calcitonin molecules secreted by the neoplastic cells.

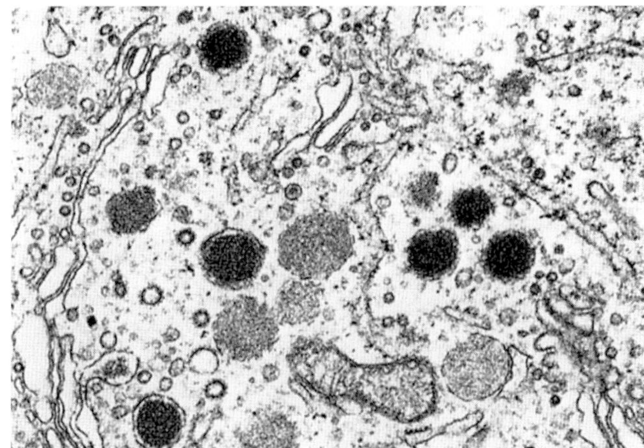

Figure 19–18 Electron micrograph of medullary thyroid carcinoma. These cells contain membrane-bound secretory granules, which are the sites of storage of calcitonin and other peptides. (Original magnification ×30,000.)

some instances, the initial manifestations are caused by the secretion of a peptide hormone (e.g., diarrhea caused by the secretion of VIP). Screening of the patient's relatives for elevated calcitonin levels or *RET* mutations permits early detection of tumors in familial cases. As discussed at the end of this chapter, all members of MEN-2 kindreds carrying *RET* mutations are offered prophylactic thyroidectomies to preempt the development of medullary carcinomas; often, the only histologic finding in the resected thyroid of these asymptomatic carriers is the presence of C cell hyperplasia or small (less than 1 cm) *micromedullary* carcinomas. Recent studies have shown that specific *RET* mutations correlate with an aggressive behavior in medullary carcinomas.

SUMMARY
Thyroid Neoplasms

- Most thyroid neoplasms manifest as *solitary thyroid nodules*, but only 1% of all thyroid nodules are neoplastic.
- *Follicular adenomas* are the most common benign neoplasms, while papillary carcinoma is the most common malignancy.
- Multiple genetic pathways are involved in *thyroid carcinogenesis*. Some of the genetic abnormalities that are fairly unique to thyroid cancers include *PAX8/PPARG* fusion (in follicular carcinoma), chromosomal rearrangements involving the *RET* oncogene (in papillary cancers), and mutations of *RET* (in medullary carcinomas).
- *Follicular adenomas and carcinomas* both are composed of well-differentiated follicular epithelial cells; the latter are distinguished by evidence of capsular and/or vascular invasion.
- *Papillary carcinomas* are recognized based on nuclear features (ground glass nuclei, pseudoinclusions) even in the absence of papillae. These neoplasms typically metastasize by way of lymphatics, but the prognosis is excellent.
- *Anaplastic carcinomas* are thought to arise by dedifferentiation of more differentiated neoplasms. They are highly aggressive, uniformly lethal cancers.
- *Medullary cancers* are nonepithelial neoplasms arising from the parafollicular C cells and can occur in either sporadic (70%) or familial (30%) settings. Multicentricity and C cell hyperplasia are features of familial cases. Amyloid deposits are a characteristic histologic finding.

PARATHYROID GLANDS

The parathyroid glands are derived from the developing pharyngeal pouches that also give rise to the thymus. They normally lie in close proximity to the upper and lower poles of each thyroid lobe but may be found anywhere along the pathway of descent of the pharyngeal pouches, including the carotid sheath and the thymus and elsewhere in the anterior mediastinum. Most of the gland is composed of *chief cells*. On hematoxylin-eosin (H&E) staining, the chief cells range from light to dark pink, depending on their glycogen content. They contain secretory granules of *parathyroid hormone* (PTH). *Oxyphil cells* are found throughout the normal parathyroid either singly or in small clusters. They are slightly larger than the chief cells, have acidophilic cytoplasm, and are tightly packed with mitochondria. *The activity of the parathyroid glands is controlled by the level of free (ionized) calcium in the bloodstream, rather than by trophic hormones secreted by the hypothalamus and pituitary.* Normally, decreased levels of free calcium stimulate the synthesis and secretion of PTH, with the following effects:

- Increase in renal tubular reabsorption of calcium
- Increase in urinary phosphate excretion, thereby lowering serum phosphate levels (since phosphate binds to ionized calcium)
- Increase in the conversion of vitamin D to its active dihydroxy form in the kidneys, which in turn augments gastrointestinal calcium absorption
- Enhancement of osteoclastic activity (i.e., bone resorption, thus releasing ionized calcium), mediated indirectly by promoting the differentiation of osteoclast progenitor cells into mature osteoclasts

The net result of these activities is an increase in the level of free calcium, which inhibits further PTH secretion. Abnormalities of the parathyroids include both hyperfunction and hypofunction. *Tumors of the parathyroid glands, unlike thyroid tumors, usually come to attention because of excessive secretion of PTH, rather than mass effects.*

HYPERPARATHYROIDISM

Hyperparathyroidism occurs in two major forms, *primary* and *secondary*, and, less commonly, as *tertiary* hyperparathyroidism. The first condition represents an autonomous, spontaneous overproduction of PTH, while the latter two conditions typically occur as secondary phenomena in patients with chronic renal insufficiency.

Primary Hyperparathyroidism

Primary hyperparathyroidism is a common endocrine disorder, and an important cause of *hypercalcemia.* There has been a dramatic increase in the detection of cases in the latter half of the last century, mainly as a result of the routine inclusion of serum calcium assays in testing for a variety of clinical conditions that bring a patient to the hospital. The frequency of occurrence of the various parathyroid lesions underlying the hyperfunction is as follows:

- Adenoma—85% to 95%
- Primary hyperplasia (diffuse or nodular)—5% to 10%
- Parathyroid carcinoma—1%

In more than 95% of cases, primary hyperparathyroidism is caused by a sporadic parathyroid adenoma or sporadic hyperplasia. The genetic defects identified in *familial primary hyperparathyroidism* include multiple endocrine neoplasia syndromes, specifically MEN-1 and MEN-2A (see further on). *Familial hypocalciuric hypercalcemia* is a rare cause of hyperparathyroidism, caused by inactivating mutations in the calcium-sensing receptor gene on parathyroid cells, leading to constitutive PTH secretion.

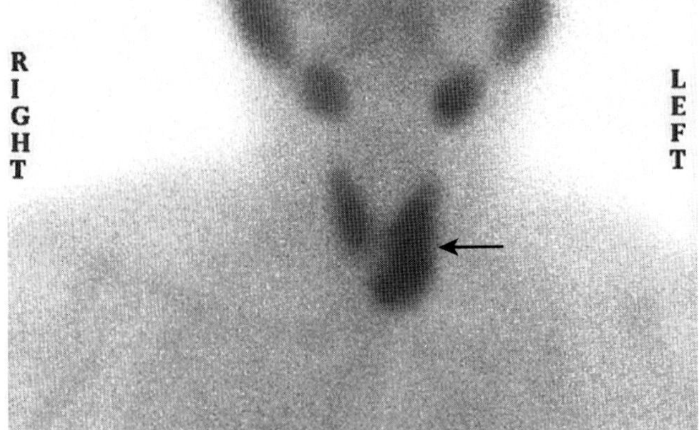

Figure 19–19 Technetium-99 radionuclide scan demonstrates an area of increased uptake corresponding to the left inferior parathyroid gland (*arrow*). This proved to be a parathyroid adenoma. Preoperative scintigraphy is useful in localizing and distinguishing adenomas from parathyroid hyperplasia, in which more than one gland will demonstrate increased uptake.

PATHOGENESIS

Although the details of genetic alterations in sporadic parathyroid tumors are beyond the scope of this discussion, abnormalities in two specific genes are commonly associated with these tumors:

- **Cyclin D1 gene inversions:** Cyclin D1 is a positive regulator of the cell cycle. A **chromosomal inversion** on chromosome 11 results in relocation of the *cyclin D1* gene (normally on 11q), so that it is now positioned adjacent to the 5′-flanking region of the *PTH* gene (on 11p), leading to abnormal expression of cyclin D1 protein and increased proliferation. Between 10% and 20% of adenomas have this clonal genetic defect. In addition, cyclin D1 is overexpressed in approximately 40% of parathyroid adenomas, suggesting that mechanisms other than *cyclin D1* gene inversion can lead to its overexpression.
- **MEN1 mutations:** Approximately 20% to 30% of parathyroid tumors not associated with the MEN-1 syndrome have mutations in both copies of the *MEN1* gene (see later). The spectrum of *MEN1* mutations in the sporadic tumors is virtually identical to that in familial parathyroid adenomas.

MORPHOLOGY

The morphologic changes seen in primary hyperparathyroidism include those in the parathyroid glands as well as those in other organs affected by elevated levels of calcium. In 75% to 80% of cases, one of the parathyroids harbors a solitary **adenoma,** which, like the normal parathyroids, may lie in close proximity to the thyroid gland or in an ectopic site (e.g., the mediastinum). The typical parathyroid adenoma is a well-circumscribed, soft, tan nodule, invested by a delicate capsule. **By definition, parathyroid adenomas are almost invariably confined to single glands** (Fig. 19–19), and the remaining glands are normal in size or somewhat shrunken, as a result of feedback inhibition by elevated serum calcium. Most parathyroid adenomas weigh between 0.5 and 5 g. On microscopic examination, parathyroid adenomas are composed predominantly of chief cells (Fig. 19–20). In most cases, at least a few nests of larger oxyphil cells also are present. A rim of compressed, non-neoplastic parathyroid tissue, generally separated by a fibrous capsule, often is visible at the edge of the adenoma. This finding constitutes a helpful internal control, since the chief cells of the adenoma are larger and show greater nuclear size variability than that typical for the normal chief cells. Cells with bizarre and pleomorphic nuclei are often seen within adenomas (so-called **endocrine atypia**) and must not be taken as a sign of malignancy. Mitotic figures are rare. In contrast with the normal parathyroid parenchyma, adipose tissue is inconspicuous within adenomas.

Parathyroid hyperplasia is typically a multiglandular process. In some cases, however, enlargement may be grossly apparent in only one or two glands, complicating the distinction between hyperplasia and adenoma. The combined weight of all glands rarely exceeds 1.0 g and often is less. Microscopically, the most common pattern seen is that of chief cell hyperplasia, which may involve the glands in a diffuse or multinodular pattern. Less commonly, the constituent cells contain abundant clear cytoplasm as a consequence of accumulation of glycogen—a condition designated "water-clear cell hyperplasia." As in the case of adenomas, stromal fat is inconspicuous within foci of hyperplasia.

Parathyroid carcinomas may be circumscribed lesions that are difficult to distinguish from adenomas, or they may be clearly invasive neoplasms. These tumors enlarge one parathyroid gland and consist of gray-white, irregular masses that sometimes exceed 10 g in weight. The cells usually are uniform and resemble normal parathyroid cells. They are arrayed in nodular or trabecular patterns with a dense, fibrous capsule enclosing the mass. There is general agreement that a **diagnosis of carcinoma based on cytologic detail is unreliable, and invasion of surrounding tissues and metastasis are the only definitive**

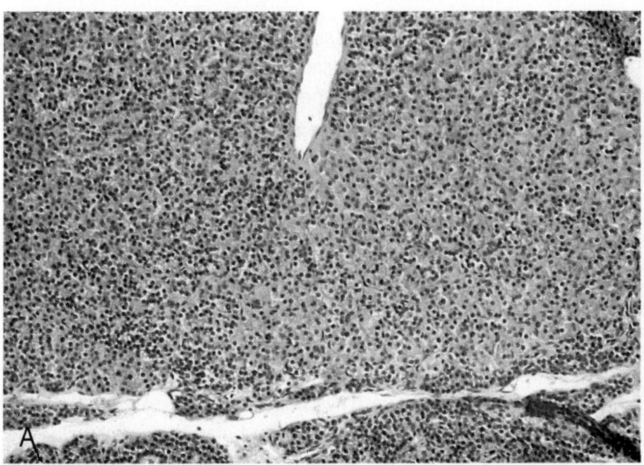

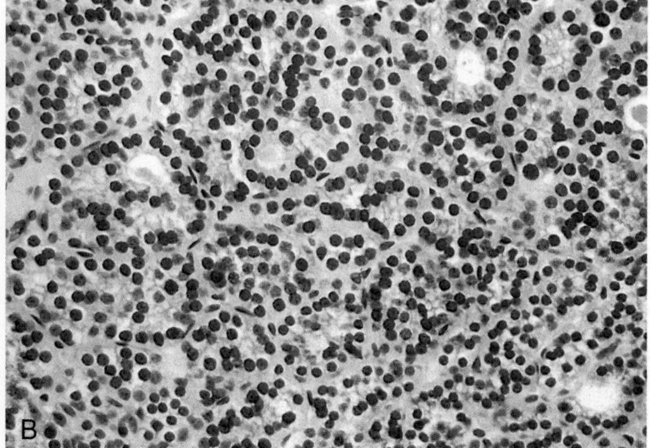

Figure 19–20 Chief cell parathyroid adenoma. **A,** On this low-power view, a solitary adenoma is clearly delineated from the residual gland below. **B,** High-power detail shows slight variation in nuclear size and tendency to follicular formation but no anaplasia.

criteria. Local recurrence occurs in one third of cases, and more distant dissemination occurs in another third.

Morphologic changes in other organs deserving special mention are found in the skeleton and kidneys. **Skeletal changes** include increased osteoclastic activity, which results in erosion of bone matrix and mobilization of calcium salts, particularly in the metaphyses of long tubular bones. Bone resorption is accompanied by increased osteoblastic activity and the formation of new bone trabeculae. In more severe cases the cortex is grossly thinned and the marrow contains increased amounts of fibrous tissue accompanied by foci of hemorrhage and cysts **(osteitis fibrosa cystica)** (Chapter 20). Aggregates of osteoclasts, reactive giant cells, and hemorrhagic debris occasionally form masses that may be mistaken for neoplasms (**brown tumors** of hyperparathyroidism). PTH-induced hypercalcemia favors the formation of urinary tract stones (nephrolithiasis) as well as calcification of the renal interstitium and tubules (nephrocalcinosis). Metastatic calcification secondary to hypercalcemia also may be seen in other sites, including the stomach, lungs, myocardium, and blood vessels.

Table 19–4 Causes of Hypercalcemia

Raised PTH	Decreased PTH
Hyperparathyroidism	Hypercalcemia of malignancy
Primary (adenoma > hyperplasia)*	Osteolytic metastases
Secondary†	PTH-rP–mediated
Tertiary†	Vitamin D toxicity
Familial hypocalciuric hypercalcemia	Immobilization
	Drugs (thiazide diuretics)
	Granulomatous diseases (sarcoidosis)

PTH, parathyroid hormone; PTH-rP, PTH-related protein.
*Primary hyperparathyroidism is the most common cause of hypercalcemia overall. Malignancy is the most common cause of *symptomatic* hypercalcemia. Primary hyperparathyroidism and malignancy together account for nearly 90% of cases of hypercalcemia.
†Secondary and tertiary hyperparathyroidism are most commonly associated with progressive renal failure.

Clinical Features

Primary hyperparathyroidism usually is a disease of adults and is much more common in women than in men (gender ratio of nearly 4:1). *The most common manifestation of primary hyperparathyroidism is an increase in serum ionized calcium.* In fact, primary hyperparathyroidism is the most common cause of *clinically silent hypercalcemia.* Of note, other conditions also may produce hypercalcemia (Table 19–4). The most common cause of clinically apparent hypercalcemia in adults is paraneoplastic syndromes associated with *malignancy* and bone metastases (Chapter 5). The prognosis for patients with malignancy-associated hypercalcemia is poor, because it often occurs in those with advanced cancers. In persons with hypercalcemia caused by parathyroid hyperfunction, serum PTH is inappropriately elevated, whereas serum PTH is low to undetectable in those with hypercalcemia caused by nonparathyroid diseases, including malignancy. Other laboratory alterations referable to PTH excess include hypophosphatemia and increased urinary excretion of both calcium and phosphate.

Primary hyperparathyroidism traditionally has been associated with a constellation of symptoms that included "painful bones, renal stones, abdominal groans, and psychic moans." Pain, secondary to fractures of bones weakened by osteoporosis or osteitis fibrosa cystica and resulting from renal stones, with obstructive uropathy, was at one time a prominent manifestation of primary hyperparathyroidism. Because serum calcium is now routinely assessed in the workup of most patients who need blood tests for unrelated conditions, clinically silent hyperparathyroidism is detected early. Hence, many of the classic clinical manifestations, particularly those referable to bone and renal disease, are seen much less frequently. Additional signs and symptoms that may be encountered in some cases include

- *Gastrointestinal disturbances,* including constipation, nausea, peptic ulcers, pancreatitis, and gallstones
- *Central nervous system alterations,* including depression, lethargy, and seizures
- *Neuromuscular abnormalities,* including weakness and hypotonia
- *Polyuria* and secondary polydipsia

Although some of these alterations, for example, polyuria and muscle weakness, are clearly related to hypercalcemia, the pathogenesis of many of the other manifestations of the disorder remains poorly understood.

Secondary Hyperparathyroidism

Secondary hyperparathyroidism is caused by any condition associated with a chronic depression in the serum calcium level, because low serum calcium leads to compensatory overactivity of the parathyroids. *Renal failure is by far the most common cause of secondary hyperparathyroidism.* The mechanisms by which chronic renal failure induces secondary hyperparathyroidism are complex and not fully understood. Chronic renal insufficiency is associated with decreased phosphate excretion, which in turn results in hyperphosphatemia. The elevated serum phosphate levels directly depress serum calcium levels and thereby stimulate parathyroid gland activity. In addition, loss of renal substances reduces the availability of α_1-hydroxylase enzyme necessary for the synthesis of the active form of vitamin D, which in turn reduces intestinal absorption of calcium (Chapter 7).

MORPHOLOGY

The parathyroid glands in secondary hyperparathyroidism are hyperplastic. As in the case of primary hyperplasia, the degree of glandular enlargement is not necessarily symmetric. On microscopic examination, the hyperplastic glands contain an increased number of chief cells, or cells with more abundant, clear cytoplasm **(water-clear cells),** in a diffuse or multinodular distribution. Fat cells are decreased in number. **Bone changes** similar to those seen in primary hyperparathyroidism also may be present. **Metastatic calcification** may be seen in many tissues.

Clinical Features

The clinical manifestations of secondary hyperparathyroidism usually are dominated by those related to chronic renal failure. Bone abnormalities (*renal osteodystrophy*) and other changes associated with PTH excess are, in general, less severe than those seen in primary hyperparathyroidism. Serum calcium remains near normal because the compensatory increase in PTH levels sustains serum calcium. The metastatic calcification of blood vessels (secondary to hyperphosphatemia) occasionally may result in significant ischemic damage to skin and other organs—a process sometimes referred to as *calciphylaxis.* In a minority of patients, parathyroid activity may become autonomous and excessive, with resultant hypercalcemia—a process sometimes termed *tertiary hyperparathyroidism.* Parathyroidectomy may be necessary to control the hyperparathyroidism in such patients.

SUMMARY

Hyperparathyroidism

- Primary hyperparathyroidism is the most common cause of asymptomatic hypercalcemia.
- In a majority of cases, primary hyperparathyroidism is caused by a sporadic parathyroid adenoma and, less commonly, by parathyroid hyperplasia.
- Parathyroid adenomas are solitary, while hyperplasia typically is a multiglandular process.
- Skeletal manifestations of hyperparathyroidism include bone resorption, *osteitis fibrosa cystica*, and *brown tumors.* Renal changes include nephrolithiasis (stones) and nephrocalcinosis.
- The clinical manifestations of hyperparathyroidism can be summarized as "painful bones, renal stones, abdominal groans, and psychic moans."
- Secondary hyperparathyroidism most often is caused by renal failure, and the parathyroid glands are hyperplastic.
- Malignancies are the most important cause of symptomatic hypercalcemia, which results from osteolytic metastases or release of PTH-related protein from nonparathyroid tumors.

HYPOPARATHYROIDISM

Hypoparathyroidism is far less common than hyperparathyroidism. The major causes of hypoparathyroidism include the following:

- *Surgically induced hypoparathyroidism*: The most common cause is inadvertent removal of parathyroids during thyroidectomy or other surgical neck dissections.
- *Congenital absence*: This occurs in conjunction with thymic aplasia (Di George syndrome) and cardiac defects, secondary to deletions on chromosome 22q11.2 (Chapter 6)
- *Autoimmune hypoparathyroidism*: This is a hereditary polyglandular deficiency syndrome arising from autoantibodies to multiple endocrine organs (parathyroid, thyroid, adrenals, and pancreas). Chronic fungal infections involving the skin and mucous membranes (mucocutaneous candidiasis) are sometimes encountered in affected persons. This condition is caused by mutations in the *autoimmune regulator* gene (*AIRE*) and is discussed more extensively later on, in the context of autoimmune adrenalitis. As one consequence of the failure of self-tolerance, some of these patients make autoantibodies against their own IL-17, accounting for the increased susceptibility to *Candida* infections (in which the T_H17 response plays an important protective role).

The major clinical manifestations of hypoparathyroidism are secondary to hypocalcemia and include *increased neuromuscular irritability* (*tingling, muscle spasms, facial grimacing,* and *sustained carpopedal spasm or tetany*), cardiac arrhythmias, and, on occasion, *increased intracranial pressures* and *seizures*. Morphologic changes generally are inconspicuous but may include cataracts, calcification of the cerebral basal ganglia, and dental abnormalities.

ENDOCRINE PANCREAS

The endocrine pancreas consists of about 1 million microscopic clusters of cells, the islets of Langerhans, which contain four major cell types—beta, alpha, delta, and PP (pancreatic polypeptide) cells. The cells can be differentiated morphologically by their staining properties, by the ultrastructural characteristics of their granules, and by their hormone content. *The beta cell produces insulin,* which is the most potent anabolic hormone known, with multiple synthetic and growth-promoting effects; *the alpha cell secretes glucagon,* inducing hyperglycemia by its glycogenolytic activity in the liver; *delta cells contain somatostatin,* which suppresses both insulin and glucagon release; and *PP cells contain a unique pancreatic polypeptide,* VIP, that exerts several gastrointestinal effects, such as stimulation of secretion of gastric and intestinal enzymes and inhibition of intestinal motility. The most important disease of the endocrine pancreas is diabetes mellitus, caused by deficient production or action of insulin.

DIABETES MELLITUS

Diabetes mellitus is not a single disease entity but rather a *group of metabolic disorders sharing the common underlying feature of hyperglycemia.* Hyperglycemia in diabetes results from defects in insulin secretion, insulin action, or, most commonly, both. The chronic hyperglycemia and attendant metabolic deregulation of diabetes mellitus may be associated with secondary damage in multiple organ systems, especially the kidneys, eyes, nerves, and blood vessels. According to the American Diabetes Association, diabetes affects over 20 million children and adults, or 7% of the population, in the United States, nearly a third of whom are currently unaware that they have hyperglycemia. Approximately 1.5 million new cases of diabetes are diagnosed each year in the United States, and diabetes is the leading cause of end-stage renal disease, adult-onset blindness, and nontraumatic lower extremity amputations. A staggering 54 million adults in this country have *prediabetes,* which is defined as elevated blood sugar that does not reach the criterion accepted for an outright diagnosis of diabetes (discussed next); persons with prediabetes have an elevated risk for development of frank diabetes.

Diagnosis

Blood glucose levels normally are maintained in a very narrow range, usually 70 to 120 mg/dL. The diagnosis of diabetes is established by elevation of blood glucose by any one of three criteria:

1. A random blood glucose concentration of 200 mg/dL or higher, with classical signs and symptoms (discussed next)
2. A fasting glucose concentration of 126 mg/dL or higher on more than one occasion
3. An abnormal oral glucose tolerance test (OGTT), in which the glucose concentration is 200 mg/dL or higher 2 hours after a standard carbohydrate load (75 g of glucose).

Derangements in carbohydrate metabolism proceed along a continuum. Persons with serum fasting glucose values less than 110 mg/dL, or less than 140 mg/dL for an OGTT, are considered to be euglycemic. However, those with serum fasting glucose greater than 110 but less than 126 mg/dL, or OGTT values of greater than 140 but less than 200 mg/dL, are considered to have *impaired glucose tolerance,* also known as *prediabetes.* Persons with impaired glucose tolerance have a significant risk for progression to overt diabetes over time, with as many as 5% to 10% advancing to full-fledged diabetes mellitus per year. In addition, those with impaired glucose tolerance are at *risk for cardiovascular disease,* as a consequence of abnormal carbohydrate metabolism and the coexistence of other risk factors (Chapter 9).

Classification

Although all forms of diabetes mellitus share hyperglycemia as a common feature, the underlying causes of hyperglycemia vary widely. *The vast majority of cases of diabetes fall into one of two broad classes:*

- *Type 1 diabetes (T1D)* is characterized by an absolute deficiency of insulin secretion caused by pancreatic beta cell destruction, usually resulting from an autoimmune attack. Type 1 diabetes accounts for approximately 10% of all cases.
- *Type 2 diabetes (T2D)* is caused by a combination of peripheral resistance to insulin action and an inadequate compensatory response of insulin secretion by the pancreatic beta cells (*relative insulin deficiency*). Approximately 80% to 90% of patients have type 2 diabetes.

A variety of monogenic and secondary causes make up the remaining cases of diabetes (Table 19–5). An important point is that although the major types of diabetes arise by different pathogenic mechanisms, *the long-term complications in kidneys, eyes, nerves, and blood vessels are the same and are the principal causes of morbidity and death.*

Normal Insulin Physiology and Glucose Homeostasis

Before discussing the pathogenesis of the two major types of diabetes, we briefly review normal insulin physiology and glucose metabolism. *Normal glucose homeostasis is tightly regulated by three interrelated processes*: (1) glucose production in the liver, (2) glucose uptake and utilization by peripheral tissues, chiefly skeletal muscle, and (3) actions of insulin and counterregulatory hormones (e.g., glucagon).

The principal metabolic function of insulin is to increase the rate of glucose transport into certain cells in the body (Fig. 19–21). These are the *striated* muscle cells (including myocardial cells) and, to a lesser extent, *adipocytes,* representing collectively about two thirds of total body weight. Glucose uptake in other peripheral tissues, most notably the brain, is insulin-independent. In muscle cells, glucose is then

Table 19–5 Classification of Diabetes Mellitus

1. Type 1 Diabetes
Beta cell destruction, usually leading to absolute insulin deficiency
2. Type 2 Diabetes
Combination of insulin resistance and beta cell dysfunction
3. Genetic Defects of Beta Cell Function
Maturity-onset diabetes of the young (MODY), caused by mutations in: Hepatocyte nuclear factor 4α gene (*HNF4A*)—MODY1 Glucokinase gene (*GCK*)—MODY2 Hepatocyte nuclear factor 1α gene (*HNF1A*)—MODY3 Pancreatic and duodenal homeobox 1 gene (*PDX1*)—MODY4 Hepatocyte nuclear factor 1β gene (*HNF1B*)—MODY5 Neurogenic differentiation factor 1 gene (*NEUROD1*)—MODY6
Maternally inherited diabetes and deafness (MIDD) due to mitochondrial DNA mutations (3243A→G)
Defects in proinsulin conversion
Insulin gene mutations
4. Genetic Defects in Insulin Action
Insulin receptor mutations
5. Exocrine Pancreatic Defects
Chronic pancreatitis
Pancreatectomy
Neoplasia
Cystic fibrosis
Hemochromatosis
Fibrocalculous pancreatopathy
6. Endocrinopathies
Growth hormone excess (acromegaly)
Cushing syndrome
Hyperthyroidism
Pheochromocytoma
Glucagonoma
7. Infections
Cytomegalovirus infection
Coxsackievirus B infection
Congenital rubella
8. Drugs
Glucocorticoids
Thyroid hormone
β-Adrenergic agonists
9. Genetic Syndromes Associated with Diabetes
Down syndrome
Klinefelter syndrome
Turner syndrome
10. Gestational Diabetes Mellitus
Diabetes associated with pregnancy

Modified from the American Diabetes Association: Position statement from the American Diabetes Association on the diagnosis and classification of diabetes mellitus. Diabetes Care 31(Suppl 1):S55–S60, 2008.

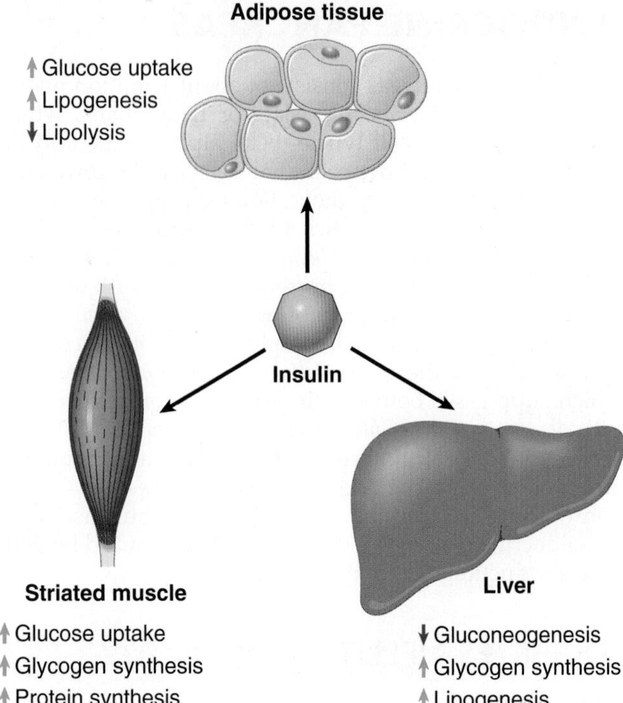

Figure 19–21 Metabolic actions of insulin in striated muscle, adipose tissue, and liver.

either stored as glycogen or oxidized to generate adenosine triphosphate (ATP). In adipose tissue, glucose is stored primarily as lipid. Besides promoting lipid synthesis (lipogenesis), insulin also inhibits lipid degradation (lipolysis) in adipocytes. Similarly, insulin promotes amino acid uptake and protein synthesis while inhibiting protein degradation. *Thus, the metabolic effects of insulin can be summarized as anabolic, with increased synthesis and reduced degradation of glycogen, lipid, and protein.* In addition to these metabolic effects, insulin has several *mitogenic* functions, including initiation of DNA synthesis in certain cells and stimulation of their growth and differentiation.

Insulin reduces the production of glucose from the liver. Insulin and glucagon have opposing regulatory effects on glucose homeostasis. During *fasting* states, low insulin and high glucagon levels facilitate hepatic gluconeogenesis and glycogenolysis (glycogen breakdown) while decreasing glycogen synthesis, thereby preventing hypoglycemia. Thus, *fasting* plasma glucose levels are determined primarily by hepatic glucose output. After a meal, insulin levels rise and glucagon levels fall in response to the large glucose load. *The most important stimulus that triggers insulin release is glucose itself, which initiates insulin synthesis in the pancreatic beta cells.* In peripheral tissues (skeletal muscle and adipose tissue), secreted insulin binds to the *insulin receptor,* triggering a number of intracellular responses that promote glucose uptake and postprandial glucose utilization, thereby maintaining glucose homeostasis. Abnormalities at various points along this complex signaling cascade, from synthesis and release of insulin by beta cells to insulin receptor interactions in peripheral tissues, can result in the diabetic phenotype.

PATHOGENESIS

Type I Diabetes Mellitus

Type I diabetes is an autoimmune disease in which islet destruction is caused primarily by immune effector cells reacting against endogenous beta cell antigens. Type I diabetes most commonly develops in childhood, becomes manifest at puberty, and progresses with age. Most patients with type I diabetes depend on exogenous insulin for survival; without insulin they develop serious metabolic complications such as ketoacidosis and coma.

Although the clinical onset of type I diabetes is abrupt, this disease in fact results from a chronic autoimmune attack on beta cells that usually starts many years before the disease becomes evident (Fig. 19–22). The classic manifestations of the disease (hyperglycemia and ketosis) occur late in its course, after more than 90% of the beta cells have been destroyed. **The fundamental immune abnormality in type I diabetes is a failure of self-tolerance in T cells.** This failure of tolerance may be a result of some combination of defective clonal deletion of self-reactive T cells in the thymus, as well as defects in the functions of regulatory T cells or resistance of effector T cells to suppression by regulatory cells. Thus, autoreactive T cells not only survive but are poised to respond to self-antigens. Not surprisingly, **autoantibodies** against a variety of beta cell antigens, including insulin and the beta cell enzyme glutamic acid decarboxylase, are detected in the blood of 70% to 80% of patients. In the rare cases in which the pancreatic lesions have been examined early in the disease process, the islets show necrosis of beta cells and lymphocytic infiltration (so-called insulitis).

As with most autoimmune diseases, the pathogenesis of type I diabetes involves the interplay of genetic susceptibility and environmental factors. Genome-wide association studies (Chapter 6) have identified over 20 susceptibility loci for type I diabetes. Of these, **the principal susceptibility locus for type I diabetes resides in the chromosomal region that encodes the class II MHC molecules on *6p21 (HLA-D)*.** Between 90% and 95% of white patients with type I diabetes have *HLA-DR3,* or *DR4,* or both, in contrast with about 40% of normal subjects, and 40% to 50% of patients are *DR3/DR4* heterozygotes, in contrast with 5% of normal subjects. Of note, despite the high relative risk in persons with particular class II alleles, most people who inherit these alleles do not develop diabetes. Several *non-HLA genes* also confer susceptibility to type I diabetes, including polymorphisms within the gene encoding insulin itself, as well as *CTLA4* and *PTPN22*. CTLA-4 is an inhibitory receptor of T cells and PTPN-22 is a protein tyrosine phosphatase; both are thought to inhibit T cell responses, so polymorphisms that interfere with their functional activity are expected to set the stage for excessive T cell activation. Polymorphisms in the insulin gene may reduce expression of this protein in the thymus, thus reducing the elimination of T cells reactive with this self protein (Chapter 4). Additional evidence suggests that **environmental factors,** especially infections, may be involved in type I diabetes. It has been proposed that certain viruses (mumps, rubella, and coxsackie B viruses, in particular) may be an initiating trigger, perhaps because some viral antigens are antigenically similar to beta cell antigens **(molecular mimicry),** leading to bystander damage to the islets, but this idea is not conclusively established.

Type 2 Diabetes Mellitus

Type 2 diabetes is a prototypical complex multifactorial disease. Environmental factors, such as a sedentary life style and dietary habits, unequivocally play a role, as described in the subsequent discussion of the association with obesity. Genetic factors are also involved in the pathogenesis, as evidenced by the disease concordance rate of 35% to 60% in monozygotic twins compared with nearly half that in dizygotic twins. Such concordance is even greater than in type I diabetes, suggesting perhaps an even larger genetic component in type 2 diabetes. **Additional evidence for a genetic basis has emerged from recent large-scale genome-wide association studies, which have identified more than a dozen susceptibility loci called "diabetogenic" genes.** Unlike type I diabetes, however, the disease is not linked to genes involved in immune tolerance and regulation (e.g., *HLA, CTLA4*), and evidence of an autoimmune basis is lacking. The two metabolic defects that characterize type 2 diabetes are (1) a decreased ability of peripheral tissues to respond to insulin (insulin resistance) and (2) beta cell dysfunction that is manifested as inadequate insulin secretion in the face of insulin resistance and hyperglycemia (Fig. 19–23). Insulin resistance predates the development of hyperglycemia and usually is accompanied by compensatory beta cell hyperfunction and hyperinsulinemia in the early stages of the evolution of diabetes.

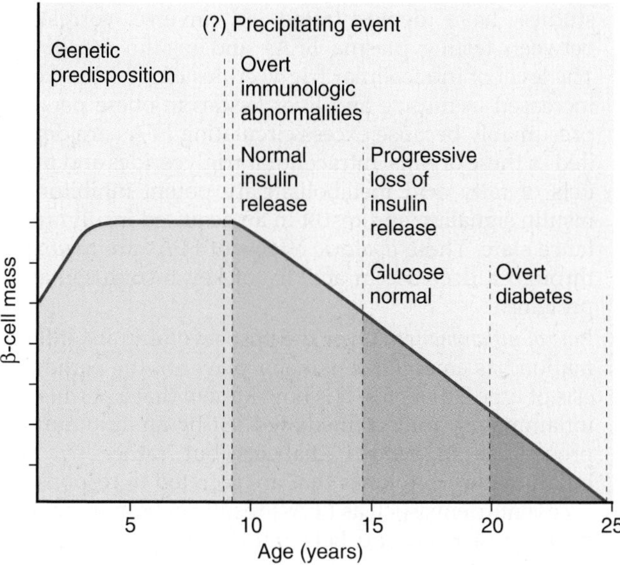

Figure 19–22 Stages in the development of type I diabetes mellitus. The stages are listed *from left to right,* and hypothetical beta cell mass is plotted against age.

(From Eisenbarth GE: Type I diabetes—a chronic autoimmune disease. N Engl J Med 314:1360, 1986.)

Insulin Resistance

Insulin resistance is defined as the failure of target tissues to respond normally to insulin. It leads to decreased uptake of glucose in muscle, reduced glycolysis and fatty acid oxidation in the liver, and an inability to suppress hepatic gluconeogenesis. A variety of functional defects have been

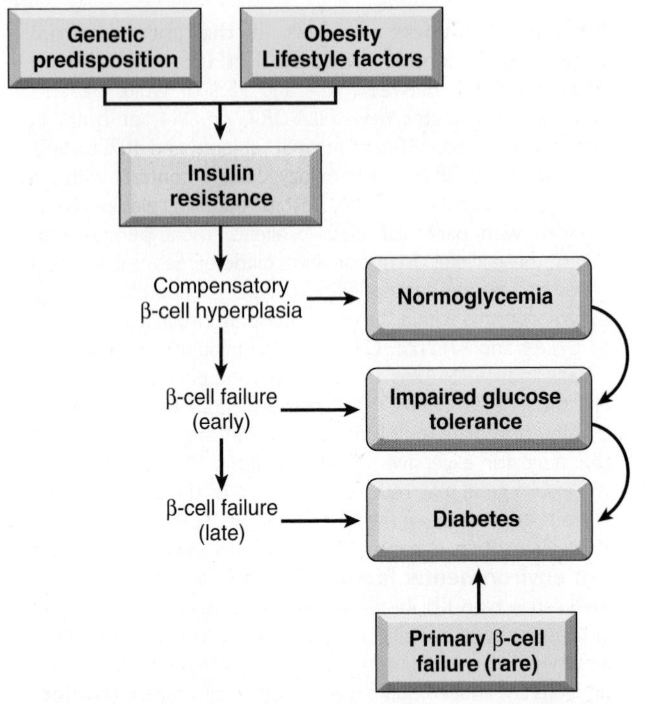

Figure 19–23 Pathogenesis of type 2 diabetes mellitus. Genetic predisposition and environmental influences converge to cause insulin resistance. Compensatory beta cell hyperplasia can maintain normoglycemia, but eventually beta cell secretory dysfunction sets in, leading to impaired glucose tolerance and, ultimately, frank diabetes. Rare instances of primary beta cell failure can lead directly to type 2 diabetes without an intervening state of insulin resistance.

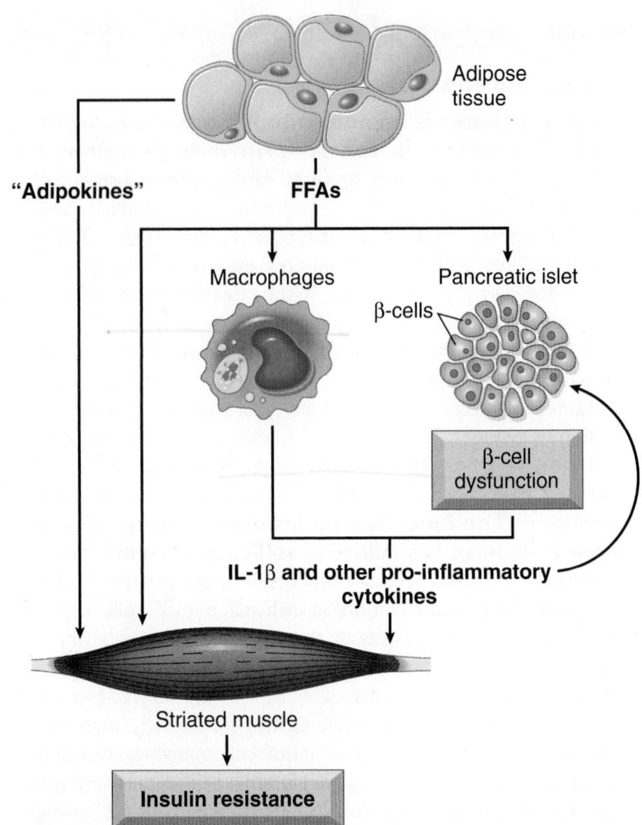

Figure 19–24 Mechanisms of beta cell dysfunction and insulin resistance in type 2 diabetes. Free fatty acids directly cause beta cell dysfunction and induce insulin resistance in target tissues (such as striated muscle, *shown here*), and also induce the secretion of pro-inflammatory cytokines that cause more beta cell dysfunction and insulin resistance.

reported in the insulin signaling pathway in states of insulin resistance (for example, reduced phosphorylation-dependent activation of the insulin receptor and its downstream components), which attenuate signal transduction. *Few factors play as important a role in the development of insulin resistance as obesity.*

Obesity and Insulin Resistance

The association of obesity with type 2 diabetes has been recognized for decades, with visceral obesity being common in a majority of affected patients. Insulin resistance is present even with simple obesity unaccompanied by hyperglycemia, indicating a fundamental abnormality of insulin signaling in states of fatty excess. In fact, the term *metabolic syndrome* has been applied to a constellation of findings dominated by visceral obesity, which is accompanied by insulin resistance, glucose intolerance, and cardiovascular risk factors such as hypertension and abnormal lipid profiles (Chapter 7). In the absence of weight loss and lifestyle modifications, persons with metabolic syndrome are at significant risk for the development of frank type 2 diabetes, underscoring the importance of obesity to the pathogenesis of this disease. The risk of diabetes increases as the body mass index (a measure of body fat content) increases, suggesting a dose-response relationship between body fat and insulin resistance. Although many details of the so-called *adipo-insulin axis* remain to be elucidated, recognition of some of the putative pathways leading to insulin resistance has increased substantially (Fig. 19–24):

- *Role of excess free fatty acids* (FFAs): Cross-sectional studies have demonstrated an inverse correlation between fasting plasma FFAs and insulin sensitivity. The level of intracellular triglycerides often is markedly increased in muscle and liver tissues in obese persons, presumably because excess circulating FFAs are deposited in these organs. Intracellular triglycerides and products of fatty acid metabolism are potent inhibitors of insulin signaling and result in an acquired insulin resistance state. These *lipotoxic* effects of FFAs are mediated through a decrease in activity of key insulin-signaling proteins.
- *Role of inflammation*: Over the past several years, inflammation has emerged as a major player in the pathogenesis of type 2 diabetes. It is now known that a permissive inflammatory milieu (mediated *not* by an autoimmune process as in type 1 diabetes but rather by pro-inflammatory cytokines that are secreted in response to excess nutrients such as FFAs) results in both peripheral insulin resistance and beta cell dysfunction (see later). Excess FFAs within macrophages and beta cells can engage the *inflammasome*, a multiprotein cytoplasmic complex that leads to secretion of the cytokine interleukin IL-1β (Chapter 2). IL-1β, in turn, mediates the

secretion of additional pro-inflammatory cytokines from macrophages, islets, and other cells that are released into the circulation and act on the major sites of insulin action to promote insulin resistance. Thus, excess FFAs can impede insulin signaling directly within peripheral tissues, as well as indirectly through the release of pro-inflammatory cytokines. Not surprisingly, there are now several ongoing trials of cytokine antagonists (particularly of IL-1β) in patients with type 2 diabetes.

- *Role of adipokines*: Adipose tissue is not merely a passive storage depot for fat; it can operate as a functional endocrine organ, releasing so-called *adipokines* in response to extracellular stimuli or changes in metabolic status. Thus, adipocytes also release IL-1β and other pro-inflammatory cytokines into the circulation in response to excess FFAs, which promote peripheral insulin resistance. By contrast, *adiponectin* is an adipokine with insulin sensitizing activity, which probably acts by dampening the inflammatory response.
- *Peroxisome proliferator-activated receptor-γ* (PPARγ): PPARγ is a nuclear receptor and transcription factor expressed in adipose tissue and plays a seminal role in adipocyte differentiation. A class of antidiabetic medications known as thiazolidinediones acts as agonist ligands for PPARγ and improves insulin sensitivity. Activation of PPARγ promotes secretion of antihyperglycemic adipokines such as adiponectin, and shifts the deposition of FFAs toward adipose tissue and away from liver and skeletal muscle.

Beta Cell Dysfunction

Beta cell dysfunction in type 2 diabetes reflects the inability of these cells to adapt themselves to the long-term demands of peripheral insulin resistance and increased insulin secretion. In states of insulin resistance, insulin secretion initially is higher for each level of glucose than in controls. This hyperinsulinemic state is a compensation for peripheral resistance and often can maintain normal plasma glucose for years. Eventually, however, beta cell compensation becomes inadequate, and there is progression to hyperglycemia, which is accompanied by an absolute loss in beta cell mass. The molecular mechanisms underlying beta cell dysfunction in type 2 diabetes are multifactorial and in many instances overlap with those implicated in insulin resistance. Thus, excess nutrients such as FFAs and glucose can promote the secretion of pro-inflammatory cytokines from beta cells, which leads to recruitment of mononuclear cells (macrophages and T cells) into the islets, resulting in more local cytokine production. The consequences of this abnormal inflammatory microenvironment are beta cell dysfunction and, ultimately, beta cell death. Amyloid replacement of islets is a characteristic finding in persons with *long-standing* type 2 diabetes and is present in more than 90% of diabetic islets examined (see later). The islet amyloid polypetide (IAPP), also known as amylin, is secreted by the beta cells in conjunction with insulin, and its abnormal aggregation results in amyloid. IAPP also engages the inflammasome and promotes IL-1β secretion, thus sustaining the inflammatory onslaught on surviving beta cells even late in the disease.

Monogenic Forms of Diabetes

Type 1 and type 2 diabetes are genetically complex, and despite the associations with multiple susceptibility loci, no single-gene defect (mutation) can account for predisposition to these entities. By contrast, monogenic forms of diabetes (Table 19–5) are uncommon examples of the *diabetic phenotype occurring as a result of loss-of-function mutations within a single gene.* Monogenic causes of diabetes include either a primary defect in beta cell function or a defect in insulin receptor signaling. The largest subgroup of patients in this category traditionally was designated as having *maturity-onset diabetes of the young (MODY)* because of its superficial resemblance to type 2 diabetes and its occurrence in younger patients; MODY can be the result of inactivating mutations in one of six genes. Other uncommon causes include *maternally inherited diabetes and bilateral deafness,* secondary to mitochondrial DNA mutations, and mutations within the *insulin* gene itself, which most commonly manifests with diabetes in the neonatal period. Finally, rare instances of *insulin receptor* mutations that affect receptor synthesis, insulin binding, or downstream signal transduction can cause severe insulin resistance, accompanied by hyperinsulinemia and diabetes.

Complications of Diabetes

Diabetes can be a devastating disease because the abnormal glucose metabolism and other metabolic derangements have serious pathologic effects on virtually all the systems of the body. The most significant complications of diabetes are vascular abnormalities, renal damage, and lesions affecting the peripheral nerves and eyes (Fig. 19–25). The pathologic findings in these tissues and their clinical consequences are described below. There is extreme variability among patients in the time of onset of these complications, their severity, and the particular organ or organs involved. In persons with tight control of their diabetes, the onset may be delayed.

The pathogenesis of the long-term complications of diabetes is multifactorial, although persistent hyperglycemia (glucotoxicity) seems to be a key mediator. At least three distinct metabolic pathways seem to be involved in the pathogenesis of long-term complications; it is likely that all of them play a role in a tissue-specific manner.

1. *Formation of advanced glycation end products* (AGEs). AGEs are formed as a result of nonenzymatic reactions between intracellular glucose-derived precursors (glyoxal, methylglyoxal, and 3-deoxyglucosone) with the amino groups of both intracellular and extracellular proteins. The natural rate of AGE formation is greatly accelerated in the presence of hyperglycemia. AGEs bind to a specific receptor (RAGE), which is expressed on inflammatory cells (macrophages and T cells) and in endothelium and vascular smooth muscle. The detrimental effects of the AGE-RAGE signaling axis within the vascular compartment include
   - Release of pro-inflammatory *cytokines and growth factors* from intimal macrophages
   - Generation of *reactive oxygen species* in endothelial cells

- Increased *procoagulant activity* on endothelial cells and macrophages
- Enhanced *proliferation of vascular smooth muscle cells and synthesis of extracellular matrix*

  In addition to receptor-mediated effects, *AGEs can directly cross-link extracellular matrix proteins,* which decreases protein removal while enhancing protein deposition. AGEs cross-linked proteins can *trap* other plasma or interstitial proteins; for example, low-density lipoprotein (LDL) gets trapped within AGE-modified large vessel walls, accelerating atherosclerosis (Chapter 9), while albumin can get trapped within capillaries, accounting in part for the basement membrane thickening that is characteristic of diabetic microangiopathy (see later).

2. *Activation of protein kinase C.* Activation of intracellular protein kinase C (PKC) by calcium ions and the second messenger diacylglycerol (DAG) is an important signal transduction pathway in many cellular systems. Intracellular hyperglycemia can stimulate the de novo synthesis of DAG from glycolytic intermediates and hence cause activation of PKC. The downstream effects of PKC activation are numerous and include production of *proangiogenic molecules* such as vascular endothelial growth factor (VEGF), implicated in the neovascularization seen in diabetic retinopathy, and profibrogenic molecules such as transforming growth factor-β, leading to increased deposition of extracellular matrix and basement membrane material.
3. *Disturbances in polyol pathways.* In some tissues that do not require insulin for glucose transport (e.g., nerves, lens, kidneys, blood vessels), hyperglycemia leads to an increase in intracellular glucose that is then metabolized by the enzyme *aldose reductase* to sorbitol, a polyol, and eventually to fructose, in a reaction that uses NADPH (the reduced form of nicotinamide dinucleotide phosphate) as a cofactor. NADPH is also required by the enzyme glutathione reductase in a reaction that regenerates reduced glutathione (GSH). As described in Chapter 1, GSH is one of the important antioxidant mechanisms in the cell, and any reduction in GSH increases cellular susceptibility to *oxidative stress.* In neurons, persistent hyperglycemia appears to be the major underlying cause of diabetic neuropathy (*glucose neurotoxicity*).

MORPHOLOGY

Diabetes and Its Late Complications

Pathologic findings in the diabetic pancreas are variable and not necessarily dramatic. The important morphologic changes are related to the many late systemic complications of diabetes. In most patients, morphologic changes are likely to be found in arteries **(macrovascular disease),** basement membranes of small vessels **(microangiopathy),** kidneys **(diabetic nephropathy),** retina **(retinopathy),** nerves **(neuropathy),** and other tissues. These changes are seen in both type 1 and type 2 diabetes (Fig. 19–25).

Pancreas. Lesions in the pancreas are inconstant and rarely of diagnostic value. One or more of the following alterations may be present:

- **Reduction in the number and size of islets.** This change most often is seen in type 1 diabetes, particularly with rapidly advancing disease. Most of the islets are small, inconspicuous, and not easily detected.
- **Leukocytic infiltration of the islets,** which are principally composed of mononuclear cells (lymphocytes and macrophages) (Fig. 19–26, *A*). Of note, both type 1 and type 2 diabetes may demonstrate islet inflammation early in the disease, although it is typically more severe in T1D. In both types inflammation is often absent by the time the disease is clinically evident.
- **Amyloid replacement of islets in long-standing type 2 diabetes,** appearing as deposition of pink, amorphous material beginning in and around capillaries and between cells. At advanced stages the islets may be virtually obliterated (Fig. 19–26, *B*); fibrosis also may be observed. While inflammation is observed early in the natural history of type 2 diabetes, amyloid deposition occurs in long-standing cases.
- **An increase in the number and size of islets, especially characteristic of nondiabetic newborns of diabetic mothers.** Presumably, fetal islets undergo hyperplasia in response to the maternal hyperglycemia.

Diabetic Macrovascular Disease. Diabetes exacts a heavy toll on the vascular system. The hallmark of diabetic macrovascular disease is accelerated atherosclerosis affecting the aorta and large and medium-sized arteries. Except for its greater severity and earlier age at onset, atherosclerosis in diabetics is indistinguishable from that in nondiabetics (Chapter 9). Myocardial infarction, caused by atherosclerosis of the coronary arteries, is the most common cause of death in diabetics. Significantly, it is almost as common in diabetic women as in diabetic men. By contrast, myocardial infarction is uncommon in nondiabetic women of reproductive age. Gangrene of the lower extremities, as a result of advanced vascular disease, is about 100 times more common in persons with diabetes than in the general population. The larger renal arteries also are subject to severe atherosclerosis, but the most damaging effect of diabetes on the kidneys is exerted at the level of the glomeruli and the microcirculation, as discussed later on.

Hyaline arteriolosclerosis, the vascular lesion associated with hypertension (Chapters 9 and 13), is both more prevalent and more severe in diabetics than in nondiabetics, but it is not specific for diabetes and may be seen in elderly persons who do not suffer from either diabetes or hypertension. It takes the form of an amorphous, hyaline thickening of the wall of the arterioles, which causes narrowing of the lumen (Fig. 19–27). Not surprisingly, in diabetic patients, its severity is related not only to the duration of the disease but also to the presence or absence of hypertension.

Diabetic Microangiopathy. One of the most consistent morphologic features of diabetes is **diffuse thickening of basement membranes.** The thickening is most evident in the capillaries of the skin, skeletal muscle, retina, renal glomeruli, and renal medulla. However, it also may be seen in such nonvascular structures as renal tubules, the Bowman

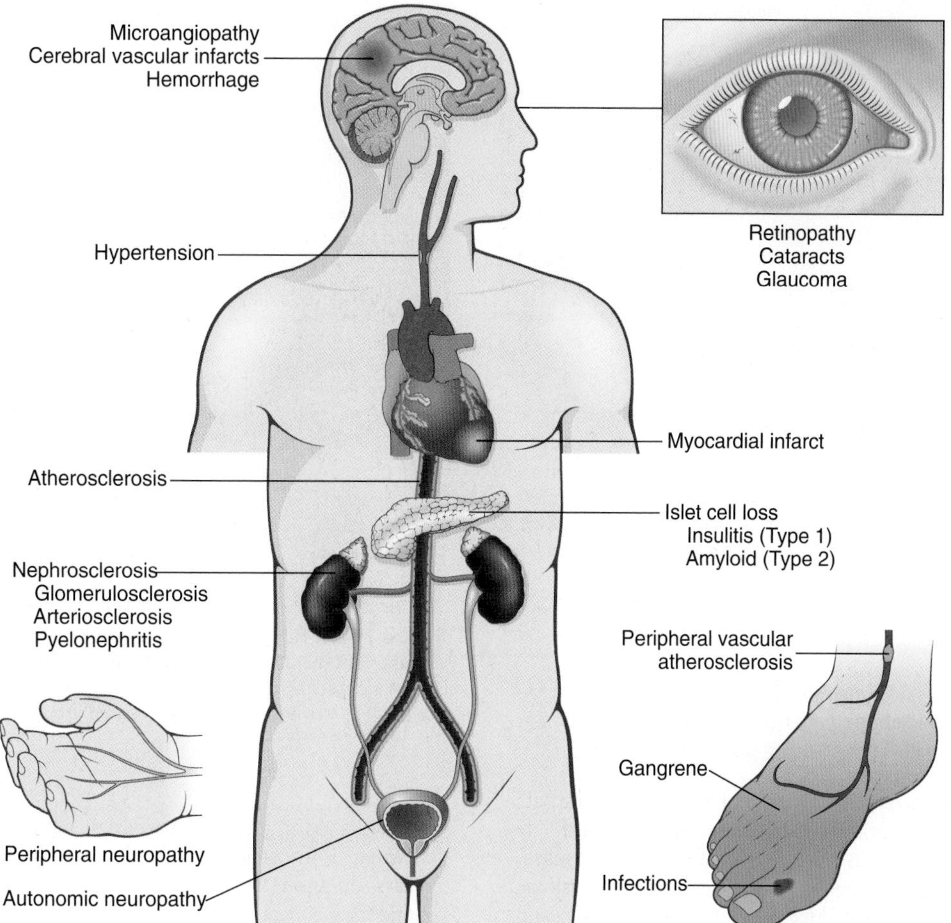

Figure 19–25 Long-term complications of diabetes.

capsule, peripheral nerves, and placenta. By both light and electron microscopy, the basal lamina separating parenchymal or endothelial cells from the surrounding tissue is markedly thickened by concentric layers of hyaline material composed predominantly of type IV collagen (Fig. 19–28). Of note, **despite the increase in the thickness of basement membranes, diabetic capillaries are more leaky than normal to plasma proteins. The microangiopathy underlies the development of diabetic nephropathy, retinopathy, and some forms of**

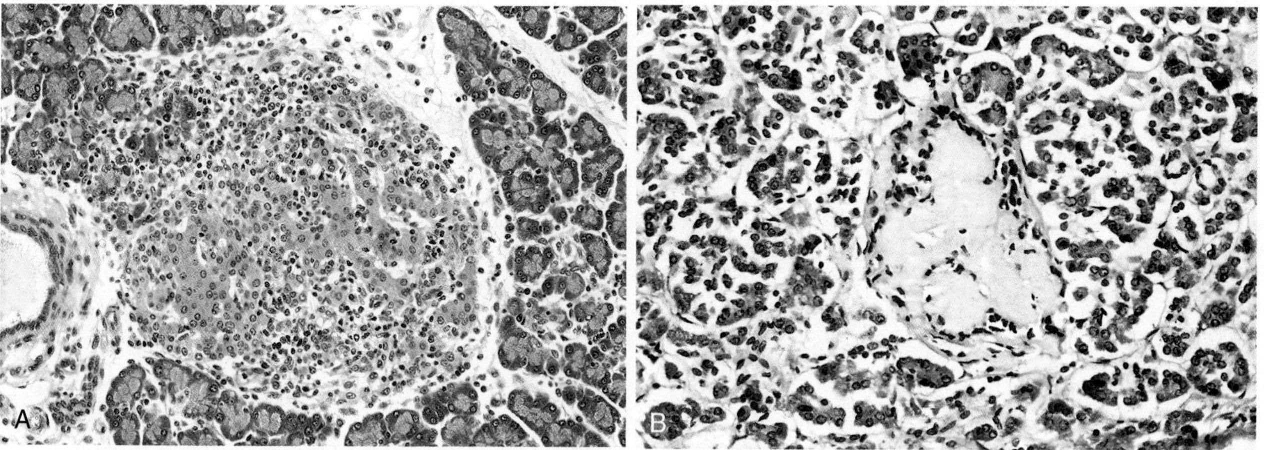

Figure 19–26 A, Autoimmune insulitis in a rat (BB) model of autoimmune diabetes. This disorder also is seen in type 1 human diabetes. **B,** Amyloidosis of a pancreatic islet in type 2 diabetes. Amyloidosis typically is observed late in the natural history of this form of diabetes, with islet inflammation noted at earlier observations.

(A, Courtesy of Dr. Arthur Like, University of Massachusetts, Worcester, Massachusetts.)

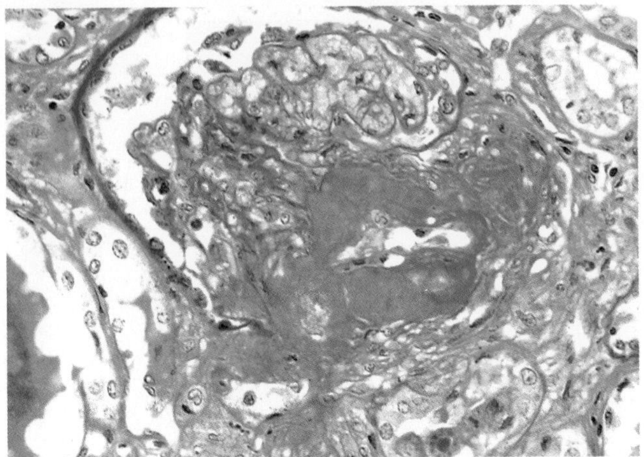

Figure 19–27 Severe renal hyaline arteriolosclerosis in a periodic acid–Schiff stained specimen. Note the markedly thickened, tortuous afferent arteriole. The amorphous nature of the thickened vascular wall is evident.
(Courtesy of Dr. M.A. Venkatachalam, Department of Pathology, University of Texas Health Science Center, San Antonio, Texas.)

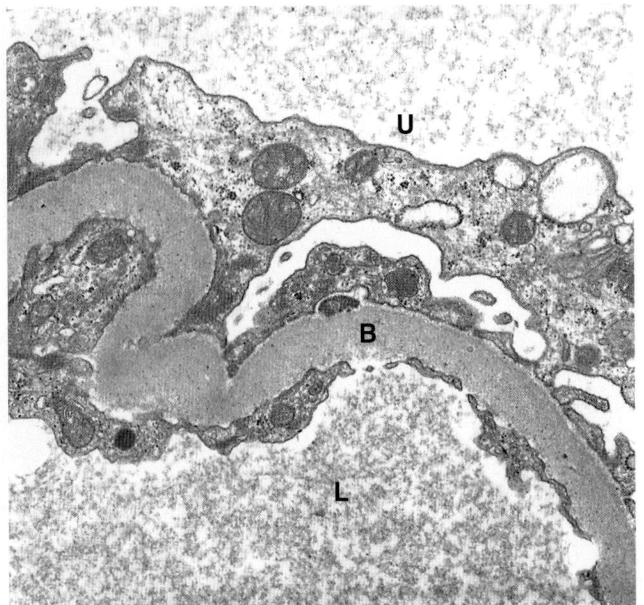

Figure 19–29 Renal glomerulus showing markedly thickened glomerular basement membrane (B) in a diabetic. L, glomerular capillary lumen; U, urinary space.
(Courtesy of Dr. Michael Kashgarian, Department of Pathology, Yale University School of Medicine, New Haven, Connecticut.)

neuropathy. An indistinguishable microangiopathy can be found in aged nondiabetic patients, but rarely to the extent seen in persons with long-standing diabetes.

Diabetic Nephropathy. The kidneys are prime targets of diabetes (see also Chapter 13). Renal failure is second only to myocardial infarction as a cause of death from this disease. Three lesions are encountered: (1) glomerular lesions; (2) renal vascular lesions, principally arteriolosclerosis; and (3) pyelonephritis, including necrotizing papillitis.

The most important glomerular lesions are capillary basement membrane thickening, diffuse mesangial sclerosis, and nodular glomerulosclerosis. The glomerular capillary basement membranes are thickened along their entire length. This change can be detected by electron microscopy within a few years of the onset of diabetes, sometimes without any associated change in renal function (Fig. 19–29).

Diffuse mesangial sclerosis consists of a diffuse increase in mesangial matrix along with mesangial cell proliferation and is always associated with basement membrane thickening. It is found in most individuals with disease of more than 10 years' duration. When glomerulosclerosis becomes marked, patients manifest the nephrotic syndrome, characterized by proteinuria, hypoalbuminemia, and edema (Chapter 13).

Nodular glomerulosclerosis describes a glomerular lesion made distinctive by ball-like deposits of a laminated matrix situated in the periphery of the glomerulus (Fig. 19–30). These nodules are PAS-positive and usually contain trapped mesangial cells. This distinctive change has been called the **Kimmelstiel-Wilson lesion,** after the two pathologists who first described it. Nodular glomerulosclerosis is encountered in approximately 15% to 30% of persons with long-term diabetes and is a major contributor to

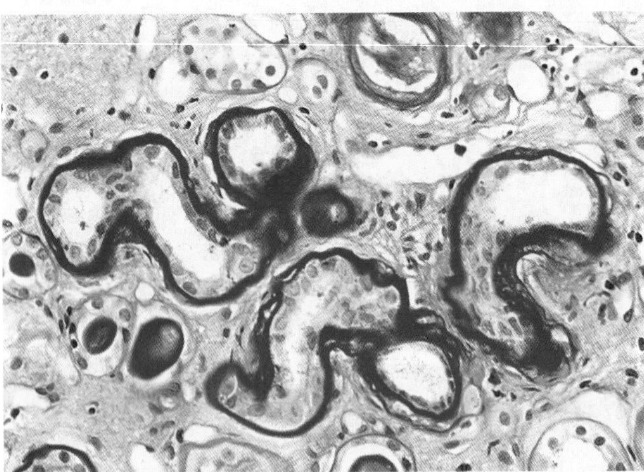

Figure 19–28 Renal cortex showing thickening of tubular basement membranes in a specimen from a diabetic patient. Periodic acid–Schiff stain.

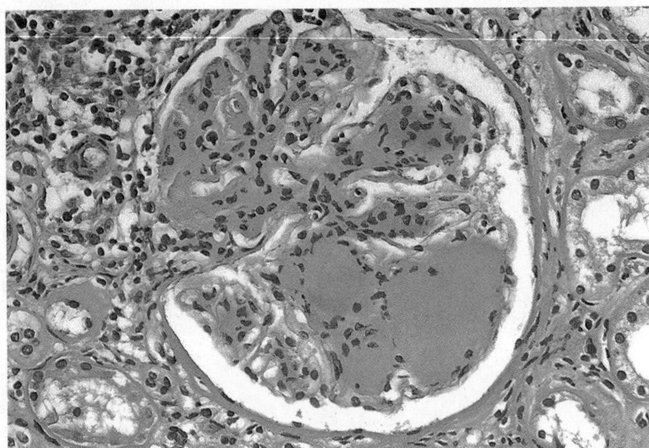

Figure 19–30 Nodular glomerulosclerosis in a renal specimen from a patient with long-standing diabetes.
(Courtesy of Dr. Lisa Yerian, Department of Pathology, University of Chicago, Chicago, Illinois.)

morbidity and mortality. Diffuse mesangial sclerosis also may be seen in association with old age and hypertension; by contrast, the nodular form of glomerulosclerosis, once certain unusual forms of nephropathies have been excluded (Chapter 13), is essentially pathognomonic of diabetes. Both the diffuse and the nodular forms of glomerulosclerosis induce sufficient ischemia to cause scarring of the kidneys, manifested by a finely granular-appearing cortical surface (Fig. 19–31).

Renal atherosclerosis and arteriolosclerosis constitute part of the macrovascular disease seen in diabetics. The kidney is one of the most frequently and severely affected organs; however, the changes in the arteries and arterioles are similar to those found throughout the body. **Hyaline arteriolosclerosis affects not only the afferent but also the efferent arterioles.** Such efferent arteriolosclerosis is rarely if ever encountered in persons who do not have diabetes.

Pyelonephritis is an acute or chronic inflammation of the kidneys that usually begins in the interstitial tissue and then spreads to involve the tubules. Both the acute and chronic forms of this disease occur in nondiabetics as well as in diabetics but are more common in persons with diabetes than in the general population; once affected, diabetics tend to have more severe involvement. One special pattern of acute pyelonephritis, **necrotizing papillitis** (or papillary necrosis), is much more prevalent in diabetics than in nondiabetics.

Ocular Complications of Diabetes. Visual impairment, sometimes even total blindness, is one of the more feared consequences of long-standing diabetes. **The ocular involvement may take the form of retinopathy, cataract formation, or glaucoma.** Retinopathy, the most common pattern, consists of a constellation of changes that together are considered by many ophthalmologists to be virtually diagnostic of the disease. **The lesion in the retina takes two forms: nonproliferative (background) retinopathy and proliferative retinopathy.**

Nonproliferative retinopathy includes intraretinal or preretinal hemorrhages, retinal exudates, microaneurysms, venous dilations, edema, and, most importantly, thickening of the retinal capillaries (microangiopathy). The retinal exudates can be either "soft" (microinfarcts) or "hard" (deposits of plasma proteins and lipids) (Fig. 19–32). The microaneurysms are discrete saccular dilations of retinal choroidal capillaries that appear through the ophthalmoscope as small red dots. Dilations tend to occur at focal points of weakening, resulting from loss of pericytes. Retinal edema presumably results from excessive capillary permeability. Underlying all of these changes is the microangiopathy, which is thought to lead to loss of capillary pericytes and hence to focal weakening of capillary structure.

The so-called proliferative retinopathy is a process of neovascularization and fibrosis. This lesion leads to serious consequences, including blindness, especially if it involves the macula. Vitreous hemorrhages can result from rupture of newly formed capillaries; the subsequent organization of the hemorrhage can pull the retina off its substratum (retinal detachment).

Diabetic Neuropathy. The central and peripheral nervous systems are not spared by diabetes. The most frequent pattern of involvement is that of a peripheral, symmetric neuropathy of the lower extremities affecting both motor and sensory function, particularly the latter. Other forms include autonomic neuropathy, which produces disturbances in bowel and bladder function and sometimes sexual

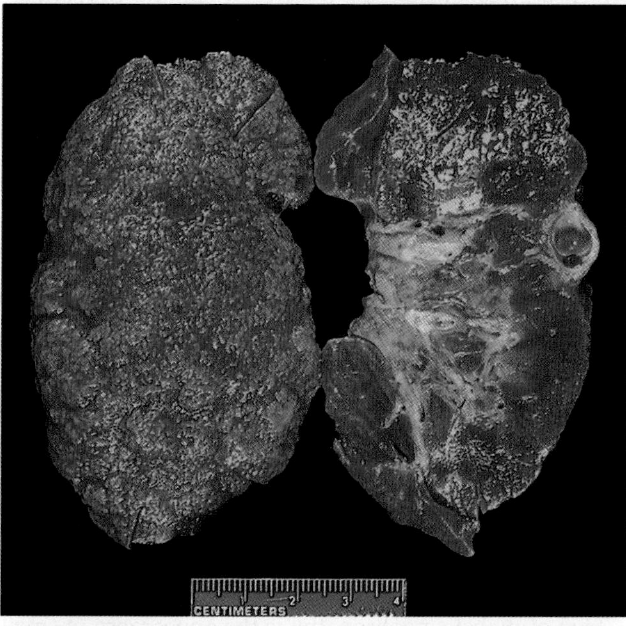

Figure 19–31 Nephrosclerosis in a patient with long-standing diabetes. The kidney has been bisected to demonstrate both diffuse granular transformation of the surface (*left*) and marked thinning of the cortical tissue (*right*). Additional features include some irregular depressions, the result of pyelonephritis, and an incidental cortical cyst (*far right*).

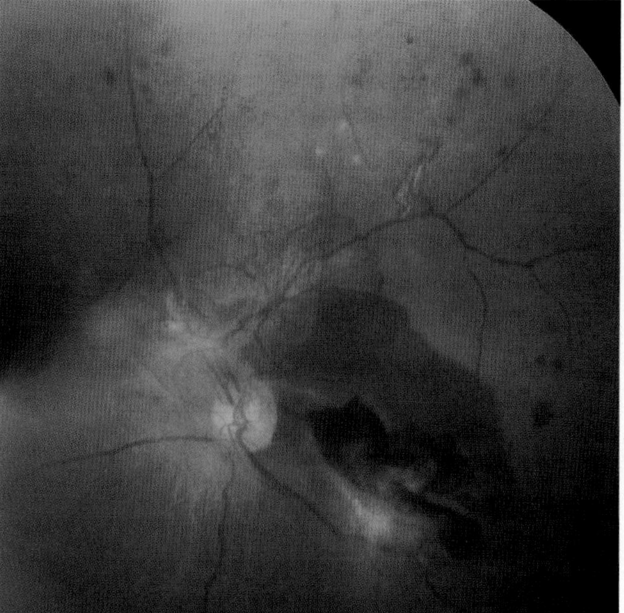

Figure 19–32 Characteristic morphologic changes of diabetic retinopathy. Features include advanced proliferative retinopathy with retinal hemorrhages, exudates, neovascularization, and tractional retinal detachment (*lower right corner*).

(Courtesy of Dr. Rajendra Apte, Washington University School of Medicine, St. Louis, Missouri.)

impotence, and diabetic mononeuropathy, which may manifest as sudden footdrop or wristdrop or isolated cranial nerve palsies. The neurologic changes may be the result of microangiopathy and increased permeability of the capillaries that supply the nerves, as well as direct axonal damage.

Clinical Features

It is difficult to discuss with brevity the diverse clinical presentations of diabetes mellitus. Only a few characteristic patterns are presented here. In the initial 1 or 2 years after manifestation of overt *type 1 diabetes* (referred to as the "honeymoon period"), exogenous insulin requirements may be minimal to none because of residual ongoing endogenous insulin secretion, but thereafter the beta cell reserve is exhausted and insulin requirements increase dramatically. Although beta cell destruction is a gradual process, the transition from impaired glucose tolerance to overt diabetes may be abrupt, heralded by an event associated with increased insulin requirements such as infection. The onset is marked by polyuria, polydipsia, polyphagia, and in severe cases, ketoacidosis, all resulting from metabolic derangements (Fig. 19–33).

Since insulin is a major anabolic hormone in the body, *deficiency of insulin results in a catabolic state that affects not only glucose metabolism but also fat and protein metabolism.* The assimilation of glucose into muscle and adipose tissue is sharply diminished or abolished. Not only does storage of glycogen in liver and muscle cease, but also reserves are depleted by glycogenolysis. The resultant hyperglycemia exceeds the renal threshold for reabsorption, and glycosuria ensues. The glycosuria induces an osmotic diuresis and, consequently, *polyuria,* causing a profound loss of water and electrolytes. The obligatory renal water loss combined with the hyperosmolarity resulting from the increased levels of glucose in the blood tends to deplete intracellular water, triggering the osmoreceptors of the thirst centers of the brain. This sequence of events generates intense thirst (*polydipsia*). With a deficiency of insulin, the scales swing from insulin-promoted anabolism to catabolism of proteins and fats. Proteolysis follows, and the gluconeogenic amino acids are removed by the liver and used as building blocks for glucose. The catabolism of proteins and fats tends to induce a negative energy balance, which in turn leads to increasing appetite (*polyphagia*), thus completing the classic triad of diabetes: *polyuria, polydipsia,* and *polyphagia.* Despite the increased appetite, catabolic effects prevail, resulting in weight loss and muscle weakness. The combination of polyphagia and weight loss is paradoxical and should always point to the diagnostic possibility of diabetes.

In patients with type 1 diabetes, deviations from normal dietary intake, unusual physical activity, infection, or any other forms of stress may rapidly influence the treacherously fragile metabolic balance, predisposing the affected person to *diabetic ketoacidosis.* The plasma glucose usually is in the range of 500 to 700 mg/dL as a result of absolute insulin deficiency and unopposed effects of counterregulatory hormones (epinephrine, glucagon). The marked hyperglycemia causes an osmotic diuresis and dehydration characteristic of the ketoacidotic state. The second major effect is activation of the ketogenic machinery. Insulin deficiency leads to activation of lipoprotein lipase, with resultant excessive breakdown of adipose stores, giving rise to increased FFAs, which are oxidized by the liver to produce *ketones.* Ketogenesis is an adaptive phenomenon in times of starvation, generating ketones as a source of energy for consumption by vital organs (e.g., brain). The rate at which ketones are formed may exceed the rate at which they can be used by peripheral tissues, leading to *ketonemia* and *ketonuria.* If the urinary excretion of ketones is compromised by dehydration, the accumulating ketones decrease blood pH, resulting in metabolic ketoacidosis.

Type 2 diabetes mellitus also may manifest with polyuria and polydipsia, but unlike in type 1 diabetes, patients often are older than 40 years and frequently are obese. Unfortunately, with the increase in obesity and sedentary life style in Western society, type 2 diabetes is now seen in children and adolescents with increasing frequency. In some cases, medical attention is sought because of unexplained weakness or weight loss. *Most frequently, however, the diagnosis is made after routine blood or urine testing in asymptomatic persons.*

In the decompensated state, patients with type 2 diabetes may develop *hyperosmolar nonketotic coma.* This syndrome is engendered by severe dehydration resulting from sustained osmotic diuresis and urinary fluid loss due to chronic hyperglycemia. Typically, the affected person is an elderly diabetic who is disabled by a stroke or an infection and is unable to maintain adequate water intake. The absence of ketoacidosis and its symptoms (nausea, vomiting, respiratory difficulties) delays recognition of the seriousness of the situation until the onset of severe dehydration and coma. Table 19–6 summarizes some of the pertinent clinical, genetic, and histopathologic features that distinguish between type 1 and type 2 diabetes.

As previously discussed, it is the long-term effects of diabetes, more than the acute metabolic complications, which are responsible for the overwhelming preponderance of morbidity and mortality attributable to this disease. In most instances, these complications appear approximately 15 to 20 years after the onset of hyperglycemia.

- In both forms of long-standing diabetes, cardiovascular events such as myocardial infarction, renal vascular insufficiency, and stroke (cerebrovascular accident) are the most common contributors to mortality. The impact of cardiovascular disease can be gauged by its involvement in as many as 80% of deaths among persons with type 2 diabetes; in fact, diabetics have a 3 to 7.5 times greater incidence of death from cardiovascular causes than nondiabetic populations. The hallmark of cardiovascular disease is accelerated atherosclerosis of the large and medium-sized arteries (i.e., macrovascular disease). The importance of obesity in the pathogenesis of insulin resistance has already been discussed, but it also is an independent risk factor for development of atherosclerosis.
- Diabetic nephropathy is a leading cause of end-stage renal disease in the United States. The earliest manifestation of diabetic nephropathy is the appearance of small amounts of albumin in the urine (greater than 30 but less than 300 mg/day—i.e., microalbuminuria). Without specific interventions, approximately 80% of patients with type 1 diabetes and 20% to 40% of those with type

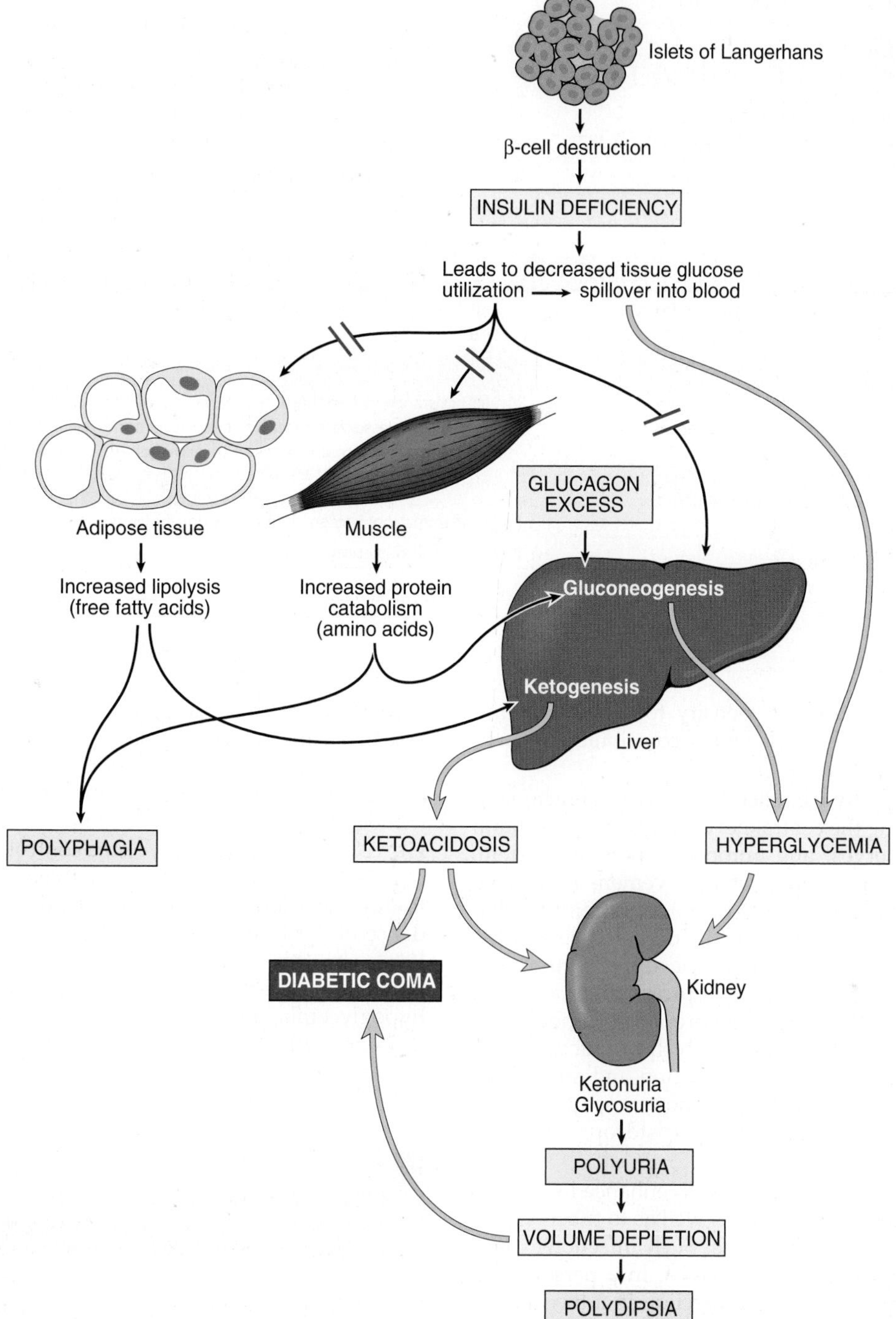

Figure 19–33 Sequence of metabolic derangements leading to diabetic coma in type 1 diabetes mellitus. An absolute insulin deficiency leads to a catabolic state, eventuating in ketoacidosis and severe volume depletion. These derangements bring about sufficient central nervous system compromise to cause coma and, eventually, death if left untreated.

2 diabetes will develop overt nephropathy with macroalbuminuria (excretion of more than 300 mg/day) over the succeeding 10 to 15 years, usually accompanied by the appearance of hypertension. The progression from overt nephropathy to end-stage renal disease can be highly variable and is evidenced by a progressive drop in glomerular filtration rate. By 20 years after diagnosis, more than 75% of persons with type 1 diabetes and about 20% of those with type 2 diabetes with overt nephropathy will develop end-stage renal disease, necessitating dialysis or renal transplantation.

- Visual impairment, sometimes even total blindness, is one of the more feared consequences of long-standing diabetes. This disease currently is the fourth leading cause of acquired blindness in the United States. Approximately 60% to 80% of patients develop some form of diabetic retinopathy approximately 15 to 20 years after diagnosis. In addition to retinopathy, diabetic patients

Table 19–6 Type 1 Versus Type 2 Diabetes Mellitus

Type 1 Diabetes Mellitus	Type 2 Diabetes Mellitus
Clinical	
Onset usually in childhood and adolescence	Onset usually in adulthood; increasing incidence in childhood and adolescence
Normal weight or weight loss preceding diagnosis	Vast majority of patients are obese (80%)
Progressive decrease in insulin levels	Increased blood insulin (early); normal or moderate decrease in insulin (late)
Circulating islet autoantibodies	No islet autoantibodies
Diabetic ketoacidosis in absence of insulin therapy	Nonketotic hyperosmolar coma
Genetics	
Major linkage to MHC class I and II genes; also linked to polymorphisms in *CTLA4* and *PTPN22*	No HLA linkage; linkage to candidate diabetogenic and obesity-related genes
Pathogenesis	
Dysfunction in regulatory T cells (Tregs) leading to breakdown in self-tolerance to islet autoantigens	Insulin resistance in peripheral tissues, failure of compensation by beta cells Multiple obesity-associated factors (circulating nonesterified fatty acids, inflammatory mediators, adipocytokines) linked to pathogenesis of insulin resistance
Pathology	
Autoimmune "insulitis"	*Early*: inflammation; *late*: amyloid deposition in islets
Beta cell depletion, islet atrophy	Mild beta cell depletion

HLA, human leukocyte antigen; MHC, major histocompatibility complex.

also have an increased propensity for glaucoma and cataract formation, both of which contribute to visual impairment in diabetes.

- Diabetic neuropathy can elicit a variety of clinical syndromes, afflicting the central nervous system, peripheral sensorimotor nerves, and autonomic nervous system. The most frequent pattern of involvement is a distal symmetric polyneuropathy of the lower extremities that affects both motor and sensory function, particularly the latter (Chapter 21). Over time, the upper extremities may be involved as well, thus approximating a "glove and stocking" pattern of polyneuropathy. Other forms include autonomic neuropathy, which produces disturbances in bowel and bladder function and sometimes sexual impotence, and diabetic mononeuropathy, which may manifest as sudden footdrop, wristdrop, or isolated cranial nerve palsies.
- Diabetic patients are plagued by an enhanced susceptibility to infections of the skin, as well as to tuberculosis, pneumonia, and pyelonephritis. Such infections cause about 5% of diabetes-related deaths. In a person with diabetic neuropathy, a trivial infection in a toe may be the first event in a long succession of complications (gangrene, bacteremia, pneumonia) that may ultimately lead to death.

Several large-scale prospective studies have convincingly demonstrated that the long-term complications, and the associated morbidity and mortality, from diabetes are attenuated by strict glycemic control. For patients with type 1 diabetes, insulin replacement therapy is the mainstay of treatment, while non-pharmacologic approaches such as dietary restrictions and exercise (which improves insulin sensitivity) are often the "first line of defense" for type 2 diabetes. Most patients with type 2 diabetes will eventually require therapeutic intervention to reduce hyperglycemia, which can be achieved by administration of a number of agents that lower glucose levels through several distinct mechanisms of action. Glycemic control is assessed clinically by measuring the percentage of glycosylated hemoglobin, also known as HbA1C, which is formed by non-enzymatic addition of glucose moieties to hemoglobin in red cells. Unlike blood glucose levels, HbA1C is a measure of glycemic control over long periods of time (2 to 3 months) and is relatively unaffected by day-to-day variations. An HbA1C below 7% is taken as evidence of tight glycemic control, but patients with HbA1C levels in this range also have an increased risk of potentially life-threatening episodes of therapy-related hypoglycemia, and "optimal" control of glucose levels in diabetic patients remains an unsettled area of clinical investigation.

SUMMARY

Diabetes Mellitus: Pathogenesis and Long-Term Complications

- Type 1 diabetes is an autoimmune disease characterized by progressive destruction of islet beta cells, leading to absolute insulin deficiency. Both autoreactive T cells and autoantibodies are involved.
- Type 2 diabetes is caused by insulin resistance and beta cell dysfunction, resulting in relative insulin deficiency. Autoimmunity is not involved.
- Obesity has an important relationship with insulin resistance (and hence type 2 diabetes), probably mediated by cytokines released from adipose tissues (adipocytokines). Other players in the *adipo-insulin axis* include FFAs (which may cause *lipotoxicity*) and the PPARγ receptor, which modulates adipocytokine levels.
- Monogenic forms of diabetes are uncommon and are caused by single-gene defects that result in primary beta cell dysfunction (e.g., *glucokinase* mutation) or lead to

abnormalities of insulin–insulin receptor signaling (e.g., insulin receptor gene mutations).

- The long-term complications of diabetes are similar in both types and affect mainly blood vessels, and the kidneys, nerves and eyes. The development of these complications is attributed to three underlying mechanisms: formation of AGEs, activation of PKC, and disturbances in polyol pathways leading to oxidative stress.

PANCREATIC NEUROENDOCRINE TUMORS

Pancreatic neuroendocrine tumors (PanNETs), also known as *islet cell tumors,* are rare in comparison with tumors of the exocrine pancreas, accounting for only 2% of all pancreatic neoplasms. PanNETs are most common in adults and may be single or multifocal; when they are malignant, the liver is the most common site of organ metastases. These tumors have a propensity to elaborate pancreatic hormones, but some are nonfunctional. The latter typically are larger lesions at diagnosis, since they come to clinical attention later in their natural history than functional PanNETs, which often present with symptoms related to excessive hormone production. All PanNETs, with the exception of insulinomas (see later), are regarded as having malignant potential, and in fact, 65% to 80% of PanNETs manifest with overtly malignant features of biologic aggressiveness, such as invasion into local tissues or distant metastases. The *proliferative rate of PanNETs* (measured using either mitotic counts or nuclear labeling with the proliferation marker Ki-67) is one of the best correlates of outcome. Genomic sequencing of sporadic PanNETs has identified recurrent somatic alterations in three major genes or pathways:

- *MEN1,* which causes familial MEN syndrome, type 1 (see later), is also mutated in many sporadic neuroendocrine tumors
- Loss-of-function mutations in tumor suppressor genes such as *PTEN* and *TSC2,* which are negative regulators of the oncogenic mammalian TOR (mTOR) signaling pathway
- Inactivating mutations in two genes, *ATRX* and *DAXX,* which have multiple cellular functions. Of note, nearly half of PanNETs have a somatic mutation in either *ATRX* or *DAXX,* but not both, suggesting that the encoded proteins function in a critical but redundant pathway.

Insulinomas

Beta cell tumors (insulinomas) are the most common type of PanNET and may be responsible for the elaboration of sufficient insulin to induce clinically significant hypoglycemia. The characteristic clinical picture is dominated by attacks of hypoglycemia, which occur when plasma blood glucose levels fall below 50 mg/dL. The attacks consist principally of such central nervous system manifestations as confusion, stupor, and loss of consciousness. They are precipitated by fasting or exercise and are promptly relieved by feeding or parenteral administration of glucose. Most insulinomas are cured by surgical resection.

MORPHOLOGY

Insulinomas exhibit favorable biologic behavior, possibly because the vast majority are identified while they are small (less than 2 cm in diameter) and localized to the pancreas. Most are solitary lesions, although multifocal tumors or tumors ectopic to the pancreas may be encountered. Malignancy in insulinomas, constituting less than 10% of cases, is diagnosed on the basis of local invasion or metastases. On histologic examination, these benign tumors look remarkably like giant islets, with preservation of the regular cords of monotonous cells and their orientation to the vasculature. Not even malignant lesions present much evidence of anaplasia, and they may be deceptively encapsulated. **Deposition of amyloid** in the extracellular tissue is a characteristic feature of many insulinomas (Fig. 19–34, *A*). Under the electron microscope, neoplastic beta cells, like their normal counterparts, display distinctive round granules (Fig. 19–34, *B*).

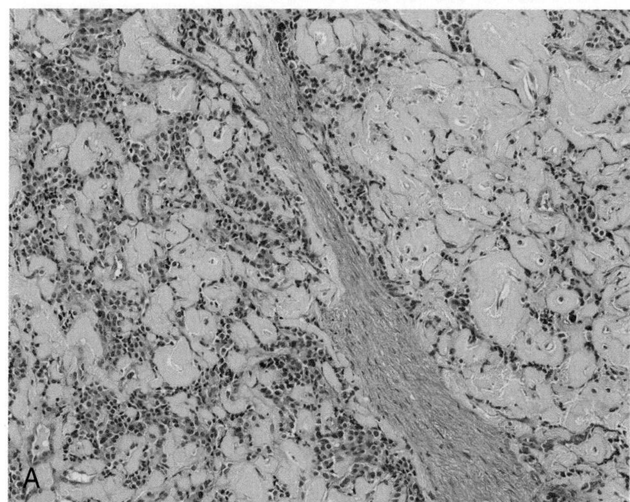

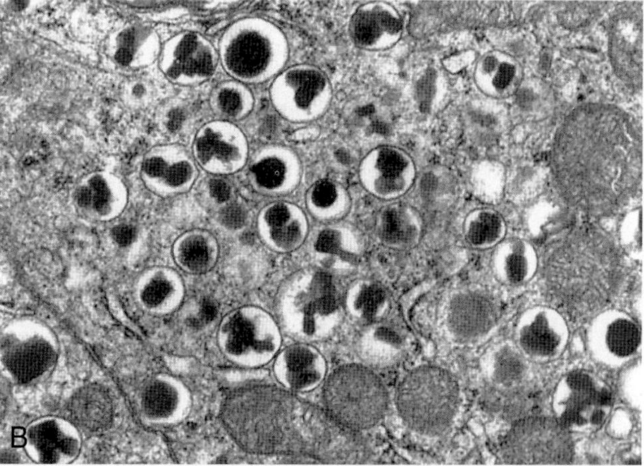

Figure 19–34 Pancreatic neuroendocrine tumor (PanNET), also called islet cell tumor. **A,** The neoplastic cells are monotonous in appearance and demonstrate minimal pleomorphism or mitotic activity. There is abundant amyloid deposition, characteristic of an insulinoma. On clinical evaluation, the patient had episodic hypoglycemia. **B,** Electron micrograph of a normal beta cell shows the characteristic membrane-bound granules, each containing a dense, often rectangular core and distinct halo. Insulinomas contain comparable granules.

Gastrinomas

Marked hypersecretion of gastrin usually has its origin in gastrin-producing tumors (*gastrinomas*), which are just as likely to arise in the duodenum and peripancreatic soft tissues as in the pancreas (the so-called gastrinoma triangle). Zollinger and Ellison first called attention to the *association of pancreatic islet cell lesions with hypersecretion of gastric acid and severe peptic ulceration,* which are present in 90% to 95% of patients with gastrinomas—the clinical hallmark of Zollinger-Ellison syndrome. In this condition, hypergastrinemia from a pancreatic or duodenal tumor stimulates extreme gastric acid secretion, which in turn causes *peptic ulceration.* The duodenal and gastric ulcers often are *multiple;* although they are identical to those found in the general population, they often are *unresponsive* to usual therapy. In addition, ulcers may occur in *unusual locations* such as the jejunum; when intractable jejunal ulcers are found, Zollinger-Ellison syndrome should be considered. More than half of the affected patients have diarrhea; in 30%, it is the presenting manifestation.

MORPHOLOGY

Gastrinomas may arise in the pancreas, the peripancreatic region, or the wall of the duodenum. **Over half of gastrin-producing tumors are locally invasive or have already metastasized at the time of diagnosis.** In approximately 25% of patients, gastrinomas arise in conjunction with other endocrine tumors, thus conforming to the MEN-1 syndrome (see further on); MEN-1–associated gastrinomas frequently are multifocal, while sporadic gastrinomas usually are single. As with insulin-secreting tumors of the pancreas, gastrin-producing tumors are histologically bland and rarely exhibit marked anaplasia.

ADRENAL CORTEX

The *adrenal glands* are paired endocrine organs consisting of two regions, the cortex and medulla, which differ in their development, structure, and function. The *cortex* consists of three layers of distinct cell types. Beneath the capsule of the adrenal is the narrow layer of zona glomerulosa. An equally narrow zona reticularis abuts the medulla. Intervening is the broad zona fasciculata, which makes up about 75% of the total cortex. The adrenal cortex synthesizes three different types of steroids:

- *Glucocorticoids* (principally cortisol), which are synthesized primarily in the zona fasciculata, with a small contribution from the zona reticularis
- *Mineralocorticoids,* the most important being aldosterone, which are generated in the zona glomerulosa
- *Sex steroids* (estrogens and androgens), which are produced largely in the zona reticularis

The *adrenal medulla* is composed of chromaffin cells, which synthesize and secrete *catecholamines,* mainly epinephrine. This section deals first with disorders of the adrenal cortex and then of the medulla. Diseases of the adrenal cortex can be conveniently divided into those associated with cortical hyperfunction and those characterized by cortical hypofunction.

ADRENOCORTICAL HYPERFUNCTION (HYPERADRENALISM)

There are three distinctive hyperadrenal clinical syndromes, each caused by abnormal production of one or more of the hormones produced by the three layers of the cortex: (1) *Cushing syndrome,* characterized by an excess of cortisol; (2) *hyperaldosteronism;* and (3) *adrenogenital* or *virilizing syndromes,* caused by an excess of androgens. The clinical features of some of these syndromes overlap somewhat because of the overlapping functions of some of the adrenal steroids.

Hypercortisolism and Cushing Syndrome

Hypercortisolism, typically manifested as *Cushing syndrome,* is caused by any condition that produces an elevation in glucocorticoid levels. In clinical practice, the vast majority of cases of Cushing syndrome are the result of administration of exogenous glucocorticoids (iatrogenic). The remaining cases are endogenous, and the three most common etiologic disorders are (Fig. 19–35):

- Primary hypothalamic-pituitary diseases associated with hypersecretion of ACTH
- The secretion of ectopic ACTH by non-pituitary neoplasms
- Primary adrenocortical neoplasms (adenoma or carcinoma) and rarely, primary cortical hyperplasia

Primary hypothalamic-pituitary disease associated with hypersecretion of ACTH, also known as *Cushing disease,* accounts for approximately 70% of cases of spontaneous, endogenous Cushing syndrome. The prevalence of this disorder is about four times higher among women than among men, and it occurs most frequently during young adulthood (the 20s and 30s). In the vast majority of cases, the *pituitary gland contains an ACTH-producing microadenoma* that does not produce mass effects in the brain; some corticotroph tumors qualify as macroadenomas (larger than 10 mm across). In the remaining patients, the anterior pituitary contains areas of *corticotroph cell hyperplasia* without a discrete adenoma. Corticotroph cell hyperplasia may be primary or, much less commonly, secondary to excessive ACTH release by a hypothalamic corticotropin-releasing hormone (CRH)–producing tumor. The adrenal glands in patients with Cushing disease are characterized by a variable degree of bilateral nodular cortical hyperplasia (discussed later), secondary to the elevated levels of ACTH ("ACTH-dependent" Cushing syndrome). The cortical hyperplasia is in turn responsible for the hypercortisolism.

Secretion of ectopic ACTH by nonpituitary tumors accounts for about 10% of cases of Cushing syndrome. In

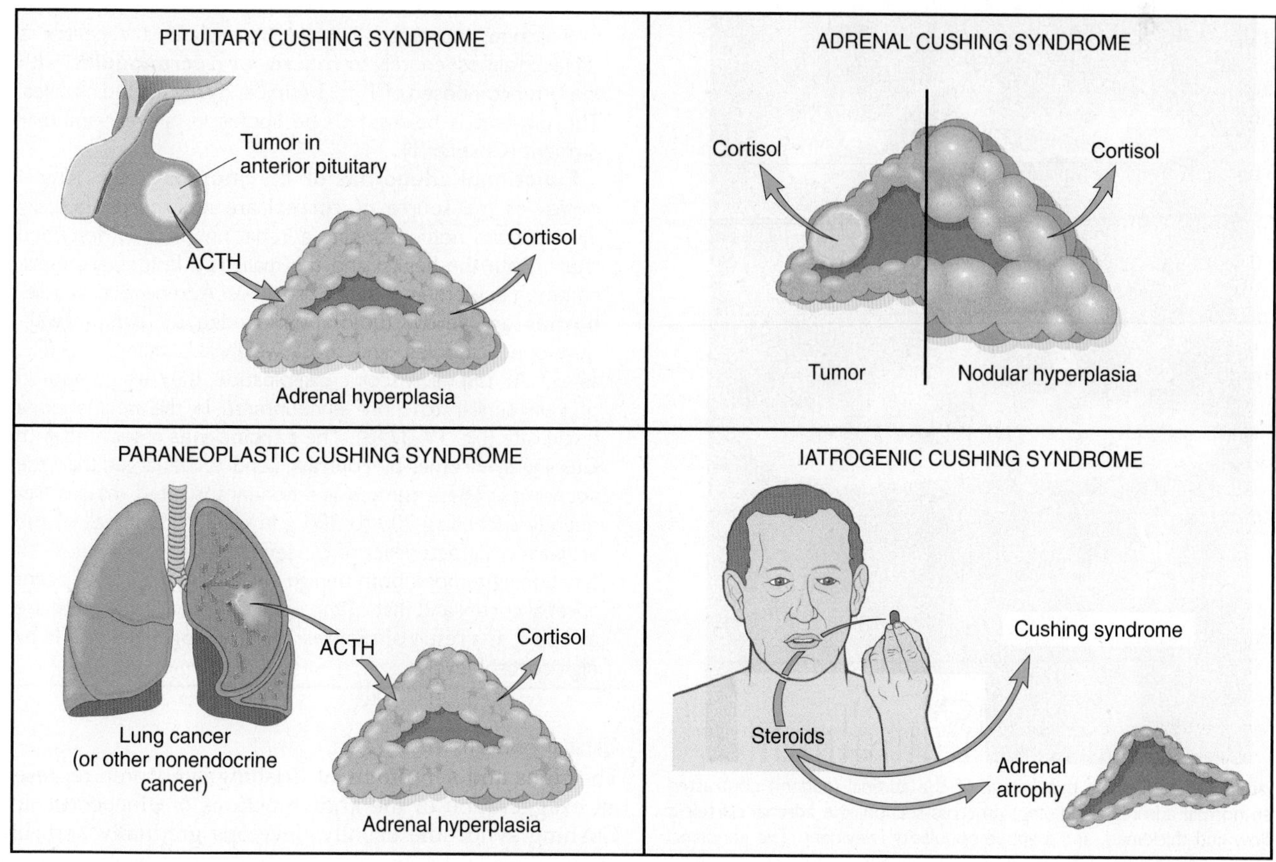

Figure 19–35 Schematic representation of the various forms of Cushing syndrome: The three endogenous forms, as well as the more common exogenous (iatrogenic) form. ACTH, adrenocorticotropic hormone.

many instances the responsible tumor is a *small cell carcinoma of the lung,* although other neoplasms, including carcinoids, medullary carcinomas of the thyroid, and PanNETs, have been associated with the syndrome. In addition to tumors that elaborate ectopic ACTH, an occasional neuroendocrine neoplasm produces ectopic CRH, which in turn causes ACTH secretion and hypercortisolism. As in the pituitary variant, the adrenal glands undergo bilateral cortical hyperplasia secondary to elevated ACTH, but the rapid downhill course of patients with these cancers often cuts short the adrenal enlargement.

Primary adrenal neoplasms, such as adrenal adenoma and carcinoma, and rarely, *primary cortical hyperplasia,* are responsible for about 15% to 20% of cases of endogenous Cushing syndrome. This form of Cushing syndrome is also designated *ACTH-independent Cushing syndrome,* or adrenal Cushing syndrome, because the adrenals function autonomously. The biochemical hallmark of adrenal Cushing syndrome is elevated levels of cortisol with low serum levels of ACTH. In most cases, adrenal Cushing syndrome is caused by a unilateral adrenocortical neoplasm, which may be either benign (adenoma) or malignant (carcinoma). The overwhelming majority of hyperplastic adrenals are ACTH-dependent, and primary cortical hyperplasia of the adrenal cortices is a rare cause of Cushing syndrome. There are two variants of this entity; the first presents as macronodules of varying sizes (3 cm or greater in diameter) and the second as micronodules (1 to 3 mm).

MORPHOLOGY

The main lesions of Cushing syndrome are found in the pituitary and adrenal glands. The **pituitary** in Cushing syndrome shows changes that vary with different causes. The most common alteration, resulting from high levels of endogenous or exogenous glucocorticoids, is termed **Crooke hyaline change.** In this condition, the normal granular, basophilic cytoplasm of the ACTH-producing cells in the anterior pituitary is replaced by homogeneous, lightly basophilic material. This alteration is the result of the accumulation of intermediate keratin filaments in the cytoplasm.

Morphologic changes in the adrenal glands also depend on the cause of the hypercortisolism and include: (1) cortical atrophy, (2) diffuse hyperplasia, (3) macronodular or micronodular hyperplasia, or (4) an adenoma or a carcinoma.

In patients in whom the syndrome results from exogenous glucocorticoids, suppression of endogenous ACTH results in bilateral **cortical atrophy,** due to a lack of stimulation of the zona fasciculata and zona reticularis by ACTH. The zona glomerulosa is of normal thickness in such cases, because this portion of the cortex functions independently of ACTH. In cases of endogenous hypercortisolism, by contrast, the adrenals either are hyperplastic or contain a cortical neoplasm. **Diffuse hyperplasia** is found in patients with ACTH-dependent Cushing syndrome (Fig. 19–36). Both glands are enlarged, either subtly or markedly, each weighing up to

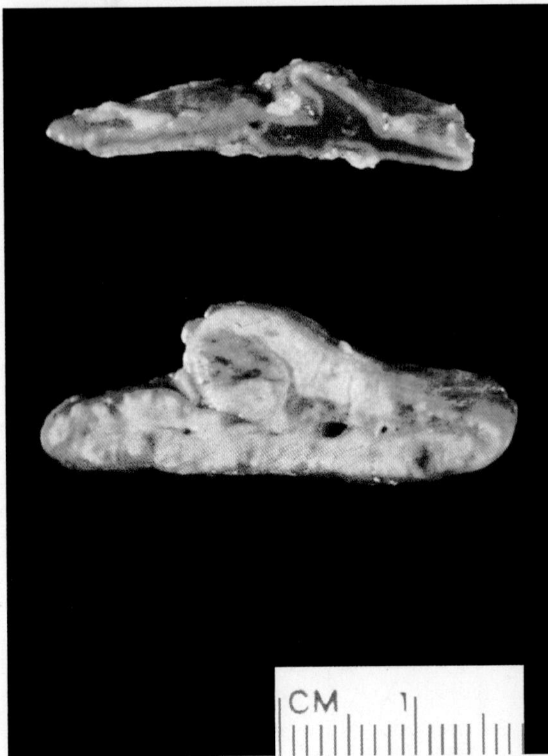

Figure 19–36 Diffuse hyperplasia of the adrenal (*bottom*) contrasted with normal adrenal gland (*top*). In cross-section, the adrenal cortex is yellow and thickened, and a subtle nodularity is evident. The abnormal gland was from a patient with ACTH-dependent Cushing syndrome, in whom both adrenals were diffusely hyperplastic. ACTH, adrenocorticotropic hormone.

30 g. The adrenal cortex is diffusely thickened and variably nodular, although the latter is not as pronounced as in cases of ACTH-independent nodular hyperplasia. The yellow color of diffusely hyperplastic glands derives from presence of **lipid-rich** cells, which appear vacuolated under the microscope. In primary cortical hyperplasia, the cortex is replaced almost entirely by **macro- or micronodules,** with the latter composed of 1- to 3-mm darkly pigmented nodules. The pigment is believed to be lipofuscin, a wear-and-tear pigment (Chapter 1).

Functional adenomas or carcinomas of the adrenal cortex as the source of cortisol are not morphologically distinct from nonfunctioning adrenal neoplasms (described later). Both the benign and the malignant lesions are more common in women in their 30s to 50s. Adrenocortical **adenomas** are yellow tumors surrounded by thin or well-developed capsules, and most weigh less than 30 g (Fig. 19–37, *A*). On microscopic examination, they are composed of cells similar to those encountered in the normal zona fasciculata (Fig. 19–37, *B*). The **carcinomas** associated with Cushing syndrome, by contrast, tend to be larger than the adenomas. These tumors are nonencapsulated masses frequently exceeding 200 to 300 g in weight, having all of the anaplastic characteristics of cancer, as detailed later on. With functioning tumors, both benign and malignant, the adjacent adrenal cortex and that of the contralateral adrenal gland are atrophic, as a result of suppression of endogenous ACTH by high cortisol levels.

Clinical Features

The signs and symptoms of Cushing syndrome represent an exaggeration of the known actions of glucocorticoids. Cushing syndrome usually develops gradually and, like many other endocrine abnormalities, may be quite subtle in its early stages. A major exception to this insidious onset is with Cushing syndrome associated with small cell carcinomas of the lung, when the rapid course of the underlying disease precludes development of many of the characteristic features. Early manifestations of Cushing syndrome include *hypertension* and *weight gain.* With time, the more characteristic centripetal distribution of adipose tissue becomes apparent, with resultant truncal obesity, "moon facies," and accumulation of fat in the posterior neck and

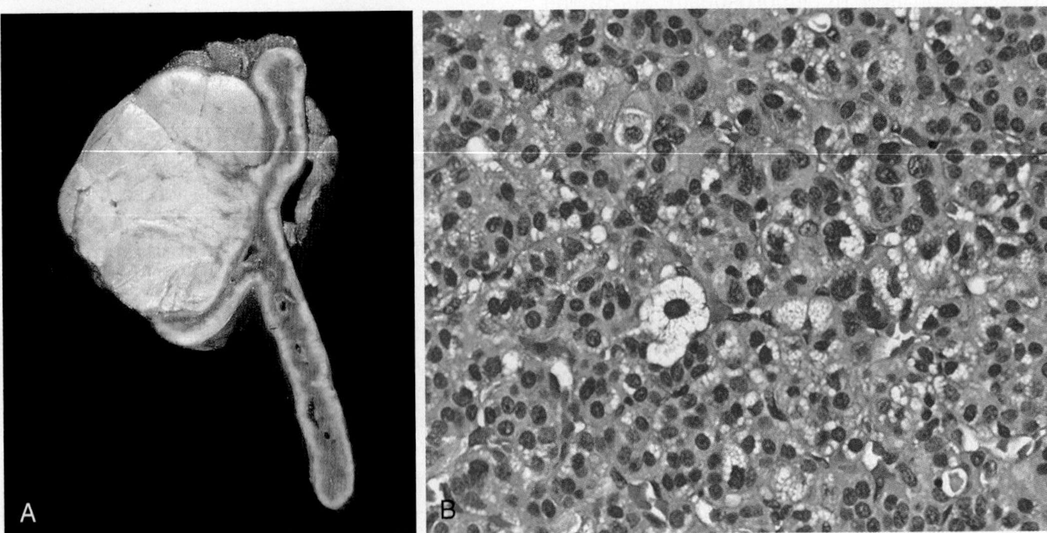

Figure 19–37 Adrenocortical adenoma. **A,** The adenoma is distinguished from nodular hyperplasia by its solitary, circumscribed nature. The functional status of an adrenocortical adenoma cannot be predicted from its gross or microscopic appearance. **B,** Histologic features of an adrenal cortical adenoma. The neoplastic cells are vacuolated because of the presence of intracytoplasmic lipid. There is mild nuclear pleomorphism. Mitotic activity and necrosis are not seen.

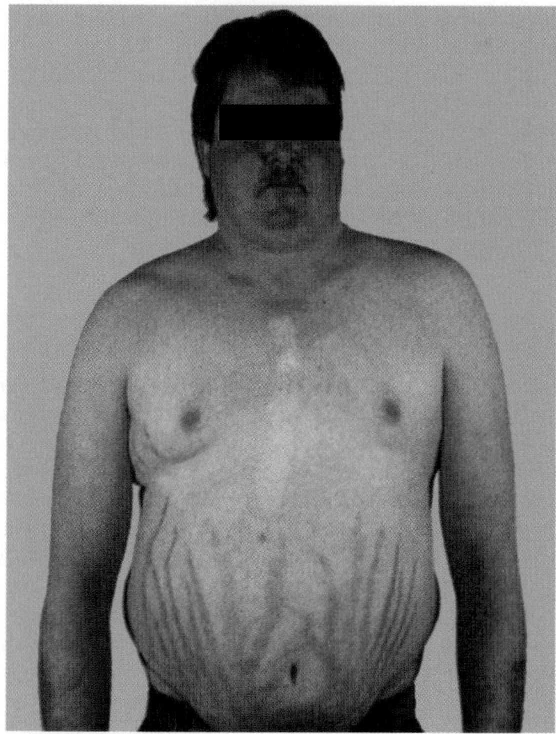

Figure 19–38 A patient with Cushing syndrome. Characteristic features include central obesity, "moon facies," and abdominal striae.
(Reproduced with permission from Lloyd RV, et al: Atlas of Nontumor Pathology: Endocrine Diseases. Washington, DC, American Registry of Pathology, 2002.)

back ("buffalo hump") (Fig. 19–38). Hypercortisolism causes selective atrophy of fast-twitch (type II) myofibers, with resultant decreased muscle mass and proximal limb weakness. Glucocorticoids induce gluconeogenesis and inhibit the uptake of glucose by cells, with resultant *hyperglycemia, glucosuria,* and *polydipsia,* mimicking diabetes mellitus. The catabolic effects on proteins cause loss of collagen and resorption of bone. Thus, the skin is thin, fragile, and easily bruised; *cutaneous striae* are particularly common in the abdominal area. Bone resorption results in the development of *osteoporosis,* with consequent increased susceptibility to fractures. Because glucocorticoids suppress the immune response, patients with Cushing syndrome also are at increased risk for a variety of infections. Additional manifestations include *hirsutism* and *menstrual abnormalities,* as well as a number of *mental disturbances,* including mood swings, depression, and frank psychosis. Extra-adrenal Cushing syndrome caused by pituitary or ectopic ACTH secretion usually is associated with increased skin pigmentation secondary to melanocyte-stimulating activity in the ACTH precursor molecule.

SUMMARY

Hypercortisolism (Cushing Syndrome)

- The most common cause of hypercortisolism is exogenous administration of steroids.
- Endogenous hypercortisolism most often is secondary to an ACTH-producing pituitary microadenoma (*Cushing disease*), followed by primary adrenal neoplasms (*ACTH-independent* hypercortisolism) and paraneoplastic ACTH production by tumors (e.g., small cell lung cancer).
- The morphologic features in the adrenal include bilateral cortical atrophy (in exogenous steroid-induced disease), bilateral diffuse or nodular hyperplasia (most common finding in endogenous Cushing syndrome), or an adrenocortical neoplasm.

Hyperaldosteronism

Hyperaldosteronism is the generic term for a group of closely related conditions characterized by chronic excess aldosterone secretion. Hyperaldosteronism may be primary, or it may be secondary to an extraadrenal cause. In *secondary hyperaldosteronism,* aldosterone release occurs in response to activation of the renin-angiotensin system. This condition is characterized by *increased levels of plasma renin* and is encountered in association with

- Decreased renal perfusion (arteriolar nephrosclerosis, renal artery stenosis)
- Arterial hypovolemia and edema (congestive heart failure, cirrhosis, nephrotic syndrome)
- Pregnancy (caused by estrogen-induced increases in plasma renin substrate)

Primary hyperaldosteronism, by contrast, indicates a primary, autonomous overproduction of aldosterone, with resultant suppression of the renin-angiotensin system and *decreased plasma renin activity.* The potential causes of primary hyperaldosteronism are:

- *Bilateral idiopathic hyperaldosteronism,* characterized by bilateral nodular hyperplasia of the adrenal glands. This mechanism is the most common underlying cause of primary hyperaldosteronism, accounting for about 60% of cases. The pathogenesis is unclear.
- *Adrenocortical neoplasm,* either an aldosterone-producing adenoma (the most common cause) or, rarely, an adrenocortical carcinoma. In approximately 35% of cases, primary hyperaldosteronism is caused by a solitary aldosterone-secreting adenoma, a condition referred to as *Conn syndrome.*
- Rarely, familial hyperaldosteronism may result from a genetic defect that leads to overactivity of the *aldosterone synthase* gene, *CYP11B2.*

MORPHOLOGY

Aldosterone-producing adenomas are almost always solitary, small (less than 2 cm in diameter), well-circumscribed lesions. They are bright yellow on cut section and, surprisingly, are composed of lipid-laden cortical cells more closely resembling fasciculata cells than glomerulosa cells (the normal source of aldosterone). In general, the cells tend to be uniform in size and shape; occasionally there is some nuclear and cellular pleomorphism. A characteristic feature of aldosterone-producing adenomas is the presence of eosinophilic, laminated cytoplasmic inclusions, known as **spironolactone bodies.** These typically are found after treatment with the antihypertensive agent spironolactone, which is the drug of choice in primary hyperaldosteronism. In contrast with cortical adenomas associated with Cushing syndrome, those associated with hyperaldosteronism do not usually suppress ACTH secretion. Therefore, the adjacent adrenal cortex and that of the contralateral gland are not atrophic. **Bilateral idiopathic hyperplasia** is marked by diffuse or focal hyperplasia of cells resembling those of the normal zona glomerulosa.

Clinical Features

The clinical hallmark of hyperaldosteronism is hypertension. With an estimated prevalence rate of 5% to 10% among unselected hypertensive patients, primary hyperaldosteronism may be the most common cause of secondary hypertension (i.e., hypertension secondary to an identifiable cause). The long-term effects of hyperaldosteronism-induced hypertension are cardiovascular compromise (e.g., left ventricular hypertrophy and reduced diastolic volumes) and an increase in the prevalence of adverse events such as stroke and myocardial infarction. *Hypokalemia* results from renal potassium wasting and, when present, can cause a variety of neuromuscular manifestations, including weakness, paresthesias, visual disturbances, and occasionally frank tetany. In primary hyperaldosteronism, the therapy varies according to cause. Adenomas are amenable to surgical excision. By contrast, surgical intervention is not very beneficial in patients with primary hyperaldosteronism due to bilateral hyperplasia, which often occurs in children and young adults. These patients are best managed medically with an *aldosterone antagonist* such as spironolactone. The treatment of secondary hyperaldosteronism rests on correcting the underlying cause of the renin-angiotensin system hyperstimulation.

Adrenogenital Syndromes

Excess of androgens may be caused by a number of diseases, including primary gonadal disorders and several primary adrenal disorders. The adrenal cortex secretes two compounds—dehydroepiandrosterone and androstenedione—which require conversion to testosterone in peripheral tissues for their androgenic effects. Unlike gonadal androgens, adrenal androgen formation is regulated by ACTH; thus, excessive secretion can present as an isolated syndrome or in combination with features of Cushing disease. The adrenal causes of androgen excess include *adrenocortical neoplasms* and an uncommon group of disorders collectively designated *congenital adrenal hyperplasia* (CAH). Adrenocortical neoplasms associated with symptoms of androgen excess (*virilization*) are more likely to be carcinomas than adenomas. They are morphologically identical to other functional or nonfunctional cortical neoplasms.

CAH represents a group of autosomal recessive disorders, each characterized by a hereditary defect in an enzyme involved in adrenal steroid biosynthesis, particularly cortisol. In these conditions, decreased cortisol production results in a compensatory increase in ACTH secretion due to absence of feedback inhibition. The resultant adrenal hyperplasia causes increased production of cortisol precursor steroids, which are then channeled into synthesis of androgens with virilizing activity. Certain enzyme defects also may impair aldosterone secretion, adding salt loss to the virilizing syndrome. *The most common enzymatic defect in CAH is 21-hydroxylase deficiency,* which accounts for more than 90% of cases. 21-Hydroxylase deficiency may range in degree from a total lack to a mild loss, depending on the nature of the underlying mutation involving the *CYP21A2* gene, which encodes this enzyme.

MORPHOLOGY

In all cases of CAH, the adrenals are **hyperplastic bilaterally,** sometimes expanding to 10 to 15 times their normal weights. The adrenal cortex is thickened and nodular, and on cut section, the widened cortex appears brown as a result of depletion of all lipid. The proliferating cells mostly are compact, eosinophilic, lipid-depleted cells, intermixed with lipid-laden clear cells. In addition to cortical abnormalities, **adrenomedullary dysplasia** also has recently been reported in patients with the salt-losing 21-hydroxylase deficiency. This is characterized by incomplete migration of the chromaffin cells to the center of the gland, with pronounced intermingling of nests of chromaffin and cortical cells in the periphery. Hyperplasia of corticotroph (ACTH-producing) cells is present in the anterior pituitary in most patients.

Clinical Features

The clinical manifestations of CAH are determined by the specific enzyme deficiency and include abnormalities related to androgen metabolism, sodium homeostasis, and (in severe cases) glucocorticoid deficiency. Depending on the nature and severity of the enzymatic defect, the onset of clinical symptoms may occur in the perinatal period, later childhood, or (less commonly) adulthood.

In 21-hydroxylase deficiency, *excessive androgenic activity* causes signs of masculinization in females, ranging from clitoral hypertrophy and pseudohermaphroditism in infants to oligomenorrhea, hirsutism, and acne in postpubertal girls. In males, androgen excess is associated with enlargement of the external genitalia and other evidence of precocious puberty in prepubertal patients and with oligospermia in older patients. In some forms of CAH (e.g., 11β-hydroxylase deficiency), the accumulated intermediary steroids have mineralocorticoid activity, with resultant *sodium retention* and *hypertension.* In other cases, however, including about one third of persons with 21-hydroxylase deficiency, the enzymatic defect is severe enough to produce mineralocorticoid deficiency, with resultant *salt (sodium) wasting.* Cortisol deficiency places persons with CAH at risk for *acute adrenal insufficiency* (discussed later).

CAH should be suspected in any neonate with ambiguous genitalia; severe enzyme deficiency in infancy can be a life-threatening condition, with vomiting, dehydration, and salt wasting. In the milder variants, women may present with delayed menarche, oligomenorrhea, or hirsutism. In all such cases, an androgen-producing ovarian neoplasm must be excluded. Treatment of CAH is with exogenous glucocorticoids, which, in addition to providing adequate levels of glucocorticoids, also suppress ACTH levels, thereby decreasing the excessive synthesis of the steroid hormones responsible for many of the clinical abnormalities.

SUMMARY

Adrenogenital Syndromes

- The adrenal cortex can secrete excess androgens in either of two settings: adrenocortical neoplasms (usually *virilizing* carcinomas) or congenital adrenal hyperplasia (CAH).
- CAH consists of a group of autosomal recessive disorders characterized by defects in steroid biosynthesis, usually cortisol; the most common subtype is caused by deficiency of the enzyme 21-hydroxylase.
- Reduction in cortisol production causes a compensatory increase in ACTH secretion, which in turn stimulates androgen production. Androgens have virilizing effects, including masculinization in females (ambiguous genitalia, oligomenorrhea, hirsutism), precocious puberty in males, and in some instances, salt (sodium) wasting and hypotension.
- Bilateral hyperplasia of the adrenal cortex is characteristic.

ADRENAL INSUFFICIENCY

Adrenocortical insufficiency, or hypofunction, may be caused by either primary adrenal disease (primary hypoadrenalism) or decreased stimulation of the adrenals resulting from a deficiency of ACTH (secondary hypoadrenalism). The patterns of adrenocortical insufficiency can be divided into three general categories: (1) primary *acute* adrenocortical insufficiency (adrenal crisis); (2) primary *chronic* adrenocortical insufficiency (*Addison disease*); and (3) secondary adrenocortical insufficiency.

Acute Adrenocortical Insufficiency

Acute adrenocortical insufficiency occurs most commonly in the clinical settings listed in Table 19–7. Persons with chronic adrenocortical insufficiency may develop an acute crisis after any stress that taxes their limited physiologic reserves. In patients maintained on exogenous corticosteroids, rapid withdrawal of steroids or failure to increase steroid doses in response to an acute stress may precipitate a similar adrenal crisis, because of the inability of the atrophic adrenals to produce glucocorticoid hormones. *Massive adrenal hemorrhage* may destroy enough of the adrenal cortex to cause acute adrenocortical insufficiency. This condition may occur in patients maintained on anticoagulant therapy, in postoperative patients who develop disseminated intravascular coagulation, during pregnancy, and in patients suffering from overwhelming sepsis; in this last setting it is known as the Waterhouse-Friderichsen syndrome (Fig. 19–39). This catastrophic syndrome is classically associated with *Neisseria meningitidis* septicemia but can also be caused by other organisms, including *Pseudomonas* spp., pneumococci, and *Haemophilus influenzae*. The pathogenesis of the Waterhouse-Friderichsen syndrome remains unclear but probably involves endotoxin-induced vascular injury with associated disseminated intravascular coagulation (Chapter 3).

Table 19–7 Causes of Adrenal Insufficiency

Acute
Waterhouse-Friderichsen syndrome
Sudden withdrawal of long-term corticosteroid therapy
Stress in patients with underlying chronic adrenal insufficiency
Chronic
Autoimmune adrenalitis (60–70% of cases in developed countries)—includes APS1 and APS2
Tuberculosis
Acquired immunodeficiency syndrome
Metastatic disease
Systemic amyloidosis
Fungal infections
Hemochromatosis
Sarcoidosis

APS1, APS2, autoimmune polyendocrine syndrome types 1 and 2.

Chronic Adrenocortical Insufficiency: Addison Disease

Addison disease, or chronic adrenocortical insufficiency, is an uncommon disorder resulting from progressive destruction of the adrenal cortex. More than 90% of all cases are attributable to one of four disorders: *autoimmune adrenalitis, tuberculosis,* the *acquired immune deficiency syndrome* (AIDS), or *metastatic cancer* (Table 19–7).

- *Autoimmune adrenalitis* accounts for 60% to 70% of cases and is by far the most common cause of primary adrenal insufficiency in developed countries. As the name implies, there is autoimmune destruction of steroid-producing cells, and autoantibodies to several key

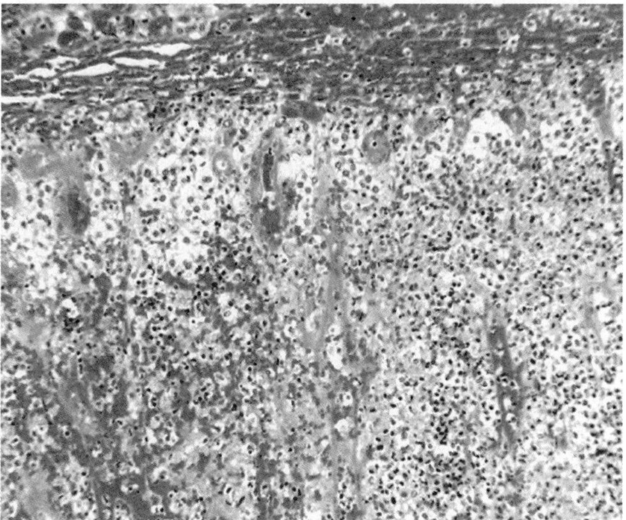

Figure 19–39 Waterhouse-Friderichsen syndrome. Bilateral adrenal hemorrhage in an infant with overwhelming sepsis, resulting in acute adrenal insufficiency. At autopsy, the adrenals were grossly hemorrhagic and shrunken; in this photomicrograph, little residual cortical architecture is discernible.

steroidogenic enzymes have been detected in affected patients. Autoimmune adrenalitis occurs in one of two *a*utoimmune *p*olyendocrine *s*yndromes: APS1, which is caused by mutations in the *autoimmune regulator (AIRE)* gene on chromosome 21 and is characterized by chronic mucocutaneous candidiasis and abnormalities of skin, dental enamel, and nails (ectodermal dystrophy) occurring in association with a combination of organ-specific autoimmune disorders (autoimmune adrenalitis, autoimmune hypoparathyroidism, idiopathic hypogonadism, pernicious anemia) that result in destruction of target organs. The AIRE protein is involved in the expression of tissue antigens in the thymus and the elimination of T cells specific for these antigens (Chapter 4). The second setting is that of APS2, which manifests in early adulthood and manifests as a combination of adrenal insufficiency and autoimmune thyroiditis or type 1 diabetes. Unlike in APS1, in APS2 mucocutaneous candidiasis, ectodermal dysplasia, and autoimmune hypoparathyroidism do not occur.

- *Infections,* particularly tuberculosis and those produced by fungi, also may cause primary chronic adrenocortical insufficiency. Tuberculous adrenalitis, which once accounted for as many as 90% of cases of Addison disease, has become less common with the advent of antituberculosis therapy. With the resurgence of tuberculosis in many urban centers, however, this cause of adrenal deficiency must be borne in mind. When present, tuberculous adrenalitis usually is associated with active infection in other sites, particularly the lungs and genitourinary tract. Among fungi, disseminated infections caused by *Histoplasma capsulatum* and *Coccidioides immitis* also may result in chronic adrenocortical insufficiency. Patients with AIDS are at risk for the development of adrenal insufficiency from several infectious (cytomegalovirus, *Mycobacterium avium-intracellulare*) and noninfectious (Kaposi sarcoma) complications of their disease.
- *Metastatic neoplasms* involving the adrenals are another potential cause of adrenal insufficiency. The adrenals are a fairly common site for metastases in patients with disseminated carcinomas. Although adrenal function is preserved in most such instances, the metastatic growths sometimes destroy sufficient adrenal cortex to produce a degree of adrenal insufficiency. Carcinomas of the lung and breast are the source of a majority of metastases in the adrenals, although many other neoplasms, including gastrointestinal carcinomas, malignant melanomas, and hematopoietic neoplasms, also may metastasize to the organ.

Secondary Adrenocortical Insufficiency

Any disorder of the hypothalamus and pituitary, such as metastatic cancer, infection, infarction, or irradiation, that reduces the output of ACTH leads to a syndrome of hypoadrenalism having many similarities to Addison disease. *With secondary disease, the hyperpigmentation of primary Addison disease is lacking because melanotropic hormone levels are low* (discussed later). ACTH deficiency may occur alone, but in some instances, it is only one part of panhypopituitarism, associated with multiple tropic hormone deficiencies. In patients with primary disease, serum ACTH levels may be normal, but the destruction of the adrenal cortex does not permit a response to exogenously administered ACTH in the form of increased plasma levels of cortisol. By contrast, secondary adrenocortical insufficiency is characterized by low serum ACTH and a prompt rise in plasma cortisol levels in response to ACTH administration.

MORPHOLOGY

The appearance of the adrenal glands varies with the cause of the adrenocortical insufficiency. In **secondary hypoadrenalism** the adrenals are reduced to small, flattened structures that usually retain their yellow color because of a small amount of residual lipid. A uniform, thin rim of atrophic yellow cortex surrounds a central, intact medulla. Histologic evaluation reveals atrophy of cortical cells with loss of cytoplasmic lipid, particularly in the zona fasciculata and zona reticularis. **Primary autoimmune adrenalitis** is characterized by irregularly shrunken glands, which may be exceedingly difficult to identify within the suprarenal adipose tissue. On histologic examination, the cortex contains only scattered residual cortical cells in a collapsed network of connective tissue. A variable lymphoid infiltrate is present in the cortex and may extend into the subjacent medulla (Fig. 19–40). The medulla is otherwise preserved. In **tuberculosis or fungal diseases,** the adrenal architecture may be effaced by a granulomatous inflammatory reaction identical to that encountered in other sites of infection. When hypoadrenalism is caused by **metastatic carcinoma,** the adrenals are enlarged, and their normal architecture is obscured by the infiltrating neoplasm.

Clinical Features

In general, clinical manifestations of adrenocortical insufficiency do not appear until at least 90% of the adrenal cortex has been compromised. The initial manifestations often include progressive weakness and easy fatigability, which may be dismissed as nonspecific complaints. *Gastrointestinal disturbances* are common and include anorexia, nausea, vomiting, weight loss, and diarrhea. In patients with primary adrenal disease, increased levels of ACTH precursor hormone stimulate melanocytes, with resultant *hyperpigmentation* of the skin and mucosal surfaces. The

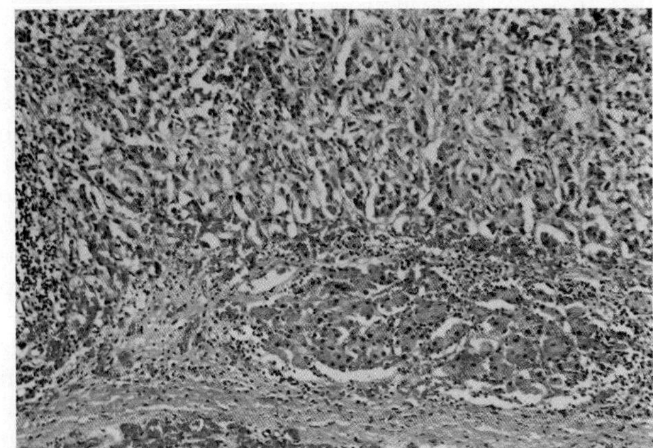

Figure 19–40 Autoimmune adrenalitis. In addition to loss of all but a subcapsular rim of cortical cells, there is an extensive mononuclear cell infiltrate.

face, axillae, nipples, areolae, and perineum are particularly common sites of hyperpigmentation. By contrast, hyperpigmentation is not seen in patients with secondary adrenocortical insufficiency. Decreased mineralocorticoid (aldosterone) activity in patients with primary adrenal insufficiency results in potassium retention and sodium loss, with consequent *hyperkalemia, hyponatremia, volume depletion,* and *hypotension,* whereas secondary hypoadrenalism is characterized by deficient cortisol and androgen output but normal or near-normal aldosterone synthesis. Hypoglycemia occasionally may occur as a result of glucocorticoid deficiency and impaired gluconeogenesis. Stresses such as infections, trauma, or surgical procedures in affected patients may precipitate an acute adrenal crisis, manifested by intractable vomiting, abdominal pain, hypotension, coma, and vascular collapse. Death follows rapidly unless corticosteroids are replaced immediately.

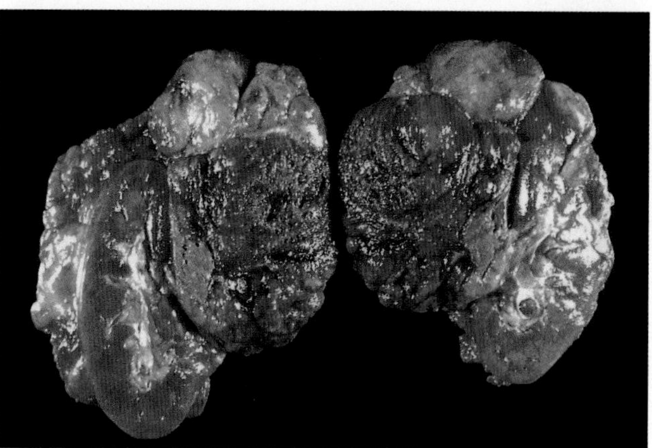

Figure 19–41 Adrenal carcinoma. The tumor dwarfs the kidney and compresses the upper pole. It is largely hemorrhagic and necrotic.

SUMMARY

Adrenocortical Insufficiency (Hypoadrenalism)

- Primary adrenocortical insufficiency can be acute (Waterhouse-Friderichsen syndrome) or chronic (Addison disease).
- Chronic adrenal insufficiency in the Western world most often is secondary to autoimmune adrenalitis, which occurs in the context of one of two autoimmune polyendocrine syndromes: APS1 (caused by mutations in the *AIRE* gene) or APS2.
- Tuberculosis and infections due to opportunistic pathogens associated with the human immunodeficiency virus and tumors metastatic to the adrenals are the other important causes of chronic hypoadrenalism.
- Patients typically present with fatigue, weakness, and gastrointestinal disturbances. Primary adrenocortical insufficiency also is characterized by high ACTH levels with associated skin pigmentation.

ADRENOCORTICAL NEOPLASMS

It should be evident from the discussion of adrenocortical hyperfunction that functional adrenal neoplasms may be responsible for any of the various forms of hyperadrenalism. While functional adenomas are most commonly associated with hyperaldosteronism and with Cushing syndrome, a virilizing neoplasm is more likely to be a carcinoma. Not all adrenocortical neoplasms, however, elaborate steroid hormones. Determination of whether a cortical neoplasm is functional or not is based on clinical evaluation and measurement of the hormone or its metabolites in the laboratory.

MORPHOLOGY

Adrenocortical adenomas were described earlier in the discussions of Cushing syndrome and hyperaldosteronism. Most cortical adenomas do not cause hyperfunction and usually are encountered as incidental findings at the time of autopsy or during abdominal imaging for an unrelated cause. In fact, the half-facetious appellation of **"adrenal incidentaloma"** has crept into the medical lexicon to describe these incidentally discovered tumors. On cut surface, adenomas usually are yellow to yellow-brown, owing to the presence of lipid within the neoplastic cells (Fig. 19–37). As a general rule they are small, averaging 1 to 2 cm in diameter. On microscopic examination, adenomas are composed of cells similar to those populating the normal adrenal cortex. The nuclei tend to be small, although some degree of pleomorphism may be encountered even in benign lesions **(endocrine atypia).** The cytoplasm of the neoplastic cells ranges from eosinophilic to vacuolated, depending on their lipid content; mitotic activity generally is inconspicuous.

Adrenocortical carcinomas are rare neoplasms that may occur at any age, including in childhood. Two rare inherited causes of adrenal cortical carcinomas are Li-Fraumeni syndrome (Chapter 5) and Beckwith-Wiedemann syndrome (Chapter 6). In most cases, adrenocortical carcinomas are large, invasive lesions that efface the native adrenal gland. On cut surface, adrenocortical carcinomas typically are variegated, poorly demarcated lesions containing areas of necrosis, hemorrhage, and cystic change (Fig. 19–41). Microscopic examination typically shows these tumors to be composed of well-differentiated cells resembling those seen in cortical adenomas or bizarre, pleomorphic cells, which may be difficult to distinguish from those of an undifferentiated carcinoma metastatic to the adrenal (Fig. 19–42). Adrenal

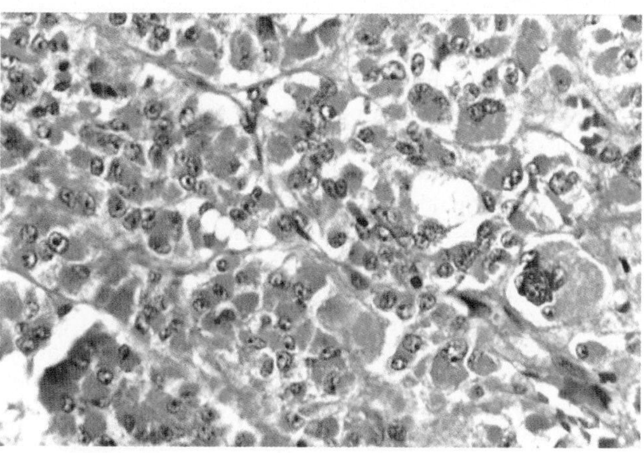

Figure 19–42 Adrenal carcinoma with marked anaplasia.

cancers have a strong tendency to invade the adrenal vein, vena cava, and lymphatics. Metastases to regional and peri-aortic nodes are common, as is distant hematogenous spread to the lungs and other viscera. Bone metastases are unusual. The median patient survival is about 2 years. Of note, carcinomas metastatic to the adrenal cortex are significantly more frequent than a primary adrenocortical carcinoma.

ADRENAL MEDULLA

The adrenal medulla is embryologically, functionally, and structurally distinct from the adrenal cortex. It is populated by cells derived from the neural crest (*chromaffin cells*) and their supporting (sustentacular) cells. The chromaffin cells, so named because of their brown-black color after exposure to potassium dichromate, synthesize and secrete catecholamines in response to signals from preganglionic nerve fibers in the sympathetic nervous system. Similar collections of cells are distributed throughout the body in the extraadrenal paraganglion system. The most important diseases of the adrenal medulla are neoplasms, which include both neuronal neoplasms (including neuroblastomas and more mature ganglion cell tumors) and neoplasms composed of chromaffin cells (pheochromocytomas).

TUMORS OF THE ADRENAL MEDULLA

Pheochromocytoma

Pheochromocytomas are neoplasms composed of chromaffin cells, which, like their non-neoplastic counterparts, synthesize and release catecholamines and, in some cases, other peptide hormones. These tumors are of special importance because although uncommon, they (like aldosterone-secreting adenomas) give rise to a surgically correctable form of hypertension.

Pheochromocytomas usually subscribe to a convenient "rule of 10s":

- *10% of pheochromocytomas are extraadrenal,* occurring in sites such as the organ of Zuckerkandl and the carotid body, where they usually are called *paragangliomas,* rather than pheochromocytomas.
- *10% of adrenal pheochromocytomas are bilateral;* this proportion may rise to 50% in cases that are associated with familial syndromes.
- *10% of adrenal pheochromocytomas are malignant,* although the associated hypertension represents a serious and potentially lethal complication of even *benign* tumors. Frank malignancy is somewhat more common in tumors arising in extraadrenal sites.
- One "traditional" 10% rule that has since been modified pertains to familial cases. It is now recognized that *as many as 25% of persons with pheochromocytomas and paragangliomas harbor a germ line mutation* in one of at least six known genes, including *RET,* which causes type 2 MEN syndromes (described later); *NF1,* which causes type 1 neurofibromatosis (Chapter 21); *VHL,* which causes von Hippel-Lindau disease (Chapters 13 and 22); and three genes encoding subunits within the succinate dehydrogenase complex (*SDHB, SDHC,* and *SDHD*), which is involved in mitochondrial oxidative phosphorylation.

MORPHOLOGY

Pheochromocytomas range in size from small, circumscribed lesions confined to the adrenal to large, hemorrhagic masses weighing several kilograms. On cut surface, smaller pheochromocytomas are yellow-tan, well-defined lesions that compress the adjacent adrenal (Fig. 19–43). Larger lesions tend to be hemorrhagic, necrotic, and cystic and typically efface the adrenal gland. Incubation of the fresh tissue with potassium dichromate solutions turns the tumor dark brown, as noted previously.

On microscopic examination, pheochromocytomas are composed of polygonal to spindle-shaped chromaffin cells and their supporting cells, compartmentalized into small nests, or **Zellballen,** by a rich vascular network (Fig. 19–44). The cytoplasm of the neoplastic cells often has a finely granular appearance, highlighted by a variety of silver stains, because of the presence of granules containing catecholamines. Electron microscopy reveals variable numbers of membrane-bound, electron-dense granules, representing catecholamines and sometimes other peptides. The nuclei of the neoplastic cells are often quite pleomorphic. Both

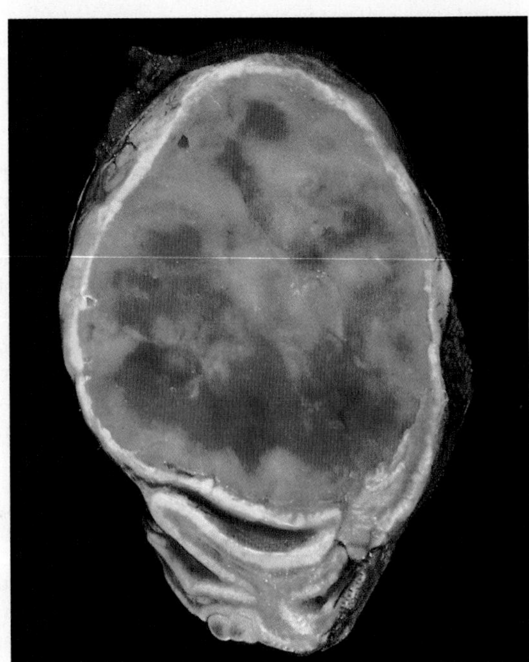

Figure 19–43 Pheochromocytoma. The tumor is enclosed within an attenuated cortex and demonstrates areas of hemorrhage. The comma-shaped residual adrenal is seen *below.*

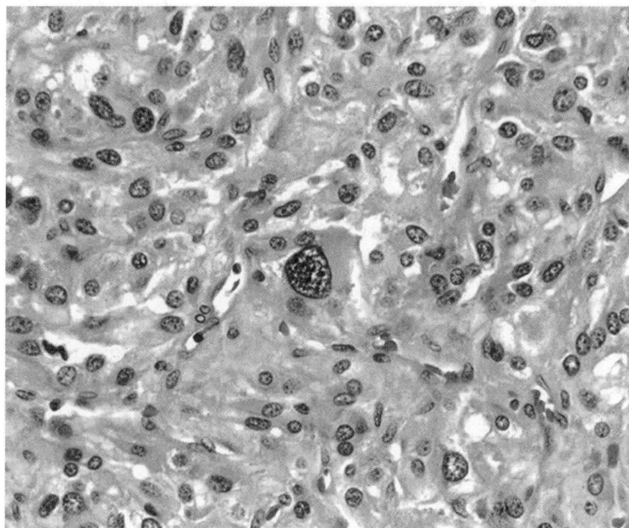

Figure 19–44 Photomicrograph of pheochromocytoma, demonstrating characteristic nests of cells (*Zellballen*) with abundant cytoplasm. Granules containing catecholamine are not visible in this preparation. It is not uncommon to find bizarre cells even in pheochromocytomas that are biologically benign, and this criterion by itself should not be used to diagnose malignancy.

capsular and vascular invasion may be encountered in benign lesions, and the mere presence of mitotic figures does not imply malignancy. **Therefore, the definitive diagnosis of malignancy in pheochromocytomas is based exclusively on the presence of metastases.** These may involve regional lymph nodes as well as more distant sites, including liver, lung, and bone.

Clinical Features

The predominant clinical manifestation of pheochromocytoma is *hypertension.* The characteristic presentation with a hypertensive episode is one of abrupt, precipitous elevation in blood pressure, associated with tachycardia, palpitations, headache, sweating, tremor, and a sense of apprehension. Such episodes also may be associated with pain in the abdomen or chest, nausea, and vomiting. In clinical practice, *isolated, paroxysmal episodes of hypertension occur in fewer than half of patients* with pheochromocytoma. In about two thirds of patients the hypertension occurs in the form of a chronic, sustained elevation in blood pressure, although an element of labile hypertension often is present as well. Whether sustained or episodic, the hypertension is associated with an increased risk of myocardial ischemia, heart failure, renal injury, and stroke (cerebrovascular accident). Sudden cardiac death may occur, probably secondary to catecholamine-induced myocardial irritability and ventricular arrhythmias. In some cases, pheochromocytomas secrete other hormones such as ACTH and somatostatin and may therefore be associated with clinical features related to the effects of these and other peptide hormones. The laboratory diagnosis of pheochromocytoma is based on demonstration of increased urinary excretion of free catecholamines and their metabolites, such as vanillylmandelic acid and metanephrines. Isolated benign pheochromocytomas are treated with surgical excision. With multifocal lesions, long-term medical treatment for hypertension may be required.

Neuroblastoma and Other Neuronal Neoplasms

Neuroblastoma is the most common extracranial solid tumor of childhood. These neoplasms occur most commonly during the first 5 years of life and may arise during infancy. Neuroblastomas may occur anywhere in the sympathetic nervous system and occasionally within the brain, but they are most common in the abdomen; a majority of these tumors arise in either the adrenal medulla or the retroperitoneal sympathetic ganglia. Most neuroblastomas are sporadic, although familial cases also have been described. These tumors are discussed in Chapter 6, along with other pediatric neoplasms.

MULTIPLE ENDOCRINE NEOPLASIA SYNDROMES

The MEN syndromes are a group of inherited diseases resulting in proliferative lesions (hyperplasias, adenomas, and carcinomas) of multiple endocrine organs. Like other inherited cancer disorders (Chapter 5), endocrine tumors arising in the context of MEN syndromes have certain distinctive features that are not shared with their sporadic counterparts:

- These tumors occur at a *younger age* than that typical for sporadic cancers.
- They arise in *multiple endocrine organs,* either *synchronously* or *metachronously.*
- Even in one organ, the tumors often are *multifocal.*
- The tumors usually are preceded by an *asymptomatic stage of endocrine hyperplasia* involving the cell of origin of the tumor (for example, patients with MEN-2 almost universally demonstrate C cell hyperplasia in the thyroid parenchyma adjacent to medullary thyroid carcinomas).
- These tumors are usually *more aggressive* and *recur* in a higher proportion of cases than similar endocrine tumors that occur sporadically.

Unraveling the genetic basis of the MEN syndromes with clinical application of this knowledge in therapeutic decision making has been one of the success stories of translational research. The salient features of the MEN syndromes are discussed next.

Multiple Endocrine Neoplasia Type 1

MEN type 1 is inherited in an autosomal dominant pattern. The gene (*MEN1*) is located at 11q13 and is a tumor suppressor gene; thus, inactivation of both alleles of the gene is believed to be the basis for tumorigenesis. Organs most commonly involved are the parathyroid, the pancreas, and the pituitary—the "3 Ps."

- *Parathyroid*: *Primary hyperparathyroidism* is the most common manifestation of MEN-1 (80% to 95% of patients) and is the initial manifestation of the disorder in most patients, appearing in almost all patients by age 40 to 50. Parathyroid abnormalities include both hyperplasia and adenomas.
- *Pancreas*: Endocrine tumors of the pancreas are the leading cause of death in MEN-1. These tumors usually are aggressive and manifest with metastatic disease. It is not uncommon to find multiple "microadenomas" scattered throughout the pancreas in conjunction with one or two dominant lesions. Pancreatic endocrine tumors often are functional (i.e., secrete hormones). Zollinger-Ellison syndrome, associated with gastrinomas, and hypoglycemia, related to insulinomas, are common endocrine manifestations. Of note, the gastrinomas arising in MEN-1 syndrome are far more likely to be located within the duodenum than in the pancreas.
- *Pituitary*: The most frequent pituitary tumor in patients with MEN-1 is a prolactin-secreting macroadenoma. In some cases, acromegaly develops in association with somatotropin-secreting tumors.

Multiple Endocrine Neoplasia Type 2

MEN type 2 actually comprises two distinct groups of disorders that are unified by the occurrence of activating (i.e., gain-of-function) mutations of the *RET* proto-oncogene at chromosomal locus 10q11.2. A strong *genotype-phenotype correlation* has been recognized for the MEN-2 syndromes, and differences in mutation patterns account for the variable features in the two subtypes. MEN-2 is inherited in an autosomal dominant pattern.

Multiple Endocrine Neoplasia Type 2A

Organs commonly involved in MEN type 2A include

- *Thyroid*: Medullary carcinoma of the thyroid develops in virtually all untreated cases, and the tumors usually occur in the first 2 decades of life. The tumors commonly are multifocal, and foci of C cell hyperplasia can be found in the adjacent thyroid. *Familial medullary thyroid cancer* is a variant of MEN-2A characterized by medullary thyroid cancers, but not the other characteristic manifestations listed here. In comparison with MEN-2, familial medullary carcinoma typically occurs at an older age and follows a more indolent course.
- *Adrenal medulla*: Adrenal pheochromocytomas develop in 50% of the patients; fortunately, no more than 10% of these tumors are malignant.
- *Parathyroid*: Approximately 10% to 20% of patients develop parathyroid gland hyperplasia with manifestations of primary hyperparathyroidism.

Multiple Endocrine Neoplasia Type 2B

Patients with MEN-2B harbor a distinct germline *RET* mutation involving a single–amino acid change. Organs commonly involved include the thyroid and the adrenal medulla. The spectrum of thyroid and adrenal medullary disease is similar to that in MEN-2A, with the following differences:

- *Primary hyperparathyroidism does not develop* in patients with MEN-2B.
- *Extraendocrine manifestations* are characteristic in patients with MEN-2B. These include ganglioneuromas of mucosal sites (gastrointestinal tract, lips, tongue) and a *marfanoid habitus*, in which overly long bones of the axial skeleton give an appearance resembling that in Marfan syndrome (Chapter 6).

Before the advent of genetic testing, relatives of patients with the MEN-2 syndrome were screened with annual biochemical tests, which often lacked sensitivity. Now, routine genetic testing identifies *RET* mutation carriers earlier and more reliably in MEN-2 kindreds; *all persons carrying germline RET mutations are advised to have prophylactic thyroidectomy to prevent the inevitable development of medullary carcinomas.*

BIBLIOGRAPHY

Akirav EM, Ruddle NH, Herold KC: The role of AIRE in human autoimmune disease. Nat Rev Endocrinol 7:25, 2011. *[A comprehensive review on the function of AIRE gene, mutations of which are responsible for autoimmune adrenalitis and other manifestations of APS1.]*

Almeida MQ, Stratakis CA: Solid tumors associated with multiple endocrine neoplasias. Cancer Genet Cytogenet 203:30, 2010. *[An expert review on the spectrum of tumors observed in various MEN subtypes.]*

Bahn RS: Graves ophthalmopathy. N Engl J Med 362:726, 2010. *[A well-rounded article on the pathogenic mechanisms and management of ocular manifestations in Graves disease.]*

Bluestone JA, Herold K, Eisenbarth G: Genetics, pathogenesis and clinical interventions in type 1 diabetes. Nature 464:1293, 2010. *[An authoritative review on multiple facets of type 1 diabetes.]*

Cibas ES: Fine-needle aspiration in the work-up of thyroid nodules. Otolaryngol Clin North Am 43:257, 2010. *[A review on the most commonly used technique for diagnosing thyroid nodules from an expert on the histopathology and cytology of this disease.]*

Donath MY, Shoelson SE: Type 2 diabetes as an inflammatory disease. Nat Rev Immunol 2011. *[An authoritative review on inflammatory mechanisms leading to beta cell dysfunction and insulin resistance in type 2 diabetes.]*

Ekeblad S: Islet cell tumors. Adv Exp Med Biol 654:771, 2010. *[A comprehensive review on pancreatic neuroendocrine tumors, including genetics, histopathology, and clinical features.]*

Klibanski A: Clinical practice: prolactinomas. N Engl J Med 362:1219, 2010. *[An up-to-date review on the most common subtype of pituitary adenomas.]*

Leavy O: IAPP stokes the pancreatic fire. Nat Rev Immunol 10:748, 2010. *[A review highlighting the pathogenic role played by islet amyloid in aggravating beta cell dysfunction in type 2 diabetes.]*

Mazzone T, Chait A, Plutzky J: Cardiovascular disease risk in type 2 diabetes mellitus: insights from mechanistic studies. Lancet 371:1800, 2008. *[A well-rounded summary of the pathogenic mechanisms influencing cardiovascular risk, one of the most important contributors to mortality in type 2 diabetes.]*

McCarthy MI: Genomics, type 2 diabetes and obesity. N Engl J Med 363:2339, 2010. *[A summary of the major "diabetogenic" loci implicated in type 2 diabetes.]*

Michels AW, Eisenbarth GS: Immunologic endocrine disorders. J Allergy Clin Immunol 125:S226, 2010. *[A broad-spectrum and well-written review on immune-mediated endocrine diseases, including several that are discussed in this chapter.]*

Nieman LK: Approach to the patient with an adrenal incidentaloma. J Clin Endocrinol Metab 95:4106, 2010. *[A comprehensive review on incidental adrenal lesions that are being increasingly identified owing to greater use of sensitive imaging techniques.]*

Pivonello R, DeMartino MC, DeLeo M: Cushing syndrome. Endocrinol Metab Clin North Am 37:135, 2008. *[A succinct clinical review on causes and manifestations of Cushing syndrome.]*

Samuel VT, Petersen KF, Shulman GI: Lipid-induced insulin resistance: unraveling the mechanism. Lancet 75:2267, 2010. *[A scholarly review on the "adipo-insulin axis," which is one of the most profound influences on type 2 diabetes.]*

Silverberg SJ, Bilzekian JP: The diagnosis and management of asymptomatic primary hyperparathyroidism. Nat Clin Pract Endocrinol Metab 2:494, 2006. *[An older but still outstanding review on primary hyperparathyroidism.]*

Tomer Y, Huber A: The etiology of autoimmune thyroid disease: a story of genes and environment. J Autoimmun 32:231, 2009. *[An outstanding review on genetic and environmental contributions to the pathogenesis of autoimmune thyroid disorders, including Graves disease and Hashimoto thyroiditis.]*

Xing M: Genetic alterations in the phosphatidylinositol-3 kinase/Akt pathway in thyroid cancer. Thyroid 20:697, 2010. *[A comprehensive review on one of the most commonly afflicted pathways in follicular neoplasms of the thyroid.]*

See Targeted Therapy available online at **studentconsult.com**

CHAPTER

Bones, Joints, and Soft Tissue Tumors 20

CHAPTER CONTENTS

The musculoskeletal system and the integrated neural connections enable locomotion by the human body. Aside from providing the fulcrums and levers against which muscles contract to allow movement, the skeleton is critical for mineral (particularly calcium) homeostasis and also protects viscera and supplies an environment conducive to both hematopoietic and mesenchymal stem cell development. The term diseases of the bones and joints embraces a large number of conditions ranging from localized, benign tumors of bone and soft tissue such as the osteochondroma and lipoma, respectively, to generalized disorders such as osteoporosis and osteogenesis imperfecta. In this chapter we will first consider some of the more common conditions affecting the bones and joints, then discuss tumors arising in the various soft tissues of the body. Diseases of the muscles and peripheral nerves are discussed in Chapter 21.

BONES

The skeletal system is composed of 206 bones that vary in size and shape and are interconnected by a variety of joints that allow for a wide range of movement and promote structural stability. Bones are composed of a unique type of mineralized connective tissue that undergoes mineralization with a distinctive admixture of organic matrix (35%) and inorganic elements (65%). The inorganic mineral component consists mainly of calcium hydroxyapatite [$Ca_{10}(PO_4)_6(OH)_2$]. This mineral gives bone strength and hardness and serves as the storehouse for 99% of the body's calcium, 85% of the body's phosphorus, and 65% of the body's sodium and magnesium. The organic component

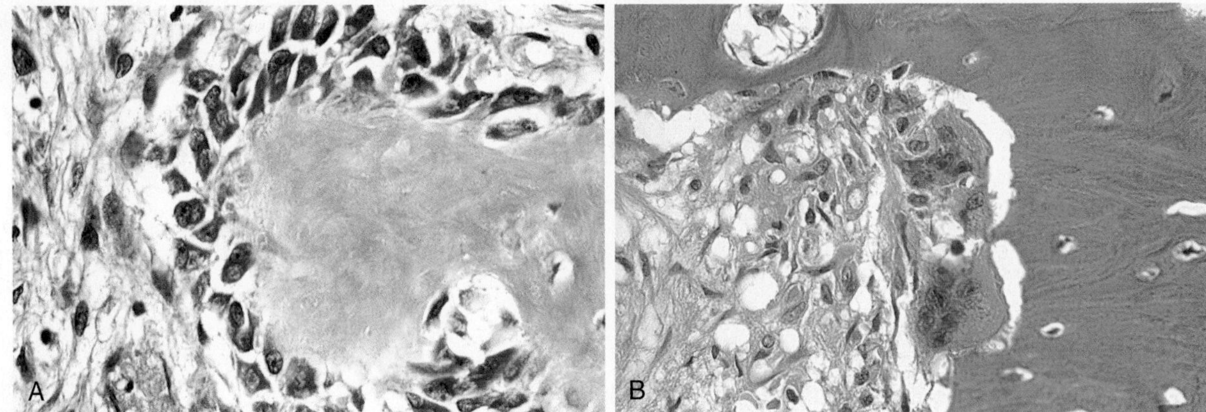

Figure 20–1 Cells of bone. **A,** Active osteoblasts synthesizing bone matrix proteins. The surrounding spindle cells are osteoprogenitor cells. **B,** Two osteoclasts resorbing bone. The smaller blue nuclei surrounded by a halo of clearing in the dense pink lamellar bone are osteocytes in their individual lacunae.

includes the cells of bone and the proteinaceous osteoid. The bone-forming cells include osteoblasts and osteocytes, while cells of the bone-digesting lineage include osteoclast precursor cells and mature functional osteoclasts (Fig. 20–1).

To the uninitiated, bone appears to be an inert, stable tissue, but in fact it is very dynamic and subject to constant breakdown and renewal, a process referred to as *remodeling*. The net effects of remodeling may be bone maintenance, bone loss, or bone deposition, with the balance being determined by the relative activities of osteoblasts, which deposit bone, and osteoclasts, which resorb bone (Fig. 20–1, *A* and *B*). As might be imagined, osteoblast and osteoclast activity is highly regulated and tightly integrated under normal circumstances, both by local crosstalk between these two cell types and by circulating factors that impact their activity, such as vitamin D and parathyroid hormone.

Among the local factors that regulate bone remodeling, the most important are RANK (receptor activator for nuclear factor-κB), RANK ligand (RANKL), and osteoprotegerin (OPG) (Fig 20–2). RANK, a member of the tumor necrosis factor (TNF) receptor family, is expressed on the cell membranes of preosteoclasts and mature osteoclasts. Its ligand, RANKL, is expressed by osteoblasts and marrow stromal cells. RANK stimulation by RANKL leads to activation of the transcription factor NF-κB, which drives the expression of genes that stimulate osteoclast formation, fusion, differentiation, function, and survival. RANKL production is upregulated by factors that stimulate osteoclastic activity. The actions of RANKL can be blocked by another member of the TNF receptor family, OPG, which is a "decoy" receptor produced by a number of tissues including bone, hematopoietic marrow, and immune cells. OPG competitively binds to RANKL, preventing RANK from interacting with RANKL. OPG production is regulated by signals similar to those that stimulate RANKL. Therefore, these molecules enable osteoblasts and stromal cells to control osteoclast development and activity and provide a mechanism for a wide variety of biologic mediators (hormones, cytokines, growth factors) to influence the homeostasis of bone tissue and bone mass.

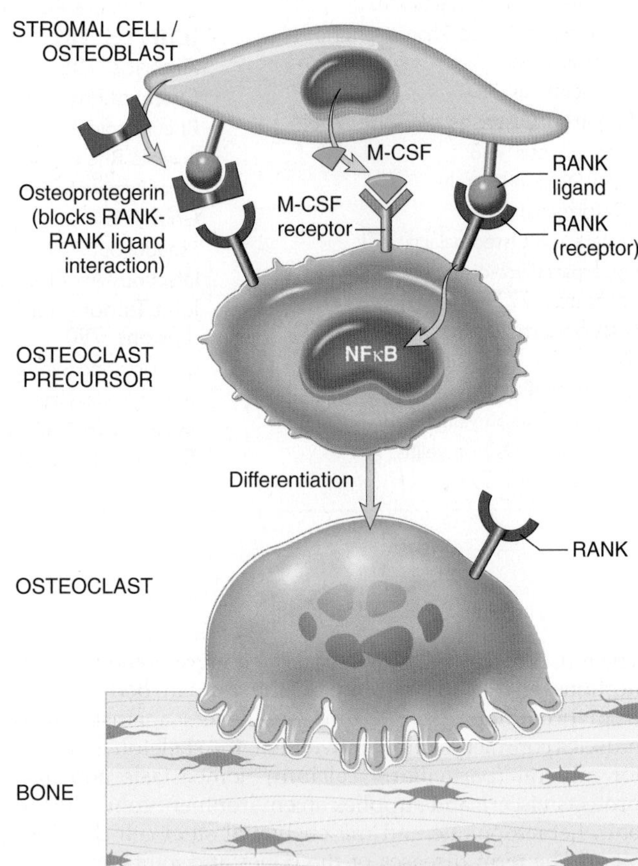

Figure 20–2 Paracrine mechanisms regulating osteoclast formation and function. Osteoclasts are derived from the same stem cells that produce macrophages. RANK (*r*eceptor *a*ctivator for *n*uclear factor-*κ*B) receptors on osteoclast precursors bind RANK ligand (RANKL) expressed by osteoblasts and marrow stromal cells. Along with macrophage colony-stimulating factor (M-CSF), the RANK-RANKL interaction drives the differentiation of functional osteoclasts. Stromal cells also secrete osteoprotegerin (OPG), which acts as a decoy receptor for RANKL, preventing it from binding the RANK receptor on osteoclast precursors. Consequently, OPG prevents bone resorption by inhibiting osteoclast differentiation.

Primary and secondary diseases of bone are varied and numerous and are classified in this chapter according to their perceived biologic defect or pathologic process.

CONGENITAL DISORDERS OF BONE AND CARTILAGE

Congenital disorders of the skeleton are various and, depending on the resulting defect, become manifest at different ages. The most severe produce developmental abnormalities that are evident from the earliest stages of skeletogenesis.

- Developmental anomalies resulting from localized problems in the migration of mesenchymal cells and the formation of condensations are called *dysostoses* and may affect individual or a group of bones and can result from mutations in specific homeobox genes. The more common lesions include *aplasia* (e.g., congenital absence of a digit or rib), the formation of extra bones (e.g., supernumerary digits or ribs), and abnormal fusion of bones (e.g., premature closure of the cranial sutures or congenital fusion of the ribs). Such malformations may occur as isolated, sporadic lesions or as components of a more complex syndrome.
- Mutations that interfere with bone or cartilage formation, growth, and/or maintenance of normal matrix components have more diffuse effects; such disorders are called *dysplasias*—more specifically, *osteodysplasias* and *chondrodysplasias*. *Dysplasia* in this context refers to abnormal growth and does not imply precancerous lesions, as it does in other tissues (Chapter 5). They number well over 350, and only select examples are discussed here.
- Other genetic metabolic disorders not usually thought of as primary skeletal diseases (e.g., mucopolysaccharidoses such as Hurler syndrome) also affect the bone matrix; such conditions are discussed briefly with other genetic disorders in Chapter 6.

Osteogenesis Imperfecta

Osteogenesis imperfecta (OI), also known as "brittle bone disease," is actually a group of genetic disorders caused by defective synthesis of type I collagen. Because type I collagen is a major component of extracellular matrix in other parts of the body, there are also numerous extraskeletal manifestations (affecting skin, joints, teeth, and eyes, for example). The mutations underlying OI characteristically involve the coding sequences for α_1 or α_2 chains of type I collagen. Because collagen synthesis and extracellular export require formation of a complete and intact triple helix, any primary defect in a collagen chain tends to disrupt the entire structure and results in its premature degradation (an example of a *dominant negative mutation*) (Chapter 6). As a consequence, most defects manifest as autosomal dominant disorders and may be associated with severe malformations. There is, however, a broad spectrum of severity, and mutations that result in qualitatively normal collagen but at only reduced levels generally have milder manifestations.

The fundamental abnormality in all forms of OI is too little bone, resulting in extreme skeletal fragility. Four major subtypes are recognized. The type II variant is uniformly fatal in utero or immediately postpartum as a consequence of multiple fractures that occur before birth. By contrast, patients with type I OI have a normal lifespan, with only a modestly increased proclivity for fractures during childhood (decreasing in frequency after puberty). The classic finding of *blue sclerae* in type I OI is attributable to decreased scleral collagen content; this deficit causes a relative transparency that allows the underlying choroid to be seen. *Hearing loss* can be related to conduction defects in the middle and inner ear bones, and *small misshapen teeth* are a result of dentin deficiency.

Achondroplasia and Thanatophoric Dwarfism

Achondroplasia is the most common form of dwarfism. It is caused by activating point mutations in fibroblast growth factor receptor 3 (FGFR3), a receptor with tyrosine kinase activity that transmits intracellular signals. Signals transmitted by FGFR3 *inhibit* the proliferation and function of growth plate chondrocytes; consequently, the growth of normal epiphyseal plates is suppressed, and the length of long bones is severely stunted. The disorder can be inherited in autosomal dominant fashion, but many cases arise from new spontaneous mutations.

Achondroplasia affects all bones that develop by enchondral ossification. The most conspicuous changes include short stature, disproportionate shortening of the proximal extremities, bowing of the legs, and frontal bossing with midface hypoplasia. The cartilage of the growth plates is disorganized and hypoplastic.

Thanatophoric dwarfism is a lethal variant of dwarfism, affecting 1 in every 20,000 live births (*thanatophoric* means "death-loving"). This disease is caused by missense or point mutations most commonly located in the extracellular domains of FGFR3. Affected heterozygotes exhibit extreme shortening of the limbs, frontal bossing of the skull, and an extremely small thorax, which is the cause of fatal respiratory failure in the perinatal period.

Osteopetrosis

Osteopetrosis is a group of rare genetic disorders characterized by defective osteoclast-mediated bone resorption. Osteopetrosis (literally, "bone-that-is-like-stone disorder") is an appropriate name, since the bones are dense, solid, and stone-like. Paradoxically, because turnover is decreased, the persisting bone tissue becomes weak over time and predisposed to fractures like a piece of chalk. Several variants are known, the two most common being an autosomal dominant adult form with mild clinical manifestations, and autosomal recessive infantile, with a severe/lethal phenotype.

The defects that cause osteopetrosis are categorized into those that disturb osteoclast function and those that interfere with osteoclast formation and differentiation. The precise nature of the osteoclast dysfunction is unknown in many cases. Nevertheless, in some cases the abnormalities have been identified. These include carbonic anhydrase II deficiency, proton pump deficiency and chloride channel defect, all of which interfere with the ability of osteoclasts to resorb bone. A mouse model of osteopetrosis is caused by mutations in the monocyte-colony stimulating factor (M-CSF), which is required for osteoclast differentiation. No comparable defect has been identified in humans.

Besides fractures, patients with osteopetrosis frequently have cranial nerve palsies (due to compression of nerves within shrunken cranial foramina), recurrent infections because of reduced marrow size and activity, and hepatosplenomegaly caused by extramedullary hematopoiesis resulting from reduced marrow space. Morphologically, the primary spongiosa, which normally is removed during growth, persists, filling the medullary cavity, and bone is deposited in increased amounts woven into the architecture. Because osteoclasts are derived from marrow monocyte precursors, hematopoietic stem cell transplantation holds the promise of repopulating recipients with progenitor cells capable of differentiating into fully functional osteoclasts. Indeed, many of the skeletal abnormalities appear to be reversible once normal precursor cells are provided.

SUMMARY

Congenital Disorders of Bone and Cartilage

- Abnormalities in a single or group of bones are called *dysostoses* and can result in the absence of bones, supernumerary bones, or inappropriately fused bones; some of these result from mutations in homeobox genes affecting localized migration and condensation of primitive mesenchymal cells.
- Abnormalities in bone or cartilage organogenesis are called *dysplasias*; these can be caused by mutations that affect signal transduction pathways or components of the extracellular matrix:
  - Achondroplasia and thanatophoric dwarfism occur as a consequence of constitutive FGFR3 activation, resulting in defective cartilage synthesis at growth plates.
  - Osteogenesis imperfecta (brittle bone disease) is a group of disorders caused by mutations in the genes for type I collagen that interfere with its normal production, with resultant bone fragility and susceptibility to fractures.
  - Osteopetrosis is caused by mutations that interfere with osteoclast function and is associated with dense but architecturally unsound bone owing to defective bone resorption.

ACQUIRED DISEASES OF BONE

Many nutritional, endocrine, and systemic disorders affect the development of the skeletal system. Nutritional deficiencies causing bone disease include deficiencies of vitamin C (involved in collagen cross-linking; deficiency causes *scurvy*) and vitamin D (involved in calcium uptake; deficiency causes *rickets* and *osteomalacia*). Both of these are discussed in greater detail with other nutritional diseases in Chapter 7. Primary and secondary forms of hyperparathyroidism (discussed in Chapter 19) also cause significant skeletal changes, which are briefly reviewed in this section. Many of these disorders are characterized by inadequate osteoid, also called *osteopenia;* the most important clinically significant osteopenia is *osteoporosis*.

Osteoporosis

Osteoporosis is an acquired condition characterized by reduced bone mass, leading to bone fragility and susceptibility to fractures. The bone loss may be confined to certain bones or regions, as in *disuse osteoporosis of a limb,* or be generalized, involving the entire skeleton. Generalized osteoporosis may be primary or occur secondary to a large variety of insults, including metabolic diseases, vitamin deficiencies, and drug exposures (Table 20–1).

Primary forms of osteoporosis are most common and may be associated with aging (senile osteoporosis) or the postmenopausal state in women. The drop in estrogen following menopause tends to exacerbate the loss of bone that occurs with aging, placing older women at high risk of osteoporosis relative to men. The risk of osteoporosis with aging is related to the peak bone mass earlier in life, which is influenced by genetic, nutritional, and environmental factors. Bone mass peaks during young adulthood; the greater the peak bone mass, the greater the delay in onset of osteoporosis. In both men and women, beginning in the third or fourth decade of life, bone resorption begins to outpace bone formation. The bone loss, averaging 0.5% per year, is a seemingly inevitable consequence of aging and is most prominent in areas containing abundant trabecular bone—namely the spine and femoral neck. The amount of bone loss with each cycle of remodeling is accelerated after menopause; hence, the vulnerability of women to osteoporosis and its complications. Regardless of the underlying cause, the progressive loss of bone mass is clinically significant because of the resultant increase in the risk of fractures. Roughly 1.5 million Americans each year experience an osteoporosis-related fracture, with those of greatest clinical significance involving the vertebrae and the hips. All told, the annual health care costs associated with osteoporosis-related fractures in the United States exceeds $18 billion.

MORPHOLOGY

The hallmark of osteoporosis is a loss of bone. The cortices are thinned, with dilated haversian canals, and the trabeculae are reduced in thickness and lose their interconnections. Osteoclastic activity is present but is not dramatically increased, and the mineral content of the bone tissue is normal. Once enough bone is lost, susceptibility to fractures increases (Fig. 20–3). In postmenopausal osteoporosis, trabecular bone loss often is severe, resulting in compression

Table 20–1 Categories of Generalized Osteoporosis

Primary
Postmenopausal
Senile
Secondary
Endocrine Disorders
Hyperparathyroidism
Hypo or hyperthyroidism
Hypogonadism
Pituitary tumors
Diabetes, type 1
Addison disease
Neoplasia
Multiple myeloma
Carcinomatosis
Gastrointestinal Disorders
Malnutrition
Malabsorption
Hepatic insufficiency
Vitamin C, D deficiencies
Idiopathic disease
Drugs
Anticoagulants
Chemotherapy
Corticosteroids
Anticonvulsants
Alcohol
Miscellaneous
Osteogenesis imperfecta
Immobilization
Pulmonary disease
Homocystinuria
Anemia

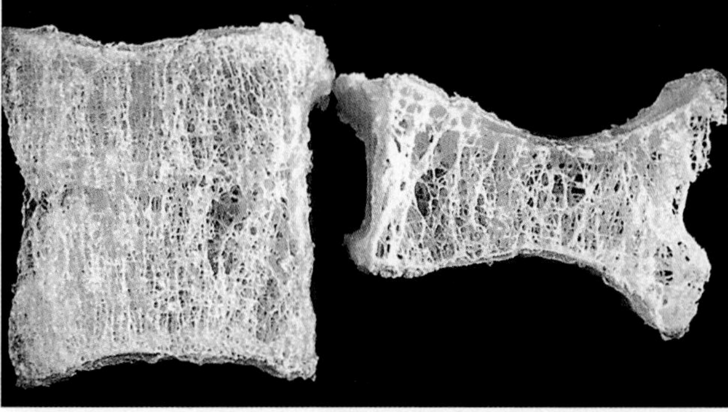

Figure 20–3 Osteoporotic vertebral body (*right*) shortened by compression fractures, compared with a normal vertebral body. The osteoporotic vertebra exhibits a characteristic loss of horizontal trabeculae and thickened vertical trabeculae.

fractures and collapse of vertebral bodies. In senile osteoporosis, cortical bone loss is prominent, predisposing to fractures in other weight-bearing bones, such as the femoral neck.

PATHOGENESIS

Osteoporosis occurs when the dynamic balance between bone formation by osteoblasts and bone resorption by osteoclasts (Fig. 20–2) tilts in favor of resorption. Several factors may tip the scales (Fig. 20–4):

- **Age-related changes.** With increasing age, the replicative and matrix production activities of osteoblasts progressively diminish. The various growth factors deposited in the extracellular matrix also diminish with time. Unfortunately, while new bone synthesis wanes with advancing age, osteoclasts retain their youthful vigor.
- **Hormonal influences.** The decline in estrogen levels associated with menopause correlates with an acceleration of cortical bone and trabecular (cancellous) bone loss. Over 30 to 40 years, this can result in the loss of up to 35% of cortical bone and 50% of trabecular bone! It is therefore not surprising that roughly half of postmenopausal women will suffer an osteoporotic fracture (compared with 2% to 3% of men of comparable age). It appears that the postmenopausal drop in estrogen leads to increased cytokine production (especially IL-1, IL-6, and TNF), presumably from cells in the bone. These stimulate RANK–RANK ligand activity and suppress OPG production (Fig. 20–2). There is some compensatory osteoblastic activity, but it is inadequate to keep pace with osteoclastic bone resorption. While estrogen replacement can ameliorate some of the bone loss, such therapy is increasingly associated with cardiovascular risks (Chapter 10).

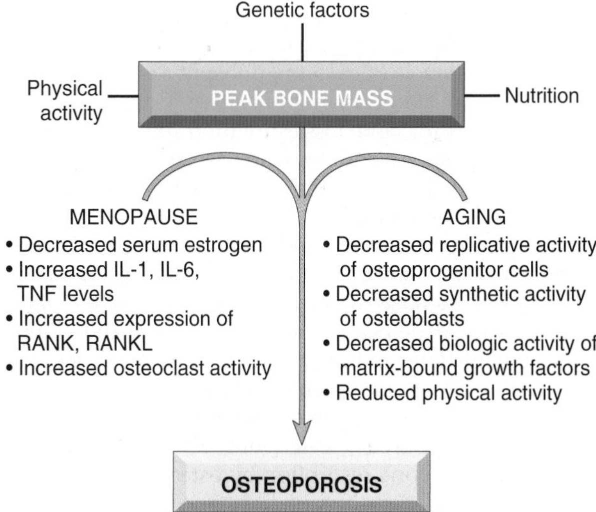

Figure 20–4 Pathophysiology of postmenopausal and senile osteoporosis (see text).

- **Physical activity.** Because mechanical forces stimulate bone remodeling, reduced physical activity increases bone loss. This effect is obvious in an immobilized limb and also occurs throughout the skeleton in astronauts working in a gravity-free environment. Decreased physical activity in older persons also contributes to senile osteoporosis. Because the magnitude of skeletal loading influences bone density more than does the number of load cycles, the type of physical activity is important. Thus, resistance exercises such as weight training increase bone mass more effectively than endurance activities such as jogging.
- **Genetic factors.** Vitamin D receptor polymorphisms appear to influence the peak bone mass early in life. Additional genetic variables can influence either calcium uptake or PTH synthesis and responses.
- **Calcium nutritional state.** A majority of adolescent girls (but not boys) have insufficient dietary calcium. Unfortunately, this calcium deficiency occurs during a period of rapid bone growth. As a result, girls typically do not achieve the peak bone mass that could be otherwise expected and are accordingly more likely to develop clinically significant osteoporosis at an earlier age than their male counterparts.
- **Secondary causes of osteoporosis.** These include prolonged glucocorticoid therapy, which increases bone resorption and reduces bone synthesis. Cigarette smoking and excess alcohol also can result in reduced bone mass.

Clinical Course

The clinical outcome with osteoporosis depends on which bones are involved. Thoracic and lumbar vertebral fractures are extremely common, leading to loss of height and various deformities, including kyphoscoliosis, which can compromise respiratory function. Pulmonary embolism and pneumonia are common complications of fractures of the femoral neck, pelvis, or spine and result in as many as 50,000 deaths annually.

Osteoporosis is difficult to diagnose because it is asymptomatic until skeletal fragility is announced with a fracture. Moreover, it cannot be reliably detected in plain radiographs until 30% to 40% of bone mass has already disappeared; serum levels of calcium, phosphorus, and alkaline phosphatase are notoriously insensitive. Current state-of-the-art methods for bone loss estimation consist of specialized radiographic techniques to assess bone mineral density, such as dual-energy absorptiometry and quantitative computed tomography.

Osteoporosis prevention and treatment begin with adequate dietary calcium intake, vitamin D supplementation, and a regular exercise regimen—starting before the age of 30—to maximize the peak bone mass. Calcium and vitamin D supplements later in life can also modestly reduce bone loss. Pharmacologic treatments include use of antiresorptive and osteoanabolic agents. The antiresorptive agents, such as bisphosphonates, calcitonin, estrogen, and denosumab, decrease bone resorption by osteoclasts. The main anabolic agent is parathyroid hormone or an analogue, given in amounts that stimulate osteoblastic activity.

Paget Disease (Osteitis Deformans)

This unique skeletal disease is characterized by repetitive episodes of frenzied, regional osteoclastic activity and bone resorption (*osteolytic stage*), followed by exuberant bone formation (*mixed osteoclastic-osteoblastic stage*), and finally by an apparent exhaustion of cellular activity (*osteosclerotic stage*). The net effect of this process is a *gain in bone mass;* however, the newly formed bone is disordered and weak, so bones may become enlarged and misshapen.

Paget disease usually presents in mid- to late adulthood. Marked variation in prevalence has been reported in different populations: The disorder is rare in Scandinavia, China, Japan, and Africa and relatively common in much of Europe, Australia, New Zealand, and the United States, affecting up to 2.5% of the adult populations. Of interest, it appears that the incidence of Paget disease is decreasing.

MORPHOLOGY

Paget disease may manifest as a solitary lesion (monostotic) or may occur at multiple sites (polyostotic) usually asynchronously. In the initial **lytic phase,** osteoclasts (and their associated Howship lacunae) are numerous, abnormally large, and have increased numbers of nuclei. Osteoclasts persist in the **mixed phase,** but the bone surfaces become lined by prominent osteoblasts. The marrow is replaced by loose connective tissue containing osteoprogenitor cells, as well as numerous blood vessels needed to meet the increased metabolic demands of the tissue. The newly formed bone may be woven or lamellar, but eventually all of it is remodeled into abnormal lamellar bone with a pathognomonic **mosaic pattern** (likened to a jigsaw puzzle) due to prominent haphazardly arranged cement lines (Fig. 20–5). As the osteoblastic activity ceases, the periosseous fibrovascular tissue recedes and is replaced by normal marrow. Although thickened, the resulting cortex is softer than normal and prone to deformation and fracture under stress.

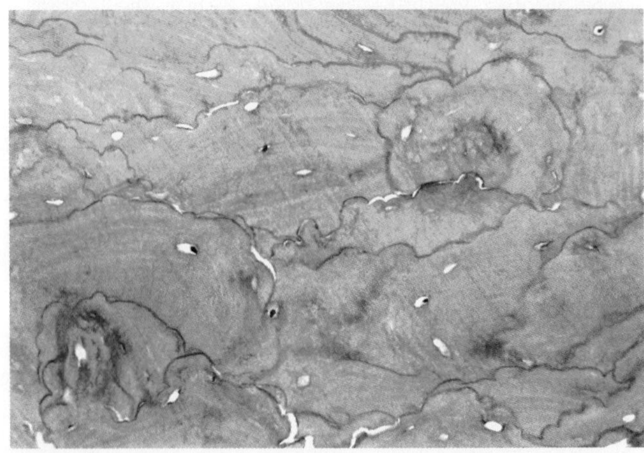

Figure 20–5 Paget disease, showing a mosaic pattern of lamellar bone.

PATHOGENESIS

When he first described the disease, Sir James Paget attributed the skeletal changes to an inflammatory process, and assigned the moniker **osteitis deformans.** After many years and multiple alternative theories, Paget's original idea may prove to be correct. It has long been postulated that a **paramyxovirus** infection (a slow virus) underlies Paget disease. Paramyxovirus antigens and particles resembling paramyxovirus can be demonstrated in osteoclasts. The causal connection is that paramyxoviruses can induce IL-1 and IL-6 secretion from infected cells, and these cytokines—as well as macrophage colony-stimulating factor (M-CSF)—are produced in large amounts in pagetic bone. As noted earlier, these potently activate osteoclasts. Nevertheless, as intriguing as these observations are, no infectious virus has been isolated from affected tissue. About 10% of affected patients have germline mutations in the gene *SQSTM1*, which encodes a protein that appears to increase osteoclastogenesis; these mutations are associated with earlier onset disease, a greater number of affected bones, and an increased incidence of fractures.

Clinical Course

The clinical findings depend on the extent and site of the disease. Paget disease is *monostotic* (tibia, ilium, femur, skull, vertebrae, and humerus) in about 15% of cases and *polyostotic* in the remainder; the axial skeleton or the proximal femur is involved in as many as 80% of cases. Involvement of the ribs, fibulae, and small bones of the hands and feet is unusual. Although Paget disease can produce a plethora of skeletal, neuromuscular, and cardiovascular complications, most cases are clinically mild, and the bone changes are discovered only incidentally in radiographs. Elevations in serum alkaline phosphatase and increased urinary excretion of hydroxyproline reflect exuberant bone turnover.

In some patients, the early hypervascular bone lesions cause warmth of the overlying skin and subcutaneous tissue. With extensive polyostotic disease, hypervascularity can result in high-output congestive heart failure. In the proliferative phase of the disease involving the skull, common symptoms attributable to nerve impingement include headache and visual and auditory disturbances. Vertebral lesions cause back pain and may be associated with disabling fractures and nerve root compression. Affected long bones in the legs often are deformed, as a consequence of the inability of pagetoid bone to remodel appropriately in response to the stress of weight bearing. Brittle long bones in particular are subject to *chalkstick fractures.*

The development of sarcoma is a dreaded but fortunately rare complication of Paget disease, occurring in only an estimated 1% of patients. The sarcomas usually are osteogenic, although other histologic variants can occur. The distribution of osteosarcoma generally parallels that of the Paget disease lesions, with the exception of vertebral bodies, which rarely harbor malignancy. The prognosis for patients who develop secondary sarcomas is exceedingly poor, but otherwise Paget disease usually follows a relatively benign course. Most patients have mild symptoms that are readily controlled with bisphosphonates, drugs that interfere with bone resorption.

Rickets and Osteomalacia

Both rickets and osteomalacia are manifestations of vitamin D deficiency or its abnormal metabolism (and are detailed in Chapter 7). The fundamental defect is an impairment of mineralization and a resultant accumulation of unmineralized matrix. This contrasts with osteoporosis, in which the mineral content of the bone is normal and the total bone mass is decreased. *Rickets* refers to the disorder in children, in which it interferes with the deposition of bone in the growth plates. *Osteomalacia* is the adult counterpart, in which bone formed during remodeling is undermineralized, resulting in predisposition to fractures.

Hyperparathyroidism

As discussed in Chapter 19, parathyroid hormone (PTH) plays a central role in calcium homeostasis through the following effects:

- Osteoclast activation, increasing bone resorption and calcium mobilization. PTH mediates the effect indirectly by increased RANKL expression on osteoblasts.
- Increased resorption of calcium by the renal tubules
- Increased urinary excretion of phosphates
- Increased synthesis of active vitamin D, 1,25$(OH)_2$-D, by the kidneys, which in turn enhances calcium absorption from the gut and mobilizes bone calcium by inducing RANKL on osteoblasts

The net result of the actions of PTH is an elevation in serum calcium, which, under normal circumstances, inhibits further PTH production. However, excessive or inappropriate levels of PTH can result from autonomous parathyroid secretion (*primary hyperparathyroidism*) or can occur in the setting of underlying renal disease (*secondary hyperparathyroidism*) (see also Chapter 19).

In either setting, *hyperparathyroidism leads to significant skeletal changes related to unabated osteoclast activity.* The entire skeleton is affected, although some sites can be more severely affected than others. PTH is directly responsible for the bone changes seen in primary hyperparathyroidism, but additional influences contribute to the development of bone disease in secondary hyperparathyroidism. In chronic renal insufficiency there is inadequate 1,25-$(OH)_2$-D synthesis, which ultimately affects gastrointestinal calcium absorption. The hyperphosphatemia of renal failure also suppresses renal α_1-hydroxylase, further impairing vitamin D synthesis; additional influences include metabolic acidosis and aluminum deposition in bone. As bone mass decreases, affected patients are increasingly susceptible to fractures, bone deformation, and joint problems. Fortunately, a reduction in PTH levels to normal can completely reverse the bone changes.

MORPHOLOGY

The hallmark of PTH excess is **increased osteoclastic activity, with bone resorption.** Cortical and trabecular bone are diminished and replaced by loose connective tissue. Bone resorption is especially pronounced in the subperiosteal regions and produces characteristic radiographic changes, best seen along the radial aspect of the middle phalanges of the second and third fingers. Microscopically, there are **increased numbers of osteoclasts boring into the centers of bony trabeculae (dissecting osteitis) and expanding haversian canals (cortical cutting cones)** (Fig. 20–6, *A*). The marrow space contains increased amounts of loose fibrovascular tissue. Hemosiderin deposits are present, reflecting episodes of hemorrhage resulting from microfractures of the weakened bone. In some instances, collections of osteoclasts, reactive giant cells, and hemorrhagic debris form a distinct mass termed a **brown tumor of hyperparathyroidism** (Fig. 20–6, *B*). Cystic change is common in such lesions (hence the name **osteitis fibrosa cystica**), which can be confused with primary bone neoplasms.

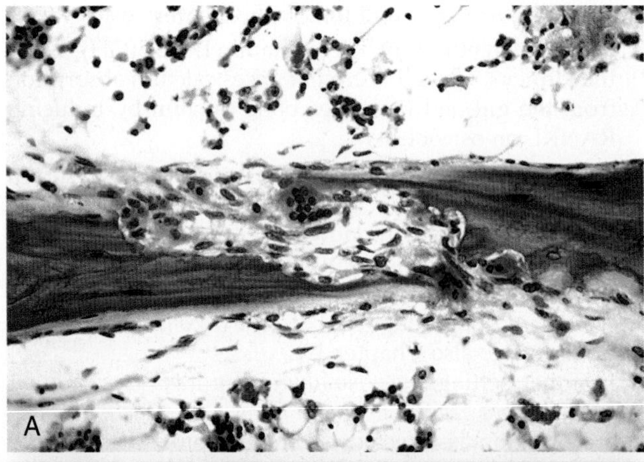

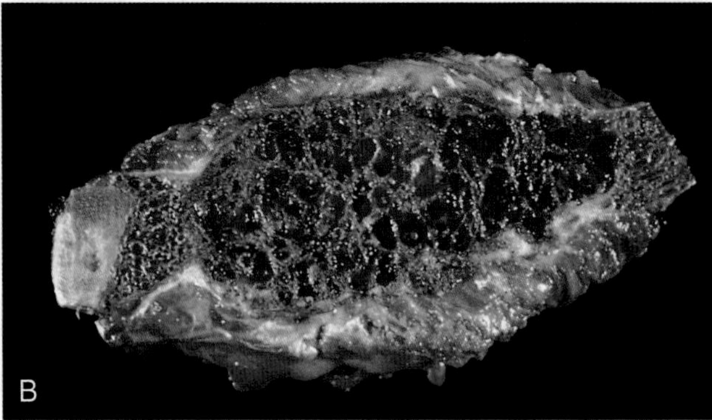

Figure 20–6 Bone manifestations of hyperparathyroidism. **A,** Osteoclasts gnawing into and disrupting lamellar bone. **B,** Resected rib, with expansile cystic mass (so-called brown tumor).

SUMMARY

Acquired Diseases of Bone Development and Mass

- Nutritional deficiencies can affect bone integrity by altering the quality of the organic matrix (e.g., vitamin C is involved in collagen cross-linking) or by influencing bone mineralization (e.g., vitamin D is involved in calcium uptake).
- Osteoporosis results from decreased bone mass and is clinically significant because it predisposes bone to fracture. Although osteoporosis is multifactorial, the two most common forms are *senile osteoporosis* due to aging-related losses of osteoblast function, and *postmenopausal osteoporosis* due to increased osteoclastic activity caused by the relative absence of estrogen.
- Paget disease may result from a paramyxovirus infection in genetically susceptible persons and is caused by aberrant and excessive osteoclast activity, followed by exuberant—but structurally unsound—osteoblast deposition of bone.
- Primary or secondary (due to renal failure) overproduction of PTH (*hyperparathyroidism*) results in increased osteoclast activity and bone resorption, leading to fractures and deformities.

FRACTURES

Fractures rank among the most common pathologic conditions of bone. They are classified as follows:

- *Complete* or *incomplete*
- *Closed,* in which the overlying tissue is intact, or *compound,* in which the fracture extends into the overlying skin
- *Comminuted,* in which the bone is splintered
- *Displaced,* in which the fractured bone is not aligned

If the break occurs at the site of previous disease (e.g., a bone cyst, a malignant tumor, or a brown tumor associated with elevated PTH), it is termed a *pathologic fracture.* A *stress fracture* develops slowly over time as a collection of microfractures associated with increased physical activity, especially with new repetitive mechanical loads on bone (as sustained in military bootcamp activities).

In all cases, the repair of a fracture is a highly regulated process that involves overlapping stages:

- The trauma of the bone fracture ruptures associated blood vessels; the resulting blood clot creates a fibrin mesh scaffold to recruit inflammatory cells, fibroblasts, and endothelium. Degranulated platelets and marauding inflammatory cells subsequently release a host of cytokines (e.g., platelet-derived growth factor, fibroblast growth factor) that activate bone progenitor cells, and within a week, the involved tissue is primed for new matrix synthesis. This *soft tissue callus* can hold the ends of the fractured bone in apposition but is noncalcified and cannot support weight bearing.
- Bone progenitors in the periosteum and medullary cavity deposit new foci of woven bone, and activated

mesenchymal cells at the fracture site differentiate into cartilage-synthesizing chondroblasts. In uncomplicated fractures, this early repair process peaks within 2 to 3 weeks. The newly formed cartilage acts as a nidus for *endochondral ossification,* recapitulating the process of bone formation in epiphyseal growth plates. This connects the cortices and trabeculae in the juxtaposed bones. With ossification, the fractured ends are bridged by a *bony callus.*

- Although excess fibrous tissue, cartilage, and bone are produced in the early callus, subsequent weight bearing leads to remodeling of the callus from nonstressed sites; at the same time there is fortification of regions that support greater loads. This process restores the original size, shape, and integrity of the bone.

The healing of a fracture can be disrupted by many factors:

- Displaced and comminuted fractures frequently result in some deformity; devitalized fragments of splintered bone require resorption, which delays healing, enlarges the callus, and requires inordinately long periods of remodeling and may never completely normalize.
- Inadequate immobilization permits constant movement at the fracture site, so that the normal constituents of callus do not form. In such instances, the healing site is composed mainly of fibrous tissue and cartilage, perpetuating the instability and resulting in delayed union and nonunion. Too much motion along the fracture gap (as in nonunion) causes the central portion of the callus to undergo cystic degeneration; the luminal surface can actually become lined by synovial-type cells, creating a false joint, or *pseudoarthrosis.* In the setting of a nonunion or pseudoarthrosis, normal healing can be achieved only if the interposed soft tissues are removed and the fracture site is stabilized.
- *Infection* (a risk in comminuted and open fractures) is a serious obstacle to fracture healing. The infection must be eradicated before successful bone reunion and remodeling can occur.
- Bone repair obviously will be impaired in the setting of inadequate levels of calcium or phosphorus, vitamin deficiencies, systemic infection, diabetes, or vascular insufficiency.

With uncomplicated fractures in children and young adults, practically perfect reconstitution is the norm. When fractures occur in older age groups or in abnormal bones (e.g., osteoporotic bone), repair frequently is less than optimal without orthopedic intervention.

OSTEONECROSIS (AVASCULAR NECROSIS)

Ischemic necrosis with resultant bone infarction occurs relatively frequently. Mechanisms contributing to bone ischemia include

- Vascular compression or disruption (e.g., after a fracture)
- Steroid administration
- Thromboembolic disease (e.g., nitrogen bubbles in caisson disease—see Chapter 3)
- Primary vessel disease (e.g., vasculitis)
- Sickle cell crisis (Chapter 11)

Most cases of bone necrosis are due to fracture or occur after corticosteroid use, but in many instances the etiology is unknown.

MORPHOLOGY

The pathologic features of bone necrosis are the same regardless of cause. Dead bone with empty lacunae is interspersed with areas of fat necrosis and insoluble calcium soaps. The cortex usually is not affected, because of collateral blood supply; in subchondral infarcts, the overlying articular cartilage also remains viable because the synovial fluid can provide nutritive support. With time, osteoclasts can resorb some of the necrotic bony trabeculae; any dead bone fragments that remain act as scaffolding for new bone formation, a process called **creeping substitution.**

Clinical Course

Symptoms depend on the size and location of injury. *Subchondral infarcts* initially present with pain during physical activity that becomes more persistent with time. *Medullary infarcts* usually are silent unless large in size (as may occur with Gaucher disease, caisson disease, or sickle cell disease). Medullary infarcts usually are stable, but subchondral infarcts often collapse and may lead to severe osteoarthritis. Roughly 50,000 joint replacements are performed each year in the United States to treat the consequences of osteonecrosis.

OSTEOMYELITIS

Osteomyelitis is defined as inflammation of bone and marrow, but in common use it is virtually synonymous with infection. Osteomyelitis can be secondary to systemic infection but more frequently occurs as a primary isolated focus of disease; it can be an acute process or a chronic, debilitating illness. Although any microorganism can cause osteomyelitis, the most common etiologic agents are pyogenic bacteria and *Mycobacterium tuberculosis.*

Pyogenic Osteomyelitis

Most cases of acute osteomyelitis are caused by bacteria. The offending organisms reach the bone by one of three routes: (1) hematogenous dissemination (most common); (2) extension from an infection in adjacent joint or soft tissue; or (3) traumatic implantation after compound fractures or orthopedic procedures. Overall, *Staphylococcus aureus* is the most frequent causative organism; its propensity to infect bone may be related to the expression of surface proteins that allow adhesion to bone matrix. *Escherichia coli* and group B streptococci are important causes of acute osteomyelitis in neonates, and *Salmonella* is an especially common pathogen in persons with sickle cell disease. Mixed bacterial infections, including anaerobes, typically are responsible for osteomyelitis secondary to bone trauma. In as many as 50% of cases, no organisms can be isolated.

MORPHOLOGY

The morphologic changes in osteomyelitis depend on the chronicity and location of the infection. Causal bacteria proliferate, inducing an acute inflammatory reaction, with consequent cell death. Entrapped bone rapidly becomes necrotic; this non-viable bone is called a **sequestrum.** Bacteria and inflammation can percolate throughout the haversian systems to reach the periosteum. In children, the periosteum is loosely attached to the cortex; therefore, sizable **subperiosteal** abscesses can form and extend for long distances along the bone surface. Lifting of the periosteum further impairs the blood supply to the affected region, and both suppurative and ischemic injury can cause segmental bone necrosis. Rupture of the periosteum can lead to abscess formation in the surrounding soft tissue that may lead to a **draining sinus.** Sometimes the sequestrum crumbles, releasing fragments that pass through the sinus tract.

In infants (and uncommonly in adults), epiphyseal infection can spread into the adjoining joint to produce suppurative arthritis, sometimes with extensive destruction of the articular cartilage and permanent disability. An analogous process can involve vertebrae, with an infection destroying intervertebral discs and spreading into adjacent vertebrae.

After the first week of infection, chronic inflammatory cells become more numerous. Leukocyte cytokine release stimulates osteoclastic bone resorption, fibrous tissue ingrowth, and bone formation in the periphery. Reactive woven or lamellar bone can be deposited; when it forms a shell of living tissue around a sequestrum, it is called an **involucrum** (Fig. 20–7). Viable organisms can persist in the sequestrum for years after the original infection.

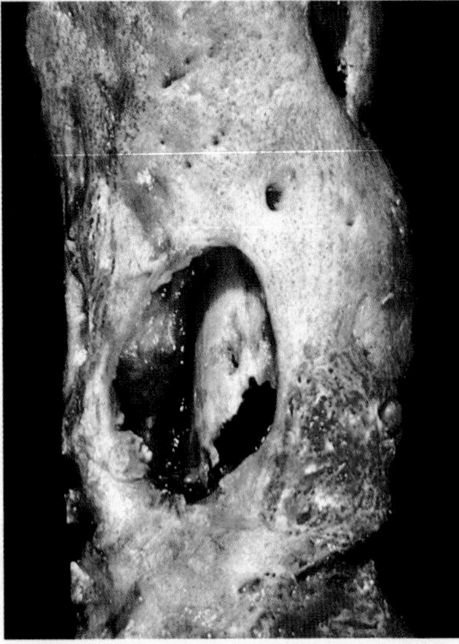

Figure 20–7 Resected femur from a patient with chronic osteomyelitis. Necrotic bone (the sequestrum) visible in the center of a draining sinus tract is surrounded by a rim of new bone (the involucrum).

Clinical Features

Osteomyelitis classically manifests as an acute systemic illness, with malaise, fever, leukocytosis, and throbbing pain over the affected region. Symptoms also can be subtle, with only unexplained fever, particularly in infants, or only localized pain in the adult. The diagnosis is suggested by characteristic radiologic findings: a destructive lytic focus surrounded by edema and a sclerotic rim. In many untreated cases, blood cultures are positive, but biopsy and bone cultures are usually required to identify the pathogen. A combination of antibiotics and surgical drainage usually is curative, but up to a quarter of cases do not resolve and persist as chronic infections. Chronicity may develop with delay in diagnosis, extensive bone necrosis, abbreviated antibiotic therapy, inadequate surgical debridement, and/or weakened host defenses. Besides occasional acute flare-ups, chronic osteomyelitis also may be complicated by pathologic fracture, secondary amyloidosis, endocarditis, sepsis, development of squamous cell carcinoma if the infection creates a sinus tract, and rarely osteosarcoma.

Tuberculous Osteomyelitis

Mycobacterial infection of bone has long been a problem in developing countries; with the resurgence of tuberculosis (due to immigration patterns and increasing numbers of immunocompromised persons) it is becoming an important disease in other countries as well.

Bone infection complicates an estimated 1% to 3% of cases of pulmonary tuberculosis. The organisms usually reach the bone through the bloodstream, although direct spread from a contiguous focus of infection (e.g., from mediastinal nodes to the vertebrae) also can occur. With hematogenous spread, *long bones and vertebrae are favored sites.* The lesions often are solitary but can be multifocal, particularly in patients with an underlying immunodeficiency. Because the tubercle bacillus is microaerophilic, the synovium, with its higher oxygen pressures, is a common site of initial infection. The infection then spreads to the adjacent epiphysis, where it elicits typical granulomatous inflammation with caseous necrosis and extensive bone destruction. *Tuberculosis of the vertebral bodies is a clinically serious form of osteomyelitis.* Infection at this site causes vertebral deformity, collapse, and posterior displacement (Pott disease), leading to neurologic deficits. Spinal deformities due to Pott disease afflicted several men of letters (including Alexander Pope and William Henley) and likely served as the inspiration for Victor Hugo's *Hunchback of Notre Dame.* Extension of the infection to the adjacent soft tissues with the development of psoas muscle abscesses is fairly common.

BONE TUMORS

Primary bone tumors are considerably less common than bone metastases from other primary sites; metastatic disease is discussed at the end of this section.

Primary bone tumors exhibit great morphologic diversity and clinical behaviors – from benign to aggressively malignant. Most are classified according to the normal cell counterpart and line of differentiation; Table 20–2 lists the salient features

Table 20–2 Tumors of Bone

Tumor Type	Common Locations	Age (yr)	Morphology
Bone-Forming			
Benign			
Osteoma	Facial bones, skull	40–50	Exophytic growths attached to bone surface; histologically similar to normal bone
Osteoid osteoma	Metaphysis of femur and tibia	10–20	Cortical tumors, characterized by pain; histologic pattern consisting of interlacing trabeculae of woven bone
Osteoblastoma	Vertebral column	10–20	Arise in vertebral transverse and spinous processes; histologically similar to osteoid osteoma
Malignant			
Primary osteosarcoma	Metaphysis of distal femur, proximal tibia, and humerus	10–20	Grow outward, lifting periosteum, and inward to the medullary cavity; microscopy shows malignant cells forming osteoid; cartilage also may be present
Secondary osteosarcoma	Femur, humerus, pelvis	>40	Complications of polyostotic Paget disease; histologically similar to primary osteosarcoma
Cartilaginous			
Benign			
Osteochondroma	Metaphysis of long tubular bones	10–30	Bony excrescences with a cartilaginous cap; may be solitary or multiple and hereditary
Enchondroma	Small bones of hands and feet	30–50	Well-circumscribed single tumors resembling normal cartilage; arise within medullary cavity of bone; uncommonly multiple and hereditary
Malignant			
Chondrosarcoma	Bones of shoulder, pelvis, proximal femur, and ribs	40–60	Arise within medullary cavity and erode cortex; microscopy shows well-differentiated cartilage-like or anaplastic features
Miscellaneous			
Giant cell tumor (usually benign)	Epiphysis of long bone	20–40	Lytic lesions that erode cortex; microscopy shows osteoclast-like giant cells and round to spindle-shaped mononuclear cells; most are benign
Ewing sarcoma	Diaphysis and metaphysis	10–20	Arise in medullary cavity; microscopy shows sheets of small round cells that contain glycogen; aggressive neoplasm

of the most common primary bone neoplasms, excluding multiple myeloma and other hematopoietic tumors. Overall, matrix-producing and fibrous tumors are the most common, and among the benign tumors, osteochondroma and fibrous cortical defect occur most frequently. Osteosarcoma is the most common primary bone cancer, followed by chondrosarcoma and Ewing sarcoma. Benign tumors greatly outnumber their malignant counterparts, particularly before the age of 40 years; bone tumors in elderly persons are much more likely to be malignant.

Most bone tumors develop during the first several decades of life and have a propensity to originate in the long bones of the extremities. Nevertheless, specific tumor types target certain age groups and anatomic sites; these associations are often helpful in arriving at the correct diagnosis. For instance, most osteosarcomas occur during adolescence, with half arising around the knee, either in the distal femur or proximal tibia. By contrast, chondrosarcomas tend to develop during mid- to late adulthood and involve the trunk, limb girdles, and proximal long bones.

Most bone tumors arise without any previous known cause. Nevertheless, genetic syndromes (e.g., Li-Fraumeni and retinoblastoma syndromes) (Chapter 5) are associated with osteosarcomas, as are (rarely) bone infarcts, chronic osteomyelitis, Paget disease, irradiation, and use of metal orthopedic devices.

In terms of clinical presentation, benign lesions frequently are asymptomatic and are detected as incidental findings. Others produce pain or a slowly growing mass. Occasionally, a pathologic fracture is the first manifestation. Radiologic imaging is critical in the evaluation of bone tumors; however, biopsy and histologic study and, in some cases, molecular tests are necessary for diagnosis.

Bone-Forming Tumors

The tumor cells in the following neoplasms all produce bone that usually is woven and variably mineralized.

Osteoma

Osteomas are benign lesions most commonly encountered in the head and neck, including the paranasal sinuses, but which can occur elsewhere as well. They typically present in middle age as solitary, slowly growing, hard, exophytic masses on a bone surface. Multiple lesions are a feature of Gardner syndrome, a hereditary condition discussed later. On histologic examination, osteomas recapitulate cortical-type bone and are composed of a mixture of woven and lamellar bone. Although they may cause local mechanical problems (e.g., obstruction of a sinus cavity) and cosmetic deformities, they are not locally aggressive and do not undergo malignant transformation.

Osteoid Osteoma and Osteoblastoma

Osteoid osteomas and *osteoblastomas* are benign neoplasms with very similar histologic features. Both lesions typically appear during the teenage years and 20s, with a male predilection (2:1 for osteoid osteomas). They are distinguished from each other primarily by their size and clinical presentation. *Osteoid osteomas* arise most often beneath the periosteum or within the cortex in the proximal femur and tibia or posterior spinal elements and are by definition less than 2 cm in diameter, whereas osteoblastomas are larger. Localized pain, most severe at night, is an almost universal complaint with osteoid osteomas, and usually is relieved by aspirin. *Osteoblastomas* arise most often in the vertebral column; they also cause pain, although it often is more difficult to localize and is not responsive to aspirin. Local excision is the treatment of choice; incompletely resected lesions can recur. Malignant transformation is rare *unless* the lesion is treated with irradiation.

MORPHOLOGY

On gross inspection, both lesions are round-to-oval masses of hemorrhagic, gritty-appearing tan tissue. A rim of sclerotic bone is present at the edge of both types of tumors; however, it is much more conspicuous in osteoid osteomas. On microscopic examination, both neoplasms are composed of interlacing trabeculae of woven bone surrounded by osteoblasts (Fig. 20–8). The intervening stroma is loose, vascular connective tissue containing variable numbers of giant cells.

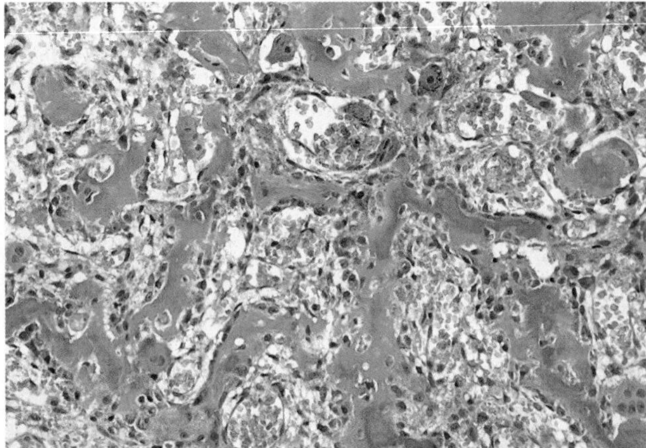

Figure 20–8 Osteoid osteoma showing randomly oriented trabeculae of woven bone rimmed by prominent osteoblasts. The intertrabecular spaces are filled by vascular loose connective tissue.

Osteosarcoma

Osteosarcoma is a bone-producing malignant mesenchymal tumor. After myeloma and lymphoma, osteosarcoma is the most common primary malignant tumor of bone, accounting for approximately 20% of primary bone cancers; a little over 2000 cases are diagnosed annually in the United States. Osteosarcomas occur in all age groups, but about 75% of patients are younger than 20 years of age, with a second peak occurring in elderly persons, usually in association with other conditions, including Paget disease, bone infarcts, and previous irradiation. Men are more commonly affected than women (1.6:1). Although any bone can be involved, most tumors arise in the metaphyseal region of the long bones of the extremities, with almost 60% occurring about the knee, 15% around the hip, 10% at the shoulder, and 8% in the jaw. Several subtypes of osteosarcoma are distinguished on the basis of the site of involvement within the bone (e.g., medullary versus cortical), degree of differentiation, number of involved sites, presence of underlying disease, and histologic features; the most common type of osteosarcoma is primary, solitary, intramedullary, and poorly differentiated, producing a predominantly bony matrix.

MORPHOLOGY

On gross evaluation, osteosarcomas are gritty-appearing, gray-white tumors, often exhibiting hemorrhage and cystic degeneration. Tumors frequently destroy the surrounding cortices, producing soft tissue masses (Fig. 20–9, *A*). They spread extensively in the medullary canal, infiltrating and replacing the marrow but only infrequently penetrating the epiphyseal plate or entering the joint space. Tumor cells vary in size and shape and frequently have large hyperchromatic

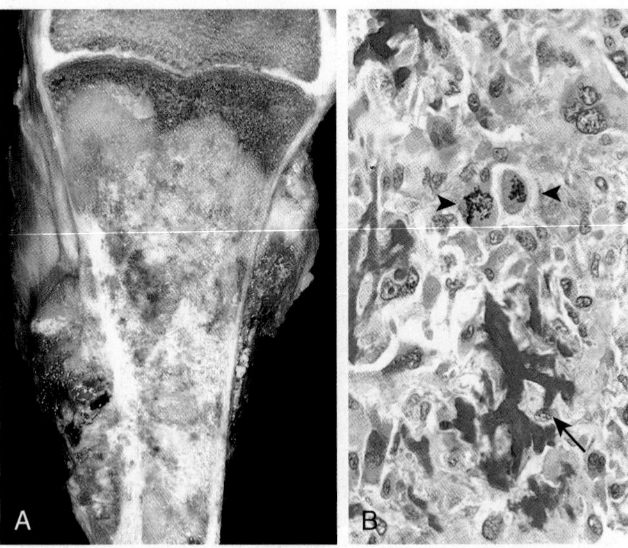

Figure 20–9 Osteosarcoma. **A,** Mass involving the upper end of the tibia. The tan-white tumor fills most of the medullary cavity of the metaphysis and proximal diaphysis. It has infiltrated through the cortex, lifted the periosteum, and formed soft tissue masses on both sides of the bone. **B,** Histologic appearance, with coarse, lacelike pattern of neoplastic bone (*arrow*) produced by anaplastic tumor cells. Note the wildly aberrant mitotic figures (*arrowheads*).

nuclei; bizarre tumor giant cells are common, as are mitotic figures. **The production of mineralized or unmineralized bone (osteoid) by malignant cells is essential for diagnosis of osteosarcoma** (Fig. 20–9, *B*). The neoplastic bone typically is coarse and lacelike but also can be deposited in broad sheets. Cartilage and fibroblastic differentiation can also be present in varying amounts. When malignant cartilage is abundant, the tumor is called a **chondroblastic osteosarcoma.** Vascular invasion is common, as is spontaneous tumor necrosis.

PATHOGENESIS

Several mutations are closely associated with the development of osteosarcoma. In particular, *RB* gene mutations occur in 60% to 70% of sporadic tumors, and persons with hereditary retinoblastomas (due to germline mutations in the *RB* gene) have a thousand-fold greater risk for development of osteosarcoma. Like many other cancers, spontaneous osteosarcomas also frequently exhibit mutations in *TP53* and in genes that regulate the cell cycle, including cyclins, cyclin-dependent kinases, and kinase inhibitors. Many osteosarcomas develop at sites of greatest bone growth, perhaps because rapidly dividing cells provide a fertile soil for mutations.

Clinical Features

Osteosarcomas typically manifest as painful enlarging masses, although a pathologic fracture can be the first sign. Radiographic imaging usually shows a large, destructive, mixed lytic and blastic mass with indistinct infiltrating margins. The tumor frequently breaks through the cortex and lifts the periosteum, resulting in reactive periosteal bone formation. A triangular shadow on the x-ray film between the cortex and raised periosteum (*Codman triangle*) is characteristic of osteosarcomas. Osteosarcomas typically spread hematogenously; at the time of diagnosis, approximately 10% to 20% of patients have demonstrable pulmonary metastases, and a larger number have microscopic metastases.

Despite aggressive behavior, standard treatment with chemotherapy and limb salvage therapy currently yields long-term survivals of 60% to 70%.

Secondary osteosarcomas occur in older adults most commonly in the setting of Paget disease or previous radiation exposure. Like primary osteosarcomas, secondary osteosarcomas are highly aggressive tumors, but they do not respond well to therapy and are usually fatal.

Cartilage-Forming Tumors

Cartilage-forming tumors produce hyaline or myxoid cartilage; fibrocartilage and elastic cartilage are rare components. Like the bone-forming tumors, cartilaginous tumors constitute a spectrum from benign, self-limited growths to highly aggressive malignancies; again, benign cartilage tumors are much more common than malignant ones. Only the more common types are discussed here.

Osteochondroma

Osteochondromas are relatively common benign, cartilage-capped tumors attached by a bony stalk to the underlying skeleton. Solitary osteochondromas typically are first diagnosed in late adolescence and early adulthood (male-to-female ratio of 3:1); multiple osteochondromas become apparent during childhood, occurring as *multiple hereditary osteochondromas,* an autosomal dominant disorder. Inactivation of both copies of the *EXT1* or *EXT2* genes through mutation and loss of heterozygosity in chondrocytes of the growth plate is implicated in both sporadic and hereditary osteochondromas. These tumor suppressor genes encode glycosyltransferases essential for polymerization of heparin sulfate, an important component of cartilage. This finding and other molecular genetic studies support the concept that osteochondromas are true neoplasms and not developmental malformations.

Osteochondromas develop only in bones of endochondral origin arising at the metaphysis near the growth plate of long tubular bones, especially about the knee; they tend to stop growing once the normal growth of the skeleton is completed (Fig. 20–10). Occasionally they develop from bones of the pelvis, scapula, and ribs and in these sites frequently are sessile. Rarely, osteochondromas arise in the short tubular bones of hands and feet.

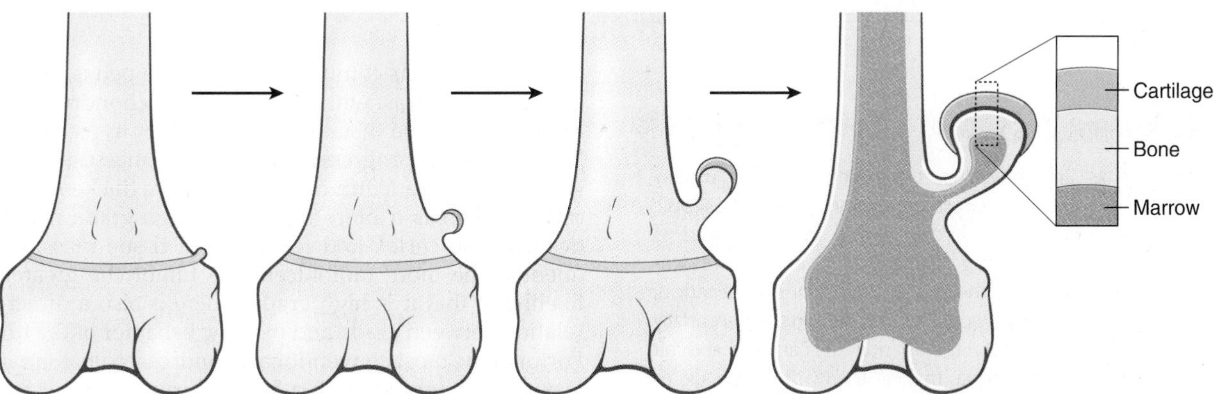

Figure 20–10 The development of an osteochondroma, beginning with an outgrowth from the epiphyseal cartilage.

associated with multiple schwannomas in which vestibular schwannomas are absent. Some cases have recently been linked to loss-of-function mutations in a tumor suppressor gene on chromosome 22 that encodes a protein that regulates chromatin structure.

MORPHOLOGY

On gross inspection, most schwannomas appear as circumscribed masses abutting an adjacent nerve. On microscopic examination, these tumors often show an admixture of dense and loose areas referred to as Antoni A and B, respectively (Fig. 21–7, *A* and *B*). They are comprised of a uniform proliferation of neoplastic Schwann cells. In the dense Antoni A areas, bland spindle cells with buckled nuclei are arranged into intersecting fascicles. These cells often align to produce nuclear palisading, resulting in alternating bands of nuclear and anuclear areas called Verocay bodies. Axons are largely excluded from the tumor. Thick-walled hyalinized vessels often are present. Hemorrhage or cystic change are also seen sometimes.

Neurofibromas

Neurofibromas are benign peripheral nerve sheath tumors. Three important subtypes are recognized:

- *Localized cutaneous neurofibromas* arise as superficial nodular or polypoid tumors. These occur either as solitary sporadic lesions or as often multiple lesions in the context of neurofibromatosis type 1 (NF1).
- *Plexiform neurofibromas* grow diffusely within the confines of a nerve or nerve plexus. Surgical enucleation of such lesions is therefore difficult and is often associated with lasting neurologic deficits. Plexiform neurofibromas are virtually pathognomonic for NF1 (discussed later on). Unlike other benign nerve sheath tumors, these tumors are associated with a small but real risk of malignant transformation.
- *Diffuse neurofibromas* are infiltrative proliferations that can take the form of large, disfiguring subcutaneous masses. These also are often associated with NF1.

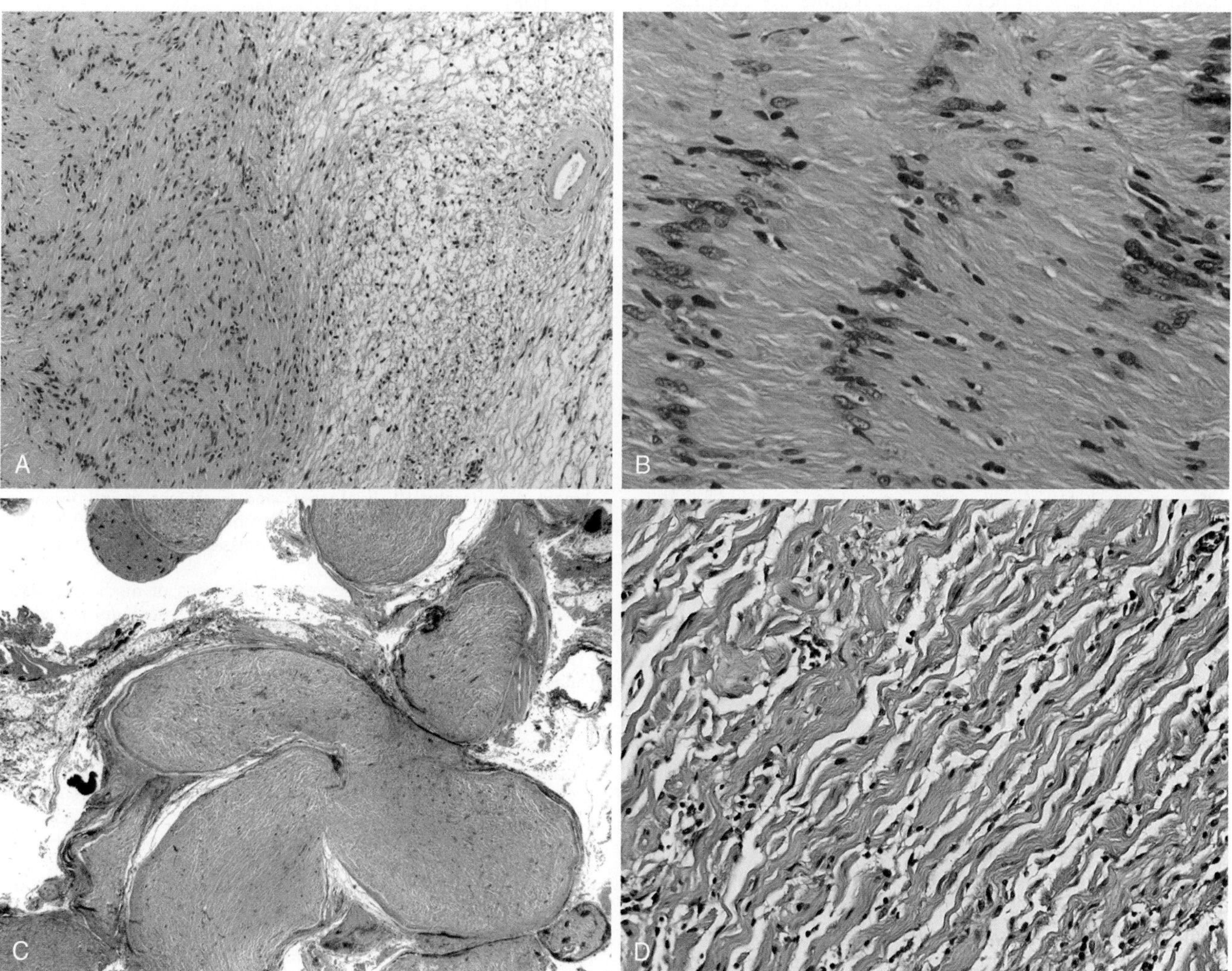

Figure 21–7 Schwannoma and plexiform neurofibroma. **A** and **B,** Schwannoma. As seen in **A,** schwannomas often contain dense pink Antoni A areas (*left*) and loose, pale Antoni B areas (*right*), as well as hyalinized blood vessels (*right*). **B,** Antoni A area with the nuclei of tumor cells aligned in palisading rows. **C** and **D,** Plexiform neurofibroma. Multiple nerve fascicles are expanded by infiltrating tumor cells **(C),** which at higher power **(D)** are seen to consist of bland spindle cells admixed with wavy collagen bundles likened to carrot shavings.

MORPHOLOGY

Unlike schwannomas, neurofibromas are not encapsulated. They may appear circumscribed, as in **localized cutaneous neurofibromas,** or exhibit a diffuse infiltrative growth pattern. Also in contrast with schwannomas, the neoplastic Schwann cells in neurofibroma are admixed with other cell types, including mast cells, fibroblast-like cells and perineurial-like cells. As a result, the cellular growth pattern of neurofibromas is more haphazard than that of schwannomas. The background stroma often contains loose wavy collagen bundles but also can be myxoid or contain dense collagen (Fig. 21–7, *D*). **Plexiform neurofibromas** involve multiple fascicles of individual affected nerves (Fig. 21–7, *C*). Residual axons are found embedded within the diffuse neoplastic Schwann cell proliferation, which expand the fascicles while leaving the perineurium intact. **Diffuse neurofibromas** show an extensive infiltrative pattern of growth within the dermis and subcutis of the skin.

Malignant Peripheral Nerve Sheath Tumors

Malignant peripheral nerve sheath tumors are neoplasms seen in adults that typically show evidence of Schwann cell derivation and sometimes a clear origin from a peripheral nerve. They may arise from transformation of a neurofibroma, usually of the plexiform type. About one half of such tumors arise in patients with NF1, and 3% to 10% of all patients with NF1 develop a malignant peripheral nerve sheath tumor during their lifetime.

MORPHOLOGY

Malignant peripheral nerve sheath tumors manifest as large, poorly defined soft tissue masses. On histologic examination, these tumors are highly cellular and exhibit features of overt malignancy, including anaplasia, necrosis, infiltrative growth pattern, pleomorphism, and high proliferative activity. The low-power view often shows alternating areas of high and low cellularity that result in an appearance described as "marble-like." Also frequently seen are perivascular areas of increased cellular density.

Neurofibromatosis Type 1

NF1 is an autosomal dominant disorder caused by mutations in the tumor suppressor neurofibromin, encoded on the long arm of chromosome 17 (17q). Neurofibromin is a negative regulator of the potent oncoprotein Ras (Chapter 5). Disruption of neurofibromin function and Ras hyperactivity appear to be a cardinal feature of NF1-associated tumors. As would be anticipated for a tumor suppressor gene, the sole normal neurofibromin allele is mutated or silenced in tumors arising in the setting of NF1, which include neurofibromas of all three main types, malignant peripheral nerve sheath tumors, optic gliomas, and other glial tumors. In addition, patients with NF1 exhibit learning disabilities, seizures, skeletal abnormalities, vascular abnormalities with arterial stenoses, pigmented nodules of the iris (*Lisch nodules*), and pigmented skin lesions (axillary freckling and café au lait spots) in various degrees.

Traumatic Neuroma

Traumatic neuroma is a non-neoplastic proliferation associated with previous injury of a peripheral nerve. Injuries that lead to the transection of axons activate a regenerative program (see Fig. 21–1) characterized by sprouting and elongation of processes from the proximal axonal stump. With severe injuries that disrupt the perineurial sheath, these new processes may "miss" their target, the distal end of the transected nerve. The misguided elongating axonal processes can induce a reactive proliferation of Schwann cells, leading to the formation of a painful localized nodule that consists of a haphazard mixture of axons, Schwann cells, and connective tissue.

SUMMARY

Peripheral Nerve Sheath Tumors

- In most peripheral nerve sheath tumors, the neoplastic cells show evidence of Schwann cell differentiation.
- Peripheral nerve sheath tumors are important features of the familial tumor syndromes neurofibromatosis type 1 (NF1) and type 2 (NF2).
- Schwannomas and neurofibromas are benign nerve sheath tumors.
- Schwannomas are circumscribed, usually encapsulated tumors that abut the nerve of origin and are a feature of NF2.
- Neurofibromas may manifest as a sporadic subcutaneous nodule, as a large, poorly defined soft tissue lesion, or as a growth within a nerve. Neurofibromas are associated with NF1.
- About 50% of malignant peripheral nerve sheath tumors occur de novo in otherwise normal persons, while the remainder arise from the malignant transformation of a preexisting NF1-associated neurofibroma.

BIBLIOGRAPHY

Amato AA, Barohn RJ: Evaluation and treatment of inflammatory myopathies. J Neurol Neurosurg Psychiatry 80:1060, 2009. *[Review of idiopathic inflammatory myopathies focused especially on clinical features and therapy.]*

Briemberg HR: Peripheral nerve complications of medical disease. Semin Neurol 29:124, 2009. *[Review of the ways medical diseases including diabetes, connective tissue diseases, cancer, and infections affect peripheral nerves.]*

Dalakas MC: Inflammatory muscle diseases: a critical review on pathogenesis and therapies. Curr Opin Pharmacol 10:346, 2010. *[Discussion of current concepts on the pathophysiology of idiopathic inflammatory myopathies.]*

Finsterer J, Stollberger C: Primary myopathies and the heart. Scand Cardiovasc J 42:9, 2008. *[Review of inherited myopathies with focus on associated cardiac involvement.]*

Gorson KC: Vasculitic neuropathies: an update. Neurologist 13:12, 2007. *[A good review of peripheral nerve disease with vasculitis.]*

Greenberg SA: Inflammatory myopathies: disease mechanisms. Curr Opin Neurol 22:516, 2009. *[Discussion of current concepts on the pathophysiology of idiopathic inflammatory myopathies.]*

Habib AA, Brannagan TH III: Therapeutic strategies for diabetic neuropathy. Curr Neurol Neurosci Rep 10:92, 2010. *[Review focused especially on clinical features and therapy of diabetic neuropathy.]*

Hewer E, Goebel HH: Myopathology of non-infectious inflammatory myopathies—the current status. Pathol Res Pract 204:609, 2008. *[Review focused on the pathologic features of inflammatory myopathies.]*

Klopstock T: Drug-induced myopathies. Curr Opin Neurol 21:590, 2008. *[Review focused especially on the effects of statins and nucleoside analogue reverse transcriptase inhibitors for HIV infection/AIDS.]*

Mahadeva B, Phillips LH, Juel VC: Autoimmune disorders of neuromuscular transmission. Semin Neurol 28:212, 2008. *[Review of myasthenia gravis and Lambert-Eaton syndrome.]*

McClatchey AI: Neurofibromatosis. Annu Rev Pathol 2:191, 2007. *[Review of features that distinguish neurofibromatosis type 1, neurofibromatosis type 2, and schwannomatosis, with a focus on the genetics.]*

Nelson SF, Crosbie RH, Miceli MC, et al: Emerging genetic therapies to treat Duchenne muscular dystrophy. Curr Opin Neurol 22:532, 2009. *[Good review of recent developments in the search for new therapies.]*

North K: What's new in congenital myopathies? Neuromuscul Disord 18:433, 2008. *[Review on new developments in congenital myopathies.]*

Obrosova IG: Diabetes and the peripheral nerve. Biochim Biophys Acta 1792:931, 2009. *[Detailed discussion of the pathophysiology of diabetic neuropathy.]*

Silberman J, Lonial S: Review of peripheral neuropathy in plasma cell disorders. Hematol Oncol 26:55, 2008. *[Review of the ways in which peripheral nerve diseases are related to plasma cell disorders and the chemotherapies used in their treatment.]*

van Adel BA, Tarnopolsky MA: Metabolic myopathies: update 2009. J Clin Neuromuscul Dis 10:97, 2009. *[Review of metabolic myopathies.]*

See Targeted Therapy available online at **studentconsult.com**

CHAPTER 22

Central Nervous System

CHAPTER CONTENTS

Degenerative, inflammatory, infectious, and neoplastic disorders of the central nervous system (CNS) are some of the most serious diseases of mankind. The pathology of these diseases has many features that reflect the unique properties of the CNS. In fact, the diagnosis and analysis of CNS disorders requires specialized expertise, a realization that has led to the creation of the field of neuropathology.

PATTERNS OF INJURY IN THE NERVOUS SYSTEM

The cells of the nervous system respond to various forms of injury with distinct morphologic changes.

MORPHOLOGY

Features of Neuronal Injury. In response to injury, a number of changes occur in neurons and their processes (axons and dendrites). Within 12 hours of an irreversible hypoxic-ischemic insult, acute neuronal injury becomes evident on routine hematoxylin and eosin (H&E) staining (Fig. 22–1, *A*). There is shrinkage of the cell body, pyknosis of the nucleus, disappearance of the nucleolus, and loss of Nissl substance, with intense eosinophilia of the cytoplasm ("red neurons"). Often, the nucleus assumes the angulated shape of the shrunken cell body. Injured axons undergo swelling and show disruption of axonal transport. The swellings **(spheroids)** can be recognized on H&E stains (Fig. 22–1, *B*) and can be highlighted by silver staining or immunohistochemistry. Axonal injury also leads to cell body enlargement and rounding, peripheral displacement of the nucleus, enlargement of the nucleolus, and peripheral dispersion of Nissl substance **(central chromatolysis)** (Fig. 22–1, *C*). In addition, acute injuries typically result in breakdown of the blood-brain barrier and variable degrees of cerebral edema (described later).

Many neurodegenerative diseases are associated with specific intracellular inclusions (e.g., Lewy bodies in Parkinson disease and tangles in Alzheimer disease), also described later. Pathogenic viruses can also form inclusions in neurons, just as they do in other cells of the body. In some neurodegenerative diseases, neuronal processes also become thickened and tortuous; these are termed **dystrophic neurites.** With age, neurons also accumulate complex lipids **(lipofuscin)** in their cytoplasm and lysosomes.

Astrocytes in Injury and Repair. Astrocytes are the principal cells responsible for repair and scar formation in the

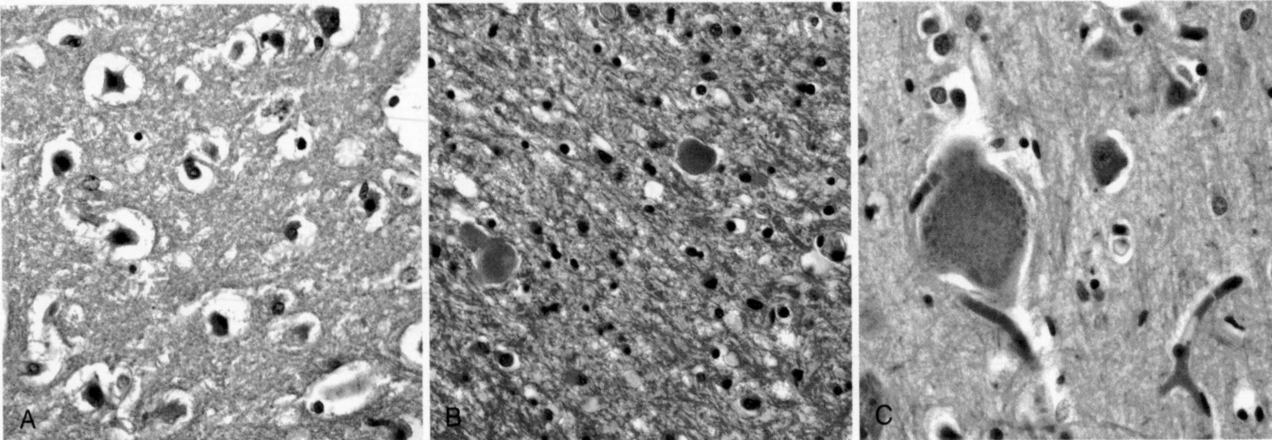

Figure 22–1 Patterns of neuronal injury. **A,** Acute hypoxic-ischemic injury in cerebral cortex, where the individual cell bodies are shrunken, along with the nuclei. They also are prominently stained by eosin ("red neurons"). **B,** Axonal spheroids are visible as bulbous swellings at points of disruption, or altered axonal transport. **C,** With axonal injury there can be swelling of the cell body and peripheral dispersal of the Nissl substance, termed chromatolysis.

brain, a process termed **gliosis.** In response to injury, astrocytes undergo both hypertrophy and hyperplasia. The nucleus enlarges and becomes vesicular, and the nucleolus becomes prominent. The previously scant cytoplasm expands and takes on a bright pink hue, and the cell extends multiple stout, ramifying processes **(gemistocytic astrocyte).** Unlike elsewhere in the body, fibroblasts participate in healing after brain injury to a limited extent except in specific settings (penetrating brain trauma or around abscesses). In long-standing gliosis, the cytoplasm of reactive astrocytes shrinks in size and the cellular processes become more tightly interwoven **(fibrillary astrocytes). Rosenthal fibers** are thick, elongated, brightly eosinophilic protein aggregates found in astrocytic processes in chronic gliosis and in some low-grade gliomas.

Changes in Other Cell Types. Oligodendrocytes, which produce myelin, exhibit a limited spectrum of specific morphologic changes in response to various injuries. In progressive multifocal leukoencephalopathy, viral inclusions can be seen in oligodendrocytes, with a smudgy, homogeneous-appearing enlarged nucleus.

Microglial cells are bone-marrow–derived cells that function as the resident phagocytes of the CNS. When activated by tissue injury, infection, or trauma, they proliferate and become more prominent histologically. Microglial cells take on the appearance of activated macrophages in areas of demyelination, organizing infarct, or hemorrhage; in other settings such as neurosyphilis or other infections, they develop elongated nuclei **(rod cells).** Aggregates of elongated microglial cells at sites of tissue injury are termed **microglial nodules.** Similar collections can be found congregating around and phagocytosing injured neurons **(neuronophagia).**

Ependymal cells line the ventricular system and the central canal of the spinal cord. Certain pathogens, particularly cytomegalovirus (CMV), can produce extensive ependymal injury, with typical viral inclusions. **Choroid plexus** is in continuity with the ependyma, and its specialized epithelial covering is responsible for the secretion of cerebrospinal fluid (CSF).

EDEMA, HERNIATION, AND HYDROCEPHALUS

The brain and spinal cord exist within the protective and rigid skull and spinal canal, with nerves and blood vessels passing through specific foramina. The advantage of housing the delicate CNS within such a protective environment is obvious, but this arrangement provides little room for brain parenchymal expansion in disease states. Disorders that may cause dangerous increases in brain volume within the fixed space of the skull include generalized cerebral edema, hydrocephalus, and mass lesions such as tumors.

Cerebral Edema

Cerebral edema is the accumulation of excess fluid within the brain parenchyma. There are two types, which often occur together particularly after generalized injury.

- *Vasogenic edema* occurs when the integrity of the normal blood-brain barrier is disrupted, allowing fluid to shift from the vascular compartment into the extracellular spaces of the brain. Vasogenic edema can be either localized (e.g., increased vascular permeability due to inflammation or in tumors) or generalized.
- *Cytotoxic edema* is an increase in intracellular fluid secondary to neuronal and glial cell membrane injury, as might follow generalized hypoxic-ischemic insult or after exposure to some toxins.

The edematous brain is softer than normal and often appears to "over fill" the cranial vault. In generalized edema the gyri are flattened, the intervening sulci are narrowed, and the ventricular cavities are compressed (Fig. 22–2).

Hydrocephalus

After being produced by the choroid plexus within the ventricles, CSF circulates through the ventricular system

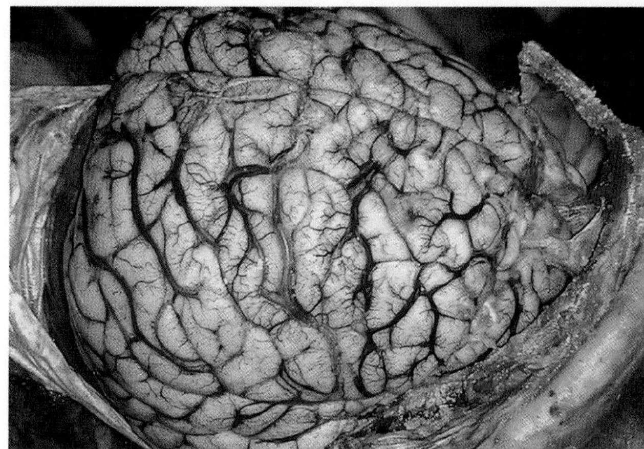

Figure 22–2 Cerebral edema. The surfaces of the gyri are flattened as a result of compression of the expanding brain by the dura mater and inner surface of the skull. Such changes are associated with a dangerous increase in intracranial pressure.

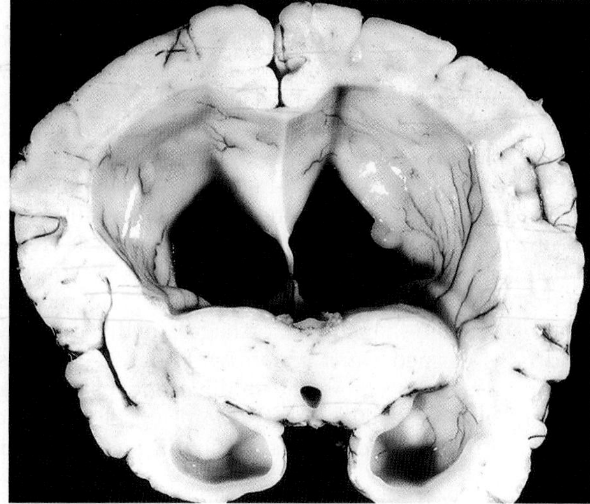

Figure 22–3 Hydrocephalus. Dilated lateral ventricles seen in a coronal section through the midthalamus.

and flows through the foramina of Luschka and Magendie into the subarachnoid space, where it is absorbed by arachnoid granulations. The balance between rates of generation and resorption regulates CSF volume.

Hydrocephalus refers to the accumulation of excessive CSF within the ventricular system. This disorder most often is a consequence of impaired flow or resorption; overproduction of CSF, typically seen with tumors of the choroid plexus, only rarely causes hydrocephalus. If there is a localized obstacle to CSF flow within the ventricular system, then a portion of the ventricles enlarges while the remainder does not. This pattern is referred to as *noncommunicating hydrocephalus* and most commonly is caused by masses obstructing the foramen of Monro or compressing the cerebral aqueduct. In *communicating hydrocephalus*, the entire ventricular system is enlarged; it is usually caused by reduced CSF resorption.

If hydrocephalus develops in infancy before closure of the cranial sutures, the head enlarges. Once the sutures fuse, hydrocephalus causes ventricular expansion and increased intracranial pressure, but no change in head circumference (Fig. 22-3). In contrast with these states, in which increased CSF volume is the primary process, a compensatory increase in CSF volume can also follow the loss of brain parenchyma (*hydrocephalus ex vacuo*), as after infarcts or with degenerative diseases.

Herniation

When the volume of tissue and fluid inside the skull increases beyond the limit permitted by compression of veins and displacement of CSF, intracranial pressure rises. The cranial vault is subdivided by rigid dural folds (falx and tentorium), and a focal expansion of the brain displaces it in relation to these partitions. If the expansion is sufficiently large, herniation occurs. Herniation often leads to "pinching" and vascular compromise of the compressed tissue, producing infarction, additional swelling, and further herniation. There are three main types of herniation (Fig. 22–4).

- *Subfalcine (cingulate)* herniation occurs when unilateral or asymmetric expansion of a cerebral hemisphere displaces the cingulate gyrus under the edge of falx. This may be associated with compression of the anterior cerebral artery.
- *Transtentorial (uncinate)* herniation occurs when the medial aspect of the temporal lobe is compressed against the free margin of the tentorium. As the temporal lobe is displaced, the third cranial nerve is compromised, resulting in pupillary dilation and impaired ocular

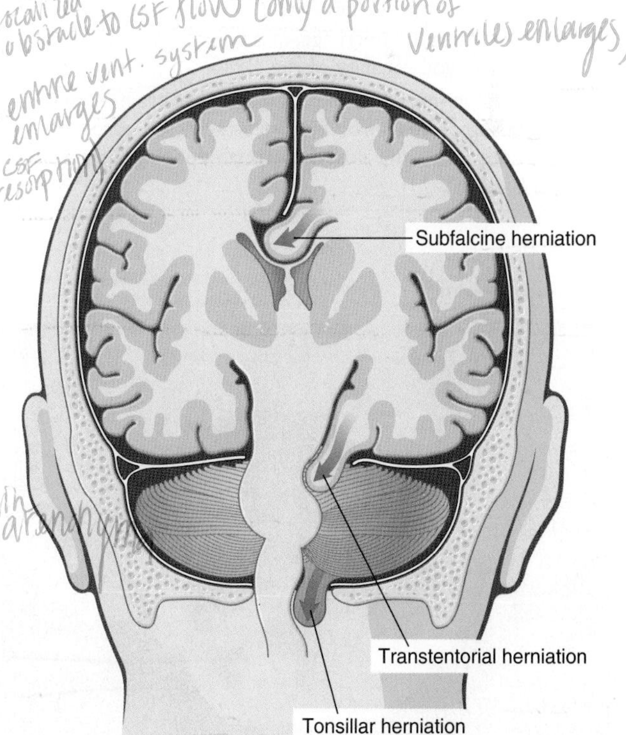

Figure 22–4 Herniation syndromes. Displacement of brain parenchyma across fixed barriers can be subfalcine, transtentorial, or tonsillar (into the foramen magnum).

movements on the side of the lesion ("blown pupil"). The posterior cerebral artery may also be compressed, resulting in ischemic injury to tissue supplied by that vessel, including the primary visual cortex. If the amount of displaced temporal lobe is large enough, the pressure on the midbrain can compress the contralateral cerebral peduncle against the tentorium, resulting in hemiparesis ipsilateral to the side of the herniation (a so-called false localizing sign). The compression of the peduncle creates a deformation known as Kernohan's notch. Progression of transtentorial herniation is often accompanied by linear or flame-shaped hemorrhages in the midbrain and pons, termed *Duret hemorrhages* (Fig. 22–5). These lesions usually occur in the midline and paramedian regions and are believed to be the result of tearing of penetrating veins and arteries supplying the upper brain stem.

- *Tonsillar* herniation refers to displacement of the cerebellar tonsils through the foramen magnum. This type of herniation is life-threatening, because it causes brain stem compression and compromises vital respiratory and cardiac centers in the medulla.

SUMMARY

Edema, Herniation, and Hydrocephalus

- Cerebral edema is the accumulation of excess fluid within the brain parenchyma. Hydrocephalus is defined as an increase in CSF volume within all or part of the ventricular system.
- Increases in brain volume (as a result of increased CSF volume, edema, hemorrhage, or tumor) raise the pressure inside the fixed capacity of the skull.
- Increases in pressure can damage the brain either by decreasing perfusion or by displacing tissue across dural partitions inside the skull or through openings in the skull (herniations).

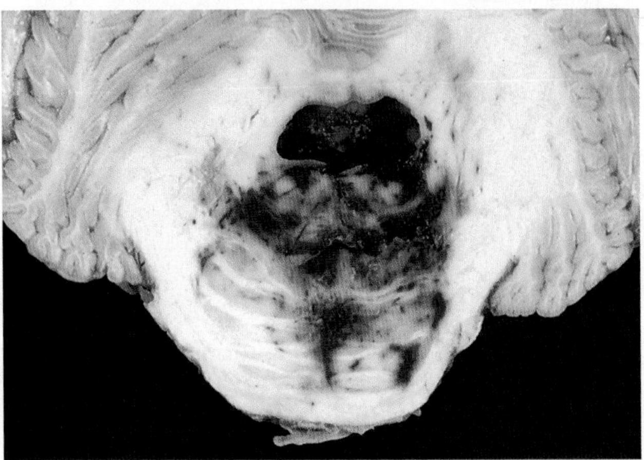

Figure 22–5 Duret hemorrhage. As mass effect displaces the brain downward, there is disruption of the vessels that enter the pons along the midline, leading to hemorrhage.

CEREBROVASCULAR DISEASES

Cerebrovascular diseases—the broad category of brain disorders caused by pathologic processes involving blood vessels—constitute a major cause of death in the developed world and are the most prevalent cause of neurologic morbidity. The three main pathogenic mechanisms are (1) thrombotic occlusion, (2) embolic occlusion, and (3) vascular rupture. *Stroke* is the clinical designation applied to all of these conditions when symptoms begin acutely. Thrombosis and embolism have similar consequences for the brain: loss of oxygen and metabolic substrates, resulting in infarction or ischemic injury of regions supplied by the affected vessel. Similar injury occurs globally when there is complete loss of perfusion, severe hypoxemia (e.g., hypovolemic shock), or profound hypoglycemia. Hemorrhage accompanies rupture of vessels and leads to direct tissue damage as well as secondary ischemic injury. Traumatic vascular injury is discussed separately in the context of trauma.

Hypoxia, Ischemia, and Infarction

The brain is a highly oxygen-dependent tissue that requires a continual supply of glucose and oxygen from the blood. Although it constitutes no more than 2% of body weight, the brain receives 15% of the resting cardiac output and is responsible for 20% of total body oxygen consumption. Cerebral blood flow normally remains stable over a wide range of blood pressure and intracranial pressure because of autoregulation of vascular resistance. The brain may be deprived of oxygen by two general mechanisms:

- *Functional hypoxia,* caused by a low partial pressure of oxygen (e.g., high altitude), impaired oxygen-carrying capacity (e.g., severe anemia, carbon monoxide poisoning), or inhibition of oxygen use by tissue (e.g., cyanide poisoning)
- *Ischemia,* either *transient* or *permanent,* due to tissue hypoperfusion, which can be caused by hypotension, vascular obstruction, or both

Global Cerebral Ischemia

Widespread ischemic-hypoxic injury can occur in the setting of severe systemic hypotension, usually when systolic pressures fall below 50 mm Hg, as in cardiac arrest, shock, and severe hypotension. The clinical outcome varies with the severity and duration of the insult. When the insult is mild, there may be only a transient postischemic confusional state, with eventual complete recovery. Neurons are more susceptible to hypoxic injury than are glial cells, and the most susceptible neurons are the pyramidal cells of the hippocampus and neocortex and Purkinje cells of the cerebellum. In some individuals, even mild or transient global ischemic insults may cause damage to these vulnerable areas. In severe global cerebral ischemia, widespread neuronal death occurs irrespective of regional vulnerability. Patients who survive often remain severely impaired neurologically and in a persistent vegetative state. Other patients meet the clinical criteria for so-called brain death, including evidence of diffuse cortical injury (isoelectric, or "flat," electroencephalogram) and brain stem damage, including absence of reflexes and respiratory drive. When patients with this form of irreversible injury are maintained on mechanical ventilation, the brain gradually undergoes autolysis, resulting in the so-called "respirator brain."

MORPHOLOGY

In the setting of global ischemia, the brain is swollen, with wide gyri and narrowed sulci. The cut surface shows poor demarcation between gray and white matter. The histopathologic changes that accompany irreversible ischemic injury (infarction) are grouped into three categories. **Early changes,** occurring 12 to 24 hours after the insult, include acute neuronal cell change (red neurons) (Fig. 22–1, *A*) characterized initially by microvacuolization, followed by cytoplasmic eosinophilia, and later nuclear pyknosis and karyorrhexis. Similar changes occur somewhat later in astrocytes and oligodendroglia. After this, the reaction to tissue damage begins with infiltration by neutrophils (Fig. 22–6, *A*). **Subacute changes,** occurring at 24 hours to 2 weeks, include necrosis of tissue, influx of macrophages, vascular proliferation, and reactive gliosis (Fig. 22–6, *B*). **Repair,** seen after 2 weeks, is characterized by removal of all necrotic tissue, loss of organized CNS structure, and gliosis (Fig. 22–6, *C*). The distribution of neuronal loss and gliosis in the neocortex typically is uneven with preservation of some layers and devastation of others—a pattern termed pseudolaminar necrosis.

Border zone ("watershed") infarcts are wedge-shaped areas of infarction that occur in regions of the brain and spinal cord that lie at the most distal portions of arterial territories. They are usually seen after hypotensive episodes. In the cerebral hemispheres, the border zone between the anterior and the middle cerebral artery distributions is at greatest risk. Damage to this region produces a band of necrosis over the cerebral convexity a few centimeters lateral to the interhemispheric fissure.

Focal Cerebral Ischemia

Cerebral arterial occlusion leads first to focal ischemia and then to infarction in the distribution of the compromised vessel. The size, location, and shape of the infarct and the extent of tissue damage that results may be modified by collateral blood flow. Specifically, collateral flow through the circle of Willis or cortical-leptomeningeal anastomoses can limit damage in some regions. By contrast, there is little if any collateral flow to structures such as the thalamus, basal ganglia, and deep white matter, which are supplied by deep penetrating vessels.

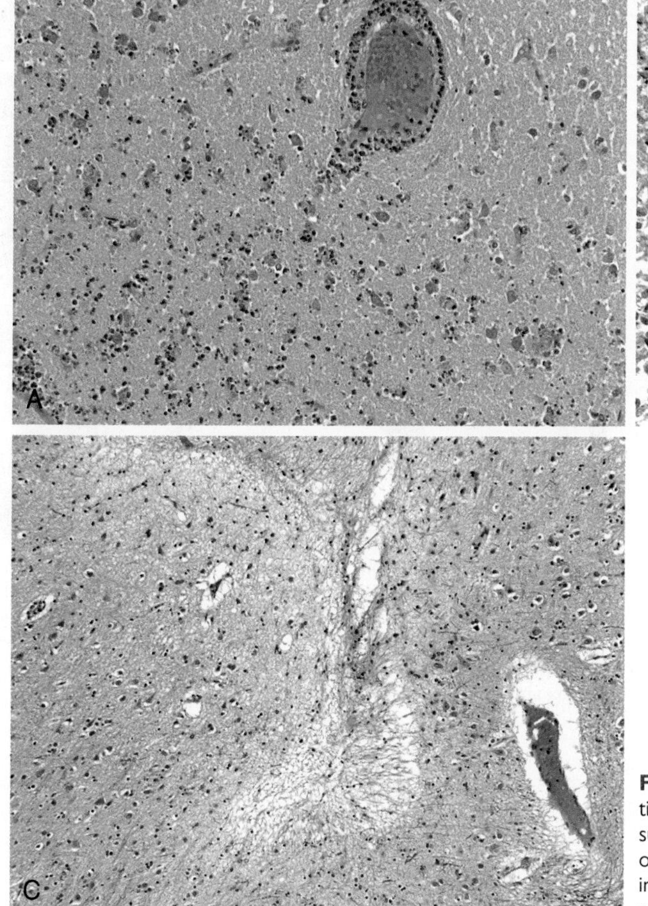

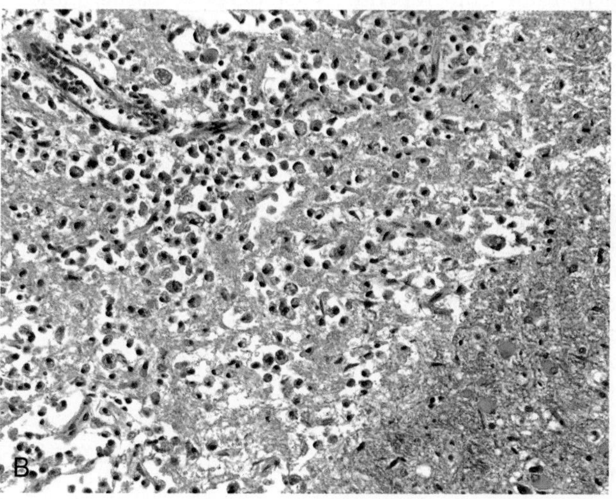

Figure 22–6 Cerebral infarction. **A,** Infiltration of a cerebral infarction by neutrophils begins at the edges of the lesion where the vascular supply is intact. **B,** By day 10, an area of infarction shows the presence of macrophages and surrounding reactive gliosis. **C,** Old intracortical infarcts are seen as areas of tissue loss with a modest amount of residual gliosis.

Embolic infarctions are more common than infarctions due to *thrombosis.* Cardiac mural thrombi are a frequent source of emboli; myocardial dysfunction, valvular disease, and atrial fibrillation are important predisposing factors. Thromboemboli also arise in arteries, most often from atheromatous plaques within the carotid arteries or aortic arch. Other emboli of venous origin cross over to the arterial circulation through cardiac defects and lodge in the brain (paradoxical embolism; see Chapter 3); these include thromboemboli from deep leg veins and fat emboli, usually following bone trauma. The territory of the middle cerebral artery, a direct extension of the internal carotid artery, is most frequently affected by embolic infarction. Emboli tend to lodge where vessels branch or in areas of stenosis, usually caused by *atherosclerosis.*

Thrombotic occlusions causing cerebral infarctions usually are superimposed on atherosclerotic plaques; common sites are the carotid bifurcation, the origin of the middle cerebral artery, and at either end of the basilar artery. These occlusions may be accompanied by anterograde extension, as well as thrombus fragmentation and distal embolization.

Infarcts can be divided into two broad groups based on their macroscopic and corresponding radiologic appearance (Fig. 22–7). *Nonhemorrhagic infarcts* result from acute vascular occlusions and can be treated with thrombolytic therapies, especially if identified shortly after presentation. This approach is contraindicated in *hemorrhagic infarcts,* which result from reperfusion of ischemic tissue, either through collaterals or after dissolution of emboli, and often produce multiple, sometimes confluent petechial hemorrhages (Fig. 22–7, *A* and *B*).

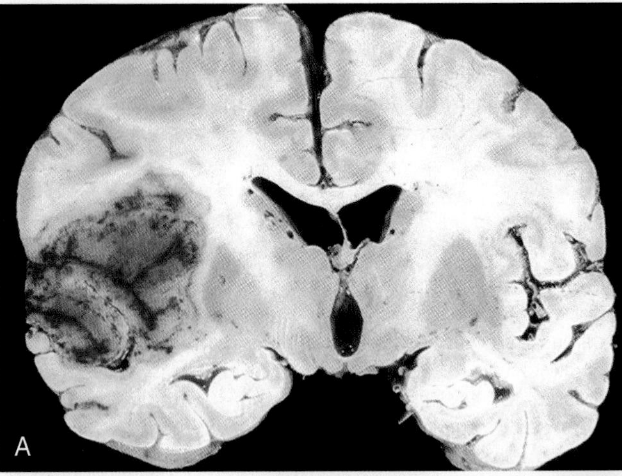

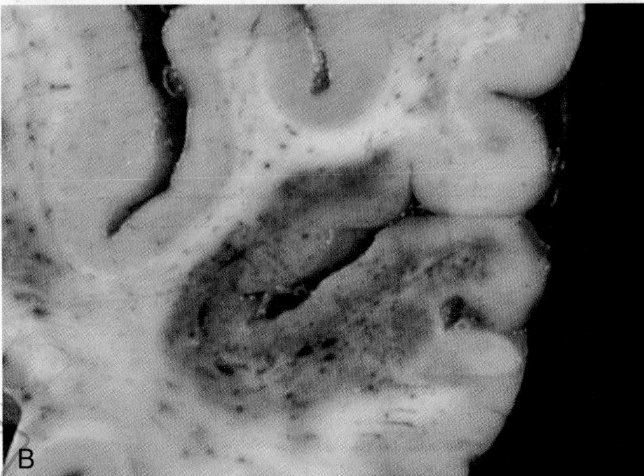

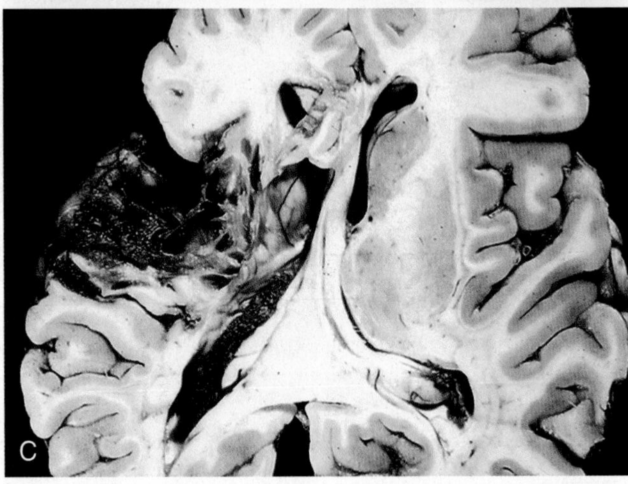

Figure 22–7 Cerebral infarction. **A,** Section of the brain showing a large, discolored, focally hemorrhagic region in the left middle cerebral artery distribution (hemorrhagic, or red, infarction). **B,** An infarct with punctate hemorrhages, consistent with ischemia-reperfusion injury, is present in the temporal lobe. **C,** Old cystic infarct shows destruction of cortex and surrounding gliosis.

MORPHOLOGY

The macroscopic appearance of a **nonhemorrhagic infarct** evolves over time. During the first 6 hours the tissue is unchanged in appearance, but by 48 hours, the tissue becomes pale, soft, and swollen. From days 2 to 10, the brain turns gelatinous and friable, and the boundary between normal and abnormal tissue becomes more distinct as edema resolves in the adjacent viable tissue. From day 10 to week 3, the tissue liquefies, eventually leaving a fluid-filled cavity lined by dark gray tissue, which gradually expands as dead tissue is resorbed (Fig. 22–7, *C*).

Microscopically, the tissue reaction follows a characteristic sequence. **After the first 12 hours,** ischemic neuronal change (red neurons) (Fig. 22–1, *A*) and cytotoxic and vasogenic edema predominate. Endothelial and glial cells, mainly astrocytes, swell, and myelinated fibers begin to disintegrate. **Up to 48 hours,** there is some neutrophilic emigration, which is followed by mononuclear phagocytic cells during the ensuing **2 to 3 weeks.** Macrophages containing myelin or red cell breakdown products may persist in the lesion for months to years. As the process of phagocytosis and liquefaction proceeds, astrocytes at the edges of the lesion progressively enlarge, divide, and develop a prominent network of cytoplasmic extensions.

After several months, the striking astrocytic nuclear and cytoplasmic enlargement regresses. In the wall of the cavity, astrocyte processes form a dense feltwork of glial fibers admixed with new capillaries and a few perivascular connective tissue fibers. In the cerebral cortex, the cavity is delimited from the meninges and subarachnoid space by a gliotic layer of tissue, derived from the molecular layer of the cortex. The pia and arachnoid are not affected and do not contribute to the healing process.

The microscopic picture and evolution of **hemorrhagic infarction** parallel those of ischemic infarction, with the addition of blood extravasation and resorption. In persons with coagulopathies, hemorrhagic infarcts may be associated with extensive intracerebral hematomas.

Intracranial Hemorrhage

Hemorrhages within the brain are associated with (1) hypertension and other diseases leading to vascular wall injury, (2) structural lesions such as arteriovenous and cavernous malformations, and (3) tumors. Subarachnoid hemorrhages most commonly are caused by ruptured aneurysms but also occur with other vascular malformations. Subdural or epidural hemorrhages usually are associated with trauma.

Primary Brain Parenchymal Hemorrhage

Spontaneous (nontraumatic) intraparenchymal hemorrhages are most common in mid- to late adult life, with a peak incidence at about 60 years of age. Most are due to the rupture of a small intraparenchymal vessel. Hypertension is the leading underlying cause, and brain hemorrhage accounts for roughly 15% of deaths among persons with chronic hypertension. Intracerebral hemorrhage can be clinically devastating when it affects large portions of the brain or extends into the ventricular system; alternatively, it can affect small regions and be clinically silent. Hypertensive intraparenchymal hemorrhages typically occur in the basal ganglia, thalamus, pons, and cerebellum (Fig. 22–8), with the location and the size of the bleed determining its clinical manifestations. If the person survives the acute event, gradual resolution of the hematoma ensues, sometimes with considerable clinical improvement.

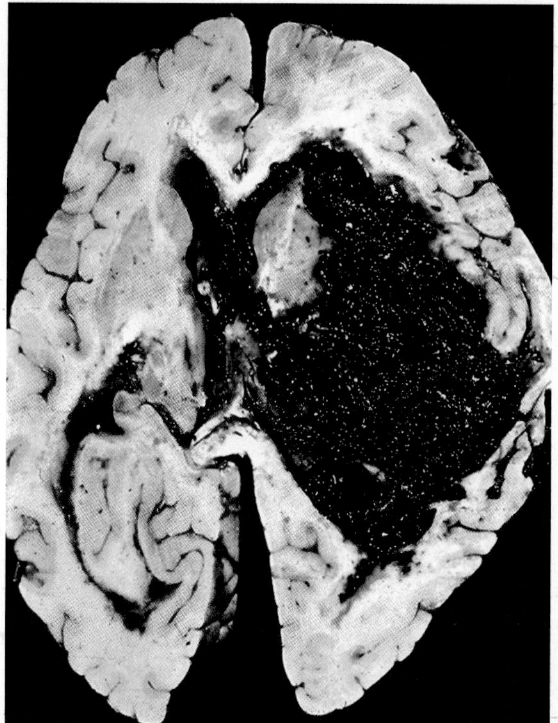

Figure 22–8 Cerebral hemorrhage. Massive hypertensive hemorrhage rupturing into a lateral ventricle.

MORPHOLOGY

Acute hemorrhages are characterized by extravasated blood, which compresses the adjacent parenchyma. With time, hemorrhages are converted to a cavity with a brown, discolored rim. On microscopic examination, early lesions consist of clotted blood surrounded by brain tissue showing anoxic neuronal and glial changes as well as edema. Eventually the edema resolves, pigment- and lipid-laden macrophages appear, and proliferation of reactive astrocytes becomes visible at the periphery of the lesion. The cellular events then follow the same time course observed after cerebral infarction.

Cerebral Amyloid Angiopathy

Cerebral amyloid angiopathy (CAA) is a disease in which amyloidogenic peptides, typically the same ones found in Alzheimer disease (discussed later), deposit in the walls of medium- and small-caliber meningeal and cortical vessels. The amyloid confers a rigid, pipelike appearance and stains with Congo red. Amyloid deposition weakens vessel walls and increases the risk of hemorrhages, which differ in distribution from those associated with hypertension. Specifically, CAA-associated hemorrhages often occur in the lobes of the cerebral cortex (*lobar hemorrhages*).

Subarachnoid Hemorrhage and Saccular Aneurysms

The most frequent cause of clinically significant nontraumatic subarachnoid hemorrhage is rupture of a *saccular (berry) aneurysm*. Hemorrhage into the subarachnoid space also may result from vascular malformation, trauma (usually associated with other signs of the injury), rupture of an intracerebral hemorrhage into the ventricular system, hematologic disturbances, and tumors.

Rupture can occur at any time, but in about one third of cases it is associated with acute increases in intracranial pressure, such as with straining at stool or sexual orgasm. Blood under arterial pressure is forced into the subarachnoid space, and the patient is stricken with sudden, excruciating headache (classically described as "the worst headache I've ever had") and rapidly loses consciousness. Between 25% and 50% of affected persons die from the first bleed, and recurrent bleeds are common in survivors. Not surprisingly, the prognosis worsens with each bleeding episode.

About 90% of saccular aneurysms occur in the anterior circulation near major arterial branch points (Fig. 22–9); multiple aneurysms exist in 20% to 30% of cases. Although they are sometimes referred to as *congenital,* they are not present at birth but develop over time because of underlying defects in the vessel media. There is an increased risk of aneurysms in patients with autosomal dominant polycystic kidney disease (Chapter 13), as well as those with genetic disorders of extracellular matrix proteins. Overall, roughly 1.3% of aneurysms bleed per year, with the

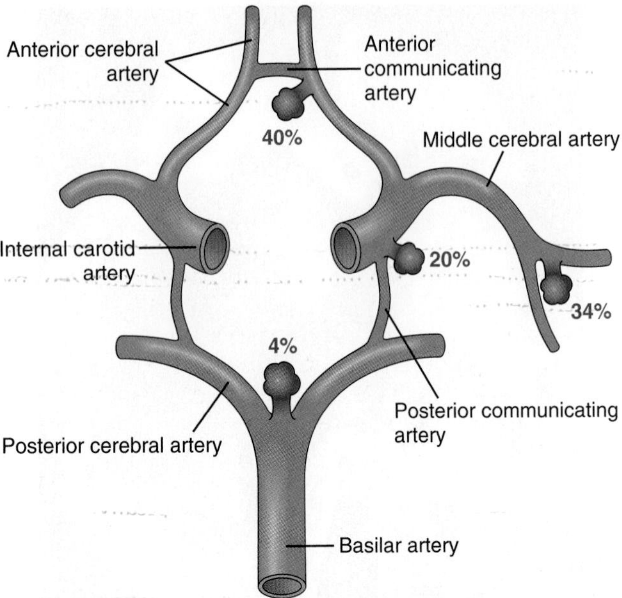

Figure 22–9 Common sites of saccular aneurysms.

probability of rupture increasing nonlinearly with size. For example, aneurysms larger than 1 cm in diameter have a roughly 50% risk of bleeding per year. In the early period after a subarachnoid hemorrhage, there is an additional risk of ischemic injury from vasospasm of other vessels. Healing and the attendant meningeal fibrosis and scarring sometimes obstruct CSF flow or disrupt CSF resorption, leading to hydrocephalus.

MORPHOLOGY

An unruptured saccular aneurysm is a thin-walled outpouching of an artery (Fig. 22–10). Beyond the neck of the aneurysm, the muscular wall and intimal elastic lamina are absent, such that the aneurysm sac is lined only by thickened hyalinized intima. The adventitia covering the sac is continuous with that of the parent artery. Rupture usually occurs at the apex of the sac, releasing blood into the subarachnoid space or the substance of the brain, or both.

In addition to saccular aneurysms, atherosclerotic, mycotic, traumatic, and dissecting aneurysms also occur intracranially. The last three types (like saccular aneurysms) most often are found in the anterior circulation, whereas atherosclerotic aneurysms frequently are fusiform and most commonly involve the basilar artery. Nonsaccular aneurysms usually manifest with cerebral infarction due to vascular occlusion instead of subarachnoid hemorrhage.

Vascular Malformations

Vascular malformations of the brain are classified into four principal types based on the nature of the abnormal vessels: *arteriovenous malformations* (AVMs), *cavernous malformations, capillary telangiectasias,* and *venous angiomas.* AVMs, the most common of these, affect males twice as frequently as females and most commonly manifest between the ages of 10 and 30 years with seizures, an intracerebral hemorrhage, or a subarachnoid hemorrhage. Large AVMs occurring in the newborn period can lead to high-output congestive heart failure because of blood shunting from arteries to veins. The risk of bleeding makes AVM the most dangerous type of vascular malformation. Multiple AVMs can be seen in the setting of hereditary hemorrhagic telangiectasia, an autosomal dominant condition often associated with mutations affecting the TGFβ pathway.

MORPHOLOGY

AVMs may involve subarachnoid vessels extending into brain parenchyma or occur exclusively within the brain. On gross inspection, they resemble a tangled network of wormlike

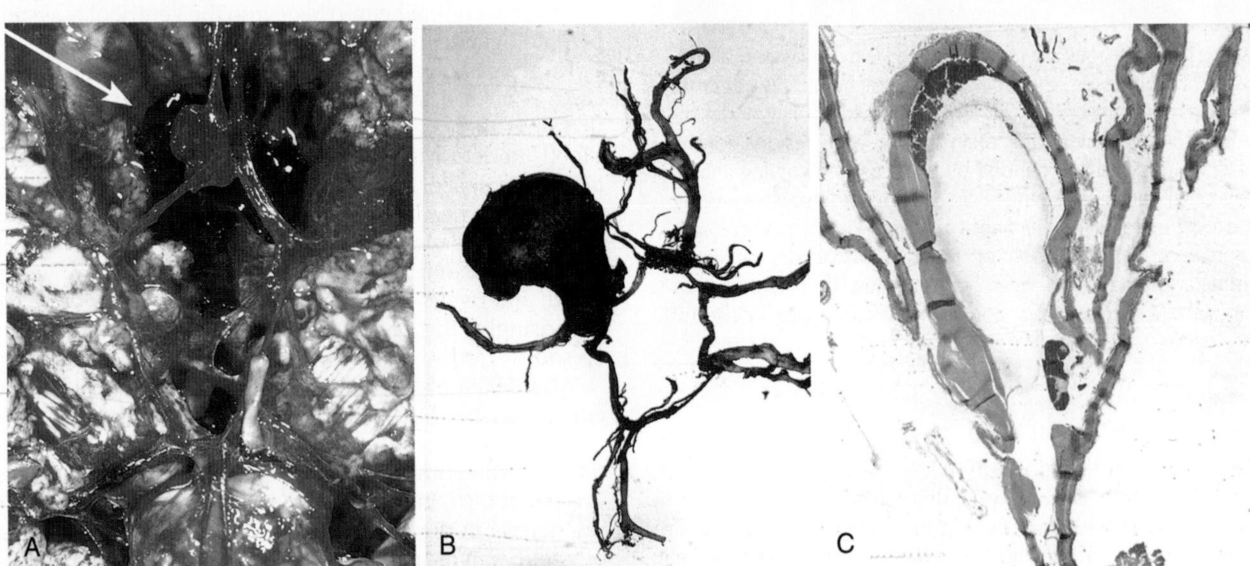

Figure 22–10 Saccular aneurysms. **A,** View of the base of the brain, dissected to show the circle of Willis with an aneurysm of the anterior cerebral artery *(arrow)*. **B,** Circle of Willis dissected to show large aneurysm. **C,** Section through a saccular aneurysm showing the hyalinized fibrous vessel wall. Hematoxylin-eosin stain.

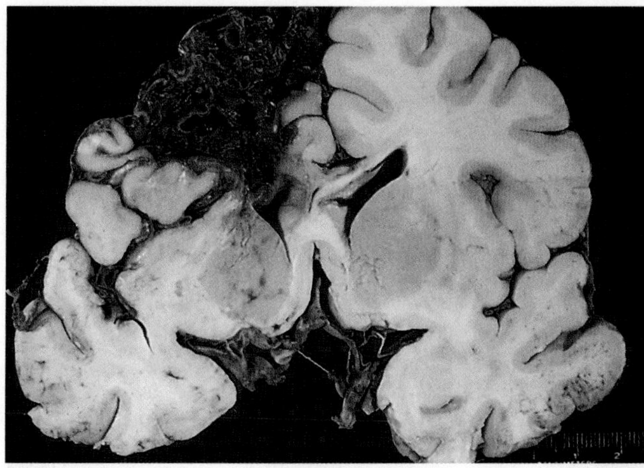

Figure 22–11 Arteriovenous malformation.

vascular channels (Fig. 22–11). Microscopic examination shows enlarged blood vessels separated by gliotic tissue, often with evidence of previous hemorrhage. Some vessels can be recognized as arteries with duplicated and fragmented internal elastic lamina, while others show marked thickening or partial replacement of the media by hyalinized connective tissue.

Cavernous malformations consist of distended, loosely organized vascular channels with thin collagenized walls without intervening nervous tissue. They occur most often in the cerebellum, pons, and subcortical regions, and have a low blood flow without significant arteriovenous shunting. Foci of old hemorrhage, infarction, and calcification frequently surround the abnormal vessels.

Capillary telangiectasias are microscopic foci of dilated thin-walled vascular channels separated by relatively normal brain parenchyma that occur most frequently in the pons. **Venous angiomas** (varices) consist of aggregates of ectatic venous channels. These latter two types of vascular malformation are unlikely to bleed or to cause symptoms, and most are incidental findings.

Other Vascular Diseases

Hypertensive Cerebrovascular Disease

Hypertension causes *hyaline arteriolar sclerosis* of the deep penetrating arteries and arterioles that supply the basal ganglia, the hemispheric white matter, and the brain stem. Affected arteriolar walls are weakened and are more vulnerable to rupture. In some instances, minute aneurysms (*Charcot-Bouchard microaneurysms*) form in vessels less than 300 μm in diameter. In addition to massive intracerebral hemorrhage (discussed earlier), several other pathologic brain processes are related to hypertension.

- *Lacunes* or *lacunar infarcts* are small cavitary infarcts, just a few millimeters in size, found most commonly in the deep gray matter (basal ganglia and thalamus), the internal capsule, the deep white matter, and the pons. They are caused by occlusion of a single penetrating branch of a large cerebral artery. Depending on their location, lacunes can be silent clinically or cause significant neurologic impairment.
- *Rupture of the small-caliber penetrating vessels* may occur, leading to the development of small hemorrhages. In time, these hemorrhages resorb, leaving behind a slitlike cavity (*slit hemorrhage*) surrounded by brownish discoloration.
- *Acute hypertensive encephalopathy* most often is associated with sudden sustained rises in diastolic blood pressure to greater than 130 mm Hg. It is characterized by increased intracranial pressure and global cerebral dysfunction, manifesting as headaches, confusion, vomiting, convulsions, and sometimes coma. Rapid therapeutic intervention to reduce the intracranial pressure is essential. Postmortem examination may show brain edema, with or without transtentorial or tonsillar herniation. Petechiae and fibrinoid necrosis of arterioles in the gray and white matter may be seen microscopically.

Vasculitis

A variety of inflammatory processes involving blood vessels may compromise blood flow and cause cerebral infarction. Infectious arteritis of small and large vessels was previously seen mainly in association with syphilis and tuberculosis, but is now more often caused by opportunistic infections (such as aspergillosis, herpes zoster, or CMV) arising in the setting of immunosuppression. Some systemic forms of vasculitis, such as polyarteritis nodosa, may involve cerebral vessels and cause single or multiple infarcts throughout the brain. *Primary angiitis of the CNS* is a form of vasculitis involving multiple small to medium-sized parenchymal and subarachnoid vessels that is characterized by chronic inflammation, multinucleate giant cells (with or without granuloma formation), and destruction of vessel walls. Affected persons present with a diffuse encephalopathy, often with cognitive dysfunction. Treatment consists of an appropriate regimen of immunosuppressive agents.

SUMMARY

Cerebrovascular Diseases

- *Stroke* is the clinical term for acute-onset neurologic deficits resulting from hemorrhagic or obstructive vascular lesions.
- Cerebral infarction follows loss of blood supply and can be widespread or focal, or affect regions with the least robust vascular supply ("watershed" infarcts).
- Focal cerebral infarcts are most commonly embolic; with subsequent dissolution of an embolism and reperfusion, a nonhemorrhagic infarct can become hemorrhagic.
- Primary intraparenchymal hemorrhages typically are due to either hypertension (most commonly in white matter, deep gray matter, or posterior fossa contents) or cerebral amyloid angiopathy.
- Spontaneous subarachnoid hemorrhage usually is caused by a structural vascular abnormality, such as an aneurysm or arteriovenous malformation.

CENTRAL NERVOUS SYSTEM TRAUMA

Trauma to the brain and spinal cord is a significant cause of death and disability. The severity and site of injury affect the outcome: injury of several cubic centimeters of brain parenchyma may be clinically silent (if in the frontal lobe), severely disabling (spinal cord), or fatal (involving the brain stem).

A blow to the head may be *penetrating* or *blunt;* it may cause an *open* or a *closed* injury. The magnitude and distribution of resulting traumatic brain lesions depend on the shape of the object causing the trauma, the force of impact, and whether the head is in motion at the time of injury. Severe brain damage can occur in the absence of external signs of head injury, and conversely, severe lacerations and even skull fractures do not necessarily indicate damage to the underlying brain. When the brain is damaged, the injuries may involve the parenchyma, the vasculature, or both.

Recent evidence suggests that repetitive episodes of trauma (such as occurs in athletes participating in contact sports) can lead to later development of neurodegenerative processes. In addition to a long-recognized association of trauma with the risk of Alzheimer disease, a distinct form of trauma-associated degeneration has been described, *chronic traumatic encephalopathy,* which is characterized by a unique pattern of intraneuronal tau protein inclusions (described later).

Traumatic Parenchymal Injuries

When an object impacts the head, brain injury may occur at the site of impact—a *coup injury*—or opposite the site of impact on the other side of the brain—a *contrecoup injury.* Both coup and contrecoup lesions are contusions, with comparable gross and microscopic appearances. A *contusion* is caused by rapid tissue displacement, disruption of vascular channels, and subsequent hemorrhage, tissue injury, and edema. Since they are closest to the skull, the crests of the gyri are the part of the brain that is most susceptible to traumatic injury. Contusions are common in regions of the brain overlying rough and irregular inner skull surfaces, such as the orbitofrontal regions and the temporal lobe tips. Penetration of the brain by a projectile such as a bullet or a skull fragment from a fracture causes a laceration, with tissue tearing, vascular disruption, and hemorrhage.

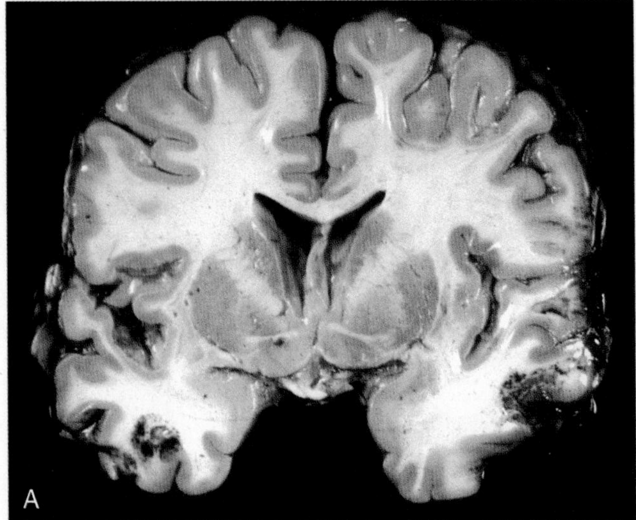

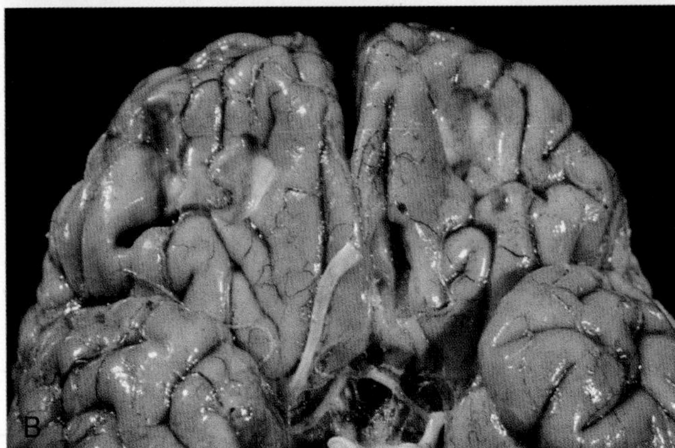

Figure 22–12 Cerebral trauma. **A,** Acute contusions are present in both temporal lobes, with areas of hemorrhage and tissue disruption. **B,** Remote contusions, seen as discolored *yellow* areas, are present on the inferior frontal surface of this brain.

MORPHOLOGY

On cross-section, contusions are wedge-shaped, with the widest aspect closest to the point of impact (Fig. 22–12, *A*). Within a few hours of injury, blood extravasates throughout the involved tissue, across the width of the cerebral cortex, and into the white matter and subarachnoid spaces. Although functional effects are seen earlier, morphologic evidence of injury in the neuronal cell body (nuclear pyknosis, cytoplasmic eosinophilia, cellular disintegration) takes about 24 hours to appear. The inflammatory response to the injured tissue follows its usual course, with neutrophils preceding the appearance of macrophages. In contrast with ischemic lesions, in which the superficial layer of cortex may be preserved, trauma affects the superficial layers most severely.

Old traumatic lesions have a characteristic macroscopic appearance: They are depressed, retracted, yellowish brown patches involving the crests of gyri (Fig. 22–12, *B*). More extensive hemorrhagic regions of brain trauma give rise to larger cavitary lesions, which can resemble remote infarcts. In sites of old contusions, gliosis and residual hemosiderin-laden macrophages predominate.

Although contusions are more easily seen, trauma can also cause more subtle but widespread injury to axons within the brain (called **diffuse axonal injury**), sometimes with devastating consequences. The movement of one region of brain relative to another is thought to disrupt axonal integrity and function. Angular acceleration, even in the absence of impact, may cause axonal injury as well as hemorrhage. As many as 50% of patients who develop coma shortly after trauma are believed to have white matter damage and diffuse axonal injury. Although these injuries may be widespread, the lesions usually are asymmetric and are most commonly found near the angles of the lateral ventricles and in the brain stem. They take the form of axonal swellings that appear within hours of the injury. These are best demonstrated with silver stains or by immunohistochemical stains for axonal proteins.

Concussion describes reversible altered consciousness from head injury in the absence of contusion. The characteristic transient neurologic dysfunction includes loss of consciousness, temporary respiratory arrest, and loss of reflexes. Although neurologic recovery is complete, amnesia for the event persists. The pathogenesis of the sudden disruption of nervous activity is unknown.

Traumatic Vascular Injury

CNS trauma often directly disrupts vessel walls, leading to hemorrhage. Depending on the affected vessel, the hemorrhage may be *epidural, subdural, subarachnoid,* or *intraparenchymal* (Fig. 22–13, *A*), occurring alone or in combination. Subarachnoid and intraparenchymal hemorrhages most often occur at sites of contusions and lacerations.

Epidural Hematoma

Dural vessels—especially the middle meningeal artery—are vulnerable to traumatic injury. In infants, traumatic displacement of the easily deformable skull may tear a vessel, even in the absence of a skull fracture. In children and adults, by contrast, tears involving dural vessels almost always stem from skull fractures. Once a vessel is torn, blood accumulating under arterial pressure can dissect the tightly applied dura away from the inner skull surface (Fig. 22–13, *B*), producing a hematoma that compresses the brain surface. *Clinically, patients can be lucid for several hours between the moment of trauma and the development of neurologic signs.* An epidural hematoma may expand rapidly and constitutes a neurosurgical emergency necessitating prompt drainage and repair to prevent death.

Subdural Hematoma

Rapid movement of the brain during trauma can tear the bridging veins that extend from the cerebral hemispheres through the subarachnoid and subdural space to the dural sinuses. Their disruption produces bleeding into the subdural space. *In patients with brain atrophy, the bridging veins are stretched out, and the brain has additional space within which to move, accounting for the higher rate of subdural hematomas in elderly persons.* Infants also are susceptible to

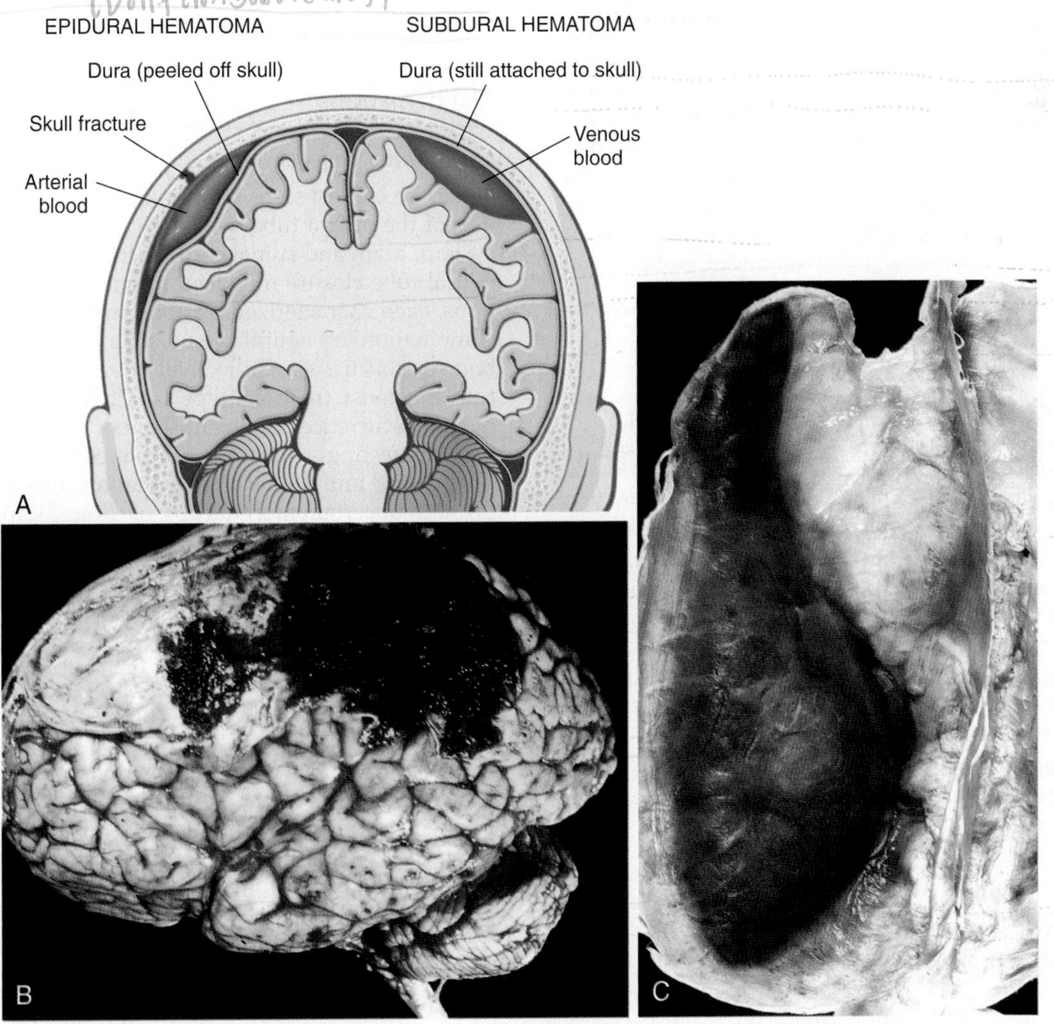

Figure 22–13 Traumatic intracranial hemorrhages. **A,** Epidural hematoma (*left*) in which rupture of a meningeal artery, usually associated with a skull fracture, has led to accumulation of arterial blood between the dura and the skull. In a subdural hematoma (*right*), damage to bridging veins between the brain and the superior sagittal sinus has led to the accumulation of blood between the dura and the arachnoid. **B,** Epidural hematoma covering a portion of the dura. **C,** Large organizing subdural hematoma attached to the dura.

(B, Courtesy of the late Dr. Raymond D. Adams, Massachusetts General Hospital, Boston, Massachusetts.)

ematomas because their bridging veins are
.

hematomas typically become manifest within ours after injury. They are most common over spects of the cerebral hemispheres and may be bilateral. Neurologic signs are attributable to the pressure exerted on the adjacent brain. Symptoms may be localizing but more often are nonlocalizing, taking the form of headache, confusion, and slowly progressive neurologic deterioration.

MORPHOLOGY

An acute subdural hematoma appears as a collection of freshly clotted blood apposed to the contour of the brain surface, without extension into the depths of sulci (Fig. 22–13, C). The underlying brain is flattened, and the subarachnoid space is often clear. Typically, venous bleeding is self-limited; breakdown and organization of the hematoma take place over time. Subdural hematomas organize by lysis of the clot (about 1 week), growth of granulation tissue from the dural surface into the hematoma (2 weeks), and fibrosis (1 to 3 months). Organized hematomas are attached to the dura, but not to the underlying arachnoid. Fibrosing lesions may eventually retract, leaving only a thin layer of connective tissue ("subdural membranes"). Subdural hematomas commonly rebleed (resulting in **chronic subdural hematomas**), presumably from the thin-walled vessels of the granulation tissue, leading to microscopic findings consistent with hemorrhages of varying age. Symptomatic subdural hematomas are treated by surgical removal of the blood and associated reactive tissue.

SUMMARY

Central Nervous System Trauma

- Physical injury to the brain can occur when the inside of the skull comes into forceful contact with the brain.
- In blunt trauma, if the head is mobile there may be brain injury both at the original point of contact (coup injury) and on the opposite side of the brain (contrecoup injury) owing to impacts with the skull.
- Rapid displacement of the head and brain can tear axons (diffuse axonal injury), often causing immediate severe, irreversible neurologic deficits.
- Traumatic tearing of blood vessels leads to epidural hematoma, subdural hematoma, or subarachnoid hemorrhage.

CONGENITAL MALFORMATIONS AND PERINATAL BRAIN INJURY

The incidence of CNS malformations, giving rise to mental retardation, cerebral palsy, or neural tube defects, is estimated at 1% to 2%. Malformations of the brain are more common in the setting of multiple birth defects. Prenatal or perinatal insults may either interfere with normal CNS development or cause tissue damage. Since different parts of the brain develop at different times during gestation, the timing of an injury will be reflected in the pattern of malformation; earlier events typically lead to more severe phenotypes. Mutations affecting genes that regulate the differentiation, maturation, or intercellular communication of neurons or glial cells can cause CNS malformation or dysfunction. Additionally, various chemicals and infectious agents have teratogenic effects.

Not all developmental disorders are characterized by specific, recognizable gross or microscopic findings, yet such disorders may nevertheless be associated with profound neuronal dysfunction. Genetic underpinnings for various forms of *autism* have emerged recently; many of the implicated genes contribute to the development or maintenance of synaptic connections. Similarly, *Rett syndrome* is an X-linked dominant disorder associated with mutations in the gene encoding methyl-CpG–binding protein-2 (MeCP2), a regulator of epigenetic modifications of chromatin. Development in affected girls initially is normal, but neurologic deficits affecting cognition and movement appear by the age of 1 to 2 years, highlighting the importance of epigenetic processes in neuronal development and synaptic plasticity.

Malformations

Neural Tube Defects

On of the earliest steps in brain development is the formation of the neural tube, which gives rise to the ventricular system, brain and spinal cord. Partial failure or reversal of neural tube closure may lead to one of several malformations, each characterized by abnormalities involving some combination of neural tissue, meninges, and overlying bone or soft tissues. Collectively, *neural tube defects* constitute the most frequent type of CNS malformation. The overall recurrence risk in subsequent pregnancies is 4% to 5%, suggesting a genetic component. Folate deficiency during the initial weeks of gestation also increases risk through uncertain mechanisms; of clinical importance, prenatal vitamins containing folate can reduce the risk of neural tube defects by up to 70%. The combination of imaging studies and maternal screening for elevated α-fetoprotein has increased the early detection of neural tube defects.

The most common defects involve the posterior end of the neural tube, from which the spinal cord forms. These can range from asymptomatic bony defects (*spina bifida occulta*) to severe malformation consisting of a flat, disorganized segment of spinal cord associated with an overlying meningeal outpouching. *Myelomeningocele* is an extension of CNS tissue through a defect in the vertebral column that occurs most commonly in the lumbosacral region (Fig. 22–14). Patients have motor and sensory deficits in the lower extremities and problems with bowel and bladder control. The clinical problems derive from the abnormal spinal cord segment and often are compounded by infections extending from the thin or ulcerated overlying skin.

At the other end of the developing CNS, *anencephaly* is a malformation of the anterior end of the neural tube that leads to the absence of the brain and the top of skull. An

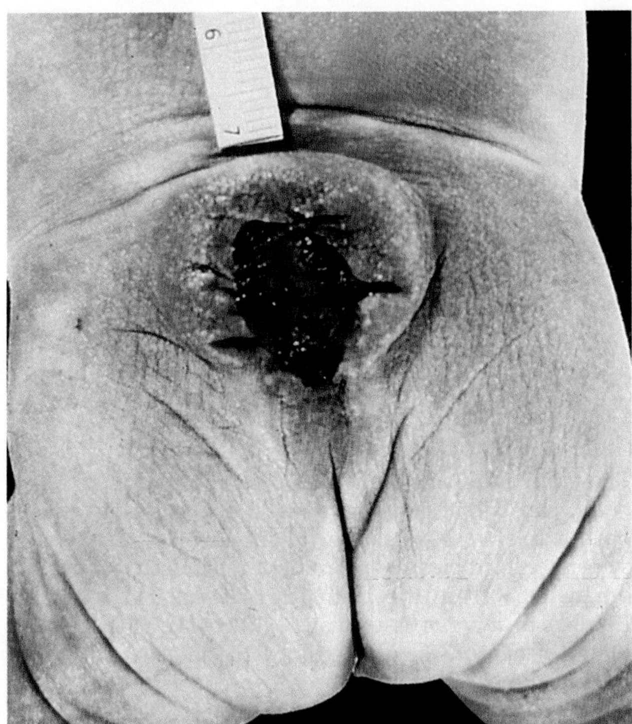

Figure 22–14 Myelomeningocele. Both meninges and spinal cord parenchyma are included in the cystlike structure visible just above the buttocks.

encephalocele is a diverticulum of malformed CNS tissue extending through a defect in the cranium. It most often involves the occipital region or the posterior fossa. When it occurs anteriorly, brain tissue can extend into the sinuses.

Forebrain Malformations

In certain malformations, the volume of the brain is abnormally large (*megalencephaly*) or small (*microencephaly*). Microencephaly, by far the more common of the two, usually is associated with a small head as well (microcephaly). It has a wide range of associations, including chromosome abnormalities, fetal alcohol syndrome, and human immunodeficiency virus type 1 (HIV-1) infection acquired in utero. The unifying feature is decreased generation of neurons destined for the cerebral cortex. During the early stages of brain development, as progenitor cells proliferate in the subependymal zone, the balance between cells leaving the progenitor population to begin migration to the cortex and those remaining in the proliferating pool affects the overall number of neurons and glial cells generated. If too many cells leave the progenitor pool prematurely, there is inadequate generation of mature neurons, leading to a small brain.

Disruption of neuronal migration and differentiation during development can lead to abnormalities of gyration and the six-layered neocortical architecture, often taking the form of neurons ending up in the wrong anatomic location. Various mutations in genes that control migration result in these malformations, which include the following:

- *Lissencephaly* (*agyria*) or, with more patchy involvement, *pachygyria,* is characterized by absent gyration leading to a smooth-surfaced brain. The cortex is abnormally thickened and usually has only four layers. Many forms of lissencephaly are associated with defects in genes that control neuronal migration.
- *Polymicrogyria* is characterized by an increased number of irregularly formed gyri that result in a bumpy or cobblestone-like surface. These changes can be focal or widespread. The normal cortical architecture can be altered in various ways, and adjacent gyri often show fusion of the superficial molecular layer.
- *Holoprosencephaly* is characterized by a disruption of the normal midline patterning. Mild forms may just show absence of the olfactory bulbs and related structures (arrhinencephaly). In severe forms the brain is not divided into hemispheres or lobes, and this anomaly may be associated with facial midline defects such as cyclopia. Holoprosencephaly as well as polymicrogyria can be the result of acquired or genetically determined disruption of normal development. Several single-gene defects including mutations in sonic hedgehog have been linked to holoprosencephaly.
- Other examples are focally disordered cortex (confusingly called *dysplastic cortex*) and neurons stranded beneath the cortex, sometimes as nodules and other times as bands.

Posterior Fossa Anomalies

The most common malformations in this region of the brain result in misplacement or absence of portions of the cerebellum. The *Arnold-Chiari malformation* (Chiari type II malformation) combines a small posterior fossa with a misshapen midline cerebellum and downward extension of the vermis through the foramen magnum; hydrocephalus and a lumbar myelomeningocele typically are also present. The far milder *Chiari type I malformation* has low-lying cerebellar tonsils that extend through the foramen magnum. Excess tissue in the foramen magnum results in partial obstruction of CSF flow and compression of the medulla, with symptoms of headache or cranial nerve deficits often manifesting only in adult life. Surgical intervention can alleviate the symptoms.

Syndromes characterized by "missing" cerebellar tissue include *Dandy-Walker malformation,* characterized by an enlarged posterior fossa, absence of the cerebellar vermis, and a large midline cyst, and *Joubert syndrome,* in which there is absence of the vermis and brain stem abnormalities resulting in eye movement problems and disrupted respiratory patterns. A range of recessive genetic lesions have been found to cause Joubert syndrome, with many involving alterations of the primary cilium.

Spinal Cord Abnormalities

In addition to neural tube defects, structural alterations of the spinal cord can occur that are not associated with abnormalities of the bony spine or overlying skin. These include expansions of the ependyma-lined central canal of the cord (*hydromyelia*) or development of fluid-filled cleft-like cavities in the inner portion of the cord (*syringomyelia, syrinx*). These lesions are surrounded by dense reactive gliosis, often with Rosenthal fibers. A syrinx also may develop after trauma or with intramedullary spinal tumors.

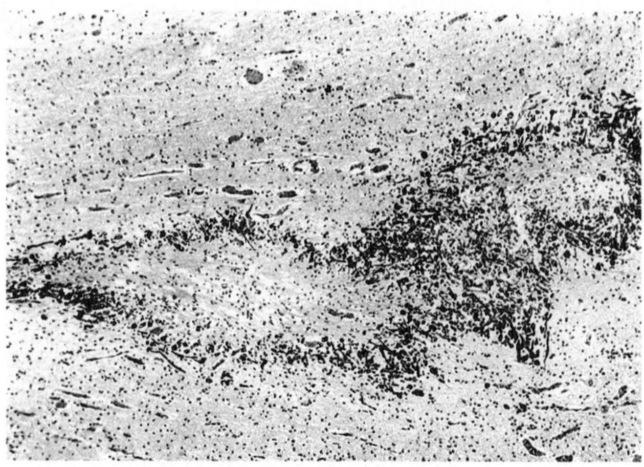

Figure 22–15 Perinatal brain injury. This specimen from a patient with periventricular leukomalacia contains a central focus of white matter necrosis with a peripheral rim of mineralized axonal processes.

Perinatal Brain Injury

A variety of exogenous factors can injure the developing brain. Injuries that occur early in gestation may destroy brain tissue without evoking reactive changes, sometimes making them difficult to distinguish from malformations. Brain injury occurring in the perinatal period is an important cause of childhood neurologic disability. *Cerebral palsy* is a term for nonprogressive neurologic motor deficits characterized by spasticity, dystonia, ataxia or athetosis, and paresis attributable to injury occurring during the prenatal and perinatal periods. Signs and symptoms may not be apparent at birth and only declare themselves later, well after the causal event.

The two major types of injury that occur in the perinatal period are hemorrhages and infarcts. These differ from the otherwise similar lesions in adults in terms of their locations and the tissue reactions they engender. In premature infants, there is an increased risk of *intraparenchymal hemorrhage* within the germinal matrix, most often adjacent to the anterior horn of the lateral ventricle. Hemorrhages may extend into the ventricular system and from there to the subarachnoid space, sometimes causing hydrocephalus. Infarcts may occur in the supratentorial periventricular white matter (*periventricular leukomalacia*), especially in premature babies. The residua of these infarcts are chalky yellow plaques consisting of discrete regions of white matter necrosis and mineralization (Fig. 22–15). When severe enough to involve the gray and white matter, large cystic lesions can develop throughout the hemispheres, a condition termed *multicystic encephalopathy*.

SUMMARY

Congenital Malformations and Perinatal Brain Injury

- Malformations of the brain can occur because of genetic factors or external insults.
- The developmental timing and position of the injury determine its pattern and characteristics.
- Various malformations stem from failure of neural tube closure, improper formation of neural structures, and altered neuronal migration.
- Perinatal brain injury mostly takes one of two forms: (1) hemorrhage, often in the region of the germinal matrix with the risk of extension into the ventricular system; and (2) ischemic infarcts, leading to periventricular leukomalacia.

INFECTIONS OF THE NERVOUS SYSTEM

The brain and its coverings, as with all other parts of the body, can be sites of infections. Some infectious agents have a relative or absolute predilection for the nervous system (e.g., rabies), while others can affect many other organs as well as the brain (e.g., *Staphylococcus aureus*). Damage to nervous tissue may be the consequence of direct injury of neurons or glial cells by the infectious agent or microbial toxins, or may be a consequence of the host innate or adaptive immune response.

Infectious agents may reach the nervous system through several routes of entry:

- *Hematogenous spread* by way of the arterial blood supply is the most common means of entry. There can also be retrograde venous spread, through the anastomoses between veins of the face and the venous sinuses of the skull.
- *Direct implantation* of microorganisms is almost invariably due to traumatic introduction of foreign material. In rare cases it can be iatrogenic, as when microbes are introduced with a lumbar puncture needle.
- *Local extension* can occur with infections of the skull or spine. Sources include air sinuses, most often the mastoid or frontal; infected teeth; cranial or spinal osteomyelitis; and congenital malformations, such as meningomyelocele.
- *Peripheral nerves* also may serve as paths of entry for a few pathogens—in particular, viruses such as the rabies and herpes zoster viruses.

Epidural and Subdural Infections

The epidural and subdural spaces can be involved by bacterial or fungal infections, usually as a consequence of direct local spread. *Epidural abscesses* arise from an adjacent focus of infection, such as sinusitis or osteomyelitis. When abscesses occur in the spinal epidural space, they may cause spinal cord compression and constitute a neurosurgical emergency. Infections of the skull or air sinuses may also spread to the subdural space, producing *subdural empyema.* The underlying arachnoid and subarachnoid spaces usually are unaffected, but a large subdural empyema may produce a mass effect. In addition, thrombophlebitis may develop in the bridging veins that cross the subdural space, resulting in venous occlusion and infarction of the brain. Most patients are febrile, with headache and neck stiffness, and if untreated may develop focal neurologic signs referable to the site of the infection, lethargy, and coma. With treatment, including surgical drainage, resolution of the empyema occurs from the dural side; if resolution is complete, a thickened dura may be the only residual finding. With prompt treatment, complete recovery is usual.

Meningitis

Meningitis is an inflammatory process involving the leptomeninges within the subarachnoid space; if the infection spreads into the underlying brain it is termed *meningoencephalitis.* Meningitis usually is caused by an infection, but *chemical meningitis* also may occur in response to a nonbacterial irritant introduced into the subarachnoid space. Infectious meningitis can be broadly divided into *acute pyogenic* (usually bacterial), *aseptic* (usually viral), and *chronic* (usually tuberculous, spirochetal, or cryptococcal) subtypes. Examination of the CSF is often useful in distinguishing between various causes of meningitis.

Acute Pyogenic Meningitis (Bacterial Meningitis)

Many bacteria can cause acute pyogenic meningitis, but the most likely organisms vary with patient age. In neonates, common organisms are *Escherichia coli* and the group B streptococci; in adolescents and in young adults, *Neisseria meningitidis* is the most common pathogen; and in older individuals, *Streptococcus pneumoniae* and *Listeria monocytogenes* are more common. In all age groups, patients typically show systemic signs of infection along with meningeal irritation and neurologic impairment, including headache, photophobia, irritability, clouding of consciousness, and neck stiffness. *Lumbar puncture reveals an increased pressure; examination of the CSF shows abundant neutrophils, elevated protein, and reduced glucose.* Bacteria may be seen on a smear or can be cultured, sometimes a few hours before the neutrophils appear. Untreated pyogenic meningitis is often fatal, but with prompt diagnosis and administration of appropriate antibiotics, many patients can be saved.

MORPHOLOGY

In acute meningitis, an exudate is evident within the leptomeninges over the surface of the brain (Fig. 22–16, *A*). The meningeal vessels are engorged and prominent. From the areas of greatest accumulation, tracts of pus can be followed along blood vessels on the brain surface. When the meningitis is fulminant, the inflammatory cells infiltrate the walls of the leptomeningeal veins and may spread into the substance of the brain (focal cerebritis), or the inflammation may extend to the ventricles, producing ventriculitis. On microscopic examination, neutrophils fill the entire subarachnoid space in severely affected areas or may be found predominantly around the leptomeningeal blood vessels in less severe cases. In untreated meningitis, Gram stain reveals varying numbers of the causative organism. Bacterial meningitis may be associated with abscesses in the brain (Fig. 22–16, *B*), discussed later. Phlebitis also may lead to venous occlusion and hemorrhagic infarction of the underlying brain. If it is treated early, there may be little or no morphologic residuum.

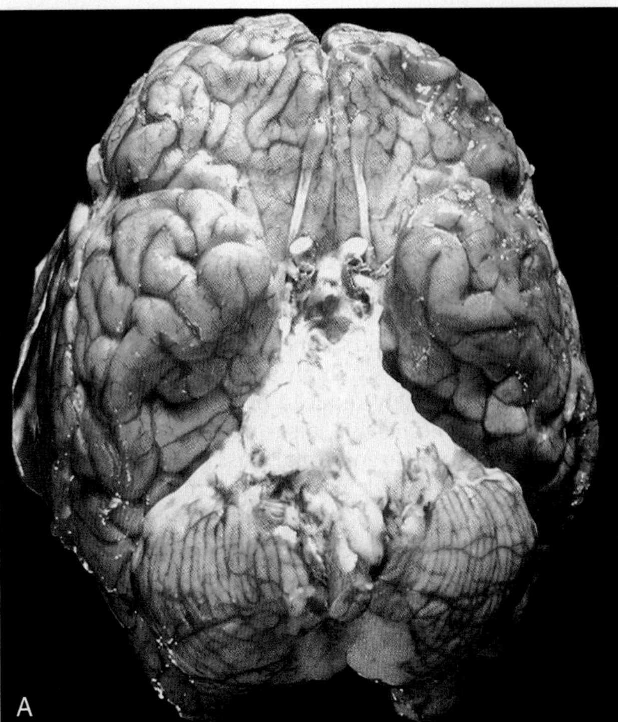

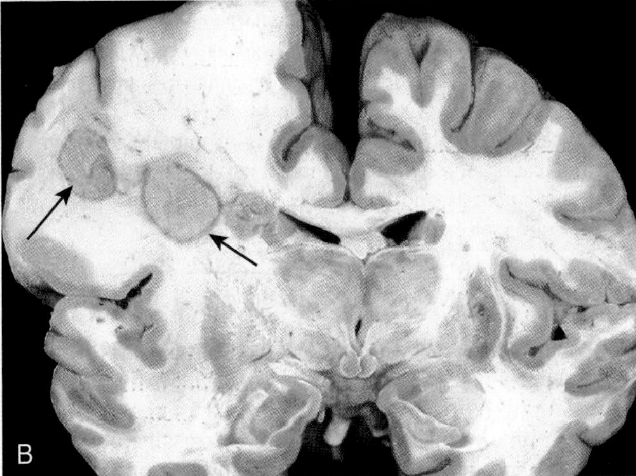

Figure 22–16 Bacterial infections. **A,** Pyogenic meningitis. A thick layer of suppurative exudate covers the brain stem and cerebellum and thickens the leptomeninges. **B,** Cerebral abscesses in the frontal lobe white matter (*arrows*).

(A, From Golden JA, Louis DN: Images in clinical medicine: acute bacterial meningitis. N Engl J Med 333:364, 1994. Copyright © 1994 Massachusetts Medical Society. All rights reserved.)

Aseptic Meningitis (Viral Meningitis)

Aseptic meningitis is a clinical term for an illness comprising meningeal irritation, fever, and alterations in consciousness of relatively acute onset. The clinical course is less fulminant than in pyogenic meningitis. In contrast to pyogenic meningitis, examination of the CSF often shows lymphocytosis, moderate protein elevation, and a normal glucose level. The disease typically is self-limiting. It is believed to be of viral origin in most cases, but it is often difficult to identify the responsible virus. There are no distinctive macroscopic characteristics except for brain swelling, seen in only some instances. On microscopic examination, there is either no recognizable abnormality or a mild to moderate leptomeningeal lymphocytic infiltrate.

Chronic Meningitis

Several pathogens, including mycobacteria and some spirochetes, are associated with chronic meningitis; infections with these organisms also may involve the brain parenchyma.

Tuberculous Meningitis

Tuberculous meningitis usually manifests with generalized signs and symptoms of headache, malaise, mental confusion, and vomiting. There is only a moderate increase in CSF cellularity, with mononuclear cells or a mixture of polymorphonuclear and mononuclear cells; the protein level is elevated, often strikingly so, and the glucose content typically is moderately reduced or normal. Infection with *Mycobacterium tuberculosis* also may result in a well-circumscribed intraparenchymal mass (*tuberculoma*), which may be associated with meningitis. Chronic tuberculous meningitis is a cause of arachnoid fibrosis, which may produce hydrocephalus.

MORPHOLOGY

The subarachnoid space contains a gelatinous or fibrinous exudate, most often at the base of the brain, obliterating the cisterns and encasing cranial nerves. There may be discrete white granules scattered over the leptomeninges. Arteries running through the subarachnoid space may show **obliterative endarteritis** with inflammatory infiltrates and marked intimal thickening. On microscopic examination there are mixtures of lymphocytes, plasma cells, and macrophages. Florid cases show well-formed granulomas, often with caseous necrosis and giant cells, similar to the lesions of tuberculosis elsewhere.

Spirochetal Infections

Neurosyphilis, a tertiary stage of syphilis, occurs in about 10% of persons with untreated *Treponema pallidum* infection. Patients with HIV infection are at increased risk for neurosyphilis, which often is more aggressive and severe in this setting. The infection can produce chronic meningitis (*meningovascular neurosyphilis*), usually involving the base of the brain, often with an obliterative endarteritis rich in plasma cells and lymphocytes. There can also be parenchymal involvement by spirochetes (*paretic neurosyphilis*), leading to neuronal loss and marked proliferation of rod-shaped microglial cells. Clinically, this form of the disease causes an insidious progressive loss of mental and physical functions, mood alterations (including delusions of grandeur), and eventually severe dementia. *Tabes dorsalis* is another form of neurosyphilis, resulting from damage to the sensory nerves in the dorsal roots that produces impaired joint position sense and ataxia (locomotor ataxia); loss of pain sensation, leading to skin and joint damage (Charcot joints); other sensory disturbances, particularly characteristic "lightning pains"; and the absence of deep tendon reflexes.

Neuroborreliosis represents involvement of the nervous system by the spirochete *Borrelia burgdorferi*, the pathogen of Lyme disease. Neurologic signs and symptoms are highly variable and include aseptic meningitis, facial nerve palsies, mild encephalopathy, and polyneuropathies.

Parenchymal Infections

The entire gamut of infectious pathogens (viruses to parasites) can potentially infect the brain, often in characteristic patterns. In general, viral infections are diffuse, bacterial infections (when not associated with meningitis) are localized, while other organisms produce mixed patterns. In immunosuppressed hosts, more widespread involvement with any agent is typical.

Brain Abscesses

Brain abscesses are nearly always caused by bacterial infections. These can arise by direct implantation of organisms, local extension from adjacent foci (mastoiditis, paranasal sinusitis), or hematogenous spread (usually from a primary site in the heart, lungs, or distal bones, or after tooth extraction). Predisposing conditions include acute bacterial endocarditis, from which septic emboli are released that may produce multiple abscesses; cyanotic congenital heart disease, associated with a right-to-left shunt and loss of pulmonary filtration of organisms; and chronic pulmonary infections, as in bronchiectasis, which provide a source of microbes that spread hematogenously.

Abscesses are destructive lesions, and patients almost invariably present with progressive focal deficits as well as general signs related to increased intracranial pressure. The CSF white cell count and protein levels are usually high, while the glucose content tends to be normal. A systemic or local source of infection may be apparent or may have ceased to be symptomatic. The increased intracranial pressure and progressive herniation can be fatal, and abscess rupture can lead to ventriculitis, meningitis, and venous sinus thrombosis. Surgery and antibiotics reduce the otherwise high mortality rate, with earlier intervention leading to better outcomes.

MORPHOLOGY

Abscesses are discrete lesions with central liquefactive necrosis and a surrounding fibrous capsule (Fig. 22–16, *B*). On microscopic examination, the necrotic center is surrounded by edema and granulation tissue, often with exuberant vascularization. Outside the fibrous capsule is a zone of reactive gliosis.

Viral Encephalitis

Viral encephalitis is a parenchymal infection of the brain that is almost invariably associated with meningeal inflammation (and therefore is better termed *meningoencephalitis*). While different viruses may show varying patterns of injury, the most characteristic histologic features are perivascular and parenchymal mononuclear cell infiltrates, microglial nodules, and neuronophagia (Fig. 22–17, *A* and *B*). Certain viruses also form characteristic inclusion bodies.

The nervous system is particularly susceptible to certain viruses such as rabies virus and poliovirus. Some viruses infect specific CNS cell types, while others preferentially involve particular brain regions (such as the medial temporal lobes, or the limbic system) that lie along the viral route of entry. Intrauterine viral infection may cause *congenital malformations*, as occurs with rubella. In addition to

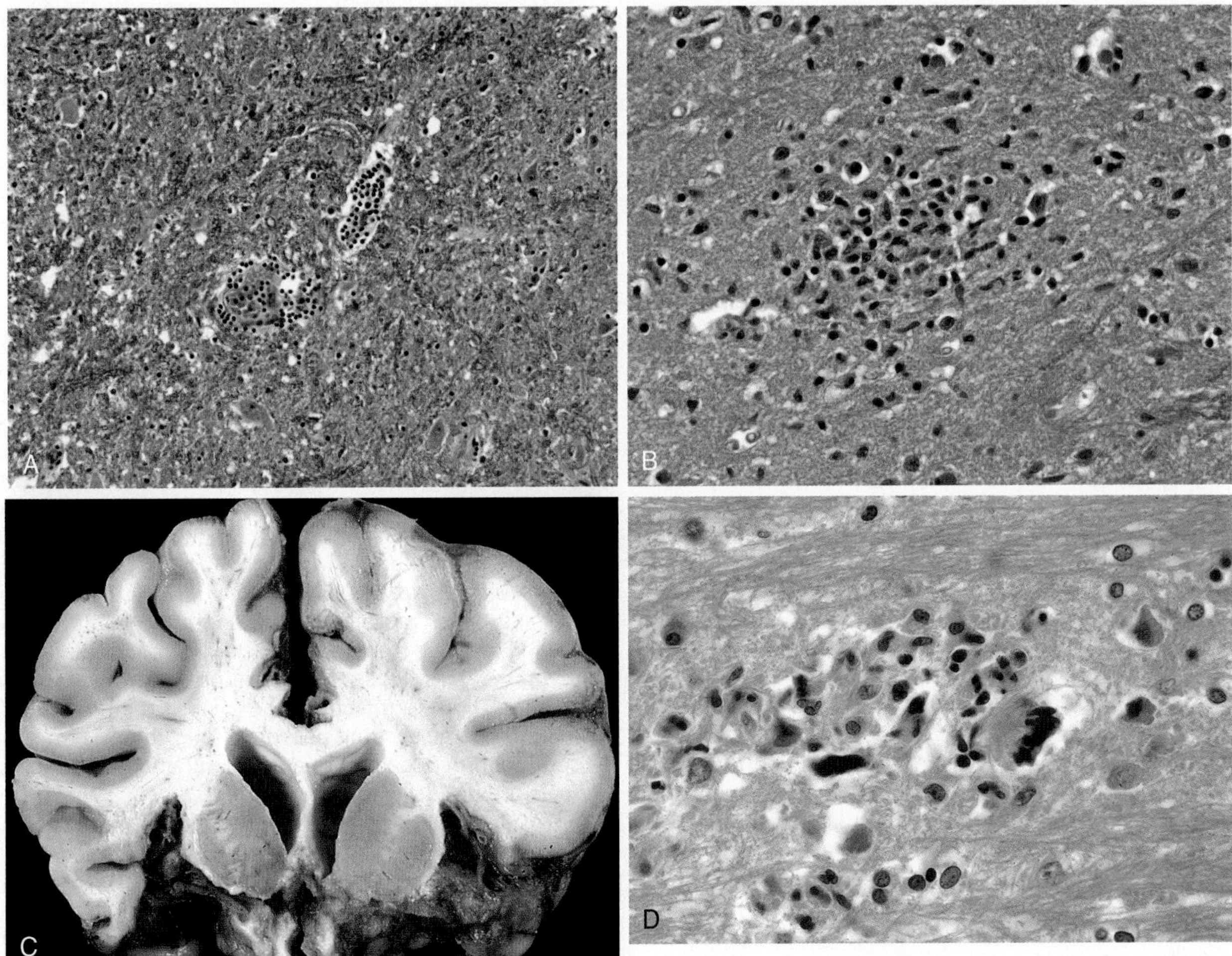

Figure 22–17 Viral infections. **A** and **B,** Characteristic findings in many forms of viral meningitis include perivascular cuffing of lymphocytes **(A)** and microglial nodules **(B). C,** Herpes encephalitis showing extensive destruction of inferior frontal and anterior temporal lobes. **D,** Human immunodeficiency virus (HIV) encephalitis. Note the accumulation of microglia forming a microglial nodule and multinucleate giant cell.

(C, Courtesy of Dr. T.W. Smith, University of Massachusetts Medical School, Worcester, Massachusetts.)

direct infection of the nervous system, the CNS also can be injured by immune mechanisms after systemic viral infections.

Arboviruses

Arboviruses (arthropod-borne viruses) are an important cause of epidemic encephalitis, especially in tropical regions of the world, and are capable of causing serious morbidity and high mortality. Among the more commonly encountered types are Eastern and Western equine encephalitis and West Nile virus infection. Patients develop generalized neurologic symptoms, such as seizures, confusion, delirium, and stupor or coma, as well as focal signs, such as reflex asymmetry and ocular palsies. The CSF usually is colorless but with a slightly elevated pressure and an early neutrophilic pleocytosis that rapidly converts to a lymphocytosis; the protein level is elevated, but the glucose is normal.

MORPHOLOGY

Arbovirus encephalitides produce a similar histopathologic picture. Characteristically, there is a perivascular lymphocytic meningoencephalitis (sometimes with neutrophils) (Fig. 22–17, *A*). Multifocal gray and white matter necrosis is seen, often associated with neuronophagia, the phagocytosis of neuronal debris, as well as localized collections of microglia termed microglial nodules (Fig. 22–17, *B*). In severe cases there may be a necrotizing vasculitis with associated focal hemorrhages.

Herpesviruses

HSV-1 encephalitis may occur in any age group but is most common in children and young adults. It typically manifests with alterations in mood, memory, and behavior, reflecting involvement of the frontal and temporal lobes. Recurrent HSV-1 encephalitis is sometimes associated with inherited mutations that interfere with Toll-like receptor signaling (specifically that of TLR-3), which has an important role in antiviral defense.

MORPHOLOGY

Herpes encephalitis starts in, and most severely involves, the inferior and medial regions of the temporal lobes and the orbital gyri of the frontal lobes (Fig. 22–17, *C*). The infection is necrotizing and often hemorrhagic in the most severely affected regions. Perivascular inflammatory infiltrates usually are present, and large eosinophilic intranuclear viral inclusions (Cowdry type A bodies) can be found in both neurons and glial cells.

HSV-2 also affects the nervous system, usually in the form of meningitis in adults. Disseminated severe encephalitis occurs in many neonates born by vaginal delivery to women with active primary HSV genital infections.

Varicella-zoster virus (VZV) causes chickenpox during primary infection, usually without any evidence of neurologic involvement. The virus establishes latent infection in neurons of dorsal root ganglia. Reactivation in adults manifests as a painful, vesicular skin eruption in the distribution of one or a few dermatomes (*shingles*). This usually is a self-limited process, but there may be a persistent pain syndrome in the affected region (*postherpetic neuralgia*). VZV also may cause a granulomatous arteritis that can lead to tissue infarcts. In immunosuppressed patients, acute herpes zoster encephalitis can occur. Inclusion bodies can be found in glial cells and neurons.

Cytomegalovirus

CMV infects the nervous system in fetuses and immunosuppressed persons. All cells within the CNS (neurons, glial cells, ependyma, and endothelium) are susceptible to infection. Intrauterine infection causes periventricular necrosis, followed later by microcephaly with periventricular calcification. When adults are infected, CMV produces a subacute encephalitis, again often most severe in the periventricular region. Lesions can be hemorrhagic and contain typical viral inclusion–bearing cells.

Poliovirus

Poliovirus is an enterovirus that most often causes a subclinical or mild gastroenteritis; in a small fraction of cases, it secondarily invades the nervous system and damages motor neurons in the spinal cord and brain stem (paralytic poliomyelitis). With loss of motor neurons, it produces a flaccid paralysis with muscle wasting and hyporeflexia in the corresponding region of the body. In the acute disease, death can occur from paralysis of respiratory muscles. Long after the infection has resolved, typically 25 to 35 years after the initial illness, a *postpolio syndrome* of progressive weakness associated with decreased muscle bulk and pain can appear. The cause of this syndrome is unclear. One hypothesis is that motor neurons that survive the initial insult sprout new nerve terminals to compensate for the death of their neighbors, and that over time the additional demands placed on these neurons leads to injury that diminishes function or causes cell death.

Rabies Virus

Rabies is a severe encephalitic infection transmitted to humans from rabid animals, usually by a bite. Various mammals are natural reservoirs. Exposure to some bat species, even without evidence of a bite, is also a risk factor. Virus enters the CNS by ascending along the peripheral nerves from the wound site, so the incubation period depends on the distance between the wound and the brain, usually taking a few months. The disease manifests initially with nonspecific symptoms of malaise, headache, and fever. As the infection advances, the patient shows extraordinary CNS excitability; the slightest touch is painful, with violent motor responses progressing to convulsions. Contracture of the pharyngeal musculature may create an aversion to swallowing even water (hydrophobia). Periods of mania and stupor progress to coma and eventually death, typically from respiratory failure.

Human Immunodeficiency Virus

In the first 15 years or so after recognition of AIDS, neuropathologic changes were demonstrated at postmortem examination in as many as 80% to 90% of cases, owing to direct effects of virus on the nervous system, opportunistic infections, and primary CNS lymphoma. Introduction of highly active antiretroviral therapy (HAART) has decreased the frequency of these secondary effects of HIV infection. However, cognitive dysfunction ranging from mild to full-blown dementia that is lumped under the umbrella term *HIV-associated neurocognitive disorder* (HAND) continues to be a source of morbidity. The cognitive symptoms are believed to stem from HIV infection of microglial cells in the brain. This leads to activation of innate immune responses, both in infected microglial cells and unaffected bystanders. The ensuing neuronal injury likely stems from a combination of cytokine-induced inflammation and toxic effects of HIV-derived proteins.

Aseptic meningitis occurs within 1 to 2 weeks of onset of primary infection by HIV in about 10% of patients; antibodies to HIV can be demonstrated, and the virus can be isolated from the CSF. The few neuropathologic studies of the early and acute phases of symptomatic or asymptomatic HIV invasion of the nervous system have shown mild lymphocytic meningitis, perivascular inflammation, and some myelin loss in the hemispheres. After the acute phase, an HIV encephalitis (HIVE) commonly can be found if affected persons come to autopsy.

MORPHOLOGY

HIV encephalitis is best characterized microscopically as a chronic inflammatory reaction with widely distributed infiltrates of **microglial nodules,** sometimes with associated foci of tissue necrosis and reactive gliosis (Fig. 22–17, *D*). The microglial nodules also are found in the vicinity of small blood vessels, which show abnormally prominent endothelial cells and perivascular foamy or pigment-laden macrophages. These changes occur especially in the subcortical white matter, diencephalon, and brain stem. An important component of the microglial nodule is the macrophage-derived **multinucleate giant cell.** In some cases, there is also a disorder of white matter characterized by multifocal or diffuse areas of myelin pallor with associated axonal swellings and gliosis. HIV is present in CD4+ mononuclear and multinucleate macrophages and microglia.

Polyomavirus and Progressive Multifocal Leukoencephalopathy

Progressive multifocal leukoencephalopathy (PML) is caused by JC virus, a polyomavirus, which preferentially infects oligodendrocytes, resulting in demyelination as these cells are injured and then die. Most people show serologic evidence of exposure to JC virus during childhood, and it is believed that PML results from virus reactivation, as the disease is restricted to immunosuppressed persons. Patients develop focal and relentlessly progressive neurologic symptoms and signs, and imaging studies show extensive, often multifocal, ring-enhancing lesions in the hemispheric or cerebellar white matter.

MORPHOLOGY

The lesions are patchy, irregular, ill-defined areas of white matter destruction that enlarge as the disease progresses (Fig. 22–18). Each lesion is an area of demyelination, in the center of which are scattered lipid-laden macrophages and a reduced number of axons. At the edges of the lesion are greatly enlarged oligodendrocyte nuclei whose chromatin is replaced by glassy-appearing amphophilic viral inclusions. The virus also infects astrocytes, leading to bizarre giant forms with irregular, hyperchromatic, sometimes multiple nuclei that can be mistaken for tumor.

Fungal Encephalitis

Fungal infections usually produce parenchymal granulomas or abscesses, often associated with meningitis. The most common fungal infections have distinctive patterns:

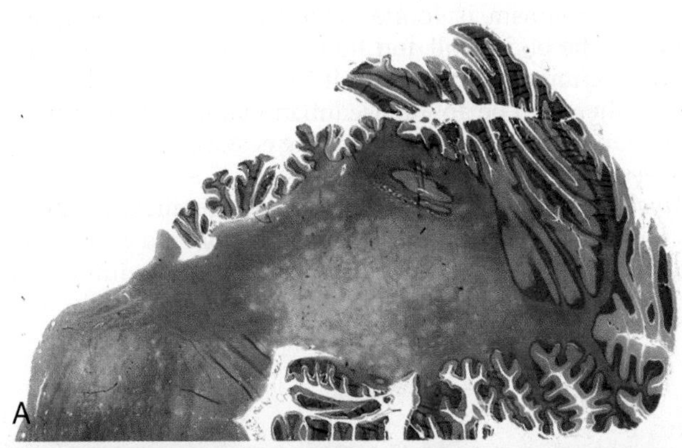

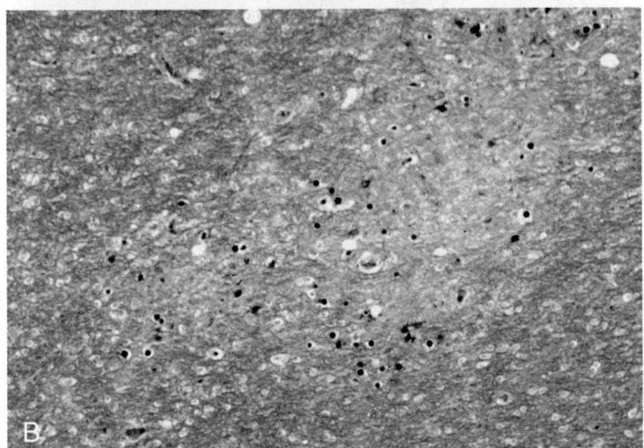

Figure 22–18 Progressive multifocal leukoencephalopathy. **A,** Section stained for myelin showing irregular, poorly defined areas of demyelination, which become confluent in places. **B,** Enlarged oligodendrocyte nuclei stained for viral antigens surround an area of early myelin loss.

- *Candida albicans* usually produces multiple microabscesses, with or without granuloma formation.
- *Mucormycosis* is the term used to describe rhinocerebral infections caused by several fungi belonging to the order Mucorales. It typically presents as an infection of the nasal cavity or sinuses of a diabetic patient with ketoacidosis. It may spread to the brain through vascular invasion or by direct extension through the cribriform plate. The proclivity of Mucor to invade the brain directly sets it apart from other fungi, which tend to reach the brain by hematogenous dissemination from distant sites.
- *Aspergillus fumigatus* tends to cause a distinctive pattern of widespread septic hemorrhagic infarctions because of its marked predilection for blood vessel wall invasion and subsequent thrombosis.
- *Cryptococcus neoformans* can cause both meningitis and meningoencephalitis, often in the setting of immunosuppression. It can be fulminant and fatal in as little as 2 weeks or may exhibit indolent behavior, evolving over months or years. The CSF may have few cells but elevated protein, and the mucoid encapsulated yeasts can be visualized on India ink preparations. Extension into the brain follows vessels in the Virchow-Robin spaces. As organisms proliferate, these spaces expand, giving rise to a "soap bubble"-like appearance (Fig. 22–19). The diagnosis is usually established by a positive test for cryptococcal antigens in the CSF or the blood.

In endemic areas, *Histoplasma capsulatum, Coccidioides immitis,* and *Blastomyces dermatitidis* also can infect the CNS, especially in the setting of immunosuppression.

Other Meningoencephalitides

While a wide range of other organisms can infect the nervous system and its covering, only three specific entities are considered here.

Cerebral Toxoplasmosis. Cerebral infection with the protozoan *Toxoplasma gondii* can occur in immunosuppressed adults or in newborns who acquire the organism transplacentally from a mother with an active infection. In adults, the clinical symptoms are subacute, evolving during a 1- or 2-week period, and may be both focal and diffuse. Due to inflammation and breakdown of the blood-brain barrier at sites of infection, computed tomography and magnetic resonance imaging studies often show edema around lesions (so-called ring enhancing lesions). In newborns who are infected in utero, the infection classically produces the triad of chorioretinitis, hydrocephalus, and intracranial calcifications. Understandably, the CNS abnormalities are most severe when the infection occurs early in gestation during critical stages of brain development. Necrosis of periventricular lesions gives rise to secondary calcifications as well as inflammation and gliosis, which can lead to obstruction of the aqueduct of Sylvius and hydrocephalus.

MORPHOLOGY

When the infection is acquired in immunosuppressed adults, the brain shows abscesses, frequently multiple, most often involving the cerebral cortex (near the gray-white junction) and deep gray nuclei. Acute lesions consist of central foci of

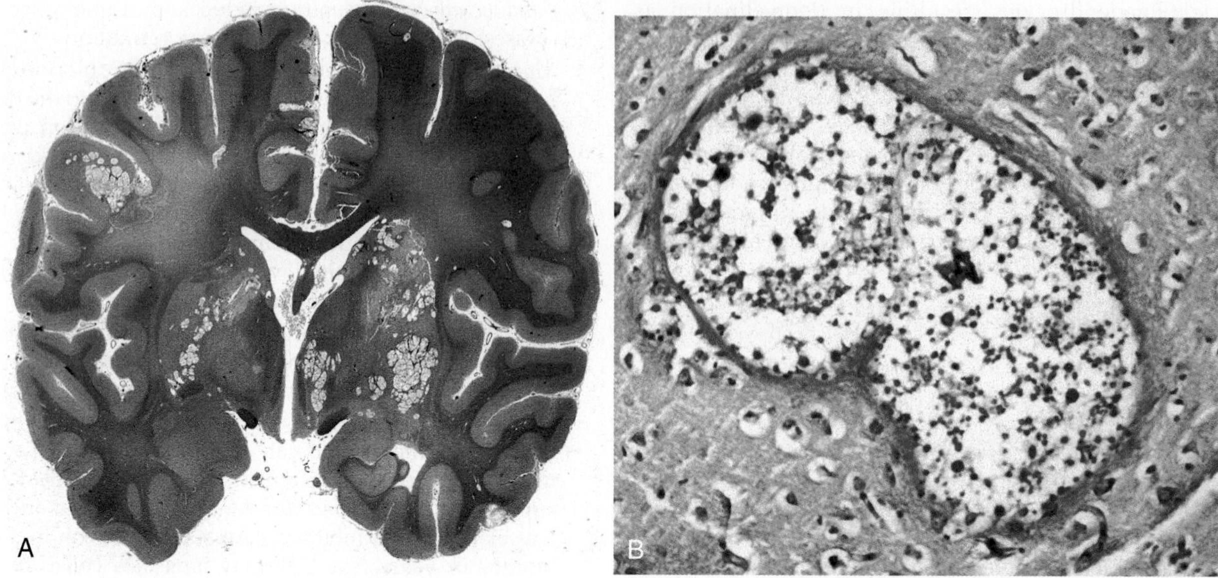

Figure 22–19 Cryptococcal infection. **A,** Whole-brain section showing the numerous areas of tissue destruction associated with the spread of organisms in the perivascular spaces. **B,** At higher magnification, it is possible to see the cryptococci in the lesions.

necrosis with variable petechiae surrounded by acute and chronic inflammation, macrophage infiltration, and vascular proliferation. Both free tachyzoites and encysted bradyzoites may be found at the periphery of the necrotic foci (Fig. 22–20).

Cysticercosis. Cysticercosis is the consequence of an end-stage infection by the tapeworm *Tenia solium.* If ingested larval organisms leave the lumen of the gastrointestinal tract, where they would otherwise develop into mature tapeworms, they encyst. Cysts can be found throughout the body but are common within the brain and subarachnoid space. Cysticercosis typically manifests as a mass lesion and can cause seizures. Symptoms can intensify when the encysted organism dies, as happens after therapy.

The organism is found within a cyst with a smooth lining. The body wall and hooklets from mouth parts are most commonly recognized. If the encysted organism has died, there can be an intense inflammatory infiltrate in the surrounding brain, often including eosinophils, which may be associated with marked gliosis.

Amebiasis. *Amebic meningoencephalitis* manifests with different clinical syndromes, depending on the responsible pathogen. *Naegleria* spp., associated with swimming in nonflowing warm fresh water, cause a rapidly fatal

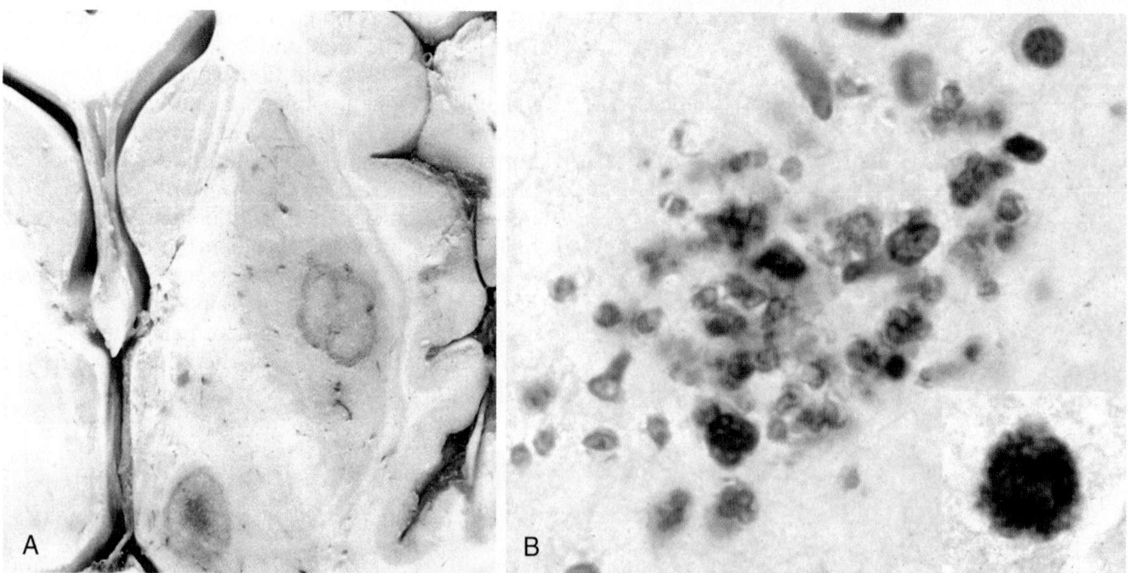

Figure 22–20 *Toxoplasma* infection. **A,** Abscesses are present in the putamen and thalamus. **B,** Free tachyzoites are demonstrated by immunohistochemical staining. *Inset,* Bradyzoites are present as a pseudocyst, again highlighted by immunohistochemical staining.

necrotizing encephalitis. By contrast, *Acanthamoeba* causes a chronic granulomatous meningoencephalitis.

Prion Diseases

Prion diseases are a group of rare but fascinating disorders that include sporadic, familial, iatrogenic, and variant forms of Creutzfeldt-Jakob disease (CJD), as well as animal diseases such as scrapie in sheep and bovine spongiform encephalopathy in cattle ("mad cow disease"). Unlike in other infectious diseases, the agent in prion diseases is an abnormal form of a cellular protein. This protein, termed prion protein (PrP), may undergo a conformational change from its normal shape (PrP^c) to an abnormal conformation called PrP^{sc} (*sc* for scrapie). PrP normally is rich in α-helices, but PrP^{sc} has a high content of β-sheets, a characteristic that makes it resistant to proteolysis (hence an alternative term for the pathogenic form, PrP^{res}—i.e., protease-resistant). More important, when PrP^{sc} physically interacts with PrP molecules it induces them to also adopt the PrP^{sc} conformation (Fig. 22–21), a property that accounts for the "infectious nature" of PrP^{sc}. Over time, this self-amplifying process leads to the accumulation of a high burden of pathogenic PrP^{sc} molecules in the brain. PrP^c also may change its conformation spontaneously (but at an extremely low rate), accounting for sporadic cases of prion disease (sCJD). Certain mutations in the gene encoding PrP^c (*PRNP*) accelerate the rate of spontaneous conformational change; these variants are associated with early-onset familial forms of prion disease (fCJD). Accumulation of PrP^{sc} in neural tissue seems to be the cause of cell injury, but the mechanisms underlying the cytopathic changes and eventual neuronal death are still unknown.

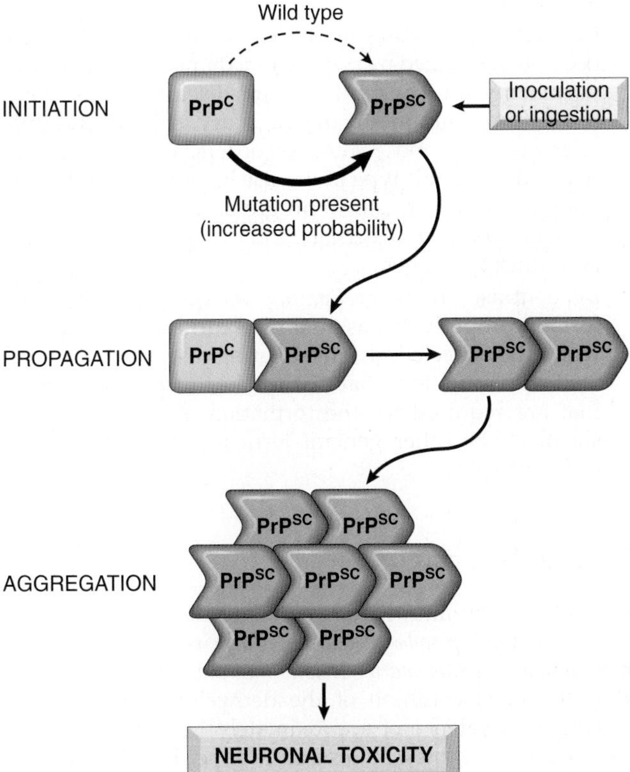

Figure 22–21 Pathogenesis of prion disease. α-Helical PrP^c may spontaneously shift to the β-sheet PrP^{sc} conformation, an event that occurs at a much higher rate in familial disease associated with germ line PrP mutations. PrP^{sc} may also be from exogenous sources, such as contaminated food, medical instrumentation, or medicines. Once present, PrP^{sc} converts additional molecules of PrP^c into PrP^{sc} through physical interaction, eventually leading to the formation of pathogenic PrP^{sc} aggregates.

Creutzfeldt-Jakob Disease

CJD is a rapidly progressive dementing illness, with a typical duration from first onset of subtle changes in memory and behavior to death in only 7 months. It is sporadic in approximately 85% of cases and has a worldwide annual incidence of about 1 per million. While commonly affecting persons older than 70 years of age, familial forms caused by mutations in *PRNP* may present in younger people. In keeping with the infectious nature of PrP^{sc}, there are well-established cases of iatrogenic transmission by contaminated deep implantation electrodes and human growth hormone preparations.

MORPHOLOGY

The progression to death in CJD usually is so rapid that there is little, if any, macroscopic evidence of brain atrophy. On microscopic examination, the pathognomonic finding is a **spongiform transformation of the cerebral cortex and deep gray matter structures** (caudate, putamen); this multifocal process results in the uneven formation of small, apparently empty, microscopic vacuoles of varying sizes within the neuropil and sometimes in the perikaryon of neurons (Fig. 22–22, *A*). In advanced cases, there is severe neuronal loss, reactive gliosis, and sometimes expansion of the vacuolated areas into cystlike spaces ("status spongiosus"). No inflammatory infiltrate is present. Immunohistochemical staining demonstrates the presence of proteinase K–resistant PrP^{sc} in tissue, while western blotting of tissue extracts after partial protease digestion allows detection of diagnostic PrP^{sc}.

Variant Creutzfeldt-Jakob Disease

Starting in 1995, cases of a CJD-like illness appeared in the United Kingdom. The neuropathologic findings and molecular features of these new cases were similar to those of CJD, suggesting a close relationship between the two illnesses, yet this new disorder differed from typical CJD in several important respects: The disease affected young adults, behavioral disorders figured prominently in early disease stages, and the neurologic syndrome progressed more slowly than in other forms of CJD. Multiple lines of evidence indicate that this new disease, termed *variant Creutzfeldt-Jakob disease* (vCJD) is a consequence of exposure to the prion disease of cattle, called bovine spongiform encephalopathy. There has now also been documentation of transmission by blood transfusion. This variant form has a similar pathologic appearance to that in other types of CJD, with spongiform change and absence of inflammation. In vCJD, however, there are abundant cortical amyloid plaques, surrounded by the spongiform change (Fig. 22–22, *B*).

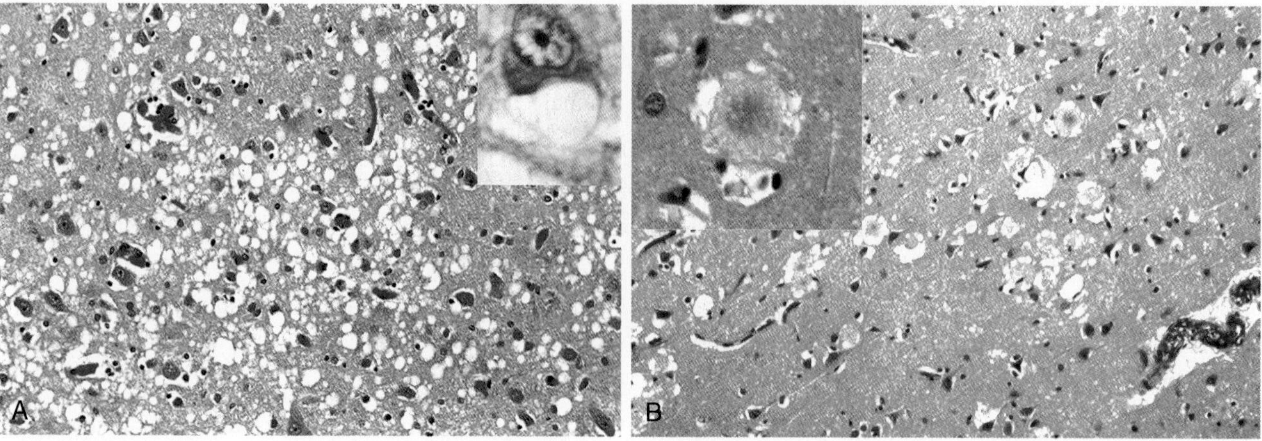

Figure 22–22 Prion disease. **A,** Histologic features of Creutzfeldt-Jakob disease (CJD) include spongiform change in the cerebral cortex. *Inset,* High magnification of neuron with vacuoles. **B,** Variant CJD (vCJD) is characterized by amyloid plaques (see *inset*) that sit in the regions of greatest spongiform change.

SUMMARY

Infections of the Nervous System

- Pathogens from viruses through parasites can infect the brain; in addition, prion disease is a protein-induced transmissible disease unique to the nervous system.
- Different pathogens use distinct routes to reach the brain, and cause different patterns of disease.
- Bacterial infections may cause meningitis, cerebral abscesses, or a chronic meningoencephalitis.
- Viral infections can cause meningitis or meningoencephalitis.
- HIV can directly cause meningoencephalitis, or indirectly affect the brain by increasing the risk of opportunistic infections (toxoplasmosis, CMV) or CNS lymphoma.
- Prion diseases are transmitted by an altered form of a normal cellular protein. They can be sporadic, transmitted, or inherited.

PRIMARY DISEASES OF MYELIN

Within the CNS, axons are tightly ensheathed by myelin, an electrical insulator that allows rapid propagation of neural impulses. Myelin consists of multiple layers of highly specialized, closely apposed plasma membranes that are assembled by oligodendrocytes. Although myelinated axons are present in all areas of the brain, they are the dominant component in the white matter; therefore, most diseases of myelin are primarily white matter disorders. The myelin in peripheral nerves is similar to the myelin in the CNS but has several important differences: (1) peripheral myelin is made by Schwann cells, not oligodendrocytes; (2) each Schwann cell in a peripheral nerve provides myelin for only one internode, while in the CNS, many internodes are created by processes coming from a single oligodendrocyte; and (3) the specialized proteins and lipids are also different. Therefore, most diseases of CNS myelin do not involve the peripheral nerves to any significant extent, and vice versa.

In general, diseases involving myelin are separated into two broad groups.

- *Demyelinating diseases* of the CNS are acquired conditions characterized by preferential damage to previously normal myelin. The most common diseases in this group result from immune-mediated injury, such as multiple sclerosis (MS) and related disorders. Other processes that can cause this type of disease include viral infection of oligodendrocytes, as in progressive multifocal leukoencephalopathy (see earlier), and injury caused by drugs and other toxic agents.
- By contrast, in *dysmyelinating diseases,* myelin is not formed properly or has abnormal turnover kinetics. As would be expected, dysmyelinating diseases are associated with mutations that disrupt the function of proteins that are required for the formation of normal myelin sheaths. The other general term for these diseases is *leukodystrophy.*

Multiple Sclerosis

MS is an autoimmune demyelinating disorder characterized by *distinct episodes of neurologic deficits, separated in time, attributable to white matter lesions that are separated in space.* It is the most common of the demyelinating disorders, having a prevalence of approximately 1 per 1000 persons in most of the United States and Europe. The disease may become clinically apparent at any age, although onset in childhood or after age 50 is relatively rare. Women are affected twice as often as men. In most patients with MS, the illness shows relapsing and remitting episodes of neurologic impairment. The frequency of relapses tends to decrease during the course of the illness, but a steady neurologic deterioration is characteristic in a subset of patients.

PATHOGENESIS

It is believed that MS, like other autoimmune diseases, is caused by a combination of environmental and genetic factors that result in a loss of tolerance to self proteins (in this case, myelin antigens). The nature of the initiating agent, often suggested to be an infectious agent, remains uncertain. Many lines of evidence indicate a significant contribution of genetic factors to the risk of developing MS. The disease risk is 15-fold higher when the disease is present in a first-degree relative, and the concordance rate for monozygotic twins is approximately 25%, with a much lower rate for dizygotic twins. A significant fraction of the genetic risk for MS is attributable to HLA-DR variants, the DR2 allele being the one that most significantly increases the risk for developing MS. Many other genetic polymorphisms have been linked to the disease by genome-wide association studies. Two that have received considerable recent interest are polymorphisms in the genes encoding receptors for the cytokines IL-2 and IL-7, which are known to control the activation and regulation of T cell–mediated immune responses.

In view of the prominence of chronic inflammatory cells within and around MS plaques as well as the genetic evidence, immune-mediated myelin destruction is thought to have a central role in MS. Evidence from human studies as well as from experimental allergic encephalomyelitis—an animal model of MS in which demyelination and inflammation occur after immunization with myelin, myelin proteins, or certain peptides from myelin proteins—has suggested that a range of immune cells contribute to lesion development in MS. A central role for CD4+ T cells has been suggested, with an increase in T_H17 and T_H1 CD4+ cells thought to be a critical component of the injury to myelin. There is also evidence for important contributions from CD8+ T cells and B cells. While MS is characterized by the presence of demyelination out of proportion to axonal loss, some injury to axons does occur. Toxic effects of lymphocytes, macrophages, and their secreted molecules have been implicated in initiating the process of axonal injury, sometimes even leading to neuronal death.

MORPHOLOGY

MS is primarily a white matter disease with affected areas showing multiple, well-circumscribed, slightly depressed, glassy-appearing, gray-tan, irregularly shaped lesions termed **plaques** (Fig. 22–23, *A*). These commonly arise near the ventricles. They also are frequent in the optic nerves and chiasm, brain stem, ascending and descending fiber tracts, cerebellum, and spinal cord. The lesions have sharply defined borders at the microscopic level (Fig. 22–23, *B*). In an **active plaque** there is evidence of ongoing myelin breakdown with abundant macrophages containing myelin debris. Lymphocytes and macrophages are present, mostly as perivascular cuffs. Small active lesions often are centered on small veins. Axons are relatively preserved but may be reduced in number.

Active plaques fall into four classes, only one of which typically is seen in a particular affected patient. The recognized microscopic patterns are **type I,** which has macrophage infiltrates with sharp margins; **type II,** which is similar to type I but also shows complement deposition (suggesting an antibody-mediated component); **type III,** with less well-defined borders and oligodendrocyte apoptosis; and **type IV,** with nonapoptotic oligodendrocyte loss. When plaques become quiescent **(inactive plaques),** the inflammation mostly disappears, leaving behind little to no myelin. Instead, astrocytic proliferation and gliosis are prominent.

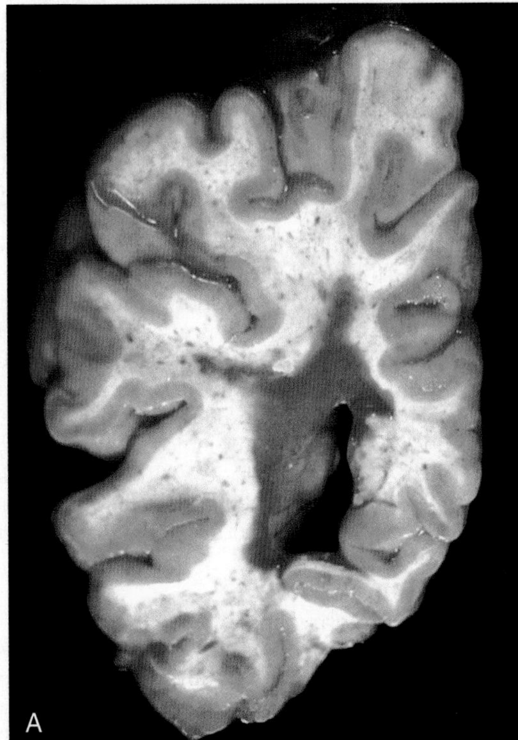

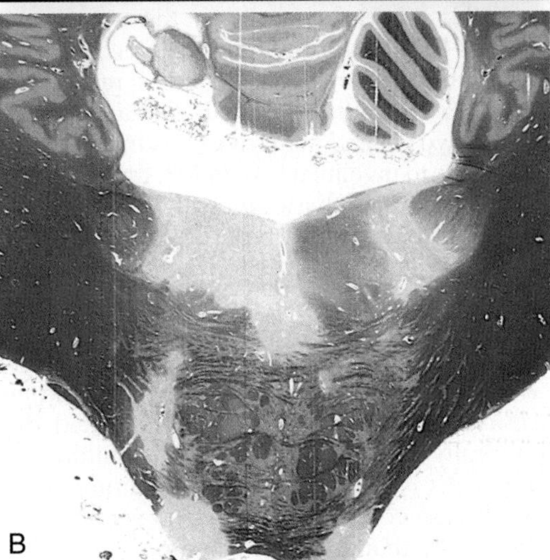

Figure 22–23 Multiple sclerosis (MS). **A,** Section of fresh brain showing a plaque around occipital horn of the lateral ventricle. **B,** Unstained regions of demyelination (MS plaques) around the fourth ventricle. Luxol fast blue–periodic acid–Schiff stain for myelin.

Clinical Features

The course of MS is variable, but commonly there are multiple *relapses* followed by episodes of *remission;* typically, recovery during remissions is not complete. As a consequence, over time there is usually a gradual, often stepwise, accumulation of neurologic deficits. Imaging studies have demonstrated that there are often more lesions in the brains of patients with MS than might be expected from the clinical examination, and that lesions can come and go much more often than was previously suspected. Changes in cognitive function can be present, but are often much milder than the other deficits. In any individual patient, it is hard to predict when the next relapse will occur; most current treatments, which are intended to control the immune response, aim at decreasing the rate and severity of relapses rather than recovering lost function.

The CSF in patients with MS shows a mildly elevated protein level with an increased proportion of immunoglobulin; in one third of cases, there is moderate pleocytosis. When the immunoglobulin is examined further, *oligoclonal bands* usually are identified. These antibodies are directed against a variety of antigenic targets and can be used as markers of disease activity. Although B cells are clearly involved in the pathogenesis of MS, the contribution of these characteristic antibodies to the disease process is unknown.

Other Acquired Demyelinating Diseases

Immune-mediated demyelination can occur after a number of systemic infectious illnesses, including relatively mild viral diseases. These are not thought to be related to direct spread of the infectious agents to the nervous system. Rather, it is believed that immune cells responding to pathogen-associated antigens are cross reactive against myelin antigens, resulting in myelin damage.

There are two general patterns of postinfectious autoimmune reactions to myelin; unlike in MS, they are associated with acute-onset monophasic illnesses. In *acute disseminated encephalomyelitis,* symptoms typically develop a week or two after an antecedent infection and are nonlocalizing (headache, lethargy, and coma), in contrast with the focal findings of MS. Symptoms progress rapidly, and the illness is fatal in as many as 20% of cases; in the remaining patients, there is complete recovery. *Acute necrotizing hemorrhagic encephalomyelitis* is a more devastating related disorder, which typically affects young adults and children.

Neuromyelitis optica (NMO) is an inflammatory demyelinating disease centered on the optic nerves and spinal cord. Previously thought to be a form of MS with stereotypic anatomic regions of susceptibility, this is now recognized to be an antibody-mediated autoimmune disorder. Antibodies to the water channel aquaporin-4 are both diagnostic and pathogenic.

Central pontine myelinolysis is a nonimmune process characterized by loss of myelin involving the center of the pons, most often after rapid correction of hyponatremia. The mechanism of oligodendroglial cell injury is uncertain, but it may be related to edema induced by sudden changes in osmotic pressure. It occurs in a variety of clinical settings including alcoholism and severe electrolyte or osmolar imbalance. Although the most characteristic lesion occurs in the pons, similar lesions can be found elsewhere in the brain. Because of the involvement of fibers in the pons carrying signals to motor neurons in the spinal cord, patients often present with rapidly evolving quadriplegia.

As discussed earlier, *progressive multifocal leukoencephalopathy* (PML) is a demyelinating disease that occurs after reactivation of JC virus in immunosuppressed patients.

Leukodystrophies

Leukodystrophies exemplify inherited dysmyelinating diseases in which the clinical symptoms derive from abnormal myelin synthesis or turnover. Some of these disorders involve lysosomal enzymes, while others involve peroxisomal enzymes; a few are associated with mutations in myelin proteins. Most are of autosomal recessive inheritance, although X-linked diseases also occur (Table 22–1).

MORPHOLOGY

Much of the pathologic change of leukodystrophy is found in the white matter, which is diffusely abnormal in color (gray and translucent) and volume (decreased). Early in their course, some diseases may show patchy involvement, while others have a predilection for occipital lobe involvement. In the end, though, nearly all of the white matter usually is affected. With the loss of white matter, the brain becomes atrophic, the ventricles enlarge, and secondary changes can be found in the gray matter. Myelin loss leads to infiltration of macrophages, which often become stuffed with lipid. Some of these diseases also show specific inclusions created by the accumulation of particular lipids.

Clinical Features

Each of the various leukodystrophies has a characteristic clinical presentation, and most can be diagnosed by genetic or biochemical methods. Despite differences in underlying mechanisms, the leukodystrophies share many features because of the common myelin target. Affected children are normal at birth but begin to miss developmental milestones during infancy and childhood. Diffuse involvement of white matter leads to deterioration in motor skills, spasticity, hypotonia, or ataxia. In general, the earlier the age at onset, the more severe the deficiency and clinical course.

Table 22–1 Selected Leukodystrophies

Metabolic Disorder	Inheritance Mode	Abnormality
Metachromatic leukodystrophy	AR	Arylsulfatase A deficiency
Krabbe disease	AR	Galactocerebroside β-galactosidase deficiency
Adrenoleukodystrophy	AR, X	Peroxisomal defects; elevated very-long-chain fatty acids
Canavan disease	AR	Aspartoacylase deficiency
Pelizaeus-Merzbacher disease	X	Mutations in proteolipid protein
Vanishing white matter disease	AR	Translation initiation factor; link to myelin unclear
Alexander disease	AR	Mutations in glial fibrillary acidic protein

AR, autosomal recessive; X, X-linked.

SUMMARY

Primary Diseases of Myelin

- Because of the critical role of myelin in nerve conduction, diseases of myelin can lead to widespread and severe neurologic deficits.
- Diseases of myelin can be grouped into *demyelinating diseases* (in which normal myelin is broken down for inappropriate reasons—often by inflammatory processes), and *dysmyelinating diseases* (metabolic disorders that include the leukodystrophies in which myelin structure or its turnover is abnormal).
- Multiple sclerosis, an autoimmune demyelinating disease, is the most common disorder of myelin, affecting young adults. It often pursues a relapsing-remitting course, with eventual progressive accumulation of neurologic deficits.
- Other, less common forms of immune-mediated demyelination often follow infections and are more acute illnesses.

ACQUIRED METABOLIC AND TOXIC DISTURBANCES

Toxic and acquired metabolic diseases are relatively common causes of neurologic illnesses. Because of its high metabolic demands, the brain is particularly vulnerable to nutritional diseases and alterations in metabolic state. Surprisingly, even though metabolic alterations might be expected to affect the entire brain uniformly, there can be very distinct clinical presentations because of unique features or requirements of different anatomic regions. A few of the more common types of injury, particularly those with distinct patterns of damage, are discussed here.

Nutritional Diseases

Thiamine Deficiency. In addition to the systemic effects of thiamine deficiency (*beriberi*), there also may be abrupt onset of confusion, abnormalities in eye movement, and ataxia—a syndrome termed *Wernicke encephalopathy*. Treatment with thiamine can reverse these deficits. If the acute stages go untreated, they are followed by largely irreversible profound memory disturbances (Korsakoff syndrome). Because the two syndromes are closely linked, the term *Wernicke-Korsakoff syndrome* is often applied.

The syndrome is particularly common in the setting of chronic alcoholism but also may be encountered in patients with thiamine deficiency resulting from gastric disorders, including carcinoma and chronic gastritis, or from persistent vomiting.

MORPHOLOGY

Wernicke encephalopathy is characterized by foci of hemorrhage and necrosis, particularly in the mammillary bodies but also adjacent to the ventricles, especially the third and fourth ventricles. Despite the presence of necrosis, there is relative preservation of many of the neurons in these structures.

Early lesions show dilated capillaries with promin thelial cells and progress to hemorrhage. As t resolve, a cystic space appears along with hemosi macrophages. Lesions in the medial dorsal nucl thalamus seem to best correlate with the memory disturbance in Korsakoff syndrome.

Vitamin B_{12} Deficiency. In addition to pernicious anemia, deficiency of vitamin B_{12} may lead to neurologic deficits associated with changes in the spinal cord, collectively termed *subacute combined degeneration of the spinal cord*. As the name implies, both ascending and descending tracts of the spinal cord are affected. Symptoms develop over weeks. Early clinical signs often include slight ataxia and lower extremity numbness and tingling, which can progress to spastic weakness of the lower extremities; sometimes even complete paraplegia ensues. Prompt vitamin replacement therapy produces clinical improvement; however, if paraplegia has developed, recovery is poor.

Metabolic Disorders

Several systemic derangements may produce CNS dysfunction; only those associated with glucose levels and liver dysfunction are considered here.

Hypoglycemia. Since the brain requires glucose as a substrate for energy production, the cellular effects of diminished glucose generally resemble those of global hypoxia. Hippocampal neurons are particularly susceptible to hypoglycemic injury, while cerebellar Purkinje cells are relatively spared. As with anoxia, if the level and duration of hypoglycemia are sufficiently severe, there may be widespread injury to many areas of the brain.

Hyperglycemia. Hyperglycemia is most common in the setting of inadequately controlled diabetes mellitus and can be associated with either ketoacidosis or hyperosmolar coma. Patients develop confusion, stupor, and eventually coma associated with intracellular dehydration caused by the hyperosmolar state. The hyperglycemia must be corrected gradually, because rapid correction can produce severe cerebral edema.

Hepatic Encephalopathy. Decreased hepatic function may be associated with depressed levels of consciousness and sometimes coma. In the early stages, patients exhibit a characteristic "flapping" tremor (asterixis) when extending the arms with palms facing the observer. Elevated levels of ammonia, which the liver normally clears through the urea cycle, in combination with inflammation and hyponatremia, cause the changes in brain function. Because it is only one contributing factor, ammonia levels in symptomatic patients vary widely. Within the CNS, ammonia metabolism occurs only in astrocytes through the action of glutamine synthetase, and in the setting of hyperammonemia, astrocytes in the cortex and basal ganglia develop swollen, pale nuclei (called *Alzheimer type II cells*).

Toxic Disorders

The list of toxins with effects on the brain is extremely long. Among the major categories of neurotoxic substances are *metals,* including lead (often causing a diffuse encephalopathy), as well as arsenic and mercury; *industrial chemicals,* including organophosphates (in pesticides) and methanol (causing blindness from retinal damage); and *environmental pollutants* such as carbon monoxide (combining hypoxia with selective injury to the globus pallidus).

Ethanol has a variety of effects on the brain. While acute intoxication is reversible, excessive intake can result in profound metabolic disturbances, including brain swelling and death. Chronic alcohol exposure leads to cerebellar dysfunction in about 1% cases, with truncal ataxia, unsteady gait, and nystagmus, associated with atrophy in the anterior vermis of the cerebellum.

Ionizing radiation, commonly used to treat intracranial tumors, can cause rapidly evolving signs and symptoms including headaches, nausea, vomiting, and papilledema, even months to years after irradiation. Affected brain regions show large areas of coagulative necrosis, adjacent edema, and blood vessels with thickened walls containing intramural fibrin-like material.

NEURODEGENERATIVE DISEASES

Degenerative diseases of the CNS are disorders characterized by the cellular degeneration of subsets of neurons that typically are related by function, rather than by physical location in the brain. Many of these disorders are associated with the accumulation of abnormal proteins, which serve as histologic hallmarks of specific disorders (Table 22–2). An important but unanswered question is why these abnormal proteins tend to accumulate in and preferentially affect particular kinds of neurons, since the involved proteins typically are widely expressed throughout the nervous system.

Subtle differences among subtypes of neurons are presumed to explain why particular neurons are affected in specific disorders. Understandably, the clinical manifestations of degenerative diseases are dictated by the pattern of neuronal dysfunction: those that affect the cerebral cortical neurons result in loss of memory, language, insight, and planning, all components of dementia; those that affect the neurons of the basal ganglia result in movement disorders; those that affect the cerebellum result in ataxia; and those that affect motor neurons result in weakness. Although many degenerative diseases have primary targets, other brain regions are often affected later in the course of the illness; thus, while Huntington disease often has movement disorders as an early symptom, later cortical involvement typically results in the development of cognitive changes as well. *Dementia* is defined as the development of memory impairment and other cognitive deficits severe enough to decrease the affected person's capacity to function at the previous level despite a normal level of consciousness. It arises during the course of many neurodegenerative diseases; it also can accompany numerous other diseases that injure the cerebral cortex (Table 22-3). Dementia is an increasing public health concern as the population ages.

Table 22–2 Protein Inclusions in Degenerative Diseases

Disease	Protein	Location
Alzheimer disease	Aβ Tau	Extracellular Neurons
Frontotemporal lobar degeneration	Tau	Neurons
Progressive supranuclear palsy	Tau	Neurons and glia
Corticobasal degeneration	Tau	Neurons and glia
Parkinson disease	α-Synuclein	Neurons
Multiple system atrophy	α-Synuclein	Glia and some neurons
Frontotemporal lobar degenerations	TDP-43	Neurons
Amyotrophic lateral sclerosis	TDP-43 SOD-1 (familial disease)	Neurons Neurons
Huntington disease	Huntingtin	Neurons
Spinocerebellar ataxias	Ataxins (various)	Neurons

SOD-1, superoxide dismutase-1; TDP-43, TAR DNA-binding protein 43.

Table 22–3 Some Causes of Dementia or Cognitive Impairment

Primary Neurodegenerative Disorders
Alzheimer disease
Frontotemporal lobar degeneration
Lewy body dementia
Huntington disease
Spinocerebellar ataxia (certain forms)
Infections
Prion disease
HIV associated neurocognitive disorder
Progressive multifocal leukoencephalopathy
Viral encephalitis
Neurosyphilis
Chronic meningitis
Vascular and Traumatic Diseases
Multifocal cerebral infarction
Severe hypertensive cerebrovascular disease
Cerebral autosomal dominant arteriopathy with subcortical infarction and leukoencephalopathy (CADASIL)
Chronic traumatic encephalopathy
Metabolic and Nutritional Diseases
Thiamine deficiency (Wernicke-Korsakoff syndrome)
Vitamin B_{12} deficiency
Niacin deficiency (pellagra)
Endocrine diseases
Miscellaneous
Neuronal storage diseases
Toxic injury (from mercury, lead, manganese, bromides, others)

Alzheimer Disease

Alzheimer disease (AD) is the most common cause of dementia in the elderly population. The disease usually manifests with the insidious onset of impaired higher intellectual function and altered mood and behavior. Later, this progresses to disorientation, memory loss, and aphasia, findings indicative of severe cortical dysfunction, and over another 5 to 10 years, the patient becomes profoundly disabled, mute, and immobile. Death usually occurs from intercurrent pneumonia or other infections. Age is an important risk factor for AD; the incidence is about 3% in persons 65 to 74 years old, 19% in those 75 to 84 years old, and 47% in those older than 84 years. Most cases of AD are sporadic, but at least 5% to 10% are familial. Sporadic cases rarely present before 50 years of age, but early onset is seen with some heritable forms.

PATHOGENESIS

Study of the familial forms of AD supports a model in which a peptide called beta amyloid, or Aβ, accumulates in the brain over time, initiating a chain of events that result in AD. Aβ is created when the transmembrane protein amyloid precursor protein (APP) is sequentially cleaved by the enzymes β-amyloid converting enzyme (BACE) and γ-secretase (Fig. 22–24). APP also can be cleaved by α-secretase and γ-secretase, which liberates a different peptide that is nonpathogenic. Mutations in APP or in components of γ-secretase (presenilin-1 or presenilin-2) lead to familial AD by increasing the rate at which Aβ is generated. The *APP* gene is located on chromosome 21, and the risk of AD also is higher in those with an extra copy of the *APP* gene, such as patients with trisomy 21 (Down syndrome) and persons with small interstitial duplications of *APP*, presumably because this too leads to greater Aβ generation. The other major genetic risk factor is a variant of apolipoprotein E called ε4 (ApoE4). Each ApoE4 allele that is present increases the risk of AD by approximately 4 fold and also appears to lower the age of onset. How ApoE4 influences Aβ accumulation is unknown; it may increase Aβ aggregation or deposition, or decrease Aβ clearance.

While large deposits of Aβ are a feature of end-stage AD, small aggregates of Aβ may also be pathogenic, as they alter neurotransmission and are toxic to neurons and synaptic endings. Large deposits, in the form of plaques, also lead to neuronal death, elicit a local inflammatory response that can result in further cell injury, and may cause altered region-to-region communication through mechanical effects on axons and dendrites.

The presence of Aβ also leads to hyperphosphorylation of the neuronal microtubule binding protein tau. This increased

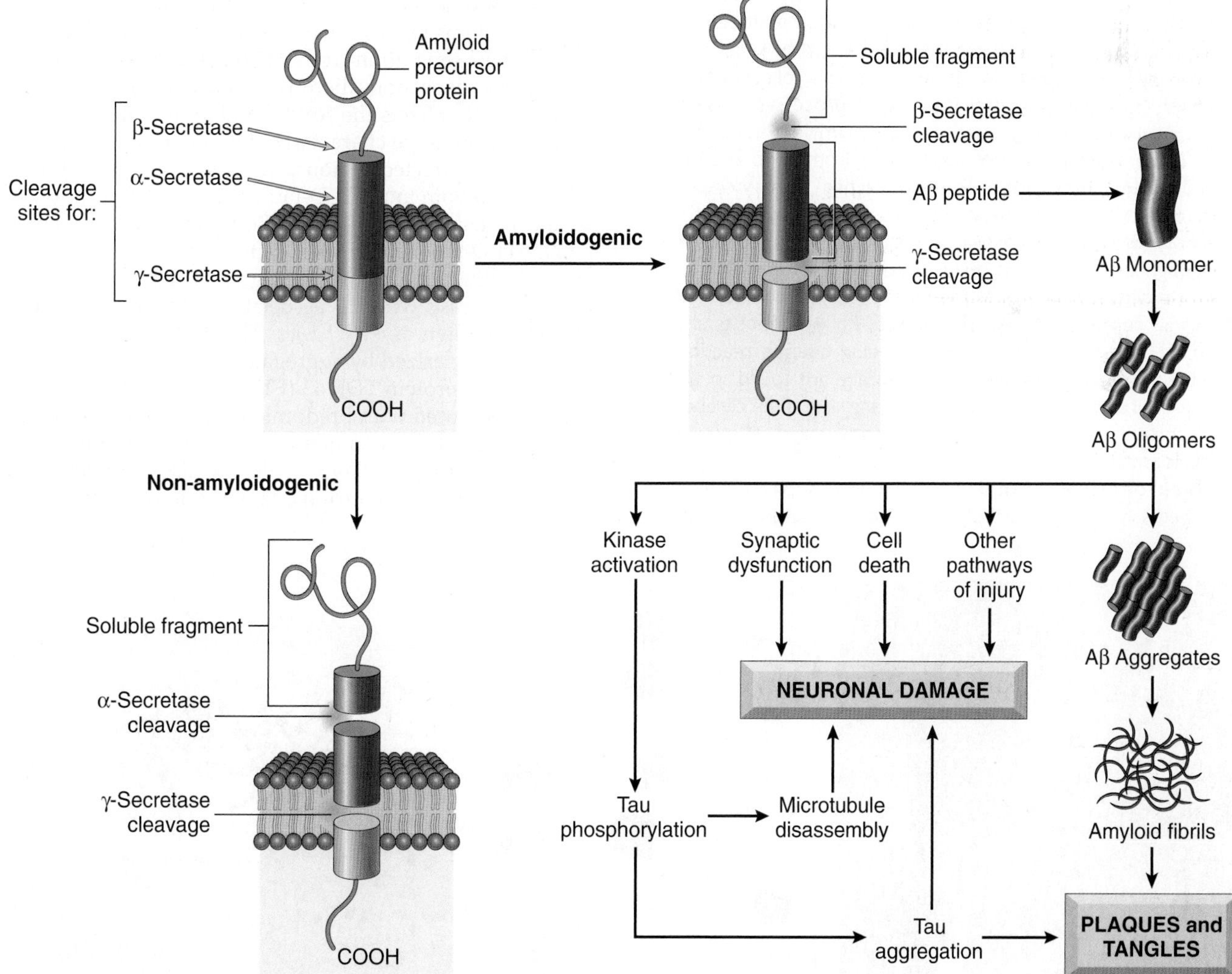

Figure 22–24 Aβ peptide genesis and consequences in Alzheimer disease. Amyloid precursor protein cleavage by α-secretase and γ-secretase produces a harmless soluble peptide, whereas amyloid precursor protein cleavage by β-amyloid–converting enzyme (BACE) and γ-secretase releases Aβ peptides, which form pathogenic aggregates and contribute to the characteristic plaques and tangles of Alzheimer disease.

level of phosphorylation causes tau to redistribute from axons into dendrites and cell bodies, where it aggregates into tangles, which also contribute to neuronal dysfunction and cell death.

MORPHOLOGY

Macroscopic examination of the brain shows a variable degree of cortical atrophy, resulting in a widening of the cerebral sulci that is most pronounced in the frontal, temporal, and parietal lobes. With significant atrophy, there is compensatory ventricular enlargement (hydrocephalus ex vacuo). At the microscopic level, AD is diagnosed by the presence of **plaques** (an extracellular lesion); and **neurofibrillary tangles** (an intracellular lesion) (Fig. 22–25). Because these may also be present to a lesser extent in the brains of elderly nondemented persons, the current criteria for a diagnosis of AD are based on a combination of clinical and pathologic features. There is a fairly constant progressive involvement of different parts of the brain: pathologic changes (specifically plaques, tangles, and the associated neuronal loss and glial reaction) are evident first in the entorhinal cortex, then in the hippocampal formation and isocortex, and finally in the neocortex. Silver staining or immunohistochemistry methods are extremely helpful in assessing the true lesional burden.

Neuritic plaques are focal, spherical collections of dilated, tortuous, silver-staining neuritic processes (dystrophic neurites), often around a central amyloid core (Fig. 22–25, *A*). Neuritic plaques range in size from 20 to 200 μm in diameter; microglial cells and reactive astrocytes are present at their periphery. Plaques can be found in the hippocampus and amygdala as well as in the neocortex, although there usually is relative sparing of primary motor and sensory cortices until late in the disease course. The amyloid core contains Aβ (Fig. 22–25, *B*). Aβ deposits also can be found that lack the surrounding neuritic reaction, termed **diffuse plaques;** these typically are found in the superficial cerebral cortex, the basal ganglia, and the cerebellar cortex and may represent an early stage of plaque development.

Neurofibrillary tangles are bundles of paired helical filaments visible as basophilic fibrillary structures in the cytoplasm of the neurons that displace or encircle the nucleus; tangles can persist after neurons die, becoming a form of extracellular pathology. They are commonly found in cortical neurons, especially in the entorhinal cortex, as well as in the pyramidal cells of the hippocampus, the amygdala, the basal forebrain, and the raphe nuclei. A major component of paired helical filaments is abnormally hyperphosphorylated **tau** (Fig. 22–25, *C*). Tangles are not specific to AD, being found in other degenerative diseases as well.

Frontotemporal Lobar Degeneration

Another major category of disease that results in dementia is called *frontotemporal lobar degeneration* (FTLD). These disorders share clinical features (progressive deterioration of language and changes in personality) stemming from the degeneration and atrophy of temporal and frontal lobes; the clinical syndromes commonly are referred to as *frontotemporal dementias.* When the frontal lobe bears the greatest burden of disease, behavioral changes often dominate, whereas when the disease begins in the temporal lobe, language problems often are the presenting complaint. These symptoms precede memory disturbances, which can assist in their separation from AD on clinical grounds.

On gross inspection, there is atrophy of the brain that predominantly affects the frontal and temporal lobes. Different subgroups are characterized by neuronal inclusions involving the affected regions. In some cases the defining inclusions contain tau (FTLD-tau), but the configuration of the tau inclusions differs from the tau-containing tangles of AD. FTLD-tau sometimes is caused by mutations in the gene encoding tau. One well-recognized subtype of FTLD-tau is *Pick disease,* which is associated with smooth, round inclusions known as *Pick bodies.* The other major form of FTLD is characterized by aggregates containing the DNA/RNA-binding protein TDP-43 (FTLD-TDP43). This form of FTLD is associated with predominantly frontal lobe cognitive impairment. It is sometimes caused by mutations in the gene encoding TDP-43, which is also mutated in a subset of cases of amyotrophic lateral sclerosis (described later).

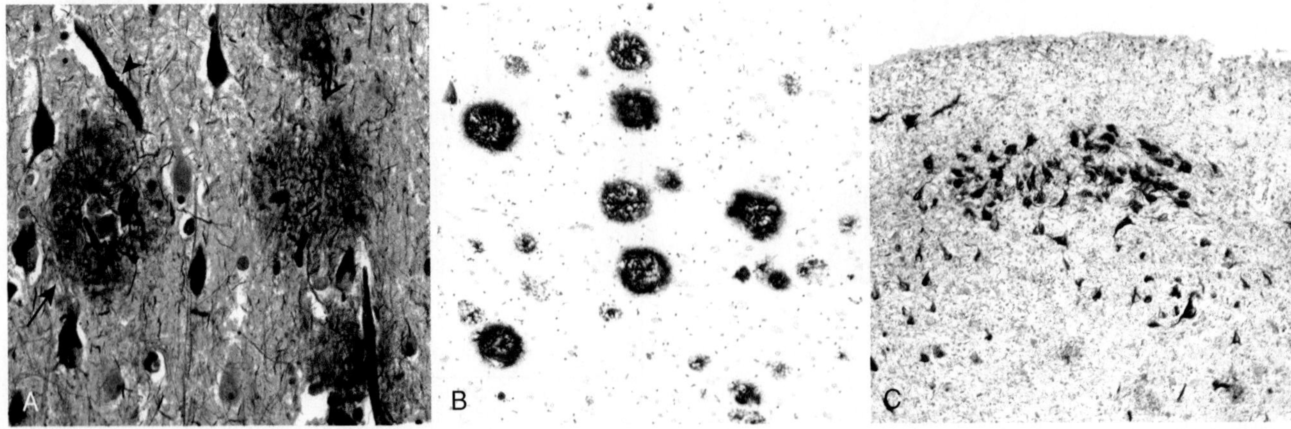

Figure 22–25 Alzheimer disease. **A,** Plaques (*arrow*) contain a central core of amyloid and a surrounding region of dystrophic neurites (Bielschowsky stain). **B,** Immunohistochemical stain for Aβ. Peptide is present in the core of the plaques as well as in the surrounding region. **C,** Neurons containing tangles stained with an antibody specific for tau.

Parkinson Disease

Parkinsonism is a clinical syndrome characterized by tremor, rigidity, bradykinesia and instability. These types of motor disturbances may be seen in a range of diseases that damage dopaminergic neurons, which project from the substantia nigra to the striatum. Parkinsonism can be induced by drugs such as dopamine antagonists or toxins that selectively injure dopaminergic neurons. Among the neurodegenerative diseases, most cases of parkinsonism are caused by *Parkinson disease* (PD), which is associated with characteristic neuronal inclusions containing α-synuclein. Other diseases in which parkinsonism may be present include *multiple system atrophy* (MSA), in which α-synuclein aggregates are found in oligodendrocytes; *progressive supranuclear palsy* (PSP) and *corticobasal degeneration* (CBD), which are both associated with tau-containing inclusions in neurons and glial cells; and *postencephalitic parkinsonism,* which was associated with the 1918 influenza pandemic.

PATHOGENESIS

While PD in most cases is sporadic, both autosomal dominant and recessive forms of the disease also exist. Point mutations and duplications of the gene encoding α-synuclein, a protein involved in synaptic transmission, cause autosomal dominant PD. Even in sporadic PD, the diagnostic feature of the disease—the Lewy body—is an inclusion containing α-synuclein. The linkage between α-synuclein and disease pathogenesis is unclear, but other genetic forms of PD provide some clues. Two other causative genetic loci encode the proteins parkin, an E3 ubiquitin ligase, and UCHL-1, an enzyme involved in recycling of ubiquitin from proteins targeted to the proteasome, suggesting that defects in protein degradation may have a pathogenic role. Another tantalizing clue comes from the association of PD with mutations in a protein kinase called LRRK2; histopathologic examination of cases associated with LRRK2 mutations may show either Lewy bodies containing α-synuclein or tangles containing tau. Finally, some forms of familial PD are associated with mutations in the *PARK7* or *PINK1* genes, both of which appear to be important for normal mitochondrial function.

MORPHOLOGY

A typical gross finding at autopsy is pallor of the substantia nigra (Fig. 22–26, *A* and *B*) and locus ceruleus. Microscopic features include loss of the pigmented, catecholaminergic neurons in these regions associated with gliosis. **Lewy bodies** (Fig. 22–26, *C*) may be found in those neurons that remain. These are single or multiple, intracytoplasmic, eosinophilic, round to elongated inclusions that often have a dense core surrounded by a pale halo. On ultrastructural examination, Lewy bodies consist of fine filaments, densely packed in the core but loose at the rim, composed of α-synuclein and other proteins, including neurofilaments and ubiquitin. The other major histologic finding is **Lewy neurites,** dystrophic neurites that also contain abnormally aggregated α-synuclein.

As implied by the occurrence of a broad array of neurologic deficits in PD, immunohistochemical staining for α-synuclein highlights more subtle Lewy bodies and Lewy neurites in many brain regions outside of the substantia nigra and in nondopaminergic neurons. These lesions appear first in the medulla and then in the pons, before involvement of the substantia nigra. As implied by the dementia, Lewy bodies and Lewy neurites eventually appear in the cerebral cortex and subcortical areas, including the cholinergic cells of the basal nucleus of Meynert and the amygdala.

Clinical Features

PD commonly manifests as a movement disorder in the absence of a toxic exposure or other known underlying etiology. The disease usually progresses over 10 to 15 years, eventually producing severe motor slowing to the point of near immobility. Death usually is the result of intercurrent infection or trauma from frequent falls caused by postural instability.

Movement symptoms of PD initially respond to L-dihydroxyphenylalanine (L-DOPA), but this treatment does not slow disease progression. Over time, L-DOPA becomes less effective and begins to cause potentially problematic fluctuations in motor function.

While the movement disorder associated with loss of the nigrostriatal dopaminergic pathway is an important feature of PD, it is clear that the disease has more extensive clinical and pathologic manifestations. Lesions can be found lower

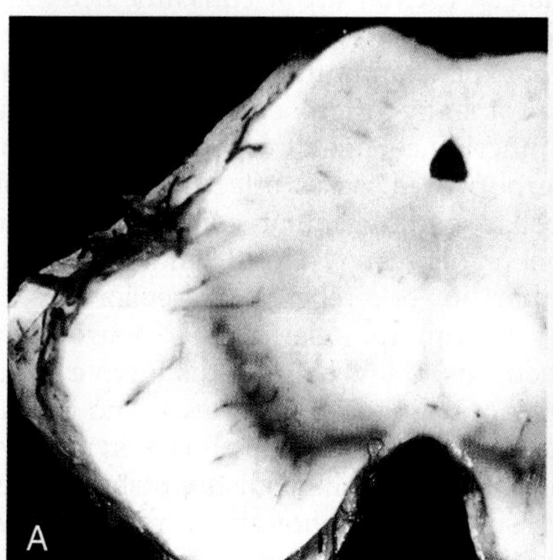

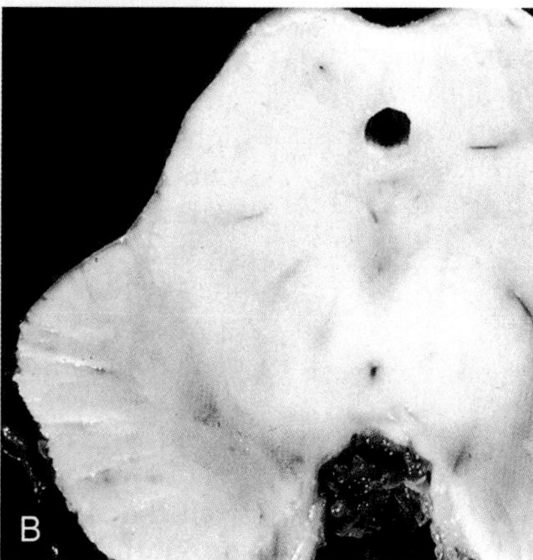

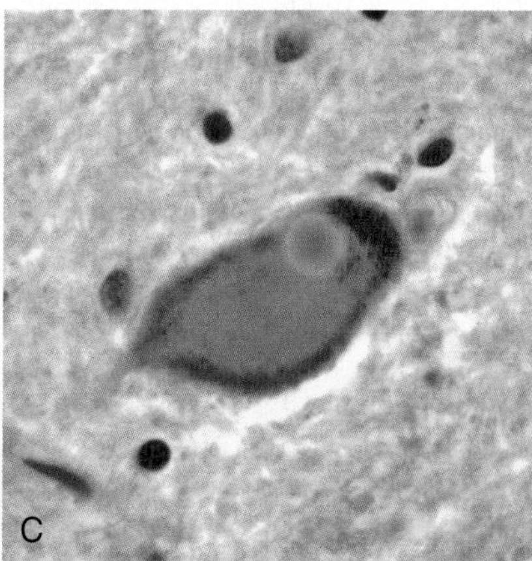

Figure 22–26 Parkinson disease. **A,** Normal substantia nigra. **B,** Depigmented substantia nigra in idiopathic Parkinson disease. **C,** Lewy body in a neuron from the substantia nigra stains *pink*.

in the brain stem (in the dorsal motor nucleus of the vagus and in the reticular formation) in advance of nigral involvement, in line with clinical studies showing that autonomic dysfunction and behavioral disorders often are present in advance of the motor problems. Dementia, typically with a mildly fluctuating course and hallucinations, emerges in many persons with PD and is attributable to involvement of the cerebral cortex. When dementia arises within 1 year of the onset of motor symptoms, it is referred to *Lewy body dementia* (LBD).

Huntington Disease

Huntington disease (HD) is an autosomal dominant movement disorder associated with degeneration of the striatum (caudate and putamen). The movement disorder is choreiform (dancelike), with increased and involuntary jerky movements of all parts of the body; writhing movements of the extremities are typical. *The disease is relentlessly progressive, resulting in death after an average course of about 15 years.* Early cognitive symptoms include forgetfulness and thought and affective disorders, and there may be progression to a severe dementia. As a part of these early behavioral changes, HD carries an increased risk of suicide.

PATHOGENESIS

HD is caused by **CAG trinucleotide repeat expansions** in a gene located on 4p16.3 that encodes the protein huntingtin. Normal alleles contain 11 to 34 copies of the repeat; in disease-causing alleles the number of repeats is increased, sometimes into the hundreds. There is strong genotype-phenotype correlation, with larger numbers of repeats resulting in earlier-onset disease. Once the symptoms appear, however, the course of the illness is not affected by repeat length. Further expansions of the pathologic CAG repeats can occur during spermatogenesis, so paternal transmission may be associated with earlier onset in the next generation, a phenomenon referred to as **anticipation** (Chapter 6).

HD appears to be caused by a toxic gain-of-function mutation somehow related to the expanded polyglutamine tract in huntingtin. The mutant protein is subject to ubiquitination and proteolysis, yielding fragments that can form large intranuclear aggregates. As in other degenerative diseases, smaller aggregates of the abnormal protein fragments are suspected to be the critical toxic agent. These aggregates may sequester transcription factors, disrupt protein degradation pathways, perturb mitochondrial function, or alter brain-derived neurotrophic factor (BDNF) signaling. It is likely that some combination of these aberrations contributes to HD pathogenesis.

MORPHOLOGY

On gross examination, the brain is small and shows striking atrophy of the caudate nucleus and, sometimes less dramatically, the putamen (Fig. 22–27). Pathologic changes develop over the course of the illness in a medial to lateral direction in the caudate and from dorsal to ventral in the putamen. The globus pallidus may be atrophied secondarily, and the lateral and third ventricles are dilated. Atrophy frequently is also seen in the frontal lobe, less often in the parietal lobe, and occasionally in the entire cortex.

Microscopic examination reveals severe loss of neurons from affected regions of the striatum. The medium-sized, spiny neurons that release the neurotransmitters γ-aminobutyric acid (GABA), enkephalin, dynorphin, and substance P are especially sensitive, disappearing early in the disease. Also seen is fibrillary gliosis, which is more extensive than in the usual reaction to neuronal loss. There is a strong correlation between the degree of degeneration in the striatum and the severity of motor symptoms; there is also an association between cortical neuronal loss and dementia. In remaining striatal neurons and in the cortex, there are intranuclear inclusions that contain aggregates of ubiquitinated huntingtin protein (Fig. 22–27, *inset*).

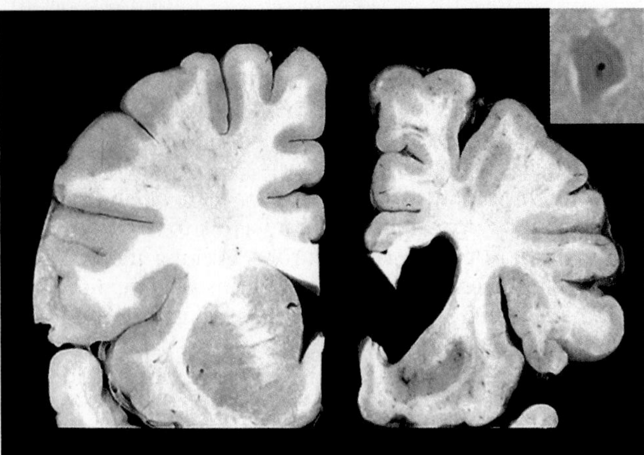

Figure 22–27 Huntington disease. Normal hemisphere on the *left* compared with the hemisphere with Huntington disease on the *right* showing atrophy of the striatum and ventricular dilation. *Inset,* An intranuclear inclusion in a cortical neuron is strongly immunoreactive for ubiquitin. *(Courtesy of Dr. J.P. Vonsattel, Columbia University, New York, New York.)*

Spinocerebellar Ataxias

Spinocerebellar ataxias (SCAs) are a clinically heterogeneous group of diseases that are frequently caused by trinucleotide repeat expansion mutations. They are distinguished from one another by differences in causative mutations, patterns of inheritance, age at onset, and signs and symptoms. This group of diseases affects, to a variable extent, the cerebellar cortex, spinal cord, other brain regions, and peripheral nerves. As a result, clinical findings may include a combination of cerebellar and sensory ataxia, spasticity, and sensorimotor peripheral neuropathy. Degeneration of neurons, often without distinctive histopathologic changes, occurs in the affected areas and is associated with mild gliosis. The additional clinical symptoms that accompany the ataxia can help distinguish between well-characterized subtypes. Although more than two dozen distinct genetic types of SCA have been identified, there remain many cases which do not fall into one of the already characterized forms.

As with Huntington disease, several forms of SCA (SCA types 1, 2, 3, 6, 7, and 17 and dentatorubropallidoluysian atrophy) are caused by CAG repeat expansions encoding polyglutamine tracts in various genes. In these forms of SCA, neuronal intranuclear inclusions are present containing the abnormal protein and there is an inverse correlation between the degree of repeat expansion and age of onset. Other SCAs are caused by trinucleotide repeat expansions in untranslated regions or by other types of mutations.

Friedreich ataxia is an autosomal recessive disorder that generally manifests in the first decade of life with gait ataxia, followed by hand clumsiness and dysarthria. Most patients develop pes cavus and kyphoscoliosis, and there is a high incidence of cardiac disease and diabetes. The disease usually is caused by a GAA trinucleotide repeat expansion in the gene encoding frataxin, a protein that regulates cellular iron levels, particularly in the mitochondria. The repeat expansion results in decreased protein levels through transcriptional silencing; rare cases in which point mutations produce a nonfunctional frataxin protein also have been described. Decreased frataxin leads to mitochondrial dysfunction as well as increased oxidative damage.

Amyotrophic Lateral Sclerosis

Amyotrophic lateral sclerosis (ALS) results from the death of lower motor neurons in the spinal cord and brain stem, and of upper motor neurons (Betz cells) in the motor cortex. The loss of lower motor neurons results in denervation of muscles, muscular atrophy (the "amyotrophy" of the condition), weakness, and fasciculations, while the loss of upper motor neurons results in paresis, hyperreflexia, and spasticity, along with a Babinski sign. An additional consequence of upper motor neuron loss is degeneration of the corticospinal tracts in the lateral portion of the spinal cord ("lateral sclerosis"). Sensation usually is unaffected, but cognitive impairment does occur, sometimes as a frontotemporal dementia.

The disease affects men slightly more frequently than women and becomes clinically manifest in the fifth decade or later, usually beginning with subtle asymmetric distal extremity weakness. As the disease progresses to involve more of the motor system, muscle strength and bulk diminish and involuntary contractions of individual motor units, termed fasciculations, occur. The disease eventually involves the respiratory muscles, leading to recurrent bouts of pulmonary infection, which is the usual cause of death. The balance between upper and lower motor neuron involvement can vary, although most patients exhibit involvement of both. In some patients, degeneration of the lower brain stem cranial motor nuclei occurs early and progresses rapidly, a pattern of disease referred to as bulbar amyotrophic lateral sclerosis. With this disease pattern, abnormalities of swallowing and speaking dominate.

PATHOGENESIS

While most cases are sporadic, 5% to 10% are familial, mostly with autosomal dominant inheritance. Familial disease begins earlier in life than sporadic disease, but once symptoms appear, the clinical course is similar in both forms. More than a dozen genes have been implicated, but the most frequent genetic cause (20% of cases) is mutations in the superoxide dismutase gene, *SOD-1*, on chromosome 21. These mutations are thought to generate abnormal misfolded forms of the SOD-1 protein, which may trigger the unfolded protein response and cause apoptotic death of neurons. The next two most common causative genes both encode DNA/RNA binding proteins, TDP-43 and FUS; how these mutations cause disease is unknown. As already mentioned, mutations in TDP-43 also can cause frontotemporal lobar degeneration (FTLD) or a disease with overlapping features of both ALS and FTLD.

MORPHOLOGY

The most striking gross changes are found in anterior roots of the spinal cord, which are thin and gray (rather than white). In especially severe cases, the precentral gyrus (motor cortex) may be mildly atrophic. Microscopic examination demonstrates a reduction in the number of anterior horn cell neurons throughout the length of the spinal cord associated with reactive gliosis and loss of anterior root myelinated fibers. Similar findings are found with involvement of motor cranial nerve nuclei except those supplying the extraocular muscles, which are spared except in very longstanding survivors. Remaining lower motor neurons often harbor cytoplasmic inclusions that contain TDP-43, except in those cases in which the underlying cause is a mutation in SOD-1.

Death of upper motor neurons—a finding that may be hard to demonstrate microscopically—results in degeneration of the descending corticospinal tracts. This is usually easily seen in the spinal cord. With the loss of innervation from the death of anterior horn cells, skeletal muscles show neurogenic atrophy.

SUMMARY

Neurodegenerative Diseases

- Neurodegenerative diseases cause symptoms that depend on the pattern of brain involvement. Cortical disease usually manifests as cognitive change, alterations in personality, and memory disturbances; basal ganglia disorders usually manifest as movement disorders.
- Many neurodegenerative diseases preferentially affect a primary set of brain regions, but other regions can be involved later in the disease course. This evolving process can change the phenotype of the disease over time—as with the appearance of cognitive impairments in people initially affected by the movement disorder of Parkinson disease.
- Many of the neurodegenerative diseases are associated with various protein aggregates, which serve as pathologic

hallmarks. It is unclear whether these striking inclusions and deposits are critical mediators of cellular degeneration. Familial forms of these diseases are associated with mutations in the genes encoding these proteins or controlling their metabolism.

TUMORS

The annual incidence of CNS tumors ranges from 10 to 17 per 100,000 persons for intracranial tumors and 1 to 2 per 100,000 persons for intraspinal tumors; about half to three quarters are primary tumors, and the rest are metastatic. Tumors of the CNS make up a larger proportion of childhood cancers, accounting for as many of 20% of all pediatric tumors. Childhood CNS tumors differ from those in adults in both histologic subtype and location. In childhood, tumors are likely to arise in the posterior fossa; in adults, they are mostly supratentorial.

Tumors of the nervous system have unique characteristics that set them apart from neoplastic processes elsewhere in the body.

- These tumors do not have detectable premalignant or in situ stages comparable to those of carcinomas.
- Even low-grade lesions may infiltrate large regions of the brain, leading to serious clinical deficits, nonresectability, and poor prognosis.
- The anatomic site of the neoplasm can influence outcome independent of histologic classification due to local effects (e.g., a benign meningioma may cause cardiorespiratory arrest from compression of the medulla) or nonresectability (e.g., brain stem gliomas).
- Even the most highly malignant gliomas rarely spread outside of the CNS; in addition to local infiltration, the subarachnoid space allows for spread to distant sites along the neuroaxis.

Gliomas

Gliomas are tumors of the brain parenchyma that are classified histologically on the basis of their resemblance to different types of glial cells. The major types of glial tumors are *astrocytomas, oligodendrogliomas,* and *ependymomas.* The most common types are highly infiltrative or "diffuse gliomas," including astrocytic, oligodendroglial, and mixed forms. In contrast, ependymomas tend to form solid masses.

Astrocytoma

Several different categories of astrocytic tumors are recognized, the most common being diffuse and pilocytic astrocytomas. Different types of astrocytomas have characteristic histologic features, anatomic distributions, and clinical features.

Diffuse Astrocytoma

Diffuse astrocytomas account for about 80% of adult gliomas. They are most frequent in the fourth through the sixth decades of life. They usually are found in the cerebral hemispheres. The most common presenting signs and symptoms are seizures, headaches, and focal neurologic deficits related to the anatomic site of involvement. They show a spectrum of histologic differentiation that correlates well with clinical course and outcome. On the basis of histologic features, they are stratified into three groups: well-differentiated astrocytoma (grade II/IV), anaplastic astrocytoma (grade III/IV), and glioblastoma (grade IV/IV), with increasingly grim prognosis as the grade increases.

Well-differentiated astrocytomas can be static for several years, but at some point they progress; the mean survival is more than 5 years. Eventually, patients suffer rapid clinical deterioration that is correlated with the appearance of anaplastic features and more rapid tumor growth. Other patients present with glioblastoma from the start. Once the histologic features of glioblastoma appear, the prognosis is very poor; with treatment (resection, radiotherapy, and chemotherapy), the median survival is only 15 months.

Astrocytomas are associated with a variety of acquired mutations, which cluster in several important pathways. In glioblastoma, loss-of-function mutations in the p53 and Rb tumor suppressor pathways and gain-of-function mutations in the oncogenic PI3K pathways have central roles in tumorigenesis. Surprisingly, mutations that alter the enzymatic activity of two isoforms of the metabolic enzyme isocitrate dehydrogenase (IDH1 and IDH2) are common in lower-grade astrocytomas. As a result, immunostaining for the mutated form of IDH1 has become an important diagnostic tool in evaluating biopsy specimens for the presence of low-grade astrocytoma.

MORPHOLOGY

Well-differentiated astrocytomas are poorly defined, gray, infiltrative tumors that expand and distort the invaded brain without forming a discrete mass (Fig. 22–28, *A*). Infiltration beyond the grossly evident margins is always present. The cut surface of the tumor is either firm or soft and gelatinous; cystic degeneration may be seen. In glioblastoma, variation in the gross appearance of the tumor from region to region is characteristic (Fig. 22–28, *B*). Some areas are firm and white, others are soft and yellow (the result of tissue necrosis), and still others show regions of cystic degeneration and hemorrhage.

Well-differentiated astrocytomas are characterized by a mild to moderate increase in the number of glial cell nuclei, somewhat variable nuclear pleomorphism, and an intervening feltwork of fine, glial fibrillary acidic protein (GFAP)-positive astrocytic cell processes that give the background a fibrillary appearance. The transition between neoplastic and normal tissue is indistinct, and tumor cells can be seen infiltrating normal tissue many centimeters from the main lesion. Anaplastic astrocytomas show regions that are more densely cellular and have greater nuclear pleomorphism; mitotic figures are present. Glioblastoma has a histologic appearance similar to that of anaplastic astrocytoma, as well as either necrosis (often with pseudopalisading nuclei) or vascular proliferation (Fig. 22–28, *C*).

Pilocytic Astrocytoma

Pilocytic astrocytomas are relatively benign tumors, typically affecting children and young adults. Most commonly

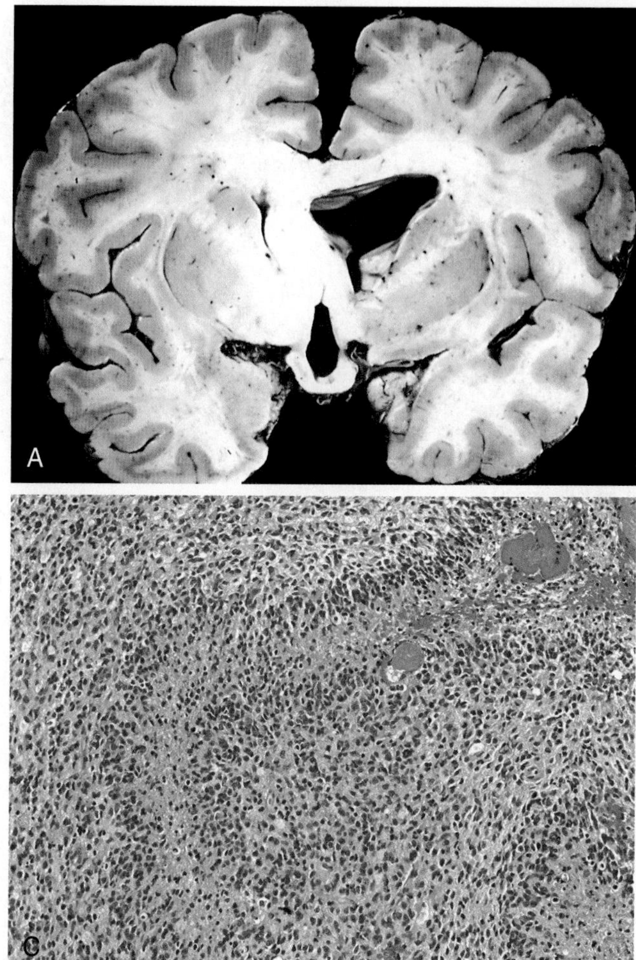

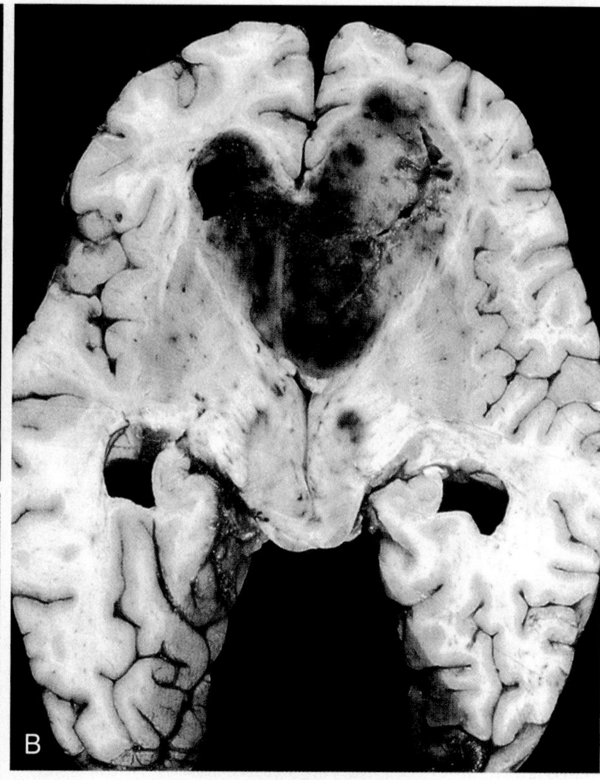

Figure 22–28 Astrocytomas. **A,** Low-grade astrocytoma is seen as expanded white matter of the left cerebral hemisphere and thickened corpus callosum and fornices. **B,** Glioblastoma appearing as a necrotic, hemorrhagic, infiltrating mass. **C,** Glioblastoma is a densely cellular tumor with necrosis and pseudopalisading of tumor cell nuclei.

located in the cerebellum, they also may involve the third ventricle, the optic pathways, spinal cord, and occasionally the cerebral hemispheres. There is often a cyst associated with the tumor, and symptomatic recurrence from incompletely resected lesions is often associated with cyst enlargement, rather than growth of the solid component. Tumors that involve the hypothalamus are especially problematic because they cannot be resected completely.

A high proportion of pilocytic astrocytomas have activating mutations in the serine-threonine kinase BRAF—either a specific point mutation (V600E) that is also found in many other cancers (Chapter 5), or more commonly a partial tandem duplication event. Mutations in IDH1 and IDH2 (common in low-grade diffuse astrocytomas) are not found in pilocytic tumors. These genetic distinctions support the division of these astrocytomas into two diagnostic categories.

MORPHOLOGY

A pilocytic astrocytoma often is cystic, with a mural nodule in the wall of the cyst; if solid, it is usually well circumscribed. The tumor is composed of bipolar cells with long, thin "hair-like" processes that are GFAP-positive. Rosenthal fibers, eosinophilic granular bodies, and microcysts are often present; necrosis and mitoses are rare.

Oligodendroglioma

Oligodendrogliomas account for 5% to 15% of gliomas and most commonly are detected in the fourth and fifth decades of life. Patients may have had several years of antecedent neurologic complaints, often including seizures. The lesions are found mostly in the cerebral hemispheres, mainly in the frontal or temporal lobes.

Patients with oligodendrogliomas enjoy a better prognosis than that for patients with astrocytomas of similar grade. Treatment with surgery, chemotherapy, and radiotherapy yields an average survival of 10 to 20 years for well-differentiated (WHO grade II) or 5 to 10 years for anaplastic (WHO grade III) oligodendrogliomas. The most common genetic findings are deletions of chromosomes 1p and 19q, alterations that typically occur together. Tumors with deletions of 1p and 19q are usually highly responsive to chemotherapy and radiotherapy.

MORPHOLOGY

Well-differentiated oligodendrogliomas (WHO grade II/IV) are infiltrative tumors that form gelatinous, gray masses and may show cysts, focal hemorrhage, and calcification. On microscopic examination, the tumor is composed of sheets of regular cells with spherical nuclei containing finely granular-appearing chromatin (similar to that in normal

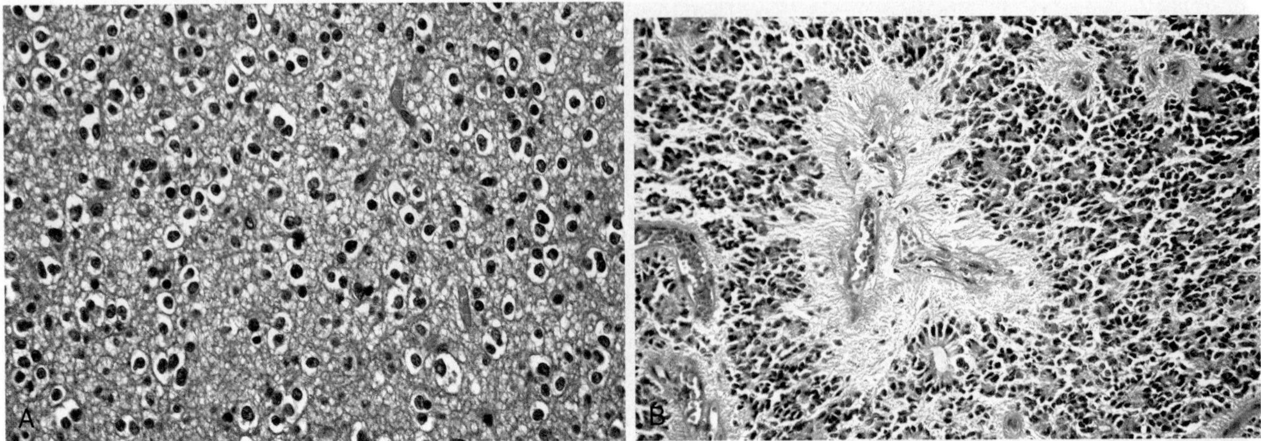

Figure 22–29 Other gliomas. **A,** In oligodendroglioma tumor cells have round nuclei, often with a cytoplasmic halo. Blood vessels in the background are thin and can form an interlacing pattern. **B,** Microscopic appearance of ependymoma.

oligodendrocytes) surrounded by a clear halo of cytoplasm (Fig. 22–29, *A*). The tumor typically contains a delicate network of anastomosing capillaries. Calcification, present in as many as 90% of these tumors, ranges in extent from microscopic foci to massive depositions. Mitotic activity usually is difficult to detect. Anaplastic oligodendroglioma (WHO grade III/IV) is a more aggressive subtype with higher cell density, nuclear anaplasia and mitotic activity.

Ependymoma

Ependymomas most often arise next to the ependyma-lined ventricular system, including the central canal of the spinal cord. In the first 2 decades of life, they typically occur near the fourth ventricle and constitute 5% to 10% of the primary brain tumors in this age group. In adults, the spinal cord is their most common location; tumors in this site are particularly frequent in the setting of neurofibromatosis type 2 (Chapter 21). The clinical outcome for completely resected supratentorial and spinal ependymomas is better than for those in the posterior fossa.

MORPHOLOGY

In the fourth ventricle, ependymomas typically are solid or papillary masses extending from the ventricular floor. The tumors are composed of cells with regular, round to oval nuclei and abundant granular chromatin. Between the nuclei is a variably dense fibrillary background. Tumor cells may form round or elongated structures **(rosettes, canals)** that resemble the embryologic ependymal canal, with long, delicate processes extending into a lumen (Fig. 23–29, *B*); more frequently present are **perivascular pseudorosettes** in which tumor cells are arranged around vessels with an intervening zone containing thin ependymal processes. Anaplastic ependymomas show increased cell density, high mitotic rates, necrosis, and less evident ependymal differentiation.

Neuronal Tumors

Central neurocytoma is a low-grade neoplasm found within and adjacent to the ventricular system (most commonly the lateral or third ventricles), characterized by evenly spaced, round, uniform nuclei and often islands of neuropil.

Gangliogliomas are tumors with a mixture of glial elements, usually a low-grade astrocytoma, and mature-appearing neurons. Most of these tumors are slow-growing, but the glial component occasionally becomes frankly anaplastic, and the disease then progresses rapidly. These lesions often manifest with seizures.

Dysembryoplastic neuroepithelial tumor is a distinctive, low-grade childhood tumor that grows slowly and carries a relatively good prognosis after resection; it often manifests as a seizure disorder. It typically is located in the superficial temporal lobe and consists of small round neuronal cells arranged in columns and around central cores of processes. These typically form multiple discrete intracortical nodules that have a myxoid background. Also present are well-differentiated "floating" neurons within pools of mucopolysaccharide-rich myxoid fluid.

Embryonal (Primitive) Neoplasms

Some tumors of neuroectodermal origin have a primitive "small round cell" appearance that is reminiscent of normal progenitor cells encountered in the developing CNS. Differentiation is often limited, but may progress along multiple lineages. The most common is the *medulloblastoma,* accounting for 20% of pediatric brain tumors.

Medulloblastoma

Medulloblastoma occurs predominantly in children and exclusively in the cerebellum. Neuronal and glial markers are nearly always expressed, at least to a limited extent. It is highly malignant, and the prognosis for untreated patients is dismal; however, medulloblastoma is exquisitely radiosensitive. With total excision, chemotherapy, and irradiation, the 5-year survival rate may be as high as 75%. Tumors of similar histologic type and a poor degree of differentiation can be found elsewhere in the nervous system, where they are called *primitive neuroectodermal tumors* (PNETs).

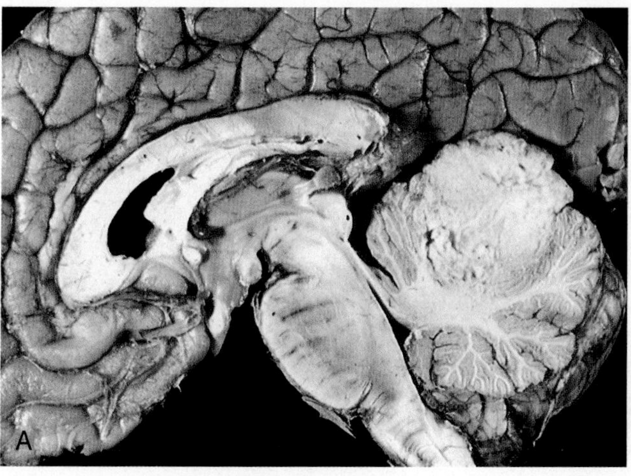

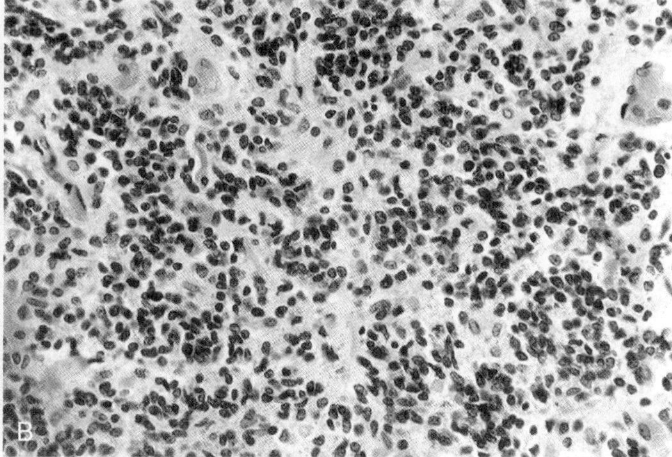

Figure 22–30 Medulloblastoma. **A,** Sagittal section of brain showing medulloblastoma with destruction of the superior midline cerebellum. **B,** Microscopic appearance of medulloblastoma.

MORPHOLOGY

In children, medulloblastomas are located in the midline of the cerebellum; lateral tumors occur more often in adults. The tumor often is well circumscribed, gray, and friable and may be seen extending to the surface of the cerebellar folia and involving the leptomeninges (Fig. 22–30, *A*). Medulloblastomas are extremely cellular, with sheets of anaplastic ("small blue") cells (Fig. 22–30, *B*). Individual tumor cells are small, with little cytoplasm and hyperchromatic nuclei; mitoses are abundant. Often, focal neuronal differentiation is seen in the form of the Homer Wright or neuroblastic rosette, which closely resembles the rosettes encountered in neuroblastomas; they are characterized by primitive tumor cells surrounding central neuropil (delicate pink material formed by neuronal processes).

Genetic analysis of medulloblastoma has revealed that morphologically similar tumors commonly exhibit distinct alterations, and that there is a relationship between the underlying mutations and outcome. In general, tumors with *MYC* amplifications are associated with poor outcomes, while those linked with mutations in genes of the WNT signaling pathway have a more favorable course. Many tumors also have mutations that activate the sonic hedgehog (shh) pathway, which has a critical role in tumorigenesis but an uncertain relationship to outcome. These genetic distinctions are beginning to be used to stratify patients into different risk groups and guide therapy. Ideally, it would be best to avoid CNS radiotherapy in young patients, and it is hoped that new therapies targeting mutated gene products will achieve this goal.

Other Parenchymal Tumors

Primary Central Nervous System Lymphoma

Primary CNS lymphoma, occurring mostly as diffuse large B cell lymphomas, accounts for 2% of extranodal lymphomas and 1% of intracranial tumors. It is the most common CNS neoplasm in immunosuppressed persons, in whom the tumors are nearly always positive for the oncogenic Epstein-Barr virus. In nonimmunosuppressed populations, the age spectrum is relatively wide, with the incidence increasing after 60 years of age. Regardless of the clinical context, primary brain lymphoma is an aggressive disease with relatively poor response to chemotherapy as compared with peripheral lymphomas.

Patients with primary brain lymphoma often are found to have multiple tumor nodules within the brain parenchyma, yet involvement outside of the CNS is an uncommon late complication. Lymphoma originating outside the CNS rarely spreads to the brain parenchyma; when it happens, tumor usually is also within the CSF or involvement of the meninges.

MORPHOLOGY

Lesions often involve deep gray structures, as well as the white matter and the cortex. Periventricular spread is common. The tumors are relatively well defined as compared with glial neoplasms but are not as discrete as metastases. EBV-associated tumors often show extensive areas of necrosis. The tumors are nearly always aggressive large B-cell lymphomas, although other histologic types can be observed rarely (Chapter 11). Microscopically, malignant cells accumulate around blood vessels and infiltrate the surrounding brain parenchyma.

Germ Cell Tumors

Primary brain *germ cell tumors* occur along the midline, most commonly in the pineal and the suprasellar regions. They account for 0.2% to 1% of brain tumors in people of European descent but as many as 10% of brain tumors in persons of Japanese ethnicity. They are a tumor of the young, with 90% occurring during the first 2 decades of life. Germ cell tumors in the pineal region show a strong male predominance. The most common primary CNS germ cell tumor is germinoma, a tumor that closely resembles testicular seminoma (Chapter 17). Secondary CNS involvement by metastatic gonadal germ cell tumors also occurs.

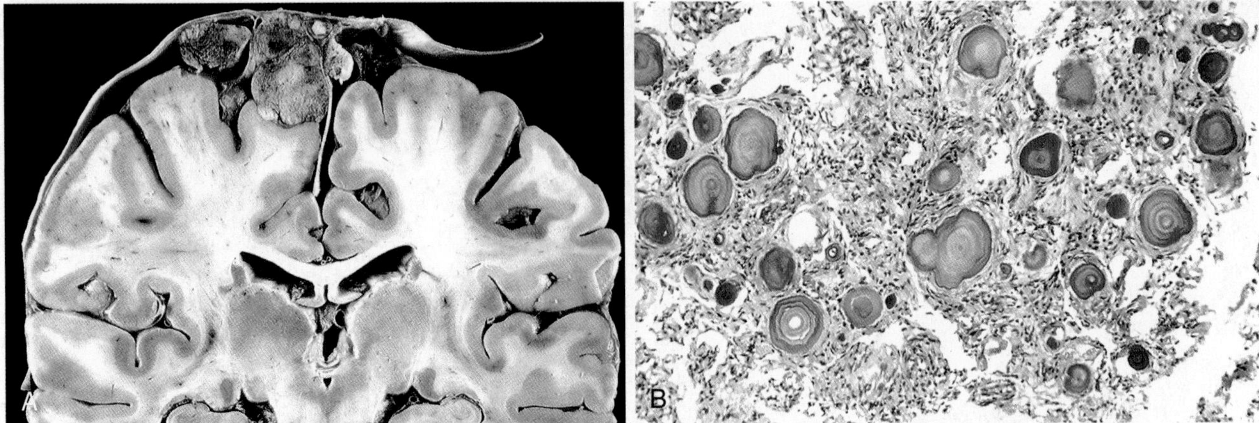

Figure 22–31 Meningioma. **A,** Parasagittal multilobular meningioma attached to the dura with compression of underlying brain. **B,** Meningioma with a whorled pattern of cell growth and psammoma bodies.

Meningiomas

Meningiomas are predominantly benign tumors that arise from arachnoid meningothelial cells. They usually occur in adults and are often attached to the dura. Meningiomas may be found along any of the external surfaces of the brain as well as within the ventricular system, where they arise from the stromal arachnoid cells of the choroid plexus. They usually come to attention because of vague nonlocalizing symptoms, or with focal findings referable to compression of adjacent brain. Although most meningiomas are easily separable from underlying brain, some tumors infiltrate the brain, a feature that is associated with an increased risk of recurrence. The overall prognosis is determined by the lesion size and location, surgical accessibility, and histologic grade.

When a person has multiple meningiomas, especially in association with eighth-nerve schwannomas or glial tumors, the diagnosis of neurofibromatosis type 2 (NF2) should be considered (Chapter 21). About half of meningiomas not associated with NF2 have acquired loss-of-function mutations in the *NF2* tumor suppressor gene on the long arm of chromosome 22 (22q). These mutations are found in all grades of meningioma, suggesting that they are involved with tumor initiation. Mutations in *NF2* are more common in tumors with certain growth patterns (fibroblastic, transitional, and psammomatous).

MORPHOLOGY

Meningiomas (WHO grade I/IV) grow as well-defined dura-based masses that may compress the brain but do not invade it (Fig. 22–31, *A*). Extension into the overlying bone may be present. Among the varied histologic patterns are **syncytial,** named for whorled clusters of cells without visible cell membranes that sit in tight groups; **fibroblastic,** with elongated cells and abundant collagen deposition between them; **transitional,** which shares features of the syncytial and fibroblastic types; **psammomatous,** with numerous psammoma bodies (Fig. 22–31, *B*); and **secretory,** with gland-like PAS-positive eosinophilic secretions known as pseudopsammoma bodies.

Atypical meningiomas (WHO grade II/IV) are recognized by the presence of certain histologic features (prominent nucleoli, increased cellularity, pattern-less growth), and often have a higher mitotic rate. These tumors demonstrate more aggressive local growth and a higher rate of recurrence; they may require therapy in addition to surgery.

Anaplastic (malignant) meningiomas (WHO grade III/IV) are highly aggressive tumors that may resemble a high-grade sarcoma or carcinoma, although there usually is some histologic evidence of a meningothelial cell origin.

Metastatic Tumors

Metastatic lesions, mostly carcinomas, account for approximately one fourth to one half of intracranial tumors. The most common primary sites are lung, breast, skin (melanoma), kidney, and gastrointestinal tract—together these account for about 80% of cases. Metastases form sharply demarcated masses, often at the gray-white junction, and elicit edema (Fig. 22–32). The boundary between tumor and brain parenchyma is sharp at the microscopic level as well, with surrounding reactive gliosis.

In addition to the direct and localized effects produced by metastases, *paraneoplastic syndromes* may involve the peripheral and central nervous systems, sometimes even preceding the clinical recognition of the malignant neoplasm. Many but not all patients with paraneoplastic syndromes have antibodies against tumor antigens. Some of the more common patterns include

- *Subacute cerebellar degeneration* resulting in ataxia, with destruction of Purkinje cells, gliosis, and a mild inflammatory infiltrate
- *Limbic encephalitis* causing a subacute dementia, with perivascular inflammatory cells, microglial nodules, some neuronal loss, and gliosis, all centered in the medial temporal lobe

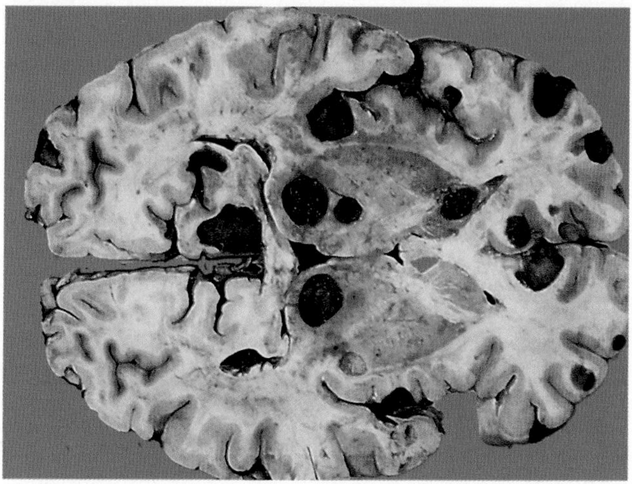

Figure 22–32 Metastatic melanoma. Metastatic lesions are distinguished grossly from most primary central nervous system tumors by their multicentricity and well-demarcated margins. The dark color of the tumor nodules in this specimen is due to the presence of melanin.

- *Subacute sensory neuropathy* leading to altered pain sensation, with loss of sensory neurons from dorsal root ganglia, in association with inflammation
- *Syndrome of rapid-onset psychosis, catatonia, epilepsy, and coma* associated with ovarian teratoma and antibodies against the *N*-methyl-D-aspartate (NMDA) receptor

Familial Tumor Syndromes

Several inherited syndromes caused by mutations in various tumor suppressor genes are associated with an increased risk of particular types of cancers. Those with particular involvement of the CNS are discussed here; familial syndromes associated with tumors of the peripheral nervous system are covered in Chapter 21.

Tuberous Sclerosis

Tuberous sclerosis (TSC) is an autosomal dominant syndrome characterized by the development of hamartomas and benign neoplasms involving the brain and other tissues. CNS hamartomas variously consist of cortical tubers and subependymal hamartomas, including a larger tumefactive form known as subependymal giant cell astrocytoma. Because of their proximity to the foramen of Monro, they often present acutely with obstructive hydrocephalus, which requires surgical intervention and/or therapy with an mTOR inhibitor (see below). Seizures are associated with cortical tubers and can be difficult to control with antiepileptic drugs. Extracerebral lesions include renal angiomyolipomas, retinal glial hamartomas, pulmonary lymphangiomyomatosis, and cardiac rhabdomyomas. Cysts may be found at various sites, including the liver, kidneys, and pancreas. Cutaneous lesions include angiofibromas, leathery thickenings in localized patches (shagreen patches), hypopigmented areas (ash leaf patches), and subungual fibromas. TSC results from disruption of either *TSC1,* which encodes hamartin, or *TSC2,* which encodes tuberin. The two TSC proteins form a dimeric complex that negatively regulates mTOR, a kinase that "senses" the cell's nutrient status and regulates cellular metabolism. Loss of either protein leads to increased mTOR activity, which disrupts nutritional signaling and increases cell growth.

MORPHOLOGY

Cortical hamartomas are firmer than normal cortex and have been likened in appearance to potatoes—hence the appellation "tubers." They are composed of haphazardly arranged large neurons that lack the normal cortical laminar architecture. These cells may exhibit a mixture of glial and neuronal features, having large vesicular nuclei with nucleoli (like neurons) and abundant eosinophilic cytoplasm (like gemistocytic astrocytes). Similar abnormal cells are present in the subependymal nodules, in which large astrocyte-like cells cluster beneath the ventricular surface.

von Hippel–Lindau Disease

In this autosomal dominant disorder, affected persons develop hemangioblastomas within the cerebellar hemispheres, retina, and, less commonly, the brain stem, spinal cord, and nerve roots. Patients also may have cysts involving the pancreas, liver, and kidneys and have an increased propensity to develop renal cell carcinoma. The disease frequency is 1 in 30,000 to 40,000. Therapy is directed at the symptomatic neoplasms, including surgical resection of cerebellar tumors and laser ablation of retinal tumors. The affected gene, the tumor suppressor *VHL,* encodes a protein that is part of a ubiquitin-ligase complex that targets the transcription factor hypoxia-inducible factor (HIF) for degradation. Tumors arising in patients with von Hippel-Lindau disease generally have lost all VHL protein function. As a result, these tumors express high levels of HIF, which drives the expression of VEGF, various growth factors, and sometimes erythropoietin, leading to a form of paraneoplastic polycythemia.

MORPHOLOGY

The cerebellar **capillary hemangioblastoma,** the principal neurologic manifestation of the disease, is a highly vascular neoplasm that occurs as a mural nodule associated with a large, fluid-filled cyst. On microscopic examination, the lesion consists of numerous capillary-sized or somewhat larger thin-walled vessels separated by intervening stromal cells with vacuolated, lightly PAS-positive, lipid-rich cytoplasm.

SUMMARY

Tumors of the Central Nervous System

- Tumors of the CNS may arise from the cells of the coverings (meningiomas), the brain (gliomas, neuronal tumors, choroid plexus tumors), or other CNS cell populations (primary CNS lymphoma, germ cell tumors), or they may originate elsewhere in the body (metastases).

- Even low-grade or benign tumors can have poor clinical outcomes, depending on where they occur in the brain.
- Distinct types of tumors affect specific brain regions (e.g., cerebellum for medulloblastoma, an intraventricular location for central neurocytoma) and specific age populations (medulloblastoma and pilocytic astrocytomas in pediatric age groups, and glioblastoma and lymphoma in older patients).
- Glial tumors are broadly classified into astrocytomas, oligodendrogliomas, and ependymomas. Increasing tumor malignancy is associated with more cytologic anaplasia, increased cell density, necrosis, and mitotic activity.
- Metastatic spread of brain tumors to other regions of the body is rare, but the brain is not comparably protected against spread of distant tumors. Carcinomas are the dominant type of systemic tumors that metastasize to the nervous system.

BIBLIOGRAPHY

In general, many areas of neuropathology and neurologic diseases are well covered in the following standard texts:

Burger PC, Scheithauer BW (eds): Tumors of the Central Nervous System. AFIP Atlas of Tumor Pathology: Series 4. Washington, DC, American Registry of Pathology, 2007.

Louis DN, Frosch MP, Mena H, et al (eds): Non-Neoplastic Diseases of the Central Nervous System. AFIP Atlas of Nontumor Pathology: Series 1. Washington, DC, American Registry of Pathology, 2009.

Louis DN, Ohgaki H, Wiestler OD, Cavenee WK (eds): WHO Classification of Tumours of the Central Nervous System (IARC), 4th ed. Geneva, World Health Organization, 2007.

Love S, Louis DN, Ellison DW (eds): Greenfield's Neuropathology, 8th ed. Oxford, Oxford University Press, 2008.

Perry A, Brat DJ: Neuropathology patterns and introduction. In: Perry A, Brat DJ (eds): Practical Surgical Neuropathology, Elsevier/Churchill Livingstone, Philadelphia, 2010.

Ropper AH, Samuels MA (eds): Adams and Victor's Principles of Neurology, 9th ed. New York, McGraw-Hill Professional, 2009.

For some topics covered in this chapter, there have been recent changes in classification, advances in understanding of pathogenesis, therapeutic interventions, and better understanding of clinicopathologic correlations. For these selected topics, additional reading recommendations are provided.

CENTRAL NERVOUS SYSTEM TRAUMA

McKee AC, Cantu RC, Nowinski CJ, et al: Chronic traumatic encephalopathy in athletes: progressive tauopathy after repetitive head injury. J Neuropathol Exp Neurol 68:709, 2009.

CONGENITAL MALFORMATIONS AND PERINATAL BRAIN INJURY

Copp AJ, Greene ND: Genetics and development of neural tube defects. J Pathol 220:217, 2010.

Diaz AL, Gleeson JG: The molecular and genetic mechanisms of neocortex development. Clin Perinatol 36:503, 2009.

Kriegstein A, Alvarez-Buylla A: The glial nature of embryonic and adult neural stem cells. Annu Rev Neurosci 32:149, 2009.

Lee JE, Gleeson JG: Cilia in the nervous system: linking cilia function and neurodevelopmental disorders. Curr Opin Neurol 24:98, 2011.

Lim Y, Golden JA: Patterning the developing diencephalon. Brain Res Rev 53:17, 2007.

Na ES, Monteggia LM: The role of MeCP2 in CNS development and function. Horm Behav 59:364, 2011.

Ten Donkelaar HJ, Lammens M: Development of the human cerebellum and its disorders. Clin Perinatol 36:513, 2009.

Thompson BL, Levitt P: The clinical-basic interface in defining pathogenesis in disorders of neurodevelopmental origin. Neuron 67:702, 2010.

Walsh CA, Morrow EM, Rubenstein JL: Autism and brain development. Cell 135:396, 2008.

INFECTIONS OF THE NERVOUS SYSTEM

Gambetti P, Cali I, Notari S, et al: Molecular biology and pathology of prion strains in sporadic human prion diseases. Acta Neuropathol 121:79, 2011.

Ironside JW: Variant Creutzfeldt-Jakob disease. Haemophilia 16(Suppl 5):175, 2010.

Johnson T, Nath A: Neurological complications of immune reconstitution in HIV-infected populations. Ann N Y Acad Sci 1184:106, 2010.

Martin-Blondel G, Delobel P, Blancher A, et al: Pathogenesis of the immune reconstitution inflammatory syndrome affecting the central nervous system in patients infected with HIV. Brain 134(Pt 4):928, 2011.

Parchi P, Strammiello R, Giese A, Kretzschmar H: Phenotypic variability of sporadic human prion disease and its molecular basis: past, present, and future. Acta Neuropathol 121:91, 2011.

Singer EJ, Valdes-Sueiras M, Commins D, Levine A: Neurologic presentations of AIDS. Neurol Clin 28:253, 2010.

Wright EJ: Neurological disease: the effects of HIV and antiretroviral therapy and the implications for early antiretroviral therapy initiation. Curr Opin HIV AIDS 4:447, 2009.

PRIMARY DISEASES OF MYELIN

Comabella M, Khoury SJ: Immunopathogenesis of multiple sclerosis. Clin Immunol 10:399, 2011.

Hu W, Lucchinetti CF: The pathological spectrum of CNS inflammatory demyelinating diseases. Semin Immunopathol 31:439, 2009.

Jarius S, Wildemann B: AQP4 antibodies in neuromyelitis optica: diagnostic and pathogenetic relevance. Nat Rev Neurol 6:383, 2010.

Oksenberg JR, Baranzini SE, Sawcer S, Hauser SL: The genetics of multiple sclerosis: SNPs to pathways to pathogenesis. Nat Rev Genet 9:516, 2008.

NEURODEGENERATIVE DISEASES

DeKosky ST, Carrillo MC, Phelps C, et al: Revision of the criteria for Alzheimer's disease: A symposium. Alzheimers Dement 7:e1, 2011.

Durr A: Autosomal dominant cerebellar ataxias: polyglutamine expansions and beyond. Lancet Neurol 9:885, 2010.

Pandolfo M: Friedreich ataxia. Arch Neurol 65:1296, 2008.

Kiernan MC, Vucic S, Cheah BC, et al: Amyotrophic lateral sclerosis. Lancet 377:942, 2011.

Ross CA, Tabrizi SJ: Huntington's disease: from molecular pathogenesis to clinical treatment. Lancet Neurol 10:83, 2011.

Selkoe DJ: Biochemistry and molecular biology of amyloid beta-protein and the mechanism of Alzheimer's disease. Handb Clin Neurol 89:245, 2008.

Storch A, Hofer A, Krüger R, et al: New developments in diagnosis and treatment of Parkinson's disease—from basic science to clinical applications. J Neurol 251(Suppl 6):VI33, 2004.

Thinakaran G, Koo EH: Amyloid precursor protein trafficking, processing, and function. J Biol Chem 283:29615, 2008.

Vidailhet M: Movement disorders in 2010: Parkinson disease-symptoms and treatments. Nat Rev Neurol 7:70, 2011.

TUMORS

Cancer Genome Atlas Research Network: Comprehensive genomic characterization defines human glioblastoma genes and core pathways. Nature 455:1061, 2008.

Cho YJ, Tsherniak A, Tamayo P, et al: Integrative genomic analysis of medulloblastoma identifies a molecular subgroup that drives poor clinical outcome. J Clin Oncol 29:1424, 2011.

Dubuc AM, Northcott PA, Mack S, et al: The genetics of pediatric brain tumors. Curr Neurol Neurosci Rep 10:215, 2010.

Maher ER, Neumann HP, Richard S: von Hippel-Lindau disease: A clinical and scientific review. Eur J Hum Genet 19:617, 2011.

Mawrin C, Perry A: Pathological classification and molecular genetics of meningiomas. J Neurooncol 99:379, 2010.

Orlova KA, Crino PB: The tuberous sclerosis complex. Ann N Y Acad Sci 1184:87, 2010.

Riemenschneider MJ, Jeuken JW, Wesseling P, Reifenberger G: Molecular diagnostics of gliomas: state of the art. Acta Neuropathol 120:567, 2010.

O

T

W

X

Y

Z